Fact Index
A-K

Scientiam non dedit natura semina scientiae nobis dedit
"Nature has given us not knowledge itself, but the seeds thereof."
Seneca

The Joy of Knowledge Encyclopaedia is affectionately
dedicated to the memory of John Beazley, 1932–1977,
Book Designer, Publisher, and Co-Founder of the
publishing house of Mitchell Beazley Limited, by all
his many friends and colleagues in the company.

The Joy of Knowledge Library

General Editor: James Mitchell
With an overall preface by Lord Butler, Master of Trinity College,
University of Cambridge

The Mitchell Beazley Joy of Knowledge Library

Fact Index
A-K

MITCHELL BEAZLEY

The Joy of Knowledge Encyclopaedia
© Mitchell Beazley Encyclopaedias Limited 1976

The Joy of Knowledge Fact Index A–K
© Mitchell Beazley Encyclopaedias Limited 1978

Artwork © Mitchell Beazley Publishers Limited
1970, 1971, 1972, 1973, 1974, 1975 and 1976
© Mitchell Beazley Encyclopaedias Limited 1976, 1977
© International Visual Resource 1972

First printed May 1978
Reprinted November 1978

ISBN 0 85533 113 5

Typesetting by G. A. Pindar and Son Ltd., England

Printed in England by Balding + Mansell

Major contributors and advisers to The Joy of Knowledge Library

Fabian Acker CEng, MIEE, MIMarE; Professor Leslie Alcock; Professor H.C. Allen MC; Leonard Amey OBE; Neil Ardley BSc; Professor H.R.V. Arnstein DSc, PhD, FIBiol; Russell Ash BA(Dunelm), FRAI; Norman Ashford PhD, CEng. MICE, MASCE, MCIT; Professor Robert Ashton; B.W. Atkinson BSc, PhD; Anthony Atmore BA; Professor Philip S. Bagwell BSc(Econ), PhD; Peter Ball MA; Edwin Banks MIOP; Professor Michael Banton; Dulan Barber; Harry Barrett; Professor J.P. Barron MA, DPhil, FSA; Professor W.G. Beasley FBA; Alan Bender PhD, MSc, DIC, ARCS; Lionel Bender BSc; Israel Berkovitch PhD, FRIC, MIChemE; David Berry MA; M.L. Bierbrier PhD; A.T.E. Binsted FBBI (Dipl); David Black; Maurice E.F. Block BA, PhD(Cantab); Richard H. Bomback BSc (London), FRPS; Basil Booth BSc (Hons), PhD, FGS, FRGS; J. Harry Bowen MA(Cantab), PhD(London); Mary Briggs MPS, FLS; John Brodrick BSc(Econ); J.M. Bruce ISO, MA, FRHistS, MRAeS; Professor D.A. Bullough MA, FSA, FRHistS; Tony Buzan BA(Hons) UBC; Dr Alan R. Cane; Paul Carmody; Dr J.G. de Casparis; Dr Jeremy Catto MA; Denis Chamberlain; E.W. Chanter MA; Professor Colin Cherry D Sc(Eng), MIEE; A.H. Christie MA, FRAI, FRAS; Dr Anthony W. Clare MPhil(London), MB, BCh, MRCPI, MRCPsych; Professor Aidan Clarke MA, PhD. FTCD; Sonia Cole; John R. Collis MA, PhD; Professor Gordon Connell-Smith BA, PhD, FRHistS; Dr A.H. Cook FRS; Professor A.H. Cook FRS; J.A.L. Cooke MA, DPhil; R.W. Cooke BSc, CEng, MICE; B.K. Cooper; Penelope J. Corfield MA; Robin Cormack MA, PhD, FSA; Nona Coxhead; Patricia Crone BA, PhD; Geoffrey P. Crow BSc(Eng), MICE, MIMunE, MInstHE, DIPTE; J.G. Crowther; Professor R.B. Cundall FRIC; Noel Currer-Briggs MA, FSG; Cristopher Cviic BA(Zagreb), BSc(Econ, London); Gordon Daniels BSc(Econ, London), DPhil(Oxon); George Darby BA; G.J. Darwin; Dr David Delvin; Robin Denselow BA; Professor Bernard L. Diamond; John Dickson; Paul Dinnage MA; M.L. Dockrill BSc(Econ), MA, PhD; Patricia Dodd BA; James Dowdall; Anne Dowson MA(Cantab); Peter M. Driver BSc, PhD, MIBiol; Rev Professor C.W. Dugmore DD; Herbert L. Edlin BSc, Dip in Forestry; Pamela Egan MA(Oxon); Major S.R. Elliot CD, BComm; Professor H.J. Eysenck PhD. DSc; Dr Peter Fenwick BA, MB, BChir, DPM, MRCPsych; Jim Flegg BSc, PhD, ARCS, MBOU; Andrew M. Flemming MA; Professor Antony Flew MA(Oxon), DLitt(Keele); Wyn K. Ford FRHistS; Paul Freeman DSc(London); G.S.P. Freeman-Grenville DPhil, FSA, FRAS, G.E. Fussell DLitt, FRHistS; Kenneth W. Gatland FRAS, FBIS; Norman Gelb BA; Gavin Gibbons; John Gilbert BA(Hons, London); Professor A.C. Gimson; John Glaves-Smith BA; David Glen; Professor S.J. Goldsack BSc, PhD, FInstP, FBCS; Richard Gombrich MA, DPhil; A.F. Gomm; Professor A. Goodwin MA; William Gould BA(Wales); Professor J.R. Gray; Christopher Green PhD; Bill Gunston; Professor A. Rupert Hall LittD; Richard Halsey BAHons(UEA); Lynette K. Hamblin BSc; Norman Hammond; Peter Harbison MA, DPhil; Professor Thomas G. Harding PhD; Professor D.W. Harkness; Richard Harris; Dr Randall P. Harrison; Cyril Hart MA, PhD, FRICS, FIFor; Anthony P. Harvey; Nigel Hawkes BA(Oxon); F.P. Heath; Peter Hebblethwaith MA(Oxon), Lic Theol; Frances Mary Heidensohn BA; Dr Alan Hill MC, FRCP; Robert Hillenbrand MA, DPhil; Catherine Hills PhD; Professor F.H. Hinsley; Dr Richard Hitchcock; Dorothy Hollingsworth OBE, BSc, FRIC, FIBiol,

FIFST, SRD; H.P. Hope BSc(Hons, Agric); Antony Hopkins CBE, FRCM, LRAM, FRSA; Brian Hook; Peter Howell BPhil, MA(Oxon); Brigadier K. Hunt; Peter Hurst BDS, FDS, LDS, RSCEd, MSc(London); Anthony Hyman MA, PhD; Professor R.S. Illingworth MD, FRCP, DPH, DCH; Oliver Impey MA, DPhil; D.E.G. Irvine PhD; L.M. Irvine BSc; E.W. Ives BA, PhD; Anne Jamieson cand mag(Copenhagen), MSc (London); Michael A. Janson BSc; G. H. Jenkins PhD; Professor P.A. Jewell BSc (Agric), MA, PhD. FIBiol; Hugh Johnson; Commander I.E. Johnston RN; I.P. Jolliffe BSc, MSc, PhD, ComplCE, FGS; Dr D.E.H. Jones ARCS, FCS; R. H. Jones PhD, BSc, CEng. MICE, FGS, MASCE; Hugh Kay; Dr Janet Kear; Sam Keen; D.R.C. Kempe BSc, DPhil, FGS; Alan Kendall MA (Cantab); Michael Kenward; John R. King BSc(Eng), DIC, CEng, MIProdE; D.G. King-Hele FRS; Professor J.F. Kirkaldy DSc; Malcolm Kitch; Michael Kitson MA; B.C. Lamb BSc, PhD; Nick Landon; Major J.C. Larminie QDG, Retd; Diana Leat BSc(Econ), PhD; Roger Lewin BSc, PhD, Harold K. Lipset; Norman Longmate MA(Oxon); John Lowry; Kenneth E. Lowther MA; Diana Lucas BA(Hons); Keith Lye BA, FRGS; Dr Peter Lyon; Dr Martin McCauley; Sean McConville BSc; D.F.M. McGregor BSc, PhD(Edin); Jean Macqueen PhD; William Baird MacQuitty MA(Hons), FRGS, FRPS; Professor Rev F.X. Martin OSA; Jonathan Martin MA; Rev Cannon E.L. Mascall DD; Christopher Maynard MSc, DTh; Professor A.J. Meadows; Dr T.B. Millar; John Miller MA, PhD; J.S.G. Miller MA, DPhil, BM, BCh; Alaric Millington BSc, DipEd, FIMA; Rosalind Mitchison MA, FRHistS; Peter L. Moldon; Patrick Moore OBE; Robin Mowat MA, DPhil; J. Michael Mullin BSc; Alistair Munroe BSc. ARCS; Professor Jacob Needleman; John Newman MA, FSA; Professor Donald M. Nicol MA PhD; Gerald Norris; Professor F.S. Northedge PhD; Caroline E. Oakman BA(Hons. Chinese); S. O'Connell MA(Cantab), MInstP; Dr Robert Orr; Michael Overman; Di Owen BSc; A.R.D. Pagden MA, FRHistS; Professor E.J. Pagel PhD; Liam de Paor MA; Carol Parker BA(Econ), MA (Internat. Aff.); Derek Parker; Julia Parker DFAstrolS; Dr Stanley Parker; Dr Colin Murray Parkes MD, FRC(Psych), DPM; Dee Parkes; Professor Geoffrey Parrinder MA, PhD, DD(London), DLitt(Lancaster); Moira Paterson; Walter C. Patterson MSc; Sir John H. Peel KCVO, MA, DM, FRCP, FRCS, FRCOG; D. J. Penn; Basil Peters MA, MInstP, FBIS; D.L. Phillips FRCR, MRCOG; B.T. Pickering PhD, DSc; John Picton; Susan Pinkus; Dr C.S. Pitcher MA, DM, FRCPath; Alfred Plaut FRCPsych; A.S. Playfair MRCS, LRCP, DObst RCOG; Dr Antony Polonsky; Joyce Pope BA; B.L. Potter NDA, MRAC, CertEd; Paulette Pratt; Antony Preston Frank J. Pycroft; Margaret Quass; Dr John Reckless; Trevor Reese BA, PhD, FRHistS; M.M. Reese MA (Oxon); Derek A. Reid BSc, PhD; Clyde Reynolds BSc; John Rivers; Peter Roberts; Colin A. Ronan MSc, FRAS; Professor Richard Rose BA(Johns Hopkins), DPhil (Oxon); Harold Rosenthal; T.G. Rosenthal MA(Cantab); Anne Ross MA, MA(Hons, Celtic Studies), PhD (Archaeol and Celtic Studies, Edin); Frank Rudman; Georgina Russell MA; Dr Charles Rycroft BA (Cantab), MB(London), FRCPsych; Susan Saunders MSc(Econ); Robert Schell PhD; Anil Seal MA, PhD(Cantab); Michael Sedgwick MA(Oxon); Martin Seymour-Smith BA(Oxon), MA(Oxon); Professor John Shearman; Dr Martin Sherwood; A.C. Simpson BSc; Nigel Sitwell; Dr Alan Sked; Julie and Kenneth Slavin FRGS, FRAI; Professor T.C. Smout; Alec Xavier Snobel BSc(Econ); Terry Snow BA, ATCL; Rodney Steel; Charles S. Steinger MA, PhD; Geoffrey Stern BSc(Econ); Maryanne Stevens BA(Cantab), MA(London); John Stevenson DPhil, MA; J. Sidworthy MA; D. Michael Stoddart BSc, PhD; Bernard Stonehouse DPhil, MA, BSc, MInstBiol; Anthony Storr FRCP, FRCPsych;

Richard Storry; Charles Stuart-Jervis; Professor John Taylor; John W.R. Taylor FRHistS, MRAeS, FSLAET; R.B. Taylor BSc(Hons, Microbiol); J. David Thomas MA, PhD; D. Thompson BSc(Econ); Harvey Tilker PhD; Don Tills PhD, MPhil, MIBiol, FIMLS; Jon Tinker; M. Tregear MA; R.W. Trender; David Trump MA, PhD, FSA; M.F. Tuke PhD; Christopher Tunney MA; Laurence Urdang Associates (authentication and fact check); Sally Walters BSc; Christopher Wardle; Dr D. Washbrook; David Watkins; George Watkins MSc; J.W.N. Watkins; Anthony J. Watts; Dr Geoff Watts; Melvyn Westlake; Anthony White MA(Oxon), MAPhil(Columbia); Dr Ruth D. Whitehouse; P.J.S. Whitmore MBE, PhD; Alan Wightman; Professor G.R. Wilkinson; Rev H.A. Williams CR; Christopher Wilson BA; Professor David M. Wilson; John B. Wilson BSc, PhD, FGS, FLS; Philip Windsor BA, DPhil(Oxon); Roy Wolfe BSc(Econ), MSc; Donald Wood MA, PhD; Dr David Woodings MA, MRCP, MRCPath; Graeme Wright; Bernard Yallop PhD, BSc, ARCS, FRAS; Professor John Yudkin MA, MD, PhD(Cantab), FRIC FIBiol, FRCP.

The General Editor wishes particularly to thank the following for all their support:
Nicolas Bentley
Bill Borchard
Adrianne Bowles
Yves Boisseau
Irv Braun
Theo Bremer
the late Dr Jacob Bronowski
Sir Humphrey Browne
Barry and Helen Cayne
Peter Chubb
William Clark
Sanford and Dorothy Cobb
Alex and Jane Comfort
Jack and Sharlie Davison
Manfred Denneler
Stephen Elliott
Stephen Feldman
Orsola Fenghi
Professor Richard Gregory
Dr Leo van Grunsven
Jan van Gulden
Graham Hearn
the late Raimund von Hofmansthal
Dr Antonio Houaiss
the late Sir Julian Huxley
Alan Isaacs
Julie Lansdowne
Professor Peter Lasko
Andrew Leithead
Richard Levin
Oscar Lewenstein
The Rt Hon Selwyn Lloyd
Warren Lynch
Simon macLachlan
George Manina
Stuart Marks
Bruce Marshall
Francis Mildner
Bill and Christine Mitchell
Janice Mitchell
Patrick Moore
Mari Pijnenborg
the late Donna Dorita de Sa Putch
Tony Ruth
Dr Jonas Salk
Stanley Schindler
Guy Schoeller
Tony Schulte
the late Dr E.F. Schumacher
Christopher Scott
Anthony Storr
Hannu Tarmio
Ludovico Terzi
Ion Trewin
Egil Tveteras
Russ Voisin
Nat Wartels
Hiroshi Watanabe
Adrian Webster
Jeremy Westwood
Harry Williams
and the dedicated staff of MB Encyclopaedias who created this Library and of MB Multimedia who made the IVR Artwork Bank.

Preface

I do not think any other group of publishers could be credited with
producing so comprehensive and modern an encyclopaedia as this.
It is quite original in form and content. A fine team of writers has been
enlisted to provide the contents. No library or place of reference would
be complete without this modern encyclopaedia, which should also
be a treasure in private hands.

The production of an encyclopaedia is often an example that a
particular literary, scientific and philosophic civilization is thriving
and groping towards further knowledge. This was certainly so when
Diderot published his famous encyclopaedia in the eighteenth century.
Since science and technology were then not so far developed, his is a
very different production from this. It depended to a certain extent on
contributions from Rousseau and Voltaire and its publication created
a school of adherents known as the encyclopaedists.

In modern times excellent encyclopaedias have been produced, but
I think there is none which has the wealth of illustrations which is
such a feature of these volumes. I was particularly struck by the
section on astronomy, where the illustrations are vivid and unusual.
This is only one example of illustrations in the work being, I would
almost say, staggering in their originality.

I think it is probable that many responsible schools will have sets,
since the publishers have carefully related much of the contents of the
encyclopaedia to school and college courses. Parents on occasion feel
that it is necessary to supplement school teaching at home, and this
encyclopaedia would be invaluable in replying to the queries of
adolescents which parents often find awkward to answer. The "two-
page-spread" system, where text and explanatory diagrams are
integrated into attractive units which relate to one another, makes this
encyclopaedia different from others and all the more easy to study.

The whole encyclopaedia will literally be a revelation in the sphere
of human and humane knowledge.

Butler

**Master of Trinity College,
Cambridge**

Fact Index/Contents

The Structure of the Library

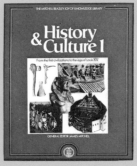

Science and The Universe	The Physical Earth	The Natural World	Man and Society	History and Culture
The growth of science	Structure of the Earth	How life began	Evolution of man	Volume 1 From the first
Mathematics	The Earth in perspective	Plants	How your body works	civilizations to the age of
Atomic theory	Weather	Animals	Illness and health	Louis XIV
Statics and dynamics	Seas and oceans	Insects	Mental health	
Heat, light and sound	Geology	Fish	Human development	The art of prehistory
Electricity	Earth's resources	Amphibians and reptiles	Man and his gods	Classical Greece
Chemistry	Agriculture	Birds	Communications	India, China and Japan
Techniques of astronomy	Cultivated plants	Mammals	Politics	Barbarian invasions
The Solar System	Flesh, fish and fowl	Prehistoric animals and	Law	The crusades
Stars and star maps		plants	Work and play	Age of exploration
Galaxies		Animals and their habitats	Economics	The Renaissance
Man in space		Conservation		The English revolution

The two *Fact Index* volumes contain more than 25,000 short factual articles that complement and supplement the eight other volumes in *The Joy of Knowledge Library*. They not only cross-refer to those volumes but also have their own internal system of cross-references to help you to build up a rounded picture of the subjects they cover.

These two volumes complete Mitchell Beazley's ten-volume library of individual books we have entitled *The Joy of Knowledge Library*—a library which forms a comprehensive encyclopaedia.

For a new generation brought up with television, words alone are no longer enough—and so we have made the *Library* a new sort of pictorial encyclopaedia for a visually oriented age, a new "family bible" of knowledge which will find acceptance in every home.

There are eight other colour volumes in the *Library*: *Man and Society*, *The Physical Earth*, *The Natural World*, *History and Culture* (two volumes), *Science and The Universe*, *Man and Machines*, and *The Modern World*. *The Modern World* is arranged alphabetically: the other volumes are organized by topic and provide a comprehensive store of general knowledge rather than isolated facts.

The two *Fact Index* volumes in the *Library* provide a different service. Split up for convenience into A-K and L-Z references, these volumes are a fact index to the whole work. They provide factual information of all kinds on peoples, places and things through more than 25,000 mostly short entries listed in alphabetical order. The entries in the A-Z volumes also act as a comprehensive index to the other eight volumes, thus turning the whole *Library* into a rounded *Encyclopaedia*, which is not only a comprehensive guide to general knowledge in volumes 1–7 but which also provides access to specific information as well in *The Modern World* and the *Fact Index* volumes.

Access to knowledge
Whether you are a systematic reader or an unrepentant browser, my aim as General Editor has been to assemble all the facts you really ought to know into a coherent and logical plan that makes it possible to build up a comprehensive general knowledge of the subject.

Depending on your needs or motives as a reader in search of knowledge, you can find things out from the seven thematic volumes in four or more ways: for example, you can simply browse pleasurably about in their pages haphazardly (and that's my way!) or you can browse in a more organized fashion if you use our "See Also" treasure hunt system of connections referring you from spread to spread. Or you can gather specific facts by using the individual volume indexes. Yet again, you can set yourself the solid task of finding out literally everything in the books in logical order by reading them from cover to cover: in this the contents lists are there to guide you.

Our basic purpose in organizing the volumes in *The Joy of Knowledge Library* into two elements—the three volumes of A-Z factual information and the seven volumes of general knowledge—was functional. We devised it this way to make it easier to gather the two different sorts of information— simple facts and wider general knowledge, respectively—in appropriate ways.

The functions of an encyclopaedia
An encyclopaedia (the Greek word means "teaching in a circle" or, as we might say, the provision of a *rounded* picture of knowledge) has to perform these two distinct functions for two sorts of users, each seeking information of different sorts.

First, many readers want simple factual answers to straightforward questions such as "Who was William Wilberforce?" They may be intrigued to learn that he was a British philanthropist who lived between 1759 and 1833, was a Member of Parliament for more than 40 years, and was a leading figure in the fight for abolition of the slave trade. Such facts are best supplied by a short entry and in the *Library* they will be found in the *Fact Index* volumes.

But secondly, for the user looking for in-depth knowledge on a subject or on a series of subjects—such as "What effect did the abolition of the slave trade have on the economies of England and the West Indies?"—short alphabetical entries alone are bitty and disjointed. What do you look up first—"England"? "West Indies"? "Slave trade"?—and do you have to read all the entries or only some? You normally have to look up lots of entries in a purely alphabetical encyclopaedia to get a comprehensive answer to such wide-ranging questions. Yet comprehensive answers are what general knowledge is all about.

A long article or linked series of longer articles, organized

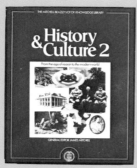

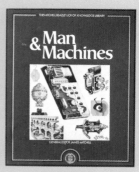

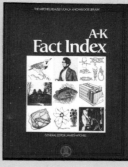

History and Culture

Volume 2 From the Age
of Reason to the
modern world

Neoclassicism
Colonizing Australasia
World War I
Ireland and independence
Twenties and the
    depression
World War II
Hollywood

Man and Machines

The growth of
    technology
Materials and techniques
Power
Machines
Transport
Weapons
Engineering
Communications
Industrial chemistry
Domestic engineering

The Modern World

Almanack
Countries of the world
Atlas
Gazetteer

Fact Index A-K

The first of two volumes
containing 25,000 mostly
short factual entries
on people, places and
things in A-Z order. The
Fact Index also acts as
an index to the eight
colour volumes. In
this volume, everything
from Aachen to Kyzyl
Kum Desert.

Fact Index L-Z

The second of the A-Z
volumes that turn the
Library into a complete
encyclopaedia. Like the
first, it acts as an
index to the eight
colour volumes. In this
volume, everything from
Ernest Laas to Zyrardow.

by related subjects, is clearly much more helpful to the
person wanting such comprehensive answers. That is why
we have adopted a logical, so-called *thematic* organization
of knowledge, with a clear system of connections relating
topics to one another, for teaching general knowledge in
the seven general knowledge volumes in the *Library*.

The spread system
The basic unit of all the general knowledge books is the
"spread"—a nickname for the two-page units that
comprise the working contents of all these books. The
spread is the heart of our approach to explaining things.

    Every spread tells a story and the spreads all work to the
same discipline, which is to tell you all you need to know in
two facing pages of text and pictures. The discipline of having
to get in all the essential and relevant facts in this
comparatively short space actually makes for better results—
text that has to get to the point without any waffle, pictures
and diagrams that illustrate the essential points in a clear and
coherent fashion, captions that really work and explain the
point of the pictures.

    The spread system is a strict discipline but once you get
used to it, I hope you'll ask yourself why you ever thought
general knowledge could be communicated in any other way.

    The structure of the spread system will also, I hope,
prove reassuring when you venture out from the things you
do know about into the unknown areas you don't know,
but want to find out about. There are many virtues in
being systematic. You will start to feel at home in all sorts
of unlikely areas of knowledge with the spread system to
guide you. The spreads are, in a sense, the building blocks
of knowledge. Like living cells which are the building
blocks of plants and animals, they are systematically
"programmed" to help you to learn more easily and to
remember better. Each spread has a main article of 850
words summarizing the subject. The article is illustrated
by an average of ten pictures and diagrams, the captions
of which both complement *and* supplement the
information in the article (so please read the captions,
incidentally, or you may miss something!). Each spread,
too, has a "key" picture or diagram in the top right-hand
corner. The purpose of the key picture is twofold: it
summarizes the story of the spread visually and it is

intended to act as a memory stimulator to help you to
recall all the integrated facts and pictures on a subject.

    Finally, each spread has a box of connections headed
"See Also" and, sometimes, "Read First". These are
cross-reference suggestions to other connecting spreads.
The "Read Firsts" normally appear only on spreads with
particularly complicated subjects and indicate that you
might like to learn to swim a little in the elementary
principles of a subject before being dropped in the deep
end of its complexities.

    The "See Alsos" are the treasure hunt features of *The
Joy of Knowledge* system and I hope you'll find them
helpful and, indeed, fun to use. They are also essential if
you want to build up a comprehensive general knowledge.
If the spreads are individual living cells, the "See Alsos"
are the secret code that tells you how to fit the cells
together into an organic whole which is the body of
general knowledge.

Level of readership
The level for which we have created *The Joy of Knowledge
Library* is intended to be a universal one. Some aspects of
knowledge are more complicated than others and so readers
will find that the level varies in different parts of the
Library. This is quite deliberate: *The Joy of Knowledge
Library* is a library for all the family.

    Whatever their level, the greatest and the best selling
popular encyclopaedias of the past have always had one
thing in common—simplicity. The ability to make even
complicated subjects clear, to distil, to extract the simple
principles from behind the complicated formulae, the gift
of getting to the heart of things: these are the elements
that make popular encyclopaedias really useful to the
people who read them. I hope we have followed these
precepts throughout the *Library*: if so our level will be
found to be truly universal.

Philosophy of the Library
The aim of *all* the books—general knowledge and *Fact
Index* volumes—in the *Library* is to make knowledge more
readily available to everyone, and to make it fun. This is
not new in encyclopaedias. The great classics enlightened
whole generations of readers with essential information,

popularly presented and positively inspired. Equally, some works in the past seem to have been extensions of an educational system that believed that unless knowledge was painfully acquired it couldn't be good for you, would be inevitably superficial, and wouldn't stick. Many of us know in our own lives the boredom and disinterest generated by such an approach at school, and most of us have seen it too in certain types of adult books. Such an approach locks up knowledge instead of liberating it.

The great educators have been the men and women who have enthralled their listeners or readers by the self-evident passion they themselves have left for their subjects. Their joy is natural and infectious. We remember what they say and cherish it for ever. The philosophy of *The Joy of Knowledge Library* is one that precisely mirrors that enthusiasm. We aim to seduce you with our pictures, absorb you with our text, entertain you with the multitude of facts we have marshalled for your pleasure—yes, *pleasure*. Why not pleasure?

There are three uses of knowledge: education (things you ought to know because they are important); pleasure (things which are intriguing or entertaining in themselves); application (things we can do with our knowledge for the world at large).

As far as education is concerned there are certain elementary facts we need to learn in our schooldays. The *Library*, with its vast store of information, is primarily designed to have an educational function—to inform, to be a constant companion and to guide everyone through school, college and other forms of higher education.

But most facts, except to the student or specialist (and these books are not only for students and specialists, they are for everyone) aren't vital to know at all. You don't *need* to know them. But discovering them can be a source of endless pleasure and delight, nonetheless, like learning the pleasures of food or wine or love or travel. Who wouldn't give a king's ransom to know when man really became man and stopped being an ape? Who wouldn't have loved to have spent a day at the feet of Leonardo or to have met the historical Jesus or to have been there when Stephenson's *Rocket* first moved? The excitement of discovering new things is like meeting new people—it is one of the great pleasures of life.

There is always the chance, too, that some of the things you find out in these pages may inspire you with a lifelong passion to apply your knowledge in an area which really interests you. My friend Patrick Moore, the astronomer, who first suggested we publish this *Library* and wrote much of the astronomy section in the volume on *Science and The Universe*, once told me that he became an astronomer through the thrill he experienced on first reading an encyclopaedia of astronomy called *The Splendour of the Heavens*, published when he was a boy. Revelation is the reward of encyclopaedists. Our job, my job, is to remind you always that the joy of knowledge knows no boundaries and can work untold miracles.

In an age when we are increasingly creators (and less creatures) of our world, the people who *know*, who have a sense of proportion, a sense of balance, above all perhaps a sense of insight (the inner as well as the outer eye) in the application of their knowledge, are the most valuable people on earth. They, and they alone, will have the capacity to save this earth as a happy and a habitable planet for all its creatures. For the true joy of knowledge lies not only in its acquisition and its enjoyment, but in its wise and living application in the service of the world.

Thus the Latin tag "Scientiam non dedit natura semina scientiae nobis dedit" on the first page of this book. It translates as "Nature has given us not knowledge itself, but the seeds thereof."

It is, in the end, up to each of us to make the most of what we find in these pages.

General Editor's Introduction
How to Use this Book

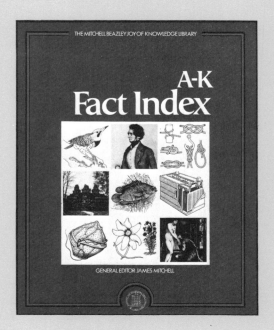

The *Fact Index* is a self-contained alphabetical encyclopaedia in its own right, but it also supplements and complements the eight other volumes in *The Joy of Knowledge Library* and provides a comprehensive index to the whole work. These two volumes should, by themselves, provide you with the basic facts about most significant people, places and things—animal, vegetable, mineral and abstract—that you are likely to come across and want to know about. In their pages you will find articles on writers, sportsmen, scientists and major historical figures; on wild and domestic animals; on the major cities of the world; and on all the "isms", schools and movements that make up the world's intellectual heritage.

Particular emphasis has been laid on articles of significance to readers in Britain and the Commonwealth, especially Australia, New Zealand, Canada and South Africa. Approximately one fifth of all the articles is devoted to the towns and cities, physical features, flora and fauna, and artists, sportsmen, statesmen and scientists of those four countries.

As well as being a source of quick reference to facts, the *Fact Index* is the first step on the "circle of knowledge" that lies at the heart of the *Library's* system. The articles not only provide basic facts: they also lead on, through cross-references, to the thematic spreads in the colour volumes. For example, someone who comes across the word "euglena" may not know whether it is an animal, a chemical, a place, a plant, a star or perhaps even a person. Reference to the *Fact Index* article **Euglena** will reveal that it is a living organism on the threshold of the plant and animal kingdoms and give references to illustrations of the creature on pages 21 and 38 of *The Natural World*.

There is a second category of cross-references in the *Fact Index* volumes. A word printed in small capital letters (eg EUGLENA) is the title of an article elsewhere in the *Fact Index*. Sometimes such references are used merely to indicate alternative spellings. For example, the entry

     Aalborg. *See* ÅLBORG.

means that information about this Danish city is given under the more common of the two spellings (Ålborg).

More often a cross-reference in small capital letters directs the reader to another article which contains additional or background information. Thus the article on Abolitionists includes the name William WILBERFORCE,

indicating that the man who was instrumental in ending Britain's involvement in the slave trade has a separate biographical article in the *Fact Index*.

The system of cross-references is fully explained on page 12 of this volume and the codes are printed at the foot of each page.

An encyclopaedia functions as a really useful reference book only if the reader can quickly and easily find the information he is seeking. We have tried to make the *Fact Index* combine readability with genuine "look-up-ability". The *Fact Index* is intended to present simple information succinctly in some 25,000 articles and 3,000 illustrations, as well as signposting the route to the relevant page or pages in other volumes of *The Joy of Knowledge Library*.

Fact Index information system

The *Fact Index* volumes of *The Joy of Knowledge Library* have been compiled to complement and to supplement the *Library's* eight colour volumes. Cross-references in the body of an article take the reader to additional information within the *Fact Index*; cross-references at the foot of an article lead to additional information in the colour volumes. Sometimes, when in the editor's view it would prove useful, cross-references are used to set a topic in context. Thus the reader may find that such a cross-reference does not provide more facts about, say, a particular person but does set that person in historical perspective, giving the background of events in which he played a prominent part or associating him with a particular set of contemporaries. The Time Chart that forms part of the two volumes on history and culture is not cross-referred to in that way, but access to it can be gained by using the indexes to the history and culture volumes. The reader should note that the construction of some articles has made it impossible to give precise cross-references to other *Fact Index* articles. For example, an article may speak of a painter as an IMPRESSIONIST painter, the word "impressionist" in small capitals being a cross-reference to an article under that heading. In fact, the article will be found under IMPRESSIONISM. Similarly, plural cross-references (eg, ANTS) lead to singular articles (eg, ANT). There are few of these exceptions to the basic system and the reader should have no difficulty in finding any desired article. The overall arrangement of *Fact Index* articles, and the way in which the cross-references work, are set out below.

The *Fact Index* volumes of *The Joy of Knowledge* are constructed in such a way that the reader can obtain the maximum information from these and all the other volumes in the *Library*. This page explains how the articles are arranged and how cross-references direct the reader to related topics.

Reference codes

References to information in other *Joy of Knowledge* volumes use one of the following codes followed by the page number:

HC1 – History and Culture Vol. 1
HC2 – History and Culture Vol. 2
MM – Man and Machines
MS – Man and Society
MW – The Modern World
NW – The Natural World
PE – The Physical Earth
SU – Science and The Universe

(The codes are printed at the foot of every *Fact Index* page.)

A page number printed in ordinary numerals indicates that additional information is contained within the text of an article —for example, NW p.123 is a reference to the text on page 123 of *The Natural World*; a page number printed in italic numerals indicates that additional information is contained in an illustration or its caption— for example, MM p.*123* is a reference to an illustration on page 123 of *Man and Machines*.

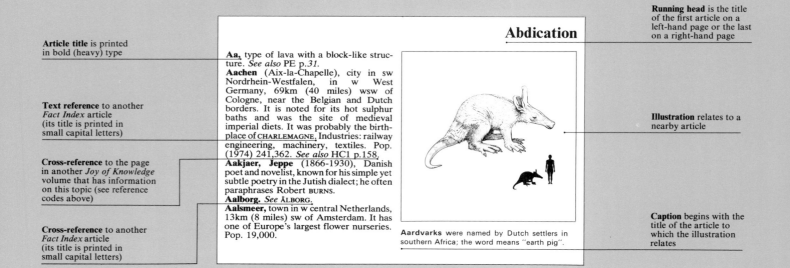

Article title is printed in bold (heavy) type

Text reference to another *Fact Index* article (its title is printed in small capital letters)

Cross-reference to the page in another *Joy of Knowledge* volume that has information on this topic (see reference codes above)

Cross-reference to another *Fact Index* article (its title is printed in small capital letters)

Abdication

Running head is the title of the first article on a left-hand page or the last on a right-hand page

Illustration relates to a nearby article

Caption begins with the title of the article to which the illustration relates

Aa, type of lava with a block-like structure. *See also* PE p.*31.*
Aachen (Aix-la-Chapelle), city in sw Nordrhein-Westfalen, in w West Germany, 69km (40 miles) wsw of Cologne, near the Belgian and Dutch borders. It is noted for its hot sulphur baths and was the site of medieval imperial diets. It was probably the birthplace of CHARLEMAGNE. Industries: railway engineering, machinery, textiles. Pop. (1974) 241,362. *See also* HC1 p.158.
Aakjaer, Jeppe (1866-1930), Danish poet and novelist, known for his simple yet subtle poetry in the Jutish dialect; he often paraphrases Robert BURNS.
Aalborg. *See* ÅLBORG.
Aalsmeer, town in w central Netherlands, 13km (8 miles) sw of Amsterdam. It has one of Europe's largest flower nurseries. Pop. 19,000.

Aardvarks were named by Dutch settlers in southern Africa; the word means "earth pig".

A

A, first letter of the Roman alphabet. It evolved from the ancient Egyptian hieroglyph representing the head of an ox through the Hebrew word *aleph*, meaning *ox*, to the Greek *alpha*. The letter *a* is a vowel. *See also* MS pp.244–245.
Aa, type of lava with a block-like structure. *See also* PE p.*31*.
Aachen (Aix-la-Chapelle), city in sw Nordrhein-Westfalen, in w West Germany, 69km (40 miles) wsw of Cologne, near the Belgian and Dutch borders. It is noted for its hot sulphur baths and was the site of medieval imperial diets. It was probably the birthplace of CHARLEMAGNE. Industries: railway engineering, machinery, textiles. Pop. (1974) 241,362. *See also* HC1 p.158.
Aakjaer, Jeppe (1866-1930), Danish poet and novelist, known for his simple yet subtle poetry in the Jutish dialect; he often paraphrases Robert BURNS.
Aalborg. *See* ÅLBORG.
Aalsmeer, town in w central Netherlands, 13km (8 miles) sw of Amsterdam. It has one of Europe's largest flower nurseries. Pop. 19,000.
Aalto, Alvar (1898–1976), Finnish architect and furniture designer, famous for his imaginative handling of floor levels and use of natural materials and irregular forms. His work includes the municipal library at Viipuri (1927–35), the sanatorium at Paimio (1929–33), the Baker House at the Massachusetts Institute of Technology (1947–49), the Säynätsalo town hall complex (1950–52) and Finlandia House, Helsinki (1967–71). *See also* INTERNATIONAL STYLE; HC2 p.206.
Aaltonen, Wäinö (1894–1966), Finnish painter who later became a pioneer in the revival of stone carving. His works in granite, classical and monumental, include important public monuments and he also produced a number of marble busts, notably one of SIBELIUS.
Aardvark, nocturnal, bristly-haired mammal of central and southern Africa; it lives on termites and ants which it scoops up with its sticky 30cm (12in) tongue. Length: up to 1.5m (5ft); weight: up to 70kg (154lb). It is the only representative of the order Tubulidentata. *See also* NW pp.*55, 62*.
Aardwolf, rare nocturnal mammal found in s and E Africa. It has soft, black-striped yellow-grey underfur, with coarse outer fur forming a crest along its back. It eats mainly termites and insect larvae. Overall length: to 1m (3.3ft). Family Hyaenidae; species *Proteles cristatus*. *See* NW p.*165*.
Aare, longest river in Switzerland, running 295km (183 miles) from the Bernese Alps to the Rhine, opposite Waldshut. It has more than 40 hydroelectric stations.
Aarestrup, Carl Ludwig Emil (1800–56), Danish poet, known chiefly for his passionate love lyrics; his favourite theme was "eternal womanhood".
Aarhus. *See* ÅRHUS.
Aaron, elder brother of MOSES and first Jewish high priest. According to the biblical book of Exodus, he helped to obtain the release of the Israelites from slavery in Egypt. He lapsed into idolatry, made a golden calf for the people to worship, but was later restored to divine favour.
Aasen, Ivar Andreas (1813–96), Norwegian philologist and poet. He used various dialects to found the literary language, Landsmål, or Nynorsk (new Norwegian).
Aba, in SE Nigeria, originally an Ibo village, both a market and a manufacturing centre for textiles, plastics, soap and palm oil. Pop. (1975 est.) 177,000.
Abaca. *See* MANILA HEMP.
Abacus, mathematical tool used in the Middle and Far East for addition and subtraction. One form of abacus (various types have been used for thousands of years) consists of beads strung on wires and arranged in columns. The Chinese abacus dates from about the 12th century. *See also* SU p.30.
Abādān, city in sw Iran, on Abādān Island at the head of the Persian Gulf. It is an important oil pipeline terminus and refining centre and, until 1951, was the site of the world's largest oil refinery, built in 1913 by the Anglo-Iranian Oil Company. Pop. 312,000.
Abakan, formerly Ust-Abakanskoye, is the capital of the Soviet autonomous oblast Khakass. Situated on the s Siberian railway, its main industries are sawmilling, metal working and textiles. It contains Bronze Age barrows and was founded as a fortress in 1707. Pop. 116,000.
Abalone, seashore gastropod MOLLUSC with a single flattened spiral shell perforated by a row of respiratory holes; it is found on Mediterranean, Atlantic and N Pacific shores and off the coasts of South Africa and Australia. Length: to 30cm (12in). Family Haliotidae; species include *Haliotis rufescens*. *See also* NW p.96.
Abascal, José Fernando de (1743–1821), viceroy of Peru (1804–16). He quelled revolts in Upper Peru and Chile during independence uprisings (1808–25) and later became a member of the Spanish War Council. *See also* HC2 p.86.
Abbadids, Moorish dynasty that ruled Seville, Spain (1023–91). After the collapse of the Córdoba caliphate, the cadi of Seville proclaimed himself king as Abbad I in 1023. His son Abbad II succeeded him in 1042 and made SEVILLE the strongest kingdom in s Spain. His successor Abbad III, who became king in 1069, was a patron of the arts. He was forced into exile in 1091 by the ALMORAVIDS.
Abbado, Claudio (1933–), Italian conductor. In 1971 he was made principal conductor of the Vienna Philharmonic Orchestra and has been permanent conductor at LA SCALA in Milan since 1969.
Abbas I (the Great) (1571–1629), Shah of Persia (1588–1629). He defeated the UZBEKS and seized Ormuz (1622) and Baghdad (1623). He founded the port of Bandar Abbas, erected buildings at Isfahan but left the SAFAVID dynasty without an heir.
Abbas II (1874–1944), last Khedive of Egypt (1892–1914). He ruled under the OTTOMAN EMPIRE but from 1894 was largely controlled by Lord Cromer and KITCHENER. Abbas was later deposed in favour of his uncle, Husain Kamil.
Abbasids, Muslim dynasty that held the caliphate from 750 to 1258. They traced their descent from al-Abbas, the uncle of MOHAMMED, and came to power by defeating the UMAYYADS. The Abbasids moved the caliphate from Damascus to Baghdad in 862, where it achieved great splendour, particularly under HARUN AR-RASHID and AL-MAMUN. After the family's downfall in 1258, one member was invited by the Mameluke sultan to Cairo, where the dynasty was recognized until the 16th century. *See also* HC1 pp.148, 151.
Abbate, or Abati, Niccolò dell' (*c*.1512–71), Italian Mannerist painter who pioneered French landscape painting. One of his best-known works is *Landscape with Orpheus and Eurydice*.
Abbeville, town in NE France, approx. 40km (25 miles) NW of Amiens. Crudely fashioned stone hand-axes were found nearby in the mid-19th century, hence Abbevillian is the name given to the earliest (pre-ACHEULEAN) hand-axe industry of Europe. The town was under English rule from 1272 for about 100 years and flourished until the Protestants had to flee after 1685. Industries: textiles, sugar refining, brewing. Pop. 24,000. *See also* MS p.*31*.
Abbey, complex of buildings that makes up a religious community directed by an abbot or abbess, the centre of which is the abbey church. Since the decline of MONASTICISM, often only the church remains. *See also* HC1 p.134.
Abbey Theatre, founded (1904) in Abbey St, Dublin, by Annie HORNIMAN to house the Irish National Theatre Company, presenting Irish actors in Irish plays. In 1924 the Abbey became the National Theatre of Ireland. Works by W.B. YEATS, Lady GREGORY, J.M. SYNGE and Sean O'CASEY have been introduced there by such actors as Sara Allgood, Arthur Sinclair and Barry Fitzgerald. *See also* NATIONAL THEATRE OF IRELAND.
Abbott, Sir John (1821–93), lawyer, educator, and Prime Minister of Canada (1891–92). He was dean of McGill Law School and a Conservative legislator who was ousted after the PACIFIC SCANDAL of 1873. In 1880 he was re-elected to Parliament and later succeeded John MACDONALD as Prime Minister.
Abbott, Lemuel Francis (*c*.1760–1803), British painter, famous for his portraits of Lord NELSON and the poet COWPER.
Abbott and Costello, Bud Abbott (1895–1974) and Lou Costello (1906–59), US music hall and film comedy team. Abbott was the straight man and Costello was the chubby fool in many films, including *Rio Rita* (1942) and *The Wistful Widow of Wagon Gap* (1947).
ABC, the Australian Broadcasting Commission, created by the Australian parliament in 1932. It has three radio networks and one television network. Its main production centres are at Sydney and Melbourne.
ABC Mediation, arbitration conducted by Argentina, Brazil and Chile to settle a dispute between Mexico and USA when US troops landed at Vera Cruz in 1914.
Abd al-Aziz IV (1878–1943), Sultan of Morocco (1894–1908), son and successor of Mulaie-Hassan. He was responsible for European influence in Morocco, a loan from France (1904), reorganization of the army, and higher taxes. He was later ousted by his brother ABD AL-HAFIZ.
Abd al-Hafiz (1875–1937), Sultan of Morocco (1908–12). He gained the throne after a coup but, faced with a rebellion, agreed to a French protectorate (1912) and abdicated.
Abd al-Malik (646–705), fifth UMAYYAD caliph (685–705). He united ISLAM by defeating the rival caliph, Abdullah ibn-al-Zubayr, and also fought against the Byzantines. He reformed the government and made Arabic the official language. *See also* HC1 pp.148-149.
Abd al-Mumim (*c*.1094–1163), successor of Mohammed ibn Tumark who founded the ALMOHAD dynasty. He conquered the MAGHREB from the ALMORAVIDS, seizing the conquests of ROGER II of Sicily in Africa as far as Tripoli. He also united the BERBERS. He rebuilt RABAT and other towns. *See also* HC1 p.171.
Abd ar-Rahman III (891–961), UMAYYAD emir (912–29) and first Caliph of Córdoba (929–61). He seized Ceuta and reclaimed other Spanish provinces, enlarged his navy, and greatly increased Córdoba's power. *See also* HC1 p.170.
Abd-el-Kader (1808–83), Algerian leader, Emir of Mascara. He displaced the French and Turks from N Algeria and in 1839 began a war against the French. He was defeated at Isly (1844).
Abd el-Krim (1882–1963), Rif leader. He fought against Spanish rule in Morocco, capturing outposts with his Rif tribesmen in 1921–22. In 1925 he attacked French Morocco but was defeated by French and Spanish troops. He surrendered in 1926 but escaped from imprisonment and was granted asylum by Egypt in 1947.
Abd er-Rahman Khan (*c*.1830–1901), Emir of Afghanistan (1880–1901). He established the border with India and began modernization of Afghanistan.
Abdication, renunciation of the throne by a ruling monarch. There have been two abdications in British history, although the first, that of JAMES II, was so only in name. The birth of a son to James on 10 June 1688 raised the possibility of a Catholic dynasty being established. Whigs and Tories therefore combined to invite WILLIAM III (William of Orange of The Netherlands) to help drive James from the throne. William's arrival in England in November sent James in flight to Sheerness. Parliament declared that by running away he had abdicated. In February 1689 the throne was declared vacant and Parliament made William and Mary joint sovereigns. In January 1936 EDWARD VIII came to the throne. His wish to marry Mrs Wallis SIMPSON, an American divorcee, raised the issue of whether the monarch might so breach the rules of the

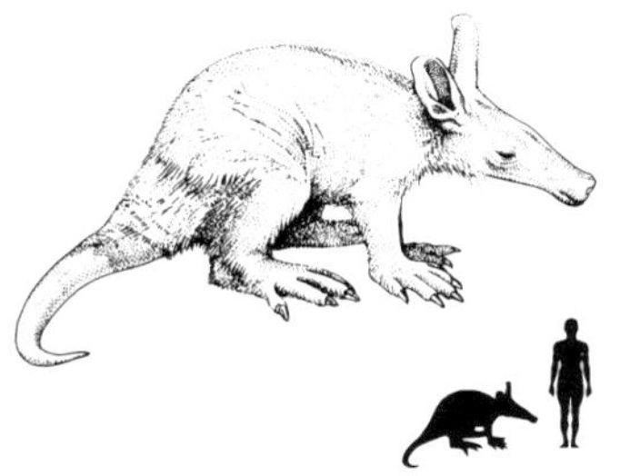

Aardvarks were named by Dutch settlers in southern Africa; the word means "earth pig".

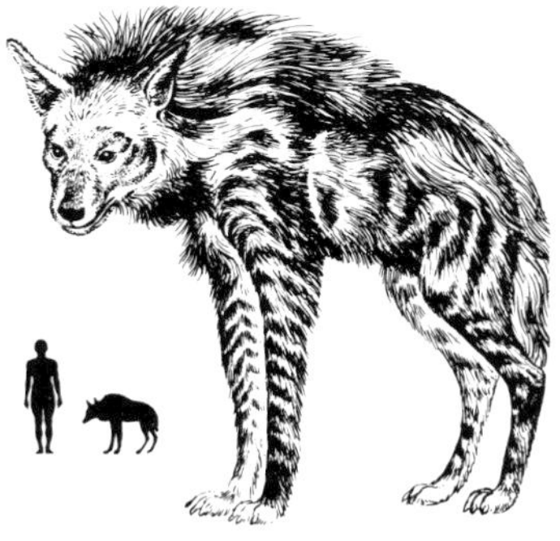

Aardwolf, a type of hyena, has small teeth and spends most of its time in burrows.

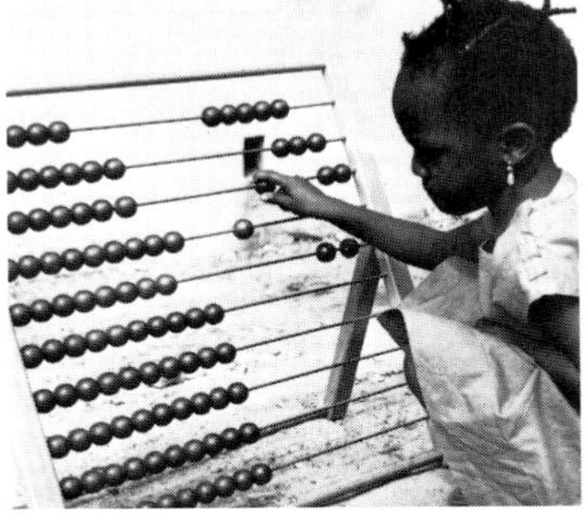

Abacus, ancient counting device still widely used. It can calculate square and cube roots.

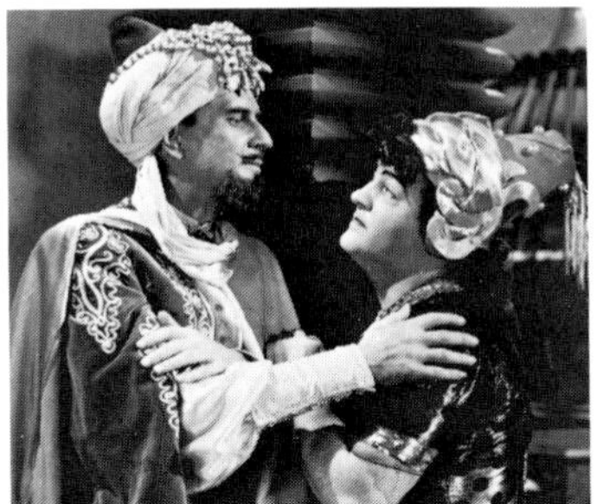

Abbott and Costello, the movie comedy duo, in a scene from *Lost in a Harem*, an MGM film.

MW = The Modern World NW = The Natural World PE = The Physical Earth SU = Science and the Universe

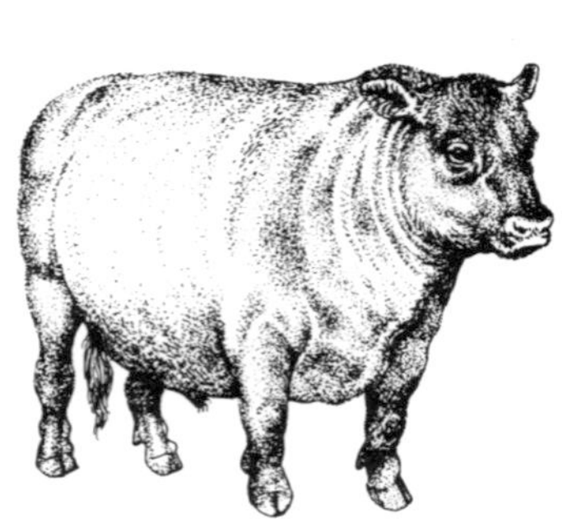

Aberdeen Angus, developed as a breed in the Scottish Highlands, is noted for its fine beef.

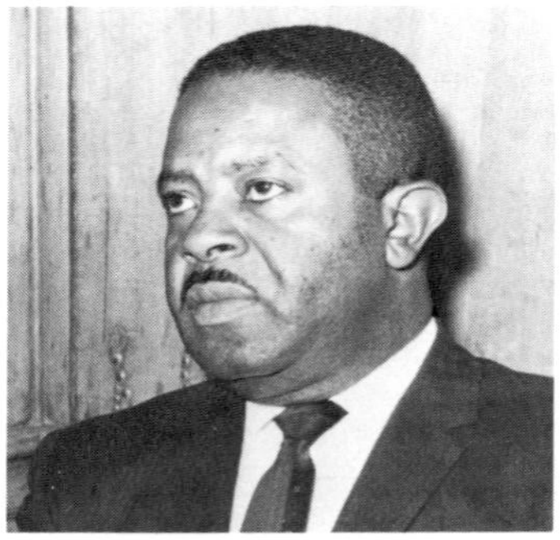

Ralph David Abernathy succeeded Martin Luther King in the civil rights movement.

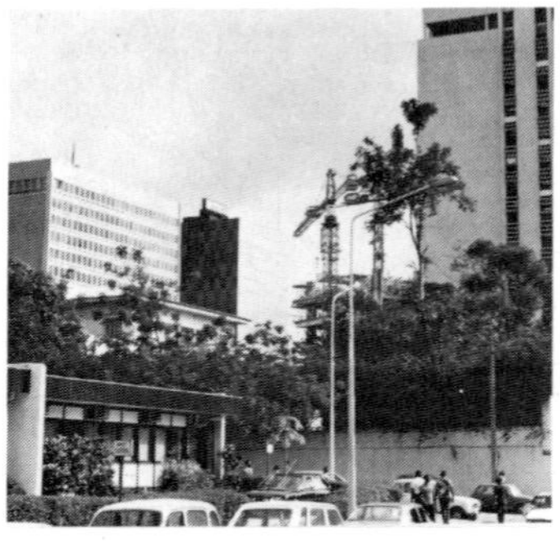

Abidjan, capital of the Ivory Coast, is the chief commercial centre and popular tourist resort.

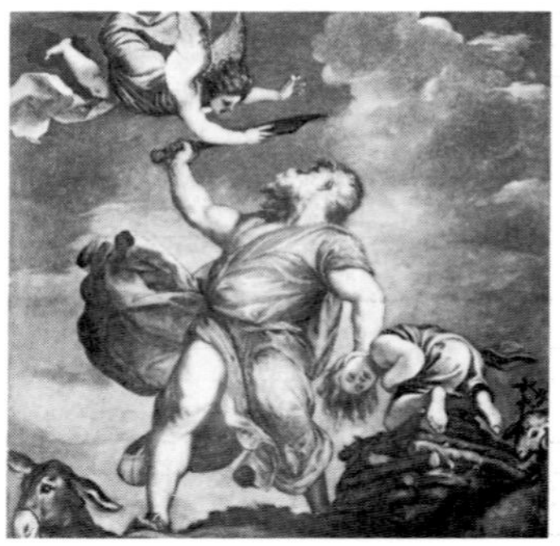

Abraham, first of the biblical patriarchs, was the traditional founder of the Hebrew people.

Church. The suggestion of a morganatic marriage (in which Mrs Simpson would not have taken any title nor any issue have the claims of an heir) was rejected. Stanley BALDWIN, the Prime Minister, insisted that the king abandon the proposed marriage or abdicate. On 10 December he announced the abdication. The throne passed to Edward's brother, the Duke of York, who became GEORGE VI. *See also* HC1 pp.292–293; HC2 p.225.

Abdomen, in vertebrates, that portion of the body between the chest and the pelvis containing the abdominal cavity and the abdominal viscera, including most of the digestive organs. In arthropods it is the posterior part of the body, containing the reproductive organs and part of the digestive system. *See also* NW pp.74–75.

Abduction, in law, forcible or fraudulent taking away or detention of a person, particularly of one – a child, for example, or an unmarried girl – who is legally in the custody of a third party.

Abdullah, Sheikh Muhammad (1905–), political leader of Muslims in Kashmir. He served as Prime Minister of Jammu and Kashmir after India's independence (1947–53) but was arrested in 1953 for advocating Kashmiri independence. Until the 1970s he was kept almost continuously in protective custody.

Abdul-Hamid II (1842–1918), Sultan of Turkey (1876–1909). He suspended the constitution and formed an alliance with Germany after the Treaty of SAN STEPHANO (1878) when Russia threatened the continuation of the OTTOMAN EMPIRE. He was deposed in 1909 after a revolt of the YOUNG TURKS. *See also* HC2 p.184.

Abel, in the Bible (Genesis), primal farmer killed by his brother CAIN, the primal hunter. *See also* MS p.184.

Abel, Sir Frederick Augustus (1827–1902), British chemist who devoted his career to the study of explosives. He was chemist to the War Department, invented cordite (with Sir James DEWAR) and wrote important works on the subject of explosives. *See also* MM pp.242–243.

Abel, Niels Henrik (1802–29), Norwegian mathematician. He studied and worked in Norway and later in France and Germany. He did research into the roots of 5th order equations and advanced the theory of elliptic functions. In 1829 he was appointed professor at Berlin but died before taking the post.

Abélard, Pierre (1079–1142), French philosopher and monk. In his famous work *Sic et Non* (*Yes and No*) he attempted to reconcile differences between the Fathers of the Church by the use of the Aristotelian method of dialectic. His views were condemned by the Council of Sens (1140). He is perhaps best known for his tragic love for Héloise, which inspired his work *A History of Misfortunes*. *See also* HC1 p.345.

Abeokuta, city in SW Nigeria, originally settled by Yoruba refugees from Fulani raiders of the Oyo Empire and from Yoruba civil strife. It was founded in *c.*1830. Pop. 226,361.

Abercrombie, Sir Leslie Patrick (1879–1957), British architect and town-planner. He was a leading consultant in the design and rebuilding of many British cities, including London, after WWII.

Abercromby, Sir Ralph (1734–1801), British general. As C-in-C in the West Indies, he captured Grenada, St Lucia, St Vincent and Trinidad. Sent to expel the French from Egypt, he defeated them at ABOUKIR (1801) but was killed in action.

Aberdeen, George Hamilton Gordon, 4th Earl of (1784–1860), British politician, Foreign Secretary under the Duke of WELLINGTON and Sir Robert PEEL. He was Prime Minister (1852–55) of the Whig-Peelite coalition that involved Britain in the CRIMEAN WAR. He resigned after Parliament voted to investigate the way the war was being waged.

Aberdeen, cathedral city in NE Scotland. It is an important economic centre and has gained prominence since the development of North Sea oil. Industries include shipbuilding and engineering. Pop. (1974) 179,575.

Aberdeen Angus, breed of beef cattle originally developed in Scotland. Small, black and hornless, they yield high-quality meat. *See also* PE p.226.

Aberdeenshire, former county in NE Scotland, now part of the Grampian Region. The area is drained by the rivers Ythan, Don and Dee, and its agricultural land is some of the finest arable and beefstock-rearing country in Scotland. Area: 5,104sq km (1,971sq miles).

Aberhart, William (1878–1943), Canadian evangelist and Social Credit premier of Alberta (1935–43). A social reformer, he unsuccessfully attempted to initiate a policy of "social dividends" and to license banks. He instituted labour legislation, tried to improve education and supported provincial autonomy.

Abernathy, Ralph David (1926–), US clergyman and civil rights leader. He succeeded Dr Martin Luther KING as the leader of the Southern Christian Leadership Conference after King's assassination in 1968 and continued to promote the non-violent civil rights movement. In 1968 he organized the Poor People's March on Washington.

Abernethy, Treaty of, the homage paid to WILLIAM I "the Conqueror" by Malcolm III of Scotland in 1072 after William had invaded Scotland to stop border raids.

Aberration, in physics, defect in lens and mirror images arising when the incident light is not at or near the centre of the lens or mirror. Spherical aberration occurs when rays falling on the periphery of a lens or mirror are not brought to the same focus as light at the centre; the image is blurred. Chromatic aberration occurs when the wavelengths of the dispersed light are not brought to the same focus; the image is falsely coloured. In astronomy, aberration is the apparent change of position of a celestial object due to the effect that the Earth's motion has on the direction of the arriving light. In medicine, aberration is a deviation from normal; mental aberration is a term used for a particular, but unspecified, mental disorder. *See also* SU p.100.

Aberystwyth, coastal borough in NW Dyfed, mid-Wales. Lying at the mouths of the Ystwyth and Rheidol rivers, it contains one of Wales' four university colleges. Pop. 10,680.

Abidjan, capital city of the Ivory Coast. Situated on the Ebire Lagoon, it is the chief port, administrative and communications centre. It is a popular tourist resort and the site of the Museum of the Ivory Coast. The important industries are chemicals and textiles. Pop. (1975) 650,000.

Abilene, city in central Texas, approx. 240km (150 miles) W of Fort Worth. It expanded rapidly when it became a cattle embarkation point on the Texas Pacific Railway. Pop. (1970) 89,653.

Ablation, in aerospace technology, the wearing away of a material by flaking, chipping, melting or vaporization. Nose-cones and leading edges of re-entry capsules and missiles are fitted with ablating material to remove excess heat. Good ablating materials such as quartz and PTFE have low thermal conductivity, high melting points, high specific heats and high heats of vaporization and fusion. Ablation, in GEOLOGY, is a measure of glacial loss through melting, evaporation, wind erosion, or calving (formation of icebergs). The term is sometimes used in geomorphology to describe erosion by the wind or by rivers or seas.

Abner, in the Bible (1 and 2 Samuel), Israelite army commander under SAUL. He transferred his loyalty from Ishbosheth, Saul's son and successor, to DAVID and was murdered by Joab, who envied Abner's close friendship with David.

Abnormal psychology, division of psychology concerned with behavioural disorders, eg psychotic disorders such as SCHIZOPHRENIA, psychoneurotic problems such as PHOBIAS, personality disorders and problems caused by brain damage or mental retardation. Unlike CLINICAL PSYCHOLOGY and PSYCHIATRY, abnormal psychology focuses on basic theory rather than on treatment. *See also* MS pp.136–143.

Åbo. *See* TURKU.

Abolitionists, people who sought to end slavery. William WILBERFORCE headed the movement that led to the abolition of Britain's role in the slave trade in 1807. Slavery was abolished throughout the British Empire by 1833. In the USA, Abolitionists were particularly active between 1820 and 1860, when they worked against the Fugitive Slave Law and helped slaves escape (through the "Underground Railroad", a series of hiding places). *See also* HC2 pp.46, 58–59, 135, 150–151.

Abomey, town in Benin, W Africa. A former slave centre and capital of the old Kingdom of DAHOMEY, it now serves as an agricultural market town. Pop. 34,000.

Abominable snowman, or Yeti, legendary ape-like creature of the HIMALAYAS. Expeditions to the area have, however, failed to find definite evidence of its existence. *See also* MS p.*21*.

Aborigines, original inhabitants of a country. Today the best known are the Australian Aborigines, who probably migrated from SE Asia about 30,000 years ago. At the beginning of European settlement in the 1780s there were about 300,000 Aborigines in Australia; by the mid-1970s there were about 110,000. Originally a semi-nomadic people who lived by hunting and gathering, many Aborigines have today become assimilated into the modern way of life. *See also* HC1 pp.124, *126*; MS pp.32–33, *35*, *250–251*, *255*; MW p.30.

Abortion, loss of a fetus from the womb before the full term of pregnancy, commonly called a miscarriage. Medically an abortion is a miscarriage that takes place within the first 28 weeks of pregnancy. A legal abortion is one sanctioned by law. In Britain, it may be deliberately induced by drugs or surgery if there is a risk to the mother's physical or mental health or if it is likely that the baby would be born with a severe abnormality.

Aboukir (Abū Qīr), village in Egypt on a promontory in the River Nile delta. In an adjoining bay Horatio NELSON defeated the French fleet on 1 Aug. 1798. Near the village NAPOLEON I defeated the Turks in 1799, and Sir Ralph ABERCROMBY defeated the French in 1801. *See also* NILE, BATTLE OF THE.

Abraham, in the Bible, progenitor of the Hebrews and founder of Judaism. Because of his dual role the expression "Abraham's bosom" gained currency among later Jews and is often used by Christians as a synonym for Heaven. He is also held in high esteem by Muslims who regard him as the ancestor, through his son Ishmael, of the Arabs.

Abraham, Plains of, Quebec City, Canada, scene of a decisive battle between the French and English. After the battle in 1759, during which both James WOLFE and Louis-Joseph de MONTCALM, the British and French commanders, were slain, the way was clear for the British to dominate eastern Canada. *See also* HC2 p.136.

Abrahams, Peter (1919–), Coloured South African novelist. Although self-exiled at the age of 20 to England and later to Jamaica, he centred most of his novels around his homeland. *Mine Boy* (1946), *The Path of Thunder* (1948), *Wild Conquest* (1951) and *A Wreath for Udomo* (1956) all deal with particular problems of South Africa.

Abrasives, hard and rough substances used to grind and polish surfaces. Some abrasives are used as fine powders, others in larger fragments with sharp, cutting edges. Most natural abrasives are minerals, eg diamond, garnet, emery, corundum, pumice, flint and quartz. Synthetic abrasives include silicon carbide, aluminium oxide, synthetic diamonds and boron carbide. Silicon carbide (called carborundum), first made in 1891, is produced by heating a mixture of pure silica sand and finely ground coke to about 2,400°C (4,530°F). Aluminium oxide, first made in 1897, is manufactured from rock bauxite (an aluminium ore) heated to over 1,100°C (2,000°F). Boron carbide is made by heating together a mixture of coke and boric acid. The manufacture of synthetic diamonds requires extremely high temperatures and pressures. *See also* MM p.43.

Abreaction, as described by Sigmund FREUD, a process of venting one's feelings after strong emotional arousal, eg a traumatic experience. He believed lack of abreaction could lead to a neurotic disorder. *See also* CATHARSIS.

Abruzzi, region in central Italy stretching from the Apennines to the Adriatic coast. It comprises four provinces; the town of L'Aquila is the capital. Its development has been restricted by its mountainous interior. Area: 10,794sq km (4,168sq miles). Pop. 1,205,100.

Absalom, name of several characters in the Bible. The most notable was the third son of DAVID, who murdered his brother Amnon because he had raped their sister. Plotting to seize the throne that SOLOMON would shortly inherit, he was killed by David's general, Joab.

Abscess, local inflammation of body tissue, caused by bacteria which destroy the body cells and leave a cavity, which then fills with pus.

Abscissa, in mathematics, the distance of a point from the *y*-axis in a CARTESIAN CO-ORDINATE SYSTEM. *See also* SU p.36.

Absinth, toxic, yellowish-green liqueur containing wormwood, anise and other aromatics. Because it can destroy the nerve centres in the brain, its production is now illegal in most Western countries.

Absolute music. *See* ILLUSTRATIVE MUSIC.

Absolute zero, the temperature at which all parts of a system are at the lowest energy permitted by the laws of quantum mechanics; zero on the KELVIN temperature scale (−273.16°C). At this temperature the entropy of the system is also zero although the total energy may be non-zero. *See also* SU pp.90–94.

Absolution, in Christian churches, formal act by a priest announcing to repentant sinners the forgiveness of sins they have confessed. The act is based on the authority given by Christ to his apostles to forgive sins (John 20:23). The Anglican, Roman Catholic and Orthodox Churches believe that this authority is transmitted to the bishops and priests and successors of the apostles (*see* APOSTOLIC SUCCESSION). The grace of forgiveness, however, flows from God, the clergy acting merely as his instruments. Absolution is pronounced either after a general CONFESSION made by the entire congregation at a public act of worship or after a private confession made by an individual to a priest (*see* PENANCE).

Absolutism, government with unlimited power vested in one individual or group. The term is primarily used to describe 18th-century European monarchies that claimed divine hereditary right to power. *See also* DIVINE RIGHT; MS pp.272–273.

Absorption, the taking in of one substance by another. Solids may absorb gases or liquids; liquids may absorb gases. In radiation the word is used of that part of radiant energy which is neither transmitted nor reflected by the surface which it hits.

Absorption Spectrum. *See* SPECTRUM.

Abstract art, art form that rejects the assumption that art must represent the external world; it is based on the belief that arrangements of colour and form can be valid in their own right as works of art. Such art may be classified as (1) semi-abstract, ie works based on nature but bearing little resemblance to natural forms; and (2) pure abstract, ie works consisting of shapes and colour wholly invented by the artist. Included in the first group are CUBISM, FUTURISM, VORTICISM, and the work of such artists as Pablo PICASSO, Paul KLEE, Henry MOORE and Alexander ARCHIPENKO. In the second group are included CONSTRUCTIVISM, DE STIJL, ACTION PAINTING, and the work of such artists as Wassily KANDINSKY, Piet MONDRIAN, Juan MIRO and Jackson POLLOCK. By 1870 the developing use of photography was already beginning to replace the need for strictly realistic painting and this, coupled with new ideas about the expressive potential of painting and sculpture, resulted in abstraction. The first paintings to achieve almost total non-representation were probably those by Kandinsky (by 1912), who freely abstracted from images inspired by landscape, myths and religious themes. The first totally abstract works were the flat, geometric compositions of the Russian painter Kasimir MALEVICH and the Dutch painter Piet Mondrian, and the glass, metal and wire constructions of the Russian artist Vladimir TATLIN. *See also* HC2 pp.152–153.

Abstract Expressionism, US art movement combining ABSTRACT ART and EXPRESSIONISM, most active in 1945–55, when it was acclaimed and emulated internationally. The paintings were generally large and abstract (sometimes with figurative elements), with dramatic colouring. The artists placed great emphasis on the process of painting, some using the technique of ACTION PAINTING. Stressing spontaneity and free expression, they rejected prescribed technical procedures, traditional aesthetic canons and the concept of a finished product. They included Willem DE KOONING, Jackson POLLOCK, Mark ROTHKO and Robert MOTHERWELL.

Abstract music. *See* ILLUSTRATIVE MUSIC.

Abstract of title, statement prepared for a purchaser or mortgagee of land and buildings summarizing documents, previous owners and other legal facts.

Absurd, Theatre of the, form of drama that developed and flourished in the 1950s, written and produced by playwrights such as Samuel BECKETT, Eugène IONESCO and Harold PINTER. Such drama attempts to abandon all logical processes and is based on unreal, absurd situations in which the characters are created deliberately out of harmony with their surroundings. Although its practitioners did not regard themselves as a school, they shared the basic belief that man's life is without meaning or purpose in a hostile universe.

Abu, isolated mountain in Rajasthan, NW India, 1,722m (5,650ft) above sea-level. It is famous for its Jain temples.

Abu al-Atahiyah (748–*c.*826), Arabic poet. A favourite at the court of HARUN AR-RASHID, he wrote sacred and ascetic verse in simple language.

Abu al-Fida (1273–1331), Arab historian and ruler. He was prince of HAMAH, Syria, from 1310 and sultan from 1320–21. He is best known for a geography, *Location of the Countries* (1321), and his *Abridgement of the History of Mankind* (1330), an Arabic history to 1329.

Abu Bakr (573–634), first Muslim caliph, successor to MOHAMMED. He accompanied Mohammed on the HEGIRA, and his daughter married the Prophet. After Mohammed's death, he became caliph. He subdued the hostile Arabian tribes, made conquests in Iraq, Iran (Persia) and Syria, and united the Arabian peninsula. He also began the extension of ISLAM as a major world religion. *See also* HC1 p.144.

Abū Dhabi (Abu Zaby), largest emirate of the UNITED ARAB EMIRATES; also the name of its capital city (pop. 46,000). Its economy is based almost entirely on the production of crude oil, extensive reserves – both onshore and in the Persian Gulf – having been discovered in the late 1950s. The centre of UAE expansion, Abū Dhabi has a new harbour and an airfield. It has been ruled since the 18th century by the Al-bu-Falah clan of the Bani Yas tribe, and there are long-standing frontier disputes with Saudi Arabia and Oman. Area: 67,340sq km (26,000sq miles). Pop. 235,700. *See also* MW p.173.

Abulcasis, or Abul Khasim (died *c.*1013), Arab physician. His most important work was a textbook of surgery and medicine, *al-Tasrif*, which was divided into sections on cautery, surgery and fractures.

Abu Nuwas (762–*c.*815), Arab poet who is known especially for love poems and wine songs. He lived mainly in Baghdad, and was a favourite of HARUN AR-RASHID.

Abū Qīr. *See* ABOUKIR.

Abu-Simbel, ancient Egyptian village on the W bank of the River Nile, and location of two temples built by RAMESSES II (*c.*1292–1225 BC). Part of the site became buried in sand and was not discovered until 1813. In the 1960s, with the construction of the new ASWAN High Dam, the temples were cut into giant blocks, raised and reassembled farther inland 60m (200ft) higher up, to prevent them being flooded by the lake behind the dam. *See also* HC1 pp.49, 331.

Abu Tammam (804–*c.*845), Arabic poet who compiled an anthology (*Hamasah*) of Arabic poets, and was himself a court poet in Baghdad.

Abu Zaby. *See* ABU DHABI.

Abydos, (Arabael Madfuna), ruined ancient city of Egypt, about 80km (50 miles) NW of THEBES and site of a series of temples dating from the 1st to the 25th dynasty (3100–*c.*664 BC) in which several stone tablets were found that contained information allowing a complete reconstruction of the succession of Egyptian PHARAOHS to be made.

Abydos (Chy), site in Phrygia, Asia Minor, opposite ancient Sestos at the narrowest point of the Dardanelles. It is near the site of an Athenian naval victory over the Spartans in 411 BC.

Abyssal fauna, animals living in the deepest ocean depths in conditions of low temperature, darkness and high pressure. They include crustaceans, fish, jellyfish and squids, many of which have adapted to their lightless environment by growing extended fins which detect food and warn of the presence of predators. As colour is no advantage in darkness most animals are either grey or black. Their expansible mouths, gullets and stomachs enable them to eat food as large as themselves, and many survive by scavenging scraps that sink from the upper ocean. *See also* NW pp.128–129, *129*.

Abyssal plain, the ocean floor below a depth of 3,000m (10,000ft) but excluding the deep OCEAN TRENCHES. The abyssal zone is characterized by stability of temperature in the range of −1°C to 5°C (30–41°F), the relative absence of water currents and the total absence of light. The slope of the floor is generally less than 1m per km (3.3ft per 1,000ft) and it is covered by deposits of biogenic oozes and non-biogenic sediments such as red clays. *See also* PE pp.82–83, *83*.

Abyssinia. Former name for Ethiopia. *See* MW p.75.

Abyssinian cat, exotic, short-haired domestic cat, probably originally from ancient Egypt. It has a wedge-shaped head; green, gold or hazel almond-shaped eyes; broad-based pointed ears; and a long, tapered tail. Its ruddy brown or brick-coloured coat has black-tipped hairs. The red variety lacks black pigment. *See also* KAFFIR CAT.

Acacia, or mimosa, evergreen shrubs and trees native to Australia and widely distributed in tropical and subtropical regions. They have small leaves and yellow or white flowers. The blossoms of one species, the WATTLE, form part of Australia's coat-of-arms. Height: 1.2–18m (4-59ft). Family Leguminosae; genus *Acacia*. *See also* NW p.200.

Académie Française, official French literary society, now part of the Institut de France. Originating as a private discussion group whose members were persuaded by Cardinal RICHELIEU to become an official body in 1635, the society is the guardian of the French language and of literary conventions. Its prestige is largely traditional and membership, gained by secret election, is no longer limited only to writers. *See also* HC2 pp.316, 317.

Academy, the name given to the school of philosophy founded by PLATO in *c.*387 BC and subsequently to institutions of learning throughout the world. Plato met his pupils in a garden outside Athens, said once to have belonged to a Greek hero called Academus. The school was known as the *Academia* and its followers as *Academists.* Plato's foundation was continued by Speusippus, Xenocrates of Chalcedon, Polemon of Athens and Crates.

Academies were formed throughout Europe in the 13th and 14th centuries, the most famous being the Academy of Floral Games, formed by troubadours in 1323, which each year awarded a golden violet to the best work of literature read by its author. In the 15th century the revival of Greek learning in Italy produced a wealth of academies, such as the Platonic Academy in Florence founded by Cosimo de'MEDICI in *c.*1400.

Between the 16th and 18th centuries

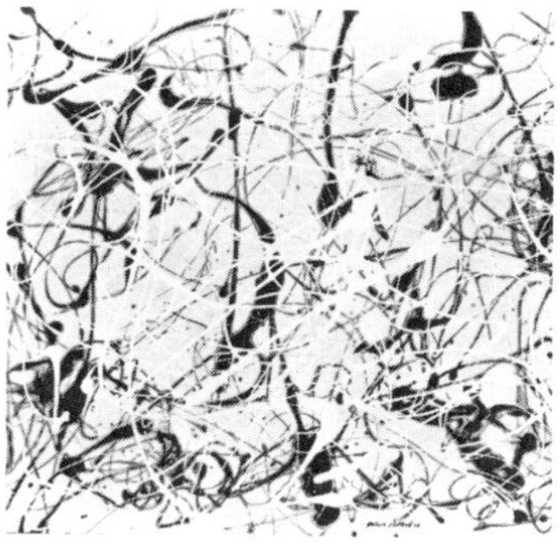

Abstract Expressionism; *Number 23,* an "action painting" by Jackson Pollock.

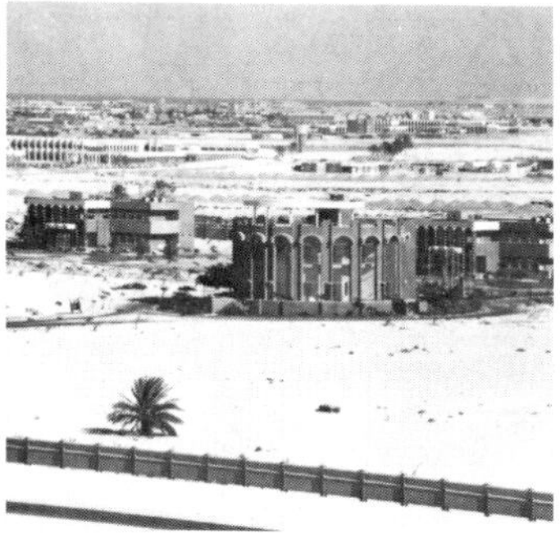

Abū Dhabi, capital of the largest of the oil-producing United Arab Emirates.

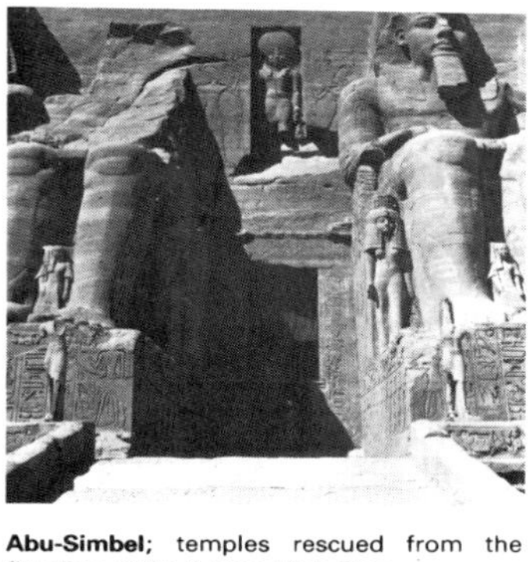

Abu-Simbel; temples rescued from the flooding at the Aswan High Dam.

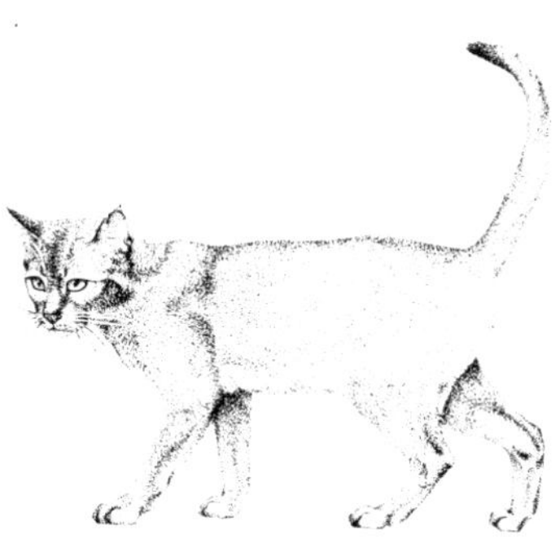

Abyssinian cats have long tapering tails, and are one of the most sensitive breeds.

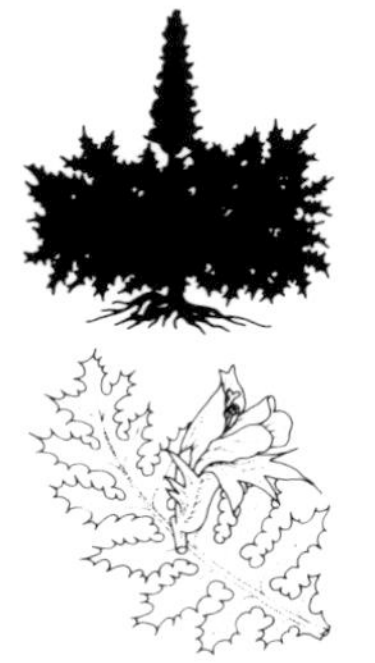

Acanthus was the plant that influenced the ornamentation on Corinthian columns.

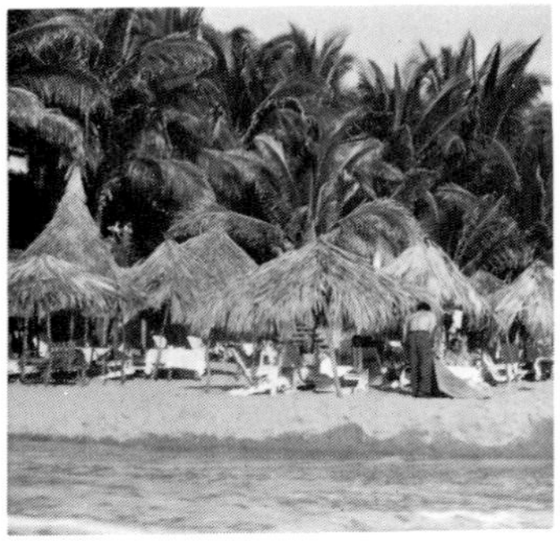

Acapulco, trading centre and popular winter resort 305km (190 miles) SW of Mexico City.

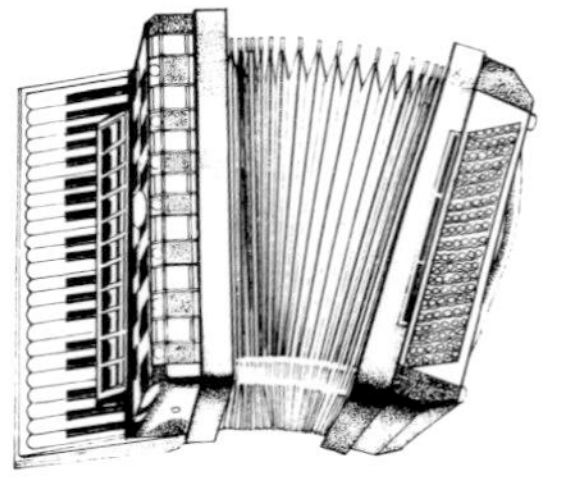

Accordions achieved great popularity as an accompaniment to folk dancing and singing.

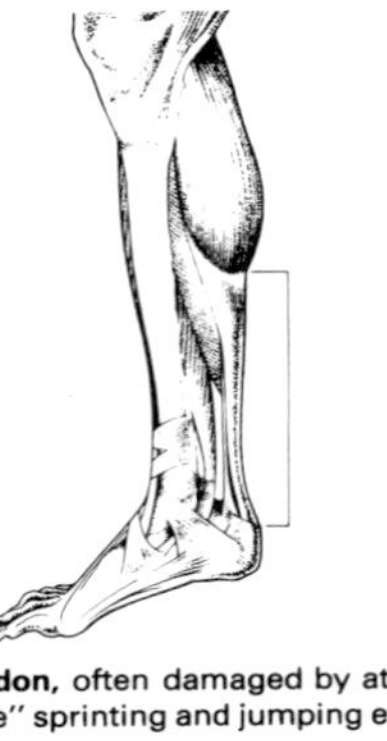

Achilles tendon, often damaged by athletes in "explosive" sprinting and jumping events.

academies changed from schools supported by private patrons to national institutions. The ACADÉMIE FRANÇAISE was founded in Paris in 1635 and the ROYAL SOCIETY in London in 1661. *See also* HC1 pp.75, 82, 302–303, 316.

Academy Awards. *See* OSCARS.

Acadia (French, Acadie), historic region in North America. It was settled by the French in the early 17th century and included present-day Nova Scotia, New Brunswick, Prince Edward Island and parts of Quebec and Maine.

Acanthocephala, phylum of spiny-headed parasitic worms once thought to be NEMATODES. They are identified by a retractable spiny proboscis and an elongated, cylindrical body. The young are parasitic in arthropods and the adults are parasitic in vertebrates, attaching themselves to the intestinal lining. Average length: 1–2cm (0.4–0.8in). *Echinorhyncus* is the main genus.

Acanthopterygii (Perciformes), perch-like fishes. The largest order of backboned animals, it contains about 8,000 species, including perches, rockfishes, sea basses, cichlids, mackerel and tunas, sunfishes, sailfishes and marlins. *See also* NW p.125.

Acanthus, thistle-like, perennial plant found in Africa, the Mediterranean region, India and Malaya. It has lobed, often spiny leaves and white or coloured flower spikes. *Acanthus spinosis* forms the pattern for the ornamentation on CORINTHIAN columns.

Acapulco, city on the sw coast of Mexico, noted for beautiful scenery, deep-sea fishing and luxurious hotels. Founded in 1550, it was for 250 years an important port on the Manila galleon route linking Spain and the Philippines. Pop. 352,673.

Accad. *See* AKKADIA.

Acceleration, rate of change of velocity. Average acceleration $\bar{\mathbf{a}}$ from velocity $\mathbf{V}_1$ to $\mathbf{V}_2$ in time t is $(\mathbf{V}_2 - \mathbf{V}_1)/t$. Instantaneous acceleration $\mathbf{a}$ is the value approached by $\bar{\mathbf{a}}$ as time t diminishes towards zero. *See also* SU p.74.

Acceleration, in economics, principle by which changes in the level of demand for consumer goods produce proportionately greater changes in the level of capital investment. This is a result of the machines' usually having a greater value than the annual output of the goods they produce, so that every £1 of additional income requires more than £1 in extra investment in replacements and additional machines. *See also* MULTIPLIER.

Accelerator, particle, device in which charged elementary particles, such as ELECTRONS or PROTONS, are accelerated so that they acquire high energies. Accelerators have a vacuum chamber (or ring) in which the particles move; the accelerating force is provided by electric and magnetic fields. Electrostatic accelerators are among the simplest; they have electrodes operating at high potential differences. An electric field produces the acceleration in field accelerators in which the particles are kept in a stable narrow beam by magnetic fields. Accelerators are used in the treatment of cancer, in the production of radioactive isotopes for medicine, research and technology, and in sterilizing food. Large, expensive high-energy accelerators are used in nuclear physics to produce other particles, such as mesons, neutrinos and anti-particles, by directing the accelerated beam at stationary targets or by causing two accelerated beams to collide. Proton synchrotron accelerators produce the highest energies so far attained. *See also* SU pp.66, 94.

Accelerometer, device used to measure acceleration. A simple example is a plumb bob suspended from the accelerating object, whose angle with the vertical is proportional to the acceleration. A more sophisticated version, used in ballistic missiles, is an electromechanical device that translates the acceleration into electric current.

Accessory, in law, a person associated with a criminal act. An accessory before the fact consults, encourages or advises the criminal. An accessory after the fact is one who, with knowledge of a crime, receives or assists the criminal.

Accolade, ceremony used in conferment of knighthood. Formerly the sovereign touched the new KNIGHT on the neck, the *accollé* (neck-blow) being given with the fist or the flat of a sword. Today the knight is tapped on each shoulder with a sword. *See also* CHIVALRY.

Accomplice, in law, person associated with another or others in the commission of a crime. Generally, unlike an ACCESSORY, he takes an active part in the crime.

Accordion, musical instrument with organ-like tone produced by air from a bellows that vibrates reeds. The melody is played on a piano-type keyboard with chordal accompaniment controlled by buttons. It was invented in 1822 and is widely used in folk music.

Accountancy, profession whose objective is to complete and be able to produce financial information for and about a company for the benefit of the management and the investing public. *See also* AUDIT; BOOK-KEEPING.

Accra, capital of Ghana, established around the three fortresses of James Fort (British), Crevecoeur (Dutch) and Christiansborg Castle (Danish). Today it is a major port and economic centre on the Gulf of Guinea. It is the site of the University of Ghana, founded in 1948, and the headquarters of the Defence Commission of the Organization of African Unity. Industries: engineering and chemicals. Pop. 851,600.

Accretion, continually growing or building up; a term frequently used to describe certain modes of geological deposition. *See* PE pp.112–113.

Acculturation, process of cultural change that occurs when one society meets another. Free acculturation results from friendly interchange and the acceptance of change by the affected society. Directed acculturation occurs when a society, by domination, forces another to change. *See also* MS pp.252–253.

Accumulator. *See* BATTERY.

Acetaldehyde (ethanal), colourless volatile inflammable liquid (CH_3CHO) made by catalytic oxidation of ethanol or catalytic hydration of acetylene. Properties: s.g. 0.788; m.p. −123.5°C (−189.4°F); b.p. 20.8°C (69.44°F). *See also* ALDEHYDE.

Acetate, salt or ester of acetic (ethanoic) acid; ie a compound containing the ion CH_3COO^- or the group CH_3COO-. It is used in synthetic acetate fibres, in lacquers and in acetate film. *See also* MM pp.54–56.

Acetic Acid (ethanoic acid), colourless corrosive liquid (CH_3COOH) made by the oxidation of ethanol, either by catalysis or by the action of bacteria. It is the active ingredient in vinegar, and has many uses in the organic chemicals industry. Properties: s.g. 1.049; m.p. 16.6°C (61.9°F); b.p. 117.9°C (244.4°F). *See also* CARBOXYLIC ACID.

Acetone (dimethyl ketone), colourless inflammable liquid (CH_3COCH_3) made by oxidizing isopropyl alcohol. It is a raw material for the manufacture of many organic chemicals and is a widely used solvent. Properties: s.g. 0.79; m.p. −94.8°C (−138.6°F); b.p. 56.2°C (133.2°F). *See also* KETONE; SU p.144.

Acetylcholine, chemical compound released by certain nerve cells that serve as a transmitter in the NERVOUS SYSTEM. Upon stimulation of a nerve cell, acetylcholine is released into a small channel (SYNAPSE) between it and the next cell, thus conducting the impulse from one cell to another. *See also* MS pp.38, 39.

Acetyl coenzyme A (acetyl Co A), derivative formed when PYRUVIC ACID is broken down during the formation of fat from carbohydrates. Co A acts as the carrier of the acetyl group which is the basic building block for the fatty acids. *See also* SU pp.154–155.

Acetylene (ethyne), colourless inflammable gas (C_2H_2), made commercially by the action of water on calcium carbide. It is used in oxy-acetylene cutting torches and as a raw material for making some organic chemicals. Properties: s.g. 0.905 (air 1.000); m.p. −80.8°C (−114.7°F). *See also* SU p.140.

Acetylsalicylic acid. *See* ASPIRIN.

Achaean League, two confederations of Greek city states formed in the area of the Peloponnese called Achaea (Akkaia). The first, founded in the 4th century BC, lasted for about 100 years. The second, founded in 280 BC, warred with Sparta, siding with Rome in 198 BC. In 146 BC Rome subjugated and dissolved the league.

Achaemenids, ruling dynasty of the first PERSIAN EMPIRE, which stretched from the River Nile as far E as modern Afghanistan. The dynasty was founded by CYRUS THE GREAT (*r.*559–529 BC) and named after his ancestor, Achaemenes. Its last ruler was DARIUS III (*r.*336–330 BC). *See also* HC1 pp.60–61, 80.

Acheampong, General Ignatius Kutu (1932–), President of Ghana from 1972. He enlisted in the army in the 1950s, serving in the UN Peace-Keeping Force in the Congo (1962–63). He led a bloodless military coup in 1972, proclaiming himself head of state.

Achebe, Chinua (1930–), Nigerian writer. His novels deal primarily with a search for identity in modern Africa and with the effect of cultural change on people's lives. *Things Fall Apart* (1958) depicts life in an African village before and after the arrival of missionaries. Other outstanding novels are *No Longer at Ease* (1960) and *Arrow of God* (1964). In 1971 he published a book of poems, *Beware Soul Brothers.*

Achernar, or Alpha Eridani, bluish-white main-sequence star in the constellation of Eridanus. Characteristics: apparent mag. 0.47; absolute mag. 1.3; spectral type B5; distance 75 light-years. *See also* SU p.226.

Acheron, in Greek mythology, a river of the underworld, one of five rivers within HADES, the realm of Pluto. CHARON carried the souls of the dead across either the Acheron or the Styx.

Acheson, Dean (1893–1971), US Secretary of State (1949–53). He was vigorously anti-Communist, and helped to develop the Marshall Plan, the Truman Doctrine and NATO. He encouraged support for Nationalist China (Taiwan) and UN involvement in Korea. *See also* HC2 p.234.

Acheson, Frank O. V. (1887–1948), New Zealand novelist, best known for *Plume of the Arawas* (1930), a historical romance of the Arawa tribe.

Acheulean culture, early Palaeolithic culture that derives its name from Saint-Acheul, near Amiens, France. The term is used in Europe for the later stages of the hand-axe tradition, and in Africa for the complete hand-axe series. *See also* MS p.31.

Achill, island off w coast of County Mayo, Republic of Ireland, connected to the mainland by bridge. It is mostly bog and heather, but is noted for its magnificent cliffs. Area: 145sq km (56sq miles). Pop. approx. 5,500.

Achilles, in Greek mythology, son of PELEUS and THETIS. A formidable warrior, he was the most fearless Greek hero of the TROJAN WAR – and of HOMER'S *Iliad.* Legend held him invulnerable from weapons because he had been dipped by Thetis in the River STYX at birth, except for the heel by which he was held. Achilles chose to seek glory by fighting at TROY, but an arrow shot by PARIS struck his heel and killed him.

Achilles tendon, strong elastic band of connective tissue in the back of the heel, also called the hamstring. It connects the gastrocnemius muscle of the calf of the leg to the heel bone. *See also* MS p.59.

Achinese, Sumatran tribe numbering some two million people. They were the dominant tribe of N Sumatra before the Dutch conquered the island in the 17th century.

Achondroplasia, hereditary disorder of the skeleton in which defective formation of cartilage (later converted to bone) results in a form of DWARFISM. It is characterized by a protruding forehead, well-developed trunk and short but strong limbs.

Achromatic vision, perception of the world in shades of white, grey and black – not in colours. It is normal in some animals

HC1 = History and Culture Vol. 1 HC2 = History and Culture Vol. 2 MS = Man and Society MM = Man and Machines

such as horses, dogs and cats, but in humans it is a defect that affects a small percentage. *See also* COLOUR BLINDNESS.
Acid, chemical compound containing hydrogen that can be replaced by a metal or other positive ion to form a SALT. Acids dissociate in water to yield hydrogen ions (H^+): the solutions are corrosive, have a sour taste, and give a red colour to litmus indicator. Strong acids are fully dissociated into ions whereas weak acids are only partly dissociated. *See also* BASE; SU p.102.
Acidosis, abnormal condition in which the blood becomes too acidic. It may be caused by a kidney complaint, diabetes or other diseases. Symptoms include muscular weakness and general malaise.
Ackermann, Rosemarie (née Witschas) (1952–), East German athlete. A high-jumper who uses the straddle technique, she won the 1975 European Championships and won the 1976 Olympic title.
Ackland, Rodney (1908–), British playwright. His plays include *Improper People* (1929); *Strange Orchestra* (1932); *The Dark River* (1943); *The Pink Room* (1952); and *A Dead Secret* (1957).
Acne, inflammatory disease of the sebaceous (or oil-producing) glands of the SKIN, probably caused by a hormonal imbalance, and resulting in skin eruptions ranging from mild blackheads and pimples to infected cysts. It is extremely common at PUBERTY, usually disappearing by the age of 20, but sometimes persists or periodically recurs later in life when a related disorder, acne rosacea (characterized by red blotchy lesions), may occur. *See also* MS pp.98, 164.
Aconcagua, mountain in the Andes range on the border between Argentina and Chile. The highest peak in the Western Hemisphere, 6,959m (22,831ft), it was first climbed in 1897.
Aconite, flowering plant of the genus *Aconitum.* Its roots provide the ALKALOID aconitine, used in medicine; in ancient times it was used as a poison. It is also called monkshood, friar's cap and wolfsbane. Family Ranunculaceae.
Acorn, the fruit of the OAK tree. The nut has some commercial value, being gathered for use as animal feed in various parts of the world. *See also* NW p.208.
Acorn worm. *See* BALANOGLOSSUS.
Acoustics, the study of the behaviour of sound waves. Architects use it in the design of public rooms such as concert and lecture halls. It assists engineers in the design of sound detectors such as microphones, and sound producers such as loud-speakers and ULTRASONIC devices. Audiologists use it to assess degrees of abnormality in the hearing of their patients. Musical acoustics is used in the design of musical instruments. *See also* SU pp.80–83.
Acquaviva, Claudio. *See* AQUAVIVA, CLAUDIO.
Acre, state in w Brazil, bordering Peru and Bolivia. Formerly a part of Bolivia, it was annexed to Brazil in 1903. The main agricultural products are coffee, rice and sugar. Area: 152,589sq km (58,915sq miles). Pop. 218,000.
Acre, unit of area measurement in English-speaking countries, equal to 4,840sq yd (0.405 hectares).
Acre (Akko), sea-port in N Israel on the Bay of Haifa, 16km (10 miles) N of Haifa. During the Crusades its possession changed hands many times, ultimately becoming the central Christian possession in Palestine. Pop. 33,900. *See also* HC1 pp.176–177.
Acridine, organic chemical compound, the molecule of which is a PYRIDINE ring held between two BENZENE rings. It is used in making drugs and dyes.
Acrilan, trademark for an acrylic fibre, chiefly acrylonitrile, made from acetylene and hydrogen cyanide. *See also* ACRYLIC; MM p.56.
Acromegaly, condition in which overproduction of PITUITARY growth hormones causes enlarged hands, feet and facial features. *See* MS p.101.
Acrophobia, irrational fear of high places, usually accompanied by obsessional thoughts of falling or jumping. People suffering from acrophobia often feel dizzy and nauseous (at times nearly paralysed) when they look down from a high place.
Acropolis, fortified high point of ancient Greek cities. The most famous one, at ATHENS, was walled before the 6th century BC and was used for religious purposes as well as defence. *See also* PARTHENON; HC1 p.73.
Acrostic, piece of prose or poetry in which the initial letters of each word or line spell a particular word or phrase: Aesthetic Conceit, Relying On Studying The Initial Characters.
Acrux, the binary star Alpha Crucis. About 270 light-years from Earth, with apparent magnitudes of 1.6 and 2.1, it is the 13th brightest star. *See also* SU pp.*260, 266.*
Acrylic, type of plastic, one of a group of synthetic, short-chain unsaturated carboxylic acid derivatives. Variation in the reagents and the method of formation yield either hard and transparent, soft and resilient, or liquid products. Their transparency, toughness and dimensional stability make acrylics useful for moulded structural parts, adhesives and paints. *See also* MM pp.54–56, 80.
Actaeon, in Greek mythology, huntsman grandson of Cadmus, King of Thebes. Turned into a stag by the goddess ARTEMIS when he surprised her bathing naked, he was torn to pieces by his own hounds.
ACTH (adrenocorticotropic hormone), protein hormone secreted by the anterior lobe of the PITUITARY GLAND at the base of the brain. It stimulates the cortex of the ADRENAL GLANDS to release steroid hormones. *See also* MS pp.64–65, 101.
Actin, protein involved in cellular contractile processes. Found mainly in muscle cells, it reacts with myosin to form actomyosin. *See also* MS pp.37, 59.
Actinide elements, group of radioactive elements with atomic numbers from 89 to 103; actinium (89), thorium, protactinium, uranium, neptunium, plutonium, americium, curium, berkelium, californium, einsteinium, fermium, mendelevium, nobelium and lawrencium (103). Each element is analogous to the corresponding LANTHANIDE SERIES element. The most important of the group is uranium.
Actinium, radioactive metallic element (symbol Ac) of the actinide group, discovered in 1899 by Andrew Debierne. It is found associated with uranium ores. Ac^{227}, a decay product of U^{235}, emits beta particles. Properties: at.no.89; s.g.10.07 (calc.); m.p.1,050°C (1,922°F); b.p. 3,200°C (5,792°F); most stable isotope Ac^{227} (half-life 21.6 yr). *See also* ACTINIDE ELEMENTS.
Actinomycosis, infection caused by the fungus *Actinomyces israeli*; it is common in cattle but also affects man. It produces multiple pus-filled abscesses usually in the sinus tracts about the neck and face, creating a swollen-jaw effect. PENICILLIN is the best treatment.
Actinopterygii, ray-finned fishes, one of the two subclasses of bony fishes (OSTEICHTHYES). They differ from the other subclass, the CROSSOPTERYGII, or tassel-finned fishes, in having fins containing little flesh and skeletal bone. The rayfins constitute 95% of all living fishes. *See also* NW pp.124–125.
Actinozoa. *See* ANTHOZOA.
Action painting, dripping and splashing paint on a canvas, on the basic assumption that the subconscious will take over and produce a work of art. The technique became widespread in the late 1940s and the 1950s. The term was first used about the work of the US artist Jackson POLLOCK. Other exponents of this style include Alan DAVIE, Robert MOTHERWELL, Mathieu EMILIO and Jean-Paul RIOPELLE. *See also* ABSTRACT EXPRESSIONISM; HC2 p.205.
Actium, Battle of (31 BC), naval battle in which the fleet of Octavian, commanded by AGRIPPA, defeated the fleets of MARK ANTONY and CLEOPATRA. After Cleopatra fled, Antony followed and Octavian captured most of his ships. Antony's army surrendered a week later, and Octavian became sole ruler of the Roman Empire. *See also* HC1 p.98.
Activator, in the life or pure sciences, agent that accelerates or augments activity, eg an impurity that increases luminescence.
Activists, The, Belgian political faction at the beginning of this century that worked for the creation of an independent Flemish state. During WWI they seemed, for a time, likely to achieve their object with the support of the German occupying forces in Belgium. But the strong hostility of the overwhelming majority of Belgians forced the Germans to abandon the plan.
Act of Congress, in the USA, statute adopted by CONGRESS. It overrides conflicting legislation from any other source, although the SUPREME COURT may rule that an Act of Congress is unconstitutional.
Act of God, in law, accident that arises from an unexpected and unforeseeable event, the result of natural causes, such as a flood or an earthquake.
Act of Parliament, statute (law) created in Britain when a Bill passed by the House of Commons and House of Lords receives Royal Assent. Embodying the supreme force of British law, an Act remains in force until it is repealed by Parliament.
Act of Supremacy, passed by the English Parliament in 1534. It made the monarch the supreme head of the Church of England and so asserted England's sovereign independence of Rome in matters both spiritual and temporal. *See also* HC1 266–267, 270.
Acton, John Emerich Edward Dalberg, 1st Baron (1834–1902), British historian of Europe-wide influence in the late 19th century. He planned the *Cambridge Modern History*, and is known for his saying "power tends to corrupt and absolute power corrupts absolutely".
Actors' Studio, theatre workshop founded by Elia KAZAN and others in New York in 1947. It became noted for the METHOD approach to acting, particularly under Lee STRASBERG, who joined in 1948 and taught many of the best young American actors. In the early 1960s, the Actors' Studio began also to produce plays on Broadway.
Acts of the Apostles, New Testament book describing the spread of the Gospel and the travels of St Paul, written by the author of St Luke's gospel.
Acupuncture, form of medical treatment in which long needles are inserted into the body at certain points. Of ancient Chinese origin, it enables surgery to be done with the patient conscious and free of pain. It has so far defied scientific explanation. *See also* MS p.123.
ACV. *See* AIR CUSHION VEHICLE.
Adad, or Hadad, in Babylonian mythology, the rain god, bringer of storms, giver of waters and withholder of the harvest. As war god he became the destroyer whose whirlwinds, thunderbolts and droughts brought havoc to the enemy.
Adadnirari, name of three Assyrian kings, the most famous of whom was Adadnirari III (*r.*810–783 BC), who in *c.*802 captured Damascus. *See also* HC2 pp.56–57.
Adalbert, Saint (*c.*956-97), first Bishop of Prague. He was elected bishop in 982 and came into conflict with the rulers of Bohemia over what he considered to be their insincere attitude towards the Church. In 994 he left to become a missionary in Prussia, where he was martyred.
Adam, in the Bible, first man and progenitor of all mankind, created from dust by God in his own image; Adam means "earth". He and his wife Eve were cast out of the Garden of Eden for sinning. Their sons were CAIN, ABEL and Seth. *See* MS pp.*184, 219.*
Adam, Adolphe Charles (1803–56), French composer of more than 60 operas and ballets, notably *Giselle.*
Adam de la Halle (or Hale) (*c.*1240–*c.*1288), French trouvère and composer, called "Le Bossu". He wrote the earliest French comedy, *Le Jeu de la Feuillée*, and the light opera *Le Jeu de Robin et Marion.*
Adam, Robert (1728–92), Scottish architect, best known of four brothers, all architects. The greatest British architect of the later 18th century, his refined neo-classical style was widely influential. He was equally brilliant as an interior decorator and furniture designer. The vast Adelphi complex, London, begun in

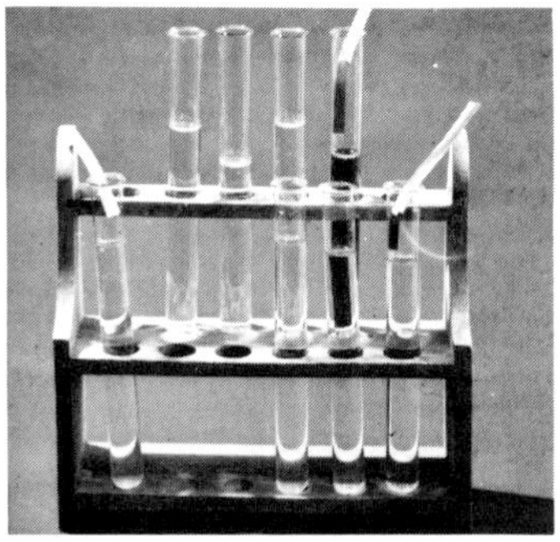

Acid is a chemical compound, often corrosive, that turns blue litmus paper red.

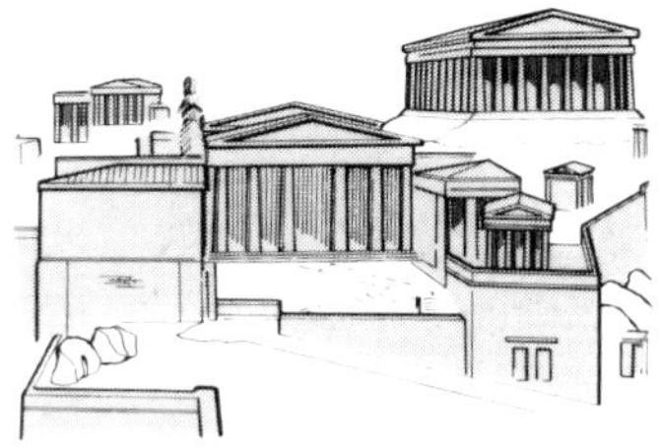

Acropolis, a fortress in ancient Greek cities, doubled as a religious and meeting place.

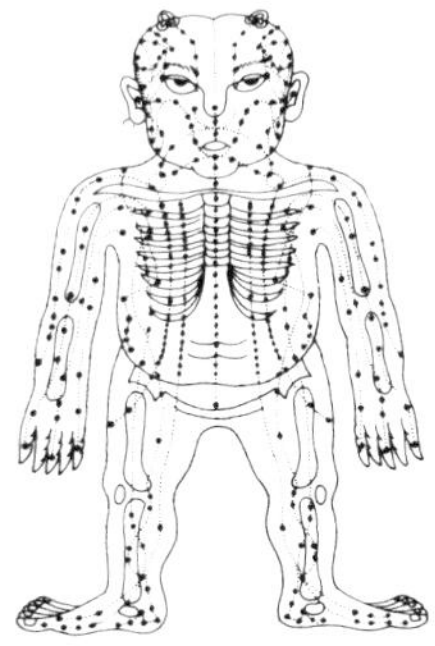

Acupuncture points, where needles are inserted, relate to different body parts.

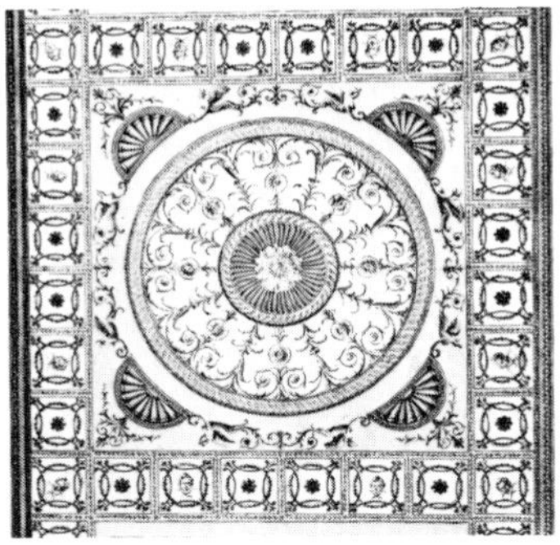

Robert Adam, architect and interior designer, won fame for delicate neoclassical designs.

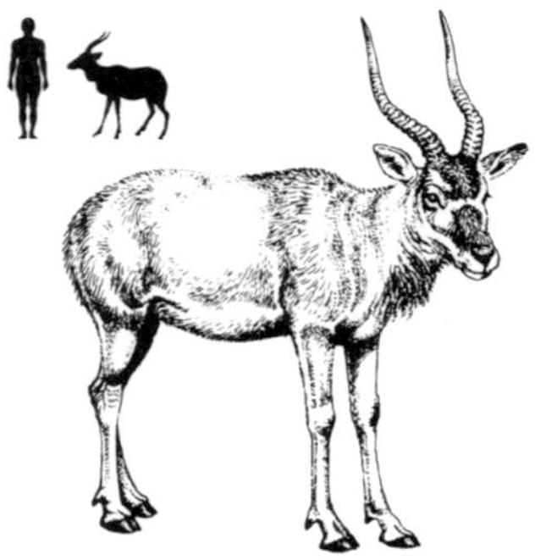

Addax, a North African desert antelope, can live without water for lengthy periods.

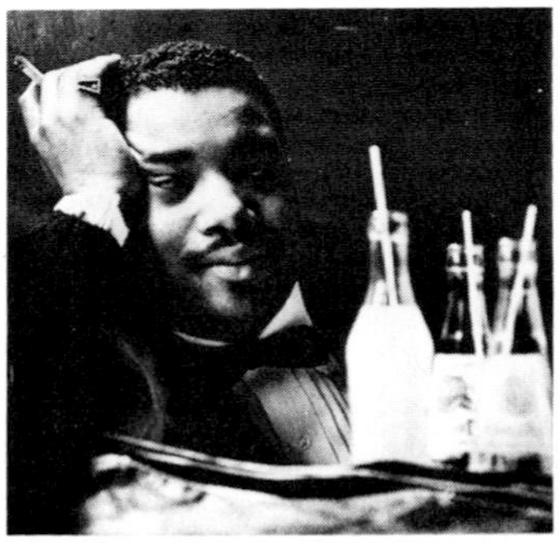

Cannonball Adderley championed "funk", a jazz style based on blues and gospel roots.

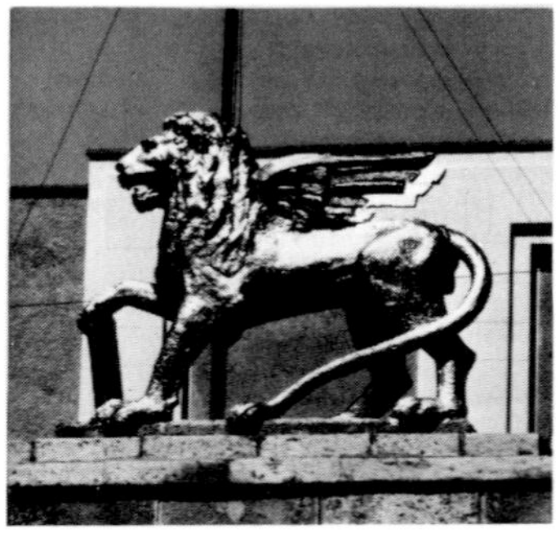

Addis Ababa, the high-altitude capital of Ethiopia, has this lion statue.

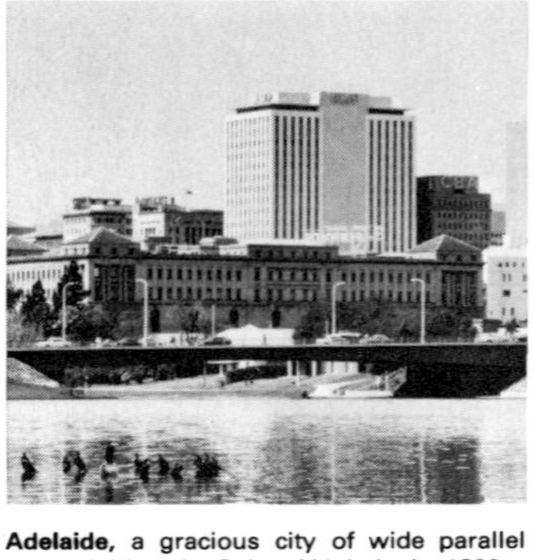

Adelaide, a gracious city of wide parallel streets laid out by Colonel Light in the 1830s.

1768, was his most ambitious project; his interior designs include Kedleston Hall, Derbyshire (1759), Kenwood House, London (1767) and Syon House, Middlesex (1762–69). *See also* HC2 pp.29, 30, 31, 71.

Adamnan, Saint (*c.*628–704), Irish monk who wrote the life of St Columba. He joined the Columbian brotherhood of Iona and became the ninth abbot there (679–704). He accepted Roman rules concerning Easter and the tonsure, but failed to implement them on Iona.

Adamov, Arthur (1908–70), Russian-born French dramatist. He pioneered the Theatre of the ABSURD, but abandoned it for Brechtian epic theatre.

Adams, Henry Brooks (1838–1918), US writer. A direct descendant of John and John Quincy ADAMS, his best-known work was *The Education of Henry Adams* (privately printed 1906, published 1918), an ironic analysis of a technological society.

Adams, James Truslow (1878–1949), US historian. He began his career on the New York Stock Exchange (1900–12), but later turned to writing. His *The Founding of New England* (1921) won the Pulitzer Prize for history.

Adams, John (1735–1826), second President of the USA (1797–1801). Stimulated by his radical cousin Samuel ADAMS, he became involved in anti-British agitation in the 1770s and helped to draft the Declaration of AMERICAN INDEPENDENCE. He served as Vice-President after 1789, and in office took a moderate Federalist position. *See also* HC2 p.64.

Adams, John Quincy (1767–1848), sixth president of the USA, son of John ADAMS. He was Secretary of State (1817–24), and helped the evolution of the MONROE DOCTRINE. He narrowly won the presidential election of 1824, but was defeated by Andrew JACKSON four years later.

Adams, Léonie (Fuller) (1899–), American metaphysical poet. Her works, which are marked with great sensitivity and a mystical view of nature, include *Those Not Elect* (1925) and *Poems* (1954).

Adams, Robert (*b.*1809), English gunmaker who patented his solid-frame, self-cocking, percussion revolving pistol in 1851. It was the English rival of the Colt. *See also* REVOLVER.

Adams, Samuel (1722–1803), American revolutionary patriot and signatory of the Declaration of AMERICAN INDEPENDENCE. As a member and clerk of the Massachusetts legislature (1765–74) he was the chief radical spokesman for revolution. He helped form several radical organizations and led the Stamp Act (1765) protest and helped to plan the BOSTON TEA PARTY of 1773. He was a delegate to the CONTINENTAL CONGRESS until 1781. *See also* HC2 p.64.

Adams, Walter Sydney (1876–1956), American astronomer, *b.*Antioch, Syria. Director of Mt Wilson Observatory from 1923, he devised a method of using the spectra of stars to measure their distances. *See also* SU p.229.

Adams, William (1564–1620), English navigator and first Englishman to reach Japan (1600). In 1613 he helped to establish an English trading factory for the East India Company. Adams remained in Japan with his Japanese wife and family, and continued his naval career with the trading company.

Adam's apple, protuberance at the front of the neck, where the LARYNX is encased in a protective surrounding of cartilage. It is more prominent in men than in women. According to fable it is part of the forbidden fruit which stuck in Adam's throat.

Adamson, Robert (1821–48), Scottish pioneer photographer. Working (1843–48) with David Octavius Hill, he made celebrated calotypes of many prominent Scots and of Edinburgh and rural scenes. *See also* MM pp.218–219.

Adana, city in S Turkey, on the Seyhan River, 48 km (30 miles) from the Mediterranean coast. Capital of Adana province, it was the scene of the Armenian massacre of 1909 and site of the Anglo-Turkish conference, led by Churchill, in 1943. Industries: tobacco, textiles, explosives. Pop. (1973) 383,046.

Adapazari, town in NW Turkey, capital of Sakarya province. It is the trading centre for the surrounding agricultural area. Pop. (1970) 101,590.

Adaptation, adjustment to the surroundings by people and other living creatures, including plants. The process is essential for survival and may be both biological and social. Some animals and plants have adapted to difficult environments by variations in structure, propagation or organization within communities. Of all mammals, man has adapted most successfully to environmental changes. As the most highly evolved of all forms of life on earth he is able to live in widely different environments and has made technological advances that have enabled him to alter his physical surroundings and exploit them to the full. Social adaptation in humans involves learning to live in interdependence with other people. *See also* ADAPTIVE RADIATION; EVOLUTION; MS pp.250–253, 262–263.

Adapter, device used in chemical or electrical apparatus. In chemistry it is a glass tube with ground-glass sockets for joining glassware. In electricity it is an attachment for connecting an appliance to a socket having a different type of terminal.

Adaptive radiation, in biology, divergent ADAPTATION, a simultaneous divergence of several populations of one parent type into different forms, each suited to a different environment. If a species in time becomes distributed over several types of surroundings, the populations of each area may develop specialized features suited to the new environment. *See also* EVOLUTION; NW p.196.

Adda, Italian river, 312km (194 miles) long, which rises in the Alps and flows through Lake Como and then SE across the Lombardy Plain to join the River Po about 11km (7 miles) W of Cremona.

Addams, Jane (1860–1935), American social reformer. In 1889 she founded Hull-House, Chicago, an early social settlement house, and she pioneered labour, housing, health and legal reforms, as well as campaigning for female suffrage, pacifism and the rights of immigrants. She shared the 1931 Nobel Peace Prize with Nicholas Murray BUTLER.

Addax, type of antelope found in the deserts of N Africa and Arabia. Noted for its long, twisting horns, the addax usually runs in herds of 5-20 animals, led by an old male. Heavily built and comparatively slow, it is becoming increasingly rare because of overhunting. Species *Addax nasomasculatus. See also* NW p.220.

Adder, any of several snakes in various parts of the world, some poisonous and others harmless. The European viper (*Vipera berus*) is called an adder in Britain. The puff adder (*Bitis arietans*) is a large African viper, and the death adder (*Acanthophis antarticus*) a dangerous Australian elapid. *See also* NW pp. 200, 205.

Adderley, Cannonball (1928–75), US jazz alto saxophonist, *b.* Julian Edwin Adderley. He came to prominence with the Miles Davis sextet in the late 1950s and then formed his own jazz group with his brother Nat, playing a popular form of jazz called "funk".

Addiction, use of a habit-forming substance, such as a drug, resulting in psychological or physiological dependence (or both). Characteristics of addiction include a tendency to increase the dosage and an overwhelming urge to continue taking the drug, without which withdrawal symptoms usually occur. One of the most common forms of addiction is ALCOHOLISM, in which someone becomes dependent on alcoholic drinks. Treatment may include group therapy (perhaps through an organization such as ALCOHOLICS ANONYMOUS) and aversion therapy with drugs such as ANTABUSE. Drug addiction is generally associated with hard drugs such as AMPHETAMINES and HEROIN; but soft drugs, such as barbiturates and tranquillizers, can also be addictive. *See also* MARIHUANA; MS pp.104–105.

Addington, Henry, Viscount Sidmouth (1757–1844), the first British Prime Minister (1801–04) not of a noble family. He later served as Home Secretary (1812–22) and became widely unpopular because of his treatment of militant working-class agitators and others pressing for parliamentary reform. The PETERLOO MASSACRE occurred during his term of office.

Addinsell, Richard Stewart (1904–), British composer noted for his film scores and incidental music, eg *Warsaw Concerto.*

Addis Ababa, capital and largest city in Ethiopia. The city, originally called Finfinnie, was chosen as the capital of the Shoa Kingdom in 1886 and became the capital of Ethiopia in 1889; its name means "new flower" in Amharic. Situated in the centre of the country, it is an important communications centre and the terminus of Ethiopia's major rail link to the sea through the Republic of Djibouti. It is the headquarters of the Organization of African Unity and has a university (1961) noted for its museum of art and ethnology. Industries: tanning, textiles and tobacco. Pop. (1975 est.) 1,167,267. *See also* MW p.75.

Addison, Christopher, 1st Viscount (1869–1951), British politician. He entered Parliament as a Liberal in 1910, but after differences with Lloyd George (1921) joined the Labour Party. An able administrator, he headed various ministries, was created a baron (1937), and was leader of the House of Lords (1945–51).

Addison, John (1920–), British composer known particularly for his theatre and film scores, as well as orchestral and chamber music. His works include the overture *Heroum Filii* (1951).

Addison, Joseph (1672–1719), English poet, essayist and politician. His outstanding essays were published in the periodicals the *Tatler* (1709–11) and the *Spectator* (1711–12 and 1714) and cover the fields of literature, philosophy, politics and morals. He worked closely in collaboration with his schoolfriend Richard STEELE. His poetry includes the verse tragedy *Cato* (1713). A Member of Parliament after 1708, he was appointed secretary of state in 1717 by the Whig government. *See also* HC2 p.34.

Addison, Thomas (1793–1860), British physician who identified the adrenal hormone deficiency known as Addison's disease (1855) and Addison's anaemia. After 1837 he worked at Guy's Hospital, London, and was the joint author of *Elements of the Practice of Medicine* (1839). *See also* ADRENAL GLANDS.

Addition, mathematical operation signified by + (plus sign), interpreted for the natural numbers, as the number of members of a set produced by combining other sets. *See also* SU p.28.

Addled Parliament, 5 April to 7 June 1614, called by JAMES I to vote finances to pay his debts. The Commons' demand that extra-parliamentary taxation, or impositions, be stopped and that the clergy deprived of their livings in 1604 be reinstated were refused and the Parliament was dissolved without any act being passed or supplies voted. *See also* HC1 pp.286–287.

Adelaide (1792–1849), Queen of Great Britain, wife of WILLIAM IV and daughter of George, Duke of Saxe-Coburg Meiningen. She married William, then Duke of Clarence, in 1818.

Adelaide, capital of the State of SOUTH AUSTRALIA. Founded in 1836, it is situated at the mouth of the Torrens River on the Gulf of St Vincent. It is especially noted for its churches and fine cathedrals. The city's natural history museum dates from 1895 and it has two universities, Adelaide (1874) and Flinders (1966). It provides port facilities for an extensive hinterland and exports wool, fruit, wine and wheat. The principal industries are engineering, electronics, chemicals and textiles. Pop. 868,000.

Adelard of Bath (*fl.* 12th century), English scholastic philosopher with great knowledge of Arabic learning, whose important work dealt with NOMINALISM and REALISM.

Aden, seaport city on the Gulf of Aden, 160km (100 miles) E of the Red Sea and capital of the People's Democratic Republic of Yemen, the former Aden

Protectorate (1936–67). A Roman trading port, its importance diminished with the discovery of the cape route around Africa to India in the 15th century. It was held by the Ottoman Turks from 1538 until *c.* 1802 when it was taken by Britain and governed by it as part of India until 1937. On becoming a free port in 1850, and with the opening of the Suez Canal in 1869, its importance greatly increased. It was made a crown colony in 1937 and the surrounding territory became the Aden Protectorate. On joining the British sponsored Federation of South Arabia in 1963, the National Liberation Front (NLF) forced the demise of the federal government and the independent republic of Southern Yemen was established (1967), known since 1970 as PDR Yemen. Industries include cigarette manufacturing, oil and salt refining. Pop. 250,000. *See also* MW p.184.

Aden, Gulf of, western arm of the Indian Ocean between Yemen and Somalia. On the west it is linked with the Red Sea by the strait known as Bab el Mandeb and is part of the trade route between the Mediterranean Sea and the Indian Ocean.

Adenauer, Konrad (1876–1967), politician, Chancellor of West Germany (1949–63). He was Lord High Mayor of Cologne from 1917 to 1933 and was later twice imprisoned by the Nazis. He helped to create the Christian Democratic Union, the dominant post-war party of West Germany, and was its leader (1946–66). In 1949 he was elected the first chancellor of the Federal Republic of Germany. As Chancellor he promoted German reconstruction, led Germany to membership of NATO (1955), and campaigned for European unity and the establishment of the COMMON MARKET (EEC). *See also* HC2 pp.234, 258.

Adenine, nitrogen-containing organic base of the PURINE group found combined in the nucleic acids. *See also* SU p.154.

Adenoids, mass of lymphoid tissue in the upper part of the THROAT behind the NOSE. When infected, they swell, interfering with breathing; they may then be surgically removed, often with the TONSILS. *See also* MS p.88.

Adenoma, type of TUMOUR (often benign) with a gland-like structure occurring in glands such as the thyroid or pituitary.

Adenosine triphosphate (ATP), nucleotide consisting of adenine, D-ribose, and three phosphate groups. Hydrolysis of ATP to give ADP (adenosine diphosphate) or AMP (adenosine monophosphate) and phosphate is accompanied by a large change in free energy. This hydrolysis is coupled to a phosphorylation reaction in biological systems to provide energy. ATP is synthesized from ADP by photosynthesis using energy from sunlight. *See also* NW p.26; SU p.154.

Adeodatus II, Saint (*d.* 676), Roman Benedictine monk, Pope from 672 to 676. He devoted much of his life to the restoration of derelict church buildings.

Ader, Clément (1841–1926), French pioneer of flight. A self-taught engineer and inventor, he was the first man to demonstrate that a heavier-than-air machine could become airborne.

Adhesion, the attraction of the molecules of one substance for the molecules of another when both substances are in contact. An adhesive is used to join substances whose molecules would not otherwise attract, although a strong joint can sometimes be made by pressing together two clean, carefully ground and matched surfaces. *See also* COHESION.

Adhesion, in medicine, fibrous band of new tissue that may bind together internal parts of the body or interfere with normal functioning by looping round and constricting the blood supply. Most adhesions result from inflammation or, more rarely, surgical operations.

Adiabatic process, thermodynamic change without any gain or loss of heat or mass into or out of a system during expansion or compression of the gas or fluid composing the system. Truly adiabatic changes must take place in short time intervals so that the heat content of the system remains unchanged, or else the system must be perfectly insulated (a practical impossibility). *See also* ISOTHERM; SU p.84.

Adige (Etsch), second longest river in Italy. It rises in the Tyrolean Alps, N Italy, and enters the Adriatic Sea S of Chioggia. A dam supplies hydroelectric power and irrigation. Length: 410km (255 miles).

Adi Granth, or Granth Sahib, sacred book of SIKHISM. It serves as the centre of devotion and worship. The book is a collection of the writings of Sikh, Hindu and Muslim religious leaders. Its compilation was begun in 1604 and it was declared holy in the 18th century.

Adipose tissue, also known as fatty tissue, connective tissue of body cells which are distended by the storage of large globules of fat.

Adirondack Mountains, circular mountain group located in NE New York State, reaching from Mohawk valley in the south to the St Lawrence River in the north. There are many scenic lakes, gorges and waterfalls. Much of the area has been set aside as the Adirondack Forest Preserve. It is noted for its resorts including Lake Placid and Lake George. Highest point: Mount Marcy, 1,629m (5,344ft).

Aditi, in Hindu mythology, the mother of the world and of the gods, sustainer of earth and sky. Her name means "free from bonds" and she is seen as the personification of the infinite.

Adjutant stork, large scavenging bird found in Africa, India and SE Asia, named for its military gait. It has white, black and grey plumage and throat pouches; it feeds on carrion. Length: up to 152cm (60in). Species *Leptoptilos crumeniferus.*

Adler, Alfred (1870–1937), Austrian psychiatrist. After working with Sigmund FREUD (1902–11), Adler broke away to found his own school of "individual psychology". Adler postulated that striving for social success and power was fundamental in human motivation. According to his theory, individuals develop problems and maladjustments when they cannot surmount feelings of inferiority acquired in childhood. Adler's concept of the "creative self" stressed the positive role that the individual plays in realizing his own goals. *See also* MS p.*149.*

Adler, Larry (1914–), US harmonica player. He played with harmonica groups in the 1930s, then appeared in solo concerts and Hollywood films. He has performed in many concerts, displaying unequalled virtuosity, and has commissioned new works by classical composers, including VAUGHAN WILLIAMS.

Admiral, naval officer equivalent in rank to an army general. There are several grades of admiral, eg rear-admiral and vice-admiral.

Admiral's Cup, international yacht-racing competition held since 1957 every two years at Cowes, Isle of Wight. Teams of three yachts from each participating country compete in four events, two offshore (Channel and Fastnet races) and two inshore during COWES Week.

Admiralty, cabinet-level department in charge of the ROYAL NAVY until 1964. Set up by HENRY VIII, it was directed by a board of five lords commissioners. The Admiralty became the Navy Department within the Ministry of Defence.

Admiralty Islands, volcanic island group in the Bismarck Archipelago, part of Papua New Guinea. Manus is the largest island in the group. They were discovered in 1616. Area: 2,072sq km (800sq miles). Pop. (1971) 23,000.

Adobe brick, building brick formed from a clay of the same name, found in SW USA. The clay is mixed with water and straw, moulded into blocks and dried in the sun. The bricks are an excellent construction material; some have lasted for thousands of years in arid climates.

Adolescence, time of life – between PUBERTY and maturity. *See* MS pp.164–167.

Adonis, in Phoenician and Greek myth, a youth of remarkable beauty. He was the favourite of APHRODITE and PERSEPHONE. ZEUS decided that Adonis should spend half of the year with Persephone, queen of the underworld, and half with Aphrodite.

Adoption, act of a person taking as his child one who is not his own by fact or law. Often in ancient times an adult male was adopted in order to continue a family line. Today's laws require that the adopting parents satisfy the authorities that they are suitable, and that the child (when over a specified age) consents to being adopted.

Adoration of the Lamb, painting by Jan van EYCK. *See* HC1 p.252.

Adoration of the Shepherds, painting by CORREGGIO. *See* HC1 p.*259.*

Adour, river in SW France, rising in the Pyrenees and flowing in a wide arc NW for 335km (208 miles) until it empties into the Bay of Biscay.

Adowa. *See* ADUWA.

ADP. *See* ADENOSINE TRIPHOSPHATE.

Adrenal glands, pair of small endocrine glands situated above the KIDNEYS. Each consists of a cortex, or outer layer, and medulla, or inner part. Essential to human life, the cortex produces many STEROIDS (including CORTISONE) that regulate the blood's salt and water balance and are concerned with carbohydrate metabolism. The medulla produces two hormones: ADRENALINE (epinephrine) during emergency or stress, which increases the immediate energy supply, blood pressure and heart rate; and noradrenalin (norepinephrine), which mediates nerve impulses. *See also* MS pp.64–65, 101.

Adrenaline, or epinephrine, chief hormone secreted by the medulla of the ADRENAL GLANDS. It stimulates the nervous system, raises metabolism, increases pulse rate and increases blood pressure when released naturally or injected intravenously. It is often administered to treat anaphylactic shock. *See also* HORMONE; MS pp.64–65.

Adrenocorticotropic hormone. *See* ACTH.

Adrian, name of six popes. One of the most notable was Adrian I (*r.* 772–95). Threats to the papal authority from the Lombards led him to seek help from CHARLEMAGNE, who confirmed PEPIN's donation of lands to the papacy and expanded its estates. Adrian IV (*r.* 1154–59), born as Nicholas Breakspear (*c.* 1100–59), was the only English pope. In 1152 he went to Scandinavia where he organized the Church. He crowned FREDERICK I (Barbarossa) Holy Roman Emperor in 1155, but their relationship was not always amicable. Adrian acknowledged the authority of William of Sicily, against the wishes of the Emperor. He was said to have given Ireland as a fief to HENRY II of England. Adrian VI (*r.* 1522–23), born as Adrian Florensz Boeyens, a Dutchman, was the last non-Italian pope. He tried to restrain the extravagance of the papal court, but died before he could make lasting reforms. *See also* HC1 p.186.

Adrian, Edgar Douglas Adrian, Baron (1889–1977), British electro-physiologist, professor of physiology at Cambridge (1937–51). His important discoveries concerning the function of nerve cells, including the "all-or-none" law, earned him a share with C. S. SHERRINGTON of the 1932 Nobel Prize in physiology and medicine. He wrote *The Mechanism of Nervous Action* in 1932.

Adrianople. *See* EDIRNE.

Adriatic Sea, shallow arm of the Mediterranean Sea between Italy and Yugoslavia. It has a comparatively high salinity and only slow-moving currents. Control of effluents is poor in the surrounding countries, particularly in Italy (the most industrially developed), and as a result the Adriatic is the most polluted part of the Mediterranean Sea. Lobsters and sardines are the chief catches of local fisheries. Length: approx. 805km (500 miles); max. depth: 1,230m (4,035ft).

Adsorption, attraction to the surface of a solid or liquid of a gas or liquid, unlike absorption which implies incorporation. The amounts adsorbed and the rate of adsorption depend on the structure exposed, the chemical identities and concentrations of the substances involved, and the temperature.

Adula massif, mountain group in the Lepontine Alps, Switzerland, rising to 3,400m (11,155ft) above sea-level.

Aduwa (Adowa), town in Ethiopia, about

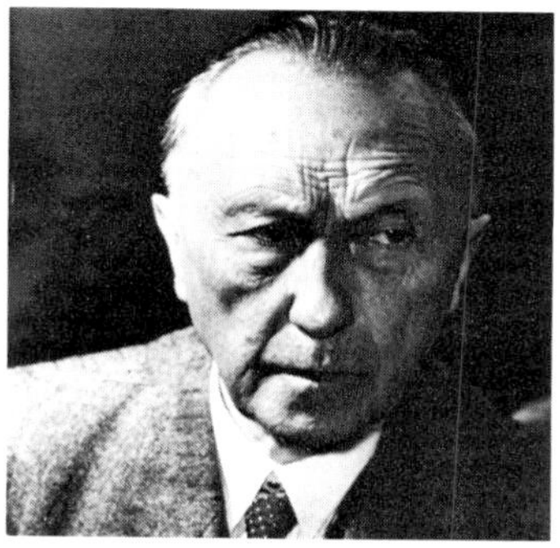

Konrad Adenauer, twice imprisoned by the Nazis, became chancellor of Germany.

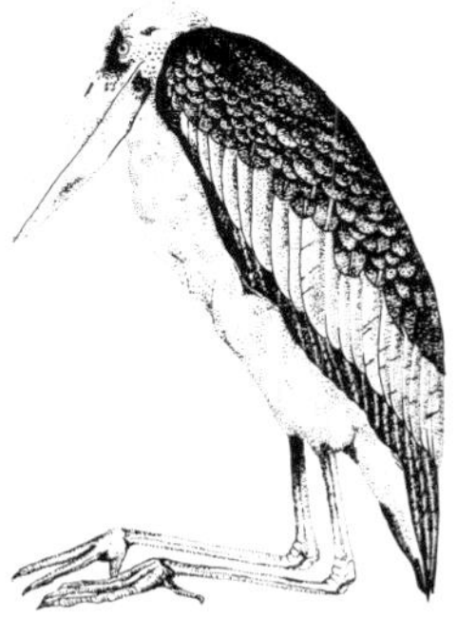

Adjutant stork, so called for its military gait, is the largest member of the stork family.

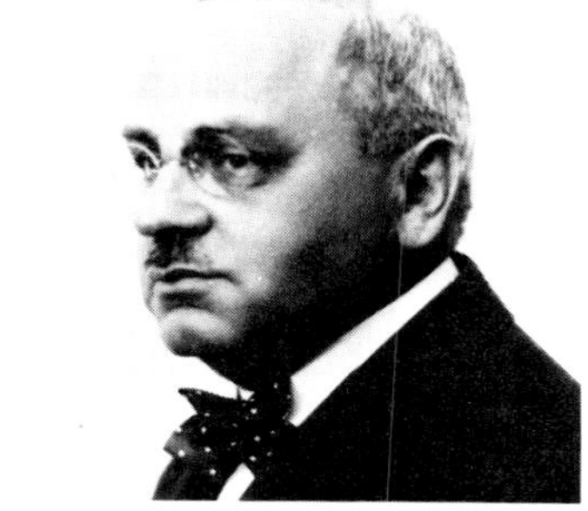

Alfred Adler, who broke away from Freud, originated the idea of "inferiority complex".

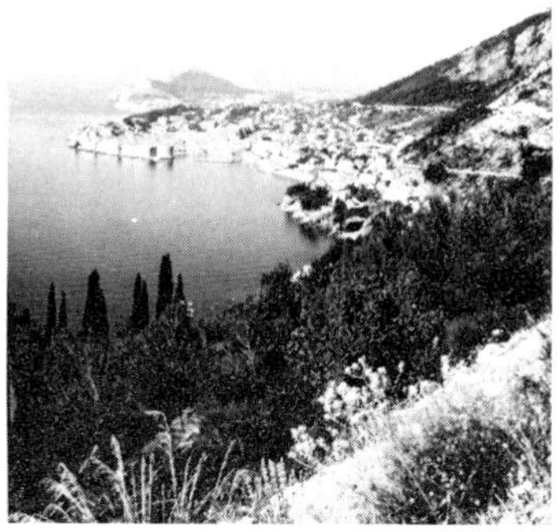

Adriatic Sea is a popular tourist region named after Adria, a once important port.

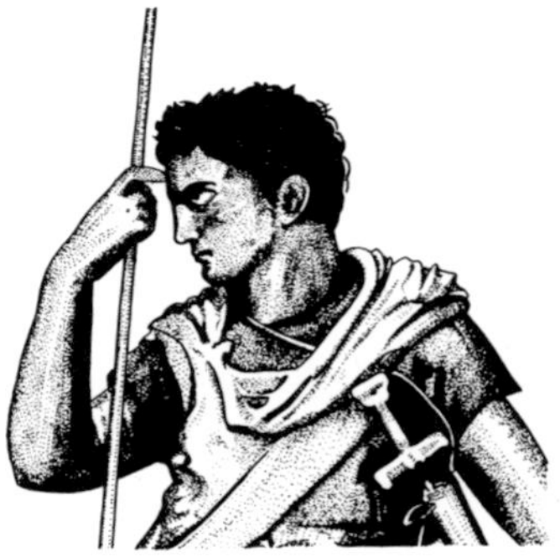

Aeneas, a mythological hero, was favoured by the gods and survived the fall of Troy.

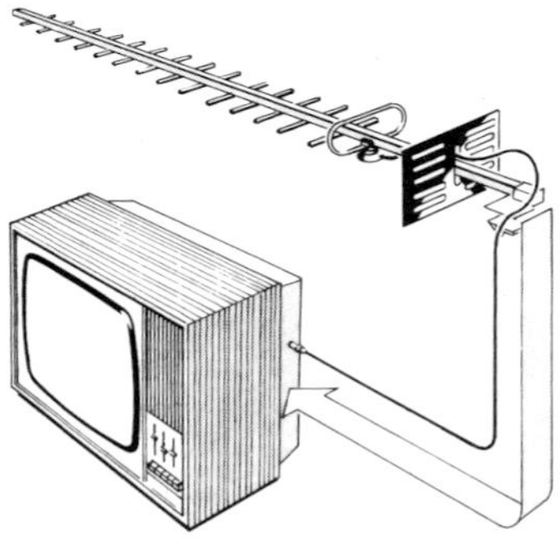

Aerials or antenna pick up TV and radio signals and relay them to the receiver.

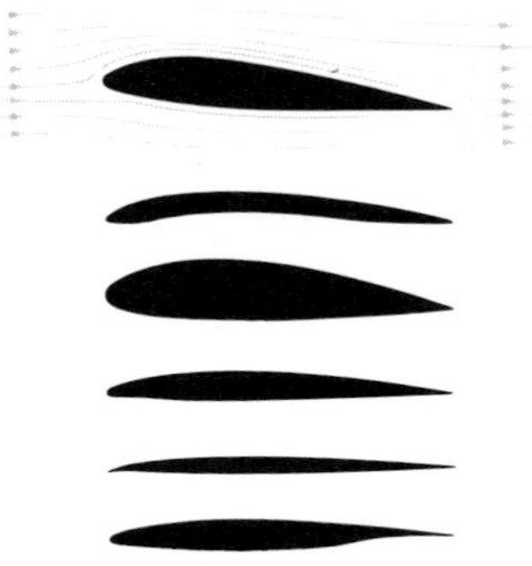

Aerofoils take a variety of forms, but all enable an aeroplane to obtain lift.

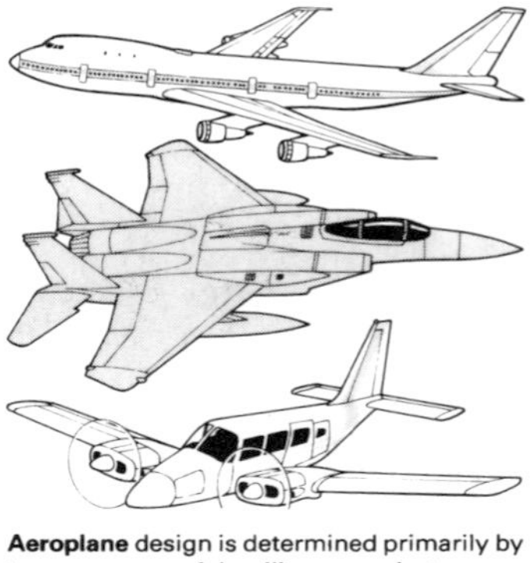

Aeroplane design is determined primarily by type – commercial, military or private.

126km (78 miles) s of Asmara. Scene of an important Italian defeat by the Ethiopians (1896), it was captured by the Italians in 1935 and restored to Ethiopia by the British in 1941. Pop. (1970 est.) 15,712.

Advent, liturgical season preceding Christmas. In the West it begins on the Sunday nearest 30 Nov. and is a time of preparation for Christmas.

Adventists, Christian sect whose distinctive belief concerns the imminent Second Coming of Christ, who will thereupon destroy evil in the world. William Miller (1782–1849) formed the first organized movement in the USA in 1831. His followers were called Millerites or Adventists. Controversies over dates of the second coming caused splits in the movement; the largest group being the SEVENTH-DAY ADVENTISTS.

Advocate, lawyer employed by a party to a civil or criminal case to represent him at a trial in court; generally called a barrister in England. The advocate's duty is to put his client's case as skilfully as the client himself would have done had he possessed the advocate's knowledge and experience of legal procedure. In a criminal case, it is not part of the advocate's function to decide whether his client is innocent or guilty; but it is considered unethical for an advocate positively to proclaim the innocence of a client who has privately admitted guilt. *See also* MS p.*286*.

A.E. (1867–1935), pseudonym of the Irish poet, artist and man of letters George Wilson Russell. A leader of the Irish literary revival, he edited the *Irish Homestead* (1905–23); his works include *The Candle of Vision* (1918) and mystical poetry. *See also* HC2 p.282.

AE Aurigae, O-type star that is moving at a high velocity (about 130km – 80 miles – per second). *See* SU p.232.

Aegean Sea, part of the Mediterranean Sea between Greece and Turkey. Bounded by Crete to the s, it is connected to the Black Sea and the Sea of Marmara by the Dardanelles to the NE. In classical times it was known as Archipelago, literally the "chief sea", and was an important trade link between the Greek city states. Oil and natural gas have been discovered in the area.

Aegina (Aiyina), island in the Aegean Sea off E central Greece, 27km (17 miles) sw of Athens. Occupied by the Dorians (1000 BC), it was conquered by Athens in 459 BC and was the site of the minting of the first Greek coin. It was the capital of Greece (1828–29). Area: 83sq km (32sq miles). Pop. 9,500.

Aegir, Norse master of the seas. He did not have the status of a god, but his relations with the Nordic gods were friendly. He was welcomed to their feasts and returned their hospitality in his marine palace. Germanic peoples believed that treasures engulfed during shipwrecks were stored in Aegir's palace.

Aegis, in Greek mythology, a sacred goatskin garment worn by ZEUS and occasionally borrowed by his daughter ATHENA. Later it came to mean a shield or breastplate which possessed the power to protect friends and terrify enemies. The aegis of Athena was patterned with a border of snakes and had a central, petrifying image of the gorgon MEDUSA.

Aegyptopithecus, fossil primate of the Oligocene period, about 30 million years ago. Together with *Propliopithecus*, it is one of the earliest known precursors of the hominoids, the group of primates that includes apes and human beings. *See also* MS p.20.

Aelfric (*c.*955–1010), Anglo-Saxon priest who composed works of religious instruction. His *Catholic Homilies* and *Lives of the Saints* were written in rhythmic, alliterative English, to appeal to poorly educated audiences. His *Colloquy* was a primer in dialogue form intended for novice monks. *See also* HC1 p.164.

Aeneas, in Greek mythology, the son of Anchises and APHRODITE. Active in the defence of Troy, he was removed by Poseidon from the city since he was destined to rule over the survivors of Troy. Aeneas led the Trojans westward to Italy. The Romans acknowledged Aeneas and his Trojan company as their ancestors.

Aeneid, poem written by the Roman poet VIRGIL between 30 and 19 BC. Written in 12 books, the *Aeneid* recounts the legendary founding of the town of Lavinium by the Trojan AENEAS. The *Aeneid* resembles the writings of Homer in both form and concepts: the first six books have been called "Virgil's *Odyssey*" and the second six, his *Iliad*. The two themes of Rome's destiny and human suffering are contained in the character of Aeneas who tries in spite of human limitations to fulfil the divine mission. The *Aeneid* was regarded by Romans as their national epic and the study of Virgil's works was widespread in the Roman Empire. *See also* HC1 pp.90, 94, 112, 113.

Aeolian harp, instrument introduced in the late 17th century, consisting of a number of strings, tuned to unison, on a wood resonance box. It is hung in a tree and the wind produces vibrations which set off the strings' HARMONICS, so producing a chord-like effect. *See also* SU pp.80–81, 82–83.

Aeolian Islands (Lipari Islands), group of volcanic Italian islands N of Sicily. There are seven main islands, including Lipari, Stromboli and Vulcano, with a total area of about 116sq km (45sq miles).

Aeolians, ancient Greek people. In the late Bronze Age, *c.*1100 BC, they settled on Lesbos and other islands. They were famous for their music and poetry. *See also* HC1 p.40.

Aeolus, in Greek mythology, the son of Poseidon and guardian of the winds. The winds lived with him on the floating island Aeolia, where they were kept in a cave. Aeolus set them free whenever he wanted to, or whenever the gods requested.

Aeration, bringing air into contact with a fluid by bubbling through or by agitation. Compressed air, providing oxygen to promote bacterial action, is blown into a reagent tank in the treatment of sewage. Aeration is also used in the fermentation and soft drinks industries, as well as in the manufacture of penicillin and other antibiotics. *See also* MM pp.202–203.

Aerial, or antenna, component of radio systems for the radiation (broadcasting) of signals and for their reception. Coiled receiving aerials are often fitted inside radio sets, but for the transmission of VHF and UHF signals, aerials must normally be placed above the heights of buildings. *See also* MM pp.228–230; 236.

Aerobatics, form of display flying in which highly manoeuvrable, usually single-seater aircraft climb, dive, roll, turn, spin, and/or loop the loop. In competition aerobatics, the manoeuvres are marked by judges; world championships began in the 1960s. The British RAF aerobatic team, the Red Arrows, earned worldwide fame with their Gnat jet aircraft.

Aerobe, minute organism that usually grows only in the presence of free atmospheric oxygen. Some aerobes can however remain alive even in the absence of oxygen and are called facultative ANAEROBES.

Aerodynamics, science of gases in motion and the forces acting on objects, such as aircraft, in motion through the air. An aircraft designer must consider four fundamental factors and their interrelationships: weight of the aircraft and the load it will carry; lift to overcome the pull of gravity; drag, or the forces that retard motion; and thrust, the driving force. A heavier-than-air craft must have sufficient thrust to propel itself at speeds high enough for its wings (or rotor) to generate enough lift to overcome the pull of gravity. Air resistance increases as the square of an object's velocity and must be minimized by streamlining to limit turbulence (which causes drag). The WIND TUNNEL is an essential tool used by the aerodynamic engineer to predict the performance of an aircraft. *See also* SU p.79; MM pp.152.

Aerofoil, any shape or surface, such as a wing, tail or propeller blade on an aircraft, that has as its major function the deflection of airflow to produce a pressure differential or lift. A typical aerofoil has a leading and trailing edge, and an upper and lower camber. *See also* MM pp.152–153.

Aerolite, stony meteorite, as opposed to an iron (SIDERITE) one. Aerolites are composed chiefly of silicate materials, with less iron and nickel than siderites.

Aeronautics, study of flight and the control of aircraft. The study developed from the principles of lighter-than-air flight of balloons and dirigibles, which mainly concerned the raising of a load by means of buoyancy, into the multi-disciplined science of heavier-than-air flight of gliders, rotorcraft (helicopters and autogyros) and aeroplanes. All aircraft share some principles of flight, but are unique in others. BALLOONS and dirigibles go aloft by displacing air with a gas, usually hydrogen, helium or hot air. Balloons have no means of propulsion, but dirigibles are powered by engines. Rotorcraft utilize lift provided by a rotating wing or rotor. A HELICOPTER propels itself forwards by tilting the plane of rotation of its powered rotor, but an AUTOGYRO (also called gyroplane) has a free-wheeling rotor which generates lift only after the autogyro has gained forward speed using a powered propeller. GLIDERS and aeroplanes use wings to provide lift, but a minimum forward speed is essential to maintain it. A glider dives in relation to the surrounding air to maintain forward motion and lift. Some modern gliders can maintain lift if they dive at angles of 30 or 40 to 1. An AEROPLANE is pulled forwards (when propeller driven) by a propeller which advances through the air as a screw through wood, or is pushed (when jet-propelled) by the reaction forces of hot expanding gases. *See also* AIRCRAFT; MM pp.146–155.

Aeronomy, study of the Earth's upper atmosphere, including its composition, density, temperature and chemical changes as recorded by rockets and satellites. *See also* PE p.66.

Aeroplane, heavier-than-air flying machine that depends upon fixed wings for its support in the air, as it moves under the thrust of its engines. This thrust may be provided by an airscrew (propeller) turned by a piston or turbine engine, or by the exhaust gases of a jet engine or rocket motor. GLIDERS differ from aeroplanes only in their complete dependence upon air currents to keep them airborne. The main body of an aeroplane is the fuselage, to which are attached the wings and tail assembly. Engines may be incorporated into or slung below the wings, but are sometimes mounted on the fuselage towards the tail or, as in some fighter aircraft, built into the fuselage near the wings. The landing gear or undercarriage, with its heavy wheels and stout shock absorbers, is usually completely retractable into the wings or fuselage. Wing design varies with the type of plane, high-speed fighters having slim, often swept-back or adjustable wings that create minimal air resistance (drag) at high speeds. At the other extreme heavy air freighters need broader wings in order to achieve the necessary lift at take-off. AUTOGYROS are rather dated aeroplanes that obtain lift not only from wings but also from a rotor similar to that on a HELICOPTER. A delta wing is a broad wing, or fuselage extension, that is aerodynamically suited for both large and small high-speed planes. An aeroplane is steered by the pilot moving flaps and ailerons on the wings and rudder and elevators on the tail assembly. This deflects the pressure of air on various aerofoil surfaces, causing the plane to rise or descend, to bank (tilt) or swing and turn in the air. A pilot needs to refer to many control instruments, including an altimeter showing height, an artificial horizon showing tilt, and indicators for air speed, ground speed, rate of climb and rate of banking and turning. Engine and airframe systems are monitored by numerous additional gauges, meters and warning lights. Radar systems aid navigation, an automatic pilot keeps the aircraft steady on a fixed course, and pressurized cabins allow passenger aeroplanes to fly at heights exceeding 10,000m (32,000 ft). *See also* MM pp. 148–155; 176–179.

Aerosol, suspension of liquid or solid particles in a gas. Fog or mist – millions of tiny water droplets suspended in air – is a liquid-based example; airborne dust or smoke is a solid-based equivalent. Manufactured aerosols are used in products such as deodorants, cosmetics, paints and household sprays. *See also* MM p.248.

Aerosport, general term for any pursuit connected with flying machines or devices. Aeroplanes take part in races, record-breaking, team displays and display and competition AEROBATICS. In GLIDING and BALLOONING there are distance, altitude and endurance events. Other aerosports include PARACHUTING ("skydiving") and HANG-GLIDING. In parachuting, there are precision events as well as events for style and relative work (team formations). HELICOPTER flying has world championship events such as precision flying, rescue and navigation.

Aerostat, another name for a BALLOON. *See* MM pp.146–147.

Aertsen, Pieter (*c.* 1508–75), Dutch painter, whose pictures of food, kitchen utensils and other everyday subjects did much to promote the development of still-life painting; he may have influenced CARAVAGGIO and VELÁZQUEZ. One of his best-known works is *Christ in the House of Martha and Mary* (1559).

Aeschines Socraticus (4th century BC), Greek philosopher and orator. He was a student of SOCRATES and present at his teacher's condemnation and death. Aeschines composed several Socratic dialogues. *See also* HC1 p.75.

Aeschylus (*c.* 525–456 BC), Greek dramatist. The earliest of the great Greek playwrights, he is said to have been responsible for the development of tragedy as a dramatic form by his addition of a second actor to the older tradition of one actor and a chorus. He was also the first to introduce scenery. His work is best remembered for its lofty and grandiloquent verse. Among his surviving works are *The Suppliants*, *The Persians*, *The Seven against Thebes* and *Prometheus Bound*, but his best-known work was the trilogy *Oresteia*, comprising *Agamemnon*, *The Choephoroe* and *The Eumenides*. These plays, on the subject of the house of Atreus, were first performed in 458 BC. *See also* HC1 p.74.

Aesir, primary group of Nordic gods who lived in ASGARD. Three of them – Woden (Odin), Thor (Donar) and Tyr (Tiw) – with a few others, were the object of a cult that extended throughout the lands inhabited by Germanic peoples. Secondary to the Aesir was a group of gods known as the Vanir.

Aesop (*c.* 620–560 BC), semi-legendary Greek fabulist. A former slave, he was the reputed creator of numerous short tales about animals, all illustrating human virtues and failings (although they were almost certainly written by several people). Aesop supposedly died at Delphi, where he angered citizens and was thrown off a cliff. Most of the fables are simple tales in which animals symbolize human characteristics to convey a moral lesson, eg *The Hare and the Tortoise* teaches "slow and steady wins the race", and *The Fox and the Crow* cautions against trusting flatterers. The fables attributed to Aesop were preserved principally through Babrius, Phaedrus and Maximus Planudes. *See also* HC1 p.334.

Aesthetic Movement, English literary and artistic movement of the 1880s, founded in protest against the "philistine" tastes of the period. "Art for art's sake" was its chief doctrine, and the periodical *The Yellow Book* its main publication. Walter PATER and Oscar WILDE were leaders of the movement, which was also represented by the poet W.B. YEATS and such artists as J.M. WHISTLER and Aubrey BEARDSLEY.

Aesthetics, study of beauty and of standards of value in judging beauty, especially in art. The term was first used in the 18th century to describe a science whose object is beauty, although philosophizing about the arts dates from the writings of PLATO and earlier. In the 1820s, G.W.F. HEGEL employed the term in its present sense. In the 20th century, aesthetics has come to be regarded as a branch of philosophy involving the study of works of art, human behaviour towards art and the enjoyment of art. *See also* MS pp.232, *233*.

Aetiology, in medicine, the science of the origins and causes of diseases. *See* MS pp.82–133.

Afars and the Issas, former name of the African nation Djibouti. *See* MW p.65.

Affenpinscher, small German "monkey dog" (TOY DOG group) known since the 17th century in Europe. It has a rounded head, short muzzle and small, pointed, erect ears. Its prominent chin, bushy whiskers and moustache, and eyebrows that hang down over its eyes, give it a distinctive expression. The black coat is hard, wiry and short, except on the legs and face, where it is more shaggy. Average height: 20–25cm (8–10in) at the shoulder. Average weight: 3–3.5kg (7–8lb).

Affiliative motive, need to associate with, and form attachments to, other living beings.

Affirmation, promise by a witness in a court of law to tell the truth, accepted from someone who for religious reasons refuses to swear an OATH on the Bible.

Affluent Society, The (1958), book by US economist John K. GALBRAITH. Its theme is that, in an advanced Western industrial society, a serious imbalance between the provision of public goods and private goods develops. According to Galbraith, as economic development progresses, more cars and leisure will necessarily mean more of such unwanted results as congestion and pollution.

Afghan hound, aristocratic hunting dog (HOUND group) originating in Egypt 4000–3000 BC and later established in Afghanistan. Aloof and dignified, it has a long, slender head and jaws; long, hanging ears; level back; arched loins; long, straight legs with large feet; and a long, tapered tail with a ring or curve at the end. The thick, silky coat is short and smooth on the back and longer over the rest of the dog. There is a long topknot on the head. Average size: 61–71cm (24–28in) high at shoulder; 23–27kg (51–60lb).

Afghanistan (Afghānestān), landlocked mountainous country in S central Asia. Area: 647,497sq km (249,999sq milesh. The economy is predominantly agricultural. Pop. 19,796,000. *See* MW p.25.

Afghan Wars, three wars fought by Britain, 1838–42, 1878–80 and 1919, in an attempt to block Russian influence in Afghanistan and so secure the northwest frontier of India. The first war began well for Britain with the capture in 1839 of Kandahar (Quandahār) and Ghazni, but the war ended with the Russian favourite, Dost Mahomed, restored to the emirate at KABUL. The second war ended with Britain having gained control of Afghanistan's foreign policy in return for guaranteeing the emir against foreign aggression and paying him a subsidy. Britain easily won the third war, but by the treaty of Rawalpindi lost foreign policy control. *See also* HC2 p.*141*.

Afonso. *See* ALFONSO.

Africa, the second largest continent, straddles the equator and lies largely within the tropics.

Land. Africa forms a large plateau between the Atlantic and Indian oceans; its highest features include the Atlas and Ahaggar mountains in the NW, the Ethiopian Highlands in the E and the Drakensberg Mountains in the S. Kilimanjaro 5,895m (19,340ft) is the continent's highest peak. The huge sunken strip in the SE is known as the East African or Great Rift Valley. The SAHARA, the largest desert in the world, stretches across the north, covering more than a quarter of the continent. The Kalahari and Namib are smaller deserts in the S and SW. The island of Madagascar off the SE coast is the world's fourth largest.

Structure and geology. The continent is largely composed of ancient metamorphic rocks overlain with Tertiary Mesozoic and Palaeozoic sediments. The mountains of the NW are folded sedimentary material, roughly contemporaneous with the Alps. The Great Rift Valley, formed by the progressive movement of the Arabian Peninsula away from Africa, is in the N largely of igneous and in the S mainly of older Precambrian rocks.

Lakes and rivers. The Rift valley contains the lakes Albert, Malawi and Tanganyika. Lake Victoria (69,484sq km; 26,828sq miles) to the E is Africa's largest. Lake Chad (Tchad), which dries to a salt pan in dry periods, lies in the southern Sahara. The Nile, at 6,653km (4,132 miles) the longest river in the world, flows from the dual sources of Lake Victoria and Lake Tana in the Ethiopian Highlands. Other major rivers are the Niger, Congo (Zaire) and Zambezi.

Climate and vegetation. Much of the continent is hot and, outside the desert areas, humid. The belt along the Equator receives more than 254cm (100in) of moisture a year and is thickly covered by tropical rain forest. The forest gives way both to the N and S to areas of acacia and brush and then through savanna grassland to desert. The northern strip of the continent and the area around the Cape have a Mediterranean climate.

Animal life. Although the continent is traditionally the home of big game hunting, strenuous efforts are being made to conserve the remnants of Africa's wild life. Game reserves have been established, mainly in E Africa, where there are vast herds of zebras and wildebeest. All the world's largest carnivores, except the tiger and the bear, are found there and the world's largest terrestrial animal, the African elephant, is indigenous. At the opposite extreme Africa has an enormous population of insects, some of which are important disease carriers and far more dangerous in terms of human mortality than the larger animals.

People. Originally the whole continent was populated by Negroid palaeolithic peoples who depended economically on hunting and gathering. In the Sahara they were replaced by Arabs who moved in from the Middle East in the 7th and 8th centuries AD. Today three-quarters of the population is rural. Of note are the Masai and Watusi tribes of E Africa who have lived for centuries as nomadic herdsmen. The pygmies of the rain forest have remained gatherers and hunters, as have the Bushmen and Hottentots of the SW deserts.

Economy. Agriculture is restricted in the central part of the continent by the large expanse of tropical rain forest, although such cash crops as cocoa, rubber and ground nuts are grown in plantations. Along the N coast Mediterranean crops such as citrus fruits, olives and cereals are grown. The Sahara is largely unproductive, supporting only a nomadic herding community. East and southern Africa are the richest areas agriculturally, containing large mixed farms and cattle ranching. Apart from South Africa the entire continent is industrially underdeveloped. Mining is most important; Zambia contains the largest deposits of copper ore in the world. Bauxite is extracted in W Africa and oil in the Libyan and Algerian deserts. South Africa is extremely rich in minerals, gold, diamonds and coal being the most important.

Recent history. At the end of the 19th century the whole continent, except for Liberia and Ethiopia, was under foreign domination by either European powers or by the Ottoman Empire. In 1977 only Rhodesia (Zimbabwe) was technically a European colony.

Area approx. 30,244,050sq km (11,677,240sq miles).
Highest mountain Kilimanjaro 5,895m (19,340ft).
Longest river Nile 6,653km (4,132 miles).
Population (1971 est.) 354,000,000.
Largest cities Cairo (6,133,000); Alexandria (2,259,000); Johannesburg (1,498,000).
See also NW pp.200–201, 212–213, 218–221; PE pp.40–43; articles on individual countries in *The Modern World*.

African art, rich and varied, especially in its sculpture, ranges from the remarkable Nok terracotta heads, Ife bronzes and BENIN ivory masks of Nigeria to rock paintings, (such as those at Tassili,

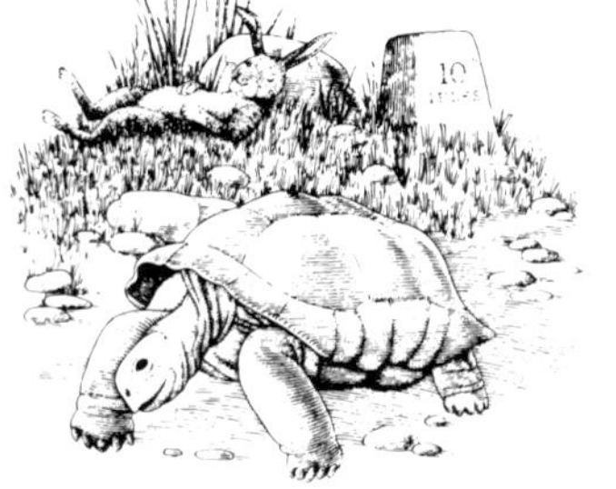

Aesop, Greek fabulist who created the moralistic tales such as *The Hare and Tortoise.*

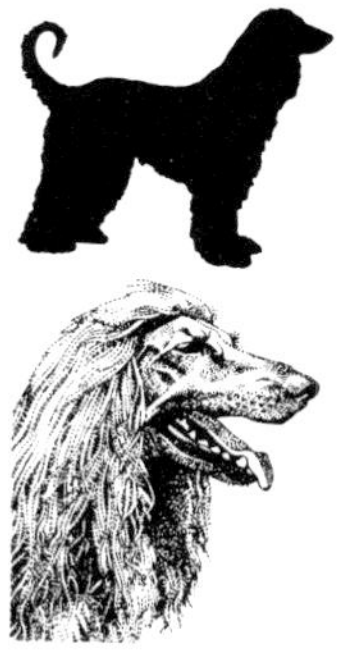

Afghan hound, now fashionable pet that was once used for hunting gazelles and leopards.

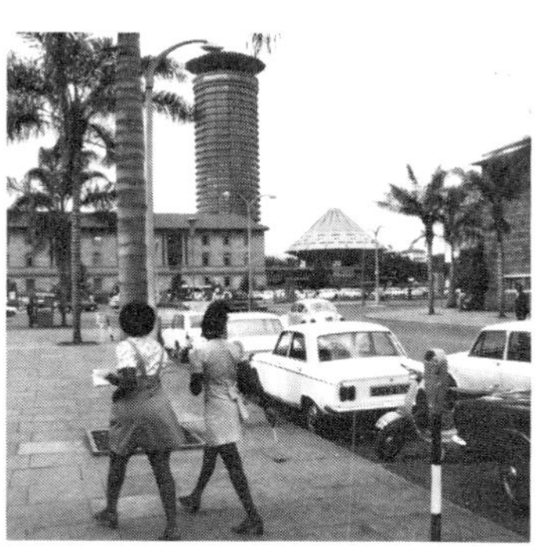

Africa; Wabera Street, Nairobi, showing the law courts and the Kenyatta centre.

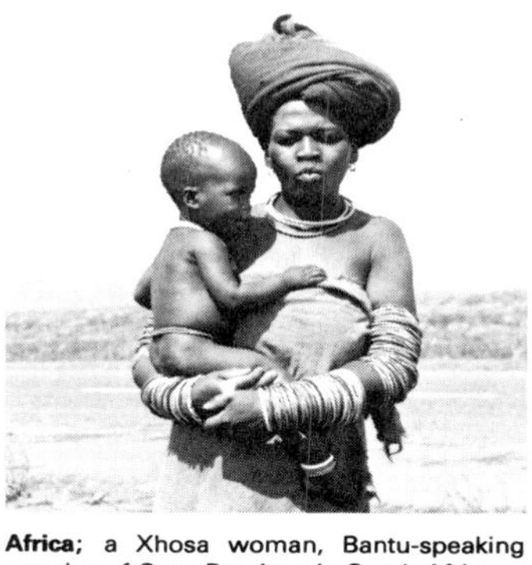

Africa; a Xhosa woman, Bantu-speaking peoples of Cape Province in South Africa.

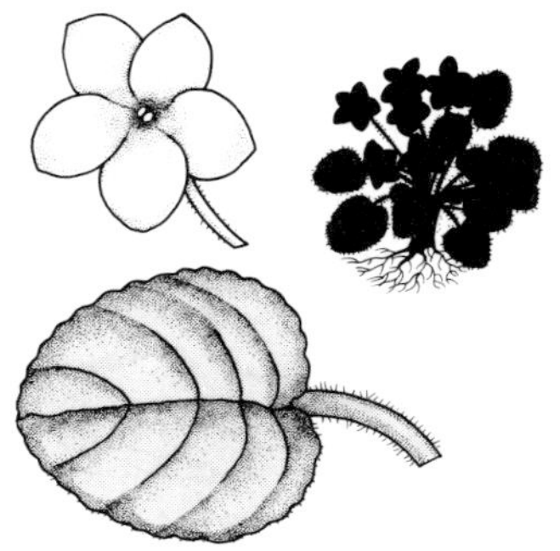

African violets display attractive purple or pink blooms in clusters around a stalk.

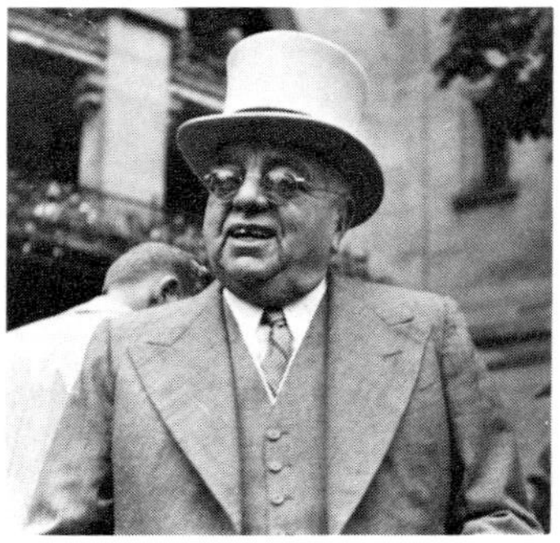

Aga Khan III, racing celebrity and descendant of an ancient line of Muslim rulers.

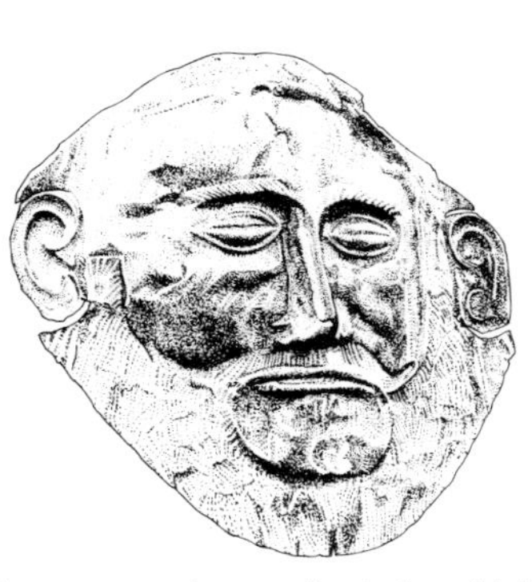

Agamemnon, who according to legend led the Greeks in the seige and capture of Troy.

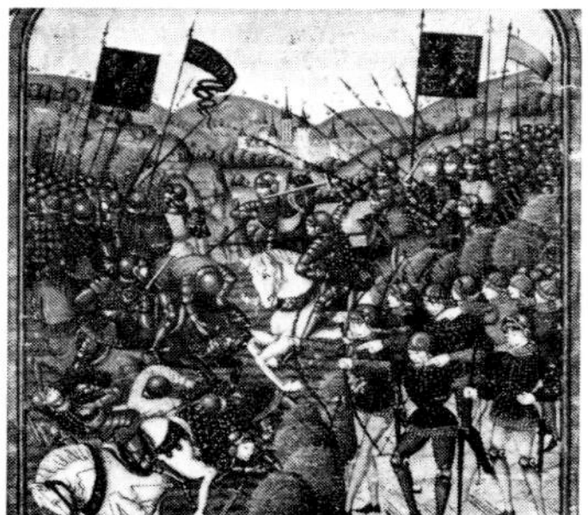

Agincourt; battle where English bowmen, outnumbered four to one, routed the French.

Sahara) spanning 5,000 years; from the complex, body painting systems of the Nuta of SE Sudan to the carved musical instruments and the stylized metal and wood "spirit guardian" figurines of tribes in Gabon. The decorative arts, particularly in textiles, murals and pottery, flourish throughout Africa. Knowledge of the origins, development and stylistic relationships of African art is at present fragmentary. Established forms evolved centuries before the arrival (in the late 15th century) of the Portuguese, the first European visitors, but because of its perishable nature – wood being the dominant material used – most early work has not survived. PICASSO, MODIGLIANI and others were influenced by African art forms. *See also* HC2 pp.60–61.

African hunting dog, wild dog found in Africa, where it hunts in packs preying on small mammals. Unlike most dogs it has only four toes on each foot. Its head is flat with a short muzzle and large ears; the coat is yellow, black and white. Height: approx. 60cm (24in) at the shoulder. Species *Lycaon pictus.*

African National Congress, South African political party, formed in 1913, banned in 1960. It worked for Black parliamentary representation and racial equality. Similar parties were formed in Rhodesia and Nyasaland. *See also* HC2 p.252.

African violet, tropical African flowering house plant. The velvety, rounded leaves grow in spreading rosettes around purple, white or pink blossoms with yellow stamens. The stems and undersides of the leaves are often purple. Propagation is by leaf cuttings or crown division. Height: 10–15cm (4–6in). Family Gesneriaceae; genus *Saintpaulia.*

Afrikaans, official language of the Republic of South Africa. It is derived from the language spoken by the original Dutch settlers of the 17th century but quickly evolved its own forms, so that it was a distinct language when the first Britons arrived in 1795. This evolution occurred unusually fast because there were no formal schools or educational institutions, and the language remained almost entirely a spoken one until the mid-19th century. Although based on Dutch, its vocabulary also shows the influence of English, German, French, Portuguese and Hottentot; the grammatical structure is based entirely on Dutch. Many original Dutch inflections have been dropped.

Afrikaans is regarded as a cultural focal point by South Africans of Dutch origin. As a result, the political struggles of the BOERS for recognition by the British in the late 19th century found expression in the self-conscious development of the Afrikaans culture, mainly in the Cape Province. This movement was led by Rev. S.J. du Toit, with encouragement from new immigrants from The Netherlands, such as Arnoldus Pannevis. By 1925 Afrikaans had replaced Dutch as one of the official languages of the South African state, education system and church.

Today the Afrikaans vocabulary is large and expanding; it has been codified and adapted to the needs of a technological society, and is spoken by almost three million people, including many detribalized Hottentots. *See also* MW p.154.

Afrika Korps, German armoured force in WWII that operated in the N African desert. Under its commander Gen. Erwin ROMMEL it had spectacular but transient success against the British 8th Army. *See also* HC2 pp.*230–231,* 231.

Afro-Asiatic languages. *See* HAMITO-SEMITIC.

Afro-Basaldella (1912–), Italian painter whose work was influenced first by CUBISM and, after WWII, by ABSTRACT ART. Among his best-known paintings is the *Garden of Hope* (1958), in the UNESCO building, Paris.

Afterbirth, PLACENTA and fetal membranes expelled from a womb after childbirth. The expulsion is carried out naturally by contraction of the womb. *See also* MS pp.78–79.

Afterimage, image retained by the brain and seen even after looking away from an object. The colour of the afterimage is the complement of that of the object viewed. Television and motion pictures use this phenomenon. *See also* MS p.48.

Afternoon of a faun. *See* APRÈS-MIDI D'UN FAUNE, L'.

Afzelius, Arvid August (1785–1871), Swedish historian and folklorist. A parish priest, he is best known for his collection of Swedish folk-songs.

Aga, title of a person of high position in the OTTOMAN EMPIRE, such as a commander or chief officer.

Agade. *See* AKKADIA.

Agadir, town in SW Morocco, Africa, 121km (75 miles) S of Mogador. It was the scene of an international incident in 1911. Pop. (1971) 61,192. *See also* HC2 p.186.

Agaja, (*c.* 1673–1740), third ruler of DAHOMEY (*r.* 1708–40). He centralized the country and added to it by war the kingdom of Allada (1724) and the state of Whydal (1727).

Aga Khan, name of the leaders of the sect of Ishmaili Muslims. Aga Khan III (1877–1957) was the best known. He succeeded his father in 1885, and headed the All-India Muslim League in support of British rule in 1906 and represented India at the World Disarmament Conference (1932) and at the League of Nations (1932; 1934–37). He moved to Europe early in his life and was known for his enormous wealth and love of racehorses. His son, Prince Karim, became Aga Khan IV in 1957; he was educated at Harvard.

Agam, Yaacov (1928–), Israeli artist, real name Yaacov Gipstein. He did pioneer work in KINETIC ART and OP ART. His work, which emphasizes change and movement and in which the component elements can often be rearranged, is typified in *Three Times Three Interplay* (1970–71).

Agamemnon, King of Mycenae, ancient Greece, brother of Menelaus. According to Homer's ILIAD, he led the Greeks at the siege of TROY. When Troy fell, Agamemnon returned home with his captive Cassandra, but was murdered by his wife CLYTEMNESTRA and her lover Aegisthus. His death was avenged by his children ORESTES and Electra.

Agamid, member of the family of iguanas and related lizards living in Africa, S and central Asia, and Australia. *See also* NW p.139.

Agammaglobulinaemia, abnormal condition in which the gamma globulin part of the blood is missing, causing a reduction in ANTIBODIES and a high susceptibility to repeated and persistent infections.

Agana, capital of Guam in the Mariana Islands, W Pacific Ocean, located NE of Apra Harbour, on the W coast. Pop. 2,100.

Agar, complex substance extracted from certain seaweeds; its powder forms a "solid" gel in solution. It is used as a thickening agent or emulsifier in foods, an adhesive, and a medium for growing bacterial cultures.

Agarics, order of fungi that includes edible mushrooms, ink caps and the poisonous AMANITAS, including the red-and-white spotted fly agaric, and the deadly destroying angel and death cap. *See also* NW pp.42, 43.

Agassiz, Jean-Louis Rodolphe (1807–73), Swiss naturalist who in 1840 proposed the theory of an Ice Age that once covered most of northern Europe. The previous year he had shown that glaciers move. He also produced an important work of zoological classification between 1840 and 1846.

Agate, James Evershed (1877–1947), British drama critic. He was critic for the *Manchester Guardian* (1907–14) and the *Sunday Times* (1923–47). He published his diary *Ego* in nine vols. (1935–49).

Agate, hard type of silica (SiO_2) with parallel bands of colour, used as a semiprecious stone and for making ornaments.

Agatha, Saint, 3rd-century Christian martyr, patron saint of Catania, Sicily, said to have been tortured by a Roman consul for repulsing him. Feast: 5 Feb.

Agathon, BILDUNGSROMAN (2 vols, 1766–67) by Christoph Martin WIELAND, set in Greece. In an idealized environment where the mind and the senses can live harmoniously, a young man abandons his fervent religious beliefs as a consequence of his experiences with a courtesan.

Agave, short-stemmed, succulent, flowering plant found in tropical, subtropical and temperate regions. Agaves have narrow, lance-shaped leaves clustered at the base of the plant, and many have large flower clusters. The well known century plant (*Agave americana*) of SW North America grows up to 7.6m (25ft) in one season. Each plant produces a flower spike once a year or less often, after which the leaves die, leaving the roots to produce a new plant. Other species are SISAL HEMP (*A. sisalana*) and the many species of YUCCA. Family Agavaceae. *See also* NW p.*68.*

Agee, James (1909–55), US writer. His works include *Let Us Now Praise Famous Men* (1941), *The Morning Watch* (1951) and *A Death in the Family* (1957), a novel which won the Pulitzer Prize.

Age of Reason, term used to describe the intellectual temper and scientific advances of the 17th century, associated especially with DESCARTES, GALILEO and NEWTON. Its ruling notions were RATIONALISM and MECHANISM, its method increasingly observation. It led to the ENLIGHTENMENT. *See also* SCIENTIFIC REVOLUTION; HC1 pp.302–303; SU pp.24–25.

Agglomerate, in geology, coarse volcanic rock that includes both rounded and angular fragments in a finer matrix, thus combining the characteristics of CONGLOMERATES and BRECCIAS.

Agglutination, clumping of BACTERIA or red blood cells by ANTIBODIES that react with ANTIGENS on the cell surface.

Agglutinative language, language in which words are composed of a series of elements representing only one grammatical category, eg Japanese and Finnish. It is also called an agglutinating language. *See also* MS p.240.

Aggregate, material such as sand, crushed and broken stone, pebbles and boiler ashes, used to form concrete by mixing with cement, lime, gypsum or other adhesive. It provides volume and resistance to wear. *See also* MM pp.46–47.

Aggregate equilibrium, in macroeconomics, the national income equilibrium for the economy. This equilibrium occurs when the economy functions in such a way that the total demand for goods and services equals the total (or aggregate) supply of goods and services. This balance means there is no tendency for prices to fall or rise or for producers to increase or decrease output.

Aggression, state of mind that is expressed in ways ranging from verbal attack to physical violence. Aggression in animals is generally regarded as instinctive. Psychologists do not agree, however, about the origin of human aggression. Some regard it as instinctive, others as entirely learned, and still others as a mixture of the two. Imitation may be a way in which children aquire aggressive behaviour. *See also* MS pp.159, 165, 186.

Agincourt, village in Pas de Calais, NE France, 53km (33 miles) W of Arras. It is the site of Henry V's decisive victory over the French in 1415 during the HUNDRED YEARS WAR. The French were more heavily armoured but the superior rate of fire of the English long-bow over the French cross-bow proved decisive. Pop. (1968) 276. *See also* HC1 pp.212–213.

Agitprop Theatre, type of drama or dramatic technique popular in the 1930s, characterized by social protest and a Marxist viewpoint. The term derives from "agitation" and "propaganda".

Agnatha, the jawless fishes. Only the LAMPREY and the HAGFISH live today, but many fossil species date from as long ago as 450 million years. *See also* NW p.123.

Agnes, Saint (*b. c.* 304), Roman Christian martyr and patron of girls. She was murdered by DIOCLETIAN. Her feast day is 21 January.

Agnew, Spiro Theodore (1918–), outspoken US politician. He was Richard Nixon's Republican vice-presidential candidate in the elections of 1968 and 1972, serving as vice-president (1969–73). In 1973 he was brought to trial on charges of bribery, conspiracy and tax evasion. He

pleaded no contest and then resigned.
Agni, fire-god in Vedic mythology, revered as god of the home and appearing in lightning and the Sun as a nature deity. He was a messenger between men and the gods when he carried consumed offerings of the sacrificial altars.
Agnon, Shmuel Yosef (1888–1970), Israeli novelist and short-story writer, *b.* Poland. He shared the 1966 Nobel Prize in literature with Nelly Sachs; his works (in Hebrew) include three epic novels on East European Jewry.
Agnosticism, theory of religious knowledge, associated with English rationalist Thomas HUXLEY (1825–95), that it is impossible either to demonstrate or to refute God's existence, on the basis of available evidence.
Agora, in ancient Greece, the central square of a city, used as a place of assembly and market place. It was usually surrounded by important public buildings. *See also* HC1 p.69.
Agoraphobia, morbid fear of open spaces, the first element of the term being derived from the Greek AGORA in its original meaning. Afflicted people are apt to panic when alone in an open or public place. *See also* MS p.*141*.
Agostini, Giacomo (1942–), Italian motorcyclist who, riding MV Augusta machines, won the 500cc world championship seven times (1966–72) and the 350cc championship once (1973). He joined the Yamaha team in 1974.
Agouti, fairly large, herbivorous rodent of Central and South America and the West Indies. Hunted as food by other animals and man, it has short ears, long legs, a minute tail and coarse fur that ranges from orange through brown to almost black. Family Dasyproctidae. *See also* PACA.
Agra, city in N central India, on the Yamuna River. It is an important rail junction and commercial and administrative centre. It was founded in 1566 by the MOGUL emperor AKBAR. Emperor SHAH JEHAN built the TAJ MAHAL there (*c.* 1632–43) as a tomb and memorial to his wife. The city's importance declined after 1658 when the Mogul capital moved to Delhi. It was annexed to the BRITISH EMPIRE in 1803 and became the capital of the North West Province during the mid-19th century. It has much fine Mogul architecture including the Pearl Mosque, the Great Mosque and Akbar's fort. Industries: glass, shoes, textiles. Pop. 592,000. *See also* MS p.*184*.
Agranulocytosis, acute and serious illness caused by chemicals or hypersensitivity to drugs, in which granular white blood cells that counter infection decrease in number. Infection may rapidly ensue, involving mouth ulcers, fever and sore throat. Cortisone and antibiotic drugs are generally used in treatment.
Agrarian revolution, term used to describe the transition in the human economy from hunting to farming, *c.* 9th–8th millennia, in western parts of Asia and Mesopotamia. *See also* AGRICULTURAL REVOLUTION; HC1 pp.26–27.
Agricola, Georgius (1494–1555), real name Georg Bauer, German mineralogist who pioneered the science with his book *De Re Metallica* (1530).
Agricola, Gnaeus Julius (AD 37–93), Roman general; conqueror and governor of Britain. As governor (*c.* 78–84), he Romanized Britain without oppression and extended Roman influence to Wales and part of Scotland. His enlightened rule was described by Tacitus, his son-in-law. *See also* HC1 p.100.
Agricultural revolution, term used by some historians to describe a variety of changes – crop rotation, new machinery, increased capital investment, scientific breeding, land reclamation and enclosure of common lands – which greatly increased the productivity of English AGRICULTURE between the early 18th and the late 19th centuries. It is also used sometimes to refer to the AGRARIAN REVOLUTION. *See also* HC2 pp.20–21.
Agriculture, the science of cultivating crops and raising livestock. Originally man hunted animals and gathered roots, berries and fruits. Later a knowledge of husbandry and crop farming enabled him to produce food on a small scale for himself and his family. Modern archaeological dating techniques suggest that the production of cereals, such as wheat and barley, and the domestication and breeding of animals were widespread thoughout E Mediterranean countries by about 7000 BC. The Egyptians and Mesopotamians (*c.* 3000 BC) were the earliest civilizations to organize agriculture on a large scale. They bred sheep and goats for meat, milk, butter and cheese, and developed new strains of cereals. They made use of irrigation techniques and used manure as fertilizer. The development of agriculture took place at differing rates in different areas but by Roman times (200 BC–AD 400) crop farming and the domestication of animals were commonplace in western Europe.
In the 1,000 years that followed, the changes that occurred were developments of techniques already known. Methods of land reclamation and drainage were developed in Europe in the 11th century and there were improvements in ploughs and in the harnesses used for the horses and oxen that pulled them. In the 17th and 18th centuries, breeding was practised to increase yields of milk and meat, and the use of the Norfolk Four Course system of crop rotation meant that plentiful fodder was produced in fields which in the past had lain fallow.
The greatest changes in agriculture, however, came with the industrial growth of the 18th century. Farm machinery was introduced during the 19th century and became widespread in the UK in the 1840s when prices were falling and labour costs were rising. In Western Europe and North America mechanization has advanced greatly and a large proportion of agricultural production is now carried out by FACTORY FARMING, involving the battery production of livestock such as pigs and poultry. The mixed farm is more common in Western Europe than elsewhere. The enormous food-producing regions of the USA mid-west and the Russian steppes consist largely of farms given over to the production of either grains or livestock. In much of the underdeveloped world, such as SE Asia, agriculture still relies heavily on labour; 75% of the world's labour force is engaged in farming. Shifting agriculture of the SLASH AND BURN method is still sometimes practised in equatorial regions. *See also* HC1 pp.26–27, *26–27;* PE pp.156–175.
Agrimony, the name of three plants: *Agrimonia* of the rose family; and *Bidens,* the bur marigold and *Eupatorium,* hemp agrimony, both of the composite family.
Agrippa, Marcus Visanius (*c.* 63–12 BC), Roman general, adviser to Octavian (who became the Emperor AUGUSTUS). After the death of Julius CAESAR in 44 BC, he helped Octavian win the throne by commanding two naval battles against Sextus Pompeius in 36 BC and helping to defeat MARK ANTONY at ACTIUM in 31 BC. Agrippa was appointed consul three times, married Augustus's daughter and became his heir designate. *See also* HC1 p.98.
Agrippa von Nettesheim, Heinrich Cornelius (*c.* 1486–1535), German philosopher and occultist. He was court secretary to Charles V and physician to Louise of Savoy, and was constantly under attack for his writings in defence of occultism, which included *De Occulta Philosophia.*
Agrippina, name of two Roman princesses. Agrippina I, Vipsania Agrippina (14 BC–*c.* AD 33), was the granddaughter of the Emperor Augustus. She married Germanicus, the heir of TIBERIUS, and after her husband's death engaged in plots against Tiberius whom she suspected of killing Germanicus. She was banished to an island near Naples in AD 29. Her daughter Agrippina II, Julia Agrippina (*c.* AD 15–59), was the mother of NERO. She married CLAUDIUS after he became emperor and persuaded him to make Nero his heir designate. She is believed to have murdered Claudius in AD 54.
Agronomy, science of soil management and improvement in the interests of agriculture. It includes the studies of particular plants and soils and their interrelationship. Agronomy has resulted in disease-resistant plants, selective breeding and the development of chemical fertilizers. *See also* PE pp.162–163, 170–171, 174–175.
Aguascalientes, city in central Mexico, 582km (364 miles) NW of Mexico City and capital of Aguascalientes State since 1835. It is a health resort noted for its mineral springs and is built over an ancient system of tunnels of advanced construction and unknown origin. It was founded in 1575 by the Spanish as a silver-mining town. Pop. 222,000.
Agulhas, Cape, southernmost point of the African continent, in South Africa, 193km (120 miles) ESE of Cape Town.
Aguti. *See* AGOUTI.
Ahab, two biblical figures. Ahab (*d. c.* 853 BC) the son of Omri, King of Israel was reprimanded by ELIJAH for allowing his wife Jezebel to worship BAAL. He was killed in a battle at Gilead. The other Ahab was a lying prophet burned to death by NEBUCHADREZZAR.
Ahaggar (Hoggar) Mountains, plateau region in the north centre of the Sahara, rising to 2,918m (9,573ft) at Mt Tahat. The main town is Tamanrasset, but most of the population are nomads, herding goats and sheep.
Ahasuerus, in Christian legend, a Jew doomed to wander forever for mocking Christ at the Crucifixion; not named as a Jew until the 18th century. The many treatments of the subject include Shelley's *Queen Mab.*
Ahidjo, Ahmadou (1924–), first President of Cameroon. After serving in the territorial government of the French Cameroons, he managed to gain independence for his country in 1960 and union with the newly independent former British Cameroons in 1961, while maintaining close ties with France.
Ahimsa, non-violence or non-injury to both men and animals, a central concept of JAINISM and BUDDHISM, important also in HINDUISM. This belief led to the condemnation of sacrificial cults by Jains and Buddhists and inspired Mahatma GANDHI's passive resistance.
Ahmadābād, city in W India, on the Sabarmati River; capital of Gujurat state. Founded in 1411, it is the cultural, commercial and transport centre of the state, with many magnificent mosques, temples and tombs, and Gujurat University (1950). It has the headquarters of the INDIAN NATIONAL CONGRESS, and GANDHI located his school for political training nearby. The city's principal industry is cotton. Pop. 1,600,000.
Ahmadnagar, city in W central India, on the River Sina. It was the birthplace of Shivaji, famed leader of the Marathas (Mahrattas). Today it is an administrative and textile manufacturing centre. Pop. 118,300
Ahmad Shah Durrani (*c.* 1722–73), Emir of Afghanistan (1747–73) and founder of the Durrani dynasty. He united the Afghan tribes and is sometimes known as the founder of modern Afghanistan. He invaded India, taking Delhi twice, in 1757 and 1760. But he was unable to hold on to the territory gained and in the 1760s he lost the Punjab to the Sikhs.
Ahmose, also Amosis, Amasis, two kings of ancient Egypt. Ahmose I (*r. c.* 1570–1546 BC) re-established THEBES as the centre of government, reconquered Nubia and expelled the HYKSOS. He was the father of AMENHOTEP I. Ahmose II (*r.* 570–525 BC) encouraged Greek trade with Egypt (founding a market town at Naucratis), but allowed his kingdom to be threatened by CYRUS THE GREAT of Persia. See also HC1 p.35.
Ahriman, or Angra Mainyu, Zoroastrian principle of evil standing in opposition to AHURA MAZDA, the omniscient God and creator of life. Like God, Ahriman is pure spirit and has with him subsidiary evil spirits such as lust and heresy. Born of infinite time along with Ahura Mazda, Ahriman will nevertheless be defeated in the end. *See also* ZOROASTRIANISM.
Ahura Mazda (Mazdah), in ZOROASTRIANISM, in early times the only God and creator. Later called Ohrmazd, Ahura

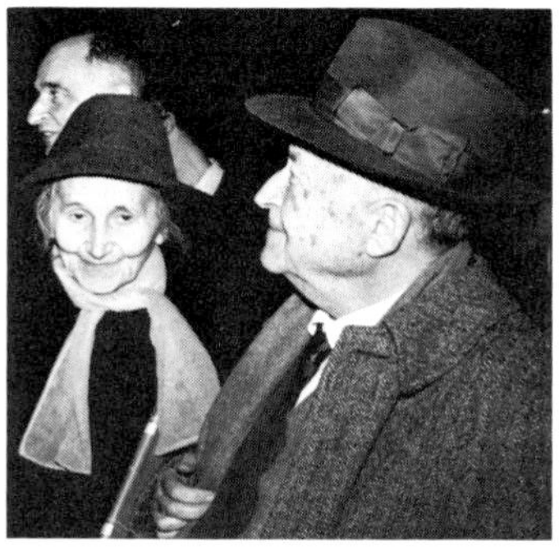

Shmuel Yosef Agnon, arriving with his wife in Stockholm to receive a 1966 Nobel Prize.

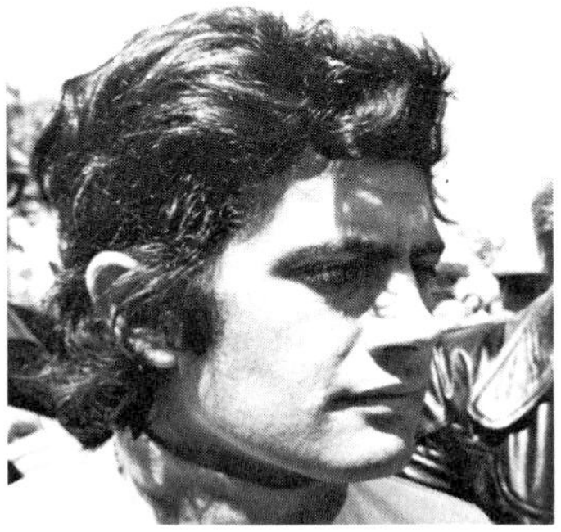

Giacomo Agostini, seven times world 500cc motorcycle champion, riding a MV Augusta.

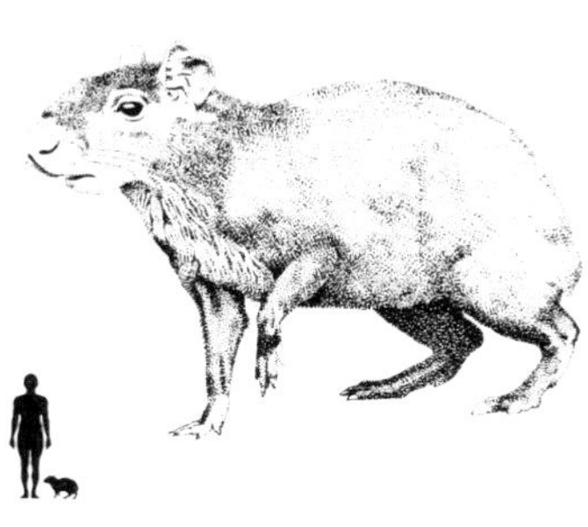

Agoutis, similar to rabbits in behaviour and diet, are hunted for their tasty white flesh.

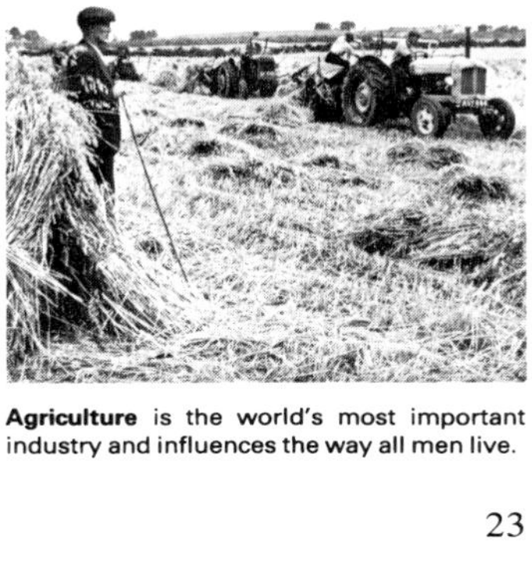

Agriculture is the world's most important industry and influences the way all men live.

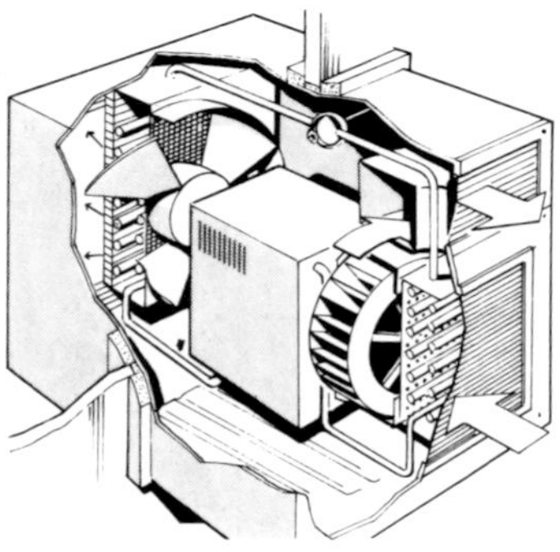

Air conditioning heats, cools or cleanses the atmosphere; the motor is equipped with fans.

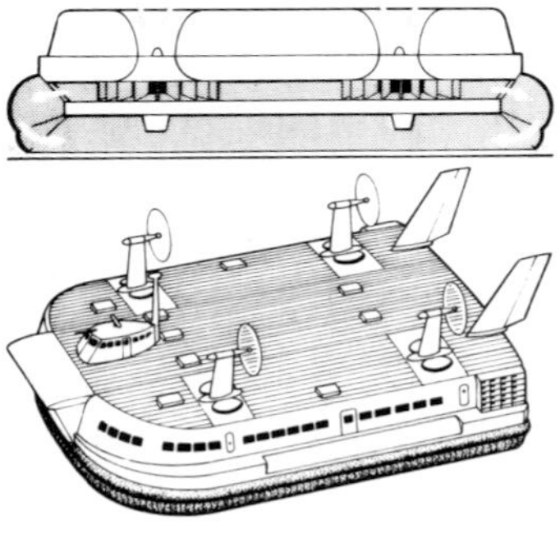

Air-cushion vehicles skim over land or water on a layer of air created by powerful fans.

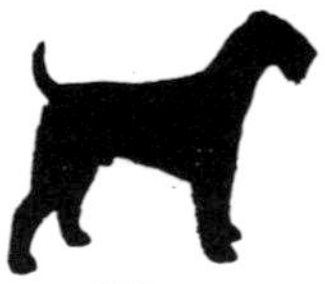

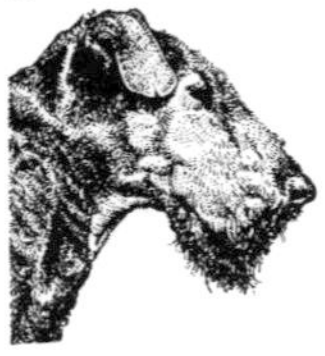

Airedale terriers are a courageous and affectionate breed; they are good swimmers.

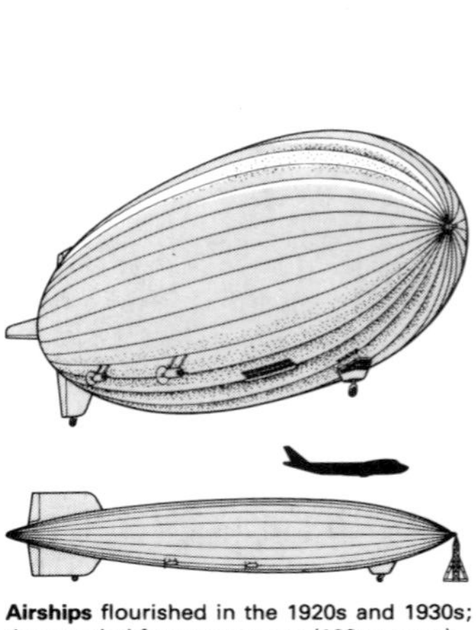

Airships flourished in the 1920s and 1930s; they carried few passengers (100 at most).

Mazda was pure goodness. Evil was attributed to an opposing principle, AHRIMAN. Ahura Mazda will defeat Ahriman in the end. The six Bounteous Immortals springing from Ahura Mazda represent godly attributes that can be acquired by righteous men. *See also* HC1 p.61.
Ahvenanmaa. *See* ÅLAND ISLANDS.
Ahvāz (Ahwāz), city in SW Iran on the Karūn River; capital of Khūzestān province. In the 12th and 13th centuries it was a flourishing Arab trading centre. It is now an important oil pipeline terminus and has petrochemical, food processing and textile industries. The ruins of the ancient Persian city remain. Pop. 302,000.
Aicard, François Victor Jean (1848–1921), French author who wrote poems, plays and novels. His most significant volume of poetry was *Poèmes de Provence* (1874); he was the author of *Maurin des Maures* (1908), a novel about Provençal life, and wrote 14 plays.
Aida (1871), tragic opera in four acts by Giuseppe VERDI (1813–1901), Italian libretto by Verdi and Antonio Ghislanzoni (1824–93). The opera was commissioned by the Khedive of Egypt for a new opera house in Cairo and concerns the love of an Egyptian hero (Rhadames) for an Ethiopian slave (Aida). *See also* HC2 p.*120.*
Aidan, Saint (*d.*651), Irish monk from Iona who *c.*635 began the conversion of Northumbria to Christianity. He became the first Bishop of Lindisfarne. *See also* HC1 pp.134, 140.
Aiken, Conrad (1889–1975), US poet, novelist and critic. His works include *Selected Poems* (1929; Pulitzer Prize 1930), *Brownstone Eclogues and Other Poems* (1942) and *Ushant* (1952), an autobiography.
Aikido, martial art based on an ancient Japanese system of self-defence. Unlike some other martial art forms, where force is met with counter-force, Aikido employs the technique of avoiding action by giving way to an opponent's impetus, thereby causing the attacker to suffer a temporary loss of balance. Forms of Aikido such as tomiki are also sports.
Aileron, hinged control surface on the outer trailing edge of each wing of an AEROPLANE. By rotating the control wheel, the pilot deflects the ailerons down or up in opposite directions to increase or decrease lift, causing the aeroplane to roll or bank. *See also* MM pp.152–153.
Ailey, Alvin (1931–), US modern dancer and choreographer. He danced with Hanya Holm and the Martha Graham Company before forming the Alvin Ailey Dance Theater in 1958, a primarily Black, modern dance group which has toured widely throughout the world.
Ailsa Craig, small island at the mouth of the CLYDE, 16km (10 miles) off the SW coast of Scotland. It has a lighthouse and a bird sanctuary.
Ain, river in E France, rising in the Jura Mountains and flowing S into the River Rhône. Length: 190km (118 miles).
Ainsworth, William Harrison (1805–82), British author of historical romances, notable for their accuracy of detail and sensational action. His most popular novel, *The Tower of London* (1840), was illustrated by the British artist George CRUICKSHANK.
Aintree, borough in Merseyside, NW England, N of Liverpool. Its race-course is famous for the annual Grand National steeplechase. Pop. (1971) 8,271.
Ainu, aboriginal people who live on Hokkaidō (N Japan), Sakhalin and the Kuril islands. Racially distinct from the Japanese, the Ainu possess certain Caucasoid features, notably heavy body and facial hair. Traditionally hunters, fishermen and trappers, they practise ANIMISM and are famed for their bear cult.
Air, the gases above the Earth's surface. *See* ATMOSPHERE; SU p.192; PE p.20.
Air bladder, abdominal sac in some fish, which fills with gas according to the density of the surrounding water in order to give the fish buoyancy.
Air compressor, machine that delivers air or gas at pressure. It is used for furnace blast systems, ventilation and refrigeration systems, pneumatic drills and for inflating vehicle tyres. Reciprocating and rotary compressors are the two basic types.
Air conditioning, process of controlling the temperature, humidity, flow and sometimes odour and dust content of air in any enclosed space. The air is cooled by refrigeration or heated by steam or hot water. Odours and dust are removed by filters and the moisture content is adjusted by humidifiers before the air is circulated by fans which also remove stale air.
Aircraft. *See* AEROPLANE; AIRSHIP; AUTOGYRO; GLIDER; HELICOPTER; MM pp.146–155; 176–179.
Aircraft carrier, military vessel with wide open deck which serves as runway for the launching and landing of aircraft. A modern nuclear-powered carrier may have a flight deck about 300m (1,000ft) long, a displacement of about 75,000 tonnes, a 4,000-man crew and carry 90 aircraft of various types – launched one a minute with each of four steam catapults. Some carriers have large, angled decks to permit launching and landing simultaneously. *See also* MM p.174.
Air-cushion vehicle, also called hovercraft, machine capable of hovering several inches to a few feet above ground or water, and of forward, backward or lateral motion. It is used to provide scheduled passenger services in many places, particularly for short sea journeys, and has been experimented with by the military. *See also* MM p.116.
Airdrie, town in Strathclyde Region, S central Scotland. Its 19th-century growth was based on local deposits of coal and iron. Industries: chemicals, electrical and electronic equipment. Pop. (1971) 37,900.
Airedale terrier, working dog, largest of the TERRIERS. This wire-haired, black-and-tan dog has a long, flat head squared off by chin whiskers. Standard size: 58cm (23in) high at the shoulder; weight: 20kg (45lb).
Air force, military force forming the primary national instrument of air power. Britain merged its Royal Flying Corps and Royal Naval Air Service into the ROYAL AIR FORCE, formed on 1 April 1918, the first independent air force. The US Air Force was created from the Army Air Force in 1947. The USSR's air power is divided between many arms including Frontal Aviation (tactical), Long-Range Aviation, Naval Aviation and the PVO (air-defence force which also includes missiles). *See also* MM pp.176–179.
Air gauge. *See* PRESSURE GAUGE.
Airglow, faint permanent glow of the Earth's ionosphere resulting from the recombination of molecules, such as oxygen and nitrogen, that have been ionized by ultra-violet radiation from the sun and probably by cosmic-ray and solar-wind particles.
Airlock, hermetically sealed passageway between two leakproof doors connecting an airless environment, eg the sea depths or outer space, with a pressurized cabin or work area. Entry is made through the outer door, which is then closed; air is pumped into the airlock until its pressure is equal to that inside and then the inner door opens.
Air New Zealand, state-owned international airline, established in 1940. Its principal routes are to Honolulu and Los Angeles, and Hong Kong and Singapore.
Air pollution. *See* POLLUTION.
Airport, tract of land upon which aircraft regularly take off and land. Airports generally contain facilities for cargo storage, maintenance and fuelling of aircraft, navigational aids, a control tower and passenger facilities. Some are huge complexes, lavishly equipped, but others are simply grass landing strips with windsocks at one end. *See also* AIR-TRAFFIC CONTROL; MM p.186.
Air pressure. *See* ATMOSPHERE.
Airscrew, or propeller, dual or multiple blade that rotates on a hub and deflects air to produce a thrust at right- angles to the blade. Airscrews are used mainly to propel aeroplanes and air cushion vehicles. *See also* MM pp.116, 152.
Airship, powered lighter-than-air craft able to control its direction of motion. A rigid airship, or Zeppelin, maintains its form with a framework of girders covered by a rubberized fabric. Non-rigid airships have no internal structure, only the pressure of the contained gas maintains the shape. A semi-rigid airship has a rigid or jointed keel to stiffen the rubberized envelope. *See also* MM pp.146–147.
Air-speed indicator, instrument that measures the speed of an aircraft relative to the air through which it passes. It measures the difference in pressures of air rushing through a pitot tube (generally mounted on the wing) and static air from a vent on the fuselage; air-speed is usually indicated in miles per hour or knots. *See also* GROUND-SPEED.
Air-speed record, the fastest speed achieved by an aircraft that can take off and land unaided. In May 1965 a Lockheed YF-12A achieved a speed of 3,331.5km/h (2,070mph), and this record stood until July 1976 when it was broken by a Lockheed SR-71A, which achieved a speed of 3,531km/h (2,194mph). Faster speeds have been achieved by rocket-powered aircraft launched in the air from a "mother" plane. In June 1964 for instance a North American Aviation X-15A-2 reached a speed of Mach 6.72 – 7,297km/h (4,534mph). The official record for the fastest piston-engined aircraft was set in Aug. 1969 by a Grumman F8F-2 Bearcat at 776.4km/h (482.5mph), although a Hawker Sea Fury in Aug. 1966 recorded a speed of 836km/h (520mph). *See also* MM p.*36.*
Air-traffic control, system of guidance to provide for the safe and orderly movement of aircraft to and from an AIRPORT, directed from the control tower. It consists of ground and local control for airport vehicles and emergency services; arrival and departure control operating from radar rooms where the "stacking" and timing of aircraft traffic to or from the runways is monitored; and a system of route control that allows controllers to "hand over" to the next control station flights that reach the limits of their airspace. *See also* MM p.186.
Airy, Sir George Biddell (1801–92), British astronomer who also made discoveries in optics, such as a cylindrical lens for correcting the eye defect ASTIGMATISM. He was Astronomer Royal from 1853 to 1881. *See also* SU p.214.
Aisne, river in France which rises near Vaubecourt and flows NW and W from the Argonne Forest to join the River Oise near Compiègne. In WWI the plateau along the river near Craonne saw bitter fighting. Length: 282km (175 miles).
Aitken, Robert Grant (1864–1951), US astronomer who discovered more than 3,000 double stars. He was director of Lick Observatory from 1930 to 1935.
Aix-en-Provence, city in SE France, 27km (17 miles) N of Marseilles. Founded in 123 BC by the Romans, its nearby mineral springs make it a popular spa. It is a cultural centre with a university (1409) and an 11th-13th-century cathedral. Paul CÉZANNE lived there. It has industries producing wine-making equipment and electrical apparatus. Pop. 102,000.
Aix-la-Chapelle. *See* AACHEN.
Aix-la-Chapelle, Treaty of (1748), diplomatic agreement, principally between France and Britain, that ended the War of the AUSTRIAN SUCCESSION (1740–48). The treaty provided for the mutual restitution of conquests made during the war, and contributed to the continuing rise of Prussian power. Britain was confirmed in its control of the trade in slaves to Spanish America. *See also* HC2 p.313.
Ajaccio, seaport town and capital of the island of CORSICA, France, on the Gulf of Ajaccio, an inlet of the Mediterranean Sea. It was founded in 1492 by Genoese colonists. NAPOLEON was born there and his home is now a national museum. The Germans occupied the town in WWII. Industries: sardine fishing, shipbuilding, cigars, wax. Pop. 42,300.
Ajanta, village in Maharashtra State, W central India. It is situated in the foothills of the Ajanta Range at an elevation of

about 400m (1,300ft). Nearby are the famous Ajanta caves consisting of 29 chambers carved out of the side of a steep ravine by the followers of Gautama BUDDHA, used for centuries as Buddhist monasteries and temples. The walls are decorated with a series of remarkable frescoes, depicting the life of Buddha through the eyes of ancient India. Pop. 3,560. *See also* HC1 p.*120*.

Ajax, in Greek mythology, name given to two heroes who fought for Greece during the TROJAN WAR. The Greater Ajax was the son of Telamon, King of Salamis; the Lesser Ajax was the son of Oileus, King of Locris. The Greater Ajax is depicted in Homer's *Iliad* as a courageous warrior who led the troops of Salamis against TROY. The lesser Ajax was so called because he was not the equal of the Telamonian Ajax. There are many versions of the manner in which he died.

Ajax (*c*.447 BC), Greek tragedy thought to be SOPHOCLES' earliest surviving play. It tells the story of Ajax who, angered when the armour of Achilles is awarded to Odysseus, offends ATHENA and is sent mad; his humiliation on recovery leads him to suicide, and a dispute ensues over the burial-honours due to him.

Ajivika, ascetic religious sect of India that flourished under Emperor ASHOKA in the 3rd century BC. The Ajivikas lived in the Bihar region in caves which had magnificent carved entrances.

Ajmer, town in NW India in the state of Rajasthan. It is an administrative town and a centre for the cotton and marble industries. Pop. (1971) 262,851.

Akaba. *See* AQABA.

Akaroa, small summer resort and fishing port in New Zealand, on French Bay. It was originally a French settlement, bought by the New Zealand government in 1849.

Akashi, city and fishing port of W Honshū Island, Japan, on the Harima Sea. Industries: electrical and farm machinery. Pop. (1974) 228,205.

Akasov, Sergei Timofeevich (1791–1859), Russian writer of humorous novels that accurately described his life and times. His sons Konstantin (1817–60) and Ivan (1823–86) were also writers.

Akbar (1542–1605), Mogul emperor of India (1556–1605). He greatly expanded the MOGUL EMPIRE, conquering Bengal, Gujarat, Kandahār, Kashmir and Sind. He reformed government, centralized banking and attempted to introduce one unifying religion. *See also* HC2 p.*48*.

À Kempis, Thomas. *See* KEMPIS, THOMAS À.

Akenside, Mark (1721–70), British poet and physician to Queen Charlotte (wife of George III). His best-known works were *The Pleasures of Imagination* (1744) and *Odes on Various Subjects*. (1745).

Akhenaton (died *c*.1362 BC), ancient Egyptian king of the 18th dynasty (reigned *c*.1379–1362 BC). He succeeded his father, AMENHOTEP III. His name at his accession was Amenhotep IV. Renouncing the old gods, he introduced worship of the sun god, Aton, and established a new capital at Akhetaten (modern Tell el Amarna). After his death Egypt rejected sun worship. *See also* HC1 p.48.

Akhmatova, Anna (1889–1967), pseudonym of Anna Andreyevna Gorenko, Soviet poet. Her simple, intense lyrics and personal themes are best represented in the volumes *The Rosary* (1914) and *The Willow Tree* (1940). Although twice denounced, in 1946 and 1957, for "bourgeois decadence", she has remained a popular poet in the Soviet Union.

Akhnaton. *See* AKHENATON.

Akihito (1933–), son of Emperor Hirohito, Crown Prince of Japan. After extensive travel abroad, he married a commoner, Michiko Shoda, in 1959. They have three children.

Akii-Bua, John (1949–), Ugandan athlete. He won the Olympic Games 400m hurdle event in 1972 in 47.8 sec., but did not defend his title in 1976, when Uganda withdrew from the Games.

Akita, town in Japan, on the Sea of Japan, capital of Akita prefecture. It is a port for the export of rice and timber and an oil-refining centre. Pop. (1974) 253,606.

Akkadia (Agade), ancient region of MESOPOTAMIA, named after the city-state of Akkad. From the mid-4th millennium BC the area's cities fought each other until SARGON united the Akkadians, Sumerians and Elamites in the 2300s. His empire reached to the Mediterranean in the W and the Black Sea in the N. Under pressure from hostile tribes, the Sumerians moved the capital from Akkad to UR. At the end of the 3rd millennium ELAM controlled the area, later known as Babylonia. *See also* SUMERIA; BABYLON; HC1 pp.30, 329.

Akkaia. *See* ACHAEAN LEAGUE.

Akko. *See* ACRE.

Akō, town in S Honshū, Japan, on the Harima Sea. It is famous for its Oishi (Shinto) Shrine and Kogakuji (Buddhist) temple. Industries include salt extraction, fishing nets and cement. Pop. 45,900.

Akosombo Dam, dam on the River Volta, Ghana, finished in 1965. It is 113m (370ft) high, stores water for irrigation, and supplies electricity for industry.

Akron, city in NE Ohio, USA, on the Cuyahoga River, 48km (30 miles) SSE of CLEVELAND. The opening of the Ohio and Erie Canal in 1827 promoted the city's growth. Places of interest include abolitionist John BROWN's home and a large dirigible airdock. Industries include rubber, plastics, engineering and chemicals. Pop. (1970) 275,425.

Aksum. *See* AXUM.

Akureyri, city in N Iceland, on the River Eyjafjördhur; the country's third largest municipality. Settled *c*.900, it is now an industrial, commercial and fishing centre. Pop. 10,800.

Alabama, state in SE USA in the chief cotton-growing region. The N of the state lies in the Appalachian Highlands, which have coal, iron ore and other mineral deposits, and the rest consists of the Gulf Coastal Plain, crossed by a wide strip of rich soil valuable for agriculture. The Mobile River (flowing S to the Gulf of Mexico) and its tributaries, the Alabama and Tombigbee, form the chief river system. The principal crops are cotton, groundnuts, soya beans and maize. Industries include chemicals, textiles and metal products. BIRMINGHAM, the largest city, is one of the nation's leading iron and steel centres. Other main cities are Montgomery, which is the state capital, Huntsville and Mobile, the chief port.

First settled by the French in 1702, the region was acquired by Britain in 1763. Most of it was ceded to the USA after the AMERICAN WAR OF INDEPENDENCE (1783). Alabama was admitted as the 22nd state of the Union in 1819, It seceded in 1861 – one of the original six states of the Confederacy – and was re-admitted to the Union in 1868. It has been the scene of many civil rights demonstrations. Area: 133,667sq km (51,609sq miles). Pop. (1975 est.) 3,614,000. *See also* HC2 p.108.

Alabama case (1872), award of $155 million compensation to the USA against the UK for damage done by Confederate ships built in England during the AMERICAN CIVIL WAR (1861–65).

Alabaster, fine-grained, massive variety of gypsum (calcium sulphate), snow-white and translucent in its natural form. It can be dyed or made opaque by heating and has been used ornamentally for centuries. *See also* GYPSUM.

Alain-Fournier (1886–1914), pseudonym of Henri-Alban Fournier, French writer, killed in action at the Battle of the Marne (1914). His reputation was secured by his only completed novel, *Le Grand Meaulnes* (1913), a lyrical account of the experiences of a schoolboy.

Alajuela, city in central Costa Rica, NW of San José; capital of Alajuela province. A former national capital (1830s), it is now a trade centre for the central plateau region. Industries include coffee, sugar, timber, flowers, hides and tourism. Pop. 29,000.

Alamanni. *See* ALEMANNI.

Alamein. *See* EL ALAMEIN.

Alamo, chapel in San Antonio, Texas, the scene of an incident in the Texas Revolution. In 1836 about 180 Texans, led by William TRAVIS, Davy CROCKETT and James BOWIE, were overwhelmed after defending heroically against superior Mexican forces. *See also* HC2 p.149.

Alanbrooke, Alan Francis Brooke, 1st Viscount (1883–1963), British general. During WWII he commanded the 2nd Army Corps in France and was Commander-in-Chief of the British Home Forces (1940–41). He was Chief of the Imperial General Staff (1941–46) and directed British tactics against Germany and co-ordinated Anglo-American strategy with Gen. EISENHOWER.

Åland (Ahvenanmaa) Islands, archipelago in the Baltic Sea between Sweden and Finland; a province of Finland. The chief town is Maarianhamina (Mariehamn), a port in Åland, the largest island. Fishing, forestry, farming and tourism are the main occupations. The islanders are Swedish speaking. Pop. (1975) 22,000.

Alanine, colourless soluble AMINO ACID, $CH_3CH(NH_2)COOH$, that occurs widely in PROTEINS, for example those derived from silk.

Alarcón, Pedro Antonio de (1833-91), Spanish novelist. His works reflected his own transition from a staunch anticleric to a devout Roman Catholic. He was wounded in a campaign in Morocco, and wrote a journal of his war experiences (1859–60). He gained international fame upon the publication of the short novel *El sombrero de tres picos* (*The Three-Cornered Hat*, *c*. 1874).

Alarcón y Mendoza, Juan Ruiz de (*c*.1581–1634), Spanish dramatist, *b*. Mexico. He is best known for his comedies, such as *La verdad sospechosa* (*c*.1619) and *Las paredes oyen*.

Alaric (*c*.370–410), King of the VISIGOTHS (395–410). His forces conquered Thrace, Macedonia and Greece and occupied Epirus (395–96). He invaded Italy in 401 and 408 and besieged (408) and sacked (410) Rome, permanently reducing the power of the Empire. He planned an invasion of Sicily and Africa, but his fleet was destroyed in a storm. *See also* HC1 p.136.

Alas, Leopoldo (1852–1910), Spanish novelist, critic and short-story writer who adopted the pen-name Clarín. In his best-known novel, *La Regenta* (1884–85), he analysed provincial life.

Alaska, state of the USA in NW North America, separated from the rest of continental USA by the province of British Columbia, Canada. About 25 per cent of Alaska lies N of the Arctic Circle. The Alaska Range includes the highest peaks in North America. The chief river is the Yukon, flowing W into the Bering Sea. The Alaskan economy is based on fish, oil and timber. The largest city is Anchorage and the capital is Juneau. Russian hunters first settled Alaska in the late 1700s. The USA purchased the area from Russia in 1867 for $7.2 million (less than two cents an acre). Fishing drew settlers and, after the gold rush of the 1890s, the population doubled in ten years. The long-standing dispute between the USA and Britain (representing Canada) over the boundary between Alaska and British Columbia was settled in 1913. Because of its strategic position and petroleum reserves, Alaska has been developed as a military area and linked to the rest of the USA by the Alaska Highway and an oil pipeline. Area: 1,518,800sq km (586,400sq miles). Pop. 352,000.

Alaskan North Slope, lowland plain in N Alaska where petroleum, discovered in the 1960s, was being developed in the mid-1970s. The land is frozen tundra for most of the year, making the extraction of oil particularly difficult.

Al Azhar, University of, in Cairo, Egypt; one of the world's oldest universities (founded 970). It is also one of the largest universities, and in 1971 had more than 20,000 students.

Alaungpaya, "the Victorious" (1711–60), also called Alompra or Aungzeya, King of Burma (1752–60). Alaungpaya refused to become a vassal of the kingdom of Mon (in the Irrawaddy Delta) when AVA, the Burmese capital, was captured in 1752. He organized resistance, recaptured Ava in 1753 and took over the Mon capital, Pegu, in 1757. He tried to conquer Siam in 1760, but died with his army in retreat.

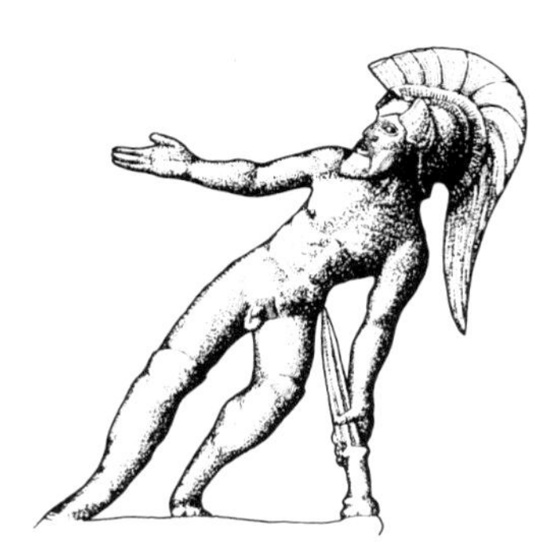

Ajax the Greater took his own life when he failed to inherit the armour of Achilles.

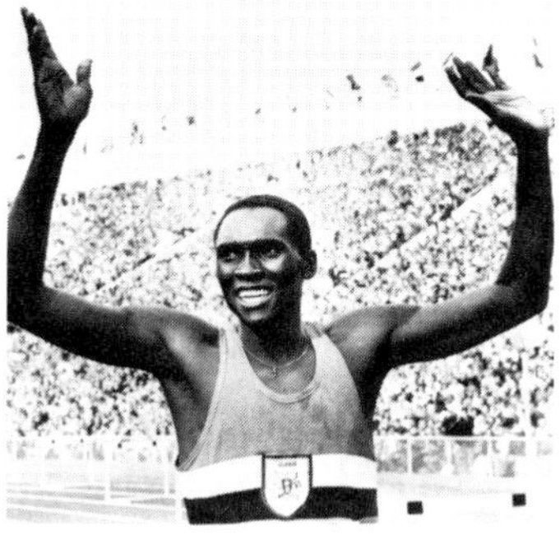

John Akii-Bua was not able to defend his title in the 1976 Olympics for political reasons.

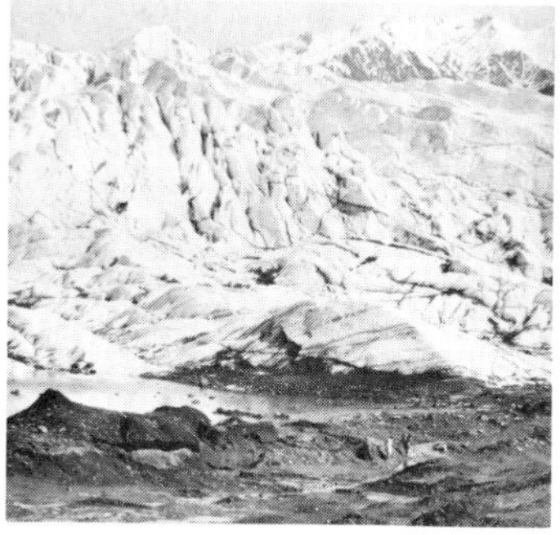

Akureyri, Iceland, is an important fishing centre at the head of the Eyjafjörd.

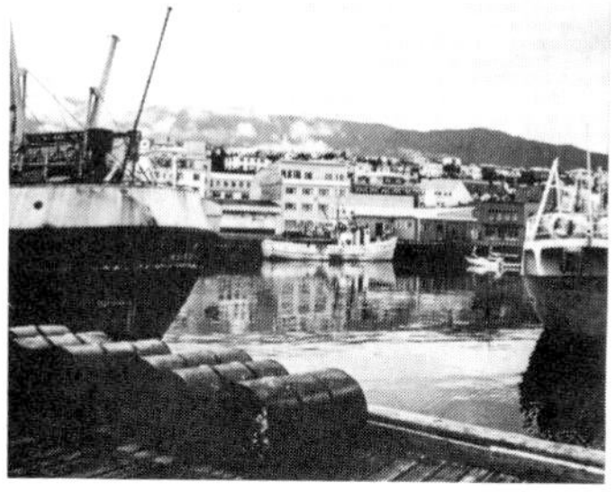

Alaska, the American state that extends into the Arctic Circle, is rich in petroleum.

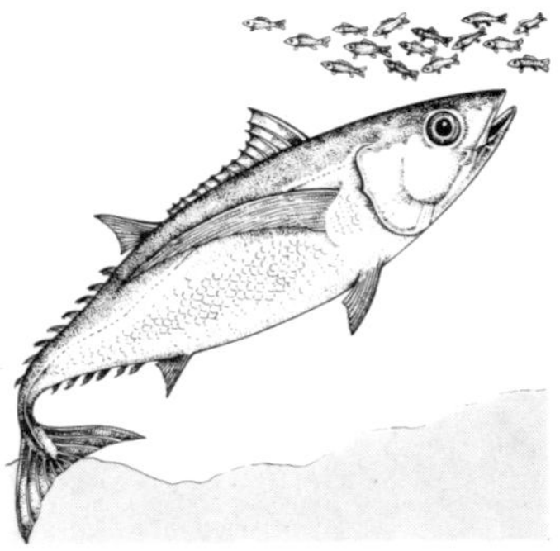

Albacores have a body temperature up to 9°C (16°F) warmer than the surrounding sea.

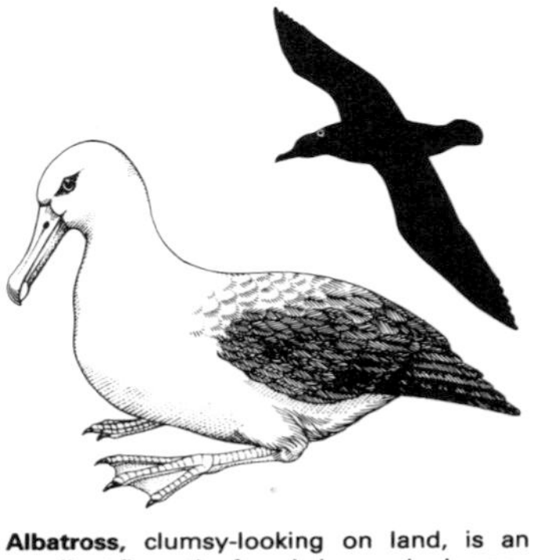

Albatross, clumsy-looking on land, is an excellent flyer; the female lays a single egg.

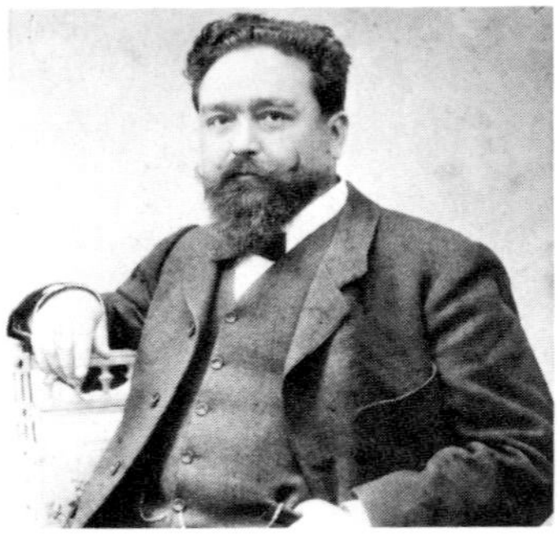

Isaac Albéniz, by often using folk tunes, wrote music that was distinctly Spanish.

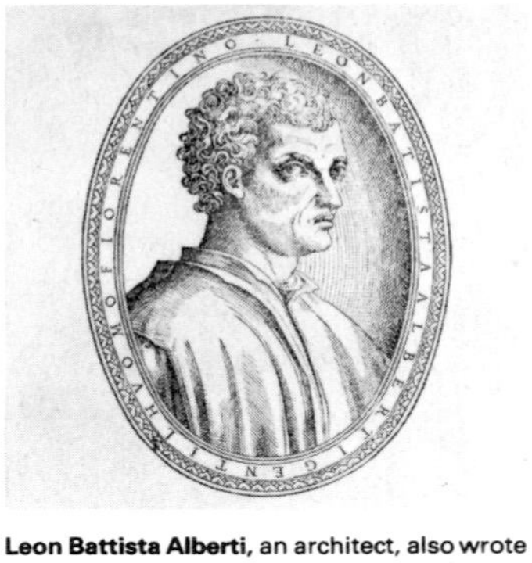

Leon Battista Alberti, an architect, also wrote on art and design, including perspective.

Alba (or Alva), Fernando Álvarez de Toledo, Duke of (1508–82), Spanish general and statesman. After successful campaigns in Germany and Italy, he was appointed regent of The Netherlands in 1567 by Philip II. He ruthlessly suppressed Protestant and nationalist opposition and thousands of people were executed. In 1572 the Dutch rose up in armed rebellion which Alba failed to suppress. He was recalled to Spain in 1573. After being out of favour for several years, in 1580 he led a successful invasion of Portugal.

Albacete, city in SE central Spain; capital of Albacete province. It has a 16th-century cathedral, Moorish remains and is an agricultural centre. Pop. (1974) 100,545.

Albacore, long-finned, fast swimming TUNA of warm seas. Cigar-shaped, with a large tail sharply divided into two lobes, it has a long pectoral fin. It is an important commercial and game fish. Length: 91cm (3ft); weight: 18-36kg (40-80lb). Family Scombridae; species *Thunnus alalugna.*

Alba Longa, city of ancient Latium near Lake Albano, 19km (12 miles) SE of Rome. According to legend it was founded *c.*1152 BC by Ascanius (son of Aeneas); it was the head of the Latin League and, as the traditional birthplace of Romulus and Remus, the mother city of Rome.

Alban, Saint (died *c.*304), first British martyr, from the Roman town of Verulamium (now St Albans). He was put to death for hiding a Christian priest from the Romans. About 500 years later King Offa founded an abbey on the site of Alban's execution.

Albanel, Charles (1616–96), French Missionary and explorer in Canada. In 1671 he established fur trading routes after exploring the Saguenay River and Hudson Bay.

Albani, Madame Emma (1847–1930), Canadian soprano. She made her first public appearance in 1870, performed first in Britain at Covent Garden in 1872, and made her debut at the Metropolitan Opera in 1890. She was a leading Wagnerian soprano of her day.

Albania, small, independent Communist republic on the Balkan Peninsula in SE Europe, on the Adriatic Sea. In 1961 it became the first European country to ally itself with China. Agriculture includes wheat, cotton, corn and tobacco, and the major industries are textiles, food processing and chemicals. Area: 28,749sq km (11,098sq miles). Pop. (1976 est.) 2,549,000. *See also* MW p.25.

Albany, dukes of, branch of the Scottish royal house, the STUARTS. The 1st Duke, Robert (*c.*1340–1420) was Regent from 1388 to 1399 and again after 1402. John (*c.*1481–1536), grandson of JAMES II, was made Regent in 1515 and heir to the throne the following year; his regency was annulled in 1524.

Albany, city and capital of New York State, on the Hudson River, 232km (145 miles) N of New York City. First settled in 1614, it replaced New York as state capital in 1797. It has many old buildings and the state capitol (1867–98). Industries include paper, machine tools, metal products and textiles. Pop. (1973) 111,373.

Albany, town in SW Western Australia, on King George Sound, 384km (240 miles) SSE of Perth. Founded in 1826 as a penal colony, it is the state's oldest settlement. It is a popular health resort and its industries include fish canning and wool. Pop. 13,000.

Albatross, large, migratory oceanic bird of the Southern Hemisphere famed for its effortless gliding flight. There are 13 species. The wandering albatross has a long, thick, hooked bill, short tail, webbed toes and the greatest wing span of any living bird – 3.5m (11.5ft) or more. After an elaborate courtship, the female lays a single white egg in a small nest on an isolated island. Length: 0.7–1.4m (2.3–4.4ft). Family Diomedeidae. *See also* NW pp.77, 148, 238.

Albatross, in golf, a term used for a hole completed in three under par. The most celebrated occasion this shot was played occurred in the 1935 US Masters at Augusta when Gene Sarazen holed his tee shot at the 15th, a 500-yard par-five, for an albatross. This shot is also referred to as a double eagle.

Albedo, the fraction of light or other radiation that is reflected from a surface. An ideal reflector has an albedo of 100%; those of real reflectors are less. The mean albedo of snow is 45 to 90%; that of the Earth, viewed from satellites, is 35%. Much has been deduced about the surfaces of planets by comparing their albedos with those of known substances.

Albee, Edward Franklin (1928–), US dramatist. His best-known play is *Who's Afraid of Virginia Woolf?* (1962). His clever, biting commentaries on American life include the plays *Tiny Alice* (1964), *A Delicate Balance* (1966) and *Seascape* (1975).

Albéniz, Isaac (1860–1909), Spanish Romantic composer and pianist. He often used Spanish folk elements in his compositions, which included the piano suite *Iberia* (1906–09). *See also* HC2 p.270.

Alberoni, Giulio (1664–1752), Italian statesman who, after the War of the SPANISH SUCCESSION (1701–14), served as premier of Spain (1716–19). He sought to drive Austrians from Italy, and to protect Spanish-American trade.

Albers, Joseph (1888–1976), German-American painter, designer and art teacher. After teaching at the BAUHAUS (1923–33) he settled in the USA, where he developed a new free abstract style and became a pioneer of OP ART. *Homage to the Square* (1949), his best-known work, is a subtle experiment in colour relationships.

Albert I (1875–1934), King of the Belgians (1909–34). Son of Philip, Count of Flanders, he succeeded his uncle, Leopold II. In 1914 he led the Belgian resistance to the Germans while the Allied defence formed. He led the Belgian and French forces through Belgium in the Allies' final general offensive of 1918. After WWI he devoted himself to the task of reconstruction.

Albert, Prince, of Saxe-Coburg-Gotha (1819–61), husband and cousin of Queen VICTORIA of England, whom he married in 1840. He was of German origin and won great respect from the British for his integrity. He was given the title of Prince Consort and advised and influenced the Queen, particularly in foreign affairs. He organized the Great Exhibition of 1851 and founded the Victoria and Albert Museum. *See also* HC2 pp.112–113.

Albert, Lake, former name of Lake Mobutu Sese Seko in E central Africa on the border between Zaire and Uganda, in the Great Rift Valley. The Semliki River and the Victoria Nile empty into the lake and it is drained by the Albert Nile. It was discovered by Samuel Baker in 1864. It is 160km (100 miles) long, has an average width of 35km (22 miles) and its maximum depth is 51m (168ft).

Alberta, province of W Canada. The Rocky Mountains lie along part of the W boundary, but most of Alberta is prairie, part of the high plains of central North America. The principal rivers are the Athabasca, Peace, North and South Saskatchewan and Milk. Lesser Slave Lake is the largest of the many lakes. The fertile plains support wheat farming and livestock (cattle, pigs, sheep and poultry). Major resources are coal, minerals and wood from the forests in the N. Oil and natural gas fields in central Alberta have been a major stimulus to the economy since WWII. Manufacturing is mostly concentrated in the areas of EDMONTON, the capital, and CALGARY, the second largest city. Industries include petroleum products, metals, chemicals, food and wood products.

The area was part of a large territory granted in 1670 by Charles II to the HUDSON'S BAY COMPANY, a fur-trading enterprise. In 1870 the government of Canada bought the region from the company. Settlement began on a large scale in the late 1800s, when migrants arrived from other Canadian provinces, the USA and Europe. A transcontinental railway was completed across the region in 1885. The area was part of the Northwest Territories and governed from Ottawa, but in 1882 this area was divided into four districts, Alberta being one. It was admitted to the then Confederation as a province in 1905. Area: 661,188sq km (255,285sq miles). Pop. (1975 est.) 1,770,000. *See also* HC2 p.136; MW p.50.

Albert Canal, waterway 130km (80 miles) long, in NE Belgium, linking the industrial city of Liège with the port of Antwerp.

Alberti, Leon Battista (1404–72), Italian architect, humanist and writer. The first major art theorist of the RENAISSANCE, he influenced its painters, sculptors and architects with his theories, contained in *On Painting* (1435). His buildings include the Rucellai Palace, Florence, the Tempio Malatestiano, Rimini, and the church of San Andrea, Mantua. *See also* HC1 p.255.

Alberti, Rafael (1902–), Spanish poet and playwright. He wrote some remarkable poetic plays, including *Concerning Angels* (1927–28). His poetry became more intimate after he joined the Communist Party, but it lacked the vivacity of some of his contemporaries' work.

Albertinelli, Mariotto (1474–1515), Florentine painter. His works sometimes resemble those of Fra BARTOLOMMEO, with whom he collaborated. His paintings include *Visitation* (1503).

Albertus Magnus, Saint (*c.*1200–80), German theologian. Introduced to Aristotle's philosophy in Padua, he became a Dominican monk in 1223, and Bishop of Regensburg in 1260. Albertus wrote *Books on the Sentences* and a *Summa Theologiae*; his work shows the influence of Aristotle's scientific writings. Thomas AQUINAS was one of his pupils. He was canonized in 1931. *See also* HC1 p.188.

Albi, town in S France, on the River Tarn; of Tarn département. The old part of the city, known as "ville rouge", has many redbrick medieval buildings. It was the birthplace of TOULOUSE-LAUTREC and a museum displays his paintings. Pop. 57,100.

Albigensians, followers of the Catharist heresy in Languedoc, southern France, in the 12th and 13th centuries. They believed in a Manichaean division between the forces of good and evil, and practised extreme ASCETICISM. INNOCENT III called for a crusade against them (started in 1209) which was led by Simon de Montfort, who mercilessly persecuted the heresy. The French crown then conquered Languedoc in 1229. *See also* HC1 p.187.

Albino, person or animal with an hereditary absence of pigment from the skin, hair and eyes. The hair is white and the eyes, which often are extremely sensitive to light, have a pink iris and a red pupil (because, in the absence of pigment, the blood vessels are visible). *See also* MS pp.61, *99.*

Albinoni, Tomaso (1671–1750), Italian violinist and composer. He was one of the first composers of CONCERTOS for a solo instrument (VIOLIN and OBOE). He also wrote nearly 50 operas.

Albion, old name for Britain or England, from the Latin *albus* (meaning white), referring to the white cliffs of Dover.

Albireo, also called Beta Cygni, a double star in the constellation Cygnus. It has a yellow primary and a greenish secondary. *See also* SU pp.*236, 259.*

Al-Biruni (973–1048), Arab scholar who worked in astronomy, mathematics and geography. His accounts of travels in India, financed by members of the Turkish Ghaznavid dynasty, provide a valuable contemporary record.

Ålborg (Aalborg), city in N Denmark, capital of Nordjylland county. It is one of the oldest cities in Denmark, and has a 14th-century church and a 16th-century castle. Today it is a major centre for industry and for transport and communications. Pop. 154,700.

Albuera, Spanish village, where in 1811 the British army, under William BERESFORD, defeated the French forces commanded by Nicolas-Jean SOULT.

Albumin, or albumen, type of soluble PROTEIN occurring in animal tissues and fluids. Principal forms are egg albumin, milk albumin and blood albumin.

Albuminuria, presence of PROTEIN (serum albumin or globulin) in the urine. It may result from eating certain foods, or from certain diseases, notably those of the kidney. *See also* MS p.93.

Albuquerque, Afonso d' (1453–1515), founder of the Portuguese empire in the East. He took control of Malacca, Calicut, the Malabar Coast, Ceylon and Goa, which he made the Portuguese capital in the East (1510). From 1506 he also explored the Madagascar and East African coasts. *See also* HC1 p.235.

Albuquerque, city in W central New Mexico, USA, on the Upper Rio Grande River; the largest city in New Mexico. Founded by the Spanish in 1706, it served as a military post until 1870. Industries: nuclear research, food processing, railway workshops. Pop. (1970) 243,751.

Alcaeus (*c.*620 BC), Greek lyric poet. He wrote political songs, hymns and love songs. He was imitated by the poet HORACE but only fragments of his poems have survived. *See also* HC1 p.75.

Alcalá Zamora, Niceto (1877–1949), Spanish politician, President of Spain (1931–36). He was instrumental in overthrowing the monarchy in 1931 and was elected first President of the Second Republic. A moderate whose policies pleased neither the left- nor right-wing, he was forced out of office in 1936.

Alcántara, town in W Spain, near the border with Portugal, on the Tagus River. It has a Roman bridge, more than 204m (670ft) long and 61m (200ft) high, which was built by TRAJAN in the second century, and the church and ruined convent of the Order of Alcántara. Pop. 5,000.

Alcatraz, island off the coast of California, in San Francisco Bay. Since its discovery by the Spanish in 1769, it has served as a fortification and then a federal prison until 1962, when it became part of the Golden Gate National Recreational Area.

Alcazar, name for Moorish palaces in Spain, reflected in the names of several towns. One of the five alcazars, Toledo, was defended by Nationalist troops in 1936 during the SPANISH CIVIL WAR; it held out for 71 days against the Republicans.

Alcestis (438 BC), Greek tragedy by EURIPIDES. The work is best known for its strong characterization of its noble heroine. Alcestis takes her husband's place in Hades so that he may live. Hercules brings her back alive, and husband and wife are reunited.

Alchemy, primitive form of chemistry practised in Western Europe from early Christian times until the 17th century, popularly supposed to involve a search for the Philosopher's Stone – capable of transmuting base metals into gold – and the elixir of life. In fact, alchemy involved a combination of practical chemistry, astrology, philosophy and mysticism, based on the concept of the unity of matter and analogous ideas of the unity of man with the universe. Similar movements existed in China and India. *See also* PARACELSUS; PHLOGISTON; SU p.24.

Alcibiades (*c.*450–404 BC) Athenian general and statesman, ward of PERICLES, intimate of SOCRATES. After inspiring a campaign to Sicily in 415 BC that was a disaster, he temporarily aided Sparta. After regaining his position in Athens, he was exiled following the Athenian defeat (in his absence) at Notium in *c.*406. *See also* HC1 p.70.

Alcmaeon (6th century BC), Greek physician and philosopher. He was a pioneer in the separation of the study of medicine from philosophy, and developed a theory of physical equilibrium to define and explain health.

Alcman (*c.*650 BC), chief lyric poet of Sparta, regarded as the founder of erotic poetry. He abandoned the hexameter and wrote in varied, simple meters. Among his known work, which survives only in fragments, is the poem *Parthenion* (a choir song for girls), which was found in Egypt in 1855 on a pre-Christian papyrus.

Alcock, George (1912–) British amateur astronomer who discovered four comets and the nova HR Delphini. *See also* SU pp.217, 241.

Alcock, Sir John William (1892–1919), pioneer British airman who, together with Arthur Whitten-Brown, was the first to fly non-stop across the Atlantic Ocean. Their transatlantic flight was in a standard twin-engined Vickers Vimy bomber biplane, in response to a £10,000 prize put up by the British newspaper *Daily Mail.* They flew from St John's, Newfoundland on 14 June 1919 and landed 16.5 hours later near Clifden, Ireland. Alcock was killed in an air crash six months later when flying from London to Paris.

Alcohol, member of a class of organic compounds having a hydroxyl (–OH) group bound to a hydrocarbon group. There are three types of alcohols: primary (RCH_2OH), secondary (RR'CHOH) and tertiary (RR'R"COH), where R is either hydrogen or a hydrocarbon group. Primary alcohols can be oxidized to aldehydes, eg ethanol $C_2H_5OH+O \rightarrow CH_3CHO$ (acetaldehyde; ethanal). An alcohol reacts with a carboxylic acid to give an ester and water: ethanol and acetic (ethanoic) acid give ethyl acetate, $C_2H_5OH+CH_3COOH \rightarrow CH_3COOC_2H_5+H_2O$. *See also* PE pp.202–203; SU p.141.

Alcoholics Anonymous, organization that seeks to help alcoholics help themselves, with the ultimate goal of rehabilitation. Founded in 1934, it has local autonomous groups in more than 90 countries. Membership is open to anyone who has the desire to stop drinking, and the group makes use of shared experiences and mutual help. *See also* MS pp.104–105.

Alcoholism, disorder caused by excessive drinking of alcohol, and the effects it can have on the nervous system and organs of the body. Intoxication (drunkenness) is acute alcoholism, experienced by anyone who has too much to drink. Its symptoms, which range from slurred speech and unsteady gait to unconsciousness, disappear as the body "burns up" the alcohol. Chronic alcoholism, in which the victim becomes dependent on alcoholic drinks, can be regarded as a form of drug ADDICTION. Perhaps prompted by a personality disorder, it results in personality changes. The heavy drinker may be rejected by his family and friends, lose his job, and rely even more heavily on alcohol to "escape" from his problems. Physical damage, such as CIRRHOSIS of the liver and inflammation of the stomach and intestines, may result. Extreme cases may lead to delirium tremens (DTS) and even death. Treatment for chronic alcoholism ranges from the prescription of sedatives and aversion drugs such as ANTABUSE to pyschotherapy. *See also* MS pp.104–105.

Alcools (1913), volume of poetry by Guillaume APOLLINAIRE. The collection, including many of his early poems, records his transition from SYMBOLISM to the early developments of CUBISM. The later poems are uncompromisingly modern in style and content.

Alcor, one partner of a double star (its companion is Mizar) in the constellation Ursa Major (the Plough). *See also* SU pp.236, *237, 256.*

Alcott, Louisa May (1832–88), US author. She is best known for her stories for children. She was a friend of EMERSON and THOREAU. Her first published book was *Flower Fables* (1855), a collection of fairy stories. Family debts led her to write the autobiographical novel *Little Women* (1868–69). Its success led her to write *An Old-Fashioned Girl* (1870), *Little Men* (1871), *Jo's Boys* (1886) and others.

Alcuin (*c.*732–804), scholar and cleric from Northumbria trained at the cathedral school at York. Invited to set up a palace school in the court of CHARLEMAGNE, he became a central figure of the CAROLINGIAN Renaissance, and inaugurated the medieval study of the seven liberal arts. His prolific writings include a corrected text of the Vulgate Bible. *See also* HC1 p.152.

Aldabra, island group in the Indian Ocean, approx. 400km (250 miles) NW of Madagascar; part of British Indian Ocean Territory and a dependency of the Seychelles. It includes Aldabra Island, the largest atoll in the Seychelles, and Assumption. Unusual flora and fauna, including the giant land tortoise, can be seen on the islands. First visited by the Portuguese in 1511, the group became British in 1810 and now has a military base.

Aldanov, Mark Alexandrovich (1886–1957), pen-name of Mark Landau, Russian author who wrote mainly about social conflict. His works include *The Thinker* (1921–27), a trilogy about the French Revolution, and *The Fifth Seal* (1939), about the Spanish Civil War.

Aldebaran, or Alpha Tauri, red giant star in the constellation of Taurus. Characteristics: apparent mag. 0.85; absolute mag. –0.7; spectral type K5; distance 76 light-years. *See also* SU p.*227.*

Aldeburgh, town in SE England on the E coast of Suffolk. It has an annual music festival founded by Benjamin BRITTEN in 1948. Pop. 2,800.

Aldehyde, member of a class of organic compounds characterized by the group –CHO. The simplest example is formaldehyde, HCOH, used as a preservative. Aldehydes can be made by oxidizing primary ALCOHOLS. They are generally reducing agents, being oxidized to carboxylic acids. Their systematic names are formed using the suffix -al; acetaldehyde, CH_3CHO, is ethanal.

Alder, Kurt (1902–58), German chemist who shared the 1950 Nobel Prize in chemistry with Otto DIELS for their development of a method of organic synthesis.

Alder, ornamental trees and shrubs of the birch family native to the Northern Hemisphere and W South America. They have toothed leaves and woody cones that remain on the branches after the nutlets are released. The bark is used in dyeing and the wood, which is water-resistant, is used for bridges. There are 30 species. The red, speckled, and European (black) alders are the best known. They are usually among the first trees to re-appear in denuded areas. Family Betulaceae; genus *Alnus.*

Alderfly, any of several species of soft-bodied flying insects commonly seen near ponds and streams. Its large aquatic larvae feed for three years on insects and then emerge to pupate on land. *See also* NW pp.106–107, *107.*

Alderman, elected or appointed member of a local legislative body that decides broad policies of municipal government. Ranking above the county or borough councillors, the aldermen elect the mayor.

Aldermaston, town in Berkshire, England, 16km (10 miles) SW of Reading. In the early 1960s its atomic energy plant became a rallying point for members of the CAMPAIGN FOR NUCLEAR DISARMAMENT (the "Aldermaston Marchers"), who made annual marches to London.

Alderney, northernmost island of the Channel Islands, separated from France by a 13km (8 mile) channel, the Race of Alderney. It is part of the Guernsey bailiwick (administrative area) and St Anne is the principal town. Early potatoes are exported, cattle are raised, and tourism is the chief industry. Area: 8sq km (3sq miles). Pop. (1971) 1,686. *See also* MW p.52.

Aldershot, town in NE Hampshire, S England, 55km (34 miles) SW of London. It has a military training camp founded in 1854. Pop. 33,400.

Aldhelm (Ealdhelm), Saint (*c.*639–709), English cleric and poet. He became abbot of Malmesbury (*c.*675) and first bishop of Sherborne in 705. He established many monasteries and churches, including the one at Bradford-on-Avon. Although his Latin works survive, none of the Old English poems that he is said to have written have been found. *See also* HC1 p.165.

Aldington, Richard (1892–1962), British writer who was a member of the IMAGIST movement (1910–18). His works include the novel *Death of a Hero* (1929), *Complete Poems* (1948) and *Lawrence of Arabia* (1955), a critical study of T. E. LAWRENCE.

Aldosterone, mineralocorticoid hormone which is secreted by the cortex (outer part) of the ADRENAL GLANDS. It regulates the salt and water balance of the body. *See also* MS pp.64–65.

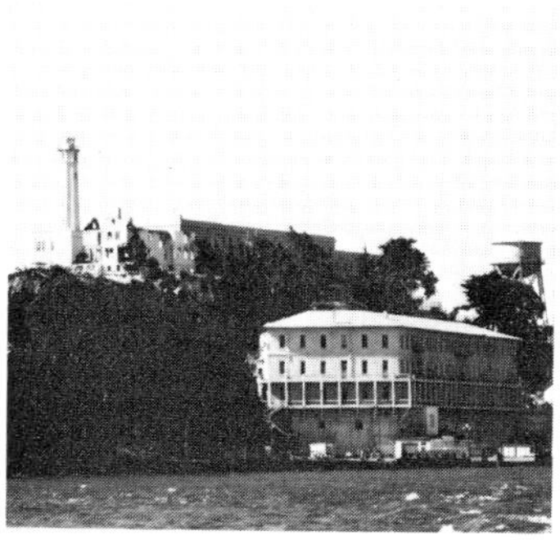

Alcatraz prison, sometimes known as "The Rock", was believed to be escape proof.

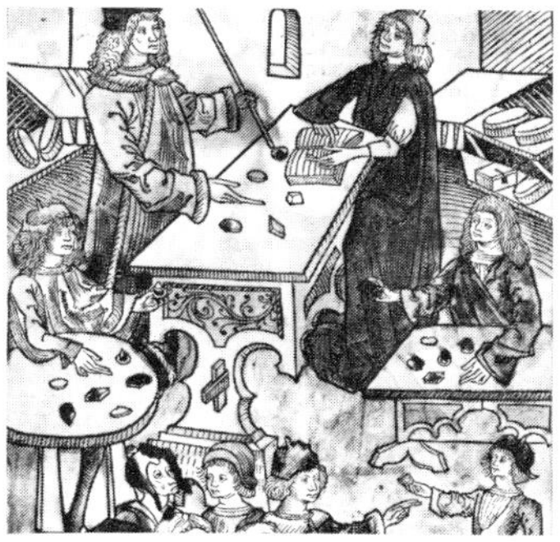

Alchemy, the study of matter and the universe, attracted scientists and fakes.

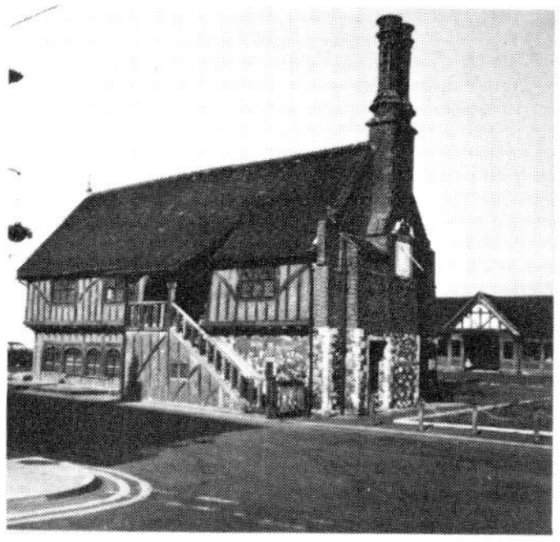

Aldeburgh, Suffolk, is the venue for the music festival founded by Benjamin Britten.

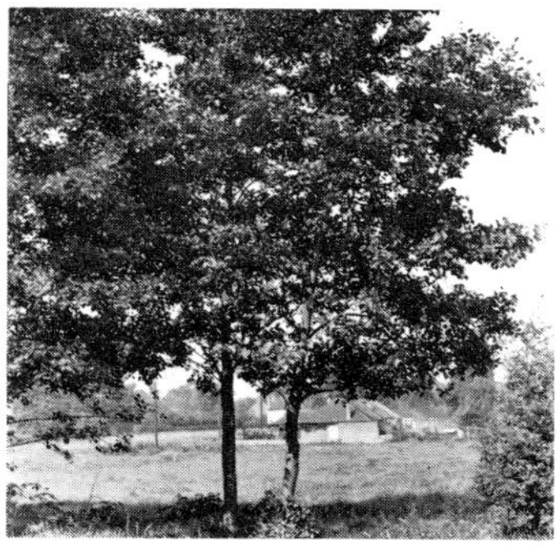

Alders make up about thirty species of trees and shrubs in the birch family.

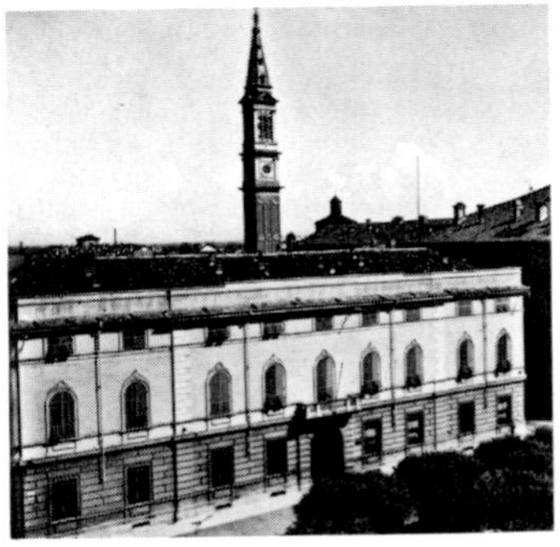

Alessandria, a hat-making town in northern Italy where the *Borsalino* hat is made.

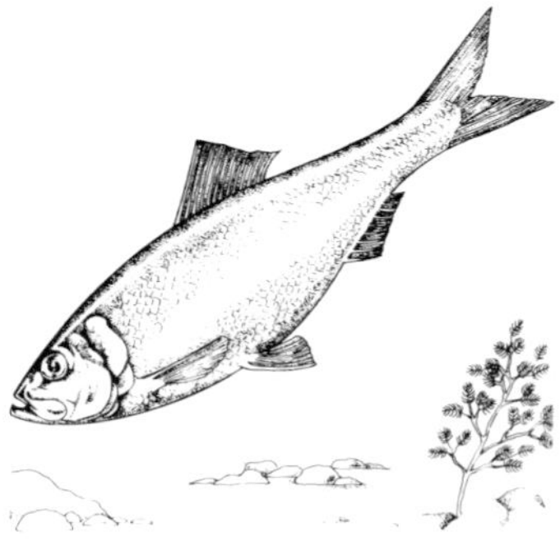

Alewife, an important food fish, returns when adult from the ocean to its native stream.

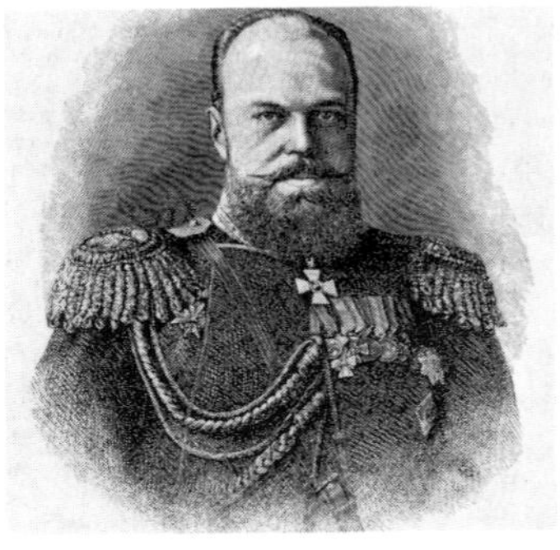

Tsar Alexander III tried to change the liberal tendencies of the previous reign.

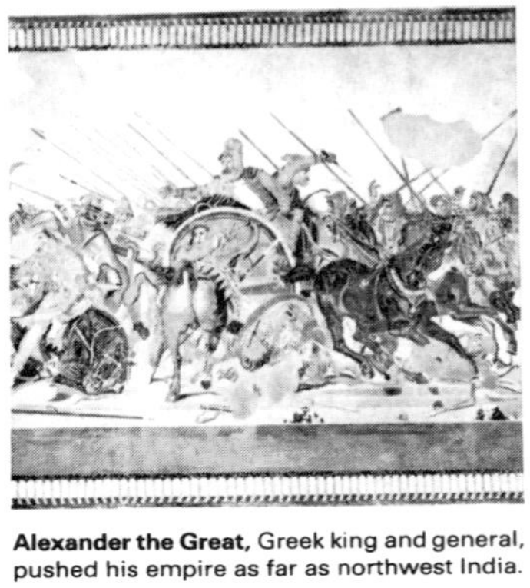

Alexander the Great, Greek king and general, pushed his empire as far as northwest India.

Aldrich, Robert (1918–), US film director. He has had box office success with often violent films – eg *The Dirty Dozen* (1968) – and has a reputation for explicit treatment of sensitive subjects, such as the lesbian theme in *The Killing of Sister George* (1970).

Aldridge, Ira Frederick (1805–67), US actor. Known as "African" Roscius, he was regarded as one of the finest actors of his time. After a triumphant London debut as Othello in 1826, he went on to great fame in England and, after 1853, elsewhere in Europe. He became a British citizen in 1863.

Aldrin, Edwin ("Buzz") (1930–), US astronaut. Aldrin piloted the Gemini XII orbital rendezvous space flight (Nov. 1966) and the lunar module for the first Moon landing (July 1969). During the landing he followed Neil ARMSTRONG to become the second man on the Moon. *See also* MM p.*159*; SU pp.180–81, *269*.

Aldrin, chlorinated naphthalene derivative (formula $C_{12}H_8Cl_6$) widely used as a contact insecticide. It is insoluble in water and is used as an emulsion or powder. It is also incorporated into plastic cable coverings to make them resistant to attack by termites.

Ale. *See* BEER; PE pp.204–205.

Aleatoric, word used to describe that music of the 20th century in which the sequence of notes is determined partly by chance, either at the time of composition or at the discretion of the performers. *See also* HC2 p.271.

Alegría, Ciro (1909–67), Peruvian novelist, the outstanding writer of the indianista (pro-Indian) movement. His best-known work is *Broad and Alien Is The World* (1941), which describes an Indian tribe's struggle against the expropriation of their land by Europeans. He was a social reform activist and was jailed twice in Peru (1931 and 1933) and exiled to Chile in 1934. He returned in 1948.

Aleichem, Shalom (1859–1916), pseudonym of Solomon Rabinowitz, Yiddish novelist, dramatist and short story writer. He was born in Russia and emigrated to the USA. He portrayed the oppression of Russian Jews with humour and compassion. His works include *The Old Country* (3rd ed. 1954) and *The Milkman (Tevye)* (*c.* 1949), adapted as the musical *Fiddler on the Roof* (*c.* 1965). He helped to establish Yiddish as a literary language.

Aleixandre, Vicente (1898–), Spanish poet. His considerable influence on younger Spanish writers derives from his original if difficult style, based on free verse and strange metaphors. Love of nature and of his fellow men are recurrent themes in his work, which includes *Historia del corazón* (1954). He was awarded the 1977 Nobel Prize in literature.

Alekhine, Alexander (1892–1946), French chess master, *b.* Moscow. He became a naturalized French citizen after the Russian Revolution of 1917, and was world chess champion 1927–35 and 1937–46.

Aleman, Mateo (1547–*c.* 1614), Spanish novelist. After a turbulent career in Spain, he emigrated to Mexico in 1608. He wrote a popular picaresque novel, *Guzmán de Alfarache* (1599–1604), which had strong moral overtones, and published a life of St Antonio de Padua.

Alemanni, or Alamanni, loose confederation of ancient Germanic tribes. It was first mentioned in AD 213 as being attacked by the Romans between the Elbe and the Danube.

Alembert, Jean Le Rond d' (1717–83), French philosopher and mathematician. He was a religious sceptic and physicist, and formulated d'Alembert's principle, used to solve certain problems in mechanics. He collaborated with DIDEROT on the French ENCYCLOPÉDIE (1751–72), for which he contributed the *Preliminary Discourse* (1851). He wrote a systematic *Treatise on Dynamics* (1743) as well as several pieces on differential equations. *See also* HC2 p.23.

Alencar, José Martiniano de (1829–77), Brazilian novelist, considered to be Brazil's first great prose writer. He is best known for three novels about his country's Indians: *O Guarani* (1857), *Iracema* (1865) and *O sertanejo* (1875). He has been praised for his vivid descriptions but criticized for romanticizing the "noble savage". Also a lawyer and journalist, he became Brazil's Minister of Justice in 1868.

Aleppo (Haleb), city in NW Syria, approx. 110km (70 miles) E of the Mediterranean coast; second largest city in Syria. It was captured from the Byzantines by the Arabs in AD 637, and then taken in 1516 by the Turks, under whom it became a great trading centre. Its commercial importance declined in the late 19th century with the opening of the Suez canal. A part of Syria since 1924, it has a 12th-century citadel, the Great Mosque (715) and a university. Industries include cotton, silk, pistachio nuts and fruit. Pop. 639,400.

Alessandria, capital city of Alessandria province, in the Piemonte region of NW Italy. Founded in the 12th century as Civitas Nova, then Cesaria, it was renamed after Pope ALEXANDER III. It is a transport and commercial centre and its industries include hat making, furniture and food processing. Pop. 105,000.

Aletsch, glacier in the Bernese Alps, S central Switzerland; the largest glacial feature of the Alps. It is 16km (10 miles) long and covers an area of 171sq km (66sq miles).

Aleutian Islands, volcanic island chain, an extension of the Aleutian Range in SW Alaska. They separate the Bering Sea from the Pacific Ocean, and were purchased with Alaska by the USA in 1867. Industries include fishing and furs. Area: approx. 17,666sq km (6,821sq miles). Pop. 8,000.

Aleutian Range, volcanic mountain system that stretches along the E coast of N Alaska. It includes Mt Katmai, 2,047m (6,716ft), and the Katmai National Monument, a recreational area. Length: approx. 970km (602 miles).

Aleuts, a branch of the Eskimo people who occupy the ALEUTIAN ISLANDS and Alaska Peninsula. They are divided into two major language groups, the Unalaska and Atka. First discovered by Vitus Bering (1681–1741) in 1741, they were forced into service as fur hunters and front-line attackers of other native peoples of the west coast. They numbered about 20,000 at that time, a total reduced to less than 1,500 a century later due to brutal treatment by the invaders. Today approx. 4,000 Aleuts live in scattered villages throughout SW Alaska. The women weave superb baskets of sea-grass that are often regarded as among the finest such articles made by native Americans. The Aleuts are racially similar to Siberians and the majority belong to the Russian Orthodox Church.

Alewife, marine commercial fish found in the N Atlantic and landlocked in large freshwater lakes. It is grey-green with dark horizontal side stripes. When canned or salted it is sold as "river herring". Length: 30cm (12in); weight: 0.4kg (14oz). Family Clupeidae; species *Pomolobus pseudoharengus.*

Alexander, name of eight POPES. Alexander III (*r.* 1159–81) was born Orlando Bandinelli (*c.* 1105–81). He was a canon lawyer who had been an associate of ADRIAN IV, but his election to the papacy was opposed by the Holy Roman Emperor FREDERICK I, who had an anti-pope, Victor IV, elected. The ensuing schism ended 17 years later with the victory of the Lombard League over Frederick at the Battle of LEGNANO. Alexander furthered the canon law and decreed that the College of Cardinals be solely responsible for the election of future popes. Alexander VI (*r.* 1492–1503) was born Rodrigo Borgia (*c.* 1431–1503). He was the father of four children, including Cesare and Lucrezia BORGIA. His use of the power of his office for personal and political ends as well as the patronage of the arts, was overt. SAVONAROLA was an outspoken critic of his pontificate.

Alexander (*c.* 886–913), Byzantine emperor. He was co-ruler with his brother Leo VI for 26 years (886–912), and sole ruler for one (912–913). During the lifetime of Leo VI, Alexander (who was a pleasure-loving man) took little part in government. His tenure as sole ruler was disastrous, for he provoked a war with the BULGARS.

Alexander, name of three Russian tsars. Alexander I (1777–1825) came to the throne in 1801, and with his chief minister Michael SPERANSKI introduced administrative and educational reforms. He repelled NAPOLEON's invasion of Russia in 1812 and led his troops across Europe and into Paris in 1814. After the war, influenced by Alexis Ararchev, he introduced many reactionary measures. His mystical interests led him to help form the HOLY ALLIANCE. He was named constitutional monarch of Poland in 1815 and annexed Finland, Georgia and Bessarabia. Alexander II (1818–81), who became Tsar in 1855, was best known for his emancipation of the serfs in 1861. Although he ended the CRIMEAN WAR in 1856, his Pan-Slavist affiliations led him to declare war on Turkey in 1877 and the Russian victory in 1878 resulted in the independence of Bulgaria from Turkey. He expanded his empire to the east despite selling Alaska to the USA in 1867. He was assassinated by revolutionaries in 1881. His successor Alexander III (1854–94) introduced reactionary policies which limited the powers of local government and extended press censorship. Arbitrary arrest and exile became common and ethnic minorities were persecuted. The principles of orthodoxy, autocracy and nationalism underlay his rule. *See also* HC2 pp.168–169.

Alexander the Great, Alexander III of Macedonia (356–323 BC), the greatest general in ancient history. Tutored by ARISTOTLE, he became king at the age of 20, destroying rivals and consolidating power in Greece. In 334 BC he began the Persian expedition, conquering western Asia Minor and storming the island of Tyre in 332 BC, his greatest military achievement. He subdued Egypt and occupied Babylon, marching north in 330 BC to Media and then conquering central Asia in 328 BC. In 327 BC he invaded India and set about consolidating his empire. While planning a voyage around Arabia he caught a fever and died at the age of 33. *See also* HC1 pp.80–81.

Alexander, the name of three kings of Scotland. Alexander I, "The Fierce" (*c.* 1080–1124), reigned between 1107 and 24. He divided the kingdom between the north and the south of the Forth river with his younger brother David. Alexander II (1198–1249) reigned between 1214 and 49 and cultivated peace with England in 1221 with HENRY III. He ruled with firm authority. Alexander III (1241–86) reigned between 1249 and 86. His great achievement was the purchase of the Hebrides and the Isle of Man from Norway in 1266. In addition, he promoted peace with England and Norway and consolidated Scottish unity.

Alexander (1893–1920), King of Greece (1917–20) after the Allies forced the abdication of his pro-German father King Constantine. Premier Venizelos approved the entry of Greece into WWI, gaining Smyrna and Thrace and hoping to form a "Greater Greece". Alexander died, from the bite of a pet monkey, before the plan could be put into operation.

Alexander I (1888–1934), King of the Serbs, Croats and Slovenes (1921–29) and King of Yugoslavia (1929–34). In his efforts to forge a united country from the rival national groups and ethnically divided political parties he created an autocratic police state. He was assassinated by a Croatian terrorist.

Alexander, Albert Victor (1885–1965), British Labour politician who became the 1st Earl Alexander of Hillsborough. He held the posts of First Lord of the Admiralty (1929–31) and Minister of Defence (1947–50).

Alexander, Frederick (1899–), Australian educationalist and author. He has travelled widely to centres of higher

education in other Commonwealth countries and the USA. Several of his books are about Australian history.
Alexander, Samuel (1859–1938), philosopher, *b.* Australia. A realist metaphysician strongly influenced by evolutionary theory, he expresses in his major work, *Space, Time and Deity* (1920), his theory of knowledge in which pure motion is held to be the basis of the universe.
Alexander Nevski (*c.* 1220–63), Russian ruler, national hero, Grand Duke of Novgorod from 1236, and from 1252 Grand Duke of Vladimir (the political centre of Russia at that time). He submitted to Mongol rule following their invasion of Russia and the Great Khan appointed him Grand Duke of Kiev. He defeated the Swedes on the Neva in 1240 (hence the name 'Nevski') and the TEUTONIC KNIGHTS in 1242. He was canonized in 1547. His exploits were the subject of a 1938 film by Sergei EISENSTEIN, with music by Sergei PROKOFIEV (later adapted as a cantata).
Alexander of Hales (*c.* 1185–1245), English theologian. He was the founder, in Paris, of the first Franciscan school of theology. The *Summa Universae theologica* attributed to him is the work of his followers. It introduced Aristotelian and Arabic elements into a basically Augustinian framework.
Alexander of Tunis, Harold Rupert Leofric George, 1st Earl (1891–1969), British military commander. He directed the British offensive in Egypt and Libya in 1942 and was Gen. Eisenhower's deputy in the victorious Tunisian campaign of 1943 before becoming Commander-in-Chief of Allied forces in Italy. He was Governor-General of Canada (1946–52) and British Minister of Defence (1952–54). *See also* HC2 p.228.
Alexander Severus, Marcus Aurelius (208–35), Roman emperor (222–35). He became emperor at the age of 14 and throughout his reign he was strongly influenced by his mother, Julia Mamaea. As a military leader, he fought the newly established Persian SASSANID Empire (231–33) and restored the Roman frontier in the Near East. On the Rhine frontier, he chose to buy peace from the Germans rather than fight them. His troops rebelled, killed Alexander and plunged the empire into military anarchy.
Alexander Island, formerly Alexander I island, off the W coast of the Antarctic Peninsula in the British Antarctic Territory and separated from the Palmer Peninsula by George VI Sound. It was discovered in 1819–21 by the Russian explorer Fabian von Bellingshausen, who named the area after his emperor. It is uninhabited. Area: 43,253sq km (16,700sq miles).
Alexandra, Queen (1844–1925), Queen Consort of EDWARD VII of Britain, daughter of Christian IX of Denmark and mother of George V. She married Edward in 1863. She began Alexandra Rose Day in 1902.
Alexandra, Princess (1936–), cousin of Queen Elizabeth II and 16th in succession to the British throne. She is the daughter of Prince George, Duke of Kent, and Princess Marina.
Alexandra, African township 13km (8 miles) N of Johannesburg, South Africa. Established early in the 1900s with facilities for 5,000 people, Alexandra's population quadrupled after WWII. It has since been extensively rebuilt. Pop. 60,000
Alexandretta. See ISKENDERUN, GULF OF.
Alexandria (Al-Iskandariya), chief port and second largest city in Egypt, situated on the western extremity of the Nile Delta. Founded by ALEXANDER THE GREAT in 332 BC, it became a centre of Hellenistic culture and contained one great library that was progressively destroyed from the time of Caesar's invasion. Under Muslim rule, the city slowly declined from 642 until the early 19th century. It contains a university, several famous museums and parks and is the Middle East Headquarters for the World Health Organization. Industries: oil refining, textiles, paper, food-processing, vegetables and plastics. Pop. 2,259,000.
Alexandrian school, group of Greek poets including Aratus (*c.* 315–*c.* 240), APOLLONIUS RHODIUS and THEOCRITUS who, between the 3rd and 1st centuries BC, worked in ALEXANDRIA.
Alexandrine, a 12-syllable line in poetry. Its name is probably derived from French medieval poetry about ALEXANDER THE GREAT. The most noted use of alexandrine is in classical French tragedy. Famous occurrences in English are Drayton's *Polyolbion* (1612-22) and the last line of the stanza form used in Spenser's *The Faerie Queene* (1589–96).
Alexeev, Vasili (1942–), Russian weightlifter. Olympic super-heavyweight champion in 1972 and 1976, Alexeev dominated the sport in the 1970s.
Alexius I Comnenus (1048-1118), Byzantine emperor (*r.* 1081–1118), founder of the Comnenian dynasty. This soldier-emperor came to the throne at a time when Byzantium was virtually destroyed, having lost vast territories to foreign invaders. During the 37 years of his reign, Alexius held off the Normans from their threatened attack on Constantinople; turned the Western armies of the First CRUSADE to his own advantage by using them to reconquer parts of Anatolia; and defeated the Patzinaks and Seljuk Turks. *See also* HC1 p.176.
Alfalfa. *See* LUCERNE.
Alfieri, Vittorio (1749–1803), Italian poet and dramatist. He sought to arouse a spirit of nationalism in his countrymen and wrote a score of verse-tragedies – among them *Filippo* (1781) and *Saul* (1782) – that proved influential.
Alfonso, name of a number of rulers of Spanish kingdoms. The kings of Aragon were not "numbered" in the same sequence as rulers of the other kingdoms. Alfonso V (994–1028) became King of León and Asturias after his supporters took the city of León following the death of the Moorish ruler in 999. He was killed in battle against the MOORS. Alfonso VIII (1155–1214) was King of Castile (1158–1214). He succeeded his father Sancho III at the age of three. He took control of his kingdom in 1166 and at first opposed both Moors and fellow-Christian kings. In 1212 he forged a coalition with the Christian rulers and won a major victory over the ALMOHADS at Las Navas de Tolosa. Alfonso X (1221–84), King of Castile and León (1252–84), was the son and successor of Ferdinand III. He continued his father's wars against the Moors but his chief ambition was to become Holy Roman Emperor. In 1257 a dissident group of German nobles named him anti-king (to Richard, Earl of Cornwall) but papal opposition kept him in Spain. A distinguished scholar, he codified the law and wrote histories of Spain and the world. He was a patron to Jewish, Moorish and Christian scholars, philosophers and scientists. Alfonso V (1396–1458) was King of Aragon (1416–58). He pursued military activity in deference to tradition, to protect his Eastern trade, and to curb Turkish power. Alfonso XIII (1886–1941) was born after the death of his father, Alfonso XII, and his mother acted as regent until 1902. Although personally popular, he could not satisfy the conflicting demands of the nationalist groups, socialists, republicans and others. In 1923 he supported the setting up of a right-wing military dictatorship under Gen. Miguel PRIMO DE RIVERA, which fell in 1930. A year later the republic was proclaimed.
Alfonso I (Afonso I) (1109–85), first King of Portugal (1139–85). He was the son of Henry of Burgundy, Count of Portugal. After his father's death (1112), his mother ruled as regent until 1128, when Alfonso deposed her. From about 1130 to 1139 he fought against the King of León and Castile and against the Moors; in 1147 he captured Lisbon. From 1139 he styled himself as King, a title ratified by Castile and the Pope in 1179. He was succeeded by his son SANCHO I.
Alfred (849-99), King of Wessex (871–99), called Alfred the Great. Warrior and scholar, he saved Wessex from the Danes and laid the foundations of a united English kingdom. Youngest of four successively reigning sons of King Ethelwulf, he became king at a time when the Danes threatened to overrun the kingdom. After the Danish invasion of Wessex in 878, he escaped to Athelney in Somerset, returning later to defeat the Danes at Edington and recover the kingdom. The legend in which he is reprimanded by a peasant woman for letting her cakes burn probably derives from this period. To strengthen Wessex against future attack he built a fleet of ships, constructed forts and reorganized the army. He instituted political reform by publishing a code of laws, translated and commissioned several Latin works into English and founded several schools. *See also* HC1 pp.154, 156, 164.
Alfreton, market town in Derbyshire, N central England. The major industries are coal mining and iron working. Pop. 21,700.
Alfvén, Hannes (1908–), Swedish astrophysicist who shared the 1970 Nobel Prize in physics with Louis Néel of France. He laid the foundation of what has become known as magnetohydrodynamics (MHD); he advanced the theory of frozen-in flux, which states that PLASMA is contained by the magnetic lines of flux through it.
Algae, large group of essentially aquatic plants found in salt and fresh water throughout the world. Algae make their own food by PHOTOSYNTHESIS, and they are the primary source of food for molluscs, fish and other aquatic animals. Algae are directly important to man as a food (especially in Japan) and as FERTILIZERS. They range in size from microscopic plants such as those that form green pond scum to huge brown KELPS more than 45m (150ft) long. The smallest algae are variously shaped single-celled organisms, some of which can move by means of whiplike "arms" called flagellae. Many-celled species – including the SEAWEEDS – grow in a variety of shapes, including cords, ruffled sheets and intricately branched structures resembling some land plants. But even the most advanced algae do not have true roots, stems or leaves like those of the higher plants. Algae are classified in 11 major botanical divisions. *See also* NW pp.46–48.
Algardi, Alessandro (1595–1654), Italian sculptor, one of the most important Italian portraitists in the 17th-century BAROQUE style. His works include the famous statue of Pope Innocent X (1645) in the Palazzo dei Conservatori, Rome. *See also* HC1 pp.304–305; 307.
Algarve, southernmost province of Portugal; the capital is Faro, on the Cabo de Santa Maria. It was first settled by the PHOENICIANS, then the MOORS, who were defeated by Alfonso III in 1253. Products: fruit, tuna and sardines. Area: 5,070sq km (1,958sq miles). Pop. (1970 est.) 266,600.
Algebra, form of arithmetic in which symbols replace numbers. Thus $3 + 5 = 8$ is a statement in arithmetic; $x + y = 8$ is one in algebra, involving the variables x and y. Boolean algebra (an example of a higher algebra) can be applied to sets and to logical propositions. *See also* MATHEMATICS; SU pp.34–40.
Algebraic fraction. *See* FRACTION.
Algeciras, seaport city in Andalusia, S Spain, on the Bay of Algeciras. It was the first Spanish town to be conquered by the MOORS (711). It was taken by Alfonso XI of Castile in 1344. Algeciras suffered great damage during the war between the Moors and the Spaniards, who rebuilt it in 1704. The city is an important resort and port. Pop. 81,700.
Algeria, independent republic in N Africa, on the Mediterranean Sea. A mostly Muslim country, it was a French colony before its independence in 1962. The chief city is ALGIERS. Industries include petroleum products (oil accounts for 70% of exports) and food processing. Agriculture is based on fruit, cereals and livestock. Area: 2,381,741sq km (919,397sq miles). Pop. 16,776,000. *See* MW p.26.
Algiers (Al-Jaza'ir), capital city of Algeria, on Algiers Bay; N Africa's chief port on the Mediterranean. At various times in its history it has been colonized by Romans, Spanish, Turks, Barbary Pirates and French. It has a Casbah (16th-century

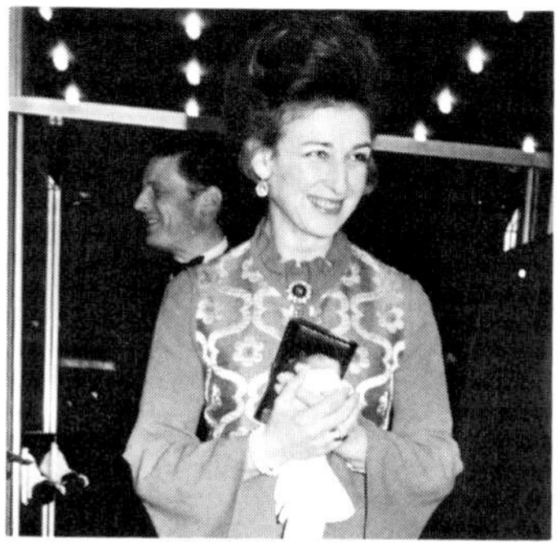

Princess Alexandra, Queen Elizabeth's cousin, is 16th in succession to the British throne.

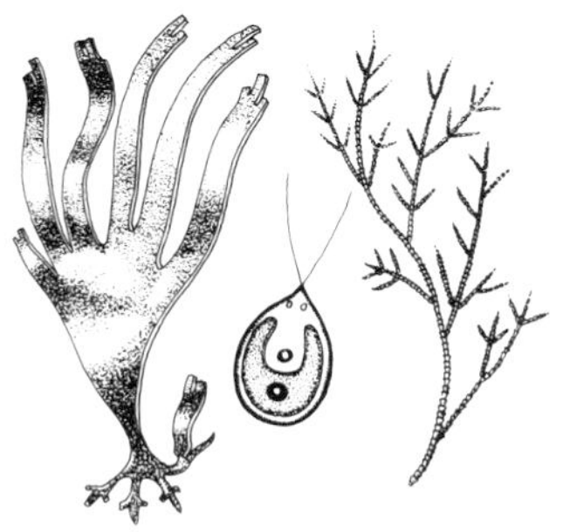

Algae, the simple organisms that purify air and water and provide food for other life.

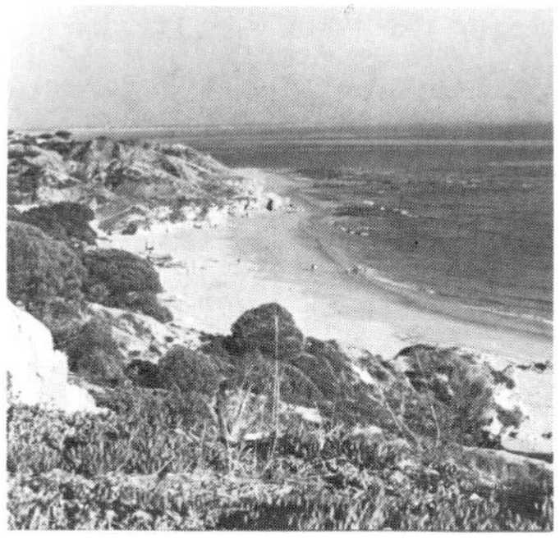

Algarve, from the Arabic meaning "the west", has about 32 small fishing seaports.

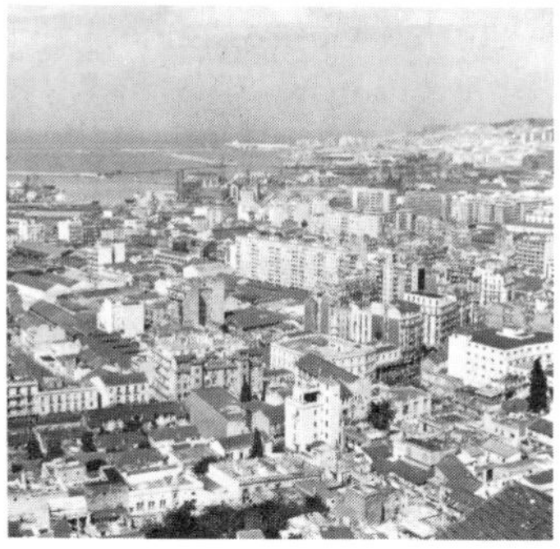

Algeria, second largest country in Africa, gained its independence from France in 1962.

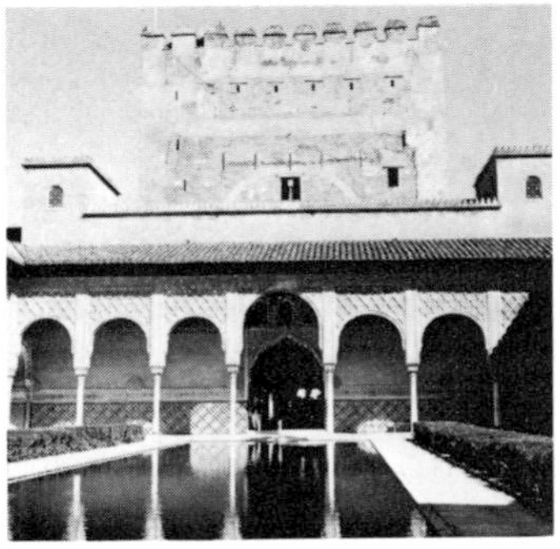

Alhambra, the palace and fortress in Granada and the last stronghold of the Moors in Spain.

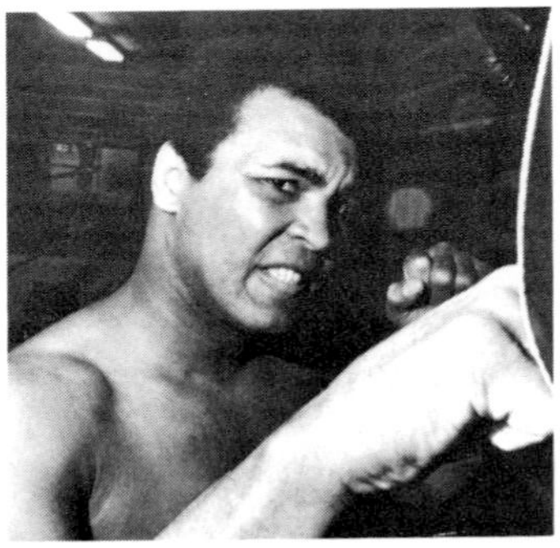

Muhammad Ali has thrilled the world with his combination of boxing and showmanship.

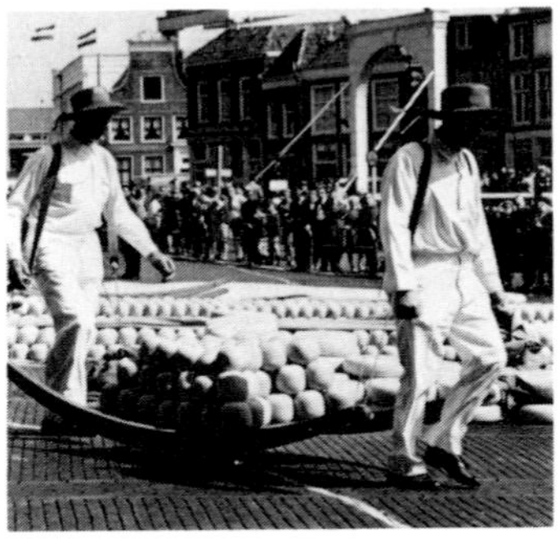

Alkmaar, the colourful town in The Netherlands, world famous for its cheese markets.

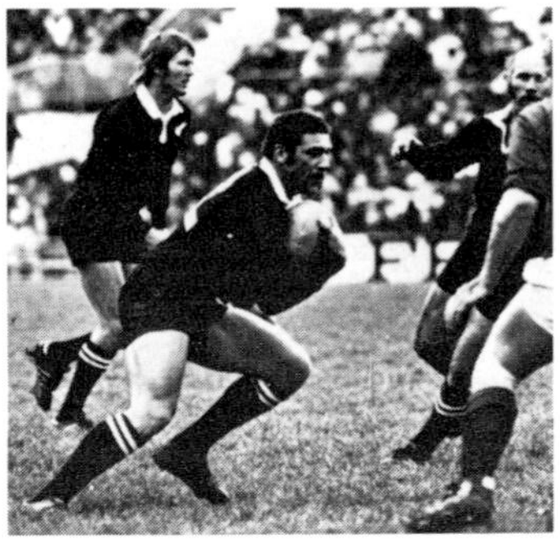

All Blacks, formidable New Zealand rugby union side in their distinctive "all black" strip.

Turkish citadel) and a Great Mosque (11th century). Industries include iron ore, food processing, cement and tobacco. Pop. (1975 est.) 1,179,000.

Algie, Sir Ronald (1888–), New Zealand politician. He founded the anti-socialist Freedom Association (1937) and sat as a Nationalist MP from 1943 to 1966.

Algin, any of a group of substances obtained from brown algae, used to stabilize emulsions and suspensions, including ice cream, chocolate and paints.

Algol (Beta Persei), eclipsing binary star in PERSEUS. *See* SU pp.*237*, 238, 255, *258*.

Algonquin, or Algonkin, group of Canadian Indian tribes that gave their name to the Algonquian languages of North America. The Algonquin people occupied the Ottawa River area *c.*AD 1600, at which time they numbered about 6,000. Driven from their home by the Iroquois in the 17th century, they were eventually absorbed into other related tribes in Canada.

Algren, Nelson (1909–), US novelist, *b.*Detroit. His works are realistic tales of petty criminals such as the hero of *The Man with the Golden Arm* (1949). The novel is best known for the way it deals with drug ADDICTION, and won the National Book Award in 1950.

Alhambra, Moorish palace and citadel overlooking Granada, Spain. Built by the Moorish rulers of Granada in the 13th–14th centuries, it is the finest example of Moorish architecture in Spain and is regarded as a masterpiece. The buildings fell into disrepair after the expulsion of the MOORS in 1492, but were restored in the 19th century. *See also* HC1 p.171.

Ali (*c.*600–61), 4th Muslim Caliph (656–61), son of Abu Talib, the Prophet MOHAMMED's cousin. Ali married Mohammed's daughter Fatima and was expected to become Caliph on the Prophet's death but had to wait 24 years before succeeding Othman. Ali crushed a revolt in Iraq but was unable to suppress Muawiya, Mohammed's former secretary who governed Syria. When Ali was murdered by fanatics his son Husan was persuaded to forgo his claim to the throne by Muawiya. The division in Islam between the SUNNI and SHIITE sects dates from this time. Ali and his wife are venerated by the Shiites, who believe Ali to have been the rightful heir of Mohammed. *See also* HC1 p.*148*.

Ali Bey (1728–73), ruler of Egypt. Although Egypt was under Ottoman control, he wielded great power, and invaded and captured Syria and Mecca (1771). He was later betrayed and fled to Syria. He tried to regain Egypt, but without success.

Ali, Muhammad (1942–) US boxer, *b.*Cassius Clay in Louisville. He won the Olympic light-heavyweight championship in 1960 and then beat Sonny Liston for the world heavyweight championship in 1964 in Miami Beach, Fla. The World Boxing Association took away Ali's title in 1967 after he refused to serve with the US Army because of his religious beliefs. In June 1971 the US Supreme Court upheld Ali's appeal on religious grounds, although upon returning to the ring in the same year he lost against Joe Frazier who was then world champion. He subsequently regained the title when he defeated George Foreman in 1974 in Zaire.

Alicante, city in SE Spain, 360km (225 miles) SE of Madrid; capital of Alicante province. It was a Roman naval base and is now an important Mediterranean port and tourist resort. The town was recaptured from the Moors *c.*1265. Falangist leader Antonio PRIMO DE RIVERA was executed there by the Republicans in 1936. It exports wine, fruit, esparto, cereals and olive oil from the fertile region surrounding it. Other industries include clay products, textiles and tobacco. Area: (province) 5,864sq km (2,264sq miles). Pop. (province) 920,100; (city) 213,143.

Alice's Adventures in Wonderland (1865), book by Lewis CARROLL. In a carefully constructed world of nonsense, a young girl, Alice, encounters such characters as the White Rabbit, the Duchess, the Cheshire Cat, the March Hare, the Mad Hatter and the Queen of Hearts. Although scholars have debated the allegorical significance and mathematical riddles of the story for years, it has remained resistant to serious interpretation.

Alice Springs, formerly Stuart, town in central Australia, on the Todd River. Founded in 1860 by McDouall Stuart, its importance increased in 1871 as a telegraph station between Adelaide and Darwin. It was the capital of the former state of Central Australia (1926–31). Industries: gold, copper and mica mining. Pop. (1968) 7,810.

Alien, in law, citizen of one country who resides in another. An alien is subject to the laws of the country he lives in but owes allegiance to his country of birth. In Britain an alien is a citizen of a non-Commonwealth country. Aliens can obtain citizenship through naturalization, which may be applied for usually only after a specified period of residence. A knowledge of the local language is normally essential for acceptance.

Alienation, in psychology, state of being alienated or diverted from normal functions. An alienated person is out of touch with reality. In drama, a term applied to plays in which audience and actors are encouraged not to identify with the characters (*see* BRECHT). *See also* MS p.144.

Alīgarh, city in Uttar Pradesh state, N central India, between the Ganges and Yamuna rivers. It is a Muslim cultural centre and is famous for its Muslim University (1920) and Alīgarh Movement, which sought to prepare Muslims for participation in political life, resulting in the All Muslim League. A market town and administrative centre, it has cotton mills and ancient Buddhist remains. Pop. 252,300.

Alimentary canal, digestive tract of an animal that begins with the MOUTH, continues through the OESOPHAGUS to the STOMACH and INTESTINES, and ends at the ANUS. It is about 9m (30ft) long in human beings. *See also* DIGESTIVE SYSTEM; MS pp.68–69.

Aliphatic compound, any organic chemical compound whose atoms are not linked to form rings. They include the alkanes (paraffins), alkenes (olefines) and alkynes (acetylenes). *See also* AROMATIC COMPOUND.

Alizarin (1,2-dihydroxyanthraquinone), red vegetable dye, first extracted from the root of the MADDER plant. A metal oxide MORDANT is used when dyeing fabrics.

Al-Jīzah. *See* GIZA.

Alkaid, star in Ursa Major. *See* SU pp.*166*, 254, 264.

Alkali, soluble BASE that reacts with an ACID to form a salt. Strong alkalis include the hydroxides of the alkali metals, and ammonium hydroxide. The carbonates of these metals, and ammonium carbonate, are weak alkalis.

Alkali elements, univalent metals forming Group IA of the periodic table: lithium, sodium, potassium, rubidium, caesium and francium. They are soft silvery-white metals that tarnish rapidly in air and react violently with water to form hydroxides, which make strongly basic solutions. *See also* SU pp.134, 146.

Alkaline-earth elements, bivalent metals forming Group IIA of the periodic table: beryllium, magnesium, calcium, strontium, barium and radium. They are all light, soft and highly reactive. All, except beryllium and magnesium, react with cold water to form hydroxides (magnesium reacts with hot water). Radium is important for its radioactivity. *See also* SU p.134.

Alkaloid, member of a class of complex nitrogen-containing organic compounds found in certain plants. Many alkaloids are tertiary amines. They are sometimes bitter and highly poisonous substances, used as DRUGS. Examples include atropine, codeine, morphine, nicotine, quinine and strychnine. *See also* MS pp.118–119.

Alkalosis, abnormal condition in which the blood becomes too alkaline. It may result from acid loss in protracted vomiting, ingestion of alkalis or a kidney complaint. Symptoms include muscle spasms and weakness.

Al-Khwarizmi (*fl.*820), Arabian mathematician. He wrote original works on ALGEBRA, which he systematized, and arithmetic. *See also* SU pp.22, 34.

Alkmaar, market city in W Netherlands, 32km (20 miles) NNW of Amsterdam. It was the first Dutch city successfully to resist the Spanish in 1573. Industry: food processing. Pop. 52,000.

Al-Kuwayt. *See* KUWAIT.

Alkyds, synthetic resins, generally of phthalic acid and glycerol. They can be moulded at high speed under low pressure and cured quickly. They are widely used as paint resins and in products where good insulation, high strength and good temperature, voltage and humidity stability are important, such as in car ignition systems. *See also* POLYESTER; MM p.54.

Alkylbenzenesulphonic acid. *See* DETERGENT; MM p.240.

Allah, Arabic term for God. The one and only God of ISLAM, Allah is the omnipresent and merciful rewarder. Unreserved surrender to Allah, as preached in the KORAN, is the very heart of the Muslim faith. *See* HC1 pp.144–145; MS pp.220–223.

Allāhābād, city in Uttar Pradesh state, N central India, at the confluence of the Rivers Ganges and Yamuna. It is a pilgrimage centre, based on the belief that the goddess Saraswati joined the two rivers at this point. It has the Kumbh Mela fair, a religious celebration that occurs every twelve years, and one of the oldest universities in India, dating from 1887. It is an agricultural trade centre. Pop. 490,600.

All-American Canal, canal in SE California, USA. Part of the irrigation system of the HOOVER DAM, it was completed in 1940 and crosses the Colorado Desert. Length: 129km (80 miles).

Allan, David (1774–96), Scottish portrait and genre painter, nicknamed the "Scottish Hogarth". His humour and gift for caricature are seen in such works as *Scottish Wedding*.

Allan, Sir Hugh (1810-82), Canadian financier and shipbuilder, *b.*Scotland. In 1856 he founded the Allan Line of steamships and later helped plan the Canadian Pacific Railroad. His donation of $350,000 to the Conservative Party of John MACDONALD resulted in the PACIFIC SCANDAL of 1873.

Allan, Sir William (1782–1850), Scottish historical painter, elected President of the Royal Scottish Academy in 1838. His paintings include scenes from the *Waverley* novels by Sir Walter SCOTT.

All Blacks, national rugby union football team of New Zealand. They get their name from their playing strip – black jerseys, shorts and socks – which became their regular uniform in 1901. The first New Zealand touring side visited the British Isles and France in 1905–06, and it was then that the term "All Blacks" was first coined. These "Original All Blacks", under the captaincy of Dave Gallaher, had a most successful tour, winning 32 of their 33 matches, with a remarkable points record of 868 against 47. This tour established the All Blacks as the leading rugby side in the world, a "title" that has been disputed vehemently over the years by the Springboks of South Africa. Of the Home Countries of the British Isles, only Wales has consistently proved to be in the same class, and it was against Wales that the All Blacks lost their only game on their first tour. Of the later touring sides, the most outstanding were the Fifth All Blacks (1963–64, captained by Wilson Whineray), who won 32 and lost only 1 of their 34 matches, and the Sixth (1967, Brian Lochore), who won 14 and drew 1 of their 15 matches. In clashes with their great rivals the Springboks, the home side has usually had the edge. The All Blacks have always dominated the Australians, but were beaten by a visiting British Isles team in 1971. *See also* FOOTBALL, RUGBY.

Allbutt, Sir Thomas Clifford (1836–1925), British physician, educated at Cambridge where he became regius professor (1892). His short clinical thermometer introduced in 1866 replaced the 30.5cm (1ft) long type previously used.

Allegheny Mountains, range in the USA extending from Pennsylvania through

Maryland, Virginia and West Virginia, where Spruce Knob (1,408m; 4,860ft) is the highest point. There are large deposits of coal and extensive forests.

Allegory, literary work in either prose or verse in which more than one level of meaning is expressed simultaneously. The fables of AESOP and of LA FONTAINE, which give human meaning to animal behaviour, are simple allegories.

Allegri, Antonio. *See* CORREGGIO.

Allegri, Gregorio (1582–1652), Italian composer. He spent much of his life in the pope's service and his *Miserere,* acclaimed as a setting of ethereal beauty, was written for the Sistine choir.

Allen, William Hervey (1889–1949), US author. His most successful novel, *Anthony Adverse* (1933), sold more than a million copies. He also wrote *Toward the Flame* (1926), *Action at Aquila* (1938), *Bedford Village* (1944) and several other novels.

Allen, Bog of, area of peat bogs in central Ireland, in Kildare, Offaly, Laoighis and Westmeath counties. Some parts are cultivated and in others peat is cut for fuel. Area: 958sq km (370sq miles).

Allen, Lough, lake in N Republic of Ireland, approx. 13km (8 miles) N of Carrick; the upper Shannon River flows through it. It is 13km (8 miles) long and 5km (3 miles) wide.

Allenby, Edmund Henry Hynman, 1st Viscount (1861–1936), English military commander. A distinguished cavalry officer, he defeated the Turkish forces in Palestine and Syria (1917–18), capturing Jerusalem, Damascus and Aleppo. He was made a Viscount in 1919 and served as British High Commissioner in Egypt and Sudan from 1919 to 1925.

Allende Gossens, Salvador (1908–73), President of Chile (1970–73). He died in a military coup in Sept. 1973. Candidate of the Popular Unity coalition, he was the first democratically elected Marxist head of state in Latin America. A doctor and active member of the Chilean Socialist Party since its formation in 1933, he was a senator from 1945 and unsuccessfully ran for the presidency in 1952, 1958 and 1964. *See also* HC2 p.256.

Allerdale, county district in NW Cumbria, England; created in 1974 under the Local Government Act (1972). Area: 1,255sq km (485sq miles). Pop. (1974 est.) 94,500.

Allergy, hypersensitive reaction of the body to certain substances (allergens) not normally considered distressing. Allergens include POLLEN, animal hair, fungi, dust, occasionally foods and increasingly drugs such as PENICILLIN. Typical allergic reactions are sneezing (HAY FEVER), "wheezing" and difficulty in breathing (ASTHMA) and skin eruptions and itching (ECZEMA). The tendency to allergic reactions is often hereditary. Treatment usually requires the identification of the allergen and its avoidance if possible, or a course of desensitization. Drugs can be useful in relieving acute symptoms. *See also* MS p.86.

Alleyn, Edward (1566–1626), English actor. He won fame and riches in tragic roles such as Marlowe's Dr Faustus (*c.* 1589), was a theatre-owner and founded Dulwich College (1613–16).

Alliance, in international relations, an agreement for furtherance of mutual or similar aims between states or other parties, sometimes arrived at by formal treaty. The North Atlantic Treaty Organization (NATO) is one such alliance.

Allied Powers. *See* ALLIES, THE.

Allier, river in S central France that flows NNW to the River Loire. It is 410km (255 miles) long.

Allies, the, term used in WWI and WWII for the forces that fought the CENTRAL POWERS and AXIS POWERS respectively. In WWI they numbered 23 and included Belgium, Britain and its empire, France, Italy, Japan, Russia and the USA. In WWII the 49 Allies included Belgium, Britain and the Commonwealth, France, The Netherlands, the USSR and the USA.

Alligator, broad-snouted reptile crocodilian found only in the United States and China. In the breeding season the female alligator lays 20–70 eggs on shore in a mound nest of leaves and mud and remains nearby to guard them. The American alligator, *Alligator mississippiensis,* is found in the SE USA; it grows up to 5.8m (19ft) long. The almost extinct smaller Chinese alligator, *A. sinensis,* is restricted to the Yangtze-Kiang river basin. Unlike the American alligator it has no webbing between its front toes. Length: up to 1.5m (5ft). Family Alligatoridea. *See also* NW pp.134, 135.

Alligator gar, primitive freshwater bony fish found in shallow weedy waters of North America, east of the Rocky Mountains. Its long cylindrical body is covered with bony diamond-shaped flat plates. It has a "snout" studded with teeth, and vertebrae resembling those of reptiles. Length: to 3.05m (10ft); weight: to 136kg (302lb). Family Lepisosteidae. *See also* NW p.*124.*

Alliluyeva, Svetlana (1926–), daughter of Joseph STALIN by his second wife, Nadezhda Alliluyeva. In 1966 she defected to the West while in India and settled in the USA the following year. She wrote an account of her experiences under various Soviet regimes, *Only One Year* (1969).

Allingham, Margery Louise (1904–66), British writer of detective novels. Her stylishly written stories included *Flowers for the Judge* (1936) and *The Mind Readers* (1965).

Allingham, William (1824–89), Irish poet. He wrote a number of attractive lyrical poems, *Up the Airy Mountain* being the best known.

Allium. *See* LILY.

Alloa, seaport town in central Scotland, on the River Forth, 40km (25 miles) NE of Glasgow. It has a 13th-century tower on Mar's Hill, which marks the seat of the Erskines, Earls of Mar. Alloa became part of the Central Region in 1975. Its major export is coal. Other industries include brewing, tiles, hosiery and bottles. Pop. (1974 est) 13,500.

Allopathy, the treatment of diseases by methods and remedies that produce effects contrasting with those caused by the disease; theoretically opposite to HOMEOPATHY.

Allori, Angelo. *See* BRONZINO, IL.

Allotropy, property of some chemical elements which enables them to exist in two or more distinct physical forms. Each form (called an allotrope) can have different chemical properties but can be changed into another allotrope – given suitable conditions. Examples of allotropes are molecular oxygen and ozone; white and yellow phosphorous; and graphite and diamond (carbon).

Alloy, mixture of two or more metals. Its properties are frequently different from those of constituent elements: alloys are generally harder, stronger and have lower melting points (those with lowest melting points are called eutectic mixtures). Most are prepared by mixing when molten. Some mixtures combining a metal with a non-metal, such as in steel, are also referred to as alloys. The proportions in which the component metals are mixed greatly affects the properties of an alloy. *See also* MM p.36; SU p.88.

All Quiet on the Western Front (1929), novel by Erich Maria REMARQUE. Based on the author's experience in WWI, it records with grim realism the horror of trench warfare. It has been adapted for several films, notably in 1930. *See also* HC2 p.276.

All Saints' Day, in the Christian liturgical calendar, the day on which all the saints are commemorated. The feast is observed on 1 November in the West and on the first Sunday after Pentecost (Whitsun) in the East. It was known as All Hallows in medieval England, and the eve of the day is celebrated in some western countries as Hallowe'en.

All Souls' Day, day of remembrance and prayer for all the departed souls, observed by Roman Catholics and High Church Anglicans on 2 Nov. or on 3 Nov. if the former falls on a Sunday. It is believed that prayers for the departed will help prepare them for heaven.

Allspice, or pimento, aromatic tree native to the West Indies and Central America. The fruits are used as a spice, in perfume and in medicine. Height: up to 12m (40ft). Family Myrtaceae; species *Pimenta officinalis, P. dioica. See also* PE p.*211.*

Allston, Washington (1779–1843), the first US artist to paint romantic landscapes. Allston experimented with colour to achieve atmospheric effects of light. His finest paintings, often fantasies of seascapes and landscapes, include *The Deluge* (1804) and *Moonlit Landscape* (1819).

All's Well That Ends Well (1602–03), comedy by William SHAKESPEARE. *See also* HC1 pp.284, *284.*

All the Talents, Ministry of (1806–07), misleading name for the government formed by Lord GRENVILLE, including Charles James FOX. It is famous for abolishing the slave trade.

Alluvium, general term that describes sediments – sand, silt and mud – deposited by flowing water along the banks, delta or flood-plain of a river or stream. Fine-textured sediments that contain organic matter form soil. *See also* PE p.112.

Alma, battle of the CRIMEAN WAR in 1854. The Russians were defeated by the British and the French but the latter failed to consolidate their victory. *See also* HC2 p.183.

Alma-Ata, largest city and capital of Kazakhistan, USSR, near the border with China; capital of Alma-Ata oblast. It was founded in 1855 as a Russian fortress and commercial centre and named Vernyi. It is now a terminus of the Turkistan-Siberian railway. Its industries include food processing, tobacco, timber and machinery. Pop. (1971) 730,000.

Almagro, Diego de (*c.* 1475–1538), Spanish conquistador. He joined Francisco PIZARRO in the initial expedition (1524–27) to Peru and was instrumental in the subjugation of the Incas. There was a land dispute between him and the Pizarro brothers and he tried to claim Cuzco, but was executed by order of Hernando Pizarro. *See also* HC1 p.234.

Alma mater (Latin, *fostering mother* or *beloved mother*), term applied by students and graduates to their college; probably first used early in the 19th century.

Al-Mamun, seventh ABBASID caliph (*r.* 813–33). Although his reign was troubled and orthodox Muslims were persecuted, it was nevertheless a period of great cultural development.

Almansa, town in SE central Spain, approx. 69km (43 miles) ESE of Albacete. It has mineral springs and a ruined Moorish castle. It is a market centre for the fertile plain around it. The major industry is textiles. Pop. 16,700.

Al-Mansur, Ahmad (1549–1603), Emir of Morocco (1578–1603). His brother Abd al-Malik defeated Sebastian of Portugal at al-Qast al-Kabir in 1578. The emir traded in slaves, gold and ivory, and built up the power of Morocco.

Alma-Tadema, Sir Lawrence (1836–1912), Netherlands-bo)n painter who settled in England (1870). He was highly popular for his idealized and colourful paintings of Greek and Roman life.

Almeida, Francisco de (1450–1510), Portuguese soldier and colonial official, first viceroy of Portuguese India (1505–09). He set up fortified trading posts and his son established a settlement on Ceylon (Sri Lanka). He was killed on his way back to Portugal.

Almeida-Garrett, Joao Batista de (1799–1854), Portuguese author and statesman. Exiled after the 1820 revolt, he was influenced by the Romantic movement in England and France. He returned to Portugal in 1832 and became a Liberal cabinet minister. His works include the heroic poems *Camoes* (1825) and the play *Frei Luis de Sousa* (1843). *See also* ROMANTICISM.

Almería, city in SE Spain, 104km (65 miles) ESE of Granada; capital of Almería province. It is an important Mediterranean seaport on the Gulf of Almería. A former Moorish naval base, it was taken by Christians in 1489. It has a Gothic cathedral and the ruins of a Moorish fort. It exports grapes and esparto and its

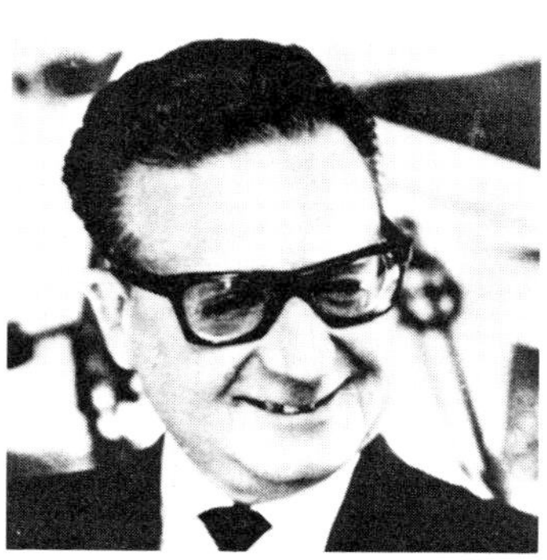

Salvador Allende, Marxist president of Chile who died in the 1973 military coup.

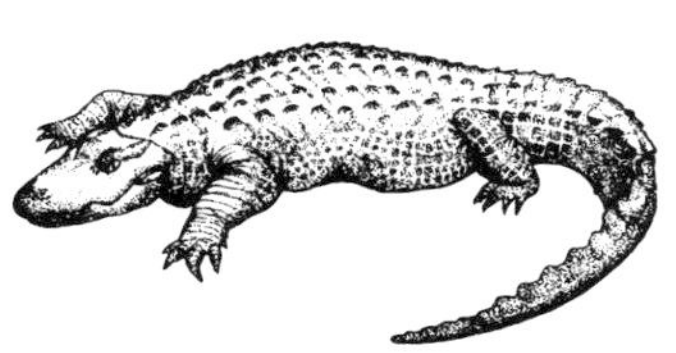

Alligators are generally much less active and vicious than crocodiles.

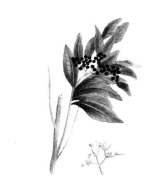

Allspice, or pimento, is a shrub whose berries provide a versatile flavouring.

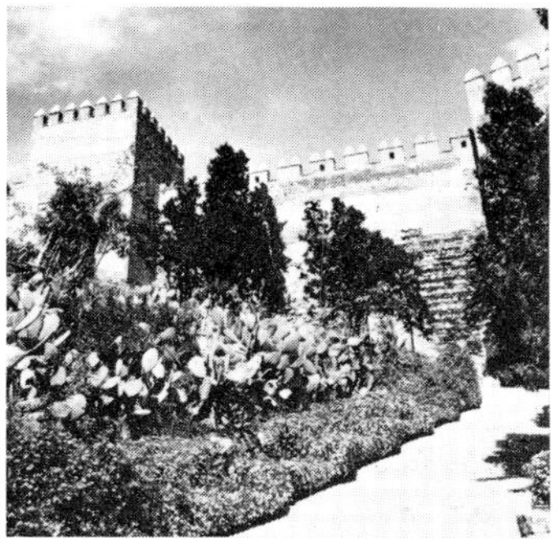

Almeria has a dazzling brightness reminiscent of a Moroccan rather than a Spanish city.

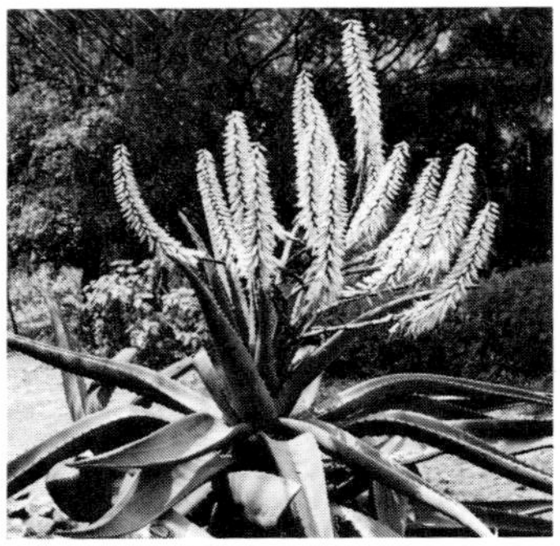

Aloe is one of a group of about 100 fleshy-leaved plants found mainly in South Africa.

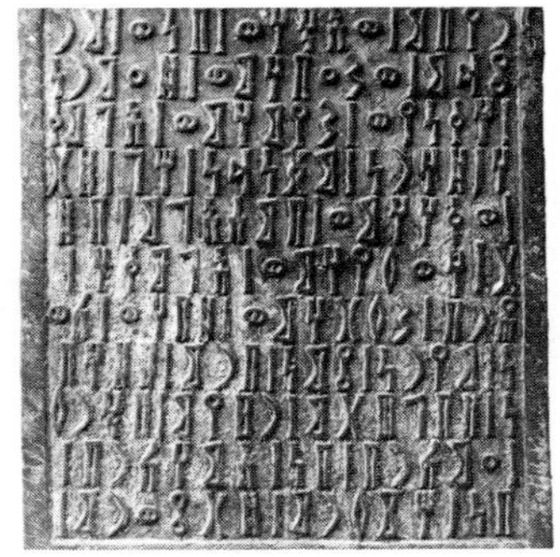

Alphabet; this Himyaritic script is developed from an earlier Phoenecian alphabet.

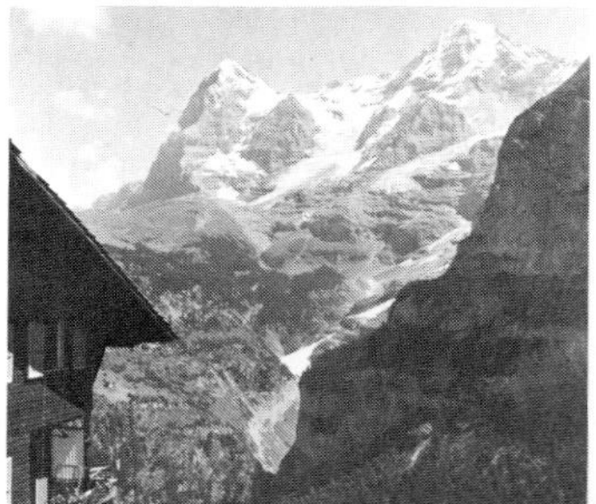

Alps; the peaks of the Eiger and Monch in Europe's greatest mountain system.

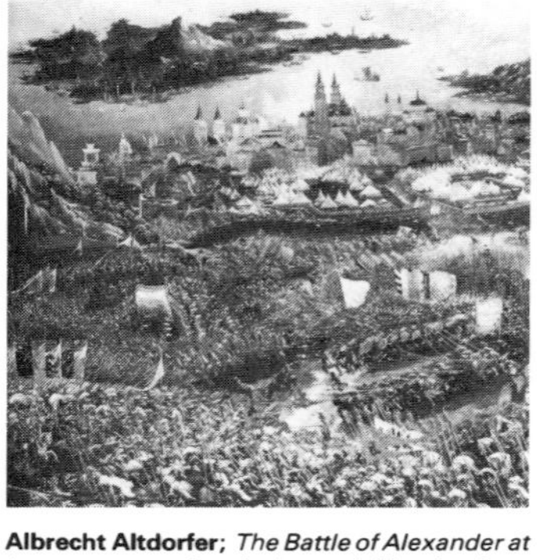

Albrecht Altdorfer; *The Battle of Alexander at Issus*, a masterpiece in dramatic illumination.

industries include oil refining, chemicals, light engineering, food processing, fishing and tourism. Pop. 125,700.

Almohads, BERBER Muslim dynasty (1145–1269) in N Africa and Spain, the followers of a monotheistic reform movement within ISLAM. Mohammed ibn-Tumart, its founder, set out from the region of the Atlas mountains to purify Islam and to oust the ALMORAVIDS from Morocco. Their conquest of the Almoravids in Spain was completed by Abd al-Mumin, Yusuf II and Yakub I. In 1212 ALFONSO VIII of Castile routed them at Las Navas de Tolosa, and in 1269 their capital Marrakesh fell to the MARINIDS. *See also* HC1 pp.170–171; 228.

Almond, small tree native to the E Mediterranean region and SW Asia; also the nut-like seed of its fruit. The tree is related to the PEACH and APRICOT but is larger and lives longer. The fruit of the sweet almond may be eaten raw or roasted; that of the bitter almond is pressed for its oil. Species *Prunnus amygdalus. See also* PE pp.214, 215, 217.

Almoravids, BERBER Muslim dynasty (1054–1145) that ruled in Morocco and Spain. It rose to power under Abdullah ibn-Yasin who converted Saharan tribes in a religious revival. Abu Bakr founded Marrakesh as the Almoravid capital in 1070; his brother Yusuf ibn-Tashufin defeated Alfonso VI of Castile in 1086. Almoravid rule was ended by the rise of the ALMOHADS. *See also* HC1 pp.121, *228*.

Almquist, Carl Jonas Love (1793–1866), Swedish writer. His enormous output, ranging from romantic, mystical verse to satirical and realistic novels, appeared chiefly in the 14-volume series *The Book of the Thorn Rose* (1832–51). He was a fugitive in the USA (1851–65) from accusations of fraud and attempted murder.

Al-Muhallah al-Kubra, city in the central Nile delta of Lower Egypt, 120km (75 miles) N of Cairo. Since 1927 it has had a cotton textile factory, which is now a major centre of the country's textile industry. Pop. (1971 est.) 263,400.

Al-Muharraq, one of four main islands, 14sq km (5.5sq miles) in area, that form the state of BAHRAIN in the Persian Gulf. Bahrain International Airport, which is able to take supersonic aircraft, is to the N of Al-Muharraq city. Pop. (1974 est.) 41,800. *See* MW p.36.

Al-Mukallā, city of the People's Democratic Republic of Yemen on the Gulf of Aden. An important fishing port, it is also a centre of trade for the surrounding region. Pop. (1976 est.) 25,000.

Alnitak. *See* ZETA.

Aloe, genus of South African plants with spiny-edged, fleshy leaves. The plants grow in dense rosettes and have drooping red, orange or yellow flower clusters. They are often grown as houseplants. Family Liliaceae. *See also* NW p.218.

Alonso, Dámaso (1898–), Spanish poet and literary critic. His works include *Essays on Spanish Poetry* (1944), *Wind and Verse* (1925) and *Children of Wrath* (1944).

Alopecia. *See* BALDNESS.

Alor Setar (Alor Star), city in Malaysia on the central Malay peninsula, on the Kedah River; capital of Kedah state. A trade centre for rice and rubber, it also has the sultan's residence. Pop. 66,260.

Aloysius, Saint (1568–91), entered the Society of Jesus (1585) against his parents' wishes and died nursing the victims of plague. Aloysius is regarded as the special protector of students and as patron of Christian youth.

Alpaca. *See* LLAMA.

Alp Arslan (1029–72), Sultan of the Seljuk Turks (*r.*1063–72). He conquered Armenia, Syria, Cilicia and Cappadocia. In 1066 he attacked the Byzantine Empire. After his decisive victory over the Byzantines at the Battle of Manzikert in 1071, Turkish domination of Asia Minor was assured.

Alpenhorn, or alphorn, simple musical instrument; a long wooden horn, played by Alpine herdsmen. Gioacchino ROSSINI (1792-1868) used a typical alpenhorn melody in the overture to his opera *William Tell.*

Alpha Aquilae. *See* ALTAIR.

Alpha Aurigae. *See* CAPELLA.

Alphabet, system of letters representing sounds of speech, used in writing; a word derived from *alpha* and *beta*, the first two letters of the Greek alphabet. In a perfect system one symbol represents just one sound, but this is rarely achieved. The International Phonetic Alphabet consists of a series of symbols devised to transcribe precisely the speech sounds for any language. The most important alphabets in use today are the Latin (Roman), Cyrillic, Greek, Arabic, Hebrew and Devanagari. Because an alphabet permits a written language it makes possible the dissemination of knowledge and its preservation. Primitive man communicated by sound, gesture and painting, and the earliest script developed from a type of picture-writing of the fourth millennium BC. Devised by the Sumerians, it evolved into cuneiform, made up of wedge-shaped characters that represented sounds. Egyptian hieroglyphics date from about 3000 BC, and by 2000 BC the Semites of Syria-Palestine were using a consonantal alphabet known as North Semite, which influenced a variety of forms throughout Asia and Europe. The Phoenicians transmitted the alphabet to the Greeks who adapted it further and added vowels. The Latin version, which grew out of the Greek by way of the Etruscans, was perfected about AD 100. It is the foundation on which Western alphabets are based. Some alphabets (eg the Devanagari of India) represent syllables rather than phonemes, and Braille and Morse code are alphabets invented to meet special needs. *See also* MS pp.244–245.

Alpha Carinae. *See* CANOPUS.

Alpha Centauri, sometimes called Rigel, Kent or Tolman, triple star composed of a binary, having a period of 80 years, and Proxima, a faint red dwarf – the nearest star to Earth. It is also the closest of the bright stars, is visible through a telescope, and is one of three stars (the others are Sirius and Procyon) in our Solar System that are more luminous than our Sun. *See also* SU pp.236, *244*, 261, 266–267.

Alpha rays, or alpha particles, stable, positively charged particles emitted spontaneously by certain radioactive isotopes (undergoing alpha decay). They were discovered by Pierre and Marie CURIE and by Ernest RUTHERFORD, who in 1899 identified them as two protons bound to two neutrons – nuclei of helium atoms. Their penetrating power is low compared with that of beta particles (electrons) but they cause intense ionization along their track. *See also* RADIOACTIVITY; SU p.62.

Alpha waves, principle slow waves produced by the human brain (frequency *c.* 10Hz), when the subject is awake but relaxed, recorded on an electroencephalogram (EEG). The state in which the brain produces Alpha waves can be induced. *See also* BRAIN WAVES; MS pp.194–195.

Alphege, Saint (954–1012), Archbishop of Canterbury (1005). Originally a monk of Deerhurst, he became Abbot of Bath, and in 984 was made Bishop of Winchester. In 1012 he was murdered by drunken Danes after he had refused to be ransomed by his impoverished tenants. His feast day is 19 April.

Alpheratz, also called Alpha Andromedae, one of the four stars included in the Square of Pegasus and linking it to Andromeda. *See also* SU p.258, *258*.

Alpine plants, small plants found above the tree line in mountain meadows and on rocky slopes, generally at altitudes above 2,300m (7,546ft). The term is frequently applied to all mountain plants, irrespective of altitude. *See also* NW pp.222–223.

Alpine sub-race, subdivision of the CAUCASIAN race, characterized by thickset stature, tawny skin, dark to pale brown hair, with facial and body hair abundant in the male. Alpinids extend across central Europe between the Cévennes and the Ukraine. *See also* MS p.32.

Alps, mountain system in S central Europe, extending approx. 1,200km (745 miles) from the Gulf of Genoa on the Mediterranean Sea through France, Italy, Switzerland, Austria, Germany and Yugoslavia. It is cut by many gaps and passes, and has a distinctive mountain landscape, the result of mountain building and glaciation. It is noted for its scenery, ski slopes and lakes, and tourism is a major source of income. Resorts include Chamonix, St Moritz, Zermatt and Interlaken. The Alps form the watershed of many of Europe's major rivers, including the Rhine, Rhône, Danube and Po, and their fast-flowing headstreams and waterfalls provide an important source of hydroelectric power. Agriculture, including fruit and vines, is limited to the valley floors and some sunny slopes of the foothills; the slopes below the snowline provide summer pasture for cattle and goats. The highest peak is Mont Blanc, 4,810m (15,781ft). *See also* PE pp.44, 104, 106, 107.

Alsace-Lorraine, region in E France, comprised of Bas-Rhin, Haut-Rhin, Moselle, Meuse, Meurthe-et-Moselle and Vosges départements. It is separated from West Germany by the River Rhine. The region has always caused friction between France and Germany. France lost it (except for Belfort) to Germany at the end of the FRANCO-PRUSSIAN WAR (1870–71), but regained it after WWI. Germany took the area during WWII but it was returned to France at the end of the war. There are rich deposits of iron ore, and industries include steel and textile mills. STRASBOURG is the leading city.

Alsatia, historical German, and later French, province in NE France between the River Rhine and the Vosges Mountains. The départements of Bas-Rhin and Haut-Rhin now cover this region, which was ruled originally by Rome, then the Franks followed by the Holy Roman Emperor. It passed to the Germans in 1871, and was incorporated in the province of ALSACE-LORRAINE.

Alsatian, breed of working dog, also known as a German shepherd. It was originally bred for herding, but is now used also as a police dog, guard dog and guide dog for the blind. It has a double coat ranging from light tan to black. Weight: 27–38kg (60–85 lb).

Alsop, Richard (1761–1815), US author and poet, known as one of the "Hartford Wits". He collaborated in the verse satire *The Echo.*

Also Sprach Zarathustra, prose-poem (1883–92) by Friedrich NIETZSCHE that inspired Richard STRAUSS's symphonic poem of the same name (1895).

Altai (Altajsk), complex mountain system in central Asia between W China and W Mongolia and between Gorno-Altajskaja autonomous oblast and Kazakhstan, USSR. A densely forested area, it is the source of the Irtyš and Ob' rivers. Highest peak: 4,620m (15,157ft).

Altair, or Alpha Aquilae, white star in the constellation of Aquila. Characteristics: apparent mag. 0.77; absolute mag. +2.3; spectral type A7; distance 16 light-years. *See also* SU pp.226, 265.

Altdorf, town in central Switzerland, 3km (2 miles) from the SE tip of Lake Lucerne; capital of Uri canton. It was the scene of the exploits of the legendary William TELL, commemorated by an annual festival and a museum. Industries: cables, rubber and tourism. Pop. 8,600.

Altdorfer, Albrecht (*c.*1480–1538), German painter and engraver. One of the first true landscape painters in Europe, he used figures in his pictures as a complement to landscape. His masterpieces include *The Battle of Alexander at Issus* (1529). *See also* HC1 p.260.

Alternating current. *See* CURRENT, ELECTRIC.

Alternation of generations, two-generation cycle by which some plants, such as MOSSES and FERNS, reproduce. The asexual (SPOROPHYTE) form produces SPORES that, in turn, grow into the sexual (GAMETOPHYTE) form. The gametophyte produces the egg cell (fern) or capsule (moss) that grows into another sporophyte. The moss gametophyte consists of the protonema, or moss plant. The fern gametophyte is the prothallus or familiar fern plant. *See also* NW pp.38, 50–52.

Alternator, electrical generator that produces an alternating current, *See* SU pp.122–125.

Altgeld, John Peter (1847–1902), US politician and Governor of Illinois (1893–97). Born in Germany, Altgeld was a man of liberal views and a champion of labour.

Althing, Icelandic Parliament, one of the oldest legislative assemblies in the world. It was first convened at Thingvellir, near Reykjavík, in 930. The 60 members (40 in the lower house and 20 in the upper house) are elected by proportional representation for four-year terms. At times the two houses act as a united Althing, as in 1944 when they voted for independence from Denmark.

Althusius, Johannes (1557–1638), Dutch Calvinist political theorist. He held that the highest power in a state is possessed by the people. The right to govern is merely delegated; the people have a legal right to resist tyranny. His *Methodical Digest of Politics* (1603) was an influential treatise against absolute royal power.

Altichiero da Zevio (*c.*1330–*c.*1395), Italian painter from Verona, whose style was influenced by the frescoes of GIOTTO at Padua. Altichiero's paintings are early examples of the use of realistic proportions in the depiction of the human figure and spatial relationships.

Altimeter, instrument that indicates the altitude of an aircraft by measuring atmospheric pressure. Essentially it is an aneroid BAROMETER calibrated in heights, and must be adjusted frequently in flight to compensate for local pressure changes.

Altiplano, high plain in the South American Andes of Peru and W Bolivia, where it is at an elevation of about 3,650m (12,000ft). *See also* PE p.65.

Altitude, in astronomy, angular height of a celestial body above the horizon, measured in degrees along a vertical circle passing through the body. Altitude and AZIMUTH are the co-ordinates used to locate the position of celestial bodies in the CELESTIAL SPHERE.

Altman, Robert (1925–), US film director. Versatile and inventive, his films include *Brewster McCloud* (1971), *M*A*S*H* (1971), *Images* (1972) and *Nashville* (1975).

Alto, in singing, the highest male voice, also called COUNTER-TENOR; or the lowest female voice, also called CONTRALTO.

Altruism, acting in others' interests. The word was coined by Comte from the Latin *altrui*, "for some one else". It is used in biology of an animal which offers itself to a predator to save its fellows.

Altwegg, Jeannette (1930–), British ice-skater. She won the 1951 world and 1952 Olympic figure-skating titles. Her best event was the compulsory figures.

Alum, double sulphate of aluminium (or another trivalent metal) and another, univalent metal. The most important is potash alum, potassium aluminium sulphate; it is used as a mordant in dyeing and as a styptic (to staunch bleeding) in medicine.

Alumina, aluminium oxide (Al_2O_3), an important mineral. Its hydrated form BAUXITE, ($Al_2O_3.2H_2O$), is the chief ore of aluminium. Other forms include corundum, two impure varieties of which are the gemstones sapphire and ruby. *See also* MM p.34; PE pp.98, 99.

Aluminium, metallic element (symbol Al) of group IIIA of the periodic table, first obtained (1827) in pure form by Friedrich WOHLER. It is the most common metal in the Earth's crust; the chief ore is BAUXITE (a hydrated oxide) from which the metal is extracted by electrolysis. Alloyed with other metals, it is extensively used in machined and moulded articles, particularly where lightness is important, as in aircraft. It is protected from oxidation by a thin, natural layer of oxide. Properties: at.no. 13; at.wt. 26.9815; s.g. 2.699; m.p. 660.21°C (1,220.38°F); b.p. 2,467°C (4,473°F); most common isotope Al^{27}. *See also* ANODIZING; MM p.34; SU p.136.

Alvarado, Pedro de (*c.*1485–1541), Spanish conquistador who accompanied Hernán CORTÉS during the conquest of Mexico (1519–21). His actions led to the death of MONTEZUMA. He became Governor and Captain-General of Guatemala in 1524. *See also* HC1 p.236.

Alvarez, Alfred (1929–), British poet and critic. An influential critic of contemporary poetry, his works include *The Shaping Spirit* (1958), a discussion of modernism in English and American poets, and *The Savage God* (1971), a study of suicide.

Alvarez, Luis Walter (1911–), US physicist and 1968 Nobel Prize-winner in the field of sub-atomic particles, in which he discovered and identified a number of extremely short-lived particles. He helped to design bubble-chambers for studying such particles, and to construct the first proton linear accelerator.

Alvarez Quintero, Serafín (1871–1938) and **Joaquín** (1873–1944), Spanish playwright brothers who collaborated on more than 200 plays, dealing mainly with life in Andalusia. Some of their best have been translated into English, including *Fortunato, A Hundred Years Old* and *The Lady from Alfqueque*, all published in 1928.

Alveolus, sac-like structure, one cell thick, that protrudes from the end of a bronchiole in the LUNGS. Each contains a network of capillary blood vessels that permit the exchange of gases between the air and the blood. *See also* MS pp.66–67.

Alwyn, William (1905–), British composer who is best known for his music for films such as *Odd Man Out* and *The Magic Box*. Other works include the symphonic prelude *The Magic Island* (1953).

Alyssum, genus of herb native to Europe. Alyssums have lance-shaped leaves, often covered with pale down, and white or yellow flowers. Species include annual *Alyssum alyssoides* and perennial golden tuft (*A. saxatile*). Height: about 30cm (12in). Family Brassicaceae.

Alzheimer's disease, degenerative condition, or atrophy, of the brain associated with mental deterioration similar to that in senile dementia, but occurring in people between 30 and 50 years of age. No cause or treatment are known. *See also* MS p.139.

Amadeus VIII (1383–1451), count and duke of Savoy who became Antipope FELIX V in 1439, but gave up the claim to Nicholas V in 1447.

Amadeus (1845–90), King of Spain (1870–73). He was the son of King Victor Emmanuel II of Italy. After Queen Isabella II of Spain was forced to abdicate in 1868, Amadeus was elected king by the Cortes. He reluctantly ruled for three years and abdicated after the CARLIST Wars started again in 1872.

Amadeus, large shallow lake in central Australia, S of the Macdonnel Ranges. It was discovered by the Australian explorer Ernest Giles in 1872. Length: approx. 145km (90 miles).

Amador Guerrero, Manuel (1833–1909), first President of Panama (1904-08). He was leader of the Panamanian movement to gain independence from Colombia. The Panama Canal Zone treaty was ratified during his period of office.

Amagasaki, city on S Honshū Island, Japan, on Osaka Bay. It has a 16th-century castle. The city was damaged by US air raids in 1945. Industries: iron, steel, chemicals, textiles. Pop. 553,700.

Amalekites, people who originally inhabited Canaan and the Sinai peninsula and who, until scattered by SAUL, waged war against the Hebrews. Some authorities identify them with the HYKSOS.

Amalgam, solid or liquid alloy of mercury with other metals. Most metals dissolve in mercury, although iron is an exception. *See also* SU p.136.

Amalthea, one of the 13 known satellites of Jupiter, discovered in 1892 by Edward Bernard. It is asteroidal in size and is closest to the planet. *See also* SU pp.212, *212*, 278, *278*.

Amanita, large, widely distributed genus of fungi, most of which are poisonous. Amanitas usually have distinct stalks and the prominent remains of a veil in a fleshy ring under the cap and at the bulbous base. *See also* NW pp.*38*, 43, *209*.

Amanullah Khan (1892–1960), ruler of Afghanistan (1919–29). He began educational and road-building projects but was forced into exile by a revolt led by Bachcheh Saqow in 1929.

Amaranth, plant from the tropics of America and Africa. The flowers, densely clustered in spikes or tassels, are often hidden by colourful foliage. The 800 species include love-lies-bleeding (*Amaranthus caudatus*) with its crimson-purple flowers. Family Amaranthaceae.

Amaryllis, any of a number of flowering plants of the genus of the same name. They have several white or coloured lily-like flowers attached to a single stem. Amaryllis is also the name of a shepherdess referred to in the poetry of Virgil and Theocritus.

Amaterasu-O-mikami, sun goddess of the SHINTO pantheon, considered to be the ancestor of the Japanese imperial clan. Because of this traditional belief, an emperor was safe on his throne; his descent from the sun prevented anyone else from holding his office. The spirit of the sun goddess is said to reside in the sacred mirror in the Grand Shrine of Ise, the most holy Shinto shrine in Japan.

Amati, family of Italian violin-makers in Cremona in the 16th and 17th centuries, including Andrea (*c.*1520–78), the founder of the Cremona school of violin-making; his two sons Antonio (*c.*1550–1638) and Girolamo (1551–1635); and Girolamo's son Niccolo (1596–1684), and grandson Girolamo (1649–1740).

Amatol, high explosive made from ammonium nitrate and TNT. *See* MM pp.242–243.

Amazon, greatest river of S America, and second longest river in the world, draining the vast rain forest of N South America. Its drainage basin, an area of 7,000,000sq km (2,700,000sq miles), includes three-quarters of Brazil and extensive areas of Colombia, Ecuador, Guyana, Peru and Venezuela. Carrying the greatest volume of water of any river in the world, the Amazon is the central artery of an extensive river system that feeds it from N, W and S. Major tributaries are the Madeira, Purus, Juruá, Ucayali, Marañón (the headstream of the Amazon), Napa, Putumayo, Japurá and Negro rivers. The river basin is flanked by the Brazilian Highlands (S), the Andes Mountains (W) and the Guyana Highlands. Cultivation of the region has been limited to the sporadic harvesting of the natural resources, dependent upon economic demand – eg, the great rubber boom of the late 19th and early 20th centuries. The development of a timber industry has been hampered by the absence of pure stands of valuable woods, the rain forest having a wide variety of trees growing side by side. The basin is sparsely inhabited, chiefly by Brazilians, who live mainly along the flood bank; a small American Indian population lives and hunts in the wider area of the rain forest. The Amazon is navigable as far W as Iquitos, Peru – more than 3,700km (2,300 miles) inland. It was first descended from Peru in 1541 by the Spaniard Francisco de Orellana. Length: approx. 6,516km (4,050 miles). *See also* MW p.40.

Amazonis Planitia. *See* MARS.

Amazons, in Greek mythology, a race of female warriors who lived in a totally matriarchal society. HERCULES, THESEUS and other Greek heroes challenged the Amazons. They were believed to have been the first to use cavalry and, as allies of the Trojans, took part in the siege of TROY, where their queen Penthesilea was slain by ACHILLES after she had killed many Greek warriors.

Ambassador, diplomatic representative of the highest rank, appointed by a head of state to represent his government abroad.

Ambato, city in central Ecuador, in a high Andean valley; capital of Tunguragua province. A wealthy resort area, it is known as the "Garden City" because of its variety of local fruits. It is a road, rail and air transport centre. Pop. 75,000.

Ambedkar, Bhim-Rao Ramji (1893–1956), Indian lawyer and politician, leader of the country's "untouchables". In 1947 he became independent India's first

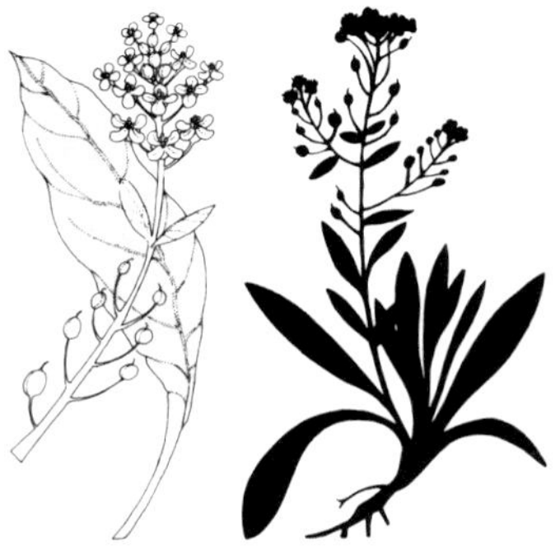

Alyssum is a hardy plant that has clusters of white or yellow flowers.

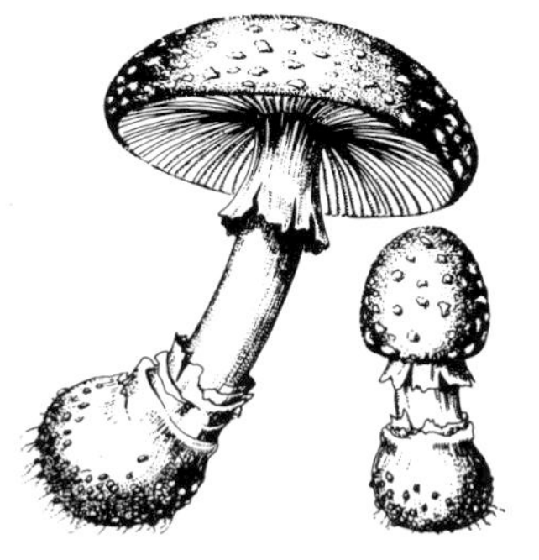

Amanita, a common genus of fungus, includes many species that are poisonous.

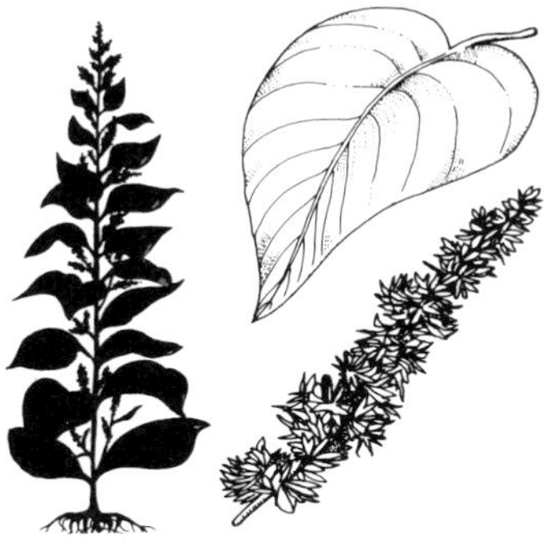

Amaranth, a plant family that flourishes in warm climates, includes garden flowers.

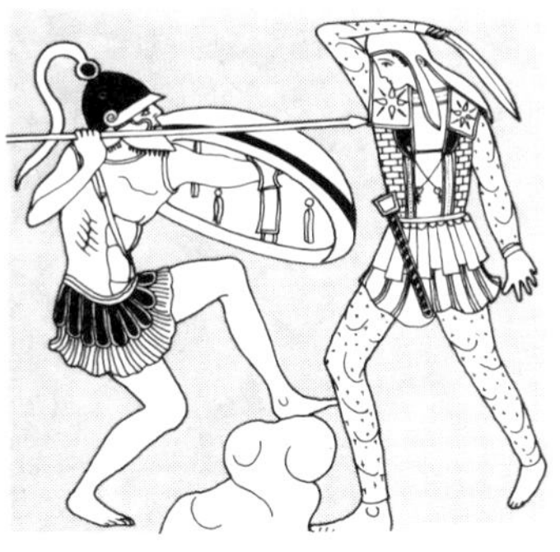

Amazons, a legendary race of female Greek warriors, enslaved any men they captured.

law minister and helped to draft the 1950 constitution which outlawed untouchability and the caste system.

Amber, hard yellow or brown, translucent fossil resin found in alluvial soils, in lignite beds or on sea-shores, especially near the Baltic Sea (where deposits represent extinct flora 50 million years old). It sometimes occurs with embedded fossil insects or plants as rods or as irregular nodules. Deeply coloured amber takes a fine polish and is prized as a gem. *See also* PE p.98.

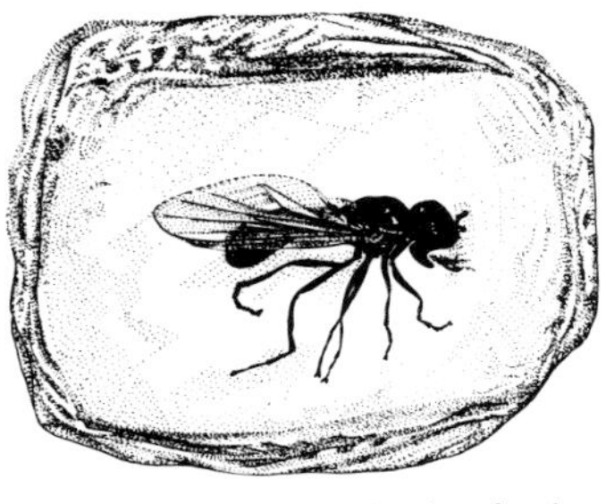

Amber, a type of fossilized resin, often has insects trapped in it.

Amberger, Christoph (*c.* 1500–*c.* 1561), German portrait painter, influenced by HOLBEIN and by the VENETIAN SCHOOL of painting. His many sitters included Emperor Charles V (1532).

Ambergris, musky, waxy, solid formed in the intestine of SPERM WHALES. It is used in perfumes as a fixative for the scent.

Ambivalence, having contradictory emotions such as love and hate towards the same person or object. It was first used in its specific psychological sense by Carl JUNG. Paul BLEULER linked ambivalent complexes to pathological behaviour.

Ambler, Eric (1909–), British writer of stories based on espionage and intrigue; one of the most popular writers of his kind. His first work was *The Dark Frontier* (1936), followed by such titles as *Journey Into Fear* (1940), *The Night-Comers* (1956) and *The Light of Day* (1965).

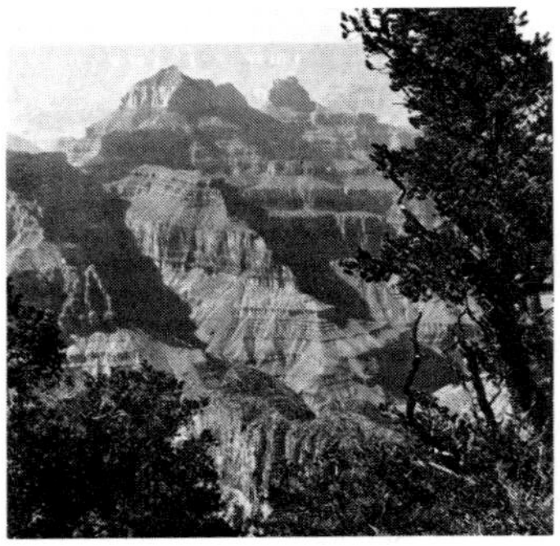

America; north rim of the Grand Canyon, one of the great natural wonders of the world.

Amboina (Ambon), one of the Moluccas (formerly the Spice Islands), Indonesia; part of the Malay archipelago. It has high mountains and active volcanoes. Its crops include tropical fruits and spices. Pop. 114,000.

Ambon, seaport city on Amboina Island in the Malay archipelago. Founded by the Portuguese in 1521, it was taken over by the Dutch East India Co. in 1605. It became part of Indonesia in 1956. Pop. 73,000.

Ambrose, Saint (*c.* 339–97), Bishop of Milan, who resisted demands to surrender Milan's churches to the Arians and refused to compromise his orthodox position. He was the author of works on theology and ethics that greatly influenced the thought of the Western Church. He also acquired a reputation for administrative skill and eloquence, and AUGUSTINE OF HIPPO attributed his own conversion to Ambrose. *See also* ARIANISM; HC2 p.*207*.

Ambrosia, divine substance eaten by gods of Greek and Roman mythology, often equated with honey. The gods kept their immortality by bathing in it or rubbing it into their skin. Without ambrosia a god became weak; a mortal who ate it became strong and immortal. Nectar, the wine of the gods, was drunk with it.

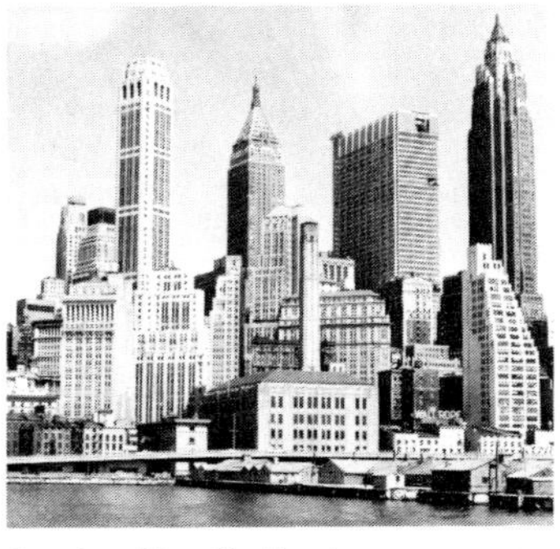

America; New York's skyscrapers, man-made wonders of 20th-century architecture.

Ambulatory, continuation of side aisles around the east (sanctuary) end of a Christian church, usually giving access to subordinate chapels. Ambulatories were originally used for processional purposes.

Amenemhet, four kings of ancient Egypt. Amenemhet I (*r.* 1991–1962 BC) overthrew the local minor monarchs, created a centralized government and founded the 12th Dynasty. His co-regent, Sesostris I, succeeded. Amenemhet II ruled with his father, Sesostris I, and with his son and successor, Sesostris II, between 1929 and 1895 BC. Amenemhet III (*r.* 1842–1797 BC) succeeded Sesostris III. He reclaimed thousands of acres in Faiyum, but his successor, Amenemhet IV (*r.* 1798–1790 BC), let the dynasty decline. *See also* HC1 p.34.

Amenhotep, or Amenophis, name of four Egyptian kings of the 18th Dynasty. (For Amenhotep IV, *see* AKHENATON.) Amenhotep I (*r.* 1546–1526 BC) succeeded his father AHMOSE I. He campaigned successfully in Syria as far as the River Euphrates and pushed Egypt's southern boundary as far as the second cataract of the River Nile, He was succeeded by THUTMOSE I. Amenhotep II (*r.* 1450–1425 BC) ruled as co-regent (*c.* 1452–1450 BC) with his father Thutmose III before becoming king. He crushed an uprising in Syria, defended Egypt's frontiers as far as the River Euphrates, invaded Nubia and completed temples to the god AMON at Karnak, central Egypt. He was succeeded by his son Thutmose IV, whose son Amenhotep III ruled Egypt 1417–1379 BC. The 18th Dynasty reached its peak during Amenhotep III's reign, and despite raids by the Hittites and Bedouin, peace was maintained. He built the Temple of Luxor and completed the Great Temple of Amon. *See also* HC1 p.48, *48*.

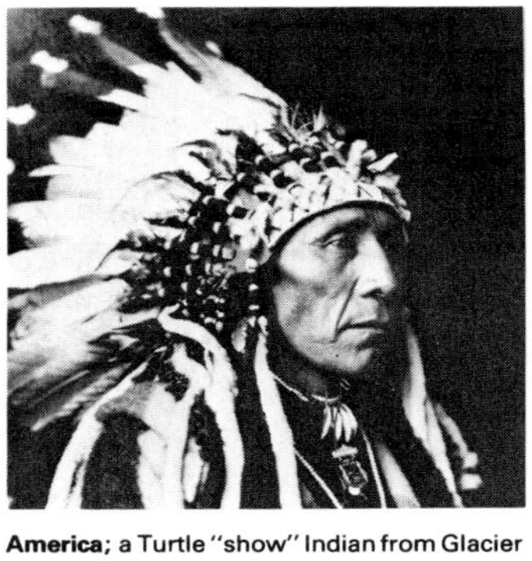

America; a Turtle "show" Indian from Glacier National Park, a great tourist attraction.

Amenorrhoea, abnormal absence of menstruation in a non-pregnant, non-lactating female between the ages of puberty and menopause. It is not a disease in itself, but the symptom of a hormonal imbalance which can arise from emotional or physiological disorders.

Amerbach, Johann (1443–1513), Swiss printer, the first of those based in Basle. His teacher and editor was the Humanist Heynlin (Johannes de Lapide), and his books reflected Humanist views.

America, comprising North and South America, extends from N of the Arctic Circle to 56°S and separates the Atlantic Ocean from the Pacific. The continents are linked by the isthmus of Panama.

Land. The continent of North America slopes up gradually from the Appalachian Mts in the E to the Rockies in the W. The highest peak is Mt McKinley in Alaska, 6,194m (20,321ft), and the lowest point is in Death Valley, California, 86m (282ft) below sea-level. The Andes of South America, towering above the rest of the continent, rise abruptly from the Amazonian Basin and the S plains and contain the highest peak of either continent – Aconcagua 7,265m (23,834ft). The Brazilian and Venezuelan highlands are the other main mountainous areas of the continent.

Structure and geology. N Canada is an old Precambrian shield area forming a saucer-shaped depression centred in the Hudson Bay and rising towards the flat-lying Palaeozoic and Mesozoic sediments of the USA. The Appalachians in the E have their origins in the Precambrian era and are composed largely of eroded metamorphic rocks. The highly complex fold mountains in the W that form the Rockies are much younger and extend the entire length of the continent, continuing in South America as the Andes. The Amazonian Basin and much of Argentina is composed of Cenozoic sediments; the highlands of Brazil and Venezuela of much older sedimentary and metamorphic rocks.

Lakes and rivers. Lake Superior is the largest lake in North America, 82,413sq km (31,820sq miles), and together with Michigan, Huron, Erie, and Ontario, makes up the Great Lakes. The St Lawrence River forms a navigable link between the Great Lakes and the Atlantic Ocean. The longest river is the combined Mississippi-Missouri system with a total length of 6,050km (3,760 miles). Other important rivers include the Yukon, Mackenzie, Colorado, Columbia, Delaware and Rio Grande. Lake Maracaibo in Venezuela, an extension of the Gulf of Venezuela, if classified as a lake, is the largest in South America with an area of 13,512sq km (5,217sq miles). The largest landlocked body of water is Lake Titicaca, in the Andes, on the border between Peru and Bolivia, covering 8,288sq km (3,200sq miles). The N part of South America is dominated by the Amazonian Basin whose many rivers feed the mighty River Amazon which flows for 6,516km (4,050 miles) and is the second longest river in the world (only the River Nile is longer). The Paraguay and Parana drain the central area, S of the Mato Grosso.

Climate and vegetation. Except for parts of the W seaboard, North America experiences hot summers and cold winters, with the most extreme ranges occurring within the plains of N USA. The natural vegetation of the plains is grass, bordered by mixed and coniferous forests in the mountains to the E, W and N. Tropical rain-forest is found in the lower areas of Central America and desert is found in the SW. The far N of Canada and Alaska is covered with tundra and permanent snow. Cypress thrive in the SE, oak and maple in the E, and giant redwoods in the W. Except in the mountains and the extreme S, the climate of South America remains generally warm and humid. Much of the N supports tropical rain-forest, while the Venezuelan highlands in the extreme N and the Brazilian highlands are areas of tropical grassland. The pampas of Uruguay are temperate grasslands. The Atacama Desert on the W coast of N Chile is the driest in the world. Pine and other temperate forests grow in the S along the W coast.

Animal life. In the W of North America bears, wolves and pumas have become scarce, but foxes remain widespread and lynxes occupy many forests. Coyotes range across the SW, and ocelots live in the S of the USA. These predators catch deer, rabbits, hares and mice. Beavers and members of the weasel family are important for their fur. There is a wide variety of bird species, and snakes – many extremely dangerous – are widespread throughout the continent. The mammals of South America include monkeys, ocelots, pumas, deer, tapirs, peccaries and coatis. Found in the Andes are small members of the camel family: llamas, alpacas and vicuñas, of which only the vicuñas are not domesticated. Many colourful birds abound, including macaws, toucans and tiny humming-birds; condors are found in the mountains. South American snakes include anacondas and boa constrictors. Many rivers of the tropical region contain alligators and piranha fish.

People. North America's first settlers probably arrived about 35,000 years ago from Asia by way of Alaska. By the time the Vikings discovered America, around AD 1000, the descendants of the original inhabitants had occupied the entire continent. Christopher COLUMBUS was the first to call them Indians when he sailed to the New World in 1492. The Spaniards settled in Mexico and the West Indies, whereas the English and French settled farther N in the USA and Canada. Swedes, Germans and the Dutch also made early settlements. Europe's political and economic problems later drove numbers of Italians, Irish and Jews to North America. Negroes were imported as slaves; Japanese and Chinese arrived with less coercion to be labourers on the W coast. Descendants of the Spanish settlers are predominant in Mexico, Central America, and some Caribbean islands and French concentrations exist in Quebec province, Canada, and parts of the West Indies. Negroes outnumber whites in many Caribbean islands. Protestantism is dominant N of Mexico, whereas Roman Catholics are more numerous in Spanish- and French-speaking areas. In South America some pure-blood INCAS (Quechuas) still remain in the Andes and some Mapuche (Araucanians) are found in Chile. However, most Indians are now of mixed blood, having interbred with the Portuguese in Brazil and the Spaniards in the rest of the continent. Brazil has a large Negroid population, descendants of slaves, as do the small countries on the N coast. Although many Germans have migrated to Argentina and some, along with the Italians, to Chile, people of Spanish and Portuguese descent remain the two main groups and theirs are the dominant languages. Roman Catholicism is the major religion.

Economy. The plains region of North America is one of the world's major grain- and livestock-producing areas. The S area produces mainly cotton, tobacco, coffee and sugar cane. The NE is heavily industrialized. In the W mining and irrigated farming are important. Fishing is conducted off most coasts but particularly in the NE. In South America livestock are reared on the grassland areas with cattle predominating in Venezuela, Brazil and Uruguay. Sheep are found mainly in the far S of Argentina. The main grain area is situated in E Argentina S of the Río de la Plata (River Plate). Valuable nitrates are found in the Atacama Desert. Copper, tin, silver and gemstones are most important; Venezuela's Maracaibo region yields petroleum. Most of these countries remain underdeveloped industrially.

Recent History. The USA and Canada have each, in recent years, been faced with a growing crisis, not yet resolved: in the USA the nascent strength of the BLACK POWER movement and in Canada the threat to the

unity of the confederation posed by the separatist movement in Québec. The separatist Parti Québecois won power in Québec in the 1976 provincial election. In Central and South America the traces of the colonial past have been almost entirely obliterated, but democracy has failed to establish itself. Military rule is in force in Argentina (since 1975), Brazil (since 1964), Chile (since 1973), Ecuador (since 1972) and Peru (since 1968). Perhaps the outstanding development has been the success of the revolution in Cuba, where 20 years of US pressure have not succeeded in toppling Fidel CASTRO.
Area 42,205,800sq km (16,295,700sq miles) North America 24,398,000sq km (9,420,100sq miles)
South America 17,807,800sq km (6,875,600sq miles)
Highest mountains North America, Mt McKinley 6,194m (20,321ft)
South America, Aconcagua 7,265m (23,834ft)
Longest rivers North America, Mississippi-Missouri 6,050km (3,760 miles)
South America, Amazon 6,516km (4,050 miles)
Population 560,933,000
North America 236,841,000
South America 324,092,000
Largest cities North America, Mexico City (8,591,750); New York City (7,567,000); Chicago (7,173,000); Los Angeles (2,747,000)
South America, São Paulo (5,869,966); Rio de Janiero (4,296,782); Santiago (3,263,000); Buenos Aires (2,976,000)
See also NW pp.198–199, 202–203, 206–209, 212–213, 216–219, 222–223, 226–227; PE pp.58–59, 62–63; indexes to HC1 and HC2; articles on individual countries in *The Modern World.*

American, The (1877), novel by Henry JAMES set in Paris in the mid-1800s. It demonstrates the interaction of two cultures as seen in the story of a wealthy American who falls in love with the daughter of an aristocratic but impoverished family.

American Ballet Theater, one of the foremost dance companies in the world, stressing modern works with US themes as well as classical pieces, founded in 1939 and called Ballet Theater. Based in New York City, it has produced the works of such notable choreographers as Michel FOKINE (1880–1942), George BALANCHINE (1904–) and Antony Tudor (1909–).

American Civil War (1861–65), the war fought in the USA between the Unionist forces of the federal government and the forces of the southern secessionist states, the CONFEDERATE STATES OF AMERICA. It began on 12 April 1861 at FORT SUMTER, South Carolina, and ended with the surrender of the Confederate commander Robert E. LEE at APPOMATTOX, Virginia, on 9 April 1865. The Confederacy collapsed and the Union was restored. *See also* HC2 pp.150–153; MW p.179.

American Constitution, the seven articles of government adopted by the delegates at the Constitutional Convention of 1787, and 26 subsequent amendments. The Convention was called to frame a constitution to replace the ARTICLES OF CONFEDERATION, which had been in force since 1781 but, in not empowering the federal government to raise taxation, for example, had left too much authority with the state governments. The federal structure of the 1781 Articles was nevertheless retained in the 1787 constitution. The chief concern of the delegates was to reach a compromise satisfactory both to the small states (who were jealous to safeguard their power against a purely democratic majority), and the large states. The solution provided two cardinal features of the constitution. The first was that in the House of Representatives (elected every two years) each state is represented according to its population, whereas in the Senate (one-third elected to a six-year term every two years) each state has two representatives. In determining the population of a state for electoral purposes, a slave was counted as three-fifths of a voter. The second salient feature of the constitution was its system of checks and balances which, from a misunderstanding of the much admired British "mixed constitution" of king, lords and commons and a devotion to the separation of powers commended by MONTESQUIEU, sharply divided the function of the judiciary (the SUPREME COURT), the executive (the President and Vice-President) and the Legislature (the two houses of CONGRESS). By late 1788 ten states had ratified the articles, and the Convention called for the first elections and set 4 March 1789 as the date on which the first President should take office. By 1790, when Rhode Island entered the Union, all 13 of the late colonies had ratified the new constitution. There have since been 26 amendments to the constitution. Important among them are the 1st (1791), which guaranteed freedom of speech, religion and peaceful assembly; the 5th (1791), which freed an accused person from the obligation of testifying against himself and guaranteed him due process of law (the equivalent of natural justice in English law); and the 13th, 14th and 15th (1865, 1868 and 1870), which abolished slavery, guaranteed that no person of whatever colour should be deprived of life, liberty or property without due process of law, and guaranteed to every citizen of whatever colour the right to vote. *See also* HC2 p.65; MW p.178.

American Independence, Declaration of (4 July 1776), statement issued by the CONTINENTAL CONGRESS announcing that the American colonies no longer considered themselves to be ruled by Britain. Drafted mainly by Thomas JEFFERSON, the Declaration restated the political notions associated with John LOCKE and the ENLIGHTENMENT, that government must rest on the consent of the governed and that when the implied contract between ruler and ruled is broken by the ruler the people have a natural right to rebel. *See also* HC2 pp.64–65.

American Independence, War of (1775–83), the successful revolt by the British colonies in America against imperial rule from London. A number of issues produced the conflict – the restrictions on trade and manufacturing imposed by the NAVIGATION ACTS, imperial control of land settlement in the virgin West, and the British attempt to raise revenue in America by such means as the Sugar Act (1764), the STAMP ACTS (1765), the Revenue Act (1767) and the Tea Act (1773) – leading to the BOSTON TEA PARTY. "No taxation without representation" became the colonial radicals' rallying cry. Each dispute narrowed to one question, whether the colonies ought to be self-governing. The British parliament's rigid adherence to at least the principle of the supremacy of parliament, embodied in the DECLARATORY ACT (1766), made war inescapable. Shots were fired first at Lexington and Concord, Massachusetts, in April 1775. In May the second CONTINENTAL CONGRESS met at PHILADELPHIA, established an army under George WASHINGTON and asumed the role of a revolutionary government. On 4 July 1776 the Declaration of Independence was proclaimed. The first decisive colonial victory, at SARATOGA in 1777, brought France into the war against Britain. Spain also entered the lists on the colonial side in 1779. When Gen. CORNWALLIS surrendered to the Americans at YORKTOWN in 1781 the war was effectively ended. It was formally ended by the PEACE OF PARIS (1783) which granted independence to America. *See also* HC2 pp.64–65; MW pp.178.

American Indians, the aboriginal peoples of North and South America, also called Amerindians. Most North American Indians are thought to be of Mongoloid stock and to have crossed from Asia via the Bering Strait or the Aleutian Islands in about 20,000 BC or even earlier. They spread throughout the continent and developed into many regional varieties with hundreds of different languages.

North American Indians can be divided into eight cultural and geographical groups: the Arctic area (Aleut, ESKIMO), the North-eastern Mackenzie area (mainly Eastern Woodland tribes), the North-west Coast area (Tlingit, Haida, Kwakiutl), the South-western area (Five Civilized Tribes, Tuscarora, Powhatan Confederacy), the Plains area (Blackfoot, Crow, Comanche, Dakota), the California- Inter-mountain area (Paiute, Shoshoni, Nez Perce), the South-western area (Pueblos, Navaho, Apache) and the Mesoamerican area (Maya, Toltec, Aztec).

South American Indians derived from North American groups that had migrated southwards. There are three main cultural and geographical groups: Indians of the Andean area, including the INCAS (a branch of the Quechua, who after 1300 dominated almost the entire region); those of the Amazon basin, mainly isolated primitive agricultural communities; and the Indians of the Pampas, including warlike nomadic tribes and the southern Araucanians, who successfully resisted both the Incas and the Spaniards. *See also* MS pp.30–31.

American National Theater and Academy (ANTA), self-supporting organization in the USA, founded in 1935. It helps to finance touring theatre companies and since 1968 has served as a performing arts centre for non-profit-making groups.

American Revolution. *See* AMERICAN INDEPENDENCE, WAR OF.

American Samoa, US territory in the E part of the Samoa island group in the S Pacific Ocean. Exports include canned fish, copra and local crafts. Area: 197sq km (76sq miles). Pop. 29,000. *See* MW p.27.

America's Cup, competition for 12-metre yachts held off Newport, Rhode Island (since 1934) between the "defender" and the "challenger" over a best-of-seven series of races. The trophy was put up in 1857 by the New York YC and named after the *America*, which had beaten the best British yachts in 1851. Most of the challenges (every few years) up to the 1950s were from British yacht clubs. Several countries now take part in an eliminating series to challenge the Americans, who were still unbeaten in the late 1970s.

Americium, radioactive metallic element (Am) in the ACTINIDE group, made by Glenn Seaborg and others by neutron bombardment of plutonium. Am^{241} is used as a source of gamma rays. Properties: at.no. 95; s.g. 13.67; m.p. 995°C (1,821°F); b.p. 2,607°C (4,725°F); most stable isotope Am^{243} (half-life 8,800 yr.).

Amerika (1927), novel by Franz KAFKA, written between 1911 and 1914 and translated in 1938.

Amerindian. *See* AMERICAN INDIANS.

Amery, Leopold Charles Maurice Stennett, (1873–1955), British Conservative politician, a minister in several administrations. In the 1930s he was a leading opponent of the policy of APPEASEMENT.

Amethyst, transparent, violet variety of crystallized QUARTZ, containing more iron oxide than other varieties, found mainly in Brazil, Uruguay, Ontario and North Carolina. It is valued as a semi-precious gem. *See also* PE p.98.

Amharic, language of the Semitic or Hamito-Semitic family. Original to the province of Amhara and Shoa, it has been the official language of Ethiopia since *c.*1300 and has many words from ancient Ghiz, the official language at the time of the conversion to Christianity in 335.

Amiens, city in N France, on the River Somme, 115km (72 miles) N of Paris; capital of the Somme département. It was the capital of the historical region of Picardy. The Germans took the city during the Franco-Prussian War, WWI and WWII. It has a fine Gothic church, the Cathedral of Notre Dame. Industries: chemicals, textiles, electrical equipment. Pop. 118,000.

Amiens, Treaty of (March 1802), peace agreement between France and her enemies in the Revolutionary Wars: Spain, Britain and the BATAVIAN REPUBLIC. France recovered most of her colonies, but evacuated the kingdom of NAPLES. Britain withdrew from Egypt, but kept Ceylon and Trinidad. The peace lasted only until May 1803. *See also* HC2 p.76.

Amin, Idi (*c.*1925–), President of

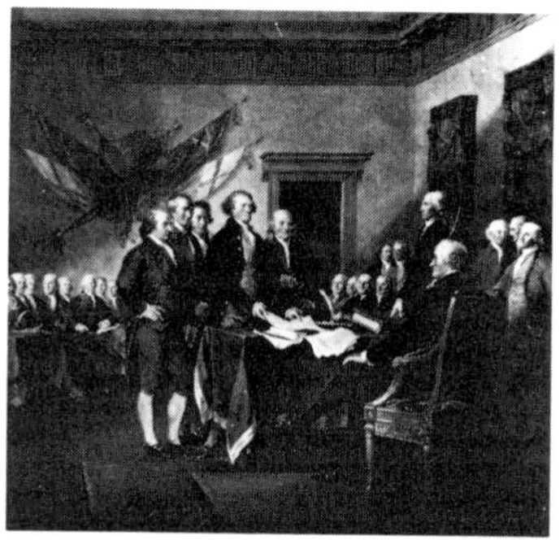

Declaration of American Independence; the document holds 56 signatures in all.

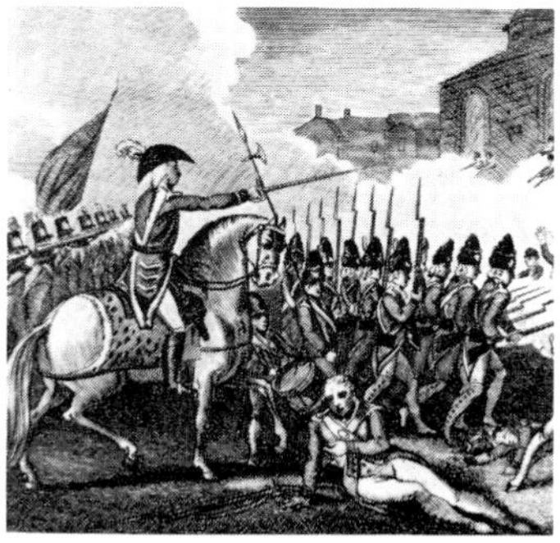

American War of Independence; first action between the British and Americans.

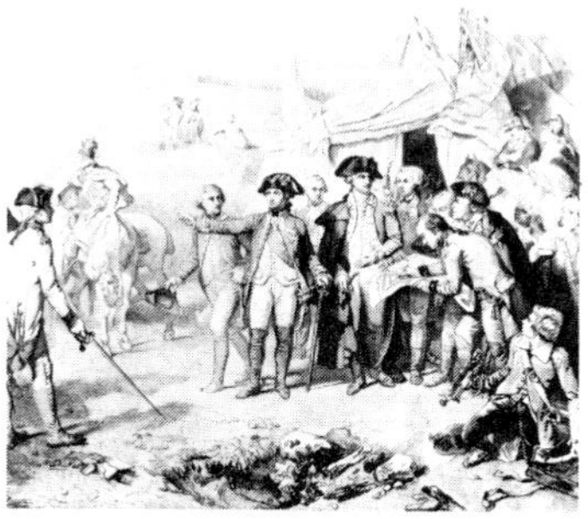

War of Independence; Washington and Rochambeau ordering the attack on Yorktown.

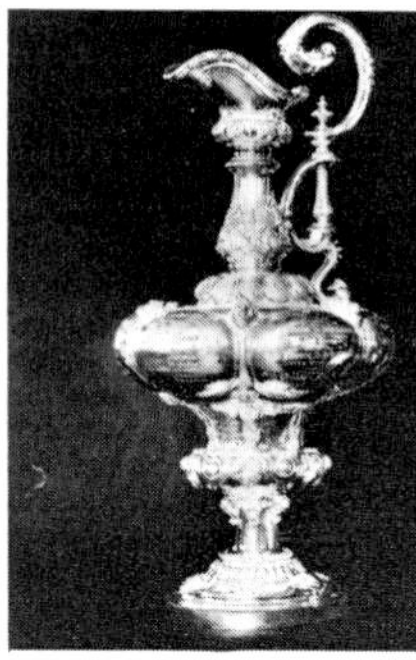

America's Cup, the yacht racing trophy held almost exclusively by the USA since 1851.

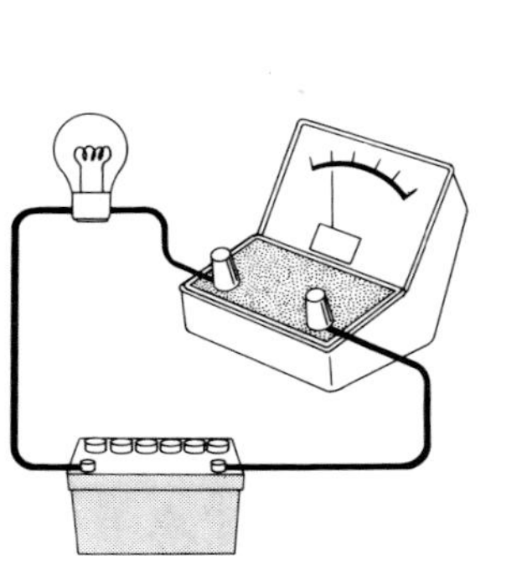

Ammeters measure, in amperes, the electric current that flows through a circuit.

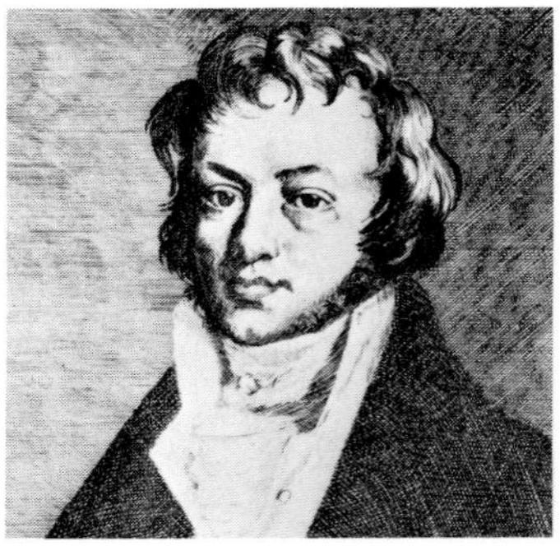

André-Marie Ampère, the father of electromagnetism, pioneered methods of measuring electricity.

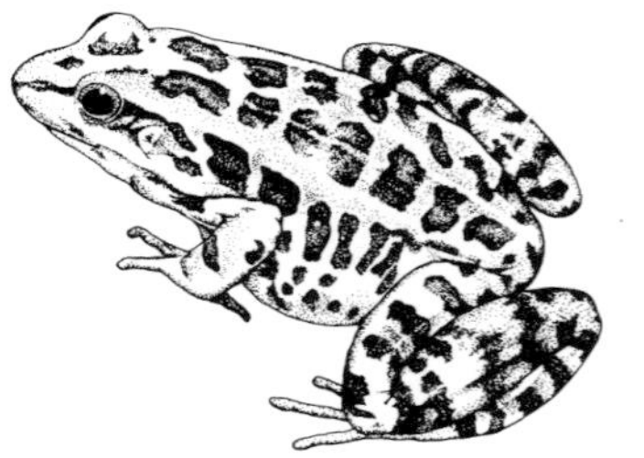

Amphibians breed in water, although adults usually spend most of their time on land.

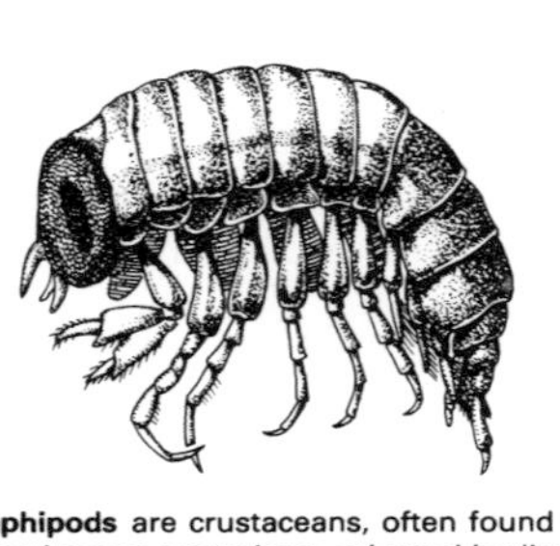

Amphipods are crustaceans, often found in coastal areas; many have coloured bodies.

Uganda (1971–). He staged a military coup in 1971, overthrowing Milton OBOTE; in 1972 he expelled about 80,000 Asian Ugandans. Both his personal behaviour and political policies have been described as flamboyant and erratic. *See also* MW p.169.

Amine, any of a group of organic compounds derived from ammonia by replacing hydrogen atoms with organic groups. Methylamine, CH_3NH_2 (a primary amine) has one hydrogen replaced. Replacement of two hydrogens gives a secondary amine and of three hydrogens, a tertiary amine. Amines are produced in the putrefaction of organic matter and are weakly basic. *See also* ALKALOID.

Amino acid, organic acid containing at least one carboxyl group (–COOH) and at least one amino group ($-NH_2$). These acids are of great biological importance because they combine together to form PROTEINS. They have the general formula $R{:}CH(NH_2)COOH$ and link to form the peptide structure –NH–CO– by condensation of the $-NH_2$ group of one acid and the –COOH of another. Proteins are cross-lined polypeptides consisting of hundreds of amino acid "building blocks". About 20 amino acids occur in proteins; not all organisms are able to synthesize all of them. Essential amino acids are those that an organism has to obtain ready-made from its environment. There are ten such essential amino acids for man. *See also* SU pp.152–156.

Amirante Islands, group of islands in the Indian Ocean, 800km (500 miles) NNE of Madagascar; a dependency of the SEYCHELLE ISLANDS. They include the African Islands. Chief product, copra.

Amis, Kingsley (1922–), British novelist. He was a university teacher until 1963 and draws on this experience in his novels. These include *Lucky Jim* (1954), *That Uncertain Feeling* (1955) and *Ending Up* (1974).

Amish, conservative Protestant sect, members of the old order Amish Mennonite Church. Followers of Jakob Ammann, a 17th-century Mennonite leader who broke away from the parent body in Europe and advocated strict community conformity, they established themselves in North America. *See also* MENNONITES.

Amitriptyline, antidepressant drug of the TRICYCLIC group. *See* MS p.144.

Amleth, hero of a Danish legend recorded in the 13th century by SAXO GRAMMATICUS and used by William SHAKESPEARE in his play *Hamlet.*

Amman, capital of Jordan, 80km (50 miles) ENE of Jerusalem. Known as Rabbath-Ammon, it was the chief city of the Ammonites. Ptolemy II Philadelphus renamed it Philadelphia, under which name it prospered as part of the Roman Empire. It became Jordan's capital in 1921. It has a university (1962), and industries include cement, textiles, tobacco and leather. Pop. 598,000. *See also* MW p.114.

Ammanati, Bartolommeo (1511–1592), Florentine MANNERIST sculptor and architect. In Florence he carved the Neptune fountain (1571–75), built the famous Bridge of the Trinity (1567–70) and made extensions to the Pitti Palace. He also designed buildings in Rome. *See also* HC1 p.265.

Ammeter, instrument for measuring electric current. In the moving-coil type (for direct current) the current to be measured passes through a coil suspended in a magnetic field and deflmcts a needle attached to the coil. In the moving-iron type (for both direct and alternating current) current through a fixed coil magnetizes two pieces of soft iron which repel each other and so deflect the needle.

Ammonia, colourless non-flammable pungent gas (NH_3) manufactured by the HABER PROCESS; it is a very important nitrogen compound because it is produced in the fixing of nitrogen for fertilizers. The gas is extremely soluble in water, forming an alkaline solution of ammonium hydroxide (NH_4OH), which can give rise to ammonium salts containing the ion NH_4^+. Chief properties: m.p. −77.7°C (−107.86°F); b.p. −33.35°C (−28.03°F). *See also* SU pp.139–141, 150.

Ammonite, any of an extinct group of shelled cephalopod MOLLUSCS. They are believed to be descended from the nautiloids (of which the pearly nautilus is the only surviving form). They are common as fossils in marine rocks. *See* NW pp.94, 178, 179.

Ammunition, any projectile launched, dropped from an aircraft or fired from a gun; also any explosive charge used in a weapon to fire a projectile. Ammunition thus includes bullets, cartridges, shells (and their cases), bombs, mortars, grenades and rockets, together with chemical and nuclear explosive warheads. *See also* MM pp.162–170; 174–180.

Amnesia, loss of memory; more particularly, partial or complete inability to recall. Selective amnesia, in which only certain unpleasant memories are eliminated, is generally caused by psychological disturbance. Amnesia caused organically is usually not selective, but also usually not total. In retrograde amnesia, memory loss extends back in time from the moment of onset (eg, a head injury). *See also* MS pp.134–135.

Amnesty, official act of pardon granted by the head of government to violators of a national law. Amnesty may be absolute or conditional. If absolute, it absolves the violator of all offences. If conditional, it stipulates certain obligations the offender must meet in order to obtain the pardon.

Amnion, membrane or sac that encloses the EMBRYO of a reptile, bird or mammal. The embryo floats in the amniotic fluid within the sac. An outer membrane, the chorion, encloses the amniotic sac. In mammals both are in the WOMB or uterus. *See also* MS pp.76–79.

Amoeba, microscopic, almost transparent protozoan animal that has a constantly changing, irregular shape. Found in ponds, damp soil and animal intestines, it consists of a thin outer membrane, a large nucleus, food and contractile vacuoles and fat globules. It reproduces by binary fission. Length: up to 3mm (0.lin). Class Sarcodina; species include the common *Amoeba proteus* and *Entamoeba histolytica,* which causes amoebic DYSENTERY. *See* NW pp*72, 81.*

Amok, murderous frenzy, usually following severe depression. Domestic problems or a grievance may lead to brooding, aand a sufferer may suddenly run "amok", killing indiscriminately.

Amon, or Amun, ancient Egyptian deity of reproduction or of the animating force. He is represented as a ram or as a ram-headed man, or a goose or snake, and often as a crowned king. Amon was worshipped at Thebes in the 12th Dynasty and later as a powerful national god renamed Amon-Re, identified with the sun. Amon's temples are at Luxor, Karnak and Thebes.

Amor, also called CUPID, Roman equivalent of EROS, the Greek god of love.

Amorites, Biblical people who lived in Canaan and were descended from an earlier dynasty of Babylon (18th century BC) whose greatest ruler was HAMMURABI. The Amorites were gradually incorporated into the ISRAELITES.

Amorphous substance, non-crystalline solid; its atoms of molecules have no regular order. Super-cooled liquids such as glass, rubber and some plastics are amorphous. Many powders appear amorphous but are microcrystalline in structure. *See also* CRYSTALS; SU p.88.

Amos, Old Testament author; third of the 12 minor prophets.

Amoy (Xiamen), seaport city in SE China, on an island in the Formosa Strait. It flourished in the 19th century after being opened for trade by the Treaty of Nanking (1842). It gained great strategic importance after the Communists took control of the Chinese mainland (1949). Pop. 308,000.

Ampère, André-Marie (1775–1836), French physicist and mathematician. He was professor of chemistry and physics at Bourg and later of mathematics at the École Polytechnique in Paris. He founded ELECTRODYNAMICS (now called ELECTROMAGNETISM) and performed numerous experiments to investigate the magnetic effects of electric currents. He was the first to devise techniques for measuring electricity, and constructed an early type of GALVANOMETER. Ampère's law – proposed by him – is a mathematical description of the magnetic force between two electric currents. His name is also commemorated in the fundamental unit of current, the ampere (A), used in the SI system of units. The ampere is defined as the current in a pair of straight and parallel conductors of equal length one metre apart that produces a force of 2×10^{-7} newton per metre of their length. This force may be measured on a current balance, which becomes the standard against which CURRENT METERS such as AMMETERS and galvanometers are calibrated. *See also* SU p.118.

Amphetamines, DRUGS that stimulate the central NERVOUS SYSTEM. Formerly used to treat psychiatric disorders, reduce appetite in people who are overweight and provide temporary stimulation and prevention of fatigue, they are now rarely prescribed. These drugs, known as "pep pills", can lead to drug abuse and dependence. After the immediate sense of well-being wears off, the user can experience fatigue and depression. Amphetamines can also cause apprehension, insomnia, dizziness, headache, digestive disturbances, confusion and even PSYCHOSIS and convulsions. *See also* ADDICTION; MS pp.105, 138, 144.

Amphibians, class of egg-laying VERTEBRATES whose larval stages are usually spent in water but whose adult life is normally spent on land. Amphibians have smooth, moist skin and are coldblooded. Larvae breathe through gills; adults usually have lungs. Amphibian eggs are shell-less and, as a result, are laid in water or humid surroundings to prevent drying out. All adults are carnivorous but larvae are frequently herbivorous. There are three living orders: Urodela – NEWTS and SALAMANDERS; Anura – FROGS and TOADS; and Apoda or CAECILIANS – an elongated, blind and burrowing form. The caecilians are the smallest and least-known group of amphibians. *See also* NW pp.73, 132–133, 138–139.

Amphibole, any of a large group of complex rock-forming minerals characterized by a double-chain silicate (Si_4O_{11}) structure. They all contain water (as OH^- ions) and usually Ca, Mg, Fe, and are found in IGNEOUS and METAMORPHIC rocks. They form wedge-shaped fragments on cleavage; their orthorhombic or monoclinic crystals are often needle-like or fibrous. Common varieties are hornblende, tremolite, actinolite and anthophyllite. Some varieties are used in commercial ASBESTOS.

Amphineura, class of MOLLUSCS that includes the CHITONS, small dwellers on rock surfaces. It also includes *Neopilina,* a small marine mollusc recently dredged from great depths which is so primitive as to show some similarities to the ANNELID worms. *See also* NW p.90.

Amphioxus, or lancelet, marine, fish-shaped animal found off sandy shores in warm seas. It has a well-developed NOTOCHORD instead of a true backbone but no distinct head region or brain. It has rudimentary eyes and tentacles round its mouth for straining food from water. Length: up to 8cm (3in). Subphylum Cephalochordata; genus *Branchiostoma. See also* NW pp.122, 123.

Amphipod, or scud, mainly marine crustacean, although some amphipods are freshwater and a few, such as the sandhopper, are semi-terrestrial. There are about 4,600 species, all of which have laterally compressed bodies. Some are parasitic. Length: 0.1–14cm (0.04–5.5in).

Amphisbaenid, or worm lizard, cylindrical, usually legless, burrowing reptile found in tropical America and Africa. Amphisbaenids resemble earthworms and have rings of scales around their bodies and tails, and no external ear openings. Some species have short front legs. Length: 20cm (20in). Formerly regarded as lizards, the 100 species are now classified as a Squamata suborder. Family

Amphisbaenidae. *See also* LIZARD; SQUAMATA; NW p.134.

Amphitheatre, in ancient Rome and the Roman Empire, a large semi-circular, elliptical or circular building used as a theatre for gladiatorial and wild-beast shows and similar events. Many ruined amphitheatres remain, the best-known being the Colosseum in Rome. The term is also used to refer to any open, banked arena, particularly for sports fields and theatres. *See also* HC1 p.107.

Amphitrite, in Greek mythology, daughter of Nereus. Wooed by the god POSEIDON, she at first rejected his proposal of marriage and fled to Atlas but was brought back by a dolphin to be made queen of the sea. Poseidon translated the dolphin to the heavens as a constellation.

Amplifier, device for changing the magnitude but not the variation of a signal, such as voltage, current or mechanical motion. Amplifiers are used in radio sets and in various kinds of audio equipment. The first electronic amplifiers were thermionic valves; the triode (invented in 1907 by Lee De Forest) was widely used but is now almost completely replaced by the TRANSISTOR. *See also* SU p.130; MM p.228.

Amplitude. *See* WAVE AMPLITUDE.

Amplitude modulation (AM), encoding a WAVE having constant amplitude (the carrier wave) with information to be transmitted, giving a single wave with varying amplitude. *See* MM. p.*228.*

Ampulla, part of the inner EAR, or any sinal membranous vesicle. *See* MS p.*50.*

Amritsar, city in Punjab state, NW India; an industrial and administrative centre. The SIKH religious centre, it was founded in 1574 on land donated by the Mogul Emperor AKBAR. The Golden Temple is especially sacred to the Sikhs. Modern Sikh nationalism began there and the city was the scene of the Amritsar Massacre in 1919. Pop. 408,000. *See also* HC2 p.216.

Amsterdam, capital and largest city in The Netherlands, on the River Amstel and linked to the North Sea by the North Sea Canal. Amsterdam was chartered in *c.*1300 and joined the HANSEATIC LEAGUE in 1369. The Dutch East India Company (1602) brought great prosperity and an influx of European refugees to the city. It also became a great centre of learning and book printing during the 17th century. Its commerce and importance declined when captured by the French in 1795 and blockaded by the British during the Napoleonic Wars. A major European port, it has an important stock exchange and diamond-cutting industry, and is one of Europe's leading cultural centres. It has many interesting buildings, including the house of REMBRANDT, the Royal Palace and a National Museum (1876–85). Industries include iron and steel, oil refining, rolling stock, food processing, chemicals, glass, and ship-building. Pop. (1970 est.) 820,400. *See also* HC1 p.197; MW pp.128, 129.

Amu Darya, river 2,540km (1,578 miles) long from its longest headstream, formed by the junction of the Vakhsh and Pandj Rivers in the Pamir Mountains of Central Asia. Originally called the Oxus, it played an important role in the early history of Persia.

Amun. *See* AMON.

Amundsen, Roald (1872–1928), Norwegian explorer and discoverer of the South Pole. From 1903–06 he sailed through the NORTH-WEST PASSAGE and, from his observations, was able to locate the exact position of the North Magnetic Pole. His next expedition took him to the ANTARCTIC, and in December 1911 (one month ahead of Capt. Robert SCOTT) he reached the South Pole. In his later years he conducted an exploration of the north polar regions by air in 1925 and 1926. His books include *North West Passage* (1908), *The South Pole* (1912), *The North East Passage* (1918–20) and *My Life as an Explorer* (1927).

Amun-Re. *See* AMON.

Amur, district of SE USSR, bounded by the Amur River to the S and the Stavanoi Range to the N. The main town is Blagoveshchensk (pop. 155,000). Industries: agriculture, coal, timber, gold-mining. Pop. (1974 est.) 849,000.

Amygdala, almond-shaped mass of nerve cells in the roof of the lateral ventricles of the BRAIN. It is concerned with emotion. *See also* MS p.41.

Amyl alcohol ($C_5H_{11}OH$), ALCOHOL which has eight isomers. Commercial amyl alcohol, a mixture of these, has a sharp odour and is used as a solvent.

Amylase, digestive enzyme secreted by the SALIVARY GLANDS (salivary amylase, or ptyalin) and the PANCREAS (pancreatic amylase, or amylopsin). It aids digestion by breaking down starch into MALTOSE and GLUCOSE. *See also* MS pp.68–69.

Amylopectin, carbohydrate organic chemical compound that makes up 80% to 90% of STARCH (the remainder being amylose).

Amyot, Jacques (1513–93), French scholar whose famous translation of PLUTARCH's *Lives* (1559) influenced the development of French classical tragedy and formed the basis of Sir Thomas North's translation into English (1557), from which Shakespeare took his Roman plots. Amyot became the tutor to the sons of Henry II of France (1552) and Bishop of Auxerre (1570).

Anabaptists, Protestant sect founded *c.*1525 by followers of ZWINGLI. Believing that infants, unaware of good and evil, were not punishable for sin, they insisted on adult baptism as an act of free choice.

Anabasis, seven-book prose narrative account by XENOPHON of the Greek mercenary soldiers who fought (401–399 BC) for Cyrus when he tried to seize the Persian throne. *See also* HC1 p.75.

Anabolism. *See* CATABOLISM.

Anacletus, Saint (died *c.*AD 88), also known as Cletus, Roman martyr and pope (*c.*76–88) who is named in the Canon of the Mass. His feast day is 26 April.

Anaconda, huge constricting SNAKE of South America, the heaviest snake in the world. Species *Eunectes murinus.* Length: up to 9m (30ft). *See also* NW p.*137*, 217.

Anacreon of Teos (*b. c.*570 BC), Greek Lyric poet, whose surviving works deal with love and the pleasures of life. He was admired by Byron and Goethe, for whom he was the "happy poet" of *Anakreonis Grab,* made into a song by Hugo WOLF.

Anaemia, condition in which there is a decrease in the amount of the pigment HAEMOGLOBIN in the red blood cells or a decline in the number of red blood cells produced. It may be caused by excessive blood loss, by a decrease in the production of haemoglobin or red blood cells, or by excessive destruction of red blood cells. Symptoms include fatigue, weakness, pallor and, in severe cases, faintness and palpitations. There are several types of anaemia. The most common is iron-deficiency anaemia. It is usually caused by poor nutrition, excessive menstrual bleeding, chronic blood loss from a minor disorder such as haemorrhoids (piles) or from more serious conditions such as CANCER or ulcers. Pernicious anaemia is an impairment of the body's ability to absorb vitamin B_{12}, a VITAMIN necessary for the normal development of red blood cells. Deficiencies in other substances, such as folic acid or other B vitamins, may also reduce blood cell production. In haemolytic anaemia there is excessive destruction of these cells. It may be due to hereditary abnormalities (such as SICKLE-CELL ANAEMIA), adverse reaction to drugs, or the production of antibodies to one's own red blood cells. Red blood cells are produced in the bone marrow and damage to it because of radiation, drugs or chemicals, cancer, etc, may also cause anaemia. *See also* MS pp.85, 91.

Anaerobe, minute organism that grows only in the absence of free atmospheric oxygen. Anaerobic BACTERIA can be a hazard in food canning because they can multiply in foods even under vacuum. *See also* AEROBE.

Anaesthetic, any drug used to numb feeling. Procaine is ordinarily used as a local anaesthetic. The most common drugs for a general anaesthesia are trichloroethylene, cyclopropane and halothane.

Anagram, word or group of words whose letters have been transposed to produce other words, such as "time", "item" and "mite" from the word "emit". A sophisticated anagram would be a transposition of letters producing a word or phrase that bears some logical relation to the original, such as "esoteric coteries".

Analgesic, DRUG that relieves or prevents pain without causing loss of consciousness. It does not cure the cause of the pain, but helps to deaden the sensation. Common analgesics include aspirin, codeine and morphine. *See also* MS pp.79, *119.*

Analog computer, type of computer that processes continuously variable information, unlike a digital computer which uses the BINARY SYSTEM. Information is converted into proportional electrical quantities which are manipulated by AMPLIFIERS and other circuits that perform the mathematical functions. *See also* COMPUTER; MM p.106.

Anan, city in E Shikoku, Japan, on the Kii Channel, 22km (14 miles) SE of Tokushima. Created in 1958 by merging the towns of Tomioka and Tachibana, it is a trade centre for the surrounding agricultural region. Industries include shipbuilding and chemicals. Pop. (1970) 58,467.

Ananda (*fl. c.*500 BC), cousin and favourite disciple of the BUDDHA, but the only close associate not to have attained enlightenment by the time of the Buddha's death. *See also* HC1 p.*123.*

Anarchy, the absence of standard forms of government. The philosophy of anarchism maintains that people will be better off if governments are abolished. The natural goodness of men will then prevail, and they can use voluntary associations to deal with any problems that may arise. Some anarchists advocate violence to overthrow and eliminate the state. *See also* MS pp.262–263; 282–283.

Anastasia (1901–*c.*1918), Grand Duchess of Russia, youngest daughter of the last tsar, Nicholas II. She was presumably murdered together with other members of the royal family in July 1918, after the Revolution. Since 1920, several women have claimed to be Anastasia, the legal heir to the ROMANOV fortune held in Swiss banks. None of the claimants has been able to prove her identity.

Anastasius, name of four POPES of the Roman Catholic Church. Anastasius I, St (*r.*399–401) attacked and condemned errors in the works of ORIGEN. Anastasius II (*r.*496–498) ruled on heresies and dealt with the prevalent belief that children could inherit souls from their parents. Anastasius III (*r.*911–913) helped to heal rifts among the German churches. Anastasius IV (*r.*1153–54) helped to reconcile the Holy Roman Emperor, FREDERICK I (Barbarossa), to the Church.

Anatomy, branch of biological science that studies the structure of an organism. The study of anatomy can be divided in several ways. On the basis of size, there is gross anatomy, studying structures with the naked eye; microscopic anatomy, studying finer detail with a light microscope; submicroscopic anatomy, studying even finer structural detail with an electron microscope; and molecular anatomy, studying with sophisticated instruments the molecular make-up of an organism. Microscopic and submicroscopic anatomy involve two closely related sciences: HISTOLOGY, the study of tissue that makes up a body organ, and CYTOLOGY, the study of cells that make up tissue. Anatomy can also be classified according to the type of organism studied, eg, plant, invertebrate, vertebrate and human anatomy. Developmental anatomy, or embryology, is the study of the origin, development and relationship of various body parts. *See also* PHYSIOLOGY; MS pp.36–69; NW pp.44–45, 74–75.

Anatomy of Melancholy, The (1621), treatise by Robert BURTON on the causes, symptoms and nature of melancholy, but ranging so widely as to be a record of human life and society.

Anaxagoras of Clazomenae (*c.*500–428 BC), Greek philosopher, the most important before SOCRATES. He was the teacher of EURIPIDES, PERICLES and, possibly, Socrates. He believed that all matter was composed of "seeds" or minute particles.

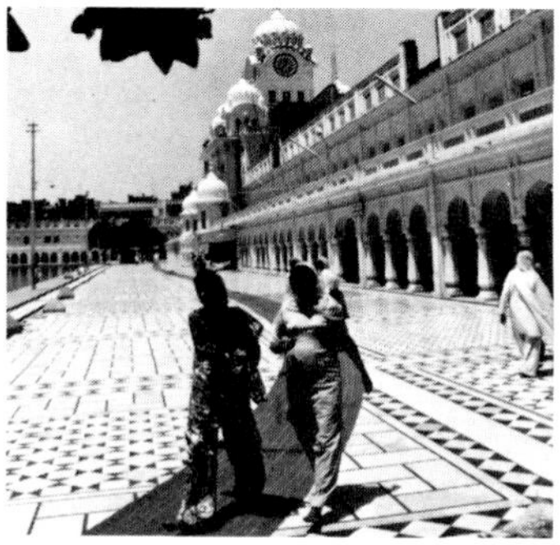

Amritsar; The Golden Temple, Sikh holy place of the large city in Punjab.

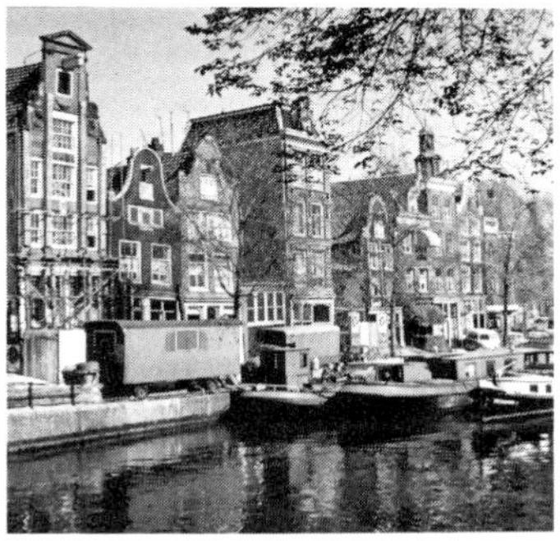

Amsterdam, a city famous for its enchanting network of canals, lies well below sea-level.

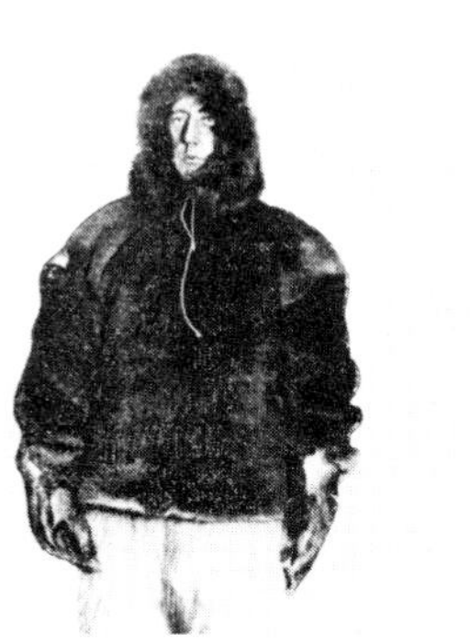

Roald Amundsen, the Norwegian explorer, was the first man to reach the South Pole.

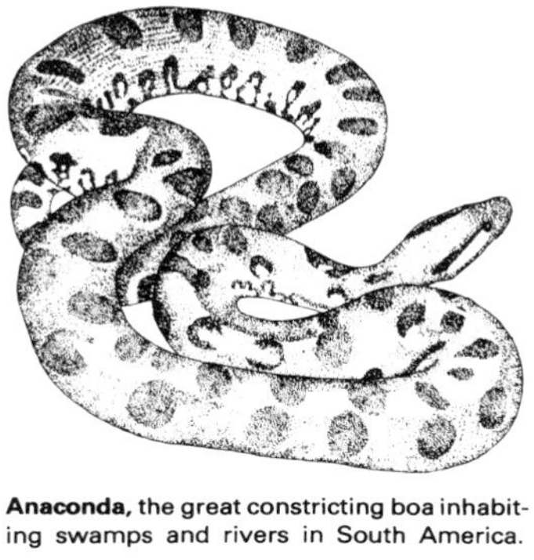

Anaconda, the great constricting boa inhabiting swamps and rivers in South America.

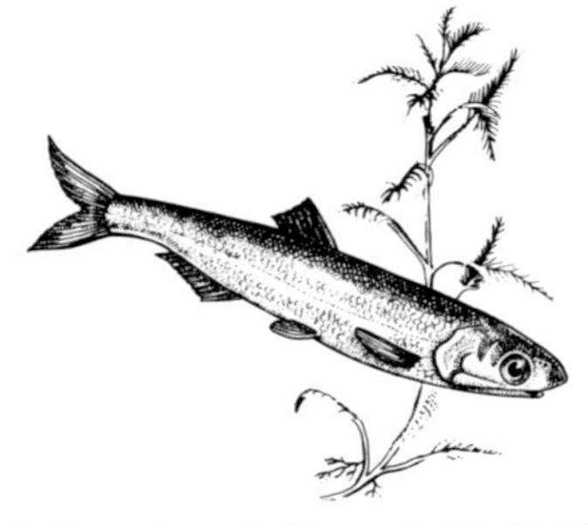

Anchovy, the valuable small fish found worldwide, is a member of the herring family.

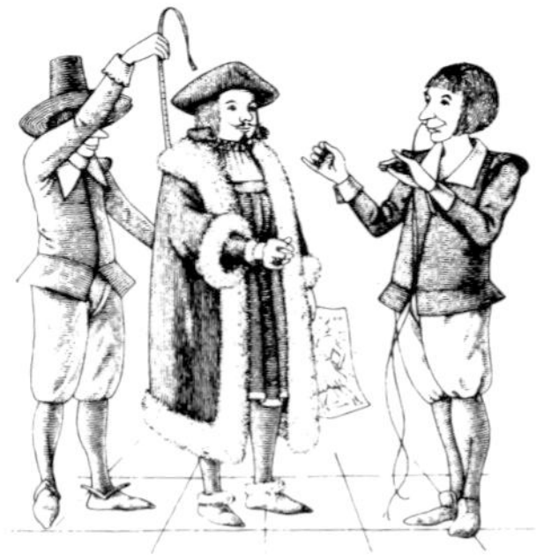

Hans Christian Andersen, creator of the famous tale *The Emperor's New Clothes.*

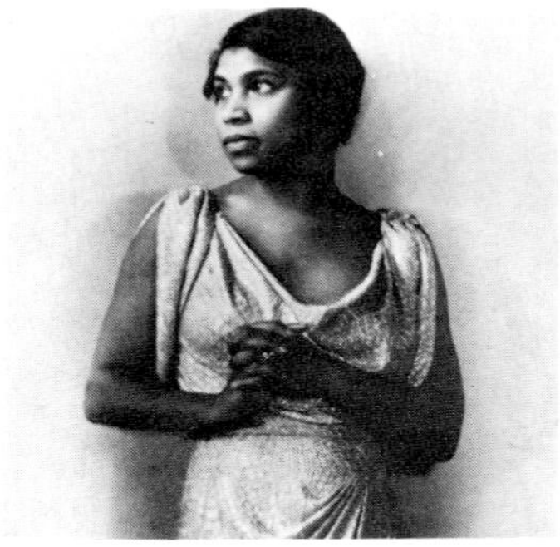

Marian Anderson became the first black singer to appear at the Metropolitan Opera.

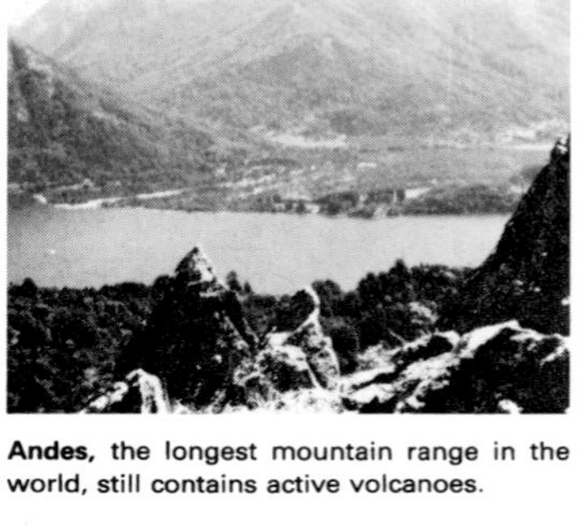

Andes, the longest mountain range in the world, still contains active volcanoes.

He explained the true nature of eclipses. Towards the end of his life he was exiled from Athens for his "impious" teaching that the sun was a white-hot stone and that the moon was composed of earth and merely reflected the sun's rays.

Anaximander (*c.*611–*c.*547 BC), Greek scientist and philosopher credited as the author of the first geometric model of the universe. His fame rests chiefly on his doctrine of a single world-principle, the starting point and origin of the cosmic process, which he identified as *apeiron* or "the infinite". *See also* HC1 p.82.

Anaximenes (*fl.*545 BC), member of the Milesian Greek philosophy, along with Anaximander and Thales. Attempting to resolve the problem of the origin and structure of the universe, he held the fundamental and most pervasive thing in the world to be air, which, being infinite, allows for the manifold processes of nature. *See also* HC1 p.82.

Ancestor worship, varieties of religious belief and practice found in societies where kinship is strong. Ancestral spirits, believed capable of good or harm, are propitiated by prayers and sacrifices. Now declining in India and the Far East, it is practised chiefly in sub-Saharan Africa and Melanesia. *See also* MS pp.222–223.

Anchieta, José de (1534–97), Portuguese missionary and educator, *b.* Canary Islands. In 1553 he was sent by the Jesuits to Brazil, where he founded the city of Sao Paulo in 1554 and wrote the first grammar of the Tupi Indian Language. He wrote the mystic poem *De Beata Virgine Dei Matre Maria* (1563), which established him as the first major writer of Brazil.

Anchorage, city in S central Alaska, 757km (470 miles) S of Fairbanks. Founded in 1914, the city grew as a railway town, becoming a supply centre for the gold and coal mining regions to the N. Its industries today include oil and natural gas and these are expected to expand further with the construction of new oil pipelines. Pop. (1970) 48,000.

Anchoveta, tropical species of ANCHOVY, used to catch tuna. Species *Cetengraulis mysticetus. See also* PE pp.240, *241.*

Anchovy, commercially valuable food marine fish found worldwide in shoals in temperate and tropical seas. There are more than 100 species, including the European anchovy *Engraulis encrasicholus.* Length: 10-25cm (4–10in). Family Engraulidae. *See also* NW p.*240*; PE p.*247.*

Ancien Régime, term used to cover the rigid political, legal and social system in France roughly from the late 16th century to the revolution of 1789. *See also* HC1 pp.300–301, 314–315, 324–325.

Ancient lights, legal right of a building's owner to prevent the obstruction of light to a window that has been unobstructed for 20 or more years.

Ancient Society (1877), book by the US anthropologist Lewis MORGAN which describes the evolution of human society. *See also* MS pp.250, *253.*

Ancona, port in E central Italy, on the Adriatic Sea; capital of Ancona province and of Marches region. Founded by Syracusan colonists *c.*39 BC, it was a flourishing port under the Romans by the 2nd century BC. In the 9th century it became a semi-independent maritime republic, nominally ruled by the popes. It came under direct papal rule in 1532. Allied bombing inflicted heavy damage during WWII. Industries include oil refining, shipbuilding, fishing and chemicals. Pop. 108,000.

Andalusia (Andalucía), southern region of Spain, crossed by the Guadalquivir river. In the N are the mountains of the Sierra Morena, which are rich in minerals, including copper, iron and zinc. Farms in the low-lying SW raise horses and cattle (including fighting bulls) and grow most of the country's cereals; other important crops are citrus fruits, olives, sugar and grapes. Sherry is made from grapes grown in the neighbourhood of Jerez de la Frontera, near Cádiz.

Andalusite, crystalline form (one of many) of aluminium silicate, occurring in contact metamorphic rock and in other deposits. It is mined commercially in the USA, USSR and South Africa to make temperature-resistant and insulating porcelains. *See also* PE pp.*96*, 97, 103.

Andaman and Nicobar Islands, territory of India comprising two chains of islands in the Bay of Bengal. *See also* MW p.27.

Andean Indians. *See* AMERICAN INDIANS.

Anders, Wladyslaw (1892–1970), Polish nationalist and army commander. In WWI he led Polish troops in the tsarist army and in WWII he fought against both Soviet and German troops. Exiled in 1946, he became a leader of the Polish forces-in-exile in Britain.

Andersen, Hans Christian (1805–1875), Danish writer of some of the world's best-loved fairy tales. He had already gained a reputation as a poet and novelist before his genius found its true expression in his humorous, delicate and fanciful stories, first published in 1835. They include *The Ugly Duckling, The Little Mermaid, The Little Match Girl* and *The Emperor's New Clothes.*

Anderson, Carl David (1905–), US physicist who shared the 1936 Nobel Prize in physics with Vidor HESS. In 1932 he discovered the first known particle of anti-matter, the POSITRON or anti-electron, while studying cosmic rays.

Anderson, Elizabeth Garrett (1836–1917), British physician and pioneer of women's rights. She had to overcome intense prejudice against women doctors to secure the right to practise. Later she became England's first woman mayor.

Anderson, Judith (1898–), Australian-born actress who, by 1924, was famous for her portrayals of classical and modern characters. Her stage roles included Lady Macbeth (her London debut, 1937) with Laurence Olivier and *Medea* (1947). She appeared in the films *Rebecca* (1939) and *Cat on a Hot Tin Roof* (1958). She was made a Dame of the British Empire in 1960.

Anderson, Keith (1898–1929), Australian airman who died while trying to rescue the aviation pioneer Sir Charles Kingsford Smith. Kingsford Smith's plane, the *Southern Cross,* had been forced down while he was trying to establish a Sydney-London record. Anderson and his mechanic joined in a search for him but crashed in the Australian desert and died of thirst.

Anderson, Lindsay (1923–), British film and theatrical director. He has worked with great distinction in both fields and has been closely associated with the plays of David STOREY. *If...* (1968) and *O Lucky Man!* (1973), his best-known films, present critical views of society in a vividly memorable form that confirms his status as a provocative and influential artist.

Anderson, Marian (1902–), US contralto. She secured her reputation as a singer by touring America and Europe in recitals (1925–35). She made her METROPOLITAN OPERA debut in 1955 as Ulrica in VERDI's *Un Ballo in Maschera;* this was the first appearance of a black singer in a leading role at the Metropolitan.

Anderson, Maxwell (1888–1959), US dramatist. He wrote a number of plays in verse, the most successful of which were *Winterset* (1935) and *High Tor* (1936), a romantic comedy. He also wrote many historical dramas including *Elizabeth the Queen* (1930) and *Valley Forge* (1934). He wrote the libretti for the Kurt WEILL musicals *Knickerbocker Holiday* (1938) and *Lost in the Stars* (1949).

Anderson, Robert Woodruff (1917–), US playwright, author of *Tea and Sympathy* (staged 1953; filmed 1956), dealing with the problems of homosexuality and its effects on a New England schoolboy. His other plays include *All Summer Long* (1955) and *Silent Night, Lonely Night* (1959).

Anderson, Sherwood (1876–1941), US short story writer and novelist. He wrote about life in the Midwest, and achieved fame with the publication of *Winesburg, Ohio* (1919). His other works include *Dark Laughter* (1925) and *Beyond Desire* (1932).

Andes, chain of mountains in South America, the longest in the world. They stretch for 8,900km (5,500 miles) along the whole W coast. At their widest, in the central area, they are about 800km (500 miles) across. There are more than 50 peaks over 6,700m (21,980ft) high, and they are the second-highest range (after the HIMALAYAS) in the world. They contain many active volcanoes, including Cotopaxi in Ecuador. Earthquakes are common, and cities such as LIMA and Callao (Peru) and VALPARAÍSO (Chile) have been severely damaged. The highest peak is Aconcagua, rising 6,959m (22,831ft) in Argentina, near the border with Chile. Lake TITICACA, the highest lake in the world, lies in the Andes at 3,810m (12,500ft) above sea-level on the Peru-Bolivia border. *See also* MW pp.28, 52, 66, 142.

Andesite, volcanic rock mineral, second in abundance only to BASALT, found in mountain folds, sills, dykes and lava streams. It is composed largely of finely crystalline FELSPARS, with occasional larger crystals called phenocrysts. *See also* PE p.101.

Andhra Pradesh, state in SE India on the Bay of Bengal, created in 1956. Although mountainous to the NE, most of the region is flat coastal plain. Its products include rice and groundnuts, and coal, chrome and manganese are mined. The capital is Hyderābād. Area: 276,814sq km (106,878sq miles). Pop. (1971) 43,502,708.

Andorra, small independent state situated high in the E Pyrenees between France and Spain. Area: 453sq km (175sq miles). Pop. (1975 est.) 27,000. *See* MW p.27.

Andrade, Edward Neville da Costa (1887–1971), British physicist who did research in atomic structure and BROWNIAN MOVEMENT and discovered a formula relating the viscosity of liquids to their temperature.

Andrássy, Count Julius (1823–90), Hungarian statesman. An ardent nationalist, he joined the abortive rebellion of 1848 against Austria and escaped execution by remaining in exile until 1857. He became the first Prime Minister of Hungary (1867–71). He was Minister of Foreign Affairs for the empire (1871–79), which he represented at the CONGRESS OF BERLIN in 1878.

André, John (1751–80), British military officer executed by the Americans for working with Benedict ARNOLD. He was caught by American soldiers as he returned from negotiations with Arnold for the betrayal of West Point.

Andrea del Castagno. *See* CASTAGNO, ANDREA DEL.

Andrea del Sarto (1486–1531), Florentine artist whose extraordinary skill as a fresco painter places him among the outstanding representatives of the High RENAISSANCE in Florence. Andrea was the first Florentine to reject the coloured drawing in favour of composition by areas of coloured light and shade. His frescoes *Birth of the Virgin* (1514) and *Madonna del Sacco* (1524) epitomize the High Renaissance style.

Andrée, Salomon August (1854–97), Swedish aeronautical engineer and arctic explorer. He was killed in an attempt to fly from Spitsbergen, Norway, to the North Pole in a balloon. His body was found 33 years later on White Island near Greenland.

Andreev, Leonid (1871–1919), Russian novelist and dramatist. He lost popularity after declaring his anti-Bolshevism, and emigrated to Finland in 1917. His work varies from the realistic to the metaphysical and includes the plays *The Red Laugh* (1904) and *The Pretty Sabine Women* (1912), and the story *The Governor* (1906).

Andreotti, Giulio (1919–), Italian journalist and politician. A leader of the Christian Democratic party, he first attained ministerial rank in 1954. He served as Prime Minister (1972–73) and formed a minority government following the elections of July 1976.

Andrew, Saint, in the New Testament, brother of Simon Peter and one of the original 12 disciples of Jesus. According to tradition he was crucified on an X-shaped cross. He is patron saint of Scotland and Russia; his feast is observed on 30 November.

Andrew, Prince (1960–), second son of Queen ELIZABETH II and Prince Philip, Duke of Edinburgh; second in succession to the British throne. *See also* ROYAL FAMILY.

Andrewes, Lancelot (1555–1626), English divine, scholar and (from 1619) Bishop of Winchester; one of the translators of the Authorized Version of the Bible. He is also remembered for his *Private Devotions*, written in Greek and Latin and published in English in 1647.

Andrews, Julie (1935–), British singer and actress, best known for her performances in the musical films *Mary Poppins* (1963), for which she was awarded an OSCAR as the best US film actress, and *The Sound of Music* (1964). She became an international star in the stage musical *The Boy Friend* (New York, 1954) and *My Fair Lady* (New York, 1956; London, 1958).

Andrews, Thomas (1813–1885), Irish physicist and chemist who established the concepts of critical temperature and pressure. He also proved that OZONE is a form of oxygen. *See also* SU p.*85*.

Andric, Ivo (1892–1975), Yugoslav writer of Serbo-Croatian novels and short stories. He was awarded the Nobel Prize for literature in 1961. He was recognized, as a writer of verse and prose, in 1918 with the publication of *Ex Ponto*, written while he was a prisoner in WWI.

Andriessen, Jurriaan (1925–), Dutch composer, conductor and pianist whose works include the *Sinfonietta concertante* and the chamber work *Homage to Milhaud*. His father, Hendrik (1892–), was the director of Utrecht Conservatory and composer of much Roman Catholic church music.

Androcles, Roman slave who ran away from his master and hid in a cave. He removed a thorn from the paw of a suffering lion. Later Androcles faced the same lion in the Roman Arena; the lion recognized him and refused to harm him. He has been immortalized in George Bernard SHAW's play *Androcles and the Lion*.

Androgen, general name for male sex HORMONES, such as TESTOSTERONE. *See also* ANDROSTERONE; MS pp.64–65.

Andromache, in Greek mythology, the daughter of Eëtion and wife of Hector. Her relatives died when TROY was taken by ACHILLES. She became the captive of Achilles' son, Neoptolemus, and bore him three sons.

Andromeda, northern constellation situated between Cassiopeia and Pegasus. It contains ALPHERATZ, or Alpha Andromedae, which is in the Square of Pegasus, and the spiral galaxy M31. It was named after the Ethiopian princess of Greek mythology who was rescued from a sea-monster by PERSEUS. *See also* SU p.258.

Andromeda Galaxy, or M31, spiral galaxy in the constellation of ANDROMEDA. It is the largest member of the local group of galaxies and, at a distance of about 2 million light-years, is the closest spiral galaxy to Earth; it is just visible to the naked eye. *See also* SU pp.246, 258.

Androsterone, STEROID hormone that produces masculine characteristics. It is obtained from the testes and from male urine, and controls the growth and function of male sexual organs and the production of secondary male sexual characteristics, such as hair growth. *See also* MS p.64.

Andrzejewski, Jerzy (1909–), Polish author. His first novel was *Ład serca* (1938); this was followed by *Ashes and Diamonds* (1948), which describes the conflicts of post-war Poland. His later works include *The Inquisitors* (1957) and a play, *Prometheus* (1972).

Anemometer, instrument using rotating cups, vanes and propellers to measure the speed or force of the wind; weather vanes indicate the direction. *See also* PE p.72.

Anemone, perennial plant found worldwide; it is also called pasqueflower and windflower. Anemones have sepals resembling petals and numerous stamens and pistils covering a central knob; two or three deeply-toothed leaves appear in a whorl midway up the stem. Many are wild flowers, including the wood anemone (*Anemone nemorosa*), with white flowers, common in Britain; and the pasqueflower (*A. patens*), with large white or blue flowers appearing before the foliage. There are 150 species. Family Ranunculaceae. *See also* BUTTERCUP; SEA ANEMONE; NW p.*209*.

Aneroid barometer. *See* BAROMETER.

Aneurin, or Aneirin (*fl.c.* AD 600), Welsh bardic poet, whose work survives in a 13th-century manuscript. His poem *Gododin* is an account of the Saxon victory at Cattraeth over the Strathclyde Britons.

Aneurysm, bulging of an artery caused by blood pressure distorting a weakened arterial wall. It can occur almost anywhere in the body, and was once a common complication of SYPHILIS and pulmonary TUBERCULOSIS. *See also* MS pp.90, 96.

Anfinsen, Christian Boehmer (1916–), American biochemist who in 1972 shared the Nobel Prize in chemistry with Stanford MOORE and William STEIN. He carried out research into the relationships between the biological function and molecular structure of PROTEINS.

Angel, spiritual being superior to man but inferior to God. In the Bible, angels appear on earth as messengers and servants of God. They are generally depicted with wings.

Angeles, Victoria de los (1923–), Spanish soprano. She gave her first public concert in 1944 in Barcelona, made her debut at the Paris Opera and LA SCALA, Milan, in 1949, and her American debut at CARNEGIE HALL in 1950. In that year she joined the METROPOLITAN OPERA COMPANY.

Angelfish, tropical fish found in the Atlantic and Indo-Pacific, popular as an aquarium fish because of its graceful, trailing fins and beautiful markings. Length: 2–10cm (0.75–4in). Family Cichlidae.

Angelica, plant of the carrot family that grows in northern temperate regions and in New Zealand. Garden angelicas (*Angelica archangelica*) grow to 1.5m (5ft) and have greenish flowers. The stems, usually crystallized, and oil from the roots and seeds, have culinary uses.

Angelico, Fra (*c.*1387–1455), Italian painter from Tuscany, noted for the spirituality of his painting. A Dominican friar, whose real name was Guido di Pietro, Fra Angelico is celebrated for his series of some 50 frescoes in the convent of S Marco, Florence, which was taken over by his Order in 1436. His paintings, all of religious subjects, show a harmonious sense of composition and a love of line and pure colour. His style was influenced by GENTILE DA FABRIANO and MASACCIO. He painted a chapel in the Vatican (*c.*1446–49) and in 1447 he painted two frescoes in Orvieto Cathedral. *See also* HC1 p.251.

Angell, Sir Norman (*c.*1872–1967), British economist and worker for international co-operation who was awarded the Nobel Peace Prize in 1933. His best known work is *The Great Illusion* (1910), in which he suggested that there would be fewer wars if nations had greater awareness of the economic ravages they caused.

Angelus (*c.*1858), popular painting by Jean François MILLET, depicting a religious aspect of peasant life.

Angelus Silesius, pseudonym of Johann Scheffler (1624–77), German poet and mystic. His *Der Cherubinische Wandersmann* (1674) embodies almost the entire range of mystic thought, expressed in epigrammatic form.

Angevins, line of English kings named after Henry II, Count of Anjou, who ascended the throne in 1154. The Angevins, also known as the PLANTAGENETS, retained the crown until 1377. *See also* HC1 p.168; HC2 p.308.

Angina pectoris, pain in the chest that may be a symptom of various disorders, often of diseased coronary arteries in the heart. It generally follows exertion or stress and may be treated with drugs such as glyceryl trinitrate. *See also* MS p.90.

Angiosperms, plants with true flowers, as distinct from GYMNOSPERMS and other non-flowering plants. They include all trees, bushes and non-woody herbs divided into two main groups: MONOCOTYLEDONS (which have one seed-leaf) and DICOTYLEDONS (which have two seed-leaves). *See also* NW pp.66–67.

Angiotensin, peptide in the blood that increases blood pressure by inducing contraction of narrow blood vessels. *See also* RENIN.

Angkor, site of several ruined capitals of the KHMER Empire; near the present city of Siem Reap. The ruins date mainly from the 10th–12th centuries and consist of temples to Hindu deities, Buddhist shrines and royal palaces. Many are grouped within the walled enclosure of Angkor Thom, the capital built 1181–95 by Jayavarman VII (*c.*1120–1215). The nearby temple complex of Angkor Wat, created by Suryavarman II (*r.*1113-50) as his sepulchre and shrine, is probably the world's most imposing religious structure. Angkor was abandoned for Phnom Penh in 1434. Its ruins were discovered in 1858 by the French. *See also* HC1 p.227; MW p.45.

Angler fish, marine fish found at the bottom of temperate and tropical seas. Its dorsal fin is modified to resemble a movable rod with lure, to attract prey. Species include goosefish, batfish and frogfish. Order Lophiiformes. *See also* NW pp.*129, 241*.

Angles, Germanic tribe from a district of Schleswig-Holstein now called Angeln. In the 5th century AD they invaded England with their neighbouring tribes, the JUTES and SAXONS. They settled in Northumbria, East and Middle Anglia. The Roman author TACITUS (AD *c.*55–120) described them as worshippers of the Scandinavian deity Nerthus. The name England derives from their name (Angle-Land). *See also* HC1 p.138.

Anglesey, Henry William Paget, Marquis of (1768–1854), British military commander who fought at the Battle of WATERLOO (where he lost a leg). He became Lord Lieutenant of Ireland (1828–29; 1830–33), where he favoured emancipation for Catholics.

Anglesey (Ynys Môn), island off the NW coast of Wales, separated from the mainland by the Menai Strait. Formerly a Welsh county, it became part of GWYNEDD in 1974. The chief town is Beaumaris. Most occupations are agricultural, particularly stock raising. Area: 718sq km (276sq miles). Pop. (1977) 63,200.

Anglican Communion, worldwide fellowship of independent national or regional churches which trace their origin to the CHURCH OF ENGLAND and are in communion with the See of CANTERBURY. The Anglican Communion does not proclaim any distinctive doctrines of its own; instead it claims to hold fast to the faith and order of the primitive, undivided Church of the first centuries. Consequently its theology contains both Catholic and Protestant elements and it permits a large measure of freedom to its members. Its liturgical worship is based on the Book of COMMON PRAYER as adapted by each national church to suit its local needs. Its structure is episcopal. The Archbishop of Canterbury is accorded a primacy of honour. Since 1867 all Anglican bishops of the world have been invited to the LAMBETH CONFERENCE, normally held every ten years. The total number of Anglicans in the world in the mid-1970s was about 45 million.

Angling. *See* FISHING.

Anglo-Boer War. *See* SOUTH AFRICAN WARS.

Anglo-Egyptian Sudan, name given to the Sudan under British and Egyptian rule set up in 1899, following their joint conquest of it in 1897–98. The Sudan gained independence in 1956. *See also* MW p.161.

Anglo-Saxon Chronicle, collection of four monastic chronicles written in England between the 890s and 1155. The original Chronicle, possibly commissioned by ALFRED the Great, attempted a history of England from the 5th century Anglo-Saxon invasions; the later chronicles updated the historical content to their own times. *See also* HC1 p.*155*.

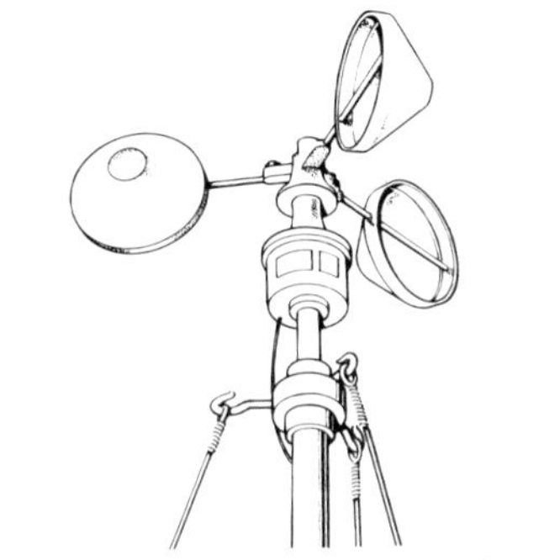

Anemometers measure wind speed by the number of revolutions the cups make.

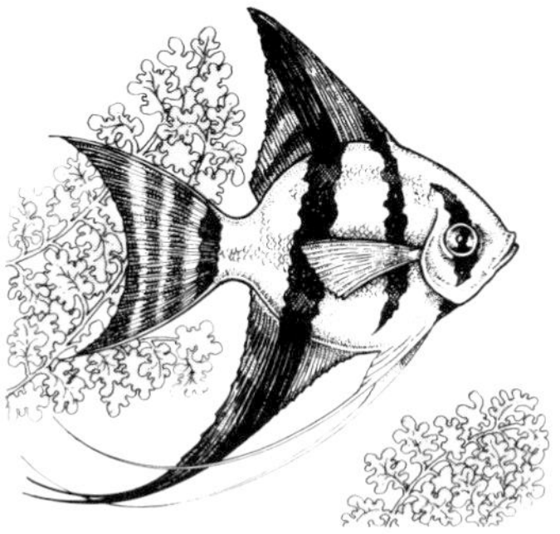

Angelfish, the colourful tropical fish popular in domestic warm-water aquaria.

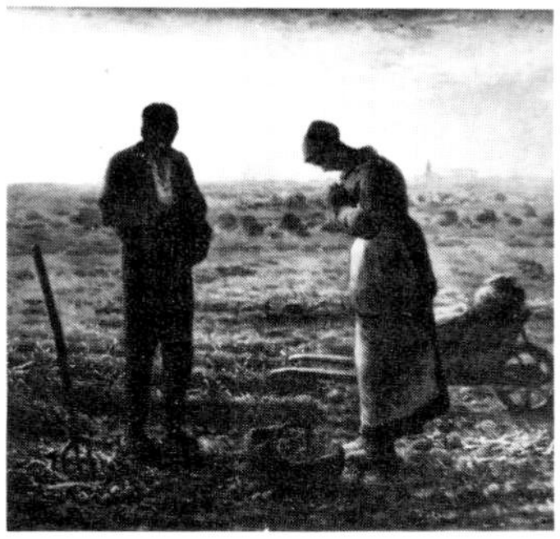

The Angelus by Millet was a firm Victorian favourite due to its religious sentimentality.

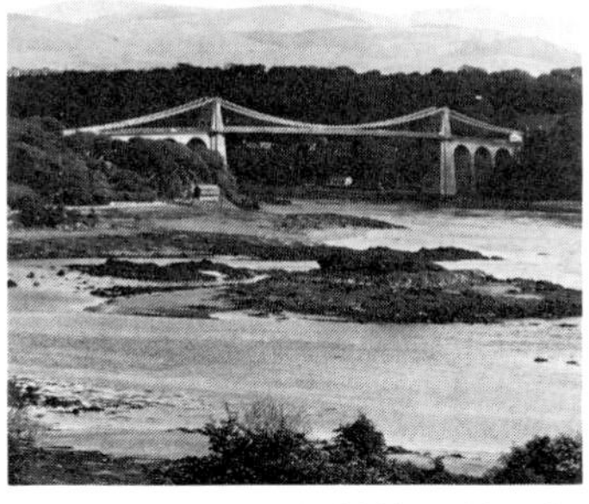

Anglesey is joined to the Welsh mainland by Telford's well-known suspension bridge.

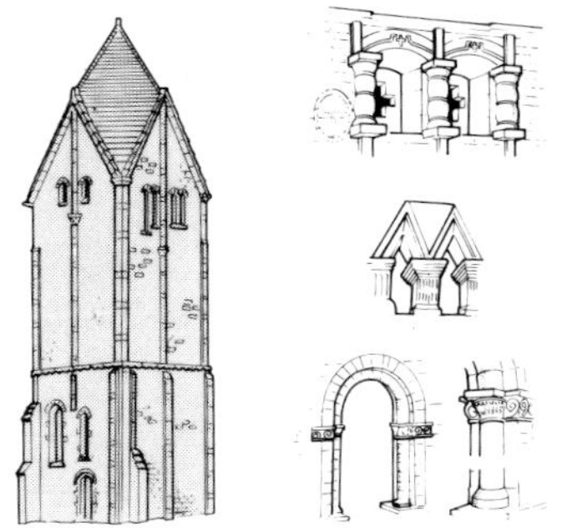

Anglo-Saxons built in a style distinguished mainly by semicircular or triangular arches.

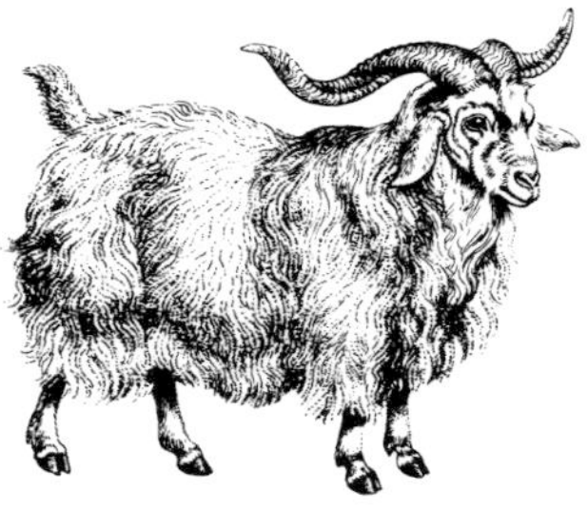

Angora goats, native to Turkey, have dense fur from which mohair is made.

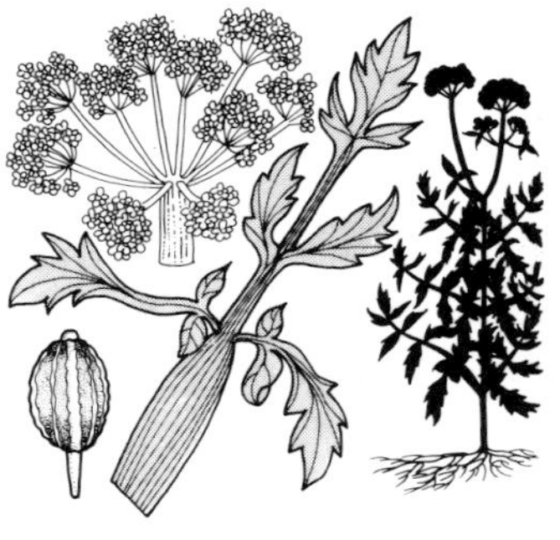

Anise is a Mediterranean herb; its seeds are used as a flavouring and to make absinth.

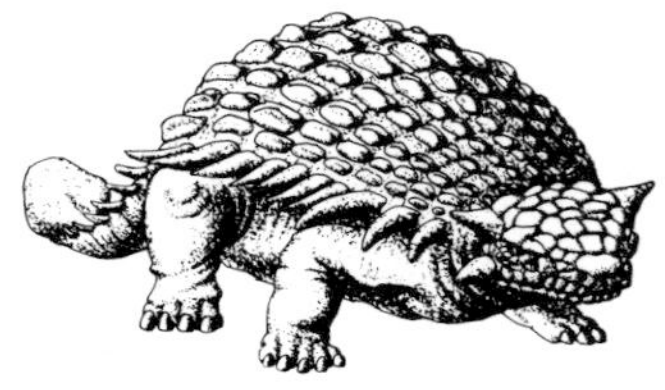

Ankylosaurus, a dinosaur of North America, was short and squat and heavily armoured.

Anglo-Saxons, peoples of Germanic origin comprising ANGLES, SAXONS and other tribes who settled in England from the mid-5th century. The term itself was first used in the late 8th century to distinguish the Saxon settlers in England from the "Old Saxons" of northern Germany. The term became synonymous with "English". *See also* HC1 pp.138, 154, 164–167.

Angola, independent nation of sw Africa, known as Portuguese West Africa until it gained its independence in 1975, after which it was torn by wars. It is a Bantu nation. The principal products are petroleum, coffee and diamonds. The capital is LUANDA. Area: 1,246,700sq km (481,250sq miles). Pop. (1975 est.) 6,761,000. *See* MW p.27.

Angora. *See* ANKARA.

Angora, domestic rabbit bred in France in the early 18th century. It produces white, black, blue and fawn wool and is also excellent as meat. Weight: (English angora) 3kg (6.6lb); (French angora) 3.5kg (8lb).

Angora cat, long-haired domestic cat with a round head, short body and tail and short, strong legs. It is also commonly called a Persian. Its large, wide-set eyes can be blue, yellow or green, depending on the colour of the fine silky coat. Smoky and black varieties, for instance, have yellow eyes. A blue-eyed white Angora is usually deaf.

Angora goat, domestic GOAT native to the Turkish province of Ankara (formerly Angora), now found also in South Africa and USA. Its body is covered with long, silky hair (MOHAIR), important in the clothing and upholstery industries.

Angostura. *See* CIUDAD BOLÍVAR.

Angostura bark, bark of a South American tree *Cusparia trifoliata*, known also as cusparia bark. It has been used in the past to treat fevers, but is now used as aromatic bitters often added to drinks.

Angry young men, term applied to a group of British writers in the 1950s, taken from Leslie Allen Paul's autobiography *Angry Young Man* (1951) and popularized through John OSBORNE's play *Look Back in Anger* (1956). All the writers and their heroes shared a working- or lower-middle-class background and a rebellious attitude towards what they saw as the hypocrisy and conventions of British society. Other writers associated with the group include Kingsley AMIS, John BRAINE, Alan SILLITOE and John WAIN.

Ångström, Anders Jonias (1814–74), Swedish astronomer and physicist, one of the founders of the science of spectroscopy. In 1861 he began to use the spectroscope and photographic plates to study the Solar System. His experiments proved that the sun contains hydrogen, and in 1868 he was able to map the entire solar spectrum. A unit for the wavelength of light is named after him – the angstrom unit, Å, equal to 10^{-8} cm. *See also* SU pp.60, 84.

Anguilla, island in the West Indies, one of the Leeward Islands. In 1967 it became part of the St Kitts-Nevis-Anguilla group, but left shortly afterwards and re-adopted British colonial status in 1971. Area: 91sq km (35sq miles). Pop. (1971 est.) 6,000 *See also* MW p.28.

Angular acceleration, rate of change of angular velocity. The average angular acceleration of an object whose angular velocity changes from ω_1 to ω_2 over a time t is $(\omega_2-\omega_1)/t$. Instantaneous angular acceleration is the value approached by ω as t becomes small. The direction of the angular acceleration VECTOR is perpendicular to the plane of motion. The tangential acceleration a_T of a particle at a distance r from a fixed point is directly proportional to the fixed magnitude of its angular acceleration α: $a_T=r_\alpha$.

Angular distance, in astronomy, apparent distance on the CELESTIAL SPHERE between two celestial bodies measured along an arc of a great circle passing through them with the observer at the centre. For example, the angular distance of the Pointers of Ursa Major (The Plough) is 5°.

Angular momentum, product of the moment of inertia I and the angular velocity ω of an object or the centre of gravity of a system of particles. Usually denoted by L, angular momentum is a VECTOR quantity that is conserved at all times.

Angular velocity, rate of change of an object's angular position relative to a fixed point. Average angular VELOCITY ω of an object moving from angle θ_2 to θ_2 in time t is $(\theta_2-\theta_1)/t$. Instantaneous angular velocity ω is the value approached by ω in succeeding instants (mathematically, as t tends to zero). The direction associated with the angular velocity of an object is perpendicular to the plane of its motion. The speed v of an object at a distance r from a fixed point is directly proportional to the magnitude ω of its angular velocity: $v=r\omega$.

Angus, former county in E Scotland, bounded by the North Sea (E) and the Firth of Tay (S). Originally Forfarshire (until 1928), it became part of the Tayside Region in 1975. Oats, barley and root crops are grown; industries include textiles and food processing. Forfar, once the county town, is the seat of authority in the district of Angus, which includes most of the former county. Area: 2,033sq km (785sq miles). Pop. (1971) 97,000.

Anhui (Anhwei), province in E central China. It is divided by the Wan Mountains into two areas: the N is an extensive plains area where agriculture is limited because of the cold winters; the S has a subtropical climate and rice and tea are grown. The capital is Hofei (Hefei). Industries: iron and steel. Area: 139,898sq km (54,015sq miles). Pop. 35,000,000.

Anhydrite, mineral form of calcium sulphate ($CaSO_4$), usually found in sediment ary rocks in salt beds. Its crystals are orthorhombic, and usually occur in large deposits. It has a glassy or pearly lustre and is colourless when pure. Properties: hardness 3–3.5; s.g. 3. *See also* GYPSUM; PE pp.96, 133.

Aniline, highly poisonous, colourless oily liquid ($C_6H_5NH_2$) made by the reduction of nitrobenzene. It is an important starting material for making organic compounds such as drugs, explosives and particularly dye-stuffs. Properties: s.g.1.02; m.p.−6.3°C (20.66°F); b.p.184.13°C (363.43°F). *See also* AMINE; SU p.142.

Animal, living organism of the animal kingdom, usually distinguishable from members of the plant kingdom by its power of locomotion (at least during some stage of its existence); a well-defined body shape; limited growth; its feeding exclusively on organic matter; the production of two different kinds of sex cells; and the formation of an embryo or larva during the developmental stage. Higher animals, such as the VERTEBRATES, are easily distinguishable from plants, but the distinction becomes blurred with the lower forms. Some one-celled organisms could easily be assigned to either category. Evolutionists believe that the difficulties in such areas point to the fact that animals and plants must have originated from a common ancestor. Scientists have classified about a million different kinds of animals. PROTOZOA, SPONGES, JELLYFISH, segmented WORMS, ARTHROPODS, MOLLUSCS, ECHINODERMS and CHORDATES make up the major phyla out of more than twenty. *See* NW pp.22–23, 72–79.

Animal behaviour. *See* ETHOLOGY.

Animal classification, systematic grouping of animals into categories based on shared characteristics. The first major classification was drawn up by Aristotle. The method now used was devised by Carl LINNAEUS, a Swedish botanist, in the 1750s.

Each animal is given a two-part Latin name, the first part indicating its GENUS, the second its SPECIES. A species is composed of animals capable of interbreeding in nature. A genus includes all sim3lar and related species. The FAMILY takes in all related genera, and an ORDER is made up of all related families. Similar orders are grouped in a CLASS, and related classes make up a PHYLUM. More than twenty separate phyla comprise the animal kingdom. For example, the dog is classified thus: phylum Chordata; class Mammalia; order Carnivora; family Canidae; genus *Canis* and species *familiaris*. *See also* NW pp.23, 72–73, 106–107, 124–125, 140–141, 154–155.

Animal Farm (1945), satirical novel by George ORWELL about the Russian Revolution and Stalinism in the Soviet Union. The animals of Manor Farm drive out their brutal, human master and elect to be governed by the pigs, whose rule grows to be just as authoritarian.

Animal Kingdom, about one million species of animals classified into about 20 major groups, or phyla. All phyla but one are invertebrate (ie lack backbones). The CHORDATE phylum includes some animals that are not true vertebrates, as well as the vertebrate fishes, amphibians, reptiles, birds and mammals. *See also* NW pp.72–73, 254.

Animal worship, various beliefs and practices dating from prehistoric times. In North America, where the bear was the chief cult animal, Indians believed each animal to be inhabited by a spirit. The bear is still sacred to the AINU of Japan. Among Australian ABORIGINES, whose TOTEMISM is highly developed, kinship links clans and animals. Ancient Egyptians believed that certain animals were divine incarnations and in Hindu literature the god VISHNU appears as a fish, wild boar and giant turtle. *See also* MS pp.213, 217.

Animation, cinema, illusion of motion created by projecting successive images of still drawings or inanimate objects. A series of drawings, each showing a stage in the motion being created, is made and photographed singly; a jointed model can be similarly photographed. Projecting the images at normal speed, normally 24 frames per second, creates an illusion of motion. *See also* MM pp.220–223.

Animatism, belief that all objects, beings and natural phenomena (such as stones, trees, water, fire, stars, thunderstorms) and animals possess a life and consciousness but not a spirit (soul). *See also* ANIMISM.

Animism, belief that within every object dwells an individual spirit capable of governing its existence. Natural objects and phenomena are regarded as possessing life, consciousness and a spirit (soul). By extension of this, the spirits of dead animals live on and, if the animals have been killed improperly, their spirits can inflict harm. These beliefs are widespread in primitive religions. *See also* ANIMATISM.

Anion, a negative ION.

Anise, annual herb native to Egypt and widely cultivated for its small, ridged liquorice-flavoured seeds. It has small white flowers. Height: up to 76cm (2.5ft). Family Umbelliferae; species *Pimpinella anisum*. *See also* PE pp.207, 210, *210*.

Anjou, region and former province in W France, bounded by the River Maine (N) Touraine (E), Poitou (S) and Brittany (W). It was ruled by HENRY II of England after his marriage to Eleanor of Aquitaine. Louis XI annexed it to the French crown in 1480. *See also* HC1 p.146.

Ankara, city in W central Turkey, at the confluence of the Cubuk and Ankara rivers; capital of Turkey and Ankara province. In ancient times it was known as Ancrya (and later Angora) and was an important commercial centre as early as the 18th century BC. It was a Roman provincial capital and flourished particularly under AUGUSTUS. The Mongol conqueror TAMERLANE took the city in 1402. In the late 19th century Ankara declined in importance until the Turkish Nationalists set up a provisional government there in 1920. It replaced Istanbul as the national capital in 1923. Industries include textiles (it is particularly noted for its angora wool and mohair products), food processing, cement and farm machinery. Pop. (1974 est.) 1,522,400.

Ankylosaurus, armoured ornithischian DINOSAUR of the upper Cretaceous period (65–136 million years ago) of W USA and Canada. It was a squat herbivore with short, massive legs and hoofed feet, and the leathery skin on its back and sides was armour-plated with bony nodules and plates arranged in geometric rows. Its tail ended in a bony club much like the head of a mace. Length: 4.5m (15ft); height: 1.2m (4ft). *See also* NW p.185.

Ankylosis, condition occurring when a joint of the body becomes or is made fixed, leaving only a limited degree of movement. Causes include inflammation and fusion of bones, often after arthritis. *See also* MS p.*86*.

Annaba, city in NE Algeria, formerly Bône; Mediterranean port and departmental capital. The city was founded by the Phoenicians and flourished as a Roman port (Hippo Regius) until approx. AD 300. It was plundered by the Vandals in 431, but rebuilt by the Arabs in the 7th century. It was a centre of early Christianity. Industries: cork production, metalworking, chemicals, food-canning. Pop. 150,000.

Anna Christie (1921), drama by US playwright Eugene O'NEILL about a prostitute whose father, a hard-drinking captain of a coal barge, sent her away as a child to protect her from the sordid life on the waterfront. The play portrays the reconciliation of Anna and her father; it won the Pulitzer Prize in 1922.

Anna Karenina, realist novel (1873–77) by Count Leo TOLSTOY in which he explores the related themes of marriage, social order and responsibility. The passionate but adulterous, and ultimately ruinous, love affair between Anna Karenina and Count Vronsky is contrasted with the routine and conventional marriage of Levin and Kitty. *See also* HC2 p.99.

Annakin, Ken (1914–), British film director. He made his name with short comedies, then switched to large-scale productions such as *The Swiss Family Robinson* (1960) and *Those Magnificent Men in their Flying Machines* (1965).

Annales Cambriae, ancient Latin annals of Welsh history by an unknown compiler. The earliest existing manuscript is from the late 10th century. They are a source for the Arthurian legend.

Annam, former kingdom on E coast of Indochina, now in Vietnam; the capital was Hué. The ancient empire fell to China in 214 BC. It regained self-government but was again ruled by China from 939 to 1428. The French obtained missionary and trade agreements in 1787, and a protectorate was established (1883–84). During WWII it was occupied by the Japanese; in 1949 it was incorporated into the Republic of Vietnam. *See also* MW p.181.

Annapolis, seaport and capital of Maryland, USA, on the S bank of the Severn River, 35km (22 miles) SSE of Baltimore. It was founded in 1649 by Puritans from Virginia, and was the scene of the signing of the peace treaty with Britain ending the War of Independence. It has many pre-Revolutionary buildings. It also has boatyards and a seafood packing industry. Pop. (1970) 30,000.

Annapurna, mountain massif in the HIMALAYAS, N central Nepal; includes two of the highest peaks in the world. Annapurna 1 in the W rises to 8,078m (26,504ft) and was first scaled in 1950 by the French expedition led by Maurice Herzog; Annapurna 2 in the E rises to 7,937m (26,041ft).

Annates, tax on the income of a benefice for one year, paid to the pope as first fruits. Originally paid only by bishoprics, they were extended to rectories and abbeys. In 1534 in England they were appropriated to the Crown by HENRY VIII as part of the REFORMATION.

Anne (1665–1714), Queen of Great Britain and Ireland (*r.* 1702–14). The second daughter of JAMES II, she was the last reigning Stuart, and after the Act of Union of 1707 the first monarch of the United Kingdom of England and Scotland. She was dependent on her favourites, Sarah Churchill, DUCHESS OF MARLBOROUGH, and Abigail MASHAM, but presided over an age of military success and cultural distinction. Despite 18 pregnancies, no child survived her. *See also* HC1 pp.312–313.

Anne, Princess (1950–), daughter of Queen ELIZABETH II and fourth in line of succession to the British throne. During the 1970s, as a noted horsewoman, she represented Britain at various international events. In 1973 she married Lt. Mark Phillips and in 1977 they had a son.

Annealing, slow heating and cooling of a metal, alloy, or glass to relieve internal stresses and make up dislocations or vacancies that may have been introduced during mechanical shaping such as rolling or extruding. Annealing increases the material's workability and durability. Machine tools, wire and sheet metal are annealed during manufacture. *See also* TEMPERING.

Anne Boleyn. *See* BOLEYN, ANNE.

Annelid, animal phylum of segmented WORMS. All have encircling grooves usually corresponding to internal partitions of the body. A digestive tube, nerves and blood vessels run through the entire body, but each segment has its own set of internal organs. Annelids form an important part of the diets of many animals. The three main classes are Polychaeta, marine worms; Oligochaeta, freshwater or terrestrial worms; and Hirudinea, LEECHES. *See also* NW pp.72, 74, 88–89.

Anne of Austria (1601–66), wife of LOUIS XIII of France, mother of LOUIS XIV. Her husband died in 1643 and she ruled France as regent with Cardinal MAZARIN until Louis XIV was crowned (1661).

Anne of Bohemia (1366–94), queen consort of RICHARD II of England. She was the daughter of Emperor CHARLES IV, and married Richard in 1382. She died of the plague 12 years later.

Anne of Cleves (1515–57), fourth wife of HENRY VIII of England. Her marriage (1540) was a political alliance joining Henry with the German protestants, and was declared null after only six months. Anne received a pension from Henry, and remained in England until her death.

Anne of Denmark (1574–1619), Queen Consort of JAMES I of England. She married James in 1589 but her extravagance and adherence to Roman Catholicism led to their separation from 1606.

Annensky, Innokenty Feodorovich (1856–1909), Russian poet who wrote about beauty and death. His verse has been published in two books: *Quiet Songs* (1904) and *The Cypress Chest* (1910).

Annihilation, in particle physics, the complete conversion of matter into energy. An ELEMENTARY PARTICLE and its antiparticle are converted, on collision, into gamma radiation. An electron and positron annihilate to produce two gamma-ray photons, travelling in opposite directions to conserve momentum. Each has an energy of 0.511 MeV, which is equivalent to the rest mass of the electron or positron. *See also* SU pp.66–67.

Annigoni, Pietro (1910–), Italian painter, especially of society portraits. He has painted portraits of Queen ELIZABETH II, Prince Philip and Princess Margaret.

Anno Domini, Latin for "in the year of our Lord" and abbreviated to AD, the location in time of a year after the supposed year in which Christ was born. Years before 1 AD are denoted BC ("before Christ"). *See also* CALENDAR.

Annual, plant that completes its life cycle in one growing season. Annuals are used in summer flower beds, window boxes, pots or winter greenhouses. Popular garden annuals include zinnias, nasturtiums, sweet peas and petunias. Some plants may be started indoors and others sown outdoors. Some, such as cosmos and marigolds, self-seed and appear as new plants the following year. *See also* BIENNIAL; PERENNIAL.

Annunciation, as recounted in the New Testament (Luke 1:26–38), the announcement made to the Virgin Mary by the Angel Gabriel that she was to be the mother of Christ. In many Christian Churches the Feast of the Annunciation is kept on 25 March, a date often called "Lady Day". The Annunciation was a common subject of painters of medieval and Renaissance times.

Annus Mirabilis (1666), poem by John DRYDEN consisting of 300 quatrains recounting the principal great events of the period Aug. 1665–Sept. 1666: the sea battles leading to the British victory over the Dutch fleet off the Dutch coast, and the FIRE OF LONDON.

Anoa, or dwarf water buffalo, smallest representative of wild CATTLE, native to Celebes and the Philippines. The young are covered with yellow woolly hair; adults are almost hairless with black or brown skin blotched with white. Height: up to 104cm (41in) at the shoulder. Family Bovidae; genus *Anoa*; there are three species. *See also* BUFFALO; OX; NW p.196.

Anode, the positive electrode, usually of an electrolytic cell or electron tube (valve). *See* ELECTROLYSIS; ELECTRON TUBE; SU pp.130–131; 148.

Anodizing, electrolytic process by which ALUMINIUM OR MAGNESIUM is coated with a thin layer of oxide by making the metal the ANODE in an acid solution. The coating, which is steamed to seal the pores, is insoluble and a good insulator. It can be dyed bright colours, many of which are resistant to sunlight. *See also* SU p.149.

Anole, arboreal LIZARD found in warm regions of North and South America and the West Indies. Enlarged finger and toe pads enable it to cling to surfaces. It is best known for its ability to change from brown to yellow and several shades of green. Males often have an expandable dewlap. Length: 13–46cm (5–18in). There are about 200 species. Family Iguanidae; genus *Anolis*. *See also* IGUANA; NW pp.136–137, *139*.

Anomalistic period, time taken for a celestial body to make one complete revolution around another, starting and finishing at the same point, such as PERIGEE OR PERIHELION. It is slightly longer than the SIDEREAL PERIOD – 27.55455 days for the Moon and 365.25964 days for the Earth.

Anopheles. *See* MALARIA; MOSQUITO.

Anorexia nervosa, abnormal loss of appetite and even a refusal to eat. It is a pathological condition, probably of psychological origin, which occurs most commonly in young females and results in emaciation, a cessation of menstruation and other disorders. *See also* MS p.142.

Anouilh, Jean (1910–), French dramatist and film writer. Like some other contemporary French writers, he has found inspiration in Greek myth, but the underlying theme of many of his plays is the contrast between innocence and bitter experience. His works include *Le Bal des Voleurs* (1938; translated as *Thieves' Carnival*, 1952); *Eurydice* (1942; *Point of Departure*, 1951); *L'Invitation au Château* (1947; *Ring Round the Moon*, 1950) and *La Waltz des Toréadors* (1952; *Waltz of the Toreadors*, 1956). *See also* HC2 p.328.

Anquetil, Jacques (1934–), French racing cyclist. A master time-triallist, he won a record five Tours de France (1957, 1961–64) and numerous other "classics".

Ansbach, town in West Germany, 40km (25 miles) SW of Nüremberg (Nürnberg), on the River Rezat. The residence of the Franconian branch of the HOHENZOLLERN family from 1331 to 1791, it passed to PRUSSIA in 1791 and to BAVARIA in 1806. Industries: electrical equipment, textiles, chemicals. Pop. 30,800.

Anschluss, the unification of Austria and Germany. Prohibited by treaty at the end of WWI, expressly to limit the strength of Germany, the Anschluss was nevertheless favoured by Germans and Austrians of all political persuasions. Unification finally took place through a show of force under HITLER (1938). The union was dissolved by the Allies in 1945, and Austria, after ten years' Allied occupation, again became an independent state. *See also* HC2 pp.226–227; MW p.35.

Anselm of Canterbury, Saint (1033–1109), English theologian, born in Italy. He was an early scholastic philosopher and became Archbishop of Canterbury in 1093. He refused to allow the king to appoint new bishops. His belief in the powers of reason led him to propose an ontological argument for the existence of God. *See also* ONTOLOGY; MS pp.231, 233.

Anseriformes, order of birds that includes ducks, geese and swans together with a small group of primitive South American wading birds called screamers. Intermediate between these is the semi-palmated goose of Australia, the most primitive of the geese. *See also* NW p.140.

Ansermet, Ernest (1883–1969), Swiss

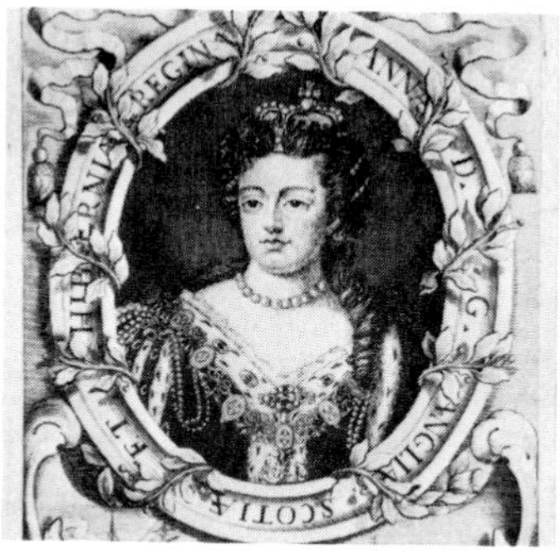

Queen Anne of England (reigned 1702–14) was the last monarch of the House of Stuart.

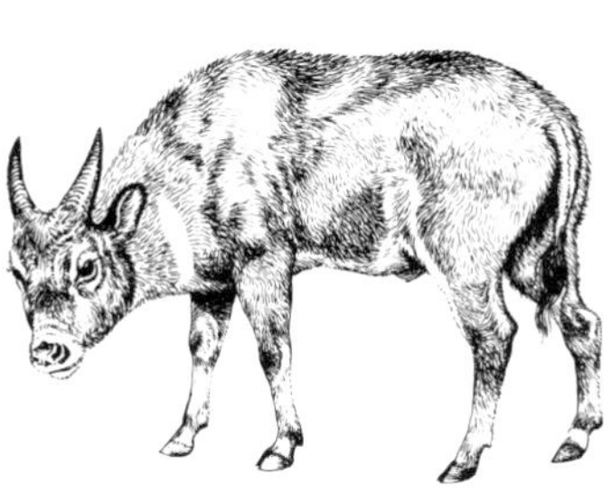

Anoa, a small type of buffalo, is ordinarily timid, but becomes dangerous if provoked.

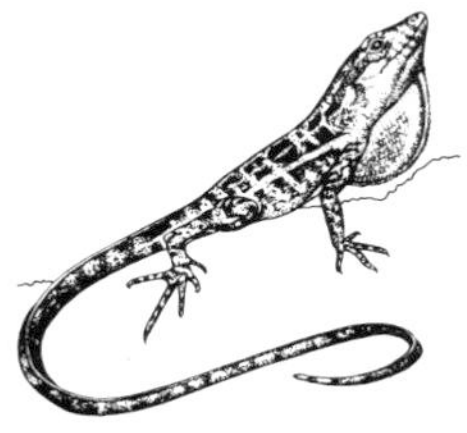

Anole, or American lizard, changes colour in response to mood, temperature and light.

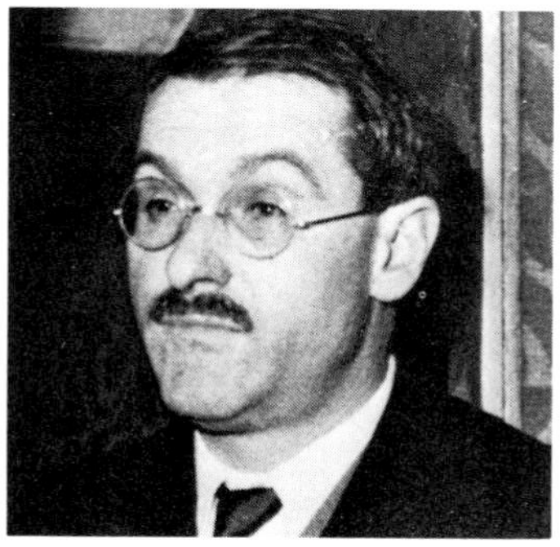

Jean Anouilh is often linked intellectually with the ideas of Camus and Sartre.

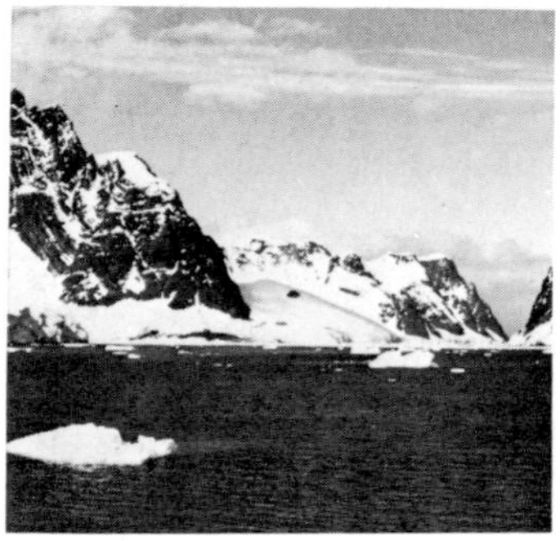

Antarctica, the fifth largest and last continent to be explored by man.

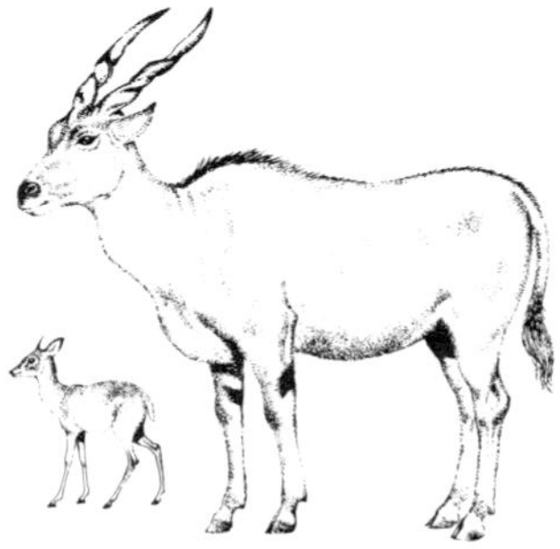

Antelope, an animal of plains, mountains, and forests, is widely hunted for its meat.

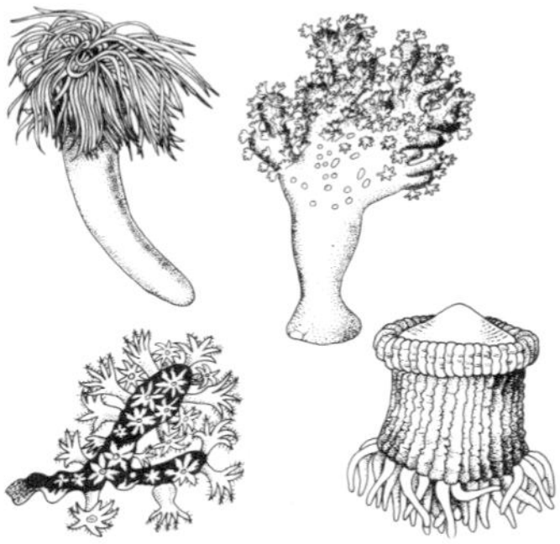

Anthozoa are often vividly coloured; many form colonies that give rise to coral.

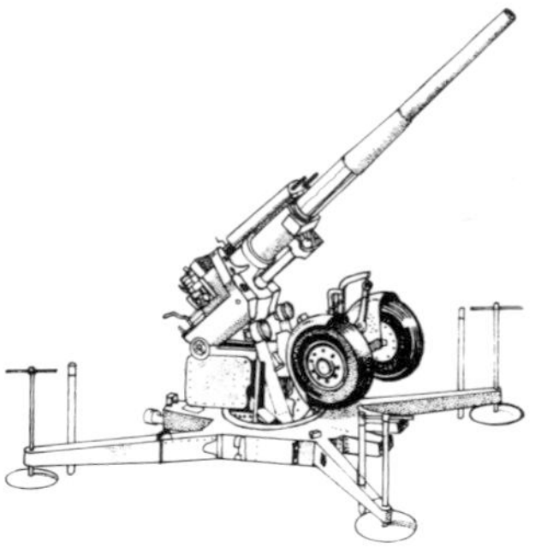

Anti-aircraft artillery in World War II consisted of mounted and often portable guns.

orchestral conductor. In 1915 he conducted for the BALLETS RUSSES on tour. In 1918 he founded the Orchestre de la Suisse Romande in Geneva, and was its permanent conductor until 1967.

Anshan, city in Manchuria, China, 96km (60 miles) SW of Shenyang (Mukden). Iron mining dates from the 10th century and the city is now the centre of China's iron and steel production. It has many blast furnaces and steel converters. Other industries include chemicals and machinery. Pop. 805,000.

Anskar, Saint, missionary in medieval Europe and the first Bishop of Hamburg. He is the patron saint of Scandinavia.

Anson, George Anson, Baron (1697–1762), British admiral who sailed around the world in 1740-44. He was made First Lord of the Admiralty in 1751, and again in 1757. He reformed naval discipline by greatly reducing corruption and inefficiency. In 1755 he created the Marine Corps.

Anstey, Frank (1865–1940), Australian trade unionist and federal MP (1910–34). A pioneer of Australian socialist thought and politics, he was elected deputy leader of the Labor Party in 1922.

Ant, social insect belonging to a family that also includes BEES and WASPS. Ants range in length from 2 to 25mm (0.08–1.0in) and are found worldwide. They feed on plants, nectar and other insects. Most ants are wingless except at times of dispersal. Family Formicidae. *See also* NW pp.78, 79, 113, 116, 199, 214, 216, 219.

ANTA. *See* AMERICAN NATIONAL THEATER AND ACADEMY.

Antabuse, drug that causes an abnormal physiological reaction to alcohol, marked by vomiting. It is sometimes used in the treatment of ALCOHOLISM.

Antakya (formerly Antioch), city in S Turkey on the Orontes River and capital of Hatay province. Founded in *c.* 300 BC by Seleucus I, it rivalled Alexandria. It was taken by Pompey (64 BC) and became an important Roman commercial, cultural and eventually Christian centre. The modern city occupies only a small part of the ancient site. The remains of an aqueduct, theatre, castle and the city walls are still visible. Industries: olives, tobacco, cotton, cereals. Pop. 66,500.

Antananarivo. *See* TANANARIVE.

Antarctica, fifth largest continent, surrounding the South Pole and surrounded by the Antarctic Ocean, the southernmost section of the Atlantic, Pacific and Indian oceans. Almost entirely within the Antarctic Circle and perpetually snow-covered, it holds strategic and scientific interest for the rest of the world. No people live permanently in Antarctica, although scientists frequently stay there for short periods for purposes of research and exploration.

Land. Resembling an open fan, with the Antarctic Peninsula as a handle, the continent is a snowy desert covering about 13,209,000sq km (5,100,000sq miles). The land is a high plateau, having an average elevation of 1,800m (6,000ft). Mountain ranges occur near the coasts. The interior, or South Polar Plateau, lies beneath about 2,000m (6,500ft) of snow, an accumulation of tens of thousands of years. Mineral deposits exist in the mountains, but their recovery has not become practicable. Coal may be plentiful, but the value of known deposits of copper, nickel, gold and iron will not repay the expenses of extracting and exporting them.

Seas and glaciers. The rivers of Antarctica are frozen, inching towards the sea, and instead of lakes there are large bodies of ice along the coasts. The great Beardmore Glacier creeps down from the South Polar Plateau and eventually becomes part of the Ross Ice Shelf. This shelf of ice is that part of the Ross Sea that never thaws. The southernmost part of the Atlantic is the portion of the Antarctic Ocean known as the Weddell Sea.

Climate and vegetation. Antarctica remains cold all year, with only a few coastal areas being free from snow or ice in summer – December to February. On most of the continent the temperature remains below freezing and in August it has been recorded at nearly −90°C (−130°F). Precipitation generally amounts to 17.5–38cm (7–15in) of snow a year, but melting is less than that, allowing a build-up over the centuries. Nevertheless, mosses manage to survive on rocks along the outer rim of the continent. Certain algae grow on the snow, and others appear in pools of fresh water when melting occurs.

Animal life. The best-known Antarctic animals are PENGUINS, especially the emperor and Adélie. Whales, such as the blue and finback, live in the icy waters, as do a few species of hair seals.

History. Islands associated with the continent were sighted in the 18th century, and in 1820 Nathaniel Palmer, an American hunting for seals, reached what is now called the Antarctic Peninsula. Charles Wilkes of the United States explored enough of the coast between 1838 and 1840 to prove that a continent existed, and James Clark Ross of Britain made coastal maps at about the same time. Towards the end of the 19th century, exploration reached inland until a race for the SOUTH POLE developed. Roald AMUNDSEN of Norway won, reaching the pole on 14 December 1911, a month before Robert SCOTT. The aeroplane brought a new era of exploration, and Richard E. Byrd of the United States became the best-known of the airborne polar explorers. In the 1970s scientists from a dozen nations studied the continent and its past. *See also* MM p. *136*; NW pp.224–225; PE pp.54–55, 118, 137.

Antares, or Alpha Scorpii, red supergiant star in the constellation of Scorpius; it has a smaller green companion. Characteristics: apparent mag. 0.92; absolute mag. –4.7; spectral type M1; distance 420 light-years. *See also* SU pp.226, 236, 262, 266.

Ant bear. *See* ANTEATER.

Anteater, or ant bear, toothless, mainly nocturnal, insect-eating mammal that lives in swamps and savannas of tropical America. It has a long, sticky tongue and powerful claws. Length: up to 152cm (60in). Family Myrmecophagidae. *See also* EDENTATE; PANGOLIN; TAMANDUA; NW pp.203, 216.

Antelami, Benedetto (*c.* 1150–1230), the major Italian sculptor before the PISANO family. He was renowned for the profoundly expressive faces of his figures and for his skilful carving of drapery. He executed a relief of the *Deposition* (1178) and other work in Parma cathedral.

Antelope, hollow-horned, speedy RUMINANT found throughout the Old World except in Madagascar, Malaya and Australasia; most antelopes occur in Africa. They range in size from that of a rabbit to that of an ox. In some species both sexes bear horns of varied shapes and sizes; in others, only the males are horned. Family Bovidae. *See also* NW pp.198, 213, 222.

Antenna, long sensory organ (usually of touch) on the heads of insects and most other arthropods. Insects have a single pair of antennae, crustaceans generally two pairs. *See also* AERIAL; NW pp. *107–109*.

Anterus, Saint, pope for a brief period in 235–236. He was executed for insisting that the acts of martyrs should be recorded in church archives.

Anthem, choral composition in Anglican and other English-speaking church services analagous to the Roman Catholic Latin MOTET. Developed in the 16th century as a verse anthem with soloists, the anthem was later performed with orchestral accompaniment and by a choir without soloists. Composers of anthems include Henry PURCELL and Ralph VAUGHAN WILLIAMS.

Anthemius of Tralles, Greek architect from Asia Minor who, with Isidorus of Miletus, designed the Byzantine cathedral HAGIA SOPHIA (532–87) in Constantinople for Justinian I. *See also* HC1 p. *143*.

Anthodite, branching, flower-like formations, often coloured by impurities, found on the roofs of some caves. Anthodites grow, like ordinary stalactites and stalagmites, from the seeping of water rich in calcium carbonate. *See also* PE p.111.

Anthony (or Antony), Saint (AD 250–355), the first Christian monk. Born of Christian parents in Egypt, he withdrew into complete solitude at the age of 20 to practise ascetic devotion. The monastic ideal, outlined in the *Life of St Anthony* attributed to St Athanasius, attracted many. By the time of his death Christian monasticism was well established.

Anthony and Cleopatra (1606–07), a tragedy by William SHAKESPEARE.

Anthozoa, also called Actinozoa, a class of COELENTERATES characterized by a columnar body, top mouth surrounded by tentacles and bottom disc for sliding or holding. There is no MEDUSA stage. The name means flower animals. They include SEA ANEMONES, CORALS and sea pens. Subphylum Cnidaria. *See also* NW pp.82–83.

Anthracene, organic chemical compound, the molecular structure of which consists of three BENZENE rings linked together. Its formula is thus $C_6H_4(CH)_2C_6H_4$. It is produced in the distillation of coal, and was used for the manufacture of dyes. *See also* MM pp.244–245.

Anthracite, form of coal consisting of almost pure carbon. It burns with the hot pale-blue flame of complete combustion. It is the final form in the series of fuels peat, lignite, bituminous coal and black coal. *See also* COAL; PE pp.136, 140; MM p.76.

Anthracnose, various fungal plant diseases that attack crops and are indicated by ulcer-like lesions of dead tissues on fruit, leaves and twigs. Spores of anthracnose fungi are commonly transmitted by insects, seeds and rain. *See also* PE p. *223*.

Anthrax, contagious disease, chiefly of grass-eating animals (but also affecting man, pigs, dogs and captive wild animals), caused by the microbe *Bacillus anthracis.* Animals catch it from contaminated feed and water and certain insects that harbour the germ. The symptoms of this fatal disease are bloody discharges, staggering and convulsions. Human beings can catch anthrax by handling infected animals or their hides. It needs early diagnosis for treatment to be effective. *See also* MS p. *85*.

Anthropology, scientific study of human beings, a method of examining how they developed and how different races are related to each other. It is concerned with the whole chronological and geographic range of human societies. Modern anthropology stems from the first half of the 19th century when a systematic racial classification was made. Public interest in cultural evolution followed the publication in 1859 of DARWIN's *Origin of Species.* Another aspect of this science, known as applied anthropology, is where specific studies are made to discover and learn about a particular community and its relationships, either collectively or individually, *See also* ETHNOGRAPHY; ETHNOLOGY; MS pp.20–34, 248–256.

Anthropometry, measurement of human physical characteristics. It was one approach to racial classification and a method used to compare humans with other primates. *See also* BERTILLON MEASUREMENT; CEPHALIC INDEX; MS p.292.

Anthropomorphism, assigning human characteristics or forms to the divine spirits of such things as winds and rivers, events such as war and death, and emotions. It is found in many primitive religions, especially Greek and Roman. *See also* ANIMISM; MS pp.206–207.

Anthroposophy, type of mystical philosophy founded in Basle in the early 1900s by the Austrian philosopher Rudolph STEINER, who made use of "non-scientific knowledge". *See also* THEOSOPHY.

Anti-aircraft artillery, ground-based weapons used against aircraft in flight. Until the end of WWII the term referred to cannon, although during the war the Germans tested rockets. Increasingly since the war the term has referred to surface-to-air missiles (or rockets). Flak, the German term for anti-aircraft shrapnel, proved effective in WWII, Korea and Vietnam.

Antibes, resort in S France, on the Riviera, 18km (11 miles) SW of Nice. Originally a

Greek colony called Antipolis (founded 340 BC), it contains the ruins of a later Roman settlement and 16th to 17th-century fortifications. Products: fruit, wines and perfume. Pop. 47,550.

Antibiotic, chemical produced by a micro-organism – eg, by specific strains of certain bacteria or moulds – that is capable, in small doses, of stopping the growth of or destroying bacteria and other disease-causing micro-organisms. The introduction of antibiotics during WWII revolutionized medical science, making possible the control, and in some cases the virtual elimination, of once widespread and often fatal diseases, including typhoid, plague, cholera and tuberculosis. Most antibiotics are selective – that is, effective only against specific micro-organisms; those effective against a large number of micro-organisms are known as broad-spectrum antibiotics. They inhibit the growth of sensitive bacteria, and some dissolve or kill bacteria. Important antibiotics include PENICILLIN, the first widely used antibiotic and effective against many infections, such as bronchitis and tonsillitis; streptomycin, effective against tuberculosis and some lung, liver and urinary infections; and the TETRACYCLINES, effective against many bacterial and rickettsial infections. Some bacteria, once sensitive to certain antibiotics, have become resistant, posing a threat to continued antibiotic therapy and giving impetus to the search for new substances for treating diseases. *See also* MS pp.88, 97, 113, 119, 120–121.

Antibody, or immunoglobulin, globular PROTEIN of the BLOOD that reacts specifically with foreign substances or organisms that enter an animal, rendering it immune to them. Pre-formed antibodies, such as tetanus ANTITOXIN, can be injected for immediate protection against disease. *See also* MS pp.114–115.

Antichrist, term that loosely refers to the greatest enemy of Christ. It is used in the letters of St JOHN to refer to a force that will appear at the end of time. Martin LUTHER and other leaders of the REFORMATION applied it to the POPE.

Anticline, fold in rock strata in the shape of an arch. Unless the formation has been overturned, the oldest rocks are found in the centre with younger rocks symmetrically on each side of it. *See* PE pp.104–105.

Anticoagulent drugs. *See* DRUGS.

Anti-Corn Law League, organization formed at Manchester in 1839 to agitate for the removal of import duties on grain. It was led by the Radical MPS Richard COBDEN and John BRIGHT. By holding mass meetings, distributing pamphlets and contesting elections it helped bring about the repeal of the CORN LAWS in 1846. *See also* HC2 pp.95, 96.

Anti-Cosmos. *See* MOHOLE.

Anticyclone, area of high atmospheric pressure around which air circulates in a clockwise direction in the Northern hemisphere and in an anticlockwise direction in the Southern hemisphere. Anticyclones are associated with slowly subsiding, stagnant air masses which bring periods of hot dry weather in summer and cold, often foggy, weather in winter. Stable belts of high pressure occur just to the N and S of the tropics. *See also* PE p.68.

Antidepressant drugs. *See* DRUGS.

Antidiuretic hormone. *See* HORMONE.

Antidote, remedy or other agent used to counter the effects of a POISON. Antidotes may be either specific or general in their effect.

Antietam, Battle of (17 Sept. 1862), also known as Sharpsburg, battle in the AMERICAN CIVIL WAR, fought at Sharpsburg, Md. Gen. George McClellan's 70,000 Union soldiers made five assaults on Gen. Robert E. LEE's 50,000 Confederates. Each side lost more than 12,000 men. Neither side won, but Lee was forced to abandon his Maryland campaign and retreat to Virginia. *See also* HC2 pp.150–151.

Antifreeze, substance dissolved in a liquid to lower its freezing point. Ethylene glycol (ethane diol, HOC_2H_4OH), is commonly used in car radiators. *See also* SU p.144.

Antigen, any substance or organism which, when injected into animal tissues, induces the production of an ANTIBODY that reacts specifically with the antigen. *See also* MS pp. *114*, 115.

Antigone, Greek mythological figure. The daughter of Oedipus and Jocasta, she accompanied her father through his banishment until his death. Despite her efforts, her brother Polynices rebelled unsuccessfully against Eteocles, another brother and ruler of Thebes. In defiance of the king, Antigone buried her brother and hanged herself rather than face the punishment of being buried alive. The tragedy *Antigone* (*c*.441 BC) by SOPHOCLES is based on the legend.

Antigonus I (*c*.382–301 BC), general of ALEXANDER THE GREAT. He became governor of Phrygia in 333 BC and, in the struggles over the regency, he defeated challengers and controlled Mesopotamia, Syria and Asia Minor. At Salamis in 306 BC he defeated his former ally, Ptolemy I, and he was himself killed at Ipsus.

Antigua, Caribbean island in the Leeward Island group. It is self-governing except for foreign policy, which is controlled by Britain. Pop. 65,525. *See also* MW p.74.

Antihistamine, any one of certain drugs that counteract or otherwise prevent the effects of histamine, a natural substance released by the body in response to injury or more often as part of an allergic reaction. Histamine can produce symptoms such as sneezing, running nose and burning eyes. *See also* HAY FEVER; MS p.89.

Anti-inflammatory drug. *See* DRUGS.

Antilogarithms, numbers having specified numbers as their LOGARITHM. Thus the antilogarithm (or antilog) of 0.4771 is 3, because $\log_{10}3 = 0.4771$ (to 4 places of decimals). *See also* SU pp.38–39.

Antill, John (1904–), Australian composer. His works include the ballet *Corroboree* (1947), an evocation of Australian aboriginal life, the opera *Endymion*, based on KEATS's poem, and the cantata *The Song of Hagar*.

Antimatter, matter made up of antiparticles, which are identical to ordinary particles in every way except charge and magnetic moment. When an antiparticle such as a positron (anti-electron), antiproton or antineutron meets its respective particle, both are annihilated. Since the PHOTON is its own antiparticle the possibility exists that there are stars or galaxies composed entirely of antimatter. *See also* SU p.*66*.

Antimony, toxic metallic element (Sb) of Group V of the periodic table. Stibnite (a sulphide) is its commonest ore. It is used in some alloys, particularly in hardening lead for batteries and type metal. The element has two allotropes: a silvery metallic form and an amorphous grey form. Properties: at.no. 51; at.wt. 121.75; s.g. 6.684; m.p. 630.5°C (1,166.9°F); b.p. 1,750°C (3,182°F); most common isotope Sb^{121} (57.25%). *See also* MM p.27.

Antineutron, in particle physics, the antiparticle of a NEUTRON. It has no electric charge, and a magnetic moment equal but opposite to that of the neutron. An antineutron is sometimes formed in a bubble chamber when a PROTON collides with an antiproton. *See also* ANTIMATTER; SU p.*66*.

Anti-novel, or non-novel, type of fiction that first became popular in France. The term was first used by Jean-Paul SARTRE in 1957 in an introduction to Nathalie SARRAUTE's *Portrait of a Man Unknown*, (first published 1947). An avant-garde approach to literature, the anti-novel is characterized by painstaking descriptions of physical and psychological details while avoiding traditional expression of the author's values, and omitting any dialogue or biographical detail that might explain the characters or develop the plot. Significant anti-novels are Sarraute's *Tropisms* (1938); Alain ROBBE-GRILLET's *The Erasers* (1953) and *The Voyeur* (1955); and Michel BUTOR's *Passing Time* (1956).

Antioch. *See* ANTAKYA.

Antiparticle. *See* ANTIMATTER.

Antipater (*c*.397–319 BC) Macedonian general and aide of PHILIP II. In 347–336 BC he negotiated peace with ATHENS and later helped ALEXANDER THE GREAT. Disliked for favouring tyranny and oligarchy, he nevertheless ruled Athens until his death in 319, which precipitated the breakup of authority in the empire.

Antiphanes (*c*.408–*c*.334 BC), Greek playwright. A leading writer of comedy, he wrote 260 plays, including parodies of myths. His style is based on wit, charm and elegance. His plays include *Creation of Man*, *Sappho* and *As Much Again*.

Antiphon, method of singing psalms or canticles, often in PLAINSONG, in which alternate verses are sung by two halves of a choir or by a priest (or deacon) and choir. The word applies also to a single verse sung by either side.

Antipodes Islands, barren uninhabited islands in the South Pacific, 740km (458 miles) SE of New Zealand, of which they are a part. Discovered in 1800 by British seamen, the islands were so named because they are antipodal or diametrically opposite to Greenwich. Area: 62sq km (24sq miles).

Antipope, name given to rivals of legitimately elected popes, generally "appointed" by unauthorized religious factions. The first was HIPPOLYTUS (217–35), a Trinitarian heretic and rival of Calixtus I. The most famous were the AVIGNON POPES, starting with Clement VII, during the Great Schism of 1378–1417.

Antipsychotic drug. *See* DRUGS.

Anti-Semitism, prejudice against Jews. Since ancient times, Jews have been persecuted for religious reasons and accused of being Christ's crucifiers. Many Jews of the Middle Ages became moneylenders and were looked upon with contempt. The growing nationalism of the 19th century further isolated the Jews who were considered racially inferior. HITLER in the 20th century used these attitudes to strengthen his own position. After WWII, anti-Zionism among the Arabs and the Soviet Union added a new dimension to anti-Semitism. *See also* HC2 pp.222, *223*.

Antiseptics, agents that destroy or arrest the growth of putrefaction-producing GERMS as distinct from DISINFECTANTS which destroy the germs that cause disease. Among commonly used antiseptics are ALCOHOL, IODINE and CHLORINE compounds. ANTIBIOTICS are the most commonly used antiseptics in surgery. *See also* MS p.126.

Anti-tank weapons, arms ranging from grenades, large-calibre rifles, high-velocity cannon and mines to rockets and missiles. Mines and grenades disable tanks by damaging their running gear; the other weapons are designed to penetrate their thick armour. *See also* MM pp.168, 171.

Antitoxin, ANTIBODY produced by the body in response to toxins. They are specific in action, and neutralize the TOXIN. Antitoxin serums are used to treat and prevent bacterial diseases such as TETANUS and DIPHTHERIA. *See also* MS pp.114-115.

Antlers, bony outgrowth on the skulls of male DEER (and female reindeer). In temperate-zone species, antlers begin to grow in early summer. They are soft, well supplied with blood and covered with thin, velvety skin. Later, the blood recedes and the dried skin is rubbed off. Antlers then serve as sexual ornaments and weapons until they are shed the following spring. First-year males grow short spikes. More branches (points) are added each year until maturity is reached. *See also* HORN.

Ant lion, larva of the neuropteran family Mymeleontidea, found in most parts of the world. Carnivorous, with large, sickle-shaped jaws, it digs a pit in dry sand where it lies waiting for ants and other insects to fall in. See also LACEWING; NEUROPTERA.

Antofagasta, major sea port on the coast of N Chile and the capital of Antofagasta province. Built in 1870 to provide port facilities for the nitrate deposits in the ATACAMA DESERT, it now has both ore refining and concentrating plants. Pop. 125,100.

Antonello da Messina (*c*.1430–79), Sicilian painter, who passed on to Giovanni BELLINI his knowledge of the Flemish technique of working in glazes of pure oil paint, and thus influenced the develop-

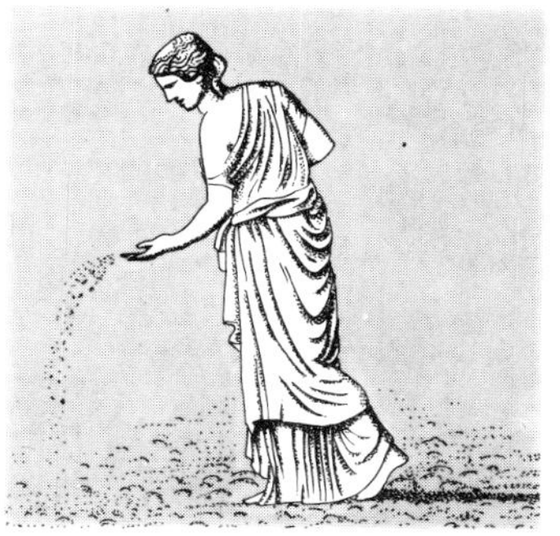

Antigone, in Greek mythology, was the daughter of Oedipus and Jocasta.

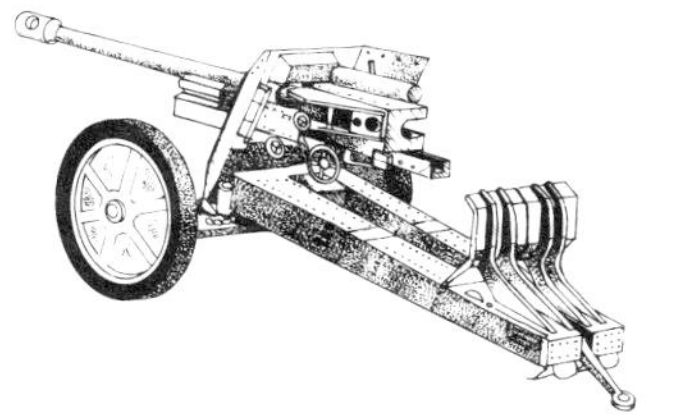

Anti-tank weapons such as mounted guns proved a valuable artillery aid in World War II.

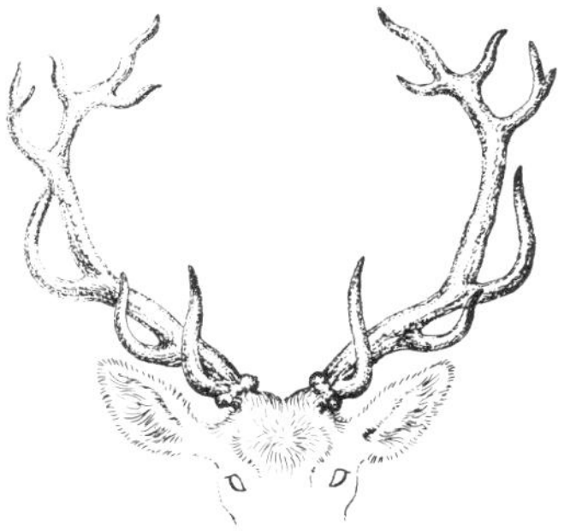

Antlers are grown and shed annually by deer; size increases with age until maturity.

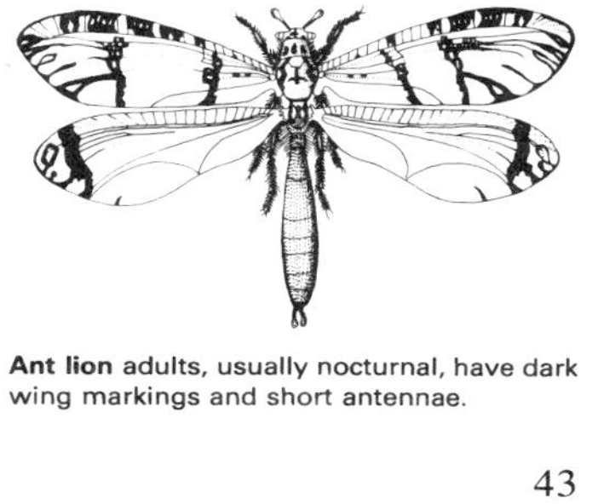

Ant lion adults, usually nocturnal, have dark wing markings and short antennae.

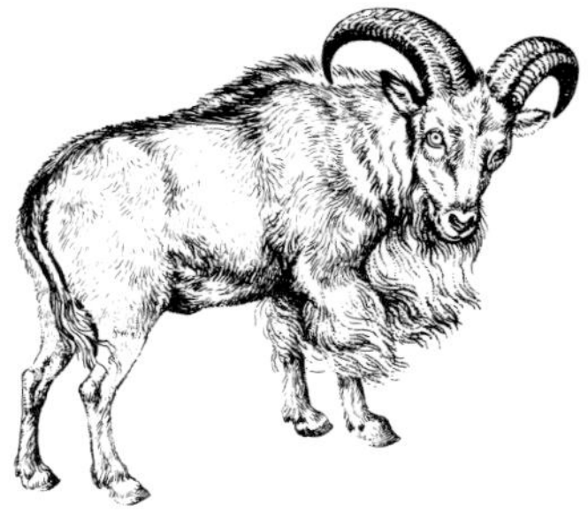

Aoudad or Barbary sheep (sometimes called udad) is the only wild sheep living in Africa.

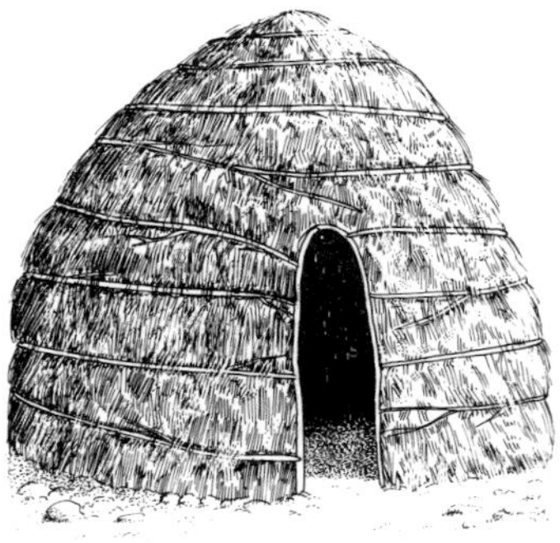

Apaches in New Mexico lived in tepees, whereas those in Arizona used brush huts.

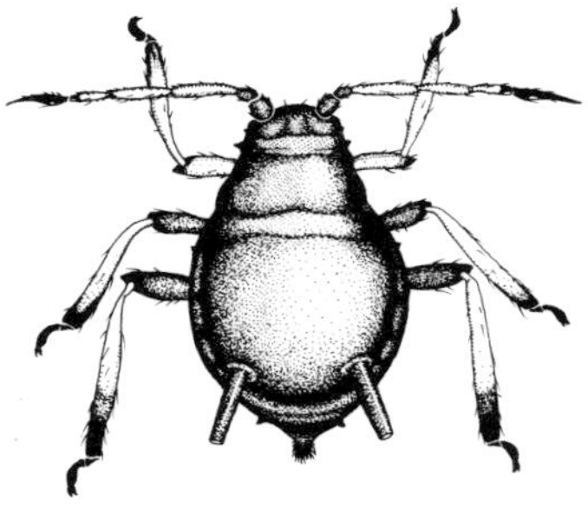

Aphids are sometimes farmed by ants for the tasty honeydew which these insects secrete.

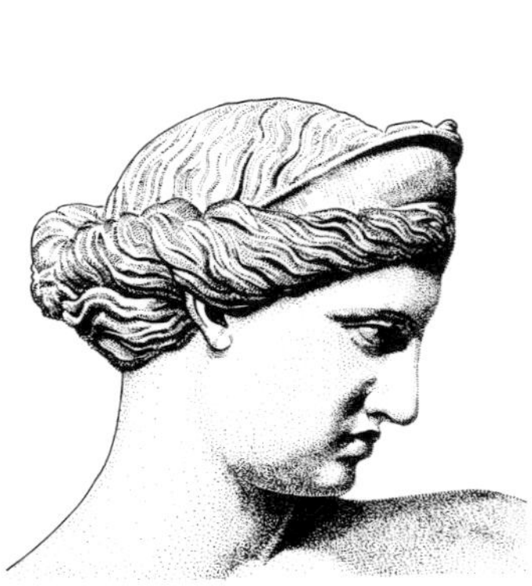

Aphrodite represented the physical and spiritual aspects of love to the ancient Greeks.

ment of Venetian painting. His works include *Portrait of a Young Man* (1472) and *The Virgin Annunciate* (1476).

Antonescu, Ion (1882–1946), Romanian general, leader of the pro-Nazi Iron Guard movement. After losing office because of his pro-Nazi sympathies, he was appointed Premier in 1940 at Germany's insistence, and in 1941 he set up a military dictatorship, forcing the abdication of King Carol II. Antonescu suppressed all opposition, modelling his regime on that of Germany and siding with the Axis powers. He was arrested during King Michael's coup in September 1944, and later executed.

Antonine Wall, Roman defensive wall built in AD 142, extending about 58.7km (36.5 miles) across Scotland from the Forth to the Clyde. Traces remain. *See also* HC1 pp.100, *182*.

Antonio (1921–), stage name of the Spanish dancer Antonio Ruiz Soler. He made his debut in Liège in 1928. Since then his performances, such as *Zapateado*, have been acclaimed all over the world.

Antrim, County, county in Northern Ireland, bounded to the N by the Atlantic Ocean and to the NE and E by the North Channel. Mainly a low basalt plateau, it is noted for perpendicular basalt columns (the Giant's Causeway). The county town is Belfast. County Antrim is chiefly an agricultural region, cereals and livestock being important. Industries include linen and shipbuilding. Area: 3,043sq km (1,175sq miles). Pop. (1971) 353,417.

Antung (Andong), port in NE China, on the Yalu (Yalujiang) River, on the North Korean boundary, 200km (125 miles) S of Mukden (Shenyang). Its importance increased after 1907 when the railway connecting Mukden with Korea was built. Industries: timber, trading, food processing. Pop. 360,000.

Antwerp (Antwerpen, Anvers), city in N Belgium, on the River Scheldt, 37km (23 miles) N of Brussels and capital of Antwerp province. Antwerp rose to commercial prominence in the 15th century and became a centre for English mercantile interests. The site of Europe's first stock exchange (1460), its commercial importance was affected adversely by the closing of the River Scheldt after the PEACE OF WESTPHALIA in 1648. The reopening of the river to traffic (1795) and improvements made by NAPOLEON I in *c.*1803 transformed Antwerp into one of the world's major ports. It is the site of the State University Centre (1965) and the Royal Museum of Fine Arts (1880-90). It possesses the fine large 14th-century Cathedral of Notre Dame. Industries: oil refining, food processing, shipyards, diamond cutting. Pop. 672,703.

Antwerp Mannerists, group of Antwerp painters, mostly unknown, who worked *c.*1510–30.

Antwerp School, school of painting that developed in the late 15th century and was strongly influenced by Italian art in its use of rich warm tones in intimate paintings. The school reached the height of its fame in the 17th century. In the early 16th century the ANTWERP MANNERISTS developed an over-elaborate Italianate style.

Anu, in Assyro-Babylonian mythology, the supreme god of the pantheon, chief of the triad Anu, Ea and Enlil. Anu is the sky-god, the ruler of destiny, and the creator of the four winds. *See also* HC1 p.329.

Anu, also Danu or Dana, in Celtic mythology, the earth mother. As the female principle in nature she was associated with the wind and with the birth and suckling of other deities. The Irish gods, and later the fairy folk of Irish folklore, were known as the people of the goddess Danu.

Anubis, jackal-headed god of the ancient Egyptians. Son of Nephthys and OSIRIS, he conducted the souls of the dead to the underworld and presided over mummification and funerals. In the myths, Anubis accompanied Osiris on his world conquest and buried him after his murder. *See also* MS p.*207*.

Anuradhapura, town in Sri Lanka on the Aruvi River and capital of the North Central province. The former capital of the Sinhalese Kingdom, it is noted for its Buddhist ruins, including several STUPAS, the Brazen Palace and the sacred bo tree. It is a famous pilgrimage centre and was founded in 437 BC. Pop. 30,000.

Anus, end of the alimentary canal, from the rectum to the exterior, through which waste material and solid excretions of undigested food are expelled from the body.

Anuszkiewicz, Richard (1930–), US painter. An originator of OP ART, he emphasizes visual sensation and optical illusion in his work, which is characterized by geometric shapes and vibrant colours. His best-known work includes *All Things Live in the Three* (1963).

Anxiety, in clinical psychology and psychiatry, emotional state similar to FEAR and involving apprehension and dread, but not associated with any specific event or stimulus. Chronic anxiety is considered to be one of the primary symptoms of NEUROSIS. *See also* EMOTION; MS pp.134, 135, 140, 141, 146.

Anyang, city in E central China. The former capital of the ancient state of the Shang dynasty (17th-11th centuries BC), it is today an important trade area. Pop. 124,900.

ANZAC, short for Australian and New Zealand Army Corps, a volunteer force of 30,000 men which played a major part in the GALLIPOLI CAMPAIGN in WWI. They spearheaded the Gallipoli landings (25 April 1915), and also fought in France and the Middle East. About 8,500 Anzac troops were killed during the war. Anzac Day (25 April) is a public holiday in Australia and New Zealand. *See also* HC2 p.*191*.

Anzengruber, Ludwig (1839–89), Austrian novelist and dramatist. He wrote dramatic works, numerous short stories and two novels. He also wrote popular comedies and tragedies for the Viennese stage, including *Das vierte Gebot* (1877), but these had limited success.

Anzio, town in E central Italy, on the Tyrrhenian Sea. Supposedly founded by Anteias, it was a favourite resort of the Romans by 341 BC, and the birthplace of Caligula and Nero. Anzio was the scene of one of the bloodiest battles of the Italian campaign in WWII, when the Allies landed there in 1944. Industries: tourism, fishing. Pop. 23,500.

ANZUS Pact (Australia-New Zealand-United States Treaty Organization), defensive alliance organized by the United States in 1951 in response to waning British power, the KOREAN WAR, and alarm at increasing Soviet influence in the Pacific. The treaty stated that an attack on any one of the three countries would be considered as an attack on them all. *See also* HC2 p.251.

Aorta, the largest ARTERY in the body. Oxygenated blood passes from the heart's left ventricle through semi-lunar valves to the aorta. Outside the heart, the aorta curves and branches to form the arteries that carry the oxygenated blood to all parts of the body (except the lungs). *See also* CIRCULATORY SYSTEM; HEART; MS pp.62,*63*.

Aosta, Prince Amedeo Umberto, Duke of (1898–1942), Italian soldier. He was Viceroy of Italian East Africa (1937–41) and commander in the East African campaign (1939–41).

Aoudad, or Barbary sheep, wild SHEEP, found in N African rocky hills. It has a uniform reddish-brown coat and long, soft mane on throat and chest. Both sexes have large, backward-pointing horns. Length: up to 1.9m (6.25ft). Family Bovidae; species *Ammotragus lervia*.

Apache, Athabascan-speaking tribe of North American Indians that live in Arizona, New Mexico and Colorado. Divided culturally into Eastern Apache, including Mescalevo and Kiowa, and Western Apache, which included Coyotero and Tonto, they migrated from the northwest in about AD 1000 with the Navajo but separated to form a distinct tribal group. They retained their earlier nomadic raiding customs, which brought them into military conflict with Mexico and the USA. They live in brush huts or tepees and are noted for their basketry. The total population is approximately 11,000. *See also* HC2 pp.148–149.

Apartheid, South Africa's policy of racial segregation, translated as "separate development" from Afrikaans. The policy was made official by Daniel F. MALAN after his Afrikaaner National Party came to power in 1948. Apartheid limits aspects of the lives of South Africa's Blacks and Coloureds (82.5% of the population), but is intended gradually to free them from economic and political subservience. South Africa left the British Commonwealth in 1961 in response to anti-apartheid criticism. *See also* HC2 p.249; MW p.154.

Apatite, phosphate mineral, usually found as calcium phosphate associated with hydroxyl, chloride or fluoride ions. It occurs in igneous rocks and sedimentary deposits, as prismatic or tabular hexagonal crystals, as granular aggregates or in massive crusts. It is usually too soft for cutting and polishing, but there are two gem varieties. Hardness 5; s.g. 3.1-3.4.

Ape, term usually applied to the anthropoid apes – PRIMATES that are man's closest relatives. There are three great apes – CHIMPANZEE, GORILLA and ORANG-UTAN – and one lesser, the GIBBON. Apes differ from MONKEYS in being larger, in having no visible tail and in possessing more complex brains. Two monkeys are also called "apes" – the BARBARY APE of N Africa and Gibraltar, and the black ape of Celebes. *See also* NW pp.168, 169.

Apeldoorn, resort city in the E Netherlands, N of Arnhem, with many beautiful gardens and Het Loo, the royal summer palace. Industries: drugs, furniture, paper, tourism. Pop. 124,000.

Aperture, in an optical instrument, the uncovered part of a lens or mirror through which light passes. In a telescope it is the clear diameter of the main mirror or objective lens and controls the instrument's light-gathering power. In a camera it is the "hole" (often called a stop) which controls the amount of light passing through the shutter to the film. Camera apertures are often variable – using a diaphragm – and are expressed as f-numbers (equal to the focal length of the lens divided by the diameter of the aperture); the larger the aperture, the smaller the f-number. *See also* MM pp. 218–223; SU p.169.

Apex, in astronomy, point on the CELESTIAL SPHERE, located in the constellation of Hercules, towards which the Sun appears to be moving. As the Sun slowly orbits the galactic centre, nearby stars (as seen from the Earth) appear to move away from it because of the Sun's relative velocity.

Aphasia, condition usually associated with brain damage involving the loss or impairment of ability to communicate through language. It can mean that a sufferer is unable to write or make signs, or is unable to understand. It is often characterized by vague and confused speech. *See also* BRAIN DISORDERS; MS p.97.

Aphid, or plant louse, winged or wingless, soft-bodied insect found throughout the world. It transmits virus diseases of plants when sucking plant juices. Females reproduce with or without mating, producing one to several generations annually. Length: to 5mm (0.2in). Family Aphididae. *See also* COTTON APHID; HOMOPTERA; NW pp. *110*, *228*.

Aphorism, concise sentence expressing an important truth. Hippocrates published his famous series of precepts under the title *Aphorisms*. One of these, later translated by Chaucer, is: "The life so short, the craft so long to learn".

Aphrodite, Greek goddess of love, beauty and fruitfulness, identified by the Romans as VENUS. She was the daughter ot ZEUS and Dione. Her husband was designated as Hephaestus (Vulcan), although she loved many gods and legendary mortals. Among these were ARES, ADONIS (whose death left her broken-hearted) and Anchises, who was the father of AENEAS. Statues of her include the Venus de Milo (Paris) and Aphrodite of Cnidus (Rome).

Apia, capital city and chief port in Western Samoa, on Upolu Island in the SW central Pacific Ocean; it is the location of

the government hospital. Robert Louis STEVENSON spent his last years there. Products: coconuts, cacao, bananas, coffee. Area: (island) 1,114sq km (430sq miles). Pop. (city) 32,600. *See also* MW p.183.
Apis, sacred bull of the Ancient Egyptians, worshipped at Memphis. The bull was sacred to OSIRIS, believed to be his incarnation, and was even mummified upon its death.
Ap Ivor, Denis (1916–), Irish-born composer of Welsh parentage, much of whose work employs the TWELVE-TONE MUSIC system. His works include the cantata *The Hollow Men* (1939; revised 1946), based on T.S. ELIOT's poem, the ballet *Blood Wedding* (1953) and the opera *Yerma* (1957–58), based on gipsy plays by F. Garcia LORCA.
Apocrine gland, odour-producing gland in human skin; restricted mainly to the armpits and groin. In response to sex and stress stimuli, they secrete a liquid which is readily decomposed by bacteria to give odour. *See also* ECCRINE GLAND; MS p.61.
Apocrypha, certain books of the OLD TESTAMENT included in the Anglican and Roman Catholic canon (although only as deuterocanonical) but not those of the Jews and Protestants. They comprise 1 and 2 Esdras, TOBIT, JUDITH, WISDOM, ECCLESIASTICUS, BARUCH, 1 and 2 MACCABEES and parts of ESTHER and DANIEL. At the end of the Roman Catholic Old Testament, the books of 3 and 4 Esdras and the Prayer of Manasseh are also to be found, although they are not in the Anglican canon. These books are hardly ever read aloud in church but are nevertheless considered useful background information.
Apodiformes, order of birds that includes HUMMING-BIRDS and SWIFTS. They are among the most aerial and aerobatic of all birds, and have weak feet which make them unable to walk or hop. Unlike humming-birds, some species of swifts are unable to perch on twigs or wires. *See also* NW. p.141.
Apogee, point in its orbit round the Earth of the Moon or an artificial satellite at which it is farthest from the Earth.
Apollinaire, Guillaume (1880–1918); *b.* Wilhelm Apollinaris de Kostrowitzky. He championed CUBISM and FUTURISM. His poetry, varying from the lyrical to the modernist, includes *Alcools* (1913) and the typographically experimental *Calligrammes* (1918). Other works are the short stories *L'Heresiarque et cie* (1910) and the play *Les Mamelles de Tiresias* (1918).
Apollo, in Greek mythology, god of the sun, archery and agriculture; patron of farmers, poets and physicians; founder of cities and giver of laws. He was the son of ZEUS and Leto, twin to Artemis. In the TROJAN WAR he sided with Troy, sending a plague against the Greeks. *See also* MS p.206.
Apollo Belvedere, sculpture, in the Vatican museum, of the Greek god of sun or light. The most famous statue of this god, it is a Roman copy of an original Greek statue, probably by Leochares, 4th century BC. It influenced MICHELANGELO and other Renaissance artists.
Apollodorus (5th century BC), Athenian painter. He was called "Sciagraphus" (Shadow Painter) because he introduced shading into his work, all of which is now lost. He also experimented with foreshortening.
Apollodorus (2nd century BC), Greek scholar who wrote about history and theology. His best-known works are *On the Gods* and *Chronicle*, a history in poetry of Greece from the fall of Troy.
Apollonius of Tyana (*fl.* 1st century AD), Greek philosopher in the school of PYTHAGORAS. He travelled widely in India and also visited Babylon and Nineveh. Many of his contemporaries regarded him as a magician.
Apollonius Rhodius (3rd century BC), Greek poet. He was a pupil of CALLIMACHUS but disagreed with the views of his teacher on epic poetry. Apollonius is best known for his epic poem *Argonautica*. *See also* ARGONAUTS; HC1 p.74.
Apollo programme, US project to land men on the Moon. Initiated in May 1961 by President John Kennedy, it achieved its objective on 21 July, 1969, when Neil ARMSTRONG set foot on the lunar surface. The programme terminated with the successful Apollo-Soyuz linkup in space during July 1975, having placed more than 30 astronauts in space and 12 on the moon. *See also* SOYUZ PROGRAMME; MM pp.156–*159*; SU pp.180, 196, 268–271.
Apologetics, branch of theology concerned with the defence of Christian truth on intellectual grounds. A famous early Apologist was ORIGEN of Alexandria, whose Greek work *Contra Celsum* appeared in the 3rd century. Two celebrated Latin Apologists were TERTULLIAN (2nd century) and LACTANTIUS (4th century).
Apomorphine, powerful narcotic drug ($C_{17}H_{17}NO_2$) prepared from the opium alkaloid morphine. It is sometimes used in medicines as an expectorant and, when injected, as an emetic, but like many alkaloids it is an addictive DRUG which must be used carefully. *See also* MS p.*146*.
Apoplexy. *See* STROKE.
Apostle, commissioned and authoritative messenger. Jesus, who taught that he had been "sent" by the Father, in turn commissioned his twelve original disciples to carry out the purpose of God for man's salvation (Mark 3:14; Matt.10:1; Luke 6:13ff). The first qualification for apostolic office was to have "seen the Lord". The twelve were the first apostles: Simon Peter, Andrew, James the son of Zebedee, John, Philip, Bartholomew (or Nathanael), Thomas, Matthew (the tax-collector), James the son of Alphaeus, Jude (Lebbaeus, or Thaddaeus), Simon the Zealot and Judas Iscariot (whose place was taken by Matthias.) The term is also applied in the New Testament to St PAUL who received his commission from Jesus in a vision on the road from Jerusalem to Damascus. In modern usage the title is sometimes given to the leader of the first Christian mission to a country, eg to St PATRICK, the "Apostle of Ireland". *See also* HC1 pp.110–111.
Apostles' Creed, statement of Christian faith, based on evidence in the New Testament and divided into three sections devoted to God the Father, his Son Jesus Christ and the Holy Spirit. The last section also affirms the tradition of the "holy Catholic Church; the communion of saints; the forgiveness of sins; the resurrection of the body; and the life everlasting". The text evolved gradually from very early times and its present form was fixed by the early 8th century. It is used widely in private and public worship in all the major Churches in the West. *See also* NICENE CREED.
Apostolic Succession, doctrine held by the Orthodox, Roman Catholic and Anglican Churches that bishops are successors of Christ's apostles, from whom they derive their commission in an unbroken chain of historic succession. The doctrine is held to be a guarantee of the continuity of the Church with the Church of the apostles.
Apothecary, pharmacist, one who prepares and sells medicines and drugs. In Britain until 1617, when the Society of Apothecaries was formed, practitioners were not distinguished from physicians. An Act of Parliament of 1815 granted licences to practise following an approved course of study.
Apotheosis, act of deifying a human being. The Greeks elevated founders of cities and colonies to the status of gods after death. The Romans deified ROMULUS, CAESAR, AUGUSTUS and others. After Christianity became the official religion of the Roman Empire, deification of emperors gradually ceased.
Appalachians, mountain system running from E Canada to Alabama, USA. They include the White Mts, Green Mts, Catskills, Alleghenies, Blue Ridge and Cumberland Mts.
Apparent movement, also called illusory movement, phi phenomenon, or the marquee effect, movement that appears to occur when two or more stimuli are turned on and off in rapid succession; if they are lights, a spot of light appears to jump from one location to another. Motion pictures, which are really a series of sequential still pictures, make use of apparent movement. *See also* MS p.46.
Appeal, in law, the review of a court's decision in an action, heard in a higher court. Normally either party to a law-suit may appeal but must generally show good reason for doing so – for example, a misinterpretation of the law by a judge. *See also* MS p.*287*.
Appeasement, policy in which one government grants unilateral concessions to another to forestall a political, economic or military threat. Appeasement of Germany at MUNICH in 1938 at the expense of Czechoslovakia is considered a classic example. *See also* MUNICH AGREEMENT; HC2 p.226.
Appel, Karel (1921–), Dutch painter, exhibited with the Cobra group from 1949 and settled in Paris (1950). His colourful paintings are in the ABSTRACT EXPRESSIONIST style. In 1960 he was awarded the International Guggenheim Award for his *Woman with an Ostrich* (1957).
Appendicitis, inflammation of the APPENDIX caused by obstruction and infection. Symptoms include severe pain in the lower right abdomen, nausea and vomiting. Acute appendicitis is generally treated by surgery. A ruptured appendix can cause peritonitis and even death.
Appendix, finger-like organ, about 10cm (4in) long, located near the junction of the small and large intestines, usually in the lower right part of the ABDOMEN. It has no known function in man but can become inflamed or infected (APPENDICITIS). *See also* MS pp.*92*, 93.
Appennines (Appennino), mountain range extending the length of Italy, a continuation of the Alps. Unselective deforestation over the years has caused deep erosion and landslides. They are the location of numerous hydroelectric plants and sheep and goats are grazed on the slopes. The highest point is Mt Corno Grande (2,914m; 9,560ft). Length: 1,350km (840 miles). *See also* PE p.*45*.
Appert, Nicholas (*c.*1750–1841), confectioner and distiller who invented a method for preserving food in sealed glass containers, regarded as the forerunner to today's food canning.
Appia, Adolphe (1862–1928), Swiss theatrical designer. He revolutionized stage effects by introducing three-dimensional sets, and by his use of light to create atmosphere. His works include *The Staging of the Wagnerian Drama* (1895) and *Music and Staging* (1899).
Appian Way, ancient military road in Italy, constructed in *c.* 312 BC by the censor Appius Claudius Caecus. Initially connecting Rome with Capua, it was later extended through Benevenum and Tarentum to Brundisium. It formed the first stage of routes to Greece and the East; portions of it remain today. Length: approx. 563km (350 miles).
Apple, common name for the most widely cultivated fruit tree of temperate climates. Developed from a tree native to Europe and sw Asia, apples are propagated by budding or grafting. From the flowers, which require cross-pollination to produce a desirable fruit, the fleshy fruit grows in a variety of sizes, shapes and acidities; it is generally roundish, 5–10cm (2–4in) in diameter, and a shade of yellow, green or red. A mature tree may yield up to 1cu m (30 bushels) of fruit in a single growing season. Europe produces 50–60% of the world's annual crop; the USA produces 16–20%; and Japan, Korea, China, India, Australia, New Zealand, Argentina and Chile are also important producers. Apples may be eaten raw, cooked or made into jams, tarts, pies, puddings, preserves or sauces. The alcoholic drink CIDER is made from fermented apple juice. Family Rosaceae; genus *Malus*. *See also* PE pp.178, *179*, 192, 193.
Applegarth, Robert (1834–1924), British trade union leader. He was secretary of the Amalgamated Society of Carpenters and Joiners in 1862, and became a leader of the "new unionism". *See also* HC2 p.89.
Appleton, Sir Edward Victor (1892–

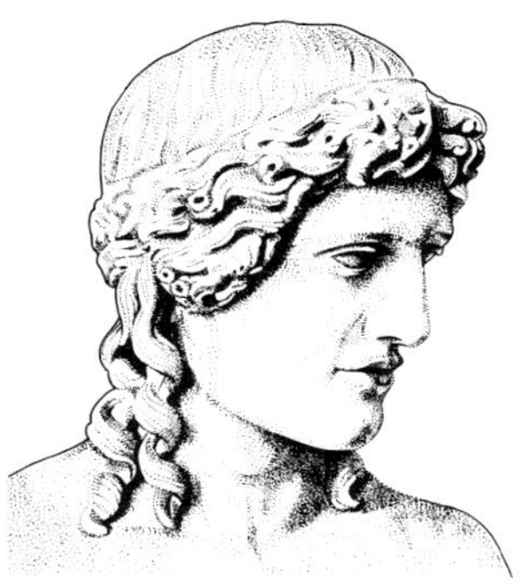

Apollo was the epitome of goodness and reason to both the Greeks and the Romans.

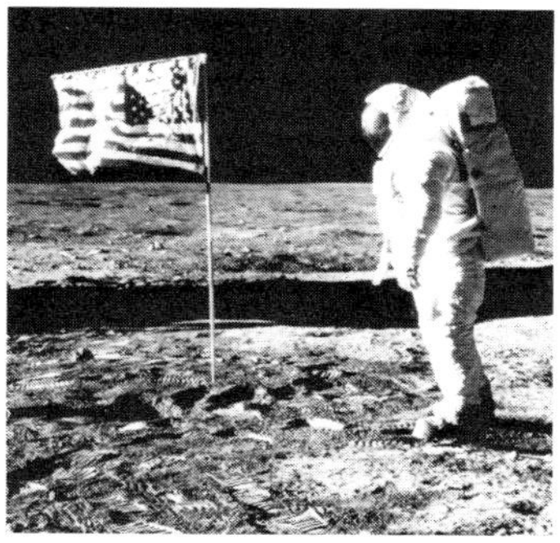

Apollo programme at its culmination; the saluting of the American flag on the Moon.

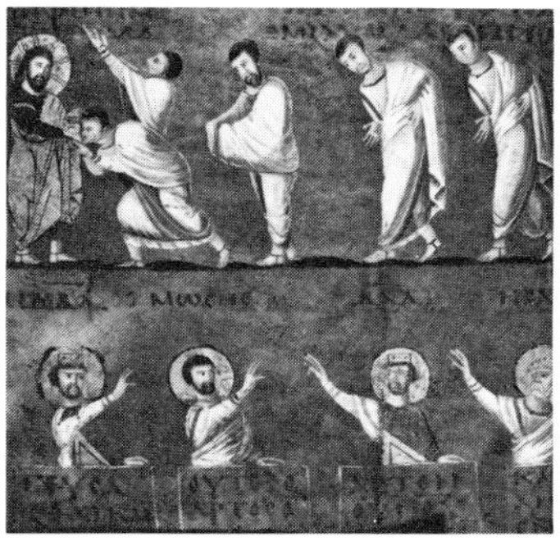

Apostles, portrayed here in a 6th-century manuscript, spread the doctrine of Christ.

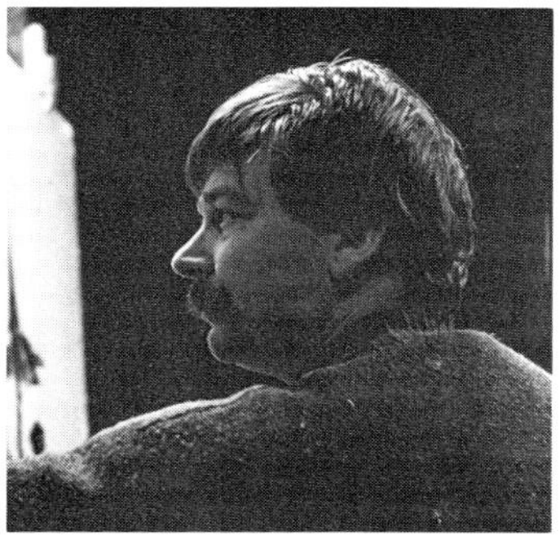

Karel Appel, whose ghostly fantasy pieces show the influence of primitive art forms.

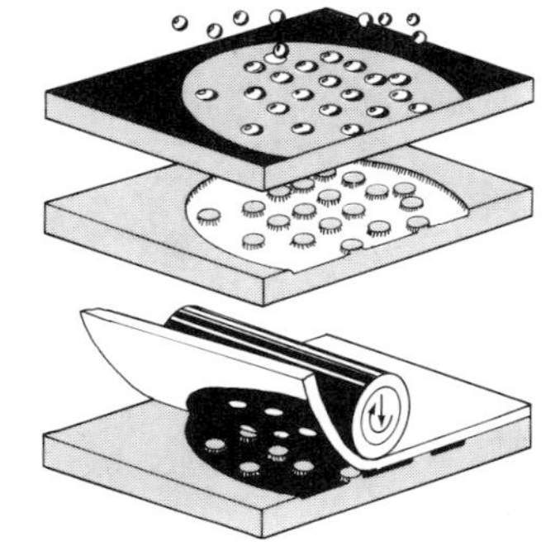

Aquatint, an engraving process designed to imitate the effect of ink or wash drawings.

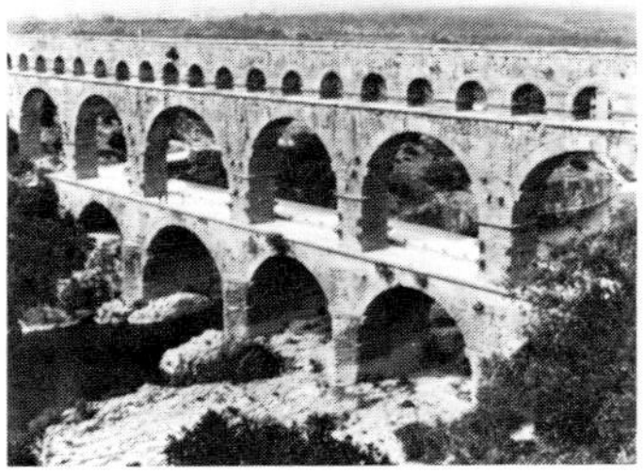

Aqueducts were a feature of Roman engineering; this is the Pont du Garde, Nîmes.

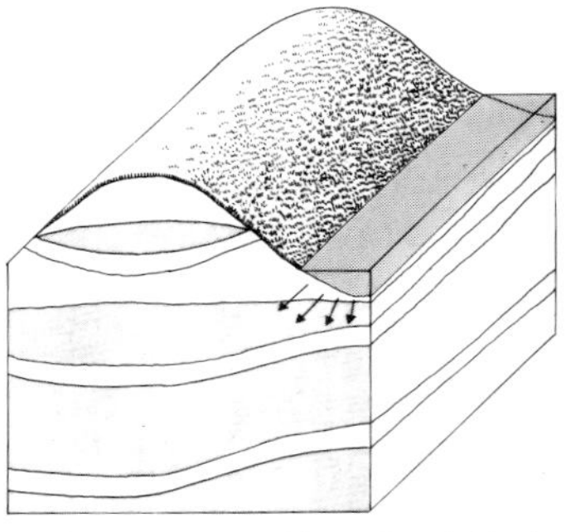

Aquifer, the geological formation vital in the provision of domestic water supply.

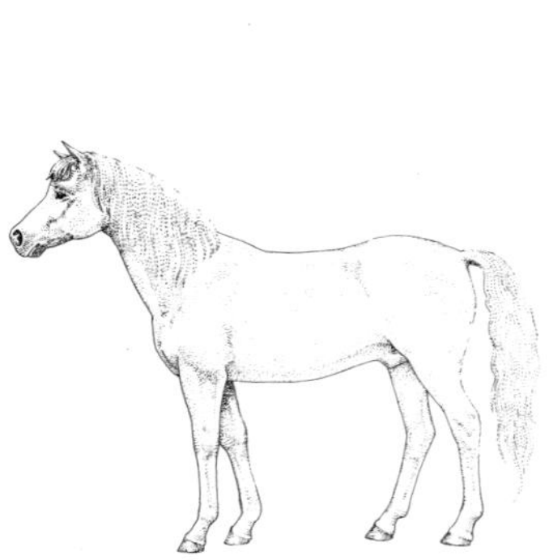

Arab horse, a slender, short-backed breed noted for their intelligence, grace and speed.

1965), British physicist. He was awarded the 1947 Nobel Prize in physics for the discovery of the Appleton layer of the IONOSPHERE. This layer reflects radio waves, and its discovery spurred the development of RADAR. *See also* MM p.229.

Applied art, use of artistic principles in objects in which art and utility are both considered. The term is generally used in distinction to fine art, such as painting and sculpture, which is judged chiefly in aesthetic terms, although the line between the two is sometimes hard to define. Examples of applied art are the design of a manufactured item, such as pottery, glass, furniture, jewellery and clothing. Illustration and graphic design are also applied arts. *See also* BAUHAUS.

Applied mathematics, application of mathematical tools in science or engineering. More generally, it is a body of knowledge and theory with a mathematical structure including the abstract entities and formal rules of "pure" MATHEMATICS together with physical measurable quantities and physical laws. It includes mechanics, statistics and relativity theory. *See also* SU pp.56–57; 106–107.

Applied psychology, use of psychological theory and techniques in problems of everyday life as diverse as industrial relations, military training, aircraft design, teaching, vocational guidance and mental health. An important task involves the determination of character traits and likely responses to given situations. *See also* MS pp.146–147, 150–151, 188–189, 288–289, 304–305.

Appliqué. *See* EMBROIDERY.

Appomattox Court House National Historical Park, area in Virginia, USA, 130km (80 miles) W of Richmond; it was established in 1954 on the site of the Confederate surrender by Gen. Robert E. LEE to the Union army under Gen. Ulysses S. GRANT (1865). The park has a restoration of the McLean house where Grant and Lee signed the terms of surrender.

Appreciation, in economics, increase in the market value of an asset. It is usually not the result of any activity on the part of the current owner: a house may appreciate in value regardless of any improvements made or not made.

Apprenticeship, term of practical instruction in a craft or trade, usually over several years. Known since ancient times, the practice became highly organized in medieval Europe under the supervision of the GUILDS. Today government-regulated apprenticeship schemes are sponsored by trade unions and professional organizations. *See also* MS p.307.

Approved school, in Britain, school for delinquent children that had been approved by the Home Secretary under the Children and Young Persons Acts (1933–1963). In 1969, under a new Children and Young Persons Act, approved schools were discontinued in favour of community homes.

Après-Midi d'un Faune, L' (1876), poem by Stéphane MALLARMÉ which inspired a piece of music by Achille-Claude DEBUSSY (1894). Vaslav NIJINSKY choreographed a ballet of the same name (1912), using Debussy's music.

Apricot, tree cultivated throughout temperate regions, which botanists believe originated in China. The large, spreading tree with dark green leaves and white blossoms bears yellow or yellowish-orange edible fruit, with a large stone. Species *Prunus armeniaca. See also* PE p.193.

April, fourth month of the year, having 30 days. Its name derives from the Latin *aperire*, "to open", either because it is the time when buds begin to open or because the ground in the Northern Hemisphere is then opened to receive seed. Until 153 BC *Aprilis* was the second month in the Roman calendar. In some countries 1 April is known as All Fool's Day and people play practical jokes on each other.

Apse, in architecture, a semicircular or polygonal space sometimes at the end of an aisle; in a church or temple it may be the place of a choir, an altar or statues.

Apsis (pl. apsides), either of the two points at the extremities of the major axis of the elliptical orbit of a planet, comet or satellite. Perihelion and aphelion are the apsides for a solar orbit.

Apterygiformes, order of birds that contains only the three living species of KIWIS. *See also* NW pp.*140*, *153*, 211.

Apterygota, sub-class of small, wingless insects, worldwide.

Apteryx. *See* KIWI.

Aptitude test, examination designed to predict how well a person is likely to perform a particular task or job. Scholastic aptitude tests assess academic abilities and performances. Vocational aptitude tests measure abilities and skills involved in specific occupations, and may be used in vocational counselling (to help people find jobs they can do well) and vocational selection (to help employers screen job applicants). *See also* MS pp.298–303.

Apuleius, Lucium (*c.*125–170), Roman author. His prose narrative *Metamorphoses* (or *The Golden Ass*) is the only classical Latin novel that has survived in its entirety. He also wrote philosophical treatises influenced by PLATO and Eastern mysticism. *See also* HC1 p.113.

Apulia (Puglia), region in SE Italy, composed of the provinces of Bari, Brindisi, Foggia, Lecce and Ionia; the capital is Bari. Colonized by the Greeks, it was conquered by the Romans in the 3rd century BC. It became part of Italy in 1861. Products: wheat, almonds, figs, tobacco, wine, salt. Area: 19,345sq km (7,470sq miles). Pop. (1971) 3,582,787.

Aqaba, only seaport of Jordan, at the head of the Gulf of Aqaba, on the NE end of the Red Sea. Once a strong Roman military post, it was an important part of medieval Palestine. In 1917 it was captured from Turkey by T.E. LAWRENCE, and ceded to Jordan in 1925. Pop. 10,000.

Aquaculture. *See* FISH FARMING.

Aquae Sulis. *See* BATH.

Aqualung, breathing apparatus for skin-divers comprising a cylinder of compressed air or oxygen and helium which supplies these gases to the diver through a valve and a flexible tube ending in a mouthpiece. A harness attaches the cylinder to the diver's back. *See also* SCUBA DIVING; PE p.*92*.

Aquaplaning, water sport, similar to WATER SKIING in that the rider is towed by a power-driven boat. In aquaplaning the rider places both feet on a board usually 1.68 by 0.76m (5.5 by 2.5ft), weighing 9–32kg (20–70lb), and slightly raised at the front. The rider achieves balance by holding two hand ropes fastened to each side of the bow of the aquaplane, and can travel at speeds of up to 100km/h (62mph). Aquaplaning originated in Florida in 1914, some eight years before water skiing.

Aqua regia, mixture of concentrated nitric and hydrochloric acids. Its Latin name means "royal water" and was given because the acid dissolves the "royal" metal gold. *See also* SU p.32.

Aquarium, tank, pond or building in which aquatic animals, usually fish, are held in captivity in fresh or salt water. Aquaria may be used for scientific research or for public or home entertainment. Fish were kept in captivity in Sumeria as early as 2500 BC, and the ancient Romans kept marine fish in large pools connected to the sea. The first indoor aquaria were developed by Chinese of the Sung Dynasty (960–1279), who kept goldfish in porcelain vessels. A UK aquarium may have minnows, sticklebacks, goldfish, axolotls and water-snails, together with a variety of useful aerating water plants. TROPICAL FISH require special care and conditions.

Aquarius, or the Water-bearer, equatorial constellation situated on the ecliptic between Capricornus and Pisces; the eleventh sign of the Zodiac. It contains the Saturn Nebula (NGC 7009), the globular cluster M2 (NGC 7089) and the Helix Nebula (NGC 7293). The brightest star is Beta Aquarii. *See also* MS p.200; SU pp.254, 262.

Aquatint, method of engraving on copper to produce transparent tones. The copper plate, etched by acid through a porous ground of granulated resin, becomes textured and produces a speckled tone when printed. *See also* PRINTMAKING.

Aquaviva (Acquaviva), Claudio (1543–1615), general of the Jesuits, who drew up a practical code of education.

Aqueduct, artificial channel or conduit, often an elevated masonry or brick structure, for conveying water from source to destination. Among ancient examples there exist traces of aqueducts built in Assyria and Egypt. The Greeks also built conduits. The most ambitious aqueducts in the classical period were built by the Romans. *See also* MM pp.197, 200, 202.

Aqueous humour, watery fluid that fills the eyeball between the lens and the CORNEA. It serves a double purpose: to nourish the eyeball and to refract, or bend, light rays, so helping them to focus on the RETINA. *See also* VITREOUS HUMOUR; MS pp.48–49.

Aquifer, rock, usually sandstone or limestone, which because of its porosity and permeability is capable of both storing and transmitting water. Much of the world depends for its water supply on aquifers, which may be exploited directly by sinking wells or by pumping the water into a reservoir. *See also* PE pp.*108–109*.

Aquilegia. *See* COLUMBINE.

Aquinas, Saint Thomas (1225–74), Roman Catholic theologian and philosopher. He played a leading part in the 13th-century movement of SCHOLASTICISM. Aquinas joined the Dominican Order and followed the Aristotelian ALBERTUS MAGNUS to Paris in 1245. Thereafter Thomas refused ecclesiastical positions in order to preach and work on his most important treatise, *Summa Universae Theologica* (1266–73). Reconciling Aristotelianism with Christian theology, he argued that revelation could not conflict with reason, and while separate, both rested on the one absolute Truth – the existence of God. He provided five proofs of God's existence. He was canonized in 1323. *See also* HC1 pp.188–189; MS pp.230, *230–233*.

Aquitaine, historical region in SW France, named after a Celtic tribe, the Aquitani, and called Aquitania by the Romans. It became an integral part of the Roman Empire in 56 BC and included all the land between the Pyrenees and the Garonne. Independent for a time during the early Middle Ages, it became part of France and then England. In the early 13th century all but the southern part (Gascony) was returned to France; the rest was returned in 1453. *See also* HC1 pp.212–213.

Arab, peoples of many nationalities found predominantly in the Middle East and North Africa, who share a common heritage in the religion of Islam and their language (Arabic). Most Arabs are either agriculturalists or city dwellers; the remainder practise pastoralism, raising camels, sheep and goats. The patriarchal family is the basic social unit in a strongly traditional culture that has been little affected by external influences, although wealth from oil is bringing rapid modernization. *See also* HC1 pp.144–145, 148–153, 170–171, 220–221; HC2 pp.190–191, 296–297; MS pp.136, 201, 223, *240*, 244–245; SU pp.22–24, 31.

Arab Emirates, Union of, also known as the United Arab Emirates, federation of seven states on the Persian Gulf. Its capital is ABU DHABI. The land is mostly desert and oil production is central to the state's economy. *See* MW p.173.

Arab horse, horse bred in Arabia before the 7th century AD and the first to be developed for endurance and speed. It was used as parental stock for many later breeds. Its coat is bay, chestnut, grey or brown. Height: 1.4–1.5m (4.6–5ft) at the shoulder.

Arabia, peninsular region of SW Asia bordered by the Persian Gulf (to the E), the Arabian Sea (S), the Syrian Desert (N) and the Red Sea (W). It was unified by the Muslims in the 7th century and dominated by Ottoman Turks after 1517. Hussein led a successful revolt against the Turks and founded an independent state in the Hejaz region in 1916, but the Saud family defeated Hussein in a violent siege and founded Saudi Arabia in 1925. Britain

had protectorates there, but after WWII British influence declined greatly and Arab nations have become increasingly independent. Area: approx. 2,600,000sq km (1,000,000sq miles) Pop. approx. 20,000,000. *See also* MW pp.100, 101, 116, 149, 173.
Arabian Nights, The, (*A Thousand and One Nights*), originally called Alf Laylah Wa Laylah. Of a variety of origins – Arab legends, Indian and Persian fairy tales and Egyptian love stories – the tales were compiled in written form from oral tradition as long ago as the 15th century in the colloquial Arabic language.
Arabian Sea, NW arm of the Indian Ocean, bordered by Somalia and the Arabian Peninsula (W), Pakistan (N), India (E) and the Indian Ocean (S). In the NW, the Gulf of Aden links it to the Red Sea, and the Gulf of Oman links it to the Persian Gulf. The River Indus is the only major river with an outlet into the Arabian Sea. Medieval trade routes between Arab kingdoms and the Chinese Empire passed through the Arabian Sea and the Persian Gulf. Area: 3,108sq km (1,200sq miles).
Arabic, Semitic language. Classical Arabic is the language of the Muslim scriptures, the KORAN. With many colloquial variations, the written form is understood in all Muslim countries across northern Africa to Iraq. Originating in the Arabian Peninsula, it spread with Islamic conquests in the 7th and 8th centuries. It is estimated that 100 million people now speak Arabic. *See also* MS p.240.
Arabic numeral, any of the common notations 0 to 9. *See* NUMERAL; SU p.30.
Arabis, or rock cress. flowering plant found growing on sand dunes, belonging to the Cruciferae (wallflower family). Cultivated species are used in rock gardens.
Arab-Israeli Wars (1948–49, 1956, 1967, 1973–74), conflicts between Israel and the Arab states. After being established in 1945 Israel made substantial gains from the Palestinians; Israeli independence (14 May 1948) saw troops from Egypt, Iraq, Lebanon, Syria and Transjordan (modern Jordan) invade the country. Initial Arab gains were halted and armistices arranged at Rhodes (Jan.–July 1949). UN security forces upheld the truce until Oct. 1956 when Israeli forces under DAYAN attacked the SINAI PENINSULA, supported a few days later by France and Britain, alarmed at the nationalization of the SUEZ CANAL. International opinion forced a ceasefire in Nov. when Israel surrendered gains after being guaranteed access to the Gulf of AQABA. In 1967 guerrilla raids led to an Israeli mobilization. In the ensuing SIX DAYS WAR, Israel captured Sinai, the GOLAN HEIGHTS on the Syrian border and the Old City of JERUSALEM. In 1973, after intermittent hostilities, the Arabs again began to prepare for war; Egyptian and Syrian forces invaded on 6 Oct. 1973, on Yom Kippur, a Jewish holiday. Israel pushed back their advance after severe losses. Disengagement talks began on 26 Dec. but fighting continued until 1974. *See also* HC2 p.296; MW pp.68, 107, 114, 117.
Arab League, organization formed in 1945 to give a collective political voice to the Arab nations. Its members include Egypt, Syria, Lebanon, Iraq, Jordan, Sudan, Algeria, Kuwait, Saudi Arabia, Libya, Morocco, Tunisia, Yemen, People's Democratic Republic of Yemen, Qatar and the United Arab Emirates. Its main sphere of activity is economic: in 1953 it set up an Arab Telecommunications Union, in 1954 a postal union was organized and in 1959 a financial organization (Arab Bank) was developed. The Arab Common Market was formed in 1965 and is open to all members. Political unity has been hampered by divisions over attitudes to the Western nations.
Arachnid, arthropod (animal with jointed limbs) of the class Arachnida, which includes SPIDERS, TICKS, MITES, SCORPIONS and HARVESTMEN. Arachnids have four pairs of jointed legs, two distinct body segments (cephalothorax and abdomen) and chelicerate jaws (consisting of clawed pincers). They lack antennae and wings. *See* NW pp.102–104.
Arad, city in W Romania, 420km (265 miles) NW of Bucharest, on the River Muresul. It passed from Turkish, to Austrian then to Hungarian rule (1699). In 1849 Hungarians used the city as their headquarters for the revolt against the Hapsburg empire. Arad, which became part of Romania in 1919, has the state theatre, a philharmonic orchestra, a museum and an 18th-century citadel. Industries: engineering, electrical equipment, textiles, distilling. Pop. 146,000.
Arafat, Yasir (1929–), leader of the Palestine Liberation Organization (PLO), one of the first Palestinians to advocate guerrilla war against Israel. In 1974 the PLO was recognized by Arab leaders as the "sole legitimate representative of the Palestinian people." *See also* HC2 p.299.
Arafura Sea, shallow stretch of water between Arnhem Land, the N central promontory of Australia, and New Guinea. It contains several Indonesian island groups. The dangerous Torres Strait at the E end links it with the Coral Sea. Area: approx. 650,000sq km (250,000sq miles).
Aragon, Louis (1897–), French novelist, poet and essayist. A founder of the Surrealist movement with the review *Littérature* (1919), Aragon advocated "automatic writing". Early poetry includes *Feu de Joie* (1920). He visited Russia in 1930, became a Communist, and turned to social realism and the dissemination of Soviet literature. Later works include a series of novels *Le monde réel* (1933–42), the autobiographical novel *Blanche ou l'oublie* (1967) and a two-volume novel about the life of the painter Henri MATISSE (1971).
Aragón, region in NE Spain, bordered by the Pyrenean mountains (to the N), the Iberian mountains (S), Catalonia (E), and Old Castile (W); formerly part of the ancient Roman province of Hispania Tarraconensis. In 1479 the Kingdom of Aragón became part of Spain, but retained its own government, currency and military forces until the early 18th century. It is an agricultural region producing grapes, wheat and sugar-beet. Industries: textiles, chemicals, iron ore, marble and limestone. Area: 47,670sq km (18,500sq miles). Pop. 1,152,700.
Arakan Coast District, division of W Burma, extending along the coast of the Bay of Bengal and bordered in the E by the Arakan Yoma range. The capital is Sittwe. Products: tobacco, rice. Area: approx. 36,500sq km (14,000sq miles). Pop. (1971) 1,847,000.
Aral Sea (Aralskoye More), formerly Lake Aral, inland sea in the USSR, central Asia. The world's fourth largest inland body of water, it has no outlet, contains many small islands, and is fed by the rivers Syrdarja in the NE and Amudarja in the S. It is generally shallow and only slightly saline, indicating its geologically recent separation from the Caspian Sea 400km (250 miles) to the E. The shores are sparsely populated, mostly in the NE in the Aralsk and Novokzalinsk areas. Area: 68,681sq km (26,518sq miles).
Aramaeans, North Semitic people who lived in Aram and northern Syria from the 11th to the 8th century BC. They were incorporated into the New Babylonian, or Chaldean, empire by the 8th century.
Aramaic, Biblical Semitic language, the original language of parts of the Old Testament. After the Babylonian captivity, it was the common written and spoken language of the Middle East until replaced by ARABIC. Minor dialects still persist today in parts of the Near and Middle East. *See also* MS pp.244, *245*.
Aran Islands, group of small islands off the W coast of Northern Ireland at the entrance to Galway Bay; the chief islands are Inishmore, Inishmaan and Inisheer. They are of pre-Christian archaeological interest. Area: 47sq km (18sq miles). Pop. 2,270.
Aranda. *See* ARUNTA.
Arany, János (1817–82), Hungarian epic poet. He was secretary of the Hungarian Academy (1865–79) and wrote many ballads and lyrics. His best-known work was an epic trilogy on the life of the hero Toldi (written 1846–79).
Ara Pacis (9 BC), Roman Altar of Peace, whose rich bas-relief carvings provide a contemporary picture of the era of AUGUSTUS. *See also* HC1 p.*106*.
Ararat, town in Victoria, Australia, at the foot of Mt Ararat, 177km (110 miles) WNW of Melbourne. Industries: textiles, wine. Pop. 8,300.
Araucanian, independent language family of South American Indians who live in Chile and Argentina. A loose confederation of Araucanian-speaking sub-tribes including the Picunche, Mapuche and Huilliche, they offered strong resistance to the Spanish invasion under Diego de ALMAGRO in 1536 and were never completely conquered, although Pedro de Valdivia set up a Spanish province in 1541. They drove the Spaniards back to the Bio-Bio River in 1598 and retained possession of interior portions of Chile to the present time. Their descendants prefer the name Mapuche, meaning "land people". The population has declined from approximately 1 million in the 16th century to about 300,000 today.
Araucaria, genus of evergreen trees native to the Southern Hemisphere. They have scale-like leaves and seed-bearing cones. Family Araucariaceae. *See also* MONKEY PUZZLE; NORFOLK ISLAND PINE; NW p.*228*.
Arawak, the largest and most widely spread South American Indian language family, at one time spoken from the Caribbean to the Gran Chaco. Some 40 Arawak tribes remain in Brazil today.
Arbitration, submission by disputing parties to a ruling made by an arbiter chosen by them to decide between them. In some countries such rulings or decisions may be enforced by the government. Arbitration is a procedure most commonly used in commercial and industrial disputes, although it may be employed to settle international disagreements – often before the United Nations International Court of Justice, based at The Hague, Netherlands. Arbitration was practised in the Middle Ages when high ecclesiastical authorities were called upon to settle controversies. *See also* MS p.*285*.
Arblay, Frances d'. *See* BURNEY, FRANCES.
Arbor Day, day celebrated by the planting of trees, usually by school children. First suggested by the US politician Julius Sterling Morton in 1872, Arbor Day occurs at different times throughout the USA because of varying planting seasons.
Arbor vitae, common name for six species of trees or shrubs of the genus *Thuja*, resinous, evergreen conifers of the cypress family native to North America and E Asia. They have thin outer bark, fibrous inner bark, and characteristically flattened branches. Family Cupressaceae.
Arbroath, town and seaport of E Tayside region, E Scotland; it is a tourist resort. Industries: fishing and engineering. Pop. 22,600.
Arbuckle, Roscoe ("Fatty") (1887–1933), US star and director of silent films who starred in Mack SENNET Keystone Comedies (1913), and became an actor-director in 1914. He later appeared in short films with Charles CHAPLIN and Buster KEATON. Charged with manslaughter over the death of a model (1920), he was acquitted (1922), but his career was ruined.
Arbuthnot, John (1667–1735), court physician to Queen ANNE from 1705 to 1714 and TORY satirist, famous for his *John Bull* pamphlets (1712). He was a member of the Scribblers Club.
Arbutus, genus of evergreen trees and tall shrubs native to the Mediterranean region and W North America. They have dark green, glossy leaves and reddish brown bark. The urn-shaped flowers are white or pink, and the strawberry-like fruit is red or orange. Family Ericaceae.
Arc, geometric, portion of a curve. For a circle, the length (s) of an arc is the product of the angle (θ) it subtends at the centre, measured in RADIANS, and the radius (r): that is $s = r\theta$.
Arcadia, ancient region in Peloponnesus, Greece, completely surrounded by mountains. The chief city, Megalopolis, was founded *c.* 370 BC. It became the centre of political activity and the capital of the Arcadian Confederacy, although by the

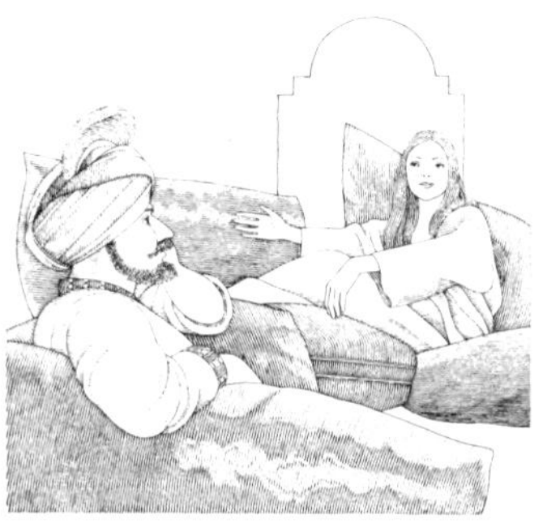
The Arabian Nights includes the tale of the sultan and Scheherazade, the story teller.

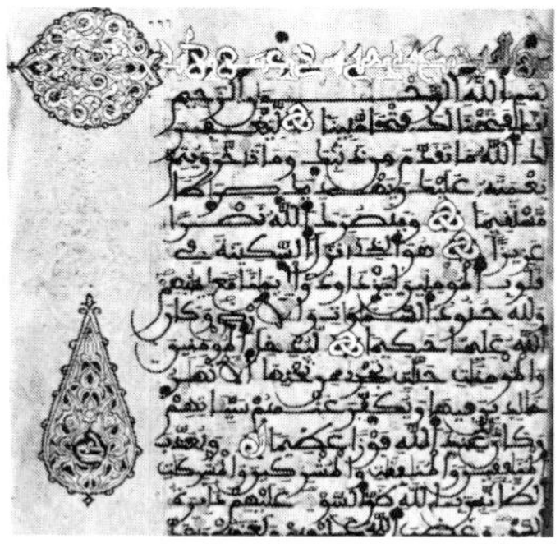
Arabic's 28 consonants read from right to left; the vowels are marked above and below.

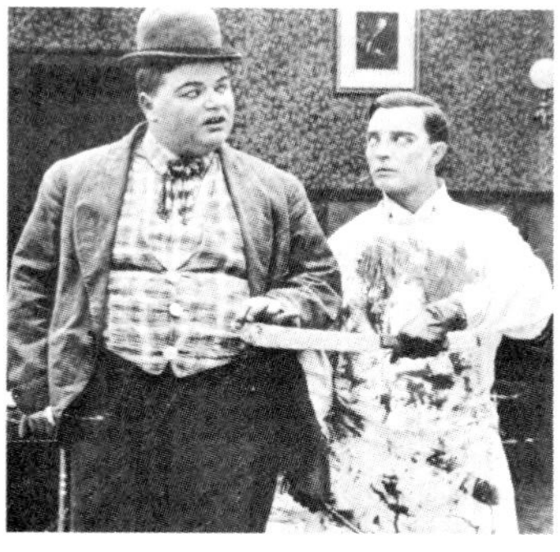
Fatty Arbuckle, seen here with Buster Keaton in a scene from *Good Night Nurse* (1918).

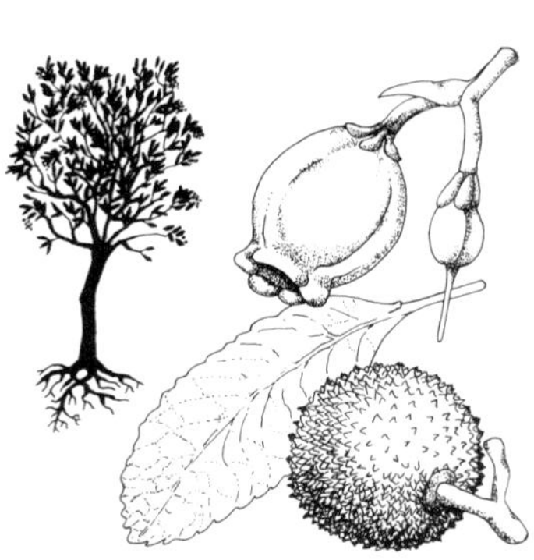
Arbutus is a member of the heath family; best-known is the strawberry tree (*A. unedo*).

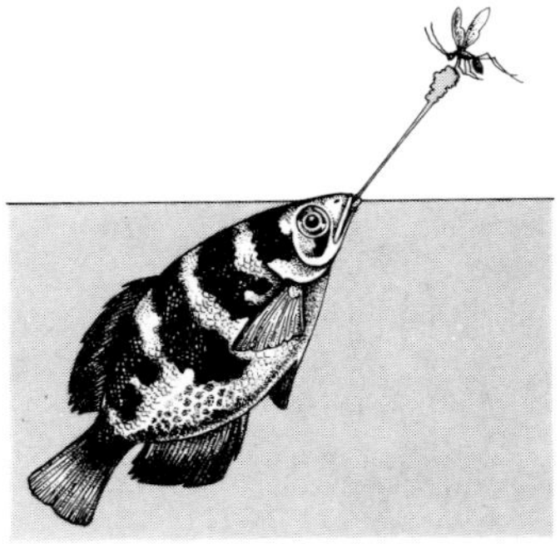

Archer fish catch flying insects by knocking them down with a forceful spit.

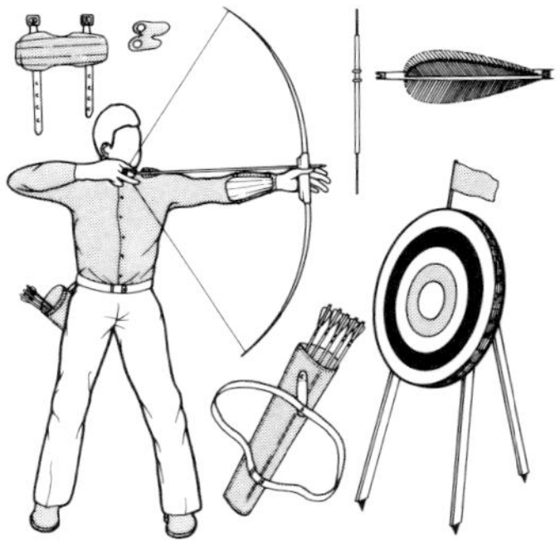

Archery, originally used in hunting and waging war, is nowadays an international sport.

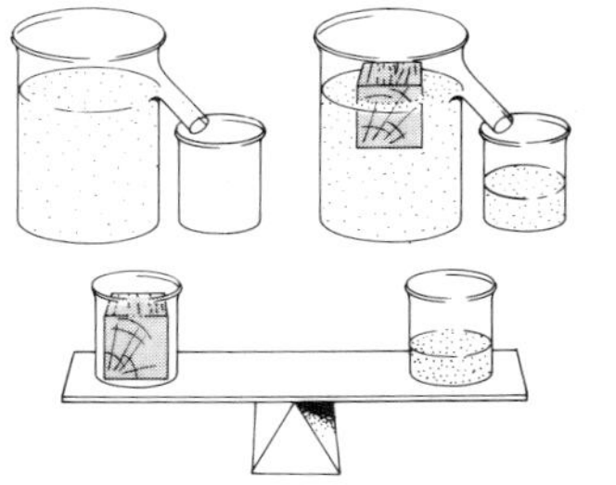

Archimedes discovered that a floating body displaces an equal weight of water.

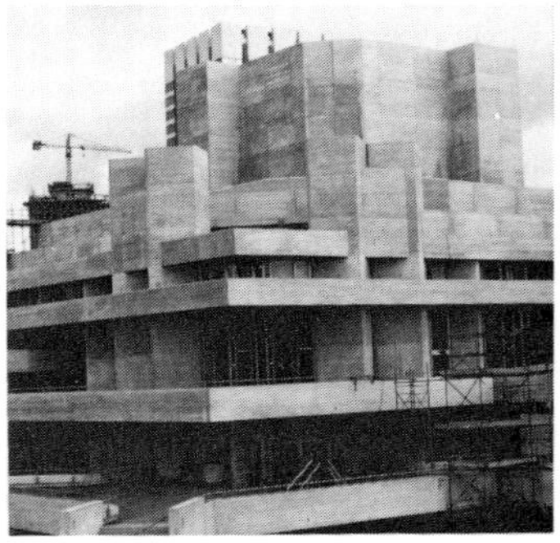

Architecture; the recently completed National Theatre, London.

end of the 2nd century AD it was in ruins.

Arcadia (1504), pastoral romance by Jacopo SANNAZZARO, consisting of 12 verse eclogues interspersed with 12 prose narratives. It influenced many authors, including Tasso, SIDNEY, SPENSER and CERVANTES. Dignified and musical in style, it is noted for the principal, autobiographical character, Sincero.

Arcadia, pastoral romance (1590) by Sir Philip SIDNEY. It consists of prose tales interspersed with verse and was intended to teach morals as well as to entertain. Three versions exist, two by Sidney and one with alterations by the Countess of Pembroke, his sister.

Arc de Triomphe, commemorative monument in Paris begun in 1806 by NAPOLEON to celebrate his victories. Completed in 1836, it still stands in the Place Charles de Gaulle, at the western end of the Champs-Élysées.

Arch, Joseph (1826–1919), British Methodist preacher and politician. In 1872 he founded the National Agricultural Labourers Union and was its first president. He was an MP in 1885–86 and 1892–1902, one of the first representatives of labour at Westminster.

Arch, in construction, curved self-supporting structure used to support a load, such as a bridge or a ceiling. A stone arch is made from wedge-shaped stones to prevent slip, and achieves its stability only after the keystone (the top-most and largest stone) is in position. The weight of each stone and the load they bear are essential for the arch's stability. The weight being supported is transmitted through adjacent stones to points called imposts on the vertical supports. Modern arches are made from steel or reinforced concrete units. *See also* MM pp.190–193.

Archaean, precambrian geological period. It ended 570 million years ago at the beginning of the Palaeozoic. *See also* PE pp.130–131.

Archaeology, scientific study of former human life and activities through material remains (fossils, artefacts and buildings). An archaeologist's work includes: excavation and retrieval of remains from the ground or sea-bed; recording and interpreting the circumstances in which objects were found (such as their level in the soil and association with other objects); thorough examination and description of their finds; and hence the building up of a picture of the culture that produced the objects. In the study of cultures that developed the art of writing, written remains supplement other material, but archaeology increasingly relies on the aid of various scientific techniques to increase knowledge about the past. *See also* HC1 pp.20–23; MS pp.20–31.

Archaeopteryx, first known bird. About the size of a crow and fully feathered, its fossilized skeleton is more like that of a reptile than a modern bird, and its beak had pronounced jaws with teeth. It was probably capable only of weak, flapping flight. *See* NW pp.*24*, 185, 186.

Archangel, superior angel. The archangels Michael, Raphael, Gabriel and Uriel stand on all sides of God's throne.

Archangel (Archangel'sk), city and port in NW USSR, at the head of the Dvina Gulf and the northern Dvina delta. During the winter icebreakers have to keep the large harbour clear. It was originally settled in the 10th century by Norsemen, but founded officially as Novo-Kholmogory in 1583. The city was opened to European trade in *c.*1600 by Boris Godunov, and it prospered as Russia's only port until 1703. The monastery of Archangel Michael was built there between 1685 and 1699. The port received Allied convoys during WWII. Industries: shipbuilding, timber, wood pulp, paper. Pop. 376,000.

Archbishop, chief bishop or metropolitan of an ecclesiastical province or archdiocese. *See also* BISHOP.

Archdeacon, in the Roman Catholic and Anglican Churches, a high-ranking diocesan official with many administrative responsibilities.

Archer, Fred (1857–86), British jockey. In 8,084 races he rode 2,748 winners, including 21 classics; he was a champion jockey for 13 consecutive seasons. He committed suicide when only 29, at the peak of his career.

Archer, William (1856–1924), British theatre critic and dramatist whose best-known play was *The Green Goddess* (1921). His translation of Ibsen's *Samfundets Støtter,* performed in London as *The Pillars of Society* (1880), occasioned much critical hostility.

Archer fish, fish found in brackish waters of SE Asia and Australia. It is yellowish-green to brown with dark markings, and catches insect prey by spitting water "bullets". Length: up to 20cm (8in). Family Toxotidae; five species include *Tdoxotes chatareus. See also* NW p.*131.*

Archery, sport that makes use of a bow and arrow. Archers try to accumulate points by shooting a specified number of arrows at a target that consists of five concentric circles, the innermost circle being the "gold". Other than target-shooting, the three other divisions of archery are field, flight and cross-bow. Archery was the prime military weapon used before the advent of gunpowder and was revived as a sport in England in 1676 by Charles II. Its popularity grew after the Grand National Archery Association, the sport's first governing body, was formed in England in 1861. *See also* MS p.*304.*

Archetype, in the psychology of Carl JUNG, primordial symbol or idea present in the "collective unconscious" and inherited from ancestors. Archetypes occur in dreams, myths, religion, art and fairy tales. The term is often used in literary criticism to describe archetypal characters, such as Mother or Hero, and archetypal situations such as Birth or Rites of Passage. *See also* MS p.*148.*

Archilochus (7th century BC), Greek poet. Fragments of his intense, personal lyrics still survive. He is considered to be the first Greek poet to write about individual experiences and emotions.

Archimedes (287–212 BC), Greek mathematician and engineer. He developed a method for expressing large numbers and made outstanding discoveries about the determination of areas and volumes, which led to a new accurate method of measuring π (pi). In his work *On Floating Bodies* he enunciated "The Principle of Archimedes", which states that a body in a fluid is buoyed up by a force equal to the weight of the fluid it displaces. An Archimedian screw is a machine used for raising water, thought to have been invented by Archimedes. It consists of a cylindrical pipe enclosing a revolving helix, with its lower end in the water. *See also* SU pp.20, 78, 86.

Archipelago, name given either to a region of ocean where many islands are clustered, or to the islands themselves.

Archipenko, Alexander (1887–1964), Russian-American sculptor, one of the first in the CUBIST style, which he later rejected in favour of abstract sculpture. His use of hollows to complement mass in depicting the human form, as in *Walking Woman* (1912), has influenced many sculptors. His many innovations have included the collage sculpture (using wood, glass, metal, etc.).

Architecture, art and science of building and an indication of a civilization's beliefs and ideas at a given time. The development of architectural style and expertise can be traced through extant examples, which serve as visual evidence of the progress of man. Architecture in its earliest form occurred in ancient Egypt and Mesopotamia, where the impulse to build was heightened by powerful dynastic and religious motivations.

Until the 20th century there were three major structural systems: the TRABEATE system, employing horizontal beams and vertical posts; the ARCH (and its developments, the VAULT and DOME); and the steel-frame system of the late 19th century. Trabeate architecture in its earliest related form is evident in Egypt's tombs (mastabas) erected before 3000 BC, and in the brick temples and palaces of the same period built by the Babylonians and Assyrians, who also constructed brick vaulted roofs. Greek temple architecture (7th–4th centuries BC) represents the trabeate system at its most perfect in proportion and subtle in detail.

The Romans combined the trabeate system and the round arch, and erected a wide variety of buildings (temples, theatres, amphitheatres, aquaducts, baths, etc.) throughout their empire. The development and extensive use of concrete enabled them to span vast areas with vaulting and to develop the dome, seen at its most impressive in the PANTHEON, Rome (AD 120). The Romans and early Christians, like the Greeks, also used wooden truss roofing in their basilican halls and churches (essentially a development of the Greek temple).

The Byzantines perfected the PENDENTIVE, which they employed so brilliantly in the dome of HAGIA SOPHIA, Constantinople. Dating from the late 9th century Romanesque architecture was characterized by massive arches and vaults of finely cut stone. Early GOTHIC architecture introduced the pointed arch (hitherto used only in Muslim building) and BUTTRESS, making the possibilities endless for taller buildings with higher vaults and windows. Gothic as a consistent style began in France *c.*1140 with the cathedrals of St Denis, Notre Dame de Paris, Amiens and Chartres. It predominated in Western Europe until the rise of RENAISSANCE architecture in the 15th century. This heralded a period of nearly five hundred years during which no major structural innovations emerged, although the forms of Antiquity (first Roman and later Greek) were revived and presented in countless permutations and styles, including MANNERIST, BAROQUE, ROCOCO and GEORGIAN. This eclecticism continued into the first half of the 19th century with NEO-CLASSICISM and the GOTHIC REVIVAL.

By mid-century architects, tiring of the long imitation of historic styles and confronted with the demands of a society being rapidly transformed by technology, industry and speed, searched for new aesthetic and structural forms. A landmark was the use of prefabricated iron and glass, notably in the CRYSTAL PALACE (1851), which inspired the great railway terminals of the era. The last great technical breakthrough of the century occurred in the 1880s in the USA with the development by W. JENNEY, H.H. RICHARDSON, BURNHAM and ROOT and Louis SULLIVAN of the steel-frame multi-storey building – ancestor of the modern SKYSCRAPER. In the 20th century this was exploited in the USA by MIES VAN DER ROHE, Frank Lloyd WRIGHT and others. Further inventions, such as reinforced concrete and pre-stressed concrete, were employed to create new forms. Distinguished European pioneers included Walter GROPIUS and LE CORBUSIER, two of the most powerful and original influences of the century. In contemporary architecture, whether in flats on stilts or the GEODESIC domes of Buckminster FULLER, innovatory ideas and designs find expression in structures still built in response to the changing needs and functional requirements of society. *See also* articles under styles, eg ART NOUVEAU; individual architects, eg Andrea PALLADIO; structural elements, eg BASILICA, etc; and indexes of *History and Culture* volumes.

Architrave. *See* ENTABLATURE.

Archives, documentary materials accumulated and preserved for their historical and literary value. The concept of archives located independently from a LIBRARY reached full development during the French Revolution.

Arciniegas, Germán (1900–), Colombian writer, politician, diplomat and educator. The theme of liberalism permeates his essays, biographies and histories. He lived in exile in the USA from 1942 to 1960 teaching at Columbia University.

Arc-lamp, device in which light is produced by an electric arc between two electrodes. Many modern arc-lamps, used as sources of intense light, have metal and oxide electrodes immersed in a gas which becomes luminous during arcing.

Arcot, town in SE India, on the Palar

River, 105km (65 miles) W of Madras. It was ceded to the British by the French in 1801. It is an agricultural market town and the chief industry is textiles. Pop. 25,000.

Arctic, vast region of icy seas and cold lands around the North Pole, often defined as extending from the Pole to the Arctic Circle, latitude 66°30″N. In areas N of this latitude the sun does not set during the height of summer nor rise during the depths of winter. Other definitions place the S limit of the Arctic proper at the tree line, the northern boundary of forest growth, or make the limit the summer isotherm of 18°C (50°F). The more southerly areas are frequently referred to as the subarctic. At the centre of the Arctic is the Arctic Ocean, with its many seas and inlets. The Bering Strait gives access to the Pacific Ocean and the Greenland and Norwegian seas provide a connecting passage to the Atlantic that is some 1,600km (1,000 miles) across. The ocean's area is about 12,257,000sq km (4,732,400sq miles). In the region around the North Pole the waters of the Arctic are permanently covered with sheet ice or a floating mass of ice debris called the ice pack, but some parts of the ocean are frozen only in winter. When the ice starts to melt in the spring it disintegrates into floes and drifting pack ice. Icebergs have their origins in fresh water glaciers flowing into the ocean from the surrounding lands.

Lands and climate. Bordering the Arctic Ocean are the most northerly lands of Asia, Europe and North America. By far the greater part of the huge frozen island of Greenland lies N of the Arctic Circle. Five-sixths of Greenland's surface is always hidden by a thick ice-cap, although arctic lands generally have a summer that is free from ice and snow. Most of the arctic tundra is flat and marshy in summer but the subsoil is permanently frozen to a considerable depth. This frozen subsoil is called permafrost. For most of the year arctic temperatures are below freezing point. In spring the sun appears, and some arctic lands have sunshine every day from March or April to September.

Plant and animal life. Mosses and lichens are the characteristic tundra vegetation, but many other kinds of plants are found too: sedges, grasses and flowers. Several kinds of trees and woody shrubs grow, but almost always in a dwarfed form. The commonest trees are willow, alder and birch. When the winter snows melt in tundra areas, the vegetation bursts into life and colour. Tundra is found in the subarctic as well as in the more northerly latitudes, but many parts of the subarctic are covered in thick evergreen forests of fir, pine, spruce and larch. Coniferous forests of this kind, called taiga, stretch seemingly endlessly across Siberia. The name taiga is also used for subarctic forests in North America. Much of the animal life of the Arctic is made up of summer visitors that move in winter, but some mammals and birds have adapted to survive arctic conditions the whole year round. The commonest land mammals include polar bears, reindeer, arctic wolves, arctic foxes, caribou, lemmings, voles, ermines and martens; whales, walruses and seals live in the sea. Land and fresh water birds include ptarmigans, snowy owls, plovers and falcons. Among sea birds the commonest is the old squaw duck; others include auks, gulls, terns and petrels.

People. Despite the severity of the climate and the restricted food resources, many peoples live in the Arctic. The most scattered are the 60,000 or so ESKIMOS spread across polar North America, including Greenland and NE Siberia. Several culturally separate groups of people live in northern Siberia. They include the Chukchi of the Chukchi Peninsula, the Kamchadals of Kamchatka, the Yakuts and the Samoyeds. In the European part of the USSR there are the numerous Zyryans and in Lapland – northern Norway, Sweden and Finland – the Lapps. Most of these peoples follow ancient traditional patterns of life, but the discovery of great mineral wealth in arctic lands, especially in Alaska and the USSR, is already bringing change to their homelands. *See also* MW pp.45, 90, 170.

Arctic fox, also called white fox or polar fox, fox found on tundra or mountains of the Arctic. It changes in winter either from grey-brown to white or grey to grey-blue. Length: 50–60cm (20–24in).

Arctic tern, sea bird whose migrations are the longest of any bird – from summer breeding areas in the far north to wintering areas in Antarctica, a round trip of about 35,500km (22,000 miles). It has grey, black and white feathers and a reddish bill and feet. It nests in colonies and lays one to four eggs in a sandy scrape nest. Length: 38cm (15in). Species *Sterna paradisaea*. *See also* NW p.*142*.

Arcturus, or Alpha Boötis, red giant star in the constellation of Boötes. Characteristics: apparent mag. −0.06; absolute mag. −0.2; spectral type K2; distance 36 light-years. *See also* SU p.226.

Ardabīl, city in NW Iran, on the Qareh Sū River; near the USSR border. It has become important as the birthplace of Safi ad-Din (founder of the Safavid Order) and site of the Safavid Shrine visited by pilgrims. Products: carpets and cereals. Pop. 90,000.

Ardashir I, King of Persia (*c*.224–41). He overthrew the last Parthian king, Artabanus V, and re-united Persia. He founded the SASSANID dynasty and established ZOROASTRIANISM. He strengthened Persia by going to war against the Roman emperor, ALEXANDER SEVERUS.

Arden, Elizabeth (1884–1966), Canadian-born US cosmetic manufacturer. She founded, and gave her name to, an international organization of health farms and beauty salons. Her organization also manufactures a complete range of world-famous beauty products.

Arden, John (1930–), British playwright, whose plays, eg *The Waters of Babylon* (1957) and *Live Like Pigs* (1958), are often an exciting mixture of poetry, prose and Brechtian ballads, used to develop universal themes. *Serjeant Musgrave's Dance* (1959), produced throughout the world, is widely accepted as a masterpiece of modern British drama.

Ardennes (Forest of Ardennes), sparsely populated wooded plateau in SE Belgium, N Luxembourg and the Ardennes département of N France. The chief towns are Charleville-Mézières and Wiltz. It was the scene of heavy fighting in both world wars, notably in the Battle of the Bulge (Dec. 1944–Jan. 1945). In the well-preserved forest areas, wild game is abundant and cleared areas support arable and dairy farming.

Ardizzone, Edward (1900–), British artist and book illustrator of great individuality and author of children's books. He was an official war artist (1940–46).

Area, two-dimensional measurement of a plane figure or body (eg this page) given in square units, such as cm^2 or in^2. The area of a rectangle of sides a and b is ab, the areas of triangles and other polygons can be determined using TRIGONOMETRY. Areas of curved figures and surfaces can be determined by integral CALCULUS. *See also* SURFACE AREA; SU pp.32–33, 48.

Areca, genus of flowering plants, commonly known as palms. It includes the areca palm, *A. catechu*, from which edible BETEL nuts are obtained.

Arecibo radiotelescope. *See* RADIO TELESCOPE.

Arensky, Anton Stepanovich (1861–1906), Russian composer. He was professor of composition at the Moscow Conservatory and in 1895 became conductor of the Imperial Chapel Choir. He is best remembered for his chamber music and songs; he also wrote operas, including *Dream on the Volga* (1892).

Areola, in anatomy a small area of the body, such as the iris of the eye or the darkened bit around the nipple of a breast.

Areopagitica (1644), pamphlet by John MILTON giving the text of a speech in defence of freedom of the press. Under the Cromwellian Commonwealth in England books required a parliamentary licence before publication. Milton called this an affront to learning and noted the parallel between such licences and the censorship imposed by the Papacy during the Inquisition. *See also* HC1 p.*290*.

Arequipa, city in S Peru and capital of Arequipa department, which extends along the Cordillera Occidental and is bounded in the W by the Pacific Ocean. The city is a regional trade centre and the site of two universities founded in 1828 and 1961. It was established in 1540 by Francisco PIZARRO on the site of an INCA settlement. Pop. 194,700.

Ares, Greek god of war, identified by the Romans as MARS. He was the son of ZEUS and HERA and the lover of APHRODITE. Ares' activities consisted of making war and love. In the TROJAN WAR he sided with the Trojans, whose leader, Hector, received his personal protection. Among his offspring were Alcippe, Harmonia and Cycnus, who was slain by HERCULES. In art Ares is often represented as a stalwart figure with a helmet, shield and spear.

Aretaeus, respected Greek physician of the 1st century in Cappadocia. He also practised in Rome and Alexandria, and was a follower of the teachings of HIPPOCRATES. *See also* MS p.100.

Arête, sharp ridge, peak or horn formed by erosion where two glaciers meet. An example is the Matterhorn on the Swiss-Italian border. *See also* PE pp.*116*, 117.

Aretino, Pietro (1492–1556), Italian Renaissance satirist. Vigorous, bawdy, often scurrilous, his six volumes of letters (1537–57) and many other works vividly portray contemporary court society. He also wrote five comedies (1534–46).

Aretino. *See* SPINELLO, ARETINO.

Arezzo, city in central Italy; capital of Arezzo province in the Toscana region. As the former Etruscan town of Arretium, it became famous for Arretine red-clay vases. There are numerous 14th-century houses and palaces, an Etruscan museum and a cathedral (1286–1510). It is an agricultural, trade and transport centre. Industries: textiles and food processing. Pop. 81,800.

Argali, or arkal, wild SHEEP native to the highlands of central Asia. The largest of all sheep, the ram has large spiral horns often more than 1m (3.3ft) long. Height: 1.3m (4.3ft) at the shoulder; weight: 140kg (310lb). Family Bovidae; species *Ovis ammon*.

Argelander, Friedrich Wilhelm August (1799–1875), German astronomer who, in 1837, became director of the observatory at the University of Bonn. The positions and brightness of about 324,000 stars are recorded in his *Bonner Durchmusterung* (1862).

Argensola brothers, Bartolomé Leonardo de (1562–1631) and Lupercio Leonardo de (1559–1613), Spanish writers. Bartolomé's best-known work is *Conquista de las Islas Molucas* (1609); Lupercio's most famous plays are *Isabela* and *Alejandra*.

Argentina, second largest country in South America (after Brazil). Formerly a Spanish possession, it has been an independent republic since 1816. Since then Argentina has been disrupted by a series of political upheavals. It has a basically agricultural economy, with the export of beef the principal earner of foreign currency. Area: 2,776,889sq km (1,072,156sq miles). Pop. (1976 est.) 25,719,000. *See* MW p.28.

Argentine Confederation, the establishment of modern Argentina by the Republican Constitution of 1853. The province of Buenos Aires at first refused to join, but was incorporated by force of arms and became the seat of government.

Arghezi, Tudor (1880–1967), real name Ion N Theodorescu, Romanian writer. He won the National Poetry Prize in 1947. His poetry includes *Cărticică de seară* (1935) and *Hore* (1939). His first two novels (1930) were *Icoane de lemn* and *Poarta neagră*.

Argon, monatomic gaseous element (Ar) of the noble gas group, discovered (1894) in air by Lord Rayleigh and Sir William Ramsay. Of the argon in the atmosphere (0.93% by volume), 99.6% is $argon^{40}$; the remainder is $argon^{36}$ (0.34%) and $argon^{38}$ (0.06%). It is obtained commercially by the fractionation of liquid air and is used in electric light bulbs, fluorescent tubes, arc

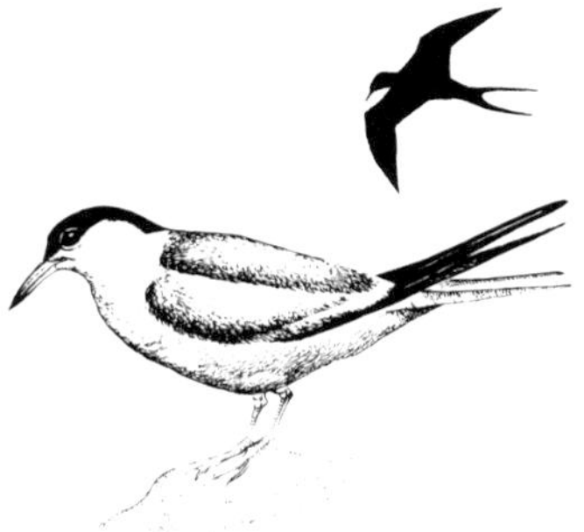

Arctic terns are renowned for their annual migration from Arctic regions to Antarctica.

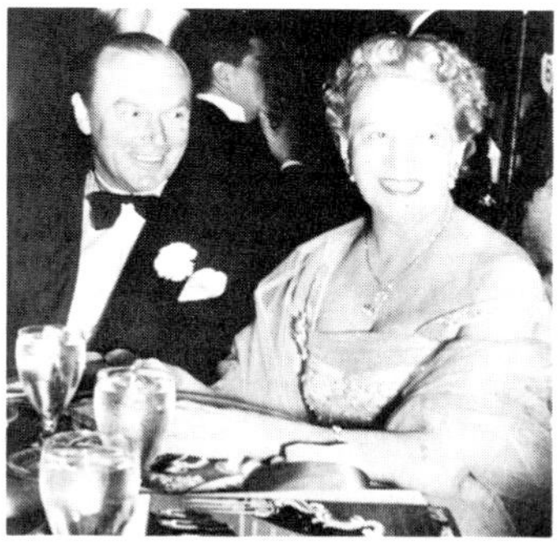

Elizabeth Arden, the beauty expert, seen here dining with Count Michael Rienwski.

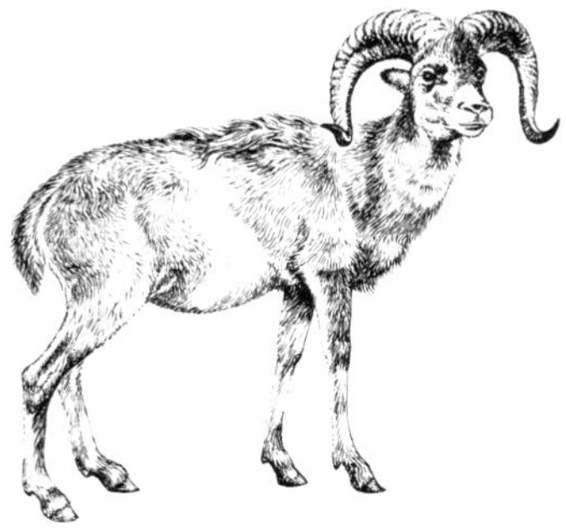

Argali sheep, the largest of all breeds, have impressive horns and inhabit mountains.

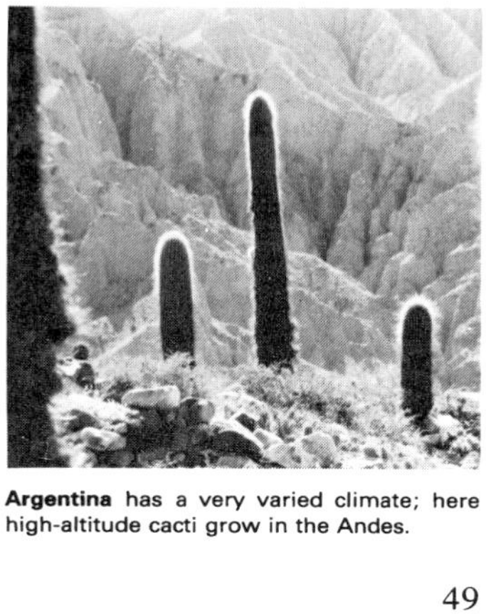

Argentina has a very varied climate; here high-altitude cacti grow in the Andes.

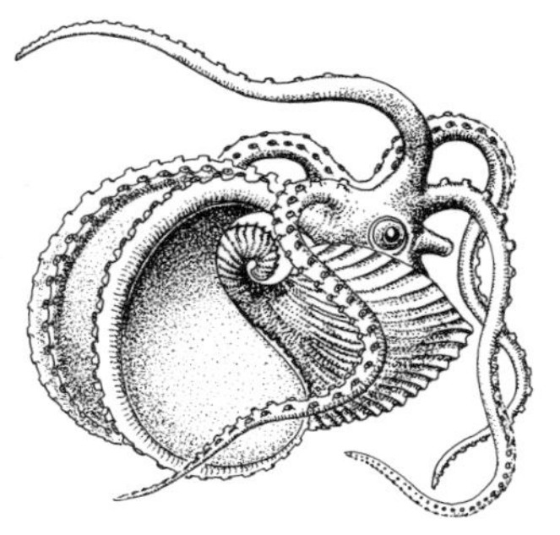
Argonauts, or paper nautiluses, live in warm seas; females are much larger than males.

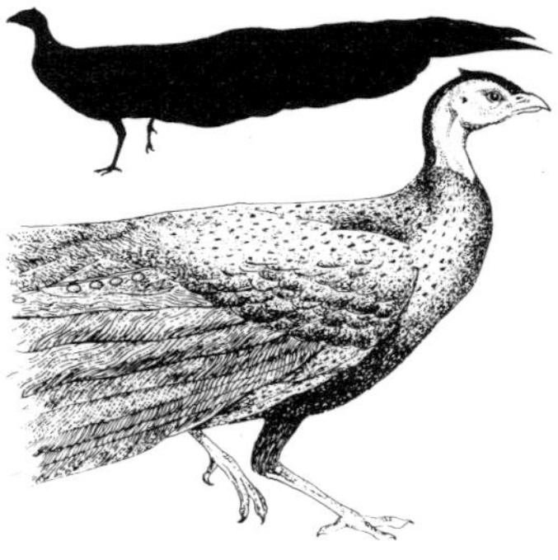
Argus pheasants have vivid colours; they can grow to 2m (6ft) from the beak to the tail.

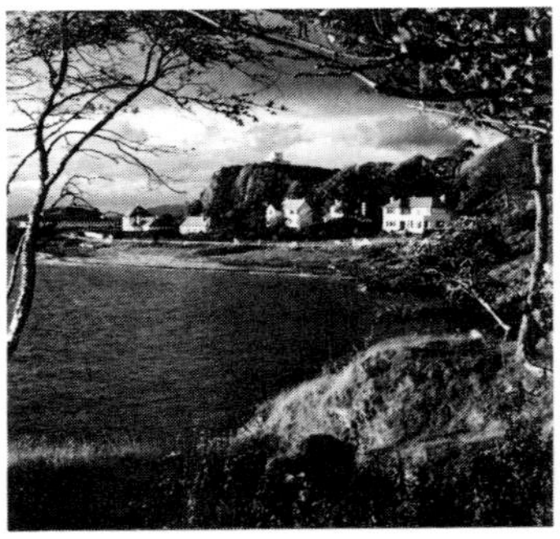
Argyllshire, with its picturesque Scottish coastline, is a favourite tourist attraction.

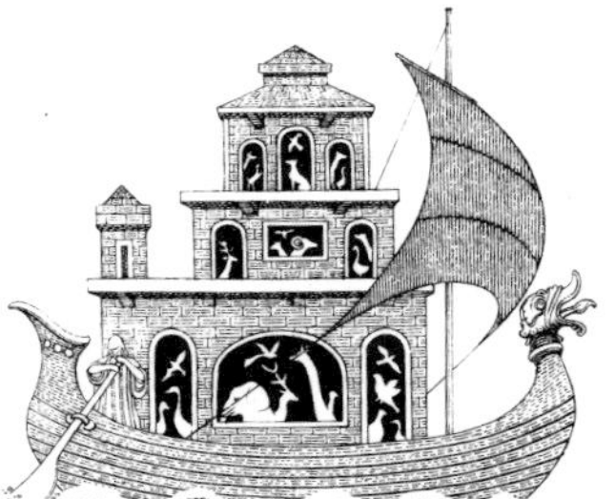
Noah's Ark preserved Noah, his family and a pair of all the species from the great flood.

welding and semiconductor preparation. The element forms no compounds. Properties: at. no. 18; at. wt.39.948; density 1.7837g cm^{-3}; m.p. (−189.4°C) (−308.9°F); b.p. −185.9°C (−302.6°F). *See also* NOBLE GASES; SU p.134.

Argonaut, or paper nautilus, ocean-dwelling cephalopod MOLLUSC found in many parts of the world. Related to the OCTOPUS, it has eight arms with suckers. Two of the female's arms are modified to secrete a coiled, paper-thin, ridged shell that is actually an egg-case. Length: to 40cm (16in). Family Argonautidae. *See also* NW p.96.

Argonauts, in Greek legend, 50 heroes who sailed the ship *Argo* to Colchis, a kingdom at the eastern end of the Black Sea, in search of the Golden Fleece. Their leader was JASON, husband of MEDEA. Many adventures and tragedies characterized their wanderings.

Argo Navis (the Ship Narvo), large group of stars once considered as a constellation but now divided into four: Carina (Keel), Puppis (Poop), Pyxis (Compass) and Vela (Sails). *See also* SU pp.255, *260*, 266.

Argonne, wooded plateau in NE France, S of the Ardennes near the Belgian border, where the Meuse-Argonne offensive of WWI took place.

Argos, town in NE Peloponnesus, Greece. It is referred to in HOMER's *Iliad* as the Kingdom of Diomed, and occupies the site of Greece's oldest city state, dating from the middle Bronze Age. It is now a small market town. Pop. 19,000.

Argus, name of three figures in Greek legend. One was a giant with 100 eyes, half of which remained open at all times. The second was the shipbuilder who built the ship Argo for JASON and became a member of the crew. Argus was also the name of the dog who recognized ULYSSES on his return to Ithaca.

Argus pheasant, colourful bird native to Malaya and Borneo. The inner wing feathers are long, broad and marked with round eyespots. At mating time the male clears a site on his forest floor and performs a courtship display, elevating his wing feathers to form "reflectors" on each side of the back. Length: 1.8m (6ft). Species *Argusiarus argus*.

Argyll, family of Scottish earls and dukes prominent in 16th- and 17th-century politics. Archibald Campbell, 5th Earl (1530–73), was a follower of KNOX in 1556 but later supported MARY, QUEEN OF SCOTS. He was implicated in the murder of her husband Lord DARNLEY in 1567. Eventually he gave his support to JAMES VI. His grand-nephew Archibald Campbell, 8th Earl and 1st Marquess (1598–1661), was a leader of the PRESBYTERIAN cause in Scotland. He won some concessions from CHARLES I in 1641 and led a Parliamentarian army during the ENGLISH CIVIL WAR. He opposed the execution of Charles and in 1651 crowned CHARLES II King of Scotland. After the failure of an invasion of England the following year, Argyll returned to the COMMONWEALTH side. After Charles's restoration, Argyll was executed for treason. His son Archibald, 9th Earl (1629–85), was a royalist, but after defending the Scottish Presbyterians against James, Duke of York (later JAMES II) was accused of treason. He fled to Holland, was implicated in the RYE HOUSE PLOT of 1683 and was executed after supporting MONMOUTH's invasion of 1685. His son Archibald, 1st Duke (*c*.1651–1703), offered the Scottish crown to William and Mary in 1689. His troops were responsible for the massacre of the MacDonalds at GLENCOE in 1692. His son John, 2nd Duke (1678–1743), promoted the Act of UNION (1707) and was later involved in political intrigue supporting both the WHIGS and the TORIES. His brother Archibald, 3rd Duke (1682–1761), was Lord High Treasurer of Scotland after 1705. He acted as WALPOLE's chief adviser in Scotland. *See also* HC1 pp.298–299.

Argyllshire, former county of W Scotland, on the Atlantic coast; now a part of the Strathclyde region. It has a deeply indented coastline and includes many islands. Much of the terrain is mountainous and forested. Industries: tourism, agriculture, manufacturing, granite quarrying, fishing, forestry. Area: 8,055sq km (3,110sq miles).

Argyll's rebellion, rising of the Campbell clan in Scotland in 1685, planned by Archibald Campbell, the 9th Earl of ARGYLL, to coincide with MONMOUTH's rebellion. It marched on Glasgow but failed through lack of support.

Argyre Dorsum, prominent ridge in the S polar region of the MOON. *See* SU p.199.

Århus (Aarhus), university city and port on the Kattegat coast of Denmark. It became an episcopal see in the 10th century and is the site of a 13th-century cathedral. The town hall was built between 1938 and 1942 of Norwegian marble. Industries include engineering, textiles and food processing. Pop. 245,212.

Aria, solo song with instrumental accompaniment; also a lyrical instrumental piece. An important element of operas, cantatas and oratorios, the aria form originated in the 16th century. *See also* HC1 pp.318–319.

Ariadne, in Greek mythology, Cretan princess who fell in love with THESEUS but was abandoned by him. She was consoled by the god BACCHUS who later married her. *See also* HC1 p.112; MS p.210.

Arianism, theological school based on the teachings of ARIUS (*c*.AD250-336), considered heretical by orthodox Christianity. Arius taught that Christ was a created being, not divine and that the Son was neither equal nor co-eternal with the Father. Arianism was condemned by the first Council of NICAEA (325). *See also* HC1 pp.134–136.

Arica-Tacna Dispute, 46-year quarrel between Chile and Peru over two former Peruvian provinces, Arica and Tacna. Chile took these over in 1883 by the Treaty of Ancón after the War of the Pacific. In 1929 it was agreed that Chile should keep Arica and Peru should have Tacna.

Ariège, river in S France. It flows through the E Pyrenees and forms the border between the Pyrénées-Orientales département and Andorra. Length: 170km (106 miles).

Aries, or the Ram, northern constellation situated on the ecliptic between Taurus and Pisces. As the first sign of the Zodiac it formerly contained the First Point of Aries, the intersection of the ecliptic and the equator marking the vernal equinox. Owing to precession this has now shifted into Pisces. The brightest star is Hamal (Alpha Arietis). *See also* MS p.200; SU pp.254, 258.

Ariosto, Ludovico (1474–1533), Italian Renaissance poet and dramatist. He was forced by financial difficulties to work as a statesman and administrator for the d'Este family. His plays were the first to imitate Latin comedy in the vernacular. His most famous work is the epic poem *Orlando Furioso* (1532). *See also* HC1 p.282.

Aristarchus of Samos (310-230 BC), Greek astronomer, supposedly the first person to put forward the theory that the Earth orbits the Sun. *See also* HC1 p.83.

Aristarchus of Samothrace (*c*.217–*c*.145 BC), member of the school of Aristophanes of Byzantium at Alexandria, leading philologist of his age. Aristarchus produced critical editions of classical authors (especially of Homer) and wrote commentaries on the classics.

Aristides the Just (*d.c.*468 BC), Athenian statesman and general. He led the Athenian forces at the Battle of MARATHON (490 BC) and, after a period of exile, fought at SALAMIS (480) and led the Athenians at PLATAEA in 479.

Aristillus, on the surface of the Moon, a prominent crater on the eastern edge of the *Mare Ibrium*. It is 56km (35 miles) in diameter. *See also* SU p.184, *184*.

Aristippus (*c*.435–366 BC), Greek founder and leader of the CYRENAICS. Basing his HEDONISM on man's ignorance of the objective world, he formulated as the goal of life prudent enjoyment of present pleasure.

Aristocracy, social system based on privilege, literally meaning "rule by the best". The term has been applied in Western Europe usually to describe the rule of a hereditary landed nobility, but could be used to include a "meritocracy" in which leaders are chosen for their ability or education. *See also* MS pp.272–277.

Aristophanes (*c*.448–*c*.388 BC), Greek writer of comedies. Eleven of his more than 40 plays survive, the only extant comedies from that period. All follow the same basic plan: realistic characters become involved in absurd situations. Graceful choral lyrics frame caustic personal attacks. A conservative, Aristophanes attacked EURIPIDES' innovations in drama, SOCRATES' philosophical radicalism and Athens' expansionist policies. His most noted plays are *The Clouds* (423), *The Birds* (414), *Lysistrata* (411) and *The Frogs* (405). *See also* HC1 p.75.

Aristotle (384–322 BC), Greek philosopher, PLATO's disciple for 20 years. His work on LOGIC founded the science and has until recently remained unchallenged. In direct opposition to Plato's idealism, Aristotle's philosophical work is based on the principle that all knowledge and theorizing must proceed directly from observation of the particular. Among his works are the *Organon*, in which he defines the SYLLOGISM and logic, *Politics*, on the conduct of the state and *Nicomachean ethics*, which he describes the virtuous life. His work was the basis of medieval SCHOLASTICISM. *See also* PE p.90; HC1 pp.63, 68, 82, 188–189, *189*; MS pp.*226–227*, 228, *229*, *232–233*, 272, *272*. HC1 pp.63, 68, 82, 188–9, 189.

Aristoxenus, Greek philosopher of the late 4th century BC and the first authority on musical theory. His interest extended to ethics and biographies, but many of his works have been lost or exist only in fragments.

Arithmetic, calculations and reckoning using numbers and such operations as addition, subtraction, multiplication and division. The study of arithmetic usually involves learning procedures for operations such as long division and extraction of square roots. *See also* MATHEMATICS; SU pp.28–30.

Arithmetical progression, sequence of numbers in which each term is produced by adding a constant term (the common difference d) to the preceding one. It has the form a, $a + d$, $a + 2d$. An example is the sequence 1, 3, 5. The sum of such a progression, $a + (a + d) + (a + 2d) + \ldots$ is an arithmetic series. For n terms it has a value $\frac{n}{2}[2a + (n - 1)d]$. *See also* SU p.38.

Arius, (*c*.250–336), heretical priest who founded ARIANISM. He supported a subordinationist teaching about the person and nature of Christ: the Son is a perfect creature, but inferior to the Father and less than divine. In 325 the Council of NICAEA condemned him.

Arizona, state in the SW USA, bordering on Mexico. The Colorado Plateau occupies the N part of the state and is cut by many steep canyons, notably the Grand Canyon, through which the Colorado River flows. Arizona's mineral resources and its grazing and farming land have long been mainstays of the economy. Mining and agriculture are still important, but since the 1950s manufacturing has been the most profitable sector. Between 1950 and 1970 Arizona's population more than doubled, and in the 1970s its annual growth rate was more than 35%. At the end of the MEXICAN WAR (1848), Mexico ceded most of the present state to the USA. Arizona became a US territory in 1863. Area: 295,025sq km (113,909sq miles). Pop. 2,224,000.

Ark, Noah's, according to Genesis 6:14-16, 18-22, the floating house Noah was ordered to build and live in with his family and one pair of each living creature during the flood. The ark was believed to have come to final rest on Mt Ararat. *See also* MS p.213.

Arkansas, state in the S central USA and one of the 11 Confederate states during the AMERICAN CIVIL WAR. In the E and S the land is low, providing excellent farmland; cotton, rice and soya beans are the main crops. The principal river is the Arkansas which, together with all the state's other rivers, drains into the Mississippi. Forests are extensive and economically important. Bauxite processing from local ore, timber and chemicals are the important industries. Most of the population are descended from immigrants who moved westwards from the S Atlantic states after 1815. Area: 137,539sq km (53,104sq miles). Pop. (1970) 1,923,295.

Ark of the Covenant, according to Jewish tradition, the chest containing the two stone tablets on which the TEN COMMANDMENTS were inscribed. It symbolized God's covenant with His chosen people. Only the high priest could look upon it; no one could touch it. The tabernacle built by King SOLOMON to house it was destroyed in 586 BC and no further record of the original Ark remains. In today's synagogues, the Ark of the Covenant is a closet or recess in which the sacred scrolls of the congregation are kept. *See also* MS pp.218–219.

Ark Royal, name of four fighting ships of the Royal Navy, separated in time by several centuries. The most famous was the third of the name, the aircraft carrier launched in 1937 (22,500 tonnes, 48 aircraft, 1,216 men) that helped to hunt and destroy the German battleship *Bismarck*. HMS *Ark Royal* was torpedoed in the W Mediterranean and sank while being towed to Gibraltar. The latest of the line, launched in 1950 (43,050 tonnes), is the largest carrier in the Royal Navy and has been much modified.

Arkwright, Sir Richard (1732–92), British inventor and industrialist. He introduced powered machinery to the textile industry with his water-driven frame for spinning; he started work on this machine in 1764 and completed it four years later, although it was not patented until the following year. He opened textile factories in Nottingham. *See also* MM p.58.

Arland, Marcel (1899–), French novelist and literary critic, influenced by André GIDE. His novels include *L'Ordre* (1929, awarded the Prix Goncourt), a study of pride and shyness, and *La Vigie* (1935).

Arlen, Harold (1905–), US composer and songwriter. His first song to achieve popularity was *Get Happy*, which appeared in the *9:15 Revue* (1928). In 1939 he received an Academy Award for his song *Over the Rainbow*, featured in the film *The Wizard of Oz*. Other film music includes *A Star is Born* (1954).

Arlen, Michael (1895–1956), British writer, *b.* Dikran Kuyumjian at Roustchouk, Bulgaria. He became a naturalized Briton in 1922 and won fame for his novel *The Green Hat* (1924).

Arles, town in S France on the River Rhône delta, 72km (45 miles) NW of Marseilles. The Romans called it Arelate and joined it by canal to the Mediterranean Sea in 103 BC. The counts of Savoy and kings of France gradually acquired the Kingdom of Arles during the 14th century. There is a 12–14th-century abbey, Montmajour, and the remains of a 2nd-century Roman amphitheatre now used for bullfighting. Industries: boat-building, metalworking, sulphur refining. Pop. 45,700.

Arlington, Henry Bennett, 1st Earl of (1618–85), English statesman. He was Secretary of State (1662–74) under Charles II and a member of the CABAL.

Arlington, city in N Virginia, across the Potomac River from Washington, DC. It is the location of the Arlington National Cemetery, Tomb of the Unknown Soldier, Pentagon and Marymount College (1950). Originally a part of the District of Columbia, it was made a county of Virginia in 1847. Pop. (1975) 102, 228.

Armada, Spanish (1588), fleet launched by the Catholic Philip II of Spain against England to overthrow the Protestant Elizabeth I. *See also* HC1 p.276.

Armadillo, nocturnal mammal found from Texas to Argentina, noted for the armour of bony plates that protects its back and sides. When attacked, some species roll into a defensive ball. It eats insects, carrion and plants. Length: 13-150cm (5-59in). Family Dasypodidae. *See* NW p.202.

Armageddon, from the Hebrew *har megiddo* ("hill of MEGIDDO"), a city of Palestine. According to Revelation 16:16, the place where the final battle between the demonic kings of the earth and the forces of God will be fought at the end of the world.

Armagh, city of Armagh district, SE Northern Ireland. It is the county town of Armagh, and the seat of Roman Catholic and Protestant archbishops. The chief industry is linen. The district of Armagh is low-lying in the N, hilly in the S, and is drained by the rivers Blackwater, Newry and Upper Bann. Much of the land is used for farming. Apart from Armagh, the main towns are Lurgan and Portadown. Pop. (city) 12,315; (district) 133,969.

Armagnac, region in SW France, formerly part of the old province of Gascony. It is an agricultural area famous for its brandy. Once part of the Roman Empire, it became a countship in the 10th century, and was annexed by France in 1607.

Armagnacs, faction supporting the Duke of Orléans in the early 15th-century civil war in France. Led by Bernard VII, Count of Armagnac, they opposed the BURGUNDIANS led by John, Duke of Burgundy, who collaborated with the English invaders in this phase of the HUNDRED YEARS' WAR. *See also* HC1 pp.203, 212.

Armaments race. *See* ARMS RACE.

Armature, central part of an electric motor or generator. In most machines the armature consists of several coils of wire on a spindle and rotates in a magnetic field. In an electric motor the armature rotates when an electric current passes through it, thus providing the driving force of the motor. *See also* SU p.122.

Armed merchant cruisers, sometimes called defensively equipped merchant ship (DEMS), fast merchant ships hastily equipped with one or two large guns, used to defend Atlantic convoys in the early stages of WWI. Merchantmen with concealed guns, "Q-ships", were also used.

Armed Neutrality, league formed by Denmark, Norway, Sweden and Russia in 1780, and later other European countries, opposing Britain's claim to have the right to search these nations' vessels during its war with the American colonies. The league was revived in 1800–01.

Armenia, ancient region of W Asia, now divided between Iran, Turkey and the USSR. It is centred on the mountainous region SE of the Black Sea and SW of the Caspian Sea and is the source of the Euphrates and Araks rivers. Strategically located between Europe and Asia, this historically important area has been the scene of repeated battles for more than 3,000 years. After enjoying prosperity under Tigranes the Great from 95 to 55 BC, Armenia came under Roman and Byzantine rule until 1064, when it fell to the Seljuk Turks. It was ravaged by Mongol forces in the 13th century and in the 16th and 17th centuries was divided between the Ottoman Turks and the Persians. The Persian sector came under Russian rule in 1828. The Turkish Armenians' fight for independence began in 1894, but this led to the almost total destruction of the Armenian population by 1915. Armenia's declaration of independence in 1918 was opposed by Russia and Turkey. The Russo-Turkish Treaty of 1921 established the present national boundaries. *See also* MW pp.100, 167, 170.

Armenia (Armanskaja Republic), smallest constituent republic of the USSR, in the S Transcaucasia. Established in 1936, it occupies the E part of ancient ARMENIA. It is a mountainous region, rising to 4,094m (13,432ft) at Mt Aragats. Jerevan is the capital, and other major cities are Leninakan and Kirovakan. Lake Sevan supports a fishing industry, and the valley of the chief river, the Araks, is an agricultural region producing cotton, fruit, rice and tobacco. Area: approx. 30,000sq km (11,500sq miles). Pop.2,842,000. *See also* MW pp.170, 173.

Armenian language, Indo-European tongue spoken in the Armenian, Georgian and Azerbaijan Soviet Socialist Republics, and in parts of the Middle East, Europe and the USA.

Armentières, town in NE France on the River Lys 13km (8 miles) NW of Lille. During WWI it was just behind the front line and was completely destroyed by various offensives. It inspired the marching song *Mademoiselle from Armentières*. Products: lace, velvet, hosiery, beer. Pop. 27,000.

Armillary sphere, skeleton sphere made up of hoops so that models of the heavenly bodies can be seen in motion through it.

Arminius Hermann (*c.*18 BC–AD 19), German tribal leader, chief of the Cherusci. In AD 9 he destroyed a Roman army commanded by Varus advancing in the Teutoburg Forest. It was the last Roman attempt to conquer lands E of the Rhine.

Arminius, Jacobus (1560–1609), Dutch theologian whose views, especially of salvation, became widespread and were known as Arminianism. He rejected CALVIN's notion of absolute PREDESTINATION in favour of conditional election and universal redemption. *See also* HC1 p.269.

Armistice Day, day of remembrance for the dead of WWI and WWII, held on 11 November, the day war ended in 1918.

Armitage, Kenneth (1916–), British sculptor. His semi-abstract figures, usually in bronze and often presented in groups, achieve an effect of movement and vitality, as in *Family Going for a Walk* (1951). He has won many prizes, including an award at the Venice Biennale (1958).

Armory Show, international exhibition of modern art held in New York City in 1913. Originally the show was intended to exhibit radical US artists, but the European section created a greater controversy. The show introduced IMPRESSIONISM, POST-IMPRESSIONISM, FAUVISM and CUBISM to the USA, beginning of modern art there.

Armour, (1) protective clothing and headgear usually made of metal or thick leather used to prevent injury to warriors in battle. Employed since antiquity, body armour, except for the helmet, ceased to be of use in Europe in the 17th century. (2) Metal plating on warships or armoured vehicles which is at least strong enough to deflect small-arms fire. Warships were first armoured in the mid-19th century, vehicles during WWI. (3) Military units having a high concentration of armoured vehicles such as TANKS, armoured personnel carriers and mechanized ARTILLERY. *See also* MM pp.28, 160, 170.

Armoured car, in military use, a wheeled armoured fighting vehicle operating primarily on firm terrain and used for reconnaissance, combat and convoy protection. *See also* TANK; MM p.170.

Arms, small, weapons that can easily be carried. Strictly, small arms include maces, swords, spears and bows and arrows, although today the term is generally used for portable firearms such as pistols and rifles. *See also* AUTOMATIC FIREARM; MM pp.160–165.

Arms race, rivalry between nations or blocs of nations to achieve supremacy in military strength. The first modern instance was the race between Germany and Britain to build up their navies before WWI, but the term refers principally to the race in nuclear weapons – atomic and hydrogen – between the USSR and the USA since WWII. The first atomic bomb was developed (1942–45) in the USA; the first used was by the USA at Hiroshima in 1945. The USSR tested its first atomic bomb in 1949. The first thermonuclear device was tested by the USA in 1952; the USSR first tested one in 1953. Four other nations – China, Britain, France and India – have tested nuclear weapons and several others have the potential to do so. As the stockpiling of nuclear weapons leaves West and East balanced, attention has increasingly turned to chemical and biological warfare. *See also* DISARMAMENT; MM pp.180–181.

Armstrong, Daniel Louis (1900–71), US jazz trumpeter, singer and bandleader, known as "Satchmo" (satchel mouth). He learned to play in New Orleans and in 1922 moved to Chicago where he joined "King" OLIVER's band. His music of the 1920s, with the Hot Five and Hot Seven, was important in the development of improvization in jazz bands. *See also* HC2 p.272.

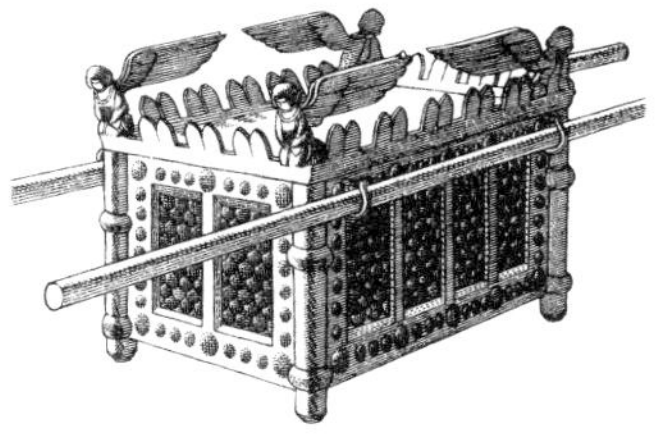

The Ark of the Covenant was a wooden chest carried on poles and decorated with gold.

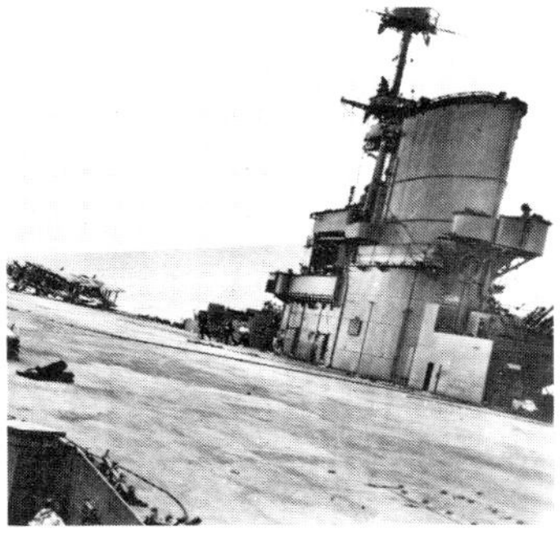

Ark Royal; the last moments on the famous warship before it sank in World War II.

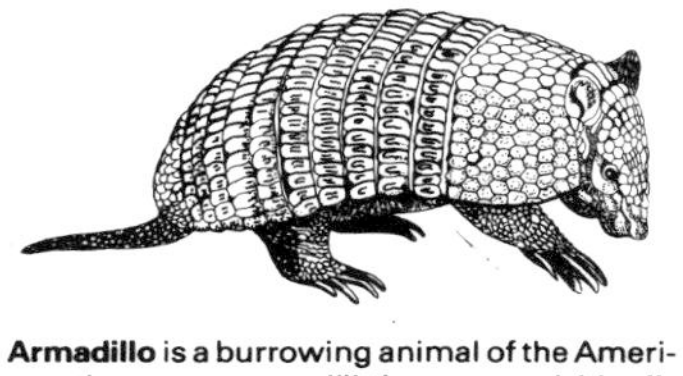

Armadillo is a burrowing animal of the Americas; the name means "little armoured thing".

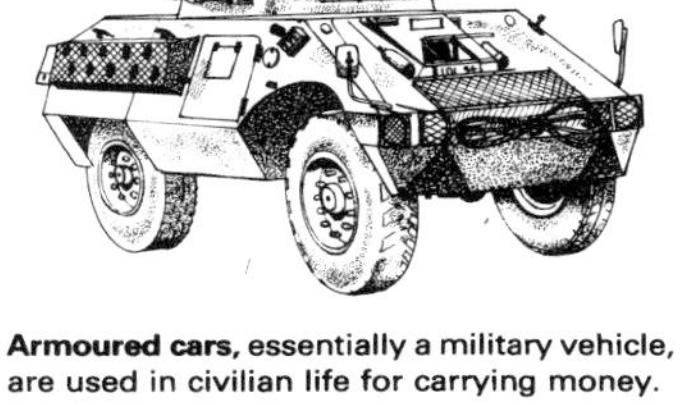

Armoured cars, essentially a military vehicle, are used in civilian life for carrying money.

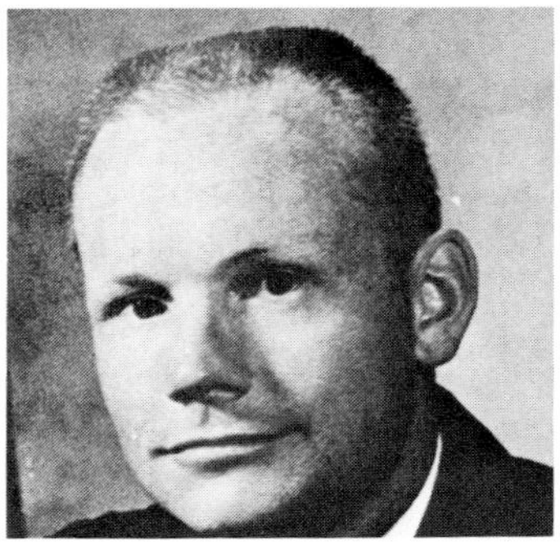

Neil Armstrong, the American astronaut, was the first man to walk on the Moon.

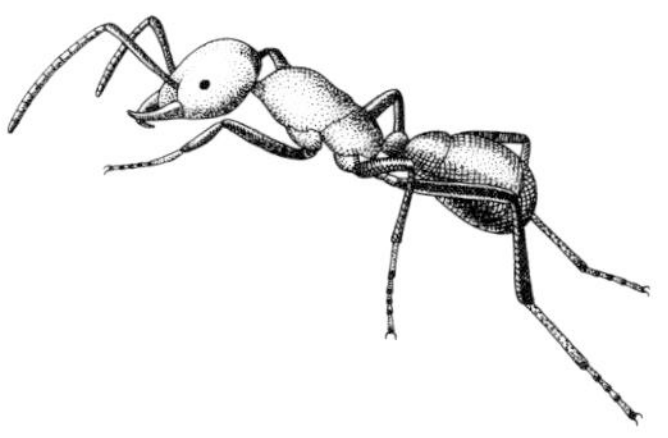

Army, or driver, ants are nomadic and do not build nests; they travel in enormous colonies.

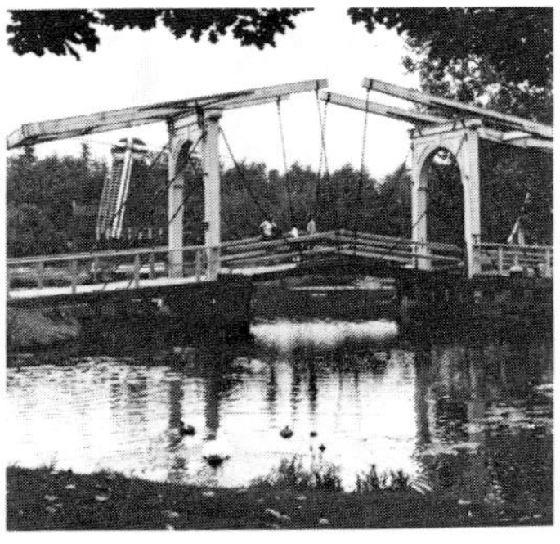

Arnhem; a typical Dutch lift bridge in the Park Museum in the town centre.

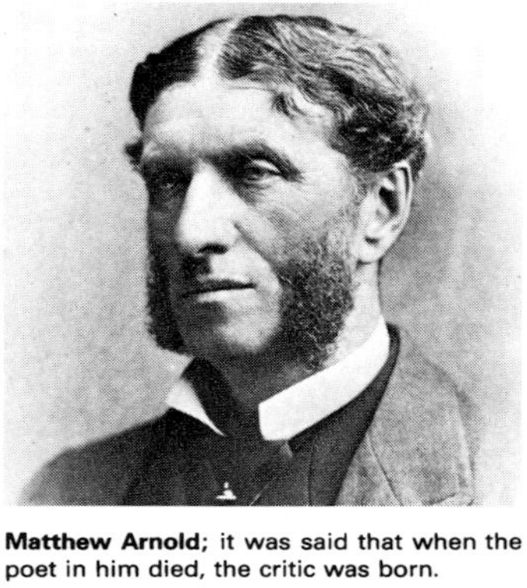

Matthew Arnold; it was said that when the poet in him died, the critic was born.

Armstrong, Henry (1912–), US boxer, real name Henry Jackson. He held the world featherweight title in 1937–38, lightweight title in 1938–39 and welterweight title in 1938–40.

Armstrong, John (1758–1843), US army officer and politician. In 1812 he was charged with the defence of New York city. As Secretary of War he received the blame for the failure of the expeditions to Canada in 1813 and the British destruction of the city of Washington.

Armstrong, Neil Alden (1930–), US astronaut. In July 1969 he became the first man to walk on the Moon. He was chosen as a NASA astronaut in 1962 and was the command pilot for the GEMINI 8 orbital flight in 1966. *See also* MM p.159.

Armstrong, William Howard (1914–), US author of children's books. His best-known work is *Sounder* (1969), the story of a black sharecropper's family during the Great DEPRESSION, which won the Newbery Medal in 1970. Other works include *Barefoot in the Grass* (1970) and *Sour Land* (1971).

Army, organized group of soldiers trained to fight on land, usually rigidly hierarchical in structure. An army can be used to maintain order and provide aid in times of civil emergency. The first evidence of an army – as opposed to a horde – comes from SUMER in the third millennium BC. The use of cavalry was a Hittite development and the Assyrians added archers and developed siege machines. The phalanx, heavily armed spearmen eight rows deep in a solid rectangle, was a tactical formation introduced by the Sumerians and also used by the Greeks, who developed such machines as the CATAPULT and BALLISTA. The phalanx was a defensive structure which could withstand a cavalry charge but it was unable to move rapidly or attack over rough ground. The Romans organized their army into divisions – legions – which were composed of 100-man groups called centuries. These had greater flexibility than phalanxes and each was in three lines of small phalanxes or cohorts. The Romans built roads and bridges to link their forts, and their intensively trained and strictly disciplined legions were thus extremely mobile.

In the Middle Ages armies used the improved armour and weapons of cavalry, and battles were won or lost by charges of heavy cavalry. The short-term feudal levy, by which these armies were raised, proved inflexible and this in turn led to the use of MERCENARIES. This change coincided with the downfall of heavy cavalry as all-important, and its replacement by a combination of infantry and archery. The end of the HUNDRED YEARS WAR saw the inception of royal standing armies and an end to the chaos caused by mercenaries. Muskets and bayonets replaced the combinations of longbow, pike and infantry, and artillery was much improved. In the FRENCH REVOLUTIONARY WARS a citizen army was raised by conscription and it contained various specialist groups such as quartermasters, ordnance troops, engineers and medical personnel. Other European armies followed suit and the age of the mass nationalist army began.

The invention of the MACHINE GUN brought about the deadlocked war, as in WWI, with masses of infantry bogged down in trenches. This deadlock was broken by the TANK, and WWII saw highly mechanized and mobile armies such that, by its end, the logistics of supply and support demanded an integration of the forces of land, sea and air. Since WWII nuclear weapons have been deployed both tactically and strategically and again the nature of its weapons has determined an army's structure. *See also* MM pp.160–170, 180–181.

Army, or driver, ant, highly predaceous ant found in tropical and subtropical parts of the world. Ranging in length from 3.25 to 43.75mm (0.13–1.75in), these ants travel in huge armies, when hunting for food and migrating. Family Formicidae; subfamily Dorylinae. *See also* HYMENOPTERA; NW pp.78, 79, 116.

Arnaud, Yvonne Germaine (1892–1958), French actress who spent most of her working life in England. She excelled in farce and musical comedy. A theatre, opened in Guildford in 1965, was named after her.

Arne, Thomas Augustine (1710–78), English composer. His first opera *Rosamond* (1733) gained him renown. Today his fame rests on his settings of Shakespearean songs, such as *Under the Greenwood Tree.* He also wrote the song *Rule, Britannia.*

Arnell, Richard Anthony Sayer (1917–), British composer. He has written five symphonies, chamber music, three operas and various concertos.

Arnhem, city in E central Netherlands, 55km (35 miles) E of Utrecht on the Neder-Rijn River; capital of Gelderland province. An important medieval trading centre, it was occupied variously by the Dutch (1585), French (1672, 1795) and Prussians (1813). An abortive Allied airborne attack of 1944 almost destroyed the city. Industries: metallurgy, textiles, electrical equipment, chemicals. Pop. 127,000.

Arnhem Land, region on the N coast of Australia, on the wide peninsula W of the Gulf of Carpentaria. Discovered in 1623 by Jan Carstensz, it is now Australia's largest Aboriginal reserve. Bauxite is mined in the region. Area: approx. 80,808sq km (31,200sq miles).

Arnim, Ludwig Achim von (1781–1831), German poet. He is best known for *Des Knaben Wunderhorn* (1805–08), written with Clemens BRENTANO, which Gustav MAHLER set to music.

Arnim, Mary Annette von (1866–1941), Australian-born writer. She married Count von Arnim of Prussia and, after his death, Earl Russell. As Elizabeth von Arnim she wrote many books, including *Elizabeth and her German Garden* (1898), *The Pastor's Wife* (1914) and *Mr Skeffington* (1940).

Arno, river in central Italy. It rises in the Apennine Mountains in Arezzo province, and enters the Ligurian Sea below Pisa. Flood control works, some planned by Leonardo da Vinci, failed to prevent the Arno causing flooding of Florence in 1966, resulting in major damage to the city's art treasures. Length: 241km (150 miles).

Arnold of Brescia (*c.*1100–55). Italian monk and church reformer. He attacked the church for owning property and from 1145 led the republican commune in Rome. He was excommunicated in 1148 and arrested and executed by FREDERICK I in 1155.

Arnold, Benedict (1741–1801), American soldier. He was placed in command of Philadelphia in 1778 after being wounded at the Battle of SARATOGA. In 1780 he became commander of West Point, a fort he planned to betray to the British for money. After the plot was discovered, Arnold fled and was made a general by the British.

Arnold, Henry Harley (1886–1950), US general, known as "Hap". He joined the aviation division of the Signal Corps in 1911, and became chief of the US Army Air Corps (1938) and chief of the US Army Air Forces in 1941. In 1949 he became the first five-star general of the independent Air Force.

Arnold, Malcolm (1921–), British composer. Formerly principal trumpet with the London Philharmonic Orchestra, he won immediate acclaim for his many compositions: symphonies, concertos, overtures (eg, *Beckus the Dandipratt,* 1943), ballets (eg, *Homage to the Queen,* 1953) and film scores.

Arnold, Matthew (1822–88), British poet and critic, the son of Thomas ARNOLD. He held the Oxford chair in poetry (1857–67) and was a school inspector (1851–86). His writings include literary criticism, such as *Essays in Criticism* (series 1, 1865; series 2, 1888), and social commentary, such as *Culture and Anarchy* (1869). *See also* HC2 p.100.

Arnold, Thomas (1795–1842), headmaster of Rugby School 1828–42. A Liberal publicist and spokesman for a "Broad Church", he raised the standard of public school education and manners, making the formation of Christian character the chief end of education.

Arnoldson, Klas Pontus (1844–1916), Swedish politician who shared with Fredrik BAJER the 1908 Nobel Peace Prize for his efforts to inspire world peace. He introduced a motion for the permanent neutrality of Sweden while he was a member (1882–87) of the Riksdag.

Arnolfini Wedding, The (1434), double portrait of great psychological insight by Jan van EYCK; (National Gallery, London). *See also* HC1 p.*252*.

Arnolfo di Cambio (*c.*1232–*c.*1310), Italian architect and sculptor, designer (*c.*1300) of Florence Cathedral. He was first architect of the Church of S. Croce, Florence, and sculpted its facade. His celebrated statue of Charles of Anjou (*c.*1277) is among the first modern portrait statues. *See also* HC1 pp.217, 250.

Aromatic compound, organic chemical compound that contains atoms of carbon (often six) joined to form a ring-shaped molecule, eg BENZENE. *See also* SU p.142.

Arp, Jean or Hans (1887–1966), Alsatian sculptor, painter and poet. He was a pioneer of abstract art and a leader in European avant-garde movements in the first half of the 20th century. In Zürich during WWI he was a founder of the DADA movement and in the 1920s joined the SURREALISTS. His works are marked with a simple exuberance, of which *Navel Shirt and Head* (1926) and *Human Concretion* (1935) are typical examples. *See also* HC2 pp.202, 204, 205

Arpino, Giuseppi Cesari (1568–1640), among the last and most conservative of Italian MANNERIST painters. He designed the mosaics for the Dome of St Peter's, Rome, and painted frescoes in S Martino, Naples. CARAVAGGIO was his pupil.

Arquebus, late 15th-century firearm and immediate precursor of the musket; it was the first type of gun to be fired from the shoulder. It had a pivoted clamp which held a slow-burning "fuse". When the trigger was pulled the fuse dipped into priming powder, which fired the main charge. *See also* MM pp.162–163.

Arrabal, Fernando (1932–), Spanish novelist and playwright. His satirical method, as in *A Picnic in the Country* (1959) and *The Car Cemetery* (1962), has made him unacceptable in Spain. He writes in French and lives in France.

Arraignment, the appearance of a person in court, the reading of the charge and the recording of his plea.

Arran, island off SW Scotland, in the Firth of Clyde; a popular tourist resort. The main town is Brodick. Area: approx. 430sq km (166sq miles). Pop. (1971) 3,576.

Arras, town in NE France on the River Scarpe, 40km (25 miles) SE of Lille; capital of Pas-de-Calais département. Settled during Roman times, it became a wealthy commercial and weaving town in the Middle Ages. By the Treaty of the Pyrenees (1659) it became part of the French crown lands. Industries: food, food processing, brewing, Pop. 48,000.

Arras, Union of (1579), pact signed by the Walloon (southern, Roman Catholic, French-speaking) provinces of the Low Countries, which separated them from the northern, Protestant provinces. In response the northern provinces formed the UNION OF UTRECHT. Although the signatories of the Union of Arras signed a peace treaty with the Spaniards, they were soon reconquered by them. The lands covered by the Union of Arras formed the basis of present-day Belgium and Luxembourg; the Utrecht Provinces led to the formation of The Netherlands. *See also* HC1 p.272.

Arrau, Claudio (1903–), Chilean pianist, best known for his interpretations of the Romantic repertoire. He made his debut in Santiago at the age of five.

Arrest, the taking into custody – usually by a policeman or other agent of the government – of a person suspected of a crime or other offence. Under COMMON LAW, the person making the arrest must have a warrant or reasonable cause for thinking that an offence has been committed. *See also* MS pp.292–293.

Arrhenius, Svante August (1859–1927), Swedish chemist and physicist, awarded the Nobel Prize in chemistry in 1903 for his theory of electrolytic dissociation. His later work was concerned with reaction rates, biochemistry, the structure of the universe and the revelation that light exerts pressure.

Arrol, Sir William (1839–1913), Scottish engineer who constructed the new Tay Bridge, the Forth Bridge and Tower Bridge. He was also a Member of Parliament (1892–96).

Arromanches-les-Bains, coastal village in the Calvados département of N France, 8km (5 miles) NNE of Bayeux. During the Allied invasion of Normandy in 1944 it was used as a landing-place.

Arrow, Kenneth Joseph (1921–), US economist who shared the 1972 Nobel Prize in economics with Sir John Richard HICKS.

Arrowhead, fresh water plant found in tropical and temperate America. Its leaves are arrow-shaped, and the flowers are white and cup-shaped. Species include the broad-leaved arrowhead (*Sagittaria latifolia*). Family Alismataceae. *See also* NW p.*66*.

Arrowroot, tropical and subtropical perennial plant found in wet habitats of North and South America. Its leaves are lance-shaped and the flowers are usually white. The dried and ground roots are used in cooking. Family Marantaceae. *See also* PRAYER PLANT; PE p.*187*.

Arrowworm. *See* CHAETOGNATHA.

Ars Amatoria, manual of seduction written by the Roman poet OVID at the beginning of the 1st century AD. The work was an obvious challenge to the moral reforms of Emperor Augustus. The first two books are addressed to men, the third to women.

Arsenic, toxic metallic element (As) of group Va of the periodic table, probably obtained (1250) by Albertus Magnus. The chief ores are realgar and orpiment (both sulphides) and mispickel (arsenopyrite, FeSAs). Arsenic is used for hardening lead and in semiconductors. Three allotropes are known: a grey metallic form, black arsenic and a yellow non-metallic form. Properties: at.no. 33; at.wt. 74.9216; m.p. 817°C (1,503°F) at 28 atms.; sublimes 613°C (1,135°F); most common isotope As^{75} (100%). *See also* SU p.128.

Arson, intentional burning of the property of another. In some countries the crime of arson is judged in degrees of seriousness, the heaviest punishment being given for actions which endanger life.

Ars Poetica or Epistle to the Pisos, verse essay written by Roman poet HORACE in *c.* 19–18 BC. His longest work, it is a survey of the history and theory of dramatic poetry.

Ars Poetica, poem by Archibald MACLEISH published in *Streets in the Moon* (1926). It presents MacLeish's thoughts on poetry, such as: "A poem should not mean/But be".

Art, treated in the *Fact Index* under the main headings of PAINTING, SCULPTURE, DRAWING and ARCHITECTURE. These articles contain numerous cross-references to related subjects. There are articles about individual artists and architects and the various movements, styles and schools are described in articles such as ART NOUVEAU, BAUHAUS, MANNERISM and ROMANESQUE art and architecture. There are articles on techniques, eg, AQUATINT and FRESCO, as well as a number of entries on famous paintings, buildings, museums and galleries.

Artaud, Antonin (1896–1948), French director and theorist of drama. He was co-founder of the Théatre Alfred Jarry, where he experimented with his idea of the "Theatre of Cruelty". His most important book was *Le Théatre et son Double* (1938).

Artaxerxes, name of three Persian kings of the Achaemenid dynasty. During the reign of Artaxerxes I (*r.* 465–425 BC) there were several revolts in his empire, including those of Egypt (459–454 BC), Bactria and Cyprus. He allowed Judaism to revive. Artaxerxes II (*r.* 404–359 BC), the successor of DARIUS II, also suffered disaffection in the empire; his brother Cyrus tried to assassinate him and several of his satraps rebelled. His son Artaxerxes III (*r.* 359–338 BC) restored the authority of the emperor by murdering most of his family, and reconquered Egypt. *See also* HC1 p.60.

Art Deco, style in the decorative arts first promoted in Paris in 1925, which flourished in the late 1920s and throughout the 1930s. It sought to create for mass-production sleek, linear, decorative and industrial designs that made use of modern technology. Glass, semi-precious stones and man-made materials, such as concrete and plastics, were used.

Artel, Soviet organization of farmers and industrialists which forms the collective farms and industrial co-operatives. The term has been extended to include groups of intellectuals and artists.

Artemis, Greek goddess, daughter of ZEUS and Leto, twin sister of APOLLO, called DIANA by the Romans. She was a virgin who assisted in childbirth and protected the young of human beings and animals. She was goddess of the hunt and deity of light, associated with the moon.

Arteriography, medical technique for examining blood vessels. A dye opaque to X-rays is injected into the patient's bloodstream and the arteries revealed in an X-ray photograph. The technique is particularly useful in detecting ARTERIOSCLEROSIS. *See also* MS p.*124*.

Arteriosclerosis, several diseases of the arteries, including ATHEROSCLEROSIS, the most common form; popularly known as "hardening of the arteries". It is caused by deposits of fatty materials and sometimes calcium on the ARTERY walls, narrowing the passage for blood; the calcium also makes the arteries less elastic. There is usually an absence of overt symptoms until the disease is well advanced. Serious cases can lead to coronary complications, when the symptoms may include sharp pains in the chest radiating to the arms or neck (ANGINA PECTORIS). So-called senile forgetfulness or confusion may occur if the brain is affected. Evidence suggests that predisposition to the disease is hereditary and that it is more likely in cigarette smokers, people who do not exercise regularly or those with high-fat diets. The favoured method of control of the disease is adherence to a low cholesterol diet and exercise. If an ANEURYSM or obstruction in the artery is identified, surgery may be needed. Anticoagulant drugs are sometimes effective on a short-term basis. *See also* MS pp.87, 90, 91, 124.

Artery, BLOOD VESSEL that carries BLOOD away from the HEART. The pulmonary artery carries deoxygenated blood to the lungs, but all other arteries carry oxygenated blood to the body's tissues. An artery is usually protected and embedded in muscle; its walls are thick, elastic and muscular and pulsate as they carry the blood. A cut artery causes rapid loss of blood. *See also* MS pp.62, *63*.

Artesian wells, wells from which water is forced out naturally under pressure. They occur where water is sandwiched between two layers of impervious rock in a reservoir, or AQUIFER, such as sandstone. If, because of the configuration of the strata, water is able to flow into the aquifer at a higher level and if a well shaft is drilled down through the upper impervious strata, water flows up to the surface (providing that the well-head is lower than the original entry point). *See* PE pp.*108–109*, 109.

Arthritis, inflammation of the joints. The most common forms are osteoarthritis and rheumatoid arthritis. Osteoarthritis, common among the elderly, occurs when joint cartilage wears away. Rheumatoid arthritis is generally more crippling and occurs most often in women. The cause is unknown but physical and emotional stress may trigger symptoms, with aching and stiffness developing into pain in the affected joints. People with chronic rheumatoid arthritis usually show swelling and deformation of the hands, feet or wrists; movement is both difficult and painful. Although often severely crippling, it rarely leads to total disablement. Treatment includes prescribed exercise, diet and rest, with analgesics to relieve pain. The most severe cases may need surgery or treatment by CORTISONE drugs. *See also* RHEUMATISM; MS pp.*86*, 87, *94*, 95.

Arthropod, member of the largest animal phylum, Arthropoda. Living forms include CRUSTACEANS, ARACHNIDS, CENTIPEDES, MILLIPEDES and INSECTS. The more than 800,000 species are thought to have evolved from ANNELIDS. All have a hard outer skin of CHITIN that is attached to the muscular system on the inside. The body is divided into segments, modified among different groups, with each segment originally carrying a pair of walking or swimming jointed legs. In some animals some of the legs have evolved into jaws, sucking organs or weapons. Arthropods have well-developed digestive, circulatory and nervous systems. Land forms use tracheae for respiration. *See* NW pp.72–75, 98–99, 104, 108–109, 178, 223.

Arthur, King. *See* KING ARTHUR.

Arthur I, Duke of Brittany (1187–1203), French duke who claimed the English crown that his uncle, JOHN, had taken. Arthur was captured in 1202 and was probably murdered by John.

Arthur, Chester Alan (1830–86), 21st President of the USA. A Republican, he became President in 1881 after the assassination of James Garfield. He tried to reform the spoils system (by which incoming presidents replaced all government staff with their own appointments). He was not renominated by his party.

Arthur's Pass, route through the Southern Alps of New Zealand, named after the explorer, Sir Arthur Dudley Dobson.

Arthur's Seat, rock (a volcanic plug) in E EDINBURGH, Scotland. According to legend, it is the place from which KING ARTHUR watched the defeat of the Picts. Height: 251m (823ft).

Artichoke, or globe artichoke, tall, thistle-like perennial plant native to the Mediterranean region, widely grown in warm parts of the world for its large, edible, immature flower heads. It has spiny, deeply-cut leaves, and its flowers are blue. Height: 0.9–1.5m (3–5ft). Family Compositae; species *Cynara scolymus*. *See also* NW p.189.

Articles of Confederation (1781), the first federal constitution of the USA, superseded in 1789. Each state had one vote in the weak central government, revenues were appropriated on the basis of the value of surveyed lands, and the states were prevented from interfering with the western territories. *See also* HC2 p.64.

Articles of the Church of England, 39 articles accepted by the synod in 1571, setting out the doctrinal orthodoxy of the Church. Their formulation was supervised by Archbishop PARKER, although they were based on earlier series of articles. They are included in the Book of COMMON PRAYER.

Artificial insemination, method of inducing PREGNANCY without sexual intercourse by artificially injecting viable SEMEN into the female genital tract. Some of the first successful insemination experiments on mammals were those of Lazzaro Spallanzani (1729–99). The artificial impregnation of livestock allows proven sires to "mate" with many females at low cost. In human reproduction the semen may be from the husband of the woman inseminated or from an anonymous donor. *See also* PE pp.225, 226.

Artificial kidney, popular term for a device operating outside the body that performs the functions of a properly functioning natural KIDNEY. *See also* DIALYSIS; MS p.102.

Artificial limbs, man-made limbs or segments thereof used to replace parts of the body lost by amputation. Made from new metals or plastics, modern artificial legs, feet, arms and hands can perform most of the original functions. *See also* MS p.*127*.

Artificial respiration, method of maintaining breathing in someone whose lungs are not working. For first aid treatment, *see* MS p.*132*.

Artillery, projectile-firing weapons with a carriage or mount. An artillery piece is generally one of four types – gun,

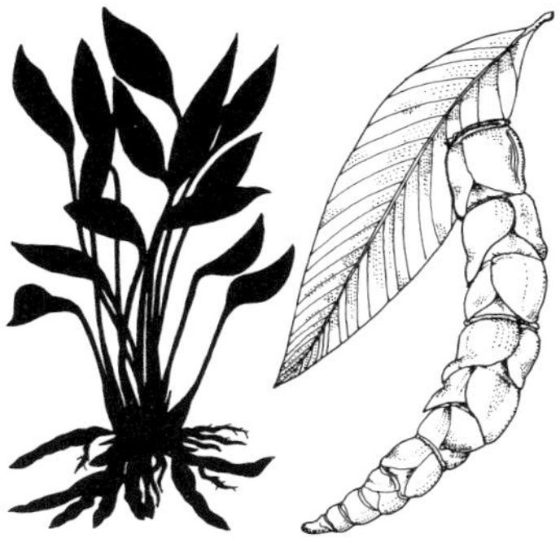

Arrowroot has large, distinctive leaves; its roots are used for culinary purposes.

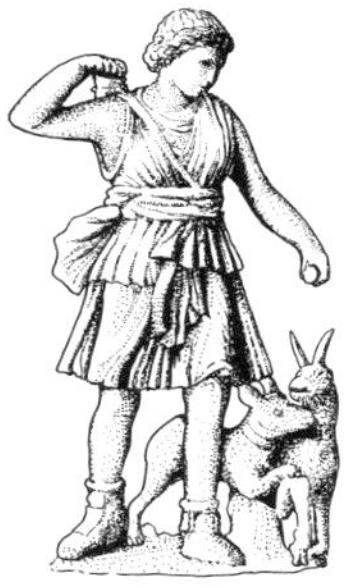

Artemis, the Greek goddess, was worshipped as the protector of animals and children.

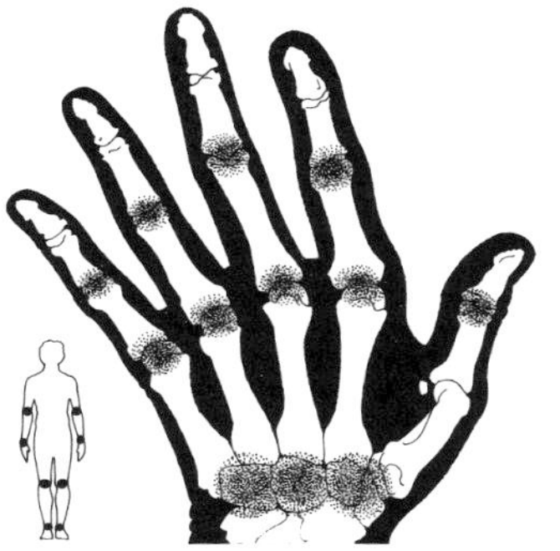

Arthritis affects the joints, especially of the hands and feet; movement is often difficult.

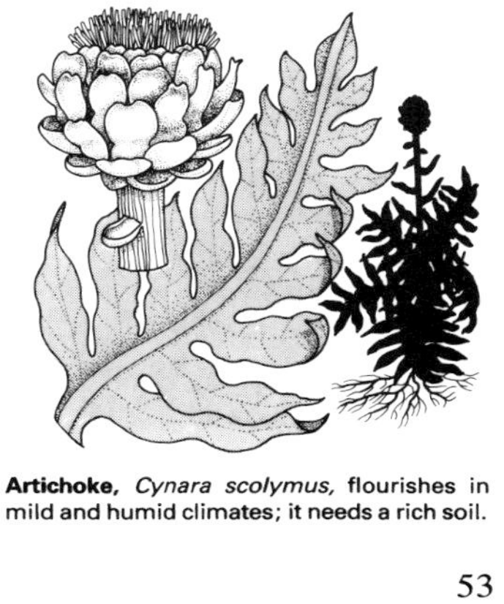

Artichoke, *Cynara scolymus,* flourishes in mild and humid climates; it needs a rich soil.

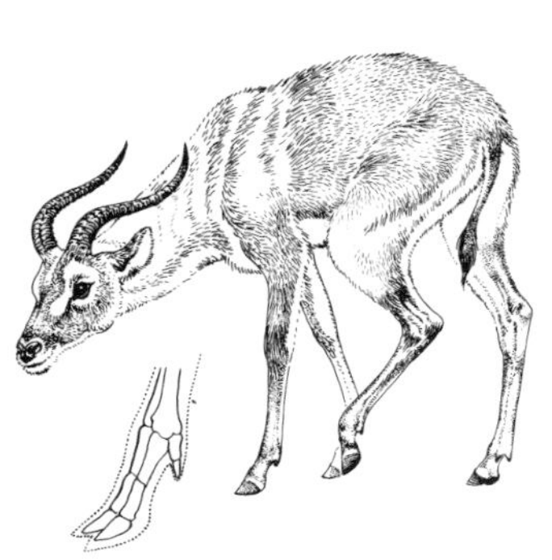

Artiodactyla is an order that includes the antelope *Kobus kob.*

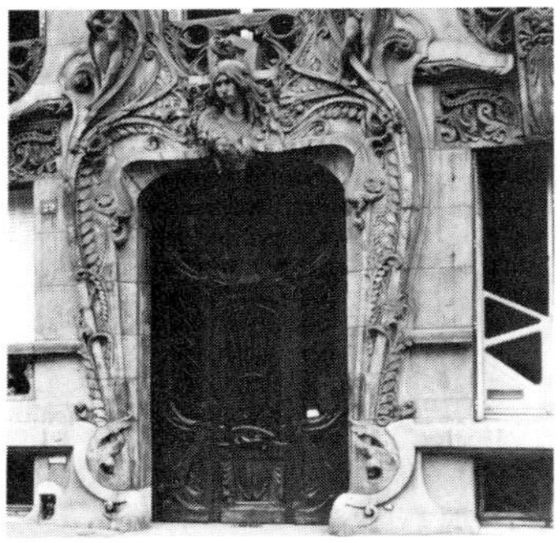

Art Nouveau is a turn of the century decorative style recently brought back into vogue.

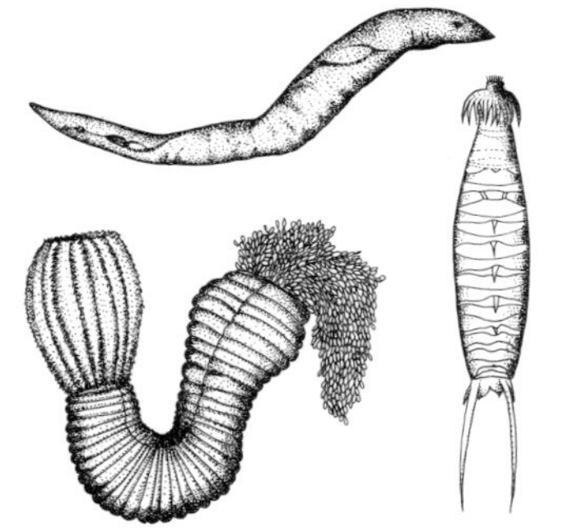

Aschelminthes are a group of worm-like animals; either aquatic or terrestrial.

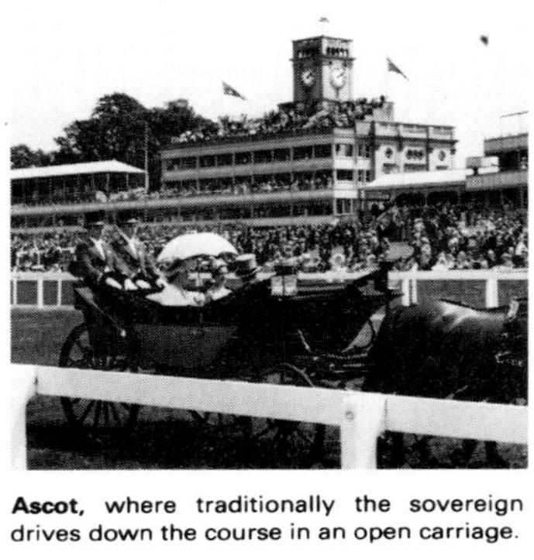

Ascot, where traditionally the sovereign drives down the course in an open carriage.

howitzer, mortar, or missile launcher. Modern artillery is classified according to calibre, ranging from under 105mm for light artillery to more than 155mm for heavy. The exact origin of artillery using gunpowder is unknown, although such weapons appeared in Europe and the Near East in the 14th century. Used by the Turks to take Constantinople in 1453, artillery changed the whole strategy and tactics of siege warfare. Advances in the 19th century, including smokeless powder, elongated shells, rifling and rapid-fire breach loading made artillery indispensable on the battlefield. *See also* MM pp.166–169.

Artiodactyla, order of mammals characterized by hoofs with an even number (2 or 4) of toes. It includes GIRAFFES, HIPPOPOTAMUSES, DEER, CATTLE, PIGS, SHEEP, GOATS and CAMELS. They are mostly of Old World origin and range in size from the 3.6kg (8lb) MOUSE DEER to the 4.5 tonne hippopotamus. *See also* NW pp.155, 162.

Art Nouveau, movement in decoration and architecture that evolved from the ARTS AND CRAFTS MOVEMENT. Starting in Britain, as a reaction against what some designers considered the poor design standards of the period, it spread through Europe and the USA, lasting until about 1910. Art Nouveau has two distinct styles, although these are often used together. One is characterized by a sinuous linearity and organic asymmetry reminiscent of writhing plant forms (as in an Aubrey BEARDSLEY drawing), the other by a severe geometry and reduced decoration (as in the architecture and interior design of C.R. MACKINTOSH). In Britain the movement's leaders included Mackintosh, A. MACKMURDO and Beardsley. In Belgium it achieved its peak in the architecture of Victor HORTA and Henri van de VELDE. In France the architect Hector GUIMARD and the designers Emile GALLÉ and René LALIQUE led the way. In Spain the architect Antoni GAUDI evolved his own unique interpretation of the style. Louis Comfort TIFFANY led the US movement with his elegant and iridescent glassware.

Artois, region in NE France, close to the English Channel. A former province between Picardy and Flanders, and once ruled by counts of Flanders, it was first annexed by France in 1180. An agricultural region, it also contains part of the Franco-Belgian coal basin.

Arts and Crafts Movement, late 19th- and early 20th-century British movement to revive the standard of the decorative arts by means of a return to the ideals of medieval craftsmanship. Inspired by William MORRIS, the movement contributed to the European renaissance in design, but was eventually transformed by acceptance of modern industrial methods.

Arts Council (of Great Britain), body established in 1946 to develop a greater knowledge, understanding and practice of the arts in Britain. It receives government aid, most of which goes to bodies or individuals involved in promotion or performance of the arts.

Artzybashev, Mikhail Petrov (1878–1927), Russian novelist, famous for *Sanine* (1907) and *Breaking-Point* (1912).

Arum. *See* LILY.

Arundel, Thomas FitzAlan (1353–1414), English churchman. He was Archbishop of Canterbury (1396), several times Chancellor, and vigorously opposed the LOLLARDS.

Arundel, Thomas Howard (1586–1646), English politician and patron of the arts. He had a celebrated collection of antiques, paintings, books and sculptures (the Arundel Marbles).

Arundel, market town in W Sussex, England, on the River Arun, with an 11th-century castle; it is the seat of the Duke of Norfolk. Pop. 2,000.

Arunta, native Australian desert people of N central Australia. They believe in pre-existence, reincarnation and totemism and live basically by food gathering. They were, and still are, noted for their art forms. *See also* ABORIGINES.

Arup, Ove (1895–), Danish consulting engineer, based in London, who worked there with the architect Berthold LUBETKIN in the 1930s to produce Highpoint apartments, the Penguin Pool and Finsbury Health Centre. He designed London's WWII air-raid shelters. Later works include the design for Somerville College, Oxford, and the construction of SYDNEY OPERA HOUSE (1959–73).

Arval Brethren, college of 12 priests in ancient Rome, selected from senatorial families and always including the emperor. They particularly worshipped Dea Dia, a goddess of agriculture.

Arvida, industrial town in S Quebec, Canada, on the Saguenay River, 8km (5 miles) W of Chicoutimi. The chief industry is aluminium smelting. Pop. 18,400.

Aryan, language of an ancient people who lived in the region between the Caspian Sea and Hindu Kush mountains. About 1500 BC one branch entered India, introducing the Sanskrit language; another branch migrated to Europe. In their racist propaganda in the 1930s the Nazis traced German descent from Aryans.

Arya Samaj, revivalist Hindu organization founded by Dayananda Saraswati (1824–83) in Bombay in 1875. Begun as an expression of absolute faith in the VEDAS, it reflected Dayananda's militant character, asserting Hindu nationalism from its stronghold in N India.

Asahikawa (Asahigawa), city in central Hokkaidō, Japan, on the Ishikari River. It is a commercial, rail and agricultural centre. Industries: timber, wood, pulp, paper. Pop. 288,500.

Asaph, Saint (died *c.* 596), first bishop of St Asaph (Llanelwy) in Clwyd, Wales. A Briton and the grandson of a chieftain, he became abbot of a monastery that had been founded by the Scottish bishop St Kentigern, whose disciple he was. Later the monastery became the centre of a bishopric.

Asbestos, fibrous naturally occurring mineral used in insulating, fireproofing and friction materials. Asbestos is used in the form of wool, fabric and various asbestos-cement compounds. Several types exist; they are varieties of amphibole, pyroxene and chrysotile minerals. Blue asbestos (crocidolite) has certain advantages over the white forms, but can cause a serious lung condition (asbestosis). *See also* MS pp.57, 59.

Asbjørnsen, Peter Christen (1812–85), Norwegian writer. He travelled around Norway with his friend and poet, Jørgen Engebretsen MOE, collecting folk tales. These appeared in a four-volume collection, *Norwegian Folk Stories* (1841–44).

Asbury, Francis (1745–1816), US Wesleyan leader, *b.* Britain. In 1771 he volunteered for service in the USA, where in 1784 he became superintendent of Methodist societies. *See also* METHODISM.

Ascari, Alberto (1918–55), Italian motor racing driver. He won the world championship in a Ferrari in 1952 and 1953, but like his father Antonio died at the wheel of his car.

Ascariasis, infestation of the intestine by a number of large roundworms, ascaris, which may migrate throughout the body. Intestinal evacuation is the first treatment, followed by special drugs. *See also* MS p.85; NW p.88.

Ascension, island in the S Atlantic Ocean, a dependency of St Helena. *See* MW p.148.

Ascension day, Christian feast that commemorates Christ's ascension into heaven. It falls on a Thursday, the 40th day after EASTER. It used to be called Holy Thursday.

Asceticism, self-denial of bodily pleasures and worldly pursuits, indulged in for religious purposes. It is practised in some form in most religions; in Christianity it is regarded as an imitation of Christ. The commonest form of ascetic discipline – and the form most often practised by lay people – is fasting. *See also* MS p.*186*.

Asch, Sholom (1880–1957), Polish-born American author. He emigrated to the USA in 1914 and wrote many novels about Jewish life. These include *Mother* (1937) and *Three Cities* (1933).

Ascham, Roger (1515–68), English writer and widely travelled classical scholar. His treatises *Toxophilus* (1545) and *The Scholemaster* (published 1570) discuss the ideal elements of a Humanist education. He believed that British scholars should write in English, but recommended a "pure" prose style based on Latin.

Aschelminthes, phylum of small worm-like animals. Rather a mixed assemblage, it consists of the Rotifers, Gastrotrichs, roundworms (Nematodes), threadworms (Nematomorphs) and a small group of marine worms, the Kinorhyncha. Each of these groups was often accorded phylum status. *See also* NW p.72.

Ascomycetes, one of the four main classes of fungi, characterized by the formation of asci, (enlarged, commonly elongated cells, in which eight spores are usually formed). Examples are yeasts, truffles and blue and green moulds. *See also* NW pp.41, 48.

Ascorbic acid. *See* VITAMINS.

Ascot, village in Berkshire, England, 10km (6 miles) SW of Windsor. A racecourse was established there in 1711 by Queen Anne. The Royal Ascot Meeting still takes place every June, although the course is used throughout the year.

Asdic. *See* SONAR.

Asellus, genus of aquatic crustaceans that includes the water louse. Most grow to about 1cm (0.4in) long. *See also* NW pp.*105, 230.*

Asen, medieval Bulgarian dynasty (1185–1257), set up after John, or Ivan, Asen I (*d.* 1196) and his brother Peter (*d.* 1197) rose against Byzantium. Their brother Kaloyan, or Joannitsa (*r.* 1197–1207) made peace with the Greeks in 1201. He took advantage of the 4th CRUSADE's capture of Constantinople in 1204 to break with the Eastern ORTHODOX CHURCH. The benevolent rule of John, or Ivan, Asen II (1218–41) marked the height of the Second Bulgarian Empire. He added Epirus, Macedonia, Thessaly and part of Albania to his realm.

Asepsis, exclusion of bacteria or germs during operations or injections. In an operating theatre, clothes, gloves, equipment and even the air are sterilized. *See also* MS pp.128–129.

Asexual reproduction, type of reproduction in organisms that does not involve the union of male and female reproductive cells. It occurs in several forms: FISSION – division of a single individual, as in bacteria and protozoa; BUDDING – growing out and eventual splitting off of a new individual, as in HYDRA; spore formation, as in YEAST; vegetative reproduction – in which a plant sends out "runners" that take root to form new plants, as in strawberries; regeneration – the regrowth of an individual from a detached part of the "parent", as in planarian worms; and PARTHENOGENESIS – the birth of young from an unfertilized female, as in APHIDS. *See also* SEXUAL REPRODUCTION; NW pp.70–71.

Asgard, in ancient Scandinavian mythology, the domain of the gods, who resided there in splendid palaces. Chief of these was VALHALLA, to which heroes slain in battle were carried in triumph.

Ash, group of mainly deciduous trees growing in temperate regions. The wood is elastic, strong and shock-resistant, and is widely used for tool handles, sporting equipment and furniture. Species include manna ash, *Fraxinus ornus,* the flowering ash of southern Europe and Asia Minor; the European ash, *F. excelsior,* which grows to 45m (148ft) tall; and *F. floribunda,* a native of the Himalayas. Family Oleaceae. *See also* NW p.209.

Ash, volcanic, fine particles of LAVA thrown up by a volcanic explosion. The cone of compound volcanoes consists of built-up layers of ash and lava. *See also* PE pp.30–31.

Ashanti, Negroid people of S and central Ghana. In the 18th century they established a powerful empire, based on trade in slaves with the Dutch and British. Conflicts with the British throughout the 19th century were finally resolved in 1902, when the Ashanti territories were declared a British Crown colony. Ashanti society is MATRILINEAL and traditionally agricultural, plantains, bananas, manioc, yams and cocoa being the chief crops. Gold and diamonds are mined and large reserves of bauxite are being developed west of Kumasi, the capital. Most Ashantis follow ethnic religions and bear allegiance to a paramount chief who is advised by his mother or sister. Their crafts include high-quality gold-work and weaving, particularly the famous gold-encrusted stool that was a symbol of their sovereignty. *See also* MW p.88.

Ashanti, administrative region in s central Ghana. A kingdom (capital Kumasi) was founded there in 1697; it came under British protection in 1896 and was part of the British Gold Coast from 1901. Products: cocoa, kola nuts, hardwoods and food crops. Industries: gold and bauxite mining. Pop. 1,477,400. *See also* MW p.88.

Ashbee, Charles Robert (1863–1942), British designer and architect, a leader of the ARTS AND CRAFTS MOVEMENT. He founded the Guild of Handicraft (1888–1913), distinguished for its fine work in the decorative arts, especially in book design.

Ashcan School, nickname given in the 1930s to a group of late 19th- and early 20th-century US artists, including George BELLOWS and Robert HENRI, who rejected academic and "aesthetic" subjects for the seamier aspects of city life (especially New York).

Ashcroft, Dame Peggy (1907–), leading British actress. Since her debut in 1926, she has covered the classical repertoire from SHAKESPEARE (notably as Desdemona in *Othello* in 1930) to PINTER. In 1968 she became a director of the ROYAL SHAKESPEARE COMPANY with whom she has appeared both at Stratford-upon-Avon and in London.

Ashdod, port in Israel, 5km (3 miles) from the Mediterranean Sea and 56km (35 miles) w of Jerusalem. It was a centre of the worship of Dagon. Revived by the Romans, the city ultimately became a centre of early Christian learning. Today it is one of the most important Israeli ports, with factories that make chemicals and synthetic fibres. Pop. 37,600.

Ashe, Arthur Robert (1943–), US tennis player. He won the US men's singles championships in 1968. In 1975 he won the World Championship Tennis title, and the Wimbledon Tournament – the first black American to do so.

Ashendene Press, important English printing concern founded in 1894, in an attempt to re-emphasize the earlier craft traditions of the trade and to adapt them to the requirements of the commercial press. Highly successful for a time, it closed in 1935.

Ashes, The, cricket trophy held by the winners of a Test series between England and Australia. It is an urn of ashes kept at Lord's, no matter which country wins the series. This sporting trophy originated in 1882 with a mock obituary notice in the *Sporting Times* about the death of English cricket after England had lost to Australia in a Test Match. The last words were "The body will be cremated and the ashes taken to Australia". The next season England won the series and a stump was burnt and the ashes presented in an urn to the English captain. *See also* CRICKET.

Ashes and Diamonds (1958), last of a trilogy of Polish films directed by Andrzej WAJDA. It is heavily symbolistic and deals with the political and social atmosphere in postwar Poland.

Ashikaga, city in central Japan, 80km (50 miles) N of Tokyo. It is an ancient silk-weaving centre and the site of a 9th-century school, containing a large collection of Chinese classics. Industries: textiles, metal products, machinery. Pop. (1970) 156,004.

Ashkenazy, Vladimir (1937–), Soviet pianist. He studied at the Central Music School of Moscow and the Conservatoire, Moscow. In 1956 he won the Queen Elizabeth International Piano Competition in Brussels, and in 1962 he shared first prize in the Tchaikovsky Piano Competition in Moscow.

Ashkhabad (Aščhabad), formerly Poltoratsk, a city in sw central Asia, USSR, near the border with Iran; capital of Turkmenistan (Turkmenskaya). It was founded in 1881 as a fortress. The city was severely damaged by an earthquake in 1948. Located on the Trans-Caspian Railway, it has factories that make textiles, glass and light machinery. Pop. 2,510,000.

Ashmole, Elias (1617–92), English antiquary who amassed a fine collection of books and other objects, which he donated (1675) to Oxford University. His collection was housed in the "Old Ashmolean" (opened 1683) and is the nucleus of the present museum (built 1841–45).

Ashmore and Cartier Islands, group of four uninhabited islands, administratively linked to Northern Territory, Australia, and lying in the Indian Ocean 320km (200 miles) NW of Western Australia. A weather station is maintained on West Island, part of the Ashmore group.

Ashoka (*c.* 274–*c.* 236 BC), Emperor of India, the first to unite most of the Indian subcontinent under a single authority. After the violent conquest of Kalinga in *c.* 261 he turned to Buddhism, which he promulgated throughout his realm in edicts which are preserved in rocks and pillars. *See also* HC1 pp.62–64.

Ashram, also called ashrama, a hermitage, retreat or settlement for a religious group, usually a GURU and his disciples. The term originated in India, but is also used for other religious communities.

Ashton, Eric (1935–), British rugby league player. One of the finest centres in the game, he captained Wigan and Great Britain, scoring more than 1,800 points in 501 appearances for his club.

Ashton, Sir Frederick (1906–), British choreographer, *b.* Ecuador. In 1935 he joined the Sadler's Wells Ballet in London (now the Royal Ballet) and was its chief choreographer until 1963, and subsequently became its director (1963–70). His classics, *Cinderella* (1948), *Ondine* (1958), *La Fille Mal Gardée* (1960), and many other works have been performed by major ballet companies around the world. *See also* HC2 p.*275*.

Ashton-Warner, Sylvia (1905–), New Zealand teacher and author who was influential in developing many progressive educational methods. Works recounting her teaching philosophy and experiences in Maori and US schools include *Teacher* (1963) and *Spearpoint: Teacher in America* (1972). Among her novels are *Spinster* (1957), *Bell Call* (1964) and *Three* (1970).

Ashur, national god of the Assyrians. A god of battle, he was depicted as eagle-headed and winged, usually in combination with the winged solar disc surmounted by a warrior. He is identified with the storm god BAAL (Bel-Marduk) of the city of Ashur, and has similarities to YAHWEH of the early Israelites.

Ashurbanipal (Assurbanipal), last great King of ASSYRIA (668–*c.* 627 BC). During his reign Assyria reached its highest level in art, architecture, literature and science. *See also* HC1 pp.28, 56.

Ashurbanipal, or Ashurnazirpal, II, King of ASSYRIA (883–859 BC). He contributed to the establishment of a more centralized Assyrian state by appointing governors to rule the western regions of the empire. *See also* HC1 pp.28, 56.

Ash Wednesday, the first day of Lent, 40 days before Easter (excluding Sundays). In Roman Catholic Churches, ashes are placed on the foreheads of members on that day, reminding them of their need for penance and forgiveness.

Ash Wednesday (1930), poem by T.S. ELIOT. Written after Eliot's conversion to Anglo-Catholicism, this six-part poem has a more traditional form and more hopeful religious theme than his earlier works.

Asia, largest continent of the world, entirely in the Eastern Hemisphere. It extends from N of the Arctic Circle in the USSR to s of the Equator in the islands of Indonesia.

Land. On the w Asia's boundary with Europe follows a line through the Ural Mountains, w of the Caspian Sea and along the Caucasus. Geographically Europe and Asia are one enormous continent – Eurasia – but historically they have always been thought of as separate continents. Asia has six districts and regions, each defined by mountain ranges.

Northern Asia includes the inhospitable region known as Siberia, extending from the Urals to the Pacific. A large part lies within the Arctic Circle forming a vast cold, treeless plain known as the TUNDRA where the soil, except on the surface, is permanently frozen to depths exceeding 700m (2,000ft). The s part of this region includes great coniferous forests (TAIGA) and the Russian steppe lands. Its s boundary runs through the Tien Shan and Yablonovy mountains and Lake Baikal, the world's deepest lake. The high plateau area of Central Asia extends s to the Himalayas and includes the w Chinese provinces of Tibet and Sinkiang as well as Mongolia. This is a region of low rainfall and very low winter temperatures. Much of the area is desert, the largest being the Gobi and Takla Makan deserts. The Tibetan plateau, entirely above 400m (1,310ft) is mostly barren.

Eastern Asia lies between the plateaus of Central Asia and the Pacific. It is a region of highlands and plains, watered by broad rivers. Off the E coast there are many islands, the most important being the Japanese islands of Hokkaido, Honshū and Kyūshū, and the Chinese island of Taiwan (Formosa). South-eastern Asia includes the Indochina Peninsula, part of which forms the Malay Peninsula, Burma and a large number of islands; the Philippines and the Indonesian islands are the most important. The N of this region is mountainous and the s mainly low-lying.

Southern Asia consists of the Indian subcontinent and the island of Sri Lanka (Ceylon). In the N it is bounded by the Hindu Kush, Pamir, Karakoram and Himalayan mountains. In the Himalayas, on the Nepal-Tibet border, is Mt Everest, 8,848m (29,029ft), the world's highest mountain. To the s of the mountains lie wide plains, crossed by rivers flowing from the Himalayas. Farther s is the Deccan, a triangular plateau that rises on its E and W edges culminating in the E and W Ghats. SW Asia includes most of the region known as the Middle East. It is made up largely of two peninsulas, Anatolia (Asia Minor) and the vast Arabian Peninsula. It is also a region of large inland seas: the Aral, Caspian, Dead and Black seas.

Structure and geology. The most striking feature of the continent is the massive range of Himalayan fold mountains that were formed when the Indo-Australian and Eurasian tectonic plates collided in the Mesozoic era. Most of China and southern USSR is composed of folded Palaeozoic and Mesozoic sediments and large expanses of central Siberia consist of flat-lying sediments of the same age, some completely exposed. The Indian subcontinent is largely Precambrian except for the Deccan Plateau which is a complex series of lava flows.

Lakes and rivers. Most of the major Asian lakes are found in the centre of the continent, and include the Caspian, which is the largest landlocked body of water in the world and is said to form the border between Europe and Asia, the Aral Sea, and lakes Balkhash and Baikal. The Chinese river Yangtze is the longest of Asia's many great rivers, 5,980km (3,716 miles) long. The Yellow River is China's other major river and until flood control measures were taken it flooded regularly, drowning thousands of people. The Indus, Brahmaputra and Ganges are the largest rivers of the Indian subcontinent, and the rivers Ob', Yenisey (Jenisej) and Lena are the continent's major N flowing streams.

Climate and vegetation. Except for the climate found on W temperate seaboards, all the world's major climatic divisions, with certain variations, are represented in the continent. The monsoonal climates of India and SE Asia are peculiar to these regions and apart from extremes of heat and cold typify the continent. Large expanses are covered by desert and semi-arid grassland with belts of coniferous forest to the N and tropical forest to the s.

Animals. The richest variety of animal life is found in the s and SE. Mammals include apes and monkeys, big cats such as tigers and leopards, and hoofed animals such as rhinoceroses and buffaloes.

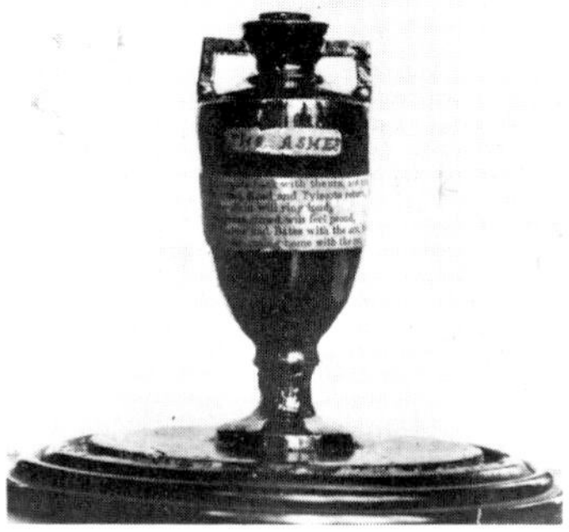

The Ashes, symbolic trophy for the winner of the England-Australia cricket test series.

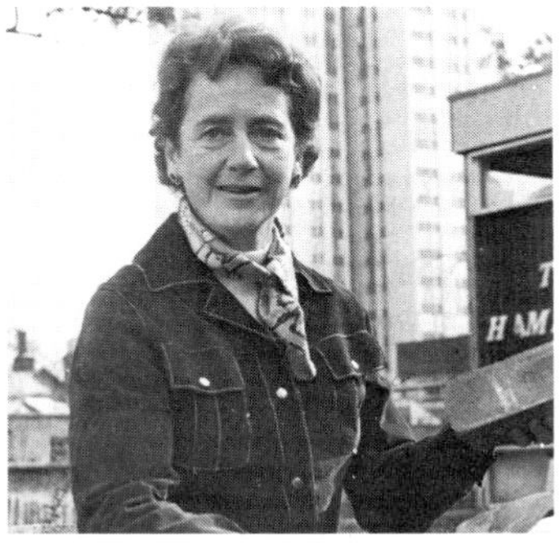

Dame Peggy Ashcroft at the reopening of the Hampstead Theatre Club in London.

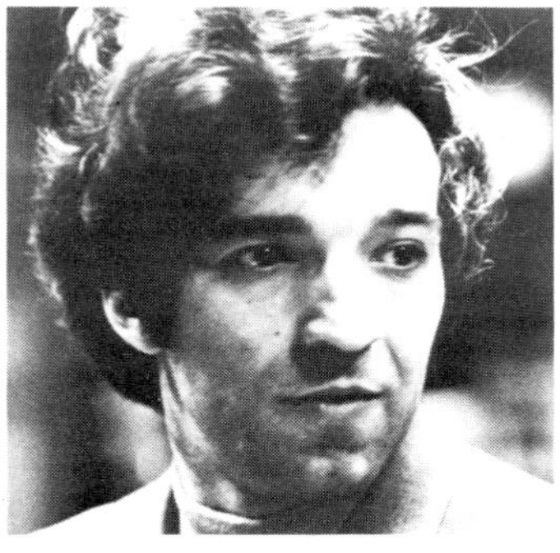

Vladimir Ashkenazy, the Soviet pianist, has been resident in Britain since 1963.

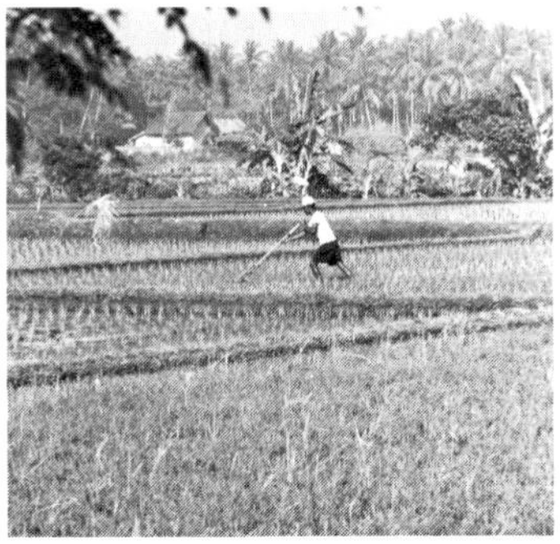

Asia has an economy founded mainly on agriculture; rice is the most important crop.

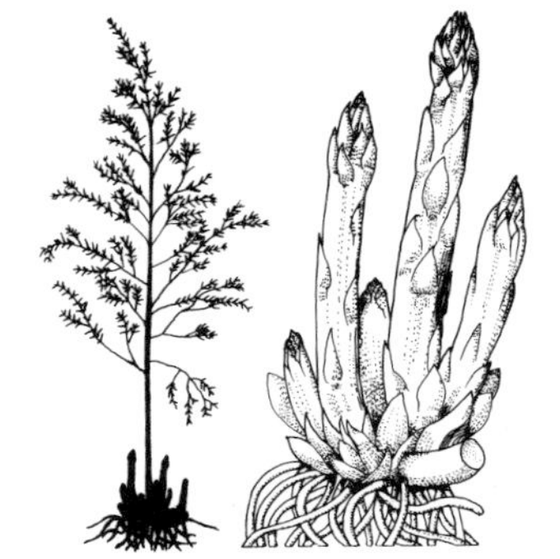

Asparagus can be grown as a vegetable or as an ornamental plant with fern-like foliage.

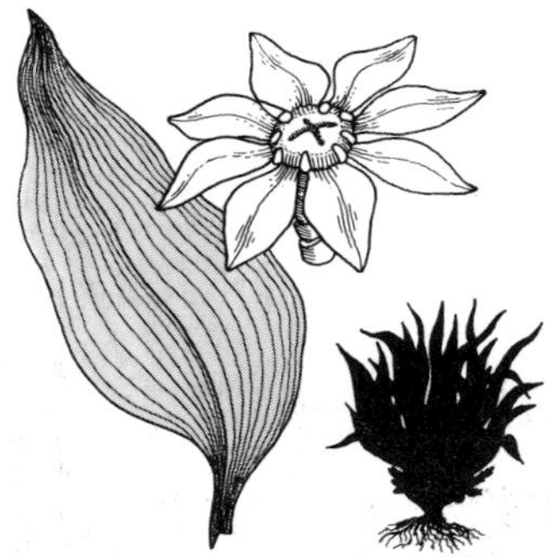

Aspidistra is widely grown indoors; it has glossy leaves and purple-brown flowers.

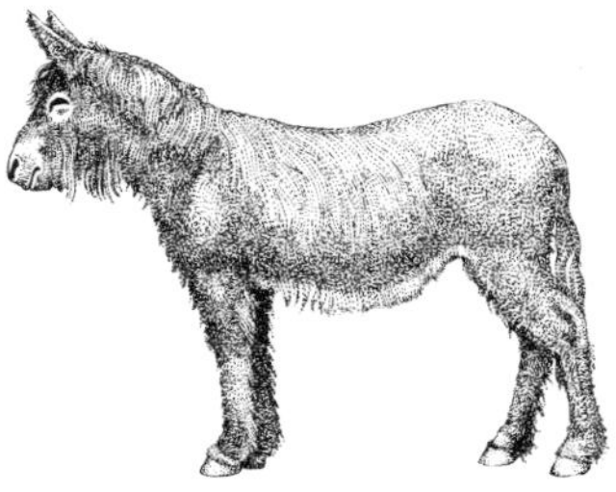

Asses survive in areas of little vegetation; the common donkey is a domesticated species.

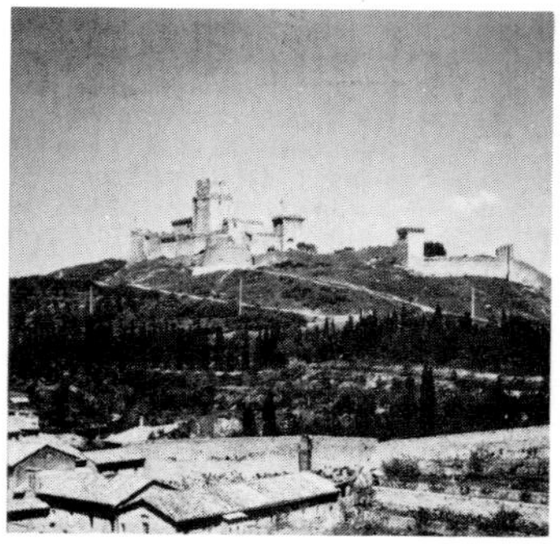

Assisi in central Italy is a historic hilltop town; St Francis was born and buried there.

There are also many poisonous creatures including snakes, scorpions, spiders and insects. Antelopes, rodents, wild asses and wild goats are common in the sw. Tibet and s China is the home of the giant panda. Wolves, reindeer, Arctic foxes, Arctic hares and lemmings roam the snows of the N. Birdlife ranges from penguins in the N to colourful tropical birds in the s.

People. Asia has half the world's population and is made up of many peoples who can be divided into two main categories: Mongoloid, inhabiting the E half of the continent, and Caucasian, whether light-skinned, (as in the USSR) or dark-skinned, (as in India), inhabiting the w. The main language groups are Indo-Aryan, Sino-Tibetan, Ural-Altaic, Malayan and Semitic. Hinduism is the religion with the most adherents, although it is confined to India and SE Asia; Islam, Confucianism, Buddhism, Shintoism, Christianity, Taoism and Judaism are also important.

Economy. Agriculture is important to most Asian countries, although less than 10% of the continent is cultivated. Rice is the major crop in the E and s, and wheat and barley are grown in the w and N. China, Japan and the USSR are the most highly industrialized countries, with India rapidly catching up. Oil is an important export of many sw Asian states.

Recent history. Since WWII the history of Asia has been dominated by two main themes: the throwing off of its Western colonial past and the steady advance of Communism. The Indian subcontinent gained its independence from Britain in 1947, when India and Pakistan became separate nations. In 1971 East Pakistan became the independent nation of Bangladesh. Malaysia achieved independence from Britain in 1957, Indonesia from Holland in 1945. The spread of Communism began with the victory of MAO TSE TUNG in China in 1949. North Korea failed during the war with South Korea (1950–53) to establish a united Communist state and Communism has been repulsed in Indonesia. Communists are now also a major power in Malaysia and have won control of Vietnam and Cambodia.

Area 44,391,206sq km (17,139,445sq miles)
Highest mountain Mt Everest (Nepal) 8,848m (29,029ft)
Longest river Yangtze (China) 5,980km (3,716 miles)
Population 2,255,458,000
Largest cities Shanghai (10,800,000); Tokyo (8,642,000); Peking (7,600,000)
See also NW pp.198–199, 206–209, 214–215, 222–223, 226–227; PE pp.48–51; articles on individual countries in *The Modern World.*

Asia Minor (Anatolia), great peninsula of w Asia making up most of modern Turkey. It is bordered by the Black Sea (N), the Mediterranean Sea (s) and by the Aegean Sea (w). The waterway made up of the Bosporus, the Sea of Marmara and the Dardanelles divides this region from Europe. Apart from a very narrow coastal plain the area is a high, arid plateau; in the SE the Taurus Range rises to more than 3,750m (12,000ft). *See also* MW p.167.

Asian Games, athletics championships for Asian countries, first held in 1951 and quadrennial since 1954. They have been dogged by political intrigue and usually dominated by Japan.

Asiento de negros, agreement, first made with Portugal in 1595 and later with Britain, by which Spain farmed out the slave trade in her colonies to foreign contractors.

Asimov, Isaac (1920–), US author and scientist, *b.* the USSR. Although he has published several serious scientific works, he first became widely known for his science fiction novels and short stories including *I, Robot* (1950) and *The Foundation Trilogy* (1963).

Asmara (Asmera), city in N Ethiopia, 64km (40 miles) sw of Mesewa; capital of Eritrean province. It was occupied by Italy in 1889, and was the main base for the Italian invasion of Ethiopia (1935–36), then called Abyssinia. It was capital of the Italian colony until captured by the British in 1941, becoming part of Ethiopia in 1952. The University of Asmara opened in 1958. Industries: meat-canning, ceramics, textiles. Pop. 318,000.

Asoka. *See* ASHOKA.

Aso-san, volcano in Japan, approx. 40km (25 miles) E of Kumamato on the island of Kyūshū It has one of the world's largest craters, between 16 and 24km (10-15 miles) across.

Asp, popular name for two species of VIPER, the asp viper of s Europe (*Vipera aspis*), and the Egyptian asp, a horned, side-winding viper of N Africa (*Cerastes cerastes*). Both are weakly venomous and eat small animals. Family: Viperidae. The asp that Cleopatra used to commit suicide was probably the Egyptian cobra (*Naja haja*; Family Elapidae). *See also* NW p.215.

Asparagus, perennial plants primarily native to Asia and Africa. They have tuberous or fleshy roots, scale-like leaves and small greenish flowers. *Asparagus officinalis* is grown widely for its edible tender shoots. Family Liliaceae. *See also* PE pp.188, 189.

Aspasia (*fl.* 440 BC), Greek noblewoman who became the mistress of the Athenian statesman PERICLES. Many famous Athenians used to meet in her house.

Aspen, one of three trees of the Poplar family, whose toothed, rounded leaves quake in the breeze. Native to temperate Eurasia, North Africa and North America, they grow up to 30m (100ft).

Asphalt, naturally occurring black or brown semi-solid bitumen, used mainly for road covering and roofing. Asphalts are found in deposits in many parts of the world, including Trinidad, Venezuela, Alabama and Texas. They are also a component of petroleum and are produced in oil refineries. They were probably produced by gradual chemical change of mineral oils. *See also* MM p.80.

Asphodel, perennial plants native to the Mediterranean region. They have white or yellow lily-like flowers. Family Liliaceae; genera *Asphodelus* and *Asphodeline.*

Aspidistra, or cast-iron plant, genus of durable house plants native to Asia, with long, broad, arching leaves. Height: to 91cm (3ft), Family Liliaceae.

Aspirin (acetylsalicylic acid), a DRUG widely used to reduce fever (antipyretic) and to relieve pain (ANALGESIC). It is effective against low-intensity pain such as headache or muscular aches, but not so effective against deep-seated internal organic pain. How it relieves pain is not fully understood. Aspirin irritates the stomach, is toxic in overdoses and can cause death. *See also* MS pp.*18–19.*

Asplenium, genus of ferns that includes spleenwort and bird's nest fern. Order Polypodiales.

Asplund, Gunnar (1885–1940), leading 20th-century Swedish architect, a major exponent in N Europe of FUNCTIONALISM, which he endowed with grace and restraint. Among his best works are the extension of the Town Hall of Goteborg (1937) and Stockholm Crematorium.

Asquith, Anthony (1902–68), British film director. Apart from well-made entertainment films, he directed stylish adaptations of stage works, such as *Pygmalion* (1938), *The Winslow Boy* (1948) and *The Importance of Being Earnest* (1952).

Asquith, Herbert Henry (1852–1918), First Earl of Oxford and Asquith, British Liberal Prime Minister (1908–16); MP for East Fife (1886–1918). His second cabinet appointment was as Chancellor of the Exchequer (1906–08), when he made the first provision for old-age pensions. His government, faced with House of Lords opposition to reforms such as Lloyd George's welfare budget of 1909, saw the passing of the Parliament Act (1911), which ended the Lords' power of veto. In 1916 he was replaced as Prime Minister by LLOYD GEORGE; he resigned as head of the Liberal party in 1926.

Asquith, Margot, Countess of Oxford and Asquith (1864–1945), second wife of Herbert Henry ASQUITH. She wrote a frank autobiography (1922) and several volumes of reminiscences.

Ass, wild, speedy, long-eared member of the HORSE family found in African and Asian desert and mountain areas. Smaller than the horse, it has a short mane and tail, small hoofs and dorsal stripes. It brays instead of neighing. The three African races (species *Equus asinus*) are the Nubian, North African and the rare Somali. Height: 90-150cm (3-5ft) at shoulder. Asian races are the KIANG and the ONAGER. Family Equidae. *See also* NW p.*222, 243.*

Assad, Hafez al- (1928–), President of Syria. He attended the Syrian Military Academy and rose through the ranks to become a general. From 1965 to 1970 he was Minister of Defence and Commander-in-Chief of the air force, positions he used to gain power and influence. In 1970 he seized power through a coup. His policies have been militantly anti-Zionist.

Assam, state in NE India, almost cut off from the rest of the country by Bangladesh and Bhutan. Ruled as part of the Ahom Empire (*c.* 1400–1826), it became part of the British Empire in 1826. Industries: tea, jute, timber. Pop. 14,857,000. *See also* MW p.95.

Assamese, language spoken in Assam by about 7 million people. It belongs to the Indic branch of the Indo-Iranian subdivision of the Indo-European family of languages.

Assassin, secret Muslim sect founded *c.* 1090 by Hasan ibn al-Sabbah. It quickly gained control of the Muslim world by spreading terror. The members were organized into two classes with the highest class as devotees. They were used as instruments of assassination, sometimes sacrificing their own lives. The order was noted in the tales of Marco POLO and the Crusaders, who brought the term "assassin" to Europe. It derives from the alleged use of hashish (a drug made from Indian hemp) by terrorists seeking ecstatic visions. *See also* HC1 p.224.

Assault, in law, an attempt by a person using force or violence and with the ability to do bodily harm to another person.

Assay, the result of determining the amount of a specific metal (especially gold, silver or platinum) in ores or metallurgical products.

Assembly line, in factory production, a process line in which each worker carries out a particular task, these culminating at the end of the line in a completely assembled complex unit – eg, a car engine or body. *See also* MM pp.94–95.

Assent, Royal, approval given by the British sovereign or his representative to a bill that has been agreed by Parliament. Once it has received the royal assent a bill becomes an ACT OF PARLIAMENT.

Asser (died *c.* 910), Welsh monk who wrote an authoritative biography of ALFRED THE GREAT. He entered the royal household in about 885 and spent much of his time teaching the king and recording the history of his reign. As a reward, he was made Bishop of Sherborne.

Asser, Tobias Michael Carel (1838–1913), Dutch jurist. He shared the 1911 Nobel Peace Prize with Alfred Hermann FRIED.

Assisi, town of Perugia province, in the Umbria region of Italy, 19km (12 miles) ESE of Perugia. Its ancient name was Asisium. The birthplace of St FRANCIS, the town contains a medieval fortress, a 12th-century cathedral and the sacred convent of St Francis. Chief industry: tourism. Pop. 24,600.

Assiut. *See* ASYUT.

Assizes, in English Common Law, courts that were held in provincial towns at regular intervals, presided over by peripatetic High Court judges. The assizes were founded by HENRY II in the 1160s. They have been replaced in England by CROWN COURTS. *See also* MS p.297.

Associated State of the United Kingdom, status which gives full internal self-government to a British colony, but control of external affairs to the UK. It was adopted first by Antigua in 1967.

Association football. *See* FOOTBALL.

Assumption, in the Roman Catholic Church, principal feast of the Blessed Virgin Mary, celebrated on 15 August.

Assurdan II, ruler of Assyria from 935 to

913 BC. He briefly restored Assyrian military authority, but by his death the empire was at its smallest extent.

Assy, village and sanatorium, about 800m (2,600ft) above sea-level, in Haute-Savoie département, E France. Its Church of Notre Dame (1937–50) was decorated by Georges BRAQUE, Henri MATISSE and others.

Assyria, ancient empire of the Middle East. It took its name from the city of ASHUR, or Assur, which was located on the River Tigris near the modern city of Mosul, Iraq. At its height, the Assyrian Empire comprised the modern nations of Iraq, Syria, Jordan, Israel and Egypt; and it included parts of Saudi Arabia, Armenia and Asia Minor (Turkey). The Assyrian Empire had its beginning in the 3rd millennium BC, reached its zenith between the 9th and 7th centuries BC, and thereafter went into swift decline and was absorbed into the Persian Empire. ASHURBANIPAL (*d.c.*627 BC) was the last great Assyrian king. Under his rule Assyrian art – particularly its great bas-relief sculpture – and Assyrian learning reached their peak. The luxuriance of Ashurbanipal's court at NINEVEH was legendary. The cost of maintaining his huge armies, added to the sumptuousness of his court, fatally weakened the empire. Two of his sons ruled briefly after his death, but with the capture of Nineveh in 612 BC, the empire fell into ruin. *See also* HC1 pp.56–57.

Assyro-Babylonian mythology described a cosmic order of heaven, earth and an underworld and populated it with some 4,000 deities and demons to direct the physical and spiritual activities of the world. The complex stories dealing with the Mesopotamian pantheon are generally regarded as literary entertainments or interesting explanations of natural occurrences and religious rituals, having little effect on the daily lives of the people. *See also* MS pp.213–214.

Astaire, Fred (1899–), US dancer and film star, real name Frederick Austerlitz. He worked with his sister, Adele, in music hall until she retired in 1932, after which he starred with Ginger ROGERS in a number of 1930s musical films outstanding for their sophisticated and exuberant choreography. His major films include *The Gay Divorcee* (1934), *Top Hat* (1935), *Swing Time* (1936), *Royal Wedding* (1951), *Funny Face* (1957) and the drama *On the Beach* (19,9). *See also* HC2 p.*268*.

Astarte, also Ashtar or Ashtoreth, Phoenician goddess of fertility and love, the equivalent of ISHTAR of the Assyro-Babylonians and APHRODITE of the Greeks. She is represented by a crescent, perhaps symbolic of the moon or the horns of a cow. The dove, gazelle and myrtle were sacred to her. *See also* HC1 p.54.

Astatine, radioactive element (At) of the HALOGEN group, first made (1940) by bombarding bismuth with alpha particles. It has been made only in trace amounts. Properties: at. no.85; m.p. 302°C (576°F); b.p. 337°C (639°F); most stable isotope At^{210} (half-life 8.3hr).

Aster, genus of mostly perennial, leafy-stemmed plants native to the Americas and Eurasia. Asters are popular garden plants and most bear daisylike flowers. The outer rays are yellow, white, blue, pink or purple and the inner discs are yellow, which turns darker with age. Family Compositae.

Asteroid, minor planet or planetoid, any of several thousand small celestial bodies orbiting the Sun in the region between Mars and Jupiter. Ranging in diameter from only a few kilometres to several hundred, asteroids may be the remains of a planet that broke up or failed to attain a stable existence. *See also* SU p.203.

Asthenosphere, the Earth's upper mantle, extending from 100 to 700km (60–430 miles) below the surface. *See also* MANTLE; PE p.20.

Asthma, disorder of the respiratory system in which the bronchial air passages narrow, making breathing difficult. It can result from infection in the lungs, nose or sinuses or, more commonly, by an allergic reaction to pollen, animals, dust, foods or drugs. Attacks may be provoked by emotional stress, climate, polluted atmospheres and fatigue. The chest feels tight and breathing is difficult, with a characteristic "wheeze" and gasping for air; sputum is also coughed up. Allergic asthma may be treated, after tests, by injections aimed at lessening sensitivity to specific allergens. Otherwise treatment is by drugs, including steroids, antibiotics and inhalers; in severe attacks hydrocortisone injections may be given. Children often get better as they grow up, although some people suddenly acquire the disease in middle age. In the acute form, the attacks are usually severe and follow longish periods of otherwise good health. The chronic condition is marked less by severe attacks than by a general breathing impairment. *See also* BRONCHITIS; EMPHYSEMA; LUNGS; MS pp.88, 89, 142.

Asti, capital of Asti province in the Piedmont region, NW Italy, 45km (28 miles) ESE of Turin (Torino). An influential medieval republic, it reached its prime in the 13th century, and was controlled by Savoy in the 16th century. Industries: chemicals, wine making, food processing. Pop. 76,150.

Astigmatism, defect of vision in which the cornea or lens is curved more strongly in one plane than another. It can usually be corrected with glasses. *See also* MS p.*49*.

Aston, Francis William (1877–1945), British scientist. He was awarded the 1922 Nobel Prize in chemistry for his work on isotopes. He invented the mass spectrograph, and proved that elements are composed of mixtures of various isotopes. *See also* SU p.151.

Astor, family of American financiers. Its founder, John Jacob Astor (1763–1848), was an immigrant from Germany who became a successful businessman in New York. He founded the American Fur Company in 1808, and after 1812 acquired a virtual monopoly of the US fur trade. He concentrated on land investment after 1834 and became the wealthiest man in the USA. His great-great-grandson William Waldorf (1879–1952) was married to Viscountess Nancy Wither Astor (1879–1964), who in 1919 became the first woman to sit in the House of Commons. William Waldorf was owner of the *Observer* newspaper. In the 1930s their country house, Cliveden, was the centre of a group that advocated APPEASEMENT of Nazi Germany. William's brother, John Jacob (1886–1971), 1st baron Astor of Hever, was owner of *The Times* newspaper from 1922 to 1966.

Astraea, Greek goddess of justice. She is usually depicted carrying scales and wearing a crown of stars. Daughter of ZEUS and Themis, she fled to the skies when men began forging weapons of war. Astraea formed the constellation VIRGO in the ZODIAC.

Astrakhan (Astrachan), city in SE European USSR and a port on the Caspian Sea approx. 378km (235 miles) SE of Volgograd. It is capital of Astrachan oblast and site of the USSR's largest fishery. A railway, airline and oil shipping terminal, it is an important trade centre. It possesses a walled kremlin (1587–89) and cathedral (1700–10). The city was expanded in the 13th century under Mongols near the site of the ancient Khazar city of Itil (8th-10th century). It became a Tartar stronghold until its capture (1554–56) by IVAN (IV) the Terrible. In the civil war (1917–20) the city remained in White Russian hands, becoming a base for the Caspian Sea conquest of 1920. Industries include shipbuilding, engineering, oil-refining, paper and food processing. Pop. (1970) 411,000.

Astringents, agents which heal mucous membranes and raw sores by narrowing the blood vessels (cocaine), abstracting water (alcohol) or making scabs (metallic astringents).

Astrodynamics, application of celestial mechanics, ballistics, mathematical perturbation theory, and the principle of observation reduction to determine, predict and correct orbits and trajectories in space. *See also* CELESTIAL MECHANICS.

Astrology, pseudoscientific study of the influence supposedly exercised by celestial bodies upon the lives of human beings. It originated in Babylon about 3,000 years ago and sought, by means of arbitrary rules, to predict an individual's fate according to the motions and positions of the Sun, Moon and planets at the time of his birth. For this purpose accurate observational records were begun which led to the exact science of ASTRONOMY. *See also* MS p.200.

Astronaut (Russian: cosmonaut), person who navigates or rides in a space vehicle; also a person selected for a training programme to fly in space vehicles. The first man in space was the Russian Yuri GAGARIN in 1961. The first man on the Moon was the American Neil ARMSTRONG in 1969. The first woman in space was the Russian Valentina Tereshkova in 1963. *See also* SU pp.180, 268.

Astronomer Royal, head of the British Royal Observatory, which was founded in 1675 at Greenwich but has been gradually moved to Herstmonceux, Sussex, since WWII. The first Astronomer Royal was John FLAMSTEED; since 1972 the position has been held by Sir Martin RYLE.

Astronomical telescope. *See* TELESCOPE.

Astronomical unit (AU), unit of length used for the measurement of distances within the solar system and as a base line for the measurement of stellar parallax. It is equal to the mean distance of the Earth from the Sun, approx. 149,600,000km (92,957,000 miles). *See also* SU p.166.

Astronomy, branch of science studied since ancient times and concerned with the universe and its components in terms of the relative motions of celestial bodies, their positions on the celestial sphere, physical and chemical structure, evolution and the phenomena occurring on them. It includes celestial mechanics, ASTROPHYSICS, COSMOLOGY and astrometry. Waves in all regions of the ELECTROMAGNETIC SPECTRUM can now be studied either with ground-based instruments or, where no atmospheric window exists, by observations and measurements made from satellites, space probes and rockets.

History. Astronomy was first used practically to develop a calendar, the units of which were determined by observing the heavens. The Chinese had a calendar in the 14th century BC. The Greeks developed astronomy significantly between 600 BC and AD 200. THALES introduced geometrical ideas and PYTHAGORAS saw the universe as a series of concentric spheres. ARISTOTLE believed the Earth to be stationary but he explained lunar eclipses correctly. ARISTARCHUS put forward a heliocentric theory. HIPPARCHUS used trigonometry to determine astronomical distances. PTOLEMY's system was a geometrical representation of the SOLAR SYSTEM that predicted the motions of the planets with great accuracy.

From then on astronomy remained dormant until the scientific revolution of the 16th and 17th centuries, when COPERNICUS' theory, that the Earth rotates on its axis and, with all the other planets, revolves round the Sun, had a profound effect upon the religion and philosophy of the day. KEPLER's laws of planetary motion refined the theory of heliocentric motion, and his contemporary, GALILEO, made use of the TELESCOPE and discovered the moons of Jupiter. Isaac NEWTON combined the sciences of astronomy and physics. His laws of motion and universal theory of GRAVITATION provided a physical basis for Kepler's laws and the work of many astronomers from then on – eg, in the prediction of HALLEY'S COMET and the discovery of the planets Uranus, Neptune and Pluto. By the early 19th century the science of celestial mechanics, the study of the motions of bodies in space as they move under the influence of their mutual gravitation, had become highly advanced and new mathematical techniques permitted the solution of the remaining problems of classical gravitation theory as applied to the Solar System. In the second half of the nineteenth century astronomy was revolutionized by the introduction of techniques based on photography and SPECTROSCOPY. These encouraged investigation into the

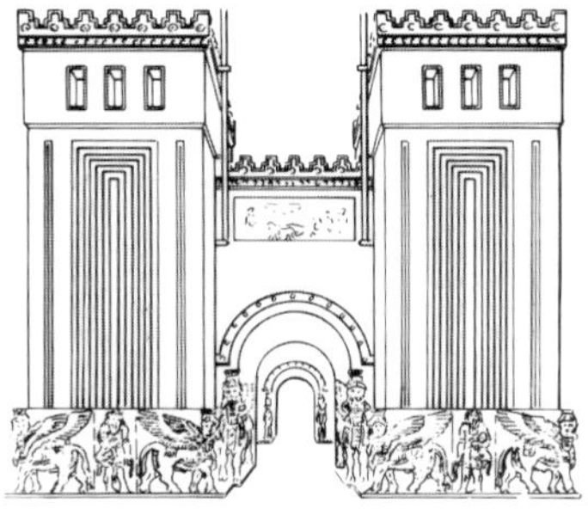

Assyria produced striking architecture; major buildings had impressive sculpture.

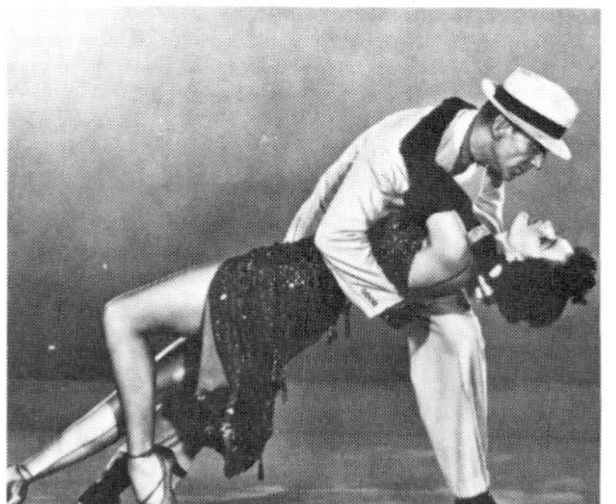

Fred Astaire, dancer supreme, partnered many famous screen stars, including Cyd Charisse.

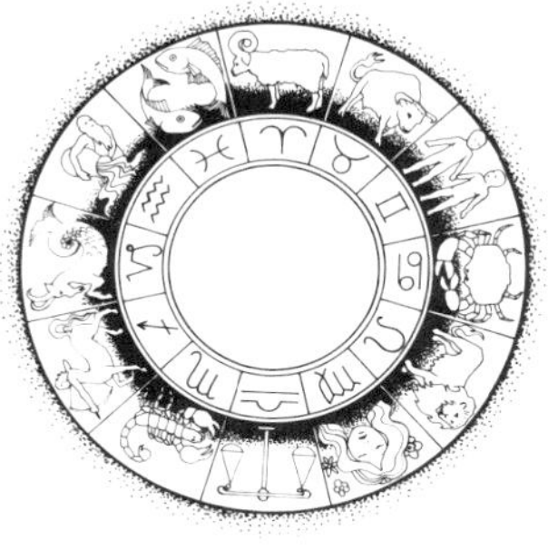

Astrology is based on the assumption that heavenly bodies influence people's lives.

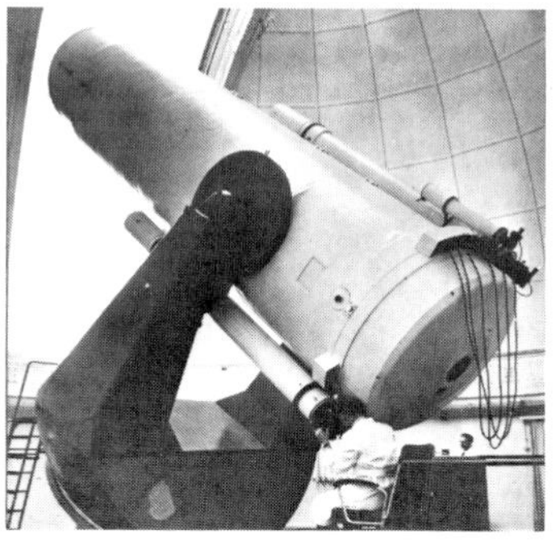

Astronomy; here scientists look out into space using a giant astronomical telescope.

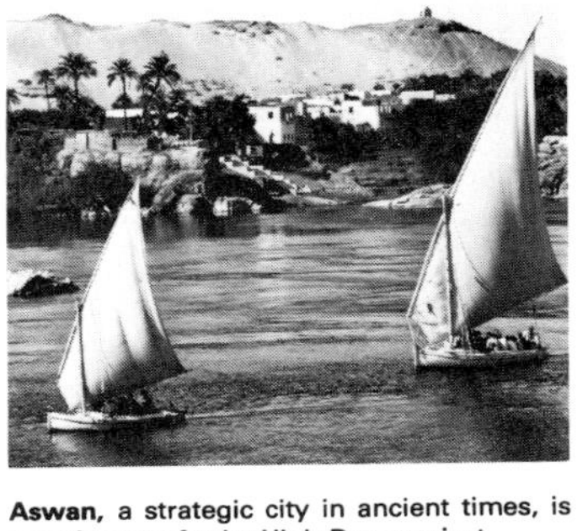

Aswan, a strategic city in ancient times, is now famous for its High Dam project.

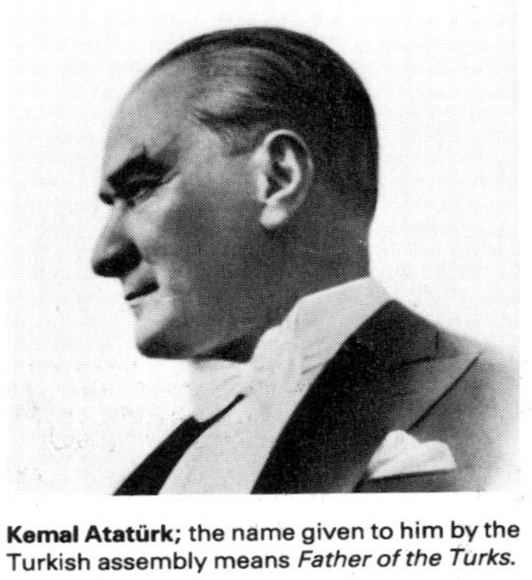

Kemal Atatürk; the name given to him by the Turkish assembly means *Father of the Turks.*

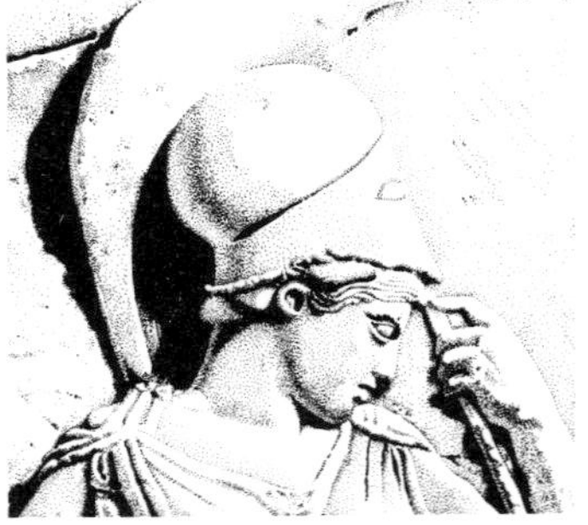

Athena was childless and was often referred to as Pallas (Maiden) or Parthenos (Virgin).

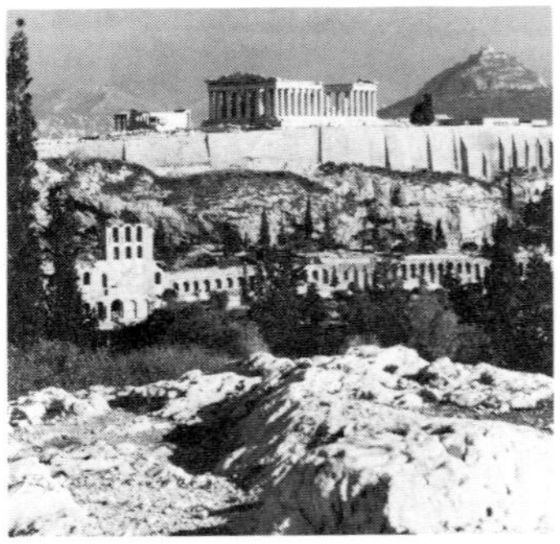

Athens; the Acropolis and the magnificent Parthenon, dedicated to the goddess Athena.

physical composition of stars, rather than their position. Ejnar HERTZSPRUNG and H. N. RUSSELL studied the relationship between the colour of a star and its luminosity. By this time also larger telescopes were being constructed, which extended the limits of the universe known to man. Harlow SHAPLEY determined the shape and size of our galaxy and E.P. HUBBLE's study of distant galaxies led to his theory of an expanding universe. The "Big Bang" and Steady State theories of the origins of the universe were formulated. In recent years space exploration and observation in different parts of the electromagnetic spectrum have contributed to the discovery and postulation of such phenomena as QUASARS, PULSARS and BLACK HOLES.

There are various branches of modern astronomy:

Gamma-ray astronomy is concerned with the study of gamma rays, which cannot penetrate the Earth's atmosphere and must be studied from satellites. The Sun is the principal source. *See* SU p.172.

Infra-red astronomy is concerned with detecting infra-red (IR) waves, determining their source and studying their spectra. Most IR radiation is absorbed by the Earth's atmosphere. The Sun and the centre of the galaxy are sources of IR radiation. *See* SU p.172.

Optical astronomy is the oldest branch which studies sources of light in space. Light rays can penetrate the atmosphere but, because of disturbances, many observations are now made from above the atmosphere. *See* SU pp.168, 170.

Radar astronomy is used to determine distance, orbital motion and surface features of objects in the solar system. Radar pulses are bounced back to Earth from the object. *See* SU p.167.

Radio astronomy uses radio telescopes to detect radio waves from space and determine their source and energy spectrum. The most powerful sources include the Sun, interstellar clouds of hot hydrogen, such as the Orion Nebula, supernova remnants and pulsars, like the Crab Nebula, quasars and radio galaxies. *See* SU p.172.

Ultra-violet astronomy studies ultraviolet (UV) waves from space, their source and spectra. Higher wavelengths can be studied from the ground but lower wavelengths must be studied from satellites and balloons. Sources include the Sun, the Orion Nebula, and Wolf-Rayet stars. *See* SU p.172.

X-ray astronomy is concerned with studying X-ray sources. X-rays are absorbed by the Earth's atmosphere so detecting instruments must be carried in satellites. Sources include the Sun, the Crab Nebula, Cygnus A and the galaxy M87. *See* SU p.172. *See also* index to *Science and the Universe*.

Astrophysics, branch of ASTRONOMY that studies the physical and chemical nature of celestial bodies and their evolution. Many branches of physics, including nuclear physics, plasma physics, relativity and spectroscopy, are used in predicting properties of celestial bodies and in interpreting the information obtained from astronomical studies of the electromagnetic spectrum, including light, X-rays and radio waves. *See also* SU p.226.

Asturias, Miguel Angel (1899–1974), Guatemalan novelist. He won the Nobel Prize in literature in 1967. His most famous novel, *El Señor Presidente* (1946), condemns dictatorship. Although it is based on conditions in Guatemala its message is universal. In it the author criticizes the change from a rural, "natural" world to an urbanized community dominated by a dictator.

Asturias, region in NW Spain, bordering the Bay of Biscay and traversed by the Cantabrian Mountains. The region was named by the Iberians in the 2nd century BC and is famous for its cider and coal mines, the richest in Spain. Industries: coal, manganese, mining, steel and non-ferrous metal production, fishing, fruit. Pop. 1,045,600.

Asunción, capital and largest city of Paraguay, located in the SW on the E bank of the River Paraguay at its junction with the River Pilcomayo. It is Paraguay's chief port and an administrative, industrial and cultural centre. Founded about 1536 as a trading post and Jesuit mission (1538), it was the scene of the Communeros rebellion against Spanish rule in 1721. It was later occupied by Brazil (1868–76). The city's features include the Panteón Nacional (a tomb for national heroes), the Encarnación Church, the National University (1889) and the Catholic University (1960). Industries: vegetable oil mills, textiles, food processing. Pop. (1975 est.) 574,000.

Aswan, city in SE Egypt, on the E bank of the River Nile just above Lake Nasser; capital of Aswan province. Originally an Egyptian settlement called Syene, meaning "market place", the city was of strategic importance to the Egyptians and Greeks because it controlled all shipping and communications above the first cataract of the Nile. The modern city is a commercial and tourist centre and has benefited greatly from the construction of the Aswan High Dam. The dam, completed in 1970, has a generating capacity of 10,000 million kilowatt-hours. The rock terrain surrounding the lake abounds in Egyptian and Greek temples and although some archaeological treasures were lost under water, the temples of ABU-SIMBEL were moved and saved. Industries: steel, textiles, tourism. Pop. 246,000.

Asynchronous transmission, the fastest method of programme execution in computers; the beginning of each operation is signalled by the stop bit at the end of the previous one.

As You Like It (1599–1600), comedy by William SHAKESPEARE.

Asyūt, city and trade centre on the River Nile in E central Egypt. Its ancient name was Lycopolis. The nearby Asyūt Barrage helps to regulate the flow of the Nile and stores water for irrigation. Industries: inorganic chemicals, textiles, ceramics, handcrafts. Pop. (1971 est.) 181,200.

Atabrine, quinacrine hydrochloride, a drug used in the prevention and treatment of MALARIA.

Atacama Desert, in N Chile, is considered to be the driest desert in the world and, except for where it is artificially irrigated, is devoid of vegetation. It was crossed in 1540 by the Spanish conquistador Pedro de Valdivia. Until the advent of synthetic fertilizers, the desert was extensively mined for sodium nitrate. Although the mining boom is over, large deposits of copper and other minerals remain.

Atahualpa (*c.*1502–33), also known as Atabalipa, last Inca ruler of Peru. The son of Huayna Capac, he fought his brother Huáscar for control of the Inca kingdom and defeated him in 1532, the year Francisco PIZARRO arrived in northern Peru. Atahualpa was later taken prisoner by Pizarro and executed. *See also* HC1 pp.232–233, 236–237.

Atalanta, in Greek mythology, a swift-footed huntress who was suckled by a she-bear. She offered to marry any man who could outrun her, and to kill those who failed. APHRODITE gave three of the golden apples of the HESPERIDES to Hippomenes, who undertook to race Atalanta. During the race he dropped them one by one, distracting and delaying his opponent. They married, but in later life ZEUS turned them into lions.

Atatürk, Kemal (1881–1938), *b.* Mustafa Kemal, founder of modern Turkey. As a youth he joined the Young Turks, a liberal movement that sought to establish a government independent of Ottoman rule. He fought against the Italians in Tripolitania in 1911 and served with distinction in WWI. In 1919 he organized a Turkish Nationalist party in E Anatolia and formed an army. He also announced the aims of an independent Turkish state and in 1921–22 he expelled the Greeks from Anatolia. He abolished the sultanate in 1922 and proclaimed the republic in 1923. Elected President in 1923 and re-elected in 1927, 1931 and 1935, he instituted sweeping reforms aimed at Westernizing Turkey.

Atavism, out-of-date term for a genetic reversion by an organism or any one of its parts to a characteristic of its ancestors after an interval of at least one generation in which the trait was absent.

Athabascan, or Athapascan, also known as Slave Indians, tribe and language group of North American Indians inhabiting NW Canada. They were forced north to the Great Slave Lake and Fort Nelson by the Cree, and their common name, Slave, derives from the domination and forced labour exacted by the Cree. The Athabascan tribe has always been closely linked to the Chipewyan people, and some authorities regard the two as one group. The Athabascan language, which derives from the tribe, covers the largest geographical area of all North American Indian groups: from the Cree in Canada to the Hupa in California, and the Navajo and Apache of the SW. The number of Athabascan-speaking Indians in North America is believed to exceed 250,000.

Athanasian Creed, Christian profession of faith, probably written in the 6th century, that explains the teachings of the Church on the Trinity and the incarnation. It is accepted as authoritative by the Roman Catholic and Anglican churches.

Athanasius, Saint (*c.* 297-373), Doctor of the Church. As Patriarch of Alexandria he confuted ARIANISM and in *Four Orations against the Arians* (357) he represented the TRINITY as three persons in one nature, thereby maintaining the divinity of Christ. He is no longer considered the author of the ATHANASIAN CREED.

Atheism, literally "without God", a system of thought developed around the denial of the existence of God. Atheism, so defined, first appeared during the ENLIGHTENMENT, the age of reason. In ancient Greece it meant refusal to worship the state deities. It is different from AGNOSTICISM, which merely expresses uncertainty about the existence of God. *See also* MS p.224.

Athelney, Isle of, historic area formerly surrounded by marshland in Somerset, SW England. In 878 King ALFRED took refuge there from the Danes and later moved from that stronghold to defeat them. He founded a Benedictine abbey on the Isle in 888 to give thanks for this victory.

Athelstan (*c.*895–939), King of England (924–939). As King of the Mercians and the West Saxons, he gained Northumbria and invaded Scotland. In 937 he confirmed his rule over most of England by his decisive victory over the Scots, Danes and Welsh at Brunanburh.

Athena (Athene), Greek goddess of war and patroness of the arts and industry (Roman, MINERVA). Athena was born fully grown and armed from the head of ZEUS. As a war goddess she emphasized skill and justice. In the TROJAN WAR she sided with the Greeks. She inspired sculptural masterpieces by Phidias and the ship Argo by Argus, for JASON and the Argonauts. Athens was named after her. *See also* MS p.206.

Athenagoras (*fl.* 2nd century), Greek philosopher and Christian apologist. His *Embassy for the Christians*, addressed to MARCUS AURELIUS, appeared in *c.* 177.

Athens (Athínai), capital city of Greece situated on the Saronic Gulf. The ancient city was built around the Acropolis, a fortified citadel, and was the greatest art and cultural centre in ancient Greece, gaining importance after the PERSIAN WARS (500–449 BC). The city prospered under Cimon and PERICLES during the 5th century BC and provided a climate in which the great classical works of PHILOSOPHY and DRAMA were created. Defeated by SPARTA in the PELOPONNESIAN WAR of 431–404 BC, Athens lost supremacy in Greece and declined under Roman domination (from 228 BC). Since Greece became an independent kingdom after the Greek War of Independence (1821–32), Athens has regained its former standing as a cultural and commercial centre. The most noted artistic treasures are the Parthenon (438 BC), created by Ictinus and Callicrates, the temple to Athena, Athena Parthenos (a Doric statue), the Erechtheum (406 BC) and the Theatre of Dionysus (*c.* 500 BC, the oldest of the Greek theatres). Modern Athens and its port of Piraeus form a major transportation and economic centre in the Mediterranean area. Industries include shipbuilding, papermills, steel machinery, textiles, breweries, chemicals, glass and tourism. Pop. (1971) 2,530,207. *See also* HC1 pp.70–71, *70–71*; MS pp.272, *278*.

Atherosclerosis, thickening of artery walls caused by fatty deposits, a common arterial disease. *See* ARTERIOSCLEROSIS; MS p.90, *91*.

Athlete's foot, contagious, fungus-caused infection that usually appears first between the last two toes. Itching, macerated skin and blisters are usual symptoms. *See also* MS p.*98*.

Athletic Park, sports stadium in Wellington, New Zealand; home of the New Zealand Rugby Union, rugby Test venue, and home ground of the Wellington provincial side.

Athletics, composite sport that includes running and hurdling events on the track, jumping and throwing field events, cross-country and long-distance road running, and walking. In the USA it is known as "track and field sports", the term "athletics" embracing all competitive sports. Men have competed with each other in tests of speed and strength for thousands of years. It is known that the ancient Greek OLYMPIC GAMES were held as early as 776 BC, and possibly as much as 600 years earlier, but it is thought that the Tailtean Games in Ireland were founded even before that, in 1829 BC. A sport called pedestrianism became popular in 17th-century England, in which wagers were struck by men of means on the road-running ability of their footmen. But it was not until the 19th century that modern athletics originated – at the Royal Military Academy, Sandhurst; in the public schools; and above all in the universities of Oxford and Cambridge, which inaugurated their annual match in 1864. The first modern Olympics were held at Athens in 1896, since when athletics has always been a predominantly amateur sport. The world's governing body, the International Amateur Athletic Federation, was established in 1912. Each athletics event has a separate article in the *Fact Index*.

Atholl, Scottish dukedom. John Murray (1635–1703), the 2nd Earl and 1st Marquess of Atholl, was a Royalist who was involved in a rising against the COMMONWEALTH in 1653 and later held office under CHARLES II. He lost royal favour after opposing the repression of the Scottish COVENANTERS by LAUDERDALE in 1678. He supported James II and flirted with the JACOBITES, was pardoned and he helped to pacify the Highlands. His son John Murray (1659–1724), 2nd Marquess and 1st Duke of Atholl, opposed the Act of Union but later rose to high office and helped to repress the JACOBITE REBELLION of 1715. *See also* HC1 pp.298–299.

Athos, Holy mountain in NE Greece, at the E end of the Acte Peninsula. It is located inside the autonomous Mt Athos community of monasteries. Height: 2,032m (6,667ft).

Atkins, Thomas, nickname for the British infantry soldier, sometimes shortened to "Tommy". The name was first used on a specimen army form in the 1800s; it is possible that it commemorates a real person.

Atkinson, Sir Harry (1831–92), New Zealand Prime Minister, *b.* Cheshire, England. He formed three governments between 1876 and 1891. He was renowned for his financial expertise and for his social welfare programme.

Atlanta, industrial city and state capital of Georgia, USA. It is a major distribution, commercial, cultural and finanical capital. The land was ceded to Georgia in 1821 by the Creek Indians and was settled in 1833; the city was founded in 1837 at the E end of the Western and Atlantic Railroad and was originally called Terminus. It served as a Confederate supply depot and communications centre during the AMERICAN CIVIL WAR. On 2 Sept. 1864, it fell to Gen. Sherman who fired it on 15 Nov. The city was rapidly rebuilt and soon recovered its former importance. It was made temporary state capital in 1868 and, by popular vote, permanent capital in 1887. During the 20th century, Atlanta has grown to become one of the USA's major cities. The site of the state legislature, it contains numerous educational and cultural institutions among which are the High Museum of Art and the Emory University, founded in 1836. Industries: textiles, chemicals, glass, paper, timber, iron and steel, electronics, agricultural machinery, car and aircraft assembly and food processing. Pop. (1973) 451, 123.

Atlantic, Battle of the (1939–43), WWII engagements arising from Germany's attempt to starve Britain into submission by U-boat attacks on merchant shipping. More than 14 million tonnes of shipping was destroyed. *See also* HC2 pp.228, *229*, 230.

Atlantic Charter, joint declaration of peace aims issued in Aug. 1941 by the US President Franklin D. ROOSEVELT and the British Prime Minister Winston CHURCHILL. It affirmed the right of all nations to choose their own form of government, promised to restore sovereignty to all nations that had lost it, and advocated the disarmament of all aggressor nations.

Atlantic Monthly, US magazine (founded 1857) of current events and reviews of high repute. James Russell LOWELL was its first editor, and William Dean HOWELLS edited the magazine from 1871 to 1881.

Atlantic Ocean, the world's second largest ocean. It stretches from the Arctic circle in the N to the Antarctic, or Southern, Ocean in the S. Its most striking feature is the Mid-Atlantic Ridge which runs N-S for its entire length. At the crest, the ridge is cleft by a deep rift valley which is frequently offset by E-W transform faults. The age of the crust steadily increases with distance from the central rift, and so there is little doubt that the rift has evolved by sea-floor spreading and is associated with the movement of the Americas away from Europe and Africa at a rate of 2–4cm (0.8–1.6in) per year.

Currents. The current pattern of the Atlantic consists of two gyres, a clockwise flowing gyre in the N and an anti-clockwise flowing gyre in the S. The N gyre is dominated by the fast flowing Gulf Stream, travelling at speeds of up to 130km (80 miles) per day, and forming the western boundary current of the gyre. The southern current gyre is atypical in having a weak western boundary current, the Brazil Current.

Resources. Apart from oil (which is found mainly in the Gulf of Guinea), sand and gravel are the most important minerals from the Atlantic. The largest single offshore mining operation in the world is located at Ocean Cay on the Grand Bahamas bank, where calcium carbonate is extracted in the form of aragonite. Valuable diamond deposits, exploited by dredging, occur off the coast of Namibia. The North Atlantic contains the most valuable fishing grounds in the world: the cod fisheries around Iceland, S Greenland and the Grand Banks of Newfoundland. The relatively unexploited fisheries of the S Atlantic are a comparatively unknown quantity and are probably less stable than those of the N. Area: 82,400sq km (31,800sq miles). *See also* PE pp.24–27, 76–85, 134–135, 240–241.

Atlantis, mythical island in the Atlantic Ocean from which a great empire is said to have tried to subdue the Mediterranean countries. It has been identified by some authorities with the Greek island of Thera, destroyed by an earthquake *c.* 1450 BC.

Atlas, in Greek mythology, the son of the Titan Iapetus and the nymph Clymene and brother of PROMETHEUS. According to Homer he was a marine being who supported the pillars that divided heaven and earth. According to Hesiod he was one who, having warred against ZEUS, was condemned to hold up the heavens.

Atlas, collection of maps and charts, usually in book form. It may contain information about climates, boundaries, geology, history and populations of the world or regions, often with pictures, facts of interest and indexes of place names. The term comes from the name of the Greek god ATLAS who was thought to support the world on his shoulders. *See also* MW p.192.

Atlas bone, the topmost vertebra of the spine, a ring of bone on which the skull sits. *See also* MS p.*56*.

Atman. *See* BRAHMAN.

Atmolysis, the process of separating mixed gases by allowing them to pass through a porous material.

Atmosphere, envelope of gases surrounding the Earth. Its shielding effect from the harsh environment of outer space and some of the gases it contains are vital to life. About 95% by weight of the Earth's atmosphere lies below the 25km (15 miles) altitude; the mixture of gases composing it is called air. The Earth is believed to have possessed three other atmospheres; the first probably consisted of hydrogen, helium, nitrogen and small amounts of argon, methane and ammonia. Hydrogen and helium drifted off but were replaced by volatile vapours including steam and carbon dioxide. These vapours, together with the remaining gases from the first atmosphere, made up the second atmosphere. As the Earth cooled, water settled and dissolved the soluble gases, leaving nitrogen, argon and carbon dioxide – the third atmosphere. The present atmosphere evolved with oxygen which replaced most of the carbon dioxide. Its composition by weight is: nitrogen 78.1%, oxygen 21%, argon 1.0% and 0.2% made up of carbon dioxide, hydrogen, the inert gases and varying amounts of water vapour. The atmosphere can be conceived as concentric shells; the first is the troposphere, in which dust and water vapour create the clouds and weather. The stratosphere extends from 10 to 55km (8–36 miles); it is cooler and clearer and contains ozone concentrated in its upper regions. Above, to a height of 70km (43 miles), is the mesosphere in which chemical reactions occur, powered by sunlight. The temperature climbs steadily in the thermosphere above, which gives way to the exosphere at about 400km (250 miles), where helium and hydrogen may dart off into space. The ionosphere ranges from about 50km (30 miles) out into the VAN ALLEN RADIATION BELTS. *See also* PE p.66.

Atoll, ring-shaped REEF of CORAL enclosing a shallow LAGOON. An atoll begins as a fringing reef surrounding a slowly subsiding island, usually volcanic. As the island sinks the coral continues to grow upwards until eventually the island is below sea-level and only a ring of coral is left at the surface. *See also* PE pp.*123*.

Atom, smallest particle of matter that can take part in a chemical reaction, every element having its own characteristic atoms. The atom, once thought indivisible, consists of a central, positively charged NUCLEUS (identified in 1911 by Ernest RUTHERFORD) which is composed of tightly packed protons and neutrons. In 1913 Niels BOHR, using quantum mechanics, suggested that electrons (known then to surround the nucleus) moved in fixed orbits. The study of wave mechanics has since modified the concept of orbits: the HEISENBERG uncertainty principle requires that electrons encompass the nucleus as a cloud whose density varies according to the probable location of the electron. The number of electrons in an atom (its atomic number) and their configuration determine its chemical properties. Removal of an atomic electron produces a positively charged ion. The nucleus occupies a small fraction only of the atomic space, but accounts for almost the whole of the mass of the atom. *See also* SU pp.60–66, 138.

Atomic bomb. *See* NUCLEAR WEAPON; MM p.180.

Atomic clock, the most accurate of clocks, keeping time to within thousandths of a second per year. It is an electric clock regulated by the natural resonance frequency of excited atoms, those of the metal caesium being most commonly used. *See also* MM pp.92–93.

Atomic energy. *See* NUCLEAR ENERGY.

Atomic nuclear reactor. *See* REACTOR, NUCLEAR.

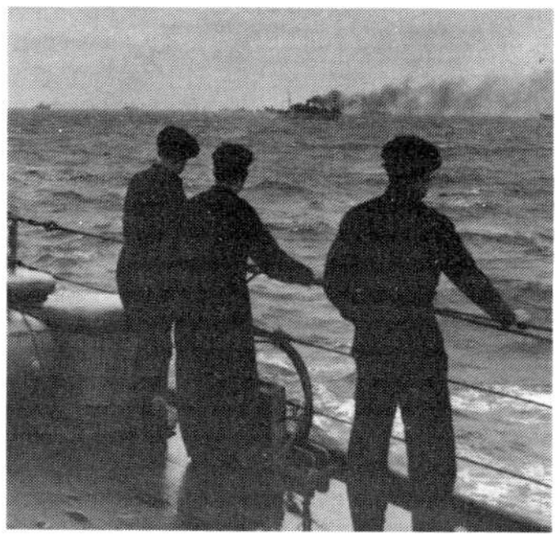

The Battle of the Atlantic was crucial in the fight for survival against Nazi Germany.

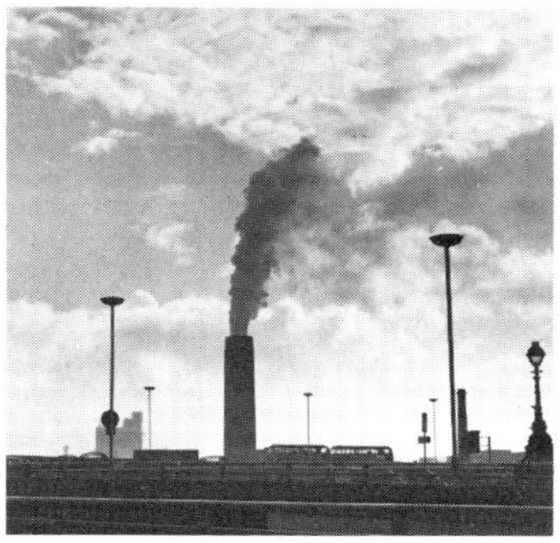

Atmosphere; the ever present danger of air pollution in the industrial world.

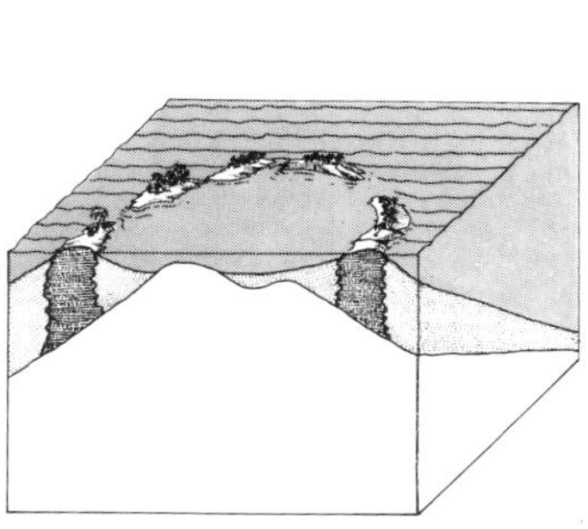

Atolls are circular coral formations above the water, common in the Pacific Ocean.

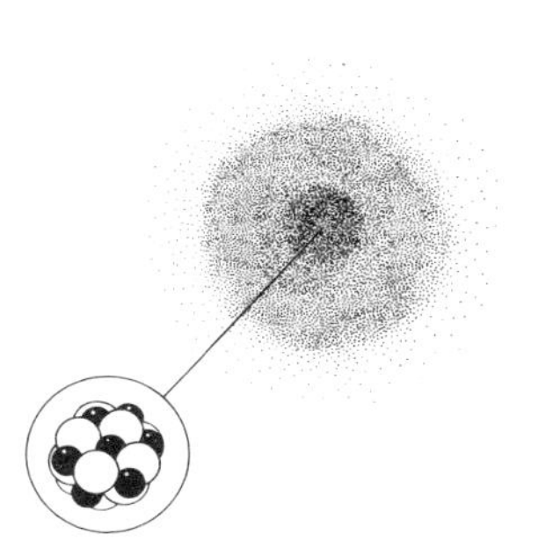

Atom, the fundamental unit of matter, consists of a nucleus surrounded by electrons.

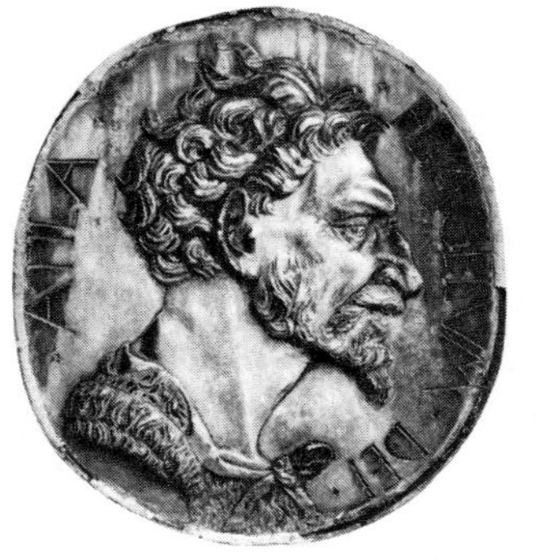

Attila the Hun forced the Romans to pay him not to attack their eastern empire.

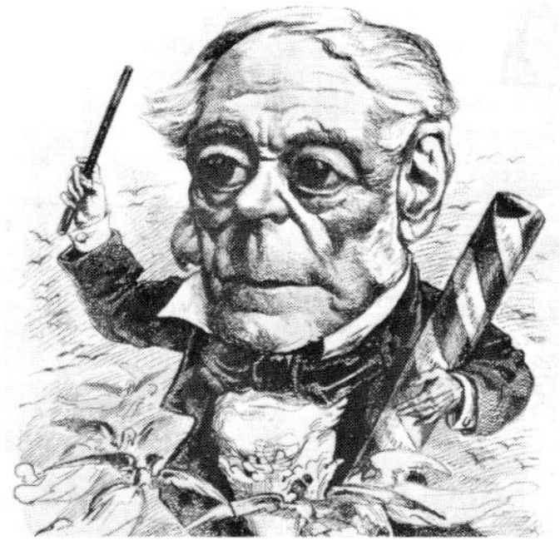

Daniel Auber's work influenced the early music of Gounod and Massenet.

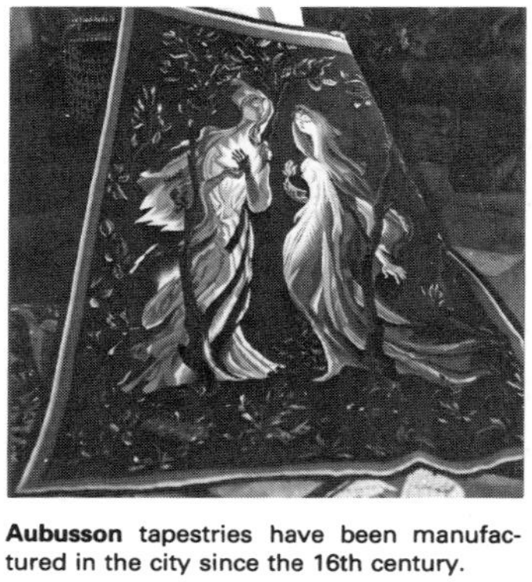

Aubusson tapestries have been manufactured in the city since the 16th century.

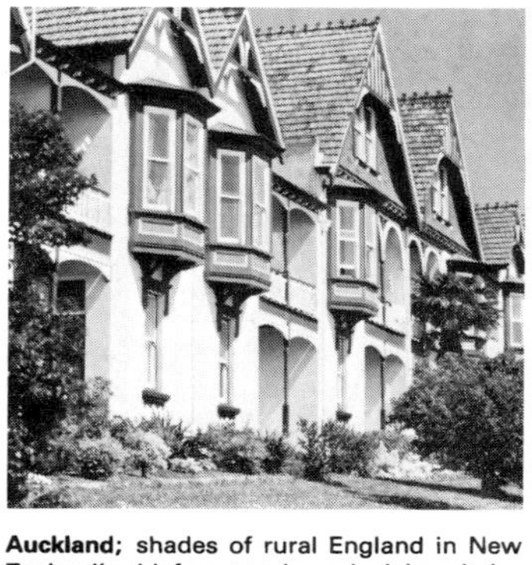

Auckland; shades of rural England in New Zealand's chief port and provincial capital.

Atomic number, number of protons in the nucleus of a neutral atom of an element or number of electrons moving around that nucleus; abbreviated to at. no. It determines the chemical properties of an element and its position in the PERIODIC TABLE. ISOTOPES of an element all have the same atomic number. *See also* SU pp.132–134.
Atomic power. *See* NUCLEAR POWER.
Atomic weapons. *See* NUCLEAR WEAPONS.
Atomic weight, mean mass of the atoms in a chemical element (assuming natural isotopic composition), expressed in atomic mass units; abbreviated to at. wt. It is the ratio of the mass of the atom in question to 1/12th the mass of the carbon–12 atom. *See also* SU pp.32–36.
Atomism, doctrine originated by Leucippus and elaborated by DEMOCRITUS in Greece during the 5th century BC, which tried to reconcile Eleatic "being" with Heraclitean change, by suggesting that everything is composed of immutable and indivisible atoms. *See also* ELEATICISM; HERACLITUS.
Aton. *See* AMUN.
Atonal. *See* TWELVE-TONE MUSIC.
Atonality, in music, composing in terms of the 12 tones of the chromatic scale without reference to traditional keys and harmony, as in *Pierrot Lunaire* (1912) by Arnold SCHOENBERG *See also* HC2 p.270.
Atonement, in religion, the process by which a sinner moves towards union with God, through prayer, fasting, sacrifice or good works. In Christian theology Jesus Christ atoned for the sins of the whole world by his sacrifice on the cross. The Jews observe the Day of Atonement (Hebrew: YOM KIPPUR) as their most sacred feast.
ATP. *See* ADENOSINE.
Atrium, interior court of an ancient Roman house; also an open court of Early Christian churches. Atrium is also the medical term for one of the upper two chambers of the HEART, which are also called auricles; in zoology, the cavity behind the pharynx of certain tunicates and Urochordata.
Atrophy, in medicine, refers to the shrinking or wasting of a cell, tissue or organ. It may be associated with a number of pathological conditions, usually muscular diseases, or with disuse. *See also* MS pp.94–95.
Atropine, poisonous ALKALOID drug ($C_{17}H_{23}O_3N$) obtained from certain plants such as *Atropa belladonna* (DEADLY NIGHTSHADE), used medicinally to regularize the heartbeat during anaesthesia and to dilate the pupil of the eye.
Atropos, in Greek mythology, one of the three Fates who shortened men's lives. She gave her name to the plant genus *Atropa,* which includes DEADLY NIGHTSHADE (belladonna).
Attainder, Act of, means by which in the 1640s the English Parliament, unable to convict STRAFFORD and LAUD by the judicial process of IMPEACHMENT, simply declared their guilt and sentenced them to death. *See also* HC1 pp.286–287.
Attar of roses, perfume made using the essential oils distilled from rose petals.
Attenborough, Sir Richard (1923–), British film actor and director. His first part was in *In Which We Serve* (1942) and he starred in *The Angry Silence* (1960) and *10 Rillington Place* (1971). *Oh What a Lovely War* (1971) was his first film as director and in 1977 he directed *A Bridge Too Far.*
Atterbom, Per Daniel Amadeus (1790–1855), Swedish poet, leader of the Uppsala school of Romantics. His greatest work was the dramatic verse fairy tale *Lycksalighetens ö* (1824–27).
Attica (Attikí), department in central Greece; the capital is Athens. According to legend, King Cecrops divided the region into 12 colonies that were united by THESEUS under the administrative control of Athens in 700 BC. Cleisthenes, a politician of Athens, reformed the aristocratic rule, classifying the people into ten tribes based on topographical divisions. Industries: lead, marble, shipping, tourism. Area: 3,375sq km (1,303sq miles). Pop. 2,060,000.
Atticus, Titus Pomponius (109–32 BC), Roman businessman who lived in Athens and to whom many of CICERO's letters were addressed.
Attila (*c.*406–53), King of the Huns (434–53), co-ruler with his elder brother Bleda until he murdered him in 445. THEODOSIUS II, eastern Roman emperor, was compelled to pay him tribute. Attila invaded Gaul in 451, although his motives for this action are unclear. His army suffered heavy losses, but he was still able to invade Italy the next year. But with his army suffering from disease and lack of provisions, he recrossed the Alps and died before he could again invade Italy. *See also* HC1 pp.136–137.
Attis, in Greek mythology, a shepherd who was loved by CYBELE, goddess of the earth, fertility and wild nature. In one version, the jealous Cybele caused Attis to lose his senses and castrate himself so that none other might have him; later she changed him into a fir-tree.
Attis, one of the longer poems by the Roman poet CATULLUS. Probably modelled on the work of Callimachus or some other Alexandrian, it tells the story of Attis, an Athenian youth who sailed to Asia Minor and mutilated himself in religious frenzy.
Attlee, Clement Richard, 1st Earl (1883–1967), British Labour politician, Prime Minister 1945–51. He began as a social worker in London's East End in 1907 and joined the FABIAN SOCIETY the same year. He was elected MP for Limehouse in 1922, and served in the first Labour government of 1924. He was Postmaster-General in MACDONALD's government of 1929, but resigned in 1931 over the formation of the NATIONAL GOVERNMENT. Elected Labour leader in 1935, he served as deputy prime minister in CHURCHILL's wartime cabinet (1940–45). As Prime Minister he was responsible for the establishment of the NATIONAL HEALTH SERVICE, an extension of national insurance, and the nationalization of the Bank of England, the railways, the coal, iron, steel, gas and electricity industries. Attlee was also involved in the granting of Indian independence. His government's majority was substantially reduced in the election of 1950 and at the next election (in Oct. 1951) Labour was narrowly defeated. Attlee continued to be Labour leader until he retired in 1955. *See also* HC2 p.236.
Attorney, person who has authority to act for another, especially in a court of law. In Britain and the USA, the Attorney General is the chief law officer. The term attorney also refers to county and state prosecutors in the USA. *See also* MS pp.286–287.
Attrition, in warfare, a gradual wearing down of an enemy, often by inflicting casualties he cannot make good and by cutting or limiting his supplies of food and material. In theology, attrition is incomplete sorrow for a sin. *See also* HC2 pp.188–191.
Attwell, Mabel Lucie (1879–1964), British illustrator of many books for children, including books of her own poems and stories. Her drawings of children have been widely reproduced.
Attwood, Thomas (1783–1856), MP for Birmingham (1832–39). A country banker of radical views, his major political achievement was to found, in 1830, the Birmingham Political Union, a focus of agitation leading to the 1832 REFORM ACT.
Atwood, Margaret (1939–), Canadian author. Most of her work is poetry that explores human relationships. Her books of poems include *The Circle Game* (1966), *The Journals of Susanna Moodie* (1970) and *Power Politics* (1971).
Aube, river in N central France which rises in the Haute-Marne département and flows W and NW into the River Seine. Length: 248km (154 miles).
Auber, Daniel François Esprit (1782–1871), French composer. He studied under Cherubini and wrote more than 40 operas, including *La Muette de Portici* (The Dumb Girl of Portici), also called *Masaniello, Manon Lescaut* and *Fra Diavolo.* He is regarded as the founder of French grand opera.
Aubergine, or eggplant, tropical plant whose egg- or pear-shaped purple fruit is eaten as a vegetable. Species *Solanum melongena. See also* PE p.188.
Aubert, Louis (1877–1968), French composer. He had a brief career as a pianist and his compositions include piano music, songs and the ballet *Fourberies* (1950).
Aubert de Gaspé, Philippe (1786–1871), Canadian author. His historical novel *Les anciens canadiens* (1863) is a valuable record of 18th-century French-Canadian social customs and folklore.
Aubignac, François-Hédelin (1604–76), French theorist of drama whose book *La Pratique du théâtre* (1657) provides an insight on the dramatic techniques of the 17th century.
Aubretia, or aubrietia, plant having showy purple flowers, seen most commonly in rock gardens. It belongs to the mustard family and comes from the Middle East.
Aubrey, John (1626–97), English antiquarian and author. His main work was *Lives of Eminent Men* (published 1813), originally collected for Anthony Wood's *Athenae Oxonienses.* Only one of his works, *Miscellanies* (1696), was published during his life.
Aubusson, town in the Creuse département in central France, on the River Creuse. It has been the home of the famous Aubusson tapestries since the 16th century, and there is a museum of tapestry and a design school. Pop. 5,700.
Auca, generic term loosely applied to several South American Indian peoples; there is no Auca tribe as such.
Auch, capital city of the Gers département in SW France, 68km (42 miles) W of Toulouse. It has a 15th-century cathedral, museum and library. Industries: tiles, tobacco, wines. Pop. 21,500.
Auchincloss, Louis (1917–), US novelist and short-story writer. His first book was *The Indifferent Children* (1947). His collections of stories include *The Romantic Egoists* (1954) and *Powers of Attorney* (1963).
Auchinleck, Sir Claude John Eyre (1884–) British field-marshal. After serving in the Middle East in WWI, he commanded operations in India in the 1930s and helped to mechanize the Indian Army. During WWII he commanded the abortive Narvik expedition, in 1940. In 1941 he succeeded Gen. WAVELL as Commander-in-Chief in the Middle East and launched an unsuccessful campaign across Libya. In 1943 he once again became Commander-in-Chief in India, where he remained until independence (1947).
Auckland, George Eden, Earl of (1784–1849), British statesman, Governor General of India (1836–42). He was a good administrator but lost the first AFGHAN WAR (1841).
Auckland, capital city of Auckland Province, New Zealand, and the country's chief port; it lies on an isthmus on NW North Island. It served as the country's capital (1840–65) and is now the chief base of New Zealand's navy and contains the War Memorial Museum and the University of Auckland (1882). Within the city's limits there are many volcanic cones. Industries: shipyards, canneries, chemicals. Pop. (1971) 649,700.
Auckland district, two statistical areas in the north island of New Zealand, formerly Auckland province. They are Central and South Auckland. The largest city is AUCKLAND. The two areas comprise about one-third of North Island.
Auction bridge, a card game similar to, and older than, CONTRACT BRIDGE. The chief difference is that in auction bridge it is not necessary to bid "game" to score it. Developed by the British in India, it has been largely superseded by contract.
Aude, river in S France which rises in the Pyrenees and flows N and E to the Mediterranean Sea. Length: 209km (130 miles).
Auden, Wystan Hugh (1907–73), British poet, who moved to the USA in 1939. Known in the 1930s for his collaborations with Christoper ISHERWOOD and for his Marxist outlook, his postwar work was more Christian in approach. His *Collected Longer Poems* were published in 1976.

Audenarde. *See* OUDENAARDE.

Audiberti, Jacques (1899–1965), French poet, novelist and dramatist. His poems, such as *Race des Hommes* (1937), show the influence of Symbolism, and his novels, including *Abraxas* (1938) and *Marie Dubois* (1952), combine nightmarish fantasy and paganism. His best-known play is *Le Mal court* (1947).

Audiometry, technique for studying differences in hearing ability. An audiometer is an instrument that measures the sensitivity of the ear to sounds; it tests hearing by giving out sounds of low but controlled intensity through headphones. *See also* MS pp.50–51.

Audio-visual aids, in teaching, the use of supplementary material (pictures, displays, slides, television, films, radio, recordings and other media) to facilitate learning. The extensive use of these media is a development of the 20th century; they have proved highly successful as an aid to the assimilation of information and often provide an effective basis for student motivation. *See also* MM p.*109*.

Audit, investigation of a company's accounting procedures to ensure that the financial statements issued by the company are in accordance with the actual expenditure, income and valuation of stock, as recorded in any one financial year (or shorter period).

Auditory canal, the 2.5cm (1in) tube in the outer EAR between the ear flap (pinna) and the eardrum. *See* MS pp.50–51.

Auditory nerve, bundle of nerves that carry impulses related to hearing and balance from the inner EAR to the brain. *See* MS pp.50–51.

Auditory ossicles, three small bones in the middle EAR that transmit vibrations from the eardrum to the cochlea in the inner ear. *See* MS pp.50–51.

Audubon, John James (1785–1851), US ornithologist and artist, whose remarkable series of some 400 watercolours of birds, often in action, were published in *Birds of America* (1827–38).

Audumulla, in Norse mythology, a cow that gave nourishment to YMIR, the first being, who was a giant created from drops of water. It fed by licking salt-covered stones, which became Buri, the grandfather of ODIN. *See also* MS p.*208*.

Auer, Leopold (1845–1930), Hungarian violinist and teacher. He was a successful concert and chamber soloist, and became a teacher in Russia until 1918, when he moved to New York City. Auer taught many of the great 20th-century violinists, including Jascha Heifetz, Mischa Elman, Efrem Zimbalist and Nathan Milstein.

Auerbach, Frank (1931–), German-born British painter, one of a group of figurative painters influenced by David BOMBERG in his use of thick heavily applied paint to achieve sculptural effects.

Auerstädt, Battle of (1806), conflict in the NAPOLEONIC WARS in which the French defeated the Prussians under Duke Charles of Brunswick. *See also* HC2 p.76.

Augean stables, in Greek mythology, the buildings in which Augeas, King of Elis, kept a large herd of cattle. The sixth labour of HERCULES was to clean the stables in one day (which he did by diverting a river through them).

Auger, Pierre Victor (1899–), French physicist who discovered the Auger effect, a change in an atom from an excited to a lower energy state with the emission of an (Auger) electron but without radiation. He became director general of the European Space Research Organization (ESRO) in 1962.

Augier, Emile (1820–89), French playwright. He is best known for *Le Gendre de Monsieur Poirier* (1854), which he wrote with Jules Sandeau.

Augsburg, city in S Germany, on the River Lech, founded by the Romans (*c.* 15 BC). It became a free imperial city in 1276, and was a prosperous banking and commercial centre in the 15th and 16th centuries. The AUGSBURG CONFESSION (1530), which was a basic statement of Lutheran beliefs, was presented there to the Imperial Diet. Augsburg is noted for its cathedral (started in 994), a 17th-century town hall and the 16th-century *Fuggerei,* a poor house. Industries: textiles, motor vehicles. Pop. 213,000.

Augsburg, League of, alliance formed in 1686 by the Roman Catholic and Protestant enemies of the French King LOUIS XIV. Composed of Spain, Sweden, the Holy Roman Empire and a number of lesser states, its formation under Emperor Leopold I was a reaction to France's encroachment on the lands bordering the Holy Roman Empire. Following the French attack on the Palatinate in 1688, a new coalition against the French, the Grand Alliance, was formed in 1689. *See also* GRAND ALLIANCE, WAR OF THE; HC1 p.314.

Augsburg Confession, summation of the Lutheran faith, formulated in 1530 from Lutheran statements of faith principally by Philip MELANCHTHON. It was denounced by the Roman Catholic Church, but became a model for later Protestant creeds. *See also* HC1 pp.268–269.

Augur, in ancient Rome, a religious official whose duty was to foretell future events and interpret the will of the gods in order to give advice on public affairs.

August, the eighth month of the year, with 31 days. It is named after the Emperor AUGUSTUS (63 BC–AD 14), who considered it his lucky month. He added one day (taken from February) to the existing 30 for parity with Julius CAESAR's month, July. Until 8 BC, the month was the sixth, called *Sextilis.*

Augusta, capital city of Maine, USA, on the Kennebec River, 72km (45 miles) from the Atlantic Ocean. It was incorporated in 1797 on the site of the Plymouth Colony trading post; the Capitol was designed by Charles Bulfinch. The governor's mansion was formerly James G. Baine's house. A dam, built across the Kennebec River in 1837, made Augusta's industry change from shipping to manufacturing. Industries: tourism, timber, textiles, paper products. Pop. (1970) 21,945.

Augustin, Jacques-Jean-Baptiste (1759–1832), French artist who revived the art of miniature painting in France. Augustin's pictures are noted for their strength and purity of colour, high finish and attention to detail, and sureness in execution.

Augustine of Canterbury, St (*d.* 604), first Archbishop of CANTERBURY. He was sent from Rome in 596 by Pope GREGORY I at the head of a mission to England. Augustine converted King ETHELBERT and introduced Roman ecclesiastical practices into England. This brought him and his monks into conflict with the Celtic monks of the British Isles whose traditions had developed in isolation from the Continent. It was not until the SYNOD OF WHITBY (663) that their disputes were settled in favour of Roman practices. *See also* HC1 pp.102, 139, 164; MS pp.232–233.

Augustine of Hippo (354–430), Christian theologian and philosopher. Augustine's *Confessions* provide an intimate psychological self-portrait of a spirit in search of ultimate purpose. This he believed he found in his conversion to Christianity in 386. As Bishop of Hippo, North Africa (396–430), he defended Christian orthodoxy against MANICHAEANISM, DONATISM and PELAGIANISM. In his *Enchiridion* (421) he tended to emphasize the corruption of human will and the freedom of the divine gift of grace. *The City of God* (426), perhaps his most enduring work, is a model of Christian apologetic literature. Of the Four Fathers of the Latin Church, who also included AMBROSE, JEROME and GREGORY I, Augustine is considered the greatest. *See also* HC1 pp.113, 134; MS pp.232–233.

Augustinians, name of two distinct and long-established Christian orders. The order of Augustinian Canons was founded in the 11th century. Based on the recommendations of ST AUGUSTINE OF HIPPO, its discipline was milder than those of full monastic orders. The mendicant order of Augustinian Hermits or Friars was founded in the 13th century and modelled on that of the DOMINICANS.

Augustus, Gaius Julius Caesar Octavianus (Octavian) (63 BC–AD 14), Emperor of Rome after 27 BC. He was the adopted son of Julius CAESAR, and returned to Rome to avenge Caesar's murder in 44 BC. He was elected consul, forming the Second Triumvirate with MARK ANTONY and Lepidus. With Antony he defeated BRUTUS and CASSIUS, who had murdered Caesar, at the battle of Philippi in 42 BC. With the assistance of AGRIPPA he beat Pompeius in 36 BC and after Agrippa's victory over Antony at the battle of ACTIUM in 31 BC, Octavian's power at Rome was assured. The Senate voted him the title of "Augustus" in 27 BC, but he himself preferred to be called "First Citizen". As emperor, he sought to stabilize the power of Rome and to foster colonization in the empire. He rebuilt much of Rome, particularly the FORUM, took general censuses of his subjects and tried to make taxation more equitable. He set up fire and police services, and was an important patron of the arts and of learning. His only defeat occurred when his legions under the command of Varus were massacred by the German troops of ARMINIUS in AD 9. He was succeeded by his stepson TIBERIUS. *See also* HC1 pp.97–99, 106–107.

Auk, squat-bodied sea bird of colder Northern Hemisphere coastlines. The flightless great auk (*Pinguinus impennis*), also called the Atlantic penguin, became extinct in the 1840s; height: 76cm (30in). The razorbill auk (*Alca torda*) is the largest of living species. Family Alcidae.

Auld Alliance, name sometimes used to describe the long-standing similarity of interests between Scotland and France in their opposition to England from the 12th to the 18th centuries.

Auld Lang Syne, traditional song with words by Robert BURNS (1759-96), in the Scottish dialect; the refrain is taken from an earlier song. It is sung at gatherings of old friends, especially on New Year's Eve.

Auld Reekie, Scottish dialect, meaning "old smoky". It was once applied to Edinburgh because of the city's dirty appearance.

Aung, San (1914–47), Burmese politician. After opposing British rule and collaborating with the Japanese (1942), he helped expel the invaders. Appointed deputy chairman of the executive council in 1946, he was assassinated the following year.

Aurangzeb. *See* AURUNGZEBE.

Aurelian (Lucius Domitius Aurelianus) (*c.*215–75), Roman Emperor (270-75). His victories against the Goths who invaded Italy, his reconquest of Palmyra and his recovery of Gaul and Britain earned him the title of "Restorer of the world". In Rome he established the Unconquered Sun God as the protective deity of the Empire. *See also* HC1 p.114.

Aurelius (Antonius), Marcus. *See* MARCUS AURELIUS.

Auric, Georges (1899–), French composer. He was artistic director of the Opéra, Paris (1962–67), and wrote effective film scores, such as those for *Caesar and Cleopatra* (1946) and *Moulin Rouge* (1952).

Auricula, genus of ten widespread species of fungus found on dead treetrunks in moist autumn conditions. Class Basidiomycetes. *See also* NW p.*41*.

Auricularia, type of larva of ECHINODERMS (starfishes and their relatives) which is rather similar to the larvae of certain protochordates, primitive members of the phylum which includes the backboned animals. This resemblance has been taken to indicate a remote relationship between the echinoderms and the CHORDATES; ie, human beings may have descended from something like a starfish. *See also* NW p.*119*.

Auriga, or the Charioteer, northern constellation in Gemini. It has several open clusters, including M36 (NGC 1960). The brightest star is Capella (Alpha Aurigae). *See also* SU pp.258, 264.

Aurignacian culture, Upper Palaeolithic group of people who lived in the Pyrenees region about 30,000 years ago. *See also* MS pp.*27, 31*.

Auriol, Vincent (1884–1966), French socialist, principal founder and president (1947–54) of the Fourth Republic. He entered Parliament in 1914 and served as

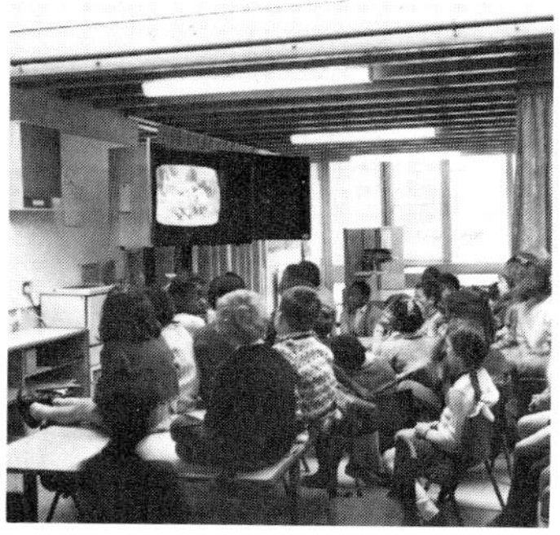

Audio-visual aids help extend the experience of the student beyond the classroom.

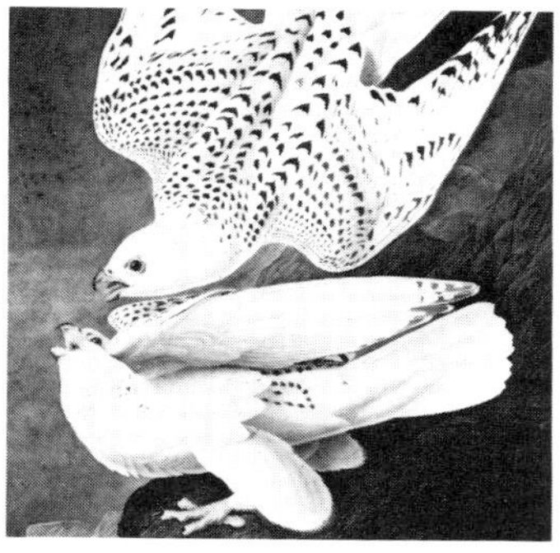

John James Audubon captured the beauty and drama of the birds of North America.

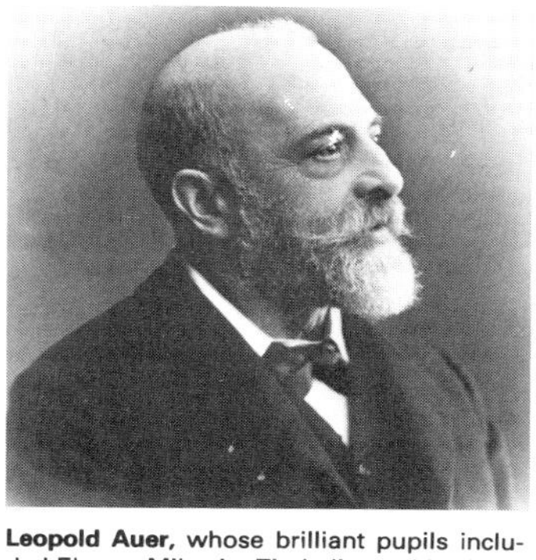

Leopold Auer, whose brilliant pupils included Elman, Milstein, Zimbalist and Heifetz.

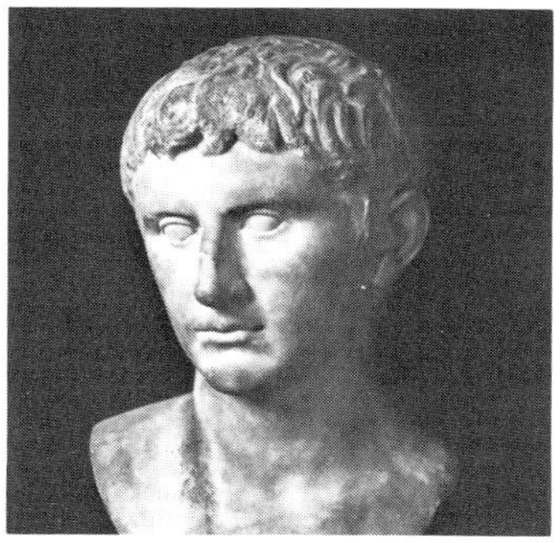

Caesar Augustus who, it was said, found Rome a city of brick and left it a city of marble.

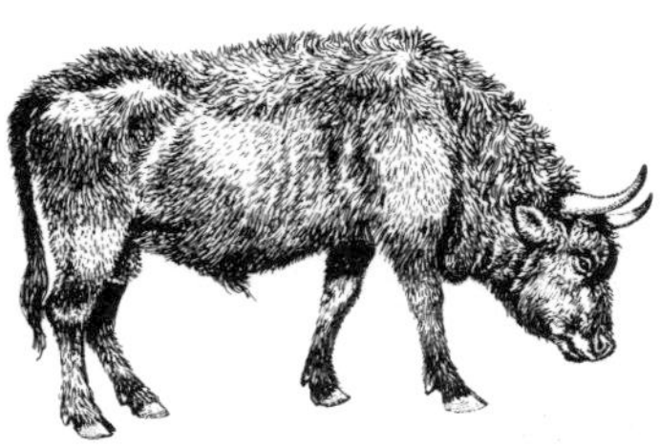

Aurochs, or urus, the now extinct wild ox of Europe, was a massive fearsome beast.

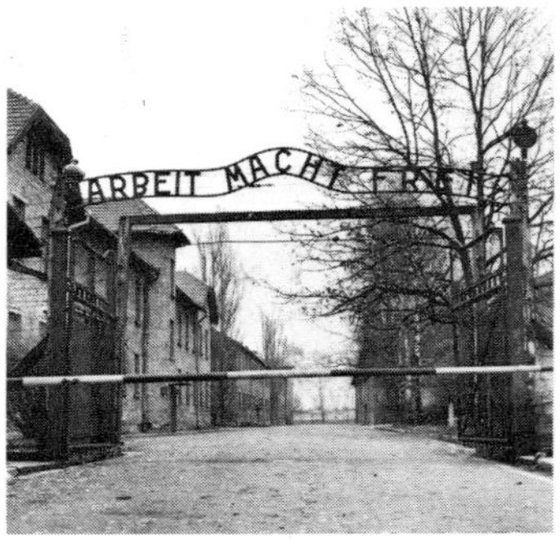

Auschwitz; the sinister motto on the gates of the death factory means "work makes free".

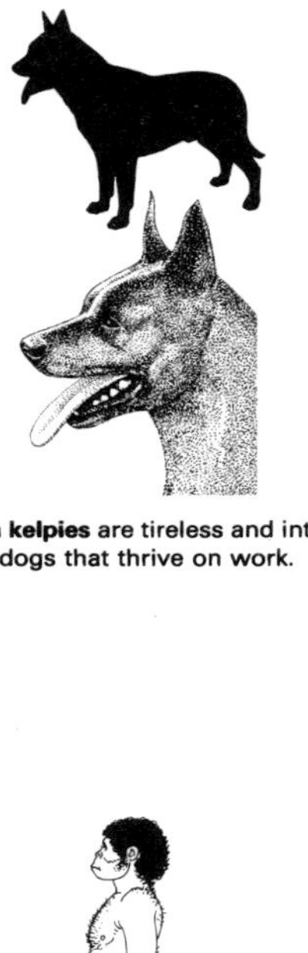

Australian kelpies are tireless and intelligent shepherd dogs that thrive on work.

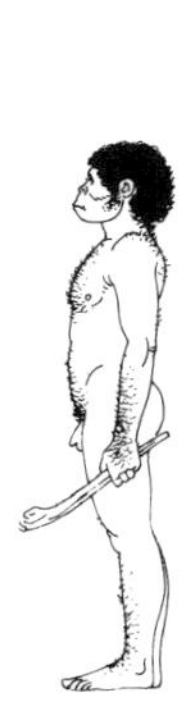

Australopithecus was an early hominid that walked upright but had only a small brain.

Minister of Finance under Leon BLUM in 1936–37. During WWII he fought in the Resistance before joining Charles DE GAULLE's Government in exile.

Aurochs, or urus, extinct European wild ox, the long-horned ancestor of modern domesticated cattle. Once found throughout the forests of Europe and central and SE Asia, it became extinct in 1627. A dark, shaggy animal, it stood up to 2m (7ft) tall at the shoulder. Family Bovidae; species *Bos primigenius*. *See also* WISENT.

Aurora, Greek goddess of the dawn. She was the daughter of Hyperion and Theia, and sister of Helios (Sun) and Selene (Moon). By Astraeus she was the mother of the winds, Boreas (North), Zephyrus (West), Notus (South) and Eurus (East), as well as the evening star Hesperus.

Aurora, sporadic, radiant display of coloured light in the night sky, caused by charged particles from the Sun interacting with air molecules in the Earth's magnetic field. A polar phenomenon, they are known as aurora borealis (N) and australis (S).

Aurungzebe (1618–1707), last of the great MOGUL emperors of India. In 1658 he had his father SHAH JEHAN imprisoned and crowned himself emperor. During his reign the Mogul empire reached its greatest size. Towards the end of this period his fanatical Muslim faith alienated many of his subjects, including the Hindus and the Marathas. *See also* HC2 p.48.

Auschwitz, town in Poland, the site of a concentration camp in WWII where between 1941 and 1945 the Nazis executed about four million prisoners, mostly Jews. Pop. (1970) 39,600.

Auscultation, diagnostic act of listening to sounds within the body. The invention of the stethoscope in 1819 replaced the former method of placing the ear against the body.

Ausgleich, constitutional compromise made in 1867 between the Austro-Hungarian Emperor Francis Joseph, who wished to centralize his empire, and the Hungarians, who wanted an independent nation-state. By it the Empire became the DUAL MONARCHY and, although Francis Joseph remained King of Hungary, the Hungarians gained control of their country's internal affairs. *See also* HC2 pp.84–85.

Ausonius, Decimus Magnus (*c.*310–*c.*395), Latin rhetorician and poet of provincial Gaul. Called to Trèves (Trier) by VALENTINIAN I to be GRATIAN's teacher, on Gratian's ascension to the throne Ausonius became prefect and then consul. His works include *Ephemeris* and *Mosella*.

Aussie, nickname for an Australian, originally applied to Australian troops in WWI.

Austen, Jane (1775–1817), English novelist. She was a clergyman's daughter and wrote six novels of great art, insight and wit, which deal with the society of upper-middle-class England. They are *Sense and Sensibility* (1811), *Pride and Prejudice* (1813), *Mansfield Park* (1814), *Emma* (1816), *Persuasion* (1818) and *Northanger Abbey* (1818). *See also* HC2 p.98.

Austerlitz, Battle of (2 Dec. 1805), battle fought in Bohemia in which the French under NAPOLEON defeated the Austrians and Russians under Gen. Mikhail Kutuzov. *See also* HC2 p.76.

Austin, Alfred (1835–1913), former British poet laureate. His official verse and works in praise of the countryside attracted much adverse criticism.

Austin, Herbert (1866–1941), first and only Baron of Longbridge, founder of the British Austin Motor Company. He spent his early life in Australia, becoming a director of the Wolesley Sheep Shearing Co. He designed and built the first three-wheeled Wolesley car in 1895 and introduced the Austin 7 in 1921, a name briefly revived for the Austin Mini in 1959. *See also* MM p.127.

Austin, John (1790–1859), British jurist. He systematized BENTHAM's legal ideas and founded the analytical school of jurisprudence. He was professor of jurisprudence at University College, London (1826–32). His greatest work was *Province of Jurisprudence Determined* (1832).

Austin, John Langshaw (1911–60), British philosopher. His work centred on the use of words and their meaning. All of his books, including *Philosophical Papers* (1961) and *Sense and Sensibilia* (1962) were published posthumously.

Austin, capital city of Texas, USA, 120km (75 miles) NE of San Antonio on the Colorado River. Originally called Waterloo, it was first settled in 1835. In 1839 it was renamed after Stephen F. Austin, the "Father of Texas". It has some fine 19th-century architecture, including the Capitol building. Industries: electronics, furniture, machinery, building materials, food processing. Pop. (1970) 251,000.

Austin Friars. *See* AUGUSTINIANS.

Austral, Florence (1894–1968), Australian soprano who won worldwide acclaim as a concert artist and in opera. She made her debut in 1921 at the Royal Opera House, Covent Garden, and then embarked on an international career.

Australasia, region that includes Australia, New Zealand and Papua New Guinea. The term Australasia is not exact, and can be defined in a number of different ways. Sometimes it is used to include various Asian countries – principally Indonesia and Malaysia – as well as Australia, New Zealand and Papua New Guinea. In a political sense, it may be extended to include also some Pacific island groups and the Australian and New Zealand territories in Antarctica – all the lands coming within a particular sphere of influence. Many botanists and zoologists use the term Australasia to mean the lands and seas to the E and S of Wallace's Line, a line drawn from the Sulu Sea S through the Celebes Sea and between Borneo and Bali on the W and Celebes Island (Sulawesi) and Lombok on the E. The native flora and fauna on one side of the line differ from those on the other. *See also* MW pp.28, 131, 141; NW p.*196*.

Australia, large island nation that is sometimes regarded as a continent. It is one homogeneous political unit. About 80 per cent of the population is of British extraction. A low plateau makes up most of the country, bounded in the E by the Great Dividing Range. Agriculturally sheep and cattle rearing dominate. The interior is exceptionally rich in minerals. The capital is Canberra, although Sydney is the largest city. Area: 7,686,848sq km (2,967,909sq miles). Pop. 13,502,000. *See also* HC2 pp.124, 126–127, 248–249.

Australia Day, annual national holiday in Australia, on the Monday following 26 Jan. It commemorates the arrival of the First Fleet (carrying the first colonists) at Port Jackson, Sydney on 26 Jan.1788.

Australian Alps, mountains in Victoria and New South Wales, SE Australia. Part of the Great Dividing Range, it forms the watershed between the Murray River system and the streams flowing into the Tasman Sea. There are many resort areas and forest reserves. The Alps were first explored in 1839–40. The highest peak is Mount Kosciusko 2,230m (7,316ft).

Australian Antarctic Territory, external territory of Australia in the ANTARCTIC. It includes all the country's Antarctic territories (except Adélie Land). Area: 6,112,406sq km (2,360,000sq miles).

Australian Capital Territory (ACT or Commonwealth Territory), a district within, but administratively independent of New South Wales, containing the Australian capital city, CANBERRA. The area was first settled in 1824 and was set aside for the capital territory in 1908. In 1915 an additional 72sq km (28sq miles) were added, making a total of 2,432sq km (939sq miles). *See also* MW p.33.

Australian cattle dog, working dog, also called the "heeler" because it herds livestock by nipping their heels. It has a V-shaped head and pricked ears, and a short, rough, mottled blue coat with a tan or red speckling. Average size: 48–51cm (19–20in) high at the shoulder; 16kg (35lb).

Australian kelpie, shepherding dog, also called the Australian collie. It has a V-shaped head, prick ears, almond-shaped eyes, and brush tail. The short, dense coat should be solid black, or as dark as possible, though it can be red, blue-grey or fawn. Average size: 46–51cm (18–20in) high at the shoulder; weight: 14kg (30lb).

Australian rules football. *See* FOOTBALL.

Australian terrier, small, rugged working dog (TERRIER group) bred from the first English dogs shipped to Australia. It has a long, flat head with a light-coloured topknot and pricked, pointed ears. It has short legs and the docked tail is carried up. The rough coat can be blue-black or silver-black mixed with tan, or red. Average size: 25cm (10in) high at the shoulder; weight: 5–6kg (10–13 lb).

Australopithecus, or "southern ape", race of extinct near-men whose fossilized bones, dating back about 3 million years, have been found in southern Africa. The Australopithecines had teeth more human than ape-like, and like man could move and stand fully erect without the help of their arms. They are therefore classified as hominids (men), and are possibly direct ancestors of modern man. *See also* PITHECANTHROPUS; MS pp.22, 24.

Austrasia, also called Ostrasia, Germanic northern and eastern part of the Frankish kingdom during the MEROVINGIAN period. Divided into the semi-independent regions of Austrasia, Neustria and Burgundy in the 6th and 7th centuries, the lands were reunited under the Austrasian Pepin family, one of whom, Charles Martel, defeated Arab invaders at POITIERS (732). From this new foundation sprang the CAROLINGIAN Empire of CHARLEMAGNE. *See also* FRANKS.

Austria (Österreich), landlocked and largely mountainous country in central Europe. It was once the centre of an extensive empire embracing much of central Europe. Vienna (Wien) is the capital. Cereals and root crops are grown in the E plains. Linz and Graz are industrial towns. Area: 83,848sq km (32,367sq miles). Pop. 7,523,000.

Austria–Hungary. *See* AUSTRO-HUNGARIAN EMPIRE.

Austrian Empire (1804–67), all lands controlled by the Hapsburg dynasty. The Holy Roman Emperor FRANCIS II proclaimed himself Francis I, Emperor of Austria, in 1806. Under Francis and his Foreign Minister, METTERNICH, the Empire opposed change at home and abroad. Despite nationalist revolts in Vienna, Bohemia and Hungary in 1848, authoritarian rule continued under FRANCIS JOSEPH and Prince Schwarzenberg. Loss of land and prestige in war with Prussia in 1866 forced the emperor to negotiate with the Hungarian nationalists, and after the AUSGLEICH (compromise) of 1867 the term "Empire of Austria" applied only to the non-Hungarian Hapsburg possessions; the area as a whole was called the AUSTRO-HUNGARIAN EMPIRE or Dual Monarchy. *See also* HC2 pp.82, 108–111.

Austrian Netherlands, first Spanish and later Austrian region roughly corresponding to modern Belgium and Luxembourg, under Hapsburg control 1477–1794. During the Eighty Years War (1568–1648) the Spanish opposed the desire for autocracy as well as the Protestant faith of this successful mercantile community.

Austrian Succession, War of the (1740–48), overall name for several related wars: the war for the Austrian succession itself, in which France supported Spain's claim to part of the Hapsburg domains; the first and second Silesian wars, in which FREDERICK II of Prussia took Silesia from Austria; and the war between France and Britain over colonial possessions (known in North America as KING GEORGE'S WAR).

Austro-Hungarian Empire, or Dual Monarchy (1867–1918), organization of the old Austrian Empire into the Kingdom of Hungary and the Empire of Austria. The Emperor of Austria and the King of Hungary was the same person but each nation had its own parliament and controlled its internal affairs. This arrangement did not take into account other nationalist minorities, nor did it please either the Hungarians who wanted complete autonomy, or the Austrians who wanted a realignment with other German states. After the death of FRANCIS JOSEPH in 1916 and defeat in WWI, Czechoslovakia and Hungary declared their independence

HC1 = History and Culture Vol. 1 HC2 = History and Culture Vol. 2 MS = Man and Society MM = Man and Machines

in 1918, Emperor Charles abdicated and Austria was declared a republic. *See also* HC2 p.86.

Austro-Prussian War (1866), conflict with PRUSSIA and Italy allied against Austria, also known as the Seven Weeks War. BISMARCK engineered the war to further Prussia's supremacy in Germany and remove Austria from the GERMAN CONFEDERATION. Defeat at Sadowa forced Austria to leave the Confederation and cede VENETIA to Italy. *See also* HC2 p.111.

Autarky, nationalist economic policy among Fascist countries, aimed at establishing self-sufficiency by reducing imports.

Authoritarianism, political philosophy that concentrates power in the hands of one person or small group of people not responsible to the population as a whole. Authoritarian systems deify the state and are based on anti-democratic principles. Modern examples are Germany under HITLER, Italy under MUSSOLINI and Spain under FRANCO. *See also* MS pp.264–265.

Authorized Version, of the BIBLE, is a translation into English first published in 1611, also called the *King James Bible.* It was authorized by King JAMES I of England and more than 50 leading scholars worked on it for seven years. It has been the most influential Bible among English-speaking Protestant churches. *See also* HC1 pp.*269, 282.*

Autism, disorder of young children characterized by failure to relate to others, failure to use language normally and ritualistic behaviour such as playing for hours with one toy. An autistic child seems to withdraw into a private world. The causes of autism are not known, but some experts believe it is genetic in origin while others regard it as primarily psychological.

Autobiography, record of a man's life written by himself. The first important one was the *Confessions* of AUGUSTINE OF HIPPO (4th century). The modern, introspective autobiography, dealing frankly with all aspects of life, is usually dated from ROUSSEAU's *Confessions* (written 1765–72; pub. 1782).

Autocracy, system of government in which a single person or small group of people wields absolute power. It is invariably imposed and generally aimed only at furthering the interests of the individual or group. Now rarely used, the term is applied to regimes before the development of modern technology and state institutions made TOTALITARIANISM possible. *See also* MS p.276.

Autocross. *See* MOTOR SPORTS.

Auto-da-fé, strictly speaking any judicial sentence of the Spanish Inquisition, but usually referring to the solemn ceremony, at the end of a session, when the convicted (mostly heretics) were publicly burned at the stake. It dates from *c.*1480.

Autogyro, heavier-than-air craft supported by a freely spinning horizontal rotor. The engine powers a tractor propeller (at the nose) for forward flight. *See also* AEROPLANE; MM p.154.

Autolycus, in Greek mythology, son of the Greek god HERMES and the mortal Chione. He received from his father the gift of making whatever he touched invisible. In this way he was able to commit numerous thefts until one day SISYPHUS, whose oxen he had stolen, caught him. Also, an astronomer and mathematician who flourished in Pitane in AEOLIA in the 4th century BC.

Automatic firearm, weapon that will continue to fire while the trigger is pressed, until it runs out of ammunition. Machine guns and machine pistols are automatic firearms. The term is also often incorrectly applied to any self-loading weapon (in which the trigger has to be pressed every time a shot is fired); most so-called "automatic" pistols are of this type. *See also* MM pp.164–165.

Automatic typesetting, system in which a machine casts and arranges individual letters (monotype) in lines or whole lines of type (linotype) as one piece of metal, generally on instructions from a punched paper or magnetic tape. By extension, modern techniques of optical typesetting (photosetting) of letters or lines of letters on photographic films are also examples of automatic typesetting. *See also* MM pp.205–207.

Automatic writing, in clinical psychology and psychiatry, a symptom of disturbed functioning: the individual writes something without being consciously aware of what he is writing or even that he is writing. In spiritualistic seances, it is a way in which departed souls may communicate with the living – ie, by causing a living person to write a message in the spirit's own handwriting. *See also* PARAPSYCHOLOGY; MS p.298.

Automation, process that feeds back data from its own operations, usually through a computer, to controls that govern the process. It can dispense with all direct manpower. *See also* MM pp.95, *95,* 104–105.

Automatism, in painting, suspension of the control of reason and allowing the release of subconscious imagery. Automatism as a technique is associated chiefly with SURREALISM, which was defined in A. Breton's *Manifeste du Surréalisme* (1924) as "pure psychic automatism".

Automobile. *See* MOTOR CAR.

Autonomic nervous system, part of the body's nervous system that, without conscious control of the brain, regulates the internal organs. It has two parts; the sympathetic and PARASYMPATHETIC systems, which work in balanced opposition. *See also* MS pp.38, *39, 65.*

Autopilot, gyroscopic device for operating the flight controls of an aeroplane with limited attention from the pilot. Systems vary from simple wing levellers in light planes to computer-operated units consisting of gyroscopes, electric servo units and accelerometers. *See also* MM p.104.

Autosuggestion, in psychology, the conscious or unconscious process by which a person can influence his own ideas. It has been proposed by psychotherapists as a method of treating some neuroses, but its effectiveness depends on the suggestibility of the patient. SUGGESTION by another person, usually under HYPNOSIS, is called heterosuggestion. *See also* MS p.196.

Autumn, the season between summer and winter. In the Northern Hemisphere, it begins at the September equinox and ends at the December solstice. In the Southern Hemisphere, it begins at the March equinox and ends at the June solstice. In many places autumn is the harvest season, and the time when the vegetation of summer begins to fail; in the USA it is usually called fall, because deciduous trees then shed their leaves. The word *autumn* comes from a Latin word meaning "maturing" or "autumnal".

Autumn crocus. *See* COLCHICUM.

Auvergne, region and former province of S France, now divided into the départements of Puy-de-Dôme, Cantal and part of Haute-Loire. In Roman times it was conquered by Julius Caesar after the fall of the Gallic leader Vercingetorix. Running N to S are the Auvergne Mountains, a scenic chain of extinct volcanoes; the highest peak is Puy de Sancy (1,886m; 6,188ft). The region also has many fine examples of Romanesque architecture.

Auxin, HORMONE produced naturally in the growing tips of plant roots and stems. Auxins accelerate plant growth by stimulating cell enlargement and interacting with other hormones. Actions include the elongation of cells in response to GEOTROPISM and PHOTOTROPISM and fruit drop and leaf fall. Synthetic auxins are also applied to plants. *See also* GIBBERELLIN.

Ava, village in central Burma, on the Irrawaddy River 10km (6 miles) SW of Mandalay. Ruins remain from when it was the capital of a dynasty of Burmese kings which moved to Amarapura in 1783.

Avalanche, tumbling down of a mass of rock or snow. It is most likely on an incline of slope greater than 35°. Any steep slope with 30cm (12in) or more of new snow may avalanche as a result of a weather change, disturbance due to vibration or through its own accumulated weight. Large avalanches can carry down thousands of tonnes of rock.

Avalon, mythical island where KING ARTHUR is supposed to have died after going there to heal his wounds. *See also* HC1 pp.20–21.

Avant-garde (French, "advance guard"), term applied to innovators in the arts, particularly those whose artistic audacity surprises their contemporaries. The phrase also has radical political overtones and derives from the military concept "vanguard".

Avars, Mongolian people who settled near the Volga River *c.* AD 460. One group remained there, and another moved to the DANUBE RIVER basin in the 6th century and occupied Dacia (modern Romania). Their domain extended from the VOLGA to the BALTIC SEA, and they exacted huge tributes from the BYZANTINE EMPIRE during this time. The Avars were finally crushed by CHARLEMAGNE in 796.

Avatar, in Hinduism, a "descent" or incarnation of God; from time to time God manifests himself in order to restore virtue. In Hindu tradition, Vishnu has ten important avatars. Avatars appear also in Buddhist and Jain traditions. *See also* HC1 p.*119.*

Avebury, John Lubbock, 1st Baron (1834–1913), Vice-Chancellor of London University (1872–80) and author of popular books on science.

Avebury, village in Wiltshire, England, 47km (29 miles) E of Bristol. The megalithic remains there are of uncertain origin but are older than STONEHENGE. There is also a medieval church and an Elizabethan manor house. Pop. 630.

Aved, Jacques (1702–66), French portrait painter who trained in Amsterdam and was influenced by REMBRANDT. Unlike most of his French contemporaries, he often painted his subjects in their normal dress and surroundings. His work is sometimes confused with that of CHARDIN.

Ave Maria, Latin phrase meaning "Hail, Mary". In the Roman Catholic Church it forms the first words of a prayer taken from the beginning of the angel GABRIEL's address to MARY (Mother of Jesus) (*Luke* 1:28). SCHUBERT and GOUNOD composed musical settings for the prayer.

Avens. *See* GEUM.

Avenue of Middelharnis (1669), painting by Meindert HOBBEMA (National Gallery, London); one of the best-known Dutch realistic landscapes.

Average, in statistics, the one score that most typifies an entire set of scores. It may be the arithmetic mean of the scores (the sum of the scores divided by their number), the mode (the one score that occurs most often), or the median (the score that divides the set of scores into upper and lower halves). Most often the "average" is the arithmetic mean.

Avercamp, Hendrick (1585–1634), Dutch painter who specialized in winter landscapes with numerous tiny figures, and who was influenced by BRUEGEL the Elder.

Averescu, Alexandru (1859–1938), Romanian general and statesman. After reorganizing the army in 1907 as Minister of War, he became Chief of the General Staff in 1912. He became Prime Minister in 1918 and conducted the first peace negotiations with the CENTRAL POWERS.

Averno (Lago d'Averno), crater lake in an extinct volcano in Italy, about 13km (8 miles) W of Naples in the Campania region. It was regarded by Virgil as the entrance to the underworld. It became a naval harbour in the 1st century BC after AGRIPPA joined it by canal to the sea. There are Roman ruins nearby at Cumae. Area: approx. 2sq km (0.8sq miles).

Averrhöes, Latin name for Abu-al-Walid Ibn-Rushd (1126–98), leading Islamic philosopher in Spain. He served as a judge after 1169 and became physician to the Caliph of Marrakesh in 1182. He was banished in 1195 to Lucena near Seville for advocating reason over religion, but soon returned to favour. His major work, *Incoherence of the Incoherence,* defends Neoplatonism and ARISTOTLE. *See also* HC1 p.188; MS p.*227.*

Aversion therapy, use of learning or conditioning procedures to develop aversive responses to certain situations or unwanted habits. The therapy consists of providing an unpleasant stimulus such as a

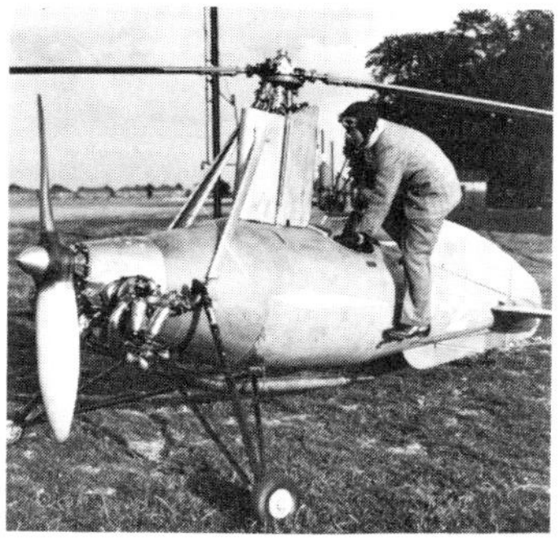

Autgyros differ from helicopters in that the rotors are not powered by an engine.

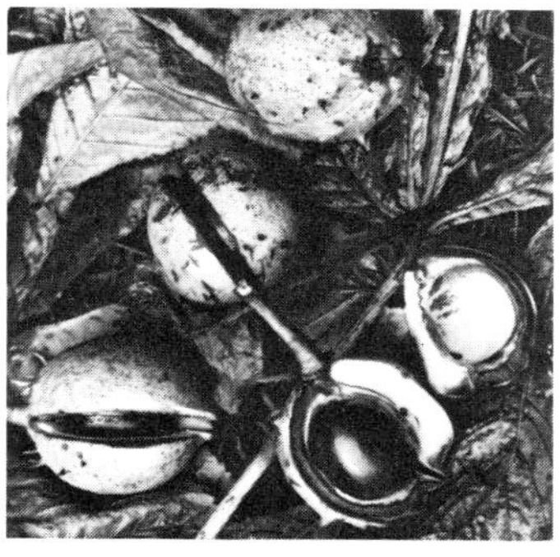

Autumn is the time for playing "conkers", the delight of the English schoolboy.

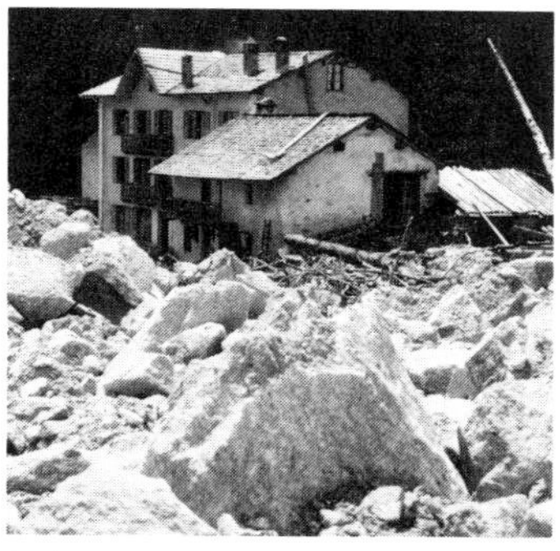

Avalanches are caused by vibrations, the wind or the ice thawing on the high glaciers.

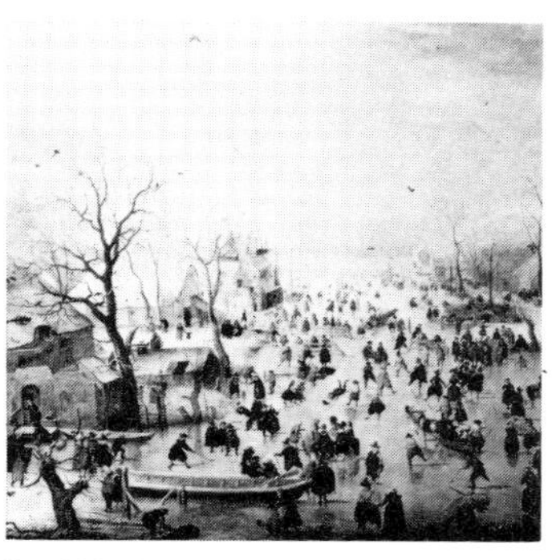

Hendrick Avercamp, whose icescapes are reminiscent of Bruegel, who influenced him.

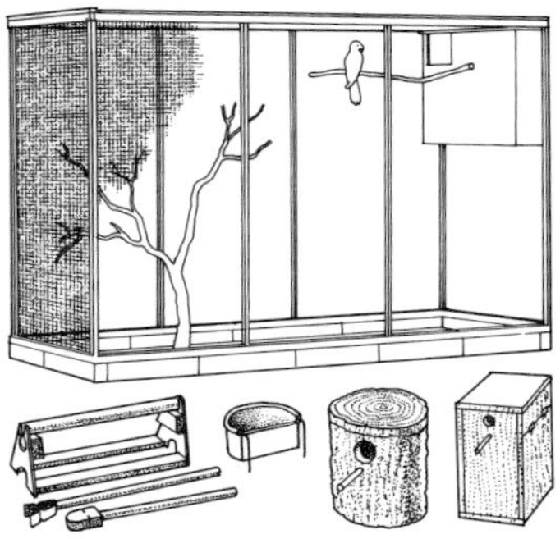

Aviaries act as both shelters and showcases for birds; spacious ones allow free flight.

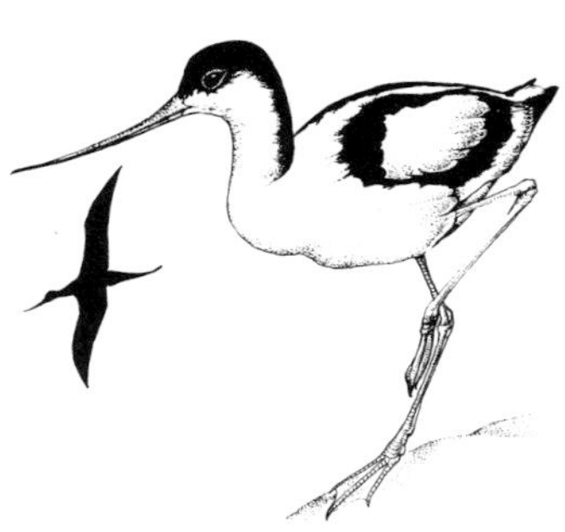

Avocet, a long-legged wader and strong swimmer, seeks food in marshy areas.

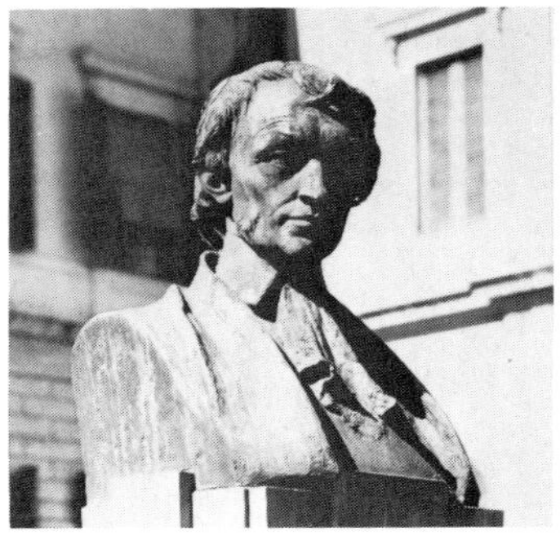

Amadeo Avogadro postulated his famous theory, now known as Avogadro's law.

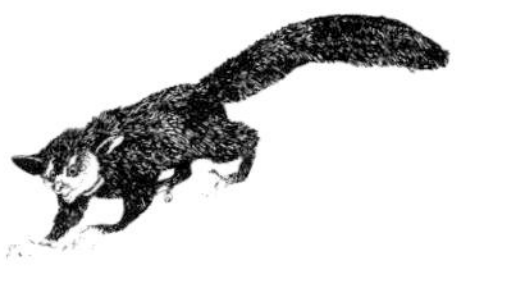

Aye-aye, a rare lemur of Madagascar, has prominent ears and eyes and a bushy tail.

bad-tasting substance when the behaviour occurs (eg, over-eating or smoking) until an aversion to that behaviour is developed. *See also* MS p.146.

Avesta, Zoroastrian scriptures. Most of the original was lost when ALEXANDER THE GREAT burned Persepolis. The Gathas, forming the oldest part, originated with Zoroaster. The other remaining parts are the Yashts, Yasna and Vendidad and prayers. *See also* ZOROASTRIANISM.

Avianus, or Avianius, Flavius (*fl.* 4th century AD), Latin author who wrote fables in elegaic verse.

Aviary, enclosure for the observation and/or breeding of captive birds. Sometimes spacious enough for flight, it is generally made of wire mesh round a metal or wood frame. Zoos usually contain large flight cages; private homes may have considerably smaller cages in the garden as an aviary. Natural botanical surroundings are preferred. *See also* NW p.252.

Avicenna (979–1037), Arab physician and philosopher whose work influenced the science of medicine for many centuries. His *Canon Medicinae* became a standard work. *See also* MS pp.226, *227, 232–233*; SU p.22.

Avignon popes, during the BABYLONIAN CAPTIVITY (1309–77), popes who resided in Avignon instead of Rome (the city was bought by CLEMENT VI in 1348). See also GREAT SCHISM; HC1 pp.*187*, 240.

Avila, city in central Spain, on the River Adaja, 85km (53 miles) NW of Madrid; the capital city of Avila province. The birthplace of St Teresa, it is a religious centre and is noted for its medieval architecture, including the Cathedral, the basilica of San Vicente and an 11th-century wall. The city was captured from the Moors in 1088 by Alfonso VI of León and Castile. Industries: flour milling, tanning, woollen goods. Area: (province) 8,047sq km (3,017 miles). Pop. (city) (1970) 30,938; (province) (1970) 203,798.

Aviz, dynasty that ruled Portugal (1385–1580). It was founded by JOHN I, who was grand master of Aviz, a knightly order. The dynasty's rule coincided with the most glorious period of Portuguese history. Its end brought a period of Spanish rule in Portugal.

Avocado, evergreen, broad-leafed tree native to the tropical New World. The name is extended to its green to dark purple, pear-shaped fruit. This has soft, greenish flesh (surrounding a single large seed) which is eaten fresh, often in salads; it has a high oil content and a nutty flavour. Weight up to 2kg (4.4lb). Species *Persea americana*.

Avocet, graceful, long-legged, black-and-white wading bird, related to the SNIPE. It has a long, slender upcurved bill with which it sifts through shallow water and mud for small fish, crustaceans and water insects. The hen lays 3–5 mottled eggs in a grass-lined scrape. Length: 45cm (18in). Genus *Recurvirostra*.

Avogadro, Amadeo (1776–1856), Italian physicist and chemist. In 1811 he put forward the hypothesis, known as Avogadro's law, stating that equal volumes of gases at the same pressure and temperature contain an equal number of molecules. This led later physicists to determine that the number of molecules in one gramme molecule (the molecular weight expressed in grammes) is constant for all gases. This number, called Avogadro's number, equals 6.02257×10^{23}. *See also* SU p.84.

Avon, Lord (1897–1977), previously Robert Anthony Eden, British politician. He served in WWI as a captain in the King's Royal Rifle Corps, winning the Military Cross, and took a first-class degree in Oriental languages at Oxford (1922). He entered the House of Commons in 1923 and in 1935 became the youngest man ever to be made Foreign Secretary. He resigned in February 1938 in protest against the APPEASEMENT policy of Neville CHAMBERLAIN. He served again as Foreign Secretary in 1940–45 and 1951–55. He was Prime Minister 1955–57, when ill health and the dissatisfaction with his handling of the SUEZ CRISIS forced him to resign.

Avon, county in SW England, on the Bristol Channel; formed in 1974 under the Local Government Act (1972) from the county boroughs of Bath and Bristol and parts of the former counties of GLOUCESTER(SHIRE) and SOMERSET. Bristol is the administrative centre. Area: 1,346sq km (520sq miles). Pop. (1976) 920,200.

Avon, name of four British rivers. The Bristol, or Lower, Avon rises in the Cotswold Hills in Gloucestershire, and flows S and then W through Bristol, entering the Severn estuary at Avonmouth. Length: 121km (75 miles). The Warwickshire, or Upper, Avon rises in Northamptonshire, and flows SW through Stratford-on-Avon to join the River Severn at Tewkesbury. Length: 155km (96 miles). The Wiltshire, or East, Avon rises near Devizes and flows S into the English Channel. Length: 77km (48 miles). The Scottish Avon flows E into the Firth of Forth. Length: 29km (18 miles).

Awami League, opposition political party originally formed in Pakistan in 1949; since 1971 the major party of Bangladesh (formerly East Pakistan); renamed Awami Peasants' and Workers' League of Bangladesh in 1975. It was led by Sheikh Mujibur Rahman from 1953 to his death in a military coup in 1975. From 1966 the party advocated a federation government for Pakistan that would give more autonomy to East Pakistan. In 1970 the party won a majority in the legislature, but the government cancelled the election and outlawed the party. Civil war broke out in early 1971 and East Pakistan won its independence, becoming Bangladesh. *See also* MW p.36.

Awe, Loch, largest lake in Scotland, drained into Loch Etive by the River Awe. Length: 38.5km (24 miles).

Awolowo, Obafemi ("Awo") (1909–), Nigerian political figure and leader of the YORUBA ethnic group of W Nigeria. In 1950 he founded the Action Group political party, and later held political offices.

Axel Heiberg Island, Canadian island in the Arctic Ocean, W of Ellesmere Island; part of the Northwest Territories. It was explored by a Norwegian, Otto Sverdrup, in 1898–1902. Area: 40,867sq km (15,779sq miles).

Axelrod, Julius (1912–), American biochemist. He shared the 1970 Nobel Prize in physiology and medicine with Ulf Svante von EULER and Sir Bernard KATZ for their work on the chemistry of nerve-impulse transmission. Axelrod discovered how the neurotransmitter noradrenalin is inactivated after it has performed its function. *See also* MS p.65.

Axholme, Isle of, lowland region, 210sq km (80sq miles) in area, in Humberside, NE England. Originally marsh and fenland, it was first drained in the 17th century and is now an area of highly fertile soil. Pop. (1971 prelim.) 14,880.

Axial planning, the placing of several buildings or parts of a building along a single line.

Axiomatic method, method of mathematical reasoning based on logical deduction from assumptions (axioms). The method is fundamental to the philosophy of modern mathematics: it was used by the Greeks and formalized early in the 20th century by the German mathematician David Hilbert (1862–1943). In an axiomatic system certain undefined entities (terms) are taken and described by a set of axioms. Other, often unsuspected, relationships (theorems) are then deduced by logical reasoning. For instance, the points, lines and angles of Euclidean geometry are connected by postulates; theorems, such as Pythagoras' theorem, can then be deduced. This geometry describes measurements of position, distance and angle in space. *See also* SU p.44.

Axis, imaginary straight line about which a body rotates, or about which rotation is conceived. In mechanics an axis runs longitudinally through the centre of an axle or rotating shaft. In geography and astronomy, it is a line through the centre of a planet or star, about which the planet or star rotates. The Earth's axis joins its two geographic poles, is 12,700km (7,900 miles) long and is inclined at an angle of 66.5° to the plane in which the Earth orbits the sun. A mathematical axis is a fixed line, such as the *x*, *y* or *z* axis, chosen for reference. *See also* SU pp.30, 50.

Axis, the bone second from the top of the neck (the second cervical vertebra), on which the first bone (atlas) pivots.

Axis deer. *See* CHITAL.

Axis powers, term applied to Germany and Italy after they signed the Rome-Berlin Axis in Oct. 1936 and to Japan, which joined them in the Tripartite Pact (27 Sept. 1940). Minor Axis powers were Hungary and Romania (1940) and Bulgaria (1941). *See also* HC2 p.222–229.

Axminster, town in Devon, SW England, on the River Axe; a market town with an old carpet industry. Pop. (1971) 15,300.

Axolotl, larval form of certain species of SALAMANDER native to western USA and Mexico. Axolotls are aquatic amphibians and they normally mature and reproduce without developing into salamanders. Length: about 25cm (10in). Family Ambystomidae. *See also* NW p.132.

Axon, that part of a nerve cell, or NEURON, that carries a nerve impulse beyond and away from the cell body, such as an impulse for movement to a muscle. There is typically only one axon per neuron, and it is generally long and unbranched. It is encased by a fatty, pearly myelin sheath (white matter) in all peripheral nerves, and in all central nerves except those of the brain and spinal cord. Axons in peripheral nerves are covered by an additional delicate sheath, a neurillemma, which helps to regenerate damaged nerves. *See also* MS p.38.

Axum (Aksum), N Ethiopian town, once the capital of a powerful empire of Semitic-Sabean origin. The empire was Christianized in the 4th century and at one time claimed to possess the Ark of the Covenant. A rich trading centre, Axum was known for its ivory, and dominated the Red Sea for centuries. Pop. 12,800.

Ayala, Francisco (1906–), Spanish scholar, critic and novelist. He founded the reviews *Realidad* in Buenos Aires and *La Torre* in Puerto Rico.

Ayala y Herrera, Adelardo Lopez de (1828–79), Spanish playwright and politician who in 1878 became President of the Cortes (state assembly). His works include *Un hombre de estado* (1851), *El tejado de vidrio* (1857) and *Consuelo* (1878).

Aye-aye, rare, primitive, squirrel-like LEMUR of Madagascar. Nocturnal and tree-dwelling, it has dark shaggy fur and an elongated third finger with which it scrapes insects and pulp from bamboo canes. Length: 40cm (16in) excluding tail. Species *Daubentonia madagascariensis*.

Ayer, Sir Alfred Jules (1910–), British philosopher. Building on the ideas of the VIENNA CIRCLE of positivists and of George Berkeley, David Hume, Bertrand Russell and Ludwig Wittgenstein, he introduced LOGICAL POSITIVISM into British and American philosophy. His works include *Language, Truth and Logic* (1936), *The Problem of Knowledge* (1956) and *Philosophy and Language* (1960).

Ayers Rock, outcrop of rock, 348m (1,142ft) high, 448km (280 miles) SW of Alice Springs, Northern Territory, Australia. It is the largest single rock in the world and the distance around its base is 9.7km (6 miles). There are many aboriginal paintings in its caves. It was discovered by European settlers in 1872.

Ayesha (Aisha) (614–678), favourite wife of the prophet MOHAMMED, daughter of ABU BAKR.

Aylesbury, county town of Buckinghamshire, SE England, 51km (32 miles) NW of London. A breed of large white ducks is named after the town. Industries: light engineering, printing, food processing. Pop. (1971) 41,266.

Aylward, Gladys (1902–1970), British missionary who went to China in 1930 and worked to spread the Christian faith. During WWII she led a hundred homeless Chinese children on a long and gruelling mountain trek to escape the Japanese invaders. Her story was told in the film *The Inn of the Sixth Happiness* (1958).

Aymará, major tribe of South American

Indians who live in the highlands of Bolivia and Peru. By 1500 they had been brought into the INCA empire, which was subsequently conquered by the Spanish. Today the Aymará number approx. 1,360,000. Their struggle to survive in a harsh, semi-desert region accounts for their drab appearance and lack of interest in traditional arts. The Aymará language is spoken by about a million people in Bolivia and 3 million in Peru.

Aymé, Marcel (1902–67), French novelist. His novels, including *The Green Mare* (1933) and *The Secret Stream* (1936), combine fantasy and satire, as do his witty short stories, such as *Across Paris and Other Stories* (1958). He also wrote several plays and children's books, such as *Les Contes du Chat Perché* (1939).

Ayr, town in E of central Queensland, Australia. It is the chief processing centre of a sugar cane region. Pop. (1971) 17,000.

Ayrshire, former county in Scotland, now part of the Strathclyde region. Metal, textile and chemical industries in the towns are linked to the important local coal mines, and there is intensive farming on the lowland areas. Area: 2,929sq km (1,131sq miles). Pop. (1971) 361,074. The port of Ayr is the former county town. Industries: heavy engineering, textiles. Pop. (1971) 47,884.

Ayrshire, common breed of dairy cattle native to Scotland. They have been introduced into Canada and to a lesser extent into the USA, South Africa and New Zealand. Medium-sized, they are predominantly red and white or brown and white. They produce less milk than Friesians but it contains more butterfat. *See also* DAIRYING; PE p.226.

Ayrton, Hertha (1854–1923), British scientist, second wife of the electrical engineer William AYRTON. She invented (1915) a fan for use against war gases.

Ayrton, Michael (1921–75), leading British figurative sculptor, painter and draughtsman who derived his subject matter largely from Greek myth, eg, Daedalus, the Minotaur and the Delphic oracle. His sculpture includes a series of bronzes of Icarus. He was also a writer, his main book being *Testament of Daedalus* (1962). *See also* HC2 p.281.

Ayrton, William Edward (1847–1908), British inventor and electrical engineer who developed the electric arc, especially for use in searchlights.

Ayton, Sir Robert (1570–1638), Scottish poet who is credited with the words to the song *Auld Lang Syne*.

Aytoun, William Edmonstoune (1813–65), Scottish poet, best known for his parodies of Alfred Tennyson and others in *Bon Gaultier Ballards* (written with Sir Theodore Martin) and of Walter Scott in *Lays of the Scottish Cavaliers*.

Ayub Khan, Muhammad (1907–74), military leader and President of Pakistan (1958–69). His military career began in 1928 and he became Commander-in-Chief of the Pakistani army in 1951. From 1954–56 he was Defence Minister, and in 1958 a military coup made him ruler of the country. He became President in 1960 and again in 1965. Although Pakistan made economic progress under Ayub Khan, student riots over suffrage restrictions and disputes with India over the boundaries of Jammu and Kashmir forced his resignation in 1969.

Ayurveda, system of medicine practised by the ancient Hindus and derived from the VEDAS. It is still practised in India.

Ayutthaya, city in S central Thailand on the Chao Phraya River. It was the capital of a Thai kingdom in the 14th century and some of the few remaining monuments of Siamese civilization can still be seen there. Today it is a market centre for the surrounding rice-growing region. Pop. (1965 est.) 40,000.

Azad, Abdul Kalman (1888–1958), Indian politician who was imprisoned several times for his part in GANDHI's civil disobedience movement that sought independence from the British.

Azalea, species of shrubs and small trees from temperate regions of Asia and North America. Mostly deciduous, they have leathery leaves and funnel-shaped red, pink, magenta, orange, yellow or white flowers, sometimes variegated. Family Ericaceae; genus *Rhododendron*..

Azaña y Díaz, Manuel (1880–1940), Spanish politician. He was Prime Minister 1931–33 and in 1936 until he was elected President of the Second Republic. He was titular head of the Republican Government during the Spanish Civil War, and resigned in 1939.

Azande, Negroid people of the Sudan, Zaire and the Central African Empire. They have a patrilineal, polygynous society noted for incorporating various ethnic minorities, and are highly skilled in crafts such as pottery, metalwork and woodwork. Azande religion is TOTEMIC and includes ancestor-worship. It holds that a man has two souls, one of which at death becomes a totemic animal.

Azariah, Vedanayakam Samuel (1874–1945), Indian Christian leader who in 1912 became the first of his people to become an Anglican bishop in India.

Azerbaijan (Azerbajdzanskaya SSR), constituent republic of the USSR. It lies largely in the lowland area of the Caucasus and extends S over the Malayjkavkaz mountains to the borders of Turkey and Iran. In the 7th century it was part of the Persian Empire. It was dominated by the Seljuk Turks in the 11th and 12th centuries, followed by the Mongols in the 13th century. It was not until 1936 that the whole area became part of the USSR. The valley and lowland areas produce grain, fruit and tobacco; sheep rearing for wool is also important. Although the region has deposits of copper, lead and iron, it is still developing industrially. Most of the inhabitants are Turkic speaking and belong to the Shiite sect of Islam. The capital is BAKU. Area: 86,600sq km (33,435sq miles). Pop. (1976) 2,842,000. *See also* MW p.170.

Azevedo, Aluízio (1857–1913), Brazilian novelist. His novel *O Mulato* (1881) helped to steer Brazilian writing towards a naturalist style. Graphically describing the harshness and violence of life among Brazil's poor, his novels have been praised for their energy and realism and criticized, like many other naturalistic works, for their lack of lyricism.

Azhar, Al, in Cairo, one of the oldest universities in the world, founded in 970 by the Fatimid army commander Jawhar. It became the centre of Islamic teaching.

Azikiwe, Benjamin Nnamdi "Zik" (1904–). Nigerian politician and author. He was President of Nigeria (1963–66). During the civil war (1967–70), he first supported BIAFRA but changed his support to the federal government in 1969.

Azilian culture, one of the earliest mesolithic cultures in Europe which sprang up in the Pyrenees region and spread to France, Belgium, Scotland and Switzerland.

Azimuth, the angle between the vertical plane on which a celestial body is located and the observer's meridian plane. It is measured, in astronomy, eastwards from the north point of the observer's horizon and, in navigation and surveying, westwards from the south point. Altitude and azimuth form an astronomical co-ordinate system for defining position.

Azo and diazo compounds, nitrogenous organic chemical compounds used widely for organic synthesis, particularly in the manufacture of dyes. An azo dye has the general formula $Ar\text{-}N{=}N\text{-}Ar$, where Ar is an aromatic group. Diazo compounds include reactive salts having the general formula $Ar\text{-}N{\equiv}N^{+}\text{-}X^{-}$, where X is the anion. *See also* MM pp.244–245.

Azores, Portuguese island group in the N Atlantic Ocean, 1,288km (800 miles) W of Portugal. They consist of nine main islands, divided into three groups. A variety of fruits and vegetables are grown for export and the islands' economy has improved with the development of tourism. Area: 2,344sq km (905sq miles). Pop. (1970 est.) 336,100.

Azorin. *See* MARTÍNEZ RUIZ, JOSÉ.

Azov, city in Rostov oblast, SW USSR. A former port on the River Don, it is today a manufacturing and trading centre and a railway terminus. Built near the site of the Greek colony of Tanaïs (3rd century BC), it was secured by Russia in 1739. Industries: fishing, textiles, timber, farm machinery. Pop. 59,000.

Aztecs, Indian civilization that rose to a position of dominance in the central valley of Mexico in about AD 1450. A warlike group, the Aztecs (also called Tenochca) settled on islands in Lake Texcoco in about 1325 and there founded their capital Tenochtitlan (now Mexico City). They established an empire that included most of modern Mexico and extended southwards as far as Guatemala. The state was theocratic, with a number of deities whose worship included human sacrifice. The Aztecs built temples, pyramids and palaces and adorned them with stone images and symbolic carvings. At the time of the Spanish conquest, Aztec society was based on the exploitation of labour. As a result, Hernán CORTÉS was able to use disaffected Indians to help him defeat the Aztecs in 1521. *See also* HC1 pp.230, 231.

Azuela, Mariano (1873–1952), Mexican novelist. He is best known for his vivid, unsentimental novels of the Mexican Revolution. A physician, he served as surgeon for Pancho Villa's revolutionary forces in 1915. His best-known novel, *The Underdogs* (1915), examines the revolution's impact on a broad cross-section of characters.

Azurite, basic copper carbonate mineral found in the oxidized parts of copper ore veins, often as earthy material with MALACHITE. The crystals are blue, brilliant and transparent but are too soft for good gemstones. They were used by the ancients as pigments in wall paintings. Hardness 3.5–4; sg 3.77–3.89.

Az-Zarqā. *See* ZERQA.

B

B, second letter of the alphabet. It is probably derived from an Egyptian hieroglyph for a house (*c.*3000 BC), which entered the Semitic alphabet about 1500 years later as the letter *beth.* From there it was taken to Greece (*c.*600 BC) to become *beta*, which was a similar shape to the modern B. *See also* MS pp.244–245.

Baade, Walter (1893–1960), German-born US astronomer. In 1925 he discovered the asteroid Hidalgo.. He held a position at the Hamburg Observatory in Germany (1919–31), and at the Mt Wilson observatory in the USA (1931–58). *See also* SU pp.204, 231. 239.

Baal, chief god of the Semitic pantheon, akin to the Greek ZEUS. In the ancient Middle East he was linked with fertility as lord of the earth, the rain and the dew. The Canaanites looked upon him as the foe of Mot, god of death and barrenness.

Baalbek, town in E Lebanon, 56km (35 miles) NW of Damascus. An early Phoenician settlement, the Greeks occupied it in 323 BC and renamed it Heliopolis (city of the sun); it was colonized by the Romans in the 1st century BC. It is noted for its Greek and Roman remains, including the Temple of Jupiter. Pop. 11,700.

Ba'ath Party, political party in Syria and Iraq, founded in 1943. Its major objectives are socialism and pan-Arabism. From 1963 the Ba'ath Party has been the only legal political party in SYRIA, but divisions within it have caused frequent changes of government. In IRAQ the party came to power in 1963 when Abdal Salam Arif became President.

Babar, group of five small islands and one large one (which is also called Babar), at the NW end of the Arafura Sea, E of Timor, Indonesia.

Baba-Yaga, in Russian folklore, a witch-like ogre who kidnaps and cooks her victims or eats the souls that Death provides for her. She travels through the air in an iron pot or a mortar, rowing with a pestle. In another aspect she is the guardian of the

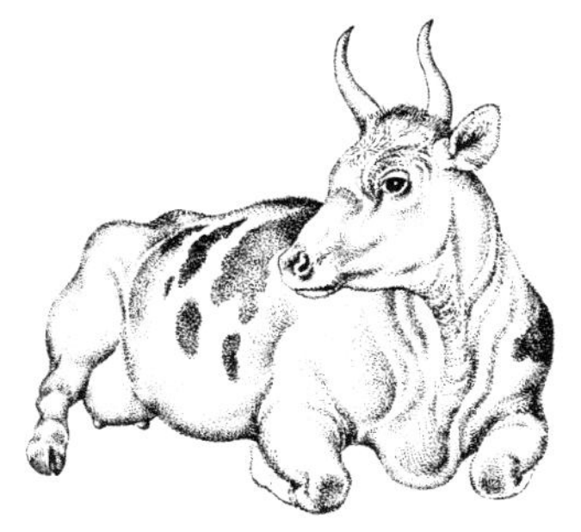

Ayrshire cattle are a rugged breed of dairy cattle that thrive in hilly country.

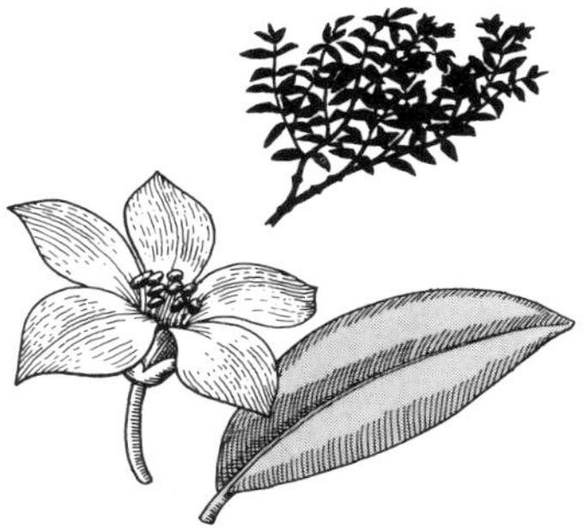

Azaleas, popular garden shrubs, have flowers of attractive colours with long pollen stalks.

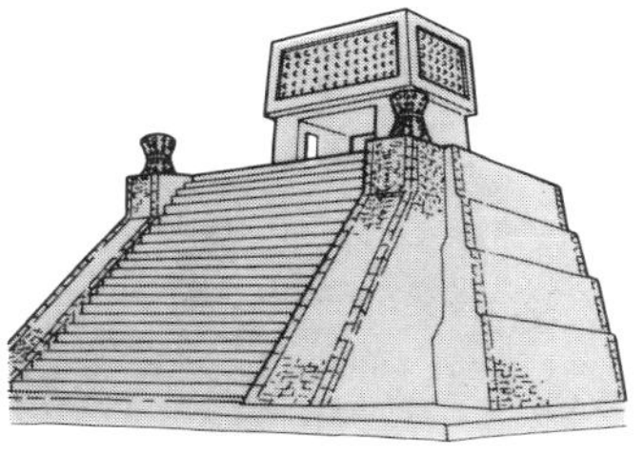

Aztecs built temples and palaces that were of impressive size; many ruins remain.

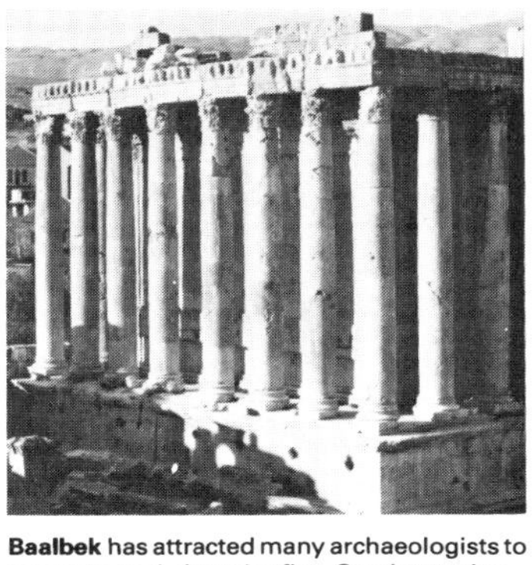

Baalbek has attracted many archaeologists to excavate and clear the fine Greek temples.

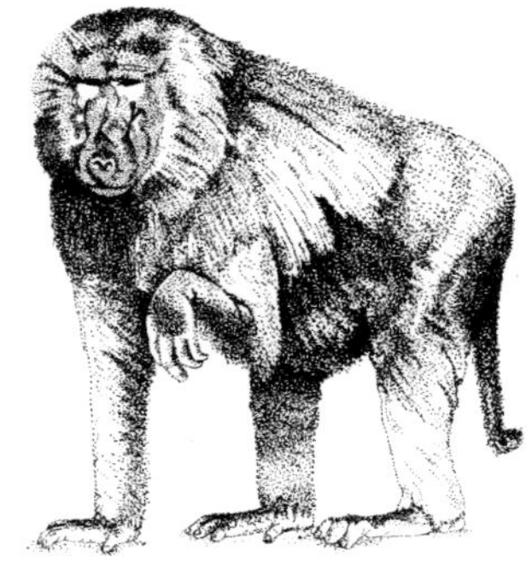

Baboon males, generally larger than the females, can sometimes be fierce fighters.

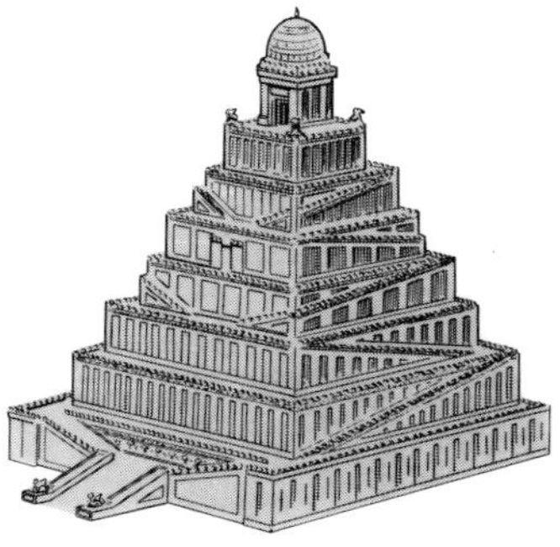

Babylonia produced some of the most beautiful temples of the ancient world.

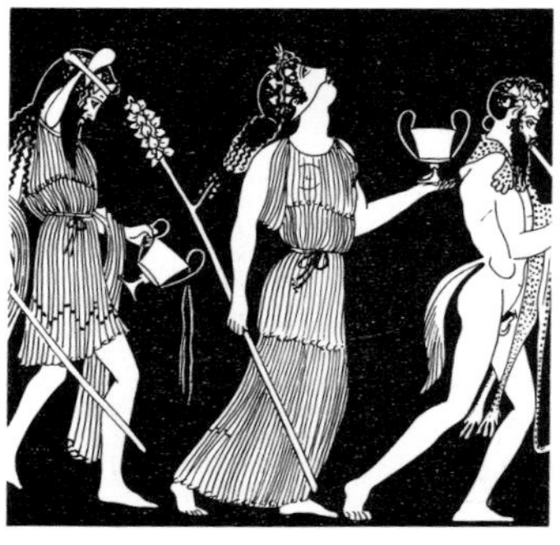

Bacchus inspired the legendary Bacchanalia, the wild drunken annual Roman festival.

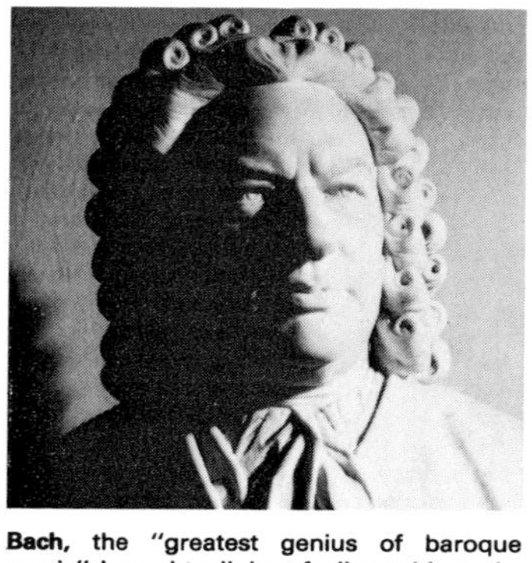

Bach, the "greatest genius of baroque music", brought religious feeling to his work.

fountain that supplies the the water of life.

Babbage, Charles (1791–1871), British mathematician. He compiled the first actuarial tables and planned a mechanical calculating machine, the forerunner of the modern computer. He failed to complete the construction of the machine because the financial support recommended by the Royal Society was refused by the government. *See also* MM p.*106*.

Babbitt, Milton (1916–), US composer, musicologist and teacher. He studied with Roger SESSIONS and has a mathematical background that influences his musical style. He analysed and systematized TWELVE-TONE MUSIC. His compositions include vocal, piano and chamber music.

Babbitt (1922), novel by Sinclair LEWIS about George Babbitt, a Mid-western American businessman and die-hard Republican, who begins to re-evaluate his life. After a brief rebellion against the deadening conformity that surrounds him, he again becomes a "good citizen".

Babbitt metal, any alloy with a high tin content as well as copper and antimony, specifically an alloy invented by Isaac Babbitt in 1839 as bearing material for steam engines.

Babcock, Harold Delos (1882–1968), US physicist and spectroscopist who developed a modern theory to account for the formation of SUNSPOTS. *See also* SU p.221.

Babcock, Stephen Moulton (1843–1931), US agricultural research chemist. In 1890 he helped to improve dairy production with his Babcock test, a method of measuring the butterfat content of milk.

Babel, Isaac Emmanuelovich (1894–1941), Russian short-story writer. His works included *Red Cavalry* (1926) and *Jewish Tales* (1927). He died a victim of Stalinist purges in a concentration camp.

Babel, Tower of, according to Genesis 11:1-9, was begun in the Babylonian city of Babel by NOAH's descendants to reach Heaven. God made the people's speech incomprehensible and scattered them throughout the world, causing the work to cease.

Bab el-Mandeb, strait connecting the Red Sea and the Gulf of Aden. It separates the SW Arabian Peninsula from Africa, and contains Barim Island (Yemen PDR). It is 32km (20 miles) wide.

Babenberg, Austrian dynasty (976–1246). Leopold I was the first Babenberg margrave of Austria. In 1156 Emperor FREDERICK I (Barbarossa) made Austria a duchy. The Babenbergs extended the authority of Austria to the E.

Babeuf, François-Noel (1760–97), called "Gracchus", political activist in the French Revolution. He supported land reform and the constitution of 1793. He was executed on the orders of the Directory after an attempted insurrection. His *Manifesto of Equals* (1796) influenced later socialists. *See also* HC2 p.74.

Babi faith, Muslim religious sect founded in 1844 in Iran (Persia) by SAYYID ALI MUHAMMED, the self-proclaimed prophet Bab (gate). Drawing on the teachings of all existing branches of ISLAM, the Babists believed in the imminent coming of the Promised One. In 1848 they declared their secession from Islam but their rebellion against the new shah was crushed and their founder was executed in 1850.

Babilée, Jean (1923–), French dancer and choreographer. He became the principal dancer of the Ballets de Paris (1947) and was director of the Ballet du Rhin (1972–73).

Babington Conspiracy (1586), plot against ELIZABETH I of England, led by Anthony Babington (1561–86), which aimed to restore Roman Catholicism by replacing Elizabeth by MARY QUEEN OF SCOTS. The conspiracy failed, and Babington was executed.

Babism. *See* BABI FAITH.

Babi Yar (1961), poem by the Soviet poet Yevgeny YEVTUSHENKO evoking the horror of the Nazi massacre of 34,000 Jews at Kiev and attacking continuing anti-Semitism in the USSR.

Baboon, large African MONKEY with a dog-like face, which walks on all fours. Its buttocks have callous-like pads surrounded by brilliantly coloured naked skin. Baboons are ground dwellers and active by day, travelling in families and larger troops led by old males, usually in open, rocky country. They eat a wide variety of food – plants, insects and small animals – carrying it, if necessary, in their cheek pouches. The males have huge canine teeth up to 5cm (2in) long. Weight: 14-41kg (30-90lb). Genus *Chaeropithecus* (or *Papio*). *See also* NW p.172.

Babur (1483–1530), first Mogul ruler of India (1526–30). He became ruler of Fergana, a principality in central Asia in 1495. He struggled with various relatives for Samarkand but failed and settled in Kabul, from where he gained control of Delhi and Agra, establishing Mogul rule in India. *See also* HC2 p.48.

Baburen, Dirck van (*c.*1590–1624), Dutch painter, leading member of the UTRECHT SCHOOL. He worked briefly in Rome, where he was influenced by CARAVAGGIO; he was one of the first to introduce Caravaggio's *chiaroscuro* technique into the Netherlands.

Babylon, ancient city, sited on the River Euphrates in MESOPOTAMIA; it rose to prominence as the capital of BABYLONIA. It was rebuilt after being destroyed by the ASSYRIANS *c.*689 BC, and its new buildings included the Hanging Gardens, one of the seven wonders of the world. This was the period, under NEBUCHADREZZAR, of the BABYLONIAN CAPTIVITY of the Jews. The city declined after 275 BC, when it was replaced in importance by Seleucia.

Babylonia, ancient region and empire of Mesopotamia, based on the city of BABYLON. The Babylonian empire was first established in the early 18th century BC by HAMMURABI the Great, but it soon declined under the impact of Hittite and Kassite invaders in about 1595 BC. After a long period of weakness and confusion, the empire eventually fell to the ASSYRIANS in the 8th century. Babylon's greatness was restored as part of the Assyrian empire, and in about 625 BC its independence was won by NABOPOLASSAR, who captured the Assyrian capital NINEVEH, with the help of the Medes and Persians. This New Babylonian, or Chaldaean, Empire defeated Egypt and took the Jews to captivity in Babylon in 586 BC; but in 538 BC it fell to the Persians, under whom it remained until the rise of ALEXANDER THE GREAT. *See also* HC1 pp.32–33.

Babylonian Captivity, exile of the Jews to BABYLON from the fall of JERUSALEM (586 BC) to the completion of the new Temple (516 BC). The term was later applied also to the exile of the popes at AVIGNON (1309–77). A line of French popes began in 1305 with the election of Clement V. The papal court returned to Rome in 1377 but two French ANTIPOPES, Clement VII and Benedict XIII, lived at Avignon during the GREAT SCHISM (1378–1417).

Baccarat, French card game, popular in gambling casinos. The game involves a banker and two players. Each player, including the banker, receives two cards with an option for a third. The object of the game is to hold two or three cards that count nine or as close to nine as possible. Picture cards rate as *baccarat*, ie zero and the first digit is disregarded from all totals above nine. *See also* CHEMIN DE FER.

Bacchae (*c.*405 BC), Greek tragedy by EURIPIDES. Dionysus assumes human form, causing grief and confusion on earth.

Bacchus, Roman god of wine, identified with the Greek god Dionysus. The son of JUPITER and SEMELE, he was reared by nymphs, shepherds and satyrs, and learned the secrets of cultivating grapes and making wine. His worshippers indulged in riotous revelry and debauchery. *See also* PE p.*199*.

Bacchylides (*c.*516–*c.*450 BC), Greek lyric poet, most of whose work exists only in fragments although in 1896 some complete poems were discovered.

Bach, German family of composers, the most outstanding of whom were Johann Sebastian (1685–1750) and four of his sons, Wilhelm Friedemann (1710–84), Carl Philipp Emanuel (1714–88), Johann Christoph Friedrich (1732–95) and Johann Christian (1735–82).

In J. S. Bach, the greatest of the family, the style of Baroque counterpoint reached its highest expression (*see* BAROQUE; COUNTERPOINT). He was renowned as a virtuoso on organ and harpsichord, and composed prolifically for these instruments and for orchestra and choir. Bach's musical career began with a short time as court musician at Weimar, after which he was organist at Arnstadt (1703–07) and at Mühlhausen (1707–08). He served again at Weimar, as court organist and chamber musician (1708–17), and was the Prince of Anhalt-Köthen's musical director (1717–23). From 1723 until his death Bach was *Kapellmeister* at the church of St Thomas, Leipzig. Much of his work was therefore sacred music – more than 200 CANTATAS, more than 300 four-part chorales, the great *Passions* and the monumental *Mass in B Minor.* His secular works include the Brandenburg Concertos, the four orchestral suites and several concertos for solo instrument and orchestra. His keyboard works include 18 preludes and fugues for organ and the harpsichord compositions, the *Well-Tempered Clavier*, the French and English suites and the two-part and three-part inventions.

Carl Philipp Emanuel Bach was an important figure in the development of the classical concerto and symphony. Whereas his father had used the baroque forms of the FUGUE and the SUITE, Carl Philipp wrote principally in SONATA form. *See also* HC2 pp.40–41.

Bache, peninsula on E Ellesmere Island in N Northwest Territories, Canada. It was explored in 1898 by Robert Peary.

Bach System (1849–59), repressive administrative policy of absolute and centralizing bureaucracy applied to the whole HAPSBURG EMPIRE. It was introduced by Alexander von Bach, the Austro-Hungarian minister of the interior. In 1851 Hungary lost its historical identity and was ruled as a province by officials from Vienna. A rigorous programme was introduced to enforce the use of the German language. *See also* AUSTRO-HUNGARIAN EMPIRE.

Bacillus, genus of aerobic, spore-forming BACTERIA present in the soil. One species, *B. anthracis*, is PATHOGENIC to man, causing ANTHRAX. *See also* NW pp.36–37.

Backcross, the offspring of a first generation HYBRID and either of its parents. Backcrosses are used by biologists as a means of testing for the dominance of one quality over another.

Backgammon, game of strategy and luck usually involving two players. There is a specially marked board divided into two halves, each containing 12 alternately coloured points. Each player receives 15 discs that are arranged in a predetermined order on the boards. Each move is determined by the throw of dice, the first player to successfully move all 15 pieces around the board into his "home" or "inner board" and then off the board, wins.

Backhaus, Wilhelm (1884–1969), German pianist. He studied in Leipzig and Frankfurt and toured as a virtuoso from 1910. He was famous as an interpreter of Beethoven; he lived in Switzerland after WWII.

Backhuysen, Ludolf (1631–1708), Dutch painter, mainly of marine subjects. The realism of his style, in particular *Boats in a Storm* (1696, Dulwich), may have influenced Joseph TURNER.

Bacolod, capital city of Negros Occidental Province on NW Negros Island, Philippines. Pop. 165,000.

Bacon, Delia Salter (1811–59), US author. In *Philosophy of the Plays of Shakespeare Unfolded* (1857) she publicized the theory that Shakespeare's plays were written by other authors such as Francis BACON and Edmund SPENSER. *See* BACONIAN THEORY.

Bacon, Francis (1561–1626), British philosopher, statesman and early advocate of the scientific method. He is also a literary figure of the first rank, especially in his essays. Successively Attorney-General, Lord Keeper and Lord Chancellor, he was forced to resign his offices in 1621 on charges of venality. None of this interrupted his efforts to break the hold of Aristotelian LOGIC and establish an inductive empiricism. He entertained the idea of cataloguing all useful knowledge in his *Advancement of Learning* (1605) and *Novum Organum* (1620). *The New Atlantis* (1627) discusses his philosophy as practised in an imaginary nation. *See also* HC1 pp.282, 302; MM pp.212, 214.

Bacon, Francis (1910–), British painter, *b.* Dublin, mainly self-taught, whose powerful images capture and freeze the fleeting expression or gesture, often violent or hallucinatory. His work is largely based on photographs, eg the screaming nurse in the film *Battleship Potemkin*, or on his favourite paintings, eg Velázquez's *Innocent X*. To Bacon painting is "the pattern of one's nervous system being projected on canvas". *See also* HC2 pp.175, *175*, 281.

Bacon, Sir Nicholas (1509–79), English lawyer, father of Francis Bacon, who in 1559 became lord chancellor under ELIZABETH I. He proposed that stern measures should be taken against MARY QUEEN OF SCOTS.

Bacon, Roger (1220–92), British philosopher and scientist. He was strongly influenced by Robert Grosseteste when studying languages, mathematics, alchemy and astronomy at Oxford. Writing the *Opus majus*, *Opus minor* and the *Opus tertium* (1267–68) for Pope CLEMENT IV, he urged that extensive studies of these areas be included in university curricula. Clement died before acting on this proposal. *See also* GROSSETESTE, ROBERT; HC1 p.188; SU p.23.

Bacon (meat). *See* PE p.234.

Baconian theory, postulate that the plays of William SHAKESPEARE were really the work of Francis BACON. The theory was championed in 1856 by William Henry Smith, although it had been suggested three years earlier by the US author Delia BACON. It is furthered by the Bacon Society (founded 1886).

Bacteria, simple unicellular microscopic organisms (class Schizomycetes), usually classified in the plant kingdom. They lack a clearly defined nucleus and most are without CHLOROPHYLL. There are three typical forms – rod-shaped (bacillus), round (coccus, eg streptococcus) and spiral (spirillum). Many are mobile, swimming about by means of whip-like flagella. Although many multiply by transverse fission, some species reproduce in different ways, chiefly by conjugation and transformation. Under adverse conditions many can remain dormant inside highly resistant SPORES with thick protective coverings. There are different kinds of metabolic functioning: AEROBIC, using free or atmospheric oxygen; ANAEROBIC, using oxygen from compounds; autotrophic, obtaining some energy from light using bacteriochlorophyll. Although PATHOGENIC bacteria are a major cause of human disease, many more are harmless or even beneficial to man by providing an important link in food chains, eg in decomposing plant and animal tissue, and in converting free nitrogen and sulphur into amino acids and other compounds that plants and animals can use. They are important too in such processes as FERMENTATION and food preservation. *See also* NW pp.*21*, 36–37; PE 150, 167, *173*, *223*; SU p.*157*.

Bacteriology, the scientific study of BACTERIA. They were first observed in the 17th century by Anton van LEEUWENHOEK, but it was not until the researches of Louis PASTEUR, the French chemist, and later Robert KOCH, a German physician, in the mid-19th century that bacteriology was established as a science.

Bacteriophage, VIRUS that lives on and infects BACTERIA, with a protein head containing DNA OR RNA and a protein tail. Since its discovery in 1915 it has been important in the study of GENETICS.

Bactria, ancient name for the region between the Hindu Kush Mts and the River Oxus in NE Afghanistan. It is mountainous but fertile, with abundant water and a mild climate. The region gave its name to the two-humped Bactrian CAMEL. The capital, Bactra, has adopted the modern name Balkh.

Badajoz, capital city of Badajoz province, on the River Guadiana in SW Spain. There is a ruined citadel dating from the flourishing Moorish period and a 13th-century cathedral. Industries: distilling, food processing. Pop. (1970) 101,700.

Baden, town in E Austria 23km (14 miles) SSW of Vienna. It has been famous since Roman times for its hot sulphur springs. Pop. 22,500.

Baden-Baden, health resort in W Baden-Württemberg state, SW West Germany, 30km (18 miles) SW of Karlsruhe in the Black Forest. The Roman mineral baths built there in the 3rd century remain a tourist attraction. Pop. 39,000.

Badenoch, wild, mountainous and densely-wooded area of NE Scotland, near the upper reaches of the River Spey; includes Lock Laggan. The mountains extend for 72km (45 miles), and the main town and tourist centre is Kingussie.

Baden-Powell of Gilwell, Robert Stephenson Smyth Baden-Powell, 1st Baron (1857–1941), British soldier and founder of the Scout movement. He held Mafeking against the Boers (1899–1900) and from 1910 he devoted the rest of his life to the BOY SCOUTS. His sister Agnes (1858–1945) founded the GIRL GUIDES (1910). His wife, Lady Olave St Clair Baden-Powell (1889–1977), also did much to promote these movements throughout the world.

Baden-Württemberg, region (*land*) in SW West Germany, formed in 1952; capital, Stuttgart. Agriculture and livestock-rearing are important, but industry is the major occupation. There are universities at Heidelberg and Freiburg, and the area is a popular tourist resort, with a spa at BADEN-BADEN. Industries: motor vehicles, machinery, textiles, glass. Area: 35,750sq km (13,803sq miles). Pop. (1970) 8,959,700.

Badger, burrowing, nocturnal mammal that lives in Eurasia, North America and Africa. It has a stocky body with short legs and tail. Eurasian badgers (*Meles meles*) have grey bodies with black-and-white striped heads. American badgers (*Taxidea taxus*) are smaller and have grey-brown to red fur with a white head stripe. Length: 41-71cm (16-28in); weight: 10-20kg (22-44lb). Family Mustelidae.

Badings, Henk (1907–), Dutch composer, *b.* Java. His is famous especially for his ELECTRONIC MUSIC, including the electronic ballet *Evolutions* (1958).

Badlands, region in SW South Dakota and NW Nebraska, USA. It is a rugged eroded area with layered sedimentary deposits containing numbers of fossils.

Badminton, game for two or four people. It enjoyed popularity in England in the 1870s, when it was called battledore and shuttlecock; afterwards it was taken to Poona in India where the first rules of the game were compiled. The game is similar to tennis and the object is to volley, with light rackets, a shuttlecock or bird (a cork base to which feathers are attached) until it is missed by an opponent or hit out of bounds. The court used for singles (indoors and out) is 5.3 by 13.4m (17 by 44ft); for doubles it is 6.1 by 13.4m (20 by 44ft). The net is 1.5m (5ft) high in the centre.

Badoglio, Pietro (1871–1956), Italian soldier and statesman. Chief of the general staff in 1919, he led the Italians at the WWI armistice talks. He was chief of staff again from 1925 to 1940. He headed the government that came to power after MUSSOLINI was overthrown and arranged the armistice (3 Sep. 1943).

Baedeker, Karl (1801–59), German publisher best known for a series of guidebooks to various cities throughout Europe. The first English editions appeared in 1861. The firm's files were destroyed during WWII, although a great-grandson of Baedeker revived the business after the war.

Baekeland, Leo Hendrik (1863–1944), US chemist, *b.* Belgium. He invented a type of photographic paper capable of being developed under artificial light. He also invented the first thermosetting plastic – BAKELITE – a substance that led to the development of the plastics industry.

Baena, Juan Alfonso de (*fl.* 1410–45), Spanish poet. He compiled an anthology – the *Cancionero de Baena* (1445) – of nearly 600 court poems, most of which were in Castilian.

Baer, Karl Ernst von (1792–1876), Estonian biologist. He described his discovery of the mammalian ovum in *De Ovi Mammalium et Hominis Genesi* (1827). He also wrote *On the Development of Animals* (2 vols. 1828, 1837).

Baer, Maximilian Adelbert (Max) (1909–59), US boxer who in 1934 beat Primo Carnera for the world heavyweight championship. He held the title for one year, being beaten by James Braddock.

Baeyer, Johann Friedrich Wilhelm Adolph von (1835–1917), German organic research chemist. He was awarded the Nobel Prize in chemistry in 1905 for his synthesis of indigo. He also investigated uric acid derivatives, discovered the phthalein dyes and devised a "strain" theory to account for the stability and conformation of carbon with five-membered and six-membered rings.

Baez, Joan (1941–), US folk singer. She first played in coffee houses and in the 1960s toured the USA and Europe (1970), and has made many recordings. She became associated with the protest movement, particularly against US involvement in Vietnam.

Baffin, William (1584–1622), English navigator and explorer. From 1612–16 he led several expeditions in search of the Northwest Passage, one of which led to the discovery of the bay between Greenland and Canada (since named after him). He was the first person to determine longitude at sea by observing the moon.

Baffin Bay, inlet of the Atlantic Ocean between Greenland and Baffin Island, Canada; connected with the Atlantic Ocean by the Davis Strait. First discovered in 1587 by John Davis, it was explored by William BAFFIN in 1616.

Baffin Island, large island at the E end of the Arctic Archipelago in the Northwest Territories, Canada; separated from Québec by the Hudson Strait. It is the fifth-largest island in the world, with largely mountainous terrain, and an almost entirely Eskimo population. Area: 476,070sq km (183,810sq miles). Pop. 3,400.

Bagatelle, billard game. It is played on a special table with nine balls. The object is to try to cue the balls in one of the nine numbered cups on the table. After playing all of the balls in turn, the players tally their score either by the number of cups filled or by the total points value of the cups that were filled.

Bagehot, Walter (1826–77), British economist and writer. Trained as a lawyer, he became a banker (1852–58) and an influential editor of *The Economist* (1860–77), which was founded by his father-in-law in 1843. His book *Lombard Street* (1873) inaugurated the modern theory of central banking. Two of his other important works were *Literary Studies* (1879) and *Economic Studies* (1880).

Baghdad, capital city of IRAQ, on the River Tigris. Established in 762 as capital of the Abbasid Caliphate, it grew into a cultural and financial centre, a focus of caravan routes between the Orient and the West. It was almost destroyed by the MONGOLS in 1258. Soon after Iraq gained its independence from the Turks, Baghdad became the capital (1921). It is now an administrative, transport and educational centre. Industries: building materials, textiles, tanning, bookbinding, tourism. Pop. (1970 est.) 2,183,000. *See also* MW p.101.

Baghdad Pact, joint defence agreement signed by Turkey, Iran, Iraq, Pakistan and Britain in 1955, as a bulwark against Soviet expansion in the Middle East. In 1959 Iraq withdrew, the headquarters were moved to Ankara, Turkey, and the name was changed to the Central Treaty Organization.

Baghdad Railway, rail link between Europe and the Middle East. In 1902 a German company was granted permission by the Ottoman Empire to extend the line from Turkey to Baghdad. Britain, Russia

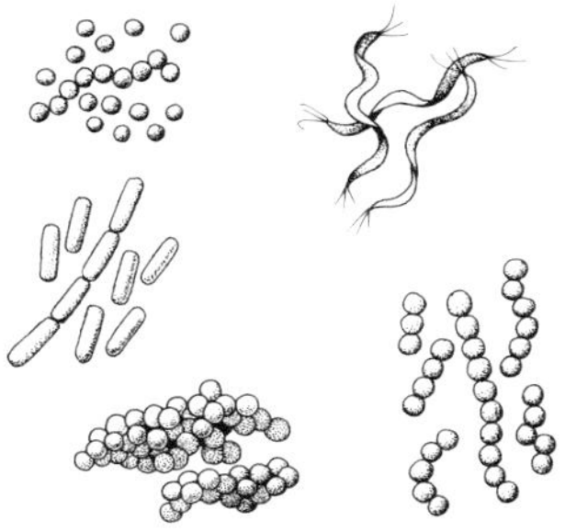

Bacteria, is found almost everywhere, can be both helpful and harmful to man.

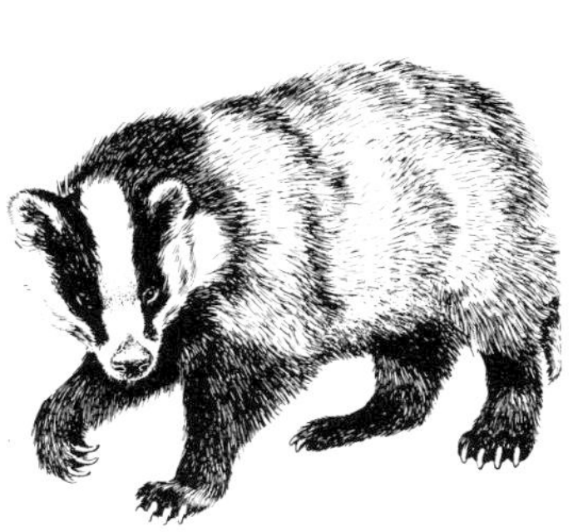

Badger, a distinctive member of the weasel family, can outdig even the mole.

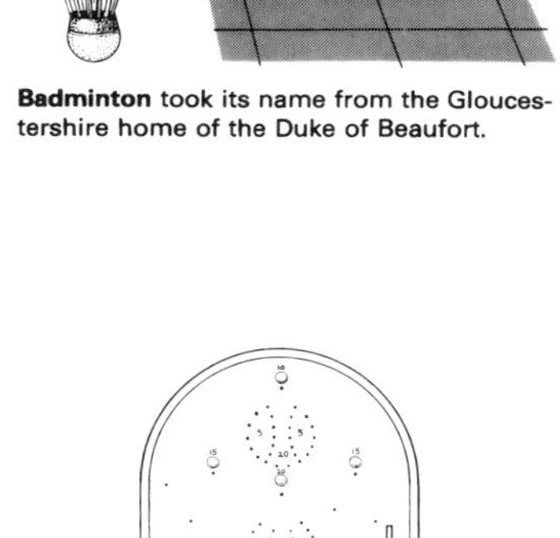

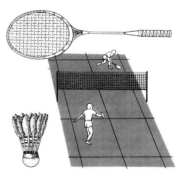

Badminton took its name from the Gloucestershire home of the Duke of Beaufort.

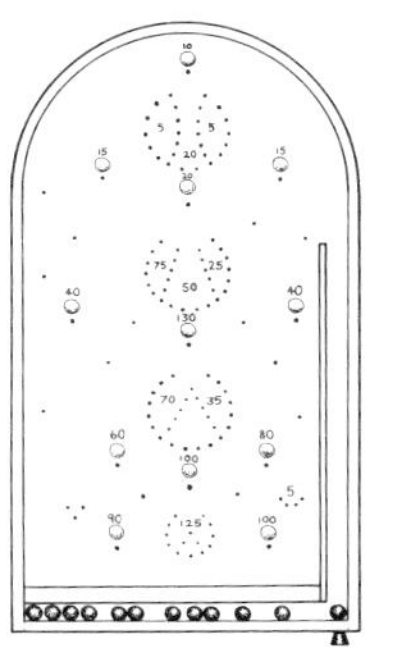

Bagatelle almost certainly gave rise to the present-day electronic pinball machine.

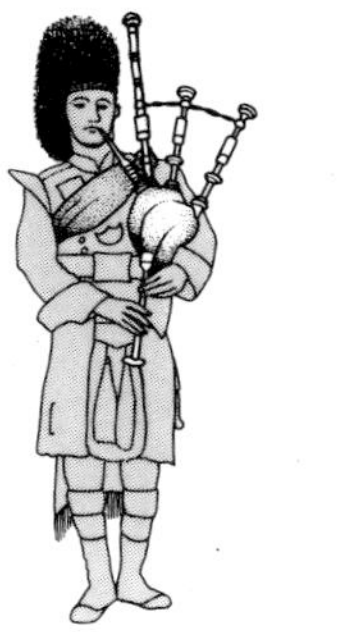

Bagpipe music is characterised by a drone harmony sustained by the air filled bag.

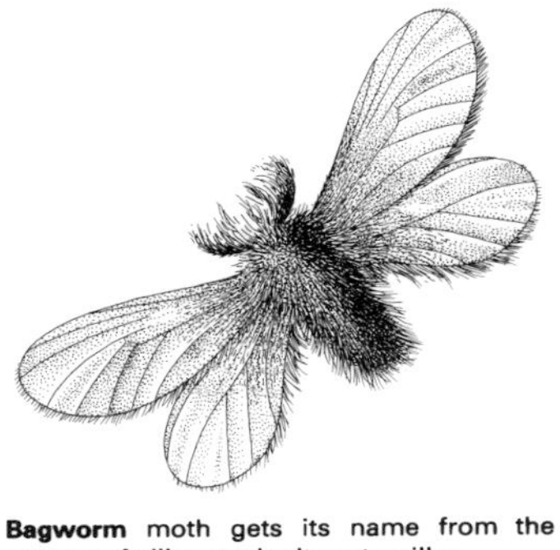

Bagworm moth gets its name from the cocoon of silk spun by its caterpillar.

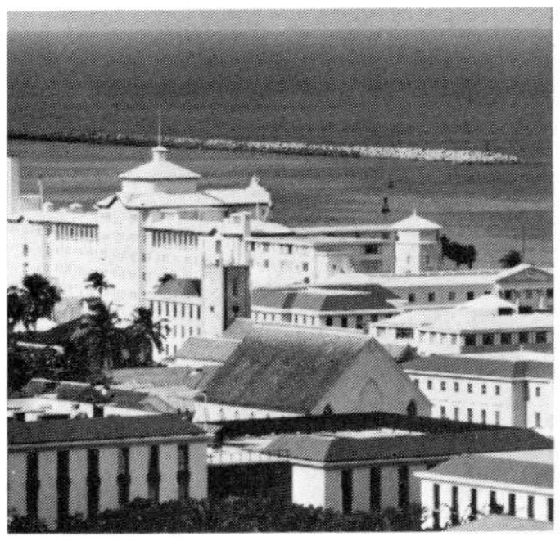

Bahamas; washed by the warm Gulf stream, the islands enjoy an almost perfect climate.

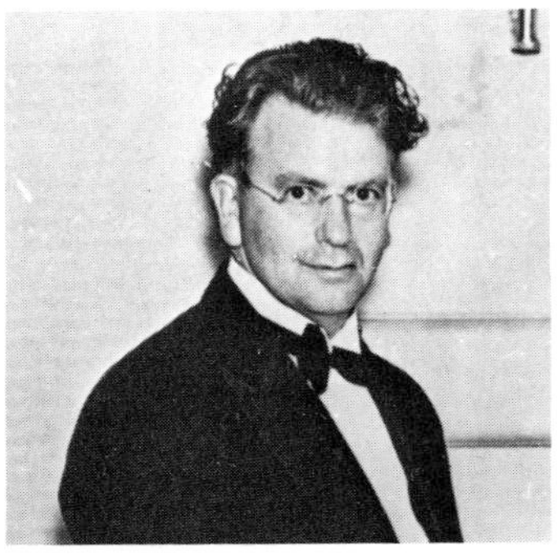

John Logie Baird, the television pioneer who demonstrated the first "true" television.

and France objected, seeing the railway as a threat to their own interests in the Middle and Far East. The resulting tension contributed to the hostility leading up to WWI.

Bagnold, Enid (1889–), British author. Her best-known novel is *National Velvet* (1935), the story of a girl and her horse. Her other work includes *The Squire* (1938), *The Loved and Envied* (1951) and the play *The Chalk Garden* (1956).

Bagot, Sir Charles (1781–1843), British colonial administrator who was minister to France (1814) and to the USA (1815–20). He helped negotiate the RUSH-BAGOT CONVENTION (1817) and in 1841 Robert Peel appointed him governor-general of Canada, an office he held until his death.

Bagpipe, musical instrument with reed pipes connected to a windbag held under the arm and filled by mouth or bellows. The chanter pipe has finger-holes for melody, while drone pipes produce monotone accompaniment. The bagpipe originated in Greece or Asia and is closely associated with Scotland and Ireland, although it is also played elsewhere in rural Europe.

Bagritsky, Eduard (1895–1934), Russian poet, real name Eduard Dzyubin. His best-known work is *Duma pro Opanasa* (1926), an epic poem set in the Russian civil war. His later poetry, which continued in a romantic style despite the official shift to social REALISM, includes the collection *Yugo-Zapad* (1928).

Bagworm, moth caterpillar that partly conceals itself in a cocoon of silk strands and particles of leaves and twigs. The common bagworm (*Thyridopteryx ephemeraeformis*) attacks trees and shrubs, especially arborvitae and CEDARS. Family Psychidae.

Bahadur Shah II (1775–1862), last Mogul Emperor of India (1837–58). He prevented Hindu-Muslim conflict in Delhi but in 1857 supported the mutiny against British rule of India and was dethroned. *See also* INDIAN MUTINY.

Bahai faith, religion founded in 1863 by BAHAULLAH as an outgrowth of the BABI FAITH. Its headquarters are in HAIFA, Israel, although it has centres throughout the world. It seeks world peace through the unification of all religions and stresses a simple life dedicated to serving others. It recognizes Bahaullah as the latest prophet of God.

Bahamas, small independent state in the W Atlantic, SE of Florida and consisting of about 700 islands of which Grand Bahama is the largest. The capital, Nassau, is situated on New Providence Island. Pop. (1976 est.) 208,000. *See* MW p.35.

Bahaullah (1817–92), Persian religious leader, original name Mirza Husayn Ali Nuri, founder of the BAHAI FAITH. He embraced the BABI FAITH in 1850 but broke with it in 1867, proclaiming himself Bahaullah ("The Glory of Allah"), the Promised One foretold by Bab. His work, the *Katabi ikan* (*The Book of Certitude*) is the Bahai holy book.

Bahāwalpur, city in E central Pakistan, on the River Sutlej; capital of the Bahāwalpur division of the Punjab province. It was the capital of the principality of Bahāwalpur in the late 18th century. Industries: machinery, textiles, food processing. Pop. (1972) 133,956.

Bahia, coastal state in E Brazil; capital, Salvador. Declared a province in 1823, it became a state in 1889. Products: cocoa, tobacco, piassava fibre, sisal, hardwoods, vegetable oils, natural gas, lead, titanium, asbestos, hydroelectricity. Area: 561,026sq km (216,612sq miles). Pop. 7,430,000.

Bahr, Hermann (1863-1934), Austrian critic, novelist and dramatist. He founded the Jungwien Group, which was influenced by French symbolism. His notable works include the novel *Die gute Schule* (1890), the essay *Zur Kritik der Moderne* (1890), which established Modernism as a literary term, and the comedies *Das Konzert* (1909) and *Der Meister* (1914).

Bahrain, island state in the Persian Gulf between the Qatar peninsula and the E coast of Arabia, named after the main island. Main exports are oil and pearls. Area: 663sq km (256sq miles). Pop. (1975 est.) 256,000. *See also* MW p.36.

Baia, small Italian holiday resort on the Gulf of Pozzuoli, 16km (10 miles) NW of Naples. Formerly called Baiae, it has warm sulphur springs, a mild climate and rich vegetation. HADRIAN died in the town, and Julius CAESAR had a villa there. Pop. 2,400.

Baikal (Baykal), lake in Siberia, the largest and deepest freshwater lake in the continent. It is fed by many small rivers but the only major outlet is the River Angara. It has a variety of fish and a unique species of seal, although some of these are threatened by the increasing pollution from lakeside factories. Area: 31,494sq km (12,160sq miles); max. depth: 1,742m (5,714ft).

Baikie, William Balfour (1825–64), British explorer and colonial administrator. He led two important explorations of the River Niger in 1854 and 1859. On the second expedition he set up a trading community at Lokoja, where he studied African languages.

Bail, in law, the granting or obtaining the release from custody of someone awaiting trial, by the deposit of a security ensuring the accused's return when required, eg in court for trial. If the person on bail does not return then the monetary value of the security, also called bail, is forfeited.

Baile Átha Cliath. *See* DUBLIN (city).

Bailey, Sir Donald Coleman (1901–), British civil engineer who designed the Bailey bridge for military use. The steel lattice girders can be assembled by groups of six men from easily manhandled component parts and cantilevered across a gap to provide a bridge to carry 70 tonnes over spans of up to 46m (150ft).

Bailey, James Anthony (1847–1906), circus impresario. He became involved with the Robinson and Lake Circus in 1863. In 1872 he became a partner in Cooper and Bailey, which merged with competitor P.T. BARNUM's in 1881. After Barnum's death in 1891, Bailey became head of the Barnum and Bailey Circus.

Bailey, Liberty Hyde (1858–1954), US botanist. He helped to establish horticulture as an applied science through the systematic study of cultivated plants. His work had an important influence on the development of GENETICS and plant pathology. He founded and directed the Bailey Hortorium at Cornell University.

Bailey, Pearl (1918–), US jazz singer. She made her stage debut in the Broadway musical *St Louis Woman* (1946) and later played in various musicals and films, including *St Louis Blues* (1957), *Porgy and Bess* (1959) and *The Landlord* (1969). In 1975 she retired from show business and was appointed to the US delegation to the United Nations.

Bailey bridge. *See* BAILEY, SIR DONALD COLEMAN.

Baillie, Dame Isobel (1895–), Scottish soprano. In 1923 she made her first London appearance and in 1933 was the first British artist to sing at the Hollywood Bowl, USA. She was professor of singing at the Royal College of Music (1955–57) and at Cornell University, USA (1960–61).

Baillie, Joanna (1762–1851), Scottish poet and playwright. Her plays include the tragedies *De Montfort* (1800) and *Family Legend* (1810). Collections of her poems, which were written in Scottish dialect, include *Fugitive Verses* (1790) and *Metrical Legends* (1821).

Bailly, Jean-Sylvain (1736–93), French astronomer and politician, author of *Histoire de l'astronomie* (1775–87). In 1789 he was elected president of the NATIONAL ASSEMBLY. He was mayor of Paris (1789–91) but lost political favour. He was guillotined in 1793.

Baily, Edward Hodges (1788–1867), British sculptor, best-known for his statue of Lord Nelson in Trafalgar Square, London.

Baily, Francis (1774–1844), British astronomer. In 1836 he discovered the phenomenon known as "Baily's beads" – spots of light seen on the edge of the Sun before and after total ECLIPSE. He calculated the Earth's mean density, using the data of Henry CAVENDISH. Baily was one of the founders of the Royal Astronomical Society and became its president.

Bain, Alexander (1818–1903), Scottish philosopher who held the chair of logic at Aberdeen University (1860–80). In the British empiricist mould, he studied the physical basis of mental events and the nervous processes of the brain.

Bainbridge, Beryl (1934–), British novelist. Her first novel, *A Weekend with Claude*, was published in 1967. She won the *Guardian* fiction award in 1974 for *The Bottle Factory Outing* and the Whitbread fiction prize in 1977.

Bainbridge, Kenneth Tompkins (1904–), US physicist who in 1945 directed the testing of the atom bomb at Alamogordo, New Mexico. He also did research into radar and in 1961 became a professor of physics at Harvard.

Bainton, Edgar Leslie (1880–1956), British composer. In 1934 he went to Australia and was director of the State Conservatory of Music, Sydney (1934–47). His many compositions include the symphony *Before Sunrise*, which won the Carnegie Trust Award in 1917.

Bainville, Jacques (1879–1936), French historian. His work includes *History of France* (1924), *Napoleon* (1931) and *The French Republic 1870–1935* (1935).

Baird, John Logie (1888–1946), Scottish engineer, the first man to transmit moving pictures. He demonstrated the first true television to members of the Royal Institution, London, in 1926; he transmitted television to a ship at sea in 1928 and was granted experimental broadcasting facilities by the BBC, London, in 1929. His mechanical television system was used alternately with an electronic system for the world's first public television service set up by the BBC in 1936. *See also* TELEVISION; MM pp.230–231.

Baireuth. *See* BAYREUTH.

Baja California (Lower California), peninsula of NW Mexico extending SSE for 1,220km (760 miles) between the Golfo de California and the Pacific Ocean. The chief product of the region is long-staple cotton and the main industry is tourism. Pop. 998,400.

Bajazet. *See* BEYAZID.

Bajer, Fredrik (1837–1922), Danish statesman. He was a Liberal member of the Danish parliament (1872–95) and did much work towards the development of Danish neutrality. In 1885 he was a delegate to the first Scandinavian peace conference and was one of the founders of the International Peace Bureau in Berne in 1891. He was president of the Bureau until 1907. He shared the 1908 Nobel Peace Prize with K.P. ARNOLDSON.

Bakelite, trade name (coined by Leo BAEKELAND) for a thermosetting plastic used for insulating purposes and in making paint. It was the first plastic made by the process called condensation, in which many molecules of two simple chemicals (in this case phenol and formaldehyde) combine to form large polymer molecules. *See also* PLASTICS; MM p.55.

Baker, Sir Benjamin (1840–1907), British civil engineer. He was the principal designer of the Forth railway bridge in Scotland, completed in 1890, which at 518m (1,700ft) had the longest bridge-span in the world until 1918. He was also responsible for the construction of much of London's underground railways and the first Aswan dam. *See also* MM p.192.

Baker, Sir Herbert (1862–1946), British architect. With Sir Edwin LUTYENS he designed legislative buildings for NEW DELHI, India; in London his buildings include India House and the Bank of England. In South Africa he designed the estate of Groote Schuur, near Cape Town, and the Union Government Buildings at Pretoria.

Baker, Janet Abbott (1933–), British mezzo-soprano. She is renowned as a singer of *Lieder* and opera. Well known at COVENT GARDEN, SADLER'S WELLS and GLYNDEBOURNE, she has toured throughout the world. In 1971, she was awarded the Shakespeare Prize in Hamburg for her services to the arts. In 1976 she became a Dame Commander of the Order of the British Empire.

Baker, Josephine (1906–75), US entertainer. After starring in Paris in *La Revue Nègre* (1925) she was based in France for most of her career and became a French citizen. She was active in humanitarian and philanthropic work, and became a member of the French Legion of Honour.

Baker, Richard Edward St Barbe (1889–), British silviculturist, founder of the worldwide Men of the Trees Society. In 1963 he launched the first Sahara Reclamation Conference at Rabat and in 1972 helped to launch the World Year of the Tree.

Baker, Sir Samuel White (1821–93), British explorer. He made discoveries in Ethiopia about the sources of the River NILE (1861–62) and discovered and named Lake ALBERT (1864). Later, as a colonial administrator, he opposed the slave trade, and led an expedition up the River Nile, claiming land and establishing trade.

Baker, Sir Stanley (1928–76), Welsh film actor. He featured in adventure dramas and thrillers, in strong masculine roles. His major films included *The Cruel Sea* (1953), *The Criminal* (1960) and *Accident* (1968). Baker had his own production company that made several films, among them *Zulu* (1964) and *Robbery* (1967).

Bakewell, Robert (1725–95), British breeder of sheep and cattle who revolutionized animal husbandry by scientific breeding. He spent all his life in Leicestershire. His methodical inbreeding and selection produced better meat animals. (Previously sheep had been raised mainly for wool, and cattle as draught animals.) *See also* HC2 pp.20, 21; PE p.226.

Bakewell, town in N Derbyshire on the River Wye, 16km (10 miles) ESE of Buxton. A spa town, it has a fine stone bridge and many old buildings. Chatsworth, the seat of the dukes of Devonshire, is 5km (3 miles) to the NE. Tourism is an important industry. Pop. (1971) 4,249.

Bakhtiari, or Bakhtyari, nomadic people of SW Iran whose leaders have been prominent in Iranian politics. Their Muslim society is noted for the freedom afforded its female members. Today there are more than 400,000 Bakhtiari, about one-third of them nomadic herders.

Baking powder, mixture used in cooking as a substitute for yeast. It contains BICARBONATE OF SODA mixed with an acid component such as tartaric acid or cream of tartar. During cooking, the acid reacts with the bicarbonate to generate carbon dioxide gas, which causes the food to rise without the fermentation effects of yeast.

Baking soda, common name for sodium bicarbonate, $NaHCO_3$, so-called because it is a constituent of BAKING POWDER. *See* BICARBONATE OF SODA.

Bakr, General Ahmad Hassan al-. *See* HASSAN AL-BAKR, GENERAL AHMAD.

Bakst, Leon (1866–1924), Russian painter, and stage designer, *b.* Lev Rosenberg. He lived in Paris from 1908, and joined Diaghilev's BALLETS RUSSES, his sets, especially for the ballets *Cléopâtre* (1909) and *Schéhérazade* (1910) causing sensations. Bakst's designs, exotic and colourful, were the first to integrate sets and costumes into a visual entity.

Baku, capital of Azerbaijan, USSR; an oil-shipping port on the W coast of the Caspian Sea. A trade and craft centre in medieval times, Baku prospered under the Shirvan shahs in the 15th century. It was ruled by the Persians from 1509 until 1723 and annexed by Russia in 1806. Commercial oil production began in the 1870s and Baku now handles more freight, mainly oil and petroleum products, than any other Soviet port. Pop. (1975) 851,547.

Bakunin, Mikhail Alexandrovich (1814–76), Russian political philosopher. He became a believer in violent revolution while in Paris in 1848, and was active in the First COMMUNIST INTERNATIONAL until expelled by MARX in 1872. His approach, known as revolutionary ANARCHY, repudiates all forms of governmental authority as fundamentally at variance with human freedom and dignity. In *God and the State* (1882) Bakunin recognized natural law alone as consistent with liberty. *See also* HC2 p.*170*.

BAL (British Anti-Lewisite), oily chemical used as an antidote for poisoning by organic arsenic compounds and certain heavy metals. (Lewisite was an arsenical poison gas developed during WWI.)

Bala, Lake (Welsh, Lyn Tegid), largest natural lake in Wales, 30km (18 miles) NE of Dolgellau. It is 7km (4 miles) long and acts as a reservoir, its waters being pumped to Merseyside.

Balaam, in the Bible, Midianite prophet hired by BALEK, King of MOAB, to curse the Israelites wandering in the wilderness. But he blessed them instead, as recounted in Numbers 22–24.

Balaclava (Balaklava), town 13km (8 miles) SE of SEBASTOPOL, Crimea, USSR. It was the scene of an inconclusive battle in 1854 in which the British, French and Turks defended against a Russian attack on their supply port of Balaclava. The battle is famous for a disastrous charge by Lord CARDIGAN's Light Brigade of cavalry to capture Russian guns. The incident was recorded in a poem by Alfred, Lord TENNYSON. *See also* CRIMEAN WAR; HC2 p.85.

Balaguer, Joaquín (1909–), lawyer, diplomat and president of the Dominican Republic (1960–62; 1966–). He was deposed after a military coup in 1962, but returned in 1966 and defeated Juan Bosch in an election for the presidency. He was elected in 1970 and again in 1974 after a violent political campaign. His rule has promoted economic stability, but has had constant opposition.

Balaguer, Victor (1824–1901), Spanish poet, historian and Catalan nationalist. He was leader of the Liberal Party in Barcelona (1843–68). His poetry, written in Catalan, was among work published in a 39-volume collection *Obras Completas* (1882–1899).

Balakirev, Mili Alexeyevich (1837–1910), Russian composer. One of the RUSSIAN FIVE dedicated to advancing Russian nationalism in 19th-century music, his best-known compositions are *Islamey* (1869) and incidental music to *King Lear* (1858–61). He founded the St Petersburg Free School of Music in 1862. *See also* HC2 p.*106*.

Balalaika, triangular-shaped musical instrument popular in the USSR. The strings (usually three) are fingered on a fretted neck and may be picked, or plucked with the fingers. It sounds similar to the MANDOLIN.

Balance of payments, overall surplus or deficit that occurs as a result of the exchange of all goods and services between one nation and the rest of the world. A country with a balance of payments deficit is in debt and this must normally be repaid, usually from the nation's gold reserves. Such deficits, if frequent, can pose a serious problem, because they cause a reduction in the reserves. This in turn leads to economic pressure for DEVALUATION in order to correct the balance. A country with a surplus is in a favourable position, but it may come under international pressure to revalue its currency in order to adjust the imbalance. *See also* MS pp.314, 315; HC2 p.300.

Balance of power, system in international affairs by which nations seek to keep peace and order by maintaining an approximate balance of forces among rivals, thereby preventing any single one from obtaining a marked advantage. *See also* HC2 pp.82–83.

Balance of trade, the surplus or deficit incurred by a country in its trading. It is the difference between the sum of its imports and the sum of its exports. *See also* BALANCE OF PAYMENTS.

Balance sheet, financial statement that sets out the assets, liabilities, profits and losses of a company or organization. It is usually produced at the end of the financial year by accountants.

Balanchine, George (1904–), US ballet dancer and choreographer. He left his native Russia in 1924 and became a principal dancer and choreographer for DIAGHILEV's BALLET RUSSES in Paris. He moved to the USA in 1933 and was director of the Metropolitan Opera ballet (1934–37). He became the first artistic director of the New York City Ballet in 1948. Works he has choreographed include *The Prodigal Son* (1929), *The Nutcracker* (1954) and *Don Quixote* (1965). *See also* HC2 p.275.

Balanoglossus, the acorn worm, a small marine animal which has a soft, ribbon-like body, an acorn-shaped proboscis and numerous gill slits. It has long been classified as a primitive CHORDATE, and so remotely related to the VERTEBRATES, but this has lately been disputed. *See also* NW p.*122*.

Balas, Iolanda (1936–), Romanian high-jumper. She completely dominated her event from 1957 to 1966, with two Olympic (1960, 1964) and two European (1958, 1962) titles and 14 world records. The last of these (1961) was 1.91m (6ft 3¼in).

Balassi, or Balassa, Balint (1554–94), Hungarian soldier and poet, the greatest Hungarian lyric poet of his time. He wrote war poems and love lyrics and created a new verse form known as the Balassi stanza. His best-known poem is *In praise of the outposts* (1589).

Balaton, lake in W central Hungary, 89km (55 miles) SW of Budapest. This shallow lake, rich in fish, is the largest in central Europe. There are many holiday resorts and vineyards along its shores. Area: 600sq km (232sq miles).

Balbás, Jerónimo (*c.* 1670–1760), Mexican architectural designer who designed large building complexes. His works are incompletely documented but include the Altar de los Reyes for the apse of the Mexico City Cathedral (1718–37).

Balboa, Vasco Núñez de (*c.* 1475–1519), Spanish conquistador and discoverer of the Pacific Ocean. He went to Hispaniola in 1500 and to Darien (Panama) ten years later, where the colonists ousted the governor and he took control. With a group of local Indians he crossed the isthmus and discovered the Pacific in September 1513. He was summoned home and executed for treason.

Balboa, town and port in the Panama Canal Zone on the Gulf of Panama, Pacific Ocean. It is the location of a US naval base and of Balboa Heights, which is the administrative headquarters for the canal. Pop. (1970) 2,568.

Balch, Emily Greene (1867–1961), US economist and sociologist. She taught at Wellesley College, Massachusetts (1897–1918). In 1915 she was a delegate to the International Congress of Women at The Hague and was one of the founders of the Women's International League for Peace and Freedom. She was secretary-treasurer of the League (1919–22; 1934–35). In 1946 she shared the Nobel Peace Prize with John Raleigh MOTT.

Balchin, Nigel Marlin (1908–70), British author. He became known after the publication of his novel *The Small Back Room* (1943), which dealt with scientific military research during WWII, an area in which Balchin worked.

Balcon, Sir Michael (1896–1977), British film producer. He exercised a powerful influence on British film-making at Gainsborough Pictures, Gaumont-British and at Ealing Studios where he controlled production from 1938 to 1955 and produced films such as *Passport to Pimlico* (1949), *The Cruel Sea* (1953) and the *The Ladykillers* (1955).

Balczo, Andras (1939–), Hungarian modern pentathlete. Five times world champion, he reached the peak of his career with an Olympic gold medal in 1972. He also won team medals in the 1960 and 1968 Olympics.

Baldassarino Belgiojoso (*fl.* 16th century), also known as Baltazarini or Balthazar de Beaujoyeulx, French violinist of Italian birth who proclaimed himself inventor of the dramatic "ballet" which was to lead gradually to the conception of opera.

Balder, Scandinavian god of light, beauty, brightness and wisdom, the much beloved son of ODIN and FRIGGA. Balder was supposedly indestructible but through the treachery of LOKI, god of evil, he was killed by a dart made of mistletoe. His death heralded the fall of ASGARD, the stronghold of the gods.

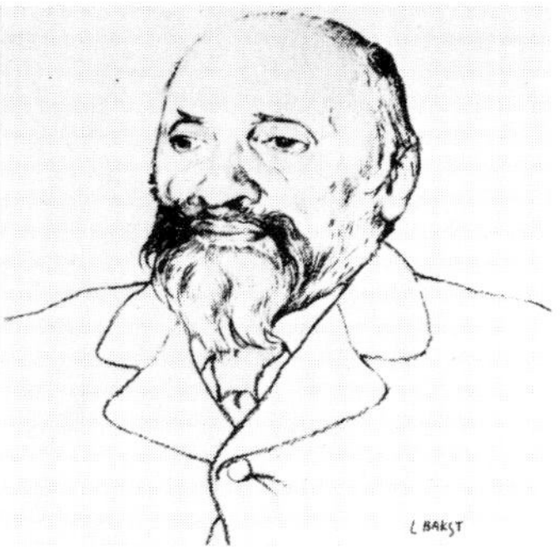

Balakirev set the course for orchestral music and lyrical song in later 19th-century Russia.

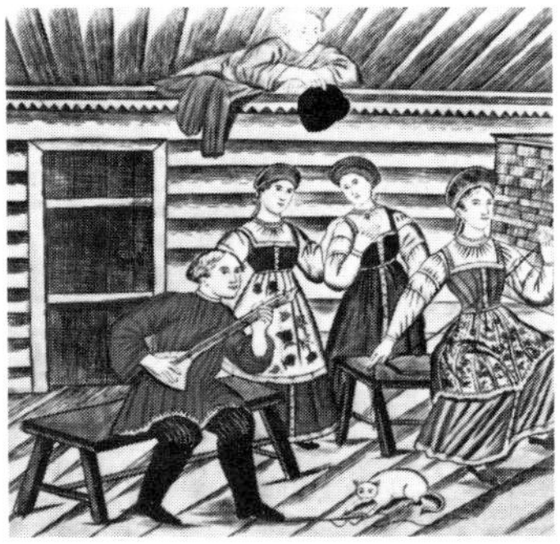

Balalaikas are made in five sizes from treble to double bass and form a whole orchestra.

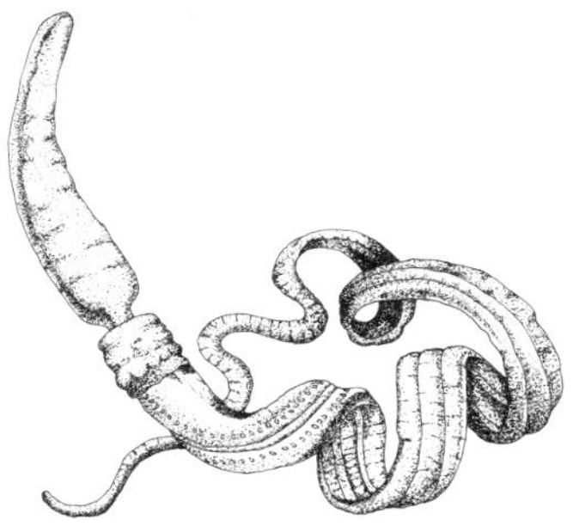

Balanoglossus, the acorn or tongue worm, lives in the mud and sand of inshore waters.

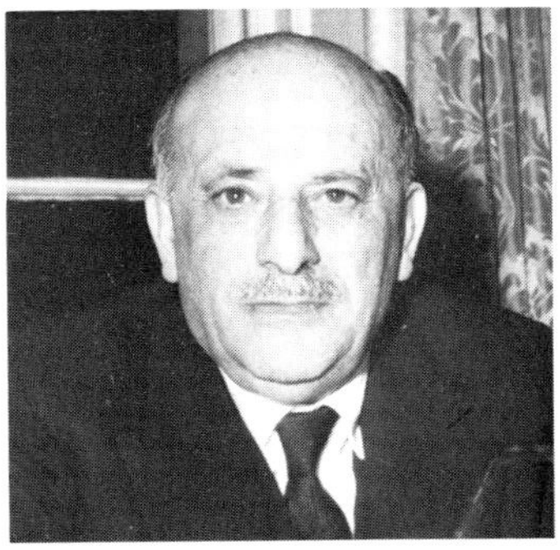

Sir Michael Balcon was a powerful influence in the success of postwar British cinema.

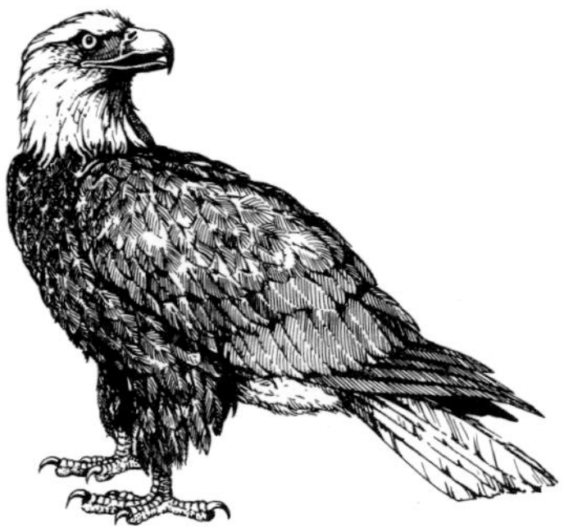

Bald-headed eagle, the national emblem of the USA, is now an endangered species.

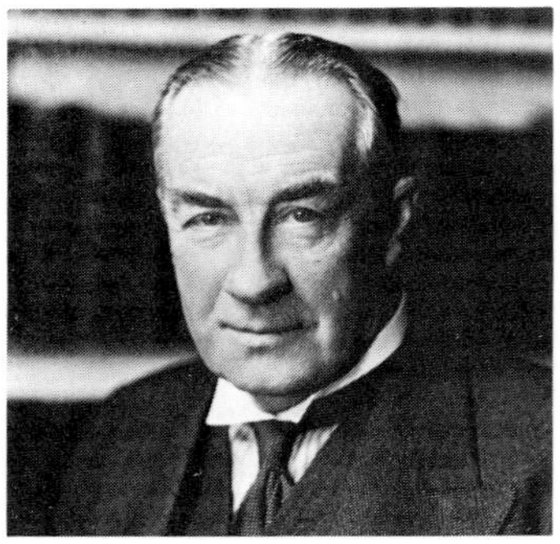

Stanley Baldwin, was three times British Prime Minister.

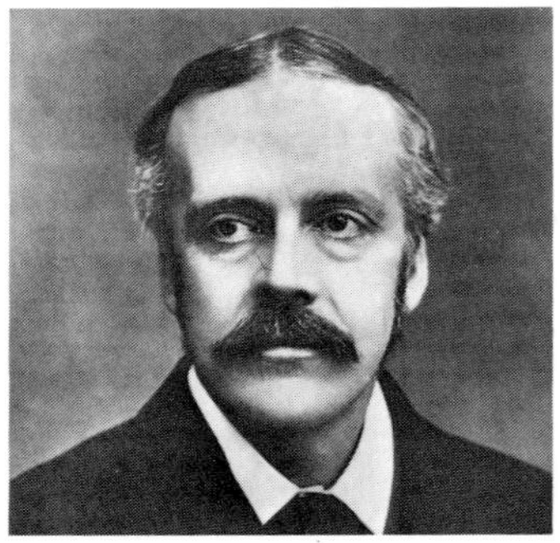

James Balfour, who pledged co-operation by founding a Jewish homeland in Palestine.

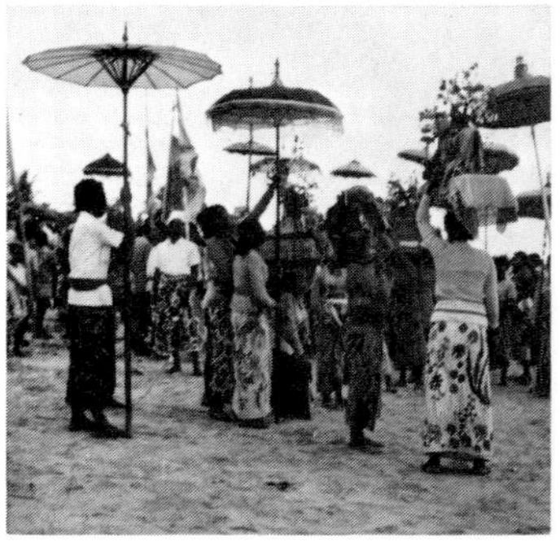

Bali is an island of great natural beauty and treasure house of old Indonesian culture.

Bald-headed eagle, large bird of prey that lives in North America, where it feeds on fish and small mammals. It is brown with a white head and tail and a yellow bill. Its tail feathers were used in the head-dresses of some American Indians, and it is the national emblem of the USA. Although now protected by law, it is an endangered species. Species *Haliaeetus leucocephalus*. *See also* NW p.207.

Baldness, or alopecia, the absence of HAIR from the areas of skin where hair was formerly present. Causes include disease (eg scarlet fever), ageing, deficiencies of diet, stress and the use of certain drugs. In some cases hair will grow back normally, but in others loss is permanent. Premature baldness, loss of hair in late adolescence or early adulthood, occurring most often in males, is believed to be hereditary. Hair loss in women occurs much later and is much less severe than in men. *See also* MS p.99.

Baldovinetti (or Balduinetti), Alleso (*c.* 1425–99), Florentine painter whose *Nativity* (1460–62), a fresco in the church of S. Annunziata, Florence, shows his interest in landscape and the sensitivity of his colour. He influenced GHIRLANDAIO.

Baldung-Grien, Hans (*c.* 1484–1545), German painter and graphic artist. His work shows the influence of Albrecht DÜRER under whom he probably studied. He painted portraits and religious subjects and designed tapestries and stained-glass. His best-known work is the altarpiece *The Coronation of the Virgin* (1512–16) in Freiburg Cathedral, Breisgau, for which he also designed the choir windows.

Baldwin, name of two Latin emperors of Constantinople. Baldwin I (*r.* 120n–05) was, as Baldwin IX of Flanders (1195–1205), a leader of the Fourth Crusade which took Constantinople in 1204. He was elected ruler of the new state. Baldwin II (*r.* 1228–61) was the last emperor of the Latin Empire. He fled from Constantinople when Michael PALAEOLOGUS captured the city and restored the Byzantine Empire.

Baldwin, name of five kings of Jerusalem. Baldwin I (1058–1118) came to the throne in 1100 after leading the first CRUSADE. He consolidated the power of the Crusader states in the Middle East. His cousin succeeded him as Baldwin II (*r.* 1118–31), after he had been Count of EDESSA. He had been captured by the SELJUK Turks in 1104 and ransomed four years later; as king he was again captured in 1123–24. His grandson, Baldwin III (1131–62), acceded to the throne in 1143 as co-ruler with his mother until he defeated her supporters in a civil war in 1151. The second Crusade occurred during his reign. Baldwin IV (1161–85), called the Leper King (*r.* 1174–83), had to contend with internal struggles as well as the attacks of SALADIN. He died of leprosy after crowning his nephew (1177–86) as Baldwin V in 1183 who, however, did not come to the throne until his uncle's death in 1185. His regent Raymond III won a truce with Saladin that lasted for four years. *See also* HC1 p.176–177.

Baldwin, James (1924–), US author. He was born in Harlem, New York, and his works deal with the problems of colour and race relations. They include the novel *Go Tell It on the Mountain* (1953); the books of essays *Notes of a Native Son* (1955), *Nobody Knows My Name* (1961) and *The Fire Next Time* (1963); and the play *Blues for Mister Charlie* (1965). *See also* HC2 p.289, *289*.

Baldwin, Robert (1804–58), Canadian statesman. He shared the first premiership of united Canada with Louis LA FONTAINE, who represented the French of Lower Canada (1841–43, 1847–1851). He advocated co-operation between French and British Canadians, organized an effective system of municipal government for Ontario, and re-organized the courts.

Baldwin, Stanley, 1st Earl Baldwin of Bewdley (1867–1947), British Conservative statesman. He ran the family iron and steel business before entering Parliament in 1908. He became Chancellor of the Exchequer (1922–23), and although his handling of the US debt was criticized, he succeeded BONAR LAW as Prime Minister (1923–24). He was Prime Minister again in 1924–29. Prime Minister for a third time (1935–37) as leader of the NATIONAL GOVERNMENT, he had to deal with the ABDICATION crisis (1936). *See also* HC2 pp.224–225.

Bâle. *See* BASEL.

Balearic Islands, Spanish resort islands in the W Mediterranean Sea, off the coast of Spain, forming the Baleares province. Successively occupied by all the Mediterranean civilizations, the Moorish kingdom of the 10th century was a base for piracy. The chief islands are MAJORCA, MINORCA and IBIZA. Industries: tourism, silverworking, olive oil, wine, fruit. Pop. (1970) 558,287.

Baleen whales, the whalebone whales – giant marine mammals in which the mouth is filled with sheets of whalebone, fringed with hairs, that act as filters to extract food from seawater. *See* NW pp.166–167.

Balewa, Sir Abubakar Tafawa (1912–66), Nigerian political leader. He was a founder and officer of the Northern People's Congress political party, and served as Nigeria's first prime minister (1957–66). After independence in 1960 his power was diminished and in 1966 he was killed in a coup.

Balfour, Arthur, James Balfour, 1st Earl of (1848–1930), British Conservative statesman, *b.* Scotland. His time as Prime Minister (1902–05) was marked by party friction. He was an energetic leader of the opposition (1906–11) and First Lord of the Admiralty (1915–16). In 1917, as Foreign Minister, he issued the BALFOUR DECLARATION in favour of founding a Jewish nation in Palestine. He played a major role in various post-war European agreements.

Balfour Declaration, letter written in 1917 by British foreign secretary Arthur BALFOUR to the British Zionist Federation pledging co-operation for the settlement of the Jews in PALESTINE. Jews were admitted to the area, a province of the OTTOMAN EMPIRE, when it became a British mandate after WWI. British forces withdrew in 1948 and the state of ISRAEL was proclaimed. *See also* HC2 p.296.

Bali, fertile, densely populated island province in Indonesia, off the E tip of Java, between the Bali Sea and the Indian Ocean; the capital is Denpasar. It was under Javanese control from the 10th to 15th century and was a Dutch possession from 1908 to 1949. It is the centre of Majaphit Hinduism, and its scenic beauty and native culture make it a popular tourist resort. Industries: rice, sweet potatoes, cassava, copra, meat processing. Area: 5,623sq km (2,171sq miles). Pop. (1970) 2,247,000.

Balikpapan, port city in SE Borneo, Indonesia, on Balikpapan Bay. It is a major oil-producing and refining centre, with a pipeline connection to the Samarinda oil-fields. It was occupied by the Japanese from 1942–45. Pop. (1975) 137,340.

Baliol, Edward de (*d.* 1364), John de BALLIOL's son, became king of Scotland in 1332. Deposed in 1333, he was restored by EDWARD III, to whom he surrendered the throne in 1356.

Baliol, John de. *See* BALLIOL, JOHN.

Balkan Mountains, major mountain range of the Balkan Peninsula extending from E Yugoslavia through central Bulgaria, a continuation of the Carpathian Mts. It is rich in minerals and forms a climatic barrier for the inland regions. The highest pass is Shipka Pass, approx. 1,270m (4,166ft), and the highest peak is Botev 2,375m (7,793ft).

Balkan Wars (1912–13), two wars involving Balkan states. In the first the Balkan League (Serbia, Bulgaria, Greece and Montenegro) conquered most of the OTTOMAN EMPIRE's European territory. The second war, mainly between Serbia and Bulgaria, arose out of dissatisfaction with the distribution of these lands; Serbia's victory added to the tension in the Balkans before WWI. *See also* HC2 p. 186.

Balkhash (Balchaš), city of SE Kazakhstan, S central USSR. It is a copper-smelting centre, served by a branch railway. Pop. (1968) 77,000. It is on the N shore of Lake Balkhash (Ozero Balchaš), a landlocked, saline lake. The lake is fed at its W end by the fresh-water River Ili, and so its salinity increases towards the E. Area: 18,907sq km (7,300sq miles). Average depth: 6m (20ft).

Ball, John (*d.* 1381), English priest and one of the leaders of the PEASANTS' REVOLT. He was imprisoned in 1360 and excommunicated (1376) for his radical preaching. In 1381 he was released from Maidstone prison by the followers of Wat TYLER, but he was recaptured and executed at St Albans. *See also* HC1 p.*215.*

Ball, Lucille (1911–), US actress and comedienne. Her film debut was in *Broadway through a Keyhole* (1933). She went on to make more than 70 films including *Mame* (1973). Her greatest success came in the television series *I Love Lucy* (1951–60).

Balla, Giacomo (1871–1958), Italian painter, a founder of FUTURISM and a signatory of the Futurist manifesto (1910). In *Dog on a Leash* (1912), a logical expression of Futurism, Balla attempted to break down the dog's running movements into separate superimposed images. Later he abandoned this naturalistic approach and began to express movement in painting in abstract terms. *See also* HC2 p.177.

Ballad, form of popular poetry, often sung, narrative in style with simple metre, rhyme and often a refrain. It dates from medieval times and typically consists of four-line stanzas. Subjects include historical events, folk-lore and love.

Ballade, non-narrative poem of three stanzas of seven or eight lines and a final stanza (envoy) of four or five lines in which the poet's conclusion or moral is drawn. A widely used form, it flourished in the Middle Ages and was often sung. Composers have used the name for instrumental pieces.

Ballad opera, English type of comic opera in which a play with a BURLESQUE plot is interspersed with songs adopted from ballads and popular folksong. Its main vogue was in the mid-18th century and the first, *The Beggar's Opera* (1728) by John GAY, remains the best.

Ballad of Reading Gaol, The (1898), long poem by Oscar WILDE. It was inspired by Wilde's own experiences while serving a two-year sentence for homosexuality.

Ballance, John (1839–93), New Zealand journalist and politician, *b.* Northern Ireland. In 1866 he emigrated to New Zealand and became editor of the *Wanganui Herald.* He entered politics and held various government posts before becoming Prime Minister (1891-93).

Ball and socket joint, type of joint that allows one part to rotate at almost any angle with respect to another. Such joints are used in machinery and occur naturally, as in the human hip joint. *See also* MS pp.56–57.

Ballantyne, David Watt (1924–), New Zealand author. His novels include *The Cunninghams* (1948), *The Last Pioneer* (1963) and *A Friend of the Family* (1966). He has worked as a journalist in New Zealand and in Britain.

Ballantyne, Robert Michael (1825-94), Scottish author of many books for boys including the well-known *The Coral Island* (1858). He worked with the Hudson's Bay Company in Canada as a young man and wrote about the experience in *Hudson's Bay, or, Every-Day Life in the Wilds of North America* (1845).

Ballarat, city in central Victoria, Australia, 113km (70 miles) NW of Melbourne. A leading sheep-breeding centre and former gold-mining boom town, it was the scene of the EUREKA STOCKADE rebellion (1854). Pop. (1971) 58,434.

Ballard, James Graham (1930–), British science fiction writer. His first story was *Prima Belladonna* (1956). It was followed by novels such as *The Wind from Nowhere* (1962), *The Drought* (1965), *The Crystal World* (1965), *Crash* (1970) and *High Rise* (1974).

Ballard, John Frederick ("Fred") (1884–1957), US dramatist who is best known for his comedies, such as *Believe*

Me and *Ladies of the Jury*.
Ball bearing, type of BEARING for machinery, consisting of two concentric rings of steel which together form a "race" for a number of steel balls positioned between them. The inner ring is fixed to a shaft and the outer one to a support.
Ballet, theatrical art form in which stylized dancing to music conveys a story or theme. It evolved from RENAISSANCE court spectacles. The first formal ballet, the *Ballet comique de la Reine*, was performed at the French court of Catherine de' MEDICI in 1581. Thoinot Arbeau wrote the first treatise on ballet, *Orchésographie* (1588). LOUIS XIV, who performed in ballet, founded the Royal Academy of Dance in 1661. Jean-Georges Noverre, the most influential choreographer and theorist of the 18th century, argued for meaningless gestures and masks to be replaced by a greater naturalism. The performance of *Les Sylphides* in Paris (1832) set the model for the Romantic ballets of the 19th century. Towards the end of the century Russian ballet began emphasizing technique and virtuosity. Subsequently, Sergei DIAGHILEV and his BALLETS RUSSES revolutionized ballet with dynamic choreography and dancing, and the mid-20th century saw a melding of elements of Classical ballet and modern dances. *See also* HC2 pp.38–39, 274–275.
Ballet, Royal, ballet company formed in 1956 from the SADLER'S WELLS Ballet and Sadler's Wells Theatre Ballet. It dates from Ninette DE VALOIS' Academy of Choreographic Art (founded in 1926) that became the Vic-Wells, and subsequently Sadler's Wells Ballet. It inherited high standards and a repute that it added to and is indisputably one of the top ballet companies in existence. Resident at the Royal Opera House, Covent Garden, it runs a ballet school and has a second company that tours and performs in London at Sadler's Wells Theatre. The Royal Ballet, strong on classics, has performed important new works such as *Ondine* (1958), *Antigone* (1959), *Enigma Variations* (1968) and *A Month in the Country* (1976). From the 1960s the partnership of Margot FONTEYN and Rudolf NUREYEV has become the most celebrated in modern ballet. *See also* Frederick ASHTON; Kenneth MACMILLAN; HC2 p.275.
Ballet, Sadler's Wells, ballet company that grew out of the Vic-Wells Ballet founded in 1931 by Ninette DE VALOIS. Alicia MARKOVA, Robert HELPMANN and Frederick ASHTON worked with the company and major productions included *Job* (1931), *Coppelia* (1933) and *Daphnis and Chloe* (1951). In 1946 a second, mainly touring, company was formed as the Sadler's Wells Theatre Ballet. Both were incorporated in the Royal Ballet in 1956. *See also* HC2 p.274.
Ballet Russe de Monte Carlo, the name of several ballet companies that succeeded the BALLETS RUSSES. One of its most successful managers was Col. W. de Basil. In 1938 René Blum and Léonide MASSINE formed their own, separate company. It inherited many of Diaghilev's choreographers and dancers, such as George BALANCHINE. It was disbanded in 1947.
Ballets Russes, dance company founded in 1909 in Paris by Sergei DIAGHILEV, with Michel FOKINE as chief choreographer. It revitalized and reshaped ballet by bringing together great dancers (PAVLOVA, NIJINSKY) and choreographers (Léonide Massine, Vaslav Nijinsky and BALANCHINE). Leading composers, such as STRAVINSKY, DEBUSSY and Richard STRAUSS composed music for the company, and top artists such as Picasso, Chagall and Matisse designed sets and costumes. It disbanded soon after Diaghilev's death in 1929; many members later joined the BALLET RUSSE DE MONTE CARLO. *See also* HC2 pp. 274–275.
Ballinrobe, town in Mayo, Republic of Ireland. It is on the River Robe near its entry to Lough Mask, 27km (17 miles) S of Castlebar. It is noted for its trout fishing. Pop. 1,300.
Balliol, Edward. *See* BALIOL, EDWARD.
Balliol, John (1249–1315), King of Scotland (1292–96). His claim to the Scottish throne was upheld by EDWARD I of England, who claimed feudal overlordship of Scotland in consequence (1291). Balliol quarrelled with Edward and Edward invaded Scotland in 1296; Balliol was captured. He died in exile in Normandy. *See also* HC1 pp.182–183.
Ballista, firing device used by the Romans and later, medieval, armies to hurl rocks and other missiles at enemy formations and fortifications. It had a range of about 400m (1,320ft) for missiles weighing up to 27kg (60lb). *See also* MM p.166.
Ballistic missile. *See* GUIDED MISSILE; MM pp.*169, 180.*
Ballistics, the science of projectiles, including bullets, shells, bombs, rockets and guided missiles. Interior ballistics deals with the propulsion and motion of the projectile within the firing device. Exterior ballistics investigates the trajectory of the projectile in flight. Terminal ballistics is concerned with the impact and effect of the projectile at the target. At each stage scientists try to maximize the performance of the gun and projectile by improving their design. It has developed along with the technology of ARTILLERY and with the invention of instruments to monitor such factors as the ignition and burning of the propellant explosive, the stresses on a gun barrel and the effect of air resistance and gravity on the trajectory. For example, a gun has its maximum range when fired at an elevation (angle between the barrel and the horizontal) of 45°. The shape of the trajectory is a PARABOLA and at less than maximum range there are two possible trajectories (one high, one low). *See also* MM pp.146–147.
Balloon, lighter-than-air craft used for recreation or for scientific or military purposes. The first balloons to fly were of the open-necked hot-air type. Unmanned military, meteorological or other scientific balloons are usually filled with hydrogen, lightest in weight of all gases but dangerously inflammable. Manned balloons are now generally filled with the safer gas helium. *See* MM pp.146–147.
Ballooning, travelling by balloon ie, suspended in a basket underneath a balloon inflated with a gas lighter than air. Now largely a leisure activity, ballooning was the method by which man first succeeded in flying. Generally credited with the achievement are the French brothers Jacques and Joseph MONTGOLFIER who devised a hot-air balloon in which Jean François Pilatre de Rozier and the Marquis d'Arlandes made the first free ascent on 21 Nov. 1783. Ten days later, another two Frenchmen made the first flight in a hydrogen-filled balloon.

Although hydrogen ballooning is considered by many to be the purest form of the sport, because it is completely silent, it has been largely superseded by the cheaper hot-air method. In this, burning propane gas is used to heat the air through an opening in the bottom of the balloon, which is usually made of nylon fabric. After the initial inflation and heating, occasional re-heating is required during flight. Descent is accomplished by releasing air slowly through a valve. In Britain passenger-carrying balloons have to be registered. *See also* MM pp.146–147.
Ballot, object used to cast a vote. The word derives from the Italian *ballotta* ("little ball"). Since 5th-century BC Athens, balls have been used to cast votes, white for yes, black for no. Today, the ballot is a sheet (or sheets) of paper, although in some countries voting machines are increasingly being used to register votes.
Ballot Act (1872), law introduced by William GLADSTONE'S first government, that required parliamentary elections to be held by secret ballot, so ending bribery at elections. *See also* REFORM ACTS.
Ballot, Australian, form of BALLOT generally used today, and originating in Victoria, Australia, in 1856. In secret, the voter indicates his choice on a printed form that lists all the candidates.
Ballpoint pen, pen that employs as its writing point a small ball-bearing that rolls against and picks up semi-solid ink from a reservoir. It was invented by John Loud in 1888 but Lazlo Biro was the first to make a reliable model in 1938, which was patented in 1943.
Ball python, small, stout-bodied West African PYTHON, which twists itself into a ball when frightened or handled. It is pale yellow with slate grey markings; it kills its prey by constriction. Length: up to 153cm (5ft). Family Boidae; species *Python regius*.
Ballymena, market town in NE Northern Ireland, on the River Braid. Industries: linen and woollen goods, carpets, tobacco. Pop. 16,500.
Balm, resin from a BALSAM plant and the name of various aromatic plants, particularly those of the genera *Melissa* and *Melittis*; also an old name for any soothing ointment.
Balmoral castle, private residence of the monarch of Britain, in the Scottish Highlands, 85km (53 miles) W of Aberdeen. It was left to Queen VICTORIA by Prince ALBERT on his death in 1861. It is served by the villages Ballater, Crathie and Braemar. *See also* HC2 p.164.
Balon, Jean (1676–1739), French ballet dancer. He first performed in 1691 and spent many years with the Académie Royale. He was noted for his exceptional lightness, and his name is often used to describe this characteristic of ballet.
Balsa, lightweight wood used particularly for modelling, eg aeroplanes, and for building rafts, obtained from a tree of South America. Species *Ochroma lagopus*.
Balsam, aromatic RESIN obtained from plants; or healing preparations, especially those with benzoic and cinnamic acid added to the resin; or balsam-yielding trees, such as the balsam fir and balsam poplar. The name is also given to numerous species of tropical succulent plants of the family Balsaminaceae that are sprawling, waterside forms with thin leaves and pendent flowers. *See also* IMPATIENS.
Baltazarini. *See* BALDASSARINO BELGIOJOSO.
Balthazar de Beaujoyeulx. *See* BALDASSARINO BELGIOJOSO.
Baltic Sea, arm of the Atlantic extending past Denmark, along the N German coast and separating Sweden from the USSR and Finland. The sea extends roughly N–S with an arm reaching out to the E. The N part is known as the Gulf of Bothnia and the E part as the Gulf of Finland. The Baltic is the largest body of brackish water in the world. Its low salinity is due to the size of its catchment area, about four times the area of the sea. Each year the sea receives a fresh water inflow of 1/40 of its volume, which being less dense floats on top of the more saline and therefore denser water. There is a constant surface out-flow of brackish water through the Danish sound which is replaced by more saline Atlantic water at a greater depth. The low salinity of the surface water accounts for the ease with which the Gulf of Bothnia freezes over in the winter. The tidal range is low and currents, flowing in a clockwise fashion, are weak. During the Middle Ages there was an important herring fishing industry. Its sudden decline at the end of the 15th century is thought to be a contributory factor in the demise of the HANSEATIC LEAGUE. Area: 414,400sq km (160,000sq miles).
Baltic, Battle of the (2 April 1801), alternative name of the Battle of COPENHAGEN in which the British defeated the Danish fleet.
Baltic states, countries of ESTONIA, LATVIA and LITHUANIA, on the E coast of the Baltic Sea. The region was settled by various tribes in the 7th century AD, but until the 20th century they remained mostly under Danish, Russian or Polish rule. Each was set up as an independent state in 1918, following the Russian Revolution, but came under the control of the USSR in 1940.
Baltimore, chief city of Maryland, USA, at the mouth of the Patapsco River, on Chesapeake Bay. Founded by the Barons of Baltimore as a tobacco port in 1729, it later began exporting wheat. Baltimore was burned down in 1904, but was rapidly rebuilt. A major port, is has steelworks, oil refineries, shipbuilding and other industries, and is a centre for insurance firms. Pop. (1973) 877,838.

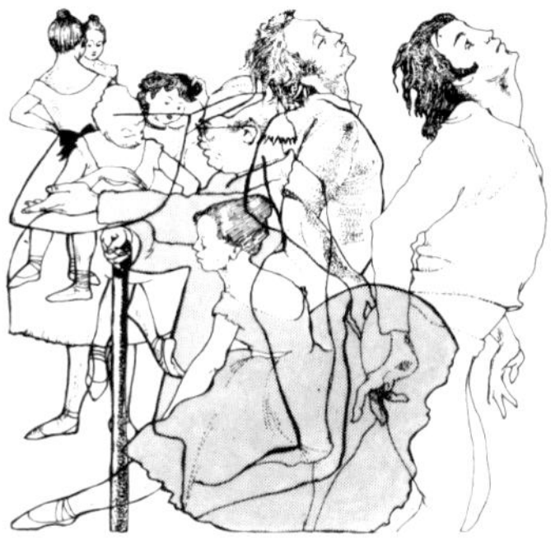

Ballet dancers express the most sublime of human emotions through their movement.

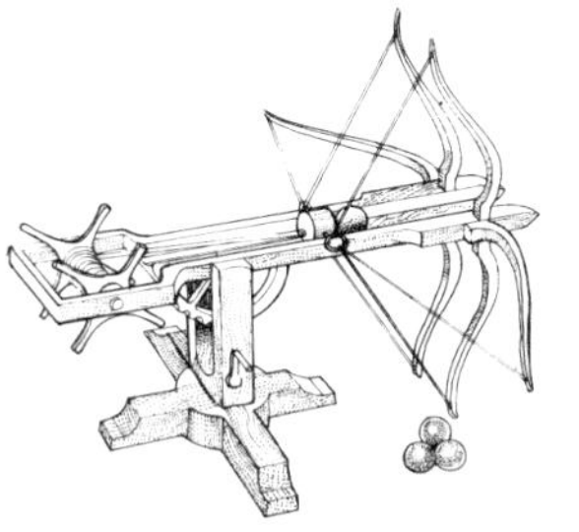

Ballista, a development of the bow, sometimes hurled dead or live prisoners.

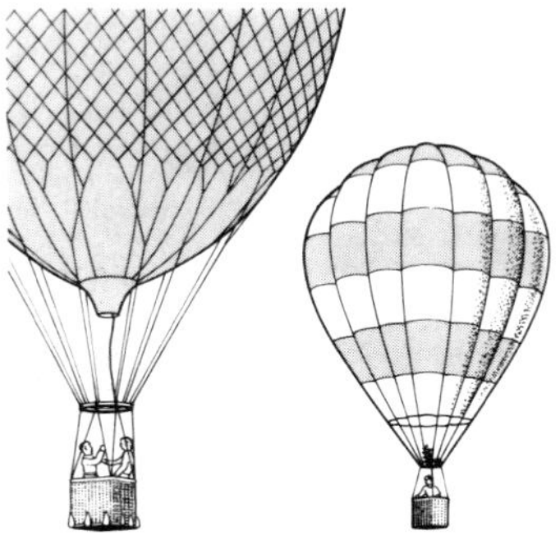

Balloon racing, a sport determining who can remain aloft longest or travel farthest.

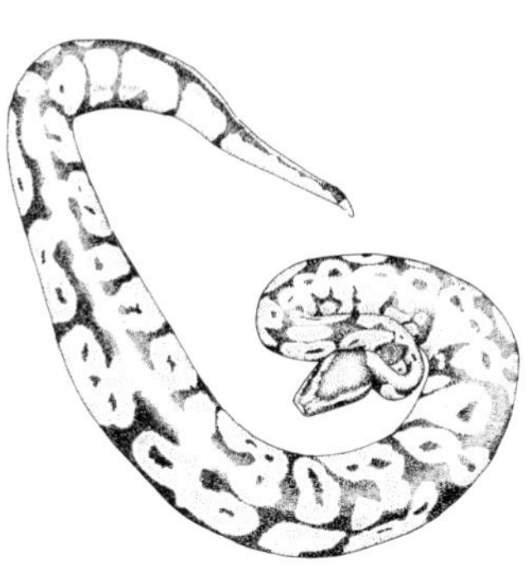

Ball pythons kill by constriction; death results from suffocation rather than crushed ribs.

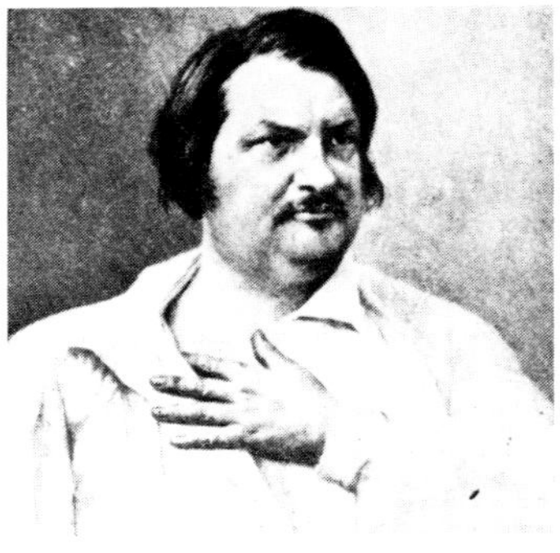

Honoré de Balzac, whose many characters depicted French bourgeois society in detail.

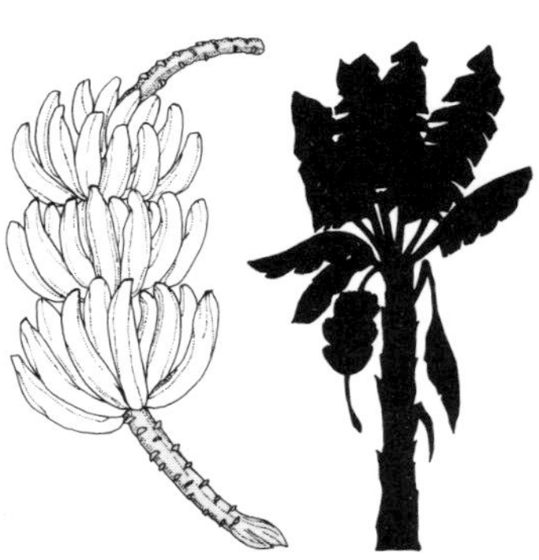

Bananas contain vitamins A, B and C and are always available fresh throughout the year.

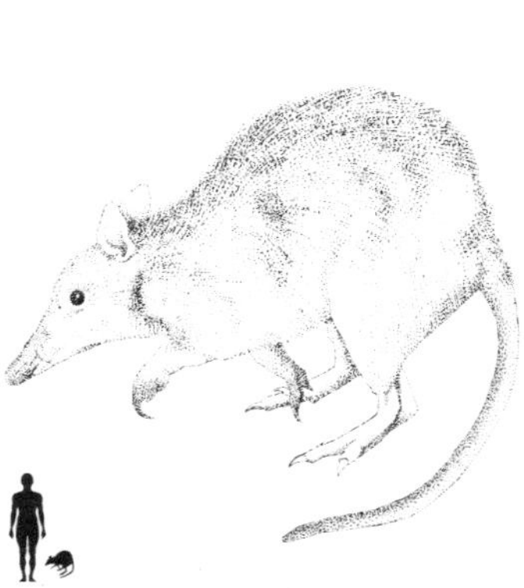

Bandicoots, unlike the kangaroos, have a pouch that opens at the bottom.

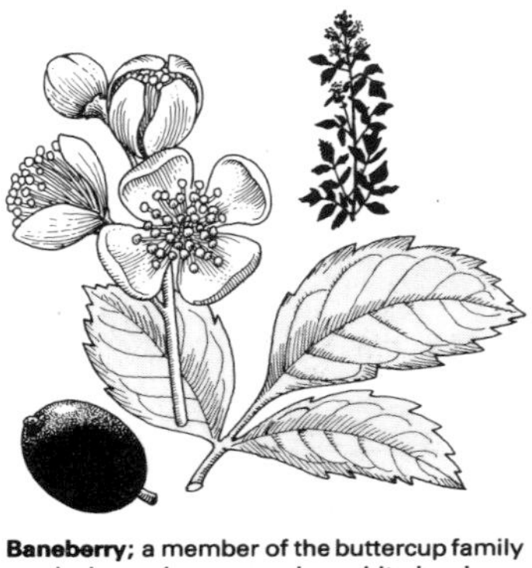

Baneberry; a member of the buttercup family producing poisonous red or white berries.

Baluchistan, region and province in central and SW PAKISTAN; bordered by Iran (W), Afghanistan (N), and the Arabian Sea. Quetta is the capital. The terrain is hilly and arid, being mostly desert, and is inhabited by a few nomadic tribes such as the Baluchi. The region was ruled by the Arabs from the 7th to the 10th centuries. It became a British dependency in 1876 and a province of India in 1887. The boundaries with Iran and Afghanistan were settled in 1885 and 1896. The region became part of Pakistan in 1947. Some cotton is grown, and fishing is the chief occupation on the coast. Natural gas is extracted and exported along with salt and fish. Area: approx. 344,747sq km (133,107sq miles). Pop. (1969 est.) 1,484,000. *See also* MW p.140.

Balzac, Honoré de (1799–1850), French novelist. Balzac began by writing thrillers in a Paris attic. His first success was *Les Chouans* (1829), and more than 90 novels and short stories followed at a prolific rate in his grand scheme – *The Human Comedy*. He devised this as a detailed, realistic study of contemporary French society. Among his best known novels are *Eugénie Grandet* (1833), *Le Père Goriot* (1834) and *La Cousine Bette* (1846). *See also* HC2 pp.98, *99*.

Balzac, Jean Louis Guez de (*c.* 1597–1654), French author who is regarded as one of the best prose writers of his time. His works include *Lettres* (1624), *Le Barbon* (1648) and *L'Aristippe* (1658).

Bamako, capital of MALI, on the River Niger 145km (90 miles) NE of the border with Guinea. Once a centre of Muslim learning (11th-15th centuries), it declined until the French occupied it in 1883 and later made it capital of the French Sudan (1908). Industries: shipping, groundnuts, meat, metal products. Pop. (1970 est.) 387,700.

Bambara, Negroid people of the upper Niger valley, MALI. Their decentralized, patrilineal society is based on subsistence farming, although cash crops such as groundnuts are also grown. Now largely intermixed with other local peoples, they are still known for their wood and metal sculpture.

Bamboo, tall, tree-like grass native to tropical and subtropical regions. The hollow, woody stems grow in branching clusters from a thick rhizome and the leaves are stalked blades. It is used in house construction and for household implements. Some bamboo shoots are eaten. The pulp and fibre may form a basis for paper production. Height to 40m (131ft). There are 1,000 species. Family Gramineae; genus *Bambusa. See also* GRASS; NW pp.66, 68.

Banana, long, curved, yellow or reddish fruit of the tree of the same name. It has soft, creamy flesh. A spike of yellow, clustered flowers grows from the centre of the crown of the tree and bends downwards and develops into bunches of 50–150 fruits or "hands" of 10–20. More than 100 varieties are cultivated. Fruits used for cooking are called cooking bananas or plantains. Height: 3–9m (10–30ft). Family Musaceae; genus *Musa. See also* NW p.210.

Banaras. *See* VĀRĀNASI.

Banbury, town in Oxfordshire, England, on the River Cherwell, 35km (22 miles) N of Oxford. Industries: food processing, electrical and metal goods. Pop. (1971) 29,216.

Bancroft, George (1800–91), US diplomat and historian. He was appointed secretary of the navy in 1845 and established the US Naval Academy at Annapolis, Maryland. He served as minister to Britain (1846-49) and to Germany (1867-74), where he became a friend of BISMARCK. His *History of the United States* (10 vols., 1834–74) studied the origins and development of the country.

Band, group of musicians, usually playing wind and percussion instruments – in contrast to an ORCHESTRA, in which stringed instruments predominate. The lineal ancestors of European bands were the Turkish military bands of the Ottoman empire, loud and raucous ensembles which were intended to terrify the enemy. From these, Europe borrowed or adapted several instruments, such as the cymbals. By the end of the 18th century many European countries had military, town and village bands. These were the forerunners of the various types of modern bands.

A modern big band normally has about 16 musicians in four sections – trumpets, trombones, saxophones and a rhythm section of piano, guitar, double bass (or bass guitar) and drums. This kind of band evolved in the swing era of JAZZ, and performs swing music. A brass band often contains only brass instruments, some rarely heard elsewhere, although percussion instruments may be added. There are 20 or more players, usually amateurs. The music may be specially written, but arrangements of well-known tunes and classical pieces are often also performed. A dance band plays in strict tempo for dancing. It has a rhythm section to provide the beat and instruments such as saxophone, trumpet and violin to play the tunes. A big band may also play for dancing. A jazz band varies according to the style of jazz. A traditional jazz band has a clarinet, trumpet and trombone playing independent melodic lines over a rhythm section. A swing band has the same "line-up" as a big band. In modern jazz, bands are small, often having only a trumpet and saxophone with a rhythm section.

A military band contains sections of brass and woodwind instruments with percussion. It plays music for marching and must itself be able to march while performing. A percussion band consists solely of percussion instruments and is mainly a musical activity for schoolchildren. It is also known as a rhythm band. A ROCK band contains a core of electric guitar, bass guitar and drums to which singers and instruments such as saxophones and keyboards may be added; all are heavily amplified.

Banda, Hastings Kamuzu (*c.* 1902–), President of MALAWI (1966–). He studied medicine in the USA and practised in England before returning to Africa in 1953. He became a nationalist political leader, guiding Nyasaland to independence as Malawi within the British Commonwealth (1964) and establishing an autocratic Presidency (1966). He has been criticized by other black African leaders for maintaining amicable relations with SOUTH AFRICA.

Bandar Abbas, town in SE Iran at the mouth of the Persian Gulf; capital of the Persian Gulf province. It was founded in 1623 and flourished as a port until the 18th century. Today it is a fishing centre. Industries: food processing, textiles. Pop. (1971 est.) 38,000.

Bandaranaike, Sirimavo (Ratwatte Dias) (1916–), Prime Minister of SRI LANKA (formerly Ceylon). She became the world's first woman Prime Minister in 1960 after her husband, the former premier, was assassinated in 1959. Her Sri Lanka Freedom Party was defeated in 1965, but returned to power in 1970. In 1971 she put down an uprising led by the Marxist People's Liberation Front. In 1972 a republican constitution was adopted and the country's name was officially changed to Sri Lanka. Mrs Bandaranaike and her party were resoundingly defeated by J.R. Jayawardene's United National Party in the July 1977 general election.

Bandaranaike, Solomon West Ridgeway Dias (1899–1959), Prime Minister of Ceylon (now Sri Lanka) from 1956–59. He made Sinhalese the official language and founded the Sri Lanka Freedom Party, which united the nationalists and socialists. Following his assassination by a dissident Buddhist monk, his wife, Mrs Sirimavo Bandaranaike, succeeded him as Prime Minister.

Bandeira, Manuel (1885–1968), Brazilian poet. His work deals mainly with his home-town in N Brazil. His first book of verse, *Ash of the Hours* (1917), had a strong influence on the development of modern Brazilian poetry.

Bandicoot, Australian MARSUPIAL about the size of a rabbit and with similarly long ears, hopping gait and burrowing habits. But it eats insects rather than vegetation and its long pointed snout is probably an adaptation for this diet. Genus *Perameles. See also* NW pp. *156, 158, 205.*

Bandinelli, Baccio (or Bartolommeo) (*c.* 1493–1560), Florentine sculptor, the rival of MICHELANGELO and Benvenuto CELLINI. He executed a series of bas-relief of apostles, prophets and saints in Florence Cathedral.

Bandjarmasin, city in S Borneo, Indonesia, on the Martapura River; it is the capital of the South Kalimantan province. A settlement established by the Dutch in 1711, it is now a trading centre. Exports: diamonds, oil, rubber products. Pop. 282,000.

Bandundu (Banningville), capital of the Bandundu Region (1966) in SW Zaire, W Africa, on the Kasai River. The region is mainly agricultural, but also yields timber from its forests. Pop. (capital) 107,000.

Bandung, capital of West Java province, Indonesia, 121km (75 miles) SE of Djakarta. The Asian-African conference took place there in 1955. Industries: canning, chemicals, quinine, textiles, food processing. Pop. 1,202,000.

Bandung Conference (1955), meeting in BANDUNG of representatives of 29 non-aligned countries of Asia and Africa, including China, to express their united opposition to colonialism and to gain recognition for the "Third World". *See also* HC2 pp.254–255.

Baneberry, any of about ten species of perennial plants (genus *Actaea*) of the buttercup family (Ranunculaceae) found throughout the Northern Hemisphere. All have poisonous berries appearing in the autumn. Height: to 61 cm (2ft).

Banff, town in SW Alberta, Canada, on the Bow River in the Rocky Mountains. It is noted for its Indian and natural history exhibits. It is a popular resort town and the home of the University of Alberta. Pop. 3,500.

Banffshire, former county of Scotland, now part of the Grampian Region. It lies S of the Moray Firth and is drained by the rivers Spey, Deveron and Avon, and contains some of the highest peaks in the Cairngorms. Industries: whisky, cattle, fishing, quarrying. Area: 1,640sq km (630sq miles).

Bangalore (Bangalur), city in S central India, 290km (180 miles) W of Madras; capital of Mysore state. Established in 1537 by the Mysore Dynasty, the city was retained by Britain as a military headquarters until 1947. It is the sixth largest city in India, and an important industrial and communications centre. Pop. (1971) 1,540,741.

Bangalore torpedo, metal pipe or tube filled with high explosive. It is used by infantry to blow up beach obstacles, cut paths through barbed wire, or explode mines.

Banghāzi (Benghazi), city in Libya, on the NE shore of the Gulf of Sidra, 650km (400 miles) E of Tripoli. Founded by the Greeks in the 6th century BC, it has been conquered and ruled by Romans, Vandals, Byzantines, Arabs and Turks. The Italians captured it in 1911 and during the 1930s developed it into a port, an air and naval base, and used it as a supply base during WWII. It is a commercial and industrial centre for Cyrenaica province and its industries include food processing, shipping and oil. Pop. 140,000.

Bangkok, capital and chief port of Thailand, on the E bank of the River Menam (or Chao Phraya) and headquarters of SEATO. A busy market centre, it is cosmopolitan, with a large Chinese minority. Bangkok became the capital in 1782 and grew quickly, with many ornate palaces and temples. Today it is Thailand's communications centre. Pop. (1976 est.) 4,349,500.

Bangladesh, formerly East PAKISTAN, country in S Asia situated on the Ganges delta and bordered on the N, E and W by India. Dacca is the capital city. The main products are jute, rice, sugar cane and tobacco. Area: 142,776sq km (55,126sq miles) Pop. (1975 est.) 76,815,000. *See* MW p.36.

Bangor, town in County Down, SE Northern Ireland, 19km (12 miles) ENE of Belfast. It is noted for its ruined abbey, founded in the 6th century by St Comgall. The town is a popular seaside resort and yachting area. Pop. (1971) 35,105.

Bangor, cathedral city and borough in Gwynedd (formerly Caernarvonshire), NW Wales, on the Menai Strait. The town, which grew up beside a Norman castle, is the home of the University College of North Wales (1884). Industries: slate quarrying, tourism. Pop. 14,500.

Bangui, capital of the CENTRAL AFRICAN EMPIRE, founded in 1890 by the French on the Ubangi (Oubangui) River, near the Zaire border. It is the nation's chief port for international trade. Industries: textiles, food processing, beer, soap. Pop. (including suburbs) 301,800.

Banja Luka (St Luke's Baths), town in Bosnia, Yugoslavia, 306km (190 miles) W of Belgrade on the River Vrbas. It has fine mosques, Christian monasteries and ruined Roman baths. There were battles there between the Turks and the Russians in 1527, 1688 and 1737. Pop. (1971) 89,866.

Banjo, musical instrument with from four to nine strings, a body of stretched parchment on a metal hoop, and a long, fretted neck. It is played with a plectrum or the fingers. Probably of African origin, it was taken to the USA by slaves. It is most often used in minstrel shows, Dixieland jazz and folk-music.

Banjul (Bathurst,) capital of GAMBIA, W Africa, on St Mary's Island, where the River Gambia enters the Atlantic Ocean. Founded by the British in 1816 as a trading post, it is the country's chief port and commercial centre. Industries: groundnut processing, hides, beeswax. Pop. (1975 est.) 42,689.

Banka, or Banga, island of Indonesia off the SE coast of Sumatra, in the Java Sea. Tin was discovered *c.*1710, since when Banka has been one of the world's major tin-producing regions. Pepper is the chief agricultural product. The capital is Pangkalpinang and the chief port is Muntok. Area: approx. 11,915sq km (4,600sq miles). Pop. (1971) 303,804.

Bankhead, Tallulah Brockman (1903–68), US stage and screen actress. She won the New York Drama Critics' Circle Award for her performance in *The Little Foxes* (1939) by Lillian HELLMAN and *The Skin of Our Teeth* (1942) by Thornton WILDER. Her flamboyant lifestyle made her a legendary star.

Bank holidays, in Britain, weekdays on which the banks are closed; schools, factories, offices and most shops also close. Traditionally they were church holy days ("holidays"): Good Friday, Easter Monday, Whit Monday, Christmas Day and Boxing Day, with August Bank Holiday included to provide a break at the beginning of that month. Now in England and Wales New Year's Day has been added, Whit Monday has become Late Spring Bank Holiday (Monday nearest 31 May) and the August Bank Holiday has moved to the end of the month. In Scotland and Northern Ireland there are some differences. *See also* MW pp.189, 190.

Banking, commercial process providing individuals, companies and institutions with a wide range of services such as holding and transferring money, providing loans and giving stability to the financial sector of the economy. Clearing banks deal with the general public; MERCHANT BANKS provide services to business and industry such as investment loans and share floatations; and the central bank, under government control, is the bankers' bank and can be used as an economic regulator. The banking system facilitates exchange through the use of cheques, and the acceptance of these as a means of payment enhances the buying and selling of goods and services. *See also* MS p.308.

Bank of England, Britain's central banking institution, founded in 1694 and situated in Threadneedle Street, City of London. Nationalized in 1946, it regulates foreign exchange, issues bank-notes, advises the government on monetary matters and acts as the government's financial agent.

Bank of Scotland, bank founded in 1695 by an Act of the Parliament of Scotland; it was the first Scottish bank. In the mid-1970s it had more than 500 branches in Scotland, with a total staff in excess of 8,000.

Bank rate, the minimum rate of interest at which a bank (in Britain the Bank of England) is prepared to discount bills of exchange. Rates of interest on deposits and loans of other banks and BUILDING SOCIETIES are based on the bank rate, which therefore is an effective means of controlling the amount of borrowing. *See also* MS p.308.

Bankruptcy, legally determined status of a person or company, usually when debts greatly exceed income and assets. A person or company may ask to be declared bankrupt by the court, or else the creditors may do so. A court-appointed receiver takes charge of the bankrupt's property with the aim of meeting, as far as possible, the bankrupt's financial obligations to his creditors.

Banks, Don (1923–), Australian composer who settled in London in 1950. He studied there under Matyas SEIBER and in Florence (1953) under Luigi DALLAPICCOLA. Works, in the TWELVE-TONE system, include a horn concerto and various chamber works; he also composed film scores.

Banks, Gordon (1937–), English footballer. Regarded as the world's best goalkeeper of his day, he won 73 international caps (1963–72) before an eye injury sustained in a car crash (1972) curtailed his career.

Banks, Sir Joseph (1743–1820), British explorer and naturalist. He studied botany on one of COOK's voyages to Australia, and was influential in promoting the sciences in Britain. He was honorary director of the Royal Botanical Gardens at KEW from 1762 and made it a centre of botanical research. He was elected president of the ROYAL SOCIETY in 1778.

Bankside, principal theatrical district of Tudor LONDON, on the opposite bank of the River Thames from the city itself. The Globe, Rose and Swan theatres were located there.

Banks Island, small wooded island in the Torres Strait, NE Australia. It was named after Sir Joseph BANKS, a botanist who travelled on HMS *Endeavour* with Capt. James Cook (1768–71). Circumference: approx. 45km (28 miles).

Banks Island, hilly, lake-dotted island in NW Northwest Territories, Canada, in the Arctic Archipelago. First circumnavigated by Sir Robert McClure in 1851, it was explored by the Canadian Vilhjalmur Stefansson in 1914–17. It has a small Eskimo population. Area: 60,166sq km (23,230sq miles).

Banks Peninsula, land that projects from the E central coast of South Island, New Zealand. Lyttelton is on the E side, Akaroa Harbour on the SE. It is 56km (35 miles) long by 40km (25 miles) wide.

Banks Strait, channel off the S coast of Australia, NE of Tasmania and S of Clark Island connecting the Bass Strait and the Tasman Sea. Width: approx. 21km (13 miles).

Banneker, Benjamin (1731–1806), US scientist, mathematician, astronomer, surveyor and clock-maker. In 1789 he became the first black presidential appointee when George WASHINGTON appointed him to the District of Columbia Commission to survey the site of the new Capitol.

Bannister, Sir Roger Gilbert (1929–), British athlete. At Oxford University he became the first man to run a mile in less than four minutes (on 6 May 1954 in a time of 3 min. 59.4sec.). He received his medical degree at St Mary's Hospital Medical School and later became a government sports adviser.

Bannockburn, town and moor in central Scotland. In the battle on the moor in 1314, Scottish troops under ROBERT THE BRUCE defeated the much larger English army led by EDWARD II. Today the town has a textile industry. Pop. 4,000.

Banteng, wild cattle that inhabit hills and forests in Asia. The size of small cows, with narrow curving horns and white stockings on their legs, bantengs are sometimes domesticated for meat and milk. Species *Bos banteng*. *See also* NW p.196.

Banting, Sir Frederick Grant (1891–1941), Canadian physician. He shared, with J.J.R. Macleod, the 1923 Nobel Prize in physiology and medicine for his work in extracting the hormone INSULIN from the PANCREAS, thus making possible the effective treatment of DIABETES MELLITUS.

Bantock, Sir Granville, (1868–1946), British composer, professor of music at the University of Birmingham (1907–34). His works include *Omar Khayyam* (1906–09), for soloists, chorus and orchestra; the unaccompanied choral symphony *Atalanta in Calydon* (1912); and *Hebridean Symphony* (1916).

Bantry, port and resort in SW Cork, Ireland, at head of Bantry Bay. The Bay is a natural anchorage and a terminus for oil tankers, including supertankers. Industries: fishing, tweed, quarrying. Pop. (1961) 3,159.

Bantu, group of African languages in the Niger-Congo branch of the Niger-Kordofanian language family. The most widely-spoken of the several hundred tongues used from the Congo Basin to South Africa are Swahili, Ruanda, Zulu and Sotho. There are more than 70 million Bantu-speakers and it is widely used in schools. They are all tonal languages, ie the same word in a different tone has a different meaning. *See also* MS pp.*35*, *255*.

Banville, Théodore-Faullain de (1823–91), French PARNASSIAN poet. His work influenced BAUDELAIRE, RIMBAUD and MALLARMÉ. He wrote many volumes of verse including *Odes funambulesques* (1857) and *Les Exiles* (1867).

Banyan, evergreen tree of E India. The branches send down aerial shoots that take root, forming new trunks. Such trunks from a single tree may form a circle up to 100m (330ft) across. Height: to 30m (100ft). Family Moraceae; species *Ficus benghalensis.*

Banzer Suarez, Hugo (1926–), Bolivian army officer who became president in 1971. He rose to power through a coalition of the National Revolutionary Movement (MNR) and the Bolivian Socialist Falange (FSB), but by 1974 the MNR had broken with him. He crushed a military coup in 1974 and suspended elections scheduled for 1975.

Baobab, tropical tree native to Africa. It has a stout trunk containing water storage tissue, and short, stubby branches with sparse foliage. Fibre from its bark is used for rope. Its gourd-like fruit has edible pulp. Height: to 18m (60ft); trunk diameter: to 12m (40ft). Family Bombacaceae; species *Adansonia digitata.*

Baoji, *See* PAOKIN.

Baptism, one of the SACRAMENTS of the Christian Church. It is a rite of initiation into the Church and is administered by the pouring of water – which symbolizes regeneration – on to the forehead or by immersion (as by the BAPTISTS), accompanied by the invocation of the TRINITY. In churches which practise infant baptism it is the occasion when children are given their names. *See also* HC1 p.110; MS pp.204–205.

Baptistery, part of a church, or a related separate building, originally used for baptism. Based on the Early Christian baptistery in the Lateran basilica at Rome, many were octagonal. Baptisteries were still built even after baptism by immersion was no longer generally practised. There are superb examples at Pisa and Florence.

Baptists, members of a Protestant denomination who profess a personal religion based on the principle of religious liberty. There is no official creed and no hierarchy, and individual churches are autonomous; they evolved from ANABAPTISTS. They practise BAPTISM of believers and regard immersion as the only legitimate form sanctioned by the NEW TESTAMENT. They reject the practice of infant baptism. Insisting on freedom of thought and expression, Baptists have developed a democratic form of church government. The Baptist World Alliance, an advisory

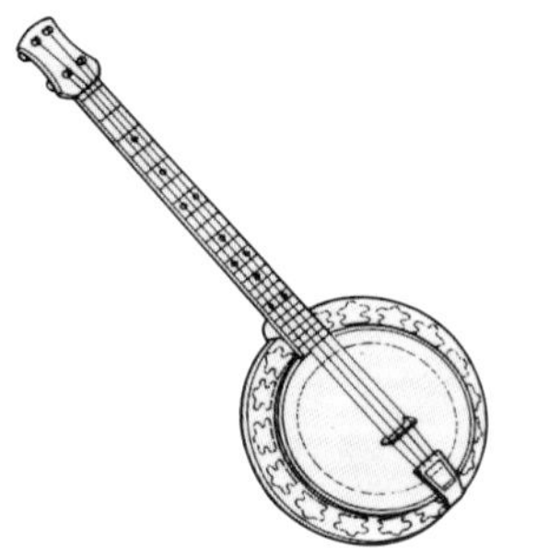

Banjos produce their percussive sound from the tightly stretched vellum resonator.

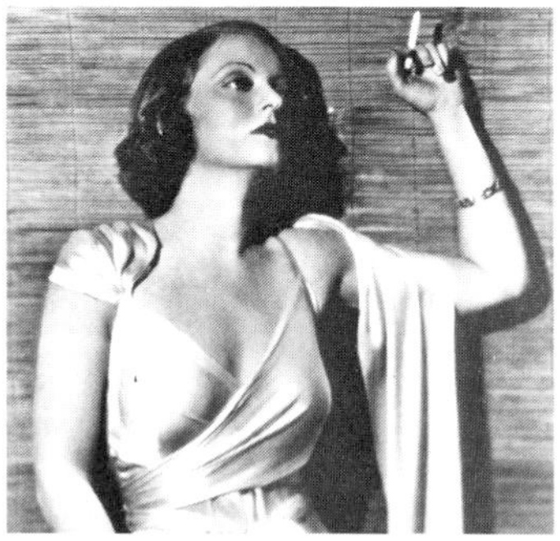

Tallulah Bankhead, as famous for her dramatic off-stage activities as her theatrical roles.

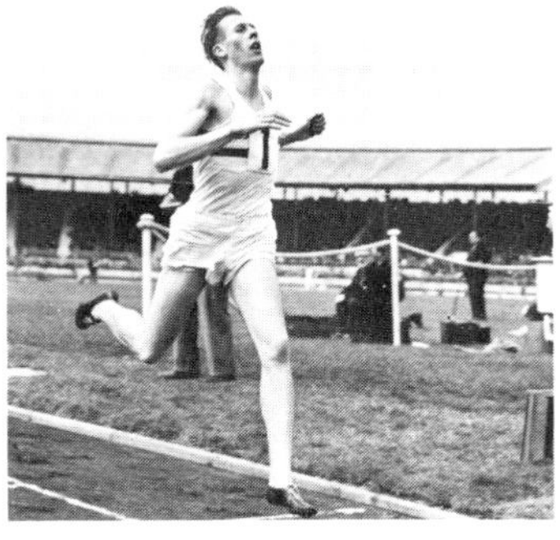

Sir Roger Bannister, who was the first man to run a mile in less than four minutes.

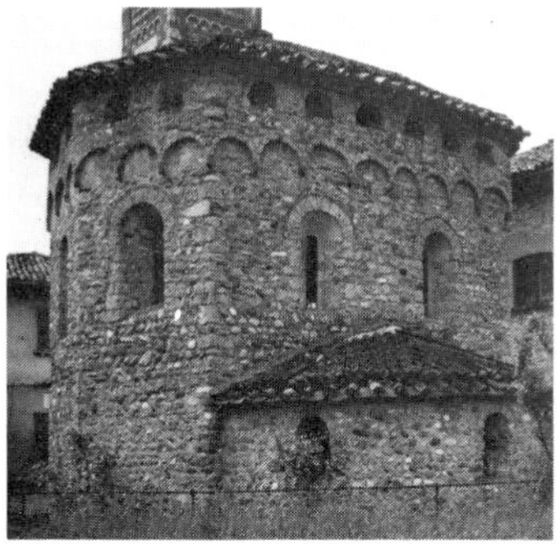

Baptistery; the octagonal plan relates to the number 8 and the idea of a new beginning.

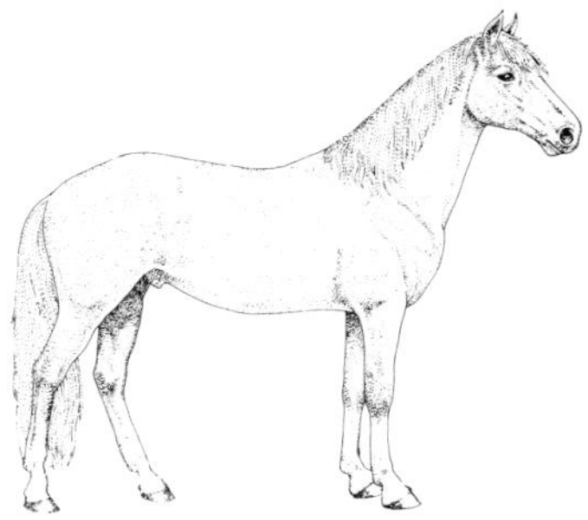

Barb; the rugged north African breed, the "heart" of the English racing thoroughbred.

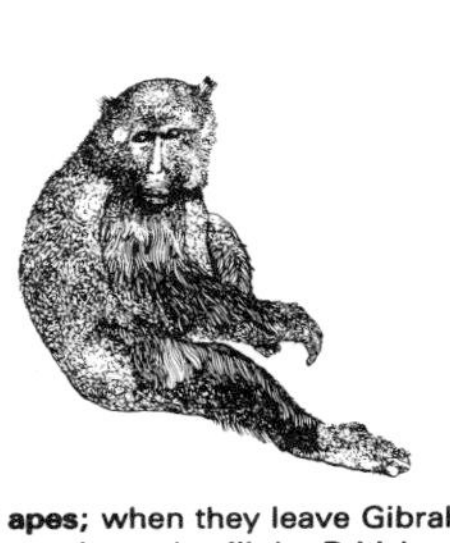

Barbary apes; when they leave Gibraltar so, according to legend, will the British.

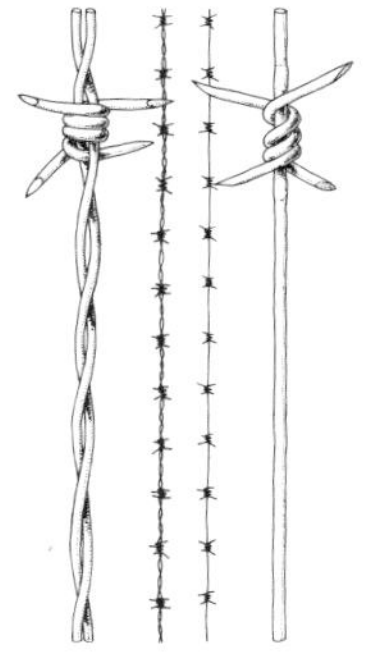

Barbed wire; the two wires twisted together allow safe expansion and contraction.

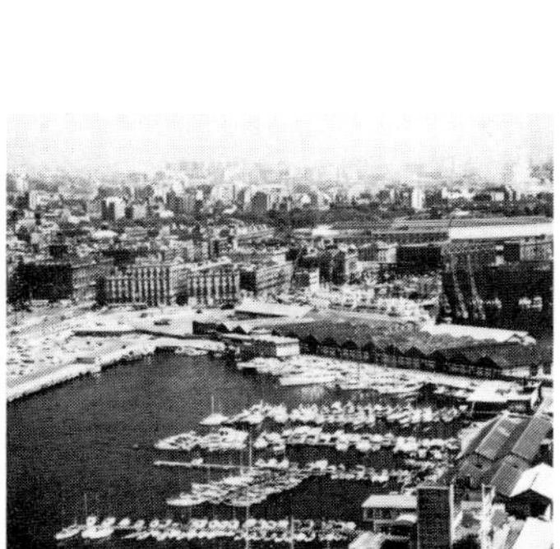

Barcelona, seaport and commercial heart of Spain's greatest industrial concentration.

body, holds regular international congresses. Baptists are active throughout the world and have suffered for their beliefs in the USSR, where they form the second largest religious group. The total number of baptists in the world in the mid-1970s was estimated at about 31 million.

Baqqarah, or Baggaras, nomadic Muslim herdsmen of Arab descent who live in E Sudan. They reached Lake Chad from Egypt in about the 16th century. Today they number about 5 million.

Bar, unit of pressure corresponding to the pressure of a column of mercury 75.007cm high. Atmospheric pressure is about 1.01325 bars, or 1,013.25 millibars.

Bar, The. *See* INNS OF COURT.

Bara, Theda (1890–1955), leading US actress of silent films, real name Theodosia Goodman. Her first major film was *A Fool There Was* (1915) and she was an immediate sensation as the first screen "vamp" or sex goddess. She made more than 40 films including *Cleopatra* (1917) and *Salome* (1918).

Barabbas, in the New Testament, convicted felon who was in prison at the time Jesus Christ stood trial before Pontius PILATE. The people, given the choice of which prisoner to set free, nominated Barabbas and Christ was crucified.

Bărány, Robert (1876–1936), Swedish physician, *b.* Austria. He was awarded the 1914 Nobel Prize in physiology and medicine for his work on the physiology and pathology of the vestibular apparatus of the EAR. His studies of the normal and abnormal functioning of this important balancing mechanism greatly advanced understanding of the ear.

Barassi, Ron (1936–), Australian Rules footballer. The Melbourne captain and ruckrover, he won the "best and fairest" awards in 1961 and 1964. His move in 1965 to the rival club Carlton as player-coach created a sensation.

Barb. *See* BARBEL.

Barb, light horse breed native to the Barbary region of N Africa. Introduced into England by King Charles II (*r.* 1660–85) to develop racing thoroughbreds, it is similar to the ARAB but has a more rugged physique. It has an average height of 14.2 hands (92cm) and may be grey, black, brown, chestnut or bay.

Barbados, island state in the West Indies. A popular tourist resort, the capital is Bridgetown. Pop. 245,000. *See also* MW p.37.

Barbari, Jacopo de (1440–1516), Venetian painter and engraver. He was consulted on style by DÜRER, whose work he influenced. Barbari was possibly the first artist to paint a signed and dated still life, which included a dead partridge, gauntlets and an arrow. His work also included engravings on copper, etchings and woodcuts. Two well known etchings are *Judith* and *St Sebastian.*

Barbarians, term given to all uncivilized tribes by the ancient Greeks and Romans. It is more specifically used to apply to the Germanic and Slavonic tribes that invaded the Roman Empire after about 50 BC and eventually overthrew it. *See also* HC1 pp.136–137.

Barbarians, Barbarian Football Club, touring British rugby union club. Formed in 1890, the Barbarians have six traditional annual fixtures in Wales and the Midlands, and since 1948 have played the final game against major touring sides. Membership is by invitation, and teams are selected from players of all countries. Famous for their open, attacking play, the Barbarians also tour abroad.

Barbarossa. *See* FREDERICK I.

Barbarossa (*c.*1466–1546), Ottoman naval commander; also called Khayr-ad-Din. In 1529 he seized Algiers from Spain for the OTTOMAN EMPIRE and later gained all the BARBARY STATES. He continued to harass European shipping and gained control of most of the Mediterranean. He was admiral of the Ottoman fleet (1533–44).

Barbary, general name for the countries of N Africa except Egypt. The name is derived apparently from the Arabic for "barbarians". The coast of the area was notorious for piracy from the 16th to the 19th centuries. Animal life in the region includes the tailless BARBARY APE. Barbary Coast is also the name given to a waterfront area of San Francisco.

Barbary ape, tailless, yellowish-brown, ape-like MONKEY native to Algeria, Morocco and introduced into Gibraltar. It is the size of a small dog. The Gibraltar Barbary apes are the only wild monkeys in Europe. According to legend, if the Barbary apes leave Gibraltar, so will the British. Species *Macaca sylvana. See also* MACAQUE, PRIMATE.

Barbary sheep. *See* AOUDAD.

Barbary States, historic coastal region of N Africa now occupied by Libya, Algeria, Tunisia and Morocco. At one time Roman and later independent Muslim states (7th–15th centuries), they became infamous pirate states under Turkish control (16th–19th centuries). The pirates raided Mediterranean trade for booty and prisoners to ransom. After many attempts, the European powers and the USA finally subdued them in the early 19th century.

Barbastelle, BAT found in Europe and Asia. It is small – up to 6cm (2.5in) long – with greyish fur; it roosts in buildings or caves. Genus *Barbastella.*

Barbed wire, form of wire fencing patented in 1873 by Joseph F. Glidden. The metal wire had barbs spaced every few inches. This simple product changed the history of the W USA by allowing the fencing of ranches, so containing livestock on the open ranges. Barbed wire is also used for defence in warfare.

Barbel, or barb, CARP-like freshwater fish of W Asia and S central Europe. A game and food fish, it has an elongated body, flattened underside and two pairs of fleshy mouth whiskers (barbels). It is a strong swimmer well adapted to fast-flowing rivers. Length: 50–90cm (19.7–35.4in); weight: 16kg (35lb). Family Cyprinidae; species *Barbus barbus.*

Barber, Samuel (1910–), US composer. He has composed works in many forms, including chamber music, two symphonies, a *Piano Concerto* (1962) and two operas, *Vanessa* (1958) and *Antony and Cleopatra* (1966). The piano concerto and the first opera each won a Pulitzer prize.

Barberini, name of an aristocratic Roman family. Maffeo Barberini (1568–1644) was elected Pope URBAN VIII in 1623 and made cardinals of his nephew Francesco, his brother Antonio the Elder, and another nephew Antonio the Younger (the patron of the Baroque artist BERNINI).

Barber of Seville, The (1816), two-act comic opera by Gioacchino ROSSINI, Italian libretto by Cesare Sterbini, after Pierre BEAUMARCHAIS's play satirizing aristocratic foibles. Figaro (baritone), a barber, helps Count Almaviva (tenor) to win Rosina (soprano) despite the efforts of her guardian Bartolo (bass) to marry her for her dowry. *See also* HC2 pp.120, 121.

Barberry. *See* BERBERIS.

Barbershop quartet, four male vocalists who sing traditional and popular songs in a style generally featuring part-singing with close harmony. The four parts are usually lead (who sings the melody), tenor, baritone and baso. It first became a popular entertainment in US barber-shops in the 1890s.

Barber's itch, ringworm of the beard, contagious skin disease affecting the bearded region of a man's face. It is caused by a fungus and is generally treated with antifungal drugs.

Barber surgeons, men who practised as both barbers and surgeons, common in Europe until well after the Renaissance. Owing mainly to the influence of GALEN, a Greek physician of the 2nd century AD, medicine became separated from surgery. The former was regarded as worthy of intelligent study whereas the latter, necessitated by the more unpleasant aspects of war and disease, was left to barbers and other professional wielders of sharp instruments. *See also* MS pp.126–127.

Barberton, town in South Africa, 290km (180 miles) E of Pretoria. Gold, nickel and asbestos are mined there. It was founded in 1886. Pop. (1967 est.) 13,200.

Barbet, brightly coloured tropical bird, known for its monotonous call. It is stout-bodied with a large head, heavy bill, beard-like bristles and short legs. It is a poor flier, although some species can climb tree trunks. It lives in the tops of trees, and eats fruit and insects. The female lays 2–5 white eggs in a nest hollowed out of a tree branch. Length: 9–30cm (3.5–12in). Family Capitonidae. Genus *Mayalaima. See also* NW p.214.

Barbirolli, Sir John (1899–1970), British conductor who won international acclaim for sensitive performances of a wide range of music. He conducted the New York Philharmonic (1937–42) and was then resident with the Hallé Orchestra, Manchester (1943–68), which he transformed into a world-class ensemble.

Barbiturates, DRUGS used as sedatives or to induce sleep or sedation. Among the common barbiturates are phenobarbital, secobarbital (Seconal) and pentobarbital (Nembutal). When taken in controlled doses, they are safe, effective medical agents. But barbiturates are also dangerous drugs: in often repeated doses they are addictive, and when combined with other drugs such as alcohol or tranquillizers can result in sudden unconsciousness and death. *See also* MS pp.104–105; 120–121.

Barbizon School, mid-19th-century French school of Romantic landscape painting that derives its name from a village SE of Paris near the forest of Fontainebleau. A group of artists, led by Théodore ROUSSEAU and Jean-François MILLET, gathered there (*c.*1840–80) to discuss art and to paint the unacademic aspects of the countryside and peasant life. In painting directly from nature they were forerunners of IMPRESSIONISM. They were inspired by CONSTABLE and 17th-century Dutch landscapists, and in turn influenced DAUMIER and COURBET.

Barbour, John (*c.*1316–1395), Scottish poet. In about 1375 he wrote *The Bruce*, Scottish literature's earliest epic, describing Scotland's fight for independence from England. It combines patriotic sentiment with historical accuracy and is widely used as an historical source.

Barb-throat. *See* NW p.217.

Barbuda, coral island in the West Indies, a dependency of ANTIGUA. The chief industry is cotton. Pop. (1960) 1,100.

Barbusse, Henri (1873–1935), French novelist and journalist. He received the Prix Goncourt for *Under Fire* (1916), a bitterly disillusioned account of the experiences of front-line soldiers in WWI. His growing Communist sympathies are evident in his later works, *Light* (1918) and *Chains* (1925).

Barcarole, musical composition derived from the type of song sung by Venetian gondoliers. Well-known examples are those composed by Jacques Offenbach and Frédéric Chopin.

Barcelona, Mediterranean port and city in Catalonia, NE Spain, 507km (315 miles) NE of Madrid; capital of Barcelona province. Founded by the Carthaginian Barca family, it became a major trading centre in the late Middle Ages. Several times the French occupied and lost it (1640–52, 1715, 1808–14). It has long been the focus of radical political and Catalan separatist movements. The autonomous Catalan government there (1932–39) was swept away by the SPANISH CIVIL WAR. Industries: cars, aircraft, textiles, machinery, electrical goods. Pop. (1970) 1,745,142.

Barcelona, city and port in N Venezuela, on the W bank of the River Nevari; capital of Anzoategui state. The surrounding areas produce petroleum, coal, cotton, beef and cocoa. Industries: food processing, textiles, sawmilling. Pop. 55,000.

Barchan dune, crescent-shaped sand hill found in sandy deserts throughout the world where the wind is constant in speed and direction. Barchans also occur fairly frequently in coastal regions; they are quickly shifted by the wind, particularly when small. *See also* DESERT; DUNE; PE p.120.

Barchester Towers (1857), by Anthony TROLLOPE, second of the "Barchester Novels", six stories examining the ecclesiastical-rural Establishment in the imaginary English county of Barsetshire.

Barclay, Alexander (*c.*1475–1552), British poet, probably of Scottish birth. He is best remembered for his adaptation of Sebastian Brant's *Narrenschiff* into the satirical poem *The Ship of Fools* (1508).
Barclay, John (1582–1621), French-born Scottish author. He wrote a number of political and satirical novels, most of them in Latin. These novels included *Euphormio nis Lusini Satyricon* (1603), an attack on the Jesuits, and *Argenis* (1621).
Barclay, Robert (1648–90), Scottish Quaker and apologist of QUAKERISM. Often imprisoned for his religious views, he was eventually befriended by the Duke of York (later JAMES II) and made nominal governor of the Quaker province of East New Jersey (1682–88) although he never visited it. His collected works were published as *Truth Triumphant* (1692).
Bard, in Celtic society, poet and singer charged with celebrating the exploits and virtues of the king or chieftain in whose court he lived. In Ireland and Wales the bards formed an hereditary order with jealously guarded privileges analogous to those of the nobility and clergy. The medieval bardic EISTEDDFOD (gathering) in Wales was revived as an annual event in the 19th century, at which the winner of a national poetry competition is "chaired" as a bard.
Bardeen, John (1908–), US physicist known for his research into SEMICONDUCTIVITY. He worked with the Bell Telephone Laboratories (1945–51) and in 1951 became professor of physics at Illinois University. In 1956 he shared the Nobel Prize in physics with William SHOCKLEY and Walter BRATTAIN for their joint invention of the TRANSISTOR. In 1972 he again won the Nobel Prize in physics, sharing it with Leon COOPER and John SCHRIEFFER, for his work on SUPERCONDUCTIVITY. *See also* SU p.131.
Bardi, Giovanni, Count of Vernio (1534–1612), Italian musician, founder of the Florentine Camerata (*c.*1580). That society of writers and musicians sought to revive Greek musical tragedy and laid the foundations of modern opera.
Bardot, Brigitte (1934–), French film actress who became a sex-symbol of the 1960s. She became famous for her roles in *And God Created Woman* (1956) and *Heaven Fell that Night* (1957), directed by her then husband, Roger Vadim. Her later films include *La Verité* (1960), *Le Mépris* (1963) and the comedy *Viva Maria!* (1965).
Barea, Arturo (1897–1957), Spanish author. He fought as a republican in the SPANISH CIVIL WAR. In 1939 he travelled to Britain where he wrote a trilogy based on his war experiences – *The Forge* (1941), *The Track* (1943) and *The Clash* (1946). The trilogy was published in Spanish as *La forja de un rebelde* (1952).
Barebone's Parliament, or Parliament of Saints (July–Dec.1653), the last Parliament of the English COMMONWEALTH. Named after the MP "Praise God" Barebone and hand-picked by CROMWELL and the Puritan army chiefs, it was intended to usher in godly rule. But religious disputes, especially about Church patronage and tithes, ruined its effectiveness and it voted its own dissolution, handing over power to Cromwell. *See also* HC1 pp.290–291.
Bareilly, city in N India; capital of Bareilly district. It became a British possession in 1801 and Bareilly College was founded there in 1837. Industries: sugar, cotton, furniture. Pop. (1971) 296,248.
Barenboim, Daniel (1942–), Israeli pianist and conductor, *b.* Argentina. He has performed with many of the world's leading orchestras, including the New York Philharmonic, the London Symphony, the Berlin Philharmonic and the Orchestre de Paris. In 1967 he married the cellist Jacqueline du Pré.
Barents Sea, part of the ARCTIC Ocean lying between Spitsbergen and Novaya Zemlya. It is named after the Dutch explorer Willem Barentz who discovered Spitzbergen (1596). The sea-bed consists of an uneven surface distribution of Quaternary sediments. The deeper older sediments bear evidence of long periods above sea-level. The fishing-grounds are particularly rich in cod and herring. Area: 1,370,360 sq km (529,096sq miles).
Barentz, or Barents, Willem (*d.*1597), Dutch navigator. He made three expeditions in search of the NORTH-EAST PASSAGE (1594–97). On his third voyage he discovered Spitzbergen, off Norway, but after rounding Novaya Zemlya was trapped by ice for the winter. He died on the return journey.
Barère de Vieuzac, Bertrand (1755–1841), French politician. During the FRENCH REVOLUTION he supported the execution of Louis XVI and was a member of the Committee of Public Safety. In 1794 he was party to the overthrow of ROBESPIERRE. Imprisoned for his part in the Terror, he escaped and later worked for NAPOLEON. *See also* HC2 pp.74–75.
Baretti, Giuseppe Marc-Antonio (1719–89), Italian writer and literary critic. In 1751 he went to London and was associated with Samuel Johnson. His writings include a *Dictionary of English and the Italian Language* (1760), and *A Journey from London to Genoa* (1770–71).
Barge, boat for carrying freight or, occasionally, passengers, usually flat bottomed and often towed by tugs or (more traditionally) by horses. Barges have long been the principal means of heavy freight transport on rivers, canals and other inland waterways. Because of its low cost, this method of transport is enjoying a new popularity in western countries. Originally a barge was a shallow-draught sailing vessel. *See also* MM p.196–197.
Bargello, Italian national art museum in Florence. Built as a high-towered civic palace-fortress in 1255, the Palazzo del Podesta became the seat of the chief of police (*bargello*) and was a prison from 1574. In 1865, it was established as a museum and today is famous for its collection of Renaissance sculpture including MICHELANGELO's unfinished *David,* and works by DONATELLO, GIOTTO, CELLINI and Della Robbia.
Bargello, type of zig-zag embroidery that originated in 17th-century Florence. It has long flat stitches, generally on a canvas-like fabric, that create a design consisting mainly of chevrons. It is also called Florentine canvas work.
Barham, Richard Harris (1788–1845), British humorist. In 1837, using the pseudonym Thomas Ingoldsby, he began a series of humorous tales that were first published in 1840 under the title *The Ingoldsby Legends.*
Bari, port city in SE Italy; capital of Bari and Apulia province. It was colonized by several peoples, such as the Romans, Saracens and the Normans. Industries: oil refining, building materials, textiles, food processing. Pop. (1975) 376,467.
Barisāl, city in the Khulna Division, S Bangladesh, in the Ganges Delta on the W bank of the Barisāl River, 118km (73 miles) S of Dacca. It is an important port and has three colleges. Pop. 79,000.
Barisan, mountain range that extends along the W coast of Sumatra, Indonesia; length: 1,600km (1,000 miles). Many lakes have formed between the two parallel chains, the largest being Lake Toba. The highest peak is Mt Kerintji (3,805m; 12,483ft).
Barisano da Trani (2nd half of the 12th century), southern Italian sculptor, famous for his bronze doors in the cathedrals of Trani (*c.*1175), Ravello (1179), and Monreale (1185).
Barite, translucent, white or yellow mineral, barium sulphate ($BaSO_4$), found in sedimentary rocks and in ore veins in limestone. It occurs as orthorhombic system tabular crystals or masses. Radiating clusters of crystals are called "barite roses". Hardness 3–3.5; s.g. 4.5. *See also* PE pp.96–97, *97.*
Baritone, name for the register of the human voice which falls between that of TENOR and BASS.
Barium, metallic element (Ba) of the alkaline-earth group, discovered in 1808 by Sir Humphry DAVY. Chief sources are heavy spar (sulphate) and witherite (carbonate). Barium sulphate is swallowed to permit X-ray examination of the stomach and intestines because barium atoms are opaque to X-rays. Properties: at.no. 56; at.wt. 137.34; s.g. 3.5; m.p. 725°C (1,337°F); b.p. 1,640°C (2,984°F); most common isotope Ba^{138} (71.66%). *See also* ALKALINE-EARTH ELEMENTS.
Bark, outer protective covering of a woody plant stem. It is made up of several layers. As food-conducting cells die, they become the inner layer. The CORK layer, waxy and waterproof, is the thickest and hardens into the tough, fissured outer covering. Spongy areas (lenticels) allow the stem to breathe. *See also* NW p.62.
Barka, Mehdi ben (1920–), Moroccan nationalist leader. He was president of the National Consultative Assembly in 1956-59. In 1959 he formed the National Union of Popular Forces. From 1960 he lived in self-imposed exile, mainly in Algeria, and launched attacks on the Moroccan government.
Bark beetle, or engraver beetle, small, brown to black beetle that tunnels through the inner bark and wood of trees. The tunnels of some species form characteristic patterns, resembling engravings.
Barker, Lady Mary Anne (1831–1911), New Zealand author. Her novels, *Station Life in New Zealand* and *Station Amusements in New Zealand,* describe 19th-century sheep farming life.
Barker, Sir Herbert Atkinson (1869–1950), British surgeon who became famous for his ability to treat orthopaedic disorders by means of manipulation, without the need for surgery.
Barking deer. *See* MUNTJAC.
Barkla, Charles Glover (1877-1944), British physicist who was awarded the 1917 Nobel Prize in physics for his discovery that elements have a characteristic X-ray spectrum, which enables them to be identified. He also formulated laws governing the scattering of X-rays and their transmission through solids.
Barkly, Sir Henry (1815–98), colonial administrator and governor of the Cape of Good Hope (1870–77). His initiative led to the solving of the Griqua-Natal dispute by Britain's annexation of Griqualland West in 1871.
Barkly Tableland, vast plateau region in N central and E Australia, extending from Northern Territory into Queensland. Beef cattle are grazed there on large cattle stations. Height: 300m (1,000ft).
Bar Kokba, Simon (*d.*135), leader of the rebellion of the Jewish community against the Romans in JERUSALEM in 131–135. At first successful, he was finally slain in battle at Bethar.
Bark painting, art form practised by Australian Aborigines, particularly along the coast of Arnhem Land. A great variety of sacred and common subjects are painted on sheets of bark that have been stripped from trees and flattened and smoothed. Pigments are made with ochres and clay; sticks dipped in the paint are used as "brushes".
Barlach, Ernst (1870–1938), German sculptor, graphic artist, writer and dramatist. He was a major pioneer of the German EXPRESSIONIST movement. The compact angularity of his forms, as in the figure *Man in a Stock* (1918), conveys intense compassion. His writings include poems and plays (some of which he illustrated) and an autobiography.
Barley, cereal GRASS native to Asia and Ethiopia, cultivated perhaps since 5000 BC. Three cultivated species are: *Hordeum distichum* commonly grown in Europe; *H. vulgare,* favoured in the USA; and *H. irregulare* or irregular barley, grown in Ethiopia. Barley is eaten by human beings and animals, and is also used in making malt beverages. Family Gramineae. *See also* PE pp.156, 180, *181,* 204–205.
Barlow, Eddie (1940–), South African cricketer. A fine, robust batsman, medium bowler and expert slip-fielder, he played for South Africa, Transvaal, Eastern Province and Western Province before emigrating to England and joining Derbyshire in 1976.
Bar Mitzvah, Jewish ceremony in which a young male (traditionally aged 13 years and 1 day) is initiated into the religious community. At the ceremony he reads a

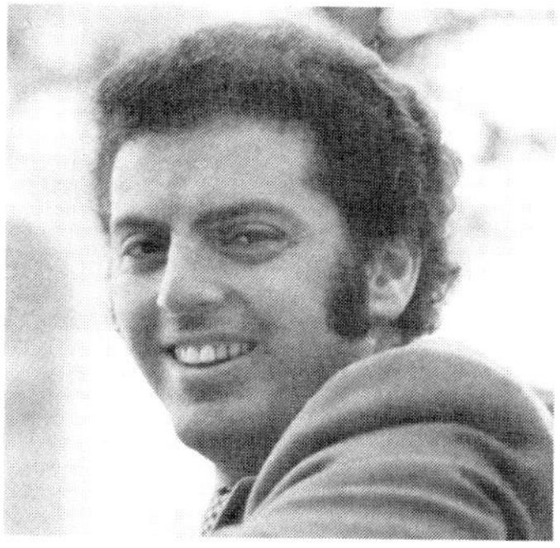

Daniel Barenboim, the Israeli conductor and pianist, is known as an interpreter of Mozart.

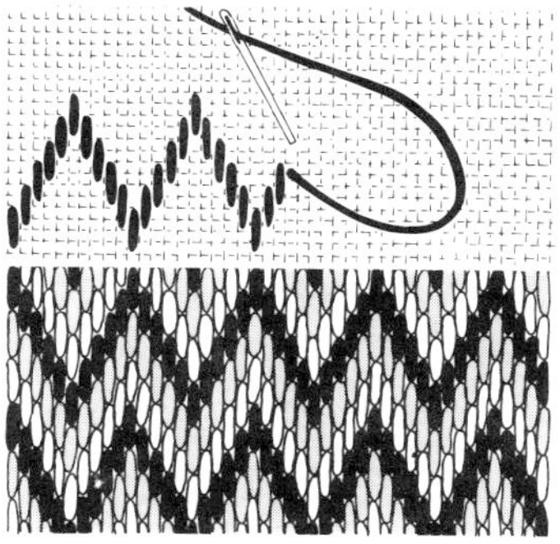

Bargello, known also as flamestitch because of the traditional colour blending.

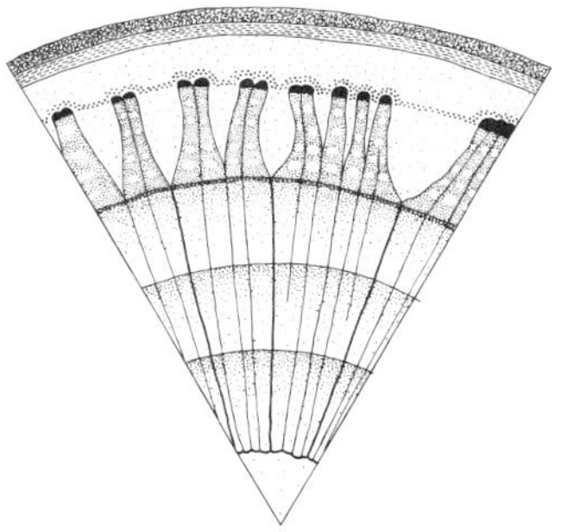

Bark, familiar in such products as cork, is also used in the preparation of medicines.

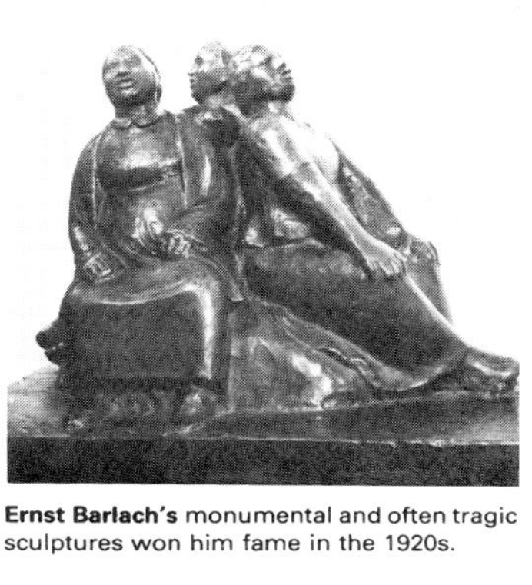

Ernst Barlach's monumental and often tragic sculptures won him fame in the 1920s.

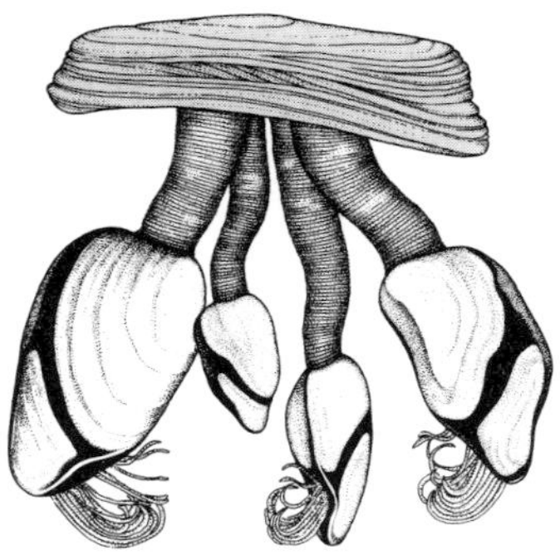

Barnacles slow any ship they cling to, which is why they are periodically scraped off.

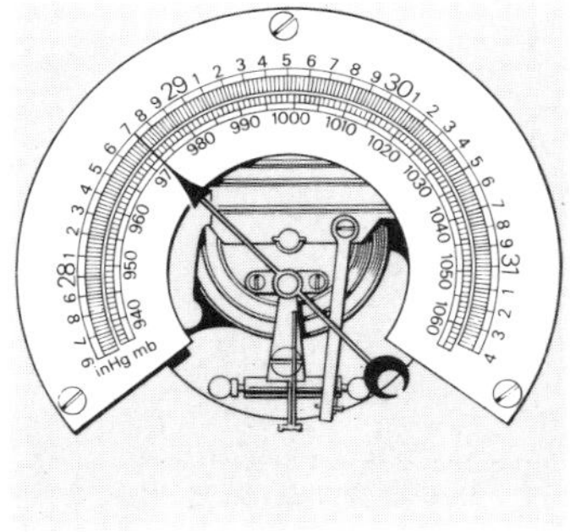

Barometer; the aneroid is more sensitive but less accurate than the mercury barometer.

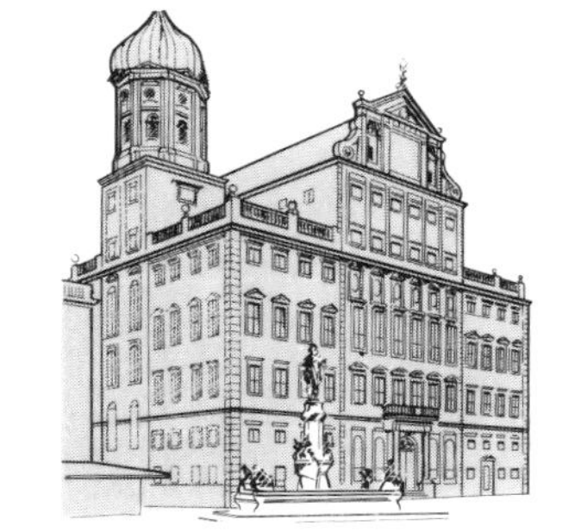

Baroque palaces, like Versailles, expressed the power of the heads of state.

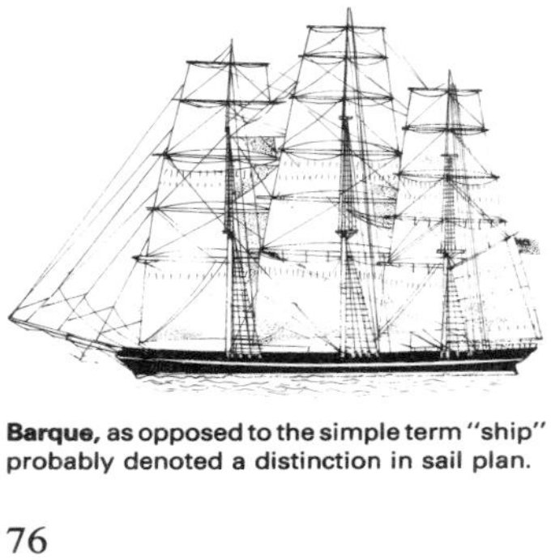

Barque, as opposed to the simple term "ship" probably denoted a distinction in sail plan.

portion of the TORAH in a synagogue. The religious rite is followed by a social celebration. *See also* MS p.165.

Barn, scientific unit of area used in nuclear physics for measuring the cross-sections of atomic nuclei; 1 barn = 10^{-24}cm^2. This area is a measure of the probability that fission will occur when a neutron moves towards a heavy nucleus. It is usually different from the geometric area of the nucleus.

Barn (building). *See* PE p.164.

Barna, Victor (1911–), Hungarian table-tennis player who won 15 world championships, including five singles (1932–35) and seven Swaythling Cup gold medals. He played 82 times for Hungary and 56 times for England (he became naturalized in 1947).

Barnaba da Modena (*fl.* 1362–83), Italian painter. He worked in Genoa and was popular there, in his attempt to combine Byzantine stylization with the freer techniques of GIOTTO's work.

Barnabas, Saint, Christian apostle of the first century, originally named Joseph. Barnabas accompanied PAUL (Saul) on two proselytizing missions to Cyprus and the European mainland. A rift developed between the two, after which Paul replaced Barnabas as head of the church in Antioch. Feast: 11 June.

Barnaby Rudge (1841), Charles DICKENS' fifth novel. One of Dickens' earlier studies of a recurrent theme involving the interplay of public and private violence, it follows the lives of a wide variety of characters against the background of London's anti-popery riots, led by Lord George GORDON in 1780.

Barnacle, CRUSTACEAN that lives mostly on rocks and floating timber. Some barnacles live on whales, turtles and fish, without being parasitic, although there are also parasitic species. The larvae swim freely until ready to become adults, when they settle permanently on their heads; their bodies become covered with calcareous plates. The adult uses its appendages to scoop food into its mouth. Two main types are those with stalks (goose barnacles) and those without (acorn barnacles). Subclass Cirripedia. *See also* NW p.*236*.

Barnard, Christiaan (1922–), South African surgeon. He was the first to perform a human heart transplant (3 Dec. 1967). In 1974 he was the first to implant a second heart in a patient and to link the circulations of the two hearts so that they worked together as one.

Barnard, Edward Emerson (1857–1923), US astronomer. He is chiefly known as an acute observer and pioneer in astronomical photography. He discovered comets, catalogued dark nebulae and made observations of BARNARD'S STAR.

Barnard Castle, town in County Durham, N England, on the River Tees. It is an ancient market town, with the ruins of a 12th-century castle and a fine European art collection in the Bowes Museum. Pop. (1971 est.) 5,200.

Barnard's star, red dwarf star in the constellation of Ophiuchus. It was discovered by the US astronomer Edward BARNARD in 1916, and is remarkable for having the greatest proper motion of any star yet observed. A companion body, perhaps an orbiting planet with a mass 1.5 times that of Jupiter, was detected near it in 1963. Characteristics: apparent mag. 9.5; absolute mag. 13.2; spectral type M5; distance 6 light-years. *See also* SU pp.226, 283.

Barnardo, Thomas John (1845–1905), British philanthropist who founded the Dr Barnardo Homes for destitute children. He was born in Ireland and in 1866 moved to London to study medicine. In 1867, while still a student, he founded the East End Mission for orphan children – the first of his famous homes. These spread rapidly through the UK and still flourish today.

Barnato, Barney (1852–97), South African mining millionaire (real name Barnet Isaacs). Born in London, he went to Kimberley in 1873 and in 1889 he formed the Johannesburg Consolidated Investment Company. Possibly fears of what an inquiry into the Jameson Raid (1895) might reveal of his financial dealings led him to drown himself in 1897.

Barnaul, capital of Altaikraj, s central USSR; a port and railway junction on the River Ob'. It is an industrial and trading centre serving local farms and mining. It also has industrial and teachers' training colleges. Pop. 502,000.

Barnave, Antoine (1761–93), French politician, member of the ESTATES-GENERAL and NATIONAL ASSEMBLY (1789). He supported constitutional monarchy and was guillotined for treasonable correspondence with the king.

Barn dance, US paired dance in quadruple time. Originally called the Military Schottische, the present name was coined from the tune which frequently accompanied it, *Dancing in a Barn.* The dance involves hops and waltz steps, and is occasionally progressive.

Barnes, Ernest William (1874–1953), British mathematician and clergyman, a friend of Bertrand RUSSELL. He became Bishop of Birmingham (1924). Many of his mathematical articles concerned special functions.

Barnes, Sydney Francis (1873–1967), British cricketer, a medium-pace bowler of unrivalled consistency. He played most of his cricket in the Minor Counties and northern leagues and in only 27 Tests took 189 wickets (average 16.43), including 17 for 159 against South Africa at the age of 41. He played as a league professional until 1940; as late as the 1938 season, when he was 65, he took 126 wickets for an average of less than 7 runs each.

Barnes, Thomas (1785-1841), English journalist and editor of *The Times* newspaper. In 1809 he became dramatic critic on *The Times* and as its editor (1817–41) aimed to make the paper independent of any political party.

Barnet, Battle of (April 1471), battle of the Wars of the ROSES, in which EDWARD IV defeated WARWICK "the King-maker" and thus prepared for the restoration of the Yorkist dynasty later in the year. *See also* HC1 p.*243*.

Barn owl, generally nocturnal bird of prey that lives mainly in the Eastern hemisphere. The widely distributed common barn owl (*Tyto alba*) has a heart-shaped face and long legs. It lives in old buildings where its acute hearing enables it to locate rodents and other prey in almost total darkness. Family Tytonidae. *See also* OWL.

Barnsley, city in South Yorkshire 19km (12 miles) N of Sheffield. Its market day (Wednesday) dates from 1249 when it was established by Henry III, and it has many old buildings. Industries: coal-mining, engineering, textiles. Pop. (1971) 75,300.

Barnuevo, Pedro de Peralta (1663–1743), Peruvian poet and playwright, best known for his epic play *The Founding of Lima* (1732). He was also a mathematician, historian and astronomer. His intellectual activities caused him to be persecuted by the Inquisition.

Barnum, Phineas Taylor (1810–91), US showman. He established the American Museum in New York City in 1842, where he presented the dwarf TOM THUMB, a bearded lady and other "freaks". In 1850 he introduced Jenny LIND to the USA for a concert tour. In 1871 he opened his circus, billed as "The Greatest Show on Earth". He merged with rival James BAILEY in 1881 to form Barnum and Bailey's Circus.

Barocci, Federico (*c.* 1526–1612), Italian MANNERIST painter, a precursor of the BAROQUE style and, after RAPHAEL, the most important painter in Urbino. His work is marked by emotional expression, as in his famous *Madonna del Popolo* (1579).

Baroda, city in Gujarat state in W India, on the fertile alluvial plain between the Mahi and Narmada rivers. Many of its palaces, gates and gardens were built by the Gaekwar princes in the 18th century. There is a state museum, gallery and university. Industries: cotton, textiles, chemicals. Pop. (1970 est.) 404,200.

Baroja y Nessi, Pio (1872–1956), Spanish novelist. He gained recognition for his bitter, humorous and pessimistic novels portraying down-and-out characters moving in a colourful but meaningless world. His works include *The Tree of Knowledge* (1911) and *Memoirs of a Man of Action* (1913-35).

Barometer, instrument for measuring atmospheric pressure. Mercury and aneroid barometers are the two basic types. They are used in WEATHER FORECASTING to predict probable local weather changes: a rising barometer (increasing pressure) presages fair weather; if pressure is falling, worse weather can be expected. In a barograph the needle of an aneroid barometer is replaced by a pen which traces variations in pressure on a revolving cylindrical chart. A barometer can also be employed in an ALTIMETER, which uses air pressure as a measure of altitude. *See also* MM pp.33, 91, 250.

Baron, in Britain, member of the lowest rank of the PEERAGE. Inheritance is usually confined to male heirs or to collateral male descendants. A baron is addressed as "Lord" and his wife as "Lady".

Baronet, member of a British hereditary order of honour made up of commoners who rank below BARONS. Baronets are designated "Sir" or "Lady" before the forename and "Bart" or "Bt" after the surname to distinguish them from KNIGHTS. *See also* PEERAGE.

Barons' Wars (1263–65), conflict between HENRY III of England and his barons, led by Simon de MONTFORT. Henry provoked war by breaking his pledge of 1258 to rule through a council of barons rather than foreign favourites. The barons defeated the king at LEWES in 1264 and summoned a "parliament" in 1265 to show the broad support for their actions. De Montfort was eventually defeated at Evesham in 1265. *See also* HC1 pp.178–179, 210–211.

Baroque, term (perhaps derived from the Portuguese *barroca*, a mis-shapen pearl) applied to the style of art and architecture that succeeded MANNERISM and lasted from the end of the 16th century into the 18th century. Baroque was at its height in Rome under BERNINI, BORROMINI and Pietro de CORTONA (*c.*1630–80) and in S Germany under Balthazar NEUMANN and FISCHER VON ERLACH (*c.*1700–50). The High Baroque at its best was a union of architecture, painting and sculpture in a blend of light, colour and movement calculated to overwhelm the spectator by a direct emotional appeal. Paintings contained visual illusions; sculpture exploited the effect of light on surface and contour. Architecture was created in series of geometrically controlled spaces (squares, circles, ovals and triangles) which enclosed, adjoined and superimposed each other to create the illusion of rhythmic movement. Buildings conforming to this design were heavily decorated with stucco ornament and free-standing sculpture. Baroque was closely linked to the COUNTER-REFORMATION and especially to the Jesuits, and therefore lasted longest in Catholic countries. Spanish and Portuguese missionaries carried the style to South America, where it was an important European influence until the late 19th century. Baroque became increasingly florid before it merged with the lighter style of ROCOCO. The AGE OF REASON eventually rejected both in favour of NEO-CLASSICISM. In music, the term Baroque is applied loosely to the period between MONTEVERDI and J. S. BACH. *See also* HC1 pp.304–307.

Barotseland (Western Province), historical region in W Zambia, central Africa. The capital is Mongu. The River Zambezi drains the province, which is primarily savanna grassland. It is a livestock-rearing and grain-growing region, with some teak forest. In 1911 it became a province of the British Protectorate of Northern Rhodesia, and was called Western Province after Zambian independence in 1964. Area: 126,386sq km (48,798sq miles). Pop. (1972 est.) 448,000.

Barque, also spelled bark, standard merchant ship on the N Atlantic during the second half of the 19th century, characterized by two square-rigged masts and a third with fore-and-aft sails. Four- and five-masted barques were also built. *See also* MM p.*113*.

Barquentine, large commercial sailing ship which came into use at the beginning of the 19th century. It had a single square-rigged mast and as many as three masts with fore-and-aft sails. *See also* SCHOONER.

Barquisimeto, city in NW Venezuela, capital of Lara state, 274km (170 miles) WSW of Caracas on the Pan American Highway. Founded in 1552, it was rebuilt after an earthquake in 1812. A university was founded there in 1968. Industries: cement, sisal rope, sugar. Pop. (1970) 291,353.

Barra, small rugged island in the Outer Hebrides, off NW Scotland; it is separated from South Uist by the Sound of Barra. The main occupations are fishing and weaving, and some people still live in crofts. The main settlement is Castlebay. Area: 91sq km (35sq miles). Pop. 1,260.

Barracouta, also called snoek, atun, or South African mackerel, commercial food fish found in tropical and temperate marine waters. A snake (deep-sea) MACKEREL, it has a laterally compressed body, elongated lower jaw and two dorsal fins. Length 1m (3.3ft); weight: 4-10kg (8.8-22.05lb). Family Gemphylidae; species *Thyrsites atun.*

Barracuda, marine fish found in tropical Atlantic and Pacific waters. Known to attack man, it has a large mouth with razor-sharp teeth; its olive green body is elongated. Length: usually 1.2–1.8m (4–6ft); weight: 1.4–22.7kg (3–50lb). Family Sphyraenidae; there are 20 species. *See also* NW p.*125.*

Barranquilla, city and major port in N Colombia, on the River Magdalena. It became a river port in the mid-19th century, and the river was deepened to take seagoing ships in 1935. Located in an agricultural region, it has two universities. Industries: textiles, food processing, chemicals, shipbuilding, glass. Pop. (1973) 661,920.

Barraqué, Jean (1928–73), French composer. He was a pupil of MESSIAEN, and one of the earliest composers of ELECTRONIC MUSIC. His best known work is his piano sonata.

Barras, Paul François Jean Nicolas, Vicomte de (1755–1829), French revolutionary leader. He joined the JACOBINS and was a member of the CONVENTION. He was a leader in the coup which brought down ROBESPIERRE in July 1794 (which, in the Revolutionary Calendar, was 9 Thermidor). By turning over his troops to the command of NAPOLEON during a royalist uprising in Paris in 1795, he helped advance Napoleon's career. He was a member of the DIRECTORY (1795–99).

Barrault, Jean-Louis (1910–), French actor and director. He is best known for his roles as Hamlet in the André Gide translation (1946) and as the mime in the film *Children of Paradise* (1944). In 1946 he formed a repertory company and later directed (1959–68) the successful Théâtre de France. In 1940, he married the actress Madeline Renaud.

Barrel jumping, sport in which an ice-skater jumps over a number of barrels. It is believed to have originated in Holland in the 17th century and now has a following in the USA.

Barrel organ, mechanical musical instrument in which pins on a rotating drum open valves that let air from a wind-chest enter organ pipes to produce the sound. MOZART and HANDEL wrote compositions for it. It has been used in village churches and by street musicians. The name is sometimes incorrectly applied to a mechanical PIANO or to a HURDY-GURDY.

Barrel tree. *See* BOTTLE TREE.

Barrès, Auguste Maurice (1862–1923), French author and politician. A prolific writer, his interest lay in the cult of the self, as depicted in the trilogy of novels *Le Culte du Moi* (1888–91), and the concept of anti-German, French nationalism, as asserted in the treatise *Scène et Doctrines du Nationalisme, Leurs Figures* (1902).

Barrett, David (1930–), Canadian politician, Prime Minister of British Columbia (1972–75). He was a social worker and entered the provincial legislature in 1960 as a member of the New Democratic Party. He was the first non-Conservative to be elected Prime Minister, but his policies were voted out in 1975.

Barrie, Sir James Matthew, (1860–1937), Scottish dramatist and novelist. Despite a degree of sentimentality, his works generally have a clever twist in their plots. J.M. Barrie re-wrote his novel *The Little Minister* (1891) into a play (1897). His other plays include *The Admirable Crichton* (1902), *What Every Woman Knows* (1908) and *Peter Pan* (1904), which remains popular to this day.

Barrier island, any long, low island of sand parallel to a shore and permanently separated from it. It may be composed of dunes, swamps and areas of vegetation. *See also* PE pp.122–123.

Barrier reef, long narrow coral reef lying some distance from and roughly parallel to the shore, but separated from it by a deep lagoon. The GREAT BARRIER REEF is the most famous. *See also* PE p.123.

Barrington, Jonah (1940–), British squash player. A left-hander, he dominated squash in the late 1960s with a game based on tenacity and supreme physical fitness. He turned professional in 1969.

Barrington, Ken (1930–), British cricketer for England and Surrey. A dour but nontheless prolific batsman, he played in 82 Test matches between 1955 and 1968 (6,806 runs, average 58.67), scoring 20 centuries. He became an England selector in 1975.

Barrios, Eduardo (1884–1963), Chilean novelist. His novels deal with abnormal psychological types. In *Los hombres del hombre* (1950) he divided the main character into several different men in order to explore the fragmented personality.

Barrister, name given in some countries to lawyers entitled to practise as advocates in the higher courts. In Britain the right to "call to the bar" is vested in the four Inns of Court.

Barrow, Errol Walton (1920–), Prime Minister of Barbados from 1966 to 1976. Co-founder of the Democratic Labour Party and the island's premier (1961–66), he became Prime Minister when the country gained independence.

Barrow, Isaac (1630–77), English philosopher. He resigned his position as professor of mathematics at Cambridge in favour of his pupil, Isaac NEWTON. He became vice-chancellor of Cambridge in 1675. He wrote *Optical Lectures,* and his *Sermons* were popular.

Barrowclough, Sir Harold (1894–), New Zealand soldier and lawyer. He fought in WWI and was New Zealand's Pacific commander in WWII. He was Chief Justice of New Zealand from 1953 to 1966.

Barrow-in-Furness, town in SW Cumbria, on the coast 84km (52 miles) N of Liverpool. It has several ironworks, but the local ore is now nearly exhausted. Industries: iron-mining, iron and steel, paper, engineering, shipbuilding. Pop. 75,300.

Barry, Sir Charles (1795–1860), British architect. In collaboration with PUGIN, he designed the Houses of Parliament at Westminster, in the Gothic style which was a term of the commission. Barry was influenced by the Italian Renaissance, as in his Travellers' Club and the Reform Club in London. *See also* HC2 p.122.

Barry, James (1741-1806), Irish painter of heroic and historical pictures. He went to London (1764), and although largely self-taught was elected an RA (1773).

Barry, John (1933–), British composer and musician. A jazz arranger and band leader, he gained fame with imaginative scores for James Bond films – eg *From Russia With Love* (1963), *Goldfinger* (1964) – and many others such as *King Rat* (1965), *Born Free* (1966) and *Midnight Cowboy* (1969).

Barrymore, famous US family of actors. Maurice (1847–1905) made his stage début in London in 1872. In 1875 he went to the USA where he married the actress Georgiana Drew. They had three children: Lionel (1878–1954), Ethel (1879–1959) and John (1882-1942). Lionel, a fine character actor, made many films, among them *Dinner at Eight* (1933) and *A Free Soul* (1931), for which he won an Academy Award. Ethel was best known for her stage performances in *A Doll's House* (1905) and *The Corn is Green* (1942). She won an Academy Award for her part in the film *None but the Lonely Heart* (1944). John's good looks quickly won him a huge following. Among his many films were *Beau Brummel* (1924), *Don Juan* (1926) and *Grand Hotel* (1932).

Barstow, Stanley (1938–), British novelist. His first novel, *A Kind of Loving,* was published in 1960. He wrote the script for *South Riding,* which won the BBC award for the best television serial in 1974. In 1976 he published *Right True End.*

Bart, Lionel (1930–), British songwriter. He began his career writing songs for Tommy Steele, and later wrote lyrics and music for musicals including *Fings Ain't Wot They Used T'Be* (1959), *Oliver!* (1960) and *Maggie May* (1964).

Bartered Bride, The (1866), three-act comic opera by Bedřich SMETANA, Czech libretto by Karel Sabina. First produced as an operetta with dialogue, it was later enlarged. Villagers Hans and Wenzel (tenors) and Marie (soprano) contend with their families and the marriage broker Kezal (bass). It was Bohemia's first important opera and established Smetana as a "nationalist" composer. *See also* HC2 pp.107, 120.

Barth, Heinrich (1821–65), German explorer and geographer. In 1845 he led a two-year expedition which explored Italy, Tunis, Barea, Egypt, Palestine and Greece. In 1851–56 he accompanied a British sponsored expedition through central Africa. *See also* HC2 pp.142–143; *142.*

Barth, John (1930–), US author. A professor of English, he has written several complex and imaginative novels. They include *The End of the Road* (1961), *The Sot-Weed Factor* (1960), *Giles Goat Boy* (1966) and three novellas entitled *Chimera* (1972), for which Barth won the 1973 US National Book Award in fiction.

Barth, Karl (1886–1968), Swiss theologian. He was a leading thinker of 20th-century PROTESTANTISM; he tried to lead theology back to principles of the REFORMATION and to emphasize the revelation of God through Jesus Christ. His school has been called dialectical theology or theology of the word. In 1935 he was suspended from his position at the University of Bonn for his anti-Nazi stance and so he returned to Switzerland. His works include *Epistle to the Romans* (1919) and *Church Dogmatics.*

Bartholdi, Frédéric Auguste (1834–1904), French sculptor, best known for his *Liberty Enlightening the World* (Statue of Liberty) in New York harbour, dedicated in 1886. His colossal *Lion of Belfort* at Belfort, France, is considered one of his best works.

Bartholin, Caspar (1585–1629), Danish physician who advanced the study of human anatomy, professor of medicine at Copenhagen University. His best-known work was *Anatomicae Institutiones Corporis Humani* (1611). His son Thomas (1616–80) and grandson Caspar (1655–1738) were also well-known physicians.

Bartholomew, Saint, according to the New Testament, one of the 12 apostles of Christ. He is mentioned in the gospels of Matthew, Mark and Luke, and is probably identical with the Nathanael of St John's Gospel. Feast: 24 Aug.

Bartholemew's Day Massacre, Saint (24 Aug. 1572), attempt by the leaders of Catholic France to extinguish French Protestantism. More than 3,000 Parisian HUGUENOTS were killed and a milder persecution followed in the provinces. It contributed to the resumption of civil war. *See also* HC1 pp.272–273, *272.*

Bartlett, Sir Frederic Charles (1886–1969), British experimental psychologist who made important contributions to the study of memory. His major works include *Remembering: A Study in Experimental and Social Psychology* (1932) and *Thinking: An Experimental and Social Study* (1958).

Bartlett, Robert Abram (1875–1946), US arctic explorer. Between 1897–1909 he accompanied Robert PEARY on his historic

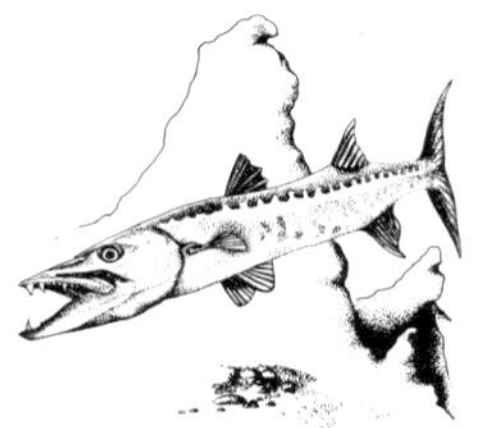

Barracuda; the "tiger of the sea", a swift and destructive fish known to attack man.

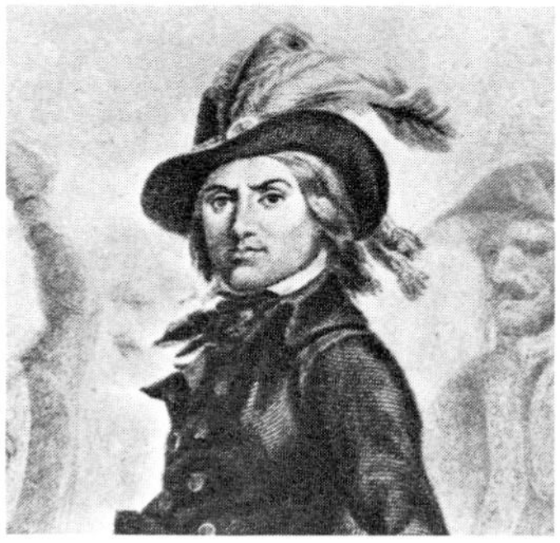

Barras, whose former mistress Josephine de Beauharnais became Napoleon's wife.

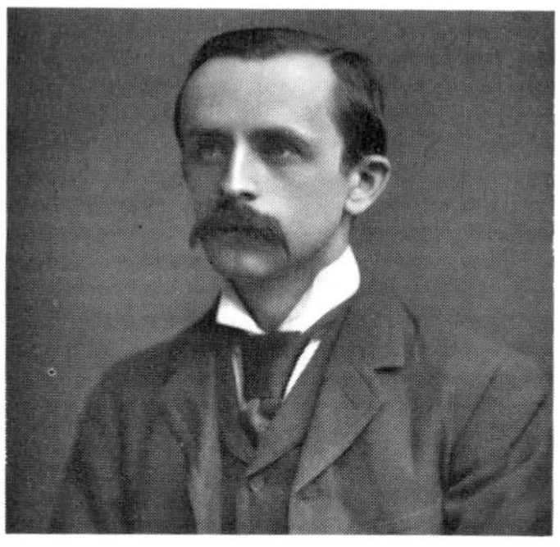

J. M. Barrie, creator of Peter Pan, a character now firmly rooted in Western mythology.

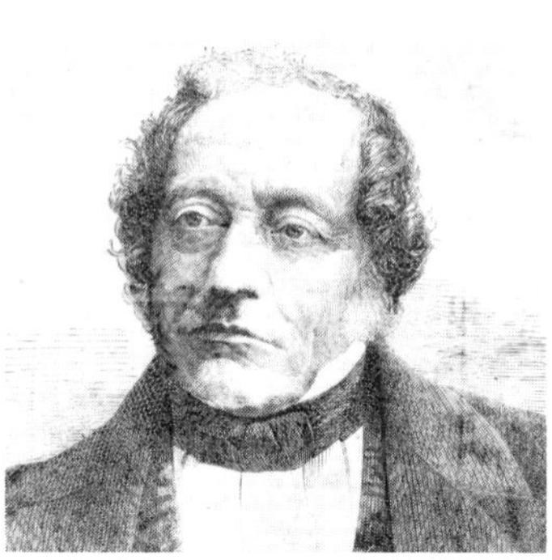

Sir Charles Barry, who designed the British Houses of Parliament and Tower Bridge.

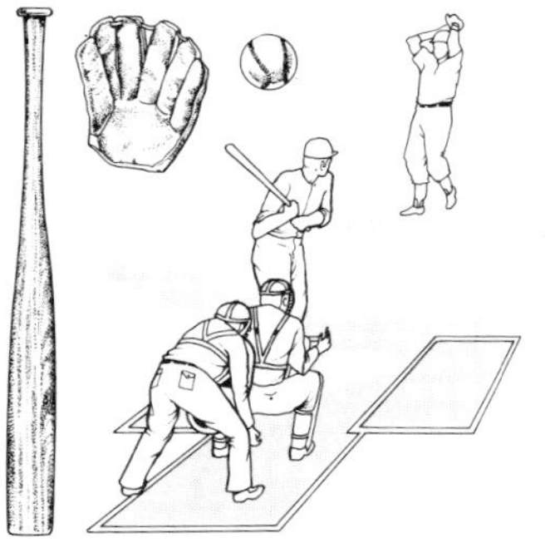

Baseball, where the focus is on the skill of the pitcher against the skill of the batter.

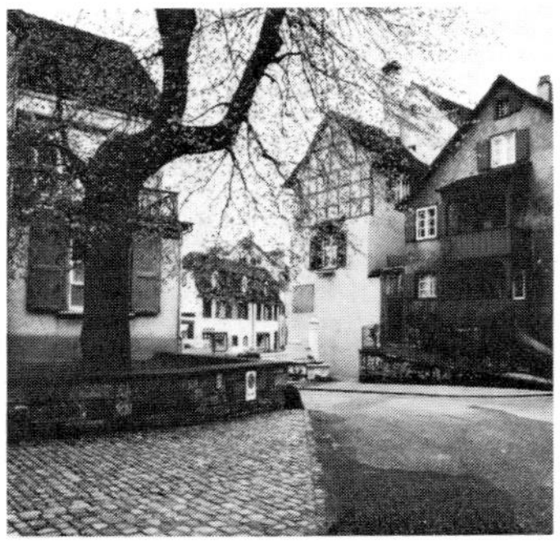

Basel; Rhine port and major industrial and communications centre of NW Switzerland.

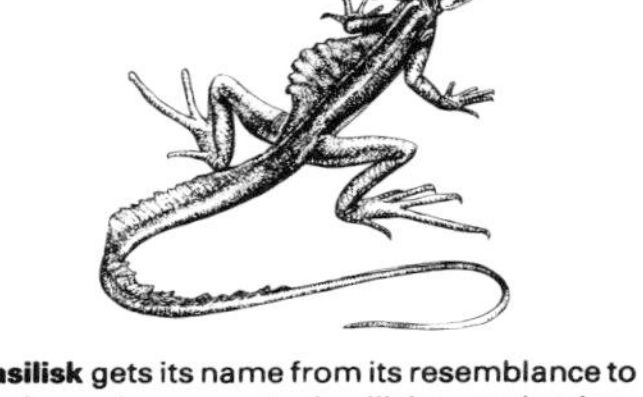

Basilisk gets its name from its resemblance to the legendary monster basilisk or cockatrice.

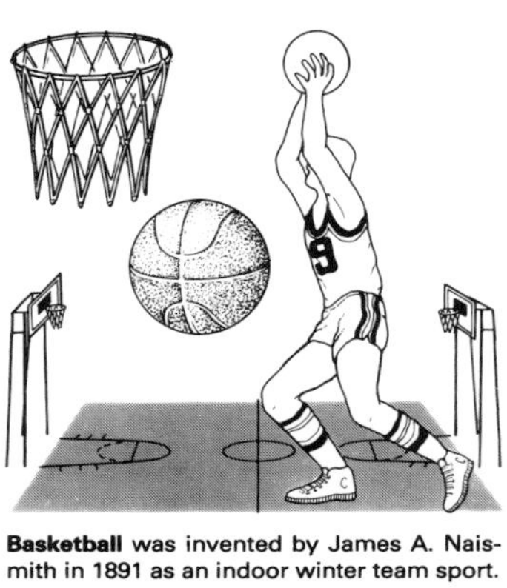

Basketball was invented by James A. Naismith in 1891 as an indoor winter team sport.

polar expeditions. Later he commanded his own expeditions to the Arctic, including voyages to Greenland, Alaska, Siberia and Labrador.

Bartók, Béla (1881–1945), Hungarian composer. With Zoltán KODÁLY, Bartók amassed a definitive collection of Hungarian folk-music that became the basis of many of his compositions. His orchestral works include *Music for Strings, Percussion, and Celesta* (1936), *Violin Concerto No.2* (1938) and *Concerto for Orchestra* (1943), and he wrote one opera *Bluebeard's Castle.* His six string quartets have been described as the finest since Beethoven. He was also a pianist and composed three piano concertos and a six-volume set of piano pieces, *Mikrokosmos. See also* HC2 pp. 121, 270–271.

Bartolommeo della Porta, Fra (1475–1517), Florentine RENAISSANCE painter and draughtsman, who collaborated (*c.*1509–12) with ALBERTINELLI. He was deeply influenced by RAPHAEL. His finest work includes *Vision of St Bernard* (1504–07).

Barton, Clara (1821–1912), US humanitarian, founder of the American National Red Cross in 1882. She was responsible for the "American amendment" at the 1884 Geneva Convention which enabled the Red Cross to be active in peacetime emergencies, such as natural disasters.

Barton, Sir Derek Harold Richard (1918–), British chemist who did innovatory research into conformational analysis – the study of the geometric structure of complex molecules. He was professor of organic chemistry at Birkbeck College, London (1953–55), professor of chemistry at Glasgow University (1955–57) and later professor of organic chemistry at Imperial College, London. He shared the 1969 Nobel Prize in chemistry with Odd HASSEL of Norway.

Barton, Sir Edmund (1849–1920), first Prime Minister of Australia (1901–03). Born in Sydney, he qualified as a barrister and became a member of the New South Wales parliament in 1879. Disliking party tensions, he soon resigned as prime minister, and served as a senior High Court judge until his death. *See also* HC2 pp.126–127.

Barton, Otis. *See* BEEBE, CHARLE WILLIAM.

Baruch, Book of, biblical book included in the APOCRYPHA. It consists of an introduction, believed to have been written by Baruch (*fl.* 600 BC), the disciple of JEREMIAH; a liturgical confession; a sermon and a set of canticles.

Baryon, any of the heavier sub-atomic ELEMENTARY PARTICLES, such as PROTONS and NEUTRONS. Their corresponding anti-particles are called antibaryons. The difference between the number of baryons and antibaryons in a system is called the baryon number. *See also* LEPTON.

Baryshnikov, Mikhail (1948–), ballet dancer, *b.* in the USSR. He was a member of the Kirov Ballet in Leningrad from 1969 to 1974, when he defected from the USSR. He has toured Australia and various European countries and performed with the AMERICAN BALLET THEATER.

Basalt, hard, fine-grained IGNEOUS ROCK, which may be INTRUSIVE or extrusive. Its colour can be dark green, brown, dark grey or black. If it originally solidified quickly it can have a glassy appearance. There are many types of basalt with different proportions of elements. It may be compact or vesicular (porous) because of gas bubbles contained in the lava while it was cooling. If the vesicles are subsequently filled with secondary minerals, eg quartz or calcite, it is called amygdaloidal basalt. Basalts are the main rocks in the world's major lava flows, eg the Deccan trap in India. *See also* PE pp.*83*, *100*, 101, 124.

Basalt ware, fine-grained unglazed stoneware, named after volcanic rock basalt. It was first manufactured (1768) by Josiah WEDGWOOD, who used it to imitate Classical originals, such as Greek vases, antique busts and jewellery.

Base, chemical compound that accepts protons, ie it has available electrons. Bases react with acids to form salts and water. Most are oxides or hydroxides of metals; others are compounds, such as ammonia and the amines, that yield hydroxide ions in water. Soluble bases (called ALKALIS) colour litmus blue. Strong bases are fully dissociated into ions; weak bases are partially dissociated in solution. *See also* ACID.

Base, in geometry, the side opposite the vertex from which an altitude is drawn in a triangle. The area of a triangle is one-half the product of the base and the height. *See also* SU pp.30, 46.

Baseball, sport popular in the USA (where it is the national game), Japan, the Caribbean and Latin America and gaining popularity in Australia. It is played by two opposing teams of nine players each – a pitcher, catcher, four infielders and three outfielders. A game is divided into nine innings; each team having three outs in an innings and runs being scored each time a player completes the circuit of four bases. Games tied at the end of nine innings are played until there is a winner. Baseball evolved from the old English game of rounders, played in the 19th century. The basic rules of the game were compiled by Alexander J. Cartwright in 1845. In the USA two leagues – the American and National – play a series of post-season games whereby the winners then compete in the World Series to decide the champion side.

Basel (Bâle, or Basle), city and river port in NW Switzerland, on the River Rhine; capital of Basel-Stadt canton. It joined the Swiss Confederation in 1501. It is an economic, financial and historically important intellectual centre. There is a cathedral, where ERASMUS is buried, a 15th-century university and a 16th-century town hall. Industries: publishing, silk, chemicals, food processing, metal goods. Pop. 212,860.

Basenji, ancient, deer-like, barkless hunting dog (hound group) native to central Africa. It has a flat head with rounded muzzle and wrinkled forehead. Standard size: 43cm (17in) at the shoulder; weight: 11kg (24lb).

Bashkir (Baškirskaja Autonomous SSR), region in the S Urals, E European USSR. A mountainous, forested area, it occupies the basins of the Belaya River and its tributary the Ufa. Its people, the Bashkirs, are mostly farmers or herdsmen and are Muslims. The capital is Ufa. There are valuable mineral deposits, including oil. Area: 141,007sq km (54,443sq miles). Pop. (1970) 3,819,000.

Bashkirtsev, Marya Konstantinovna (1860–84), Russian painter and author, a friend of Guy de MAUPASSANT. Her works include the pastel *Meeting* (1884) and her best-known writing was *Journal* (1887).

Basidiomycetes, class of FUNGI, including the jelly fungus, the bird's nest fungus, the ear fungus and mushrooms. They reproduce by sexual spores.

Basie, Count (1904–), US jazz bandleader, pianist and composer. He formed his own band in 1935, became a leading figure in the "swing" era, and has remained a popular performer. Many of his compositions, including *One O'Clock Jump,* have entered the jazz repertoire.

Basil, name of two Byzantine emperors, Basil I (*r.* 867–86) and Basil II (*r.* 960–1025). Basil I was the founder of the Macedonian dynasty. He was befriended by Emperor MICHAEL III, who assisted him in his rise to power. After Michael designated him co-emperor, Basil had his former patron murdered and assumed sole power in BYZANTIUM. Basil converted the Bulgars to Orthodox Christianity rather than Roman Catholicism. Basil II annexed Bulgaria in 1018 and later expanded the BYZANTINE EMPIRE by extending its eastern frontier to the Caucasus. *See also* HC1 pp.142–143, *147*.

Basil, common name for a tropical plant of the MINT family (Labiatae). It has white or purple flowers, and its dried leaves are used for flavouring. Species *Ocimum basilicum. See also* PE pp.*191*, *212*.

Basilar membrane, part of the COCHLEA, a structure in the inner EAR. *See* MS p.50.

Basildon, urban district in Essex, SE England, 40km (25 miles) ENE of London. The S part is a planned new town with factories nearby. Industries: milk bottling, printing, clothing, light engineering, chemicals. Pop. (1973) 135,720.

Basilica, in Roman architecture, a public hall used as a market or court-room and with the similar rectangular plan as a Greek temple. In Early Christian and later church architecture, it is a building consisting of a nave and aisles, with windows above the level of the aisle roofs.

Basilisk, semi-aquatic LIZARD found in trees near streams of tropical America. It has a compressed greenish body, whiplike tail, a crest along its back and an inflatable pouch on its head. It can run over water for short distances on its hindlegs, and eats plants and insects. Length: up to 61cm (2ft). Family Iguanidae; genus *Basiliscus. See also* NW p.134.

Basil the Great, Saint (*c.*330–79), Bishop of Caesarea and one of the three Cappadocian Fathers. He is recognized in both East and West as a Doctor of the Church. He is principally known for establishing the orthodoxy of the NICENE CREED over ARIANISM in Asia Minor and for laying down rules for monastic orders. Feast: 2 Jan. in the West; 1 Jan. in the East.

Basingstoke, town in N Hampshire, 74km (46 miles) WSW of London. For centuries a market town, it now has industries producing farm machinery, leather goods, textiles and clothing. Pop. (1971) 52,500.

Baskerville, John (1706–75), British printer and type designer. In 1750 he began experimenting with typefaces and in 1757 set up his own printing house. In 1758 he became printer to Cambridge University and produced many excellent books including editions of the Bible (1763) and Latin authors (1772–73). His typefaces remain in common use.

Basketball, ball game, originating in the USA, but now played throughout the world. It is played by two teams of five people, usually indoors on a court up to 28.7m (94ft) long and 15.2m (50ft) wide. At each end of the court is a backboard to which a bottomless netting basket is attached at right angles 3m (10ft) above the floor. The object of the game is to get the ball to drop down through the opposing team's basket, thus scoring a goal. Each field goal (thrown during normal play) counts two points and a successful free throw (unimpeded shot taken as a result of a penalty) counts as one point. The game was devised in 1891 by Dr James Naismith, a US physical education instructor. It has been part of the Olympic Games since 1936. *See also* MS p.*304*.

Baskin, Leonard (1922–), US sculptor and printmaker. His massive figures are sculpted in limestone, bronze and wood. His well-known works include *Blake* (1955), *Barlach Dead* (1959) and *Seated Man With Owl* (1959).

Basle. *See* BASEL.

Basov, Nikolai Gennadiyevich (1922–), Soviet physicist who did pioneer work on the development of MASERS, which led in turn to LASERS. For this contribution to science Basov and his co-worker Alexandr PROKHOROV shared the 1964 Nobel Prize in physics with the US physicist Charles TOWNES (who had made similar discoveries independently).

Basques, indigenous people of N Spain and SW France, numbering about 3,900,000. Their language is not related to any other European tongue. Throughout history they have tenaciously maintained their cultural identity. The kingdom of NAVARRE, which existed for 350 years, was the home of most of the Basques; after its dissolution in 1512 most of the Spanpsh Basques enjoyed a degree of political autonomy. This autonomy was taken away in 1873, and Basque unrest followed. In 1977 the Spanish government promised renewed autonomy to the Basques.

Basra (al-Basrah), city and only port in Iraq, on the River Shatt al-Arab; capital of Basra province. After harbour renovations, the building of a railway link to Baghdad and the discovery of large oil-fields nearby in the early 20th century, it has thriven as a commercial and industrial centre. Industries include oil refining, flour milling, wool. Pop. (1965) 313,327.

Bass, George (*c.*1771–*c.*1803), British explorer. With Matthew FLINDERS he explored parts of the coast near Sydney, Australia, that were as yet unmapped, and in 1798 they circumnavigated Tasmania. The dividing strait they found is now named BASS STRAIT. In 1803 Bass disappeared while on a voyage to South America. *See also* HC2 pp.124–125, *125.*
Bass, Sam (1851–78), US bandit. He led a band of bank and train robbers in Texas, but had little success until 1877 when his gang stole $60,000 in gold from a Union Pacific train at Big Springs. One of his men betrayed him to the Texas Rangers, and he was killed at Round Rock in a shootout with the Rangers.
Bass, term denoting low or deep pitch, used of the lowest-pitched part of a composition, or the lowest-pitched member of a family of instruments, and of a male singing voice that descends to the F below the bass stave.
Bass, any of several bony fishes, both freshwater and marine, and not all closely related. They include the white, black, striped, rock and calico basses. *See also* PE p.*244, 246,* 247.
Bassani, Giorgio (1916–), Italian novelist. He examined the life of Ferrara's Jews under FASCISM in the collection of short stories *A Prospect of Ferrara* (1955) and the novel *The Garden of the Finzi-Continis* (1962). His other works include *The Gold-Rimmed Spectacles* (1958) and a collection of poetry, *L'alba ai vetri* (1942–50).
Bassano, Jacopo (*c.*1517–92), Venetian painter of the late RENAISSANCE, the most talented of a family of five painters. After 1540 he was heavily influenced by the Florentine and Roman MANNERISTS. His portraits and religious paintings are noted for the realism of their landscape settings. His works include *Flight into Egypt* (1536) and *Adoration of the Shepherds* (*c.*1540).
Bass drum. *See* DRUM.
Bassein, city and river port in SW Burma, on the Irrawaddy Delta, approx. 145km (90 miles) W of Rangoon; it is the capital of Bassein district and the Irrawaddy division. Captured by the Japanese in 1942, it was retaken by Allied forces in 1945. Industries: rice mills, machine shops and fancy goods. Pop. 175,000.
Basse-Terre, city and port in the French West Indies; it is the capital of Guadeloupe département. Founded by the French in 1643, it is an important trade centre serving the surrounding agricultural region. Pop. 16,000.
Basseterre, town in the West Indies, on St Kitts island in the Leeward Islands group; capital of the British Associated State of St Kitts-Nevis. Founded in 1627, it is an important commercial centre, with a sugar-refining industry. Pop. 14,000.
Basset horn, musical instrument resembling a bass CLARINET in appearance but without the horizontal mouthpiece. MOZART wrote chamber music for the instrument and Richard Strauss employed it in some of his operas. The basset horn is usually replaced in modern performances by the alto clarinet.
Basset hound, short-legged hunting dog (a type of HOUND) originally bred in France to flush out game such as rabbits and pheasants from thick ground cover. After the BLOODHOUND, it has the most highly developed sense of smell among dogs. Bassets have long bodies and long floppy ears which, when the dog is following a scent, touch the ground. The short coat is generally tan and white. Standard size: 30–38cm (12–15in) at the shoulder; weight: 11.3–22.7kg (25–50lb).
Bassoon, bass WOODWIND instrument with a range of three octaves, corresponding to that of the CELLO. It has a double-reed mouthpiece and a conical bore, the tube bending back on itself to reduce the instrument's length. Bassoons are used in symphonic and chamber music.
Bass Rock, small island in the Firth of Forth, Scotland; the lava plug of an extinct volcano. It provides a nesting ground for many kinds of sea-birds. St Baldred lived there until his death in 756.
Bass Strait, channel between Tasmania and Victoria, SE Australia. In 1798 Matthew FLINDERS and George BASS discovered the Strait, thus proving that Tasmania was not part of the Australian continent. It has natural gas and oil deposits and rich fishing grounds. Width: 129–241km (80–150 miles).
Bast, also Bastet and Pasht, ancient Egyptian goddess of the city of Bubastis, depicted as a lion-headed woman crowned with the solar disc and sacred asp, or as a cat-headed goddess with the sistrum, or ritual rattle; in the latter form she is Pasht, the personification of life and fecundity. Two festivals were held in her honour, one at Bubastis and the second and lesser at Memphis.
Bast, type of vegetable fibre or matting made from the inner bark (phloem) of plants. Examples include JUTE, HEMP and FLAX. *See also* PE p.216.
Bastard feudalism. *See* FEUDAL SYSTEM.
Bastia, city in NE Corsica, France, on the Tyrrhenian Sea, 35km (22 miles) S of Cape Corse. Founded in the 14th century by the Genoese, it was the Corsican capital until 1791 and is still the chief commercial city. It has a citadel built in the 16th-17th centuries and many old buildings. Industries: tourism, food processing, timber. Pop. (1968) 49,375.
Bastien-Lepage, Jules (1848–84), French painter who produced mainly peasant scenes, although his best-known work is probably *Jeanne d'Arc.*
Bastille, 14th-century fort and prison in Paris. Political prisoners were often incarcerated there and it became a symbol of royal oppression in the 18th century. On 14 July 1789 a Parisian mob stormed it, captured the ammunition store and released its prisoners (only seven, none of whom was political). Its governor was killed, its troops surrendered and the fort was pulled down. The incident marked the beginning of the FRENCH REVOLUTION and its anniversary (14 July) is celebrated as the major holiday in France. *See also* HC2 pp.74–75.
Basutoland. *See* LESOTHO.
Bat, only MAMMAL that has controlled flight (although a few others can glide). Bats are nocturnal and found in all tropical and temperate regions. Most are brown, grey or black. A bat's wing is formed by a sheet of skin stretched over a frame of greatly elongated "arm" and "hand" bones. Bats are able to navigate in complete darkness by means of a kind of SONAR, which uses echoes of the bat's own supersonic squeaks to locate obstacles and prey. Many bats live largely on insects, some are carnivorous, some drink blood, some live on nectar and pollen and one group – the flying foxes – subsists on fruit. Most are small, although they range in wingspan from 25 to as much as 147cm (10–58in). The 178 genera of bats make up the order Chiroptera. *See also* NW pp.161, *206,* 211, *228.*
Bataan, province of the Philippines, on the peninsula of Luzon Island that extends S from the W central coast, shielding Manila Bay from the South China Sea; the capital is Balangos. Densely forested on the W side, the population is concentrated in the E. There was heavy fighting there during WWII. Products: rice, sugar cane. Area: 1,373sq km (530sq miles). Pop. (1970) 214,100.
Batak, people (five tribes) and language of Sumatra, Indonesia, centred around Lake Toba; part of the Malay group of peoples and languages. They have a christianized, patrilineal, agricultural society and grow mainly rice and maize. The language has a very simple phonetic structure.
Batambang (Bătdâmbăng), second-largest town in Cambodia and the capital of Batambang province, W Cambodia. It was ceded to Thailand in 1809, became part of French Indo-China in 1907, and was returned to Cambodia in 1946. It is a market centre in a major rice-producing area. Pop. 39,000.
Batangas, province of the Philippines, on the SW tip of Luzon Island; the capital is Batangas. Mountainous and largely forested, it contains Lake Taal, 243sq km (94sq miles) in area, and a nearby volcano that erupted in 1965 causing many deaths. Products: rice, cocoa, coffee, timber. Area: 3,165sq km (1,222sq miles). Pop. (1970) 926,308.
Batan Islands (Batanese), island group between Luzon Island, Philippines, and Formosa; it is the northernmost province of the Philippines. The main islands are Itbayat, Sabtang and Batan, which has the capital, Basco. Industries: corn, rice, coal-mining. Area: 205sq km (80sq miles). Pop. 11,000.
Batavi (Batavians), ancient Germanic tribe that settled in the Rhine-Meuse delta in the 1st century BC. Famous as warriors, they served in the Roman army. In about AD 70 Claudius Civilis led them in an unsuccessful revolt against Roman rule. In the 4th century they were displaced by the Salian Franks.
Batavia. *See* DJAKARTA.
Batavian Republic, name of The Netherlands when it was reorganized and occupied by French forces from 1795 to 1806.
Bates, Alan (1934–), British actor. He has won acclaim for his sensitive performances on stage and in films. His main films include *The Caretaker* (1963), *The Fixer* (1968), *Women in Love* (1970) and *The Go-Between* (1971).
Bates, Daisy (*c.*1860–1951), British welfare worker who spent 35 years of her life among the Australian ABORIGINES. She wrote *The Passing of the Aborigines* (1938).
Bates, Henry Walter (1825–92), British naturalist. His work on the natural selection in animal MIMICRY lent support to Charles Darwin's theory of evolution. Bates collected 14,712 unknown species of insects on a trip to the Amazon (1848–59) and recounted his experiences in *The Naturalist on the River Amazon* (1863). *See also* NATURAL SELECTION.
Bates, Herbert Ernest (1905–74), British novelist and short-story writer, notable for his descriptions of England and its countryside. His novels include *Fair Stood the Wind for France* (1944), *The Jacaranda Tree* (1949), *The Darling Buds of May* (1958) and *Oh! To Be in England* (1963).
Bateson, William (1861–1926), British biologist. He founded and named the science of GENETICS. Bateson translated much of Gregor MENDEL's pioneering work on inheritance in plants, so bringing it recognition. By his own experiments he also extended Mendel's theories to animals, which provided a foundation for the modern understanding of heredity. *See also* NW pp.30–35.
Bath, city in Avon, SW England, situated on the River Avon, 19km (12 miles) SE of Bristol. Hot springs were discovered there by the Romans in the 1st century AD and have been used ever since to treat rheumatism, arthritis and gout. In the 18th century the city became a fashionable resort. Many fine Georgian streets remain from the city's expansion at that time. Each June a festival of music and drama is held. Industries: printing, electrical engineering and clothing. Pop. (1970 est.) 84,800.
Bath, Knights of the, second highest order of knighthood in Britain. Founded by Henry IV in 1399, it fell into disuse but was revived by George I in 1725. The sovereign confers the title on members of the armed forces, scientists, artists, scholars and other distinguished citizens. Women were first admitted to the order in 1971. *See also* GARTER, ORDER OF THE.
Batholith, huge mass of igneous rock at the earth's surface that has an exposed surface of more than 104sq km (40sq miles). It may have originated as an intrusive igneous structure that was gradually eroded and which became surface material. *See also* PE pp.100, 101.
Báthory, noble Hungarian family. Its most notable member was Stephen, King of Poland (1575–86). Stephen's brother Christoph succeeded him as Prince of Transylvania (1575–81). Christoph's son Sigismund (1572–1613), Prince of Transylvania from 1581, abdicated in favour of Emperor Rudolf in 1598 and later tried unsuccessfully to regain his throne. Stephen's son, Gabriel, was ousted from the throne and murdered in 1613.

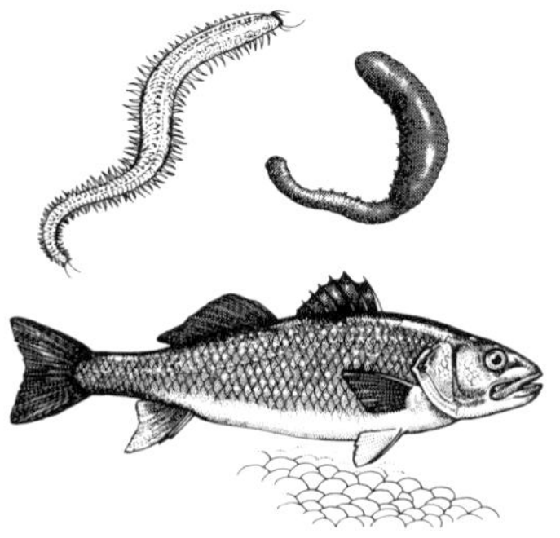

Bass; name of several sea and freshwater fish caught by fishermen around the world.

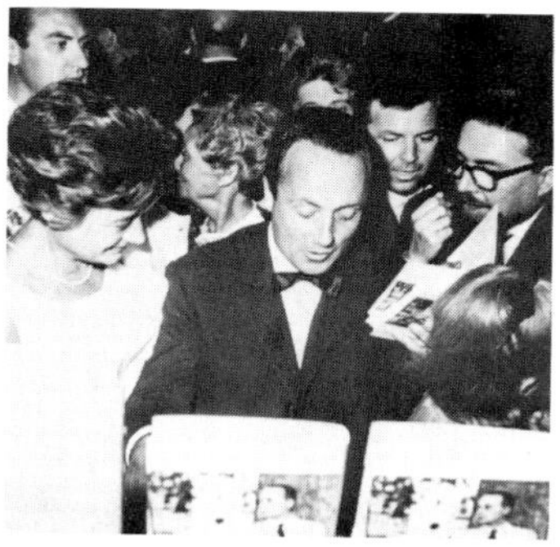

Giorgio Bassani, the Italian novelist who wrote *The Garden of the Finzi-Continis.*

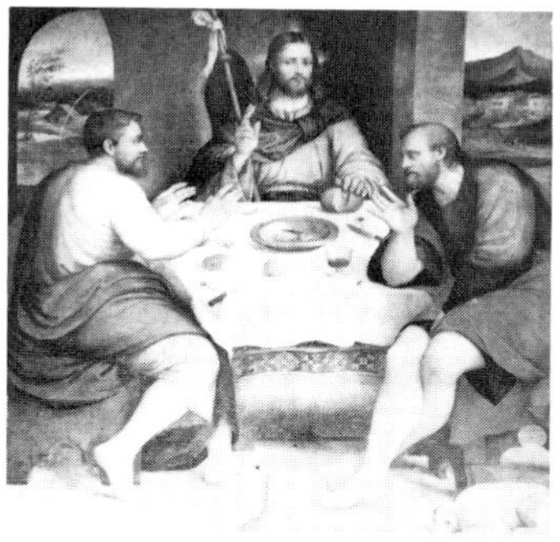

Jacopo Bassano, whose genuine works are rare; this is his *Supper at Emmaus.*

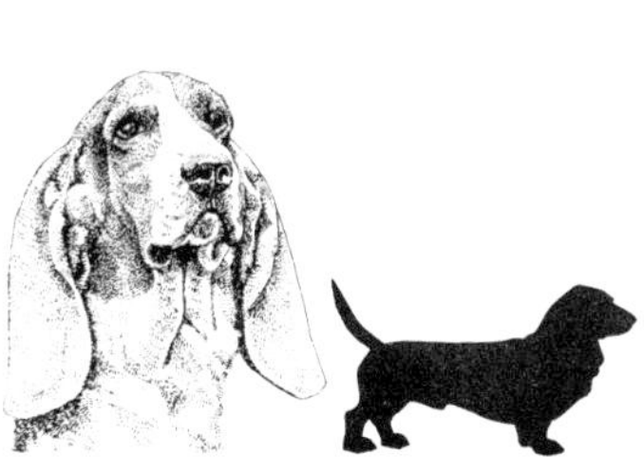

Basset hounds were bred originally in the 1700s by the Abbots of St Hubert in France.

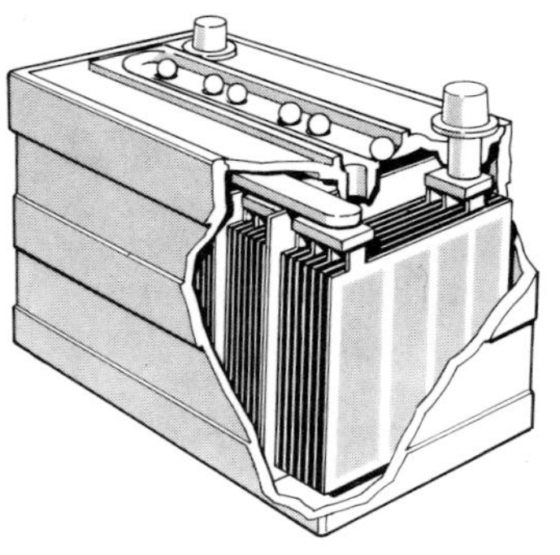

Batteries of the lead-acid automobile type are re-charged by current from the dynamo.

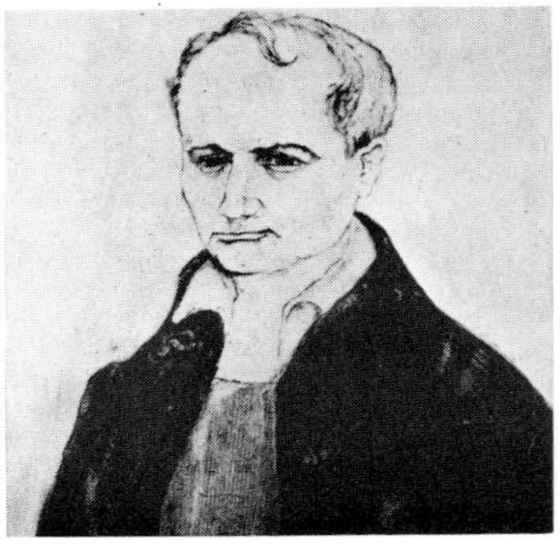

Charles Baudelaire, poet who explored the irrational and symbolic elements of man.

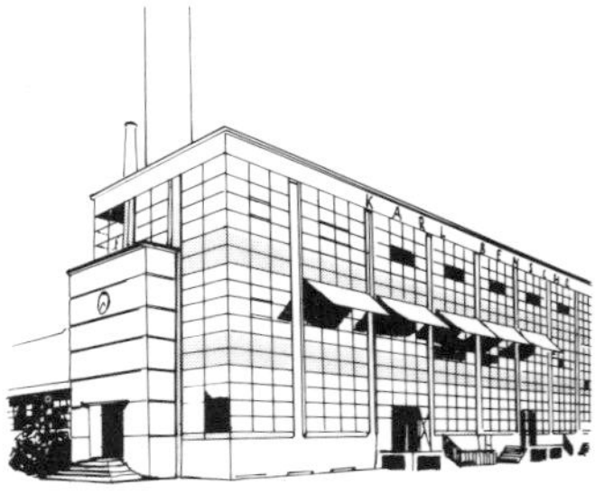

Bauhaus; German school of design which has influenced art education everywhere.

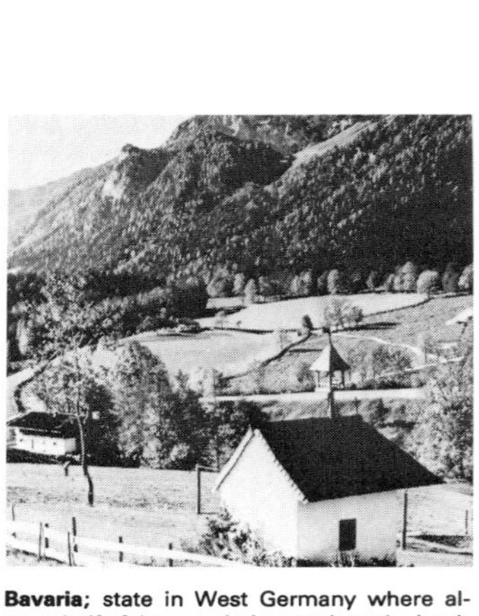

Bavaria; state in West Germany where almost half of the population work on the land.

Baths, public bathing facilities. Originally public baths were probably related to religious ritual. The first baths were made in ancient Egypt and the Indus River Valley. The ancient Greeks built elaborate public baths, which were copied and further embellished with mosaics and gilt details by the Romans. Water, brought by a system of pipelines and aqueducts from reservoirs, was heated in pipes. The grandest Roman baths, now ruined, were built by three emperors: TITUS in AD 81, CARACALLA in 217, and DIOCLETIAN in 302. Even more richly designed baths were built in Islamic lands, including the baths of the Alhambra in Granada, Spain, which were built in the 14th century. *See also* HC1 pp.*94*, 104, 108.

Bathsheba, in the Bible, wife of Uriah the Hittite and, later, wife of DAVID, who arranged Uriah's death in battle. SOLOMON was one of her sons by David.

Bathurst (Gambia). *See* BANJUL.

Bathurst, city in New South Wales, SE Australia, on the Macquarie River. Founded in 1815, this tourist centre is noted for its trout fishing. Industries: mining, fruit growing, food processing, tobacco, wheat. Pop. 17,200.

Bathurst, town in NE New Brunswick, Canada, on Nepisiguit Bay. Founded in 1818 as St Peters, becoming Bathurst in 1826, it is a popular holiday resort. Industries: paper, mining, fishing. Pop. (1971) 16,404.

Bathyal zone, region of the ocean floor from the edge of the continental shelf, about 133m (436ft) in depth, to about 2,000m (6,560ft), where the ABYSSAL PLAIN begins. Only a feeble light penetrates to the upper layers of this zone. *See also* PE pp.90–91.

Bathysphere and bathyscaphe, manned vehicles for deep-sea exploration. The bathysphere, invented by Otis Barton in the USA, has steel walls and toughened glass windows several inches thick. Used mainly during the 1930s it was released from a surface vessel and descended to depths greater than 900m (2,950ft). The bathyscaphe, an improved version invented by August PICCARD of Switzerland, has the bathysphere slung below a tank which can be sunk or made buoyant in a controlled manner. This reached even greater depths. *See also* MM p.119; PE pp.92–93.

Bathythermograph, instrument that simultaneously measures the temperature and depth of the sea to a depth of 300m (1,000ft). *See also* PE p.91.

Batik, method of decorating textiles, practised for centuries in Indonesia and introduced into Europe by Dutch traders. Molten wax is applied to the parts of a fabric that are to remain undyed, before the fabric is dipped into cool vegetable dye. The fabric is then dipped in hot water to remove the wax from the undyed areas. The process may be repeated, using different coloured dyes.

Batista y Zaldivar, Fulgencio (1901–73), Cuban political leader. A sergeant in the army, he led a successful coup in 1933. From then until 1940 he ruled through figurehead presidents. In 1940 he was elected president. He retired in 1944 and moved to Florida, but in 1952 a military coup returned him to power. In 1959 he was overthrown by Fidel CASTRO.

Batlle y Ordóñez, José (1856–1929), Uruguayan President (1903–07; 1911–15), and leader of the Colorado Party. He initiated an extensive social welfare programme, and at his urging the country adopted a nine-man National Council of Administration that shared power with the President (1917). *See also* URUGUAY.

Batoidei, or Batoidea. *See* RAY.

Battambang. *See* BATAMBANG.

Batten, Jean Gardner (1909–), New Zealand aviator who in 1935 became the first woman to make the solo flight from Australia to Britain (having made the Britain-Australia flight the year before). She also flew solo across the S Atlantic Ocean to South America and in 1936 and 1937 established records for the fastest flights between Britain and Australia.

Battenberg, German family. In the 19th century the titles Prince or Princess of Battenberg were bestowed on the grandchildren of the Grand Duke of Hesse-Darmstadt. One of them, Louis Battenberg (1854–1921), became an English admiral, was created marquess of Milford Haven, and married a grand-daughter of Queen VICTORIA. The English branch of the Battenbergs anglicized the name to Mountbatten during WWI. Prince PHILIP, Duke of Edinburgh, is a Mountbatten.

Battery, collection of cells that convert energy, usually chemical, into direct current electricity. Primary batteries, such as those in a torch, are not rechargeable; storage batteries (accumulators) are recharged when a current in the reverse direction restores the original chemical state. *See also* SU pp.*68*, 115, 148.

Battery, in law, illegal violent beating of one person by another. In some cases the use of reasonable force is permissible, eg in self-defence or when punishing a child. *See also* ASSAULT.

Batthyány, Lajos (*c.* 1806–49), premier of the first Hungarian ministry, a leader of the revolution of 1848 who tried to prevent a total break with Austria. He was executed on 6 Oct. 1849.

Battleaxe, broad-headed hewing weapon, used particularly in the early Middle Ages. *See* MM pp.160–161.

Battlecruiser. *See* CRUISER.

Battle of the Books, The (1704), prose satire by Jonathan SWIFT in defence of the "ancients". In it books representing ancient and modern authors "battle" to decide if the ancients should continue to take precedence on Mt Parnassus.

Battle of... *See* second part of name.

Battleship, most powerful type of naval warship in use during the late 19th and early 20th centuries, the largest displacing 72,000 tonnes. Battleships combined the thickest armour and the most powerful naval guns. In addition to their main gun batteries, housed in armoured turrets, most were armed with smaller batteries for combating lighter enemy warships and, later, automatic weapons for defence against aircraft. *See also* AIRCRAFT CARRIER; MM p.174.

Battleship Potemkin (1925), film directed by S. M. EISENSTEIN and starring A. Antonov, Vladimir Barski and Grigori Alexandrov. Made to commemorate the 1905 Russian revolution, it has great dramatic power and startling effects, and immediately won world acclaim. *See also* HC2 p.*201*.

Batu, group of islands in Indonesia, in the Indian Ocean off the W coast of Sumatra. There are three main islands, Pini, Tanahmasa and Tanahbala, and approx. 50 islets. The land is low-lying and forested. Products: copra, coconut oil. Area: 1,200sq km (463sq miles). Pop. 13,100.

Batumi (Batum), city and major port in SW Georgia, USSR, on the Black Sea near the Turkish border; capital of Adzhar ASSR. The Russians annexed it from the Turks in 1878. It is a commercial centre with an oil pipeline terminus and a Soviet naval base. Industries: oil refining, shipbuilding, food processing, engineering. Pop. (1970 prelim.) 101,000.

Bat Yam, city in W central Israel, a suburb of Tel Aviv-Jaffa (Yafo), on the Mediterranean Sea. It is an industrial area and a tourist resort. Industries: engineering, printing, publishing. Pop. (1970 est.) 83,500.

Baudelaire, Charles Pierre (1821–67), French poet and critic. His first volume of poetry, *Les Fleurs du Mal* (1857), was the introduction of SYMBOLISM. The poetic theory of correspondences – of scent, sound, colour – was explored and the aesthetic creed of the inseparability of beauty and corruption proclaimed. The poems were condemned by the censor and six of them suppressed. Baudelaire was much influenced by Edgar Allan POE, whose poetry he translated and whose works figure prominently in his major pieces of criticism, *Curiosités Esthetiques* (1868) and *L'Art Romantique* (1868). *See also* HC2 pp.100–101.

Baudot, Jean-Maurice-Emile (1845–1903), French electrical engineer who devised a telegraph code that used the presence or absence of an electrical pulse, rather than the short and long pulses of the MORSE CODE. He also invented a distributor system which permitted several messages to be transmitted along the same wire. *See also* MM p.225.

Baudouin (1930–), King of Belgium (1951–). During WWII he was interned by the Germans and after the war joined his father, Leopold III, in exile (1945–50) in Switzerland. His father abdicated in 1951 and Baudouin became king. He granted independence to the Belgian Congo in 1960.

Bauhaus, school for architects and artists founded in 1919 at Weimar, Germany by Walter GROPIUS. Such diverse talents as those of Marcel BREUER, Paul KLEE, Wassily KANDINSKY, Lazlo MOHOLY-NAGY and Ludwig MIES VAN DER ROHE worked together to produce a distinctly modern approach to design. The Bauhaus style emphasized craftsmanship and its architecture, in particular, was severely functional. In 1925 the Bauhaus moved to Dessau where its buildings, designed by Gropius, exemplified its ideals. In 1928 Mies van der Rohe succeeded as director. The Bauhaus was closed by the Nazis in 1933. Many of its members moved to the USA, where Chicago became the Bauhaus centre, with Moholy-Nagy as its new director (1937). *See also* HC2 pp.179, *325*.

Bauhin, Gaspard (1560–1624), Swiss anatomist and botanist. He gave a scientific binomial system of classification to anatomy and botany and was the first to describe the ileocaecal valve (Bauhin's valve) between the large and small intestines.

Baum, Vicki (1888–1960), US author, *b.* Austria. Her best-known works include *Grand Hotel* (1929), a novel that became both a successful play and a film, and *Grand Opera* (1942).

Baumé, Antoine (1728–1804), French chemist. He invented the Baumé hydrometer which utilized the Baumé scales (one scale is used for liquids less dense than water, one for liquids denser than water). He also improved bleaching and saltpetre purification processes.

Baumgarten, Alexander Gottlieb (1714–62), German philosopher, considered to be a disciple of Christian WOLFF. His ambitious system is now chiefly remembered for the *Aesthetica* (1750–58). The word AESTHETICS, in its modern use, was devised by him.

Bauxite, the mineral from which nearly all aluminium is extracted. Chemically it is an hydrated aluminium oxide (ALUMINA), $Al_2O_3.2H_2O$. Large deposits occur in France, Hungary, the USA, Guyana, Jamaica, Surinam, Italy, Greece and the USSR. *See also* MM pp.34–35; PE pp.*97*, 133.

Bavaria (Bayern), largest state in West Germany, bounded by East Germany in the N, Hesse and Baden-Württemberg in the W, Austria in the S and Czechoslovakia in the E; Munich is the capital. Part of the Roman Empire until the 6th century, it was taken by CHARLEMAGNE in 788 and formed part of the Holy Roman Empire until the 10th century. Incorporated into Germany in 1871, it became a state within the German Federal Republic in 1946. Industries: glass, porcelain and brewing. Area: 70,511sq km (26,224sq miles). Pop. 10,820,900.

Bax, Sir Arnold (1883–1953), British composer. His works include symphonies, three symphonic poems (which made his reputation) and piano and chamber compositions. He was knighted in 1937 and became Master of the King's Musick in 1941.

Baxter, James Keir (1926–72), New Zealand poet, critic and dramatist. His several verse collections include *The Fallen House* (1953) and *Pig Island Letters* (1966). Among his other works are *Recent Trends in New Zealand Poetry* (1951) and *The Iron Breadboard* (1957).

Bay, tree or shrub of the laurel family, the leaves of some varieties being commonly used as flavouring in cooking. In the Classical tradition, head wreaths of bay leaves were awarded as tokens of honour to conquerors and bards. Bay should not be confused with the cherry laurel, a common evergreen shrub of another family, the leaves of which are poisonous. Family Lauraceae; species *Laurus nobilis*. *See also* NW p.*65*.

Bayamón, town in NE Puerto Rico, 8km (5 miles) SW of the capital San Juan. Founded in 1772, it is one of the island's oldest settlements. Situated in a fertile fruit-growing region, it is a residential suburb of the capital. Pop. (1970) 147,552.

Bayard, Pierre de Terrail, Seigneur de (*c.*1473–1524), French military hero of the Italian wars. In 1521, against overwhelming odds, he held Mézières against an attack by the forces of Emperor Charles V. He was known as the *Chevalier sans peur et sans reproche* (knight without fear or reproach).

Bayern. *See* BAVARIA.

Bayeux tapestry (*c.*1080), strip of linen embroidered in wool, measuring 70m × 48cm (231ft × 19in) and depicting in more than 70 scenes the life of King Harold of England and the NORMAN CONQUEST. An unfounded tradition attributes its design to Matilda, wife of William the Conqueror, but it was probably commissioned by William's half-brother Odo, Bishop of Bayeux. *See also* HC1 pp.*165, 168*.

Baykal, Lake. *See* BAIKAL.

Bayle, Pierre (1647–1706), French Protestant philosopher. Forced into exile, he taught philosophy at Rotterdam (1681). He argued against superstition in *Thoughts on the Comet* (1682) and advocated toleration and PYRRHONIAN scepticism in the erudite *Historical and Critical Dictionary* (1690–1702). The French ENLIGHTENMENT claimed Bayle's critical approach to tradition as an inspiration.

Baylis, Lilian Mary (1874–1937), British theatrical manager. From 1898 she managed the Royal Victoria Coffee Music Hall, where in 1912 she created the Old Vic Company. She produced both opera and drama, and in 1914 began the regular Shakespearean seasons which established her reputation. In 1931 she took over SADLER'S WELLS for the production of opera and ballet exclusively.

Bayliss, Sir William Maddock (1860–1924), British physiologist. He studied blood pressure, circulation and digestion, and with Professor Ernest H. Starling discovered (1902) secretin, a hormone secreted by the DUODENUM.

Bay of Islands, on the NE coast of New Zealand's North Island, has about 150 tiny islands, some Maori reserves. Tourist attractions include big-game fishing. The main towns include RUSSELL, New Zealand's first capital.

Bay of Pigs invasion (1961), unsuccessful effort by Cuban exiles to overthrow Fidel CASTRO by invading the S coast of CUBA near the Bay of Pigs. About 1,500 Cubans, trained, equipped and transported by the USA, were involved. John KENNEDY, the US president, initially denied but then accepted US involvement in the invasion attempt. *See also* HC2 p.*255*.

Bayreuth, city in Bavaria, West Germany, where the WAGNER Festival is held at intervals. The festivals are held in the *Festspielhaus*, which was built to Wagner's specification, for the performance of his music dramas. The first festival was held in 1876.

Bazaine, Achille François (1811–88), French army officer. He served in the Crimean War (1854–56) and in Mexico in 1863. He commanded French troops in the Franco-Prussian War (1870–71), although his incompetence led to the disaster at Sedan, in which Emperor Napoleon III and his army were captured. Convicted of treason in 1873 – for intrigues with the Germans during the war – Bazaine escaped and lived thereafter in exile. *See also* FRANCO-PRUSSIAN WAR.

Bazin, René Francois Nicolas Marie (1853–1932), French novelist and biographer, who also wrote books on travel. His writings portrayed the realities, beauty and social problems of simple rural dwellers in France.

Bazooka, portable rocket launcher with a calibre of 60mm (2.36in), developed in the USA during WWII. It was used with considerable success by infantry against tanks and small fortified emplacements. *See also* MM p.169.

BBC (British Broadcasting Corporation), state-financed radio and television network. Its directors are appointed by the government, but in terms of policy and content, the BBC is largely independent. It was set up in 1927 to replace the British Broadcasting Company that had been in operation since 1922. Its first director-general (1927–38) was Lord REITH, whose philosophy of the BBC as an instrument of education and civilization has greatly shaped the policies of the corporation.

BCG (Bacillus Calmette-Guérin), vaccine against tuberculosis. It was named after its discoverers, the French bacteriologists Albert Calmette and Camille Guérin.

Beach, the gently sloping zone of the shore, covered by sediment, sand or pebbles, that extends from the low-water line to the limit of the highest storm waves. The sediment is derived from coastal erosion or river alluvium. Waves breaking on the beach move the sediment back and forth so the heavier pebbles remain on the upper beach and the sand works downwards towards the water.

Beach Boys, US rock group, formed in 1961, which made its name with records about surfing. Their main hits included *Surfin' USA* (1963), *I Get Around* (1964), *Help Me Rhonda* (1965) and *Good Vibrations* (1966).

Beachy Head, promontory on the S coast of England, between Eastbourne and Seaford, on the English Channel. There is a chalk cliff 175m (575ft) high and a famous lighthouse. In 1690 the French defeated the English and Dutch forces there. *See also* MW p.69.

Beacon, radio, navigational aid for ships and aircraft. It consists of a transmitter and an aerial which broadcast radio signals of a fixed frequency, peculiar to one beacon only. A navigator can find his position from the bearings of two beacons, using a DIRECTIONAL AERIAL to receive the signals. *See also* MM p.*187*.

Beaconsfield, Earl of *See* DISRAELI.

Beaconsfield, residential town in Buckinghamshire, S central England, 35km (22 miles) NW of London. Edmund WALLER and Edmund BURKE both lived there, as did Benjamin DISRAELI, who became the Earl of Beaconsfield in 1876. Pop. (1971) 11,900.

Beadle, George Wells (1903–) US biologist. During his study of mutations in the bread mould *Neurospora crassa*, he and Edward TATUM found that genes are responsible for ENZYME synthesis and that these enzymes control each step of all biochemical reactions occurring in an organism. For this discovery they shared with J. Lederberg the 1958 Nobel Prize in physiology and medicine.

Beagle, hunting DOG, (HOUND group) used in packs to chase and follow small game. Of ancient origin, the modern breed was developed in England in the mid-1800s. It has a long, slightly domed head with a medium, square-cut muzzle, long, hanging ears and widely set, large, gentle eyes. Average size: (two varieties) up to 33cm (13in) at the shoulder and not exceeding 38cm (15in); weight: 8–14kg (18–31lb).

Beagle, HMS, British survey ship that carried Charles DARWIN as ship's naturalist on his famous expedition. The *Beagle* left England in Dec. 1831 and for five years explored parts of South America and the Pacific islands. *See also* NW pp.32–33.

Beaglehole, John Cawte (1901–71), New Zealand historian. His works include *The Exploration of the Pacific* (1934), *The Discovery of New Zealand* (1939) and an edition of the journals of James COOK. He became professor of Commonwealth history at Wellington's Victoria University in 1963.

Beak, or bill, horny or stiff animal mouthparts, projecting or pointed. Beaks are found among cephalopods, some insects, some fish and all egg-laying mammals, including some whales and turtles and birds. Bird bills are adapted to many functions: grasping, preening, seed-cracking, piercing, tearing, nectar-sipping, stabbing and display. *See also* NW p.*143*.

Beaked whale, small to medium-sized toothed WHALE with a distinct beak. It dives swiftly and deep for fish and CEPHALOPODS. It is also called the bottle-nosed whale. Length: 4–13m (13–44ft). Family, Hyperoodontidae. *See also* DOLPHIN; PORPOISE; NW p.*167*.

Beaker culture, distinctive culture that spread throughout Europe in the late 3rd millennium BC. It was characterized by its single-grave burials in round barrows, and a common type of decorated beaker-shaped pot accompanying the burial. It is likely that the diffusion of this culture represented a gradual spread of new ideas to existing groups, rather than the migration of large numbers of people. *See also* HC1 p.84, *84*.

Beale, Dorothea (1831–1906), British educationalist, a pioneer in women's education and a leading figure in the struggle for female suffrage. In 1858 she became headmistress of the Ladies' College at Cheltenham.

Beamon, Robert (1946–), US long-jumper. He won the Olympic gold medal in 1968 with a jump of 8.90m (29ft 2½in), which beat the world record by 55cm (21½in), more than the cumulative improvements of the previous 40 years.

Bean, Roy (*c.*1825–1903), US frontier judge. After the Civil War he followed the construction camps of the Southern Pacific Railroad as a saloon-keeper and a gambler. In 1882 he settled in Vinegaroon, Texas, where as justice of the peace he kept order in court with his six-guns and dispensed harsh but just sentences.

Bean, plant grown for its edible seeds and seed pods; species include broad, string, kidney and runner beans. The broad bean (*Vicia faba*) is native to N Africa. The string bean (*Phaseolus vulgaris*) is native to tropical South America and is common in the USA; several varieties are cultivated. Its long pods or kidney-shaped seeds are eaten as vegetables. The scarlet runner (*Phaseolus coccineus*) has scarlet, rather than white or lilac flowers, and shorter, broader seeds. Family Leguminosae. *See also* SOYA BEAN; PE pp.*173, 178*, 184–185, 188.

Bean weevil, stout-bodied, dull grey or brown beetle found throughout the world. It lays eggs on bean pods and the hatched larvae bore into the beans. It can breed all the year round in stored dried beans. Length: up to 5mm (0.2in). Family Bruchidae; species *Acanthoscelides obtectus*.

Bear, large, omnivorous mammal with a stocky body, thick coarse fur and a short tail. Bears are native to the Americas and Eurasia. The sun bear is the smallest species, the Kodiak brown bear the largest. Bears have poor sight and only fair hearing, but an excellent sense of smell. Except for the polar bear, which lives almost exclusively on fish, walruses and seals, bears eat a wide variety of plant and animal foods. They kill their prey with a blow from their powerful fore-paws. In cold regions most bears doze or hibernate in winter. Length: 1.3–3m (4–10ft); weight: 45–725kg (100–1,600lb). Order Carnivora; family Ursidae; there are approximately nine species. *See also* NW pp.*164*, 206, *214*, 224, *243*.

Bear, Great and Little, constellations in the northern sky, that help in the recognition of other groups. Two stars in the Great Bear (Ursa Major) align so that they point to Polaris, the NORTH STAR, which is in the Little Bear (Ursa Minor). *See also* SU pp.*165–166, 237, 264–265*.

Bear baiting, popular pastime in England (11th-19th century) in which dogs were let loose on a tethered bear. The "bait" continued until either the supply of dogs ran out or the bear was too badly injured.

Bearden, Romare (1914–), US painter and collage artist, a founder (1963) of the Spiral Group of black artists. His pictures, often with religious or musical themes, are in flat planes of glowing colour.

Beardsley, Aubrey (1872–98), British illustrator. His highly-wrought, stylized black-and-white drawings epitomize the English ART NOUVEAU style. Associated with the Decadent writers of the 1890s, he illustrated the first four volumes of the *Yellow Book* (1894–95), which contained their work. All his work was done in the

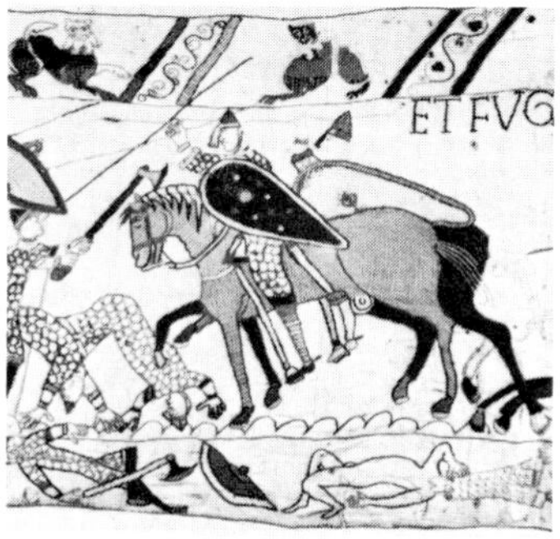

Bayeux tapestry (11th century); a detail from this important and historical document.

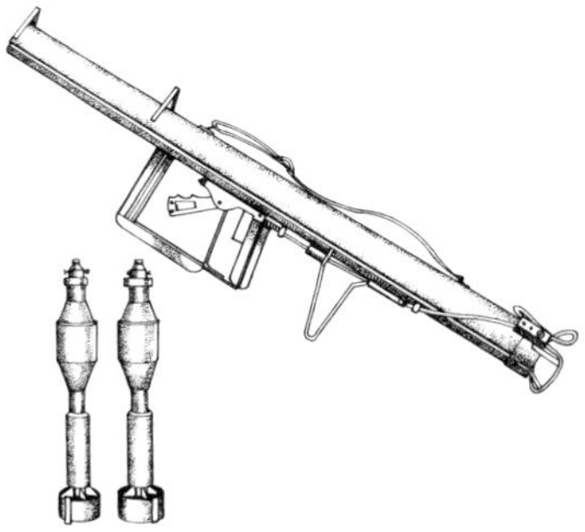

Bazookas have a range of up to 460m (1,500ft) and can pierce 30cm (1ft) armour plating.

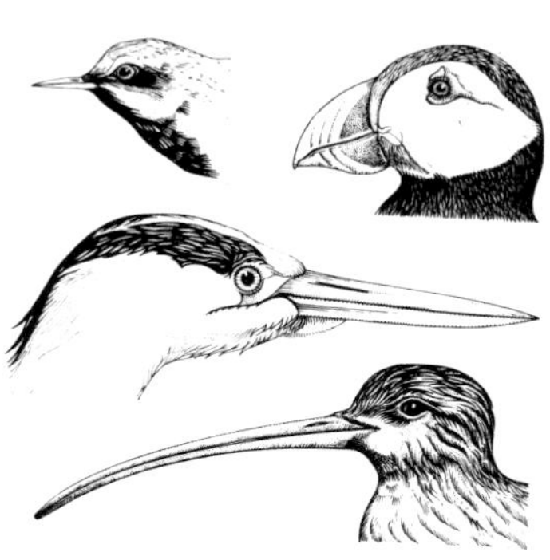

Beaks, or bills, vary greatly in design and structure according to their function.

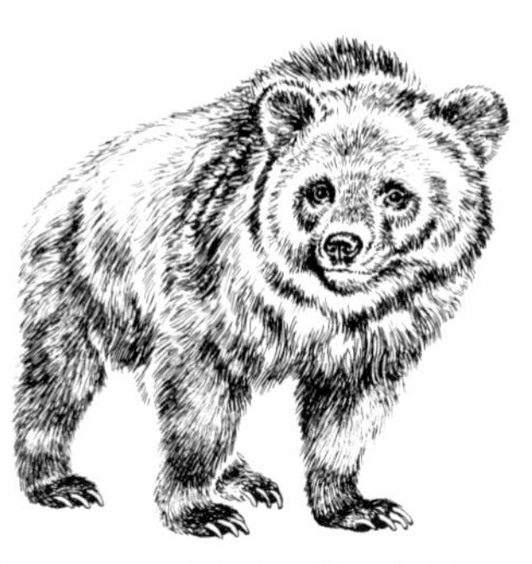

Bears swim and climb well, and can run at speeds of up to 50km/h (30mph).

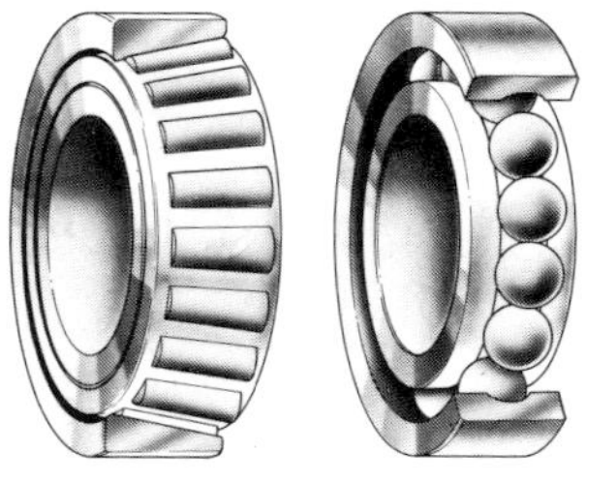

Bearings on axles are of two main types: roller-bearings (left) and ball-bearings.

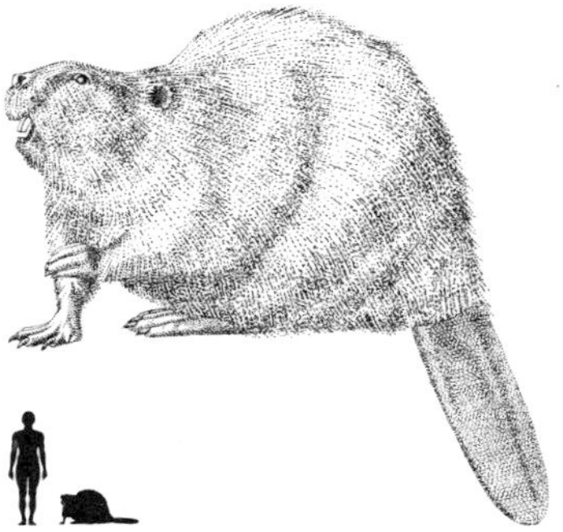

Beavers repair their lodges and keep their dams in good condition for many years.

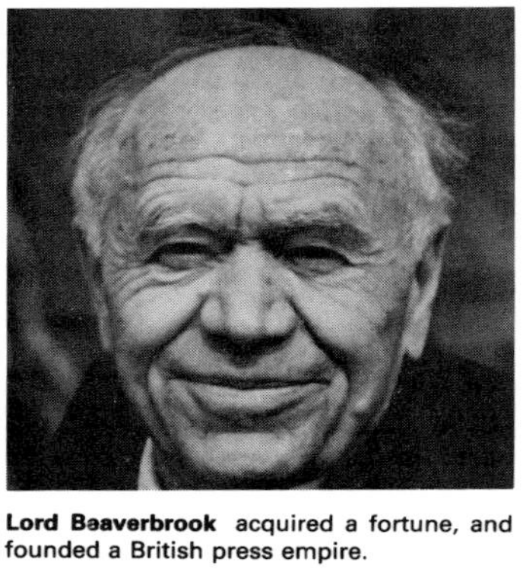

Lord Beaverbrook acquired a fortune, and founded a British press empire.

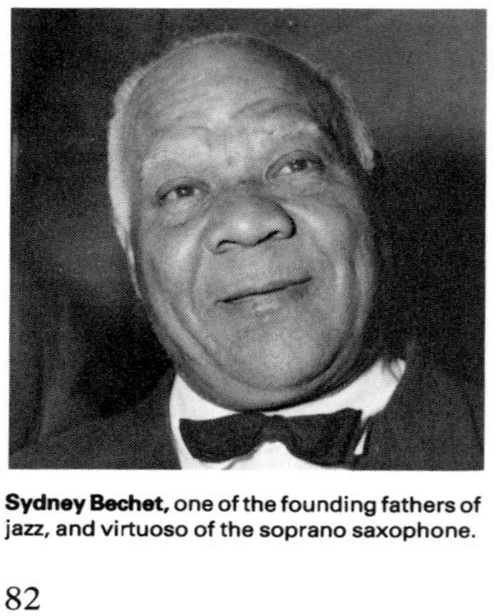

Sydney Bechet, one of the founding fathers of jazz, and virtuoso of the soprano saxophone.

period 1892–98. Many people condemned him for his eroticism.

Bearing, supporting component, usually of a resistant metal alloy, used to minimize friction between moving parts of machines. Some bearings are cylindrical shells which separate the surfaces of moving parts by trapping a thin film of lubricant between them. BALL BEARINGS use balls confined to a race to reduce the areas in contact; ROLLER-BEARINGS use rollers. *See also* MM p.*32*.

Beas, river in NW India, rising in the Himalayas and flowing SW through the Kulu Valley and the Siwalik Hills into the Sutlej River. It is one of the "five rivers" that gave the Punjab its name. Length: approx. 466km (290 miles).

Beat frequency oscillator, device in which an OSCILLATOR is designed to mix a variable radio frequency with a fixed one to give a pulsating beat frequency that can be amplified to give an audible sound.

Beat Generation, term applied to a group of US writers in the 1950s who rejected middle-class values and commercialism. They included the poets Allen GINSBERG, Gregory CORSO and Laurence FERLINGHETTI and novelists Jack KEROUAC and William BURROUGHS. Ferlinghetti's City Lights Press in San Francisco published works of many of the Beat writers. *See also* HC2 pp.289, *289*.

Beating the bounds, ancient English ceremony to mark the boundaries of each parish and offer prayers for good crops. Every year the priests and villagers would walk around the parish boundaries, beating the route, buildings or trees with sticks. The custom is still practised in some parts of England.

Beatitudes, blessings spoken by Jesus at the opening of the SERMON ON THE MOUNT upon those worthy of admission to the Kingdom of God. They are found in simple form in Luke 6:20–23 but are recorded most fully in Matt. 5:3–12.

Beatles, British pop music group consisting of John Lennon (1940–), Paul McCartney (1942–), George Harrison (1943–) and Ringo Starr (real name Richard Starkey) (1940–). From Liverpool, the Beatles based their style on US RHYTHM-AND-BLUES influences which, blended with their song-writing talent and attractive harmony, raised pop music to a new level of sophistication. The group disbanded in 1971 to pursue individual careers. The Beatles' many records included *Rubber Soul* (1965), *Revolver* (1966) and *Sergeant Pepper's Lonely Hearts Club Band* (1967). They also made some successful films, including *Hard Day's Night* (1964) and *Help!* (1965).

Beatnik, name applied in the early 1960s to young people who adopted unconventional dress, hairstyles and behaviour to set themselves apart from the society of the time. The term originally applied to members of the US BEAT GENERATION. *See also* MS pp.164–167.

Beaton, Sir Cecil Walter Hardy (1904–), British photographer, costume and stage designer, and writer. He commenced his career in the 1920s as a fashion photographer, and took up stage designing in the 1930s. His WWII photographs recorded the endurance of wartime hardship by the British people. His film and stage designs include *Gigi* (film, 1951), *My Fair Lady* (stage, 1956; film, 1964) and *Coco* (1969). Beaton's books include *The Wandering Years* (1962) and *Memoirs of the 40s* (1973).

Beaton, or Bethune, David (*c.*1494–1546), Scottish Roman Catholic prelate. Created cardinal (1538) and Archbishop of St Andrews (1539), Beaton opposed an English alliance and became Chancellor of Scotland in 1543. He was murdered in reprisal for the execution of George Wishart, a Reformation supporter.

Beatrice and Benedict (1862), opera by BERLIOZ, based on the story of Shakespeare's play *Much Ado about Nothing*. The libretto was written by the composer.

Beatrix (1938–), Crown Princess of The Netherlands. Married to Claus von Amsberg, she has three sons (after three generations of only female heirs to the Dutch throne).

Beattie, James (1735–1803), Scottish philosopher. Like Thomas REID, he opposed Hume's moral philosophy. In the *Essay on the Nature and Immutability of Truth* (1770) he argues for the "universality and immutability of moral sentiment". Poetical works by Beattie were popular.

Beatty, David, 1st Earl (1871–1936), British admiral. He served in Egypt and the Sudan (1896–98) and in the China War (1900). In WWI he commanded naval actions at Heligoland Bight, Dogger Bank and the Battle of Jutland. He became Commander-in-Chief of the Grand Fleet in 1916 and First Sea Lord in 1919.

Beaufort wind scale, range of numbers from 0 to 17 representing the force of winds, together with descriptions of the corresponding land or sea effects. The Beaufort number 0 means calm, wind less than 1km/h (1mph), with smoke rising vertically. Beaufort 3 means light breeze, 12–19km/h (8–12mph), with leaves in constant motion. Beaufort 11 is storm, 103–116km/h (64–72mph) and Beaufort 12–17 is hurricane, 117.5–219+ km/h (73–136+ mph), with devastation.

Beauharnais, Alexandre, Vicomte de (1760–94), French general who served in the American War of Independence. In 1789 he was a deputy of the nobility in the revolutionary French States-General. He was guillotined during the Reign of Terror and his widow, JOSÉPHINE, later married NAPOLEON I. Joséphine's son, Eugène (1781–1824), served with his stepfather at the battles of Marengo and Lutzen. He was later adopted by Napoleon and in 1805 became viceroy of Italy. He went to live in Bavaria after Napoleon's downfall.

Beauharnais, Josephine. *See* JOSÉPHINE.

Beauharnois, Marquis de (Charles de la Boische) (1670–1749), Governor of French Canada (1726–46). A successful naval commander, he attempted to improve relations with Canadian Indians, thus falling out with the intendant, Claude-Thomas Dupuy. He backed Pierre de Vérendrye's explorations and rose to the rank of Lieut.-Gen. after his retirement from politics.

Beaujolais, former region in central France on the W bank of the River Saône, N of Lyon in the Rhône département. The region was formed around the small village of Beaujeu and became famous for its fine Beaujolais wines.

Beaulieu, Victor-Lévy (1945–), Canadian author. His novels, which are written in French, deal with modern urban life. They include the trilogy *Race de monde* (1969), *Jos Connaissant* (1970) and *Les grands-pères* (1972).

Beaumarchais, Pierre Augustin Caron de (1722–99), French dramatist whose related plays, *The Barber of Seville* (1775) and *The Marriage of Figaro* (1778) were made into operas by ROSSINI and MOZART respectively. A cosmopolitan adventurer, Beaumarchais satirized the court society into which he had married. *See also* BARBER OF SEVILLE, THE; MARRIAGE OF FIGARO, THE.

Beaumont, Francis (*c.*1584–1616), English dramatist closely associated with the dramatist John FLETCHER. Between 1607 and 1613 they produced at least ten outstanding plays including *Philaster, The Maid's Tragedy* and *A King and No King*. Beaumont is usually credited with sole authorship of two plays, *The Woman Hater* (1607) and *The Knight of the Burning Pestle* (*c.*1607). *See also* HC1 p.285.

Beaune, town in France 37km (23 miles) SW of Dijon, known for some of the finest Burgundy wines. It is the home of the Hotel-Dieu, a hospital founded in 1443 for the poor, which is supported by the proceeds of its vineyards. Industries: wine, textiles, cutlery, leather. Pop. (1968) 16,874.

Beauneveû André (*c.*1330–1410), French architect, sculptor, miniaturist and illuminator. One of the last great wandering artists of the Middle Ages, his work survives in four figures on the royal tombs at St Denis, France, and in the miniatures at the beginning of the *Psalter of the Duke of Berry*.

Beauport, town in Canada on the St Lawrence River, 8km (5 miles) NE of Québec. It was settled in 1634 and is one of the oldest towns in the country. Montcalm had his headquarters there in 1759. Pop. (1971) 14,739.

Beauregard, Pierre Gustave Toutant de (1818–93), US Confederate general. He served in the Mexican War and was superintendent of West Point when the Civil War broke out in 1861. On 13 April 1861 he forced the Union surrender of Ft Sumter in the first action of the war.

Beauséjour, Fort, in the Fort Beauséjour National Historic Park (1926) in SE New Brunswick, Canada, was established by the French in 1751 and occupied by the British in 1755. It had strategic importance in the American War of Independence and the War of 1812.

Beauvoir, Simone de (1908–), French novelist and essayist. *She Came to Stay* (1943) and *The Mandarins* (1954) are portraits of the existentialist intellectual circle of which she and her close companion, Jean-Paul SARTRE, were members. Her best-known work remains the feminist essay *The Second Sex* (1949). Other significant works include *The Prime of Life* (1960), *A Very Easy Death* (1964) and *Old Age* (1972).

Beaux-Arts, École des, national art school of France, founded as the *Académie d'Architecture* in 1671 by COLBERT. It merged with the *Académie Royale de Peinture et de Sculpture* in 1793 and acquired its present casts of antiquities and old-master drawings.

Beaux' Stratagem, The (1707), comedy by the English playwright George Farquhar. The plot involves Aimwell and Archer, two young rakes whose scheme to marry well provokes intrigue and deception. It combines Restoration cynicism with 18th-century sentimentality and is notable for its realism and geniality.

Beaver, large RODENT with fine brown to black fur, webbed hind feet, and a broad scaly tail; it lives in streams and lakes of Europe, North America and Asia. Beavers eat parts of trees, shrubs and other plants. They build "lodges" of trees and branches above water-level and dam streams and rivers with stones, sticks and mud. In many places they are hunted for their fur. Length: to 1.2m (4ft); weight: up to 32kg (70lb). Family Castoridae; species *Castor fiber*. *See also* NW pp.206, *207*.

Beaverbrook, William Maxwell Aitken, 1st Baron (1879–1964), British newspaper proprietor and politician, *b.* Canada. He arrived in England in 1910 after making a fortune in stockbroking. He entered Parliament in the same year and was made a peer in 1917. He was CHANCELLOR OF THE DUCHY OF LANCASTER (1918–22) and a member of CHURCHILL's war cabinet (1940–45). He bought a majority interest in the *Daily Express* newspaper in 1916 and afterwards founded the *Sunday Express* and the *Evening Standard*.

Beavogui, Louis Lansana (1923–), Guinean politician. He was minister of trade and industry (1957–58), of economic affairs (1958–61, 1969–72) and of foreign affairs (1961–69) before becoming Prime Minister in 1972.

Bebop, or bop, form of jazz with subtle harmonies and shifting rhythm. It arose in the late 1940s as a development from the simpler "SWING" style. *See also* HC2 p.272, *272*.

Bebel, Ferdinand August (1840–1913), German politician. One of the founders of the German Social Democratic Party (SPD) in 1869, he was its leader for more than 40 years and, by 1912, had made it the largest single party in the state.

Beccafumi, Domenico (1486–1551), Siennese MANNERIST painter and sculptor. His masterpiece is the mosaic for the pavement in the cathedral, Sienna. He also worked in Genoa and Pisa. He was influenced by the pictorial composition of RAPHAEL and the boldness and vigour of MICHELANGELO.

Beccaria, Cesare di (1738–94), Italian philosopher and criminologist. He wrote *On Crime and Punishments* (1764), advocating penal reform and the creation of an enlightened judicial code.

Bechet, Sidney (1897–1959), US JAZZ

clarinettist and soprano saxophonist. A New Orleans-born Creole, Bechet was noted for his broad vibrato and sweeping phrases, especially on soprano sax. A professional from 14, he worked in New Orleans with Joe "King" OLIVER, and in 1919 toured Europe with the Southern Syncopated Orchestra, where he was praised by the Swiss conductor Ernest ANSERMET.

Bechstein, Friedrich Wilhelm Carl (1826–1900), German piano-maker. He began his own business in 1856 and quickly won a reputation as a master craftsman. His company soon had branches in France, Russia and Britain, and built the Wigmore Hall, in London in 1901.

Bechuanaland, former name of BOTSWANA. *See* MW p.40.

Beck, Józef (1894–1944), Polish statesman. He served in WWI and as military attaché in Paris (1922–23). As Foreign Minister (1932–39) he firmly rejected HITLER's demands for concessions in the Polish Corridor and Danzig, although he tried to remain on friendly terms with Hitler. On 6 April, 1939 he signed an alliance with Britain that later resulted in Britain's declaring war on Germany – the start of WWII – in Poland's defence.

Beckenbauer, Franz (1945–), West German footballer. He was captain of Bayern Munich when it won the EUROPEAN CUP (1974, 1975, 1976) and of West Germany when it won the WORLD CUP (1974). His roving, attacking style has become the ideal for a centre half-back. He joined the New York Cosmos in 1977.

Becket, Thomas à (*c.*1118–70), English clergyman and statesman. He was appointed Chancellor of England (1155), became a friend of HENRY II and vigorously pursued the interests of the Crown. In 1162 he became Archbishop of Canterbury. Resigning the Chancellorship that year, he devoted all his energies to Church affairs. Conflict with Henry over clerical privileges and the independence of ecclesiastical courts followed and Becket fled from England and sought support from the Pope. Returning to Canterbury after six years' exile, he was murdered there by four of Henry's knights. He was acclaimed a martyr and canonized in 1173. *See also* HC1 pp.186, *194*.

Beckett, Samuel (1906–), Irish novelist and playwright. Based in Paris since 1937, he writes in both English and French. His mastery of the Theatre of the ABSURD is shown in such plays as *Waiting for Godot* (1952), *Endgame* (1957), *Krapp's Last Tape* (1958) and *Not I* (1973). His novels, such as *Murphy* (1938), *Malone Dies* (1951) and *Watt* (1953) humorously study the plight of the alienated individual. He was awarded the 1969 Nobel Prize in literature. *See also* HC2 p.*283*.

Beckford, William Thomas (1760–1844), British writer and traveller. He achieved note with the baroque Arabian romance *The History of the Caliph Vathek* (1786), which he wrote in French. He collected books and paintings, and built a GOTHIC folly at Fonthill, Bath.

Becklin's object, invisible body detected inside the Orion Nebula by infra-red techniques. It is concealed by nebular dust through which only infra-red radiation can pass. *See also* SU pp.173, 230, 232.

Beckmann, Max (1884–1950), German EXPRESSIONIST painter. His work is unique in its constricted treatment of space, primitive angular forms, vividness of colour, and the staring intensity of its faces. Condemned as a decadent artist in 1933, Beckmann left Germany in 1938 and eventually settled in the USA. His most famous work, nine triptychs painted after 1932, includes the monumental *Departure*. *See also* HC2 p.175.

Becknell, William (*c.*1790–*c.*1832), US trader and explorer. He established the trading route known as the SANTÉ FE TRAIL (1821–22), which was used for 50 years and has become part of US legend.

Beckwith, Julia Catherine (1796–1867), Canadian author. Her romance *St. Ursula's Convent; or The Nun of Canada* (2 vols., 1824) was the first novel to be written by a native-born English-speaking Canadian and published in Canada. She wrote the novel while in her teens.

Bécquer, Gustavo Adolfo (1836–70), Spanish lyrical poet. He is best remembered for his melancholy *Rimas* collection, posthumously published in 1871, which assured him a place amongst the finest Spanish lyrical writers.

Becquerel, Antoine Henri (1852–1908), French physicist. He was Professor of Physics at the Paris Museum of Natural History and later at the Ecole Polytechnique. In 1896 he discovered RADIOACTIVITY in uranium salts,for which he shared the 1903 Nobel prize for physics with Pierre and Marie CURIE. He was also concerned with the rotation of the plane of polarized light in a magnetic field. *See also* SU pp.62–64.

Bed, in geology, a layer of rock. It underlies the surface material (regolith) except where regolith has been removed by erosion. Bedrocks can be classified according to their origins as igneous, sedimentary or metamorphic. SEDIMENTARY ROCKS are formed on the surface, IGNEOUS may be formed on the surface or within the Earth's interior, and METAMORPHIC are formed only deep inside the Earth.

Bedding plane, in geology, layers in which sedimentary material is deposited. It may also describe the layering of other, non-sedimentary material such as an ore. *See also* PE p.103.

Bedbug, broad, flat, wingless BUG found worldwide. It feeds by sucking blood from mammals, including human beings. Bedbugs usually gorge themselves at night and remain hidden during the day. Length: to 6mm (0.25in). Family Cimicidae; species *Cimex lectularius.*

Bede, Saint (*c.*673–735), the Venerable Bede, monk and scholar from Northumbria who spent his entire life in the monasteries of Wearmouth at Sunderland and Jarrow. The most important of his many works on science, grammar, history and theology is the *Ecclesiastical History of the English Nation*, which remains an indispensable primary source for English history from 54 BC–AD 597. *See also* HC1 pp.20, 138, 139, 164, 165.

Bedford, county town of BEDFORDSHIRE, on the River Ouse, 77km (48 miles) NNW of London. It is noted for its public school, dating from the 16th century, and a chapel in memory of John BUNYAN who preached there in the 17th century. Industries: electrical equipment, agricultural machinery, diesel engines. Pop. (1971) 73,064.

Bedford Level, low-lying area of about 3,000sq km (1,200sq miles) in SE England, S of the Wash. Drained in the 17th century, it is now a rich agricultural area which yields vegetables, fruit and flowers.

Bedford, Master of the Duke of (*fl.*1405–30), French painter. Working for the Duke of Bedford, regent of France (1423–35) during the English occupation, he illuminated a breviary and *The Bedford Book of Hours.*

Bedfordshire, county in central S England. The land is mostly flat with low chalk hills, the Chilterns, in the S. The region, drained by the River Ouse, is fertile and agriculture is the chief economic activity. Agriculture includes growing of cereal crops, cattle raising and market gardening. Industries include the manufacture of motor vehicles, electrical equipment and precision instruments. The main towns are BEDFORD (the county town), Luton and Dunstable. Area: 1,235sq km (477sq miles). Pop. 463,500.

Bedi, Bishen (1946–), Indian cricketer. A slow left-arm spinner with N Punjab and Delhi, he made his Test debut in 1966–67. Ten years later he was India's captain and leading wicket-taker, with 168 in Tests. He played for Northants 1972–77.

Bedlam, popular name for Bethlem Royal Hospital, London, an institution for the insane. Founded as a priory of the Order of the Star of Bethlehem in 1247, it was converted to its later use in *c.*1400. Its present site is Croydon. *See also* MS p.*137*.

Bedlington terrier, graceful, lamb-like breed of dog (TERRIER group) established in the 1880s. It has a pear-shaped head, hanging ears, long legs and a gracefully curved 23–28cm (9–11in) tail. The coat can be blue, liver, sandy or a combination of any two of these colours. Standard size: 39cm (15in) high at the shoulder; 8–11kg (18–24lb).

Bedouin, nomadic, desert-dwelling ARAB peoples of the Middle East and followers of ISLAM. Traditionally they live in tents, moving with their herds of camels, goats, sheep and sometimes cattle across vast areas of arid land in search of the sparse grazing. Their society is patrilineal and they are renowned for their hospitality, honesty and fierce independence. In the 20th century many Bedouin have been forced to abandon the nomadic way of life and work in agriculture or in towns.

Bedser, Alec and **Eric** (1918–), British twin brothers who both played cricket for Surrey. Alec was a fast bowler who played for England in 51 Test matches, in which he took a total of 236 wickets. After retiring as a player he became chairman of the England selectors.

Bedsore, ulcerous sore that results from prolonged pressure on the skin, as in a patient who has to lie in one position in bed during a long illness. Bedsores can be prevented by a frequent change of the patient's position. Cloth pads and air cushions can also help to prevent sores, as can frequent bathing and dusting pressure points with antiseptic powder.

Bedstraw, small wildflower found from tropical to temperate regions. Once used as a mattress filling, this plant has tiny, clustered flowers, slender square stems and stalkless, whorled leaves. Family Rubiaceae; genus *Galium.*

Bee, insect distinguished from other members of the order Hymenoptera, such as ants and wasps, by the presence of specially adapted hairs, with which they collect POLLEN; all bees feed their young NECTAR and pollen. The body is usually quite hairy and the hairs are multibranched (plumose). Although HONEYBEES and BUMBLEBEES are social insects living in well-organised colonies, many other bees are solitary, and some species even live in the colonies of other bees. Found throughout the world except near the N and S poles, they are important pollinators of flowers. Entomologists recognize about 12,000 species, but only the honeybee provides the HONEY used by man. It also builds combs of six-sided cells from wax produced within its body. A honeybee colony may consist of up to 60,000 individuals. *See also* NW pp.78–79, *108*, 109, *113*, *116*.

Beebe, Charles William (1877–1962), US naturalist and explorer, Curator of Ornithology (1899–1919) at the New York Zoological Gardens and Director of Tropical Research (1919–52) at the New York Zoological Society. He led explorations in central and S America, the West Indies and the Orient. His numerous books include *Galápagos* (1923) and *Beneath Tropic Seas* (1928).

Beeby, Clarence Edward (1902–), New Zealand educationalist, *b.* England. Director of education in New Zealand from 1940 to 1960, he was Assistant Director-General of UNESCO (1948–49), becoming chairman of its executive board in 1963.

Beech, deciduous tree native to the Northern Hemisphere. Beeches have wide-spreading branches, smooth grey bark and alternate, coarse-toothed leaves. Male flowers hang from thin stems; pairs of female flowers hang on hairy stems and develop into triangular, edible nuts enclosed by burs. The American beech (*Fagus grandifolia*) is an important timber tree used for furniture and tool handles. Height: to 36m (117ft). Family Fagaceae; there are 10 species. *See also* NW p.*65*.

Beecham, Sir Thomas (1879–1961), British conductor, one of the greatest of his day. He founded the New Symphony Orchestra in 1906, the London Philharmonic in 1932 and the Royal Philharmonic in 1947. He became artistic director of Covent Garden Opera in 1933, introduced the operas of Richard Strauss into England, and was widely known as an interpreter of such composers as Frederick DELIUS and Jean SIBELIUS.

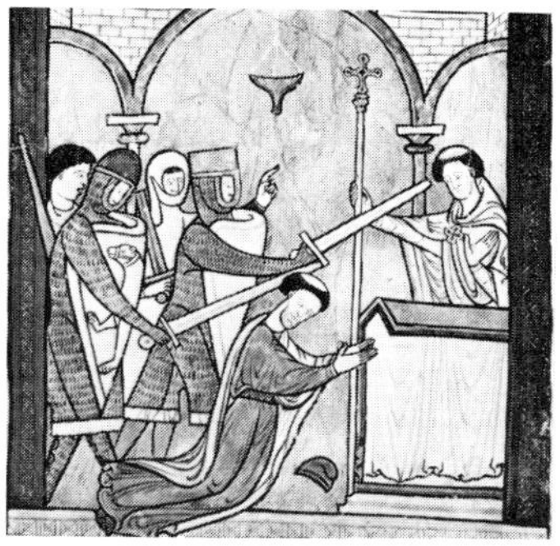

Thomas à Becket, murdered while in the Cathedral by four of King Henry's knights.

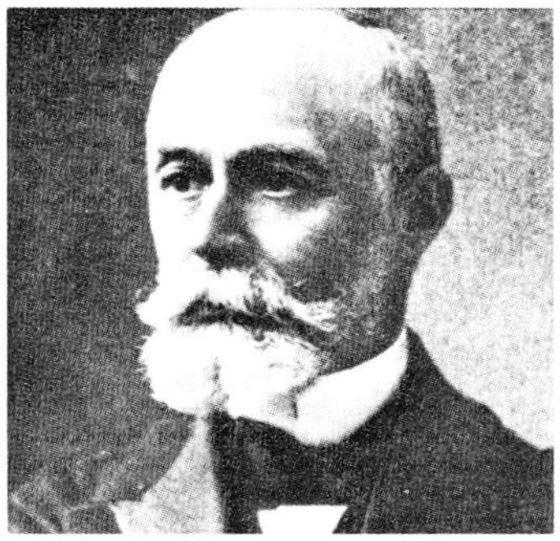

Henri Becquerel shared the 1903 Nobel Prize for the discovery of natural radioactivity.

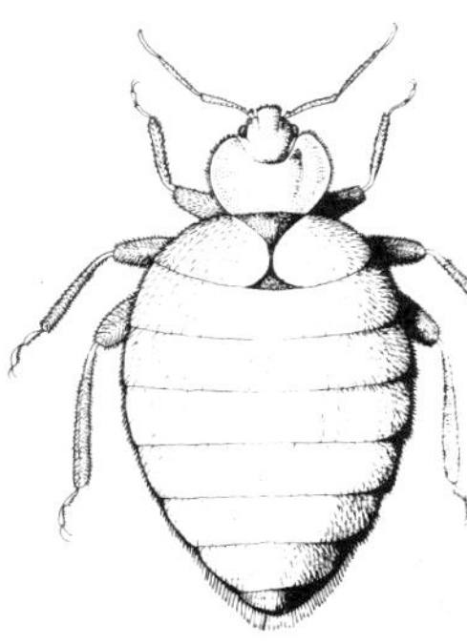

Bedbugs, because of their flat shape, can hide, by day, in the tiniest cracks and crevices.

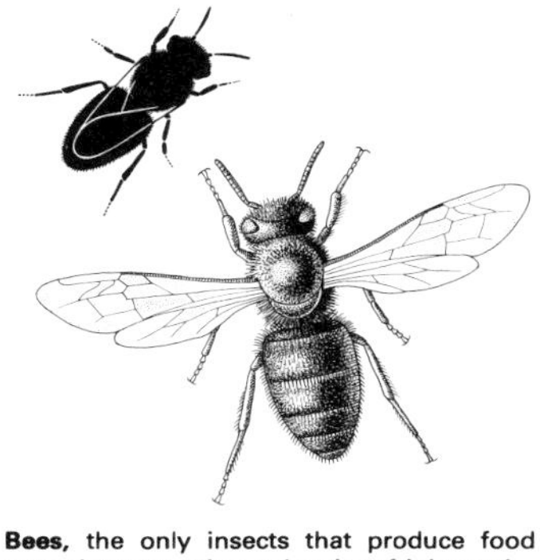

Bees, the only insects that produce food eaten by man, sting only when frightened.

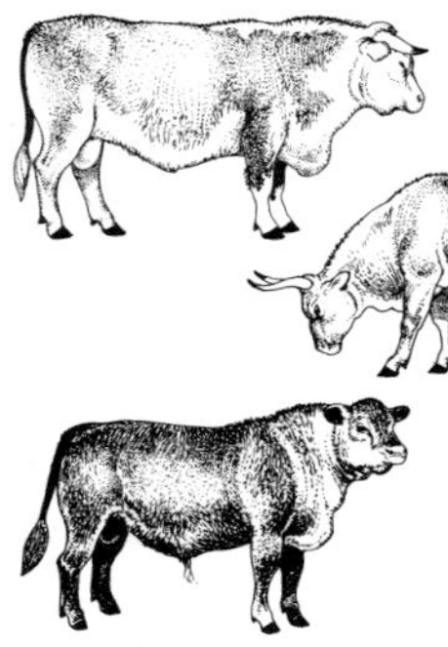

Beef cattle, generally larger than dairy breeds, convert most of their food into flesh.

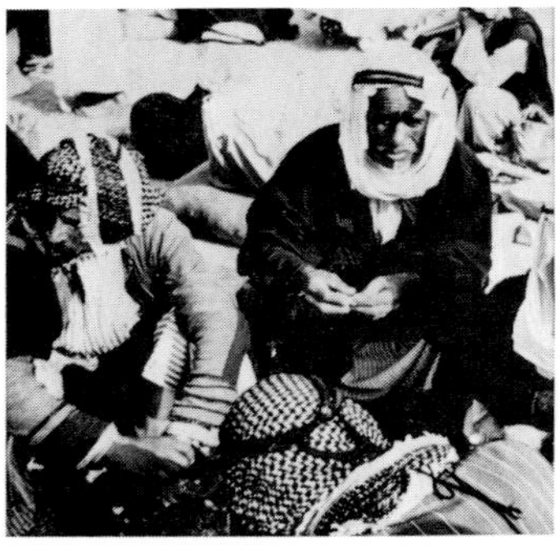

Beersheba, a thriving town in modern Israel, is the place where Abraham first settled.

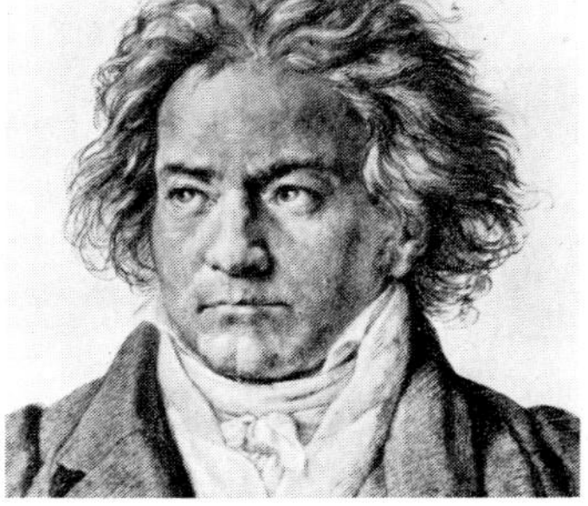

Beethoven; one of the greatest, if not *the* greatest composer in music history.

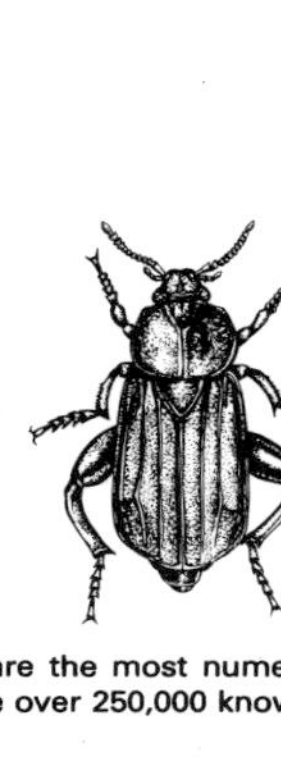

Beetles are the most numerous of insects. There are over 250,000 known species.

Beeching, Richard, Baron (1913–), British industrialist. As chairman of the British Transport Commission and of the British Railways Board (1961–63) he was responsible for the re-shaping of Britain's railways.

Bee eater, tropical BIRD of the Eastern Hemisphere that swoops to catch bees and wasps. It has a long, curved beak, bright, colourful plumage and a long tail. It nests in large colonies and builds a tunnel to its egg chamber. Length: 15–38cm (6–15in). Family Meropidae. *See also* NW p.*205*.

Beef cattle, breeds of domesticated cattle reared primarily for meat. Generally larger than DAIRY CATTLE, they are chunky and rectangular in appearance and convert most of their food into flesh. Beef production includes three distinct agricultural phases: breeding, a period of growth and final fattening. Some farmers do all three but the modern trend is towards specialization, concentrating on one phase of production. Breeds include Aberdeen Angus, Brahman, Charolais, Hereford, Longhorn and Shorthorn. *See also* PE pp.*159*, 226–227, *232*.

Beefeater. *See* YEOMEN OF THE GUARD.

Beekeeping. *See* PE p.196.

Beelzebub, or more properly Beelzebul ("Lord of demons"), corrupted deliberately in Syrian texts and the (Latin) Vulgate Bible to Beelzebub ("Lord of the flies") as a gesture of contempt. Originally an aspect of BAAL, it was later merely another name for SATAN or the Devil – as in Matt. 10:25 and 12:24, 27; Mark 3:22, and Luke 11:15, 18, 19. Despite this, Beelzebub also appears as one of Satan's henchmen in Milton's *Paradise Lost*.

Beer, alcoholic beverage produced by brewing and fermentation of a cereal extract (malt), which is flavoured with a bitter substance (hops). Other ingredients are water, sugar and yeast. The alcohol content of beer ranges from about 3.5 to 12% by weight. Among the types of beer are ales, which are pale or brown in colour; stouts, very dark brown and bitter; and porter, a sweeter stout. Beer is especially popular in Britain, the USA and Germany. *See also* PE p.204.

Beerbohm, Sir Max (1872–1956), British caricaturist and drama critic. His writings include *A Christmas Garland* (1912), parodies on contemporary writers, and *Around Theatre* (1930; 1953). He also wrote a novel *Zuleika Dobson* (1911), an amusing satire set in Oxford. Some of his caricatures were published in *Rossetti and His Circle* (1922).

Beernaert, Auguste (1829–1912), Belgian politician, a member of the Christian Social Party. He served in several cabinet posts before becoming Prime Minister (1884–94). He was a delegate at the Hague peace conferences of 1899 and 1907 and in 1909 he shared the Nobel Peace Prize with ESTOURNELLES DE CONSTANT.

Beersheba (Be'er Sheva'), chief city of the Negev Desert, in S Israel, approx. 88km (55 miles) S of Tel Aviv. It was the most southerly point of biblical PALESTINE. It flourished under Byzantine rule, but declined thereafter until re-established by the Ottoman Turks *c.*1900 as a market centre for the BEDOUIN tribes of the Negev. In 1917, it became the first city to be taken by the British in the Palestine campaign of WWI. Industries: chemicals, textiles, ceramics. Pop. (1970 est.) 77,400.

Beet, vegetable native to Europe and parts of Asia, and cultivated in most cool regions. Its leaves are green or red and edible, although it is generally grown for its thick red or golden root. Beets thrive on sandy loam or in a sunny area. Some varieties are eaten as a vegetable, others are a source of sugar and some are used as fodder. Family Chenopodiaceae; species *Beta vulgaris*. *See also* SUGAR-BEET; PE p.188.

Beethoven, Ludwig van (1770–1827), German composer who exerted a profound influence on the development of musical styles. Despite the onset of deafness, which finally became total, he wrote many masterpieces that are among the finest and most popular of their type. He provides a link between the formal classical style of HAYDN and MOZART and the romanticism of WAGNER, BRAHMS and BRUCKNER. Born in Bonn, Beethoven visited Vienna in 1787 and was taught briefly by Mozart; he made Vienna his home from 1792 and took lessons from Haydn. He was a proud, determined and independent man. Unlike his predecessors he was never directly employed by a European ruler, aristocrat or Church; he did get support from men of means, but he wrote to satisfy his own inclinations. As a result he liberated music from many of the conventions then current. His music is ultimately optimistic, although sometimes involving dark, gloomy struggle. With the onset of deafness from about 1800 Beethoven became difficult, unpredictable and suspicious, alternately cheerful and moody, tender and boisterous. He composed nine symphonies, five piano concertos, a violin concerto, one opera (*Fidelio*), more than 30 piano sonatas and a sizeable body of chamber music. He is best known for having made the symphony a dramatic form; he also expanded the size of the orchestra and wrote compositions that were considered long. His output is often divided into three periods. Until 1800 he generally followed the convention of Haydn and Mozart; from about 1800–14 he wrote passionate works, now among his most popular, including the third and fifth symphonies, the violin concerto and *Appassionata* piano sonata; and from 1814 date his most sublime compositions, among them the last five string quartets, the ninth symphony and the *Missa Solemnis*. *See also* HC2 p.106.

Beetle, insect characterized by horny front wings that serve as protective covers for the membranous hind wings and are not used in flight. These protective sheaths are often brightly coloured. Beetles are widely distributed in every continent except Antarctica. Most live on land, but some are aquatic and several are parasitic on plants and other animals. Beetles are usually stout-bodied and their mouthparts are adapted for biting and chewing. They are poor fliers but, like all insects, are protected from injury and drying up – which can be a serious hazard – by an EXOSKELETON.

Beetles are the most numerous of the insects, and more than 250,000 species are known and new ones are still being discovered. Most feed on plants, some prey on small animals, including other insects, whereas others are scavengers. Beetles undergo complete METAMORPHOSIS. Their larvae, called grubs, usually have three pairs of legs. Unlike caterpillars and worms, the grubs have distinct heads, usually dark in colour. Length: 0.5mm–16cm (0.02–6.3in). Order Coleoptera. *See also* NW pp.114–115, *208*.

Beeton, Mrs (1836–65), compiler of *Mrs Beeton's Household Management* (1861), probably the world's most famous cookery book. It was originally published in monthly parts between 1860 and 1861.

Beetroot, edible bulbous root of the cultivated red BEET (*Beta vulgaris*). Widely grown in temperate regions, it is usually boiled and eaten cold as a salad vegetable. Beetroot is also canned, whole or diced.

Beggar's Opera, The, opera with libretto by John GAY and popular music of the day arranged by J.C. Pepusch, first performed in England in 1728. Very popular in its time, it is one of the few successful "ballad" operas, and formed the basis of the 20th-century comic opera *The Threepenny Opera* (1928).

Begonia, family of plants, shrubs or trees native to tropical America and SE Asia. Those popular as house plants have leaves of various sizes and shapes; white, pink or red flowers; and often hairy stems. There are three types: rex, with ornamental leaves that combine green, red and silver colours; rhizomatous, with fleshy, creeping stems and glossy leaves; and basket, with trailing stems and brightly coloured leaves. Family Begoniaceae: genus *Begonia*. *See also* PE p.*179*.

Beguines, religious societies of women which began to be formed in Europe in the 12th century to perform good works. They took no formal vows, but were guided by the canons regular, laying great emphasis on the sacrament.

Behan, Brendan (1923–64), Irish writer, notorious for his riotous lifestyle. He became a member of the IRA at the age of 14 and served several years in borstal and prison, which he described in his autobiography *Borstal Boy* (1958). His first play, *The Quare Fellow* (1956), was also based on his experiences in prison. His second, and last complete, play was *The Hostage* (1959).

Behavioural ecology, study of the interactions between a natural environment and the animal behaviour that takes place within it. Drawing on biology, behavioural ecologists study such topics as the ways in which an organism adapts to its habitat. Human behaviour is also studied in this way. *See also* ECOLOGY; ETHOLOGY.

Behavioural sink, term applied by John Calhoun, a US behavioural sociologist, to conditions that develop where there is severe overcrowding. His studies with experimental animals suggest that overcrowding leads to a breakdown of normal social patterns, an increase in aggression, and a decline in normal reproductive and maternal behaviour. *See also* OVERPOPULATION.

Behaviour in animals. *See* ETHOLOGY.

Behaviourism, school of psychology that seeks to explain all animal and human behaviour primarily in terms of observable and measurable responses to stimuli. It uses objective, scientific methods, particularly laboratory experiments. Pavlov's work on conditioned reflexes was a source for the early behaviourists such as the American J.B. Watson. Accepting the basic emotions of fear, rage and love, they rejected the evidence introspection gives of feelings, motives and will. Later behaviourists such as B.F. SKINNER explain learning and development by "operant conditioning". *See also* MS pp.146–147, 150–151, 187.

Behaviour Therapy (Behaviour Modification), treatment of psychological disorders by using principles and methods of BEHAVIOURISM. It assumes that abnormal, like normal, behaviour is learned through conditioning and reinforcement. The therapy is designed to reward desirable, constructive behaviour whereas abnormal behaviour is ignored or punished. *See also* MS pp.146–147.

Behn, Aphra (1640–89), playwright, poet and novelist. After a childhood in Dutch Guiana and marriage to a London merchant she acted as unpaid spy for CHARLES II in Antwerp. She produced 15 risqué comic plays in London, as well as writing excellent poetry and philosophical novels, notably *Oroonoko*.

Behrens, Peter (1868–1940), German architect, painter and designer, one of the first artists to consider the commercial manufacturing process as something worthy of original design rather than adaptation. As adviser to the electrical firm AEG in Berlin (1907–12), he produced designs for factories, offices and shops and controlled product design. His turbine factory for AEG (1909) is widely acknowledged as "the first modern building". He was director of Dusseldorf School of Art (1903–07). *See also* HC2 pp.178, 281.

Behring, Emil Adolph von (1854–1917), German bacteriologist and pioneer immunologist. In 1901 he was awarded the first Nobel Prize in physiology and medicine for his work on serum therapy, especially for developing immunization against DIPHTHERIA (1890) and TETANUS (1892) by injections of antitoxins, a word he introduced. His discoveries led to the treatment of many childhood diseases.

Behring, Vitus Jonassen. *See* BERING, VITUS JONASSEN.

Beiderbecke, Bix (1903–31), US jazz cornetist, pianist and composer; real name Leon Bismarck Beiderbecke. He played with Paul Whiteman's band (1928–30), but his best recordings were made with his own bands such as the Wolverines, and with the saxophonist Frankie Trumbauer. The piano solo, *In a Mist* (1927) is one of his finest compositions.

Beijing. *See* PEKING.

Beilby, Sir George Thomas (1850–1924),

British chemist who developed the manufacture of potassium CYANIDE on an industrial scale for use in extracting gold and silver from ores of low yield. He was president of the Institute of Chemistry from 1909 to 1912.

Beinum, Eduard van (1901–59), Dutch conductor. He was conductor of the Concertgebouw Orchestra of Amsterdam from 1931 and musical director of the Los Angeles Philharmonic from 1956 until shortly before his death.

Beira, port city on the SE coast of Mozambique; capital of the Manica and Sofala District. Developed in 1891 as a railway terminus to the interior, it is now a centre for trade and commerce and a tourist resort. Products: minerals, tobacco, cotton, sugar. Pop. 59,000.

Beirut (Bayrūt), capital of the LEBANON. It is situated on the Mediterranean coast on the site of the ancient Phoenician city of Berytus. Under the Romans it was an important colony and the site of a prominent law school (AD 3). The city was taken by the Arabs in AD 635 and by the Ottoman Turks in 1516. Before the devastating civil war of 1975–76 the city was an important banking, trading and cultural centre. Pop. 702,000.

Beit-Lahm. *See* BETHLEHEM.

Béja, town in s Portugal, 137km (85 miles) SE of Lisbon; capital of Béja district and Baixo Alentajo. It flourished under Roman rule and was used by the Moors as a fortress. Today, mining and farming are the chief occupations. Pop. 28,100.

Béja, town in N Tunisia, 105km (65 miles) W of Tunis. Once a Moorish fortress city, it was reconquered by the Portuguese in 1162. It was the scene of fighting in WWII (1943). Chief export: wheat. Pop. 28,100.

Bejaia (Bougie), town in Algeria, 185km (115 miles) E of Algiers. A former centre for the Barbary pirates, it is now the chief oil-exporting port of the W Mediterranean, being the N terminus of the Hassi Messaoud pipeline. Other exports include phosphates, iron ore, olive oil and fruit. Pop. 49,900.

Béjart, Maurice Jean (1928–), French BALLET dancer and choreographer. He added avant-garde modern dance techniques and acrobatics to classical movements to become one of the most innovative choreographers. He founded the Ballet of the 20th Century in Brussels (1960). Works include *Nijinksy, Clown of God* (1971) and *The Truimphs of Petrarch* (1977).

Beke, Charles Tilstone (1800–74), British explorer and geographer. He was the first man scientifically to chart the course of the BLUE NILE. He published a series of works on the languages of Ethiopia and the sources of the Nile (1847–65), and later produced several books on biblical geography.

Bekesy, Georg von (1899–1972), US biophysicist, *b.*Hungary. As director of the Hungarian Telephone System Research Laboratory (1923–46), he worked on problems of communication and the mechanics of human hearing. At Harvard University (1949–66) he carried on his research on the COCHLEA of the EAR, for which work he received the 1961 Nobel Prize in physiology and medicine.

Béla, name of four kings of Hungary. Béla III (*r.*1173–96), of the Árpád dynasty, introduced Greek culture to Hungary and laid the foundations for feudalism. Béla IV (1206–70), of the same dynasty, became king in 1235; Hungary was overrun by the MONGOLS during his reign.

Belafonte, Harry (1927–), US singer and actor. He appeared on Broadway, and in films and television programmes. He gained fame with calypso recordings and was a CIVIL RIGHTS worker.

Belalcazar, Sebastián de. *See* BENALCAZAR, SEBASTIÁN DEL.

Bel and the Dragon, two stories added to the book of DANIEL after its recognition as part of the canon of the Bible. The story of Bel shows the error of idolatry through Daniel's guidance. In the second story, Daniel is thrown into the lions' den and remains unharmed because of his faith.

Belasco, David (1853–1931), US actor, producer and playwright. He was responsible for innovations in scenic realism and stage lighting and encouraged US writers and performers such as Mrs Leslie Carter, David Warfield and Ina Claire.

Bel canto, Italian for "beautiful song", used to describe the flowing, lyrical style of solo song that was developed in Italian opera in the 17th and 18th centuries, in contrast to the more declamatory, dramatic style of the 19th century.

Belem (Pará), port and capital city of Pará state in N Brazil, on the Pará River. It was founded in 1616 and was a notable exporter of sugar and, later, rubber until the early 20th century. Products: cocoa, tobacco, rubber. Industries: saw-milling, engineering. Pop. (1970) 642,514.

Belemnite, extinct squid-like CEPHALOPOD, related to the AMMONITES. Its shell, shaped like a rifle bullet, is found fossilized. *See also* NW pp.*175, 179.*

Belfast, capital city of Northern Ireland, in County Antrim and County Down, at the mouth of the River Legan on Belfast Lough, an inlet of the Irish Sea. The city was founded in 1177 but did not develop until after the INDUSTRIAL REVOLUTION, when French Huguenots stimulated the growth of the linen industry. Belfast is now the centre for the manuacture of Irish linen. Since the 19th century the city has been the scene of bitter strife between Catholics and Protestants resulting from religious and political differences, and violence has intensified in recent years. The shipbuilding industry is of great importance in Belfast, and its large harbour includes the Harland and Wolff yard, which has produced many of the world's largest liners. Other industries include aircraft, machinery, food processing, tobacco. Pop. (1972) 362,400. *See also* HC2 pp.294–295; MW p.136.

Belgae, Germanic and Celtic tribes who banded together about 2,000 years ago and lived in what is now Belgium, The Netherlands, Germany and N France. The German tribes overcame and mixed with the Celts. Julius CAESAR, who called them the bravest of the Gauls, conquered them in 57 BC. Many Belgae then went to and settled in Britain. *See also* HC1 p.85.

Belgian sheepdog, sheep-herding dog (working group) developed in Belgium in the 1880s. It has a flat head with a pointed muzzle, triangular erect ears and a long tail. Its black coat is long and straight, with shorter hair on the head and lower legs. Average size: 56–66cm (22–26in) at the shoulder; 22.5–27kg (50–60lb).

Belgium (Belgique, België), a small densely-populated country in NW Europe. The country is intensively farmed; cereals and root crops are most important. BRUSSELS is the capital. Area: 30,513sq km (11,781sq miles). Pop. 9,804,000. *See* MW p.37.

Belgrade (Beograd), capital city of YUGOSLAVIA, situated at the junction of the Sava and Danube rivers. It was incorporated into the area which came to be known as Yugoslavia in 1929, and during German occupation in WWII suffered much damage. Industries: chemicals, metals, machine tools, textiles. Pop. 870,000.

Belgrano, Manuel (1770–1820), Argentine independence leader. He participated in the revolution of 1810 and led Argentine forces against Paraguay in 1811. As commander of one of the Argentine armies, he defeated royalist forces in 1812 and 1814. At the Congress of Tucumán in 1816 he recommended an INCA monarchy for Argentina.

Belinski, Vissarion Grigoryevich (1811–48), Russian writer and critic. He wrote for the journals *Notes from the Fatherland* and *Contemporary* and condoned the Russian social order, but after 1840 he advocated literature that expressed social and political ideas, as in his *Letter to Gogol* (1847).

Belisarius (*c.* 505–65), Byzantine general. Under Justinian I he waged campaigns against the Germanic tribes that threatened Byzantium on its western frontiers. He subjugated the Vandals in northern Africa and the Ostrogoths in Italy. *See also* HC1 p.142.

Belitung, island in Indonesia, off the SE coast of Sumatra in the Java Sea. The chief port is Tandjungpandan. It has large tin deposits, which have been worked since 1860. Area: 4,850sq km (1,872sq miles). Pop. 102,000.

Belize, town and former capital of Belize, central America, on the Caribbean Sea 80km (50 miles) NW of the new capital Belmopan. It was almost totally destroyed by a hurricane in 1961, but is still the largest town and the principal port. On the mouth of the Belize River, it is a trading centre for timber, fruit and coconuts. Industries: food processing, saw-milling. Pop. (1970) 39,050. *See also* MW p.37.

Bell, Alexander Graham (1847–1922), inventor of the telephone. Born in Scotland, he first worked with his father, inventor of a system for educating the deaf. The family moved to Canada in 1870, and Bell taught speech at Boston University (1873–77). His work on the transmission of sound by electricity led to the first demonstration of the telephone in 1876. A year later he founded the Bell Telephone Company. His many other inventions included the photophone (an instrument for transmitting sound by light vibrations) and the wax cylinder for phonographs. *See also* MM p.226.

Bell, Arthur Clive Howard (1881–1964), British literary critic. His essays included *Since Cézanne* (1922) and *Art* (1923). His wife, Vanessa (1879–1961), was the sister of Virginia WOOLF and a fellow-member of the BLOOMSBURY GROUP.

Bell, Sir Charles (1774–1842), Scottish anatomist and surgeon, the first man to distinguish between sensory and motor nerves in the brain and to describe the facial paralysis known as Bell's palsy. He was professor of anatomy and surgery at the Royal College of Surgeons, London, and from 1836 was professor of surgery at Edinburgh University.

Bell, Sir Francis Henry Dillon (1861–1936) New Zealand politician. Elected to parliament in 1893, he became a minister in 1912. In 1925 he was Prime Minister for a short period.

Bell, Gertrude Margaret Lowthian (1868–1926), British writer, archaeologist, traveller and a founder of modern Iraq. She travelled widely in the Middle East, joined the British Intelligence Service and advised the Arab Bureau of Iraq. Chiefly responsible for the selection of Faisal I as King, she also founded and directed the Iraq National Museum. Her works include *The Desert and the Sown* (1907), *Amurath to Amurath* (1911) and *Palace and Mosque at Ukhaidr* (1914).

Bell, Henry (1767–1830), Scottish engineer and pioneer of steam navigation in Europe. He designed and ran, on the River Clyde (1812–20), the steamboat *Comet,* which developed 3hp.

Bell, John (1799–1868), Canadian explorer and fur trader, *b.* Scotland. He was associated with the NORTHWEST COMPANY and HUDSON'S BAY COMPANY (1818–21), and explored the Winnipeg (1821–24) and Mackenzie River districts. He explored extensively in the Arctic, establishing fur-trading posts at Lake Athabasca and Seven Isles.

Bell, John Joy (1871–1934), Scottish writer. He wrote a number of stories and plays, mostly humorous and many of them in Glaswegian dialect. His most famous story is *Wee MacGreegor* (1902).

Bell, Patrick (1799–1869), Scottish inventor of a mechanical reaper which came into widespread use in the 1850s. It was gradually replaced by the more practical machine of the American Cyrus McCormick. *See also* MM p.*22.*

Bell, percussion musical instrument, originally of random pitch, but since the 9th century tuned and arranged in series called chimes or carillons. They were first used in Christian churches in the 6th century. The largest bell was cast in Moscow in 1733 and weighed 180 tonnes.

Bell, electric, bell that works using ELECTROMAGNETISM. When the button of an electric doorbell is pressed, a mains or battery current is made to flow through and energize an electromagnet. This pulls a spring-loaded striker against the bell, but the movement also cuts off the current, so that the striker at once springs back again,

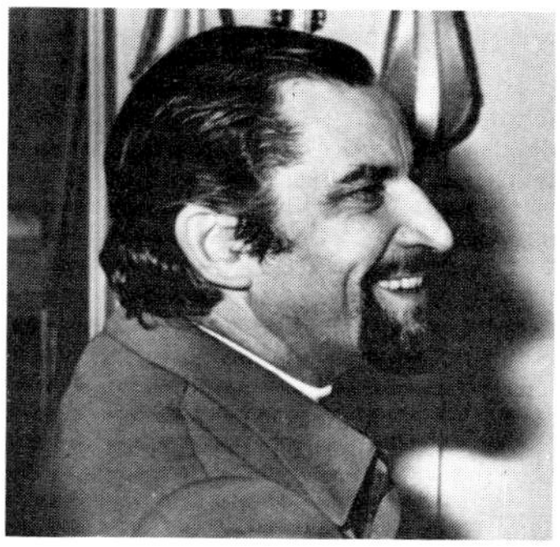

Maurice Béjart, choreographer and founder of the Ballet of the 20th Century in Brussels.

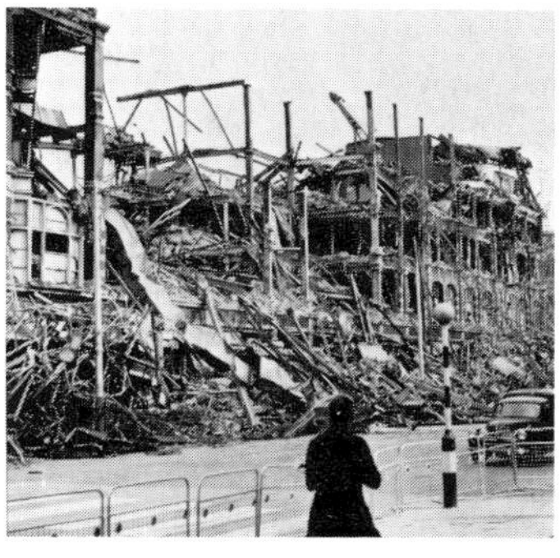

Belfast; a scene in the war-torn Northern Ireland capital after terrorist bomb explosions.

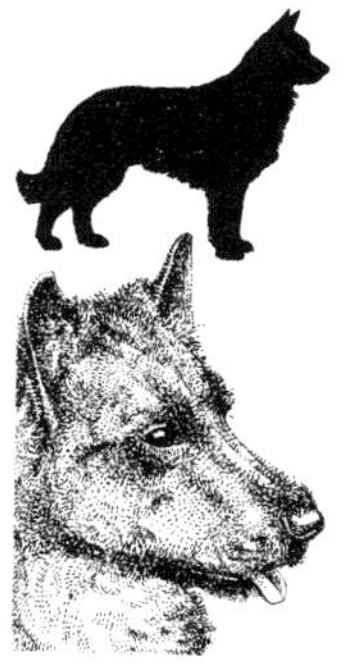

Belgian sheepdog, native to Groenendael, has a long neck ruff and a plumed tail.

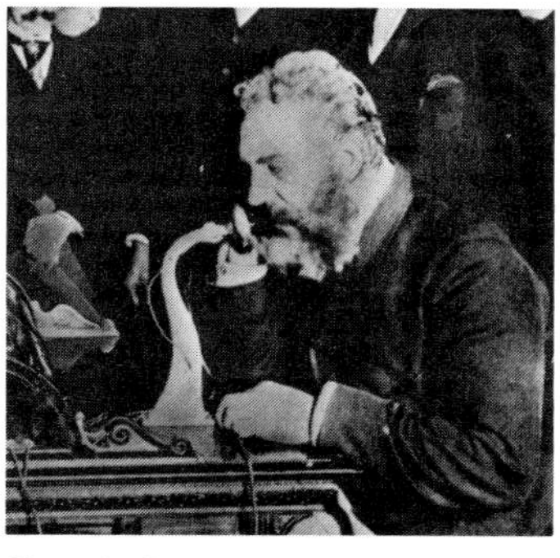

Alexander Graham Bell inaugurating the New York to Chicago telephone line in 1892.

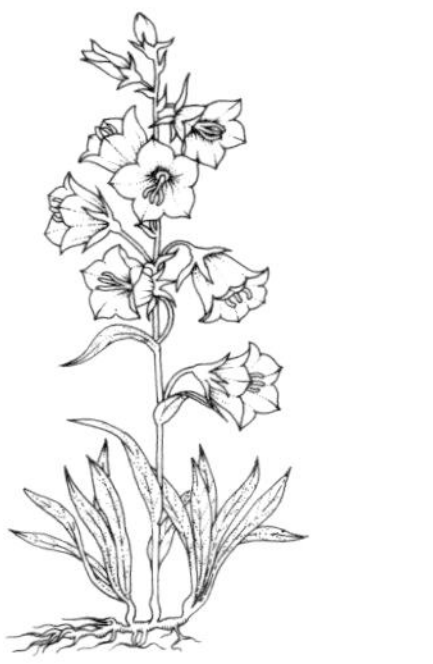

Bellflower; the drooping bell-shaped flowers bloom in shades of violet and blue.

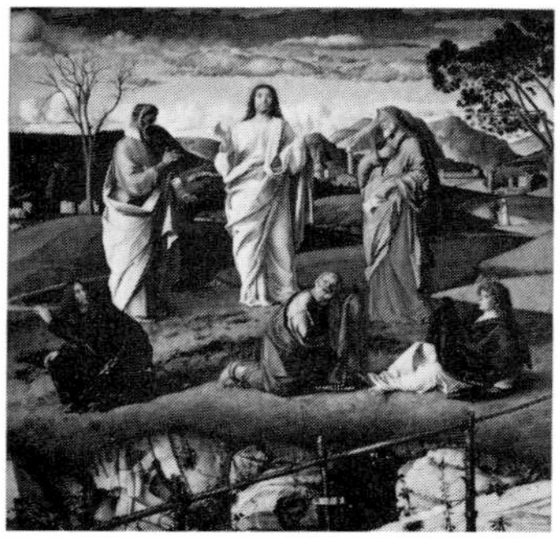

Giovanni Bellini; detail from *Transfiguration,* showing his balance of picture elements.

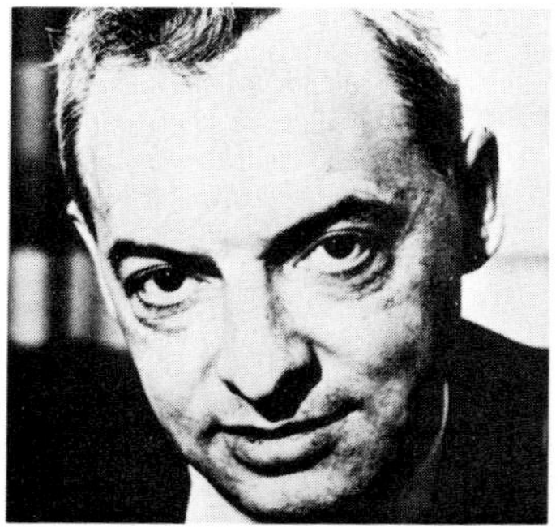

Saul Bellow, who won the 1976 Pulitzer Prize for his novel *Humbolt's Gift.*

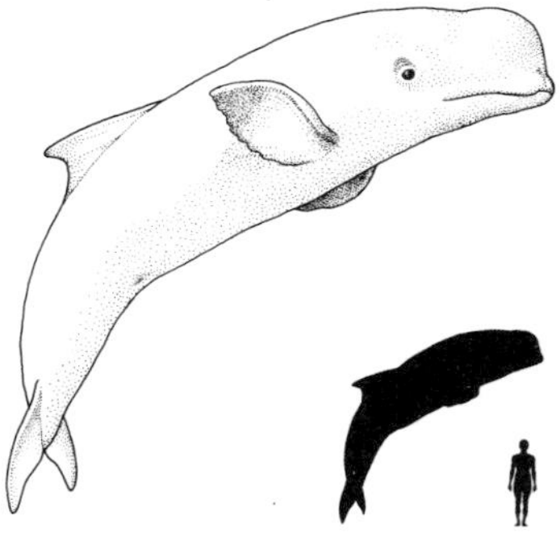

Belugas are sometimes called sea canaries because of the trilling sounds they make.

resuming contact. Quickly repeated movements of this kind account for the ringing sound of the electric bell. *See* SU p.*119*.

Bella Bella, Kwakiutl American Indian tribe of British Columbia. Because of an excellent local harbour, they were among the earliest Alaskan Indians to be visited regularly by European sailors, who described them as a warlike people. About 900 now live in the Milbank Sound region of British Columbia.

Bella Coola, the northernmost Salish-speaking tribe of North American Indians, living in British Columbia. They have taken on many of the traits of the KWAKIUTL tribe. Only about 350 survive today.

Belladonna. *See* ATROPINE; NIGHTSHADE.

Belladonna lily, southern African plant that grows from a bulb and is cultivated for its fragrant rose-pink flowers. Family Amaryllidaceae; species *Amaryllis belladonna.*

Bellarmine, Roberto Francesco Romolo, Saint (1542–1621), Italian theologian and ecclesiastic. He was a Jesuit and a prominent figure in the COUNTER-REFORMATION. From 1602 to 1605 he was archbishop of Capua. He was canonized by Pope PIUS XI in 1930.

Bellay, Joachim du. *See* PLÉIADE, LA.

Bellbird. *See* COTINGA.

Belleau, Rémi. *See* PLÉIADE, LA.

Belle Dame Sans Merci, La, poem by John KEATS, written in 1819 and first published in 1820. It has twelve quatrains, written in the IAMBIC metre. The title is perhaps from the Alain Chartier poem (1424) of the same name.

Belleek ware, pottery from Belleek, Co. Fermanagh, Northern Ireland, first made in 1857 by David McBinney and Robert Armstrong. It is used for statuary and decorative objects, such as open-work baskets, as well as utilitarian ware. It is characterized by a lustrous white eggshell glaze and the use of modelled shells as ornamentation.

Belle Isle, Strait of, channel in Canada between Newfoundland and SE Labrador. It is the northernmost entrance to the Gulf of St Lawrence, and is ice-bound from November to June. Length: 145km (90 miles); width: approx. 25km (15 miles).

Bellerophon, in Greek legend, the son of Glaucus, King of Corinth and grandson of SISYPHUS. Iobates, King of Lycia, sent him to slay the fire-breathing dragon Chimera. Previously Bellerophon had captured and tamed the winged horse PEGASUS, and by riding above the dragon he was able to attack and kill it.

Belles-lettres, type of literature that is valued more for its elegant style than for the information it contains. The term comes from the French, meaning "fine letters", and once applied to the whole of literature.

Bellflower, annual, perennial or biennial plant native to northern temperate regions and tropical mountains, now widely cultivated. Bellflowers have bell-shaped flowers, alternate leaves and milky sap. There are 250-300 species. Family *Campanulaceae*; genus Campanula.

Belli, Giuseppe Gioacchino (1791–1863), Italian poet, one of the Italian representatives of Romantic realism. His early poetry was undistinguished but his best, written between 1830 and 1849 and describing daily life in Rome, gained deserved popularity.

Bellini, family of Italian painters, Jacopo and his sons Gentile and Giovanni, who created the VENETIAN SCHOOL of painting. Jacopo (*c.*1400–*c.*1470) was a pupil of GENTILE DA FABRIANO. His major surviving works are two sketch books, the source of many ideas used by his sons and by his son-in-law MANTEGNA. Gentile (*c.*1429–1507) was famous for his narrative works (eg *The Procession in the Piazza of San Marco* and *The Miracle of the True Cross*) which became the prototype of the genre in Venice. Giovanni (*c.*1430–1516) was possibly the greatest of Venetian Madonna painters. His early paintings interpreted nature with precise realism. Gradually, however, his composition became more monumental and his handling of light and colour more poetic. He frequently included landscape backgrounds in his portraits (eg, those of the Doges), and in his allegorical paintings and altarpieces (such as that for S. Giobbe) he often used architectural settings, within which the figures were bathed in light. In Padua (1458–60) he was influenced by Mantegna, although his work remained less severe than Mantegna's. He was one of the greatest teachers of his generation and his pupils included GIORGIONE and TITIAN. *See also* HC1 pp.*143*, 255.

Bellini, Vincenzo (1801–35), Italian composer of operas, most notably *Norma* and *La Sonnambula* (both in 1831) and *I Puritani* (1835). His characteristically flowing melodies require great vocal skill. The BEL CANTO operas were widely popular during the 19th century, and since WWII have come back into favour. *See also* HC2 p.120.

Bell Island, Canadian island off the SE coast of Newfoundland, in Conception Bay. It was noted for its underwater iron-ore mines, worked from 1895 until 1966. The island is 10km (6 miles) long and 5km (3 miles) wide. Pop. 8,200.

Bello, Andrés (1781–1865), Chilean poet. His *Gramática de la lengue Castellana* (1847), which unified American and European Spanish, reflected his desire for an intellectually independent yet sophisticated Latin America.

Belloc, Joseph Hilaire Pierre (1870–1953), British author, *b.* France. A versatile writer, he is remembered chiefly for his light verse, especially *Cautionary Tales* (1908). He wrote several satirical novels in collaboration with G.K. CHESTERTON. He was a Liberal MP (1906–10).

Bellona, Roman goddess of war. She was an associate of Mars, possibly his sister, wife or daughter. She may have originally been an Asian goddess of war, worshipped in Cappadocia and Phrygia, and introduced to Rome by the dictator SULLA.

Bellotto, Bernardo (1720–80), Italian landscape painter, the nephew and pupil of CANALETTO. In his later works his style is more realistic and foreshadows that of the 19th century. His finest paintings are views of Dresden, Königstein and, especially, Warsaw which he executed for the Polish king.

Bellow, Saul (1915–), US writer, *b.* Canada. Bellow's work shows an intense, moral preoccupation with the plight of the individual in modern society. A novelist, short story writer and playwright, his first novel, *The Dangling Man,* appeared in 1944. Subsequent novels include *The Adventures of Augie March* (1953), *Herzog* (1964) and *Mr Sammler's Planet* (1970). He was awarded the Nobel Prize for literature in 1976. *See also* HC2 p.289.

Bellows, George (1882–1925), US illustrator and painter. Influenced by the ASH-CAN SCHOOL, he painted many fine portraits, as well as pictures of prize fights, street scenes, prayer meetings and rallies.

Bell-ringing, art of playing bells, probably originating in Asia and by the 8th century also a Christian practice. Apart from the specifically English practice of CHANGE RINGING, the most common forms of bell-ringing are by the carillon and chime. These differ only in size. A chime contains no more than 15 bells (tuned to the intervals of a major scale), whereas a carillon can have as many as 70 bells. Both may be played from a type of keyboard.

Bell Rock. *See* INCHCAPE ROCK.

Bell's palsy, paralysis of the muscles of the face caused by a disorder of the facial nerve. Spontaneous recovery can occur, although the condition may become permanent. It is named after the Scottish physiologist Charles BELL (1774–1842).

Bell Telephone Company, trading company established in 1877 by Alexander Graham BELL in the USA to manufacture the newly invented telephone. Today it is a large, diversified business. *See also* MM pp.226–227; SU pp.*173*, 253.

Belmopan, capital of BELIZE (formerly British Honduras) since 1970, when it replaced the city of Belize as capital. The latter had been largely destroyed by a hurricane in 1961. Belmopan is on the Belize River, 80km (50 miles) upstream from Belize. When it was incorporated in 1970 its official population was only 274.

Belo Horizonte, city in E Brazil, 354km (220 miles) N of Rio de Janeiro; capital of Minas Gerais state. It was built between 1895–97, and was Brazil's first planned city. Today it is a popular resort and the distribution and processing centre for a prosperous farming and mining region whose mineral deposits include iron ore, manganese and diamonds. Industries: steel, textiles. Pop. (1970) 1,106,722.

Belorussia (Belorusskaja SSR), Soviet W republic in USSR, also called White Russia, bordered by Poland (W), Latvia and Lithuania (N), Russian SFSR (E) and the Ukraine (S). It is a low-lying region drained by the Dnieper, Dvina, Beresina and Pripyat rivers. Much of the land is swampy, and peat is a valuable resource. Farmers grow sugar-beet, cereals, flax and potatoes. One-third of the region is forest and there is an important timber industry. Other industries include mining (clay, chalk, rock phosphate and potassium salt), motor vehicles, textiles, chemicals and electrical equipment. The capital is MINSK. Area: 207,600sq km (80,155sq miles). Pop. (1976) 9,384,000.

Belsen, site of one of the most notorious of the German concentration camps established by the Nazi government in WWII, at which 30,000 people are estimated to have died. The camp was liberated by the British army in spring 1945.

Belshazzar, described in the Biblical Book of DANIEL as the son of NEBUCHADNEZZAR and last King of BABYLON, although scholars now think that he was not a historic character. William WALTON's oratorio, *Belshazzar's Feast,* dramatizes the great feast during which Babylon's downfall was foretold.

Beltane, one of the four principal Celtic feasts, a spring festival held at the beginning of May. It was marked by agricultural fertility rites. Dancers carried burning torches across the fields to invoke the Sun and, to guard against livestock losses, animals were herded between ritual fires.

Beluga, pale Eurasian freshwater STURGEON, especially the giant beluga of the Caspian and Black seas and the River Volga. This fish is prized for its roe, which is used to make CAVIARE, and its air bladder is used in the ISINGLASS industry. Length: to 8m (26ft); weight: to 1,300kg (2,865lb). Family Acipenseridae; species *Huso huso.*

Beluga, or white whale, small, toothed Arctic WHALE that is milky white when mature. It preys on fish, squids and crustaceans and is valued by Eskimos for its meat, hide and blubber. Length: to about 4m (13ft). Species: *Delphinapterus leucas. See also* NW pp.166–167, *166–167.*

Bely, Andrei (1880–1934), Russian poet and novelist, a leading SYMBOLIST. His poems are included in collections such as *Gold in Azure* (1904) and *Ashes* (1909). His best-known novels are *The Silver Dove* (1910) and *Petersburg* (1912).

Bemba, Negroid warrior people of NE Zambia, Zaire and Zimbabwe (Rhodesia). Their society is traditionally matrilineal, based on subsistence agriculture, and characterized by an absence of craft skills and material possessions. Many are now migrant labourers in the copper mines.

Bembo, Pietro (1470–1547), Italian Renaissance scholar. His writings, especially *Discussion of the Italian Language* (1525), helped to establish the supremacy of Tuscan as a language over Latin and Dantesque Italian. He also wrote poetic imitations of PETRARCH and stylized prose pieces such as *The People of Asolo* (1505).

Benalcázar, or Belalcázar, Sebastián de (*c.* 1479–1551), Spanish conquistador. He accompanied Christopher COLUMBUS on his third voyage (1498) and was with Francisco PIZARRO during the conquest of Peru (1532). He founded settlements in Colombia while searching for the legendary EL DORADO, and in 1541 became governor of Popayán province.

Benarés. *See* VĀRĀNASI.

Benaud, Richie (1930–), Australian cricketer. An outstanding all-rounder and captain of state (NSW) and country (1958–63) teams, he scored 2,201 runs and took 248 wickets in 63 Tests (1952–64). A leg-break bowler, aggressive batsman and brilliant fielder, he was an astute captain whose policy of attack rekindled Australia's enthusiasm for the game.

Benavente y Martínez, Jacinto (1866–1954), Spanish playwright. His plays were most often social satires: on the aristocracy (*Gente conocida*, 1896), the middle class (*La losa de los sueños*, 1911) and the peasantry (*Señora ama*, 1908). He won the Nobel Prize in literature in 1922.

Benbecula, island off NW Scotland, in the Outer HEBRIDES. It is linked to South Uist by bridge and North Uist by causeway. Bonnie Prince Charlie escaped from there in 1746 dressed as Flora MacDonald's maid. Area: 93sq km (36sq miles).

Ben Bella, Ahmed (1919–), Algerian statesman. After WWII, he joined the movement for Algerian independence from France. After helping to found the *Front de Libération Nationale* (1954), he was imprisoned (1956–62). Following independence in 1962, he became Algeria's first premier. He was overthrown in a coup in 1965. *See also* HC2 p.246.

Benbow, John (1653–1702), English admiral. In 1702 he engaged the French in the West Indies and, although the captains of four of his seven vessels mutinied, continued fighting for five days until a fatal leg wound forced him to return to Jamaica.

Benchley, Peter (1940–), US author, son of Robert Benchley. A reporter and magazine writer, he wrote *Jaws* (1974), an immensely popular novel about a shark that terrorizes a seaside resort. The film of the book was equally successful.

Benchley, Robert Charles (1889–1945), US humorist and drama critic, renowned for his wit. His books include *Pluck and Luck* (1925) and *From Bed to Worse* (1934).

Benda, Julien (1867–1956), French writer. His most famous work, *La Trahison des Clercs* (*The Treason of the Intellectuals*) was published in 1927.

Bender-Gestalt test, in psychology, test devised by Lauretta Bender to help to diagnose mental and neurological disorders. The patient is told to copy, as accurately as possible, nine geometrical designs. The test indicates the level of development of a child's eye/hand coordination and may detect organic brain disorders and personality difficulties.

Bendigo (1811–80), ring name of William Thompson, British prize-fighter. Probably the first "southpaw", he was little more than a middleweight, yet won the championship of England (1839, 1845). He later became an evangelist.

Bendigo, city in central Victoria state, SE Australia. Founded i 1851, when gold was discovered there, it was the centre of the largest goldfield in Victoria. Now a commercial and railway centre for a dairy farming region, it has iron, textile and brick industries. Pop. (1971 prelim.) 32,000.

Bends, or decompression sickness, physical disorder, characterized by pain in the joints, dizziness, nausea and paralysis, caused by the release of nitrogen bubbles into the tissues and blood. This occurs if there is a too rapid return to normal atmospheric pressure after a period of breathing high-pressure air (when the body absorbs more nitrogen). It is an occupational hazard of divers and deep tunnel workers. The treatment requires recompression and then slow decompression. *See also* PE p.92, *92*.

Bene Beraq, city in W central Israel, suburb of Tel Aviv-Yafo. It was famous for its academy under the direction of Rabbi Akiba. Its industries include textiles and diamond cutting and polishing. Pop. (1972 est.) 72,100.

Benedict, name of fifteen popes and two antipopes, the most notable being: Benedict XI (*r.*1303–04), *b.* Niccolò Boccasini (*c.*1240–1304). A member of the Dominican order, he was created cardinal in 1298 and served on missions to England and France. He was noted for his sanctity and administrative abilities. He was beatified by Pope Clement XII in 1 36. Benedict XIII antipope (*r.*1394–1423), *b.* Pedro de Luna (1328–1423), was elected antipope mainly because of his promise to end the GREAT SCHISM, which he failed to do. Benedict XIV (*r.*1740–58), *b.* Prospero Lambertini (1675–1758), sought to improve the lot of all classes of people and to reform the Church. Benedict XV (*r.*1914–22), *b.* Giacomo della Chiesa (1854–1922). During WWI he strove for peace among nations. He made changes in the Curia and revised CANON LAW.

Benedict Biscop (*c.*628–90), English scholar. Five trips to Rome gave him contact with learning and the books to furnish great libraries at the monasteries he founded at Wearmouth (674) and Jarrow (682). He may thus be considered the father of Northumbrian learning. The Venerable BEDE was his pupil. *See also* HC1 pp.164–165.

Benedict, Ruth Fulton (1887–1948), US anthropologist. She conducted extensive fieldwork among the SW Indian tribes of the USA, the Serrano of California and the Canadian Blackfoot. Her best-known work is *Patterns of Culture* (1934), which described cultural behaviour patterns. Other works include *Zuni Mythology* (1935) and *The Chrysanthemum and the Sword: Patterns of Japanese Culture* (1946).

Benedictines, members of a monastic order who follow the Rule laid down by St BENEDICT OF NURSIA in the 6th century. The order played a leading role in bringing Christianity and civilization to western Europe in the 7th century and in preserving the traditions of Christianity throughout the Middle Ages. After the Reformation the order was confined to the Roman Catholic Church until its revival in the Church of England in 1914. The centre of the Anglican Benedictine community is Nashdom Abbey in Buckinghamshire, England. *See also* HC1 pp.134–135, 187.

Benedict of Nursia, Saint (*c.*480–*c.*547), known mainly through St Gregory's *Dialogues*, lived as an ascetic in a cave at Subiaco, where he acquired a reputation for austerity. A community gradually grew up round him and he established twelve monasteries, each under an abbot appointed by himself. In *c.*525 he moved to Monte Cassino, where he remained until his death. It was there that he composed his Rule which became the basis of the BENEDICTINE order named after him. Feast: 11 July in the West; 14 March in the East. *See also* HC1 pp.134–135, 187.

Benefit of clergy, legal term for the right claimed by some Christian churches for clerics to be tried in ecclesiastical courts even in civil matters. Today few countries admit such a right. Its scope was limited in England by HENRY II, but it was not abolished until 1827.

Bene Israel, Jews of India. Found mostly around Bombay, they are of unknown origin. When rediscovered by Western Jews in the 18th century, they were found to have retained some Jewish rites and festivals but were ignorant of Hebrew and had borrowed many customs and rituals from their HINDU neighbours. In the mid-1970s only about 10,000 of them were left in India, more than half having emigrated to Israel after 1948.

Benelux, customs union of Belgium, The Netherlands and Luxembourg, established in 1948. The earliest "common market" in Europe, it abolished trade restrictions between its members. It also has wider aims – the standardization of prices, wages, taxes and social security – but these have to some extent been merged in the aspirations of the EEC, of which the Benelux countries are also members. *See also* HC2 pp.258–259.

Beneš, Eduard (1884–1948), Czechoslovak statesman. A disciple of Tomáš MASARYK, he promoted Czech independence during WWI and became the first foreign minister of the new state (1918–35). Benes was President of Czechoslovakia from 1935 to 1938, when he resigned in protest against the German occupation of the Sudetenland. He was re-elected President in 1946, but resigned in 1948 after the Communist takeover.

Benét, Stephen Vincent (1898–1943), US author noted for his poetry and short stories. He won a Pulitzer Prize in 1929 for his epic poem on the American Civil War, *John Brown's Body* (1928).

Benevolences, gifts of money to the Crown expressive of the donors' goodwill. In fact a form of taxation, they were raised often by EDWARD IV to pay for wars, but were last raised by JAMES I in 1622.

Bengal, former province of India and now a region of the Indian subcontinent that includes West Bengal state in India and BANGLADESH. Much of the area lies in the deltas of the Ganges and the Brahmaputra rivers. In AD 750 it was a kingdom, ruled by King Gopala, who founded the Pala dynasty and spread BUDDHISM throughout the region. The Senas, a Hindu people, followed in the 11th century. The area was re-organized in the 12th century under the Muslim leader, Mohammed Khalji. The Mogul emperor Akbar ruled in the 16th century when Bengal became the richest region in his empire. Conquered by the British in 1757, Bengal became the centre of the British Indian Empire, with Calcutta as the capital city. It was made an autonomous region in 1937 and the present boundaries fixed in 1947. Area: 200,575sq km (77,442sq miles).

Bengal, Bay of, NE gulf of the Indian Ocean, bounded by India and Sri Lanka (W), India and Bangladesh (N), Burma (E) and the Indian Ocean (S). Many rivers empty into the Bay, including the Ganges, Brahmaputra, Krishna and Mahānadi.

Benghazi. *See* BANGHĀZĪ.

Bengtsson, Stellan (1952–), Swedish table tennis player. A powerful left-hander, he broke Asian dominance of the sport by winning the 1971 world singles championship, and helped Sweden to win the Swaythling Cup in 1973.

Benguela, port in W Angola on the Atlantic coast, 29km (18 miles) S of Lobito; capital of Benguela province. It is a rail terminus, and a commercial and fishing centre; it exports agricultural products. Founded in 1617, it once played an important part in the slave trade. Pop. (1969 est.) 35,000.

Benguela Current, current in the S hemisphere flowing N in the S Atlantic Ocean along the W coast of southern Africa and merging with the South Equatorial Current at approx. 15° S. It is a cold current produced by the prevailing southerly winds, and its waters are rich in plankton, making it an excellent fishing ground. *See also* PE p.79.

Ben-Gurion, David (1886–1973), Israeli politician (Mapai or Labour Party), born in Poland. A leader in the campaign for an independent Jewish state, he was made Israel's first Prime Minister in 1948. He resigned in 1953, but was Prime Minister again from 1955 to 1963. *See also* HC2 p.297, *297*.

Ben Hur (1880), novel by US author Lew WALLACE. It tells of the persecution, and ultimate conversion to Christianity, of Judah Ben-Hur after he is wrongly accused of the attempted murder of the Roman governor of Judea. It has been made into a film several times; the most notable was produced in 1926, and re-issued in 1931. *See also* HC2 p.289.

Benin, independent country in W Africa, formerly the French protectorate of Dahomey. The capital is Porto-Novo. Area: 112,622sq km (43,474sq miles). Pop. (1975 est.) 3,112,000. *See* MW p.38.

Benin, kingdom in W Nigeria that flourished 14–17th centuries AD. It is remembered chiefly for its bronze sculptures and wood and ivory carvings, considered among the finest African art. *See also* HC1 pp.*228–29*, 229, *351*.

Benitoite, glassy, blue to violet mineral, barium titanium silicate, $BaTi(SiO_3)_3$, found in San Benito, USA. It forms hexagonal system tabular, triangular crystals and is a valuable gem when transparent and without flaws. Hardness 6-6.5; s.g. 3.6.

Benjamin, in the Bible (Genesis), youngest son of JACOB, born to RACHEL who died during childbirth. His tribe settled between JUDAH and EPHRAIM. According to the New Testament, the apostle PAUL descended from this tribe.

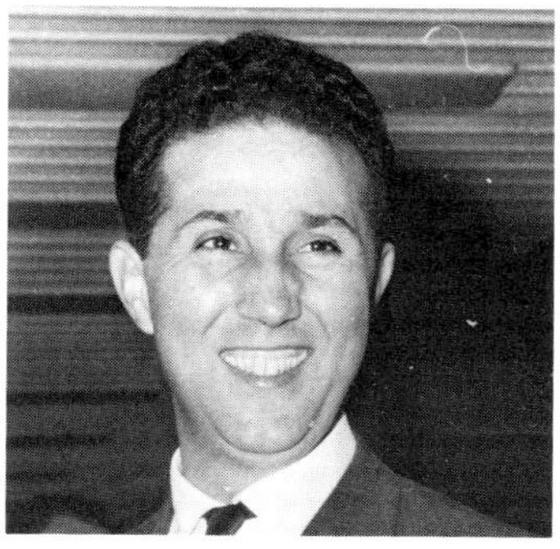

Ahmed Ben Bella was the first President of Algeria following independence in 1962.

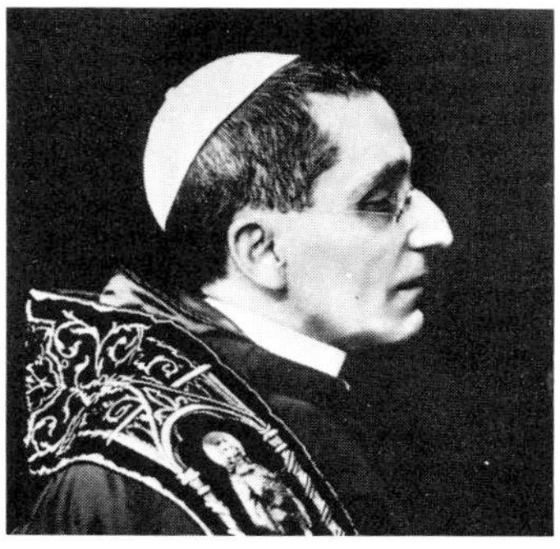

Benedict XV, whose papacy was concerned with the problems that arose from WWI.

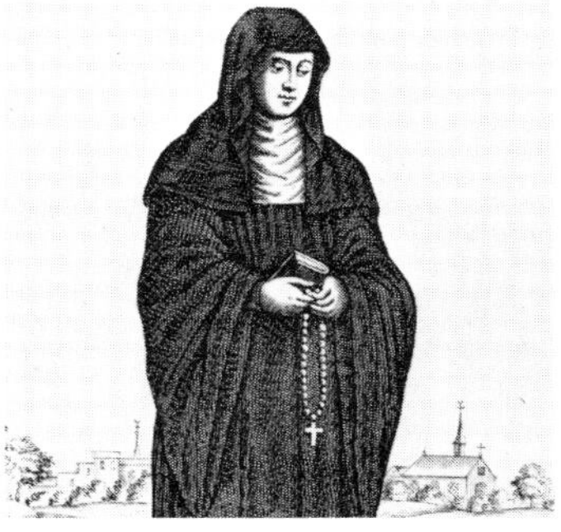

Benedictine nun of the "black" order, whose patroness was the virgin sister of St Benedict.

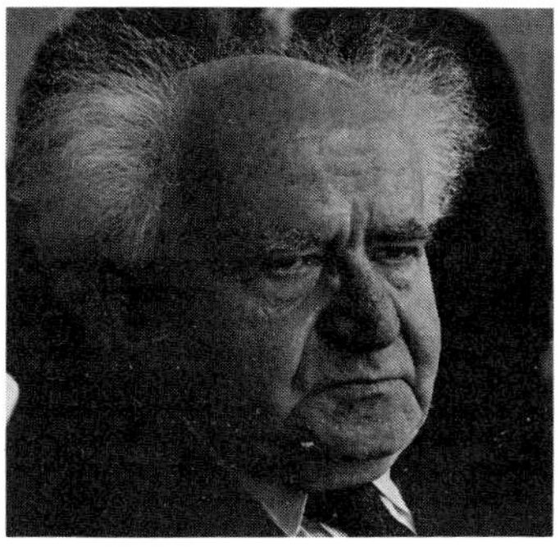

David Ben-Gurion, first Prime Minister and one of the founders of the State of Israel.

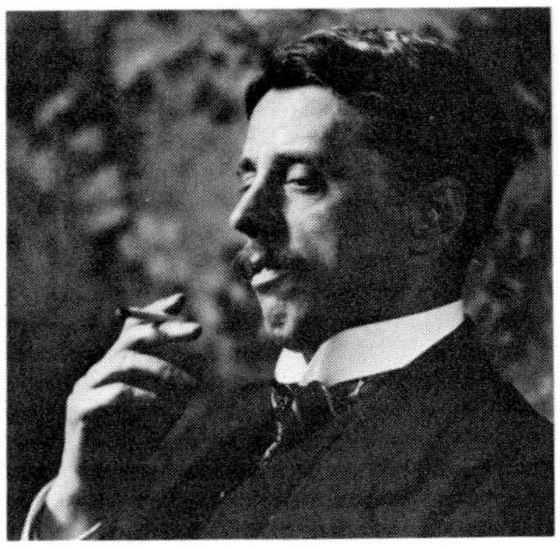

Arnold Bennet, whose writing explores the conflict between idealism and reality.

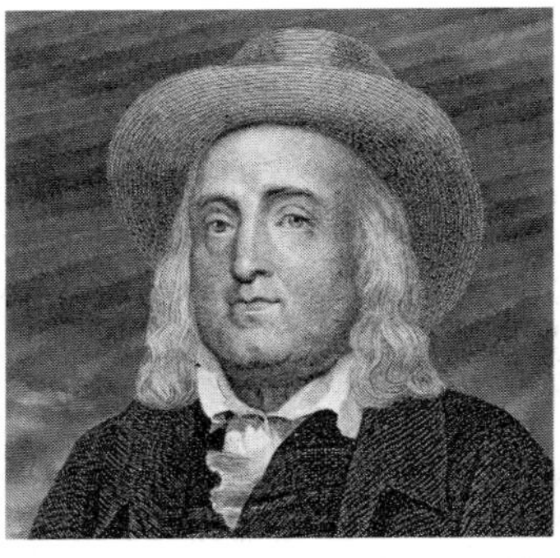

Jeremy Bentham attempted to measure happiness in "felicific calculus".

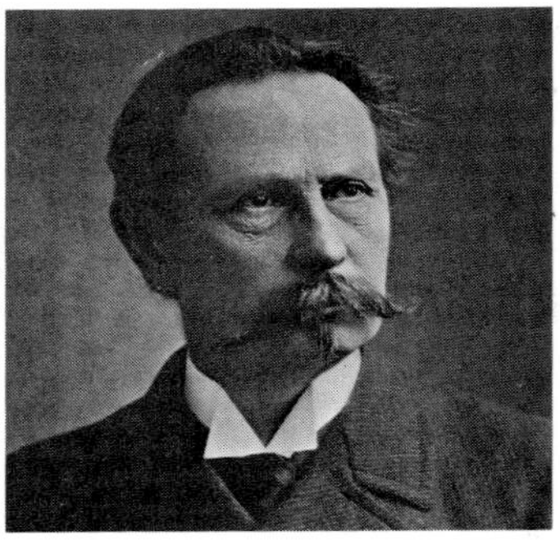

Karl Benz, who designed and built the first commercially successful motor car.

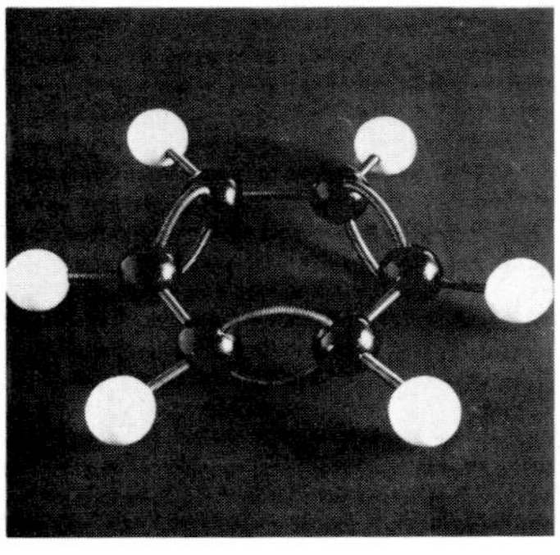

Benzene was discovered by Faraday, who called it "bicarburet of hydrogen".

Benjamin, Arthur (1893–1960), Australian composer who taught at the Royal College of Music in London. His works include the opera *The Tale of Two Cities* (1957) and the popular orchestral work *Jamaican Rhumba*.

Benjamin of Tudela (*d.* 1173), Spanish Jew who travelled from Saragossa, Spain, through Europe as far as China, returning through Egypt and Sicily (1159–73). His account – *Masse'oth Rabbi Binyamin* – was the first description by a European of the Far East.

Benmore dam, earth dam on the Waitaki River, South Island, New Zealand. Completed in 1965, the dam feeds power to the North Island via an underwater cable across Cook Strait approximately 32km (20 miles).

Benn, Anthony Neil Wedgwood (1925–), British Labour politician. He was elected to Parliament in 1950 and in 1963 disclaimed his hereditary peerage in order to remain in the House of Commons. He was Postmaster-General (1964–66) and Minister of Technology (1966–70) and was made Secretary of State for Energy in 1975.

Benn, Gottfried (1886–1956), German poet, essayist and physician whose work was banned by the NAZIS. His poetry, such as *Morgue* (1912), *Flesh* (1917) and *Intoxicated Tide* (1949), varied from the ecstatic and sensuous to the refined and intellectual. His essays include *After Nihilism* (1932) and *The Ptolemean* (1949).

Bennett, Sir Charles Moihi (1913–), New Zealand soldier. He commanded the Maori Battalion in WWII and, as High Commissioner for Malaya (1958–61), was the first Maori to serve his government overseas.

Bennett, Air Vice-Marshal Donald Clifford Tyndall (1910–), Australian airman who holds the world long-distance seaplane record (set in 1938) and who made the first non-stop flights from Britain to South Africa and Canada. In WWII he commanded the RAF Pathfinder Force.

Bennett, Enoch Arnold (1867–1931), British author. He documented realistically the provincial life of the industrial Midlands, where he was born, in his novels of the "Five Towns", such as *Anna of the Five Towns* (1902), *The Old Wives' Tale* (1908) and the trilogy *Clayhanger* (1910), *Hilda Lessways* (1911) and *These Twain* (1916).

Bennett, Floyd (1890–1928), US airman who accompanied Richard BYRD on his expedition to Greenland in 1925 and on his flight over the North Pole (9 May 1926), for which he was awarded the Congressional Medal of Honour.

Bennett, Henry Gordon (1887–1962), Australian major-general who commanded the 8th division of the Australian Imperial Force (1940). In 1941 he commanded all Australian forces in Malaya. A year later he escaped from Singapore and was made lieutenant-general.

Bennett, James Gordon (1795–1872), Scottish-born US editor and publisher. He founded the *New York Herald* in 1835. His innovations included telegraphed reports from correspondents.

Bennett, Richard Bedford (1870–1947), Canadian politician. In 1927 he became leader of the Conservative Party. During his time as Prime Minister (1930–35), he advocated preferential tariff agreements within the British Commonwealth. He led the Conservative opposition until his retirement from politics in 1938.

Bennett, Richard Rodney (1936–), British pianist and composer. He has written several operas, including *The Mines of Sulphur* (1965), a ghost story; a horn concerto and various pieces for piano.

Bennett, Tony (1926–), US singer. He has enjoyed popular success for more than 25 years and specializes in ballads. His hits include *Stranger in Paradise* (1954) and *I left my Heart in San Francisco* (1962).

Bennett, Sir William Sterndale (1816–75), British pianist and composer. From 1856 to 1866 he was conductor of the Philharmonic Society. In 1856 he was appointed professor of music at Cambridge. His works are rarely performed.

Ben Nevis, mountain in the central Grampian Mountains of w central Scotland, in the Highland Region near Fort William, overlooking Glen Nevis. It is the highest point in Britain, rising to 1,343m (4,406ft).

Bennington, Battle of (16 Aug. 1777) battle in the American War of Independence in which mainly British forces, under Col. F. Baume, were defeated by American forces under Gen. John Stark while they attempted to seize much-needed supplies in Vermont. The battle, the beginning of the defeat of the British was a turning point in the war. *See also* HC2 p.64.

Benny, Jack (1894–1974), US comedian, real name, Benjamin Kubelsky. He began his career in music hall at the age of 18, using a violin as a comic prop. He appeared in films and in *The Jack Benny Show* on radio (1932–55) and television (1950–65).

Benois, Alexandre (1870–1960), Russian theatre art director and ballet librettist. With DIAGHILEV he founded the WORLD OF ART movement and the Diaghilev ballet. He collaborated with STRAVINSKY and FOKINE and was a pioneer of modern ballet.

Benoit, Pierre (1886–1962), French novelist. He wrote novels of adventure and "romantic" love, including *Koenigsmark* (1918), *L'Atlantide* (1919) and *Axelle* (1928). In 1931 he was elected to the French Academy.

Benoni, town in Transvaal, NE South Africa, 32km (20 miles) E of Johannesburg. It is the distribution centre for a gold-mining area. Fierce fighting occurred there in 1922 during the Witwatersrand miners' strike. Industries: iron founding, electrical equipment. Pop. (1970) 149,563.

Benson, Sir Frank Robert (1858–1939), British actor-manager. In 1882 he made his first professional appearance in *Romeo and Juliet*, at the Lyceum Theatre, London. He formed his own company, devoting himself mainly to Shakespearean plays. In 1916 he was knighted on stage at the Drury Lane Theatre, London.

Benson and Hedges Cup, sponsored cricket tournament, held annually in England since 1972. The 17 first-class counties take part together with three minor counties and university sides. They are divided into four zones, in which they play each other once, the top two going into the quarter-finals. The final is played at Lord's in July. All fixtures are "one-day" matches played for a maximum of 55 overs per innings.

Bentham, George (1800–84), British botanist. His classification of seed-plants provided a foundation for modern systems. With W.J. HOOKER he wrote the multi-volume *Genera Plantarum* (1862–83), a definitive work in its time. Bentham also wrote *Handbook of British Flora* (1858).

Bentham, Jeremy (1748–1832), British philosopher, jurist and social reformer. He trained as a lawyer but never practised. Bentham developed the theory of UTILITARIANISM based on the premise that "the greatest happiness of the greatest number" should be the object of individual and government action. This philosophy was defined in his *Introduction to the Principles of Morals and Legislation* (1789). His followers were responsible for much of England's early reform legislation. *See also* MS pp.*232–233, 235*.

Benthic division, all of the ocean bottom from the high-tide line to the greatest depths. It is divided into two main systems, the littoral and the deep-sea. The littoral system is subdivided into eulittoral and sublittoral zones, and the deep-sea system into the bathyal and abyssal zones.

Benthos, flora and fauna of the deepest ocean. They include sedentary forms such as sponges, creeping creatures such as crabs and snails, and burrowing animals such as worms. *See also* PE pp.82–83.

Benti, Brig.-Gen. Teferi (1921–), Ethiopian politician. He is the chairman of the Provisional Military Administrative Council which, after the overthrow of Emperor Haile SELASSIE in 1974, became the ruling body in Ethiopia.

Bentinck, Lord William George Frederick Cavendish (1802–48), British politician. He led the Conservative attack on Robert PEEL and the repeal of the Corn Laws. From 1846 to 1847 he was the leader of the Protectionist party in the Commons.

Bentinck, Lord William Henry Cavendish (1774–1839), British administrator in India. He was Governor of Madras (1803–07) and in 1827 he became Governor-General of Bengal and then of India (until 1935). He introduced reforms, including the abolition of SUTTEE, and campaigned against the THUGS.

Bentley, Edmund Clerihew (1875–1956), British journalist and writer; originator of the "clerihew", a humorous biographical rhyme. He is best remembered for *Trent's Last Case* (1913), perhaps the first "modern" detective novel.

Bentley, John Francis (1839–1902), British church architect who designed in a Gothic style (English Gothic). His best-known work is the Roman Catholic cathedral in Westminster, London.

Bentley, Phyllis Eleanor (1894–), British author who wrote novels set in Yorkshire, including *The Spinner of the Years* (1928), *Freedom Farewell!* (1936) and *Manhold* (1941).

Bentley, Richard (1662–1742), English clergyman and Classical scholar, Master of Trinity College, Cambridge. He was a critic of classical texts and his most notable work was *Dissertation upon the Epistles of Phalaris* (1699).

Bentley, Walter Owen (1888–1971), car designer and manufacturer. He produced a series of stylish and successful sports and racing cars between 1921–31.

Benton, Thomas Hart (1889–1975), US regional painter, best known for his paintings of rural and small-town life and for his many murals, including those for the Whitney Museum of American Art and the New School for Social Research, New York. He taught Jackson POLLOCK.

Ben Yehudah, Eliezer (1858–1922), Hebrew scholar and Zionist, *b.* Lithuania. He modernized the Hebrew language and encouraged its adoption as the ordinary language of the people.

Benz, Karl (1844–1929), German pioneer of the internal combustion ENGINE. After some success with an earlier two-stroke engine, Benz built a four-stroke in 1885 that was first applied to a tricycle, and achieved great success when installed in a four-wheel vehicle in 1893. Benz was the first to make and sell light, self-propelled vehicles built to a standardized pattern. Hundreds had been built by 1900. *See also* MM p.126.

Benzaldehyde, C_6H_5CHO, the simplest of the aromatic chemical compounds in which the aldehyde group, $-CHO$, is attached directly to a benzene ring. It is a colourless liquid having a smell of bitter almonds; it is used as a chemical reagent, flavouring material and for making perfumes and dyes.

Benzedrine. *See* AMPHETAMINES.

Benzene, colourless, volatile, sweet-smelling inflammable liquid hydrocarbon (C_6H_6), a product of petroleum refining. Benzene is the simplest aromatic hydrocarbon; its molecule is a hexagonal ring of unsaturated carbon atoms (benzene ring). It is a raw material for manufacturing many organic chemicals and is widely used as a solvent. Properties: s.g. 0.879; m.p. 5.5°C (41.9°F); b.p. 80.1°C (176.2°F). *See also* BENZINE; SU pp.139, 142, *144*.

Benzine, mixture of hydrocarbon compounds obtained as a fraction in the distillation of petroleum. It is an inflammable liquid used as a solvent, motor fuel and for dry cleaning. It should not be confused with BENZENE.

Benzoic acid, white, crystalline weak CARBOXYLIC ACID (C_6H_5COOH) made from toluene. It is used to make dye-stuffs and for preserving fruit juices. Properties: s.g. 1.266 (15°C); m.p. 122.4°C (252.3°F); b.p. 249°C (480.2°F).

Benzoin, resinous polymer obtained from asiatic trees or made synthetically. It is used in perfumery and as an antiseptic.

Benzpyrene, or benzopyrene, aromatic hydrocarbon, $C_{20}H_{12}$, found in coal tar and cigarette smoke. More than any other compound it has been implicated as a cause of cancer, its carcinogenetic properties having been established during laboratory tests.

Ben-zvi, Itzhak (1884–1963), Israeli statesman. After fleeing his native Russia, he settled in PALESTINE in 1907. Exiled from 1915 to 1918, he worked with David BEN-GURION and other Zionist leaders to create the institutions basic to the formation of the state of Israel, including Histadrut, the leading labour organization, and the Mapai party, the leading political force. He was elected President of Israel in 1952, an office he held until his death. *See also* HC2 p.296.

Beograd. *See* BELGRADE.

Beothuk, now-extinct people once inhabiting Newfoundland, perhaps the first American Indians to be seen by white explorers. They were noted for their custom of painting their bodies with red ochre. The few who survived colonization apparently crossed the Belle Isle Strait and intermixed with the Montagnais.

Beowulf (*c.* 8th century), the oldest English epic poem and the most important example of ANGLO-SAXON verse. It tells how the young prince, Beowulf, slays the monster Grendel and his vengeful mother. Fifty years later the aged Beowulf, now King of the Geats, in Sweden, fights and slays a fire-breathing dragon but dies of his wounds. The poem ends with Beowulf's funeral and a lament. The text was transcribed by more than one hand and the many explicitly Christian interpretations were probably added by monks. *See also* HC1 pp.*139*, 164, *164*, 206.

Béranger, Pierre Jean de (1780–1857), French poet. His lively and satirical poems about everyday life and politics earned him general popularity but also resulted in short spells of imprisonment for his republican sympathies.

Berard, Christian (1902–49), French neo-Romantic painter and set designer. He is best known for his designs for the BALLET RUSSE DE MONTE CARLO company.

Berberis, genus of about 400 species of shrubs native to temperate regions, commonly called barberry. The bark and wood are yellow, and the golden flowers give way to sour blue berries. The sensitive stamens spring erect when touched. It is host for the plant disease rust. Family Berberidaceae.

Berbers, Caucasian Muslim people of N Africa and the Sahara Desert. Some are herdsmen and subsistence farmers; others, like the Tuareg, roam the desert with their great animal herds. The farmers live in independent villages, governed by meetings of male tribesmen. Their remarkably stable culture dates back to before 2400 BC and, after the Arab conquest of the 7th century, there were Berber empires in the 11th and 12th century. Berber languages are spoken by more than 10 million people.

Berceo, Gonzalo de (*c.* 1195–*c.* 1264), earliest-known Spanish poet. He was a BENEDICTINE monk and produced thousands of devotional verses. He also wrote *Milagros de Nuestra Señora*, a collection of poems about the Virgin Mary.

Berchet, Giovanni (1783–1851), Italian poet whose *Lettera semiseria di Grisostomo* (1816) was the leading expression of Italian Romanticism. He published his best-known poems such as *Le fantasie* (1829) in London, where he was a political exile (1821–48).

Berchtesgaden, town in the Bavarian Alps of West Germany, 16km (10 miles) S of Salzburg, Austria. Salt has been mined there since the 12th century. During WWII Adolph HITLER had a villa there, which was bombed by the Allies in March 1945. Pop. 4,500.

Berchtold, Count Leopold von (1863–1942), Austro-Hungarian statesman who, as Foreign Minister (1912–15), sent the ultimatum to Serbia in 1914 after the assassination of Archduke Francis Ferdinand at Sarajevo. This action precipitated WWI. *See also* HC2 pp.186–187, *187*.

Berdyaev, Nicholay (1874–1948), Russian theologian and religious philosopher. In his most influential book, *Freedom and the Spirit*, he put an anti-Marxist defence of the traditional orthodoxy of the Russian church.

Berenson, Bernard (1865–1959), US art critic, *b.* Lithuania. He was taken to the USA as a child. An authority on Italian RENAISSANCE art, he published a number of books on the subject. For most of his life he lived in Italy at his home, I Tatti, a gathering place for intellectuals.

Beresford, Jack (1899–1977), British oarsman. Principally a sculler, he competed in five Olympics (1920–36), winning three gold and two silver medals, including the 1920 single sculls. His Henley record is unparalleled, with wins in the five major events, including four in the Diamond Sculls and two in the "Grand" (eights).

Beresford, John (1738–1805), Irish statesman who served in Parliament from 1760 to 1802. As Commissioner of Revenue from 1770, he reformed fiscal collection. He was Prime Minister PITT's chief adviser on Irish matters, helping to bring about the union of Britain and Ireland.

Beresford, William Carr Beresford, Viscount (1768–1854), British general. His career included fighting in Egypt (1801–03) and capturing Cape Colony (1806). He successfully reorganized the Portuguese army in the PENINSULAR WAR.

Berg, Alban (1885–1935), Austrian composer. A student of Arnold SCHOENBERG, he composed most of his works in a complex, highly individualized style based on Schoenberg's 12-tone technique. His opera *Wozzeck* (1925) is regarded as one of the masterpieces of 20th-century opera. He also composed a violin concerto (1935) and began another opera *Lulu*, which was unfinished at his death. *See also* TWELVE-TONE MUSIC; WOZZECK; HC2 pp.*121*, 270.

Bergama. *See* PERGAMUM.

Bergamot, herb of the genus *Monarda*, including horsemint and Oswego tea; or the pear-shaped fruit of *Citrus bergamia*, grown in Italy for its oil, which is used in perfumery.

Berganza, Teresa (1936–), Spanish mezzo-soprano. She studied at the Madrid Conservatory, made her debut in Madrid in 1955 and appeared at the Metropolitan Opera in 1967.

Bergen, port in SW Norway on the N Atlantic Ocean; second-largest city in Norway and capital of Hordaland county. Founded in the 11th century, Bergen was Norway's chief city and the residence of several medieval kings. It is now an industrial and cultural centre with a university (1948), a national theatre (1850), several museums and a 13th-century Viking hall (*Haakonshallen*). Industries include shipbuilding, textiles, fish processing and electrical equipment. Pop. 214,000.

Bergius, Friedrich (1884–1949), German chemist who developed a method of treating coal with hydrogen, under high pressure, to produce oil. It became known as the Bergius process, and in 1931 Bergius shared the Nobel Prize in chemistry with Carl BOSCH. He also developed a process for converting wood into sugar by hydrolysis.

Bergman, Ingmar (1918–), Swedish stage and film writer-director. With a versatile company of artists and a strong personal vision, he has created dark allegories, sex satires and complex studies of human relationships. His major films include *The Seventh Seal* (1956), *Wild Strawberries* (1957), *The Virgin Spring* (1960), *Persona* (1966), *Scenes from a Marriage* (1974) and *The Magic Flute* (1975). *See also* HC2 p.277.

Bergman, Ingrid (1915–), Swedish actress whose acclaimed stage performances – *Joan of Lorraine* (1947), *Liliom* (1940) and *Anna Christie* (1941) – led to a long and varied film career in Hollywood. She won Academy Awards for *Gaslight* (1944), *Anastasia* (1956) and *Murder on the Orient Express* (1974).

Bergman, Torbern Olof (1735–1784), Swedish chemist who introduced improvements in chemical analysis, did important research into crystal structure and developed a table of chemical affinity.

Bergmann, Richard (1918–70), Anglo-Austrian table tennis player. Four times world singles champion (1937, 1939, 1948, 1950), he won Swaythling Cup gold medals with both Austria (1936) and England (1953). He had a fierce competitive temperament, and resisted even the finest attacks with his acrobatic retrieving.

Bergschrund, deep, wide crevasse or a series of parallel narrow crevasses in a glacier. It is produced by tension within the ice, often at the point where the moving ice separates from the immobile or apron ice. The formation is more common in old or retreating glaciers. *See also* PE p.116, *116*.

Bergson, Henri (1859–1941), French philosopher of evolution. He saw existence as a struggle between man's life-force (élan vital) and the material world. Man perceives the material through the use of his intellect whereas the life-force is perceived through intuition. Bergson received the Nobel Prize in literature in 1927. His works include *Time and Free Will* (1889) and the particularly significant *Creative Evolution* (1907).

Beria, Lavrenti Pavlovich (1899–1953), head of the Soviet secret police (NKVD). He took part in Stalin's purges and controlled internal security (1938–53). When Stalin died he was arrested and executed for treason. *See also* HC2 p.240.

Beriberi, disease caused by a deficiency of vitamin B_1, or thiamine, and other vitamins in the diet. The symptoms include weakness of the limbs, general swelling of the body and gastric disorders. Therapeutic doses of B complex vitamins are the usual treatment. *See also* MS pp.84–85.

Bering, Vitus Jonassen (1680–1741), Danish navigator who discovered Alaska and gave his name to the Bering Strait and Bering Sea. In 1728 he sailed north from Kamchatka, NE Siberia, through the Bering Strait, but failed to sight land. In 1741 he again set out from Kamchatka towards N America. He sighted Alaska but was shipwrecked on what is now Bering Island.

Beringia, one of many land bridges formed in the last glacial period, when the sea-level was much lower than now. Beringia is thought to have linked E Siberia with Alaska, enabling *Homo sapiens sapiens* to reach the Americas. *See also* MS p.30.

Bering Sea, northernmost reach of the Pacific Ocean, bounded by Siberia (NW) and Alaska (NE), and separated from the Pacific Ocean by the Aleutian Islands; it is connected to the Arctic Ocean by the Bering Strait. It is ice-bound in winter months. Exploration for Russia by the Danish navigator Vitus BERING in the early 18th century drew great attention to the fur-seal resource. International disagreement concerning the protection of seals resulted in the Bering Sea Controversy in 1886. Agreement was reached in 1893 and seal hunting was regulated. Area: approx. 2,292,000sq km (885,000sq miles).

Bering Strait, channel N of the Bering Sea separating W Alaska from E Siberia (which were once joined) and connecting the Bering Sea to the Arctic Ocean. It was named after the Danish explorer Vitus BERING who sailed through it in 1728. Width: 85km (53 miles) at narrowest point.

Berio, Luciano (1925–), Italian composer. He is in the forefront of avant-garde composers and uses electronic and "chance" effects in many of his works, which include *Nones* (1953), *Différences* (1958–60), *Visage* (1961) and *Opera* (1970).

Beriosova, Svetlana (1932–), Soviet-born prima ballerina. She joined Sadlers Wells Ballet in the 1952 and has danced both classical and modern roles. One of the most distinguished of modern dancers, her *Giselle* has won special praise.

Berkeley, Busby (1895–1977), US film choreographer, real name William Berkeley Enos. In 1930 he went to Hollywood to stage dance numbers for the musical *Whoopee*. He is best known for the elaborately planned and extravagant dance sequences in Warner Brothers musicals such as *42nd Street* (1953) and

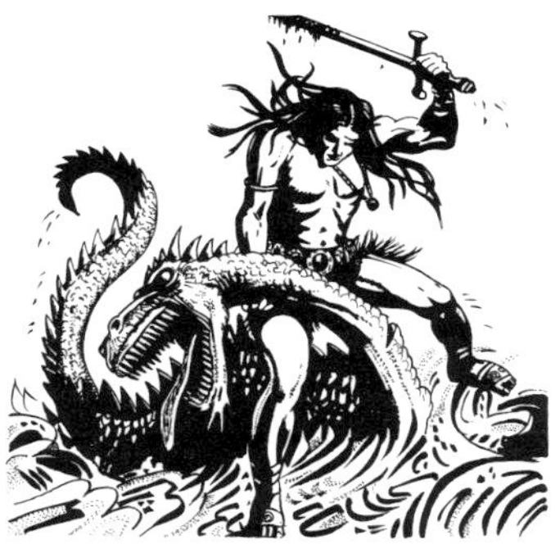

Beowulf; a surviving single manuscript of this epic is in the British Museum, London.

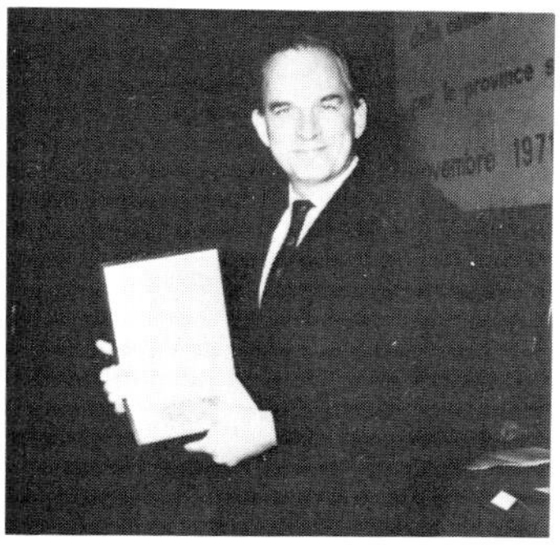

Ingmar Bergman, whose complex symbolic films explore themes of guilt and morality.

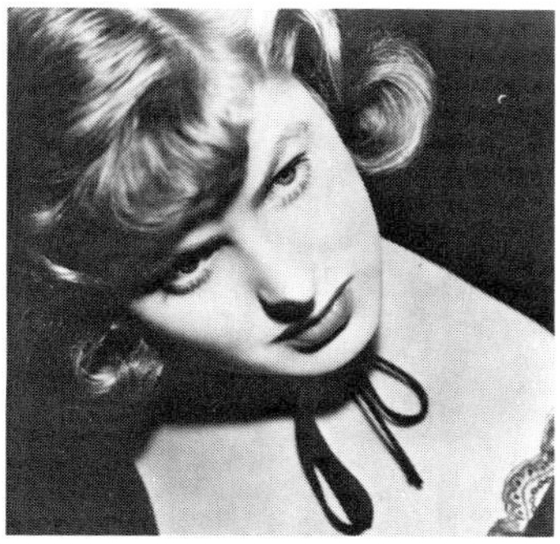

Ingrid Bergman has won three Academy Awards for her film roles.

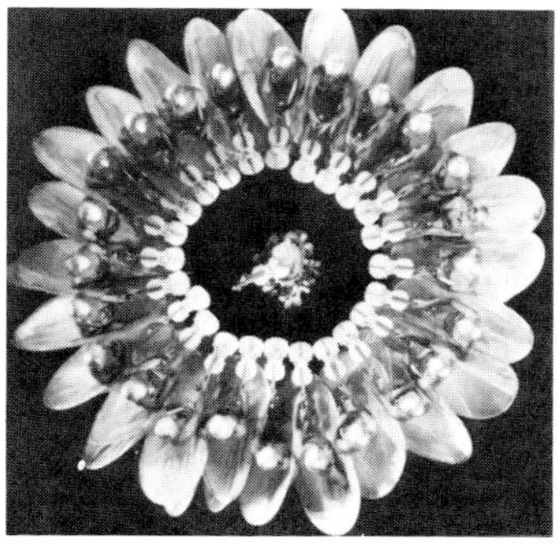

Busby Berkeley used dancers to create fantastic patterns in his screen musicals.

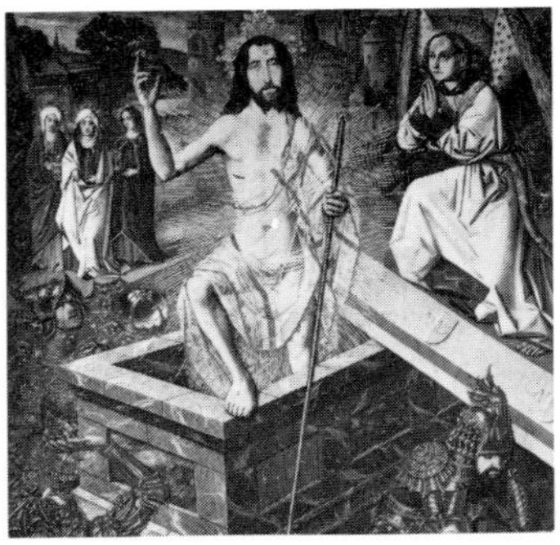

Bartolomé Bermejo took the Flemish style to Spain; this is his *Resurrection of Christ*.

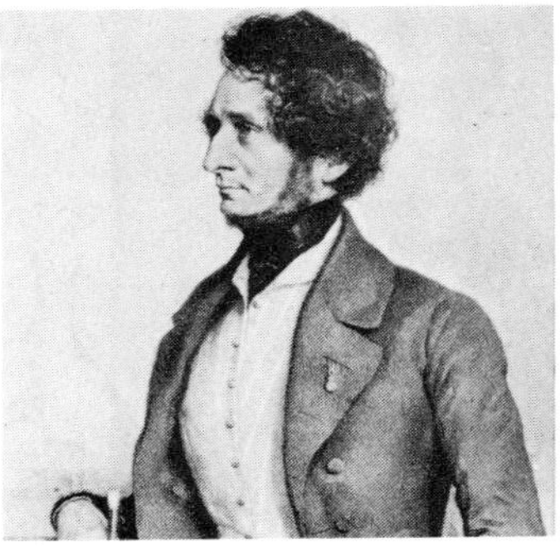

Berlioz related his compositions to stories and ideas; this is called "programme music".

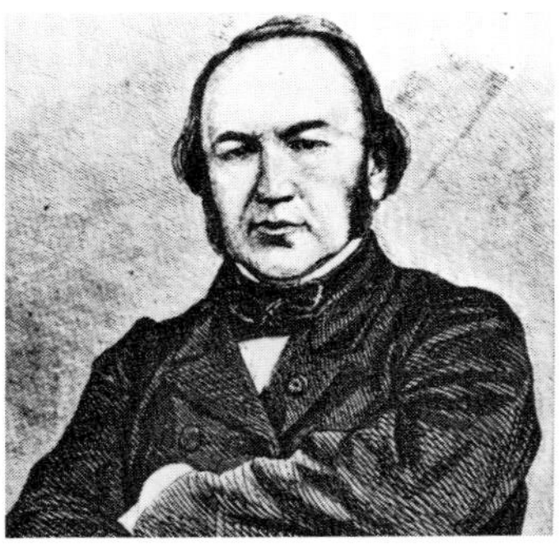

Claude Bernard, who became the foremost French physiologist of his day.

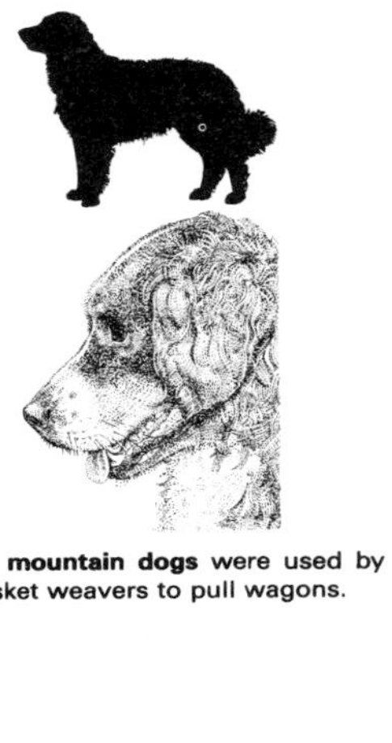

Bernese mountain dogs were used by the local basket weavers to pull wagons.

the series *The Gold Diggers* (1933–37).

Berkeley, George (1685–1753), Irish philosopher and churchman. He discussed the meaning of "existence" of objects in terms of their ability to be perceived by a mind. He became Bishop of Cloyne in 1734 and wrote extensively on philosophical matters. *See also* EMPIRICISM; MATERIALISM.

Berkeley, Sir Lennox Randal Francis (1903–), British composer. A pupil of Nadia BOULANGER from 1927 to 1933, he was thus little affected by the prevailing influence of folk music on British composers. His *Serenade for Strings* and *Symphony* (1939–40) bear the mark of STRAVINSKY. His major choral work is the *Stabat Mater* (1946); he also wrote four operas. The most often performed work is the horn trio.

Berkeley, Miles Joseph (1803–89), British botanist who was a leading authority on fungi and plant disease. He recorded more than 6,000 species of fungi, and his *Outlines of British Fungology* (1860) was an important contribution to knowledge of the subject.

Berkelium, radioactive metallic element (Bk), one of the ACTINIDE ELEMENTS. It does not occur in nature and was first made (1949) by alpha-particle bombardment of americium-241. Properties: at.no. 97; at.wt. 243.07; most stable isotope Bk^{247} (half-life 1.4×10^3 yr).

Berkshire, county in s central England, almost entirely within the river basin of the Thames, which marks the northern border. The Berkshire Downs run across the county. It is a fertile area: dairy cattle and poultry are important and barley is the main crop. Industries include nuclear research. The county town is Reading. Area: 1,255sq km (485sq miles). Pop. (1976) 659,000.

Berlage, Hendrik Petrus (1856–1934), Dutch architect who designed the Amsterdam Stock Exchange (1898–1903), establishing modern architecture in The Netherlands.

Berle, Milton (1908–), US comedian, real name Milton Berlinger. He began his career in music hall and later appeared on Broadway, in films and on television.

Berlin, Irving (1888–), US composer of musicals and more than 800 songs. His successful Broadway musicals include *Annie Get Your Gun* (1946) and *Call Me Madam* (1950). He also composed the scores for the films *Easter Parade* (1948) and *White Christmas* (1954). His most popular songs include *Alexander's Ragtime Band* and *White Christmas.*

Berlin, Sir Isaiah (1909–), British political scientist. He was the Chichele Professor of Social and Political Theory, Oxford (1957–67). From 1966 to 1975 he was President of Wolfson College, Oxford. His *The Hedgehog and the Fox* (1953) is a classic study of politics.

Berlin, city situated within East Germany and divided into two parts, East and West. East Berlin is the capital of the German Democratic Republic (East Germany) and West Berlin is a state and city belonging to the German Federal Republic (West Germany). Berlin rose to prominence in the 18th century as a manufacturing town and became the capital of the newly formed state of Germany in 1871. The city continued to expand and gain importance economically, industrially and culturally, reflecting Prussian pre-eminence in the newly formed state. In the early 20th century Berlin was the second-largest city in Europe. Virtually destroyed at the end of WWII, the city was divided into four sectors; British, French, US and Soviet. On the formation of East Germany the Soviet sector became East Berlin and the rest West Berlin. East Berlin industries: chemicals, electrical goods and foodstuffs. Pop. (1976 est.) 1,098,000. West Berlin industries: electrical goods, engineering and clothing. Pop. (1976) 2,024,000. *See also* MW p.83.

Berlin airlift (1948–49), 15-month operation to supply BERLIN with food and other basic necessities after the USSR closed all road and rail links between the city and West Germany. Britain and the USA flew more than 270,000 flights, delivering cargo and transporting Berlin's manufactured goods to markets elsewhere. *See also* HC2 *p.235.*

Berlin, Congress of (1878), meeting of European powers to revise the Treaty of SAN STEFANO by which Russia had ended the Russo-Turkish war. At the Congress, which was presided over by BISMARCK, Austria-Hungary was given military occupation of BOSNIA-HERCEGOVINA (which had gained independence in the earlier treaty), Bulgaria was divided and Russia's naval expansion limited. *See also* HC2 pp.84–85, 184, *184.*

Berlin Wall, heavily fortified and defended wall 49km (29 miles) long, dividing East and West BERLIN. It was built in 1961 by the East Germans to stop a continuing flood of refugees to West Germany. Limited passage across the frontier was again permitted after 1963. *See also* HC2 p.243.

Berliner, Emile (1851–1929), US engineer, *b.* Germany. Among his many inventions were a "gramophone" (patented in 1887) – which used a flat, spiralled disc record – and a light, rotating-cylinder internal-combustion engine, used later in aeroplanes. *See also* MM p.232.

Berlioz, Louis-Hector (1803–69), pre-eminent French Romantic composer noted for innovative, highly progressive orchestral writing, the use of large forces and the emphasis he laid on orchestral colour. His best-known works include the *Symphonie Fantastique* (1830), *Harold in Italy* for viola and orchestra (1834), the operas *Benvenuto Cellini* (1838) and *The Trojans* (1855–58), and the *Requiem* (1837). He also wrote an extremely influential treatise on orchestration (1844). *See also* ROMANTIC music; HC2 p.106.

Bermejo, Bartolomé (*fl.c.*1474–95), Spanish painter and designer of stained glass said to have introduced oil painting to Spain. His most famous work is in Barcelona Cathedral.

Bermuda, self-governing British colony, formerly Somers Islands, in the w Atlantic Ocean; consists of approx. 300 islands. The capital is Hamilton on Bermuda Island. Area: 52sq km (20sq miles). Pop. (1975 est.) 56,000. *See* MW p.38.

Bern (Berne), capital of SWITZERLAND, on the River Aare, 95km (59 miles) sw of Zurich; capital of Bern canton. Founded in 1191 as a military post, it became part of the Swiss Confederation in 1353. Bern was occupied by French troops during the French Revolutionary Wars (1798). It is noted for its Gothic architecture. Industries: precision instruments, chemicals, tourism. Pop. (1976 est.) 162,405. *See also* MW p.163.

Bernadette of Lourdes, Saint (1844–79), full name Marie Bernarde Soubirous. The daughter of a poor French miller, she began to see visions of the Virgin Mary in 1858, who revealed to her the healing shrine of LOURDES. In 1866 she became a member of the Sisters of Charity at Nevers where, in declining health, she spent her last days. *See also* MS p.122.

Bernadotte, Count Folke (1895–1948), Swedish diplomat. In May 1948, as head of the Swedish Red Cross, he was appointed UN mediator to negotiate a truce between the newly created state of Israel and the Arab countries. On 17 Sept., while negotiating a permanent armistice, he was killed by Israeli partisans in Jerusalem.

Bernadotte, Jean Baptiste Jules, Prince (1763–1844), French general and King of Sweden and Norway (1818–44). He was NAPOLEON'S deputy in the Italian Campaign of 1797. In 1810 he accepted the title of Crown Prince of Sweden. He finally broke with Napoleon in 1813 at the Battle of Leipzig and thereafter devoted himself entirely to the affairs of Sweden. *See also* CHARLES XIV, JOHN.

Bernal, John Desmond (1901–71), Irish physicist, remembered for his work in the field of X-ray crystallography; he used the technique to study atomic structures. He was professor of physics, and then of crystallography, at London University between 1938 and 1968.

Bernanos, Georges (1888–1948), French novelist and political essayist. His novels *Sons le Soleil de Satan* (1926) and *Diary of a Country Priest* (1937) reflect his ardent Roman Catholicism. His political writings denounced FRANCO'S régime in Spain and the Vichy government in France.

Bernard, Claude (1813–78), French physiologist. He defined the role of the PANCREAS in digestion, the glycogenic function of the LIVER and the regulation of blood supply by vasomotor nerves.

Bernard, Émile (1868–1941), French painter. He experimented with POINTILLISM and claimed to have developed CLOISONNISM, the style used by GAUGUIN. Bernard was a leader of the SYNTHETIST movement in painting. He was a friend of van GOGH, and of CÉZANNE, who wrote him the famous letter about treating nature in painting "by means of the cylinder, the sphere and the cone".

Bernard, Jean-Jacques (1888–1972), French playwright. *Martine* (1922) is a fine example of his work and his fascination for the "drama of the unexpressed", in which the dialogue does not convey the real feelings of the characters.

Bernard de Ventadour (*d.c.*1195), Provençal troubadour. His work is executed delicately and simply and with powerful emotion; 45 short love lyrics and 19 tunes still survive. He is known to have travelled in England in 1152–55.

Bernardin de Saint-Pierre, Jacques-Henri (1737–1814), French author who spent three years (1768–71) in Mauritius (then known as Île de France), after which he wrote *Voyage à l'Île de France.* An early contributor to the French Romantic movement, his best-known work is *Paul et Virginie* (1788).

Bernard of Clairvaux, Saint (1090–1153), French mystic and religious leader. He was abbot of the Cistercian monastery of Clairvaux from 1115 until his death, and steadfastly refused all offers of higher positions. Under his direction nearly 100 new monasteries were founded. His reputation for miraculous cures made him a renowned and powerful religious influence in France. In 1130 his views were sought during a contested papal election, and afterwards he became an adviser to several popes. He actively fought heresy and advocated the Second Crusade in 1147. Bernard's devotion to the Virgin Mary and the Infant Christ greatly influenced the future of the Roman Catholic Church. He was canonized in 1174.

Bernard of Cluny, Benedictine monk at the Abbey of Cluny, N France, during the 12th century. He wrote many sermons, but his best-known work is the long poem *De Contemptu Mundi,* which criticized some aspects of contemporary monasticism. Many hymns have been based on the poem, including *Jerusalem the Golden* by John Neale.

Bernard of Menthon, Saint (923–1008), Italian Catholic priest who *c.*962 founded hospices on the alpine peaks Great and Little St Bernard. He is the patron saint of Alpine climbers.

Bern Convention (1887), agreement between various countries (but excluding the USA) that the copyright of a printed work in one of the countries should be effective in any of the others. The USA did not enter into such an agreement until the Universal Copyright Convention of 1952.

Berne. *See* BERN.

Bernese mountain dog, Swiss draught dog (working group) taken to Switzerland 2,000 years ago by Roman soldiers. It has a flat head with a strong muzzle and hanging lips, and a thick, medium-length tail. Its long silky coat is black with brown and white markings. Average size: 58.5–70cm (23–27.5in); 23–32kg (50–70lb).

Bernhard of Lippe-Biesterfeld, Prince (1911–), prince consort of The Netherlands, who married Juliana of Orange in 1937 and became prince consort when she became queen in 1948. Interested in animal conservation, he has helped ensure survival of endangered species.

Bernhardt, Sarah (1844–1923), *b.* Rosine Bernard, French actress of legendary international stature, known as the greatest tragedienne of her day. Her superb portrayals in *King Lear* (1867), *Ruy Blas* (1872), *Phèdre* (1874) and

Hernani (1877) earned her the title "Divine Sarah". She also toured Europe and the USA and managed the Théâtre Sarah Bernhardt in Paris (1899), where she played Hamlet.

Bernicia, Anglo-Saxon kingdom between the Tyne and the Forth, founded by King Ida in the mid-6th century and later joined with DEIRA to form NORTHUMBRIA.

Bernini, Gianlorenzo (1598–1680), Italian architect and sculptor, one of the fathers of Roman BAROQUE. By the age of 22 he had startled Rome with his sculpture, eg such psychological portrait studies as the *Vigevano* bust (1617–18) and the *Montoya* (*c.* 1621). He was also a skilful painter. His architecture was splendid in conception, lavish in use of marble and dramatic lighting, and often grand in scale. As the favourite of several popes, he was given unparalleled design opportunities. His large-scale commissions in and around St Peter's include the baldacchino (canopy) above the high altar (1633), and the Barbarini Palace (1638), the Cathedra Petri (1657–66) and (from 1656 onwards) the great elliptical piazza and enclosing colonnades in front of St Peter's. Other notable works are the fountain in the Piazza Novana (1647–52) and Sant'Andrea del Quirinale (1658–70), which he regarded as his most perfect creation. Bernini, more than any other architect, gave Rome its Baroque character. *See also* HC1 pp.304–305.

Bernoulli, Daniel (1700–82), Swiss mathematician and physicist, member of a famous family of mathematicians. His work on hydrodynamics demonstrated that fluid pressure decreases as the velocity of fluid flow increases; this fact has become known as Bernoulli's principle. Bernoulli's equation states that $p + 1/2\rho v^2 + \rho g y$ =constant, where p is the pressure, ρ the density, v the velocity, g the acceleration due to gravity and y is the height of the fluid at any point. This equation makes it possible to measure the pressure at two points, as with a MANOMETER or Pitot tube. Bernoulli also attempted the first statement of the KINETIC THEORY of gases. *See also* SU p.79.

Bernstein, Leonard (1918–), US conductor, composer and pianist. He was a conductor with the New York Philharmonic (1957–58) and then musical director (1958–69), winning large audiences and world fame mainly through recordings. His compositions include three symphonies, the oratorio *Kaddish* (1963), the *Chichester Psalms* (1965) and the *Mass* (1971), ballets, and music for the shows *Candide* (1956) and *West Side Story* (1957).

Berrigan, Daniel (1921–) and **Philip Francis** (1923–), US political activists dedicated to the peace and civil rights movements. Daniel, a Jesuit, and his brother Philip, a Roman Catholic priest, gained prominence in 1968 by burning government files in protest against the VIETNAM WAR.

Berruguete, Alonso (*c.* 1488–1561), Spanish sculptor. He studied in Italy (1504–17) and became the foremost Spanish sculptor, famous for figures in the MANNERIST style.

Berry, small, fleshy fruit containing many seeds. It consists of an outer skin, fleshy middle and an inner membrane enclosing the seeds. Often juicy and edible, a true berry develops from a flower ovary with petals attached underneath (superior ovary). Berries include TOMATO, GRAPE, BANANA and red PEPPER (capsicum); CITRUS fruits are also modified berries. False berries are fruits (such as the cucumber) formed from the matured ovary wall and other flower parts, often the floral tube. *See also* PE p.214.

Berry, Chuck (1926–), US rock and blues singer, real name Charles Edward Anderson Berry. A ROCK-AND-ROLL star with hits such as *Maybellene* (1955), *Roll over Beethoven* (1956) and *Sweet Little Sixteen* (1958), he sang music that voiced the frustration of 1950s youth, and many of his songs were subsequently sung by the ROLLING STONES and the BEATLES. He later concentrated on blues.

Berry, Jean de France, Duc de (1340–1416), French prince and patron of the arts. During the HUNDRED YEARS WAR his heavy taxation to support the wars led to a peasant revolt in 1381. His art treasures included tapestries and illuminated manuscripts. *See also* HC1 pp.*218*, 252.

Berserker, name given to Scandinavian warriors dedicated to the god ODIN, so called because they wore bearskin shirts into battle rather than armour, which contributed to werewolf legends in Europe. Berserkers drove themselves into a martial frenzy and fought ferociously.

Berthelot, Pierre Eugène Marcelin (1827–1907), French chemist. By making in the laboratory some organic compounds, including ethyl alcohol, methyl alcohol, benzene and methane, he showed that the distinction between organic compounds as substances formed only in living things and inorganic compounds was wrong. In the 1860s he did important work in THERMOCHEMISTRY. In 1895 he became Foreign Secretary of France.

Berthier, Louis Alexandre, Prince de Wagram (1753–1815), NAPOLEON's trusted assistant and chief of staff of the Grande Armée, sovereign prince of Neuchâtel. He fought during the American and French revolutions, Napoleon's first reign (when he acquired his titles), and served Louis XVIII until Napoleon's return from Elba.

Berthold (*c.* 1210–72), German FRANCISCAN preacher. He preached throughout Germany, and travelled extensively in Europe. His sermons are a valuable record of aspects of medieval life.

Berthollet, Claude Louis, Comte (1749–1822), French chemist. He discovered the structure of ammonia, showed the bleaching ability of chlorine and predicted the law of mass action, although his views were ignored on this subject.

Bertillon measurement, system of measuring human physical characteristics (eg, length of the middle finger), evolved by Alphonse Bertillon (1853–1914) for criminal identification and now used extensively by physical anthropologists. *See also* ANTHROPOMETRY; MS p.*292.*

Bertolucci, Bernardo (1940–), Italian director. He began working in films as an assistant to director Pier Pasolini on *Accatone* (1961). The first film he directed on his own was *La commare secca* (1962). Others included *La Strategia del ragno* (1970) and the controversial *Last Tango in Paris* (1972).

Bertrand, Henri-Gratien, Comte (1773–1844), French general and friend of NAPOLEON Bonaparte. He joined the army as an engineer and met Napoleon in Italy in 1797. In 1804 he became Napoleon's aide-de-camp and accompanied him into exile on Elba and St Helena (1814–15, 1815–21).

Bertrand de Born (*c.* 1140–*c.* 1214), French troubadour and soldier whose poems described (and encouraged) the rebelliousness of the sons of Henry II of England. DANTE, in the *Inferno*, refers to Bertrand's role in the quarrels.

Berwick, James Fitzjames, Duke of (1670–1734), illegitimate son of James II of England, was a soldier in the French army. He fought against the Hungarians and Ottoman Turks and in 1706 was made a marshal of France. He fought for Philip V of Spain in the War of the Spanish Succession and captured Barcelona (1714). He was killed at Philippsburg while commanding a French army during the War of the Polish Succession.

Berwickshire, former county in SE Scotland (now part of the BORDERS Region) made up of the Lammermuir Hills (NW), the hilly Lauderdales (W) and the fertile Merse region (SE). Sheep graze on the hills and, on the lower land, farmers grow cereal crops, sugar-beet and potatoes. Fishing is a major industry. The main rivers are the Blackadder, Eye, Whiteadder and Tweed. The administrative centre is Duns. Area: 1,184sq km (457sq miles). Pop. (1971) 20,750.

Beryl, mineral, beryllium silicate. Its crystals are usually hexagonal prisms of the hexagonal system. Gemstone varieties are aquamarine (pale blue-green) from Brazil; emerald (deep green) from Colombia; and morganite (pink) from Madagascar. Cut stones have little brilliance, but are valued for their intense colour. Hardness 8; s.g.2.6–2.8. *See also* PE pp.*94*, 98–99, *99*.

Beryllium, strong, light silver-grey metallic ALKALINE-EARTH ELEMENT (Be), first isolated in 1828 by Friedrich Wöhler. It occurs in many minerals including aquamarine, emerald and morganite (all forms of BERYL) and is used in alloys that combine lightness with rigidity. Beryllium and its oxide are also used as moderators in nuclear reactors. Properties: at.no. 4; at.wt. 9.01218; s.g.1.85 (20°C); m.p.1,285°C (2,345°F); b.p.2,970°C (5,378°F); most common isotope Be^9 (100%). *Se also* ALKALINE-EARTH ELEMENTS; SU p.136.

Berzelius, Baron Jöns Jakob (1779–1848), Swedish chemist, one of the founders of modern chemistry. His accomplishments include the discovery of the elements cerium, selenium and thorium; the isolation of the elements silicon, zirconium and titanium; the determination of atomic weights; and the devising of a modern system of chemical symbols. He prepared the first table of atomic weights and he contributed to the founding of the theory of radicals. *See also* PERIODIC TABLE.

Bes, god of ancient Egypt, in the form of a large-headed dwarf. A god of childbirth and children, he also gave protection from evil spirits.

Besant, Annie (1847–1933), British theosophist and social reformer. A supporter of birth control and free thought, she joined the Theosophical Society in 1889, serving as its president from 1907 until her death. She lived for many years in India, where she established in 1898 the Central Hindu College at Benares. She was later active in the movement for Indian self-government and was president of the Indian National Congress in 1917. *See also* THEOSOPHY.

Besant, Sir Walter (1836–1901), British author. His early works, written with James Rice, included the Romantic novels *The Golden Butterfly* (1876) and *The Seamy Side* (1881). His later works commented on contemporary social problems, such as *All Sorts and Conditions of Men* (1882) and *Children of Gibeon* (1886).

Bessarabia, historical region in SW European USSR; now in the Moldavian Republic (Moldavskaja SSR). The capital is Kišin'ov. It is a fertile agricultural region and produces grain, tobacco, sugar-beet and fruit. Greek colonists settled the Black Sea coast in the 7th century BC. By the 7th century Slavs had settled in the region and the Kievan Russians held control during the 9th–11th centuries. It was ceded to Russia by the Turks (1812) and made an autonomous republic in 1917. It renounced Soviet ties in 1918 and declared itself part of Romania, with which it has certain ethnic affinities. After WWII it was annexed to the USSR.

Bessel, Friedrich Wilhelm (1784–1846), German astronomer and mathematician. He devised a system for analysing and reducing astronomical observations, made the first accepted measurements of the distance of a star (61 Cygni) and carried out observations which led him to make predictions (since confirmed) that SIRIUS and PROCYON are binary stars. He devised Bessel functions, a type of mathematical function named after him, after observing perturbations of the planets. *See also* SU pp.165, 167.

Bessemer process, first method for mass-producing steel, patented by the British engineer Henry Bessemer in 1856. In a Bessemer converter, cast iron is converted into steel by blowing air through the molten iron until all carbon and silicon are burned out. A little carbon is then added along with other metals to give the desired properties to the steel. The converter is tilted to pour the molten steel. Sir Henry Bessemer (1813–98), son of a French engineer, trained as a designer. He not only made many contributions to iron and steel manufacture, but also was a prolific inventor and improver in many other fields, eg graphite pencils, telephones and

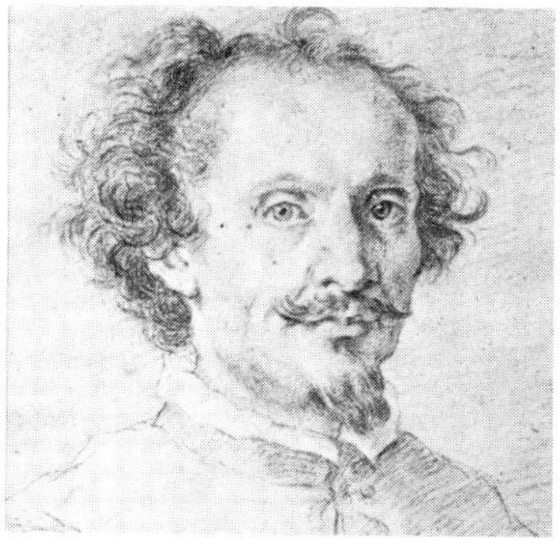

Bernini; sculptor, architect and painter, foremost artist of the 17th century.

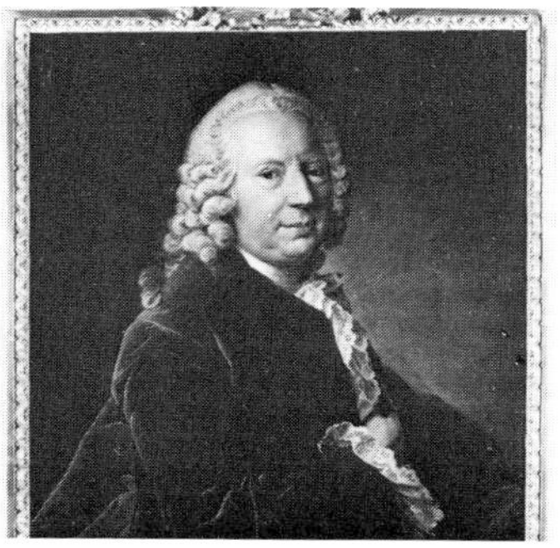

Daniel Bernouilli, whose famous principle explains the lift of an aeroplane.

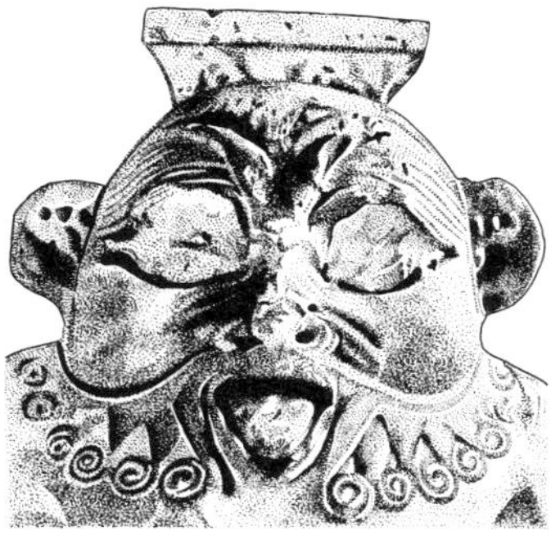

Bes, the Egyptian God of re-creation, was supposed to scare away evil spirits.

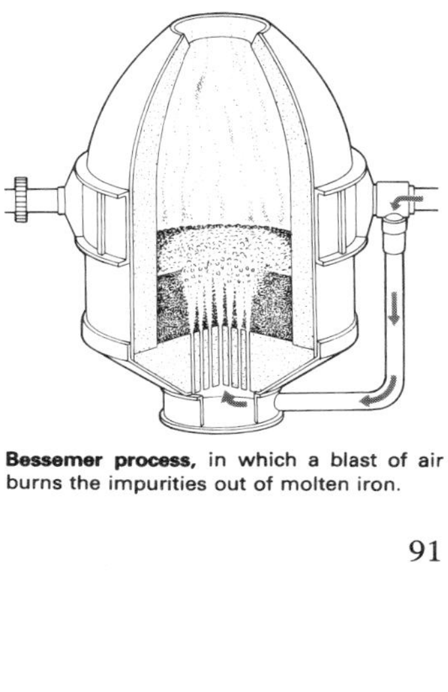

Bessemer process, in which a blast of air burns the impurities out of molten iron.

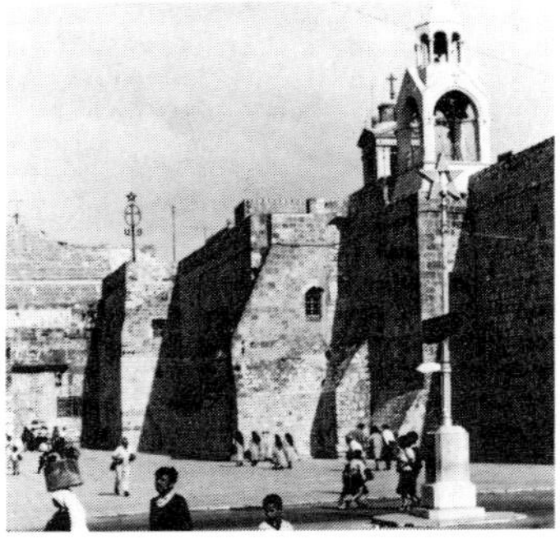

Bethlehem, the Church of the Nativity in the Jordan town now under Israeli occupation.

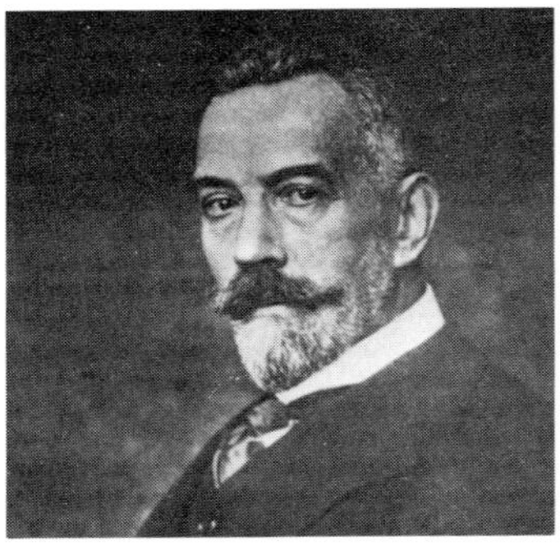

Bethmann-Hollweg, the author of the cynical phrase "fighting for a scrap of paper".

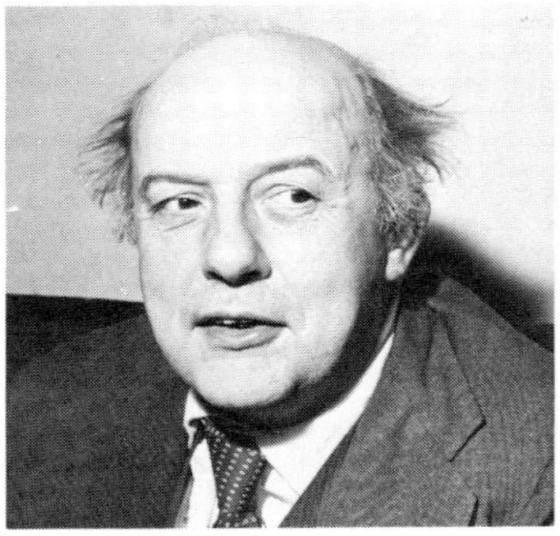

Sir John Betjeman, who is active in preserving buildings of architectural interest.

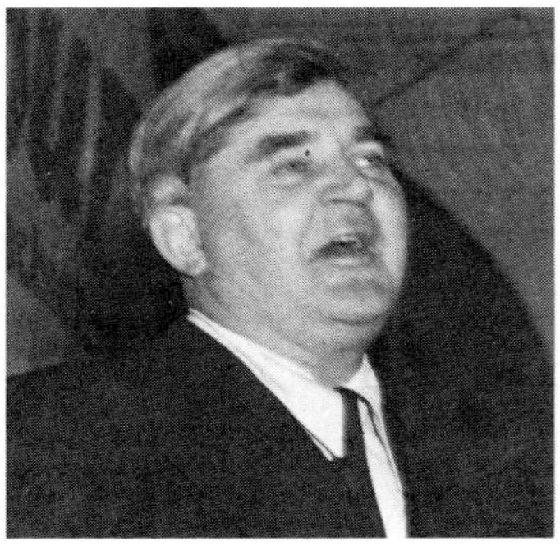

Aneurin Bevan, who was the architect of the British National Health Service.

typecasting. *See also* HC2 pp.88–89, 158–159; MM p.31.

Bessette, Gérard (1920–), Canadian author. A university professor, his novels about French-Canadian culture include *La bagarre* (1958), *Les pédagogues* (1961), and *L'incubation* (1965; *tr.* 1967, *Incubation*).

Best, Charles Herbert (1899–), Canadian physiologist. He and F. G. BANTING discovered INSULIN in 1921. From 1929–65 he was head of the department of physiology at the University of Toronto and chief of the Banting-Best department of medical research there after Banting's death in 1941. In collaboration with N.B. Taylor, he wrote *The Physiological Basis of Medical Practice* (1936).

Best, George (1946–), British footballer, *b.* Northern Ireland. He played for Manchester United and Fulham in the English League and for Northern Ireland internationally. He played his first match in the first division at the age of 17. He was a forward noted for his speed, ball control and goal-scoring ability. In 1968 he was the European footballer of the year. In 1977 he began a new football career in the USA.

Bet. *See* GAMBLING.

Beta Centauri, Agena, or Hadar, bluish-white giant star in the constellation of CENTAURUS. It has a 9th-magnitude companion. Characteristics: apparent mag. 0.61; absolute mag. 4.3; spectral type B1; distance 391 light-years. *See also* SU pp.226, 261, 266.

Beta Crucis, or Mimosa, blue-white giant star in the constellation of Crux (the SOUTHERN CROSS). Characteristics: apparent mag. 1.3; absolute mag. 4.7; spectral type B0; distance 489 light years. *See also* SU pp.226, 260, 266.

Beta-rays, or beta particles, energetic electrons emitted spontaneously by certain radioactive ISOTOPES. Beta decay results from the breakdown of a neutron to a proton, electron and antineutrino. *See also* RADIOACTIVITY; SU p.62.

Betatron, type of particle ACCELERATOR consisting of a hollow, evacuated circular ring in which ELECTRONS are confined and accelerated by a rapidly changing magnetic field. When they reach very high energies, of the order of 350MeV, they are focused magnetically to strike a target. The output beam can be either an electron beam or secondarily-produced X-rays. *See also* SU p.67.

Betelgeuse, or Alpha Orionis, red supergiant star and the second-brightest in the constellation of Orion. It is a pulsating variable whose diameter fluctuates between 300 and 400 times that of the Sun. Characteristics: apparent mag. 0.85 (mean); absolute mag. −5.5 (mean); spectral type M2; distance 500 light-years. *See also* SU pp.226, 239, 240, 257, *264*.

Betel palm, or areca, tall slender PALM tree native to the Philippines, planted throughout SE Asia and the Pacific islands. It has small feather-shaped leaves. Its seeds (betel nuts) are chewed as a stimulant or narcotic; they redden the saliva and gums. Height: to 15m (50ft). Family Palmaceae; species *Areca catechu*.

Bethany, (Al-'Ayzarīgah), village in Jordan, 3km (2 miles) E of Jerusalem, at foot of the Mt of Olives. It is the biblical home of Mary, Martha and Lazarus, and the traditional site of Christ's Ascension and the raising of Lazarus from the dead.

Bethe, Hans Albrecht (1906–), US nuclear physicist, *b.* Germany. Educated in Germany, he left with the advent of Hitler, going first to Britain and then to the USA. He worked on stellar energy processes and helped to develop the ATOMIC BOMB. He is noted for his theories on atomic properties and was awarded the 1967 Nobel Prize in physics for his work on the origin of solar and stellar energy.

Bethell, Mary Ursula (1874–1945), New Zealand poet. Her most important collection, *From a Garden in the Antipodes* (1929), shows her realism and fascination with religious themes.

Bethlehem (Bayt Lahm), town in Israeli-occupied Jordan (since 1967), 8km (5 miles) SSW of Jerusalem (Yerushalayim). The traditional birthplace of JESUS CHRIST, it was the early home of King David and the site of the biblical Massacre of the Innocents. The Church of the Nativity, built by Constantine in AD 330, is the oldest Christian church still in use. Under the rule of the Ottoman Empire from 1571 until 1916, it was part of the British Palestine mandate until 1948 when it became part of Jordan. Tourism is the main industry. Pop. 16,300.

Bethmann-Hollweg, Theobald von (1856–1921), German statesman. He succeeded BÜLOW as Chancellor of the German Empire (1909–17). In 1914 he referred to the treaty ensuring Belgian neutrality as a "scrap of paper". Hindenburg and Ludendorff forced him to resign (1917) after he advocated a restriction of submarine warfare and an end to the war. *See also* HC2 p.186.

Beti, Mongo (1932–), pen-name of the African novelist Alexandre Biyidi. An important figure in the NEGRITUDE movement, he explored modern African life and the effects of colonialism, often through satire. Among his works are *The Poor Christ of Bomba* (1956) and *Mission to Kala* (1958).

Betjeman, Sir John (1906–), English poet. He became Poet Laureate in 1972. His verse, traditional in form, considers the details and oddities of English domestic life. *Summoned by Bells* (1960) is a verse autobiography of his early years. He is also a noted authority on Victorian and Edwardian architecture. Recent books include *A Nip in the Air* (1974) and *A Few Late Chrysanthemums* (1975).

Betony, common name for colourful herbs of the MINT family (Labiatae), including *Stachys grandiflora* and *S. officinalis*. Flowers of this perennial from Asia Minor are white or purple and arranged in showy clusters. Betony grows in damp, shady places.

Bettelheim, Bruno (1903–), US psychologist, *b.* Vienna. He applied the psychoanalytic approach to emotionally disturbed children, detailing the roles that parents play in the development of their children's personalities. His books include *Love is not Enough* (1950) and *The Empty Fortress* (1967).

Betterton, Thomas (*c.* 1635–1710), English actor and theatre manager. He was one of the finest actors of the RESTORATION period, his most notable roles being Hamlet and Sir Toby Belch. He also successfully adapted plays and managed his own theatre company in what is now Her Majesty's Theatre, London.

Betti, Ugo (1892–1953), Italian poet and dramatist. He wrote collections of verse including *Il re pensioroso* (1922) and many plays including *La padrona* (1927) and *Corruzione al palazzo di giustizia* (1944).

Betting. *See* GAMBLING.

Betty, William Henry West (1791–1874), English actor, known as the Young Roscius. In 1804 he appeared at Covent Garden, London, and for a season had enormous success as a child prodigy, acting in Shakespeare's main tragic roles. He retired in 1808.

BeV, abbreviation for US billion electron volts, a unit of energy equal to a thousand million (10^9) electron volts

Bevan, Aneurin (1897–1960), British socialist politician. An active trade unionist, he became a Labour MP in 1929 and gradually assumed leadership of the Labour Party left wing, whose views he expressed in *Tribune* magazine, which he edited (1940–45). He became Minister of Health in 1945 and introduced the National Health Service in 1946. His book, *In Place of Fear,* was published in 1952.

Bevan, Brian (1925–), Australian rugby league player. A winger who forsook his native land to join Warrington, he became the most prolific try-scorer of his time. The "galloping ghost" scored 834 tries, including 72 in the 1952–53 season and seven in a match twice.

Bevatron, particle ACCELERATOR, the proton synchrotron, in which PROTONS are accelerated magnetically to high energies in a circular path, then focused on a target for "atom smashing" experiments. *See also* SU p.*67*.

Beveridge, William, 1st Baron (1879–1963), British academic and social reformer. He was sub-warden of Toynbee Hall (1903-05) and Director of the Labour Exchanges (1909–16). He was Director of the London School of Economics (1919–37) and Master of University College, Oxford (1937–45). As Chairman of the Committee on Social Insurance and Allied Services (1941–42), he wrote the report which was the basis for the creation of the welfare state after 1945. *See also* HC2 pp.*211,* 225.

Beverley, market town in N Humberside, NE England, 11km (7 miles) NNW of Hull. It was an important centre of the medieval cloth trade, and has a 13th-century minster. Industries: tanning, agricultural machinery. Pop. (1971 prelim.) 17,100.

Beverley Hills, city on the slopes of the Santa Monica Mts, S California, USA; completely surrounded by the city of Los Angeles. It is a fashionable residential area and the home of many film and television stars. Pop. (1970) 33,400.

Bevin, Ernest (1881–1951), British trade unionist and Labour politician. Organizer of the Dockers' Union (1910–21) and General Secretary of the Transport and General Workers' Union (1922–40), Bevin planned the GENERAL STRIKE (1926). He was Minister of Labour and National Service (1940–45), and as Foreign Secretary (1945–51) he assisted in Europe's economic recovery and helped to establish NATO. *See also* HC2 p.*234*.

Bewick, Thomas (1753–1828), British wood engraver and illustrator. He revived a method of white-line engraving on wood which restored wood engraving to popularity. His best illustrations were published in natural history books (1784–1804).

Beyazid, name of two Ottoman sultans. Beyazid I (*c.*1347–1403), who was sultan 1389–1402, besieged Constantinople for several years but suffered defeat by TAMERLANE at Ankara in 1402, who took him prisoner the same year. Beyazid II (1447–1512), who ruled 1481–1512, fought an intermittent war with the Mamelukes (1485–91) and established the Ottomans as a major naval power, but failed to defeat the SAFAVIDS of Persia. He abdicated in favour of his son Selim.

Beyle, Marie Henri, real name of the French author STENDHAL.

Beyond Good and Evil. *See* NIETZSCHE.

Beyrout. *See* BEIRUT.

Beza (de Bèsze), Theodore de (1519–1605), French theologian. In 1548 he joined CALVIN's Protestant church in GENEVA, acting as Calvin's assistant. He succeeded Calvin in 1564 as leader of the Genevan theocratic community. His editions of the New Testament influenced English versions. *See also* HC1 p.269.

Bezique, card game for two or more players. Most popular is the two-handed version played with 64 cards from two packs. The game was developed in France and England in the 1860s. The cards in each suit rank ace, 10, king, queen, jack, nine, eight, seven (the twos to the sixes are not used). Each player is dealt eight cards; another card is turned up to establish trumps. A player other than the dealer leads and the others follow. The highest card of the suit led or trump wins the trick. More cards are drawn from the deck and the game continues until all cards have been played.

Bhagavad Gita, "The Song of the Lord", a popular episode in the sixth book of the Hindu epic, the *Mahābhārata*. Probably composed shortly before the Christian era, it presents Krishna as the Supreme God who, if worshipped, will save men. The Gita begins with a battle between two related but hostile clans. The archer Arjuna, seeing his relatives in the opposing army, hesitates until Krishna reminds him of his duty to fight. Devotion and faith towards the Lord is the central theme. *See also* MS p.222.

Bhaktapur (Bhadgaon), city in central Nepal, in the Himalayan Mts. It is a Hindu pilgrimage centre with many fine temples, including that of Changu Narayan, a fine example of Newar religious architecture. Pop. (1968 est.) 35,500.

Bharal, also called blue sheep, is a sheep-like animal that lives in the Himalayas and mountains of Mongolia. It is intermediate between goats and true wild sheep. The pygmy blue sheep was first discovered in 1934. Species *Pseudois nayaur. See also* NW p.*222.*

Bhārat, Sanskrit name for INDIA; derived from Bhārata, a legendary monarch. *See also* MW p.95.

Bhartrhari (*c.*570–651), Hindu philosopher and poet of noble birth. He is the author of the Vakyapadiya, an important study of the philosophy of language. His life was spent struggling against his taste for luxurious living, until he finally became a yogi.

Bhave, Acharya Vinoba (1895–), Indian social reformer, selected by GANDHI to lead the independence movement in 1940. In 1951 he began walking tours urging landowners to give their land to the poor. He walked thousands of miles and his movement (Bhoodan Yayna) obtained 1,700,000ha (4,250,000 acres) of land by 1967.

Bhopāl, city in central India; capital of Madhya Pradesh state. Founded in 1728, it is noted for its terraced lakes and ancient mosques. It is a trade centre with food processing, electrical engineering and cotton textile industries. Pop. (1970 est.) 326,000.

Bhubaneswar, city in E central India; capital of Orissa state. It is famous for its numerous shrines and temples displaying many aspects of Hindu and Buddhist art and architecture. It is an administrative centre and has rolling mills and wire-cable works. Pop. 105,500.

Bhumibol (or Phumiphon) Adulyadej (1927–), King of Thailand (1946–). He succeeded to the throne in 1946 but ruled with a regent until 1950 when he became King in his own right, as Rama IX.

Bhutan, kingdom in the Himalayan Mountains, on the NE border of India and the S border of China. The capital is Thimbu. The economy is based on agriculture, with some craft industries such as metal and leather work. Area: 47,000sq km (18,147sq miles). Pop. (1976 est.) 1,202,000. *See* MW p.38.

Bhutto, Zulfikar Ali (1928–), Pakistani political leader. As leader of the Pakistan People's Party since 1967, he refused to co-operate with the East Pakistani AWAMI LEAGUE, which had won a majority in the Legislature in 1970. After BANGLADESH (East Pakistan) gained independence in the ensuing civil war, Bhutto became President in 1971 of what remained of Pakistan. Under the 1973 Constitution he became Prime Minister. Disorderly elections early in 1977 prompted a military coup, as a result of which he was imprisoned. *See also* MW p.140.

Biafra, former state in W Africa, formed from the eastern region of Nigeria; now divided into East-Central, South-Eastern and River states. It was established under Colonel Odumegwu Ojukwu in May 1967, when the Ibos attempted to secede from Nigeria. All economic aid was cut off by Nigeria and a bitter civil war followed in which Biafra lost territory, oil fields, (its main source of income) and many lives. The war ended in January 1970, when Biafra surrendered and was re-incorporated into Nigeria. *See also* MW p.135.

Bialik, Hayyim Nahman (1873–1934), Hebrew poet, teacher and translator who worked in the modern Hebrew language to express the feelings of the Jewish people. Born in the Ukraine, he later travelled to Germany, Vienna and finally to Tel Aviv.

Białystok, city in NE Poland, approx. 160km (100 miles) NE of Warsaw (Warszawa); capital of Białystok province. It is an important transport and industrial centre. Industries include textiles, precision instruments, metal goods and food processing. Pop. (1974) 187,100.

Biard, Pierre (1567–1622), French Jesuit missionary in Canada. He accompanied Père Masse to Acadia in 1611. His colony at St Sauveur was destroyed by Samuel Argall, acting on a commission from the Governor of Virginia.

Biathlon, sport involving cross-country skiing and target shooting which originated in Scandinavia. Each competitor is required to ski 20km (12.4 miles), stopping four times during the race to fire at fixed targets with a rifle. A miss results in the addition of a time penalty. The competitor with the lowest corrected time wins the contest.

Bibaud, Michel (1782–1857), French-Canadian author. A journalist and editor, he published the first book of poems by a French-Canadian (1830) and wrote a two-volume history of Canada (1837, 1844).

Bibesco, Princess Marthe Lucie (1887–1973), member of the Romanian Royal family (wife of Prince George Valentin Bibesco), who wrote novels under the pen-name Lucile Decaux. She also wrote, in French and under her real name, *The Eight Paradises* (1905), an account of her Asian travels. During WWI she ran a Red Cross hospital.

Bibiena, Galli da, family of Italian theatre architects and designers: Ferdinando (1657–1743) and Francesco (1659–1739). Ferdinando's son Giuseppe (1696–1757) and his grandson Carlo (1728–87) also produced work in this field in the Baroque style.

Bible, sacred scriptures of Judaism and Christianity. In part a history of the tribes of Israel, it is regarded as a source of divine revelation and of prescriptions and prohibitions for moral living. The OLD TESTAMENT, excluding the APOCRYPHA, is accepted as sacred by both Jews and Christians. The Roman Catholic and Eastern Orthodox Churches accept parts of the Apocrypha as sacred, while Jews and Protestants do not. The NEW TESTAMENT is accepted as sacred only by Christians.

Books of the Bible

Old Testament

Genesis	2 Chronicles	Daniel
Exodus	Ezra	Hosea
Leviticus	Nehemiah	Joel
Numbers	Esther	Amos
Deuteronomy	Job	Obadiah
Joshua	Psalms	Jonah
Judges	Proverbs	Micha
Ruth	Ecclesiastes	Nahum
1 Samuel	S. of Solomon	Habakkuk
2 Samuel	Isaiah	Zephaniah
1 Kings	Jeremiah	Haggai
2 Kings	Lamentations	Zechariah
1 Chronicles	Ezekiel	Malachi

New Testament

Matthew	Ephesians	Hebrews
Mark	Philippians	James
Luke	Colossians	1 Peter
John	1 Thessalonians	2 Peter
Acts	2 Thessalonians	1 John
Romans	1 Timothy	2 John
1 Corinthians	2 Timothy	3 John
2 Corinthians	Titus	Jude
Galatians	Philemon	Revelation

See also HC1 pp.58, 110, *174,* 195, *199, 260, 269,* 270, *282;* HC2 pp.*166,* 286.

Bible societies, Protestant organizations for spreading knowledge of the Bible. An early example was the Bible Society founded in England in 1780 to supply free Bibles to soldiers and sailors. The British and Foreign Bible Society was formed in London in 1804.

Bibliography, system of listing books and articles, described and arranged for easy reference. The Swiss naturalist Konrad von Gesner (1516–65) is credited with the first modern bibliography, *Universal Bibliography* (1545), a listing of European writers and their works in Latin, Greek and Hebrew. For a bibliography of *The Joy of Knowledge Encyclopaedia, see* end of *Fact Index L–Z.*

Bibliothèque Nationale, national library of France, in Paris. One of the oldest existing libraries, its basis was the library of Charles V (1364–80) and was first opened to the public in 1692. It receives a copy of every book published in France.

Bicameral system, legislative system that has two chambers or branches. It has its origins in the House of Commons and House of Lords in the English Parliament. Usually, members of the lower house are elected by popular vote whereas members of the upper house are appointed, or elected on a different basis.

Bicarbonate of soda, sodium bicarbonate, ($NaHCO_3$), a white, crystalline salt which decomposes in acid or on heating to release carbon dioxide gas, which explains its use in baking powder. It has a slightly alkaline reaction, hence its other main application as an ingredient of indigestion powders and tablets.

Biceps, large muscle on the front of the upper arm, easily felt when the arm is bent. It contracts to raise the forearm towards the upper arm, and also contracts to turn the inturned hand outwards (flexion). *See also* MS p.*58.*

Bichat, Marie François Xavier (1771–1802), French anatomist, pathologist and physiologist. His study and classification of tissues laid the foundations of modern HISTOLOGY.

Bichir, primitive freshwater fish that lives in Africa. It has large horny scales and a row of finlets along its back. A two-part swim bladder enables it to breath air at the surface of the water. Length: 61–91cm (2–3ft). Family Polypteridae; genus *Polypterus. See also* NW p.*232.*

Bicycle, first made (1817) by Karl von Drais in Germany and developed as an important means of transport and recreation in many countries. An Englishman, J. Starley, demonstrated the first successful chain drive in 1871. *See also* MM p.122.

Bicycle racing, sport involving a variety of events, from the sprint to the internationally known Tour de France (begun in 1903), in which the world's best cyclists compete annually in a road race about 4,800km (3,000 miles) long. The sport has become the accepted national summer sport of France, Belgium and the Netherlands and has increased in popularity in Italy, Spain, Germany and Scandinavia. Now a regular event at the Olympic Games, racing first became popular with the invention of the pneumatic tyre in 1888 by John DUNLOP, a Scottish veterinary surgeon.

Bidault, Georges (1899–), French political leader. He is known for his leadership of the underground resistance movement during WWII. Following the war he headed the provisional government in 1946 and was foreign minister in 1947–48 and 1953–54. In 1958 he founded the Christian Democratic Party, which opposed independence for Algeria. *See also* HC2 p.*234.*

Biddle, John (1615–62), founder of English UNITARIANISM. His *Twelve Arguments Against the Deity of the Holy Ghost* (1644) denied the Trinitarian doctrine. Biddle was arrested in 1645 and the book publicly burned in 1647.

Biedermeier, phase of German culture and a style of furniture (1816–48), characterized by simplicity and sober realism. Its name was derived from Papa Biedermeier, a humorous fictional character who epitomized middle-class conservatism. Furniture designs were simplified versions of French EMPIRE and DIRECTOIRE styles, black lacquer being substituted for the expensive ebony of the originals.

Biel, lake in NW Switzerland, bordering the cantons of Bern and Neuchâtel. It is connected by canals to the lake of Neuchâtel (to the SW) and the River Aare (NE). It contains St Pierre Island, which was the home of Jean-Jacques ROUSSEAU in 1765. Area: 41sq km (16sq miles).

Bielorussia. *See* BELORUSSIA.

Bielostok. *See* BIALYSTOK.

Bielsko-Biała, city in the province of Katowice, S Poland. It has been an important centre of the wool trade since medieval times. The city was formed in 1951 by the merger of two settlements on the River Biała. The chief industry is textiles. Pop. 105,600.

Bien Hoa, manufacturing city in S Vietnam, 32km (20 miles) NNE of Saigon (Ho Chi Min City). It was once the capital of Cambodia and, more recently, it had a US air force base in the Vietnam War. It is now an industrial city. Pop. (1971 est.) 177,500.

Bienne. *See* BIEL.

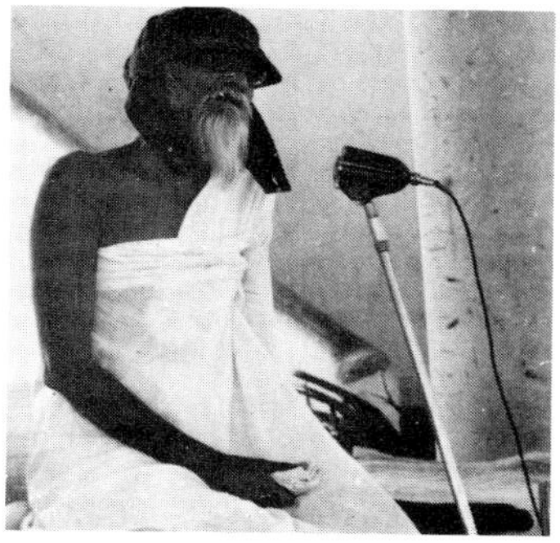

Vinoba Bhave, the Indian social reformer who championed the cause of the landless poor.

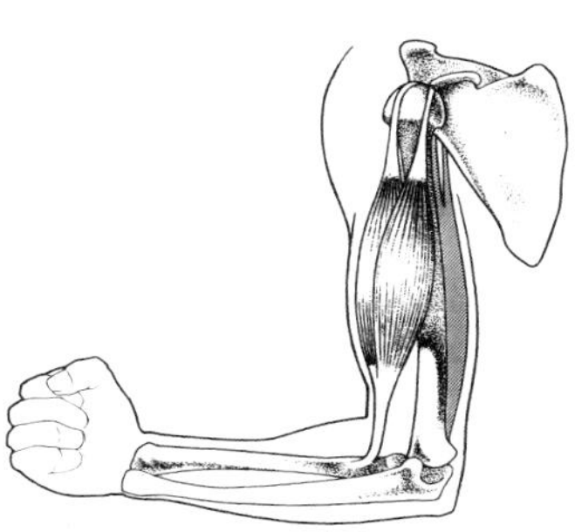

Biceps, the muscles with which we associate the idea of manly "strength".

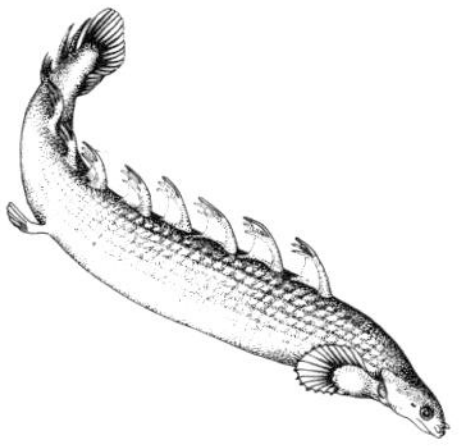

Bichirs live in marshy areas and take in the air they need at the surface of the water.

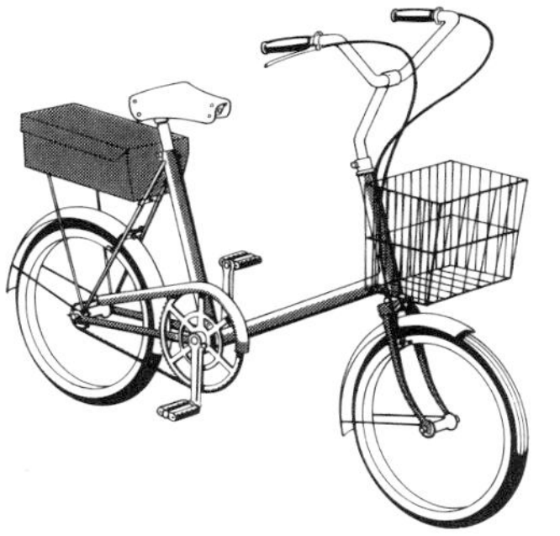

Bicycle; the versatile vehicle of self-transportation, recreation and sport.

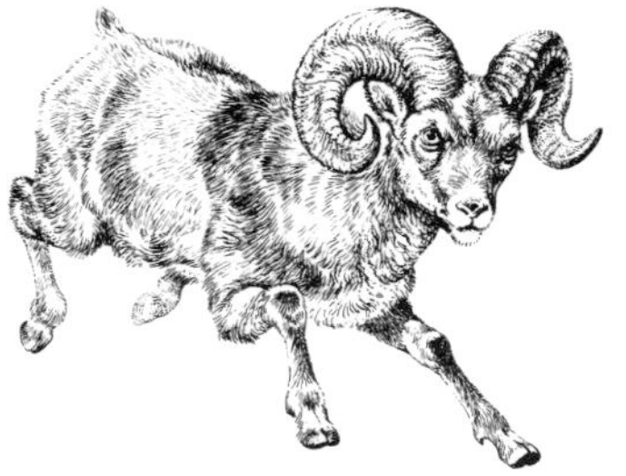

Bighorn, or Rocky Mountain sheep climb easily in the most dangerous of places.

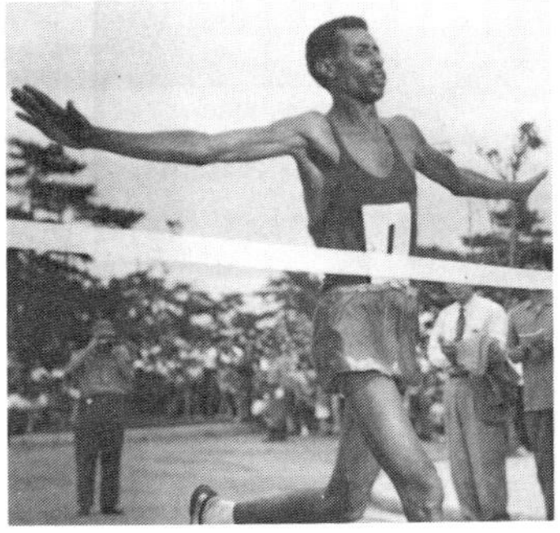

Abebe Bikila, the marathon runner whose life ended tragically in a wheelchair.

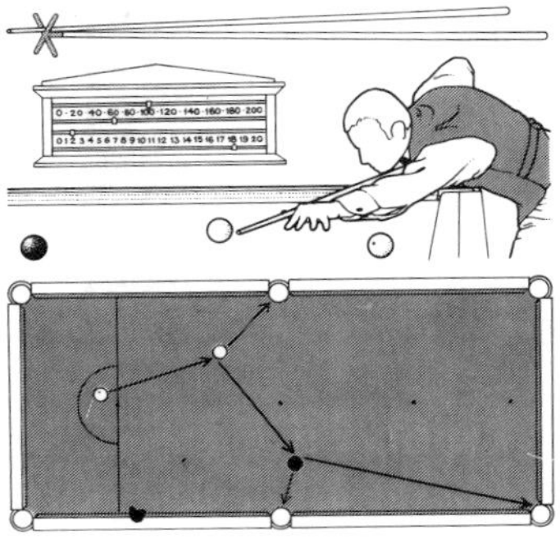

Billiards has an obscure origin; it is probably a development of several different games.

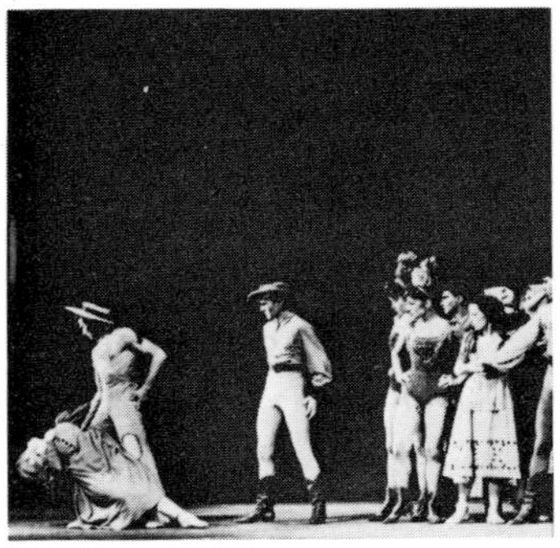

Billy the Kid was the subject of a one-act ballet by Eugene Loring.

Biennial, plant that completes its life cycle in two years, producing flowers and seed during the second year. This distinguishes it from an ANNUAL, which germinates, flowers, fruits and dies in one season, and a PERENNIAL, which is a plant that lives for three years or more. Some biennial seeds planted in early spring bloom the same year, but most are sown from June to August and bloom the following year. Popular garden biennials include FOXGLOVE, CANTERBURY BELL and WALLFLOWER.

Bienville, Jean Baptiste Le Moyne, Sieur de (1680–1768), French colonizer of Louisiana, *b.* Canada. In 1698 he accompanied his brother, Sieur d'Iberville, from Canada to the mouth of the Mississippi River. He founded Mobile (1711) and New Orleans (1718).

Bierbaum, Otto Julius (1865–1910), German poet and novelist. He was co-founder of the art journal *Pan* and the literary journal *Die Insel.* His writings include a collection of lyric verse *Irrgarten der Liebe* (1901) and a novel, *Prinz Kuckuck* (3 vols. 1906–07).

Bierce, Ambrose Gwinett (1842–*c.*1914), US satirical writer and journalist. He published several collections of short stories, but is best remembered for the collection of epigrammatic definitions, *The Devil's Dictionary* (1906).

Bigamy, according to the law in most countries, the criminal offence of entering into a second marriage when a first marriage is still in lawful existence.

Big-bang theory, postulate that all the matter and energy of the universe was once concentrated in a whole at near infinite density and was subsequently hurled in all directions at great speed by an explosion. Recently discovered microwave cosmic radiation (thought to be a remnant of the big bang) is evidence for this theory. *See also* SU p.252.

Big Ben, bell in the clock tower forming part of the Houses of Parliament at Westminster, London. It was named after Sir Benjamin Hall who was commissioner of works in 1859 when the bell was installed. The name is commonly used to refer to the clock and, by extension, to the tower.

Big Four, name applied to the main WWII Allies: Britain, USA, USSR and China. The term was extended to apply to the leaders of these countries, the US president Franklin D. ROOSEVELT (succeeded by Harry S. TRUMAN in 1944), the British prime minister Winston CHURCHILL, Soviet premier Joseph STALIN and Chinese president CHIANG KAI-SHEK. *See also* HC2 p.235.

Big game hunting. *See* HUNTING.

Bighorn, or Rocky Mountain sheep, wild SHEEP, native to the mountains of W North America. It has a brown or fawn short-haired coat; the males have long curved horns. Living in herds of about 50, their great climbing ability is aided by elastic food pads. Height: 1m (39in) at the shoulder; weight: to 155kg (340lb). Family Bovidae; species *Ovis canadensis.*

Bignonia, genus of woody climbing vines native to North America and Asia. They have showy, orange or yellow tubular flowers and are often cultivated as ornamental plants. Family Bignoniaceae.

Bihar, state in NE India, bordered by Nepal (to the N), West Bengal (E), Orissa and Madhya Pradesh (S) and Uttar Pradesh (W); the capital is Patna. The area is drained by the River Ganges and is a rich agricultural area. Other products: mica, coal, iron ore. Area: 174,006sq km (67,184sq miles). Pop. 56,387,300.

Bijāpur, city in Karnataka state, SW India, capital of the Bijāpur district. It was once capital of the Deccan Kingdom of Bijāpur and has many famous temples. Industries: textiles, food processing. Pop. (1971 prelim.) 103,300.

Bikila, Abebe (1932–73), Ethiopian road runner. The first man to win two Olympic marathons (1960, 1964), he was virtually unknown when he won in Rome, running in bare feet. In Tokyo, only six weeks after having his appendix removed, he won by more than 4 min. He spent the last years of his life in a wheelchair after a serious car accident in 1969.

Bikini Atoll, group of about 36 islands in the W central Pacific and part of the US-administered Marshall Islands. The USA used the area to conduct atomic weapons tests between 1946 and 1956. The islands were affected by fallout but considered to be safe for habitation after 1969.

Bilateralism, agreement between two states to pursue common interests jointly. Bilateral agreements are usually such that the value of trade each way is equally beneficial.

Bilbao, capital city of Vizcaya province in N central Spain, on the estuary of the River Nervión, near the Bay of Biscay. It was founded *c.*1300 and is now one of Spain's most important ports and commercial centres. It is the home of the University of Bilbao (1968). Industries: iron and steel, fishing, shipbuilding, chemicals. Pop. (1970) 410,490.

Bilberry, also called blueberry, blaeberry or whortleberry, deciduous evergreen shrub native to N Europe and E North America, which produces a small, dark purple fruit. There are two types: the cultivated high-bush, raised commercially, which grows best in damp, acid soil; and the wild low-bush, which grows best in sandy, acid soil. Family Ericaceae; genus *Vaccinium.*

Bildungsroman, German "educational novel" of which the prototype is GOETHE's *Wilhelm Meister,* in which someone with an artistic temperament is taught by experience how to come to terms with reality. Gottfried KELLER's *Der Grüne Heinrich* (1854–55) is the last direct example, and Thomas MANN's *The Magic Mountain* (1924) is a good example of an ironical parody of this traditional form. *See also* HC1 pp.72–73.

Bile, bitter yellow, brown or green alkaline fluid, secreted by the LIVER and stored in the GALL BLADDER, which is important in digestion. It enters the duodenum via the bile duct. It has two functions in digestion: the bile salts it contains emulsify fats (allowing their easier absorption) and it neutralizes stomach acids. Bile also contains excreted products, notably CHOLESTEROL and BILIRUBIN. The latter, a bile pigment, is a breakdown product of HAEMOGLOBIN with a green-orange colour. It is this that causes the skin yellowing in JAUNDICE, which can be caused by the inflammation or blockage of the gall bladder. *See also* MS p.69, *69.*

Bilharzia, bilharziasis, or schistosomiasis, one of the world's most widespread and prevalent tropical diseases, caused by infection by blood (flukes, small flatworms of the genus *Schistosomum.* In many hot countries it affects more than 90% of the inhabitants, and hundreds of millions of people suffer from the disease. Infection comes from drinking or bathing in contaminated water. The worms spend part of their life cycle as parasites in water snails, and the main hope for control of the disease is elimination of the snails. *See also* MS p.107; NW p.86.

Bilirubin, pigment derived from blood. When red blood cells have reached the end of their useful lives, they are broken down, mainly by the LIVER. Useful materials, such as the haem of HAEMOGLOBIN, are recycled in the body. Among the waste materials is the green-orange pigment bilirubin, which is converted into stercobilin, the colouring matter of faeces. *See also* MS pp.92, 93.

Bilk, Acker (1929–), English traditional jazz clarinettist, real name Bernard Bilk. In 1954 he joined Ken COLYER's jazz band and in 1958 formed his own group – the Paramount Jazz Band. He made various successful records including *Summer Set* (1960) and the solo *Stranger on the Shore* (1962).

Bill, Max (1908–), Swiss sculptor who was also active as a painter, designer and architect. He was influenced by the design principles of the BAUHAUS, where he studied (1927–29). From 1951 he taught at Ulm for six years, exerting great influence on German artists. His writings include essays on Kandinsky and on mathematical aspects of modern art.

Bill, birds, the horny jaws or BEAK.

Bill, draft of a proposed law. It must be approved by the legislature before it can become law. A bill is drawn up by law-draughtsmen in the civil service on the basis of instructions from a minister. Changes may be made to the bill during discussion and scrutiny in the legislature. *See also* ACT OF PARLIAMENT.

Billiards, game with three balls (two white and one red) played by striking one's own of the two whites against the red, using a long tapering cue, on a table with six pockets. Points are scored in four ways: sinking the white or an opponent's red in a pocket (a "pot"); sinking one's own white off the opponent's or the red (an "in-off"); hitting both the red and the opponent's white with one's own white (a cannon); and by means of penalty points. A variation in the USA uses 15 numbered balls; *See* POOL.

Billingsgate, fish-market in the City of London, on the N bank of the River Thames between London Bridge and the Tower of London. It dates from Saxon times and takes its name from a river gate in the old city wall. The fish-porters are noted for their hats, strengthened with wood, with which they carry heavy loads on their heads.

Billion, in Britain and most countries other than the USA, 1 million million, or 1,000,000,000,000. In the USA and France it is 1 thousand million, or 1,000,000,000. *See also* SU p.31.

Billiton. *See* BELITUNG.

Bill of exchange, unconditional written order from one person to another calling on him to pay on demand, or at a specified date, a sum of money to a particular person or to the bearer. A cheque and a postal order are both bills of exchange. *See also* HC1 p.238.

Bill of Rights (1689), British statute enshrining the constitutional principles won during the GLORIOUS REVOLUTION. It confirmed the abdication of JAMES II; offered the throne to WILLIAM III and MARY II; excluded Roman Catholics from the succession; outlawed certain of James' abuses of the Royal Prerogative, such as his control of the legal system and use of a standing army; set out the subjects' civil and political rights; assured the freedom of speech in Parliament and guaranteed the supremacy of that institution over the Crown. *See also* HC1 pp.293, 312.

Bill of sale, formal written document by which the sale or mortgage of goods is recorded, although possession is unaffected. It is often used as a means of securing a loan.

Billy Budd (1924), novella by Herman MELVILLE, published posthumously (1924), on which Benjamin BRITTEN based his opera (1951). Billy, an innocent young sailor, accidentally kills Claggart, the evil master-at-arms who had persecuted him. Capt. Vere, commander of the ship, sympathizes with Billy but feels he must still hang him. In 1962 Peter USTINOV directed and starred in a film of the book.

Billy the Kid (1859–81), US frontier outlaw, also known as William H. Bonney. Traditionally 21 murders are ascribed to him but there is no reliable evidence for this figure. In 1878 he killed a sheriff and led a gang of cattle rustlers. He was sentenced in 1880. He escaped from jail, but was caught and killed by Sheriff Pat F. Garrett. The one-act ballet *Billy the Kid* (1938) by Eugene Loring has music by Aaron Copland, based on cowboy melodies.

Bimetallic strip, device used in THERMOSTATS and mechanical thermometers. It consists of bonded strips of two metals with dissimilar coefficients of thermal expansion. When heated the bimetallic strip bends because one metal expands more than the other. This, reversible, distortion is used to move a dial pointer or to open or close a switch in an electrical circuit.

Bimetallism, policy of defining a country's money in terms of two metals, usually gold and silver, according to a fixed weight ratio. Each metal is accepted for the manufacture of coins, which become legal tender. The system was used in Europe and the USA in the 19th century. Its great drawback was that the market price for the metals kept changing, so that if a metal had a commercial value higher than its face value as money, coins tended to go out of circulation as they were hoarded for their intrinsic value.

Binary star, stellar system consisting of two separate stars orbiting around a common centre of gravity. Visual binaries are those whose components can be seen as separate stars with the naked eye or through a telescope. Spectroscopic binaries are visually unresolvable but show redshifts and blueshifts in their spectra as the individual stars move towards or away from the observer.

Binary system, in mathematics, number system having a base of 2 (the decimal system has a base of 10), most appropriate to computers since it is simple and corresponds to the open (0), and the closed (1) states of switch, or logic gate, on which computers are based. *See also* MM pp.106–107; SU p.31.

Binding energy, energy that holds an atomic nucleus together. This amount of energy must be supplied to a nucleus before it will "split" – undergo fission (except during radioactive decay). *See also* NUCLEAR ENERGY. SU pp.64–65.

Bindweed, climbing plant with white or pink trumpet-shaped flowers. Species include *Calystegia sepium*, or hedge bindweed, and *Convolvulus arvensis*, field bindweed. Family Convolvulaceae.

Binet, Alfred (1857–1911), French psychologist. He established the first French psychology laboratory in 1889 and the first French psychology journal in 1895. His best-known achievement was devising the first practical intelligence tests 1905–11, which profoundly influenced the assessment of abilities in psychology and education. *See also* MS p.*143*.

Bing, Sir Rudolf (1902–), Austrian-born impresario, In 1933 he went to England and in 1947 founded the Edinburgh Festival, From 1950 to 1972 he was the director of the Metropolitan Opera in New York.

Bingham, Hiram (1875–1956), US archaeologist. His discovery in 1912, of the INCA mountain city of MACHU PICCHU in the Peruvian Andes helped historians to unravel the story of Peru before the Spanish conquest. He led many expeditions to South America and wrote *Inca Land* (1922), *Machu Picchu* (1930) and *Lost City of the Incas* (1948). *See also* HC1 pp.*23*, 232–233.

Bingo, board game, usually played by a large number of people for cash prizes. Each player purchases one or more boards containing differently-numbered squares, together with some small discs with which to cover the numbers. A "caller" draws numbered balls at random, and the first contestant to cover a straight row of numbers on the board with numbers called is the winner.

Binoculars, optical instrument, used with both eyes simultaneously, that produces a magnified image of a distant object or scene. It consists of a pair of identical telescopes, one for each eye, both containing an objective lens and an eye-piece lens and an optical system (usually prisms), to form an upright image. *See also* SU p.100.

Binomial nomenclature, system of naming organisms by giving them a two-part Latin name. The first part of the name is the GENUS and the second part the SPECIES, eg *Homo sapiens* is the binomial name for human beings. The system was developed by the Swedish botanist Carl LINNAEUS in the 18th century. *See also* TAXONOMY; NW p.23.

Binomial theorem, mathematical rule for expanding (as a series) an algebraic expression of the form $(x+y)^n$, where x and y are monomials and n is a positive integer. Its expansion is

$$(x+y)^n = x^n + \frac{n\,x^{n-1}}{1!}y + \frac{n\,(n-1)}{2!}x^{n-2}y^2 + \frac{n\,(n-1)\,(n-2)}{3!}x^{n-3}y^3 \ldots y^n.$$

Binturong, mammal of the civet family, also related to mongooses. It lives in the forests of SE Asia, spending much of its time in trees, eating their fruits and leaves. It has a shaggy black coat and grows to approx. 1.7m (5.6ft) long, including a bushy prehensile tail of almost half this length. Species *Arctitis binturong*. *See also* NW pp.214, 215.

Binyon, Robert Laurence (1869–1943), English poet and literary critic. His elegy *For the Fallen*, remembering the dead in WWI, was widely acclaimed, but much of his work was more academic. He also produced a notable translation of DANTE's *Divine Comedy* in 1933–43.

Binzerte. *See* BIZERTE.

Bío-Bío, river in S central Chile, flowing generally NW from the Andes through the provinces of Cautín, Bío-Bío and Concepción. It enters the Pacific Ocean near the city of Concepción. Length: approx. 383km (238 miles).

Biochemical engineering, the production or modification of materials arising from living organisms, often on an industrial scale. Particularly important has been the production of moulds and bacteria as sources of ANTIBIOTICS, VITAMINS and ENZYMES. The many applications of enzymes in the manufacture of food and chemicals is another important aspect of biochemical engineering, as also is the growing "manufacture" of bacteria and yeasts as animal foods.

Biochemistry, science of the chemistry of life. It attempts to use the methods and concepts of organic and physical chemistry to investigate living matter and systems. Biochemists study both the structure and properties of all the constituents of living matter – eg, fats, proteins, enzymes, hormones, vitamins, DNA, cells, membranes, organs etc. – together with the complex reactions and pathways of these in metabolism. *See also* NW pp.26–31, 36–37, SU pp.152–155.

Bio-degradability, property of a substance that enables it to be decomposed by micro-organisms into stable, simple compounds (such as water and carbon dioxide). This property is being designed into products such as plastics to aid refuse disposal.

Bio-electricity, electricity originating in plants or animals. Different electrical potentials are built up within the organism by the process of ionic separation across a membrane in association with nerve impulses and muscle contractions. *See also* SU pp.112, 112–13, 148; MS pp.39–40.

Bio-engineering, application of engineering techniques to medical and biological problems. Also, the engineering of devices to aid or replace defective or inadequate body organs, for example, artificial limbs and hearing aids. *See also* MS p.*127*; MM p.*105*.

Bio-feedback, from "biological feedback", voluntary control of normally involuntary states using sensitive electronic instruments. People train themselves to control their internal functioning by observing the monitoring signals of the parameters such as their heart rate, blood pressure and brain-wave patterns, and consciously respond to them and eventually control them. The method holds promise for treating headaches, hypertension and other disorders related to the activities of the AUTONOMIC NERVOUS SYSTEM. *See also* MS pp.123, 192.

Biogenesis, long-held principle in biology (originally opposed to the idea of spontaneous generation of life) that maintains that all living organisms derive from parent(s) generally similar to themselves. On the whole, it still holds good despite variations in individuals caused by mutations, hybridization and other genetic effects. *See also* GENETICS.

Biography, literary form which describes the events of a person's life. Any fragment may be biographical, but the first known complete biographies were PLUTARCH's *Lives* (2nd century). In English literature the first biographical works appeared in the 17th century, notably WALTON's *Lives* and AUBREY's *Lives*. The first modern biography was BOSWELL's *Life of Samuel Johnson* (1791), rich in detail. Since its publication, the biography has become a sophisticated and highly popular form of literature, aiming at a critically balanced assessment of its subject's life.

Biological oxygen demand. *See* BOD.

Biological rhythm, regular pattern of changes in metabolism or activity in living things, usually synchronized with daily, monthly, seasonal or annual changes in their environment. Examples of daily, or CIRCADIAN, rhythms are the opening and closing of flowers, feeding cycles of animals during the day or the night, the response of marine organism to the tides and, in man, changes in body temperature and blood pressure. Monthly changes include the menstrual cycle in women. Annual rhythms include hibernation, migration and reproductive activity. If an organism is isolated from its environment, the rhythms continue as though by a biological clock (as in the phenomenon known as JET LAG). The internal mechanism of these rhythms is not yet fully understood.

Biological shield, thick wall containing such materials as concrete, steel, magnetite and lead, used to protect workers in nuclear power stations and radiochemical laboratories from the possible harmful effects of radiation. In remote-handling "caves" the biological shield contains a viewing window approx. 30cm (12in) thick, also with radiation absorbers.

Biological warfare, the use of disease microbes and their toxins in warfare. Since WWII the USA, USSR, Britain and other European countries have all maintained costly research programmes for the production of virulent (sometimes hyper-virulent) bacteria (and possibly viruses also) and for the discovery of more effective antidotes to their pathogenic effects. These microbes include plant pathogens for the destruction of food crops. None has yet been used, although US forces employed a variety of biological warfare in Vietnam when they defoliated forests. *See also* MM pp.180–181.

Biology, science of life and living things. Its branches include botany, zoology, ecology, morphology, phsyiology, cytology, histology, genetics, taxonomy, embryology and microbiology. These sciences deal with the origin, history, structure, development and function of living things, their relationships to each other and their environment, and the differences between the living and the non-living. *See also The Natural World*.

Bioluminescence, production of light, without heat, by living organisms. Its biological function is varied: in some species, eg fireflies, it is a recognition signal in mating; in others, eg squids, it is a method of diverting predators for protection; and in many deep-sea fish it is simply a form of illumination. The light-emitting substance (luciferin) in most species is an organic molecule that emits light when it is oxidized by molecular oxygen in the presence of an enzyme (luciferase). Each species has different forms of luciferin and luciferase. *See also* NW pp.95, 128, *241*.

Biome, natural and extensive community of animals and plants whose make-up is determined by the type of soil and the climate. There is generally distinctive, dominant vegetation and a characteristic climate and type of animal life. Ecologists divide the earth (including the seas, lakes and rivers) into ten biomes. *See* NW p.*195*.

Bionomics, the study of living organisms as they relate to their environments; synonymous with ECOLOGY.

Biophysics, study of biological phenomena in terms of the laws and techniques of physics. Subjects studied include the structure and function of biological molecules such as proteins and nucleic acids; the conduction of electricity by nerves; the transport of molecules across cell membranes; muscle contraction (using electron microscopy); energy transformations in living organisms; and the function of hormones in the body (using radioisotopes as tracers).

Biopsy, the removal of a small piece of living tissue from a patient for subsequent laboratory examination to aid in the diagnosis of disease. Most common is the cervix biopsy (smear test) done for the early diagnosis of womb cancer or a pre-cancerous condition. *See also* MS p.103.

Biosociology (biological sociology), the study of social forms and behaviour in

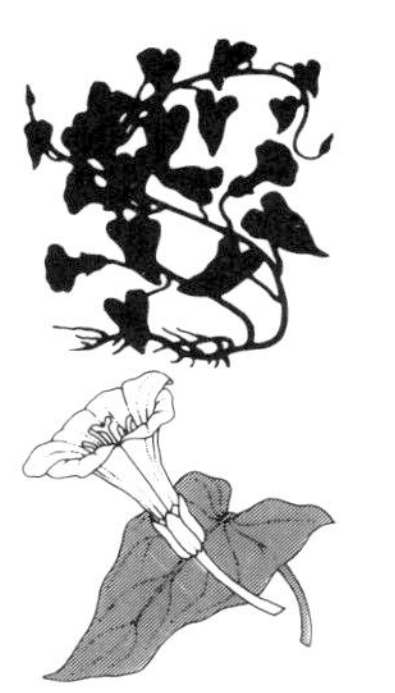

Bindweed flowers open in the early morning but close again in the later bright sunlight.

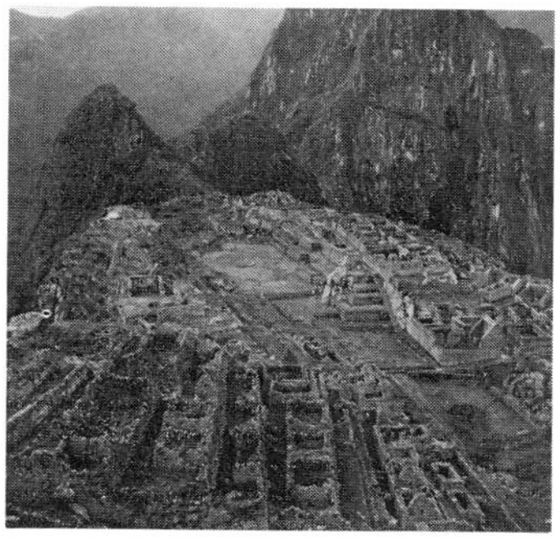

Hiram Bingham discovered the "lost city" of Macchu Picchu in the Andes Mts in 1911.

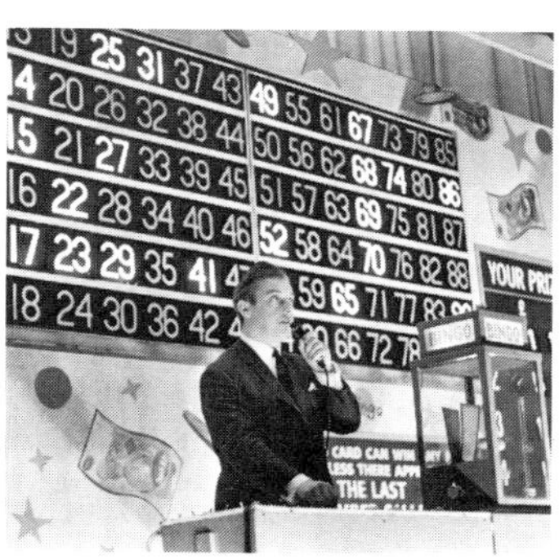

Bingo; 14 million club members spent over £11m a year during the craze of the 1960s.

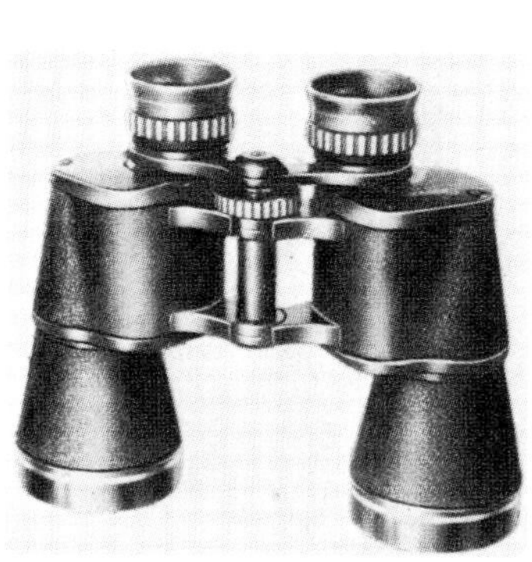

Binoculars, with reflecting prisms, produce a greatly improved stereoscopic effect.

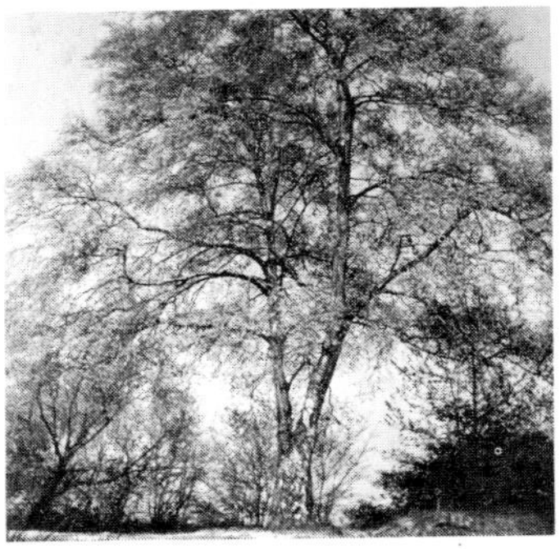

Birch bark is used by the North American Indians to cover the frames of their canoes.

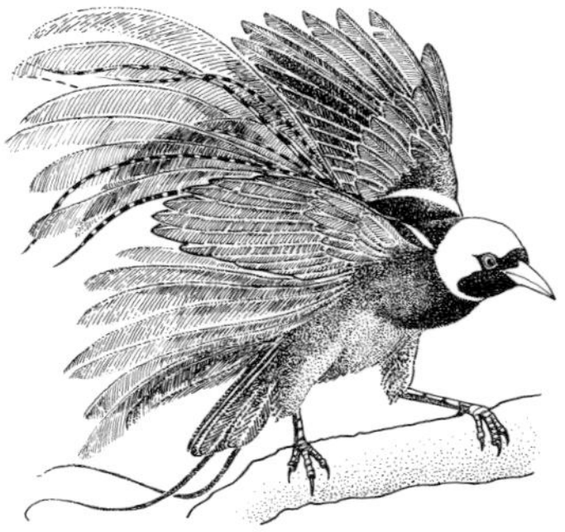

Bird of paradise; the male bird has vivid plumes which stand erect during display.

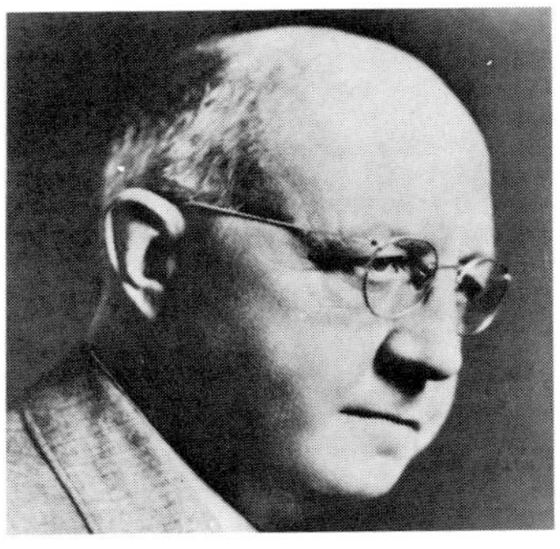

Clarence Birdseye, who invented and developed techniques for deep-freezing food.

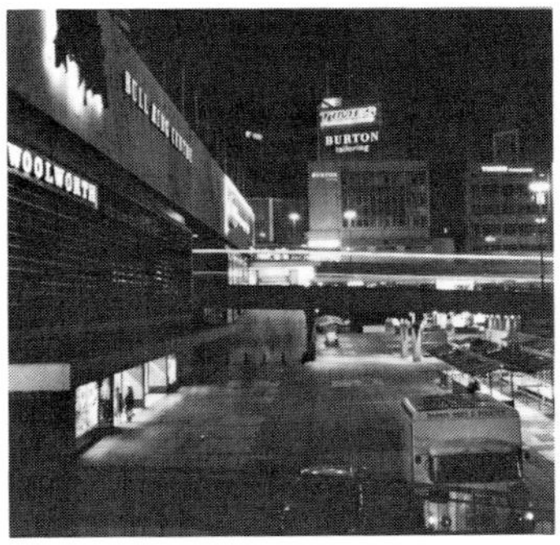

Birmingham; the Bull Ring shopping precinct in the heart of Britain's second largest city.

terms analogous to the study of organisms and biological processes. Paying special attention to the interactions between man's biological make-up and his social behaviour, it tries to avoid a simplified view of the roles of heredity and environment in human development. *See also* MS pp.150–179.

Biosphere, or zone of life, that portion of the earth from its crust to the surrounding atmosphere, encompassing and including all living organisms, animal and vegetable. It is self-sufficient except for energy and extends a few kilometres above and below sea-level.

Biosynthesis, the genetic process in living cells by which complex chemical substances, such as PROTEINS, are made from simpler substances. A GENE, part of the DNA of the chromosomes of the cell nucleus, "orders" a particular protein to be made. The "order" is a particular molecule of RNA. On the RIBOSOMES of the cell, the protein is built up from molecules of AMINO ACIDS, in accordance with the specification of the genetic code carried by the RNA. *See also* NW pp.28–29; SU cp.156–157.

Biot, Jean Baptiste (1774–1862), French astronomer, mathematician and physicist who made fundamental discoveries about POLARIZED LIGHT. He developed the technique of estimating the concentration of certain organic substances (particularly sugars) by measuring the angle through which they rotate the plane of polarization of light.

Biotin, member of the vitamin B complex ($C_{10}H_{16}O_3N_2S$). It is vital to the body, but is needed in only minute quantities, which are synthetized by intestinal bacteria. *See also* VITAMIN.

Biotite, common mineral of the MICA group. It is a silicate of aluminium, iron, potassium and magnesium. Its colour ranges from greenish-brown to black. Its lustrous, monoclinic crystals are opaque to translucent, and cleave to form elastic sheets. It is found in igneous and metamorphic rocks. *See also* PE p.97.

Birch, any of about 40 species of trees and shrubs native to cooler areas of the Northern Hemisphere. The smooth resinous bark peels off in papery sheets. The double-toothed leaves are oval or triangular with blunt bases and are arranged alternately along the branches. The male catkins droop whereas the smaller female catkins stand upright and develop into conelike clusters with tiny one-seeded nuts. Some well-known species are the grey, sweet and yellow birches. Height: up to 30m (98ft). Family Betulaceae; genus *Betula*. *See also* NW pp.*64*, *209*, 226; PE p.218.

Bird, any one of about 8,600 species of feathered vertebrates that occupy every conceivable natural habitat from deserts and tropics to polar wastes. Birds are warm-blooded and have forelimbs modified to wings, hind-limbs for walking and jaws elongated into a toothless beak. They lay eggs in nests, incubate the eggs and care for young. They feed on seeds, nectar, fruit and carrion and hunt live prey ranging from insects to lambs. Sight is the dominant sense with smell the poorest. Size ranges from the bee hummingbird, 6.4cm (2.5in) to the wandering albatross, whose wingspread reaches 3.5m (11.5ft). The 2.4m (8ft) tall ostrich is the largest of living birds, but several extinct flightless birds were even bigger. Of the 27 orders of birds, the perching birds (Passeriformes) include more species than all others combined. A bird's body is built primarily for flight, with all its parts modified accordingly. There are several groups of large flightless land birds, including the ostrich, rhea, emu, cassowary, kiwi and penguin. There are also some flightless members of typically flighted groups, such as the rail and the cormorant. Birds are descended from Theocodonts (reptiles), and the first fossil bird, *Archaeopteryx*, dates from late Jurassic times. Class Aves. *See* NW pp.73, 140–153.

Bird cherry, small wild cherry tree that grows in most temperate parts of the world, although it was probably originally native to E Asia. It has small bitter fruit. Family Rosaceae, genus *Prunus*. *See also* PE p.192.

Bird louse, also called chewing LOUSE, any of about 3,000 species of small, flattened insects of the order Mallophaga that are distinguished from the sucking lice because they do not suck blood and so are not so harmful as transmitters of disease. Despite their name more than 300 species are parasites of mammals.

Bird migration. *See* MIGRATION.

Bird of paradise, brightly coloured, ornately plumed, perching bird of N Australia, New Guinea forests and nearby regions. Most species have stocky bodies, rounded wings, short legs and a squarish tail. The males' plumes are black, orange, red, yellow, blue or green and become erect during elaborate courtship displays and rituals. Length: 12.5–100cm (5–40in). Family Paradisaeidae.

Bird-of-paradise flower, ornamental plant native to Southern Africa. It grows from RHIZOMES and has stiff, leathery, oblong leaves. The flowers are brilliant orange and blue held in a boat-shaped, green bract. Height: to 1.5m (5ft). Family Musaceae; species *Strelitzia reginae*.

Bird of prey, bird having a sharp, hooked beak and curved talons with which it captures its prey. Two groups of birds fit this description: the hawks, falcons, eagles, vultures and secretary bird (order Falconiformes), and the owls (order Strigiformes). *See also* NW pp.140–141.

Birds, The (414 BC), Greek comedy by ARISTOPHANES. Disgusted with their world, a group of men persuade the birds to create a city half-way between heaven and earth in which they will have complete control of gods and men. The play is a satire on men's search for an ideal society.

Birdseye, Clarence (1886–1956), US industrialist and inventor who developed a technique for deep-freezing foods. He began experiments on freezing food in 1917 and marketed frozen fish in 1924. He was a founder of General Foods Corporation, and found new ways of reducing the time to freeze foods.

Birendra Bir Bikram Shah Dev (1945–), King of Nepal. He was educated in India, England, Japan and the US and travelled extensively through Europe, N and S America, Asia and Africa. In 1964 he became colonel-in-chief of the Royal Nepalese Army and in 1972 succeeded his father Mahendra to the throne.

Biringuccio, Vannoccio (1480–1539), Italian metallurgist. In 1538 he became director of the papal arsenal. He wrote *De la pirotechnia*, published posthumously in 1540, the first comprehensive, practical work on metallurgy.

Birkbeck, George (1776–1841), British physician and natural philosopher. As Professor of Philosophy at the Andersonian University in Glasgow (1799–1804), he began classes for workmen which gave rise to the Glasgow Mechanics' Institute. In 1823 he founded a similar college in London, now Birkbeck College.

Birkenhead, Frederick Edwin Smith, 1st Earl of (1872–1930), British Conservative politician. He entered Parliament in 1906 and gained prominence as a defender of ULSTER during the Irish Home Rule crisis. As Attorney-General (1915–19) he was responsible for the prosecution of Roger CASEMENT. He later became Lord Chancellor (1919–22).

Birkenhead, town and port in Merseyside, NW England, on the Wirral Peninsula, overlooking the River Mersey and connected to Liverpool by road and railway tunnels. Industries: engineering, shipbuilding, food processing. Pop. 136,000.

Birkett, William Norman, Baron (1883–1962), British lawyer. Called to the Bar in 1913, he gained a brilliant reputation by 1930. He was a judge of the King's Bench (1941–50), a judge at the Nuremberg Trials (1945–46) and a Lord Justice of Appeal (1950–57).

Birmingham, George A. (1865–1950), pseudonym of James Owen Hannay, Irish clergyman and novelist. In 1889 he became a priest and served in Ireland and England. Using his pseudonym he wrote many novels including *Spanish Gold* (1908) and *Wild Justice* (1930).

Birmingham, city in West Midlands Metropolitan County, central England; second largest city in Britain. In the 17th and 18th centuries Birmingham's industrial development and population growth accelerated. James WATT designed and built his steam-engine there. Later it became known for the manufacture of cheap goods ("Brummagem ware"). The Birmingham Repertory Theatre, opened in 1913, has a justly high reputation. An important centre for rail, road and water transport, it has motor-vehicle, locomotive, mechanical and electrical engineering, food processing and metallurgical industries. Pop. 1,013,400.

Birmingham, largest city in Alabama, USA. It was founded in 1871 as a rail junction at the centre of a mineral-rich region. It has a university and three colleges. Industries: iron and steel, metalworking, construction materials and transport equipment. Pop. (1970) 300,910.

Birmingham Riots (July 1791), attacks by "Church and King" mobs on Dissenters and supposed supporters of the FRENCH REVOLUTION. The house of the Unitarian Joseph Priestly was sacked.

Birney, (Alfred) Earle (1904–), Canadian poet and novelist. He has tried to work within the Canadian idiom and his collections of verse include *David and Other Poems* (1942), *The Strait of Anian* (1948), *Ice Cod Bell or Stone* and *False Creek Mouth* (1964).

Birth, the bringing forth of live, partly or fully formed offspring. All mammals, except the echidna and the platypus, some reptiles and sharks, and various insects and other invertebrate animals give birth to live young. All birds, most reptiles, amphibians and fishes, and the majority of invertebrates lay eggs from which the live young are later born, this process being called hatching. *See also* MS pp.78–79; NW pp.76–77, 144–145.

Birth, breech, also called breech delivery, birth in which the baby presents its buttocks (or breech) and not its head to the birth canal of the mother. *See also* MS pp.78–79.

Birth, caesarian, delivery of a baby by a surgical incision made through the abdomen and womb of the mother, named after Julius Caesar, who is reputed to have been born this way. It is carried out for various medical reasons; the mother usually recovers quickly, without complications. *See also* MS pp.78–79.

Birth control, or contraception, procedures adopted by men and women to prevent pregnancy. Methods range from the PILL, a hormone preparation that alters the sequence of physiological events in a woman's body to prevent her conceiving, through the wearing of contraceptive devices such as the coil (women) and the condom (men), to the unreliable use of spermicidal creams and douches and the almost completely ineffective method of *coitus interruptus*. Contraceptive pills are now being developed for men, and the sterilization of men and women is a growing practice. *See also* MS pp.80–81.

Birthmark, or naevus, area of pigment, usually red, purple, yellow or brown, that appears on the skin at birth or shortly after. Some birthmarks are caused by concentrations of melanin; others (strawberry marks) by raised blood vessels. Some fade or disappear with maturity.

Birth of a Nation (1915), US film. This US civil war melodrama was directed by D.W. GRIFFITH who adapted the script with Frank Woods from Thomas Dixon's novel *The Clansman*. The film incorporated many technical innovations that were widely adopted later, and brought world renown to its star Lillian Gish. Its sympathetic treatment of the early Ku Klux Klan caused Griffith to be characterized as a bigot. *See also* HC2 p.*200*.

Birth rate, statistic that gives the number of births in a given area, age group, socio-economic stratum or time period. The most common is the crude birth rate, which is the number of births per thousand population per year. *See also* MS p.*81*.

Birth rites, ceremonies performed at the birth of a child eg, christening. They celebrate a safe birth and stress that the child is

now a member of the society. The ceremonies usually involve relations with the spiritual world and are virtually universal.
Birthstone, gemstone associated with the month of one's birth and worn as a talisman. January, garnet; February, amethyst; March, bloodstone or aquamarine; April, diamond; May, emerald or agate; June, pearl; July, ruby or onyx; August, sardonyx or alexandrite; September, sapphire; October, opal or beryll; November, topaz; December, turquoise, tourmaline or zircon. *See also* PE pp.98–99.
Birtwistle, Harrison (1934–), English composer. He has written a wide variety of works that have consolidated his position as a leading composer of the modern school. His works include the instrumental motet *The World is Discovered* (1960), the one-act opera *Punch and Judy* (1967) and *Verses for Ensembles* (1970).
Biscay, Bay of, inlet of the Atlantic Ocean, W of France and N of Spain. It is noted for its strong currents and sudden storms, and for its sardine fishing grounds. The chief ports are Bilbao, San Sebastián and Santander in Spain, and Bayonne, La Rochelle and St-Nazaire in France. There is a resort area along the French coast.
Biscuit, crisp, unleavened and often sweet pastry made lightweight by the addition of baking powder or soda, sometimes covered with chocolate or including fruit such as currants.
Biscuit ware, pottery that has been fired in a kiln but not glazed; either the fired piece, yet to be glazed, or a finished product.
Bishop, in Christian churches, the highest order in the ministry. Bishops are distinguished from priests chiefly by their powers to confer holy orders and to administer the rite of CONFIRMATION. They usually exercise pastoral oversight of a DIOCESE. *See also* APOSTOLIC SUCCESSION.
Bishop, Sir Henry Rowley (1786–1855), English composer and conductor, one of the original members of the Philharmonic Society (1813). Except for *Home Sweet Home*, his music is now mostly forgotten.
Bishop, William Avery "Billy" (1894–1956), Canadian pilot who received the highest awards for bravery in WWI. During WWII he was director of the Royal Canadian Air Force.
Bishops' Wars (1639, 1640), campaigns by CHARLES I of England against the Scots. Charles aimed to strengthen episcopacy by imposing English church ritual on Scotland; the COVENANT of 1638 pledged the Scots to defend PRESBYTERIANISM. By the treaty of Ripon 1640, Charles was forced to pay an indemnity to the invading Scots. *See also* HC1 pp.287, 298.
Bishop's-weed. *See* GROUND ELDER.
Bismarck, Otto von (1815–98), German statesman. He was born into a wealthy Prussian family and in 1862 WILHELM I named him Chancellor of Prussia. Victory in the FRANCO-PRUSSIAN WAR (1870–71) brought the southern German states into the Prussian-led confederation, and in 1871 Wilhelm I was proclaimed German Emperor and Bismarck the first Chancellor of the Empire. In 1882 he formed the TRIPLE ALLIANCE with Austro-Hungary and Italy. Bismarck encouraged industrialization and a paternalist programme of social welfare at home, and colonization overseas. He found it difficult to work with WILHELM II, and in 1890 the "Iron Chancellor" was forced to resign. *See also* HC2 p.110–111; 180–181.
Bismarck, German WWII battleship. It was built to raid the Atlantic shipping lanes and was renowned for its firepower. It was sunk at heavy cost by the British on 27 May 1941 off the coast of France, three days after it had sunk the British battleship HMS *Hood* near Greenland.
Bismarck Archipelago, group of volcanic islands off NE New Guinea, in the W Pacific Ocean. The group comprises many islands, including New Britain and New Ireland. All were once under the administration of Australia, but are now a part of Papua, New Guinea. Pop. approx. 200,000.
Bismuth, metallic element (Bi) of group Va of the PERIODIC TABLE, first identified as a separate element in 1753. The chief ores are bismite (oxide) and bismuthnite or bismuth glance (sulphide). To extract the metal, the oxide is reduced with carbon and the sulphide is roasted in the presence of charcoal and metallic iron (to remove the sulphur). Bismuth expands when it solidifies, a property exploited in several bismuth alloys used in making castings. Properties: a.n. 83; a.w. 208.9806; s.g. 9.75 (20°C); m.p. 271.3°C (520°F); b.p. 1,560°C (2,840°F); most common isotope Bi^{209} (100%).
Bison, two species of wild oxen formerly ranging over the grasslands and open woodlands of most of North America and all of Europe. Once numbered in millions, the American bison (sometimes incorrectly called "buffalo") is now almost extinct in the wild. The wisent (European bison) was reduced to two herds by the 18th century. Both species are now found in protected areas. The American species is not as massive or as shaggy as the European. Length: to 3.5m (138in); height: to 3m (118in); weight: to 1,350kg (2,976lb). Family Bovidae; species American *Bison bison*; wisent *Bison bonasus*. *See also* BUFFALO; OX; NW pp.*191*, 198, 206–207.
Bissau, port town and capital of Guinea-Bissau, W Africa, on the Geba Channel. Established in 1687 by the Portuguese as a slave-trading centre, it became a free port in 1869. Industries: oil processing. Pop. 25,000.
Bithynia, ancient region of NW Asia Minor. Originally occupied by THRACIANS, it was incorporated into the Persian Empire by CYRUS the Great. After 300 BC it evolved into a strong, independent kingdom. In 74 BC, in accordance with the will of its last king, it became a Roman province.
Bitter Lakes, two lakes in NE Egypt. The Great Bitter Lake and the Little Bitter Lake are connected and crossed by the Suez Canal. They were originally situated in the ancient bed of the Red Sea.
Bitterling, deep-bodied fresh-water fish native to Asia Minor and central Europe. The female deposits her eggs in the mantle cavities of clams and mussels for hatching. Length: to 7.5cm (3in). Family Cyprinidae; species *Rhodeus sericeus*.
Bittern, solitary heron-like wading bird with a characteristic booming call found in marshes around the world. A heavy-bodied bird, it is brownish with streaks and spots which help to hide it in swamplands. The female lays 3–6 brownish eggs. Length: 25–90cm (10in–3ft). Family Ardeidae, species *Botaurus stellaris*.
Bittersweet. *See* NIGHTSHADE.
Bitumen, or asphalt, mixture of hydrocarbons and other organic chemical compounds, occurring naturally, eg in the pitch lakes of Trinidad, or made by distilling tar from coal or wood. Small amounts are made during the refining of petroleum. It is used for roadmaking and for proofing timber against rot. *See also* MM pp.80–81, 182–183.
Bivalve, animal that has a shell with two halves or parts hinged together. The term applies to animals of the phylum BRACHIOPODA (lamp shells) with dorsal and ventral shells and to a class of molluscs – Pelecypoda or Lamellibranchiata – with left and right shells, eg. clams, cockles, mussels and oysters. Length: 2mm-1.2m (0.17in–4ft). *See also* NW pp.92–93, 96–97.
Biwa-ko, lake in W central Honshū, Japan, and namesake of the Japanese musical instrument whose shape it resembles. It is the largest lake in Japan and yields fresh-water fish. Length: 64km (40 miles); width 3–19km (2–12 miles); depth; 96m (315ft).
Biya, Paul (1933–), Cameroon political figure. He held various government posts (1962–68) and in 1968 was appointed Minister of State and Secretary-General to the Cameroon President, Ahmadou Ahidjo. In 1975 he became Prime Minister of Cameroon.
Bizerte, port in Tunisia, 60km (37 miles) NNW of Tunis. Strategically placed at the narrowest part of the Mediterranean Sea, it was a naval station under the French, who fortified the outer harbour and deepened the channel to Lake Bizerte. It was a German base in WWII and was heavily bombed by the Allies in 1943. In 1963 France evacuated its base there; it is now an international shipyard. Pop. 51,700.
Bizet, Georges (1838–75), French Romantic composer. His opera *Carmen* (1875), although a failure at its first performance, has become one of the most popular. Bizet also composed other operas and orchestral works, including a symphony in C (1855) and the *L'Arlésienne Suites* (1872).
Bjerknes, Vilhelm Frimann Koren (1862–1951), Norwegian physicist who laid the foundation of a revolution in weather forecasting by applying theories of fluid forces and motions to the circulation of the atmosphere with the development of air masses, fronts and cyclones.
Björling, Jussi (1911–60), Swedish tenor who, beginning his career with the Royal Opera, Stockholm (1931–39), sang in most of the world's opera houses. His best-known roles were in Italian and French operas.
Björneborg. *See* PORI.
Bjørnson, Bjørnstjerne (1832–1910), Norwegian poet, novelist and dramatist. A great public figure and prolific writer, his works included the novels *Trust and Trial* (1858) and *The Heritage of the Kurts* (1844), the plays *Lame Hulda* (1858) and *The Bankrupt* (1874), and *Poems and Songs* (1870). He lectured throughout Europe and was awarded the Nobel Prize in literature in 1903.
Björnsson, Sveinn (1881–1952), Icelandic statesman. He became Regent of Iceland in 1941 and was elected President when the country was proclaimed a constitutional republic in 1944, a post he held until death.
Black, Davidson (1884–1934), Canadian anthropologist who first discovered the remains of Peking man (*Homo erectus pekinensis*). In 1927, at Chou-k'ou-tien near Peking, he discovered a single tooth belonging to this previously unknown form of early man which he named *Sinanthropus pekinensis*. *See also* MS p. 24, *24*.
Black, Joseph (1728–99), British chemist and physicist. Rediscovering "fixed air" (carbon dioxide), he found that this gas is produced by respiration, burning of charcoal and FERMENTATION, that it behaves as an ACID, and that it is probably found in the atmosphere. He investigated LATENT HEAT and the concept of SPECIFIC HEAT but was unable to reconcile it with the PHLOGISTON theory. *See also* SU pp.24–25, *25*.
Black and Tans, special constables (12,000 in all) sent from England to assist the Royal Irish Constabulary in the Irish Civil War (1919–21). Their name derived from the colours of their temporary dress (khaki uniform and black and green belts and caps). *See also* HC2 p.*295*.
Blackbeard (*d.* 1718), British pirate, real name Edward Teach, who in 1716 began attacking shipping off the N American coast and in the Caribbean. He was killed when two ships sent by the governor of Virginia attacked his ship, *Queen Anne's Revenge*.
Black Beauty (1877), children's book by Anna SEWELL. Despite the sentimentality of this story of a horse passing from owner to owner in 19th-century England, the popularity of the book started a trend in children's literature towards stories about animals.
Black Belt, in judo, grade given to those who have proved certain fighting ability. There are five black-belt ratings, progressing from first to fifth Dan (degree).
Blackberry, or bramble, fruit-bearing bush, native to northern temperate regions. The prickly stems may be erect or trailing, the leaves oval and toothed, and the blossoms white, pink or red. The edible berries are black or dark red. Family Rosaceae; genus *Rubus*. *See also* DEWBERRY; PE p.214.
Blackbird, songbird of the THRUSH family, common in gardens and woodland throughout most of Europe, the Near East, Australia and New Zealand. The male has jet-black plumage and a bright orange bill. The female is a dark, ruddy

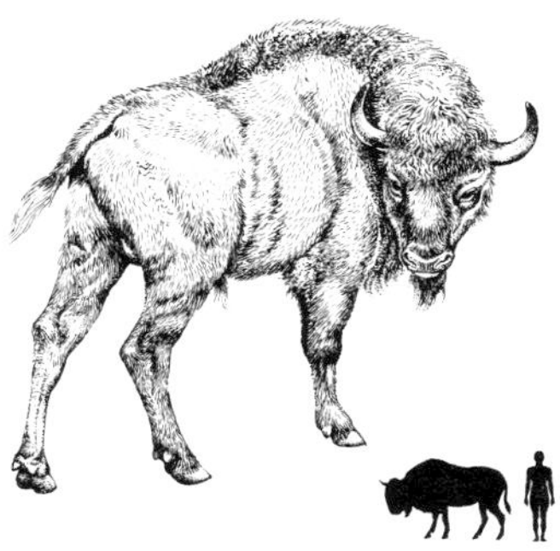
Bison, the animal (incorrectly called buffalo) which has been hunted almost to extinction.

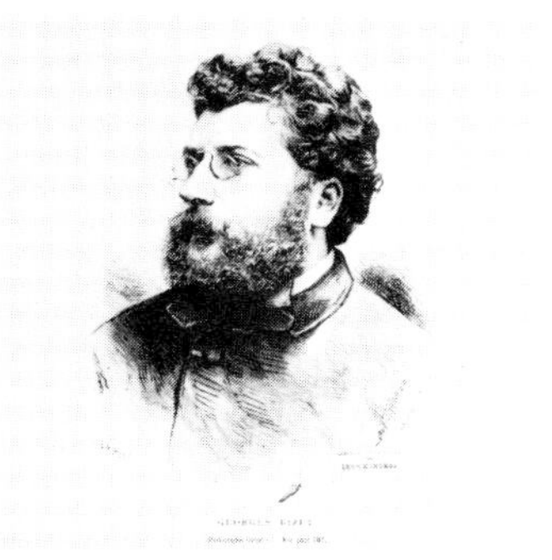
Bizet's last (and finest) work, *Carmen,* was a failure at its first performance in Paris.

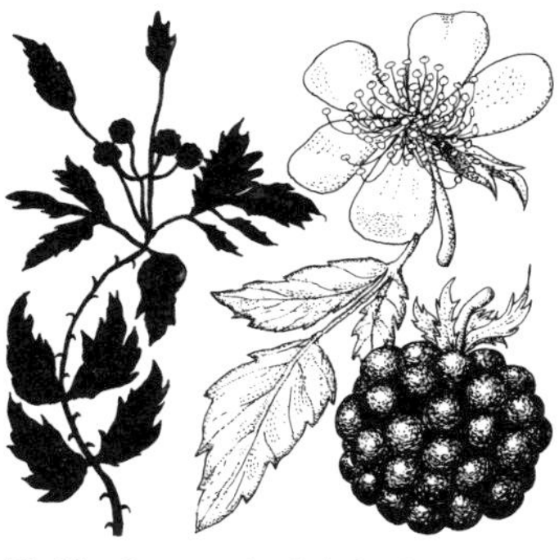
Blackberries, popular fruit for jam-making, grow wild in the hedgerows of Britain.

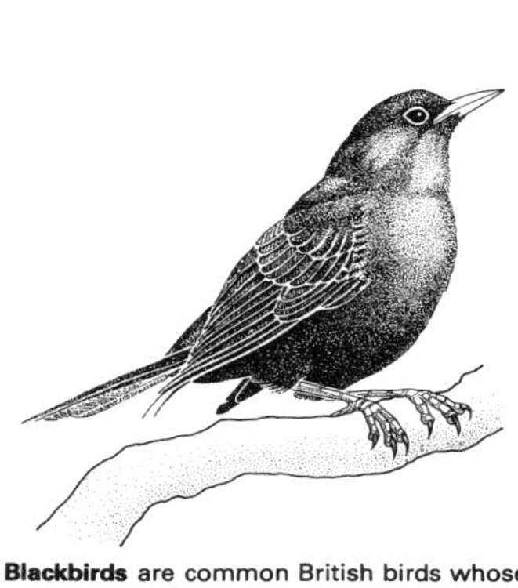
Blackbirds are common British birds whose song is distinctive and enchanting.

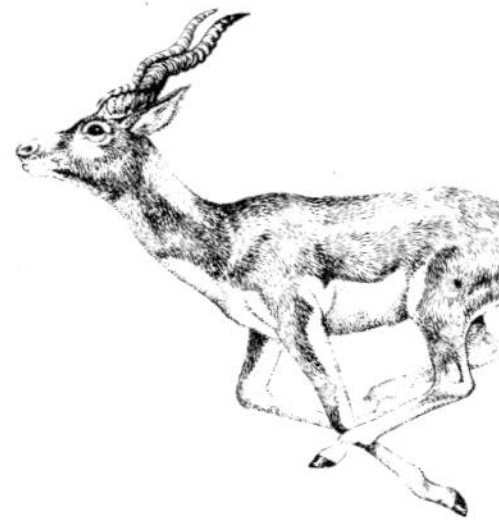

Blackbuck males have spirally twisting horns. They are hunted by trained cheetahs.

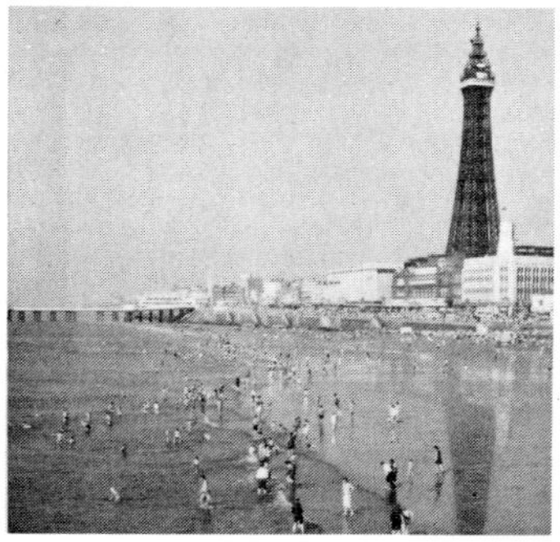

Blackpool's 160m (520ft) tower was built in 1895, modelled on the Eiffel Tower in Paris.

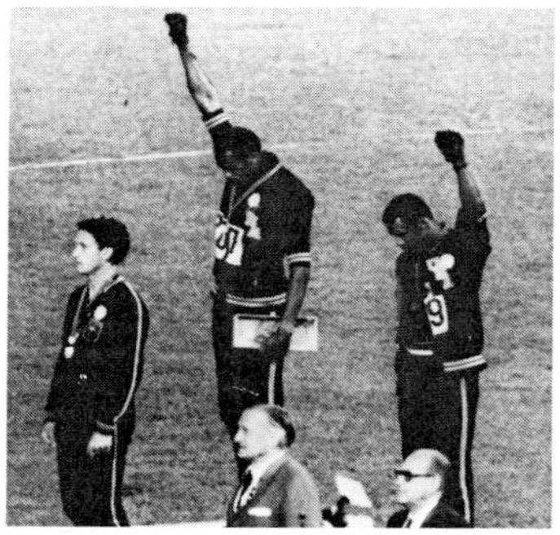

Black Power salutes at the 1968 Olympics, a reminder of the political nature of sport.

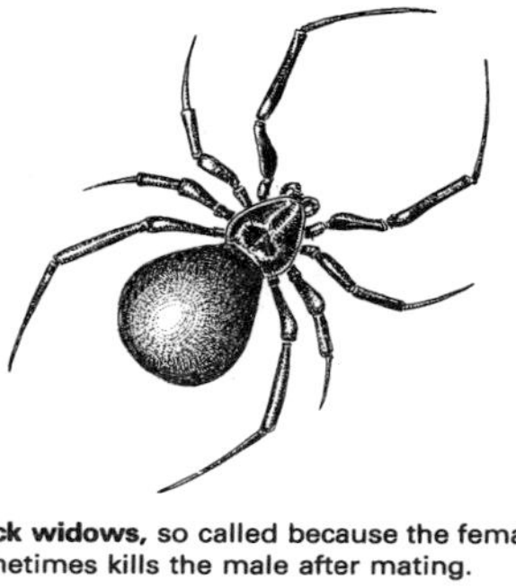

Black widows, so called because the female sometimes kills the male after mating.

brown. The blackbird feeds on earthworms and other invertebrates. Length: to 25cm (10in). Species *Turdus merula.*

Black body, in physics, an ideal body that absorbs all incident radiation and reflects none. Such a body would look "perfectly" black – hence the name. The study of black bodies has been important in the history of physics. Wien's law, Stefan's law and Planck's law of black body radiation grew out of this study, as did Planck's discoveries in quantum mechanics.

Black bottom, popular US dance of the 1920s. Similar to the CHARLESTON, it was originally danced by southern Blacks at the turn of the 20th century. It became a national craze after Ann Pennington's performance of it in the show *Scandals of 1926.*

Blackbuck, or Indian antelope, medium-sized, long-horned ANTELOPE native to the open plains of India. Females and young are fawn coloured and males are dark, becoming almost black at maturity. The underparts are white and there are also patches of white on the muzzle and round the eyes. Only males carry long, spiral horns. Blackbuck are hunted for sport by trained cheetahs. Length: to 1.2m (47in); height: to 81cm (32in) at the shoulder. Family Bovidae; species *Antilope cervicapra. See also* PE p.*238.*

Blackburn, town in Lancashire, NW England, on the Leeds-Liverpool Canal, 34km (21 miles) NW of Manchester. The area has been a textiles centre since the 17th century and, more recently, has yielded coal. Industries: textiles, electrical equipment. Pop. (1973) 101,670.

Blackcap, perching bird with a black, caplike crown. The European blackcap is a small warbler, *Sylvia atricapilla.* In the USA the chickadee is sometimes called a blackcap. Family *Muscicapidae.*

Black Country, region in England in the W Midlands, formerly comprised of S Staffordshire and N Warwickshire. The name derives from the smoke and soot of the original heavy industries. It includes the industrial towns of Birmingham, Wolverhampton, West Bromwich and Wednesbury.

Black Death (1348–50), plague, both bubonic and pneumonic, that killed between 25% and 50% of the population of Europe. It was first taken to Mediterranean ports from the Crimea and spread throughout Europe, carried by rats and fleas. It recurred in 1361–63, 1369–71, 1374–75, 1390 and 1400, and reappeared consistently until the 18th century. *See also* HC1 pp.209, *215.*

Black earth, or chernozem, type of soil rich in HUMUS and prized for its agricultural qualities such as good structure and high nutrient content. It is mostly found in regions that have hot summers and cold winters.

Blackett, Patrick Maynard Stuart, Baron (1897–1974), English physicist who was awarded the 1948 Nobel Prize in physics for his research on cosmic radiation. He spent 10 years at the Cavendish laboratory developing the Wilson cloud chamber into an instrument for the study of cosmic radiation. He was professor of physics at Manchester University (1937–53) and in 1953 became professor of physics at Imperial College, London.

Blackfeet or Blackfoot, nomadic, warlike North American Indian tribes. They are made up of three Algonquin-speaking tribes: the Siksika, or Blackfeet proper; the Kainah; and the Pikuni, or Piegan. Living on the N Great Plains E of the Rockies, they depended largely on the bison (buffalo), which was hunted on horseback. Something of their richly ceremonial culture survives among the 8,850 Blackfeet living today on reservations in Alberta and Montana.

Blackfish, freshwater fish from Siberia and Alaska (*Dallia pectoralis*); or any of a number of dark-coloured marine fishes, including sea basses; or a small toothed whale of the genus *Globicephala.*

Blackfly. *See* APHIS.

Black Forest (Schwarzwald), mountainous region in Baden-Württemburg state, SW West Germany, between the rivers Rhine and Neckar. It is heavily forested in the higher areas around the sources of the Danube and the Neckar. The highest peak is Feldberg. Industries: timber, clocks. Area: 6.009sq km (2,320sq miles).

Blackfriars Theatre, the name of two separate London theatres built within the boundaries of the old Blackfriars monastery, the second of which was acquired in 1597 by Richard BURBAGE. It was considered the best patronized of pre-Restoration theatres, and was demolished in 1655.

Black Friday (24 Sept. 1869), day of financial panic in the USA. The financiers Jay Gould and James Fisk attempted to corner the gold market and drove the price of gold up. The price fell after the US government sold part of its gold reserve, and many speculators were ruined.

Blackheath, suburb of London whose common was a gathering place for highwaymen in the Middle Ages. From it Wat TYLER in 1381 and Jack CADE in 1450 launched their attacks on London. *See also* HC1 p.*215.*

Black hole, postulated end-product of the total gravitational collapse of a massive star into itself following exhaustion of its nuclear fuel; the matter inside is crushed to unimaginably high density. It is an empty region of distorted space-time that acts as a centre of gravitational attraction; matter is drawn towards it and once inside nothing can escape. Its boundary (the event horizon) is a demarcation line, rather than a material surface. *See also* SU pp.107, 234–235, *235.*

Black Hole of Calcutta, prison in which about 64 British soldiers were placed by the Nawab Siraj-ad-Dawlah on 20 June 1756. The cell was 5.5 by 4.5m (18 by 15ft) and had only two small windows and many of the soldiers died of suffocation.

Blackjack, gambling card game. Each player gets one card face down and bets that this card plus one or more cards dealt face up will beat the dealer's hand without exceeding 21. An ace counts as 11 or 1, picture cards as 10, and all others at their face value. A score of 21 on the first two cards dealt to a player is called blackjack.

Blackmail, in law, the act of making a demand of someone by threatening unwarranted consequences if the demand is not met. It can involve extortion of money or criminal acts, or anything likely to damage a person's standing.

Blackmail. *See* HITCHCOCK, ALFRED.

Black market, illegal or profiteering trade in goods whose supply is restricted, eg because of rationing, or in goods subject to a legal price limit. Black markets are common in currency-exchange transactions when the official exchange rate is unrealistic.

Blackmore, Richard Doddridge (1825–1900), English novelist and poet. He studied law but gave it up through ill-health and turned to writing. He wrote several novels, the best known of which is *Lorna Doone* (1869), and many volumes of poetry.

Black Mountains, range of mountains in Powys, S Wales, to the E of the River Usk. It forms part of the Brecon Beacons National Park. The highest peak, Waun Fach, is 811m (2,660ft) high.

Black Muslims, US religious movement, officially called the Nation of Islam, founded in Detroit in 1930 by W.D. Fard, who was succeeded in 1933 by Elijah Muhammad. The Black Muslims adhere strictly to the KORAN's moral codes and maintain their own schools, farms and businesses, living as independently as possible from the larger society. Elijah Muhammed died in 1975 and was succeeded by his son Wallace, who called for radical changes including the welcoming of whites into the movement and association with non-Muslim religious groups.

Blackout, in physiology, the total loss of vision encountered by test pilots and astronauts during rapid acceleration caused by insufficient oxygen supply to the eyes. Blackout is the opposite of *redout,* a reddish haze caused by engorged blood vessels in the eyes encountered at zero-g or negative-g conditions.

Black Pagoda, 13th-century Hindu temple to the sun, in Konarak, India, and the largest temple in the region. It once had a 60m (200ft) tower, but only the main hall remains.

Black Panthers. *See* BLACK POWER.

Blackpool, town in Lancashire, England, on the Irish Sea, 24km (15 miles) WNW of Preston. One of Britain's most popular resorts, it has 11km (7 miles) of sandy beaches, a 158m (520ft) tower (built in 1895), many indoor and outdoor entertainments and a promenade which is illuminated every autumn. Industries: confectionery; tourism. Pop. (1973) 150,940.

Black Power, doctrine of radical Black movements in the USA, probably first used by Stokeley CARMICHAEL in 1965. Its principal organizations have been SNCC, the BLACK MUSLIMS, the Organization of Afro-American Unity and the Black Panther party. The Black Power movement rejects the policy of non-violent civil disobedience associated with Martin Luther KING and advocates armed preparedness and Black nationalism.

Black Prince (1330–76), eldest son of Edward III of England. He was made Duke of Cornwall (England's first duke) in 1337 and Prince of Wales in 1343. His part in the victory at Crécy (1346) made him a hero; he commanded at the victory of Poitiers (1356).

Black rat snake. *See* BLACK SNAKE.

Black Sea, inland sea between Europe and Asia, connected to the Aegean Sea by the Bosporus, the Sea of Marmara and the Dardanelles. It is bordered by the USSR (to the N and E), Turkey (S) and Bulgaria and Romania (W). It receives many rivers, including the Danube, and is a major outlet for Soviet shipping. The Black Sea, which is subject to violent storms in winter, yields large quantities of fish, especially sturgeon. It is almost free of ice except in the remote NW area. It is comprised of two layers of water. The upper layer has lower salinity and supports most of the marine life, the lower layer supports anaerobic bacteria only. Area: 422,170sq km (163,000sq miles).

Black Shirts, common name of the members of the *Fasci di combattimento* units of the fascist organization founded in Italy in 1919 by Benito MUSSOLINI. Their uniform included black shirts. It later came to mean any group of militant fascists. *See also* HC2 pp.222–223.

Black snake, wide-ranging North American rat snake. A good climber, it is shiny black, sometimes with small, light spots between its scales; it has a paler belly. Length: to 2.5m (8.2ft). Family Colubridae; species *Elaphe obsoleta. See also* COLUBRID.

Black spot, any of various fungus diseases that cause black spots of the leaves of plants, particularly members of the rose family. It can be treated or, better, prevented by fungicide sprays. *See also* ANTHRACNOSE.

Blackstone, Sir William (1723–80), English jurist. As a Fellow of All Souls' College, Oxford, he introduced the first English law course into an English university. His *Commentaries on the Laws of England* (1765–69) is a classic study.

Blackthorn, tree or shrub of the rose family which bears its white flowers early in the year and has small plum-like fruits (sloes) and long black thorns that give it its name. Species *Prunus spinosa.*

Blackwater fever, tropical disease that results from contracting malaria. Red blood cells are destroyed, causing darkened urine and giving rise to fever and jaundice. The patient is put to bed, steroid drugs may be prescribed and blood transfusions may be needed.

Blackwell, Elizabeth (1821–1910), US physician, *b.* England. In 1847 she began to study medicine at the Geneva Medical College in New York. She graduated in 1849, becoming the first woman doctor in the USA. She established the New York Infirmary (1857), which combined health services and medical training.

Black widow, common name for a small, American SPIDER. It is black and has a red hour-glass-shaped mark on the underside. Its bite is poisonous, though rarely fatal to humans. Several closely related species are found in other parts of the world.

Length: 25mm (1in); the male is smaller. Family Theridiidae; genus *Latrodectus*.

Blackwood's Edinburgh Magazine, Tory journal established by William Blackwood (1776–1834) in 1817 as a rival to the Whig *Edinburgh Review*. Since 1850 it has declined in influence, but it is still published.

Bladder, urinary, large pouch in the lower abdomen in which urine is stored. Urine, a kidney secretion containing waste products and water extracted from the blood, is passed through two narrow tubes (ureters) to the bladder, where it is stored until the pressure becomes too great and nervous impulses signal that the bladder has to be emptied. Urine leaves the bladder through a tube called the URETHRA. *See also* MS p.*68*.

Bladderwort, mat-like, aquatic plant found in bogs and ponds. It has feathery thread-like leaves with small bladders in which insects and other small creatures are trapped and drowned. Upright stems bear purple or dark pink flowers. Family Lentibulariaceae. *See also* NW p.59.

Blaebury. *See* BILBERRY.

Blair, David (1932–76), British ballet dancer. He joined the Sadler's Wells ballet in 1945 and became its principal dancer in 1955. He retired in 1973.

Blair, Eric Arthur, real name of the British author George ORWELL.

Blais, Marie-Claire (1939–), Canadian novelist. Her novels, which deal with isolation and lack of love, include *La Belle Bête* (1959), *Tête Blanche* (1960) and *Une saison dans la vie d'Emmanuel* (1965).

Blake, Robert (1599–1657), British admiral. During the Civil War, he destroyed the Royalists' naval power under Prince RUPERT. He won a series of encounters during the First Dutch War (1652–54) and annihilated a Spanish treasure fleet at Tenerife (1657).

Blake, William (1757–1827), British poet, painter and engraver. His work is characterized by the prophetic and mystical visions he experienced. *Poetical Sketches* (1783) was followed by *Songs of Innocence* (1789), *The Marriage of Heaven and Hell* (1790) and *Songs of Experience* (1794). His prophetic books, portraying his private mythologies, include *The Book of Urizen* (1794), *The Four Zoas* (1797), *Milton* (1804–08) and *Jerusalem* (1804–20). In addition to his own works, Blake illustrated *The Book of Job* (adapted as a masque for dancing by Ralph VAUGHAN WILLIAMS) and DANTE's *Divine Comedy*. *See also* HC2 pp.80–81.

Blakelock, Ralph Albert (1847–1919), US painter. His works depict the American landscape, especially the West, and the daily life of the American Indian. They include *The Chase* (1879) and *Moonlight* (*c.* 1885).

Blamey, Sir Thomas (1884–1951), Australian general. In 1939 he became commander of Australian forces in the Middle East. In 1942 he was appointed Commander-in-Chief of Allied Land Forces in Australia and in 1945 was present at the Japanese surrender.

Blanc, Louis (1811–82), French socialist and historian, *b.* Spain. His part in the revolution of 1848 forced him into exile, where he wrote a history of the FRENCH REVOLUTION. He returned to France in 1870 and was elected to the Chamber of Deputies.

Blanc, Mont. *See* MONT BLANC.

Blanchard, Jean-Pierre (1753–1809), French balloonist. He made the first balloon ascents in England in 1784 and in the US in 1793. In 1785, with the US balloonist John JEFFRIES, he made the first air crossing of the English Channel.

Blanchflower, Danny (1926–), Irish footballer. An intelligent and subtle wing-half, he captained the famous Spurs "double" side of 1960–61. He won a record 56 international caps for Northern Ireland, many as captain. In 1976 he became manager of Northern Ireland.

Blanching, in gardening, covering of vegetables from light so that they become white. In cooking and food preservation, it is an initial stage of preparation; almonds, for example, are placed in boiling water until the coverings soften and can be peeled off; vegetables are lightly boiled before freezing so they retain their texture when cooked.

Blankers-Koen, Francina (Fanny) (1918–), South African sportswoman who won nine gold medals in various international events. One of the greatest all-round women athletes, she set world records in sprint events, hurdles, high jump, long jump and pentathlon. She won four gold medals in the 1948 Olympics.

Blank verse, unrhymed verse, especially iambic pentameter or unrhymed HEROIC; widely used in English dramatic and epic poetry. Henry HOWARD, Earl of Surrey, introduced blank verse into England in the 16th century with his translation of Virgil's *Aeneid*. The form was also used by Christopher Marlowe, William Shakespeare, John Milton, William Wordsworth and Alfred Lord Tennyson, among others.

Blanqui, (Louis) Auguste (1805–81), French socialist leader. He participated in the February Revolution of 1848 and the overthrow of NAPOLEON III in 1870. During one of his many prison terms, he devised the idea of a "dictatorship of the proletariat".

Blarney, village in central County Cork, in SW Ireland. It is noted for its 15th-century castle which contains the Blarney Stone. Those who kiss the stone are supposedly endowed with "the blarney" – fluent persuasive speech. Pop. (1971) 1,128.

Blasco Ibáñez, Vicente (1867–1928), Spanish novelist, influenced by ZOLA and MAUPASSANT, whose best works such as *The Cabin* (1898) and *Reeds and Mud* (1902) deal with rural life in Valencia and express his fervent Republican beliefs. *Blood and Sand* (1908) and *The Four Horsemen of the Apocalypse* (1916), a war novel, established his international reputation.

Blasis, Carlo, (1803–1878), Italian ballet teacher and choreographer. In 1837 he was appointed director of the ballet school at La Scala, Milan. His two textbooks on ballet, *An Elementary Treatise* (1820) and *The Code of Terpsichore* (1830), have remained the backbone of pure traditional and classic dance technique.

Blasphemy, speech or action manifesting contempt for God or religion. Severe penalties were prescribed for it in the Old Testament and also by medieval CANON LAW. The secular statute books of many countries still include laws against blasphemy, perhaps because an attack on religion may imply an attack on the State. It is now commonly regarded as an offence against the religious feelings of society.

Blast furnace, cylindrical smelting furnace, narrower at the top and bottom, used in the extraction of metals, (mainly iron and copper) from their ores. The ore is mixed with coke and a FLUX. A blast of hot compressed air is piped in at the bottom to force combustion up to temperatures where the reduction of the oxide ore occurs. The molten metal sinks to the bottom and is tapped off. Waste "slag" floats to the top and is piped off. *See also* MM pp.21, 29, *30*.

Blastula, stage in the development of the EMBRYO in animals. It consists of a hollow cavity (blastocoele) surrounded by one or more spherical layers of cells. Commonly called the hollow ball of cells stage, it occurs at or near the end of cleavage and precedes the gastrulation stage.

Blaue Reiter, Der, loosely-organized group of German EXPRESSIONIST painters, formed in 1911, which took its name from a picture painted (1903) by KANDINSKY, one of the group's leading members. Other members included Alexei von JAWLENSKY, Paul KLEE, August MACKE and Franz MARC. Influenced by CUBISM, the group, which was the most important manifestation of German modern art before WWI, sought in their paintings to stress inner impulses, which they felt that the IMPRESSIONISTS had overlooked.

Blavatsky, Helena Petrovna (1831–91), Russian spiritualist. In 1875, with Colonel Henry Olcott, she founded the THEOSOPHICAL SOCIETY in New York. In 1878 she went to India. She outlined her beliefs in *Isis Unveiled* (1877).

Bleaching, process of whitening various products eg, textiles, wood pulp, flour, straw, petroleum, oil, fats, hair and wood. It was originally achieved by exposure to the sun and soaking in an alkaline solution. It is now done chemically, usually by OXIDATION using chlorine and its derivatives, but is also achieved by reduction using sulphur dioxide and by adsorption using bone-charcoal.

Bleak House (1853), novel by Charles DICKENS. It shows the influence of Wilkie COLLINS in the mystery and intrigue of its plot. Dickens uses double narrative and extensive symbolism to unite the novel's different themes. This satire on the abuses of the Chancery Court focused on the need for law reform.

Bledisloe, Sir Charles Bathurst, Viscount (1867–1958), Governor-General of New Zealand (1930–35) and one of the most respected holders of that office.

Bleeding, loss of blood following a cut or wound to the skin. Menstrual bleeding in women is the monthly shedding of the lining of the uterus. Bleeding can also occur internally and may be revealed by paleness or breathlessness, or blood may be coughed up, vomited or passed in the urine. For centuries the practice of bleeding or blood-letting was used to cure ills. Leeches, whose salivary glands contain an anticoagulant, were used to prevent blood-clotting. *See also* MS p.83.

Blenheim, chief town of Marlborough district, South Island, New Zealand and an important agricultural centre. Industries: engineering, furniture. Pop. 15,000.

Blenheim, Battle of (13 Aug. 1704), decisive battle in the War of the SPANISH SUCCESSION at which the Duke of MARLBOROUGH and Eugene of Savoy defeated the French at Blenheim (Blindheim), Bavaria. Vienna was saved and Bavaria taken by the anti-French allies. *See also* HC1 pp.312–313.

Blenheim Palace, English country seat of the Dukes of Marlborough, near Woodstock in Oxfordshire. It was built by VANBRUGH and HAWKSMOOR and presented by the nation to the Duke of MARLBOROUGH after his victory over the French at BLENHEIM, Bavaria in 1704. *See also* HC1 pp.*297*, *313*.

Blenny, marine fish in shallow and offshore waters of all tropical and temperate seas. Often scaleless, with a long dorsal fin, it is olive green with varicoloured markings. Length: to 30.5cm (12in). Family Blenniidae. *See also* NW p.*131*.

Blepharitis, inflammation of the border of the eyelid caused by bacteria. It takes the form of white scales and can be accompanied by ulceration and discharge. It is sometimes associated with CONJUNCTIVITIS.

Blériot, Louis (1872–1936), French aircraft designer and aviator. He was the first man to fly an aircraft across the English Channel (1909). The flight from Calais to Dover took 37 minutes. As a designer Blériot was responsible for a number of innovations, including a system by which the pilot could operate ailerons by remote control. *See also* MM p.*148*.

Blesbok, small South African antelope which has a large white mark on its face. Both sexes have horns that grow up to 50cm (20in) long. They are raised successfully as livestock. Family Bovidae, species *Damaliscus aorcas*.

Blesmol, practically blind burrowing RODENT found in Africa south of the Sahara. The tunnels which they dig to seek their food – roots, bulbs, tubers and invertebrate animals – include chambers for storage and sleep. Length (excluding tail) to 33cm (13in). Family Bathyergidae; genus *Cryptomys*.

Blessington, Marguerite, Countess of (1789–1849), Irish beauty. She knew the leading figures of the day and established a highly fashionable literary salon in London. She wrote novels and *Conversations with Lord Byron* (1834).

Bleuler, Eugen (1857–1939), Swiss psychiatrist, pioneer in the diagnosis and treatment of PSYCHOSES. He coined the term SCHIZOPHRENIA and, unlike his predecessors, attributed the symptoms to psychological, not physiological, origins. *See also* MS pp.138–139.

Blida, town in N Algeria 16km (10 miles)

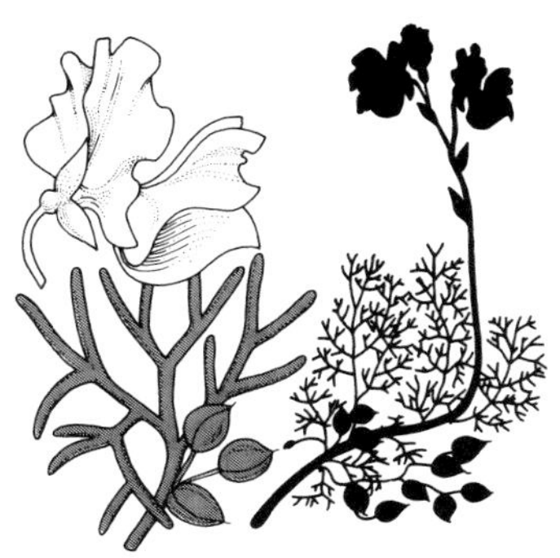

Bladderworts are known as carniverous plants because they trap small insects.

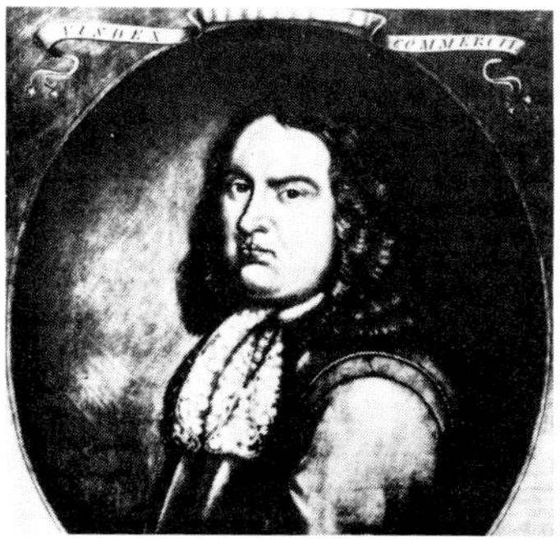

Robert Blake won dramatic actions at sea and reorganized the Commonwealth navy.

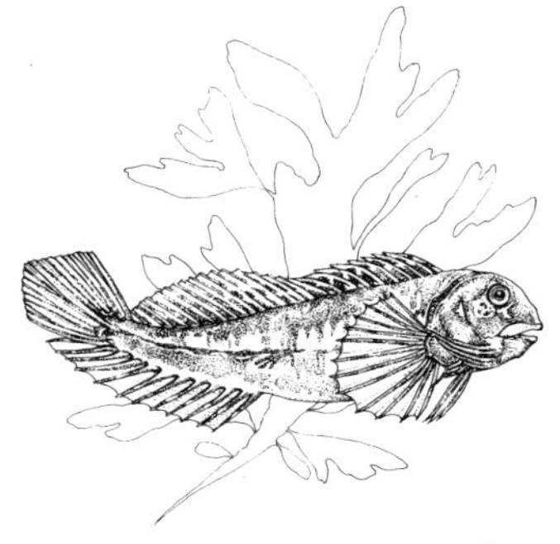

Blennies have long dorsal fins; they are usually olive green with varicoloured marks.

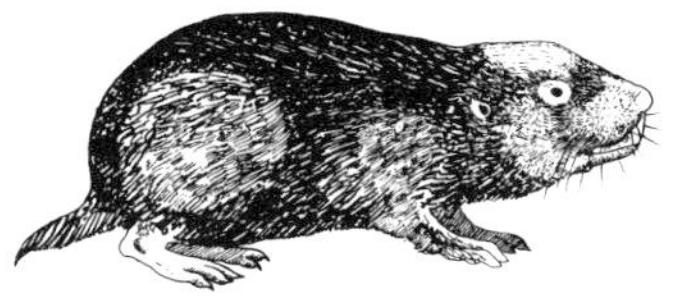

Blesmols tunnel in the earth for roots, bulbs, tubers and small invertebrate animals.

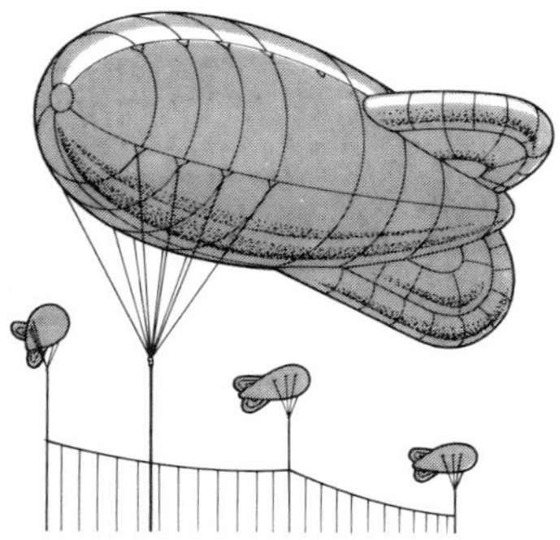

Blimps were called "limps" in WWI, the most common type being "B" – hence the name.

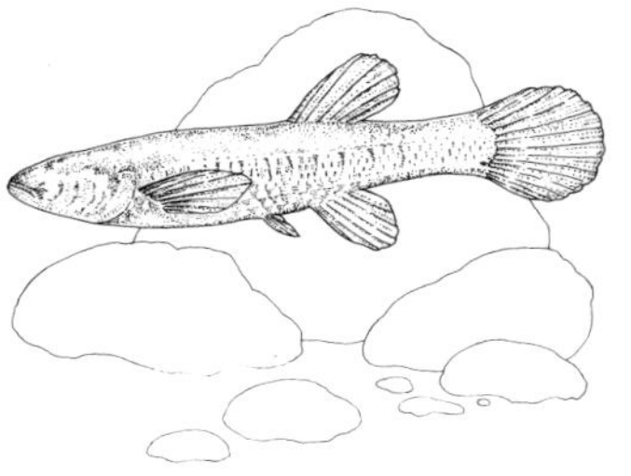

Blindfish have small projections on their heads and bodies which are touch sensitive.

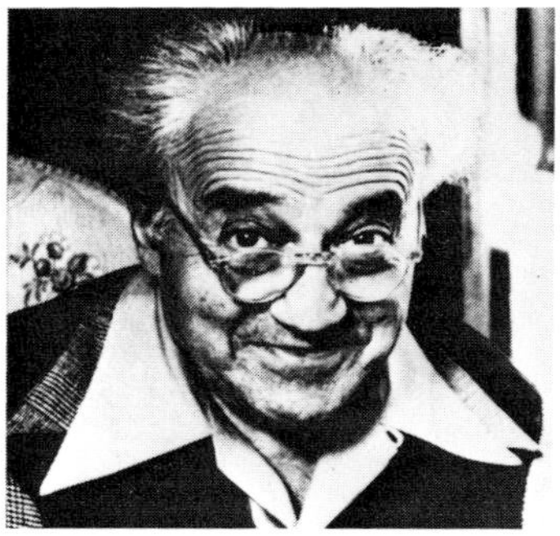

Ernest Bloch, much of whose music reflects the aspirations of the Jewish people.

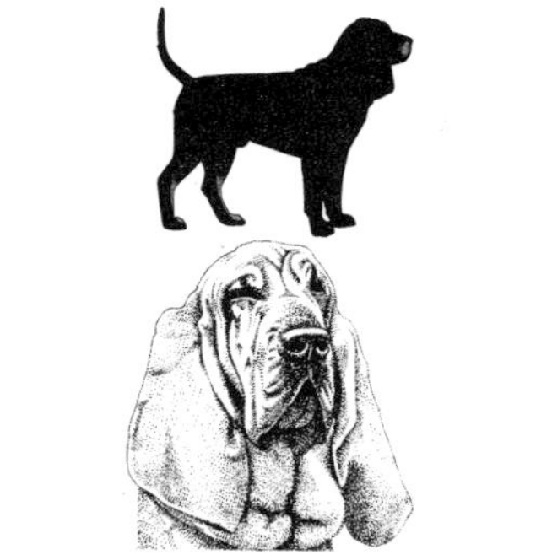

Bloodhounds, despite their name, have no aggressive instincts or inclination for blood.

SW of Algiers, at the foot of the Atlas Mts. Founded in the 1550s by Andalusians, most of the old town was destroyed by earthquakes in 1825 and 1867. Today it is an administrative and trading centre of a fertile region that produces oranges, flowers and almonds. Pop. 85,700.

Bligh, William (1754–1817), British admiral. He was captain of HMS *Bounty* in 1789 but survived the famous mutiny, sailing nearly 6,440km (4,000 miles) in the ship's longboat. While Governor of New South Wales (1805–08) he was imprisoned by army mutineers led by John MacArthur in the Rum Rebellion of 1808.

Blight, John (1914–), Australian poet. In 1945 he published *The Old Pianist.* His collected poems, 1939–75, were published in 1976. He won the Myer award for Australian poetry (1964) and the Patrick White award for Australian literature (1976).

Blight, the yellowing, browning and withering of plant tissues caused by various diseases; alternatively, the diseases themselves. Blights may be caused by micro-organisms, such as bacteria and fungi, or by environmental factors such as drought. Common blights induced by micro-organisms include fire blight, bean blight and late blight. They typically affect leaves more severely than other parts.

Blighty, soldiers' name for Britain or a wound necessitating a return to Britain. It is derived from the Hindi word *bilayati,* meaning "foreign".

Blimp, non-rigid AIRSHIP; it is smaller and lighter than the semi-rigid and the rigid types. They are usually powered by small, light aero-engines and are steerable. Blimps were used during WWI and WWII for antisubmarine warfare and coastal patrol. *See also* MM pp.146–147.

Blindfish, or blind cave-fish, freshwater fish found mainly in cave waters of North America. Usually white, some species are blind, others are partly sighted. Length: up to 13cm (5in). Family Characidae, species include *Anoptichthys jordani*; and Family Amblyopsidae; species *Amblyopsis spelaeus.*

Blindness, is the inability to perform any work for which eyesight is essential. Blindness occurs most frequently in people more than 55 years old, with the greatest percentage caused by senile cataract (clouding of the lens) and glaucoma (hardening of the eye due to pressure within the eyeball). Other causes of blindness include diseases such as measles or syphilis; diseases such as diabetes; nutritional deficiencies; injuries; and congenital anomalies, which include inherited defects. Blindness as a result of disease and accident is being reduced rapidly with progress in research, early diagnosis and accident prevention.

Blind snake, burrowing, almost sightless, legless reptile with the vestiges of a pelvic girdle. The Typhlopidae (blind snakes) and Leptotyphlopidae (slender blind snakes) are found throughout the world in tropical and temperate areas. Length: up to 30cm (12in). *See also* NW p.*139.*

Blind spot, small area on the retina of the eye where there is no visual reception because of the absence of rods and cones. It is the area where optic nerve processes converge and where blood vessels enter and leave the eye. *See also* MS pp.48–49.

Blindworm. *See* SLOW-WORM.

Blink comparator, instrument for detecting slight differences, such as the position or brightness of a star, by comparing two photographs of the same area of the sky. The photographs are viewed alternately in rapid succession by means of a mechanical device and any difference is observed as a flickering of the image.

Bliss, Sir Arthur (1891–1975), British composer. He was the pupil of STANFORD, VAUGHAN WILLIAMS and HOLST. His works include the *Colour Symphony* (1932), quintets for oboe (1927) and clarinet (1931), a piano concerto (1938), two operas and a number of choral works. They are all written in the ROMANTIC tradition. From 1953 until his death he was MASTER OF THE QUEEN'S MUSICK.

Blister beetle, medium-sized beetle that secretes cantharadin, an irritant which causes blisters on human skin. Believed to be a diuretic and aphrodisiac, cantharadin was formerly made from the European blister beetle or Spanish fly (*Lytta vesicatoria*). Family Meloidae.

Blitz, the name used by the British to describe the night bombings of British cities by the German Luftwaffe in 1940–41. *See also* HC2 p.232.

Blitzkreig, type of fast-moving warfare developed by the Germans during WWII. It means "lightning war", and was used in their invasion of Poland in 1939. Tanks and mechanized troops smashed through enemy lines, often supported by dive-bombers. The British amended the term to BLITZ. *See also* HC2 p.228.

Blixen, Karen. *See* DINESEN, ISAK.

BL Lacertae, extraordinary object with a strong infra-red emission, of unknown category; recent indications (as yet unconfirmed) are that it may be a quasar embedded in a normal galaxy. *See also* SU p.251.

Bloch, Ernest (1880–1959), Swiss-born US composer. He was well known for his orchestral compositions, which included *Schelomo* (1916) for cello and orchestra. He also composed concertos, chamber music, an opera, *Macbeth* (1909) and *Sacred Service* (1933).

Bloch, Ernst (1885–1977), German philosopher. A Marxist, he left Nazi Germany in 1933 and wrote most of his major work, *The Hope Principle* (1954–59), in the USA. He returned to East Germany in 1948, where his Marxist revisionism became suspect to Party authorities. Unable to get his works published, he defected to West Germany in 1961.

Bloch, Felix (1905–), Swiss-born US nuclear physicist. From 1934 he was professor of theoretical physics at Stanford University, USA, becoming a naturalized American in 1939. With the US physicist Edward Mills PURCELL he shared the 1952 Nobel prize in physics for their separate development of the nuclear induction or nuclear resonance method of measuring the magnetic fields of atomic nuclei.

Bloch, Konrad Emil (1912–), German-born US biochemist. He studied fat metabolism, and in particular the way CHOLESTEROL is synthesized in the body. He shared the 1964 Nobel prize for physiology and medicine with Feodor LYNEN.

Blockade, military tactic aimed at closing ports to commerce or obstructing communications and movement in and out of a territory.

Bloemaert, Abraham (1564–1651). Dutch MANNERIST painter of historical and allegorical themes, still lifes and portraits; influenced by the chiaroscuro of CARAVAGGIO. He played an important role in the founding of the UTRECHT SCHOOL.

Bloemfontein, city and judicial capital of South Africa, 475km (295 miles) W of Durban, and capital of the Orange Free State province. Dutch farmers settled there in the early 19th century. The modern city is a centre for education. Industries: furniture, plastics. Pop. (1970) 148,282.

Blok, Alexander Aleksandrovich (1880–1921), Russian poet, the leading member of the SYMBOLIST school. His most famous early work is *Verses About the Lady Beautiful* (1904). He is best known for his pro-Revolutionary epic poem, *The Twelve* (1918).

Blondel, originally called Blondel de Nesle, French minstrel who became a legend. He lived in the late 12th century and is generally associated with RICHARD I.

Blondin, pseudonym of Jean-Francois Gravelet (1824–97), French acrobat and tightrope walker. He gained an international reputation by crossing Niagara Falls several times on a tightrope, the first time in 1859. The rope, drawn 160ft above the water, was 1,100ft long.

Blood, Colonel Thomas (*c.*1618–80), Irish adventurer. In 1671 he and three accomplices stole the crown jewels from the Tower of London. He was arrested and imprisoned, but later pardoned by Charles II who visited him in prison.

Blood, fluid tissue circulating in the bodies of animals that transports oxygen, water, nutrients and metabolites. In a healthy human being, its normal temperature is approx. 37°C (98.6°F) and it constitutes about 9% of the body's total weight. By volume, it comprises about 5.5litres (9.7pt) of which 54% is the yellowish, transparent liquid called plasma and 46% the microscopic cells it contains. *See also* MS pp.62–63.

Blood cells comprise red cells (erythrocytes) delivering oxygen to body tissues through their HAEMOGLOBIN content, white cells (leukocytes) protecting the body from infection and PLATELETS, the blood's vital clotting agents. *See also* MS pp.*62.*

Blood clotting, protective physiological mechanism that prevents loss of blood after injury or other causes of haemorrhage. A mesh of tight fibres coagulates at the site of injury through a complex series of chemical reactions; normal clotting takes place within five minutes. *See also* MS pp.*62,* 63, 91, *114,* 115.

Blood groups are classified into four major types: A, B, AB or O, according to the blood's basic protein content present in its red cells as agglutinogens A and B. The RHESUS FACTOR (Rh) further classifies groups as Rh-positive or Rh-negative. Group identification is essential before BLOOD TRANSFUSION can take place. *See also* LANDSTEINER; MS pp.62, *62,* 126.

Bloodhound, hunting DOG with long tapered head, loose hanging jowls and ears, and a characteristically wrinkled skin. The body is strong and the legs muscular, and the dog weighs up to 50kg (110lbs). The smooth coat may be black, tan, or red and tan. Height: (at shoulder) up to 69cm (27in). *See also* HOUND.

Blood poisoning (septicaemia), the prolonged invasion of the bloodstream by pathogenic bacteria. Such microbes may enter the body through a cut or materialize as toxins produced after an infectious disease. Symptoms include sudden chills and fever, sweating and pains in the joints; ANTIBIOTICS are the normal treatment. *See also* MS pp.84–85, *85.*

Blood pressure, force exerted on artery walls, is usually taken as two readings: first when the heart is contracting and then when it is at rest between beats. An average young adult's pressure is thus quoted as 120/80mm, the two heights of a SPHYGMOMANOMETER's mercury column the blood can support. *See also* MS pp.*90,* 91.

Blood tests, examination of blood, taken usually from a vein in the inner elbow. Tests include blood grouping, counts of red and white cells, detection of abnormal cells such as those indicating a type of cancer, and estimation of the clotting power and the levels of various proteins, including antibodies against disease. *See also* MS pp.62–63, 76, 112, 128.

Blood transfusion, supplying blood into a patient's circulation, most often to counteract shock caused by loss of blood, which can otherwise prove fatal. The BLOOD GROUP of the donor must be compatible with that of the recipient, to avoid dangerous or even fatal clotting in the recipient's blood vessels. The donor's blood must also be free from agents of disease. *See also* MS pp.62–63, 127.

Blood type. *See* BLOOD GROUPS.

Blood vessels, closed tube-like channels that circulate blood throughout the body. There are three major types of blood vessels: arteries, which carry blood away from the heart; veins, which carry blood towards the heart; and capillaries, the smallest, in which gases and dissolved substances diffuse in and out of the blood. *See also* MS pp.62–63, 87, *90, 91.*

Blood Wedding, one of three folk tragedies by GARCIA LORCA; it was published in 1933 as *Bodas de Sangre* and followed by *Yerma* (1934) and *La Casa de Bernarda Alba* (1936; *The House of Bernarda Alba*). These three works are filled with the energy of revolt against the middle-class theatre in Madrid at the time.

Bloody Assizes (1685), trials held in the West Country of England following MONMOUTH's rebellion. Judge JEFFREYS, who presided, conducted the trials with notorious severity and sentenced 200 people to be hanged, about 800 to transportation, and hundreds more to flogging, imprisonment or fines. *See also* HC1 p.*293.*

Bloom, Claire (1931–), British actress best known for her role as the ballet dancer in Charlie CHAPLIN's film, *Limelight* (1952). In the theatre, she won particular acclaim for her performances in plays by IBSEN and in Tennessee WILLIAMS' *A Streetcar Named Desire.*

Bloomer, Amelia Jenks (1818–94), US women's rights campaigner. She published *Lily,* the first US magazine for women. She continued as editor and wrote articles on education, marriage laws and female suffrage. As part of her campaign for the emancipation of women she popularized the full trousers for women that became known as "bloomers".

Bloomsbury Group, intellectuals who met in Bloomsbury, central London, from about 1907. They included the art critics Roger FRY and Clive BELL; novelists E.M. FORSTER and Virginia WOOLF; her husband Leonard, a publisher; economist John Maynard KEYNES and biographer Lytton STRACHEY. The group's attitudes were influenced by the philosopher G.E. MOORE, and are contained in his statement that "the rational ultimate end of human progress consists in the pleasures of human intercourse and the enjoyment of beautiful objects".

Blow, John (*c.*1648–1708), English composer, organist at Westminster Abbey and the Chapel Royal, London. He wrote many anthems, a masque, *Venus and Adonis* (1685), and taught PURCELL.

Blowfly. *See* BLUEBOTTLE.

Blowpipe, or blowgun, accurate weapon consisting of a tube through which a pellet or poisoned dart is ejected by force of breath. It is widely used by people in South and Central America and SE Asia for hunting small game.

Blücher, Gebhard Leberecht von (1742–1819), Prussian field-marshal. He distinguished himself during the NAPOLEONIC WARS, fighting against France (1793–94), and in the campaign of 1805–06. He led the Prussian troops at the battle of Lützen and helped to defeat Napoleon at LEIPZIG (1813). In 1815 he was defeated at Ligny but arrived at WATERLOO in time to secure British victory over Napoleon. *See also* HC2 pp.76, *77.*

Blue, honour conferred on those representing their universities in sporting competitions. These were originally conferred by Oxford and Cambridge whose identifying colours are dark blue and light blue respectively.

Blue baby, child born with a defect of the heart or incompletely expanded lungs, either or both of which causes its blood to be deficient in oxygen. It leads to a bluish skin colour (cyanosis).

Bluebeard, folk tale character, murderer of a succession of wives who became too curious about a locked room in his castle. In the story by Charles PERRAULT, Bluebeard is a rich nobleman. His wife manages to open the locked door and sees the bodies of several women inside. She is saved from death by the arrival of her brothers who thereupon kill her husband.

Bluebeard's Castle, only opera by Béla BARTÓK, written in 1911 and produced in Budapest in 1918. It has extraordinary richness and power and is a superb handling of the Bluebeard legend.

Bluebell, spring-flowering blue flower, native throughout Europe. It grows from a bulb, especially in woodlands. Height: 20–50cm (8–20in). Family Liliaceae; species *Endymion non-scriptus. See also* NW pp.*67, 209.*

Blueberry. *See* BILBERRY.

Bluebottle, black or metallic blue-green fly, slightly larger but similar in habits to the HOUSE FLY. The larvae (maggots) usually feed on carrion and refuse containing meat. Like the greenbottle, it is often also called a blowfly. Family Calliphoridae. Genus *Musca.* Length: 6–11mm (0.23–0.43in).

Bluebuck, another name for the NILGAI, an Indian antelope.

Bluefields, town in SE Nicaragua, on Bluefields Bay at the mouth of the Escondido River. It is the capital of Zelaya department and Nicaragua's chief port on the Caribbean Sea. Products: bananas, hardwoods, coconuts. Pop. (1970 est.) 23,000.

Bluefish, marine fish found in most tropical and temperate seas. A voracious predator, it travels in large schools. Fished widely for food and sport, it has an elongated blue or green body and a large mouth with sharp, strong teeth. Length: to 1.2m (4ft). Family Pomatomidae; species *Pomatomus saltatrix.*

Bluegrass, type of grass that grows in temperate and Arctic regions and is used extensively for food by grazing animals. Family Gramineae; genus *Poa.*

Blue-green algae, unicellular or two-celled plants which live on moist surfaces or on water; they reproduce by spores. Class Cyanophyta. *See also* ALGAE.

Blue Mountains (Blue Plateau), range in New South Wales, SE Australia; part of the Great Dividing Range and a barrier to westward colonial expansion until 1813. The area is popular with walkers and mountaineers. Height: 610–1,100m (2,000–3,600ft).

Blue Mountain, highest peak in the Blue Mountain range in E Jamaica, West Indies; it is 2,253m (7,388ft) high. The range is thickly covered by vegetation and the well-known Blue Mountain coffee is grown on its slopes.

Blue Nile, river in NW Ethiopia, rising near Lake Tana and flowing SE and W into the Sudan. It merges with the White Nile to form the River Nile. Two dams on its course through the Sudan irrigate 400,000 ha (1,000,000 acres) of land. Length: approx. 1,368km (850 miles).

Blueprint, photographic image on paper with white lines against a blue background, frequently used for engineering drawings. The paper is coated with a solution of ammonium ferric citrate and potassium ferricyanide and exposed to intense light under the sheet of drawings to be copied. The blueprint is "developed" in water. *See also* MM p.208.

Blue Rider. *See* BLAUE REITER, DER.

Blues, musical form used in jazz and related music. It may have developed from Scottish folk tunes; by the early 20th century, in the hands of Negro musicians, such as W. C. HANDY it had become a fairly strict harmonic progression, usually over 12 bars. An authentically American Negro form, it was the basis of many songs (often pessimistic) and was used for instrumental improvization in which the use of "blue notes" (flattened thirds and sevenths) was an important melodic device. The blues and the styles of playing associated with it have influenced much 20th-century music. *See also* HC2 pp.272–273.

Bluestocking, pejorative term applied to women with literary pretensions. It dates from the 18th century when a London women's literary circle was attended by Benjamin Stillingfleet, who wore ordinary blue worsted stockings rather than the black silk of evening dress.

Blue whale, the largest animal that has ever lived, now in danger of extinction. Species *Sibbaldus musculus. See also* NW p.166, *167.*

Bluff, southernmost port of South Island, New Zealand. It has a large harbour with automatic loading facilities, and exports wool and fish. Pop. (1972 est.) 3,250.

Blum, Léon (1872–1950), French politician. He served in the Chamber of Deputies (1919–40) as a leader of the Socialist Party. He was Prime Minister (1936–37) and deputy prime minister (1938), leading the opposition to the MUNICH AGREEMENT. Interned by the VICHY GOVERNMENT (1940–45) he was released by the Allies and led the provisional government of 1946–47 before the elections held by the new Fourth Republic.

Blumberg, Baruch Samuel (1925–), US research physician. From 1964 he worked with the American Institute for Cancer Research. He shared the 1975 Nobel Prize in physiology and medicine with Daniel C. GAJDUSEK for discoveries concerning new mechanisms for the origin and dissemination of infectious diseases.

Blumenbach, Johann Friedrich (1752–1840), German zoologist and anthropologist, often called the "father of physical anthropology". He proposed one of the earliest classifications of man. His study of cranium measurements led him to propose that there are five families of man – Caucasian, Mongolian, Malayan, Ethiopian and American.

Blundell, Sir Edward Denis (1907–) New Zealand lawyer and diplomat. He was high commissioner for New Zealand in London (1968-72) and in 1972 he was appointed governor-general of New Zealand.

Blunden, Edmund Charles (1896–1974), English poet and author. His poetry, including that written during wartime, is marked by a deep love of the traditions of rural England. His most celebrated work is the prose narrative *Undertones of War* (1928), a classic account of his experiences in WWI. In 1966–68 he was professor of poetry at Oxford.

Blunt, Wilfred Scawen (1840–1922), English poet. He supported Egyptian and Irish nationalism and in 1887 was imprisoned for his political activity in support of Irish independence. His poems include *The Love Sonnets of Proteus* (1875–92).

Boa, constricting SNAKE which gives birth to live young. The boa constrictor (*Constrictor constrictor*) of the American tropics can grow to 3.7m (12ft), although the iridescent rainbow boa, the emerald tree boa and the rosy boa are smaller species. Most boas are tree-dwellers, but the rubber boa of the W USA is a burrowing species. Family Boidae. *See also* NW pp.*73,* 137, 217.

BOAC. *See* BRITISH AIRWAYS.

Boadicea (*d.* AD 62), British Queen of the ICENI in East Britain. She was the wife of King Prasutagus who, on his death, left his daughters and the Roman emperor as co-heirs. The Romans seized his domain and Boadicea led a revolt against them. Defeated, she took poison. *See also* HC1 pp.100–101.

Boar, male domestic pig (particularly one that has not been castrated) or, more specifically, the wild pig of Europe, Africa and Asia. In almost all its habitats it is hunted, either for food or merely for sport. The European wild boar is species *Sus scrofa. See also* NW p.206; PE p.*234.*

Boat, vehicle for passenger and freight transport by water. Today the term "boat" is often reserved for a small craft that can easily be taken out of the water; larger vessels are called SHIPS. The first boats, made in prehistoric times, included hollowed-out logs and rafts and boats made from plaited reeds. Among the first maritime peoples were the Phoenicians, who built fleets of galleys for their extensive trading in the Mediterranean and adjoining areas. These galleys, and the later ones of the Greeks and Romans, were propelled by sails, supplemented by oars usually plied by slaves. The later Viking long-boats, also square-sailed, were slimmer and speedier, their oars being plied by strong fighting men. Lateen (triangular) sails were probably imported from the Persian Gulf, and introduced to the west by the empire-building Arabs. Modern boats include SAILING vessels, generally used mainly for pleasure, MOTOR-BOATS and launches. *See also* LIFE-BOAT; MM pp.110–113.

Boatbill, or boat-billed heron, nocturnal wading bird of tropical America, related to the night herons but having a much broader bill. Family Ardeidae; species *Cochlearius cochlearius. See also* NW p.*233.*

Boat Race, annual rowing contest between Oxford and Cambridge eights, first held in 1829. It is rowed on a 6.8km (4$\frac{1}{4}$mile) course on the Thames, from Putney to Mortlake. The race, first held on the present course in 1845, takes place in March or April.

Boatswain. *See* BO'SUN.

Boaz, in the Bible, Bethlehemite related to NAOMI's husband Elimelech. He married their daughter-in-law Ruth, inheriting her deceased husband's estates.

Bobadilla, Francisco de (*d.* 1502), Spanish colonial administrator. He replaced Christopher COLUMBUS as Governor of the West Indies in 1500, sending Columbus back to Spain in chains. He was recalled to Spain in 1502 but died at sea.

Bobcat. *See* LYNX.

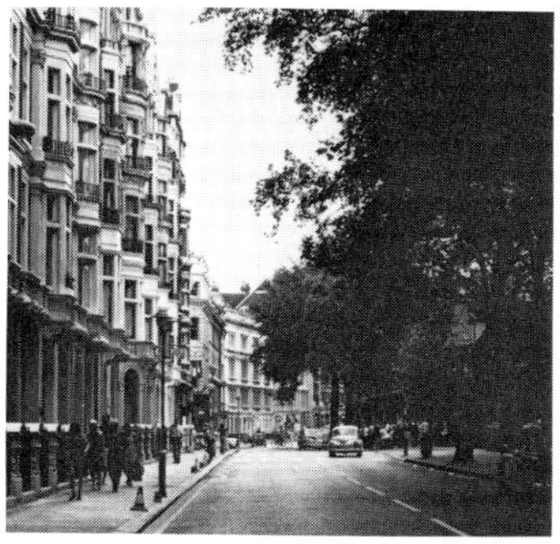

Bloomsbury, London, where a group of intellectuals met informally in their homes.

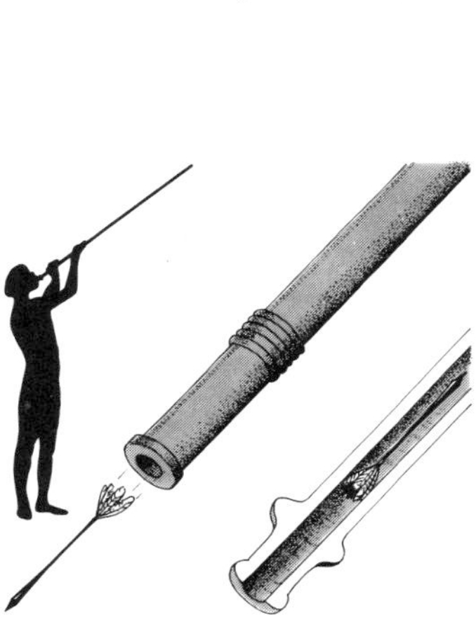

Blowpipes are accurate deadly weapons which can shoot poison darts at game.

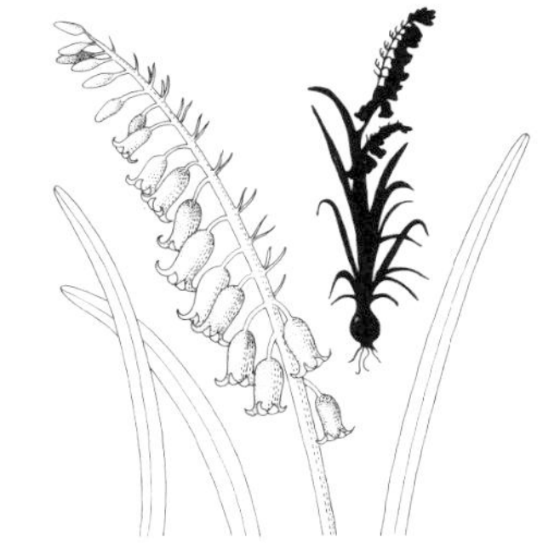

Bluebells have strong stems which bear rows of fragrant, hanging bell-shaped flowers.

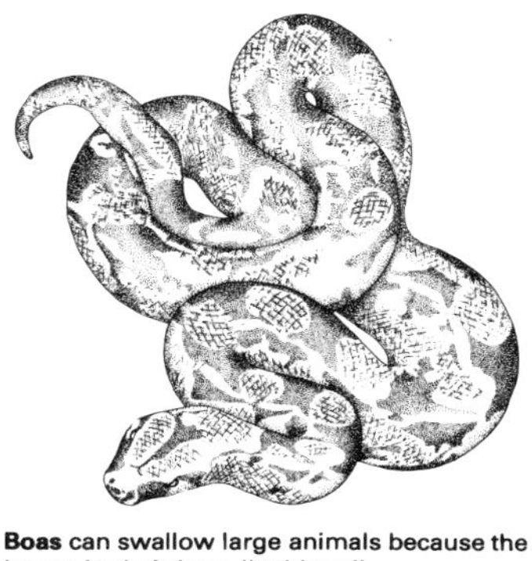

Boas can swallow large animals because the bones in their jaws "unhinge".

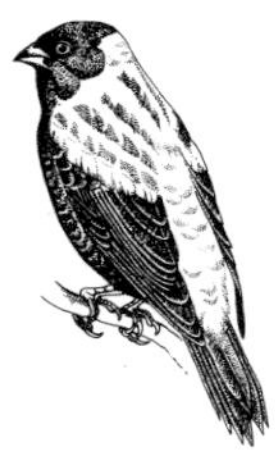

Bobolink, a relative of the European blackbird, gets its name from its distinctive call.

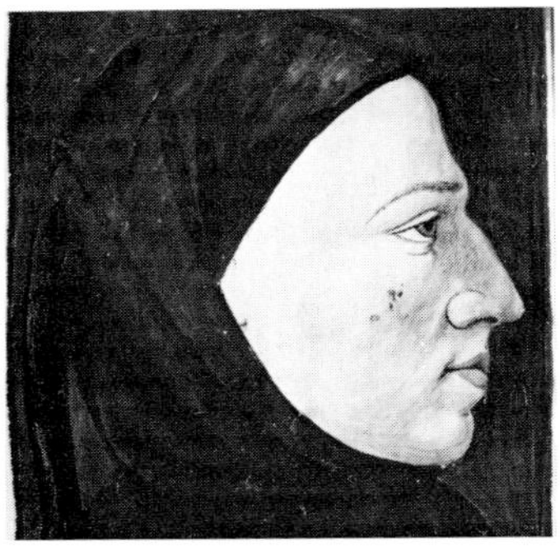

Boccaccio's Decameron states that man, to be truly noble, must accept life as it is.

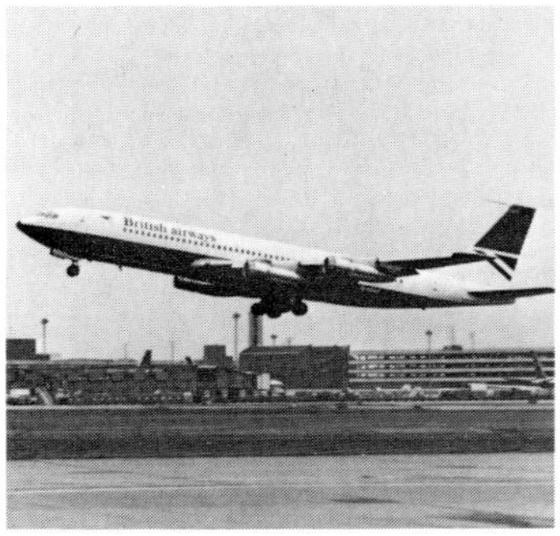

Boeing 707, first of several successful jet liners from one of America's largest companies.

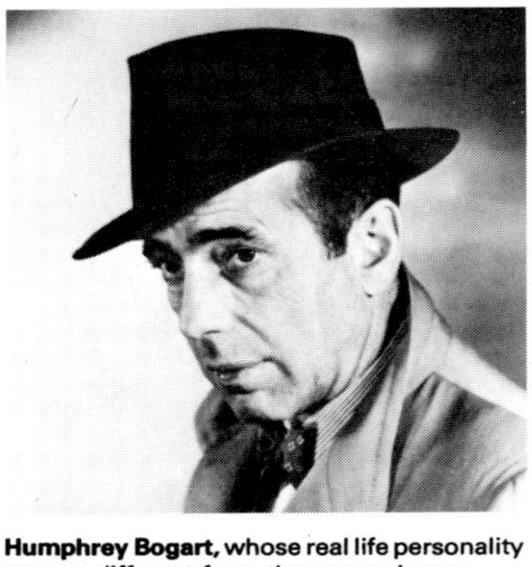

Humphrey Bogart, whose real life personality was so different from the screen image.

Bobolink, songbird found in Canada and N USA, which winters in South America. Males have a tawny neck, buff back and black underparts in spring. The brown female lays up to seven spotted eggs in a ground nest. Species *Dolichonyx oryzivorus.*

Bobsleigh, long metal sledge for two or four people which is ridden down a steep, twisting ice-covered course in one of the fastest winter sports. Developed in Switzerland in the 19th century, bobsleighing has been included as an Olympic event since 1924. One of the most famous courses is the CRESTA RUN.

Boccaccio, Giovanni (1313–75), Italian poet. His early work, the *Filocolo* (*c.* 1340) is sometimes considered the first European novel, but he is best known for the *Decameron* (1348–53), a series of stories of contemporary mores, and for *La Fiammetta*, a romance. He knew and imitated DANTE, and with his friend PETRARCH he is considered to be one of the founders of the Italian RENAISSANCE. *See also* HC1 p.*207.*

Boccherini, Luigi (1743–1805), Italian composer. He was an accomplished concert cellist and a prolific composer of chamber music in the emerging classical manner. He wrote over 60 string trios and more than 200 string quartets and quintets.

Boccie. *See* BOWLS.

Boccioni, Umberto (1882–1916), Italian FUTURIST painter, sculptor and writer, a signatory of the FUTURIST MANIFESTO (1910). His paintings (eg *Street Noises Penetrate into the House*; 1911), and sculpture (eg *Unique Forms of Continuity in Space*; 1913), try to depict complete ranges of sensations and impressions simultaneously. *See also* HC2 p.177.

Bochum, city in West Germany, 16km (10 miles) E of Essen, in the heart of the industrial Ruhr district. The city, containing a 16th-century church, was once an important producer of coal. Industries: engineering, iron and steel, textiles, Pop. (1970 est.) 343,968.

Bock, Hieronymus (*c.* 1498–1554), German botanist. He constructed a system of plant classification based on physical characteristics. His description of German plants, *Neu Kreutterbuch* (1539), was a great improvement on any of the earlier herbals.

BOD, or biological oxygen demand, chemical test for determining the level of pollution of water by organic matter. Two equal samples of water are taken, and the first is treated chemically to "mop up" any dissolved oxygen. Both samples are then incubated in the dark for some days, after which the second sample is given a similar chemical treatment. This allows the amount of "mopped-up" oxygen to be estimated. The difference between the two estimations represents the amount of oxygen that has been used up by living and dead organic matter in the water during the period of storage. *See also* MM p.203; PE pp.150–151.

Bode's law, empirical numerical relationship for the mean distances of the planets from the Sun. It is named after the German astronomer Johann Bode, who popularized it in the late 18th century. If the number 4 is added to 0, 3, 6, 12, 24, 48, 96 and 192, and each sum is divided by 10, the figure arrived at is the mean distance in astronomical units of the planets from the Sun from Mercury to Uranus, including the asteroid belt. The law does not work for Neptune and Pluto.

Boden See. *See* CONSTANCE, LAKE.

Bodh Gaya. *See* BUDDH GAYA.

Bodhidharma (*fl.* 6th century AD), Indian Buddhist monk who founded, in China, ZEN (or Ch'an) Buddhism.

Bodhista, also called bodhisatta and bodhisattva, in HĪNAYANĀ BUDDHISM, an individual who is about to reach NIRVANA, such as Gautama prior to his enlightenment. In MAHAYANA BUDDHISM, the term is used to denote an individual on the verge of enlightenment who delays his salvation in order to help mankind. *See also* HC1 pp.64–65.

Bodin, Jean (1530–96), French lawyer and political philosopher. In *Six Books of the Commonwealth* (1576) he treated anarchy as the supreme political evil and order as the supreme human need. He therefore supported absolute monarchy and was an early proponent of the modern notion of unrestricted secular sovereignty residing in the state.

Bodleian Library, large collection of books founded at Oxford University in 1602 by Sir Thomas Bodley (1545–1613), a scholar and diplomat, who donated to it many volumes and manuscripts. The library's collection has more than 2,500,000 volumes and it can accommodate 17,000 readers in the central and dependent libraries.

Bodley, George Frederick (1827–1907), British architect in the GOTHIC REVIVAL manner. He is best-known for his churches, the most famous of which is the chapel of Queen's College, Cambridge.

Bodø, town in N Norway, N of the Arctic Circle, 161km (100 miles) SW of Narvik. It experiences the midnight sun between 1 and 12 July. Industries: copper and marble distribution, fishing. Pop. (1974) 29,123.

Bodoni, Giambattista (1740–1813), Italian printer, one of the originators of the first modern, Roman style typeface. He published editions of HOMER, VIRGIL and HORACE in the new typeface. His editions were considered elegant and imitative of classical styles of writing.

Body snatchers, criminals who stole newly dead bodies to sell to anatomists when there was no legal supply of human corpses for dissection. After the sensational trial (1828–29) of William Burke and William Hare, who murdered people in order to sell the bodies, Britain passed the Anatomy Act in 1832 that permitted medical schools to acquire unclaimed bodies. *See also* BURKE AND HARE.

Boece. *See* BOETHIUS.

Boehm, or Böhm, Theobald (1794–1881), German flautist, composer and inventor. A flute virtuoso, he devised a new key system that involved blocking the flute holes with keys instead of the fingers. This improved the sound of the instrument and has been universally accepted in the manufacture of modern woodwind instruments. Boehm's system was later used on other woodwind instruments.

Boehme, Jakob (1575–1624), German philosophical mystic. A shoemaker by trade, he began to have mystical experiences in 1600. In his books *The Aurora* (1612) and *The Way to Christ* (1623) he exhorted Christians to make their lives a genuine imitation of Christ's suffering and triumph.

Boeing Airplane Company, formed in 1917 by William Edward Boeing from the Pacific Aero Products Company. The company made several famous military aeroplanes which were used during WWII, but it is most famous for its passenger jets, the first of which is the Boeing 707 of 1957. The large-capacity 747, or jumbo jet, was introduced in 1970. *See also* MM p.*151.*

Boeotia, department in central Greece, on the N shore of the Gulf of Corinth; the capital is Levádhia. Formed in the 7th century BC, the Boeotian League of ancient Greek cities was dominated by Thebes. It was disbanded after 479 BC. Heinrich Schliemann excavated the Treasury of Minyas there in the 19th century. Area 3,211sq km (1,240sq miles). Pop. 114,300.

Boer, also known as Afrikaner, Dutch and French Huguenot settler, who from 1652 settled in the area which is now the Republic of South Africa. Boer means "farmer" in Afrikaans. *See also* HC2 pp.128–129, 142, 319, 323.

Boer Wars. *See* SOUTH AFRICAN WARS.

Boerhaave, Hermann (1668–1738), Dutch physician who introduced the bedside method of teaching. From 1701 he taught medicine at Leiden University and later also taught botany and chemistry. His works included *Institutiones Medicae* (1708).

Boethius (Anicius Manlius Severinus) (*c.* 480–524), Roman statesman and philosopher under the Emperor Theodoric. He attempted to eliminate governmental corruption, but was finally imprisoned on a charge of conspiracy. In prison at Pavia, where he was subsequently tortured and executed, he wrote *On the Consolation of Philosophy* (523), a dialogue based on NEO-PLATONIST and ARISTOTELIAN principles, and next to the Bible medieval Europe's most influential book.

Boëthus (*fl.* 2nd century BC), Greek sculptor. Regarded as a member of the Alexandrian school, he is noted for his carvings of children. A bronze statue in the Louvre, of a boy strangling a goose, may be a copy of a sculpture by Boëthus, who also worked in silver.

Bog, spongy wet soil consisting of decayed vegetable matter; often called a peat bog. It develops in a depression with little or no drainage, where the water is cold and acidic and almost devoid of oxygen and nitrogen. A bog rarely has standing water like a marsh, but plants such as cranberry and sundew readily grow there.

Bogarde, Dirk (1921–), British film actor, real name Derek Niven van den Bogaerde. He made his film debut in *Esther Waters* (1947) and after his success in *The Blue Lamp* (1950) became a leading British film star. His later and most notable films include *Victim* (1961), *The Servant* (1963), *Darling* (1965), *Accident* (1967) and *Death in Venice* (1971). He published his autobiography in 1976.

Bogardus, James (1800–74), US architect. He was one of the first to use cast iron in the facades of buildings. In 1848 he built his own factory in New York City to make prefabricated cast iron frames. One of his best known works is the Iron Building in New York City. *See also* HC2 p.*122.*

Bogart, Humphrey de Forest (1899–1957), US film actor. He is best known for his portrayal of rather tough, cynical characters. His films include *The Petrified Forest* (1936), *The Maltese Falcon* (1941), *Casablanca* (1942), *The Big Sleep* (1946), *Treasure of the Sierra Madre* (1948), *The African Queen* (1951), for which he won an Academy Award as best actor, and *The Caine Mutiny* (1954).

Boğazköy, in Turkey, the site of the ancient capital, Hattusa, of the HITTITES who flourished in Anatolia and N Syria in the 2nd millennium BC. It remained the capital throughout the history of the Hittite empire, and was destroyed when the empire fell *c.* 1190 BC.

Bogdanovich, Peter (1939–), US film director and critic. He worked with director Roger Corman on *Wild Angels* (1966) and directed his first film *Targets* (1968) with Corman's backing. His other films include *The Last Picture Show* (1971), a nostalgic look at a Texas town in the mid-1950s, *What's Up, Doc?* (1972), *Paper Moon* (1973), *At Long Last Love* (1975) and *Nickelodeon* (1976).

Bog myrtle, or sweet gale, flowering shrub of wetlands. Its aromatic, resinous leaves have been used in medicines. Family Myricaceae; species *Gale belgica.*

Bogomils, 10th–15th-century heretical Christian sect, founded by Bogomil, a priest. This starkly ascetic group originated in Bulgaria *c.* 950, spread to other Slavic countries and to France, where it influenced the ALBIGENSIAN heresy. Bogomils believed that materialism, or Satan, God's first and fallen son, was uppermost in the world but with the redeeming help of Christ, God's second son, this bondage could be broken and evil destroyed.

Bogotá, capital of Colombia in the centre of the country, 483km (300 miles) N of the Equator. It was founded in 1538 by the Spanish near the Chibcha Indians, on a fertile plateau 2,640m (8,563ft) above sea-level. In 1819 it became the capital of Greater Columbia, part of which later became Colombia. Today it is a centre for culture, education and finance. Industries: tobacco, sugar, flour, textiles. Pop. (1976 est.) 3,153,000.

Bohème, La, opera in four acts by Giacomo PUCCINI, libretto by Giacosa and Illica. It was first produced at Turin in 1896. The story is taken from the novel by Henri Murger, *Scènes de la Vie de Bohème.*

Bohemia, historic region, now forming W Czechoslovakia; its capital is PRAGUE.

Bohemia was first unified in the 10th century and became part of the HOLY ROMAN EMPIRE in 950. It was the centre of several heretical and nationalist revolts, including the HUSSITES, and Protestant opposition to the Emperor in Prague led to the start of the THIRTY YEARS WAR in 1618. Bohemia had become a HAPSBURG possession in 1526, and won its independence from the AUSTRO-HUNGARIAN EMPIRE in 1918, when it became the core of Czechoslovakia. *See also* HC1 pp.162–163, 273; HC2 pp.84–85; MW p.62–63.

Bohemian school, 14th-century group of artists based in Prague. Their most important achievements lie in panel paintings and frescoes by exponents such as Theodoricus of Prague (*fl.* 1360–80) and the Master of Wittingau (*fl.* 1380–90), who were initially influenced by Italian models but developed a specifically Bohemian SOFT STYLE. Through Charles IV, King of Bohemia (1346–78) and Holy Roman Emperor (1355–78), they influenced later Gothic art in Germany.

Bohemond I (*c.* 1056–1111), Norman Crusader. In 1096 he joined the First Crusade and played a key role in the capture of Antioch in 1098, of which he became prince in 1099. He was held captive by the Turks (1100–03).

Böhm, Karl (1894–), Austrian conductor, famous for his interpretations of MOZART and STRAUSS. In 1921 Bruno WALTER engaged him for the Munich State Opera and in 1934 he became musical director of the Dresden Opera. He was principal conductor of the Vienna Philharmonic Orchestra from 1933.

Bohr, Aage Niels (1922–), Danish physicist. From 1956 he was professor of physics at Copenhagen University. In 1963 he became director of the Nordic Institute for Theoretical Nuclear Physics (NORDITA). With Benjamin MOTTELSON (also of NORDITA) and James RAINWATER of the USA he shared the 1975 Nobel Prize in physics for their discovery of the connection between collective motion and particle motion in atomic nuclei.

Bohr, Niels (1885–1962), Danish physicist. He worked with J.J. THOMSON and Ernest RUTHERFORD in Britain before teaching theoretical physics at the University of Copenhagen. He used the QUANTUM THEORY to explain the spectrum of hydrogen and devised the atomic model that bears his name. He escaped from German-occupied Denmark during WWII and helped to develop the atom bomb in the USA. He later returned to Copenhagen and worked for international cooperation. He was awarded the Nobel Prize for physics in 1922 for his work on atomic structure. *See also* SU pp.62–63.

Bohun, Humphrey V de (*d.* 1275) and Humphrey VII de (1276–1322), 1st and 3rd earls of Essex. The 1st earl was one of the baronial opponents of HENRY III who drew up the PROVISION OF OXFORD. The 3rd earl was one of the lords ordainers who opposed EDWARD II.

Boiardo, Matteo Maria (1441–94), Italian poet. His incomplete *Orlando innamorato* revived the Italian epic, chiefly by inspiring Ludovico ARIOSTO, whereas *Three Books on Love* (1499), for Antonia Caprara, is among the best lyric poetry.

Boil, or furuncle, localized infection of the skin and subcutaneous tissue, often formed around hair follicles on the neck, face or buttocks. Most boils are caused by friction, which irritates the roots of the hair, and the growth of the microorganism STAPHYLOCOCCUS.

Boileau-Despréaux, Nicolas (1636–1711), French poet and critic. In *L'Art poétique* (1674), he expounded classical standards for poetry, and his criticisms gained him both friends and enemies. He was royal historian to Louis XIV of France in 1677. *See also* HC1 pp.316–317.

Boiler, vessel for heating and converting water to steam, an essential part of steam-engines and turbines. It consists of a furnace for burning fuel and a compartment where water is evaporated into steam. *See also* MM pp.64–67.

Boiling-point, temperature at which a substance changes phase from a liquid to a vapour or gas. The boiling-point is higher or lower as the external pressure increases or decreases. It is usually measured at standard pressure (760mm of mercury).

Boito, Arrigo (1842–1918), Italian composer and librettist. His principal work as a composer was the opera *Mefistofele* (1868, revised 1875), but more significant were the librettos he wrote for VERDI's operas *Otello* and *Falstaff.*

Boksburg, city of NE South Africa, 24km (15 miles) E of Johannesburg. It was established in 1887 and became an important gold-mining area. Industries: gold, electrical equipment, clay products, food processing. Pop. (1968 est.) 108,800.

Bolas, missile hunting-weapon of South American Indians, consisting of two or more stone balls tied to the end of thongs and thrown in such a manner as to entangle the legs of the prey. It is used mainly in the open country of the Patagonian and Pampas zones. *See also* MM p.160.

Boldrewood, Rolf (1826–1915), British-born Australian novelist, pseudonym of Thomas Alexander Browne. In Australia he was first a squatter and later an inspector of goldfields. Using his pseudonym he wrote adventure stories including *Robbery Under Arms* (1882) and *The Miner's Right* (1890).

Boleslav, name of five Polish rulers of the PIAST dynasty. Boleslav I (*c.* 966–1025), "the Mighty" (*r.* 992–1025) and the founder of the Polish monarchy, gained independence from Germany and greatly expanded Polish territory. Boleslav II (1039–81), "the Generous", ruled as king from 1058 to 1079 until noble opposition forced him to flee to Hungary. Boleslav III (1086–1138), "the Bold", (*r.* 1102–38) Christianized Pomerania and repulsed an invasion by the Emperor HENRY V but in his division of the country into four separate duchies for his sons created two centuries of internal conflict. Boleslav IV (1127–73), "the Curly", (*r.* 1146–73) saw his country invaded twice by FREDERICK BARBAROSSA. Boleslav V (1221–79), "the Chaste", ruled from 1227 to 1279. *See also* HC1 pp.162, *162.*

Boletus, genus of terrestrial fungi whose spore-bearing parts are tubes instead of the usual gills. There are many species, all of which have a fleshy cap on a central stem and some of which are edible. Many poisonous kinds have red tube mouths. *See also* NW p.*43.*

Boleyn, Anne (*c.* 1507–1536), second wife of HENRY VIII and mother of ELIZABETH I who became the king's mistress some time after 1526 and his queen in 1533. Moves to enable Henry to break with Rome and allow his childless marriage to Catherine of Aragon to be annulled were intensified in 1533 when Anne became pregnant and married Henry secretly. Her own failure to produce a male heir led to her trial and execution on charges of adultery and incest. *See also* HC1 p.270.

Bolingbroke. *See* HENRY IV (of England).

Bolingbroke, Henry St John, Viscount (1678–1751), English politician and propagandist. A TORY member of Parliament (1701–14), he became Secretary for War in 1704 under Queen ANNE. His *Idea of a Patriot King* (1749) was thought to have influenced the "PHILOSOPHES".

Bolívar, Simón (1783–1830), Venezuelan soldier and statesman whose experiences in Napoleonic Europe influenced his persistent attempts to free South America of Spanish rule. He achieved no real success, however, until he established an inland base in 1819 from where he succeeded in liberating New Granada (later Colombia) in 1821. The liberation of Venezuela (1821), Ecuador (1822), Peru (1824) and Upper Peru (1825) followed, the latter renaming itself Bolivia in his honour. Despite this complete removal of Spanish hegemony from the continent, his hopes of uniting South America into one continental alliance were dashed by the inevitable rivalry between the new states. *See also* HC2 pp.86, *87.*

Bolivia, inland nation in W central South America. It has rich mineral deposits, including tin, gold and silver, but it is nevertheless one of the poorest nations of the continent. Sucre is the official capital, but La Paz is the seat of government. Area: 1,098,581sq km (424,162sq miles). Pop. (1976 est.) 4,687,618. *See* MW p.39.

Böll, Heinrich (1917–), German novelist and short-story writer. His works include *Where Were You, Adam?* (1951), *Acquainted with the Night* (1953), *The Clown* (1963), *Absent Without Leave* (1964) and *Group Portrait with Lady* (1971). A concern for Catholic authenticity and a critical view of German society pervades his stories. He was awarded the Nobel Prize for literature in 1972.

Boll weevil, small black beetle common in the USA. Adults and larvae feed on cotton plants, especially the bolls, and cause serious crop damage. Species *Anthonomus grandis. See also* NW p.113.

Bollworm, caterpillar found in many areas where cotton is grown; it is cream or slightly pink in colour and feeds mainly on the green cotton bolls. The adult resembles the CLOTHES MOTH. Length: 12mm (0.5in). There are various species.

Bologna city in N central Italy, at the foot of Apennines, capital of Bologna and Emilia-Romagna province. Originally an Etruscan town, Felsina, it was colonized by Rome in the 2nd century BC. It has an 11th-century university, the uncompleted Church of San Petronio (1390), and the Palazzo Comunale (13th, 15th, 16th centuries). Industries: mechanical and electrical engineering, food processing. Pop. (1975 est.) 491,330.

Bolometer, instrument for detecting and measuring electromagnetic radiation such as light and heat. One type uses a thin blackened metal strip whose electrical resistance varies according to the amount of radiation falling on it. Bolometers are often mounted in telescopes to measure the energy given off by stars.

Bolsheviks, MARXISTS led by LENIN who obtained and held power by the RUSSIAN REVOLUTION. Their name ("the majority") distinguished them from the MENSHEVIKS ("the minority"), whom they narrowly defeated at the Second Congress of the All-Russian Soviet Democratic Workers' Party in London in 1903. The split, on tactics as much as doctrine, centred on the means of achieving revolution, the Bolsheviks believing it could be obtained only by professional revolutionaries leading the PROLETARIAT, their more liberal Menshevik opponents led by Julius Martov holding a less doctrinaire, more democratic approach which included cooperation with other parties including those in the DUMA. Numerically in a minority in 1917, the Bolsheviks were nevertheless able to overthrow the Provisional government of KERENSKY through their support in the SOVIETS of Moscow and Petrograd led by Leon TROTSKY. *See also* HC2 pp.196–197, *196–197.*

Bolshoi Ballet, one of the world's leading companies which was founded in 1776. Based at the BOLSHOI THEATRE, its choreographers have included Marius PETIPA and Alexander Gorsky and its leading dancers Galina ULANOVA and Mikhial Lavrovsky.

Bolshoi Opera, leading Russian opera company, founded in 1780 in Moscow. It performs mostly Russian works and a few foreign operas translated into Russian.

Bolshoi Theatre, home of the BOLSHOI BALLET and Bolshoi Opera. The present building dates from 1856 and seats more than 2,000.

Bolt, Robert Oxton (1924–), British dramatist whose reputation was established with *Flowering Cherry* (1957) and consolidated with *A Man for All Seasons* (1960), about the life of Sir Thomas MORE. Later plays include *Vivat, Vivat Regina!* (1970), about ELIZABETH I, and State of Revolution (1977), which explored the politics of LENIN.

Bolton, town in Greater Manchester Metropolitan County, NW England, 18km (11 miles) NW of Manchester. Since the late 18th century it has been a cotton and textile-manufacturing centre. Crompton's SPINNING MULE was invented there in 1779. Other industries: chemicals, textile machinery. Pop. (1971) 154,000.

Boltwood, Bertram Borden (1870–1927), US chemist and physicist who did important research in radioactivity which led to

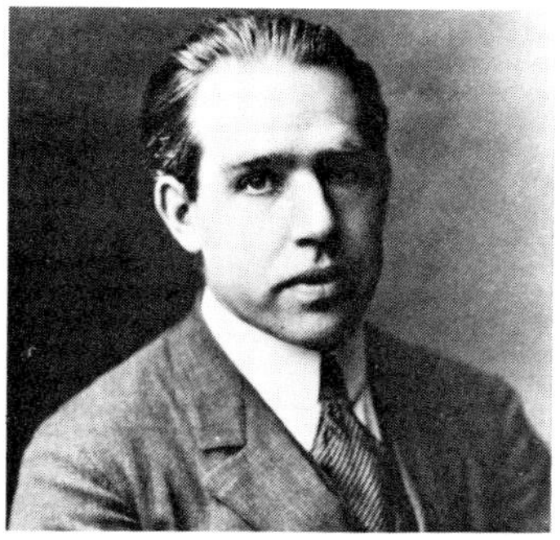

Niels Bohr, Danish physicist who worked as an adviser on the atom bomb project.

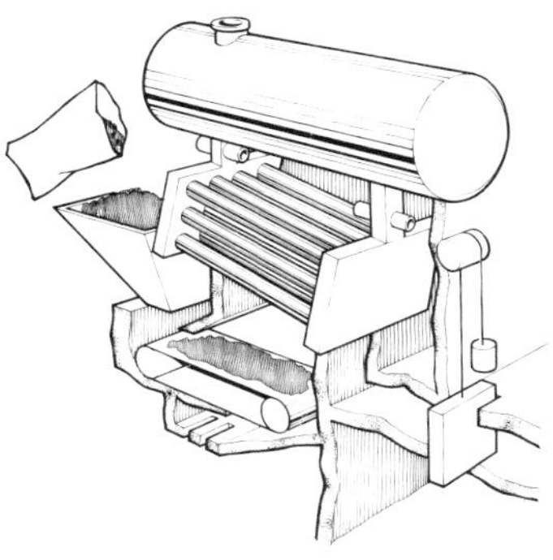

Boilers convert liquids into vapour to drive engines or for heating systems.

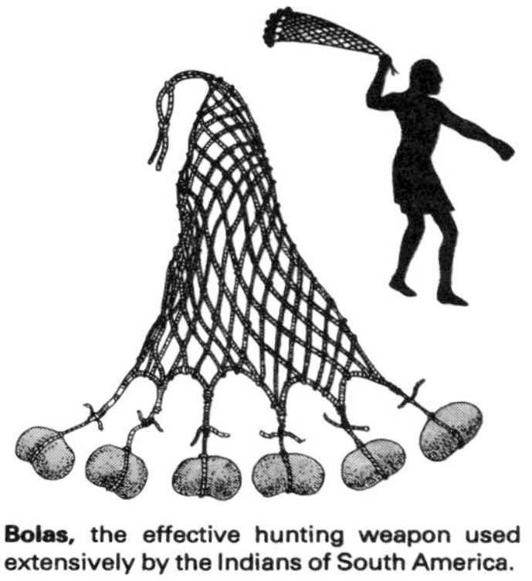

Bolas, the effective hunting weapon used extensively by the Indians of South America.

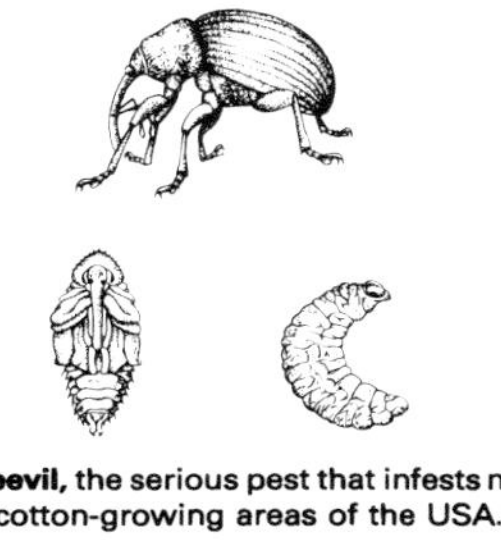

Boll weevil, the serious pest that infests most of the cotton-growing areas of the USA.

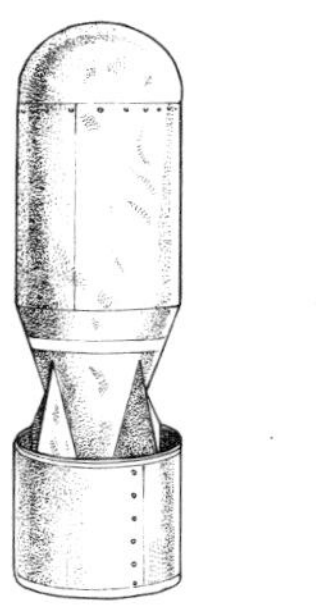

Bombs; the phases of destruction are blast, vacuum pressure, fragmentation and shock.

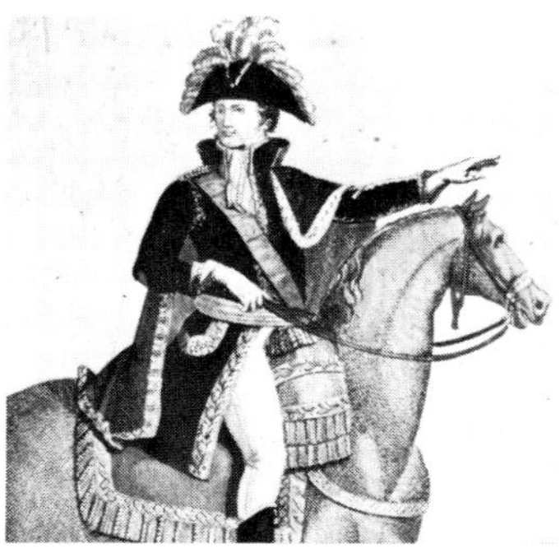

Joseph Bonaparte, who was placed on the Spanish throne by his brother, the Emperor.

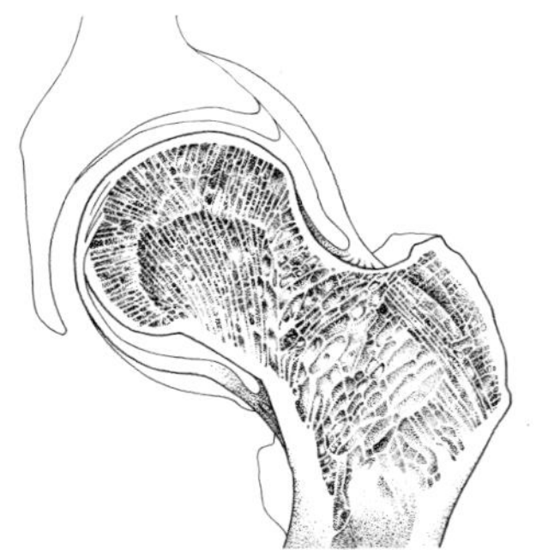

Bones form the skeleton of most vertebrates and contain blood-forming bone marrow.

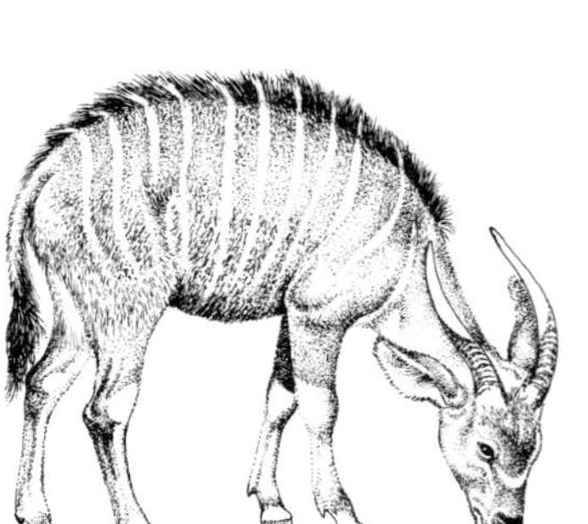

Bongo; both the male and female carry large horns that spiral with one complete twist.

the development of the theory of ISOTOPES. In 1904 he discovered ionium (a radioactive isotope of thorium). He was professor of radiochemistry at Yale University in the US (1910–27).

Boltzmann, Ludwig (1844–1906), Austrian physicist who made fundamental contributions to the kinetic theory of gases and to statistical mechanics. Using the work of Josef Stefan he also demonstrated the law of radiation from a black body, now known as the Stefan-Boltzmann law. From 1866 he held professorships at the universities of Graz, Vienna, Munich and Leipzig.

Boma, port and city in W Zaïre, central Africa, on the estuary of the River Congo. It was founded as a slave-market and is now the commercial centre of central Africa. Products: timber, cocoa, bananas. Pop. (1967 est.) 79,200.

Bomb, projectile filled with an explosive charge exploded by a fuse or by impact, and used as a weapon to cause destruction and death. Originally dropped on attackers from the walls of a castle, bombs are now usually dropped from aircraft. The many specialized types include atomic bombs, high-explosive bombs, smoke bombs to provide a smoke-screen, gas bombs to spread poison gas and fire bombs that scatter burning napalm (a thickened fuel). *See also* MM pp.*33*, 74, *75*, 180, *181*, *242*, *243*.

Bomb, volcanic, piece of solid material, usually cooled lava, ejected by a volcano. Volcanic bombs are usually greater than 32mm (1.3in) in diameter, and may be very large. *See also* PE pp.30–31.

Bombardon, term adopted early in the 19th century in Austria for a type of bass TUBA, now obsolete. Its fundamental note may be E♭ , F or B♭ . It had three valves. Today, a related instrument in circular form which fits round a marching player is usually called a helicon.

Bombay, largest city in India and capital of Maharashtra state. It is located on an island off the W coast and as a port it is second only to Calcutta. It was founded in 1534 by the Portuguese, and was ceded to England in 1661 as part of Catherine of Braganza's dowry to Charles II. After 1941, a population boom occurred due to immigration and an increasing birth-rate. The city was enlarged through re-zoning in 1951. It is a cultural, educational, trade and financial centre, the site of the University of Bombay (1857) and the Indian Institute of Technology (1958). Industries: chemicals, textiles. Exports: cotton, manganese. Pop. 5,970,575.

Bomber, aircraft designed to carry bombs and to drop them either on enemy troops or enemy-occupied territory during combat, or in large quantities from a relatively high altitude on the enemy's supply areas or strategically selected railways and roads. The first bombers, including the British de Havilland DH-4 and the German G-IV, appeared towards the end of WWI. In WWII several four-engined types were developed. They had a greater load-carrying capacity and range combined with higher speed. After WWII jet bombers were introduced; today these incorporate sophisticated electronic equipment. Modern defence techniques have, however, raised questions on the value of bombers in warfare. *See also* MM pp.176–179.

Bomberg, David (1890–1957), British painter of landscapes, figures and still-lifes, a leading member of the LONDON GROUP. His work was influenced both by CUBISM and EXPRESSIONISM. As a teacher at Borough Polytechnic, London (1946–53), he inspired the Borough Group of young painters.

Bombois, Camille (1883–1970), French primitive painter. Largely self-taught, he is best known for his street scenes. One of his most famous works is *Before Entering the Ring* (1930–35), now in the Museum of Modern Art in New York.

Bona fide, legal term meaning "in good faith", "without intent to defraud or deceive". It can also be used to mean "genuine", "not assumed".

Bonaparte (Buonaparte), family of Italian origin that lived in Corsica. Carlo (1746–85), a lawyer, and Maria Letizia Ramolino (1750–1836), known as Madame Mère, were parents of a large family whose members were raised to distinction by their second and famous son, NAPOLEON I. Joseph (1768–1844), the eldest son, became King of Spain (1808–13). Lucien (1775–1840), the third son (known as Prince Canino) opposed Napoleon's despotic rule and lived in exile in Italy. Maria Anna Elisa (Elisa) (1777–1820) became Duchess of Tuscany. Louis (1778–1846) was created King of Holland in 1806. He married Hortense de Beauharnais and their son became NAPOLEON III. Maria Paulina (originally Carlotta, 1780–1825) was first married to General LeClerc and later to Prince Camillo Borghese. Carolina (1782–1839) married Marshal Joachim Murat, who became King of Naples. Jerome Bonaparte (1784–1844), youngest brother of NAPOLEON, was king of Westphalia from 1807 to 1813. He fought in the campaign against Russia and at WATERLOO.

Bonar, Horatius (1808–89), Scottish clergyman and writer of hymns. In 1843 his congregation at Kelso seceded from the established Church and founded the Free Church. His three series of *Hymns of Faith and Hope* (1857–66) include the hymn *I Heard the Voice of Jesus Say.*

Bonar Law, Andrew (1858–1923), British politician, born in Canada. He entered Parliament in 1900 and in 1911 became the first leader of the CONSERVATIVE PARTY to come from a manufacturing background. He was chancellor of the exchequer from 1916 to 1919 and prime minister from 1922 to 1923.

Bonaventure, Saint (*c.* 1217–74), Italian theologian, *b.* Giovanni di Fidanza. He studied at the University of Paris and was a contemporary of St. Thomas Aquinas. He was elected minister-general of the Franciscan Order in 1257 and became Cardinal Bishop of Albano in 1273. He played a prominent part in the Council of Lyons of 1274. His essentially mystical theory of knowledge is set forth in his *Journey of the Soul to God. See also* HC1 p.*188*.

Bond, Edward (1935–), British playwright. His first successful play *Saved* (1965) was considered controversial for its scenes of violence. His other plays include *Early Morning* (1968), which was heavily censored, *The Pope's Wedding* (1962), *Passion* (1971), *Black Mass* (1971), *Lear* (1972), *The Sea* (1973) and *A-A-merica* (1976).

Bond, James, character created by novelist Ian FLEMING. A British Secret Service agent, code-named 007, he appeared in 12 best-selling novels from 1953 and later in highly successful films. He was suave and enterprising with a refined taste in food, wine and women.

Bond, William Cranch (1789–1859), American astronomer who discovered Hyperion, Saturn's eighth satellite, and the Crêpe Ring, the faint innermost ring around the planet. Both discoveries were made with the assistance of his son George. He produced a recognizable daguerreotype of the Moon in 1850. *See also* SU p.*210*.

Bondfield, Margaret Grace (1873–1953), English political figure and trade unionist. She was a Labour MP (1923–24; 1926–31). In 1923 she became chairman of the Trades Union Congress (TUC). She was Minister of Labour (1923–31), the first British woman to hold cabinet office.

Bonding, in chemistry, the forces that hold atoms together in molecules. It is electrostatic in nature but takes various forms. Atoms in strong acids, alkalis and their salts are bonded weakly by the donation of electrons by some atoms and their reception by other atoms. This is called ionic bonding, the individual charged atoms being known as IONS. Many less reactive compounds are bonded by the sharing of electron pairs, one from each atom; this is called covalent bonding. In a somewhat intermediate form, co-ordinate bonding, both bonding electrons are donated by one of the combining atoms. *See* SU pp.138–139.

Bone, Sir Muirhead (1876–1953), Scottish draughtsman and etcher. His *Portfolio*, a series of etchings (1899), was an immediate success, as were *Glasgow, Fifty Drawings* (1911) and *Old Spain* (1936).

Bône. *See* ANNABA.

Bone, type of connective tissue that forms the skeleton of the body, protects its internal organs, serves as a lever for muscles and stores calcium and phosphorus. Bone is composed of a strong, compact layer of collagen and calcium phosphate and a lighter, porous inner spongy layer containing marrow, in which red and some white blood cells are produced. Most bones are sheathed by the periosteum, a tough protective membrane. *See also* MS pp.56–57, 94–95.

Bone china, hard-paste porcelain with a body of kaolin, china stone and bone ash, the standard English porcelain paste since the early 19th century. Josiah SPODE is credited with the perfection of bone china, which is valued for its translucency, cheapness of manufacture and suitability for underglaze decoration.

Boneset, any of about 600 species of plants in the genus *Eupatorium*, found in the USA. It has wrinkled, lance-shaped leaves and small white flowers in flat clusters. Height: to 1.8m (6ft). Family Compositae.

Bongo, Omar (1935–), President of Gabon (1967–). He began government service in 1958 and came to hold several cabinet ministries in addition to the presidency.

Bongo, large African antelope of humid forests; both sexes are red-brown with white vertical stripes and carry horns. Height: up to 1.3m (4.2ft) Family Bovidae; species *Taurotragus* eurycerus. *See also* NW p.*212*.

Bongos. *See* DRUM.

Bonham-Carter, Lady Violet (1887–1969), daughter of Herbert ASQUITH and Liberal spokesman. President of the LIBERAL PARTY in 1944–45, she twice failed to enter Parliament, at Wells (1945) and at Colne Valley (1951). In 1963 she was the first woman to deliver the Romanes lecture at Oxford.

Bonheur, Rosa (1822–99), French painter and sculptor, acclaimed in her lifetime for her sympathetic and accurate depiction of animals. She exhibited regularly at the Paris Salon from 1841 with animal paintings and later with sculpture. Her best-known works include *The Horse Fair* (1853–55).

Bonhoeffer, Dietrich (1906–45), German theologian. He was a Lutheran pastor and opposed the rise of National Socialism in Germany. Arrested in 1943, he was executed for treason. Among his works, most published posthumously, are *Letters from Prison* (1951) and *Christology* (1966). Bonhoeffer's theology is Christocentric and opposed to reparation of Church and the world. *See also* HC2 pp.304–305.

Boniface, Saint (*c.* 675–754), English missionary. He left England in 716 to convert the pagan Germans. For his success he was rewarded with the Archbishopric of Mainz in 751. In 754, however, he was martyred by pagans in Friesland. He is buried in Fulda and venerated as the Apostle of Germany. See also HC1 pp.134–135.

Boniface, name of nine POPES, of whom the most notable included Boniface VIII (*r.* 1294–1303), *b.* Benedetto Caetani *c.* 1235. He faced considerable factional dispute in Rome on his accession, and asserted throughout his reign that the clergy could not be taxed by a secular prince without the consent of the Pope. Boniface IX (*r.* 1389–1404) *b.* Pietro Tomacelli in *c.* 1355. He was elected Pope in Rome during the GREAT SCHISM, and tried to restore the prestige and fortunes of the papacy, but met considerable opposition.

Bonin Islands (Ogasaware-Guntō), group of approximately 30 islands in the W central Pacific Ocean, 966km (600 miles) SSW of Japan and part of the Tokyo prefecture. They were discovered by the Japanese in the 16th century and claimed by Britain in the early 19th century. Area: approx. 104sq km (40sq miles). Pop. 205.

Bonington, Richard Parkes (1802–28), English painter who lived and worked mainly in Calais. One of the first artists to break with the Classical tradition of Jacques-Louis DAVID, Bonington was influential with his landscape scenes – views of harbours, beaches and seas, often painted in watercolours – in developing a new French school of ROMANTIC painting. His works include *Normandy Coast* (1824). *See also* HC2 p.119.
Bonito, speedy streamlined tuna-like fish found in all warm and temperate waters, usually in schools. Bonitos are blue, black and silver and highly valued as food and game fish. The ocean bonito (*Katsuwonus pelamis*) is also called skipjack tuna or bluefin. Family Scombridae. *See also* NW pp.*240*, 241.
Bonjour Tristesse (1954), novel by Françoise SAGAN. Cécile's over-possessiveness towards her father leads her into scheming to prevent his remarriage. She involves her lover and her father's mistress, with tragic consequences.
Bonn, city and capital of West Germany, on the River Rhine, 26km (16 miles) SSE of Cologne. Founded in the 1st century AD as a Roman camp, it was awarded to Prussia by the Congress of Vienna (1815). There is some fine architecture including a Romanesque cathedral and Poppelsdorf Palace; BEETHOVEN was born there. It was chosen as the capital in 1949. Industries: engineering, laboratory equipment. Pop. (1976) 283,900.
Bonnard, Pierre (1867–1947), French painter. His early work, mainly of domestic scenes, was in the style of Paul GAUGUIN and Paul SERUSIER. In the 1890s he was a member of the NABIS. He received favourable reviews for his entries in the Salon des Indépendants, Paris, in 1891, and about a year later for *The Terrasse Family*. Other notable works include *Luncheon* (1922) and *Martha in a Red Blouse* (1928).
Bonneville Salt Flats, flat barren saltland in NW Utah, once part of the Pleistocene Lake Bonneville. It is now used for motor-racing and speed trials. Area: approx. 259sq km (100sq miles).
Bonnie and Clyde, American couple, Bonnie Parker and Clyde Barrow, who robbed banks and shops during the Depression era. The story was filmed in 1967 by Arthur Penn. Although his depiction of their violent life and death was considered extreme, the film developed a cult following.
Bonny Prince Charlie. *See* STUART, CHARLES EDWARD.
Bonsai, Japanese art of dwarfing woody plants and shrubs by pruning and restraining root growth; they are primarily outdoor plants and occur naturally in cliff areas. This art, which has been practised for centuries in the Orient, is most successful with plants that have a substantial tapering trunk, naturally twisted branches and small leaves. Bonsais can be 5–60cm (2–24in) tall, depending on the plant used. *See also* NW p.*63*.
Bontemps, Arna Wendell (1902–73), US writer. He was identified with the Harlem Renaissance of the 1920s, and wrote extensively on the black experience. He wrote poetry, novels including *God Sends Sunday* (1931) and *Black Thunder* (1935), children's books, biographies and anthologies of black poetry, music, folklore, and slave narratives.
Booby. *See* GANNET.
Boogie-woogie, type of JAZZ popular in the 1930s. It has a rapid, driving beat, uses BLUES themes and is generally played on the piano. The melody is played over a consistently repeated bass motif.
Book, nowadays primarily a bound volume of printed pages, but may also be a division within a book (as in the Bible) and a statement of accounts. It must be long enough to be distinguished from a pamphlet and single-minded enough to be distinguished from a journal. The first books, properly called, were the Egyptian writings on papyrus, of which the BOOK OF THE DEAD is usually considered the first. Roman books were mostly in the form of rolls. In the Middle Ages vellum, a fine parchment from the Middle East, became the standard material for writing. Modern printed books date from GUTENBERG's invention of movable metal type in 1454. The first printed book was a German Latin Bible of 1455. *See also* MM pp.204–215.
Bookbinding, assembling and covering a number of sheets of paper, parchment or vellum to form a BOOK. The craft began when rolls and scrolls were replaced by the CODEX; the earliest elaborate examples were for use in churches. Modern books are often assembled from folded sections (signatures) generally of 16, 32 or 48 pages, which are then sewn together, trimmed and covered. Commercial binding methods include side-sewing, where a machine drills and sews through the edge of the assembled sections; and perfect binding, where the individual sheets are clamped, glued along the spine, covered and trimmed. *See also* MM p.*213*.
Book-keeping, regular and systematic recording in ledgers of the amounts of money involved in business transactions. These records provide the basis for accountancy, which is the practice of classifying and summarizing transactions and interpreting the results. *See also* AUDIT.
Booklouse, transparent to white, usually wingless insect found throughout the world. It feeds on moulds in hot, humid, dusty places such as shelves, books and behind loose wallpaper. Length: to 5mm (0.2in). Order Psocoptera; genus *Liposcelis*.
Book of Changes, ancient Chinese book of wisdom, also known as the *I Ching*. Although the oldest parts of the text are thought to pre-date CONFUCIUS, he is credited with the commentaries which form a part of the collection. *See also* HC1 pp.124–125.
Book of Common Prayer. *See* COMMON PRAYER, BOOK OF.
Book of Healing, The. massive encyclopaedia by AVICENNA (980–1037). It dealt with philosophical and medical matters, including logic, the natural sciences and mathematics.
Book of Hours, book containing the prescribed order of prayers, rites for the canonical hours and readings from the Bible. Such books, developed in the 1300s, were often lavishly decorated by miniaturists and served as status symbols. The most celebrated of these to survive is the *Très riches heures du duc de Berry*, illustrated in part by the LIMBOURG BROTHERS. *See also* HC1 pp.218, *219*.
Book of Kells, illuminated manuscript of the four GOSPELS in Latin. Probably begun in the late 8th century at the Irish monastery of Iona, it was taken to the monastery of Kells, County Meath, Ireland. Its intricate illumination and superb penmanship have earned it the title of "the most beautiful book in the world". It is now in Trinity College, Dublin. *See also* HC1 pp.*140*, *164*.
Book of Martyrs, written in 1563 by John FOXE whilst exiled in Strasburg and Basel. It is an account of the English Protestant movement since the fourteenth century and its persecution by the Catholics. *See also* HC1 p.*271*.
Book of Nonsense (1846), children's book by Edward Lear. It includes jingles, rhymed alphabets, ballads and limericks, accompanied by entertaining drawings.
Book of Taliesin, one of the great Welsh poetic works, named after a little-known character who may have been a bard or, according to another theory, a Celtic mythical figure. Although tradition places him in the 6th century, the collection exists only in a 13th-century form.
Book of the Dead, collection of Old Egyptian texts dating from the 16th century BC. The papyrus texts, which have many different versions, were placed in the tombs of the dead in order to help them combat the dangers of the underworld. *See also* MS pp.*212*, *214*, *222*.
Book of the Dun Cow, Irish manuscript of uncertain age but dating from before 1106. Said to have been first recorded on cow hide, it contains several myths, including the *Cattle Raid of Cooley*.
Boole, George (1815–64), English mathematician. Largely self-taught, he was appointed professor of mathematics of Cork University in 1849. He is remembered for his invention of a set of symbols to represent logical operations. Using symbols he developed a form of algebra (Boolean algebra) in which the symbols can be manipulated with logical consistency. *See also* SU p.40.
Boom, floating, breakwater that stills or absorbs the force of waves on the surface of water. A boom may be used across a harbour mouth, to contain oil slicks, or even to harness waves as a source of power for man. *See also* MM pp.*70*, 71.
Boomerang, sharp-edged throwing stick used for hunting, warfare and sport. It is a flat, angled or curved piece of wood, shaped aerodynamically so that it flies in an arc or in a circle. These and non-returning boomerangs are used mainly by the ABORIGINES of Australia.
Boomslang, venomous snake of the savannas of Africa. It is green or brown with a slender body and a small head. Commonly found in a tree or bush, it lies in wait for lizards and small birds, often with the front portion of its body extended motionless in mid-air. Length: to 1.5m (4.9ft). Species *Dispholidus typus*. *See also* NW p.*137*.
Boone, Daniel (1734–1820), US pioneer. In 1775 he blazed the famous Wilderness Road from Virginia to Kentucky and founded the settlement of Boonsborough. During the American War of Independence he was captured by Shawnee Indians but escaped and reached Boonsborough in time to prevent its capture.
Booster engine, rocket engine which powers a missile or space vehicle in the early stages of its flight and then drops off, reducing deadweight. Several booster engines may be attached to the first stage of a launch vehicle for extra power. *See also* CLUSTER, ROCKET; ROCKET ENGINE.
Boot, Sir Jesse, 1st Baron Trent (1850–1931), British pharmacist, founder of one of the largest retail pharmacists in the world. In 1877 he opened his first chemist shop in Nottingham. By 1883 he had ten shops. In 1892 he began to manufacture drugs on a large scale and by 1931 had more than 1,000 retail outlets.
Boötes, in astronomy, a constellation beside the Great Bear in the northern sky; it contains the bright orange star Arcturus. The name, derived from the Greek, means ox-driver, or herdsman. *See also* SU pp.*256*, 256.
Booth, Charles (1840–1916), English social reformer who pioneered the method of social survey in his *Life and Labour of the People in London* (1891–1903). He was helped in this work by the English Fabian, Beatrice WEBB. He was instrumental in gaining the passage of the Old Age Pensions Act in 1908.
Booth, John Wilkes (1838–65), US actor and assassin of Abraham LINCOLN. He was a Confederate sympathizer. On 14 April 1865 at Ford's Theater in Washington DC he shot Lincoln, who died the next day. Booth escaped but was either shot, or killed himself, two weeks later.
Booth, William (1829–1912), English religious leader, founder and first General (leader) of the SALVATION ARMY. He was a Methodist revivalist preacher from 1852 to 1861. He then started his own revivalist movement, which undertook evangelistic and social work among the poor. It became known as the Salvation Army in 1878 and gradually spread to many countries. In 1912 Booth was succeeded as General by his son William Bramwell Booth.
Boothe, Clare (1903–), US author. She worked as an editor on the magazine *Vogue* and wrote various plays including *The Women* (1936) and *Kiss the Boys Goodbye* (1938). Her novels include *European Spring* (1940).
Boothia Peninsula, virtually uninhabited peninsula in Northwest Territory, Canada. The area was first explored by John Ross, a British explorer, in 1829–33. He also established the original position of the North Magnetic Pole. Area: 32,331sq km (12,483sq miles).
Bootlegging, sale of alcoholic drinks in countries or areas where it is prohibited by

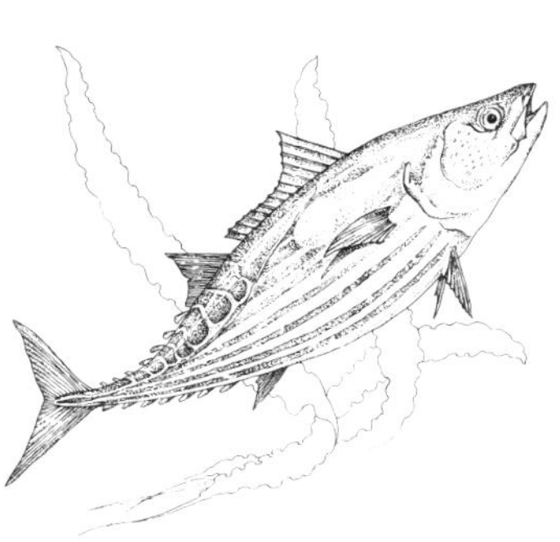

Bonitos live in both the Atlantic and Pacific oceans; they feed on squid and small fish.

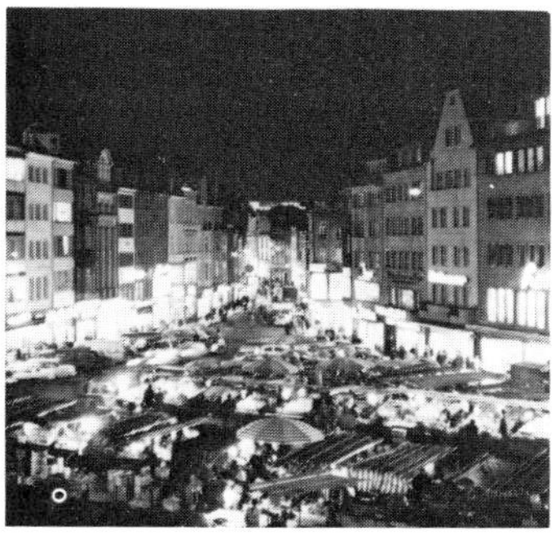

Bonn, the quiet university town that became the capital of the German Federal Republic.

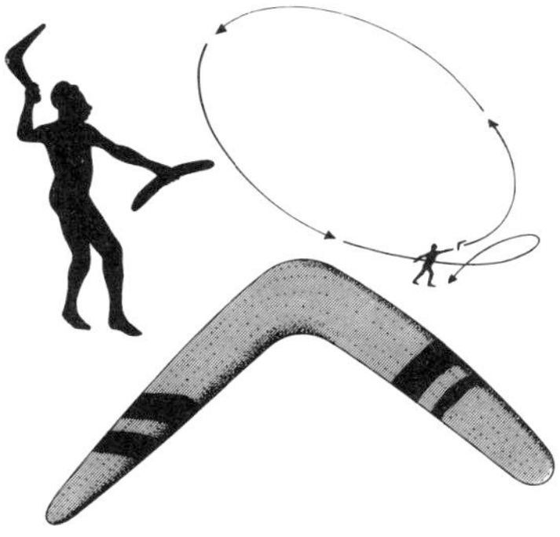

Boomerangs spin in flight and return because their ends are skewed in opposite directions.

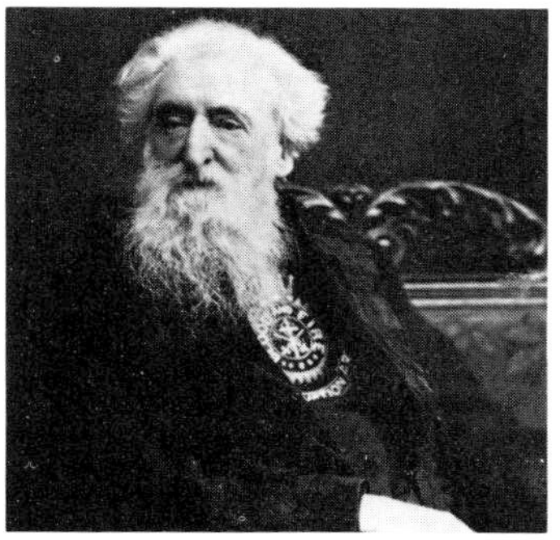

William Booth had experience of human misery when apprenticed to a pawnbroker.

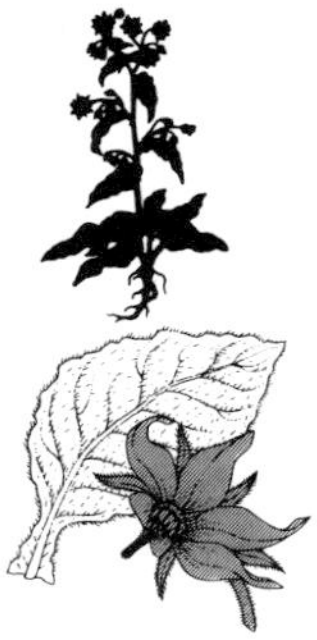

Borage; a medicinal and honey plant which is also used in salads and for flavouring drinks.

law, or the sale of alcohol in a way that evades tax. The name is said to derive from the practice of American frontier traders carrying bottles of illicit liquor in the tops of their boots. During PROHIBITION in the USA, many gangster fortunes were made by bootlegging.

Bop. *See* BEBOP.

Borage, hairy annual plant native to S Europe. It has rough oblong leaves and drooping clusters of pale blue flowers and is cultivated as a food and flavouring. Height: up to 60cm (2ft). Family Boraginaceae, species *Borago officinalis. See also* PE p.*213.*

Borås, city on the River Viskan, SW Sweden; in Älvsborg county. It was founded in 1632 by Gustavus II and is today a centre for cotton and woollen textiles. Pop. (1970) 73,475.

Borate, any salt of boric acid (H_3BO_3) or of more complex oxyacids of boron. Borates are inorganic compounds; many exist as minerals, the most important of which are BORAX, colemanite and kernite – all used as sources of boron compounds.

Borax, the most common BORATE mineral (hydrated sodium borate), used in making glass and as a mild alkali. It is found in large deposits in dried-up alkaline lakes in arid regions as crusts or masses of prismatic crystals (monoclinic system). It may be colourless or white, transparent or opaque.

Bordeaux, port and capital of the Gironde département in SW France, on the River Garonne and serving an area famous for its fine wines and brandies. Once a thriving Roman settlement, it is a good deep-water inland port and has many 18th-century buildings. Industries: shipbuilding, oil refining, flour, textiles, glass. Pop. (1968) 266,700.

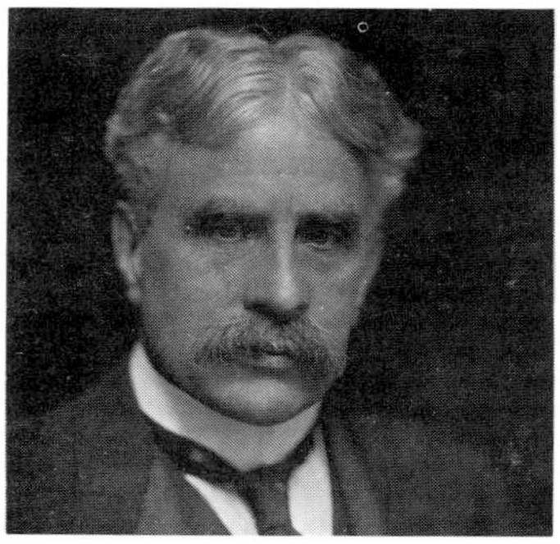

Sir Robert Laird Borden helped Canada win a more independent role in world affairs.

Borden, Lizzie (1860–1927), American who in 1892 was accused of murdering her father and stepmother, but was acquitted in a sensational trial. Many books were written about the case, and she and her trial have become part of legend.

Borden, Sir Robert Laird (1854–1937), Canadian politician. A successful lawyer, he led the Conservative Party from 1901 and was Prime Minister from 1911 to 1920. Borden worked for civil service reform, public ownership of telephone and telegraph services, and a say in imperial policy-making. He also sought to keep Canada economically independent of the USA.

Border collie, breed of COLLIE, a popular sheepdog that has been used in Britain for about 300 years. It has a narrow tapering head and erect ears that droop forwards at the tips. Its long coat is generally black and white. Height: to 51cm (20in) at the shoulder.

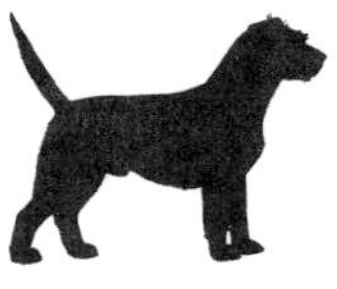

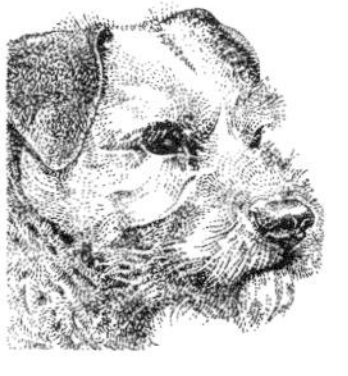

Border terriers are hunting dogs from the border country of northern England.

Borders, region in SE Scotland, formed in 1974 from the former counties of BERWICKSHIRE, PEEBLES, ROXBURGH and SELKIRK, and a small part of MIDLOTHIAN; bounded by England (S), the North Sea (NE), Lothian (N), Strathclyde (NW) and Dumfries and Galloway (W). The main towns are Hawick and Berwick-on-Tweed. The area was the scene of many battles between the English and the Scots. Area: about 4,671sq km (1,803sq miles). Pop. (1975 est.) 99,400.

Border terrier, breed of short-haired terrier used in Scotland and northern England to hunt foxes. It has a grey or reddish coat, floppy ears and stands about 30cm (12in) high at the shoulder.

Bordet, Jules Jean Baptiste Vincent (1870–1961), Belgian bacteriologist and immunologist. He was awarded the 1919 Nobel Prize for physiology and medicine for his development of the complement-fixation test, an important method of diagnosis for immunology. He identified the whooping cough bacillus in 1906.

Bordone, Paris (1500–71), Venetian artist who was influenced by TITIAN and GIORGIONE. His most famous work is *A Fishman Consigning a Ring to the Doge* (1540).

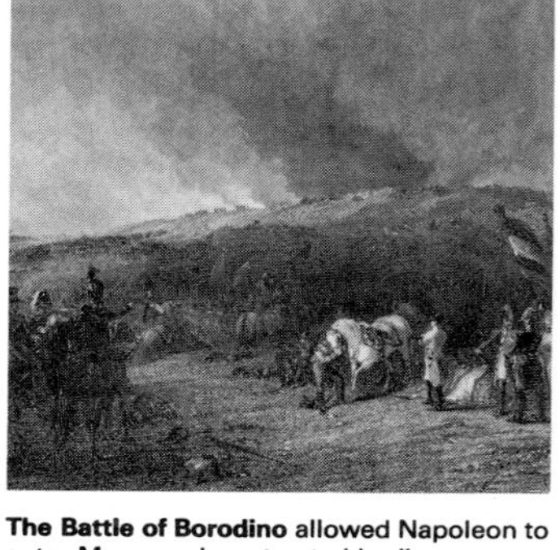

The Battle of Borodino allowed Napoleon to enter Moscow; he retreated in disaster.

Bore, tidal, turbulent, wall-like wave of water that rushes up a narrowing estuary, bay or tidal river. It is thought to be caused by a combination of the incoming tidal wave, the slope and shape of the channel, and by the river flow. *See also* PE p.81.

Boreal forest, wooded zone with a cold dry climate and a poor sandy soil; it consists primarily of conifers and stretches like a broad ribbon across the Northern Hemisphere. Its northern edge is bordered by frozen tundra. *See also* NW pp.206, *207.*

Borges, Jorge Luis (1899–), Argentinian writer, poet and critic educated in Europe until 1921. He is best known for his short stories, which include the collections *El hacedor* (1960) and *Informe sobre Brodie* (1970). They often use intellectual puzzles to dramatize what Borges believes is the extreme difficulty of achieving knowledge. *See also* HC2 p.*290.*

Borghese, Italian princely family, originally of Siena but later of Rome. Camillo Borghese (1552–1621) became pope as Paul V in 1605. Another Camillo (1775–1832) married Marie Pauline Bonaparte, the sister of NAPOLEON I, and was made governor of Piedmont. The Borghese Palace (1590) is one of Rome's most splendid buildings. The former summer residence, the Villa Borghese, Rome, has a magnificent art collection.

Borgia, family notorious in 15th- and 16th-century Italian politics. The family originated in Spain and went to Rome with the first Borgia pope, Calixtus III (1455–58). His nephew Rodrigo became Pope ALEXANDER VI in 1492 and was the father of Cesare (*c.*1476–1507) and Lucrezia (1480–1519), both notorious for their ruthless attitude to politics. Cesare was probably the model for MACHIAVELLI's *The Prince.* By alliances with the French, use of papal patronage, strategic marriages and treachery, the family sought to acquire political control over the PAPAL STATES and throughout central Italy. Alexander's death in 1503, Cesare's illness at the same time, and the election of the Borgias' enemy Giuliano della Rovere as Pope JULIUS II conspired to defeat these aspirations.

Borglum, John Gutzon (1867–1941), US sculptor. From a six-ton marble block he fashioned a head of Abraham LINCOLN, which now stands in the Capitol rotunda in Washington, DC. His last project was the carving of the heads of WASHINGTON, JEFFERSON, Lincoln and ROOSEVELT in a rock-face at Mt Rushmore, South Dakota; the final details were completed by his son.

Boric acid, soft white crystalline solid (H_3BO_3) which occurs naturally in certain volcanic hot springs. It is used as a metallurgical flux, preservative and antiseptic.

Boris, name of three Bulgarian rulers. Boris I (*d.*907) ruled from 852 to 889, when he abdicated and retired to a monastery. He introduced the Eastern form of Christianity to Bulgaria. Boris II (*r.*969–72) also abdicated. Boris III (1894–1943) was the Tsar of Bulgaria from 1918 to 1943; after 1938 he established a dictatorship. He sided with the AXIS powers in 1941 and died in unknown circumstances.

Boris Godunov (*c.*1551–1605), Tsar of Russia. The chief minister of IVAN the Terrible, he became regent to Ivan's son FEODOR after Ivan's death and was popularly supposed to have murdered Feodor's brother and heir, Dmitri, in 1591. On Feodor's death in 1598 Boris was elected Tsar and gained recognition of the Russian Orthodox Church as an independent patriarchate. A pretender, the false DMITRI, invaded in 1604 and became Tsar after Boris's death. *See also* HC1 p.321.

Boris Godunov (1874), four-act opera by Modest MUSSORGSKY based on a play by PUSHKIN and the histories of Nikolai KARAMZIN about BORIS GODUNOV and the false DMITRI. It was heavily reworked by Nikolai RIMSKY-KORSAKOV in 1896. *See also* HC2 p.*120.*

Borlaug, Norman Ernest (1914–), US agronomist. As a director of the Rockefeller Foundation in Mexico, he led a team of scientists experimenting with the improvement of cereal crops. He was awarded the Nobel Peace Prize in 1970 for his accomplishments in the "GREEN REVOLUTION", developing improved wheat seed, a higher-yielding rice and better ways of using fertilizer and water.

Bormann, Martin Ludwig (1900–45), German National Socialist Party leader. He joined the Nazis in 1925 and was important in the Party hierarchy. In 1941 he succeeded Rudolf HESS as deputy leader. He disappeared in 1945 and was sentenced to death *in absentia* during the NUREMBERG TRIALS. In 1973, after identification of his skeleton, he was formally pronounced dead as a result of suicide in 1945.

Born, Bertrand de. *See* BERTRAND DE BORN.

Born, Max (1882–1970), German-born British physicist. He was professor of physics at Göttingen University from 1921 but left Germany in 1933 and went to Britain. He taught natural philosophy at the University of Edinburgh. For his work in QUANTUM MECHANICS, the basis of atomic and nuclear physics, he was awarded the 1954 Nobel Prize in physics, which he shared with Walter BOTHE.

Borneo, island in the Malay Archipelago, South-East Asia, 640km (400 miles) E of Singapore, Mostly undeveloped, Borneo is the world's third-largest island, and is divided into four political regions: Sarawak state (W) and Sabah state (N) are Malaysian; Brunei state (NW) is a British protectorate; Kalimantan state (E, central and S) covers 70% of the island and is part of Indonesia. Industries: timber, fishing, oil and coal extraction. Area: 743,330sq km (287,000sq miles). Pop. (1971 est.) 6,968,000. *See also* MW p.39.

Bornholm, Danish island group in the Baltic Sea, near Sweden; Bornholm is the largest island. After Germany's surrender in May 1945, some German forces made a desperate stand there, but Soviet troops forced them to surrender. Industries: farming, fishing, tourism. Exports: granite, kaolin. Pop. (1971) 47,241.

Bornite, also called peacock ore, a common copper mineral, copper iron sulphide (Cu_5FeS_4). It generally occurs in masses, sometimes as crystals (cubic system) in intrusive igneous rocks and metamorphic rocks. It is opaque and bronze with an irridescent purple tarnish. Hardness 3; s.g. 5.0.

Bornu, province in NE Nigeria, SW of Lake Chad; the capital is Maiduguri. From the 14th to the 19th centuries it was the centre of a powerful Muslim empire, which exported slaves and fabrics to N Africa. Industries: agricultural products, mining. Area: 105,000sq km (40,500sq miles). Pop. 2,850,000.

Borobudur, ruins of a Buddhist monument in Central Java, built under the SAILENDRA dynasty *c.*AD 800. It comprises the stupa (a relic mound), the mandala (ritual diagrams) and the temple mountain, all forms in Indian GUPTA religious art. *See also* HC1 pp.*65,* 226.

Borodin, Alexander Porfirevich (1833–87), Russian composer and chemist, one of "The Five" group of composers. His most popular works include the tone poem *In the Steppes of Central Asia* (1880) and the *Polovtsian Dances* from his opera *Prince Igor* (completed after his death by GLAZUNOV and RIMSKY-KORSAKOV). *See also* HC2 pp.107, 121.

Borodino, Battle of (1812), French victory over the Russians under KUTUZOV about 70 miles W of Moscow. It allowed Napoleon to take the city with ease but heavy casualties on both sides totalled over 75,000. The battle is vividly described in Leo TOLSTOY's WAR AND PEACE. *See also* HC2 pp.76–77, *76–77.*

Boron, non-metallic element (symbol B) of group III of the PERIODIC TABLE, first isolated in 1808 by Sir Humphry DAVY. It occurs in several minerals, notably borax and kernite (its chief ore). Amorphous boron, an impure powder, is made by reducing the oxide with magnesium. Pure boron is obtained as a hard crystalline material by decomposing boron tribromide vapour on a hot metal filament. The element is used in semiconductor devices and the stable isotope B^{10} is a good neutron absorber, used in nuclear reactors and particle counters. Properties: at. no. 5; at. wt. 10.81; s.g. 2.34 (cryst.), 2.37 (amorph.); m.p. 2,300°C (4,172°F); b.p. 2,550°C, (4,622°F); most common isotope B^{11} (80.22%). *See also* SU p.136.

Borotra, Jean (1898–), French tennis player. Known as the "Bounding Basque", he was immediately recognizable on court by his blue beret. He reached the Wimbledon singles final five times in the 1920s, winning twice (1924, 1926), and continued to play into his seventies.

Borough, originally, in medieval England, a town which had a charter granting privileges and autonomy; today an urban area granted a charter of incorporation and administered internally. Large metropolitan areas, such as London, may be divided into separate boroughs. *See also* LOCAL GOVERNMENT.

Borromeo, Charles, Saint (1538–84), Italian church reformer. He was created cardinal by his uncle Pope PIUS IV in 1560 and then appointed Archbishop of Milan. He was largely responsible for the reconvening of the Council of TRENT. During the plague of 1576–78 he heroically administered to the needs of the populace.

Borromini, Francesco (1599–1667), Italian architect and sculptor, with BERNINI and Pietro da CORTONA, one of the three giants of the BAROQUE style in Rome. His palace and church designs were based on geometric forms (especially ovals and triangles) hitherto not generally used in architecture. Borromini was a dominant influence in Italy and northern Europe; he named his own sources of inspiration as "Nature, Antiquity and Michelangelo". His masterpieces are *S. Carlo alle Quattro Fontane* (1638–41) and *S. Ivo della Sapienza* (1642), both in Rome. *See also* HC1 p.305.

Borrow, George Henry (1803–81), British author. He travelled widely in England, Europe and Russia. Much of his writing is based on his experiences and on his knowledge of gypsies whom he met on his travels. His best-known works include *The Zincali: or, An Account of the Gypsies of Spain* (1841), *The Bible in Spain* (1843) and *The* ROMANY RYE (1857).

Borrowdale, valley in the Lake District in Cumbria, NW England. It stretches S from Derwent Water and is drained by the River Derwent. The narrow pass at the S end is called the Jaws of Borrowdale.

Borstal, British system of rehabilitation for juvenile offenders between the ages of 16 and 21. The idea originated in 1895 with the Gladstone Committee, and the first institution was established at Borstal Prison, Kent, in 1902. Borstals are residential, providing education, vocational training, regular work and group counselling. *See also* MS pp.296–297.

Boru, Brian (*c*.940–1014), King of Munster and Ireland (*r*.1002–14). He died at the Battle of CLONTARF, in which his forces drove the Norse Vikings from Ireland. *See also* HC1 p.180, *180*.

Borzoi, keen-sighted speedy hunting DOG, also called Russian wolfhound; it has a long narrow head and powerful jaws. The body is deep and streamlined and the legs are long, as is the curved tail. The coat is long and silky and is usually white with darker markings. Height: (at shoulder) up to 79cm (31in). *See also* HOUND.

Borzov, Valeriy (1949–), Russian sprinter. The first European to win the Olympic men's sprint double (1972), he is said to have the ideal characteristics for starting as a sprinter.

Boscán, Juan (*c*.1495–1542), Catalan lyric poet. He helped to introduce Italian metre and verse forms into Spanish poetry. His poems were published, with those of Garcilaso de la Vega, in 1543. Boscan also translated works from Italian, eg Baldassare CASTIGLIONE's *The Courtier*.

Boscawen, Edward (1711–61), English admiral, sometimes known as "Old Dreadnought". He won renown for his victories against the French at Porto Bello in 1739, Cape Finisterre in 1747 and Lagos Bay in 1759.

Bosch, Hieronymus (*c*.1450–1516), Flemish painter of weird and fantastic visions with emphasis on the grotesque. His pictures contain many references to folk-legends of his time and frequently combine a number of unrelated incidents. His concern for the depraved state of man is seen in *The Garden of Earthly Delights*, and his anti-clericism in *Adoration of the Magi*. *See also* MS *p.217*.

Bosch, Karl (Carl) (1874–1940), German industrial chemist who adapted Fritz HABER's method of synthesizing ammonia to an industrial scale. His work involved finding metallic catalysts that could promote this high-pressure synthesis. His invention of the Bosch process (in which water gas and steam at high temperatures are passed over a catalyst) aided the large-scale preparation of hydrogen. Bosch was awarded the 1931 Nobel Prize in chemistry, with Friedrich BERGIUS, for his high-pressure techniques.

Bose, Sir Jagadis Chandra (1858–1937), Indian plant physiologist and physicist. He invented highly sensitive instruments capable of detecting tissue responses of plants to external stimuli. His automatic recorder, which regulated extremely slight movementss allowed him to demonstrate apparent feeling in plants and to anticipate parallelism between plant and animal tissue.

Bose, Satyendranath (1894–1974), Indian physicist and mathematician who significantly extended one of Albert EINSTEIN's theories of QUANTUM MECHANICS concerning the gas-like properties of ELECTROMAGNETIC RADIATION. He developed a statistical model for the behaviour of a collection of sub-atomic particles.

Boshier, Derek (1937–), British artist. Prominent in the emergence of POP ART, he became an avant-garde painter in the mid-1960s with his love of vivid optical effects.

Bosnia-Hercegovina, constituent republic of central Yugoslavia drained by the rivers Sava and Neretva, in the Dinaric Alps, comprising the regions of Bosnia in the N and Hercegovina in the S; the capital is Sarajevo. Originally settled by the Serbs, it came under Turkish rule in 1463 and was partly converted to Islam. It declined into a feudal backwater, but after the peasant nationalist revolt of 1875 it came under Hungarian control. It became part of Yugoslavia in 1918 and again in 1946, after a period of German occupation. Products: grain, potatoes, copper, iron, manganese, lignite. Area: 51,129sq km (19,741sq miles). Pop. (1971 prelim.) 3,743,000.

Bosporus (Karadeniz Bogazi), narrow strait joining the Sea of Marmara with the Black Sea, and separating European and Asiatic Turkey. It is an important strategic and commercial waterway, controlled by the Turks since 1452, and refortified by them after the Montreux Convention of 1936. Length: 30km (19 miles).

Bossuet, Jacques Bénigne (1627–1704), French theologian. He was the most respected preacher at the court of LOUIS XIV. His *Politics Drawn from Holy Scripture* was an apology for the DIVINE RIGHT OF KINGS. He vigorously opposed both JANSENISM and QUIETISM in favour of traditional Catholicism.

Boston, William John ("Billy"), (1935–), British rugby league player. A fast and powerful winger for Wigan and Great Britain (36 Tests, 78 tries), he scored 563 tries in his career, including seven in a match twice.

Boston, Ralph (1939–), American Negro long-jumper. He broke the 25-year-old world record in 1960, shortly before winning the Olympic title. His sixth and last world mark, set in 1965, was 8.35m (27ft 5in).

Boston, seaport city and capital of Massachusetts, USA, at the mouth of the Charles River on Massachusetts Bay. Founded in 1630, it became a Puritan stonghold and the scene of several events that led to the American Revolution. A noted religious and cultural centre, Boston is the home of important educational establishments, including Harvard University and the Massachusetts Institute of Technology. Industries: publishing, shipbuilding, electronics, fishing. Pop. (1970) 641,071.

Boston Tea Party (1773), protest by a group of American colonists, disguised as Indians and led by Sam ADAMS, against the British policy of taxing tea and, more generally, against "taxation without representation". Tea from ships was thrown into Boston harbour after Governor Thomas Hutchinson had refused to let the ships leave without paying tax. *See also* HC2 p.64, *64*.

Boston terrier, American DOG bred from the English bulldog and the white English TERRIER. It has a flat square head, a blunt wide muzzle and a short wide-chested body; the tail is short. The smooth coat is usually brindle with a specific pattern of white marks. Height: (at shoulder) up to 43 cm (17in).

Bo'sun, abbreviation of boatswain, a naval warrant officer who is in charge of anchors and anchor gear, rigging, boats and cargo-handling equipment. He also instructs the ship's crew in the practicalities of seamanship.

Boswell, James (1740–95), Scottish biographer and author. He travelled widely in Europe, meeting VOLTAIRE and Jean-Jacques ROUSSEAU. His works include *Account of Corsica* (1768) and *The Journal of a Tour to the Hebrides* (1785), an account of his travels with Samuel JOHNSON. He was a friend of Johnson and a fellow member of the Literary Club. His *Life of Samuel Johnson* (2 vols, 1791) is regarded as one of the best biographies in English.

Bosworth. *See* MARKET BOSWORTH.

Botany, the study of plants and plant life, including the classification, structure, physiology, reproduction and evolution of plants. By tradition, the plant kingdom has been studied in two halves: lower (non-flowering) plants, including ALGAE, MOSSES and FERNS, and higher (seed bearing) plants, including most flowers, trees and shrubs. Botany also studies the importance of plants to man. *See also* NW pp.38–70; PE pp.180–222.

Botany Bay, large, shallow inlet immediately S of Port Jackson, Sydney Harbour, New South Wales, Australia. It was visited in 1700 by Captain James COOK, who named it because of its flora. It is fed by the Georges and Woronora rivers and is about 1.6km (1 mile) wide at its mouth. A penal colony named Botany Bay was in fact sited at Port Jackson.

Botev, Khristo (1848–76), Bulgarian poet. He joined the Bulgarian revolutionary emigrés in Romania in 1867 and worked for Bulgarian independence through satirical journals, such as *Duma* (1871) and *Zname* (1874). His poems were collected in *Pesni u stihove* (1875). He was killed fighting against the Turks.

Botfly, any of several families of stout, hairy, black-and-white to grey fly. It is a parasite of livestock, small animals and even human beings. Usually eggs are laid on the host and the larvae cause damage to the host's skin or internal systems. The botfly that attacks deer is possibly the swiftest insect, flying at 80km/h (50mph). Order Diptera; family Oestridae.

Botha, Louis (1862–1919), South African political and military figure. During the SOUTH AFRICAN (Boer) WAR (1899–1902) he was one of the exceptional military commanders. He was Prime Minister of South Africa (1910–19). *See also* HC2 pp.129, 252.

Bothe, Walther Wilhelm Georg Franz (1891–1957), German physicist. From 1934 he was director of the Max Planck Institute, Heidelberg and in 1946 was professor of physics at the university there. During WWII he worked on Germany's nuclear energy project and built Germany's first cyclotron. He shared the 1954 Nobel Prize in physics with Max BORN for his development of the coincidence method, which can detect two particles emitted simultaneously from the same nucleus during radioactive decay.

Bothnia, Gulf of, main arm of the Baltic Sea, N of the Åland Islands, between Sweden (W) and Finland (E). It freezes over for part of the year and has timber-shipping ports. Length: approx. 644km (400 miles).

Bothwell, James Hepburn, 4th Earl of (*c*.1535–78), Scottish nobleman, third husband of MARY, QUEEN OF SCOTS. He made many enemies in Scotland's turbulent politics but supported the Queen, winning her affection. He was implicated in the murder of Lord DARNLEY

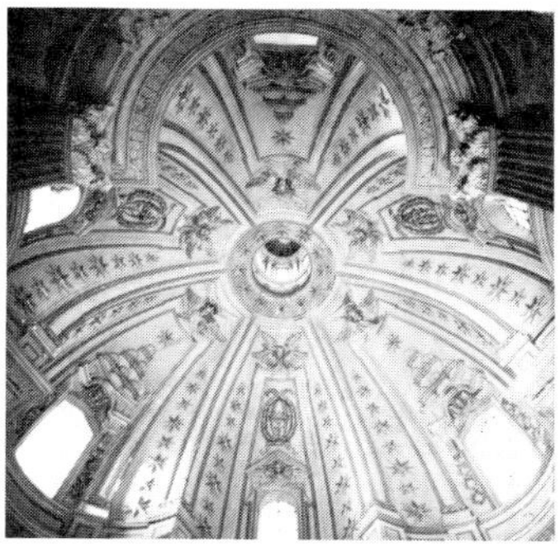

Francesco Borromini; this is the baroque ceiling at S Ivo della Sapienza, Rome.

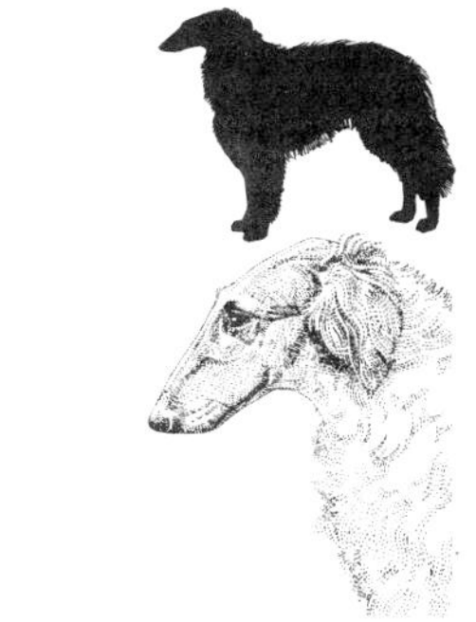

Borzoi or Russian wolfhound, the elegant hunting dog (Borzoi is Russian for *swift*).

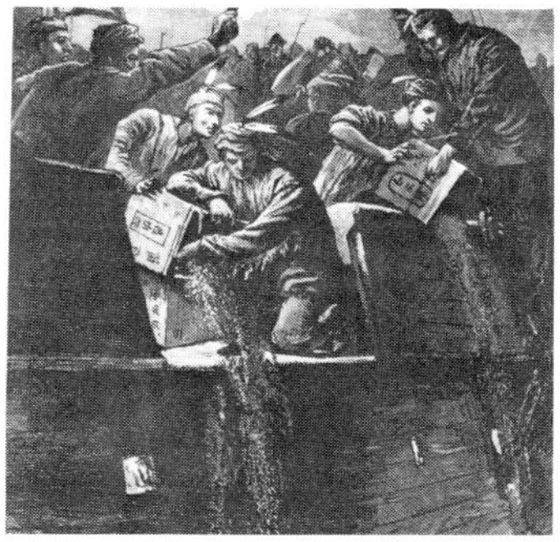

The Boston Tea Party, one incident that led to the American War of Independence.

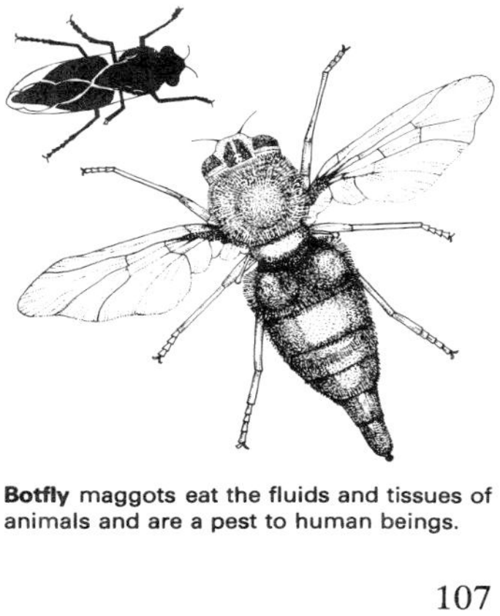

Botfly maggots eat the fluids and tissues of animals and are a pest to human beings.

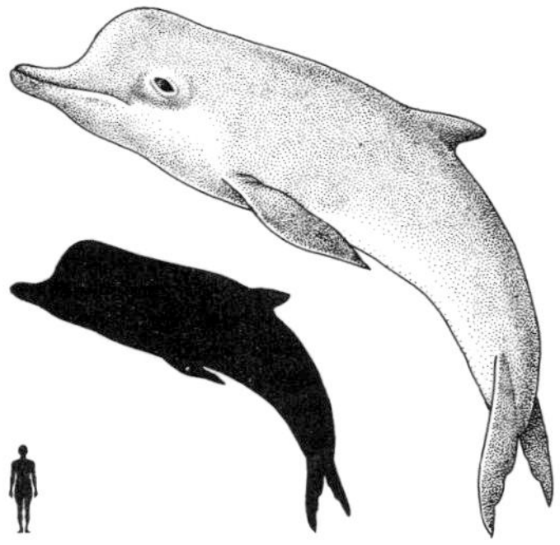

Bottle-nosed whales have only one or two pairs of teeth; they feed on fish and squid.

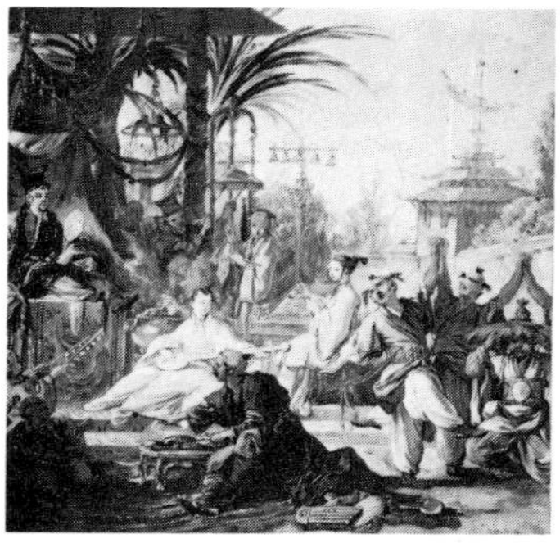

François Boucher, master of 18th-century French rococo, painted *Chinese Dance.*

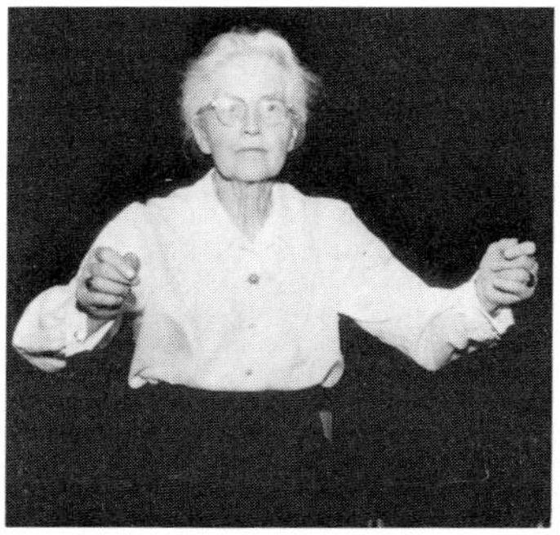

Nadia Boulanger, French concert organist, in rehearsal with the Boston Symphony.

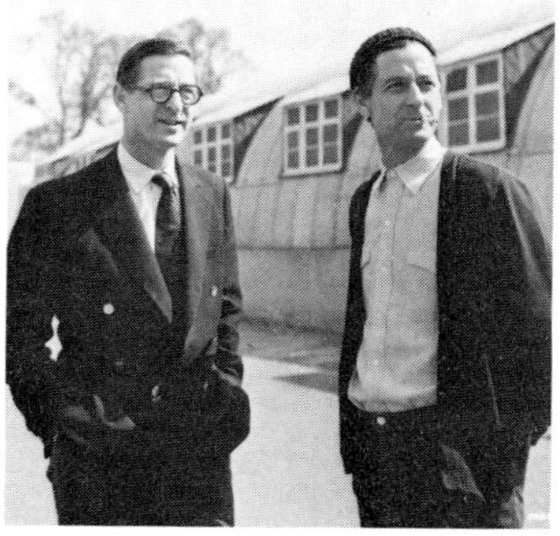

John and Roy Boulting, who produced and directed many successful British films.

(1567), and subsequently married Mary. Faced by a rebellion of Scottish nobles he fled abroad, and died insane in a Danish prison.

Botocudo, tribe of about 4,000 South American Indians occupying the Rio Pardo region of the Matto Grosso, Brazil. They have a custom of wearing large carved wooden plugs in their lips and ears.

Bo tree, Indian tree regarded as sacred by Buddhists. There is generally one near each temple to commemorate the fact that BUDDHA (Gautama) found enlightenment under a bo tree at Bodh Gaya. Its long-stalked leaves rustle in the slightest breeze. Also called pipal, it is a member of the family Moraceae; genus *Ficus.*

Botswana, republic of central S Africa, formerly known as Bechuanaland until it gained its independence from Britain in 1966, when it was one of the poorest nations in the world. In the late 1960s valuable mineral deposits were discovered and have contributed greatly to the growth rate of the traditionally agrarian economy. The capital is Gaborone. Area: 569,583sq km (219,916sq miles). Pop. (1975 est.) 691,000. *See* MW p.40.

Bottesini, Giovanni (1821–89), Italian composer, conductor and one of the greatest double bass players. He played and conducted in Paris and London, and from 1871 was director of the Parma Conservatory. His compositions include the opera *Cristoforo Colombo* (1847) and the oratorio *Garden of Olivet* (1887).

Botticelli, Sandro (*c.*1444–1510), Italian painter of the Florentine RENAISSANCE. He was influenced by Piero POLLAIUOLO with whom he worked on a series of *Seven Virtues* (1470) and by Filippo LIPPI and VERROCCHIO. In Florence he was patronized by the leading families, including the Medicis, whose portraits he included in *Adoration of the Magi.* In 1481 he assisted in the decoration of the Sistine Chapel, Rome. After his return to Florence, he painted a number of mythological pictures, including *Birth of Venus, Primavera* and *Pallas and the Centaur* (all now in the Uffizi, Florence). He is renowned for his masterful use of colour, and graceful lines. His themes are considered important in the transition from religious to non-religious subjects. *See also* HC1 pp.255–256; MS p.*219.*

Bottle-nosed whale, beaked WHALE found in Atlantic waters. Length: to 13m (40ft); species: N Atlantic *Hyperoodon ampullatus;* S Atlantic *Hyperoodon planifrons. See also* BEAKED WHALE; NW p.*166.*

Bottle, or barrel, tree, tropical and subtropical semi-deciduous tree found in drier parts of Australia. It has a dense crown and a bottle-shaped trunk. Height: to 18m (59ft); lower trunk diameter: to 1.8m (6ft). Family Sterculiaceae; species *Brachychiton rupestris.*

Bottling, domestic method of preserving foods such as fruits, jams, pickles and purées by airless sealing in bottles while hot. The term is also used to describe the mechanized or automated bottling of liquid and solid foods on a factory line. *See also* PE pp.250–251.

Botulism, form of food-poisoning caused by a bacterial toxin that interferes with the transmission of nerve impulses, leading to respiratory paralysis and, ultimately, suffocation. Early symptoms include lassitude, vision and speech impairments, difficulty in swallowing, and sometimes nausea and vomiting. Hospitalization is necessary – death can occur within hours. The bacteria can grow only in an oxygen-free atmosphere, such as canned food, and the most frequent source of botulism is imperfectly prepared home-preserved food.

Botvinnik, Mikhail Moiseievich (1911–), Russian chess master. World champion 1948–57, 1958–60 and 1961–63, he retired from world competition in 1963. His game was marked by great depth of strategy, and he would often accept positional inferiority for tactical initiative.

Bouake (Bwake), city in the central Ivory Coast, W Africa. Now a commercial and communications centre, it was once a meeting point of caravan routes. Gold and manganese deposits are mined nearby. Products: tobacco, cotton. Pop. 53,000.

Boucher, François (1703–70), French painter, decorator and engraver. Working in the ROCOCO style of the Louis XV period, he was immensely popular and widely imitated throughout Europe. He painted historical, mythological, genre and landscape works, executing more than 1,000 paintings, 10,000 drawings and 180 engravings. Boucher became director of the GOBELINS tapestry works in 1755, and was also First Painter to Louis XV.

Boucher de Crèvecoeur de Perthes, Jacques (1788–1868), French archaeologist and writer. His discovery in 1837 of PALAEOLITHIC flint artefacts near Abbeville, France, enabled him to demonstrate that man had existed in the PLEISTOCENE period, long before the traditionally accepted limit of 4000 BC.

Boucicault, Dionysius Lardner (*c.*1822–90), Irish actor and dramatist who lived in London and New York. He wrote numerous romantic melodramas, including *London Assurance* (1841). In *The Octoroon* (1859) he attempted a serious stage treatment of an American Negro theme, creating a popular standard piece for touring US repertory companies.

Boucicaut, Master (*fl.* late 14th century), Flemish illustrator whose prolific and skilful illuminated manuscripts were influential in the development of Flemish painting.

Boudicca. *See* BOADICEA.

Boudin, Eugène Louis (1824–98), French landscape painter whose style represents the link between that of COROT and IMPRESSIONISM. He was famous for his pictures of fashionable seaside resorts, eg *On the Beach at Deauville* (1869). Boudin, who painted out-of-doors, introduced MONET to this method. He exhibited at the first Impressionist exhibition (1874).

Bougainville, Louis Antoine de (1729–1811), French navigator. An army veteran of the French and Indian wars, in 1763 he joined the navy and commanded the first French naval force to circumnavigate the globe (1766–69), making botanical and astronomical studies. He published an account of the journey in 1771–72. *See also* HC2 p.*124.*

Bougainville, largest of the Solomon Islands group, in the SW Pacific Ocean, E of New Guinea; a territory of Papua New Guinea. Kieta is the chief port. Discovered in 1768 by Louis de Bougainville, the island was under German control from 1884 and then came under Australian administration after 1914, and again in 1945 after the Japanese wartime occupation. Products: coconuts, coffee, cacao. Exports: copra, timber, Area: 10,049sq km (3,880sq miles). Pop. (1970 est.) 78,000 *See also* MW p.141.

Bougainvillea, tropical, flowering woody vine often grown as a garden plant in warm climates. Its inconspicuous flowers have showy purple or red bracts. It was named after the French explorer Louis de BOUGAINVILLE. Family Nyctaginaceae; species *Bougainvillea spectabilis.*

Boughton, Rutland (1878–1960), British composer. His plan to make Glastonbury the home of an annual festival of his operas failed. *The Immortal Hour* (1913) was a great, although short-lived, success.

Bougie. *See* BEJAÏA.

Bouguer anomaly, the observation that gravity measured on a great rock mass, such as a mountain range, is higher than average. This is due to the gravitational force exerted by the rock mass itself. It is named after its discoverer, the French mathematician Pierre Bouguer (1698–1758). *See also* PE pp.32–33.

Boulanger, Nadia (1887–), French music-teacher. She was the foremost teacher of composition of the 20th century and taught such composers as Aaron COPLAND, Darius MILHAUD and Jean Françaix. In the 1930s she became the first woman to conduct the Boston Symphony Orchestra and the New York Philharmonic.

Boules, group of French games similar to bowls but played with metal bowls usually thrown through the air. Various forms of the game are played in different regions of France. The *cochonnet* (target ball or jack) is of white-painted wood and 25–35mm (1–1.4in) in diameter. The metal bowls, usually steel, are 7–8cm (2.75–3.1in) in diameter and are not biased. The game may be played as singles (3 or 4 bowls each), doubles (3), or trebles (2). The object is to get one's bowls as near to the target ball as possible. The bowls may be thrown high to drop dead (*plomber*), rolled (*rouler*), or thrown to knock away an opponent's bowl (*tirer*).

Boulez, Pierre (1925–), French conductor and composer. His works for voice and orchestra have received much attention, especially *Le Marteau sans maître* (1954) and *Pli selon pli* (1960). Renowned for conducting complex 20th-century works, Boulez became director of the French Institute for Acoustic and Musical Research in 1975.

Boulle or Buhl, André Charles (1642–1732), French cabinetmaker, one of a number of skilled craftsmen maintained in the Louvre Palace by Louis XIV to design furniture and art objects for the court. Boulle created a distinctive MARQUETRY of tortoiseshell and gilded brass, to which he gave his name. Examples of his art exist at Versailles and the Louvre.

Boulle, Pierre (1912–), French novelist. He is best known for *The Bridge on the River Kwai* (1954), drawn from his years in SE Asia, and for $E = mc^2$ (1957) and *The Planet of the Apes* (1964).

Boult, Sir Adrian (1889–), British conductor, widely known for his interpretation of modern English composers, such as Gustav HOLST and Ralph VAUGHAN WILLIAMS. He was musical director and principal conductor of the BBC Symphony Orchestra (1930–50) and principal conductor of the London Philharmonic Orchestra (1950–57).

Boulting brothers, the (1913–), twins John and Roy who worked together as film directors and producers from the late 1940s. Their earlier films included *Brighton Rock* (1946) and *Fame is the Spur* (1946). From 1955 they made realistic satirical comedies such as *Lucky Jim* (1957) and *I'm All Right Jack* (1959).

Boulton, Matthew (1728–1809), British engineer and manufacturer. In 1762 he built the Soho iron works near Birmingham. In 1775 he went into partnership with James WATT and began manufacturing Watt's steam engines on a commercial basis. In 1790 he patented a steam-powered coining press and introduced a new copper coinage into Britain in 1797.

Boumédienne, Houari (*c.*1925–), Algerian politician. In the Algerian war for independence from France he commanded guerrilla forces around Oran in 1955–60. He served as Vice-President from the achievement of independence in 1962 to 1965, when he overthrew President Ben Bella, his former ally, and became President and Prime Minister himself. He has maintained a strongly anti-Israel policy. *See also* MW p.000.

Bounty Islands, group of approx. 12 small uninhabited islands in the S Pacific Ocean 668km (415 miles) ESE of Dunedin, New Zealand; administered by New Zealand. They were discovered in 1788 by Captain William BLIGH, the year before the mutiny on his ship, HMS *Bounty.*

Bounty, Mutiny on the (28 April 1789), revolt led by the master's mate Fletcher Christian against Lieut. William BLIGH of HMS *Bounty* off Tahiti. Christian and nine other mutineers subsequently went on to colonize the island of Pitcairn. *See also* MW p.143.

Bourbon, House of, European dynastic family, descendants of the CAPETS. The ducal title was created in 1327 and continued until 1527. A cadet branch, the Bourbon-Vendôme line, won the kingdom of Navarre, so that when Henry of Navarre became King of France as HENRY IV in 1589, the Bourbons became France's ruling family until 1789. Two members of the family, LOUIS XVIII and CHARLES X, ruled from 1814 to 1830.

The Bourbons became the ruling family of Spain in 1700 when PHILIP V, grandson of LOUIS XIV of France, assumed the throne. His descendants mostly continued

to rule Spain until 1931, when the Second Republic was declared. JUAN CARLOS I, a Bourbon, was restored to the Spanish throne in 1975.
Bourbonnais, former province in central France. It was gradually put together by the counts of BOURBON, one of whom married into the family of LOUIS IX of France, and the throne thus passed into the Bourbon family in 1589.
Bourgeois Gentillhomme, Le (*The Would-be Gentleman*) (1670), satirical comedy by the French dramatist MOLIÈRE. It follows the progress of M. Jourdain, a wealthy social climber whose desire to be considered a gentleman becomes an obsession and, finally, a delusion.
Bourgeois, Léon Victor Auguste (1851–1925), French statesman. He was Prime Minister of France (1895–96) and, as a determined proponent of the LEAGUE OF NATIONS, he represented France there until 1923. He won the Nobel Peace Prize in 1920.
Bourgeoisie, the middle class. The term originally referred to artisans and craftsmen who lived in medieval French towns. Up to the late 18th century it was a propertied but relatively unprivileged class, often of urban merchants and tradesmen, who helped speed the decline of feudalism. Since then it has expanded greatly, and can be divided into the high bourgeoisie (industrialists and financiers) and the petty bourgeoisie (tradesmen, white-collar workers and those in the professions). The name has come to imply an outlook of narrow materialism and impoverished culture. *See also* HC1 pp.288–289,; HC2 pp.66–67, 88–89.
Bourguiba, Habib (*c.*1903–), Tunisian politician, President since 1957. In 1934 he founded the Neo-Destour Party. In 1954 he began the negotiations that culminated in independence in 1956. He became Prime Minister but in 1957 he deposed the bey. In foreign policy he has favoured negotiations between the Arab states and Israel. *See also* MW p.167.
Bourne, William (*d.*1583), English mathematician and writer on naval subjects. In 1578 his *Inventions or Devises* was published. It contained the first serious discussion of the submarine, a submersible craft to be navigated underwater; there is no evidence that his craft ever sailed. *See also* MM pp.118–119.
Bournemouth, town in Hampshire, S England, on the English Channel at the mouth of the River Bourne. A small fishing village until the mid-19th century, it has grown into a popular resort with sandy beaches and fine parks. Pop. (1973) 147,460.
Bournonville, Auguste (1805–79), Danish ballet dancer and choreographer. He want to Paris in 1823 and danced with the Paris Opera Company for two years. After joining the Royal Danish Ballet as director and choreographer in 1830, he stayed with the company after his retirement as a dancer in 1848. He choreographed more than 50 ballets, which combined Romanticism with technical precision. *See also* HC2 pp.*274*, 275.
Bournville, district 6km (4 miles) SW of Birmingham in West Midlands, England. It was built in 1879 by George CADBURY as a garden city for the workers in his chocolate and cocoa factories. As such it is one of the first examples of town planning, and is now owned and managed by the Bournville Village Trust.
Bouts, Dirk (*c.*1420–75), Dutch painter and pioneer of woodcuts. His individualistic and detailed style is best shown in his altarpiece for St Peter's, Louvain, and in the panels of *Justice of Emperor Otto.*
Bouzouki, musical instrument that is lute-backed, fretted and usually has three double metal strings. Probably of Persian origin, it is played mostly in Greece.
Bovet, Daniele (1907–), Italian pharmacologist. He was awarded the 1957 Nobel Prize for physiology and medicine for his pioneering work on the development of antihistamines and the muscle relaxants used in surgery. He also studied the effects of mental illness on the chemistry of the brain.
Bow, Clara (1905–65), US film star. Known as the "It" girl, she was a vivacious actress who personified the "flapper" in *Dancing Mothers, Mantrap* (1926), *It* (1927) and *The Wild Party* (1929). Her much publicized personal life and her difficulty in adjusting to acting in sound films led to a sharp decline in her popularity.
Bow and arrow, weapon consisting of a length of wood, horn (or today metal) flexed and held in tension by a string, and a flighted pointed shaft which it fires. Probably developed in the Upper Palaeolithic Age about 300,000 years ago, it is still used by some primitive communities for hunting and warfare. *See also* ARCHERY; MM pp.160–161; MS pp.25–31.
Bow bells, peal of bells in the church of St Mary-le-Bow in the centre of the City of London, England. According to tradition only those who are born within the sound of the bells are true COCKNEYS.
Bowden cable, device for the flexible transmission of small mechanical movements, generally to the controls of a machine. It consists of a strong steel cable (usually multi-stranded and lubricated) in a flexible outer tube, often made in the form of a long coiled spring. The outer tube is anchored at the ends so that the inner cable can move independently. Bowden cables are commonly used for throttle (accelerator), clutch, choke and sometimes brake controls on cars and motor-cycles.
Bowdler, Thomas (1754–1825), English editor, famous for his popular expurgated version of SHAKESPEARE, *The Family Shakespeare* (1818). He also published an expurgated edition of the Old Testament (1823) and Gibbon's *History of the Decline and Fall of the Roman Empire* (1826). The term "bowdlerize", meaning to omit or change indelicate sections of a work, is derived from his name.
Bowell, Sir Mackenzie (1823–1917), Prime Minister of Canada (1894–96). As leader of the Conservative Party he defended the Protestant interest. He served as Minister of Customs and colonel of militia before becoming Prime Minister and then leader of the opposition (1896–1906).
Bowen, Elizabeth (1899–1973), British novelist. Her numerous works are noted for their psychological insight into restless, unhappy, and primarily upper-middle-class characters. Her novels include *The Hotel* (1927), *The House of Paris* (1935), *The Heat of the Day* (1949) and *Changing Scenes* (1969).
Bowen, Marjorie (1886–1952), pseudonym of Gabrielle Margaret Vere Long, *b.* Campbell, British writer of popular historical fiction. Her first novel was published in 1906 and her first best-seller was a romantic novel set in Renaissance Italy, *The Viper of Milan* (1917). *Windfalls* (1923) was also successful. She also used the pen-names Joseph Shearing, George R. Preedy, Robert Page and John Winch, and wrote a large number of historical biographies.
Bowen, Norman Levi (1887–1956), Canadian petrologist and mineralogist. His contributions to the study of the origins, structure and chemistry of rocks were outstanding. His most important book is *The Evolution of Igneous Rocks* (1928). *See also* PE pp.100–101.
Bowerbird, forest bird of New Guinea and Australia. The male builds a simple but brightly ornamented bower to attract the female. After mating, the female lays 1–3 eggs in a cup-shaped nest. Adults, mainly terrestrial, have short wings and legs and variously coloured plumage. Length: 25–38 cm (10–15in). Family Ptilonorhynchidae. *See also* NW pp.144, 149, *211.*
Bowering, George (1935–), Canadian poet and novelist. His many books of poetry include *Sticks and Stones* (1963), *Two Police Poems* (1968), *Rocky Mountain Foot* (1969), and *The Gangs of Kosmos* (1969). He has also written a novel, *Mirror on the Floor* (1967).
Bowery, The, area of lower Manhattan, New York City, centred round the street of the name. *Bouwerie* is Dutch for farm, and in the 17th century the street (then an unmade road) led to the farm of Peter Stuyvesant, governor of New Amsterdam.
Bowie, David (1947–), British pop singer, real name David Jones. Fusing a bizarre theatricality to progressive pop, he graduated to international stardom with his record *Ziggy Stardust* (1972). His subsequent work embraced many styles. He made his film debut in *The Man Who Fell to Earth* (1976).
Bowie, James (*c.*1796–1836), US frontiersman. He moved to Texas from Louisiana in 1828 and married the daughter of the Mexican Vice-Governor. By 1832 he had joined the US colonists who opposed the Mexican government. He was appointed a colonel in the Texas army in 1835, and was killed at the ALAMO in 1836.
Bowles, William Lisle (1762–1850), English poet and clergyman. His first work *Fourteen Sonnets* (1789) was admired by the poets Samuel Coleridge and William Wordsworth. His later poems included *The Battle of the Nile* (1799) and *St John in Patmos* (1832).
Bowling. *See* TENPIN BOWLING.
Bowls, game in which a bowl (wood) is delivered underarm to stop as close as possible to a small white ball (jack) at the farthest end of the playing area (rink). A point is scored for each bowl closer the jack than the best opposition bowl. Lawn bowls is played on a level green, in singles, pairs, triples or fours; crown green bowls is played on a green that is raised in the centre, generally as singles but sometimes in pairs. Indoor bowls is played on a matting surface.
Bowra, Sir (Cecil) Maurice (1898–1871), English classical scholar, He was vice-chancellor of Oxford University (1951–54) and wrote many books including *Greek Lyric Poetry* (1936) and *The Greek Experience* (1957).
Bow Street Runners, semi-official police and detective force, organized in London in 1748 by the Bow Street magistrate, Henry Fielding, and later by his half-brother Sir John Fielding. They were assisted by a government grant from 1757 and allowed to extend their activities beyond Westminster and Middlesex.
Box, evergreen tree or shrub found in tropical and temperate regions in Europe, North American and W Asia. The shrub is popular for TOPIARY, and box wood is used for musical instruments. The 100 species include English or common *Buxus sempervirens* and larger Buxus balearica that grows to 24m (80ft). Family *Euphorbiaceae.*
Box and Cox, two people who alternate in the same place, never meeting, from the old French farce in which two men rent the same room by day and by night respectively. The story was made into a comic opera called *Cox and Box*, by Burnand and SULLIVAN in 1867.
Boxer, smooth-haired working DOG bred originally in Germany. It has a broad head with a deep, short, square muzzle, and its deep-chested body is set on strong, medium-length legs. The tail is commonly docked, and its coat is generally red or brindle, with black and white markings. Height: to 61cm (24in) at the shoulder.
Boxer Rebellion (1900), violent Chinese uprising to oust all foreigners from China. Forces led by the secret society of Boxers (Righteous and Harmonious Fists) that attacked Europeans and Chinese Christians besieged Peking's foreign legations enclave for two months. An international expeditionary force put down the uprising. *See also* HC2 p.145.
Boxing, sport of fist fighting between two men wearing gloves in a roped-in square (ring). Boxers, who are matched according to weight, are classified into eight divisions: flyweight, bantamweight, featherweight, lightweight, welterweight, middleweight, light-heavyweight and heavyweight. Professional bouts can be from 4 to 15 rounds of three minutes' duration. A fight is controlled by a referee in the ring and ends when there is a knock-down (where a boxer is unable to get to his feet by the count of ten), or a technical knockout (one fighter is too seriously injured to continue). If both boxers finish the scheduled number of rounds, a decision is generally made by the referee; under International Rules, this decision

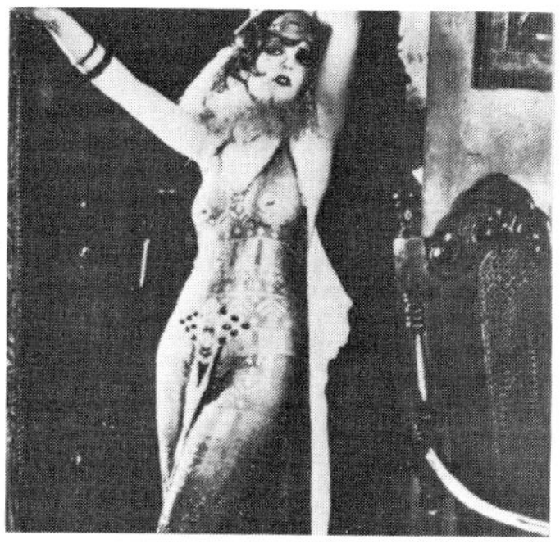
Clara Bow, the wide-eyed "flapper" with the cupid-bow lips, silent screen star of the 1920s.

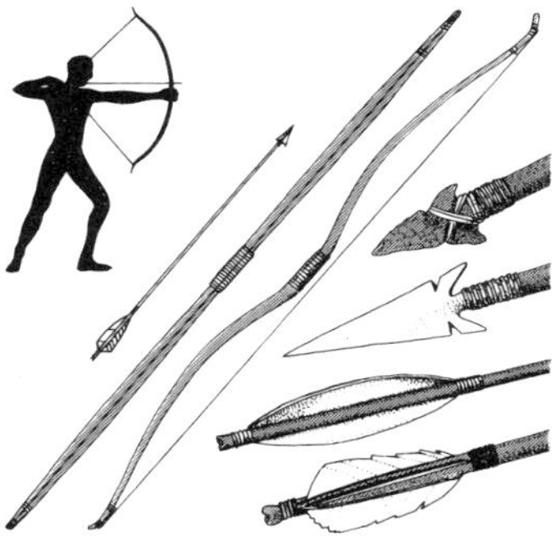
Bow and arrow; in 16th century England, firearms superseded the bow as a weapon.

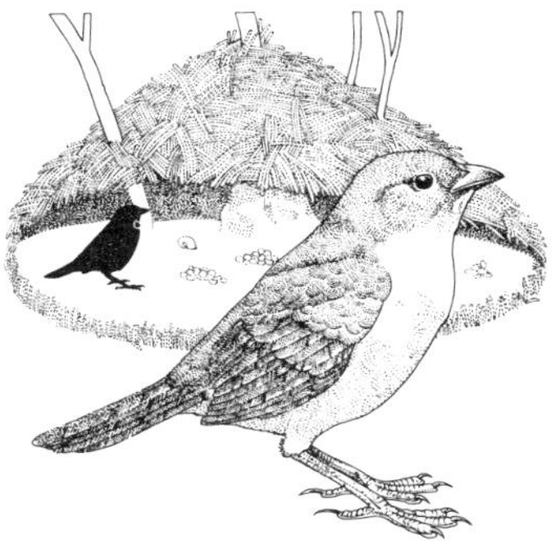
Bowerbirds plant bright attractive objects to lure the female into the bower for courtship.

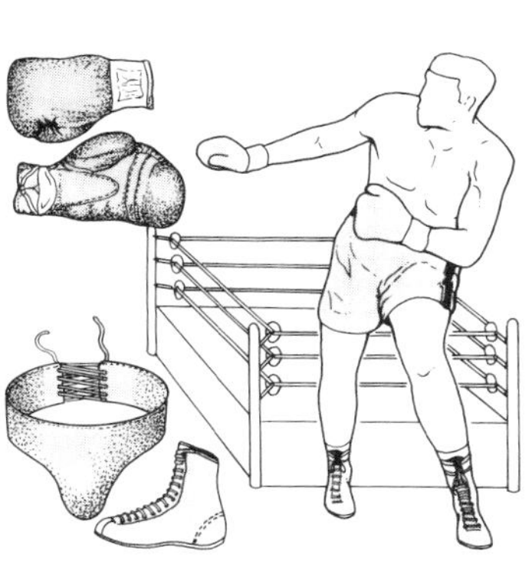
Boxing, the "noble art" of attack and defence under the Marquess of Queensbury Rules.

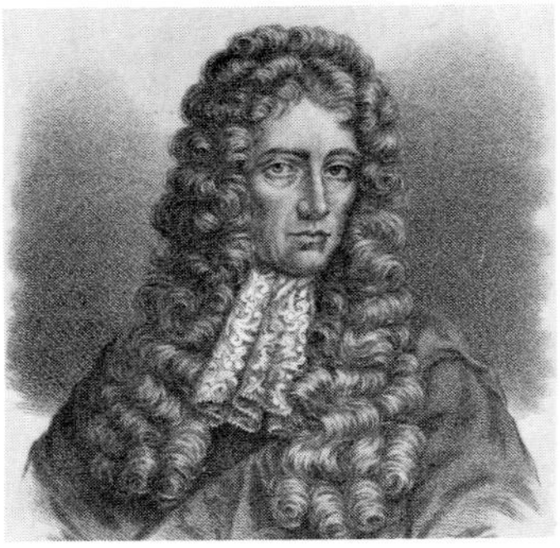

Robert Boyle, the "natural philosopher" regarded as the father of modern chemistry.

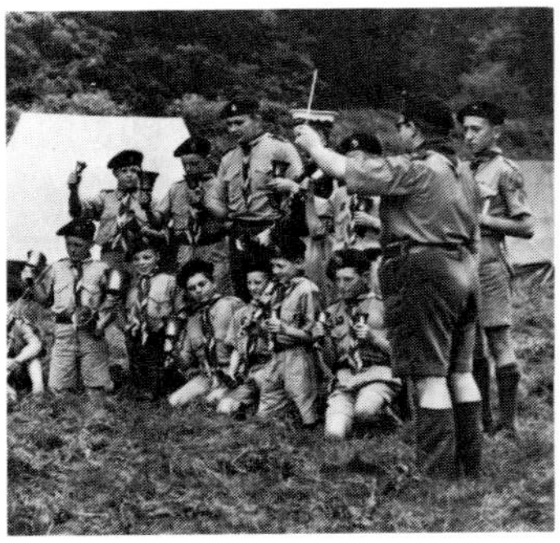

Boy Scouts make a promise, obey a law, and pursue the skills of outdoor activities.

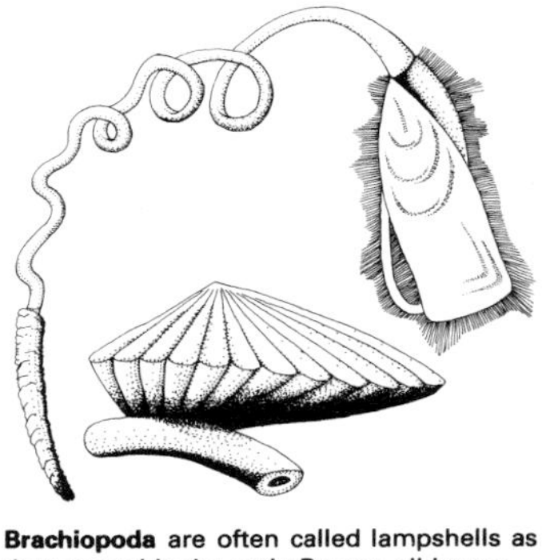

Brachiopoda are often called lampshells as they resemble the early Roman oil lamps.

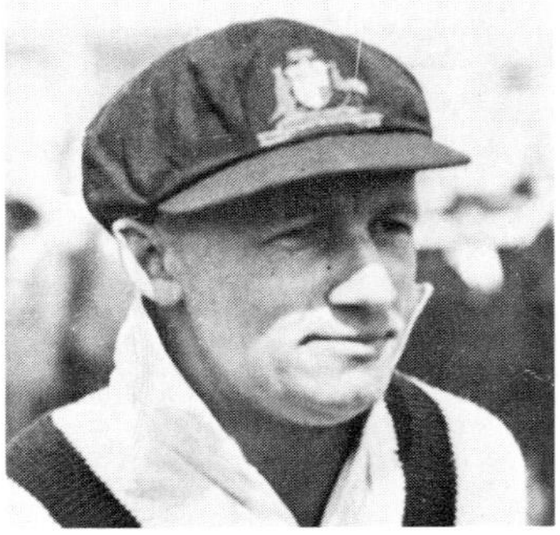

Sir Donald Bradman, the greatest batsman the game of cricket has ever known.

is made by three judges outside the ring.

Box lacrosse, game similar to LACROSSE, played mainly in Canada. It is played by two teams of six people in a boarded-in area (indoors or outdoors) with maximum dimensions of 61 by 27m (200 by 90ft). The rules are similar to those of (field) lacrosse, except that the ball may be played off the surrounding boards.

Boyacá, Battle of, was fought on 7 Aug. 1819 between revolutionary forces (led by Simon BOLÍVAR) and the Spaniards. Bolívar's victory confirmed the independence of Venezuela and Colombia. *See also* HC2 p.*87*.

Boyars, higher nobility of medieval Russia, originally warriors but increasingly important as great landowners. After long disputes over the respective powers of the boyars and the tsar, the title was abolished in the late 17th century by PETER I. *See also* HC1 pp.320–323.

Boyce, William (1710–1779), English composer and organist. He compiled *Cathedral Music* (3 vols, 1760–78), and composed symphonies, overtures and vocal works as well as pieces for the organ.

Boycott, Geoffrey (1940–), English cricketer. He was made captain of Yorkshire in 1971, the year in which he became the first batsman to average over 100 in an English first-class season. In 1977, during the Headingley Test against Australia, he became the 18th player to make 100 first-class centuries.

Boycott, refusal to have dealings with a person, organization or country. The term originated in 1880 when Irish tenant farmers refused to work for, supply or speak with a man named Capt. Charles Boycott who was an agent of their landlord.

Boyd, Arthur Merric Bloomfield (1920–), Australian painter and ceramic sculptor. He studied under his grandfather, Arthur Boyd, and began painting landscapes at age 17. His EXPRESSIONIST paintings are evocative of CHAGALL and Stanley SPENCER.

Boyd, William. *See* HOPALONG CASSIDY.

Boydell, Brian Patrick, (1917–), Irish musician and composer. His works show a reaction against the strong influence folk music exerted on his contemporaries. Compositions include *Five Joyce Strings* (1946) and *Meditation and Fugue* (1956).

Boyd Orr, John, 1st Baron (1880–1971), Scottish nutritionist. In 1936 he published *Food, Health and Income,* a report on income-related diet in Britain which formed the basis for food rationing during WWII. He founded the Imperial Bureau of Animal Nutrition at Aberdeen in 1929 and in 1945 became the first director-general of the UN Food and Agricultural Organization (FAO). He was awarded the Nobel Peace Prize in 1949.

Boyer, Charles, (1899–), French actor who went to Hollywood in 1929, and who established a reputation as one of the screen's "great lovers" in a career which included leading roles in *Mayerling* (1937), *All This and Heaven Too* (1940) and *Barefoot in the Park* (1968).

Boyle, Charles, 4th Earl of Orrery (1676–1731), Anglo-Irish scholar and soldier. In 1695 he edited a version of the letters of the Greek tyrant Phalaris. These were later proved to be forgeries by the scholar Richard Bentley and were satirized by Jonathan SWIFT in his *Battle of the Books* (1704).

Boyle, Kay (1903–), US author. She spent many years in France and used them as the basis for much of her writing. Her work includes the novels *Plagued by the Nightingale* (1931) and *Gentlemen, I Address You Privately* (1933) and the poems *A Glad Day* (1938) and *American Citizen* (1944).

Boyle, Robert (1627–91), Anglo-Irish scientist, often regarded as the father of modern chemistry. Working at Oxford (1656–68), he made an efficient vacuum pump and used it in 1662 to establish that the volume of a gas is inversely proportional to its pressure at a constant temperature; this relationship is known as Boyle's law. An advocate of experimental methods, he freed chemistry from Aristotelian theory and formulated the chemical definitions of an element and a reaction. He also researched into the calcination of metals, combustion, acids and bases, the nature of colours and the propagation of sound in air. He later worked in London (1668–91) and was a founding Fellow of the ROYAL SOCIETY. *See also* HC1 pp.*292,* 303; PE p.90; SU pp.24–25, 84–85.

Boylston, Zabdiel (1679–1766), US physician who introduced smallpox inoculation into the USA. In 1721, during a smallpox epidemic, he was encouraged by the clergyman Cotton MATHER to introduce the technique. He vaccinated more than 200 patients, nearly all of whom survived. Despite his success, there was a public outcry and his life was threatened.

Boyne, Battle of the (1690), engagement that took place near Drogheda, Ireland, in which the forces of the Protestant WILLIAM III defeated those of the Catholic JAMES II.

Boy Scouts, worldwide organization for boys that stresses outdoor knowledge and good citizenship, founded in Britain in 1908 by Sir Robert BADEN-POWELL. Boy Scouts are divided into community groups called troops, which are subdivided into patrols. Scouts can advance through several grades and earn merit badges for proficiency in various activities; the classes of Scouts are: Scout standard, Advanced Scout standard and Chief Scout's award. The Cub Scouts and Venture Scouts are organized within the Scout movement, the first for boys under 12, the second for older teenagers.

Brabançonne, La, Belgian national anthem. Written in 1830, the original words are by Jenneval and the music by François van Campenhout. The Brabançons of the title were renowned warriors in 12th-century Europe.

Brabant, Sir Edward (1839–1914), South African soldier and politician, *b.* England. He went to the Cape as an ensign in 1855. He was a member of the Assembly between 1873 and 1907. In 1878 he raised a force known as Brabant's Horse and revived it for the SOUTH AFRICAN (Boer) WAR.

Brabant, province of central Belgium; capital, Brussels. Mainly Flemish-speaking, it is densely populated and fertile agricultural region. Industries: chemicals, metallurgy, food processing. Area: 3,372sq km (1,302sq miles). Pop. (1970 est.) 2,178,000.

Brabazon of Tara, John Theodore Cuthbert Moore-Brabazon, 1st Baron (1884–1964), British pilot, the first man to hold a pilot's licence. He had a distinguished career in WWI and introduced new methods of aerial photography. In 1940 he was made Minister of Transport.

Brabham, Jack (1926–), Australian racing driver and designer. He won the World Drivers' Championship three times (1959, 1960 and 1966). He was the first driver to win the world championship in his own car (1966), the Brabham, which he raced for the first time in the German grand prix in 1962. He was the first Australian driver to make his name in European racing. He retired in 1970 after racing in 126 grand prix events.

Brace, Charles Loring (1826–90), US social reformer. In 1853 he founded the Children's Aid Society of New York City, which pioneered modern child care.

Bracegirdle, Anne (*c.* 1663–1748), English actress. She was trained by Thomas BETTERTON and became the leading actress of her day. She gave her greatest performances in the plays of William CONGREVE and retired in 1707.

Brachiopoda, lamp shells, a phylum of about 260 species of small, bottom-dwelling, marine invertebrates, similar in appearance to bivalve molluscs. They are identified by a shell with two halves, a characteristic lophophore – a tentacled organ for feeding – and a stalk in some species. They live attached to rocks or buried in mud or sand and reproduce sexually. There are 75 genera including *Lingula,* the oldest known animal genus. Most modern brachiopods are less than 5cm (2in) across, but more than 30,000 fossil species have been found and described. *See also* NW pp.*22, 121.*

Brachycephalic. *See* CEPHALIC INDEX.

Bracken, Thomas (1843–98), New Zealand journalist and poet, *b.* Ireland. He wrote the national anthem *God Defend New Zealand.*

Bracken, persistent weedy FERN found throughout the world. It has an underground stem that can travel 1.8m (6ft) and sends up fronds that may reach 4.6m (15ft) in some climates. The *typica* variety is widespread in Britain. Species *Pteridium aquilinum. See also* NW p.52.

Bracton, Henry de (*d.* 1268), English jurist, whose *De Legibus et Consuetudinibus Angliae* is the best medieval statement of the limited sovereignty of feudal and divine kingship.

Bradbury, Ray Douglas (1920–), US science-fiction writer. His works include the novel *Fahrenheit 451* (1953), the play *The Halloween Tree* (1968), and *The Martian Chronicles* (1950), *The Illustrated Man* (1951) and *The Autumn People* (1965), all short story collections.

Bradford, William (1590–1657), American colonial governor and signatory of the Mayflower Compact. He emigrated to America as one of the PILGRIM FATHERS on the MAYFLOWER in 1620, and was elected Governor of Plymouth Colony in 1621. He helped draw up a body of laws for the colony in 1636, and wrote a *History of Plymouth Plantation, 1620–46.*

Bradford, city in West Yorkshire, N England, in the Aire Valley, 14km (9 miles) W of Leeds. Since the 14th century it has been a centre for woollen and worsted manufacturing. Industries: textiles, textile engineering, electrical engineering, motor-cars. Pop. 292,340.

Bradford-on-Avon, town in Wiltshire, SW England, 10km (6 miles) E of Bath. It is noted for its medieval architecture, including an 8th-century Saxon church and a 13th-century stone bridge over the River Avon. Industries: wool, rubber processing. Pop. 8,000.

Bradley, Francis Herbert (1846–1924), British philosopher. Bradley's idealism was Hegelian in inspiration. *Appearance and Reality* (1893) contained his famous theory of "the degrees of truth". Dialectical analysis distinguished his *Principles of Logic* (1883).

Bradley, Henry (1845–1923), English philologist and lexicographer. In 1889 he became an editor of the *Oxford English Dictionary* and was its senior editor (1915–23).

Bradley, Omar Nelson (1893–), US general. In WWII he commanded the 2nd Corps in N Africa and during the invasion of Sicily (1943), and led the 1st Army in the Normandy invasion (1944). After the war he served as Chief-of-Staff of the US Army (1948–49) and was appointed first chairman of the joint Chiefs of Staff (1949–53).

Bradman, Sir Donald (1908–), Australian cricketer and sports administrator, regarded as one of the finest batsmen the game has known. His record in Test matches was 6,996 runs in 52 games (average 99.94), including 29 centuries and a highest score of 334 (against England at Leeds in 1930). During his career in first class cricket, playing for Australia, New South Wales and South Australia, he made a total of 28,067 runs (average 95.14), including 117 centuries and a highest score of 452 not out (for New South Wales against Queensland at Sydney, 1929–30). He played for Australia from 1928 to 1948, and was its captain from the 1936–37 season.

Bradshaw, George (1801–53), English printer and the originator of railway guides. In 1839 he published *Bradshaw's Railway Time-Tables* which was developed into the series *Bradshaw's Monthly Railway Guide.*

Bradycardia, slow, arhythmic heart rate defined by a pulse of less than 60 beats per minute. It is caused by disturbance of the primary pacemaker and is also common in healthy athletes whose performances are partly related to respiratory variation. *See also* MS pp.62–63, 90–91.

Braemar Gathering, best known of the HIGHLAND GAMES, a Scottish athletics meeting.

Braga (Bracara Augusta), town in Minho province, NW Portugal, approx. 48km (30 miles) NNE of Oporto; the capital of Braga district. It was the location of a powerful Episcopal See in the Middle Ages. Industries: engineering, cutlery, guns, jewellery. Pop. 47,000.

Bragança, town in NE Portugal, the capital of Bragança district. It is the seat of the Braganza family, who ruled Portugal from 1640 to 1910. Industries: textiles, hats, chocolate. Pop. 34,000.

Braganza, dynasty that ruled Portugal from 1640 until 1910; a branch of the house ruled as emperors of Brazil from 1822 to 1889. The dynasty was founded by the Duke of Braganza, who ruled as John IV (1640–56). During the NAPOLEONIC WARS, the royal family fled to Brazil, then a Portuguese colony.

Bragg, Sir William Lawrence (1890–1971), English physicist, *b.* Australia. With his father, Sir William Henry, he determined the mathematics involved in X-ray diffraction, showed how to compute X-ray wavelengths, and studied CRYSTAL STRUCTURE by X-ray DIFFRACTION. In 1915, they were jointly awarded the Nobel Prize in physics.

Brahe, Tycho (1546–1601), Danish astronomer. Educated in law at Copenhagen and Leipzig, he became interested in astronomy and devoted himself to improving observational technique. He built an observatory on the island of Hven (1576). The most accurate observer of his time, he discovered a NOVA (1572) and advanced the solar theory of COPERNICUS. His calculations were used by Johannes KEPLER. *See also* HC1 pp.164–165

Brahma, creator god in HINDUISM, one of the three gods in the TRIMURTI. Although Brahma is equal to the gods VISHNU and SHIVA, there is only one major temple to him, at Pushkar in India.

Brahman, or Atman, in HINDUISM the supreme soul of the universe. The omnipresent Brahman sustains the earth. According to the UPANISHADS, the individual soul is identified with Brahman. Brahman is not God, but rather is *neti neti*, "not this, not that", or indescribable.

Brahmanas, ancient Hindu writings of the pre-Upanishadic period (*c.*900–*c.*700 BC). They interpret the VEDAS and contain social doctrines, instructions for ritual sacrifice as the means of achieving salvation and myths of the Hindu pantheon of gods. *See also* HINDUISM; UPANISHADS.

Brahman cattle, or zebu, many domestic varieties of a species of ox native to India. Tan, grey or black with a hump over the shoulders, brahmans have drooping ears and a large dewlap. Family Bovidae; species *Bos indicus. See also* PE p.*226*

Brahmanism, term used to denote the early phase of HINDUISM. It was characterized by acceptance of the VEDA as divine revelation. The BRAHMANAS, the major text of Brahmanism, are the ritualistic books comprising the greater portion of Vedic literature. They were complemented by the UPANISHADS. In the course of time deities of post-Vedic origin began to be worshipped and the influence of Brahmin priests declined. This led to a newer, popular form of Hinduism which superseded Brahmanism.

Brahmaputra, river in S Asia; it flows E across Tibet into SW China, S into India, WSW across India into Bangledesh where it becomes the River Jamuna, and S to the Bay of Bengal, forming, with the rivers Ganges and Meghna, a vast delta mouth. Length: approx. 2,900km (1,800 miles).

Brahma Sutra, "Aphorisms about Brahman", sometimes called the Vedanta Sutra, is the root text of the VEDANTA school of HINDU philosophy. Probably composed in the 2nd or 3rd century AD, it includes an interpretation of the UPANISHADS and relates it to the conclusions of other schools.

Brahmin. *See* BRAHMANISM.

Brahms, Johannes (1833–97), German composer. Encouraged by his friends Robert and Clara SCHUMANN, he began to earn his living as a composer at the age of 30. He followed classical models of form and was a master of contrapuntal HARMONY. He composed in all major musical forms except OPERA. Among his works are the *German Requiem* (1868), the *Variations on a Theme by Paganini* (1863), the *Violin Concerto in D* (1878) and two piano concertos (1858 and 1881). His best-known works include the orchestral *Hungarian Dances* (1873) and the *Lullaby* (1868). He wrote four symphonies between 1876 and 1885. *See also* HC2 pp.106–107.

Braided stream, network of small, shallow interlacing streams. It forms whan a river deposits sediment, causing it to divide up into new channels, which then redivide and rejoin, looking like a braided cord.

Braila, city and port in Romania, 19km (12 miles) S of Galati on the River Danube. It is a major industrial and commercial centre, important for its grain exporting. Industries: food processing, metal products, fishing. Pop. 165,803.

Braille, Louis (1809–52), French inventor of the Braille system of reading for the blind (he was himself blinded at the age of three). A scholar, and later a teacher, at the National Institute of Blind Youth in Paris, Braille developed a system of embossed dots to enable the blind to read by touch. This was first published in 1829, and a more complete form appeared in 1837. There are also Braille codes for music and mathematics. *See also* MS p.*243.*

Brain, Dennis (1921–57), British horn player. He was principal horn player of the Royal Philharmonic and the Philharmonia orchestras. Benjamin BRITTEN and Paul HINDEMITH composed works for him. He died in a car crash.

Brain, Walter Russell, 1st Baron of Eynsham (1895–1966), English neurologist. He was president of the Royal College of Physicians (1950–57) and in 1960 became president of the Association of British Neurologists. He wrote extensively on neurology and from 1954 was editor of the magazine *Brain.*

Brain, principal structure of the CENTRAL NERVOUS SYSTEM which regulates observable behaviour and governs the organ systems of the body. Weighing approx. 1.5kg (3.3lb), the adult human brain is about the size of two clenched fists, most of which consists of two hemispheres known collectively as the cerebrum. Its heavily convoluted surface contains innumerable nerve cells and has areas associated with one or more functions, eg sight or taste. *See also* MS pp.*24*, 26–27, *31*, 36–37, 38, 40–43, 52–55, 194–195.

Brain damage, sometimes caused by external injury or partial asphyxiation, may also be related to delayed or incomplete brain development, brain trauma suffered during or after birth, or psychiatric or social disturbances. It is the possible cause of lack of co-ordination, such as difficulties in muscular control, and diseases such as EPILEPSY. Whether treatment is likely to prove beneficial depends on accurate individual diagnosis. *See also* MS pp.96–97, 104, 134, 139.

Brain disorders, mental disturbances caused by an impairment of brain tissue function and associated with a deterioration of "thinking" processes. *See also* MS pp.84, 96–97, 104, 134, 176–177.

Braine, John Gerard (1922–), British novelist. One of the ANGRY YOUNG MEN, his novels include *Room at the Top* (1957), *Life at the Top* (1962), *The Crying Game* (1968) and *Stay with Me Till Morning* (1970).

Brain storage, in neuropsychology, the capacity of the mind and brain to store information or memories. The term is most often related to physiological theories of changes that take place in the brain during cognitive learning processes. *See also* MS pp.44–45, 152–153.

Brains Trust, BBC programme in which a panel of eminent authorities answered listeners' questions on all manner of topics. It began as a radio show (1941–47) and was later revived on TV in the 1950s.

Braintree, town in Essex, E England, on the rivers Brain and Blackwater, and on the Roman Stane Street. Stones from the road were used in the construction of its 13th-century church. Industries: textiles, plastics. Pop. (1971) 24,839.

Brainwashing, technique of coercive persuasion used to alter a person's basic beliefs and attitudes without his consent. Such techniques involve attempts to render a victim's beliefs so useless that he substitutes new values for his old ones, while specific procedures (including isolation, starvation, physical abuse and threats of death) are designed to make the subject dependent on his captors and receptive to new ideas.

Brain waves, fluctuations in the electrical activity of selected areas of the brain which can be recorded on an electroencephalograph (EEG). Electrodes are placed on the scalp, amplifying their output and recording the resulting patterns which can be used to "read" various states of consciousness. *See also* MS pp.194–195.

Braithwaite, Dame Lillian (1873–1948), English actress. Her most famous roles included Florence Lancaster in *The Vortex* (1924), Elizabeth I in *Elisabeth La Femme Sans Homme* (1938) and Abby Brewster in *Arsenic and Old Lace* (1942).

Braithwaite, Warwick (1896–), New Zealand conductor. He conducted the Sadler's Wells Opera Co., London (1932–40 and from 1960), and New Zealand's National Orchestra (1953–54).

Brake, device for slowing the speed of a vehicle by reducing the speed at which the wheels turn. It can be accomplished by mechanical, hydraulic or pneumatic systems that press a non-rotating member into contact with a rotating wheel o shaft, so that friction stops the motion. *See also* MM pp.130–131.

Braking, atmospheric, drag exerted on a space vehicle as it re-enters the Earth's atmosphere and encounters increased air density. The friction slows down the vehicle, which must be built to withstand the intense heat created. *See also* ABLATION; MM pp.156–157.

Braking parachute, or drogue, device used to slow down space vehicles during landing; several are used together. Some high-speed aircraft and even cars, such as "dragsters", also use them to decelerate. *See also* MM pp.156–157.

Brakpan, town in Transvaal, NE South Africa, 36km (23 miles) E of Johannesburg at an altitude of 1,637m (5,371ft). Industries: gold and coal-mining, electrical engineering. Pop. 64,000.

Bramah, Joseph (1748–1814) British engineer and inventor. He ran a lock-manufacturing shop which became the basis of the machine-tool industry in Britain, furthering the expansion of manufacturing in Britain in the 19th century. His inventions included an almost pick-proof lock, a hydraulic press and a numbering machine for the printing trade.

Bramante, Donato (1444–1514), Italian architect. He trained first as a painter but is famous for his buildings, which are distinguished by their Roman grandeur and beauty of proportion. His Roman buildings are classic examples of the High RENAISSANCE style. His plan was the basis for the basilica of St Peter's, Rome. *See also* HC1 pp.256–257.

Bramble. *See* BLACKBERRY.

Brambling, or bramble-finch, small FINCH that lives in Europe and Asia. It is brightly coloured and resembles a chaffinch. Species *Fringilla montifringilla. See also* NW p.*206.*

Bramwell, George William Wilshere, Baron (1808–92), English judge who introduced the term "limited" for companies of limited liability. He helped to draft the Common Law Procedure Act (1852) and was partly responsible for the Companies Act (1862).

Branching, growth extension of vascular plants. A branch develops from the stem and consists of the growth from the previous year (branchlet) and new growth (twig). New twigs are produced during the next season of growth, both from the terminal bud at the end of the twig and from lateral buds in leaf axils along it. *See also* NW pp.54–69.

Brand, Hennig (*d.c.*1692), German alchemist who in 1669 discovered the element PHOSPHORUS. *See* SU p.*137.*

Brand, Sir John Henry (1823–88), South African politician. Other forms of his

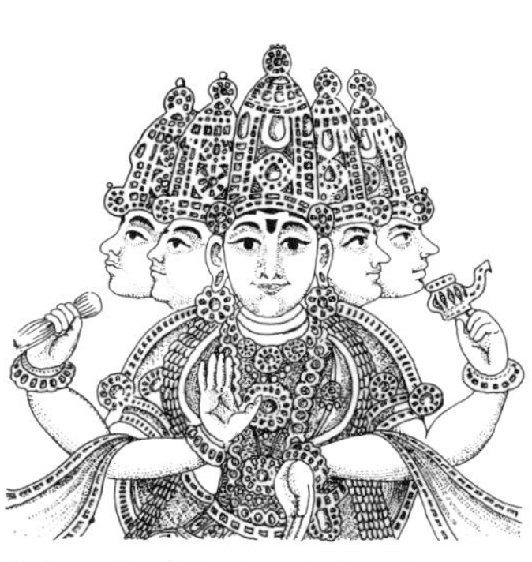

Brahma, the divine force believed by Hindus to be the creative soul of the universe.

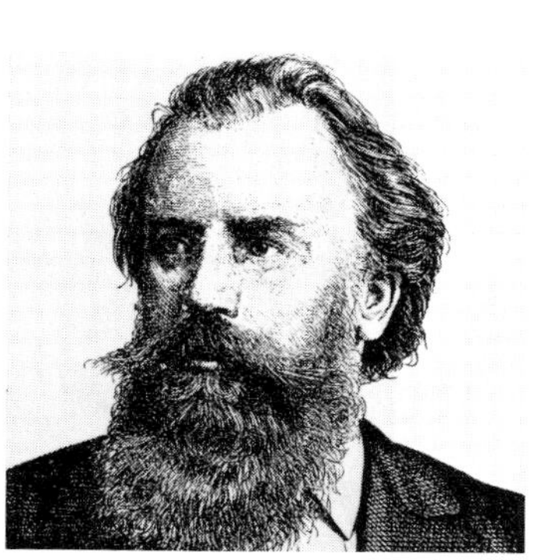

Brahms, romantic composer and third (after Bach and Beethoven) of the three great "Bs".

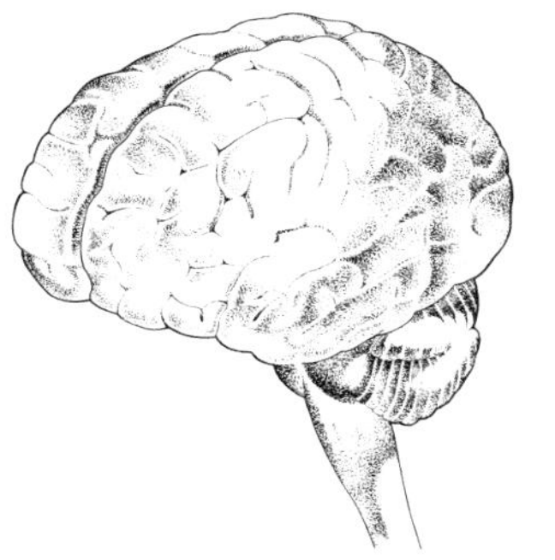

Brain, the highly complex organ that controls all mental and physical processes.

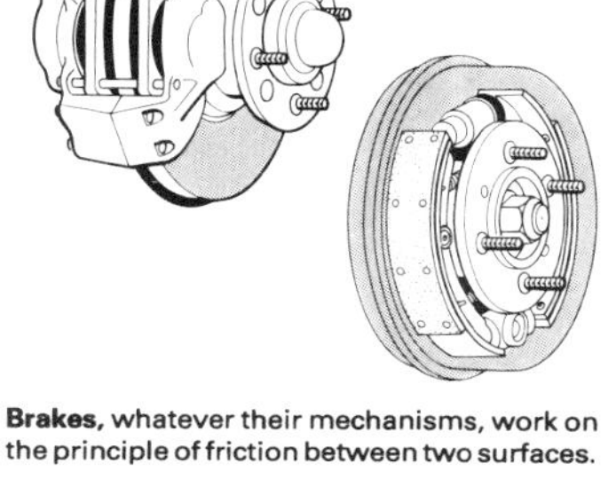

Brakes, whatever their mechanisms, work on the principle of friction between two surfaces.

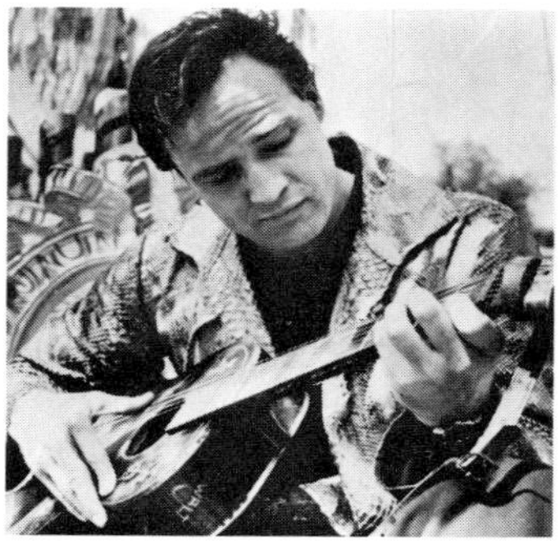

Marlon Brando, whose early films had a great influence on acting in Europe and America.

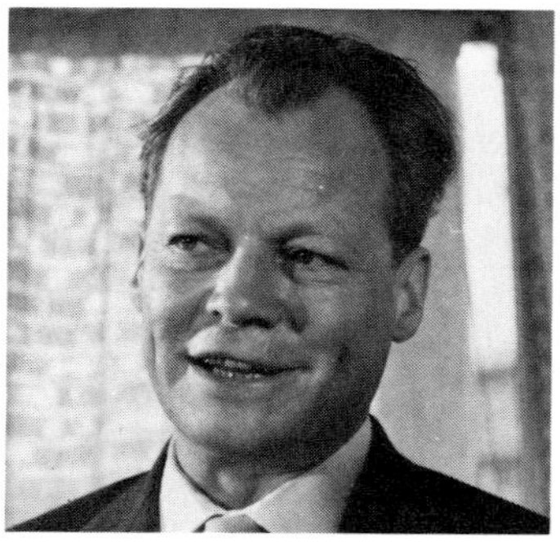

Willy Brandt, who resigned when it was found his aide was an East German spy.

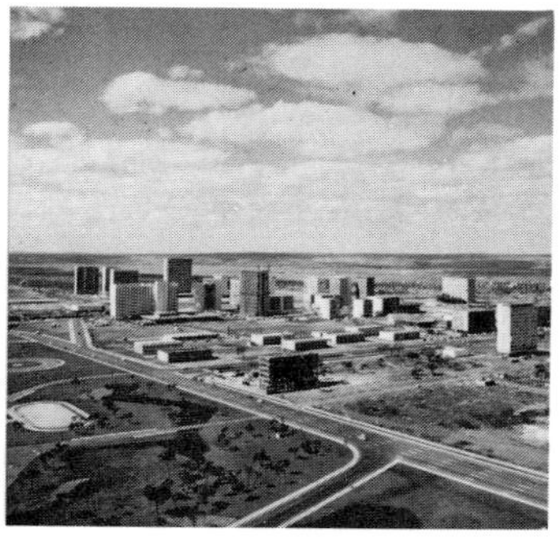

Brasília, with its architectural wonders, was created to develop the vast interior of Brazil.

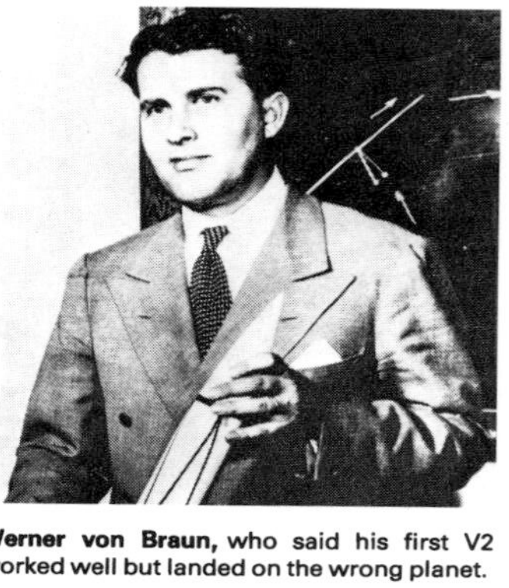

Werner von Braun, who said his first V2 worked well but landed on the wrong planet.

name are Jan Hendrik Brand and Johannes Henricus Brand. He was elected President of the ORANGE FREE STATE in 1864 and served until his death.

Brandenburg, city and canal port in Potsdam district, central East Germany, on the River Havel, 61km (38 miles) WSW of Berlin; former capital of the old state of the same name, now part of East Germany. The state was founded by the German King Henry I (*r.*916–36), and later formed the nucleus of the Kingdom of PRUSSIA. Both city and province have Wendish origins. Industries: steel, engineering, chemicals, textiles. Pop. (1970 est.) 94,000.

Brandenburg Concertos, six pieces of the CONCERTO GROSSO type by J.S. BACH, dedicated in 1721 to Christian Ludwig, Margrave of BRANDENBURG. All but Nos 3 and 6 have solo parts; all but No. 1 have three movements although the middle movement of No.3 consists of only two chords. They were probably not written as a set. They are often regarded as the finest examples of the BAROQUE concerto. *See also* HC2 pp.40–41.

Brandes, Georg Morris Cohen (1842–1927), Danish writer and critic. The radical views expressed in *Main Currents in 19th Century Literature* (1871–87), *Aesthetic Studies* (1868) and *Danish Poets* (1877) aroused hostility among conservative Danes.

Brando, Marlon (1924–), US film star, renowned for his "method" style of acting. His first major film success was in *A Streetcar Named Desire* (1951). Other notable films included *The Wild One* (1954), *On the Waterfront* (1954), *One-eyed Jacks* (1961), *Mutiny on the Bounty* (1962), *The Godfather* (1971), *Last Tango in Paris* (1972) and *The Missouri Breaks* (1976).

Brandt, Georg (1694–1768), Swedish chemist who discovered, isolated and named COBALT in 1730. In 1727 he was a research director for the Council of Mines, Stockholm, and later became the warden of the Swedish Mint. He rejected alchemy and discredited many spurious processes for the production of gold.

Brandt, Willy (1913–), German Social Democrat politician. His real name was Karl Herbert Frahm. He fled to Norway and then Sweden during the Nazi era and adopted the name "Willy Brandt". He returned to Germany after WWII and was elected Mayor of West Berlin in 1957. In 1969 he became Chancellor of West Germany. He initiated a programme of co-operation with the Communist bloc nations. In 1971 he was awarded the Nobel Peace Prize. He resigned in 1974 after a close aide was exposed as an East German spy. *See also* HC2 p.307.

Brandy, any alcoholic spirit made by distilling wine or the fermented juice of a fruit. Armagnac and cognac are famous French wine brandies, with an alcohol content of 42%–44%. Marc is a French brandy distilled from grape mush or pomace. Applejack and calvados are brandies distilled from fermented apple juice. Other well known fruit brandies are kirsch (cherries), slivovitz (plums) and peach, apricot, cherry and blackberry brandies. *See also* PE pp.206–207.

Brandywine creek, in SE Pennsylvania, USA, scene of a battle (11 Sept. 1777) in the American War of Independence in which the American troops under George WASHINGTON were defeated by the British who later marched, under Gen. Howe, into Philadelphia. *See also* HC2 p.*65*.

Brangwyn, Sir Frank (1867–1956), Welsh painter and draughtsman. His huge murals, in vivid and brilliantly handled colour, are to be seen in Skinners' Hall, the Royal Exchange and Lloyd's Register (all in London); the Rockefeller Center, New York; Missouri State Capitol and elsewhere. Bruges (his birthplace) and Orange in southern France have museums devoted to his work.

Brant, Joseph (1742–1807), Mohawk Indian chief. He served in the French and Indian War and in PONTIAC's Rebellion. He attended an Anglican school for Indians (1761) and became interpreter to a missionary. He was commissioned a captain in the British army in 1775 and fought on the British side in the American War of Independence. He translated the Book of COMMON PRAYER and the Gospel of St MARK into Mohawk.

Brant, Sebastien (1457–1521), German satirical writer and poet. He is noted for his long moral satire *Das Narrenschiff* (1494), in a verse form which became popular in 16th-century Europe. His other works include several Latin translations and theoretical musings on the lives of the saints.

Brantford, industrial city in SE Ontario, Canada, approx. 96 km (60 miles) SE of Toronto, on the River Grand. It was named after the Mohawk Indian chief Joseph BRANT who established the Six Nations of the Iroquois tribes there in 1784. Pop. 64,000.

Brant goose. *See* BRENT GOOSE.

Branting, Karl Hjalmar (1860–1925), Swedish politician. He was the first Social Democrat elected to the Riksdag (1896). He was Minister of Finance in 1917 and three times Prime Minister (1920, 1921–23, 1924–25). He was a delegate to the Paris Peace Conference (1919) and shared the Nobel Peace Prize in 1921 with Christian LANGE.

Brantôme, Pierre de Bourdeille, abbé and seigneur de (*c.*1540–1614), French soldier and chronicler. He fought against the HUGUENOTS in France, for the Spanish in Africa, and accompanied MARY QUEEN OF SCOTS to Scotland. His memoirs were published in 1665–66.

Braque, Georges (1882–1963), French painter, printmaker and sculptor. His early work, during the years 1907–09, foreshadowed CUBISM and had a great influence on early COLLAGE. *Head of a Woman* (1909) and *Violin and Palette* (1909-10) are transitional works between early and analytical Cubism. After WWI his style became less three-dimensional and his colour stronger, as in *The Table* (1918). *Woman with a Mandolin* (1937) typifies his more diverse style of the 1930s and 1940s. *See also* HC2 pp.176–177.

Brasch, Charles Orwell (1909–76), New Zealand poet. He was a careful, meticulous craftsman; his published volumes include *Disputed Ground* (1948) and *Ambulando* (1964). In 1947 he founded *Landfall*, an influential literary periodical that he edited for many years.

Brasília, capital city of Brazil and a Federal district, in W central Brazil, 933 km (580 miles) NW of Rio de Janeiro (the former capital). Although the city was originally suggested in 1891, building did not start until 1956. The city was laid out in the shape of an aircraft by the Brazilian architect Lúcio Costa, and Oscar Niermeyer designed the modernistic public buildings. Inaugurated as the capital in 1960, its economic purpose is to develop the interior of Brazil. Pop. 272,000.

Brasov, city in Brasov district, E central Romania, at the foot of the Transylvanian Alps. It has a 14th-century church and a 15th-16th century citadel. Industries: oil refining, building materials, textiles. Pop. 199,000.

Brass, alloy of copper (55%–95%) and zinc (5%–45%). It is yellowish, malleable and ductile, and can be machined or cast. Its properties can be altered by varying the amounts of copper and zinc, or by adding other metals such as tin. It has many uses eg in plumbing fixtures, coinage and ornamental metalwork. *See also* MM p.32, *32*.

Brass, family of musical wind instruments made of metal and played by means of a cupped or funnel-shaped mouthpiece. The chief brass instruments of a symphony orchestra are the trumpet, French horn, trombone and tuba. Other members of the family include the cornet and the bugle. *See also* HC2 p.105.

Brass band. *See* BAND.

Brassica, genus of plants with edible roots or leaves including cabbages, cauliflowers, brussels sprouts (all sub-species of *Brassica oleracea*), turnip (*B. rapa*), swede (*B. napobrassica*). Some, such as broccoli, have edible flowerheads, whereas both the root and leaves of kohlrabi (*B. caulorapa*) may be eaten. The species may vary considerably in appearance; they are mostly hardy and can withstand cold winters. *See also* PE p.188.

Brass rubbing, technique of making reproductions of the designs of flat, brass plaques found on monuments. A sheet of paper is laid over the brass, held in position with adhesive tape and lightly pressed into the outlines of the design. The surface of the paper is rubbed with cobbler's heel ball or wax crayon. The wax adheres to the paper where the brass is raised and smooth, and the engraved areas of the design remain unwaxed. Some 7,000 monument brasses survive in British churches, principally in Kent and East Anglia.

Bratby, John (1928–), British painter and novelist, a member of the realist "kitchen sink" school of painting in the 1950s. His best-known novel is *Breakdown* (1960).

Bratislava, city in S central Czechoslovakia, on the River Danube, 48km (30 miles) E of Vienna; capital of Slovak SR. It became part of Hungary after the 13th century and of Czechoslovakia in 1918. It has an important refinery for oil from the USSR. Other industries: shipping and manufacturing. Pop. (1974) 328, 765.

Brattain, Walter Houser (1902–), US physicist. From 1929 he worked as a research physicist with the Bell Telephone Laboratories and concentrated on research into solid-state physics. In 1956, with John BARDEEN and William SHOCKLEY, he was awarded the Nobel Prize in physics for research into semiconductivity and the development of the transistor. In 1967 he became professor at Whitman College, Washington.

Brauchitsch, Heinrich Alfred Walther von (1881–1948), German field marshal. In 1939 he directed the occupation of Austria, Czechoslovakia and Poland. In 1941 he was relieved of his command by Adolf Hitler.

Braun, Eva (1912–45), mistress of Adolf HITLER. A photographer's assistant, she met Hitler in the early 1930 and lived with him for the rest of their lives. As far as is known, she never exercised any political influence. She and Hitler were married in Berlin the day before they committed suicide together.

Braun, Karl Ferdinand (1850–1918), German physicist. From 1895 he was professor of physics and director of the Physical Institute, Strasbourg. In 1897 he invented the oscilloscope – using a CATHODE RAY TUBE known as the Braun tube, the forerunner of the television tube. In 1909, with Guglielmo MARCONI, he shared the Nobel Prize in physics for the development of wireless telegraphy.

Braun, Wernher von (1912–77), US rocket engineer, *b.* Germany. By 1937 he was director of a rocket research station at Peenemünde, where he perfected the V-2 rocket missiles in the early 1940s. At the end of WWII he went to the USA, becoming a US citizen in 1955. In 1958 von Braun was largely responsible for launching the first US satellite, *Explorer I.* He later worked on the development of the *Saturn* rocket (for the Apollo programme) and was deputy associate administrator of NASA (1970–72).

Braunau, town in N Austria, on the River Inn, approx. 50 km. (31 miles) N of Salzburg. It has many old houses and churches and was the birth place of Adolf HITLER. Industries: aluminium processing, wood products. Pop. 16,400.

Brave New World (1932), satirical novel by Aldous HUXLEY. The novel presents a future totalitarian society with technologically developed leisure industries, genetic manipulation and sterile promiscuity.

Brazil, largest country of South America, a former Portuguese colony. Despite large and varied mineral deposits and the vast hardwood forests of the Amazon Basin, Brazil's economic development has been hampered by poor communications, little money and a lack of trained technologists. The largest manufacturing industry is the production of textiles; nearly half the population live off the land. The capital is BRASÍLIA. Area: 8,511,685sq km (3,286,365sq miles). Pop. (1976 est.) 109,181,000. *See* MW p.40.

Brazil current, warm current in the S Atlantic Ocean, and a branch of the S Equatorial current, which flows southwards along the E coast of South America. It forms part of the weak-flowing western boundary of the S Atlantic current gyre.

Brazil nut, seed of an evergreen tree which has leathery leaves and grows to 41m (135ft) tall. Its flowers produce a thick-walled fruit 10–30.5cm (4–12in) in diameter which contain 25–40 large seeds – the Brazil nut. Family Lecythidaceae; species *Bertholletia excelsa. See also* PE p.215.

Brazing, process in which metallic parts are joined by the fusion of alloys that have lower melting points than the parts themselves. The bonding alloy is either pre-placed or fed into the joint as the parts are heated. Brazed joints are very reliable and are used extensively in the aerospace industry. *See also* MM p.41.

Brazzaville, capital and largest city of the Congo, on the River Congo, below Stanley Pool. It was the former capital of French Equatorial Africa (1910–59). It is a major port, connected by rail to the main Atlantic seaport of Pointe-Noire. Industries: foundries, food processing. Pop. 289,700. *See also* MW p.60.

Breach of contract, in legal terms, when a party to a CONTRACT fails to perform in accordance with the terms of the contract. When one party breaches a contract, the other has the legal right to treat his own obligation under the contract as discharged. In addition, the innocent party has a right to damages or to demand compensatory action.

Breach of the peace, in law, disrupting public order either by an act of violence or by an act that would provoke violence. Riots and assaults are included in this type of offence.

Bread, staple food made by mixing wheat flour (containing a little yeast, salt and sugar) with water to make a spongy dough, allowing the yeast to ferment carbohydrates in the mixture (thus providing carbon dioxide gas which raises, or leavens, the bread), and finally baking the product to firmness in an oven. The yeast fermentation not only lightens the texture of the bread but also adds to its taste. Bicarbonate of soda ($NaHCO_3$) may be used instead of yeast. Unleavened bread, favoured in many Asian countries, is flat in shape and heavy-textured by comparison. *See also* PE pp.182–183.

Breadalbane, John Campbell, 1st Earl of (*c.* 1635–1717), Scottish leader. He assisted MONCK in the restoration of CHARLES II (1660) and helped to negotiate the submission of the Scottish chiefs to the Crown.

Breadfruit, the starchy fruit of a tree of the MULBERRY family native to SE Asia. The pulp is eaten fresh or cooked, or ground up and baked to made a bread. Genus *Atocarpus. See also* PE p.*195*.

Break-even analysis, in economics, a technique for determining at what point a company's costs equal its revenue.

Breaking and entering, in law, entry by forceable means either into a home or business with intent to commit a crime on the premises.

Breakspear, Nicholas. *See* ADRIAN (IV).

Bream, Julian Alexander (1933–), British guitarist and lutanist. He studied at the Royal College of Music 1945–48. An outstanding classical guitarist, he has transcribed lute music for the guitar.

Bream, freshwater fish of E and N Europe. Its stocky body is green-brown and silver, and anglers prize it for its tasty flesh. Length: 30–50cm (12–20in); weight: 4–6kg (9–13lb). Family Cyprinidae; species *Abramis brama. See also* NW p.*231*.

Breasley, Scobie (1914–), Australian jockey. He won more than 3,000 races in a career spanning 40 years – 18 of them in Britain, where he was champion jockey four times (1957, 1961, 1962 and 1963). He won four English CLASSICS, including the Derby twice – on *Santa Claus* in 1964 and on *Charlottown* in 1966. He also won Australia's Caulfield Cup five times, the Sydney Cup twice and the French Prix de l'Arc de Triomphe on *Ballymoss* (1958). He retired in 1968 and became a trainer.

Breast, or mammary gland, organ of a female mammal that secretes milk to nourish new-born young. In males the glands are rudimentary and non-functional. The human female breast, which develops during puberty, is made up of about 15–20 irregular-shaped lobes separated by connective and fat tissues. Lactiferous ducts lead from each lobe to the nipple, a small cone-shaped structure in the centre of the breast. *See also* MS pp.*61*, 76–77.

Breathing, in land animals, the use of the lungs for inhaling and exhaling air during respiration. When man and other mammals breathe, oxygen from the air passes into the blood through tiny air sacs in the lungs, which also remove carbon dioxide from the bloodstream. Respiratory movements of the lungs are partly consciously controlled by the brain but are also under unconscious control. Damage to the part of the brain concerned, the medulla, leads to death by asphyxiation. *See also* MS pp.66–67; NW pp.44–45, 75.

Brébeuf, St Jean de (1593–1649), French missionary in Canada. Ordained a Jesuit in 1623, Brébeuf travelled extensively after 1625 among the Huron Indians of Georgian Bay and Lake Huron. He was tortured to death by the Iroquois. His annual narratives are found in *The Jesuit Relations and Allied Documents* (1896–1901) by R. G. Thwaites.

Breccia, rock formed by the cementation of sharp-angled fragments in a finer matrix of the same or different material. Its origin varies: some is formed under the earth by movements of the crust, some from scree slopes, and some from volcanic material. *See also* CONGLOMERATE; PE pp.102–103.

Brecht, Bertolt (1898–1956), German dramatist. His notable works include *The Threepenny Opera* (with music by Kurt WEILL, 1928), *The Rise and Fall of the City of Mahagonny* (with music by Kurt Weill, 1930), *The Caucasian Chalk Circle* (1st version, with music by Paul DESSAU, 1948) and *The Resistible Rise of Arturo Ui* (published posthumously, 1957). After HITLER came to power in Germany in 1933, Brecht lived abroad, first in Scandinavia, then in the USA. In 1947 he returned to Europe, first to Switzerland, then to East Berlin. There he directed the Berliner Ensemble.

Brecknockshire (Breconshire or Brycheiniog), former county of SE Wales. Mountainous, with the Brecon Beacons reaching almost 886m (2,906ft), it is drained by the rivers Usk and Wye. Since 1974 it has been a part of Powys.

Breconshire. *See* BRECKNOCKSHIRE.

Breda, city in Noord-Brabant province, S Netherlands, 23km (14 miles) W of Tilburg on the River Merk. Being strategically positioned, it has often changed hands. The Compromise of Breda (1566), for example, concluded a Dutch rebellion against Spanish rule. Industries: engineering, textiles, food processing. Pop. 118,594.

Breda, Declaration of (1660), statement made by CHARLES II of England while in exile in Holland, promising religious toleration and an amnesty to former enemies of the Stuarts. He was thereupon invited to take the throne. *See also* HC1 p.298.

Breda, Treaty of (1667), peace agreement which ended the Second Anglo-Dutch War. Britain gave up its claim to the Dutch East Indies but gained control of New York and New Jersey.

Breech birth. *See* BIRTH, BREECH.

Breeder reactor, nuclear fission reactor in which more fissile material is produced than is consumed. In it, surplus high-energy neutrons transmute a "breeding blanket" of nonfissile Uranium-238 into fissile Plutonium-239. *See also* MM pp.74–75; SU p.65.

Breeding, science of changing or promoting certain GENETIC characteristics in animals or plants through careful selection and combination of the parent stock. Breeding may involve CROSS-BREEDING or INBREEDING to produce the desired characteristics in the offspring. Scientific breeding has resulted in disease-resistant strains of crops and in animals that give improved food yields. *See also* NW pp.30–31, PE pp.225, 227, 230–231.

Bremen, city in N West Germany, on the River Weser approx. 96km (60 miles) SW of Hamburg; capital of Bremen state and second-largest port in West Germany. The city suffered severe damage during WWII, but many of its original buildings, including the Gothic city hall, survived. Industries: shipbuilding, electrical equipment, textiles, food processing. Pop. (1974) 584,265.

Bremerhaven, seaport city in Bremen state, N West Germany, at the mouth of the River Weser, 56km (35 miles) N of Bremen. Founded in 1827, it became an important emigrant port in the late 19th and early 20th centuries. Today it is West Germany's largest fishing port. Other industries: shipbuilding, engineering. Pop. (1969 est.) 149,250.

Bremsstrahlung, electromagnetic radiation with a continuous range of energies, in the X-RAY wavelength region of the ELECTROMAGNETIC SPECTRUM. It is emitted when high-speed electrons decelerate on passing close to a positively-charged nucleus. It takes its energy from the electron's lost KINETIC ENERGY.

Brendan, Saint (*c.* 484–577), also known as St Brenainn. He was Abbot of Clonfert in County Galway, Ireland. A legend popular in the Middle Ages described his visit to the "northern and western islands", probably the Orkneys and Hebrides or possibly Iceland, Greenland and even North America. In 1977 a group of men sailed a leather boat (of the type used in St Brendan's time) along that route to North America, so proving the possibility of such a journey.

Brendel, Alfred (1931–), Moravia-born pianist. One of the world's most critically acclaimed and widely travelled concert artists, he is especially noted for his interpretation of Beethoven and of Schubert.

Bren gun, air-cooled light MACHINE GUN. It was once highly regarded, issued to nearly all the Allied armies, and is the best-known machine gun of WWII; one of the later models is still in use today. Mounted on a bipod and fed from a 28-round magazine, it is capable of short accurate bursts of fire at a rate of more than 500 rounds per minute. *See also* MM p.*165*.

Brennan, Christopher John (1870–1932), Australian poet. Although he wrote lyrical verse, most of his output was abstract and highly symbolic, and dealt with universal, rather than narrowly Australian, themes

Brenner Pass, lowest of the main Alpine passes, it connects Bolzano in Italy with Innsbruck in Austria; an important Roman invasion route. The first trans-alpine road was built over it in 1772, and a railway in 1867. Height: 1,370m (4,495ft); length: 95km (59 miles).

Brentano, Clemens (1778–1842), German poet, novelist and dramatist. While a student in Heidelberg he founded with his brother-in-law, Achim von Arnim, a school of Romantics devoted to the study of German folklore. *Des Knaben Wunderhorn* (1805–08) and *Godwi* (1801) are among his best works.

Brentano, Franz (1838–1917), German philosopher. He classified psychic phenomena according to "acts" and "intentions". His notion of psychology as an analysis of behaviour is explored in *Psychology from an Empirical Standpoint* (1874) and *Inquiry into Sense Psychology* (1907).

Brentano, Lujo (1844–1931), German political economist. In 1868 he made a thorough study of trade unionism in England and wrote *Die Arbeitergilden der Gegenwart* (1871–72), in which he linked modern trade unions to medieval guilds. From 1871 he was professor at various German and Austrian universities including Munich. He was a pacifist and opposed the rise of German militarism. In 1927 he was awarded the Nobel Peace Prize.

Brent goose, small, dark-coloured wild goose that lives in Europe and North America. It is also called brant goose and is closely related to the barnacle goose.

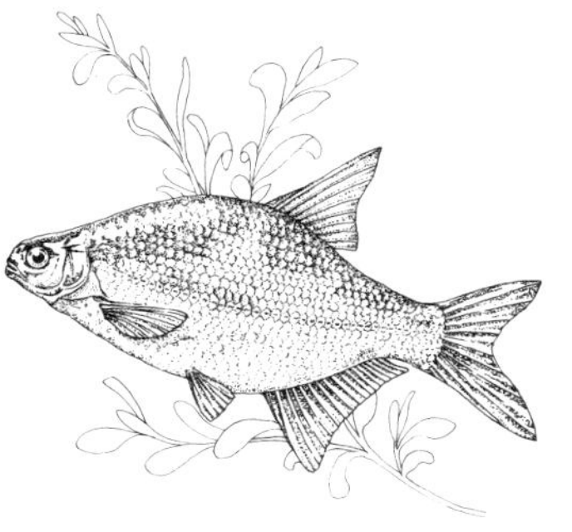

Bream, the carp-like freshwater fish prized by anglers for their extremely tasty flesh.

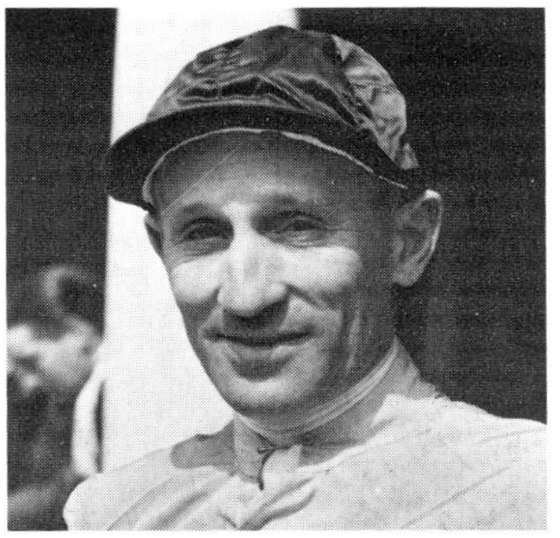

Scobie Breasly, champion jockey four times and winner of the Derby in 1964 and 1966.

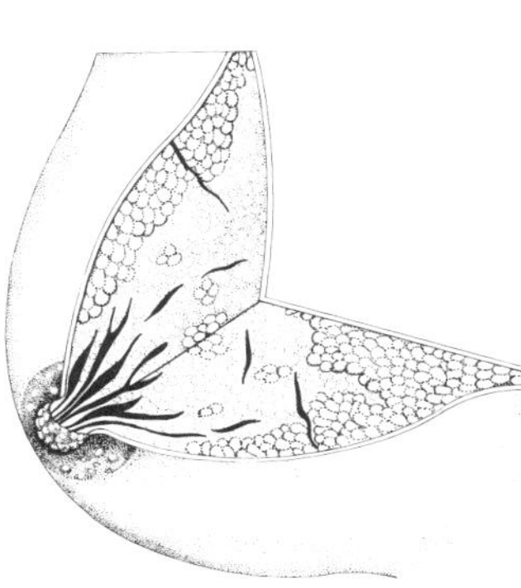

Breasts of female mammals secrete milk to nourish the new-born young.

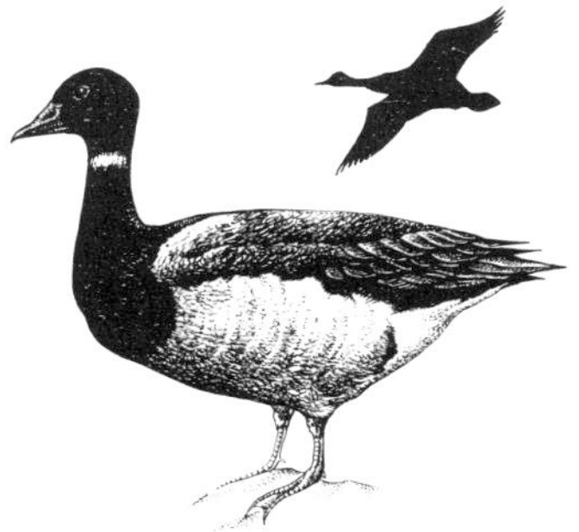

Brent geese, the wild sea geese usually found near salt water, do not fly in a V formation.

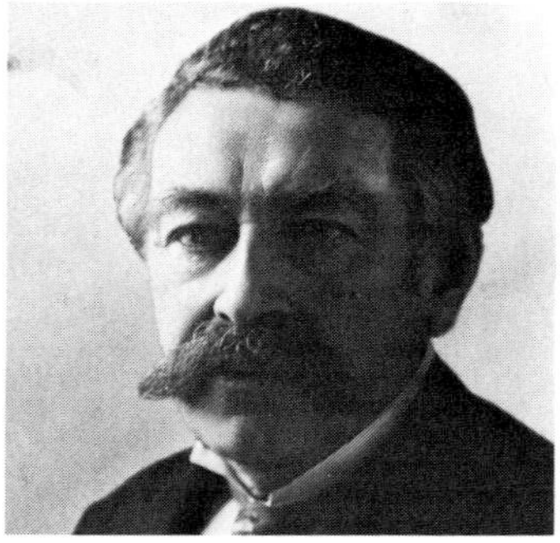

Aristide Briand was a socialist politician who served 11 times as the premier of France.

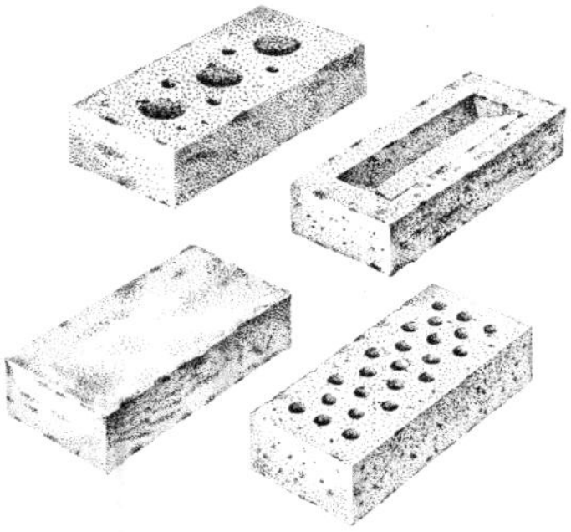

Bricks used in building must resist fire and frost, and bond well with the mortar.

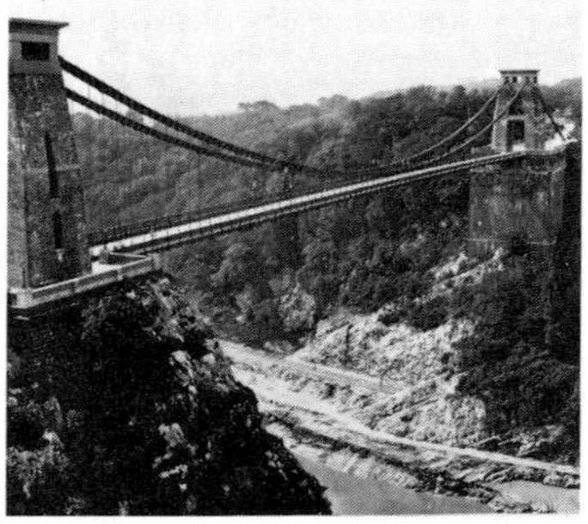

Bridges of all kinds span obstacles the world over. This is the Clifton Suspension Bridge.

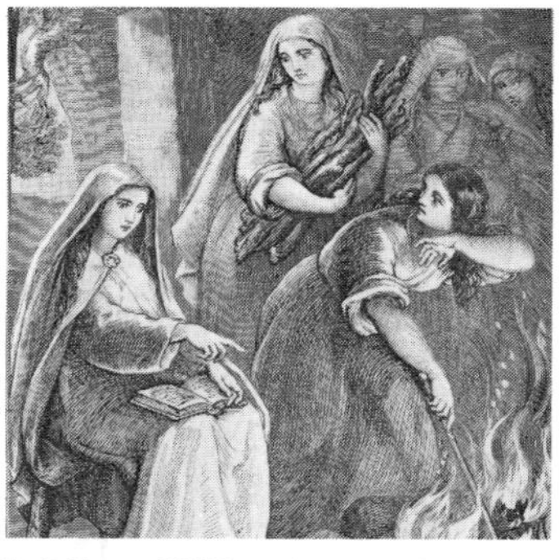

St Bridget of Kildare, the beautiful woman whose prayer to be ugly was answered.

Species *Branta bernicla. See also* NW pp. *227*, 235.

Brescia, city in N Italy, in Lombardy region; capital of Brescia province. The city was sacked by ATTILA in 452, and it repeatedly changed rulers, passing to Austria in 1815 and joining Italy in 1860. The city's many art treasures include the Roman bronze *Winged Victory*. It also has the 13th-century Broletto and the Loggia (15th-16th century). A transport and agricultural trade centre, it has iron and steel, aerospace engineering and textile industries. Pop. (1970) 210,000.

Breslau. *See* WROCLAW.

Brest, city and port in Brittany, W France. An important naval base, the town was severely damaged in WWII. Industries now include shipbuilding and repair, chemical manufacture, and trade in wine, fruit, coal and timber. Pop. (1971 est.) 163,800. *See also* HC2 p.*44*, 45.

Brest-Litovsk, Treaty of (Feb.-March 1918), treaty between Russia and the CENTRAL POWERS that ended WWI for Russia. Under its provisions, the Ukraine and Georgia were made independent, Russian power was reduced in Poland and the Baltic, and much of BELORUSSIA given up to Germany and Austria-Hungary. The treaty, which was declared void later in 1918, was negotiated by TROTSKY for the Russian BOLSHEVIKS, who had promised to take Russia out of the war at any diplomatic cost. *See also* HC2 p.196.

Brétigny, Peace of (1360), treaty between England and France during the HUNDRED YEARS WAR. Edward III of England abandoned his claim to the French throne, in return for which his large territorial holdings in SW France were freed from French sovereignty. The treaty, which was never ratified, was followed by the Treaty of Calais, but war was soon resumed. *See also* HC1 p.212.

Breton, André (1896–1966), French poet and theorist. A founder of the SURREALIST movement, he wrote *Manifeste du surréalisme* (1924) and *Le Surréalisme et la peinture* (1928). His fictional works, including a partly autobiographical novel *Nadja* (1928), *Les vases communicants* (1932), *L'Amour fou* (1937) and *Poèmes* (1948), reflect Surrealist theories.

Breton, Celtic language spoken in Brittany, on the NW coast of France. It is a descendant of British, an old Celtic language, and is closely related to Welsh. Its one million users usually also speak French, which is rapidly replacing it.

Bretton Woods Conference, United Nations' Monetary and Financial Conference meeting at Bretton Woods, New Hampshire, USA in July 1944. The representatives of the 44 United Nations agreed to establish the International Monetary Fund and the International Bank for Reconstruction and Development, which were ratified by Dec. 1945. *See also* MS p.316; HC2 p.300.

Breuer, Josef (1842–1925), Austrian physiologist and associate of Sigmund FREUD. Breuer's discovery that under hypnosis some neurotic patients reveal unconscious feelings and their symptoms disappear became basic to the psychoanalytic movement, and inspired Freud to pursue further his researches into the unconscious.

Breuer, Marcel (1902–), US architect, *b.* Hungary. He studied and taught at the BAUHAUS (1920–28), where he designed his famous tubular steel chair. He designed the UNESCO building in Paris (with Pier Nervi and Bernard Zehrfuss 1953–58) and the Whitney Museum of American Art in New York City (1966).

Breuil, Henri-Édouard-Prosper (1877–1961), French priest and archaeologist; a notable authority on palaeolithic art. His discovery of cave paintings at Les Eyzies in the Dordogne region of SW France led to the authentication of others at La Mouthe in the same region, and also of those at Altamira in N Spain. *See also* HC1 p.24–25.

Breviary, liturgical book containing prayers, psalms, hymns and scriptural lessons, required to be recited by Roman Catholic priests at specific hours of the day.

Brewer, E. Cobham (1810–97), British clergyman and writer, whose best known work is his *Dictionary of Phrase and Fable* (1870).

Brewing, the preparation of beer and stout by the alcoholic fermentation by yeast of liquors containing malt and hops. The making of vinegar and acid sauces by a further process of fermentation to yield acetic acid is sometimes also called brewing. In beer brewing, a malt liquor (wort) is made from crushed germinated barley grains. Hops are added to the boiling wort both to impart an attractive, bitter flavour, and also to help to clarify the beer and keep it free from spoilage microbes. The clear, filtered wort is cooled and inoculated with brewer's yeast, which then ferments part of the sugar from the malt to alcohol. *See also* PE pp.204–205.

Brewster, Sir David (1781–1868), Scottish physicist who performed significant experiments in OPTICS and POLARIZED LIGHT. He discovered Brewster's law, which relates the polarizing angle (the angle at which light strikes a substance) to the refractive index of the substance.

Brewster, William (1567–1644), English religious leader, signatory of the Mayflower Compact. He withdrew from the Anglican Church in 1606, formed the Separatists and with them fled from persecution in England to Holland, where they became known as Pilgrims. He helped to organize the Pilgrim migration to America and became a leader of the church in PLYMOUTH COLONY.

Brezhnev, Leonid Ilyich (1906–), Soviet political leader. In 1952 he became secretary to the central committee of the Soviet Communist Party. In 1957 he became a member of the presidium (later politburo) of the central committee. He helped to plan the downfall of Nikita KHRUSHCHEV in 1964 and soon emerged as one of the two chief rulers of the USSR, sharing power with Alexei KOSYGIN. Brezhnev was named First Secretary and Kosygin became Premier. By the late 1960s, Brezhnev was acknowledged as the sole ruler, although Kosygin remained as premier. *See also* HC2 p.*241*.

Brian Boru. *See* BORU, BRIAN.

Brian, William Havergal (1876–1972), British composer. Despite poverty and, until his last years, an indifferent public, he devoted most of his life to composition. His 33 symphonies make him the most prolific symphonist since Haydn; he also wrote five operas, choral works and more than 100 songs. Most of his music is complex and often requires large groups.

Briand, Aristide (1862–1932), French radical and socialist politician. He was prime minister in 1909–11, 1913, 1915–17, 1921–22, 1925–26 and 1929. In 1904 he founded *L'Humanité* with Jean JAURÈS. He is best known for his advocacy of international co-operation in the interwar years, one of the fruits of which was the KELLOGG-BRIAND PACT (1928). He shared the Nobel Peace Prize in 1926 with Gustav STRESEMANN.

Briar, wild rose or any other prickly bush of the ROSE family; also the smoking pipe made from the root of an unrelated plant, the tree heath (genus *Erica*).

Briard, breed of working DOG, French in origin, originally used to herd sheep, now used also as a police dog. It has a long, wavy coat of a solid colour, usually black, grey or tawny. Height: 22–27in (60–69cm); weight: 70–80lb (32–36kg).

Bribri, Talamancan-speaking tribe of American Indians who live on the border of Costa Rica and Panama. They provide the main link between pre-Columbian and contemporary Indian customs. Pop. approx. 900.

Brick, hardened block of clay used for building and paving. Usually rectangular, bricks are made in standard sizes by machines that either mould bricks or cut off extruded sections of stiff clay which are conveyed into a continuously operating kiln. The first, sun-dried bricks were used in the Tigris-Euphrates basin about 5,000 years ago. Mechanized processes replaced the old hand-moulding methods during the 19th century. *See also* MM pp.46–47.

Bride price, recompense made at the time of marriage by the husband or his family to that of the wife in compensation for her leaving their family. Widespread among African tribes, bride price is usually paid in the form of property, but is sometimes rendered in months or even years of labour by the husband to his wife's family. *See also* DOWRY.

Brideshead Revisited, novel by Evelyn WAUGH, first published in 1945. Considered by many to be his masterpiece, it traces the effect of declining fortunes on the faith of the various members of a wealthy Roman Catholic family.

Bridge, Frank (1879–1941), British composer and conductor. He was a pupil of STANFORD. His best works were written for voice or chamber groups. He is best remembered by a work of his pupil, Benjamin BRITTEN, *Variations on a Theme of Frank Bridge*.

Bridge, structure providing a continuous passage over a body of water, roadway or valley for man, vehicles, pipelines or power transmission lines. Bridges are prehistoric in origin, the first probably being merely logs over rivers or chasms. Modern bridges take a great variety of forms – movable bridges, pontoon bridges, overpasses, causeways, aqueducts, suspension bridges and cantilever bridges. *See also* MM pp.190–193.

Bridge. *See* AUCTION BRIDGE; CONTRACT BRIDGE.

Bridge, in dentistry, a partial denture held in place by anchorage to adjacent teeth. Depending on the situation it may be permanently installed or removable; anchorages are of various sorts. Usually, only one or a few teeth in a series are artificially replaced in this manner. *See also* MS p.130.

Bridge of San Luis Rey, The, novel by Thornton WILDER, first published in 1927. The book tells of five people who plunged to their deaths off a collapsing footbridge in Peru and then skilfully recounts the events leading up to their presence on the bridge. Wilder won one of his three PULITZER PRIZES for this novel.

Bridge on the River Kwai, The (1957), English film. Adapted by Carl Foreman from Pierre BOULLE's novel about prisoners of war building the Burma railway during WWII, it was directed by David LEAN and starred Alec GUINNESS and Sessue Hayakawa.

Bridges, Calvin Blackman (1889–1938), US geneticist. He helped to prove the chromosomal basis of heredity and sex. His work with Thomas Hunt MORGAN on the fruit fly (*Drosophila*) proved that inheritable variations could be traced to observable changes in the chromosomes. These experiments resulted in the construction of "gene maps", which proved the chromosome theory of heredity.

Bridges, Robert Seymour (1844–1930), British poet. He practised medicine before turning to full-time writing in 1882. Numerous volumes appeared, but worldwide recognition did not come until his *Poetical Works* were published in 1912, the year before he was appointed Poet Laureate. His philosophical poem *The Testament of Beauty* appeared in 1929.

Bridget of Kildare, Saint (*c*.452–523), also known as St Brigid, St Bride or St Bridget, founder of a great monastery in Kildare. She is one of the patron saints of Ireland. Feast day: 1 Feb.

Bridget of Sweden, Saint (*c*.1303–1373), one of the great saints of Scandinavia. A noblewoman at court, she became a nun after her husband's death and founded a religious order known as the Brigittines. She went to Rome in 1349 and devoted herself to the reform of religious life in Italy. She is the patron saint of Sweden. Feast: 23 July.

Bridgetown, capital and chief port of Barbados. Founded in 1628, it is the seat of the Parliament and has a constituent college of the University of the West Indies. Industries: rum distilling, sugar processing. Pop. (1970 est.) 8,800.

Bridgewater, Francis Egerton, 3rd Duke of (1736–1803), British canal builder. In 1760, with the engineer James BRINDLEY, he built England's first canal from his collieries at Worsley, Lancashire, to Manchester and subsequently to Runcorn on the River Mersey.

Bridgman, Percy Williams (1882–1961), US physicist. From 1919 he was a professor at Harvard University. He was awarded the 1946 Nobel Prize in physics for his work in high-pressure physics. He is known also for his work on crystal properties and for his writings on the philosophy of science. His books include *The Nature of Modern Physics* (1927); his collected papers were published in 1964.

Bridie, James (1888–1951), Scottish dramatist and doctor, real name Osborne Henry Mavor. His first major London success was *The Anatomist* (1931). His later plays included *Mr Bolfry* (1943), *Daphne Laureola* (1949) and *The Queen's Comedy* (1950). He was one of the founders of the Glasgow Citizens Theatre.

Brie, region in the Marne and Seine-et-Marne départements of N France, E of Paris. This fertile agricultural area, with its large imposing farmhouses, is famous for its vineyards and for Brie cheese.

Brief, in English law, document prepared by a solicitor setting out his client's case for the benefit of counsel. The information contained in the brief will form the basis of the advocate's legal argument and influence his strategy in court.

Brig, two-masted sailing vessel, square-rigged on both masts and with fore-and-aft stay sails. Brigs were used commercially from about 1700 until 1860 as cargo ships and as small, fast warships with about ten guns. They needed large crews. Length: 27–30m (90–100ft); displacement; up to 350 tonnes. *See also* MM p.*113*.

Brigantine, sailing ship in use from the 18th-20th century. It has two masts with mainsails and staysails on the mainmast, and a square rig on the foremast. *See also* MM p.*113*.

Briggs, Barry (1934–), New Zealand speedway rider. World champion four times (1957, 1958, 1964, 1966), he accumulated more than 200 points in a record 18 appearances in finals. He went to England at age 17 and rode for Wimbledon, New Cross, Southampton and Swindon.

Briggs, Henry (1561–1630), English mathematician who introduced common LOGARITHMS. In 1614, with John NAPIER's agreement, he suggested that Napier's logarithms be altered to a base of 10. In 1624 he p ıblished *Arithmetica Logarithmica. See also* SU pp.38–39.

Bright, Sir Charles Tilston (1832–88), British engineer who helped to develop submarine telegraph cables. In 1856 he became engineer-in-chief of the Atlantic Telegraph Co. and in 1858 supervised the laying of the first transatlantic cable from Ireland to Newfoundland. With the engineer Joseph Clark he also invented an asphalt covering for submarine cables.

Bright, John (1811–89), British politician and parliamentary reformer. With Richard COBDEN he founded the ANTI-CORN LAW LEAGUE (1839). A Member of Parliament (1843–57) he lost his seat because of his opposition to the CRIMEAN WAR but was re-elected the following year and sat until 1889. *See also* HC2 pp.*96, 182*.

Bright, Richard (1789–1858), British physician who was the first to describe the kidney disorder sometimes called BRIGHT's DISEASE. He graduated in Edinburgh in 1813 and became a physician at Guy's Hospital, London, in 1820.

Brightener, substance added to detergents to whiten fabrics. Optical brighteners are left in the fibres where they absorb ultra-violet light. The excited molecules later re-emit a faint blue light, which counteracts the yellowish caste developed by white fabrics. An older method was to use blue dye. *See also* MM pp.240–241.

Brighton, resort town in East Sussex, S England, on the English Channel, 80km (50 miles) S of London. Originally a fishing village, it was popularized as a resort by the Prince Regent (GEORGE IV) who had the Royal Pavilion rebuilt there in oriental style (1817), and by Dr Russell, who advocated sea-bathing. It is the seat of the University of Sussex. Industries: food processing, shoes, paint, tourism. Pop. (1971 prelim.) 166,000.

Bright's disease, term, no longer in widespread use, describing any of several kidney diseases characterized by albumin in urine. *See also* NEPHRITIS; MS p.102.

Brill, flatfish similar to and related to the TURBOT. Species *Scophthalmus rhombus*.

Brillat-Savarin, Jean-Anthelme (1755–1826), French author on gastronomy. He was a member of the National Assembly in the French Revolution and wrote *Physiologie du goût* (1825), an amusing book about eating.

Brindley, James (1716–72), British engineer and pioneer canal-builder who constructed the first economically viable major canal in England, from Worsley, Lancashire to Manchester. He was eventually responsible for a network of about 565km (350 miles) of canals, an advancement which helped to hasten the INDUSTRIAL REVOLUTION. None of his written records or working drawings has survived.

Brinell, Johann August (1849–1925), Swedish metallurgist who devised a safe rapid test to determine the hardness of metals, which was first exhibited in Paris in 1900. It involves the measurement of the indentation made by a hardened steel ball after it has been pressed into the metal with predetermined force. A version of the test is still in use today.

Brisbane, Sir Thomas Makdougall (1773–1860). British astronomer and colonial administrator. He was Governor of New South Wales (1821–25) and helped to develop the colony's economy. He founded observatories in Sydney in 1822 and in Scotland in 1841. Brisbane, Australia, is named after him.

Brisbane, seaport city in E Australia, on the Brisbane River. First settled in 1824, it became capital of Queensland in 1859. It is the location of Parliament House (1869) and the University of Queensland (1909) and is a major shipping and rail centre. Industries: oil refining, shipbuilding, car assembly, railway engineering, chemicals. Pop. (1976 est.) 911,000. *See also* MW p.34.

Brissot de Warville, Jacques Pierre (1754–93), French revolutionary. He founded the *Amis des Noirs*, a society for the abolition of slave trade, and edited the paper *Patriote Français*, which became the Girondist publication when he aligned himself with the GIRONDINS. He was executed following the war with Austria.

Bristleworm. *See* RAGWORM.

Bristol, university city in the county of Avon, England, on the River Avon, 11km (7 miles) from the Bristol Channel. An important seaport since the 12th century, it is the location of BRUNEL's Clifton Suspension Bridge (1864). The main port facilities are now at Avonmouth. Industries: aircraft engineering, chemicals, tobacco, food processing. Pop. (1971) 425,200.

Bristol Channel, inlet of the Atlantic Ocean that extends 137km (85 miles) between S Wales and SW England, narrowing from 69km (43 miles) to 8km (5 miles). Its northern (Welsh) shore is highly industrialized, its southern shore agricultural.

Britain, Ancient, the period of British history from the cutting of the land bridge to Europe in *c.*5500 BC to the Roman invasion of 55 BC. It covers four ages of social development: MESOLITHIC (middle stone age), NEOLITHIC (new stone age), BRONZE and IRON ages. At the end of the period Britain was culturally and economically greatly inferior to its Roman conquerors. *See also* HC1 pp.42–43, 84–85.

Britain, Battle of, (July–Oct. 1940), series of air battles fought over Britain during WWII between the German LUFTWAFFE and the ROYAL AIR FORCE (RAF). The Germans hoped to destroy Britain's industry and military installations and shatter civilian morale by bombing, as a prelude to invasion. Although outnumbered, the defending RAF fighter pilots inflicted such heavy losses that the strategy was abandoned. *See also* HC2 pp.228, 230.

Britannia, Roman name for the province of Britain before the Saxon period, and later a female personification of Britain or the British Empire, usually represented on coins as a woman seated on a rock or a globe, with standard, spear, sceptre or trident, and a shield.

Britannia metal, tin alloy used for tableware, similar to pewter but containing approx. 7% antimony, 2% copper but no lead. It is a lustrous, hard, malleable alloy that is easy to cast.

British Airways, company formed in 1974 from the merger of BOAC, BEA and their subsidiary companies. In 1976–77 it flew 30,143 million passenger-km and 716 million freight-tonne-km and employed more than 59,000 people.

British American Tobacco Company, formed in 1902, is today among the largest British-based enterprises. In the mid-1970s it employed more than 230,000 people in various countries and dealt mainly in tobacco, paper and cosmetics.

British Antarctic Territory, British colony in Antarctica comprising the mainland and islands within a triangular area bounded by latitude 60° S and longitudes 20° and 80° W. It includes the South Shetland Islands, South Orkney Islands and Graham Land. Formerly part of the Falkland Islands, the territory became a British Crown colony in 1962, although today Argentina and Chile claim parts of it. There are no permanent settlements, but teams of scientists man the meteorological stations and other establishments of the British Antarctic Survey. Area: 1,725,000sq km (666,000sq miles).

British Association for the Advancement of Science, organization founded in 1831 for furthering the sciences and bringing them to the attention of the general public. Each year it holds a conference in a different university town, which is the major gathering where all branches of science are brought together.

British Broadcasting Corporation. *See* BBC.

British Cameroon, former region of W Africa. Once a German protectorate, it came under the League of Nations in 1922 and then under the United Nations before its northern and southern peoples voted (1961) to join Nigeria and Cameroon.

British Columbia, province of W Canada, on the Pacific coast, bounded by the USA to the N (Alaska) and S. The Rocky Mts run N to S through the province. The many rivers, principal of which is the Fraser, provide abundant hydroelectric power. Three-quarters of the land is forested, making timber an important industry. Mineral deposits include copper, silver, gold, lead, zinc and asbestos. Dairying and fruit growing are the chief farming activities, practised mainly in the S. Industries include fishing, paper making, tourism, transport equipment, chemicals and food processing. The chief cities are Victoria (the capital) and Vancouver.

The region was first sighted by Sir Francis DRAKE in 1578; Capt. James COOK landed there in 1778, and George VANCOUVER took possession of the island that bears his name for Britain in 1794. The two areas of Vancouver Island and New Caledonia were united as British Columbia in 1866 and admitted to the Canadian Confederation in 1871. Completion of the CANADIAN PACIFIC RAILWAY in 1885 spurred the development of the province. Area: 948,600sq km (366,255sq miles). Pop. (1971) 2,184,621. *See also* MW p.45.

British Commonwealth of Nations. *See* COMMONWEALTH OF NATIONS; HC2 pp.220–221.

British Council, organization that promotes the teaching of English overseas and arranges for the exchange of cultural and scientific missions between Britain and other countries. It offers a number of annual postgraduate scholarships for overseas scholars in Britain and maintains numerous libraries abroad. Founded in 1934, it is financed from public funds.

British East Africa, former name of the African countries of Kenya, Tanganyika, Uganda, and Zanzibar (now united with Tanganyika as Tanzania), which were once all united as part of the British Empire.

British Empire, overseas territories ruled by Britain, originating in the activities of

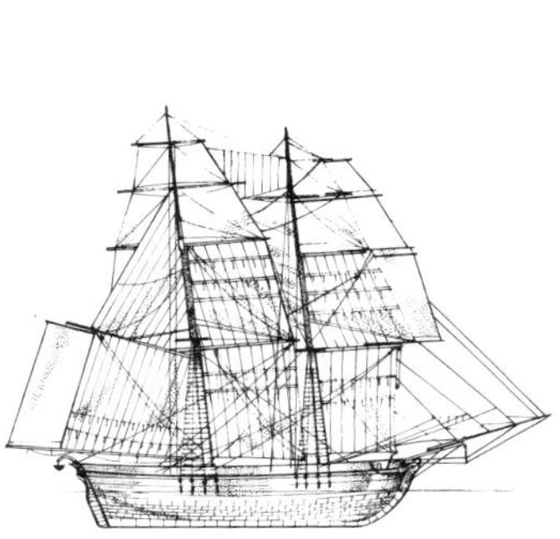

Brig, the speedy, two-masted sailing ship used for carrying cargo and as a warship.

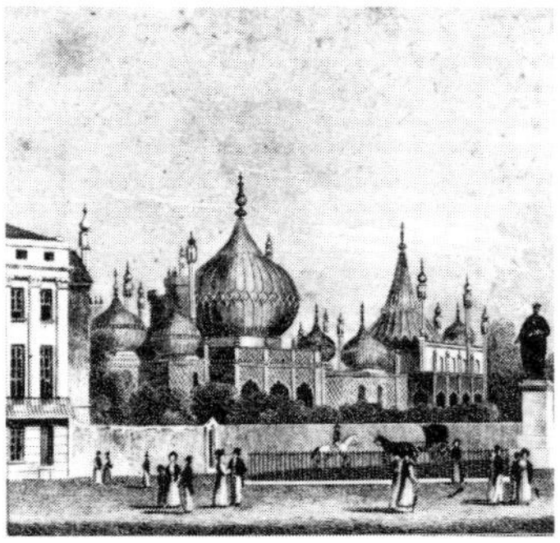

Brighton Pavilion, built for the Prince Regent in Italian style with a Chinese interior.

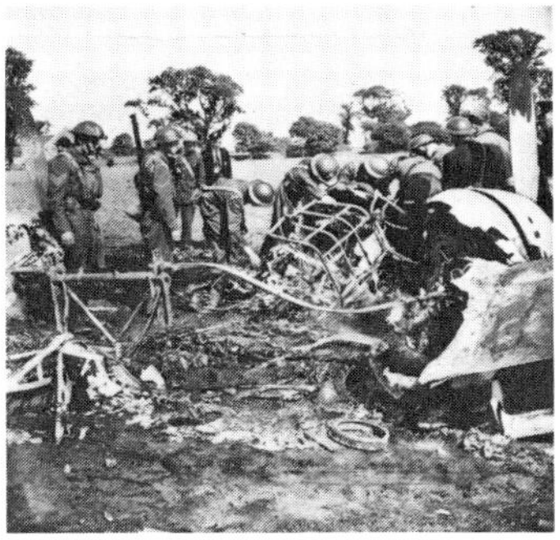

Battle of Britain; soldiers inspecting the wreckage of a Messerschmidt 110.

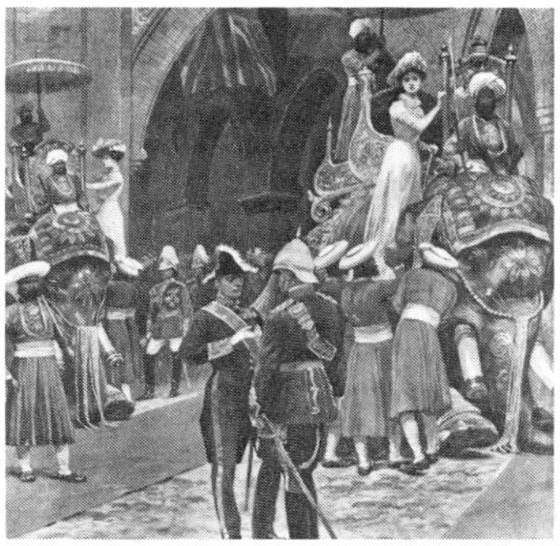

British Empire; ruling dignitaries about to mount their state elephant in Delhi 1902.

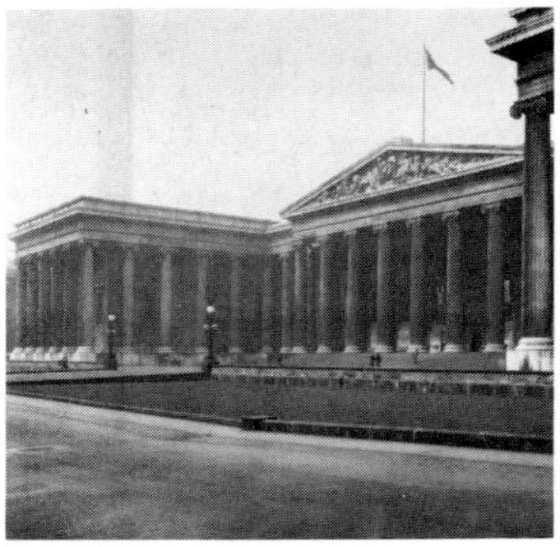

British Museum; the building opened in 1847 on the site of the old Montagu House.

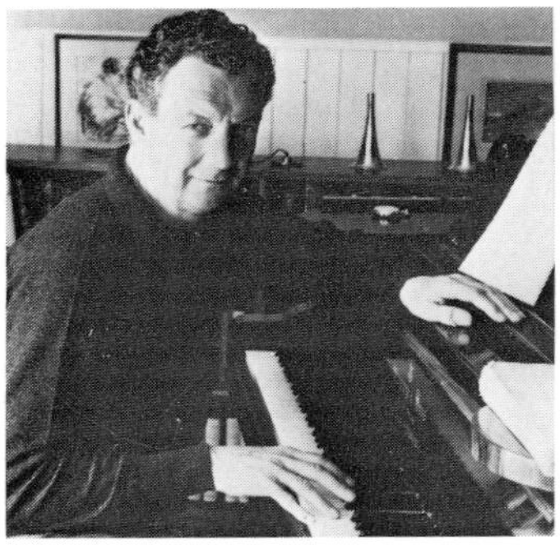

Benjamin Britten, famous for his operas, wrote much of his music to interest children.

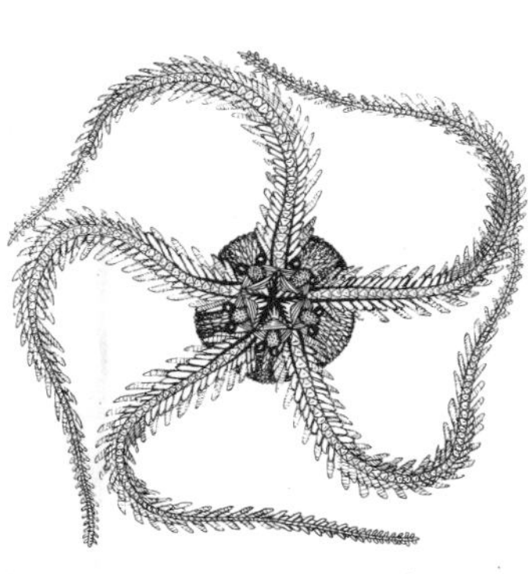

Brittle stars can grow new arms if they lose one through being handled or disturbed.

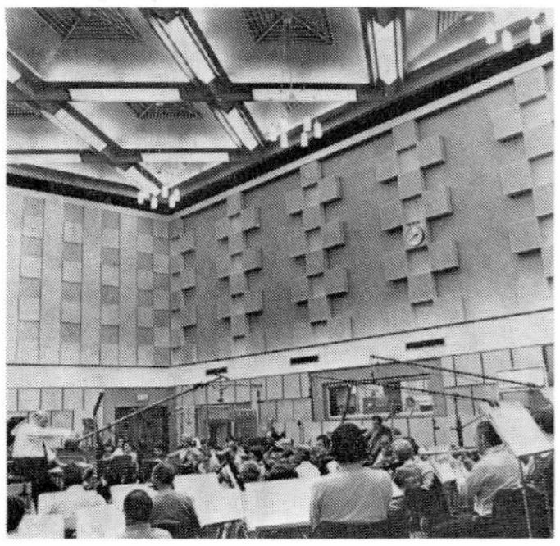

Broadcasting from the BBC's main radio orchestra studio at Pebble Mill, Birmingham.

the 16th-century trading companies. The first empire, centred on the N Atlantic, was ended by the independence of the American colonies by 1783. The second empire, won mainly in the 19th century, was more widespread and by 1914 covered about 25% of the land surface of the earth. By 1970 most of the empire had been granted independence. *See also* relevant articles in HC1; HC2.

British Empire, Order of the, military and civil order or knighthood bestowed as a reward for public service to the COMMONWEALTH OF NATIONS. Created in 1917, it has five different classes for men and women: Knights (or Dames) Grand Cross, Knights (or Dames) Commander, Commanders, Officers and Members.

British Expeditionary Force (BEF), the original British Army in both WWI and WWII. The BEF in WWI, under General Sir John French (later Earl of YPRES), originally comprised six divisions but grew into an army of more than one million men; in WWII the 13-division army in France was evacuated from DUNKIRK in 1940. *See also* HC2 pp.188–191; 228–231.

British Film Institute, organization founded in 1933, originally having a strong bias towards educational films. Its Information Department and Book Library now contains one of the largest collections of printed material on films in the world. Its own cinema, the NATIONAL FILM THEATREχ WAS ESTABLISHED IN αδθατϖ

British Guiana. *See* GUYANA.

British Honduras. *See* BELIZE.

British Indian Ocean Territory, island colony in Indian Ocean. *See* MW p.41.

British Isles, group of islands off the NW coast of Europe, made up of the United Kingdom of Great Britain and Northern Ireland, and Eire. It includes England, Scotland and Wales on the island of Great Britain; Northern Ireland and Eire on the island of Ireland; the Isle of Man in the Irish Sea, a self-governing island but part of the UK; and the Channel Islands in the English Channel, which are also self-governing but a dependency of the British Crown. *See* MW pp.68, 102, 136, 150, 174, 182.

British Legion, organization of ex-service men and women for helping disabled and unemployed war veterans, their widows and families. Founded in 1921 by Earl Haig, the Legion adopted the Flanders poppy as its emblem. Each year during the week preceding Remembrance Day (the Sunday nearest to 11 Nov.) millions of artificial poppies (made by disabled Legion members) are sold to commemorate the dead of two world wars and raise funds for the Legion.

British Lion, production-distribution company founded in 1927 and incorporated as British Lion Film Corporation. London Films acquired control of the company in 1946 and Alexander KORDA ran the Shepperton studios, although by 1954 losses forced its closure. A new company, British Lion Films Ltd., was formed a year later and was for a time run by Sir Michael Balcon. It was taken over by Barclay Securities in 1972. It merged with EMI in 1976.

British Lions, name of the British Isles Rugby Union team, a touring side composed of players from England, Scotland, Wales and Ireland (joint). Their first tour was in 1888; the name was coined in 1924 from the symbol on the official tie.

British Medical Association (BMA), professional body founded in 1832; two-thirds of all doctors in Britain are members. The BMA was set up originally to advance the medical sciences. Since the establishment of the NATIONAL HEALTH SERVICE in 1948 it has also negotiated over pay and conditions for hospital doctors and general practitioners.

British Museum, established by an Act of Parliament as a storehouse of knowledge for the benefit of the "learned and curious", was opened in London in 1759. The original collection was purchased (1753) by Sir Hans SLOANE. Later additions included the ROSETTA STONE and the ELGIN MARBLES. The Museum's departments include the Museum of Mankind and the Department of Prints and Drawings, which houses 20,000 drawings by Turner in addition to works by Rembrandt, Rubens, Michelangelo, Dürer and others.

British North America Act (1867), legislation of the British Parliament that created the Dominion of Canada from the provinces of Nova Scotia, New Brunswick and Canada. The Act provided for a Constitution similar to that of Britain, a bicameral Parliament, the re-establishment of Ontario and Quebec as separate provinces and a legal system for Canada. *See also* MW p.49.

British Petroleum Company, international corporation, based in Britain, that drills for oil and produces petroleum products and chemicals. It employs about 78,000 people throughout the world. BP was the first company to strike oil in Britain's prospecting area of the North Sea.

British Solomon Islands, self-governing protectorate in SW Pacific Ocean, 850km (530 miles) E of New Guinea. The main island is Guadalcanal, which has the capital (Honiara). The protectorate was formed in 1898. The chief product is copra. Area: 29,800sq km (11,505sq miles). Pop. (1975 est.) 190,000. *See also* MW p.41.

British Standards Institute (BSI), the recognized body in Britain for the harmonization of technical standards for education and industry. Its scope includes the publication of glossaries of terms, definitions, quantities, units and symbols, test methods and specifications for quality, safety, performance and codes of practice. It certifies and approves manufactured products that comply with its standards.

British Steel Corporation, British company re-nationalized in 1967 from 13 steel companies. It undertakes exploration, mining and processing of more than 90% of the nation's crude iron and steel. *See also* MM pp.30–31.

British Summer Time (BST). *See* SUMMER TIME.

British thermal unit (BTU), the amount of heat energy necessary to raise the temperature of a pound of water from 59.5°F to 60.5°F. One BTU is the equivalent of 778.3 foot-pounds, 252 CALORIES or 1,055 JOULES. It has been largely superseded by the metric system.

British Virgin Islands, British colony in the West Indies; part of the Lesser Antilles group between the Caribbean Sea and the Atlantic Ocean. The colony comprises 36 islands, the chief ones being Tortola, which has the capital (Road Town), Anngada and Virgin Gorda. The main economic activities are tourism, fishing and farming. Area: 155sq km (60sq miles). Pop. (1975 est.) 11,000. *See also* MW p.41.

Brittain, Vera Mary (*c*.1893–1970), British writer and lecturer. During WWI she worked as a nurse, and in 1933 wrote *Testament of Youth*, which was based on her war experiences. She toured the USA on several occasions giving lectures.

Brittany (Bretagne), region and former duchy and province in NW France, on the peninsula between the Bay of Biscay and the English Channel. Under Roman rule from 56 BC to the 5th century, it was then settled by Celtic Britons who gave it its name, its language (BRETON) and its distinctive costume and culture. England and France hotly disputed its possession until 1532, when it became part of France. Industries: tourism, farming, fishing.

Britten, Edward Benjamin (1913–76), English composer. Although he wrote in all forms, he is best known for his operas, which rank him among the foremost opera composers of the 20th century. He also wrote numerous songs, many especially for Peter PEARS. Britten's operas include *Peter Grimes* (1945), *Albert Herring* (1947), *Let's Make an Opera* (for children, 1949), *Billy Budd* (1951), *A Midsummer Night's Dream* (1960) and *Death in Venice* (1973). Other significant works include the popular *Young Person's Guide to the Orchestra* (1945) and the impressive *War Requiem* (1962). In 1948 he established the music festival held annually at his home town of Aldeburgh, on the Suffolk coast. He was made a peer in 1976. *See also* HC2 pp.*121*, *271*.

Brittle star, or serpent star, marine ECHINODERM with a small central disc body and long, sinuous arms; these break off easily and are replaced by regeneration. Class Ophiuroidea; genera include the phosphorescent *Amphiopholis* and the small *Ophiactis*. *See also* NW pp.*22*, 118–119.

Brno (Brünn), second largest city of Czechoslovakia and capital of central Jihomoravský (Moravia) region, 185km (115 miles) SE of Praha (Prague). Founded in the 10th century; it has a 15th-century cathedral. The BREN GUN was designed there. Industries: armaments, engineering. Pop. 336,000.

Broad, Charles Dunbar (1887–1971), British philosopher. He was a professor at Cambridge from 1933 to 1953 and president of the Society for Psychical Research in 1935. He published *Perception, Physics and Reality* (1914).

Broad bean. *See* BEAN.

Broadcasting, transmission of sound or images by radio waves to a widely dispersed audience through RADIO or TELEVISION receivers. The British Broadcasting Corporation (BBC), founded in 1922 and given a charter in 1927, enjoyed a monopoly in radio broadcasting in the United Kingdom until the "pirates" (unlicensed radio stations operating offshore) forced the introduction of commercial and local radio broadcasts. Television broadcasting in the UK started with the BBC in 1936 from Alexandra Palace, London on one channel, or station, which used 405 lines to build up an image. A second channel (ITV) run by the Independent Television Authority, and later a third (BBC2) were introduced. All three channels may now be received on sets which use 625 lines. Latest advances in broadcasting include stereo radio, simultaneous stereo sound with colour pictures, and quadrophony. *See also* MM pp.228–233.

Broadmoor, village ten miles from Reading in SE Berkshire, England. Since 1863 it has been the site of a special hospital for the criminally insane which, in 1949, was transferred from the control of the Prison Commission to that of the Ministry of Health.

Broads, Norfolk, region of shallow lakes and waterways in E England, connected by the rivers Waveney, Yare and Bure, between Norwich and the coast. It is a resort area and wildlife sanctuary, with 320km (200 miles) of navigable waterways.

Broadsheet, large sheet of paper printed on one side only. It was the standard method of publishing popular ballads, lampoons and political propaganda in Britain in the 17th and 18th centuries.

Broadway, major thoroughfare of New York City that began as the principal north-south street of the old town. It runs from the southern tip of Manhattan to the northern city limit in the Bronx. In the vicinity of Times Square it contains theatres and cinemas, for which it is known worldwide as the "show centre" of the USA. *See also* HC2 p.*289*.

Broadwood, British family of piano makers, beginning with John (1732–1812). Broadwood is the world's oldest firm of keyboard instrument makers, and in 1911 it patented the bar-less grand piano.

Broccoli, variety of CAULIFLOWER with large, lobed leaves and thick stems. Tiny green, white or purple flower buds 23cm (9in) compact heads that are eaten. Family Cruciferae; species *Brassica oleracea botrytis*.

Broch, Hermann (1886–1951), Austrian novelist and poet. He emigrated to the USA in 1938 to continue his philosophical and psychological researches. He wrote a play, short stories, and critical essays, but his most important works were the novels *The Sleepwalkers* (1931–32, a trilogy) and *The Death of Virgil* (1945).

Broch, circular stone tower used as a fortified homestead, built in Britain during the early Christian era. There are about 400 brochs in the N and W of Scotland. They were built with a central court, and thick hollow walls containing rooms and a stairway to an upper floor or a roof walk. The most famous and best preserved is the Broch of Mousa, in the Shetland Islands.

Brock, Sir Isaac (1769–1812), English

general. Brock was sent to Canada in 1802, and became administrator of Upper Canada in 1811. A brilliant strategist in the WAR OF 1812, he defeated US General William Hull at Detroit and died in the battle at Queenston Heights.

Brock, Sir Thomas (1847–1922), British sculptor, best known for his memorial to Queen Victoria which stands in the Mall, London, outside Buckingham Palace.

Brockes, Barthold Heinrich (1680–1747), German poet, one of the earliest of the German ENLIGHTENMENT. His work includes *Irdisches Vergnügen in Gott* (9 vols, 1721–48) and translations of the English poets James THOMSON and Alexander POPE.

Brocket deer, or cariacu, small DEER ranging from s Mexico to Paraguay. Stout with slender limbs and an arched back, they are timid and live alone or in pairs. Length: to 91cm (3ft); weight: to 21kg (46lb). Family Cervidae; genus *Mazama*; there are ten species. *See also* NW p.216.

Brockway, Archibald Fenner, 1st Baron (1888–), British Labour politician. He entered Parliament in 1929 and devoted his career to working for international peace and colonial liberation. He wrote extensively on these subjects.

Brod, Max (1884–1968), Czech novelist, critic and philosopher, important for bringing Franz KAFKA to the attention of the public. He settled in Palestine as a refugee in 1939, and later became director of the Habina Theatre.

Brodie, Sir Israel (1895–), Chief Rabbi of the United Hebrew Congregations of the British Commonwealth of Nations (1948–65). He was Senior Jewish Chaplain to the Armed Forces (1944–48). In the 1964 dispute over orthodoxy he championed the conservative viewpoint.

Broglie, Prince Louis Victor de (1892–), French physicist who put forward the theory that all ELEMENTARY PARTICLES have an associated wave and devised the formula that predicts this wavelength. With Erwin SCHRÖDINGER he later developed the form of QUANTUM MECHANICS, called WAVE MECHANICS, for which he was awarded the Nobel Prize in physics in 1929. *See also* SU pp.63, *63*.

Broiler house, also called brooder house, farm-building for intensive stockrearing, particularly of chickens but also of pigs and calves. A typical chick brooder contains tens of thousands of birds. Heating and ventilation are automatically controlled and feeding and removal of wastes are fully mechanized. *See also* PE pp.*162*, 236–238.

Broken Hill, town in w New South Wales, SE Australia, in the Main Barrier Range. Founded in 1884, it is a major silver, lead and zinc mining centre. Pop. (1971) 29,743.

Bromberg. *See* BYDGOSZCZ.

Bromeliad, any of the 1,700 species of the pineapple family. Most are plants native to the tropics and subtropics and, beside the PINEAPPLE itself, include many of the larger EPIPHYTES of trees of the rain forests. *See also* NW pp.*68*.

Bromfield, Louis (1896–1956), US novelist, playwright and essayist. His early works are the best known and include *The Green Bay Tree* (1924), *Possession* (1925), and *Early Autumn* (1926), which won the Pulitzer Prize in 1927.

Bromide, salt of hydrobromic acid or certain organic compounds containing bromine. The bromides of ammonium, sodium, potassium and certain other metals were once extensively used medically as sedatives. Silver bromide is light-sensitive and is used in photography.

Bromination, introduction of a bromine atom into a chemical compound, either by reaction with an unsaturated molecule or by replacing hydrogen, as in the preparation of bromobenzene from BENZENE. Organic bromides are widely used as intermediates in dye and drug syntheses, alkali metal bromides as sedatives, and silver bromide in photography.

Bromine, volatile liquid element (symbol Br) of the HALOGEN group, first isolated by A.J. Balard in 1826. It is extracted by treating sea-water or natural brines with chlorine. It is a red-brown liquid used in making a range of commercially useful compounds. Chemically it resembles chlorine but is less reactive. Properties: at. no. 35; at. wt. 79.904; s.g. 3.12; m.p. −7.2°C; (19.04°F); b.p. 58.78°C (137.8°F); the most common isotope is Br^{79} (50.54%). *See also* SU pp.94, *135*.

Bromine processing, extraction of the halogen element bromine from soluble bromides, especially magnesium bromide, found in sea-water. The bromine is displaced by the more active halogen chlorine and is extracted as a by-product from the saline concentrates left after crystallization of the main salt products.

Bronchitis, an inflammation of the bronchial tubes caused most frequently by irritation from chemicals or pollutants, or by a viral infection such as the common cold or influenza. Symptoms include coughing and the expectoration of mucus. It can be acute (sudden and shortlived) or chronic (persistent). In its worst form it may lead to pneumonia; it is the cause of many deaths, particularly of old people, each year. *See also* MS p.88.

Bronchus, one of two branches into which the TRACHEA or windpipe divides, with one branch leading to each LUNG. The bronchus divides into smaller and smaller branches, called bronchioles, which extend throughout the lung. These open into the lung's air sacs or ALVEOLI, where air is diffused into the blood. *See also* MS p.66.

Bronowski, Jacob (1908–75), British biologist and man of letters. He lectured at many US universities and was made a fellow of Jesus College, Cambridge, in 1967. Among his books are *Science and Human Values* (1958), *Nature and Knowledge* (1969) and three studies of William Blake. His celebrated BBC television series on man's intellectual history was published as *The Ascent of Man* (1973).

Brontë, name of three English novelists, the sisters, Charlotte (1816–55), Emily (1818–48) and Anne (1820–49). They spent most of their lives at Haworth, Yorkshire where their father Patrick was curate. From the earliest the family was beset by poverty and personal unhappiness; their mother died of cancer and two older sisters, Elizabeth and Maria, of tuberculosis; their brother Branwell, a writer and painter, declined into alcoholism and opium addiction. Charlotte's first published novel, *Jane Eyre* (1847), was a great success; her earlier work, *The Professor* (1857), was written in 1846 but rejected. Anne's *Agnes Gray*, reflecting her experience as a governess, and Emily's only novel *Wuthering Heights*, which established her as a writer of major importance, were also published in 1847. Anne's second and last novel *The Tenant of Wildfell Hall* was published in 1848. Only after Charlotte's *Shirley* (1849) had appeared were the identities of the three sisters made public. Before then, in 1848, Branwell and Emily had died and in the following year Anne died. In 1854 Charlotte married, but she died within a year. *See also* HC2 p.98.

Brontosaurus, DINOSAUR that lived in North America during the Jurassic and early Cretaceous periods. It had a long neck and tail, and a small head with the eyes and nostrils on the top so that it could remain almost completely immersed in water. Length: 21m (70ft); weight: to 30 tonnes. *See also* NW pp.186–187.

Bronx, The, mainland borough of N New York City, NE of the River Harlem, connected to the island boroughs of Manhattan and Queens by a network of bridges. Founded in 1641 by Jonas Bronck for the Dutch West India Company, it is now a crowded residential area with 129km (80 miles) of waterfront lined with factories, warehouses and markets. Pop. (1970) 1,472,000.

Bronze, traditionally an alloy of copper and tin containing no more than 33% tin. It is hard and resistant to corrosion, but easy to work. It has long been used in sculpture and in bell-casting. Other metals are often added for specific properties and uses eg. aluminium in aircraft parts and tubing, silicon in marine hardware and chemical equipment and phosphorus in springs, gunmetal and electrical parts. *See also* MM pp.21, 26–27, 33, 36.

Bronze Age, period between the first introduction of bronze tools and the discovery of iron-working techniques. In Mesopotamia the Bronze Age began *c.*3700 BC and lasted until *c.*2000 BC. In Britain bronze was used after 2000 BC, and iron technology did not become widespread until *c.*500 BC. *See also* HC1 pp.28–31, 84–85; MM pp. 26–27.

Bronzino, Il (1503–72), Florentine painter, one of the most influential of all MANNERIST portraitists, whose work exemplifies the school's cool elegance and elongation of the human figure. He was court painter to Cosimo I de MEDICI, for whom he undertook many court portraits. His work includes *Young Man with the Lute* (1540) and *Ascension* (1552). *See also* HC1 p.265.

Brook, Peter Stephen Paul (1925–), British director of theatre, opera and film. He directed at COVENT GARDEN (1947–50) and was appointed co-director of the ROYAL SHAKESPEARE COMPANY in 1962, for which he directed *King Lear* (1962) and Peter WEISS's *Marat/Sade* (1964). He described his ideas on modern theatre in *The Empty Space* (1968). In 1970 he worked in Paris with the experimental International Centre for Theatre Research.

Brooke, Sir James (1803–68), English soldier who in 1841 became the Rajah of SARAWAK on the island of Borneo. He received the title for helping Rajah Muda Hassim of Borneo crush a rebellion in Sarawak in 1840. He was subsequently appointed governor of Labuan (1847–57) and consul-general for Borneo by the British government. He introduced many reforms and was succeeded by his nephew, Charles Anthony Johnson Brooke (1829–1917), who abolished slavery in Sarawak.

Brooke, Rupert Chawner (1887–1915), English poet. His early works, such as *Poems* (1911), were highly patriotic and his personal charm made him almost a contemporary legend. He died on a hospital ship during WWI off the island of Skiros, where he is buried.

Brookeborough, Basil Stanlake Brooke, 1st Viscount (1888–1973), Prime Minister of Northern Ireland (1943–63). He served as Minister of Agriculture for Northern Ireland (1933–41) and Minister of Commerce (1941–45) before becoming Prime Minister. He developed the economy and improved relations with the Republic of Ireland, although he was an uncompromising Unionist.

Brooklands, English motor racing circuit at Weybridge, Surrey, the first specially built for the sport. Scores of car and motorcycling records were set on the track between the time of its opening in 1907 and its closure during WWII.

Brooklyn, borough of New York City and capital of Kings County in SW Long Island; it is connected to Manhattan and Staten Island by bridges, underground railways and ferries. First settled in 1645, it became a borough in 1898. It is the home of Brooklyn College (1930), Prospect Park and Coney Island. Industries: shipbuilding, warehousing, brewing. Area: 184sq km (71sq miles). Pop. (1970) 2,601,852.

Brooks, Sir Basil. *See* BROOKEBOROUGH.

Brooks, Gwendolyn (1917–), US poet. She wrote sensitively of Northern ghetto life, and in 1950 became the first black woman to win the Pulitzer Prize (for *Annie Allen*). Her collected verse was published in *The World of Gwendolyn Brooks* (1971).

Brooks, James (1906–), US painter. He is a leading artist of ACTION PAINTING, whose style is influenced by CUBISM. He was a member of the team that worked on the Federal Art Project during the Depression in the late 1930s.

Brooks, Mel (*c.*1926–), US film director and scriptwriter. Formerly a writer for television comedy shows, he made films that combine satire, slapstick and parody in effervescent style. *The Producers* (1968) won an Oscar, and *Blazing Saddles* (1974) and *Silent Movie* (1976) were both highly successful.

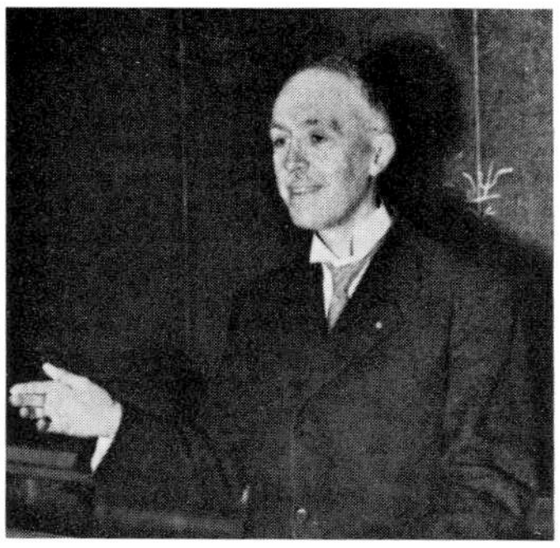

Louis Victor de Broglie won a Nobel Prize for discovering the wave nature of the electron.

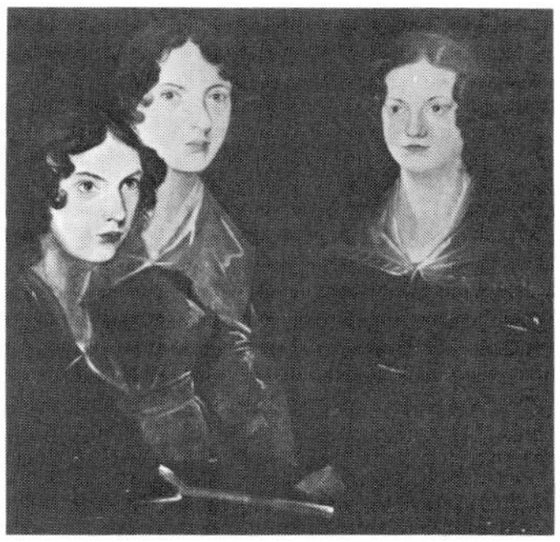

Brontë Sisters, Anne, Charlotte and Emily, from a portrait by their brother, Branwell.

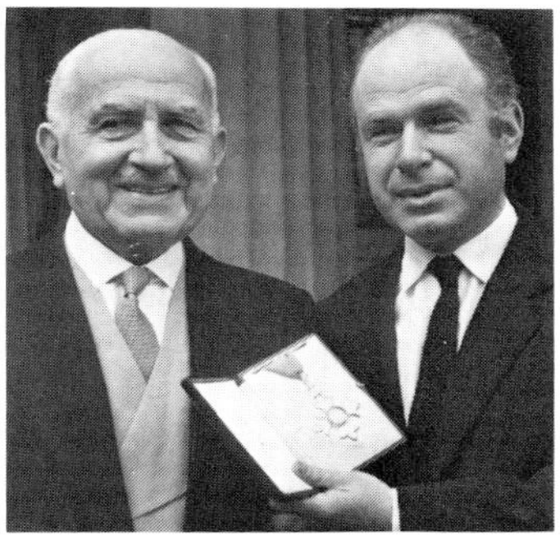

Peter Brook with his father, Simon, after receiving the OBE at Buckingham Palace.

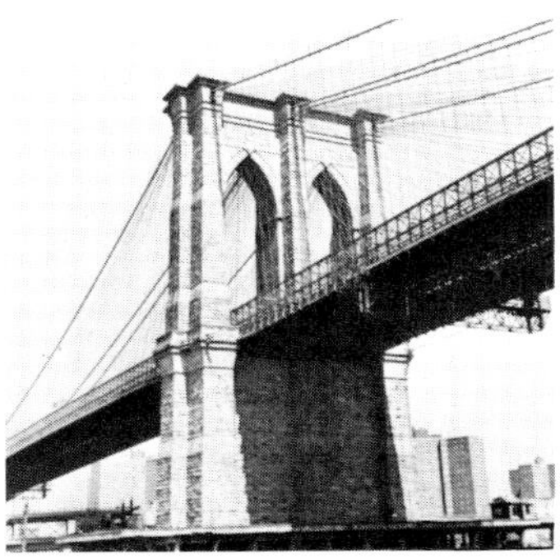

Brooklyn Bridge, which connects Brooklyn to the island of Manhattan, was opened in 1883.

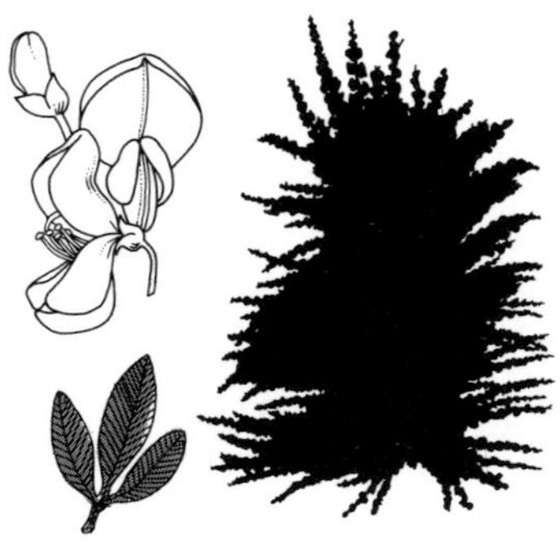

Broom scatters its pollen by a mechanism triggered by a bee landing on a flower.

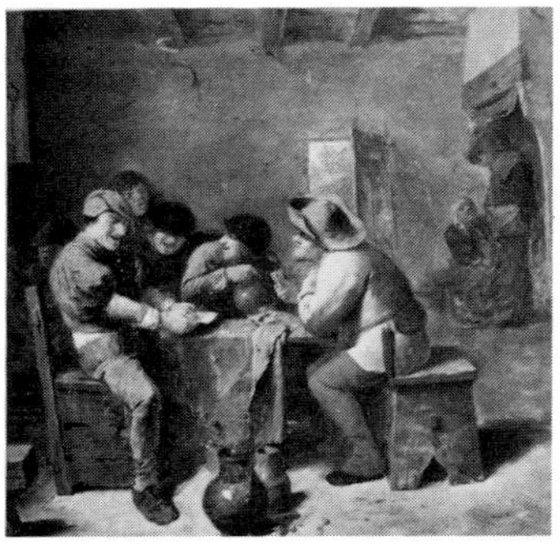

Adriaen Brouwer, who painted scenes of coarse peasant life in a delicate sensitive way.

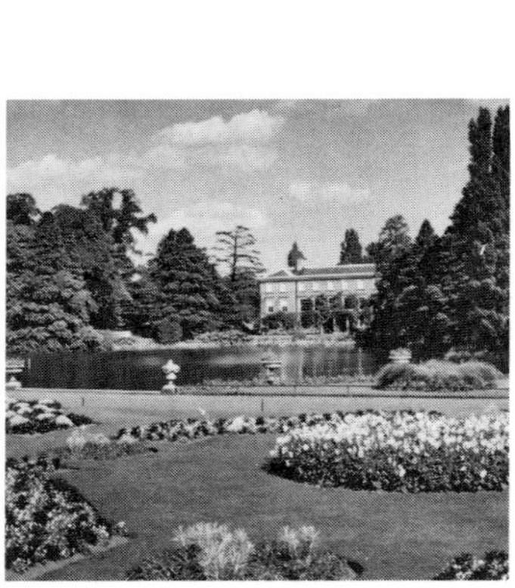

Capability Brown laid out the beautiful gardens of the Royal Botanical Society, Kew.

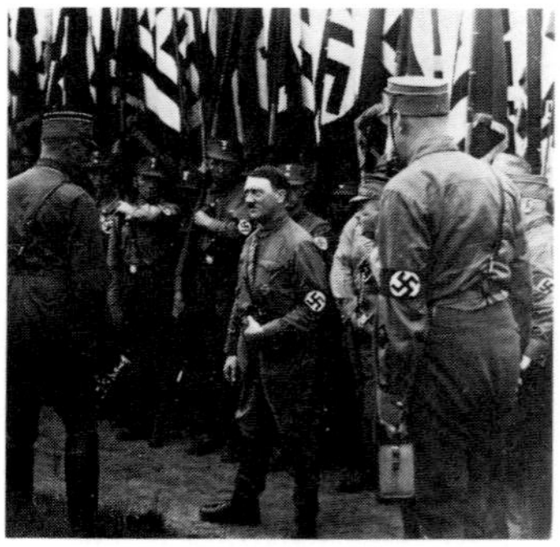

Brownshirts, Hitler's private army which helped him until he liquidated their leaders.

Brook trout. *See* CHAR.

Broom, any of various deciduous shrubs of the PEA family. They have yellow, purple or white flowers, usually in clusters. Many belong to the genus *Genista,* which gave its name to the Plantagenate kings of England (from the Latin *Planta genista*), who used the broom as their emblem.

Broom corn. *See* SORGHUM.

Broome, David (1940–), British show-jumper. World champion in 1970 on *Beethoven,* he won the European title three times, on *Sunsalve* (1961) and *Mister Softee* (1967, 1969). In 1977, on *Philco,* he created a record by winning the King George V Gold Cup for the fourth time.

Broonzy, Big Bill (1893–1958), US blues singer, guitarist and songwriter, real name William Lee Conley Broonzyo. He composed many classic blues songs, performed at Carnegie Hall in 1938 and toured Europe in 1951.

Brothers Karamazov, The (1879–80), novel by Fyodor DOSTOEVSKY. Its intense psychological drama culminates in the murder by his sons of the father, Fyodor Karamazov, symbolizing man's revolt against his heavenly father.

Brough, Louise (1923–), American tennis player. Expert at the serve-and-volley technique, she won 36 major titles, including four Wimbledon singles (1948–50, 1955). With Margaret Osborne, she won the US doubles nine times in a row (1942–50) and 12 times in all.

Brougham, Henry Peter, 1st Baron Brougham and Vaux (1778–1868), Scottish politician. He became MP for Camelford in 1810 and fought for liberal reforms in the House of Commons. As Lord Chancellor (1830–34), he reformed legal procedure and helped pass the REFORM ACT (1832). He was a founder of the University of London (1828) and designed the brougham four-wheeled closed carriage. *See also* MM p.*121.*

Brouwer, Adriaen (*c.*1606–38), Flemish painter, influential in the development of Dutch and Flemish painting. He is best known for his depictions of peasant life and for his humorous treatment of figures sleeping, drinking, smoking and fighting. A well-known example is *The Smokers. See also* HC1 p.*310.*

Brown, Sir Arthur Whitten (1886–1948), British aviator. With Sir John ALCOCK he completed the first non-stop trans-Atlantic flight in 1919.

Brown, Charles Brockden (1771–1810), US author who gained acclaim for his Gothic romances. His best-known novels included *Wieland* (1798), *Ormond* (1799), *Arthur Mervyn* (1799–1800), *Edgar Huntly* (1799), *Clara Howard* (1801) and *Jane Talbot* (1801).

Brown, Dave Australian rugby league player. The "Bradman of football", he was a prolific scorer. A centre for the Kangaroos on the 1933–34 tour of England, he scored 285 points (19 tries, 114 goals); in the 1935 Sydney Premiership he scored 244 points for Eastern Suburbs, including a record 38 tries. He later played for the English Club Warrington.

Brown, Ford Madox (1821–93), English painter, deeply influenced by the PRE-RAPHAELITES, as may be seen in *The Last of England* (1855) and *Work* (1852–63), although he was never a member of the Brotherhood. He was the grandfather of the writer Ford Madox FORD.

Brown, George (1818–80), Canadian journalist and politician, *b.* Scotland. He went to Canada in 1844 and began the Toronto *Globe* newspaper to advocate responsible government. He founded the "Clear Grit" (Liberal) Party and was an MP from 1851 to 1867. He took a prominent part in the conferences that produced Canadian confederation.

Brown, James Nathaniel ("Jimmy") (1936–), US football player. He was considered one of the greatest full-backs in the history of the game. He played for the Cleveland Browns in the National Football League (1957–65) and scored 126 touchdowns. After his retirement, he became a film actor.

Brown, Joe E. (1892–1973), US comedian, especially popular during the 1930s and 1940s as a film comedian. His clown-like features were sometimes referred to in the titles of his films, eg *You Said a Mouthful* (1933) and *Shut my Big Mouth* (1941). His later films include *Some Like it Hot* (1959) and *Comedy of Terrors* (1963).

Brown, John (1800–59), American anti-slavery leader who, with 21 cohorts, took possession of the US arsenal at Harper's Ferry, Virginia. He was captured, tried and hanged. The trial raised North–South tensions on the eve of the Civil War. He is the hero of the song *John Brown's Body.*

Brown, Lancelot "Capability" (1715–83), English landscape gardener who revolutionized garden and parkland layout in the 1700s. He designed or remodelled nearly 150 estates, including gardens at Blenheim and Kew. He worked to achieve casual effects, with scattered groups of trees and gently rolling hills. He earned his nickname from a habit of saying that a place had "capabilities of improvement".

Brown, Robert (1773–1858), Scottish botanist. He went on an expedition to Australia (1801–05), returning to England with valuable botanical collections. He described the flora of Australia in *Prodomus Florae Novae Hollandiae et Insulae Van Diemen* (1810). He is best known for establishing, in *A Brief Account of Microscopical Observations* (1828), that minute particles suspended in a liquid or gas are continuously in motion. This motion has since been called "BROWNIAN MOVEMENT".

Brown, Thomas Alexander. *See* BOLDREWOOD, ROLF.

Brown algae, group of almost exclusively marine ALGAE that includes the kelps, the largest kinds of seaweed, which may grow more than 30m (100ft) long. Division Phaeophyta. *See also* NW p.*46.*

Brown bear. *See* BEAR.

Browne, Elliot Martin (1900–), British theatre director, known for his revival of verse drama. His productions include T.S. ELIOT's *Murder in the Cathedral* (1935). He revived the York cycle of MYSTERY PLAYS in 1951.

Browne, Robert (*c.*1550–1633), English religious leader. While young, he tried to form Presbyterian congregations outside the established Church of England. His followers were called BROWNISTS. He was imprisoned for this act, and after his release went with his followers to Holland in 1581, where he published what later became the basic tenets of CONGREGATIONALISM. He returned to England via Scotland in 1584, made a submission to the Church of England and spent his last 42 years (1591–1633) as rector of Achurch, Northamptonshire.

Browne, Sir Thomas (1605–82), English author. He studied medicine in England at Oxford University, in Italy and in The Netherlands, and practised in England. His works include *Religio Medici* (1642), *Vulgar Errors* (1646), *Hydriotaphia: Urn-Burial* (1658) and *The Garden of Cyrus* (1658).

Brownian movement, random, zig-zag movement of particles suspended in a fluid. It is caused by the unequal bombardment of the particles, from different sides, by the molecules of the fluid. It is observable up to a particle size of 3×10^{-3}mm. It is named after the botanist Robert BROWN, who observed the movement of plant spores floating in water in 1828. *See also* SU pp.*84,* 85.

Browning, Elizabeth Barrett (1806–61), English poet. In 1846 she married Robert Browning, and from 1847 lived in Florence. She began to write verse early in life; *The Battle of Marathon,* her first volume, was published in 1820. *The Seraphim and Other Poems* (1838) and *A Drama of Exile* (1845) established her widespread popularity. *Aurora Leigh* (1857) is considered her last important poem.

Browning, Robert (1812–89), English poet. *Pauline,* his first published poem, appeared anonymously in 1833. Later poems, *My last Duchess* and *Soliloquy of the Spanish Cloister,* both published in *Bells and Pomegranates* (1846), display his characteristic use of dramatic monologue. In 1846 he married Elizabeth Barrett (BROWNING) and moved to Italy, where he lived until she died in 1861. While there he published the volumes *Christmas Eve and Easter Day* (1850) and *Men and Women* (1855). Returning to London, he became popular with *Dramatis Personae* (1864) and *The Ring and the Book* (1868–69), a series of dramatic dialogues that many consider his masterpiece. *See also* HC2 p.100.

Brownists, followers of Robert Browne (*c.*1550–1633), an English clergyman who founded the Separatist movement. That movement asserted the authority of the congregation in matters of ecclesiastical organization. It therefore opposed the existing episcopal structure of the Church and the discipline of the ecclesiastical courts. The Brownists moved to Middelburg, Zeeland, in 1581. They were the forerunners of the INDEPENDENTS and the CONGREGATIONALISTS.

Brownshirts, the *Sturm-Abteilung,* or SA, HITLER's private army, one of the many to flourish in Weimar Germany. After 1933 it became a source of potential rivalry to Hitler and on 29 June 1934 the SA leaders, including Ernst ROEHM, were shot.

Brubeck, David Warren (1920–), US jazz pianist and composer. In 1951 the Dave Brubeck Quartet was formed, consisting of Brubeck, Paul Desmond (alto sax), Joe Morello (drums) and Eugene Wright (bass). The group enjoyed great popularity in the 1960s. Brubeck's compositions include cantatas and orchestral works.

Bruce, Edward (*d.*1318), Scottish King of Ireland (1315–18). He helped his brother, ROBERT I, become Scotland's king. In Ireland he led the local people against their English overlords, before being killed in battle.

Bruce, James (1730–94), Scottish explorer. In 1770, he reached the source of the Blue Nile and was the first to follow it to its confluence with the White Nile. He also made archaeological discoveries in N Africa, Rhodes, Cyprus and Syria. *See also* HC2 p.*142.*

Bruce, Robert (1274–1329), Robert I of Scotland and securer of Scotland's independence from the English. He was crowned at Scone on 27 March 1306, and immediately began a campaign to wrest from EDWARD I those Scottish castles and towns in English hands. Bruce's victory at BANNOCKBURN in 1314 marked the defeat of the English. *See also* HC1 pp.182–183.

Bruce, Stanley Melbourne, 1st Viscount, (1883–1967), Australian politician. He entered the Australian legislature in 1918 and was a representative to the LEAGUE OF NATIONS in 1921. He served in W.M. HUGHES' Cabinet (1921–23) as treasurer. He was prime minister (1923–29) and encouraged reforms such as unemployment insurance and health legislation. From 1933–45 he was High Commissioner for Australia in London. In 1947 he became a viscount and was the first Australian to sit in the British House of Lords.

Bruce, Thomas, Earl of Elgin. *See* ELGIN MARBLES.

Brucellosis, or undulant fever, infectious disease passed from farm animals to man, often in unpasteurized milk. In man the symptoms include headache, weakness and intermittent fever. Pasteurization of milk, vaccination of young animals and the destruction of infected animals make the disease rare. *See also* MS p.*110–111.*

Bruch, Max (1838–1920), German Romantic composer. He composed operas and was a prominent conductor, but he is remembered primarily for three orchestral works – the *Violin Concerto No. 1, Scottish Fantasy* for violin and orchestra and the *Kol Nidrei* for cello and orchestra. *See also* HC2 pp.106, *106,* 107.

Brucite, mineral form of magnesium hydroxide ($Mg_3(OH)_6$), derived from periclase. The crystals are either glassy or waxy, can be white, pale green, grey or blue, and occur in fibrous masses or plate aggregates. It is found in SCHISTS, SERPENTINE and METAMORPHIC rocks. It is used to make magnesia refractory materials.

Brücke, Die (1905–1913), first group of German EXPRESSIONIST painters, founded in Dresden by Ernst KIRCHNER. Other members of the group were Karl SCHMIDT-ROTTLUFF, E. NOLDE and Erich Heckel. They thought of their art as a bridge between the contemporary academic style of painting and a freer style. Inspired by MUNCH, van GOGH and GAUGUIN, their work was characterized by linear, rhythmical expression and simplification of colour and form. Their extensive use of woodcut raised it to a significant 20th-century medium. *See also* HC2 pp.174–175.

Bruckner, Anton (1824–96), Austrian Romantic composer. An intensely pious man, he wrote a great deal of church music – cantatas, masses and a *Te Deum* (1881–84) – and nine symphonies. His compositions are especially noted for their massive scale: the symphonies are lengthy, monumental creations in which the lush Romanticism of WAGNER, whom Bruckner admired, is apparent. His use of complex musical form infuses his work, in which folk tunes are often employed. *See also* HC1 p.107.

Bruegel, Pieter the Elder (*c.*1525–69), last of the early Flemish painters, the most important moralist in the Netherlands after BOSCH and one of the greatest landscape painters. When most of his contemporaries were being influenced by Italian painting, Bruegel stayed closer to the Flemish tradition, although transcending it. Using his powers of minute observation, he depicted a world of peasants working and playing in a rural landscape, shown in every season and mood; often his paintings have satirical and allegorical meaning. His best known pictures are *Peasant Wedding* (*c.*1567) and his series *The Months* (1565). His son, Pieter the Younger (1564–1637), sometimes copied his father's work. Another son, Jan (1568–1625), specialized in highly detailed flower paintings which earned him the nickname "Velvet Bruegel". *See also* HC1 pp.261, *261, 300;* MS pp.*169, 191.*

Bruges, (Brugge), city in NW Belgium 88km (55 miles) WNW of Brussels; the capital of West Flanders province. Built on a network of canals, it was a great trading centre in the 15th century. Declining after 1500, its trade revived when the Zeebrugge ship canal was opened in 1907. Industries: engineering, brewing, lace, tourism. Pop. (1970 est.) 51,000.

Brugge. *See* BRUGES.

Bruhn, Erik (1928–), Danish dancer. He joined the Royal Danish Ballet Company in 1947 and was a guest soloist with many major dance companies in the USA, Europe and Australia.

Bruise, or contusion, an injury to the deeper parts of the SKIN and underlying tissues caused by a blow or pressure. Small blood vessels under the surface are ruptured and internal bleeding causes tenderness and discoloration of the skin. Bruising often accompanies a FRACTURE.

Brulé, Étienne (*c.*1592–1633), Canadian explorer. Brulé travelled to Quebec from France with Samuel de CHAMPLAIN in 1608. In the next 20 years he explored the Great Lakes and Georgian Bay, guiding French expeditions and befriending the HURON Indians who eventually killed and ate him.

Brumel, Valeriy (1942–), Russian athlete. He established a world record in the high jump of 2.30m (7ft 5.75in) in 1963. He won a gold medal in the same event at the 1964 Olympics, but a broken leg in 1965 retarded his career.

Brummell, George Byran ("Beau") (1778–1840), English dandy renowned for his restrainedly elegant style of dress. He was a friend of the Prince Regent, later GEORGE IV, and enjoyed an enormous social success. By 1816 his debts caused him to leave England.

Brundage, Avery (1887–1975), US sportsman, *b.* Detroit. He was a staunch advocate of keeping "professionalism" out of amateur sports, and served as president of the International Olympic Committee (1952–72).

Brunei, self-governing British protectorate in N Borneo, SE Asia; the capital is Bandar Seri Begawan. Recent finds of offshore natural gas and oil are replacing the oil found at Seria in 1929. Products: oil, rubber, timber, rice. Area: 5,765sq km (2,225sq miles). Pop. (1975 est.) 147,000.

Brunel, Isambard Kingdom (1806–59), British engineer, son of Sir Marc BRUNEL. In 1829 he designed the Clifton Suspension Bridge (completed in 1864) and in 1833 he became chief engineer for the Great Western Railway, for whom he designed the Royal Albert Bridge across the River Tamar. He is also famous for his ships: *Great Western* (designed 1837), the first trans-Atlantic wooden steamship, *Great Britain* (1843), the first iron-hulled screw-driven steamship, and *Great Eastern* (1858), a steamship powered by screws and paddles, the largest vessel of its time.

Brunel, Sir Marc Isambard (1769–1849), engineer, *b.* France. A refugee from the FRENCH REVOLUTION, he went to the USA in 1793 and was chief engineer of New York. He went to England in 1799, where he invented machinery for making ships' blocks. He was responsible for the construction of the first tunnel under the River Thames (1825–42).

Brunelleschi, Filippo (1377–1446), Florentine architect, first of the great RENAISSANCE architects and a pioneer in the scientific use of perspective. He influenced many later architects, including MICHELANGELO. In 1420 he began to design the dome of Florence Cathedral, the largest dome since HAGIA SOPHIA, Constantinople. His other works include the Ospedale degl' Innocenti (1419–26), the first completed Renaissance building, the Basilica of S. Lorenzo (begun 1421) and the Pazzi Chapel (*c.*1440), all in Florence. *See also* HCl pp.250–251.

Brunfels, Otto (1488–1534), German botanist. His *Herbarium Vivae Eicones* (1530–40) helped to change botany from a lore of medieval herbalism towards a modern science. The text, a record of the properties of plants, was distinguished by accurate descriptions.

Brunhoff, Jean de (1899–1937), French creator of the *Babar the Elephant* books for children. He wrote and illustrated the first story, *The Story of Babar the Little Elephant,* in 1931. Six more books in the series followed. Since 1947 his son Laurent has continued the Babar saga.

Brünn. *See* BRNO.

Brunner, Sir John Tomlinson (1842–1919), British industrialist. In 1873 he founded, with Ludwig MOND, a chemical firm called Brunner, Mond and Company which was incorporated into Imperial Chemical Industries (ICI) in 1926.

Bruno, Saint (*c.*1030–1101), German founder of the CARTHUSIAN order of monks. He founded the monastery at the Grande Chartreuse in the Alps in 1084, and laid emphasis on austerity and rigid observation of harsh monastic customs. In 1090 he returned to Rome for a short time to be a counsellor to Urban II. *See also* HCl p.187.

Bruno, Giordano (1548–1600), Italian philosopher. A fierce opponent of dogmatism and a supporter of the relativity of perception, his pantheistic belief in a deity manifest in the cosmos led to his censure for unorthodoxy and his death at the stake. He had a profound influence on Spinoza, Leibniz, Hegel and Schelling.

Brunswick (Braunschweig), city in E West Germany on the River Oker 145km (90 miles) SSE of Hamburg. It is the capital of Lower Saxony state, and is the former capital of the old Duchy of Brunswick that was ruled by the Brunswick-Lüneburg line (later Hanover) until 1884. Industries: food processing, printing, pianos, optical equipment. Pop. 219,000.

Brusa. *See* BURSA.

Brush drawing, in Chinese art, method in which there is no sharp demarcation between calligraphy and drawing. In the Middle Ages it was used for miniatures and for under-drawing of paintings. Dürer's *Praying Hands* was drawn with a fine brush point; Rembrandt used brush drawing to sketch his large compositions, as did Degas and Picasso.

Brussels (Bruxelles), capital of Belgium, 42km (26 miles) S of Antwerp; capital of Brabant province. The main commercial, financial, cultural and administrative centre of Belgium, it is also the headquarters of the European Economic Community (EEC) and of NATO. Two languages are spoken: French and Flemish. Industries: textiles, chemicals, electrical goods, brewing. Pop. (1970 est.) 161,000. *See also* MW p.37.

Brussels sprout, member of the CABBAGE family, first grown in Belgium. Stem buds develop into miniature, globular heads that are eaten as a vegetable. Height: 60–90cm (24–36in). Family Cruciferae; species *Brassica oleracea gemmifera. See also* PE p.188.

Brussels, Treaty of (1948), agreement by which Britain, Belgium, The Netherlands, Luxembourg and France established the European Union for co-operation in defence, politics, economics and cultural affairs for 50 years. The defence agreement was merged in NATO in 1950. In 1954, Italy and West Germany joined, the name being changed to the Western European Union.

Brut (*c.*1200), early Middle English verse history of Britain by LAYAMON. Based on the works of GEOFFREY OF MONMOUTH and Robert WACE, the *Brut* contains the earliest mention in English of KING ARTHUR, King Lear, and Cymbeline (CUNOBELINUS).

Brutalism, widespread architectural movement which originated in Britain in the 1950s in the work of Alison and Peter SMITHSON, who coined the phrase "the new brutalism". Setting as their standard the uncompromising simplicity of MIES VAN DER ROHE and LE CORBUSIER, they emphasized the honest presentation of structural materials in modern building by leaving steel girders exposed and concrete and brick walls undisguised by plaster or stone facing. The Smithsons' school at Hunstanton (1954) was a landmark in the movement.

Brutus, Lucius Junius (*fl.* late 6th century BC), founder of the Roman Republic. He led the Romans in the expulsion of the last Etruscan king in 509 BC after his kinswoman Lucretia (Lucrece) had been raped by the king's son. He executed his own two sons for plotting to restore the Tarquins.

Brutus, Marcus Junius (*c.*85–42 BC), Roman republican politician, one of the principal assassins of the dictator Julius CAESAR. He sided first with POMPEY against Caesar, but Caesar forgave him and made him governor of Cisalpine Gaul in 46 BC and city praetor in 44 BC. After Caesar's murder in 44 BC, he went to Greece where he raised an army. He was defeated at Philippi in 42 BC, by MARK ANTONY and Octavian (AUGUSTUS), and committed suicide. *See also* HCl p.97.

Bruxelles. *See* BRUSSELS.

Bryant, Sir Arthur (1899–), British historian, author of numerous historical works, including a trilogy on British history between 1793 and 1822: *The Years of Endurance* (1942), *Years of Victory* (1944) and *The Age of Elegance* (1950). He edited Viscount Alanbrooke's diaries in *The Turn of the Tide* (1957) and *Triumph in the West* (1959). Other works include books on Samuel Pepys, Charles II and George V.

Bryhtnoth (*d.*991), known also as Byrhtnoth, alderman of the East Saxons. He led the Saxon forces against the Danish invaders at the Battle of MALDON, where he was killed. He was buried at Ely.

Brynner, Yul (1915–), US film actor, *b.* Russia. He made his film debut in *Port of New York* (1949) and had his first major success in the screen musical *The King and I* (1956). His later films include *The Magnificent Seven* (1960).

Bryony, either of two quite unrelated plants, both of which are climbers in hedgerows in Britain, Europe and elsewhere. White bryony, *Bryonia dioica,* is a member of the GOURD family, with large hand-shaped leaves. Black bryony, *Tamus communis,* is a member of the YAM family and has heart-shaped leaves. *See also* NW p.*61.*

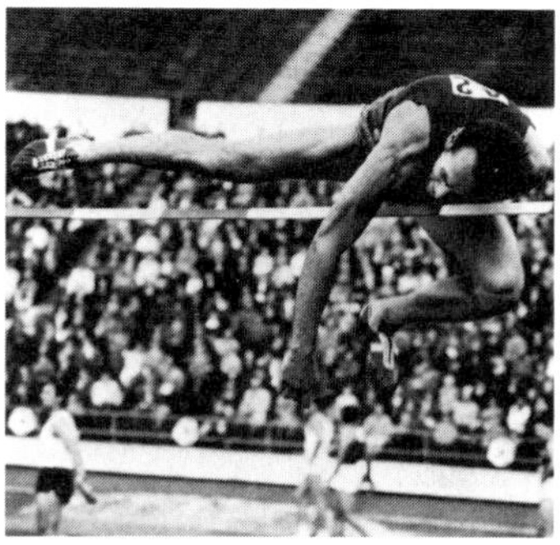

Valeriy Brumel, the Russian high jumper who established a record of 2.30m in 1963.

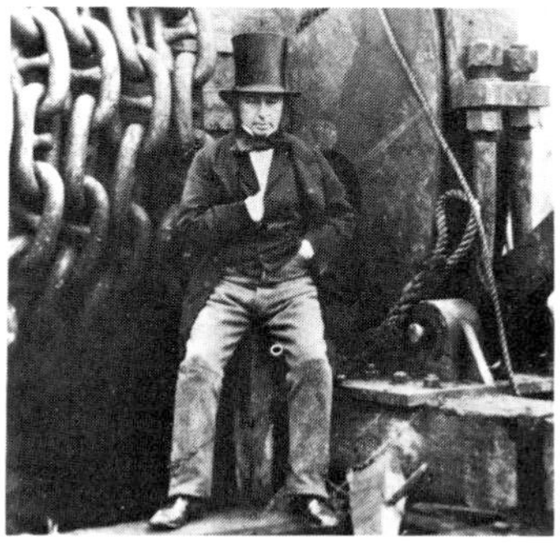

Isambard Brunel, whose engineering feats reflect the energy of the Victorian age.

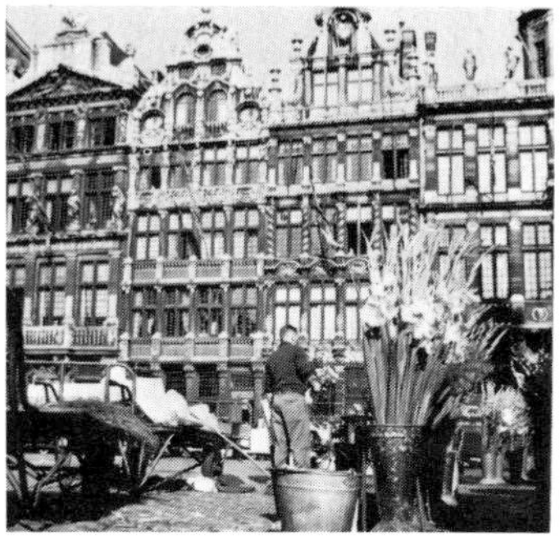

Brussels; the Belgian capital which is now the headquarters of the EEC.

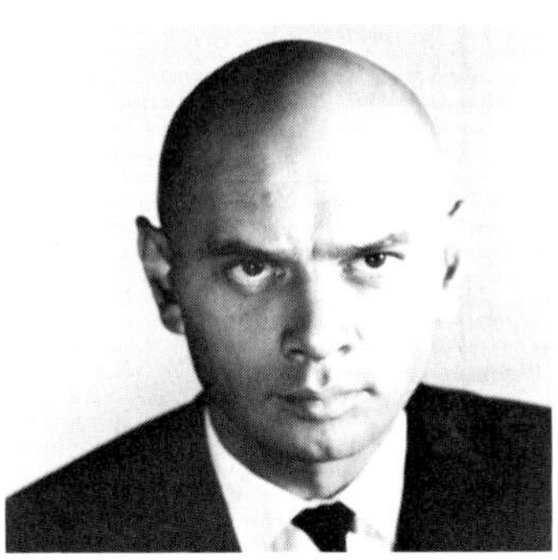

Yul Brynner, whose greatest success was in the screen musical *The King and I* (1956).

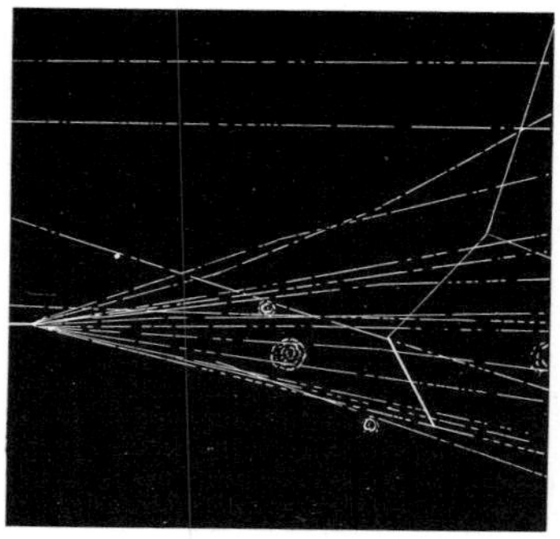

Bubble chambers enable physicists to photograph the tracks of sub-atomic particles.

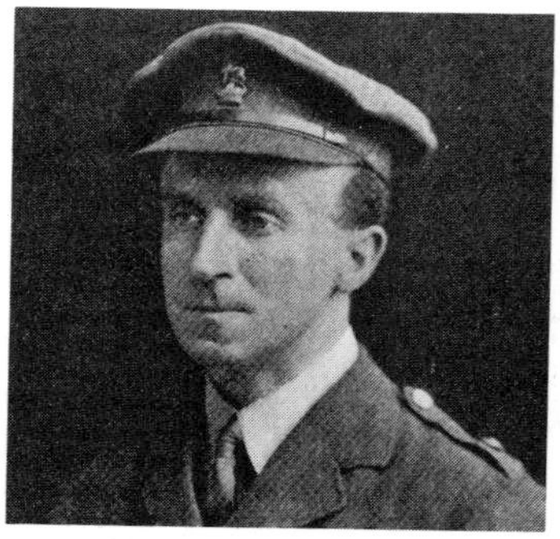

John Buchan had an equal reputation in his lifetime as a creative writer and statesman.

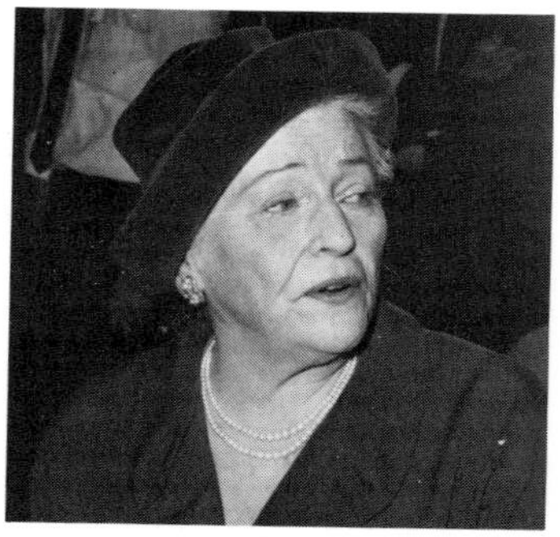

Pearl Buck was brought up in China, where her parents were Presbyterian missionaries.

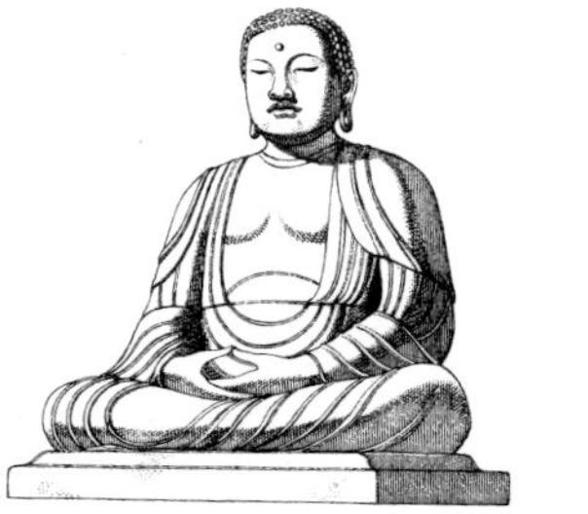

Buddha, the "Enlightened", is thought to have lived in northern India around 400 BC.

Bryophyte, group of small green plants (division Bryophyta) consisting of the MOSSES and LIVERWORTS. Bryophytes grow on damp surfaces exposed to light, including rocks and tree bark, almost everywhere from the Arctic to the Antarctic. *See also* ALTERNATION OF GENERATIONS; NW pp.50–51.

Bryozoan, or moss animal, term used to describe members of the phylum of invertebrate animals known as Ectoprocta, but formerly also an old name for the phylum Endoprocta.

Brythonic, group of languages belonging to the CELTIC subfamily of the Indo-European family of languages. Its two existing members are Welsh and Breton. A third Brythonic language, Cornish, virtually died out in the 18th century, although there are still Cornish speakers in Cornwall. The separate languages emerged from an ancient Celtic British root in the 6th century after the Germanic invasions.

Bubble chamber, device for detecting and identifying sub-atomic particles. It consists of a sealed chamber filled with liquid hydrogen or helium kept just below its boiling point by the high pressure in the chamber. When the pressure is released the boiling point is lowered and a charged particle passing through the superheated liquid leaves a trail of tiny gas bubbles that can be illuminated and photographed before the pressure is restored. If a magnetic field is applied to the chamber, the tracks are curved according to the charge, mass and velocity of the particles, which can thus be identified. It was developed by D. GLASER in 1952 from the CLOUD CHAMBER. *See also* SU *p.60.*

Buber, Martin (1878–1965), Jewish philosopher, theologian and political activist, *b.* Vienna. He was an ardent early ZIONIST, and edited *Der Jude* (1916–24), the leading journal of German-speaking Jewish intellectuals. He defiantly opposed the Nazis in Germany until forced to move to Palestine in 1938. His most important published work is *I and Thou* (1923), on the directness of the relationship between man and God within the traditions of HASIDISM. He has also written on the ideals of the state of Israel.

Bubonic plague. *See* BLACK DEATH.

Bucaramanga, commercial city in N central Colombia, in the E Andes highlands at an altitude of 1,018m (3,340ft). Crops: coffee, tobacco, cocoa, cotton. Industries: cigars, cigarettes, textiles. Pop. 292,000.

Buccaneer, pirate operating mostly on the SPANISH MAIN in the 16th and 17th centuries. Many buccaneers, such as Henry MORGAN (*c.*1635–88), were British or French, confined their raids to Spanish property, and often took their booty home to their mother countries. As buccaneers began to attack ships of all nations indiscriminately, they became indistinguishable from ordinary pirates. *See also* HC1 pp.278–279; HC2 p.134.

Bucephalus, horse of ALEXANDER THE GREAT. When Bucephalus died in 326 BC in India, Alexander had him buried on the banks of the Hydaspes (now JHELUM) River and built the city of Bucephala in his memory. *See also* HC1 pp.80–81.

Bucer, Martin (1491–1551), German Protestant reformer who attempted to reconcile the viewpoints of Martin LUTHER and Ulrich ZWINGLI. In 1549 he became Regius professor of divinity at Cambridge University.

Buchan, Alexander (1829–1907), Scottish meteorologist, whose achievements included the collation and analysis of massive quantities of meteorological data. He identified the series (named after him) of nine spells of weather that consistently deviated from the normal between certain dates each year in the period 1857–66.

Buchan, John, 1st Baron Tweedsmuir (1875–1940), British author and statesman. He was famous for his adventure novels, which included *The Thirty-Nine Steps* (1915) and *Sick Heart River* (1941). He also wrote a four-volume history of WWI and biographies of Julius Caesar, Walter Scott and Oliver Cromwell. He served as Governor-General of Canada from 1935 until his death.

Buchanan, Colin Douglas (1907–), British transport expert. He worked (1935–39) at the Ministry of Transport; served in the Royal Engineers during WWII; and worked (1946–61) at the Ministry of Town and Country Planning. He was Urban Planning Adviser (1961–63) to the Ministry of Transport, for which he prepared a report called *Traffic in Towns* (1963).

Buchanan, Jack (1891–1957), British comedy actor best known for playing the lead in musical comedies of the 1920s and 1930s. He also appeared in several films, including *The Band Wagon* (1953).

Buchanan, James (1791–1868), 15th president of the USA. A Democrat, he was elected President in 1857, and attempted to maintain a balance between the pro- and anti-slavery states. He reluctantly supported the establishment of the federal garrison at Fort SUMTER, and civil war broke out shortly after he left office in 1861. *See also* HC2 p.150.

Buchan Ness, most easterly point of Scotland in Grampian Region, 40km (25 miles) NNE of Aberdeen. Buchan stretches from Fraserburgh to Turriff; the name is generally used to refer to all the low-lying land of NE Scotland.

Buchara (Bukhara), ancient city in W Uzbekistan, USSR; capital of the Buchara region. Founded in about the 1st century AD, it was conquered by Arabs (7th-9th century), by Turks and Mongols (12th-15th century) and annexed to Russia in 1868; it was included in Uzbekistan in 1924. It is an important Asian trade and cultural centre. Monuments there include the 10th-century mausoleum of Ismail Samani and the Ulugbek (1417–18). Industries: silk and wool processing, rugs, handicrafts, textiles. Pop. (1970) 112,000.

Bucharest (Bucureşti), capital and largest city of Romania, on the River Dimbovita. It became capital in 1862, was occupied by Germany in both world wars and finally by Russia in 1944. The seat of the Patriarch of the Romanian Orthodox Church, it is an industrial, commercial and cultural centre. Pop. (1969 est.) 1,526,000.

Buchenwald, site of a Nazi concentration camp, outside Weimar in Germany. It was notorious especially for the medical experiments conducted on its inmates. It was liberated by the Allies in 1945.

Buchman, Frank Nathan Daniel (1878–1961), US founder of the Moral Re-Armament (MRA) movement. An ordained Lutheran minister, he began propagating his ethical views in 1921 at Hartford, and later at Oxford and Cambridge universities. He was decorated by eight governments for services rendered by his worldwide MRA programme.

Buchner, Eduard (1860–1917), German biochemist. He became professor at Berlin, Breslau and finally at Würzburg, having been awarded the Nobel Prize in chemistry in 1907 for his work on fermentation. His work indicated that it was not the actual yeast cells, but rather the enzymes contained within them, that actively caused alcoholic sugar fermentation. He was killed in WWI. *See also* FERMENTATION.

Büchner, Georg (1813–37), German dramatist. He studied medicine and became involved in politics, fleeing to Zurich where he died. His best-known works are *Danton's Death* (1835), *Woyzeck* (1850), which was used by the composer Alban Berg as the basis for his opera *Wozzeck* (1925), and *Leonce and Lena* (1850).

Buck, Pearl S. (1892–1973), US novelist. She was brought up in China, which she used as the setting for many of her novels. Her first book appeared in 1930. In 1931 *The Good Earth*, a novel about Chinese peasants, was published; it won the Pulitzer Prize in 1932. Her other works include *Sons* (1932), *The Mother* (1934), *A House Divided* (1935) and *Dragon Seed* (1942). In 1938 she was awarded the Nobel Prize in literature.

Buck, Sir Peter (1880–1951), New Zealand MAORI leader and anthropologist. He became an MP (1908) and Minister of Maori affairs (1912), and served as a medical officer in WWI. Buck's Maori name was Te Rangi Hiroa.

Buckingham, George Villiers, 1st Duke of (1592–1628), English courtier. As JAMES I's favourite from 1614 he became rich and influential; he also dominated Charles I. His missions to Spain and France were disasters, largely because of his incompetence and arrogance. Parliament's two attempts to impeach him (1626, 1628) were blocked by Charles I. His son, the 2nd Duke (1628–87), was educated with Charles I's sons and supported Charles II in the final battle of the Civil War (1651). He was a privy councillor (1660–74) and then a major opposition figure (1675–80). *See also* CABAL.

Buckingham Palace, London residence of British sovereigns since 1837. Formerly owned by the dukes of Buckingham, it was purchased by George III in 1761 and remodelled into a 600-room palace by John NASH in 1825. Sir Aston WEBB redesigned the east front in 1913. The changing of the guard takes place there daily.

Buckinghamshire, county in SE central England; the chief town is Aylesbury. In the Vale of Aylesbury to the N cereal crops and beans are grown, and livestock and poultry are kept in the S. Beechwood furniture is still made there. Area: 1,882sq km (727sq miles). Pop. (1976) 512,000.

Buckle, Henry Thomas (1812–62), English historian. He emphasized the influence of the physical environment on the behaviour of nations. *History of Civilization in England* (2 vols, 1857–61) is his most important work.

Buckthorn, any of several trees or shrubs of the genus *Rhamnus*, family Rhamnaceae. *R.catharticus* is a many-branched shrub with black bark, spine-like branchlets, and oval, toothed leaves. The succulent fruit is used medicinally and the bark is used to produce a yellow dye.

Buckwheat, Asian cereal plant cultivated throughout the world; it is well adapted to cool arid areas and is an important animal food and cooking ingredient. Cultivated buckwheat (*Fagopyrum esculentum*) has heart-shaped leaves attached to swollen sheaths, white flowers and triangular seeds. Height: up to 1.5m (5ft). Family Polygonaceae.

Bud, in plants, a small swelling or projection consisting of a short stem with overlapping, immature leaves covered by scales. Leaf buds develop into leafy twigs; flower buds develop into blossoms; and mixed buds develop into twigs and flowers, as on apple and lilac trees. A bud at the tip of a twig is a terminal bud and contains the growing point; lateral buds develop in leaf axils along a twig.

Budapest, capital city of Hungary, on the River Danube, created in 1873 by uniting the towns of Buda and Pest on opposite banks of the river. After this it became one of two capitals of the AUSTRO-HUNGARIAN EMPIRE; it made rapid industrial and commercial progress in the early 20th century. It was declared capital of an independent Hungary in 1918, and was seized by the USSR in 1945. Industries: iron and steel, chemicals, textiles. Pop. (1970 prelim.) 1,940,000.

Buddenbrooks (1901), novel by Thomas MANN (with his elder brother Heinrich). Showing the influences of Friedrich Nietzche and Richard Wagner, the story depicts the decline of a wealthy merchant family caused by an increase in spiritual and artistic refinement.

Buddha, the "Enlightened" or "Awakened One", a person who has come to have knowledge of the truth. Originally describing Gautama, the founder of BUDDHISM, the term was later used by Mahayana Buddhists to describe a variety of Buddha-figures, which are all manifestations of the Buddha-Nature that pervades the universe. *See also* HC1 pp.64–65; MS p.221.

Buddh Gaya (Bodh Gaya), town in NE India. The Temple of Vishnu there marks the place where, according to tradition, BUDDHA received enlightenment under the sacred Bo tree. Pop.7,000.

Buddhism, religion founded in India *c.*528 BC by Gautama Siddhartha, the

BUDDHA. Buddhism is based on Four Noble Truths: existence is suffering; the cause of suffering is craving and attachment; cessation of suffering is possible through NIRVANA; Nirvana is attained through the Eightfold Path, which consists of the right views, resolve, speech, action, livelihood, effort, mindfulness and concentration. The total number of Buddhists in the world in the mid-1970s was estimated at about 220 million. They are concentrated most heavily in Burma, Sri Lanka, Indochina and Japan. *See also* HC1 pp.64–65; MS p.221.

Budding, or gemmation, method of asexual reproduction that produces a new organism from an outgrowth of the parent. Hydras often bud in spring and summer. A small bulge appears on the parent and grows until it breaks away as a new individual. In cooler weather many hydras reproduce sexually and lay eggs, which hatch only when conditions are again favourable. *See also* NW pp.82–83.

Budding, grafting a bud from one woody plant to another in the same or a closely related species. It can be done to improve the quality of the root or stem, to increase hardiness or resistance to disease, or to dwarf the plant. Commonly used in the cultivation of stone fruit trees, budding is most successful when done in the spring. *See also* PE p.*179*.

Buddleia, flowering shrub, often conspicuous because of the butterflies attracted to its purple or yellow flowers. Buddleias used to be classified as members of the logania family, native to the tropics, but are now considered to be a separate family.

Budenny, Semyon Mikhailovich (1883–1973), Soviet marshal (1935–41). He entered the Imperial Russian Cavalry in 1903 and joined the Communists in 1919, organizing the first Red cavalry armies, which in 1920 broke the Polish lines in the Soviet-Polish war. In 1941 he commanded the Soviet forces in the SW sector against the German invasion, but they were heavily defeated and he was replaced.

Budge, Donald (1915–), US tennis player. Regarded by most experts as one of the two greatest players of all time (with TILDEN), he was the first man to complete the "Grand Slam" of the four major singles (Wimbledon, USA, Australia, France) in one year (1938), after which he turned professional. He was triple Wimbledon and US champion in both 1937 and 1938.

Budgerigar, also called parakeet, small brightly coloured seed-eating PARROT native to Australia, and a popular pet. It can be taught to mimic speech. The sexes look alike but the coloration of the cere may differ seasonally. Size: 19cm (7.5in) long. Species *Melopsittacus undulatus*. *See also* NW pp.205, *221*.

Budget, annual financial statement "brought down" by the British Chancellor of the Exchequer, usually in the early spring, in which the expected outlays and the proposed means of supplying them are introduced in the House of Commons. The complexity of modern trade and finance has recently forced upon governments the making of two or more budgets in a single year.

Buena Vista, Battle of (Feb. 1847), MEXICAN WAR battle, in which US troops under Zachary TAYLOR were attacked by SANTA ANNA's Mexican army. After an indecisive battle lasting for two days, Santa Anna withdrew, giving the USA control of northern Mexico.

Bueno, Maria (1939–), Brazilian tennis player. A majestic, graceful player, she could hit the ball with power. She won three Wimbledon (1959, 1960, 1964) and four US (1959, 1963, 1964, 1966) singles and 11 major doubles titles with a variety of partners.

Buenos Aires, capital of Argentina, on the estuary of the Río de la Plata, 240km (150 miles) from the Atlantic Ocean. The largest city in the Southern Hemisphere, it was originally colonized by Spain in 1536. It then became a separate federal district in 1880. The seat of the national University (1821), it is a political, cultural and commercial centre. Industries: meat processing, flour milling, textiles, metal works, car assembly, oil refining. Pop. (1975 est.) 2,976,000. *See also* MW p.28.

Buerger's disease (*thromboangiitis obliterans*), inflammation of the arteries and veins that occurs particularly in men between adolescence and middle age. Pain and pallor of the affected part are the usual symptoms and treatment includes exercise of the affected limbs. *See also* MS pp.90–91.

Buffalo Bill. *See* CODY, WILLIAM.

Buffalo, industrial city and port in W New York State, on the E shore of Lake Erie. Settled 1803 by the Holland Land Company, the city's 19th-century industrial growth was due to its being the W terminus of the Erie Canal, opened in 1825. It was the scene of the assassination of President MCKINLEY in 1901 at the Pan-American Exposition. Industries include flour milling, motor-cars, chemicals and railway engineering. Pop. (1970) 462,768.

Buffalo, any of several horned mammals and a misnomer for the North American BISON. The massive ox-like Indian, or water, buffalo (*Bubalus bubalis*) is often domesticated for milk and hides. When wounded, the similar Cape, or African, buffalo (*Syncerus caffer*) is regarded as one of the animals most dangerous to man. Height: 1.5m (5ft). Family Bovidae. *See also* ANOA; NW pp.*72*, *163*, *196*, *198*, *200*, 207.

Buffer solution, solution to which a moderate quantity of a strong acid or a strong base can be added without making a significant change in its pH value (acidity or alkalinity). Buffer solutions usually consist of a mixture of a weak acid and one of its salts, a mixture of an acid salt and its normal salt or a mixture of two acid salts.

Buffet, Bernard (1928–) French painter. His most powerful works – harshly realistic still lifes, portraits and landscapes in monochromatic colours, painted in the 1950s and early 1960s – were a visual documentation of the philosophy of EXISTENTIALISM. His later work, the product of highly paid commissions, tends to be largely decorative.

Buffon, Georges-Louis Leclerc, Comte de (1707–88), French naturalist. From 1739, as keeper of the Jardin du Roi (now Jardin des Plantes) in Paris, he began to collect data for the monumental *Histoire naturelle* (44 vols, 1749–1804), a popular compendium of natural history. *See also* HC2 pp.*23*, 32; NW pp.22, 32.

Bug, any member of the order of insects Hemiptera, although in the USA any insect is commonly called a bug. True bugs are flattened insects which undergo gradual or incomplete metamorphosis, have two pairs of wings and use piercing and sucking mouthparts. Most feed on plant juices – greenfly being the best known – although a number attack animals and are important carriers of disease. *See also* APHIS; NW pp.110, *114*, *115*.

Bug, two rivers in the USSR. The western Bug rises in the Ukraine, flows N and then NW through Poland to join the River Vistula near Warsaw. Length: approx. 774km (481 miles). The southern Bug rises in the Ukraine and flows SE to the Black Sea. Length: approx. 856km (532 miles).

Bug, in espionage (spying), concealed electronic device used to listen in on private conversations. It is a microphone and may be connected to a radio transmitter, tape-recorder or telephone link, and may be hidden on a person or in a room. Most bugs are miniaturized, making use of the latest micro-electronic circuits. *See also* MS pp.*292–293*.

Bugaku, dances performed in the Japanese Imperial court with traditional exactitude, characterized by movements in ritualized patterns. They were imported from India and China in the 7th century.

Buganda, region of SE Uganda, E Africa. For centuries it was a powerful independent kingdom trading in slaves and ivory, but it gradually lost autonomy with the growth of British colonial influence. It was finally made part of Uganda in 1967. The Ganda tribe are its chief inhabitants. Area: 66,384sq km (25,631sq miles). Pop. (1971 est.) 2,854,000.

Bugatti, Ettore (1881–1947), Italian builder of motor vehicles and racing cars. He established a factory at Molsheim, Germany, in 1909 and there built a successful racer for LE MANS. The Bugatti Royale was one of the largest cars ever made, although production costs limited the total number to six. *See also* MM p.*129*.

Buggy, light carriage usually drawn by one horse. Buggies were a common form of transport before the advent of the motor-car, and there were various types. The gig was a two-wheeled, hooded vehicle with front seats for a driver and passenger. Coupés, sometimes called broughams, resembled coaches with the front part removed; the driver sat on an open seat in front of an enclosed passenger section. *See also* MM pp.120–121.

Bugle, brass wind instrument resembling a small TRUMPET without valves, capable of playing notes of only one harmonic series. Because its penetrating tones carry great distances, it is used for military signalling, as in calls to arms, réveille and retreat.

Bugle, or bugleweed, any of various species of flowering plants of the MINT family. The carpet bugle (*Ajuga reptans*) is common in Britain. It has a creeping stem and produces whorls of white or blue flowers.

Bugloss, wild flowering plant of the BORAGE family, with bright purplish-blue flowers. The genus *Echium* includes viper's bugloss, a common meadow plant, and genus *Lithospermum* contains the rarer flower also called blue cromwell.

Bugs Bunny, cartoon character. Created in 1936 by Chuck Jones and Fritz Freleng, and voiced by Mel Blanc, he starred in numerous hectic cartoon adventures.

Buhl. *See* BOULLE, ANDRÉ CHARLES.

Building Society, institution for providing mortgage loans to house-buyers. The money comes from savings invested by the public in deposits and shares. There have been building societies in Britain for more than 200 years, but the great period of their growth has been since WWII. The conduct of the societies is governed by Building Societies Acts and supervised by the Registrar of FRIENDLY SOCIETIES. There are about 330 societies in Britain, but most of the business is controlled by the ten largest firms.

Building techniques, methods of construction influenced by location, which affects climate and local customs, and the available technology. Some techniques still used for small structures are refinements of those used by early man. Walls of timber, mud stone, or mortar made from straw and mud may be used to support a roof. Another method uses supporting poles or columns and nonsupporting walls; yet another uses a skeletal framework which is covered with light material. Many large modern buildings have a central supporting column and a light surrounding framework. *See also* MM pp.46–49.

Buisson, Ferdinand-Édouard (1841–1932), French educationist. As director of elementary education (1879–96) he helped to re-organize French primary education. He taught at the Sorbonne University (1896–1902) and was a member of the chamber of deputies (1902–14; 1919–23). He was a pacifist and in 1898 helped to found the League of Human Rights, of which he was president (1913–26). In 1927, with Ludwig QUIDDE, he was awarded the Nobel Peace Prize.

Bujumbura, formerly Usumbura; capital and chief lake port of Burundi, E central Africa, at N end of Lake Tanganyika. It was the capital of Belgian Ruanda-Urundi after WWI, and remained so after independence in 1962. It is an administrative and commercial centre. Industries: textiles, food processing, tourism. Pop. (1976 est.) 110,000.

Bukavu, formerly Costermansville; port city of E Zaire, at S end of Lake Kivu. Capital of the Kivu region, it is an administrative, agricultural and trade centre. Industries: food processing, brewing, tourism. Pop. (1974) 181,774.

Bukhara. *See* BUCHARA.

Bukharest. *See* BUCHAREST.

Bukharin, Nikolai Ivanovich (1888–

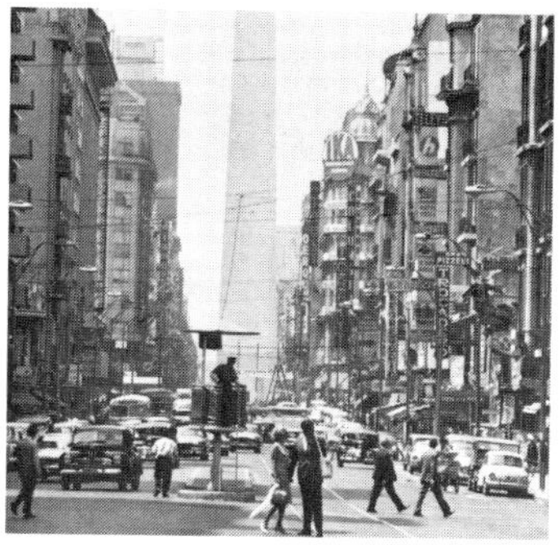

Buenos Aires, the home of one in four Argentinians, means *fair winds* in Spanish.

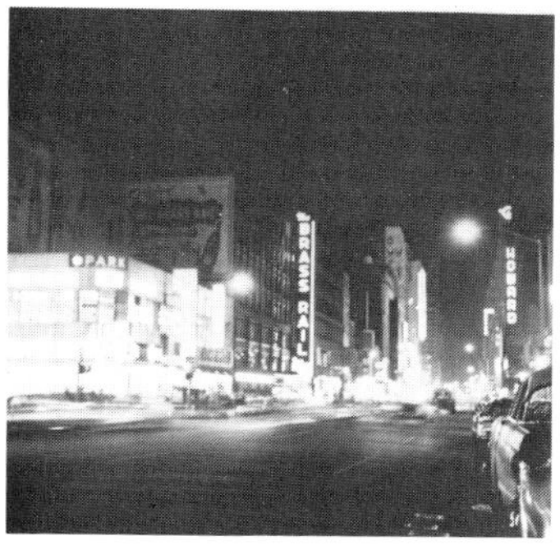

Buffalo receives much of its power as hydroelectricity from nearby Niagara Falls.

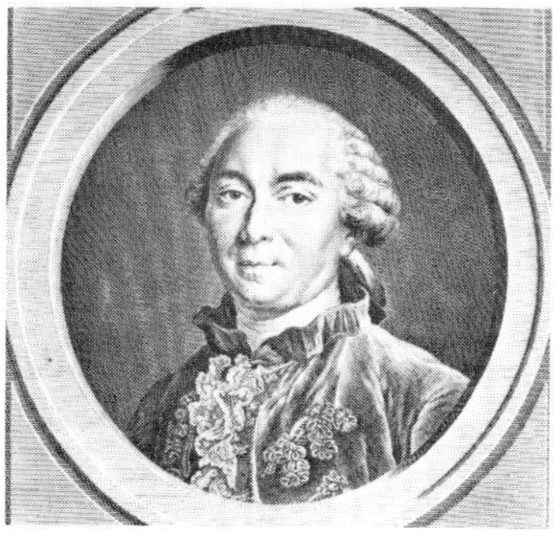

Georges Buffon organized the facts of natural history in comprehensible form.

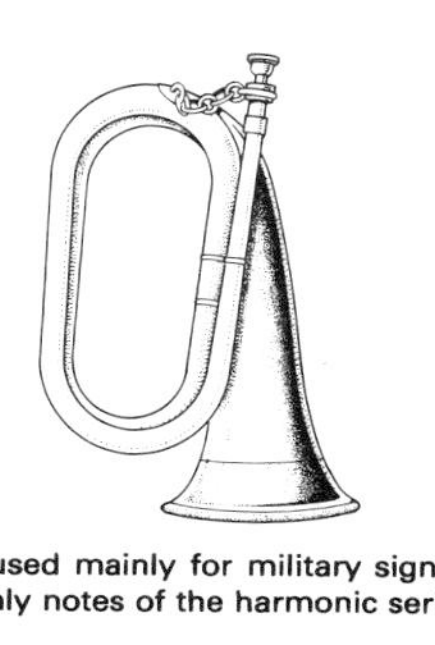

Bugles, used mainly for military signalling, sound only notes of the harmonic series.

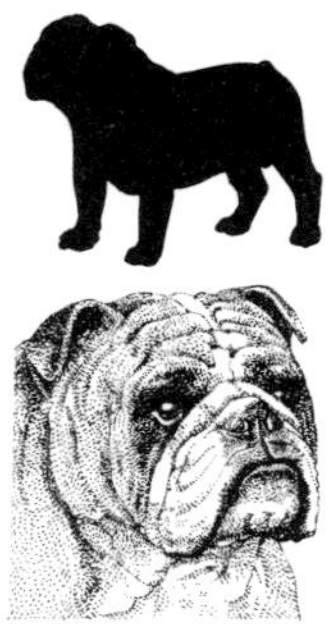

Bulldog; when the animal bites its upper and lower jaws lock tightly together.

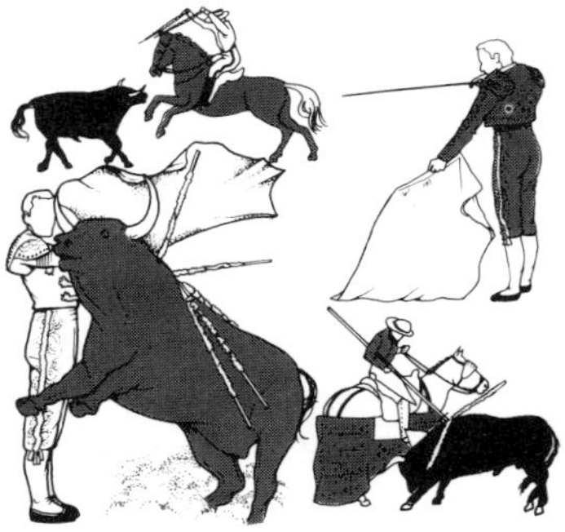

Bullfighting has been discouraged without much success by many of the rulers of Spain.

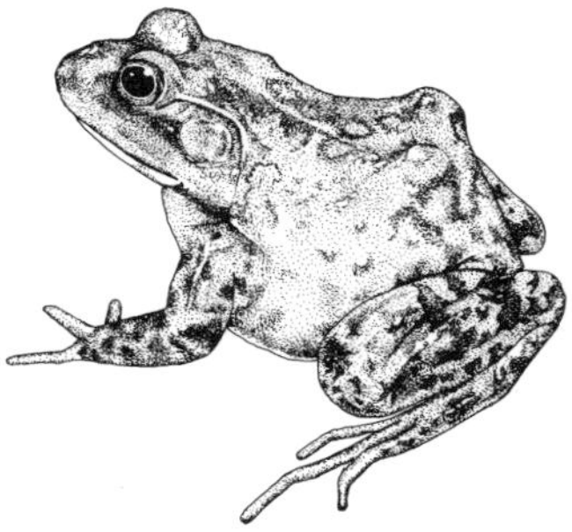

Bullfrogs are heard mainly at night in the spring and summer; the females are silent.

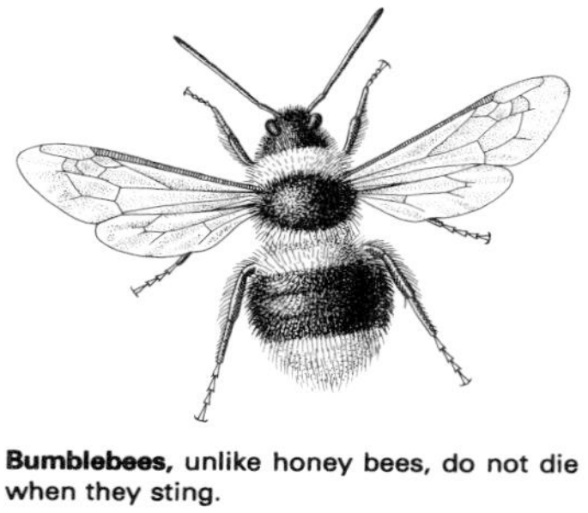

Bumblebees, unlike honey bees, do not die when they sting.

1938), Russian politician. In 1916 he edited the Leninist *Novy Mir* in New York. After the 1917 revolution he became a leading member of the Comintern and editor of *Pravda*, and in 1924 he was made a member of the Politburo. He opposed agricultural collectivisation and was executed for treason by STALIN in 1938.

Bukovina, historic region in NE Romania, extending into w Ukraine, USSR; the chief city is Chernovtsy. It was originally ceded to Romania by the treaties of Saint-Germain (1919) and Sèvres (1920), but the Romanian Peace Treaty of 1947 gave N Bukovina to the Russians. Products: timber, textiles, oil, salt, iron, copper, grain and livestock. Area: 10,440sq km (4,031sq miles).

Bulawayo, city in sw Rhodesia (Zimbabwe) 386km (240 miles) sw of Salisbury. It was founded by the British in 1893, and the Matabele revolt took place there in 1896. It is the second-largest city in the country and a major industrial centre. Industries: textiles, motor vehicles, cement. Pop. 281,000.

Bulb, underground bud consisting of a short stem and enlarged fleshy leaf scales; it produces a plant. Food is stored in the scales which are either layered in a series of rings, as in the onion, or loosely attached to the stem, as in some lilies. Smaller bulbs are produced in the axils of the outer leaf scales. When the offsets are mature they can be planted and will increase in size until capable of producing plants. *See also* NW pp.70–71.

Bulb, electric. *See* LAMP.

Bulbul, any of numerous species of songbirds of Africa and s Asia, where they are kept as cage birds. They are short-necked dull-coloured birds, ranging in size from 15 to 30cm (6–12in). They feed on berries and other fruits and build a grass nest for 3–5 eggs. Family Pycnonotidae; there are about 120 species. *See also* NW p.*214*.

Bulfinch, Thomas (1796–1867), US author who wrote a number of popular works on fable and legend. These include *The Age of Fable* (1855), *The Age of Chivalry* (1858), *Legends of Charlemagne* (1863) and *Oregon and Eldorado* (1866).

Bulgakov, Mikhail Afanasyevich (1891–1940), Russian novelist and dramatist. His most famous novels are *The White Guard* (1925) and *The Master and Margarita*, which he wrote between 1928 and his death.

Bulganin, Nikolai (1895–1975), Soviet military and political leader. He became Defence Minister (1947–49; 1953–55) and rose from being a Central Committee member to become Premier of the USSR (1948). He was expelled from the Presidium for opposing KHRUSHCHEV in 1958. *See also* HC2 p.241.

Bulgaria, country in SE Europe on the Balkan peninsula. Since WWII it has been one of the Communist bloc nations under the domination of the Soviet Union. Traditionally it has an agrarian economy, although efforts have been made by the Communist government to stimulate industrialization. Area: 110,911sq km (42,823sq miles). Pop. (1975 est.) 8,722,000. *See* MW p.42.

Bulgars, ancient Turkic people originating in the region to the N and E of the Black Sea, which divided *c.* AD 650 into two separate states. The western part moved to present-day Bulgaria, where it was assimilated into the Slavic population and adopted Christianity in 865. The other group moved to the VOLGA region where they set up a Bulgar state. They were converted to ISLAM and ruled by the MUSCOVITES in the 15th century.

Bulge, Battle of the, final German offensive in WWII. The US lines along the borders of France and Germany were thin when the Germans launched an attack on them in Dec. 1944. They pushed the Allies back into Belgium, but the US forces held Bastogne against their attack. A combined Allied counter-attack from the NW and from the S led to eventual German defeat (Jan. 1945). *See also* HC2 p.228.

Bulk modulus, physical constant of solids and fluids that indicates their elastic properties when they are under pressure over their entire surfaces. The bulk modulus is also called the incompressibility: if a solid or a fluid (liquid or gas) has a high bulk modulus, then it is difficult to compress.

Bull, Jacob Martin Luther Olaf (1883–1933), one of Norway's leading poets. His finest collection was *Metope* (1927).

Bull, John (*c.* 1562–1628), English composer and organist, the writer of some 150 pieces for organ and virginals. He became organist of the Chapel Royal in 1591, and later was professor of music at GRESHAM'S COLLEGE. He left England in 1613, and after working in Brussels for some years became organist at Antwerp cathedral, a post he held until his death.

Bull, Papal. *See* PAPAL BULL.

Bullace, small wild PLUM tree that flowers in hedges and scrubland in Britain from March to mid-May. The bullace fruit or plum is only about 2cm (0.75in) in diameter, purple or yellow in colour, and is borne in small clusters. Species *Prunus institia*.

Bullard, Sir Edward Crisp (1907–), English geophysicist. He is noted for his work in GEOMAGNETISM, especially his theory of the geomagnetic dynamo, based on convective motion in the Earth's core.

Bull-baiting, popular pastime in England (11th–19th centuries) in which dogs were set on a tethered bull. Another version was bull-running, in which a bull was chased from one end of a town to the other by the townspeople with sticks and eventually killed and eaten.

Bulldog, English bull-baiting breed of DOG with a distinctive large head, a short upturned muzzle and a projecting lower jaw. The body is large with muscular shoulders, a broad chest and short stout legs; the tail is short. The smooth coat may be white, tan or brindle. Height: (at shoulder) up to 38cm (15in).

Bulldozer, tractor fitted with caterpillar tracks and a large vertical blade at the front. It is used for levelling ground, clearing debris and removing boulders. *See also* MM pp.98–99.

Buller, Charles (1806–48), British Radical politician. He was secretary to Lord DURHAM on the mission to report on Canada in 1838, and his belief in the need to grant responsible government to the Canadian colonies was influential in producing the radical recommendations of the DURHAM REPORT. *See also* HC2 pp.132–133, 136–137.

Buller, Sir Redvers Henry (1839–1908), British general. He began his career in China, took part in the Red River expedition against the RIEL rebellion in Canada, and won the Victoria Cross in the ZULU WAR (1879). He was Commander-in-Chief in the SOUTH AFRICAN WAR from 1899–1900.

Bullfighting, sport popular in Latin America and Spain, where it is the national sport. Usually there are six bulls and three matadors who are assigned two bulls each. Each matador has five assistants – two *picadors* (who are mounted on armoured horses) and three *peones* or *banderilleros*. A bullfight starts when the picadors stab the bull four times with their lances to weaken it. The *peones* then plant banderillas (barbed sticks) on the withers of the bull. The matador makes several passes with his red cape (muleta) before attempting to kill the bull by thrusting a sword into its heart.

Bullfinch, European finch, with a stout, rounded beak. Males have a crimson and grey body and a black head; females have duller colours. Species *Pyrrhula pyrrhula*. Bullfinch is also the name given by horse-riders to a stout, high hedge that is difficult to jump.

Bullfrog, FROG found in streams and ponds in the USA; it is green or brown and breeds in the spring. The largest North American frog, it can jump long distances; it gets its name from its loud bass voice. Family Ranidae, genus *Rana*. Length: up to 20cm (8in).

Bullion, precious metal such as gold or silver in the form of ingots, plate or coins not in legal use, when valued simply for the weight of metal.

Bull mastiff, English watchdog bred from the MASTIFF and BULLDOG, with a large head and a broad deep muzzle. The body is compact; the wide-set legs are straight and strong and the tail is tapered and set high. The smooth dense coat is red, tan or brindle. Height: (at shoulder) up to 68.5cm (27in).

Bullroarer, flat piece of wood or bone attached to a string which, when swung in the air, produces a roaring sound. It originated in primitive societies.

Bull Run, Virginia, site of two battles in the American Civil War. The first battle (21 July 1861), saw the defeat of the Union troops under McDowell at the hands of the Confederates led by Beauregard and JACKSON, who won his nickname "Stonewall" on this occasion. The second battle (29 Aug. to 1 Sept. 1862) was also a Confederate victory won by Robert E. LEE. *See also* HC2 p.150–151.

Bull terrier, strongly-built sporting DOG once used for bear-baiting; it has a large oval head with small erect ears. The broad-chested body is set on strong big-boned legs and the tail is short. The "coloured" variety can be any colour, but the "white" is always pure white, often with darker head markings. Height: (at shoulder) up to 56cm (22in).

Bülow, Bernhard von, Prince (1849–1929), German statesman and imperial Chancellor from 1900-09. He was a careful conservative in domestic policy, but his aggressiveness in foreign policy left Germany isolated and heightened the tensions leading up to WWI. He lost the favour of the emperor in 1908 and was forced to resign the next year.

Bülow, Friedrich Wilhelm, Freiherr von (1755–1816), Prussian general. In the NAPOLEONIC WARS he defeated the French at the battles of Grossbeeren and Dennewitz (1813), and was made a count. He also participated in the victories at LEIPZIG (1813) and WATERLOO (1815).

Bülow, Hans Guido, Freiherr von (1830–94), German pianist and conductor. In 1857 he married LISZT's daughter, Cosima, who later left him for WAGNER. Although highly regarded as a piano virtuoso (he was taught by Liszt) he became best known as a conductor of German music and a champion of BEETHOVEN, Wagner and BRAHMS. He conducted the first performance of several Wagner operas.

Bulrush, grass-like plant of the SEDGE family found in marshes or beside water in Europe, Africa and North America. The common British bulrush, or reed mace, *Typha latifolia*, reaches 1.8–2.1m (6–7ft) and bears both male and female flowers. Family Cyperaceae. *See also* NW p.*69*.

Bultmann, Rudolf (Karl) (1884–), German theologian. He is one of the most controversial and influential New Testament scholars of the 20th century. His EXISTENTIALIST interpretations, which systematically "remove" mythology from the New Testament, are found in *The Theology of the New Testament* (1948–53). *See also* HC2 p.*305*.

Bulwer-Lytton. *See* LYTTON.

Bumblebee, also called humble bee, robust hairy black BEE with broad yellow or orange stripes. Two genera, *Bombus* and its parasite *Psithyrus*, occur widely in Britain. Bombus live in organized groups in ground or tree nests, where the fertile queen lays her first eggs after the winter hibernation. These become worker bees. Later, the queen lays eggs to produce drones (males) and new queens which develop before the colony dies. The cycle is then repeated. Length: up to 2.5cm (1in). Order Hymenoptera; family Apidae. *See also* NW p.108.

Bumbry, Grace (1937–), US mezzo-soprano. She studied with Lotte LEHMANN and made her debut in Paris in 1960. After many successes in Europe and at the Carnegie Hall, she made her Metropolitan Opera debut in 1965.

Bunbury, port in sw Western Australia, on Geographe Bay at the junction of the Collie and Preston rivers. It is a resort area and a major outlet for the export of timber, farm products, fruit, coal and other minerals. Pop. (1971) 17,762.

Bunche, Ralph Johnson (1904–71), US

statesman and diplomat. He entered the UN in 1947, where he held several posts, eg under-secretary for special political affairs. He helped negotiate a ceasefire in the Arab-Israeli conflict (1949), for which he received the Nobel Peace Prize (1950) – the first black American to do so.
Bundaberg, port in SE Queensland, Australia, on the Burnett River, 322km (200 miles) N of Brisbane. It is the centre of a sugar area – plantations were established there in the 1870s. Industries: sugar refining and distilling, dairying. Pop. (1971) 26,570.
Bundesrat, upper house of the West German parliament. It is composed of voting representatives elected by the federal states, and of non-voting West Berliners. The Bundesrat acts on measures sent from the more powerful BUNDESTAG. It was the federal chamber of the German Empire (1871–1918). The upper house of the Austrian Parliament is also known as the Bundesrat. *See also* BUNDESTAG.
Bundestag, lower house of the West German parliament, responsible for initiating legislation, ratifying important treaties and electing the chancellor. With an equal number of representatives from the state parliaments, it elects the federal president. It also includes non-voting members from West Berlin. *See also* BUNDESRAT.
Bunin, Ivan Alekseyevich (1870–1953), Russian writer. He was opposed to the 1917 Revolution and left Russia to settle in France. Influenced by TURGENEV, his works lament the passing of the old Russian order. They include the novel *The Village* (1910) and the short story *The Gentleman from San Francisco* (1915). He was awarded the Nobel Prize for literature in 1933.
Bunion, form of BURSITIS occurring at the base of the big toe's first joint. The swelling involved becomes covered with thickened skin due to friction, and prolonged pressure on the toe forces it painfully towards its neighbour. It can be treated by surgery.
Bunker Hill, Battle of, battle in the AMERICAN WAR OF INDEPENDENCE that took place on 17 June 1775 on Boston's Charlestown peninsula. The first large-scale battle of the war, it was fought S of Bunker Hill on Breed's Hill. Although technically defeated, the Americans won a moral victory by inflicting heavy losses on the British. *See also* HC2 pp.64–65.
Bunsen, Robert Wilhelm (1811–99), German chemist, professor at Heidelberg (1852–99). During his early work on arsenic compounds he lost an eye in an explosion and was badly poisoned. He discovered an arsenic poisoning antidote and evolved a method of gas analysis. With his assistant, Gustav KIRCHHOFF, he used spectroscopy to discover two new elements (caesium and rubidium). He invented various kinds of laboratory equipment, such as the Bunsen cell, a carbon-zinc electric cell. He also improved a gas burner that was later named after him. The Bunsen burner consists of a tube with a variable air inlet that controls the intensity of its smokeless, blue flame.
Bunting, Edward (1773–1843), Irish organist and folksong collector. His great achievement was to collect, in three volumes (1796, 1809 and 1840), uncorrupted harpists' tunes from all over Ireland.
Bunting, FINCH found throughout most of the world. Males of the genus *Passerina* are brightly coloured, whereas the females are smaller and duller. Members of the genus *Emberiza* are larger and dull coloured, although the snow bunting is almost white. Most build cup-shaped nests for their eggs. Family Fringillidae.
Buñuel, Luis (1900–), Spanish film-maker who has worked mostly outside Spain. His films are concerned with harsh criticism of the Church and social hypocrisies by means of a surrealist comic vision. Among his major works are *Un chien andalou* (1928), *Viridiana* (1961), *Belle de jour* (1966), *The Discreet Charm of the Bourgeoisie* (1972) and *The Phantom of Liberty* (1974). *See also* SURREALISM.
Bunyan, John (1628–88), English preacher and author. During the ENGLISH CIVIL WAR he was a Parliamentarian soldier. In 1655 he became a Puritan minister, and twice suffered imprisonment for his nonconformist religious activities. His writings were popular and colloquial in style. They included *Grace Abounding* (1666), and *The Pilgrim's Progress* (1678), his best-known work. *See also* HC1 354L.
Bunyan, Paul, legendary US folk hero, a gigantic lumberjack. Tales about him and his blue ox, Babe, first appeared in the early 20th century lumber camps of the Midwest. He was credited with the creation of the Black Hills and the Grand Canyon.
Bunyoro, former kingdom in E Africa, bordering Lake Albert. It was established by northern intruders who subjugated the local Bantu people. It lost territory to Buganda and was absorbed into the British protectorate of Uganda in 1896.
Buoyancy, upward pressure exerted on an object by the fluid in which it is immersed. The object is subjected to pressure from all sides, but the pressure on its lower part is greatest because of the increasing depth of the fluid. The result of all these forces is a force acting upwards, which is equal to the weight of the fluid displaced. *See also* ARCHIMEDES' PRINCIPLE: SU pp.78, 86.
Buraydah, town in N central Saudi Arabia, 338km (210 miles) NW of Riyadh (Ar-Riyād). It is a commercial centre with cattle and camel markets and date palm groves. Pop. 50,000.
Burbage, family of Elizabethan actors. James (1531–97) one of the Earl of Leicester's players, leased land for the first English playhouse, the Theatre, in Shoreditch (1576). His son, Richard (*c.* 1567–1619), has been called the first great English actor. He was the leading tragedian in the King's Men, and first played the title roles in Shakespeare's *Hamlet*, *King Lear*, *Othello* and *Richard III*. In 1598, his brother Cuthbert moved the Theatre to Bankside, and with Shakespeare as partner, founded the famous Globe Theatre. *See also* HC1 pp.*284–285*.
Burbank, Luther (1849–1926), US horticulturalist. He experimented with thousands of varieties of plants and, by means of revolutionary breeding methods, he developed more than 800 new strains of fruits, grains and flowers. His great efforts helped to elevate plant-breeding into a modern science.
Burbot, bottom-dwelling fresh-water COD found in colder waters of Asia, N America and Europe. It is a slender brown fish that spawns in winter. Length: to 110cm (38in); weight: to 16kg (36lb). Order Gadiformes; family Gadidae; species *Lota lota*. *See also* NW p.131.
Burbridge, Eleanor Margaret (*c.* 1925–), British astronomer. She was professor of astronomy at the University of California, San Diego, from 1965 until 1972, and director of the Royal Greenwich Observatory (1972–73). She contributed significantly to the study of QUASARS.
Burchfield, Charles Ephraim (1893–1967), US painter. His works merged a realistic and Romantic style with occasional elements of SURREALISM. His works include *Night Wind* (1918), *The Four Seasons* (1949–60) and *An April Mood* (1946–55).
Burckhardt, Jacob Christoph (1818–97), Swiss cultural and art historian. He emphasized cultural values, rather than political factors, an attitude influential in the development of the modern approach to history. His chief work was *The Civilization of the Renaissance in Italy* (1860).
Burden of proof, in law, the obligation to provide evidence which the judge or jury could reasonably believe, in the settlement of a case. More generally, it is the obligation to establish the truth of an alleged fact.
Burdett, Sir Francis (1770–1844), British political figure. In 1810 he was imprisoned for defending a radical orator in William Cobbett's *Weekly Register*. In 1820 he was imprisoned again for opposing government action at the PETERLOO MASSACRE. His daughter, Angela Georgina Burdett-Coutts (1814–1906), was a wealthy philanthropist who spent much of her money on housing and education for the needy in London.
Burdock, oil-yielding weed found throughout Europe, North Africa and North America. It has large basal leaves and thistle-like purple flowerheads covered by stiff, hooked bracts. Common burdock, *Arctium pubens*, is biennial and grows to 0.9m (3ft). Family Compositae.
Bureaucracy, the administrative structure of any large organization, public or private. A hierarchic, compartmental administration should be efficient and responsible. In practice it often turns out to be rigid and incompetent, duplicating work and sticking inflexibly to the rules. *See also* MS pp.280–281, 302.
Burford, Battle of (752), victory of Cuthbert of Wessex over Ethelbert of Mercia. The battle probably secured Wessex's independence from the more powerful Mercian kingdom.
Burgage, tenure of the sovereign's or the lord of the manor's property by a burgess, or freeman of a town, in Britain from Anglo-Saxon times. The payment of rent, and not necessarily the owner's favour, secured the tenure. Until the Municipal Corporations Act (1835) it conferred a special electoral FRANCHISE.
Burgas, major Black Sea port of SE Bulgaria. Capital of Burgas province, it is a developing resort. Industries: fishing, canning, oil refining, agricultural machinery. Pop. (1970 est.) 136,000.
Burgenland, province of E Austria, extending from the River Danube southwards along the W border of Hungary from which it was transferred after WWI. Industries: agriculture, timber, mining. Area: 3,965sq km (1,531sq miles). Pop. (1971) 272,000.
Burgess, Anthony (John Burgess Wilson) (1917–), English novelist. Malaya, where he lived from 1954 to 1959, is the setting for the trilogy *Time for a Tiger* (1956), *The Enemy in the Blanket* (1958) and *Beds in the East* (1959). In later novels he shows an interest in social trends, linguistic effects and religious symbolism, as in *A Clockwork Orange* (1962), the *Enderby* trilogy (1963–74) and *Abba, Abba* (1977).
Burgh, Hubert de (*d.* 1243) Justiciar of England (1215–32) and effective ruler of the country during the minority and early reign of HENRY III. His ship led the fleet in England's first great naval victory, over the French near Sandwich, in 1217.
Burgh, former Scottish administrative area, finally abolished in 1975. Royal burghs were incorporated by royal charter and parliamentary burghs elected their own MPS. The burgh was the equivalent of the English BOROUGH, and was pronounced in the same way.
Burghley, William Cecil, 1st Baron (1520–98), English statesman. He began his career under the Protector SOMERSET and served ELIZABETH I for 40 years, as secretary (1558–72) and lord treasurer (1572–98). He resolutely suppressed all Catholic plots against Elizabeth's rule. *See also* HC1 pp.274–275.
Burgkmair, Hans, the Elder (1473–1531), German painter and woodcut designer. He was one of the first artists in Germany to be influenced by the Italian RENAISSANCE style. His works include *The Triumphs of the Emperor Maximilian I* (*c.* 1509) and *The Lovers Surprised by Death* (1510).
Burglar alarm, device that gives warning of an actual or attempted illegal entry to premises. In a typical system electrified metal tape is placed at all doors and other entrances to a building. The tape is in circuit with an electromechanical relay, which trips and so energizes an alarm if any tape is disturbed or broken. Other alarm systems employ photoelectric cells (magic eyes), ultrasonic sensors or laser beams. *See also* MM p.*103*.
Burgos, capital of Burgos province, Old Castile, N Spain, 212km (132 miles) N of Madrid. It has a Gothic cathedral (1221), and is the burial place of El Cid. It is an important trade and tourist centre. Industries: fabrics, soap, furniture, footwear, wine, paper. Pop. (1970) 119,915.

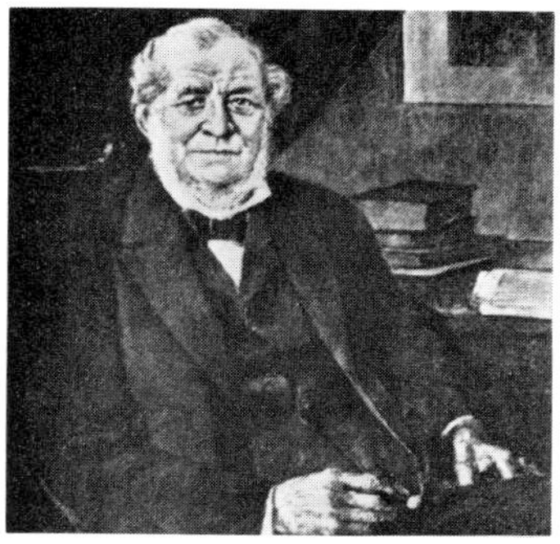

Robert Wilhelm Bunsen developed the gas burner which gives a hot smokeless flame.

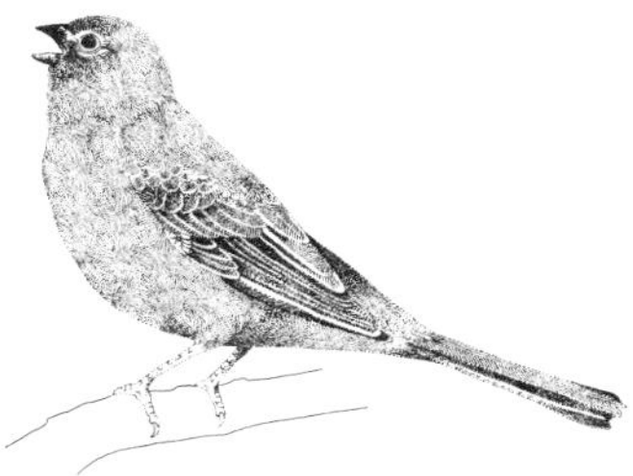

Bunting, a group of seed-eating birds of the finch family; this is the Indigo bunting.

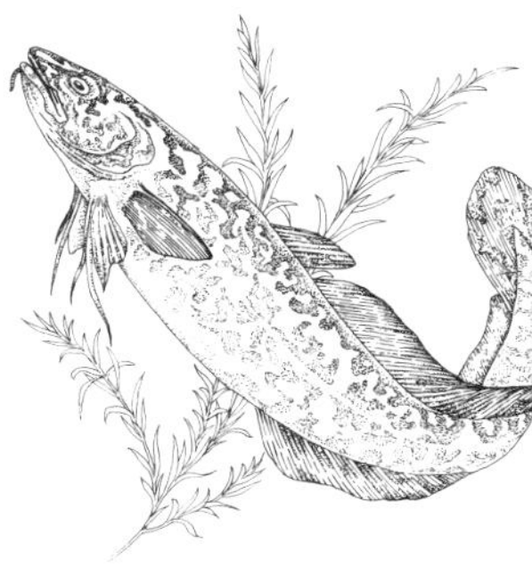

Burbot, the only freshwater member of the cod family, lives close to the bottom.

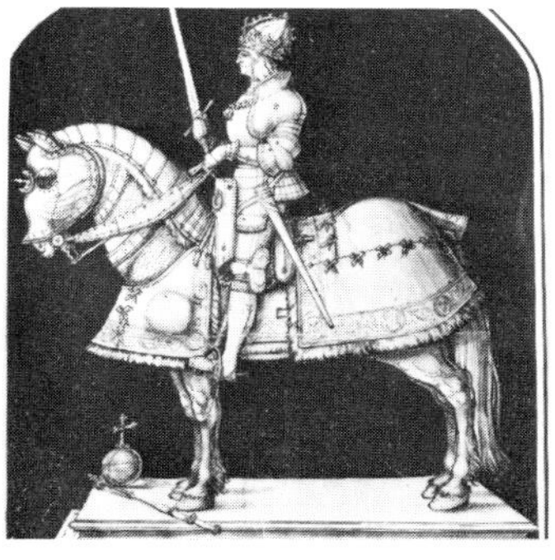

Hans Burgkmair the Elder; his design for the portrait of the Emperor Maximilian.

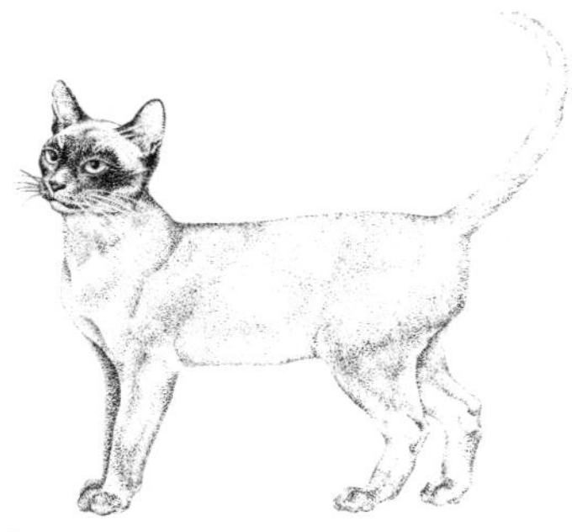

Burmese cats are related to the Siamese and are probably a domesticated oriental wildcat.

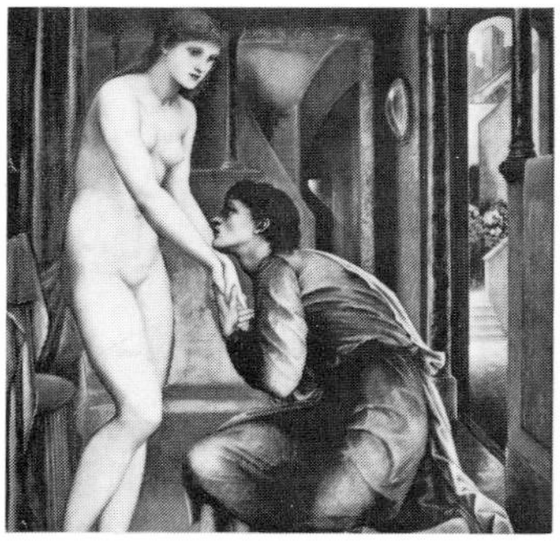

Edward Burne-Jones; *Pygmalion* (detail) the sculptor who falls in love with his creation.

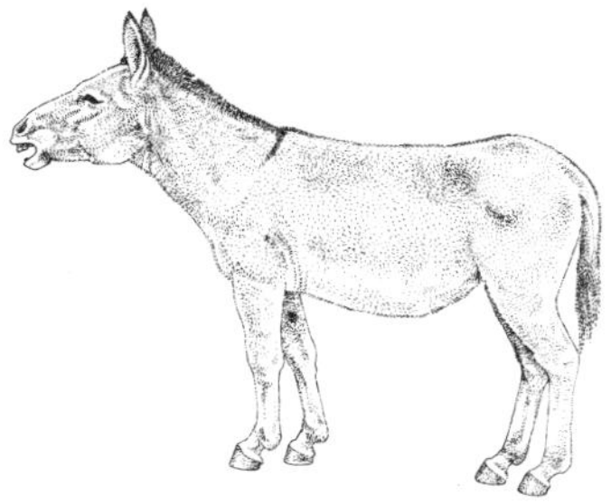

Burro; the domesticated ass used as a pack animal in south-western USA and Mexico.

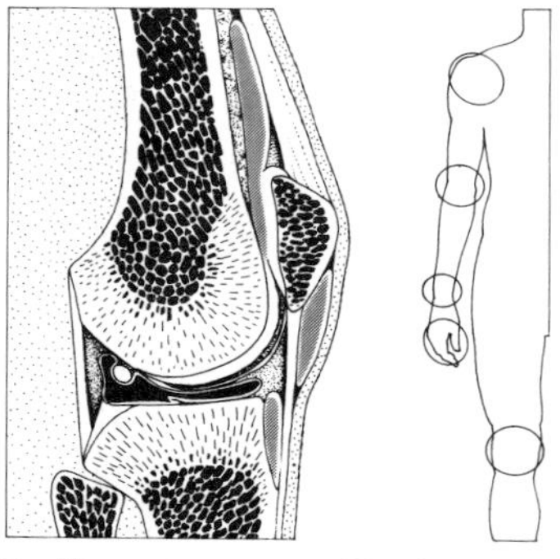

Bursitis; a common condition known by familiar names such as "housemaid's knee".

Burgoyne, John (1722–92), British general during the American War of Independence. He served as major-general in Canada (1776) and campaigned in New York State, securing Crown Point and Fort Ticonderoga. He was finally forced to surrender his troops at Saratoga in October 1777. *See also* HC2 p.65.

Burgundy, historical region of E central France that now includes the départements of Yonne, Côte-d'Or, Saône-et-Loire, Ain, and Nièvre. The region has many Romanesque churches. Dijon is the historical capital. A rich agricultural region, it has long been known for its wine. Burgundy's golden age began in 1364 when John II of France made his son, Philip the Bold, Duke of Burgundy. The succeeding dukes created a state that extended across the Rhine and included the Low Countries. They dominated French politics in the early 15th century. The last reigning duke, Charles the Bold (*r.* 1467–77) failed to have himself crowned king by the Holy Roman Emperor, and Burgundy was dismembered after his death, France annexing the largest part.

Burh. *See* BOROUGH.

Burial customs, ceremonies performed for the dead. Men have interred corpses for various reasons: to propitiate the gods; to speed the soul of the dead on its transcendent journey; or to honour the dead. The Greeks buried each person with a coin as payment to the ferryman, Charon, for carrying his soul across the river of death. The Western habit of wearing mourning black comes from the Romans. Embalming comes from the Egyptians, who believed that, by preserving the body of a dead person, they helped his soul to live. *See also* MS pp.*26–27*, 180–181.

Buriat, region in central Asia inhabited by the Buriat people. It is now part of the USSR, with its capital at Ulan-Ude. Its western boundary is Lake Baikal. The region is mostly steppe-land; its inhabitants raise cattle.

Burke, Edmund (1729–97), British statesman and writer. He played a major part in the reduction of royal influence in the House of Commons. With Charles James FOX he sought better treatment for the Catholics and Americans. He instigated the impeachment of Warren HASTINGS in an attempt to reform India's government in 1788. Burke believed in liberty based on order, with change being gradual; his horror at the radicalism of the FRENCH REVOLUTION is shown in *Reflections on the Revolution in France* (1790). *See also* HC2 pp.*25*, 27, 68, *68*, *94*, 170.

Burke, Robert O'Hara (1820–61), Irish explorer. With W. J. WILLS he led an expedition across Australia from south to north in 1860. Starting in Melbourne, he left most of his party at the River Barcoo, continuing to N Australia (reached in 1861) with a party of three. On the return trip he and two of his companions died; a fourth (King) was finally rescued.

Burke and Hare, Irish murderers. William Burke helped William Hare, his landlord in Edinburgh, sell the body of a deceased tenant (1827) to anatomists. They then murdered at least 15 people for their bodies. When caught, Hare turned king's evidence and Burke was hanged. *See also* BODY SNATCHERS.

Burke's Peerage, book produced each year since 1826, proper title *Genealogical and Heraldic History of the Peerage, Baronetage, and Knightage of the United Kingdom.* It lists details of all the British nobility and was first produced by John Burke (1787–1848).

Burlesque, form of literary or dramatic entertainment that achieves its effect by caricature, ridicule and distortion, often of celebrated literary works. The word is derived from the Italian, *burla*, "ridicule". A later American form became generally synonymous with strip shows.

Burlington, Richard Boyle, 3rd Earl of (1694–1753), English architect. He was an advocate of the PALLADIAN style. His most important building in that style is the Assembly Room at York (1730).

Burma, nation in SE Asia. Although it is rich in natural resources, including gem stones and teak, many of these have yet to be fully exploited, and the economy is largely agrarian; major cash crops are rubber, tea, tobacco and jute. Area: 678,033sq km (261,789sq miles). Pop. (1975 est.) 31,240,000. *See* MW p.43.

Burma Road, 1,154km (717 mile) road from Lashio, Burma, to K'un-ming, China, built in 1937–38 to carry supplies when China's seaports were blockaded by Japan. It was used in WWII to carry Allied war supplies but was closed by the Japanese in 1942.

Burmese cat, short-haired domestic cat. It has a well-rounded head, yellow or gold eyes and a coat that may be sable, blue, red or tortoiseshell. The ears are wide-set and the body is muscular. It is related to the Siamese.

Burn, injury produced by fire, steam, chemicals, hot metals, electricity or radiation. Burns are classified according to the depth of the tissue injury. First-degree burns involve only superficial skin damage; second- and third-degree burns go progressively deeper. Treatment includes relief of pain, control of infection and prevention of shock. *See also* SKIN; SKIN GRAFTING; MS p.*133*.

Burne-Jones, Sir Edward Coley (1833–98), English painter and designer. Influenced by Dante Gabriel ROSSETTI and William MORRIS, he began painting in 1855 and was associated with PRE-RAPHAELITE Romanticism and escapism. An early work is *Merlin and Nimue*; his later, more literary work is typified in *King Cophetua and the Beggar Maid* (1884).

Burnet, perennial plant native to N temperate regions, whose leaves are used to give a cucumber flavour to salads. Long-stamened pink flowers are borne on tall stalks. Family Rosaceae; genus *Sanguisorba. See also* PE pp.*191*, *213*.

Burnet, Gilbert (1643–1715), British churchman and historian. His 3-vol. *History of the Reformation in England* (1679–1715), based on original sources, and his *History of His Own Time* (published 1723–24) are invaluable studies of 17th-century Britain.

Burnet, Sir (Frank) Macfarlane (1899–), Australian virologist and immunologist. Burnet proposed that under certain conditions tissues and organs could be successfully transplanted from one animal to another. This idea was called "acquired immunological tolerance". As a result of this discovery he shared the 1960 Nobel Prize in physiology and medicine with Peter MEDAWAR.

Burnett, Frances (1849–1924), US author, *b.* England, real name Eliza Hodgson. She is most noted for *Little Lord Fauntleroy* (1886), a rags-to-riches tale. She is also remembered for her notable book, *The Secret Garden* (1911).

Burnett, William Riley (1899–), US author. His novels about gangsters and prize-fighters include *Little Caesar* (1929), which was made into a film starring Edward G. Robinson (1930), *Dark Hazard* (1933) and *The Asphalt Jungle* (1949).

Burney, Fanny (1752–1840), English novelist and diarist. Her most successful novel, *Evelina* (1778), was followed by *Camilla* (1796) and *The Wanderer* (1814). Her diaries and letters vividly describe English culture and society from 1768–1840. *See also* HC2 p.34.

Burnham, Daniel Hudson (1846–1912), US architect and city planner. With his partner John W. ROOT he was a pioneer in the development of early steel-frame and modern commercial architecture, designing buildings such as the Reliance Building (1890) and the 20-storey Masonic Temple Building (1891), both in Chicago.

Burnham, Forbes (1923–), Prime Minister of Guyana (1964–). Leader of the People's National Congress (1957–), Burnham was chief executive when British Guiana attained independence in 1966 and became a republic (1970). His party increased its majority in 1973.

Burnley, town in Lancashire, NW England, on the Leeds-Liverpool Canal and the River Calder. Industries: coalmining, chemicals, textile machinery, textiles. Pop. (1971) 76,500.

Burnout, rocket, the point on a rocket's trajectory at which the fuel supply is exhausted or cut off. In solid fuel rockets, controlled burnout is achieved by lowering the pressure in the combustion chamber or by opening vents to drop the temperature below the combustion point. In liquid fuel rockets the fuel supply is simply turned off. *See also* MM p.156.

Burns, George (1896–), US comedian. With his wife Gracie Allen he starred in music hall, on radio and on television in the *Burns and Allen Show* (1950–58). In 1975 he received an Academy Award for his acting in the film *The Sunshine Boys.*

Burns, John (1858–1943), British Labour politician who was an MP for 26 years (1892–1918). From 1905 he was a cabinet minister and was president of the Board of Trade at the outbreak of WWI, when he resigned.

Burns, Robert (1759–96), Scottish lyric poet. The success of *Poems, Chiefly in the Scottish Dialect* (1786), including *The Holy Fair* and *To a Mouse*, enabled him to move to Edinburgh. Although popular he could not support himself solely on his poems, so he became an excise officer. Scotland's unofficial poet laureate, his best-known works are *Tam o'Shanter* (1790) and the song *Auld Lang Syne. See also* HC2 p.31, *31*.

Burns, Tommy (1881–1955), Canadian boxer, real name Noah Brusso. He claimed the world heavyweight championship in 1906 when he beat Marvin Hart in Los Angeles.

Burra, Edward John (1905–76), British painter. After studying in London he worked in Paris, where the underworld formed the inspiration for much of his painting. His later work, such as *Soldiers* and *War in the Sun*, was strongly influenced by the Spanish Civil War and WWII.

Bur-reed, marsh plant that has hard, dry, prickly fruits and long grass-like leaves. Genus *Sparganium. See also* NW p.69.

Burro, small domesticated ASS used as a pack animal in SW USA and Mexico; it is a long-eared sturdy animal derived from the Nubian wild ass and may be brown, grey or black. Family Equidae; species *Equus asinus asinus.*

Burroughs, Edgar Rice (1875–1950), US author of adventure novels. A prolific writer, he is noted for the Tarzan books, the first of which was *Tarzan of the Apes* (1914). He also wrote science fiction.

Burroughs, William (1914–), US novelist, regarded as a founder of the BEAT GENERATION. His most notable work, *Naked Lunch* (1959) deals in part with his addiction to heroin. Other works, experimental in style, include *The Ticket That Exploded* (1962) and *The Wild Boys* (1971). *See also* HC2 p.289.

Burrows, Abe (1910–), US playwright, director and humorist. He appeared on radio and television as well as in theatres and nightclubs. He wrote the Broadway plays *Can Can* (1953) and *Say, Darling* (1958), and received the New York Drama Critics' Award as co-author of *Guys and Dolls* (1950) and *How to Succeed in Business Without Really Trying* (1961), for which he also received the Pulitzer Prize and a Tony Award.

Bursa, formerly Brusa, capital of Bursa province in NW Turkey, 26km (16 miles) SE of the Sea of Marmara. Site of the ancient Bithynian city of Prusa, it became the Ottoman capital (1327–1413). It is an important transport centre. Industries: silk, carpets, tobacco. Pop. 318,209.

Bur Sa'id. *See* PORT SAID.

Bursitis, inflammation of a sac or cavity (bursa) located (usually) near a joint. It is characterized by pain, swelling and difficulty in movement; treatment generally includes rest, heat and mild exercise. "Housemaid's knee" and "tennis elbow" are common forms of bursitis, as is a BUNION. *See also* MS pp.94–95.

Burslem, town in Staffordshire, W central England. Incorporated into STOKE-ON-TRENT in 1910, it is in the area known as the Potteries. Josiah WEDGWOOD was born there in 1730, and the Wedgwood Institute contains a museum. The town's main industry is ceramics.

Bur Sudan. *See* PORT SAID.
Burt, Sir Cyril Lodowic (1883–1971), British psychologist who pioneered the use of psychological testing and the theory of factor analysis for the measurement of intelligence. His intelligence and aptitude tests have been used in education and in the study of juvenile delinquency.
Burton, Beryl (1937–), British amateur cyclist. She dominated British women's cycling until well into her thirties, competing with and regularly beating even male time-triallists. She won five world pursuit titles and two on the road.
Burton, Gary (1943–), US jazz musician. He is a self-taught vibraphone player who developed a unique four-mallet technique. After working with Stan GETZ he led his own group and won a Grammy award for the best solo jazz performance of 1972.
Burton, Sir Richard Francis (1821–90), English explorer, writer, linguist and diplomat. In 1853, in disguise, he travelled to Medina and Mecca, being one of the first Europeans to visit those cities. On his second trip to E Africa, with John Speke in 1857, he discovered Lake Tanganyika. The author of many books, he was best known for his translation of the *Arabian Nights* (1885–88). *See also* MS p.248.
Burton, Richard (1925–), Welsh actor, real name Richard Jenkins. By the 1950s he had a reputation as a leading Shakespearian actor. He made his film debut in *The Last Days of Dolwyn* (1948). From 1952 he concentrated on cinema, appearing in such films as *The Robe* (1953), *Look Back in Anger* (1959) and *Becket* (1964). He also made a number of films with Elizabeth TAYLOR, notably *Who's Afraid of Virginia Woolf?* (1966).
Burton, Robert (1577–1640), English author. He wrote a comedy in Latin, *Philosophaster* (1606), but his most famous work is *The Anatomy of Melancholy* (1621), which was written under the pen-name of Democritus Junior. *See also* ANATOMY OF MELANCHOLY.
Burundi, republic in E central Africa. Until 1962 it was, with Rwanda, part of the Belgian League of Nations mandate (Ruanda-Urundi). Most of its people are subsistence farmers. The chief cash crops are coffee, cotton and tea. The capital is Bujumbura. Area: 27,865sq km (10,747sq miles). Pop. (1975 est.) 3,400,44. *See* MW p.44.
Bury, Pol (1922–), Belgian painter and sculptor, whose painting was associated first with SURREALISM and later with the free abstraction of the COBRA group. From 1952 onwards he concentrated on sculpture, producing mobiles into which he eventually incorporated small motors. His mobiles, which move almost imperceptibly, give the impression of being both gently humorous and significant.
Bury, town in Greater Manchester Metropolitan County, NW England, on the River Irwell, 16km (10 miles) N of Manchester. Industries: engineering, chemicals, textiles. Pop. (1971) 67,800.
Burying beetle, medium-sized BEETLE found in temperate regions. It digs under the carcasses of small animals, burying them, and lays its eggs in them. It is also called carrion beetle. Family Silphidae; genus *Necrophorus.*
Bury St Edmunds, town in West Suffolk, on the River Lark, 35km (22 miles) NW of Ipswich. It was named after King Edmund, who was killed by the Danes and buried in the town's abbey in 903. Industries: engineering, brewing, food processing, timber. Pop. (1971) 25,600.
Bus, large, public passenger-carrying road vehicle; the name comes from the Latin word omnibus, meaning "for all". A horse-drawn bus service started in Britan in 1829 and motor buses were introduced in the late 19th century. Buses are usually driven by petrol or diesel engines, but have also been run from an overhead electricity supply (a trolleybus).
Busby, James (1801–71), first British Resident in New Zealand (1833). He was sent from New South Wales to keep law and order but failed for lack of support.
Busby, Sir Matt (1909–), Scottish footballer and manager. After a fine career as a player (Manchester City, Liverpool, Scotland), he became manager of Manchester Utd (1945–69), guiding them to many honours. He survived the 1958 Munich air disaster, in which most of the famous "Busby Babes" died, to build his third great side, the first English club to win the European Cup (1968).
Busch, family name of two German musicians. Adolf (1891–1952), a violinist and composer of chamber and choral works, founded the Busch String Quartet and the Busch Trio. Fritz (1890–1951) was a conductor, chiefly of operas. He led the Glyndebourne Festival for several years and in 1945 became a conductor of the Metropolitan Opera, New York.
Bush, Alan Dudley (1900–), British composer. His *Dialectic* for string quartet (first performed in 1935) gained him notice. He has written several operas including *Wat Tyler* (1950) and *Men of Blackmoor* (1956), three symphonies, a violin concerto and various choral works.
Bush, Geoffrey (1920–), British composer. He has written three operas, the most recent of which is *The Equation (x=o)*, first performed in London in 1968. But he is best known for his chamber works, especially the two song cycles, *Five Spring Songs* (1944) and *Greek Love Songs* (1964).
Bushbaby, primitive squirrel-like PRIMATE of African forests and bushlands. It is usually grey or brown with a white stripe between its large eyes. Also called a GALAGO, it is a gregarious nocturnal tree-dweller which can be domesticated as a pet. Length: (excluding tail) to 38cm (15in). Family Lorisidae; genus *Galago. See also* NW pp.168, *212.*
Bush Ballad, early Australian verse celebrating the exploits of convicts, pioneers and bushrangers. It has been called the first true Australian literary form. Frequently sung, bush ballads were transmitted orally and usually have a recurring refrain set to a simple lively rhythm. Well-known ballads such as *The Wild Colonial Boy* and *Botany Bay* have become part of Australian folklore. *See* PATERSON, Banjo; LAWSON, Henry.
Bushbuck, small, often striped ANTELOPE found in forested or brushy areas of sub-Saharan Africa. Family Bovidae; species *Tragelaphus scriptus. See also* NW p.213.
Bushehr (Bushire), city in SW Iran, near the head of the Persian Gulf and 185km (115 miles) SW of Shiraz. Founded in 1736, it was the chief Iranian port until the rise of ABADAN. Imports: sugar, steel, cement. Exports: carpets, cotton. Pop. (1972 est.) 45,000.
Bushel, unit of dry measure equal in volume to eight imperial gallons of water (36.5l), and to four pecks. It is traditionally used to measure grain and fruit. The name comes from a word in Old French for a much smaller measure, "the amount one can hold in the hand".
Bushell's case (1670), English legal case which established the immunity of juries from fines for verdicts contrary to the evidence and the direction of the court. Bushell was acquitted on a charge of the non-payment of a fine levied for returning a verdict contrary to the evidence. This case was instrumental in the formulation of the HABEAS CORPUS ACT (1679).
Bushido, the "Way of the Samurai", a moral discipline important in Japan between 1603 and 1868 which arose from a fusion of Confucian ethics and Japanese feudalism. Requiring loyalty, courage, honour, politeness and benevolence, Bushido paralleled European chivalry. Although not a religion, Bushido involved family worship and SHINTO rites.
Bushmaster, largest PIT VIPER, found in central USA and N South America. It has long fangs and large venom glands, and is pinkish and brown with a diamond pattern. Length: up to 3.7m (12ft). Family Viperidae; sub family *Crotalidae.*
Bushmen, or San, Khoisan-speaking people of southern Africa. Typically, they are short, with a leathery yellowish skin, flat faces and high cheekbones. Until recently they had a hunting and gathering culture, with little regard for material possessions. About half of them now follow the traditional ways, mostly in the Kalahari region; others have become assimilated into white and Bantu agricultural society as hired labourers. *See also* MS pp.33, 35, *250, 252.*
Bushnell, David, American inventor (*c.*1742–1824) who in 1776 built the first underwater vessel to be used in war. Called "Bushnell's turtle", it carried two essential features of the modern SUBMARINE – a closed hull and screw propulsion – and could be operated by one crew member. *See also* MM pp.118–19.
Bushrangers, bandits who terrorized the Australian outback in the late 18th and 19th centuries. Many were escaped convicts, others were adventurers who after 1850 attacked gold convoys. The gang led by Ned KELLY was wiped out in 1880.
Buskerud, county in SE Norway, bounded by those of Oslo and Telemark; capital Drammen. Industries: farming, forest products, textiles. Area: 14,802sq km (5,765sq miles). Pop. 201,400.
Busking, street entertainment of cinema or theatre queues, or passers-by, by dancing, singing, playing musical instruments or performing tricks. The entertainer afterwards begs money from his audience.
Busoni, Ferruccio Benvenuto (1866–1924). Italian pianist and composer. He was a virtuoso concert pianist in the LISZT tradition and the influence of Liszt shows in his large piano concerto. He wrote several operas, including *Doktor Faust* (1916–24) and *Turandot* (1917).
Bustamante, Sir William Alexander (1884–1977), Prime Minister of Jamaica (1962–67), founder and president of the Jamaica Labour Party (1943). As leader of the opposition (1955–62), he favoured Jamaica's withdrawal from the West Indies Federation. Illness caused him to retire from politics in 1967.
Bustard, large, shy bird found in arid areas of the Eastern Hemisphere. Its plumage is grey, black, brown and white and its neck and legs are long; in appearance it is quite ostrich-like. A swift runner and a strong, though reluctant flier, it feeds on small animals and lays up to five eggs. Family Otidae. Height: 1.3m (4.3ft).
Bustle, pad or cushion worn under the back of a woman's skirt to make it stick out behind. The bustle was made of horsehair or stiffened ruffles. Popular in the late 19th century, it later evolved into a flounce of material half way down the back of the skirt.
Butadiene, (1,3-butadiene), (CH_2:CH-CH:CH_2) gaseous flammable hydrocarbon made from butenes or by "cracking" NAPHTHA. It is copolymerized with STYRENE to produce synthetic rubbers. Properties: s.g. 0.62; m.p. −108.9°C (−164.0°F); b.p. −4.4°C (24.1°F). *See also* MM p.54.
Butane, (C_4H_{10}) gaseous flammable colourless hydrocarbon. It is obtained as a by-product of PETROLEUM refining and from natural gas. It can be liquefied under pressure at normal temperatures, and is used as a fuel gas and in the manufacture of synthetic rubber. Properties: m.p. −138.3°C (−217.0°F); b.p. −0.5°C (31.1°F). *See also* MM p.79.
Bute, John Stuart, 3rd Earl of (1713–92), tutor of GEORGE III, who appointed him Prime Minister in 1762. He had great influence over the king during the first five years of his reign (1760–65). He was widely disliked, and although he negotiated the peace that ended the Seven Years War (1756–63), he was unable to establish a stable administration. Having failed to gain parliamentary support, he resigned in 1763. *See also* HC2 pp.68–69.
Bute, island off SW Scotland, in the Firth of Clyde and separated from the mainland by the Kyles of Bute. Formerly the chief island of Buteshire, it is now part of the Strathclyde Region. It has important prehistoric and early Christian remains. The principal town, Rothesay, is the main tourist centre. Its mild climate favours agriculture. Area: 119sq km (246sq miles). Pop. (1974 est) 7,956.
Butenandt, Adolf Friedrich Johann (1903–), German biochemist who did important research into sex hormones. In

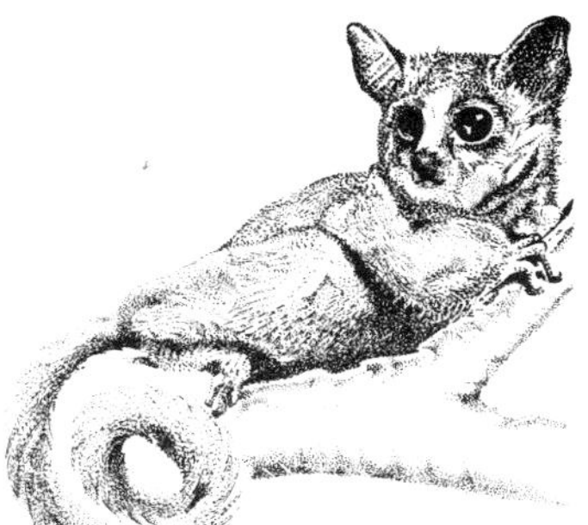
Bushbabies are extremely agile tree dwellers and have the ability to fold up their ears.

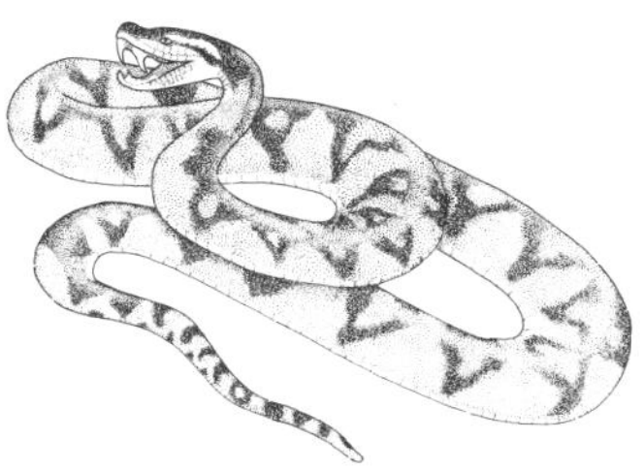
Bushmaster; the poisonous pit viper whose fangs may grow up to 2.5cm (1in) long.

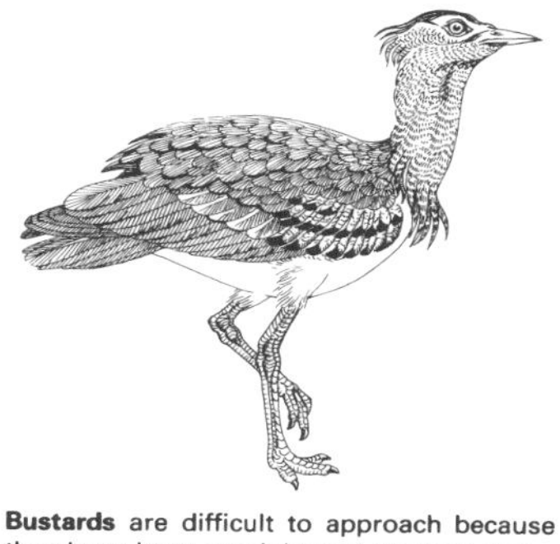
Bustards are difficult to approach because they have keen eyesight and are very shy.

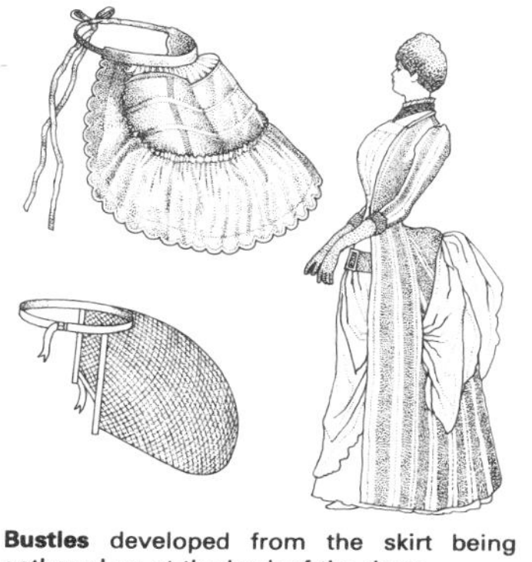
Bustles developed from the skirt being gathered up at the back of the dress.

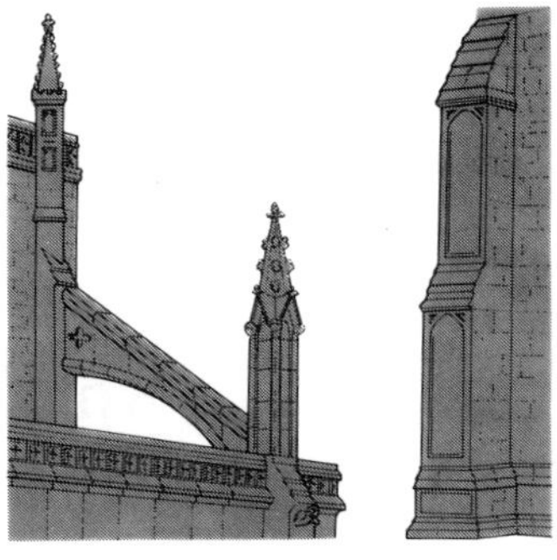

Buttresses achieved their most spectacular form in the Gothic "flying buttresses".

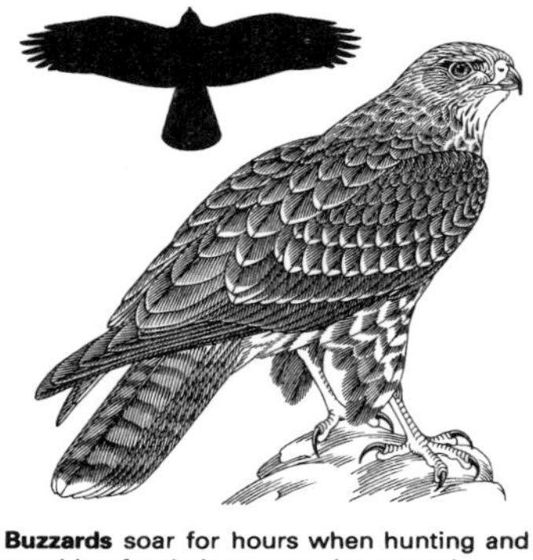

Buzzards soar for hours when hunting and watching for their prey on the ground.

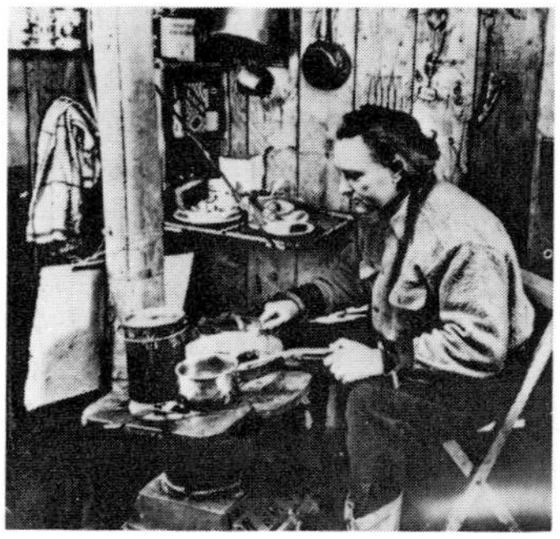

Richard Eveleyn Byrd, the aviator who explored and surveyed much of Antarctica.

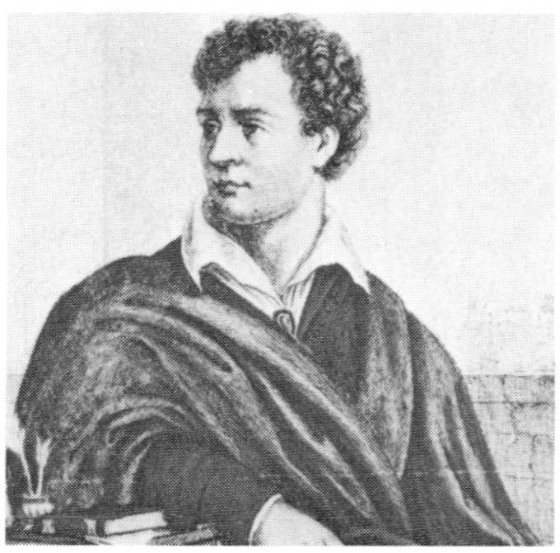

Lord Byron, the romantic poet whose adventurous private life aroused equal interest.

1931 he isolated the male SEX HORMONE ANDROSTERONE and in 1934 investigated the chemical structure and properties of the female sex hormone PROGESTERONE. For this work he was awarded the 1939 Nobel Prize in chemistry, but had to decline the award because of a Nazi decree prohibiting acceptance.

Butene (butylene), any of three hydrocarbon gases having the general formula C_4H_8: butene-1 [CH_3-CH_2-CH=CH_2], butene-2 [CH_3-CH=CH-CH_3] and isobutene [$(CH_3)_2C$=CH_2]. Butene is made from petroleum and used as a starting material for other organic compounds.

Butler, Earls and Dukes of Ormonde. *See* ORMONDE.

Butler, Josephine Elizabeth, (1828–1906), British social reformer. From 1869 she campaigned against the Contagious Diseases Act, whereby prostitutes in military towns were subject to state or other official control. The Act was repealed in 1886.

Butler, Sir Milo Boughton (1906–), since 1973 Governor-General of the Bahamas. Before that he was Minister of Labour, Welfare, Agriculture and Fisheries (1968–72) and minister without portfolio (1972–73).

Butler, Nicholas Murray (1862–1947), US educationalist. He was president of Columbia University (1902–45) and helped to establish the Carnegie Endowment for International Peace (becoming its president from 1925 to 1945). With Jane ADDAMS he shared the 1931 Nobel Peace Prize.

Butler, Reginald (1913–), English sculptor and architect. In 1953 he won first prize in the international competition for a monument to *The Unknown Political Prisoner.* Butler was influenced in his early work by CONSTRUCTIVISM, but later evolved a highly sensual language to interpret his delicate figurative sculpture, often of girls.

Butler, Richard Austen, Baron Butler of Saffron Walden (1902–), British politician. He entered Parliament in 1929 as a Conservative and was Minister of Education (1941–45). During this time he was responsible for the Education Act (1944) which provided free primary and secondary education for all. He held major cabinet posts (1951–64), before being named master of Trinity College, Cambridge (1965–).

Butler, Samuel (1612–80), English satirical poet. His verse, dating from the 1660s and 1670s, includes *The Elephant on the Moon, Characters* and *Hudibras.*

Butler, Samuel, (1835–1902), British satirical writer. His novel *Erewhon* (1872), a utopian criticism of contemporary social and economic injustice, made him famous. It was written while he was a sheep farmer (1860–64) in New Zealand. He opposed DARWIN's theory of evolution and expounded his own ideas in several of his works. His autobiographical *The Way of All Flesh* (1903) is a biting attack on Victorian life and his own upbringing.

Butlin, Sir William ("Billy") (1899–), British HOLIDAY CAMP pioneer. Born in Cape Town, he was named William Edmund Heygate Colbourne Butlin. In 1921 he arrived in England from Canada, and in 1936 opened his first holiday camp at Skegness. After WWII he developed a chain of such camps. He was knighted in 1964.

Butor, Michel (1926–), French novelist. His contributions to the *nouveau roman* or ANTI-NOVEL examined the intricacies of human psychology and relationships within a limited framework of action. His novels include *Passage de Milan* (1954), *La Modification* (1957: tr. as *Second Thoughts, 1958) and Niagara* (1969).

Butt, Dame Clara Ellen (1872–1936), British contralto. One of the best-loved singers of her age, she was especially famous for her singing of Liddell's *Abide With Me.* Elgar wrote the song cycle *Sea Pictures* for her in 1900.

Butt, Isaac (1813–79), Irish political figure. As a Member of Parliament, he demanded land tenure reform and led the Home Rule movement in Parliament in the 1870s until he was supplanted by Charles Stewart PARNELL. *See also* IRISH HOME RULE; HC2 p.162.

Butte, isolated, flat-topped, steep-sided hill. It is formed when a remnant of hard rock overlies and protects softer rock underneath from being worn down, while the surrounding areas continue to be eroded. *See also* PE pp.*115, 120.*

Butter, edible fat made from milk by a churning process in which the milk is converted from a water-in-oil emulsion to an oil-in-water emulsion. The fat (oil) globules of the milk coalesce into butter, thus separating out from the more watery whey. To assist this process a "starter" of a bacterial culture may first be added; this helps to coalesce, or ripen, the cream. Commercial butter contains about 80% fat, 1–3% added salt, 1% milk solids and 16% water. *See also* PE p.228.

Buttercup, herbaceous flowering plant found throughout the world; the many species vary considerably according to habitat, but usually have yellow or white flowers and deeply-cut leaves. Family Ranunculaceae. *See also* CROWFOOT; NW pp.*39, 58, 70,* 222.

Butterfield, Sir William (1814–1900), British architect who designed in the Gothic style. His best-known works are the chapel at Rugby School and Keble College, Oxford University.

Butterfly, day-flying INSECT of the order Lepidoptera. The adult has two pairs of membranous scale-covered wings that are often brightly coloured and held erect when at rest. The female lays eggs on a selected food source and the LARVAE (CATERPILLARS) emerge within days or even hours. The larvae have chewing mouth-parts and often do great damage to crops until they reach the "resting phase" of the life cycle, the pupa (chrysalis). Within the pupa the adult (imago) is formed with wings, wing muscles, antennae, a slender body and sucking mouth-parts. The adults mate soon after emerging from the chrysalis, and the four-stage life cycle begins again. *See also* METAMORPHOSIS; NW pp.*73,* 106–107, *106–107, 109,* 112, *116–117,* 247, *247.*

Buttermilk, fermented milk drink originating with the nomads of central Asia, who often made it in a goatskin bag hung at the door of their tents. Cultured buttermilk is now made by selectively souring skimmed low-fat milk, using a bacterial culture or "starter", and cooling the product to stop fermentation at the desired acidity. *See also* PE p.228.

Butterwort, large group of carnivorous bog plants that trap and digest insects in a sticky secretion on their leaves. They bear single white, purple or yellow flowers on a leafless stalk. Family Lentibulariaceae; species *Pinguicula. See also* NW p.59.

Butterworth, George Stainton Kage (1885–1916), British composer who was killed during WWI at the battle of the Somme. He studied at the Royal College of Music and was active in the revival of English folk song and dance. Among his compositions are *A Shropshire Lad* (1912), an orchestral rhapsody based on Alfred Housman's poetry, and *The Banks of Green Willow* (1913).

Button, Richard Totten ("Dick") (1929–), US figure-skater. He won the US senior figure-skating championship at the age of 16, the world figure-skating title (1948–52) and two Olympic gold medals (1948, 1952).

Buttress, mass of masonry built against a wall to add support or reinforcement. Used since ancient times in Mesopotamia, buttresses became increasingly complex and decorative in Christian cathedral architecture.

Butylene, C_4H_8. *See* BUTENE.

Buxtehude, Diderik (1637–1707), Danish organist and composer known for his organ and church music. While an organist at Lübeck he gave recitals that won him fame. J. S. BACH travelled some 320km (200 miles) on one occasion to hear him.

Buysse, Cyriel (1859–1932), Flemish novelist and playwright who wrote mainly in Flemish. A realist, his first major novel was *The Right of the Strongest* (1893); his plays include *The Paemel Family* (1893).

Buzău, capital of Buzău district in the Danube plain of SE Romania, 100km (60 miles) NE of Bucharest. It has been an important trade centre since the 15th century. Industries: metallurgy, plastics, brewing, textiles. Pop. (1971 est.) 71,300.

Buzzard, slow-flying bird with broad rounded wings, fan-shaped tail, sharp hooked beak and sharp talons. It is an imprecise term applied to many BIRDS OF PREY and used widely in North America for hawks and vultures. Family Accipitridae; genus *Buteo. See also* NW *p.245.*

Byblos, ancient city of the Phoenicians, now in Lebanon, 27km (17 miles) N of BEIRUT. Byblos became a centre of Phoenician trade with Egypt in the late 2nd millennium BC, and was particularly known for its PAPYRUS. The Greek word for "book" was derived from its name. In the late 10th century BC the city declined and Hiram I moved the Phoenician capital to Tyre. *See also* HC1 p.54, *54.*

Bydgoszcz (Bromberg), city in N central Poland; capital of Bydgoszcz province. It was controlled by Prussia from 1772 to 1919. Industries: mechanical engineering, chemicals, textiles, food processing. Pop. (1970) 281,000.

Byelobog, in Slavonic mythology, white god of light and day, the creative force, the god of good, antithetical to Črnobog. In popular legends Byelobog was depicted as an old man with a white beard, whose actions were always benevolent.

Byelorussia. *See* BELORUSSIA.

Byng, John (1704–57), British admiral. In 1756 he was sent to protect Britain's base on the island of Minorca where, believing himself to be outmanned, he failed to drive off a blockading French fleet. He withdrew to Gibraltar, where he was court-martialled, found guilty and shot.

Byng, Julian Hedworth George, 1st Viscount (1862–1935), British general and Governor-General of Canada (1921–26). He became a Viscount after his defeat of the Germans at Vimy Ridge (1917) – one of the most famous Canadian victories of WWI. In 1918 his army broke the Hindenburg Line. From 1928 to 1931 he was Commissioner of London's Metropolitan Police Force.

Byrd, Richard Evelyn (1888–1957), US rear admiral and the first man to fly over both the North Pole (1926) and the South Pole (1929). In 1927 he flew the first transatlantic air mail from New York to France. He also led five major expeditions to the Antarctic (1928–57), discovering and surveying more than 2,200,000sq km (845,000sq miles).

Byrd, William (1543–1623), English composer. He was appointed by ELIZABETH I to be joint organist of the Chapel Royal with Thomas TALLIS, whom he succeeded in 1585. With Tallis, he was granted England's first monopoly to print music. Byrd was a master of all the musical forms of his day, celebrated for his madrigals and church music. *See also* HC1 p.249.

Byron, George Gordon Noel Byron, 6th Baron (1788–1824), British poet. He is remembered as much for his flamboyant, romantic life as for his poetry. The handicap of a clubfoot and maltreatment by his mother resulted in an unhappy childhood. *English Bards and Scotch Reviewers* (1809) established his reputation, and in 1812 the first two cantos of *Childe Harold's Pilgrimage* appeared, to widespread acclaim. His dissolute lifestyle and numerous affairs with women excited great popular interest. In 1816, a social outcast, he left England for good. Abroad, Byron wrote Cantos III and IV of *Childe Harold* (1816, 1818) and *Don Juan* (1819–24) an epic satire often regarded as his masterpiece. In 1823 he travelled to Greece to fight for Greek independence against the Turks. *See also* HC2 pp.*73, 84,* 100, *182.*

Bytom, (Beuthen), city in S Poland, 13km (8 miles) NW of Katowice. It was part of Prussia from 1742 but was assigned to Poland by the Potsdam Conference (1945). Industries: metalworking, mining of zinc and lead. Pop. (1970) 187,000.

Byzantine Empire, known also as the Eastern Roman Empire, or Medieval Greek Empire. The history of the Byzantine Empire spanned the long period from AD 330 when its capital city of Constantinople (ISTANBUL) was established by the Roman Emperor CONSTANTINE the Great (as part of the attempt to modify the structure of the Roman Empire to deal with barbarian invasions), to the year 1453, when the same city was captured by the OTTOMAN Turks.

Constantinople, a well-fortified city on the BOSPORUS, commanded one of the most important routes between the European and Asian continents. The city was the heart of the Byzantine empire, the outer boundaries of which were constantly changing, as the empire annexed foreign territories and was in turn invaded. It generally comprised large parts of Anatolia, or Asia Minor, and the Balkans, as well as (for varying lengths of time during periods of expansion) southern Italy and Ravenna, Greece, Syria, Egypt and portions of Spain and the N African coast. Although the Byzantines referred to themselves as "Romans", their society was made up of many other elements. The traditions of Imperial Rome shaped their governmental institutions; the language and customs of Classical Greece moulded their cultural life; and orthodox Christianity, within which a series of heresies occurred, determined their religion.

The Byzantine state was, in theory, a continuation of the Roman Empire. While the Roman Empire in the W had fallen into decline after the Germanic invasions, the E provinces remained a centralized state. The Emperor JUSTINIAN I (*r.* 527–65) reconquered much of the Mediterranean territory of the old Roman Empire and codified Byzantine law. Under the Heraclian emperors (610–717), the empire defeated its Persian enemies, but also faced the rise of Arab power, which continued to threaten its control of the Middle East. During the age of the ICONOCLASTIC CONTROVERSY (717–843), the Isaurian and Amorian rulers dealt with severe internal crises. The Macedonian epoch (867–1025) is known as the Golden Age of the Byzantine Empire; it was a time of territorial consolidation and cultural flowering. The emperors of the Comnenian and Angelian dynasties (1081–1204) had to deal with the unpredictable and rapacious Crusaders, who besieged and stormed Constantinople in 1204. These crusaders ruled Byzantium during the dominion of the LATIN EMPIRE OF THE EAST (1204–61). MICHAEL VIII, restorer of the Greek Empire, founded the Palaeologan dynasty (1261–1453). The area of the empire shrank rapidly under the attacks of the Ottoman Turks, who finally took Constantinople itself in 1453. *See also* HC1 pp.*115*, 136–137, *142–143*, 220.

Byzantium, former name of Constantinople, during the BYZANTINE EMPIRE.

C

C, third letter of the alphabet, derived from the Greek *gamma* and the Semitic *gimel.* It originally had a hard sound (like a *k*), but before *e*, *i* or *y* took on a sibilant sound (like *s*), or had an *h* added to create the *ch* sound. Followed by *a*, *o*, *u* or any consonant (except *h*) *c* normally has a hard sound in English.

Cabal, advisers to CHARLES II of England in 1667–74. The five members of this group, which is sometimes considered the first cabinet, were CLIFFORD, ARLINGTON, BUCKINGHAM, Ashley (later earl of SHAFTESBURY) and LAUDERDALE; the first letters of their names spelt "cabal". When it became known that two of them plotted with the king to tolerate Catholicism, the Cabal split up. *See also* HC1 pp.292–293.

Caballé, Montserrat (1933–), Spanish soprano. She studied at the Liceo Conservatory in Barcelona and made her debut as Mimi in Puccini's *La Bohème* in 1957. She performed at the Metropolitan Opera in 1965, and has appeared in many of the world's leading opera houses.

Caballero, Fernán (1796–1877), Spanish novelist, real name Cecilia Böhl de Faber. She wrote of peasant tales and customs from Andalusia, and inspired the regional school in Spanish literature.

Cabaret, originally the name of any French restaurant where musical theatre, often of a satirical nature, was performed. The term has since been applied to the performances of singers, dancers and comedians who appear in modern nightclubs, either as solo performers or in lavish productions.

Cabaret, musical play with songs by John Kander and Fred Ebb, first produced on Broadway in 1966. Based loosely on Christopher ISHERWOOD's Berlin novels, it is set in pre-Nazi Germany and portrays the decadence of the times. It was made into a highly successful film in 1972.

Cabbage, low, stout vegetable of the genus *Brassica*, first grown domestically in the E Mediterranean about 4,000 years ago and possibly taken to Europe by pre-Christian Celtic warriors. Members of the genus include Brussels sprouts, cauliflowers, broccoli and crops such as kohlrabi, rape and turnips. They are all biennials that produce "heads" one year and flowers the next. The common cabbage (*Brassica oleracea capitata*) is noted for its edible head and large, fleshy leaves. It is grown in a wide range of varieties classifiable by the shape of their heads, their growth cycle or their colour. They grow best in well-fertilized, amply watered soil in regions with a temperate climate. Early varieties develop heads about two months after seedlings have been planted out, whereas late varieties take about four months to mature. Family: Cruciferae. *See also* PE pp.188, *188*, 191.

Cabbage palm, any of several species of PALM whose young leaves are eaten as vegetables. They include cabbage palmetto (*Sabal palmetto*), which grows to 27m (90ft) tall and is native to the SE USA and the West Indies. *See also* NW p.190.

Cabbage rose, flowering perennial cultivated in Europe since medieval times, especially in the Grasse district of S France where attar of roses (rosewater) is manufactured from its petals. Family Rosaceae; species *Rosa centifolia.*

Cabbage Tree, largest plant of the LILY family, native to tropical and subtropical parts of the world. Palm-like in appearance, it has bushy crowns of long narrow leathery leaves at the end of its branches which are used for making paper. It produces fragrant cream flowers and white berries, and its decaying leaves are phosphorescent at night. Height: to 12m (40ft). Species *Cordyline australis.*

Cabbage white butterfly, BUTTERFLY, the green caterpillar of which is a common pest on plants of the cabbage family. The female adult is almost completely white except for black spots on its wings; the male has no forewing spots. Species *Pieris brassicae. See also* NW p.*112*.

Cabbala. *See* KABBALA.

Cabell, James Branch (1879–1958), US author who wrote a long sequence of novels set in an imaginary medieval kingdom called Poictesme. The best-known is *Jurgen* (1919); others include *The Cream of the Jest* (1917), *Figures of Earth* (1921) and *The Silver Stallion* (1926).

Caber, Tossing the, athletic event popular at Scottish games. Cabers (trimmed tree-trunks) are not of any specified size but all are large and heavy, sometimes weighing 54kg (119lb) and 6m (19ft) long. The athlete holds the caber upright in his hands using his shoulder and head to support it. In a perfect throw ("12 o'clock toss") the caber turns end over end in the air and comes to rest with the top pointing in a straight line away from the competitor.

Cabet, Etienne (1788–1856), French political idealist. Elected to the French assembly (1831) he was convicted for treason because of fiery anti-government speeches. He went into exile in Britain (1834–39), where he developed communistic ideas, and later in the USA. His *Voyage en Icarie* (1840) won adherents and several Icarian (utopian) communities were set up in the USA.

Cabeza de Vaca, Alvar Nunez (*c.* 1490–*c.* 1557), Spanish explorer. In 1528 he was shipwrecked off the Texas coast and with three other survivors was the first European to explore the American Southwest. He recorded his explorations in *The Shipwrecked Men* (1542). His *Comentarios* (1555) recounts hardships endured in South America, where he served as governor of the Río de la Plata region (1542–45).

Cabimas, town in NW Venezuela, on the NE shore of Lake Maracaibo. An important centre for petroleum products, it is situated in the Ambosio oilfields, N of La Salina refinery. Pop. (1970 est.) 147,250.

Cabinet, body of the official advisors of a nation's chief executive, each of whom has the management of a department of state. It derives from Britain in the 18th century, when it slowly evolved from the king's council. In Britain cabinet ministers are chosen by the prime minister, but officially appointed by the Crown. A cabinet minister need not sit in either House of Parliament, but since the government is accountable to Parliament, he usually does. Most present-day cabinets have about 20 members. *See also* HC1 p.64; HC2 p.264; MS pp.276, 280.

Cabinet of Dr Caligari, The (1919), silent film directed by Robert Wiene starring Werner Krauss, Conrad Veidt and Lil Dagover. It was highly influential in the evolution of German EXPRESSIONISM, representing emotional anguish with the aid of bizarre sets, ambiguous story and odd camera angles.

Cabiri, group of deities, protectors of seafarers, usually associated with Thebes and Samothrace. Strange and powerful, they were approached, through ORPHEUS' intercession, by JASON, who hoped that they would protect his expedition.

Cable, in civil and mechanical engineering, a rope made by twisting together strands of (usually steel) wire. Cables vary in size from small ones in BOWDEN CABLES to the massive ones from which the deck of a suspension bridge is hung. Originally, particularly on ships, cables were merely strong ropes, and a cable is a unit of length equal to a tenth of a nautical mile, approx. 185m (608ft). In electrical engineering a cable is a conductor consisting of two or more insulated wires, which may be either single or multiple stranded. They also vary greatly in size, from the small cables used for domestic wiring to the large armoured cables of submarine telegraph and telephone lines. This latter use gave rise to the term "cable" for a telegram. In a COAXIAL CABLE one conductor is cylindrical and surrounds the other. *See also* MM pp.84–85, *191*, *193*, 224–227.

Cable, coaxial. *See* COAXIAL CABLE.

Cable car, passenger vehicle for ascending and descending mountains, often used as a tourist facility. A car is slung from a trolley pulley running on a steel cable. It is moved along by a steel traction cable, continuously looped around terminal drums which are turned by an electric motor. In the USA a tram "powered" by a moving cable beneath the tracks is called a cable car.

Cabot, family name of two Italian-born British navigators and explorers. The father, John Cabot (*c.* 1450–*c.* 1498), sailed from England in search of a western route to India and landed at Nova Scotia and Newfoundland in 1497. On a second voyage in 1498 it is generally assumed that he reached America, although evidence is scanty. His son, Sebastian (1474–1557), accompanied his father in 1497. He continued to explore the Americas, and in 1509 reached Hudson Bay. He also directed an expedition to Russia. *See also* HC1 pp.*234*, 278, *278*.

Cabral, Luis de Almeida (1929–), West African politician. He founded the African Party for the Independence of Guinea and Cape Verde with his brother Amilcar in 1956 and worked for it until GUINEA-BISSAU became independent in 1974. He then became the country's first president.

Cabral, Pedro Alvares (*c.* 1467–*c.* 1520), Portuguese navigator who discovered Brazil. In 1500 King Manuel I of Portugal sent him with a fleet of ships to the East

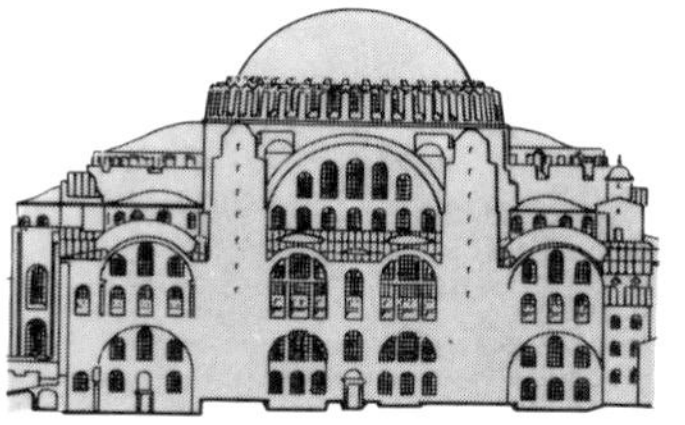

Byzantine architecture combined Eastern imagination with the ideas of the Romans.

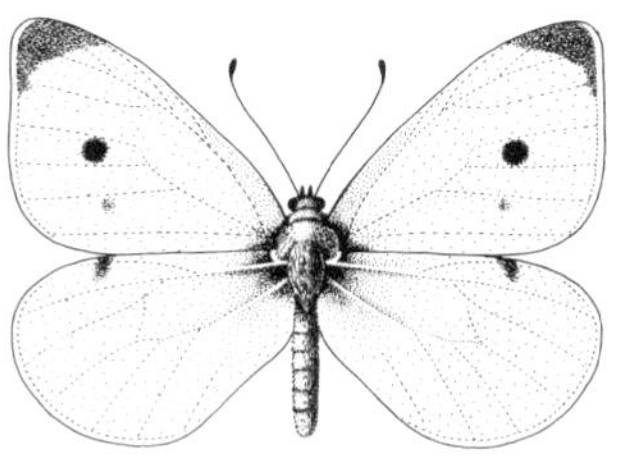

Cabbage white, the most common English butterfly. The male has no spots on the wings.

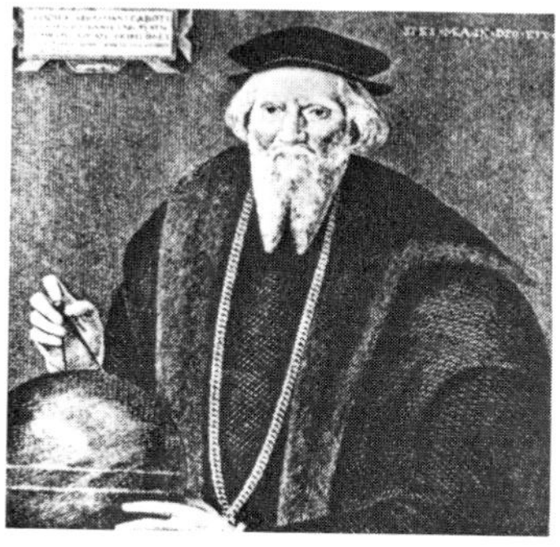

Sebastian Cabot conducted naval expeditions for the kings of both England and Spain.

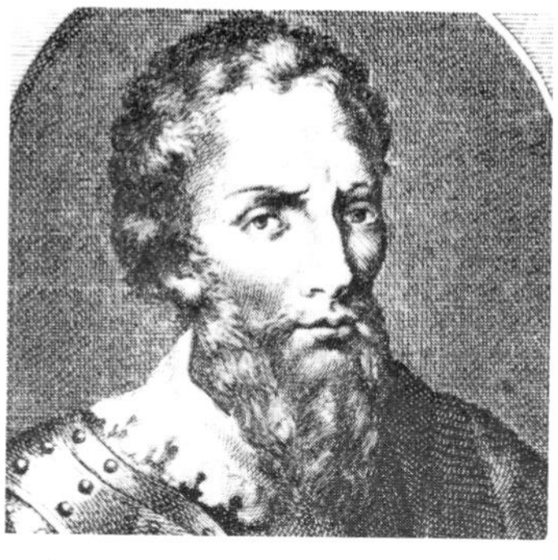

Pedro Cabral, the Portugese navigator who sighted the coast of Brazil on 22 April 1500.

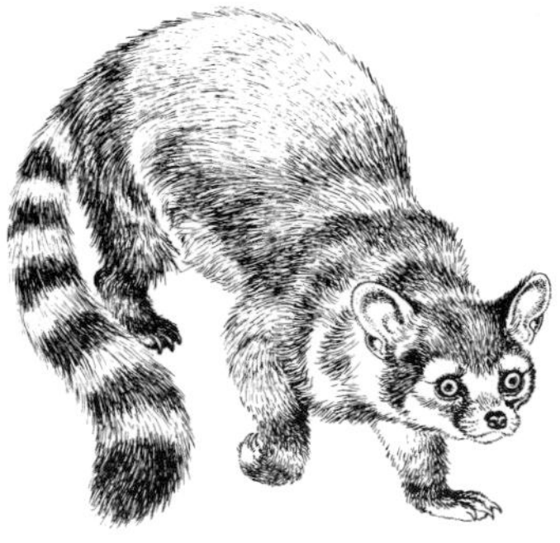

Cacomistles feed on fruit, mice, lizards, birds and insects; they make a barking sound.

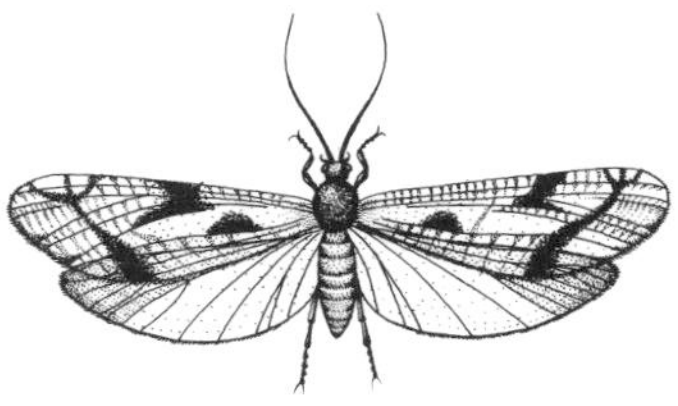

Caddisflies make up a large and important segment of the life of aquatic communities.

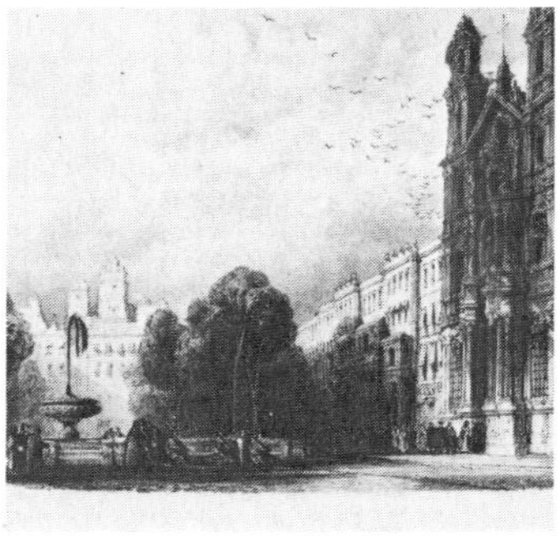

Cádiz; a 19th-century print of The Avenue of Poplars in the great Spanish port.

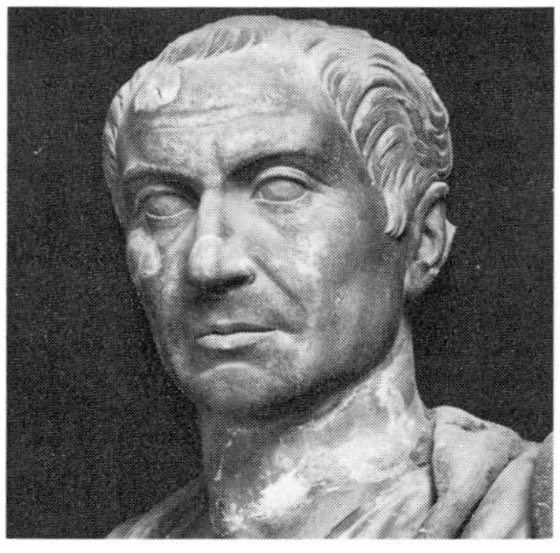

Julius Caesar became established as a military genius in the Gaul campaigns.

Indies. To avoid the Gulf of Guinea Cabral sailed westwards and reached Brazil, which he claimed for Portugal.

Cabrera Infante, Guillermo (1929–), Cuban novelist and short-story writer. His novel *Tres tristes tigres* (1967), about Havana nightlife, was a satire on BATISTA's Cuba. His collection of short stories, *Así en la paz como en la guerra* (1960), is also set in the 1950s.

Cabrini, Frances, Saint (1850–1917), US foundress of numerous orphanages, hospitals, schools and convents, *b.* Italy. She became a nun in 1877, Prioress of an Institute of Missionary Sisters of the Sacred Heart in 1880, and went to the USA in 1889. She founded charitable establishments throughout the USA and Latin America. She was canonized in 1946. Feast: 13 Nov.

Cacao. *See* COCOA.

Caccini, Giulio (*c.*1550–1618), Italian composer, one of the CAMERATA group of Florence which pioneered OPERA. His opera *Euridice* was the first to be printed (probably in Jan. 1601), and his *Le Nuove Musiche* (1602) was one of the most influential collections of vocal music in the new monodic or homophonic style.

Cachalot. *See* SPERM-WHALE.

Cacomistle, large-eyed, long-tailed, omnivorous member of the RACCOON family (Procyonidae). It has grey-brown fur with black and white rings on its bushy tail, and is both nocturnal and aboreal. Adult cacomistles grow to 76cm (30in) long. Species *Bassariscus astutus.*

Cactus, any of more than 2,000 species of succulent plants, found particularly in hot desert regions of the Western Hemisphere from Canada to Chile. The roots of the cactus are adapted to absorb moisture from desert terrains and the fleshy, well-developed stems are adapted for water storage. The green stems function as leaves and a waxy coating helps to restrict water evaporation. Cactus stems are usually spiny and cylindrical and often branched. Cactus flowers are usually borne singly and range in colour from white to red, purple and orange. Their height can range from less than 2.5cm (1in) to more than 15m (50ft). Cacti have become popular houseplants. Family Cactaceae. *See also* XEROPHYTE; NW p.*218.*

Cactus moth, small yellow or white moth with dark markings. A member of the Pyralidae family, its orange-red caterpillar destroys cactus plants and was introduced into Australia in 1925 as a biological control against prickly pear. Species *Cactoblastis cactorum. See also* NW p.246.

Cadbury, George (1839–1922), British manufacturer and social reformer. In 1879 he moved the family cocoa and chocolate factory to Bourneville, where he built a garden village for his employees. Its success influenced the GARDEN CITY movement. He also supported the movement for national insurance and pensions.

Caddisfly, any of several moth-like insects of the order Trichoptera. Adults have long, many-jointed antennae, hold their wings tent-like over the body and usually grow about 25mm (1in) long. Their larvae live in fresh water and are an important fish food. *See also* NW pp.79, *107, 226, 230, 231.*

Cade, Jack (*d.*1450), English rebel who led a rising in 1450 in Kent and Sussex (Cade's Rebellion) against HENRY VI. Claiming to be a cousin of the Duke of York, and captain of Kent, he proposed administrative reforms. In May and June he and 40,000 followers marched on London, which they took over for two days. Cade returned to Sussex but was hunted, wounded and captured; he died while being taken back to London.

Cadence, in music, ending of a melodic phrase and/or its accompanying CHORD progression. In Western classical theory, the main kinds of chordal cadence are: perfect (dominant to tonic chords); imperfect (tonic or other chord to dominant); plagal (subdominant to tonic); and interrupted (dominant to chord other than tonic, eg submediant).

Cadenza, solo passage, usually before the final CADENCE of a musical movement or piece (eg CONCERTO, ARIA), in which an instrument or voice shows its virtuosity. Many early cadenzas were improvised; in modern performances they are usually written out.

Cadillac, Sieur de, Antoine de la Mothe (1658–1730), French colonial administrator who went to North America in 1683. In 1701 he founded Detroit and served as its commandant (1704–10). Cadillac was governor of Louisiana (1710–16) until he fell into disfavour; he was recalled to Paris and imprisoned in the Bastille.

Cádiz, port in SW Spain, on the Gulf of Cádiz; capital of Cádiz province. Founded in 1100 BC by the Phoenicians, it was successively conquered by the Carthaginians, Romans, Goths and Moors. In 1493 COLUMBUS sailed from Cádiz on his second journey to the New World. It has a 13th-century cathedral, art and archaeological museums and the tomb of composer Manuel de FALLA. Industries: chemicals, paper, textiles, salt, shipbuilding, fishing. Pop. 135,700.

Cadmium, metallic element (symbol Cd) in group IIB of the periodic table, first isolated in 1817 by Friedrich Stromeyer. It is found in greenockite (a sulphide) but is mainly obtained as a by-product in the extraction of zinc and lead. Its main use is as a protective electroplated coating. Chemically it resembles zinc. Properties: at.no. 48; at.wt. 112.4; s.g. 8.65; m.p. 320.9°C (609.6°F); b.p. 765°C (1,409°F); most common isotope Cd^{114} (28.86%).

Cadmium processing, recovery of the rare metallic element cadmium from zinc and lead ores, in which it occurs as an impurity. It is obtained from the fumes eliminated during the heating of zinc concentrates, from the dust collected from gases from lead-blasting furnaces, and from various purification stages during the electrolytic refining of zinc.

Cadogan, William, 1st Earl (1672–1726), English soldier and diplomat. A close associate of the Duke of MARLBOROUGH, he fought in the War of the Spanish Succession, helped to put down the Jacobite uprising in 1716 and became army commander in 1722. As a diplomat, he helped to arrange the accession of GEORGE I.

Cadre, military term for a nucleus of officers and key enlisted men who train and lead a larger unit. In political and social science, a cadre is the trained and motivated core of a movement or party; the term is also applied to individual members of the group.

Cadwalader (*d.*1171), Welsh prince, son of King Gruffydd of North Wales (Gwynedd). After having been exiled by his brother Owain to Ireland he returned with an army which mutinied after Cadwalader made peace with his brother. He was blinded by his troops.

Caecilian, underground burrowing amphibian found in central and South America, S Asia and Africa. Its worm-like body varies from approx. 18 to 135cm (7–53in) in length and its colour from black to pink. There is a sensory organ between the eyes, which are tiny and often useless. *See also* NW pp.73, 132–133.

Caecum, in human beings, the pouch at the beginning of the large intestine. It opens to admit partly digested food from the small intestine and closes to prevent it passing back. The APPENDIX joins the caecum. *See also* MS pp.68, 69.

Caedmon (*fl.*670), earliest-known English poet. According to Bede, he was an illiterate herdsman of Whitby Abbey, Yorkshire, who was commanded in a vision to turn the scriptures into poetry. His only surviving authentic work is probably the brief *Hymn on the Creation.*

Caen, city and port in N France, on the Orne River; capital of Calvados département. Many of its buildings were destroyed in WWII, although the 11th-century Abbaye Aux Hommes (burial place of WILLIAM THE CONQUEROR) survived. The university (founded in 1432) had to be rebuilt. Industries: iron ore mining, textiles, motor vehicles, electronic equipment. Pop. (1968) 110,260.

Caerleon, town on the River Usk in SE Wales, on the outskirts of Newport. In Roman times it was the military fortress of Isca, and there are remains of the amphitheatre, baths and soldiers' quarters. Caerleon is considered by some people to be CAMELOT. *See also* HC1 p.*184.*

Caernarvon, market town in NW Wales, on the Menai Strait; formerly the county town of Caernarvonshire, which became part of Gwynedd in 1974. It has the ruins of a Roman fortress (AD 70–80) and a 13th-century castle built by Edward I in which his son Edward II was born in 1284 and crowned the first Prince of Wales in 1301. The Princes of Wales are now invested there. The principal industry is tourism. Pop. 9,300. *See also* HC1 p.205.

Caernarvonshire (Caernaerfon), former county in N Wales, now part of GWYNEDD. Livestock rearing is the most important activity as much of the terrain is mountainous and therefore agriculturally unproductive. Tourism and slate quarrying are also valuable sources of income.

Caerphilly (Caerffili), market town in Mid Glamorgan, S Wales. It has a Norman castle and was noted for its cheese-making industry (now ceased). It has light industry. Pop. (1971) 40,700.

Caesalpinus, Andreas. *See* CESALPINO, ANDREA.

Caesar, name of classical Roman family of the patrician Julian gens, or clan. The most illustrious representative was Julius CAESAR. The name became the title for the Roman emperor in 27 BC on the accession of Octavius (later AUGUSTUS), who had acquired it by adoption from Julius, in 44 BC. The name was retained by Augustus' successors until the time of HADRIAN, who made Augustus the name for the emperor. Caesar then became the name for the heir apparent. The Russian *Tsar* and German *Kaiser* are derived from it.

Caesar, Gaius Julius (100–44 BC), Roman general and statesman. He married Cornelia, daughter of Cinna, an associate of MARIUS, and after the death of SULLA Caesar became military tribune and leader of the popular party against the Senate. As *pontifex maximus* he directed reforms in 63 BC that resulted in the Julian calendar. He formed the first Triumvirate in 60 BC with POMPEY and CRASSUS, and instituted agrarian reforms, created a patrician-plebeian alliance and successfully conquered Gaul for Rome in 58–49 BC. In 54 BC Caesar led a successful military campaign in Britain. He refused Senate demands that he disband his army and engaged in civil war with Pompey, defeating him at Pharsalus in 48 BC. He pursued Pompey to Egypt where he met CLEOPATRA. He returned to Rome in 45 BC using the title of *dictator,* but refusing that of king. He was assassinated in the Senate on 15 March 44 BC by a conspiracy led by CASSIUS and Marcus BRUTUS, and he bequeathed his wealth and power on his grandnephew Octavian (later AUGUSTUS) who, with Mark ANTONY, avenged his murder. *See also* HC1 pp.96–97, 100.

Caesarea, ancient city of Israel, on the Mediterranean Sea, 35km (22 miles) S of Haifa (Hefa). It was a Roman capital of Palestine and the site of St Paul's imprisonment (57–59 AD). In 66 AD it was the scene of a massacre of Jews who demanded Roman citizenship. The Saracens destroyed the city in 1291. It is noted for its Roman theatre.

Caesarean section. *See* BIRTH, CAESAREAN.

Caesium, rare metallic element (symbol Cs) of the alkali-metal group, discovered in 1860. Caesium has a few commercial uses. Chemically it is an extremely reactive electropositive element. The decay rate of the isotope Cs^{133}, is used in defining the second. Properties: at.no. 55; at.wt. 132.9055; s.g. 1.87; m.p.28.5°C (83.3°F); b.p. 690.0°C (1,274°F); most common isotope Cs^{133} (100 %). *See also* ALKALI ELEMENTS; ATOMIC CLOCK.

Caffrelli (1710–83), real name Gaetano Majorano, Italian CASTRATO. Although quarrelsome and consistently bad-mannered, he was a superb soprano, widely celebrated in the opera houses of Europe. He amassed a huge fortune that enabled him to purchase a dukedom.

Caffeine ($C_8H_{10}N_4O_2$), white, bitter ALKALOID that occurs in coffee, tea and other substances such as cola nuts, ilex (holly) plants and cocoa. In beverages it acts as a mild and harmless stimulant, although an excess dose can cause insomnia and delirium.

Cágaba, or Kágaba, Chibchá-speaking tribe of about 2,000 South American Indians occupying parts of NE Colombia. They are thought to be descendants of the pre-Columbian TAIRONA. They are noted for their weaving.

Cage, John (1912–), controversial US avant-garde composer. Two of his ideas are the concept of "total soundspace" (that all sounds, including noises, and silence, are valid compositional materials) and the use of chance composition. His compositions include *Bacchanale* (1938) and *Sonatas and Interludes* (1946–48) for "prepared piano" (modified by fixing objects to the strings); *Imaginary Landscape* (1951) for 12 randomly-tuned radios; and *Reunion* (1968), electronic sounds created by chess moves on an electric board. *See also* HC2 p.271.

Cagliari, port in S Sardinia (Sardegna), Italy; capital of Cagliari province and of Sardegna region. Vital naval and air bases at Cagliari were destroyed by Allied bombing during WWII. Historical landmarks include a Roman amphitheatre, the Cathedral of St Cecilia (1257–1312) and a 5th–6th-century church. Industries: ceramics, petrochemicals, textiles, building materials. Pop. (1971 prelim) 231,670.

Cagliostro, Count Alessandro di (1743–95), Italian freemason and self-styled alchemist. He earned a reputation throughout Europe for his supposed powers of prediction and knowledge of the elixir of youth. In 1789 he was charged with heresy and died in prison.

Cagney, James (1899–), US actor. He began his career as an actor and dancer and became a Broadway success in *Maggie the Magnificent* (1929) and in *Penny Arcade* (1930). He made many films and is possibly best-known for his gangster role in *Public Enemy* (1930), which launched his film career. He won an Academy Award in 1942 for his portrayal of the US showman George M. Cohan in *Yankee Doodle Dandy*.

Cagoulards, also called Hooded Men, secret, masked French terrorist organization. Its full name was the Comité Secret d'Action Révolutionnaire (CSAR). It was set up in the 1930s by Henri Dorgeres to support extreme right-wing causes.

Caguas, municipality and city in E central Puerto Rico. The products of the municipality, 150sq km (58sq miles) in area, include tobacco, fruits and vegetables. The industries of the city, which is the country's largest inland settlement, include glass, plastics and electronics. Pop. (1970) Mun. 94,959; city 62,807.

Cahokia mounds, large prehistoric American earthworks, situated in Illinois and named after the Cahokia tribe who inhabited the area in ancient times. They are in a group of about 85, the highest at 30.5m (100ft) (Monks' Mound) taking the form of a four-sided pyramid.

Caiman, or cayman, any of several species of Central and N and E South American reptiles of the ALLIGATOR family. They include the small, heavily-armoured smooth cayman (*Paleosuchus trigonatus*) and dwarf cayman (*P. palpebrosus*); the spectacled cayman (*Caiman crocodilus*); and the large, fierce black cayman (*Melanosuchus niger*).

Cain, in the Bible (Genesis), first-born son of ADAM and EVE and brother of ABEL. Because God accepted Abel's offering in preference to his own, Cain murdered Abel in anger. Driven from the Garden of EDEN, he lived in exile with his family. *See also* MS p.*184*.

Cain, James Mallahan (1892–), US author, noted for his realistic novels of crime and violence. These include *The Postman Always Rings Twice* (1934) and *Double Indemnity* (1936). Many of his novels have been made into films.

Caine, Sir Thomas Henry Hall (1853–1931), British novelist who lived in the Isle of Man. He was secretary to the poet Dante Gabriel Rossetti and wrote *Recollections of Rossetti* (1882). His novels include *The Deemster* (1887), *The Eternal City* (1901) and *The Prodigal Son* (1904).

Caine Mutiny, The (1951), novel by Herman WOUK. It deals with a mutiny against a paranoid captain on a US minesweeper and the subsequent court martial of an officer involved in the mutiny. It was dramatized as *The Caine Mutiny Court Martial* (1954) and made into a film (1954).

Caingang (Kaingang), Ge-speaking tribe of about 25,000 South American Indians. They inhabit the states of São Paulo, Santa Catarina and Rio Grande do Sul in BRAZIL.

Cainozoic. *See* CENOZOIC PERIOD.

Cairn, rough heap of stones, usually cone-shaped. In the Neolithic and Bronze ages more complex cairns were built over burial places. Found throughout the world, their other uses include landmarks, road markers, makeshift altars (in the Middle Ages) and monuments.

Cairngorms, range of mountains in NE central Scotland, in Grampian region. The highest peak is Ben Macdhui, 1,309m (4,296ft), the second highest point in the British Isles.

Cairns, port in Queensland, NE Australia, on Trinity Bay. Its proximity to the Great Barrier Reef has made it a popular tourist resort. Its industries include sugar, timber and tobacco. Pop. (1975) 35,200.

Cairn terrier, small working dog bred in W Scotland to resemble the terriers of Skye, and renowned for its hunting of foxes and badgers. Standing about 25cm (10in) high at the shoulder, cairns have small, broad heads, short legs and coats of almost any shade, and weigh about 6.5kg (14lb).

Cairo (Al-Qāhirah), capital city of Egypt, and port on the River Nile near the head of the delta. It includes two islands in the Nile, Zamalik and Rawdah, which are linked to the mainland by bridges. Cairo was founded in AD 968 and includes Old Cairo, a Roman fortress city. Built on high ground to avoid the Nile floods, the city became the capital in 969. It is the site of the sphinx and pyramids of Giza dating from 2,500 BC. There are more than 400 museums, temples, palaces and mosques. Industries: textiles, iron and steel, sugar refining. Pop. (1974) 5,715,000.

Caisson, watertight structure or chamber used in underwater excavation or construction. It allows men to work underwater and makes it easier to remove excavated material. Caissons are frequently used in building bridges, where they keep out water during the construction of a foundation. They may be open, with "walls" that project above the surface of the water, or closed at the top and submerged (pneumatic caissons), using air pressure to exclude water.

Caisson disease. *See* BENDS.

Caithness, former county in NE Scotland, now part of Highland Region; the county town was Wick. it has a rugged moorland terrain and the main occupations are sheep farming and fishing. Area: 1,784sq km (686sq miles). Pop.27,481.

Caius, also Gaius, Christian priest in late 3rd-century Rome. His reference to the "trophies of the apostles", cited by the ancient church historian EUSEBIUS, has played an important role in the discussions about the excavations under ST PETER'S Basilica in Rome.

Caius, John (1510–73), English physician and anatomist; court physician and president of the College of Physicians. In 1557 he endowed Gonville Hall, Cambridge, re-naming it Gonville and Caius College.

Cajal, Santiago Ramón y. *See* RAMÓN Y CAJAL, SANTIAGO.

Cakchiquel, major division of the QUICHÉ MAYA Indians, living N and NE of Lake Atitlan and Guatemala City in Central America. Numbering approx. 340,000 and inhabiting villages in the Guatemala highlands, they are renowned weavers and retain many of their ancient traditions.

Cakewalk, US dance popular at the turn of the 20th century. Originated by southern Blacks, it is characterized by fanciful strutting. Its name probably comes from the custom of awarding a pastry prize to the performer of the most complex steps.

Cakobau, Ratu Sir George (1911–), Fijian politician. He was minister for foreign affairs and local government (1970–71), and minister without portfolio (1971–72). In 1973 he was knighted and made governor-general of Fiji.

Calabash gourd, or bottle gourd, fast-growing, tropical annual vine with oval leaves, white flowers and a musky smell. It reaches a length of 9–12m (30–40ft). Its smooth, hard fruit is bottle-shaped and grows to 180cm (6ft) long. Species *Lagenaria vulgaris*. *See also* NW p.*61*.

Calabria, region in S Italy, including the provinces of Catanzaro, Cosenza and Reggio di Calabria. The capital is Reggio di Calabria. The area was colonized by the Greeks, but its fortunes declined under Roman rule. Economic development has been hampered by rugged terrain, poor communications and the feudal landholding system. Products: grain, citrus fruits, olives, figs, wool, hydro-electric power. Area: 15,080sq km (5,822sq miles). Pop. (1971 est.) 1,508,000.

Caladium, genus of tropical American plants of the ARUM family. They are cultivated (often as houseplants) for their brilliantly coloured and variegated, triangular or arrow-shaped leaves. These are veined and mottled in various shades of red, green and yellow, and are carried on long stems from underground tubers.

Calais, city in N France, on the Strait of Dover. It has been a major commercial centre and port since the Middle Ages. It fell to the English in 1347 and a Rodin monument commemorates the six burghers who offered their lives to save the town. It was returned to the French in 1558. Heavy fighting during WWII destroyed much of its fine architecture. Industries: lace making, chemicals, paper. Pop. 70,000. *See also* HC1 pp.212,276.

Calamity Jane (*c.* 1852–1903), US frontier figure, real name Martha Jane Canary. She worked in mining and railroad camps in the western USA and with the US cavalry as a guide and scout. She was a fine horsewoman and expert shot, and featured in various Wild West shows.

Calceolaria, genus of shrubby or other herbaceous plants with colourful, slipper-shaped flowers; commonly called slipper-flower. Members of the FIGWORT family, calceolarias are native to the Andes of Chile and Peru, but are now widespread garden and houseplants.

Calciferol (vitamin D_2), fat-soluble VITAMIN formed by the action of sunlight on the skin and further converted into compounds necessary for the intestinal uptake of dietary calcium for bone formation. *See also* MS pp. 56, 57.

Calcination, process of heating solids to high temperatures (but not to their fusion point) to remove volatile substances, partially to oxidize them, or to render them friable. Lead, zinc, calcium, copper and iron ores calcine to agglomerated oxides, used as coloured pigments or as intermediates in metal extraction.

Calcite, mineral, calcium carbonate ($CaCO_3$). It is found in many kinds of rock, eg limestone. The crystals are in the hexagonal system and vary in form from tabular (rare) to prismatic or needle-like. Calcite may be glassy white and fluoresces red, pink or yellow; hardness 3; s.g. 2.7. A transparent variety is used in optical instruments. *See also* PE pp.*96–97*.

Calcium, common metallic element (symbol Ca) of the ALKALINE-EARTH group, first isolated in 1808 by Sir Humphry DAVY. It occurs in many rocks and minerals, notably LIMESTONE and GYPSUM, and in bone. The metal has few commercial applications but its compounds are widely used. Chemically it is a reactive element, combining readily with oxygen, nitrogen and other non-metals. Properties: at.no. 20; at.wt. 40.08; s.g. 1.55; m.p. 839°C (1,542°F); b.p. 1,487°C (2,709°F); most common isotope Ca^{40} (96.95 per cent).

Calcium bicarbonate, salt that is responsible for temporary HARDNESS of water, ie, the hardness removed when the water is heated. Insoluble calcium carbonate then precipitates from the water (forming a "fur" inside pipes and kettles), as it does also when water drips inside caves: STALAGMITES and STALAGTITES are thus formed. *See also* PE pp.110–111.

Calcium carbide, CaC_2, chemical made by

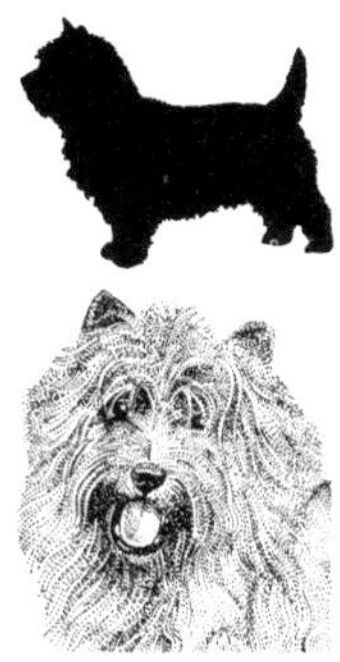

Cairn terriers were named for their ability to dig under the heaps of stones called cairns.

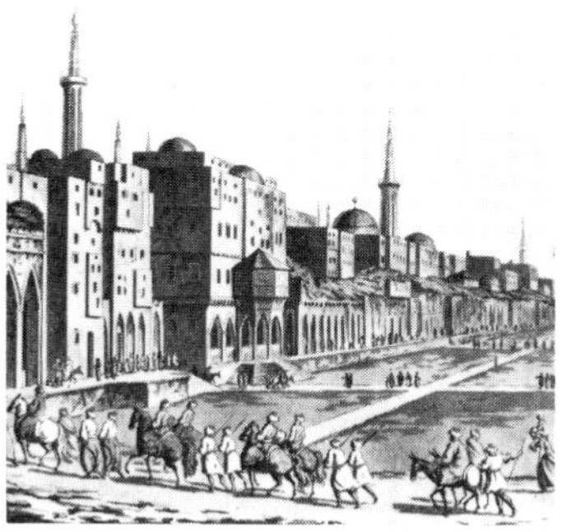

Cairo; an early 19th-century print of the main square of Africa's most populous city.

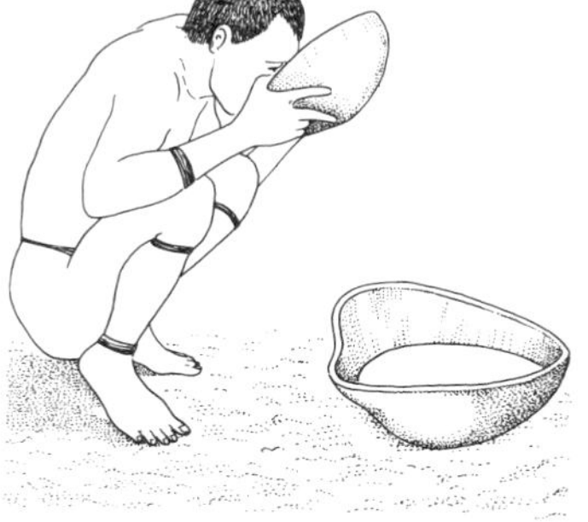

Calabash gourds' hard, tough outer shells can be used as cooking pots over an open fire.

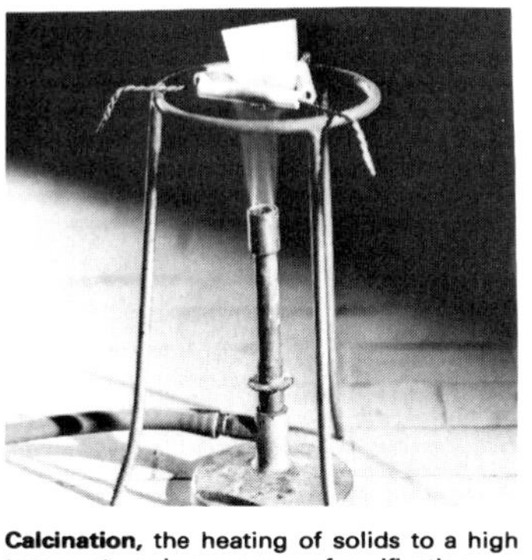

Calcination, the heating of solids to a high temperature, is a process of purification.

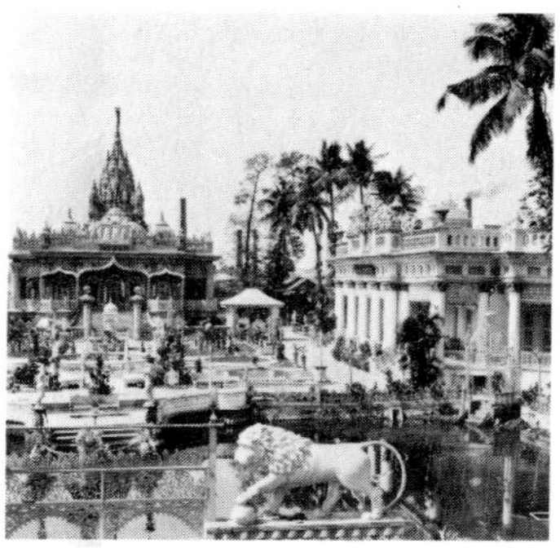

Calcutta; a peaceful oasis in this desperately populous city is the Jain Temple of Badri Das.

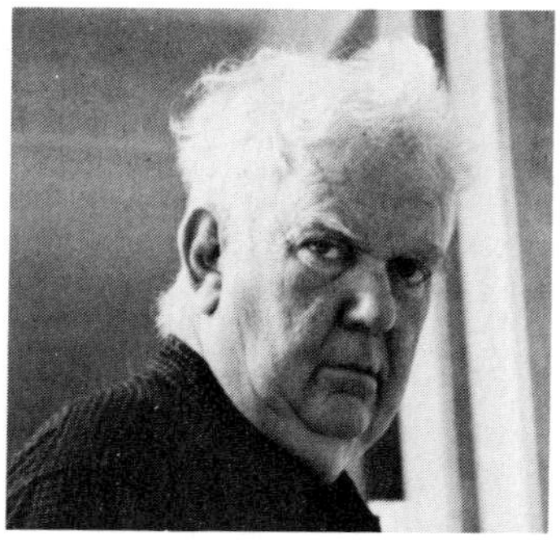

Alexander Calder's work reflects the vision of an artist who was originally an engineer.

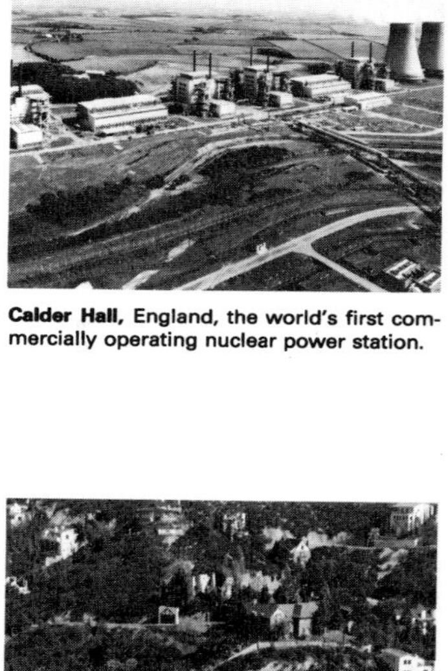

Calder Hall, England, the world's first commercially operating nuclear power station.

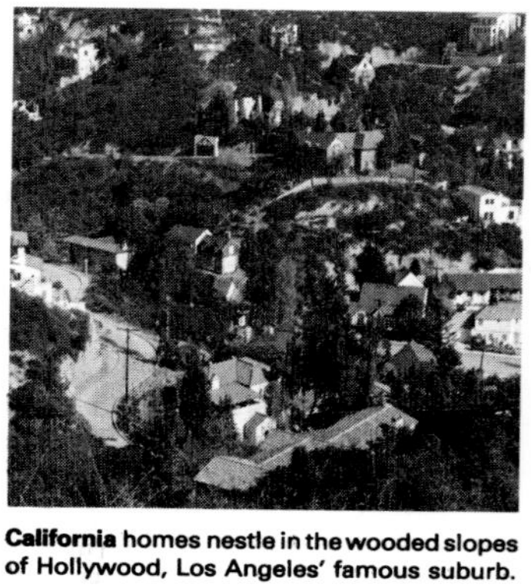

California homes nestle in the wooded slopes of Hollywood, Los Angeles' famous suburb.

heating coke and lime in a furnace. It is used mainly for the manufacture of acetic (ethanoic) acid and acetaldehyde (ethanal). It reacts with water to release the gas ACETYLENE, which burns with a luminous flame; for this reason it was once much used in carriage and engine lamps.

Calcium carbonate, $CaCO_3$, white compound, insoluble in water, that occurs naturally as marble, chalk, limestone, calcite, "kettle fur", etc. It is used in the manufacture of cement and lime, and as a constituent of antacids and dentifrices. Properties: s.g. 2.7–2.93 (calcite); decomposes at 825°C (1,517°F).

Calcium oxide, CaO, quicklime or unslaked lime, a white solid used industrially mainly for making bleaching powder, caustic soda, mortar and cement, and in the recovery of AMMONIA from the ammonia-soda process. It reacts with water to form calcium hydroxide, or slaked lime, $Ca(OH)_2$, much used in laboratories for the detection of carbon dioxide gas, CO_2. Calcium oxide was used in the 19th century for producing limelight illumination, an incandescence that occurs when coal-gas is burned in air against a block of quicklime.

Calcium sulphate, $CaSO_4$, chemical that occurs naturally as the mineral ANHYDRITE. The hydrated form, $CaSO_4.2H_2O$, is the mineral GYPSUM, which, when heated, loses water to form the half-hydrate $2CaSO_4.H_2O$, or PLASTER OF PARIS. This, when mixed with water, quickly sets hard to a crystalline form of the hydrate. *See also* PE pp.110–111.

Calculating machines. *See* COMPUTER.

Calculus, branch of higher mathematics involving the operations of differentiation and INTEGRATION. It has two branches: differential calculus and integral calculus, both concerned with the limiting values of a function as the increment of a variable tends to zero. Differential calculus enables the calculation of the rate at which one quantity changes with respect to another. It is used in finding slopes of curves, velocities, accelerations, etc. Integral calculus is used in finding the areas enclosed by curves and in solving related problems. *See also* SU pp.42–43.

Calcutta, city in E India, on the Hooghly River; capital of West Bengal state; second largest city and chief port in India. Founded *c.*1690 by the EAST INDIA COMPANY, it was the capital of India under the British from 1772 until 1912. It has a university (1857), an Indian Museum, and the Maidan, a large riverside park which is one of the more attractive parts of a city that suffers much overcrowding and poverty. The major industrial and transport centre of E India, Calcutta is one of the world's largest jute-milling centres. Its other industries include electrical equipment, cotton textiles and food processing. Pop. 3,148,746. *See also* HC2 p.217.

Calcutta Cup, trophy awarded to the winner of the annual England-Scotland rugby union international. If a draw results, the holder retains the cup. It was given in 1878 by the Calcutta (India) club. England (1951–63) holds record tenure.

Caldecott, Randolph (1846–86), English illustrator. His illustrations of Washington IRVING's books enjoyed enormous popularity. He also illustrated a series of 16 children's books in colour including *The House that Jack Built* and *John Gilpin* (1878).

Calder, Alexander (1898–1976), US sculptor, creator of the MOBILE, a delicate, colourful, KINETIC sculpture with parts that move either by motors or air currents. In Paris in the 1930s Calder was influenced by Joan MIRO and Piet MONDRIAN and broke new ground with his "stabiles", wire figure sculptures that did not move. These led to the development of the mobile, a famous example of which is *.125* at Kennedy Airport, N.Y.

Calder, Peter Ritchie-Calder, Baron Ritchie, (1906–), British author, scientific, social and political journalist and broadcaster. Originally a newspaper reporter (1922–41) he went on to work for many other publications and gained a reputation as a popularizer of scientific subjects. He has worked in several universities and has had a distinguished career in international relations, working for UNESCO, WHO and other UNITED NATIONS organisations.

Calder Hall, English nuclear power station in Cumbria. The world's first commercially operating nuclear reactor, work started on it in 1953 and it opened in October 1956. It is gas-cooled and uses a graphite moderator. It is called a "Magnox" station because the natural uranium fuel rods are encased in a magnesium alloy.

Caldera, large shallow crater formed when a volcano subsides due to the migration of the MAGMA under the earth's crust. The caldera of an extinct volcano, if fed by floodwater, rain or springs, can become a crater lake. *See also* PE p.30.

Calderón de la Barca, Pedro (1600–81), Spanish dramatist and priest. In 1635 he became court playwright to Philip IV and wrote for the court, church and public theatre. His *Autos sacramentales,* religious dramas for the festival of Corpus Christi, are among his finest works. His best-known plays include *La vida es sueño* (*c.*1638) (Life is a dream) and *El alcalde de Zalamea* (*c.*1640) (The Mayor of Zalamea).

Calderón, Ventura García. *See* GARCÍA, CALDERÓN, VENTURA.

Caldwell, Erskine (1903–), US author, noted for his humorous novels and short stories dealing with the impoverished country people of the southern states of the USA. Some of his best-known works are *Tobacco Road* (1932) and *God's Little Acre* (1933).

Caldwell, Zoë (1933–), Australian-born actress. She starred in many plays at the Shakespeare Theatre at Stratford-on-Avon in England, and in 1966 made her Broadway debut in *Slapstick,* for which she won the New York Drama Critics' Award. In 1968 she won the award again for her role in *The Prime of Miss Jean Brodie.*

Caldy Island (Ynys Byr), island 3.6km (2.3 miles) off the SW coast of Wales, in Carmarthen Bay. It is owned and inhabited by Cistercian monks. Area: 200 hectares (500 acres).

Caledonia, ancient Roman name for northern Britain, now used poetically for the Highlands or for the whole of Scotland. It was invaded by the Roman general AGRICOLA in AD 82. The word was first used in the writings of Lucan in the 1st century AD.

Caledonian Canal, waterway running SW to NE across Scotland, through the Great Glen from Loch Linnhe to the Moray Firth. A series of canals link lochs Lochy, Oich, Elia and Ness. Length: 97km (60 miles).

Calendar, way of reckoning time for regulating religious, commercial and civil life, and for dating events in the past and future. Calendars have been in use since the earliest times: the Ancient Egyptians had a system based on the movement of the star Sirius and on the seasons. Calendars are based on natural and astronomical regularities: the tides and seasons, the movements of the Sun and Earth and the phases of the Moon. The basic units are the day, month and year. The Earth turns once a day on its axis; the Moon goes round the Earth once a lunar or synodic month (29.53059 days); the Earth takes one year to complete a revolution round the Sun – reckoned as a TROPICAL YEAR this is 365.242199 days. The main difficulty in compiling a calendar is that the month is not an exact number of days and the year not an exact number of months. For convenience, months and days are assigned a whole number of days, and extra days (called intercalations) are added at intervals to compensate. In the modern Gregorian calendar an extra day (29 Feb.) is added every four years (leap years). The Gregorian or New Style calendar was based on the Julian or Old Style solar calendar. This was introduced by Julius Caesar in the 1st century BC and was developed from an earlier Roman moon-based calendar. *See also* MW pp.188–190.

Calgary, city in S Alberta, Canada, at the confluence of the Bow and Elbow rivers. It was founded in 1875 as a post of the Royal Canadian Mounted Police. It is noted for the Calgary Stampede, an annual rodeo. An industrial and commercial centre, it has a university (1945) and its industries include flour milling, timber, brick, cement and oil refining. Pop. (1974) 403,320.

Cali, city in W Colombia on the River Cali; founded in 1536. It was damaged in 1885 by an earthquake. The Cauca Valley Authority was established in 1954 to develop land reclamation, electric power and control flooding. The city has an old aqueduct, a cathedral and two universities. Industries: tourism, tobacco, textiles, paper. Pop. 898,253.

Calibration, testing of scientific instruments for the purpose of affixing measuring scales. For example, thermometers are calibrated in degrees of Fahrenheit, Celsius or Kelvin, and pressure gauges are calibrated in lb/sq ft or kg/sq m. All calibrations are based on fundamental standard units of length, temperature, etc., most particularly the SI, or International System, of units.

Calico, plain woven cotton cloth, often white but also dyed and block-printed. It is named after its place of origin, Calicut, India. It became a general term for Oriental plain weave cottons. Calico was the staple textile product of the early Industrial revolution in England.

California, state in W USA on the Pacific coast; the largest state by population and the third largest in area. There are Coast Ranges running N to S, paralleled by the high Sierra Nevada in the E, between which lies the fertile Central Valley, drained by the Sacramento and San Joaquin rivers. In the SE is a broad desert area. With an all-year growing season and vast irrigation projects, the state is the leading producer of many crops, including a wide variety of fruit and vegetables. Poultry and dairy produce are also important, as is the fishing industry. Forests covering about 40% of the land support an important timber industry. Mineral deposits include oil and natural gas, and a variety of ores valuable in manufacturing, which is the largest sector of the economy. Industries include aircraft, aerospace equipment, electronic components, missiles, motor vehicles, communications equipment, chemical and petroleum products, cement and paper. Tourism is also an important industry. The capital is Sacramento, and the major cities are Los Angeles, San Francisco, Oakland and San Diego. The Spanish explored the coast in 1542, but the first settlement was in 1769, when Spaniards from Mexico founded a Franciscan mission at San Diego. The area became part of Mexico, then a Spanish colony, and government land grants were used to establish huge cattle ranches. Settlers came from the USA and in 1846, early in the Mexican War (1846–48), US forces occupied California, which was ceded to the USA at the war's end. After gold was discovered in 1848, the GOLD RUSH swelled the population from 15,000 to 250,000 in four years. In 1850 California joined the Union. Since the turn of the century, the discovery of oil and the development of service industries have attracted more and more settlers to California. Area: 411,013sq km (158,693sq miles). Pop. (1975 est.) 21,185,000.

California, Lower. *See* BAJA CALIFORNIA.

California Current, Pacific Ocean current that flows S along the W coast of North America. It is part of a clockwise current of the entire N Pacific, and carries cool water from the Aleutian current. *See also* PE p.79.

Californian poppy, plant native to the western seaboard of the USA, having a glossy red or orange flower 5cm (2in) or more in diameter. It grows up to 1m (3.2ft) tall. It was brought into general cultivation as a result of the work of David Douglas (1798–1834). Family Papaveraceae; species *Eschscholtzia californica.*

California redwood, *Sequoia sempervirens,* conifer related to the swamp cypresses that grows to a height of more than 100m (330ft) and is thus one of the tallest of all trees. Its close relative, also from California, is the less common big tree or wellingtonia (*Sequoiadendron gigan-*

teum), which is the heaviest tree in the Western world. Sequoias live to be more than 4,000 years old. *See also* NW p.56.

Californium, radioactive metallic element (symbol Cf) of the ACTINIDE group, first made in 1950 at the University of California, Berkeley, by alpha-particle bombardment of Curium-242. Properties: at.no. 98; most stable isotope Cf^{251} (half-life 800 yr).

Caligula, Gaius Caesar (AD 12–41), Roman emperor (*r.* AD 37–41), great-nephew of TIBERIUS. The Senate and army made him emperor, but he became mentally disturbed, and his reign was cruel and absurd. Solders of his bodyguard killed him and made CLAUDIUS I emperor. *See also* HC1 p.98.

Caliph, leader of the Muslim community. After the death of MOHAMMED, ABU-BAKR was chosen to be his caliph (successor). Later the caliphate moved often, and was controlled by the dominant dynasty within Islam at the time. The title remained with the Ottoman sultans (1517–1924), after which it was abolished. *See also* HC1 pp.144–145, 148–149.

Calixtus, name of three POPES. Calixtus I (*r.* 217–22) a former slave, was attacked for his leniency towards sinners, but formed the Church's doctrine of penance. Calixtus II (*r.* 1119–24), a Burgundian, engaged in conflicts with the Holy Roman Emperor over lay investiture, and came to a compromise with him on the issue in the Concordat of WORMS in 1122. Calixtus III (*r.* 1455–58), *b.* Alfonso de BORGIA (1378–1458), a Spaniard, proclaimed an abortive crusade in 1455 and, by favouring members of his own family, established the influence of the Borgias.

Callaghan, Leonard James (1912–), British Labour politician. He entered Parliament as member for Cardiff South in 1945 and sat for Cardiff South-east from 1950. He was elected leader of the LABOUR PARTY and became Prime Minister in April 1976. He is the only Prime Minister in British history to have held all three of the major offices of state: Chancellor of the Exchequer (1964–67), Home Secretary (1967–70) and Foreign Secretary (1974–76).

Callaghan, Morley Edward (1903–), Canadian author. He was a friend of Ernest HEMINGWAY (who encouraged him to write) and later met Scott FITZGERALD in Paris. His first novel was *Strange Fugitive* (1928); later novels included *More Joy in Heaven* (1937), *The Loved and the Lost* (1951) and *That Summer in Paris* (1963).

Calla lily, flowering plant of the ARUM family (Araceae) native to South Africa. It has brilliant white flowers and arrow-shaped leaves, and is a popular house-plant. It grows to a height of 90cm (3ft) or more. Genus *Zantedeschia*. *See also* LILY.

Callao, city on the central W coast of Peru, approx. 13km (8 miles) W of Lima; it is Peru's chief port. Founded in 1537 by Francisco Pizarro, the original city was destroyed by a tidal wave and earthquake in 1746. Today it is a commercial centre, with flour milling, brewing and sugar refining industries. Pop. (1970 est.) 335,400.

Callard, Sir Jack (1913–), British industrialist. He joined ICI in 1935 and was appointed chairman of the company in 1971. In the same year he became a member of the Royal Institution and a fellow of the Royal Society of Arts.

Callas, Maria (1923–77), Greek soprano. She studied at the Athens Conservatory and made her debut in Verona in 1947. Her successes at La Scala Opera House, Milan, from 1951, and at Covent Garden, from 1952, established her reputation as a leading singing actress. She made her Metropolitan Opera debut in 1956 in *Norma*. Noted for her stormy personality, she made infrequent appearances after 1960.

Callicrates (5th century BC), Greek architect. With the architect Ictinus, he designed and directed the building of the PARTHENON at Athens (447–438 BC). He also designed the Temple of Athena Nike. *See also* HC1 p.78.

Calligrammes, collection of poems by Guillaume APOLLINAIRE (1880–1918) written during 1913–16, published in 1918. The poems are experimental, often lack conventional punctuation, and sometimes use pictorial typography eg, in *Il Pleut* the printed letters trickle down the page like water.

Callimachus (*c.* 300–240 BC) Greek poet, the most important of the Hellenistic period. Among his best-known works were the *Aetia*, or *Causes*, a discussion of the origins of myths, legends, and rituals, and the *Lock of Berenice*, a celebration of the Egyptian Queen Berenice.

Calliope, Greek muse of epic poetry. One of the nine daughters of ZEUS and Mnemosyne, she had two daughters by APOLLO, and was the mother of ORPHEUS.

Callisthenes of Olynthus (*c.* 360–*c.* 328 BC), Greek philosopher and historian. He was a nephew of Aristotle and accompanied Alexander the Great into Asia as historian. He later criticized Alexander, was accused of plotting against him, and died in prison. His works include a history of Greece from 386–355.

Callisto, satellite of Jupiter; one of the satellites first seen by Galileo. Its diameter is 5,720km (3,553 miles); its mean distance from the planet 1,070,000km (665,000 miles); and its mean sidereal period 16.75 days. *See* SU p.212, *212*.

Call Me Madam, musical play with songs by Irving BERLIN and book by Russel Crouse and Howard Lindsay, first produced on Broadway in 1950, starring Ethel MERMAN.

Call of the Wild, The (1903), novel by Jack LONDON. It tells of a dog, Buck, and his conflicts with man and nature as it journeys farther and farther north. When its last master is killed, Buck responds to the call of nature and joins a wolf pack.

Callot, Jacques (1592–1635), French engraver and master of the technique of etching, a form of print-making that he learned in Italy and later popularized in France. His work ranges from battles, crowd scenes and court festivities to grotesque portrait figures, but he is best known for his *Les Grandes Misères de La Guerre* (1633), illustrating the brutalities of the THIRTY YEAR WAR.

Calomel, mercurous chloride, Hg_2Cl_2, chemical used in medicine as a purgative. Its use has declined as it may dissociate into mercury and the poisonous mercuric chloride, corrosive sublimate $HgCl_2$.

Caloocan, city in Luzon, the Philippines. Incorporated in 1963, it is actually part of Greater Manila and its primary function is that of a dormitory suburb. It is now developing its own industries. Pop. (1975) 364,126.

Calorie, measure of heat energy: the amount of heat required to raise one gram of water one degree Celsius between the temperatures of 14.5 and 15.5°C. In the SI system the calorie is replaced by the JOULE (1 calorie = 4.1855 joules). The large or kilocalorie (Cal) is used in nutritional studies. *See also* SU p.91.

Calorimeter, apparatus used for experiments involving heat measurements, typically having a conducting container, thermally insulated, and means of supplying heat and measuring temperature. There are many types, each designed for a special purpose, eg, measurement of specific heat capacities, latent heats, heats of reaction and heats of formation.

Calumet, or peace pipe, ceremonial tobacco-pipe of American Indians, smoked on ceremonial occasions or as a devotional exercise. The pipe was symbolically decorated, and the smoke was considered a medium of communication with the spirit world.

Calvados, apple brandy made in the Calvados département of NE France. The health-giving qualities of this liqueur are particularly acclaimed. Cider and the cheeses of CAMEMBERT and Pont l'Evêque are also produced in this region.

Calvary, place where Jesus was crucified. It was called Calvary by St Luke. St John, St Matthew and St Mark refer to it as Golgotha. Calvary has most often been located near the Church of the Holy Sepulchre in Jerusalem, but a small hill called "Gordon's Calvary" has also been proposed as the site.

Calvert, Edward (1799–1883), British painter and engraver. His work is marked by sensitivity and rich detail. His works include the engravings *The Return Home*, *The Ploughman* and *The Bride*, all of which were produced from the 1820s onwards.

Calvin, John (Jean) (1509–64), French theologian of the Reformation. He first prepared for a career in the Catholic Church but then turned to the study of classics. Around 1533 he became a protestant and began work on his *Institutes of the Christian Religion*. In this work he presented the basics of what came to be known as Calvinism. To avoid persecution, he went in 1536 to stay in Geneva, where he advanced the Reformation. *See also* HC1 pp.269, 316.

Calvin, Melvin (1911–), US chemist who did fundamental research into the mechanism of PHOTOSYNTHESIS, for which he was awarded the 1961 Nobel Prize in chemistry.

Calvinism, doctrines and attitudes derived from or strongly influenced by the Protestant theologian John CALVIN (1509–64), as expounded in his *Institutes of the Christian Religion* and propagated by the Churches (Reformed and Presbyterian) established in his tradition. Rejecting papal authority and relying on the Bible as the source of religious truth, Calvinism stresses the utter sovereignty of God and the PREDESTINATION of every person either to election to bliss in harmony with God or to damnation in separation from Him. It politically subordinates State to Church and cultivates austere morality, family piety, business enterprise, education and science.

The development of these doctrines, particularly predestination and the rejection of CONSUBSTANTIATION in its eucharistic teaching, caused a split in PROTESTANTISM between the LUTHERAN CHURCH and what became the Reformed and PRESBYTERIAN CHURCHES. The influence of Calvinism spread rapidly. Important Calvinist leaders include John KNOX (1505–72) in Scotland and Jonathan EDWARDS (1703–58) in North America. *See also* HC1 pp.269, 316.

Calvinistic Methodist Church, religious group, originally followers of George WHITEFIELD (an English preacher) and Welsh preachers in the 18th century. In 1795 formal secession from the Church of England was considered, and in 1811 the Calvinistic Methodist Connexion was officially recognized and ordinations begun. Their Confession of Faith in 44 articles was published in 1823, and a ministerial training college was opened in Bala in 1837. Constitutionally, the Church combines features of PRESBYTERIANISM and CONGREGATIONALISM.

Calypso, folksong that originated in the West Indies, sung on plantations by African slaves. It is highly rhythmic and the words are often improvised. Calypso carnivals are held regularly in the Caribbean. A commercialized form was widely popular in English-speaking countries after WWII.

Cam, mechanical device consisting of an eccentric projection on a rotating shaft, shaped so as to give some desired reciprocating linear motion to another component. Cams are used in many different kinds of machinery, eg car engines. *See also* MM p.86.

Camagüey, city in E central Cuba; capital of Camagüey province. It is an important commercial and transport centre, with industries based on agriculture and cattle rearing, including meat-packing and dairy-food processing. Pop. (1970) 197,720.

Camargo, Marie-Anne (1710–70), French ballerina. She revolutionized ballet, being one of the first to shorten her skirts and remove the heels of her shoes. *See also* HC2 p.39.

Camberwell, municipality in S Victoria, Australia. It is a residential suburb of Melbourne, situated 8km (5 miles) E of the main city. Pop. (1976) 98,227.

Cambium, continuous layer of actively dividing cells, responsible for the growth in diameter of woody plant stems and

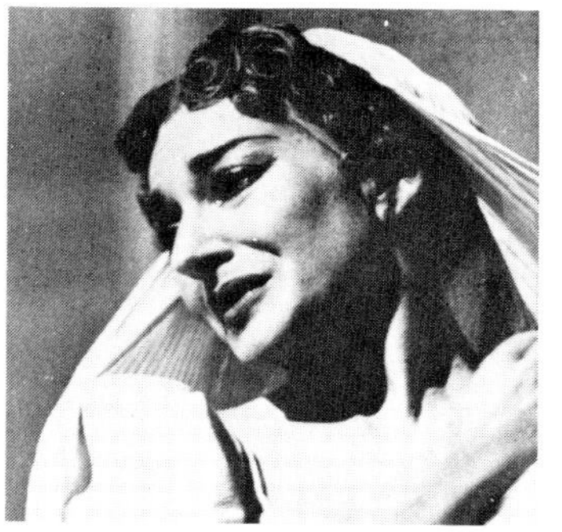

Maria Callas, the world famous soprano whose life and art were filled with drama.

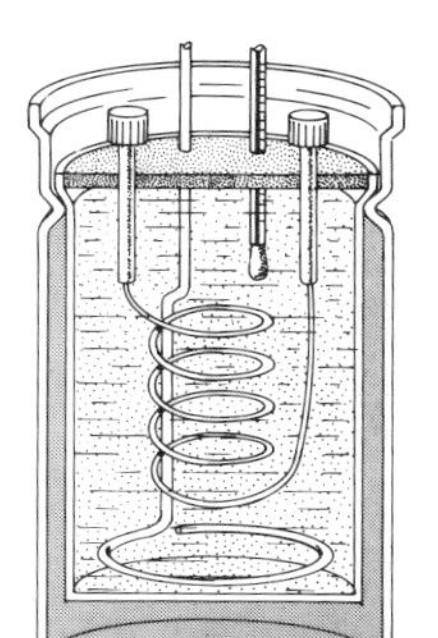

Calorimeters measure quantities of heat; thermometers only measure temperature.

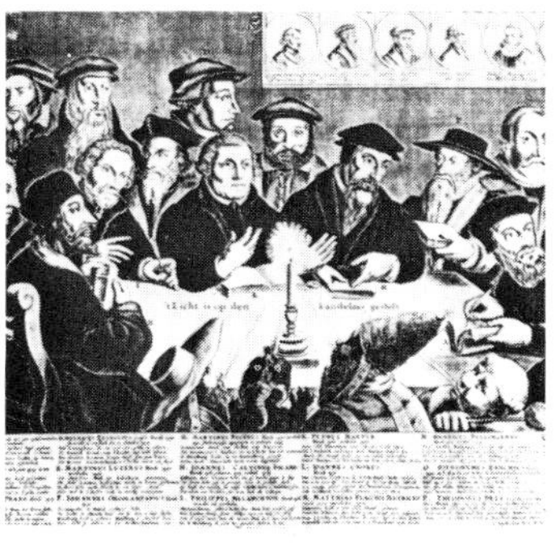

Calvin (right) and Luther, the two great lights of the reformation in 16th-century Europe.

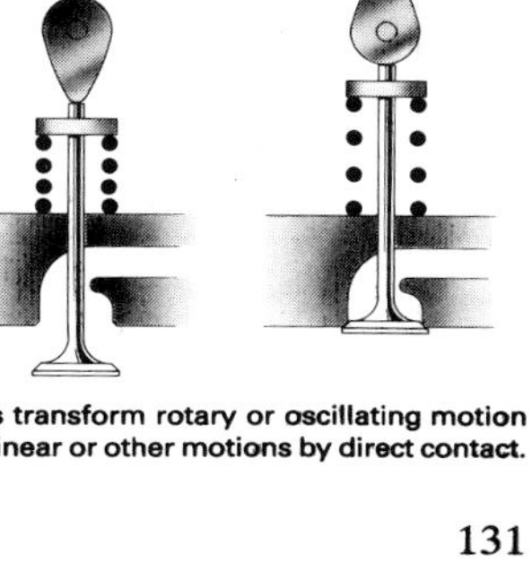

Cams transform rotary or oscillating motion into linear or other motions by direct contact.

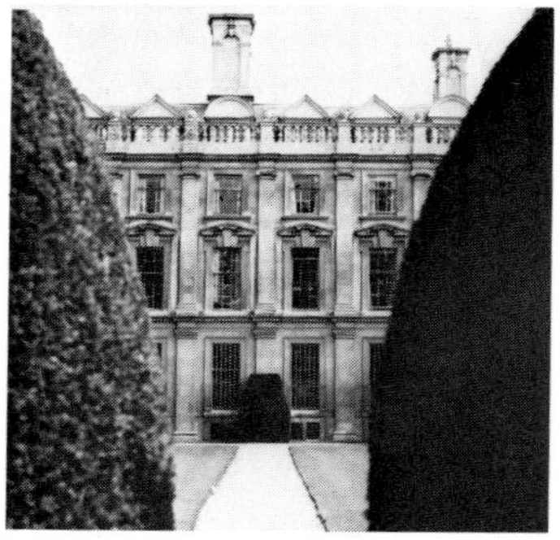

Cambridge, England; Clare College, one of the many historic university buildings.

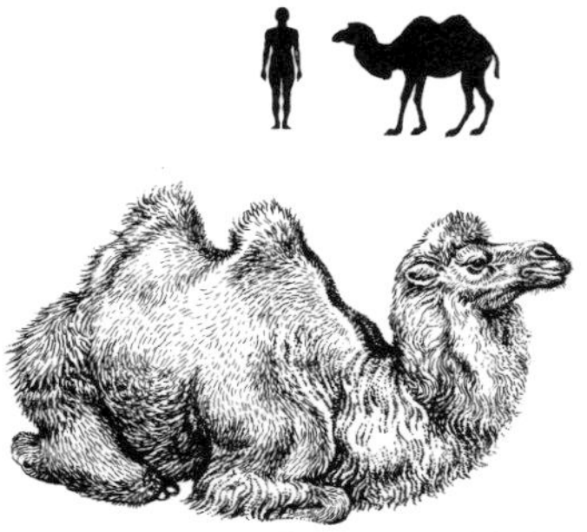

Camels can change their body temperature by as much as 6°C (11°F) without harm.

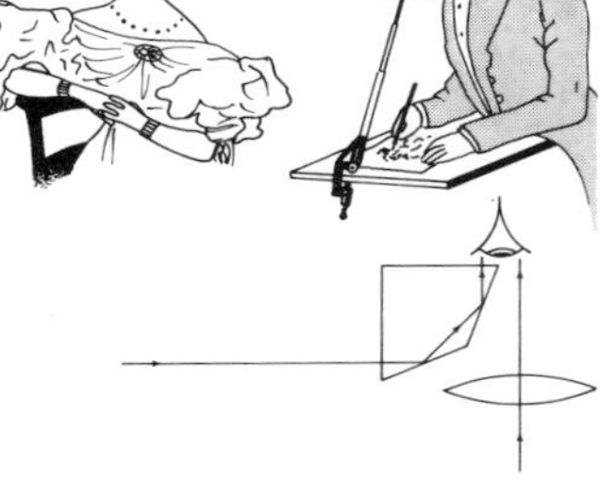

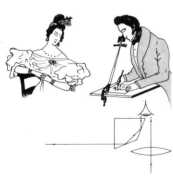

Camera lucida, where the observer sees a reflected image on his drawing paper.

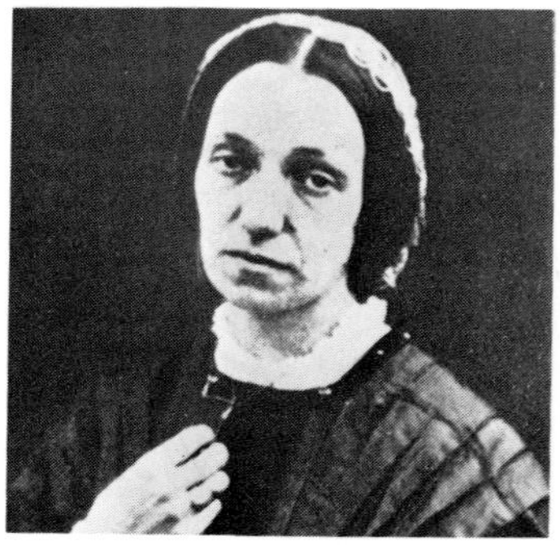

Julia Margaret Cameron produced photographic portraits of leading Victorians.

roots. After division, one cell remains part of the cambial layer whereas the other becomes a water-conducting XYLEM element or a food-conducting PHLOEM factor. *See also* NW p.62, *62*.

Cambodia, nation in SE Asia on the Indochina peninsula, formerly the Khmer Republic. Much of the country is in the basin of the Mekong River and more than half the cultivated land is devoted to the growing of rice. The main cash crops are rubber, pepper, maize, soya beans, cotton and bananas. Industry is conducted on a small scale and is mainly concerned with food processing and timber. Cambodia has felt the effects of the recent war in SE Asia and now has a communist government. The capital is Phnom Penh. Area: 181,035sq km (69,898sq miles). Pop. (1975 est.) 8,110,000. *See also* HC2 p.293; MW pp.44–45.

Cambrai, town and port in N France on the Escaut River, 55km (34 miles) SSE of Lille. It was ruled by the bishops of the HOLY ROMAN EMPIRE until taken by Spain in the 16th century and France in 1678. The Germans occupied the town during both World Wars (on 20 Nov. 1917 tanks were first used in warfare at a battle at Cambrai). It has long been known for its textiles and gave its name to cambric. Pop. (1968) 37,532.

Cambrian period, the earliest period of the PALEOZOIC ERA, lasting from about 570 million to 500 million years ago. The earliest geological period, its rocks contain a large variety of fossils, including all the animal phyla with the exception of the vertebrates. At that time the animals lived in the seas, while the land was barren. The commonest animal forms were trilobites, brachiopods, sponges and snails. Plant life consisted mainly of seaweeds. *See also* PE pp.124–131; NW 24, *25*.

Cambridge, city in Cambridgeshire, E England, on the River Cam, 77km (48 miles) NE of London. It was an important medieval river port. It is noted for the 12th century CAMBRIDGE UNIVERSITY which has many buildings of historic and architectural interest. Industries: precision engineering, printing and publishing, food processing. Pop. (1970) 100,361.

Cambridge, city in E Massachusetts USA, on the Charles River. It has Harvard University (1636), Radcliffe College (1879) and the Massachusetts Institute of Technology. Industries include printing and publishing, and electronic and scientific instruments. Pop. (1970) 100,360. *See also* HC2 p.63.

Cambridgeshire and Isle of Ely, former county in E central England, since 1974 part of the new county of Cambridgeshire. The area is mostly fenland with chalk hills to the S and is drained by the Ouse and Nene rivers and their tributaries. Agriculture is most important: the area produces wheat, barley and oats, and there is some market gardening.

Cambridge University, founded in 1209 (with claims for an earlier origin), is one of the oldest scholarly establishments in England. It has 26 colleges, the oldest Peterhouse (1284) and the most recently-founded Robinson (1977); it also includes several non-collegiate and post-graduate institutions. A centre of Renaissance learning and theological debate in the Reformation, it now has faculties for studying almost every discipline. In this century it has excelled in scientific research. Until 1948 it elected two members of Parliament.

Cambyses II (*d*.522 BC), King of Persia, son of CYRUS the Great. His main achievement was the conquest of Egypt. His other campaigns failed and he died in Syria. *See also* HC1 p.60.

Camden, William (1551–1623), English antiquary. As headmaster of Westminster School he encouraged the revival of Anglo-Saxon scholarship. His chief works are *Britannia* (1586) and *Annales rerum Anglicarum et Hibernicarum regnante Elizabetha*. *See also* HC1 p.*22*.

Camden Society, historical society founded in Britain in 1838 to further research, named after the Elizabethan antiquary William CAMDEN. Its chief contribution has been the publication of many documents of historical importance.

Camden Town Group, informal group of young British painters who, after 1905, met in the studio of Walter SICKERT. The group was only formally named in 1911. Influenced by the French post-impressionists their main subject was urban life. Its members included Harold Gilman, Robert Bevan and Charles Ginner.

Camel, large, hump-backed, UNGULATE mammal of the family Camelidae. There are two species – the two-humped Bactrian of central Asia and the single-humped Arabian camel. Its broad, padded feet, load-bearing capacity and supreme adaptability to local climatic conditions (eg, its ability to go for long periods without water) make the camel a useful desert animal. Genus *Camelus*. *See also* NW pp.162, *191*, 220, *221*.

Camellia, genus of evergreen trees or shrubs of the family Theaceae, native to E Asia (especially Japan) and popular as a garden plant. It has oval, dark green leaves and waxy, rose-like flowers which may be pink, red, white or variegated. *Camellia japonica* is the most common species.

Camelot, in English mythology, the seat of King ARTHUR's court. Its site is not known, although many people believe it was at Cadbury Castle, Somerset. *See also* HC1 pp.20–21.

Camembert, soft cheese made from whole cow's milk. After inoculation with a penicillium mould the milk is curdled and portions are set on straw mats to drain. The cheese is named after the village of Camembert in Normandy, NE France, where it was traditionally made. Normandy cheeses have been famous since the 12th century.

Cameo, relief carving, usually on striated gemstones or semi-precious stones, such as onyx, sardonyx, or agate, or on shell. The decoration, often a portrait head, is generally cut on the light-coloured vein, the dark vein being left as a background. Cameos were common among the Ancient Egyptians, Greeks and Etruscans, whose carved stone seals bearing the mystic symbol of the scarab beetle were the origin of the cameo. Interest in cameos revived during the Renaissance and continues to the present.

Camera, apparatus for taking photographs, consisting essentially of a light-tight box in which photographic film is positioned. When a shutter is briefly opened light from the scene outside is focused by a lens system on to the film. The amount of light falling on the film is controlled by the shutter speed, often variable, and by the diameter of the lens aperture, which can also often be varied using an adjustable diaphragm. Many cameras also have a rangefinder, enabling a focused image to be produced for a given object distance, and a built-in exposure meter, used to determine correct combination of shutter speed and aperture for the prevailing light conditions. *See also* MM *102*, *103*, 218–219, 220–221, *220*.

Camera lucida, apparatus for drawing and copying in perspective, developed in 1812 by W. H. Wollaston. A prism is set between the draftsman's eye and the paper in such a way that light is reflected from the object he is copying to form an image on the paper.

Camera obscura, optical device consisting of a darkened room into which an inverted image is thrown through a convex lens. A portable version of this was used by 17th- and 18th-century artists to trace scenes from nature. By the 19th century it had become a box, fitted with a lens and mirror and placed on a tripod. It eventually developed into the modern camera.

Cameron, Julia Margaret (1815–79), British pioneer photographer. In 1863 she began to take photographs of her friends including many leading figures of the day – Robert Browning, Charles Darwin, Henry Wadsworth Longfellow and Ellen Terry. Her works are imaginative, perceptive and superbly composed.

Cameron, Richard (*c*.1648–80), Scottish Covenanter. A Presbyterian convert, he preached in Scotland, then fled fo Rotterdam in 1679, returning to Scotland soon afterwards to continue preaching. He opposed the Stuarts for what he saw as their usurping of Christ's prerogatives and was killed by dragoons at Ayrsmoss. The CAMERONIANS are named after him.

Cameronians, numerically small but historically important Presbyterian communion in Scotland. They fought for religious liberty against the Stuarts and became (1743) the Reformed Presbytery under John MACMILLAN, a group which refused to recognize or participate in civil government in any way. Despite a majority of the group merging with the Church of Scotland in 1929, a minority still formed a synod in the Scottish lowlands about 600 strong in 1960.

Cameroon, republic in W Africa, extending from the Gulf of Guinea to Lake Chad, with a diverse population that includes more than 200 ethnic groups. It is a country of rain forest (S) and savanna (N). Most of its inhabitants are subsistence farmers. Coffee, cocoa and bauxite are exported. It became independent in 1961. The capital is Yaoundé. Area: 475,441sq km (183,568sq miles). Pop. (1975 est.) 6,398,000. *See* MW p.45.

Camisards, French Protestants of the Cévennes region who rebelled against LOUIS XIV in 1702. Although few in number, they were at first successful under their leader, Jean Cavalier, but by 1705 their revolt had all but ended.

Camoes, Luís Vaz de (*c*.1524–80), Portuguese poet. A courtier and soldier, he served in North Africa, where he lost an eye, and in India (1553–70). In 1572 he published *Os Lusíadas*, which soon became Portugal's national epic. He also wrote love lyrics and a few comic dramas.

Camomile, or chamomile, low-growing yellow or white herb of the genus *Anthemis* and family Asteraceae. Several species are cultivated as ground cover; the flowers of the perennial European camomile (*Anthemis nobilis*) can be used to make a medicinal tea.

Camouflage, technique used to conceal military personnel and equipment from observation by disguising them or making them blend with their natural surroundings. For example, nets are used to break up angular silhouettes and desert tanks are painted the colour of sand. Many animals and insects have natural camouflage, either to conceal them from their prey or to protect them from predators. The CHAMELEON, which changes colour at will, is the most versatile exponent.

Camp, Holiday. *See* HOLIDAY CAMP.

Campa, ARAWAK-speaking tribe of about 25,000 South American Indians. They inhabit the headwaters of the rivers Ucayali, Urubamba and Apurimac in PERU.

Campagna di Roma, lowland region 2,070sq km (800sq miles) in area, surrounding the city of Rome, central Italy. Although archaeological evidence shows the region to have been popular in Roman times, it was abandoned as marsh land in the Middle Ages. It was reclaimed in the 19th century and used for crop growing.

Campaign for Nuclear Disarmament (CND), mass-protest movement in Britain. It was founded by its president, Bertrand RUSSELL and Canon John Collins in 1958. It organized an annual Easter march between the atomic research centre at ALDERMASTON, Berkshire, and Trafalgar Square, London. In members and activity it has declined from its 1960 peak, when it influenced the LABOUR PARTY conference to pass a resolution in favour of unilateral disarmament. *See also* HC2 p.*237*.

Campana, Dino (1885–1932), Italian poet. He was emotionally unstable and published only one collection, *Canti orfici* (1914), whose spiritual and symbolic qualities considerably influenced later modern Italian poetry. *Inediti* (1941–42) a supplementary work, was not published until after his death.

Campanella, Tommaso (1568–1639), Italian philosopher and poet. A heterodox Dominican, he was active against the Spanish domination of south Italy. His most famous work is the utopian *The City* *of the Sun* (1602). He spent 26 years in prison.

Campania, region of sw Italy on the Tyrrhenian Sea, including the provinces of Avellino, Benevento, Caserta, Napoli and Salerno; the capital is Naples (Napoli). Settled by the Greeks and Etruscans, it prospered under Roman rule in the 4th century BC. It was conquered by Goths, Byzantines, Lombards and Normans and became part of Italy in 1860. It is a mountainous area with fertile plains. Products, wheat, corn, potatoes, fruit, nuts, tobacco, hemp, flowers, wine, fish, timber. Area: 13,595sq km (5,249sq miles). Pop. 5,132,860.

Campanile, Italian term for a bell-tower, often free-standing. Bell-towers originated in the 6th century and were the first church spires in Europe. A notable example is the campanile in Piazza San Marco, Venice.

Campanulaceae, the bellflower family of herbaceous flowering plants. There are about 300 species, including HAREBELL, CANTERBURY BELL, Coventry bell, peach bellflower and clustered bellflower. These and many other bellflowers are cultivated extensively for their delicate blossoms, often a pale or purplish blue in colour. Rampion is a bellflower cultivated for its leaves and root, which are used in salads.

Campbell, Sir Colin. *See* CLYDE, COLIN CAMPBELL, 1ST BARON.

Campbell, Colen (*c.*1673–1729), Scottish architect who contributed to the English revival of PALLADIAN architecture by compiling a book of engravings of classical architecture, notably that of Inigo JONES, in England (*Vitruvius Britannicus*). His major buildings include Mereworth Castle, Kent (1723), Houghton Hall, Norfolk (1722–26) and the remodelling of Burlington House, London (1717).

Campbell, David (1915–), Australian poet. He published selected poems from 1942 to 1968, and was the editor of *Modern Australian Poetry* (1970).

Campbell, Donald Malcolm (1921–67), British land and water speed record-holder. Son of Sir Malcolm Campbell, he set six new records on water, attaining 444.7km/h (276.3mph) in 1964. Also in 1964 he set a new land speed record of 648.72km/h (403mph). He was killed trying to set a new water speed record when his boat *Bluebird* sank.

Campbell, Sir Malcolm (1885–1948), British high-speed champion of both cars and speed-boats. In 1935 he became the first man to reach a land speed of 483km/h (300mph), which he accomplished in *Bluebird* at the Bonneville Salt Flats in the USA. He also set a speedboat record of 227km/h (141mph), on Coniston Water, Lancs. He was knighted in 1931.

Campbell, Mrs Patrick (1865–1940), British actress, born Beatrice Stella Tanner. She was a fine actress, her first major role being the lead in *The Second Mrs Tanqueray* (1893). She had a close platonic relationship with the playwright George Bernard SHAW, who wrote the part of Eliza Doolittle in *Pygmalion* (1914) especially for her.

Campbell, Robert (1808–94), Scottish-born Canadian fur trader and explorer. He worked for the HUDSON'S BAY COMPANY exploring the Yukon River and established posts at Fort Frances (1843), Pelly Banks (1844) and Fort Selkirk (1848).

Campbell, Roy (1901–57), South African poet. With William Plomer he founded *Voorslag*, a short-lived literary magazine, then left for Europe where he fought for Gen. Franco in the Spanish Civil War. He later settled in Britain and was acknowledged as South Africa's leading poet. His important poems include *The Flaming Terrapin* and *The Wayzegoose.*

Campbell, Thomas (1777–1844), Scottish poet who is best remembered for his war songs, such as *Ye Mariners of England, Hohenlinden* and *The Battle of the Baltic,* and for the ballad *Lord Ullin's Daughter.* His poetry includes *The Pleasures of Hope* (1799), *Gertrude of Wyoming* (1809) and *Theodoric* (1824).

Campbell-Bannerman, Sir Henry (1836–1908), British politician. He entered Parliament in 1868, and held minor posts until he became secretary of state for war in 1886. In 1901 he denounced British policy against the Boers in South Africa. As prime minister (1905–08) and leader of the Liberal Party he formed a strong reforming government before ill-health forced his retirement.

Camperdown, Battle of (1797), naval battle fought off the coast of Holland in which a British fleet under the command of Admiral Adam Duncan defeated the Dutch.

Camphor, $C_{10}H_{16}O$, organic chemical compound the molecule of which has a complex ring structure. It has a strong odour, which also occurs in the wood and leaves of the camphor tree, *Cinammonum camphora,* native to Taiwan. Camphor is used in medicine for liniments, in the polymercindustry as a plasticizer and as an ingredient of mothballs.

Campi, family of Italian painters, the most notable of whom was Giulio (*c.*1502–*c.*1572). Influenced by Giulio Romano and Pordenone, he studied the works of RAPHAEL and painted many fine altarpieces and frescoes in Cremona, eg *Madonna appearing to Franceso and Bianca Sforza* (1540).

Campinas, city in SE Brazil, 109km (68 miles) NW of São Paulo. A major centre of coffee production in the 19th century, it is now the processing and distribution centre for the mixed agriculture of the surrounding region. Industries: agricultural and railway equipment. Pop. (1970) 328,629.

Camping, leisure activity in which individuals or groups live in tents. Originally used by the military to accommodate troops, it has gained universal appeal as an inexpensive form of holiday-making, and the production and selling of camping equipment is a major business. Camp sites vary from an isolated field to planned areas with modern facilities. *See also* CARAVAN.

Campion, Saint Edmund (1540–81), one of the Forty Martyrs of England and Wales canonized in 1970. He was ordained deacon in the Church of England in 1569, but became a Roman Catholic in 1571 and subsequently joined the Jesuit Order. He spent some years on the European continent and taught in Prague until 1580, when he returned to England as a Jesuit missionary. In 1581 he published his pamphlet *Decem Rationes* defending the Roman Catholic position against Protestantism. He was charged with treason and executed at Tyburn in 1581. Feast: 1st December.

Campion, Thomas (1567–1620), English physician, poet and composer. He published a book of Latin epigrams, *Poemata* (1595), a treatise on *The Art of English Poesie* (1602), and four books of *Ayres* complete with music. He also wrote masques for the court of JAMES I.

Campion, annual, biennial or perennial garden plant of the CARNATION family (Caryophyllaceae), found throughout the world and comprising about 500 species. It has red, white or pink flowers. The wild flower CATCHFLY is also a campion. Genus *Silene. See also* NW p.*35.*

Campobello, island in SW New Brunswick, Canada, at the entrance of Passamaquoddy Bay, just off the coast of Maine, USA, to which it is connected by the Roosevelt Memorial Bridge (1962). Pres. Franklin D. Roosevelt had a summer home there. Area: 696 hectares (1,720 acres).

Campodeid (campodeiform larva), type of beetle larva that is a slim, actively moving insect resembling a SILVERFISH and not at all like the more worm-like beetle larvae. Like them and all other beetle larvae, however, campodeids eventually pupate and metamorphose into adult beetles. *See also* NW p.*106.*

Campoli, Alfredo (1906–), British violinist, *b.* Italy. He won many prizes before he was 20 years old . In 1950 he made an extensive concert tour of Australia and New Zealand.

Campra, André (1660–1744), French composer. He held musical posts at Notre-Dame cathedral, Paris (1694–1700), and the Chapel Royal (1722–44). Highly esteemed for lively dramatic compositions, he wrote more than 40 stage works, most of them opera-ballets.

Camps, Professor Francis Edward (1905–72), British pathologist who became interested in forensic medicine, particularly poisons and drugs, in the 1930s. He built up a renowned department of forensic medicine at the London Hospital Medical College, and was a founder of the British Association of Forensic Medicine, serving as its president from 1958–60. His fame rests on his association with many criminal cases.

Camus, Albert (1913–60), French novelist, playwright and essayist. During WWII he was one of the leaders of the French Resistance. His outlook is humanitarian yet he sees man's condition as absurd. He achieved recognition with his first novel *The Stranger* (1942). His writings also include the novels *The Plague* (1947) and *The Fall* (1956), and the essay *The Rebel* (1951). He was awarded the 1957 Nobel Prize in literature.

Camus, Marcel (1912–), French film director. His films are often shot in colourful locations, such as Brazil for *Os Bandeirantes* (*The Pioneers,* 1960) and Cambodia for *L'Oiseau de Paradis* (1962). The celebrated *Orfeu Negro* (*Black Orpheus,* 1958) portrayed Brazilian carnival scenes in a spectacular manner.

Canaan, historical region of Palestine and W Syria, Phoenician after 1200 BC, with a Semitic population and culture. It had vigorous trade and became extremely prosperous, before being subjugated by the Israelites on their return from Egypt (who regarded Canaan as the Promised Land). Biblical Hebrew has historical links with the area.

Canada, nation in N America, the second-largest country in the world in terms of area, occupying most of the N half of the continent, and bounded by the Atlantic, Arctic and Pacific oceans, and the USA. A member of the COMMON WEALTH OF NATIONS, it acknowledges the British monarch as head of state, and has a federal system of government, with Ottawa the capital. A country of great contrasts, it has the lofty Rockies in the W, vast rolling prairies, the forest of the CANADIAN SHIELD and the icefields of the Arctic. Timber is of great economic importance and Canada's mineral deposits are some of the richest in the world, including gold, silver, nickel, zinc and lead. It has oilfields in the central plains. The prairies yield much wheat, and cattle are also raised there. Area: 9,976,139sq km (3,851,809sq miles). Pop. (1975 est.) 22,831,000. *See* MW pp.45–50.

Canada East, official title of LOWER CANADA after the creation of a single British province of Canada in 1841. In 1867 the region became known as QUEBEC, when Canada was federated as a group of states. *See also* HC2 p.136.

Canada goose, bird native to North America where it is migratory. It has been successfully introduced into Europe and has a distinctive long black neck and white cheek pouches. It nests on the banks of streams and on tundra. Length: 58–109cm (22–43in); weight: 3–6.5kg (6.6–14lb). Family Anatidae; species *Branta canadensis.*

Canada West, official title of UPPER CANADA, after the creation of a single British province of Canada in 1841. In 1867 the region became known as ONTARIO, when Canada was federated as a group of states. *See also* HC2 p.136.

Canadian fivepins, version of TENPIN BOWLING that originated in Toronto in 1909. Played on a tenpin alley, 18m (60ft) long, it has a ball 13cm (5in) in diameter without fingerholes and five squat pins arranged in a triangular shape. Pins vary in value and a strike (when all five pins are knocked down with the first ball) is worth 15 points.

Canadian football. *See* FOOTBALL.

Canadian Pacific Railway, privately owned railway system in Canada. It stretches from St John, New Brunswick, to Vancouver, British Columbia. It was begun in 1872 and, after long delays caused by a political scandal, the main line from Montreal to the Pacific

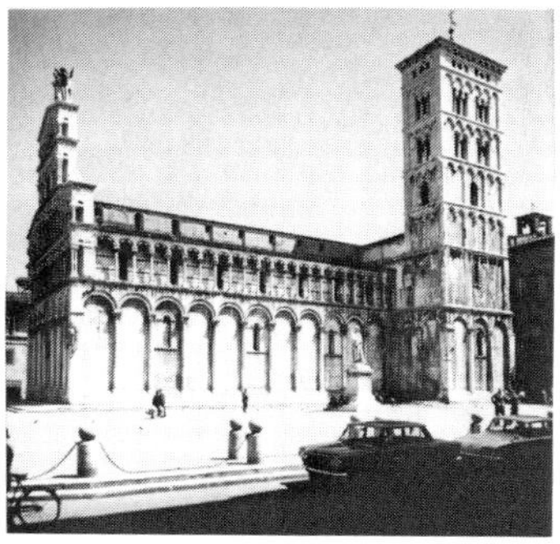

Campaniles are the tall towers built to hold bells that summon worshippers to church.

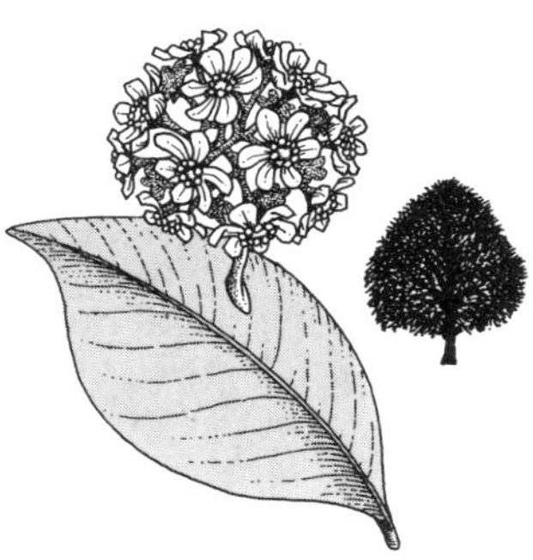

Camphor trees grow in the Far East; the camphor is removed by steaming.

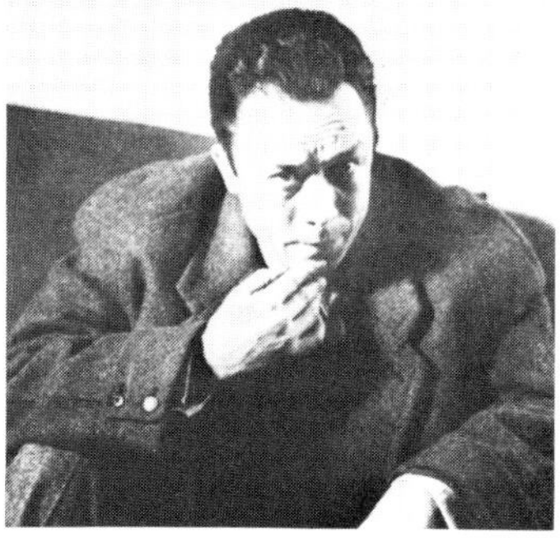

Albert Camus considered suicide to be "the one truly serious philosophical problem".

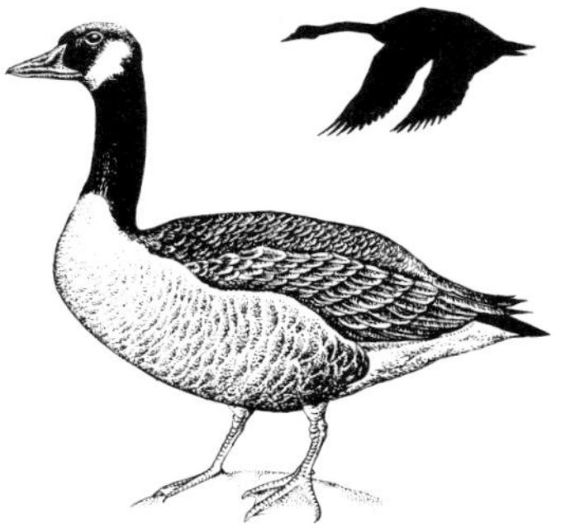

Canada geese are the common wild geese of North America. They fly south for winter.

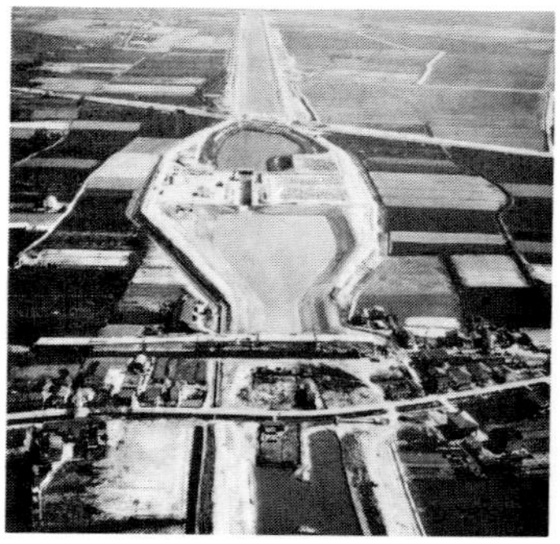

Canals, artificial waterways created mostly to connect natural oceans, rivers and lakes.

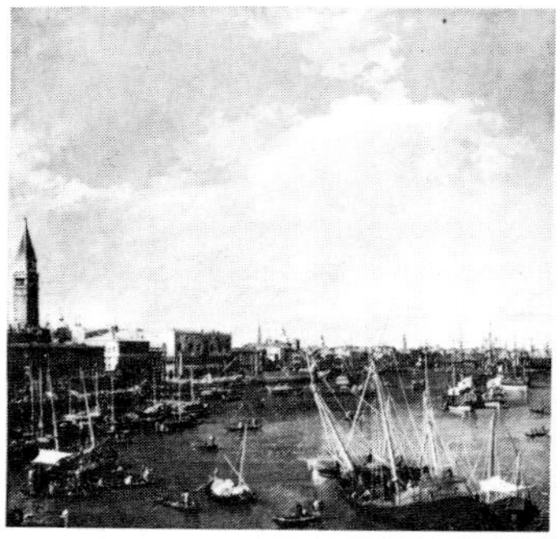

Canaletto received many commissions for paintings from English tourists in Venice.

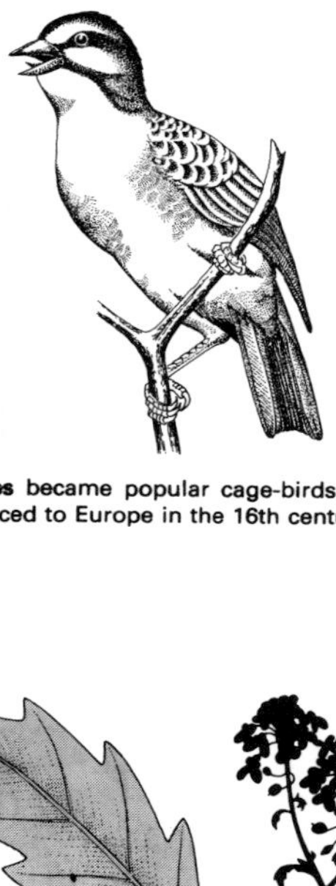

Canaries became popular cage-birds when introduced to Europe in the 16th century.

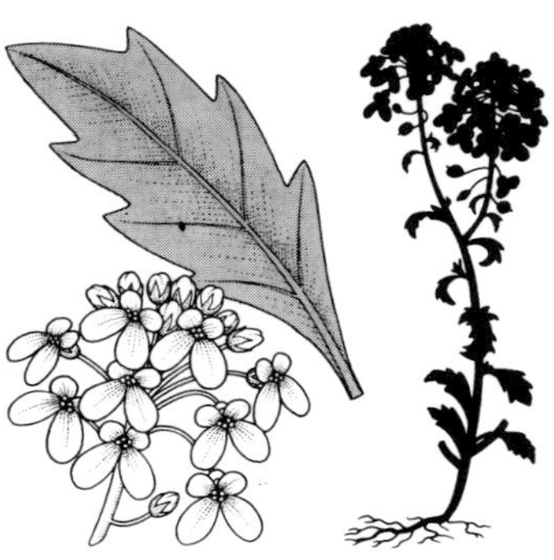

Candytuft blooms in shades ranging from white to violet. There are about 30 species.

coast was completed in 1885. *See also* HC2 p.137.

Canadian Shield, or Laurentian Highlands, great plateau of Canada, roughly outlining the Hudson Bay; extends from Mackenzie River Basin SE through S Ontario and S Quebec (including the Great Lakes region of central North America), and NE to the Labrador Sea. It is an area of extensive forests (S) and tundra (N) and is largely undeveloped.

Canal, artificial waterway constructed for irrigation, drainage, navigation or in conjunction with hydroelectric dams. Many canals serve multiple purposes. Canals were known 4,000 years ago in Ancient Mesopotamia. The longest canal able to accommodate large ships today connects the Baltic and White seas in the USSR and is 227km (141 miles) long. The heyday of canal building and use in England was the late 18th and early 19th century. *See also* MM pp.188, 196–197.

Canal du Midi, artificial waterway in S France, linking Toulouse and Sete. It was built in 1666–92 to carry oceangoing ships between the Atlantic Ocean and the Mediterranean Sea. It runs for 250km (155 miles) through rugged terrain, and includes 106 locks, one tunnel and three major aqueducts. It is now used only for barge traffic. *See also* MM p.*196*.

Canaletto (Giovanni Antonio Canal) (1697–1768), Italian painter of the VENETIAN SCHOOL, famous for his views of Venice. His work was very popular in the 1720s and 30s, especially with visiting English collectors. In 1746 he went to England, where he painted many London scenes. Canaletto's treatment of landscape – the shimmering effect of light touching water, sky and buildings – have influenced painters and illustrators to the present day.

Canal Zone, the area astride the Panama Canal. The name is also sometimes given to the region occupied by the Suez Canal. *See* MW p.51.

Canaries Current, cold current of the N Atlantic Ocean; flows SW from Spain along the NW coast of Africa. It joins with the North Equatorial current at approx. 20° N. *See also* PE p.79.

Canary, popular cage-bird that lives wild in the Azores, Canary and Madeira islands. These yellowish FINCHES feed on fruit, seeds and insects, and lay spotted greenish-blue eggs in cup-shaped nests. The pure yellow varieties have been domesticated since the 16th century, although they are difficult to breed in captivity. Family Fringillidae; species *Serinus canarius*.

Canary Islands, group of islands in the N Atlantic Ocean, approx. 113km (70 miles) off the NW coast of Africa. They constitute two provinces of Spain, Las Palmas and Santa Cruz de Tenerife. The main cities are Santa Cruz de Tenerife and Las Palmas de Gran Canaria. The islands are mountainous and the climate warm, with little rainfall. Irrigation allows the cultivation of sugar cane, bananas, fruits, tobacco, nuts and vegetables. Fishing and tourism are important industries. Area: 7,273sq km (2,808sq miles). Pop. (1975 est.) 1,275,643.

Canasta, card game for two to six players. The game, a version of RUMMY, is generally played by two sets of partners using two standard packs of cards and four jokers. The object is to accumulate sets of like-numbered cards. Seven cards or more of one number is called a canasta. The cards have different point values, and 3,000 points is usually the total needed to win.

Canberra, capital city of Australia, in Australian Capital Territory, SE Australia, 249km (155 miles) SW of Sydney, on the Molonglo River. Settled *c.* 1824, it was chosen in 1908 as the new site for Australia's capital, succeeding Melbourne. The transfer of all governmental agencies was not, however, complete until after WWII. The city has the Australian National University (1946), Royal Australian Mint (1965), The Royal Military College, Stromlo Observatory and other scientific institutions. Most of the residents are employed by the federal government. Pop. (1973) 185,000.

Canberra bomber, English two-seater, twin-engined jet fighter-bomber. The prototype first flew in May 1949 and was in service by late 1950. It soon saw active service in the Korean War. Many variants, eg for training, were developed, but by the 1970s it was being phased out. Altogether 925 were built by English Electric, BAC and other manufacturers.

Cancan (also called chahut), saucy French dance usually in quick 4/4 time, performed with much high-kicking by women in frilly skirts. Popular in the 1830s as a Parisian show dance, it was used by J. OFFENBACH in his operetta *Orpheus in the Underworld* and later depicted by TOULOUSE-LAUTREC in many famous paintings and lithographs.

Cancer, the unchecked production of abnormal cells in the body which leads to the growth of malignant tissues and possibly death unless diagnosed at an early stage. Treatment can consist of surgery, chemical therapy or radiation and classification is by the type of tissue affected – the most prevalent being CARCINOMA and SARCOMA – and the type of cell from which it is derived. Cancer can attack almost any organ and, whereas no specific cause has been fully determined, environmental factors and irritants such as cigarette smoking may play a large part in causing it. *See also* MS pp.86, 87, *87*, 89, 113, 125.

Cancer, Tropic of, parallel of latitude, approx. 23.5° N of the equator which marks the northern boundary of the TROPICS. It indicates the farthest northern position at which the sun appears directly overhead at noon. The sun is vertical over the Tropic of Cancer on about 21 June, which is the summer SOLSTICE in the Northern Hemisphere.

Cancer, in astrology, a sign of the zodiac, symbolised by a crab. It is the sun-sign for those born between 23 June and 23 July. A feminine sign, its element is water and its ruling planet is the Moon. The crab symbolism is Babylonian in origin.

Cancer, or the Crab, northern constellation between Gemini and Leo. It contains two open clusters: M44, the Praesepe or Beehive Nebula (NGC 2632), and M67 (NGC 2692). The brightest star is Beta Cancri. *See also* SU pp.254, 257.

Cancer Ward (1968), novel by Soviet author Alexander SOLZHENITSYN, who suffered from cancer throughout his prison sentence. The author examines the reactions of several men, particularly Kostoglotov and Rusanov, faced with the prospect of imminent death from cancer.

Candela, or new international candle, standard unit of luminous intensity defined as the luminous intensity of a BLACKBODY of surface area 1/60sq cm at the temperature of solidification of platinum (1,772°C) and at atmospheric pressure. Symbol: cd.

Candela, Félix (1910–), Spanish architect and engineer who settled in Mexico (1939), where he developed the use of shell vaulting. Using thin curved planes of concrete, he created roofs of great elegance and lightness which allowed him to cover large buildings economically. The Church of the Miraculous Virgin, Mexico (1953) is a fine example of his style.

Candelabra tree. *See* EUPHORBIA.

Candida. *See* CRETE.

Candide (1759), short novel by VOLTAIRE. A farcical satire on contemporary complacency, it deals with the series of misfortunes encountered by Candide, who had been taught that "all is for the best in this the best of all possible worlds". After a series of swift-moving, disastrous and violent adventures, Candide and his entourage become disillusioned and decide to take no further part in the world beyond cultivating their garden.

Candidiasis, also known as moniliasis, it is an infectious disease caused by the fungus *Candida albicans*. It may occur in the mouth or vagina, where it is known as THRUSH, and also in the lungs, intestinal tract, skin or nails.

Candle, column (usually cylindrical) of wax or tallow surrounding a fibrous wick used as a light source. Candles were known to the ancient Egyptians, who used tallow wax. Later the more pleasant-smelling beeswax and spermaceti were used. Modern candles are generally made of a mixture of paraffin wax and stearic acid with a little added beeswax. In physics, candle is the name given to a unit of luminous intensity.

Candlefish. *See* EULACHON.

Candlemas (2 Feb.), Christian festival commemorating the Purification of the Blessed Virgin and the Presentation of Christ in the Temple. In the Roman Catholic church it is the day when the candles are blessed. Its name derives from the procession of candles symbolizing the entry of Christ – in Simeon's words "a light to lighten the gentiles" (Luke 2.32) – in to the temple.

Candytuft, any of several species of annual and perennial plants native to Spain and popular in temperate climates as garden flowers. They have large, dome-like clusters of white, red or violet flowers. Height: to 30cm (12in). Family Cruciferae; genus *Iberis*.

Cane, term applied to the stems of stalks of a wide variety of plants. Certain species of BAMBOO and reed are referred to commonly as "cane", although in botany the name should be properly restricted to members of the palm family known as rattans. *See also* NW p.*69*.

Canea. *See* KHANIA.

Canidae, family of mammals whose members include dogs, wolves, jackals, coyotes and foxes, all belonging to the genus *Canis* and sharing features suited to their natural hunting lives. The DOG is the oldest domesticated animal. *See also* NW pp.164, 201, *204*, 205, *206*, 207.

Canine, any one of four sharp "stabbing" teeth in the frontal dentition of most mammals. In human beings they are also called eye teeth. *See* TEETH.

Canis Major, or the Great Dog, southern constellation situated S of Monoceros. It contains the bright open cluster M41 (NGC 2287). The brightest star is Alpha Canis Majoris or Sirius, the brightest star in the sky, also called the Dog star. *See also* SU p.260.

Canker, disease involving areas of dying plant tissue which attacks fruit or forest trees. It can be caused by various agents but most commonly by fungi such as *Nectria galligena,* which attacks apple and pear trees.

Canker, ulcerous sore, usually occurring on the inner surface of the lips or around the mouth. Causes may include injury, allergy or hormonal reaction, although the cause of most cankers is still unknown. They usually heal spontaneously.

Canna, or Indian shot, flowering plant native to tropical America and Asia. It is raised as an ornamental plant, and has large red, pink, yellow or white flowers and large, broad leaves. Height: 60–240cm (2–8ft). Among the 50 species is *Canna indica*. Family Cannaceae.

Cannabis, resin from the leaves or stem of the Indian hemp plant, *Cannabis sativa*. It is taken as a psychotropic drug in many parts of the world, being either smoked or eaten under such names as hashish, marijuana, bhang, kif and ghanga, when it produces a NARCOTIC effect allied with a feeling of well-being and perhaps mild hallucinations. There is no evidence to show that it is harmfully addictive in the way of "hard" drugs such as heroin. *See also* MS p.105.

Cannae, ancient town in SE Italy, on the Ofanto River, in Bari province. In 216 BC Hannibal led the Carthaginians to a crushing defeat of the Romans at the Battle of Cannae.

Cannel coal, variety of coal formed from organic matter rich in spores and algae. It contains a high percentage of the lighter HYDROCARBONS and burns easily, and is thus a good domestic coal. Unlike other coals, which appear banded, cannel coal is without any visible structure. *See also* PE p.*136*.

Cannery Row (1944), novel by John Steinbeck. A return to the style of *Tortilla Flat* (1935), it is the whimsical story of six happy-go-lucky idlers in Monterey, California, who set out to catch frogs for a lonely but sympathetic biologist called "Doc". There are portraits of other local characters.

Cannes, resort in SE France on the French Riviera, 29km (18 miles) SW of Nice. The old part of the city has a 16th–17th century church. An international film festival is held there each spring. Industries: tourism, flowers. Pop. 67,000.

Cannibalism, the practice of eating human flesh as food or for ritual purposes. It was once widespread but is now almost extinct, although the practice still exists in remote parts of New Guinea. People were eaten to satisfy vengeance or as a supposed means of acquiring their strength and powers. *See also* MAGIC.

Canning, Charles John, Earl (1812–62), British politician, the son of George CANNING. As governor-general of India (1856–58) he repressed the INDIAN MUTINY, and followed a policy of conciliation towards the Indians that earned him the nickname "Clemency Canning". He was viceroy of India (1858–62). *See also* HC2 pp.140–141.

Canning, George (1770–1827), English politician. He was foreign minister (1807–09) and supported the PENINSULAR WAR but resigned after a duel with Viscount CASTLEREAGH. He was president of the Board of Control for India (1816–20) and later served a second term as foreign minister (1822–27). He was a Tory and supported free trade; he opposed the HOLY ALLIANCE. He became prime minister four months before his death. *See also* HC2 pp.182–183.

Canning, Stratford, Viscount Stratford de Redcliffe (1786–1880), British politician and diplomat, cousin of George CANNING. He was a member of Parliament from 1828 to 1841. Most of his diplomatic career was in Turkey, where he conducted negotiations in the CRIMEAN WAR.

Canning, method of preserving food by sealing it under hygienic conditions into cans made from tin-plated steel sheet. Any bacteria present in the food are killed, either by dry heat or by steam heat – a temperature of about 100°C being necessary for fruit, and somewhat higher temperatures for meat and vegetables. Once a can is sealed it must remain airtight to prevent infection by bacteria, particularly those that cause FOOD POISONING. *See also* PE pp.250–251.

Canning Basin (Desert Basin), arid region of Western Australia, approx. 145km (90 miles) NNE of Perth. Area: approx. 518,000sq km (200,000sq miles).

Cannizzaro, Stanislao (1826–1910), Italian chemist who showed how to determine atomic weights using Avogadro's law, and distinguished between molecular and atomic weights. In the early 1850s he discovered the Cannizzaro reaction for obtaining alcohols from aldehydes.

Cannon, artillery piece consisting of a metal tube, used to aim and fire missiles propelled by the explosion of gunpowder in the closed end of the cylinder. Cannon, first used in the 14th century, were originally made of bronze or iron. Major improvements in the 19th century included the introduction of steel barrels, more powerful chemical propellants, breech-loading mechanisms and standardized parts. By WWI recoil devices were employed to absorb the shock of firing. *See also* MM pp.*29*, 166, *167*, 173.

Cano, Alonso (1601–67), Spanish architect, sculptor and court painter. Called the "Spanish Michelangelo" because of his versatility, he executed both the sculpture and paintings for his monumental altarpieces. His Virgin sculptures are among his best works, including *Maternity of Mary* (1638–44) in multi-coloured wood.

Cano, Juan Sebastian del (*c.*1476–1526), Spanish navigator who was first to circumnavigate the globe. He commanded one of the five vessels in Ferdinand MAGELLAN's voyage of discovery and assumed control in 1521 after Magellan's death, returning to Spain in 1522. *See also* HC1 p.234.

Canoe, light shallow-draft boat, with a curved bow-shaped hull, propelled by one or more paddles. Primitive types were dug out of logs or made of skin or bark stretched over wooden frames. Modern types are made of wood, metal, fibreglass or plastics. Canoes can also be double-hulled, fitted with a sail or equipped with an outrigger. *See also* CORACLE; KAYAK.

Canoeing, boating sport popular in Europe and N America. It includes many different types of events for one or more people. The sport began in England in 1865 when John MacGregor, a lawyer, founded The Royal Canoe Club. It became a part of the Olympics in 1936.

Canon, in music, form of COUNTERPOINT using strict imitation: all the voices or parts have the same melody, starting at different times, at the same or different pitches. A round, or perpetual canon, can be repeated endlessly. In a crab canon, the 1st part is performed backwards to make the 2nd part. The earliest written canon, *Sumer is Icumen In*, dates from 13th-century England.

Canon, in Christian Churches, a term with several meanings: (1) title of secular clergy belonging to a cathedral or collegiate church and usually responsible for the maintenance of its services, fabric etc.; (2) the most solemn part of the Roman MASS, which includes the prayer of consecration; (3) rules and regulations pertaining to ecclesiastical discipline (*see* CANON LAW); (4) CANON OF SCRIPTURE.

Canonical hours, in the Roman Catholic Church, periods set aside each day for devotion. They are matins and lauds, prime, terce, sext, nones, vespers and compline.

Canonization, in the Roman Catholic Church, creation of one of its members as a saint. Today the results of an investigation into a candidate's life and virtues are submitted to the Congregation for the Causes of Saints, and after their findings are ratified by the pope the candidate is beatified. Proof of further miracles is required before full canonization.

Canon Law, in the Roman Catholic, Anglican and Orthodox churches, a body of ecclesiastical laws relating to faith, morals and discipline. Based partly on custom and partly on regulations laid down by church councils (ecumenical or local), popes or bishops, it grew up gradually and was codified from time to time. The most recent compilation in the Roman Catholic Church is the *Codex Iuris Canonici*, issued in 1917, and a revision (begun in 1963) was still in progress in the mid-1970s. In the post-Reformation Church of England the main body of canonical legislation was long contained in the *Book of Canons*, first issued in 1604, but it was replaced by a new code promulgated in two parts in 1964 and 1969.

Canon of Scripture, collection of books of the Old and New Testaments, believed by Christians to be inspired and to contain divine revelation, as distinct from other religious writings not included in the BIBLE. The concept of a canon of Scripture dates back to the OLD TESTAMENT times, when Judaism gradually accepted certain books as canonical. The definition of the NEW TESTAMENT canon was a slow process culminating in the Council of TRENT's dogmatic pronouncement of 1547. The principle that only the Church has the right to declare a book canonical is recognized by all the major Christian Churches. *See also* APOCRYPHA.

Canopus, or Alpha Carinae, yellowish super-giant in the constellation of Carina, the second brightest star visible from earth. Its characteristics are apparent mag. −0.7; absolute mag. −4.7; spectral type FO; distance 196 light-years. *See also* SU pp.226, 260, 266–*267*.

Canova, Antonio (1757–1822), Italian sculptor. A foremost Neo-Classical artist, his works include *Eurydice* (1773), *Orpheus* (1776), *Venus Victrix* (1803–07) and a *Cupid and Psyche* group. He went to Paris in the early 1800s to sculpt a bust of Napoleon from life. He also executed a number of other Napoleonic statues.

Cantaloup, trailing annual vine derived from the musk MELON and native to S Asia. It has roundish, hairy leaves and small, yellow flowers. The musky fruit is round, with yellow, white or red flesh. Family Cucurbitaceae; species *Cucumis melo cantalupensis*. *See also* PE pp.193, *193*.

Cantata, musical work consisting of vocal solos and choruses, often with passages of RECITATIVE, and accompanied by an orchestra. It was a popular form in the 17th and 18th centuries, when Alessandro Scarlatti and J. S. Bach wrote numerous cantatas, both secular and religious.

Canterbury, city in Kent, SE England, on the Great Stour River, 80km (50 miles) ESE of London. The present cathedral, built in the 11th–15th centuries, replaced a St Augustine Abbey and an earlier cathedral that was burned. It is the seat of the archbishop and primate of the Anglican Church. The murder of Thomas à BECKET took place in the cathedral in 1170 and is commemorated by a tablet. After Becket's canonization, Canterbury became a major pilgrimage centre. CHAUCER'S CANTERBURY TALES (14th century) describe the pilgrims. The city is the home of the University of Kent (1964). Tourism is a major industry. Pop. 33,000.

Canterbury, municipality in New South Wales, SE Australia. It is a suburb of Sydney situated 13km (8 miles) WSW of the city centre. It is a manufacturing centre for knitted goods. Pop. (1971) 130,334.

Canterbury, New Zealand's third largest district, occupying E central South Island. The CANTERBURY PLAINS, descending SE from the SOUTHERN ALPS, include some of New Zealand's richest farmland. Chief towns: CHRISTCHURCH, Timaru, Ashburton, Rangiora. Area: 43,467sq km (16,769sq miles).

Canterbury, Archbishop of, Primate of All England and leader of the worldwide ANGLICAN COMMUNION. The archbishopric was established when Pope GREGORY I sent a mission to England in 597 to convert the Anglo-Saxons. St AUGUSTINE, leader of the mission, became the first Archbishop of Canterbury. During the Reformation Archbishop Thomas CRANMER accepted the decision of the English Crown in 1534 to end papal jurisdiction in England. The Archbishop of Canterbury traditionally crowns British monarchs and officiates at other religious ceremonies of national importance. He presides over the LAMBETH CONFERENCE of all Anglican bishops of the world, but he exercises no jurisdiction outside his own ecclesiastical province.

Canterbury bell, biennial bellflower of the family CAMPANULACEAE. and native to S Europe. It is widely cultivated as a garden plant and grows up to 1m (3.2ft) tall. Its large spikes of upright, cup-shaped, pink, blue or white flowers appear in late spring and early summer. Species *Campanula medium*.

Canterbury Bight, wide inlet of the Pacific Ocean, on the E central coast of South Island, New Zealand, S of the Banks Peninsula. Width: 185km (115 miles).

Canterbury Plains, grassland district of South Island, New Zealand, famous for the fat lambs (for meat) reared there. Area: approx. 25,900sq km (10,000sq miles).

Canterbury Tales (*c.*1385–1400), collection of narrative poems by Geoffrey CHAUCER, each told by one of a party of pilgrims to Canterbury. They range from the courtly *The Knight's Tale* to the bawdy *The Miller's Tale*, from the charming *The Nun's Priest's Tale* to the exuberant characterizations in *The Wife of Bath's Tale*. *See also* HC1 pp.*207*, 214–215.

Cantharides, also called cantharis or cantharidin, drug obtained from the dried bodies of the cantharis, or Spanish fly (*Lytta vesicatoria*), a species of BLISTER BEETLE. The drug was used to cause blisters and as an aphrodisiac.

Cantilever bridge, type of bridge in which the main span gets its support by being "built in" at each end; unlike a beam bridge it does not rely on the intrinsic strength of the material forming the span. *See also* MM 192–193.

Cantinflas (1911–), Mexican film comedian, real name Mario Moreno. His urchin characterizations and his comic interpretations of Romeo and D'Artagnan made him famous. He portrayed Passepartout in *Around the World in 80 Days* (1956).

Canton, city in E central Ohio, USA, 32km (20 miles) SSE of Akron. It was the home of President William McKinley, whose

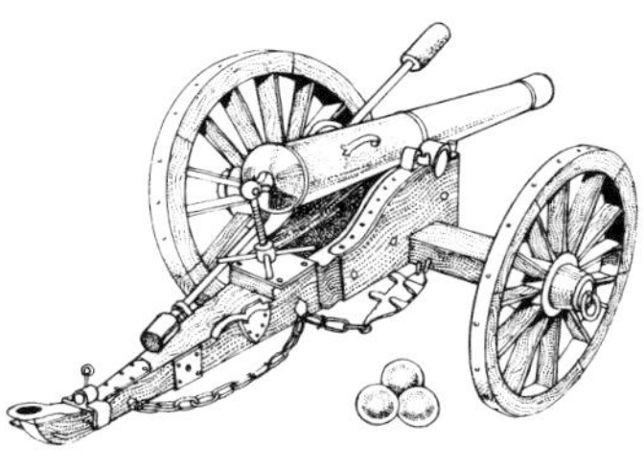

Cannon, guns now called artillery. The word comes from the Latin *canna*, a reed or tube.

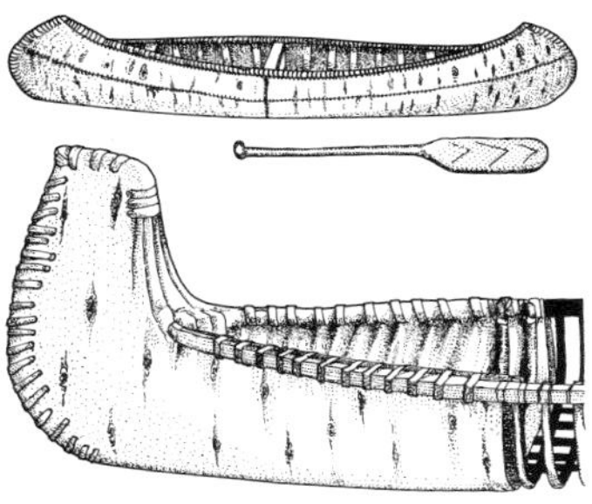

Canoes are bow-shaped, giving them great strength in relation to their weight.

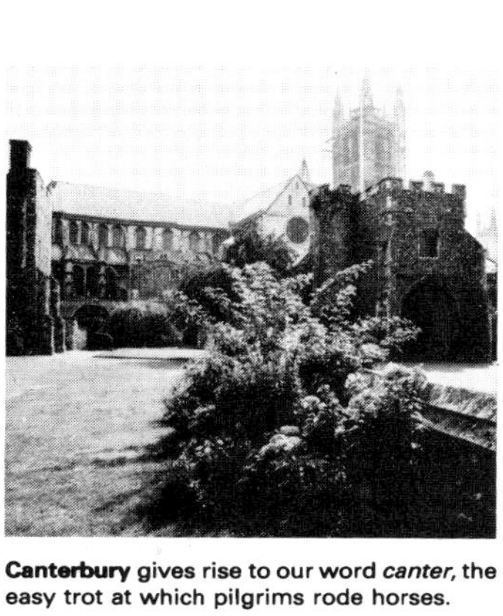

Canterbury gives rise to our word *canter*, the easy trot at which pilgrims rode horses.

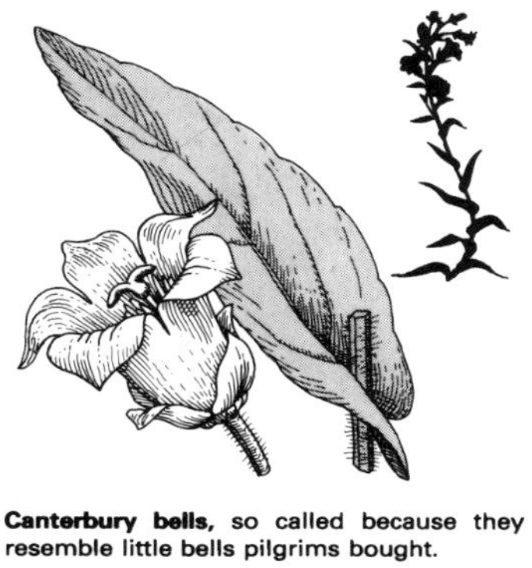

Canterbury bells, so called because they resemble little bells pilgrims bought.

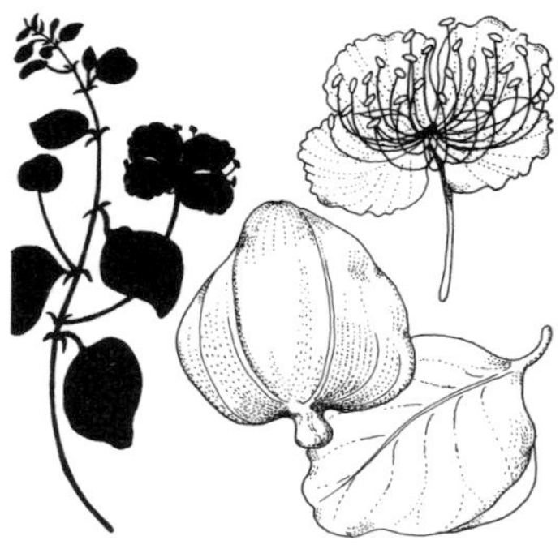

Caper flowers are pinkish-white with four petals and long stamen tassels.

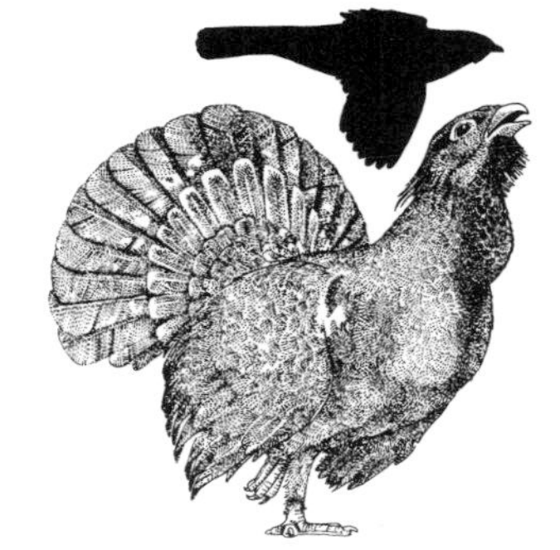

Capercaillies feed on pine leaves in winter, giving their flesh a taste of turpentine.

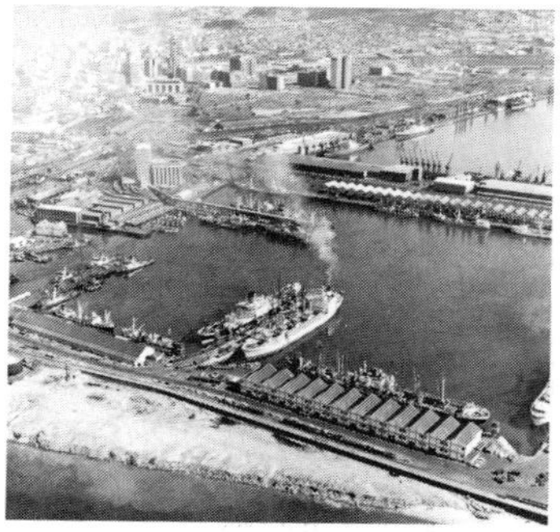

Cape Town has always been a port of call for ships travelling to India and beyond.

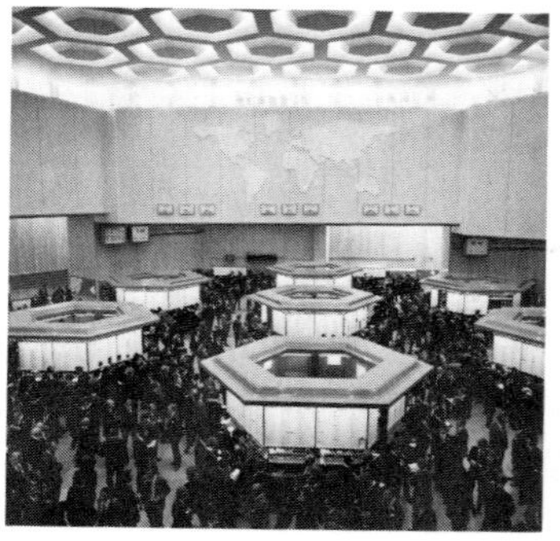

Capitalism; interior of the new Stock Exchange in London's financial centre.

grave is in the National McKinley Memorial. Industries: iron and steel, roller bearings, machinery, office equipment. Pop. (1970) 110,053.

Canton, one of the units of government and administration that make up the Swiss Confederation or Switzerland. Each canton sends two members to the Council of State which, with the National Council, forms the country's federal parliament. *See also* MW p.163.

Canton and Enderbury, two coral islands in the W central Pacific Ocean. Claimed by both the USA and Britain in the 1930s, Canton atoll was the subject of an agreement by both powers in which they established a joint administration for the atoll and nearby Enderbury Island until 1989.

Cantor, Eddie (1892–1964), US comedian and singer, real name Edward Israel Iskowitz, noted for his large mobile eyes. He appeared in Ziegfeld's "Follies" (1916–19), and in the musicals *Kid Boots* (1923–26) and *Roman Scandals* (1933). He also appeared in films and on radio and television.

Cantor, Georg (1845–1918), German mathematician, *b.* Russia. Obtaining his PhD in Göttingen, he later became professor at Halle. His work on the concept of infinity led to a highly original theory of sets for series of integers.

Cantor, solo singer who performs in religious services. Anglican and Roman Catholic cantors intone the opening words of hymns, responses and psalms. In the Jewish religion, they recite the scriptures by cantillation.

Cantos, unfinished poetic work by Ezra POUND. Complex, erudite but sometimes obscure, *The Cantos* is epic in scope, sweeping through the history of civilization (especially China, Renaissance Italy and the USA). It ranges from the intensely lyrical and personal to the public and didactic. *See also* HC2 p.*289*.

Canute, or Cnut, name of two kings of Denmark and England. Canute I (994–1035) began his conquest of England with his father SWEYN in 1013, and was accepted as sole ruler of the country in 1016. He became king of Denmark in 1018, and led several expeditions to Norway. He established a code of laws, and upheld the traditional Anglo-Saxon society and Church. His son Canute II (1019–42), also known as Hardicanute, became King of Denmark in 1035 and of England in 1040, after he had driven out his brother HAROLD HAREFOOT. *See also* HC1 p.155.

Canyon, deep, narrow depression in the Earth's crust. Land canyons are the result of erosion by rivers of comparatively recent origin flowing through arid terrain. Marine canyons may be formed when a river-bed and the surrounding terrain is submerged or by turbulence produced by deep water currents. *See also* PE pp.*82*, 83, *115*.

Capa, Robert (1913–54), US photographer, *b.* Hungary. He specialized in taking pictures of war victims and made his name during the SPANISH CIVIL WAR.

Capablanca, José Raul (1888–1942), Cuban chess player. He was the champion of Cuba at the age of 12 and became world champion in 1921 when he defeated Emanuel Lasker, retaining the title until 1927.

Capacitance, property of an electrical circuit or component that allows it to store charge. It is measured in farads (a capacitance that requires a charge of 1 coulomb to raise its potential by 1 volt). *See also* CAPACITOR; SU p.126.

Capacitor, also called a condenser, electrical circuit component that has CAPACITANCE. Used principally in AC circuits, there are various types, such as parallel plate condensers and electrolytic capacitors. *See* SU p.126.

Cape Barren Island, 34km (21 miles) off the NE coast of Tasmania, Australia, is the second largest of the Furneaux Group. The main industry is tin mining. Area: 943sq km (364sq miles). Pop. 164.

Cape Breton Island, rocky island in NE Nova Scotia, Canada, separated from the mainland by the Strait of Canso. It has the Cape Breton Highlands National Park, numerous summer resorts and North Barren, at 537m (1,747ft) the highest peak in Nova Scotia. Industries: timber, fishing, coal mining. Pop. 167,000.

Cape Buffalo. *See* BUFFALO.

Cape Canaveral, low sandy promontory in E Florida, USA, extending E into the Atlantic Ocean. It is the site of NASA's John F. Kennedy Space Centre, which since 1950 has been the main US launch site for space flights and long-range missiles.

Cape Coast, city in S Ghana, W Africa, 120km (75 miles) WSW of Accra, on the Gulf of Guinea; capital of Central Region. Settled in 1610 by the Portuguese, it was the capital of the GOLD COAST until succeeded by Accra in 1877. Fishing is the chief industry. Pop. 51,800.

Cape Cod, hook-shaped sandy peninsula in SE Massachusetts, USA. Of glacial origin, it extends into the Atlantic Ocean, forming Cape Cod Bay. It was originally a centre for fishing, whaling and salt extraction, but tourism is now the major industry.

Cape Colony, British colony in South Africa, around the CAPE OF GOOD HOPE, founded in 1806 after the area had been captured from the Dutch. The Boers left the colony in the GREAT TREK of 1835. The colony became a province of the Union of South Africa in 1910. *See also* HC2 pp.128–129; MW pp.154–158.

Cape Coloured, or simply Coloured, legal class of South African citizens of mixed racial origin. They are placed on a separate electoral roll and elect four Whites to the national House of Assembly. They have also their own Coloured Persons Representative Council. Since 1958 the South African government has included a Department of Coloured Affairs. *See also* MW pp.154, 156.

Cape Horn, southernmost point of South America in S Chile. It was sighted by Francis Drake in 1578, and first rounded in 1616 by Cornelis van Schouten. It is noted for its severe storms.

Čapek, Karel (1890–1938), Czech novelist, playwright and essayist. Most of his works portrayed man's struggle against fate, especially in a scientific world. His writings included *R.U.R.,* a play about robots (1920), and the novel *War with the Newts* (1936).

Capella, or Alpha Aurigae, spectroscopic binary star in the constellation of Auriga; both components are yellow giants. Its characteristics are: apparent mag. +0.09 (combined); absolute mag. −0.6 (Capella A), 0.37 (Capella B); spectral type G8 (Capella A), G0 (Capella B); distance 45 light-years. See also SU pp.226, 258, 264–265.

Cape of Good Hope, peninsula lying 48km (30 miles) S of Cape Town, Africa. The first European to sail around it was Bartolomew DIAZ in 1488 who, according to tradition, named it *Cabo da Boa Esperança*. The Cape sea route between India and Europe was established by Vasco da GAMA in 1497–99. *See also* HC1 p.234.

Cape Province, formerly Cape Colony, province in South Africa, bordered by the Indian Ocean (SE) and the Atlantic Ocean (W); the capital is Cape Town. A colony was first established by the Dutch in 1652. Slaves were imported from 1658 onwards, but slavery was abolished in 1833 by the British. Diamonds were discovered there in 1867. The colony became a province of the Union of South Africa in 1910. Industries: wine, diamonds, wool, asbestos. Area: 721,005sq km (278,380sq miles). Pop. 6,199,634. *See* HC2 pp.128–129, 132, 253; MW pp.154–158.

Caper, flower bud, generally pickled in vinegar, of a shrub native to Sicily and other Mediterranean countries, used as a condiment and to make sauces. Family cruciferae; species *Capparis spinosa.*

Capercaillie, largest grouse of Eurasian evergreen forests and a prized game bird. The male is mostly black and the smaller brownish female lays up to 8 eggs in a ground nest. Length: to 86cm (34in). Species *Tetrao urogallus. See also* NW p.206.

Cape St Vincent, promontory of SW Portugal. A battle was fought off the cape in 1797, in which the English, under Jervis and Nelson, defeated the Spanish fleet which was trying to raise a blockade on the ports of France. *See also* HC2 p.78.

Capet, surname given to King Hugh of France (*r.* 987–96) and his descendants, to whom the throne was passed in direct line until 1328. The Capetians gradually extended their rule from the two counties of Paris and Orleans to the whole of France. Philip II Augustus (*r.* 1180–1223) dispossessed the English king of Normandy, Anjou and Maine. *See also* HC1 p.202, *202*.

Cape Town, city in South Africa, at the foot of Table Mountain; the legislative capital of South Africa and the capital of Cape province. Places of interest include the Union Parliament, a 17th-century castle and the National Historic Museum. It has the University of Cape Town and the University College Western Cape, for Coloureds. Industries: clothing, engineering equipment, motor vehicles. Pop. 818,100.

Cape Verde Islands, republic in the E Atlantic Ocean. It is made up of about 15 volcanic islands divided into two groups, the Windward Islands to the N and the Leeward Islands. The capital is Praia on São Tiago island in the Leewards. The economy is based on the production of coffee, tobacco, suger cane, oranges and groundnuts and the mining of salt and coal. An overseas province of Portugal, the islands became independent in 1975. Area: 4,033sq km (1,557sq miles). Pop. (1975 est.) 294,000. *See also* MW p.51.

Cape York, peninsula in Australia forming the NE section of Queensland. The northernmost point is Cape York on the Torres Strait. Length: 725km (450 miles).

Capillarity, movement of a liquid in a narrow opening caused by the surface tensional between the liquid and the surrounding material. This is most often seen in a vertical narrow glass capillary tube but also occurs in various directions – as when a sponge or blotting paper soaks up water.

Capillary, microscopic blood-vessel connecting arteries and veins and situated close to living body cells. Oxygen and other nutrients in the blood are passed to these cells through the thin capillary walls at the same time as carbon dioxide and other waste matter is diffused back into the blood in the capillaries. *See also* MS p.*62*.

Capillary constant, measure of surface tension defined, for two immiscible fluids in contact, by $2T/g(D-d)$, where T is the surface tension for the interface, g is the acceleration due to gravity and D and d are the densities of the fluids. Usually one of these is air. The capillary constant is equal to the rise of a liquid in a capillary tube multiplied by the radius of the tube. *See also* SU p.87.

Capital, in architecture, the wide piece of masonry at the top of a column. In classical architecture, the design of the capital is characteristic of the ORDER to which it belongs.

Capital, in ECONOMICS, different forms of wealth. It ranges from business assets such as buildings, machinery and stock, to a person's invested savings. Fixed capital refers to such things as buildings, tools and equipment; working capital includes raw materials, stock and cash.

Capital gain, the difference between the buying price for a CAPITAL asset and the price received when selling it at a profit. Long-term capital gains, where the asset has been held for longer than a certain period, are generally taxed less heavily than short-term capital gains.

Capitalism, economic system in which property and the means of production are privately owned. Its development in modern times dates from the INDUSTRIAL REVOLUTION, which saw the rise to prominence of industrialists and financiers. Capitalism embraces the notions of freedom of choice, the profit motive, individual enterprise and efficiency through competition. In practice, however, governments actively participate in economic regulation under a capitalist system, although to a much lesser extent than under COMMUNISM or SOCIALISM.

Capital offence, criminal act that is punishable by death. In some countries murder carries the death penalty but death for a crime such as treason is more usual. *See also* CAPITAL PUNISHMENT; MS p.*165*.

Capital punishment, the punishing of a criminal offence by death. Most ancient societies inflicted the death penalty, using methods such as decapitation, drowning, boiling in oil, flaying alive and burning (this last being practised in Europe until the 18th century). In the Middle Ages crimes against state and church carried the death penalty and in early 19th-century Britain more than 220 crimes, such as sheep-stealing, the coining of false money and picking pockets, were still capital offences. In the 20th century the usual methods of execution have been by hanging, electrocution or firing squad. The death penalty is now abolished in many countries, although in most it can be enforced for exceptional crimes such as treason. Some states in the USA prescribe death for rape, armed robbery and kidnapping. Britain abolished capital punishment (except for treason) in the 1960s, as did some Commonwealth countries; in 1972 the US Supreme Court declared capital punishment as it was then being applied to be unconstitutional. Those that campaigned against capital punishment stressed the primitive nature of the practice, its ineffectiveness as a deterrent and its finality, which means that a miscarriage of justice could not be rectified. *See also* MS pp.296–297.

Capitol, building in WASHINGTON, DC, in which the US Congress convenes. The original architect was William Thornton and in 1793 George Washington laid the cornerstone. In 1814 it was burned to the ground by the British. The central section of the modern building covers 1.4 hectares (3.5 acres), and the dome reaches a height of 88m (288ft).

Capone, Alphonse (1899–1947), Italian-born US gangster of the PROHIBITION era. He grew up in Brooklyn, New York City, and was bodyguard to the gang leader Johnny Torio from whom he inherited a vast crime empire. He was eventually convicted of income tax evasion (1931) and imprisoned.

Capote, Truman (1924–), US author. His first novel, *Other Voices, Other Rooms,* appeared in 1948. Other works include a novella, *Breakfast at Tiffany's* (1958), *The Grass Harp* (1951) and *In Cold Blood* (1966), with which Capote stated he had introduced a new literary genre, the non-fiction novel.

Capp, Al (1909–), US cartoonist, born Alfred Caplin. He gained worldwide popularity with Li'l Abner, a hill-billy character around whom a cartoon strip was built (1934). He scripted the film *Li'l Abner* (1940) and wrote books from the cartoon strip such as *Fearless Fosdick* (1956) and *The Hardhat's Bedtime Story Book* (1971).

Capp, Andy, cartoon character invented in 1957 by Reg Smythe, featured each day in the British newspaper the *Daily Mirror.* Andy is a cloth-capped northern Englishman with a liking for beer and an aversion to work. He spends much of his time trying to avoid the demands of his long-suffering wife, Flo.

Cappadocia, ancient plateau region of Asia Minor. Cuneiform tablets found at Kültepe indicate that the region traded with ASSYRIA before 1800 BC. It was part of the PERSIAN EMPIRE from the 6th century. After a brief period of semi-independence (3rd century BC), it was allied to Rome and was finally annexed by the emperor TIBERIUS in AD 17.

Capra, Frank (1897–), Italian-born US film director. He was noted for his comedies which included *Platinum Blonde* (1931), *It Happened One Night* (1934) and *You Can't Take It With You* (1938). During WWII he directed propaganda films. Post-war films included *A Hole in the Head* (1959) and *A Pocketful of Miracles* (1961).

Capri, island in the Bay of Naples, S Italy. A popular Roman resort, the Roman Emperor Augustus lived there, and it has the remains of Tiberius' palace. It passed from French to British rule several times during the Napoleonic Wars, and was returned to the Kingdom of the Two Sicilies in 1813. It has the ruins of two medieval castles, the Villa San Michele and The Blue Grotto, a famous cave on the coast. Industries: tourism, fishing. Area: 10sq km (4sq miles). Pop. (1971 prelim) 8,000.

Capricorn, in astrology, a sign of the zodiac, symbolized by a goat. It is the sun-sign for those born between 23 December and 19 January. A feminine sign, its element is Earth and its ruling planet is Saturn. The goat symbol probably derives from PAN.

Capricorn, Tropic of, parallel of latitude, approx. 23.5° S of the equator which marks the southern boundary of the TROPICS. It indicates the farthest southern position at which the sun appears directly overhead at noon. The sun is vertical over the Tropic of Capricorn on about 22 December, which is the summer SOLSTICE in the Southern Hemisphere.

Capricornus, or the Sea Goat, southern constellation on the ecliptic between Sagittarius and Aquarius. Known as Capricorn for astrological purposes, this constellation contains the faint GLOBULAR CLUSTER M30 (NGC 7099), and a double star visible to the naked eye, Alpha or Al Giedi. *See also* MS p.200; SU pp.254, 262.

Caprimulgiformes, order of birds whose best-known representatives are the NIGHTJARS, nocturnal, wide-mouthed, insect-eaters with an incessant, distinctive call. Other families include the South American OILBIRD, the only bird to navigate its flight by echo-location. Like bats, it can fly in the pitchdark caves in which it lives. An Australian family, the owlet nightjars, provide some evidence of a link with the owls. *See also* NW p.141.

Caprivi Strip, narrow strip of land in NE Namibia (South-West Africa), bounded by Botswana (S) and Zambia and Angola (N). It was named after the German Chancellor Leo von Caprivi, who obtained the region from the British, and thereby gained access to the Zambezi River. It is an extremely arid region, but some farming is carried out in the easternmost section of the strip, where the Zambezi River is used for irrigation. Length: 483km (300 miles); width: 64km (40 miles).

Capsian culture, MESOLITHIC culture (*c*.8th–3rd centuries BC) of inland N Africa. Its most characteristic sites are in the salt-lake region of present-day southern Tunisia, the best of them being Jabal al-Maqta, near Qafsah. It was a post-glacial culture, distinguished by the variety of its microlithic (tiny-flaked-blade) tools and its development of geometrically shaped tools. Probable rock paintings of the culture survive.

Capsicum. *See* PEPPER.

Capsule, space, that part of a spacecraft that carries the payload, which may be a crew of astronauts or a variety of scientific instruments. A space capsule is designed to withstand extremes of temperature and pressure, shocks and vibration during acceleration, spinning or tumbling, radiation and meteoric impacts, while maintaining a stable environment for the payload. Some of the features that help to achieve these ends are an ABLATION heat shield for re-entering the atmosphere; slow, continuous rotation to reduce exposure to the Sun; and highly reflecting exteriors. The capsule of a manned spacecraft contains the flight controls, and television cameras and instruments for monitoring the activities of the crew and controlling their environment. *See also* SU pp.268–270; MM p.158.

Captain Beefheart (1941–), stage name of Don Van Vliet, US singer and leader of The Magic Band. They made their first recording *Diddy Wah Diddy* in 1966, but Beefheart is known better for several LPs including *Safe as Milk* (1967), *Trout Mask Replica* (1969) and *Clear Spot* (1973).

Capuchin, small diurnal monkey found in South and Central America, a popular pet in Europe and the USA. It is generally brown or black and is a tree-dweller with a furry prehensile tail. Omnivorous, but preferring fruit, it may grow to 55cm (22in) with a tail of the same length. Family Cebidae. *See also* NW p.*216*.

Capuchins, Roman Catholic religious order, founded by Matteo da Bassi in 1525 as an offshoot of the FRANCISCAN Order. Its official title is Order of Friars Minor of St Francis Capuchin (O.F.M.Cap.). The Capuchins are so called because of the pointed cowl (*capuche*) which forms part of their habit. They re-emphasized the Franciscan ideals of poverty and austerity and played an important role in the COUNTER-REFORMATION, particularly through their missionary activities.

Capybara, largest living RODENT, native to Central and South America; it is semi-aquatic with webbed feet, a large, nearly hairless, body, short legs and a tiny tail. Length: 1.2m (4ft). Species *Hydrochoerus hydrochoeris. See also* NW pp.*160, 216.*

Car. *See* MOTOR CAR.

Caracal, also called Persian lynx, short-haired carnivore of the CAT family Felidae, native to Africa and parts of Asia and India. Mainly nocturnal, it is quick and agile and has a slender red body and long pointed ears with black tufts. Length: 1m (3.3ft). Species *Lynx caracal. See also* NW pp.164–165.

Caracalla, Marcus Aurelius Antoninus (AD 188–217), Roman emperor (211–17). His name came from the fact that he wore a Gallic tunic (caracalla). He resented sharing rule with his brother, Geta, whom he murdered along with many of Geta's supporters (212). He erected the Baths of Caracalla. Macrinus killed him in Asia and succeeded him as emperor.

Caracara, comparatively slow-moving ground-dwelling bird of prey of the FALCON family that lives on the grasslands of South America. It feeds on insects, carrion and birds eggs. *See also* NW p.*203.*

Caracas, capital city of Venezuela, on the Guaire River. The city was under Spanish rule until 1821.mIt was the birthplace of Simón BOLÍVAR, the leader of the revolt against Spain. The city grew after 1930, encouraged by the exploitation of oil. It has the Central University of Venezuela (1725) and a colonial cathedral (1614). Industries: motor vehicles, oil, brewing, rubber. Pop. (1976 est.) 2,576,000.

Caractacus (*d.c.* AD 54), British chieftan who led the tribes of SE Britain against the Romans (43–51). He was defeated and sent to Rome, but so impressed Emperor Claudius that he released him. *See also* HC1 p.100.

Carat, unit of weight used for gemstones. Traditionally it varied from country to country, perhaps because of its method of origin: the name carat derives from that of the seeds of the Mediterranean locust tree, which were once used to weigh gemstones. By 1913 the carat was fixed internationally at 200 milligrams. The carat measure of gold alloys (usually gold-silver or gold-copper) indicates the number of parts of gold in 24 parts. Thus 22-carat gold contains 22 parts of gold in 24 parts of the alloy. *See also* PE p.99

Caravaggio, Michelangelo Merisi da (1573–1610), Italian painter. A powerful innovator, he worked directly on canvas from live models, in contrast to the current practice and idealized Renaissance style. He also made original use of dramatic CHIAROSCURO effects. Many earlier works, such as *The Fortune Teller,* are genre pieces, but in later years he mainly produced portraits and religious paintings, such as *The Martyrdom of St Matthew.* Caravaggio influenced many painters, including REMBRANDT. *See also* HC1 pp.*301*, 305, *309. 310–311, 352–353.*

Caravan, vehicle used as a mobile home. Gypsy caravans were traditionally horse-drawn, large-wheeled wagons with a barrel-shaped roof. They were known for their colourful decorations, and caravans of similar design are still used in parts of Ireland. Small-wheeled lightweight metal caravans towed by a car or motorized caravans are now widely used by holiday-makers as a more comfortable alternative to CAMPING.

Caravel, small sailing ship, two- or three-masted, with square and lateen sails and a high bow and stern. It originated in the Mediterranean but was

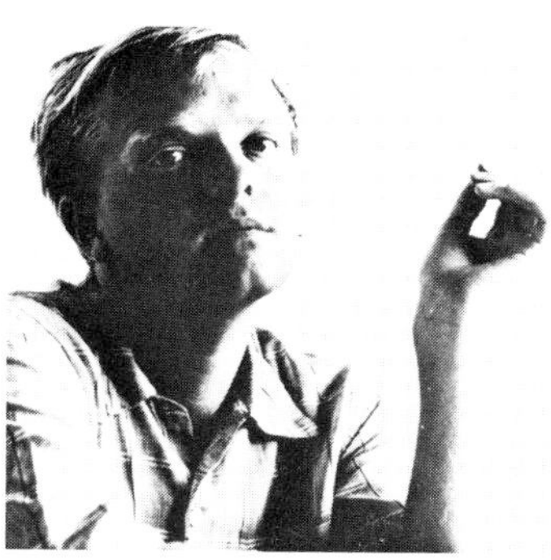

Truman Capote's novel *In Cold Blood* combined journalistic and literary styles.

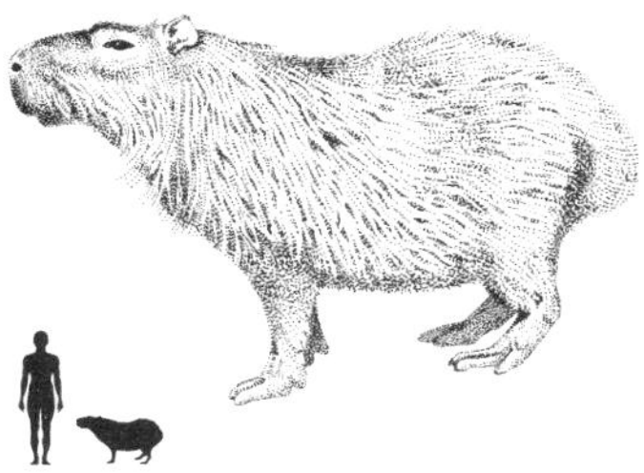

Capybara, the largest living rodent, is a timid animal that takes to the water when alarmed.

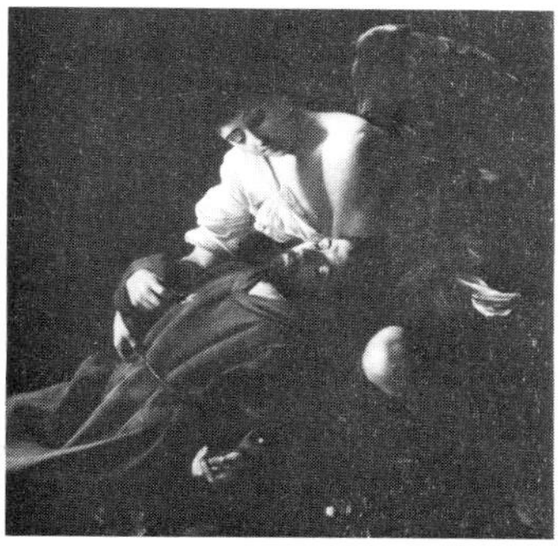

Caravaggio heightened the emotional impact of his work by the dramatic use of light.

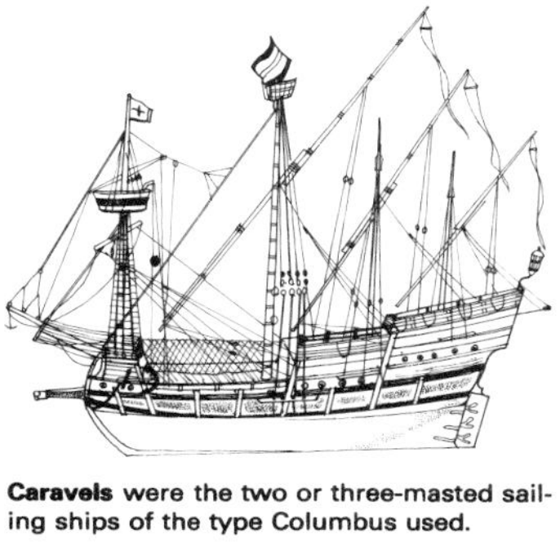

Caravels were the two or three-masted sailing ships of the type Columbus used.

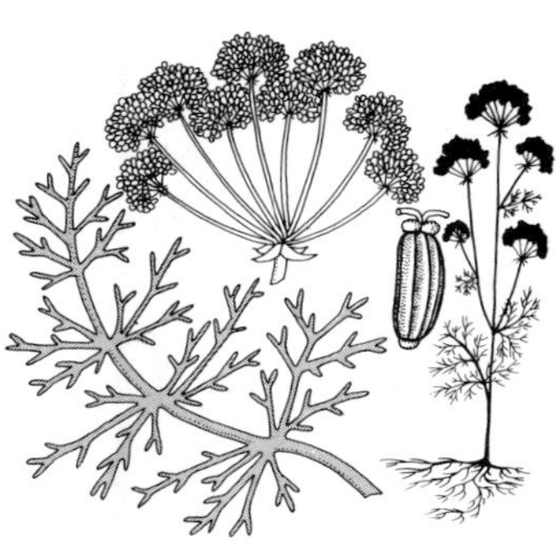

Caraway is a member of the parsley family whose seeds are much used for flavouring.

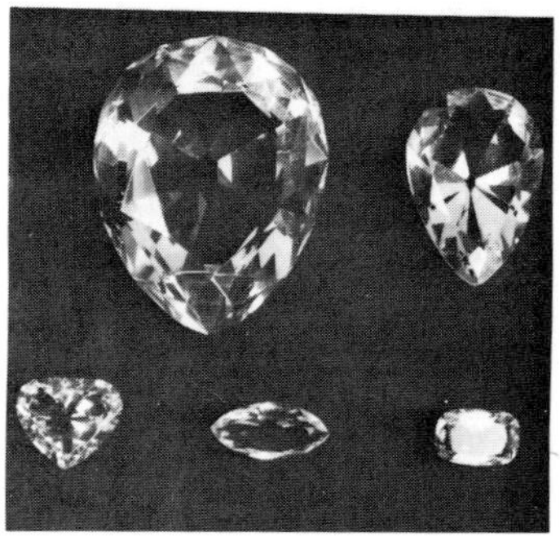

Carbon is present in all living things. Diamond is a pure crystalline form of this element.

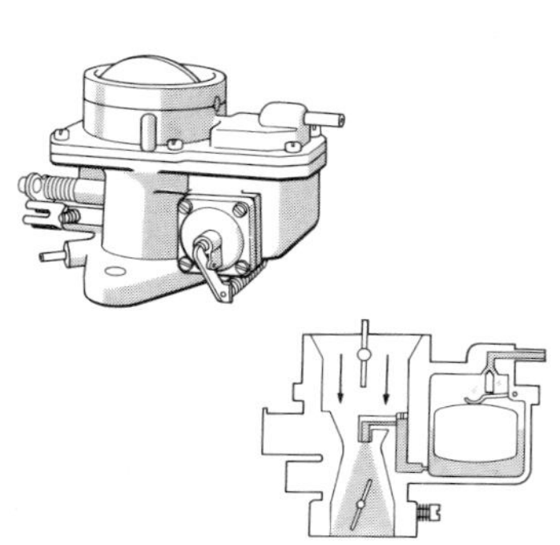

Carburettor forms the mixture of air and petrol for an internal combustion engine.

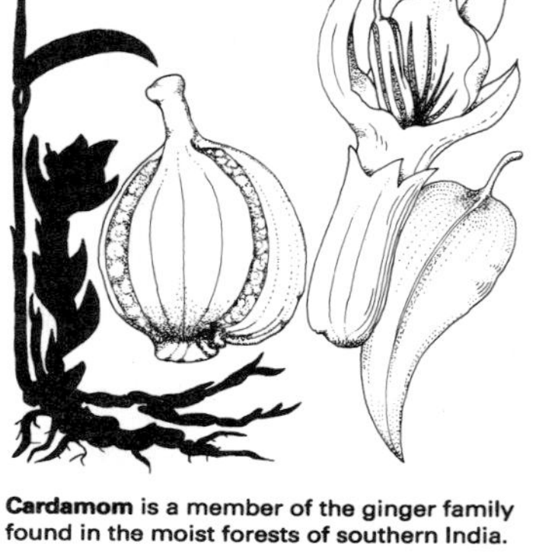

Cardamom is a member of the ginger family found in the moist forests of southern India.

adapted by Portuguese mariners of the 15th century for voyages of exploration along the African coast. Columbus's caravels were NIÑA and PINTA.

Caraway, biennial herb native to Eurasia and cultivated for its small, brown seedlike fruits that are used for flavouring foods. It has feathery leaves and white flowers. Family Umbelliferae; species *Curum carni. See also* PE pp.*210*, 211.

Carbide, inorganic compound of carbon and a more electropositive element. BORON and SILICON both form extremely hard carbides which are used as abrasives. Many TRANSITION METALS also form carbides, in which the carbon atoms occupy interstitial positions in the metal lattice. Some electropositive metals form ionic carbon compounds; the best-known is CALCIUM CARBIDE (CaC_2), which reacts with water to give ACETYLENE.

Carbine, short-barrelled RIFLE originally introduced at the end of the 16th century for use by cavalry. By WWII the term was used for a short-range automatic infantry weapon (such as the Sten gun). *See also* MM p.162.

Carbohydrate, organic compound of carbon, hydrogen and oxygen and a constituent of many kinds of foods. The simplest carbohydrates are the sugars, usually with five or six carbon atoms in each molecule. Glucose and fructose are naturally occurring sugars; they have the same formula, $C_6H_{12}O_6$, but different structures. One molecule of each combines with the loss of water to make cane sugar (sucrose, $C_{12}H_{22}O_{11}$), which also occurs naturally in sugarcane and sugar-beet. Starch and cellulose are carbohydrates consisting of hundreds of glucose molecules linked together. *See also* SACCHARIDE; SU p.152, *152*.

Carbolic acid. *See* PHENOL.

Carbon, common non-metallic element (symbol C) of group IV of the periodic table. There are two crystalline allotropes; GRAPHITE, a soft black solid, and DIAMOND, the hardest naturally occurring material known (used for gems). Various amorphous (non-crystalline) forms of carbon also exist, such as soot and lampblack. Industrial diamonds are used in rock drills and in cutting and polishing tools. Graphite is a lubricant and is also used in making electrodes, crucibles and pencils. Amorphous carbon has many uses, for example as pigment for inks and a filler for rubber for vehicle tyres. Carbon forms a vast number of compounds with hydrogen (hydrocarbons) – the subject of ORGANIC CHEMISTRY – and other non-metals. Properties: at.no. 6; at. wt. 12.011; s.g. 1.9–2.3 (graphite), 3.15–3.53 (diamond); m.p. approx. 3,550°C (6,422°F); sublimes at 3,367°C (6,093°F); most common isotope C^{12} (98.89 per cent). *See also* SU pp.136–142, 152.

Carbon-13, one of the seven ISOTOPES of carbon, the only one other than the common isotope carbon-12 that is stable. Carbon-13 (at.wt. 13) occurs naturally in very minute quantities.

Carbon-14, the most important radioisotope of carbon, the ISOTOPE detected and measured in CARBON DATING. It is formed on Earth when cosmic rays from outer space hit nitrogen atoms in the upper atmosphere. This transmutes the nitrogen into carbon-14, which then breaks down again into nitrogen; the half-life of carbon-14 is 5,730 years.

Carbonari, members of an early 19th-century Italian secret society advocating liberal, nationalist reforms. They were opposed to conservative regimes imposed on Italy after the Council of Vienna (1815) and were a model for Giuseppi MAZZINI's Young Italy Movement.

Carbonates, salts of CARBONIC ACID, which is formed when carbon dioxide (CO_2) dissolves in water. Carbonic acid is an extremely weak acid and both it and many of its salts are unstable, decomposing readily to release carbon dioxide. Nevertheless, large parts of the Earth's crust are made up of carbonates: CHALK and LIMESTONE are examples of calcium carbonate, MAGNESITE is a magnesium carbonate and DOLOMITE a magnesium-calcium carbonate. Seashells are also calcium carbonate. *See also* NW pp.96–97; PE pp.110–111.

Carbon black, form of the element CARBON made by heating or burning hydrocarbon gases in a restricted supply of air. The product contains a little hydrogen, oxygen and sulphur as well as carbon. Carbon black is used to reinforce rubber (for vehicle tyres) and other materials, and in various dark pigments for paint and inks.

Carbon cycle, circulation of carbon in the biosphere. It is a complex cycle of events in which the most important are the taking up of carbon dioxide by green plants from the atmosphere during PHOTOSYNTHESIS, and the return of carbon dioxide to the atmosphere by the respiration and eventual decomposition of animals which eat the plants. *See also* SU p.*153*.

Carbon dating (radiocarbon dating), method of determining the age of organic materials by measuring the amount of radioactive decay of an ISOTOPE of carbon, carbon-14, or C^{14}. This radio-isotope decays to form nitrogen, its half-life being about 5,730 years. When a living organism dies, it ceases to take carbon dioxide into its body, so that the amount of carbon-14 it contains is fixed as a known quantity relative to its total weight. Over the centuries, this quantity diminishes in accordance with radioactive decay, and refined chemical and physical analysis is used to determine the exact amount remaining, and from this the age of a specimen is deduced. *See also* PE p.131.

Carbon dioxide, colourless odourless gas (CO_2) that occurs in the atmosphere (0.03 per cent) and as a product of the combustion of fossil fuels and in metabolic processes. In its solid form (dry ice) it is used in refrigeration; as a gas it is used in carbonated beverages, as a fire extinguisher and to provide an inert atmosphere for welding. Properties: density 1.527 (air = 1); m.p. (5.2 atm) −56.6°C (−69.9°F); sublimes −78.5°C (−109.5°F). *See also* SU pp.92, *140*, 153–155.

Carbon dwarf star, very "late" type of red dwarf star belonging to either of two spectral classes designated N and R. The absorption lines in the spectra of these stars are due chiefly to carbon compounds and their surface temperatures range downwards from about 2600°K to 1700°K. *See also* SU p.226.

Carbon fibre, fibrous form of carbon made by heating textile fibres to high temperatures. The result is fibres (typically 0.001cm in diameter) which are, weight for weight, some of the strongest of all fibres. They are too short to be woven into a super-strong yarn. Instead they are incorporated into plastics, ceramics and glass, which give the materials great strength and resistance to breakage. *See also* MM p.37.

Carbonic acid, H_2CO_3, extremely weak acid formed when carbon dioxide (CO_2) dissolves in water. Its salts, the CARBONATES, are of great importance in nature both in rock formations and in the shells of various animals. *See also* PE pp.110, 112.

Carboniferous Period, fifth geologic division of the PALEOZOIC ERA, lasting from 345 to 280 million years ago. It is often called the "Age of Coal" because of its extensive swampy forests of conifers and tree ferns that turned into most of today's coal deposits. Amphibians flourished, marine life abounded in warm shallow inland seas, and the first reptiles appeared. *See also* PE pp.*130–131*, 136, *137*.

Carbon microphone. *See* MICROPHONE.

Carbon monoxide, colourless, odourless poisonous gas (CO) formed during the incomplete combustion of fossil fuels, occurring for example in coal gas and the exhaust gases of internal-combustion engines. Carbon monoxide poisons by starving the body of vital oxygen with which it combines to form the more stable carbon dioxide. It is used in PRODUCER GAS, metallurgy and the manufacture of chemicals. Properties: density 0.968 (air = 1); m.p. 205°C (−337°F); b.p. −191.5°C (−312.7°F).

Carbon tetrachloride (tetrachloromethane), colourless non-inflammable liquid with a characteristic odour (CCl_4), prepared by the chlorination of methane or the catalytic reaction of carbon disulphide and chlorine. It is used as a refrigerant, insecticide, degreaser and dry-cleaning fluid. Properties: s.g. 1.59; m.p. −23°C (−9.4°F); b.p. 76.8°C (170.2°F). *See also* SU p.*151*.

Carborundum, originally a trade name for silicon carbide (SiC) abrasives and refractories prepared by heating silica (SiO_2) with carbon in an electric furnace. It is used in grinding wheels, grinding papers, abrasive grains and powders, valve-grinding compounds, and in refractory bricks and blocks. Nearly as hard as diamond, it oxidizes slowly at temperatures above 1,000°C (1,832°F).

Carboxylic acid, member of a class of organic chemical compounds containing the group −CO.OH. The commonest example is acetic (ethanoic) acid, CH_3COOH, which is present in vinegar. These acids are weakly acidic, forming salts with bases and esters with alcohols. Esters of high-molecular weight carboxylic acids, such as stearic, lauric and oleic acids, are present in animal and vegetable fats; for this reason carboxylic acids are often called fatty acids. The systematic names are formed using the suffix -oic. *See also* FATTY ACIDS.

Carbuncle, large localized inflammation of the subcutaneous tissue; it is an aggregation of adjacent boils, or furuncles. Carbuncles most commonly appear on the neck and may need no treatment, even though they are extremely painful.

Carburation, the mixing of air and fuel vapour in the correct proportions for an internal combustion engine. In a petrol engine air sucked into the cylinders passes through the CARBURETTOR, creating a partial vacuum which draws petrol in through a jet. The resulting air/petrol mixture rapidly burns in the cylinders and the expansion of the gases produced provides the power. In broad terms, the speed of the engine regulates the amount of air – and hence the amount of petrol – drawn into the carburettor. A throttle valve, controlled by the accelerator pedal, determines how much fuel mixture reaches the cylinders, and thus controls the engine's speed. The choke is an air-restricting device used by the driver when starting the engine from cold to enable him to feed the engine with a mixture richer in petrol. *See also* MM pp.68, 69, 130–131.

Carburettor, component of petrol-powered internal-combustion engines, used to vaporize and mix fuel with air in the correct proportion for proper combustion. Generally steady speed requires a ratio of 15:1 air to fuel. Richer ratios of 10:1 air to fuel are necessary for starting cold engines. Efficient CARBURATION is essential for smooth running and efficient engine performance. *See also* MM pp.*69*.

Carchemish, ancient city on the River EUPHRATES, near Jarablus, Syria. It was the centre of an important kingdom in the 9th century BC, and was the scene of a decisive defeat of the Egyptians by the Babylonians in 605 BC. The British Museum carried out excavations there in 1878–81 and 1911–14. *See also* HC1 pp.49, 52.

Carcinogen, external substance or agent that causes CANCER, including chemicals, radiation and some viruses. Many different chemical carcinogens have been found to cause cancer in animals, but more research is needed to confirm their ability to cause cancer in man. It is thought that carcinogenic hydrocarbons in tobacco smoke cause lung cancer. *See also* MS pp.87, 89, 113.

Carcinoma, one of the two major forms of CANCER; the other is sarcoma. It is a malignant growth of epithelial cells which can invade surrounding tissues. *See also* MS pp.*87*, 89, 113.

Cardamom, pungent spice made from seeds of a plant of the GINGER family (Zingiberaceae), often mixed with TURMERIC to make a type of curry. Species *Elettaria cardamomum. See also* PE p.210.

Cardano, Girolamo (1501–76), Italian mathematician and physician. His books on mathematics were influential; *De Subtilitate Rerum* (1550) summarized existing scientific beliefs.

Cardew, Cornelius (1936–), British

avant-garde composer. He studied at the Royal Academy of Music and between 1958 and 1960 studied electronic music and collaborated with STOCKHAUSEN. He has composed for orchestra and piano.

Cardew, Michael (1901–), British potter. A pupil of Bernard LEACH from 1923–26, he had a pottery at Winchcombe, Gloucestershire, until 1939. He then worked in Ghana (1942–48) and Nigeria (1951–65), and then returned to his pottery at Wenford Bridge, Cornwall.

Card games, leisure or gambling activities in which one or more players employ a regulated number of playing cards. Cards are reputed to date from the Chinese T'ANG DYNASTY and were known in Europe by the 13th century, when they were used for divination as much as for gaming. There are four principal kinds, each with many varieties. Games featuring bidding and the trumping of tricks – such as BRIDGE, WHIST and BEZIQUE – demand of players concentration, wit, shrewdness and good manners, the latter quality being inessential for POKER, the patriarch of gambling games, in which the cards' values are determined by pattern and stakes are raised by bluff. Of less intensity are the variants, GIN RUMMY and CANASTA, whereas PATIENCE is a singular pursuit, as its alternative name, SOLITAIRE, suggests.

Cardiac cycle, process by which the HEART pumps blood. Blood enters the heart while it is relaxed, filling the atria and ventricles. Contraction of the ventricles forces blood out of the heart and, at the end of the contraction, the ventricles again relax and the heart starts to fill again, ready for the next cycle. *See also* MS pp.62–63.

Cardiff (Caerdydd), capital of Wales and a major port in s Glamorgan, on the River Severn estuary at the mouth of the rivers Taff, Rhymney and Ely. The construction of docks in 1839 led to the rapid growth of Cardiff and, until the beginning of the 20th century, it was a major coal exporting centre. It is the seat of the University College of South Wales and Monmouthshire, and has an 11th-century castle. Industries: shipbuilding and repairing, steel, engineering, chemicals, food processing. Pop. 287,000.

Cardigan, James Thomas Brudenell, 7th Earl of (1797–1868), British cavalry officer who led the disastrous charge of the Light Brigade (1854) at the Battle of BALACLAVA in the CRIMEAN WAR.

Cardiganshire (Ceredigion), former county in w Wales; since 1974 it has been part of Dyfed. It is an area of moorland with fertile valleys and a narrow coastal plain along Cardigan Bay. The county town was Cardigan but Aberystwyth is the most important town.

Cardigan Welsh corgi, guard and cattle dog; it has a wide flat head with a tapered muzzle, a long strong body, short bowed legs and a long fox-brush tail. The smooth, moderately long coat may be red, sable or black with white markings. Height: 30.5cm (12in); weight: up to 12kg (26lb).

Cardinal, highest rank in the hierarchy of the Roman Catholic Church after the POPE. Some cardinals are heads of departments of the Roman CURIA, whereas others are PRIMATES of national churches or other senior bishops. They are nominated by the pope, whom they advise and assist in the performance of his duties. On the death of a pope they meet in a secret CONCLAVE to elect his successor, a privilege which has been exclusively theirs since 1179. They are collectively called the Sacred College of Cardinals.

Cardinal number, number expressing the content of a SET but not the order of its members. For example, six is a cardinal number in "six books". Two sets have the same cardinal number if their members can be put in one-to-one correspondence – a concept that allows the idea of cardinal numbers of infinite sets. The set of integers is said to have cardinal number $\aleph_0$ (aleph-null). The set of all real numbers cannot be put into one-to-one correspondence with aleph-null and is a "larger" infinite set. *See also* ORDINAL NUMBER; SU p.40.

Cardoon, vegetable, the parts eaten being the crisp inner leaves, stalks and main roots. It is a perennial herb native to the Mediterranean which, since its introduction to South America, has spread widely across the pampas. Family Compositae; species *Cynara cardunculus.*

Carducci, name of two Italian painters who settled in Spain in 1585. Bartolommeo (1560–1608) painted frescoes in the library of the ESCORIAL and altarpieces in the Church of San Felipe el Real, introducing the BAROQUE style to Spain. His brother Vincenzo (*c.*1576–1638) painted *The Martyrdom of St Andrew* in Toledo cathedral and a series of paintings for El Paular monastery. He also wrote *De las Excelencias de la Pintura* (1633).

Carducci, Giosuè (1835–1907), Italian poet who was professor of literature at Bologna University (1860–1904). He was a patriot and advocated a return to Classical and Renaissance literary values in *Inno a Satana* (1865), and *Odi Barbarai* (1887–1889), and in his critical works. He was awarded the Nobel prize in literature in 1906. *See also* HC2 pp.100–101.

Cardus, Sir Neville (1889–1975), noted British music critic and writer on cricket. He joined the *Manchester Guardian* in 1917 and was later appointed its chief music critic. He wrote for the *Sydney Morning Herald* from 1941 to 1947. He was knighted in 1967.

Caretaker, The, second full-length play by the British dramatist Harold PINTER. It was first performed in 1960 and it established his reputation; it was later made into a film.

Carew, Thomas (*c.*1595–*c.*1639), English poet. His poetry was largely influenced by Ben JONSON and John DONNE, to whom he wrote an elegy. His work includes the largely licentious *A Rapture* and the masque *Coelum Britannicum* (1634).

Carey, Henry (*c.*1687–1743), English dramatist and song writer, best known for his ballad *Sally in our Alley.* In 1713 he published his first collection of poems and later wrote many songs, burlesques and comic dramas.

Carey Street, former location of the Bankruptcy Court in London, which was housed in the Thomas More building of the Royal Courts of Justice. "To be in Carey Street" means, in popular usage, to be in straitened circumstances.

Cargill, William Walter (1784–1860), Scottish-born New Zealand settler who founded OTAGO in 1848. He was elected superintendent of Otago in 1852. INVERCARGILL is named after him.

Cargo cult, mainly Melanesian religious and political movement where local people have been suddenly confronted by white civilization. They expect their ancestors to return in planes or ships laden with modern goods and to free them from white control and the need to work. As part of the cult they prepare runways and landing areas for the expected cargoes.

Carib, major language group of warlike American Indians (from whom the word "cannibal" is derived). They entered the Caribbean region as relatively late arrivals from NE South Americas. About 500 Caribs still live on the island of Dominica; 5,000 migrated to the eastern coast of Central America, notably around Honduras, where their descendants still live.

Caribbean Sea, extension of the N Atlantic Ocean, bounded by South America (s), Central America (w) and the West Indies (N and E); linked to the Gulf of Mexico by the Yucatan Channel and to the Pacific Ocean by the Panama Canal. The major rivers flowing into it are the Magdalena and Atrato from Columbia, and the San Juan Grande and Coco from Nicaragua. The Caribbean was discovered by Christopher Columbus in 1492 and was named after the Carib Indians. Thereafter it lay on the route of many Spanish expeditions and was later notorious for piracy, particularly after other European powers had established colonies on the islands of the West Indies. With the opening of the Panama Canal in 1914 its strategic importance increased. Area: 2,718,208sq km (1,049,500sq miles).

Caribou. *See* REINDEER.

Caricature (from the Italian "caricare", to load or surcharge), a painting or drawing in which a person is presented in a comic, often ridiculous, light by the distortion or exaggeration of his most obvious features. Caricature may be used to interpret the personality and character of a person, event or age, eg the crowd figures in a ROWLANDSON illustration. The word and genre first appeared in the late 16th century. BERNINI was an excellent caricaturist. HOGARTH attempted to distinguish between depicting character (his forte) and comic likeness, but the two traditions merged. DAUMIER, the 19th-century French artist was a particularly skilful political caricaturist. In the 20th century many popular graphic artists have combined caricature with social and political satire, and today most political "cartoons" in newspapers and periodicals are caricatures.

Caries, decay of teeth or, less commonly, of bones. Tooth decay is caused principally by bacteria living in the mouth. Some feed on food sugars, producing an acid which eats through the hard, outer layers of the teeth, permitting infection with decay bacteria. Brushing the teeth prevents this decay by removing from the teeth a composite plaque of food and bacteria. *See also* MS pp.130–131.

Carinatae, old term for all birds except ratites (ostriches, emus and their relatives). The name refers to the keeled (carinated) breastbone of nearly all birds. *See also* NW pp.140–141.

Carinthia (Kärnten), province in s Austria, on the border with Italy and Yugoslavia. Originally inhabited by Celts, it was taken by the HAPSBURGS in 1276, and became part of the Austrian crown lands in 1335. It has several summer resorts. Klagenfurt is the capital. Agriculture is based on rye, oats and livestock raising, and the chief industries are zinc, iron and lead mining. Pop. (1971) 526,000.

Carisbrooke Castle, castle on the ISLE OF WIGHT, built on the site of a 3rd-century Roman fort. It shows three main building periods – Roman, Norman and Elizabethan. CHARLES I was imprisoned in it by the Parliamentarians in 1647–48.

Carissimi, Giacomo (1605–74), Italian composer, the teacher of A. SCARLATTI. He wrote chamber CANTATAS, but was important especially as one of the early writers of ORATORIOS, of which *Jephtha* is the best known.

Carl XVI Gustaf (1946–), King of Sweden since September 1973, when he succeeded his grandfather Gustaf VI Adolf. He immediately renounced all (except purely formal) powers of monarchy, a renunciation incorporated in Sweden's 1975 constitution. In June 1976, he married Silvia Sommerlath, the daughter of a West German businessman.

Carleton, Guy, 1st Baron Dorchester (1724–1808), British soldier and colonial administrator. He served in North America during the SEVEN YEARS WAR, and became lieutenant governor of Quebec in 1766 and governor in 1768. His policies were confirmed by the Quebec Act passed by the British Parliament in 1774. He became British military commander in Canada in 1775 and, after initial setbacks, defeated the US forces during the Quebec campaign (1775–76). He was made a baron and was governor-in-chief of British North America (1786–96).

Carlevaris, Luca (1663–1731), Italian painter and engraver. He was the first notable painter of Venetian views, a precursor of CANALETTO and GUARDI.

Carlile, Wilson (1847–1942), clergyman of the Church of England who founded the CHURCH ARMY in 1882. A successful businessman before becoming a priest, he combined his work for the Church Army with several parochial appointments.

Carlisle, city in Cumbria, NW England, on the River Eden, 13km (8 miles) from its mouth on the Solway Firth. Mary Queen of Scots was imprisoned there in 1568. An important rail centre, its industries include agricultural engineering, textiles, food processing. Pop. (1971) 71,497.

Carlists, Spanish faction that favoured the royal claims of Don Carlos (1788–1855) and his successors. They were beaten in

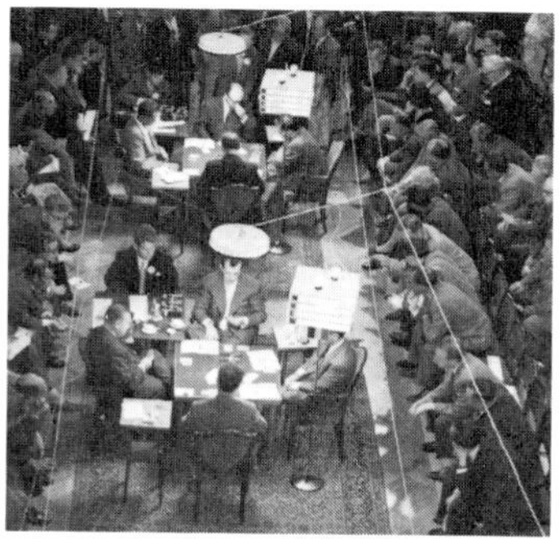

Card games; international bridge competitions are followed with great enthusiasm.

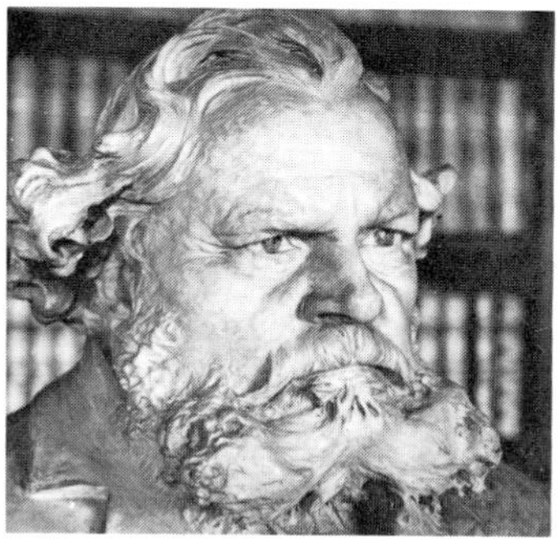

Giosuè Carducci, the Italian poet who rebelled against the Romanticism of his age.

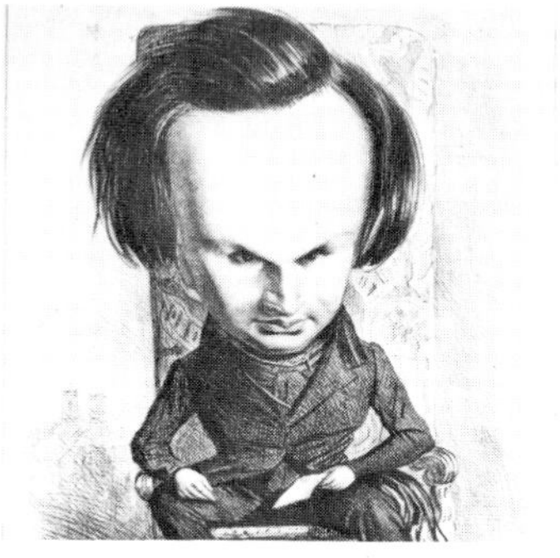

Caricature; drawing of Victor Hugo in which the size of the head is greatly exaggerated.

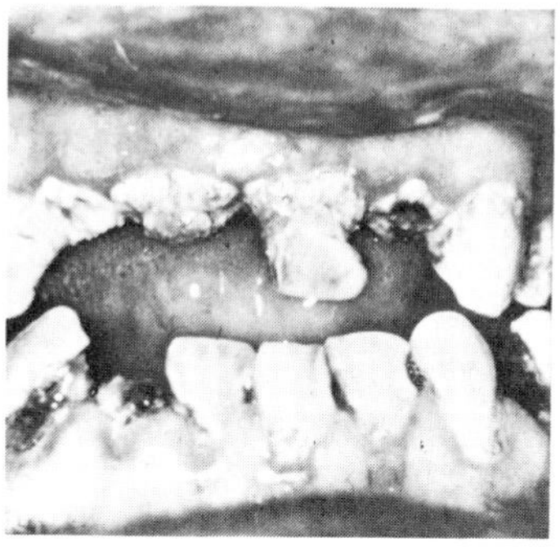

Caries; lack of oral hygiene may cause tooth decay from destructive bacteria.

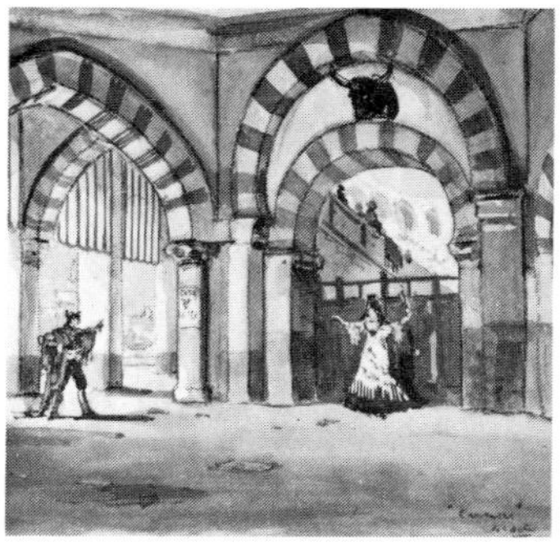

Carmen; an original costume and set design for the fourth act of Bizet's opera (1875).

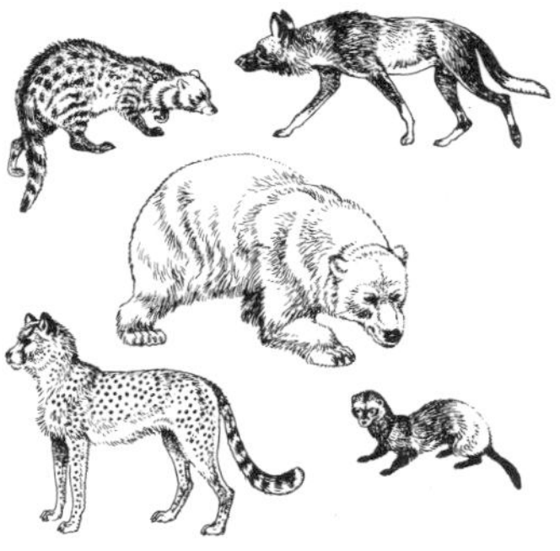

Carnivores prey mainly on herbivores and help to preserve the balance of nature.

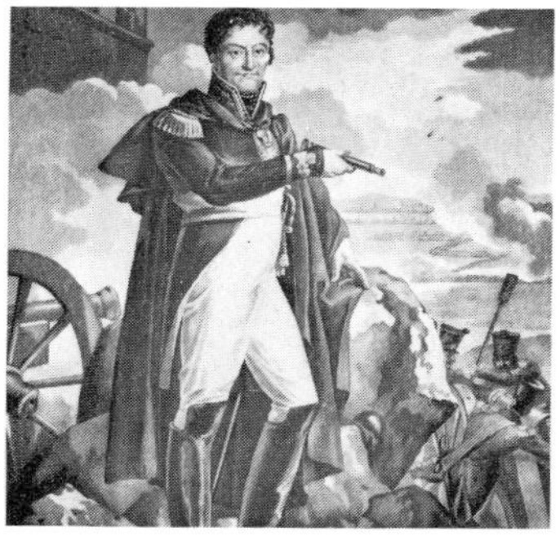

Lazare Carnot; Napoleon said to him "Monsieur Carnot, I have known you too late".

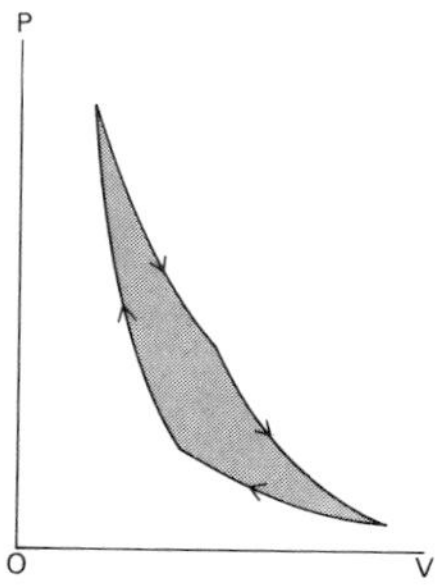

Carnot cycle, which proves theoretically the impossibility of perpetual motion.

the civil war (1834–39), but Carlist sentiments persisted and they seized considerable territory in N Spain in 1873. That uprising was defeated in 1876, but the Carlists, mainly conservative and nationalist, survive to the present.

Carlos I, King of Portugal. *See* CHARLES I (CARLOS).

Carlos, Juan. *See* JUAN CARLOS.

Carlos, kings of Spain. *See* CHARLES, KINGS OF SPAIN.

Carlos, Don, tragedy by Friedrich von SCHILLER (1787) and opera by Giuseppe VERDI (1867). Don Carlos (1545–68), son of Philip II of Spain, had fits of insanity and was jailed for planning to murder his father. Schiller portrayed him as a champion of liberty in love with his stepmother, and the play formed the basis for Verdi's opera.

Carlow, market town in SE Republic of Ireland, at the confluence of the Barrow and Burren rivers; county town of Carlow County. It has the ruins of a 12th-century castle. Industries: food processing, brewing. Pop. 9,400.

Carlsbad. *See* KARLOVY VARY.

Carlson, Chester (1906–68), US physicist, inventor of XEROGRAPHY (1938). He patented it in 1940, but had great difficulty in convincing anyone of its commercial value. Finally, in 1947, he signed an agreement with the Haloid Company (now the Xerox Corporation). His royalties made him a multi-millionaire.

Carlsund, Otto Gustaf (1897–1948), Swedish artist, a pioneer of avant-garde painting in Sweden. He worked in Paris (1924) under LEGER and was later influenced by MONDRIAN. From 1931 to 1944 he abandoned painting for art criticism.

Carlyle, Thomas (1795–1881), Scottish philosopher, critic and historian. His most successful work, *Sartor Resartus* (1836), combined philosophy and autobiography. His histories include *The French Revolution* (three vols 1837), and a study of Frederick II of Prussia (six vols 1858–65). He studied Goethe and the German Romantics. He was anti-democratic in his political thought and expressed his preference for strong heroes or leaders in a series of lectures *On Heroes, Hero Worship and the Heroic in History* (1841).

Carman, William Bliss (1861–1929), Canadian poet. He settled in New York, USA, in 1890 and with the poet Richard Hovey produced the series *Songs from Vagabondia* (1894–1901). His later poetry included *The Pipes of Pan* (5 vols 1905), and *Far Horizons* (1925).

Carmarthen (Caerfyrddin), market town in SW Wales, on the River Towy, 13km (8 miles) from Carmarthen Bay on the Bristol Channel. It is the administrative centre for Dyfed and was formerly the county town of Carmarthenshire. Pop. 13,000.

Carmarthenshire (Sirgaerfyrddin), former county in SW Wales; since 1974 it has been part of Dyfed; the largest of the former Welsh counties. It is a hilly area and dairy farming is the chief occupation. The county town was Carmarthen.

Carmel, Mount, mountain ridge in NW Israel extending 24km (15 miles) from the Esdraelon plain to the Mediterranean Sea at Haifa (Hefa). It is associated with the prophets Elijah and Elisha. In 1931–32 archaeologists discovered there the remains of a type of Neanderthal Man, previously unknown. *See also* MS p.27.

Carmelites, common name for members of the Order of Our Lady of Mount Carmel, founded by St BERTHOLD in Palestine about 1154. An order of Carmelite sisters was founded in 1452. The Carmelites devote themselves to contemplation and missionary work.

Carmen (1875), opera in four acts by Georges BIZET, with French libretto by Henri Meilhac and Ludovic Halévy after Prosper Mérimée's novel. Carmen (mezzo-soprano), a *femme fatale*, induces Don José (tenor), a corporal of the guard, to join the gypsy smugglers, then deserts him for the toreador Escamillo (baritone) and is killed by Don José. *See also* HC2 p.121.

Carmichael, Hoagy (1899–), US popular composer. He wrote many songs that have become "standards", among them *Stardust* (dedicated to Bix BEIDERBECKE) and *Two Sleepy People*; he received an Oscar for *In the Cool, Cool, Cool of the Evening*. He has written film scores, made recordings and appeared on radio and television programmes.

Carmichael, Stokely (1942–), West Indian-born US black activist and leader in the BLACK POWER movement. He was chairman of a civil rights group, the Student Nonviolent Co-ordinating Committee in 1966 and in 1967 joined the more militant Black Panther party. He served as its prime minister until 1969. He left the Panthers as a protest against their association with white radicals and lived in self-imposed exile in Africa.

Carmina Burana, collection of popular 13th century Latin poems from a Bavarian monastery; the lyrics were set to music by Carl ORFF in 1935–36. Probably composed by minstrels and students, many of the poems tell of gambling and drinking, but some have moral or religious themes.

Carnac, village in Brittany, NW France. It is noted for its Megalithic monuments, in particular its menhirs (standing stones), which extend along the coast in 11 parallel rows and probably antedate the Druids. The village also has the remains of a Gallo-Roman villa.

Carnap, Rudolph (1891–1970), German philosopher. He was a member of the VIENNA CIRCLE and is often considered to be a founder of LOGICAL POSITIVISM. He went to the US from Europe in 1936. He wrote extensively on the theory of probability, theory of knowledge, mathematical logic and the philosophy of science.

Carnarvon. *See* CAERNARVON.

Carnarvonshire. *See* CAERNARVONSHIRE.

Carnation, slender-stemmed herbaceous plant native to Europe. It has narrow leaves, characteristic swollen stem joints, and produces several dense blooms with serrated (pinked) petals which range from white to yellow, pink and red. Family Caryophyllaceae; species *Dianthus caryophyllus.*

Carné, Marcel (1909–), French film director. He is best known for his work with screenwriter Jacques PRÉVERT, as in *Quai des Brumes* (1938), *Le Jour se Lève* (1939), *Les Enfants du Paradis* (1943) and *Les Jeunes Loups* (1968), all of which show careful attention to atmosphere and detail.

Carnegie, Andrew (1835–1919), Scottish-born US industrialist and philanthropist. He began as a telegraph operator with the Pennsylvania Railroad (1853–65) but foresaw the demand for iron and steel and started the Keystone Bridge Company. From 1873 he concentrated on steel and by 1901, when his Carnegie Steel Company was sold, it was producing 25% of US steel. He endowed 2,800 libraries and donated more than $350,000,000 to various foundations. *See also* HC2 p.152.

Carnegie Hall, New York concert hall named after Andrew Carnegie, its principal benefactor, and opened in 1891. It has excellent acoustics and until the Lincoln Center opened in 1962 it was the best concert hall in New York.

Carnegie Trust. *See* CARNEGIE, ANDREW.

Carniola, administrative unit of the Austrian empire. Once part of the Roman province of Pannonia, Carniola was occupied during the 6th century by the SLOVENES. It belonged to Ottokar II of Bohemia (1269–1276), and passed to the Hapsburgs in 1335. In 1918 most of the region was awarded to Yugoslavia.

Carnival, celebration, usually of a religious nature, with parades, masques, pageants and other forms of revelry with origins in pre-Christian fertility rites. It often occurs in conjunction with a religious feast. The term also refers generally to a local festival or bazaar.

Carnivore, any member of the order of flesh-eating mammals. Weasels, martens, minks and the wolverine make up the largest family. The cats are the most specialized killers among the carnivores; dogs, bears and raccoons are much less exclusively meat eaters; and civets, mongooses and their relatives also have a mixed diet. Related to the civets, but in a separate family, are the hyenas, large dog-like scavengers. More distantly related to living land carnivores are the seals, sea lions and walruses; they evolved from the ancient land carnivores which also gave rise to early weasel-like or civet-like forms. Other extinct carnivores include the sabretooth cats, which died out during the Pliocene Epoch about 2 million years ago. *See also* NW pp.164–165.

Carnot, Lazare Nicolas Marguerite (1753–1823), French general whose brilliant planning was largely responsible for French victories during the REVOLUTIONARY WARS. In 1800 he became minister of war and served under NAPOLEON Bonaparte.

Carnot, Nicolas Léonard Sadi (1796–1832), French army officer and engineer. His major work, *Réflexions sur la puissance motrice du feu* (1824), provided the first theoretical background to the steam engine and introduced the concepts of reversible cycles and the second law of thermodynamics. His work was ignored until it was quoted and extended by the railway engineer Emile Clapeyron in 1834. *See also* SU pp.92–93.

Carnot cycle, in thermodynamics, a cycle of events that demonstrates the impossibility of total efficiency in heat engines. It was named after Nicholas Carnot (1796–1832). In brief, the Carnot cycle shows how an engine can never convert all the heat energy supplied to it from its burning fuel into mechanical energy. Some heat energy always remains unused in a "cold sink" which in, say, an internal combustion engine, can be thought of as the engine itself; more properly, the cold sink is the entire universe. *See also* SU p.92.

Carnotite, secondary vanadate mineral, potassium uranium vanadate $[K_2(UO_2)_2(VO_4)_2.nH_2O]$, an ore of uranium and radium, important for atomic energy. It occurs in the Colorado Plateau, Australia, and Congo as yellow-green crusts or cavity fillings in sandstone and in fossilized wood. It is finely crystalline (monoclinic), dull or earthy; s.g. 3–5.

Caro, Anthony (1924–), British sculptor, whose open-form painted "structures", which he evolved after a visit to the USA in 1959, go beyond pure CONSTRUCTIVISM in their expressiveness. He was an assistant to Henry MOORE (1951–53), then taught at St Martin's School of Art (1953–64) and at Bennington Coll., Vermont, USA (1963–65). Both as teacher and practising sculptor Caro has been a major influence on recent English sculptors.

Carob tree, plant of the eastern Mediterranean. It belongs to the pea family (LEGUMINOSAE) and bears typically leguminous fruits – long juicy pods which have been used as food for people and animals. Species *Ceratonia siliqua.*

Carol, name of two kings of Romania. Carol I (1838–1914) was a prince of the HOHENZOLLERN dynasty, Prince of Romania (1866–81) and Romania's first king (1881–1914). During the RUSSO-TURKISH WAR (1877–78) he sided with Russia and at the BERLIN CONGRESS (1878) won independence for Romania. By 1913 he had made Romania the strongest Balkan power. His grand-nephew, Carol II (1893–1953), also became king (1930–40). In 1938 he assumed dictatorial powers in a struggle against the Fascist IRON GUARD but was later deposed. *See also* HC2 pp.184–185, *184–185*, 223.

Carol, traditional English song usually of religious joy, especially associated with Christmas. Earliest examples date from the 14th century.

Carolan. *See* O'CAROLAN, TURLOUGH.

Carolina, municipality and town in NE Puerto Rico, 18km (11 miles) ESE of San Juan. It is a market centre for tobacco and sugar; its industries include textiles. Pop. (1970): mun. 107,600; town 94,300.

Carolina. *See* NORTH CAROLINA; SOUTH CAROLINA.

Caroline Islands, archipelago of more than 600 volcanic islands, coral islets and reefs in the W Pacific Ocean, N of the equator; part of the US Trust Territory of the Pacific Islands since 1947. The larger

islands include Palau, Ponape, Truk and Yap. Copra is the chief export. Area: 1,130sq km (450sq miles). Pop. 67,000.
Caroline of Ansbach (1683–1737), wife of GEORGE II of England. After George II became king in 1727 she helped keep Robert WALPOLE in power and exerted considerable political influence.
Caroline of Brunswick (1768–1821), wife of GEORGE IV of England. They separated in 1796 but on George's accession in 1820 she claimed her rank of queen. A divorce bill was introduced but Caroline won public sympathy and retained her title, but was prevented from attending the coronation.
Carolingian minuscule, script devised in the reign of Charlemagne (8th to 9th centuries) that gained general acceptance throughout Latin-speaking Europe. It evolved over the centuries and by the 13th was known as Gothic script. *See also* MS p.247, *247*.
Carolingians, Frankish dynasty in early medieval Europe. Founded in the 7th century by Pepin of Landen, they rose to power over the Franks as major domos (mayors of the palace) under the weak kingship of the later MEROVINGIANS. In 732 Pepin's great-grandson CHARLES MARTEL defeated the Muslims at Poitiers; in 751 Charle's son PEPIN THE SHORT deposed the last Merovingian and became King of the Franks. The dynasty reached its peak under Pepin's son CHARLEMAGNE, who united the Frankish dominions and was crowned as HOLY ROMAN EMPEROR by the pope in 800. The Treaty of Verdun (843) divided the empire into three parts: an E part (Germany), a W part (France) and a central part including Italy. Each part was ruled by one of Charlemagne's grandsons: Charles the Bald in the W; Louis the German in the E; and Lothair I, inheriting the title of emperor, in the centre. The Carolingian era saw the rise of FEUDALISM in W Europe and, under Charlmagne, a temporary revival of learning known as the Carolingian Renaissance. *See also* HC1 pp.152–153, 160–161.
Carossa, Hans (1878–1956), German novelist and doctor. In *Doctor Bürger's Fate* (1913) and *Der Arzt Gion* (1932), he attempted to reconcile a visionary faith in life with his knowledge of medicine. His autobiographical work, influenced in style and philosophy by GOETHE, expressed his quest for a harmonious existence.
Carotene, plant pigment that is converted to vitamin A by the liver. It occurs in various fruits and vegetables (such as carrots).
Carotenoid, one of a group of fat-soluble plant pigments ranging in colour from yellow to red. Carotenoids also occur in some animal fats. They include isomers of CAROTENE, a pigment that is converted in the liver into vitamin A, necessary for normal vision and healthy skin.
Carothers, Wallace Hume (1896–1937), US chemist who discovered the synthetic polyamide fibre now called NYLON. *See also* MM pp.56–57.
Carp, fresh-water fish farmed in Japan, native to temperate waters and those warmed by hot springs. It is brown or golden and has four fleshy mouth whiskers. The mirror carp has only a few scales and the leather carp has none. Length: to 1m (3.2ft). Family Cyprinidae; species *Cyprinus carpio*. *See also* NW p.231; PE pp.242–243.
Carpaccio, Vittore (*c*.1460–1525), Venetian painter, who was influenced by Giovanni BELLINI and possibly by GIORGIONE. A story-teller of great inventiveness, he related the incidents in his many narrative paintings to backgrounds of an idealized Venice. He did this with exceptional success in his cycle of scenes from the legend of St Ursula (Accademia, Venice). Always a popular painter, and one whose work has gained critical interest in recent times, Carpaccio's range of subjects varied from religious paintings, eg *The Presentation of Christ in the Temple*, to the enchanting *Two Venetian Ladies* (Correr Museum, Venice), said to be a painting of two courtesans. *See also* HC1 p.*135*.
Carpathian Mountains, range in central and E Europe, extending from central Czechoslovakia NE to the Polish-Czechoslovakian border. The N Carpathians (Beskids and Tatra) run E along the border and SE through W Ukraine, USSR; the S Carpathians (Transylvanian Alps) extend SW to the Danube River. The highest peak is Gerlachovka, 2,655m (8,711ft). It is a sparsely populated area except for the valleys in the S. Industries: timber, mining, tourism. Length: 1,530km (950 miles).
Carpeaux, Jean Baptiste (1827–75), French sculptor and painter. His individual and realistic approach to sculpture was in contrast to the pseudo-Classicism of his time. His most famous work is *The Dance* (1869), a group sculpture for the Paris Opéra.
Carpentaria, Gulf of, large inlet of the Arafura Sea, indenting the N coast of Australia, bounded by Arnhem Land (W) and Cape York Peninsula (E). Area: 310,800sq km (120,000sq miles).
Carpentier, Alejo (1904–), Cuban novelist and musicologist. In *La musica en Cuba* (1946), he captured the flavour of Afro-Cuban music. His novels, structured around myths, are concerned with the conflict between the sophisticated and the primitive, as in *Los pasos perdidos* (1953).
Carpentier, Georges (1894–1975), French boxer, world light-heavyweight champion (1920–22). He lost a heavyweight championship fight to Jack Dempsey (1921) in Jersey City, USA, in the sport's first million-dollar gate. It was the first time a commentary of a championship was broadcast by radio.
Carpentry, craft of cutting, shaping and joining wood. Today the term is generally applied to the bulkier type of woodwork for structural and functional purposes; house construction and its associated woodwork such as rafters, joists, roofs, floors, gates and moulds for concrete are examples of work classed as carpentry. The basic tools of carpentry are the saw, chisel and plane (for cutting and shaping) and the drill, hammer and nails (for joining). Although a carpenter sometimes works from detailed plans, his technique is largely freehand: essential dimensions of a mould, for example, are maintained but the external appearance is unimportant. Joinery and cabinet-making are more specialized types of carpentry. They concern the finer, more precise and visually attractive woodwork: a joiner specializes in making articles such as staircases, shelves, doors, windows and cupboards; a cabinet-maker makes furniture. *See also* MM pp.38–39, 46–47.
Carpet, floor-covering of soft and durable fabric. Carpets are made from a variety of materials, including wool, cotton and synthetic fibres, synthetics being used in more than 80% of the carpets manufactured today. Most carpets are produced by weaving, tufting, knitting or electrostatic flocking. Pile carpets, in which the cut ends of threads form the upper surface (pile), are woven on power looms using one of four main types of weave: Wilton, Axminster, Velvet, and Chenille. The pattern of a woven carpet is produced by the various colours of the threads. In tufting, which can produce up to 670sq m (800sq yd) per day on one machine, pile yarn is stitched to a previously made backing, often of jute; the carpet can then be printed or dyed. In electrostatic flocking, chopped fibres are "glued" to a backing fabric.
Carpetbaggers, term used after the US Civil War to refer to Northern whites affiliated with the Republican Party who went to the South to participate in its reconstruction. The name referred to the carpet-bag in which many of them carried their belongings. Their opportunism made the phrase a term of abuse. *See also* HC2 p.152.
Carpetsweeper, hand-operated device for the removal of surface dirt from rugs and carpets invented by Melville Reuben Bissell (1843–89) and patented in 1876. It consists of a long-handled metal or wooden case on wheels. The case contains a cylindrical brush and two pans. When the sweeper is pushed back and forth, the brush rotates, picking up dirt, which drops into the pans.
Carpi, Ugo da (*c*.1479–*c*.1525), Italian designer of woodcuts. He introduced the CHIAROSCURO technique, which requires the use of several blocks, inked separately, to superimpose colours in printing, achieving a three-dimensional effect.
Carpini, Giovanni da Pian del (*c*.1180–1252), Italian traveller and churchman. He was sent by Pope INNOCENT IV to the Mongol court in 1245, and on his return to Italy wrote a history of the Mongols in which he discredited many of the contemporary rumours concerning Mongol atrocities. He was then made Archbishop of Antivari.
Carr, Edwin (1926–), New Zealand composer. He has studied with Carl ORFF and Benjamin Frankel and his compositions include an opera, *Nastasya* (1972), a symphony (1952), song cycles, concertos and ballet music.
Carrà, Carlo (1881–1966), Italian painter, a founder of FUTURISM, whose early work is in that style. After WWI he was influenced by the "metaphysical" style of CHIRICO and from the 1920s he worked in a more naturalistic style, apparently inspired by the paintings of GIOTTO.
Carracci, family of three painters from Bologna who founded the Carracci Academy, one of the most important 16th-century schools of painting. They revolted against the MANNERISM of the time and sought a more naturalistic style akin to the masters of the High Renaissance. Lodovico (1555–1619) specialized in large altarpieces, eg *The Bargellini Madonna* (1588). Agostino (1557–1602) whose masterpieces include *The Last Communion of St Jerome* (*c*.1594), was also an important art theorist and famous engraver. Annibale (1560–1609), the greatest artist of the three, painted the frescoes in the Farnese Palace, Rome. These were a prelude to the BAROQUE style of RUBENS and BERNINI.
Carrack, small wooden sailing ship first used in the Middle Ages and characterized by one or two large square-rigged main masts, one or two smaller lateen mizzen or rear masts, and a rear rudder. One example was the SANTA MARIA used by Christopher Columbus on his voyage to America. *See also* LATEEN; RIG; MM p.112.
Carrel, Alexis (1873–1944), French surgeon who was awarded the 1912 Nobel Prize in physiology and medicine for his development of a surgical technique for stitching together blood vessels end-to-end. He also contributed to tissue culture research. *See also* MS p.177.
Carrera brothers, José Miguel (1785–1821), Juan José and Luis, Chilean independence leaders and political rivals of Bernardo O'HIGGINS. José became effectively the president of Chile in 1811 and again in 1814. All three were executed by the Spanish when they reconquered the country, José in 1821 and his brothers in 1818.
Carrero Blanco, Luis (1903–73), Spanish admiral and political figure. He fought with the Nationalists in the SPANISH CIVIL WAR and became closely associated with the Francisco FRANCO regime. He was vice-premier (1967–73). In 1973 he was named premier and was expected to succeed Franco but was assassinated, apparently by Basque nationalists.
Carriage, horse-drawn passenger-carrying vehicle. The Romans were the first to develop a practical four-wheeled carriage, but it was in the 19th century – with the great advances in road-building – that carriages became popular. A wide variety of designs appeared, ranging from the purely functional to the magnificent and luxurious carriages of the wealthy. Carriages declined in popularity after WWI with the introduction of MOTOR CARS. *See also* COACH; MM pp.120–121.
Carrier, apparently healthy person who harbours a disease which, while it does not affect him, can be transmitted to other people. Carriers are difficult to detect and are often unaware of the infection they carry.
Carrier, Jean Baptiste (1756–94), extreme Jacobin in the FRENCH REVOLU-

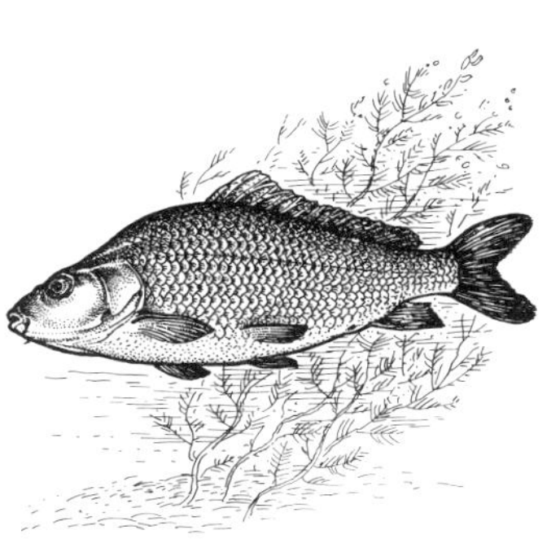
Carp are an ideal species of fish for farming in artificial freshwater ponds.

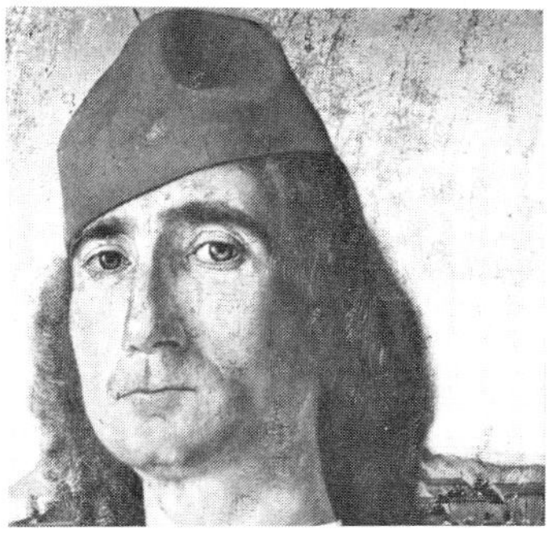
Vittore Carpaccio; a detail from his portrait of a *Young man in a Red Beret*.

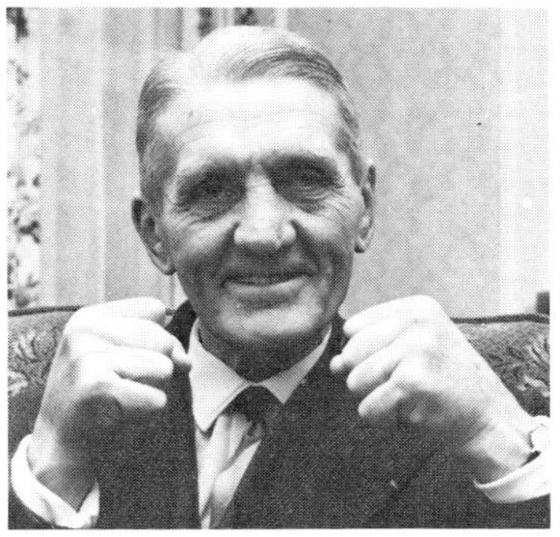
Georges Carpentier's contest with Jack Dempsey was the first to be broadcast.

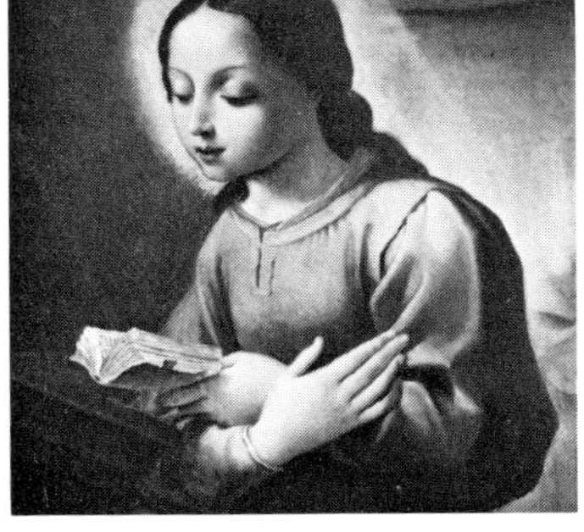
Carracci Academy included the painter Ludovico; this is his *Annunciation*.

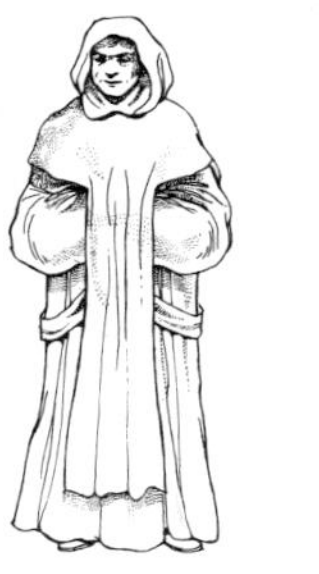

Carthusian vocation makes severe tests of physical and psychological endurance.

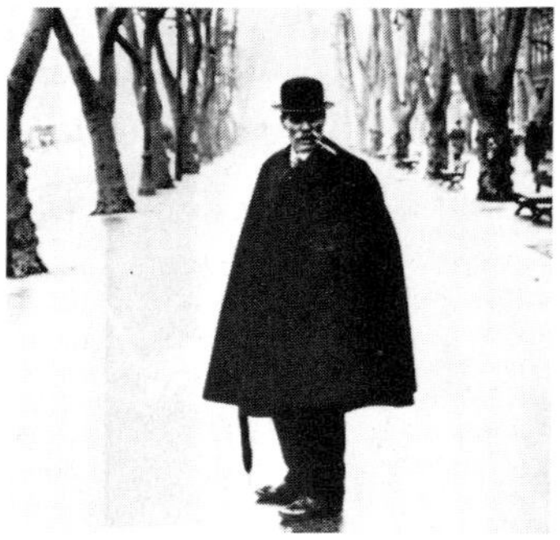

Henri Cartier-Bresson produced photographs of great merit using 35mm cameras.

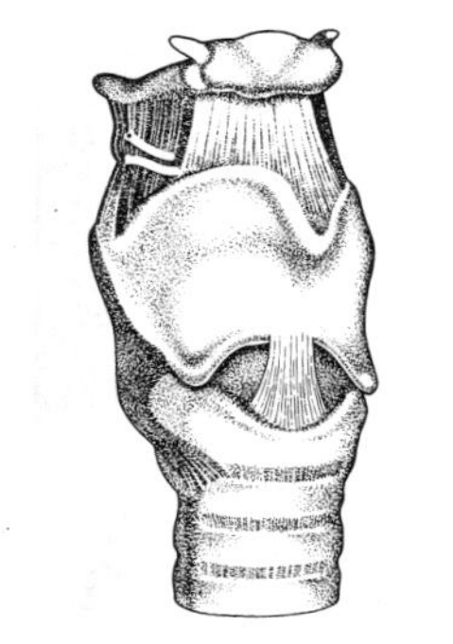

Cartilage plays an important and continuing role in the formation of the body skeleton.

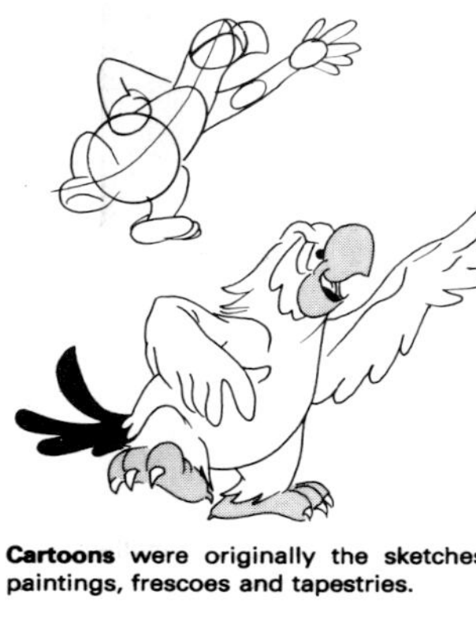

Cartoons were originally the sketches for paintings, frescoes and tapestries.

TION. His contribution to the Terror was to introduce the drowning of political opponents. He was executed in the Thermidorian reaction.

Carrier, Roch (1937–), Canadian novelist. His realistic, often violent, novels of Quebec life include *La Guerre, Yes Sir!* (1968), *Floralie où es-tu?* (1969) and *Il est par là, le soleil* (1970).

Carrier wave, high frequency electromagnetic wave which carries information signals from a radio or television transmitter. The fixed wavelength and frequency of the transmitter's wave is the signal, or channel, to which a receiver must be tuned in order to receive its broadcast. To prevent interference, transmitter carrier waves are separated by clean channels of 10 kHz frequency. *See also* MM p.*228*.

Carroll, Sir James (1853–1926), New Zealand politician. Elected to parliament in 1887, he was Minister of Maori Affairs from 1899 to 1912, in which time he was twice acting Prime Minister.

Carroll, Lewis (1832–98), British mathematician, photographer and writer, real name Charles Lutwidge Dodgson. He is especially remembered for *Alice's Adventures in Wonderland* (1865) and its sequel, *Through the Looking Glass* (1872), which have attracted much serious scholarly criticism as well as being popular children's classics.

Carroll, Paul Vincent (1900–68), Irish dramatist. His best-known play was *Shadow and Substance* (1937), first performed at the ABBEY THEATRE, Dublin. His other plays include *Things That Are Caesar's* (1932), *The White Steed* (1939), *The Strings, My Lord, Are False* (1942) and *The Wayward Saint* (1955).

Carronade, short-barrelled CANNON that fired iron balls weighing up to 31kg (68lb). Invented in 1759 by Sir Robert Melville, it was used in the British, French and US navies between 1779 and 1850 and proved to be extremely effective at short ranges, especially fired over the stern of a ship. *See also* MM p.173.

Carrot, herbaceous, generally biennial, root vegetable native to Afghanistan and cultivated widely as a food crop. The edible orange taproot is the plant's store of food for the following year. The plant is topped by delicate fern-like leaves and white or pink flower clusters. The carrot family, UMBELLIFERAE. Species *Daucus carota. See also* PE p.*189*.

Carse of Gowrie, fertile low-lying plain 24km (15 miles) long in the Perth and Kinross and Dundee City districts, Tayside region, Scotland, bordering the Firth of Tay. It is one of the country's most productive agricultural areas.

Carson, Edward Henry (1854–1935), British political figure. He was an MP (1892–1921), and fought against home rule for Ireland. He organized the paramilitary Ulster Volunteers (1912–13) and forced the Government to keep most of Ulster in Britain. He served in the war cabinet during WWI and became an appeal judge (1921–29). *See also* HC2 p.163.

Carson, Kit (1809–68), US guide and soldier. He originally lived as a trapper and hunter but achieved fame for his work as a guide for John C. FRÉMONT's expeditions (1842–46). In 1854 he became US Indian agent at Taos, New Mexico, and in 1861 became a colonel in the US army, fighting against Confederate and Indian forces. In 1868 he became superintendent of Indian affairs for Colorado Territory.

Carson, Rachel Louise (1907–1964), US biologist and science writer. She is best known for her widely popular and influential books on pollution, wild life and the sea. Her works include *The Sea Around Us* (1951), which won a National Book Award, *Silent Spring* (1962), about the dangers of pollution, *Under the Sea Wind* (1941) and *The Edge of the Sea* (1955).

Carson City, capital city of Nevada, USA, 50km (30 miles) S of Reno. The city grew rapidly after silver was discovered in the Comstock Lode in 1859. It was named after Kit CARSON. Gambling is the main industry. Pop. (1970) 15,468.

Cartagena, city and port in NW Colombia, on the Bay of Cartagena in the Caribbean Sea. It was an important city under the Spanish in the 17th century, and is today the principal oil port of Colombia. There is a university (founded in 1824). Industries: oil refining, sugar, tobacco, hides, textiles, tourism. Pop. (1975) 292,512.

Cartago, city in central Costa Rica, at the foot of the volcano Irazú 23km (14 miles) SE of San José; capital of Cartago province. It served as the capital of Costa Rica until independence was won from Spain in 1823. Industries: coffee production, livestock raising. Pop. 22,000.

Carte, Richard D'Oyly (1844–1901), British impresario and producer of the operas of Sir William S. GILBERT and Sir Arthur SULLIVAN. He founded the Savoy Theatre in London (1881) – the first to be lighted electrically – especially for staging Gilbert and Sullivan's works.

Cartel, formal agreement among the producers of a particular product to fix the price and divide the market among themselves. Such an arrangement usually results in higher prices for consumers and extra profits for the producers. Cartels are illegal in many countries.

Carter, Elizabeth (1717–1806), British poet, one of the BLUESTOCKINGS. Her poems were published in two major collections (1738, 1762); she also translated (1758) works of the Greek stoic philosopher EPICTETUS.

Carter, Elliott Cook Jr (1908–), US composer, widely regarded as the leading modern American composer. His works, notable for their elaborate counterpoint and use of tempo as an aspect of form, include a piano (1946) and cello (1948) sonata, *Variations* (1953–55) and a concerto (1970) for orchestra, and three string quartets (1951, 1959 and 1973). He received a Pulitzer Prize for his second string quarter in 1960.

Carter, Howard (1873–1939), British Egyptologist. He discovered the tombs of Hatshepsut and Thutmose IV in the VALLEY OF THE KINGS in Luxor, Egypt, and supervised excavations for Lord Carnarvon. He helped find the tomb of TUTANKHAMEN in 1922. *See also* HC1 p.22

Carter, James Earl (1924–), US politician and 39th president. He graduated from the US Naval Academy and served in the navy until 1953. He then devoted himself to managing his family's extensive peanut farms. He was a senator for the state of Georgia (1962–66) and governor of the state (1971–74). He was elected President as the DEMOCRATIC candidate in 1976, when he defeated the Republican incumbent, Gerald FORD. His vice-president was Walter MONDALE. He is the first president since the Civil War to come from the "Old South".

Cartesian co-ordinate system, system in which the position of a point is specified by its distances from intersecting lines (the axes). In the simplest type – RECTANGULAR CO-ORDINATES in two dimensions – two axes are used at right angles: the y-axis and the x-axis. The position of a point is then given by a pair of numbers (x,y). The abscissa, x, is the point's distance from the y-axis, measured along the x-axis and the ordinate, y, is the distance from the x-axis. The axes in such a system need not be at right angles. Three axes represent three dimensions. *See also* SU p.34.

Cartesian philosophy, doctrine of the 17th century French philosopher René DESCARTES. Cartesians agreed with Descartes that all human knowledge could be established with mathematical certainty on the basis of indubitable first truths. The thinking self alone, working on its own clear and distinct ideas, could establish the reality of the world. Matter (extended substance) and mind (thinking substance) constituted the fullness of reality, while the former, always in motion, was the sole object of scientific study. *See also* RATIONALISM; MS p.230.

Carthage, ancient port in N Africa, on a peninsula in the Bay of Tunis. It was founded in the 9th century BC by Phoenician colonists who fought the Punic Wars against Rome. Carthage was destroyed during the Third Punic War 149–146 BC, but was rebuilt by Caesar in 29 BC. It was the capital of the Vandals (439–553 AD), and was destroyed by the Arabs in 698. Today a small town surrounds the ancient remains. *See also* HC1 pp.55, 88, 90–91.

Carthusians, monastic order founded by St BRUNO in 1084 at the Grande CHARTREUSE monastery near Grenoble, France. A mainly contemplative order, the monks are vowed to silence and solitude. The order includes nuns. *See also* HC1 p.*187*.

Cartier, Sir George Etienne (1814–73), Prime Minister of Canada who did much to encourage French Canadians to accept federation at the Quebec conference in 1864. He represented Montreal in the Legislative Assembly (1848–73) and was prime minister jointly with John A. MACDONALD (1858–62).

Cartier, Jacques (1491–1557), French explorer who discovered the St Lawrence River. He made three Canadian voyages, primarily looking for the NORTHWEST PASSAGE and for natural resources. On his first voyage in 1534 he discovered the Magdalen Islands and Prince Edward Island and explored the Gulf of St Lawrence. In 1535–36 he sailed up the St Lawrence River to the site of Montreal. His explorations formed the chief basis for later French claims on Canada. *See also* HC2 p.136, *136*.

Cartier-Bresson, Henri (1908–), French photojournalist. His photographs reflect the modern world and have won international acclaim for their superb composition and sense of timing. His many books include *The Decisive Moment* (1952), *The World of Henri Cartier-Bresson* (1968) and *About Russia* (1974).

Cartilage, flexible supporting tissue of the body. It has a tensile strength and consistency enabling it to bear weight although comparatively elastic. In man, the nose, ears and windpipe are made of cartilaginous tissue. *See also* MS pp.56–57.

Cartography, the science of making MAPS, representing all or a part of the earth's surface to a specified scale. Maps are usually printed on a flat surface using various kinds of projections. The most common type is topographical; it indicates hills and valleys with contour lines. Relief maps, usually used in civil engineering planning, are the clearest method of demonstrating the three-dimensional nature of the terrain. *See also* PE p.34.

Cartoon, term with two meanings. In its original sense it described a preparatory drawing for a tapestry, painting, fresco or stained-glass window. The design may be drawn in chalk, charcoal, colourwash or pencil. Italian Renaissance painters made very thorough cartoons, famous examples of which are RAPHAEL's cartoons for the Sistine Chapel (seven of which are in the Victoria and Albert Museum). The use of the word "cartoon" for a humorous drawing is derived from a 19th-century competition for fresco designs for Parliament parodied in *Punch* magazine.

Cartridge, case of a bullet or shell, containing the explosive and the detonator. In small arms the term is used for a complete round of AMMUNITION, including the bullet or shot. *See also* MM p.*163*.

Cartwright, Edmund (1743–1823), British inventor. Originally a clergyman, Cartwright invented the power loom (patented 1785) after visiting Sir Richard ARKWRIGHT's cotton spinning mill, although it was not used commercially until early in the following century. He also invented a wool-combing machine (patented 1789) and an alcohol engine (1797).

Cartwright, John (1740–1824), British radical reformer. He was the brother of Edmund CARTWRIGHT, and came to prominence with his pamphlets in favour of American independence. He wrote on many topics, including the abolition of slavery and the need for parliamentary reform. *See also* HC2 p.160.

Caruso, Enrico (1873–1921), Italian tenor, one of the most famous and widely-acclaimed opera singers of all time. He made his debut in Naples in 1894; his fame began in 1902 when he sang at Monte Carlo. In 1903 he sang in Verdi's *Rigoletto* at the Metropolitan Opera in the USA, where he centred his career for the next 17 years. He also appeared in the leading European opera houses and made many recordings.

Carver, George Washington (1864–1943), US agricultural chemist and experimenter, best known for his scientific research on the peanut, from which he derived more than 300 products. His primary intent was to aid impoverished farmers of the American South.

Carver, Robert (*b.*1487), Scottish composer. Although little is known about his life, seven pieces of his music are known to have survived. These are five masses and two motets, which show highly accomplished polyphonic writing.

Cary, Arthur Joyce Lunel (1888–1957), British novelist. At the age of 16 he studied art in Edinburgh and Paris, and from 1909–12 he studied law at Oxford University. His experiences in colonial political service in Nigeria (1914–20) are reflected in *Mister Johnson* (1939). He also wrote two trilogies, the first of which contains *The Horse's Mouth* (1944), his best-known novel.

Casablanca, city in W Morocco, on the Atlantic coast. The site was resettled in 1515 by the Portuguese after their destruction of the previous town of Anfa. An earthquake damaged the city in 1755 and it was rebuilt in its present form by Muhammad XVI two years later. Today it is a thriving commercial centre, exporting phosphates and importing petroleum products. Local industries include textiles, glass and bricks. Pop. 1,395,000.

Casablanca Conference (Jan. 1943), meeting of the US president Franklin D. ROOSEVELT and British prime minister Winston CHURCHILL at Casablanca, Morocco. The Allied leaders pledged to fight the AXIS POWERS until they won an unconditional surrender. *See also* HC2 pp.228–231.

Casals, Pablo (Pau) (1876–1973), Spanish cellist and conductor. He organized his own orchestra in Barcelona in 1919, directed the Prades Music Festivals in southern France from 1950, and organized the annual Casals Festival in Puerto Rico from 1957. His virtuoso playing influenced many other cellists.

Casanova de Seingalt, Giovanni Giacomo (Jacopo) (1725–98), Italian adventurer. From 1750 he travelled through Europe leading a dissolute existence. In 1755 he was imprisoned in Venice but made a daring escape to Paris, where he amassed a fortune and mixed with the leading men and women of the day. After 1785 he became a librarian. He is remembered for his memoirs, which were not published in unexpurgated form until 1960.

Cascade Range, mountains in W USA, extending from NE California N across Oregon and Washington into Canada. The Cascade Tunnel, at 13km (8 miles) the longest rail tunnel in the USA, passes through them. Crater Lake National Park is in the Cascades. The highest peak is Mt Ranier, 4,395m (14,410ft).

Cascarilla, vegetable extract used as a laxative. It is obtained from the bark of *Croton elveria,* a shrub of the spurge family native to the West Indies.

Casein, principal protein in milk, containing 0.71% phosphorus, 0.72% sulphur and about 15 amino acids. It constitutes about 80% of the proteins in cow's milk and about 40% in human milk. Obtained from milk by the addition of either acid or rennet, casein is used to make plastics, paper coatings, adhesives, paints, textile sizing, and animal feed.

Casella, Alfredo (1883–1947), Italian composer, teacher, pianist and conductor. His compositions, conservative in style, include three operas, two symphonies, the mass *Missa Solemnis* (1944), piano and ballet music and songs.

Casement, Sir Roger David (1864–1916), Irish humanitarian and patriot. While a British consul (1895–1912) he exposed the brutal exploitation of Congolese rubber-gatherers by agents of the Belgian king. For this and for similar exposures in S America, he received a British knighthood. But in WWI he sought aid in the USA and then in Germany for an Irish uprising, and was executed for treason by the British. To blacken his name, British agents revealed his diaries which showed him to be homosexual. The authenticity of these diaries has sometimes been questioned.

Caserta, city in Campania, SW Italy; capital of Caserta province. The surrender of German forces in Italy was signed there in 1945. It has the "Versailles of Naples", and a Bourbon royal palace (1752). An agricultural trade centre, it has manufacturing and food processing industries. Pop. 59,000.

Casey, Richard Gardiner, Lord (1890–), Governor-General of Australia (1965–69). He held many cabinet posts – including federal treasurer (1935–39), minister for external affairs (1951–60) – and was also minister to the USA (1940–42), minister of state resident in the Middle East (1942–43) and Governor of Bengal (1944–46).

Cash crop, agricultural crop cultivated for its commercial value, as opposed to one grown for subsistence or for use on the farm. Fruit, vegetables, maize and olives for oil are examples of cash crops in European farming. Hay, in contrast, is generally grown as feed for animals. *See also* PE pp.158–159.

Cashew, evergreen shrub or tree grown in the tropics, chiefly important for its nuts. It is used for making boxes and boats, and as charcoal, and it produces a gum similar to gum arabic. Height: to 12m (39ft). Family Anacardiaceae; species *Anacardium occidentale. See also* PE pp.214–215, *215.*

Cash flow, money going into a business (earnings) and money going out (expenditure or costs). The amount of incoming funds compared with outgoing funds determines how much ready cash a company has for its day-to-day operations.

Cashmere, the woolly hair of a goat native to Kashmir, India. It was first used there to make the cashmere shawls that became famous throughout the world. The warm but lightweight wool was later woven into textiles for coats and sweaters.

Casket Letters, letters and sonnets given in evidence at the inquiries of York and Westminster in 1568 into the murder of Lord DARLEY. They were submitted by the Earl of MORAY, regent of Scotland, who claimed that they were found in a casket of the Earl of BOTHWELL, husband of MARY QUEEN OF SCOTS. They apparently proved the complicity of Mary in the murder, but the originals were lost in 1584.

Caslavska, Vera (1942–), Czechoslovak gymnast. She enraptured millions by winning four Olympic gold medals in 1968. It was the climax of a career in which she won seven Olympic, four world and 11 European titles.

Caslon, William (1692–1766), English printer and typefounder. In 1716 he began work in London as an engraver of guns but soon started his own typefoundry. He developed a distinctive typeface which became popular throughout Europe. Although it lost favour during the 1800s, Caslon's typeface was revived and is still used in book printing.

Caspian Sea, shallow salt lake mostly in the USSR; S edge forms the N border of Iran; the world's largest inland body of water. The water level fluctuates as a result of evaporation and the fluctuating volume of its tributaries. It is fed mainly by the Volga River but also receives the Ural, Emba, Kura and Terek rivers; there is no outlet. The chief USSR ports are Baku, an oil-shipping centre, and ASTRAKHAN. An important trade route for centuries, the Caspian Sea was part of a medieval Mongol-Baltic route for goods from Asia. It still has important fisheries and sealeries. Area: 393,896sq km (152,083sq miles).

Cassandra, in Classical mythology, a Trojan skilled in the art of prophecy, but condemned by APOLLO never to be taken seriously. Her warning that the Greeks would capture Troy went unheeded. She was raped by the Greek Ajax the lesser, carried off by AGAMEMNON, and murdered by CLYTEMNESTRA and Aegisthus.

Cassatt, Mary (1845–1926), US-born painter and printmaker, who lived in Paris, where she was influenced by DEGAS and the IMPRESSIONISTS. Her finest paintings include *The Bath* (1892). She also made many fine DRY POINT and AQUATINT studies of domestic life, and a series of Japanese-influenced colour prints.

Cassava, also called manioc, a TAPIOCA plant native to Brazil. It is a tall woody shrub with small clustered flowers. A valuable cereal substitute is obtained by processing the tuberous roots. Height: up to 2.7m (9ft). Family Euphorbiaceae; species *Manihot utilissima. See also* PE pp.156–157, 186–187.

Cassavetes, John (1929–), US film actor and director. As an actor he appeared in *A Man is Ten Feet Tall* (1957), *The Dirty Dozen* (1967) and *Rosemary's Baby* (1968). His first independent production *Shadows* (1960) greatly influenced other low-budget film makers. Other productions included *Faces* (1968) and *Minnie and Moskowitz* (1971).

Cassel. *See* KASSEL.

Cassia, sweet aromatic spice derived from the bark of a cinnamon plant, *Cinnamomum cassia,* found in Asia. Ground cassia is red-brown in colour and is used to produce drugs, liqueurs and incense. *Cassia* is also the name of a large genus of leguminous plants, from which SENNA and other medicinal substances are obtained.

Cassin, René (1887–), French statesman. He was a professor of international law in Paris and in 1924 joined the French delegation to the League of Nations. In 1946 he became a member, and later chairman, of the United Nations Human Rights Commission and helped to found UNESCO. From 1965 he was president of the Council of Europe. He was awarded the 1968 Nobel Peace Prize.

Cassini, Giovanni Domenico (1625–1712), Italian-born French astronomer. He is chiefly remembered for being the first to detect, in 1675, the dark cleft between Saturn's two outer rings known as Cassini's Division. He also discovered four of Saturn's moons. *See also* SU pp.166, 210, *210.*

Cassino, town in the Lazio region, central Italy, on the River Rapido. Formerly known as San Germano, it was a medieval centre of arts and learning. During WWII it was the scene of fierce fighting in 1944 when the Germans attempted to halt the Allied advance on Rome. They failed and the town and nearby Benedictine abbey of Monte Cassino were destroyed. Today it is an agricultural and commercial centre and manufactures toys. Pop. 25,000.

Cassiodorus, Flavius Magnus Aurelius (*c.*490–*c.*585), Roman writer and statesman. He served under THEODORIC and Athalaric, and founded several monasteries. His major work, a history of the GOTHS, has been lost.

Cassiopeia, northern circumpolar constellation in the Milky Way N of Andromeda and characterized by the W shape of its five brightest stars. In addition to several clusters and variables, Cassiopeia contains two radio sources: Cassiopeia A, the remains of a SUPERNOVA of 1700, and Cassiopeia B, the remnant of Tycho Brahe's supernova of 1572. *See also* SU p.258.

Cassirer, Ernst (1874–1945), German philosopher. Strongly influenced by Immanuel KANT, he is particularly known for his study of cultural values. His works include *The Philosophy of Symbolic Forms* (1923–29), *Language and Myth* (1925), *An Essay of Man* (1944), and *The Myth of the State* (1946).

Cassiterite, translucent black, yellow or white mineral, tin oxide (SnO_2); the major ore of tin. It occurs in PLACER DEPOSITS, chiefly in the Malay peninsula and in PEGMATITES and other intrusive igneous rocks. It occurs as short tetragonal prismatic crystals, or masses and radiating fibres. Hardness 6–7; s.g.7. *See also* PE p.96.

Cassius Longinus, Gaius (*d.* 42 BC), Roman general who led the plot to assassinate Julius CAESAR. He sided with POMPEY during the war against Caesar but was pardoned in 48 BC after Caesar defeated Pompey at Pharsalus (48 BC). After the assassination of Caesar in 44 BC he left for Sicily. In 42 BC he and Marcus BRUTUS fought against Mark ANTONY and Octavian (AUGUSTUS) at Philippi. Cassius, thinking the battle was lost, committed suicide.

Cassivellaunus (1st century BC), British chieftain. He ruled north of the River

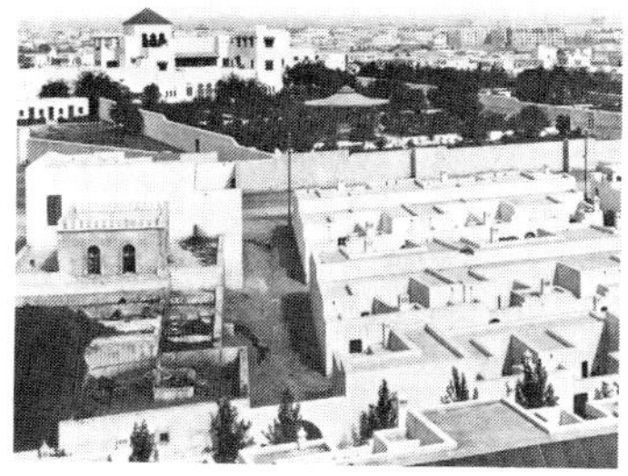

Casablanca; Moorish town and Sultan's palace with the European city in the distance.

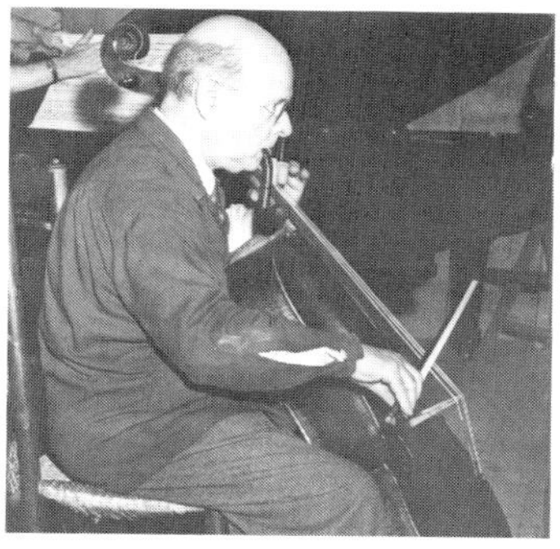

Pablo Casals was one of the great virtuosi of the cello and also a noted conductor.

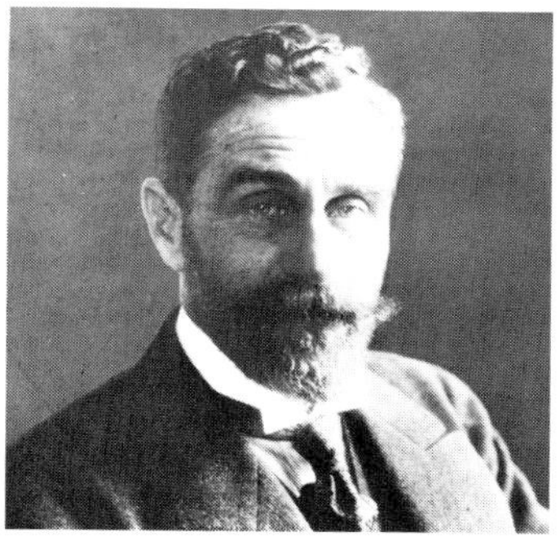

Roger Casement, the Irish patriot, sought German support for Irish independence.

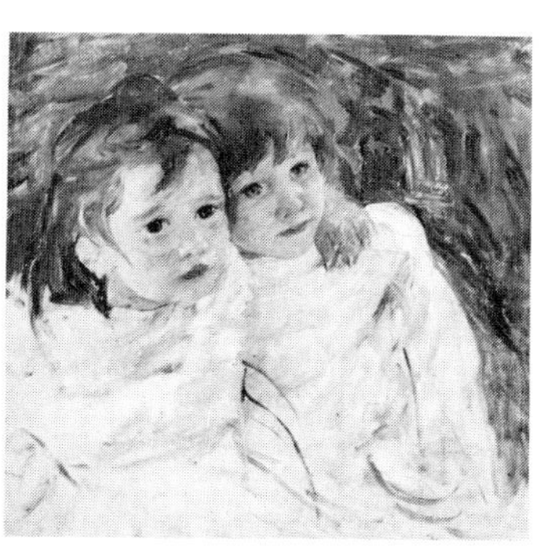

Mary Cassett's paintings of motherhood made her a popular painter.

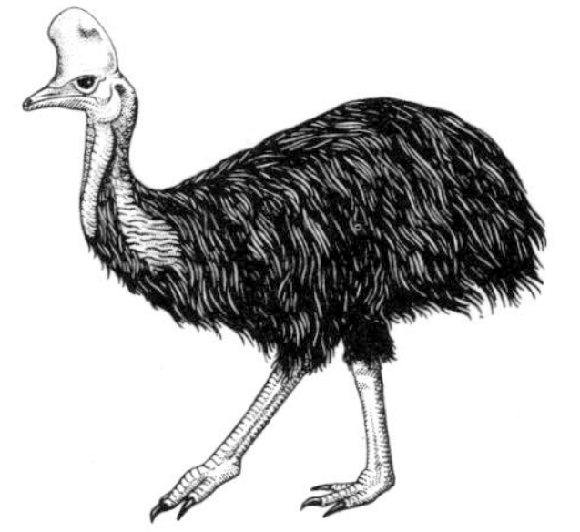

Cassowaries can fatally injure a man with a blow from their powerful sharp claws.

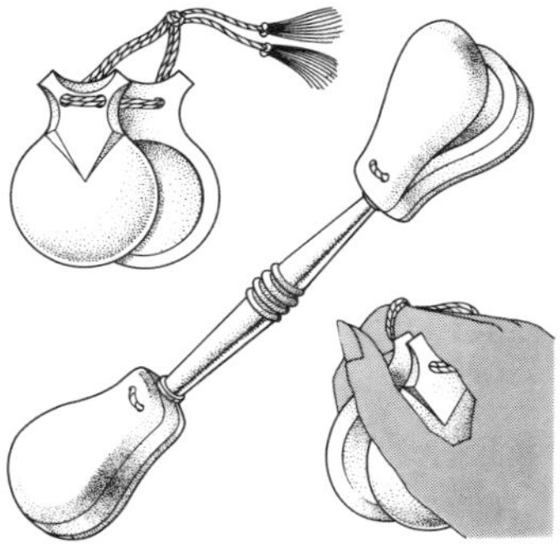

Castanets are named from the Spanish for chestnuts, which they resemble in shape.

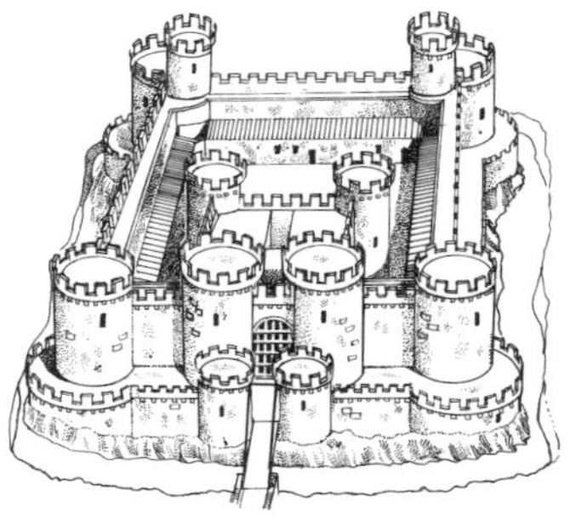

Castles reflect the state of almost constant war that prevailed in feudal Europe.

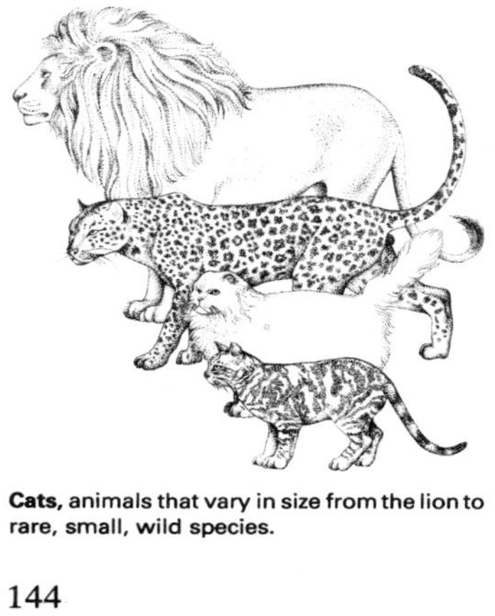

Cats, animals that vary in size from the lion to rare, small, wild species.

Thames and fought Julius CAESAR in the invasion of 54 BC, but was defeated and forced to pay tribute.

Casson, Sir Hugh (1910–), British architect. Director of Architecture (1948–51) at the FESTIVAL OF BRITAIN, he was knighted in 1952. He was Professor of Interior Design at the Royal College of Art from 1953 to 1975.

Casson, Sir Lewis (1875–1969), British actor and manager. In 1908 he joined the Gaiety Theatre, Manchester, and was its director (1911–14). From 1922 he concentrated mainly on the production of plays by George Bernard Shaw and Shakespeare. He continued acting, however, and gave notable performances in *The Linden Tree* (1947) and *Eighty in the Shade* (1959). He often worked with his wife, Dame Sybil THORNDIKE.

Cassowary, powerful flightless bird of rain forests in Australia and Malaysia. It has coarse black plumage, a horny crest on its brightly coloured head, large feet and sharp claws. The male incubates the eggs in a nest on the forest floor. Height: to 1.6m (65in). Family Casuariidae; species *Casuarius casuarius. See also* NW pp.140–141.

Castagno, Andrea del (*c*.1423–57), Florentine painter. He was first influenced by MASACIO, then by DONATELLO and UCELLO. He was noted for his realistic figure drawing, which greatly influenced later Florentines, including LEONARDO da Vinci and MICHELANGELO. Castagno's masterpiece is his *Last Supper,* a fresco of enormous power.

Castanets, percussion instrument consisting of two pairs of hinged hardwood shells, usually held in the hands, which produce clicking sounds. They are used in orchestral music and percussion bands, but principally in Spanish dancing.

Caste, formal, rigid system of social stratification based on factors beyond individual control (eg race, sex, or religious heritage) and sanctioned by tradition. This kind of system is called ascriptive because the individual is born into his or her position and cannot change it. *See also* STRATIFICATION; MS pp.264, 270.

Castel Gandolfo, town on Lake Albano in Roma province, Latium, central Italy. It became a realm of the Holy See in 1608. It is the summer residence of the Pope and the Villa Barberini houses the Vatican observatory. Fishing is the main occupation. Pop. 5,000.

Castelnuovo-Tedesco, Mario (1895–1968), Italian composer who emigrated to the USA in 1939. He composed many works including songs, operas, chamber music and solo piano and guitar music. One of his most popular works is the *Guitar Concerto in D* (1939).

Castelo-Branco, Camilo (1825–90), Portuguese novelist and short story writer. His works are realistically romantic and include the novel *Fatal Love* (1862) and the short stories *Novelas do Minho* (1875–77).

Castiglione, Baldassare (1478–1529), Italian Renaissance diplomat and writer. As a diplomat he served in Rome at the court of URBINO (1507–13) and with the papal court. He subsequently served as papal nuncio to CHARLES V in Spain. He produced a famous work on court etiquette, IL CORTEGIANO (1528). *See also* HC1 p.248.

Castile, region and former kingdom in central Spain, traditionally comprising Old Castile (N) and New Castile (S). The name is said to derive from the many castles built during the Christian reconquest of the area from the MOORS in the 8th century. Old Castile was originally part of the kingdom of LEON and did not become part of Castile proper until 1230. The Castilian kings were responsible for the capture of New Castile from the MOORS at this time. Queen ISABELLA established the union with ARAGON in 1479 and in the 16th century Castile became the most influential power in Spain and the core of the Spanish monarchy. Today the region remains underdeveloped with few traditional industries surviving.

Castilho, António Feliciano de (1800–75), Portuguese poet, who was blind from the age of six. He was initially a ROMANTIC, in poems such as *A Noite do Castelo* (1836) and *Os Ciúmes do Bardo* (1838), but later repudiated Romanticism in the *Revista Universal Lisbonense* (1842).

Casting, metal, forming metal objects by pouring molten metal into moulds of specified shapes and allowing it to solidify. Most castings are made by pouring metal into sand or clay moulds. Specialized processes, such as plastic moulding, composite moulding, CIRE-PERDU (or lost-wax process), and die casting give greater dimensional accuracy, smoother surfaces and finer detail. *See also* MM pp.26, 42.

Cast iron, general term applied to various grades of iron, especially grey iron and pig iron (directly out of a blast furnace). It includes a wide range of iron-carbon-silicon alloys containing from 1.7 to 4.5 per cent carbon with varying amounts of other elements. Grey iron (so-called because its fracture looks greyish) is the most widely used for casting vehicle engines, machinery parts and many other products. *See also* MM pp.*23,* 28–34.

Cast-iron plant. *See* ASPIDISTRA.

Castle, fortified residence of a king or noble in the Middle Ages, often providing a centre of refuge for people living in the surrounding area. Built of wood or masonry, located on a site dominating its environment and often surrounded by a water-filled moat, castles were enclosed by high walls protecting those inside from attack. Turrets were usually found at the angles of the walls and occasionally interspersed along the exterior walls. The walls were built thick enough to withstand bombardment and wide enough at the top to allow the defenders to manoeuvre behind the protection afforded by the parapets that capped them. Inside the walls were the living quarters, the stables, the arsenal and the storage space for the daily provisions. *See also* HC1 p.205.

Castle, The (1926), novel by Franz KAFKA. The central character, K, attempts to take up a job in a strange village where he alone is convinced he has been appointed. The castle, evil and inexplicable, dominates the story by creating uncertainty and fear in this world of unreality.

Castlemaine, Lady. *See* CLEVELAND, DUCHESS OF.

Castlemaine, town in Central Victoria, Australia. It was the site of an early gold mine (1851). Industries: iron, textiles. Pop. 7,000.

Castlereagh, Robert Stewart, 2nd Viscount (1769–1822), British politician. He was Chief Secretary of Ireland (1799–1801) and helped secure the passage of the Act of Union with Britain in 1800. As British War Secretary (1805–06, 1807–09) he vigorously opposed NAPOLEON but resigned after a duel with George CANNING. Castlereagh was a brilliant Foreign Secretary (1812–22), backing WELLINGTON in war and helping to secure long-term peace in Europe at the Congress of Vienna (1814–15). *See also* HC2 pp.82, *83,* 182.

Castletown, urban district and historic capital of the Isle of Man, on Castletown Bay. The old House of Keys, seat of the Manx parliament until 26 Nov. 1874 (when it was removed to Douglas) is in this area. Pop. (1971 prelim.) 2,820.

Castor and Pollux, in Classical mythology, the youthful, athletic and inseparable twin sons of LEDA. They were invoked by sailors seeking favourable winds. ZEUS, father of Pollux, transformed them into the Gemini constellation after Castor, who was mortal, died and Pollux refused to be parted from him.

Castoreum. *See* CASTOR.

Castor oil, viscous yellow oil, sometimes used as a laxative or as an industrial lubricant. It is obtained from the seeds of the CASTOR PLANT.

Castor plant, also called castor bean, plant that in hot countries grows into a tree, but which remains a bushy herb in temperate climates. It belongs to the SPURGE family and bears pods containing castor beans, the source of castor oil. *See also* PE p.*217.*

Castration, removal of the sexual glands from an animal or human being – the testes in a male, the ovaries in a female. In human beings it has been a form of punishment, a way of sexually incapacitating slaves to produce EUNUCHS or artificially creating soprano voices (see CASTRATO) and as a way of stopping the spread of cancerous growths. It can make livestock animals tamer and improve the quality of their meat. In pets it prevents breeding.

Castrato, voice of the soprano register. Produced in adult males by castration during boyhood, it was in vogue in the 17th and 18th centuries. The most famous castrato was FARINELLI. *See* COUNTER TENOR, FALSETTO.

Castries, port and capital of Saint Lucia in the Windward Islands. It was founded in 1650 by the French. It has the Church of the Immaculate Conception. Exports include sugar, bananas and citrus fruits. Pop. 5,000. *See also* MW p.149.

Castro Alves, Antônio de (1847–71), Brazilian poet whose verse, devoted to the issues of slavery and social justice, earned him the title of "the poet of the slaves". He is most famous for *Gonzaga, or the Revolution at Minas* (1875), *Voices of Africa* (1880) and *The Slaves* (1883).

Castro, Fidel (1926–), Cuban revolutionary leader and prime minister (1959–). In 1953 he was sentenced to 15 years' imprisonment after an unsuccessful coup against BATISTA's regime. Two years later he was granted an amnesty and began, in Mexico, his association with Che GUEVARA. In 1959, barely two years after Castro's return to Cuba, his guerrilla forces deposed Batista and he became *de facto* ruler. He collectivized agriculture, dispossessed foreign companies and established close connections with communist countries. In 1961 he declared himself a Marxist-Leninist, aligning his country with the Third World nations. *See also* HC2 pp.*255–256,* 257; MW p.61.

Cat, carnivorous, often solitary, mainly nocturnal mammal of the family Felidae, ranging in size from the rare Siberian tiger to the domestic cat. It has specialized teeth and claws for hunting, a keen sense of smell, acute hearing, highly sensitive vision, and it balances well with its long tail (only the manx cat has no tail at all). Cats walk on their toes and all have fully retractile claws, except for the cheetah which needs greater purchase on the ground to run at high speeds. The lineage of the Felidae is one of the most easily traced to prehistoric ancestors, among them the sabre-toothed cats. One of the first animals to be domesticated by man, cats have appeared frequently in myth and religion. Today there are many domestic breeds, all popular as pets. British and American short-haired breeds include Siamese, Burmese, Abyssinian, Rex and Manx; the Persian varieties are long-haired. Most common domestic cats are a mixture of breeds. Order Carnivora. *See also* NW pp.164–165.

Catabolism (also spelled katabolism), metabolic process in living things. Complex substances are chemically changed into waste products with simpler compositions during the release of energy. It is the opposite of anabolism, in which complex substances are formed from simpler ones and energy is stored. *See also* METABOLISM.

Catacombs, early Christian (and some Jewish) subterranean cemeteries, often used as refuges from persecution and as shrines. The extensive catacombs of Rome are the best-known, but remains of others have been found elsewhere in Europe, N Africa and Syria. Built between the 1st and 5th centuries, those in Rome are a complex of galleries as deep as 8m (25ft) below ground-level with burial niches, vaults and rooms along the sides covered with inscribed tablets.

Catalepsy, abnormal condition in which parts of the body remain in any position in which they are placed. Causes may be organic, psychological or the result of hypnosis.

Catalonia (Cataluña), region in NE Spain extending from the French border to the Mediterranean Sea; it includes Barcelona, Gerona, Lérida and Tarragona provinces. United with Aragón in 1137, it kept its own laws and language. It became an important medieval trading centre, but declined after the union of Castile and Aragón in 1479. During the 20th century it has been a centre for anarchist movements. During the Spanish Civil War Barcelona was a Loyalist capital, but the region fell to Franco in 1939, since when there has been a separatist movement. Products: grain, fruit, olive oil, wool, wine. Area: 31,932sq km (12,329sq miles). Pop. (1970) 5,122,500.

Catalpa, ornamental tree found in North America and the West Indies. It has large heart-shaped leaves, showy white or purple flowers and bean-like fruit pods containing many seeds. Common catalpa (*Catalpa bignonioides*) is also called the Indian bean. Height: up to 18m (60ft). Family Bignoniaceae.

Catalyst, chemical compound that accelerates or inhibits the rate of a chemical reaction without itself being consumed. Many industrial processes rely on catalysts. Inhibitors are commonly antioxidants, often used to prevent degradation of organic compounds, especially in air. Metals or their compounds catalyze by adsorbing gases to their surface, forming intermediates that then readily react to form the desired product while regenerating the original catalytic surface. Development of life forms is impossible without catalysts, since many specific-acting enzymes select and follow only one of a large number of metabolic pathways, acting much faster than nonbiological catalysts. *See also* SU pp.147, 154.

Catamaran, swift, bridged-over, twin-hulled boat, powered by sails or engine, popular in sports. Originally, a raft of Indian and Indonesian waters developed for cargo carrying and for long voyages by Melanesians and Polynesians. The design has great stability and was adopted in the 1870s by western boatbuilders.

Catamaran racing. *See* YACHT RACING.

Catania, port in E Sicily, Italy, at the foot of Mount Etna; capital of Catania province. Ancient Catania was founded by Greeks in 729 BC, and repeatedly invaded. It suffered a devastating volcanic eruption in 1669 and an earthquake in 1693, after which it was rebuilt. It has Greek and Roman ruins, a Norman Cathedral (1091), and the first Sicilian university (1444). Industries: chemicals, cement, textiles. Pop. (1968) 409,000.

Cataplexy, temporary loss of muscular control, without loss of consciousness. It is sometimes confused with CATALEPSY.

Catapult, device for hurling projectiles. Originally a handheld hunting weapon, it had developed into a massive war machine by Roman times. It is now used to launch aircraft from ships. *See also* MM. pp.*166*, 174.

Cataract, opacity in the lens of an eye. It is usually caused by degenerative changes in old age or by a condition such as diabetes. Symptom is a gradual but painless loss of vision. The cataract may be removed by surgery and corrective lenses are sometimes prescribed. *See also* MS p.*49*.

Cataract, in physical geography, term usually applied to that section of a rapidly flowing river where the running water falls suddenly in a sheer drop. When the drop is less steep, the fall is known as a cascade.

Catarrh, imprecise term that often indicates quite unrelated events in the body, such as "bronchial catarrh" and "stomach catarrh". It generally refers to the copious discharge of mucus from mucous membranes, particularly of the nose, following irritation or infection such as the common cold. *See also* MS p.88.

Catarrhini, old name for the Old World MONKEYS, indicating their downward-pointing nostrils, contrasting with the forward-pointing nostrils of the New World monkeys, or PLATYRRHINI. *See also* MS p.20.

Catch 22 (1961), novel by Joseph HELLER. Set in a US airbase during WWII, its farcical humour blackly contrasts with the realism of the fighting, high-lighting the meaninglessness and absurdity of the war.

Catcher in the Rye (1951), novel by J. D. SALINGER. It deals with several days in the life of Holden Caulfield, a teenage boy who is disillusioned by the hypocrisy and "phoniness" of the adult world.

Catchfly, another name for several species of CAMPION found throughout Europe and W Asia; especially the red catchfly (*Lychnis viscaria*). It has red flowers and a sticky hairy stem which is said to protect the plant against ants and other insects. Family Caryophyllaceae; genus *Silene*.

Catchpole, Kenneth William (1939–), Australian rugby union footballer. He played more than 20 games for the Wallabies in the 1960s and was regarded as one of the world's best half-backs. He had great agility and gave his back line speedy service from scrums and lineouts.

Catechism, a manual of instruction in Church teachings intended for use by candidates in preparation of membership of a Church or for instruction of baptized members. It is frequently in the form of questions and answers.

Catechol, organic chemical compound, dihydroxbenzene, $C_6H_4(OH)_2$. It forms clear aqueous solutions which soon turn brown because, under the influence of light, they react strongly with oxygen. For these reasons catechol is used to protect stored materials against oxidation, and in photographic developers. It also has uses in making dyes. *See also* SU p.*142*.

Catechu, extract of any of several acacia plants, particularly *Acacia catechu* from Malaysia. It is a brown or blackish brittle substance containing tannins, used in medicine to combat diarrhoea and in dyeing and tanning.

Caterpillar, work-like larva of a butterfly or moth; it has a segmented body, short antennae, simple eyes, three pairs of true legs and chewing mouthparts. Nearly all caterpillars feed voraciously on plants and thus constitute a serious danger to crops; they sometimes need to be controlled. *See also* NW p.112, *112*; PE pp.172–173.

Caterpillar tractor. *See* TRACTORS.

Catesby, Robert (1573–1605), English Roman Catholic conspirator. He took part in ESSEX's rebellion against ELIZABETH I (1601) and in the RYE HOUSE PLOT (1603). He was the chief organizer of the GUNPOWDER PLOT (1605) and was killed while resisting arrest.

Catfish, any member of a large family of slow-swimming scaleless fish found in tropical and subtropical waters; it has fleshy "whiskers" on the upper jaw, sometimes with venomous spines. Most species live in fresh water and some may be farmed. Length: up to 3.3m (10ft). Order Siluriformes. *See also* NW pp.*73*, *125*, *130–131*; PE pp.242–243.

Cathars. *See* ALBIGENSES.

Catharsis, in psychology, expression of repressed feelings during the treatment of neurotic disorders. Sigmund FREUD and Josef BREUER pioneered the "Cathartic Method", in which hypnotized patients were encouraged to remember and tell about repressed experiences. Freud later abandoned hypnosis, but retained the basic form of psychoanalytic treatment.

Cathay, medieval and poetic name for China, taken to Europe by Marco POLO's writings and early missionaries. It is probably derived from the Khitai, a mongolian people of S Manchuria. It generally refers to China N of the Yangtze River.

Cathedral (from Greek *kathedra*, a throne or seat), the main church of a bishop's province, the church containing his throne. The plan of a cathedral, as with most churches, usually follows the shape of a cross. The longest arm of the cross is the nave, the two lateral arms form the left and right transepts, and the top arm of the cross (usually the eastern arm) contains the choir and terminates in a circular or polygonal recess known as an apse. Many of the greatest cathedrals date from the Middle Ages and the ROMANESQUE and GOTHIC periods in architecture. Some of the finest English examples, such as Canterbury, Durham, Ely, Lincoln, Peterborough and York, combine Romanesque and Gothic features. Salisbury is wholly Gothic, while the BAROQUE St Paul's London, replaced a NORMAN building. The greatest French Gothic cathedrals include those at Amiens, Bourges, Chartres, Reims, Strasbourg and Notre Dame, Paris. Beauvais, with its choir rising 48m (157ft) is the highest of all cathedrals. Italian cathedrals, magnificent in materials and workmanship, include Florence, Milan, Pisa and Sienna. St Mark's, Venice, is a magnificent BYZANTINE example. Spanish cathedrals often combine Romanesque, French, German and Moorish features. Barcelona, Burgos, Córdoba and Toledo are notable examples. Seville Cathedral is the largest medieval church in Europe. In Germany, Cologne, Freiburg, Mainz and Speyer are of particular interest. In Latin America, cathedrals are often of Portuguese or Spanish RENAISSANCE and BAROQUE origin. The Episcopal Cathedral of St John the Divine in New York is the world's largest Gothic cathedral.

Catherine I (1684–1727), Empress of Russia (1725–27). She was born a peasant but became the mistress of Prince Menshikov and later of Peter I whom she married in 1712. She was crowned in 1724 and during her reign the Supreme Privy Council was established.

Catherine II, the Great (1729–96), Empress of Russia (1762–96), *b.* Germany. She married Peter III in 1745 and in 1762 organized a rebellion ending in his assassination. She began as an "enlightened autocrat", with ambitious plans for reform, but few were carried out. She became rigidly conservative after the Pugachev peasant revolt (1773–74) and FRENCH REVOLUTION, and gave the nobility absolute power over the peasants (1785). She increased Russia's territory and international prestige but was a notorious libertine. *See also* HC1 pp.322–323.

Catherine de' Medici (1519–89), Queen of France, wife of HENRY II, daughter of Lorenzo de' MEDICI. She exerted considerable influence over her sons, CHARLES IX and HENRY III. Her tolerance of the Protestant Huguenots gave way in the 1560s to dependence on the Roman Catholic GUISE party, whose growing power she failed to control. *See also* HC1 p.*272*.

Catherine of Aragon (1485–1536), Spanish-born first queen of HENRY VIII of England, whom she married in 1509. Their only living child was a daughter (later MARY I). Henry used her former marriage to his brother Arthur as an excuse to end the marriage, and it was annulled in 1533. *See also* HC1 p.270.

Catherine of Braganza (1638–1705), Queen of England, wife of CHARLES II. She was the daughter of the King of Portugal, and married Charles in 1662. England was given Tangier and BOMBAY as part of her dowry. Her Catholic faith made her unpopular and she returned to Portugal in 1692.

Catherine of Siena, Saint (1347–80), Italian Catholic nun. She joined the Third Order of St DOMINIC at the age of 16 and for three years devoted herself to contemplation, the service of the sick and the conversion of sinners. In 1376 she went to AVIGNON to persuade Pope GREGORY XI to return to Rome. She was canonized in 1461 and declared a Doctor of the Church in 1970. Feast: 29 (formerly 30) April.

Catherine of Valois (1401–37), French queen, daughter of CHARLES VI. In 1420 she became Queen of England upon her marriage to HENRY V. Their son, the future Henry VI, was born in 1421. In 1422 Henry V died, and she later married Owen Tudor. Their son Edmund, Duke of Richmond, was the father of HENRY VII, the first TUDOR king of England.

Catheter, long, slim, hollow surgical instrument for insertion into narrow passages of the body, including the URETHRA, where it is employed for such purposes as obtaining a specimen (BIOPSY) from the bladder, and to wash it out.

Cathode, negative electrode of an electrolytic cell or ELECTRON TUBE. It is the electrode from which electrons enter a system. *See* ELECTROLYSIS; SU p.148.

Cathode rays, radiation emitted by the cathode of a thermionic electron tube containing a gas at low pressure. The rays were identified in 1897 by J. J. THOMSON as streams of charged elementary particles having extremely low mass, later called electrons. Some electrons are emitted because the cathode is heated, but most because of collisions between the cathode positive ions formed in the tube. *See also*

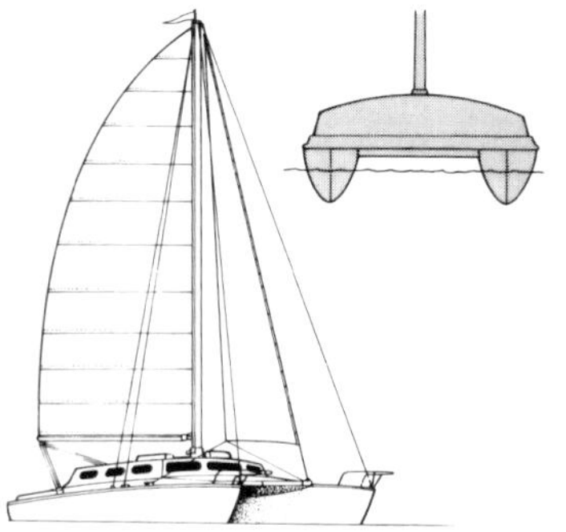

Catamarans, twin-hulled boats, are often made with a third hull – the *trimaran*.

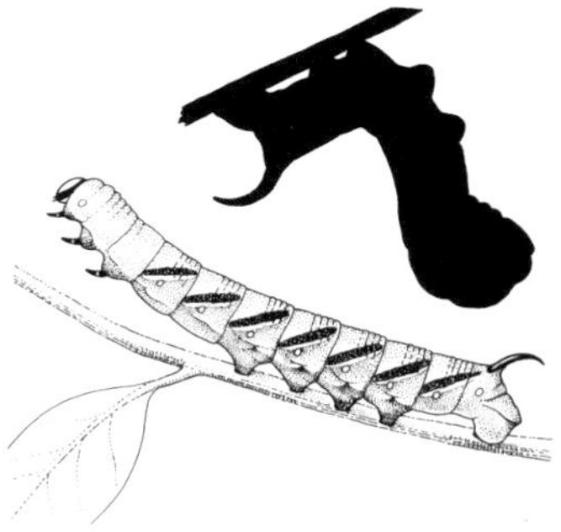

Caterpillars are the second stage in the life cycle of the moth and the butterfly.

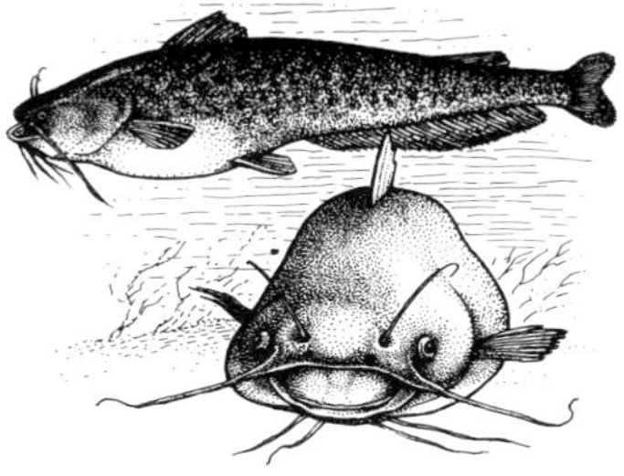

Catfish, considered a delicacy by some, include species that can "walk" on land.

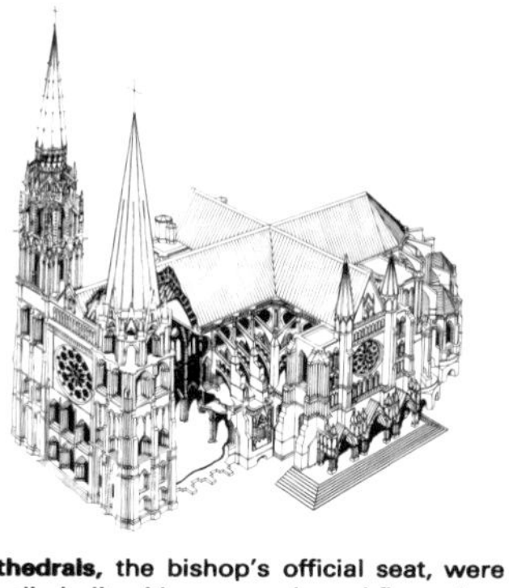

Cathedrals, the bishop's official seat, were usually built with a cross-shaped floor plan.

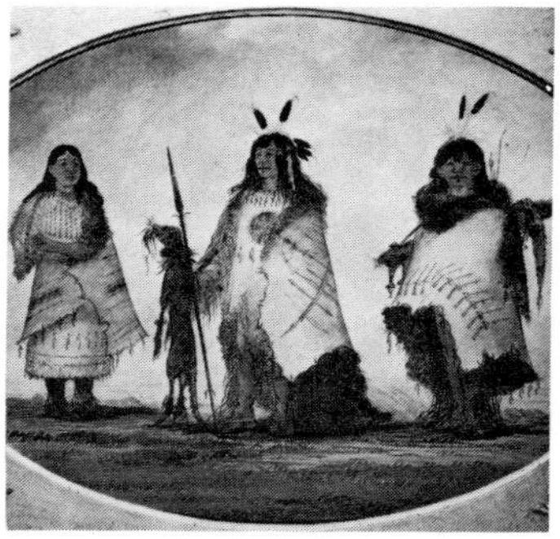

George Catlin's books and paintings provide detailed knowledge of American Indians.

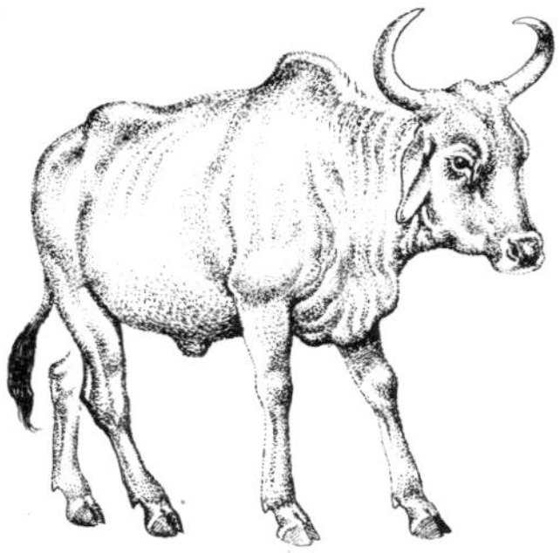

Cattle which need to thrive in hot regions are often bred with the Brahman, native of India.

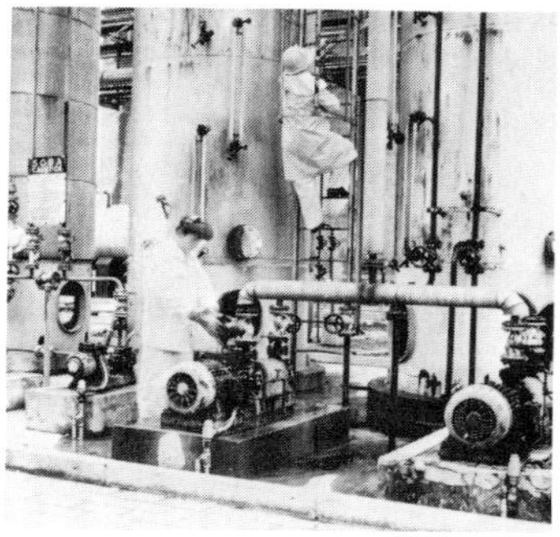

Caustic soda; plant for the large-scale commercial production of this valuable alkali.

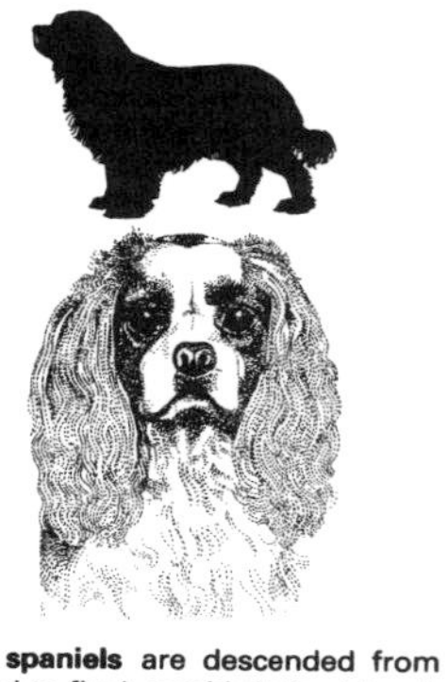

Cavalier spaniels are descended from the dogs used to flush out birds for falconing.

CATHODE-RAY TUBE; SU pp.62–63, 114.

Cathode ray tube, evacuated electron tube used for television picture tubes, oscilloscopes and display screens in radar sets and computers. An electron gun shoots a beam of electrons, focused by a grid. The electrons strike a fluorescent screen and produce a spot of light. In a television tube, an electrostatic or magnetic field deflects the beam so that it scans a number of lines on the screen, controlled by the incoming picture signals. *See also* MM pp.108–109, 230–231, 234, 237.

Catholic Apostolic Church (Irvingites), Christian religious body which originated in Britain in the 1830s. It owed its origin partly to the teaching of the Scottish minister Edward IRVING (1792–1834) and partly to a revivalist circle which had gathered around Henry Drummond (1786–1860) in London. The members of the group believed in the imminent SECOND COMING of Christ, in preparation of which they re-established the primitive offices of the Church: those of apostles, prophets, evangelists, pastors and teachers. They no longer have much influence in Britain but still command a number of adherents in the USA and in Germany.

Catholic Church, in Christian usage, a term with several connotations: (1) the Universal Church, as distinct from local churches; (2) the Church holding "orthodox" doctrines, defined by St VINCENT OF LÉRINS as doctrines which have been held "everywhere, always, and by all" – in this sense the term is used to distinguish the Church from heretical bodies; (3) the undivided Church before the GREAT SCHISM of East and West in 1054, after which the Western Church called itself "Catholic", the Eastern Church preferring the term "Orthodox" to describe itself; (4) since the REFORMATION the term has usually been used to denote the ROMAN CATHOLIC CHURCH, although the ANGLICAN COMMUNION and the OLD CATHOLIC CHURCHES use it to cover themselves as well as the Roman Catholic Church and ORTHODOX CHURCHES, these being the branches of Christendom possessing the historic episcopate (*see* APOSTOLIC SUCCESSION).

Catholic Emancipation, Act of (1829), measure by which the statutes barring Roman Catholics in Britain from holding civil office or sitting in Parliament were repealed. The concession was wrung from the Duke of WELLINGTON's government by a mass campaign of the Irish peasantry led by Daniel O'CONNELL and the Catholic Association. Catholics remained barred from holding commissions in the services. The Act's passing split the TORY Party and led to the fall of Britain's last Tory government. *See also* HC2 pp.162–163.

Catiline, or Catilina, Lucius Sergius (*c.* 108–62 BC), Roman political figure. He was made praetor in 68 BC and governor of Africa in 67 BC. In 63 BC, in an attempt to obtain the consulship, he conspired against CICERO, who accused him in the Senate. Catiline escaped but died in battle at Pistoia, in Tuscany.

Catlin, George (1796–1872), US painter, whose pictures of Indian life are valuable both to art and to history. His work, painted in the 1830s, shows 45 different tribal groups.

Catmint, also called catnip, an aromatic herb of the mint family Labiatae. It was introduced from Europe to the USA where it now grows wild. Cats are attracted and excited by the aroma of this plant. Height: up to 91cm (36in). Species *Nepeta cataria.*

Cat on a Hot Tin Roof (1955), drama by Tennessee WILLIAMS. A Mississippi Delta family is brought together to celebrate Big Daddy's 65th birthday and vie for possession of his plantation on his death. It won Williams his second Pulitzer Prize and was made into a successful film (1958).

Cato the Elder, Marcus Porcius (234–149 BC), Roman statesman, orator and writer. He was an officer in the Second PUNIC WAR. From 204 BC he held many important posts in Rome. In 184 he was appointed censor (magistrate) and worked to restore the old ideals of Rome – courage, honesty and simple living. He urged the destruction of Carthage and lived to see the Third Punic War begin. His *De Agricultura* (*c.* 160 BC), is the earliest fully extant Latin literary work. But only fragments of his *Origines* remain. *See also* HC1 p.112.

Cato the Younger, Marcus Porcius Cato Uticensis (95–46 BC), Roman patriot; great-grandson of CATO THE ELDER. He supported republican government and his opposition to Julius CAESAR led to the foundation of the first triumvirate. He became military tribune of Macedonia in 67 and quaestor in 65; he was made tribune in 62 and praetor in 54. He favoured POMPEY against Caesar in 49 and, after Pompey's defeat, committed suicide.

Cats, Jacob (1577–1660), Dutch poet, also known as Father Cats. He was a successful lawyer and diplomat but is best known for his emblem books – illustrated moralistic poems based on Biblical and classical sources.

Catskill Mountains, plateau of the Appalachian system in SE New York State, USA, on the W bank of the Hudson River. The highest peak is Slide Mountain, 1,282m (4,204ft). It is an area of forests and lakes, and is a popular resort area for the New York City metropolitan area.

Cattle, large ruminant mammals of the family Bovidae, including all the varieties of modern domestic cattle (*Bos taurus*), the Brahman (*Bos indicus*) and crosses of these two species. The family also includes the wild or domesticated YAK, the wild GAUR, the wild BANTENG and the KOUPREY. A number of different terms are used to indicate the sex and age of domestic cattle. The male is born as a bull calf and becomes a bull if left intact; if it is castrated it becomes a steer, also called a bullock or an ox if used as a draught animal. The female is a heifer calf, growing to become a heifer and, after calving, a cow. Horns, sometimes appearing only on the male, are permanent, hollow and unbranched. Domestic cattle are raised for meat, milk and other dairy products. Leather, glue, gelatin and fertilizers are made from the carcasses. Oxen are still used as work animals. *See also* NW pp.162–163, 196; PE pp.224–227, 232–233.

Catullus, Gaius Valerius (*c.* 84–*c.* 54 BC), Roman lyric poet. He is best known for his short love lyrics, the most famous of which refer to Lesbia, depicting the Roman woman, Clodia, with whom Catullus was in love. His longer works are the poems *Attis* and *The Marriage of Peleus and Thetis. See also* HC1 pp.112, *112.*

Catuvellauni, BELGIC tribe of ancient Britain, led by King CASSIVELLAUNUS. They originally lived just N of the River Thames, with headquarters at Wheathampstead, but after being defeated by the Romans at the River Stour in 55 BC, they expanded to the NW and moved their capital to VERULAMIUM (St Albans). They were an agricultural people.

Caucasian, one of the major human racial groupings. Physical characteristics include light skin; narrow, high-bridged noses; hair varying between straight and curly; heavy body hair and a high incidence of the Rh-negative blood type. Since AD 1500, Caucasoids have spread from their European, Near Eastern and North African homelands, displacing aboriginal populations in many parts of the world. *See also* MS p.32.

Caucasian Chalk Circle, The, play by Bertolt BRECHT with music by P. Dessau. Written in 1943–44, it was first performed in Nourse Little Theatre, Northfield, USA, in 1948. The German premiere was in Berlin in 1954. It is partly based on the 13th century parable *The Chalk Circle* by Li Hsing Tao.

Caucasus (Bol'šoj Kavkaz), mountain system and region in SE European USSR, extending from the mouth of the Kuban River on the Black Sea SE to the Apscheron Peninsula on the Caspian Sea. The system includes two major regions, the N Caucasia (steppes) and Transcaucasia, and it forms a natural barrier between Asia and Europe. There are deposits of oil, iron and manganese, and cotton, fruit and cereal crops are grown. The highest peak is Mt Elbrus, 5,637m (18,493ft). Length: 1,210km (750 miles).

Cauchy, Augustin-Louis, Baron (1789–1857), French mathematician noted for his work on the theory of substitution groups. He was a member of the Académie des Sciences and in 1816 won the Grand Prix of the Institut de France for a paper that has become a classic in HYDRODYNAMICS.

Caucus, private meeting of members of a political party to discuss issues, tactics and inform the leadership of rank-and-file feeling. In parliamentary democracies the term refers to the party's members in Parliament.

Caudillo, type of political leader prevalent in Latin America during the 19th century (Spanish, *chief*). A civilian who rode on horseback, he was supported by a paramilitary force. The aim of the caudillo band was to gain wealth; the tactic usually violence. Some caudillos dominated only small area; others an entire nation.

Caulfield, Patrick (1936–), British painter, whose work has been influenced by US painters such as Roy LICHTENSTEIN and by the art and architecture of the 1930s. He often uses popular illustrations and images, which he treats in a PAINTERLY – rather than a literary – manner.

Caulfield, municipality in S Victoria, SE Australia. It is a suburb of Melbourne, situated 10km (6 miles) SE of the main city, and has given its name to one of the highlights of the Australian horse-racing calendar, the Caulfield cup. Pop. (1976) 83,750.

Cauliflower, form of CABBAGE with a short thick stem, large lobed leaves and edible white or purplish flower clusters that form tightly compressed heads. Family Brassicaceae; species *Brassica oleracea. See also* PE pp.188–189.

Causalgia, sensation of burning pain, which may be real or imagined, usually felt in the palms of the hands or the soles of the feet. The causalgia syndrome is usually seen after nerve damage and is associated with changes in the vasomotor system and in the skin of the affected parts.

Caustic soda, sodium hydroxide (NaOH), a strong ALKALI prepared industrially by the electrolysis of brine (salt solution). It is used in many industries on a large scale, eg in soap-making to saponify fats and in bauxite processing in the manufacture of ALUMINIUM. Petroleum refining, plastics manufacture and dye-making also use caustic soda. It is a white solid that burns the skin, with a slippery feel because it absorbs moisture from the air. It also absorbs atmospheric carbon dioxide, so forming a crust of sodium carbonate. *See also* MM p.240.

Cavafy, Constantine (1863–1933), Egyptian-born Greek poet, real name Konstantínos Pétrou Kaváfis. Most of his poetry was written after his 40th year; it expressed his sceptical opposition to traditional values such as Christianity.

Cavalcanti, Guido (*c.* 1255–1300), Italian lyric poet. He was a personal friend of DANTE Alighieri and is mentioned in the *Inferno* and in the dedication of the *Vita Nuova.* Although he was a philosopher and treated love as an impersonal principle, he was nevertheless often personal and expressive in his poetry. His most famous poem is *Donna mi Prega.*

Cavalier (from the French *chevalier,* meaning *horseman*), name adopted by the Royalists during the English Civil War of the 1640s (in opposition to the Parliamentarian ROUNDHEADS). The court party retained the name after the restoration of the Stuart monarchy in 1660, whence the name CAVALIER PARLIAMENT (1661–79). By the end of the 17th century the name for the court party had become TORY. *See also* HC1 288–289.

Cavalier King Charles spaniel, small hunting dog descended from the toy spaniel that was popular during the reign of Charles II; it has a flat head with a short tapered muzzle, wide-set ears and eyes and a square deep-chested body. The coat is long and silky and is black and tan or solid red. Height: 30.5 cm (12in) (at the shoulder); weight: 4.5–8kg (10–18lb).

Cavalier Parliament, (1661–79), so-called for its fervent royalism when it was first called to create the institutions of the Restoration monarchy. The longer it sat, the more critical its members became of CHARLES II. The king eventually dissolved it in Feb. 1679. *See also* HC1 pp.*289*, 292, *292*.

Cavalleria Rusticana (1890), one-act opera by Pietro MASCAGNI, Italian libretto based on Giovanni Verga's play. Santuzza (soprano), rejected by Turiddu (tenor), tells Alfio (baritone) that his wife Lola (mezzo-soprano) is Turiddu's lover. Alfio and Turiddu duel and Turiddu is killed.

Cavalli, Francesco (1602–76), Italian composer. Successively chorister, organist and choirmaster at St Mark's, Venice, he became highly esteemed, especially for his more than 40 operas, which had rare verve and brilliance.

Cavallini, Pietro (*c.* 1250–*c.* 1330), Italian painter whose work reflects the movement away from the flat Byzantine style and into the three-dimensional and naturalistic.

Cavalry, mounted troops. It was used by most ancient civilizations from the time of the Egyptians; the first use of cavalry in Europe dates from the invasions of the Huns, Magyars and Mongols. The last prominent use of cavalry occurred in the AMERICAN CIVIL WAR.

Cavan, county in N Republic of Ireland, drained by the Erne and Annalee rivers. It is a hilly and infertile area with many bogs and lakes. Pastoral agriculture is the main occupation. Cavan is the county town. Area: 1,890sq km (730sq miles). Pop. (1971) 52,700.

Cave, Edward (1691–1754), English printer and publisher who produced the first modern English magazine. He wrote and published *The Gentleman's Magazine* (1731–1907), a collection of news and political essays. One of his contributors was Samuel JOHNSON.

Cave, natural underground cavity. There are several kinds of cave, including coastal caves, formed by wave erosion, ice caves, formed in glaciers, and lava caves. By far the largest caves are, however, formed in carbonate rocks such as limestone. Such rocks are impervious but dissolve in underground streams or ground water formed by rain. *See also* PE pp.110–111, *117*, 122–123.

Caveat Emptor, legal term meaning "let the buyer beware". When a customer purchases goods he should examine them before agreeing to buy, otherwise he does so at his own risk unless the item is covered by warranty, guarantee or a legal requirement (such as the Sale of Goods Act in Britain).

Cave fish. *See* BLIND FISH.

Cavell, Edith (1865–1915), British nurse. She established modern nursing in Belgium but was arrested by the Germans and executed by a firing squad for aiding and sheltering Allied soldiers during WWI.

Cavendish, Lord Frederick Charles (1836–82), British Liberal politician. He was made chief secretary for Ireland in 1882, but the day after arriving in Dublin on 5 May 1882, was assassinated by Irish nationalists in Phoenix Park.

Cavendish, Henry (1731–1810), British physicist and chemist. He discovered hydrogen and the composition of water, determined the composition of air, and estimated the earth's mass and density by a method now known as the Cavendish experiment. He also discovered nitric acid, the specific gravity of carbon dioxide and hydrogen, and stated the inverse square law for the interaction of charged particles. The Cavendish Laboratory at CAMBRIDGE UNIVERSITY is named after him. *See also* SU pp.72, *72*.

Cavendish, Thomas (1560–92), English navigator. In 1585 he took part in Sir Richard GRENVILLE's expedition to Virginia, North America. In 1586 he sailed from Plymouth on a voyage around the world. He crossed from W Africa to South America and continued via the Philippines, East Indies and the Cape of Good Hope, returning to England in 1588. *See also* HC1 p.279.

Caviare, the roe of a sturgeon which, when salted and seasoned, is considered to be a great delicacy. The roe is extracted from the fish before it can spawn. *See also* NW pp.244.

Cavour, Camillo Benso, Conte di (1810–61), Piedmontese statesman and nationalist who was instrumental in uniting Italy under Savoy rule. From 1852 he was prime minister under VICTOR EMMANUEL II. From 1856 he engineered Italian liberation from Austria with French aid, then expelled the French with the help of Guiseppe GARIBALDI, and finally neutralised Garibaldi's influence. This led to the formation of the kingdom of Italy in 1861. *See also* HC2 pp.110–111.

Cavy, also called wild guinea-pig, South American rodent from which domestic guinea-pigs are descended; it is a small dark plant-eater which emerges at dawn or dusk to feed. Cavies live in burrows and often form large colonies for protection. Family Caviidae; species *Cavia aperea*. *See also* NW pp.203, *203*.

Cawdor, village in Highlands Region, NE Scotland. Its castle is the reputed scene of Prince Macbeth's murder of King Duncan in 1040. Pop. (1961) 849.

Cawley, Evonne (née Goolagong), (1951–), Australian tennis player. She won the French and British (1971) and Australian (1974 and 1975) women's singles championships. She was the first Australian Aborigine to represent Australia in tennis.

Cawnpore. *See* KĀNPUR.

Cawthron Institute, in Nelson, New Zealand, is a leading centre for research into crops, insect pests and soils.

Caxton, William (*c.* 1422–91), the first English printer. Following a period in Cologne (1470–72), where he learned printing, he set up his own printing press in 1476 at Westminster. He published more than 100 items, many of them his own translations from French, Latin and Dutch. His books, carefully edited, are fine examples of superb craftsmanship. *See also* HC1 p.*242*.

Cayapa, Chibcha language tribe of about 2,000 South American Indians in the coastal lowlands of Manabi province, Ecuador. Along with the Colorado, they are among the last few surviving aboriginal groups in Ecuador.

Cayenne, capital city of French Guiana, NW South America, on an island in the Cayenne River. It was founded by the French in 1643. Its Pasteur Institute (1940) specializes in the study of tropical diseases. Timber, rum and gold are exported. Pop. (1967) 19,700. *See also* MW p.81.

Cayenne pepper, hot spicy condiment made from the dried fruits of the sweet pepper plant, a variety of *Capsicum annuum*, native to Mexico and Central America. The plant may be successfully grown in greenhouses in more moderate climates. *See also* PE pp.188, *189*.

Cayley, Arthur (1821–95), British mathematician, famous for founding the British school of pure mathematics. He held the Sadlerian chair of pure mathematics at Cambridge University and published many papers on the subject, including the theory of matrices and the theory of invariants.

Cayley, Sir George (1773–1857), British inventor who founded the science of aerodynamics. He built the first glider to carry a man successfully and developed the basic form of the early aeroplane. He also invented a caterpillar tractor and founded London's Regent Polytechnic.

Cayman. *See* CAIMAN.

Cayman Islands, British islands in the West Indies belonging to the Greater Antilles group of islands, approx. 325km (200 miles) NW of Jamaica, in the Caribbean Sea; includes Grand Cayman, Little Cayman and Cayman Brac. The islands were discovered by COLUMBUS in 1503 and colonized *c.* 1734. The capital is Georgetown on Grand Cayman. Industries: tourism, turtle and shark fishing, timber, coconuts, shipbuilding. Area: 200sq km (125sq miles). Pop. (1974) 11,363.

CBI, Confederation of British Industry, an organization founded in Aug. 1965 to promote the prosperity and interests of British industry. It is financed by subscription, and more than 1,400 employers' associations, 85 national associations and 10,000 companies are affiliated to it. The CBI advises and negotiates directly with the Government and the TUC.

CBS (Columbia Broadcasting System), US communications corporation. It operates the largest broadcasting network in the USA. CBS and its subsidiaries make records, musical instruments and toys, produce educational films, and publish books and magazines.

Ceausescu, Nicolae (1918–), Romanian politician. He became a member of the politburo (1955), general secretary of the Romanian Communist Party (1965) and head of state (1967). He has aimed at fostering Romanian nationalism, achieving greater independence from the USSR and encouraging trade with the West.

Cebu, province in central Philippines, made up of the Visayan group of islands including Cebu, Camotes, Bantayan and other smaller ones. Cebu is by far the largest island – 224km (139 miles) in length and up to 32km (20 miles) wide. A mountain range extends N-S the length of the island. The island was discovered in 1521 by Ferdinand MAGELLAN, and is the oldest Spanish settlement in the Philippines (1565). The capital is the city of Cebu, which is an important port and trading centre for the islands. Products: rice, corn, coconuts, tobacco, coal. Area (island): 4,421sq km (1,707sq miles). Pop. (1970) 1,632,642.

Cebus. *See* CAPUCHIN MONKEY.

Cecil, Edgar Algernon Robert, 1st Viscount Cecil of Chelwood (1864–1958), British statesman. He was a Conservative member of Parliament (1906–23) and held the posts of under-secretary in 1915, minister of blockade in 1916 and assistant secretary of state in 1918. He helped draft the LEAGUE OF NATIONS covenant and was president of the League of Nations union (1923–45). He won the 1937 Nobel Peace Prize. His works include *The Way of Peace* (1928) and *A Real Peace* (1941).

Cecil, Robert, 1st Earl of Salisbury (1563–1612), English statesman, son of BURGHLEY. He became secretary of state to ELIZABETH I on his father's retirement in 1596, and after negotiating the accession of JAMES I, served the new king as well. He was known for his financial skill, and became lord treasurer in 1608. He built Hatfield House in Hertfordshire. *See also* HC1 pp.280, *281*, 286.

Cecilia, Saint, (2nd or 3rd century), patroness of music. According to legend she converted her pagan husband, Valerian, and his brother, Tiburtius, to Christianity. One of the most venerated martyrs in the early Roman Church, she is buried in the church named after her in Trastevere in Rome. Feast: 22 Nov.

Cecrops, in Greek mythology, the founder of Athens. He had a man's body and a snake's tail, and became the first king of ATTICA. Cecrops brought 12 Greek cities under his control, made ATHENA the patron deity, and acknowledged ZEUS as the supreme god.

Cedar, evergreen tree native to the Mediterranean and Asia, but found in warm temperate regions throughout the world; it has clustered needle-like leaves, long cones and fragrant, durable wood. It is a popular ornamental tree. Height: 30–55m (98–180ft). Family Pinaceae; genus *Cedrus*.

Celadon, semi-transparent bluish or greyish-green glazes used in Chinese and Korean porcelain. Celadon wares were first produced in Chekiang province, China, during the Sung dynasty (10th–13th centuries). The most popular celadons are the Sung Lung-ch'üan wares, which continued to be made into the Ming dynasty (1368–1644).

Celan, Paul (1920–70), German-Jewish poet, one of the leading post-war poets. He was influenced by EXPRESSIONISM and SURREALISM. His poetry includes *Poppy and Memory* (1952) and *From Step to Step* (1955).

Celandine, herb common to Britain and the USA; it has serrated leaves, yellow flowers and narrow seed pods. Its yellow sap was once thought to have the power to cure warts. Family Papaveraceae; species *Chelidonium majus*.

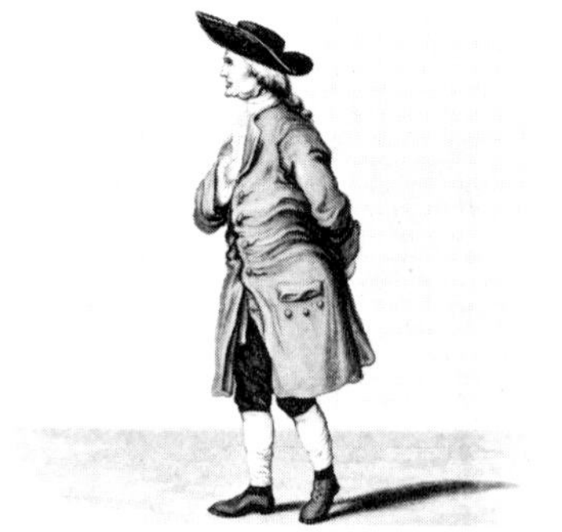

Henry Cavendish, who discovered water to be a mixture of hydrogen and oxygen (H_2O).

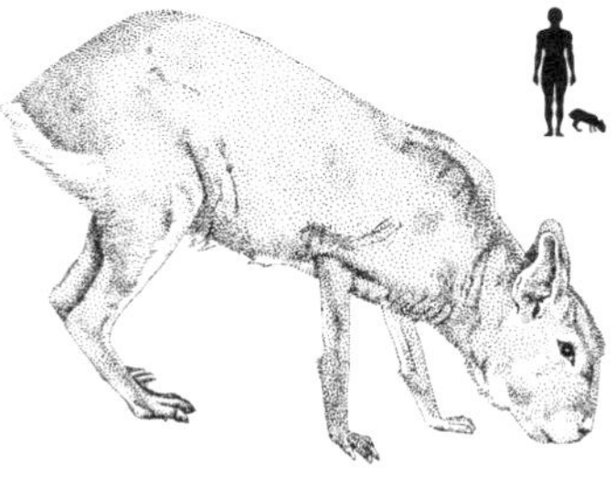

Cavies are South American rodents, the best known of which are the guinea-pigs.

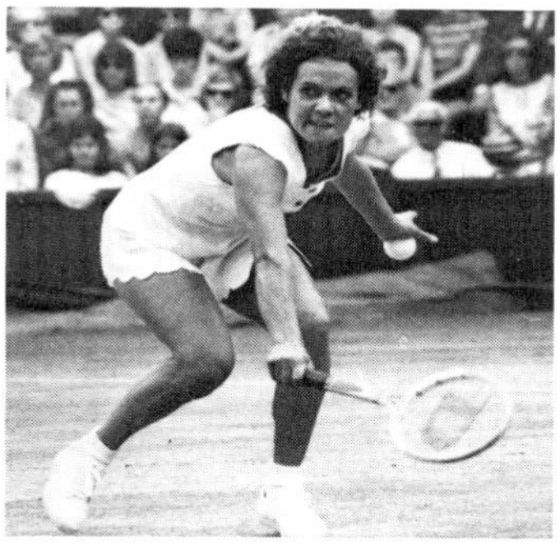

Evonne Cawley, Wimbledon champion and first Aborigine to represent Australia.

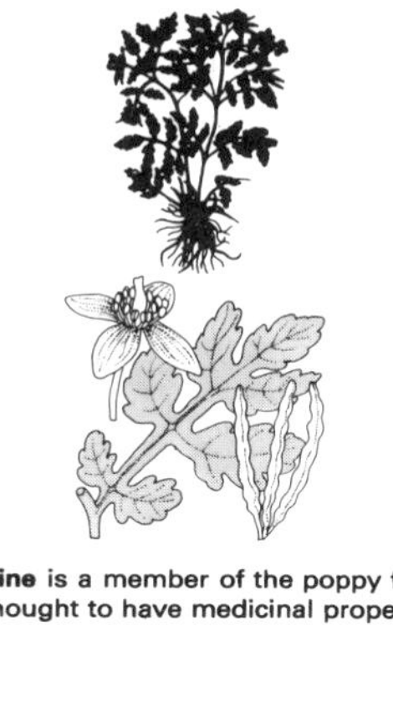

Celandine is a member of the poppy family once thought to have medicinal properties.

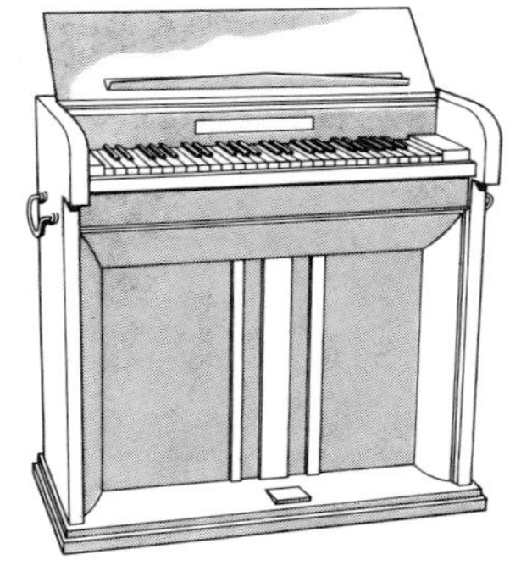

Celesta; the small piano-like instrument that produces tinkling notes from steel bars.

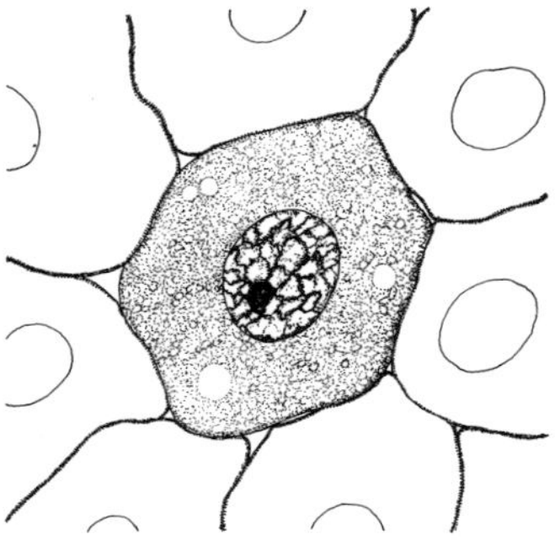

Cells, the basic units of all living things, grow, reproduce and eventually die.

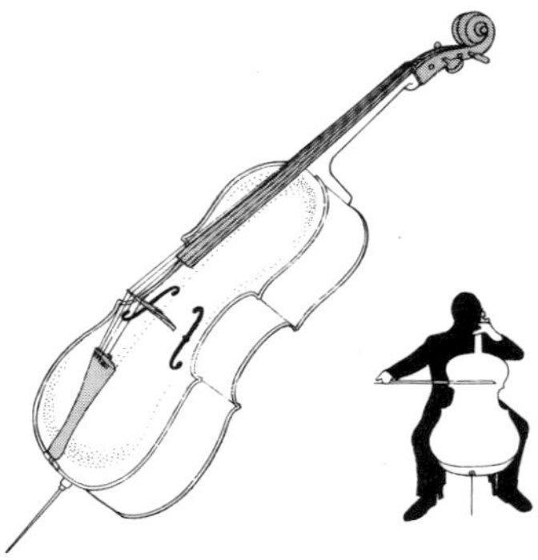

Cellos, tuned an octave below the viola, have a rich, mellow and somewhat mournful tone.

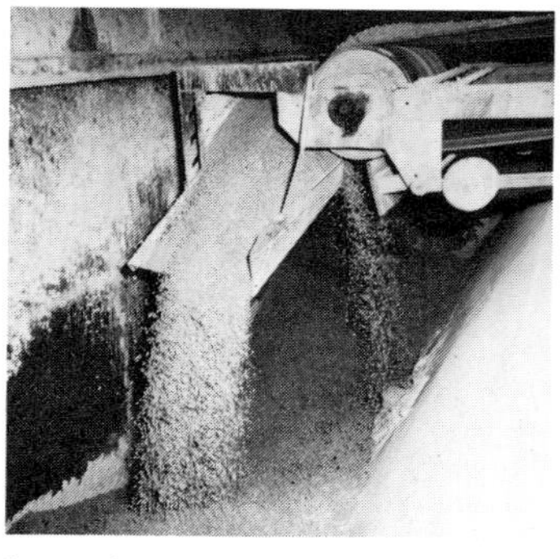

Cement, known to the Romans, was a lost art until its rediscovery in the 18th century.

Celebes, or Sulawesi Island, largest island in E Indonesia, E of Borneo. It is irregular in shape, consisting of four peninsulas separated by the Tomini (NE), Tolo (SE) and Boni (S) gulfs. The island is mountainous, having many volcanoes, and is almost entirely covered by forest. There is some farming in the few inland valleys, although fishing is the main occupation. The largest city is Makasar. Area: 189,034sq km (72,986sq miles). Pop. (1970 est.) 8,925,000.

Celeriac, or knob celery, variety of CELERY with a swollen, underground stem that is cooked and eaten.

Celery, biennial plant native to the Mediterranean and widely cultivated for its long stalks used as a vegetable or salad. Its fruits are used as food flavouring and in medicine. It has white flowers. Family Umbelliferae; species *Apium graveolens*. *See also* PE pp.*189, 190, 210, 213.*

Celesta, or céleste, percussion instrument played by keyboard, with a range of four octaves. Like the GLOCKENSPIEL it consists of steel bars that are struck. Invented by Auguste Mustel in Paris (1886), its clear, tinkling tones were used by TCHAIKOVSKY for the "Dance of the Sugar Plum Fairy" in the *Nutcracker Suite* (1892).

Celestial body, any object, including the Sun, Moon, planets, asteroids, comets, stars, galaxies, nebulae and interstellar dust, to be found in space.

Celestial equator, great circle on the CELESTIAL SPHERE, lying midway between the celestial poles in the same plane as the earth's equator.

Celestial mechanics, branch of ASTRONOMY concerned with the relative motions of CELESTIAL BODIES that are associated in systems, such as the Solar System or a binary star system, by gravitational fields. Introduced by Isaac NEWTON in the 17th century on the basis of his law of gravitation and KEPLER's laws of planetary motion, celestial mechanics, rather than general RELATIVITY, is usually sufficient to calculate the various factors determining the motion of planets, satellites, comets, stars and galaxies around a centre of gravitational attraction.

Celestial meridian, circle on the CELESTIAL SPHERE passing through the CELESTIAL POLES, the ZENITH and the NADIR and crossing the horizon at the N and S points.

Celestial poles, two diametrically opposite points at which the extension of the earth's axis meets the CELESTIAL SPHERE. The celestial sphere rotates about a line through the celestial poles.

Celestial sphere, imaginary sphere of infinite radius used to define the positions of celestial bodies as seen from Earth, at the centre of the sphere. The sphere rotates, once in 24 hours, about a line that is an extension of the earth's axis. The position of a celestial body is the point at which a radial line through it meets the surface of the sphere. The position is defined in terms of coordinates, such as declination and right ascension or altitude and azimuth, which refer to great circles on the sphere, such as the CELESTIAL EQUATOR or the ecliptic.

Celestine, name of five popes. Celestine I (*r.* 422–32), was involved in the NESTORIAN CONTROVERSY, in which he vigorously asserted the authority of his see. Celestine II (*r.* 1143–44) was a former student of ABELARD and a learned scholar, but held papal office for only six months. Celestine III (*r.* 1191–98) was a skilled diplomat, although he could only temporize in his relations with a recalcitrant Europe. Celestine IV (*r.* 1241) was the first pope to be elected by a conclave, but he died less than three weeks later. Celestine V (St Celestine) (*r.* 1294), an ascetic who founded a group of hermits, was in his 80s when elected after a two-year papal vacancy. A weak administrator, he resigned after five months – the first pope to do so. He was canonized in 1313. Feast: 19 May.

Celestite, mineral, strontium sulphate ($SrSO_4$), with distinctive pale blue or white, glassy orthorhombic crystals, sometimes occurring in fibrous masses. It is found chiefly in sedimentary rocks and also as gangue material in ore veins. There are deposits in Britain, Sicily and the USA. It is an important source of STRONTIUM and some of its compounds.

Céline, Louis-Ferdinand (1894–1961), pen-name of Louis-Ferdinand Destouches, French novelist. His works are noted for their cynical and pessimistic misanthropy. Céline's novels include *Journey to the End of the Night* (1932), *Death on the Instalment Plan* (1936) and the trilogy *Rigodon* (1969).

Cell, smallest unit of life that can exist and sustain life independently; all living things are made up of one or more cells, most of which consist of a membrane surrounding jelly-like cytoplasm with a central nucleus. The nucleus is the main structure in which genetic information is stored. Animal cells vary widely in shape. In the liver they are polyhedral and in bone they are spiky. Usually they reproduce, grow and metabolize within their membrane. Blue-green algae and bacteria cells do not have nuclei; instead, they have large chromosomes floating in the cytoplasm. *See also* NW pp.20–21, 26–29.

Cell, electrochemical, device from which electricity is obtained due to a chemical reaction. A cell consists of two electrodes (a positive anode and a negative cathode) immersed in a solution (electrolyte). The chemical reaction takes place between the electrolyte and one of the electrodes. In a primary cell, current is produced from an irreversible chemical reaction, and the chemicals must be renewed at intervals. In a secondary cell (battery), the chemical reaction is reversible and the cell can be charged by passing a current through it. *See also* SU p.148.

Cell division, process by which living cells reproduce and thereby allow an organism to grow. The methods of its division include nuclear division (occurring by mitosis and meiosis) the fission of cytoplasm (cytokinesis). *See also* NW p.26.

Cellini, Benvenuto (1500–71), Florentine sculptor, goldsmith and adventurer best known for his *Autobiography* (1558–62), an entertaining and informative record of life in Renaissance Italy. As an artist, Cellini was profoundly influenced by MICHELANGELO. Between 1537 and 1545 he twice visited the court of Francis I of France, for whom he made a famous gold salt-celler (1540) and the bronze *Nymph of Fontainebleau* (1543). *See also* HC1 pp.263–265, *265.*

Cello, or violoncello, member of the violin family of musical instruments, with a soft, mellow tone, one octave below the viola, and a range of 2½ octaves. It has four strings and is played with a bow; the seated player supports it with his knees. Developed in the 16th century by the AMATI family, the cello has had many famous players, the most important of the 20th century including Pablo CASALS and Mstislav ROSTROPOVICH. *See also* HC2 pp.104–105, *104–105.*

Cellophane, flexible, transparent film made of regenerated CELLULOSE and used mostly as a wrapping material. It is made by dissolving wood-pulp or other plant material in an alkali, to which carbon disulphide is added to form viscose. This is then forced through a narrow slit into a dilute acid where it precipitates as a film of a simpler form of cellulose.

Cell potential, the potential difference between the electrodes of an electric cell. It depends on the internal resistance (r) of the cell and the external resistance (R) through which the current flows. It is given by the formula $ER/(r + R)$, where E is the ELECTROMOTIVE FORCE (emf) on open circuit. *See also* SU pp.114–115, 148.

Celluloid, hard, synthetic plastic invented in 1869 and made by mixing cellulose nitrate with pigments and fillers in a solution of camphor and alcohol. It was the first important plastic, replacing expensive natural materials in a wide range of domestic uses. It is highly inflammable and has been superseded by other plastics. *See also* MM p.55.

Cellulose, polysaccharide carbohydrate that is the structural constituent of plant cells and fibres [$(C_6H_{10}O_5)_n$]. Consisting of parallel unbranched chains of glucose units cross-linked together into a stable structure, it forms the basic material of the paper and textile industries. It is most easily obtained in the pure form by treating cotton with alkalis and acids. Its uses include paper, rayon, plastics and explosives. *See also* NW pp.44; SU pp.152, 156; MM pp.55–61.

Cellulose nitrate, also called nitrocellulose or guncotton, an organic compound made by reacting the natural polymer cellulose with nitric acid. It was chiefly used in the 19th and 20th centuries (together with camphor) to make celluloid – one of the first plastics – or as a propellant explosive (called cordite in Britain). *See also* MM pp.163, 242.

Celsius, Anders (1701–44), Swedish astronomer who invented the Celsius or centigrade scale in 1742. He also published a collection of 316 observations of the Aurora Borealis in 1733 made by himself and other astronomers.

Celsius, temperature scale established in 1742 by the Swedish astronomer Anders CELSIUS. On such a scale the difference between the reference temperatures of the freezing and boiling points of water is divided into 100 degrees, hence it is commonly called the CENTIGRADE scale. To convert a temperature from degrees Celcius to degrees Fahrenheit, multiply by 9/5 and add 32.

Celsus, Aulus Cornelius (*fl.* AD 14) Roman encyclopaedist, author of a comprehensive work covering several topics. Only the section dealing with medicine survived. *De re medicina,* consisting of eight books, is the most complete Roman medical text extant. Most of what is known about Hellenistic medical practices is based on Celsus' description.

Celt, someone who speaks a CELTIC LANGAGE or is descended from a Celtic language area. After 2000 BC, the early Celts spread from E France and W Germany over much of W Europe, including Britain. They developed a village-based, heirarchical society headed by nobles and by priests called DRUIDS, and elaborate, decorative styles of art. Conquered first by the Romans, the Celts were then pushed into "fringe" regions by Germanic peoples. But their culture remained vigorous, and the Celtic churches were important in the early spread of Christianity in N Europe.

Celtic fields, general name in Britain for the traces of ancient fields, generally rectangular and about 0.2–0.6 hectares (0.5–1.5 acres) in area. Although all such fields are called Celtic, the system is probably pre-Celtic in origin, dating from *c.* 1500 BC. Most are from the Roman and Anglo-Saxon periods (*c.* 500 BC–AD500).

Celtic languages, group of languages spoken in parts of Britain, Ireland and France, forming a subdivision of the Indo-European family. There are two branches: Brythonic, which includes WELSH, BRETON and the virtually extinct CORNISH, and Goidelic, including GAELIC and MANX, which died out only recently. The Celtic languages were dominant in Britain until the 5th century AD. *See also* MS p.240.

Cement, manufactured powder that hardens after mixing with water, used in building as an adhesive binding material. It is made by heating a mixture of limestone and clay, grinding it, and adding gypsum. This process of making portland cement was patented in 1824 by Joseph Aspdin, an English bricklayer, although natural cement had been known since Greek and Roman times. *See also* CONCRETE; MM pp.51, 192.

Cementite, hard iron-carbon compound (Fe_3C) present as a major component of steel. The first of all steel-making processes, practised in the Hittite civilization of the 2nd millennium BC, is the cementite process; the ancient smiths beat carbon from hot wood ashes into wrought iron, so forming cementite. *See also* MM p.30.

Cendrars, Blaise (1887–1961), French author, real name Frédéric Sauser. He wrote a number of books based on his frequent trips abroad. His novels *L'Or* (1925), *Moravagine* (1926) and *Dan Yack* (1927–29) also dealt with the theme of existential man.

Cenotaph, originally a Greek word meaning "empty tomb", a monument in memory of a person buried elsewhere. Though often found in churches and cathedrals, such as Westminster Abbey, London, and Santa Croce, Florence, the term is commonly reserved for national war memorials, eg the London Cenotaph, Whitehall, by Sir Edwin LUTYENS (1920).
Cenozoic Era, most recent major division of geological time, beginning about 65 million years ago and extending up to the present. It is subdivided into the TERTIARY and QUATERNARY periods in North America, and the Paleogene and Neogene periods in Europe. It is the period during which the modern world with its present geographical features and plants and animals developed. *See also* NW pp.*25*, 190–191; PE pp.44, *57*.
Censor, magistrate of ancient Rome. Two censors were elected for 18-month terms to take the census; supervise public works, finance and morals; and fill senate vacancies. The office lasted from 443 BC to 22 BC.
Censorship, system whereby a government-appointed body or official claims the right to protect the public interest by influencing the release of any item of mass communication, such as books, newspapers, films and plays. Censorship most often involves two broad categories – politics and sex. Material may be censored before publication or it may be seized by the authorities or a performance banned.
Census, survey conducted by a government to collect facts about the society it governs. In addition to ascertaining up-to-date population counts, most censuses seek information about marital status, age and sex, numbers of children, occupation, education, housing and annual income. Such information helps a government to formulate policy.
Centaur, in Greek mythology, a creature half-human and half-horse, one of a warlike and sensual race of mountain-dwellers, sometimes associated with DIONYSUS or EROS. *See also* MS p.*206*.
Centaurus, or the Centaur, brilliant southern constellation situated N of Crux. It contains the Sun's nearest stellar neighbours, Alpha Centauri, or Rigil Kent, and its companion, Proxima Centauri. Beta Centauri is also very bright. Also to be found in this region of the sky are the brilliant GLOBULAR CLUSTER Omega (NGC 5139), and the radio galaxy Centaurus A (NGC 5128). *See also* SU pp.260–261, 266–267.
Centaury, any plant of the genus *Centaurium* (or *Centaurea*) of the GENTIAN family (Gentianaceae). Garden varieties are small plants with flat clusters of reddish flowers. The name originates in Greek legend, the centaur Chiron having discovered curative properties in the plants.
Centigrade. *See* CELSIUS.
Centipede, common name for many arthropods of the class Chilopoda. Found in warm and temperate regions, they have flattened, segmented bodies. Most centipedes have about 70 legs (35 pairs, one pair per segment), rather than 100 as their name suggests. Many tropical species are 15–30cm (6–12in) long; temperate ones are about 2.5cm (1in). They eat small insects and other invertebrates. *See also* NW pp.*104, 208, 213*.
Cento. *See* CENTRAL TREATY ORGANIZATION.
Central African Empire, formerly the Central African Republic (until 1976), a landlocked nation that for the most part consists of a plateau covered with savanna. Most of the people are subsistence farmers. Important crops, and chief exports, are coffee and cotton. Development of the economy is hampered by poor communications. The capital is Bangui. Area: 624,977sq km (241,304sq miles). Pop. (1975 est.) 1,800,000. *See also* MW p.51.
Central Criminal Court, housed in the Old Bailey whose sessions it replaced in 1834 with the Central Criminal Court Act while continuing to try the same offences. The 1834 act was repealed with the Administration of Justice Act (1964) under which the Central Criminal Court had jurisdiction to try all offences committed in Greater London. In 1971, as a result of the Courts Act, the Central Criminal Court became a CROWN COURT.
Central heating, method of heating the rooms in a home using only one central-ized heating unit. In its original form, central heating made use of a boiler that supplied steam or hot water which flowed through pipes to heat radiators. The term has been extended to include electric heating systems, such as those using underfloor heating elements or individual storage, convector or radiant-type heaters. Electricity, oil or gas may also be used to fuel a boiler for generating hot air that is ducted to various rooms.
Central Intelligence Agency. *See* CIA.
Central nervous system (CNS), division of the nervous system comprising the brain and spinal cord (protected by the skull and spinal column), as opposed to the peripheral system of nerves extending from them. *See also* MS pp.*38–39*.
Central Powers, WWI alliance of Germany, Austria-Hungary, Bulgaria and Turkey, so-called because they were opposed to the W by Britain, France and Belgium (and lat¡r, the USA) and to the E by Russian (joined later by Serbia).
Central Treaty Organization (CENTO), defensive alliance signed by Iraq, Turkey, Iran, Britain and Pakistan. Originally known as the BAGHDAD PACT, the organization was formed in 1955 largely as an anti-communist body and with US support. When Iraq left in 1959 the present name was adopted, and its headquarters were shifted from Baghdad to Ankara.
Centre of gravity, point in or near an object or system of objects through which passes the resultant force of all the gravitational forces acting on each particle of the object or system. It is the point at which the weight of the object may be considered to act. In a uniform gravitational field it is the same as the CENTRE OF MASS. *See also* SU p.70; PE p.32.
Centre of mass, point in or near an object or system of objects such that, when it moves, the acceleration of this point multiplied by the total mass of the system equals the total resultant force acting on it. Isaac NEWTON first verified his law of gravitation by assuming that respective masses of the Earth and Moon were located at their centres. *See also* CENTRE OF GRAVITY.
Centrifugal force. *See* CENTRIPETAL FORCE.
Centrifuge, mechanical device, usually a rapidly spun container, used in many laboratory and industrial processes to separate substances of varying density. Examples of its use include the removal of water (in a washing machine), and the separation of cream from milk, red blood cells from PLASMA, and sugar from syrup. *See also* SU p.76.
Centriole, dense body consisting of micro-tubules near the nucleus of a cell. It occurs in all cells except those of ANGIOSPERMS and the sperm cells of ferns and GYMNOSPERMS. During cell division centrioles reproduce before the rest of the cell and move to each pole to form the spindle. *See also* NW p.27.
Centripetal force, in circular or curved motion, the force acting on a body pushing it towards the centre of the circular path. On a planet orbiting the Sun it is gravitational; on an electron orbiting a nucleus it is electrical; on a ball twirled on a string it is mechanical. In accordance with NEWTON'S LAWS, the reaction to this, the CENTRIFUGAL FORCE, is equal in magnitude and opposite in direction. *See also* SU p.76.
Centurion, military officer of ancient Rome. The LEGION was divided into ten cohorts each comprising six centuries of 100 men, commanded by a centurion. Centurions were usually foot-soldiers who had risen from the ranks, and were well paid to maintain discipline.
Ceorl, in Anglo-Saxon England, a middle-order free peasant with a WERGILD of 200s. They farmed small-holdings of varying sizes. Although personally free they had various obligations: military service, payment of church dues and royal taxes, and attendance at the local court or moot. With their decline after the Norman invasion, "churl" became a derogatory term.
Cephalic index, measurement of the head, used in physical ANTHROPOLOGY. The maximum width of the skull is divided by the maximum length and the result expressed as a percentage. The classifications are dolichocephalic (long-headed; less than 75%); mesocephalic, or mesaticephalic (median; 75–80%); brachycephalic (broad-headed; more than 80%). *See also* MS p.34.
Cephalochordates, lancelets or Amphioxus, small marine animals that look and swim rather like fish but have no head or paired fins. They are related to vertebrates, having a NOTOCHORD throughout their lives. Their method of filter-feeding is, however, much more like that of many animals without backbones. Lancelets inhabit shallow, temperate and tropical sea-water. *See also* CHORDATE; NW pp.122–123.
Cephalonia, largest of the IONIAN Islands, off the W coast of Greece. It has a largely mountainous terrain rising to Mt Ainos 1,628m (5,341ft) in the SE. Manufactured goods include lace and basketwork and, although agriculture is limited, fruit and cotton are produced and currants are exported through the main port of Argostolion. Area: 780sq km (300sq miles). Pop. (1971) 31,787.
Cephalopoda, highest class of predatory marine molluscs including the SQUID, NAUTILUS, OCTOPUS and CUTTLEFISH. Each has eight or more arms surrounding the mouth, which has a parrot-like beak. The nervous system is well developed, permitting great speed and alertness; the large eyes have an image-forming ability equal to that of vertebrates. Most can squirt an inky fluid to alarm attackers. Cephalopods move by squirting water from their mantle edge. Their heavily-yolked eggs develop into larval young that resemble the adults. Members of this class vary dramatically in size from 4cm (1.5in) to the giant squid, which may reach 20m (65ft). There are over 600 species. *See also* NW pp.*94–95*; PE pp.248–249.
Cephalosporins, group of ANTIBIOTIC drugs derived from fungi of the genus *Cephalosporium*. Related to PENICILLIN, they act against a wide variety of BACTERIA by preventing cell-wall synthesis. Cephalosporins are useful for treating patients who are allergic to penicillin and for infections caused by penicillin-resistant PATHOGENS. *See also* MS p.121.
Cepheid variable, type of regular pulsating variable star whose maximum luminosity is directly proportional to the time between one maximum brightness and the next. Such stars, whose prototype is Delta Cephei in the northern constellation of Cepheus, are generally extremely regular in their light variations, thus allowing their distances to be very accurately measured. Classical Cepheids, of POPULATION I, have periods of one to 50 days. Their discovery in external GALAXIES has been a major aid in determining intergalactic distances. *See also* SU pp.227, 238, 246–247, 249.
Ceramics, in art, objects shaped out of moistened clay and then baked. EARTHENWARE, TERRA-COTTA, brick, tile, FAIENCE, MAJOLICA, STONEWARE and PORCELAIN are all ceramics.

The clay may be shaped by hand, using a coil or slab technique, a mould or a potter's wheel. Ceramic ware may be ornamented with clay inlays, by relief modelling on the surface, or by incized, stamped or impressed designs. A creamy mixture of clay and water (SLIP) can be used to coat the ware before firing. Ceramic ware is baked in a kiln, until it has hardened into its "biscuit" stage. Glaze, thin transparent oil pigment, is then applied to the clay surface and fused to it during firing, to make the pottery non-porous and to give it a smooth, colourful, decorative surface.

The ancient Egypt and neolithic communities of Europe were familiar with terra-cotta vessels. The Egyptians developed a FAIENCE with a glaze, and the Mesopotamians and Persians used architectural tiles with coloured glazes. The Greeks developed red, black, and white glazed decorated pottery; the Romans

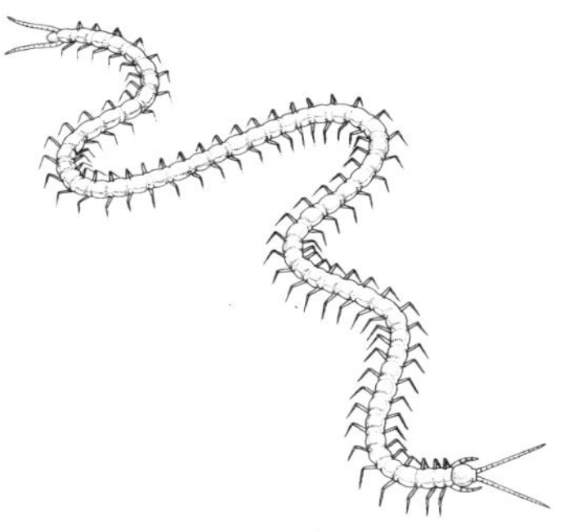

Centipedes have a pair of poison claws with which they kill their prey.

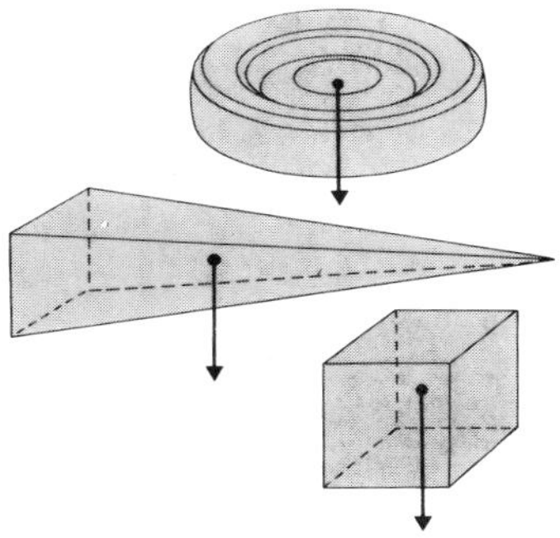

Centre of gravity; the lower this is in an object or vehicle, the greater is stability.

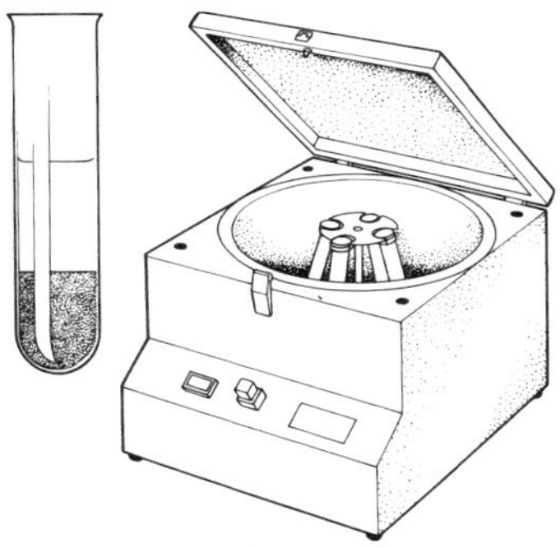

Centrifuges separate liquids of different densities or solids suspended in the liquid.

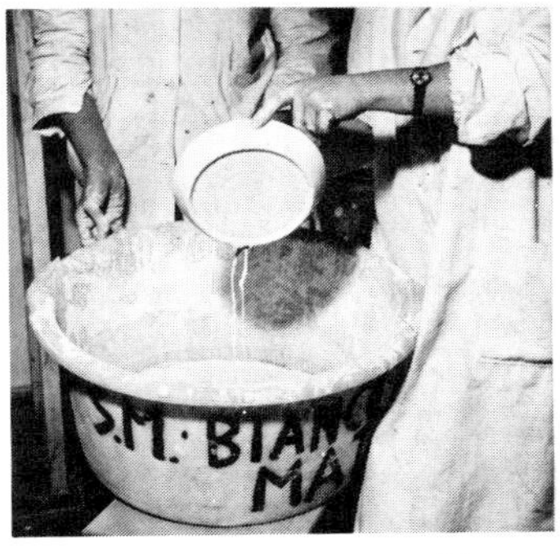

Ceramics form an important material source of domestic and industrial products.

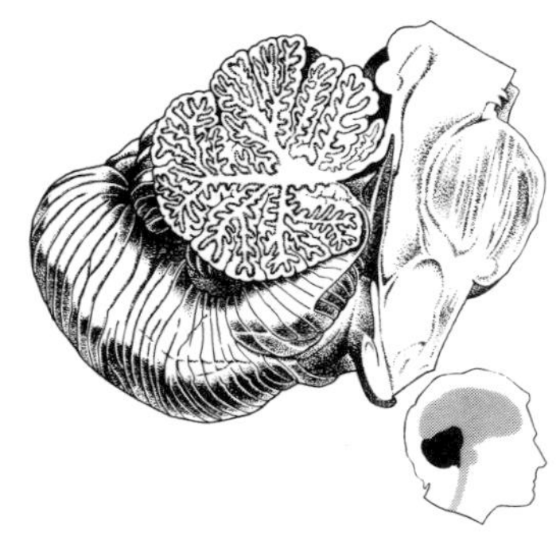

Cerebellum; the part of the brain that controls the positions and movements of the body.

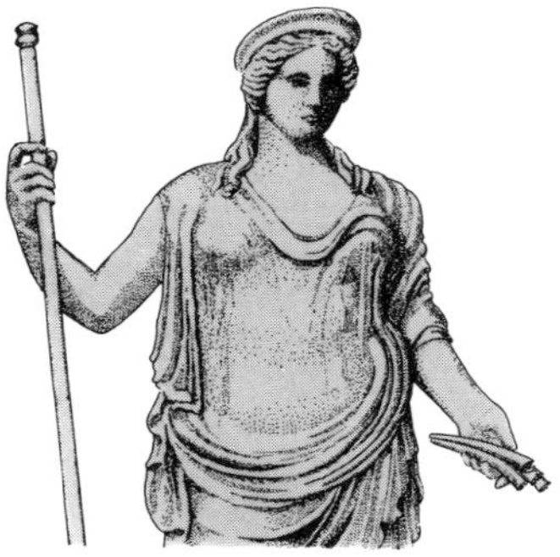

Ceres, the Roman goddess of agriculture after whom the largest asteroid was named.

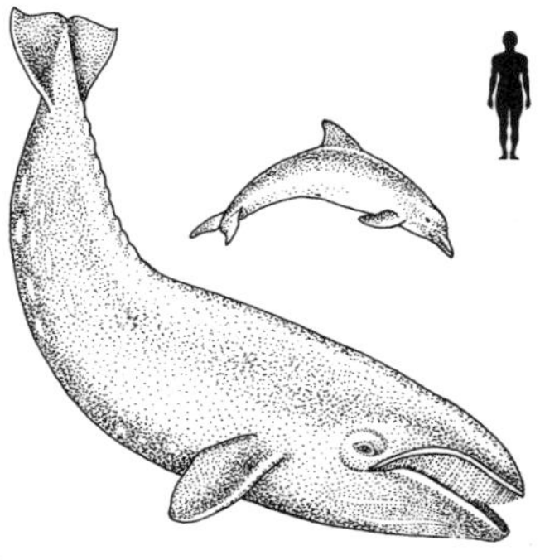

Cetacea are the aquatic mammals which include whales, dolphins and porpoises.

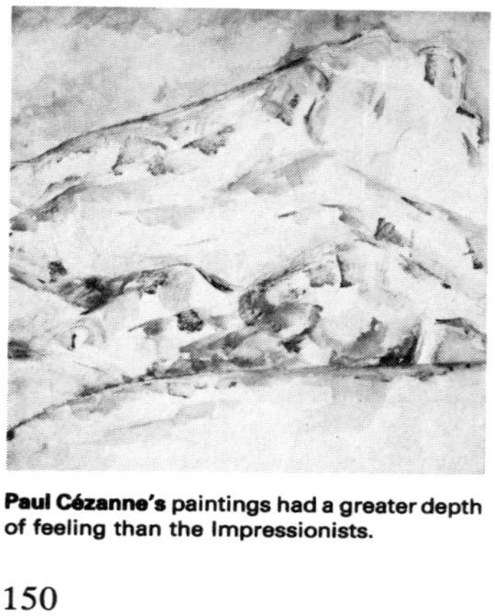

Paul Cézanne's paintings had a greater depth of feeling than the Impressionists.

used relief decoration on theirs. In Spain, LUSTREWARE, the first sophisticated ceramics of the modern era, was produced by the Moors. Italian majolica, Dutch DELFT ware, German MEISSEN, and English WEDGWOOD were further refinements of the product. Chinese porcelain dates from the T'ang dynasty, and Chinese stoneware can be dated from *c.* 2000 BC. *See also* MM pp.44–45.

Cerberus, in Greek mythology, a three-headed dog who guarded the entrance to HADES. *See also* MS p.*206*.

Cercopithecine. *See* BABOON.

Cereal, any grain of the grass family (Gramineae) grown as a food crop. Wheat, corn, rye, oats and barley are grown in temperate regions but rice, millet, sorghum and maize require more tropical climates. The discovery of cereal cultivation (ie farming) was the basis of civilization and cereals developed over the years into high-yielding strains, remain the world's most important food source. *See also* NW p.68; PE pp. 180–181.

Cerebellum, part of the brain, often known as the "little brain", located at the base of the CEREBRUM. It co-ordinates voluntary muscular activity and regulates muscle tone for proper posture and balance. It also modifies CEREBRAL CORTEX activity. *See also* MS pp.40–41.

Cerebral cortex, outer layer of the brain, most highly developed in human beings, which suggests that it governs the higher nerve activity usually termed the human intellect. The cortex has intricate connections with most other neural structures in the body. *See also* MS pp.40, *41*.

Cerebral haemorrhage, rupture of a blood vessel in the BRAIN usually caused by ARTERIOSCLEROSIS, less often by injury or disease. Symptoms are headache, vomiting, then coma. A major haemorrhage is fatal; recovery from a minor haemorrhage may take months. *See also* MS p.96.

Cerebral hemispheres, the two lateral halves of the CEREBRUM, the largest parts of the BRAIN and sites of higher thought. Due to the crossing-over of nerve fibres from one cerebral hemisphere to another, the right side controls most of the movements and sensation on the left side of the body, and vice versa. Damage to the cerebral hemispheres often produces personality changes. *See also* MS pp.40–43.

Cerebral palsy, disease caused by damage to the BRAIN. The damage may result from disease or injury before birth, from difficulties during childbirth or, in later life, from infection, circulatory diseases or head injury. Symptoms include spastic movements of the arms and legs, and sometimes convulsions and impared speech and hearing. Signs of mental abnormality that often accompany the disease may reflect difficulty in communication rather than mental retardation.

Cerebrospinal fluid, fluid found in the space between the arachnoid and the pia-mater layers of the MENINGES, the membranes that protect the brain and spinal cord from shocks. The fluid acts as a protective cushion. A sample of the fluid can aid diagnosis of diseases affecting the meninges. *See also* MS p.38.

Cerebrum, the major part of the BRAIN. It is divided into two dome-shaped hemispheres, each of which has four lobes. Each hemisphere is made up of an outer greyish layer (grey matter) known as the CEREBRAL CORTEX; cortical white matter, made up of nerve fibres; and grey basal ganglia that are connected with other areas of the cerebrum and other parts of the brain. *See also* MS p.40.

Cerenkov, or Cherenkov, radiation, light emitted when energetic particles travel through a transparent medium of fairly high refractive index (such as water) at a speed higher than the velocity of light in that medium. It is analogous to the SONIC BOOM in sound, and a cone of light is emitted trailing the path of the particle. *See also* SU pp.104–105.

Ceres, largest of the asteroids or minor planets. It was the first to be sighted, in 1801 by Giuseppe Piazzi. It has a diameter of between 1,000 and 1,200km (600 – 750 miles), and its mean distance from the Sun is 413,400,000km (256,762,000 miles). It has a mean sidereal period of 4.6 years. *See also* SU pp.204, *205*.

Cereus, genus of CACTUS native to the West Indies and E South America. Its stems are long, cylindrical and ribbed, and may be tree-like or trailing. Height: to 12m (39ft). There are about 25 species. Family Cactaceae, genus *Cereus*.

Cerium, soft, ductile, iron-grey metallic element (symbol Ce) of the LANTHANIDE group, first isolated in 1803. The chief ore is monazite. It is used in alloys, eg lighter flints, in catalysts and as the core of carbon electrodes in arc lamps. Properties: at.no. 58; at.wt 140.120; s.g. 6.7; m.p. 798°C (1,468°F); b.p. 3,257°C (5,895°F). The most common isotope is Ce^{140} (88.48%).

Cermet, strong heat-resistant combination of ceramic material and powdered metal, produced by powder metallurgy and used in the manufacturing of drilling tools, heat shields and turbine blades.

CERN (European Council for Nuclear Research), nuclear research centre sited on the Franco-Swiss border W of Geneva. It was founded in 1954 as an intergovernmental organization, and its activities are now sponsored by 13 European countries. It is the principal European centre for research into high-energy nuclear physics. *See also* SU pp.*67, 95*.

Cernan, Eugene Andrew (1934–), US astronaut who made three space flights. The first was in GEMINI 9 (1966) and the second in APOLLO 10 (1969). Finally, in 1972 as commander of Apollo 17, he landed on the moon with Ronald EVANS, making extensive explorations and collecting samples. *See also* MM pp.188–189.

Certiorari, legal document issued by a superior court for the review of a decision by a lower court, particularly ones that have no regular means of appeal.

Ceruminous gland, part of the ear that produces the yellow wax (cerumen) that helps to protect the sensitive external ear canal. Too much wax can be produced by the glands, blocking the canal; the wax has then to be softened and removed by syringing with warm water. *See also* MS pp.50–51.

Cervantes, Miguel de (1547–1616), Spanish novelist, poet and dramatist. He joined the army in 1570 and was wounded in the Battle of Lepanto in 1571. While returning to Spain in 1575, he was captured and kept as a slave in Algiers. He was ransomed in 1580 and settled in Madrid. Cervantes' works include *Don Quixote de la Mancha* (1605, 1615) and *Novelas Ejemplares* (1613).

Cervix, neck of the womb (uterus); it is the narrow part leading from the vagina into the womb. Cancer of the cervix is one of the commonest cancers found in women. Most often found amongst middle-aged women with several children, it can be successfully treated if detected at an early stage through a cervical smear. *See also* MS pp.74, *75*, 113.

Césaire, Aimé (1913–), West Indian poet *b.* Martinique. He writes in French and introduced the term NÉGRITUDE in his *Return to My Native Land* (1939). He has also held a number of government positions in Martinique.

Cesalpino, Andrea (1519–1603), Italian physiologist and botanist. His *De plantis* (1583) was one of the first attempts to classify plants according to their flowers and fruits and was based on a comparative study of his own large collection.

César (Baldacchini) (1921–), French sculptor. Working in metal and scrap from refuse dumps, he used these *objets trouvés* in abstract compositions and in witty sculptures of birds and human beings.

Céspedes, Carlos Manuel de (1819–74), lawyer and Cuban revolutionary. He issued the first proclamation of independence from Spanish rule (*El Grito de Yara*) and led the armed revolt that began the Ten Years War (1868–78).

Cessna Aircraft Company, US industry with international sales and distribution of aircraft, mainly light passenger planes. Cessna also produces fluid power systems and defence products.

Cestodes, TAPEWORMS that are inner parasites of man and animals. Usually they live in the intestines, holding on to its lining by terminal hooks. They have no mouths and absorb their food through the body wall from their hosts. They are HERMAPHRODITE, one segment fertilizing another. Ripe segments drop off and are voided by the host after which, to survive, they usually need to be eaten by a second host. For this reason their life cycles are often complex. *See also* MS p.85; NW p.87.

Cetacea, order of aquatic mammals found in all oceans and some rivers. The larger cetaceans are called WHALES, the smaller ones are known as PORPOISES OR DOLPHINS. Cetaceans are streamlined, with a pair of front flippers and horizontal tail flukes. Their bodies are insulated by a thick layer of blubber. Length: from 1.5m (4.9ft) to more than 30m (100ft); weight: from 36kg (80lb) to 100 tonnes. *See also* NW pp.155, 157, 166–167.

Cetewayo, or Cetshwayo (*c.* 1826–84), King of the Zulus (1873–79). British demands for him to disarm led to the ZULU WAR (1879), in which he was defeated. He lost the loyalty of his subjects, and was forced into exile.

Cetus, constellation of the equatorial zone adjacent to the constallations ARIES, PISCES and TAURUS. It contains the binary star MIRA CETI which, in the early 17th century, was the first variable star to be recognized; its magnitude varies from 1.7 to 10. *See also* SU pp.255, 262, 263.

Ceuta, city in NW Africa on the Strait of Gibraltar. Built by the Phoenicians, it was in turn held by the Carthaginians, Romans, Vandals, Byzantines, Arabs and Portuguese. It has been a territory of Spain since 1580 and is part of Cadiz province. It forms one of the PILLARS OF HERCULES. Today, it is an important refuelling port, and has shipping, fishing and food processing industries. Pop. (1970) 67,187.

Cévennes, mountain range in S France W of the Rhône Valley and bordering the Massif Central; extending SW from St Étienne to the Canal du Midi. Cévennes was once known for its breeding of silkworms, but the silk manufacturing industry has declined and coal mining and sheep rearing are now the main occupations. The highest peak is Mont Mézenc, 1,754m (5,755ft).

Ceylon. *See* SRI LANKA.

Cézanne, Paul (1839–1906), French painter. A friend of PISSARRO, by whom he was influenced, Cézanne exhibited at the first Impressionist show in 1874. *House of the Hanged Man* (1873–74) is characteristic of his Impressionist period. He later developed away from IMPRESSIONISM in favour of a deeper, more analytical approach using colour to model and express form, which he depicted in geometric terms – cubes, cones and cylinders. Figure paintings, eg *The Card Players* (1890–92), *Madame Cézanne* (*c.* 1885) and *The Bathers* (1895–1905), as well as landscapes, eg *Mont Sainte-Victoire* (1904–06), and still-lifes were painted on this principle. Cézanne ranks as one of the great influences in modern art, especially CUBISM. *See also* POST-IMPRESSIONISM; HC2 pp.118–119, 176.

CG. *See* CHORIONIC GONADOTROPIN.

CGS system, system of metric units based on the centimeter, gramme and second. The dyne is the unit of force, the erg the unit of energy. It has been largely superseded by the SI and MKS SYSTEMS. *See also* SU p.33.

Chaadayev, Piotr Yakovlevich (1794–1856), Russian philosopher. His idealistic philosophy stressed the importance of unity at all levels, the immorality of egoism, the idea of Russia's divine mission and the importance of Christianity for understanding history. An aristocratic army officer in his early years, he travelled in Europe (1823–26) and in 1829 began writing eight *Philosophical Letters* expressing his views.

Chabanel, Noël (1613–49), French Jesuit missionary who worked among the Huron Indians in North America and was captured and killed by Iroquois. He was canonized in 1930. Feast: 26 Sept. or (among the Jesuits) 19 Oct.

Chablis, name of a French wine of distinc-

tion produced near the village of Chablis, Burgundy. Pale greenish-gold in colour, it has a clean dry taste. Chablis Grand Cru is produced in limited quantities from vineyards only 155sq km (60sq miles) in area. Although the name is often used for more inferior wines, true Chablis is at its best after about ten years.
Chabrier, Alexis Emmanuel (1841–94), French composer of orchestral and piano works, most notably *España* (1883) and *Joyeuse Marche* (1888) for orchestra and the opera *Le Roi malgré lui* (1887). His music had considerable influence on such French composers as Ravel and Satie. *See also* HC2 p.102.
Chacabuco, Battle of (12 Feb. 1817), first major engagement in the Chilean War of Independence, after SAN MARTÍN crossed the Andes from Argentina to Chile. The royalists suffered heavy losses and withdrew from the Santiago area. *See also* HC2 p.87.
Cha cha, dance popular in the 1950s. It has a 4/4 rhythm and its basic movements are similar to those of the MAMBO. It allows the dancers to improvise freely.
Chacma. *See* BABOON.
Chaco, extensive lowland plain in central S America, that has three principle divisions: Chaco Boreal in N Paraguay and S Bolivia, Chaco Central in NE Argentina and Chaco Austral in central W Argentina. The area is sparsely inhabited. Industries: timber, cotton, cattle grazing, oil prospecting, tannin extraction. Area: 777,000sq km (300,000sq miles).
Chaconne, dance popular in 17th-century Europe and often included in baroque dance SUITES. A moderately slow dance in 3/4 time, it was a series of variations on a GROUND BASS usually of eight bars. The operas of LULLY customarily ended with a chaconne and J.S. Bach used the dance in his *Violin Suite in D minor.* The PASSACAGLIA is a very similar form.
Chaco War, (1932–35), conflict between Paraguay and Bolivia over possession of the CHACO. Bolivia, landlocked since the War of the Pacific, sought a route to the sea via the Rio de la Plata. Most of the disputed territory was ceded to Paraguay in 1938.
Chad, Saint. *See* CEADDA, SAINT.
Chad (Tchad), lake in N central Africa; mainly in the Republic of Chad, partly in Nigeria, Cameroon and Niger. The chief tributary is the Chari River; the lake has no outlet. Depending on the season, the area of the surface varies from approx. 10,000–26,000sq km (3,850–10,000sq miles). Max. depth: 7.6m (25ft). *See also* PE p.47.
Chad, landlocked republic in N central Africa formerly a French colony that gained its independence in 1960. The N half of the country is desert, inhabited by nomads. In the S the land is farmed, the chief crop, and chief export, being cotton. Cattle are raised near Lake Chad. The capital is Ndjamena. Area: 1,284,000sq km (495,752sq miles). Pop. (1975 est.) 4,030,000. *See also* MW p.51.
Chadwick, Sir Edwin (1800–90), British sanitation reformer. He was a pupil of Jeremy BENTHAM, and pioneered the introduction of modern urban drainage systems with his book *The Sanitary Conditions of the Labouring Population* (1842). He was influential in the passing of the Public Health Act of 1848 and the setting up of a new drinking water system in London. *See also* HC2 p.96.
Chadwick, Florence May (1918–), US swimmer. In 1950 and 1951 she was the first woman to swim the English Channel both ways. She broke the time record for swimming the Catalina Channel, the Straits of Gibralter, the Dardanelles and the Hellespont.
Chadwick, Sir James (1891–1974), British physicist. In 1932 he discovered the NEUTRON by bombarding beryllium with alpha particles. He examined the change of these materials into different chemical elements. This work on NUCLEAR STRUCTURE led him to discover the neutron and determine its mass. For that work he was awarded the 1935 Nobel Prize in physics.
Chadwick, Lynn (1914–), British sculptor. He emerged in the 1950s as a leader among the group of British sculptors whose linear constructions were in direct contrast to the monumental style of Henry MOORE.
Chaetognatha, arrow worms, a phylum of small marine animals not at all closely related to any other group. They are between 3mm and 10cm ($\frac{1}{8}$–4in) long, and have narrow bodies, with bristly jaws for siezing their prey (small crustaceans of the PLANKTON). Although invertebrate animals, they swim like fishes by means of fins. They are HERMAPHRODITES. Some species are useful indicator organisms for marine biologists because they are sensitive to the temperature, salinity and depth of the water in which they live.
Chaetopoda, obsolete term for most of the classes of ANNELID worms.
Chafer, any of a large number of beetles, particularly of the SCARAB family (Scarabaeidae), that feed on the leaves of plants. They include shining leaf chafers and rose chafers. *See also* NW p.114.
Chaffinch, small songbird common throughout Europe. It generally perches on low trees, bushes and fences near houses, feeding on plants and insects. The blue and buff colours and pink breast belong to the male only, although the drab female shares his white markings. In winter flocks consisting solely of males can be seen. Family Fringillidae; species *Fringilla coelebs.*
Chagall, Marc (1887–), Russian-French painter. His paintings, with their dreamlike imagery – poetic evocations of Russian village life and Jewish tradition – considerably influenced the SURREALISTS. His work ranged from ceramics and mosaics to tapestry and theatre design. It included stained-glass windows for Hadassah-Hebrew Medical Centre, Jerusalem (1962), murals for the Metropolitan Opera House, New York (1966), and mosaics and tapestries for the Knesset in Jerusalem (1969) and Nice University (1968).
Chagas' disease, infectious disease transmitted by a protozoan parasite, *Trypanosoma cruzi,* in insect faeces, primarily in South America. Swelling at entry point, fever and malaise are early symptoms; heart damage is typical of the chronic form. *See also* MS p.*107.*
Chain, Sir Ernst Boris (1906–), British biochemist, *b.* Germany. Leaving Germany in 1933, he went to England to conduct research at Cambridge and Oxford universities. He shared the 1945 Nobel Prize in physiology and medicine with Howard FLOREY and Alexander FLEMING for the isolation and development of penicillin as an antibiotic. He also studied spreading factor, an enzyme that aids the dispersal of fluids in tissue. *See also* MS p.120.
Chainmail, form of ARMOUR, consisting of small metal rings which either interlock or are sewn onto a backing cloth. Flexible, relatively light and easy to manufacture, chainmail garments were extensively used in the early Middle Ages. The hauberks (mailed tunics) worn by Norman knights and their foes at the Battle of Hastings were typical. From the 13th century chainmail was gradually superseded by the stronger plate armour. *See also* HC1 p.*167*; MM p.161.
Chain reaction, self-sustaining molecular or nuclear reaction in which one reaction is the cause of a second, the second of a third and so on. The initial conditions are often critical, eg in a nuclear chain reaction the quantity of fissionable material must exceed the CRITICAL MASS. *See also* MM pp.74–75; SU pp.64–65.
Chaitanya (Caitanya) (1485–1533), Hindu mystic and theistic reformer, worshipped as the incarnation of Krishna. Moved by a religious experience at Bodh-Gaya calling him to a life of total commitment, he founded a cult devoted to the worship of the God Vishnu in his form as Krishna and played an important part in the Vishnuism (Vaishnavism) movement in Bengal. His cult was characterized by the performance of chanting and eurhythmic movements and for its emphasis on equality of treatment to all castes. Temples were built after his death at the traditional site of Vishnuism at Brindaban, which he visited and which is still the site of pilgrimages and festivals.
Chaka or Shaka (*d.*1828), chief of the Zulus (1800–28). He raised a large army and extended his control over many neighbouring tribes, subjugating all of what is now Natal. He later became insane and was murdered by his half-brother.
Chalcanthite, mineral which consists mainly of hydrated copper sulphate ($CuSO_4.5H_2O$), although it is rarely used as a source of copper. It occurs as greenish-blue triclinic crystals or as fibrous veins or stalactites. It is soluble in water and has a nauseating taste. Hardness 2.5; s.g. 2.25.
Chalcedon, Council of, meeting of all the bishops of the Christian Church, held in 451 in the city of Chalcedon in Asia Minor. It was convoked by the Emperor Marcian to settle controversial theological questions relating to CHRISTOLOGY. It reaffirmed the doctrine of two natures (divine and human) in Christ and condemned NESTORIANISM.
Chalcedony, fine-grained variety of quartz used by gem engravers and as ornaments when cut and polished. It is waxy, lustrous and there are white, grey, blue and brown varieties. It is often coloured by artificial methods. Other varieties contain impurities giving a distinctive appearance, eg AGATE (coloured bands), BLOODSTONE (dark green with red flecks), CARNELIAN (dark red) and ONYX (striped). *See also* PE p.98.
Chalcid, any member of the insect superfamily Chalcidoidea, related to bees, ants and ichneumon flies (order Hymenoptera). Many are predators on or parasites of other insects. Like some other hymenopterans, some chalcids are so small as to be hyperparasites – parasites of parasites.
Chalcocite, dark grey, metallic, soft mineral, copper sulphide (Cu_2S); one of the chalcocite group. It is a major ore of copper, found mainly in sulphur deposits. The crystals occur in orthorhombic granular masses, or rarely in prismatic form. Hardness 2.5 to 3.0; s.g. 5.7.
Chalcolithic Age, period in which man discovered how to extract copper by heating its ore with charcoal. This art was known in the Middle East before 3500 BC. A subsequent important development was the alloying of copper with tin to produce bronze. *See also* BRONZE AGE; MM p.26.
Chalcopyrite, or copper pyrites, opaque, brass-coloured, metallic, brittle mineral, copper iron sulphide ($CuFeS_2$); the most important copper ore. It is found in sulphide veins and in igneous and contact metamorphic rocks. The crystals are tetragonal but often occur in masses. Hardness 3.5–4; s.g. 4.2. *See also* PE p.94.
Chaldaea. *See* BABYLONIA.
Chaleur Bay, inlet of the Gulf of St Lawrence in SE Quebec, Canada. It was discovered in 1534 by Jacques Cartier. It is a noted fishing ground for herring, cod, mackerel and salmon. Length: approx. 137km (85 miles).
Chaliapin, Fyodor Ivanovich (1873–1938), Russian operatic bass of international fame. He made his debut at La Scala in Milan in 1901 and at the Metropolitan Opera, New York, in 1907. His differences with the Soviet government caused him to leave Russia in 1921, when he joined the Metropolitan. He was particularly noted for his role in Mussorgsky's opera *Boris Godunov.*
Chalice, in Christian Churches, cup used at celebrations of the EUCHARIST to hold the consecrated wine. Chalices are usually made of precious metals and consist of a bowl with a stem.
Chalk, mineral, mainly calcium carbonate ($CaCO_3$), formed from the shells of minute marine organisms. It varies in properties and appearance; pure forms, such as calcite, contain up to 99% calcium carbonate. It is used in making putty, plaster and cement, and harder forms are occasionally used for building. Blackboard chalk is calcium sulphate.
Challenger Expedition (1872–76), British expedition for oceanic research whose findings laid the foundations of the science of oceanography. HMS *Challenger,*

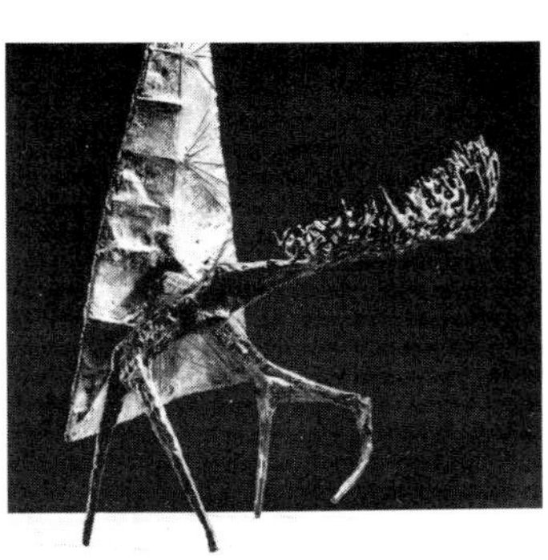

Lynn Chadwick's early sculpture included Calder-like "mobiles"; this is *The Seasons.*

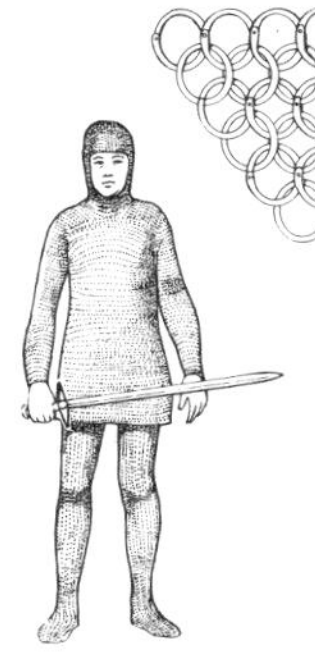

Chainmail, worn extensively in the Middle Ages, was also used by Roman soldiers.

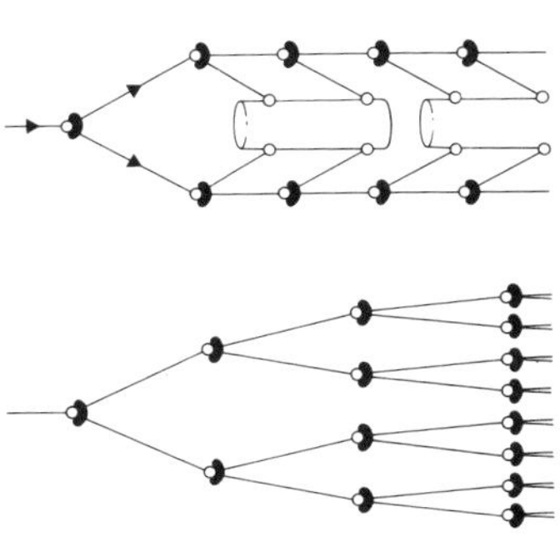

Chain reaction; self-sustaining, explosive process following "splitting" of an atom.

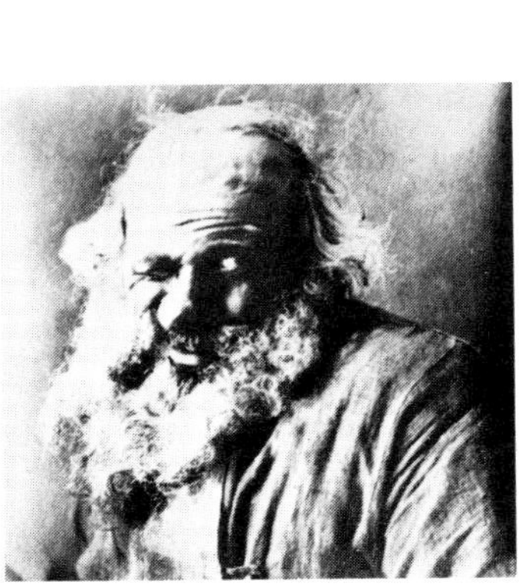

Fyodor Chaliapin, the great Russian bass, as he appeared as Varlaam in *Boris Godunov.*

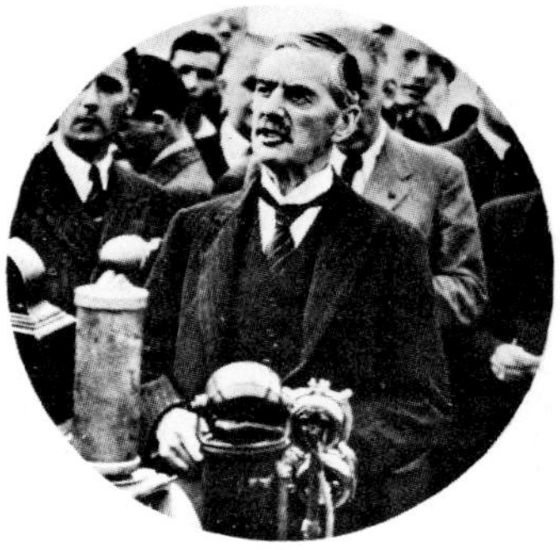

Neville Chamberlain; his illusions that Hitler's demands were limited were shattered.

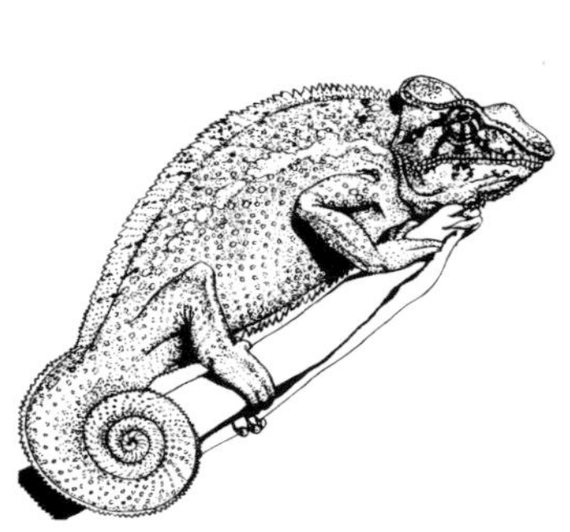

Chameleons of the larger species are known to catch small birds with their long tongues.

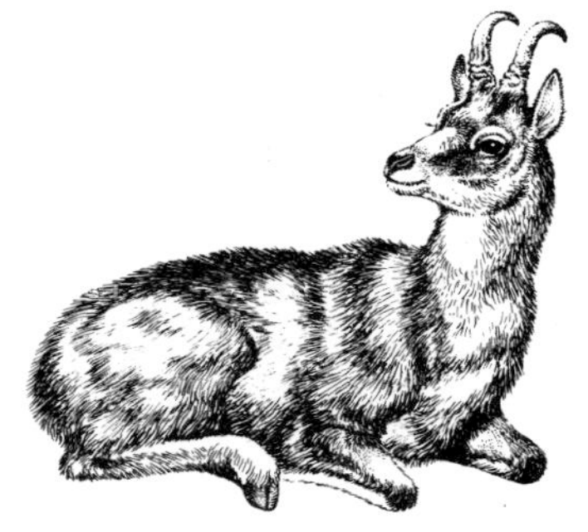

Chamois are widely hunted for their meat but they are amazingly agile and evasive.

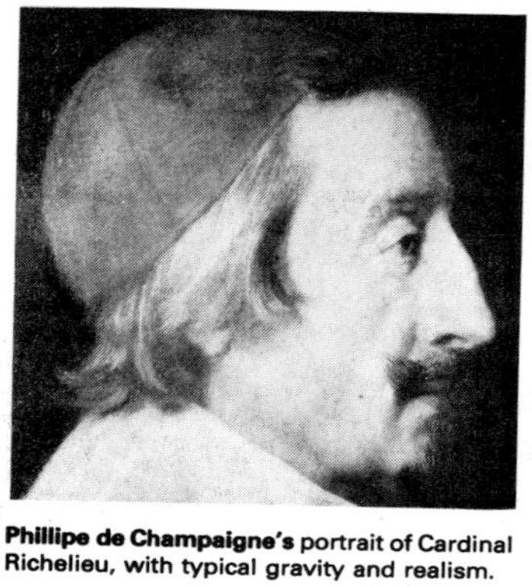

Phillipe de Champaigne's portrait of Cardinal Richelieu, with typical gravity and realism.

a steam corvette of 2,306 tonnes, was commanded by George Nares and had a staff of six naturalists headed by Professor Charles Wyville Thompson. The expedition travelled nearly 128,000km (69,000 nautical miles) and made studies of the life, water and beds of the Atlantic, Pacific and Indian oceans. *See also* PE pp.90–91.

Challis, James (1803–82), British scientist who aimed to co-ordinate all the known facts of science in one general theory of physical action. He was Cambridge Plumian professor of astronomy and experimental philosophy and director of the Cambridge Observatory from 1836. Most famous for his unconscious discovery of Neptune in 1845, he also invented the meteoroscope (1848) and the transit reducer (1849).

Chalybes, ancient people of NE Asia Minor, who lived on the SE shore of the Black Sea. Described by Aeschylus and Strabo, to whom they were semi-legendary, the Chalybes were miners and metal workers. Early iron workings, attributed to the Chalybes, have been found in the mountains above Trebizond.

Cham, Malayo-Polynesian people, inhabiting central Vietnam and Cambodia; descendants of the inhabitants of the ancient kingdom of Champa. Their society is based on agriculture, the main crops being rice and millet.

Chamberlain, Arthur Neville (1869–1940), British politician, son of Joseph CHAMBERLAIN and half-brother of Austen CHAMBERLAIN. He turned from business to local politics in 1911 and in 1915 became mayor of Birmingham. In 1918 he was elected to Parliament as a Conservative. He was chancellor of the exchequer (1923–24) and minister of health (1924–29). At the latter office he distinguished himself by a thorough reform of the social services which brought about a simplification of local government. As prime minister (1937–40) he conducted the policy of APPEASEMENT and signed the MUNICH AGREEMENT in 1938. German successes at the beginning of WWII led to criticism of his leadership and he resigned in May, 1940. *See also* HC2 p.226.

Chamberlain, Houston Stewart (1855–1927), Anglo-German author. He settled in Germany in 1907, married Richard Wagner's daughter and became a German citizen. Much of his writing, particularly *The Foundations of the Nineteenth Century* (1911), argued for a uniquely pure and superior "Teutonic race", a theme that later appeared in NAZI propaganda.

Chamberlain, Joseph (1836–1914), British politician. After being elected to Parliament (1876) he served as Liberal president of the Board of Trade (1880–85) and president of the Local Government Board (1886) but resigned (1886) and joined the Liberal-Unionists. As colonial secretary (1895–1903), in the Conservative/Liberal-Unionist government (1895–1906), Chamberlain advocated both social reform and a vigorous colonial policy. *See also* HC2 p.180.

Chamberlain, Sir Joseph Austen (1863–1937), British political figure. He entered Parliament in 1892 and was postmaster general (1902), chancellor of the exchequer (1903–05, 1919–21), secretary of state for India (1915–17), lord privy seal (1921–22), Conservative Party leader (1921–22), foreign secretary (1924–29) and first lord of the admiralty (1931). As foreign secretary he was one of the main architects of the Locarno Pact of 1925 by which France, Germany and Belgium accepted their existing frontiers and Britain and France agreed to guarantee these frontiers. He received the 1925 Nobel Peace Prize (with Charles G. Dawes) for his work on the pact.

Chamberlain, Owen (1920–), US physicist. After working on the development of the ATOM BOMB between 1942 and 1946 he became professor of physics at the University of California, Berkeley. With Emilio Segrè, using the bevatron particle accelerator, he confirmed the existence of the antiproton and was awarded the Nobel Prize in physics in 1959.

Chamberlain, Thomas Chrowder (1843–1928), US geologist who founded the *Journal of Geology* in 1894. His research into the causes of glaciers and into atmospheric composition led him to formulate, with Forest MOULTON, the PLANETESIMAL HYPOTHESIS of the origin of the solar system. *See also* SU pp.174–175.

Chamberlain's Men, Elizabethan company of actors, formed in 1594; it included William SHAKESPEARE and Richard BURBAGE. The Lord Chamberlain, Henry Carey, was their patron, succeeded by his son Richard in 1596. They acted at Court and in the Inns and theatres of London. In 1599 they gained a part share in the GLOBE THEATRE, where they performed the works of Shakespeare and other dramatists. They became the King's Men in 1603.

Chamberlain, Lord, head of a sovereign's household. The first Lord Chamberlain was appointed in 1360 and until the 20th century the office had political importance, its incumbent taking part in government business. During the reign of George II the Lord Chamberlain took over the licensing of all plays presented in Britain. Confirmed by an Act of 1844, this function was abolished in 1968.

Chamberlain, Lord Great, officer in the English parliamentary system. In the 11th century the Lord Great Chamberlain was the chief finance officer of the Crown. By the 12th century his functions were mainly ceremonial, but developed with the growth of the parliamentary system itself to comprise the government of the Palace of Westminster and of the House of Lords during parliamentary sessions.

Chamber music, instrumental music for two or more instruments, each taking one part. Two to eight instruments is the usual number, and the string quartet (for two violins, viola and cello) the most common arrangement. The term dates from the 17th century and was applied to music suitable for intimate surroundings which was played privately in the homes of wealthy patrons. *See also* HC2 pp.40, 104.

Chamber of Commerce, local association of companies formed to improve their community and promote their commercial interests. The first Chamber of Commerce was formed in Marseille in 1599, and they spread rapidly throughout Europe and to the USA. The International Chamber of Commerce was founded in 1920 and advises governments on economic issues.

Chambers, Ephraim (*c.*1680–1740), English encyclopaedist, founder of modern encyclopaedias. In 1728 he published his comprehensive *Cyclopaedia,* which later influenced the production of the French *Encyclopédie* (1751–71) and the first *Encyclopaedia Britannica* (1768–71). *See also* MM p.214.

Chambers, Sir William (1726–96) British architect, *b.*Sweden. In opposition to the light and gracious style of his contemporary Robert ADAM, his work was robustly Classical. He designed Somerset House, London (1776–86), and Duddingston House, Edinburgh (1762–64).

Chambly, town in S Quebec, Canada, 23km (14 miles) E of Montreal. It is the site of a French fort dating from 1665. It was the headquarters for the British generals Carleton and Burgoyne 1776–77. Industries: paper, canned food, chemicals. Pop. 11,400.

Chameleon, arboreal LIZARD, found chiefly in Madagascar, Africa and Asia, best known for its ability to change colour. The compressed body has a curled, prehensile tail and bulging eyes that move independently. Length: 17–60cm (7–24in). Family Chamaeleontidae; genus *Chamaeleo*; there are 80 species. *See also* NW pp.*135, 139.*

Chaminade, Cécile Louise Stephanie (1857–1944) French concert pianist and composer. Her most successful compositions are small-scale works, including songs and piano pieces.

Chamois, nimble, goat-like RUMINANT that lives in mountain ranges of Europe and W Asia. It has coarse, reddish-brown fur with black tail and horns. Its skin is made into the familiar polishing chamois leather. Length: up to 1.3m (50in); weight: 25–50kg (55–110lb). Family Bovidae; species *Rupicapra rupicapra.*

Chamorro, indigenous people of Guam, of mixed Spanish and Filipino descent; most are Roman Catholics. Their livelihood is based on agriculture, with crops including rice, tobacco and copra.

Champagne, district in NE France, made up of the Aube, Marne, Haute-Marne and Ardennes départements. The major city is Reims, where the early French kings were crowned. Trade fairs in the 11th to 13th centuries made the district a centre of European trade and commerce. There was heavy fighting there during WWI along the Marne River. It is a rather arid region but it produces all world's champagne.

Champagne, sparkling wine, usually white, produced in CHAMPAGNE. Wine is bottled before fermentation ends, and a secondary fermentation produces carbon dioxide under pressure. When the bottle is opened, the gas escapes as bubbles. *See also* PE pp.198–203.

Champaigne Philippe de (1602–74), French painter, *b.* Brussels. He worked in Paris with POUSSIN on the Luxembourg Palace. In 1628 he became artist to Queen Marie de' Medici, and did many portraits and religious paintings for her and Cardinal RICHELIEU. From 1643 he was involved with JANSENISM and produced religious paintings characterized by a serene realism. His best-known works include portraits and frescoes at Vincennes and in the Tuileries.

Champlain, Samuel de (1567–1635), French explorer, founder of New France (Canada). In 1603 he went on an expedition to the Gulf of St Lawrence, where he explored the St Lawrence River. He later (1604–07) led settlers to Port Royal (now Annapolis Royal, Nova Scotia) and explored the Atlantic coast from Nova Scotia to Massachusetts Bay and beyond. Champlain founded Quebec in 1608 and explored northern New York state, where he discovered Lake Champlain in 1609. He also explored the Ottawa River in 1613 and the Great Lakes in 1615. *See also* HC2 p.62.

Champlain, lake on the border of New York State and Vermont, USA, and extending into Quebec, Canada. Linked to the Hudson River by the Champlain division of the Barge Canal, it serves as a link in the Hudson-St Lawrence waterway. Discovered by Samuel de Champlain in 1609, it was the scene of many battles in the French and Indian wars and the American Revolution, and the defeat of the British by Thomas MacDonough in the War of 1812. Today it is a popular resort area with swimming, fishing, boating and winter sports facilities. Areas: 1,101sq km (435sq miles).

Champollion, Jean François (1790–1832), French egyptologist. He was curator of Egyptian antiquities for the Louvre and is generally considered the creator of egyptology. He helped to decode the Rosetta Stone, the key to all Egyptian hieroglyphics.

Chancay, centre of the Cuismancu Empire in central Peru that lasted from *c.*1000–1476, when it was conquered by the Inca. Located in the Chancay, Ancón, Huaura and Chillón valleys the Chancay people built impressive cities and were expert weavers and woodworkers.

Chancellor, Richard (*d.*1556), English navigator. In 1553 he commanded a ship on an expedition to find a north-east passage to Asia, and reached Moscow. By his negotiations with Ivan the Terrible he laid the foundations for English trade with Russia. *See also* HC1 p.278.

Chancellor, Lord High, head of the British legal system. The medieval chancellor was the king's chief minister, who sat in both the CURIA REGIS and the Court of EXCHEQUER. He travelled with the king and all petitions for the king were seen by him. He was the keeper of the GREAT SEAL. Of all the posts in the medieval HOUSEHOLD, the chancellorship alone has retained its political importance. The office is still of cabinet rank.

Chancellor of the Duchy of Lancaster, office deriving from the 14th century, when the duchy was made a county palatine (1351) with its own courts free of royal jurisdiction. Its rights passed to the crown in 1399. The office is now used to accommodate a cabinet minister without portfolio.

Chancellor of the Exchequer, minister responsible for the national finances in Britain. The office evolved from the 13th-century clerk of the Court of EXCHEQUER, assistant to the CHANCELLOR, who, as administration became more complex, withdrew from the Exchequer, leaving the clerk to acquire special responsibility for finance. Until the mid-19th century the office was departmentally inferior to the first lord of the treasury. Since GLADSTONE's tenure of the office in 1850s, however, it has been a major office of state with cabinet rank.

Chancellorsville, Battle of (2–4 May, 1863), American Civil War defeat for the Unionists after the Confederate commander Robert E. Lee sent "Stonewall" JACKSON to surprise the Union rear. Jackson was accidentally killed by a Confederate patrol. *See also* HC2 pp.150–151.

Chancery, Court of, court developed in the 15th century for the Lord Chancellor to deal with petitions, passed on from the king-in-council, from aggrieved persons for redress when no remedy was available in the common law courts. By the middle of the 17th century Chancery had become a second system of law (equity) rather than a reforming agency. By the Supreme Court of Judicature Act of 1925 the court of Chancery was merged into the High Court, of which it is now known as the Chancery Divison.

Chand, Prem (1880–1936), pen-name of Dhanpat Rai Schrivastava, an Indian novelist and short-story writer. Until 1914 he wrote in Urdu and is credited with having given the Urdu short story its form, after which he wrote in Hindi. Chand wrote more than 250 short stories and 12 novels in Hindi; his last novel, *Godan* (*The Gift of a Cow*; 1936), is generally regarded as his best.

Chandelle, in aviation, an abrupt climbing turn in which an aircraft uses its momentum to gain altitude and change direction at once. *See also* MM pp.152–153.

Chandigarh, city in NW India, at the foot of the Siwalik Hills; capital of Punjab and Haryana states. It is one of India's planned cities, designed by LE CORBUSIER, and built in the 1950s. It has the Punjab University (1947), and the garden of Pinjora, a replica of Srinigar's Shalimar gardens. Pop. 257,000.

Chandler, Raymond Thornton (1888–1959), US author. His detective fiction, featuring the tough private eye Philip Marlowe, includes *The Big Sleep* (1939), *Farewell, My Lovely* (1940) and *The Long Goodbye* (1953), all of which were made into films.

Chandragupta (Candragupta), (*c.*321–297 BC), founder of the MAURYA Empire, the first great empire of India. He seized the throne of Magadha kingdom from the Nanda dynasty and extended their territories to include much of N India and parts of Afghanistan. *See also* HC1 p.62.

Chandra Gupta, name of two Indian emperors of the GUPTA dynasty. Chandragupta I (*r.c.* AD 320–*c.*330), the founder of the dynasty, ruled all Bihar and part of Bengal. Chandra Gupta II (*r.c.*375–415), the third and greatest Gupta, expanded the empire and codified its laws. He presided over a period of peaceful prosperity and cultural achievement.

Chanel, Gabrielle (Coco) (*c.*1883–1971), French fashion designer. She revolutionized women's FASHION beginning in the 1920s with a straight, simple, uncorseted line; many elements of her designs were borrowed from men's clothing. She is associated with short hair, costume jewellery, the Chanel suit, jersey dresses, bell-bottom trousers, trench coats and Chanel No.5 perfume.

Chang Chih-tung (1837–1909), traditional Confucian scholar who became one of the key modernizers and regional leaders in China. As a governor in the S (1884–89), he helped build modern armed forces and military academies and organized industrial development by establishing modern iron and steel works.

Changchun. *See* HSINKING.

Chang Heng (AD 78–139), Chinese scientist and poet. He designed astronomical and weather instruments and wrote *Two Capitals*, which compared the imperial cities of the HAN DYNASTY. *See also* HC1 pp.117, 123.

Ch'ang O, in Chinese mythology, the beautiful Moon goddess. Her festival was celebrated on the 15th day of the eighth lunar month. According to one legend, she fled to the Moon to avoid punishment after she stole the drug of immortality.

Change-ringing, art of bell-ringing which was developed in England in the 17th century. "Peals" or sets of from four to 12 bells, tuned to notes of the diatonic scale (usually in the major), are rung in different sequences, with no repetition; each new sequence is a "change". The bells are attached to bellropes and are swung full circle, being struck by internal clappers.

Channel Islands, group of islands at the SW end of the English Channel, approx. 16km (10 miles) off the W coast of France. Part of the United Kingdom, the main islands are Jersey, Guernsey, Alderney and Sark. The chief towns are St Helier on Jersey and St Peter Port on Guernsey. The islands have a warm, sunny climate and fertile soil so the major industries are tourism and agriculture, in particular the raising of dairy cattle. Dairy produce is exported along with spring vegetables and fruit. Area: 194sq km (75sq miles). Pop. (1975 est.) 128,000. *See also* MW p.52.

Channel swimming. *See* SWIMMING.

Channel Tunnel, any of several schemes to link Britain and France by a tunnel under the English Channel. The first was proposed in 1802 by a French engineer; no work began until the late 19th century when a short tunnel was started but soon abandoned for political reasons. In 1973 another project was started but this was also discontinued (in 1975) due to increasing costs. *See also* MM p.189.

Chanson de Roland, French epic by an unknown author of the late 11th century. It describes the defeat of Charlemagne's rearguard at Roncesvalles Pass in the Pyrenees on 15 August 778. As in the typical CHANSONS DE GESTE (songs of deeds), the poem alters historical fact to develop the personal and tragic elements of a situation. *See also* HC1 p.206.

Chansons de geste, French epic poems of the period between the 11th and 14th centuries, generally dealing with the campaigns of Charlemagne and his lieutenants. These anonymously written narratives describe imaginary events in the lives of Guillaume of Orange, Girart de Rousillon, Roland and others. *See also* HC1 p.206.

Chant, unaccompanied liturgical music. The Anglican chant developed from the earlier Gregorian tones, which were melody formulas defining only pitch relationships. After the Reformation harmonies were added and note values designated to English texts of the psalms. The chant is adjustable in length to fit the different psalm verses by repeating one note for any number of words. *See also* HC1 p.*207*.

Chanterelle, medium-sized, edible, fleshy, terrestrial MUSHROOM, which has long been highly prized. It occurs in beech and oakwoods in autumn. It has a bright yellow, funnel-shaped cap with prominent gills continuing down the stem. Family Cantharellaceae; species *Cantharellus cibarius*.

Chantilly, town N of Paris celebrated for its picturesque racecourse. It is the venue of the Prix du Jockey-Club, (the French Derby). The town is also famous for its 14th century chateau and for its lace. Pop.(1968) 10,156.

Chantrey, Sir Francis Legatt (1781–1841), British painter and sculptor. His early work included painted portraits but after 1804 he concentrated exclusively on sculpture. Famous for his portrait busts, his output was prolific and included a marble bust of Sir Walter Scott (1820) at Abbotsford and the statue of William Pitt in Hanover Square, London.

Chantry, in the Roman Catholic Church, the office or the benefice maintained to celebrate MASS for the repose of the souls of the founder and his friends. The term is also used to denote the chapels in which such masses were said. Chantries originated in the Middle Ages but it was not until the 14th and 15th centuries that they became widespread. They were suppressed in England during the Reformation.

Chanukah. *See* HANUKKAH.

Chanute, Octave (1832–1910), US airman who greatly aided the invention and development of the aeroplane. Trained as a engineer, he built railways before turning to aviation. Chanute organized a glider camp from which he and his associates made about 2,000 glides in machines which he had designed.

Chao Kuang-yin (927–976), founder of the Chinese Sung dynasty (960–1279). He was a scholarly general who eliminated regional military control, established a paid army and laid the basis for three centuries of cultural advance in China.

Chao Meng-fu (1254–1322), Chinese painter, calligrapher, and descendant of the Imperial family of the Sung dynasty. His paintings of landscapes and horses are well known, and his calligraphy is considered among the best.

Chaos, in Greek cosmology, the gaping space that preceded creation, also associated with the lowest region of the underworld, TARTARUS. The term is now used to denote utter confusion or disorder.

Chapais, Sir Joseph Amable Thomas (1858–1946), Canadian historian and politician. Editor of *Le Courrier du Canada* (1884–1901), he served in Maurice Duplessis' cabinet and the Senate. Chapais wrote extensively about Jean Talon, Gen. Montcalm, and the history of NEW FRANCE; he was president of the Royal Society of Canada in 1923.

Chapbook, cheap and popular pamphlet, forerunner of the inexpensive book or magazine. Chapbooks were sold by a chapman (pedlar) between the 15th and 18th centuries, and contained popular fiction, newletters, comics and easy-to-read Bible stories, all written in the vernacular.

Chapel Royal, clergy, choir and organist that perform church services for English royalty. Dating from the early 12th century, it was an integral part of the court. In its heyday, the 16th and 17th centuries, it included the most celebrated composers of the age, such as William BYRD and Henry PURCELL.

Chaplin, Sir Charles Edward Spencer ("Charlie") (1889–1977), British actor and film-maker, considered by many to be the greatest comedian of the silent film era. In his short films such as *The Immigrant* (1917) and *A Dog's Life* (1918) he developed his famous role – a jaunty, wistful and often pathetic soul in baggy trousers, bowler hat and a moustache. His major films included *The Kid* (1920), *The Gold Rush* (1924), *City Lights* (1931), *Modern Times* (1936), *The Great Dictator* (1940), *Monsieur Verdoux* (1947) and *Limelight* (1952). He was attacked for his politics and in 1952 left the USA to live in Switzerland. *See also* HC2 p.200–201, *201*.

Chapman, George (*c.*1560–1634), English poet, dramatist and translator. He completed Christopher Marlowe's unfinished poem *Hero and Leander* (1598). His works include the poem *The Shadow of Night* (1594), the plays *The Blind Beggar of Alexandria* (1598) and *Bussy D'Ambois* (1604), and famous translations of Homer's *Iliad* (1611) and *Odyssey* (1614–15).

Chapman, Herbert (1873–1934), Yorkshire-born football manager. An unremarkable player, he became a skilful, innovative manager. In the 1920s he made an ordinary Huddersfield team League champions, then created the great Arsenal side of the 1930s, devising the third-back game and W-formation.

Chappe, Claude (1763–1805), French engineer who, with his brother, Ignace, invented a SEMAPHORE telegraph in 1791. During the French Revolutionary Wars they used their telegraphs on towers to relay information about the state of the war between France and Austria, this method being much faster than other

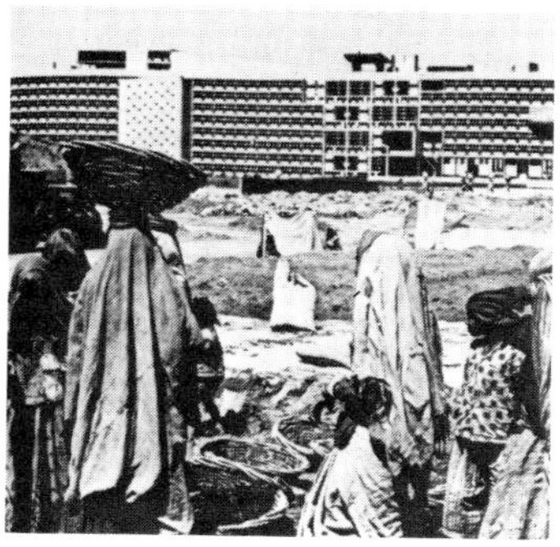

Chandigarh, where traditional Indian life contrasts with the architecture of Le Corbusier.

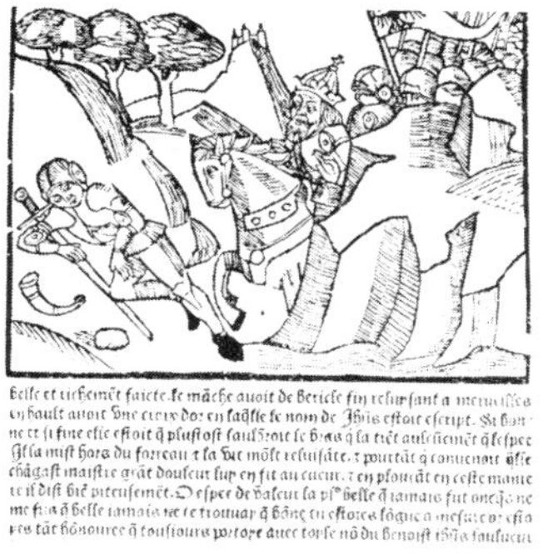

Chanson de Roland, best known of the epic poems of the barons in medieval France.

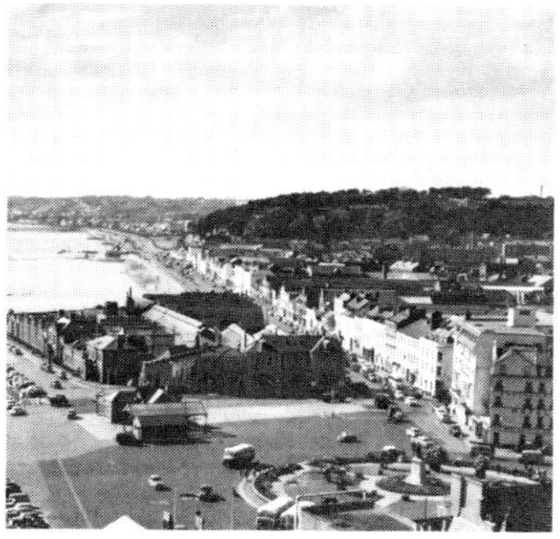

Channel Islands; the harbour at St Helier, Jersey, where French is the official language.

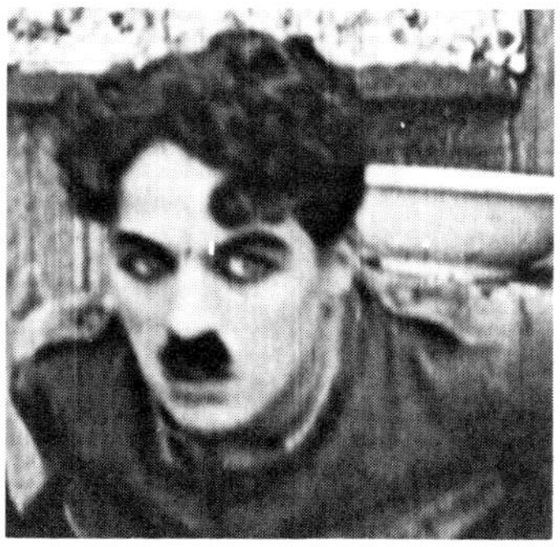

Charlie Chaplin lived in the USA for more than 40 years, never becoming a US citizen.

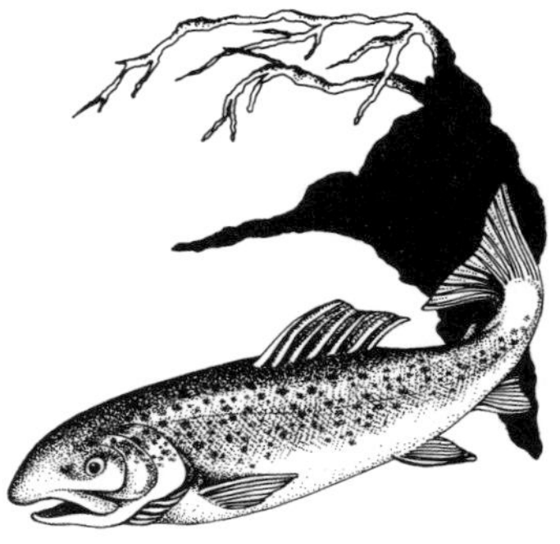

Char; there are four main types of this game fish, a member of the salmon family.

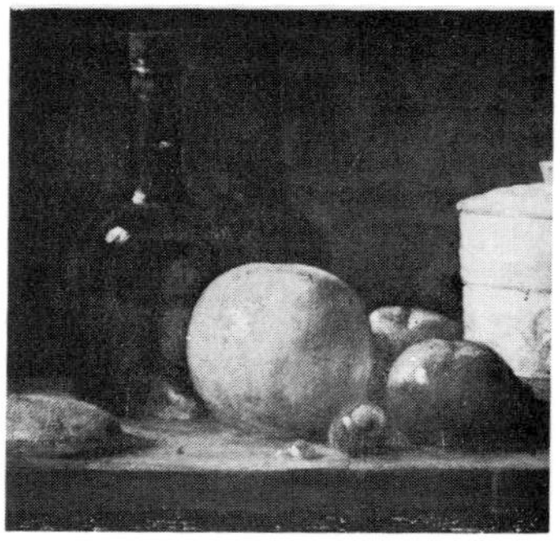

Chardin's career as a painter began humbly when he painted shop signs for tradesmen.

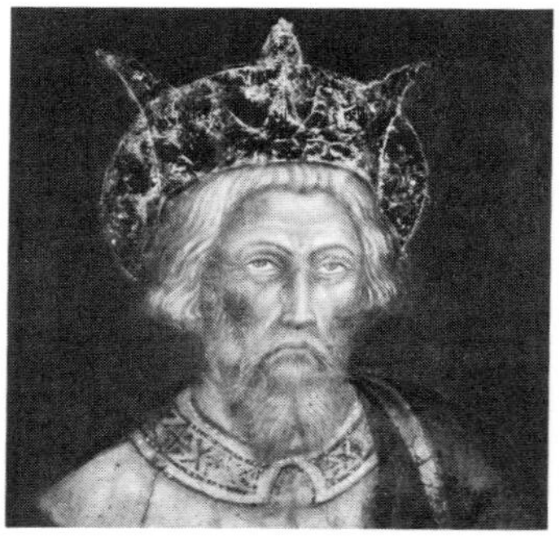

Charlemagne was already inspiring heroic legends long before his death.

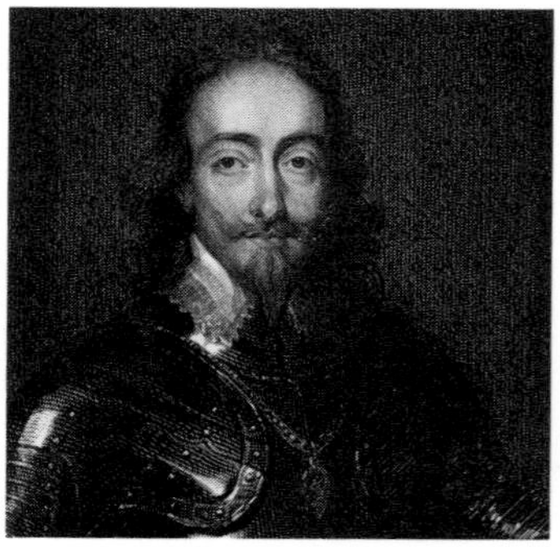

Charles I had a high sense of royal duty but was unable to deal with Parliament.

existing forms of communication. *See also* MM p.224.

Chappell, name of two brothers who played cricket for Australia. Ian (1943–) appeared for South Australia and was a forceful batsman. He captained Australia (1971–75), creating a team of much talent. He played in 72 Test matches, scoring 5,187 runs at an average of 42.86. Greg (1948–), a tall, elegant batsman, played for South Australia, Somerset and Queensland. He succeeded his brother as Australia's captain in 1975. He played in 51 Tests (1970–77), scoring 4,097 runs at an average of 53.20.

Char, name of several species of freshwater game fish belonging to the genus *Salvelinus* of the SALMON family (Salmonidae). There are various European kinds; North American species include the brook, or speckled, trout and the Dolly Varden, or bull trout. *See also* PE p.244.

Charadriiformes, varied order of birds, many of which are shore-dwellers, that live in most areas of the world. They include gulls, terns and auks, guillemots and puffins, plovers, curlews, snipe and phalaropes, and the South American jacanas and sheathbills. *See also* NW p.141.

Charbonneau, Jean (1875–1960), Canadian poet. He wrote imaginative poetry in French which included *Les blessures* (1912), *L'age de sang* (1921), and *Sur la born pensive* (1952). In his work he moved away from the patriotic themes of earlier French-Canadian verse to follow the French Parnassians' principle of art for art's sake.

Charcoal, porous form of CARBON, made traditionally by heating wood in the absence of air, and used in western Europe until late medieval times for smelting iron ore. Today charcoal is chiefly used for its absorptive properties, to decolourize food liquids such as syrups, and to separate one chemical from another. Artists also used charcoal sticks for sketching.

Charcot, Jean-Martin (1825–93), French physician, known as the "father of neurology". He made classical studies of hypnosis and hysteria and taught Pierre JANET and Sigmund FREUD. His work centred on discovering how behavioural symptoms of patients related to diseases of the nervous system. *See also* MS pp.*123*, 137.

Chardin, Jean-Bartiste Siméon (1699–1779), French painter, a great master of genre and still life. His modest choice of subject matter and understated brilliance were overshadowed in that age of BOUCHER and FRAGONARD, but his still lifes and his pictures of kitchen-maids at work greatly influenced many 19th-century painters, especially MANET. *See also* HC2 pp.36,*37*.

Charge, in law, a formal complaint, information or indictment filed against the accused. It is the basic document of any court case. A judge's instruction to the jury is also known as a charge.

Chargé d'affaires, diplomatic representative who works in an embassy or consulate. The post is of lesser status than that of an AMBASSADOR, who is the personal representative of a sovereign or other head of state. A chargé d'affaires is accredited to the government department that deals with foreign affairs (in Britain the Foreign Office).

Charge, electric, quantity of electricity. The crackle of freshly laundered nylon and dry hair being brushed are everyday examples of electric charge and discharge. The ancient Greeks also knew the phenomenon, as the crackle of fur rubbed with amber; their word for amber, *elektron*, was adapted for the whole of a branch of physics, electricity. Electric charges are either positive or negative. They can be stored on insulated metal spheres (as in Van de Graaf machines), on insulated plates (as in capacitors and condensers) and in chemical solutions (as in electric batteries). *See also* SU pp.42–43; 148–149.

Charge of the Light Brigade (25 Oct. 1854), British cavalry charge in the CRIMEAN WAR, one of the most notorious mistakes in British military history. It stemmed from Lord Lucan's misreading of an ambiguous order by the British commander, Lord RAGLAN. As a result Lord Cardigan led the unsupported Light Brigade (at a steady trot rather than a "charge") straight at a battery of some 30 Russian guns. More than 600 men took part, and nearly half of them were killed, wounded or captured.

Charing Cross, district within the city of Westminster, London, lying around the mainline railway station of the same name. Although the present stone cross is modern it marks one of the resting-places of the coffin of EDWARD I's queen, ELEANOR, on its journey to Westminster Abbey.

Chariot, light, two- or four-wheeled vehicle drawn by two or more horses harnessed side by side. The body of a chariot was a small floor-space, with a waist-high guard in front and at the sides. Scythes sometimes projected from the wheels. First employed in warfare *c.* 1700 BC by the HYKSÖS who invaded Egypt, it spread throughout Europe and Asia because it provided a stable and mobile platform for a warrior. By the beginning of the Christian era, its disadvantages on rough ground made it practically obsolete in war, although it was used for racing by the Romans. *See also* MM p.*110*.

Charity Commission, British organization established in 1837 to give administrative and legal advice to the trustees of charities and to investigate possible abuses in such trusts. The Charities Act of 1960 recognized the need to bring the Commission up to date in giving it wider powers and relating its work more closely to that of the welfare services.

Charlemagne (742–814), King of the Franks, (768–814) and Holy Roman Emperor (800–14). The eldest son of PEPIN the Short, he inherited Neustria, the NW half of the Frankish kingdom, in 768 and annexed the remainder on his brother Carloman's death in 771. Responding to Lombard threats against the papacy, he led two armies into Italy and took the Lombard throne in 773. He undertook a long (772–804) and brutal conquest of Saxony, which he forcibly converted to Christianity. He also annexed Bavaria in 788 and defeated the AVARS of the middle Danube (791–96, 804). After regular campaigns against the Muslims, he had established the Spanish march in N Spain by 811. He was crowned Emperor of the West by Pope Leo II in 800, thus reviving the concept of the Roman Empire, and completing the West's split with the Byzantine Empire. A man of great forcefulness, he initiated the intellectual awakening of the Carolingian Renaissance. He set up a strong central authority and kept control of his lands by means of regular visits by his officials, but the empire lacked sufficient coherence to maintain its unity after his death. *See also* HC1 pp.152–153; 158–159.

Charlemagne Prize, annual award made by the city of Aachen to someone who makes a major contribution to the cause of European unity and co-operation. It was first awarded in 1950; in 1963 Edward HEATH was the recipient.

Charleroi, town in SW Belgium on the River Sambre, 50km (31 miles) S of Brussels. The medieval village of Charnoy, it was renamed after Charles II of Spain. A commercial and transport centre, its industries include steel, glass, chemicals and food processing. It is also a centre of coal and iron ore mining. Pop. (1969 est.) 23,900.

Charles I (1600–49), King of England, Scotland and Ireland (*r.* 1625–49). Charles was the second son of JAMES I of England and became heir apparent on the death of his brother Henry in 1612. He inherited his father's reliance on the counsel of the unpopular Buckingham, and was attacked for his marriage in 1625 to the Catholic HENRIETTA MARIA. Charles' unpopular foreign policy and his literal interpretation of the DIVINE RIGHT OF KINGS made him mistrust Parliament, and led him to rule without it for 11 years (1629–40) and to resort to feudal impositions to raise revenue. The attempt of his minister LAUD to impose High Church liturgy on Scotland led to a rebellion in that country in 1639, which necessitated the recall of Parliament. Charles allowed Parliament to impeach Laud and to execute his chief adviser STRAFFORD in 1641, but he attempted a coup against the Commons in 1642 when he tried to arrest the five leading members of his opposition. The incident was the trigger for English Civil War. Charles took command of the royalist army and made his headquarters in Oxford. Following his defeat at NASEBY in 1645, Charles surrendered and was imprisoned by the parliamentary army which tried to establish a constitutional monarchy. Disputes over its form, and plots by Charles, led in Dec. 1648 to a purge of Parliament of all but those most hostile to Charles; he was tried for treason, although he refused to recognize the court, and he was executed on 30 Jan. 1649. *See also* HC1 pp.286–288.

Charles II (1630–85), King of England, Scotland and Ireland (*r.* 1660–85). When his father CHARLES I was defeated in 1646 he fled to France where Thomas HOBBES acted as his tutor. He was crowned King of Scots in 1651, but after the failure of his Scottish uprising in that year he again went into exile in France and Holland. He issued a declaration at BREDA in 1660 that included an indemnity for all those involved in the civil wars, and he was invited to return to the throne the same year. His reign was marked by his attempts to manoeuvre towards a more autocratic monarchy and to introduce greater religious toleration. Initially he relied on the advice of the Earl of CLARENDON; in the late 1670s his harmonious relationship with Parliament broke up as fears arose that he sympathized with Roman Catholicism. Parliamentary opposition reached a peak during the POPISH PLOT and Exclusion Crisis of 1679–81, when attempts were made to exclude Charles's brother, the Catholic Duke of York (later JAMES II) from the succession. Charles survived the crisis and in the last years of his reign rooted out much of the opposition in the boroughs. Although Charles had many mistresses, and was known as the Merry Monarch, he had no legitimate children. He was a patron of the arts and incorporated the ROYAL SOCIETY in 1662. *See also* HC1 pp.292–294, 298.

Charles, Prince of Wales (1948–) eldest son of ELIZABETH II, heir to the British throne. He was educated at Cambridge University (1967–70) and trained as an air force pilot before becoming a naval officer in 1971. He was invested with the title Prince of Wales in 1969.

Charles, name of seven Holy Roman emperors. For Charles I *see* CHARLEMAGNE. Charles II (823–77), the Bald, became King of the West Franks in 843 and Emperor in 875. He signed the Treaty of VERDUN in 843. Charles III (839–88), the Fat, became Emperor in 881, King of the East Franks in 882 and of the West Franks in 884. Charles IV (1316–78) became King of Bohemia in 1346 and Emperor in 1355. He opposed papal influence in the election of emperors and promoted the independence of BOHEMIA. Charles V (1500–58), the greatest of the HAPSBURG kings, was King of Spain 1516–56 and Emperor 1519–56, and also controlled The Netherlands, Sicily and Naples and Spanish America. He was constantly thwarted in his attempts to unify his empire by his rivalry with the VALOIS kings of France, and by the emergence of the REFORMATION in the 1520s. He became leader of the Catholic cause, but after constant opposition within the empire, he abdicated his various thrones in the mid-1550s and retired to the monastery of Yuste in Spain. Charles VI (1685–1740) became Emperor in 1711, and was the last direct Hapsburg emperor. His claim to the Spanish throne was supported by England in the War of the SPANISH SUCCESSION, in which he won The Netherlands. Charles VII (1697–1745) became Emperor in 1742, but his throne was disputed in the War of the AUSTRIAN SUCCESSION. *See also* index to *History and Culture 1.*

Charles I (1887–1922), Austrian emperor

(*r.* 1916–18), and King (as Charles IV) of Hungary (*r.* 1916–18), the last Hapsburg ruler. When Hungary and Czechoslovakia declared their independence in 1918, Charles was forced into exile in Switzerland. In 1921 he twice attempted unsuccessfully to regain the Hungarian throne.

Charles, name of ten kings of France. For Charles I, *see* CHARLEMAGNE; for Charles II (the Bald) and III (the Fat), *See* CHARLES (Holy Roman emperors). Charles III (879–929), known as Charles the Simple (*r.* 893–922), ceded Normandy to the Norsemen in 911 and gained Lorraine. Charles IV (1294–1328), Charles the Fair, succeeded to the throne in 1322, and was the last king of the CAPET family. He won part of Guienne (AQUITAINE) from England in 1327. Charles V (1338–80), who came to the throne in 1364, was called the Wise, and regained much territory lost to the English in the HUNDRED YEARS WAR; he built a strong army and navy, as well as increasing royal control of taxation and patronizing the arts. His son Charles VI (1368–1422), known as Charles the Well-Beloved or Charles the Mad, was under the unpopular influence of his uncle until 1388 and from 1392 suffered from bouts of insanity. Following the invasions of HENRY V of England, Charles was compelled by the Treaty of TROYES (1420) to recognize Henry as his successor. Nevertheless, Charles's son, Charles VII (1403–61), took the title of king on his father's death and ruled S of the Loire. He was prompted to oppose the English by JOAN OF ARC in 1429. He signed the Treaty of ARRAS in 1435 and won Paris the next year. By 1453 he finally secured the complete withdrawal of English troops from France, thus ending the Hundred Years War. Charles VIII (1470–98) came to the throne in 1483. He invaded Italy in 1494 to capture Naples but was driven out of Naples the next year. This expedition was important in introducing the Italian Renaissance to France. Charles IX (1550–74) became king at the age of 10, under the regency of his mother Catherine de' MEDICI. After he fell under the influence of the HUGUENOT leader COLIGNY in 1571, Catherine forced Charles to instigate the MASSACRE OF ST BARTHOLEMEW in 1572. Charles X (1757–1836) fled France in 1789, went into the Austrian Netherlands, Turin, Prussia and Russia, and finally went into exile in England until 1814. After the assassination of Louis XVIII in 1824 Charles succeeded to the throne. In 1830 he abolished the liberal chamber of deputies and restricted press freedom. He was forced to abdicate in the ensuing JULY REVOLUTION. *See also* index to *History and Culture* volumes.

Charles, name of three kings of Naples. Charles I (1226–85) was made King of Naples and Sicily by the pope in 1246 in return for political support. The SICILIAN VESPERS rebellion of 1282 was supported by the ARAGON king who captured his son Charles II (1254–1309) shortly before his father's death. After his release, Charles restored peace to Sicily in 1302. Charles III (1345–86) became King of Naples in 1381 and Hungary in 1385.

Charles I (Carlos) (1863–1908), King of Portugal (1889–1908). Unable to compete with British and German expansion in Africa, Charles was criticized at home for his weak attitude to the Portuguese empire. After a revolt in 1906, he ruled arbitrarily. In another revolt Charles and the heir apparent were assassinated.

Charles, name of four kings of Spain. For Charles I, *see* CHARLES V, Holy Roman Emperor. Charles II (1661–1700), the last Spanish Hapsburg, came to the throne in 1665 and was mentally incompetent. His death led to the War of the SPANISH SUCCESSION. Charles III (1716–88) inherited the Spanish throne in 1759. He won Louisiana from the French in 1763, and was considered one of Europe's great "enlightened despots". Charles IV (1748–1819), his son, succeeded him. By an alliance with France in 1796 Spain became involved in war with England. Occupation by French troops in 1808 was met by a popular Spanish uprising and Charles was forced to abdicate. He spent the rest of his life in exile. *See also* HC1 p.325, HC2 p.77.

Charles, name of 16 kings of Sweden, the first six of whom may be legendary. The first of whom it is possible to speak with confidence was Charles VII (*c.* 1161–67), who was murdered by Erik Jedvardsson, a rival for the throne. Charles VIII reigned with two short intervals from 1448 to 1470. In 1449-50 he was also King of Norway. Charles IX (*r.* 1604–11) restored the Protestant faith to Sweden while ruling as regent before his accession. He began the long war with Poland in 1600 and the war with Denmark in 1611. Charles X Gustav (*r.* 1654–60) became king on the abdication of his cousin Christina. He invaded and conquered Poland in 1655–56 and won back lands of southern Sweden from Denmark by the Treaty of Roskilde (1658). His son, Charles XI (*r.*1660–97), greatly increased the power of the monarchy and centralized the Swedish nation state. He expanded the navy and the army, forced the nobility to surrender lands to the crown, and in 1693 was granted near-absolute power. Charles XII (*r.* 1697–1718) was called the "Alexander of the North" and the "Madman of the North". He spent much of his reign at war against Russia, Denmark and Poland. He was killed in the invasion of Norway at the siege of Fredrikshald. Charles XIII (*r.* 1809–18) presided over the union of Sweden and Norway in 1814. In 1809 he was forced to give up Finland and the Åland Islands to Russia. Charles XIV John (*r.*1818–44), French-born, served in the army during the FRENCH REVOLUTION and in NAPOLEON's diplomatic service. Charles XV (*r.* 1859–72) granted the country a two-chamber parliament and did much to reform the legal system. *See also* CARL XVI GUSTAF.

Charles, five dukes of Lorraine. Charles I (953–*c.* 992) disputed with Hugh CAPET for the French throne. Charles II (1365–1431) united Bar and Lorraine. Charles III (1543–1608), who became duke in 1545, took the Catholic side in the French Wars of Religion. His war (1592–94) with Henry IV ended after Henry's conversion to Catholicism. Charles IV (1604–75) succeeded to the duchy in 1624. He lost and regained the duchy several times during the THIRTY YEARS WAR and was finally removed by Louis XIV in 1670. Charles V (1643–90) was also refused the duchy in 1675 by Louis. He fought for the Holy Roman Emperor and the Dutch against France, but failed to regain Lorraine.

Charles, Bob (1936–), New Zealand professional golfer. One of the finest left-handers in the world, he has won the British Open (1963) and Canadian Open (1968) championships and many other titles.

Charles, Jacques (1746–1823), French physicist, inventor and mathematician who was the first to use a hydrogen balloon. He discovered the law relating the expansion of a gas to its temperature rise. GAY-LUSSAC published Charles's work 15 years later and the law is known both as CHARLES'S LAW and as Gay-Lussac's law.

Charles, John (1930–), Welsh footballer known as "the gentle giant". A world-class centre-forward or centre-half, he was at 18 Wales's youngest international. He was with Leeds United until 1957, when he went to Juventus (Turin, Italy) to win fame and honours. He also played for Roma and Cardiff City.

Charles, Ray (1932–), US singer and pianist, full name Ray Charles Robinson. Blind since the age of six, he played and sang with various bands until his first hit recording *I Got a Woman* (1955), which launched him to stardom. He has recorded many albums.

Charles, Thomas (1755–1814), Welsh churchman and educator. He was ordained to the Anglican priesthood in 1780 but became a Methodist in 1784. In 1785 he established the first of many Welsh language schools. In 1806 he published the first Welsh bible and his biblical dictionary appeared between 1805 and 1811, with his Welsh catechism.

Charles Albert (1798–1849), King of Sardinia-Piedmont (1831–49). He was a liberal reformist, opposed Austria and sought Italian liberation; but after defeat in a war against Austria (1848–49), he abdicated in favour of his son, VICTOR EMMANUEL II, and went to Portugal in exile. *See also* HC2 p.108.

Charles Augustus (1757–1828), Duke of Saxe-Weimar-Eisenach (1775–1828). He fought against Napoleon I and was an important member of the Congress of VIENNA. He was the patron of SCHILLER and GOETHE.

Charles Edward Stuart. *See* STUART, CHARLES EDWARD.

Charles Emmanuel IV (1751–1819), King of Sardinia-Piedmont (*r.* 1796–1802). Forced to cede his mainland possessions to France (1798), he abdicated in favour of his brother, VICTOR EMMANUEL I.

Charles Emmanuel, name of three dukes of Savoy. Charles Emmanuel I (1562–1630), who became duke in 1580, constantly varied his allegiance between France and Spain in an attempt to capture Geneva and Saluzzo, but had little success. Charles Emmanuel II (1634–75) became duke at the age of four. His mother, a sister of the French king, acted as regent, and throughout his reign Savoy was closely tied to French policy. Charles Emmanuel III (1701–73) also became King of Sardinia in 1730. He sided with France and Spain in the War of the POLISH SUCCESSION and against Spain in the War of the AUSTRIAN SUCCESSION.

Charles' law, in physics, states that the volume of a gas at constant pressure is directly proportional to its temperature. This phenomenon was discovered by the French scientist Jacques Charles about 1787. The law is a special case of the IDEAL GAS LAW. *See also* SU pp.84–85.

Charles Martel (*c.* 688–741), Frankish ruler, grandfather of CHARLEMAGNE. Upon the death of his father in 714, he seized control of the Frankish kingdoms of Austrasia and Neustria. He later conquered Burgundy, Aquitaine and Provence and subjugated many German tribes E of the Rhine. In 732 at POITIERS he halted the advance of the Muslims from Spain. *See also* HC1 p.152.

Charles the Bold (1433–77), last reigning Duke of Burgundy (*r.* 1467–77). He was allied with England by marriage and was ruler of the Low Countries, Luxembourg, Burgundy and Franche-Comté. He seized Nancy in 1475, and subsequently attacked the Swiss, who killed him in 1477. Burgundy's resistance to France ended with his death.

Charleston, capital of West Virginia, USA, on the Kanawha River. The city grew around Fort Lee (1788), home of Daniel Boone. It is an important trade and transport centre for the highly industrialized Kanawha Valley. Industries: chemicals, glass, metallurgy, timber, oil, coal. Pop. (1970) 71,505.

Charleston, port in SE South Carolina, USA. Founded in 1680 by William Sayle, it soon became and remained the major seaport of the SE and a leading centre of wealth and culture in the S. The South Carolina Ordinance of Secession was signed there in 1860 and the firing on Fort Sumter was the first engagement of the AMERICAN CIVIL WAR. It has many fine colonial buildings and the Fort Sumter National Monument. Industries: paper, textiles, chemicals, steel. Pop. (1970) 66,945.

Charleston, popular dance of the 1920s. Originated in the USA by southern Blacks around the turn of the 20th century, it was used in music hall and musical shows. It was a precursor of the jitterbug.

Charles Town, town in NE West Virginia, USA. John Brown was executed there in 1859. The chief industry is limestone quarrying. Pop. (1970) 3,023.

Charlevoix, Pierre François Xavier de (1682–1761), Canadian historian and explorer, *b.* France. He canoed up the St Lawrence River in 1720 to the Great Lakes, and eventually reached New Orleans.

Charley's Aunt (1892), three-act farce by Brandon THOMAS. After its London première (1892) it ran for a record 1,466

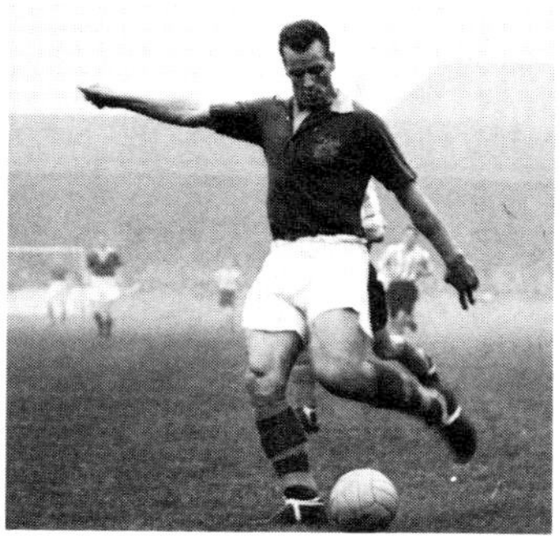

John Charles was one of the most exciting and versatile British soccer stars of the 1950s.

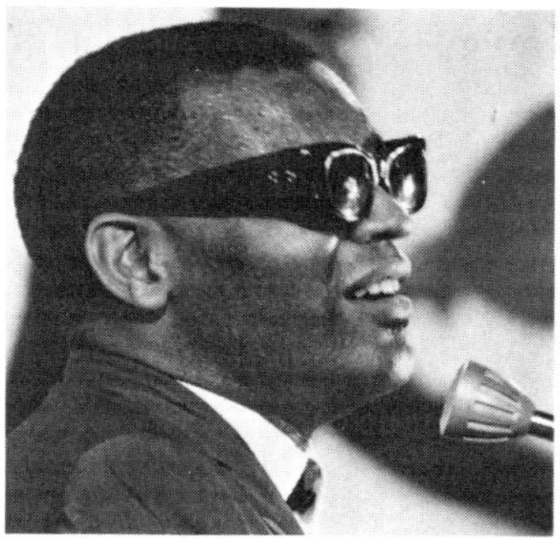

Ray Charles, blind since the age of six, is a popular American entertainer.

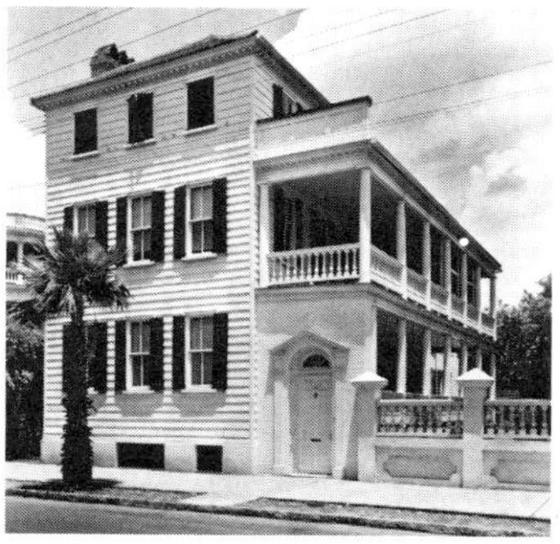

Charleston, South Carolina; a typical false-front house at 64 Meeting Street.

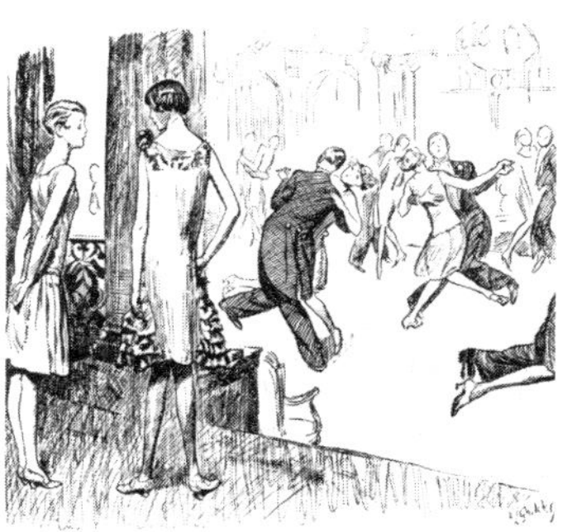

Charleston; "It's a pity you don't Charleston, Audrey, your knees are simply made for it".

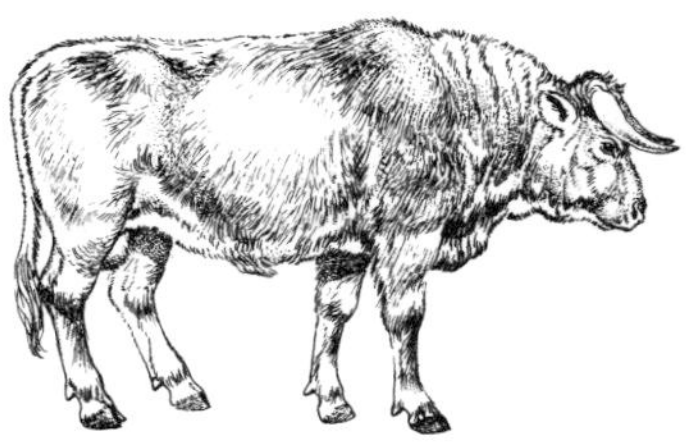
Charolais, the famous white oxen, a French breed of beef cattle of increasing popularity.

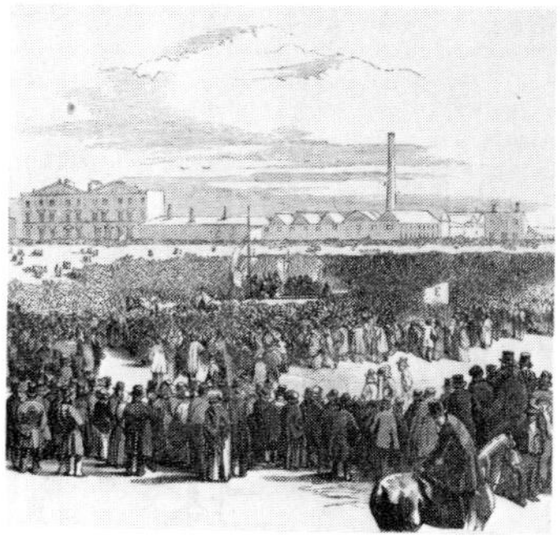
Chartism, the working-class 19th-century movement, sought electoral reforms.

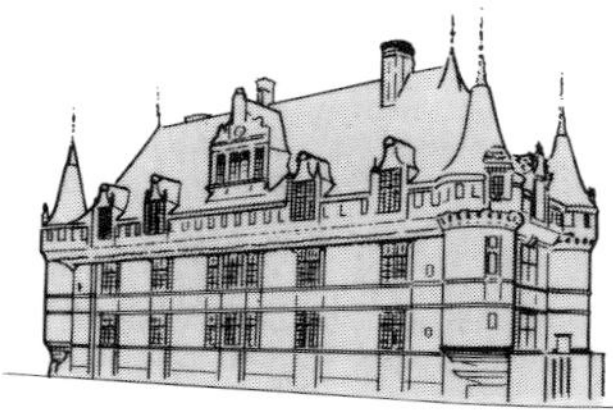
Châteaux, the grand French country houses which developed from the fortified castles.

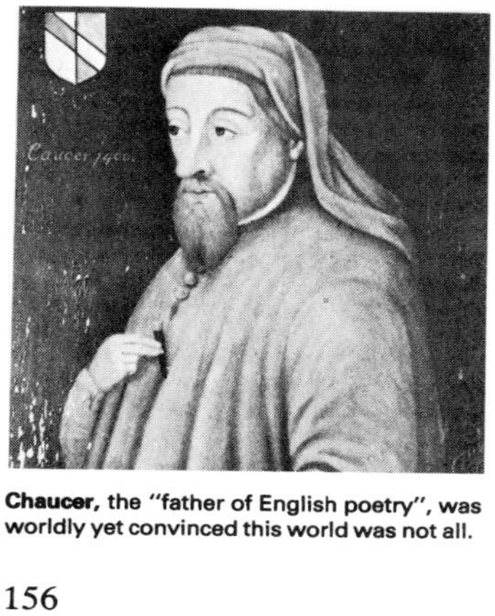

Chaucer, the "father of English poetry", was worldly yet convinced this world was not all.

performances. It is frequently revived.

Charlock, yellow-flowered, troublesome weed of the MUSTARD family common in Europe. Species *Sinapis arvensis.*

Charlotte, largest city in North Carolina, USA. It has two universities and three colleges, and was the birthplace of President James K. Polk. It is the distribution centre for the Carolina manufacturing belt. Industries: mechanical engineering, chemicals, textiles, food processing. Pop. (1970) 241,178.

Charlotte Amalie, port and capital of the Virgin Islands of the USA, on St Thomas Island. It was a Danish colonial centre, reflected in its architecture, and an important trading centre in the American Civil War. Pop. (1970) 12,372.

Charlottetown, capital and port of Prince Edward Island, Canada. Founded by the French in 1720, it has the University of Prince Edward Island (1969). Industries: food processing, fishing, tourism. Pop. 19,000.

Charlton, Robert ("Bobby") (1937–), British footballer who played for Manchester United and England. He won 106 caps between 1957 and 1970.

Charnwood Forest, upland region in NW Leicestershire, England. The area is largely barren, with patches of woodland and bracken. In the past it has been extensively quarried for roadstone. The highest point is Barden Hill, which rises to 278m (912ft).

Charolais, creamy white breed of BEEF CATTLE, originally developed in France. The breed's great size and the speed with which the calves develop has made it popular for cross-breeding purposes. *See also* PE pp.*226*, 227.

Charon, in Greek mythology, boatman of the Lower World who ferried the souls of the dead across the River STYX to HADES. The fare was a bronze coin called an *obolus,* which was placed under the corpse's tongue during the burial service.

Charpentier, Gustave (1860–1956), French composer. He was taught by Jules MASSENET and his best-known compositions are the opera *Louise* (1900) and *Impressions Fausses* (1895).

Charron, Pierre (1541–1603), French philosopher. His principal book, *De la sagesse,* was published in 1601. In this three-volume work inspired by MONTAIGNE, whom he met in 1589, he contrasted inadequate rational knowledge with true knowledge acquired by divine revelation.

Charter, document which grants specified rights to an individual or a corporation. The term implies the existence of a sovereign power which surrenders its sovereignty in a specific area. Medieval kings, for example, often gave a town a charter which freed it from some feudal dues and gave its citizens certain rights. MAGNA CARTA is one of the best-known charters. *See also* HC1 p.*192.*

Chartier, Alain (*c.*1390–1440), French poet, prose-writer and diplomat. His prose work *Le Quadrilogue invectif* (1422) was an analysis of the social and political climate of his day, but he is best known for his ballades and rondeaux. *La Belle Dame sans merci* (1424) was widely influential.

Chartism, British working-class movement 1838–48. Combining the discontent of the industrial workers in a period of depression with the demands of radical artisans, the movement was united under the People's Charter, drawn up in 1838 by William Lovett, which demanded electoral reform including universal male suffrage. As well as local riots and strikes, the Chartists organized three mass petitions (1839, 1842, 1848), but after a period of national organization led by the Irishman Feargus O'Connor, the movement became quiescent until 1848 when it briefly revived in the wake of the European revolutions of that year. *See also* HC2 pp.*95,* 160.

Chartres, town in NW France, on the Eure River, 80km (50 miles) SW of Paris; capital of Eure-et-Loir département. An 11th-century, wooden-roofed Basilica stood on the site now occupied by the 12th-13th century GOTHIC Cathedral of Notre Dame, whose stained glass and sculptures make it one of Europe's finest cathedrals. Industries: brewing, leather, agricultural equipment, radio and television parts. Pop. 34,000. *See* HC1 pp.*198–201.*

Chartreuse, La Grande, mother house of the CARTHUSIAN ORDER, situated in the Dauphine Alps in SE France. The present monastery on the site dates from the 17th century and has housed Carthusian monks since then, except for an interval of 38 years between 1903 and 1941. Chartreuse liqueur originated there.

Charybdis, in Greek mythology, a female monster in the Straits of Messina who lay opposite SCYLLA. Daughter of POSEIDON and GAEA, Charybdis had stolen HERCULES' cattle, for which ZEUS hurled her into the sea. She created a whirlpool which swallowed up many ships, but both JASON and ODYSSEUS escaped.

Chase, Stuart (1888–), US economist. He was investigator for the Federal Trade Commission (1917–22) and consultant to the Labor Bureau (1922–39). He founded the Consumers' Union and wrote *Tragedy of Waste* (1925), *Your Money's Worth* (1927), *A New Deal* (1932) and *Rich Land Poor Land* (1936).

Chasing, in metalwork, technique used to define forms of design and to heighten relief. The design is traced onto the surface and adjacent areas are hammered from the front with punches of varying shapes. Flat chasing, with small blunt tools, was popular in 18th-century European silverwork, producing low-relief ornamentation.

Chasuble, outermost vestment worn by Christian clergy in celebrating the EUCHARIST. It is used universally in the Roman Catholic Churches and widely by High Church Anglican priests and in the Lutheran Churches of Scandinavia. Its equivalent in the Eastern Orthodox Church is the phelonion.

Chat, any of several birds of the WARBLER group, including the North American yellow-breasted chat (*Icteria virens*) known for its mimicking ability, and the red-breasted chat (*Granatellus venustus*) of Central America.

Château, fortified residence that was the French equivalent of the English castle in medieval times. In the 15th century changes in methods of warfare and in the feudal system made the heavily fortified château obsolete. Lightly fortified, luxurious country houses, such as Amboise, Blois, Chambord and Chenonceaux, mark the transition between medieval fortress and country mansion.

Chateaubriand, François-René Vicomte de (1768–1848), French writer and diplomat whose works contributed to the growth of French ROMANTICISM. *The Genius of Christianity* (1802) was a reaction to ENLIGHTENMENT attacks on Catholicism and established his literary reputation; *Atala* (1801) and *René* (1805) are tragic love stories set in the American wilderness where he had travelled before the Revolution broke out and he had returned to France to fight with the emigré army. He lived in England between 1793 and 1800. After 1803 he held important diplomatic posts for both Napoleon and the Bourbons and was minister of foreign affairs (1823–24). In 1830 he resigned from politics and spent his last years with Mme RÉCAMIER working on his *Memoirs from Beyond the Grave,* which were published in 1849–50.

Château Gaillard, 12th-century French ruin on a rock above the River Seine at Les Andelys, 32km (20 miles) SE of Rouen. It was built in 1196–98 by RICHARD I of England to defend Rouen and his Norman territories from French attack.

Châteaugay, Battle of (1813), engagement in the WAR OF 1812, in which 4,000 US soldiers under Gen. Wade Hampton unsuccessfully attacked 1,600 Canadian Indian troops under Lieut.-Col. Charles de Salaberry who were defending the approaches to Montreal.

Chatelperronian Culture, the first of the Upper Paleolithic cultures, flourishing in Châtelperron in the Périgord region of central France in about 35,000 BC. Responsible for the earliest known blade culture, its people produced knives made of flint blades with one straight razor-like edge, arrows, javelin points and scrapers.

Chatham, William Pitt, 1st Earl of (1708–78), English statesman also known as William Pitt the Elder. He became known in Parliament after 1735 for his speeches advocating that England should concentrate on commerce and colonial development. He became secretary of state in 1756 following a crisis in the SEVEN YEARS WAR, and the next year headed a coalition with the Duke of Newcastle. He subsidized Frederick the Great, expanded the navy and continually harassed the French. His main effort was devoted to the successful capture of much of India and Canada. He resigned in 1761 when GEORGE III refused to declare war on Spain, and opposed the Treaty of PARIS as inadequate. He denounced the prosecution of WILKES in 1763 and attacked the STAMP ACT in 1765. He was created Earl of Chatham in 1766 and nominally headed a ministry in 1766–68, but it was weak and divided, partly on account of his physical and mental illnesses. He retired from active politics in 1768 but continued to argue for any peace settlement with the American colonies short of granting independence. *See also* HC2 p.*68.*

Chattanooga, city in SE Tennessee, on the Tennessee River. It was an important strategic centre in the American Civil War. The Battle of Chattanooga (Nov. 1863) was an important Union victory for the troops of SHERMAN. Since 1935 it has been the headquarters of the Tennessee Valley Authority. Industries: iron and steel, food processing, synthetic fibres, tourism. Pop. (1970) 119,082. *See also* HC2 p.*151.*

Chatterji, Bankim Chandra (1838–94), Indian author who created an Indian school of prose-writing on the European model. He wrote several popular novels and in 1872 began a newspaper advocating Hindu nationalism, for which he is considered a leading spokesman.

Chatterton, Thomas (1752–70), English poet and forger of antiquities. He wrote comic opera and poems such as *Bristowe Tragedie* and *Mynstrelles Songe,* supposedly composed by Thomas Rowley, an imaginary 15th-century monk. *See also* HC2 p.72.

Chaucer, Geoffrey (1345–1400), the greatest English medieval poet. He was the son of a wine merchant and served at court and on diplomatic missions before being appointed controller of customs in London (1374–86). His writings are remarkable for their range, narrative sense, power of characterization and humour. They include *The Book of the Duchesse,* (1369), *The House of Fame,* (*c.*1375) *The Parliament of Fowls,* (*c.*1385) *Troilus and Criseyde,* (*c.*1385) and *The Canterbury Tales* (*c.*1385–1400). *See also* HC1 pp.214–215.

Chaudhuri, Nirad Chandra (1897–), Indian author, editor and journalist. His work includes *The Autobiography of an Unknown Indian* (1951), *A Passage to England* (1959), which was written after a visit to England in 1955, and *Continent of Circe* (1965).

Chaudière, river in S Quebec, Canada. It rises in Lac Mégantic and flows N to the St Lawrence River, opposite Quebec. There is a hydroelectric power plant at Chaudière Falls. Length: 193km (120 miles).

Chaulmoogra, Asian tree of the genus *Hydnocarpus* whose seeds contain chaulmoogra oil. For centuries the oil was the only treatment for LEPROSY, but it has now been superseded by diaminodiphenylsulphone drugs.

Chausson, Ernest Amédée (1855–99), French composer whose orchestral, chamber, and operatic works combined elements of romanticism and impressionism. His best-known works are *Poème* (1896) for violin and orchestra and *Symphony in B flat* (*c.*1890).

Chauvinism, term first used to describe intense admiration for NAPOLEON I, after Nicolas Chauvin, a soldier in Napoleon's armies. The term was soon applied to any exclusive and exaggerated nationalist sentiments, in the 1960s was used to describe men unsympathetic to the idea of female equality.

Chavez, Carlos (1899–), Mexican composer and conductor. He used elements of Mexican Indian music in works such as *Sinfonia Indiá* (1936) and *Xochipilli-Macuilxochitl* (1940), and later works include his Sixth Symphony (1964) and *Invention* (1965) for string trio.

Chavín, one of the earliest prehistoric culture periods in Peru, lasting from *c.*1000 to *c.*200 BC. Named after the Chavín de Huántar in N Peru, the people of the culture developed excellent stone sculpture, the earliest goldwork yet found in the Americas and some ceramics that, whether judged by technological or aesthetic standards, were remarkable. *See also* HC1 p.46–47.

Chayefsky, Paddy (1923–), US writer active in the theatre, television and films. He received OSCARS for his screenplays for *Marty* (1955), *The Hospital* (1971) and *Network* (1976).

Cheapside, street running from St Paul's Cathedral to Poultry in the City of London, England. In the 13th century it was the site of a "cheap", a permanent fair and market.

Checkers. *See* DRAUGHTS.

Cheddar, village in Somerset, SW England. It is located in a dairy farming region and is noted for its cheese, a type now also produced in many other places. The nearby Cheddar Gorge is a popular tourist attraction. Pop. 3,000.

Cheese, food made by curdling milk and then processing the curd. Generally cows' milk is used, although cheese can also be made from the milk of goats, sheep and even yaks. Blue cheeses such as Stilton and Gorgonzola are made by piercing the curd with needles, which allows air to react with a fungus previously introduced; this produces the blue veins, odour and tangy taste. Roquefort and Camembert are made using the spores of *Penicillium* species of fungus. *See also* PE pp.225–229.

Cheetah, or hunting leopard, spotted large CAT found in hot, arid areas of Africa, the Middle East and India. A long-legged animal with blunt, non-retractable claws, it has a tawny brown coat with round black spots. Capable of running at more than 95km/h (60mph), it hunts gazelles and antelopes by sight. Length: body: 140–150cm (55–59in); tail: 75–80cm (29.6–31.5in); weight: 60kg (132lb). Family Felidae; subfamily Acinonchinae; species *Acinonyx jubatus. See also* NW pp.164, 220–221.

Cheiromancy. *See* PALMISTRY.

Cheka, early secret police of Soviet Russia. Formed in 1917, soon after the Bolshevik take-over, it had a wide-ranging role during the next four years of civil war. The ferocious reign of terror implemented by its director, F.E. Dzerzhinsky, alienated many local Bolshevik organizations, however, and it was disbanded in 1922, to be replaced by the GPU. *See also* HC2 p.197.

Cheke, Sir John (1514–57), English classicist and professor of Greek at Cambridge. Tutor to EDWARD VI and secretary to Lady Jane GREY, he was imprisoned by MARY I.

Chekhov, Anton Pavlovich (1860–1904), Russian dramatist who worked closely with Konstantin STANILAVSKY at the MOSCOW ART THEATRE and whose chief works, *The Seagull* (1896), *Uncle Vanya* (1897), *The Three Sisters* (1901) and *The Cherry Orchard* (1903), display a deep understanding of human nature and a fine blend of the comic and the tragic. Detailed and realistic portraits of provincial life, their main action invariably takes place off-stage and their characters reveal as much by what they leave unsaid as by the subtleties of their dialogue. *See also* HC2 pp.101, *101*.

Chekiang (Zhejiang), province in E China, on the E China Sea, including the Chushan archipelago; capital is Hangchow (Hangzhou). It was the royal capital under the Southern Sung dynasty in the 12th and 13th centuries. Agriculture is important in the N plain region where cotton, wheat and hemp are produced. Industries: fishing, cotton textiles, rice, tea and silk. Area: 101,830sq km (39,300sq miles). Pop. approx. 31 million.

Chelation, chemical reaction in which a certain type of organic compound, termed a chelating agent, combines with a metal ion by forming CO-ORDINATE bonds with two or more atoms of the organic compound. Tartaric acid (CH.OH.COOH)$_2$ and ethylenediamine ($CH_2.NH_2$)$_2$ are chelating agents. *See also* SU p.*143*.

Chellean, name formerly given to the early STONE AGE industry characterized by crude hand-axes, originally found near Chelles, France, but now more usually known as ABBEVILLEAN. Today the term more commonly refers to the genus of man whose complete skull was found in OLDUVAI GORGE, Tanzania, by Louis LEAKEY in 1960. He classified it as belonging to HOMO ERECTUS and dated it as being slightly more than half a million years old. The find seems to suggest Chellean Man was a direct ancestor of AUSTRALOPITHECUS. *See also* HC1 p.23; MS pp.24–26, *24–26, 31*.

Chelm, town in E Poland from where the country was declared a republic in 1944 and the site of two WWII German extermination camps where between 100,000 and 300,000 were killed. Industries: smelting, brewing. Pop. (1974 est.) 44,000.

Chelmsford, Frederick John Napier Thesiger, 1st Viscount (1868–1933), British colonial administrator who helped to prepare the Montagu-Chelmsford Report (1918) which advocated a measure of self-rule for India.

Chelmsford, county town of Essex, SE England, 48km (30 miles) NE of London. A market town for the surrounding agricultural area and a dormitory town for people who work in London, its industries include electronics, electrical and farm machinery. Pop. (1973est.) 58,300.

Chelonia, order of reptiles that includes TORTOISES and TURTLES. This ancient group has flourished since the Triassic period, more than 200 million years ago and before the dinosaurs. All chelonia live inside large shells, those of most tortoises being calcareous whereas those of turtles are mainly leathery. Turtles, including the small TERRAPINS, have webbed feet or flippers. *See also* NW pp.134–138.

Chelsea Pensioners, old soldiers who live in the Royal Hospital, Chelsea, which was founded in 1682 by Charles II and designed by Sir Christopher WREN. To qualify for residency single men must hold either a long service or disability army pension. Easily recognized by their scarlet uniforms, there are about 500 Chelsea Pensioners.

Chelseaware, soft-paste porcelain produced at the Chelsea factory, London, between about 1745 and 1770, after which the firm transferred to Derby. The earliest examples were primarily utilitarian pieces such as cups and teapots. From 1750, the MEISSEN and SÈVRES influence was felt. Other items were "Chelsea toys", small bottles and boxes.

Chemical balance, apparatus for making accurate weighings, often to within a tenth of a milligramme (0.0001g). Early types of chemical balances were merely finely made beam balances. As the importance of accuracy increased, designers had to introduce some form of damping to shorten the time the balance took to oscillate to a stop when it was nearly counterpoised. Often this takes the form of air-damping, in which air is compressed between a "piston" and a surrounding cylinder to slow the balance. The latest types of single-beam balances are fully automatic. *See also* MM p.*91*; SU p.150.

Chemical bonds, several mechanisms that hold together atoms to form molecules. There are several types which arise either from the attraction of unlike charges or by forming stable configurations through electron-sharing. The number of bonds an atom can form depends upon its VALENCY. The main types are IONIC, COVALENT, METALLIC and HYDROGEN bonds. *See also* SU pp.137–139, 156–157.

Chemical engineering, the application of engineering principles to the making of chemical products on an industrial scale. Unit processes of chemical engineering include oxidation and reduction, nitration and sulphonation, electrolysis, polymerization, ion exchange and fermentation. *See also* MM pp.80–81; 238–246.

Chemical equation, set of symbols used to represent a CHEMICAL REACTION. Equations show how atoms are rearranged as a result of a reaction: eg $2H_2 + O_2 \rightarrow 2H_2O$ represents the formation of water from hydrogen and oxygen. An arrow ($\rightarrow$) shows the direction of a reaction, ($\rightleftharpoons$) is a REVERSIBLE REACTION and ($\uparrow$) represents the libration of a gas. *See also* SU pp.138–139.

Chemical equilibrium, condition of balance in a REVERSIBLE REACTION, when two opposing reactions proceed at constant equal rates with no net change in the system. The initial rate of the reactions falls off as the concentrations of reactants decrease and the build-up of products causes the rate of the reverse reaction to increase. *See also* SU p.86.

Chemical kinetics, branch of chemistry concerned with the measurement and study of reaction rates and their dependence on factors such as concentration, temperature and pressure.

Chemical reaction, any change or process in which one or more chemical substances are converted into other substances. Reactions involve the breaking and formation of chemical bonds. There are several kinds of reaction mechanism of which ENDOTHERMIC, EXOTHERMIC, replacement, combination, decomposition and oxidation reactions are examples.

Chemical stabilizer, compound added during manufacturing processes to prevent chemical reactions that would otherwise interfere with the desired end product. The term is most often employed in the plastics and rubber industries. *See also* MM pp.54–55.

Chemical symbols, symbols standing for chemical elements, consisting of the capital letters of their English or Latin names, eg H for hydrogen, K for potassium (*kalium*), or a capital letter with a small letter, eg Cl for chlorine. Small superscripts denote either an ion, eg Na^+ (the sodium ion) or the atomic weight, eg He^4. Symbols may be combined to give the chemical formulas of MOLECULES, with small subscripts indicating the number of atoms involved; for example, H_2O is the formula for water (whose molecules each contain two hydrogen atoms combined with one oxygen atom). The system was devised in part in 1813 by J. J. BERZELIUS. *See also* SU pp.134–137.

Chemical warfare, employment of chemical weapons such as poison and nerve gases, defoliants and herbicides, over large areas. The term can also be extended to include smoke bombs, incendiaries and flame-throwers, which were first used in the 5th century BC. *See also* MM pp.180–181.

Chemin de Fer, card game, version of BACCARAT that differs from the original game in that the bank moves from player to player in rotation.

Chemistry, branch of physical science concerned with the properties, structure and composition of substances and their reactions with one another. Today it is a vast body of knowledge with a number of subdivisions. The major division is between inorganic and organic chemistry. PHYSICAL CHEMISTRY deals with the physical properties of substances, such as their magnetic behaviour. Its subdivisions include ELECTROCHEMISTRY, THERMOCHEMISTRY and CHEMICAL KINETICS. *See also* SU pp.132–157.

Chemistry, colour. *See* COLOUR CHEMISTRY.

Chemistry, inorganic, the science that deals with the preparation, properties and reactions of all the chemical elements and their compounds except those of carbon. This definition needs the minor proviso that such simple carbon compounds as carbonates, carbides and carbon oxides come within the province of inorganic chemistry. The historic separation from organic chemistry is, in any case, a false one, because many "inorganic" com-

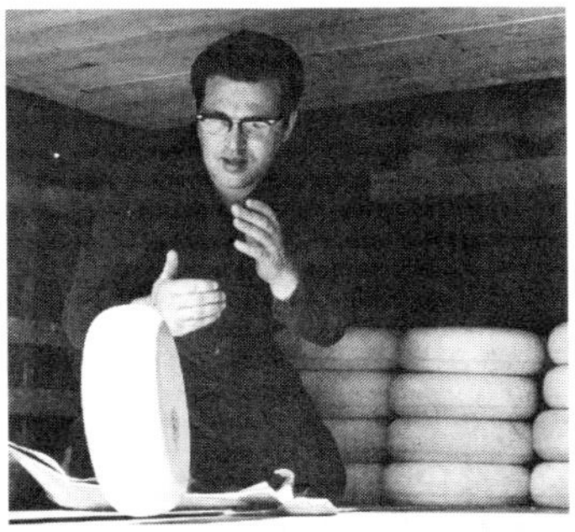

Cheeses are made in various shapes and sizes from the milk of many different animals.

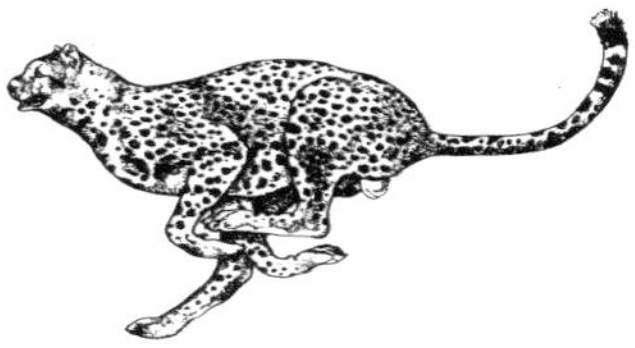

Cheetahs, the fastest animals over short distances, can reach speeds of 100km/h.

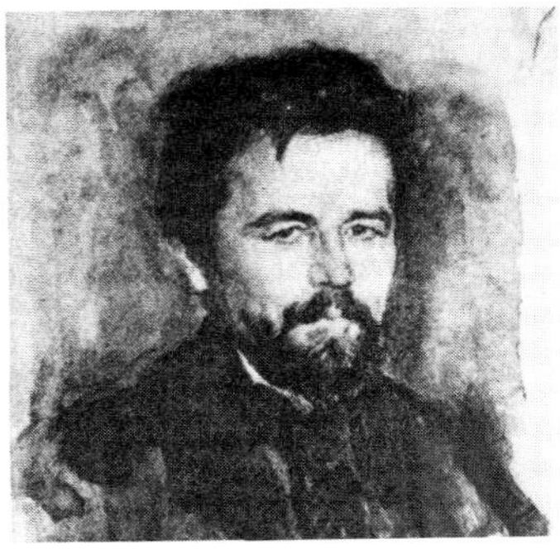

Anton Chekhov depicted the frustrations of Russian society in the final years of tsarism.

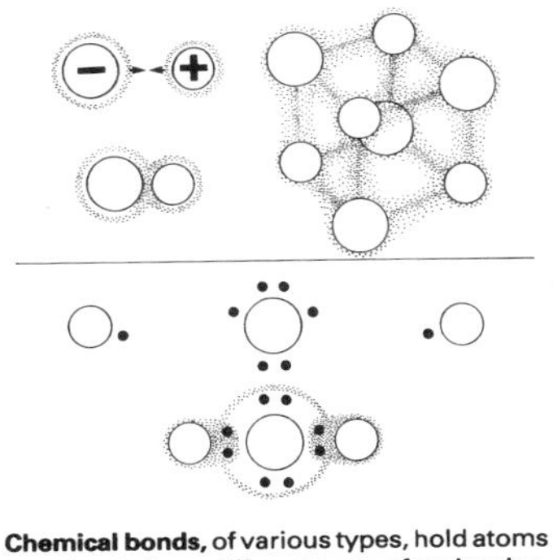

Chemical bonds, of various types, hold atoms together to form different sorts of molecules.

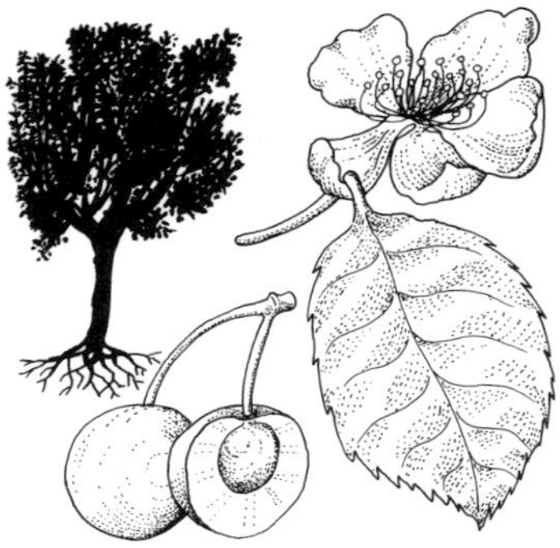

Cherry trees produce beautiful clusters of white and pink blossoms in the spring.

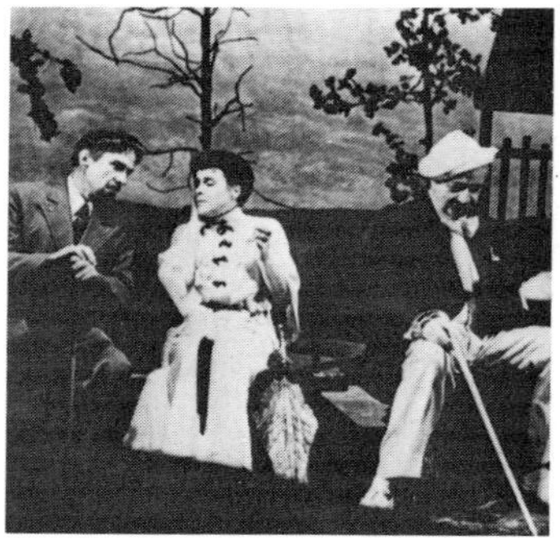

The Cherry Orchard, considered a comedy, deals with the passing of the old order.

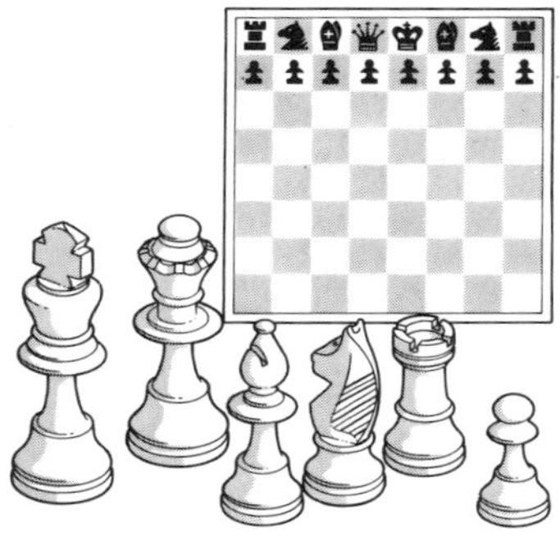

Chess, the "royal game", is thought to have originated in India around the 7th century.

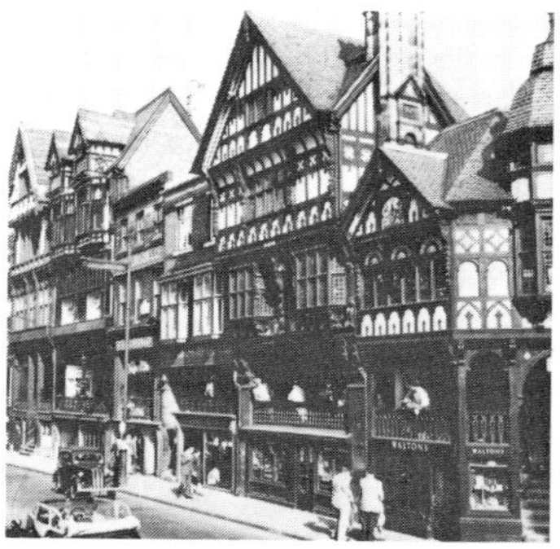

Chester; "The Rows", 16th and 17th-century double-tier shops, unique to the town.

pounds are found in living organisms, one example being the common salt (NaCl) in human blood. In education and industry, however, the distinction is frequently still made. *See also* SU pp.132–151.

Chemistry, organic, the science of the reactions of carbon compounds. Because of its unique ability to bond repeatedly with itself to form chains and rings of atoms (silicon is the only other element that has this property to any degree), carbon is able to form compounds of extreme complexity. For this reason it is predominantly the element of life, forming the "backbone" structures of such compounds as proteins, fats and carbohydrates. Organic chemistry also deals with an immense variety of smaller molecules, including those of industrial compounds such as plastics, rubbers, dyes, drugs and solvents. *See also* MM pp.54–55, 240–241, 244–245; MS pp.120–121; SU pp.132–133, 152–156.

Chemnitz. *See* KARL-MARX-STADT.

Chemotherapy, treatment of a disease by DRUGS that kill or impair disease-producing organisms in the body without damaging the patient. The concept of specific drug treatment was first introduced in the early 1900s by German bacteriologist Paul EHRLICH. *See also* MS pp.*120*.

Chemulpo. *See* INCH'ON.

Chengdu (Chengtu), city in SW China, on the River Min, 274km (170 miles) NW of Chungking (Chonqing); capital of Sweshwan (Sichuan) province. It was the capital of the Shu Han dynasty in the 3rd century AD. Today it is an agricultural trading centre and has iron-mining, food processing, machinery and chemical industries. Pop. 2,000,000.

Chengtu. *See* CHENGDU.

Chénier, André Marie de (1762–94), Turkish-born French poet. He was secretary to the French ambassador in London (1787–90) but returned to Paris and was guillotined for his anti-Jacobin attitudes. His work, which included *Bucoliques*, showed a love of ancient Greece and influenced the NEO-CLASSICISTS. Nearly all his work was published posthumously between 1795 and 1819.

Chennault, Claire Lee (1890–1958), US general. He served in WWI, then trained pilots until his retirement in 1937. He was adviser to CHIANG KAI-SHEK in 1937 and formed the Flying Tigers, a volunteer air corps set up to aid the Nationalist forces. He was made major-general in 1943.

Chenopod, any plant of the goosefoot family, including many weeds (such as *Chenopodium*) and a number of useful plants such as beet, spinach and quinoa.

Ch'en Yi (1901–72), Chinese communist general and administrator. He joined the Communist Party in the 1920s, rising to command the New Fourth Army. A close associate of Chou En-lai, he was mayor of Shanghai (1949–58) and subsequently Foreign Minister until 1966.

Cheops, or Khufu, ancient king of Egypt (*c.*2600 BC) who is remembered for his tomb, the Great Pyramid at Giza, near Cairo. The largest and most famous of the pyramids, it is about 146m (480ft) high and 236.2m (776ft) square. It is made up of 2.3 million limestone blocks each weighing 2.5 tonnes, and all fitted together with astonishing precision. The pyramid was one of the SEVEN WONDERS OF THE WORLD. *See also* HC1 p.*35*.

Cheque, authorization to a bank from one of its depositors to pay or transfer money from his account to another named person or another bank account; it is a form of BILL OF EXCHANGE. Often (although not necessarily) written on a standard form, a cheque must bear the date and the drawer's signature; it is not valid until that date but may be drawn upon up to six months afterwards. If it is "crossed" with two parallel lines and marked "& Co." it is not negotiable, ie it can be paid only into the account named on the cheque. *See also* BANKING; MS pp.308–309.

Chequers, Tudor mansion and estate near Wendover, Buckinghamshire, in S central England. It has been the official country residence of British prime ministers since 1921, when it was donated to the nation by Viscount Lee of Fareham.

Cheret, Jules (1836–1932), French painter and lithographer. He was a master of POSTER art and introduced colour LITHOGRAPHY into France in the 1860s.

Chéri (1920), novel by COLETTE, which describes a love-affair between an older woman and a beautiful but selfish young man, Chéri. It is notable for its refined sensuality and delicate descriptions of changing moods. A sequel, *La Fin de Chéri,* was published in 1926.

Cherimoya, tree and its fruit native to Central and South America and cultivated in California. The tree grows up to 9m (30ft) tall and produces yellow flowers. Its large, pale-green fruit contains a few black seeds in a delicious white pulp. Species *Annona cherimola. See also* PE p.*195*.

Cherkassky, Shura (1911–), Russian-born pianist, who emigrated to the USA in 1922. He is a regular performer at the Salzburg Festival.

Chernov, Viktor (1876–1952), Russian revolutionary, one of the founders of the Socialist Revolutionary Party. In 1917 he was minister of agriculture in the KERENSKY government and briefly headed the constitutional assembly of 1918. He was an anti-Bolshevik and tried to establish a moderate government in the city of Samara (now Kuibyshev). He went into exile in 1920. *Seh also* HC2 pp.196–197.

Chernozem, humus-rich type of dark soil typical of the grasslands of the steppes of Eurasia and the prairies of North America. *See* PE pp.*166–167*.

Cherokee, largest tribe of Indians in the SE USA, members of the great Iroquoian language family. They migrated south into the Appalachian region of Tennessee, Georgia and the Carolinas. The Cherokee sided with the British during the American War of Independence. When gold was discovered on their land in Georgia in the 1830s, they were forced to move west over the tragic Trail of Tears (1838) further reducing their population by one quarter. Today some 47,000 Cherokee descendents live in Oklahoma and about 3,000 remain in North Carolina.

Cherry, widely-grown fruit tree of temperate regions, probably native to W Asia and E Europe. Various types of cherry trees are grown for their edible fruit – round yellow, red or almost black with a single round stone. Sweet cherries are eaten fresh, and all varieties can be canned or frozen. Cherry wood is used in making furniture. Height: to 30m (100ft). Family Rosaceae; genus *Prunus*; there are about 50 species. *See also* PE p.*192*.

Cherry laurel, any of several evergreen shrubs native to SE Europe and grown ornamentally in various parts of the world. They have glossy leaves and white flowers. Height: to 5.4m (18ft). Family Rosaceae; species *Prunus laurocerasus*.

Cherry Orchard, The (1904), four-act drama, last and best-known play by Anton CHEKHOV. A bankrupt family, symbol of decaying tsarist society, fails to save its estate as their cherry orchard is cleared for commercial housing by the new owner, Lopakhin, enterprising son of a serf.

Chert, impure, brittle type of flint. A cryptocrystalline variety of SILICA, its colour can be white, yellow, grey or brown. It occurs mainly in limestone and DOLOMITE although its origin is unknown.

Cherubini, Maria Luigi Carlo Zenobio Salvatore (1760–1842), Italian composer, living in Paris from 1788 and director of the Conservatoire from 1822. He was a master of COUNTERPOINT and a prolific writer of OPERA, notably *Medée* (1797), and church music.

Chervil, annual herb of the PARSLEY family, native to Eurasia; it is cultivated for its aromatic leaves which are used for food flavouring. Height: to 61cm (24in). Family Umbelliferae, species *Anthriscus cerefolium. See also* PE pp.*212*, 213.

Cherwell, river in central England. It rises in Northamptonshire and flows S through Oxfordshire to join the Thames at Oxford. Length: 48km (30 miles).

Chesapeake Bay, inlet of the Atlantic Ocean in Virginia (S) and Maryland (N), USA, at the mouth of the Susquehanna River; it is linked to the Delaware River by the Chesapeake and Delaware Canal. The first permanent English settlement in what was later to be the USA was on Chesapeake Bay, at Jamestown, Virginia, in 1607. In 1608 John Smith explored and charted the bay. Length: 311km (193 miles); width: 5–40km (3–25 miles).

Chesapeake Bay retriever, US sporting dog. Its colour ranges from dark brown to light tan. Its webbed feet and oily coat make it an excellent retriever in icy water; it was bred to retrieve ducks. Height: to 61cm (2ft); weight: to 29kg (65lb).

Cheshire, county in NW England, bounded by Wales (W) and Greater Manchester and Merseyside (N); drained by the Mersey, Weaver and Dee rivers. Chester is the county town. It is an important dairy farming and industrial region, being particularly noted for its cheese. Other industries include salt mining, chemicals, textiles, railway machinery and oil refining. Area: 2,629sq km (1,015sq miles). Pop. (1971) 1,542,624.

Cheshire Archers, royal bodyguard in England from at least the reign of EDWARD III. At the end of the 14th century, when in RICHARD II's army of retainers, they adopted his badge of the white hart.

Chesil Bank, shingle bank extending 14km (9 miles) along the coast of Dorset, S England, from Abbotsbury to Portland, separated from the mainland by the Fleet inlet. It is a prime example of a SPIT.

Chesnutt, Charles Waddell (1858–1932), US lawyer and writer. He had an active law career and also wrote many stories and novels about Black culture. These included *The Conjure Woman* (1899) and *The Colonel's Dream* (1905).

Chess, universal board game, analogous to war, played on a 64-square chequered board, two-players starting with 16 pieces each, white or black, set out along the back two ranks. With the black corner square to his left, white's pieces are set out: rook, knight, bishop, queen, king, bishop, knight, rook. Black's pieces align directly opposite. Pawns stand on the 2nd rank. White enjoys first move, then players move alternately on the rank (horizontal), file (vertical), or diagonal accorded to their pieces: rooks in a straight line on rank or file, bishops along a diagonal, queen on file, rank, or digaonal, knight 1 square along rank or file plus 1 diagonal from its point of origin, king 1 square. A pawn moves 1 square on its file except when capturing, then it moves 1 square diagonally. Only pawns cannot move backwards. Any piece can capture a hostile piece by occupying its square, the captured piece being removed from the board. The object is to put the opposing king in a position of checkmate. If the king's capture is threatened, he is in "check" and the threat must be relieved; if this is impossible, the king is in "checkmate" and the game completed. At international level, there are individual and team world championships.

Chest. *See* THORAX.

Chester, city and county district in Cheshire, NW England. The city, on the River Dee, was a Roman garrison town and has been of strategic importance throughout British history. It was a major port until the Dee became silted and Liverpool's port facilities were expanded. Chester is the only English town with a complete city wall. The county district was created in 1974 under the Local Government Act (1972). Area: 448sq km (173sq miles). Pop. (1974 est.) 117,300.

Chesterfield, city and county district in Derbyshire, N England. It is on the River Rother and is famous for its 14th-century cathedral, which has a twisted spire. The county district was created in 1974 under the Local Government Act (1972). Area: 66sq km (25sq miles). Pop. (1974 est.) 95,000.

Chesterfield Inlet, inlet of the Hudson Bay in North-West Territories, Canada, which extends inland into Baker Lake. Length: 225km (140 miles).

Chester Plays, The, medieval cycle of 25 plays, one of four such outstanding N English cycles of MYSTERY PLAYS. They outline the message of the Bible, from the Creation to the Day of Judgement, and were probably first compiled around 1325 but greatly revised towards the end of the 15th century. The cycle took three days to perform in its entirety. The last stage performance was in 1575, but they were adapted for British television in 1976.

Chesterton, Gilbert Keith (1874–1936), British essayist, novelist and poet. His Father Brown stories, concerning the detective work of a worldly-wise priest, first appeared in 1911. He also wrote essays on social and political themes. His novels include *The Napoleon of Notting Hill* (1904) and *The Man who was Thursday* (1908). He became a Catholic in 1922 and published *St Francis of Assisi* (1923) and *St Thomas Aquinas* (1933).

Chestnut, deciduous tree native to temperate areas of the Northern Hemisphere. It has lance-shaped leaves and furrowed bark. Male flowers hang in long catkins, females are solitary or clustered at base of catkins. The prickly husked fruits open to reveal two to three edible nuts. Family Fagaceae; genus *Castanea*; there are four species. *See also* HORSE CHESTNUT; WATER CHESTNUT.

Chevalier, Albert (1862–1923), British music-hall entertainer. From 1891 he appeared as a music-hall singer and was particularly well-known for his cockney costermonger ballads, most of which he wrote himself. His best-known compositions include *My Old Dutch* and *Knocked 'Em in the Old Kent Road.*

Chevalier, Maurice (1888–1972), French singer and actor. A star of the French music-halls, he first appeared in London in *Hullo, America* (1919). His manner was breezy and casual and he usually wore a jauntily tipped straw hat to sing songs such as *Louise* and *Mimi.* Among his latest films were the musicals *Gigi* (1958), *Can-Can* (1960), and *Fanny* (1961).

Cheviot Hills, range running 56km (35 miles) SW to NE along the England-Scotland border. Sheep farming is the chief occupation of the region. Since WWII much of it has been re-forested and it is now a National Park area. The highest point is The Cheviot in Northumberland, rising to 816m (2,676ft).

Chevreul, Michel-Eugène (1786–1889), French chemist and proponent of theories on colour that influenced the painter DELACROIX and the NEO-IMPRESSIONISTS. He studied the properties of animal fats and helped to develop the commercial manufacture of soap.

Chevrotain, or mouse deer, small, even-toed, hoofed mammal from central Africa and SE Asia. Resembling DEER (but not a true deer), it has a small, hornless head, a pointed snout and slim legs. The males have small upper tusks. Chevrotains are the world's smallest RUMINANTS. Length: 1m (3.3ft); height: 30cm (1ft) at the shoulder. Family Tragulidae; genera *Hyemoschus* and *Tragulus*; there are four species. *See also* NW pp.*163, 212.*

Chevy Chase, Ballad of, English ballad, printed in Capell's *Prolusions* (1760), thought to date from the 15th century. It describes the rivalry between both England and Scotland and the Percy and Douglas families, which culiminated in a fierce battle.

Chewing gum, confection originally from the CHICLE, a gummy latex exuded from the central American SAPODILLA tree. It is now usually made from synthetic substances.

Cheyenne, large Algonquian-speaking North American Indian tribe whose home was originally in Minnesota but who spread into Dakota and areas of the Arkansas and Platte rivers. In the mid-18th century they allied with the Arapaho and in the mid-19th century split evenly into the northern and southern Cheyenne. The northern Cheyenne live in Montana, numbering about 2,000; the southern group settled in Oklahoma, where approx. 3,500 Cheyenne-Arapaho live.

Chiai, city in W Taiwan. It is a commercial and transportation centre, serving the surrounding agricultural region, which produces rice, vegetables and timber. It also houses the headquarters of the local irrigation scheme. Pop. (1970) 238,713.

Chiang Ch'ing (*c.* 1914–), the third wife of MAO TSE-TUNG. A former Shanghai actress, she joined Mao in Yenan during the war against Japan. She emerged from relative obscurity in the 1960s to become a high-ranking party official and the leader of the CULTURAL REVOLUTION. After Mao's death she was accused of treason and expelled from the Communist Party. *See also* HC2 p.245.

Chiang Kai-shek (1887–1975), Chinese politician. After training in a Japanese military academy (1909) he joined the Chinese KUOMINTANG (Nationalist Party), and succeeded SUN YAT-SEN as its leader in 1925 and in 1927 violently purged the KMT of MAO's Communist followers, although Chiang managed to maintain some unity leadership had led to civil war. His international status rose during WWII when he led the fight against Japan, and he was elected president of China in 1948. By 1949 Communist victories drove his government to TAIWAN, where he accepted US aid and launched a series of attacks on mainland China. *See also* HC2 pp.214–215, 244; MW pp.58, 165.

Chiang Kai-Shek, Madame (*c.* 1897–), Chinese politician. A member of the prominent SOONG family, she married CHIANG KAI-SHEK in 1927 and was active in the KUOMINTANG after 1940, especially in attempting to secure foreign support for its war against the Communists.

Chiang Mai, city in N Thailand, near the Burmese border. It is the commercial, cultural and religious centre of the northern region. It has air, rail and road links with the capital and is an export point for local produce. The city's own manufactures include pottery, silk and wooden articles. Pop. (1970) 89,272.

Chiaroscuro, (from Italian "light-dark"), term for the opposition of light and dark in painting and drawing. REMBRANDT and CARAVAGGIO were masters of the dramatic use of chiaroscuro.

Chiastolite, variety of andalusite, aluminium silicate (Al_2OSiO_4), found in metamorphic rocks. It has elongated prismatic crystals, which in cross-section show a black cross on a grey ground. Hardness 7.5; s.g. 3.1–3.2.

Chiba, city in Japan, on Tōkyō Bay, central Honshū Island; capital of Chiba prefecture. It has an 8th-century Buddhist temple and a university (1949). Industries: textiles, paper. Pop. (1970) 482,100.

Chicago, city in NE Illinois, on the SW shore of Lake Michigan; the second largest city in the USA. It is the major industrial, commercial, cultural and shipping centre of the Midwest. In the late 1700s it was a trading post and then became Fort Dearborn military post (1803). With the construction of the Erie Canal and railways, and the opening up of the prairies, Chicago attracted settlers and industry. It became a noted cultural centre in the late 19th and early 20th centuries with the establishment of the Chicago Symphony Orchestra (1891) and several literary magazines. It also achieved notoriety in the 1920s as the home of gangsters, in particular Al CAPONE. It has many colleges and universities, the largest rail terminal in the world and the busiest airport (O'Hare). Industries: steel, chemicals, machinery, food processing, metal working. Pop. 3,173,000. *See also* MM p.*187.*

Chicago School, architects led by Louis SULLIVAN whose steel-framed, multi-storeyed commercial buildings, erected after the 1871 Chicago fire, established the principles of SKYSCRAPER construction. *See also* HC2 pp.*153,* 178.

Chich. *See* CHICKPEA.

Chichén Itzá, chief city and shrine of the TOLTEC and MAYA peoples in Yucatán, Mexico, between the 11th and the 13th centuries AD. Remains include temple-pyramids, court for ball games and a sacrificial well. After 1200 Chichén Itzá lost its pre-eminence to nearby Mayapan. *See also* HC1 p.231, *231.*

Chichester, county town of West Sussex, S England, 26km (16 miles) E of Portsmouth. It is a market centre for the agriculture and livestock of the surrounding region and has a sheltered harbour. There are Roman remains, a Norman cathedral and a modern theatre. Pop. 21,547.

Chickadee, any of several North American birds whose calls resemble a whistled "chick-a-dee". Chickadees are small and plump, with short rounded wings, stubby bills, dark caps and bibs and light cheeks. The typical black-capped chickadee (*Parus atricapillus*) of E North America is an active, easily tamed bird that feeds on seeds and insects. Family Paridae.

Chickasaw, Muskhogean-speaking American Indians who originated in Mississippi-Tennessee around the present site of Memphis and whose economy was based on intensive maize cultivation. Along with the Choctaw, Creek, Cherokee and Seminole peoples they were recognized as the Five Civilized Tribes by the US government who in 1786 established the Ohio as their northern boundary by the Hopewell Treaty. In the 1830s the Chickasaw were forcibly resettled in Indian Territory (the present Oklahoma) when their numbers were about 5,000. Today their population is about 9,000.

Chicken. *See* POULTRY.

Chickenpox, or varicella, contagious disease which most often attacks children and usually lasts for about a fortnight. Early symptoms include a mild headache and high temperature which are followed within a day by red skin marks which develop into blisters. Recovery is rapid, with little or no scarring. Antihistamine may relieve itching. *See also* MS p.*99.*

Chickpea, also called dwarf pea, garbanzo, chich and gram, bushy annual plant cultivated from antiquity in S Europe and Asia for its pea-like seeds. It is now also grown widely in the Western Hemisphere. The seeds are eaten boiled or roasted. Family Leguminosae; species *Cicer arietinum. See also* PE p.*185.*

Chickweed, common name for a spreading annual plant native to Europe and naturalized throughout temperate regions of the world. Its drooping stems grow to about 30cm (12in) long. It has opposite oblong leaves and small white flowers. Family Caryophyllaceae; species *Stellaria media.*

Chiclayo, city in NW Peru, capital of Lambayeque department, in the coastal desert area between the Andes and the Pacific Ocean. It has a university (1962) and an agricultural college (1963). Industries: cotton, leather goods, brewing, rice, sugar cane, soap. Pop. (1972) 187,809.

Chicle, natural gum, available in reddish-brown pieces and consisting of the coagulated milky juice of the SAPODILLA (*Achras zapota).* Chicle became the chief ingredient of CHEWING GUM by the end of the 19th century but in the 1940s it began to be replaced by synthetics and now has little commercial value.

Chicory, perennial weedy plant whose leaves are cooked and eaten, or served raw in salads. The fleshy roots are dried and ground for mixing with or used as a substitute for coffee. Chicory has bright blue, daisy-like flowers. Height: 1.5m (5ft). Family Compositae; species *Chichorium intybus. See also* PE pp.188, *188,* 190, *190.*

Chidley Cape, headland at the N tip of Labrador, E Canada, on Killinek Island on the S side of the entrance to the Hudson Strait.

Chiefdom societies, in anthropology, type of social system more complex and hierarchical than tribes, but less static than kingdoms. *See also* MS pp.252–253.

Chief justice, presiding judge of the US SUPREME COURT who is appointed by the President. He administers the presidential inaugural oath and under the American Constitution is responsible for presiding at the impeachment of a president.

Ch'ien Lung (*r.* 1735–96), title of the MANCHU emperor of China, Hung-li (1711–99), during his reign. He increased China to its greatest size under the Manchus by taking Tibet and other regions. He was a patron of the arts and had some contact with European traders but refused to expand diplomatic ties with Britain in 1793. In his time, he was a powerful and influential monarch. Recently, historians have concluded that despite his contemporary success, he left the empire seriously weakened, and unable to withstand

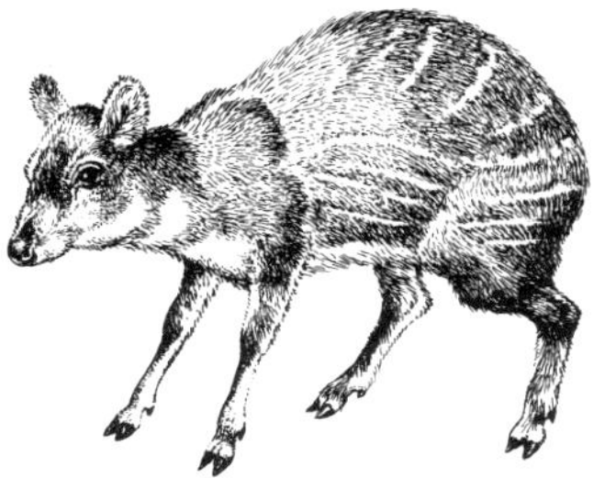

Chevrotains, or mouse deer, are reddish brown with paler spots and irregular stripes.

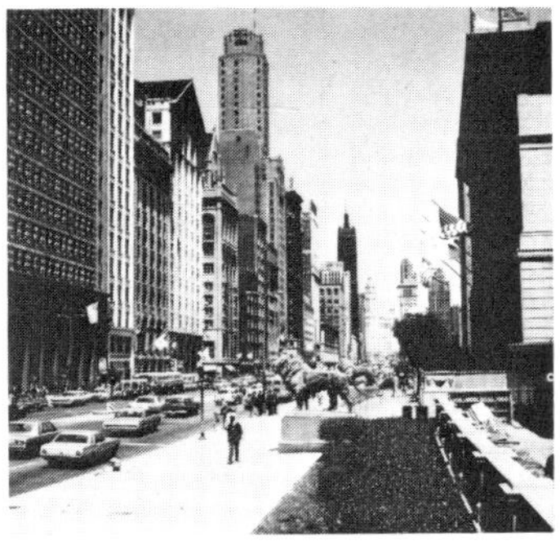

Chicago's lakeside position gives it a very varied and changeable climate.

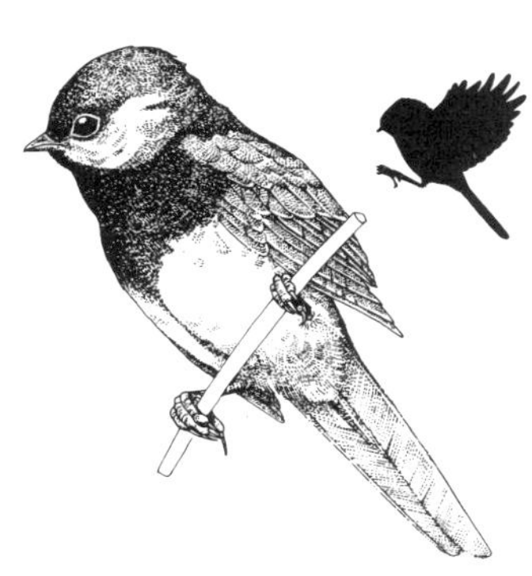

Chickadee is the American name for the little bird known in Britain as the willow tit.

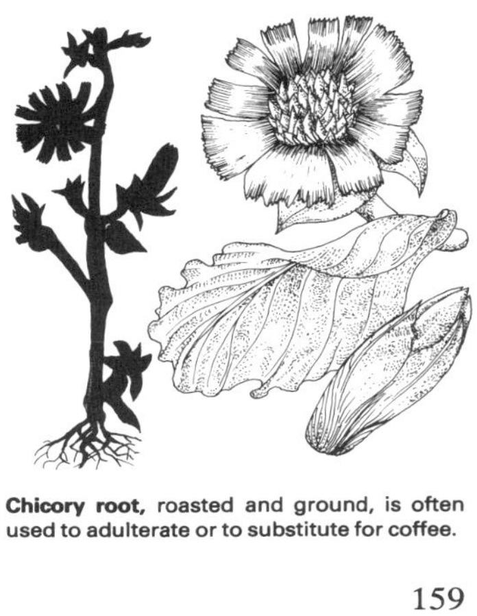

Chicory root, roasted and ground, is often used to adulterate or to substitute for coffee.

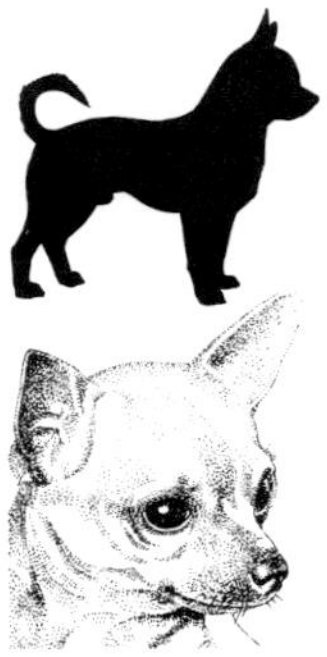

Chihuahuas, the tiniest of all dogs, are a pure American breed, probably from Mexico.

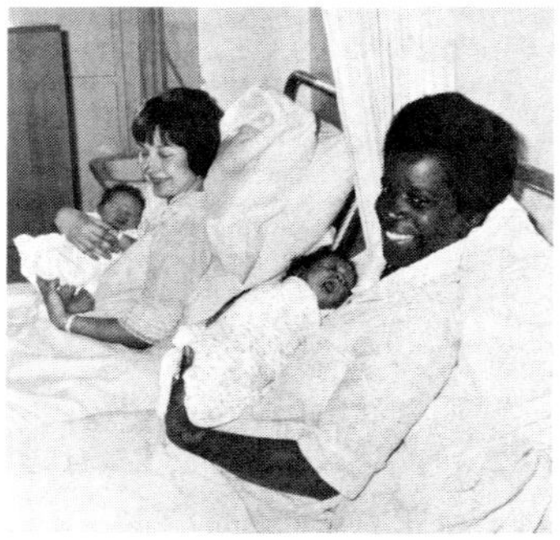

Childbirth; two happy mothers whose infants arrived in the first minutes of the new year.

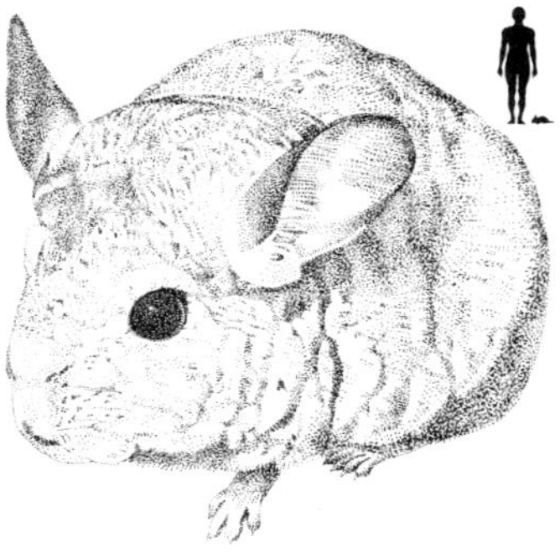

Chinchilla; over a hundred of their pelts are required to make one full-length coat.

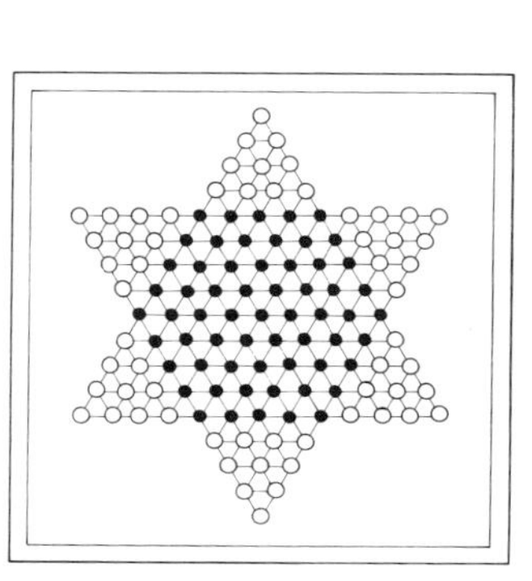

Chinese checkers, a board game not acutally from China that became popular in the 1930s.

the European incursions of the 19th century. *See also* HC2 pp.52–53.

Chiffchaff, greenish-brown warbler of the family Sylviidae, named after its distinctive two-note call. It hunts insects in trees, and nests near the ground. This sky bird is a summer visitor to Britain. Length: 11cm (4.5in). Species *Phylloscopus collybita. See also* NW p.144.

Chifley, Joseph Benedict (1885–1951), Labor Australian Prime Minister (1945–49). A former locomotive driver, he became defence minister (1929–31) then Federal Treasurer (1941–45). He increased federal involvement in education and welfare but failed to nationalize the Australian banking system.

Chigger, also called harvest mite or red bug, tiny, red larva of some kinds of MITES found worldwide. Adults lay eggs on plants and hatched larvae find a host, animal or human, on whom their bites cause a severe rash and itching. Length: 0.1–16mm (0.004–0.6in). Order Acarina; family Trombiculidae.

Chignecto Bay, inlet at the N end of the Bay of Fundy between New Brunswick and Nova Scotia, Canada. It is noted for its extremely high tides rising to 15m (50ft). Fundy National Park is on the N shore. Length: 80km (50 miles).

Chihuahua, largest state in Mexico, on the N Mexican plateau. The climate and terrain vary from cool mountains (W) to arid desert (E). The city of Chihuahua, the state capital, has a Spanish colonial cathedral and is a famous breeding centre for the miniature Mexican dogs named after the city. Industries: zinc, lead, silver, gold-mining, forestry, livestock raising, tourism, cotton, oats, potatoes, fruit. Area (state) 247,086sq km (95,400sq miles). Pop. (state) 1,730,012; (city) (1975) 346,003.

Chihuahua, tiny dog (TOY group) probably first bred in Central America. It has large, wide-set eyes and large erect ears. The long, stickle-shaped tail is held in a loop over the back. There are two types of coat – short-haired and long-haired – which may be any colour. Average size: 12.7cm (5in) at the shoulder; weight: up to 2.7kg (6lb).

Chikamatsu Monzaemon (1653–1724), Japanese dramatist. He wrote mainly for the puppet theatre and produced more than 150 plays. Most of his writings were historical romances and domestic tragedies, including *The Love Suicides at Amijima* (1720) and *The Battles of Coxinga* (1715), based on actual events.

Chilblain, soreness and swelling caused by cold; most often affected areas are toes, fingers and ears. Itching or "burning" sensations may occur. It accompanies poor circulation, and relief is usually gained by warming exercise.

Child. *See* MS pp.150–163.

Childbirth, the birth of a baby. After about 280 days following fertilization of an ovum (conception), the regular contractions of a woman's womb tell her that the baby is about to be born. Labour takes place in three stages. First the neck of the womb dilates, or opens, to let the baby's head pass through. Then the baby passes through the birth canal to the outside – it is born. The third and final stage of birth is the expulsion of the placenta, or afterbirth. *See* MS pp.78–79.

Childe, Vere Gordon (1892–1957). Australian prehistorian. His study of the cultures of the western world in the second and third millennia BC led to *The Danube in Prehistory* (1929). Other influential works include *Man Makes Himself* (1936) and *The Dawn of European Civilization* (1925). *See also* HC1 p.23.

Childe Harold's Pilgrimage (1812–18), autobiographical, romantic poem by Lord BYRON, divided into four cantos, in Spenserian stanzas. The poem tells of a young man's disillusionment with his easy life and his wanderings through Europe.

Childe Roland, character in a poem by Robert BROWNING, *Childe Roland to the Dark Tower Came,* published in 1855. "Childe" is a medieval title meaning a young nobleman. The hero of the poem, Childe Roland, is in quest of a dark tower that many others have failed to find.

Children's Crusade (1212), movement to regain the Holy Land, preached by two boys. Thousands of French children and many adult vagabonds went to Marseilles. They were offered free transport to Palestine, but were sold as slaves in Africa instead. Although the movement ended in disaster, it renewed religious fervour.

Chile, republic extending 2,450km (7,740 miles) along the Pacific coast of South America with a landscape dominated by the Andes Mts. In 1973, the Marxist president, ALLENDE, was overthrown by a military junta. The economy is based on mineral deposits. Copper accounts for 80% of exports and other minerals include nitrates, iron, gold, silver and manganese. The forests are also of economic importance and timber, pulp and paper are exported. The capital is Santiago. Area: 756,945sq km (292,256sq miles). Pop. (1975 est.) 10,253,000. *See* MW pp.52–53.

Chili, or chilli, hot red PEPPER grown commercially in Mexico and the SW USA. CAYENNE PEPPER comes from the same plant. It is an annual with oval leaves and white or greenish-white flowers that produce seedpods. When dried, the pods are ground into the condiment. Height: 2–2.5m (6–8ft). Family Solanaceae; species *Capsicum frutescens. See also* PE pp.210–211.

Chillida, Eduardo (1924–), Spanish sculptor in iron and granite. His work, abstract compositions in smooth angular strips and in rows of block shapes joined together, has a monumental, open quality.

Chilopoda, centipedes, an order of arthropod animals that have long, flat, segmented bodies, each bearing one pair of legs (the total number of legs being much less than 100, despite the name). The head has a large pair of claws with which the centipede seizes its prey and injects it with venom. *See also* NW pp.104, 208, 213.

Chilperic, name of two MEROVINGIAN kings. Chilperic I (539–84) inherited the West Frankish kingdom on the death of CLOTAR I (561). Civil wars failed to gain him the whole Frankish realm. Chilperic II (*c.*675–721) became king of the West Franks in 715, of the whole kingdom in 719.

Chiltern Hills, range of chalk hills in S central England, extending NE from the Goring Gap in the Thames Valley to the East Anglian Heights. A local furniture industry is centred on High Wycombe. The highest point is Coombe Hill, 260m (852ft). Length: 89km (55 miles).

Chiltern Hundreds, obsolete administrative district in Buckinghamshire. The stewardship of the district is still a nominal salaried office under the Crown and therefore incompatible with a parliamentary seat. MPs who wish to resign therefore apply for it.

Chilung, city in N Taiwan on the East China Sea. An important commercial centre, it is also a natural port and the country's principal naval base. Its industries include fishing and shipbuilding. Pop. (1970) 324,040.

Chimaera, also called ghost shark, cartilaginous deep-sea fish with a long poisonous dorsal spine and a slender tail. Some species have an elongated snout. An oil, derived from its liver, is used as a lubricant in precision equipment. Length: 2m (80in). Families Chimaeridae, Collorhinchidae and Rhinochimaeridae.

Chimborazo, highest mountain in Ecuador. An inactive volcano, its peak is always snow-capped. Explored in 1802 by Alexander von HUMBOLDT, it was first scaled in 1880 by the British mountaineer Edward Whymper. Height: 6,267m (20,561ft).

Chimbote, port on the coast of W central Peru, approx. 400km (250 miles) NNW of Lima. It suffered severe damage in an earthquake in 1970. Industries: steel, fishing, fish meal. Pop. (1969 est.) 97,100.

Chimera, in Greek mythology, beast that was part dragon, part lion and part goat. He was the son of TYPO and ECHIDNA and the brother of CERBERUS, HYDRA and the SPHINX. He was slain by BELLEROPHON, with the aid of the flying horse, PEGASUS.

Chimpanzee, gregarious, intelligent great APE of tropical Africa. Chimpanzees are mostly black and powerfully built. A smaller chimpanzee of the Congo region is sometimes classified as a separate species. Chimpanzees often nest in trees but most of their time is spent on the ground searching for fruit and nuts. They are communicative and, in controlled situations, have learned a limited human vocabulary in sign language. Height: approx. 1.3m (4.5ft); weight: approx. 68kg (150lb). Species *Pan troglodytes,* Congo *Pan paniscus.* Family Pongidae. *See also* PRIMATES; MS p.*238*; NW pp.172–173, *173*.

Chimú, large pre-Columbian kingdom of South American Indians in N Peru. Its centre and capital was the great city of Chan Chan near modern Trujillo, with a population of more than 100,000 inhabitants. From AD 1200 to 1465, when it was conquered by the INCA, Chimú was the largest and most important pre-Inca kingdom. It is noted for ceramics, weaving and goldwork. *See also* HC1 pp.231–232.

China, People's Republic of, nation of Asia, also known as Communist China; the third largest and most populous country in the world. It has a communist government. Occupying one-fifth of the area of Asia, it has large mineral deposits including coal, oil, iron ore, tin, tungsten, aluminium, manganese and mercury. Under the communist government a series of five-year plans have aimed at increasing industrial development. Iron and steel manufacture is the most important heavy industry. The manufacture of machinery and tools and textiles is also important. The rural population is organized into communes which farm the land in common. China is the world's leading producer of rice and third-largest producer of wheat. The capital is Peking (Beijing). Area: 9,597,700 sq km (3,704,000sq miles). Pop. (1975 est.) 838,803,000. *See* MW pp.53–58.

China, Republic of, official name of Taiwan. *See* MW p.165.

China clay. *See* KAOLIN.

China stone, partially decomposed granite, frequently used as a flux to produce vitrification and translucency, or mixed with silica and lime to form a glaze in the manufacture of PORCELAIN.

Chinchilla, genus of small, soft-furred RODENT native to South America. Chinchillas were hunted almost to extinction. They are now bred in captivity for their fur, the most expensive of all animal furs, which is long and close-textured and soft to the touch. 23–38cm (9–15in); weight; 450-900g (1–2lb). Family Chinchillidae.

Chindits, popular name for special force troops from the 3rd Indian Division, guerrillas who were commanded by Brigadier Orde WINGATE in the 1943–45 Burma campaign. They were also known as "Wingate's raiders" and managed in part to implement his idea of causing confusion behind Japanese front lines. The name most probably comes from Chinthé, a beast of Burmese mythology.

Chindwin, river in W Burma. A major tributary of the Irrawaddy, it rises in the hills of N Burma and flows generally S along the border with India to join the Irrawaddy at Myingyan. It is navigable for 644km (400 miles). Length: approx. 840km (520 miles).

Ch'in dynasty (221–207 BC), ruling Chinese house whose main achievement was the establishment of a unified sovereign state which survived as an empire until 1911. Originating in NW China, the Ch'in led by SHIH HUANG TI conquered the feuding states of the CHOU dynasty and maintained an effective administration along feudal lines to govern their vast territory. Two dynasties with the name "Chin" ruled from 265 to 419 and from 1122 to 1234 AD. *See also* HC1 pp.122–123, *122–123*; MW p.56.

Chinese checkers, board game, similar to draughts. The object is to move a set of pegs or marbles on a star-shaped board to the opposite corner. The pieces may advance by jumping over others but, unlike draughts, no pieces are taken off the board. The first player to fill the corner opposite his starting point is the winner.

Chinese lantern plant, or winter cherry,

perennial plant native to Japan and widely cultivated in gardens. The creeping stems bear large, long-stalked leaves and small white flowers; these produce a red berry surrounded by a papery, lantern-like red calyx. Height: up to 61cm (2ft). Family Solanaceae; species *Physalis alke bengi.*

Ch'ing dynasty (1644–1912), also known as the Manchu dynasty, the last dynasty of imperial China. The Manchus were a tribe from MANCHURIA who, by capturing Peking in 1644, established control over the whole country. Their rule was consolidated by K'ANG HSI and for a long time they retained their cultural identity, encouraging the development of the arts, in particular the production of porcelain which was popular in 18th-century Europe. In the 20th century the dynasty's failure to deal adequately with Western imperialism and to institute reforms led to its overthrow by nationalists led by SUN YAT-SEN. *See also* HC2 pp.52–55, 144–145.

Chingola, city in N central Zambia. Its main activity is the provision of administrative and governmental services to the nearby copper-mining community of Nchanga. Pop. (1972 est.) 214,000.

Chinnamp'o. *See* NAMP'O.

Chinnery, Ernest William Pearson (1887–), Australian anthropologist. He was adviser to the Australian government on Native Affairs (1937–47), and explored previously unknown areas of New Guinea.

Chinoiserie, European style of furniture and decorative art that reflected fanciful and poetic notions of China, based on imports of Chinese ceramics, textiles and travellers' tales.

Chinook, or Flathead (from their custom of deforming infants' heads as a sign of free birth), American Indians living along the Pacific coast from the Columbia River to The Dalles, Oregon. Although numbering fewer than 1,000, the Chinook travelled widely and their language was used by many Indians and whites during the settlement of the West. They have now fused with the Chedalis Indians.

Chinook, warm, dry FÖHN WIND experienced on the eastern side of the Rocky Mountains in Canada and the USA. It blows commonly during the winter and spring, and its warming effect can allow grazing of cattle during the winter. *See also* PE pp.67–68.

Chinquapin. *See* CHESTNUT.

Chios (Khíos), island in E Greece, W of Turkey, in the Aegean Sea. It was first colonized by the Ionians and then occupied by the Persians, 494–479 BC. It joined the Delian League in 478 BC. It flourished under the Romans and the Byzantines then passed to the Genoese, Ottomans and finally to Greece in 1912. It is reputed to be the birthplace of Homer. Products: figs, olives, marble. Area: 906sq km (350sq miles). Pop. (1971) 53,942.

Chipboard, man-made constructional material, an artificial wood made in sheets from small chips of wood embedded in a thermosetting plastic resin. It can be sawn, planed and drilled like natural wood and can be fixed using nails or screws. It is commonly used, sometimes surfaced with a veneer of hardwood or plastics, for making furniture and covering floors.

Chipewyan, Fort, fur-trading post in NE Alberta, Canada, on NW Lake Athabaska. The original fort was established in 1788 on SW Lake Athabaska by Alexander Mackenzie as the headquarters for his expeditions to the Arctic and Pacific oceans. This was later abandoned, and the modern post was established in 1821 by the North West Company.

Chipmunk, small, ground-dwelling SQUIRREL native to North America and Asia. It carries food (nuts, berries, seeds) in cheek pouches and stores it underground. Most chipmunks are brown with one or more black-bordered, light stripes. Active tree-climbers in summer, they sleep for much of the winter. Length: 13–15cm (5–6in) excluding the tail. Family Sciuridae; genera *Eutamias* and *Tamias.*

Chippendale, Thomas (*c.* 1718–79), British furniture designer. Although he was one of the great English craftsmen, much of his fame rested upon the wide circulation of his *The Gentleman and Cabinet-Maker's Director* (1754–62), a trade catalogue illustrating the designs of his factory. Many of Chippendale's finest pieces were marquetry and inlaid items in the Neo-Classical vein.

Chippewa. *See* OJIBWA.

Chirico, Giorgio de (1888–), Greek-born Italian painter, founder of the quasi-SURREALIST "metaphysical painting" movement, who painted still lifes and empty, dream-like landscapes in exaggerated perspective. In the 1930s he repudiated all modern art in favour of paintings in the style of the Old Masters. *See also* HC2 p.*202.*

Chiron, in Greek mythology, wisest and most famous of the CENTAURS. He taught many of the lesser gods and heroes, including ACHILLES and ASCLEPIUS, and was accidently killed by HERCULES with a poisoned arrow. He was placed among the stars by ZEUS.

Chiropodist, medical practitioner who specializes in treating minor disorders of the feet and hands. Typical conditions treated by a chiropodist include ATHLETE'S FOOT and CORNS.

Chiropractic, non-orthodox medical practice based on the theory that the nervous system integrates all of the body's functions, including defence against disease. With any "nerve interference", caused, for example, by a slightly misplaced vertebra, there is decreased resistance to disease and pain. Chiropractors aim to remove nerve interference by manipulations of the affected musculo-skeletal parts, particularly in the spinal region.

Chiroptera. *See* BAT.

Chisolm, Jesse (*c.* 1806–68), US trader. In 1866 he drove a wagon train through Indian territory, now Oklahoma, from Texas to Kansas. The route he took became the Chisolm Trail, over which Texas longhorn cattle were driven to railheads in Kansas.

Chital, or axis deer, comparatively common diurnal DEER of India and Sri Lanka. Its coat is red and brown, irregularly but profusely spotted with white throughout the year. Herds of 100 or more may be seen in the wild. Height: 91cm (3ft) at the shoulder. Family Cervidae; species *Axis axis.*

Chitin, hard, tough substance that occurs widely in nature, particularly in the hard shells (exoskeletons) of arthropod animals such as shrimps, crabs, insects, spiders and their relatives. The walls of hyphae – the microscopic tubes of fungi – are also composed of chitin, although this is not identical with animal chitin. Chemically chitin is, like cellulose, a natural polymer. More specifically it is a polymer of *N*-acetyl-glucosamine, a derivative of the sugar glucose.

Chiton, or coat-of-mail shell, MOLLUSC that lives attached to or creeping on rocks along marine shores. Bilaterally symmetrical, its upper surface has eight overlapping shells. Underneath is a large fleshy foot, a degenerate head with mouth, gills and a mantle. Length: to 33cm (13in). Class Amphineura; order Polyplacophora; family Chitonidae. *See also* NW p.90.

Chitral, town, district and former state in the North-western Frontier Province, Pakistan. The district is bordered by Afghanistan (N) and the Hindu Kush (W). Cereals and fruits are grown and there are mineral deposits, although these are thought too inaccessible to be mined commercially. District area: 14,833sq km (5,727sq miles). Pop. (est.)159,000.

Chittagong, principal port and capital of Chittagong division, Bangladesh, S Asia, on the Karnaphuli River near the Bay of Bengal. Under Mogul rule in the 17th century, it was ceded to the East India Company in 1760. Its port facilities were damaged in the war in 1971 between India and Pakistan. Industries: jute, tea, oil, engineering. Pop. 889,760.

Chivalry, code of ethics and behaviour for knights in Western Europe between about the 11th and the 14th centuries. The term comes from the French word for knighthood, *chevalerie.* Combining Christian virtues with armed prowess, a knight was expected to show courage, piety, honour, adventure, devotion to a lady of his choice, loyalty, generosity, honesty and skilled in courtly love. Although a combination of these virtues was probably rare in reality, the literature of the Middle Ages abounds with embodiments of the ideal. *See also* HC1 pp.204–205, *205.*

Chives, perennial herb whose long hollow leaves have an onion-like flavour and are used as a seasoning. The flowers grow in rose-purple clusters. Family Liliaceae; species *Allium schoenoprasum.*

Chladni, Ernst Florens Friedrich (1756–1827), German physicist who made studies of sound, particularly the way in which it vibrates metal plates and diaphragms. Patterns produced in fine powders on sound-vibrated plates are called Chladni's figures.

Chlamydomonas, microscopic, single-celled green ALGA that can be so common in ponds as to turn the water bright green. The cell of *Chlamydomonas* is only about 20 microns (20 millionths of a metre) across and has two flagella, which the cell beats to swim. It is thus one of the great group of algae known as FLAGELLATES.

Chloral hydrate, drug that in therapeutic doses produces natural-like sleep but with repeated use becomes addictive. Mixed with alcohol or taken in large doses it is dangerous and can result in death.

Chlorate, salt of chloric acid, containing the ion ClO_3^-. Chlorate salts are good oxidizing agents and are a useful source of oxygen, which they give off when heated. Sodium and potassium chlorates are used in explosives and also as weedkillers. They are manufactured by electrolysis.

Chlorella, microscopic, single-celled green ALGA occuring singly or in masses in fresh water and on damp soil, and as a symbiotic partner in the bodies of many small water animals including the green hydra and the fresh-water sponge (which it turns green). This alga is easy to grow, reproduces quickly and is rich in proteins and vitamins; for these reasons it has been used as plant protein for animal foods.

Chloride, salt of HYDROCHLORIC ACID or some organic compounds containing chlorine. The best-known example is common table salt, sodium chloride (NaCl). Most chlorides are soluble in water, except mercurous and silver chlorides.

Chlorine, common non-metallic element (symbol Cl) in the HALOGEN group, first discovered in 1774 by the Swedish chemist K. W. Scheele. It occurs in common salt (NaCl), carnallite and sylvite. It is a greenish-yellow gas extracted by the electrolysis of brine and is widely used in purifying drinking water, bleaching wood pulp and in the manufacture of a vast range of compounds. Chemically it is a reactive element, and combines with most metals. Properties: at.wt. 35.453; s.g. 1.56 (−33.6°C); m.p. −100.98°C (−149.76°F); b.p. −34.6°C (−30.28°F). The most common isotope is Cl^{35} (75.53%). *See also* SU pp.139, *148,* 149.

Chloroform (trichloromethane), colourless, volatile, sweet-smelling liquid ($CHCl_3$) prepared by the chlorination of methane or of acetone or ethanol in an alkaline solution. It is used in the manufacture of fluorocarbons, for insect bites and as a solvent. Properties: s.g. 1.48 at 20°C (68°F); m.p. −62°C (−80°F); b.p. 61.2°C (142.2°F). *See also* SU p.*144.*

Chloromycetin, trade name for the antibiotic drug chloramphenicol, originally found as a metabolic product of the bacterium *Streptomyces venezuelae.* Now synthesized chemically, it is used to control various bacteria.

Chlorophyll, group of green pigments present in the CHLOROPLASTS of plants that absorb light for PHOTOSYNTHESIS. There are five types: chlorophyll *a* ($C_{55}H_{72}O_5N_4Mg$) is present in all photosynthetic plants except bacteria; chlorophyll *b* ($C_{55}H_{70}O_6N_4Mg$) occurs in higher plants and green algae; and chlorophylls *c, d* and *e* present in some algae. It has a similar structure to HAEMOGLOBIN, with a magnesium atom replacing an iron atom. *See also* NW pp.44–47; SU p.155.

Chloroplast, microscopic green structure

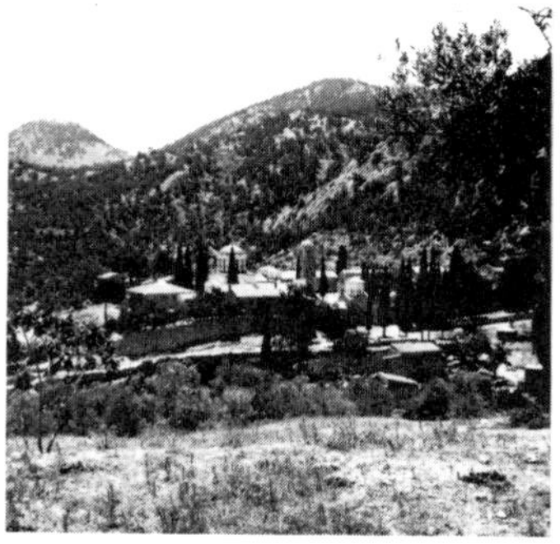

Chios has been occupied by Romans, Persians, Genoese, Turks and Germans.

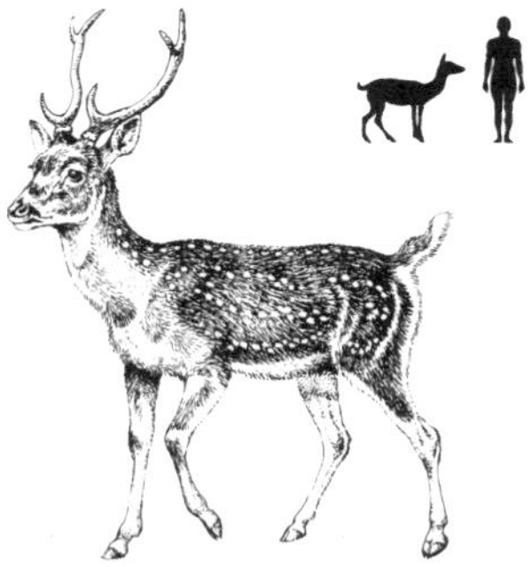

Chital or axis deer are reddish-fawn coloured with numbers of white spots on their sides.

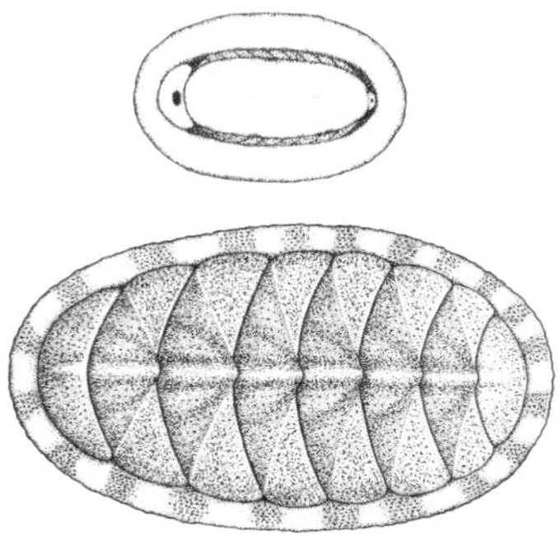

Chitons curl up tightly when they are dislodged from the rocks on which they live.

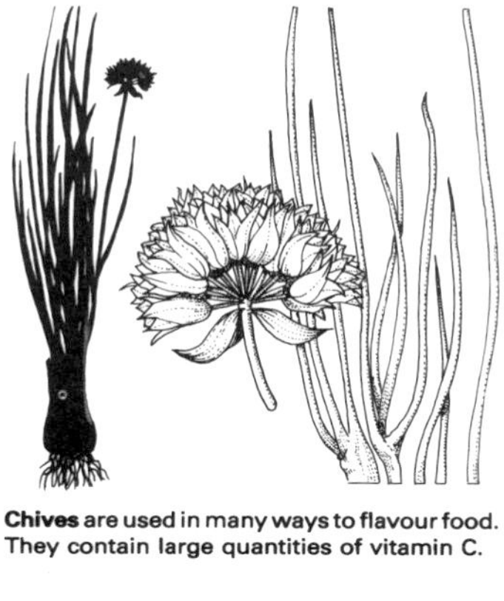

Chives are used in many ways to flavour food. They contain large quantities of vitamin C.

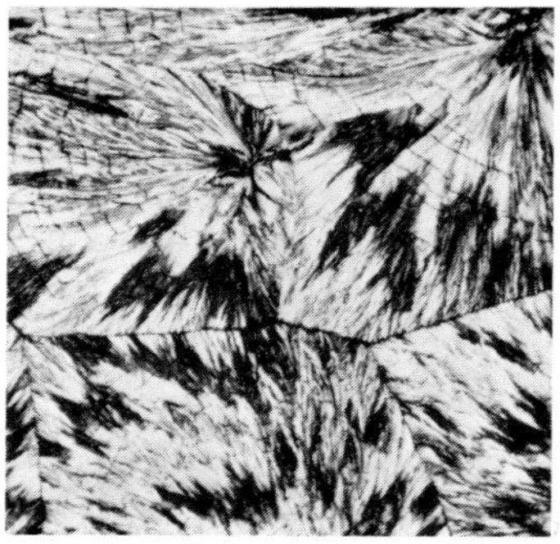

Cholesterol formed by an excessively rich diet is thought to contribute to heart disease.

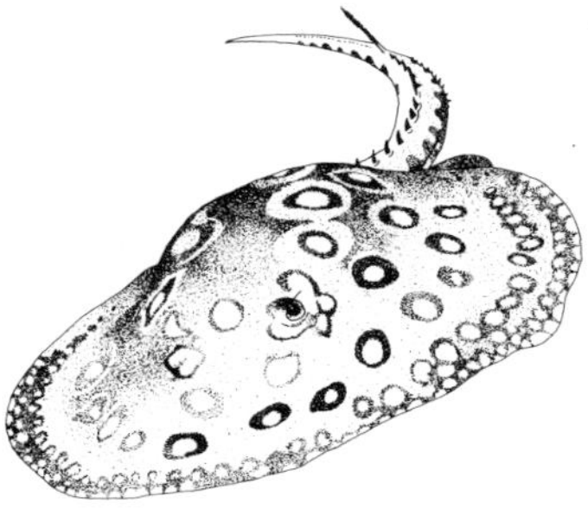

Condrichthyes is the class of fish whose skeletons are made of cartilage.

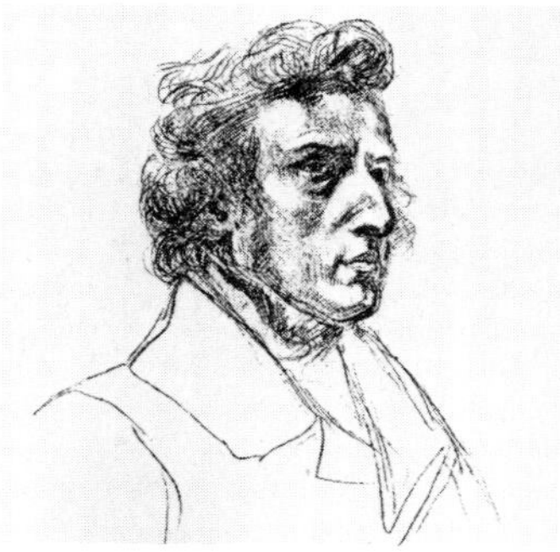

Chopin's music is closely related to the nature of the piano as an expressive instrument.

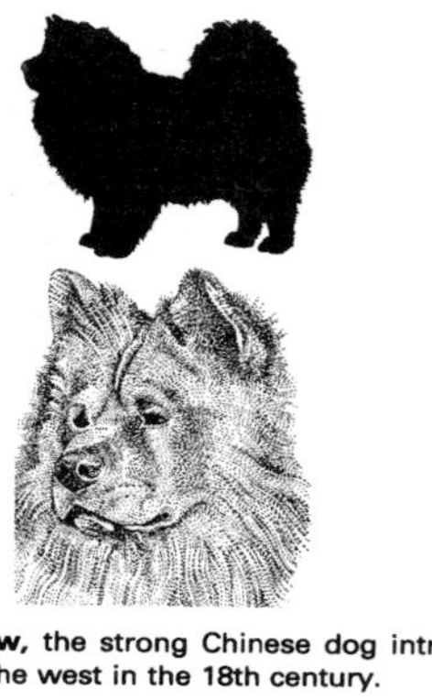

Chow-chow, the strong Chinese dog introduced to the west in the 18th century.

within a plant cell in which PHOTOSYNTHESIS takes place. The chloroplast is enclosed in an external unit membrane and contains internal membranes. The pigments providing the green colour (chlorophyll *a* and chlorophyll *b*) absorb the light energy that is converted to chemical energy. *See also* CHLOROPHYLL.

Chloroquine, synthetic drug used mainly to treat MALARIA and HEPATITIS. It can have marked side-effects, such as blurred vision.

Chlorpromazine, synthetic drug, first developed as an anti-nauseant but subsequently found to calm the central nervous system. An important and potent tranquillizer, it is used under close medical supervision in the treatment of psychoses and cases of severe anxiety or other mental illnesses. *See also* MS pp.137, 144.

Choanichthyes, sub-class of fish that includes the Crossopterygii (COELACANTH) and Dipnoi (LUNGFISH). Common during the Devonian period (395–345 million years ago), most members of this group are now extinct. They have bony skeletons, paired fins and well-developed air bladders. Class Osteichthyes.

Chocolate. *See* COCOA.

Chodowiecki, Daniel Nikolaus (1726–1801), German painter, engraver and book illustrator. He achieved great popularity with his etchings and vignettes, and in 1797 became the director of the Berlin Academy of Art.

Choir, group of singers. The earliest choirs were ecclesiastical and originally sang the plainsong in church services. After the development of polyphonic composition, some 16th century works, especially those of GABRIELI, required multiple choirs and as many as 40 parts. The beginnings of opera marked the development of the secular choir, or CHORUS.

Choking, restricted breathing caused by an obstruction in the throat or a ligature round the neck (strangulation). For first-aid treatment, *see* MS *p.132.*

Chola, medieval dynasty of S India. The Cholas established a kingdom around Tenjore in the 2nd century AD, but did not rise to prominence until the 9th century. They replaced the PALLAVAS on the E coast of S India in 888, and between 985 and 1024 established an empire that included Ceylon, Bengal, parts of Sumatra and Malaya. The dynasty declined and ended in 1279. The Cholas brought a great period of Hindu culture to S India. *See also* HC1 pp.118–119.

Cholecystitis, inflammation of the GALL BLADDER, most often associated with GALLSTONES. In mild forms it produces indigestion, sometimes with nausea and vomiting, after eating fried or greasy foods. More severe attacks, with sharp pain, usually require surgery. *See also* MS *p.92.*

Cholera, acute infectious disease caused by the bacterium *Vibrio cholerae* and occurring in epidemic form in tropical and subtropical areas with poor sanitation and hygiene. It is generally contracted by eating food or drinking water contaminated by the faeces of infected people. Cholera produces almost continuous, watery diarrhoea often accompanied by vomiting and muscle cramp, and leads to severe dehydration. Untreated it can be fatal,, but proper care, including fluid replacement and antibiotics, can result in a high recovery rate. *See also* MS pp.*107, 109.*

Cholesterol, white, fatty STEROID ($C_{27}H_{45}OH$), found in the tissues of vertebrates. It occurs in large concentrations in the brain, spinal cord and liver. It is synthesized in the liver, intestines and skin and is an intermediate in the synthesis of vitamin D and many hormones. GALLSTONES are composed mainly of cholesterol. A diet rich in animal products may produce an excess of cholesterol which possibly contributes to heart disease. *See also* SU pp.152–153.

Choline, sometimes classified as a B vitamin. It is necessary for the synthesis of ACETYCHOLINE and fatty acids by the liver. Its dietary sources are egg yolk and some vegetable oils. It can be synthesized in the body from the amino acid serine.

Cholinesterase, enzyme that breaks down and inactivates the nerve transmitter ACETYLCHOLINE at the nerve synapse. *See also* MS p.31.

Chomo Lhāri, peak in the Himalayas on Bhutan's NW border with China. Sacred to people of Tibet, the mountain was first scaled in 1937 by Lt.-Col. F. Spencer Chapman and the Sherpa Pasang Dawa Lama. Height: 7,314m (23,997ft).

Chomsky, Avram Noam (1928–), US linguist. His book *Syntactic Structures* (1957) and other writings have revolutionized modern linguistic theory. His ideas have also had considerable impact on psychologists concerned with language acquisition. Chomsky believes that the human capacity for language is partially innate, in contrast to the concept of BEHAVIOURISM. *See also* LINGUISTICS; MS pp.154–155.

Chondrichthyes, class of cartilaginous fish including Elasmobranchii (SHARK, RAY and SKATE) and Holocephali (chimaera). These marine fish have cartilaginous skeletons, a well-developed lower jaw, paired fins, separate gill openings, no air bladder, bony teeth and plate-like (placoid) scales. Chondrichthyes evolved during the late DEVONIAN period. *See also* NW pp.124, 180.

Ch'ŏngjin, city of NE North Korea on the Sea of Japan. From 1910 to 1945 it was controlled by the Japanese, who developed the Musan iron mines during the 1930s. The city was severely damaged during the Korean War. Industries: iron, steel, sardines. Pop. 265,000.

Ch'ŏngju, city in central South Korea, 113km (70 miles) SSE of Seoul. It is a market centre for the surrounding agricultural region. Industries: rice, tobacco, cotton, textiles. Pop. (1970) 143,944.

Chongqing. *See* CHUNGKING.

Chŏnju, city in SW South Korea. Situated in an area of high population and intensive agricultural production, it serves as a transportation centre. Industries include food processing and textiles. Pop. (1970) 257,530.

Chonos Islands (Archipiélago de los Chonos), large island chain off the S coast of Chile. They are sparsely inhabited by the Chonos Indians. Length: approx. 209km (130 miles).

Chopin, Frédéric François (1810–49), Polish-French composer for the piano. He studied in Warsaw and moved to Paris in 1831. He later became a close friend of George SAND and Eugène DELACROIX. Although he wrote two piano concertos and three piano sonatas, Chopin's best-known works are numerous short solo pieces – ballades, études, nocturnes, waltzes, preludes, impromptus. His Polish background and the stirring of Polish nationalism inspired a large number of mazurkas and polonaises. *See also* HC2 p.*107.*

Chopper culture, early PALAEOLITHIC culture widely distributed in the Eastern Hemisphere and particularly associated with PEKING MAN, the best site being at Choukoutien, near Peking. It is marked by the use of circular flint discs and pebbles whose circumference is flaked to a sharp, cutting edge.

Choral music, music for several voices, originally religious, such as CANTATAS and ORATORIOS. The foremost composer of cantatas was BACH, of oratorios HANDEL. Secular choral works range from MADRIGALS to large works such as ELGAR's *Dream of Gerontius* (1900).

Chordata, name of a large phylum of VERTEBRATES and some marine invertebrates, all of which at some stage in their lives have rod-like, cartilaginous supporting structures called NOTOCHORDS. Other shared features are gill slits, a hollow nerve cord along the back, a bilaterally symmetrical body and segmented muscles and nerves. Invertebrate chordates are subdivided into three subphyla: Urochordata–TUNICATES or seasquirts; Cephalochordata–AMPHIOXUS and Hemichordata. Vertebrates have notochords surrounded by bony or cartilaginous vertebrae (spinal columns). *See also* NW pp.75, 122, *123.*

Chorea, any of several diseases involving involuntary jerking movements of parts of the body. One type, Sydenham's chorea, or St Vitus's dance, occurs in children (more often in girls) and is marked by irregular muscular movements and abrupt jerks. Often accompanied by an emotional disorder, it usually subsides in a few weeks. It may be associated with rheumatic fever. Another form of chorea, Huntington's disease, is a rare hereditary complaint that starts in early middle life with lack of muscular co-ordination and progresses with emotional outbursts and mental deterioration, and ends in death.

Chorion, outermost of three protective membranes of the embryonic system of birds, reptiles or mammals, or of the insect egg. In birds it is the moist lining between the shell and allantois (organ for respiration and discharge of carbon dioxide). It contributes to placenta formation in placental mammals, and the embryo receives nourishment, oxygen and water through it.

Chorionic gonadotropin (CG), HORMONE produced by the placenta in the womb of a pregnant woman and present in her urine. The detection of this hormone is the basis of most methods of pregnancy testing. *See also* MS. p.76.

Chorus, term derived from the Greek *choros,* meaning those who danced and chanted comments on the action in Greek drama. In modern usage a chorus is a group of singers (as distinct from soloists). Major works with parts for a chorus include CANTATAS, OPERAS and ORATORIOS. A CHOIR is also a type of chorus.

Chorzow, city in S Poland, formerly known as Krolewska Huta. Situated in the Katowice mining and industrial region, it has iron and steel foundries and chemical plants. Pop. (1974) 154,500.

Chou dynasty (*c.*1030–221 BC), Chinese dynasty responsible for the creation of much of the Chinese society and culture. It overthrew the SHANG DYNASTY, after the Chou people had moved out of their homelands N of the HWANG-HO river. Chinese civilization spread under the Chou to most parts of modern China, but the dynasty never established effective control over the regions. CONFUCIUS and LAO TZE achieved the greatest of the many cultural glories of Chou China. *See also* HC1 pp.122–123.

Chou En-lai (1898–1976), Chinese politician. He was educated in Japan and Europe and worked for the nationalist KUOMINTANG (1924–27), after which he joined the Communist Party. He participated in the LONG MARCH, and acted as second-in-command to MAO TSE-TUNG. He negotiated the eventual Communist victory, and became prime minister (1949–76) and foreign minister (1949–58). He was the country's chief international spokesman until his death. *See also* HC2 pp.244–245.

Chough, bird of the CROW family, slightly larger than a jackdaw and also having black plumage, but easily distinguished by its bright red, slender, curved beak and red legs. It is a rare bird of mountains and rocky shores of Europe. The Alpine chough, *Pyrrhocorax graculus,* inhabits inland mountains, is smaller, and has a yellow bill. Family Corvidae.

Choukoutien, archaeological site near Peking, China, where the remains of Peking man, *Sinanthropus pekinensis,* were found in 1927–37. The caves where they were found show the earliest known use of fire. *See also* MS pp.24–25, *24.*

Chou-shan. *See* CHUSHAN.

Chow-chow, ancient Chinese breed of dog (originally raised for meat), introduced to the West in 1780. The only dog with a blue-black tongue, it has a massive head with a short, broad muzzle and full, hanging lips. The dense, coarse coat forms a ruff round the neck. Average size: 45.5–51cm (18–20in) height at the shoulder; weight: 23–27kg (50–60lb).

Chrétien de Troyes (*fl.*1165–80), romance writer of northern France, noted for his tales of King Arthur and his knights, which influenced both Geoffrey CHAUCER and Thomas MALORY. He wrote at least six romances, including *Lancelot, Yvain* and *Perceval.* Although deriving his subject-matter from popular legend and history, his contributions to romance literature include elaboration of plot structure and character development. *See also* HC1 pp.206, *206*.

Christ. *See* JESUS CHRIST.

Christadelphians (Christ's brethren), Christian sect founded in America in 1848 by John Thomas (1805–71). Christadelphians hold the Bible to be inspired and infallible, administer BAPTISM by immersion, reject the doctrine of the TRINITY, and believe in the SECOND COMING of Christ in glory to set up the kingdom of God on earth. They have no clergy.

Christchurch, city in E South Island, New Zealand, on the Banks Peninsula, main town of CANTERBURY. It was founded in 1850 as a Church of England settlement. Canterbury College (1873), now the University of Canterbury, and its School of Art (1882) are there. Industries: fertilizers, rubber, woollen goods, electrical goods, furniture. Pop. (1976 est.) 171,800.

Christening. *See* BAPTISM.

Christian, name of ten kings of Denmark and Norway. Christian I (1426–81) became King of Denmark in 1448 and of Norway in 1450. He controlled Sweden 1457–64. Christian II (1481–1559), the Cruel, came to the throne in 1513. He ruled Sweden in 1520–23 and was driven out of Denmark in 1523 by the nobility, who resisted his reforms. Christian III (1503–59) was elected king of Denmark and Norway in 1534. He established LUTHERANISM and weakened the HANSEATIC LEAGUE. Christian IV (1577–1648) became king in 1588. He invaded Germany in the THIRTY YEARS WAR in 1625 with little success. Christian V (1646–99) became king in 1670 and was made absolute monarch by his minister Griffenfeld. Christian VI (1699–1746) was crowned in 1730. Christian VII (1749–1808), who came to the throne in 1766, was mentally ill and his doctor, Struensee, controlled the government from 1770–1772. Liberal reforms were begun during his reign. Christian VIII (1786–1848) was elected King of Norway in 1814 but expelled the same year for refusing a union with Sweden. He became King of Denmark 1839–48. Christian IX (1818–1906) became King of Denmark in 1863. He lost Schleswig-Holstein to Prussia and Austria in 1864. Christian X (1870–1947) was king of Denmark (1912–47) and of Iceland (1912–44). He led Danish resistance to the Nazi occupation.

Christian, name by which a follower of JESUS CHRIST is known. The major Christian Churches regard affirmation of belief in the divinity of Christ *see* TRINITY as the minimum requirement for being called Christian. This definition excludes religious bodies such as the UNITARIANS. In modern popular usage, however, the term has tended to lose all credal significance and has come to imply only that which is morally noble (eg a Christian deed).

Christian Action, group founded in 1946 by Canon John Collins in London to work for radical political and social reforms on the basis of Christian principles. It has campaigned for causes such as European union, racial equality, nuclear disarmament and the abolition of capital punishment. It is also active in social welfare work such as providing homes to needy families.

Christian Democrats, centrist political parties in several Roman Catholic countries of Europe and in West Germany. They share allegiance to the doctrine of Christianity and an antipathy to the goals of SOCIALISM and COMMUNISM. They uphold the specifically Roman Catholic political position of the defence of confessional schools and strong opposition to divorce and abortion. Their origin lies in the Roman Catholic revival and quarrel with LIBERALISM in the second half of the 19th century, although all have long since broken their ties with ULTRAMONTISM. All of them have, in the pursuit of electoral success, acknowledged the necessity for schemes of social welfare.

Since the end of WWII the most successful Christian Democratic parties have been those of West Germany and Italy. The first chancellor of the reformed West German Republic was Konrad ADENAUER, the leader of the Christian Democratic Union. He remained chancellor until 1963 and was followed by two more Christian Democrats, Ludwig ERHARD (until 1966) and Kurt-Georg KIESINGER (until 1969). It is indicative of the modern latitude of Christian Democratic parties that Erhard was a Protestant. The first post-war leader in Italy was Alcide de Gasperi, whose Christian Democratic party remained an important force in Italian politics, often holding office in coalition with smaller parties. In Switzerland there is an official Christian Democratic party but Belgium and Luxembourg the equivalent parties are called the Christian Social parties. Austria, despite an overwhelmingly Roman Catholic population, has since the war been dominated by the left; the Christian Socialists, however, are in fact a centrist darty. France has never had a Christian Democratic party, although the Popular Republican Movement has similar policies.

Christian Democracy has spread beyond the borders of Europe, for instance to Chile, where a Christian Democratic party took office in 1964.

Christianity, religion based on faith in JESUS CHRIST as the Son of God. The essence of the orthodox Christian faith is summarized in the Apostles' and NICENE CREEDS which affirm belief in the TRINITY and in Christ's INCARNATION, atoning death on the cross, RESURRECTION and ASCENSION. The moral teachings of Jesus, centred on love of God and of one's neighbour, are contained in the NEW TESTAMENT, particularly in passages such as the SERMON ON THE MOUNT. The first major schism in Christianity took place in 1054 when the eastern and western churches separated. The next occurred at the time of the 16th century REFORMATION, when western Christendom split into PROTESTANTISM and ROMAN CATHOLICISM. Further divisions among Protestants occurred in succeeding centuries, but in recent times the ECUMENICAL MOVEMENT, which aims at the reunion of all Christians, has been gaining strength. Christianity has exercised a powerful influence on many aspects of world history: political, social and cultural. The number of Christians in the world in the mid-1970s was estimated at more than a thousand million. *See also* HC1 pp.110–111, 134–135; HC2 pp.138–139, 304–305; MS pp.218–219.

Christian Science, religious movement founded by the American Mary Baker EDDY (1821–1910). Its followers believe that the physical and moral problems of mankind can be solved solely by means of prayer. Instruction is based on the Bible and Mrs Eddy's book *Science and Health with Key to the Scriptures.* Divine Mind is used as a synonym for God; and man, as the "image and likeness of God", is regarded as the complete and flawless manifestation of this Mind.

Christian Socialism, movement to ally the working class and the Church to combat the alleged evils of CAPITALISM. It was begun in England in the late 1840s, principally by Frederick Denison MAURICE and Charles KINGSLEY. They wrote pamphlets, encouraged the foundation of working men's associations and founded a working men's college in 1854. The movement spread to the USA in the 1880s. The Society of Christian Socialists was founded there in 1889. In the twentieth century Christian Socialism lost much of its organizational strength, but found new, powerful advocacy in the writings of theologians such as Reinhold Niebuhr and Paul Tillich.

Christie, Dame Agatha (1891–1976), British author, a prolific and popular writer of detective stories. Her novels include *The Mysterious Affair at Styles* (1920), which introduced her most famous character, the Belgian detective Hercule Poirot, *The Murder of Roger Ackroyd* (1926), *Murder at the Vicarage* (1930), *Murder on the Orient Express* (1934), *And Then There Were None* (1940), and *Curtain* (1975). She also wrote plays, including *The Mousetrap* (1952), which held a world record for the longest continuous run at one theatre.

Christie, John (1882–1962), founder of the GLYNDEBOURNE opera. A member of a family of organ-makers and married to the soprano Audrey Mildmay, he built a small opera hall on his Sussex estate where, since 1934, world-class opera has been staged.

Christie's, popular name for Christie, Manson & Woods Ltd, a leading British fine arts auctioneers. The firm which was founded by James Christie in 1766, has its head office in London.

Christina (1626–89), Queen of Sweden (1632–54). After the regency of OXENSTIERNA (1632–44) she ruled eccentrically, giving away Crown lands. She attracted foreign scholars, including DESCARTES, to her court. She abdicated in 1654 and travelled widely, trying unsuccessfully to obtain the crown of Poland on John Casimir's abdication in 1667.

Christmas, feast in celebration of the birth of Jesus Christ. The observance of the feast does not seem to have become general in Christendom until the 4th century. The exact date of Christ's birth is unknown, but the feast has traditionally been celebrated in the West on 25 December. This date was probably chosen to oppose the pagan feast of the birth of the Roman god, Mithras, the "Sun of Righteousness", whose observance had spread to other parts of western Christendom. In the East the closely related feast of the EPIPHANY (6 January) was originally the more important but by the late 4th century it was linked with the birth of Christ. By the middle of the 5th century most Eastern Churches had adopted 25 December as the date for Christmas, but some have continued to observe it on 6 January. The feast is also celebrated socially as a season of joy lasting several days and as an occasion for the exchange of greetings and presents.

Christmas Carol, A (1843), short novel by Charles DICKENS. Ebenezer Scrooge, a miser who believes Christmas to be an unnecessary festival, is converted to generosity and benevolence by frightening visions of his past, present and future.

Christmas Island, largest atoll in the Pacific Ocean; part of the Gilbert and Ellice Islands. It was charted by Capt. James COOK in 1777 and annexed to Britain in 1888. It was the site of nuclear tests by Britain (1956–62) and the USA (1962). Sovereignty is claimed by both Britain and the USA. Area: 575sq km (222sq miles). Pop. (1968) 367.

Christmas Island, island in the E Indian Ocean, 320km (200 miles) S of Java. Once under British domination, it was annexed to Australia in 1958. It has important lime phosphate deposits. Area: 135sq km (52sq miles). Pop. (1975 est.) 3,000. *See also* MW p.58.

Christmas rose. *See* HELLEBORE.

Christoff, Boris (1919–), Bulgarian bass. Since making his opera debut in 1946 (Rome) he has sung with great success in all the major opera houses. He is particularly noted for the authority of his interpretation of Russian songs and of such roles as Boris Godunov and Ivan the Terrible.

Christology, doctrines relating to the person of Christ and, in particular, to the union in Him of the divine and human natures. Most of the theological controversies in the first centuries of Christendom centred on Christology and were debated at several ecumenical councils. *See also* ARIANISM; CHALCEDON, COUNCIL OF; COPTIC CHURCH; MONOPHYSITISM; MONOTHELITISM; NESTORIANISM; NICAEA, COUNCILS OF; NICENE CREED.

Christophe, Henri (1767–1820), Haitian revolutionary leader, president (1806–11) and king (1811–20). Born a free black on the island of Grenada, he participated in the armed struggle against the French in Haiti and fought a civil war with the partisans of the mulatto Pétion. Christophe ordered the construction of the citadel of La Ferrière, a fort overlooking Cap Haitien, the building of which cost many Haitian lives.

Christopher, Saint patron of ferrymen and travellers. There are many legends about this early martyr, who probably died

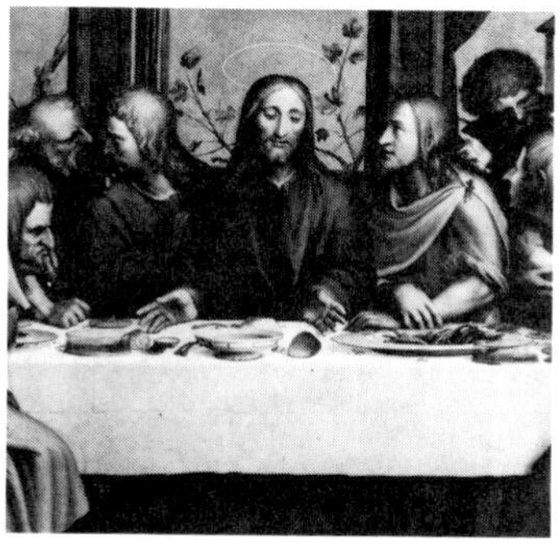

Christianity; Jesus prepares his disciples for what is to come at The Last Supper (Holbein)

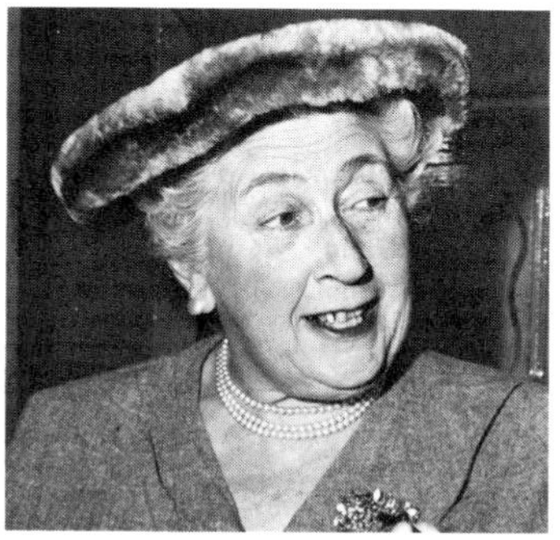

Agatha Christie's play *The Mousetrap* in 1978 entered its 25th year in London's West End.

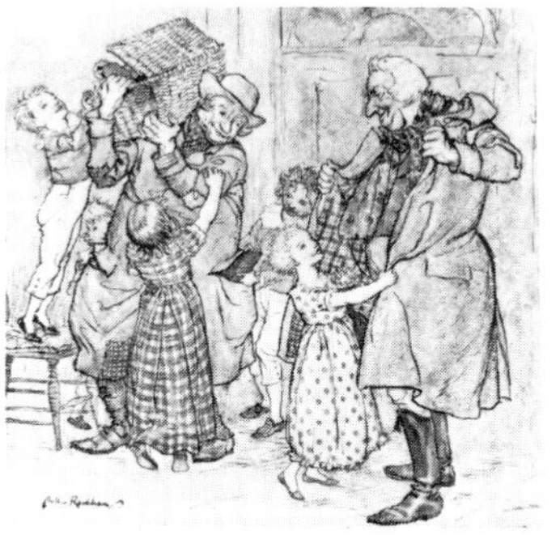

A Christmas Carol, Dickens' popular moral tale and a regular seasonal favourite.

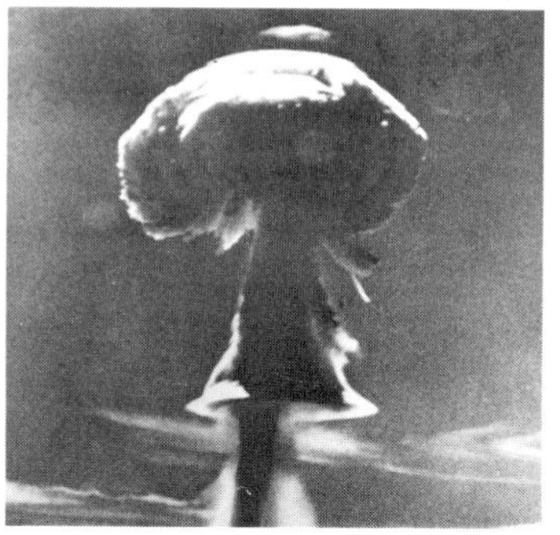

Christmas Island, where the third of Britain's hydrogen bombs was tested on 19 June 1957.

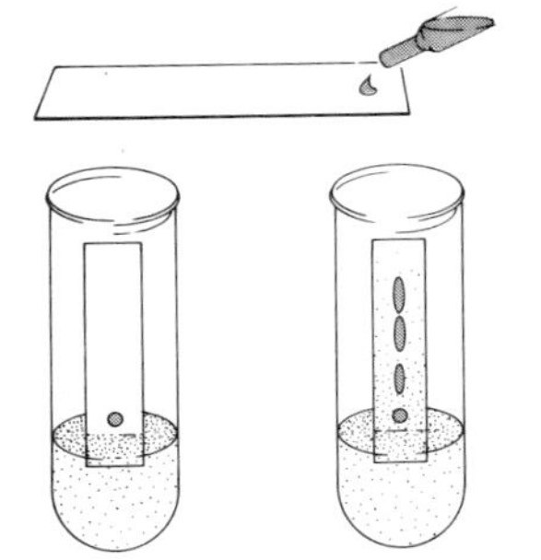

Chromatography is a process for separating and analysing mixtures of substances.

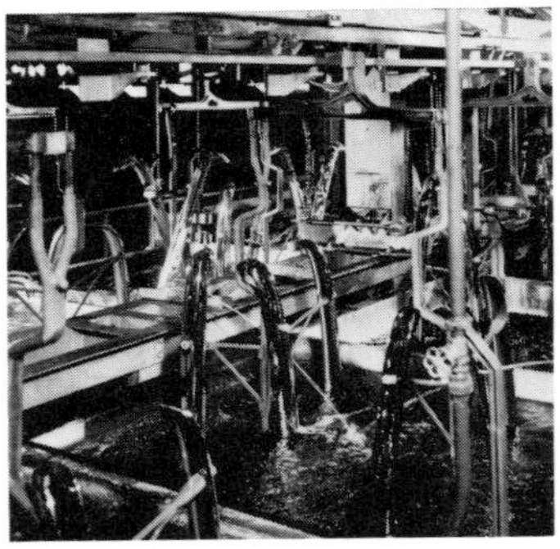

Chromium plating car bumpers; the chromium polishes well and resists corrosion.

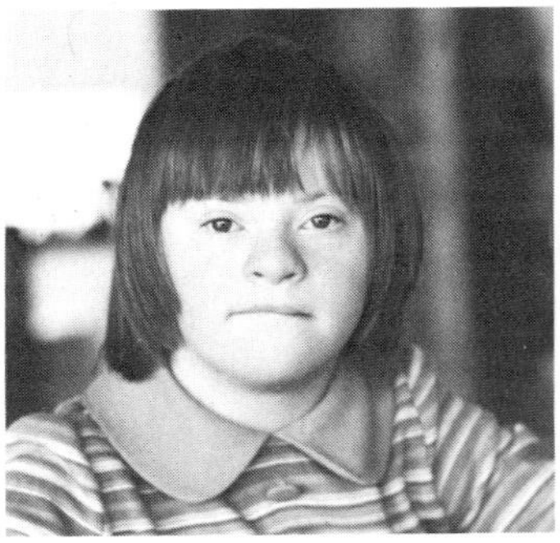

Chromosomal aberration; mongolism is associated with an extra chromosome.

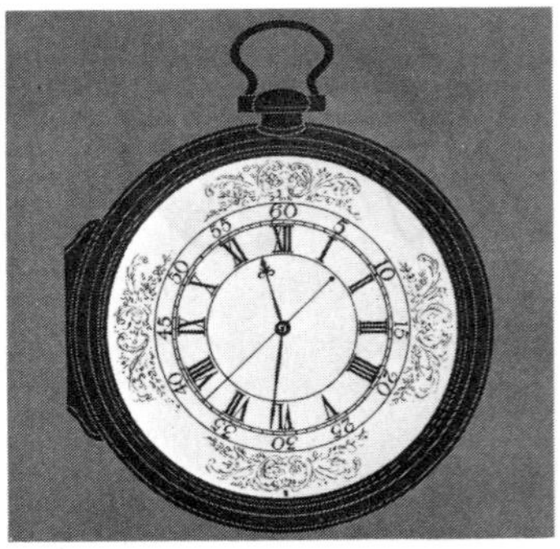

Chronometer; John Harrison's timepiece (1757) was left unaffected by ships' motion.

during DECIUS' persecution, *c.*250. According to one legend, he carried travellers across a river as a work of charity, and on one occasion Christ in the form of a child was among his passengers. His feast, 25 July, was omitted from the Roman Catholic calendar of 1969 and is no longer officially recognized, but it may be observed locally.

Christus, Petrus (*c.*1422–1473), Flemish painter whose works resemble those of Jan van EYCK, by whom he was influenced. Christus is best known for his success in depicting perspective. His sensitive portraits and religious subjects, include *Lamentation* and *Portrait of a Lady.*

Chromatic, in music, term used in melodic and harmonic analysis to refer to notes which do not occur in the scale of the key of the passage. Such notes are marked with accidentals and hence the chords in which they occur are also termed chromatic. Use of the term depends on the definition of the key of the passage.

Chromatography, techniques of chemical analysis by which substances are separated from one another, identified and measured. It is used extensively in organic chemistry and biochemistry. The various methods all rely on a principle of partition: components of a mixture separate as they flow at different speeds along a surface or column of specially chosen material, and are carried in a fluid (gas or liquid) called the eluent. The name chromatography comes from early methods of identifying separated components by their colour, but many colourless compounds are now identified using the technique. *See also* SU pp.*144, 147,* 151.

Chromite, black metallic mineral, ferrous chromic oxide ($FeO.Cr_2O_3$), the only important ore of chromium. It separates from magma when igneous rocks first form. It occurs as octahedral crystals and as granular masses. Chromite is weakly magnetic and opaque; hardness 5.5; s.g. 4.6. *See also* PE p.132.

Chromium, metallic element (Cr) of the first transition series, first isolated in 1797. Chief ore is chromite ($FeO.Cr_2O_3$). Chromium is a dull grey metal but takes a high polish and is extensively used as an electroplated coating. It is also an ingredient of many special steels. Properties: at.no. 24; at.wt. 51.996; s.g. 7.19; m.p. 1,890°C (3,434°F); b.p. 2,482°C (4,500°F); most common isotope Cr^{52} (83.76 per cent). *See also* TRANSITION ELEMENTS.

Chromosomal aberration, any abnormality in the chromosomes of a cell, such as a variation in the normal number or a change in the normal arrangement of the genetic material, which may produce an unexpected characteristic. Down's syndrome (mongolism), for example, is associated with an extra chromosome. Some malformations have been associated with the absence of sections of certain chromosomes. *See also* MS p.14.

Chromosome, microscopic thread-like bodies, usually in the cell nucleus, that carry the genetic code for an organism. Each species of plant or animal usually has a characteristic number of chromosomes made up of units called GENES. See also HEREDITY; DNA; NW pp.28–29.

Chromosphere, region of the Sun's atmosphere closest to the solar surface or PHOTOSPHERE, extending upward for some 6,000km (3,700 miles) and increasing in temperature from 6,000°C to more than 50,000°C. The chromosphere merges into the tenuous CORONA and is the source of many solar phenomena, including flares, prominences and spicules. *See also* SU pp.222–223.

Chronicles, two historical books of the Old Testament. They trace the history of ISRAEL and JUDAH from the CREATION to the return from Exile under CYRUS (538 BC).

Chronometer, instrument for accurately measuring time, an essential navigational aid for ships before the advent of radio. The ATOMIC CLOCK is the most precise instrument to date; it is used for measuring time scientifically. *See also* MM p.93.

Chrysalis, intermediate or pupal stage in the life cycle of all insects that undergo complete metamorphosis. The chrysalis is usually covered with a hard case, but some pupae, such as that of the silk moth, spin a silk cocoon around themselves. Within the chrysalis feeding and locomotion stop and the final stages of the development take place. *See also* LEPIDOPTERA; NW p.112.

Chrysanthemum, large genus of annual and perennial plants native to temperate Eurasia and now widely cultivated. Centuries of selective breeding have modified the original plain daisy-like flowers, and most species have large white, yellow, bronze, pink or red flower-heads. Family Compositae.

Chrysler, Walter Percy (1875–1940), US industrialist. He began his career as a railway machinist; by 1912 he was in the car industry, first as manager then as president of General Motors Corporation. From 1925 he was president of the Chrysler Corporation, producing not only Chrysler cars but also Dodge, Plymouth and Dart vehicles. From 1935 he was chairman of the corporation.

Chrysolite. *See* OLIVINE.

Chrysophyte. *See* GOLDEN-BROWN ALGAE.

Chrysostum, Saint John. *See* JOHN CHRYSOSTUM, SAINT.

Chrysotile, fibrous serpentine mineral, from which comes most of the world's supply of ASBESTOS. Serpentines are hydrated magnesium silicates ($3MgO.2SiO_2.2H_2O$). The variety called chrysotile has crystalline, tubular fibres that are particularly suitable for spinning and weaving into heat-resistant fabrics.

Chuang Chou, or Chuang Tze (*c.*369–*c.*286 BC), Chinese philosopher. His book of paradoxical anecdotes, known as the *Chuang Tze,* is a fundamental work of TAOISM and stresses the relativity of all human ideas.

Chuang Tse-tung (1942–), Chinese table tennis player. He dominated the sport, winning world singles titles in 1961, 1963 and 1965 and sharing in China's Swaythling Cup victories of those years. He won a fourth team gold medal in 1971.

Chuang Tze. *See* CHUANG CHOU.

Chub, fresh-water CARP found in flowing waters. It has a large head, wide mouth and is grey-brown. Length 10–60cm (4–25in). Family Cyprinidae. Chub is also the name of a marine fish of warm seas – oval-shaped with a small mouth and bright colours. Family Kyphosidae. *See also* PE p.*245.*

Chubb crater, officially known as Le Cratère du Nouveau-Québec, ancient meteor crater situated between Hudson and Ungava bays in Quebec, Canada. It measures 3.2km (2 miles) in diameter and is 411m (1,350ft) deep.

Chu-Chin-Chow, musical tale of the East, based loosely on the story of Ali Baba. The music was written by Frederick Norton. It was first performed in London in 1916 and had unparalleled success, running for 2,238 consecutive performances.

Chugach Mountains, range in S Alaska, extending E from Cook Inlet to the St Elias Mountains. It has the Chugach National Forest. The highest peak is Mt Marcus Baker, 4,039m (13,250ft). Length: approx. 450km (280 miles).

Chu-jan (*fl.*mid-10th century), Chinese painter who, like his master TUNG YUAN, specialized in landscapes. A Buddhist monk at the court of the Sung emperor, Chu-jan painted (often on a monumental scale) misty scenes of towering mountains surrounded by smaller hills.

Chukchi, a people who inhabit the Chukchi Peninsula in NE USSR. They are divided into the semi-nomadic reindeer herders of the tundra and the fishing communities on the coast, which also mine coal and ores of tin, tungsten, mercury and gold.

Chulalongkorn, Somdeth Phra Paraminda Maha (1853–1910), King of Siam as Rama V (1868–1910). He abolished slavery and modernized the courts, built railways and advanced education and technology. He visited Europe in 1897 and 1907 and appointed many Europeans to government posts. He was frequently in conflict with the French in neighbouring Indochina.

Ch'unch'ŏn, city in N South Korea, on the Pukhan River, 72km (45 miles) NE of Seoul (Sŏul). It is a market town for an agricultural region producing rice, millet and soybeans. Industries: textiles and tungsten and mica mining. Pop. 122,700.

Chung, Raymond Arthur (1918–), president of GUYANA. The son of a Chinese farmer, he studied law and became a judge of the High Court in 1962. He was elected the first president of the republic of Guyana in 1970.

Ch'ung-ch'ing. *See* CHUNGKING.

Chungking (Chongqing, or Ch'ung-ch'ing), city in S China, on the YANGTZE (Changjiang) river. It was the headquarters of the ancient Kingdom of Pa, which was overtaken by the Chin dynasty in the 3rd century BC. It was the wartime capital of China (1937–45) after Nanking (Nanjing) was besieged during the Japanese invasion. It is a transport and shipping centre with chemicals, steel, iron, silk, cotton textiles and plastics industries. Pop. 2,300,000.

Chuquicamata, town in N Chile, on the W slopes of the Andes Mountains. It has one of world's largest copper mines. Pop. 27,800. *See also* MW p.52.

Chur, town in E Switzerland, 119km (74 miles) SE of Zürich on the River Plessur; capital of Grisons canton. It has many buildings of historic interest including an 8th-century church, the Renaissance episcopal palace and the Rhaetian museum of folklore. Industries: tourism, woodworking, textiles, beer, chocolate. Pop. (1970) 31,193.

Church, Richard (1893–1972), English author who wrote poetry, novels, essays and children's stories. His best-known work includes his three-volume autobiography *Over the Bridge* (1955), which won the *Sunday Times* prize for literature, *Golden Sovereign* (1957) and *The Voyage Home* (1964).

Church, in theology, the community of Christian believers; in architecture, the building in which Christians worship. The characteristics of the Church as a community have been described in the NICENE CREED as one, holy, catholic (in the sense of universal) and apostolic. In the 20th century the ECUMENICAL MOVEMENT has been trying to restore the Church unity.

Church Army, Anglican organization of lay volunteers, founded in London in 1882 by Wilson CARLILE, a clergyman. Modelled on the SALVATION ARMY, its activities include evangelism as well as social welfare work among the poor, the lonely, the elderly and the handicapped.

Church Assembly. *See* GENERAL SYNOD.

Church Commissioners, body consisting of the archbishops and bishops of England and representatives of priests and laity which manages the estates and revenues of the Church of England. The Church Commissioners also have the responsibility for the periodical review and reorganization of the legal structure of PARISHES and RURAL DEANERIES.

Church Congress, unofficial gathering of Anglican churchmen in England held at regular intervals between 1861 and 1938. It declined because of the emergence of other avenues of expression of church life such as the Church Assembly, established in 1920, and the General Synod which superseded it in 1970.

Churchill, Charles (1731–64), British poet and satirist. His works include *Rosciad* (1761), which made him famous; *The Prophecy of Famine* (1763), a political satire; and *An Epistle to William Hogarth* (1763).

Churchill, Clive (1927–), Australian rugby league player. He was a spirited, controversial fullback, 32 of whose 34 appearances for Australia (1948–56) were consecutive. He was a rugged, feared tackler and an inspiring captain; later a respected coach.

Churchill, John. *See* MARLBOROUGH, JOHN C., DUKE OF.

Churchill, Lord Randolph Henry Spencer (1849–95), British political figure, father of Winston CHURCHILL. He entered Parliament in 1874 as a Conservative and was secretary of state for India (1885–86) and chancellor of the exchequer (1886). He resigned from office in 1886 but stayed in the Commons and attacked GLADSTONE's plans for Irish Home Rule.

Churchill, Sarah Jennings, Duchess of Marlborough. *See* MARLBOROUGH, Sarah Jennings, Churchill, Duchess of.
Churchill, Sir Winston Leonard Spencer (1874–1965), British statesman, son of Lord Randolph CHURCHILL. As a reporter in the SOUTH AFRICAN (Boer) WAR he was captured in 1899 but escaped. He was elected to Parliament in 1900 as a Conservative, but joined the Liberals in 1904. As home secretary (1910–11) he introduced important pension Acts, but suppressed labour unrest. He was first lord of the admiralty (1911–15), minister of munitions (1917–18), secretary of state for war and for air (1919–21) and colonial secretary (1921–22). He was chancellor of the exchequer (1924–29) and was out of office 1929–39, but spoke constantly against the rising threat of Nazi Germany. He was first lord of the admiralty (1939–40), and acted as prime minister and minister of defence in the War Cabinet (1940–45). His inspiring oratory made him a great war leader. He established close contact with US president F. D. ROOSEVELT, and was principal architect of the grand alliance of Britain, the USA and the USSR. He was prime minister again 1951–55, after which he retired from politics. He wrote extensively, his major works being *The World Crisis* (1923–31), *The Second World War* (1948–54) and the *History of the English-Speaking Peoples* (1956–58). He was awarded the Nobel Prize in literature in 1953. *See also* HC2 pp.211, 218–219, 234–237.
Churchill Peaks, twin peaks of Mt McKinley in S central Alaska, USA. Height: (N peak) 5,934m (19,470ft); (S peak) 6,194m (20,320ft). The S peak is the highest point of North America.
Churchill River, river rising in NW Saskatchewan, Canada; flows from Methy Lake through several lakes into the Hudson Bay at Churchill, NE Manitoba. It was once a fur-trade route. There is a hydroelectric power plant on its upper course. Length: 1,610km (1,000 miles).
Churchill River, river in Newfoundland, Canada; rises as the Ashuanipi River in SW Labrador and flows through a series of lakes to the Atlantic Ocean near Rigolet. Formerly known as the Hamilton River, it was renamed in 1965 after Sir Winston Churchill. There is a large hydroelectric power station at Churchill Falls. Length: 965km (600 miles).
Church of Christ Scientist. *See* CHRISTIAN SCIENCE.
Church of England, name by which the Christian Church in England, established by law in the sixteenth century, is known. Although closely interwoven with the state the Church in England before that date was not a national church but gave fundamental allegiance to Rome. However, during the REFORMATION, a period of turmoil and controversy spanning several reigns, it declared itself independent of papal jurisdiction and finally adopted the Elizabethan Settlement which, while espousing Protestantism, aimed at preserving religious unity by shaping a national Church acceptable to all persons of moderate theological views. This middle course found expression in the doctrinal formulary known as the Thirty-nine ARTICLES (1571). The liturgy of the Church of England is contained in the BOOK OF COMMON PRAYER of 1662, but since the 1960s alternative forms of worship have been coming into use. The sovereign bears the title Supreme Governor of the Church of England, and formally nominates the bishops, but this does not confer on the sovereign any spiritual powers. The Church is episcopally governed, but priests and laity share in all major decisions by virtue of their representation in the General Synod. Territorially the Church is divided into the two provinces of CANTERBURY and YORK, the archbishop of Canterbury being the Primate of All England. The overseas expansion of the Church of England during the period of the growth of the British Empire resulted in the gradual development of the worldwide ANGLICAN COMMUNION. The Church of England is the only part of the Anglican Communion still established by law as an official state church.
Church of Ireland, name by which the Anglican Church in Ireland is known. It claims to be the heir to the ancient Church of the land. At the time of the REFORMATION it ended papal jurisdiction and introduced doctrinal and disciplinary reforms similar to those in the CHURCH OF ENGLAND. It is territorially divided into two provinces, ARMAGH and Dublin. The Archbishop of Armagh bears the title "Primate of All Ireland", while the Archbishop of Dublin is styled "Primate of Ireland". The Church of Ireland was the legally established Church of the land until 1869.
Church of Scotland, name by which the reformed Church of Scotland, established by law, is known. After a period of turmoil during the REFORMATION, when it went through several changes, the Presbyterian system was finally established in the Church of Scotland by 1690. The character of the Church has been greatly influenced by John KNOX, who led the Calvinist party in the Scottish Reformation. The doctrinal position of the Church is based on the SCOTTISH CONFESSION of 1560, drawn up largely by Knox, and the Westminster Confession of 1643 which superseded it. highest authority of the Church of Scotland resides in the General Assembly, presided over by a moderator, who is elected annually. The spiritual independence of the Church was recognized by an Act of Parliament in 1921 although this did not affect its status as the established Church in Scotland, *See also* CALVIN; PRESBYTERIAN CHURCH; HC1 pp.298–299.
Churl. *See* CEORL.
Churriguera, family of Spanish architects after whom the "Churrigueresque" style of Spanish BAROQUE is named. Chief among them were the brothers José (1665–1725), Joaquin (1674–1724) and Alberto (1676–1750), whose masterpieces are in Salamanca. The style, characterized by twisted columns and ornate stucco decoration, reached its greatest extremes in Spanish Mexico.
Chushan (Chou-shan or Zhoushan), group of islands in E China, off the NE coast of Chekiang (Zhejiang) province, in the East China Sea at the entrance to Hangchow (Hangzhou) Bay; includes main island of Chushan and approx. 100 smaller ones. It is in one of China's richest fishing grounds.
Chu Ta (Pa-ta Shan-jen) (1626–1705), Chinese ink-painter and Buddhist monk. He was famous for his eccentricity, which is reflected in his paintings – small studies of birds, fishes, and animals, often misshapen and touched with human qualities, and landscapes with an air of mystery.
Chu Teh (1886–1976), Chinese Communist military leader. In 1911 he helped overthrow the MANCHUS. He joined with MAO TSE-TUNG in 1928 to form the Fourth Red Army and establish a base in Kiangsi. He was a key leader during the LONG MARCH (1934–35) and the military planner for the final Communist victory in China. He served as deputy chairman of the government until 1959 and then as chairman of the National People's Congress.
Chuvash (Chuvash ASSR), autonomous republic in E central European USSR. It is a region of forested steppe with most of the population engaged in agriculture, producing cereals, potatoes and fruit. Timber is also important. Oil and gas refining industries have been developed recently. Area: 18,301sq km (7,066sq miles). Pop. (1970) 1,224,000.
Ch'ü Yüan (*c.*343–*c.*289 BC), Chinese poet. His great poem *On Encountering Sorrow*, is allegorical, moving from an account of the disappointments in his personal life to a mythical search for the perfect wife. He is regarded as the father of Chinese poetry.
Chyle, fine emulsion of neutral fats found in LYMPH vessels in the intestine. It results from the absorption of fats during DIGESTION. After absorption it travels through the lymphatic system and enters the blood via the thoracic duct in the neck.
Chyme, mixture of partly digested food and digestive juices. It passes from the stomach into the small intestine and is a pulpy mush. *See also* DIGESTION; DIGESTIVE SYSTEM; MS p.68.
Chymotrypsin, substance produced in the body that aids in the digestion of food. Chymotrypsin is an ENZYME which breaks down proteins. It is made in the small intestine, by complex chemical reactions, from chymotrypsinogen. This, together with other digestive substances, is secreted by the pancreas through the pancreatic duct into the duodenum which lies between the stomach and the small intestine. The secretion is controlled partly by the vagus nerve and partly by hormones which are released automatically when food enters the duodenum. *See also* TRYPSIN.
Chymotrypsinogen. *See* CHYMOTRYPSIN.
CIA (Central Intelligence Agency), US government agency set up in 1947 to report information from abroad to the US president on questions of national security and to co-ordinate the various intelligence operations of government departments. It is responsible to the National Security Council but does not have to account for its budget. The CIA became increasingly drawn into direct intervention in the internal politics of foreign countries, and investigating security matters within the USA itself, and was subjected to heavy criticism in the 1960s and 1970s.
Ciano, Galeazzo, Conte di Cortellazzo (1903–44), Italian statesman and Fascist leader. In 1922 he took part in the Fascist March on Rome and in 1930 married Benito MUSSOLINI's daughter Edda. He became Foreign Minister in 1936 and was instrumental in Italy's entry into WWII (1940). Axis defeats led to conflict with Mussolini on foreign policy and in 1943 he was among those who forced Mussolini's resignation. He was executed for treason.
Ciba Geigy, international industrial corporation, based in Switzerland. It manufactures dyestuffs, chemicals, plastics and pharmaceuticals, and in the mid-1970s employed about 80,000 people.
Cibber, Colley (1671–1757), English actor-manager, dramatist and poet laureate. His first play *Love's Last Shift* (1696) began the fashion for sentimental comedy. Other successful plays included *The Careless Husband* (1704) and *The Non-Juror* (1717). He wrote a famous autobiography, *An Apology for the Life of Mr Colley Cibber, Comedian* (1740).
Cicada, also called 17-year locust or dog-day cicada, large, fly-like insect found in most parts of the world. It makes a loud sound by the vibration of a pair of plates on its abdomen. Females lay eggs in tree twigs, often causing damage to the twigs. The dog-day cicada appears annually in summer. The 17-year locust, or periodical cicada, appears every 13–17 years. Cicada larvae spend up to 17 years in the ground feeding on roots and live only a week as winged adults. Length: up to 50mm (2in).
Cicero, Marcus Tullius, or Tully (106–43 BC), Roman politician, philospher and orator. A leader of the senate, he exposed CATILINE's conspiracy and prosecuted his supporters. He opposed Julius CAESAR but took no part in his assassination. He criticised Mark ANTONY in the senate and when OCTAVIAN came to power, Antony persuaded him to have Cicero executed. Among Cicero's greatest speeches were *Orations Against Catiline* and the *Phillipics*. He also wrote a number of books on rhetoric and philosophical works including *De Amicitia* and *De Officiis*. *See also* HC1 pp.112, *113*.
Cichlid, any of a family of tropical freshwater fish related to PERCHES, found mainly in South America, Africa and southern Asia. Cichlids are popular aquarium fish because of their brilliant colours. Many are mouth breeders, the female harbouring the unfertilized eggs inside her mouth. Family Cichlidae. *See also* NW pp.*128*, 129, *131*.
Ciconiiformes, order of about 100 species of wading birds, including flamingos, herons, ibises, storks and spoonbills. They have long legs and necks and are found worldwide, except in polar regions.

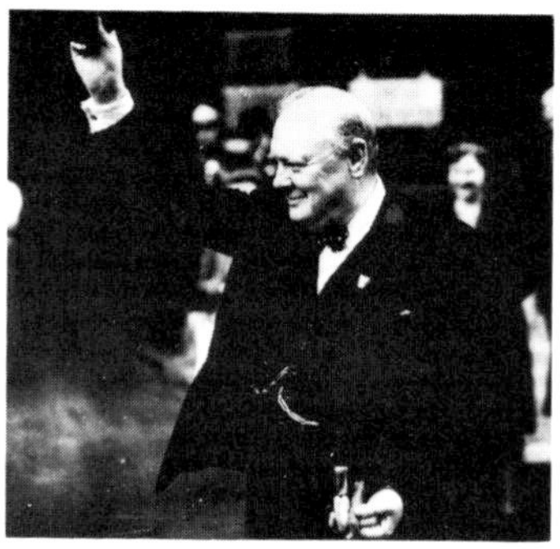
Winston Churchill, great wartime leader and the personification of resistance to fascism.

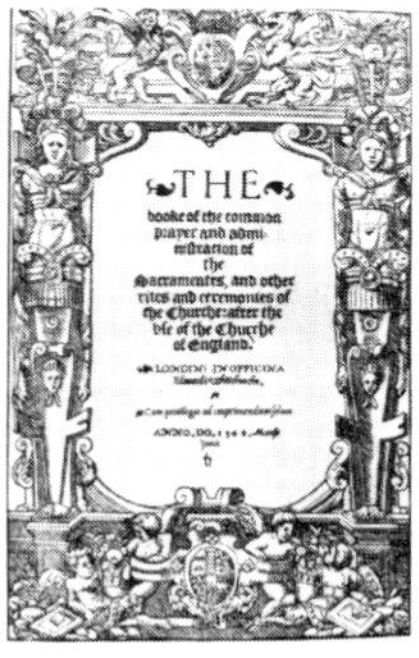
THE
booke of the common
prayer and admi-
nistration of
the
Sacramentes, and other
rites and ceremonies of
the Churche: after the
use of the Churche
of England.

Church of England; Whitchurch's edition of the first Book of Common Prayer (1549).

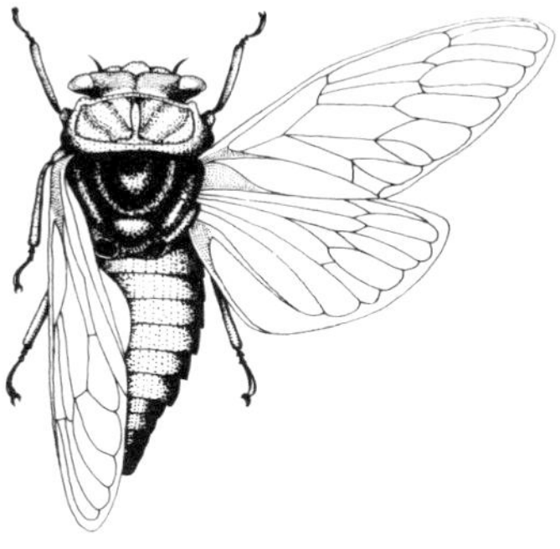
Cicadas can be religious symbols, are eaten for food and, in some places, kept as pets.

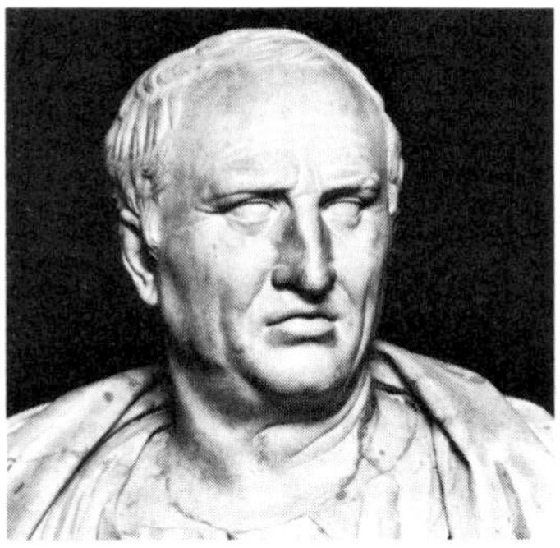
Cicero's oratory entailed a study of speech rhythms appealing to an audience.

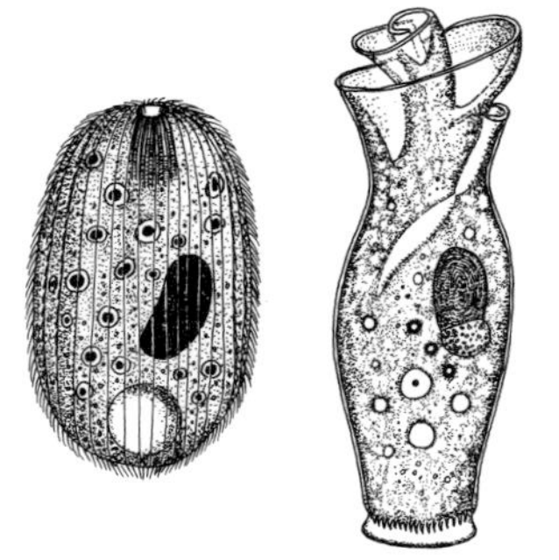

Ciliate; the class of protozoa which use numerous hair-like cilia for propulsion.

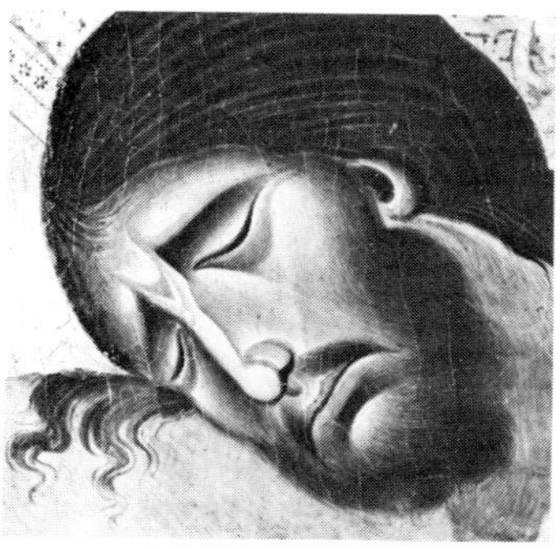

Giovanni Cimabue; a detail from the great *Crucifixion* at S Croce, Florence.

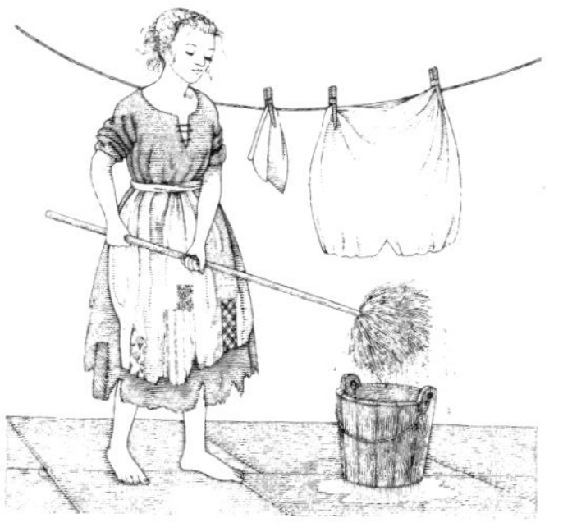

Cinderella, the universal heroine who triumphs over the jealousy of her ugly sisters.

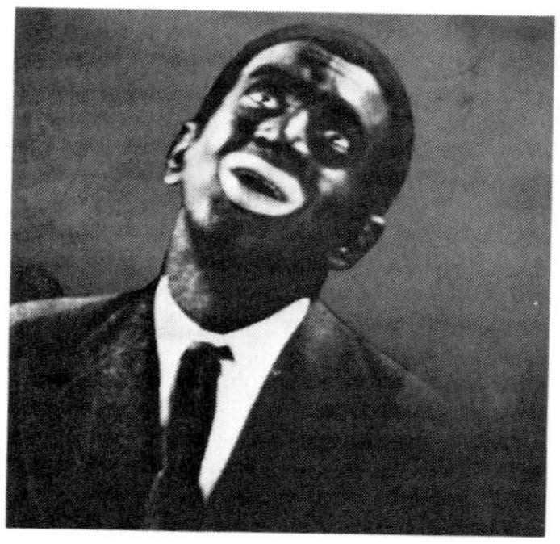

Cinema; Al Jolson as he appeared in the first "talking" picture, *The Jazz Singer.*

CID (Criminal Investigation Department), branch of the London Metropolitan Police dealing with the prevention and investigation of crime, and with the preparation of information on criminal trends. It was established in 1878 and today has a force numbering approximately 1,600, all of whom are recruited from the uniformed branch (CID officers do not wear uniform, but operate instead in so-called plain clothes). The headquarters are at NEW SCOTLAND YARD, but officers may operate from local stations within the Metropolitan District. On request, the CID also offers advice and assistance to provincial forces.

Cid, Rodrigo Díaz de Vivar, "El Cid" (*c.* 1043–99), Spanish national hero in the wars against the Moors. He was a knight in the service of the king of Castile, but was banished in 1081 and joined the Moorish king of Saragossa. He conquered Valencia in 1094 and ruled it until his death, but the Moors took the kingdom in 1102. His various exploits have been romanticized in Spanish legend. *See also* HC1 p.170.

Cider, fermented apple juice. In the USA, unfermented apple juice is sometimes marketed as non-alcoholic cider. In the manufacture of alcoholic apple cider the fruit is crushed to a pomace which is squeezed to express the juice, about 50 litres (11 gals) being obtained from 100kg (220lb) of apples, and the juice is fermented in wooden vats or casks. For sweet ciders FERMENTATION is stopped after about three weeks; for dry ciders it is allowed to go to completion. For still ciders the carbon dioxide made by the yeast is allowed to escape; for fizzy ciders the gas is retained (champagne process) or the cider is carbonated before bottling. Perry is a similar type of drink, but uses pears in place of apples. *See also* PE pp.202–207.

Cienfuegos, port on the S coast of W central Cuba, on Cienfuegos Bay. It is a market centre for a region producing sugar cane, coffee, tobacco and rice. Exports: sugar, rum. Pop. (1970) 85,248.

Cierva, Juan de la (1896–1936), Spanish engineer who in 1923 invented the AUTOGYRO, an aircraft which gets most of its lift from a freely rotating (unpowered) horizontal rotor. *See also* MM p.154.

Cigar, small, tight roll of cured TOBACCO leaves prepared for smoking. Selected leaves are bound together to form a filler, then more leaves are wound round as an outer wrapper. When Christopher Columbus and his crews landed in the West Indies in 1492 they discovered the local inhabitants smoking crude cigars in tribal rites. As a result, cigars became established in Spain as a luxury product by about 1600 but were not widely smoked elsewhere until the 19th century.

Cigarette cards, small, rectangular, illustrated cards enclosed by the manufacturers in packets of CIGARETTES. They were common in Britain until WWII and depicted a variety of subjects from film stars to wildlife, usually in colour. They were issued in sets, with one or two in each packet, and the aim was to complete favourite sets. Early cards and complete sets are now collectors' items, and some rare examples command high prices.

Cigarettes, convenient form of smoking tobacco which first became popular in Britain after the Crimean War, when soldiers became familiar with the Turkish variety. In 1976 some 130,600 million cigarettes were sold in Britain alone. The consequences to the nation's health have since the 1950s become notorious. Manufacture today starts with shredding and blending of tobacco leaf, mostly the Virginian variety, that has been matured and cured for up to two months. The subsequent packing, cutting to length, wrapping into foil, boxing and cartoning is all done by machines.

Cilea, Francesco (1866–1950), Italian composer. He is best known for several charming operas, especially *L'Arlesiana* (1897), in which Enrico CARUSO scored his first major success, and *Adriana Lecouvreur* (1902), which was internationally popular.

Cilia, protruding hair-like filaments characteristic of the group of single-celled protozoan animals called Ciliata. The animals beat the cilia rhythmically to move through the water in which they live; a typical example is *Paramecium. See also* NW pp.80–81.

Ciliate, one of a large class of PROTOZOA found in fresh water, characterized by hair-like cilia used for locomotion and food collecting. Subclasses include the Holotrichs, with cilia over the entire body (*Paramecium*); Spirotrichs, with fused cilia around the mouth (*Stentor*); and Peritrichs, with cilia around the mouth and possessing a stalk for attachment (*Vorticella*). *See also* NW p.80.

Cilicia, ancient region of SE Asia Minor, (now in Turkey), between the Taurus Mts and the Mediterranean Sea. Its chief city was Tarsus. The region was dominated by the Assyrians and Persians before being hellenized in the 4th century BC. It was conquered by Rome in 67 BC, and was invaded by the Arabs in the 8th century AD. An Armenian state was set up there in 1080 and the region fell to the Turks in 1375.

Cima, Giovanni Battista (*c.*1460–1518), called Cima da Conegliano, Italian painter of the Venetian School, best known for his half-length Madonnas. He also painted mythological scenes.

Cimabue, Giovanni, 13th-century Florentine painter, an important transitional link between the rigid Byzantine style of painting and the greater realism of the 14th-century FLORENTINE SCHOOL. His best-known work is *Madonna and Child Enthroned* (Uffizi Gallery, Florence). Much of Cimabue's work has been spoilt by time or accident. The frescoes at the Church of St Francis, Assisi, and the mosaic at Pisa Cathedral are in poor condition and the great *Crucifixion* at S. Croce, Florence, was damaged in the flood of 1966. Cimabue is said to have been the teacher of GIOTTO. *See also* HC1 p.217, *217.*

Cimarosa, Domenico (1749–1801), Italian composer, chiefly of OPERAS, of which he wrote more than 60. His first, *Le Stravaganze del Conte,* was performed at Naples in 1772. He also wrote seven CANTATAS and six ORATORIOS.

Cimon (*d.* 449 BC), Athenian statesman and general. His numerous military and political successes made him leader of the aristocrats opposing THEMISTOCLES and later PERICLES. His greatest military success was the destruction of a Persian fleet *c.* 468 BC. *See also* HC1 p.70.

Cinchona, genus of evergreen trees native to the Andes and grown in South America, Indonesia and Zaire. The dried bark of the trees is a source of QUININE and other medicinal products. Family Rubiaceae. *See also* MS pp.*118,* 119.

Cincinnati, city and port of entry in SW Ohio, USA, on the Ohio River; third largest city in Ohio. Originally named Losantiville, it grew around Fort Washington, established in 1789 by the US government to quell Indian attacks. Development was spurred by the steamboat trade on the Ohio River and the completion of the Miami and Erie Canal in 1832, making the city a shipping centre for farm produce. In order to compete with the growing cities of Chicago and St Louis, Cincinnati built its own railway in 1880, connecting with Chattanooga, Tennessee, and it is still the only US city to own and lease its own railway. In 1925 a city manager was appointed and a city council was established to counter widespread corruption in politics. The city has a university (1819) and several other colleges. Industries: machine tools, soap products, brewing, meat packing, aircraft engines, metal goods. Pop. (1973) 426,245.

Cincinnatus Lucius Quinctius (*c.* 519–438 BC), legendary Roman hero. Consul in 460, he was named dictator by the Senate in 458. A farmer, he left his land, defeated the Aequians in 16 days and then renounced his post to return to his farm. According to legend he was recalled to the dictatorship in 439 to defeat the traitor Spurius Melius.

Cinder cone, conical hill or mountain composed largely of unconsolidated material, mostly ash ejected by a volcano. It is characteristic of volcanoes that produce large amounts of gas and ash rather than lava. The coarser the ejected material, the steeper the sides of the cone. *See also* PE pp.30–31.

Cinderella, folk-tale of international derivation. More than 500 versions of the story are known in Europe alone. All the variations involve a youngest daughter, Cinderella, who is badly treated by a jealous stepmother and stepsisters; however, she is helped by a fairy godmother, and finally gets married to a rich prince.

Cine camera, apparatus that takes a number of consecutive still photographs or frames, on film, at the rate of about 24 frames per second. The illusion of motion is created when the developed film is projected on to a screen. If the motor of the cine camera is speeded up so that more frames are shot each second, the resulting film projected at normal speed is in slow motion. Conversely, a slowed-down cine camera produces speeded-up action. Big-screen cine cameras use 70mm cine film, most professional cameras 35mm, and some smaller cameras 16mm or 8mm. *See also* CINEMA; CINEMATOGRAPHY; MM pp.222–*223.*

Cinema, motion pictures as an industry and artistic pursuit. For much of its history it has been dominated commercially by the USA. Public showings of (silent) moving pictures began in the 1890s, but not until *The Jazz Singer* (1927) was speech heard in a full-length film. By then the cinema was big business with mass appeal, and before long pure entertainment was being produced very largely by a cluster of Hollywood companies. In Germany and Russia, meanwhile, startling technical innovations showed the creative possibilities of the medium. The 1930s, which saw the widespread introduction of colour and the lavish musical with elaborate sets and squads of pretty dancers, concluded with *Gone with the Wind* (1939), a huge money-spinner with lasting appeal. The growth of television in the USA in the 1940s (a decade later in Europe) profoundly altered film economics. With the decline of Hollywood came the rise of the independent producer and director. Films now were fewer but more spectacular, with a multiplicity of stars, and backed by international finance. In Europe after WWII film-makers explored social and psychological themes with often disturbing candour, and although the British cinema flourished in the 1950s and early 1960s with well-produced comedies and studies of working class life, it suffered thereafter for want of finance. *See also* ANIMATION; CINE CAMERA; CINEMATOGRAPHY; DOCUMENTARY FILM; HC2 pp.200–201; 268–269; 276–277.

Cinemascope, wide-screen cinema projection system (using an anamorphic lens originally invented by the French physicist Henri Chrétien), developed from 1952 at the studios of Twentieth Century-Fox in the USA.

Cinematography, technique of taking and projecting cine film motion pictures (movies), the basis of the CINEMA industry. Based on experiments and inventions of the 1880s and 1890s (by such people as Thomas EDISON in the USA and the LUMIÈRE brothers in France), cinematography was applied professionally to the taking and showing of films soon after the turn of the century. Sound films were introduced with the making of *The Jazz Singer* in 1927 and cinematography became a popular hobby for amateurs from the 1930s onwards. For technical details of cinematography, *see* MM pp.222–223.

Cinema-verité, style of film-making first practised by Dziga VERTOV in the 1920s, but which became popular in the 1960s. It attempted to record truthful action within a documentary-like style and avoid the distance between audience and subject imposed by traditional camera work. It represented a conscious rejection of the conventions of Hollywood narration. The style was used both in dramas, particularly by TRUFFAUT and GODARD, and in documentaries which often contained direct and explicit content that was politi-

cal, both in its inference and its presentation.
Cinerama, motion picture wide-screen system. Invented in the 1950s by Fred Waller, it used three electronically synchronized cameras and projectors to shoot the film on a large screen which partly surrounded the audience. It was later abandoned for a single-lens system. *See also* MOTION PICTURE; WIDE SCREEN.
Cineraria, or florist's cineraria, perennial hothouse plant native to the Canary Islands. It has heart-shaped leaves and large clusters of white, pink, blue or purple daisy-like flowers. Family Compositae, species *Senecio cruentus.*
Cinnabar, deep red, brilliant-to-dull mineral, mercuric sulphide (HgS), the major ore of mercury, found in hydrothermal veins (formed by water at high temperature) and volcanic deposits. It occurs in the rhombohedral crystal system as hexagonal crystals, often twinned, and as granular masses. The ore is reduced to mercury by roasting. Hardness 2–2.5; s.g. 8.1.
Cinnamon, light-brown SPICE made from the dried inner bark of the cinnamon tree. Its delicate aroma and sweet flavour make it a common ingredient in baked foods, and was once extremely expensive. It was also used for religious rites and witchcraft. The tree is a bushy evergreen native to India and Burma and now cultivated in the West Indies and South America. Family Lauraceae; species *Cinnamomun zeylanicum. See also* PE pp.210, *211.*
Cino da Pistoia (*c.*1270–*c.*1336), Italian jurist and poet. He was a friend of his younger contemporary PETRARCH, on whom his lyric verse dealing with loneliness and love had a great influence.
Cinquefoil, any of various annual and perennial plants and shrubs of the rose family, native to the temperate and cold regions of the world. The leaves are composed of three leaflets, and the small white, yellow or red flowers have five petals. Family Rosaceae; genus *Potentilla.*
Cinque Ports, association of certain ports (originally five) in SE England, with special privileges granted in return for responsibility for defending the S coast. The grouping of Dover, Hastings, Hythe, Romney and Sandwich began under the Anglo-Saxons and was expanded by the Norman kings. The association, to which Winchelsea and Rye were added in the 12th century, reached its height during the first half of the HUNDRED YEARS WAR, after which the influence of the ports declined.
Circadian rhythm, aspect of body function that varies regularly in a cycle lasting about 24 hours. Examples are waking and sleeping, and variations in temperature, blood pressure, pulse rate, glandular secretions, blood-sugar levels and the rate of growth of body cells. *See also* MS p.*135;* BIOLOGICAL RHYTHM; JET LAG.
Circassians, Muslim people native to the Caucasus Mts. During the 19th century, they unsuccessfully resisted the Russian government's take-over of the Caucasus. They often figure in Russian literature, such as in Mikhail Lermontov's *Hero of our Times* (1840).
Circe, in Greek mythology, seductive but baleful enchantress whose spells could change men into animals. Mistress of the island of Aeaea, she kept Odysseus with her for a year, changing his men into swine until, protected by Hermes, he forced her to transform them back again.
Circuit, electric, system of electric conductors and appliances or electronic components connected together so that they form a continuously conducting path. In modern electronic devices, circuits are often printed in copper on to a plastic card (a printed circuit) to which the transistors, capacitors and other components are soldered. Smaller devices use INTEGRATED CIRCUITS, in which a chip of semiconductor is treated in such a way that it consists of a number of components connected together. *See also* SU pp.118, 124–130.
Circuit breaker, automatic switch in an electrical circuit that functions like a FUSE, disconnecting the circuit if abnormal conditions, such as overloads, occur. It is not destroyed in operation and can be re-closed (re-set). Circuit breakers on transmission lines are controlled by precise relays that locate failures and cause only the needed breakers to operate, thus isolating a specific section. *See also* SU p.*114.*
Circular motion, in physics, any type of movement that can be related to or analysed in terms of the motion of an object around a circle. *See* SU pp.76–77.
Circulation. *See* CIRCULATORY SYSTEM.
Circulation, atmospheric, flow of the atmosphere around the earth. It is caused by temperature differences in the atmosphere and the rotation of the earth, which transfers heat from warm zones (the tropics) to cooler zones (towards the poles). The poleward circulation due to heat transference, usually called convection, gives rise to large-scale eddies such as CYCLONES and ANTICYCLONES, low-pressure troughs and high-pressure ridges. The eddies also take part in the longitudinal atmospheric circulation around the earth, with the earth's rotation maintaining easterly winds towards the equator and westerlies towards the poles. Narrow JET STREAMS blow swiftly over middle latitudes, usually horizontally east in the STRATOSPHERE, and move farther towards the poles during the summer. *See also* PE p.68.
Circulatory system, the means by which oxygen and products of digested food are carried to the body's tissues and carbon dioxide and other waste products are removed from them. It consists of BLOOD VESSELS that carry the BLOOD, propelled by the pumping action of the HEART. Mammals, birds and some reptiles have two circulatory systems: the pulmonary (lung) and the systemic (bodily). Blood travels to the lungs, picks up OXYGEN and gives off CARBON DIOXIDE, then flows into the HEART which pumps it into the AORTA, which branches into arteries and capillaries. The blood picks up waste products in the capillaries, which join to form veins leading back to the heart. It is then pumped back to the lungs and the entire cycle is repeated. *See also* MS pp.*62–63.*
Circumcision, operation of cutting away the whole or part of the foreskin of the penis or removal of the clitoris, which is sometimes called excision. Male circumcision is done for sanitary reasons or as a ritual among ethnic groups, where it often signifies the formal introduction of a man into his group or the achievement of status; female circumcision is intended to reduce sexual pleasure. *See also* PUBERTY RITES.
Circumcision, Feast of the, in the Christian liturgical calendar, the commemoration of the circumcision of Christ, based on the account in Luke 2:21. The feast is traditionally kept on the eighth day after Christmas – 1 Jan.
Circumference, distance round the boundary of a plane geometric figure, nearly always applied to a circle, for which it has the value $2\pi r$, where r is the radius. *See also* SU p.44.
Circumnavigation, process of navigating round something, usually with reference to sailing round the world. This was first accomplished by a Spanish expedition commanded by the Portuguese navigator, Ferdinand MAGELLAN (1519–22). Magellan discovered and sailed the length of the strait at the S tip of South America that bears his name, and crossed the Pacific. One ship, the *Victoria,* out of the original five, completed the round voyage to Spain, but Magellan himself was killed en route. See also HC1 p.*234.*
Circumstantial evidence, in law, indirect evidence arrived at by providing proof of other events and supporting facts related to an issue. An example is the discovery of a defendant's fingerprints at the scene of a crime. *See also* MS p.286.
Circus, form of entertainment featuring trained animals, acrobats and clowns, usually performed by travelling companies in outdoor tents or "big tops". Circuses originated in the Roman arena, where chariot races and gladiatorial battles took place. The first modern circus was staged in London in 1768 by Philip Astley, and today the circus is a popular entertainment that attracts large crowds. In the USA circuses are often associated with the name Phineas T. BARNUM (1810–91).
Circus Maximus (*c.*6th century BC), oldest and largest of the Roman stadia used for horse and chariot races, now no longer standing. According to tradition it was erected by Tarquin I, the first Etruscan king of Rome, substantially rebuilt by Julius Caesar and enlarged by later emperors. At its greatest it was 610m (2,000ft) long and 190m (623ft) wide, and is said to have seated 230,000.
Cire perdue, literally "lost wax", method of casting metal objects – usually bronzes – used at least since classical antiquity. First, the object is moulded in clay or plaster in roughly the desired shape but slightly smaller. This core is covered in wax not more than a $^1/_2$ inch in thickness, and further modelling is undertaken. Straws of wax pipes are fitted to admit the molten metal and release hot gases. The whole is then covered in a heat proof mould, the wax melted away and the metal poured into the space it occupied. The other method of hollow casting, SAND-CASTING, is most often used in industrial processes. *See also* MM p.27.
Cirl bunting, small seed-eating bird with a brown back and yellow underparts, originally a Mediterranean species. Length: 15cm (6in). *See also* BUNTING.
Cirque, or corrie, bowl-shaped, steep-sided hollow in rock formed through erosion by ice. It is typical of a glaciated mountain region. The eroded area is usually cut by repeated freezing and thawing, or it may result from glacial movement. After a glacier has retreated, many cirques become round lakes fed by water from the melting glacier. *See also* PE pp.116–117.
Cirrhosis, degenerative disease in which bands of fibrous tissue form in organs, usually the LIVER. The liver becomes hard, blood-flow through it is impaired and some cells die. Blood vessels may rupture and the liver is unable to detoxify harmful material, leading to serious and often fatal consequences. It is usually associated with ALCOHOLISM but may be caused by poor diet, viral hepatitis or rare disorders. Generally weakness and a loss of appetite are followed by jaundice, tendency to bleed and, in women, failbre to menstruate. Early treatment can arrest its development. *See also* MS pp.93, *105.*
Cirripedia, class of invertebrate animals, including the shell-backed BARNACLE and some non-shelled members. They are a subclass of CRUSTACEA.
Cisalpine Republic, state established in northern Italy by NAPOLEON in 1797. It was the first unification of the northern states in modern Italian history. It became the Italian Republic in 1802 and the Kingdom of Italy in 1805.
Cistercians, religious order of monks founded by St Robert of Molesme in 1098, based on ideals of strict and primitive Benedictinism. A cloistered community dedicated to contemplation, the Cistercians were noted agricultural pioneers. In the 17th century came the Strict Observance reform, whose supporters are popularly known as TRAPPISTS. *See also* HC1 p.187; *187.*
Cithaeron (Kithairón), mountain range in central Greece, bounded by Boeotia (N) and Attica (S), rising to 1,400m (4,620ft). It was sacred to Dionysus and the Muses in Green legend. Length: 16km (10 miles).
Cithara, Cithern. *See* CITTERN.
Citizen Kane, US film (1941). Written, produced and directed by Orson WELLES from Herman J. Mankiewicz's screenplay and photographed by Gregg Toland. This film described the career of a newspaper tycoon markedly similar to William Randolph Hearst. It starred Welles, Everett Sloane, Joseph Cotton and Agnes Moorehead. Inventive and unorthodox, it remains one of the most powerful films in cinematic history. *See also* HC2 p.276.
Citizen of the World, satirical essays by Oliver GOLDSMITH, which established his name when they appeared as the *Chinese Letters* in *The Public Ledger* in 1760–61. They were published as a collection under their new name in 1762.

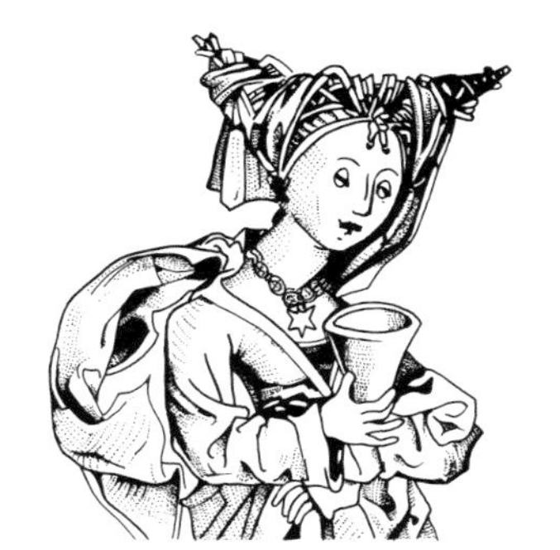
Circe surrounded her palace with the men she had changed magically into animals.

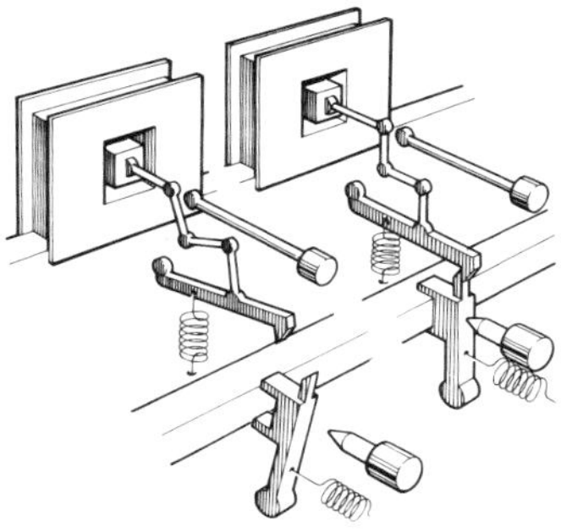
Circuit breakers protect an electrical circuit from damage due to sudden overloads.

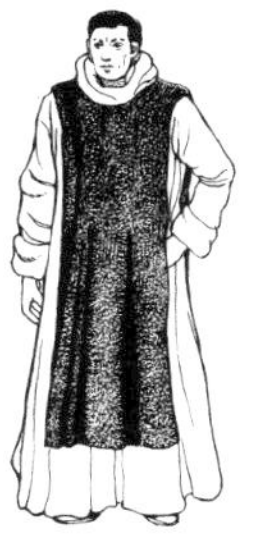
Cistercians expanded their order in the 12th century under St Bernard's influence.

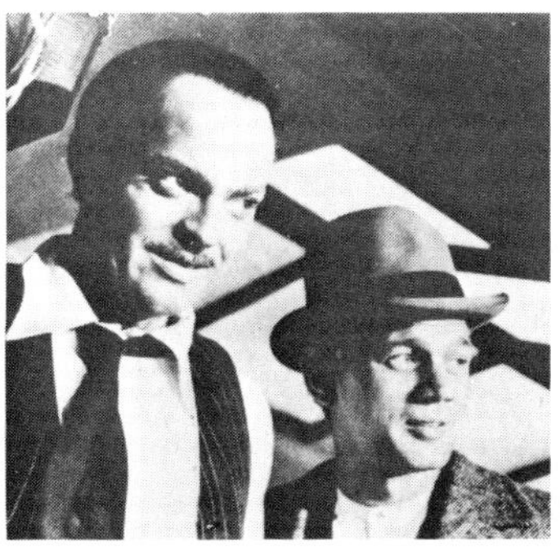
Citizen Kane; highly acclaimed film which caused a great scandal when it was released.

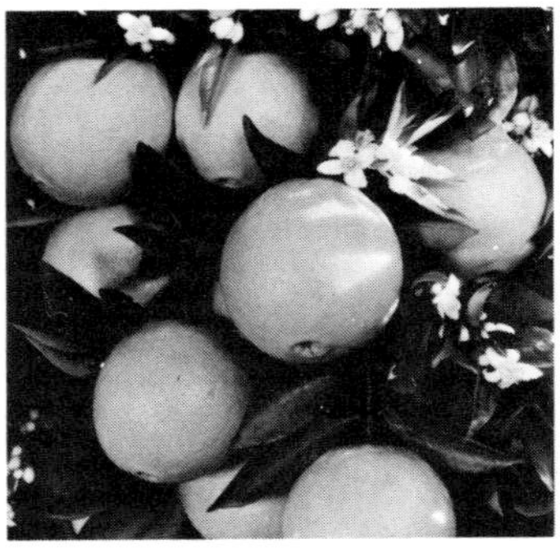

Citrus; thorny evergreen trees producing a variety of fruit and fragrant white blossom.

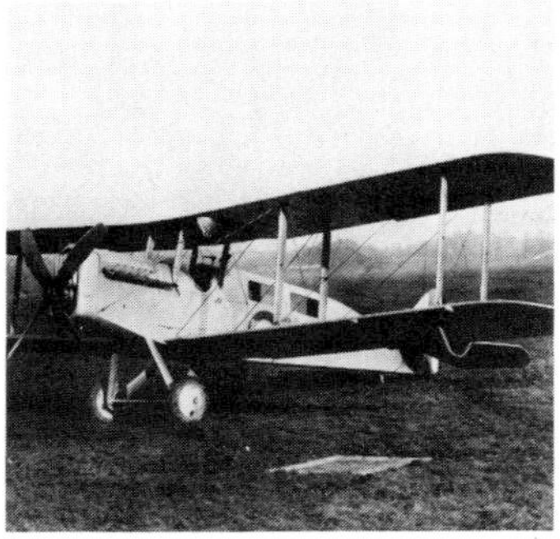

Civil aviation; a converted de Havilland bomber flew the first scheduled air service.

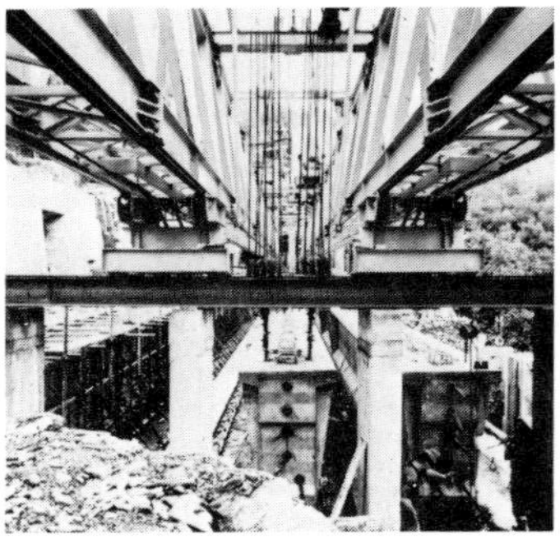

Civil engineering changes natural landscapes into modern man-made environment.

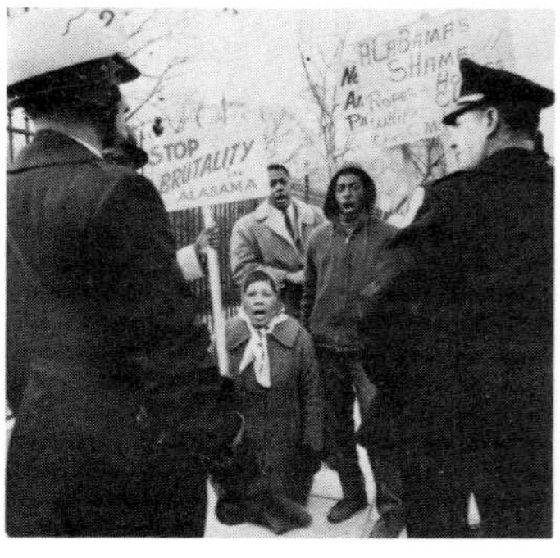

Civil rights; demonstrators picket the White House during the protests of the 1960s.

Citlaltépetl (in Spanish, Orizaba), inactive volcanic peak in E Mexico, 97km (60 miles) E of Puebla. It is the highest point in Mexico, rising to a height of 5,700m (18,701ft).

Citric acid, colourless crystalline solid ($C_6H_8O_7$) with a sour taste. It is found in a free form in citrus fruits such as lemons and limes, and is used for flavouring, in effervescent salts, and as a mordant in dyeing. Properties: s.g. 1.54; m.p. 153°C (307.4°F). *See also* SU p.154.

Citric acid cycle, or Krebs cycle, also called tricarboxylic acid cycle, biochemical pathway by which most living organisms obtain much of their energy from their food. It is also the process of cell respiration which releases the carbon dioxide breathed out by plants and animals. It comprises a cycle of complex chemical reactions, many of which release energy in the form of ATP (adenosine triphosphate) which provides chemical energy for metabolic reactions. *See also* SU pp.155, *155*.

Citrine, semi-precious stone, a glassy wine-yellow variety of QUARTZ. It is translucent and has an appearance similar to TOPAZ. It is also known as false topaz or topaz quartz.

Citron, evergreen shrub or small tree of the RUE family, native to Asia. It has short spines and oval leaves. The large oblong fruit is lemon yellow and its fragrant rind is often candied. Height: up to 3.5m (11.5ft). Family Rutaceae; species *Citron medica*. *See also* PE p.*194*.

Citrus, important group of trees and shrubs of the genus *Citrus* in the rue family. They include GRAPEFRUIT, KUMQUAT, LEMON, LIME, ORANGE, TANGERINE and UGLI. Native to subtropical regions, they are widely cultivated wherever there is plenty of sun and moisture. The stems are usually thorny, the leaves bright green, shiny and pointed. The flowers are usually white, waxy and fragrant. The fruit is usually ovoid with a thick, aromatic rind. The inside of the fruit is pulpy and juicy and is divided into segments that contain the seeds. Most citrus fruits contain significant amounts of vitamin C. Family Rutaceae. *See also* PE p.192.

Cittern, musical instrument popular in western Europe in the 16th to 18th centuries. A shallow flat-backed instrument, its four pairs of wire strings were normally plucked with the fingers.

City, any urban complex larger or more important than a town. In Britain the word is not used to denote any particular form of government, but is applied to all towns that have cathedrals; the title of city has also been granted to other large towns by royal charter. In the USA the term has a precise meaning, and is applied to any incorporated municipality. Cities have been central to social, cultural and political development since earliest times, and city life has increasingly become divorced from the countryside since the Industrial Revolution.

City, The. *See* LONDON.

City of God, The, religious and philosophical work by ST AUGUSTINE OF HIPPO. Begun about two years after the Visigoths sacked Rome in 410 and completed in 426, it was a reply to charges that the influence of Christianity had caused the fall of the city. It elaborates a Christian philosophy of history from the fall of Adam to the end of time. History is viewed as the development of two opposing powers, the city of God and the city of the world, the latter being a place of conflict and confusion. All mankind must eventually belong to one or other of these cities. After the Last Judgement the city of God becomes heaven and the city of the world hell.

City-state, self-governing political unit comprising an independent city and its adjacent hinterland. Historically, city-states have occurred when economic conditions favoured the creation of towns. Other influences have been the combination of geographical features (eg poor land communications) or political factors (eg no strong central government) that permitted the existence of many small autonomous states, as in classical Greece and renaissance Italy. Many, like ancient Athens and medieval Florence, flourished as commercial and cultural centres. *See also* HC1 pp.68, 72; MS pp.272, 278.

City Temple, London, United Reformed church, the major Nonconformist church in London. It was founded some time before 1640 when the first known pastor was Dr Thomas Goodwin, chaplain to Oliver Cromwell. It was moved to Holborn in 1874. In 1941 it was burned down, and was rebuilt in 1958.

Ciudad Bolívar, city and port in E Venezuela; capital of Bolívar state, on the River Orinoco. It was founded in 1764 as Angostura. It has the longest suspension bridge in South America, the Angostura, which is 712m (2,336ft) long. Industries: wood products, leather. Pop. (1971) 103,728.

Ciudad Guayana. *See* SANTO TOMÉ DE GUAYANA.

Ciudad Juárez, city in Chihuahua state, N Mexico, on the Rio Bravo del Norte (Río Grande); on the border of Mexico and the USA, it is connected by bridges to El Paso, Texas, USA. It has the church of the Mission of Our Lady of Guadalupe (1659). The city was named after Mexico's President Benito Juárez (1888). Today it is a commercial centre and has processing industries for the surrounding cotton-growing region. Industries: textiles, food processing. Pop. (1975) 520,500.

Ciudad Ojeda (Lagunillas), city in NW Venezuela, on the NE shore of Lake Maracaibo. Situated N of the Lagunillas oil field, the city is an important oil centre. Pop.(1971) 83,083.

Ciudad Rodrigo, town in Spain, scene of two battles during the Napoleonic Wars. In 1810 Marshal NEY took the town for the French after a long siege; WELLINGTON's army recaptured it for the anti-French coalition in 1812.

Ciudad Trujillo. *See* SANTO DOMINGO.

Civet, or civet cat, small, nocturnal, carnivorous animal, related to the genet and mongoose, found in Africa, Asia and S Europe. It has a small head and narrow body set on long legs and its coat is a brindled grey-yellow with black markings. There are about 20 species including the forest-dwelling African civet (*Civetticus civetta*). The substance known as civet (musk) is a fatty secretion from the animal's scent glands and was once used as a base for perfumes. Length: (overall) 53cm (21in) to 150cm (59in). Family Viverridae. *See also* MM p.*246*; NW p.213.

Civetone, chemical compound smelling strongly of musk, obtained from the perianal glands of civets and used in perfumery. Chemically it is a ketone, containing the group $=C=O$. *See also* MM p.*246*.

Civil action, in law, suit in which a plaintiff sues a defendant for breach of a law relating to their mutual affairs. A typical example is breach of CONTRACT. Civil actions are different from criminal ones, in which the Crown takes the role of prosecutor.

Civil aviation, term used to describe the whole of the aircraft industry excluding military applications. It includes the design and manufacture of passenger and freight aircraft and the organization and running of airlines. *See also* AIRPORT; AIR-TRAFFIC CONTROL; MM pp.148–155, 186–187.

Civil defence, non-military organization for maintaining the necessities of life in a national emergency. The British Civil Defence during WWII had 1.8 million workers, mostly voluntary, employed in firefighting, ambulance services and rescue parties and organized by local authorities and industries. The Civil Defence was abolished in 1945 but set up again three years later. Its chief concern then was the organization of resources after possible nuclear attack. Ten civil defence regions were set up in England and one in Wales to create effective chains of command in the event of the breakdown of central government, and local authorities were empowered to set up civil defence organizations. This Civil Defence Corps was abolished in 1968; since then local authorities have been voted an annual budget (£14.5 million in 1976) to extend their services to prepare for war emergencies. Most of the Civil Defence Act was repealed in 1976.

Civil disobedience, passive resistance to law or authority, usually associated with an act of conscience. The term originated with Henry Thoreau's essay *Resistance to Civil Government* (1849), in which he argued that disobeying a law is preferable to disobeying one's own conscience. It was practised in India by the supporters of Mahatma K. Gandhi and in the USA by the followers of Martin Luther King, Jr.

Civil engineering, field of engineering that deals with the creation, improvement and protection of the communal environment. Civil engineers provide facilities for living, industry and transportation, including large buildings, roads, bridges, canals, airports, water-supply systems, dams, harbours, docks, aqueducts, tunnels and other constructions. Civil engineering requires a thorough knowledge of surveying, construction, material properties, soil properties and hydraulics. Important divisions of the field are architectural, irrigation, transportation, soil and foundation, geodetic, hydraulic and coastal and ocean engineering. *See also* MM pp.48, 182–200.

Civil law, legal system derived from ROMAN LAW. It is different from COMMON LAW, the system generally adhered to in England and some other English-speaking countries. Civil law is based on a system of codes, the most famous of which is the CODE NAPOLÉON (1804), and decisions are precisely worked out from general basic principles *a priori* – ie, the civil law judge follows the evidence and is bound by the conditions of the written LAW and not by previous judicial interpretation. Civil law influences common law in jurisprudence and in admiralty, testamentary and domestic relations; it is also the basis for the system of equity. It is prevalent in continental Europe and in Louisiana (USA), Quebec Province (Canada), and Latin America. *See also* MS p.282.

Civil liberties, basic rights that every citizen possesses and governments must respect in a democracy. In some countries, the courts ensure freedom from government control or restraint, except as the public good may require. *See also* CIVIL RIGHTS and LIBERTIES.

Civil List, annual grant of money voted by Parliament to supply the expenses of the royal establishment in Britain. The money comes from the Consolidated Fund. The list has its origin in the parliamentary grant made to WILLIAM III in 1698 to supplement his hereditary revenues. It got its name, early in the 18th century, from the practice of charging the salaries of judges and government officers to the list, a practice which was abandoned in 1831. It now defrays no governmental expenses. The amount voted may differ each year, as may the specific appropriations to the several members of the royal family. Since 1975 the sum has been reviewed annually and in 1977 was about £1,905,000.

Civil List pensions, money rewards given by the British Crown, originally to people out of the CIVIL LIST. In the 18th century they were part of the patronage system used by the Crown to secure political support. In 1782 the award of secret pensions was made illegal. In 1831 the maximum sum available for pensions was set at £75,000. When Queen Victoria came to the throne pensions were separated from the Civil List and the Crown was directed to award them to major contributors to the arts and sciences.

Civil rights, certain rights conferred legally upon the individual by the state, therefore varying from country to country. In Anglo-Saxon democracies such rights include, in the absence of special disqualifications, trial by jury, HABEAS CORPUS and the right to vote. The modern use of the phrase is principally American and refers, not so much to relations between the state and the individual as to relations between individuals, both men and women and in particular Blacks and Whites. The recent history of the Civil Rights movement in the USA dates from the Supreme Court decision against segregation in schools (1954), a decision which President EISENHOWER used federal troops to enforce in Little Rock, Arkansas, in 1957. The Civil Rights Act of 1957 established the Civil Rights Commission, whose duty it is to see that no person is deprived of the vote by poll taxes, literacy tests or any other means. The 1964 Civil Rights Act prohibits discrimination on the ground of race in employment and housing. It is similar in intent to the British RACE RELATIONS ACT. *See also* PETITION OF RIGHT; BILL OF RIGHTS; MS p.271.

Civil Service, administrative establishment for carrying on the work of government in a country. In Britain the origin of the Civil Service is the personal household of the medieval monarchy. The modern service was developed in the years 1780 to 1830 and by the acts of 1855 and 1870. It was then that it became civil, not political. It also became permanent, its personnel not changing with a change of monarch or ministers. As the Crown moved out of active politics to become a constitutional monarchy, so the Crown's administrative servants abandoned their political roles to become a constitutional bureaucracy. By a series of acts the holding of a non-ministerial, salaried office under the Crown became incompatible with a seat in Parliament. At the same time the weight of parliamentary business became too heavy for ministers to attend to both policy-making and administration of the day-to-day affairs of their departments. The TREASURY got its first permanent secretary in 1805, the COLONIAL OFFICE a permanent official in 1825. Originally the service was housed in Whitehall, London. That remains its centre, but the service has now grown so vast that it is housed throughout the country.

Civil war, war between political factions or regions within the same country, nation or state to decide which of them shall exercise powers of government over the whole. *See also* AMERICAN CIVIL WAR; ENGLISH CIVIL WAR; SPANISH CIVIL WAR.

Civitavecchia, town in Roma province, Latium, W central Italy, on the Tyrrhenian Sea; chief port for Rome. It was sacked by the Saracens in 828. The construction of its citadel was supervised by MICHELANGELO. It has an arsenal built by BERNINI (1508). Main industry: building materials. Pop. (1971 est.) 48,500.

Cizek, Franz (1865–1947), Czechoslovakian art teacher, famous for his methods of teaching children. In 1893 he started a school for juveniles at which children were encouraged to draw whatever they wished. Their work was exhibited abroad.

Clackmannanshire, former county in central Scotland, now part of Central Region. It was the smallest county in Scotland, lying between the Ochil Hills (N) and the River Forth (SW). The county town was Alloa. Industries: coal-mining, woollens, brewing. Area: 142sq km (55sq miles).

Clacton-on-Sea, town in Essex, England, 21km (13 miles) SE of Colchester, mainly known as a seaside resort. An important Palaeolithic stone-working site has been found there, the earliest such in Britain. Pop.(1971 est.) 38,000.

Cladoselache, extinct SHARK of the Devonian Period (350 million years ago), exemplary among backboned animals in showing an early but complete development of jaws, teeth and paired fins.

Clair, René (1898–), French filmmaker. His early work was influenced by Surrealism but his later films concentrated more on complex characterization. His films include *The Italian Straw Hat* (1927), *À nous la Liberté!* (1931), *The Flame of New Orleans* (1940), *Les belles de nuit* (1952) and *Les Fêtes Galantes* (1965). *See also* HC2 pp.276–77.

Clairvoyance, supernatural or extra-sensory power to see objects or witness events removed in time and space from the observer, a form of extra-sensory perception. Clairvoyant-like experiences may be induced with drugs. *See also* PARAPSYCHOLOGY; PRECOGNITION; MS p.198.

Clam, bivalve mollusc found mainly in marine waters. It is usually partially buried in sand or mud with the two parts of its shell slightly open for feeding. With a large foot for burrowing, its soft, flat body lies between two muscles for opening and closing the shells. A fleshy part called the mantle, lies next to the shells. Clams feed on PLANKTON. Class Pelecypoda. *See also* NW pp.*22, 96.*

Clan, unilineal descent group, in which KINSHIP is recognized either through the male line (patrilineal) or through the female line (matrilineal). A notable example is the Highland clans of Scotland, which stress mutual obligations and duties. *See also* MATRIARCHY; PATRIARCHY; MS p.256.

Clapham Junction, railway station in south London, serving passengers in the commuter belt south of the capital. It is one of the world's busiest stations; more than 2,500 trains pass through it each day.

Clapham Sect, group of Evangelical reformers in Britain in the years *c.* 1790–*c.* 1830. Their name derived from the meetings in Clapham of William WILBERFORCE and his friends. Originally known as the "Saints", they were especially influential in prison reform and the abolition of slavery. *See also* HC2 pp.47, 135.

Clapton, Eric (1945–), British ROCK guitarist much admired for his virtuosity. He has played in several groups, notably Cream (1966–68) and Derek and the Dominos (1970–72). His records include *Wheels of Fire* (1968) and *Layla* (1970).

Clare, Saint (1194–1253), Italian nun, founder with St FRANCIS OF ASSISI of the Franciscan nuns (1215). They were also called Poor Clares. A strict order which placed special emphasis on the vow of poverty, it spread throughout Europe in the 13th and 14th centuries. She was canonized in 1255. Feast: 12 Aug.

Clare, John (1793–1864), British nature poet. The son of a labourer, his poetry is notable for its descriptions of nature and the countryside. His works include *Poems Descriptive of Rural Life and Scenery* (1820), *The Village Minstrel* (1821), *The Shepherd's Calendar* (1827) and *The Rural Muse* (1835). He was declared insane in 1837.

Clare, county in W Republic of Ireland, in Munster province, on the W coast between Galway Bay and the River Shannon estuary. The area is hilly and infertile. The chief crops are oats and potatoes; sheep, cattle, pigs and poultry are raised; and fishing is important. Ennis is the county town. Area: 3,188sq km (1,231sq miles). Pop. 75,000.

Clare Island, small island off the W coast of the Republic of Ireland, at the mouth of Clew Bay. It is noted for the ruins of a 13th-century abbey and 16th-century castle. Area: 16sq km (6sq miles). Pop. (1971) 168.

Clarence, Dukes of, English peers. The title was first granted in 1362 to Lionel (1338–68), third son of Edward II. Other holders include: Thomas, second son of Henry IV, George (1449–78), third son of Richard of York, William IV (1765–1837) before his accession, and Prince Albert (1864–92).

Clarence, George Plantaganet, Duke of (1449–78), Irish-born younger brother of EDWARD IV of England. He joined his father-in-law, the Earl of WARWICK, in revolt against Edward (1469–70) but in 1471 rejoined his brother. In 1478 he was accused of treason and secretly executed in the Tower of London.

Clarendon, Edward Hyde, 1st Earl of (1609–74), English statesman and historian. He was initially critical of CHARLES I, but became a leading royal adviser in 1641 and negotiated the RESTORATION in 1660. As CHARLES II's chief minister, his caution made him unpopular. He was forced into exile in 1667, where he wrote his *History of the Rebellion* about the English Civil War. *See also* HC1 p.292.

Clarendon, George William Frederick Villiers, 4th Earl of (1800–70), British statesman and diplomat. He was Lord-Lieutenant of Ireland (1847–52) during the Famine, and Foreign Secretary 1853–58, 1865–66 and 1868–70.

Clarendon, Constitutions of (1164), 16 articles issued by HENRY II of England to limit the temporal and judicial powers of the Church. The most controversial article was the one requiring members of the clergy who had been convicted in church courts to be surrendered to secular courts for punishment. Thomas à BECKET initially accepted the articles, but repudiated them after the Pope criticized them. *See also* HC1 pp.194–195.

Clarendon Code, four English statutes passed (1661–65) under CHARLES II's minister CLARENDON (but opposed by him) to strengthen the Church of England. Nonconformists were hampered by restrictions on the size of their gatherings and the movement of their ministers. Municipal and church officers were required to be professed Anglicans, and all ministers were forced to use the Book of Common Prayer.

Claret, red table WINE of Bordeaux, France. The name is sometimes loosely applied to dry red wines produced in other countries, but genuine claret comes from the districts of Graves, Médoc, Pomerol and St-Émilion, and should be 5 to 25 years old or more.

Clarinet, single-reed woodwind musical instrument with a cylindrical tube. It is commonly pitched in B♭ (also A), with the alto clarinet in F or E♭, and has a range of 3½ octaves. The clarinet dates from about 1700 and quickly found a place in the orchestra. It has been popular in jazz since around 1920. *See also* HC2 p.105.

Clark, Alvan Graham (1832–97), US astronomer who in 1863 helped to build the 66cm (26in) telescope at Washington DC, and with it discovered the white dwarf star that is a companion of Sirius, and various double stars. *See also* SU pp.*171*, *229*.

Clark, Desmond (1916–), British archaeologist. He conducted many excavations in S and E Africa, studying the development of early man, and proposed that there was more than one line of *Australopithecus*. His publications include *The Prehistory of Africa* (1970). *See also* MS p.*23*.

Clark, Jim (1936–68), Scottish racing driver. Greatly respected by his contemporaries, he was world champion for Lotus in 1963 (winning seven grands prix) and 1965 (winning six, including the INDIANAPOLIS). He won his record 25th grand prix in 1968 but in April of that year was fatally injured in a race at Hockenheim, West Germany.

Clark, Sir Kenneth McKenzie (1903–), British art historian. He was a professor at Oxford University, director of the NATIONAL GALLERY in London (1934–45) and chairman of the ARTS COUNCIL of Great Britain (1953–60). His writings include *Leonardo da Vinci* (1939), *Rembrandt and the Italian Renaissance* (1966) and *The Romantic Rebellion* (1973).

Clark, Mark Wayne (1896–), US general. He graduated from WEST POINT in 1917 and fought in France in WWI. During WWII he commanded the US ground forces in Europe in 1942 and the fifth Army in 1943 during the Italian campaign. He led the US forces in occupied Austria and became supreme commander of the UN forces in Korea in 1952. He retired in 1953, after the Korean War.

Clark, Sir Wilfred Edward, Le Gros (1895–1971), British anatomist. His studies of the development of human anatomy have led him to propose a theory of human evolution in his *The Antecedents of Man* (1959), in which he specified the evolutionary trends of primates. *See also* MS p.*23*.

Clarke, Arthur Charles (1917–), British science-fiction writer. He is noted for the scientific background in his works, which include *Childhood's End* (1953), *A Fall of Moondust* (1961), and *Voices from the Sky* (1965). Stanley KUBRICK's film *2001: A Space Odyssey* (1969) was based on his short story *The Sentinel.*

Clarke, Don (1933–), New Zealand rugby player. He was a renowned goal-kicker and one of the greatest fullbacks in the history of the game. He played nearly 100 matches for the All Blacks and in 226 first-class games scored more than 1,800 points, of which 781 were for his country.

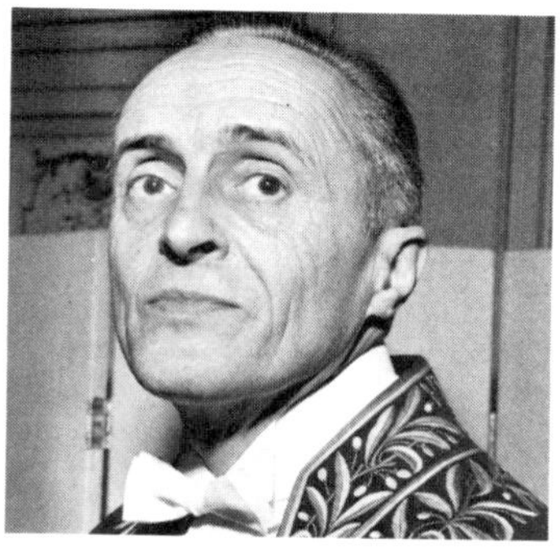

René Clair, French film director who is one of the outstanding figures of the cinema.

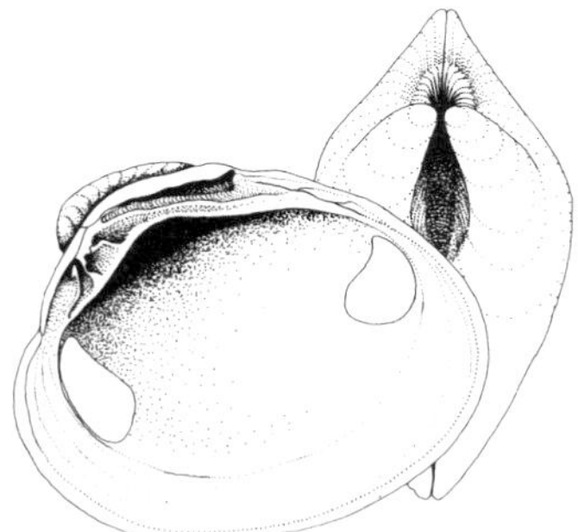

Clams; numerous species of molluscs whose two shells close tightly together.

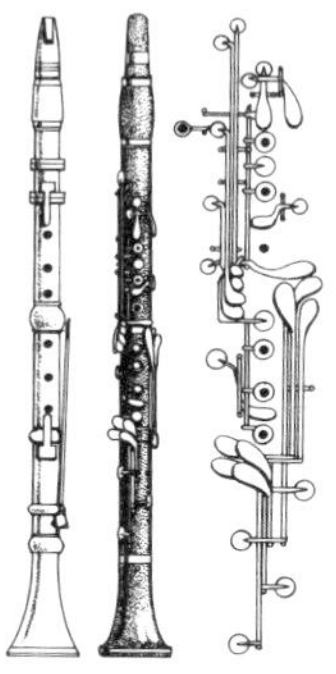

Clarinets developed into their modern form around the middle of the last century.

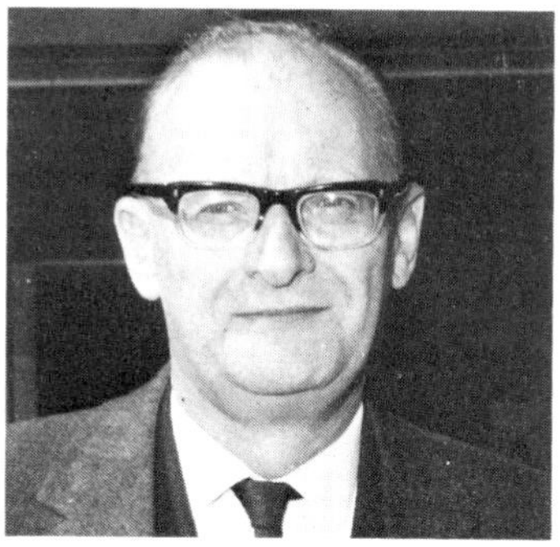

Arthur Clarke, the science fiction writer whose *The Sentinel* inspired the film *2001.*

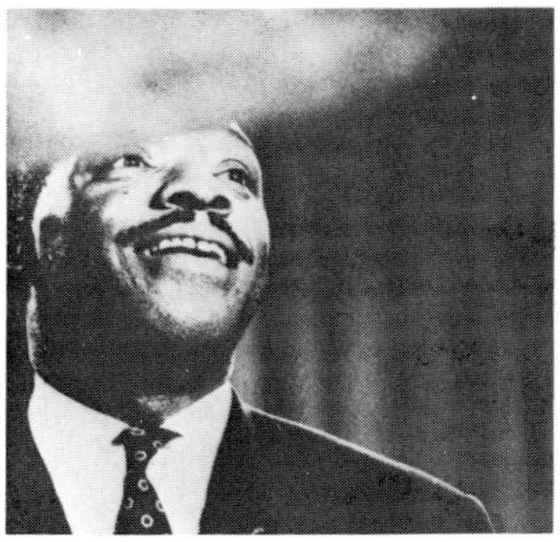
Kenny Clarke, the American Jazz drummer, founded the Modern Jazz Quartet in 1952.

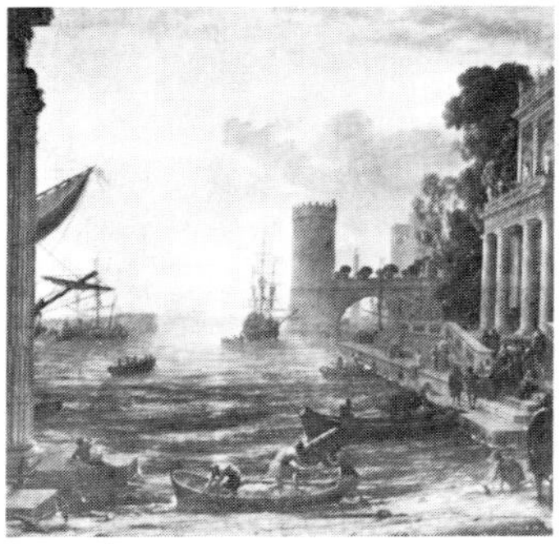
Claude Lorrain; his harbour scene depicting *The Embarkation of the Queen of Sheba.*

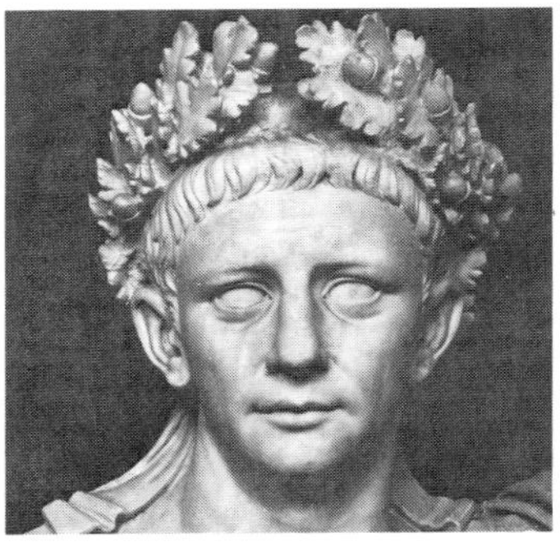
Claudius I, whose style of government was alternately humane and vindictive.

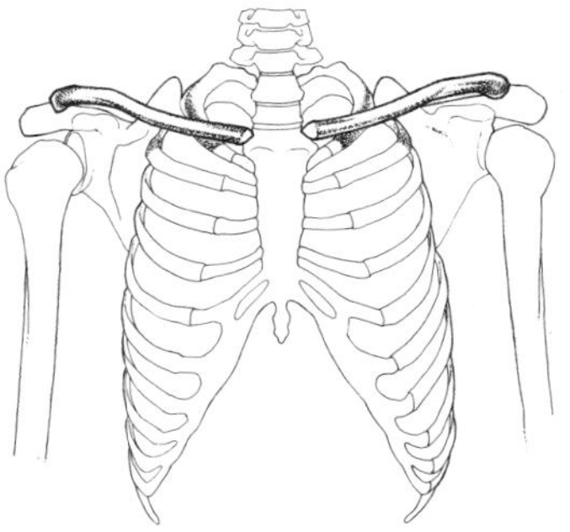
Clavicle, or collar bone, which, with the shoulder-blade, makes up the shoulder joint.

Clarke, Sir Ellis (1917–), President of TRINIDAD AND TOBAGO after independence was granted in 1976. He had previously been Governor General.

Clarke, Jeremiah (*c.* 1673–1707), English organist and composer. He was organist at St Paul's cathedral and the CHAPEL ROYAL, and choirmaster at St Paul's. He wrote choral and church music, but is best known for *The Prince of Denmark's March*, a harpsichord piece long known as *Trumpet Voluntary* and ascribed to Henry PURCELL.

Clarke, Kenneth Spearman, "Kenny" (1914–), US jazz drummer, bandleader and composer. He played with Dizzy GILLESPIE, Sidney BECHET, and Red Allen in the 1940s and helped develop the BEBOP jazz style. In 1952 he founded the Modern Jazz Quartet with John Lewis.

Clarke, Marcus Andrew Hislop (1846–81), Australian novelist. He left London for Australia at the age of 17 and worked as a journalist. His best-known work is *For the Term of his Natural Life* (1874), about convicts in Tasmania.

Clarkia, genus of annual plants related to EVENING PRIMROSE and native to W North America. They have purple or rose-pink flowers. Family Onagraceae.

Clarkson, Thomas (1760–1846), British deacon and campaigner against slavery. Working with WILBERFORCE and other ABOLITIONISTS, he devoted his life to securing abolition and its enforcement. He published a history of the trade in 1808.

Class, term used to mean a section of society, supposedly classifiable by virtue of the similar economic status of the members who compose it. The notion of class – in its simplest form including three groups, lower, middle and upper – first became widely used in the early 19th century, in response to the Industrial Revolution's making distinct the hostile interests of capital and labour. It gradually replaced the earlier notion of "interest", which supposed a society divided vertically by economic sector – agriculture, trade, commerce – not horizontally by economic status. In a biological context, a class refers to a group of animals or plants that is larger than an order, but smaller than a phylum.

Classical, term for the arts and literature of ancient Greece and Rome. These are distinguished by the emphasis on simplicity, harmony and good proportion, in contrast to the values of ROMANTICISM. The classical style of Rome was revived in RENAISSANCE Italy and it influenced the development of the arts, especially architecture, until the 18th century. NEO-CLASSICISM grew out of the rediscovery of ancient Greece. In music, classical properly refers to music of 1600–1900. *See also* index to *History and Culture* volumes.

Classical revival, art and architecture in the style of the Ancient Greeks and Romans. In general, the style reflects a simplicity, harmony and balance. The Italian RENAISSANCE and the NEO-CLASSICAL style of the early 19th century are examples of classical revivals.

Classics, The, generic term applied to celebrated horse races. The five English classics are the 2,000 and 1,000 Guineas, run at Newmarket in April or May, the DERBY and OAKS, at Epsom in June, and the ST LEGER, at Doncaster in September. Entries are for 3-year-olds only, and the 1,000 Guineas and the Oaks are further restricted to fillies. Ireland has equivalent classics, the USA three and France 17.

Classification, biological, or taxonomy, organization of plants and animals into categories based on similarities of appearance, structure, or evolution. The categories, ranging from the most inclusive to the exclusive, are kingdom, phylum, class, order, family, genus, species and sometimes variety. There are also subphyla, subfamilies, etc, in some categories. Ancient and extinct animals and plants are included in detailed classifications. *See also* NW pp.23, 72–73, 106–107, 124–125, 140–141, 154–155, *254*.

Classification, Dewey. *See* DEWEY DECIMAL CLASSIFICATION.

Claude, Albert (1899–), US cell biologist, *b.* Belgium. He shared the 1974 Nobel Prize in physiology and medicine with Christian R. de DUVE and George E. PALADE for his pioneering use of the electron microscope to study the detailed anatomy of the cell. He also pioneered the use of the centrifuge to separate various cell components. *See also* NW pp.26–27.

Claudel, Paul (1868–1955), French poet and dramatist. His conversion to Roman Catholicism in 1886 influenced his works, most of which are a form of proselytizing. They include the play *L'annonce faite à Marie* (1912; trans. *Tidings brought to Mary* 1916) and the poetry *Cinq grandes odes* (1910; *Five Noble Odes*) and *Poèmes de guerre 1914–1916* (1922).

Claude Lorrain (1600–82), French painter, real name Claude Gellée. He settled in Rome in 1627, and produced many idealized landscapes within the classical tradition. Towards the end of his career he concentrated on problems of space and light. He also made many paintings of harbours, often in late evening light. TURNER greatly admired his work.

Claudian (or Claudius) Claudianus (*d. c.* 408), last of the great Latin poets, he probably came to Rome from Alexandria. His early poems were in Greek. Several of his EPICS and official eulogies survive.

Claudius I (10 BC–AD54), Roman emperor (*r.* 41–54), nephew of TIBERIUS, the first emperor chosen by the army. He had military successes in Germany, conquered Britain in 43, and built both the harbour at OSTIA at the mouth of the Tiber and the Claudian aqueduct. AGRIPPINA, his fourth wife, poisoned him and made her son NERO emperor. *See also* HC1 pp.98, 100, 103.

Claudius II Gothicus Marcus Aurelius (214–70), Roman emperor (*r.* 268–70). He decisively defeated the barbarian invaders of Italy in 268 and the Gothic invaders of the Balkans in 269; he was given the title Gothicus ("Conqueror of the Goths").

Clausewitz, Carl von (1780–1831), Prussian soldier and military theorist. He served in the Napoleonic Wars against France, and wrote on the theory of large-scale warfare in *On War*, which was published a year after his death. His best-known theory is that war is simply an extension of politics by other means.

Clausius, Rudolf Julius Emanuel (1822–88), German physicist. He is regarded as the founder of THERMODYNAMICS and, using the work of the physicist Nicholas CARNOT, was the first to formulate the second law of thermodynamics. He also introduced the concept of ENTROPY. *See also* SU pp.92–93.

Claverhouse, John Graham, 1st Viscount Dundee (*c.* 1649–89), Scottish soldier. Known as "Bonnie Dundee", he distinguished himself serving WILLIAM OF ORANGE, CHARLES II and JAMES II. He was killed fighting for James against William and Mary.

Claves, Cuban musical instrument consisting of two round hardwood sticks beaten together to produce a percussion accompaniment for popular tunes.

Clavichord, earliest stringed musical instrument with mechanical action controlled by a keyboard. Possibly originating in the 13th century, it was used extensively from the 16th to 18th centuries. The clavichord has a soft, delicate, expressive tone; it was superseded by the HARPSICHORD and then by the PIANO. *See also* HC1 p.249.

Clavicle, or collarbone, thin, slightly curved bone attached by ligaments to the top of the STERNUM (breast-bone). The clavicle and shoulder-blade make up the SHOULDER girdle, linking the arms to the axis of the body.

Clavier, general term for stringed musical instruments played with a keyboard, such as the harpsichord, clavichord and later the piano.

Clay, Cassius. *See* ALI, MUHAMMAD.

Clay, Frederick Emes (1838–89), British composer. He was famous in his time as the composer of stage music and light songs such as *She wandered down the mountainside* and *The Sands of Dee.*

Clay, Lucius DuBignon (1897–), US general. He was commander of US forces in Europe and military governor of the US Zone in Germany 1947–49, and successfully organized the BERLIN AIRLIFT.

Clay, group of aluminium silicate rocks of various compositions, including kaolinite and halloysite, usually mixed with some quartz, calcite or gypsum. It is formed by the weathering of surface granite or the chemical decomposition of feldspar. Soft when wet, it hardens on firing and is used to make pottery, stoneware, tiles, bricks and moulds, and as a filler for paper, rubber and paint. In developing countries it is used to clad the walls of simple buildings and to make pavements for threshing cereals. *See also* PE p.102; MM p.44.

Clayhanger, the first of a trilogy of novels by Arnold BENNETT, published in 1910, the others being *Hilda Lessways* (1911) and *These Twain* (1916). Like the best of his work, it presents a picture of provincial life in the "Five Towns" potteries district of N Staffordshire.

Clay pigeon shooting, sport in which spinning, saucer-shaped targets, propelled into the air from a mechanised trap, are fired at with 12-bore shotguns. The black target, approx. 11cm (4.25in) in diameter, simulates the flight of pigeons, which were first used when the sport began in London about 1790. The modern version dates from 1880. Two types, trench and skeet, are contested to Olympic and world championship class. Trench, or down-the-line, has squads of five alternating at fixed firing positions; skeet, invented by an American in 1932, positions shooters round an arc to fire at targets coming from high and low traps.

Clayton, Jack (1921–), British film director and producer. His first feature film, *Room at the Top* (1958), was outstanding for its picture of provincial life in Britian. His other films include *The Pumpkin Eater* (1964), *Our Mother's House* (1967) and *The Great Gatsby* (1974).

Clayton, Philip Thomas Bayard "Tubby" (1885–1972), Church of England chaplain who founded an interdenominational association for Christian social service, called Toc H. The name is signallers' jargon for the letters TH, the initials of Talbot House, which was the original soldiers' club set up in the Flemish town of Poperinghe in 1915.

Clean Air Act (1956), British Act of Parliament which banned the production of large quantities of smoke. It required furnaces to be equipped against the emission of smoke, dust and grit. It also empowered local authorities to create "smokeless zones".

Cleanthes (*fl.* 3rd century BC), Greek philosopher. A disciple of ZENO of Citium, he was the second Master of the STOICS. Of the fragments of his works that survive, the principal one is the philosophical poem *Hymn to Zeus.* Cleanthes stressed the religious aspect of Stoicism.

Clearing house, institution established by businesses engaged in similar activities to facilitate transactions among them. Bank clearing houses, for example, aid in the exchange of cheques, drafts, notes, etc. without the actual transfer of cash. In industry or trade, a clearing house is a building in which the products of two or more companies are combined for distribution or sale.

Cleavage, in embryology, progressive series of cell divisions that transform a fertilized egg into the earliest embryonic stage or BLASTULA. The egg is divided into blastomeres (smaller cells), each containing a diploid number of chromosomes. In mammals, the second division is generally at right-angles to the first and the third at right-angles to the previous two.

Clee Hills, range of hills in Salop, W central England, extending 23km (14 miles) N from Ludlow. The highest point is Brown Clee Hill, which rises to a height of 546m (1,792ft).

Cleft palate, congenital deformity in which there is an opening in the palate (roof of the mouth) causing direct communication between the nasal and mouth cavities. It is often associated with HARE-LIP and makes normal speech difficult. Usual treatment includes surgical correction of the deformity, followed by special dental care and speech therapy if necessary. *See also* MS p.131.

Cleistogamous flower, small, closed, self-fertilizing flower. Cleistogamous fertilization takes place within a flower that does not open, and enables seed production in the absence of normal cross-pollination. Sweet violet, oxalis and impatiens are examples of such flowers.

Cleland, John (1709–89), British novelist. Frequently destitute, he wrote FANNY HILL (1748–49) to save himself from starving. His other works include the novel *Memoirs of a Coxcomb* (1751) and the play *Titus Vespasian* (1755).

Clematis, genus of about 400 species of perennial, mostly climbing shrubs found worldwide. Many have attractive deep blue, violet, white, pink or red flowers or flower clusters. The leaves are usually compound. Well-known species are woodbine and old-man's-beard. Family Ranunculaceae.

Clemenceau, Georges (1841–1929), French politician, nicknamed "the Tiger". He served in the Chamber of Deputies from 1876 to 1893. After ten years of journalism he returned to the Senate in 1902 and was twice premier (1906–09, 1917–20). He led the French delegation at the PARIS PEACE CONFERENCE at the end of WWI. *See also* HC2 p.192.

Clemens, Samuel Longhorne. *See* Twain, Mark.

Clement, name of 14 popes, of whom the most notable include: St Clement I (*r.c.* AD 88–*c.*97). He suffered martyrdom for refusing to pledge allegiance to the Roman emperor. Clement III (*r.*1187–91) born as Paolo Scolari, preached the Third CRUSADE in 1187. Clement IV (*r.*1265–68), a Frenchman, stressed papal authority against the HOHENSTAUFEN emperors and attacked corruption. Clement V (*f.*1305–14), born as Bertrand de Got in 1260, lived in France throughout his pontificate, moving to AVIGNON in 1309. The papacy became subject to the French crown during his time. Clement VI (*r.*1342–52) was another Frenchman, Pierre Roger (*c.*1291–1352), who enhanced the papal court at Avignon. Clement VII (*r.*1523–34), a Florentine, born as Guiliano de' Medici in 1478, did little to combat Protestantism that emerged in the Empire in the 1520s. He was a patron of MICHELANGELO and RAPHAEL. Clement VIII (*r.*1592–1605), born as Ippolito Aldobrandini in 1536, allied the papacy with France and was noted for his piety and concern for the poor. Clement XI (*r.*1700–21), born as Giovanni Francesco Albani (1649–1721) had to deal with JANSENISM, and was known for his intellectual ability. Clement XIV (*r.*1769–74), born as Giovanni Vincenzo Antonio Ganganelli (1705–74), was forced by political alliances to suppress the JESUITS.

Clement, name of three ANTIPOPES. Clement III (*r.*1080–1100) (Guibert of Ravenna), was a supporter of the Holy Roman Emperor HENRY IV, who proclaimed himself pope after the existing pope GREGORY VII had excommunicated Henry in 1080. Guibert was crowned pope in Rome in 1084. Clement VII was antipope 1378–94. He was elected pope by the college of cardinals immediately after they had elected URBAN VI. He went to Avignon, initiating the GREAT SCHISM. He was recognized by several countries, including France, but failed to win general support. Clement VIII was elected pope in Spain in 1423. Backed by King Alfonso of Aragon, he opposed Martin V, the Roman pope. However, after the reconciliation of Alfonso and Martin in 1429 he abdicated and his cardinals recognised Martin, thus ending the Great Schism.

Clément, René (1913–), French film director. His two best films, *La Bataille du Rail* (1946) and *Les Jeux Interdits* (1952), are war stories in which he used non-professional actors. His later work, which was less well received, includes *Gervaise*, an adaptation of ZOLA's *L'Assommoir*, and *Is Paris Burning?* (1965).

Clementi, Muzio (1752–1832), Italian pianist and composer who settled in England. He was an accomplished piano virtuoso whose development of early techniques earned him the soubriquet "father of the piano". His compositions include many sonatas and the instructional pieces, *Gradus ad Parnassum* (1817). *See also* HC2 p.41.

Clement of Alexandria, St (*c.*150–*c.*215), Greek church father, full name was Titus Flavius Clemens. He studied in Alexandria, where he founded a school that became a centre of learning. Several of his writings have survived, including *Exhortation to the Greeks* and *The Tutor*.

Clements, Sir John Selby (1910–), British actor and director. His first stage appearance was in 1930. He is noted for his revivals of 17th- and 18th-century comedies.

Cleon (*d.*422 BC), Athenian politician. In 429 BC, after the death of PERICLES, he spurned Sparta's peace proposals and successfully continued the PELOPONNESIAN WAR. An unprincipled demagogue and inconsistent soldier, he was killed in action against the Spartans at Anphipolis.

Cleopatra (69–30 BC), Queen of Egypt (51–30 BC). In 48 BC, with the aid of Julius CAESAR, she overthrew her husband, brother and co-ruler PTOLEMY XIII. She became Caesar's mistress, but returned to Egypt after his assassination in 44 BC. In 41 BC she won Mark ANTONY's love and they were married in 37 BC. Octavian Caesar (later AUGUSTUS) determined to destroy them and in 31 BC their fleet was defeated at Actium. They fled and Antony killed himself; Cleopatra surrendered and, after she failed to win Octavian's affections, killed herself with an asp. *See also* HC1 p.97.

Cleopatra's Needle, Egyptian obelisk that stands on the Thames Embankment in London. Nearly 21m (70ft) tall and weighing about 180 tonnes, it is one of a pair erected by King Thutmose III in Egypt in the 15th century BC. The other one now stands in New York's Central Park. Both are made of red granite and were acquired separately in the 1800s.

Clepsydra. *See* CLOCKS.

Clerestory, in church architecture, row of windows in an upper storey of a nave, particularly above the roof level of any aisles along the sides of the nave.

Clergy Reserves, income from land grants to support Protestant churches in Canada. The Canadian Constitutional Act (1791) set aside one-seventh of the Crown lands in Canada for the support of Protestant churches. The reserves, dominated by the Church of England, became a source of religious and political dispute until 1854, when the lands were secularized.

Clerihew, short verse describing the character or life work of a famous person, named after Edmund Clerihew BENTLEY (1875–1956). Sometimes witty, sometimes nonsensical, a clerihew is usually written in two rhymed couplets in which each line is often longer than the preceding one, eg:

John Stuart Mill
By a mighty effort of will
Overcame his natural bonhomie
And wrote *Principles of Political Economy.*

Clerk, Sir Dugald (1854–1932), Scottish engineer. He invented the Clerk cycle or two-stroke internal-combustion engine (patented 1881), much used on light-weight motorcycles. Director of engineering research for the British Admiralty 1916, he wrote *The Gas, Petrol, and Oil Engine* (2 vols, 1909 and 1913).

Clerke, Agnes Mary (1842–1907), British astronomer and scientific writer, *b.* Ireland. She worked in Italy from 1867 to 1877 and received the Actonian Prize in 1893. Her books include *A Popular History of Astronomy in the 19th Century* (1885), *The System of the Stars* (1890) and *Problems in Astrophysics* (1903).

Clerk Maxwell, James (1831–79), Scottish theoretical physicist who in 1865 predicted the existence of radio waves and other then undiscovered forms of ELECTROMAGNETIC WAVES. His theories were published as *Treatise on Electricity and Magnetism* (1873). *See also* MM p.228.

Clermont-Ferrand, city in S central France; capital of Puy-de-Dôme département, formed by the union of the towns of Clermont and Montferrand (1731). It was the scene of the Church Council (1095) that initiated the First CRUSADE. It has a university (1854) and a Gothic cathedral. Industries: rubber goods, textiles, Pop. (1971 est.) 160,800.

Clermont-Ganneau, Charles (1846–1923), French archaeologist. He excavated many biblical sites, and improved modern knowledge of several ancient Middle Eastern languages.

Cleveland, Barbara Villiers, Duchess of (1641–1709), wife of Roger Palmer, Earl of Castlemaine. The favourite mistress of Charles II (1660–74), she wielded considerable political influence. In 1670 she was created Duchess of Cleveland.

Cleveland, Stephen Grover (1837–1908), US President in 1885–89 and 1893–97. He rose to national prominence as the reforming DEMOCRATIC mayor of Buffalo (1881–82) and governor of New York (1883–84). In his second term as president he repealed the Sherman Silver Purchase Act of 1890 and used troops to break the Chicago Pullman strike.

Cleveland, county in NE England, created by the Local Government Act of 1972, which became effective in 1974. It is made up of parts of the former counties of Durham and Yorkshire, and the county boroughs of Hartlepool and Teeside. Area: 583sq km (225sq miles). Pop. (1976) 567,900.

Cleveland, city and port of entry in NE Ohio, USA, at the mouth of the Cuyahoga River on Lake Erie; largest city in Ohio. It is a leading port for ore and Great Lakes shipping. It is one of the leading iron and steel centres in the USA. Founded in 1796 by Moses Cleaveland, it grew rapidly with the opening of the Ohio and Erie Canal and the arrival of the railway in 1851. John D. ROCKEFELLER founded the Standard Oil Company there in 1870. NASA maintains a research centre there. Industries: chemicals, oil refining, food processing, engineering. Pop. (1973) 678,615.

Cleveland bay, breed of light HORSE developed in the Cleveland district of Yorkshire, England, for riding, driving and farm use. It is large for a light horse, and its colour is bay, with black legs. To qualify for entry in the stud-book, it must stand at least 1.6m (5.3ft) at the shoulder.

Cleveland Hills, range of hills on the border of Cleveland and northern Yorkshire, N England. They are part of the North York Moors National Park and rise to 427m (1,400ft).

Cleves, Duchy of, former state lying on both sides of the River Rhine, bordering The Netherlands. It figured prominently in German history until it passed to the electors of BRANDENBURG in 1614.

Click-beetle, or skipjack, or snapping beetle, any of a group of beetles that turn over by snapping their bodies and throwing themselves into the air. They make an audible click in the process. Their long, cylindrical larvae are called WIREWORMS.

Click language, unusual language unique to parts of southern Africa, found chiefly in the Khoisan group. A clicking sound is made by a sudden intake of air and the action of the tongue on the roof of the mouth. The sound functions as a consonant, and is also found in some languages of the Bantu group.

Clifden, Irish town and port, in Galway on the W coast. ALCOCK and Brown landed nearby on 15 June 1919, at the end of the first non-stop Atlantic flight.

Cliff, geological formation consisting of a steep slope, sometimes of exposed rock. Cliffs can be nearly vertical or even overhanging. They may result from the exposure of rock strata due to geological faults (see ESCARPMENT) or, as in the case of shore-line cliffs, they may be caused by water and weather erosion.

Cliff dwellers. *See* PUEBLO INDIANS.

Clifford, Hubert John (1904–), Australian-born composer. He was a professor at the Royal Academy of Music, London, for many years and his compositions include *A Kentish Suite* (1935), scores for films and four *sketches* for Shakespeare's *As You Like It.*

Clifford, William Kingdon (1845–79), British mathematician and philosopher. His theory about biquaternions

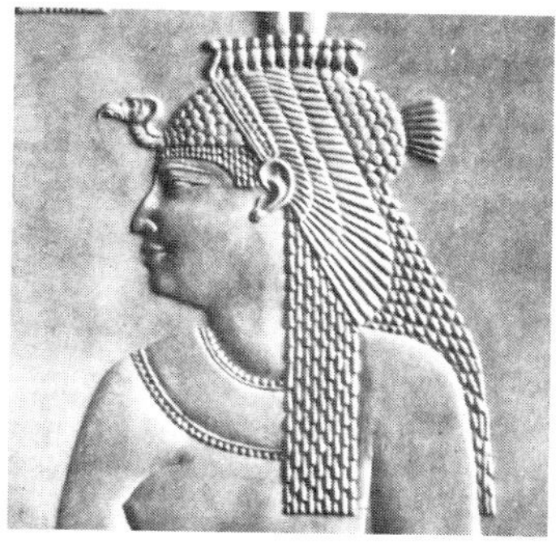

Cleopatra, representing the goddess of love on a bas relief at the Temple of Hathor.

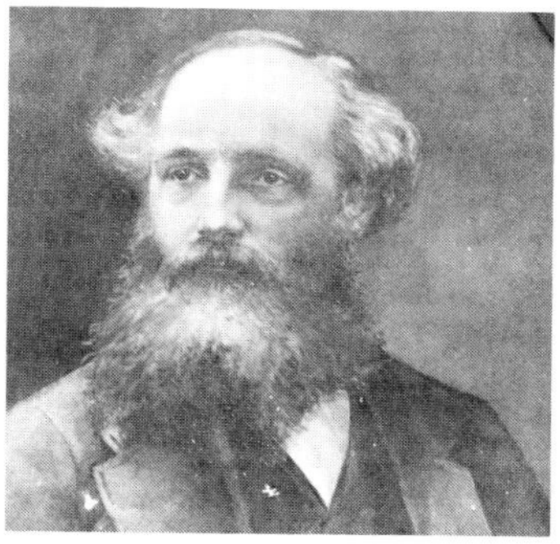

James Clerk Maxwell, who predicted the existence of electromagnetic (radio) waves.

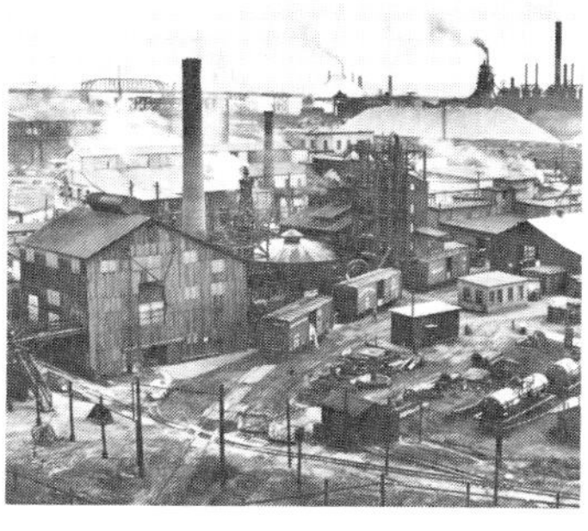

Cleveland, Ohio; a view of the heavy industrial area of the city known as the "Flats".

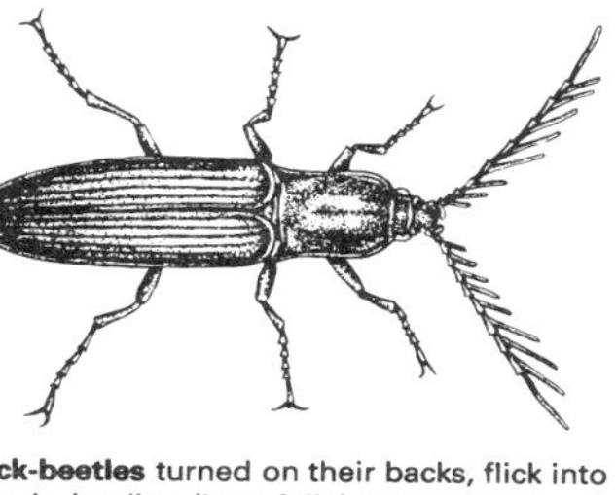

Click-beetles turned on their backs, flick into the air, landing (hopefully) on their feet.

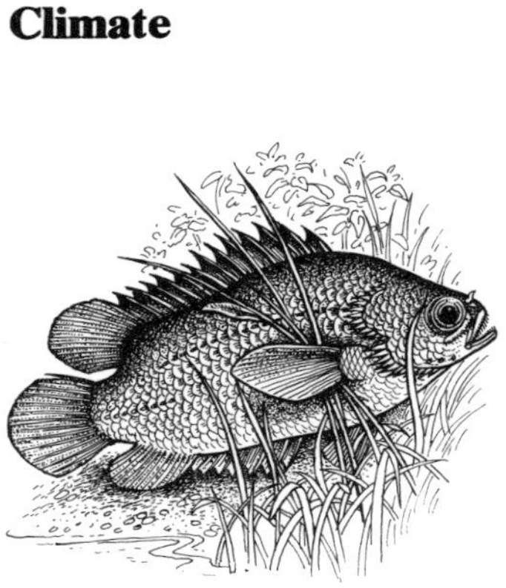

Climbing perch use their extended gill covers to "walk" on land for short distances.

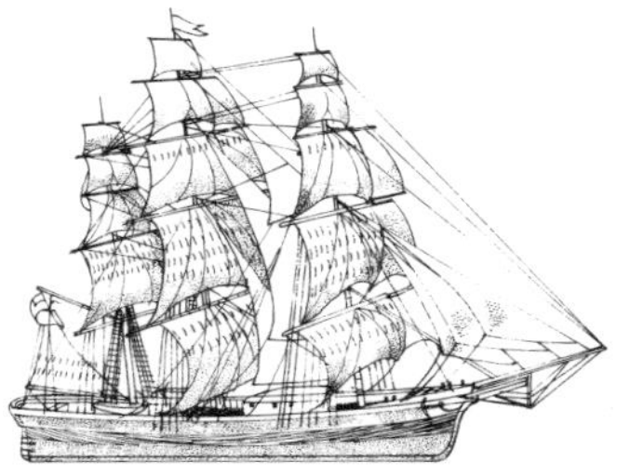

Clippers were the extremely fast and attractive sailing ships of the last century.

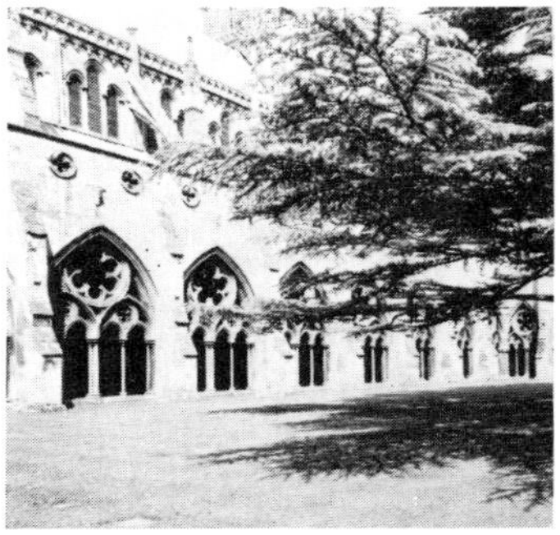

Cloisters at Salisbury Cathedral, England, around which the main buildings are ranged.

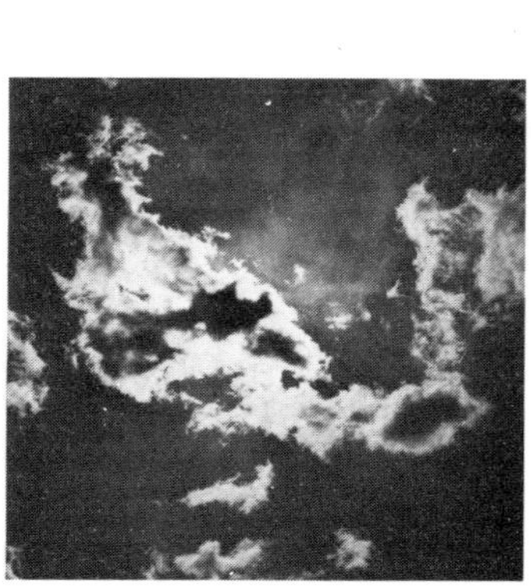

Clouds; these high-altitude cirrus clouds are composed almost exclusively of ice crystals.

generalised Sir W. R. HAMILTON's theory of quaternions, linking them with more general associative algebras. His book *On the Space-Theory of Matter* (1870) anticipated Einsteinian relativity with the idea that energy and matter are different kinds of space curve.

Climate, weather conditions of a place or region prevailing over a long time. The major factors influencing climate are surface and atmospheric temperatures, the movements of air masses in the atmosphere, incoming and outgoing radiation and the cycle and transportation of moisture both vertically and horizontally. Climates are defined on different scales, ranging from macroclimates which cover the broad climatic zones of the globe, down to microclimates which refer to the conditions in a small area such as a wood or a field. *See also* PE pp.74–75.

Climatology, scientific study of the earth's climates. Physical climatology investigates relationships between temperature, pressure, winds, precipitation and other weather phenomena. Regional climatology considers latitude and other geographical factors, eg the influence of large land masses in the climatic study of a particular place or region. *See also* PE pp.74–75.

Climatron, greenhouse in the Missouri Botanical Garden, St Louis, USA. It is the world's first greenhouse to provide a scientifically controllcd environment exactly simulating the natural conditions of tropical and sub-tropical plants. Covering 0.3 hectares (0.7 acres), the climatron consists of a GEODESIC DOM lined with clear plastic. Planned by Frits W. Went, the climatron was built in 1960.

Climbing mouse, nocturnal RODENT found in damp grassland, reedbeds and bushy regions south of the Sahara, and always near water. Its tail is partly prehensile, and it feeds on fruit, insects, small reptiles and eggs. Length of body: to 10cm (3.9in); tail length: to 11.7cm (4.6in). Family Muridae; genus *Dendromus.*

Climbing perch, tropical fresh water fish found in SE Asia. Not a true perch, it is popular in aquariums. It is grey-brown or green and uses extended gill covers to "walk" on land for short distances. Length: to 25.4cm (10in). Family Anabantideae; species *Anabas testudineus.*

Clinical psychology, field of psychology concerned with diagnosis and treatment of behavioural disorders. The term also refers to a method of investigating behaviour pioneered by Jean PIAGET. Methods of treatment include BEHAVIOUR THERAPY and PERSONALITY change. Clinical psychologists may work with psychiatrists.

Clink, district in Southwark, London. In the 13th century there was a prison for heretics at Clink, and today *clink* is a slang term for jail.

Clint, naturally occurring block of limestone produced by rain-water erosion of the surface of limestone features. *See also* PE p.*110.*

Clinton, Sir Henry (*c.*1738–95), British general. Sent to the American colonies in 1775, he became commander-in-chief in 1778 and in 1780 captured Charleston and the southern army. He resigned his post in 1781. From 1794 he served as governor of Gibraltar.

Clipper, commercial sailing vessel used during the mid-19th century. Built primarily for speed, clippers had a long slim hull, generally three masts and many square-rigged sails. One of the fastest, the American *Flying Cloud,* sailed from New York to San Francisco via Cape Horn in only 89 days. The *Cutty Sark* is a clipper preserved in a dry-dock at Greenwich, London. *See also* MM p.113.

Clive, Robert, Baron Clive of Plassey (1725–74), British soldier and colonial administrator. He went to India as an official of the British East India Company (1743) and successfully resisted growing French power in India with his capture of ARCOT (1751). By taking Calcutta and defeating the pro-French Nawab of Bengal at PLASSEY in 1757 he effectively assured British control of northern India, and was Governor of Bengal 1757–60 and 1765–67. He was acquitted of embezzling state funds in 1773. *See also* HC2 p.49.

Cliveden, the Astor family's seat in Kent, meeting place of the "Cliveden set" in the 1930s, which included Lady Astor, Geoffrey Dawson, editor of *The Times* and J.L. Garvin, editor of the *Observer.* Garvin's pro-German views have been held partly responsible for the policy of APPEASEMENT.

Clochemerle (1934), novel by the French author Gabriel Chevallier (1895–   ). A great popular success, this comic novel portrays events in a Beaujolais village between WWI and WWII. It uses caricature and maintains a broad view of all its characters, at the same time providing an excellent documentary picture of village life.

Clocks, instruments for measuring time. The earliest timekeeping instruments had no moving parts, being designed to measure the positions of the Sun, Moon and stars in their cyclic movements. Examples include neolithic stone columns, ancient Egyptian shadow clocks and their modern descendant the sundial. The ancient Egyptians also used water clocks, which are pottery bowls bearing graduated time-marks from which water slowly leaked. Candle clocks and sandglasses (hourglasses) were later types of non-mechanical clocks. The first mechanical clocks were probably falling-weight clocks. The central feature of these and all other mechanical clocks is the ESCAPEMENT mechanism, which enables a clock to tick off time at discrete intervals. This movement is transmitted through a series of gears to the hands which are pushed forward a small distance with every escapement movement. Various types of escapement mechanism were developed, culminating in the lever escapement of the 19th century. Motive power for mechanical clocks has been provided variously by falling weights, pendulums and coiled springs. In many modern wristwatches the coiled spring is rewound continually by natural wrist movements. Other modern clocks include those powered by electric motors, and those using an electrically oscillated quartz crystal as the basis of the time-division. The latter are accurate, but even more accurate are atomic clocks, which rely upon the natural oscillations of atoms – usually those of the metal caesium – and which measure time to an accuracy of thousandths of a second per year. *See also* SU pp.*22*–23, *24, 31, 76,* 106; MM pp.90, 92–93.

Cloete, Stuart (1897–1976), South African author born in Paris. Educated in Lancing College, Sussex, he later joined the Coldstream Guards and served in WWI. He is best known for his novel on the GREAT TREK, *Turning Wheels* (1937). He has also written a number of short stories.

Cloisonné, enamelling technique in which the design is constructed out of wires soldered to a plate, and the cells (cloisons) thus formed are filled with coloured enamel paste which, when fired, develops translucency and brilliant colours. The technique was developed in Mycenaean Greece, but reached its first full flowering in Byzantine art of the 10th and 11th centuries. Byzantine and Islamic cloisonné work was imported into Mongol China, where the technique was adopted and flourished in the Ming and Ching dynasties. It was also adopted in Japan, where the best examples are of the 18th and 19th centuries. *See also* ENAMEL.

Cloisonnism, also known as synthetism, style of painting evolved by Emile BERNARD, and Paul GAUGHIN. Named after its resemblance to CLOISONNÉ enamels, it uses strong, flat forms outlined in black or blue and vividly painted.

Cloister, covered arcade around a quadrangle, usually connecting a monastic church to the domestic buildings of a monastery. Notable examples are at Salisbury Cathedral, England, and St John Lateran, Rome.

Clone, set of organisms obtained from a single original parent through some form of ASEXUAL REPRODUCTION, such as MITOSIS in micro-organisms, vegetative propagation in plants or PARTHENOGENESIS in animals. Clones are genetically identical, and so cloning is often used in plant propagation to produce new plants from parents with desirable qualities, eg high yield. *See also* PE p.178.

Clontarf, suburb of DUBLIN in E Republic of Ireland. On 23 April 1014 a battle at Clontarf ended in a decisive victory for Irish forces under Brian BORU over the Norse and their allies, effectively ending Norse rule in Ireland. *See also* HC1 p.*180.*

Closed-circuit television, television system in which the television camera, receiver and associated controls are most often directly linked by cables. It has many applications, eg monitoring machinery, watching customers in shops, surveillance of military installations or hospital patients, in education, etc. Cable television is an extended form of closed-circuit television. *See also* MM p.230–231.

Closed shop, place of work at which employees (usually excluding management staff) are required to be members of one or more trade unions as a condition of employment. There are two types of closed shop. In a "pre-entry" closed shop all employees must in principle belong to the designated union(s). In a "post-entry" closed shop, those who are already employed when a closed shop agreement is negotiated are exempted from union membership if they do not wish to join, whereas all new employees must join the relevant union(s). In countries where closed shops are legal, there are usually exemptions allowing employees in a closed shop not to join a union if they have conscientious or religious objections.

Closet drama, genre of play, usually in verse, designed to be read rather than produced on stage. Some, however, have been performed successfully – eg Tennyson's *Becket* (1893), which Henry IRVING produced with much acclaim.

Clotar, name of two Merovingian kings of the FRANKS. Clotar I (*c.*497–561) ruled the NW Frankish lands after the death of CLOVIS in 511 and the whole kingdom after 558. Clotar II ruled the whole of the kingdom from 613 until his death in 629. *See also* HC1 pp.136–137.

Cloth. *See* TEXTILES.

Clothes moth, three species of small MOTH whose larvae (caterpillars) attack woollen fabrics and furs. The most destructive is the case-making *Tinea pellionella,* which builds and lives in a small portable case. Wingspan: 1.2cm (0.5in). Family Tineidae.

Clotho, in Greek mythology, one of the three FATES, who controlled men's lives. She was the spinner of the thread of life. She restored to life Pelops who had been killed by his father, Tantalus, to feed the gods at a banquet.

Cloud, visible mass of tiny water droplets or ice particles in the atmosphere, formed by the condensation of water vapour around condensation nuclei, which are usually dust particles. This happens when the temperature falls below a critical level called the DEW-POINT. Clouds are classified in many groups by meteorologists according to their appearance and formation. *See also* PE pp.70–71.

Cloud chamber, instrument for detecting and identifying charged particles, invented in the 1890s by C. T. R. Wilson to study ALPHA PARTICLES or protons. The principle is the same as the BUBBLE CHAMBER, except that the liquefied gas is replaced by air supersaturated with water or alcohol vapour, and the tracks left are droplets which form around the ionizing particle. They are deflected by a magnetic field and photographed for analysis. In the diffusion cloud chamber, which operates continuously, the air is supersaturated with vapour introduced at the top of the chamber. A large temperature difference is maintained between the top and bottom of the chamber. The air vapour cools as it diffuses towards the bottom, becoming supersaturated, and allowing tracks to form. *See also* SU p.60.

Cloud cover, or cloudiness, the proportion of the sky covered by clouds, usually measured in terms of tenths of total sky. The weather is called "clear" when the sky is less than three-tenths clouded.

Clouded leopard, small, rare cat found in forests of India, SE Asia, Sumatra and

Borneo. A nocturnal prowler, its coat is ochre-yellow marked with dark stripes and spots. It is an expert climber and has the longest canine teeth of any cat. Length: body 75–105cm (29–41in); tail: 61–90cm (27.5–35.4in); weight: 16–23kg (35–50lb). Family Felidae; species *Leo nebulosa*.

Clouds, The (423 BC), Greek comedy by ARISTOPHANES. A satire on the Sophists and SOCRATES, there has been much controversy over whether the portrayal of Socrates is an accurate one.

Cloud seeding, addition of materials to clouds to alter their natural development and initiate or increase the PRECIPITATION, or rain. Granulated solid carbon dioxide and fine silver iodide crystals have been used. These are seeded into the clouds from aircraft, flares or exploding rockets and the particles act as nuclei for the condensation of water droplets. Mixed results have been obtained from many cloud-seeding experiments, and the technique is not yet under predictable control.

Clouet, Jean (*c*.1485–*c*.1540), French painter in the court of Francis I. The oil portraits and striking crayon sketches attributed to him demonstrate great ability in rendering detail.

Clough, Arthur Hugh (1819–61), British poet. He was a fellow of Oriel College, Oxford, (1841–48). His first published poem, *The Bothie of Toper-na-Vuolich*, a narrative written in hexameters, appeared in 1848. In 1849 he published *Ambarvilia*, a collection of early lyric poems. His best-known poem is *Say not the Struggle Naught Availeth*.

Clouzot, Henri-Georges (1907–77), French film director renowned for the technical brilliance of the thrillers which he both wrote and directed. These include *Quai des Orfèvres* (1947), *The Wages of Fear* (1953) and *Les Diaboliques* (1955). He also made *Le Mystère Picasso* (1956), a study of the artist at work.

Clove, tall, aromatic, evergreen tree native to the Moluccan Islands. The small purple flowers appear in clusters; the dried flower buds are the cloves widely used in cooking as a flavouring. Oil of cloves is distilled from the stems. Height: to 12m (40ft). Family Myrtaceae; species *Eugenia caryophyllata*.

Clover, low-growing annual, biennial and perennial plants, native to temperate and warm regions of the N Hemisphere. The leaves have three leaflets, occasionally four, and the dense flower clusters are white, red, purple, pink or yellow. These plants restore nitrogen to the soil. Family Leguminosae; genus *Trifolium*.

Clovis I, or Chlodowech (465–511), King of the Franks. Clovis invoked the aid of Christianity during a battle near Cologne in 497 and, after his victory, he and his troops were baptized. By the time of his death he controlled most of Gaul, and had firmly established MEROVINGIAN power in Europe. *See also* HC1 pp.134, 137.

Clown, comic character who entertains by jokes and tricks in the theatre or circus. Many of Shakespeare's plays include such a character (eg, Touchstone in *As You Like It*), who is descended from the Old Vice of medieval liturgical plays. The modern circus or pantomime clown originated with Joseph GRIMALDI (1779–1837) and developed from the tradition of the COMMEDIA DELL' ARTE.

Clownfish, marine fish, often called anemone-fish, damselfish or clown triggerfish. Found in shallow Indo-Pacific waters it is orange, brown or yellow, sometimes with white stripes. Length: up to 8cm (3in). Family Pomacentridae; species *Amphiprion percula*. *See also* NW p.*128*.

Club, hand weapon for belabouring enemies and lawbreakers. A rough wooden club, made out of the branch of a tree, or the base of a young tree trunk with branches removed, was the earliest form. Since then the basic concept has undergone many refinements and variations – such as the fearsome Scots knobkerry of the Middle Ages, equipped with metal spikes, and the various forms of truncheons and batons used by modern police forces. Pairs of Indian clubs, made out of polished wood, are used for exercising.

Club, association of people for various purposes, eg common interests such as sports, hobbies, arts and politics, or simply for social reasons. London is noted for its many clubs, which grew out of its 18th-century coffee-houses and taverns. Until recently clubs have largely excluded women and minority groups. This is changing under pressure of anti-discriminatory legislation.

Club-foot, congenital deformity in which the foot twists inward and downward. It may be corrected by enclosing the foot in a cast in the normal position or by surgical intervention. In a few cases club-foot occurs after birth as the result of neurological or muscular disease.

Club moss, any of about 200 species of small evergreen seedless plants which, unlike the more primitive true MOSSES, have specialized tissues for transporting water, food and minerals. They are related to FERNS and HORSETAILS. The stems of some species are erect, whereas those of others creep along the ground and bear erect branches. Family Lycopodiaceae.

Clubroot, disease of cabbages, cauliflowers, turnips and related plants of the mustard family, characterized by club-like swellings of the roots. It is caused by the fungus *Plasmodiophora brassicae*, and can be avoided by using disease-free and resistant plants and uncontaminated soils.

Cluj, city NW central Romania, on the River Someşul in Transylvania; capital of Cluj district. It was founded in the 12th century by German colonists. Formerly part of Austria-Hungary, it became a Romanian city in 1920. It is noted for its 14th-century Gothic church and botanical gardens. Industries: chemicals, textiles. Pop. (1974) 218,703.

Clumber spaniel, slow-working finder and breed of retrieving dog developed in England by the Duke of Newcastle at Clumber Park. A sedate, heavy-looking dog, it has a massive head with upper lips overhanging the lower jaw. The long, low body is set on short, heavy legs. Average size: about 46cm (18in) high at the shoulder; weight 25–31kg (55–70lb).

Cluniac Order. *See* CLUNY, ORDER OF.

Cluny, Order of, religious order founded by William the Pious, Duke of Aquitaine, in 910 at the Monastery of Cluny near Mâcon, France. It was known from its beginning for its high standards, reflected in strict observance of the Benedictine rule and emphasis on dignified worship, a personal spiritual life and sound economics. Its influence spread throughout southern France and Italy, reaching its climax in the 12th century. The monastery at Cluny survived until 1790. *See also* HC1 pp.135, *135*, 154, 186, *187*.

Cluster, galaxy. *See* GALAXY CLUSTER.

Cluster, rocket, group of identical rocket engines bolted together to give increased thrust. Not only can more power be obtained than is technologically feasible in a single engine, there is a margin of safety if one engine fails. There are difficulties in simultaneous ignition and the engine nozzles must be carefully arranged to avoid overheating.

Cluster, stellar, any of innumerable collections of gravitationally associated stars occurring within galaxies. Stellar clusters are of two main types: OPEN CLUSTERS. (or galactic clusters) and GLOBULAR CLUSTERS. Open clusters, usually found in the spiral arms of galaxies, consist of up to several thousand young stars belonging to POPULATION I; globular clusters, which are much more concentrated, are found in the halo surrounding the centres of galaxies and consist of old POPULATION II stars. *See also* SU pp.242–243.

Clutch, any device placed between the rotating parts of an engine or motor and the drive-shaft to facilitate their quick connection or disconnection. In a car, for example, temporary disengagement of the engine is essential during gear-changes. The clutch usually consists of a pair of friction plates, although there are fluid clutches as well. *See also* MM p.*130*.

Clutch, electromagnetic, device that uses magnetic attraction to connect two rotating shafts. Some forms are disc clutches with energized coils and magnetic clutch plates. Eddy current clutches induce rotational movement in the shaft to be engaged and rotated. Hysteresis clutches also transmit rotation without slip. Other electromagnetic clutches employ magnetic metal particles, either flowing dryly or suspended in a liquid, to induce torque. *See also* SU p.*121*.

Clutha River, river of South Island, New Zealand; rises in Lake Wanaka, flows SE to the Pacific Ocean. There is a hydroelectric power station at Luggate. Length: 338km (210 miles).

Clutsam, George (1866–1951), Australian-born composer, pianist and critic. He composed mainly for the stage – *A Summer Night* (1910), *Konig Harlekin* (1912) – and came to concentrate mainly on musical comedy. His biggest success was *Lilac Time* (1923).

Clwyd, county in N Wales, formed in 1974 from the former counties of Flintshire, part of Denbigh and the NE corner of Merioneth; borders on the Irish Sea, Cheshire, Salop, Powys and Gwynedd; drained chiefly by the Dee, Conway and Clwyd rivers. The Vale of Clwyd is a rich agricultural region. Mold is the main town. Industries: coal-mining, iron and steel, tourism, chemicals, quarrying. Area 2,426sq km (937sq miles). Pop. (1975 est.) 374,800.

Clyde, 1st Baron, Colin Campbell (1792–1863), British soldier. In a long career he fought in the PENINSULAR WAR, the CRIMEAN WAR and in India, where he commanded the Army during the INDIAN MUTINY.

Clyde, river in SW Scotland; rises in the southern uplands; flows N, then NW, passing over the Falls of Clyde, which provide hydroelectric power, near Lanark and widening into the Firth of Clyde at Dumbarton. It is noted for its shipbuilding yards below Glasgow. Length: 170km (106 miles).

Clyde, Firth of, estuary of the River Clyde in SW Scotland, extending W and S from Dumbarton to Ailsa Craig. It contains the Bute, Arran and Cumbraes islands, and is a popular area for tourists. Length: 104km (65 miles).

Clydebank, town in Strathclyde Region, W central Scotland, on the N bank of the River Clyde, part of the Glasgow conurbation. It has important shipyards. Pop. (1971) 48,300.

Clydesdale, breed of draught HORSE developed in the valley of the River Clyde in Scotland, from Flemish and English horses. A massive horse with distinctive style and action, it has characteristic flowing, long hair below the knee and hock called "feathers". The Clydesdale is coloured bay or brown with white marks. Height: 163–173cm (64–68in) at the shoulder; weight 770–860kg (1,700–1,900lb).

Clynes, John Robert (1869–1949), pioneer of the British Labour movement. Born at Oldham, he started work in a cotton mill at the age of 10. He educated himself and became prominent in local politics before entering Parliament in 1910. He was Lord Privy Seal in the first Labour cabinet and Home Secretary 1929–31.

Clytemnestra, in Greek legend, the unfaithful wife of AGAMEMNON, King of Mycenae, and mother of his son ORESTES. On Agamemnon's return from TROY he was murdered by Clytemnestra and her lover Aegisthus, who usurped the throne until Orestes returned to exact vengeance.

CND. *See* CAMPAIGN FOR NUCLEAR DISARMAMENT.

Cnidaria, phylum of marine invertebrates, having about 9,000 species, including corals, jellyfish and sea anemones.

Cnidus (Cnidos), ancient Greek city of Caria, on the Resadiye Peninsula, SW Turkey. It was a member of the Dorian Hexapolis but was conquered by the Persians in 540 BC. It was the home of a famous statue of Aphrodite by Praxiteles.

CNS. *See* CENTRAL NERVOUS SYSTEM.

Cnut. *See* CANUTE.

Coach, horse-drawn, generally four-wheeled vehicle for carrying passengers. The term is also applied to a motor vehicle for passengers, generally more luxuriously appointed than a bus, and to a passenger-

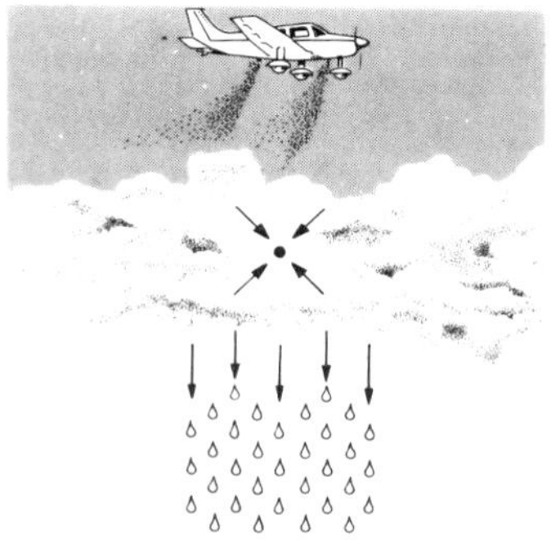

Cloud seeding is an attempt to produce rain artificially in arid areas.

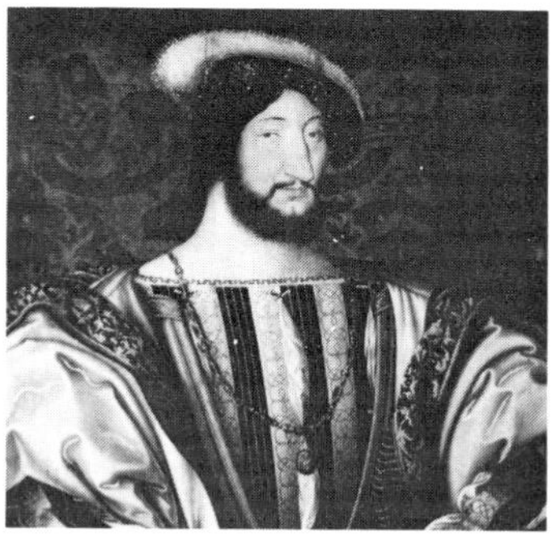

Jean Clouet's detailed portraits provide a visual record of court life; this is Francis I.

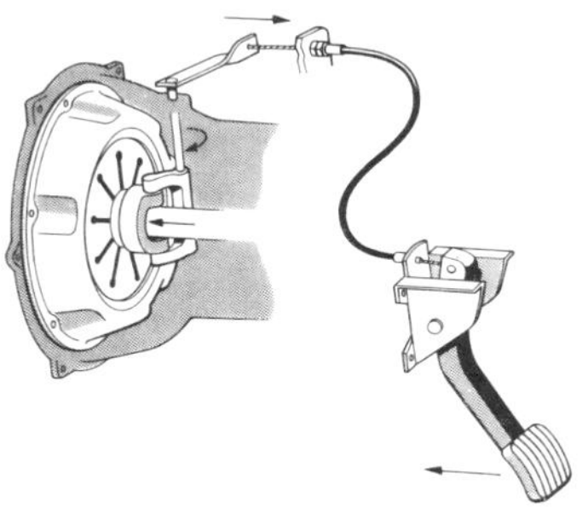

Clutch; the coupling device by which rotating parts may be connected or disconnected.

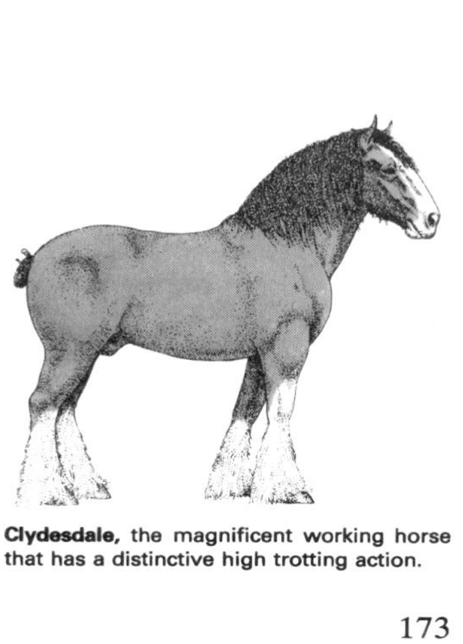

Clydesdale, the magnificent working horse that has a distinctive high trotting action.

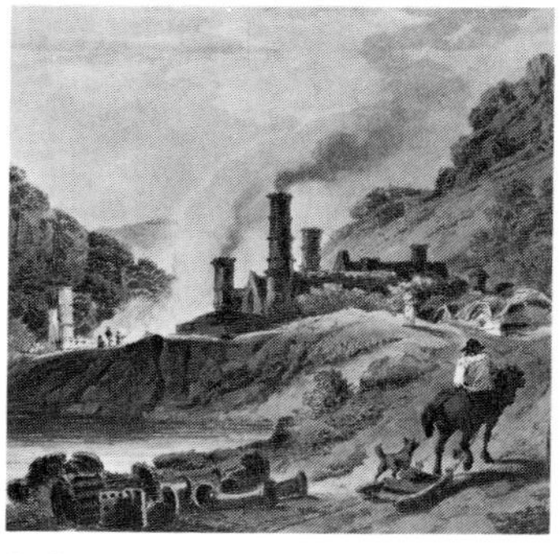

Coalbrookdale, where the Darby family virtually started the Industrial Revolution.

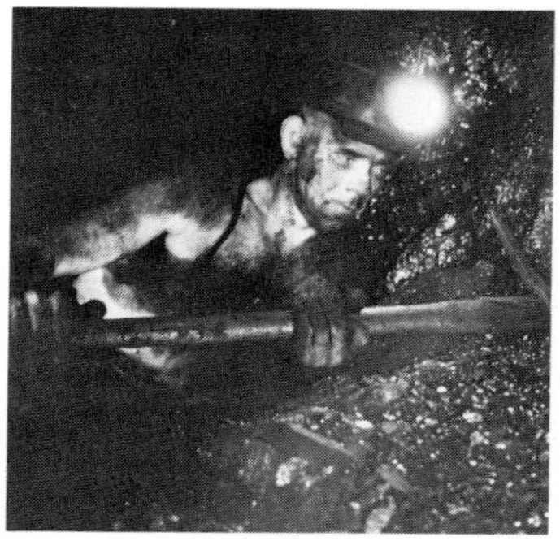

Coal-mining; stripped to the waist in the heat of a deep mine near Dover in Kent.

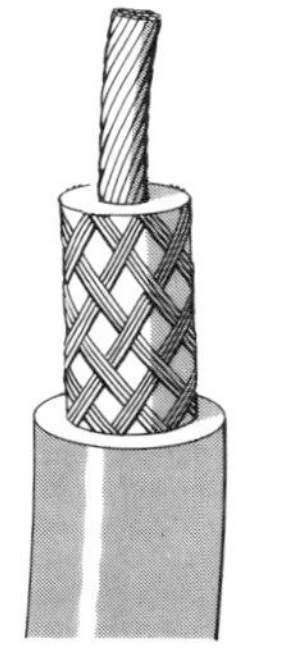

Coaxial cables, in which several channels of information are transmitted via one cable.

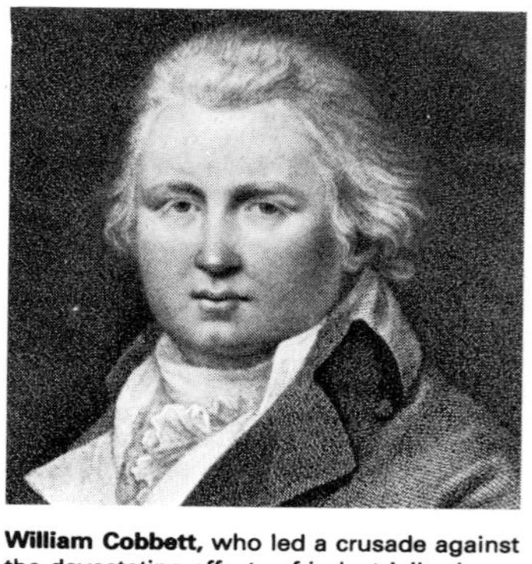

William Cobbett, who led a crusade against the devastating effects of industrialization.

carrying railway vehicle. *See also* MM pp.120–121, 134–135, 143.

Coaching, guidance in the development of technique and skills, usually related to sports but applicable to other fields, eg acting. The coach helps athletes reach and maintain fitness, corrects faults, improves skills and instils confidence. Both team and individual sports employ coaches to dictate strategy. Coaching of adults has grown in importance with the growth of professionalism and the "professional approach" in amateur sport.

Coal, blackish fuel composed of petrified vegetable matter. In the Carboniferous and Tertiary periods vegetation in swamp regions subsided to form peat bogs. Sedimentary deposits covered the bogs and applied pressure which, as it (and the consequent heat) increased, produced lignite, then bituminous coal and finally anthracite. Coal is classified by its fixed carbon content and by its volatile components. Lignite (brown coal), which has a low carbon content, is a poorer fuel than anthracite, which has a high one. Most coal seams are inter-stratified with shales, clays, sandstones and sometimes limestones. *See also* MM. pp.76–77, 82, *83,* 84; PE pp.*126–127,* 136–137, 140–141, *143,* 144.

Coalbrookdale, village in Salop, W central England, on the River Severn. It was at Coalbrookdale that, in 1711, Abraham DARBY first smelted pig iron using coke, producing a good-quality cast iron suitable for forging. In 1779 the first cast-iron bridge was constructed there over the Severn. It is still used as a footbridge *See also* MM pp.28, *28,* 190.

Coal gas, fuel once supplied to most homes and factories but now largely replaced by the safer and more calorific natural gas (mostly methane). Coal gas is made by heating coal to about 900°C (1,650°F) in a closed retort and collecting the volatile matter; COKE remains as a residue. Coal tar is condensed out, and other valuable materials are removed by dissolving them out with water. The remaining mixture of gases, containing methane, carbon monoxide and hydrogen together with nitrogen and small amounts of other gases, is coal gas. *See also* MM p.*83.*

Coal-mining, process of removing coal from the ground, by an excavation or mine. Two principal systems are used: strip mining (also called surface, open-pit or open-cast mining), a form of quarrying used when the seam of coal is near the surface; and underground (deep) mining in which the seam is reached through shafts or tunnels. Power machines such as drills, cutters and hydraulic jacks have replaced traditional hand tools. In longwall mining, an early underground method developed at the end of the 17th century, a section of coal sometimes 180m (600ft) long is worked at once. In other underground methods the seam is broken up by explosive charges or by machines. About 3,000 million tonnes of coal are mined annually. See also PE pp.136–140.

Coal tar, volatile by-product of the destructive distillation of bituminous coal during the manufacture of COKE. Coal tar is important for its organic chemical constituents which are extracted by further distillation. Such chemicals (called coal-tar crudes) include xylene, toluene, naphthalene and phenanthrene; they are the basic ingredients from which many products such as explosives, dyes, drugs and perfumes are synthetized. *See also* SU p.142.

Coastal Command, shore-based air patrol group operated jointly by the Royal Navy and the Royal Air Force during WWII. Formed in 1939, the command provided air support for British convoys, effected aerial bombardment of enemy shipping and monitored the enemy's movements at sea. It operated over British coastal waters, the North Sea, the North Atlantic and the Mediterranean Sea from stations around the British Isles, one in Gibraltar and one in Iceland.

Coast guard, organization assisting ships and people in danger on the coasts. The British coast guard was set up in 1822, originally intended to prevent smuggling, and came under the ADMIRALTY in 1856. It is now financed by the Department of Trade, and its members work to prevent accidents and assist those in difficulty.

Coasting, spacecraft, period of unpowered flight, when the spacecraft moves under momentum. For trips to the Moon or planets, this period is considerably longer than the powered-flight, or burning period, which gives it the impulse for coasting. During the coasting period, the craft is affected only by gravitational forces.

Coast Mts, mountain range in British Columbia, Canada; an extension of the CASCADE Range, running parallel to the Pacific Coast. The highest peak is Mt Waddington, 4,042m (13,260ft). One of Canada's largest hydroelectric power stations is at Kemano. Length: approx. 1,600km (1,000 miles).

Coast Ranges, mountain ranges parallel to the Pacific coast of North America, extending from S California, N through Oregon and Washington into British Columbia, Canada, and Alaska. They are composed of folded and sometimes faulted sedimentary rocks. In some valleys in the S grapes, fruit and vegetables are grown; in the N timber is important, in particular redwood, spruce and Douglas fir trees.

Coates, Eric (1886–1958), British composer. In 1912 he became leader of the Queen's Hall Orchestra under Sir Henry WOOD. From 1918 he devoted himself largely to his own compositions, which included *London Suite* (1933), *Four Centuries* (1941) and the theme for the film of *The Dam Busters* (1954).

Coates, Joseph Gordon (1878–1943), New Zealand politician and Prime Minister (1925–28). He led the agrarian Reform Party and served as minister in the United-Reform coalition (1931–35), but his policies, in the depth of depression, satisfied few. He later served in the War Cabinet (1940–43).

Coati, or coatimundi, three species of raccoon-like rodents of the SW USA and South America. Most have long, slender reddish-brown to black bodies with tapering snouts and long ringed tails. Head and body length: 67cm (26in); weight: 11.3kg (25llb). Family Procyonidae; genus Nasua. *See also* NW p.216.

Coat-of-mail shell. *See* CHITON.

Coats Land, region in ANTARTICA discovered by the Scottish explorer William Bruce in 1904. It is the site of a British research station; Argentina, Britain and Norway claim different parts of it.

Coaxial cable, a device for the simultaneous transmission of multiple radio, television and telephone signals, particularly at high frequencies. It consists of an insulated wire surrounded by a copper tube. A simple cable may house 20 or more coaxials held together by an insulated covering. *See also* MM pp.226–227.

Cobalt, metallic element (symbol Co) in the first transition series, discovered in *c.*1735. It is found in cobaltite (CoAsS) and smaltite, but most is obtained as a by-product during the processing of other ores. It is used in high-temperature steels, and as a ferromagnetic constituent in some alloys. Co^{60} (half-life 5.26yr) is an artificial isotope used as a source of gamma rays in radiotherapy, tracer studies, etc. Properties: at. no. 27; at. wt. 58.9332; s.g. 8.9; m.p. 1,495°C (2,723°F); b.p. 2,870°C (5,198°F); most common isotope Co^{59} (100 %). *See also* SU p.*136.*

Cobb, John Rhodes (1899–1952), British racing driver. He enjoyed a successful racing career, and established new land-speed records in his twin-engined Railton-Mobil in 1938 and again in 1939. In 1947 he attained a speed of 634km/h (394mph), a record which remained unbeaten until 1964. He died while attempting a water-speed record on Loch Ness, Scotland.

Cobb, Tyrus Raymond (1886–1961), US baseball player. The game's greatest hitter and base-stealer, Cobb played for the Detroit Tigers (1905–26) and the Philadelphia Athletics (1927–28), compiling a record 4,191 hits and 892 stolen bases. In 1936 was elected the first member of the Baseball Hall of Fame.

Cobbett, William (1763–1835), British political essayist and reformer. From a poor farming background, Cobbett joined the army and in 1792 was forced to flee to the US after denouncing army injustices. He returned to England and edited the *Political Register* (1802), which from 1804 was the leading voice for social and parliamentary reform despite repressive measures such as the GAGGING ACTS (1817). He became deeply concerned with the rural effects of industrialization as shown in his *Rural Rides* (1830). *See also* HC2 pp.21, 94, 160.

Cobden, Richard (1804–65), British Radical politician. He led the campaign for the repeal of the CORN LAWS and as an MP in 1841–57 and 1859–65 was the chief spokesman for the "Manchester School" of *laissez-faire* manufacturers and economists. His belief in free trade and international co-operation led him to oppose Britain's participation in the CRIMEAN WAR, opposition that led to his defeat at the 1857 elections. He negotiated the 1860 reciprocal trading agreement with France. *See also* HC2 pp.96, 182.

Cobden-Sanderson, Thomas James (1840–1922), British bookbinder and printer. He trained as a barrister but, influenced by William MORRIS, turned to bookbinding in 1883 and established the Doves bindery where he printed the Doves Bible (1903–05).

Cobham, Sir Alan John (1894–1973), British aviator who pioneered the technique of refuelling in the air. A Londoner, Cobham served with distinction in WWI in the Royal Flying Corps. He later became a civil airline pilot and took part in inaugural flights to various parts of the world. In the 1930s he became celebrated for his "flying circus", a team of talented pilots who gave exhibitions of stunt flying.

Cobham, Viscount (1909–), Governor-General of New Zealand (1957–62), who helped to establish the Outward Bound movement in New Zealand. He was also vice-captain of the MCC team that toured there in 1935 and 1936.

COBOL (Common Business Orientated Language), COMPUTER LANGUAGE first developed for business use in 1959. Revised and improved since then, it is widely used.

Coborn, Charles (1852–1945), British music-hall star, real name Colin Whitton McCallum. His best-known songs include *Two Lovely Black Eyes* (1886) and *The Man Who Broke the Bank at Monte Carlo,* and he appeared in many films including *Say it with Flowers* (1934).

Cobourg Peninsula, peninsula in N Northern Territory, Australia, E of Melville Island and N of the Van Diemen Gulf. Width: 32km (20 miles). Length: 80km (50 miles).

Cobra, any of several highly poisonous snakes in the family Elapidae, including MAMBAS, CORAL SNAKES, KRAITS and true cobras. It can expand its neck ribs to form a characteristic hood. Found primarily in Africa and Asia, they are the favourite of snake charmers and feed on rats, toads and small birds. The king cobra (*Ophiophagus hannah*) reaches 5.5m (18ft) in length, and is the largest venomous snake in the world. The Indian cobra, *Naja naja* with the spectacle-like markings on its hood, frequents houses at night to search for rats; it kills several thousand humans annually. Some African species have forward-facing fangs and can spit venom into a victim's eyes from more than 2m (7ft), causing temporary or permanent blindness. See also NW pp.*135, 137.*

Cobra, international art group that existed in Europe from 1948 to 1951. It took its name from the initials of Copenhagen, Brussels and Amsterdam, where the original members of the group were living. These included Karel APPEL, the Belgian painter Corneille (1922–) and Asger JORN. Cobra artists' work testified to their interest in folk and primitive art and spontaneous expression.

Coburg, town in Bavaria, West Germany on the River Itz; capital of the state of Saxe-Coburg-Gotha (1826–1918) and home town of Prince ALBERT, husband of Queen VICTORIA. Martin LUTHER lived in the town's castle in 1530. Today the chief industries are glass and ceramics. Pop. (1970) 42,619.

Coca, shrub native to Colombia and Peru which contains the ALKALOID drug COCAINE, used as a local anaesthetic. Local Indians chew the leaves for pleasure, to quell hunger and to stimulate the nervous system. The plant has yellow-white flowers growing in clusters, and red berries. Height: about 2.4m (8ft). Species *Erythroxylon coca. See also* MS p.*117.*

Coca-Cola, trade name of the world's largest-selling soft drink. The first bottle of Coca-Cola was produced in the USA in 1886, and today it is sold to almost every part of the world. With headquarters in Atlanta, the Coca-Cola Company in the mid-1970s employed about 30,000 workers and its sales were worth about $2,870 million annually.

Cocaine, white crystalline ALKALOID extracted from the leaves of the coca plant. It is used as a drug, with stimulant and hallucinatory effects. It is psychologically habit-forming, but increasing doses are not needed, as the body does not develop tolerance to it. Habitual use results in physical and nervous deterioration, and subsequent withdrawal results in severe depression. *See also* MS pp.104, *117.*

Coccidiodomycosis, infection caused by a fungus (*Coccidioides immitis*) that produces cough, fever and aches; in more severe cases abscesses form under the skin. It often disappears spontaneously, but if the infection spreads, and is untreated, death can result. It occurs mainly in SW USA and South America.

Coccolith, any microsocpic, single-celled flagellate of the Coccolithophorida, a class of ALGAE of the phylum Chrysophyta. The cell is covered with round, chalky platelets only one or two thousandths of a millimetre in diameter. Many limestone and chalk cliffs are made up entirely of the remains of such platelets. *See also* PE p.*83.*

Coccyx, triangular bone at the lower end of the vertebral column. It is formed by the fusion of three to five small VERTEBRAE. *See also* SPINE; MS p.*56.*

Cochabamba, city in W central Bolivia, 230km (143 miles) SE of La Paz; second largest city of Bolivia and capital of Cochabamba department. The city has a cathedral and a university. The chief industry is oil refining, and the city is a commercial centre for the surrounding area, where cereal crops and fruit are grown and cattle are raised. Pop. (1975) 184,340.

Cochet, Henri (1901–), French tennis player. A member of the squad that won the Davis Cup for France (1928–31), he was an instinctive genius, a master of the volley and half-volley. He won the Wimbledon singles in 1927 and 1929, the US title in 1928 and the French singles in 1922, 1926, 1928, 1930, 1932.

Cochin, port in Kerala state, SW India, on the Malabar coast. It was the earliest European settlement in India, dating from 1502 when Vasco da GAMA established a Portuguese trading post there. It has a naval base, fishing and paper industries and exports coconut products such as coir. Pop. (1971) 438,420.

Cochin China (Cochinchine), historical region in Vietnam, South-East Asia, including the greater part of South Vietnam; bounded by Cambodia (NW), the Annam region of Vietnam (NE), the South China Sea (SE) and the Gulf of Siam (SW). This flat alluvial plain of the Mekong River delta is one of the world's foremost rice-producing areas. It was ceded by Annam to France in 1862 under the terms of the Treaty of Saigon, and became part of French Indochina in 1887. It was incorporated into Vietnam in 1949, and became part of South Vietnam in 1954.

Cochineal, crimson dye produced from the pulverised dried bodies of certain female scale insects. These soft-bodied, cactus-eating insects are found in Mexico and Central America. The dye is still used in cosmetics and foodstuffs although in most applications it is being replaced by aniline dyes. Length: 3mm (0.1in). Species: *Dactylopius coccus. See also* MM p.*244.*

Cochlea, cavity filled with fluid in the inner EAR. It has the shape of a coiled shell and its nerve cells transmit impulses to the BRAIN as a result of sound vibrations entering the ear, thus giving hearing. *See also* MS pp.50–51.

Cochran, Sir Charles Blake (1872–1951), British theatrical producer, the leading impressario of the 1920s and 1930s. He was noted for a series of spectacular revues which he produced at the London Pavilion between 1918 and 1931. He also produced some of Noel COWARD's work, including *Bitter Sweet* (1929) and *Cavalcade* (1931).

Cockatiel, small Australian PARROT, with a yellow, crested head and a long tail. Family Psittacidae; species *Nymphicus hollandicus. See also* NW pp.*205, 221.*

Cockatoo, large PARROT with a long, erectile crest. Cockatoos live mainly in Australia, SW Asia and nearby islands. Most are mainly white, tinged with pink or yellow. They spend most of their time in treetops feeding on fruit and seeds. Females lay 1–4 white eggs in a tree hole nest. Length: 38cm (15in). Family Psittacidae.

Cockburn, Henry Thomas, Lord Cockburn (1779–1854), Scottish judge. In 1830 he was made Solicitor-General for Scotland and in 1837 became a lord of the judiciary. He supported parliamentary reform and played a major role in drafting the Scottish Reform Bill. He also wrote the notable *Life of Jeffrey* (1852).

Cockchafer, any of various large, scarabeid beetles whose grubs live underground and feed on the roots of plants. European species are particularly harmful to trees. Family Melolonthidae.

Cockcroft, Sir John Douglas (1897–1967), British physicist whose research dealt with particle acceleration in an electric field. Working with Ernest Walton, he constructed a voltage multiplier capable of accelerating protons to higher energy levels. The Cockcroft-Walton generator was utilized in the disintegration of lithium atoms by bombarding them with protons. The 1951 Nobel prize in physics was awarded to both men for their use of particle accelerators to study atomic nuclei. Cockcroft also contributed to the development of nuclear reactors.

Cockerell, Charles Robert (1788–1863), British architect. In 1819 he succeeded his father as surveyor of St Paul's Cathedral and he later became architect to the Bank of England. His most famous buildings, displaying the influence of the CLASSICAL REVIVAL include the Ashmolean Museum, Oxford and the Sun Fire Insurance Office, London.

Cockerell, Sir Christopher Sydney (1910–), British engineer, designer and inventor of the hovercraft. During WWII he worked on the development of radar and other radio aids. In 1948 he started a boat-building business and in the early 1950s began research into the development of air-cushion vehicles. By 1954 he had developed the hovercraft; he filed his first patent in 1955. In 1959 the first SRN1 hovercraft crossed the English Channel. *See also* MM pp.116–117.

Cocker spaniel, gun dog so-called because of its proficiency in flushing woodcock. It has a rounded head and a broad, square muzzle; the well-feathered ears are long and set at eye level. The coat can be black and white or a golden brown and the sturdy, compact body is set on straight, strongly boned legs; the tail is docked. Average size: 35.5–38cm (14–15in) high at the shoulder; weight: about 10–13kg (22–29lb).

Cockfighting, sport, popular in Latin America and Asia, in which two gamecocks are pitted against each other in a fight. The cocks – bred for fighting – are placed in a small circular pit. To enhance the action, metal spurs are sometimes attached to the bird's natural spurs. The match goes on until one of the cocks refuses to fight or is killed.

Cockle, bivalve mollusc found in marine waters. Its varicoloured, heart-shaped shell has 20–24 strong, radiating ribs. Of the 200 or so species that are recognized, many are edible. Average length: 4–8cm (1.5–3in). Class Bivalvia; family Cardiidae; species include *Cardium aculeatum.*

Cocklebur, popular name for a genus of coarse weeds, bearing prickly, clinging fruits that give the plants their name. Family Compositae; genus *Xanthium.*

Cockney, native of the City of London, traditionally one born within the sound of Bow bells, the bells of St Mary-le-Bow church; often extended to mean any Londoner. Cockneys have a reputation for chirpy toughness, a quality that was admirably displayed during the WWII Blitz on London. Cockney rhyming slang is often a feature of their distinctive dialect.

Cock-of-the-rock, fruit-eating, brightly coloured, parrot-like bird of tropical South America. It grows to a length of 30cm (12in) and has a large, erect crest which almost hides its bill. The birds build their mud nests among rocks or in caves, lining them with leaves and moss. The males perform communal and ritualistic courtship dances and, after mating, the females lay two eggs. Genus *Rupicola.*

Cockroach, or roach, or croton bug, insect with long antennae and a flat, soft body found worldwide, but mostly in the tropics. Its head is hidden under a shield (pronotum) and it may be winged or wingless. Some species are serious household pests. Length: 13–50mm ($^1/_2$–2in). Family Blattidae. *See also* ORTHOPTERA.

Cocktail, American term that originated in the late eighteenth century to describe a drink, usually alcoholic, made up of a number of ingredients. Gin is often added to a fortified wine, and other ingredients such as bitters, sugar and ice are added.

Cocoa, drink obtained from the tropical American evergreen tree whose Latin name reflects the fact that cocoa and chocolate contain the ALKALOID theobromine. The seeds are beans contained in an elliptical pod; they do not have the flavour or colour of chocolate until they have undergone a long process of fermentation followed by roasting. The beans are then ground up to make chocolate powder. Bitter chocolate is a liquid separated from this powder; cocoa is the powder minus some fatty substances. To make milk chocolate, milk solids are added to the powder. Family Sterculiaceae; species *Theobroma cacao. See also* PE p.209.

Cocoa butter, yellowish solid fat with a taste of chocolate, obtained by pressing roasted cocoa beans. It is used in making soap, confectionary, cosmetics and medicines. Chocolate contains about 55% of cocoa butter. *See also* PE p.209.

Coco de mer, also called double coconut, palm and its fruit of the Seychelles Islands. The large fruit, which takes ten years to mature and may weigh 20kg (50lb), has a fleshy fibrous covering over a double-lobed, edible, coconut-like centre. The flowers are borne on a large fleshy SPADIX. Species *Lodoicea maldivica.*

Coconut oil, semi-solid fat with a characteristic odour, consisting principally of the glyceride of lauric acid, $CH_3(CH_2)_{10}COOH$. The oil is extracted from pressed boiled coconut "meat" and used to manufacture soaps, vegetable fats, candles and cosmetics.

Coconut palm, or copra plant, tall palm tree native to the shores of the Indo-Pacific region and the Pacific coast of South America; commercially the most important of all palms. Growing to 30.5m (100ft) tall, it has a leaning trunk and a crown of feather-shaped leaves. The dried kernel or "meat" of the coconut fruit, called copra, is the valuable source of coconut oil used in the manufacture of margarine, soap and cooking oil. Family Palmaceae; species *Cocos nucifera. See also* PE pp.*194, 217.*

Cocoon, case or wrapping produced by larval forms of animals (such as some moths, butterflies and wasps) for the resting or pupal stage in their life cycle. Some spiders spin a cocoon that protects their eggs. Most cocoons are made of silk, and those of the domestic silkworms provide most of the world's commercial silk. *See also* CHRYSALIS; MOTH; PUPA.

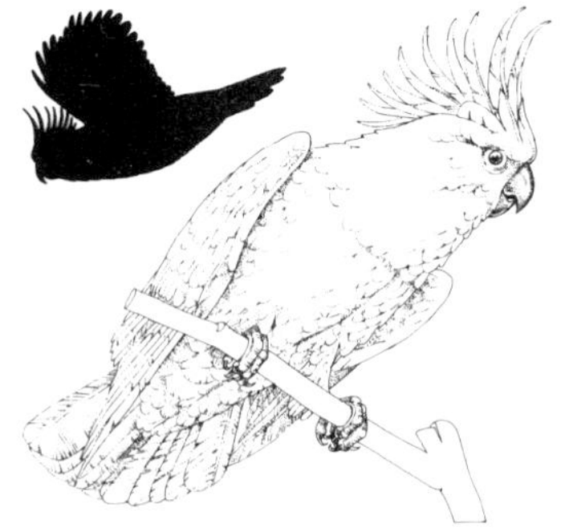

Cockatoos are the spectacular, mainly white parrots from Australia and SW Asia.

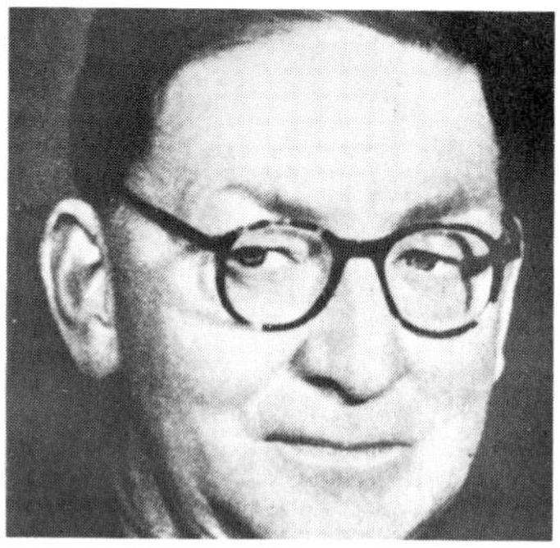

Sir John Cockcroft, joint Nobel Prize winner for his work in the study of atomic nuclei.

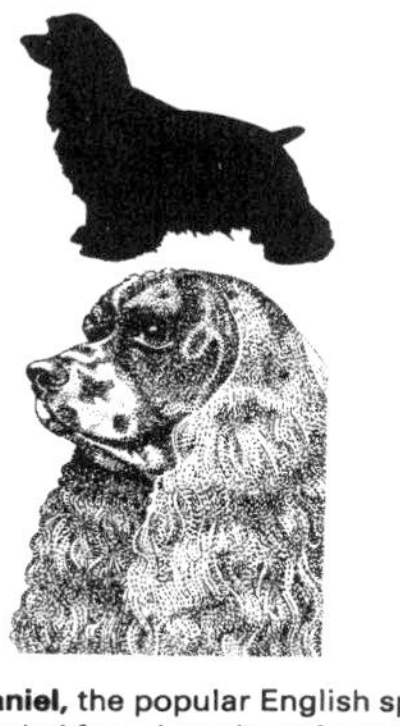

Cocker spaniel, the popular English sporting dog descended from breeds native to Spain.

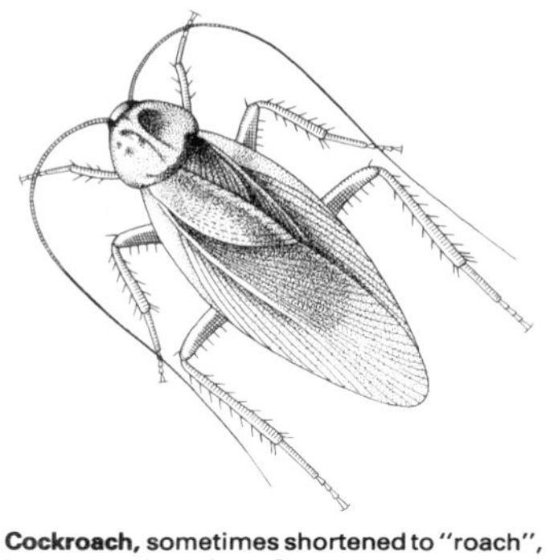

Cockroach, sometimes shortened to "roach", is a corruption of the Spanish *cucaracha.*

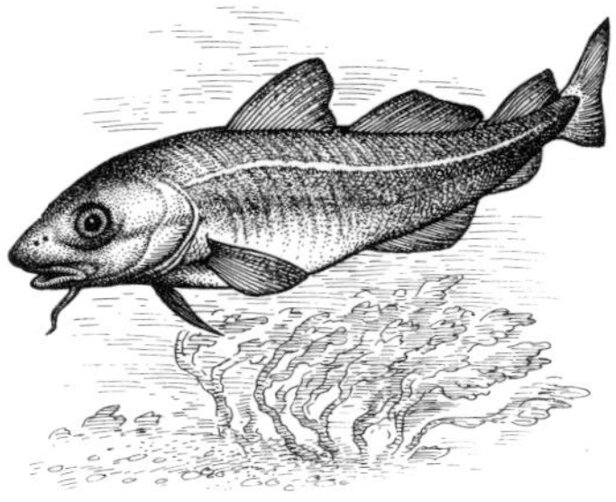

Cod; the valuable food fish that lives on or near the bottom of the colder northern seas.

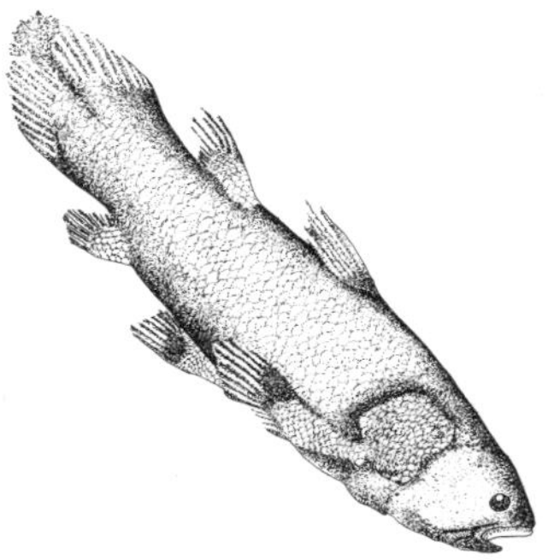

Coelacanths, thought extinct millions of years ago, turned up alive in 1938 and 1952.

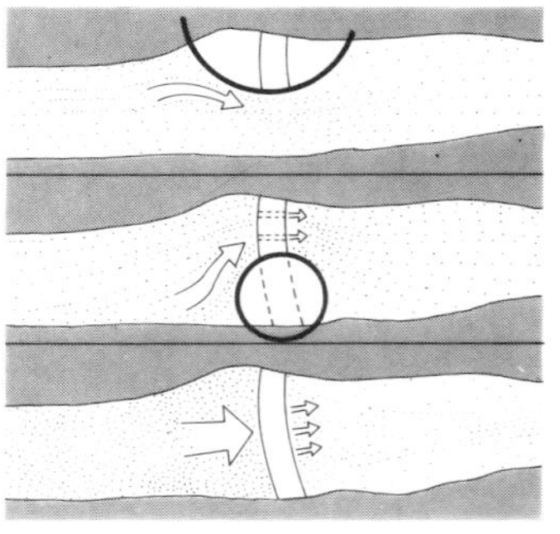

Coffer dams provide a water-free location for the excavation of the main dam foundations.

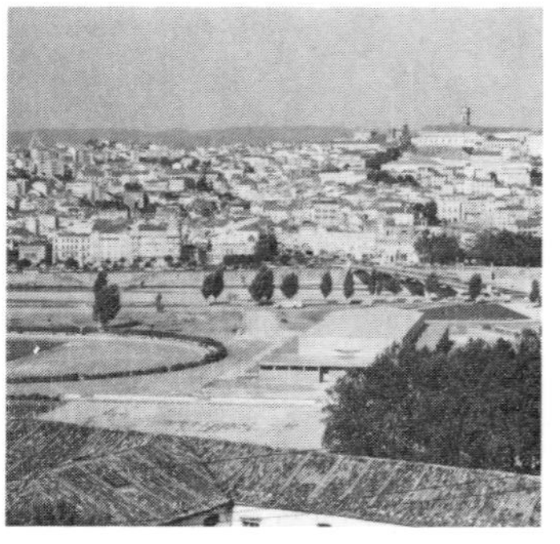

Coimbra is a Portuguese university city in the province of Beira Litoral, NE of Lisbon.

Cocos Islands, group of 28 small coral islands in the Indian Ocean, 1,200km (750 miles) SW of Java. They were discovered by William Keeling in 1609. They came under British control in 1857, but since 1955 have been a protectorate of Australia. Area 13sq km (5sq miles). Pop. (1975 est.) 1,000. *See also* MW p.58.

Cocteau, Jean (1889–1963), French writer and filmmaker, whose experimental work made him a leader of the French AVANT-GARDE in the 1920s. He was associated with many leading figures such as APOLLINAIRE, PICASSO, DIAGHILEV and STRAVINSKY. His many successful works, filled with SURREALIST fantasy, include the novel *Les enfants terribles* (1929; filmed, 1950); the dramatic work *Orphée* (1928; filmed, 1949) and other films such as *Le sang d'un poete* (1933) and *La belle et la bête* (1946). Other works include ballets, monologues, frescoes and drawings.

Cod, bottom-dwelling, marine food fish found in cold to temperate waters of the Northern Hemisphere. It is grey, green, brown or red with darker speckled markings. Cod is one of the chief food fishes although its cost must often reflect that of reaching far-off fishing grounds. Length: up to 1.8m (6ft). Family Gadidae. *See also* NW p.*131,* PE p.246, *246.*

Coda, Italian word for "tail", used to describe the added final section of a musical work, especially in the sonatas of MOZART and BEETHOVEN, although its origin lies in the BAROQUE era, above all in the music of François COUPERIN.

Codeine, white crystalline ALKALOID extracted from OPIUM by the methylation of MORPHINE, and with the properties of weak morphine. It is used in medicine as an analgesic and in the treatment of coughs, sleeplessness, neuralgia and asthma. See also MS p.119.

Code Napoléon (1804), still operative French legal code. It was intended to end the disunity of French law, and was based on Roman law. It was applied to all countries under Napoleon's control. It banned social inequality, permitted freedom of person and contract and upheld the right to own private property. *See also* MS p.*283.*

Code of Hammurabi, collection of laws compiled by HAMMURABI the Great of BABYLONIA in the 18th century BC. The code was inscribed on a column found at Susa. *See also* HC1 pp. 32, *33.*

Codex, the earliest manuscripts, bound in book form, especially classical works or the scriptures. From the Latin word meaning tree-trunk, the most famous codices are Biblical manuscripts, such as the 4th-century CODEX SINAITICUS and Codex Vaticanus and the 5th-century Codex Alexandricus. The term may also refer to a collection of laws.

Codex Sinaiticus, 4th-century manuscript of the Greek Bible found in two parts in 1849 and 1859. It contains all the New Testament and about a third of the Old Testament, and was bought by the British Museum in 1933.

Codicil, document that amends, alters, qualifies or revokes specific provisions in a WILL. It is supplementary to the main document and all laws that apply to a will apply also to its codicils.

Codling moth, small grey moth found wherever apples are grown. The larvae (caterpillars) are pale pink with brown head markings. They cause serious damage to crops by burrowing into the fruit to feed. Species *Carpocapsa pomonella. See also* PE p.172–173.

Cod liver oil, oil rich in vitamins A and D obtained from the fresh livers of cod. It is used to prevent RICKETS in children and for other nutritional purposes. Although still an important nutrient, it has largely been replaced by man-made sources of the equivalent amounts of vitamins A and D.

Cody, Samuel Franklin (1862–1913). US-born pioneer aviator. In 1896 he went to England where he subsequently took out British citizenship. He experimented with man-lifting kites and helped to plan and build the first British dirigible or steerable airship. In 1908 he built his own aeroplane. He was killed in a flying accident.

Cody, William Frederick, ("Buffalo Bill") (1846–1917), US frontiersman, scout and showman. Ned Buntline made Cody famous in his semi-fictional novels about his exploits. In 1883 Cody organized the "Wild West" exhibition with Annie Oakley and Chief Sitting Bull among his star performers.

Coeducation, teaching male and female students in the same classes. In ancient and medieval times, girls were taught separately, if at all. In Europe boys and girls began to attend the same elementary classes after the REFORMATION. In the USA, Britain and Commonwealth countries coeducation is generally accepted, although many secondary schools are single-sex establishments.

Coefficient, term multiplying a specified unknown quantity in an algebraic expression. In $5x$, 5 is the coefficient of x. In physics, it is a ratio that yields a pure number or a quantity with dimensions. *See also* SU p.34.

Coefficient of expansion. *See* EXPANSION, COEFFICIENT OF.

Coefficient of friction. *See*: FRICTION, COEFFICIENT OF

Coelacanth, bony fish of the genus *Latimeria.* Thought to be extinct for more than 60 million years, it was found in deep waters off the African coast in 1938. It is grey-brown with lobed fins that have fleshy bases. The scales and bony plates are unlike those of modern fish. Length: 1.5m (5ft). Order Crosopterygii; species *Latimeria chalumnae. See also* NW p.124, *124.*

Coelenterata, phylum of aquatic animals which include JELLYFISH, SEA ANEMONES, CORALS and hydroids. Characterized by a digestive cavity that forms the main body cavity, they were the first animal group to reach the tissue level of organization. Coelenterates are radially symmetrical, jelly-like, and have a nerve net and one body opening. Reproduction is sexual and asexual; regeneration also occurs. There are about 9,000 species. *See also* NW pp.*72,* 82–83, *82–83.*

Coelom, true body cavity, or space between an inner digestive tube and outer body wall, that provides room for additional organs. Indications of a coelom appear in roundworms but the first true coelom appears among earthworms and other segmented worms. *See also* NW pp.74–75.

Coelostat, mirror attachment for fixed astronomical telescopes which, driven by a motor so that it moves on an axis parallel to the Earth's axis of rotation, continuously reflects the same portion of sky into the telescope.

Coenzyme, a non-protein organic molecule, usually containing a vitamin and phosphorus. When combined with an apoenzyme, a protein molecule, it activates an ENZYME. A coenzyme always regains its original structure even though it may have been altered during a reaction. *See also* SU p.*154.*

Coffee, plant and the popular caffeine beverage produced from its seeds (coffee beans). The coffee plants of the genus *Coffea* are evergreen and have white flowers. More than 100 different kinds of coffee beans are marketed; some are used to produce "instant" coffee. Family Rubiaceae. *See also* PE pp.208–209.

Coffer dam, usually, but not always, temporary watertight enclosure from which water is pumped to permit construction or excavation of a main dam. Coffer dams are usually constructed of pile-driven steel sheeting and posts. *See also* MM p.*199.*

Coggan, Frederick Donald (1909–), Archbishop of Centerbury since 1974. He was Bishop of Bradford (1956–61) and Archbishop of York (1961–74). He is a New Testament scholar and was Professor of New Testament at Wycliffe College, Toronto (1937–44).

Coghill, Nevill Henry Kendal Aylmer (1899–), British university professor and theatrical producer. He is noted for his dramatic productions which include *A Midsummer Night's Dream* (1945), *Pilgrim's Progress* (1951) and *Dr Faustus* (1966). He was professor of English literature at Oxford University (1957–66).

Cognac, town in W France, on the Charente River, 37km (23 miles) W of Angoulême, in Charente département. FRANCIS I was born there. In the 16th century it was a HUGUENOT stronghold. Cognac brandy was first made in the 18th century, and has been produced there ever since. Cognac distilling is the major industry. Casks and bottles are made locally. Pop. 22,000.

Cognitive development theory, in developmental psychology, a theory concerned with growth in the processes of perceiving, thinking and knowing. Swiss psychologist Jean PIAGET holds that cognitive processes develop through four stages from birth to adolescence. During the first stage the child is most concerned with objects around him. Not until the final stage can a person make full use of symbols and logic. *See also* MS p.152.

Cognitive dissonance, social psychology theory developed by the psychologist Leon Festinger in the 1950s. Its basic idea is that a person strives for consistency between his beliefs, attitudes and behaviour. When conflicts or "dissonance" occur, he tries to reduce the resulting discomfort by altering his beliefs to fit his behaviour, or vice versa.

Cognitive psychology, broad area of psychology concerned with perceiving, thinking and knowing. It investigates such matters as the way in which people perceive information by sight or hearing; how they organize, store, remember and use information; and the use they make of language; *See also* COGNITIVE DEVELOPMENT THEORY.

Cohen, Harriet (1901–1967), British pianist. VAUGHAN WILLIAMS, FRICKER and Arnold BAX each wrote a concerto for her. She injured her right hand in 1948 and Bax wrote his *Concertino* for left hand, the first performance of which she gave in 1950.

Cohen, Leonard Norman (1934–), Canadian writer and singer. His poetry includes *The Spice-Box of Earth* (1961), *Flowers for Hitler* (1964), and *Parasites of Heaven* (1966). He also was popular as a singer during the 1960s. He has written two novels: *The Favourite Game* (1963) and *Beautiful Losers* (1966).

Cohesion, the attraction of the atoms, ions or molecules of a substance for each other. Weak cohesive forces permit the fluidity of liquids; those of solids are much stronger. *See also* ADHESION.

Cohn, Ferdinand Julius (1828–98), German botanist, one of the founders of BACTERIOLOGY as a separate discipline. He began to study bacteria in 1868 and edited *Contributions to the Biology of Plants* in 1870. He conducted research into the bacterial causes of infectious disease.

Cohnheim, Julius Friedrich (1839–84), German pathologist known for his work in determining changes occurring in tissues of diseased animals. He also developed the now-standard technique of freezing tissue before slicing it for examination under a microscope.

Coimbatore, city in S India, in Tamil Nadu state, on the River Noyil; 451km (280 miles) SW of Madras. It occupies a strategic position at the E entrance to Pālghāt Gap, a major break in the Western Ghāts. It is the site of the ancient Hindu pagoda of Perur. Industries: textiles, tanning, food processing, manufacture of machinery. Pop. (1971) 356,368.

Coimbra, city in W central Portugal, 174km (108 miles) NNE of Lisbon, on the River Mondego; capital of Coimbra district. It is a market centre for the region. It has Roman and Moorish ruins, a 12th-century cathedral and a university (1290). Pop. 108,000.

Coins, small stamped metal discs of standard sizes used as tokens of money in commercial transactions. The earliest coins are of Lydian origin, and date to the 7th century BC. Coins of early date have also been found in China and India. Ancient coins usually contained a specific quantity of precious metal, normally gold or silver; they were stamped with the symbol of the issuing authority, monarch and die, in order to verify the quality and weight of the metal. Coins were the only objects used regularly for trade in the ancient world, and the distribution of coins outside the area in which they were issued is often taken as an indication of the wealth and standing of that region. The use of coins for everyday transactions was greatly reduced after the fall of the Roman Empire with the growth of a manorial economy and the weak monarchies, but in England the Anglo-Saxons had a complex system of both gold and silver coins, produced on dies in many parts of the country under the strict supervision of the king. Monarchs throughout the Middle Ages regarded control of the coinage as an important privilege of kingship, and although they issued severe punishments to individuals "clipping' the coins or lessening the gold or silver content, such debasement of the coinage was occasionally used by the kings themselves, such as Henry VIII in the 1540s, to raise revenue. With the introduction of banknotes in the late 17th century, and the gradual decline of the quantity of precious metal in each coin to tiny amounts, the role of coins changed. They acquired only notional value, and became used merely for smaller money transactions. All coins in mainland Britain since the mid-19th century have been produced at the ROYAL MINT. *See also* index to *History and Culture 1*; MS pp.*261*, *308*.

Coir, fibre made from the husks of COCONUTS. It is used in making cords, ropes, mats and baskets. *See also* PE pp.194, 216.

Coke, Sir Edward (1552–1634), English jurist. He became attorney-general in 1594, and chief justice of the Common Pleas in 1606. As chief justice of the King's Bench (1613), he championed the COMMON LAW, and in Parliament after 1620 developed it to oppose the king's assumption of DIVINE RIGHT. He helped to draft the PETITION OF RIGHT (1628). *See also* HC1 p.*286*.

Coke, Thomas William, Earl of Leicester, "Coke of Holkham" (1752–1842), British agriculturist who introduced revolutionary new methods of arable farming and cattle breeding. He converted NW Norfolk from a rye-growing region into a wheat-growing district and introduced improved breeds of sheep, cattle and pigs. An advocate of parliamentary reform, he was Whig MP for Norfolk several times between 1776 and 1833. *See also* HC2 p.286.

Coke, solid fuel left behind as a residue in coking ovens after coal has been heated without air to drive off most of the volatile matter. It is used mainly in steelmaking for fuelling blast furnaces. Its high calorific value is due to the high carbon content – more than 90%. Coke is a stiff, porous, grey mass of carbon mixed with small amounts of minerals, sulphur and residual volatiles; the exact proportions of these depend on the type of coal used and the temperature to which it is heated. A temperature of 900–1,150°C (1,650–2,100°F) is required to produce coke for blast furnaces and for domestic heating; for foundry coke, 750–900°C (1,400–1650°F). Petroleum coke is the solid residue from the cracking of oil in refineries. *See also* MM pp.21, 29, 77, *77*.

Col, low smooth depression in a mountain range, often forming a pass through it. It is generally caused by the action of two opposing glaciers, the heads of which are commonly separated by an ARÊTE a sharp-crested ridge between the two CIRQUES (valleys) formed by the glaciers.

Colbert, Jean Baptiste (1619–83), French statesman, the principal exponent of MERCANTILISM in economic policy. He became controller-general to Louis XIV in 1665, and tried to reform the taxes. His major effort was to encourage the growth of French industry and trade; his tariffs led to economic conflict with the Netherlands. *See also* HC1 pp.314, 315.

Colborne, Sir John, 1st Baron Seaton (1778–1863), Canadian soldier and administrator. His career began in the British army, and he served as lieutenant governor of Upper Canada (1828–36). He commanded the loyalist forces against the rebels in 1837 and was appointed governor-in-chief of Canada in 1839.

Colchester, town in Essex, SE England, on the River Colne, 80km (50 miles) NE of London. It is a market centre for the surrounding agricultural and horticultural area. The first Roman colony in Britain was settled there in AD 43 and was attacked by BOADICEA (Boudicca) in AD 61. It has a Roman wall and a fine Norman castle. Industries: food processing, agricultural engineering, footwear. Pop. 76,000. *See also* HC1 pp.100–101.

Colchicum, genus of about 30 species of flowering plants, including *C. autumnale*, the autumn crocus or meadow saffron. Species grow throughout Eurasia, and have pink, white, blue or purple crocus-like flowers which appear in the autumn. The swollen underground stem contains the ALKALOID colchicine, used to treat rheumatism and gout. It is also employed in genetic and cellular research, as it inhibits MITOSIS (cell division). This property makes colchicine valuable in cancer research and as an IMMUNOSUPPRESSIVE DRUG. Family Liliaceae.

Colchis, ancient country in the Caucasus region on the E side of the Black Sea. In Greek legend it was the home of MEDEA. It was dominated successively by Persia, Greece and Rome and in the 6th century AD was disputed between Byzantium and Persia. Today it is part of Georgia, USSR.

Cold, common, mild, contagious virus infection of the upper respiratory tract. Symptoms include obstruction and inflammation of the nose, headache, sore throat, a cough and hoarseness. A cold usually disappears within a few days. Fever-reducing and pain-relieving drugs, as well as decongestants, may relieve symptoms and bring comfort; rest is recommended for heavy colds. Antibiotics may be prescribed where a bacterial infection is also present.

Cold Comfort Farm (1932), novel by Stella Gibbons (1902–). Very popular when published, it is a hilarious parody on the over-serious treatment of rural life in English fiction of the day.

Cold cream, cosmetic especially used for removing make-up. It consists of a perfumed emulsion of mineral oil, or paraffin wax, and water; the cooling effect on the skin is produced when the water evaporates.

Cold sore, also called fever blister, a small sore, often found around the lips, sometimes on the cheeks, ears or genitals. It first appears as a tiny fluid-filled blister on a red skin patch, sometimes becomes pus-filled, and then dries up, leaving a yellowish or brownish crust for a week or two. Caused by a virus – *Herpes simplex* – it is often associated with a cold, sometimes with other febrile diseases, sunburn or pneumonia.

Coldstream, Sir William Menzies (1908–), British painter who exhibited with and became a member of the LONDON GROUP in 1934. In 1937 he founded, with Victor PASMORE, the EUSTON ROAD SCHOOL of Drawing and Painting; in 1943 he was appointed an Official War Artist. His work shows the strong influence of nature and has developed towards NATURALISM.

Coldstream, town in the Borders Region SE Scotland, on the English border. Gen. MONCK's troups (later named the Coldstream Guards) marched from there into England in 1660. Pop. 1,300.

Coldstream Guards, royal regiment in the British Household Brigade. It was first raised at Coldstream, Scotland, *c.*1650 and played an important role in the restoration of CHARLES II.

Cold war, political, ideological and economic confrontation between the USA and USSR and their allies after 1945. Despite incidents such as the BERLIN blockade (1948–49) and the CUBAN MISSILE CRISIS, and many threats of retaliatory war by both sides, open warfare never occurred. Each side built up worldwide power blocs, which began to break up in the mid-1960s. *See also* HC2 pp.234–235, 306–307.

Cole, George Douglas Howard (1889–1959), British socialist, economist and historian. He was an exponent of guild socialism in the 1920s and was chairman of the Fabian Society (1939–46). He held a professorship at Oxford (1944–57). His many works include *A Short History of the British Working-Class Movement* (1927) and *A History of Socialist Thought* (1953–70).

Cole, Nat King (1919–65), US singer and pianist, *b.* Nathaniel Adams Cole. He was a jazz pianist in the King Cole Trio from 1939 but in the 1950s achieved popularity as a singer of many hit songs. These included *Unforgettable*, *Mona Lisa* and *Nature Boy*.

Cole, Thomas (1801–48) US landscape painter, *b.* England. A founder of the HUDSON RIVER SCHOOL, he revelled in the grandeur of the Hudson River valley and the Catskill Mts, subjects of many of his Romantic landscapes.

Colechurch, Peter de, priest who was the architect of the first London Bridge. A multi-storey construction built on piers across the River Thames, it took thirty years to build and was completed in 1209. *See also* MM p.191.

Coleman, Ornette (1930–), US jazz alto saxophonist and composer. From the late 1950s he played in a controversial, original style with his own groups and occasionally with John COLTRANE and Eric Dolphy. He was important in the development of jazz in the 1960s and 1970s.

Colenso, John William (1814–83), British Bishop of Natal from 1853 to 1869. His published denial of the literal truth of the Bible and his opposition to the doctrine of eternal punishment made a *cause célèbre*. He was deposed in 1869 but refused to leave his cathedral (to which he was entitled by law) even after excommunication by the Archbishop of Cape Town.

Coleoptera, largest order of the animal kingdom, the BEETLES. They are insects which have complete metamorphosis. Most possess two pairs of wings, the forward pair usually being hard covers which fold over the flying pair. More than 350,000 species are known, many of them pests called WEEVILS. Beetles include some of the largest and many of the smallest of all insects. Their larvae are either maggot-like, or elongated with six legs. *See* NW pp.106–107, 114.

Coleridge, Samuel Taylor (1772–1834), British Romantic poet and critic. His literary output was mainly criticism, political journalism and philosophy, but he is chiefly remembered for the poems *The Rime of the Ancient Mariner*, *Kubla Khan* and *Christabel*. In 1798 he and WORDSWORTH published *Lyrical Ballads*, a fundamental work of the English Romantic movement. His Shakespearean criticism, his work on critical theory, *Biographia Literaria* (1817), and his writings on German metaphysics were influential during the 19th century. *See also* HC2 p.100.

Coleridge-Taylor, Samuel (1875–1912), British composer. He wrote concertos, chamber and choral music and earned world fame for his *Hiawatha* trilogy (1898–1900), which excited great interest for its infectious rhythm, strong melody and colourful orchestration.

Coles Colossus, lorry made to carry cranes, powered by a Rolls-Royce 300bhp turbo-charged diesel; extra parts can be added to turn it into a tower crane. The vehicle has hydro-pneumatic suspension. *See also* MM p.*137*.

Colet, John (*c.*1467–1519), English humanist and theologian. He was appointed Dean of ST PAUL'S in 1504. In 1509 he planned and endowed St Paul's School. With William Lily he wrote the Latin grammar that became known as the Eton grammar and was used in the teaching of Latin for generations. *See also* HC1 pp.268, 282.

Colette (1873–1954), French novelist, real name Sidonie Gabrielle. Her first works, including the first four *Claudine* novels (1900–03), were published under her first husband's pseudonym, Willy. Most of her novels contain strong autobiographical elements, and have a notably sensitive lyricism. Among her best known works are *Chéri* (1920), *The Last of Chéri* (1926) and *Gigi* (1944).

Coleus, genus of bushy house or garden plants of the mint family native to Africa and Indonesia, noted for their oval,

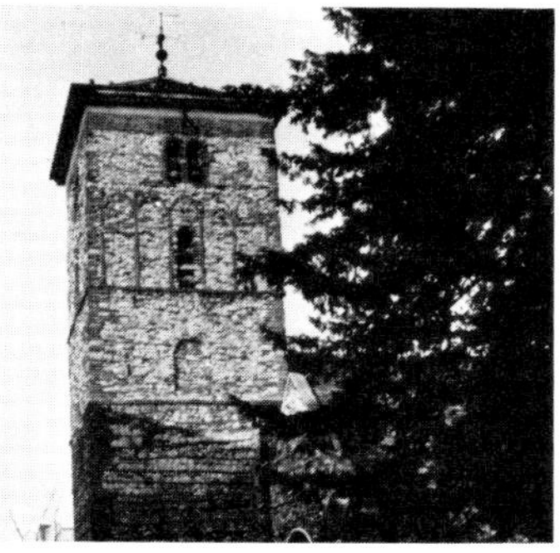

Colchester was the site of the first Roman colony in England, settled in AD 43.

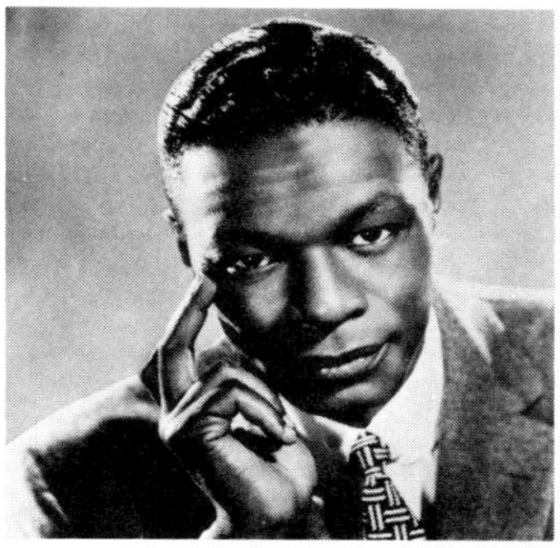

Nat King Cole, the singer whose voice was once likened to "a cat walking on velvet".

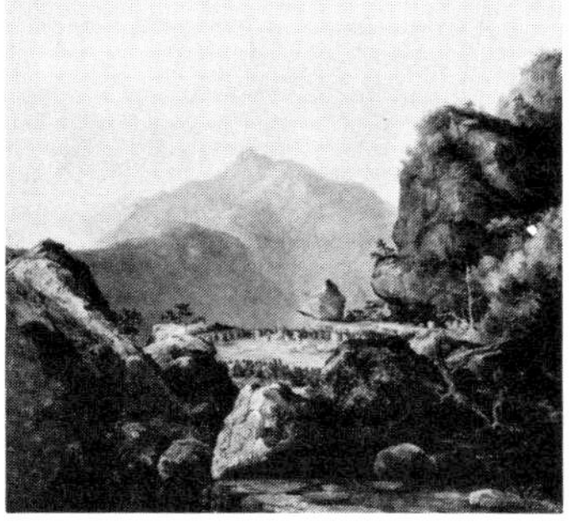

Thomas Cole; a scene from *Last of the Mohicans* by the English-born US painter.

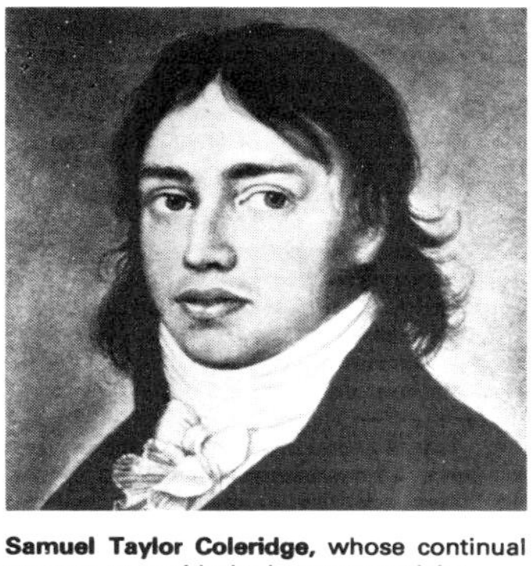

Samuel Taylor Coleridge, whose continual concern was with the human creativity.

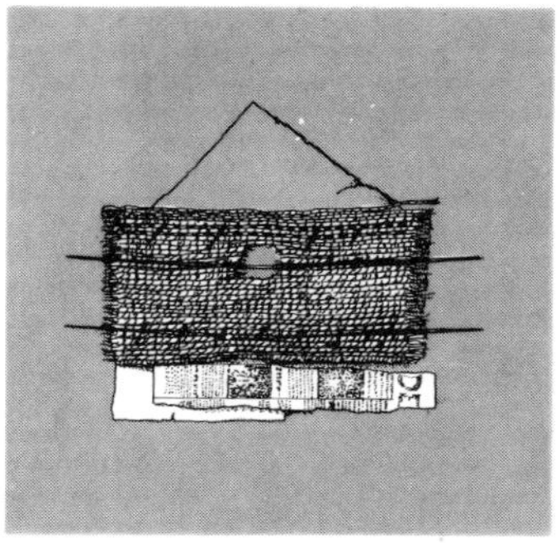

Collage was important in that it broke the bounds of two-dimensional painting.

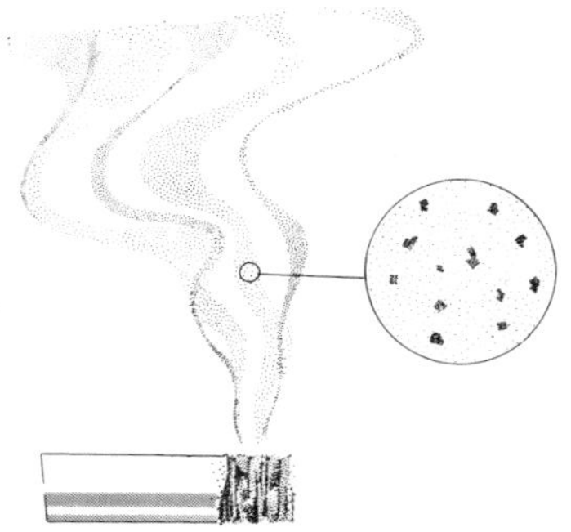

Colloids take the form of extremely fine particles; smoke is a good example.

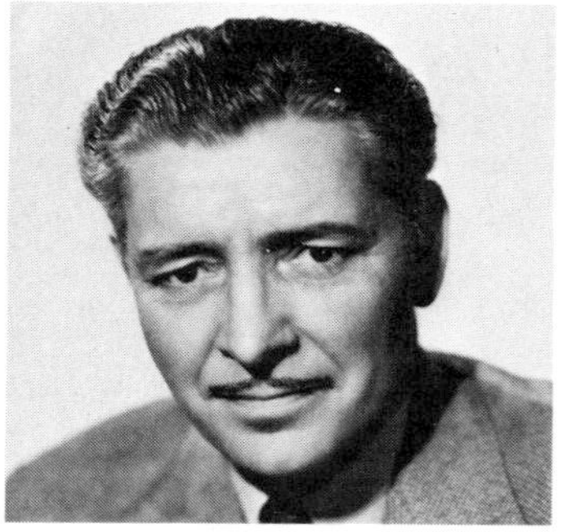

Ronald Colman, film star of the 1920s and 1930s, played the sophisticated leading man.

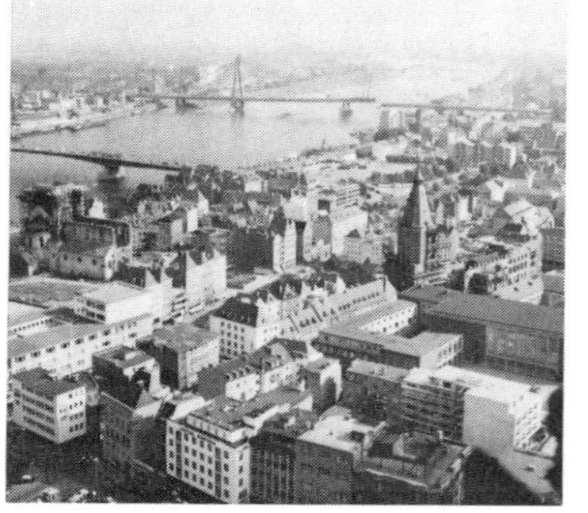

Cologne lies at the junction of the east-west, north-south trade routes of Europe.

serrated leaves of reddish, green or yellow combinations. They are propagated by stem cuttings or by seeds. Height: to 90cm (36in). Family Labiatae.

Colic, spasmodic, cramp-like pain in the abdomen usually becoming intense, subsiding and then recurring. It may be associated with the gall bladder (biliary colic), kidney or ureter (renal colic), intestines (intestinal colic) or other abdominal organs. *See also* MS p.*93*.

Coligny, Gaspard de, Comte de Châtillon (1519–72), French Protestant leader. He served France in Italy and Spain in the 1540s and 1550s and became leader of the HUGUENOT faction in 1569. He became adviser to Charles IX in 1571, but was opposed by the king's mother Catherine de'Medici, who may have persuaded Charles to order the MASSACRE OF ST BARTHOLOMEW, in which Coligny was killed.

Colitis, inflammation of the lining of the colon, or large intestine, that produces bowel changes, usually diarrhoea and cramp-like pains. It may be acute and caused by infection, or chronic and often due to an emotional problem. In severe chronic ulcerative colitis, the colon lining ulcerates and bleeds. *See also* MS pp.92–93.

Collage, composition made up of various materials – cardboard, string, fabrics, etc – which are pasted on to a canvas or other background. It was developed (1912) by PICASSO and BRAQUE, perfected by Juan GRIS, and much favoured by CUBISTS, DADAISTS and later artists. *See also* HC2 pp.176–177, 202.

Collagen, protein substance that is the main constituent of bones, tendons, cartilage, connective tissue and skin. It is made up of inelastic fibres. *See also* MS p.*57*.

Collateral, the assets that are put up by a borrower to secure a loan. Most financial institutions will not provide loans without some form of collateral.

Collective bargaining, process through which wages and other conditions of employment are determined by workers who belong to a trade union. Representatives of the workers and their employer's management meet to negotiate terms for an agreement, which is usually to remain in force for a specified period. If negotiations break down the matter may be put before a body for ARBITRATION or, in the last resort, a strike or lockout may result.

Collective farms, large co-operative farms whose policy is determined by the state. The term usually refers to farms in the USSR, where enfofced COLLECTIVIZATION or privately owned peasant holdings was begun by Joseph STALIN in 1929. Dissatisfaction led to modifications of the policy, so allowing members to own some livestock and a plot of land. By 1938 more than 90% of formerly private land had been collectivized in 235,000 units. By 1972 further amalgamation of collective farms had reduced the number to 32,000. The state owns the farm's land and equipment and pays guaranteed prices for produce, although farmers can keep part of the proceeds from their private plots. *See also* HC2 p.198.

Collective security, method by which a group of nations pledge mutual support in the event of attack from an outside power. Originally collective security agreements were global in scope (eg, the League of Nations, the United Nations), although neither of these organizations has been able to operate one principle successfully.

Collectivism, political and economic theory taken up by Socialist, Communist and Fascist states. Each member of the state is subordinated to a social collectivity such as a state or social class, an idea carried to its extreme in Communist systems with a minimum of private ownership and a totally planned economy.

Collectivization, agricultural policy initiated in the USSR in the 1920s and in China after the Communist takeover of 1949. With the object of modernizing agriculture and making it more efficient, small peasant holdings were combined and agriculture brought under state control.

College of Arms. *See* COLLEGE OF HERALDS.

College of Heralds, English heraldic body founded (1484) by Richard III and incorporating the heralds of the Royal HOUSEHOLD. The college was reincorporated (1555) by Royal Charter, issued by Mary Tudor and Philip II. The college's three Kings of Arms, six Heralds and four Pursuivants specialize in heraldic and genealogical research. The college has the right to bear arms and the Kings of Arms grant arms by letters patent.

Collembola, small, wingless insects, commonly called springtails, which inhabit dark, moist places. *See also* NW p.106.

Collett, Charles (1863–1925) French painter and etcher. He is best known for his scenes of peasant and maritime life, such as *Au Pays de la Mer* (1898).

Collie, smooth-coated or long-haired working dog, originally bred in Scotland. It has a lean, wedge-shaped head with small triangular ears. The long body is set on strong straight legs and the tail is long and curved. The coat, usually black-and-white or tan, may be rough or smooth Height: to 66cm (26in) at the shoulder.

Collier, Arthur (1680–1732), English philosopher. In his principal work, *Clavis Universalis* (1713), Collier advocated a form of idealism similar to that held by George BERKELEY.

Collimator, lens system used to produce a parallel or near parallel beam of light, sub-atomic particles or other radiation. Light passing through a fine slit at the focus of a convex lens will be rendered parallel by the lens. A collimated beam is essential for many optical purposes.

Colling, name of two British brothers who developed new breeds of cattle. From 1782 Charles (1751–1826) and later Robert (1749–1820) began work to improve the quality of cattle in the Tees River valley. They were the first to breed Shorthorn or Durham beef cattle.

Collingwood, Cuthbert, Lord (1748–1810), British naval commander. In 1797 he became a rear-admiral and was made vice-admiral in 1804. He took part in the Battle of the Glorious First of June off Brest in 1794 and off Cape St Vincent in 1797. In 1805 he was Nelson's second-in-command at Trafalgar, taking command after Nelson's death in battle.

Collingwood, Robin George (1889–1943), British philosopher and historian. He tried to integrate philosophy and history, which he saw as interdependent. He was also an expert on Roman history and archaeology. His works include *Speculum Mentis* (1924), *The Principles of Art* (1937) and *The Idea of History* (1946).

Collins, Lewis John, Canon (1905–), British clergyman. From 1948 he was Canon of St Paul's Cathedral, London. He caused some controversy by his involvement in nuclear disarmament and other political movements as chairman of the Campaign for Nuclear Disarmament (CND) (1958–64).

Collins, Lottie (1866–1910), British music-hall artist who was renowned for her presentation of the song *Ta-Ra-Ra-Boom-De-Ay*. She first performed the song and accompanying high-kick dance in the London pantomime *Dick Whittington* in 1891.

Collins, Michael (1890–1922), Irish revolutionary. He fought in the EASTER RISING in 1916 and helped to establish the Irish Assembly (Dáil) in 1918. He became intelligence director for the SINN FEIN and helped to negotiate self-government for southern Ireland in 1921. He was killed in the ensuing civil war. *See also* HC2 p.*163*.

Collins, William (1721–59), British poet. His work foreshadowed Romanticism, and he wrote some fine lyrical verse, notably his *Ode to Evening* and *How Sleep the Brave* (1746). He later became insane.

Collins, William Wilkie (1824–89), British novelist. He made important contributions to the development of the genre of the detective story in books such as *The Woman in White* (1860) and *The Moonstone* (1868)and *No Name* (1862). collaborated with Charles DICKENS in writing many stories, including *The Wreck of the Golden Mary*.

Collodi, Carlo (1826–90), Italian journalist and newspaper editor, real name Carlo Lorenzini. The founder of two satirical journals, he is remembered as the author of the classic children's story PINOCCHIO (1881; English translation 1892), a tale of a marionette turned into a boy.

Colloid, substance composed of fine particles which can be readily dispersed in a continuous phase. A solid dispersed in a liquid is termed a sol, a solid or a liquid in a gas an aerosol, a liquid in a liquid an emulsion, and a gas in either a liquid or a solid a foam. Chemists identify three main types: reversible, irreversible, and association colloids. Reversible colloids – including cellulose, proteins, haemoglobin, nylon, polystyrene and vulcanized rubber – form true solutions spontaneously when a dry colloid and a dispersion medium are brought together. Sols (dilute suspensions), emulsions, aerosols, foams and pastes (concentrated suspensions) are irreversible colloidal suspensions. Soaps, detergents and some dyes are examples of association colloids.

Colloidal condensation, technique for preparing irreversible sols. A supersaturated solution may be condensed so that a large number of small particles are produced, rather than a crystallization into large agglomerates. Electrodialysis has been used to control the deposition.

Colloidal dispersion, technique for preparing a colloidal system such as an emulsion or a foam. Emulsions are stabilized by an emulsifying agent, such as proteins or clay; foams are stabilized by foaming agents. Oil-in-water emulsions are used in polishes, cosmetic preparations and foodstuffs such as margarine and mayonnaise. Meringue and fire-fighting preparations are examples of foams.

Colloidal particle, a solid or liquid droplet measuring between 10^{-6} and 10^{-3}mm in diameter and composed of an aggregate of molecules or a single giant molecule. Such particles may be formed by breaking-down macroscopic particles by mechanical or chemical dissociation (known as peptizing) or by preparing a supersaturated solution which then aggregates.

Collotype, photo-mechanical printing process popular in Europe at the end of the 19th century. The only process which reproduces photographic documents without using a screen (resulting in minute dots on the printed impression), its use has been revived for high quality reproduction either in black or colour of posters, paintings and transparent illustrations.

Colman, George ("the Elder") (1732–94), British playwright and manager. His best-known plays were *The Jealous Wife* (1761) and *The Clandestine Marriage* (1766), which he wrote with David Garrick. He managed Covent Garden (1767–74) and in 1776 took over the Haymarket theatre.

Colman, Ronald (1891–1958), British cinema actor. After making films in England he went to the USA in 1920, where he soon achieved success by appearing as the leading man opposite Lilian GISH in *White Sister* (1925). He gave typically suave performances in *A Tale of Two Cities* (1935) and *The Prisoner of Zenda* (1937).

Colobus, also called guereza, large monkey of equatorial Africa. It is a diurnal tree-dweller that feeds on leaves and uses its hind legs for precise leaps between branches. The three species have been hunted almost to the point of extinction for their decorative fur. *See also* NW pp.*168, 213*.

Cologne (Köln), city in Nordrhein-Westfalen state, W central West Germany on the River Rhine (Rhein), 32km (20 miles) S of Düsseldorf. It is a commercial, industrial and transportation centre and a river port. The Romans established a fortress at Cologne in AD 50 and it remained in their control until the 5th century. The city was made an archbishopric by Charlemagne in 785. It declined towards the end of the Middle Ages and was ceded to Prussia in 1815. It has a cathedral (started in 1248, completed 1880), and the Gürzenich, a Renaissance patrician's house. Industries: oil refining, petrochemicals, chemicals, engineering, textiles, food processing. Pop. (1975 est.) 1,022,075

Colombe, Jean Michel. *See* TRÈS RICHES HENRES.

Colombia, republic in NW South America. It has high Andean peaks and lowland equatorial swamplands and a wide range of climate. Agriculture is the basis of the economy and Columbia ranks second only to Brazil in the production of coffee. Other major crops include beans, rice, maize, cotton, sugar cane and bananas. There are important mineral deposits, including gold, platinum and emeralds. Oil is becoming increasingly important. Industries include chemicals and food processing. The capital is Bogotá. The country's development has been hampered by internal violence. Area: 1,138,914sq km (439,735sq miles). Pop. (1975 est.) 23,542,000. *See* MW pp.58.

Columbo, capital and largest city of SRI LANKA, on the Indian Ocean at the mouth of the River Kelani. Previously ruled by the Portuguese and the Dutch, it became capital of the British Crown Colony of Ceylon in 1802. A major port, Colombo's industries also include gem cutting, chemicals, and ivory carving. Pop. (1974 est.) 592,000.

Colombo Plan, organization which seeks to foster the co-operative economic development of countries in S and SE Asia. It was started by the COMMONWEALTH in 1951, originally for six years, and now includes 24 nations, including the USA. It fosters bilateral agreements providing various kinds of aid, including educational, technical and financial.

Colón, port in central Panama at the Caribbean end of the Panama Canal; second largest city in Panama. It is an important commercial centre and was made a free trade zone in 1953. It was founded in 1850 as Aspinwall by Americans working on a trans-Panama railway. Its name was changed to Colón in 1890. Pop. (1970) 67,695.

Colon, the large intestine, that part of the digestive tract that extends from the small intestine to the rectum. It begins at a blind pouch, the caecum, passes upward (the ascending colon) along the right side of the abdomen, then across (the transverse colon) and downward (the descending colon). It then curves and opens into the rectum, where the contents are held until defecation. The colon absorbs water from digested food and allows bacterial action for the formation of faeces. *See also* DIGESTIVE SYSTEM; MS p.*68*.

Colonialism, control by one country over a dependent area or people. Although it is associated with modern political history, the practice is ancient. In Western colonial history, economic, political, military, cultural and psychological factors have been involved in the desire to colonize. After WWII the term came to imply exploitation, and in the West numerous former colonies became independent nations. *See also* IMPERIALISM; HC2 pp.46–47, 124–125, 246–247.

Colonial Office, defunct department of the British government. The first secretary of state for the American colonies was appointed in 1768, but from 1782 to 1812 his duties were discharged by the HOME OFFICE, and then combined with the WAR DEPARTMENT. In 1812 military and colonial affairs were separated, and in 1854 the Office became an independent department, until 1966, when it was joined to the Commonwealth Relations Office to form the COMMONWEALTH OFFICE. *See also* HC2 p.*132*.

Colonnade, series of columns placed at regular intervals. When in front of a building, a colonnade is called a portico. A colonnade surrounding a building or an open court within a building is called a peristyle, an extended roofed one, a stoa.

Colonne, Judas "Édouard" (1838–1910), French musician. He was leading violin of the Paris Opéra until 1873, when he founded his own orchestra.

Colophon, method in early printed works by which a printer detailed his role in the creation of a book, usually in a paragraph at the end. It has since come to mean a short statement giving the printer's name, the typeface and paper used, generally on the reverse of the title page. The term also denotes any publisher's symbol.

Colorado, state in W USA; highest state in the nation, with an average elevation of 2,073m (6,800ft). In the W half of the state are the ranges of the Rocky Mts, and in the E the W part of the Great Plains. Major rivers are the Colorado, Rio Grande, Arkansas and South Platte. The most important agricultural activity is the raising of sheep and cattle on the Plains. Sugar-beet, maize and hay are grown using extensive irrigation. Industries include food processing, transport and electrical equipment, chemicals and timber. Tourism also plays a vital role in the state's economy. The major towns are Denver, the state capital, Colorado Springs and Pueblo.

The USA acquired the E part of the state from France in the Louisiana Purchase in 1803. The remaindir was ceded by Mexico in 1848 after the Mexican War. The discovery of gold and silver promoted immigration from other states and Colorado became a territory in 1861. It joined the Union in 1876. The building of the railways after 1870 also led to an increase in the number of settlers. Area: 270,000sq km (104,247sq miles). Pop. (1975 est.) 2,534,000. *See also* MW pp.175; *176*.

Colorado potato beetle, oval beetle that is a major pest of potatoes and other members of the potato family, including the tomato and aubergine. Adults are similar in shape to ladybirds but twice as long and are yellow with black stripes or spots. They are becoming established across Europe, despite the use of insecticides such as lead arsenate. Species: *Leptinotarsa decemlineata*. *See also* NW p.113.

Colorado River, major river in SW USA; rises in the Rocky Mts in N Colorado, flows generally SW into the Gulf of California, passing through the Grand Canyon. There are many national parks and irrigation and hydroelectric power schemes along the river's course. Length: 2,333km (1,450 miles). *See also* PE p.*124*.

Coloratura, term used to describe music of an elaborate, highly "coloured" kind, decorated with trills and runs. It is also used to refer to a soprano whose voice is of the technical ability required to sing music of this kind, especially of the Baroque and Classical periods.

Colosseum, ampitheatre in Rome built AD 72–81 by the Emperor Vespasian and his sons Titus and Domitian. Oval in shape, measuring 189 × 156m (620 × 513ft) by 45.7m (150ft) high, and seating 45,000, it was used for gladiatorial contests. The Colosseum is remarkable for its size and the way in which limestone and concrete were used in its architecture – only its ornamentation being of marble – and for its superimposed use of the architectural ORDERS – Doric, Ionic and Corinthian – on the exterior. According to tradition Christians were used in the gladiatorial games there. *See also* HC1 p.*107*.

Colossians, Epistle to the, one of the epistles in the NEW TESTAMENT written by the apostle PAUL and addressed to the Church at Colossae, a city in SW Phrygia (now central Turkey).

Colossus of Rhodes. *See* RHODES, COLOSSUS OF.

Colostrum, milk-like fluid produced by the female mammary glands immediately following the birth of offspring; it precedes true milk, which is produced after about three days. Colostrum is rich in protein, and the antibodies give the suckling some immunity from infection.

Colour, sensation experienced when light of sufficient brightness and of a particular wavelength strikes the retina of the eye. Normal daylight (white light) is composed of a spectrum of pure (primary) colours, each of which has a different wavelength. The primary colours can be placed in seven bands – red, orange, yellow, green, blue, indigo and violet – of decreasing wavelength. A pure spectral colour is called a hue. If the colour is not pure but contains some white it is "desaturated" and is called a tint. Saturation is the degree to which a colour departs from white and approaches a pure hue. A colour may also have luminosity, or brightness, which determines its shade. Any colour is perceived as a mixture of three primary colours: red, green and blue-violet; red and green light mix to produce yellow; red and green paint (complementary colours) mix to produce brown. *See also* SU p.98.

Colour bar. *See* APARTHEID.

Colour blindness, general term for several disorders of colour vision. The most common involves red-green vision, a hereditary defect affecting males almost exclusively, in which the person cannot tell red from green. Total colour blindness is a very rare inherited disorder in which the person sees only black, white and grey. *See also* MS p.*49*.

Colour chemistry, in colourimetric analysis, estimation of the concentration of dissolved coloured substances by comparing the colours of their solutions with those of known strength. In spectrophotometric colourimetry, light passing through a solution of unknown strength is split into its primary optical colours, the amounts of which are then measured using photoelectric cells. *See also* MM pp.244–245.

Colour coding, in electronic and electrical engineering, system of marking components, especially resistors and capacitors, so that their values appear encoded in a series of colours. It is done partly for legibility, and partly for simplicity in manufacture. *See also* SU p.130.

Colour film, photographic film available either as positive film for projection or as negative film for making colour prints. It contains three layers of light-sensitive chemicals which respond, in turn, to the optical primary colours (roughly red, green and blue) present in the light passing through the lens of the camera. Polaroid colour film contains additionally a number of coloured dyes which are released by the light-sensitive chemicals as they react to the optical primaries, so developing a colour print directly. *See also* MM pp.*219*, 230, *245*.

Colourimetry, scientific methods in which an unknown colour is compared with known colours. It is used in chemical analysis, and for checking the colour of products such as paints, dyes and pharmaceuticals. *See also* COLOUR CHEMISTRY.

Colourpoint, or Himalayan, breed of cat produced by crossing a SIAMESE with a long-haired cat and then selectively breeding the offspring. It is stocky, short-legged and round-headed. It has the light colour and dark points of the Siamese.

Colours, military, flags or standards traditionally carried by each army regiment in battle, bearing in Britain the Union Flag, the regimental crest and the name of the major battles in which the regiment had been involved. Colours originally served as a rallying point for the regiment in the confusion of battle.

Colour vision, ability of the eye to detect the different wavelengths (colours) of light. This is achieved by three types of cone cell in the retina, "red",, "green" and "blue", which respond to light of those colours. The cone cells secrete one of three different pigments that break down and generate nerve impulses which the brain then interprets to give the range of colours we perceive. *See also* MS pp.48–49.

Colquhoun, Robert (1914–63), British painter. His work, which shows the influences of Jankel Adler and Pablo PICASSO, includes *Woman with Leaping Cat* (1945) and *Woman with Still Life* (1958).

Colt, Samuel (1814–62), US inventor of the Colt revolver. A single-barrelled firearm with a revolving set of chambers, brought successively into alignment with the barrel, the Colt was patented in Europe in 1835 and in the US in 1836. Colt also invented the submarine battery and utilized the first telegraph cable underwater. He established his own plant in Hartford in 1847 at the site of the present Colt plant where the first assembly-line procedure was developed. *See also* MM p.163.

Coltrane, John William (1926–67), US jazz saxophonist, one of the leading innovators of the 1950s and 1960s. He played with Dizzy GILLESPIE (1949–51) and Miles DAVIS (1955–57) and established a reputation as an outstanding musician, noted for his use of scales rather than chord notes.

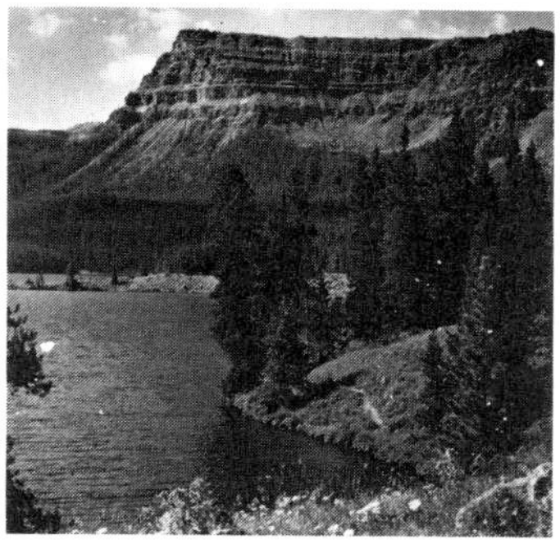

Colorado; the Amphitheatre and Trapper's Lake in the White River national forest.

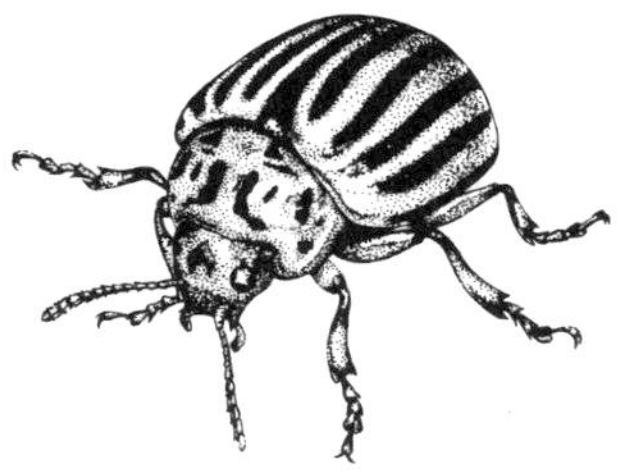

Colorado beetle prompted a ban on American potato imports in the 19th century.

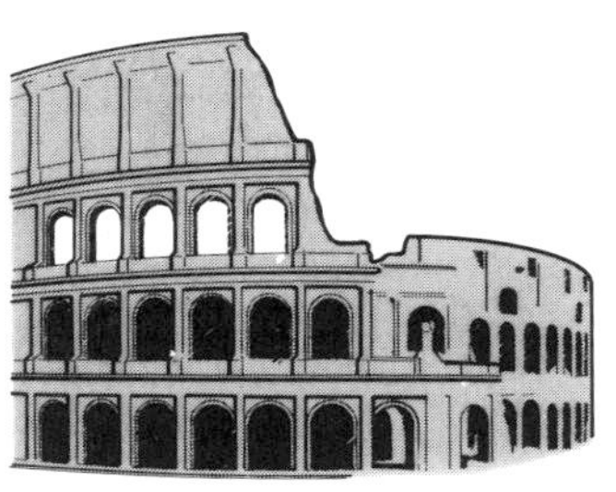

Colosseum; this Roman amphitheatre probably seated about fifty thousand people.

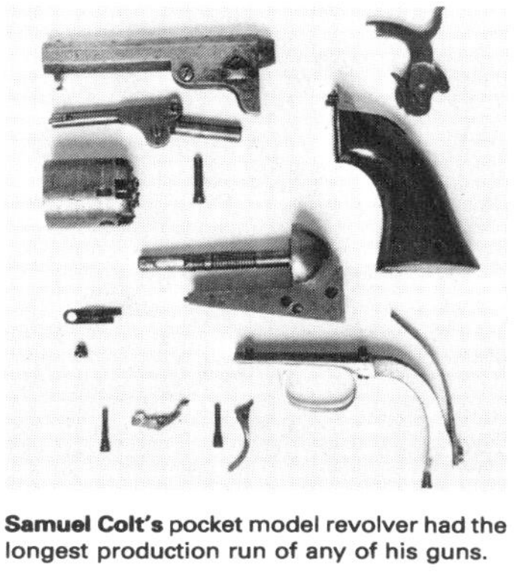

Samuel Colt's pocket model revolver had the longest production run of any of his guns.

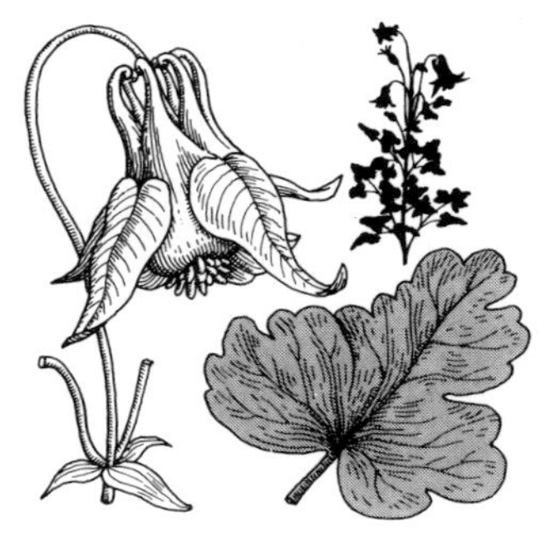

Columbine grows in thickets and woods and is one of the most beautiful of wild flowers.

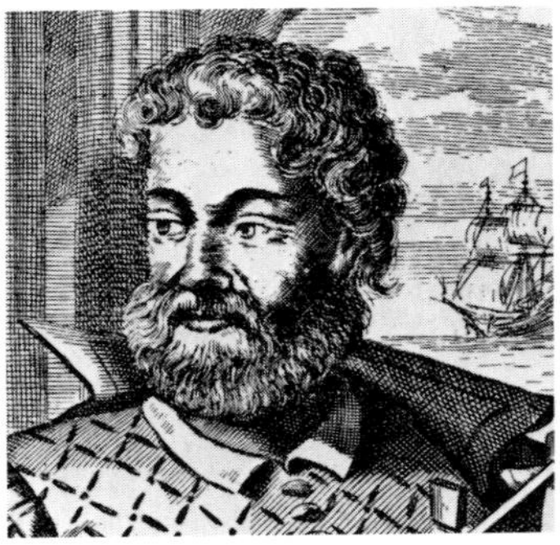

Colombus discovered the New World believing he had the western route to the Orient.

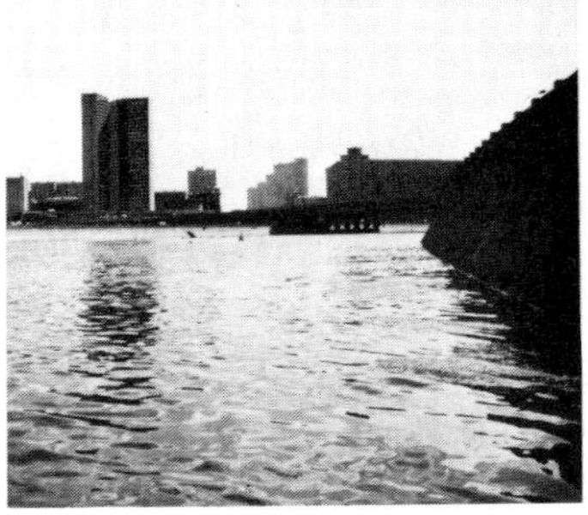

COMECON building in Moscow, centre of the Soviet bloc trading organisation.

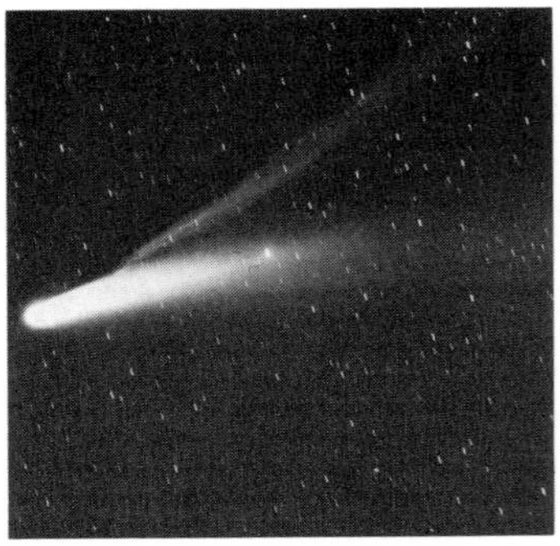

Comet, from the Greek word for "hair", conveys the image of the tail as flowing locks.

Coltsfoot, weed of the family Compositae, native to Europe but now widespread. It has small yellow flowers, and leaves whose shape gave the plant its common name. Species *Tusilago farfara. See* NW p.*59.*

Colubrid, any of about 2,500 species of mostly non-poisonous snakes of the family Colubridae, which includes about more than threequarters of the world's species of snakes. Most colubrids have terrestrial, aquatic or arboreal habitats, although a few species live underground. All lack pelvic girdles and hind limbs, and have only one lung. The few that are venomous are relatively harmless to man. *See also* SNAKE; NW pp.136–137.

Colugo. *See* FLYING LEMUR.

Colum, Padraic (1881–1972), Irish author, an associate of James JOYCE and a key figure of the IRISH LITERARY RENAISSANCE. One of Colum's many poems, *She Passed Through the Fair,* became a popular Irish song. He spent the latter part of his life in the USA, where he developed an interest in myth and folklore.

Columba, Saint (*c.*521–97), Irish missionary. He became a priest (*c.*551) and founded an important monastery at Iona (563). From his position as abbot of Iona, he strove to convert the Picts of northern Scotland to Christianity. *See also* HC1 134, 140.

Columban, or Columbanus, Saint (543–615), Irish missionary. He left Ireland *c.*590 for Gaul, accompanied by 12 monks. They settled in the Vosges, where he founded the monasteries of Luxovium and Fontaines. His adherence to Celtic practices led to his expulsion from there in 610. In 612 he founded the monastery of Bobbio in Italy.

Columbia, US film company. Founded (1920) by Harry and Jack Cohn and Joseph Brandt, it had a run of successes in the 1930s directed by Frank CAPRA. From the 1950s it financed top independent film-makers (eg, Sam Spiegel, David Lean) and produced such films as *On The Waterfront* (1954), *Lawrence of Arabia* (1962) and *Easy Rider* (1969). Screen Gems, a subsidiary, makes TV shows.

Columbia Broadcasting System. *See* CBS.

Columbia River, river in SW Canada and NW USA. It flows from Columbia Lake in British Columbia, Canada, through Washington and Oregon, USA, and enters the Pacific Ocean N of Portland. It has one of the largest drainage basins on the continent, approx. 668,220sq km (258,000sq miles) in area. Length: 1,953km (1,214 miles).

Columbia, District of. *See* DISTRICT OF COLUMBIA.

Columbiformes, order of birds containing the PIGEONS and DOVES and also the SANDGROUSE. Another member, largest of all, was the DODO. Pigeons are the only birds able to suck up water, and are also notable for feeding their young on "pigeon's milk", a white liquid regurgitated from the crop. *See also* NW p.*141.*

Columbine, any of about 100 species of perennial herbaceous plant native to cool climates of the Northern Hemisphere. They have five-petalled, spurred flowers and notched leaflets. Height: to 90cm (3ft). Family Ranunculaceae; genus *Aquilegia.*

Columbine, character in the HARLEQUINADE, evolved from Columbina, a maidservant first found in 16th-century COMMEDIA DELL'ARTE. The daughter, ward, or sometimes wife of the old man PANTALOON, she falls in love with HARLEQUIN and she eventually elopes with him.

Columbium. *See* NIOBIUM.

Columbite, black oxide mineral of IRON, MANGANESE and NIOBIUM (Fe,Mn)Nb_2O_6. Niobium is replaced by TANTALUM to form tantalite, with similar properties to columbite but denser. They are found in granite PEGMATITES in W Australia and Madagascar. Columbite crystallizes in the orthorhombic system, forming prismatic crystals with one distinct cleavage. Hardness: 6.0 to 6.5; s.g. 5.2 (columbite) to 8.0 (tantalite).

Columbus, Christopher (1451–1506), Italian-born explorer often, although erroneously, credited with the discovery of America. After seeking Portuguese sponsorship he went to Spain in 1484, where he found support for a voyage in search of a western route to China. In Oct. 1492 he landed in the Bahamas, the first European to reach the Americas, and called the people found there "Indians". He had made three other journeys by 1503, but without reaching the North American mainland. He died in poverty, still thinking he had found a route to the East. *See also* BRENDAN, SAINT; VESPUCCI, AMERIGO; HC1 p.234, *234.*

Columbus, city and capital of Ohio, USA, on the Scioto River, 156km (97 miles) NE of Cincinnati. It is a major transport, industrial and trading centre for a rich agricultural region. During the American Civil War, Camp Jackson (now Fort Hayes) served as a recruiting centre, and a Union arsenal was built there in 1863. The city has numerous universities and colleges and the Battelle Memorial Institute (1929) which conducts scientific, technological and economic research, the largest private research organization of its kind in the world. Industries: machinery, aircraft, printing, publishing, glassware. Pop. (1973) 540,933.

Colyer, Ken (1928–), British jazz trumpeter and guitarist with a fundamentalist approach to New Orleans jazz. He taught himself to play the trumpet in 1945 while in the navy, and formed his own group, Ken Colyer's Jazzmen, in 1953. He has influenced many British jazz musicians, including Acker BILK and Alexis Korner.

Coma, state of unconsciousness brought about by a head injury, brain disease, drugs or lack of blood supply to the brain.

Coma Berenices, or Berenice's Hair, northern constellation between Leo and Boötes and N of Virgo. It has few bright stars but numerous galaxies and clusters of galaxies. The N galactic pole is located in Coma Berenices. *See also* SU p.257.

Comanche, major Shoshonean-speaking American Indian tribe which separated from the parent SHOSHONI in the distant past and migrated from E Wyoming into Kansas. Riding Mexican horses, they raided southwards until they became widely known and feared throughout Texas and Mexico. Numbering at most 15,000, they were famous as daring horsemen and for introducing the horse to the Northern Plains tribes. Today approx. 3,500 Comanche live on reservations in SW Oklahoma.

Comaneci, Nadia (1962–), Romanian gymnast. At the 1976 Olympics, she displayed unparalleled precision of technique, receiving six perfect scores and winning three gold medals, a silver and bronze. In 1975, aged 13, she was Europe's youngest-ever champion, winning four golds and a silver.

Combat neurosis, also called battle fatigue, form of TRAUMATIC NEUROSIS that develops under conditions of military combat, usually after injury or a close escape from injury. Poor sleep, loss of appetite, moodiness, anxiety, and strong feelings of vulnerability usually occur. Symptoms often subside when the victim is removed from battle, but return again when he re-enters a combat zone.

Combination Acts, acts of parliament of 1799 and 1800 making combinations (or trade unions) of workers in Britain illegal. They were passed because the TORY government of William PITT feared that such combinations would be covers for politically subversive clubs. Despite the acts, trade unions multiplied after 1815 and in 1824, on the recommendation of a select committee, the acts were repealed. Another Combination Act was passed in 1825. It left trade unions legal, but severely restricted their ability to strike. *See also* HC2 pp.94–95.

Combine. *See* COMBINE HARVESTER.

Combine harvester, agricultural machine that cuts, threshes, cleans and gathers cereal crops. Modern combines cut only the top, fruited section (head) of a cereal stalk, beat it to release the grain and separate the grain from the chaff. *See also* PE pp.159, 164, *164.*

Combined operations, modern military term used to describe the combined use of sea, air and land forces. In WWII there were large-scale combined operations, notably on D-DAY. Troops especially trained for combined operations were often called COMMANDOS.

Comb jellies, also called sea gooseberries or sea walnuts, jellyfish-like animals, members of the phylum CTENOPHORA. They move in the sea by beating their stiff, hairlike cilia contained in eight combplates. They are hermaphrodites, producing both eggs and sperm. They are also carnivorous, catching their prey with a pair of branched tentacles. Genus *Pleurobrachia. See* NW pp.72, 85.

Combustion, fast chemical reaction emitting heat and light, commonly involving oxygen. In solids and liquids the reaction speed may be controlled both by the rate of oxygen flow to the surface, and by catalysts. Industrial techniques harness the energy produced using combustion chambers and furnaces. *See also* SPONTANEOUS COMBUSTION.

Combustion chamber, rocket, part of a rocket engine in which the propellant is burned. It must be strong enough to withstand high pressures and temperatures, yet not be too heavy. High-strength steel or titanium is used for solid-propellant rockets; aluminium-steel alloys are sufficient for liquid-propellant rockets. *See also* ROCKET ENGINE.

COMECON, Council for Mutual Economic Assistance, a trade organization formed in 1949 by the USSR and East European Communist nations in response to the MARSHALL PLAN in Western Europe. Its members are the USSR, Bulgaria, Czechoslovakia, Hungary, Poland, Romania, East Germany, Cuba and Mongolia. Instead of setting up one large market, it established a series of bilateral trade agreements, but provided for no uniform price system. *See also* HC2 pp.235, 242.

Comédie-Française, French national theatre, founded in 1680. It is organized according to a charter granted by LOUIS XIV and revised by NAPOLEON. There are two kinds of members: *pensionnaire,* chosen by audition, and *sociétaire,* to which the *pensionnaire* can be elevated only upon the death, retirement or resignation of a *sociétaire.*

Comédie Humaine, La, about 90 novels and stories of BALZAC, written between 1829 and 1850 and given the collective name by the author. They mirror every class of French society. The most famous are *Eugénie Grandet* (1833), Le PÈRE GORIOT (1834) and *César Birotteau* (1837).

Comedy, one of the two main types of drama. It differs from the other, TRAGEDY, by having a light style and theme, and usually a happy ending. It originated in early Greek fertility rites and, in modern usage, refers to any humorous play.

Comedy of Errors, The, (*c.* 1592), five-act farce by William SHAKESPEARE.

Comenius, John Amos (1592–1670), Czech religious leader and educational reformer, who influenced the growth of modern education. Comenius believed in equal education for all children. His best-known book, *Orbis Sensualum Pictus* (*The Visible World in Pictures,* 1658), used many pictures and related Latin to the vernacular.

Comet, small body orbiting the Sun, often with an elliptical, long-period orbit. Solar radiation vaporizes the icy nucleus producing a luminous, gaseous envelope, the coma, which surrounds the nucleus, and a luminous tail of gas and dust, up to millions of miles long, that always points away from the Sun. The origin of comets is uncertain; it is thought they may be projected into the Solar System from a region (Oort's cloud) which is bound to the Sun. *See* SU pp.216–17.

Comfort, Alexander (1920–), British medical biologist. He was director of research in the department of gerontology at University College, London, from 1966 to 1973. In 1973 he became a senior fellow at the Centre for the Study of Democratic Institutions at Santa Barbara, California. His books include *Authority and Delinquency in the Modern State* (1950), *Sex and Society* (1963) and *A Good Age* (1977).

Comfrey, any plant of the genus *Symphytum* of the BORAGE family, native to Eurasia. Comfreys have small yellow or purple flowers and hairy leaves. Boiled concoctions of *S. officinale* were once used to treat wounds.

Comic Opera, musico-dramatic work with some spoken dialogue and a light or amusing plot. The term is used indiscriminately and includes MUSICAL COMEDY and OPERETTA. In relation to operatic works, it approximates most closely to the early 18th century OPERA BUFFA (notably the operas of PERGOLESI), but bears little relation to the French OPÉRA COMIQUE (which may include serious or even tragic elements).

Comics, magazines primarily for the young, containing stories told by means of strip cartoons with "balloons" giving the characters' speech. They evolved from the comic-strip in the 1930s, and those in book-form concern themselves with adventure, war or crime, whereas the weekly ones are more usually collections of sport, school and family-life stories.

Comilla, town in E Bangladesh on the River Gumti. Situated on the main rail and road routes between Chittagong and Dacca, it is a market centre for the surrounding area, responsible for the export of hides and skins. Pop. (1972 est.) 65,400.

Comines, Philippe de (*c.*1447–1511), also known as Commines, or Commynes, French statesman and historian. He served successively with Charles the Bold of Burgundy, Louis XI and Charles VIII. His *Mémoires* (1524) are an important source of medieval history and provide a wealth of detail about the period.

Cominform (Communist Information Bureau), organization established in 1947 to co-ordinate and provide information to the Communist parties of the USSR, Bulgaria, Czechoslovakia, Hungary, Poland, Romania, Yugoslavia, France and Italy. It replaced the Comintern, which had been abolished in 1943. Yugoslavia was expelled in 1948, and the organization was dissolved in 1956.

Comintern. *See* COMMUNIST INTERNATIONAL.

Commando, originally a unit of the Boer army during the Boer War (1899–1902). In 1940, commando units were formed in the British army to undertake dangerous small-scale missions. During WWII their exploits included a raid on Rommel's headquarters (1941) and on the port of St Nazaire (1942).

Commedia dell' arte, style of Italian comedy, popular in the 16th–18th centuries, which spread throughout Europe. Professional players performed on street stages or at court functions. The plays were comic, often crude and coarse and improvised on briefly outlined scenarios. An extremely popular form, with masked characters, the Commedia produced several now familiar standard characters: Harlequin (the clown), the Capitano (a braggart soldier), Pantalone (the deceived father or cuckolded husband), Colombina (the maid) and Inamorato (the lover).

Commensalism, relationship between two species in the interests of sharing food or providing locomotion, shelter or support. Often the relationship is mutually beneficial and harms neither. *See also* SYMBIOSIS.

Commercial law, body of laws that apply to most business transactions (except those relating to carriage of goods). An outgrowth of ROMAN LAW, it was administered by special courts in trading cities during the RENAISSANCE. "Law Merchant", a term applied to principles and procedure, evolved into effective municipal laws. These were incorporated into English COMMON LAW in the 18th century.

Commissioners for Oaths, persons who administer oaths in Britain. Originally they were masters in CHANCERY. In 1677 COMMON LAW judges were empowered to appoint commissioners. In 1853 it was enacted that solicitors should be appointed by the Lord CHANCELLOR. Any solicitor with a licence to practise is eligible for the office.

Commission, Royal, extra-parliamentary committee appointed by the British Crown to enquire into and make reports on matters of public policy. DOMESDAY BOOK may be considered the first. Under HENRY II such commissions became regular. EDWARD I'S QUO WARRANTO proceedings were the most extensive medieval inquiry. Medieval commissions, concerned chiefly with property and taxation, were like a modern census. The modern commission into a particular subject dates from the Tudors. Since the early 19th century social and economic questions have increasingly been the subject of inquiry.

Committee of Public Safety, political organization of the French Revolution. Formed in 1793 to defend the state and to supervize executive government, it controlled the country during the REIGN OF TERROR. Both DANTON and ROBESPIERRE were at different times prominent members.

Commodity market, market organized by traders in which promises of immediate and future delivery are made. The commodities themselves are not brought to the market-place; only contracts (futures) are sold. Commodity markets deal in items that are subject to sampling and grading, such as grapes, sugar, coffee, tea, wool, cotton, rubber and copper.

Common Business Oriented Language. *See* COBOL.

Common cold. *See* COLD, COMMON.

Common denominator. *See* DENOMINATOR, COMMON.

Common lands, land on an estate on which, by a tradition dating from medieval times, the tenants of the estate are free to grow their own crops and pasture their own livestock. There are hardly any common lands still remaining, most having been swallowed up in the ENCLOSURE movement of the late 18th and 19th centuries.

Common law, system of law developed in England and adopted in most English-speaking countries. Distinguished from CIVIL LAW (a codified system based on statutes), its chief characteristics are judicial precedents, trial by jury and the doctrine of the supremacy of LAW. Based originally on the king's court, "common to the whole realm", rather than local or manorial courts, it dates back to the constitutions of CLARENDON (1164) and is the customary and traditional element in the law accumulating from court decisions. Swift changes in society and public opinion have resulted in a proliferation of statutes which have come to supersede common law. *See also* ROMAN LAW; MS p.*283*.

Common law marriage, marriage by verbal agreement of the parties involved without a civil or religious ceremony. It does not require a licence and in Britain is regarded as legal if followed by cohabitation of the partners as man and wife.

Common Market. *See* EEC.

Common Prayer, Book of, official LITURGY of the Church of England. It was prepared originally as a reformed version of the old Catholic liturgy for Henry VIII by Thomas CRANMER and was accepted by Parliament in 1549. Three years later it underwent thorough revision under the more Protestant government of the young Edward VI. Accordingly, the MASS was transformed from an act of sacrifice into one of commemoration, and was called the Lord's Supper or Holy Communion. After the intervening reign of the Catholic Mary, a combination of the 1549 and 1552 prayer books was produced by Elizabeth's Archbishop Matthew Parker, reincorporating much of Cranmer's liberalism. It is this version – with slight liturgical improvements and not finally published until 1662 after suppression during the Commonwealth – that in many churches is still in use.

Commons, The, in Britain the third ESTATE of the realm – everyone who is not at least a baron (and so entitled to sit in the House of Lords). The term is often used to mean the HOUSE OF COMMONS of the British PARLIAMENT. It derives from the Latin *communitas*; the *communitas regni* ("community of the realm") meant in feudal times that larger political nation than simply the tenants-in-chief. It included the knights of the shire and the burgesses of the towns which, from the 13th century, sent representatives to PARLIAMENT.

Common Sense, pamphlet published in January 1776 by Thomas PAINE. It attacked the British monarchy as being chiefly responsible for the restrictive measures against the American colonists, and was the first clear call for American independence from Britain. *See also* HC2 p.*65*.

Common Sense Realism, school of early 18th century Scottish philosophers, founded by Thomas REID, which advanced a theory of knowledge founded upon the self-evident "principles of the man in the street".

Commonwealth (1649–60), official name of the republic established in England after the execution of CHARLES I in 1649. After a series of unsuccessful attempts to find a suitable constitution, the PROTECTORATE was set up in 1653, in which Oliver CROMWELL was given almost regal powers. The Commonwealth continued until the RESTORATION of CHARLES II in 1660. *See also* HC1 pp.288–91, 296.

Commonwealth Conferences, irregular meetings of Commonwealth heads, the offspring of the Imperial conferences of 1911–37. The first was held at London in 1944. They are now held about every two years to discuss matters of common interest at places throughout the Commonwealth. The first one not held at London was in Lagos in 1966.

Commonwealth Day, in Britain and most member countries of the COMMONWEALTH OF NATIONS, holiday to celebrate the foundation of the Commonwealth. The festival was first held in Canada in 1901 and was known as Empire Day until 1958.

Commonwealth Development Corporation, name given in 1963 to the Colonial Development Corporation, a British organization founded in 1948 to foster the growth of the economics of British colonies. It seeks to provide technical and managerial assistance for Commonwealth countries and to encourage and co-ordinate overseas investment in their industries.

Commonwealth Games, sports series originated as the British Empire Games in 1930. The competitors are members of the COMMONWEALTH OF NATIONS. Based on the Olympic Games, they are held every four years and must include athletics and swimming and seven other sports selected from the following: archery, badminton, bowls, boxing, cycling, fencing, gymnastics, rowing/canoeing, shooting, weight-lifting and wrestling.

Commonwealth Institute, organization housed in Kensington, London, which has a permanent exhibition of the life and culture of the various members of the COMMONWEALTH OF NATIONS.

Commonwealth of Nations, voluntary association of states consisting of Britain and independent countries that were once its dependencies. Since the transition to independent status of many of the members, the Commonwealth has stressed cultural and economic co-operation and consultation on political issues of mutual concern. The British sovereign is head of the Commonwealth, and those member states that are dominions, such as Canada, recognize her as queen; they are outnumbered by republics, such as India and Malaysia, that have their own head of state. Commonwealth heads of government meet regularly for talks. In 1965 a Commonwealth Secretariat was set up, with headquarters in London. *See also* BRITISH EMPIRE; HC2 pp .220–221.

Commonwealth Relations Office, former department of the British government, established in 1947, when the secretary of state for Dominion affairs became the secretary of state for Commonwealth relations. The office was responsible for relations between Britain and Commonwealth countries and relations with the Republic of Ireland. In 1965 it was merged with the COLONIAL OFFICE, which became part of the FOREIGN AND COMMONWEALTH OFFICE in 1968.

Commonwealth Territory. *See* AUSTRALIAN CAPITAL TERRITORY.

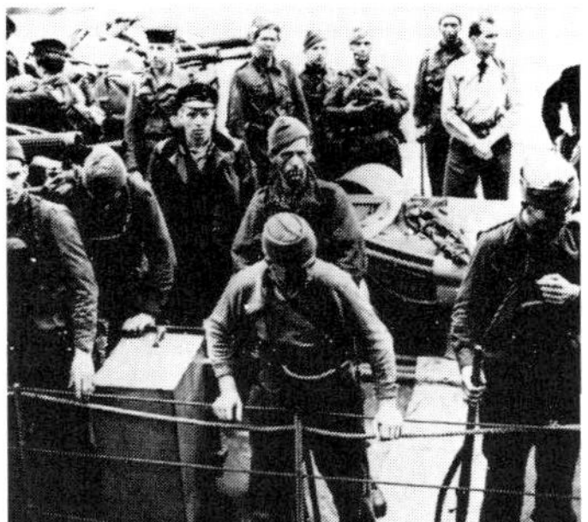

Commandos; the special service troops landing at Dieppe in the famous raid in WWII.

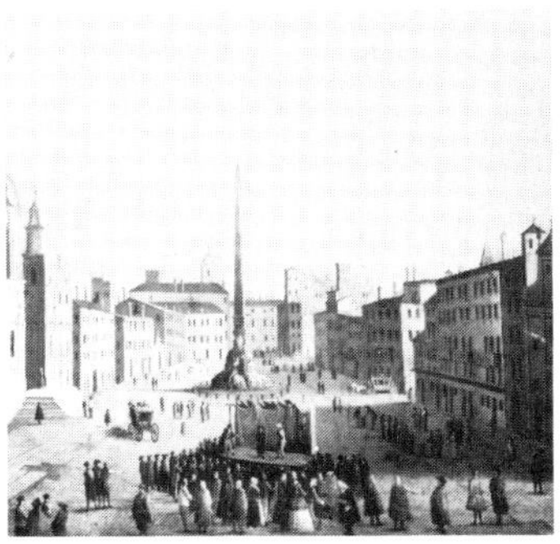

Commedia dell' arte, the renaissance theatre which brought us characters like Harlequin.

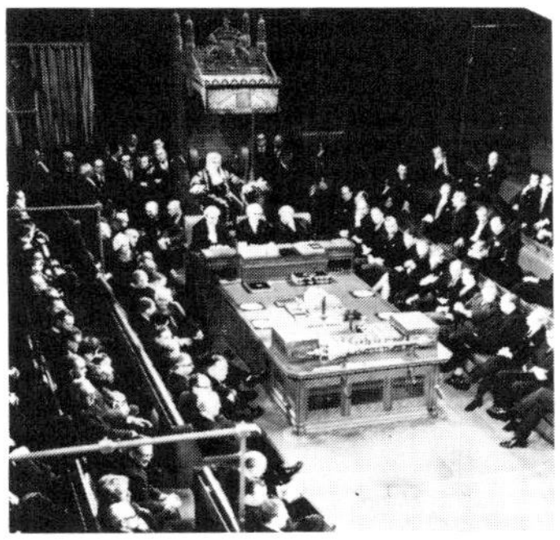

The Commons; the first televised state opening of the British Parliament in 1966.

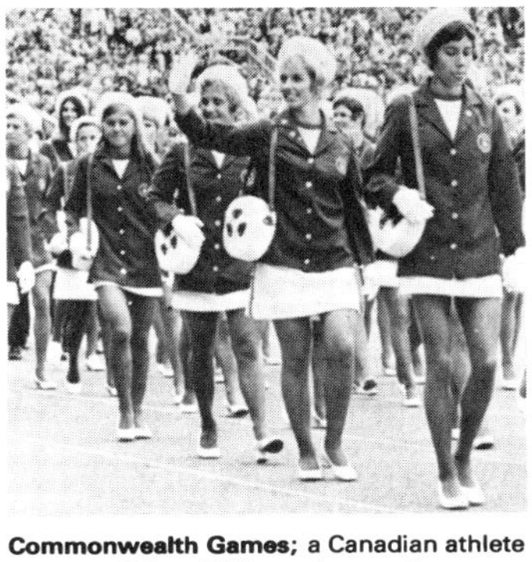

Commonwealth Games; a Canadian athlete waves to Prince Philip at the opening.

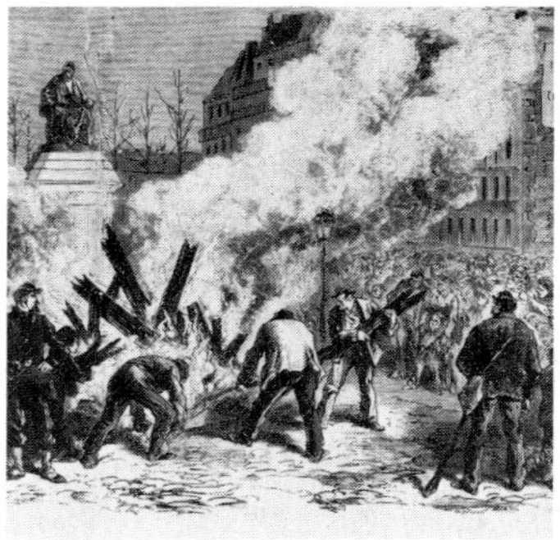

Commune of Paris; the symbolic burning of the guillotine during the 1871 uprising.

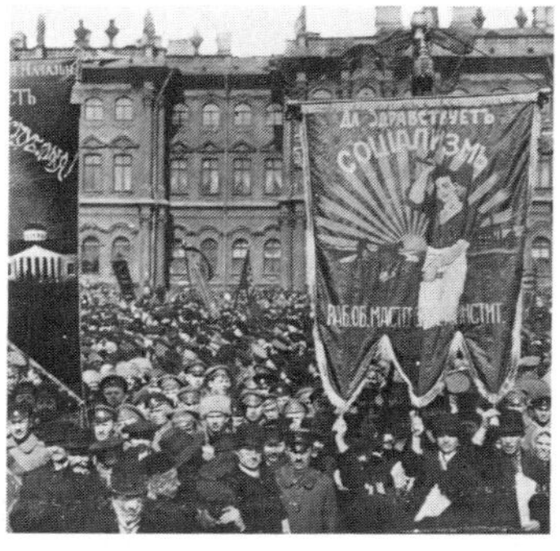

Communism; a Bolshevik demonstration at the Winter Palace in Petrograd in 1917.

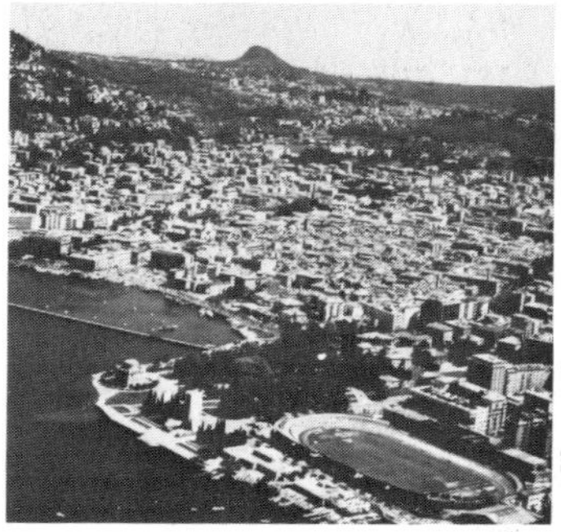

Como is the home of the Italian National Institute of Silk, the city's main industry.

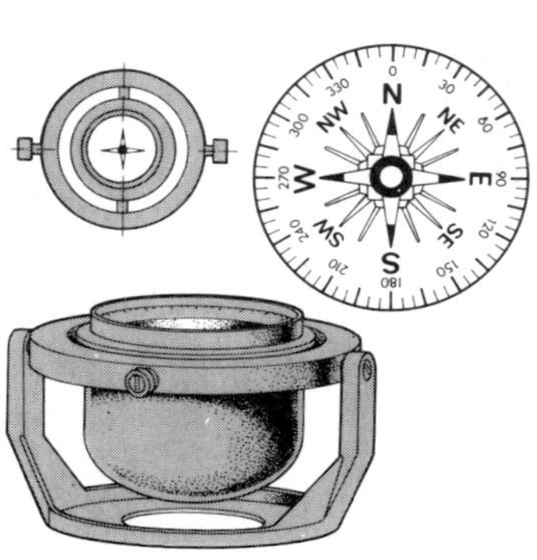

Compass; its direction finding power is because the Earth behaves like a magnet.

Communards, supporters of the COMMUNE OF PARIS (1871). The Communards represented JACOBIN and patriotic feeling as well as socialist and anarchist ideals. They relied for their defence on the Parisian national guard.
Commune, usually a community of people who choose to live together for a shared purpose. In the 19th century many communes tried to put utopian socialist ideals into practice. In the 1960s hippies and others formed communes that were intended to be co-operative, self-supporting and free of what were held to be the undesirable values of conventional society. In China farming communes have been set up, similar to the state farms of the USSR. The communes own the land and a production brigade determines what is grown. Farmers have been granted small private plots of land to grow what they like; they themselves may either use the produce they grow or sell it.
Commune of Paris (1871), insurrection against the French national government, which was accepting a humiliating peace following the FRANCO-PRUSSIAN WAR. The Parisians, spurred on by radicals, anarchists and Marxists, decided to continue the fight and organized their own defences. The French government, based in Versailles, besieged the city (March-May 1871) and put down the revolt with great brutality. *See also* HC2 p.*180*.
Communications Satellite Corporation (Comsat), a private company created by the US Congress to develop a worldwide communications network. Thirteen other nations participate in the project, which was started with the launch of the EARLY BIRD satellite in 1965.
Communism, the political theory of Karl MARX and Friedrich ENGELS, but also sometimes used to mean the institutions (the COMMUNIST PARTY and the COMMUNIST INTERNATIONAL, developed by those people claiming allegiance to the theory. Like many theories Communism, or Marxism, is sometimes self-contradictory; nevertheless its essential articles, as laid forth in the COMMUNIST MANIFESTO and DAS KAPITAL, may be outlined.

The theory is derived from the interpretation which Marx and Engels placed upon the course of human history. That interpretation asserted that all human phemomena rest upon economic facts, the most important of which are the changes that occur in the relationship between the means of production and their ownership. All wealth is produced by labour (the labour theory of value) and hence labour is wealth. Yet in the CAPITALIST system of Europe in the 18th and 19th centuries the workers owned neither their own labour nor the means of production. Hence they did not reap the fruits of their labour, which went to the capitalist owners of the means of production. Thus labour became alienated from capital and production. Capitalism, however, was asserted to be merely a transient stage in the progress of human institutions.

Marx's theory of history led him to prediction. Borrowing HEGEL's idea of the dialectic he developed, with Engels, the notion of DIALECTICAL MATERIALISM, which in social terms meant the war of classes. Marx postulated that just as the feudal aristocracy of Europe had inevitably been supplanted as the ruling class by the capitalist BOURGEOISIE, so the bourgeoisie (by the nature of its operations) brought into being the urban proletariat, or working class, which must overthrow it and establish the dictatorship of the proletariat.

Marx claimed that his SOCIALISM was scientific – as opposed to the Utopian socialism of men such as Robert OWEN – because it was based on inflexible economic forces which determine the course of human history. There was, however, no scientific basis to his historical interpretation, nor to his visionary expectation that the triumph of the proletariat would necessarily usher in a classless society. And in direct contradiction of his theory Communist parties have come to power, not in highly industrialized countries with a large urban working class, but in agricultural, peasant countries such as pre-Revolutionary Russia, China, Indonesia and Cuba. *See also* HC2 pp.240–245; MS p.277.
Communist International, or Comintern, also known as the Third International, Communist organization founded by LENIN in 1919. He feared that the reformist Second International might re-emerge and he wished to secure his control of the world socialist movement. The Comintern was made up mainly of Russians, and failed to organize a successful revolution in Europe in the 1920s and 1930s. The USSR abolished the Comintern in 1943 to placate its allies in WWII. *See also* HC2 p.198.
Communist Manifesto (1848), political tract by Karl MARX and Friedrich ENGELS. Essentially it states that economic factors determine social relations. The authors believed that the inevitability of class warfare would substitute a classless Communist society for the inequalities of a capitalist one. *See also* HC2 p.171.
Communist Party, name of numerous political parties in the world, each of them confessing with more or less strictness to Marxist, Marxist-Leninist or Maoist principles. It is the ruling party in the USSR, China, Albania and the COMECON countries.

The first Communist Party was founded at Minsk in 1898; led by LENIN, it was called the Russian Social Democratic Party. At the Brussels-London conference (1903) it affirmed three leading principles: that the party should accept all decisions made by its leaders, that all party members should be "activists" and that they should be prepared for a revolutionary seizure of power. Lenin's wing of the party, the BOLSHEVIKS, seized power in 1917. Since then the party has remained in power, under the successive leadership of Lenin, STALIN, MALENKOV, BULGANIN, KRUSHCHEV and BREZHNEV. Under Communist rule Russia has been a one-party state, in which the controlling body is the secretariat, which selects and supervises all persons appointed to positions in the party organization. Through the secretariat the distinction between party and government posts has been obliterated.

The Chinese Communist Party was formed under the leadership of Ch'en Tu-hsui and Li Ta-chao in 1921. After decades of civil war, it gained power in 1949 and proclaimed the People's Republic of China. Since then China, (like all Communist-ruled countries) has been a one-party state, led until 1976 by MAO TSE-TUNG, whose death was followed by a struggle for power.

The British Communist Party was formed in 1920. It has twice had two MPS, in 1922–23 and 1949–50. *See also* index to *History and Culture 2.*
Community, group of people, usually living in the same area, who are bound together by similar customs, beliefs and outlook. Hunting and gathering bands of early men, farming villages, monasteries and cities are examples of communities.
Community medicine, broad term that includes all aspects of public health and social services within a community. *See also* MS pp.110–111.
Commutation, in law, reduction in the severity of a punishment. It does not eradicate guilt. Commutation is neither a pardon (which terminates punishment) nor a reprieve (which temporarily witholds sentence or temporarily suspends its execution).
Commutative law, rule of combination in mathematics; it requires that an operation on two terms is independent of the order of the terms. Addition and multiplication of numbers in commutative, since $a \times b = b \times a$, and $a + b = b + a$. Vector cross-multiplication does not obey the commutative law. *See also* SU p.28.
Commutator, cylinder made up from copper bars, part of DC ELECTRIC MOTOR or GENERATOR. It makes contact via brushes between the electric terminals and the rotary ARMATURE winding. It also serves to reverse the current in these windings. *See also* SU pp.122–123.
Comnenus family, influential Byzantine family, possibly of Italian origin. In the 10th–12th centuries members of the family included six Byzantine emperors (1057–1185), statesmen and authors, such as historian Anna Comnena (1083–*c.* 1150). All the emperors of Trebizond (1204–1461) were of the family. The last one, David Comnenus, was executed in 1461 by Mehmet II. Attempts to link the Bonaparte family with a Corsican branch of the Comnenus family proved unsuccessful. *See also* HC1 pp.142, 176.
Como, city in N Italy, at the SW end of Lake Como; capital of Como province in Lombardy region. Originally a Roman colony, it became a free commune in the 11th century. It was liberated from Austrian rule by Garibaldi in 1859. Mussolini was executed there in 1945. Monuments include a 18th-century cathedral of Sta Maria Maggiore. Industries: silk, tourism. Pop. (1971) 97,395.
Comorin, Cape, southernmost point of the subcontinent of India. A rugged headland, it is the site of an ancient temple dedicated to SHIVA, which is a Hindu pilgrimage centre.
Comoro Islands (Comores), independent republic off the E coast of Africa between Mozambique and Madagascar in the Indian Ocean, made up of a group of volcanic islands. The three major islands are Grande Comore (on which is the capital, Moroni), Anjouan and Mohéli. The islands are mountainous, the climate is tropical and the soil fertile. Farming is the chief occupation, and coconuts, vanilla, copra, cocoa and sisal are the main crops and exports. France acquired the islands between 1841 and 1909. They gained their independence in 1975. Area: 1,797sq km (694sq miles). Pop. (1975 est.) 292,000, *See also* MW p.59.
Companies Act. *See* LIMITED LIABILITY.
Companions of Honour, exclusive order of chivalry in Britain, founded in 1917. Membership of the order, which allows the member to put CH after his or her name, is limited to 65 men or women.
Company, group of people who agree to work together as a firm or business. The legal responsibility of running a company rests with its board of directors which, if the business has raised finance by selling shares in the company, has to account to its shareholders. In a private company the directors sell shares to whom ever they please (sometimes the only shareholders are the directors themselves). The shares of a public company can be bought and sold by anyone through a stock exchange. In a limited company, the legal liability of its shareholders is limited to the value of their shares. There is a special branch of the law, company law, that applies to such businesses. *See also* AUDIT; CORPORATION.
Comparative law, the study and comparison of the legal systems and laws of different countries and cultures. A relatively new discipline in legal studies, its growth has been linked to several factors: the needs of international business, the establishment of international laws, the promotion of international understanding, and the improvement of legal systems.
Comparative psychology, field of biology that compares the behaviours of various animal species. Comparative psychologists study animals to learn more about all species and to aid their understanding of human behaviour. *See also* ETHOLOGY.
Comparator, measuring device used to inspect a manufactured component for deviation from a specified value, normally by direct matching or by comparing it with a master part against pre-set tolerances. The decision to accept or reject a part may be done by an operator or the comparator makes the decision automatically.
Compass, magnetic, direction-finding instrument consisting of a magnetic needle freely suspended or pivoted so that in the earth's magnetic field it can turn to align itself with the magnetic north and south poles. Adjustments can be made to give true north. The first use of the magnetic compass was once attributed to the Ancient Chinese, although this now seems unlikely. It was not until the 12th century that it was used in Europe, when the "needle" was a piece of LODESTONE. In navigation today the magnetic compass

has largely been replaced by the GYROCOMPASS. *See also* SU pp.116–117.
Compass plant, large coarse perennial plant native to North America. It has a tall flower stalk with a number of large, solitary, yellow flowers and long deeply cut leaves which are said to point to north and south. Height: 3.5m (11ft). Family Compositae; species *Silphium laciniatum.*
Compiègne, town in Oise département, NE France, 72km (45 miles) NE of Paris, on the River Oise. Joan of Arc was captured there by the Burgundians in 1430. The armistice ending WWI was signed on 11 Nov. 1918 in a railway carriage in the Compiègne forest. Hitler forced the French to sign the 1940 armistice in the same carriage. Industries: chemicals, soap. Pop. (1968) 29,700.
Compleat Angler, The (1653), literary discourse on fishing by Izaak WALTON in the form of a dialogue between Piscator (Fisherman), Venator (Hunter) and Auceps (Fowler). It combines humour, pastoral description, verse and practical instruction.
Complementary angles, two angles whose sum is 90°, or a right-angle. Supplementary angles have a sum of 180°.
Complementary colours, in the light spectrum, any two colours which combine to make white light. This involves the mixture of at least three primary colours. Thus green (a mixture of the primaries blue and yellow) mixed with red (another primary) gives white. Green is therefore the complement of red. In painting adding different colours together has the reverse effect: combinations get darker, not lighter. *See also* SU pp.98–99.
Complex, in psychology, collection of repressed memories and desires that have a powerful emotional charge. When this charge remains in the unconscious, it can exert a dominating influence on behaviour. The term was introduced by Carl JUNG, who deduced from research that certain associations were repressed because of their immoral or disagreeable content. Such associations can give rise to various NEUROSES.
Complex compounds, in chemistry, compounds in which some atoms of the molecule are held by polar bonds and others by co-ordinate bonds. They are also known as co-ordination compounds. They can form complex IONS such as chloropentammineplatinum, $Pt(NH_3)_5Cl^{3+}$, because of the co-ordinate bonding. In such compounds a metal atom is often surrounded by non-metal atoms, so that it does not manifest its metal character. *See also* CHEMICAL BONDS; CHELATE; LIGANDS; SU p.141.
Complex fraction. *See* FRACTION, COMPLEX.
Complex number. *See* NUMBER, COMPLEX.
Composite, material such as concrete, fibreglass or plywood, made by combining two or more other materials. A composite usually has qualities superior to those of the materials from which it is made. *See also* MM pp.37, 47.
Composite family, family (Compositae) of nearly 20,000 species of plants in which the "flower" is actually a composite flower-head made up of a cluster of many, usually tiny, individual flowers, called florets. In a typical composite such as the DAISY, the flower-head has a central yellow disc, consisting of a cluster of tiny bisexual florets lacking visible petals. The outer ring of female ray florets has relatively large white petals. In composites such as the dandelion and endive, the flower-head consists entirely of ray florets. Others, such as thistles, consist entirely of disc florets. Composites make up by far the largest family of plants, with a great variety of forms and sizes. They include food plants, such as artichokes, and many popular garden flowers. *See also* NW pp.58, *59, 61.*
Compost, mass of rotted plant and animal matter used as a FERTILIZER. When properly prepared, with the addition of nitrogen compounds during decomposition, it is crumbly, does not have an offensive smell and does not compete with plants for nitrogen. Large amounts have to be used to compensate for its relatively low nutrient content (compared with artificial fertilizers), but the structure of soil is greatly improved after several seasons of composting. *See also* PE pp.174–175.
Compound, substance formed by chemical combination of two or more elements. Compounds are produced by the rearrangement of valency electrons seeking to attain more stable configurations, and usually have properties quite different from those of their constituent elements. Ionic compounds have ionic bonds – they are collections of oppositely charged ions in which no distinct molecules exist. Covalent bonding produces two types of compound. In one, covalent compounds, a solid is formed in which the bonds extend throughout the crystal. Such compounds, eg, boron nitride, are hard and have high melting points. In the other, molecular compounds, groups of atoms are bound in distinct molecules. Such compounds tend to be volatile, soluble in non-polar solvents and have low melting points. *See also* MOLECULE; SU pp.138–142.
Compound eye, eye made up of from 12 to more than 1,000 simple eyes, each having light-sensitive cells, nerve fibres and a corneal lens. It is found in insects and most other arthropods.
Compound interest, interest that is earned not only on the principal (the sum originally invested) but also on any previous interest that has been added to the principal. Simple interest is earned only on the principal. *See also* INTEREST.
Compressed air, air kept at pressures much higher than that of the atmosphere (1 atmos.). It is prepared by pumping air into a reservoir from a pump or compressor, and is used extensively as a source of power for machines such as PNEUMATIC HAMMERS and other moving tools. It is easily transported in metal "bottles", and many factories have their own compressors.
Compression-ignition engine. *See* DIESEL ENGINE; ENGINE.
Compression of gases, reduction in volume of gases achieved by applying external pressure. Unlike liquids and solids, gases can be compressed to a considerable extent. Some, including carbon dioxide, can be liquefied by pressure alone at room temperatures. Many other gases must be cooled before they can be liquefied by pressure; the temperature above which they will not do so is called the critical temperature. *See also* AIR COMPRESSOR; CRITICAL POINT; SU pp.84–85.
Compressor. *See* AIR COMPRESSOR.
Compton, Arthur Holly (1892–1962), US physicist. He was head of the physics department at Washington University (1920–23) and at the University of Chicago (1923–45). He worked in the field of X-rays and discovered the scattering process known as the Compton effect, for which he was awarded the 1927 Nobel Prize in physics jointly with C. T. R. WILSON. As head of the early phase of the Manhattan Project, he helped create its first sustained nuclear CHAIN REACTION.
Compton, Denis Charles Scott (1918–), British cricketer. He played 78 times for England 1937–57 (5,807 runs at an average of 50.06), his cavalier batting for England and Middlesex winning many admirers. He once scored 300 for MCC. In football, he won England, FA Cup, and League honours with Arsenal.
Compton, Fay (1894–), British actress, full name Lillian Emmeline Compton, sister of Sir Compton MACKENZIE. She made her stage debut in 1911 and later visited the USA and toured Europe. During a long career, she gave many notable performances both in the classics and in contemporary plays.
Compton-Burnett, Dame Ivy (1892–1969), British novelist. Her novels, written mainly in dialogue, take place in upper-middle-class society in Edwardian England. They include *Pastors and Masters* (1925), *A House and its Head* (1935), *Elders and Betters* (1944) and *Mother and Son* (1955).
Compton effect, the scattering of waves such as X-RAYS and GAMMA RAYS into packets of energy called quanta (photons). The effect was discovered (1923) by the US physicist Arthur H. COMPTON, and is evidence for the dual nature of energy, ie wave and particle. It is observed as an increase in the wavelength of waves as they collide with electrons.
Compulsive personality, personality disturbance marked by obsessive concerns and rigid, ritualistic behaviour, making for an inhibited, orderly and stubborn person. Such a person has a huge capacity for work but finds it difficult to relax. Compulsive personalities show little spontaneity. They try and arrange their whole lives to fit into a set plan.
Computer, electronic calculating and problem-solving machine which originated in mechanical calculating machines of the 19th century, (such as the projected Difference Engine and Analytical Engine of Charles BABBAGE). The first modern electronic computer, which used 18,000 vacuum tubes (radio valves), was built at the University of Pennsylvania in 1946 and could perform 5,000 additions or several hundred multiplications each second. In later electronic computers, vacuum tubes and wiring were replaced by TRANSISTORS and PRINTED CIRCUITS. The latest computers use even more compact INTEGRATED CIRCUITS, which allow them to be of such complexity and efficiency that they can perform several million arithmetic operations each second. Computers are of two main types; analog and digital. Analog computers represent numbers by analogous quantities which can be varied continuously. In electronic computers this is on electric voltage, but strictly speaking, analog computers also include such simple devices as the slide rule, which represents numbers by lengths. Digital computers represent numbers discretely, not continuously – a simple example is an ABACUS, in which numbers are represented by movable beads. In a modern electronic digital computer numbers are represented by a magnetized or unmagnetized states of metal components. Analog computers are, in general, even faster than digital computers but are not as accurate. They are employed principally for such operations as designing aeroplanes, where continuously varying properties require to be assessed one against the other. All computers employed commercially, and most for scientific and technological calculations, are digital machines. They consist of a central processing unit in which information is stored and manipulated, an input unit which feeds programed information to the central unit, and an output unit which delivers the processed data for inspection. Programs are written in one or another special computer language, eg Cobol and Fortran, in which both the data and the required manipulation of it are specified. The program is fed into the computer (typically it is typed by the operator on a machine which produces punched tape) and is read by the computer at high speed. Output information is typically printed out or drawn graphically; it is frequently also displayed on a cathode ray tube. The magnetic discs and tapes are for the storage and manipulation of data. *See also* MM pp.*95*, 106–109.
Computer language, set of words and rules that enable a programmer to instruct a computer. The computer itself performs its operations using the BINARY SYSTEM in a machine code or language, which it is too time-consuming to program directly. So the computer translates an assembly or programming language into the machine code. There are several kinds of programming language designed for different purposes. For example, FORTRAN is for scientific and mathematical use, COBOL for business use, ALGOL for mathematical use, PL/1 for general use. *See also* MM pp.*95*, 106–109, *211, 216*, 217, *239.*
Computer memory, part of a computer that stores information in "words" or their "bits", each of which has an identification number (address) assigned to it for immediate use by the central processing unit. It may consist of magnetic cores, tapes, drums or discs. Developments in integrated chip circuits have revolutionized computer memory technology, permitting greater retrieval speeds and miniaturization. *See also* MM pp.106–109.

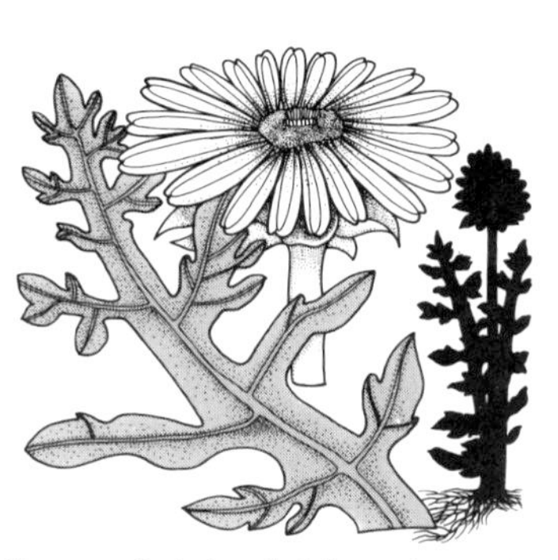

Compass plants turn their leaves in a north-south plane to avoid the harsh midday sun.

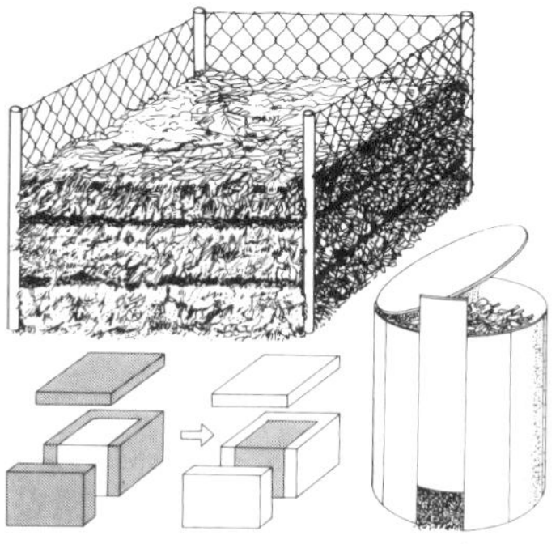

Compost, a natural fertilizer, is nutritionally lower than "artificial" chemical fertilizers.

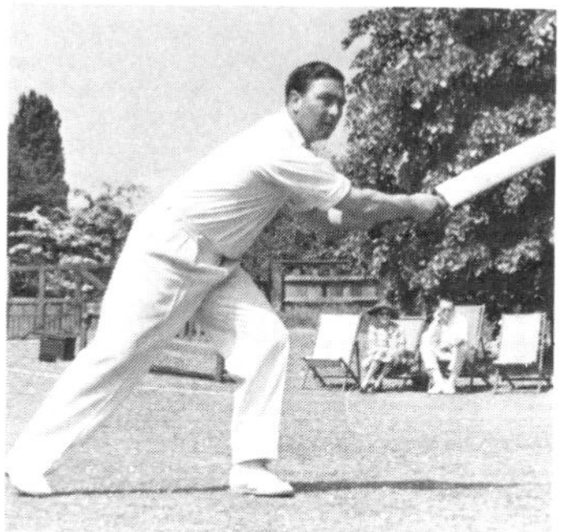

Denis Compton, the English test cricketer, also played soccer for his country.

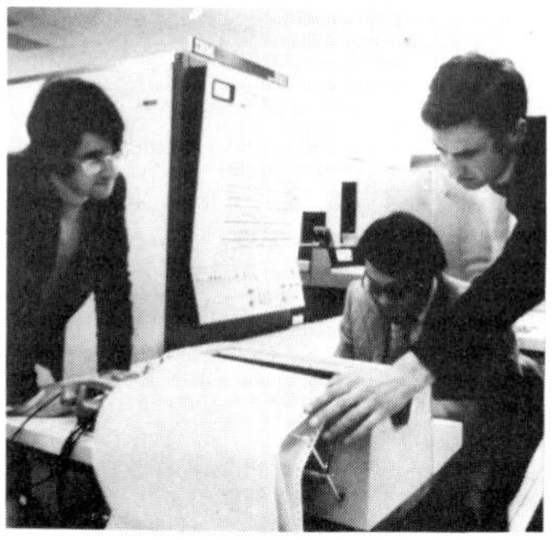

Computers calculate at high speeds and store enormous quantities of information.

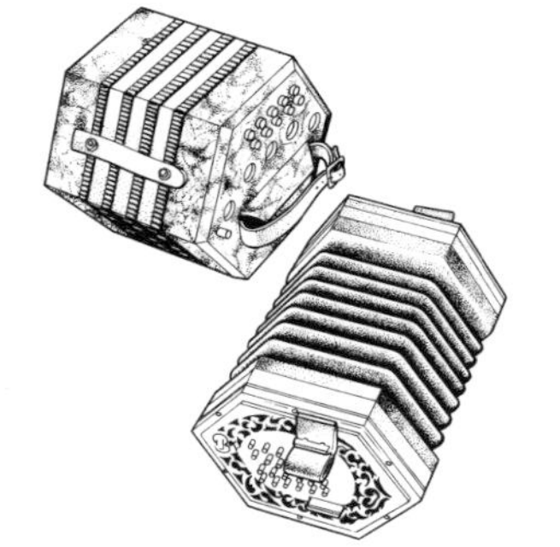

Concertinas are commonly associated with sailor's sea shanties and shipboard music.

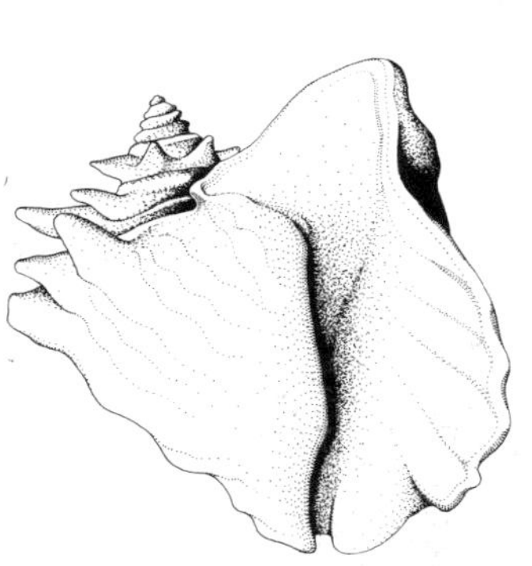

Conches are often used as horns, like the fabled shell trumpet of the Tritons.

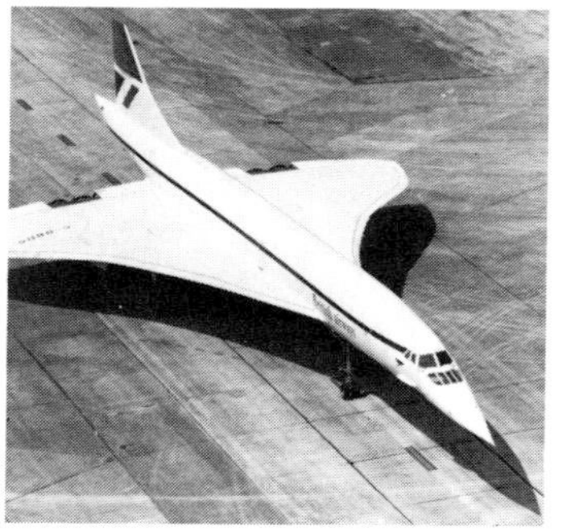

Concorde halves average journey times but has caused great controversy.

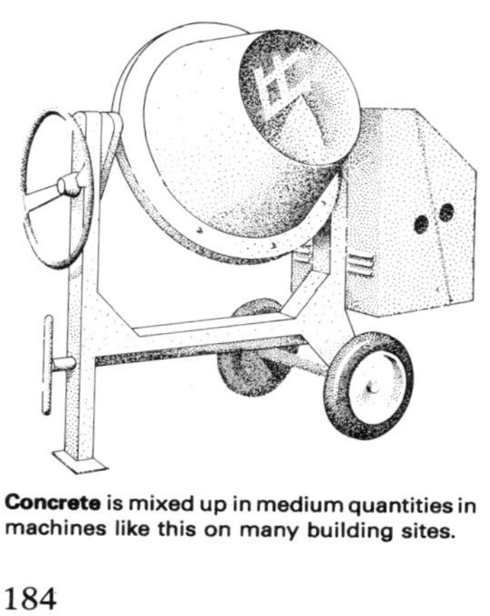

Concrete is mixed up in medium quantities in machines like this on many building sites.

Comte, Auguste (1798–1857), French philosopher, the founder of POSITIVISM. Comte proposed the law of the three stages – theological, metaphysical and positive – that represent the development of the human race. In the first two stages the human mind finds religious or abstract causes to explain phenomena, while in the third, explanation of a phenomenon is found in a scientific law. His philosophy influenced British thinkers such as J. S. MILL and Frederick HARRISON. His works include *Positive Philosophy* (1830–42) and *System of Positive Polity* (1851–54). *See also* HC2 pp.172–173; MS p.263.

Comus, pastoral entertainment by John MILTON, first performed in 1634 and published in 1637. The work describes the rescue of a chaste lady captured by Comus, the orgiastic son of Bacchus and Circe.

Conakry, capital city of Guinea, w Africa, on Tombo Island, in the Atlantic Ocean. Founded in 1884, it is a major port with a deep-water harbour and is the administrative and commercial centre of Guinea. It has an airport and is the terminus of the country's only railway. It exports alumina and bananas and has food processing industries. Pop. (1972 est.) 290,000.

Concentration camp, centre for the segregation and detention of people considered by the authorities to be objectionable or dangerous because of their politics, race, religion or nationality. Concentration camps were established by the British during the SOUTH AFRICAN (Boer) WAR and by many TOTALITARIAN regimes. During WWII a number of such camps were established by Hitler's Nazi Party and became infamous for the harsh treatment and extermination of Jews, Slavs, gypsies, criminals, homosexuals and other prisoners. *See also* AUSCHWITZ; BELSEN; DACHAU; HC2 p.326

Concentric circles, two or more circles lying in the same plane and having the same point as their centre.

Concepción, city in s central Chile; capital of Concepción province. Founded in 1550 by Pedro de VALDIVIA, it has been destroyed on several occasions by earthquakes and was severely damaged in 1960. An important commercial centre in a rich agricultural region, its industries include coal mining, oil refining, chemicals, textiles, food processing, brewing. Pop. (1975) 169,570.

Conception, start of pregnancy. The term is used to describe the fertilization of an egg cell by the male SPERM, or the implantation of the fertilized egg in the wall of the WOMB. *See also* MS p.*75.*

Concept learning, type of learning characterized by considering the qualities, aspects and relations of objects and events, which then allows comparison, generalization, abstraction and reasoning. It enables a person to classify his experiences. Words and language form the basis of concept learning and they develop alongside each other in a child. *See also* MS pp.150–155, 162–163.

Conceptual art, avant-garde philosophy of art dating from the mid-1960s and rejecting the physical art object in order to emphasize the artist's intellect, not his aesthetic ability. It is also called con art, idea art, impossible art and post-object art. Conceptual artists create works invisible to the human senses, such as exhibits of inert gases or electromagnetic waves that can be detected only by instrument readings.

Conceptualism, philosophical theory in which the universal is found in the particular. A position between NOMINALISM (which analyses universals into particulars) and REALISM (in which universals are real apart from all particulars), conceptualism includes both universals and particulars. Essentially, it holds that the mind is the individual that universalizes by experiencing particulars, finding common factors in them, and then conceptualizing these common factors as universals. *See also* MS pp.226–227.

Concertina, portable wind instrument patented by the British scientist Charles WHEATSTONE in 1829. Similar in principle to an ACCORDION, it consists of two (generally hexagonal) panels of buttons (keys) separated by bellows. The notes are produced by vibrating metal reeds.

Concerto, musical work for instrumental soloist accompanied by orchestra. Concertos usually have three movements, and may be written for two or three soloists (double and triple concertos). The best-known concertos are those written for violin, piano or cello and are often virtuoso works.

Concerto grosso, musical form in which a small section of soloists on various instruments is contrasted with the full orchestra. Alessandro Stradella is now accredited with originating the form, although Giuseppe TORELLI (1658–1709) and Antonio VIVALDI (1675–1741) are better known for early examples.

Conch, GASTROPOD MOLLUSC found throughout the world in warm seas; it has a large, tapering, helical shell. The queen conch (*Strombus gigas*) of Florida is up to 30cm (12in) across and is regarded as a gourmet's delicacy. Family Strombidae.

Conclave, originally a place of assembly, then the assembly itself. More particularly the term denotes the assembly of CARDINALS meeting to elect a new POPE.

Concord, town in E Massachusetts, USA, 31km (19 miles) NW of Boston on the Concord River. There was a battle at Concord in 1775 during the Revolutionary War when British forces were sent from Boston to destroy ammunition and supplies stockpiled in Concord, and were met by the MINUTE MEN. It was a literary centre in the mid-19th century and a number of writers lived there, including EMERSON, THOREAU and HAWTHORNE. Industries include furniture, iron and precision instruments. Pop. (1970) 16,148. *See also* HC2 p.64.

Concordance, alphabetical or thematic index of all or only the principal words of a book, giving a reference to their location and citing the context. Alexander CRUDEN (1701–70) compiled a concordance to the Authorized Version of the Bible which is still in use. There have been later concordances to the works of famous authors.

Concordat, agreement between Church and State regulating relations between them on matters of common concern. The term is usually applied to treaties between individual states and the VATICAN.

Concorde, supersonic transport (SST) aircraft developed and built jointly by the British Aircraft Corporation and Aerospatiale of France. *See also* MM p.*151.*

Concrete, hard, strong building material made by mixing CEMENT, sand, gravel and water. It is strengthened by embedding steel rods in it, giving reinforced concrete. Its modern use dates from the early 19th century, although the Romans made a natural form of concrete. *See also* MM pp.46–47, 51, 183, 192.

Concrete, reinforced, building material made by casting strengthening steel rods in concrete – a mixture of CEMENT, an aggregate such as fine gravel or coarse sand and water. The cement binds the mixture into a solid mass. Without reinforcement, concrete slabs or columns can withstand limited stress, but when reinforced are among the strongest and cheapest building materials. *See also* MM pp.46–49, *51,* 183, 192.

Concrete Art, term coined in 1930 by Theo van DOESBURG as an alternative for ABSTRACT ART – which suggested a separation from reality. To Concrete Artists, a work of art was a "concretion of the creative spirit" using elements of natural phenomena (eg space, light and form). Popular as a term in Switzerland and Latin America, its best-known representative was Max BILL. Although it survived WWII, the term has seldom been used since 1950.

Concubinage, cohabitation of a man and a woman not married to each other. In some societies concubinage is actually a socially recognized relationship into which a couple enters instead of marriage or which exists in addition to the man's marriage. In most legal systems children of such a union cannot inherit property as of right.

Concussion, temporary brain malfunction due to a blow to the head. It results in loss of consciousness for a few seconds or minutes, and later in intermittent headache and brief giddiness or difficulty in concentrating. Treatment consists of rest and close observation to ensure that there are no serious head injuries.

Condé, House of (1530–1830), branch of the French House of BOURBON. Notable members of the line included the first prince, Louis I de Bourbon (1530–69), a HUGUENOT leader. The third prince was Henry II (1588–1646), a Catholic, who was arrested for blackmail and sedition (1616), but was later rewarded for loyalty to LOUIS XIII. Louis II, the Great Condé (1621–86), was involved in the FRONDE uprisings (1648–53), and later became one of LOUIS XIV's greatest generals. Louis Joseph de Bourbon (1736–1818) led émigré forces during the FRENCH REVOLUTIONARY WARS.

Condensation, formation of a liquid from a gas or vapour caused by cooling or an increase in pressure. More particularly it is the changing of water vapour in the air into water droplets, forming mist, cloud, rain or drops on cold surfaces. *See also* PE pp.70–71, 146; SU pp.84–87, 90–91.

Condensation, colloidal. *See*: COLLOIDAL CONDENSATION.

Condensation nucleus, small liquid or solid particle, such as dust, on which water vapour in the atmosphere begins to condense in tiny water droplets or ice crystals with cloud formation. *See also* PE p.70.

Condensation trail. *See*: CONTRAIL.

Condenser. *See*: CAPACITOR.

Condenser, steam, device for changing steam to water by cooling. Condensers are used in steam-power plants where the steam from a turbine or steam engine must be condensed to water, which may then by pumped back for re-use in the boiler. *See also* MM pp.64–66.

Conder, Charles Edward (1868–1909), British artist. He began to paint while in Australia where he was born, later moving to Paris and London. Conder is known principally for his watercolours on silk and his designs for painted fans.

Condillac, Étienne Bonnot de (1715–80), French philosopher. Condillac was a prominent member of the school of sensationalists, who believed that human understanding can be reduced to the articulation and comparison of sensations derived from experience. He wrote *Treatise on Systems* (1749) and *Treatise on Sensations* (1754).

Conditioned reflex, in psychology, new or modified response elicited by a stimulus after CONDITIONING. *See also* MS pp.146–147, 152–153.

Condition Humaine, La, novel by the French writer, André MALRAUX, published in 1933. It is set against the background of Chiang Kai-Shek's coup against the Chinese Communists in 1927. It is an early expression of the ABSURD in French literature.

Conditioning, in psychology, method of controlling or modifying behaviour. Most of the procedures and terminology stem from the work of Ivan PAVLOV. A response elicited by a provided stimulus is called a conditioned reflex. Operant conditioning, first described by B. F. SKINNER in the 1930s, involves rewarding or punishing certain actions to positively or negatively reinforce behaviour. It can give rise to new behavioural patterns, unlike classical conditioning, the basis of Pavlov's work, which can modify only the existing behavioural repertoire of a human being or animal. Operant conditioning occurs naturally. Many emotional responses are learned on this principle. *See also* MS pp.146–147, 152–153.

Condliffe, John Bell (1891–), Australian economist. He was professor of economics at the University of California from 1940 to 1959, when he became professor emeritus.

Condominium, joint sovereignty over a single territory by two or more states. In Roman law condominium was common ownership by two or more persons of a single property, and still has this meaning in Canadian and US civil law. The term developed, however, to include political sovereignty, especially during the age of European colonialism. From 1899 to

1935, for example, Britain and Egypt ruled jointly as a condominium in the Sudan.

Condor, common name for two species of American VULTURES; the black Andean condor (*Vultur gryphus*) and the rare grey-brown California condor (*Gymnogyps californianus*). They are two of the largest flying birds and feed on partly rotted carrion. Length: up to 127cm (50in). Wing-span: up to 3.5m (10ft).

Condorcet, Marie Jean Antoine Nicholas de Caritat, Marquis de (1743–94), French philosopher and mathematician noted for his *Essay on the Application of Analysis to the Probability of Majority Decisions* (1785). He suggested the progress of man to ultimate perfection in his *Sketch for a Historical Picture of the Progress of the Human Mind* (1795).

Condor Legion, force sent by Nazi Germany to assist the Nationalist forces of Gen. FRANCO during the SPANISH CIVIL WAR (1936–39). It comprised almost 100 bomber and fighter aircraft and gave the Nationalists air supremacy; it was responsible for the bombing of GUERNICA.

Condottieri, leaders of mercenary armies hired to fight the numerous wars among the Italian states in the 14th–16th centuries. Both they and their armies were often foreign. By the late 14th century the *condottieri* had begun conquering principalities for themselves. Famous among the *condottieri* were the Englishman John Hawkwood (1320–1394) and Francesco Sforza, who annexed Milan in 1450.

Conductance, ability of a material to conduct electricity. In a direct-current circuit, it is the reciprocal of resistance. In an alternating-current circuit, it is the resistance divided by the square of impedance. Units of conductance are siemens.

Conduction, transfer of heat within a body. If one end of a metal rod is placed in a flame, the heat energy received causes increased vibratory motion of the molecules in that end. These molecules bump into others further along the rod, and the increased motion is passed along until finally the end not in the flame becomes hot. *See also* HEAT EXCHANGE; SU p.90.

Conductivity, in physics, a measure of the ease with which a material allows electricity or heat to pass through it. For a solid substance, the electrical conductivity is the conductance between the opposite faces of a unit cube at a specific temperature. It is the reciprocal of RESISTIVITY and is expressed in mhos (ohms^{-1}). For an ELECTROLYTIC SOLUTION, conductivity is the ratio of the current density to the field strength. The coefficient of thermal conductivity of a solid substance is the amount of heat that flows between the faces of a unit cube of it in one second when the temperature difference across its faces is one degree. *See also* SU pp.*90*, 112–115.

Conductor, in physics, substance or body allowing easy passage of free electrons. Conductors have a low electrical resistance. Metals are the best conductors; they have free electrons which constitute a current when they are made to flow. The resistance of a metallic conductor increases with temperature as the vibrations of lattice atoms increase, hindering the motion of the electrons. *See also* SU pp.112, 114.

Conductor, in music, person who controls a group of players or singers, generally a band, orchestra or choir. The conductor's task is to co-ordinate a performance and to direct and inspire the interpretation of the music. Before the 19th century a harpsichordist or first violinist "led" or "directed" orchestral playing, but with the growth in size of orchestras the practice evolved of a musician standing before the players and conducting with a baton. Many small orchestras have reverted to the traditional practice of direction by the first violinist or a solo pianist or violinist. *See also* HC2 p.105.

Cone, in botany, conical, spheroidal or cylindrical fruit- or seed-bearing structure borne by CONIFER trees and comprising clusters of stiff, overlapping, woody scales which separate to release seeds from naked ovules developed at their base. *See* NW pp.54–57, *54–57*.

Cone shell, any of about 500 species of GASTROPOD MOLLUSCS found in tropical seas; it has a heavy cone-shaped shell with vivid markings and colours. Most feed on small worms or fish and some species can inflict serious or even fatal stings. Length: to 13cm (5in). Family Conidae. *See also* NW p.*96*.

Coney Island, resort area of New York, USA, famous for its fun fairs. It has been redeveloped since the 1950s and many amusement arcades have now been replaced by high rise flats.

Confectionery, delicacies or sweetmeats based on sugar, also known as sweets or candy. Sweetmeats, long ago known to the ancient Egyptians and in the Orient, were candied fruits made with honey. One of the earliest functions of confectionery was in making unpleasant medicines more palatable. In the 19th century the manufacture of sweets became extensive. There are two types, hard or soft, depending on the stage of crystallization of the sugar.

Confederate Constitution, adopted on 9 February 1861, by the CONFEDERATE STATES of America in Montgomery, Alabama. It greatly resembled the US Constitution, except that it emphasized the rights of individual states and the right to own slaves. *See also* HC2 pp.150–151.

Confederate States of America (CSA), government formed in February 1861 by the first seven states to secede from the USA. They were South Carolina, Mississippi, Florida, Alabama, Georgia, Louisiana and Texas. Virginia, Arkansas, North Carolina and Tennessee joined the CSA soon after. Jefferson DAVIS was elected president. The capital was located originally at Montgomery, but later moved to Richmond. The government was dissolved in April 1865. *See also* HC2 pp.150–151.

Confederation of British Industry. *See*: CBI.

Confession, in Jewish-Christian tradition, the acknowledgement of sins. It may be made by a congregation in the course of worship or by individual penitents in public or private confession. It is customary in Catholic Christendom for individuals to confess their sins privately to a priest at regular intervals. The term is also used to denote a statement of religious belief, common during the Protestant Reformation.

Confessions of an English Opium Eater (1822), autobiographical work which brought Thomas de QUINCEY to eminence. He describes with imaginative force the pleasures and pains of taking LAUDANUM.

Configuration, electron, the arrangement of electrons around an atom. It is usually written in a notation using 1, 2, 3, etc for the principal shell and *s, p, d* and *f* for the subshell. The number of electrons is written as a superscript. The electron configuration of the helium atom is $1s^2$; that of the sodium atom is $1s^22s^22p^63s^1$. *See also* SU pp.62, 132–137.

Confirmation, sacrament of the Christian Church: the "outward and visible sign of an inward and spiritual grace". Today a candidate for confirmation takes the baptismal vows previously made on his behalf by godparents, and confirms that he means to keep them. As a token of renewed welcome to the congregation, a bishop lays his hands upon the head of the candidate. Candidates may be children (aged seven in the Roman Catholic Church) or adults (in other Churches). In the Eastern Orthodox Church, confirmation, baptism and first communion are combined in a single rite.

Conformity, adherence of an individual to the social norm of behaviour. The desire to conform is often taken as a basic motive in human behaviour, and studies have shown that people do tend to stick to the norm, especially when they are anxious, uncertain or under pressure. *See also* MS pp.264–271.

Conformity, in geology, the undisturbed, continuous layering of sediments in even strata with no evidence of folding, faulting, intrusion of new materials or erosion by wind or water.

Confucianism, philosophy that dominated China until the early 20th century and still has many followers, mainly in Asia. It is based on the ANALECTS, sayings attributed to CONFUCIUS (*c*.551–479 BC). At first strictly an ethical system to ensure a smooth-running society, it gradually acquired quasi-religious characteristics. Confucianism views man as potentially the most perfect form of *li*, the ultimate embodiment of good. It stresses the responsibility of sovereign to subject, of family members to each other and of friend to friend. Politically, it helped to preserve the existing order, upholding the status of the mandarins, highly educated Confucians who ran the Chinese bureaucracy. When the monarchy was overthrown (1911–12) Confucian institutions were ended, but since the Communist revolution in China (1949), many traditional Confucian elements have apparently been incorporated in Maoism. *See also* HC1 pp.124–125; MS p.*235*.

Confucius (*c*.551–479 BC), founder of Confucianism. Born in the Chinese province of Lu of aristocratic parents, he was largely self-educated. An excellent scholar, he became an influential teacher of the sons of wealthy families and is said to have been prime minister of Lu but resigned when he realized the post carried no real authority. In his later years he sought a return to the political morality of the early CHOU DYNASTY, but found no support. He died a frustrated man, but his ethical concepts dominated Chinese society for 2,000 years. Some of his teachings are recorded in the *Analects*. *See also* HC1 pp.124–125; MS p.*235*.

Conga, Latin American dance in 4/4 time, in which a file of dancers accent the fourth beat with a kick. Also the name for a narrow drum originally used in such music, about 90cm (36in) high, played with the hands.

Congenital disorders, abnormal or pathological conditions of the body caused by infection or injury of the foetus in its mother's womb or during birth. They are therefore distinct from HEREDITARY DISORDERS. Important examples of congenital disorders are congenital venereal disease, including syphilis and gonorrhoeal conjunctivitis, and abnormalities such as deafness caused by German measles and rudimentary limb development caused by drugs such as THALIDOMIDE. *See also* MS p.84.

Conger eel. *See* EELS.

Congestion, in medicine, increased amount of blood in the vessels of a tissue or organ. It is usually an early sign of inflammation, but may also be due to a circulatory disorder. Increased production of MUCUS by the cells lining the respiratory tract is also called congestion, and is a symptom of a respiratory disease or of breathing polluted air.

Conglomerate, in geology, a sedimentary rock made up of rounded pebbles embedded in a fine matrix of sand or silt. Formerly called "pudding stone", conglomerates are commonly formed along beaches or on river beds. The term is usually restricted to water-laid deposits. *See also* PE p.102.

Congo, officially named People's Republic of the Congo, an independent nation in w central Africa. Formerly French Congo, it was proclaimed a Communist state in 1970. The chief commercial crops and leading exports are sugar cane, cocoa, coffee and tobacco. There is some manufacturing. The capital is Brazzaville. Area: 342,000sq km (132,046sq miles). Pop. (1975 est.) 1,345,000. *See* MW p.60.

Congo, Belgian. *See* ZAIRE.

Congo river. *See*: ZAIRE RIVER.

Congregationalism, Christian Church denomination in which each local church is autonomous and independent; members have at various times also been called Brownists, Separatists and Independents. It is based on the belief that Christ is the head of the Church and all members are God's priests. Modern Congregationalism began in England in about 1580. Congregationalists were prominent in Oliver CROMWELL's English army and government and a major political force in American colonies. They settled PLYMOUTH COLONY in 1620 and established

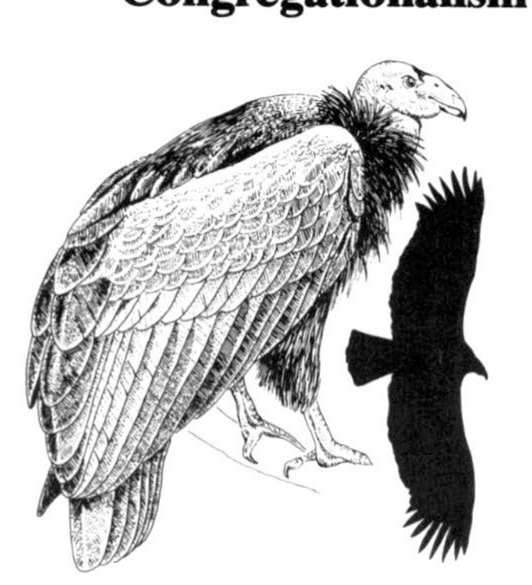

Condors differ from other birds of prey in that the female is the smaller of the two.

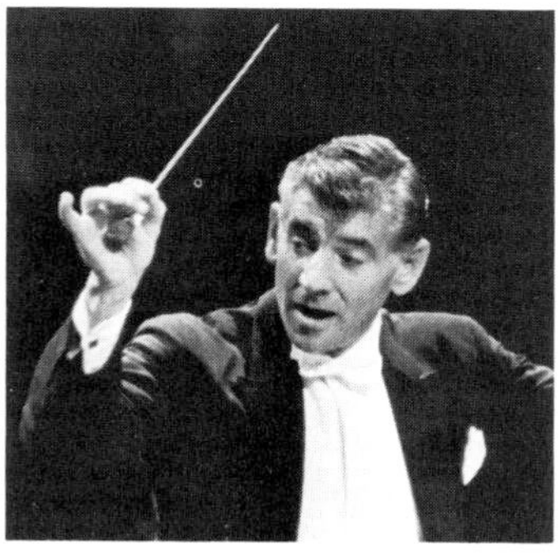

Conductor; Leonard Bernstein at the opening of Philharmonic Hall, Lincoln Centre, 1962.

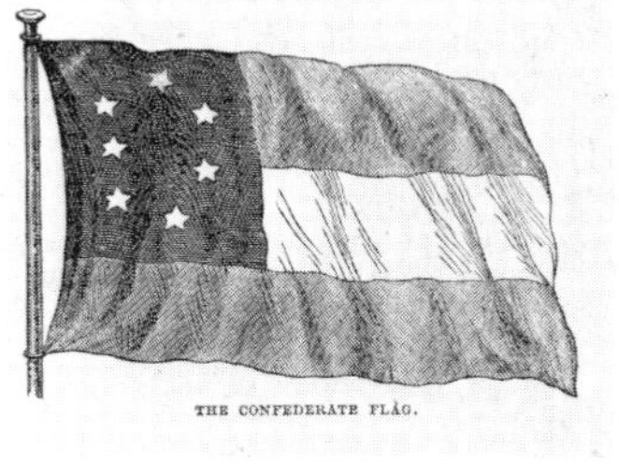

Confederate States of America; their first flag the "Stars and Bars", 4 March 1891.

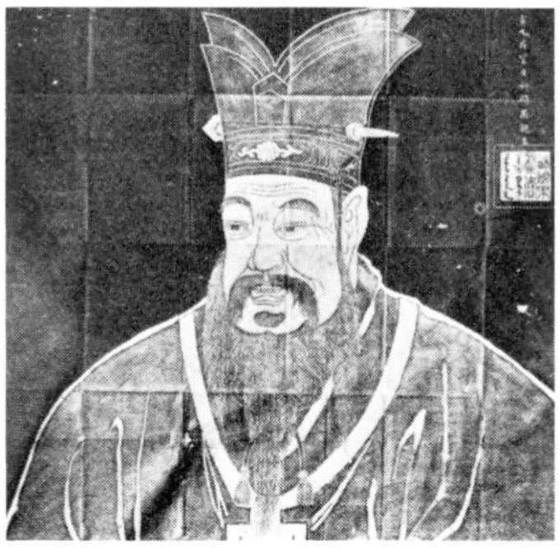

Confucius, whose humanitarian ideas were threatening to the despotic rulers of his day.

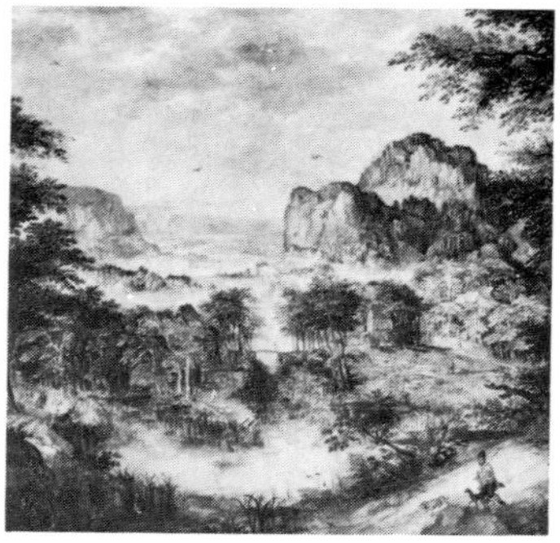

Coninxloo's landscapes combine realistic detail with fantastic points of view.

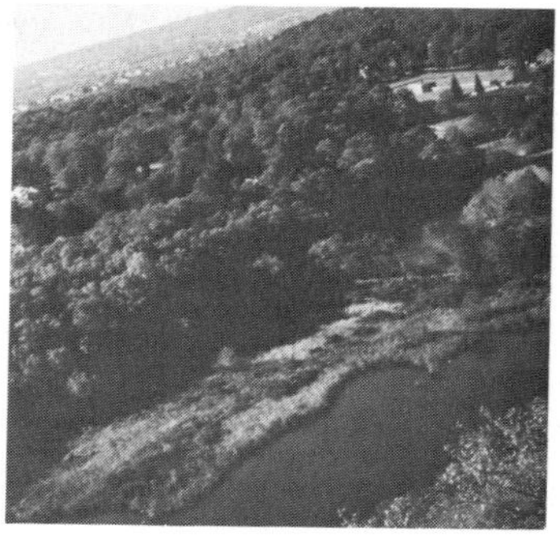

Connecticut, although a highly urbanized state, still has over half its land area forested.

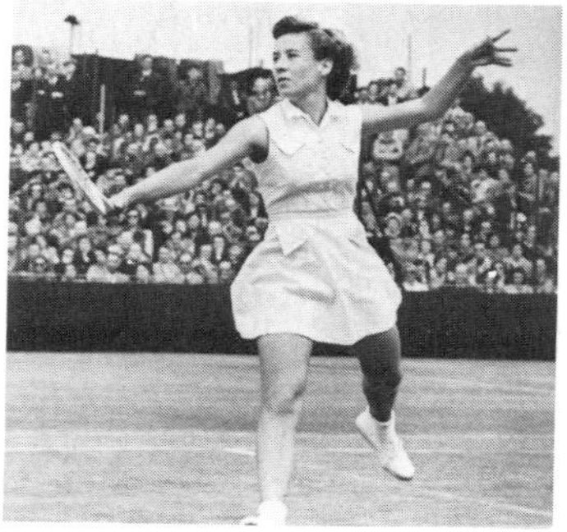

Maureen Connolly, "Little Mo", considered to be one of the greatest women tennis players.

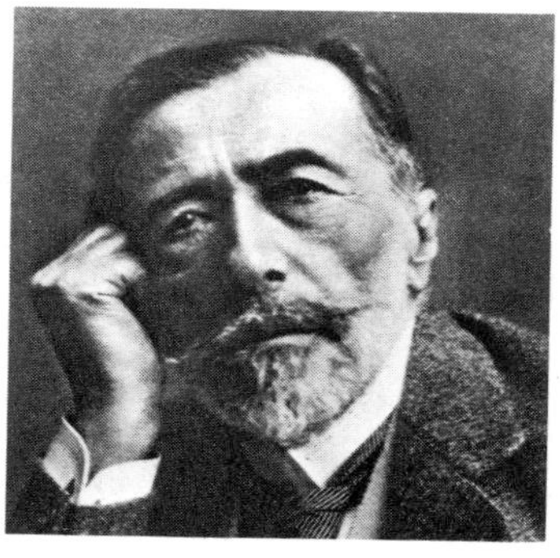

Joseph Conrad presents a deeply pessimistic view of human life in his many fine novels.

Harvard College in 1636. In 1972 the Congregational Church in England and Wales united with the Presbyterian Church of England to form the United Reformed Church. A similar union was effected in the USA in 1957; the Congregational Christian Churches united with the Evangelical and Reformed Church to form the United Church of Christ.

Congress, American, the legislative branch of the federal government consisting of the SENATE and the HOUSE OF REPRESENTATIVES. It first met in 1789. The Senate is composed of two elected members from each state; the House totals 435 members elected from each state in proportion to population. A resident commissioner from Puerto Rico is a non-voting member. Powers of Congress include the right to assess and collect taxes, regulate commerce, coin money, declare war, propose constitutional changes and raise and maintain defence forces. Legislation must be passed by both houses and be signed by the president to become law. The Constitution requires that Congress meet at least once a year.

Congress Party, official name Indian National Congress, oldest political party in India and, until 1977, the only party to hold national office since Indian independence in 1947. It was founded in 1885, but did not become powerful until after WWI, when Mahatma GANDHI transformed it into a mass movement agitating by means of civil disobedience for independence from Britain. It was the party of the Hindus (as opposed to the MUSLIM LEAGUE). At the provincial elections of 1937 it gained power in many states. During WWII it declined to support Britain, who had refused to grant immediate self-government. Since independence it has provided three prime ministers of India: Jawaharlal NEHRU, Lal Bahadur SHASTRI and Indira GANDHI. The Congress suffered a landslide defeat at the elections of 1977. *See also* HC2 pp.216–217.

Congreve, William (1670–1729), English dramatist who wrote comedies such as *Love for Love* (1695) and *The Way of the World* (1700). His elegant satire represents the peak of RESTORATION DRAMA. He also wrote a tragedy, *The Mourning Bride* (1697).

Conic, or conic section, curve found by the intersection of a plane with a cone. Circles, ellipses, parabolas, or hyperbolas are conic sections. Alternatively a conic is the locus of a point that moves so that the ratio of its distances from a fixed point (the focus) and a fixed line (the directrix) is constant. This ratio is called the eccentricity (e): $e = 1$ gives a parabola, $e > 1$ a hyperbola, $e < 1$ an ellipse and $e = 0$ a circle. *See also* SU pp.36–37, *36–37.*

Conifers, CONE-bearing trees, generally evergreen, such as pines, firs and redwoods (most larches, which are also conifers, are DECIDUOUS). The earth's largest plants, they reach heights of up to 99m (325ft) and are a major natural resource of the Northern Hemisphere. Their forests supply softwoods for building and wood pulp for papermaking and other important products such as synthetic fibres based on cellulose. Conifers lack elaborate flowers but their foliage and colour make them popular ornamental plants. *See also* GYMNOSPERM; NW pp.54–57, *54–57*; PE pp.218–219.

Coningham, Sir Arthur (1895–1948), RAF officer. In WWII he commanded the Allied attack in Tunisia (1941–43) and British and US air units in the Normandy invasion (1944–45). He was Air Marshal (1946) and commander of the Flying Training Command (1945–47).

Coninxloo, Gillis van (1544–1607) Flemish painter, a link between BRUEGEL and early 17th-century Dutch realist landscape painting. His landscapes combine realism with fantasy. RUBENS was among those he influenced.

Conjugation, sexual reproduction by fusion of gametes. It is characteristic of certain simple animals, lower plants and bacteria. In some algae, for example, a temporary conjugation tube forms a passageway for the contents of one cell to enter another. *See also* NW p.*37.*

Conjunctivitis, inflammation of the conjunctiva, the mucous membrane lining of the eyelid. It can be caused by infection, usually bacterial, by exposure to irritants, or by allergy, and produces watery, burning and itching eyelids. The contagious form is known as pink-eye.

Conklin, Edwin Grant (1863–1952), US biologist. He was professor of biology at Princeton University from 1908 to 1933. He is famous for his pioneering research in embryology and for his work in the processes of evolution and heredity.

Connacht (Connaught), province in W Republic of Ireland, including the counties of Mayo, Galway, Leitrim, Roscommon and Sligo. It was a kingdom of the O'Connors in ancient times and was invaded by the English in the 12th century. Area 17,122sq km (6,611sq miles). Pop. (1971 prelim.) 389,800.

Connaught, Arthur Frederick Patrick Albert, Prince (1883–1938), grandson of Queen VICTORIA. He was a personal aide to EDWARD VII and GEORGE V and aide-de-camp to Field Marshal FRENCH in 1914–15. He was Governor-General of the Union of South Africa from 1920 to 1923.

Connaught, Arthur William Patrick Albert, Duke of (1850–1942), 3rd son of Queen VICTORIA. He held commands in India (1886–90), was commander-in-chief in Ireland (1900–04) and the Mediterranean (1907–09), and governor-general of Canada (1911–16).

Connecticut, state in NE USA; southernmost state of New England. The Connecticut River valley separates the western and eastern highland regions. The state's economy is based on its manufacturing industries, which include transportation equipment, machinery, chemicals and metallurgy. Insurance is a major service industry, and Hartford is one of the world's leading insurance centres. Dairy produce, eggs and tobacco are the main farm products. Fishing is also important. The main cities are Hartford (the state capital and largest city), Bridgeport and New Haven. One of the original thirteen colonies, Connecticut was first settled by the English in the 1630s. Many Puritans flocked to the area, and in 1662 the colony received a charter from King Charles II of England. Many colonists later moved west but European immigrant workers took their place. Connecticut was one of the first states to ratify the US Constitution and was admitted to the Union in 1788. Area 12,973sq km (5,009sq miles). Pop. (1975 est.) 3,095,000. *See also* MW p.175.

Connecticut, river in New England, USA. It rises in Connecticut Lakes, N New Hampshire, flows S (forming the border between New Hampshire and Vermont) and continues through W central Massachusetts and central Connecticut to empty into Long Island Sound near Old Saybrook. It has 23 tributaries and has hydroelectric power plants and flood control and irrigation schemes. It was discovered in 1614 by the Dutch explorer Adrian Block. Length: 655km (407 miles).

Connecticut Wits, US writers in Hartford, Conn. at the turn of the 18th century, who produced satirical verses reflecting their conservative political views. Joel Barlow, John Trumbull, Timothy Dwight and David Humphreys were members of the group, also known as the Hartford Wits.

Connective tissue, supporting and packing that helps to maintain the body's form and holds it together. Bones, ligaments, cartilage and skin are all types of connective tissue. *See also* MS p.56.

Connelly, Marcus Cook (1890–), US dramatist. Early in his career he collaborated with George S. Kaufman on the comedy *To the Ladies* (1922). He won a Pulitzer prize for *The Green Pastures* (1930), a humorous dramatization of biblical tales in the Southern black folk idiom.

Connemara, region in Galway, on the W coast of the Republic of Ireland. Wild and mountainous and having many lakes and streams, it is particularly popular as a holiday area. Most settlement is on the coast, the chief town being Clifden.

Connery, Seán (1930–), Scottish film actor, best-known for his role as James Bond in the films of the Ian FLEMING spy stories. These included *Dr No* (1962) and *Diamonds are Forever* (1971).

Connolly, Cyril Vernon (1903–74), British author, critic and journalist. From 1927 he contributed to the magazine *New Statesman* and to the newspapers the *Sunday Times* and *Observer*. Co-founder with Stephen SPENDER of the magazine *Horizon* (1940–49), his books include *The Unquiet Grave* (1944) and *The Rock Pool* (1963), his only novel.

Connolly, James (1870–1916), Irish nationalist leader. He went to the USA in 1903 and helped to establish the INDUSTRIAL WORKERS OF THE WORLD. He helped to organize the Dublin transport workers' strike in 1913. For his part in the EASTER RISING of 1916 he was executed. *See also* HC2 pp.162–163.

Connolly, Maureen ("Little Mo") (1934–69), US tennis player. At 16, she won the US national singles championship, a title she later successfully defended (1952–53). She won the Wimbledon ladies singles championship (1952–54) and in 1953 won the grand slam of tennis by capturing also the French and Australian championships. She was forced to retire after a riding accident in 1954.

Connor, Ralph (1860–1937), Canadian clergyman and novelist, real name Charles William Gordon. He wrote adventure stories based on his experiences as a clergyman in the Canadian timber and mining camps. His novels included *Black Rock* (1898), *The Sky Pilot* (1899) and *The Man from Glengarry* (1901).

Connors, James Scott ("Jimmy") (1952–), US tennis player. He won the US, Australian and Wimbledon singles championships (1974) and the Wimbledon (1973) and US (1974) doubles titles with Ilie Nastase. In 1977 he won the Grand Prix Masters singles tournament held in New York.

Conodont, any of numerous kinds of tooth-like microfossils composed of calcium phosphate; they occur in marine deposits of the PALAEOZOIC and early MESOZOIC eras. Although their origin is uncertain, they have been classified in great detail and are used extensively in STRATIGRAPHY. *See also* NW pp.174–179; PE pp.124–127.

Conon (died *c.* 390 BC), Athenian admiral who, with the help of the Persian fleet, devastated the Spartan fleet at CNIDUS (394 BC).

Conquest, George Robert Acworth (1917–), British poet and novelist. He worked in the foreign service (1946–56) and taught in Britain and the USA. He edited the verse anthologies *New Lines* (1956, 1963). His own volumes of poetry include *Poems* (1955), *Between Mars and Venus* (1962) and *Arias from a Love Opera* (1969).

Conquistador, Spaniard who participated in the conquest of the New World in the 16th century. The term is Spanish for "conqueror". Conquistadores were professional or semi-professional soldiers, usually from Castile. PIZARRO and CORTÉS were the most famous. *See also* HC1 pp.236–237.

Conrad, name of four German kings. Conrad I (*r.* 911–18) suffered continual opposition and lost control of Lorraine. Conrad II (*c.* 990–1039) became the first SALIAN king in 1024. He consolidated his kingdom and was crowned Holy Roman Emperor in 1027. Conrad III (1093–1152) became the first king of the HOHENSTAUFEN dynasty on his accession in 1138. Disputes with the Welf family developed into GUELPH and GHIBELLINE factional warfare in Italy. Conrad IV (1228–54) was elected king in 1237 but suffered constant opposition from the pope. From 1251 he ruled mainly in Sicily. *See also* HC1 pp.160–161.

Conrad, Charles Jr (1930–), US astronaut. In 1953 he joined the US navy and became a test pilot and instructor. In 1962 he was co-pilot on the Gemini 5 space flight and in 1966 was command pilot on the Gemini 11 flight. In 1969, with Richard Gordon and Alan Bean, he commanded the Apollo 12 flight to the Moon.

Conrad, Joseph (1857–1924), British

novelist, *b.* Józef Teodor Kōnrad Korzeniowski in Poland. His years as a ship's officer in Asian, African and Latin American waters suggested the exotic settings of many of his novels. His works include *The Nigger of the Narcissus* (1897), *Lord Jim* (1900), *Heart of Darkness* (1902), *Nostromo* (1904), *The Secret Agent* (1907), *Under Western Eyes* (1911) and *Victory* (1915).

Cons, Emma (1838–1912), British social reformer. In 1880 she took over the Royal Victoria Hall, known as the "OLD VIC", as a temperance music hall. Subsequently her niece Lilian BAYLIS turned it into the theatrical home for Shakespearean plays.

Consanguinity, relationship between kin which is defined in terms of blood-ties rather than marriage. It is particularly important in legal and genetic contexts because of the inheritance of property, on the one hand, and of hereditary characteristics, on the other.

Conscience, Hendrik (1812–83), Flemish Romantic novelist. He initially wrote in French, but later virtually created the Flemish novel form. A prolific writer, his novels include the epic *The Lion of Flanders* (1853–57), *Wooden Clara* (1850) and *The Conscript* (1864).

Conscience, ability of an individual to know the difference between what is morally right and wrong. Children develop a moral sense mainly through learning from others. *See also* SUPEREGO; MS pp.160–161.

Conscientious objectors, people who on the grounds of pacifist conscience refuse to acknowledge the right of the state to require military service. During WWII in Britain, about 59,000 men and women applied to be registered as conscientious objectors. Some 3,000 were given unconditional exemption and about 43,500 were accepted on condition that they took up approved war work. About 3,000 were prosecuted and most imprisoned.

Conscription, compulsory enlistment of people for service in the armed forces. Obligatory military service existed in ancient Greece and Rome, as it did in Anglo-Saxon England, but it was short-term and local. Modern national conscription dates from the French Revolution. In Britain conscription was used in WWI and WWII; peacetime conscription was first introduced in May 1939 and continued between 1945 and 1962, when it was abolished. Peacetime conscription was abolished in the USA in 1973.

Conservation, term that has come to mean a number of different, if associated, things in the preservation of habitats, species, natural amenities and agricultural fertility. It can mean the preservation of landscape from change due to natural erosion or to soil denudation caused by overcropping. The use of soil conditioners and artificial fertilizers to maintain soil fertility against the effects of large-scale cultivation can also be called conservation. So can the protection of particular areas (such as marshes) against changes, such as drainage, which would drastically alter their fauna and flora. The replacing of topsoil and landscaping of spoiled land, such as opencast mining areas, is also a form of conservation. Finally, individual species of animals and plants, threatened with reduction or extinction, can be conserved by law or in wildlife parks or reservations. *See* NW pp.242–253.

Conservation, laws of, physical laws stating that some property of a closed system is unaltered by changes in the system. The most important are the laws of conservation of matter and of energy. The former states that matter can be neither created nor destroyed; the total mass remains constant when chemical changes occur. The total energy of a system also remains the same; energy is converted from one form into another. Mass and energy are interconvertible according to the equation $E = mc^2$. What is conserved is the total mass and its equivalent in energy. *See also* SU p.146; MM p.22.

Conservatism, political outlook that seeks to maintain the stability of society by preserving the historic continuity of its laws, customs, social structure and institutions. Its modern expression derives from the reaction, first in Germany, against the liberal doctrines of the ENLIGHTENMENT and the FRENCH REVOLUTION. Against the liberal's faith in the abstract rights of man and his willingness to undertake sweeping reforms, the conservative places his trust in the national experience and prefers to remove practical grievances by gradual, piecemeal reform. *See also* CHRISTIAN DEMOCRATS; CONSERVATIVE PARTY; TORY PARTY; HC2 p.170.

Conservative Party, or Conservative and Unionist Party, the oldest political party in Britain. Its origins lie in the transformation of the early 19th-century Tory Party into the Conservative Party under Sir Robert PEEL in the 1830s. Until late in the 19th century it was preponderantly a party of landed interests and depended electorally on the county constituencies. After the REFORM ACT of 1867 (passed by a Conservative government led by Lord DERBY) and the establishment of a Central Office in 1870, the urban and commercial element in the party increased. In 1886 the split in the Liberal party over Irish Home Rule brought Liberal Unionists into the party and led to the most successful period in Conservative history. Under Lord SALISBURY and Arthur BALFOUR the Conservatives held office for all but two years between 1886 and 1906. Before 1945, the party held office both in coalitions (the Liberal government of 1915–22 and the National governments of 1931–45) and twice in its own right (1922–24, 1924–29). Since 1945 it has held office singly from 1951 to 1964 and from 1970 to 1974. Its postwar leaders have been Winston CHURCHILL, Anthony Eden (later Lord AVON), Harold MACMILLAN, Alec Douglas HOME, Edward HEATH and Margaret THATCHER.

Conshelf, underwater habitats built under the supervision of Jacques-Yves COUSTEAU. In 1963 he lived for seven days 10m (33ft) under the Mediterranean in Conshelf I. Conshelf II was a similar experiment in 1964. In 1965 six men lived in Conshelf III at a depth of 100m (328ft) in the Mediterranean Sea for 27 days. *See also* PE p.93.

Consols, abbreviation for Consolidated Stock, or annuities in Britain. From 1748–51 and then in 1787 various public debts, incurred at different times, were consolidated into one Funded Debt. Various sources of revenue were at the same time made into a fund pledged as security for payment of interest to holders of consols. Consols are not, strictly, a loan, since the government need not repay the money; the investor in consols buys only the right to a perpetual annuity.

Conspiracy, agreement by two or more people to commit an illegal act. People may be guilty of conspiracy even though the planned crime was not committed.

Constable, John (1776–1837) British painter, one of the world's major landscapists of the 19th century. Constable was happiest painting the landscape of his native Suffolk, where he learnt what he called "the natural history of the skies". After a period in London (1795–1802) during which he attended the Royal Academy and studied the paintings of CLAUDE LORRAIN, Constable returned to Suffolk and, rejecting the fashionable Italianate paintings of the time, studied every effect of clouds and light on water – often using broken colour and a thick IMPASTO texture. His first success came when *The Hay Wain* (1821) and *View on the Stour* (1817) were shown at the 1824 Paris Salon and were acclaimed by French Romantic artists, especially DELACROIX. The success of his paintings imported into France had a considerable influence on the development of the BARBIZON SCHOOL. In England Constable was neglected until the oil sketches on which his large works were based were shown publicly after their bequest to the Victoria and Albert Museum, London, in 1888. These are much admired and are rated as among his best work. *See also* HC2 p.103, *103*.

Constance (Bodensee), lake bordering on Austria, West Germany and Switzerland. Fed and drained by the River Rhine, it divides into two arms near the city of Constance (Konstanz). It contains the remains of prehistoric lake dwellings. Area: 543sq km (210sq miles).

Constance, Council of (1414–18), gathering of bishops convoked by Antipope John XXIII to end the GREAT SCHISM between Rome (Pope Gregory XII) and AVIGNON (Pope Benedict XIII) and to combat heresy, notably that of JOHN HUSS. The council favoured the resignation of all three "popes" and elected Martin V as the new pope in 1417. John Huss was condemned and burned at the stake as a heretic.

Constant, in mathematics and science, a quantity or factor that does not change. It may be universal, eg the ratio of the circumfrence of a circle to its diameter (π); it may apply only to a particular circumstance, eg a symbol that has a fixed value in an algebraic equation; or it may be characteristic of an instrument or substance, eg BOLTZMAN's constant for gases.

Constanţa, city in E Romania, in the Constanţa district, on the Black Sea. Founded in the 7th century BC as a Greek colony, it was taken by the Romans in 72 BC and named in the 4th century AD by Constantine. It is Romania's chief port and a major trade centre. It has Roman and Byzantine ruins, several mosques and a naval and air base. Pop. (1970 est.) 172,500.

Constantan, high-melting point alloy containing 45% nickel and 55% copper. It is used in THERMOCOUPLES and in conjunction with iron and copper to form BIMETALLIC STRIPS – the sensing element in some thermostats. *See also* SU pp.*91*, *121*.

Constant de Rebecque, Henri Benjamin (1762–1830), Swiss-born French political writer. He was a member of NAPOLEON's tribunate (1799–1802), but went into exile in 1803. After the BOURBON restoration he was leader of the liberal opposition (1819–22; 1824–30). His chief work was the psychological novel *Adolphe* (1816).

Constantine, name of 11 Roman and Byzantine emperors: Constantine I (*c.*285–337; *r.*305–37); Constantine II (*c.*317–40; *r.*337–40); Constantine III (*d.*411; *r.*409–11); Constantine IV (652–85; *r.*668–85); Constantine V (718–75; *r.*741–75); Constantine VI (770–97; *r.*780–97); Constantine VII (Porphyrogenitus) (905–59; *r.*913–59); Constantine VIII (*c.*960–1028; *r.*1025–28); Constantine IX (Monomachus) (*c.*1000–55; *r.*1042–55); Constantine X (*c.*1007–67; *r.*1059–67); Constantine XI (Palaeologus) (*d.*1453; *r.*1449–53). For Constantine I *see* CONSTANTINE THE GREAT. Constantine II, his son, inherited the western third of the Roman Empire. Constantine III was a usurping emperor of the Western Empire. Constantine IV defeated the Arabs decisively at Constantinople in 678, and Constantine V was a leader of the anti-monastic party in the ICONOCLASTIC controversy. Constantine VI was emperor when the second Council of Nicaea (787) was convened. Constantine VII was an important patron of the arts, and wrote on politics. The final schism between the Eastern and Western churches occurred in 1054, in the ineffectual reign of Constantine IX, and Constantine XI was the last Byzantine emperor, killed during the successful Turkish siege of Constantinople. *See also* HC1 pp.142–143.

Constantine, name of a pope and an anti-pope. Constantine (*d.*715) was pope from 708 to 715. His principal achievement was to uphold the authority of the Roman see against Ravenna's claim to independence. His quarrel with the usurper-emperor PHILIPPICUS was the beginning of the MONOTHELITE controversy. Constantine II was anti-pope from 767 to 768. He was not canonically elected and failed to win the support of the FRANKS or LOMBARDS. He was deposed in 768 by the Lombards and after 769 nothing more was heard of him.

Constantine I, or Constantine the Great (*c.*285–337), Roman Emperor (*r.*305–37). In the early part of his reign he had to contend with rivals for his throne, and during the decisive battle of Milvian Bridge against Maxentius he was said to

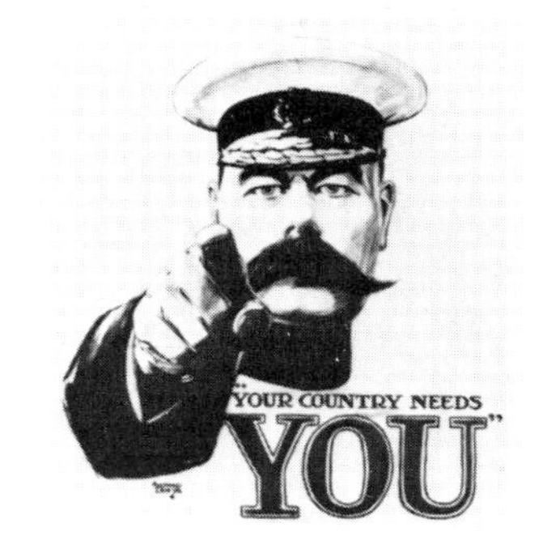

Conscription; prior to compulsory service patriotic appeals were made for volunteers.

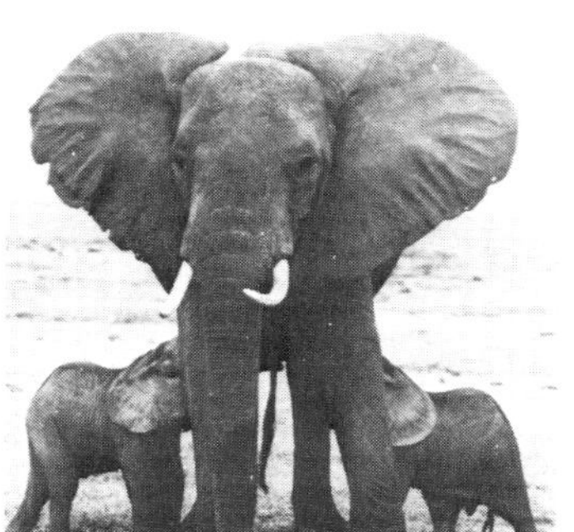

Conservation involves the protection of many endangered species in game reserves.

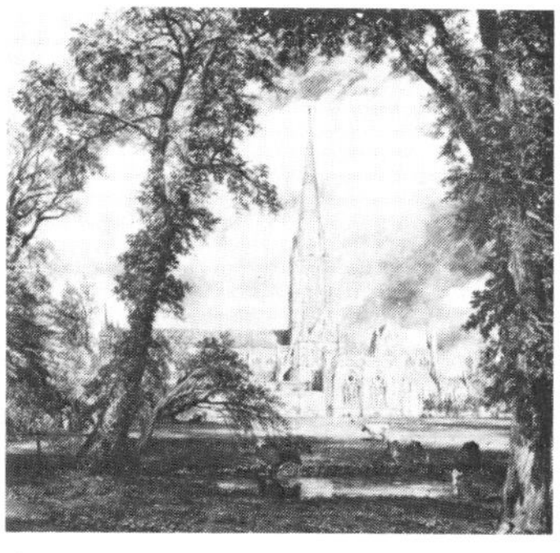

John Constable's *Salisbury Cathedral* used new techniques in landscape painting.

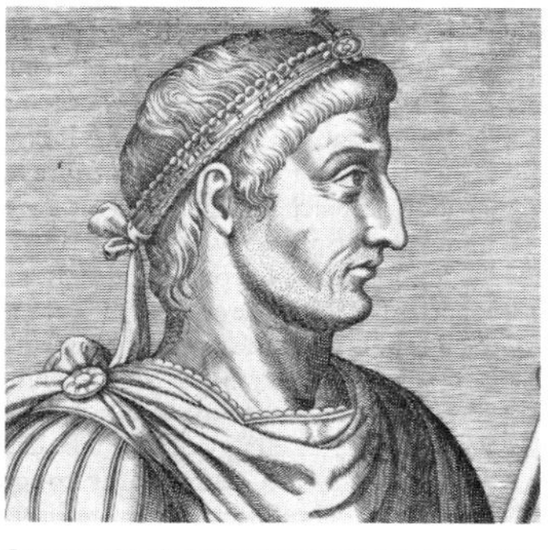

Constantine I claimed he saw a vision of the Cross while contemplating a military attack.

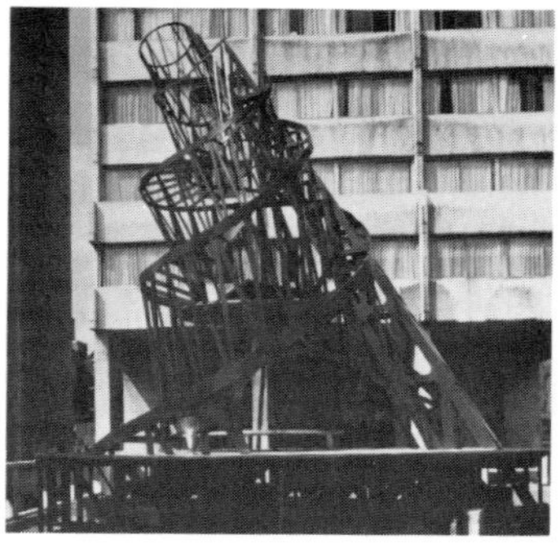

Constructivism; a reconstruction of Tatlin's monument to the third international.

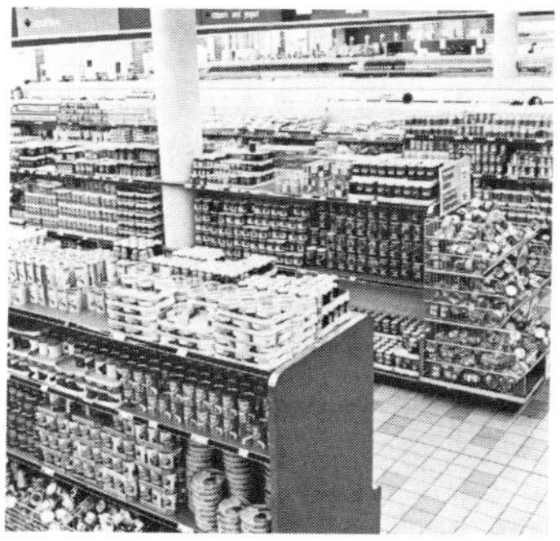

Consumer goods; their abundance reflects the material standards of Western nations.

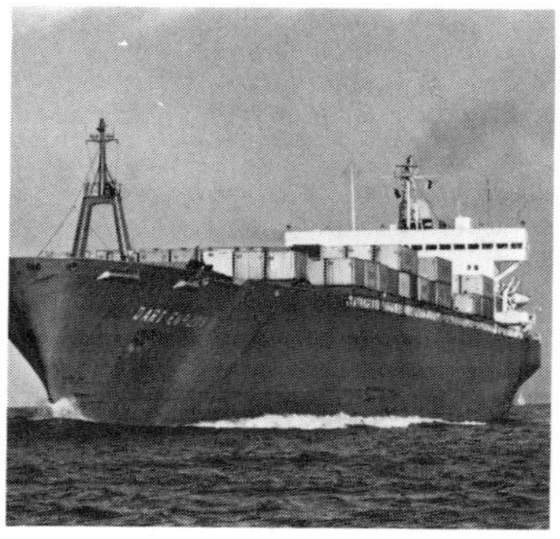

Container transportation has accelerated the international movement of large cargoes.

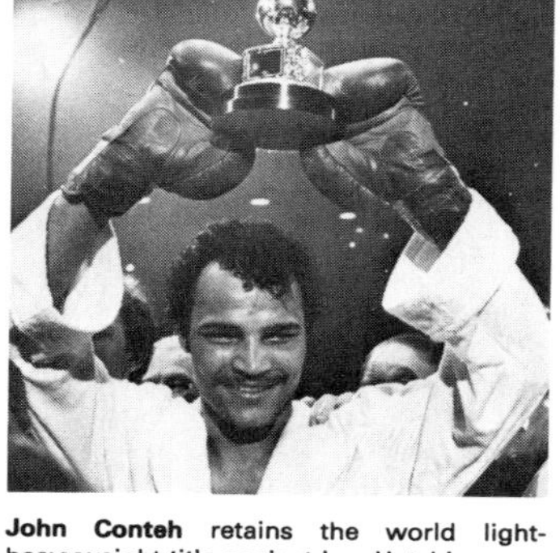

John Conteh retains the world light-heavyweight title against Len Hutchins.

have indicated his conversion to Christianity (312). In 313 he extended toleration to the Christians of the Empire by the Edict of Milan, perhaps seeing it as a means to achieve political unity. In 324 Constantine at last won sole control of the Empire, and he convened the Council of NICAEA in 325. He rebuilt BYZANTIUM, which was dedicated in 330, and renamed it Constantinople. He introduced legal reforms but ruled autocratically. He was baptized on his deathbed. *See also* HC1 pp.115, 142.

Constantine II (1940–), King of the Hellenes from 1964 to 1973. In 1967 he went into exile having failed to overthrow the then ruling military junta, who proclaimed him deposed in 1973. This was confirmed by the republic established in 1974.

Constantine, Learie Nicholas Constantine, Lord (1901–71), Trinidadian cricketer who played for the West Indies in the 1920s and 1930s. He was Trinidad's high commissioner to London from 1962 to 1964 and in 1969 he was elevated to the peerage. He was the first black to sit in the House of Lords.

Constantine, ancient fortified city and department capital in NE Algeria, on the River Rhumel. Founded by the Carthaginians as Sarim Batim, its name later changed to Cirta when it was a trading centre and capital of Numidia. It was a wealthy grain-exporting port under the Romans. Destroyed in AD 311, it was rebuilt by Emperor Constantine. Today it is Algeria's largest inland city. It has a university and a Muslim school. Industries: textiles, leather goods, food processing, tourism. Pop. 245,600.

Constantinople. *See* ISTANBUL.

Constantinople, Councils of, four gatherings of bishops held at Constantinople. The first (381) was convened by the Emperor Theodosius I to unite the Eastern Church at the end of the controversies relating to ARIANISM. It promulgated the Nicene Creed. The second (553) was convoked by the Emperor Justinian to settle controversies relating to NESTORIANISM. The third (680–81) was summoned by the Emperor Constantine IV to combat the heresy of MONOTHELITISM. The fourth (869–70) dealt with the PHOTIAN SCHISM.

Constantinople, Latin Empire of, formed after April 1204 when the armies of the Fourth CRUSADE captured the city of Constantinople and divided the former Byzantine territories among themselves. Western European feudal organizations were imposed upon some of the newly-formed states, and Constantinople was placed under the control of BALDWIN, Count of Flanders. The Latin Empire was constantly under attack and ended in 1261 when the Geeek Empire was restored by Michael Palaeologus. *See also* HC1 pp.142–143, 146–147, 176–177.

Constellation, in astronomy, traditional grouping of conspicuous stars forming a pattern as viewed from the Earth. There are a number of such groupings and each is an optical illusion, because individual stars may be at different distances from the Earth. Constellations visible in the northern and equatorial regions were named by ancient astronomers after animals or mythological figures, and some assumed importance in ASTROLOGY. Southern constellations remained unnamed by Europeans until the 16th and 17th centuries, and are often called after objects connected with navigation and science.

Constipation, incomplete or infrequent evacuation of stools that are hard and difficult to pass. It may be caused by an obstruction of the bowel passages or by a variety of digestive tract disorders, but is most often caused by improper diet or emotional stress. Treatment depends on the cause, but dietary change (with plenty of roughage and fluids) often helps. Cathartics may also be needed in stubborn cases.

Constitution, code of laws or collection of customary practices delineating the powers and organization of the various organs of government within a nation, and some of the rights and obligations of its citizens. Constitutions, like that of the USA, can be written in one document, and subsequently amended by specific rules laid down in the constitution itself, or, like that of Britain, they can evolve from the historical development of the customs, government and law of the land, and never be collected into written form. *See also* MS pp. 272–283.

Constitutional government, system in which the various elements of government (executive, legislature and judiciary, for example) have clearly defined and limited roles, as opposed to the constraints applied by the physical problems of asserting authority. In classical Greece, the idea that the form and powers of government could be a conscious choice for a polity was formalized by philosophers such as ARISTOTLE. Modern theories of constitutional government date from the 17th century, when government by constitution was frequently invoked to resist the claims of monarchs to absolutism: in England an unwritten, agreed constitution was in force after the GLORIOUS REVOLUTION of 1689. From the late 18th century, written constitutions were established in many countries, notably the USA and France. Since WWI, and the general acceptance of DEMOCRACY as a desirable form of political organization, constitutions enshrining democracy have been the rule in most countries.

Constitutional law, set of procedures and doctrines defining the operation of the constitution of a state. In modern states with a written constitution, courts often have specific powers relating to the constitution and likely points of conflict. In the USA, for example, where there is a federal system of government, the SUPREME COURT has often had to resolve conflicts between the individual states and the central government. In countries without a written constitution, such as Britain, constitutional law is more imprecise and problems are normally resolved within the political process.

Constrictor. *See* BOA.

Constructionalism, in psychology, school which maintains that basic sensations derive from unconscious neurological processes. The opposite view, ATOMISM, holds that perception is in units of simple sensations. *See also* MS p.46.

Construction engineering, branch of civil engineering responsible for preparing the site, directing the placement of materials and organizing personnel and equipment.

Constructivism, Russian abstract art movement founded *c.*1913 by Vladimir TATLIN, who created the first free geometric sculptural constructions in space. Other leading members of the movement were the brothers Naum GABO and Antoine PEVSNER whose sculpture, influenced by CUBISM and FUTURISM but less purely abstract in concept than Tatlin's, attempted to relate to the technology of the society in which they were created. From 1921 the Soviet regime officially condemned the movement and Gabo and Pevsner left Russia. Through them, and other exiles, Constructivism spread beyond the USSR and influenced modern European architecture and sculpture. Pioneer achievements in typography, through El Lissitzky, and poster and exhibition design, were also influenced. *See also* HC2 pp.204, 205.

Consubstantiation, in the Christian doctrine of the EUCHARIST, the belief that after the consecration the substances of bread and wine continue to co-exist along with the body and blood of Christ. The doctrine, attributed to MARTIN LUTHER, is opposed to that of TRANSUBSTANTIATION.

Consul, one of the two chief magistrates of ancient Rome. The office was said to have been established in 510 BC. Consuls were elected each year to administer civil and military matters. After 367 BC, one consul was a PATRICIAN, the other a PLEBIAN, and each had the power to veto the other's decisions. *See also* HC1 p.92.

Consul, government representative stationed abroad to protect his country's citizens and commercial interests. Consular services include issuing visas, birth and death certificates and the regulation of passports. Consuls are established under reciprocal bilateral treaties, and enjoy conditional immunity from the laws of the country in which they work. They are not covered by diplomatic immunity, but have some freedom from the jurisdiction of the state where they serve.

Consulate (1799–1804), name given to the French Republic's government after the end of the DIRECTORY. There were three consuls but government was actually dominated completely by NAPOLEON, who became first consul for life in 1802. *See also* HC2 p.76.

Consumer Council, National, state-financed but independent body in Britain, formed in 1961 to protect consumers. It does not deal directly with individual complaints, but as the consumers' representative applies pressure on central and local government and on manufacturers and retailers, according to complaints that it receives. It also seeks to raise the general level of consumer understanding.

Consumer durables. *See*: DURABLE GOODS.

Consumer goods, in economics, final goods produced for consumption by the domestic market. Consumer goods are classified as DURABLE GOODS if their useful life exceeds one year, eg. motor cars. If their life is less than one year, they are classified as non-durables, eg, food. Consumer goods plus services make up total consumption.

Consumer protection, intended to protect buyers in their purchase of manufactured goods, an idea that gained much force in the 1960s with the movement in the USA pioneered by Ralph NADER. Many countries now have consumer organizations, such as the British Consumers Association which passes on advice to its members through its magazine *Which?*.

Consumer psychology, special field of psychology that studies the way consumers use their time and spend their money on goods and services. It examines their needs and their attitudes toward such matters as product quality, advertising and the public image of corporations and government agencies.

Consumption. *See* TUBERCULOSIS.

Contact dermatitis, acute or chronic inflammation of the SKIN produced by contact with certain natural or synthetic substances, eg wool, poison ivy, detergent. It most usually appears as skin redness and swelling, but sometimes occurs as an oozing vesicle. *See also* ALLERGY.

Contact lenses, lenses worn on the eye to aid or correct defective vision. The earliest contact lenses were made of glass, but since 1938 plastic has generally been used. In the early 1970s "soft" lenses were introduced. Until 1950, lenses were made by taking impressions of the eye. Smaller lenses are now made, shaped to measurements taken from the eye. They cover only the cornea and float on a layer of tears. *See also* MS p.*49*.

Contactor, device for the repeated switching on and off of electrical circuits. Often, contactors contain a magnetic coil which diverts and extinguishes the electrical arc formed when a circuit is opened. *See also* SU p.*121*.

Container transportation, late 1960s development, chiefly in ocean shipping but also in air freight, that has greatly speeded cargo-moving. Ships have compartments above and below decks to hold large containers. In port, the containers are loaded and unloaded with specialized automated equipment. Usually, filled containers leave the factory by truck, are loaded on to railroad cars, and then on to a ship. *See also* MM p.114.

Contarini, noble Venetian family, dating from at least the 7th century AD. Its members included eight doges and many important statesmen and scholars. Domenico was the first Contarini doge (1043–71), and Andrea (*r.*1367–82) donated his wealth to the state. Gasparo (1483–1542) was a humanist scholar, diplomat, theologian and cardinal. Other notable Contarini were Ambrogio (*d.*1499), a great traveller; Giovanni (*d.*1603), a painter; and Marco (*d.*1689), a patron of music.

Conteh, John (1951–), British boxer. A hard-hitting coloured middleweight, he won British and Commonwealth amateur titles before turning professional in 1971. In 1974 he won the World Boxing Council version of the world light-heavyweight crown, only to be stripped of his title for failing to defend it in 1977.

Contempt, in law, disorderly conduct in a court or legislative body, or action performed elsewhere that tends to obstruct the work of a court or legislative body or bring it into disrepute. Contempt is usually punishable by a fine, imprisonment or public reprimand.

Contempt of Parliament, any action, by an MP or any other person, in breach of the privileges (the rules and habitual customs) of either house of Parliament. The offender may be committed, tried and imprisoned. The most famous instance of the offence in Britain was the regular publication of parliamentary proceedings before the practice was made legal early in the 19th century.

Conti, Italia (1874–1946), British actress, founder of a school for child actors. In 1911 she trained the children appearing in *Where the Rainbow Ends.* Subsequently she appeared on stage only occasionally, devoting most of her time to her school, which produced such actors as Noël COWARD and Gertrude LAWRENCE.

Conti family, younger branch of French royal family in the BOURBON House of CONDÉ. The family began its continuous line with Armand de Bourbon, Prince de Conti (1629–66), who took the name from the town of Conti, near AMIENS. The line ended with Louis François Joseph de Bourbon (1734–1814), who was exiled after the French Revolution.

Continent, land mass on the Earth. The continents are Europe and Asia (or Eurasia), Africa, North America, South America, Australia and Antarctica. They are not evenly distributed over the surface of the Earth; more than two-thirds of the continental area is in the N hemisphere. They cover approx. 29% of the Earth above sea-level and extend below sea-level forming CONTINENTAL SHELVES. Continental masses are found on opposite sides of the Earth to ocean basins. Geologically, they are complex formations, but they usually have extensive interior plains or plateaus of igneous or metamorphic rocks of the PRECAMBRIAN age. These areas are very often surrounded by mountain ranges composed of much younger, sedimentary rocks which have been folded or faulted, and frequently display volcanic activity. The origin of the continents is still uncertain but it is believed that the oldest rocks, in the central shield areas, were formed when the Earth's crust first solidified, and that continental formation, or accretion, continues now. This is occurring at the edges of the continents where large plates of the Earth's crust are converging, a process known as PLATE TECTONICS. The continents are composed for the most part of granitic rocks called sial, under which are denser basaltic rocks called sima. These two form the crust of the Earth. Below the crust is the region known as the mantle, which is believed to be semi-molten. The continents appear to be floating on this mantle. This belief has lent support to the theory of CONTINENTAL DRIFT, which suggests that the continents were once joined together, and have drifted apart. *See also* PE pp.26, 32, 82.

Continental Congress (1774–89), federal legislature of the American colonies, during the war of Independence and the period of Confederation. Its first meeting, at Philadelphia in Sept-Oct 1774, created the earliest unified opposition to British rule, and agreed on a boycott of trade with Britain. The meeting was adjourned until May 1775. The Congress reconvened shortly after the battles of LEXINGTON and CONCORD, and it appointed WASHINGTON to be commander of the American army. It considered a British peace plan, defied certain aspects of the NAVIGATION ACTS, and in July 1776 adopted the AMERICAN DECLARATION OF INDEPENDENCE. The Congress continued to meet until 1789, but its powers after the end of the war were few. *See also* HC2 pp.64–65.

Continental divide, line of separation running the length of a continent which determines to which side of the continent rivers flow. Such divides exist in the USA, Canada, s America and Australia.

Continental drift, theory which proposes that at one time all present-day land masses were joined in one supercontinent called Pangaea, but that about 200 million years ago it began to break up and the resulting land masses, roughly the continents of today, began to move over the Earth's surface. The idea was first suggested in 1912 by the German meteorologist Alfred Wegener but the theory was not fully accepted, until the 1960s, when the development of such theories as sea-floor spreading and PLATE TECTONICS, techniques such as radiocarbon dating, and the study of the distribution of fossils, geological formations, fauna and flora, all provided evidence for Wegener's original theory. *See* PE pp.26, 47.

Continental margin, region of the ocean floor that lies between the shoreline and the abyssal ocean floor. It includes the CONTINENTAL SHELF, the CONTINENTAL SLOPE and the CONTINENTAL RISE.

Continental rise, gently sloping region of the CONTINENTAL MARGIN at the foot of the CONTINENTAL SLOPE. It is an area of thick deposits of sediments carried down by currents off the CONTINENTAL SHELF. *See* PE p.82.

Continental shelf, the almost flat part of the CONTINENTAL MARGIN between the shoreline and the CONTINENTAL SLOPE. Such shelves lie at an average depth of 200m (656ft) and have an average width of 75km (45 miles). They yield most of the world's marine food resources, some of the petroleum and natural gas, and large quantities of sand and gravel. *See also* PE p.82.

Continental slope, relatively steep slope in the sea-bed that lies between the CONTINENTAL SHELF and the CONTINENTAL RISE leading into the areas of much deeper water. The slope marks the boundary of the continental crust and the oceanic crust. *See* PE p.83.

Continuo, or thorough bass, system of accompaniment usually played on a harpsichord or organ, to such musical forms as recitatives, cantatas and oratorios. It was employed in music of the 17th and 18th centuries.

Continuous wave radiotelegraphy, emergency frequency used internationally for transmitting distress messages only from ships at sea. Other frequencies are allocated for regular ship-to-shore transmissions.

Contour, in cartography, a line on a map joining places of equal elevation. Closely spaced contours indicate a steep slope, few or no contours mean flat or almost flat ground. *See also* PE p.35.

Contour farming, practice of tilling moderately sloping land along lines of equal elevation, to prevent excessive run-off and reduce loss from surface erosion. It also helps to conserve water in the furrows.

Contraband, war materials which neutrals may not sell to belligerents. The definition of what constitutes war material has always been imprecise and is often determined by the decision of a power capable of enforcing its own interpretation.

Contrabassoon. *See* DOUBLE BASSOON.

Contraception. *See* BIRTH CONTROL.

Contract, in law, an agreement between parties that can be legally enforced. A contract creates rights and obligations, and if the obligations are not satisfied they can be enforced by law. Before an agreement is a legal contract, five elements must be present: it must be between parties who have the right to make it; they must have reached mutual assent; the arrangement must be within the law; consideration (eg, the exchange of money) must be involved; and the agreement must be in the proper form (eg, some contracts must be signed in front of witnesses).

Contract bridge, card game for four people, evolving from AUCTION BRIDGE. Known simply as bridge, it is the most international of card games, with Olympiads and world championships. Basically, the game has two parts: bidding and playing. All 52 cards are dealt, opposite players being partners, and they bid in turn clockwise, the highest bid securing the contract. In ascending order, the suits are clubs, diamonds, hearts, spades and "no trumps". "One heart", for example, means that a partnership contracts to make seven tricks with hearts as trumps. The player who first bids the suit "plays" the hand, and after the lead by the defender on his left, his partner's hand is displayed as dummy. *See also* WHIST.

Contraction, in physiology, shortening, as of the length of a MUSCLE, or reduction in diameter, as of the pupil of the EYE.

Contrail, or condensation trail, condensed vapours appearing as streamers of cloud behind aircraft – particularly noticeable when flying through clear and damp air.

Contralto, lowest range (below SOPRANO and MEZZO-SOPRANO) of the female singing voice. A male voice in this range is called a COUNTER-TENOR. *See also* ALTO.

Control column, main steering component in aircraft which controls roll and pitch. In both aeroplanes (joystick) and helicopters (collective pitch stick) it combines with foot controls which change direction above the vertical axis. Vertical movement in helicopters is controlled by the cyclic pitch stick. *See also* MM pp.152–155.

Control rocket, small rocket engine used to make fine adjustments to a spacecraft's attitude or orbit. Attitude control jets use compressed gas to alter the craft's orientation. Vernier engines make adjustments to the craft's speed to change its orbit. *See also* VERNIER ROCKET.

Control tower, at an airport, centre responsible for controlling the movements of all aircraft within a specified area. From the tower a controller can direct aircraft to and from runways and service areas. Communication is usually by radio, using reserved frequencies, but may be by light signals. *See also* AIR-TRAFFIC CONTROL; pp.186–187, *187.*

Convection, transfer of heat by flow currents within fluids (gases or liquids). Warm fluids have a natural tendency to rise whereas cooler fluids tend to fall. This movement subsides when all areas of the fluid are at the same temperature. Convection in the form of winds is the main method of heat transfer along the Earth's surface. Liquid convection is employed in, for example, a car's cooling system or in some domestic central heating systems. *See also* HEAT EXCHANGE; SU pp.90–91.

Convection current, in geology, a slow "turn over" of rock (like convection in a heated liquid). It occurs when large masses of deeply-buried rock are heated, over geological periods of time, and the heat cannot escape or be distributed evenly by CONDUCTION. This hypothesis has been put forward to explain mountain-building by buckling of the convected rock as it cools at the Earth's surface. *See also* PE p.24.

Convent, community of monks or nuns occupying a MONASTERY or other monastic domicile, or the building in which such a religious community is housed. The characteristic form of convents was established in 3rd-century Egypt and introduced into Europe in the 4th century. Today the name tends to be restricted to houses of nuns.

Convention, the revolutionary assembly of France from 1792 (after the collapse of the 1791 constitution) to the rule of the DIRECTORY in 1795. It was the Convention which abolished the monarchy, established the republic and inaugurated mass conscription. *See also* HC2 pp.74–75.

Convention of 1818, agreement that established the 49th parallel as the boundary between the USA and Canada from Minnesota to the Rocky Mts; the status of Oregon was undecided.

Convergence, in mathematics, property of an infinite series (or sequence) having a finite limiting value. Thus, for the series $1 + 1/2 + 1/2^2 + 1/2^3 + \ldots$ the sum of the first two terms is 1.5, the first three 1.75, and the first four 1.875; as more and more terms are taken the sum approaches 2, called the limit of the series. Such a series is said to converge. *See also* DIVERGENCE.

Convergent evolution, the tendency of

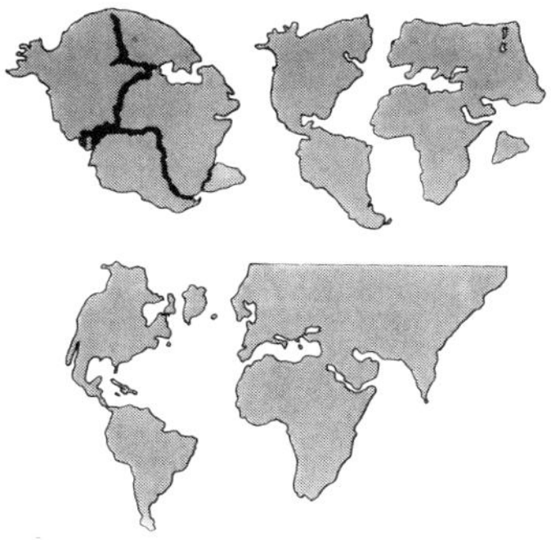

Continental drift; modern dating techniques now support a theory first proposed in 1912.

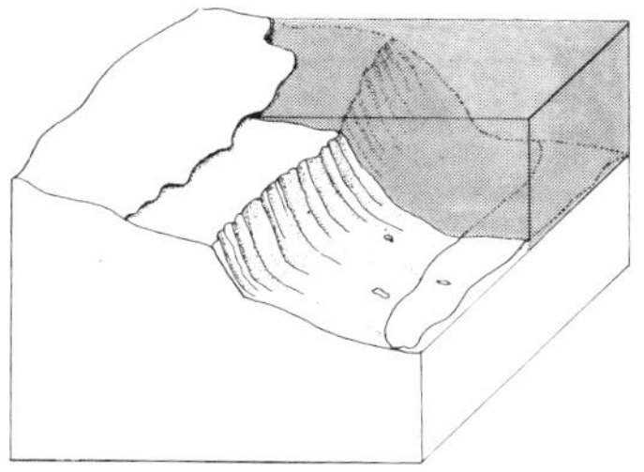

Continental shelves are the shallow zones between the coast and the deep ocean.

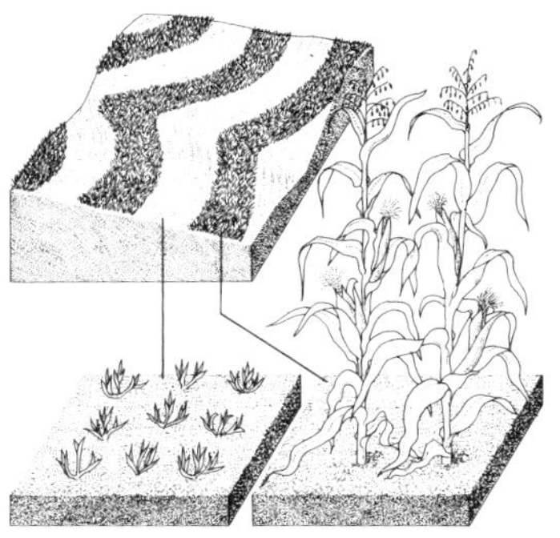

Contour farming, where the plough follows paths analogous to map contours.

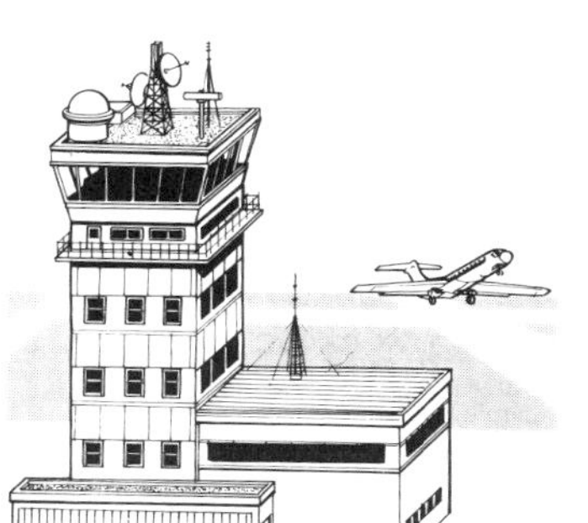

Control towers are the nerve centres for the safe and orderly movement of every aircraft.

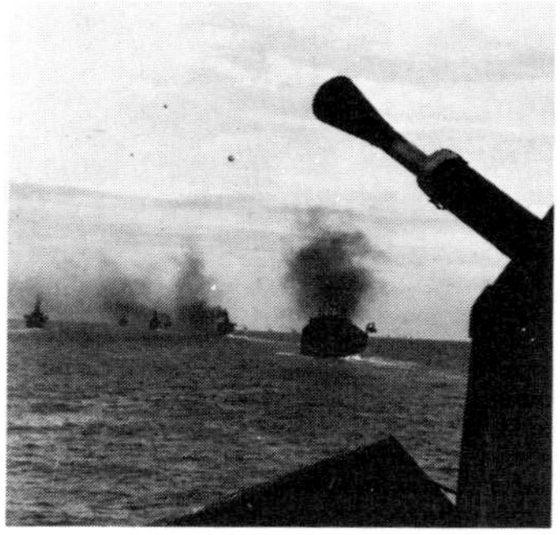

Convoys, to remain grouped, travelled at the speed of their slowest member.

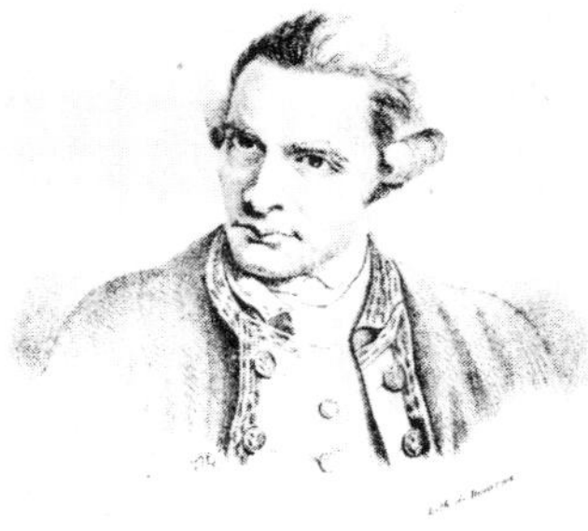

James Cook was one of the first of the truly scientific navigators and explorers.

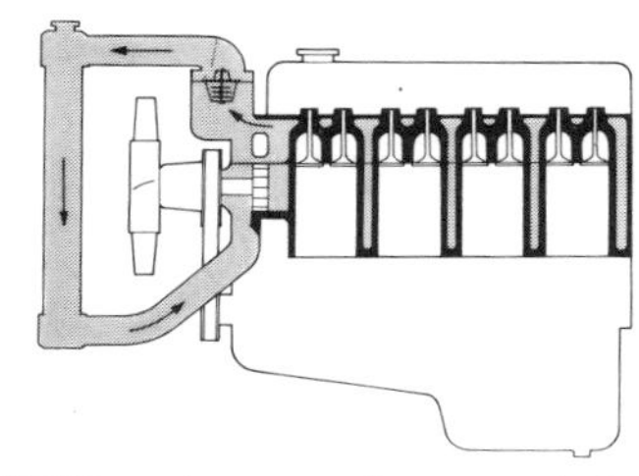

Cooling systems are often pressurized to raise the boiling point of the coolant.

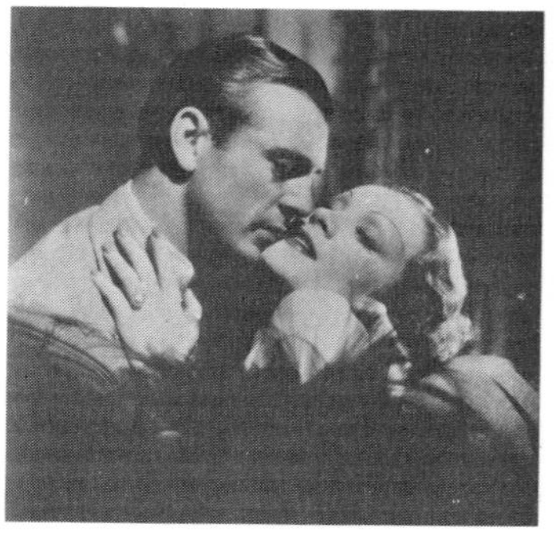

Gary Cooper, remembered as the tough hero, also played romantic roles.

several different species to resemble each other and to develop similar characteristics in their attempt to adapt to similar environments. *See also* NW pp.*35,* 140.

Convertible currency, currency that can be exchanged for other currencies for any purpose and without penalty. In order for a currency to be convertible, it must be defined in terms of an accepted standard of value, eg, gold under a gold standard. *See also* EXCHANGE RATES; HC2 p.300.

Convertive hysteria, in psychology, manifestations of HYSTERIA as physical disturbances such as blindness, deafness and paralysis. Conversion is a primitive mechanism for dealing with difficult situations and evoking sympathy. Hysterics are not malingerers; although they may be responsible for their illness, they are unaware that they are doing so. *See also* MS pp.140–141.

Conveyance, in law, the transfer of a legal title of land or property fron one person, company or institution to another.

Conveyor, machine for carrying objects from one place to another within a given area. Lifts, hoists, cranes, escalators and forklift and dump trucks are all types of conveyors, although the term is used more particularly for endless conveyors. These include looped belts moving on rollers, overhead trolleys moving on looped chains, scraper conveyors for moving loose material such as coal and ores, and fluidized-bed conveyors which transport granular or lightweight materials on a cushion of air. *See also* MM pp. *76, 96–97.*

Conveyor belt. *See* MASS PRODUCTION.

Colvolvulus. *See* BIDWEED.

Convoy, grouping of ships sailing under armed naval escort in wartime. Convoys of merchant ships were originally formed as a protection against pirates. The system was used in both world wars to safeguard merchant shipping against German U-BOATS. Overland convoys are used for military transport, over difficult or dangerous terrain.

Convulsion, bodily malfunction which results in violent, involuntary spasms of the muscles, sometimes accompanied by loss of consciousness. Such a seizure may indicate EPILEPSY, insulin overdose in a diabetic, or any of several brain disorders.

Conway Castle (Conwy), fortress in Wales built by EDWARD I in 1283 as part of his attempt to subdue Wales. During the Civil War the castle was garrisoned by forces of Charles I, but in 1646, after a three-month siege. it was surrendered to the parliamentarians.

Conzinc Rio Tinto, Australia's largest mineral company. It was founded in 1959 in Victoria as the Rio Tinto company and took its present name in 1962 when it merged with the Consolidated Zinc Corporation.

Cooch Behar district of West Bengal, India. It was established as a separate state ruled over by a maharajah in the 16th century, and became part of W Bengal in 1947. Its chief town is Cooch Behar. Pop. (1971 est.) 53,700.

Cook, James (1728–79), British naval officer and explorer. In 1768–71 he led a scientific expedition to Tahiti to observe the transit of Venus, and also surveyed the coast of New Zealand. On the same voyage he charted the E coast of Australia, naming it New South Wales and claiming it for England. On a second expedition to the S Pacific (1772–75), Cook mapped much of the S Hemisphere and sailed further south than anyone before him. On his last voyage (1776–79) he discovered the Sandwich (Hawaiian) Islands, where he was killed. *See also* HC2 pp.32, 124; MS p.248.

Cook, Sir Joseph (1860–1947), Australian politician. He emerged in 1908 as a leader of the Free Trade Party in New South Wales. As national defence minister (1909–10) he helped to set up the Australian Navy: he was prime minister (1913–14) and minister of the navy (1917–21). Cook was a delegate to the VERSAILLES Peace Conference (1919).

Cook, Thomas (1808–92), British founder of worldwide tourist agency, Thomas Cook and Son. Originally a missionary, he began to arrange the first group tours for temperance organizations (1841–44). He opened his own firm in 1845, providing his customers with railway discounts and travel guides. He first offered foreign tours in 1855, the grand tour of Europe in 1856, and the first around-the-world tour in 1872.

Cook, Mount, mountain in W central South Island, New Zealand, in the Southern Alps; the highest peak in New Zealand. It is in Mount Cook National Park and has the Tasman Glacier on its SE slope. Height: 3,764m (12,349ft).

Cooke, Alfred Alistair (1908–), British writer and broadcaster on American affairs. He was chief correspondent for *The Guardian* (1948–72). He produced a highly successful television documentary *America: A Personal History of the United States* (1972–73).

Cooke, Sir William Fothergill (1806–79), British electrical engineer. He collaborated with the physicist Charles WHEATSTONE to develop the first commercial electric telegraph in 1839. In 1845 they patented a single-needle apparatus. *See also* MM pp.*224.*

Cooking, the preparation of food for eating by the action of heat. The traditional methods are roasting on a fire, baking in an oven, boiling in water and frying in a pan. The most recently developed method, as yet scarcely extended to domestic use, is cooking by MICRO-WAVES. It is believed by anthropologists that cooking was discovered by cavemen who came upon flesh burnt in a forest fire. When man learned to produce fire by the rubbing of sticks or stones, cooking became established. Cooking by boiling in water was a later development, which came only after the making of the first fireproof pots by MESOLITHIC man.

Cook Islands, group of about 15 islands in the S Pacific Ocean, 3,000km (1,870 miles) NE of New Zealand, made up of the Northern Cook (or Manihiki) Islands and the Southern (or Lower) Cook Islands. Discovered by Capt. James Cook in 1773, they became a British protectorate in 1888 and were annexed to New Zealand in 1901. Products: copra, citrus fruits. Area: 240sq km (93sq miles). Pop. (1975) 25,000. *See also* MW p.60.

Cook Strait, channel between North and South Islands of New Zealand. It was discovered in 1770 by Capt. James Cook. Width: 26–145km (16–90 miles).

Coolant. liquid or gas used to transfer heat from a hot to a cool region or to remove excess heat. For example, in a nuclear power station heat is transferred from the core to the generator by liquid sodium, pressurized water or by a gas.

Coolidge, John Calvin (1872–1933), 30th President of the USA. He trained as a lawyer and became governor of Massachusetts in 1919. He became Republican vice-president in 1920 and president in 1923 after the death of Warren Harding. He was re-elected (1924–28), and his conservative presidency did little to curb the instability that brought the financial crash of 1929.

Coolidge, William David (1873–1975), US physicist who in 1908 developed a method for drawing tungsten into filaments for making light bulbs and radio valves. In 1916 he patented an X-ray tube (Coolidge tube) capable of producing accurate amounts of radiation. He also devised portable X-ray units and worked on construction techniques for industrial quality control. During WWII he devised a submarine-detection system with Irving Langmuir, and he also worked on atom bomb research.

Cooling, method of controlling the running temperature of the engines of cars, motor-cycles and aircraft, generally achieved by means of a flow of water or air. Most cars are water-cooled. In the most common cooling system, a pump driven by the engine, either through gears or by means of the fan belt, circulates water cooled in the radiator. In high-performance piston engines of WWII aircraft, the coolant contained or was composed of ethylene glycol. *See also* COOLANT; MM p.130.

Cooling tower, tall construction that uses atmospheric air to cool warm water in refrigeration and steam-power generation systems. There are three types of towers: atmospheric cooling towers, which depend on wind currents; natural draught towers, which depend on natural convection currents; and mechanical draught towers, which use fans to provide forced or induced convection.

Coon, Carleton Stevens (1904–), US anthropologist who worked in N Africa and the Middle East (1925–39). He published many works on the development of human races, including *Origin of Races* (1962), in which he argued that different races evolved at different speeds.

Cooper, Alfred Duff, 1st Viscount Norwich of Aldwick (1890–1954), British diplomat and Conservative statesman. He resigned his cabinet post in protest at the MUNICH AGREEMENT. He was minister of information (1940–41) and served as an ambassador in the Far East and France until 1947.

Cooper, Anthony Ashley. *See* SHAFTESBURY, ANTHONY ASHLEY COOPER.

Cooper, Gary (1901–61), US film star, real name Frank James Cooper. He was most famous for his laconic portrayal of western heroes. His films included *It* (1927), *The Virginian* (1929), *Morocco* (1930), *Sergeant York* (1941) and *High Noon* (1952).

Cooper, Dame Gladys (1888–1971), distinguished British actress who began her career in musical comedy. Her best-known roles were in *The Chalk Garden* (1955) and Noel COWARD's *Relative Values* (1951).

Cooper, Henry (1934–), British heavyweight boxer. He was British and Empire titleholder (1959–69) and European champion (1968–70). He twice fought MUHAMMAD ALI (then Cassius Clay) but on each occasion an eye injury shortened the contest.

Cooper, James Fenimore (1789–1851), US novelist. His most successful works were the romantic Leatherstocking Tales, of which the best-known are *The Pioneers* (1823) and *The Last of the Mohicans* (1826). He was one of the earliest American novelists and was much influenced by Walter SCOTT. He also wrote a number of novels about life at sea, including *The Pilot* (1823), and works of social criticism. *See also* HC2 p.288.

Cooper, Leon N. (1930–), US physicist and Nobel Prize winner. From 1974 he was professor at Brown University, Rhode Island. With John BARDEEN and John Robert SCHRIEFFER he shared the 1972 Nobel Prize in physics for research in SUPERCONDUCTIVITY. They demonstrated that negatively-charged electrons in a superconductor arrange themselves in so-called "Cooper pairs", rather than randomly dispersing energy and momentum.

Cooper, Samuel (1609–72), English portrait miniaturist whose paintings, dating from *c.* 1642, of royalty and of such notables as Oliver Cromwell, are highly valued for both aesthetic and historical content. His highly technical skill combined broad and free brushwork with modelling of the face through use of light and shadow. Horace Walpole claimed that Cooper "first gave the strength and freedom of oil to the miniature". *See also* HC1 p.297, *297.*

Co-operative Commonwealth Federation. *See* NEW DEMOCRATIC PARTY.

Co-operative farming, organizing of farmers into producer's CO-OPERATIVES. Land may be pooled, farm assets jointly owned, and buying and marketing undertaken collectively. The trading profits are then shared. *See also* PE pp.160–163.

Co-operative movement, variety of organizations, throughout the world, founded to run non-profit economic enterprises for the benefit of their members. The first such movement was founded in England in 1844 by the ROCHDALE PIONEERS, who established a co-operative retail society to eliminate the middleman and share profits among its members. That movement had its origin in the socialist propaganda of Robert OWEN. The co-operative movement has been extended to include co-operative agriculture, co-operative manufacturing (in which the workers own and manage their own plant) and co-operative banking and finance. Co-operative agriculture does not necessarily entail the common ownership of land, but does usually include the common ownership of machinery and pooled retailing. It usually also links farmers to credit unions for the purpose of borrowing. The co-operative movement is strongest in France, Scandinavia, Israel and China. In France more than 80% of grain is sold through co-operatives. In China all agriculture and most manufacturing is co-operative. The Scandinavian Wholesale Co-operative Society was founded in 1918. *See also* CO-OPERATIVE PARTY; CO-OPERATIVE WHOLESALE SOCIETY.

Co-operative Party, British political party, formed in 1917 as the political wing of the Co-operative Union. It is associated with the LABOUR PARTY and since 1946 all its parliamentary candidates have stood for election jointly as Labour co-operative candidates. Since 1959 it has limited the number of its candidates to 30.

Co-operative societies, non-profit-making voluntary enterprises owned and operated by their membership. Consumers' co-operatives distribute goods directly from the producer to the consumer. The first such society was the Rochdale Society of Equitable Pioneers (1844). Co-operative societies now operate in most countries. *See also* HC2 p.95.

Co-operative Wholesale Society, organization formed in the north of England in 1863 to provide for consumer co-operation. It was a development from the early co-operative experiments of Robert OWEN and the ROCHDALE PIONEERS, which encouraged consumers to form their own retail societies and share the profits among themselves, so eliminating the middleman. Modern Co-operative retail shops derive directly from the society.

Co-optimists, The, musical revue, written by various hands, first produced on the London stage from 1921–27, then revived in 1929 and 1935. It starred many famous names of the musical theatre, including Stanley Holloway and Melville Gideon, who also wrote the music.

Co-ordinate geometry, or algebraical geometry, branch of mathematics combining the methods of pure GEOMETRY with those of algebra. Any geometrical point can be given an algebraical value by relating it to co-ordinates, marked off from a frame of reference. Thus, if a point is marked on a square grid so that it is x_1 squares along the x-axis and y_1 squares along the y-axis, it has the co-ordinates (x_1, y_1). Circular, or polar, co-ordinates can also be used. *See also* CARTESIAN COORDINATE SYSTEM; SU p.*41*.

Co-ordinate system, reference system used to locate a point in space. A point can be defined by numbers representing distances or angles measured from lines or points of reference. In a CARTESIAN CO-ORDINATE SYSTEM a point is defined by distances from intersecting axes. In a polar co-ordinate system, distance from a fixed point is used together with angular distance from a reference line. Two numbers are required to define a position in a plane: three numbers are required in three-dimensional space. A co-ordinate system enables curves or surfaces to be defined algebraically. *See also* SU p.*34*..

Co-ordinate systems, astronomical, co-ordinate systems used to locate the positions of celestial bodies on the CELESTIAL SPHERE, each system using a different great circle on the sphere as a reference plane. Equatorial co-ordinates – right ascension (or hour angle) and declination – refer to the celestial equator; horizon co-ordinates – azimuth and altitude – refer to the observer's horizon; ecliptic co-ordinates – celestial latitude and longitude – refer to the ecliptic; and galactic co-ordinates – galactic latitude and longitude – refer to the plane of the Galaxy.

Co-ordination complex, type of compound in which one or more groups or molecules form co-ordinate bonds with a central metal atom, usually a transition metal. The complex may be either a complex ion or a neutral molecule, as in nickel tetracarbonyl $Ni(CO)_4$. The co-ordinating species are known as LIGANDS. Inorganic chemistry is mainly concerned with the study of such compounds: some, such as heme and chlorophyll, have biochemical importance. *See also* ION, COMPLEX COMPOUNDS; CHELATION; SU pp.139, 142.

Co-ordination number, number of chemical bonds made to a central atom in a specified complex salt: eg, the number of anions surrounding a cation.

Coorg, former state in sw India, annexed by the British in 1834 and administered by them until independence in 1947. The region now produces timber, coffee and rice. Area: 4,110sq km (1,587sq miles).

Coornhert, Dirck Volckertszoon (1522–90), Dutch author. His works include a translation of the *Odyssey* (1561); short songs, *Liedekens* (1575) and a moral treatise, *The Polite Art* (1586). He was imprisoned in 1586 for his opposition to religious intolerance.

Coot, aquatic bird of freshwater marshes. Related to the RAILS, it takes flight awkwardly but is a strong swimmer and diver and feeds in or near water. All coots have white bills and foreheads. The female lays 8–12 buff-coloured, brown-spotted eggs on floating reed nests. Family Rallidae; genus *Fulica*.

Coote, Sir Eyre (1726–83), British soldier. In 1754 he was a captain in the first British regiment sent to India. He fought at the battle of Plassey in 1757, at Wandiwash in 1760 and Pondicherry in 1761. In 1778 he was made Commander-in-Chief in India and in 1781 defeated Haydar Ali at Porto Novo.

Copán, second largest Maya city of the Classic Period (about AD 300–900). Its ruins, in w Honduras, 56km (35 miles) w of Santa Rosa at an altitude of 600m (2,000ft), are notable for the high artistic quality of its remains – portrait sculpture, friezes and statuary. By the 8th century, Copán's astronomers had calculated the Mayas most accurate solar calender.

Cope, in the Anglican, Roman Catholic, Orthodox and in some Scandinavian Lutheran Churches, a liturgical vestment in the shape of a semicircular cloak, worn by clergy at solemn religious ceremonies when the CHASUBLE is not used.

Copeau, Jacques (1879–1949), French critic and stage director. In 1909 he founded, with GIDE and others, *La Nouvelle Revue Française.* In 1913 he founded the Théâtre de Vieux Colombier, which sought to combat the prevailing realism of contemporary drama.

Copenhagen (København), capital city of Denmark on E Sjaelland and N Amager islands in the Øresund. A trading and fishing centre by the early 12th century, the city was often in conflict with the HANSEATIC LEAGUE. It became Denmark's capital in 1443. It suffered great damage by British troops during the NAPOLEONIC WARS and was occupied by the Germans during WWII. It has a university (1479), a 17th-century stock exchange and Amalienborg Square, which includes the royal palace. The commerical and cultural centre of the nation, it has food processing, shipbuilding, chemicals, brewing and car assembly industries. Pop. (1975) 756,256.

Copenhagen, Battle of (1801), naval battle between the English, under Sir Hyde Parker, and the Danes who had recently joined the league of ARMED NEUTRALITY. The Danish fleet was destroyed – partly because, according to legend, NELSON claimed, by putting a telescope to his blind eye, not to see an order to retreat.

Copepod, marine or freshwater CRUSTACEAN. Some copepods are parasitic on aquatic animals, especially fish. Their segmented, cylindrical bodies have a single median eye and no carapace. Length: 0.5–2mm (0.02–0.08in); length of parasitic forms may be more than 30.5cm (1ft). There are 7,500 species. Subclass Copepoda. *See also* NW p.100, *105*.

Copernicus, Nicholas, or Mikotaj Kopernik (1473–1543), Polish astronomer. He studied initially at Cracow and also in Italy, where he studied law and medicine as well as astronomy. He was appointed canon of the cathedral at Frauenberg, E Prussia, in 1497. His work *De Revolutionibus Orbium Caelestium,* which laid the foundations of modern astronomy, was probably written in 1530 but not published until 1543. *See also* HC1 p.302; SU pp.24, 164.

Copland, Aaron (1900–), US composer, especially known for combining folk and jazz elements with 20th-century symphonic techniques. His highly popular ballet music includes *Billy the Kid* (1938), *Rodeo* (1942) and *Appalachian Spring* (1944), which won the Pulitzer prize. He has written symphonies, chamber music and overtly patriotic pieces such as *A Lincoln Portrait.* Less well known are Copland's experiments with serial techniques, as in *Piano Fantasy* (1957). Among many film scores is *The Heiress* (1949). His postwar work includes the opera, *The Tender Land* (1954) and *Nonet* (1960). *See also* HC2 pp.270–271.

Copley, John Singleton (1738–1815), US painter, the finest portraitist of the colonial period. He had little academic training but was a working artist at 15, and was an extraordinarily gifted draughtsman and colourist. He settled in England in 1774.

Coppée, François (1842–1908), French poet and dramatist. He wrote about the poor in his works which include the poems collected in *Intimités* (1868) and *Le Cahier Rouge* (1874), the comedy *Le Passant* (1869) and the verse drama *Les Jacobites* (1885). He was notorious for his anti-semitism, particularly during the Dreyfus Trial.

Coppélia (1870), ballet in two acts by Arthur St Léon; music by Léo DELIBES. It is famous for introducing folk dance into ballet, and tells how a girl tricks a toymaker into thinking that she is one of his creations come to life.

Copper, metallic element (Cu) of the first transition series. It occurs native (free or uncombined) and in several ores including cuprite (an oxide) and chalcopyrite (a sulphide). The metal is extracted by smelting and is purified by electrolysis. It is a good thermal and electrical conductor, second only to silver, and is extensively used in boilers, pipes, electrical equipment and alloys. Copper tarnishes in air, oxidizes at high temperatures and is attacked only by oxidizing acids. Properties: at.no. 29; at.wt. 63.546; s.g. 8.96; m.p. 1.083°C (1,981°F); b.p. 2,595°C (4,703°F); most common isotope Cu^{63} (69.09%). *See also* TRANSITION ELEMENTS; SU pp.136, 140–141; MM pp.32, 36.

Copper Age. *See* CHALCOLITHIC AGE.

Copper carbonate, $CuCO_3.Cu(OH)_2$, green salt which occurs naturally as the mineral malachite. Pure copper carbonate, $CuCO_3$, does not exist.

Copperhead, any of various species of snakes, so-called because of their head colour. The N American copperhead is a pit viper, rarely over 1m (3ft) long. The Australian copperhead is a venomous snake of the cobra family, often reaching 1.5m (5ft) in length. The Indian copperhead is a rat snake.

Copper oxide, chemical compound of copper and oxygen which exists in two forms: cuprous or copper (I) oxide, Cu_2O, a brilliant red powder found in nature as the mineral cuprite; and cupric or copper (II) oxide, CuO, which is black and decomposes into copper (I) oxide and oxygen when heated. It is added to furnace melts as an oxidant.

Copper plating, by ELECTRODEPOSITION, is used to prepare steel for a top coating (also by ELECTROPLATING) of nickel, chromium or silver, as a surface treatment of steel and brass in the production of decorative oxidized copper finishes and as a coating on steel to prevent surface hardening. The main copper salts used in electroplating solutions are copper sulphate and copper cyanide in the form of complexes such as potassium cuprocyanide, $K_2Cu(CN)_3$. *See also* MM pp.32–33.

Copper processing, the recovery of the pure metal from its commercial ores. The ores, which contain mainly copper oxides and sulphides, are separated from the surrounding rock and are then concentrated. They are smelted into a molten mass, called matte, and pure copper (blister copper) is extracted by oxidizing

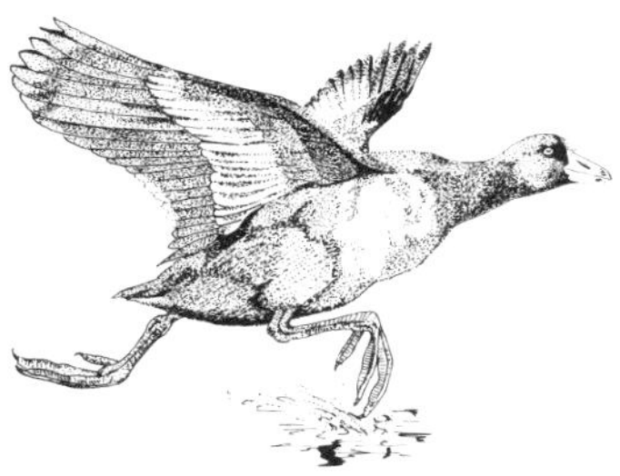

Coots, who feed mainly on water plants and seeds, will sometimes chase mice on land.

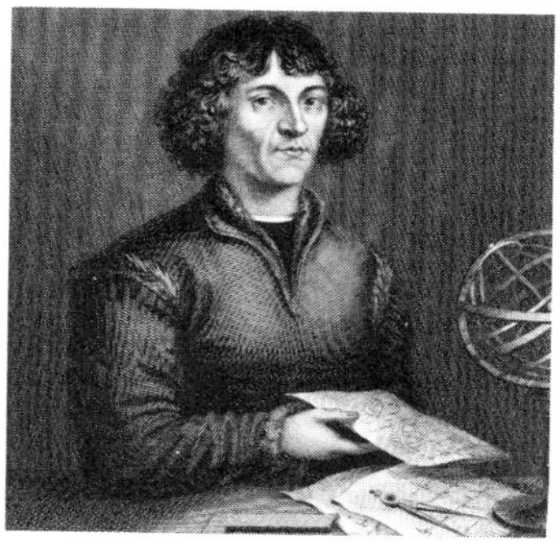

Copernicus, whose heliocentric theory shattered man's view of his place in nature.

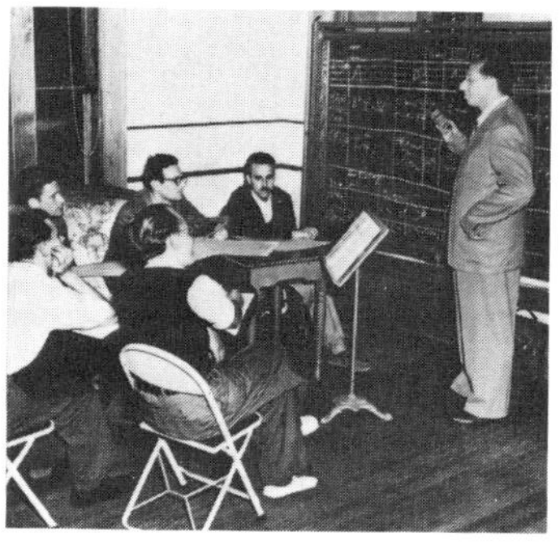

Aaron Copland wrote symphonic music dealing mainly with American themes.

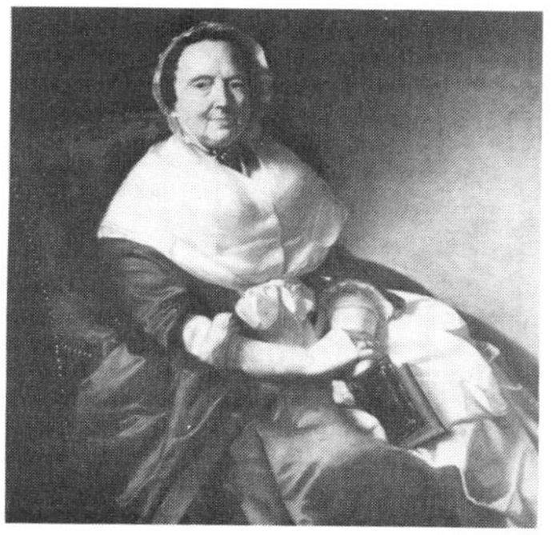

John Singleton Copley painted this portrait of *Mrs Sylvannus Bonme.*

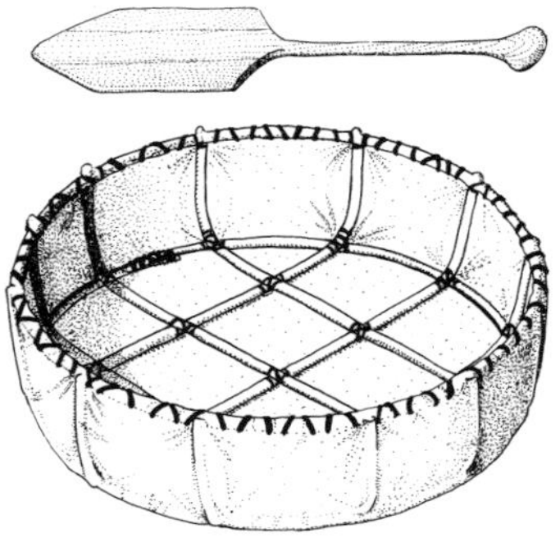

Coracles, one of the most primitive of all craft, are still used in the British Isles.

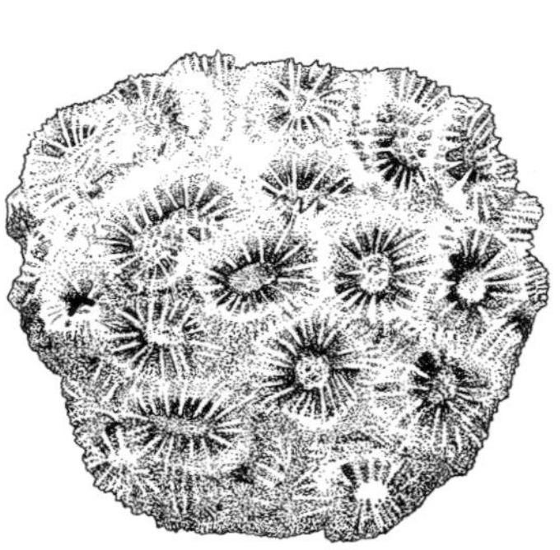

Coral is the hard accumulation of the limestone skeletons of tiny marine animals.

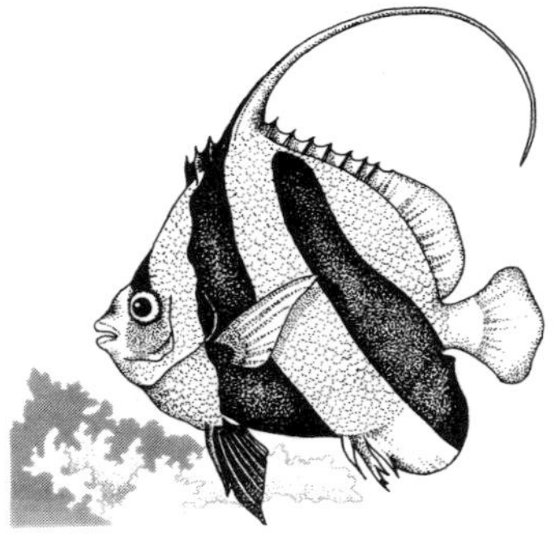

Coral fish are the exotic little creatures common in many warm water aquaria.

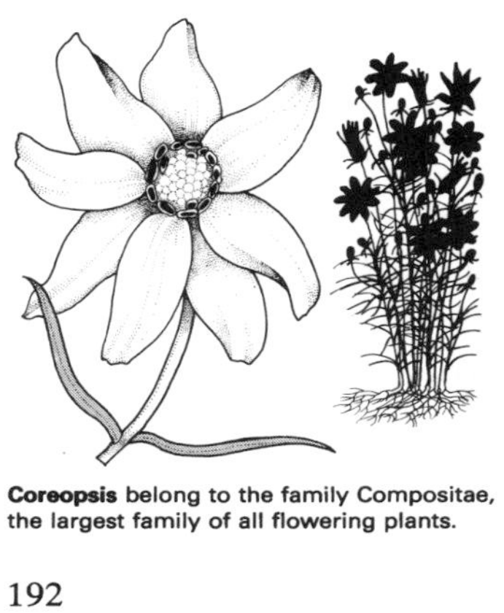

Coreopsis belong to the family Compositae, the largest family of all flowering plants.

the impurities with air. Ores are often treated with acids and the copper recovered by electrolysis. *See also* MM p.32.

Copper sulphate, chemical compound which exists in two forms. Cuprous or copper (I) sulphate, Cu_2SO_4, is a light grey powder that reacts instantly with atmospheric moisture to produce cupric or copper (II) sulphate. This is usually seen as the bright blue crystals of the pentahydrate, blue vitriol, $CuSO_4.5H_2O$, used for copper plating, for preserving wood and for killing algae in ponds. It can be dehydrated to the colourless anhydrous salt $CuSO_4$, which, because it absorbs water and turns blue, is used as a dessicant and, more widely, as a MOISTURE INDICATOR. *See also* SU p.141.

Copper sulphide, compound of COPPER and sulphur which exists in two forms. Cuprous, or copper (I), sulphide (Cu_2S) is found in nature as copper glance and, together with iron, as copper pyrites. Cupric, or copper (II), sulphide (CuS) is a black powder which on heating decomposes to copper (I) sulphide.

Copra, the dried kernel or "meat" of the COCONUT and the principal commerical product of that nut. The husk is usually removed and the exposed kernel dried by the sun and later by artificial heat. The oil is pressed out and the residue, copra, sold as animal feed.

Coprolites, fossilized excreta of many kinds of animals of a great range of sizes, relationships and geological ages. They are useful to geologists and biologists because they often contain undigested plant seeds and tissues.

Coptic art, general term to cover the visual arts of the Christian, or Coptic, minority of Egypt from the 3rd to the 12th centuries. In addition to painting, it includes especially tapestry-making and ceramics. *See also* COPTS.

Coptic Church, the ancient Church of Egypt and Ethiopia, claiming St Mark the Evangelist as its founder. It did not accept the pronouncements of the Council of CHALCEDON (451) on CHRISTOLOGY. After that council it formally embraced MONOPHYSITISM. The spiritual leadership of the Coptic Church is exercised by the Patriarch of Alexandria. The number of Copts in the mid-1970s was estimated at about 3½ million.

Copts, members of the Christian Church in Egypt, comprising between five and ten per cent of the population. A few Copts are Catholics, but the majority adhere to the Monophysite creed, declared heretical in 451, which denies the humanity of Christ. The head of the Coptic Church is the patriarch of Alexandria. In its rites the Church follows eastern customs, except that it circumsises children before baptism and obeys some Mosaic dietary traditions. The Coptic language is dead.

Copyhold, form of land tenure in Britain, now extinct. It arose in the middle ages, when VILLEINS were permitted to hold land at the pleasure of the lord of the manor. A copy of the holder's right (not title) was placed in the manorial COURT ROLL. The copyholder's rights depended entirely on the custom of the manor until, in the 17th century, he was given some legal protection. A copyhold franchise was included in the 1832 REFORM ACT. Copyholds were gradually converted into FREEHOLDS or LEASEHOLDS, and all traces of them finally disappeared with the Property Act (1925).

Copyright, legal authority granted to an individual or company to reproduce or perform works of art, literature and music. The earliest copyright act in Britain protected authors (1710). By the end of the 19th century all branches of the arts had received legislative protection. Copyright normally lasts during the lifetime of an author and for 50 years after his death. In 1956, film, radio and television performances were also covered by copyright.

Coques, Gonzales (1614–84), Flemish painter, nicknamed "Little van Dyck" because his style so resembled that of his contemporary. He is best known for his portraits.

Coracle, small, easily portable boat, consisting of a wooden framework covered with animal skins or canvas, used on inland or inshore waters. Types of coracle are still used in parts of Britain and the USA.

Coral, small coelenterate marine animal found in colonies in marine waters. The limestone skeletons secreted by each animal polyp accumulate to form CORAL REEFS. Reef-building corals are found only in waters with temperatures in excess of 20°C (68°F). Soft corals secrete a fleshy material, horny corals (sea fans) secrete fan-shaped supports, and stony corals secrete limestone cups. Class Anthozoa. *See also* NW pp.82, *83*, 179.

Coral atoll, ring-shaped island surrounding a shallow lagoon. It is built up from great depths, yet the corals that built them cannot grow in depths of more than 45m (150ft). *See also* PE p.56.

Coral, or reef, fish, brilliantly coloured tropical fish that lives among coral reefs and similar formations. Its flat, round body, large tail and short fins give it the great manoeuvrability its habitat demands. Coral fishes include the butterfly, angle, cardinal, damsel and parrot fishes. *See also* NW pp.128, *128*.

Coralli, Jean (1779–1854), French ballet dancer and choreographer. In 1802 he made his debut in Paris and later danced also in Italy and Portugal. He was choreographer at the Paris Academy (1831–45), creating the choreography for such ballets as *La Tarentule* (1839), *Giselle* (1841) and *Le Peri* (1843).

Coralline. *See* MOSS ANIMALS.

Coral reef, rock formation found in shallow tropical seas. Such reefs are formed from the calcium carbonate secreted by the living coral organisms as protection against predators and wave action. The way in which the coral, and therefore the reef, grows is strongly influenced by the prevailing currents and the temperature of the surrounding sea-water. The main types are fringing reefs and barrier reefs. *See also* PE p.123.

Coral Sea, arm of the SW Pacific Ocean between the Great Barrier Reef off the E coast of Australia, the New Hebrides (E) and New Guinea (NW). It was the scene of a US victory over the Japanese in 1942.

Coral Sea, Battle of the (May 1942), WWII naval and air battle in the SW Pacific. The US Navy inflicted heavy losses on the Japanese fleet and checked Japan's progress towards Australia. *See also* HC2 pp.228–229, *250*.

Coral snake, poisonous burrowing snake of the Americas and South-East Asia. It is secretive and docile, but its venom can be fatal to human beings. Most species, including the Eastern coral snake (*Micrurus fulvius*), are brightly coloured, ringed with red, yellow and black. It feeds on lizards, frogs and other snakes. Family Elapidae.

Coram, Thomas (*c.*1668–1751), English seaman and philanthropist. From 1693 to 1704 he lived in the colony of Massachusetts. He returned to London and in 1735 was involved in founding a colony in Nova Scotia for unemployed English artisans. In 1739 he established the Foundling Hospital for abandoned London children.

Cor anglais, or English horn, reed instrument of the OBOE family. It is longer than the oboe, its range is a fifth lower, its bell is pear-shaped and its double reed is inserted in a curved metal mouthpiece. It is used as a modern counterpart for the curved oboe da caccia in the music of J. S. Bach, and parts have been scored for it in many Romantic works, especially by Berlioz and Wagner. *See also* HC2 p.*105*.

Corbett, Harvey Wiley (1873–1954), US architect. He planned many early skyscrapers and is best known for his collaboration with Raymond Hood on the ROCKEFELLER CENTER, New York.

Corbett, James John ("Gentleman Jim") (1866–1933), US boxer. In 1892 he won the world heavy-weight championship from John L. Sullivan in New Orleans, in the first championship contest ever fought with boxing gloves. He lost the title to Bob Fitzsimmons (1897) in Carson City, Nev.

Corbière, Édouard Joachim, known as Tristan (1845–75), French poet. Son of a Breton fisherman, he was crippled by arthrtis while young and died of tuberculosis at 30. Scorning Romanticism, he described his admiration for Breton seafaring life in the symbolist poems *Gens de mer* (1873).

Corbillon Cup, trophy donated by Marcel Corbillon of France in 1934 for the winner of the women's team event at the world table tennis championships. European countries dominated the early years but since the 1950s it has been mainly the preserve of Asian nations.

Corbusier, Le. *See* LE CORBUSIER.

Corday, Charlotte (1768–93), French patriot. A noblewoman with the full name Marie-Anne-Charlotte Corday d'Armont, she stabbed the JACOBIN Jean-Paul MARAT to death in his bath on 13 July 1793 and was guillotined on 17 July. She was a GIRONDIN who disagreed with the radical policies espoused by Marat.

Cordierite, or iolite, silicate of aluminium, magnesium and iron, which occurs mostly in metamorphic rocks. It forms crystals in the orthorhombic system. Hardness 7, s.g. 2.6. *See also* PE p.*98*.

Cordite, smokeless, high-explosive shell and bullet propellant made by mixing cellulose nitrate (gun-cotton) – a highly nitrated form of cellulose – and nitroglycerine, both of which are themselves explosives. For stability, mineral jelly and acetone are added in small amounts. Cordite is generally manufactured in strands or cords, which give it its name. *See also* MM pp.163, 242.

Córdoba, city in central Argentina, 623km (387 miles) NW of Buenos Aires; capital of Córdoba district. It is the third largest city in Argentina. Córdoba is a cultural and commercial centre, and exports farm produce from the surrounding irrigated region. Founded in 1573, the city flourished during the colonial era, being on a trade route from Buenos Aires to Chile. It has a university, founded in 1613. Industries: leather, textiles, glass, cement. Pop. 798,663.

Córdoba, city in S Spain, on the Guadalquivir River; capital of Córdoba province. It has been ruled by Iberians, Romans, Vigoths and Moors, and it flourished under Caliph Abd ar-Rahman III, the first caliph of Córdoba. In 1236 Ferdinand III of Castile captured Cordoba and imposed Christian culture on the city. It has an 8th-century mosque, a Moorish bridge and a fine art museum. Industries: coal and lead mining, engineering, building materials, textiles, food processing. Pop. (1974) 249,515. *See also* HC1 pp.*151*, 170.

Core, in geology, a cylindrical rock sample that has been gathered by drilling; on land usually by a rotary drill, from the sea often by a metal cylinder, with a cutter on the bottom, which is forced into the rock. The core is used to identify the various layers in the rock or sediment. The mechanism for collecting the core is called a corer. *See also* PE pp.25, 90, 91, *91*.

Core, Earth, the interior of the Earth, under the Gutenberg discontinuity. Information concerning the composition of the core is obtained from seismic measurements. The core may be a plasma, dense compressed material comprised of atoms in which the electrons have been pushed towards the nuclei. The core makes up 16% of the Earth's volume and has 31% of its mass. Layers exist in the core: the outer one is relatively liquid; the inner is probably a mixture of iron and nickel. *See also* PE pp.20–21.

Corelli, Arcangelo (1653–1713), Italian BAROGUE composer who achieved early distinction as a violinist under the guidance of Giovanni Benvenuti. He helped to develop the concerto grosso, composed many sonatas and did much to consolidate the principles behind modern violin playing. *See also* HC2 p.40.

Corelli, Marie (1855–1924), British writer of popular romantic novels. Her first novel *The Romance of Two Worlds* (1886) was so successful that she went on to write many others, including *Thelma* (1887), *Barabbas* (1893) and *The Master Christian* (1900).

Corepsis, large genus of about 100 annual

and perennial plants cultivated for their daisy-like yellow or variegated flowers, which occur in single or branched clusters; it is also known as tickseed. Height: to 90cm (3ft). Family Compositae.

Corfe Castle, town in Dorset, SW England, dominated by a ruined castle in which Edward the Martyr was killed in 978. The castle was almost destroyed by CROMWELL after a long siege in 1646. The ruins are now a tourist attraction.

Corfu (Kérkyra), island in NW Greece, second largest of the Ionian island group; with Paxos (Paxoí) Island, it forms a department of Greece; Corfu is the capital. It was the scene of the first recorded naval battle *c.* 665 BC, with Corinth for possession of Epidamnus and was allied with Athens in 433 BC against Corinth. The Romans held the island from 229 BC and it was part of the Byzantine Empire until the 11th century. It was occupied by the Venetians from 1386 until 1797, and then under British protection from 1809 until 1864, when it passed to Greece. The Germans occupied the island during WWII. Products: olives, olive oil, fruit, livestock, wine. Tourism and fishing are important industries Area: 593sq km (229sq miles). Pop. (1971) 89,664.

Corgi, or Welsh corgi, small, short-legged WORKING DOG, some types of which are related to the Dutch SCHIPPERKE. Like the COLLIE, the corgi was used for herding, but is now principally a house dog. It has a short, pointed head and its coat may be of almost any colour except all white. Average height at the shoulder: 30cm (12in).

Cori, Carl Ferdinand (1896–), US biochemist, *b.* Czechoslovakia. He went to USA in 1922, and was naturalized in 1928. He shared the 1947 Nobel Prize in physiology and medicine with his wife Gerty Theresa (1896–1957) for their discovery of how the chemical energy of GLYCOGEN, a carbohydrate stored in the liver and muscle, is broken down into a form that can be used by the body. The 1947 prize was also shared by B. A. HOUSSAY, the Argentine physiologist.

Coriander, strong-smelling herb of the CARROT family native to the Mediterranean and Near East. Oil from the seeds is used as an aromatic flavouring in foods, medicines and liqueurs; the leaves are used in soups, especially by the Chinese. Family Umbelliferae; species *Coriandrum sativum.*

Corinth, Lovis (1858–1925), German painter and graphic artist. A member of the SEZESSIONISTS, Corinth opposed EXPRESSIONISM at first but his late portraits and landscapes show its influence, in the use of dramatic subject matter, IMPASTO paint and very lively brushwork.

Corinth (Kórinthos), city in NE Peloponnesos, Greece, at the SW tip of the Isthmus of Corinth; capital of Corinthia department. Corinth was one of the largest and most powerful cities of Ancient Greece, traditionally a rival of Athens and ally of Sparta, with which it fought in the Peloponnesian War (431–404 BC). It did, however, join with Athens, Thebes and Argos against Sparta during the Corinthian War (395–387 BC). In the mid-3rd century BC it was a leading member of the ACHAEAN LEAGUE but was destroyed by the Romans in 243. Caesar rebuilt the city in 44 BC. It was ruled by the Venetians from 1687 until 1715, then by the Turks until 1822, when it became part of Greece. It is 5km (3 miles) NE of the ruins of the ancient city of Corinth, which was destroyed by an earthquake in 1858. The ruins include a temple of APOLLO, the market-place and an amphitheatre. The present city is a major transport centre (it is at one end of the Corinth Canal) and has food processing, chemicals and wine-making industries. Pop. 20,733. *See also* HC1 pp.69, 70, 72, 76–77.

Corinth, Gulf of (Korinthiakós Kólpos), formerly Gulf of Lepanto, inlet of the Mediterranean Sea between central Greece (N) and Peloponnesos (S), connecting the Gulf of Patras to the Corinth Canal. Length: 130km (80 miles); width: 5–32km (3–20 miles).

Corinth Canal, artificial waterway across the Isthmus of Corinth, connecting the Aegean Sea to the Adriatic Sea. It was built between 1881 and 1893. Running parallel to the canal are the ruins of the ancient Isthmian Wall, restored by Byzantine emperors between the 3rd and 6th centuries.

Corinthian, latest and most ornate of the Classical ORDERS of architecture, developed by the Greeks in the 4th century BC but used more extensively in Roman architecture. A typical Corinthian column has a high base, sometimes with a pedestal; a slim, fluted column and a bell-shaped capital with acanthus-leaf ornament. *See also* HC1 pp.*78*, 79.

Corinthians, Epistles to the, NEW TESTAMENT epistles of St PAUL addressed to the Christian Church in Corinth. They were written from Ephesus *c.* 57–58.

Coriolanus (1607), five-act tragedy by William SHAKESPEARE, based on Plutarch's *Life of Coriolanus.*

Coriolis, Gaspard Gustave de (1792–1843), French mathematician who explained the effect of the earth's rotation on objects moving above its surface in terms of the force or effect bearing his name. *See also* CORIOLIS FORCE; SU p.68.

Coriolis force, or effect, apparent force on particles or objects due to the rotation of the Earth under them. The motion of the particles or objects is deflected towards the right in the Northern Hemisphere and towards the left in the Southern Hemisphere, but their speed is unaffected. The direction of water swirling round in a drain or whirlpool demonstrates this force. *See also* PE pp.68, 78, *79.*

Cork, county in S Republic of Ireland. It has a hilly and rugged terrain with fertile valleys. The chief occupations are farming (dairying, grain, livestock and sugar-beet) and fishing along the rocky coastline. The county town is Cork, a port at the mouth of the River Lee. The town was occupied by Oliver CROMWELL in 1649. Many public buildings were destroyed in nationalist uprisings in 1920. It exports farm produce and has brewing, motor vehicle, leather and food processing industries. Area (county): 7,462sq km (2,881sq miles). Pop. (1971) (county) 351,735; (town) 128,235. *See also* MW pp.102–105.

Cork, outer layer of the BARK of woody plants, cellular in structure but waterproof. This dead layer of tissue is formed by cork cambium. The bark of the cork oak, a tree native to the Mediterranean countries, is the chief source of commercial cork, used for making bottle stoppers and insulating and floor covering materials. Species *Quercus suber.*

Corm, fleshy underground stem that produces a plant such as the GLADIOLUS or CROCUS; it has more stem tissue and fewer leaf scales than a BULB. In most plants, new corms form on top of old ones, which last for one season.

Corman, Roger (1926–), US film director, writer and producer. Particularly noted for his numerous and popular low-budget productions starring Vincent PRICE, he has strongly influenced the careers of directors such as Peter BOGDANOVICH and Francis Ford Coppola.

Cormorant, aquatic bird found in coastal and inland waters throughout the world. It has a hooked bill, black plumage, a long body and webbed feet. It dives well and is sometimes used by man to catch fish. Length: to 1m (3.3ft). Family Phalacrocoracidae; genus *Phalacrocorax. See also* NW p.*149.*

Corn, in medicine, a raised, painful thickening of the skin. It usually occurs at a point of sustained pressure or pinching, most often on a toe.

Corn. *See* MAIZE.

Corn belt, common term for the area in the USA in which the crops most commonly grown are corn (maize) and soya beans. Roughly including Illinois, Iowa, Missouri, E Nebraska and Kansas and W Indiana, corn belt has soils rich in nitrogen and organic matter and the area has a well distributed rainfall. These and other favourable factors have provided perfect conditions for the growing of maize and other cereal crops for feeding livestock. *See also* PE p.180.

Corncrake, bird of the RAIL family common in grain fields of N Europe. It has a brown body and a short bill, and its specific name describes its call. Family Rallidae; species *Crex crex.*

Cornea, part of the SCLERA, or outer layer of the EYE, that forms a transparent protective covering over the IRIS. Injury or disease of the cornea can cause ASTIGMATISM. *See also* MS pp.48–49.

Corneille, Pierre (1606–84), first of the great French classical dramatists. His plays include the tragedy *Médée* (1635), the epic *Le Cid* (1637) and a comedy *Le Menteur* (1643). He was elected to the French Academy in 1647. Among his last works were *Sophonisbe* (1663) and *Attila* (1667). *See also* HC1 p.316.

Cornelius, Saint (d. 253), pope from 251 to 253. He was elected to the papacy after the see of Rome had been vacant for 14 months because of DECIUS' persecution of the Church. His rival, NOVATIAN, became antipope. Cornelius is believed to have died as a martyr. Feast: 16 September.

Cornelius, Peter von (1783–1867), German painter. In 1811 he went to Rome where he joined the Nazarene group of German painters. He returned to Germany, where his most notable works include his frescoes in the Munich Glyptothek and his fresco *The Last Judgment* in the Ludwigskirche, Munich.

Cornet, brass musical instrument similar to a trumpet. It was included in scores by 19th-century French and Italian composers, by Malcolm Arnold in *Beckus the Dandipratt* (1943) and in early jazz by King OLIVER. Its range is about the same as a trumpet's, but its tone is mellower and less penetrating.

Cornflour, or cornstarch, flour made from maize, or Indian corn, used widely in cooking. It is extracted from the grains of the corncob by a complex process in which the starchy materials are separated from the embryo or germ for which they are food, the embryo itself being used as a source of corn oil. The starchy material is then pulverized and the cornflour separated from gluten and other substances which together go to make animal feed. By further processing, cornflour is prepared for the market as a nearly pure form of starch. *See also* PE p.180.

Cornflower, or Bachelor's button, annual of the composite family common in many parts of Europe (Germany's national flower). The ray-like flowers are usually a brilliant blue, and the hairy leaves are toothed or divided. Family Compositae; species *Centaurea cyanus.*

Cornforth, John Warcup (1917–), Australian research scientist. He worked with the British Medical Research Council (1946–62) and was head of the Milstead Laboratory, Kent (1962–75). In 1975 he shared the Nobel Prize in chemistry with Vladimir PRELOG for his work on the stereochemistry of enzyme-catalysed reactions and for his demonstration of how CHOLESTEROL is made in the body.

Cornhill Magazine, quarterly literary journal first published by George Smith in 1860. Its first editor was THACKERAY. It took its name from being published at 65 Cornhill, London. It attracted the most distinguished list of any 19th-century journal. It ceased publication in 1975.

Cornice, in classical architecture, the top band of an entablature supported by a row of stone columns. Today the term generally refers to the horizontal bands in the angle between a wall and ceiling, or above a door or window.

Cornish language, member of the Celtic group of languages, closely related to BRETON and WELSH. These three together form the British branch of the CELTIC LANGUAGE group. It died out in the late 18th century, although traces remain today in Cornish place names. The earliest written records of Cornish date from the 10th century. There have been recent attempts to revive the language, but with little success.

Corn Laws, series of acts regulating the import and export of grain in Britain. Records mention their existence as early as the 12th century. The most important was the 1815 act, which virtually prohibited the entry of foreign corn. It was thus held to keep British food prices high and

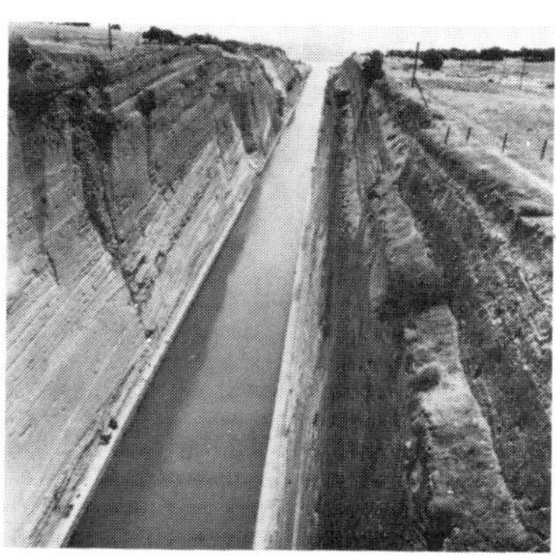

Corinth Canal, which connects the Aegean and Adriatic seas, was begun in 1881.

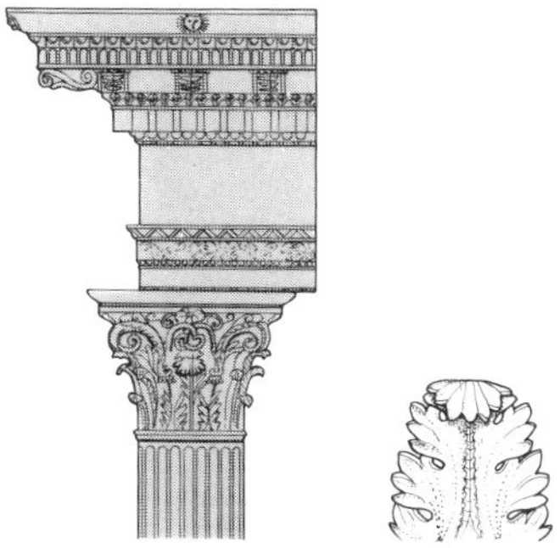

Corinthian is the latest and most ornate of the three orders of classical architecture.

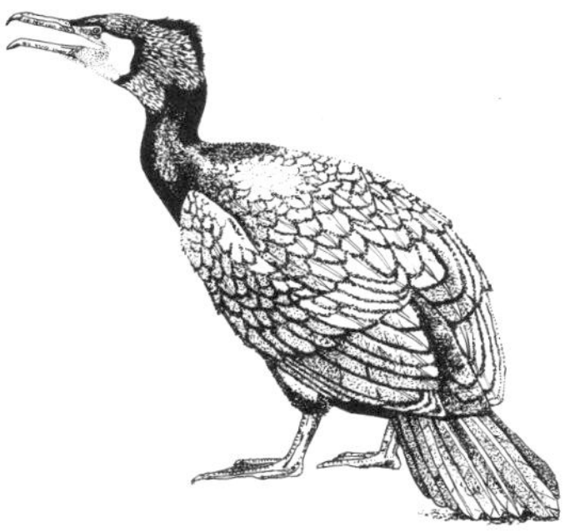

Cormorants were once taken from their nests and trained to catch fish for their masters.

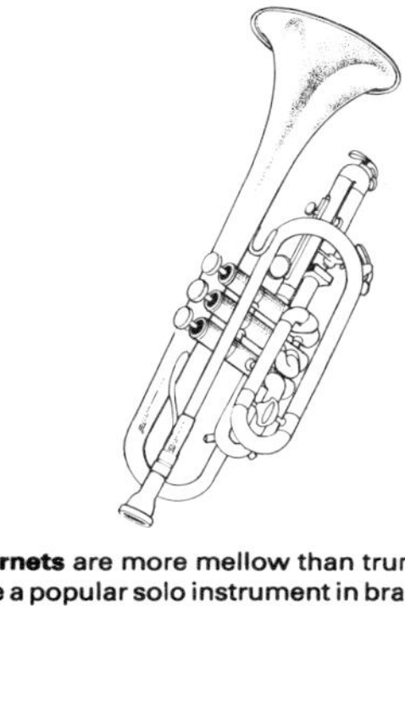

Cornets are more mellow than trumpets and are a popular solo instrument in brass bands.

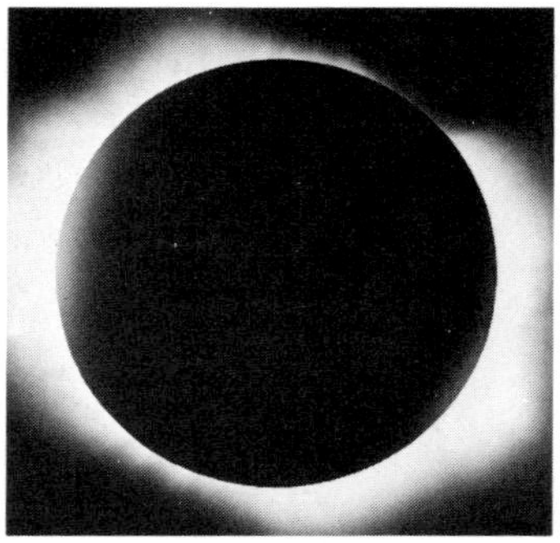

Corona, photographed during a total eclipse of the Sun in 1929 (exposure 20 sec).

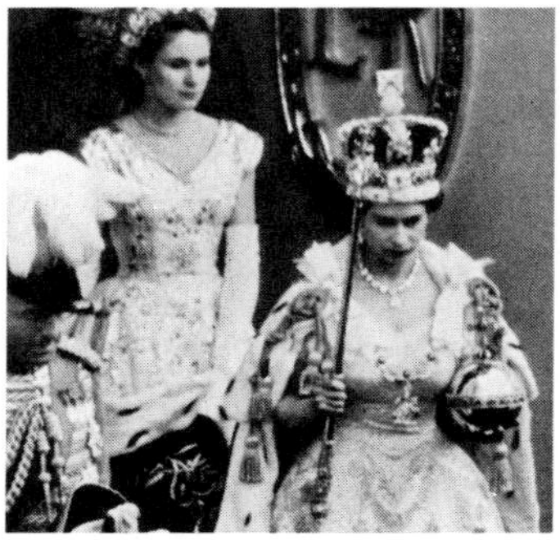

Coronation; the newly crowned Elizabeth II leaving Westminster Abbey in June 1953.

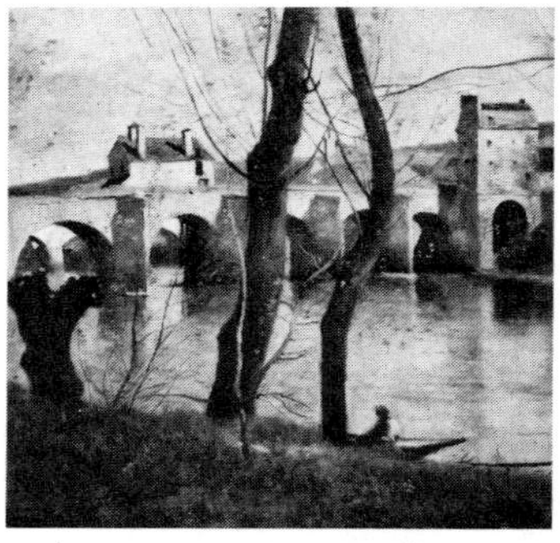

Corot, popular and important 19th-century landscape painter; *Bridge at Nantes* (detail).

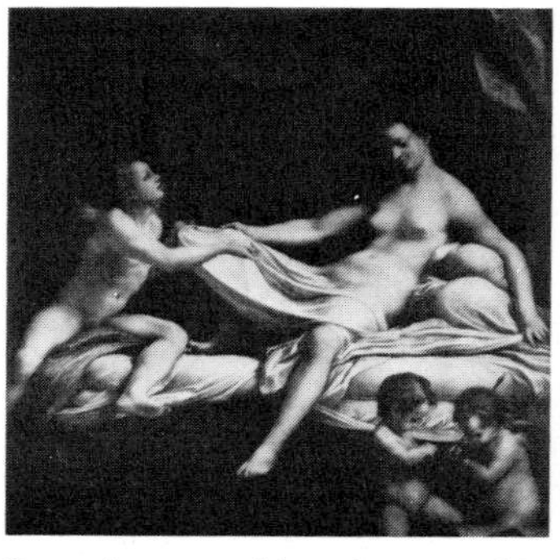

Correggio was one of the great masters of the Italian High Renaissance; *Danae* (detail).

led to a 30-year campaign for free trade, which ended with the repeal of the Corn Laws in 1846. *See also* HC2 pp.22–21, *96*, 112, 132.

Cornu, Marie Alfred (1841–1902), French physicist who worked mainly in optics and astronomy. He devised a photographical method of measuring light intensities in diffraction patterns and calculated the velocity of light.

Cornwall, county in sw England, on a peninsula bounded by the Atlantic Ocean, the English Channel and Devon. It has a rocky indented coast with hills and moors inland, and is drained by the Camel, Fowey, Tamar and Fal rivers. Its mild climate and picturesque coastline make it a popular tourist attraction. The chief towns are Bodmin (the county town), Truro, St Austell and Camborne-Redruth. Area: (including Scilly Isles) 3,512sq km (1,356sq miles). Pop. (including Scilly Isles) (1971) 379,892.

Cornwall, Duchy of, English estate consisting of lands in Cornwall and Devon granted by EDWARD III to the BLACK PRINCE in 1337 when he created him Duke of Cornwall. The lands have remained the possession of the monarch's eldest son, in the absence of whom they revert to the Crown. The duchy was administered from 1863 by a vice-warden of the stannaries court, the jurisdiction passing in 1896 to the county court.

Cornwallis, Charles Cornwallis, 1st Marquess (1738–1805), British soldier and administrator. At first a successful commander for the British in the American Revolution, he was forced to surrender at Yorktown (1781). As governor-general of India (1786–93, 1805), he reformed the administration, law and army and suppressed Tippoo Sahib's revolt. Cornwallis was also viceroy of Ireland (1798–1801), where he defeated the 1798 revolt and carried through reforms and parliamentary union with Britain. *See also* HC2 pp.47, 64–65.

Cornwallis, Sir William (1744–1819), British admiral. He served in the British West Indies until 1787; was commodore in the East Indies (1789–93); and commanded the Channel fleet during the French Revolutionary Wars.

Cornwell, David. *See* LE CARRÉ, JOHN.

Cornwell, John Travers (1900–16), British boy seaman. He joined the navy in 1915 and was killed at the Battle of JUTLAND in the following year. For his bravery on the *Chester* he was awarded the Victoria Cross posthumously.

Corollary, in mathematics, a proposition or theorem which is incidentally proved in proving some other theorem or proposition. More generally, it is an immediate or natural consequence or an easily drawn conclusion.

Coromandel Coast, rugged coastline of SE India, extending from Point Calimere (s) to the Krishna River (N). The rough seas off the coast during the monsoon season are a major hazard to shipping. Madras, Cuddalore and Nellore are the chief ports along the coast. Length: 724km (450 miles).

Corona, outer atmosphere of the Sun, visible as a pearly halo during a total eclipse. It extends outwards from about 5,000km (3,100 miles) above the PHOTOSPHERE and consists chiefly of highly ionized hydrogen, nickel, calcium and iron atoms at a temperature of 2,000,000°K or more. *See also* SU pp.*222*, 224–225.

Corona Borealis, or the Northern Crown, northern constellations between Hercules and Boötes. It contains the recurrent nova T Coronae Borealis and the irregular variable R CORONAE Borealis, the prototype and the brightest example of its class. *See also* SU p.256.

Coronal hole, low-density, low-temperature region of the Sun's CORONA, first observed in 1973, from which the emission of X-rays is apparently minimal. Such regions appear on X-ray photographs as extensive dark areas, often originating near the Sun's poles. They are associated with disturbances in the solar wind. *See also* SU p.*225*.

Coronary occlusion, blocking of a coronary blood vessel, especially of a coronary artery supplying blood to the HEART. It is almost always caused by a blood clot in the artery and may result in a heart attack. *See also* CORONARY THROMBOSIS; MS p.90.

Coronary thrombosis, blood clot in an artery to the HEART, preventing blood (and with it oxygen and nutrients) from reaching the heart. Known as a heart attack, it is marked by chest pains, perspiration and sometimes collapse. Severe heart attacks can be fatal. *See also* MS p.*90*.

Coronation, ceremony of crowning a monarch. The form of coronation used in Britain, which includes the election of the monarch by the peers and his assumption of the religious duties of the office, was first drafted by St DUNSTAN, who crowned king EDGAR in 973. The MEROVINGIAN kings of France were probably the first to introduce Christian coronation to Europe. *See also* HC1 p.*155*.

Coronel, Battle of (Nov. 1914), WWI victory of the German fleet, under Admiral von SPEE, over the British, under Rear-Admiral Cradock, off Coronel on the Chilean coast. The British flagship *Good Hope* and the cruiser *Monmouth* were sunk.

Coroner, public official who inquires into deaths having apparent unnatural causes. In Britain the office dates from shortly before the appearance in the Articles of Eyre of 1194 of the keeper of the Crown's pleas (hence the name from the Latin *corona* for "crown"). He was a high-ranking officer who not only collected and recorded evidence relating to unusual deaths but protected the king's property against possible encroachment by the sheriffs. As the judicial structure became more complex, their role became limited. The Coroners Act of 1887 prohibited them from holding pleas of the Crown. By the Coroners Amendment Act (1926), a coroner, whose only duty became that of conducting inquests, must be a barrister, solicitor or medical practitioner of five years' standing.

Coronet, small crown worn on state occasions by peers of the realm in Britain. They were worn by dukes at least as early as the 14th century. In the reign of ELIZABETH I they were worn by all other ranks except barons. In 1661 barons were also granted their own insignia.

Coronograph, telescopic device for viewing the Sun's CORONA during daylight, at which time it is normally invisible. Mounted at a high altitude, it consists of a high-quality dust-free optical system and a filter (Lyot filter) through which only a very narrow wavelength band can pass. Thus individual emission lines of the coronal spectrum can be viewed without being obscured by the much more intense radiation from the Sun's surface. *See also* SU pp.223, 225.

Corot, Jean-Baptiste Camille (1796–1875), French landscape and portrait painter, one of the most important 19th-century artists. He trained academically and travelled widely, making small oil sketches on the spot and later producing large salon paintings based on them. Critical evaluation of Corot's immense output has varied. His misty landscapes, highly popular in his time, were once considered his best work; current preference is for sketches and portraits. His landscapes influenced CÉZANNE and other POST-IMPRESSIONISTS.

Corporate state, concept of government in which workers and employers from similar industries are organized into corporations; these together with other corporations select representatives who determine national policy. Fascist Italy adopted features of the corporate state, with Benito MUSSOLINI setting himself up as the final arbitrator of differences among the various corporate units.

Corporation, business organization that is legally a separate entity, which gives it limited liability as compared to a proprietorship or partnership. The owners or shareholders are not individually responsible for the legal dealings of the corporation, except to the extent of their holdings. The corporation form is most usual in large organizations, especially in the USA. In Britain the term COMPANY is often used.

Corpus Christi, feast of thanksgiving for the institution of the EUCHARIST, observed by the Roman Catholic Church and many high church Anglicans. It is kept on the Thursday after Trinity Sunday.

Corpus Juris Civilis, legal term meaning "body of the civil law". The name was originally given to the systematic compilation of ROMAN LAW drawn up in the 6th century which subsequently formed the basis of European law. Corpus Juris Canonici is the "body of the canon law".

Corpus luteum, mass of yellow tissue formed by the follicle in the OVARY of a mammal after the OVUM (egg cell) is released. If the ovum is fertilized, the corpus luteum secretes progesterone, a hormone needed to prepare the womb for pregnancy. If the ovum is not fertilized, the corpus luteum becomes inactive. *See also* MS p.*75*.

Correggio, full name Antonio Allegri da Correggio (*c.*1490–1534), Italian painter from Correggio who worked mainly in Parma. In his oil painting and especially in his frescoes (notably those at Parma Cathedral) he made ingenious use of the available space and produced daring, although anatomically exact, foreshortening effects inspired by those of MICHELANGELO and RAPHAEL. A soft golden haze (an effect learned from the paintings of LEONARDO) characterize the major works of Correggio. One of the first painters to experiment with the dramatic effects of artificial light, he is the major link between the early illusionist painter MANTEGNA and the great BAROQUE ceiling painters. *See also* HC1 pp.258–259.

Corregidor, small island at the mouth of Manila Bay, Philippines. It was fortified by Spain in the 18th century and taken by the USA in 1898. An Allied stronghold during WWII, it surrendered to the Japanese in May 1942, but was retaken by US troops in February 1945. It was annexed to the Philippines in 1947. Area: 5sq km (2sq miles).

Correlation, in geology, method of linking rock strata of the same age. Geologists do this by comparing similar rocks in different (and sometimes widely separated) outcrops or by studying the FOSSILS they contain. *See also* PALAEONTOLOGY; PE pp.125, 128–129.

Correlation, in statistics, a number that summarizes the direction and degree of relationship between two or more dimensions or variables. Correlations range between 0 (no relationship) and 1.00 (a perfect relationship), and may be positive (as one variable increases, so does the other) or negative (as one variable increases, the other decreases). When two variables are highly correlated, as is IQ with school achievement, one may be used to predict the other. Thus, IQ tests have traditionally been used in schools to predict the likelihood of success. *See also* INTELLIGENCE TESTS; STATISTICS.

Correns, Karl Erich (1864–1933), German botanist and geneticist. In 1900 he rediscovered, along with two others, the works of Gregor MENDEL outlining the principles of heredity. Correns conducted experiments to determine the validity of Mendel's laws and helped to provide evidence that proved his theories.

Corrie, or cirque, enlarged head of a valley where a glacier forms. The enlargement is caused by the movement of firm (compacted snow), which travels out of the valley and down the mountain. *See also* PE pp.*116*–117.

Corroboree, Australian Aboriginal assembly for important dance rituals and festivals, particularly for initiating young men to adulthood by circumcision. Women were not permitted to attend corroborees, which were often held on special sites and provided the occasion for wild enjoyment. The term has since come to be used for all sorts of Aboriginal entertainment.

Corrosion, slow gradual tarnishing of surface or major structural decomposition by chemical action on solids, especially metals and alloys. It commonly appears as a greenish deposit on copper and brass, the reddish-brown deposit (RUST) on iron or the grey deposit that quickly coats freshly exposed aluminium, zinc and magnesium. Rust is the most important form of corrosion because of the extensive use of iron and its susceptibility to attack. Like many other forms of corrosion, it relies on an electrolytic process which occurs in moist conditions, especially sea-water. The net result may be explained in terms of an OXIDATION-REDUCTION reaction; some metals such as aluminium and magnesium corrode readily forming the respective oxide which protects the under-surface from further corrosion.

Corrosive sublimate, mercuric chloride, $HgCl_2$, a highly poisonous salt. It is used as an insecticide and in the preservation of skins, furs and wood. It has also been used in very small doses as an antiseptic. *See also* CALOMEL.

Corsica (Corse), mountainous island in the Mediterranean Sea, about 160km (100 miles) SE of the French coast. Until 1768, when France purchased all rights to the island, it was under the control of a series of Italian rulers, having been a Roman colony from the 3rd century BC to the 5th century AD. Napoleon was born there in 1769. In 1794 Britain took the island, but Napoleon retrieved it for France. It was occupied by Germany in 1942–43. The capital is Ajaccio. Products: grapes, olives, mutton, cheese, wool, fish. Area: 8,681sq km (3,352sq miles). Pop. (1968) 269,830.

Corso, Gregory (1930–), US author and poet of the BEAT GENERATION. His volumes of verse include *The Vestal Lady on Brattle* (1955), *Gasoline* (1958), *Long Live Man* (1962) and *The Mutation of the Spirit* (1964).

Cort, Henry (1740–1800), British engineer who invented a process for purifying iron by puddling (stirring molten pig iron from a blast furnace). He also developed a method of shaping and finishing iron by passing it through rollers.

Cortázar, Julio (1914–), Argentine novelist and short-story writer, *b.* Belgium. His early short stories are concerned with the monster in man; the collection *Bestiario* (1951) describes several nightmares. His later work, while still surrealistic, also emphasizes structural literary innovation.

Corte-Real, Gaspar (*c.* 1450–*c.* 1501), Portuguese explorer. Sent by King Manuel I in 1500 to search for the Northwest Passage, he explored the coast of Canada and is believed to have discovered Greenland. In 1501 he made a second expedition, but failed to return.

Cortes, the legislature of Spain. Local cortes were set up in the 12th and 13th centuries as various regions were reconquered from the Moors. The first national Cortes met in 1810. It became the Spanish parliament during the Second Republic (1931–39) and during the period of FALANGE rule (1942–76), when its members were appointed by government agencies. Free elections to the Cortes recommenced in June 1977.

Cortés, Hernán (1485–1547), central figure in the Spanish conquest and colonization of Mexico. Under the patronage of Diego de Velásquez, Cortés sailed for central America with 550 men in 1518. He declared himself independent of Velásquez, gave himself the official standing and legal authority to colonize and marched inland toward the Aztec capital. Converting many of the local American Indians into allies of his cause, Cortés was able to capture Tenochtitlán in 1521. Cortés's personal power, symbolized by his titles and estates, was gradually eroded by the crown. He died in Spain, but his remains were transferred to Mexico in 1562. *See also* HC1 p.236.

Cortex, in animal and plant anatomy, outer layer of a gland or tissue. Examples are the cortex of the adrenal glands, which is quite distinct from, and makes different hormones from, the central part, or MEDULLA; the cerebral cortex or outer layer of the brain; and the cortical layers of tissue in plant roots and stems lying between the bark or epidermis and the hardwood.

Cortisone, HORMONE produced by the cortex of the adrenal glands and essential for carbohydrate, protein and fat metabolism, kidney function and disease resistance. Synthetic cortisone is used to treat adrenal insufficiency, rheumatoid arthritis and other inflammatory diseases, rheumatic fever and skin complaints. A potent, versatile drug, it can have unwanted side-effects such as body swelling.

Cortona, Pietro Berrettini da (1596–1669), Italian painter and architect, with BERNINI and BORROMINI the creator of the BAROQUE style in Rome. Cortona's mastery of illusionistic decoration is shown in the ceilings of the Barberini and Pitti palaces, Rome. His architectural masterpiece is the façade of the church of Maria della Pace, Rome.

Cortot, Alfred-Denis (1877–1962), French pianist, conductor and renowned teacher. He founded the Paris Orchestra Philharmonique and in 1905 formed a celebrated trio with Jacques Thibaud and Pablo CASALS.

Corumbá, chief commercial city of MATO GROSSO, SW Brazil. Standing on the River Paraguay, it flanks a region which is believed to hold the world's largest reserves of manganese. Its main communications are by river. Pop. (1975 est.) 95,234.

Corundum, translucent to transparent mineral in many hues, aluminium oxide (Al_2O_3). It is found in igneous, pegmatitic and metamorphic rocks occurring as pyramidal or prismatic crystals in the rhombohedral system and as granular masses. It is the hardest natural substance after diamond. Gemstone varieties are sapphire and ruby; star sapphires reflect light in a six-pointed star. It is also used in watches and motors. Hardness 9; s.g. 4. *See also* PE pp.99, *98.*

Corunna, Battle of (1809), engagement between Britain and France in the PENINSULAR WAR. The British commander, Sir John MOORE, was killed, but the French failed to prevent the British army from retreating and escaping from Spain.

Corvette, modern anti-submarine warship or, historically, and used interchangeably with "sloop", a small sailing vessel. Towards the end of WWII corvettes were replaced by FRIGATES which were faster and better armed. *See also* MM p.175.

Corvidae, family of about 100 species of passerine (perching) birds, commonly known as the crow family, including CROWS, JACKDAWS, JAYS, MAGPIES, NUTCRACKERS, RAVENS and ROOKS. Crows are agile and aggressive in the air and will often mob birds of prey.

Corvo, Baron. *See* ROLFE, FREDERICK.

Coryphaena, genus of fish known commonly and confusingly as dolphins, this name also being used for several types of small whales. They are widespread, especially in tropical waters. Dolphin fish are fast swimmers and are brilliantly coloured. Species *Coryphaena hippurus. See also* NW p.*240.*

Cos. *See* KOS.

Cosa, Juan de la, (*c.* 1460–1510), Spanish navigator. Under Columbus he was the master of the *Santa Maria*, the ship which he ran aground in 1492. In 1500 he made the first large map of the New World, of great value to other cartographers.

Cosecant, ratio of the length of the hypotenuse to the length of the side opposite to an acute angle in a right-angled triangle. The cosecant of angle A is usually abbreviated "cosec A" and is equal to the reciprocal of its SINE. *See also* SU p.46.

Cosgrave, Liam (1920–), Irish lawyer and politician. Elected to the Dail Eireann for the Fine Gael party in 1943, he was external affairs minister (1954–57), becoming party leader (1965) and prime minister in 1973. He supported the British Government's plans for a Council of Ireland to link the governments of the Republic and the North. *See also* HC2 p.295.

Cosgrave, William Thomas (1880–1965), Irish nationalist. He fought in the 1916 rebellion against Britain and helped win independence. Cosgrave was president of the IRISH FREE STATE (1922–32). His party, Cumann na nGaedheal, lost the election of 1932 to EAMON DE VALERA's FIANNA FÁIL. Soon after, Cosgrave helped found the moderate Fine Gael Party, from which he resigned in 1948. *See also* HC2 p.294, *294.*

Così Fan Tutte (1790), two-act comic opera by Wolfgang Amadeus MOZART, Italian libretto by Lorenzo da PONTE. Commissioned by Emperor Joseph II, it was first performed in Vienna. In a frivolous court farce, two disguised officers, Guglielmo (baritone) and Ferrando (tenor), test the fidelity of their ladies Fiordiligi and Dorabella (sopranos) to settle a wager. *See also* HC1 p.319.

Co-signer, person whose signature appears along with the "maker" of a commercial document. The document is signed with the understanding that should the "maker" default the co-signer is responsible for the obligations incurred.

Cosine, ratio of the length of the side adjacent to an acute angle to the length of the hypotenuse in a right-angled triangle. The cosine of angle A is usually abbreviated "cos A". *See also* SU p.46.

Cosmetics, preparations applied to the body to beautify the wearer. From the Greek word meaning "skilled in adornment", such preparations are as old as mankind. The earliest were derived from vegetable colourings, and the ancient Egyptians used eye paints made of lead, antimony and copper ores. Galen, the Greek physician of the second century AD, created a cold cream which is still the basis for most cosmetic creams. The Italians led the modern development of cosmetics, the range of which was extended enormously by the discovery of aniline dyes in the mid-nineteenth century. There are now three main types of cosmetics: those for skin care (cleansing, stimulation and lubrication), make-up (pigmented foundation, rouge, face powder, lipstick and eye colourants), and such products as bath oils, deodorants and depilatories. *See also* MM pp.246–247.

Cosmetic surgery. *See* PLASTIC SURGERY.

Cosmic dust, very fine particles of solid matter in any part of the universe, including meteoric dust and interstellar material that can absorb starlight to form dark nebulae in galaxies. Spherical dust particles about 0.05mm (0.002in) in diameter, found in certain marine sediments, are thought to be the remains of some 5,000 tonnes of cosmic dust that fall to Earth each year.

Cosmic radiation, or rays, high energy radiation reaching the earth from space, the majority of which comes from the sun. Primary cosmic radiation consists of particles of extremely high energies which are usually protons, although the nuclei of atoms as heavy as nickel have been detected. When these particles strike the molecules of the atmosphere many other particles are produced, such as muons, pions and other mesons, leptons such as electrons and neutrinos and nucleons such as protons and neutrons, in addition to various HYPERONS. This process is secondary cosmic radiation and it leads to further nuclear reactions, or cascades. *See also* SU p.67.

Cosmology, branch of astronomy concerned with the origin, evolution and characteristics of the universe. Once considered the province of theologians and philosophers, it is now a science based on theoretical physics and mathematics. Experimental data are now available for testing various theories, including the "BIG BANG" theory (with the associated oscillating theory) and the STEADY-STATE theory.

Cosmonaut. *See* ASTRONAUT.

Cosmos, from the Greek *kosmos*, meaning "order", the universe considered as an ordered whole. PLATO and ARISTOTLE conceived of the universe as ordered by an intelligent principle. The conviction of an ordered nature became the basis of modern natural science.

Cosmos, summer-flowering plant, native to tropical America and cultivated in temperate climates. It has fern-like leaves and red or yellow disc florets; the ray florets occur in various colours. Common garden cosmos (*Cosmos bipinnatus*) may grow up to 3m (10ft) fall. Family Compositae.

Cossacks, community in S Russia, originating before the 16th century from

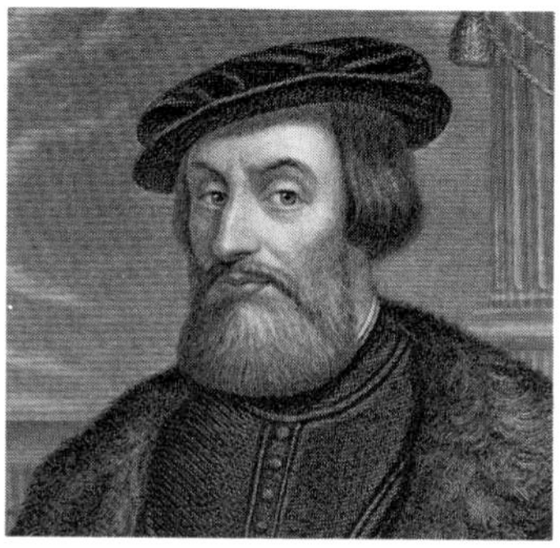

Cortés was nobly received by Montezuma, who believed he was an Aztec god.

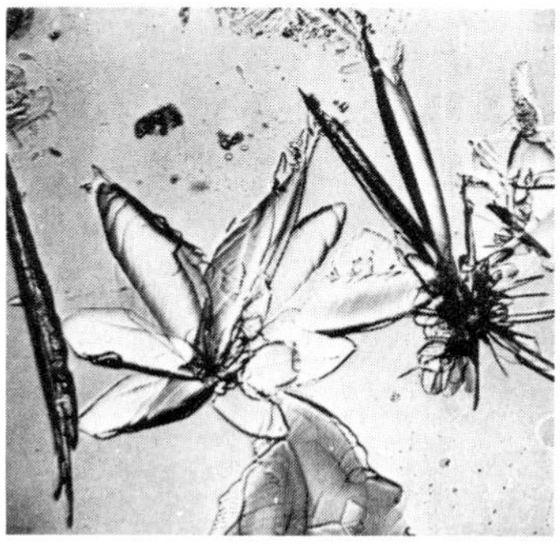

Cortisone crystals, their structure clearly visible when illuminated with polarized light.

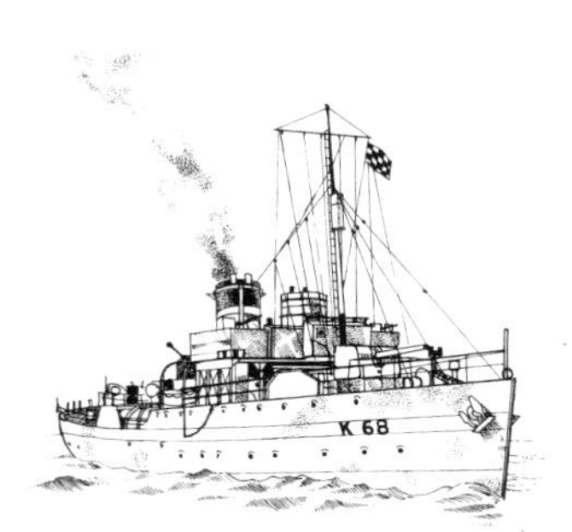

Corvette, the fast, highly manoeuvrable anti-submarine vessel of World War II.

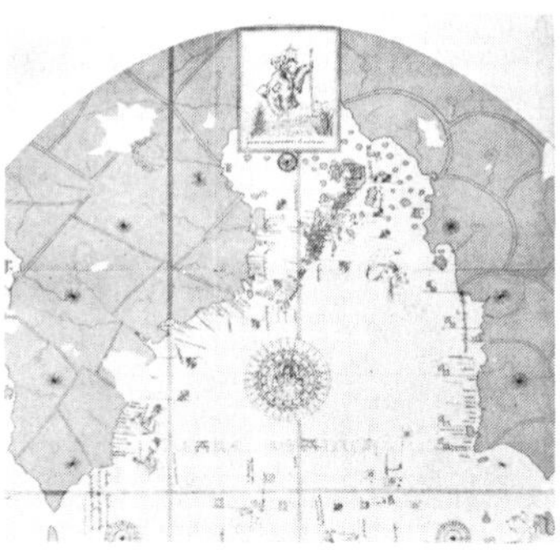

Juan de la Cosa; the western part of his great map of the New World made in 1500.

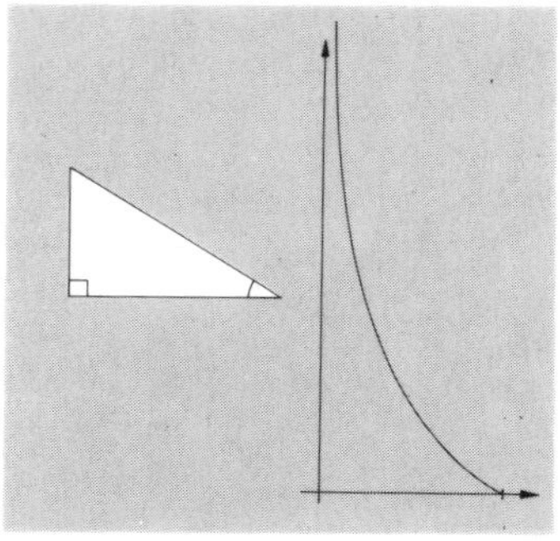

Cotangents and other trigonometrical ratios can be worked out on pocket calculators.

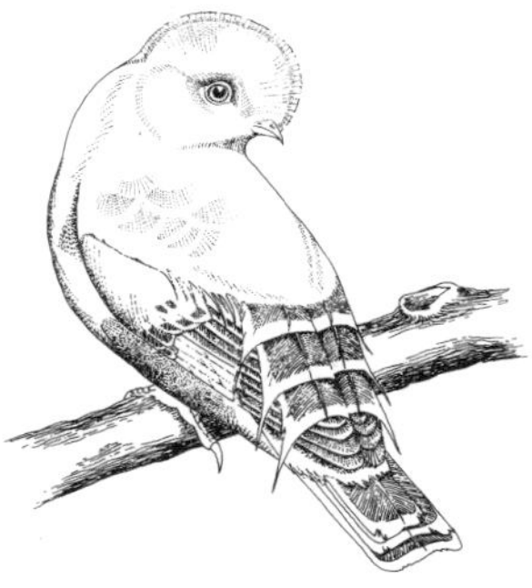

Cotinga; family of birds which includes the cock-of-the-rock (*Rupicola rupicola*)

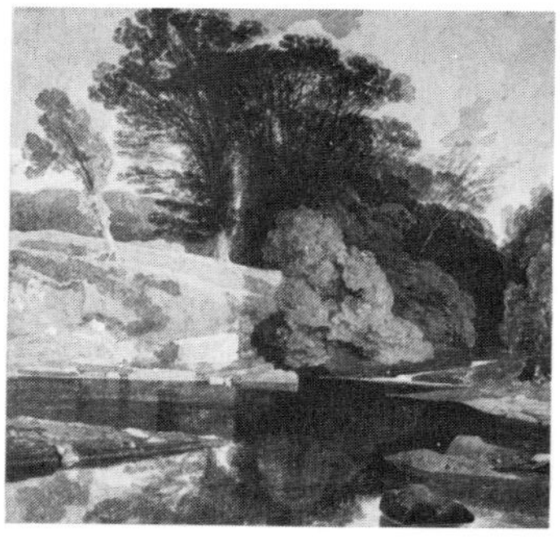

John Sell Cotman was the best watercolourist of the Norwich school (*Shady Pool*, detail).

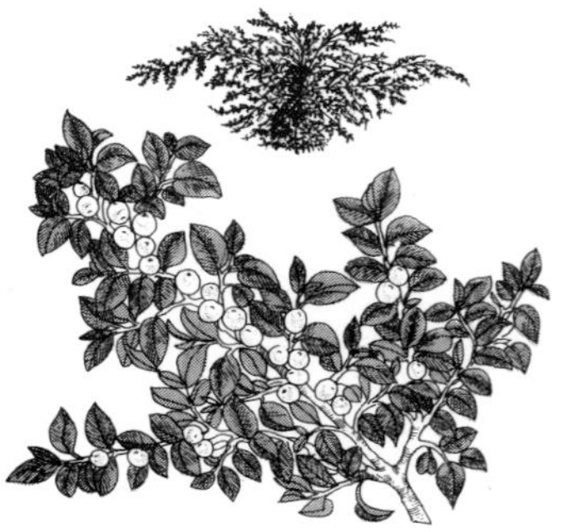

Cotoneaster's apple-like berries reveal the relationship between the rose and the apple.

escaped serfs and Tartar bands. The name comes from the Turkic *Kazak*, or adventurer. By the 16th century they had evolved into four main groups, with a militaristic society based on self-governing village communities and communal land-holding. Their relationship with the expanding Russian state was complex, and they took part in the revolts of Stenka Razin and PUGACHEV. By the 19th century their privileges had been curtailed and the tsar used them to suppress rebellions. During the civil war of 1918–20 most opposed the BOLSHEVIKS; they strongly resisted collectivization. Their separate identity was suppressed by STALIN.

Costa, Lorenzo (*c.*1460–1535), Italian painter who decorated the Sentivoglio Palace, Bologna. He succeeded Andrea Mantegna as court painter at Mantua, where he painted two *Allegories* for Isabella d'Este.

Costa, Lúcio (1920–), Brazilian architect who designed the town plan for Brasilia, which is still in the course of its execution. Costa was responsible for inviting LE CORBUSIER to design the Ministry of Health building in Rio de Janeiro, which greatly influenced Brazilian architecture.

Costa Brava, coastal strip in Gerona province, NE Spain, in Catalonia region, on the Mediterranean Sea near the border with France. Since WWII the area has developed a very important tourist industry and has many resorts along the coast.

Costa-Gavras, Costi (1933–), French film director, *b.* Greece, whose best-known works include the thrillers *Compartiment tueurs* (1956) and *Z* (1968). He also directed *L'aveu* (1970) and *État de siège* (1974), which have a political background, and *Section Spéciale* (1975).

Costa Rica, nation in Central America between Nicaragua and Panama. The chief products are coffee, cocoa, bananas and sugar cane which are grown along the hot, coastal plains where most of the inhabitants live. Manufactured goods are imported. The capital is San José. Area: 50,898sq km (19,652sq miles). Pop. (1975 est.) 1,986,000. *See* MW pp.60–61.

Costello, John Aloysius (1891–1976), Irish politician. As leader of the FINE GAEL party he was Prime Minister in two coalition governments (1948–51, 1954–57). His first government took the Irish republic out of the COMMONWEALTH. He resigned the leadership of Fine Gael in 1959.

Coster, Charles Theodore Henri de (1827–79), Belgian writer. His most famous work is *La Légende et les Aventures héroïques de Thyl Ulenspiegel et de Lamme Goedzak* (1868), written in deliberately archaic style. He also wrote *Légendes flamandes* (1858).

Coster, Laurens Janszoon (1370–1440), Dutch printer who is sometimes credited with having invented movable type which, after Coster's death, a worker took to Johann GUTENBERG at Mainz.

Cost of living, money necessary to purchase a certain level of goods and services. Most countries publish information that charts family spending on such basics as food, clothing, heating, lighting and rent.

Costume, in the THEATRE, clothing worn by actors during a performance. Early theatrical costume was closely related to religious ceremony and tended to be highly symbolic. The simplicity of medieval costume was replaced later by lavish splendour of dress especially in the courts of 16th- and 17th-century Europe. In the 18th and 19th centuries authentic detail in elaborate period costumes mirrored the concern for historical accuracy. Today the effectiveness of stage costume depends on the designer's ability to interpret the director's approach to a production.

Cosway, Richard (1742–1821), British painter famous for his miniatures. He used an unusual method, transparent watercolours on ivory, to give a translucent effect. He also painted portraits in oils and was elected a full academician of the Royal Academy in 1771.

Cotangent, ratio of the length of the side adjacent to an acute angle to the length of the side opposite to the angle in a right-angled triangle. The cotangent of angle *A* is usually abbreviated "cot *A*" and is equal to the reciprocal of its TANGENT. *See also* TRIGONOMETRIC FUNCTIONS; SU p.46.

Cotinga, any of about 90 species tropical birds, of whom the males are generally brightly coloured and bizarrely ornamented. Examples are the COCK-OF-THE-ROCK and the UMBRELLA BIRD. There are also some plain and dull-coloured species. Most cotingas live in the Amazon forests. Family Cotingidae.

Cotman, John Sell (1782–1842), British landscape painter and etcher, co-founder, with John CROME, of the NORWICH SCHOOL. His etchings of architecture in Normandy and England are important. Though not valued during his life. Cotman's watercolours – austere landscapes in broad washes of yellow, browns, blues and greens – are now highly prized, eg *Greta Bridge* and *Chirk Aqueduct*.

Cotoneaster, genus of about 50 species of deciduous shrubs of the ROSE family, mostly native to China. They have small white flowers and small, red or black, round, berry-like fruit, and are often cultivated as ornamental plants.

Cotonou, city in s Benin, w Africa, approx. 24km (15 miles) sw of Porto Novo. The former capital and largest city in Benin, it is the main port and an important transport centre for the country. Oil is drilled offshore and Cotonou is the distribution centre for petroleum products. Industries: food processing, textiles, motor vehicle assembly. Pop. 175,000.

Cotopaxi, active volcano in N central Ecuador 65km (40 miles) s of Quito, in the Andes Mountains. The highest continually active volcano in the world, its frequent eruptions have caused severe damage. It was first scaled in 1872 by Wilhelm Reid. Height: 5,896m (19,344ft).

Cotswolds, range of limestone hills lying mainly in Gloucestershire, w England and extending 80km (50 miles) NE from Bath. The local stone is widely used as a building material and the region is also known for its breed of sheep. The highest point on the hills is Cleeve Cloud, 314m (1,031ft).

Cotton, Thomas Henry (1907–), British golfer. His victory in the 1934 British Open ended 10 years of US domination, and two more Open titles (1937, 1948) established him as the foremost British golfer of his era. He won further renown as a writer and adviser on golf-course architecture.

Cotton, annual shrubby plant native to subtropical regions. Some species can be tree-like or ornamental, most cotton is grown for the fibres that develop in the seeds and are made into fabric. The leaves are lobed and flowers are yellow, white, pink or purple. Cotton needs a long, warm growing season, with ample moisture, except at harvest time. COTTON SEED is also commercially valuable. Family Malvaceae. *See also* PE pp.216–217.

Cotton aphid, also called melon aphid or cotton louse, small, soft-bodied insect that is green to black and may be winged or wingless. It feeds on cotton, squashes, melons or lilies and spreads the disease that attacks crops of Easter lily bulbs in the USA. Length: 3mm (0.125in). Family Aphididae; species *Aphis gossypii*. *See also* APHIS.

Cotton family, English antiquarians, important in the development of libraries. Sir Robert Bruce Cotton (1571–1631) collected many documents, including Hebrew and Greek manuscripts and Anglo-Saxon charters. His son Sir Thomas Cotton (1597–1662) increased the collection, which was transferred to the nation in 1700 by Sir Robert's great-grandson. Sir John Cotton (1679–1731). The collection became part of the original BRITISH MUSEUM in 1753.

Cotton gin, machine used for separating cotton lint from seeds. The gin patented in 1794 by Eli WHITNEY (which could clean 22kg – 50lb – per day) consisted of a toothed cylinder which revolved and extracted the cotton the seeds from a grate-like container.

Cotton industry, growing, harvesting, treating and weaving of cotton fibres from the fruits of the cotton plant (*Gossypium SP*). The fibres are harvested, mostly by machine, and seeds and impurities such as leaf debris and dirt are separated from the lint, also by machine. The raw lint is graded, baled and transported to the mills, where the lint is further cleaned, blended, carded to align the fibres in the same direction, and then spun into threads or yarn on bobbins or spools. The cotton yarn can then be woven into fabrics, often together with synthetic yarns. Further treatment of the cotton includes fulling, or shrinking and thickening the fibres. Finishing operations include bleaching, dyeing and printing. As a crop, cotton is one of the world's largest: because of its low production cost it is grown in most tropical and subtropical countries where the terrain is suitable. Cotton seed, which is the greater part of the fruit by weight, is also a major crop, being processed to make edible oil, cattle cake and other products. *See also* MM pp.56–59.

Cotton louse. *See* COTTON APHID.

Cotton mills, the cotton-spinning factories in Britain which emerged during the INDUSTRIAL REVOLUTION. Cotton manufacture was by far the largest industry between 1780 and 1850 and was the first to make a large-scale move from domestic, or cottage, industry (in which piece-work was distributed to hand-loom spinners in their homes) to factory industry, in which people left their homes to work steam-powered looms in the mills. *See also* HC2 pp.88–89; MM pp.58–59.

Cottonseed, seed of the COTTON plant from which cottonseed oil is extracted. This oil is used in salad oil, margarine, soap and paint. The seed hulls, or outer coverings, are ground and used as a livestock feed and fertilizers.

Cotton-tail, small RABBIT with a fluffy white tail from which it gets its name. It lives in widely varying habitats from s Canada to Argentina and relies on its speed and ability to "freeze" to survive in the presence of many carnivorous neighbours. Length: 27.5–50cm (11–20in). Genus *Sylvilagus*. *See also* NW p.*155*.

Cottrell, Sir Alan Howard (1919–), British metallurgical scientist, who became master of Jesus College, Cambridge, in 1974. He has won numerous prizes for his work, most recently the Harvey Science Prize from the Technion Israel Institute. His publications include *Theoretical Structural Metallurgy* (1948) and *The Mechanical Properties of Matter* (1964).

Cottrell, Leonard (1913–), British writer and archaeologist. He worked for the BBC (1942–59) before devoting himself to writing. His books include *The Bull of Minos* (1958), *The Concise Encyclopaedia of Archaeology* (1965) and *Lost Civilizations* (1974).

Cotyledon, first leaf or pair of leaves produced by the embryo of a flowering plant. In most species this seed leaf is small, but those of the common bean plant, for example, are easily visible at germination. The function of the cotyledon is to store and digest food for the embryo plant. *See also* DICOTYLEDON; MONOCOTYLEDON.

Coubertin, Baron Pierre de (1863–1937), French educator and sportsman. He is remembered for his untiring efforts to organize a modern version of the ancient Greek OLYMPIC GAMES. As a result, the first modern Games were held in Athens in 1896 and have continued ever since.

Coucal. *See* CUCKOO.

Couch grass, or quack grass, or twitch, persistent, perennial GRASS that spreads rapidly by rhizomes, or underground stems. It is a common weed in the Northern Hemisphere. Species *Agropyron repens*.

Coué, Emile (1857–1926), French spiritual healer who made use of hypnotism and auto-suggestion. The chief principle of "Couéism", popular in the 1920s, was his adage "Every day, and in every way, I am becoming better and better".

Cough, the sudden and noisy expulsion of air from the lungs. It is a reflex action of the body to try and dislodge an obstruction or irritant in the respiratory system. A common symptom, a cough can be associated with a wide variety of conditions, from a mild COLD to childhood diseases such as WHOOPING COUGH and more serious illnesses such as PNEUMONIA and EMPHYSEMA.

Coulomb, Charles Augustin de (1736–1806), French physicist. After serving as a military engineer in the West Indies, he returned to Paris shortly before the Revolution. His invention of the TORSION BALANCE led to his experiments in electrostatics and the discovery of the inverse-square law that bears his name. The unit of electric charge is named after him. *See also* COULOMB'S LAW.

Coulomb's law, one of the basic inverse square laws of physics. It states that the force between two point electric charges is proportional to the product of the charges and inversely proportional to the square of the distance between them. It can be stated mathematically as $F = Q_1Q_2/4\pi\varepsilon d^2$ where F is the force, Q_1 and Q_2 are the charges and d is the distance between them; ε is a constant called the permitivity of the medium between the charges.

Council, general term to describe a variety of bodies, elected and appointed, which carry out advisory, legislative or executive functions. In post-conquest Britain the council of medieval kings was the CURIA REGIS, from which sprang the PRIVY COUNCIL. The barons and officers of state called to it were expected to give counsel or advice. The most obvious public use of the word today is for the elected BOROUGH and COUNTY COUNCILS.

Council for Mutual Economic Assistance. *See* COMECON.

Council of Europe, organization formed in 1949 to work for the greater political and cultural unity of Europe. Its member states are Austria, Belgium, Britain, Cyprus, Denmark, France, West Germany, Greece, Iceland, Ireland, Italy, Luxembourg, Malta, The Netherlands, Norway, Sweden, Switzerland and Turkey. In 1958 it established the European Court of Human Rights to protect individuals against the arbitrary acts of national governments. Since matters of defence are the function of NATO and economic affairs the function of the EEC, the Council is primarily concerned with social and cultural affairs. *See also* HC2 pp.258–259.

Council of Ministers (EEC), policy-making body of the European Economic Community, composed usually of the foreign ministers of each member nation. Representing the interests of the individual member states, the council generally acts only on proposals from the EEC's executive organ, which represents the community as a whole.

Council of Ministers (Soviet), highest executive and administrative organ of the USSR, empowered to establish and oversee the monetary system, law and order, civil rights policy and the organization of the armed forces. It also acts as foreign policy adviser. It is responsible to the Supreme Soviet, which appoints its members, or to the PRESIDIUM.

Countdown, final period preceding a rocket flight during which systems and components are checked on a pre-arranged schedule. A failure of one component results in either an interruption ("hold") of the countdown or the abandoning ("scrubbing") of the flight.

Counter culture, term used to describe the life-style of young people in the USA and in Europe who, in reaction against traditional Western values, adopted Eastern religion, communal living, drugs and other signs that they had "dropped out" of bourgeois society.

Counter-espionage, branch of a government's intelligence organization concerned with protecting a country from espionage. Counter-espionage also includes protection from other acts that might endanger a country's security, such as theft, sabotage, kidnapping and assassination. In Britain counter-espionage is run by the Security Service, generally known as MI5 (M16 is the Secret Service, which controls espionage abroad). MI5 may collaborate with other government departments and with the Special Branch of the Metropolitan Police.

Counterfeiting, the illegal manufacture of coins or printed "money". Although counterfeiting is a form of forgery, it is considered more serious since it is regarded as an offence against the government. In England counterfeiting was treated as treasonable from the 14th century until 1936.

Counterpoint, in music, technique in composition involving independent melodic lines that are sung or played simultaneously to produce HARMONY. The term, originally meaning "note against note", derives from the practice in the Middle Ages of adding an accompanying note to each note of a melody. Contrapuntal writing reached its apogee in the 16th century in the work of BYRD, LASSO and PALESTRINA, and in the organ compositions of BACH in the 18th century.

Counter-Reformation, revival of the spiritual and theological life of the Roman Catholic Church in Europe during the 16th and early 17th centuries. It began as a reaction to the Protestant REFORMATION. The Counter-Reformation strove to remove many of the abuses that had crept into the late medieval Church and won new prestige for the papacy and the Church. A leading part was played in the movement by new monastic orders, particularly by the Society of Jesus (JESUITS), founded by St Ignatius of LOYOLA. The Council of TRENT (1545–63) clarified Roman Catholic teaching on the major theological controversies of the period and initiated internal Church reforms.

Counter tenor, male alto voice of the same register as the female CONTRALTO. It is produced by the use of FALSETTO and is most common in British church choirs. Alfred DELLER began its secular revival in the 1940s.

Countess of Huntingdon's Connexion, Calvinist Methodist denomination founded in England by Selina, Countess of Huntingdon, in the middle of the 18th century. It was affiliated to the Congregational Churches of England and Wales until this became the United Reformed Church in 1972.

Count of Monte Cristo, The (1844), novel by Alexandre DUMAS the elder. Edmond Dantès, a young sailor, is wrongfully imprisoned for 14 years in the Château d'If; there he is befriended by the Abbé Faria who dies leaving Dantès his fortune. Escaping disguised as Faria's corpse, he finds the money and uses it to avenge himself on his enemies.

Country and Western music, popular music originally associated with the rural and mountainous areas of S USA. The music now typically features sentimental lyrics and instrumental music played with stringed instruments such as the guitar, banjo or fiddle. Its origins were in the folk music of British immigrants, although in Texas Negro blues were also an influence. Nashville, Tennessee, is considered the commercial centre of country music in the USA. *See also* HC2 pp.272–273.

Country dancing. *See* FOLK DANCING.

Country rock, in geology, rock adjacent to mineral veins, or that has an igneous intrusion. The general term "gneiss" was applied to this type of rock formation in older mining technology. It is metamorphic rock, usually banded and made up of coarse-grained material.

County, one of the main administrative divisions of the government of a state. In Britain and the Republic of Ireland it is a division of LOCAL GOVERNMENT. Counties based on historic boundaries are known as geographical counties; those with a function in local government are called administrative counties. Local government in Northern Ireland is administered through six geographical counties, which are sub-divided into borough, urban and rural districts. In the early 1970s changes were made in the old county boundaries of England and Wales for administrative purposes. *See also* articles on individual counties and MW p.70.

County Borough. *See* BOROUGH.

County Championship, England's premier cricket competition, contested by the 17 first-class counties in a series of three-day matches. Championship rules were first applied to nine counties in 1873, when Gloucestershire and Nottinghamshire tied for the title, although Surrey (winners in 1864, when sporting newspapers decided the championship) are held to be the first champions. Since then Yorkshire have wone the most titles, followed by Surrey. The authorities have made several innovations, such as bonus points and limiting the first innings to a combined total of 200 overs, in an attempt to attract spectators. Perhaps the most significant contribution to a competition lacking public support was its first-ever sponsorship, in 1977, by Cadbury Schweppes.

County council, chief administrative body of the local government division of county in Britain. The county is the principal administrative district for local government. Each council consists of a chairman and councillors. It is elected every three years. It has both legislative and executive powers (as in the levying of rates). County councils derive from Anglo-Saxon and medieval shire courts. Historically they had no jurisdiction over large boroughs within their boundaries, but since the reorganization of local government in 1974, the power of borough councils has largely disappeared. There are 59 county councils (including metropolitan areas like greater London and greater Manchester) in England and Wales.

County Court, British court which has its origin in the shire court of Anglo-Saxon times. The modern courts date from the County Courts Act of 1846. At that time the main business of the court, presided over by a paid magistrate (it had previously been the sheriff), was the recovery of small debts. Since then its jurisdiction has expanded. By the 1959 act it is concurrent with the High Court in matters of COMMON LAW, EQUITY and PROBATE. There are more than 300 county courts.

Coup d'état, swift stroke of policy, either against the ruling power of a state or by the state against an element within it. Of the first kind, the most usual is a military take-over of civilian government, such as that by "the Colonels" in Greece in 1967. An example of the second kind is HITLER'S murder of the Sturmabteilung leaders on 30 June 1934. Today the term is often shortened merely to "coup".

Couperin, François (1668–1733), French composer. He was organist and harpsichordist at the court of LOUIS XIV. "Le Grand", as he was known, was the greatest of a large and long-lived family of brilliant musicians. Although now principally remembered for his many harpsichord pieces, his book on the technique of harpsichord-playing was influential in his day. *See also* HC2 pp.*40–41*.

Courbet, Gustave (1819–77), the leading French realist painter of his time. Largely self-taught, through his studies of great works in the Louvre, Courbet rejected traditional subject matter and instead painted monumental peasant groups, scenes from life in Paris and still lifes. His nudes, splendid in their richness of colour and textural contrast, and ranging from the mildly to the highly erotic, aroused shocked criticism – as did much of his work. His equally controversial political activity forced him into exile (1873) in Switzerland, where he spent his remaining years. Courbet's rejection of both Romantic and Classical ideals prepared the way for MILLET, DEGAS and the IMPRESSIONISTS. *See also* HC2 pp.116–118.

Cournand, André (1895–), French-born US physiologist. He shared the 1956 Nobel Prize in physiology and medicine with Dickinson Woodruff RICHARDS and Werner FORSSMANN for their discoveries concerning heart catheterization and pathological changes in the circulatory system.

Cournot, Antoine-Augustin (1801–77), French philosopher and mathematician. He applied mathematics to the study of economics and contributed to the theories of supply and demand and monopoly. His most important work was *Researches Into the Mathematical Principles of the Theory of Wealth* (1838).

Coursing, ancient and controversial field sport in which two specially bred greyhounds race after a hare driven by beaters

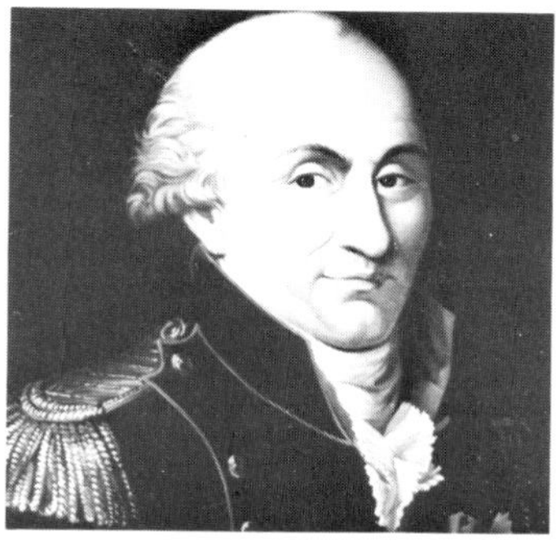

Coulomb showed that an electrostatic charge is confined to the surface of a conductor.

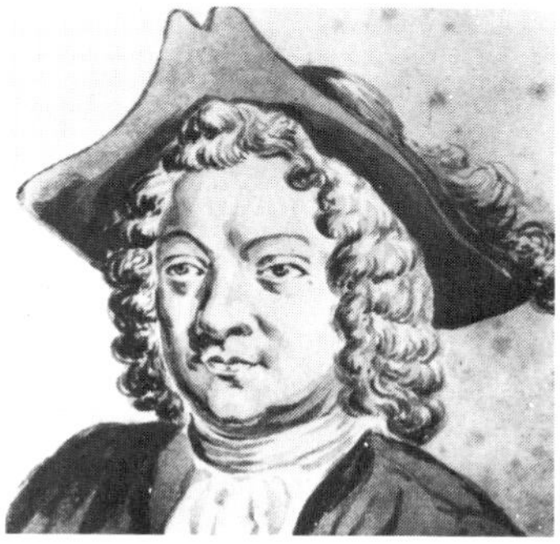

Francois Couperin taught music to the royal children at the court of Louis XIV.

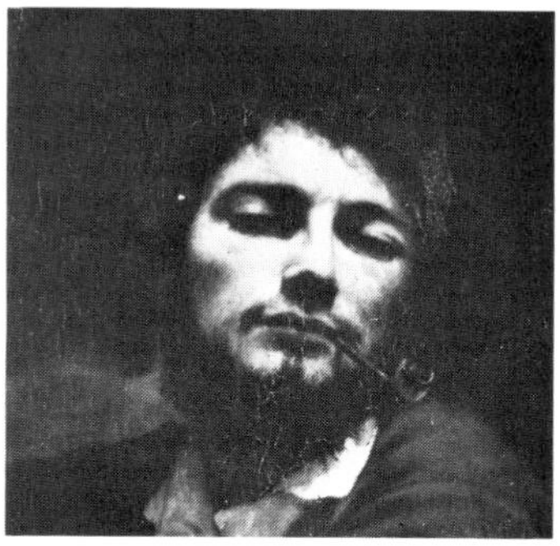

Courbet's paintings and politics shocked the conservative Parisians (self-portrait).

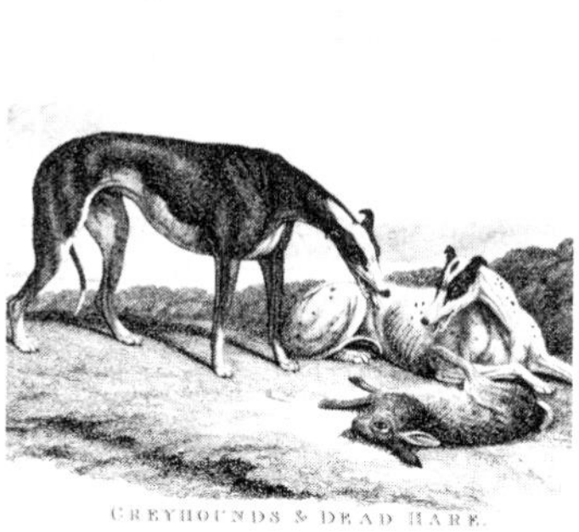

Coursing is one of several controversial bloodsports still actively pursued in Britain.

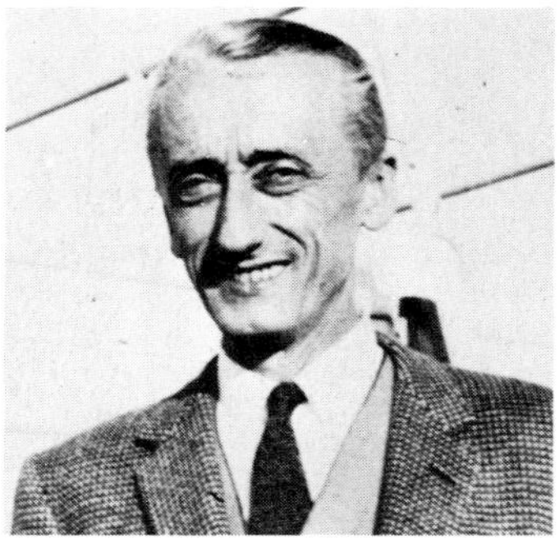

Jacques Cousteau introduced the magic of underwater life to a worldwide audience.

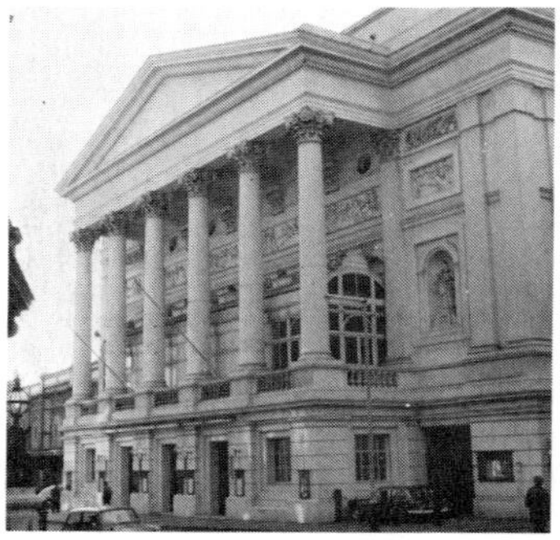

Covent Garden lost a little of its charm when the market was relocated at Nine Elms.

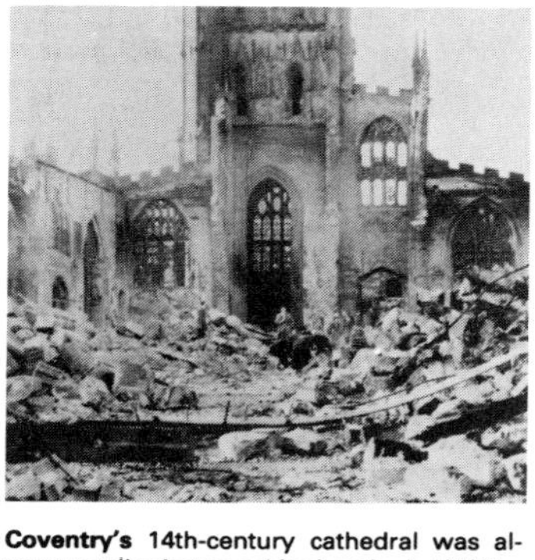

Coventry's 14th-century cathedral was almost totally destroyed by bombs in WWII.

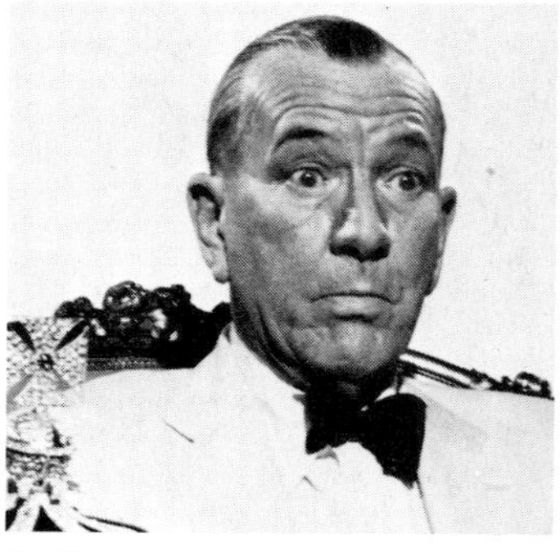

Sir Noel Coward, the brilliantly versatile actor, writer, composer and "Englishman".

into a closed area. The dogs are released some 73m (240ft) behind the hare and are awarded points for speed and agility, turning the hare, knocking it off its feet and, occasionally, for the kill. In Britain, where rules were formulated in the 16th century, the coursing season runs from September to March with the WATERLOO CUP, held near Liverpool, its blue riband. Entrants for courses are restricted to "stakes" of 8, 16, 32 or 64 and drawn in pairs, the knockout system being used to determine the finalists.

Court, Margaret Smith (1942–), Australian tennis player. She won the US amateur singles title (1962; 1965; 1968–69), US open singles (1969–70; 1973), and Wimbledon (1963; 1965; 1970), Australian (1960–66; 1969–71) and French (1962; 1964; 1969–70) ladies singles championships. In 1970 she equalled Maureen Connolly's record of winning all these titles in the same year.

Court, law. *See* LAW COURTS.

Court, ward of. *See* WARD OF COURT.

Courtauld, Samuel (1793–1881), British industrialist of Huguenot descent. He founded the firm of Courtaulds in 1816 at Bocking, Essex, which at first specialized in the production of silks, and from 1904 developed the production of viscose rayon. He promoted the nylon industry in Britain and pioneered other man-made fibres. His great nephew Samuel (1876–1947) was chairman of the company from 1921. In 1931 he bequeathed his London house (Home House), and his fine collection of 19th-century French painting to the University of London to form a department for the research and study of art (the Courtauld Institute). Courtauld's gift of paintings was later augmented by the donation of other private collections.

Courtenay, Thomas (1937–), British actor. A stage actor from 1960, he is known chiefly for his film appearances in *The Loneliness of the Long Distance Runner* (1962), *Billy Liar* (1963), *King and Country* (1964) and *Doctor Zhivago* (1965).

Court leet, court of record in Britain. It was established in a MANOR, HUNDRED or lordship by royal charter. At its annual session it reviewed the FRANKPLEDGE and tried offenders for crimes committed within its area of jurisdiction. Courts leet fell into disuse with the Summary Jurisdiction Act of 1848, but a few have survived to the present day.

Court martial, court of the armed services for trial both of accused service persons and of certain civilians who are subject to the Services Discipline Acts. The origin of military courts is to be found in the Court of Constable and Marshal, part of the CURIA REGIS established in England by WILLIAM THE CONQUEROR. Modern status derives from Mutiny Act 1689. Current authorities are the Army Act 1955, Air Force Act 1955, and Naval Discipline Act 1957, as amended. Members of the court are serving officers, in certain cases advised by a judge advocate.

Courtneidge, Dame Cicely (1893–), British film and stage actress. She began her stage career in Manchester in 1901 and made her first film in 1929. At the age of 78 she appeared in London in the play *Move Over Mrs Markham.*

Court of Arches, archbishop's court for the administration of ecclesiastical law in the province of Canterbury, in the Church of England. In some cases appeals are allowed from lower church courts to the Court of Arches.

Court of Chancery. *See* CHANCERY.

Court of Common Pleas, sometimes called Common Bench, superior court of British COMMON LAW, now defunct. It came into being in the late 12th century to hear civil disputes between individuals as opposed to litigation in which the Crown was a party. In the later Middle Ages it also supervised lower courts but its judgments were subject to review by the King's Bench. In 1880 it was united with QUEEN'S BENCH.

Court of Criminal Appeal, British court founded in 1907 by the Criminal Appeal Act and abolished in 1966, when its jurisdiction was transferred to the Criminal Division of the Court of Appeal. Its judges were the Lord Chief Justice and the KING'S BENCH. Appeals could by made to it by a person convicted on indictment, either on a question of law or, with the leave of the judge who tried him, on a question of fact. Appeals against sentence were also heard.

Court of Session, supreme court of civil jurisdiction in Scotland. It derives from the 15th century, when JAMES I called together the Chancellor and certain lords three times a year to settle disputes. JAMES IV turned their sessions into a regular court of law. The court has the same judges as the criminal High Court of Judiciary and is presided over by the Lord President.

Court of Star Chamber, medieval court of EQUITY in the Palace of Westminster, which derived its name from stars painted on the ceiling. It was used in the 15th and 16th centuries to assert royal power, but its authority was disputed by COMMON LAW lawyers, who disliked its swift and sometimes harsh proceedings. The Stuarts used it for ecclesiastical cases and to enforce the PREROGATIVE. It was absolished by the LONG PARLIAMENT in 1641.

Court of the Lord Lyon, Scottish body which controls all arms, badges and signs armorial, the granting of certificates of change of name and the execution of royal proclamations. Under the Lord Lyon, the chief officer of arms, are three heralds and three pursuivants.

Courtois, Jacques (1621–75), French painter who worked mainly in Italy. Influenced by Guido RENI and Francesco Albani, he is known principally for his paintings of battles.

Court Roll, written record of the proceedings in any court, but applying especially to the manor courts of medieval Britain. In the roll were recorded wills, grants, surrenders and admissions of tenure (in particular COPYHOLD), and also any matters pertaining to services and duties attached to the manor (such as COMMON LAND rights).

Courtship, in human society, the period before marriage in which a man woos a woman. In many societies this not only involves the participants emotionally but can include fixed customs and rituals, such as the exchange of gifts, which are often presented to the woman's parents as well. In some cultures, where marriage is arranged (as in India), the couple do not meet before the marriage. In animals, courtship includes various forms of pre-mating activity. *See also* MS pp.168–169; NW p.150.

Cousin, Jean, name of two French artists. Jean the Elder (1490–1560), a painter and designer, designed stained-glass windows in the St Eutrope chapel at Sens Cathedral and painted the first great French nude, *Eva prima Pandora* (Louvre). His son was Jean the Younger (1522–94).

Cousteau, Jacques Yves (1910–), French oceanographer. Best known as the co-inventor (with Emile Gagnan) of the AQUALUNG – an independent diving unit permitting divers underwater mobility – he also invented a process of underwater television and conducted a series of undersea living experiments (CONSHELF I-III, 1962–65). Many of the expeditions made by his research ship *Calypso* were filmed by him for television and cinema. *See also* PE p.92.

Coutts, Thomas (1735–1822), British banker who, with his brother James, established Coutts & Co., at which George III and every successive British monarch have had banking accounts. They took over an existing business in the Strand, London, at premises which the bank still occupies.

Couvade, variety of customs in which the father simulates the experiences of childbirth during the final stages of the mother's pregnancy. It involves such customs as fasting, retiring to bed and miming birth pains. It occurs in ethnic groups and cultures throughout the world.

Covalent bond, type of CHEMICAL BOND in which two atoms share a pair of electrons; both electrons move in the combined field of the two nuclei. Most compounds with covalent bonds have discrete molecules. They tend to have low melting points and to be soluble in non-polar solvents. Covalent bonding is most common in organic compounds. *See also* SU pp.137–138; *138–139.*

Covalent radius, effective radius of an atom that is part of a covalent bond. It is computed in a way analogous to that for the IONIC RADIUS in ionic compounds, by considering the atoms as regularly packed spheres.

Covenant, in Jewish and Christian theology, a mutual agreement between God and his people. The Old Testament form of the bond, symbolized by the ARK OF THE COVENANT, was the rendering of sacrifices by the people of Israel in return for God's favour. The New Testament stresses the new and perfect form of covenant by which men receive the free gift of God's grace through faith and the life and death of Christ.

Covenant, Ark of the. *See* ARK OF THE COVENANT.

Covenanters, Presbyterians in Scotland in the 17th century, pledged by the National Covenant (1638) to uphold their religion. They opposed CHARLES I but supported the parliamentarians only after they had agreed to introduce Presbyterianism in England and Ireland as well as Scotland. When the English parliament refused to implement this agreement, the Covenanters allied with the future CHARLES II, only to be defeated at DUNBAR and WORCESTER. Despite further persecution after Charles's restoration, Presbyterianism was restored in Scotland in 1688. *See also* HC1 pp.298–299.

Covent Garden, leading opera house of England, founded in 1732 in the heart of a produce market in London, located in its present building since 1858; from 1946 also the home of the ROYAL BALLET. In the late 19th century the ROYAL OPERA COMPANY achieved world fame through many great singing stars. After a decline in the early 20th century Covent Garden again became one of the world's foremost opera houses. Joan SUTHERLAND achieved world renown there and musical directors since WWII have included Rafael Kubelik (1955–58), Georg SOLTI (1961–71) and Colin DAVIS. There was also a fruit and vegetable market at Covent Garden until 1974, when it moved to Nine Elms.

Coventry, city in West Midlands, central England, (18 miles) ESE of Birmingham. It was an important medieval market town and weaving centre. The city centre was badly damaged by bombs during WWII and the 14th-century cathedral of St Michael was destroyed; a new cathedral, designed by Sir Basil SPENCE, was completed in 1962. It is the home of the University of Warwick. Industries: motor vehicles, mechanical and electrical engineering. Pop. (1973) 334,440.

Coverdale, Miles (1488–1569), English priest who issued the first printed English Bible (1535) and the "Great Bible" (1539). He was Bishop of Exeter (1551–53), in exile (1554–59) and rector of St Magnus, London (1564–66). *See also* GREAT BIBLE; HC1 p.282.

Cow, name for mature female CATTLE that have borne at least one calf. It is also applied to other female mammals, such as elephants and seals.

Cowan, James (1870–1943), New Zealand writer on the MAORIS and New Zealand pioneer days. He wrote *Maoris in New Zealand and Legends of the Maori.*

Coward, Sir Noel Pierce (1899–1973), British playwright, composer and performer. He first attracted notice as a playwright with his drama *The Vortex* (1924) and later for his highly polished comedies such as *Hay Fever* (1925), *Bitter Sweet* (1929), *Private Lives* (1930), *Present Laughter* (1939) and *Blithe Spirit* (1941). Other works written by him include the films *In Which we Serve* (1942) and *Brief Encounter* (1946). He also composed hundreds of songs, including *Mad Dogs and Englishmen* and *Mad About the Boy*, performing many of them in cabaret and revues.

Cowbird, bird that follows herds of cattle, sometimes perching on the animals to feed on ticks. It lives in the USA and South

America. The female of most species lays its eggs in the nest of another bird, leaving the "host" bird to rear the young. Length: to 20cm (8in). Family Icteridae.

Cowboy, or cowhand, US ranch hand, usually mounted on a horse, who tends large herds of cattle. Traditionally living and working in the West, cowboys came into prominence after the Civil War, in the late 1860s. They have been romanticized in song and story and today are a symbol of the rugged independence, colour and vigour of the old "Wild West". Expert horsemen and rope men, they saw the commercial possibilities in the herds of horses and cattle that wandered the plains. *See also* GAUCHO.

Cowdrey, Michael Colin (1932–), English cricketer. He first played for Kent in 1951 and was captain of the county from 1957 to 1971. He played in 114 TEST MATCHES for England (27 as captain) and went on 11 overseas tours. He made 107 centuries in first-class cricket (22 in Test matches) and on his retirement in 1976 held the English record for the highest number of Test runs and the world record for Test catches.

Cowell, Henry Dixon (1887–1965), US composer. His large output included 20 symphonies; some of his compositions are influenced by non-Western music. He created "tone clusters" (dissonance produced by striking piano keys with the fist or forearm) and other piano pieces are played directly on the strings by rubbing, plucking or striking.

Cowes, town on the N coast of the Isle of Wight, renowned for its regatta at the beginning of August, called Cowes Week. Royal patronage has ensured its place in the social as well as the yachting calendar. Every two years the international ADMIRAL'S CUP series is held there.

Cowfish, or trunkfish, bony marine fish found on both sides of the tropical Atlantic. Its triangular body has netlike markings and spines projecting from the top of the head. The scales are fused. Length: up to 50cm (18in). Family Ostraciidae; species *Acanthostracian quadricornis.*

Cowley, Abraham (1618–67), English poet and a founder of the Royal Society. His work, marking the transition between METAPHYSICAL and AUGUSTAN poetic styles, includes *The Mistress, or Love Poems* (1647), *The Davideis* and *Pindaric Odes* (1656).

Cowley Fathers, popular name for priests of the Society of St John the Evangelist (SSJE), an Anglican society of mission priests and laymen founded in 1866 by the British cleric R.M. Benson, then vicar of St James's, Cowley, near Oxford. The first monastic community for men to be established in the Church of England since the Reformation, it now extends to several countries.

Cowpea, also called black-eyed pea, bushy annual plant native to Asia. It has edible bean pods measuring as much as 30cm (12in) long, and is grown mainly for hay, green manure or as cattle feed. Family Leguminosae; species *Vigna sinensis.*

Cowper, William (1731–1800), British poet and hymn writer. He was subject to intermittent depression, but during his lucid periods wrote a variety of prose and poetry, such as the long blank-verse poem *The Task* (1785), which is full of descriptive detail and love of the countryside. *See also* TASK, THE.

Cowpox, contagious disease in cows. It is caused by a virus, and symptoms are pustular eruptions on the teats and udder. Cowpox pus was used by Edward JENNER to develop a vaccine against SMALLPOX. *See also* HC2 p.*33.*

Cowrie, or cowry, gastropod MOLLUSC identified by an ovoid, highly polished shell with a long toothed opening and varied markings. It is found on tropical coral shores. Length: 8.3–152mm (0.33–6in). Family Cypraeidae; more than 160 species, including the map cowry *Cypraea mappa.*

Cowslip, herb of the PRIMROSE family, with a hanging yellow flower. Familiar in British meadows, it is not so widespread as it once was; species *Primula veris.* In the US the name cowslip is given to the marsh marigold or kingcup, a member of the BUTTERCUP family.

Cox, David (1783–1859), British landscape artist, regarded as one of the country's best watercolourists and known particularly for his paintings of North Wales. In 1836 he began painting on coarse wrapping paper which he found particularly suitable for absorbing the washes quickly.

Cox, Mark (1943–), British tennis player. He developed a solid left-hander's game to rank as Britain's No. 1 in the mid-1970s, when he was a consistent performer on the lucrative international circuit. He won the Dewar Cup in 1969.

Coxswain, person who steers a boat or ship. In rowing competitions, such as between Oxford and Cambridge universities, he not only steers the boat but also directs the rhythm of the crew's strokes.

Coxwell, Henry Tracey (1819–1900), British balloonist who made his first ascent in 1844. In 1870, during the Franco-Prussian War, he helped to form a corps of balloonists for the German forces.

Coyote, wild DOG, resembling a small WOLF, originally native to W North America. Coyotes have moved into many eastern areas of the US formerly inhabited by wolves, including New England. Usually greyish-brown, they have pointed muzzles, big ears and bushy tails. Length: 90cm (35in); weight: about 12kg (26lb). Species *Canis latrans. See also* CANIDAE.

Coypu, large aquatic RODENT, native to South America. It now also lives in North America and parts of Europe, both wild and on fur farms. Coypus have brown outer fur and soft grey underfur, commercially known as nutria. Overall length: 1.06m (3.5ft); weight: 8kg (18lb). Species *Myocastor coypus.*

Cozens, Alexander (*c.* 1717–86), British painter, *b.* Russia; one of the earliest English landscapists in watercolours. Cozens is best known for his "blot drawing", a system of drawing in which dots of colour are randomly placed on paper and then integrated into a sketch.

Cozens, John Robert (1752–97), British painter of watercolour landscapes, a pupil of his father Alexander COZENS. Described by Constable as "the greatest genius that ever touched landscape", Cozens painted landscapes of a poetic rather than an exact topographical character and in doing so influenced TURNER, GIRTIN and other English landscapists. *See also* HC2 p.102, *102.*

Crab, flattened, triangular, or oval DECAPOD CRUSTACEAN covered with a hard shell. Primarily marine, some crabs are found in fresh water and a few are terrestrial. Their short abdomen, often called a tail, is bent under. Most have a pair of large foreclaws, a pair of movable eyestalks and a segmented mouth. Crabs usually move sideways. Many of the 4,500 species are edible. Size: pea-sized to 3m (12ft) from leg tip to opposite leg tip. Order Decapoda. *See also* NW pp.100–101, *105, 237.*

Crab apple, small sour fruit produced by certain apple trees. The various species grow in Europe, North America and Asia. The fruit is used in making preserves and jelly. Family Rosaceae; genus *Malus.*

Crabbe, George (1754–1832), British poet. His poetry is imbued with the atmosphere of his native Suffolk and is unflinchingly realistic, as in *The Village* (1783), *The Parish Register* (1807) and *Tales of the Hall* (1819).

Crab nebula, bright emission nebula in the constellation of TAURUS, the still expanding remnant of a supernova first observed by Chinese and Japanese astronomers in 1054. Its structure consists of gaseous filaments. The Crab is a powerful radio and X-ray source, with a pulsar located at its centre. *See also* SU pp.172–173, *173,* 229, 232–233, 234–235, 258.

Crabs, name commonly given to the condition of being infested with the crab louse, *Phthirus pubis,* in the hair of pubis and armpit. Crabs is caused by poor hygiene and crowded living conditions. Treatment includes shaving of the infested hair followed by the application of ointment containing DDT.

Crab spider, webless SPIDER that moves sideways like a crab and is found throughout the world. Crab spiders hide on flowers whose colour they imitate, and grab their prey as it comes to feed. They inject venom into the victim's nervous system or blood, or both. Length: 20mm (0.8in). Family Thomisidae.

Cracking, stage in oil-refining during which the products of the first distillation are treated to break up the hydrocarbons into smaller molecules by the controlled use of heat, catalysts and often pressure. The cracking of petroleum yields heavy oils, petrol, and such gases as ethane, ethylene and propylene, which are used in the manufacture of plastics, textiles, detergents and agricultural chemicals. Cracking is therefore a means of yielding greater amounts of the lighter hydrocarbons, which are in greater demand, from heavier fractions such as lubricating oil.

Cracow. *See* KRAKOW.

Cradle, Mt, mountain in NW central Tasmania, Australia, on a spur of the central highlands. Height: 1,545m (5,069ft).

Craig, Edward Gordon (1872–1966), British scenic designer. Son of actress Ellen Terry, he was a successful actor before turning to production and design. In *On the Art of the Theatre* (1905) he proposed that actors become "supermarionettes" controlled by the director-designer-creator. Among his numerous productions were Purcell's *Dido and Aeneas* (1900), Ibsen's *Rosmersholm* (1906) and *Hamlet* (1912).

Craig, Sir James Henry (1748–1812), British governor-general of Canada (1807–11). A career soldier, he fought in the American Revolution. He was unable to work harmoniously with the Canadian Legislative Assembly and in 1810 he alienated the French Canadians by suppression of *Le Canadien.*

Craigavon, James Craig, 1st Viscount (1871–1940), Northern Irish soldier and politician, first prime minister of Northern Ireland (1921–40). He was an extreme Unionist and helped Sir Edward CARSON to keep the province in Britain. *See also* HC2 p.295.

Craigie, Sir William Alexander (1867–1957), Scottish lexicographer and philologist. He was joint editor of the *Oxford English Dictionary* (1901–33), then professor at the University of Chicago. His works include *Icelandic Sagas* (1913) and *The Study of American English* (1927).

Craik, Dinah Maria (1826–87), British authoress. The moralistic novel *John Halifax, Gentleman* (1856) is her most famous work, but she also wrote stories for children, including *The Little Lame Prince* (1875).

Craiova, city in S Romania, 180km (112 miles) W of Bucharest (Bucuresti), on the Jiu River; capital of Dolj district. It was destroyed by an earthquake in 1790 and burned by the Turks in 1802. It is at the centre of Oltenia region, which has rich farmlands; Craiova is a grain market and administrative centre for the region. Its industries include food processing, machinery and electrical equipment. Pop. 175,450.

Crake. *See* RAIL.

Cramer, Johann Baptist (1771–1858), German pianist, composer and music publisher. He wrote principally for the keyboard – piano studies, SONATAS and CONCERTOS – and as a pianist he was praised by BEETHOVEN. Cramer founded a music publishing house in London in 1824.

Cramp, involuntary persistent contraction of a MUSCLE producing sharp pain. It may occur in almost any muscle as a result of over-exertion – as in athletics – chronic strain, or from normal physiological causes such as menstruation. Leg and abdominal cramp are the most common types.

Crampton, Bruce (1935–), Australian golfer. He joined the US circuit in 1957 and after then became Australia's leading money-winner, earning more than $1 million and capturing 15 tournament

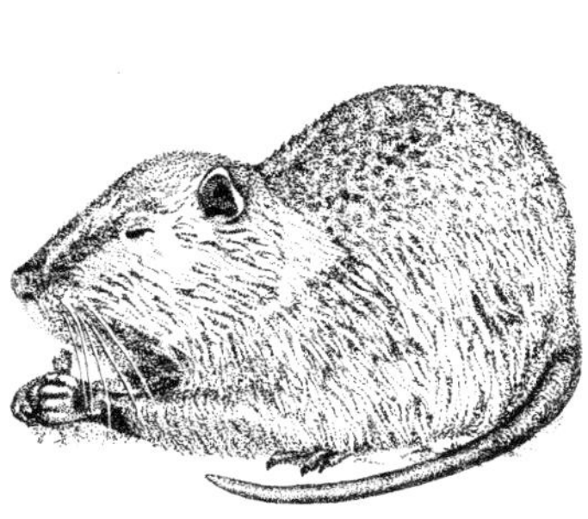

Coypu fur, known as nutria, resembles beaver and is used to make coats.

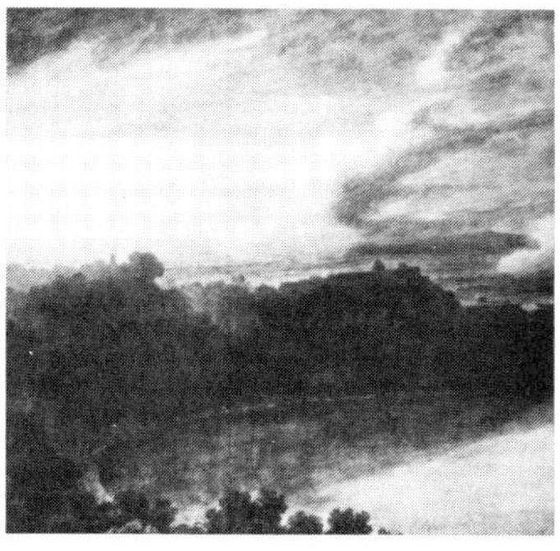

John Robert Cozen's landscapes made a very great impression on John Constable.

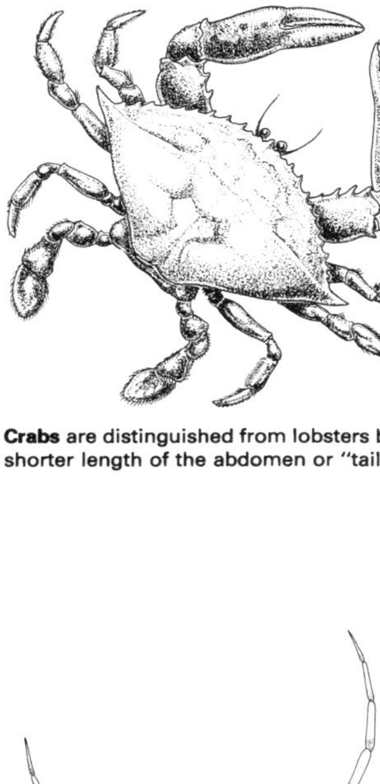

Crabs are distinguished from lobsters by the shorter length of the abdomen or "tail".

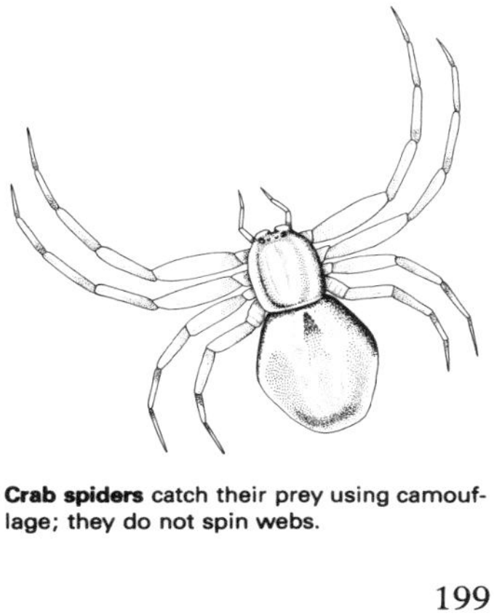

Crab spiders catch their prey using camouflage; they do not spin webs.

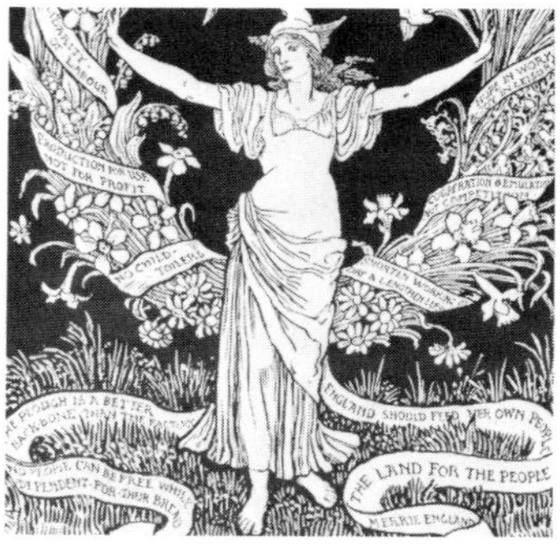

Walter Crane, much influenced by the Pre-Raphaelites, was a successful illustrator.

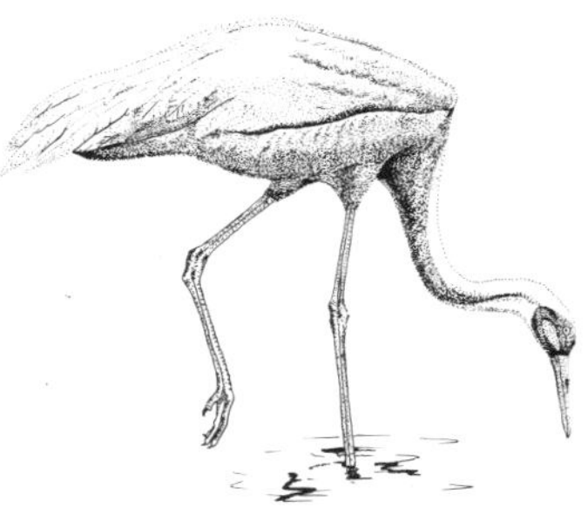

Cranes fly with their long necks stretched out in front and their legs trailing behind.

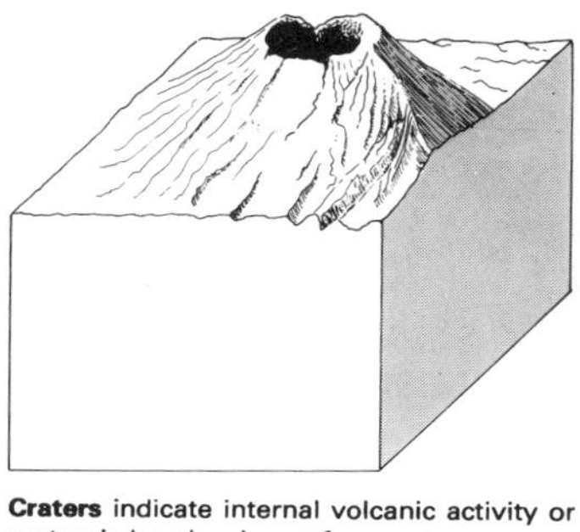

Craters indicate internal volcanic activity or meteoric bombardment from outer space.

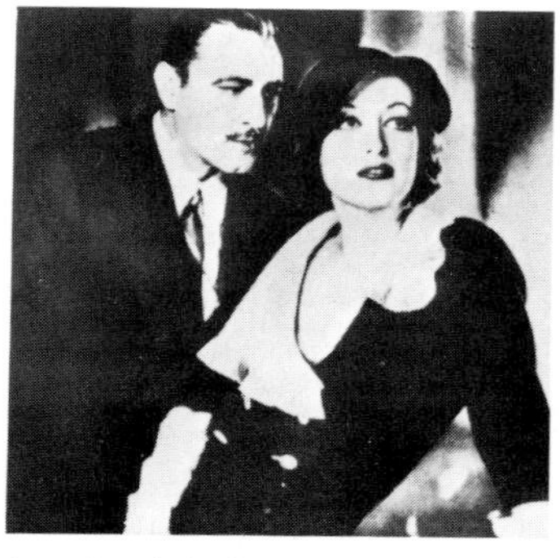

Joan Crawford with John Barrymore in a scene from the star-studded film *Grand Hotel.*

titles, three of them consecutively in 1965.

Cranach, Lucas, the Elder (1472–1553) German painter and engraver, court painter to the Electors of Saxony. A friend and follower of Martin Luther, Cranach designed many propaganda woodcuts for the Protestant cause. His portrait paintings, eg those of Luther and of Henry of Saxony, were among the first full-length portraits. He also developed a style of painting highly erotic female nudes in a glossy, enamel-like finish, new to German art, in such paintings as *Adam and Eve* and *The Judgement of Paris. See also* MS pp.*179, 184, 219.*

Cranach, Lucas, the Younger (1515–86), German painter who, following the death of his father, CRANACH THE ELDER in 1522, directed the family workshop in Weimar. Attribution of paintings to him is difficult as he derived his style from that of his father but the *Fountain of Youth* (1546) is generally accredited to him.

Cranberry, plant of the HEATH family, distributed widely in N temperate regions. It is a creeping or trailing shrub and bears red berries with an acid taste. The berries are used to make cranberry sauce. Genus *Vaccinium. See also* PE p.214.

Crane, Stephen (1871–1900), US novelist, short story writer, poet and war correspondent. His best-known work is *The Red Badge of Courage* (1895), a realistic story of the thoughts of a soldier in the Civil War. Other works include *Maggie: A Girl of the Streets* (1893), *The Black Riders and Other Lines* (1895), *The Open Boat and Other Tales of Adventure* (1898) and *War is Kind* (1899), a volume of verse.

Crane, Walter (1845–1915), British painter, designer and illustrator. He was influenced by the PRE-RAPHAELITES and became an associate of William MORRIS in designing textiles and wallpapers. A superb illustrator, one of his finest works was an edition of Spenser's *Faerie Queene* (1894–96).

Crane, any of several species of tall wading birds found in most parts of the world except S America. This long-legged bird has brownish, greyish or white plumage with a bright ornamental head. It flies with its long neck straight out and feeds on almost anything. After courtship dances, the female lays two eggs in a bulky nest of vegetation on the ground or over water. Height: to 150cm (60in). Family Gruidae. *See also* NW p.244.

Crane, machine for lifting and placing heavy loads. The large tower cranes seen on docksides have a long horizontal jib counterbalanced by a short heavy arm. Other heavy cranes, such as those moving on wheels or rails in foundries, or those in railway goods yards, form a bridge over the load. Climbing and crawling cranes are used in the construction of high-rise buildings and large bridges. Small cranes, or hoists, are frequently mounted on road vehicles for breakdown work. *See also* MM pp.96–*97,* 101, *137, 155.*

Crane-fly. *See* DADDY LONG-LEGS.

Cranesbill, common name for the wild GERANIUM.

Cranford, comic novel of manners by the British writer Elizabeth GASKELL, published in Dickens' magazine *Household Words* in 1853. *Cranford* is a series of sketches of village life, based on the author's childhood in Knutsford, Cheshire. It remains one of the most popular English novels.

Cranial index. *See* CEPHALIC INDEX.

Cranial nerves, 12 pairs of nerves that originate in different areas of the brain; they carry information from the head and control muscle-action mainly in the head and neck. The olfactory nerve is concerned with smell; the optic with vision; the oculomotor, trochlear and abducens with the movement of certain eye muscles; the trigeminal with sensation in parts of the face and with movement of jaw muscles in chewing; the facial with the sense of taste and with face, scalp, ear and neck muscle movement and salivary gland secretion; the auditory with hearing and balance; the glossopharyngeal with taste, touch and temperature in visceral-area organs, pharnyx muscle movement and salivary gland secretion; the vagus with muscle movement in the larynx and pharynx, stimulation of gastric and pancreatic secretion, and muscle movement in the heart, bronchi, oesophagus, stomach, small intestine and other organs; the accessory with muscle movement in the neck; and the hypoglossal with movement of tongue muscle and of small muscles in the neck. *See also* MS pp.38–39.

Craniostenosis, premature closing of the fontanelles, where the bones of the skull are joined. It commonly causes retardation and skull deformity, both of which can be minimized by surgery in the first two years of life. *See also* MS p.143.

Cranium, part of the skull; dome-shaped, solid, hard bone structure that surrounds and protects the brain and the organs of sight, hearing and smell. It is composed of a number of bones that are fused together. *See also* MS pp.*56, 57.*

Cranko, John (1927–73), British choreographer, *b.* South Africa. He was a member of Sadlers Wells Theatre Ballet (1946–57). In 1956, he choreographed the first British-commissioned three-act ballet, *The Prince of the Pagodas.* His *Romeo and Juliet* (1962), with the Stuttgart Ballet, was considered his best work. In 1968 he became ballet director of the Bavarian State Opera, Munich.

Cranmer, Thomas (1489–1556), English prelate and religious reformer. He was a distinguished theologian, and was appointed Archbishop of Canterbury by HENRY VIII in 1533. He secured the annulment of Henry's marriage with Catherine of Aragon despite opposition from the pope. Cranmer, a friend of Thomas CROMWELL, promoted the introduction of Protestantism into England, encouraging the translation and dissemination of the "Great Bible" in 1539 and compiling the first Book of COMMON PRAYER in 1548. After the accession of MARY in 1553, Cranmer was burnt at the stake. *See also* HC1 p.270.

Crannog, dwelling area built on artificial firm ground (made of peat, brushwood and timber) in shallow lakes or marshes. They were inhabited in Ireland from the Bronze Age to the 17th century. *See also* HC2 p.*24.*

Crapp, Lorraine (1938–), Australian swimmer. She won the 400m freestyle event at the 1956 Olympics and at the 1954 Commonwealth Games took the gold medal in the 110yds and 440yds freestyle events. She was the first woman to swim 400m in less than five minutes.

Craps, most popular DICE and gambling game in the USA. Played with a pair of matched dice and any number of players, it is based on the fact that a 7 is the most probable throw. If the shooter's first throw totals 7 or 11 (a "natural"), he wins and continues to throw if he wishes. With 2, 3 or 12 ("craps"), he loses. If he throws 4, 5, 6, 8, 9 or 10 that number becomes his point and he carries on until it turn up again, when he wins and retains the dice. But if he throws a 7 at this stage he loses and gives up the dice.

Crashaw, Richard (*c.*1612–49), English poet. The son of a Puritan preacher, he first taught at Cambridge University (1635–43) then in 1643 fled to France, where he became a Roman Catholic, and later went to Italy. His religious poetry, especially in *Steps to the Temple. Sacred Poems, With Other Delights of the Muses* (1646), is notable for its ornate and exuberant imagery, which reflects BAROQUE art.

Crassus, Marcus Licinius (*c.*115–53 BC), Roman politician. He commanded an army for SULLA in 83 BC and amassed a vast personal fortune in urban and rural property. He suppressed the slave rebellion led by SPARTACUS in 71 BC, financing six new legions. Crassus served as consul with his rival POMPEY in 70 BC, and in 60 BC Julius CAESAR formed with them the first triumvirate. He acted mainly in alliance with Caesar, and became governor of Syria in 54 BC. He was killed fighting the Parthians at Carrhae. *See also* HC1 pp. 96–97.

Crater, roughly circular depression in the surface of the Earth or the Moon, usually with steep sides. It is formed either by meteoric impact, when shock waves blast out a hole in the ground, or at the vent of a volcano, when lava is expelled explosively. Space probes have revealed similar craters on the surfaces of other planets. *See also* PE p.30, SU pp.182–187, *219.*

Crater lake, accumulation of water, usually by precipitation of rain or snow but sometimes ground water, in a volcanic crater or caldera. A noted example is Crater Lake in Oregon, USA. Should an eruption occur, the resulting mud flow, or lahar, is often more destructive than a lava flow, owing to its greater speed.

Crates, name of four different Greek philosophers: Crates of Thebes (4th century BC), a CYNIC disciple of DIOGENES; Crates of Athens (3rd century BC), a philosopher and head of the Old Academy; Crates of Mallus (2nd century BC), a STOIC philosopher and grammarian; and Crates of Tarsus (2nd century BC), an academic philosopher.

Crawfish. *See* CRAYFISH.

Crawford, Joan (1908–77), US film star, real name Lucille le Sueur. She remained a glamorous star for nearly half a century. Her major films include *Our Dancing Daughters* (1928), *Grand Hotel* (1932), *The Women* (1939) and *Mildred Pierce* (1945).

Crawford, Osbert Guy Stanhope (1886–1957), British archaeologist. During WWI he pioneered the techniques of aerial photography as a tool of archaeology. He founded and was the first editor of the magazine *Antiquity* (1927–57).

Crawford, Thomas (1814–57), US sculptor who studied in Rome and brought a Neo-Classical style to his art. His most famous works are his equestrian statue of George WASHINGTON and his enormous *Freedom* statue on top of the dome of the US Capitol.

Crayfish, edible freshwater ten-legged CRUSTACEAN that lives in rivers and streams of temperate regions. Smaller than lobsters, crayfish burrow into the banks of streams and feed on animal and vegetable matter. Some cave-dwelling species are blind. Length: normally 8–10cm (3–4in). Families Astacidae (Northern Hemisphere), Parastacidae (Southern Hemisphere), Austroastacidae (Australia). *See also* NW p.*101.*

Crazing, or crackling, method of decorative glazing of ceramics, in which fine cracks in the glaze result from different shrinkage rates of the clay and the glaze during firing. It was originated by the Chinese.

Crazy Horse (*c.*1842–77), American Indian chief of the Oglala SIOUX tribe. He was a leader of the Sioux resistance to the advance of white settlers in the Black Hills, and assisted SITTING BULL in the massacre of George CUSTER's force at the LITTLE BIG HORN in 1876. After surrendering in May 1877, he was killed possibly while trying to escape.

Creatine, amino acid found mostly in the muscle tissue of vertebrate animals. Combined with phosphoric acid, it plays an important part in muscle contraction.

Creation, in most mythologies and religions, an account of the origin of the world, as well as of man and all the other creatures on earth. There is a remarkable similarity in the creation stories as recounted in the holy books of major religions, such as the Bible and the Koran, and in the myths and legends of comparatively small ethnic groups, such as Australian Aborigines and American Indians.

Creation, The, (1796–98), oratorio by Franz Joseph HAYDN. The text was selected and adapted from the bibilical book of Genesis and Milton's *Paradise Lost,* and the composition contains vivid musical pictures of the Creation. First performed privately in Vienna (1798), with Haydn presiding over the orchestra, it was an instant success.

Crébillon, Prosper Jolyot de (1674–1762), French dramatist who wrote Senecan tragedies. His plays, such as *Électre* (1708), *Rhadamiste et Zénobie* (1711), *Xerxès* (1714) and *Pyrrhus* (1726), enjoyed great success. He was considered a rival of Voltaire.

Crèche, day nursery for the children of working mothers. It may be organized by the management of the place of employment or run as a service by licensed individuals. Crèches first appeared in France in the 1840s.

Crécy, battle of (Aug 1346), first major battle of the HUNDRED YEARS WAR. Although the French forces, led by PHILIP VI, were greater in number, the English won a clear victory through their use of the longbow, and their superior strategy. As a result of this victory, the English, led by EDWARD III, were subsequently able to capture the strategically important port of Calais. *See also* HC1 pp.212–213.

Credit, exchange of goods in return for future payment. Credit allows consumers to purchase goods before they have the required funds and permits businesses to expand while deferring payment.

Credit, in accounting, an entry on the right-hand side of an account. Credit entries are required when assets are decreased and when liabilities and capital are increased. Credit entries are made to reflect increases in revenue accounts.

Credit, letter of, document issued by a bank allowing the holder to draw upon an amount of money at another institution. Liability is assumed by the issuing bank. There are several types of letters of credit, of which travellers' cheques are a type. They are widely used in international commercial transactions.

Cree, one of the largest divisions of the Algonquian language family of North American Indians, ranging from James Bay to the Saskatchewan River in Canada. Like the closely related Chippewa, the Cree served as guides and hunters for French and British traders and were a lifeline of the HUDSON'S BAY COMPANY for decades. Today about 1,000 live on reservations in Montana and Manitoba and more than 30,000 on reserves elsewhere in Canada.

Creed, in Christian Churches, term used for personal yet formal statement of commitment to doctrinal belief (Latin *credo*, "I believe"). The three most commonly said are the APOSTLES' CREED, the ATHANASIAN CREED and the NICENE CREED.

Creek Indians, confederation of American Indian tribes speaking the Muskogean tongue. One of the largest tribal groups to live in SE USA, they ranged from coastal Georgia to Alabama. They had an agricultural society and within the confederacy individual settlements had a large degree of autonomy. Land was communally owned. After the Creek Wars (1813–14), they were removed to Oklahoma, where the majority of the approximately 17,000 surviving Creeks now live.

Creep, in geology, slow downward movement of material. This slow movement of earth is not associated with erosion. It may occur on all sorts of slopes including those that are covered with vegetation. The steady downflow of earth and rock carries the vegetation with it. Creep may be caused by the growth of plant roots, the burrowing of small animals or trampling of larger creatures, frost movement, or successive drying and wetting that leads to shrinkage and swelling of the soil.

Creep, in metallurgy, continuing deformation of a metal under stress so that is appears to flow like an extremely viscous liquid. Metal components can be tested for "creep rate" – the percentage elongation per 1,000 hours at a particular temperature. Engineers have to consider both the applied stress and the temperature of metal structures to avoid possible failure through creep, *See also* SU p.*89*.

Creeper, in botany, any plant that puts out tendrils or adventitious (false) roots as it grows, to creep over the ground or up neighbouring plants, fences or walls. In ornithology, the name refers to any small bird that creeps up and down tree-trunks, usually in search of insect food.

Creevey, Thomas (1768–1838), British gossip and diarist. He was a WHIG member of Parliament from 1802 to 1832. His letters and journals, published as *The Creevey Papers* (1903), are a lively source for late Georgian history.

Cremation, disposal of a corpse by burning it. It was a common custom in many parts of the ancient civilized world and is still the only funeral practice among Hindus and Buddhists. The early Christians discarded cremation as a result of their belief in the physical resurrection of the body. It was not until the 19th century that it was revived in the western world, mainly in free-thinking circles. Its legitimacy is recognized by all Christian Churches; the Roman Catholic Church rescinded its prohibition of cremation in 1963.

Crémazie, Joseph Octave (1822–79), Canadian poet, regarded as the father of French-Canadian poetry. He was a founder of the *Mouvement littéraire de Québec* (*c.*1852), a group that stimulated French-Canadian literary development. Many of his poems were patriotic, including *Le Vieux Soldat Canadien* (1855), about an old soldier who awaits the return of the French. He moved to France in 1862.

Cremer, William Randal (1838–1908), English politician, trade unionist and pacifist. He organized the Carpenters and Joiners Union (1860) and founded the Workmen's Peace Association (which later developed into the International Arbitration League). As its secretary (1871–1908), he travelled widely to advocate international arbitration. From 1899 to 1908 he edited the peace journal *Arbitrator.* He won the Nobel Peace Prize in 1903.

Cremona, city of N Italy, in Lombardia region; capital of Cremona province. Founded in 218 BC by the Romans, it was a centre of learning in the Middle Ages and had a Renaissance school of painting. In the 17th and 18th centuries it was famous for violins made by the Amati, Guarneri and Stradivari families. It has a 12th–16th century cathedral and a 13th-century city hall. A market centre, it has textiles, precision engineering and brick industries. Pop. (1968 est.) 80,800.

Creole, person born in the West Indies or southern USA but of foreign descent. Generally a Creole's ancestors were either African slaves or French, Spanish or English settlers. In the USA the term is also used for someone of mixed European and Negro blood. The Creole language is a debased form of that of the dominant colonists: English in the USA, French in Haiti, and Spanish and Portuguese in Curaçao.

Creosote bush, or greasewood, shrub of the caltrop family, found in deserts of North and Central America. Its blackish stems, dark green leaves and small yellow flowers exude an odour of cresote or tar. Height: to 3m (10ft). Family Zygophyllaceae, species *Larrea tridentata.*

Crerar, Henry Duncan Graham (1888–1965), Canadian soldier and diplomat. He proved to be a brilliant artillery tactician in WWII and was made chief of general staff in 1940. He served in NW Europe in 1944–45. He retired in 1946 but represented Canada in several post-war peace conferences.

Crescent, symbol of the MOON in its first quarter. The symbol has many historical associations. It has been associated with ISLAM, with or without a star, since the capture of Constantinople by the Ottoman Turks in 1453. It appears on the Turkish standard and also in the flags of several other Islamic nations, such as those of Algeria and Pakistan. In heraldry it usually appears with the horns pointing upwards.

Crespin, Regine (1927–), French soprano. She made her opera debut in 1951 as Elsa in *Lohengrin* at the Paris Opéra and as Tosca at the Opéra Comique. In 1960 she sang at LA SCALA in Pizzetti's *Fèdra*, and in 1962 she appeared at the New York METROPOLITAN OPERA in *Der Rosenkavalier.*

Cress, any of several small, pungent-leaved plants of the mustard family, generally used in salads and as garnishes. The best known of these is WATERCRESS, a perennial plant that grows in clear, running water. Genus *Rorippa*, species *nasturtium officinale.*

Cressida, in Greek legend, a daughter of the Trojan priest Calchas. Her fame rests upon the story of her affair with TROILUS, a valiant Trojan warrior, and her desertion of him for DIOMEDES, a Greek soldier.

Cresta Run, the banked, winding track of ice for one-man BOBSLEIGHS at St Moritz, Switzerland. The Grand National course is 1,212m (3,977ft) long; the Curzon Cup course starts at Junction, a point 887.9m (2,913ft) from the finish. Riders, prone and head first, average speeds of around 80km/h (50mph) and can reach around 145km/h (90mph).

Cretaceous period, last period of the MESOZOIC PERIOD, lasting from 135 to about 65 million years ago. Dinosaurs flourished until the end of this period, when they became extinct. The first true PLACENTAL and MARSUPIAL MAMMALS appeared and modern flowering plants were common. *See also* PE p.130, NW pp.25, *25*, 177, 185–187.

Crete (Kríti), the largest island of Greece, in the E Mediterranean Sea, SSE of the Greek mainland. The chief cities are Iráklion the capital, and Khaniá. Crete has a mountainous terrain upon which sheep and goats are raised. The mild climate supports the cultivation of cereals, grapes, olives and oranges. Minoan civilization was flourishing on Crete from 2000 BC, and the ruined palace of Knossos was built *c.*1600 BC. For reasons not fully understood, the Cretan kingdom declined. After 1125 BC the Dorian Greeks controlled Crete and established city states. It remained an important trade centre, but played no role in the political history of Ancient Greece. Crete was conquered by Rome in 68-67 BC and later came under Byzantine (AD 395) and Arab (826) rule. In 1669, Crete fell to Turkey. Foreign intervention forced Turkey to evacuate Crete in 1898 and Crete became an autonomous state under Turkish sovereignty. In 1908, Cretans proclaimed union with Greece which was confirmed by the Treaty of London (1913). Products: wool, hides, cheese, olive oil, wine. Area: 8,259sq km (3,189sq miles). Pop. (1971 est.) 456,208.

Cretinism, disorder present at birth, or beginning in early childhood through lack of iodine or disease of the THYROID GLAND, in which a deficiency of thyroid hormones produces retarded physical and mental development. Symptoms include poor appetite, breathing difficulties, low body temperature, dry and thickened skin, decreased vigour and activity and a failure to grow and develop. It is treated with iodine or thyroid hormones. *See also* MENTAL RETARDATION.

Crevasse, deep crack in a glacier. It is the result of stress within the glacier or the movement of the glacier over uneven terrain. *See also* PE pp.116–117.

Crèvecoeur, Michel-Guillaume-Jean de (1735–1813), often known as J. Hector St John; US author, *b.* France. He moved to America in 1754 and became known as an agriculturist, writing articles under the name Agricola. His *Letters from an American Farmer* (1782) recorded life in early America.

Cribbage, card game for two, three or four players. A 52-card pack is used together with a cribbage board (scoring device) consisting of a wood or plastic board with rows of holes and four pegs. Each player receives five or six cards (depending on the number of players) and discards one or two into a separate pile called the "crib" or "box". Picture cards and tens count as ten points, aces as one each and the other cards their face values. The first card in the deck (the undealt cards) is turned face upwards. The object is to reach 31 points or as close as possible without exceeding the total, additional points being scored during play for various combinations of exposed cards.

Crichton, James (1560–82), Scottish man of learning, known as "the Admirable Crichton". He was a renowned scholar and linguist. In Paris, Padua, Venice and Genoa he earned a reputation as a skilled debater on scientific, philosophical and mathematical questions.

Crick, Francis Harry Compton (1916–), British biophysicist. He worked in the USA in the 1950s and in association with James

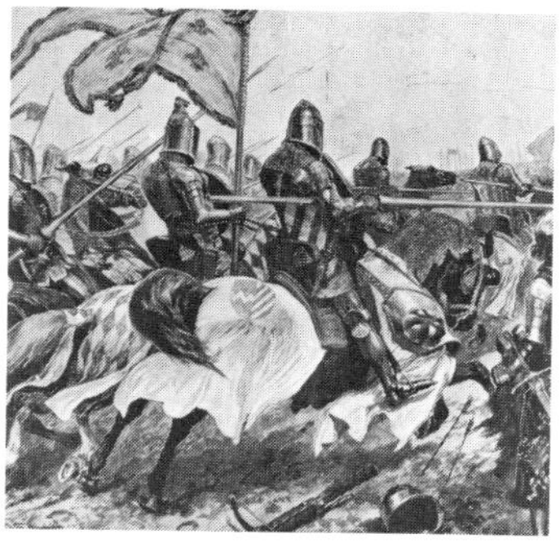

Battle of Crécy; French chivalry charge on the English bowmen who finally won the day.

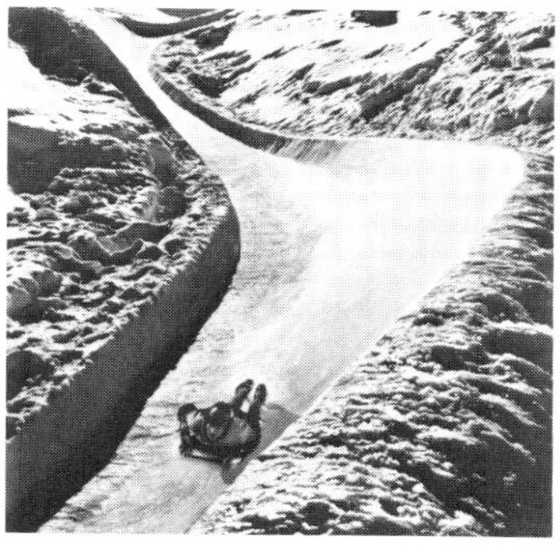

Cresta run; the course was modified recently to reduce the growing number of accidents.

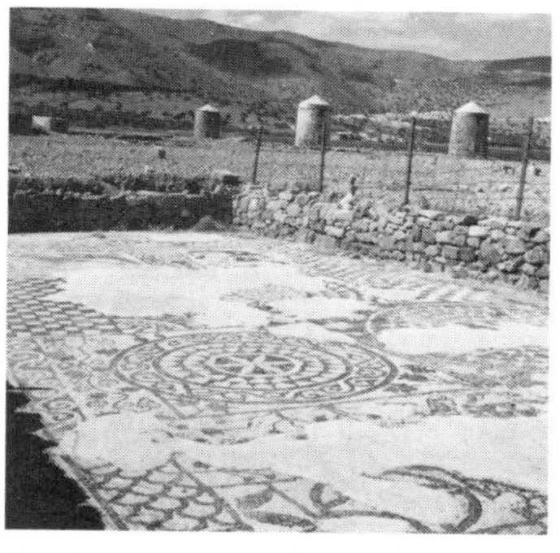

Crete's archaeological remains include Minoan towns and these Roman mosaics.

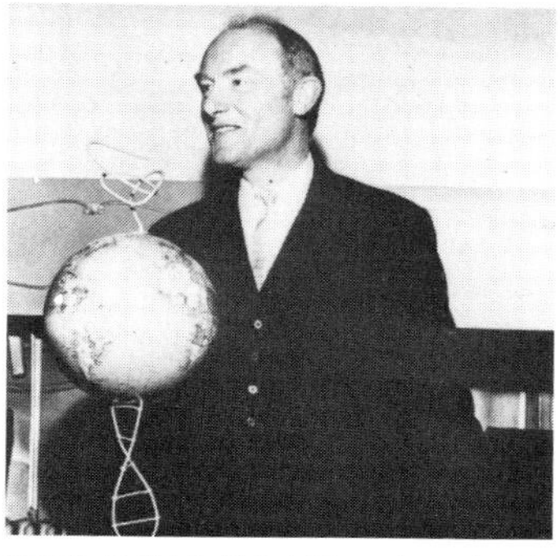

Francis H. Crick, Nobel Prize winner for his work on the structure of the DNA molecule.

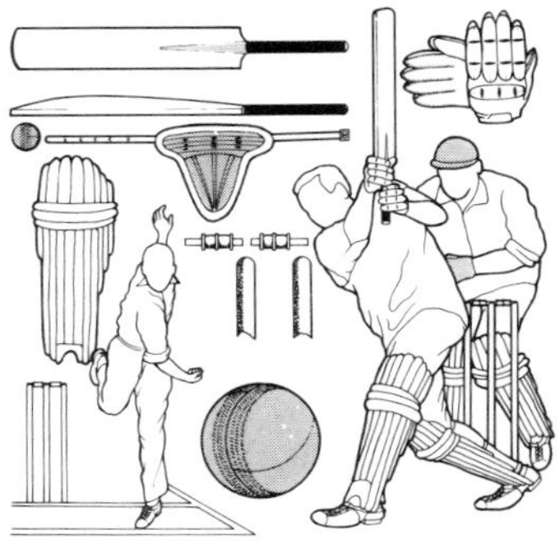

Cricket's governing bodies are now under attack from private commercial interests.

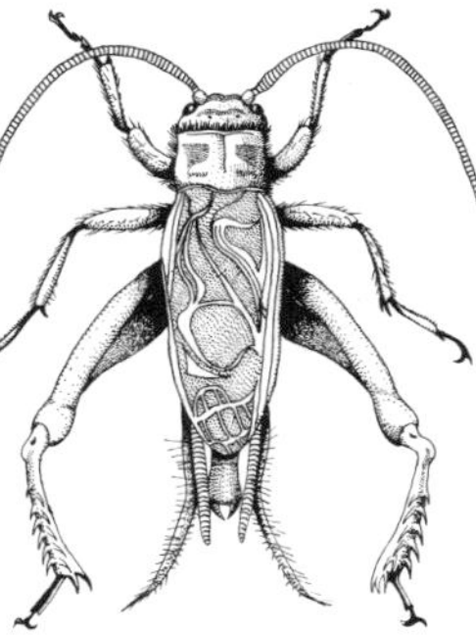

Crickets chirp both to attract the interest of the females and to repel other males.

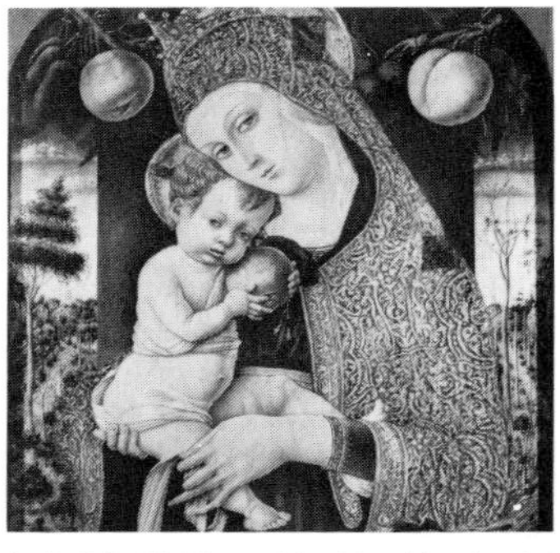

Carlo Crivelli; his work is rich with colourful ornamentation; this is *Madonna and Child.*

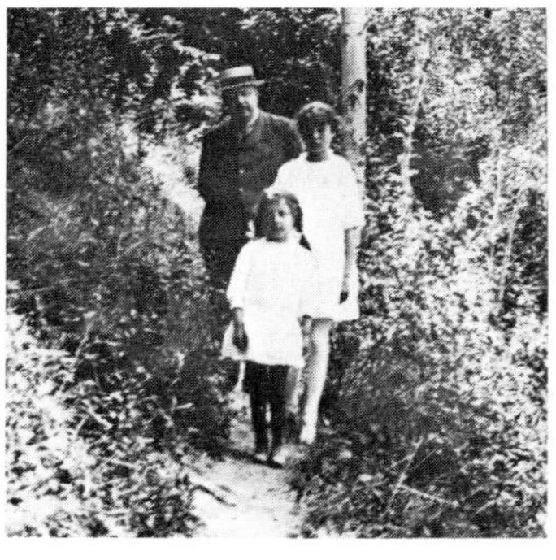

Benedetto Croce, in his analysis of philosophy, saw art as the "dawn" of knowledge.

WATSON and Maurice WILKINS he established the molecular structure of deoxyribonucleic acid (DNA). They were jointly awarded the Nobel prize in physiology and medicine in 1962. *See also* NW p.29.

Cricket, sport popular in Britain and other Commonwealth nations, the national summer sport of England, where it was played before 1700. It is played by two teams of 11 players each, on an oval field generally about 160m (525ft) across. A game, which may take several days to complete, consists of one or two innings. In an innings all the players of one team bat once in turn, with two batsmen on the field of play at a time; the other team fields, providing the bowlers and a wicket-keeper. The game is controlled by two umpires, and the team scoring the most runs wins. Except for injury, no substitutions are allowed, and then the substitute is not allowed to bat or bowl. Batsmen and the wicket-keeper wear gloves and leg protectors (pads), and the fielders are positioned around the outlying areas of the field of play. The game revolves around two wickets, which are placed near the middle of the field, 20.1m (66ft) apart. A wicket is made of three wooden stumps 71.1cm (28in) high with two small cross-pieces (bails), balanced in grooves in the top of the stumps. At each wicket a batsman stands at a crease – a line marked on the pitch (1.2m; 4ft) in front of the wicket – using a cane-handled bat made of willow. The bowler, who runs up to a point just beyond one of the wickets, has six or (in some countries) eight bowls at the farther wicket, defended by a batsman. He delivers the hard, leather-covered ball, overarm with a straight arm action, usually allowing it to bounce once. Runs are scored each time a batsman exchanges ends with his partner. A ball hit over the boundary of the pitch scores four runs, or six runs (if it does not bounce) without the need for the batsmen to run. After the "over" of six or eight bowls, another bowler begins the next over from the opposite wicket. A batsman can be "out" (dismissed) in a number of ways, for instance by being bowled (when the ball delivered by the bowler hits the wicket, with or without touching the bat), by being caught (when the ball struck by the batsman is caught before it bounces by any fielder) or by being run out (when a fielder dislodges the bails with the ball before the batsman reaches the opposite crease or returns to his own). *See also* ASHES, THE; COUNTY CHAMPIONSHIP; TEST MATCH.

Cricket, brown to black insect with long antennae and hind legs adapted for jumping, found worldwide. The field and house crickets are the best known of this family. Males produce a chirping sound by rubbing their wings together. Length: 3–50mm (0.8–2in). Family Gryllidae. *See also* MOLE CRICKET; TREE CRICKET.

Crimea (Krym), peninsula that extends into the Black Sea from SW USSR; W of the Azov Sea and joined to the mainland by the Perekop Isthmus. It is a sub-division of the Ukrainian Republic (Ukrainskaja SSR); Simferopol' is the capital. The Crimea was inhabited from the 10th to the 8th centuries BC by the Cimmerians. During the 5th century it was colonized by the Greeks and then, over the next hundreds of years, by Romans, Ostrogoths, Huns, Mongols, Byzantines and Turks, before being annexed to Russia in 1783. It was the scene of the CRIMEAN WAR (1854–56) in which the English, French, Turks and Sardinians opposed the Russians. The area was occupied by the Germans during WWII. It became the Krymskaja oblast in 1954. Area: approx. 27,000sq km (10,425sq miles). Pop. (1970 prelim.) 1,814,000.

Crime and Punishment (1866), novel by Fyodor DOSTOEVSKY which examines the nature of crime and guilt. Raskolnikov, a penniless student, kills an old pawnbroker for her money but flees without it. Suffering from remorse, he repents, gives himself up and is redeemed by suffering.

Crimean War (1853–56), war fought by Britain, France and Turkey, with later support from Sardinia-Piedmont, against Russia. Russian ambitions for expansion in the Middle East led the other powers to fear for the future independence of the Ottoman Empire. They occupied the Crimean Peninsula in 1854 to capture SEVASTOPOL, after the Russians had claimed a protectorate over Orthodox Christians in the Holy Land and seized two Turkish dependencies. The war was marked on both sides by incompetent leadership and organization. There were many deaths from disease and infection, despite the pioneering work of Florence NIGHTINGALE in introducing modern nursing methods. Most of the war was centred on the capture of Sevastopol, which was finally evacuated in 1855. On the accession of ALEXANDER II, Russia sued for peace, which was achieved at the Congress of Paris in 1856. The war ended Russian dominance in SE Europe. *See also* HC2 pp.85, 168.

Criminal Injuries Compensation Board, body established in Britain in 1964 to provide compensation for the victims of crime. Anyone who suffers personal injury from a crime or from attempting to prevent one may apply, as may the dependants of an innocent person killed during a crime.

Criminal Investigation Department. *See* CID.

Criminal law, body of law which defines crimes, lays down rules of procedure for dealing with them and establishes penalties for those convicted of them. Broadly, a crime is distinguished from a TORT by its being deemed an action injurious to the state, whereas a tort is deemed to be a private injury. In many countries the criminal law has been codified. Among the best-known modern codes are the *Constitutio Criminalis Carolina* (1532), promulgated by CHARLES V for the Holy Roman Empire, JOSEPH II's code for Austria (1786) and the CODE NAPOLEON. In Britain the law has never been codified. Criminal law remains what it was originally, a part of the COMMON LAW, although since the 18th century it has been greatly added to by STATUTE Law.

Criminology, the study of the causes and prevention of crime. It embraces various aspects of sociology, psychology and the law, and investigates such aspects as the factors that lead to criminal behaviour, case histories, methods of treating offenders and methods of preventing crime. *See also* LAW; PENOLOGY; MS pp.288–297.

Crinoid, class of primitive ECHINODERMS that includes the sea-lily and the feather star. A crinoid's mouth, on a small disc with the other main organs, is surrounded by long feathery arms. It feeds on particles that fall through the water and respires by means of its tube-feet. Class Crinoidea. *See also* NW pp.*22*, 118, *118*.

Crinoline, type of underskirt first in vogue in the 1840s. Its purpose was to stiffen and hold out the skirts. Originally made of whalebone and horsehair, it later developed into a metal frame worn under the skirts. It was modified to become the BUSTLE and gradually died out in the 1870s.

Crippen, Hawley Harvey (1862–1910), US doctor hanged for poisoning his wife. He settled in London (1900) and began an extra-marital affair. His wife went missing in Jan. 1910 and although he fled with his mistress he was traced to the SS *Montrose*, which was notified using the recently installed radio. (This is believed to be the first use of wireless telegraphy for police purposes.) Crippen was arrested before the ship reached Quebec and returned to London, where he was convicted and executed.

Cripps, Sir Richard Stafford (1889–1952), British socialist politician. He joined the Labour Party and entered Parliament in 1931. He was expelled from the Labour Party in 1939 for co-operating with the Communist Party against the Fascists. He was ambassador to Russia (1940–42) and Minister of Aircraft Production (1942–45). He was readmitted to the Labour Party in 1945 and joined Attlee's cabinet. He worked on the settlement for India (1946), and was Chancellor of the Exchequer (1947–50).

Crispi, Francesco (1819–1901), Italian statesman. He served in GARIBALDI's army in 1860 and, as a leftist and anti-clericalist, served as President of the Chamber of Deputies in 1876, Minister of the Interior (1877–78) and Prime Minister (1887–91, 1893–96). *See also* HC2 pp.110–111.

Crispin and Crispinian, Saints (died *c.* 287), patron saints of shoemakers. According to legend they were two Christian brothers of noble Roman birth who went to Gaul and worked as shoemakers, accepting for their work only such money as was voluntarily offered to them. They are believed to have died as martyrs during the persecutions of DIOCLETIAN. Feast day: 25 Oct.

Critical mass, minimum mass of fissionable material required in a fission bomb or nuclear reactor to sustain a CHAIN REACTION. The fissionable material of a fission bomb is divided into portions less than the critical mass; when brought together at the moment of detonation they exceed the critical mass. *See also* NUCLEAR FISSION: SU p.64; MM p.74.

Critical point, temperature and pressure above which a liquid and its vapour phase (a gas) can no longer coexist. If a gas is slowly compressed at temperatures above the critical temperature, or cooled at pressures above the critical pressure, it changes gradually from gas to liquid, rather than suddenly separating into two phases. *See also* SU p.84.

Critique of Pure Reason (1781), treatise on epistemology by Immanuel KANT. In this greatly influential work Kant hoped to defend mathematics and science from the incursions of David HUME's scepticism. Its principal point was that consciousness, rather than sense-data (as Hume had argued), was fundamental to man's understanding. It includes "categories" (such as cause and effect) that are essential to experience and which can neither be proved nor disproved by experience. *See also* MS pp.228, *229*, 234–235.

Crivelli, Carlo (*c.* 1430–*c.* 1493), Venetian painter who worked in the Venetian tradition in Ancona, Ascoli Piceno and other towns of the Umbrian Marches, where his painted altarpieces survive. A highly original artist, Crivelli combined in his work such elements as simple direct piety with an intensely decorative style of drawing, resembling that of BOTTICELLI. His best-known works include his *Madonna and Child* (1485) and *The Annunciation* (1486).

Croagh Patrick, mountain in W Republic of Ireland, in S county Mayo, on the S shore of Clew Bay. It is traditionally the place where St Patrick first preached and is now a place of pilgrimage. Height: 765m (2,510ft).

Croaker. *See* DRUMFISH.

Croatia (Hrvatska), federal unit and republic in NW Yugoslavia; it includes Croatia proper, Slavonia, Dalmatia and a major part of Istria. A former kingdom, Croatia came under the rule of Hungary in 1102. After the fall of the Austro-Hungarian Empire in 1918, a kingdom was formed by Serbs, Croats and Slovenes. Political conflicts resulted in the assassination in 1928 of Stefan Radić, the leader of the Croatian Peasant Party, and his successor formed a separate Croatian state. In 1945, Croatia became a Yugoslav republic. Products: maize, grapes, wool, fish, oil, lignite, iron. Area: 56,538sq km (21,829sq miles). Pop. (1971) 4,422,564. *See* MW p.185.

Croce, Benedetto (1866–1952), Italian philosopher and historian. He was a senator (1910–20) and Minister of Education (1920–21). In protest against Fascism he retired from politics when MUSSOLINI came to power until 1943, when he became head of the Liberal Party. His idealistic *Philosophy of the Spirit* (1902–17) is concerned with aesthetics, logic and linguistics, ethics and historiography. *See also* MS pp.*232–233*.

Crocheting, form of knitting with a hook. Crochet stitches may be a single loop, a double loop or a combination of the two. In making the chain or single loop, lengths of yarn or thread are drawn through other, preceding loops. Crochet is used for complete articles such as hats and shawls or for decorative edging to other articles.

Crockett, David (1786–1836), US frontiersman. He served in the US Congress (1827–31, 1833–35) as a Whig, and shrewdly cultivated the image of a rough frontiersman. He moved to Texas in 1835 and died at the ALAMO.

Crockett, Samuel Rutherford (1860–1914), Scottish novelist. He left the ministry and devoted himself to writing Romantic novels such as *The Raiders* (1894), *Mad Sir Uchtred* (1894) and *Man of the Mountain* (1909).

Crocodile, flesh-eating, lizard-like REPTILE found in warm parts of every continent except Europe. Most crocodiles have a longer, more pointed snout than members of the ALLIGATOR family. All lay hard-shelled eggs in nests. Length: up to 7m (23ft). There are about 12 species including two dwarf species in Africa. The Asian salt water crocodile (*Crocodylus porosus*) sometimes attacks humans. Family Crocodylidae. *See also* NW pp.134, 135, 137, 246.

Crocodile bird, or Egyptian plover, African bird that feeds on insects, often those infesting crocodiles. It is grey, black and white, with greenish markings. The female lays two or three dark-speckled, cream eggs and buries them in sand. Length: 23cm (9in). Species *Pluvianus aegyptius.*

Crocus, hardy perennial flowering plant native to the Mediterranean and Near East and widely cultivated. It is low-growing with a single tubular flower and grass-like leaves rising from an underground corm. It blooms in early spring or autumn. There are 75 species. Family Iridaceae; genus *Crocus.*

Croesus, King of Lydia in Asia Minor (*r.* 560–546 BC). Renowned for his wealth, he gave rise to the expression "rich as Croesus". He kept friendly relations with the Greeks but was overthrown by CYRUS the Great of Persia.

Crofting, method of subsistence farming in Scotland which is becoming less and less frequent as more of the land comes under the control of the large landowners. A crofter grows cereal crops and has some sheep or goats as livestock. A croft, the crofter's dwelling, is a small stone cottage built on the land allotted to him.

Crofts, Freeman Wills (1879–1957), Irish civil engineer who gained wider fame as a writer of detective novels. Among his many stories are *Inspector French's Greatest Case, The Box Office Murders* and *Fatal Venture.*

Croker, Richard (1841–1922), US politician. From 1886–1902 he dominated TAMMANY HALL and the New York City Democrats, after having opposed William ("Boss") Tweed. He served as alderman (1868–70) and coroner (1873–79) in the city administration before finally retiring to Ireland.

Cro-Magnon Man, tall, erect, Upper Paleolithic race of men, possibly the earliest representatives of *Homo sapiens.* They settled in Europe around 35,000 years ago. Cro-Magnon Man was part of the Aurignacian culture and manufactured a variety of sophisticated flint tools, as well as bone, shell and ivory jewellery and artifacts. He was the first to develop a flexible form of language. Cro-Magnon artists produced the cave-paintings of France and northern Spain. Cro-Magnon remains were first found in 1868 in the rock shelter of Cro-Magnon in Les Eyzies-de-Tayac, Dordogne, France. *See also* MS pp.*21, 26–27.*

Cromarty. *See* ROSS AND CROMARTY.

Crome, John (1768–1821), British landscape painter, sometimes called "Old Crome". He was the leader of the NORWICH SCHOOL. Influenced by GAINSBOROUGH and HOBBEMA, his serene, powerfully imaginative paintings are almost all scenes of rural Norwich. *Moonrise on the Marshes of the Yare* and *Mousehold Heath* are among the best known. His son, John Bernay (1794–1842), called "Young Crome", painted mainly scenes of rivers and coasts.

Cromer, Evelyn Baring, Earl of (1841–1917), British administrator. His rule as consul-general in Egypt (1883–1907) influenced the development of modern Egypt. He encouraged extensive development of railways, agriculture and irrigation at the expense of political and intellectual progress.

Crome Yellow (1921) novel by Aldous HUXLEY (1894–1963). His first book, it is a novel of ideas rather than action. It is set in a country house, from which the book takes its name, which was modelled on Garsington, home of Lady Ottoline Morrell. It contains caricatures of prominent members of the BLOOMSBURY group.

Cromford, cotton mill founded on the river Derwent, Derbyshire, by James ARKWRIGHT in 1771 in partnership with Strutt and Need. It was the first factory to use a water-powered spinning frame and a perpetual revolving cloth, called a feeder.

Cromlech, term usually applied to a MEGALITHIC stone circle such as STONEHENGE. The term, which derives from the Welsh, meaning "crooked stone", was originally used for a megalithic burial chamber.

Crompton, Richmal (1890–1969), British writer. Born Richmal Crompton Lamburn, she created William, the scruffy, adventurous schoolboy who was always in trouble. She wrote more than 30 William novels.

Crompton, Samuel (1753–1827), British inventor. His spinning machine (1779) proved a boon to the textile industry as it reduced the amount of thread-breakage that occurred with the spinning jenny and made possible the production of very fine yarn. He called his machine the spinning mule, was too poor to patent it and sold the rights for about £60. The House of Commons later voted him compensation of £5,000, which he lost in unsuccessful business ventures. *See also* HC2 pp.66–67, *315.*

Cromwell, Henry (1628–74), Governor of Ireland (1657–59). The fourth son of Oliver CROMWELL, he was appointed head of the English forces in Ireland (1654) and then made lieutenant and Governor-general. He followed moderate policies compared with those of his predecessor but was dismissed in 1659.

Cromwell, Oliver (1599–1658), English politician, Lord Protector (1653–58). He was a landowner from Huntingdon, and an MP after 1628. He rose to prominence as a commander of the parliamentarian army in the Civil War, and after the war he was a key figure in the negotiations about a new constitution, since he had the confidence of the army leaders. He eventually supported PRIDE'S PURGE and led the demand for the execution of CHARLES I After the proclamation of the COMMONWEALTH, he was unofficially ruler of the country, and commanded the army in campaigns in Ireland (1649) and Scotland (1650–51). He attempted various constitutional measures until 1653, when he accepted the title of Lord Protector. In 1657 he refused the offer of the throne. His domestic policy was typified by an attempt to restore social stability although relying on the radical army, and his foreign policy was aggressively anti-Spanish. He was succeeded on his death by his son Richard. *See also* HC1 pp.288–291.

Cromwell, Richard (1626–1712), Lord Protector of England (1658–59). The son of Oliver CROMWELL, Richard was an able administrator but an incapable politician. He was ousted from power after eight months in which the central government lost all authority, and spent 20 years in exile before returning to England in 1680.

Cromwell, Thomas, Earl of Essex (*c.* 1485–1540), English statesman. He was originally a wool merchant, and came to HENRY VIII's attention as secretary to WOLSEY. After his master's fall, he became the king's chief adviser in 1532, and was responsible for the achievement of the break with Rome and the dissolution of the monasteries. He also reorganized the royal administration. He fell from power after the failure of Henry's marriage with ANNE OF CLEVES, which he had promoted, and he was executed in 1540. *See also* HC1 pp.267, 270.

Cronin, Archibald Joseph (1896–), Scottish novelist. He was a medical inspector of mines and physician until the success of his first work, *Hatter's Castle* (1931) allowed him to devote all his time to writing popular, melodramatic novels, such as *The Citadel* (1937).

Cronje, Piet Arnoldus (*c.* 1835–1911), South African military commander. He defeated the JAMESON RAID and fought against the British in the South African (Boer) War but was forced to surrender in 1900. *See also* HC2 pp.128–129.

Cronkite, Walter Leland, Jr (1916–), US journalist and broadcaster. His newspaper career began in the 1930s and in 1950 he joined the staff of the CBS news as a political commentator.

Crookes, Sir William (1832–1919), British scientist. He was a lecturer in chemistry at Chester College when he inherited a fortune, enabling him to devote himself to private research. He invented the RADIOMETER and the CROOKES TUBE, which led to the discovery of X-RAYS. He was the first to suggest that CATHODE RAYS consist of negatively-charged particles. He also discovered the element THALLIUM. *See also* SU p.*109.*

Crookes tube, highly evacuated tube developed by Sir William CROOKES for the study of electrical discharges at low pressure. It was used in 1897 by J. J. Thomson to demonstrate the existence of the ELECTRON, and was also used to generate X-rays. *See also* SU p.*109.*

Crop rotation, practice of successively growing different crops on the same field. Rotated crops generally complement each other, each providing nutrients required by the others. *See also* PE pp.158, 174.

Croquet, lawn game, popular in Britain and the USA, in which four wooden balls (coloured blue, red, black and yellow) are hit with wooden mallets through a series of six wire hoops towards a peg. The first player to complete all 12 hoops (each hoop in both directions) and reach the peg with each ball in the correct order wins the game. Croquet had developed in France by the 17th century.

Crosby, Harry Lillis ("Bing") (1904–77), US popular singer and actor. After 1930 he became one of the most successful singers in the USA. In 1944 he won an Academy Award for the film *Going My Way.* His recording of Irving BERLIN's *White Christmas* (1942) is the best-selling record of all time.

Cross, Henri Edmond, pseudonym of Henri Edmond Delacroix (1856–1910), French painter of realistic landscapes and portraits. He was a member of the POINTILLIST movement led by Georges SEURAT. Cross's brilliant colour and solid form influenced MATISSE and FAUVISM.

Cross, Joan (1900–), British soprano. One of the greatest opera singers of her day, she was closely linked with the music of Benjamin BRITTEN. She was a founder member of the English Opera Group, (1946) took leading roles in such Britten operas as *Gloriana, The Rape of Lucretia* and *Albert Herring,* and was a Director of Opera at Sadler's Wells (1941–45).

Cross, ancient symbol with different significance to many cultures. In Christianity it is associated with Christ's sacrificial death on the cross for the redemption of mankind. A cross is usually placed on, above or near the altar in churches and is often carried in religious processions. Many Christians make the sign of the cross with their right hand as a symbol of their acceptance of the Christian faith. Other crosses are still used as religious or secular symbols: St George's Cross, St Andrew's Cross, Victoria Cross, Red Cross, etc. As a religious symbol it existed in one form or another in ancient Egypt, Babylonia and Assyria. In the Christian liturgical calendar the feast of the Exaltation of the Holy Cross is kept on 14 Sept.

Cross-bedding, in geology, sand deposited on the underwater slopes of a delta or the formation that results when sand dunes advance over each other. With dunes the tops are gradually removed, preserving the bedding on their down-wind side. *See also* PE pp.*126,* 128.

Crossbill, parrot-like forest FINCH found

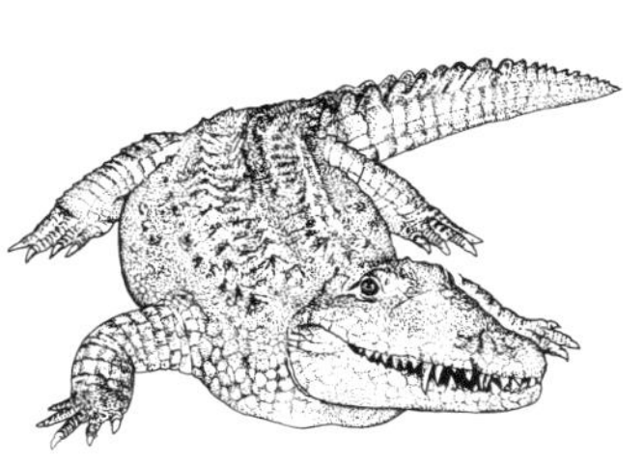

Crocodiles, unable actually to chew with their jaws, grind their food inside their stomachs.

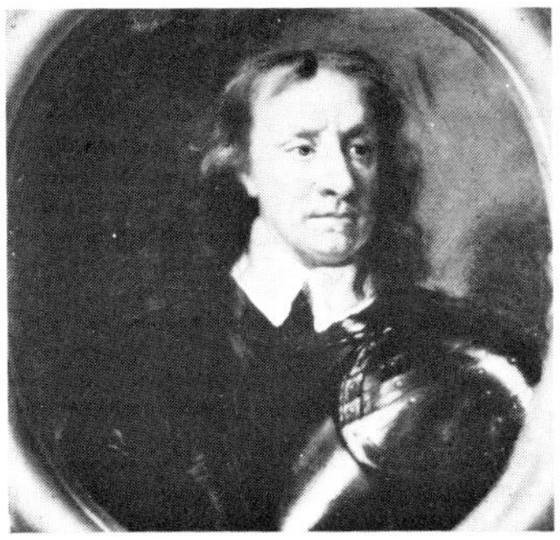

Cromwell's strict military discipline gave rise to the false idea that he was a cruel tyrant.

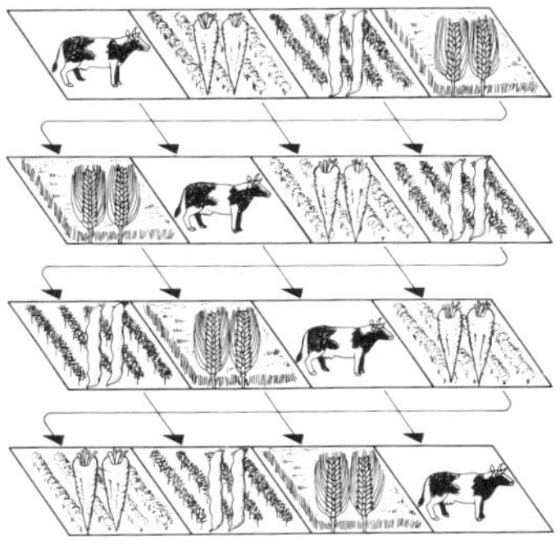

Crop rotation was introduced in the Middle Ages by way of the three-field system.

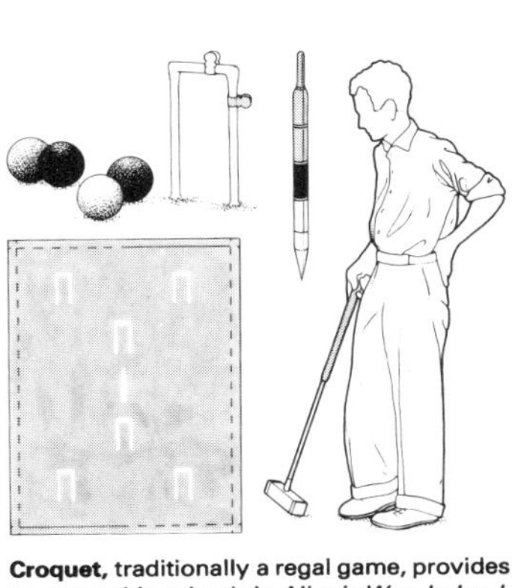

Croquet, traditionally a regal game, provides a memorable episode in *Alice in Wonderland.*

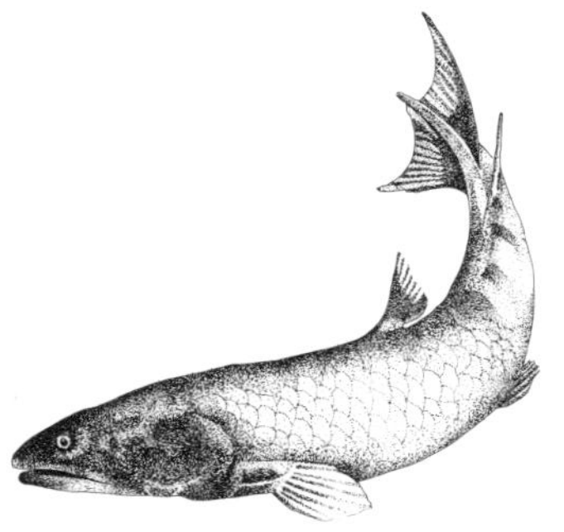

Crossopterygian; group of fish long thought extinct until the discovery of the Coelacanth.

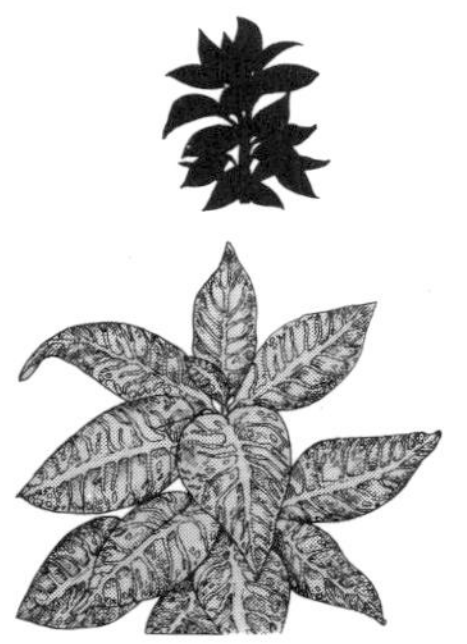

Croton produces an oil once used as a powerful purgative and counter-irritant.

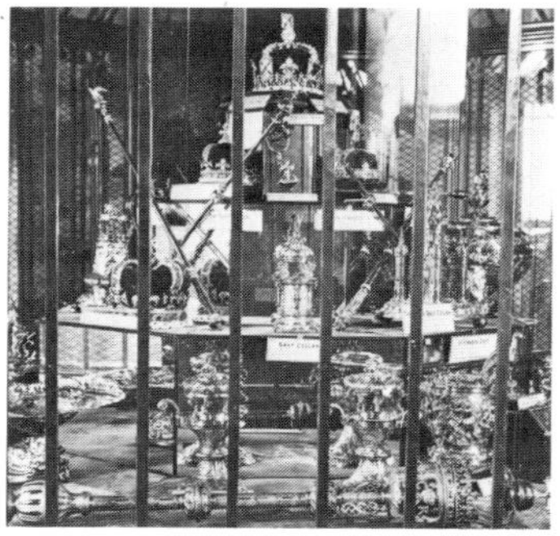

Crown Jewels, suitably protected, as seen by the public in the Tower of London.

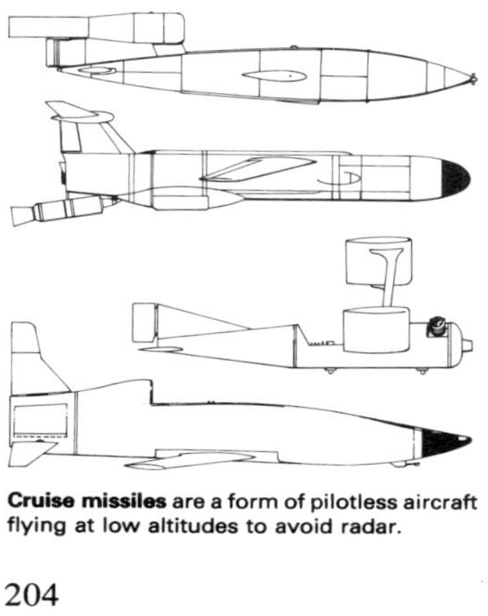

Cruise missiles are a form of pilotless aircraft flying at low altitudes to avoid radar.

mainly in the north of the Northern Hemisphere. It has a heavy, curved, scissor-like bill in which the upper and lower mandibles cross over, and which it uses to pry seeds from cones of evergreens. Length: 15cm (6in). Family Fringillidae; genus *Loxia*.

Crossbow. *See* BOW.

Crossbreeding, or outbreeding, the crossing or mixing of two unlike parents to produce a HYBRID, eg crossing a horse and a donkey to produce a mule. Most hybrids are either sterile or extremely difficult to breed from.

Cross-country running, winter pursuit by athletes over a country course with natural obstacles. Competitions are also held on racecourses with hurdles as obstacles. International championships, for teams and individuals, are contested over at least 12km (men), and 2–5km (women). British events are 7–9 miles (men) and 2–3 miles (women). It began in the early 19th century in English public schools. A cross-country event is included in the Olympic pentathlon.

Cross-examination, in law, questioning of a witness by opposing counsel (eg a prosecution witness may be cross-examined by defence counsel). The purpose of cross-examination is to test a witness's evidence or to elicit additional information.

Cross-eye. *See* STRABISMUS.

Crossing the Bar (1889), lyric poem by Alfred TENNYSON in which, himself approaching 80, he uses the analogy of embarking on a sea journey to suggest the imminence of death.

Crossopterygian, lobe-finned fish of the sub-class Crossopterygii, which flourished during the Devonian period (345–395 million years ago) and provided the evolutionary stock for land vertebrates. The COELACANTH is the only surviving member of the group. Fossil forms have fins that show the transition towards limbs for terrestrial locomotion; their trunks and tails resemble those of AMPHIBIANS. *See also* NW pp.124, *124*.

Cross-pollination, transfer of pollen from the flower of one plant to another. The process may be used by man to hybridize different plant species whose genetic make-up is compatible, thus producing "synthetic" varieties. The result of the process is called a HYBRID. *See also* PE pp.177, *178–179*.

Crossword, word puzzle arranged according to a particular design, usually a square or a rectangle, which is subdivided into smaller blank and shaded squares. Two lists of numbered clues are provided, one for words that run across the figure, the other for words that run down. The relevant letters are inserted in the blank squares only. The puzzle is completed when all the clues have been solved and the squares correctly filled in. Modern crosswords date from the early 1920s.

Croton, also called variegated laurel, any of several tropical shrubs or trees native to Australia and islands of the South Pacific. *Codiaeum variegatum pictum* is the most popular, with long leaves variegated with green, red, yellow and white. It grows to 1.8m (6ft). Family Euphorbiaceae.

Croton bug. *See* COCKROACH.

Croup, respiratory disorder most common in young children caused by inflammation of the LARYNX. It can be triggered by bacterial or viral infection, local irritation or allergy. Symptoms are a harsh, deep-sounding cough, difficult breathing and fever. Steam inhalation is often helpful although severe cases may require hospital treatment.

Crow, large, black bird found in woodlands and farm areas worldwide except in polar regions, South America and some Pacific islands. Living in large flocks, crows prey on small animals and eat plants and carrion. They can be crop pests. They are intelligent birds and can sometimes be taught to repeat phrases. They build stick-and-twig nests in tall trees, where the female lays three to six greenish eggs. Family Corvidae. *See also* CHOUGH, JAY, MAGPIE, RAVEN, ROOK.

Crowberry, or crakeberry, prostrate shrub of N and Alpine regions. Its spreading branches bear cylindrical leaves, the insides of which are hairy. The flowers develop into small, black, edible berries. Species *Empetrum nigrum*.

Crowfoot, plant of the BUTTERCUP family. There are several species, the ones which grow in woods and meadows having typical yellow flowers; aquatic species, which grow in the margins of ponds and in ditches, generally have white flowers. Genus *Ranunculus*. *See also* NW pp.*58, 70, 230*.

Crow Indians, large tribe of Siouan-speaking American Plains Indians who separated in the early 18th century from the HIDATSA. They migrated into the Rocky Mountains region from the upper Missouri River, and today occupy a large reservation area in Montana. They are noted for their fine costume, artistic culture and complex social system with humane child-rearing methods. Their population in the mid-1970s was about 5,000.

Crown, circular head ornament worn as a symbol of rank, generally royal, since the time of the ancient Egyptians. Since the Middle Ages the crowns of Western monarchies have usually consisted of an elaborate diadem (closed at the top by one or more arched bands over a cap, usually surmounted by an orb and cross), made of metal and thickly decorated with jewels. Among the most famous are the Lombard iron crown and the crown of St Stephen of Hungary. There are two crowns used by the British monarchy, both modern: a replica of the crown of EDWARD THE CONFESSOR (destroyed by Oliver CROMWELL), used at the CORONATION, and the imperial state crown, worn on state occasions. *See also* CROWN JEWELS.

Crown, in dentistry, the part of the tooth that protrudes above the gum. Artificial crowns made of porcelain or gold are used when teeth are badly decayed or broken, but still solidly rooted. They are also employed for anchorage when making a dental BRIDGE. *See also* MS p.*131*.

Crown Agents, full name Crown Agents for Overseas Governments and Administrations, business and financial agents who look after the affairs in Britain of foreign governments and public bodies. They were first appointed in 1833, when they were known as Joint Agents General for the Crown Colonies. They draw their funds entirely from the fees charged to their clients.

Crown colonies, overseas dependencies of the British government which do not enjoy full self-government. They are administered by the FOREIGN AND COMMONWEALTH OFFICE. Executive power is usually vested in a governor, appointed by the Crown. Since the end of WWII the number of crown colonies has steadily fallen. There are now only 15 of them, including Hong Kong, Gibraltar, British Indian Ocean Territory, the Seychelles, the Falkland Is. and six Caribbean colonies.

Crown Courts, British courts established in 1971 to replace the ASSIZE courts and courts of quarter session. They are superior courts, with a general jurisdiction, presided over by High Court judges.

Crown Estate Commissioners, since 1956 the official name for the agents who administer Crown lands in Britain. Since the reign of GEORGE III the Crown has surrendered its hereditary lands for life and the sale, purchase and development of such lands are discharged by the Commissioners. Forest land is managed by the FORESTRY COMMISSION, established in 1919.

Crown-green bowls. *See* BOWLS.

Crown Jewels, the crown, orb and sceptre, and other precious objects belonging to the British monarchy and kept on display in the TOWER OF LONDON. They include St Edward's crown which weighs more than 2kg (5lb), the Imperial Crown of State, weighing 1.6kg (3.5lb), and many other objects of symbolic significance. The Scottish jewels, called the Honours of Scotland, are kept in Edinburgh castle.

Crown land, property belonging to the British sovereign, most of which has been surrendered to Parliament since the reign of George III (1760–1820) in return for a fixed annual sum. The lands are managed by commissioners who may lease or sell them.

Crown Proceedings Act (1947), act of the British Parliament making the Crown liable to be sued in CONTRACT or TORT as if it were a private individual. Actions are brought against either the appropriate department of state or the attorney-general.

Crown rot, disease that affects the crown of a plant, the part near the soil-line. It is generally caused by a fungus and most commonly attacks grasses and cereal crops.

Crowther, Geoffrey (1907–72), British economist and journalist. He was editor of *The Economist* from 1938 to 1956. He published *Ways and Means* in 1936 and *An Outline of Money* in 1941. He was made a life peer in 1968.

Crucible process, method of making high-quality steel, invented in 1740 by Benjamin Huntsman. Steel, charcoal and wrought-iron are melted in a fire-clay crucible. Coke fires were once used but were replaced after 1870 by the Siemens gas furnace, which could heat 100 crucibles to over 1,700°C (3,100°F). Electric furnaces have now replaced this process. *See also* MM pp.31–32, *32*.

Crucifer, any of about 2,000 annual and perennial plants of the MUSTARD or CRESS family, which have a flower with four petals in the shape of a cross. Many are important food plants, notably the CABBAGE in all its varieties. STOCKS and WALLFLOWERS are cruciferous garden flowers, as also are AUBRIETIA, rock cress, CANDY TUFT and ALYSSUM.

Crucifix, representation of the Cross bearing an image of the crucified Christ. Crucifixes are used widely in the West as objects of public and private devotion. After the Reformation their use declined among Protestants except in Lutheran churches. They were revived in the Church of England in the 19th century. Their place is taken in the East by crosses with flat likenesses, ie a form of ICON.

Cruden, Alexander (1701–70), Scottish author and bookseller (in London) whose *Complete Concordance to the Holy Scriptures* (1737) became the basis for many later concordances. He suffered from mental illness for much of his life.

Cruel Sea, The (1951), adventure story by Nicholas MONSARRAT. It tells the story of the crew of a corvette crossing the Atlantic Ocean in a convoy during WWII. It was made into a successful film (1953).

Cruelty, Theatre of, movement in France in the late 1920s, developed under the influence of theoretician Antonin ARTAUD. His ideas include the staging of elemental emotions in order to involve the audience and excite strong reactions in them. Artaud's theories emphasize ritual and the surreal, and the performance itself is considered more important than the texts used.

Cruft, Charles (1852–1938), British breeder of dogs and showman. He held his first dog show in 1886 and since that time the annual show in London, called Cruft's, has been the premier event of the dog season.

Cruikshank, George (1792–1878), British illustrator and cartoonist, who first gained fame with his caricatures of the leading figures in George IV's divorce proceedings. Besides political and theatrical illustrations, Cruikshank illustrated over 800 books, of which the best-known are Dickens' *Sketches by Boz* and *Oliver Twist*. Cruikshank's drawings for the translated edition of fairy-tales by the GRIMM brothers are perhaps the best testimony to his flair for the grotesque.

Cruise missile, also called aerodynamic missile, a self-propelled missile that travels under its own power, generally at low altitudes following the contours of the terrain. Unlike a BALLISTIC MISSILE it must be aerodynamically designed (like a conventional high-speed aircraft) to minimize atmospheric drag. It has the advantage of being able to fly low enough, following the contours of the land, to avoid conventional radar defences.

Cruiser, warship smaller, lighter and faster than a BATTLESHIP, ranging in size from 7,500 to 21,000 tonnes. Arms limitation treaties after WWI restricted the large guns of cruisers to 200mm (8in). Few cruisers have been built since 1945, although the USS *Long Beach*, the world's first nuclear-powered surface warship, launched in 1961, is a cruiser.

Crusades, series of military enterprises undertaken by western Christendom to capture Palestine from the SELJUK Turks. The First Crusade (1096–99), which followed a chaotic Peasants' Crusade (1095–96) from France and Germany, captured much of the E Mediterranean coast and took Jerusalem in 1099. The second Crusade (1147–49) failed to capture Damascus. The Third Crusade (1189–91) was jointly commanded by PHILIP II of France and RICHARD I of England; the latter negotiated with the Turkish leader SALADIN for Christians to have access to Jerusalem. The Fourth Crusade (1202–04) sacked Constantinople and set up the LATIN EMPIRE OF THE EAST. The CHILDREN'S CRUSADE (1212) was followed by the unsuccessful Fifth Crusade (1218–21) which attacked Egypt. The Sixth Crusade (1228–29) was not a military expedition, but the Emperor FREDERICK II negotiated a new truce with the Turks. The Seventh Crusade (1248–50) was ineffectual, led by LOUIS IX of France, who was killed on the Eighth Crusade (1270). After the Ninth Crusade (1271–72), Acre, the last crusader kingdom in the Middle East, was taken by the Turks in 1291. *See also* HC1 pp.176–177.

Crust, in geology, outermost layer of the earth varying in thickness from 40km (25 miles) to 5km (3 miles) under the seafloor. The continental crust is mostly granite, composed of silica and aluminium (sial), while the oceanic crust is essentially basalt, rich in silica and magnesium (sima), which underlies the continental crust. The continents tend to float in the sima like islands. Beneath the crust is the mantle. *See also* PE pp.20–21.

Crustacea, large class of more than 30,000 species of invertebrate animals in the phylum Arthropoda. The class includes the decapods (crabs, lobsters, shrimps and crayfish), isopods (pill millipedes and woodlice) and many varied forms, most of which are not distinguished by common names. Most crustaceans are aquatic, (marine or fresh water) or live in damp surroundings; they breathe through gills or the body surface. They are typically covered by a hard exoskeleton. The Japanese spider crab is the largest member, measuring up to 4m (13ft) across; the ocean plankton, as little as 1mm (0.04in) in diameter, is the smallest. *See also* NW pp.100–101, 104–105; PE pp.248–249.

Crux Australis. *See* SOUTHERN CROSS.

Cruyff, Johan (1947–), Dutch footballer. Transferred from European champions Ajax to Barcelona for almost £400,000 in 1973, he became the world's most expensive footballer. Gifted with the skills to create and score goals, he led The Netherlands to the 1974 World Cup final.

Cruz, Sor Juana Inés de la (1648–95), Mexican poetess. She is considered one of the greatest lyric poets of the Spanish colonial period. Her poems often reflected a tension between religious obedience and a passion for the new learning of the period.

Cruz e Sousa, João de (1861–98), Brazilian Negro poet who lamented Brazil's heritage of slavery. He was the outstanding Portuguese-language poet of the SYMBOLIST movement, which stressed the mystical and spontaneous. His books of verse include *Broquéis* (1893).

Cryogenic fuels, liquid rocket fuels that operate at low temperatures. Efficient liquid fuels such as oxygen and hydrogen have extremely low boiling points and must be refrigerated until shortly before the rocket is launched.

Cryogenics, branch of physics which studies materials and effects at temperatures approaching ABSOLUTE ZERO. Some materials exhibit highly unusual properties at such temperatures: they become SUPERCONDUCTING (ie they can carry an electrical current indefinitely), or they exhibit SUPERFLUIDITY ("creep" over boundaries, apparently defying the laws of gravity). *See also* SU p.94.

Cryolite, or kryolite, brittle, icy-looking red, brown or black halide mineral, sodium-aluminium fluoride (Na_3AlF_6) found in pegmatite dykes (Greenland has the only large deposit) and used in aluminium processing. It occurs as crystals in the monoclinic system, occasionally the cubic system, or as granular masses. The crystals are frequently twinned. Cryolite is used mainly as a flux in the smelting of aluminium, and also as a source of aluminium salts and fluorides.

Cryosurgery, surgery carried out using a freezing probe, cooled by liquid nitrogen, that destroys diseased tissue on contact. It is particularly effective in treating PARKINSON'S DISEASE and in the removal of tumours, cataracts and tonsils.

Cryptococcosis, often fatal fungus (*Cryptococcus neoformans*) infection, occurring mainly in middle age; affecting men twice as often as women. It attacks the central nervous system, including the membranes of the brain, and sometimes the lungs, skin and other organs. The fungus has been isolated in pigeon droppings. When it infects the lungs, its symptoms are fever, cough and general discomfort.

Cryptogam, early botanical term for plants with no flowers or seeds but which reproduce by spores, such as mosses, liverworts and ferns. Flowering plants were called PHANEROGAMS.

Cryptography, the science of secret writing. The message is translated into codes and cyphers. (Cyphers use substitutions for single letters, whereas codes use substitutions for whole words, phrases or sentences.) It is most often used in business, diplomacy and military operations. The science of code breaking is cryptanalysis. *See also* MS pp.242–243.

Cryptomeria, or Japanese cedar, evergreen cone-bearing tree of the pine family native to eastern Asia. It has a reddish-brown bark, whorled branches and fragrant wood. Family Taxodiaceae; species *Cryptomeria japonica.*

Crystal, solid with a regular geometrical form and with characteristic angles between its faces. The structure of a crystal is based upon a regular array of atoms, molecules or ions. The outward symmetry is a reflection of the internal order of the constituents. Most pure solid substances can be obtained in crystalline form. Crystals are produced when a substance passes from the gaseous or liquid phase to the solid state or comes out of solution by evaporation or precipitation. The rate of crystallization and the solvent used determine the type and size of crystal. Crystals vary in their physical properties. *See also* PE pp.94–96; SU pp.88–89.

Crystal counter, type of particle counter in which the detector is a crystal with a high potential difference applied across it. A high-energy particle hitting the crystal induces a transient increase in its electrical conductivity, thus producing a pulse of current that is registered and displayed on the counter.

Crystal defect, any deviation from perfect order in the lattice of a crystalline substance. Most crystals have some defects, which may be of different types. Point defects are single-atom faults with either a missing atom (crystal vacuity) or an extra atom in an unusual position (crystal interstitial). Dislocations also extend over many atoms, as when part of a line or plane of atoms may be missing or one plane may be displaced relative to another. *See also* SU p.*89*.

Crystal dislocation. *See* CRYSTAL DEFECT.

Crystal glass, glass of a fine, hard quality, so called because it has the clarity of rock crystal (a type of quartz). Lead crystal glass is made with lead oxide; lime crystal is made with calcium oxide.

Crystal index, set of three numbers that characterize the type of planar configuration of atoms in a lattice. The three integers give the ratio of the reciprocals of the intercepts of the planes on three axes. *See also* PE pp.94–96; SU pp.88–89.

Crystal interstitial. *See* CRYSTAL DEFECT.

Crystal lattice, three-dimensional arrangement of atoms, ions, or molecules in a crystalline substance. The term is sometimes used in a more restricted sense to denote the diagrammatic abstraction of the pattern in which the atoms, ions or molecules are positioned. *See also* PE pp.94–96; SU pp.88–89.

Crystalline substance, solid substance in which the atoms or molecules form a regular ordered lattice. Most solids exist in the crystalline state, which is more stable, but it does not follow that they have crystals in the usual sense; metallic copper, for example, is crystalline only in that the copper atoms are arranged in a regular lattice. The BONDS in crystals can be any of the major types. *See also* AMORPHOUS SUBSTANCE; PE pp.94–96; SU pp.88–89.

Crystallization, process of forming crystals by a substance passing from a gas or liquid to the solid state (SUBLIMATION or fusion) or coming out of solution (PRECIPITATION or EVAPORATION). In the fusion method a solid is melted by heating (ie fused), and crystals form as the melt cools and solidifies. Ice crystals and monoclinic sulphur are formed in this way. Crystallization is an important laboratory and industrial technique for purifying and separating compounds. *See also* PE pp.94–96; SU pp.88–89.

Crystallography, study of the formation and structure of crystalline substances. It includes the study of crystal formation, chemical bonding in crystals and the physical properties of solids. In particular, crystallography is concerned with determining the internal structure of crystals. In X-ray crystallography the lattice arrangement is calculated from the patterns produced by the DIFFRACTION of X-rays. POLARIZED LIGHT is also used, and its effects observed under a microscope. *See also* PE pp.94–96; SU pp.88–89.

Crystal optics, optical properties of crystals. The transmission of light by crystals differs from that by glass since the REFRACTIVE INDEX may depend on the direction of incidence of the light (crystals are not, in general, ISOTROPIC). Uniaxial crystals (belonging to the tetragonal, hexagonal and trigonal systems) have two principal refractive indices and display double refraction. Biaxial crystals (orthorhombic, monoclinic, triclinic) have three principal refractive indices. *See also* SU p.*88*.

Crystal packing, manner in which atoms, ions or molecules are packed together in a crystal. In simple terms, crystal structures can often be considered geometrically, as regularly arranged spheres of equal diameter. The most efficient ways of packing spheres are the arrangements known as hexagonal and cubic close-packing. In these packing configurations every sphere has 12 nearest neighbours and 73 per cent of the available space is filled. *See also* PE pp.94–96; SU pp.88–89.

Crystal Palace, first building of its size, 124 × 564m (408 × 1,850ft), to be made of glass and iron. Designed by Sir Joseph PAXTON for the Great Exhibition of 1851, held in Hyde Park, London, it was prefabricated in sections and assembled on site. Developed by Paxton from his work in greenhouse construction, the Crystal Palace greatly influenced railway station design. After the exhibition it was dismantled and re-erected on Sydenham Hill, SE London, where it stood until accidentally destroyed by fire in 1936. *See also* HC2 pp.88–*89*, 123.

Crystal structure, regular arrangement of atoms, linked together by CHEMICAL BONDS in repeating patterns. Because of this regularity, and sometimes a corresponding asymmetry, the physical properties of a crystal, such as strength and conductivity, vary in a regular manner depending on the crystal axis along which they are measured. Single crystals are distinguished from non-crystalline (amorphous) and from polycrystalline materials, the physical properties of which are either invariant (because of complete mixing) or vary in an irregular manner. *See also* SU pp.*88, 89;* PE pp.94–99.

Crystal systems, seven types of crystal structure which are grouped from the 32 classes of crystal symmetry. The elements of symmetry found in crystals are axes,

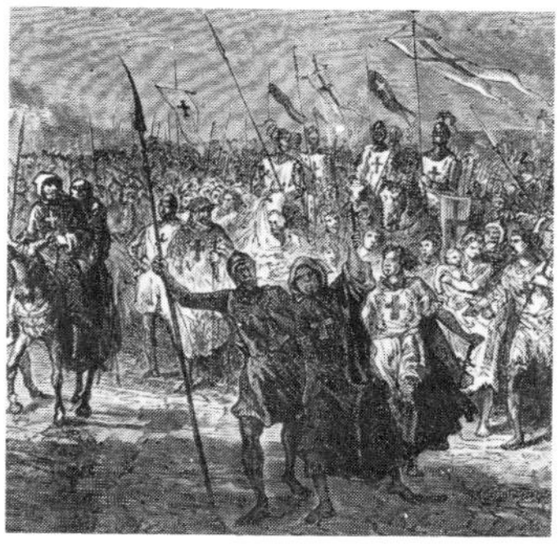

Crusades forced a religious conservatism into a hitherto enlightened Arab culture.

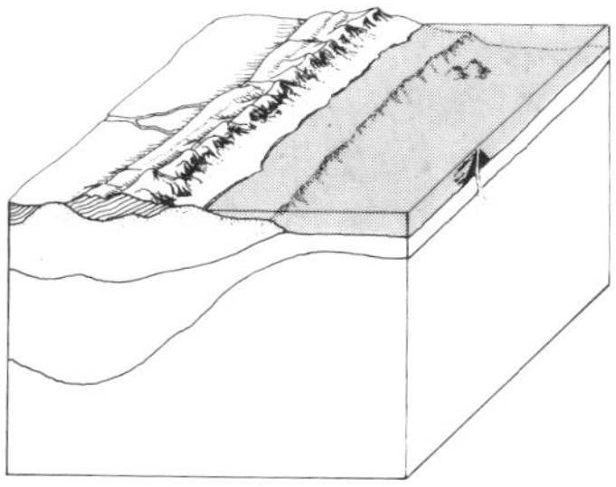

Crust; if the world were an egg, the crust would represent the thickness of the shell.

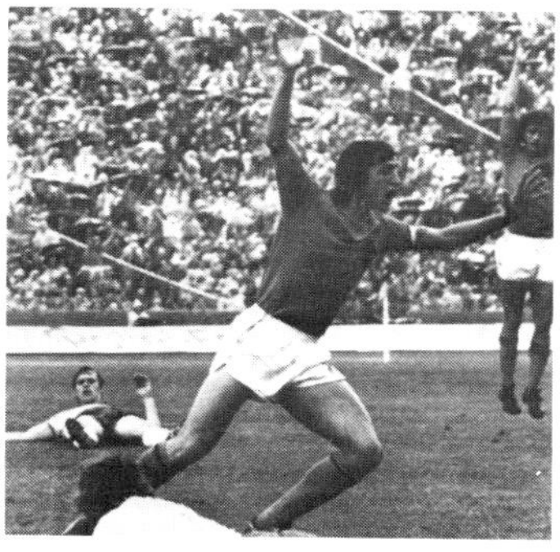

Johan Cruyff, whose solo dribble brought the first goal in the 1974 World Cup final.

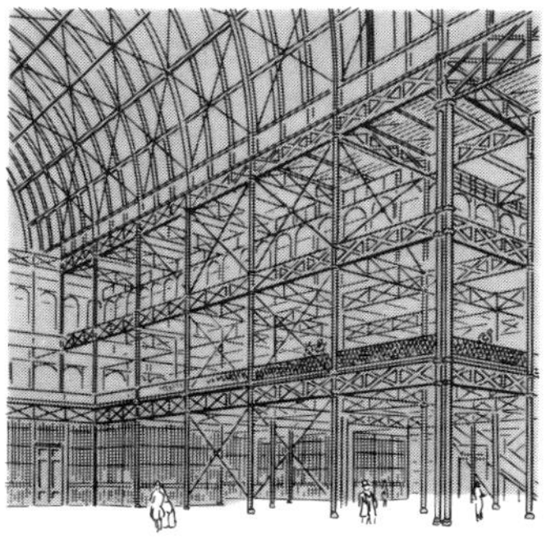

Crystal Palace, a design that celebrated the possibilities of new building techniques.

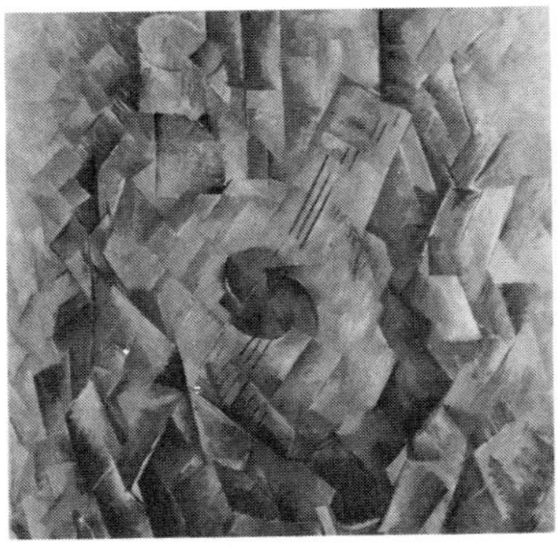

Cubism can be said to introduce the element of time into painting; *Mandolin* by Braque.

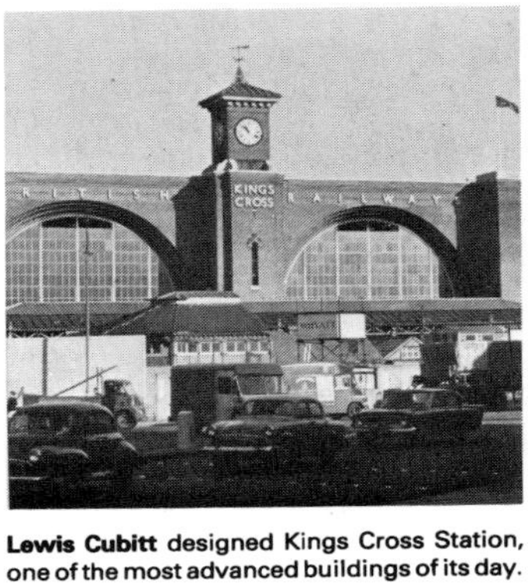

Lewis Cubitt designed Kings Cross Station, one of the most advanced buildings of its day.

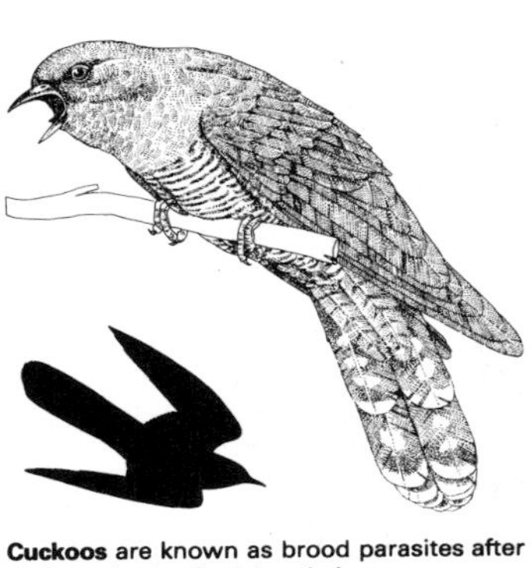

Cuckoos are known as brood parasites after their methods of raising their young.

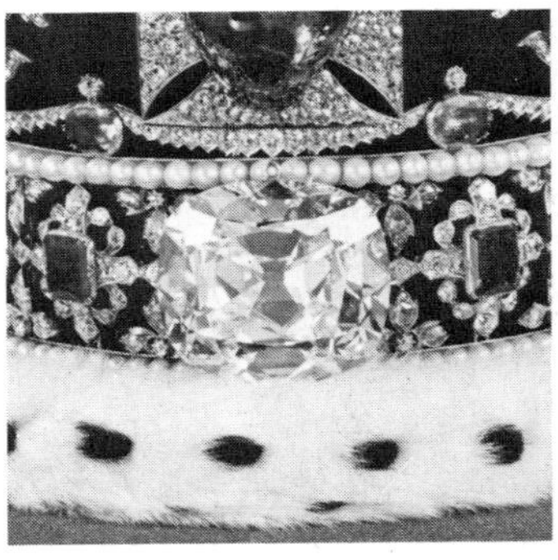

Cullinan diamond; The Star of Africa, one of the gems in the Imperial State Crown.

planes and centres. The seven systems are: cubic, trigonal, tetragonal, hexagonal, orthorhombic, monoclinic and triclinic. *See also* PE pp.94–96; SU pp.88–89.

Crystal unit cell, simplest part of a CRYSTAL LATTICE characteristic of the crystal structure. The structure is formed of repeated unit cells. In a simple cubic lattice, for example, the crystal unit cell is a cube with an atom at each corner. Unit cells conform to the seven basic shapes of the CRYSTAL SYSTEMS. *See also* PE pp.94–96; SU pp.88–89.

Cry the Beloved Country (1948), novel by Alan PATON, in which he deals with the racial conflict in South Africa from a sensitive, humanitarian viewpoint.

Ctenophore. *See* COMB JELLY.

Ctesiphon, ancient Parthian city on the River Tigris, SE of modern Baghdad in Iraq. It was the winter capital of the Parthian Empire and is now noted for the remains of a gigantic vaulted hall, the Taq-e Kisra. Arabs took the city in AD 637 and used the Taq-e Kisra as a mosque, but they deserted it in 763 upon the founding of Baghdad.

Cuala Press, private printing company founded in 1908, an offshoot of the Dun Emer Press (1902), by Elizabeth and Lily Yeats, sisters of W. B. YEATS. The firm was established to provide work for Irish women and to produce classic and contemporary Irish literature. It published work by W. B. YEATS, Lady Gregory and John MASEFIELD. It closed down in 1948.

Cuauhtémoc (*c.* 1495–1525), last Aztec ruler of Mexico, who unsuccessfully defended the capital Tenochtitlàn against Cortés' siege. Four years later, forced to accompany Cortés on an expedition to Honduras, Cuauhtémoc was implicated in a plot to kill the Spaniards and was executed.

Cuba, independent nation on the largest island in the West Indies. Since a revolution in 1959 it has been a communist state under the rule of Fidel CASTRO and reliant on Soviet aid. The mainstay of the economy is sugar, two-thirds of the cultivated land being devoted to sugar cane. Sugar is exported together with rum, molasses, tobacco (mainly cigars) and nickel, which is one of many minerals mined. Other food products, chemicals and machinery are imported from Communist bloc countries. The capital is Havana. Area: 114,524sq km (44,218sq miles). Pop.(1974 est.) 9,194,000. *See* MW p.61.

Cuban Missile Crisis (1962), USA–USSR confrontation over the installation in Cuba of Soviet nuclear rockets. Photographs taken by US reconnaissance aircraft revealed the construction of missile bases in Cuba, and a study was made of photographs of the cargo being carried on the decks of Cuba-bound Soviet ships. President John KENNEDY protested to Premier Nikita KHRUSHCHEV about the threat that such bases posed to the Western Hemisphere and, after increasingly hostile exchanges, Khrushchev ordered the bases to be dismantled.

Cube, in mathematics, the result of multiplying a given number by itself three times. Thus the cube of a is $a \times a \times a$, written a^3. The cube is also described as the third power of a number. Cube is also the name of a regular six-sided solid figure (all its edges are equal in length and all its faces are squares).

Cube root, number that must be multiplied by itself twice over to give a specified number. For example, the cube root of 27 is 3, since $3 \times 3 \times 3 = 27$. Cube roots are written in the form $\sqrt[3]{27}$ or 27.333. In algebraic terms, the cube root of x^3 is x and the cube root of x is $\sqrt[3]{x}$.

Cubic equation, equation of the third degree, ie one in which the highest power of the unknown variable is three. An example is $2x^3 + x^2 + 7 = 0$. Cubic equations have three ROOTS, two of which may be imaginary.

Cubism, early abstract art style. It originated with Pablo PICASSO and Georges BRAQUE, who were later joined by Juan GRIS, Fernand LEGER, Jean METZINGER, Albert GLEIZES and others. Cubism, a term coined by the art critic Louis Vauxcelles, was a conscious reaction to the Romanticism of Ferdinand DELACROIX, the primarily sensuous appeal of the IMPRESSIONISTS and the decorative approach of the FAUVES. The favourite form of the Cubists was STILL LIFE, seen as a composition of quasi-geometric forms without atmosphere or light, with restricted colours verging toward the monochromatic, and without movement. Natural perspective was abandoned, and a new perspective of overlapping, interlocking, semi-transparent planes was used in an attempt to present the solidity and volume of the subject two-dimensionally, from many different aspects simultaneously. Cubism in its early phase (1907–09) was influenced by African and Iberian art and, above all, by Cézanne's advice to "deal with nature by means of the cylinder, the sphere and the cone". Its second phase (1910–12) showed a breakdown of form, and a use of simultaneity – fragmented objects depicted from all angles and open from inside. The third, so-called "synthetic" phase (1913–14) developed by GRIS, discarded imitation completely and sought to re-create the object by means of "emblems" similar to a metaphor in a poem. Gris did not distort the object but painted an analogous construction. Picasso's *Les Demoiselles d'Avignon* (1907) is regarded as the source picture of Cubism. *See also* HC2 pp.176–177.

Cubitt, James (1914–), British architect, who practised privately from 1948 onwards. His principal works include schools in Hertfordshire and Yorkshire, and he has also designed many public buildings and houses in Ghana. During the early 1970s he worked in Nigeria, Ghana and Libya.

Cubitt, Lewis (1799–1883), British architect who designed King's Cross Station, one of the most advanced buildings of its time. With his brothers, Thomas and Joseph, he collaborated in the design of several London streets in Bloomsbury and Belgravia.

Cubo-Futurism, term applied to a phase of Russian art immediately before WWI. One of many short-lived movements which were inspired by CUBIST ideas, it aimed to combine Cubist and FUTURIST elements in a style somewhat resembling the early Cubist curvilinear work of Fernand LÉGER. Figurative material was depicted as a composite of shining cylindrical components expressive of a jagged mechanical rhythm. The leading exponent of the style was Kasimir MALEVICH, who later proceeded to the pure abstraction of SUPREMATISM.

Cúchulainn, Irish legendary hero. He was King of Ulster during the 1st century BC and the hero of the legend *The Cattle Raid of Cooley*, in which he defended his kingdom against the rest of Ireland. The CUILLIN HILLS are named after him.

Cuckoo, widely distributed forest bird. Related species are the ani, ROADRUNNER and coucal. True Old World cuckoos are generally brownish, although a few species are brightly coloured. Their chief food is insects. A brood parasite, the female removes one egg of another species and lays her egg in the nest. Soon after the cuckoo chick has hatched, it throws out any other eggs or young. It is then fed by the foster mother. Length: 15–75cm (6–30in). Family Cuculidae; genus *Cuculus*. *See also* NW p.*145*.

Cuckoo Flower. *See* LADY'S SMOCK

Cuckoo pint, also called wake robin or lords-and-ladies, tuberous plant native to Europe. It has arrow-shaped leaves and sends up stout SPATHES, each of which unfurls to reveal a SPADIX that gives off a fetid carrion scent, which is attractive to insects. Later red poisonous berries form and are revealed as the spathe dies off. Family Araceae; species *Arum maculatum*. *See also* NW p.*70*.

Cuckoo spit, white froth often seen on the stems of plants. It is made by larvae of FROG HOPPERS, hopping insects belonging to the order HOMOPTERA. The larva feeds on the plant's juices and expels a watery froth to cover itself completely, and so hide from its enemies.

Cuculiformes, small order of birds that includes CUCKOOS, ROADRUNNERS, TOURACOS and various related birds.

Cucumber, trailing annual vine covered in coarse hairs; it has yellowish flowers and the immature fruit is eaten raw or pickled. The plant needs a warm climate or a protective frame because it is sensitive to frost and pests. Family Cucurbitaceae; species *Cucumis sativus*. *See also* NW p.*61*; PE pp.188–191.

Cúcuta, city in NE Columbia, near the border with Venezuela; capital of Norte de Santander department. Founded in 1733, it was captured by Simón BOLÍVAR on his march to Caracas. It was rebuilt after an earthquake in 1875. It is the centre of a coffee and oil producing region and has an oil refining industry. Pop. 167,400.

Cudworth, Ralph (1617–88), English philosopher. He studied at Cambridge where he joined a group of theologians known as the Cambridge Platonists. His *Treatise Concerning Eternal and Immutable Morality* (published 1731) opposed Thomas HOBBES and the theory of determinism, and argued that there are eternal, immutable moral ideas.

Cuenca, city in s central Ecuador. Founded in 1557, it is known as the "marble city" because of its many fine buildings. It is situated in one of the richest agricultural areas in the Andes, and is a major commercial centre. The main industry is the weaving of Panama hats. Pop. (1971 est.) 77,300.

Cugnot, Nicolas Joseph (1725–1804) French engineer who in 1769 invented the first self-propelled road vehicle. It was a three-wheeled, two-cylinder steam tractor designed to pull guns, and travelled at nearly 5km/h (3mph). *See also* MM p.*126*.

Cui, César Antonovich (1835–1918), Russian composer and critic. He is best known for his dramatic musical works, including the operas *The Captive in the Caucasus* and *William Ratcliffe* and for the articles he wrote on Russian music.

Cuillin Hills, range of hills on the Isle of Skye, Highland Region, off the NW coast of Scotland. The highest peak is Sgurr Alasdair, which rises to 1,009m (3,309ft).

Cukor, George (1899–), US stage and film director. He is noted for stylish comedies and literary dramas. His major films include *Camille* (1936), *The Women* (1939), *The Philadelphia Story* (1940), *Born Yesterday* (1950), *A Star is Born* (1954) and *My Fair Lady* (1961). Many of his films featured Katharine HEPBURN (often teamed with Spencer TRACY).

Culdees, Irish and Scottish hermits in the 8th and following centuries who banded together, usually in groups of thirteen on the analogy of Christ and his twelve apostles. They were probably the last remnants of the ancient indigenous Celtic Christianity of the British Isles which was finally superseded by continental Catholicism.

Culiacán, city in NW Mexico, on the Culiacán River; capital of Sinaloa state. Founded in 1531 by Nuño de Guzmán, it was the headquarters for Coronado's expedition in 1540 to the Gulf of California. It is situated on the coastal plain where tropical fruits, maize, cotton and sugar cane are grown and cattle raised. Pop. (1970 prelim.) 358,800.

Culicidae, family comprising MOSQUITOES, small, dipterous flies which lay eggs in water. The larvae hang from the surface film by their breathing-tails and undergo complete METAMORPHOSIS within a PUPA, emerging as the familiar slender, humpbacked adult.

Cullinan, Sir Thomas (1862–1936), South African diamond prospector and building contractor. He established the Premier Mine, the largest in the world, in which the CULLINAN DIAMOND was discovered. He was knighted in 1910 and was a member of the Union Parliament (1910–15; 1920–21).

Cullinan diamond, diamond found in 1905 in the Premier Mine of South Africa, the largest gem ever found; it weighed 3,106 carats (0.6kg; 1.33lb). It was bought by the Transvaal Government who presented it to Edward VII, and was subsequently cut into nine large and 96 small stones, the largest of which is the largest cut diamond in the world. *See also* CULLINAN, SIR THOMAS.

Culloden, Battle of (1746), decisive battle of the Second JACOBITE rising, in which the army of Charles Edward STUART (Bonnie Prince Charlie) was defeated by forces under the Duke of CUMBERLAND. Culloden ended the Stuart attempts to regain the throne by force. The battle was followed by a ruthless subjugation of the Scottish Highland CLANS who had provided most of Prince Charles Edward's army. *See also* HC2 p.28, *28*.

Culpeper, Nicholas (1616–54), English physician and astrologer who in 1649 published *A Physical Directory*, which was an unauthorized translation of the pharmacopoeia of the Royal College of Physicians. Despite its enormous popularity, this book (and his Puritan views) made him many enemies. *See also* MS p.*116*.

Culpeper's Rebellion (1677), uprising by North Carolina colonists against British trade policies. John Culpeper and George Durant led the colonists who jailed the British governor and replaced him with Culpeper. He ruled until 1679, when the British reasserted their authority. The rebellion is regarded as the first uprising in the American colonies.

Cultural lag, in anthropology, a theory describing the gap between the initial effects of innovations on a culture, and their longer term effects. It is used specifically to describe the impact of western technology on primitive societies.

Cultural Revolution, The, officially the Great Proletarian Cultural Revolution, campaign led by MAO TSE-TUNG to purge the Chinese Communist Party of his opponents and to instil correct revolutionary social and political attitudes in the population. It was intended to combat the counter-revolution in domestic affairs which, in the early 1960s, had introduced incentives meant to promote efficiency in Chinese industry. It began with an attack on the moderates written by Mao and published in a Shanghai newspaper in November 1965. Senior party officials were removed from their posts and a series of open-air rallies, attended by millions of Mao's new youth corps, the RED GUARDS, was begun in August 1966. The revolution then spread throughout China and became a mass movement to defend the revolution against "bourgeois revisionism". It reached its peak in the autumn of 1968, when LIU SHAO-CHI, previously Mao's second-in-command, was relieved of all his posts. It was then that LIN PIAO was raised to the position of second most important official in China's political hierarchy. Throughout 1967 and 1968 the established local Communist Party authorities were replaced by Maoist Revolutionary Committees. *See also* HC2 pp.215, 244–245.

Culture, in ANTHROPOLOGY, all knowledge that is acquired by man by virtue of his membership of a society. A culture incorporates all the shared knowledge, expectations and beliefs of a group. Culture in general distinguishes men from animals since only man can pass on accumulated knowledge due to his mastery of language and other symbolic systems. Only man develops and uses culture consistently in the form of tools.

Cumae, ancient city in Campania region, SW Italy. It is believed to be the oldest Greek colony in Italy or Sicily, having been founded *c.*750 BC. It successfully resisted attack from the Etruscans, but was defeated by the Samnites in the 5th century BC. It came under Roman control in 338 BC, but from then on its fortunes declined and the town was destroyed in the 13th century AD. There are Greek and Roman ruins on the site and the cavern where the Cumaean Sybil, a priestess of Apollo, pronounced her prophecies.

Cumaná, port in NE Venezuela, on the Manzanares River, approx. 227km (185 miles) E of Caracas; capital of Sucre state. It was settled by the Spanish in 1520 in order to exploit the pearl fisheries near Margarita Island, and is the oldest European settlement in South America. It was raided by the native Carib Indians, the French and Dutch, and has been damaged by several earthquakes. It exports coffee, cacao, sugar and tobacco and has fish canning industries. Pop. 100,500.

Cumans, Turkic people originating in N Asiatic Russia. They conquered S Russia in the 11th century AD, set up a state on the coast of the Black Sea and traded with the Byzantine Empire and Hungary. After they had been defeated by the Mongols in *c.*1240, many Cumans moved to Hungary.

Cumberland, William Augustus, Duke of (1721–65) British general, second son of George II. He brutally suppressed the JACOBITES after defeating them at the Battle of CULLODEN (1746). His subsequent continental commands (1747–48, 1757) during the war of AUSTRIAN SUCCESSION and the SEVEN YEARS WAR were unsuccessful. *See also* HC2 p.28.

Cumberland. *See* CUMBRIA.

Cumbernauld, town in Strathclyde Region, central Scotland, 21km (13 miles) ENE of Glasgow. It was designated a "new town" in 1956 to accommodate people from Glasgow and was the first such town in Britain to cater adequately for road traffic and separate it from pedestrian ways. Its industries include machinery and food processing. Pop. 31,784.

Cumbria, county in NW England, formed in 1974 from the former counties of CUMBERLAND, WESTMORLAND and parts of YORKSHIRE and LANCASHIRE; bounded by the Solway Firth (N) and the Irish Sea (W). The region includes the LAKE DISTRICT. Carlisle is the main town. Area: 6,808sq km (2,629sq miles). Pop. 473,800.

Cumin, annual herb native to the Middle East and widely cultivated for its seed-like fruit used as a food flavouring. It has a branching stem and small pink or white flowers. Height: to 15cm (6in). Family Umbelliferae; species *Cuminum cyminum*. *See also* PE p.210.

Cummings, Edward Estlin (1894–1962), US poet whose first work, *The Enormous Room* (1922), was a novel. His poetry, usually exhibiting either sentimental emotion or cynical realism or a combination of both, is characterized by unconventional spelling and punctuation. His verse includes *Tulips and Chimneys* (1923).

Cundall, Charles (1890–1971), British painter of portraits and landscapes. He was especially skilled at painting crowd scenes. During WWII he was an official war artist; his paintings in this period include *The Withdrawal from Dunkirk*.

Cuneiform, system of writing developed in Mesopotamia around 3000 BC in which all symbols are made up of wedge-shaped strokes, derived from the practice of writing on soft clay with a triangular stylus as a "pen". Developed from pictograms (which actually illustrated the meaning) the Cuneiform "alphabet" eventually comprised over 500 characters, most as words but including also some syllables and a phonetic system. Inscriptions and clay tablets have been found representing many languages in Cuneiform; Babylonian and Assyrian are the most common, although the ancient Persians also used the script. *See also* MS p.*246*.

Cunha, Euclides da (1866–1909), Brazilian author. *Os Sertões (Rebellion in the Backlands)* (1902), his most famous work. grew out of a newspaper assignment about a pitiful rural insurrection by followers of a religious fanatic. Its sense of the tragic caused some critics to acclaim it as "the most Brazilian" of all books.

Cunningham, Allan (1784–1842), Scottish poet. He was apprenticed to his brother (a stonemason) but went to London and contributed to the *London Magazine*. From 1814 to 1841 he was clerk of works (manager) at Chantrey's studio. He published several books of poems (which he called "songs") and *The Lives of the Most Eminent British Painters, Sculptors, and Architects* (1829–33).

Cunningham, Andrew Browne, 1st Viscount Cunningham of Hyndhope (1883–1963), British admiral. He was commander-in-chief of the naval forces in the Mediterranean (1939–43) and first sea lord and chief of the naval staff (1943–46).

Cunningham, Sir John (1885–1962), British admiral. He took part in the evacuation of Norway in 1940. He was commander-in-chief of the Mediterranean (1943–46), first sea lord (1946–48) and admiral of the fleet (1948–62).

Cunningham, Merce (1919–), US modern dancer and choreographer. He was with the Martha Graham Dance Company (1940–45) and in 1952 formed the highly acclaimed Merce Cunningham Dance Company. His productions are highly experimental and controversial and include *Antic Meet* (1958) and *How to Pass, Kick, Fall and Run* (1965).

Cunninghame Graham, Robert Bontine (1852–1936), Scottish author and politician. He travelled widely in South America, returned to Britain and became a Liberal MP (1886–92) and leader of the Nationalist movement in Scotland. He later travelled in Spain and North Africa and wrote many books about his journeys.

Cunobelinus, or Cymbeline (*d.c.* AD 42), ancient British king. He was leader of the CATUVELLAUNI tribe, with his capital at Colchester, and he conquered the TRINOVANTES, to become the strongest ruler of SE Britain. CARACTACUS was his son.

Cupid, Roman god of love, corresponding to the Greek EROS. Depicted as a winged boy carrying a bow and arrows of desire, he was the youngest and most mischievous of the gods, playing wanton tricks on both men and other gods. He was an attendant figure in much Roman love poetry and in sculpture.

Cupisnique, early prehistoric culture period of South American Indians in N Peru. This was a major division of the greater CHAVÍN period, which lasted from *c.*1000–*c.*200 BC, and is noted for particularly well-formed and modelled ceramics. *See also* CHAVÍN.

Cupola, small dome shaped like an onion, crowning a roof or turret, at the intersection of the arms of a building or on the corners of a square plan. Cupolas are most often found in the Middle East, but some famous examples exist in Europe, as in the Gésu Church in Rome.

Cupressus. *See* CYPRESS.

Cuprite, red to reddish-brown, brittle, translucent oxide mineral, cuprous oxide (Cu_2O). It is formed by the weathering of other ores like copper sulphide and so is commonly found near the surface. Its octahedral, dodecahedral and cubic crystals occur in the cubic system, and it also occurs in grains and earthy masses. Hardness 3.5–4; s.g. 6.1.

Cupronickel, alloy containing 75 parts of copper to 25 parts of nickel, widely used for coins. In 1947 it replaced the silver alloy used until that time for non-copper coins in the United Kingdom.

Curaçao, largest island of the NETHERLANDS ANTILLES in the West Indies, in the S Caribbean Sea. Most inhabitants are descended from African slaves imported during the 17th and 18th centuries, and the original Arawak Indians are now extinct. The island derives most of its income from refining Venezuelan oil and tourism. The capital is Willemstad. Products: aloes, divi-divi, groundnuts, tropical fruits, Curaçao liqueur, phosphates. Area: 471sq km (182sq miles). Pop. 144,000. *See also* MW p.130.

Curaçao, LIQUEUR originally produced by Dutch settlers on the island of CURAÇAO by distilling the bitter peel of unripened oranges. Today curaçao is made by macerating orange peel in brandy or rum, distilling it and then sweetening the product. The liqueur is 60% to 80% proof.

Curare, poisonous resinous extract obtained from various tropical South American plants of the genera *Chondodendron* and *Strychnos*. Most of its active elements are ALKALOIDS, notably D-tubocurarine. It is used on the poisoned arrows of South American Indians, and produces muscle paralysis by acting on the nervous system. It now has several medical uses, notably as a muscle relaxant in abdominal surgery and setting fractures, and in treating spastic paralysis and some mental disorders. *See also* MS p.*119*.

Curassow, large, crested, long-tailed, turkey-like game bird that lives in Central and South American forests. It feeds on

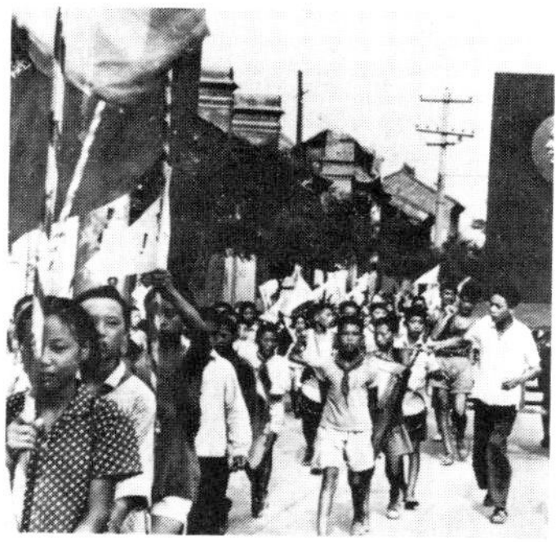

Cultural Revolution; Mao's young Red Guards parade through the streets of Peking.

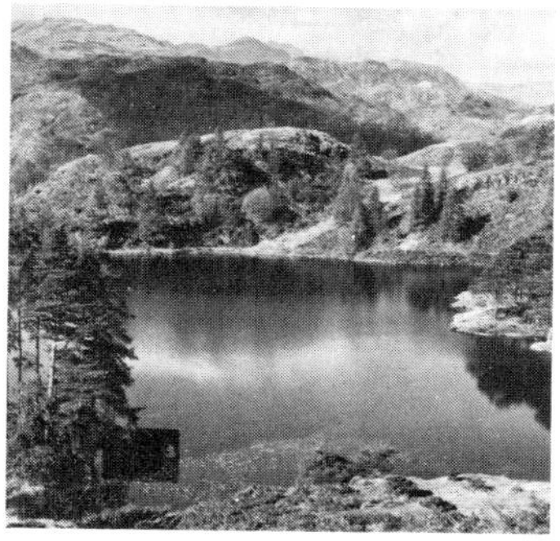

Cumbria includes the English Lake District, a region of unparallelled scenic beauty.

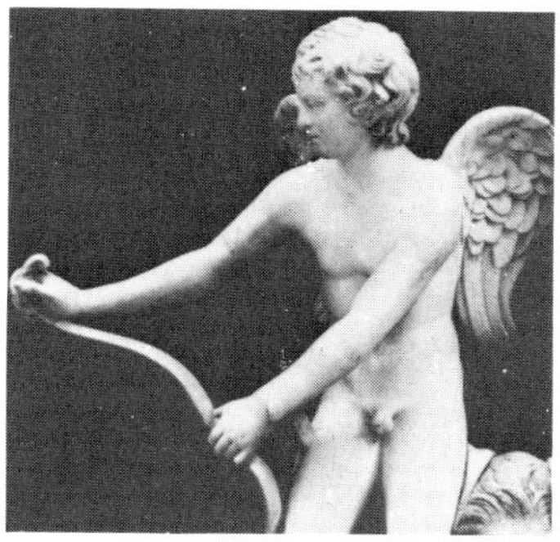

Cupid corresponds to the Greek god Eros, the centre of attraction in London's West End.

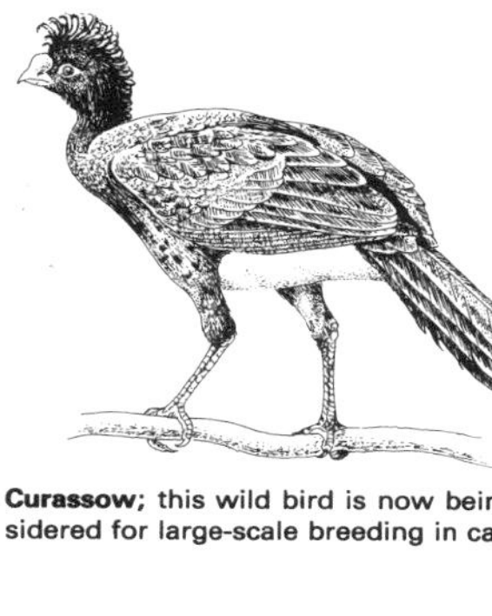

Curassow; this wild bird is now being considered for large-scale breeding in captivity.

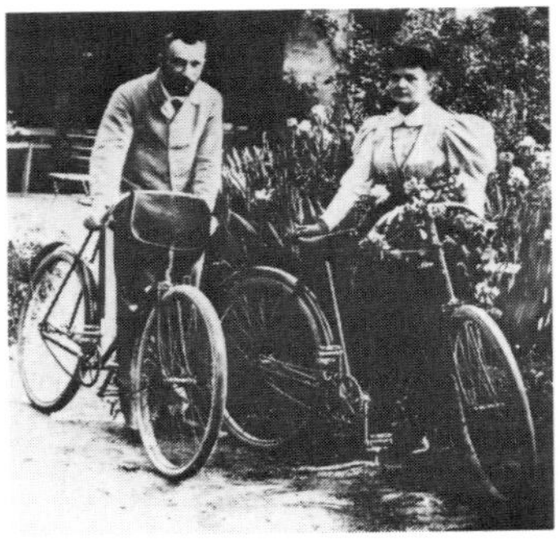

Marie and Pierre Curie shared a 1903 Nobel Prize for their discoveries in radioactivity.

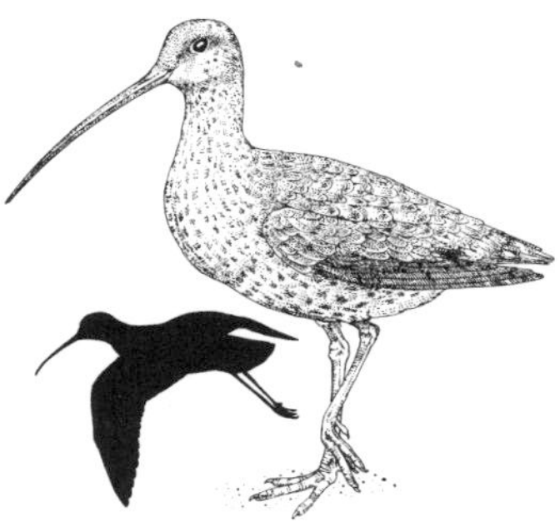

Curlews can fly powerfully, necessary for their long journeys south for the winter.

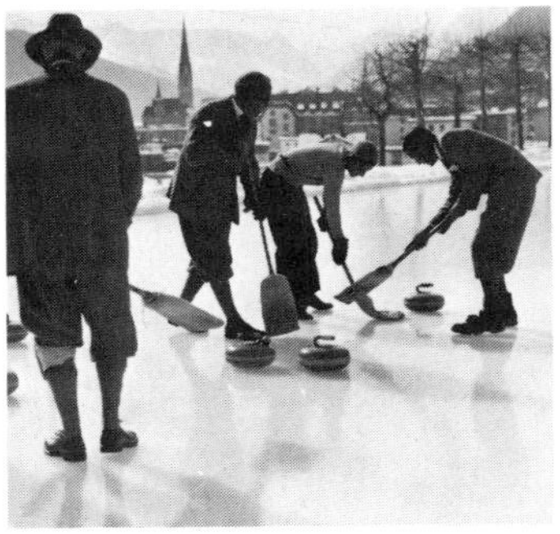

Curling is an ancient winter game which dates back at least to the 16th century.

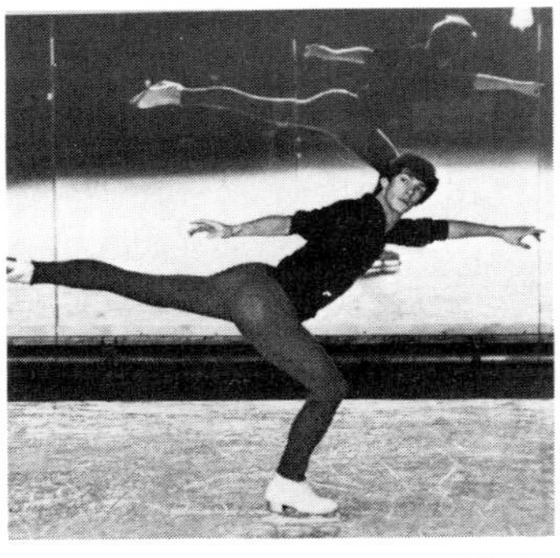

John Curry took his individual style of skating from the Olympic arena to the London stage.

insects and vegetable matter. Curassows lay 2–3 white eggs in nests built on branches near water. They live almost entirely in trees and their flesh is a delicacy. Length: to 1m (3.3ft). Family Cracidae.

Curate, in modern usage, a clergyman who assists the incumbent of a parish in the performance of his duties. The term was originally used to denote a priest who had the charge ("cure") of a parish, ie in England a vicar or rector.

Curepipe, town and health resort in central Mauritius, 16km (10 miles) s of Port Louis. Most people work in the nearby tea plantations. Pop. (1969 est.) 51,500.

Curia, political division of ancient Rome, composed of patrician and plebeian family units. Military service and electoral function were based on the *Curia,* which came to mean any public meeting-place. In medieval Europe the term was used for a court, and the modern papal court is still called the *Curia.*

Curia Regis, the great council to which kings in medieval England summoned their tenants-in-chief in fulfilment of their feudal obligation to give suit of court. There they gave counsel and, although the Curia's primary function was judicial, it is considered the origin of PARLIAMENT.

Curia Romana, official administrative body of the Roman Catholic Church. It is based in the Vatican and consists of a court of officials through which the pope governs the Church. It includes three groups – congregations, tribunals and curial offices – and is concerned with all aspects of the life of the Church and its members. In 1967 Pope PAUL VI began to modernize its structures and procedures.

Curie, name of two French scientists: Pierre (1859–1906) and his wife Marie (née Sklodowska), (1867–1934). Pierre's early work concerned the electrical and magnetic properties of crystals, from which he formulated a law relating magnetism to temperature. In 1895 he married Marie, and joined in her important work on RADIOACTIVITY. Together they discovered RADIUM and POLONIUM in 1898. In 1903 they shared the Nobel Prize in physics with A.H. BECQUEREL. In 1911 Marie became the first person to be awarded a second Nobel Prize, this time in chemistry, for her work on radium and its compounds. *See also* MM p.23; MS pp.124–125; HC2 p.*157.*

Curie, unit (symbol Ci) used to measure the activity of a radioactive substance. It is used for all radioactive isotopes and is defined as that quantity of a radioactive isotope which decays at the rate of 3.7×10^{10} disintegrations per second. It was named after Madame Marie CURIE.

Curitiba, city in SE Brazil, capital of Paraná state. Its development dates from the influx of European immigrants in the late 19th century, when it became a distribution centre for the surrounding agricultural region. Pop. (1970) 608,417.

Curium, radioactive metallic element (symbol Cm) of the ACTINIDE group, first made in 1944 by G.T. Seaborg and others by the alpha particle bombardment of Plutonium-239 in a cyclotron. It is chemically reactive and most of its halogen compounds have been prepared. It is also intensely radioactive and is toxic if absorbed by the body. Properties: at. no. 96; s.g. 13.51; m.p. 1,340°C (2,444°F); 13 isotopes, most stable Cm^{247} (half-life 1.6×10^7 years).

Curlew, long-legged shorebird with long down-curved bill and mottled brown plumage. Often migrating long distances, it is a wader and lives in open areas near water. It feeds on small animals, insects and seeds, and nests on the ground, laying two to four eggs. Length: to 48.4cm (19–25in). Species *Numenius arquata.*

Curling, game resembling bowls on ice that is a major winter sport of Scotland, and popular in Canada and the N USA. It may have originated as early as the 16th century. The game is played by two teams of four players on an ice surface 42m (138ft) long by 4.3m (14ft) wide. Each player has two circular smooth stones – dished at the base and on top and having a handle – each weighing 18–20kg (40–44lb). Players are also provided with a *crampit* (a spiked metal foot-plate). At each end of the ice is a circular target with an area in the centre known as the *tee.* While one player sends his stone towards the tee, another player uses a broom to sweep the surface in front of it to give it a smoother surface over which to glide. Each player delivers two stones, alternately with his opponent. One point is scored for each stone lying nearer the tee than an opponent's stone. A game is 10 or 12 rounds (16 stones per round).

Curly-coated retriever, sporting dog with a dense, tightly-curled coat of black or deep brown. It is able to retrieve on both land and water. It is thought to be descended from the water spaniel. Height: 58cm (23in); weight: 30kg (65lb).

Curnow, Allen (1911–), New Zealand poet, a leading literary nationalist. He is best known for his collections *Not in Narrow Seas* (1939) and *Island and Time* (1941). He was the editor of the *Penguin Book of New Zealand Verse* (1960).

Curragh "Mutiny" (March, 1914), refusal of officers of the 3rd Cavalry and some infantry officers, stationed at the Curragh, near Dublin, to fight (if required) in Ulster in order to enforce the Liberal government's Home Rule proposals for Ireland. The chief organizer was Gen. Hubert Gough. The affair forced the resignation of the war minister, J.E.B. Seely.

Curran, John Philpot (1750–1817), Irish lawyer and orator. Noted for his wit and eloquence, he is best known for his defence of rebels arrested for the 1798 insurrection. As King's counsel in 1782 and member of the opposition in the Irish Parliament (from 1783), he supported the rights of Catholics (although a Protestant himself) and opposed the Union (1800).

Currant, any of several mainly deciduous shrubs and their fruits, which are rich in vitamin C. Black, red and white currants are included in the genus *Ribes*; they are popular plants and are cultivated widely. The fruits are used in pies, preserves and syrups. *See also* PE p.214, *214.*

Currant moth. *See* MAGPIE MOTH.

Currency. *See* MONEY.

Current, broad, slow drift of water moving in a certain direction, distinguishable from the water surrounding it by differences in temperature and/or salinity. A current can be caused by prevailing winds which sweep surface water along forming drift currents. Such currents are affected by the CORIOLIS FORCE, by the shape of the ocean bed or by nearby land masses. Currents at a deeper level are the result of variation in density of the water which in turn varies according to temperature and salinity. *See* PE p.78.

Current, electric, flow of electrons along a conductor (or of ions through an ELECTROLYTE or gaseous discharge). By convention the direction of current flow is from a positive to a negative terminal, although electrons flow along a wire in the opposite direction. It is measured in AMPERES and its symbol is I. Direct current (DC) flows continuously in one direction, whereas alternating current (AC) regularly reverses direction. Mains AC reverses 120 times/sec. in North America and 100 times/sec. in most European countries (corresponding to supply frequencies of 60Hz and 50Hz). *See also* SU pp.112–115, 124–127.

Current value, market value of goods and services as measured in current monetary prices. During inflationary periods, the market value of a product increases as its price increases even though the quantity is constant. The current value of all final goods and services is the GROSS NATIONAL PRODUCT (GNP).

Currie, Sir Arthur William (1875–1933), Canadian soldier and educationalist. After holding a succession of commands during WWI, he became general-in-command of the Canadian corps in France in 1917. In 1919 he became Canada's first full general. From 1920 to 1933 he was principal and vice-chancellor of McGill University.

Currie Cup, two trophies donated by shipowner Sir Donald Currie for South African inter-provincial rugby and cricket competition. The cricket cup, first contested in 1889–90, was given for this express purpose. The rugby cup was originally for the team providing best opposition to the 1891 British touring side. It went to Griqualand West, who gave it as a trophy for the inter-provincial tournament begun in 1889.

Curry, John (1949–), British ice-skater. He was the British men's champion from 1973 to 1976. In 1976 he won the European, Olympic and World gold medals. He then turned professional and founded the Theatre of Ice Skating.

Cursor Mundi (*c.* 1300), English poem of unknown authorship. Its 24,000 lines, written in a northern English dialect, tell the history of the world from the Creation to Doomsday and are based somewhat on the paraphrase of Genesis which has been attributed to the English poet CAEDMON.

Curtain wall, originally a non-load-bearing wall, such as a fortified wall around a castle. In modern building, curtain-walling is a technique which adds a wall (generally prefabricated) to a structure erected in "skeleton" form.

Curtin, John (1885–1945), Australian political figure. A newspaper editor before first entering Parliament in 1928, he was leader of the Labour Party from 1935 until his death and prime minister and minister of defence from 1941.

Curtis, Lionel (1872–1955), British colonial official who in 1916 introduced the term "Commonwealth of Nations" when advocating federation for the members of the British Empire. He was influential in the unification of South Africa.

Curtis, Tony (1925–), real name Bernard Schwarz, US film actor. He served in the Navy in WWII and made his first film, *Criss Cross,* in 1948. Since then he has played leading roles in many films, including *Trapeze* (1956), *The Defiant Ones* (1958), *Some Like it Hot* (1959) and *The Boston Strangler* (1968).

Curtis Cup, biennial amateur golf fixture for ladies' teams representing the British Isles and the USA. First contested in 1932, it has been dominated by the USA.

Curtiss, Glen Hammond (1878–1930), US aviator. He began, as did the WRIGHT brothers, by building bicycles. By 1908 he made the first US flight of more than 1km (0.6 miles). He built planes during WWI and his JN-4 ("Jenny") was a well-known trainer. Curtiss' company and that of the Wrights merged to become the Curtiss-Wright Corporation.

Curvature of the spine, exaggerated shaping of the SPINE, which is usually gently curved. There are three major types. Scoliosis, or lateral curvature, can be due to bad posture or to a pre-birth abnormality. Lordosis, an accentuation of the inward curve of the neck region or more commonly of the lower back region, results in a sway-back appearance. Kyphosis, an accentuation of the outward curve behind the chest, can in severe form result in a HUNCHBACK appearance.

Curve, commonly, a continuously bending line without angles. In mathematical terms a straight line is also a curve, and in analytic geometry, a curve is the locus of points that satisfy a mathematical equation. *See also* SU pp.34–37.

Curwen, John (1816–80), British Congregational minister who devised the TONIC SOL-FA method of teaching sight-singing. Although officially frowned on for many years his methods eventually triumphed.

Curwen Press, printing company originally set up in the 1860s by the Rev. John Curwen. It was taken over just before WWI by Harold Curwen, who transformed the press into one producing quality illustrated books, featuring the work of such artists as Paul NASH, Graham ARDIZZONE In 1975 it presented more than 750 prints to the TATE GALLERY.

Curzon, Clifford (1907–), British pianist. He studied at the Royal Academy and made his debut in 1923. Later he studied with Artur SCHNABEL and Nadia BOULANGER. He was professor at the Royal Academy until 1932, when he embarked on his concert career, touring the world. He became known for his performances of SCHUBERT's piano music.

Curzon Line, (1919), demarcation by the LEAGUE OF NATIONS which established the eastern frontier of Poland and awarded the city of Vilna to Lithuania and large areas of Poland to Russia. The Poles invaded the USSR and recovered the territory in 1921. The YALTA CONFERENCE of 1945 recognized the Curzon line.

Curzon of Kedleston, George Nathaniel Curzon, 1st Marquess of (1859–1925), British Conservative statesman. He entered Parliament in 1886 and travelled widely in the East before becoming Viceroy of India (1899–1905). There he carried out many reforms before his resignation was engineered as a result of an argument with Lord KITCHENER. He served in the war cabinet (1915–19) and as foreign secretary (1919–24).

Cuscus, tree-dwelling MARSUPIAL related to the PHALANGERS and OPOSSUMS, native to Australia and New Guinea. It grows to the size of a large domestic cat and has a prehensile tail which it wraps round branches during nocturnal rambles through the treetops in search of insects and vegetable food. Family Phalangeridae, species *Phalanger vestitus* and *P. maculatus.*

Cush, Kingdom of. *See* KUSH, KINGDOM OF.

Cushing, Harvey (1869–1939), US surgeon. His pioneering techniques for surgery on the brain and spinal cord helped advance NEUROSURGERY. He also first described the syndrome produced by oversecretion of adrenal hormones that is now known as CUSHING'S SYNDROME.

Cushing's syndrome, rare disease marked by obesity of the body, facial redness and in women an increase in body hair and menstrual disturbances. It is often associated with high BLOOD PRESSURE, DIABETES MELLITUS, brittle bones and psychological factors. It is caused by an excessive amount of ADRENAL hormones, which can be stimulated by a tumour and occasionally by administration of the drug CORTISONE. *See also* MS p.101.

Cushioncraft. *See* HOVERCRAFT.

Cusp, in geology, a crescent-shaped depression of shingle that occasionally forms in a regularly spaced series along a beach. Cusps may vary in length from a few feet to hundreds of feet. No good explanation of them has yet been found.

Cusp, in astronomy, either of the two horned extremities of the crescent phase of the MOON, MERCURY or VENUS.

Custard apple, family of partly evergreen trees grown in tropical and subtropical America. The leaves are lance-shaped, and the yellow flowers produce large, red to brown, heart-shaped fruits with an edible custard-like pulp. Height: to 7.5m (25ft). Of the many species the CHERIMOYA, sweetsop and soursop are specially cultivated for their fruit. Family Annonaceae. *See also* PE pp.*194–195.*

Custer, George Armstrong (1839–76), US soldier who was made a major-general in the Union army in 1864 and after the Civil War became acting commander of the 7th Cavalry in 1866. He was court-martialled and suspended for a year in 1867. In 1868 he returned to service and led attacks on the Cheyenne. In 1876, at the Battle of the LITTLE BIGHORN he misjudged Indian strength, and he and his immediate command were wiped out by the Sioux and Cheyenne under SITTING BULL.

Customs and excise, taxes on goods: the first on imports, the second on goods consumed within the country of manufacture. The development of the customs system in England dates from 1266, when Edward I levied taxes on the merchandise of all traders, but because of widespread opposition this was discontinued in 1274. Customs were administered by the EXCHEQUER until 1605. The Commissioners of Excise were appointed in 1643 but did not obtain direct control of taxes until 1671. Customs and excise came under the control of one board in 1909.

Customs union, trading area within which goods may cross boundaries, whether national or provincial, without duty having to be paid. The EEC is, among other things, a customs union or common market. The most famous customs union in modern history is the German ZOLLVEREIN (1834). *See also* BENELUX.

Cut, break in the skin that results in bleeding or, in severe cases, haemorrhage. Bleeding is best stopped by applying pressure to the wound. *For* first aid treatment, *see* MS pp.132–133.

Cuthbert, Saint (*c.*635–87), English monk and bishop. He entered the monastery of Melrose under the Abbot, St Eata, in 651. He is believed to have performed miracles on Farne Island; he became Bishop of Lindisfarne in 685. He is buried in Durham Cathedral. Feast: 20 March. *See also* HC1 p.*139.*

Cuthbert, Betty (1938–), Australian athlete. The "Golden Girl" of the 1956 Olympics, she won three gold medals (100m, 200m and 4 × 100m). In 1964 she won the Olympic 400m event.

Cuticle, exposed outer layer of an animal; in human beings the epidermis, especially the dead skin at the edge of fingers.

Cutter, a small, fast-sailing boat with a single mast rigged fore and aft, carrying a mainsail and at least two headsails; similar to the SLOOP. Traditionally, the deep and narrow hull has a sharply raked stern and a sliding bowsprit. They were used to pursue smugglers in the early 19th century. The name is also used for heavy rowing boats carried on large ships.

Cutting, piece of a plant used to start a complete new plant of the same kind. Like other methods of vegetative (asexual) propagation, cuttings have the advantage of producing plants that are genetically identical to the parent plants. Cuttings are most commonly taken from young stems, although leaves and pieces of root can also be used. Cuttings of woody twigs, including those of apples and grapes, are usually taken during the winter and stored under cool moist conditions until spring, when they are planted in sandy, damp soil to develop their roots. *See also* PE pp.178–179, *178–179,* 220–221, *220–221.*

Cuttlefish, CEPHALOPOD MOLLUSCS related to SQUIDS and OCTOPUSES. Like squids cuttle-fish swim rapidly by the propulsion of a jet of water forced out through a siphon. They have ten sucker-covered arms on the head, two being much longer than the others. Their flattened bodies contain the familiar chalky cuttle-bone. Capable of rapid colour changes, they can also eject blue-black "ink" as a means of protection. Family Sepiidae; species *Sepia officinalis. See also* NW pp.*76,* 94–95.

Cutworm, mainly nocturnal caterpillar (larva), especially of the moth genus *Agrotis,* which attacks plants and crops, cutting through their stems at ground-level. Some species attack the roots of plants. Length: to 5cm (2in). Order Lepidoptera; family Noctuidae.

Cuvier, Georges, Baron de (1769–1832), French geologist and zoologist, a founder of the disciplines of comparative anatomy and palaeontology. His scheme of classification stressed the form of organs and their correlation within the body. He applied this system of classification to fossils, and came to reject the theory of the gradual development of the earth and animals, favouring instead a theory of catastrophic changes.

Cuvilliès, François de (1695–1768), French architect and decorator. He was the foremost ROCOCO artist in Germany, appointed architect to Emperor Charles VII in 1742. He built the Residenz-Theater, Munich (1751–53).

Cuyp (or Kuyp), Aelbert (1620–91), Dutch painter, one of a family of artists, best known for his animal studies and calm, colourful landscapes. His father, Jacob Gerritsz Cuyp (1594–*c.*1651) was a portrait and landscape painter. Jacob's half-brother Benjamin Gerritsz Cuyp (1612–52) was a genre painter, influenced by REMBRANDT.

Cuyp, Jacob Gerritsz (1594–*c.*1651), Dutch painter known principally for his portraits, especially of children. He also painted landscapes which influenced his son Aelbert, and his nephew Benjamin, both painters.

Cuza, Alexander John (1820–73), Romanian ruler. He was elected Prince of Walachia and Moldavia in 1859, and recognized by the Turks in 1861, when his principalities were united into the state of Romania. Cuza introduced social reforms including the emancipation of the serfs in 1864 and the foundation of universities. He was forced to abdicate in 1866. *See also* HC2 p.85.

Cuzco, city in S central Peru, 563km (350 miles) SE of Lima; capital of Cuzco deparment. An ancient capital of the Inca Empire, it is a centre of archaeological research; nearby sites include the fortress of Sacsahuáman, Inca terraces at Pisac, and the Inca city of Machu Picchu. It was founded in the 11th century and fell to the Spaniards in 1533. Cuzco was destroyed by earthquakes in 1650, and then rebuilt. It is a market centre with textile industries. Pop. (1969 est.) 105,400.

Cwmbran, urban district in Gwent, SE Wales, approx. 24km (15 miles) NNE of Cardiff. It was established under the New Towns Act of 1946 to house steelworkers. Pop. (1970) 31,600.

Cyanide, salt or ester of hydrocyanic acid (prussic acid), HCN. The most important cyanides are sodium cyanide (NaCN) and potassium cyanide (KCN), both of which are deadly poisonous and have a characteristic smell of almonds. Cyanides have many industrial uses – in electroplating, for the heat treatment of metals, in the extraction of silver and gold, in photography, and in insecticides and pigments.

Cyanophyta. *See* BLUE-GREEN ALGAE.

Cybele, in Greek mythology, an earth goddess, borrowed from PHRYGIA, whose cult was merged with that of RHEA. She was probably the mother of MIDAS. Patroness of wild beasts, especially lions, she personified the wild, primeval aspects of nature.

Cybernetics, study of communication and control systems in animals, organizations and machines. The term was first used in this sense in 1948 by the American mathematician Norbert WIENER. Cybernetics makes analogies between the brain and nervous system and computers and other electronic systems, analysing, for example, the mechanisms of FEEDBACK and data processing in both. Thus a household thermostat might be compared with the body's mechanisms for temperature control and respiration. Cybernetics combines aspects of mathematics, neurophysiology, computer technology, INFORMATION THEORY and psychology. *See also* MM p.105.

Cycads, family of primitive palm-like shrubs and trees that grow in tropical and subtropical regions. Feathery leaves which are poisonous in most species, crown a stout columnar stem. These plants first flourished about 225 million years ago. Most of the 100 or so surviving species are less than 6.1m (20ft) tall. Family Cycadaceae.

Cyclades, (Kikládhes), large group of islands off SE Greece, in the S Aegean Sea; a department of Greece, the capital is Hermoúpolis, on Síros Island. The name is derived from the Greek *kyklos,* meaning ring. During the Middle Ages, most of the islands were incorporated into the Venetian Duchy of the Archipelago. They were annexed to Greece in 1829 from the Ottoman Empire. Mineral deposits include bauxite, lead and sulphur. Products: wheat, grapes, fish, olive oil, tobacco, marble. Area: 2,572sq km (993sq miles). Pop. (1971) 86,084.

Cycladic art, art of the Greek islands, especially marble statuary. It reached its peak in the 7th century BC, with great centres at Naxos, Peros, Delos and Melos.

Cyclamates, white, odourless, soluble crystalline salts, calcium cyclamate, $(C_6H_{11}NHSO_3)_2Ca.2H_2O$ and sodium cyclamate, $CH_6H_{11}NHSO_3Na$. They have about 30 times the sweetening power of ordinary sugar (SUCROSE). Both were used as artificial sweeteners until they were shown to produce undesirable side-effects.

Cyclamen, genus of 20 species of low-growing perennial herbs, native to central Europe and the Mediterranean region and grown widely by florists. They have swollen, tuberous, turnip-like roots, and heart- or kidney-shaped leaves, often marbled or ribbed. The drooping blooms are white, pink, lilac or crimson, and appear in the autumn and winter. Family Primulaceae.

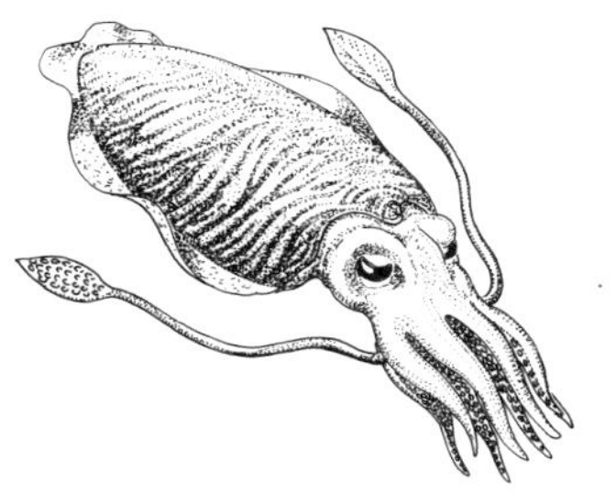

Cuttlefish are often caught at night, lured to the surface by the fishermen's lights.

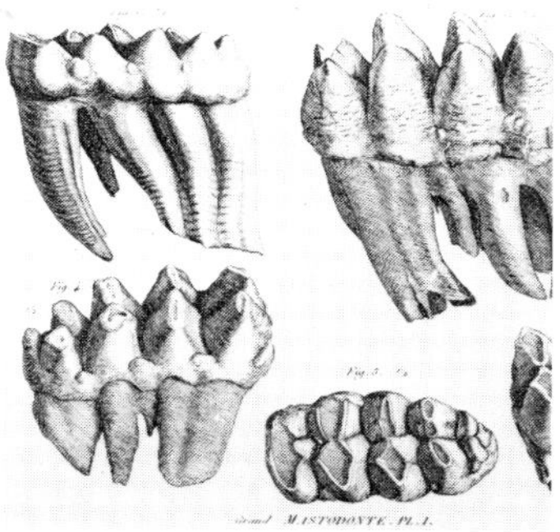

Georges Cuvier formed his illustrative style as a child by copying the works of Buffon.

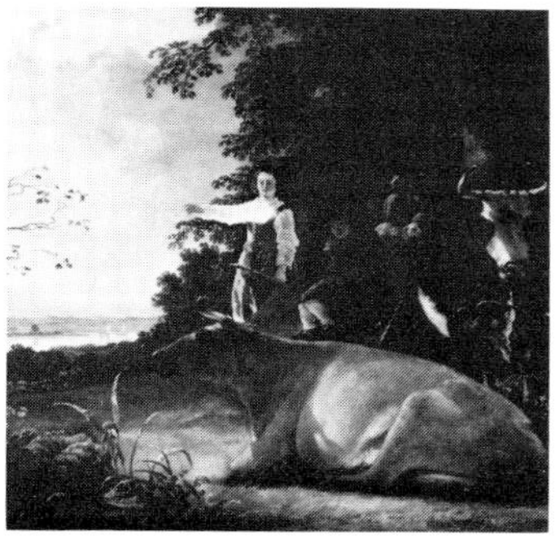

Aelbert Cuyp; *Landscape with Shepherds and Cows,* typical of his pastoral scenes.

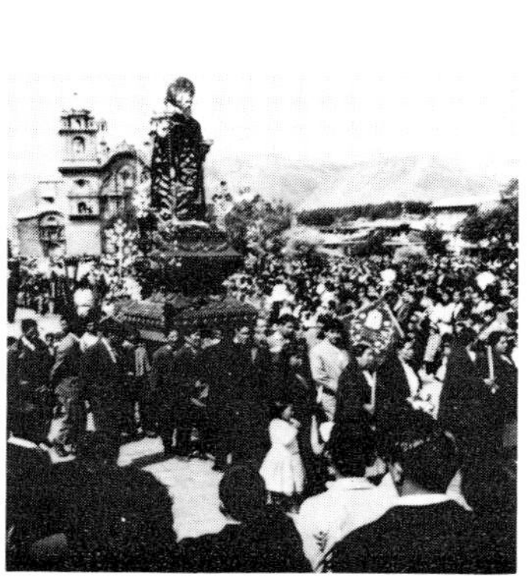

Cuzco, once capital of the ancient Inca empire, parades a Catholic European saint.

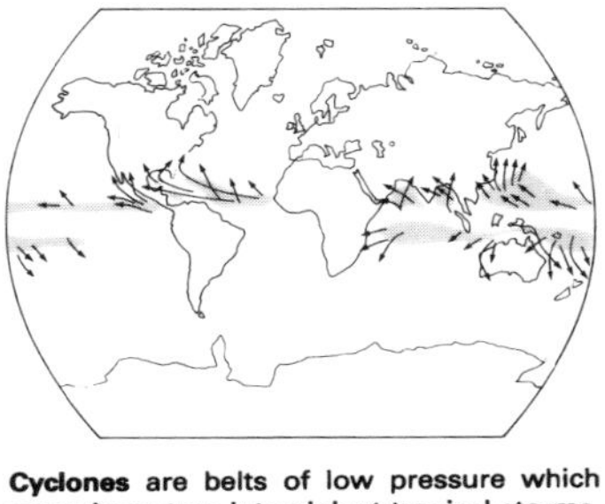

Cyclones are belts of low pressure which sometimes turn into violent tropical storms.

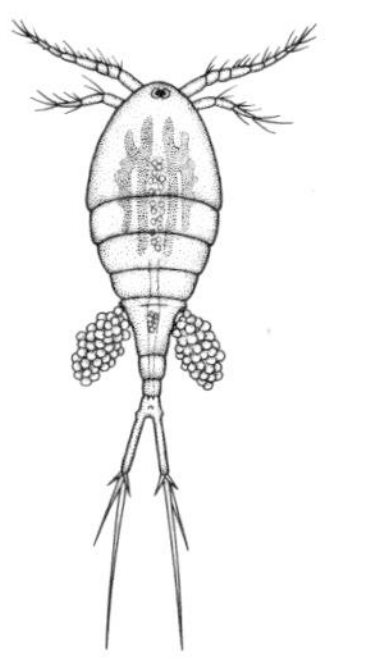

Cyclops; this freshwater creature gets it name from its large, single median eye.

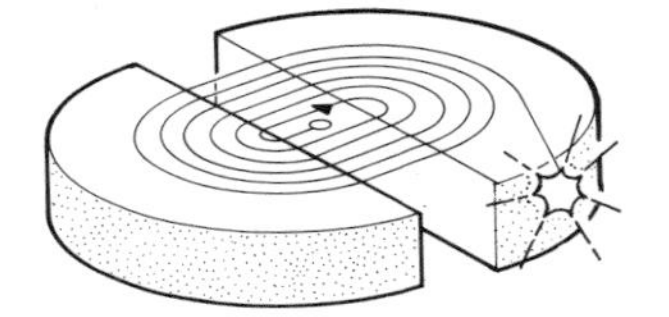

Cyclotrons, or atom smashers, accelerate nuclear particles to extremely high speeds.

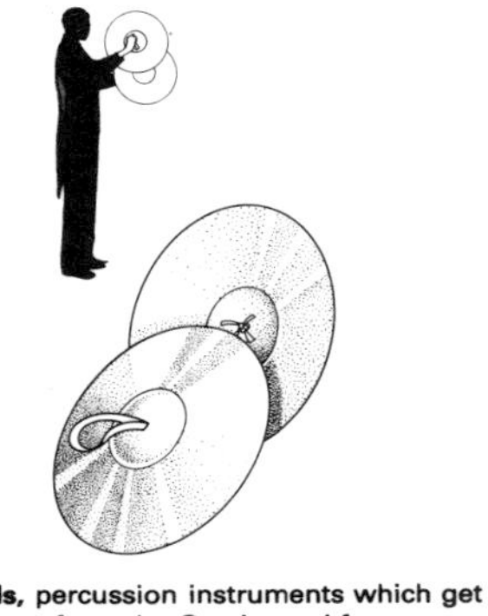

Cymbals, percussion instruments which get their name from the Greek word for cup.

Cycle, series of changes through which any system passes which brings it back to its original state. For example, alternating current starts from zero voltage, rises to a maximum, declines through zero to a minimum and rises again to zero. In the internal combustion engine the two-stroke engine completes one cycle each downward plunge and return; the four-stroke cycle takes two such movements. *See also* MM p.132; SU pp.126–127.
Cycle racing. *See* BICYCLE RACING.
Cycling. *See* BICYCLE RACING.
Cyclo-cross, cycling's equivalent of cross-country running. Competitors ride where possible; otherwise they run, bikes on shoulders, over fields, woodland and hills often worsened by winter conditions. Artificial hazards can be added to the natural ones. A race covers 16-24km (10-15 miles) over a circuit usually 0.8–3.2km (0.5–2 miles). Obscure in origins, the sport is most popular in Europe, with annual world championships. These were open events until 1966 but there are now separate ones for amateurs and professionals.
Cyclohexane, colourless liquid hydrocarbon (C_6H_{12}) which occurs naturally in crude oil, but is made commercially by combining hydrogen with benzene, using a catalyst. It is one of a type of chemical compound called conformations; they can exist in two forms differing only in the arrangement of their bonds, and may "flip" from one form to the other. M.p. 6°C (43°F); b.p. 81°C (178°F). *See also* SU p.*141*.
Cyclone, or "low", system of winds, or a storm, that rotates inwards around a centre of low atmospheric pressure, anticlockwise in the Northern Hemisphere and clockwise in the Southern Hemisphere. It is associated with cloudiness and high humidity. Strong tropical cyclones, originating near the equator, give rise to hurricanes. Although having the same spiral motion, cyclones are distinguished from small-scale systems such as tornadoes and waterspouts. They do not have FRONTS which are associated with middle-latitude wave cyclones. *See also* PE pp.68–60, 72, 75.
Cyclonite, also called RDX, T_4 or hexogen, a high explosive discovered in 1899 by Hans Hemming, formula $(CH_2N.NO_2)_3$. A colourless, crystalline solid, it is made by first mixing formaldehyde and ammonia and then nitrating the product. It was not used until WWII, when most of the combatants employed it. It is sensitive to striking, and so its main peacetime use is in blasting caps. *See also* MM pp.242–243.
Cyclopaedia, early English encyclopaedia published by the writer and translator, Ephraim CHAMBERS (*d.* 1740) in 1728. It was the first encyclopaedia to embody cross-references. The *Cyclopaedia* was translated into French and it was originally hoped that it would form the basis of DIDEROT's famous *Encyclopédie* (1751–72). But in the event, little of the *Cyclopaedia* was used. *See also* MM p.214.
Cyclopes, in Greek mythology, three storm gods, each having one eye in the centre of its forehead, who forged the thunderbolts of ZEUS. They were later depicted by Homer as hideous giant herdsmen living on an island and eating humans. ODYSSEUS escaped one by blinding him.
Cyclopropane (C_3H_6), colourless hydrocarbon gas. It is a cyclic alkane with three carbon atoms joined in a "strained" ring. It is widely used as an anaesthetic that does not irritate the lungs and is a good muscle relaxant.
Cyclops, genus of common freshwater predatory COPEPOD CRUSTACEAN. Transparent and bullet-shaped, it derives its name from its large median eye. Gravid females carry two large egg sacs. Length: under 1.6mm (0.06in). *See also* NW pp.*89*, *100*, 101.
Cyclorama, a large, concave screen, sometimes curving at the top, developed at the beginning of the century and used in stage design as a background, often lit with coloured lights. It is also a circular room or gallery having a series of paintings or photographs so arranged as to give an all-round view of a scene.
Cyclostomata, sub-class of primitive jawless fish found in temperate to cold waters. It includes the parasitic LAMPREY and the scavenging HAGFISH. Both have eel-like bodies supported by cartilage and a notocord, and sucking mouths with sharp teeth. The lamprey feeds by sucking blood from its host, and the hagfish feeds on dead and dying fish with the aid of its rasping tongue. *See also* NW p.123, *123*.
Cyclothymic personality, in psychology, personality disturbance characterized by abnormal and irregular alternations of sadness and elation. In its extreme form, with mania and severe depression, it is the main symptom of MANIC-DEPRESSIVE psychosis. The state is highly resistant to change; treatment consists of symptom alleviation with drugs. *See also* MS p.140.
Cyclotron, particle accelerator, or atom smasher, in which charged particles such as PROTONS or heavier ions are accelerated outwards in a spiral. It has two semicircular or D-shaped ELECTRODES across which is applied an alternating voltage. The charged particles are attracted by electrostatic forces to the electrode of opposite charge, but since the polarity alternates, the particles are swung outwards at increasing speed. *See also* SU p.*67*.
Cygnus. *See* NORTHERN CROSS.
Cygnus Loop, bright nebula in the constellation of Cygnus. It is made up of several separately catalogued portions, including the Veil Nebula (NGC 6992) and appears as wispy filaments forming roughly circular arcs. The Cygnus Loop is believed to be the remnant of an ancient supernova and is a powerful source of radio waves and X-rays. *See also* SU p.233.
Cylinder, engine, one of the cylindrical chambers in an internal combustion engine. Inside each, a tightly-fitting piston is pushed down by the pressure of the expansive force of burning fuel. The movement of the piston is lubricated by oil from the sump. The cylinders become hot in use and can be cooled either by air or water cooling systems. *See also* MM pp.130–131, *131*, 132.
Cymbal, saucer-shaped, percussion instrument of brass with a small dome in the centre, usually without definite pitch. It is played by clashing together a pair held in both hands or by striking a suspended cymbal with a beater. It is used in symphony orchestras, brass bands and as part of the drum kit in most jazz and rock groups.
Cymbeline. *See* CUNOBELINUS.
Cymbeline (1609), play by William SHAKESPEARE. Derived from a combination of British history and a story from BOCCACCIO's DECAMERON, the plot concerns the secret marriage of Cymbeline's daughter Imogen to Leonatus Posthumus. Typical of Shakespeare's late romances, the play ends on a note of general reconciliation.
Cymmrodorion, Honourable Society of, Welsh society serving a variety of purposes. The first society (1751–87) was founded for philanthropic ends by Welsh men living in London. The second (1820–37) worked to foster Welsh nationalism, especially through the EISTEDDFOD. The third (1873–   ) is a patron of Welsh culture, history and arts.
Cynewulf (*fl.* 800), English poet, presumed to be the author of *Elene*, *Fates of the Apostles*, *The Ascension*, and *Juliana*. Little is known about him, but the poems suggest that he was a priest in Mercia or Northumbria. Cynewulf's work shows a clarity of narrative unusual in Old English poetry.
Cynicism, philosophical way of life begun by Antisthenes, a pupil of SOCRATES. This goal of life requires self-sufficiency, as exemplified in the life of Diogenes of Sinope (*c.* 412–323 BC), a contemporary of Alexander the Great. With the succession of individuals who "lived" its precepts, great variation developed in its interpretation. The word *cynic* was derived from the Greek word meaning dog-like.
Cypher, method of disguising a message in which each letter is replaced by a sign or another letter or numeral according to a prearranged system. Cyphers are distinguished from codes, in which each word is replaced by a sign, another word or a group of numbers. "Codes" such as MORSE CODE or the flag semaphore are, strictly speaking, cyphers. Cyphers have been used since Renaissance times, particularly for military messages, and machines for producing complex cyphers were developed in the 19th century. *See also* MS pp.242–243.
Cypress, tall, evergreen tree native to North America and Eurasia, and growing best in warmer climates. It has scale-like leaves, roundish cones and a distinctive symmetrical shape. The wood is durable and fragrant, and is of value commercially. Height: 6–24m (20–80ft). Family Cupressaceae; genus *Cupressus*. There are about 20 species. *See also* NW p.*56*.
Cyprian, Saint (*c.* 200–258), bishop of Carthage. He was a pagan rhetorician who was converted to Christianity *c.* 246 and elected bishop of Carthage *c.* 248. He suffered for his faith in the persecutions carried out by the Roman emperors DECIUS and VALERIAN, and was martyred in 258. He wrote many theological treatises including *The Unity of the Catholic Church* (251), which he wrote after the schism of NOVATIANUS. Feast day: 16 September.
Cyprinodont, any of a family of about 400 species of small soft-finned fishes that live in fresh and brackish tropical and subtropical waters of North America and Africa. The best known are the SWORD TAILS and killifishes. Family Cyprinodontidae.
Cyprinoid, any of a family of about 1,500 species of freshwater fish, many of which are familiar to the angler, including carp, dace, bream, roach, tench, barbel, minnow, gudgeon, rudd and chub. Family Cyprinoidea.
Cyprus, island republic in the E Mediterranean Sea, which became independent in 1960. It is inhabited by both Greeks and Turks, between whom there has been much strife. The capital is Nicosia (Levkosía). Cyprus is predominantly agricultural, the main crops being wheat and barley, fruit (including grapes for wine) and potatoes. There is some light industry. Area: 9,251sq km (3,571sq miles). Pop. (1976 est.) 639,000. *See* MW pp.61–62.
Cyprus. *See* CYPRESS.
Cyrano de Bergerac, Savinien (1619–55), French writer. His novels and plays combine free thinking, humour and burlesque romance. He wrote two prose fantasies, *Journey to the Moon* (1657) and *The Comical Tale of the States and Empires of the Sun* (1662), which contain many scientific predictions. He was famous for his swagger.
Cyrano de Bergerac (1897), five-act drama by Edmond Rostand. It remains popular today and was made into a film in 1950 and a television play in 1968. Cyrano, afflicted with an enormous nose, writes love letters to Roxane for his friend Christian, although he loves her himself. When Christian is killed in battle, Roxane enters a convent. Years later she discovers Cyrano's love for her on the day he dies.
Cyrenaica, historic region in NE Libya, on the Mediterranean Sea. Colonized by the Greeks in the 7th century BC, it was bequeathed to Rome in 96 BC, and conquered by the Arabs in AD 642. It became part of the Ottoman Empire after the mid-16th century. An Italian colony in the 1930s, it was the scene of many battles during WWII. Area: 855,368sq km (330,258sq miles).
Cyrenaic School, school of hedonistic philosophy founded by Aristippus (*fl.* late 4th and early 3rd century BC). It maintained that happiness lies not in slavery to, but in mastery over, pleasure. Its importance in philosophy declined in favour of the later version of EPICURUS.
Cyril, Saint (*fl.* 9th century), with his brother, Methodius, one of the two so-called "Apostles to the Slavs" who did missionary work among the Khazars and Moravians. He invented an alphabet from the Greek, upon which the CYRILLIC alphabet is based.
Cyril of Alexandria, Saint (*c.* 375–444),

Greek theologian and patriarch of Alexandria from *c.*412. He upheld the Christological orthodoxy (which emphasizes the inseparable humanity and divinity of Christ, with Mary as the mother of God) against NESTORIUS.
Cyrillic alphabet. *See* ALPHABET.
Cyrus the Great (*c.*600–529 BC), King of Persia, founder of the ACHAEMENID dynasty and the Persian Empire in 549 BC. He took over Media, defeated and captured King CROESUS of Lydia (*c.*546 BC), captured BABYLON in 539 BC and the Greek cities in Asia Minor, but failed to conquer Egypt. He delivered the Jews from captivity, giving them Palestine to rule. While fighting the Massagetae, a tribe NW of the Caspian Sea, he was killed. *See also* HC1 pp.60–61.
Cyst, abnormal growth in the form of a sac that contains solid or liquid material. It may occur in a glandular organ, such as breast or prostate, or in the skin. A cyst may be malignant (cancerous) or benign; the former may interfere with normal physical functions and need to be removed. The latter are also sometimes removed for cosmetic purposes.
Cysteine, $(HS.CH_2CH.NH_2.COOH)$ crystalline AMINO ACID that occurs in animal proteins, especially those in the hair, hooves and the keratin of the skin. The hydrogen and sulphur group in it make it the catalytic element in some enzymes. *See also* SU pp.153, *153,* 154–157.
Cystic fibrosis, hereditary glandular disease most often occurring in childhood, in which the body produces abnormally thick mucus that often obstructs the breathing passages, causing chronic lung disease. There is a deficiency of pancreatic enzymes, an abnormally high salt concentration in the sweat, and loss of weight. The disease is treated with antibiotics, salt replacement and a high-protein diet. Severe cases may be fatal.
Cystitis, inflammation of the urinary bladder due to acute or chronic infection, more common in women, usually caused by bacteria. Symptoms include frequent and difficult urination, a burning sensation during and after urination, low back pain and slight fever. Treatment consists of antibiotics and increasing the intake of fluids. *See also* MS p.*102.*
Cytochemistry. *See* CYTOLOGY.
Cytochromes, proteins containing haem, an iron group, as in HAEMOGLOBIN. They are fundamental to the process of respiration in all living cells that need atmospheric oxygen. *See also* SU pp.154–156.
Cytology, study of living cells and their structure, behaviour and function. It began with Robert HOOKE's microscopic studies of cork in 1665 and the various forms of microscope are still the main tools of cytology. In the 19th century, Matthias SCHLEIDEN and Theodor SCHWANN developed the cell theory, which has since been frequently confirmed and is one of the fundamental concepts of cytology. Recently the chemistry of cell components, cytochemistry, has been a major area of research.
Cytoplasm, jelly-like, non-particulate matter inside a CELL and surrounding the nucleus. The proteins needed for cell growth and repair are produced in the cytoplasm. *See also* NW p.26, *26.*
Cytosine, organic base, first isolated in 1894. Derivatives of cytosine made in the body are important in cellular metabolism and in the formation of RNA and DNA, thus being vital for the retention of genetic characteristics. *See also* SU p.*153.*
Czar. *See* TSAR.
Czartoryski, Adam Jerzy (1770–1861) Polish politician of an ancient family that had effectively ruled Poland in the 18th century. He served in the Russian court from 1795, but became disillusioned with Russian ambitions in Poland and returned home to lead the Polish insurrection of 1830. After its failure he lived in exile in Paris, where he planned an insurrection which eventually took place in 1863.
Czechoslovakia, landlocked nation in central Europe, a member of the Communist bloc. It is one of the most industrialized nations of central Europe, the main industries being iron and steel, chemicals, motor vehicles and textiles. There are deposits of coal and iron but many raw materials are imported. The chief crops, produced mostly on co-operative farms, are sugar-beet, cereals and potatoes. The capital is Prague. Area: 127,869sq km (49,370sq miles). Pop. (1976 est.) 14,862,000. *See* MW pp.62–63.
Czerny, Karl (1791–1857), Austrian pianist, teacher and composer. A pupil of BEETHOVEN, he later taught LISZT. His piano studies are still popular.
Częstochowa, city in Katowice province, s Poland, on the Warta River, approx. 200km (125 miles) sw of Warsaw (Warszawa). An ancient monastery stands on Jasna Gora (Mountain of Light) and contains an image of the Virgin painted by St Luke, which was brought to Częstochowa in the 14th century and successfully defended against Swedish attacks in 1655 and 1705. It became a symbol of national strength and unity. The city was taken by Germany in both world wars. Industries: iron and steel, textiles, paper making. Pop. (1974) 195,400.

D

D, the fourth letter of the alphabet, derived from the Semitic *daleth* and the Greek *delta*. In Roman numerals, D stands for 500.
Dab, marine FLATFISH of the order Pleuronectifomes; a valuable food fish. The upper, "sighted" side is brown with darker spots; the underside is almost white. Length: to 25cm (10in). Species *Pleuronectes limanda. See also* NW p.*130.*
Dabchick, also called little GREBE, small, round-bodied, fresh-water diving bird with lobed, rather than webbed, feet and dark plumage. It is the smallest of the grebes and is common in Britain. It is a good flier and nests on floating vegetation. Length: approx. 27cm (10.5in). Family Podicipedidae; species *Podiceps ruficollis.*
Dablon, Claude (*c.*1619–97), French missionary in Canada. A Jesuit, he went to Canada in 1655 and accompanied Claude Jean Allouez to Wisconsin in 1670 and was a superior of Jesuit missions (1671–80, 1686–93).
Dacca, port and capital of Bangladesh, 129km (80 miles) NE of Khulna. Pakistan formally surrendered to India in Dacca in 1971. It has the University of Dacca, founded in 1921. In the centre of the world's greatest jute-producing area, Dacca has engineering, textiles, printing and chemical industries; it is also noted for cottage industries that produce handicrafts. Pop. (1974) 1,730,253.
Dace, any of several small fresh-water fishes of the CARP family, Cyprinidae. The common European dace (*Leuciscus leuciscus)* is silvery and may grow 30cm (12in) long. The Moapa dace (*Moapa coriacea*) is recognized as an endangered species. *See also* NW p.*246.*
Dachau, town in Bavaria, sw Germany, the site of a CONCENTRATION CAMP established by the Nazis (1933–45). More than 32,000 people lost their lives there.
Dachshund, small German hunting dog bred to follow badgers to earth. It has a long tapered head and rounded pendulous ears; the long body is set on short legs and the tail is held in line with the back. Its coat may be smooth, wiry or long. There are two types, standard and miniature. Height: (at shoulder) up to 23cm (9in).
Dacia, ancient region of Europe (now in Romania). Its inhabitants were thought of as wealthy and independent by the Greeks and Romans until they were colonized by Trajan in 101–106. Dacia was later overrun by Goths, Huns and Avars, but the Romance language of the area was retained and became the basis for modern Romanian. *See also* HC1 p.*99.*
Dacoit, term used in India and Burma for an armed bandit, usually one of a gang. Although at its worst in the 18th and 19th centuries, dacoity has remained a problem since independence in 1947.
Dacron, trade name for long-chain polyester fibre made from glycol and terephthalic acid, known as Terylene in Britain. It has high elastic recovery and low moisture absorption and is not combustible, but melts at about 260°C (500°F). It is used extensively in ropes and in crease-resisting fabrics. *See also* MM pp.56–57.
Dactyl, in poetry, metrical foot consisting of a stressed, followed by two unstressed syllables, or a long followed by two shorts, as in the word "mannikin". The meter is called dactylic.
Dada, or Dadaism, movement in literature and the visual arts that was started in Zürich in 1916 by a group of artists and writers which included Tristan TZARA, Marcel JANCO, Richard HUELSENBECK, Hugo Ball, Jean (Hans) ARP and others. The group, repelled by war and bored with the prevalent CUBIST art styles, promulgated complete nihilism, espoused satire and ridiculed civilization. Dadaists participated in deliberately irreverent behaviour, designed to shock a complacent public. They stressed the illogical or absurd and the importance of the irrational unconscious mind. In the 1920s SURREALISM developed from Dadaism. *See also* HC2 pp.202, *202,* 203.
Daddah, Moktar Ould (1924–), the first president (from 1961) of Mauritania. His authoritarian rule maintained a precarious national unity.
Daddi, Bernardo (*c.*1290–1348), Italian painter, a major Florentine artist of the generation after GIOTTO, whose influence is evident in Daddi's frescoes *The Martyrdom of St Laurence* and *The Martyrdom of St Stephen* (in Sta Croce, Florence). Daddi's later work, such as the altarpiece of S. Pancrazio (Uffizi, Florence), was influenced by Sienese painting, especially that of the LORENZETTI brothers.
Daddy-long-legs, fly of the order Diptera. It has a slender body, long fragile legs and one pair of wings. The hindwings are reduced to special balancing organs called halteres. Length to 3cm (1.2in). Family Tipulidae; species *Tipula simplex*. The name is also given to the HARVESTMAN spider. *See also* NW p.*112.*
Daedalus, in Greek mythology, a masterly architect and sculptor. He constructed the LABYRINTH for King MINOS of Crete. Imprisoned for offending the king, he made wings of wax and feathers to escape with his son ICARUS. The attempt ended in the death of his son.
Daffodil, bulbous flowering ornamental plant of the family Amaryllidaceae. The long rush-like leaves grow from the base and the single flowers are yellow or yellow and white, with a bell-like central cup and oval surrounding petals. Height: to 45cm (18in). Genus *Narcissus. See also* PE p.*178.*
Dagda, one of the two greatest kings of the Tuatha Dé Danann in Irish mythology. A successful military leader of superhuman capacity, he could invoke the seasons with a harp that played by itself. He had a cauldron of plenty (called Undry) and a massive club that dealt out death or life.
Dagger, short sword or double-edged knife used for stabbing, or thrown from a short distance. Its design varies in different countries. It is called a stiletto in Italy, a poniard in France and a dirk in Scotland. The blade can be between 10 and 50cm (4–20in) long, tapered to a sharp point, or broad and pointed; the handle, or hilt, may be ornately designed, and is usually fitted with a guard. Daggers are used in close combat by many armies, particularly in guerrilla fighting. *See also* MM pp.160–161; SU p.*21.*
Daghestan (Dagestanskaja ASSR), autonomous republic in the SE European USSR, bounded on the E by the CASPIAN SEA. The region is mountainous and divided by valleys, although there are irrigated lowlands to the N. These support wheat, maize and grapes and the rivers Samur and Sulak now provide hydroelectric power. Difficulty of access has left the mineral resources untapped and local industries concentrate on canned fruit, glassworking

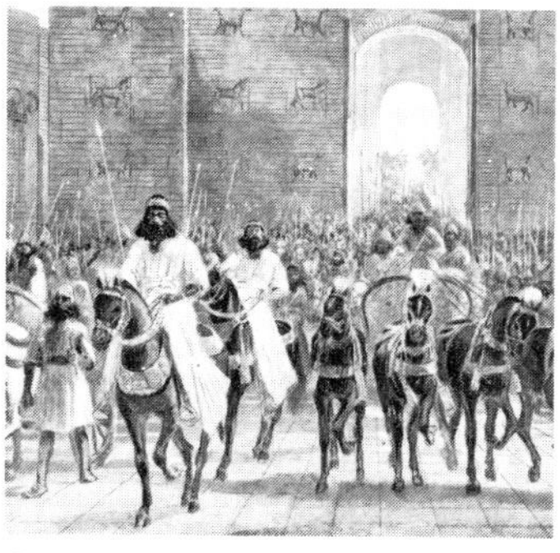

Cyrus the Great, the Persian king, triumphantly entering Babylon captured in 539 BC.

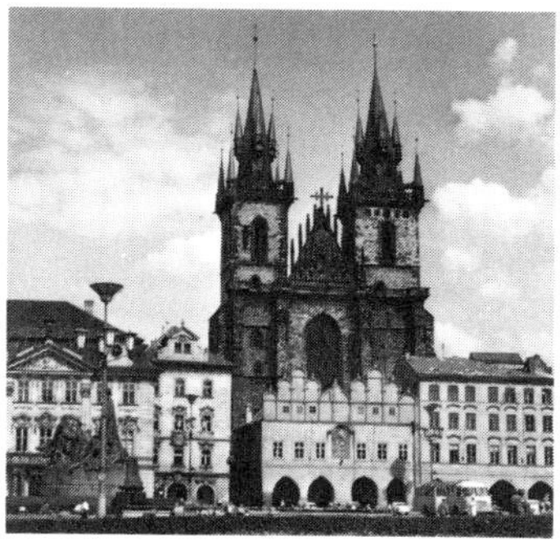

Czechoslovakia; the Tyn church towering behind the Kinski Palace in Prague.

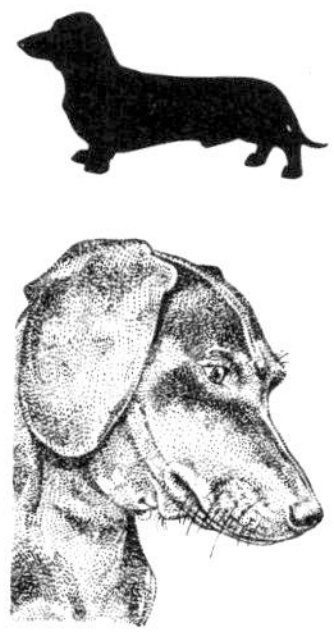

Dachshund, the small, strong German dog bred specially for following badgers to earth.

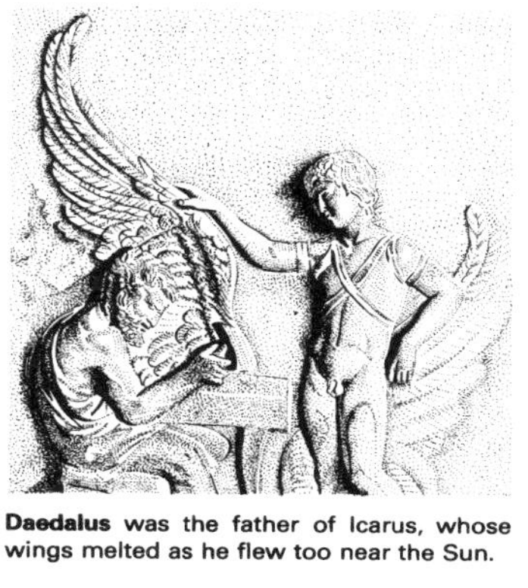

Daedalus was the father of Icarus, whose wings melted as he flew too near the Sun.

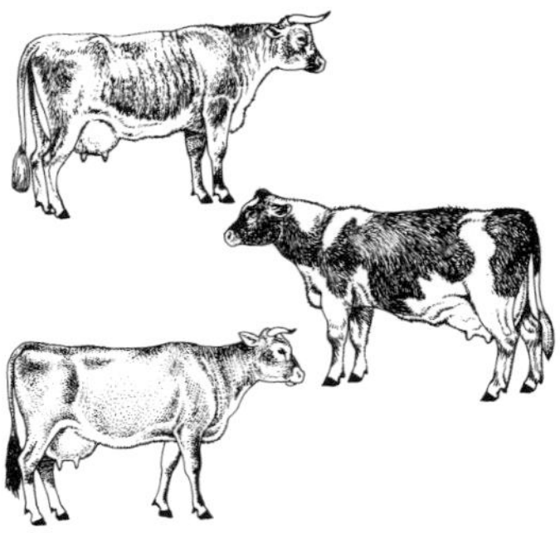

Dairy cattle are milked regularly once in the morning and once in the evening.

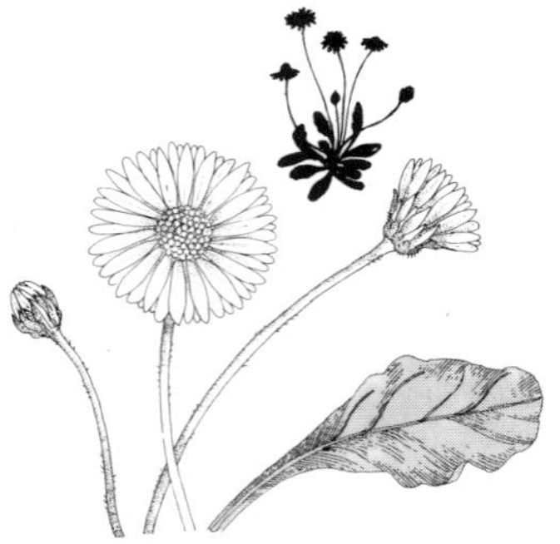

Daisies close at night, a fact revealed in the origin of the name, "day's eye".

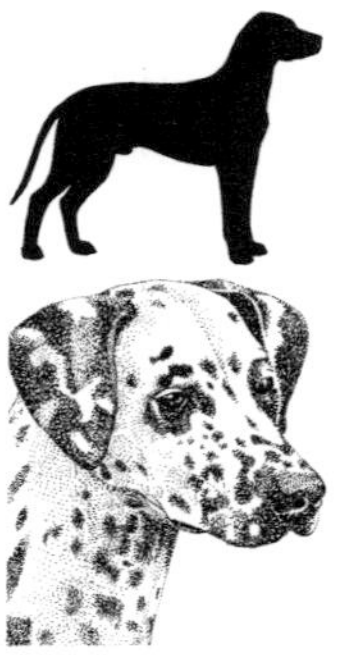

Dalmation puppies are born white, their spots appearing after about a month.

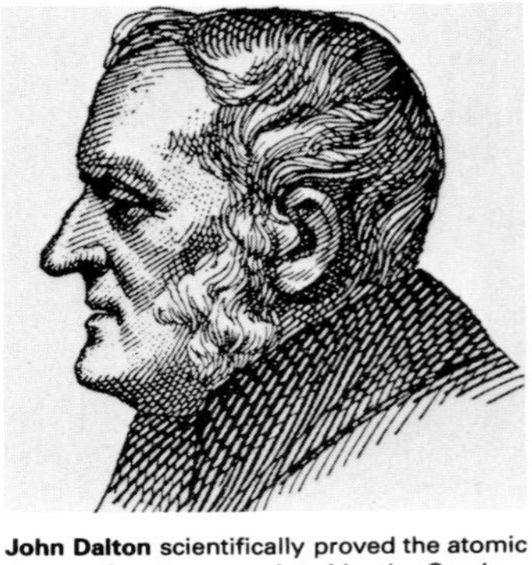

John Dalton scientifically proved the atomic theory of matter speculated by the Greeks.

and wood products. The capital is Makhachkala. Area: 50,300sq km (19,421sq miles). Pop. (1970) 1,429,000.

Daguerre, Louis Jacques Mandé (1789–1851), French painter and inventor of the daguerreotype, an early photographic process in which a delicate image is produced on a copper plate coated with silver iodide developed with mercury vapour. In 1829 he joined Nicéphore NIEPCE in photographic experiments. Their process was announced in 1839 at about the same time that William Fox TALBOT developed his calotype in England. *See also* MM p.218.

Dahl, Michael (1656–1743), Swedish portrait painter. He lived in England after 1689 and was a popular rival to Sir Godfrey KNELLER at the court of Queen Anne.

Dahl, Roald (1913–), British writer, chiefly of short stories. His first publication was the collection *Over to You* (1945). He won the Edgar Allan Poe award in the USA in 1954 and 1959.

Dahlak Archipelago, island group in the Red Sea off Mesewa (Massaua), Ethiopia, to which it belongs. Part of the province of Eritrea, it is made up of two large islands and more than 100 smaller ones, which are mostly uninhabited; the area is noted for its pearl fisheries. Area: 1,165sq km (450sq miles).

Dahlberg, Erik, Count (1625–1703), Swedish soldier, architect and graphic artist who distinguished himself as a military engineer in Sweden's war with Denmark (1675–79) and later in the Great Northern War (1700–21).

Dahlia, genus of popular, late-blooming, perennial plants with tuberous roots. The common garden dahlia (*Dahlia pinnata*) has been developed into more than 2,000 varieties with a wide range of flower heads usually white, red, purple or bicoloured. Height: to 1.5m (5ft). Family Compositae. *See also* NW p.*60*.

Dahomey, former region of W Africa, forming modern Benin and part of Ghana. The Dahomey tribal group emerged in the 17th century and won great prosperity by conquering local tribes and selling them to the Europeans as slaves. The region became a French protectorate in 1863, which became independent as Benin in 1960. *See also* MW pp.38, 87.

Dahrendorf, Ralf (1929–), German sociologist who believes that conflict is a basic element of society. His works include *Class and Conflict in Industrial Society* (1959) and *Essays in the Theory of Society* (1967).

Daibutsu, Japanese name for giant statues of BUDDHA, the most famous of which are the two extant sculptures at Nara and Kamakura and the one at Kyoto, destroyed and now represented by a wooden replica.

Dáil Éireann, popularly elected house of the two-chamber parliament of the Republic of Ireland. (The upper house is called the Seanad Eireann.) Its first members were elected in 1918 and assembled at Dublin in January 1919.

Daimler, Gottlieb (1834–1900), German engineer and motor-car manufacturer. In 1822, with Wilhelm MAYBACH, he established a research laboratory where a year later they developed a lightweight petrol engine. Daimler then used this to power a motor-cycle and then his first car (1886). In 1890 he founded the Daimler Motor Co., which made Mercedes cars, and became (1926) Daimler-Benz & Co. *See also* BENZ; MM pp.124–127.

Daimler-Benz, international vehicle-manufacturing corporation based in West Germany, with several foreign subsidiaries. It produces Mercedes-Benz cars and lorries and in 1976 employed about 168,800 people throughout the world. It was formed in 1926 when the two German pioneering car manufacturers of DAIMLER and BENZ were merged. *See also* MM pp.122, 126.

Dairen. *See* LUDA.

Dairy cattle, domesticated cattle raised mainly for milk and products derived from it. Cows have large udders and produce more milk than is needed for nursing their calves, which are weaned a few days after birth. An efficient cycle has been evolved in which manure from the animals replaces nutrients taken from the soil by feed crops. *See also* PE pp.224–229.

Daisy, any of several members of the family Compositae, especially the common English garden daisy, *Bellis perennis*. It has basal leaves and long stalks bearing solitary flower heads; each of which has a large, yellow, central disc and small radiating white petals tinged with pink. There are also many cultivated varieties.

Dakar, capital and largest city in Senegal, W Africa, on the S tip of Cap Vert, on the Atlantic coast. Founded in 1857 as a French fort, the city grew rapidly after the completion of a railway in 1885 linking it to Saint-Louis on the Senegal River. There is a Roman Catholic cathedral and a presidential palace. Dakar is a modern city with excellent educational and medical facilities, which include the Pasteur Institute. Industries: food processing, textiles, oil-refining, brewing. Pop. 799,000.

Dakota. *See* NORTH DAKOTA; SOUTH DAKOTA.

Dakota Indians. *See* SIOUX.

Daladier, Édouard (1884–1970), French statesman, radical leader and minister of war. Prime minister in 1933, 1934 and in 1938–40, he signed the Munich Pact in 1938 and declared war on Germany a year later. He was interned by the Vichy Government in 1942 and deported to Germany until his release in 1945.

Dalai Lama, Grand LAMA of the Yellow Hat Buddhist monastery at Lhasa, given the title "Dalai" (meaning "oceanwide") in the 16th century. The Grand Lama was made temporal and spiritual ruler of Tibet in 1642. The spiritual supremacy was later shared with the PANCHEN LAMA, while the Dalai Lama retained the temporal leadership until the Tibetan revolt against the Chinese in 1959, when he went into exile in India. The Dalai Lama is believed by Tibetan Buddhists to be a divine reincarnation of the BODHISTA Avalokitesvara, ancestor of the Tibetan people. On the death of a Dalai Lama his soul is believed to pass into the body of an infant, born 49 days later, whose identity is determined as a result of elaborate tests.

Da-lat, city in the central highlands of S Vietnam, 225km (140 miles) NE of Saigon. Developed by the French as a health resort and hunting centre, it is a modern city with a university. Products: coffee, tea, rubber. Pop. (1971 est.) 86,600.

Dal Cais, Irish clan which flourished in Munster in the late 10th and early 11th centuries. Its two most powerful kings were Mathgamain, who gained control of Munster in *c.*964 and gained Limerick from the Norsemen in 968, and Brian BORU, who became king of all Ireland in 1002 and destroyed the Norse threat at the Battle of CLONTARF in 1014. *See also* HC1 p.180.

Dalcroze, Émile Jaques. *See* JAQUES-DALCROZE, ÉMILE.

Dale, Sir Henry Hallett (1875–1968), British physiologist who shared the 1936 Nobel Prize in physiology and medicine with Otto Loewi for discoveries relating to the chemical transmission of nerve impulses. Dale found that the chemical acetylcholine served to transmit nerve impulses across the tiny gap from one nerve cell to another. His writings include *Adventures in Physiology* (1953) and *An Autumn Gleaning* (1954).

D'Alembert, Jean le Rond. *See* ALEMBERT, JEAN LE ROND D'.

Dalén, Niels Gustav (1869–1937), Swedish engineer responsible for the development of automatic lighting for lighthouses and railway signals by means of a "sun-valve", a switch responsive to the sun's radiation. Dalén was awarded the Nobel Prize in physics in 1912, but was blinded in a laboratory explosion a year later. He also invented a substance that absorbs acetylene and prevents the risk of explosion in acetylene tanks.

Dalgarno, George (*c.*1626–87), Scottish educator. In *Ars Signorum* (1661) he advocated a language made up of letters that stood for ideas, and *Didascalocophus* (1680) proposed a hand alphabet for the deaf and dumb.

Dalhousie, James Andrew Broun Ramsay, Marquis of (1812–60), British colonial administrator, *b.* Scotland. He became Lord Ramsay upon the death of his brother and was governor-general of India (1847–56); he defeated the Sikhs, annexed the Punjab and installed John Lawrence as its ruler. His annexations and style of government angered the Indian princes, though his administration helped to develop India's transport system.

Dali, Salvador (1904–), Spanish artist whose achievements have received enormous publicity. His style, a blend of meticulous realism and hallucinatory transformations of form and space, made him an influential surrealist. Dali has also designed jewellery, fabrics, furniture and stage décor. *See also* HC2 p.202.

Dalin, Olof von (1709–63), Swedish author. He was exiled for political activities in 1756 and during his exile, which lasted until 1761, he completed his *History of the Swedish Kingdom*.

Dallapiccola, Luigi (1904–), Italian composer. He has used the 12-tone system of SCHOENBERG, and was the first Italian composer of atonal music. He was persecuted by Mussolini during WWII because his wife is Jewish. He was keenly interested in vocal music; *Canti de Prigonia* established him as a mature composer.

Dallas, city in NE Texas, USA; the state's second-largest city and one of the fastest-growing in the nation. A leading commercial, financial and transport centre of SW USA, it was founded *c.*1841. Dallas became an important cotton market in the 1880s and in the 20th century has boomed with the development of the Texan oilfields. President John F. Kennedy was assassinated there on 22 Nov. 1963. It has oil refining, electronic equipment, clothing and aircraft industries. Pop. (1970) 844,401.

Dalmatia, historic region of Yugoslavia, between Bosnia and Herzegovina and the Adriatic Sea. An important Roman province in the 1st-5th centuries it became part of the Byzantine Empire in the 6th century. It was taken by Austria in 1815. After WWII, it became part of the Federal Republic of Hrvatska (Croatia) under the Yugoslav Government. Split is its regional capital. Products: cement, bauxite, wine, fish. Tourism is a major industry. Area: 12,732sq km (4,916sq miles).

Dalmatian,, dog characterized by its white coat with black or liver spots. It has a long flat head with a long muzzle and high-set ears. Its powerful body is set on strong legs and the tail is long and tapered. It is believed to have an instinct for working with horses. Height: to 58cm (23in) at the shoulder.

Dalou, Aimé-Jules (1838–1902), French sculptor who created monumental decorative works during the Third Republic. His masterpiece is the *Triumph of the Republic* in the Place de la Nation, Paris.

Dalriada, ancient British kingdom comprising part of Antrim, N Ireland, and Argyll, in Scotland. The kingdom emerged in the 5th century AD as many tribesmen from Ireland ("Scoti") moved to Argyll. The kingdom declined following Viking raids in the 9th century. *See also* HC1 p.182.

Dalrymple, John, 1st Earl of Stair. *See* STAIR, JOHN DALRYMPLE, 1ST EARL OF.

Dalrymple, John, 2nd Earl of Stair. *See* STAIR, JOHN DALRYMPLE, 2ND EARL OF.

Dalton, Hugh, Baron Dalton of Forest and Frith (1887–1962), British statesman. He was a Labour member of Parliament (1921–31, 1935–59), and the Bank of England was nationalized while he was chancellor of the exchequer (1945–47).

Dalton, John (1766–1844), British chemist and physicist. His early interest in meteorology yielded important information on the trade winds, the cause of rain and the Aurora Borealis. He described colour blindness (sometimes called Daltonism) based on his own experiences and those of his brother. His study of gases led to Dalton's law of partial pressures. His atomic theory states that each element is made up of indestructible, identical, small particles; he also constructed a table of atomic weights. *See also* SU pp.62, 66, *132*.

Dalton's law, in physics, states that the pressure exerted by each gas in a mixture of gases does not depend on the pressures of the other gases, provided no chemical reaction occurs. The total pressure of such a mixture is therefore the sum of the partial pressures exerted by each gas.

Daly, John Augustin (1838–99), US playwright and theatrical manager, who began his career as a critic for New York newspapers. In 1869 he opened the Fifth Avenue Theater and established the famous Daly's Theater on Broadway (1879).

Dam, Carl Peter Henrik (1895–1976), Danish biologist. In 1939 he isolated vitamin K, the fat-soluble vitamin needed for blood clotting. For this work, he received the 1943 Nobel Prize in physiology and medicine, which he shared with E.A. DOISY. In addition he examined the roles of other vitamins and lipids.

Dam, barrier built across a stream, river, estuary or part of the sea to confine or check the flow of water for irrigation, flood control or electricity generation. The first dams were probably constructed by the Egyptians at least 4,500 years ago. Common types are gravity, arch and buttress dams. Gravity dams are anchored by their own weight. Arch dams are of two types: single-arch and multiple-arch. Single-arch dams are curved (convex to the water they retain) and are supported at each end by the river banks. Multiple-arch and buttress dams are supported by buttresses rooted in the bedrock. The highest dam is the USSR's Nurek, 317m (1,040ft) high. The Fort Peck Dam in Montana, USA, has a record volume of 96,000,000cu m (125,568,000cu yd). The cheapest source of electricity that is used commercially comes from hydroelectric schemes made possible by dams such as the Aswan High Dam in Egypt. *See also* MM pp.198–199.

Damages, in CIVIL LAW, an award of money to a plaintiff in compensation for civil injury, such as breach of contract or slander. In addition to straightforward awards, in which compensation is made as fairly as may be in relation to the injury, there are two special types of award. The first is exemplary, or punitive, damages, in which the unsparing amount awarded is intended to be not a just compensation for the injury, but a punishment of the offender. It is reserved for acts of malice or wantonness. The other is nominal damages, in which, although the plaintiff's action is sustained, the injury is too trifling to warrant substantial compensation. *See also* CRIMINAL INJURIES COMPENSATION BOARD.

Damaraland, historic area and modern administrative region of Namibia (South West Africa), extending between the Namib and Kalahari deserts (W and E) and from Ovamboland (N) to Great Namaqualand (S).

Damas, Léon (1912–), Guinean poet. An early supporter of NÉGRITUDE, his collections of verse, *Pigments* (1937) and *Black Label* (1956), contain sensitive portrayals of village life in Guinea.

Damascus, capital of Syria, standing in an oasis on the edge of the Syrian desert, 137km (85 miles) NE of Haifa. It is thought to be the oldest continuously occupied city in the world and has belonged to, in turn, the Egyptians, Persians, Byzantines, Arabs, Seljuk Turks, Mongols, and Ottoman Turks. After WWI it became the capital of one of the French Levant States, and the capital of independent Syria in 1941. It is Syria's administrative and financial centre, and local industries include textiles, metalware and refined sugar. Pop. (1975 est.) 1,049,500.

Damask, patterned, woven fabric of wool, linen, silk, cotton or man-made fibre. The name is derived from the Damascus weavers who first made it. True damasks are reversible. *See also* MM pp.56–59.

Damasus I, Saint (*c.*304–84), pope (*r.*366–84), whose election was challenged by the ARIANS, who chose Ursinus as antipope. Both were consecrated by bishops, although eventually Emperor Valentinian I expelled Ursinus from Rome. Damasus asserted that a pope could be tried only by ecclesiastical courts. St JEROME produced a revised Latin translation of the Bible under his supervision.

Dame, legal title of the wife or widow of a KNIGHT or BARONET. It is also the title accorded to women appointed to the 1st or 2nd class of the Order of the BRITISH EMPIRE.

Dame aux Camélias, La (1848), novel by Alexandre DUMAS (FILS) based on his love affair with Marie Duplessis, a courtesan. When transferred to the stage (1852) it proved hugely successful. Giuseppe VERDI used the story for *La Traviata* (1853).

Damien, Father (Joseph de Veuster) (1840–89), Belgian Roman Catholic missionary. He was sent to Hawaii by the Fathers of the Sacred Heart, where he joined a community of lepers on Molokai Island to administer to their needs.

Damocles, in Greek mythology, a courtier of Dionysius I of Syracuse (Sicily). His eulogies of the king made him a well-known figure at court. At a banquet Dionysius suspended a sword hanging by a fragile thread above his head. Damocles was thus made to realize that the wealth and power he praised were ephemeral and did not bring happiness.

Damon and Pythias (Phintias), famous friends in Roman legend. Pythias plotted against Dionysius of Syracuse (*c.*430–367 BC) and was condemned to death, but Damon agreed to take his place in prison until the day of his execution so Pythias could settle his affairs. Pythias did return on the day of his execution, and Dionysius was so impressed with the loyalty of the two that he pardoned Pythias.

Dampier, William (1651–1715), English navigator and buccaneer. An adventurous early career included a buccaneering expedition against Spanish America and a journey across the Pacific Ocean, after which he was marooned. Sent by England in 1699 to the south seas, he explored the coasts of Australia, New Guinea and New Britain and gave his name to Dampier Archipelago and Dampier Strait. *See also* HC2 p.124.

Damselfish, any of 250 species of small lively marine fish, found in tropical waters of the Atlantic and Indo-Pacific oceans. It is brilliantly coloured, deep bodied and generally has a forked tail. It has a single nostril on each side. Length: to 15cm (6in). Family Pomacentridae.

Damselfly, delicate weak-flying insect resembling the DRAGONFLY. Almost all have a slender, elongated, blue abdomen and one pair of membranous wings that are held vertically (not flat) over the body when at rest. Length: to 5cm (2in). Order Odonata. *See also* NW p.*230*.

Damson, small tree and its edible fruit. The name is now applied to varieties of plum (*Prunus domestica*), especially *P. insititia.* The oval fruit, a drupe, is generally borne in clusters, and has a tart flavour and is made into jam. Family Rosaceae. *See also* PE pp.192–193.

Dan, in the Bible (Genesis), fifth son of JACOB, born to Bilhah the maid of his wife, Rachel. His tribe settled north of Judah near the Mediterranean Sea.

Dana, Richard Henry (1815–82), US author. In 1834 he sailed as a common sailor on the brig *Pilgrim* around Cape Horn to California and back. From that experience he wrote *Two Years Before the Mast* (1840), a classic in American literature of the sea.

Danaë, in Greek mythology, the daughter of Acrisius of Argos. ZEUS appeared to Danaë in a shower of gold and she bore his son PERSEUS, who killed the GORGON Medusa and also, in fulfilment of a prophecy, his grandfather Acrisius.

Da-nang city in central Vietnam with a port on the South China Sea. It is a commercial shipping, rail and air-transport centre. The first European settlers landed at Da-nang Bay in 1535 and it was ceded to France by Annam in 1787. There was a huge US military base at Da-nang during the Vietnamese war. Industries: soap, cotton, silk production. Pop. 334,200.

Danby, Francis (1793–1861), Irish painter who worked in England and Switzerland. His early paintings – small landscapes such as *Blaise Castle* (*c.*1822) – have a charming realism, but he was later influenced by TURNER's Romanticism.

Danby, Thomas Osborne, Earl of (1632–1712) (subsequently Marquess of Carmarthen, Duke of Leeds), English Tory politician who was Charles II's treasurer and chief minister (1673–78). He built up an Anglican court party in Parliament, but was impeached and imprisoned (1679–84) by them when a secret subsidy he had negotiated with Louis XIV was made public. Danby organized Tory support for William and Mary, invited them to seize the crown and became their chief minister (1690–95) until he was again impeached on a charge of bribery.

Dance, English word derived via French from Old High German *dansōn*, to stretch. Dancing is the ancient art of ordered stylized body movements coupled with leaps, measured steps and other actions, normally performed to the accompaniment of music or voices. The purpose of a dance may be religious, artistic, a means to communicate emotions, entertainment or as a form of popular expression. At its most primitive form, the dance was probably part of courtship and religious ritual. Other forms of dancing originated in China, Japan and India, where mime was the distinctive feature. The dances of Africa are quite different from those of Asia; they are characterized by rapid, athletic movements whereas Asian dances are more graceful. In the 18th century Bach and Handel composed music for gavottes and minuets. The waltz also became popular early in the 19th century. The Spanish style of dancing has assimilated Arab and gypsy influences and is accompanied by the guitar. Ballroom dancing (waltz, foxtrot, tango, quickstep etc.) became popular in the 19th and early 20th centuries, and from the 1950s came the introduction of such dances as rock 'n' roll, the jive and the twist.

Dance of Death, theme which probably originated in 13th or 14th century morality poems and plays. These, as recited and performed, accorded with popular beliefs that the dead rose up at night to attract the curious and unsuspecting and to dance them to their deaths. This superstition was reinforced with stylized dance pageants, paintings, illustrations and verse in which the dance symbolized the inevitability and equalizing nature of death.

Dance Theatre of Harlem, primarily black ballet company founded by Arthur Mitchell in 1968. Based in New York City, the company performs a varied repertoire of works ranging from classical ballets by George Balanchine to modern ethnic choreography by Talley Beatty.

Dancing. *See* DANCE.

D and C operation, abbreviation of dilation and curettage, in which the inside of the womb is scraped to remove abnormal tissue, to obtain a sample for testing or to procure an abortion.

Dandelion, one of the most widespread perennial weeds. It has deeply-cut basal leaves and yellow flowers, and reproduces by means of parachute seeds. The leaves are sometimes used in salads and the flower heads in making wine. Family Compositae; species *Taraxacum officinale. See also* NW p.*61*; PE p.*191*.

Dandie Dinmont, Scottish hunting terrier. It has a massive head with a distinctive topknot, large hazel eyes and pendulous ears. Its long body has a downward curve and is set on short legs. The pepper-coloured coat is hard but not wiry. Height: to 28cm (11in) at the shoulder.

Dandolo family, Ventian family that became rich and powerful by the 11th century, was at its height in the 12th-14th centuries and held high offices in Venetian government until the fall of the republic. Prominent members included Enrico (*c.*1192–1205), doge of Venice who took Constantinople in 1204; Giovanni (doge, 1280–89); Francesco (doge, 1329–39); and the last Dandolo doge Andrea (doge, 1343–54), who joined the crusade against the Turks (1343–46) and also waged war on Hungary and Genoa.

Dandruff, dead scalp skin that appears as white or yellowish flakes in the hair. It is

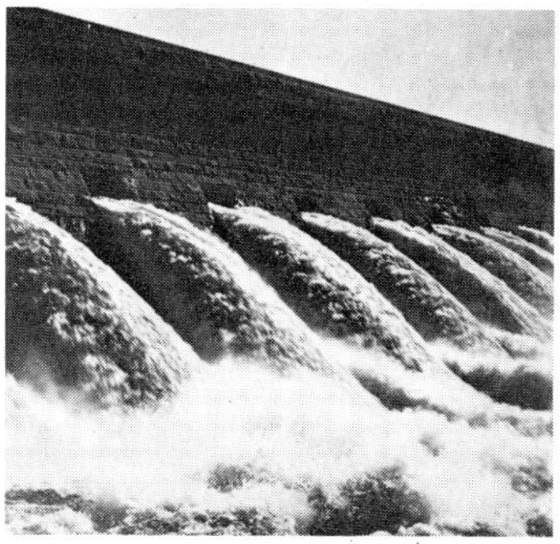

Dam; vital water supplies and hydroelectric power flow from the High Dam at Aswan.

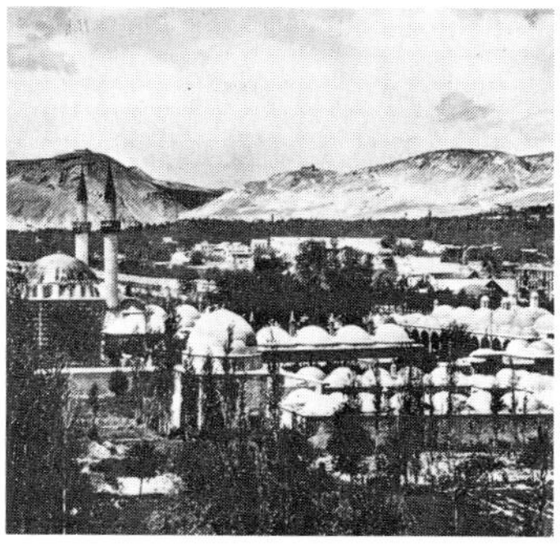

Damascus is thought to be one of the oldest continuously occupied cities of the world.

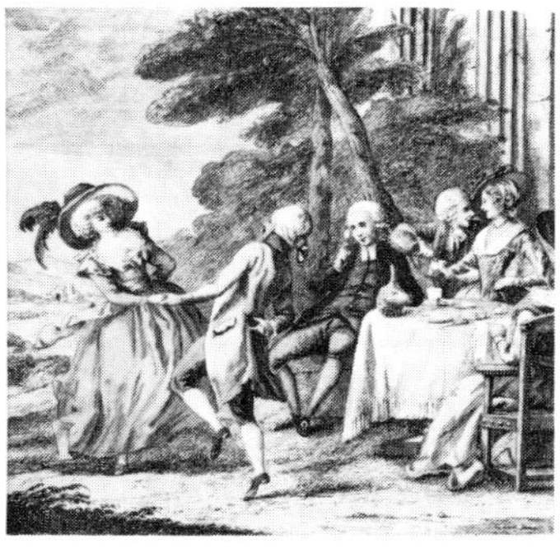

Dance, whose style and form generally reflects the popular music of the day.

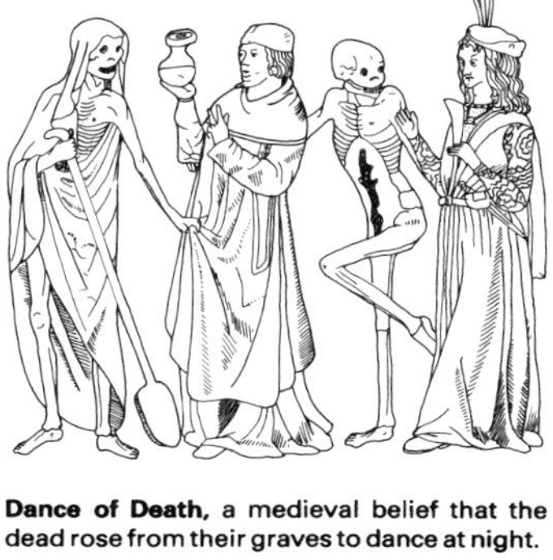

Dance of Death, a medieval belief that the dead rose from their graves to dance at night.

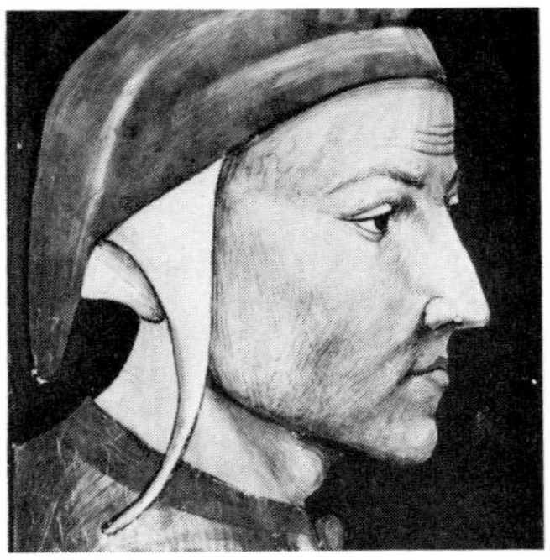

Dante's *Divine Comedy* is considered one of the greatest works of medieval literature.

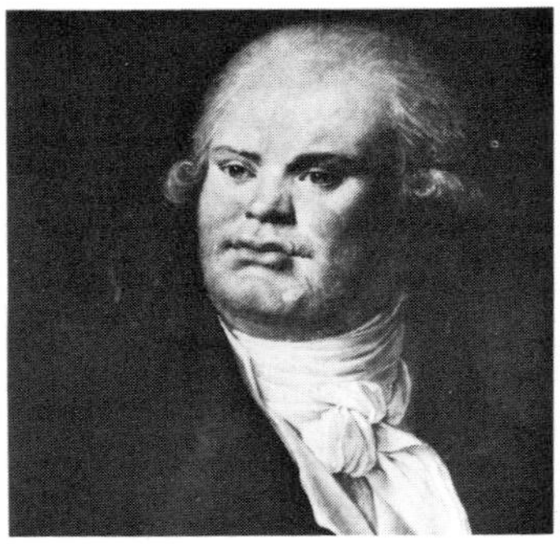

Danton eventually fell victim to the Revolution he had led boldly.

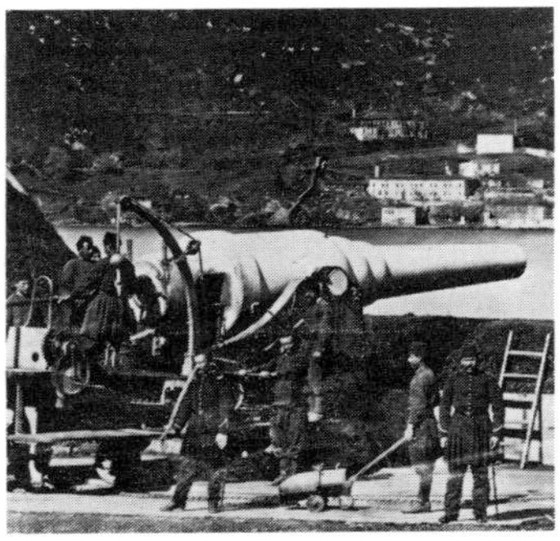

Dardanelles, known to the ancients as the Hellespont, under Turkish guns in WW1.

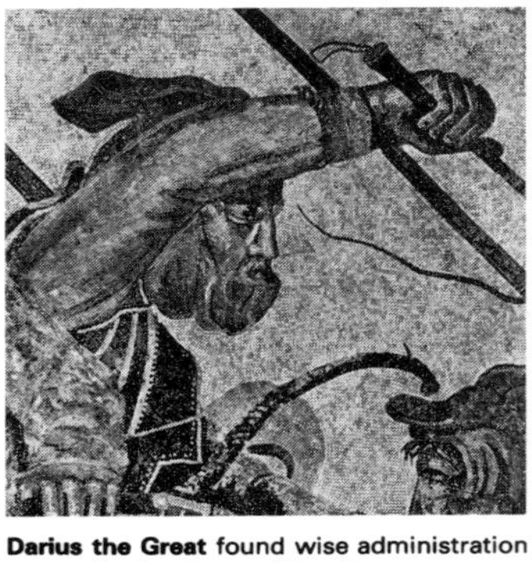

Darius the Great found wise administration more effective than military force.

made noticeable by oiliness and dense growth of hair, and is sometimes aggravated by inflammation, commonly seborrhoeic DERMATITIS.

Dane, Clemence (1888–1965), pseudonym of Winifred Ashton, British novelist and playwright. Her first novel was *Regiment of Women* (1917), a fictional account of teachers at a girls' school. Dane also wrote detective stories, plays and essays.

Danegeld, land tax levied in Anglo-Saxon England. It was first raised by ALFRED the Great to pay off the Danish invaders, and became a regular payment in 991 in the reign of ETHELRED. Payments to the Danes ceased in the 11th century, but the tax was still collected until 1162. *See also* HC1 p.155.

Danelaw, area in England occupied by Danes after a treaty in 886 between Guthrum and ALFRED. The region was soon reconquered by the Anglo-Saxons, although Danish law prevailed there until the 11th century. It included East Anglia, Essex, part of Mercia, and Northumbria between the Thames and the Tees and was bounded in the W by Watling Street. *See also* HC1 p.*155*.

Danes, North Germanic peoples who first settled in the JUTLAND peninsula about 10,000 BC. Their history is vague until about AD 800 when they played an important part in the VIKING raids on Western Europe. In the 9th–11th centuries they invaded England and established kingdoms in Yorkshire and in East Anglia. Unification of DENMARK was completed by Harold Bluetooth, and his grandson CANUTE added Norway and England to his kingdom. *See also* HC1 p.156–7.

Dangerfield, Thomas (*c.*1650–85), English conspirator. Employed to aid Roman Catholic suspects in the POPISH PLOT by defaming the Protestants, he betrayed his employers. He was killed after two days in the pillory.

Daniel, biblical hero and visionary, and prophetic book bearing his name. The book, probably written in about 165 BC, relates events in the legendary Daniel's life (6th century BC) during what is represented as the BABYLONIAN CAPTIVITY.

Daniel, Samuel (*c.*1562–1619), English poet and dramatist. His works include the sonnet sequence *Delia* (1592), *A Defence of Rhyme* (1603) and the play *The Queen's Arcadia* (1605).

Daniel, Yuri M. (1925–), pseudonym of Nikolai Arzak, Soviet writer. Most of his works have been published pseudonymously in Western Europe. Characterized by satire and fantasy, and largely directed against the Soviet regime, they include the stories *This is Moscow speaking* (1962), *Redemption*, and *A Man from Minap.* Arrested (1966) for allegedly writing anti-Soviet propaganda, he was sentenced to five years' hard labour.

Danish Royal Ballet, leading ballet company of Denmark, based at Copenhagen. Its origins are obscure, but it dates from the 16th century. It gained its international reputation under the direction of August Bounonville (1805–78).

Dankworth, John (1927–), British composer and saxophonist. He formed a large jazz orchestra in 1953, but frequently works with small jazz combos; his wife, the singer Cleo LAINE has often appeared with him. He has composed many works for combined jazz and classical musicians, and is a leading film composer his scores include *Saturday Night and Sunday Morning* (1960), *The Servant* (1963), *Darling* (1965) and *Accident* (1967).

Danse macabre. *See* DANCE OF DEATH.

Dante Alighieri (1265–1321), Italian poet famous for the *Divine Comedy*, written in *terza rima*. In his early years he wrote many *canzoni* to Beatrice Portinari, whom he admired from afar. In 1300 he became one of the rulers of the city-state of Florence, and during this time was responsible for the exile of his friend, Guido CAVALCANTI, who had been a great influence on his early writing. Later Dante himself was exiled and wrote his inspired and majestic works under the patronage of various nobles until he died in poverty in Ravenna. Other works include *La Vita Nuova* (*The New Life*), *Convivio* (*Banquet*), *De Monarchia* (*On Monarchy*) and *De Vulgari Eloquentia*, a treatise appealing for the use of the vernacular in literature. *See also* HC1 pp.206, 207, *207*.

Danton, Georges Jacques (1759–94), French statesman and controversial official of the revolution. He played the role of moderate in the turbulent 1790s, seeking conciliation between the GIRONDINS and MONTAGNARDS. Briefly leader of the JACOBINS (1793) and a member of the Committee of Public Safety, he was arrested during the Reign of Terror and guillotined.

Danu. *See* ANU.

Danube (Donau), second-longest river in Europe. It rises in the Black Forest of West Germany, flows NE then SE across Austria to form the border between Czechoslovakia and Hungary, then S into Yugoslavia, SE and E to form part of the borders of Romania with Yugoslavia and Bulgaria and continues N across SE Romania to enter the Black Sea. It was made an international waterway in 1923 and is today under the control of the Danube Commission, which has its headquarters in Budapest, Hungary. Length: approx. 2,859km (1,770 miles).

Danube school, number of painters of the early 16th century who did not form a compact group; the term refers more to the supremacy of landscape painting in the Danube region at the time than to any coherent artistic philosophy. Much of their work emphasized a romantic, expressive style of landscape painting. Among the artists involved were ALTDORFER and CRANACH. *See also* MS pp.*179, 184, 219*; HC1 p.260.

Danzig. *See* GDANSK.

Daoud Khan, Sandar Mohammed (1909–), Afghanistan military and political figure. He served as prime minister (1953–63) under Emir Mohammed Zahir Shah. Returning to the army, he overthrew Zahir Shah in 1973, proclaimed Afghanistan a republic and appointed himself president.

Daphne, genus of 70 species of flowering plants of the family Thymelaceae distributed throughout the world. It is the most important ornamental genus and includes the spurge laurel (*Daphne laureola*), mezereon (*Daphne mezereum*).

Daphne, nymph in Greek mythology. APOLLO, struck by one of EROS' gold-tipped arrows, fell in love with Daphne. But she had been shot with one of Eros' leaden-points, and so scorned all men. To protect her from Apollo, the gods transformed Daphne into a laurel tree. Thereafter Apollo wore a laurel branch on his head as a symbol of his love and grief.

Daphnia, also called waterflea, tiny fresh-water crustacean which can reproduce sexually or parthenogenetically. Length: to 0.75cm (0.3in). Order Cladocera of the subclass Branchiopoda. *See also* NW pp.*100, 105, 230*.

Daphnis, in Greek mythology, the inventor of pastoral poetry. The son of HERMES and a Sicilian nymph, Daphnis was taught by PAN to be a minstrel to APOLLO. Daphnis pledged his love to the jealous nymph NOMEIA, but was seduced by the nymph CHIMAERA. Nomeia blinded him for his unfaithfulness.

Daphnis and Chloe, ballet in three scenes by Michel FOKINE with music by Maurice RAVEL. Originally produced in 1912 in Paris, it starred Tamara Karsavina and Vaslav NIJINSKY. It tells of the love of the shepherdess Chloe and the goat herd Daphnis. When Chloe is kidnapped Daphnis invokes the aid of Pan, who frightens away the kidnappers and reunites the lovers.

Da Ponte, Lorenzo. *See* PONTE, LORENZO DA.

D'Arblay, Madame. *See* BURNEY, FANNY.

Darby, Abraham (1678–1717), English ore-smelting expert and manufacturer. He recognized the disadvantages of smelting iron with charcoal and from his experience of smelting copper with coke, Darby founded the Bristol Iron Company in 1708 and one year later, became the first to make good quality iron with coke. Abraham Darby III (1750–91) designed and built (1779) the world's first iron bridge, which stands at Coalbrookdale, England. *See also* MM pp.21 *23, 29*, 191.

Darby, John Nelson (1800–82), British religious leader. He joined the PLYMOUTH BRETHREN *c.*1830 and in 1847 led a breakaway group which established themselves as the "Darbyites". Like the Brethren they rejected all outward church forms and offices.

Darcy, Thomas, Lord (1467–1537), English soldier and political intriguer. He served in military expeditions for Henry VIII. During the PILGRIMAGE OF GRACE, he yielded Pontefract Castle to the rebels and joined them. He was executed for treason.

Dardanelles, narrow strait between the Sea of Marmara and the Aegean Sea, and separating the Canakkale district in Asian Turkey from the Gallipoli peninsula in European Turkey. With the Bosporus Strait, the Dardanelles forms a waterway from the Black Sea to the Aegean. It was crossed by means of a bridge of boats by Xerxes I in 480 BC and by Alexander the Great in 334 BC. Throughout the history of the Byzantine and Ottoman empires, and during both world wars, the Dardanelles was of strategic importance in the defence of Constantinople. Length: 61km (38 miles); width: 1.2 – 6km (0.75 – 4 miles). *See also* HC2 p.188, 190–191.

Dare, Virginia (*b.*1587), first English child born in America, in the Roanoke Island Colony. The granddaughter of Governor John White, she disappeared after an Indian attack. Her fate, and that of the rest of the colony, are unknown.

Dar-el-Beida. *See* CASABLANCA.

Dar-es-Salaam, capital and chief port of Tanzania, in central E Tanzania, on the Indian Ocean S of the Zanzibar Channel. Modern, with several colleges, Dar-es-Salaam is Tanzania's commercial centre and largest city. Industries: textiles, cement, building materials, glass. Exports: agricultural products, diamonds, minerals. Pop. (1975 est.) 517,000.

Dargomyzhky, Alexander Sergeyevich (1813–69), Russian composer and pianist. He wrote orchestral music, songs and operas, the best-known being *Russalka* (1856) and *The Stone Guest* (completed by friends in 1872).

Darien, eastern region of Panama, lying between the Gulf of Darien and the Gulf of San Miguel. Originally the word meant the whole of Panama, settled in 1510 by an expedition led by BALBOA (not, as Keats had it in *On First Looking into Chapman's Homer*, CORTÉS). It was the first Spanish settlement in Central America and the base for the exploration of the mainland between 1511 and 1519.

Darién, Gulf of, inlet of Caribbean Sea between E Panama and NW Colombia; it receives the Atrato River. The Spanish settled on its shores in the 16th century.

Darien Scheme (1695–99), unsuccessful Scottish project to colonize the Isthmus of Panama. The Scottish parliament, disowned by the English government and opposed by the Spaniards, invested heavily in the scheme. The failure of the settlements was taken as a demonstration of Scotland's commercial weakness and helped to secure the Act of Union (1707) with England.

Dario, Ruben (1867–1916), Nicaraguan poet. The father of the Modernista movement, he influenced both Latin American and Spanish writers. His finest book of verse, *Songs of Life and Hope* (1905), is noted for its universality and eloquence.

Darius, name of three ACHAEMENID kings of Persia. For Darius I, *see* DARIUS THE GREAT. Darius II (*r.*423–404 BC) faced uprisings in much of his empire, and lost Egypt in 410 BC. Darius III (*r.*336–330 BC) was feated by Alexander the Great at the Battle of Issus in 333 BC and at Gaugamela in 331 BC. He fled to Bacteria where he was murdered. The Achaemenid empire ended with his death. *See also* HC1 pp.61, 80.

Darius the Great (548–486 BC), Achaemenid king of Persia (*r.*521–486), also known as Darius I. He divided his lands into satrapies (provinces) with a degree of regional autonomy but responsible to Darius himself. He also fixed an annual taxation, consolidated his frontiers in both India and Thrace, and linked the Nile with the Red Sea by canal. He invaded Greece to punish the Greeks for aiding an Ionian revolt (499–494 BC), but he was defeated at Marathon (490 BC). He also restored much of the power of the kingdom of JUDAH. *See also* HC1 pp.60–61.

Darjeeling, town in West Bengal, NE India, at the foot of the Himalayas. It is noted for its scenic views of Mt Kānchenjunga and Mt Everest. The centre of a tea-producing region, it is a market for grain, fruit and vegetables and an administrative centre. Pop. (1971 est.) 42,700.

Dark, Eleanor O'Reilly (1901–), Australian novelist. She was the first novelist to examine Australian urban life and its social and psychological effect on human behaviour, as in *Prelude to Christopher* (1934) and *Return to Coolami* (1936).

Dark adaptation, the slow change in sensitivity of the human eye that takes place when someone passes into dim light from bright light. It is caused by a shift in functional dominance from cone cells to rod cells in the retina of the eye as the overall illumination is reduced. The complete process takes 35-40 minutes. *See also* MS pp.48–49.

Dark Ages, the period of European history from the BARBARIAN invasions of the ROMAN EMPIRE to the beginning of the 11th century. Now out of fashion, the term refers to the alleged stagnation of science and learning which followed the decline of Greek civilization and the political instability which resulted after the demise of Roman rule. The social and political upheavals of the period and the migrations and conquests of the Germanic tribes produced the merger of northern European tribal culture and classical culture which became the basis of mediaeval European society. It was also the period in which the West was converted to Christianity, a change which produced new uniquely Christian forms of art and literature. *See also* HC1 pp.136–137, 152–153, 158–159, 160–161, 172–173.

Darkness at Noon (1940), novel by Arthur KOESTLER. Drawing on the author's own experience of imprisonment during the Spanish Civil War, it describes the thoughts of an old Bolshevik, Rubashov, who awaits his execution by a government he helped to put into power.

Darley, George (1795–1846), British poet and mathematician, *b.* Dublin. He wrote prose tales, some collected in *Labours of Idleness* (1826). His poems included *The Errors of Ecstasie* (1822), *Nepenthe* (1835) and the pastoral drama *Sylvia* (1827).

Darling, Grace Horsley (1815–42), British heroine, the daughter of a lighthouse-keeper at Longstone, off the NE coast of England. Together with her father she took out a small boat in a stormy sea to rescue the survivors of the wrecked steamship *Forfarshire* (1838).

Darling, river in SE Australia. It rises in the Eastern Highlands in S Queensland and N in New South Wales, then SW into the Murray River. It is the longest river in Australia and is used for irrigation schemes. Length: 2,740km (1,702 miles).

Darling Downs, plateau in SE Queensland, Australia, W of the Great Dividing Range. First settled in 1840 by sheep herders, the area is now important for farming, especially for dairy produce. It is also in Australia's wheat belt. Area: 71,510sq km (27,610sq miles).

Darling Range, mountain range in W Australia running parallel to the SW coast. The suburbs of Perth are located on its slopes, and gold and tin are mined there. The highest point is Mt Cooke, rising to 583m (1,910ft). Length: 880km (500 miles).

Darlington, town in Durham, NE England, on the River Skerne, 21km (13 miles) W of Middlesbrough. It was one terminus of the world's first passenger railway service opened in 1825 from Stockton. Industries: railway engineering, textiles. Pop. 85,900.

Darmstadt, city in central West Germany, 19km (12 miles) E of the River Rhine (Rhein). The old town, or Altstadt, dates from the Middle Ages. The city was severely damaged during WWII. Industries: chemicals, steel, machinery. Pop. 141,224.

Darnley, Henry Stuart (or Stewart), Lord (1545–67), Scottish noble, second husband of MARY, QUEEN OF SCOTS. Born and educated in England, he was a claimant to the English succession. He went to Scotland in 1565 to marry Queen Mary. Weak and vicious, Darnley was involved in the murder of Mary's aide Rizzio (1566). Mary was probably party to Darnley's murder after the birth of their son, the future JAMES I OF ENGLAND.

Darrow, Clarence Seward (1857–1938), US lawyer. He became famous for his successful defence of William Haywood (1906), accused of assassinating a former Governor of Idaho. He was also renowned for his role as defence counsel in other notorious cases. He wrote *Crime, Its Cause and Treatment* (1922).

Dart, Robert Thurston (1921–71), British harpsichordist, pianist and conductor. He was appointed professor of music at Cambridge University in 1947 and at London University in 1964. With other artists he made fine recordings of English and continental Baroque music.

Dartchery. *See* ARCHERY.

Darter, any of 100 species of freshwater, bottom-dwelling fish found in clear streams of E North America. It is slender, brightly coloured and capable of darting quickly through the water. It feeds mainly on small aquatic animals. Length: to 23cm (9in). Family Percidae.

Dartmoor, moorland region in S Devon, SW England, composed mainly of granite which gives rise to many stark outcrops. The area was established as a National Park in 1951. The highest point is High Willhays, rising to 621m (3,039ft). Sheep- and cattle-raising are the chief farming activities; tourism is also an important industry. The prison at Princetown was built in 1806 originally for French captives. Area 945sq km (365sq miles).

Darts, game particularly popular in the USA and Britain, developed in England in the 15th century. It is played with three weighted wooden or metal darts 12.7–15.2cm (5-6in) long. The darts are thrown at a board, 45.7cm (18in) in diameter. Players generally stand 2.4m (8ft) away. There are several variations of play, as well as types of targets. The object in the 20-point board is to start with a certain score (201, 301, 501, 1,001), according to the number of players, and to reach zero by subtracting the amount of points scored from the number indicated. Generally each player has to begin and end on a "double".

Darwin, Sir Charles Galton (1887–1962), British physicist who trained under Ernest RUTHERFORD at Manchester. At Cambridge Darwin and R. H. Fowler developed the new methods of statistical mechanics that later served as a foundation for QUANTUM MECHANICS.

Darwin, Charles Robert (1809–82), British naturalist, originator of a firm theory of organic evolution. In 1831 he joined an expedition in HMS *Beagle*, which explored the South American coast. The observations made of the flora and fauna there, and in particular on the Galapagos Islands, formed the basis of his future work on animal variations. He considered various earlier theories on the subject of evolution and compared them with his own research. The development of a theory similar to Darwin's own by A. R. WALLACE led Darwin to present his ideas to a meeting of the Linnean Society in 1858, and he published *The Origin of Species*, a detailed exposition of EVOLUTION, in 1859. His ideas reached a wider public with the publication of *The Descent of Man* (1871), and other works. *See also* HC2 p.156; NW pp.32–33.

Darwin, Erasmus (1731–1802), British physician, grandfather of Charles DARWIN. His *Zoonomia, or the Laws of Organic Life* (1794–96) advanced the theory of evolution.

Darwin, Sir Francis (1848–1925), British botanist and son of Charles DARWIN. He edited his father's letters (1887 and 1903) and was knighted in 1913. He lectured in botany at Cambridge and became a Fellow of the Royal Society in 1882.

Darwin, Sir George Howard (1845–1912), British astronomer and mathematician and second son of Charles DARWIN. He was professor of astronomy at Cambridge and was distinguished for his work on tidal friction and the equilibrium of rotating masses. *See also* SU p.178.

Darwin, port and capital of Northern Territory, N Australia, at the entrance to Port Darwin, an inlet of the Timor Sea. It was the headquarters of the Allies in N Australia during WWII, and was bombed by the Japanese in 1942. In 1974 90% of the city was destroyed by a cyclone. A five-year reconstruction plan included housing construction that will withstand cyclone-force winds. Darwin's harbour is the major shipping point for the sparsely populated and relatively undeveloped N region of Australia. Pop. (1971 est.) 35,281.

Darwin finch, any of 14 species of finches (in three genera) of the Galapagos Islands; they provided Charles DARWIN with a valuable clue to his theory of EVOLUTION. He noted that they had all evolved from a seed-eating species of South American finch and had adapted differently to be able to feed efficiently in differing habitats: trees, cacti or on the ground. Some have large beaks to deal with larger seeds; others have smaller beaks for smaller seeds, or finer beaks for insects. *Camarhynchus pallidus* forces insects out of crevices with a cactus spine or a small twig. The various species can no longer interbreed. Family Fringillidae, subfamily Geospizinae. *See also* NW pp.32–33, 148.

Darwinism. *See* EVOLUTION.

Das Kapital. *See* KAPITAL, DAS.

Dasyurus, genus of mainly nocturnal, carnivorous MARSUPIALS found in Australia, New Guinea and Tasmania; they have large canine teeth, separate digits and long tails. The female's pouch is normally shallow. Family Dasyuridae.

Data processing, systematic sequence of operations performed on data, especially by a computer, in order to calculate new information or revise or update existing information stored on magnetic tape, punch cards or microfiche. The data may be in the form of numerical values representing measurements, scientific or technical facts, or lists of names, places or book titles. The main processing operations performed by a computer are arithmetical addition, subtraction, multiplication, and division, and logical operations, which involve decision making based on comparison of data, as in: "if condition *a* holds then follow programmed instruction P; if *a* does not hold then follow instruction Q". Modern computers are capable of rapid data processing, such as the "renovation" of television pictures sent back from outer space. *See also* MM pp.106–108, 216.

Data storage. *See* COMPUTER MEMORY.

Data terminal, computer, station remote from a computer, but connected to it through a transmission path (commonly by telephone line) for entering or receiving data. It normally consists of at least one combined input and output component, such as a teleprinter with its associated electronics. More complex terminals may have a cathode-ray unit for visual display, or an *X-Y* plotter for graphs. The system is favoured by small-scale users who find it economical to share the services of one computer simultaneously with other users. *See also* MM pp.106–108.

Data transmission, computer, supply of information to or from a computer via hard wire (telephone lines) or microwave broadcast (from earth-stations or satellites). DATA TERMINALS at each end of the transmission path regulate the information by encoding, decoding and synchronizing the transmitted signals. *See also* MM pp.106–107.

Date palm, tree native to the Near East

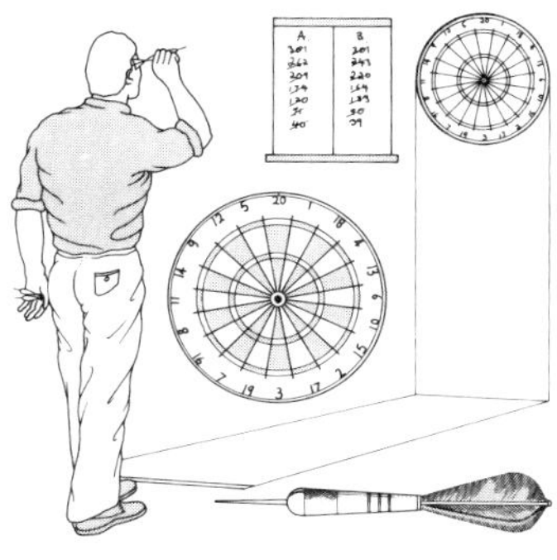

Darts; the Pilgrim Fathers were reported to have played darts on the *Mayflower* in 1620.

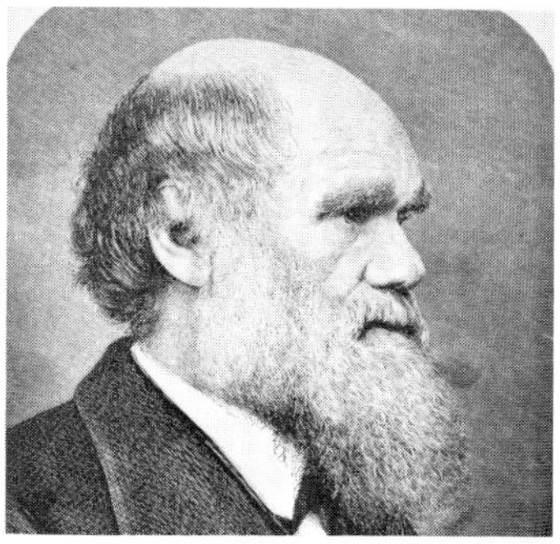

Charles Darwin's revolutionary theory undermined even his own deep religious beliefs.

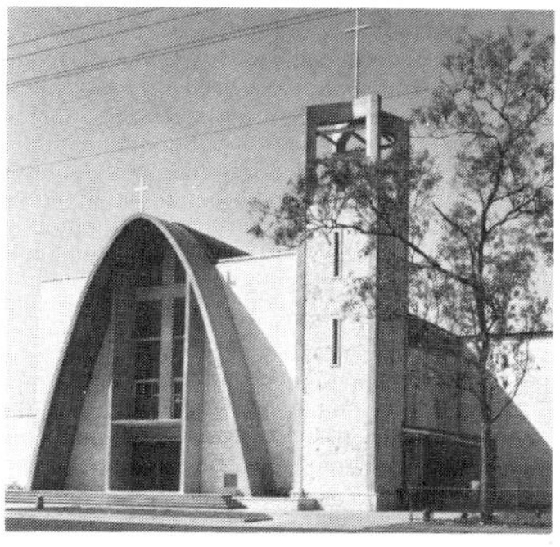

Darwin; the Roman Catholic Cathedral, destroyed with the rest of the city in 1974.

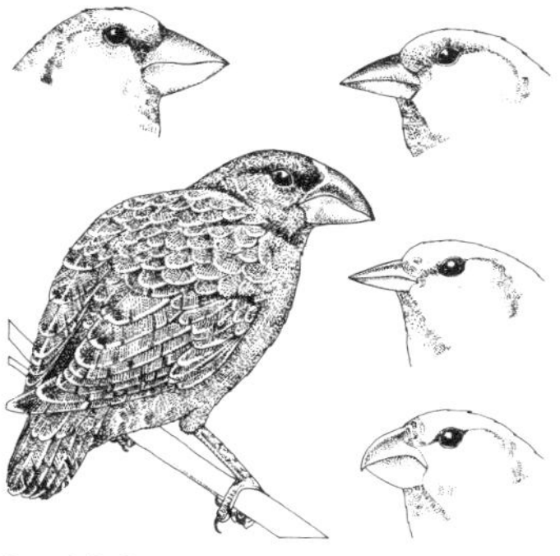

Darwin's finch, the little bird that provided a vital clue to Darwin's theory of evolution.

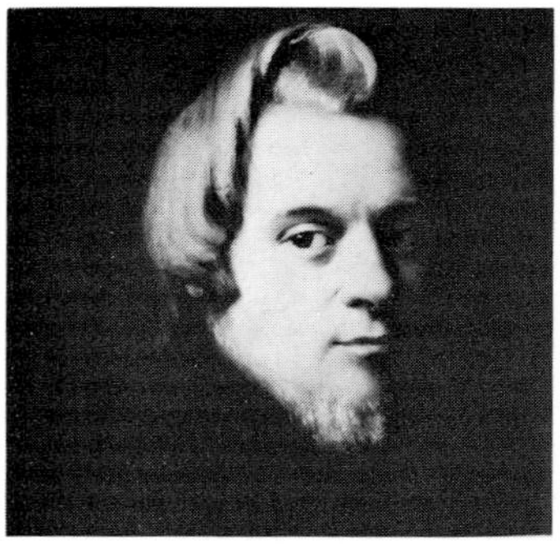

Daumier combined true artistic genius with a biting satirical comment; *Self portrait.*

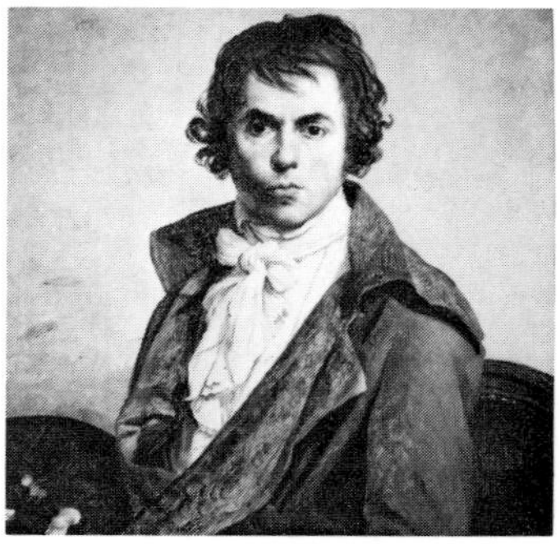

Jacques-Louis David's style captures the spirit of the Napoleonic era; *Self portrait.*

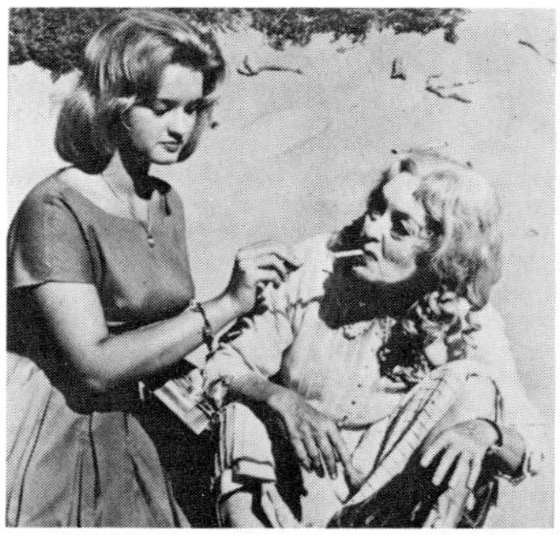

Bette Davis brings a moving, sometimes disturbing power to all her many film characters.

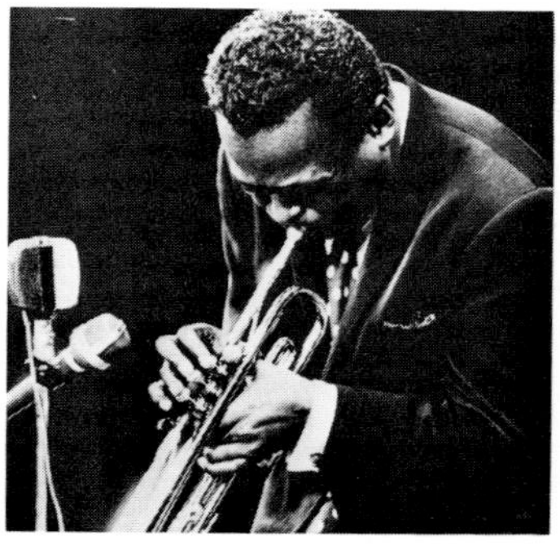

Miles Davis successfully blended jazz virtuosity with the energy of rock music.

and economically one of the most important palms. It has feather-shaped leaves and large flower clusters that produce the popular fruit. Height: up to 30.5m (100ft). Family Palmae. *See also* NW p.62.

Datolite, colourless or white orthosilicate mineral, basic calcium borosilicate, $CaBSi:O_4(OH)$, found in cavities in trap-rock. It occurs as monoclinic system crystals or, rarely, as granular masses. Hardness 5–5.5; s.g. 2.9.

Datura, genus of plants. Some produce useful drugs, others are ornamentals. The flowers are large, trumpet-shaped and sweet-smelling. Thorn-apple, or jimson-weed, (*Datura stramonium*) is the source of a crude narcotic. Family Solanaceae (the NIGHTSHADES).

Daubenton, Louis Jean-Marie (1716–1800), French comparative anatomist. He assisted Georges BUFFON with *Histoire Naturelle* (1749–1804). His research on mammalian skeletal structure aided the development of comparative anatomy into a special branch of study.

Daubigny, Charles-François (1817–78), French landscape painter, associated with the BARBIZON SCHOOL. Many of Daubigny's paintings are atmospheric oils of the Seine and Oise river areas, eg *River Scene with Ducks,* but he also worked in Britain, Holland, Italy and Spain.

Daudet, Alphonse (1840–97), French novelist. His works include the sketches *Lettres de mon moulin* (1869), *Aventures Prodigieuses de Tartarin de Tarascon* (1872), one of a series of burlesque tales, and the novels *Les Rois en exil* (1879) and *L'Immortel* (1888).

Daughters of the American Revolution (DAR), US patriotic society founded in 1890. Its members are female lineal descendants of activists in the cause of American independence. The DAR was chartered by the US Congress in 1895. In the 1970s there were 2,800 local chapters and about 188,000 members.

Daumier, Honoré (1808–79), French painter, sculptor and caricaturist. His great achievement was the lampooning of French middle-class society in more than 4,000 lithographs, worked in a realist style.

Dauphin, title of heir of the French monarch from 1350 to 1830. The name was originally that of the rulers of Viennois, SE France, lands known as the Dauphiné, which were sold to the French crown in 1349. Lands in Auvergne were also so named and passed to the French crown in 1693.

Davao, port and largest city on Mindanao island, in the Philippines, on the Davao Gulf, in the Davao Del Sur province. The city was taken by the Japanese in WWII. During the 1960s Davao's industry grew and its population more than doubled. It is now the commercial centre of a prosperous farming region. Products: hemp, timber, rice, copra, tobacco. Pop. 463,700.

Davenant or D'Avenant, Sir William (1606–68), English poet, dramatist and poet laureate (1638–68), rumoured to have been Shakespeare's son. His *Siege of Rhodes* (1656) was the first English opera. Other works include the epic *Gondibert* and the plays *The Tragedy of Albovine* and *The Wits.*

David, Saint (*d. c.*600), patron saint of Wales. A great ascetic in the tradition of early British Christianity, he founded many churches in S Wales. Feast: 1 March.

David, King of Israel (*r.c.*1000–962 BC), ruler who came to prominence by defeating the PHILISTINE champion Goliath. He became one of the greatest kings and heroes of the Jews, unifying the tribes and moving the capital from Hebron to JERUSALEM. His history is related in several versions in the Old Testament, and many of the psalms are attributed to him. *See also* HC1 p.58, *58.*

David, name of two kings of Scotland. David I (1084–1153) came to the throne in 1124. His interests in Cumbria and Northumbria involved him in the English civil war on the side of MATILDA against STEPHEN, who defeated him in 1138. He introduced Anglo-Norman feudalism to Scotland and strengthened the towns. David II (1324–71) became king in 1329 and was defeated by EDWARD III of England at Halidon Hill in 1333. He was exiled to France, and was again defeated in England in 1346 following his return to Scotland in 1341. He was released on ransom in 1357. *See also* HC1 pp.182–183, 244, *245.*

David, Gerard, or Gheerardt (*c.*1460–1523), Flemish painter who succeeded MEMLING as the most important painter of the school. Though influenced by Van EYCK and Van der WEYDEN, David has an austere grace that is distinctive. He was commissioned by the town of Bruges to paint several works, including two to warn officials of the retribution for injustice, *The Judgement of Cambyses* and *The Flaying of Sisamnes.* Among his other works are *Madonna Enthroned* and *Annunciation.*

David, Jacques-Louis (1748–1825), French painter of historical scenes and portraits. As leader of the Neo-classical movement, he had a great influence on art and fashion. Influenced by POUSSIN and Greek and Roman art, David's work was involved with his Jacobin views and support of Napoleon. His most famous work is *Oath of the Horati* (Horatii) and his many masterpieces include *Death of Marat, Mm Recamier* and *Death of Socrates. See also* HC2 pp.43, *43,* 80.

David, Pierre-Jean (David d'Angers) (1788–1856), French sculptor whose works include the statue of the Grand Conde at Versailles and statues of Lafayette and Jefferson in Washington, D.C.

David (1504), sculpture by MICHELANGELO, commissioned by the city of Florence in 1501. It was sculpted from a piece of white marble abandoned by an earlier sculptor, and epitomizes the confidence and idealism of the high Renaissance.

David Copperfield (1849–50), semi-autobiographical novel by Charles DICKENS, which he called his "favourite child". Copperfield retrospectively relates his adventures, misfortunes and eventual success and happiness.

Davidson, John (1857–1909), Scottish writer. His novels, plays and poems, including two series of *Fleet Street Eclogues* (1893, 1896), won critical acclaim but were not commercial successes. He committed suicide after a life of poverty in London.

Davidson, Thomas (1840–1900), Scottish-born US philosopher and lecturer. In 1883 he founded the Fellowship of the New Life, from which the FABIAN SOCIETY developed. He also started lecture classes for workers and a summer school in New York State. His many books include *Aristotle and Ancient Educational Ideals* (1892) and *History of Education* (1900).

Davie, Alan (1920–), Scottish painter, lithographer and jazz musician, influenced by ACTION PAINTING and especially Jackson POLLOCK. Davie's own experience as a goldsmith and jazz musician and his interest in Zen Buddhism enabled him to use colour in a sensual, freely improvized fashion, full of rhythm and movement.

Davie, Donald (1922–), British poet and critic. His collections of poetry include *Brides of Reason* (1955), *Events and Wisdoms* (1964) and *The Shires* (1975). His critical works include *Articulate Energy* (1957) and *Thomas Hardy and British Poetry* (1972).

Davies, Arthur Bowen (1862–1928), US painter of romantic landscapes with whimsical figures. A member of the EIGHT and president of the Society of Independent Artists, Davies organized the 1913 ARMORY SHOW, introducing modern European art to the USA.

Davies, Sir Henry Walford (1869–1941), British composer and organist who became famous for his popular radio talks. He was organist at Temple Church, London (1898–1918), and St George's Chapel, Windsor (1927–32). He was made Master of the King's Musick in 1934.

Davies, Sir John (1569–1626), English poet and government official, attorney-general for Ireland (1606–19). His poetry, which was often a vehicle for his philosophical reflections, includes *Orchestra* (1596), *Nosce Teipsum* (1599) and *Hymns of Astraea* (1599).

Davies, Lynn (1942–), Welsh long-jumper; the first Welsh Olympic gold medallist when, at Tokyo in 1964, his jump of 8.07m (26ft 5¾) beat established favourites. In 1966 he won European and Commonwealth golds to complete a unique treble, retaining his Commonwealth title in 1970.

Davies, Peter Maxwell (1934–), British composer. His first published work was the trumpet sonata of 1955. He is a prolific and varied composer, who has made much use of jazz rhythms and idioms. He wrote film music for *The Devils* (1971) and two operas, *Taverner* (1970) and *The Martyrdom Of St Magnus* (1977).

Davies, Rhys (1903–), Welsh novelist and short-story writer. He writes on Welsh themes, with lyrical beauty. His novels include *The Withered Root* (1927) and *Girl Waiting in the Shade* (1960). He has published a play, *No Escape* (1954), and many story collections, including *Pig in a Poke* (1931).

Davies, Robertson (1913–), Canadian novelist, dramatist and journalist. His sharp wit and polished satire are developed to the fullest in his novel *A Mixture of Frailties* (1958).

Davies, William Henry (1871–1940), Welsh poet. After living as a tramp in Britain and the USA he wrote his *Autobiography of a Super Tramp* (1907). Thereafter he wrote many volumes of simple, unaffected verse.

Davin, Dan (1913–), New Zealand-born writer resident in Britain. Most of his novels deal with New Zealand or New Zealanders abroad. They include *Cliffs of Fall* (1945), *Roads from Home* (1949) and *Not Here Not Now* (1970). He also wrote *Crete,* a volume of WWII military history.

Da Vinci. *See* LEONARDO DA VINCI.

Davis, Bette (1908–), US film actress, real name Ruth Elizabeth Davis. She is well known for her intense roles in such films as *Of Human Bondage* (1934), *Dangerous* (1935), *The Petrified Forest* (1936), *Jezebel* (1938), *The Old Maid* (1939) and *All About Eve* (1950).

Davis, Colin (1927–), British conductor. In 1971 he was appointed musical director of the Royal Opera, COVENT GARDEN. He was principal conductor of the BBC Symphony Orchestra from 1967 to 1971.

Davis, Dwight Filley (1879–1945), US public official, champion tennis player and donor of the DAVIS CUP. He enlisted in the army in WWI and rose from the rank of private to lieutenant-colonel. He was secretary of war (1925–29) and governor-general of the Philippines (1929–32).

Davis, Jefferson (1808–89), President of the Confederate States of America (1861–65). He was elected to Congress in 1845 but resigned to fight in the Mexican War in 1846. He was made secretary of war in 1853 but resigned from the Senate when Mississippi seceded from the Union, and he became president of the Confederate States. He served two years in prison and was indicted for treason in 1866, but never tried. *See also* HC2 pp.150–151, *151.*

Davis, Joe (1901–), British billiards and snooker professional, the first to hold both world titles at once; billiards 1928–33, snooker 1927–47. His best championship break at billiards was 2,052 in 1930, and in 1955 he achieved snooker's maximum break of 147.

Davis (or Davys), John (*c.*1550–1605), English explorer and inventor of the Davis quadrant. He made three voyages to Canada in search of a NORTH-WEST PASSAGE (1585–87) and explored the Davis Strait, Cumberland Gulf and Baffin Bay. In 1588 he fought against the Spanish Armada. *See also* HC1 p.278.

Davis, Miles Dewey Jr (1926–), US jazz trumpeter, one of the most influential of modern jazz players. During the 1940s he played with such musicians as Charlie PARKER, contributing to BEBOP. He developed an introspective style during the 1950s and 1960s with his own small

216

HC1 = History and Culture Vol. 1 HC2 = History and Culture Vol. 2 MS = Man and Society MM = Man and Machines

groups and made some notable recordings with the arranger Gil EVANS. During the 1970s his style changed to a blend of jazz and rock.

Davis, Paulina Wright (1813–76), US suffragette. She lectured to women on anatomy and physiology and helped to open the medical profession to them. She founded the first US women's rights newspaper, *Una* (1853), and wrote *A History of the National Women's Rights Movement* (1871).

Davis, Sammy, Jr (1925–), US singer, dancer and actor. In 1930 he joined his father and uncle in a music hall act. He appeared in several shows on Broadway, including *Mr Wonderful* (1956) and *Golden Boy* (1964), and in many films, such as *Porgy and Bess* (1959).

Davis, Stuart (1894–1964), US painter. His work depicted modern city life in a style influenced by FAUVISM and CUBISM. In 1927 he began a series of still-lifes on the theme of an eggbeater.

Davis Cup, men's international tennis team competition conceived by the American Dwight F. DAVIS and first contested in 1900. The holders met the foremost challenger annually until 1971 when the Challenge Round was replaced by a zonal knock-out producing two finalists.

Davisson, Clinton Joseph (1881–1958), US physicist, who worked on thermionics, electron DIFFRACTION and the electron MICROSCOPE for the Bell Telephone Laboratories. In 1927, working with L. H. Germer, he was able to confirm by means of diffraction by crystals the wave nature of moving electrons, which had been hypothesized by Louis DE BROGLIE. He shared the Nobel Prize in physics with G. P. THOMSON in 1937.

Davitt, Michael (1846–1906), Irish nationalist. He became a Fenian and was imprisoned in 1870. Released in 1877 he established the Irish Land League two years later to help tenants against absentee landlords. He favoured the nationalization of land and as a result was opposed to Charles PARNELL. *See also* HC2 pp.162–163.

Davy, Sir Humphry, (1778–1829), British chemist whose studies in electrolytic cells convinced him that they produce electricity by chemical means, and led to his isolation of the elements SODIUM and POTASSIUM. He proved that all acids contain hydrogen and that this is responsible for their acidic properties, and he explained the BLEACHING action of chlorine. As a result of an investigation of the conditions under which FIREDAMP (methane and other gases) and air explode, he invented the miner's safety lamp which is named after him. He was created a baronet in 1818. *See also* SU pp.134, 148.

Davy Jones, malevolent spirit or personification of the sea. "Davy Jones's locker" is the bottom of the ocean or the grave of men drowned or buried at sea. The origin of the phrase is unknown, but it may refer to Jonah (or Jonas) the prophet.

Dawe, Donald Bruce (1930–), Australian poet. He was a labourer and postman until 1962, when he published *No Fixed Address.* He has also published *An Eye for a Tooth* (1968) and *Beyond the Subdivision* (1969).

Dawes, Charles Gates (1865–1951), US politician. He was a lawyer and banker, and served as comptroller of the currency under William MCKINLEY. In 1923 he headed the financial commission that drew up the DAWES PLAN (1924) to restructure the German economy, for which he received the 1925 Nobel Peace Prize. He was vice-president (1925–29) to Calvin COOLIDGE.

Dawes, John (1940–), Welsh rugby union player. A centre with London Welsh, he played 22 times for Wales (1964–71) and in 1971 captained the British Lions to unprecedented victory in New Zealand. He coached Wales and the 1977 Lions in New Zealand.

Dawes, William Jr (1745–99), US patriot. He rode from Boston to Lexington and Concord on 18 April 1775 to warn the colonists of the arrival of British troops. He was joined on the way by Paul REVERE and Dr Sam PRESCOTT.

Dawes Plan (1924), financial measure devised by Charles DAWES to collect and distribute WWI reparations payments. It established a schedule of payments that Germany could bear and arranged for a loan of 800 million marks by US bankers to the German Government to stabilize German currency.

Dawson, Peter (1882–1961), Australian baritone. Although he sang in opera, it was as a recording artist (from 1904) and concert singer that he achieved renown. He recorded about 2,500 songs, one of the most popular being *The Road to Mandalay.*

Dawson (Dawson City), town in W Yukon Territory, Canada, at the confluence of the Yukon and Klondike rivers, 80km (50 miles) E of the Alaskan border. It was a boom town during the Yukon gold rush in 1896 and the capital of Yukon Territory from 1898 until 1952. Pop. 750.

Day, Doris (1924–), US singer and actress, *b.* Doris Kappelhof. Her recordings sold millions in the 1940s and 1950s – eg, *Sentimental Journey* (1945), *Secret Love* (1954) – and her fresh ebullience enhanced such films as *Calamity Jane* (1953), *Pajama Game* (1957), *The Man Who Knew Too Much* (1956) and *Send Me No Flowers* (1964).

Day, John (*c.* 1574–1640), English dramatist. Much of his work has been lost and he is best remembered for *The Parliament of Bees* (*c.* 1607), an allegorical masque made up of a series of six "characters" in dialogue form.

Dayaks, number of tribes in BORNEO, probably descendants of the original Indian settlers of the Malay archipelago. The family is the chief unit of social life, and they practise ANCESTOR WORSHIP; their main crop is rice. They are famous for their carved shields and masks, which are used in ceremonial dances, and also for their wood and bone carvings of people and animals.

Dayananda Sarasvati (1824–83), Indian religious leader, *b.* Mula Sankara. Discontented with the HINDUISM of his day, he became the major spokesman for a return to the authority of the VEDAS. He condemned idol worship, child marriage and the low status of women, advocated many social reforms and founded the ARYA SAMAJ (Society of Nobles) in 1875.

Daydreaming, indulging in fantasy and reverie while awake. The mind is allowed to wander aimlessly, usually through pleasurable or gratifying events or images. It is said to be motivated by unfulfilled and often unconscious desires. It is also a way of briefly overcoming frustration.

Day-Lewis, Cecil (1904–72), British poet and critic. His concern for social justice and socialist causes is evident in his poetry, which includes *Transitional Poem* (1929), *Magnetic Mountain* (1933), *Overtures to Death* (1938) and *Collected Poems* (1954). He was poet laureate (1968–72). He also wrote detective stories under the pen-name Nicholas Blake.

Dayr az-Zawr, town in E Syria, on the River Euphrates; capital of Dayr az-Zawr governorate. The town was taken by the British in 1941 and became part of independent Syria in 1946. Today it is a trading and transport centre for a large farming region. Pop. 42,036.

Dayton, city in SW Ohio, USA, at the confluence of the Great Miami and Stillwater rivers, 75km (47 miles) N of Cincinnati. It is a commercial centre for the surrounding agricultural region. Its industries include domestic appliances and cash registers. Pop. (1970) 243,601.

Dazbog, in Slavonic mythology, the sun god, son of the sky god SVAROG. Dazbog was often described as riding in a magnificent chariot and became a symbol of prosperity and power. With the advent of Christianity, he sometimes became identified with the Devil, in Serbian folklore.

D-Day (6 June 1944), code-name for the Allied invasion of Normandy during WWII. The Americans and British, commanded by EISENHOWER overall and with MONTGOMERY in charge of the land forces, landed on the coast between Cherbourg and Le Havre in a combined air and sea invasion. Despite severe opposition, they established their bridgeheads by 9 June and from there captured the whole of N France. *See also* HC2 pp.228–231.

DDT, dichlorodiphenyltrichloroethane, colourless crystalline organic halogen compound, first used as an INSECTICIDE in 1939 against the Colorado potato beetle. It acts as a contact poison, disorganizing the nervous system. It kills fleas, moths, beetles and other destructive insects, and is effective against the anopheles mosquito, which carries MALARIA. Many species, however, have successfully developed resistant populations. Birds and fish feeding on affected insects suffer toxic effects, as do many animals and man if those birds and fish are eaten; as it is not easily degraded into non-toxic components DDT may persist in FOOD CHAINS for a long time. The use of DDT has consequently been banned in many countries.

Deacon, ordained priest's assistant in the ministry of the Christian church. The institution of the deaconate can be traced to the New Testament, which describes the ordination of seven deacons, including St STEPHEN and St PHILIP (Acts 6: 1–6), to carry out the administrative work of the early Church allowing others more time for evangelical work.

Deadly nightshade, also called belladonna, poisonous perennial plant native to Europe and western Asia. It has large leaves, dull purple flowers and shiny black berries. Alkaloids such as ATROPINE have been obtained from the roots and leaves, and eating the fruits can be fatal. Family Solanaceae; species *Atropa belladonna. See also* MS pp.*86*, *117*, 119.

Deadnettle, tall flowering plant of the genus *Lamium*; it closely resembles the stinging NETTLE, but the leaf, though hairy, has no sting. It has pointed, oval, toothed leaves and yellow or purple flowers. Family Labiatae.

Dead reckoning, navigational method that determines the position and speed of a ship or aircraft without the help of celestial observation (sighting of the sun, stars or moon). Calculations are made from the records of the course, distance and time already covered using the log and a compass; they also take into account drift due to wind or currents.

Dead Sea (Al-Bahr-al-Mayyit), salt lake on the border of Jordan and Israel, fed by the River Jordan and several small streams. The surface, 396m (1,302ft) below sea-level, is the lowest point on earth. It is situated in a hot, dry region and much water is lost through evaporation; input has also been reduced by the use of the Jordan's waters for irrigation purposes, so the water level fluctuates throughout the year. One of the saltiest waters in the world, it supports no life, and large quantities of salts (potash, bromides and chlorides) are commercially extracted.

Dead Sea Scrolls, manuscripts of leather and papyrus discovered in and after 1947 in caves and ruins near the Dead Sea, mostly around QUMRAN. These documents, written in Hebrew or Aramaic, most of them between 100 BC and AD 50, provide valuable information about the culture in which early Christianity spread. They include versions of most of the Old Testament, many apocryphal and pseudographical works, biblical commentaries and other documents. *See also* HC1 p *110*; MS p.*246*.

Dead Souls (1842), novel by Nikolai GOGOL. Chichikov, an impoverished nobleman, buys "dead souls" – serfs registered on the last census but who have since died. The landowners sell as they have to pay a tax on the souls until the next census and Chichikov profits by being able to raise a mortgage on them.

Deadwood, town in the Black Hills of W South Dakota, USA, which was settled in 1876 after the discovery of gold. Wild Bill Hickok and Calamity Jane are buried there. Industries: tourism, mining, timber. Pop. (1970) 2,409.

Deafness, part or total lack of the sense of hearing. The congenitally deaf people are born deaf; the adventitiously deaf are born with normal hearing but lose it later in life. There are three major types of

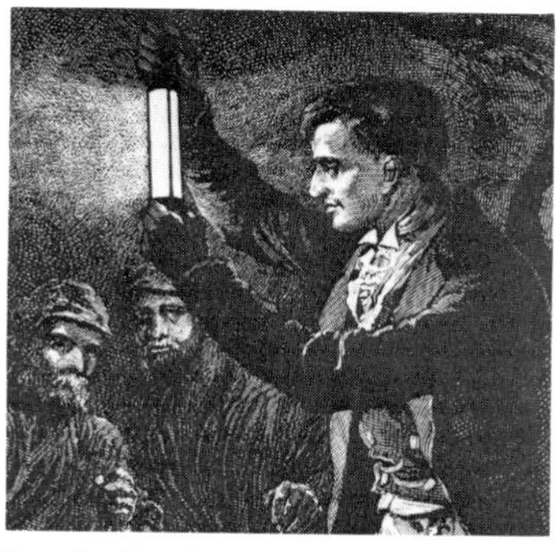

Humphry Davy's lamp, which prevented the ignition of explosive gases in coal mines.

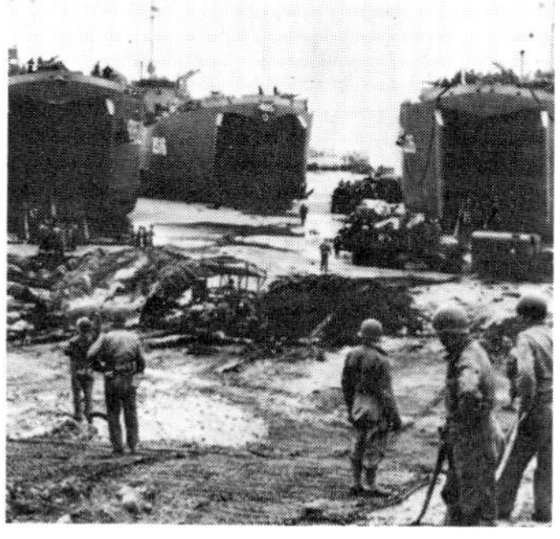

D-Day; allied troops land on the beaches of France to begin the liberation of Nazi Europe.

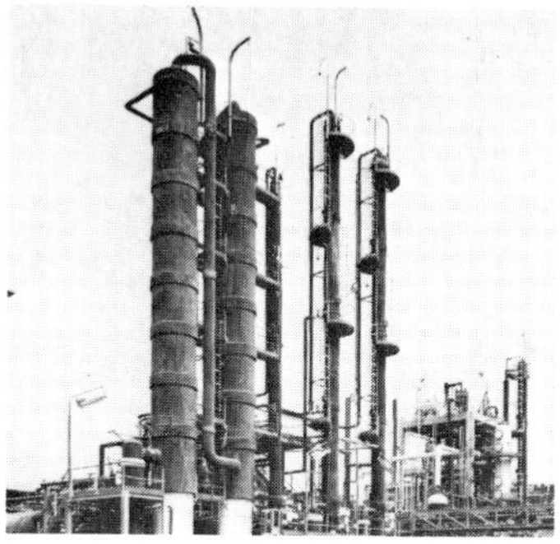

DDT; large-scale production of the insecticide which is now feared to be harmful to man.

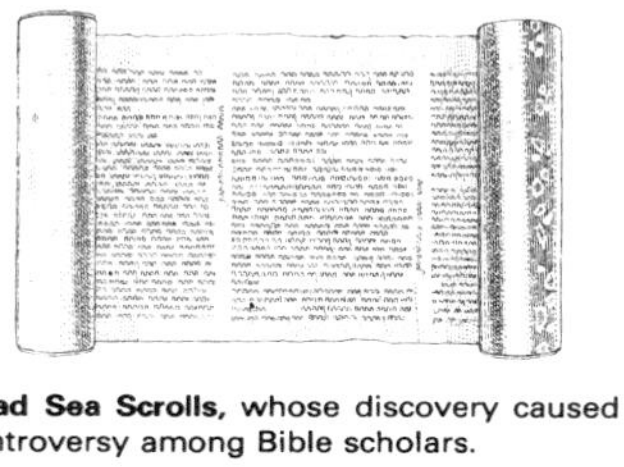

Dead Sea Scrolls, whose discovery caused controversy among Bible scholars.

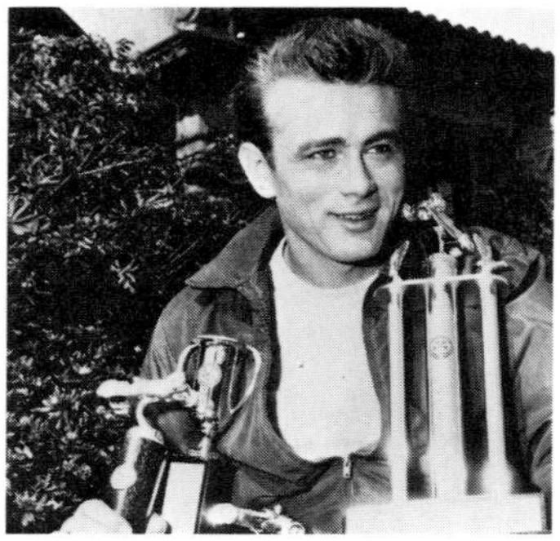

James Dean, the teenage cult movie star, proudly displays his motor racing trophies.

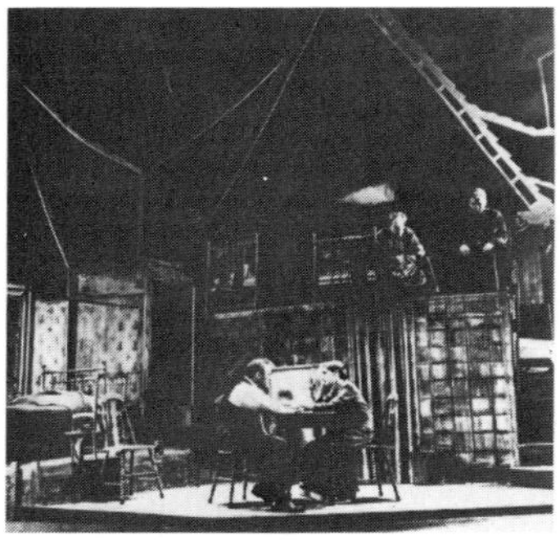

Death of a Salesman explores the tragedy of man in a hopelessly materialistic society.

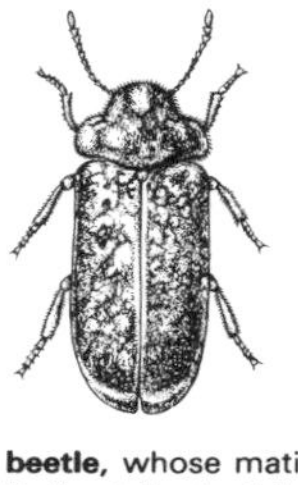

Deathwatch beetle, whose mating call was once believed to foretell a death in the family.

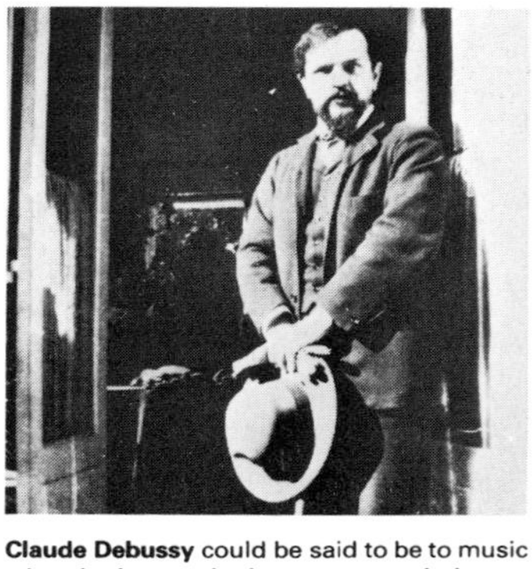

Claude Debussy could be said to be to music what the impressionists were to painting.

deafness: (1) conductive hearing loss (the most prevalent), in which there is interference with the transmission of sound to the sense organs in the middle or inner ear, often as a result of a childhood infection or the development of bony abnormalities later in life. (2) Sensory-neural hearing loss, usually occurring at birth due to intra-uterine infection, Rh incompatibility or other nerve damage, or developing in later life as a result of neural degeneration and advancing age. (3) Central hearing loss or abnormality in the central nervous system, occurring because of brain damage or disease, or various psychogenic disorders. The treatment of deafness depends on its cause and ranges from the removal of impacted wax and the administration of drugs to combat infection to delicate surgical and microsurgical procedures that can, for instance, correct some congenital malformations and bony growths. Electronic hearing aids that amplify sound help many who are hard-of-hearing, and the use of sign language and speech reading or lip-reading techniques help the deaf to lead a normal life. *See also* MS pp.50–51, 239.

Deakin, Alfred (1856–1919), Australian politician. A leader of the Liberal Party, he was prime minister of Australia in 1903–04, 1905–08 and 1909–10. He pressed for social reforms in various areas. In 1901 he became the first attorney-general of Australia. *See also* HC2 p.*127*.

Deal, town in Kent, SE England, 13km (8 miles) NE of Dover on the Straits of Dover. It was one of the CINQUE PORTS. It is a port for ship and hovercraft services to Calais and other French towns. The chief industries are tourism and fishing. Pop. 25,400.

Dean, title of various church officials. For example, the dean of a cathedral controls its services and supervises its fabric and property. Rural deans assist a BISHOP in his administrative duties. The heads of collegiate churches such as Westminster Abbey are also called deans.

Dean, Basil (1888–1971), British theatrical producer and actor. During WWII he founded and directed ENSA (Entertainments National Service Association).

Dean, Bill ("Dixie") (1907–), British association footballer, a strongly built centre-forward who played for Everton, Nottingham County and Tranmere Rovers. With Everton in 1927–28 he scored 60 goals in Division I, a Football League record. He appeared 16 times for England (1927–32), scoring 18 goals.

Dean, James (1931–55), US film actor. In 1954, he played the restless son in the film adaptation of John Steinbeck's novel *East of Eden*, and in 1955 appeared as a misunderstood drag-racing teenager in *Rebel Without a Cause*. He was killed in a car crash the year before the release of his final film *Giant* and became a cult hero. *See also* MS p.*166*.

Dean, Forest of, ancient royal forest 32km (20 miles) long and 16km (10 miles) wide in Gloucestershire, W England, situated between the Severn and Wye rivers. The remains of Roman coal mines have been found there and mining continues today. In 1938 it became the first of the National Forest Parks of Britain.

Dearborn, Henry (1751–1829), US general who distinguished himself in the American War of Independence. He fought at Bunker Hill, marched against Quebec, served in the Saratoga, Valley Forge and Monmouth campaigns and at Yorktown.

Dearborn, Fort, fort in NE Illinois, USA. It was built by the US Government in 1803 on the S bank of the Chicago River and became the nucleus of present-day Chicago. It was abandoned during the war of 1812 and destroyed by Indians, but was rebuilt in 1816–17.

Dease, Peter Warren (1788–1863), Canadian fur trader and explorer. He was employed by the Northwest and Hudson's Bay companies and explored the Mackenzie River, Point Barrow, Athabasca, New Caledonia and the Great Bear Lake.

Death, cessation of the body's physical life. The definition of death has become controversial in recent years with advances in medicine. It is now possible to revive people in the minutes after somatic death, ie, the stopping of the heart and of breathing, with few ill effects if recovery follows. Also, the need for organs for transplant from the recently dead has led to death being defined in terms of the complete cessation of all levels of activity in the nervous system. *See also* MS pp.180–181.

Death, Be Not Proud, religious sonnet by John DONNE, expressing faith that after the Last Judgement death itself shall die.

Death cap, also called deadly amanita, highly poisonous FUNGUS that grows in wooded areas, especially under beech or oak trees. It has a yellowish-green, indistinctly streaky cap about 9cm (3.5in) across. The gills are white, like the stem, which bears a pendulous ring and has a sheathed base. If eaten, the poison may take eight hours to show any effect, after which time it may cause great pain, serious liver damage and, in most cases, death. Species *Amanita phalloides*. *See also* NW p.*43*.

Death in Venice (1911), novella by Thomas Mann. In it he used the conflict between spirituality and weariness in a great writer to symbolize the decay of Western art. It was made into a film in 1971 by Luchino VISCONTI, and an opera by Benjamin BRITTEN (1973).

Death of a Salesman (1949), two-act drama by Arthur MILLER. It tells the story of a well-meaning salesman whose career and family life are nevertheless a failure, and he kills himself so that his family can receive his insurance money.

Death penalty. *See* CAPITAL PUNISHMENT.

Death rate, or mortality rate, statistic that gives the number of deaths in a population. The most common type is the crude death rate, or the number of deaths per 1,000 population per year. Death rates can also be correlated with age groups, classes, geographical distribution and causes of death. *See also* MS pp.108–109.

Death rites, rituals performed after a person's death, often to sustain their passage from life to the realm of the dead. The form of the rites varies enormously from culture to culture and may last several weeks or a few minutes. Although the rites perform a function for the dead, eg, providing symbolic food for their passage or offering prayers for the deceased spirit, they also have a function for the living in helping them through mourning. *See also* MS pp.180–181, 204–205, 214–215.

Death's head hawk-moth, large European HAWK-MOTH named after the skull-like markings on the back of its thorax. It has a short proboscis and often feeds on honey from beehives. It makes a squeaking sound that can be detected by the human ear. Order Lepidoptera; species *Acherontia atropos*.

Death Valley, large desert in E California, USA, almost surrounded by high mountains, the Panamint Range (W) and the Armagosa Range (E). It has the lowest point in the western hemisphere, 86m (282ft) below sea-level. It was so named in 1849 by gold-seekers, many of whom were lost trying to cross it. Summer temperatures can reach 56.7°C (134°F), the highest in the USA. Gold and silver were mined there in the 1850s and borax was mined in large quantities in the late 19th century. Length: 225km (140 miles).

Deathwatch beetle, small beetle that tunnels through wood, especially in old buildings. It makes a faint ticking sound which was once said to presage the death of one of the occupants of the building. The sound is actually the mating signal of the female as it taps its head against the wood. Length: to 0.9cm (0.3in). Family Anobiidae; species *Xestobium rufovillosum*.

De Beers Consolidated Mines Ltd, diamond-mining company founded by Cecil RHODES in 1888. It was formed by a merger of Rhodes' De Beers mines and the Kimberley mines of Barney BARNATO. It is South Africa's largest company in sales, profits and assets and it controls almost 80 per cent of the world's diamond sales.

Debentures, loans to companies with a promise to pay back a particular amount of money on a specific date at a certain rate of interest. Debentures are usually very secure; if the company fails to repay the loan the debenture holders can sell the company's assets to obtain payment.

Debit, in accounting, an entry on the left side of an account. Expenditure is recorded through a debit entry. The term "charge" is sometimes used interchangeably with the term "debit".

Debrecen, city in E Hungary, 193km (120 miles) E of Budapest. The city was named the "Calvinist Rome" because of its Great Protestant Church which was a stronghold of Hungarian Protestantism in the 16th century. Louis Kossuth proclaimed Hungary's independence there in 1849. Industries: food processing, farm machinery, furniture. Pop. (1974) 179,755.

Debrett, John (*c.*1750–1822), British publisher. In 1802 he published a complete reference guide to the British peerage. Up-to-date editions have continued to be published and still bear the title *Debrett's Peerage and Baronetage*.

Debriefing, process whereby information is obtained from soldiers or astronauts after returning from a mission.

De Broglie, Louis Victor, and Maurice, French physicists. Louis Victor (1892–) in 1924 hypothesized that particles should manifest certain wave-like properties, such as frequency and diffraction effects, for which, in 1929 he received the Nobel Prize in physics. He was elected to the French Academy of Sciences in 1933. Maurice (1875–1960), brother of Louis Victor, contributed notable work in the fields of X-rays, electricity and atomic physics.

Debt, National, public debt of a government, usually guaranteed by the national revenue. In Britain it has been accumulated historically by borrowing from the British people; more recently the main lenders have been overseas countries and the INTERNATIONAL MONETARY FUND. It is divided into two kinds: the funded debt, which is converted into bonds and annuities, and the floating debt, short-term loans repaid from taxation. The national debt assumed a permanent form in 1694, when it stood at about £14 million. It grew rapidly in the 18th century, when the government had to finance its anti-French wars. By 1818 it stood at £840 million, the interest being more than 7% of national income. Since 1918 Britain has been, internationally, a debtor nation. The current debt, to both international and national creditors, stands at about £35,000 million.

Debussy, Claude Achille (1862–1918), French composer, exponent of the Impressionist movement in music. Contrary to the trends of his time, Debussy wrote highly original music that was delicate, soft and suggestive rather than dramatic and direct. He explored new techniques of harmony and orchestral colour. Some critics mark Debussy's *Prélude à l'Après-midi d'un Faune* (1894) as the beginning of 20th-century music. His orchestral works also include *Nocturnes* (1899), *La Mer* (1905) and *Images* (1909). His piano works, among the most important in the piano repertoire, include the *Suite Bergamasque* (1905, containing the famous *Clair de lune*). His one opera is *Pelléas and Mélisande* (1902). *See also* HC2 pp.107, 121.

Debye, Peter Joseph Wilhelm (1884–1966), US physical chemist, *b.* The Netherlands. He is best known for his work on molecular structure and ionization in solution. He also pioneered X-ray powder crystallography. He was awarded the 1936 Nobel Prize in chemistry.

Decadents, term applied to writers of the late 19th century who believed in the artist's freedom from social and moral restraint. Influenced by Charles BAUDELAIRE, French decadents included the poets VERLAINE, MALLARMÉ and RIMBAUD. Verlaine contributed to the review *Le Décadent* (1886–89). English decadents, including Oscar WILDE and Aubrey BEARDSLEY, published much of their work in *The Yellow Book* (1894–97).

Decalogue. *See* TEN COMMANDMENTS.

Decameron (*c.*1348–53), collection of 100 stories by the Italian writer and poet Giovanni BOCCACCIO. The stories are writ-

ten as if narrated by ten young men and women who have escaped from the Florentine plague of 1348 and pass the time for ten days telling one another anecdotes, fabliaux, and fairy tales, many of them bawdy. *See also* HC1 pp.207, *207*.
Decapod, any of about 8,500 species of mainly marine, higher crustaceans, including shrimps, lobsters and crabs. They have ten legs including the chelae (pincers), which are enlarged modified legs. The order Decapoda has been represented since the Permian or Triassic period. *See also* NW pp.100–101, 104; PE pp.248–249.
Decathlon, sporting event made up of ten different track and field events. It takes place over a two-day period and is considered the most demanding in athletics. On the first day the individual must compete in a 100m race, long jump, shot put, high jump and a 400m race. The second day includes the 110m hurdles, discus, pole vault, javelin and 1,500m race. It was introduced as a three-day event in the Olympic Games of 1912.
Deccan, plateau in central India, S of the Narmada River. On its E and W edges it rises to ranges of hills called the Ghats. The plateau is covered with rich volcanic soils and cotton and cereal crops are grown there. In the S there are coffee and tea plantations. It was in the Deccan in the early 18th century that the Hindus began to regain their political power. Later in the century the British defeated the French there in their struggle for India.
Decembrists, name given to group of Russian officers and noblemen who staged an unsuccessful revolt against Tsar NICHOLAS I in December 1825. They were members of the Northern Society, a secret society demanding representative democracy. The Decembrists gathered 3,000 troops in Senate Square, St Petersburg, but they were ill-organized, and the tsar's troops quickly dispersed them.
Decibel (dB), logarithmic unit, one tenth of a bel, used for comparing two power levels. It is frequently used for expressing the loudness of a sound in terms of a particular reference level. The decibel difference between two sounds is given by $dB = 10 \log_{10} (P_1/P_2)$ where P_1 and P_2 are the power levels of the sounds. The faintest audible sound (2×10^{-5} PASCAL) is arbitrarily given a value of 0 dB. The human THRESHOLD OF PAIN is about 120 dB, and ordinary conversations occur at about 50 to 60 dB. *See also* SU p.80.
Deciduous, term describing the annual or seasonal loss of all leaves from a tree; it is the opposite of EVERGREEN. First, or milk, teeth in human beings are also referred to as deciduous.
Deciduous forest, area of vegetation composed mainly of DECIDUOUS trees, which lose all their leaves during one season. Such woodland is often dominated by oaks, chestnuts, birches, elms, beeches and larches. In tropical regions it is known as a MONSOON FOREST. *See also* NW pp.62–65, 206–209.
Decimal fractions, numbers in the DECIMAL SYSTEM (based on 10) that are written as digits to the right of a decimal point. The number 52.437 represents an integer (whole number, 52) added to a decimal fraction (0.437). It is composed of $52 + (4 \times 10^{-1}) + (3 \times 10^{-2}) + (7 \times 10^{-3})$, which may also be written $52 + (4/10 + 3/100 + 7/1000)$, $52 + 437/1000$, or 52,437/1000. Decimal fractions are added, subtracted, multiplied and divided like integers, but the decimal point must be correctly positioned after each operation. *See also* SU p.29.
Decimal system, commonly used system of writing numbers using a base ten and the Arabic numerals 0 to 9. It is a positional number system, each position to the left representing an extra power of ten. Thus 6,741 is $(6 \times 10^3) + (7 \times 10^2) + (4 \times 10^1) + (1 \times 10^0)$. Note that $10^0 = 1$. Decimal fractions are represented by negative powers of ten placed to the right of a decimal point. Thus, 3,145 is $3 + (1 \times 10^{-1}) + (4 \times 10^{-2}) + (5 \times 10^{-3})$, or $3 + 1/10 + 4/100 + 5/1000$. *See also* SU pp.30–31.
Decius, Gaius Messius Quintus Trajanus (AD 200–51), Roman emperor (*r.* 249–51). In an attempt to strengthen the state religion he was responsible for the especially cruel and methodical persecution of Christians in the empire. *See also* HC1 p.114, *114*.
Declaration of Independence. *See* AMERICAN INDEPENDENCE, DECLARATION OF.
Declaration of Rights. *See* BILL OF RIGHTS.
Declaration of the Rights of Man and Citizen (1789), statement of the principles of the FRENCH REVOLUTION. It was adopted by the National Assembly, accepted by LOUIS XVI, and included in the constitution of 1791. Influenced by the AMERICAN DECLARATION OF INDEPENDENCE and the ideas of ROUSSEAU, it established the sovereignty of the people and the restrictions for social consideration embodied in "liberty, equality, and fraternity". *See also* HC2 pp.74–75.
Declaratory Act (1766), law in which the British Parliament asserted its right to legislate for the American colonies if it so wished, after the repeal of the STAMP ACT. *See also* HC2 pp.64–65.
Declension, term for a particular class of noun in a specified language, classified according to the system by which the noun inflects to indicate gender, number and case. The term also describes the system of inflection involved: the various genders and the case endings, which also take account of singular and plural, and any alternative. In many languages pronouns, adjectives, prepositions and even articles undergo declension.
Declination, angular distance of a CELESTIAL BODY N or S of the CELESTIAL EQUATOR (N is positive, S is negative), measured in degrees along a line passing through the body and the CELESTIAL POLES. Declination and right ascension form the axes of the co-ordinate system used with reference to the celestial equator.
Declination, magnetic, angle between the magnetic lines of force and the meridians of latitude. Declination is measured positively in degrees east or negatively west of magnetic north, which is the place pointed to by a compass. Lines of equal declination are isogonic lines, and the line of zero declination is the agonic line. *See also* PE p.22.
Decline and Fall of the Roman Empire, The History of the (1776–88), historical work in six volumes by Edward GIBBON. Written partly in Lausanne, it covers the periods from the reign of Trajan to the capture of Constantinople in 1453. The work is regarded as a masterpiece of literature as well as of history.
Decompression, rapid decrease in atmospheric pressure, experienced when the pressurized cabin of an aircraft is ruptured, or when a diver returns to the surface too quickly (giving rise to the BENDS). When someone works under pressures greater than atmospheric pressure, the respiratory gases are compressed and abnormally large amounts are dissolved in the blood and tissues. Sudden release of this pressure causes the gases to bubble off and interrupt the oxygen supply.
Decompression chamber, air-tight compartment capable of withstanding high pressures, used to house one or more divers or other personnel working in pressurized environments while they are gradually returned to normal atmospheric pressure. Compression chambers are necessary to avoid decompression sickness (the BENDS). Deep-sea divers usually work in teams so that work progresses while divers who have been relieved are progressively decompressed in submerged chambers at various depths. *See also* DECOMPRESSION; PE p.*92*.
Decompression sickness. *See* BENDS.
Decorated style, term used to describe the middle phase of GOTHIC architecture in England from about 1250 to 1350. Characteristic of the style was the use of vaulted portals and richly designed windows using narrow strips of stone in gently curved tracery, such as at Exeter Cathedral. Ribs in the vaults of portals became more purely decorative. *See also* HC1 p.216.
De Coster, Charles. *See* COSTER CHARLES..
Découpage, form of COLLAGE in which wood, metal or glass surfaces are decorated with paper cutouts or similar material and then permanently preserved by thin coats of varnish or lacquer. The technique is simple and has gained popularity as an easily accessible art form.
Decree, equivalent in a court of EQUITY of a judgement in a court of law. However, whereas a judgement is always given against one party, in equity a decree may bind both parties. In particular a decree may be an injunction upon one or both parties to behave in a certain way. The injunction may then be enforced by proceedings for CONTEMPT of court. The most common decree is the decree *nisi*, which dissolves a marriage and may award alimony.
Deductive logic, reasoning method, opposite to induction, where the conclusion follows necessarily from the premises (which, of course, need not be empirically true). The classical form of this method is in Aristotle's syllogisms. For example: "No green books are worth reading. All war books are green. Thus no war books are worth reading." (Green is known as the middle term in this syllogism.) The deductive method was greatly extended by the development of symbolic logic.
Deductive method. *See* AXIOMATIC METHOD.
Dee, John (1527–1608), English mathematician and occultist. He was an associate of the alchemist Edward Kelley and was a favourite of Queen Elizabeth I. He also did preparatory work on the Gregorian CALENDAR.
Dee, common British river name. The most well known is in Scotland; it rises in the Cairngorms, flows E through the Grampian Region, and enters the North Sea at Aberdeen. It is noted for its salmon. Length: 140km (87 miles).
Deed, in law a written document, the instrument authorizing the transfer of title to real property. It must be signed, sealed and (in Britain) delivered. There are two kinds of deed. A deed indented, or indenture, is one which binds two or more parties. Its name comes from the original practice, in the Middle Ages, of indenting each copy given to each party in order to make them tally with one another. A deed poll binds only one party and gets its name from its paper being polled, or shaven, to give it a clean-cut edge. Examples of deeds are conveyances and mortgages.
Deep freezing, method of FOOD PRESERVATION, usually at −5°C (23°F) or below. Some foods can last for years if properly frozen. Three methods are widely used for commercial deep freezing: in blast freezing, a flow of cold air is passed over the food; in contact freezing, the food is placed between refrigerated plates, or in a refrigerated alcohol bath; and in vapour freezing, liquid nitrogen, or solid carbon dioxide (dry ice) is made to vapourize in the food compartment. In home freezing, various refrigerated cabinets are used.
Deep scattering layer, (DSL), sound-reflecting layers in ocean water that are distinct enough at times to create a "false bottom". Various layers that can be detected during the day by sonar equipment disappear at night. Shoals of small deep-dwelling fish, crustaceans and squid that feed on the water surface at night seem to be the cause. DSLs occur in all oceans of the world and are found most commonly at depths of 400m to 800m during the daytime.
Deep-sea drilling project (project mohole). *See* DSDP.
Deep-sea reversing thermometer. *See* DSRT.
Deer, four-toed, long-legged, hoofed, RUMINANT mammal. There are 53 species in 17 genera distributed throughout the world in forests, arctic tundra, deserts, open bush and swamps. In most species the male (buck or stag) bears antlers formed from bone and covered, while growing, with a skin called "velvet"; they are grown and shed yearly and the male's age may often be estimated from the relative size and complexity of its antlers. Deer often gather in herds. They are generally brown, with spotted young (called fawns).

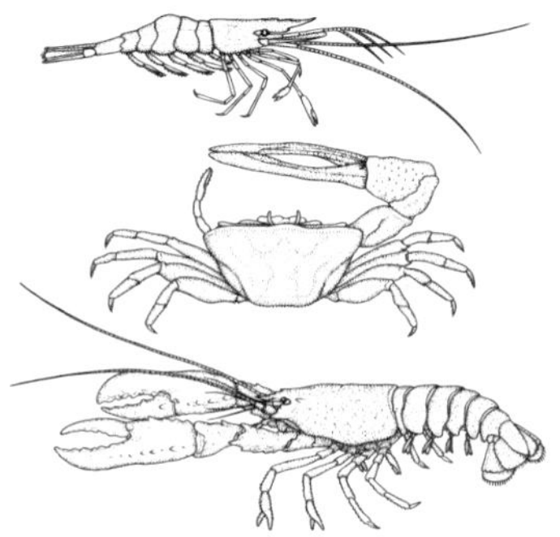
Decapods are the group of crustaceans which include the shrimps, lobsters and crabs.

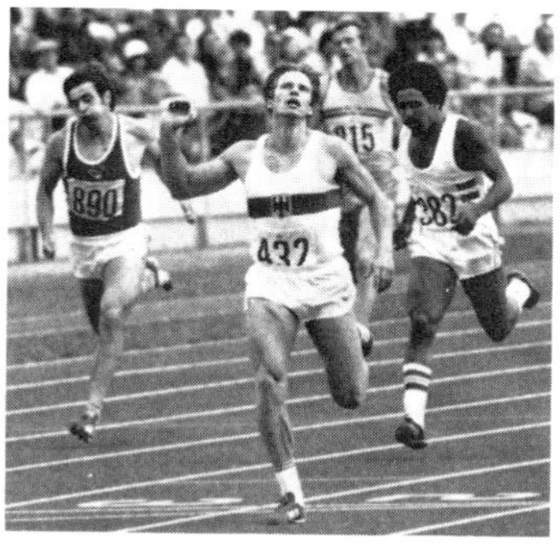
Decathalon athletes finishing the punishing 400m at the Montreal Olympic Games.

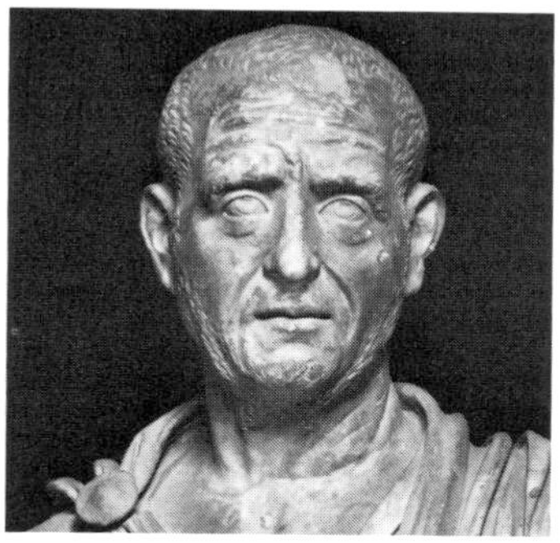
Decius used the Christians as scapegoats for his political and economic failures.

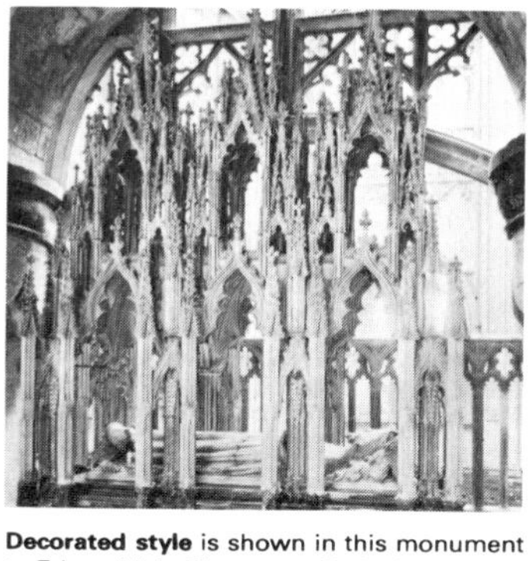
Decorated style is shown in this monument to Edward II in Gloucester Cathedral.

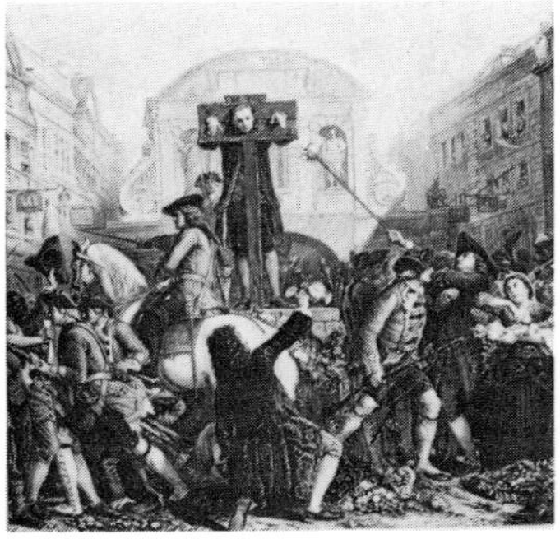

Daniel Defoe; a satirical print in which he is pilloried for his attitudes to religion.

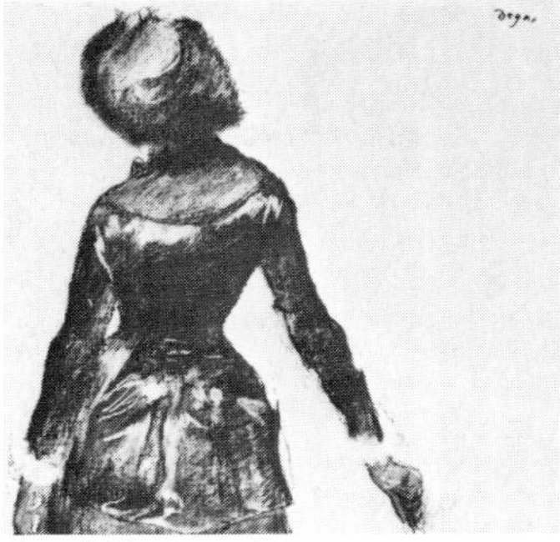

Edgar Degas was a superb sensitive draughtsman.

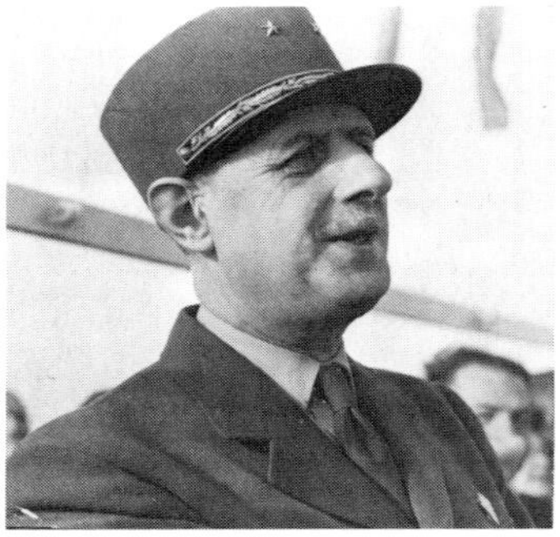

Charles de Gaulle's broadcasts from England inspired the people of occupied France.

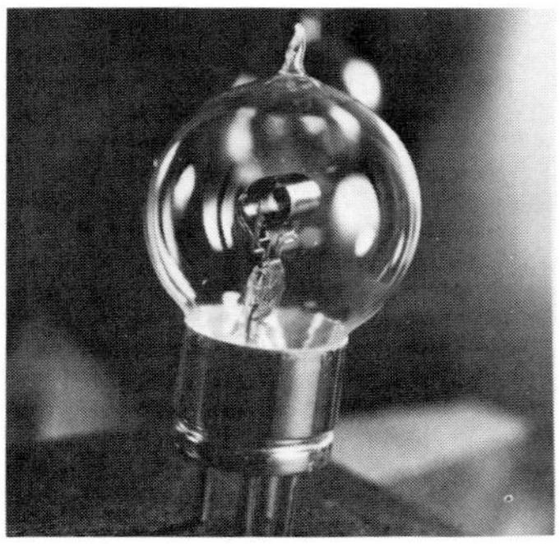

Lee De Forest's triode valve (1907) marked a crucial advance in early radio broadcasting.

They eat the bark of trees, young shoots, twigs and grass. Man exploits them for their meat (venison), hides and the antlers which are regarded as hunting trophies. The deer family Cervidae is known to have existed since the Oligocene epoch. Today the Chinese water deer is the smallest, measuring only 55cm (22in) tall at the shoulder; the moose, at 2m (6.5ft), is the largest. *See also* NW pp.162–163; PE pp.238–239, *253*.

Deere, John (1804–86), American blacksmith, industrialist and manufacturer of agricultural equipment. In 1837, in partnership with Leonard Andrus, he made one of the first steel ploughs. He went on to found his own firm, still making ploughs.

Deerhound, hunting-dog originally bred in Scotland and one of the oldest breeds in Britain; it has a long tapering head with low-set ears. Its long slim body is set on strong straight legs. The thick ragged coat may be grey or brindle. Height: over 76cm (30in) at the shoulder.

De facto, in law, condition in which a person or company acts with apparent right and under pretence of appointment or election, but is not legally qualified to do so. De facto acts are usually valid.

De Falla, Manuel. *See* FALLA, MANUEL DE.

Defamation. *See* LIBEL; SLANDER.

Default, in legal proceedings, the failure of a defendant or plaintiff to appear in court within a stated time. It is also the failure of a person to fulfil a legal obligation.

Defence, Ministry of, British department of state. It was first formed in 1940. In 1964 it was reorganized to combine in one department the old War office, ADMIRALTY and Air Ministry. It is presided over by a secretary of state, under whom there are two ministers of state, one for administration and one for equipment.

Defence mechanism, unconscious or involuntary reaction adopted by a person to protect him from the painful "effect" of a mental or physical event. A wide range of such mechanisms, from repression to mannerisms, is included in the term.

Defendant, in law, the person or persons against whom charges have been brought. A defendant may be either civil (not subject to arrest) or criminal (subject to arrest).

Defender of the Faith or Fidei Defensor, title adopted by the monarchs of England since 1521. The title was first given to Henry VIII by Pope Leo X after the publication of a book by Henry attacking Martin LUTHER.

Defenestration of Prague (May 1618), event that marked the outbreak of the THIRTY YEARS WAR. The Protestant Bohemian subjects of the HAPSBURG Ferdinand resented his Catholic rule. Two Hapsburg regents were thrown from the windows of the Prague council chamber; the Bohemian throne was offered to the Protestant Frederick, the Elector Palatine. *See also* HC1 p.273, *273*.

Deficiency disease, condition caused by an inadequate intake of vitamins or other essential diet factors. Pernicious anaemia is caused by a lack of vitamin B_{12}, scurvy by the lack of vitamin C and pellagra by the deficiency of niacin (nicotinic acid) in the diet. Night blindness is a result of a lack of vitamin A, a source of which is carrots, which gives some truth to the old saying that eating carrots helps one to see in the dark. A vegetarian diet can contain all the necessary dietary elements except vitamin B_{12}.

Deficit borrowing, large-scale borrowing employed by a government as a budgetary measure to offset a situation requiring large expenditure, such as widespread unemployment. With the growth of government expenditure in most countries deficits have become a common feature. The three main borrowing sources are the central bank, the commercial banks and the public.

Definite integral. *See* INTEGRAL.

Deflation, falling prices, the opposite of INFLATION. It normally occurs during a recession or depression and it can be measured by the price index in the same way that inflation is measured. Excess production capacity within the economy is usually the cause of deflation. Excess capacity leads to an excess of supply, in which manufacturers wish to supply more goods at full employment than consumers wish to buy. *See also* MS pp.312–315, *315*; HC2 p.208.

Deflationary gap, condition in which the total demand for goods and services in the economy is less than the total supply that can be produced at the full employment level of income. Such a gap is generally reflected by a relatively high rate of unemployment. *See also* STAGNATION.

Defoe, Daniel (1660–1731), English journalist and novelist. He joined the Duke of MONMOUTH's rebellion in 1685 and William III's army in 1688. He supported William in the poem *The True-born Englishman* (1701) and was imprisoned for his pamphlet *The Shortest Way with the Dissenters* (1702). His works include *Robinson Crusoe* (1719), *Moll Flanders* (1722), *A Journal of the Plague Year* (1722) and *Roxana* (1724). *See also* HC2 pp.*23*, 34-35.

Defoliant, any chemical that affects the metabolism of plants and causes their leaves to drop off. Cacodylic acid, 2,4,5-T,, picloran and 2,4-D are common defoliants. Sometimes used to facilitate harvesting, defoliants gained notoriety in the Vietnam War when they were used by the Americans to destroy food crops and large areas of jungle, resulting in massive disruption of the fragile jungle ECOSYSTEM.

De Forest, Lee (1873–1961), US inventor who in 1907 developed the audion vacuum-tube (triode valve), a device that made live radio broadcasting possible. It remained the key component of radio, television, radar, telephone and computer systems until the transistor was invented in 1947. *See also* SU p.131.

Deforestation, clearing away of forests and their ECOSYSTEMS, usually on a large scale, by man. It may be done to create open areas for farming or building, or to make use of the timber from the trees. There is an immediate danger that the vital topsoil will be eroded by wind (as in the DUST BOWL in the USA in the 1930s) or, in hilly areas, by rain. Proposals to clear whole regions of the rain-forests of Amazonia in Brazil which play a key role in maintaining the oxygen balance of the Earth, could, if implemented, cause a global catastrophe. *See also* PE pp.149, 154.

Degas, Hilaire-Germain Edgar (1834–1917), French painter and sculptor. Classically trained and a lifelong admirer of Jean INGRES, Degas was a perfectionist whose achievement was to combine the discipline of classic art with the immediacy of the modern. After meeting Édouard MANET and Émile ZOLA, he showed his work at the IMPRESSIONIST exhibitions. Sharing their interest in everyday life, he began painting ballet, café and racing scenes. A brilliant draughtsman, influenced by Japanese prints and photography, he introduced unusual angles and off-centre composition into his work. To master movement, he made sculptures of dancers and horses. His use of colour and light always subtle, became concentrated in his later pastels. *See also* HC2 pp. 118–119, *118*.

De Gaulle, Charles André Joseph Marie (1890–1970), French general and politician. A graduate of the *Ecole Spéciale Militaire* of Saint-Cyr, he fought in WWI and was wounded and captured in 1916. In 1924 he graduated from the *Ecole Supérieure de Guerre* and served in the occupation of the Rhineland and in Lebanon. He was made a brigadier-general in charge of the fourth Armoured Division in 1940. When the VICHY GOVERNMENT was created, he went to England as the self-declared head of the Free French forces and was sentenced to death by court martial in France. He was later head of the French Committee of National Liberation in Algiers. After the war, he made two partially successful attempts to reorganize the French government (1945–46) and following a period of retirement was elected president of the Fifth Republic in 1958. He settled the Algerian crisis and made France a nuclear power. He resigned after defeat in the referendum on administrative reform in 1969. *See also* HC2 pp.*258*, 259, 306–307.

Degaussing, demagnetization of a magnetized substance, performed by surrounding the substance with a coil carrying an alternating electric current of decreasing magnitude. The name is derived from the cgs unit of magnetic flux, the gauss.

Degenerative disease, progressive wasting ailment in which a patient's condition deteriorates at a greater or lesser rate, depending on the treatment used and the response to it; often such a condition can be arrested, althought it cannot be reversed. Various degenerative diseases are glaucoma, osteo-arthritis and carcinomas of the lymphatic system.

Degradation, in geology, wearing away or general reduction or EROSION of earth. Examples are the carrying-off of rocky material by wind, water or ice; the action of a stream as it cuts its channel; and the DENUDATION of slopes or the transport of material. *See also* PE p.*148*.

Degree, in mathematics, unit of angular measure equal to one three-hundred-and-sixtieth (1/360) of a complete revolution. One degree is written 1°, and can be divided into 60 parts called minutes (eg 20′), which may in turn be divided into 60 parts called seconds (eg 25″). Three hundred and sixty degrees are equal to 2 π radians; using this fact, angular measurements can be converted into linear measurements since π is a transcendental number. In physics and engineering, a degree is one unit on any of various scales, such as the Celsius temperature scale or the Baumé scale of specific gravity.

Degree, academic, title conferred by universities or colleges as an indication of the successful completion of a course of study. Undergraduate degrees are awarded at the end of an undergraduate course in the arts, sciences or other subjects or professions, eg Bachelor of Arts (BA) and Bachelor of Science (BSC). They are usually graded according to the standard achieved. Postgraduate degrees vary according to the amount of original thought and research they involve; the highest in Britain is that of Doctor of Philosophy (PhD), or its equivalent, which usually takes three or more years to complete.

De Havilland, Sir Geoffrey (1882–1965), British aircraft designer. He built his first plane in 1908 and during WWI he designed military aircraft creating the DH series. He was a director of the company that bears his name, a firm which has produced many famous and innovative aircraft, including the TIGER MOTH and the MOSQUITO.

Dehiwala-Mount Lavinia, city on the SW coast of Sri Lanka, 13km (8 miles) S of Colombo. It is a commercial centre and resort. Products: fish, coconuts, rice. Pop. 122,000.

Dehumanization, process, both psychological and social, by which people are made to feel alienated from a full sense of humanity. Assembly lines in factories are called dehumanizing because they compel people to function as if they were parts of a machine.

Dehydration, removal or loss of water from a substance or tissue. Water molecules can be removed by heat or a dehydrating agent such as concentrated sulphuric acid, which removes hydrogen and oxygen, in the form of water from another chemical. Dehydration (drying) is used to preserve foodstuffs. In medicine, dehydration is the excessive drying of the body due to water loss, often a symptom or result of disease or injury.

De-icing, aircraft, prevention and removal of ice which forms on the leading edges of wings, tail and propellers of aircraft in flight. Rubber "boots" along the leading edges of exposed surfaces are pulsated, or edges are heated, to dislodge or melt ice as it is formed.

Deimos, smaller of Mars' two satellites, discovered in 1877 by Asaph Hall. Diameter 12km (7.5miles); mean distance from planet 23,500km (14,600 miles); mean sidereal period 1.26 days. *See also* SU pp.202–203.

Deira, northern Anglo-Saxon kingdom

between the rivers Humber and Tyne. In the late 7th century it was united with its neighbour to the N, BERNICIA, to form the kingdom of NORTHUMBRIA.

Deirdre, a tragic figure in Irish mythology. Conchobar, the king of Ulster, kidnapped the supremely beautiful Deirdre intending to marry her, but she fled with Naoise to Scotland. After many adventures, they were permitted to return to Ulster, but Naoise and his two brothers were treacherously murdered; Deirdre killed herself almost immediately.

Deism, system of natural religion which was first developed in England in the late 17th and 18th centuries. It affirmed belief in one God, but held that he detached himself from the universe after its creation and made no revelation. Reason was man's only guide. The deists opposed revealed religion in general and Christianity in particular. The most influential deist writings were John Toland's *Christianity not Mysterious* (1696) and Matthew Tindal's *Christianity as Old as the Creation* (1730). Deism did not become popular in England, but it exercised a great influence on the ENLIGHTENMENT in France where VOLTAIRE, J.-J. ROUSSEAU and the ENCYCLOPEDISTS were its chief exponents.

Déjà vu (French, "already seen"), feeling that one has encountered the same situation before, when in reality it is new. One explanation is that the situation is very similar to a previous one that is no longer consciously remembered. It tends to occur more often when people are tired.

Déjeuner sur l'Herbe (1863), painting by MANET that raised a controversy in the Paris art world and which inspired young artists later to form the nucleus of the IMPRESSIONISTS. The painting, in bold colours, depicts a seated nude female figure gazing at the viewer, two male figures fully clothed in modern dress, and another scantily clad female figure in the background.

De jure, legal term from Latin meaning "by right", or "by lawful right". It enables companies and persons to perform duties and acts legally attributed to them. It is used to acknowledge the existence and respectability of governments.

Dekker, Thomas (1572–1632), English dramatist best known for his comedy *The Shoemaker's Holiday* (1599). He also wrote *The Gull's Hornbook* (1609), a satirical pamphlet containing incidental details of contemporary London theatre.

De Kooning, Willem (1904–), Dutch-born US painter, an important ABSTRACT EXPRESSIONIST. Although influenced by Pablo Picasso and Maxim Gorky, de Kooning's paintings are distinctive and original, marked by organic shapes in harsh colours or white on black and executed with energetic, almost violent, brushwork.

De la Beche, Sir Henry Thomas (1796–1855), British geologist. He set out, on his own initiative, to prepare a geological map of England; this prompted the British government in 1835 to form the Geological Survey, of which he was the director.

Delacroix, Eugène (1798–1863), French painter, draughtsman and writer, a leader of the Romantic movement. GÉRICAULT, CONSTABLE and other contemporaries influenced him, as well as past masters such as MICHELANGELO, POUSSIN and RUBENS. A master of colour, he was original in his use of related (as opposed to purely local) colour, and of complementary colours. His paintings, brilliant compositions full of superbly modelled and juxtaposed figures painted in broken colour and very free brushwork, deeply influenced later realists and the IMPRESSIONISTS. *Massacre of Chios* (1823) and *Liberty leading the People* (1830) are among his best known works. *See also* HC2 pp.80–81, *81, 83, 182.*

Delacroix, Henri Edmond. *See* CROSS, HENRI EDMOND.

Delafield, E.M. (1890–1943), pen-name of British novelist Elizabeth Monica Dashwood. She wrote plays, short stories and novels of manners, of which the best known is *Diary of a Provincial Lady* (1931).

Delagoa Bay, inlet on the SE coast of Mozambique, an island off SE Africa, in the Indian Ocean. It was discovered by Antonio do Campo in 1502. Length: 88km (55 miles).

De la Hunty, Shirley (née **Strickland**) (1925–), Australian sprinter and hurdler. She competed in three Olympic Games (1948, 1952, 1956), winning three gold medals (1952: 80m hurdles; 1956 80m hurdles, 4 by 100m), one silver and four bronze, the most Olympic medals won by a woman. She also won three golds at the 1950 Empire Games.

De la Mare, Walter (1873–1956), British poet, short-story writer and anthologist. His collections of poems include *Songs of Childhood* (1902), *Peacock Pie* (1913) and *Poems for Children* (1930). Of his poetry anthologies, *Come Hither* (1923) is outstanding. His prose includes the novel *Memoirs of a Midget* (1921) and the collection of stories *On the Edge* (1930). He wrote imaginative stories for children.

Delane, John Thaddeus (1817–79), British journalist. Under his editorship (1841–77) *The Times* gained its reputation as the voice of Britain.

Delaney, Shelagh (1939–), British dramatist. Her first play, *A Taste of Honey* (1959), was staged in London and won the Charles Henry Foyle New Play Award. A second play, *The Lion in Love* (1960), also won a prize. Her other works include *Sweetly Sings the Donkey* (1964), a collection of short stories.

Delarey or De la Ray, Jacobus Hercules (1847–1914), Boer military commander and political figure. He was a general in the SOUTH AFRICAN BOER WAR (1899–1902) and later helped South Africa recover, serving as a legislator (1907–14). When WWI broke out in 1914 he organized a Boer rebellion but was killed before it began by a police patrol rounding up dissidents.

De la Roche, Mazo (1885–1961), Canadian novelist. She wrote a series of best-selling novels chronicling the Whiteoaks, a matriarchal country family who have been described as a transatlantic version of GALSWORTHY's Forsytes.

De la Rue, Warren (1815–89), British astronomer. In 1858 he invented the photoheliograph, an instrument for taking photographs of the sun. In 1860 he observed the solar prominences and demonstrated their origin. *See also* SU p.222, *222.*

Delaunay, Robert (1885–1941), French painter, the founder of ORPHISM, which extended the CUBIST technique of fragmentation into the realm of colour. He deeply influenced the BLAUE REITER group and by 1914 was one of the most influential artists in Paris.

Delaunay-Terk, Sonia (1885–), Russian-French painter, with her husband Robert DELAUNAY a pioneer of ORPHISM. After WWI she became a highly successful and versatile designer of rugs, fabrics, scenery and costumes of great originality and beautiful colouring. In the 1930s she returned to painting, which she was still doing when in her eighties.

De Laurentiis, Dino (1919–), Italian film producer. He financed a number of artistically important films, such as *Bitter Rice* (1949) and *La Strada* (1956). He subsequently participated in multinational productions such as *War and Peace* (1956), *The Bible* (1966), *Waterloo* (1970) and *King Kong* (1976).

Delaware, state in E USA on the coast of the Atlantic Ocean, occupying a peninsula between Chesapeake Bay and Delaware Bay. The fourth smallest US state (after the District of Columbia, Hawaii and Rhode Island), most of its land is coastal plain. The Delaware River, an important shipping route to Pennsylvania and New Jersey, forms part of the E boundary. Delaware is primarily an industrial state, but agriculture is important: the chief products are cereal crops, potatoes, soya beans and dairy produce. Industry is concentrated in the N of the state and includes chemicals, food processing, rubber, plastics and metallurgy. The state capital is Dover, but the only large city is Wilmington in the N.

Delaware was first settled by Swedes at Wilmington (Fort Christina) in 1638. It passed to the Dutch in 1655 and then the English in 1664. One of the original 13 colonies to declare independence from Britain, Delaware ratified the US Constitution within three months of its being drawn up. The state remained loyal to the Union during the *American Civil War,* although there were some slaves within its borders. Area: 5,328sq km (2,057sq miles). Pop. (1975 est.) 579,000. *See also* MW p.175.

Delaware Indians, tribe of Algonquin-speaking North American Indians named after Lord De la Warr. The tribe, divided into three major divisions, the Unami, Munsee and Unalachtigo, lived in New Jersey, Long Island, E Pennsylvania and N Delaware. Most of the original 8,000 Delaware were forced to move in the early 19th century to Indian Territory (now Oklahoma).

De La Warr, Thomas West, Baron (1577–1618), English colonial governor of Virginia. He was the first governor of the JAMESTOWN Colony (1610–11). When he arrived the colonists were discouraged and ready to leave, but under his rule the colony was strengthened. Delaware state, river and bay are all named after him.

Delbrück, Max (1906–), US biologist, *b.* Germany. He shared the 1969 Nobel Prize in physiology and medicine with A. D. HERSHEY and S.E. LURIA for his discovery that bacterial viruses reproduce sexually, thus showing that genetic recombination occurs.

Delderfield, Ronald Frederick (1912–72), British novelist. His best-known work is a trilogy dealing with life in the English countryside at the end of the Victorian era – *God is an Englishman* (1970); *Theirs Was the Kingdom* (1971); *Give Us This Day* (1973).

Deledda, Grazia (1875–1936), Italian novelist. Most of her novels are dominated by the rugged landscape of her native Sardinia and deal with the struggle for survival of Sardinia's people. Her best-known novel is *Ashes* (1904). She won the Nobel Prize for literature in 1926.

Delft, city in SW Netherlands, in South Holland province. Founded in the 11th century, it was an important commercial centre until the 17th century, when it was superseded by Rotterdam. The subject of Jan Vermeer's painting *View of Delft,* it has a 13th-century Gothic church, as well as a 15th-century Gothic church (Nieuwe Kerk), which contains the tombs of Hugo Grotius and William the Silent, who was assassinated there in 1584. Industries: Delftware (pottery), ceramics, china, tiles. Pop. (1970) 83,700.

Delftware, fine, tin-glazed earthenware pottery, for which the Dutch town of Delft became famous in the 17th century, although many English examples of this pottery (which initially imitated Chinese blue-and-white wares) antedate the rise of Delft. In England the term Delftware is used for both Dutch and English examples. Delftware in England was made in Lambeth, Liverpool and Bristol.

Delhi, former capital city of India, in the union territory of Delhi, N central India, on the River Yamuna, NNE of the present capital of New Delhi. The region of Delhi has held a key position throughout India's history and the city is built on the site of at least seven past cities dating back more than 2,000 years. The city became the capital of British India in 1912, replacing Calcutta, and remained so until independence in 1947. Within the city walls are the Red Fort, which housed the imperial Mogul palace, and the Rajghat, a sacred shrine where Gandhi was cremated. Industries: cotton textiles, handicrafts, tourism. Pop. (1971) 3,287,883.

Delhi sultanate (1192–1398), powerful MUSLIM state in India. Muhammad of Ghur defeated the Hindus at Tarain in 1192, establishing the sultanate, which lasted until the Mogul Empire was established. It included five successive dynasties, the Turco-Afghans, Khaljis, Tughluks, Sayyids and Lodis. *See also* HC1 pp.118–119; HC2 p.48.

Delibes, Clément Philibert Léo (1836–91), French composer. He is best known

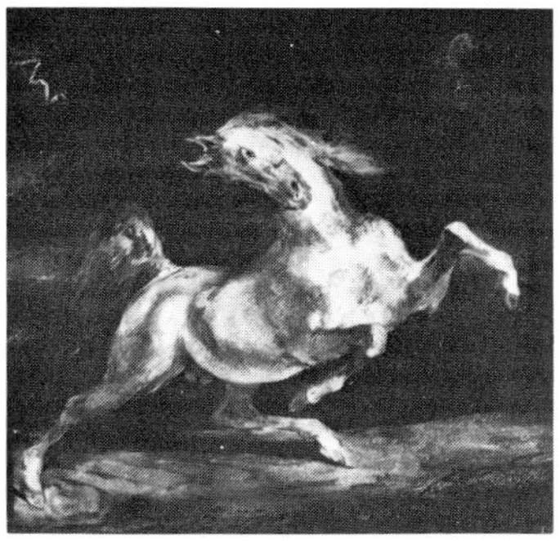

Eugène Delacroix: *Horse Frightened by a Storm,*one of the artist's many fine studies.

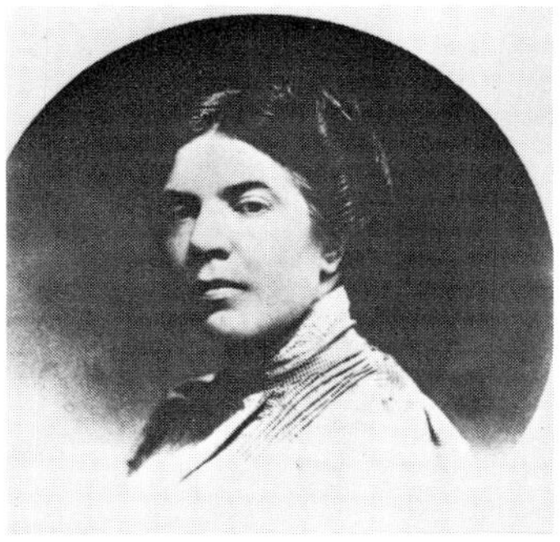

Grazia Deledda, the Italian novelist who won the 1926 Nobel Prize in literature.

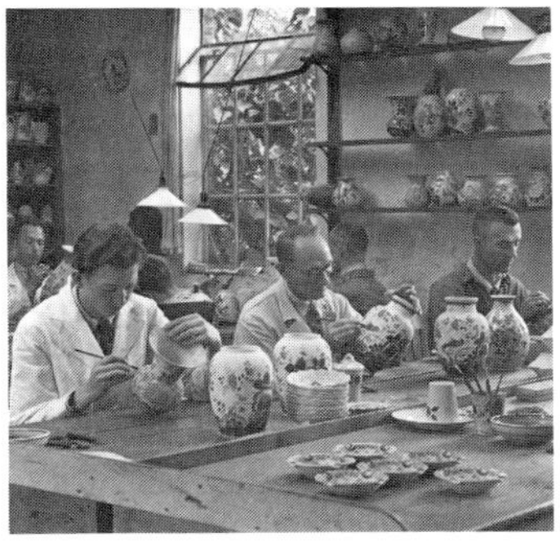

Delft; artists working on the famous Delft blue pottery, painted entirely by hand.

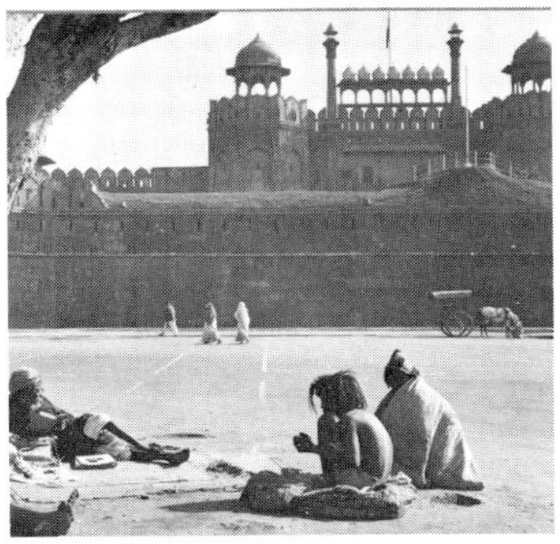

Delhi; a view of the Red Fort, built during the reign of Shah Jahan in the 17th century.

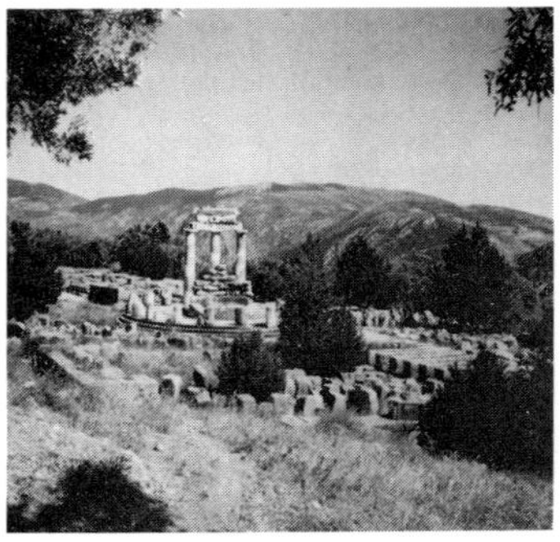
Delphic Oracle; influenced Greek politics and religion from Mount Parnassus.

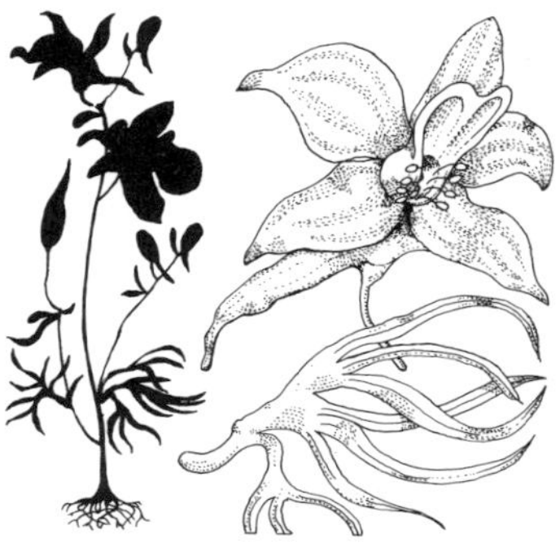
Delphinium; the wild woodland species of this perennial flower is called larkspur.

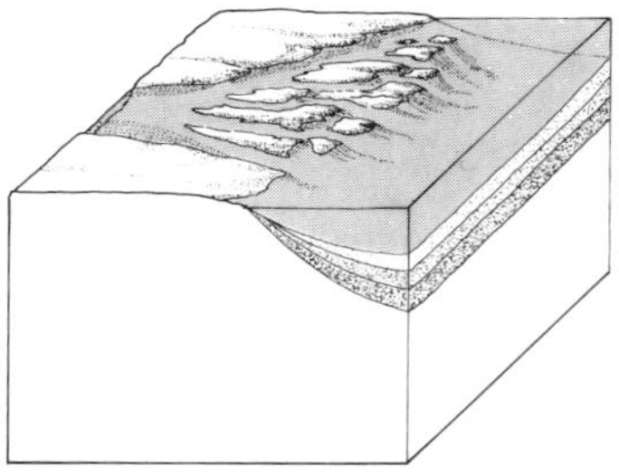
Delta; usually the slower the flow of a river, the larger is the area of its delta.

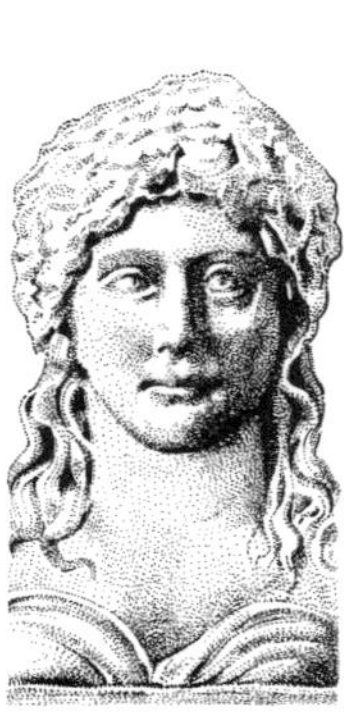
Demeter, Goddess whom the Greeks believed taught man the arts of agriculture.

for his ballets, especially *Coppélia* (1870), but also the altogether grander *Sylvia* (1876). He also wrote several OPERA and choral works, sacred and secular.

Delict, Law of, in many countries the part of the civil law which corresponds to the Anglo-Saxon law of TORT. It derives from Roman law, before the separation of criminal and civil law in the 3rd century. It meant simply the obligation to pay monetary compensation to the victim of a crime. Theft, robbery, physical injury and damage to property all came under the law of delict.

Delilah, Old Testament figure who betrayed SAMSON to the Philistines. Having learnt that his strength lay in his hair, she cut it while he slept. She has become a symbol in literature of female treachery, as in Milton's *Samson Agonistes.*

Delinquency, term covering antisocial acts, misdeeds and crimes, most often applied to the behaviour of juvenile offenders. *See also* MS p.288.

Delinquency, juvenile, sociological and legal term for offences committed by children and adolescents that would be termed criminal if committed by adults. It is only since the turn of the century that juvenile courts have developed, and these courts emphasize correction and rehabilitation rather than punishment, in such institutions as borstals and foster homes. Theft is the most common offence among children, and juvenile delinquency has a great number of socio-economic causes such as emotional maladjustment, broken homes and economic deprivation. It is higher in the more developed countries.

Delirium, symptom of many disorders, ranging from exhaustion, sunstroke, infectious diseases and high fever to metabolic dysfunction and extreme intoxication (delirium tremens, DTS). It is characterized by mental confusion, rambling statements, obsessive thoughts and poor judgment. The delirium may range from whimsicality to mania, but the patient is usually quickly tired by it and falls into an uneasy sleep, although sometimes he must be quieted with suitable drugs.

Delirium tremens. *See* DTS.

Delisle, Guillaume (1675–1726), French scientist, one of the founders of modern cartography. He used astronomical observations and accurate measurements to compile the 90 or so maps he published during his lifetime. His first important work – maps of the continents and a globe – was published in 1700. He was geographer to the French king in 1718; his brother was the French astronomer Joseph Nicolas DELISLE.

Delisle, Joseph (1688–1768), French astronomer. He pioneered the study of the sun and in 1725 he was invited to St Petersburg by Peter the Great, where he founded a school of astronomy.

Delius, Frederick (1862–1934), British composer of orchestral, operatic and chamber works. He combined elements of romanticism with IMPRESSIONISM, most notably in numerous orchestral pieces, including *Brigg Fair* (1907) and *On Hearing the First Cuckoo in Spring* (1912). Recognition of his genius came later in life in Britain, where Sir Thomas BEECHAM was among his most ardent champions. *See also* ROMANTICISM.

Dell, Ethel M. (1881–1939), British writer of romantic stories. She achieved tremendous popularity with her highly emotional novels, which included *Way of an Eagle* (1912), *The Keeper of the Door* (1915) and *Storm Drift* (1930).

Della Casa-Debeljevic, Lisa (1919–), Swiss SOPRANO. She has sung with the Metropolitan Opera, the Munich and Vienna State Operas and at La Scala, Milan. In 1970 she received the Cross of Honour, Austria's highest medal of achievement.

Della Francesca, Piero. *See* PIERO DELLA FRANCESCA.

Della Porta, Giacomo (1537–1602), Italian architect and sculptor. A pupil of VIGNOLA he completed the cupola of St Peter's, which had been left unfinished by MICHELANGELO. Of the palaces he designed the most notable was the Villa Aldobrandini.

Deller, Alfred George (1912–), British singer who, through his unique natural vocal register and musicianship, revived the art of the COUNTER TENOR. He is famous for his interpretations of Henry PURCELL, and had works written especially for him by Benjamin BRITTEN.

Delos (Dhílos), smallest of the Greek Cyclades (Kikládhos) islands in the S Aegean Sea. In Greek mythology, it was considered the birthplace of Apollo and Artemis. Its rulers became treasurers of the Delian League from 478 to 454 BC. Declared a free port by Rome in 166 BC, it prospered as an important shipping and slave centre. The island was sacked during the Mithridatic Wars in 87 BC. French excavations since 1877 have uncovered remains of temples, theatres and commercial buildings.

De los Angeles, Victoria. *See* ANGELES, VICTORIA DE LOS.

De Loutherbourg, Jacques Philippe (1740–1812), French Romantic landscape painter who settled in London in 1771, where as a stage designer he won fame for his large-scale dramatic sets of nature and his picturesque scenes.

Delphic Oracle, most famous of the ancient Greek oracles, at Delphi. It was housed in the temple of APOLLO, built in the 7th century BC, although it was first associated with the worship of the earth goddess Ge. It was famous for the ambivalent prophecies uttered by a priestess sitting on a golden tripod. The messages were usually translated by a priest and delivered in verse. The temple was destroyed and rebuilt twice.

Delphi forecasting, management procedure employing a forecast or prediction based upon answers given by experts in the field. Instead of them all meeting to reach a decision, the Delphi technique involves sequential interviews.

Delphinium, also called larkspur, any of about 250 species of herbaceous plants native to temperate areas. It has compound palmate leaves and loosely clustered purple, blue or white flowers. Garden larkspurs are varieties of *Delphinium elatum*, a hardier Asian plant. Family Ranunculaceae.

Delta, fan-shaped body of alluvium deposited at the mouth of a river. A delta is formed when a river deposits sediment as its speed decreases while it enters the sea, and the waves, tides and currents are not sufficiently strong to carry the material away. Most deltas are extremely fertile areas, but are subject to frequent flooding. The term was used by Herodotus in the 5th century BC to describe the land at the mouth of the Nile, which resembled the Greek letter "delta". *See also* PE pp.113, *125*, *127*.

Deltoid muscle, triangular muscle over the shoulder joint. Contraction of the deltoid draws the arm upwards and the shoulder backwards and outwards. *See also* MS pp.58–59.

Deluc, Jean André (1727–1817), Swiss geologist and physicist. He invented the dry pile, a type of battery, and a form of HYGROMETER. Deluc also researched the atmosphere and published the first correct rules for calculating the height of a mountain by using a BAROMETER.

Deluge, The, story of the Great Flood. In one of its earliest pre-biblical versions, reconstructed from a broken clay tablet from Mesopotamia, some of the gods decided to destroy mankind. But one of them, EA (Enki), thinking this harsh, counselled a mortal, Ziûsadra, to build a boat to save the seed of mankind. The flood lasted seven days, after which the sun shone and the earth reappeared. Thereupon the gods, pleased with his obedience, made Ziûsadra immortal.

Delusion, false or irrational belief based upon a misinterpretation of reality. Mild delusions are quite common in normal people, but fixed delusions, resistant to reason, are a form of PARANOIA. Such psychotic delusions include persecution delusions, in which the person feels himself to be hunted or persecuted by someone; delusions of grandeur, in which the person images himself to be someone of great importance, eg. Napoleon or even God; and influence delusions, in which the person thinks himself controlled by some remote force such as cosmic rays or magnetism. *See also* MS pp.134, 138, *139*.

Delvaux, Paul (1897–), Belgian painter, influenced in the 1930s by CHIRICO and the SURREALISTS. In characteristic paintings he arranges nude women and clothed men in incongruous settings reminiscent of Chirico's "metaphysical painting".

Demand, in economics, schedule of prices and the quantities that would be purchased by consumers at those prices. For most goods, the normal relationship between price and quantity is inverse, that is, as the price of the goods increases, the quantity demanded by consumers declines. The demand for goods is determined by a number of factors, however, including purchaser's income, price of competing goods and consumer tastes and preferences. *See also* MS pp.*310–311*.

Demand and supply. *See* SUPPLY AND DEMAND.

Dementia praecox, term used by Emil KRAEPELIN at the turn of the century to describe what is now called SCHIZOPHRENIA. Literally, it means "early insanity" but is insufficiently exact to describe the condition fully. *See also* MS pp.138–139.

Demerara, river in E Guyana, NE South America; it rises in the Guiana Highlands, and flows N to the Atlantic Ocean. Georgetown, Guyana's main port, is at the mouth. Length: approx. 322km (200 miles).

Demesne, in a feudal system, land enjoyed by the king or the nobles, rather than being leased out to their feudal tenants. Originally, peasants owed labour services to the lord on his demesne, but during the 14th century it became common for the demesne to be leased out to tenant farmers for fixed rents. *See also* HC1 pp.*158*, 190–191, 196–197.

Demeter, ancient Greek nature goddess, sister of ZEUS and mother of PERSEPHONE. Although specifically the goddess of corn, she presided over all crops and fruits and over human health and fertility. She was usually depicted as bountiful and gentle. *See also* MS pp.*206*, 212.

Demetrius, name of two kings of Macedonia. Demetrius I (*c.*336–283 BC) became king in 294 after defeating Ptolemy I in 306 and taking Athens in 294. He invaded Asia in 287 but was defeated. Demetrius II (*c.*276–229 BC) became king in 239 and was defeated in a war with the Aetolian and Achaean leagues.

Demetrius I Soter (187–150 BC), King of Syria (162–150 BC). He became king after overthrowing his cousin, Antiochus V. As king he crushed the revolt of Timarchus in Babylon and attempted to subdue the Maccabees in Jerusalem.

De Mille, Cecil Blount (1881–1959), US film producer and director, noted for his lavish dramatic presentations. With his first film, *The Squaw Man* (1913), he established Hollywood as the US film-production capital. Much of De Mille's best-known work covered biblical themes such as the films *The Ten Commandments* (two versions, 1923, 1956) and *King of Kings* (1927). Other major films include *Forbidden Fruit* (1921), *Union Pacific* (1939) and *The Greatest Show on Earth* (1952), which won an Academy award. *See also* HC2 p.*201*.

Demirel, Suleyman, (1924–), Turkish politician. He became leader of the Justice party in 1964 and prime minister the following year. His government fell in 1971 following left-wing agitation, but he was re-elected prime minister in 1975.

Democracy, political system in which people are involved in some way in the ruling of society. In one form the will of the people is expressed indirectly, through elected representatives. Democracy stresses that all men are endowed with basic civil rights. In the British system, in which the executive and legislative branches of government are unified, ministers keep their executive positions through majority support in the Commons. An election is usually called if that support is lost. *See also* MS p.276.

Democratic Centralists (Democratic Centre). French conservative party opposed to policies of Charles De Gaulle, including the former Mouvement Républicain Populaire.

Democratic Party, US political party, the descendant of the Anti-Federalist and Democratic-Republican Parties. From the election of Thomas JEFFERSON as president in 1801 until James Buchanan's election in 1857, the party was strong, gathering its support mainly from farmers, small businessmen and the professional classes. Party strength declined after the Civil War until 1932, when Franklin D. ROOSEVELT was elected. After that, it remained strong until 1952. In 1960, Democratic candidate John F. KENNEDY won the presidential election beginning "the New Frontier" era that stressed US world responsibilities for peace and economic growth at home. Lyndon B. JOHNSON succeeded Kennedy. *See also* DEMOCRATIC-REPUBLICAN PARTY; HC2 pp.150, 264.

Democratic-Republican Party, US political party, originally called the Anti-Federalist party, or Republicans, that was formed in the late 1790s. Led by Thomas JEFFERSON, James MADISON and James MONROE, the party opposed strong central government and Alexander HAMILTON's economic policies. It supported the French revolution, advocated an agrarian democracy, strict construction of the Constitution and other measures to minimize aristocratic control of government. *See also* DEMOCRATIC PARTY.

Democratic Socialism, political belief based on the twin assumptions that evolution rather than revolution is the best way to introduce the socialist economy and that democratic practices must be followed before and after socialism is introduced. British socialists, for example, have always operated entirely within the democratic system. *See also* SOCIALISM; HC2 pp.210–213.

Democritus of Adbera (*c.*460–370 BC), Greek philosopher. Although none of his books have survived he is best remembered for his atomic theory. He suggested that all matter consisted of tiny, indivisible particles, that various atoms differed physically and that atoms' motions were determined by laws of nature, not the actions of gods. *See also* ATOMISM; SU pp.62, *132*.

Demographic transition theory, or theory of the vital revolution, social theory that relates population patterns to the degree of social development. In pre-industrial societies, DEATH and BIRTH RATES are high. Modernization decreases the death rate, but not the birth rate, causing a temporary acceleration in population growth. With more advanced development, the birthrate also drops and population growth stabilizes.

Demography, term introduced in 1855 by the Frenchman Achille Guillard for the scientific study of human POPULATIONS, their changes, movements, size, distribution and structure. It began with the work of Englishman John Graunt, who published the first mortality table in 1662. Demographic methods are primarily statistical and quantitative, and they are used by government and business for ascertaining public needs.

Demoiselle crane, one of the smallest cranes, found from SE Europe to central Asia; it winters in Africa or India. Unlike most cranes, it prefers dry grassy areas to marshland and eats a varied animal and vegetable diet. Length: up to 96cm (38in). Family Gruidae; species *Anthropoides virgo*.

Demonetization, the ending of the practice whereby the value of a nation's currency is defined in terms of a precious metal such as gold or silver. Such metal, coins and paper money become no longer freely interchangeable. Such currency reform became widespread after WWI. The term also refers to the withdrawal from circulation of certain kinds of currency, which then cease to be legal tender.

De Morgan, Augustus (1806–71), British mathematician. He wrote a number of textbooks, including *Elements of Arithmetic* (1830), and with his contemporary, George BOOLE, contributed to the renaissance of studies in LOGIC.

De Morgan, William Frend (1839–1917), British potter. He revived many techniques of Oriental pottery, making brightly-coloured tiles and vases. Associated with the PRE-RAPHAELITE circle, he also wrote popular novels.

Demosthenes (*c.*383–322 BC), Athenian orator and statesman. He achieved fame as a public speaker and devoted his life to speaking and fighting on behalf of the Greek states in their resistance to Philip of Macedon. His speeches include the *Philippics* and *On the Crown*. *See also* HC1 pp.71, 75.

Dempsey, Jack (1895–), US boxer, real name William Harrison Dempsey. He won the world heavyweight title from Jess Willard (1919) in Toledo, and lost it to Gene Tunney (1926) in Chicago. In a re-match with Tunney (1927), he lost after flooring Tunney because he did not go immediately to a neutral corner, which delayed the start of the referee's count.

Denbighshire (Dinbych), former county of N Wales and now part of Clwyd. Although it is a mountainous area, the fertile valleys of the rivers Conway, Dee and Clwyd produce cereal crops and potatoes. Cattle, sheep, pigs and poultry are also raised there. Industries include tourism, timber and iron and steel. The county town is Denbigh, but Wrexham, as a mining and manufacturing centre, is more important. Pop. (1971) 184,824.

Dendrite, short branching projection from a nerve cell or NEURON. It carries impulses to the cell body and transmits impulses to other nerve cells over short gaps called SYNAPSES. There may be more than one dendrite per neuron.

Dendritic drainage, tree-like branching pattern of streams and their tributaries. The pattern is common in regions where the land is essentially flat and the rock is homogeneous.

Dendrochronology, means of estimating time by examination of the growth rings in trees. This data can be related to wood used in buildings, for instance, and to the hydrology of the region where the tree it came from grew, thus fixing points in the climatic history of that region. Chronology based on the bristlecomb pine extends back over 7,000 years. *See also* PE p.*131*.

Deneb, or Alpha Cygni, remote and very luminous white supergiant star in the constellation of Cygnus. Characteristics: apparent mag. 1.26; absolute mag. −7.0; spectral type A2; distance 1,500 light-years. *See also* SU pp.226–227, 259, 265, 267.

Denebola, second magnitude star in the constellation Leo (the lion), most easily seen during spring in the Northern Hemisphere. It is used as a reference star in navigation. *See also* SU p.257.

Dengue, infectious virus disease transmitted by the *Aedes aegypti* mosquito. Occurring in the tropics and in the warm months in temperate areas, it produces fever, headache and fatigue, followed by severe joint pains, aching muscles and the appearance of a reddish rash. Recovery usually follows, although relapses are common. *See also* MS p.106.

Den Haag. *See* HAGUE, THE.

Denier system, measure of the fineness of silk and nylon yarns. It is defined as the number of grammes weight of 9,000 metres of yarn.

Denis, Saint (*c.*3rd century AD), patron saint of France. According to tradition, he was the first bishop of Paris and was martyred in Montmartre. He is often represented carrying his severed head in his hands. Feast: 9 October.

Denis, Maurice (1870–1943), French painter. An important theorist, he joined in the NABIS' reaction against IMPRESSIONISM. He introduced symbolism into his work and gradually devoted himself to religious art.

Denitrification, process that chemically reduces nitrites or nitrates to yield free nitrogen, nitrites, nitrogen oxides or ammonia. Denitrifying BACTERIA change the nitrogen of ammonia into free nitrogen that enters the atmosphere or soil. *See also* NITROGEN CYCLE.

Denmark, small monarchy in W Europe occupying a peninsula and nearly 500 islands (100 inhabited). Although Denmark is known for its farm produce, it exports twice as many manufactured articles. The major industries are food processing, engineering, iron and steel and chemicals. The chief agricultural activity is the raising of pigs and cattle. Dairy produce is also important, as is the cultivation of grain, sugar-beet and potatoes. Fishing and tourism are other important economic activities. The capital is Copenhagen (København). Area: 43,068sq km (16,628sq miles). Pop. (1975 est.) 5,060,000. *See* MW p.63.

Denmark Strait, sea passage between SE Greenland and Iceland, linking the Arctic Ocean with the N Atlantic Ocean. In May 1941 the British battleship HMS *Hood* was sunk there by the German battleship *Bismarck*. Width: 209km (130 miles); length: 483km (300 miles).

Denner, Johann Christoph (1655–1707), Polish maker of musical instruments. He improved the sureness of the flute's intonation and invented the modern clarinet in *c.*1690–1700.

Dennis, Nigel (1912–), British author. His work includes the novels *Boys and Girls Come Out to Play* (1949) and *Cards of Identity* (1955) and the dramatic essay *Jonathan Swift* (1964). His most successful play, *August for the People* (1962), is about the power of the press. *Exotics*, a volume of poetry, appeared in 1970.

Denominator, common, number that is a multiple of the divisors of two or more fractions, and that allows the addition or subtraction of otherwise incomparable fractions. For example, for $\frac{1}{2}$ and $\frac{1}{5}$ the common denominator is 10, allowing the same fractions to be represented as $\frac{5}{10}$ and $\frac{2}{10}$ which can then be added or subtracted. Likewise the common denominator of $\frac{1}{2}$, $\frac{1}{3}$, $\frac{1}{4}$ and $\frac{1}{6}$ is 12; the common denominator of $\frac{1}{4}$ and $\frac{1}{2}$ is 8.

Denonville, Jacques René de Brisay, Marquis de (1637–1710), governor of New France, Canada (1685–89). In 1687 he led an army against the Iroquois Indians and laid waste their settlements. Following this he invited a number of Iroquois to a peace conference, but sparked off further troubles when, albeit reluctantly, he captured and enslaved them.

Densitometer, instrument for measuring the optical transmission or reflection (optical density) of a material such as a photographic film or plate. It is used in spectroscopy to determine the positions of spectral lines and bands and to measure their RELATIVE DENSITIES, and thus intensities.

Density, mass per unit volume of a substance; it is an indication of the concentration of particles within a material. The density of a solid or liquid changes little over a wide range of temperatures and pressures. Related to density is specific gravity, which is the ratio of the density of one substance to that of a reference substance (usually water) at the same temperature and pressure. The density of a gas depends strongly on both pressure and temperature. *See also* SU pp.*85*, 86.

Dent, Joseph Malaby (1849–1926), British publisher. With his son Hugh he planned EVERYMAN'S LIBRARY of 1,000 classics of literature.

Dentine, hard yellow matter of all TEETH, which consists of crystals of calcium and phosphate. Man and other higher animals have tubular dentine, so-called because a line of dentine-producing cells (odontoblasts) surrounding the pulp, sends out tubules into the dentine; these transmit sensations to the nerve.

Dentistry, profession concerned with the care and treatment of the mouth, particularly the teeth and their supporting tissues. As well as general practice, dentistry includes such specialities as oral surgery, prosthodontics, periodontics, orthodontics and public health. Scientific dentistry started in the 16th and 17th centuries in Germany and France when it became recognized as a separate profession; university courses were initiated and dental textbooks were published. Before that time barbers had performed most dental

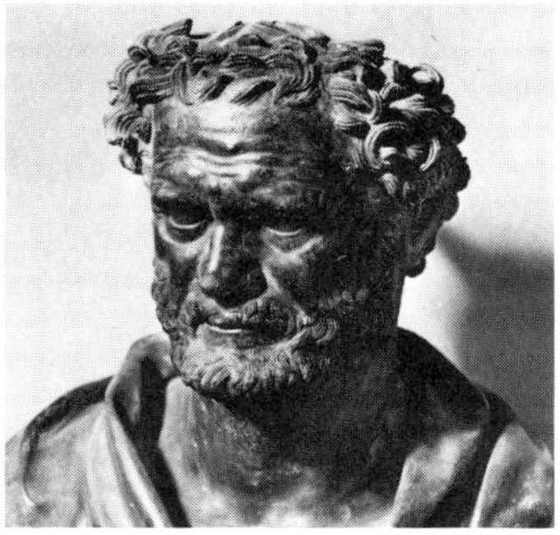

Democritus speculated at an atomic theory confirmed scientifically centuries later.

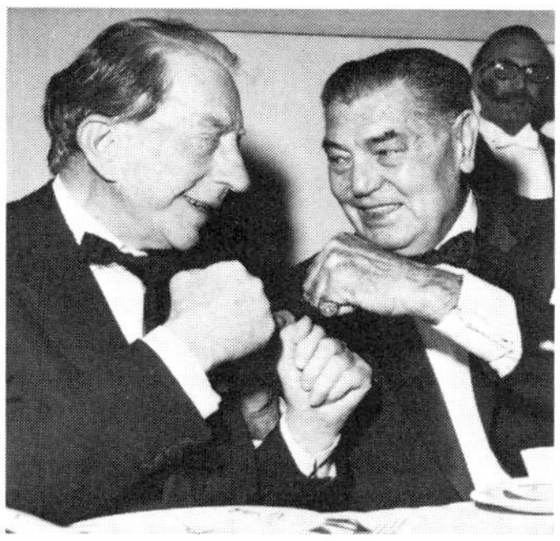

Jack Dempsey squares up to Paul Getty at an Anglo-American sporting club dinner in 1967.

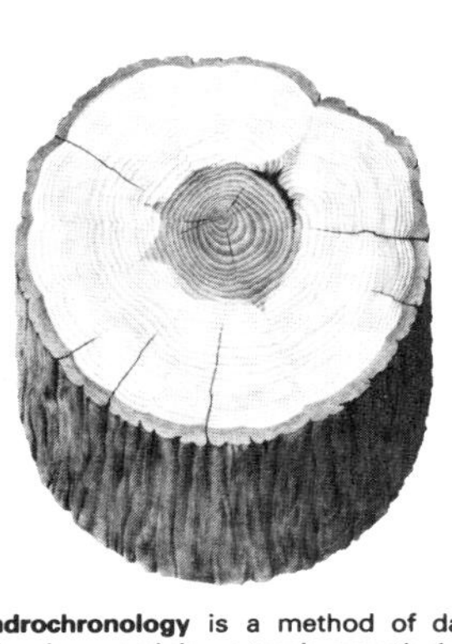

Dendrochronology is a method of dating timber by examining a tree's growth rings.

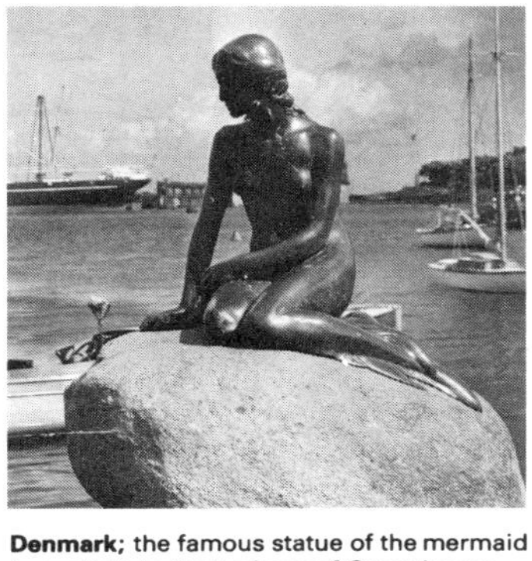

Denmark; the famous statue of the mermaid Langelinie in the harbour of Copenhagen.

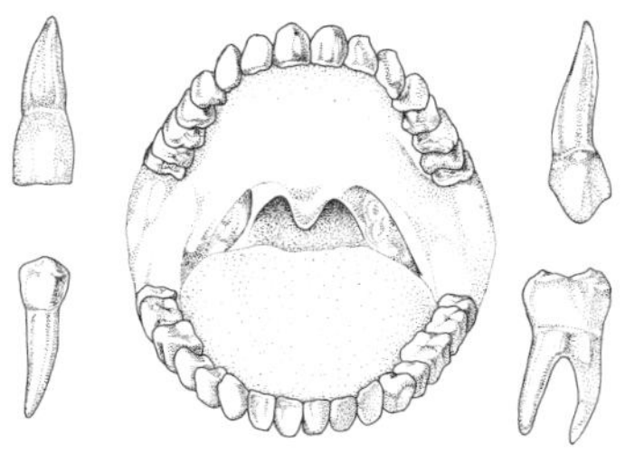

Dentition is the arrangement and classification of the teeth in humans and animals.

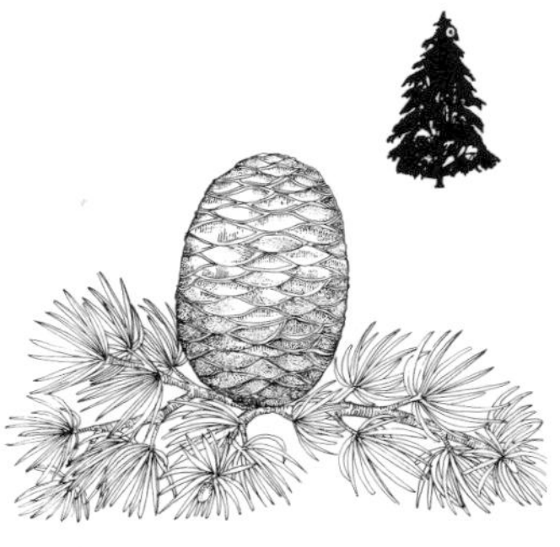

Deodar is a very valuable timber tree known also as the Indian cedar or God tree.

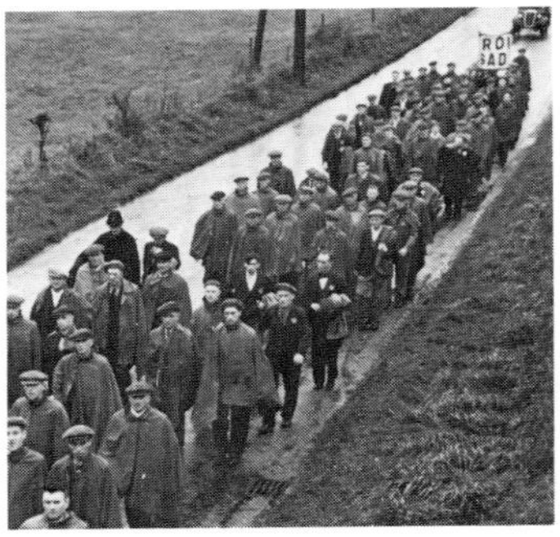

Depression; in 1936, 200 men marched to London protesting against unemployment.

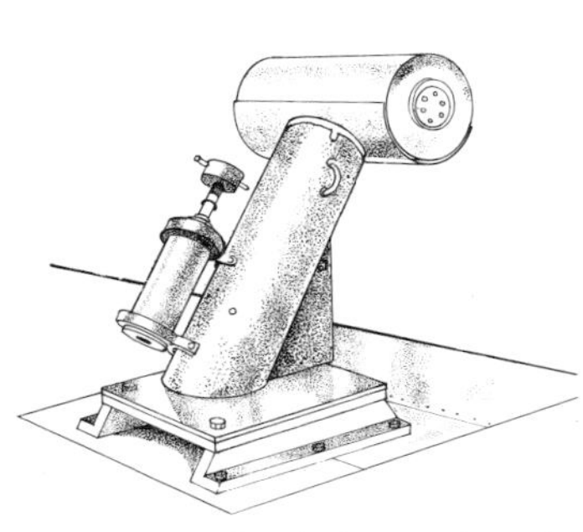

Depth charge; the shock wave from the explosion causes a submarine to collapse.

services. Today the practice of dentistry is strictly controlled; there are special educational requirements and licensing procedures in all countries. *See also* MS pp.130–131.

Dentition, the type, number and arrangement of teeth. An adult human being has 32 teeth: in each jaw are four incisors; two canines; four premolars, or bicuspids; four molars; and, in most people over 18 years of age, two wisdom teeth. Man's teeth cut, grind and tear and are not adapted to any particular type of diet. *See also* TOOTH; MS pp.130–131.

Denture, artificial substitute for teeth, usually made of plastic and occasionally reinforced with metal. Well-fitted and designed dentures can improve the appearance of the wearer as well as enabling him to chew food. A partial denture is also called a BRIDGE. *See also* MS pp.130–131.

Denudation, in geology, all processes that result in the gradual wearing away or lowering of the surface material covering the base rock. It includes erosion, mass wasting and transport of material by water or wind.

Denver, largest city and capital of Colorado state, USA, on the South Platte River. Two settlements founded in 1858, Auraria and St Charles, were united in 1860 and named after the governor, James W. Denver. Today the city is the financial centre of the Rockies, and industries include tourism, machinery, meat packing and rubber goods. Population (1973) 515,593.

Deodar, also called Indian cedar and by Hindus, the Tree of God. An evergreen native to the Himalayas, it also grows well in temperate climates. Its wood is used for timber and it yields a fragrant oil. Height: to 61m (200ft). Family Pinaceae: species *Cedrus deodara.*

Deodorant, substance used to mask or destroy unpleasant odours. Cosmetic deodorants contain perfumes and mild germicides to inhibit the bacterial decomposition of sweat. They are usually combined with antiperspirants, substances such as aluminium chlorhydrate that prevent sweating. Household deodorants are used in the form of sprays (aerosols) or slowly evaporating solids or liquids.

Deontology, term used by Immanuel KANT to denote an ethical theory which holds that the rightness of an action is not necessarily dependent on the goodness it might produce. Deontology has been contrasted with UTILITARIANISM.

Deoxyribonncleic acid. *See* DNA.

Dependence, in psychology, the extent to which an individual needs others in order to function, as opposed to independence, functioning on one's own. Infants are totally dependent on their parents for satisfying basic survival needs, but most children progress towards some degree of independence as they grow up.

Depersonalization, in psychology a feeling, often pathological, of personal and sometimes general unreality. In sociology it refers to feelings of alienation from society, especially in industrial society. In philosophy, depersonalization is the rejection of beliefs in supernatural causes of natural phenomena.

Depilatory, substance used to remove body hair. Most depilatories are creams or pastes containing calcium thiocollate, a compound that breaks up the chemical structure of hair. They are also employed in tanning for removing hair from hides.

Deportation, expulsion from a country of an alien by a branch of the executive, in Britain by the HOME OFFICE. From the 15th century until 19th- and 20th-century penal reforms it was used as an alternative to capital punishment by several European countries, particularly Portugal, England and France.

Deposition, in geology, layering or placing of any material which may become rock. It is the accumulation of sediment, ore deposits and organic material by any natural agent that would result in stratification of rock-forming material. See also PE p.112.

Deposition, act of removing an individual, usually a monarch from office. In Britain, kings such as Edward II (1327) and Richard II (1399) were deposed for what was held to be unconstitutional conduct.

Depreciation, decline in the value of an asset as it is spread over its economic life. It includes the decrease in value or usefulness because of wear and tear, obsolescence, or fall in market prices but does not cover unexpected losses due to accident or natural disaster. It is a way of measuring an asset's actual cost and actual value to the owner, either a business or an individual.

Depressants, variety of drugs which impair the functioning of the body, either by affecting a particular organ or by depressing the nervous system as a whole. They may be used to slow the action of the heart, to induce sleep, to mitigate pain or to relieve emotional tension.

Depression, term to describe a period of economic hardship, more severe than a recession. It is commonly measured by a fall in economic output per head of population, a decline in trade and a rise in unemployment. It may be accompanied by either falling or rising prices, although before the 1970s the coincidence of unemployment and inflation in industrialized western nations was rare. The term is almost always used to describe conditions in an industrial society which is subject to capitalism's cycle of growth and stagnation, although it may, as in Britain from 1875 to 1895, have special reference to agriculture. The first classical example of a capitalist depression occurred in Britain in the late 1830s and early 1840s, the so-called "Hungry Forties". The most severe and widespread depression was the Great Depression of the 1930s. *See also* HC2 pp.208–209.

Depression, emotional state characterized by feelings of guilt, failure, worthlessness or rejection. Frequently a response to a difficult or boring situation, depression leads to remorse, self-recrimination and obsessive thoughts. Insomnia, loss of appetite and fatigue often occur. MANIC-DEPRESSION alternates periods of intense excitement with those of acute depression. Suicide is an extreme manifestation of the self-abnegation of depression.

Depression, in meteorology, a region of low atmospheric pressure with the lowest pressure at the centre. It usually brings unsettled or stormy weather. In the Northern Hemisphere, winds circulate anticlockwise in a depression; they circulate clockwise in the Southern Hemisphere.

Depressive neurosis. *See* NEUROSIS.

Depressive psychosis. *See* PSYCHOSIS.

Depressive reaction, psychological disorder with severe DEPRESSION as its main symptom. It occurs after an individual has experienced a stressful or disturbing event, eg, loss of a loved one. He or she typically withdraws, feels helpless and worthless and may be unable to cope with daily life. This disorder responds to treatment with drugs and the support of sympathetic people. More severe forms may lead to attempted suicide and thus require more intensive treatment. *See also* MS pp.138–141.

De Profundis, personal essay of confession and reminiscence by Oscar WILDE published in extracts in 1905, and in full in 1962. The title is a Latin phrase which means "out of the depths" and is a cry of wretchedness. It is taken from the first two words of Psalm 130 in the Latin version.

Depth charge, explosive cannister detonated underwater by time fuses at predetermined depths and used by naval vessels and aircraft to attack submerged submarines.

Depth perception, ability of the eyes to locate the position of objects in three-dimensional space. The RETINA is two-dimensional, and information about depth is created in the brain. The brain uses "depth clues" which include such factors as linear perspective, PARALLAX, relative size and the slightly different view each eye has of the object. *See also* MS pp.48–49.

De Quincey, Thomas (1785–1859), English essayist and critic. In 1822 he published his famous work *Confessions of an English Opium Eater* describing his opium habit, which began while he was at Oxford University, and the effects of opium itself.

Derain, André (1880–1954), French FAUVE painter, influenced by VLAMINCK, CÉZANNE and MATISSE, whose landscape paintings, before 1914, were painted in brilliant colour and Pointillist technique. His later style was influenced by Italian masters, and his subjects became precisely drawn in subdued colours. *See also* HC2 pp.174, *174.*

Derby, Edward George Geoffrey Smith Stanley, 14th Earl of (1799–1869), leader of the British CONSERVATIVE PARTY from 1846 to 1868 and three times Prime Minister (1852, 1858–59, 1866–68). He resigned from PEEL's cabinet in 1845 in protest against the repeal of the CORN LAWS. His last government introduced the 1867 REFORM ACT.

Derby, Thomas Stanley, 1st Earl of (1435–1504), English noble. At BOSWORTH FIELD (1485) his large force was nominally on the side of Richard III, but took no part in the fighting. After the battle he crowned his stepson, the victorious Henry VII, King of England and in 1486 was made an earl.

Derby, town in Derbyshire, N England on the River Derwent 60km (37 miles) NNE of Birmingham. England's first silk mill was built there in 1719. Today it is an important railway junction and its industries include railway and aerospace engineering, textiles, ceramics and food processing. Rolls-Royce cars are made there. Pop. (1971 prelim.) 219,300

Derby, The, English horse race. The most important of the CLASSICS, it is run in June over a 2.4km (1.5 mile) course at Epsom, and is open to three-year-old colts and fillies. It was first run in 1780 and was named after the Earl of Derby, who won the right to put his name to it on the toss of a coin. The race has given its name to events in other countries, such as the Irish Derby and the Kentucky Derby (USA).

Derbyshire, county in N central England. Low-lying in the S, it rises to the PEAK DISTRICT in the N, and is drained by the River Trent and its tributaries the Dove, Derwent and Wye. Agriculture is important and includes dairy farming, sheep and cattle rearing, wheat, oats and market gardening. There are coal deposits in the E, and other industries include steel, textiles, paper and pottery. The main towns are Derby, Chesterfield and Alfreton. Area: 2,631sq km (1,016sq miles). Pop. 887,600.

Derg, Lough, either of two lakes in the Republic of Ireland. One is in Galway, Tipperary and Clare counties, on the Shannon River and is 40km (25 miles) long by 3 to 9.5km (2 to 6 miles) wide. The other is in SE county Donegal with an area of approx. 26sq km (10sq miles).

Derivative, rate of change of a mathematical function with respect to a change in the independent variable. The derivative is an expression of the instantaneous rate of change of the function: in general it is itself a function of the variable. An example is obtaining the velocity and acceleration of an object that moves distance x in time t according to the equation $x=at^2$. In such motion the velocity increases with time (the object accelerates). The expression dx/dt, called the first derivative of distance with respect to time, is equal to the velocity of the object; in this example it equals $2at$. The result is obtained by considering a small time interval δt, over which the average velocity is $\delta x/\delta t$, and taking the limit of this as t becomes vanishingly small; the operation is called differentiation. The second derivative, written d^2x/dt^2, is equal to the acceleration. Derivatives can similarly be used to find the slope of a curve at a particular point. *See also* CALCULUS; DIFFERENTIAL EQUATION; LIMIT.

Dermaptera. *See* EARWIG.

Dermatitis, inflammation of the skin. In acute form it produces redness, itching and blisters or oozing; in chronic form it causes a thickening and darkening of the skin and scales. In CONTACT DERMATITIS contact with a particular substance, such as soap or nettles, produces the reaction.

In atopic dermatitis (often associated with hay-fever and ASTHMA) excessive dryness occurs, with redness at the neck, elbows and knees. In stasis dermatitis heavy pigmentation and sometimes ulcers develop on the inner sides of the lower legs as a result of poor circulation. In neurodermatitis there is no known cause except the patient's repeated rubbing and scratching of the area. The term is also sometimes used for ECZEMA. *See also* MS pp.98–99.

Dermatology, branch of medicine that deals with the diagnosis and treatment of skin diseases. *See also* MS pp.98–99.

Dermis, the inner of the two main layers of the SKIN. Also known as the true skin, it is made up of connective tissue containing fibres that provide strength and toughness. It is richly supplied with blood vessels and contains many nerve endings, sensory organs and numerous glands. *See also* MS pp.60–61.

Derrick, hoisting apparatus using a tackle rigged at the end of a beam. The name is derived from a 17th-century English hangman. In building construction, a derrick is a tall, three-legged structure, erected to support a hoisting crane. In the petroleum industry, it is the tower over a bore hole that supports the tackle for drilling and hoisting. *See also* MM pp.78, 79, 86–87, 88–89, 96–97.

Derry. *See* LONDONDERRY.

Dervish, member of a Muslim fraternity, not necessarily mendicant, resembling a Christian monastic order. The communities arose within SUFISM and by the 12th century had established themselves strongly in the Middle East. The Bektashi order of Dervishes acted as companion to the Ottoman JANISSARIES, although as the Empire went into decline they became regarded as a reactionary influence and were eventually suppressed by ATATÜRK. A group of Bektashi are officially recognized in Albania, and were granted independent status after 1945. The chief devotion of the Dervish is *dhikr*, the remembering of God, a meditative rite used to remind the Dervish of his dependence on the invisible world of the spirit. Its encouragement of emotional display and hypnotic-like trances has earned the Dervish the epithets "whirling" and "dancing".

Derwentwater, lake in the Lake District in Cumbria, NW England, formed by a widening of the River Derwent. It contains the islands Rampsholme, Derwins, Lord's and St Hubert's. Length: approx. 5km (3 miles); width: 2km (1.25 miles).

Dery, Tibor (1894–1977), Hungarian writer. His works reflect his strong Socialist commitment and he was imprisoned 1957–60. They include the novel *Felelet* (1950–52), and the short stories *Odysseus* (1956).

DES. *See* DIETHYLSTILBESTROL.

Desaguadero, river in W Bolivia. It rises in Lake Titicaca in the Andes and flows SE to the saline Lake Poopó; its upper course is used for irrigation. Length: approx. 322km (200 miles).

Desai Morarji Ranchodji (1896–), Indian politician. From 1930 he devoted himself to the movement for Indian independence and was jailed by the British several times. After independence (1947) he was chief minister of Bombay (1952–56), minister of commerce and industry (1956–58), minister of finance (1958–63, 1967–69) and deputy prime minister (1967–69). In 1969 he was ousted by Prime Minister Indira GANDHI and became a leader of the opposition.

Desalination, extraction of pure water for drinking, industrial and chemical uses, or for irrigation, from water containing dissolved salts (usually sea water). The commonest and oldest method is to evaporate the water from a salt solution by DISTILLATION, and condense the vapour to form water. Another method is to freeze the salt solution; salt is excluded from the ice crystals which can then be melted. In the method of reverse osmosis, pure water only passes through a semipermeable membrane against which salt water is pressurized. Other methods are based on the migration of ions between electrodes. *See also* SU pp.144, *145*; MM pp.*50*, 201.

Descant, in music, a high part (generally sung) that harmonises with the melody, often used to provide a variation in the singing of consecutive verses of a hymn.

Descartes, René (1596–1650), French philosopher and mathematician who was educated by Jesuits. He founded analytic geometry; he introduced CARTESIAN COORDINATES in the treatise that prefaced the *Discourse on Method* (1637). Here, and in his *Meditations* (1641), Descartes' method of deduction and intuition, later known as Carthesianism, lead to modern metaphysics. By doubting all his ideas, he found that he reached one indubitable proposition: "I am thinking" and from this it followed that he existed, hence *cogito, ergo sum* – "I think therefore I am". Although mind and matter are distinct so that only ideas can be perceived, Descartes deduced the existence of an external world from his proofs of the existence of a perfect and consequently undeceiving God. *See also* DUALISM; MS pp.230–231; HC1 p.*302*.

Descent of Man and Selection in Relation to Sex, The, biological treatise published by Charles DARWIN in 1871. It explains his theory that man evolved from lower forms of life, primarily from ape-like ancestors. It did not cause the widespread outcry that his ORIGIN OF SPECIES occasioned 12 years before, since that book's evolutionary thesis implied much of what the later work propounded.

Dese, town in central Ethiopia, capital of Elo province. Of strategic importance in the war between Ethiopia and Italy in the 1930s, it was taken by Italy in 1936 but restored to Ethiopia in 1941. Pop. (1970) 45,700.

Desegregation, elimination of laws or customs that separate people on such grounds as sex, age, race or religion. *See also* APARTHEID.

Desensitization, medical procedure in which someone who is allergic to a certain substance (an allergen) is injected with it in a series of gradually increasing dosages in order to desensitize him or decrease his sensitivity. The term desensitization is also used to describe a type of treatment in psychotherapy. *See* MS p.146.

Desert, arid region of the Earth, in any latitude, characterized by scant, intermittent rainfall (25cm (10in) or less per year) and little or no vegetation. Cold deserts, areas almost permanently covered with snow or ice, extend over one-sixth of the Earth's surface, and hot deserts over one-fifth. Most desert regions lie between 20° and 30° N and S of the Equator, either where mountains form a barrier to prevailing winds, or where high pressure prevents precipitation. The SAHARA in Africa is the largest desert in the world. The term is more often applied to hot deserts, where agents of erosion have produced landforms unique to these areas of the Earth. *See also* NW pp.218–221; PE pp.120–121, 149.

Deserted Village, The, celebrated long poem (1770) by Oliver GOLDSMITH. It describes the peaceful English countryside and defends rural and conservative values against Whig imperialism.

Desert Fathers, early group of Christian hermits in Egypt, considered to be the first exponents of Christian monasticism. They preached the value of complete withdrawal from the world, and included St Antony and St Pachomius.

Desert pavement, coarse material, usually pebbles and gravel, that is generally unmoved by wind, forming a residual sheet on the rocky desert floor which can help prevent removal of finer material.

Desert Rats, popular name for the British 8th Army. The name comes from the jerboa (desert rodent) on the shoulder-flash of the 7th Armoured Division. They became famous for their part in WWII, especially at the Battle of EL ALAMEIN (October 1942) and the subsequent expulsion of the German forces from N Africa.

Desert Song, The operetta with lyrics by Oscar HAMMERSTEIN II and Otto Harbach and music by Sigmund ROMBERG. Originally produced on Broadway in 1926, it was made into films in 1929, 1944 and 1953. It contains many well known songs.

De Sica, Vittorio (1901–74), Italian film director and actor. He is noted for his use of amateur actors in biting, realistic drama. Notable films directed by him include *Bicycle Thieves* (1948), *Umberto D* (1952), *Indiscretion of an American Wife* (1953), *Two Women* (1961) and *A Brief Vacation* (1975). He acted in *General Della Rovere* (1959).

Desiccator, chemical apparatus used for drying substances or for keeping them dry. It consists of a glass vessel with a tight-fitting lid. Specimens are supported on a perforated platform above a lower chamber containing a desiccant, such as anhydrous calcium chloride.

Design Centre, name of two centres run by the DESIGN COUNCIL as showcases for modern British consumer goods. The centre in London was opened in 1956, that in Glasgow in 1957. Both also feature exhibitions on specialist themes, eg RECYCLING and dental health.

Design Council, body set up to "promote by all practicable means the improvement in design of the product of British industry". Founded (1944) as The Council of Industrial Design, it adopted its present title in 1972, by which date it was also involved in engineering design. The council runs the DESIGN CENTRES, maintains a design advisory and consultancy service and publishes the journals *Design* and *Engineering*. It also administers scholarships, organizes competitions and award schemes and works closely with other bodies in the field of design education.

Desman, aquatic mole-like animal with a flexible tubular snout, webbed hind feet and a vertically flattened scaly tail. It eats fish, insects and molluscs. Length: to 41cm (16in). Family Talpidae. *See also* NW p.*242*.

Desmid, any of a group of tiny, freshwater, single-celled green algae. Desmids are characterized by perforations in the cell wall and highly symmetrical shapes not unlike those of DIATOMS; they have no silica skeleton. Order Zygnematales. *See also* NW pp.46–47, *46*; PE p.*150*.

Des Moines, capital city of Iowa, USA, near the confluence of the Des Moines and Raccoon rivers. Founded in 1843 as a fort, it is now an industrial and transport centre for the Corn Belt. The city is protected from flooding by a system of dams and reservoirs. Industries: mechanical and aerospace engineering, chemicals, food processing. Pop. (1970) 201, 404.

Desmoulins, Camille (1760–94), journalist in the French Revolution. His pamphlets such as *Révolutions de France et de Brabant* (1789) were widely read and contributed to the rising which led to the fall of the BASTILLE. He aligned with Georges DANTON and was guillotined during the REIGN OF TERROR.

Despensers, English noble family of wealth and influence in the late 13th and early 14th centuries. Hugh the elder (1261–1326) the principal adviser of EDWARD II after 1312 and with his son, Hugh the younger (*d.* 1326), used royal favour to build up their estates and gain the earldom of Winchester. They were principal objects of attack when ISABELLA and MORTIMER invaded in 1326 and were beheaded after Edward had been deposed.

Desportes, Phillippe (1546–1606), French poet, disciple of the PLÉIADE. The melodic rhythms of his verse showed a strong Italian influence. His translated the Psalms and received several benefices from his patron, Henry III of France.

Despotism, absolute or autocratic rule by an individual, without legal sanction or popular consent. The term originated in ancient Greece and has been applied to dictatorial systems under which power was tyrannically and arbitrarily imposed and personal freedoms severely curtailed. The 18th century has been called the Age of ENLIGHTENED DESPOTISM, when a number of rulers, such as FREDERICK II of Prussia and CATHERINE II of Russia, exercised absolute power claiming that their regimes sought the improvement of the people they governed. *See also* MS p.276; HC1 p.324.

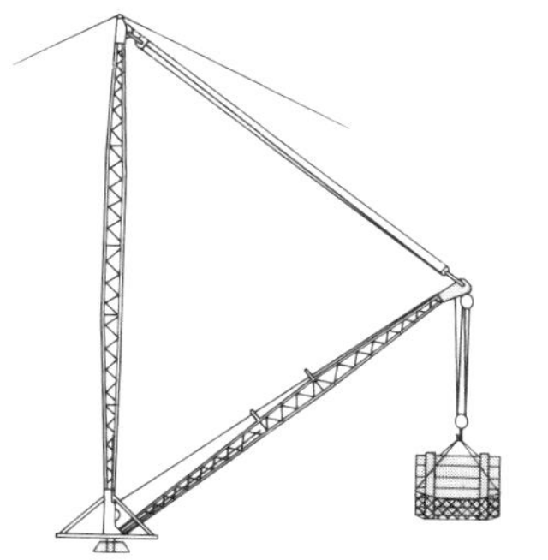

Derrick, the lifting device which in its simplest form uses a pole and supporting ropes.

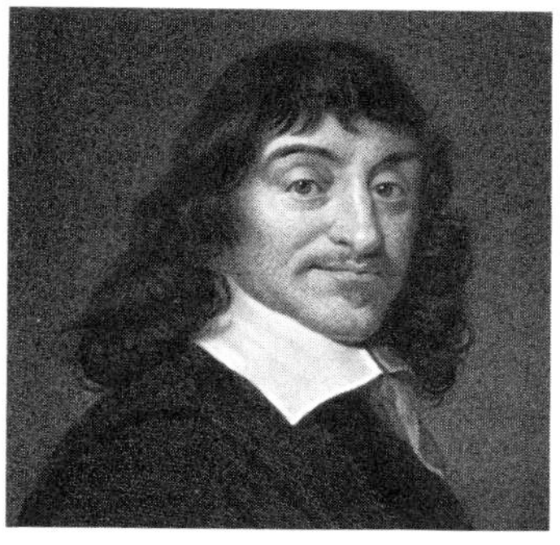

Descartes' proof of the existence of God ultimately turned out to be a circular argument.

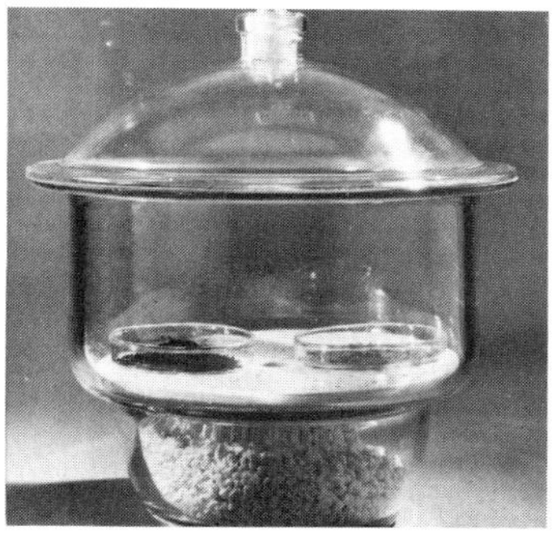

Desiccators utilize the properties of certain chemicals to absorb all traces of moisture.

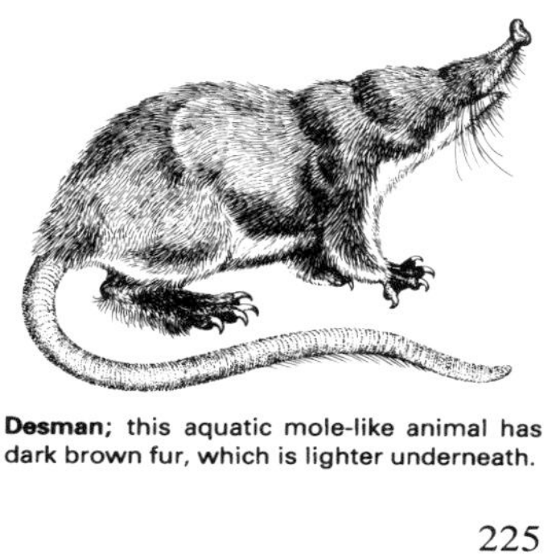

Desman; this aquatic mole-like animal has dark brown fur, which is lighter underneath.

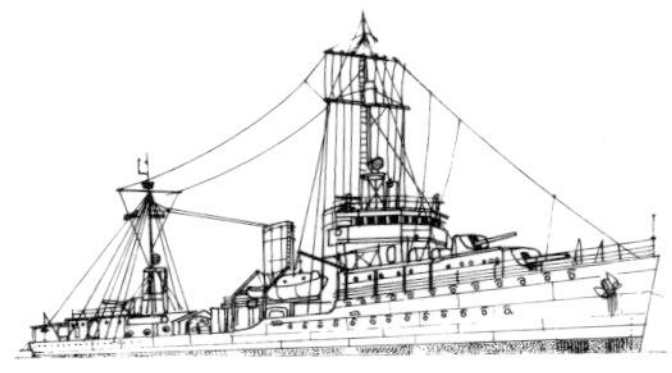

Destroyers are small naval vessels armed with torpedoes, guns and depth charges.

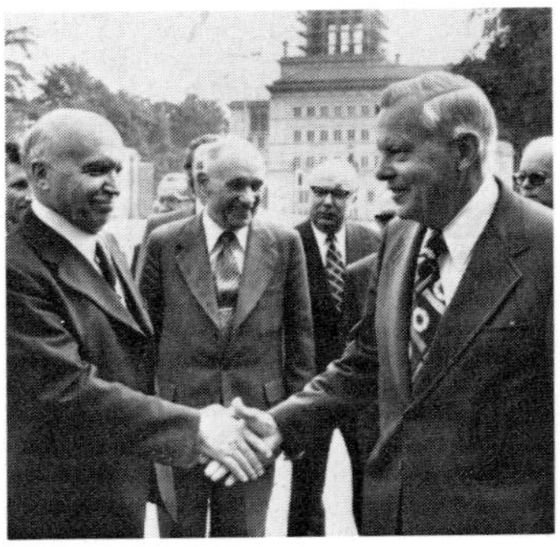

Detente; Russian and American delegates at the resumption of the SALT talks in 1976.

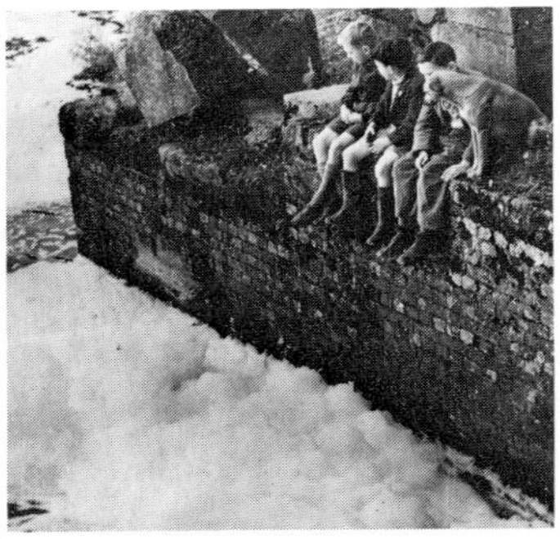

Detergent pollution forced the development of chemicals that bacteria break down.

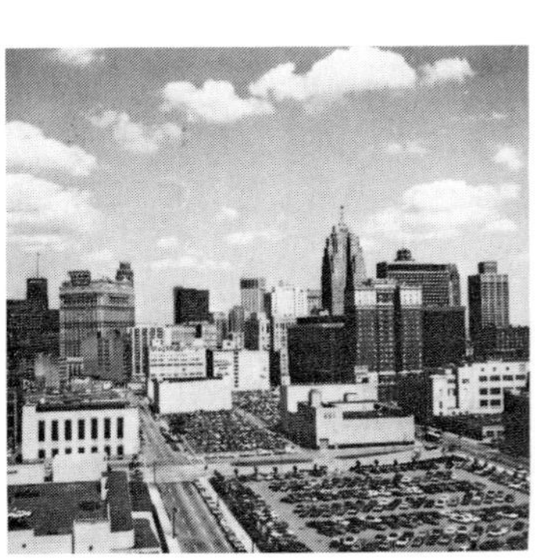

Detroit has a major problem of racial tension as almost half the city's population is black.

Des Prés, or Deprez, Josquin, or Josse (*c.*1445–1521), Flemish composer of church and secular music. A member of the papal choir in Rome (1486–94), he later entered the service of LOUIS XII of France. He wrote three books of Masses, more than 100 motets, and several secular songs. *See also* HC1 p.248.

Dessalines, Jean Jacques (1758–1806), Haitian revolutionary and leader of the independence movement after the capture of TOUSSAINT L'OUVERTURE. In 1803 he drove out the French and declared independence in 1804, changing the country's name from St Domingue to Haiti. As Emperor Jacques, his despotic rule lasted from 1804–06.

Dessau, city and river port in East Germany at the confluence of the rivers Elbe and Mulde. It was the site of Walter Gropius' BAUHAUS (school of architectural design) from 1925 until 1932. The city was almost destroyed in WWII. Industries: machinery, chemicals, paper, food processing. Pop. (1970 est.) 98,300.

Dessau, Paul (1894–), German composer and conductor. His works include films and orchestral music and the opera *The Trial of Lucullus* (1951) with libretto by Bertolt BRECHT, in honour of whom Dessau composed *In Memoriam Bertolt Brecht* (1957).

Dessoir, Max (1867–1947), German philosopher. He saw a moral and social need for a general "science of art", in which the arts would be systematically classified and their relevance to other cultural areas investigated.

D'Estaing, Valéry Giscard. *See* ESTAING VALÉRY GISCARD D'.

De Stijl. *See* STIJL, DE.

Destroyer, warship, smaller than a CRUISER, usually equipped with guns, torpedoes, depth charges and missiles. It was evolved from torpedo boats by the Royal Navy in the 1890s and played a major role in both world wars convoying Allied merchant ships. The first nuclear-powered destroyer was built by the USA in 1962.

Detective fiction, literary form in which a crime (almost always murder) is solved by a detective, usually amateur, who is the hero of the story. The form achieved its peak interest, especially in Britain, in the years between WWI and WWII. The first great detective-story writer was Edgar Allan POE, whose hero, C. Auguste Dupin, first appeared in *The Murders of the Rue Morgue* (1841). In Britain the first great detective novel was Wilkie COLLINS' *The Moonstone* (1868). The most famous and popular of 19th-century writers was Arthur Conan DOYLE, whose hero the vain and imperturbable Sherlock Holmes, first appeared in a *A Study in Scarlet* (1887). Since then a succession of detectives have become household names: G.K. CHESTERTON's Father Brown, Agatha CHRISTIE's Hercule Poirot and Miss Marple, E.S. GARDNER's Perry Mason and Dorothy SAYERS' Peter Wimsey.

Detente, term in international relations, signifying the reduction of tension between states. It was utilized in the 1960s to describe the effort of the USA and the USSR to end the COLD WAR and, after the events of the CUBAN MISSILE CRISIS, to establish closer links of mutual understanding. Since 1969 detente between the two superpowers has been marked by the two Strategic Arms Limitation Agreements (SALT). The preliminary SALT II agreement was announced at Okeanskaya, near Vladivostok in 1974, and was detailed in early 1975. That was followed by the Helsinki agreement of 1975, by which 35 nations of Europe and North America agreed to uphold fundamental HUMAN RIGHTS and freedoms and to permit the free exchange of people and ideas. *See also* DISARMAMENT; HC2 pp.306–307.

Detergent, substance used for cleansing. Strictly, detergents include SOAPS as well as synthetic detergents (syndets), both of which have molecules that possess a long hydrocarbon chain attached to an ionized group. The hydrocarbon chain attaches to grease and other non-polar substances; the ionized group has an affinity for water. Substances of this type lower surface tensions, ie they are surface active. The term is often used in the more restricted sense of synthetic detergents, of which there are several types; the commonest are salts of organic sulphonic acids. Domestic detergents often contain additives such as perfume and bleach. *See also* SURFACTANT; SU pp.86–87, *86*, 144, *144*; MM pp.240–241.

Detergent pollution, visual and chemical WATER POLLUTION of rivers and streams mostly by detergents used domestically. Seen as a thick foam on the surface, it is detrimental to water life and contributes to algal bloom. This type of detergent, usually high in phosphate, is being replaced by biodegradable detergents, which are decomposed in sewage-treatment plants. *See also* EUTROPHICATION; MM p.241.

Determinism, philosophical thesis that every event is the necessary result of its causes. Everything has a cause; no event is purely accidental. It involves the notion that the human will is not free, that choice is illusory, and that how people act is determined. The thesis cannot be proved or disproved. Some theories of psychology are deterministic in seeing an individual as controlled entirely by his history.

Deterrence, in criminology, theory that the punishment of criminals serves as an example and makes others less likely to commit crimes. Arguments about the death penalty and imprisonment turn on the question of how far such measures deter potential criminals. Most criminologists believe that the certainty of being caught and punished is a better deterrent than the severity of punishment of those who are caught. *See also* MS pp.292–293, 296–297.

Detonator, device using sensitive chemicals (initiating explosives) to set off less sensitive main charges (high explosives). The detonating charge is generally housed in a thin-walled metal or plastic, waterproof capsule, such as the "cap" at the base of a rifle cartridge. Detonators may be exploded electrically, by mechanical shock, or by igniting a fuse. *See also* MM pp.162, 242–243.

Detritus, in geology, SEDIMENT deposited by natural forces. It is classed by the size of the particles. *See also* ALLUVIUM.

Detroit, port in SE Michigan, USA, on the Detroit River just W of Lake St Clair; largest city in the state. It was founded as a French fort and trading post in 1701 and named Fort Pontchartrain. The British captured it in 1760 and used it as a base during the American War of Independence. Detroit served as territorial then state capital from 1805 to 1847. It suffered a severe fire in 1805, and was then rebuilt to a plan of the governor. It was lost to Britain in the WAR OF 1812, but retaken by American forces in 1813. A major Great Lakes port and rail centre, Detroit is the headquarters of General Motors, Chrysler and the Ford Motor Company. Industries: steel, pharmaceuticals, food processing, machine tools, tyres, paint and motor vehicles. Pop. (1970) 1,512,893.

Dettingen, Battle of (27 June 1743), engagement in the War of the AUSTRIAN SUCCESSION in which Anglo-German forces, led by GEORGE II of Britain, defeated the French army. It was the last occasion on which a British monarch went into battle in person.

Deus ex Machina, Latin term meaning "the god from the machine". It refers to the device in Greek and Roman drama by which a god appears to resolve the plot. The "machine" was a crane which raised and lowered the actor involved.

Deus, João de (1830–96), Portuguese poet. His volumes of poetry include *Flores do campo* (1869) and *Campo do flores* (1893), and his primer, *Cartilha maternal* (1876), is still used to teach reading in Portugal.

Deuterium oxide. *See* HEAVY WATER

Deuterium, isotope (D or H^2) of hydrogen whose nuclei contain a neutron in addition to a proton. Every million hydrogen atoms in nature contain about 156 deuterium atoms. Deuterium occurs in water as D_2O (heavy water), from which it is obtained by electrolysis. Heavy water is used as a moderator in some fission reactors and it could become a fuel in fusion reactors. Mass no. 2; at. wt. 2.0144. *See also* SU pp.64–65, 132–134.

Deuteron, nucleus of a DEUTERIUM (heavy hydrogen) atom, consisting of one proton and one neutron. The nucleus of ordinary hydrogen contains one proton only. *See also* SU pp.64–65.

Deuteronomy, biblical book, fifth and last of the PENTATEUCH. Three discourses ascribed to MOSES shortly before he died frame a code of civil and religious laws. The book attempts to explain the religious meaning of the events described in the previous books, GENESIS, EXODUS, LEVITICUS and NUMBERS, and appeals for fidelity to the Mosaic Law.

Deutsch, Otto Erich (1883–1967), Austrian-born British musical biographer and bibliographer. He was an authority on Handel, Mozart and, especially, Schubert, for whom he produced a complete catalogue.

Deutzia, genus of flowering plants, mostly shrubs native to Asia and cultivated elsewhere as ornamentals; they are related to the HYDRANGEA. They bear clusters of white single or double flowers. The leaves are oval and pointed, with a slightly toothed edge. Family Hydrangeaceae.

Deva, the all-encompassing word for god in the VEDAS, the earliest religious texts of India. There were 33 of these gods, 11 for each of the three world categories – sky, air, and earth. Some of the nature gods of Vedic poems appear in present-day HINDUISM; they include Surya (the sun) and Varuna (the sky).

De Valera, Eamon (1882–1975), US-born Irish statesman. He was active in the movement for Irish independence and after the Easter Rebellion of 1916 was elected president of the SINN FEIN Party while imprisoned in England. He opposed William COSGRAVE's Irish Free State ministry and founded the FIANNA FÁIL Party in 1924. He defeated Cosgrave in 1932 and remained head of Ireland's government (with two brief interruptions) until 1959, when he became president of the Republic of Ireland. He retired in 1973. *See also* HC2 pp.294–295, *294*.

De Valois, Dame Ninette (1898–), Irish-born ballerina and choreographer, real name Edris Stannus. She danced with Diaghilev's BALLETS RUSSES (1923–26) and was appointed ballet director of Dublin's Abbey Theatre. In 1931, she founded the Sadler's Wells Ballet School, which later became the Royal Ballet which she directed (1956–63).

Devaluation, lowering the value of one nation's currency with respect to that of another or to gold. The decision to adjust the currency downwards is made by the central government when the nation is having balance-of-payments problems. Devaluation stimulates a nation's exports and decreases its imports by increasing the purchasing power of foreign currencies.

Devanagari, or Nagari, Indian script developed in the 7th century AD and used for Sanskrit, Hindi and Marathi, among other languages. It is written from left to right, and although it has vowels and consonants it is often written syllabically without the use of vowels.

Developed countries, term used to describe those countries where industrial development has made possible a standard of living which may be termed affluent. In such countries the literacy rates are high as are the gross national products and per capita incomes, with an even spread of wealth rather than the extreme differences seen in developing or third world countries. The developed countries are chiefly the nations of North America, Europe and Australasia.

Developer, photographic, solution that converts the invisible image formed on a photographic emulsion during exposure into a visible image. The developer works by converting the silver salts in the emulsion of the film or plate into metallic silver. Commonly used developers consist of a solution of metal ($CH_3NH.C_6H_4OH$) and hydroquinone, $C_6H_4(OH)_2$, to which a preservative, an alkali and a restrainer are added. The preservative arrests deterioration of the developer and the restrainer reduces fogging during development. Various formulations are used for specific purposes. *See also* MM pp.218–219.

Developing countries. *See* THIRD WORLD.

Deventer, Sir Jacob Louis van (*c.*1874–1922), Boer military commander. He was a guerrilla leader in the South African War (1899–1902) and later worked for the unity of the various South African states. He fought against the Germans in South-West Africa and E Africa during WWI.

Devereux, Robert, 2nd Earl of Essex. *See* ESSEX, ROBERT DEVEREUX, 2ND EARL OF.

Devi, supreme HINDU goddess. She is also known by the names Uma, Parvati and Ambika (in her benevolent aspects) and Kali (in her destructive aspect).

Deviance, in the social sciences, anything that departs from or conflicts with the standard norm. Deviant behaviour differs markedly from socially accepted attitudes, moral standards and general behaviour. In considering both "deviation" and "norm", the group context must be taken into consideration, eg members of a teenage gang might consider respect for the law to be "deviant". *See also* MS pp.262–267.

Deviated septum, abnormality of the muscular wall (septum) that separates two cavities. Such an abnormality can interfere with the normal functioning of an affected organ, and may require surgery as in the case of a deviated heart septum.

Deviation, standard, in statistics, an average measure of the variability of a set of numerical values from the MEAN of the set. If the values are bunched together around the mean, the deviation tends to be small; if they are widely dispersed, the deviation tends to be large.

Devil, in many religions an evil spirit. In Christianity the devil is the chief of the fallen angels cast out of heaven for their pride, or some other sin. There was little mention of the devil in the Old Testament, but from the biblical account of Christ's temptation in the desert it became common to regard the devil as the tempter who sought to win men's souls away from God. In the Middle Ages it was believed that the power of the devil could be manifested physically, and that he presided over Hell, where souls were made to suffer for their sins.

De Villiers, Dawie (1940–), South African rugby union halfback whose 25 international appearances (1962–70) included a record 22 as captain. A graduate of Stellenbosch University, where he studied for the ministry, he represented Western Province.

Devils, The, or The Possessed (1872; trans. 1914), novel by DOSTOEVSKY about a group of revolutionaries whose beliefs lead them to commit arson, murder and suicide.

Devil's coach horse, large, dark-coloured beetle and the largest member of the family Staphylinidae. It has strong concealed wings and is found in or near decaying organic matter including carrion and dung. Length: to 2.8cm (1.1in). Species *Ocypus olens.*

Devil's Island (Île du Diable), smallest and southernmost of the Îles de Salut in the Caribbean Sea, off the coast of French Guiana. It was a French penal colony from 1852 until 1938.

Devine, George (1910–65), British actor, director and theatre manager, noted for his part in founding the English Stage Company, which he directed at the ROYAL COURT THEATRE London, from 1956 to 1965.

Devis, Arthur (1711–87), British painter of decorative portraits and conversation pieces, often portraying squires with their families in gardens or parks.

Devlin, Josephine Bernadette (1947–), Northern Irish politician. A radical socialist and Catholic Irish nationalist, she sat as the Independent Unity representative for Mid-Ulster at Westminster from 1969 to 1974.

Devolution, War of (1667–68), conflict over the Spanish Netherlands, engineered by LOUIS XIV using a dispute over his dowry from Marie Thérèse (daughter of the King of Spain) as a pretext. After an easy French victory, the Dutch joined England and Sweden in the TRIPLE ALLIANCE and forced the return of much of the territory to Spain. *See also* HC1 p.314, *314.*

Devon, county in SW England, bounded by the English Channel (S) and the Bristol Channel (N). It is a hilly region that includes Dartmoor and Exmoor, and the principal rivers are the Ex, Tamar, Dart and Teign. Beef and dairy cattle are important and industries include tourism, fishing, textiles, pottery and clay-mining. The county town is Exeter. Area: 6,711sq km (2,591sq miles). Pop. 942,000.

Devon cattle, breed of horned, dark-red domesticated cattle reared for both meat and milk, yields of which are fair. The breed was originally developed in Devonshire, England, and has been introduced to the USA and Argentina. *See also* PE pp.226–227.

Devonian period, the fourth-oldest period of the PALAEOZOIC era, lasting from 395 to 345 million years ago. It PALAEOZOIC ERA, lasting from 395 to 345 million years ago. It is sometimes called the Age of Fishes. Numerous marine and freshwater remains include jawless fishes and forerunners of today's bony and cartilaginous fishes. The first known land vertebrate, the amphibian *Ichthyostega*, appeared at this time. Land arthropods included scorpions, mites, spiders and the first insects. Land plants consisted of tall CLUB MOSSES, scouring rushes and ferns. *See also* PE pp.119, *119, 130 131*; NW p.24

Devon Island, arctic island off the extreme N coast of Canada. Lying at the head of Baffin Bay S of Ellesmere Island and N of Baffin Island it forms part of the Northwest Territories. Area: approx. 54,030sq km (20,861sq miles).

De Vries, Hugo (1848–1935), Dutch botanist who introduced the concept of MUTATION into the study of GENETICS. In 1900, with Karl Correns and Erich Tschermak, he rediscovered Gregor MENDEL's work on heredity. He later wrote *The Mutation Theory* (1901–03), which influenced later concepts of the role of mutation in evolution. *See also* NW pp.34–35.

De Vries, Peter (1910–), US novelist and poet, frequent contributor to *The New Yorker.* His first publication was *No, But I Saw the Movie* (1952); in 1974 he published *The Glory and the Hummingbird.*

Dew, water droplets formed, usually at night, by condensation on vegetation and other surfaces near the ground. Hoar frost is formed when temperatures are below freezing. Fog also deposits moisture on exposed surfaces.

Dewar, Sir James (1842–1923), Scottish chemist and physicist who carried out research into materials at extremely low temperatures. He built a device that could produce liquid oxygen. He invented Dewar flasks (household varieties are Thermos flasks), which were capable of storing low-temperature liquid oxygen for longer periods than was previously possible. He first liquified and solidified hydrogen, and reached a temperature of 14° above absolute zero.

Dewberry, perennial fruit-bearing plant of the family Rosaceae, similar to a blackberry but with weaker trailing stems. The fruit, a source of iron and vitamin C, is thought to possess a finer flavour than that of the blackberry. Species *Rubus caesius. See also* PE pp.214–215.

De Wet, Christian Rudolph (1854–1922), Boer general and political figure. A skillful guerrilla commander, under CRONJE during The SOUTH AFRICAN WAR (1899–1902), he later held office in the South African Government and championed Boer nationalism.

Dewey, John (1859–1952), US educator, philosopher and psychologist, who worked at Columbia University (1904–29). He was a founder of PRAGMATISM and modern FUNCTIONALISM, and strove to make the social sciences deal with the practical problems of education and mental disturbance. He had a profound impact on US educational practice and the development of applied psychology. His books include *The School and Society* (1899) and *Experience and Education* (1938).

Dewey, Melvil (1851–1931), US librarian, who created the DEWEY DECIMAL SYSTEM. He established the first library training school of Columbia College and was its librarian (1883–89). He was also a founder of the American Library Association (1876).

Dewey decimal system, means of classifying books, created by Melvil DEWEY in 1876, based on the decimal principle. It is popular because of its subject currency and simplicity. There have been 18 revisions in the system. *See also* MM p.216.

Dewi. *See* DAVID, SAINT.

De Wint, Peter (1784–1849), British landscape painter in oils and watercolour, influenced by Thomas GIRTIN. De Wint's watercolour landscapes approach those of COX in their quality and subtle variations of light.

Dew point, the temperature at which a vapour begins to condense, as when water vapour in the air condenses into cloud when the air becomes saturated with the vapour.

Dew pond, water that collects in a hollow through the accumulation of dew, moisture that condenses from the air on a cool night. Farmers sometimes deliberately create a dew pond by spreading straw or leaves in a natural hollow, on which dew can condense.

Dexter, John (1925–), British theatrical director. Notably, he has produced many of Arnold WESKER's plays, including *Chips with Everything* (1963). He has also been responsible for several spectacular stage productions.

Dexter, Ted (1935–), British cricketer. A majestic batsman who hit the ball with tremendous power, he played in 62 Test Matches 1958–68 (4,502 runs; average 47.89), 34 times as captain. A useful bowler and brilliant fielder, he played for Cambridge University and Sussex.

Dextran, stable, water-soluble polysaccharide sugar. It is used as a substitute or extender for blood plasma in transfusions.

Dhahran (Az-Zahrān) town in E Saudi Arabia on a headland in the Persian Gulf. Oil was discovered there in 1938 and it is a terminus of the Transarabian pipeline and the headquarters of the Arabian American Oil Company. Pop. 12,500.

Dharma, sacred law or duty in Hindu tradition. Virtue lies in following one's Dharma, which varies with one's caste and stage in life. In BUDDHISM the Dharma is the doctrine of Buddha; in JAINISM it is The Good as the principle of motion. *See also* HINDUISM.

Dhaulagiri, Mt, fifth-highest peak in the world, in the Himalayan Mts, N central Nepal. It was first climbed in 1960 by a Swiss expedition led by Max Eiselin. Various rivers, including the Gandak, rise on its slopes. Height: 8,177m (26,827ft).

Dhole, rare, yellow, brown or grey wild dog native to central and E Asia; it preys chiefly on rodents and other small animals, but packs have been known to attack larger mammals such as deer and even to drive tigers from their prey. Length: (without tail) to 1m (3.3ft). Family Canidae; species *Cuon alpinus.*

Dhow, sharp-bowed Arab sailing craft, with one or two masts and slanting triangular (lateen) sails, used in the Indian Ocean and the Red Sea. In larger dhows, called baggalas, the mainsail is much larger than the mizzen sail.

Diabetes insipidus, disease characterized by extreme thirst and excessive output of very dilute urine. It is caused by a decrease in the secretion of the hormone VASOPRESSIN, also known as the antidiuretic hormone (ADH), which may be due to damage to the HYPOTHALAMUS. Left untreated by antidiuretic drugs it can result in dehydration, reduced blood volume, shock and even death. *See also* MS pp.100–101.

Diabetes mellitus, common metabolic disorder in which the body's inability to produce adequate amounts of the hormone INSULIN results in a disease characterized by inability to process carbohydrates. It may also affect many other body organs

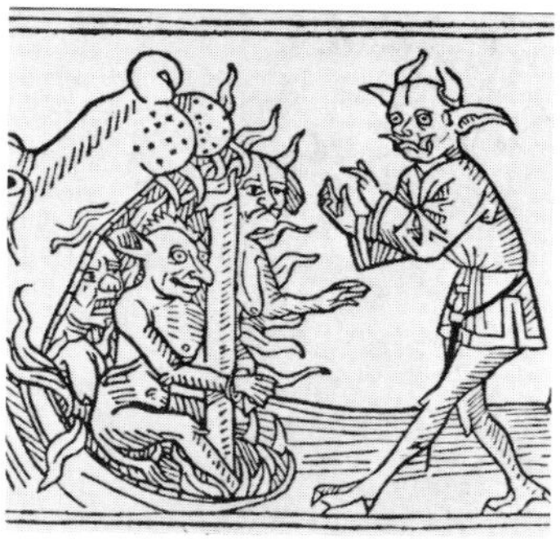

Devil; a 15th century woodcut showing the devil Belial before the gates of hell.

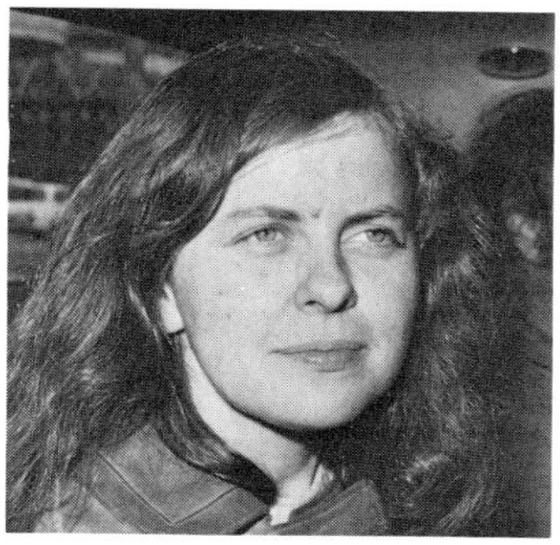

Bernadette Devlin broke a parliamentary rule when she delivered her maiden speech.

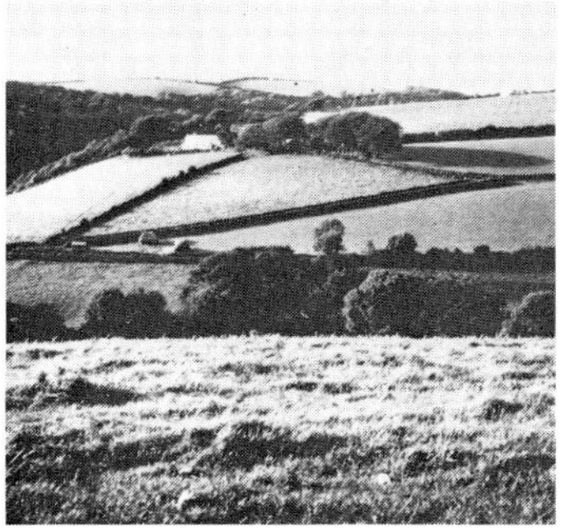

Devon countryside is more suitable to small farming than large mechanical cultivation.

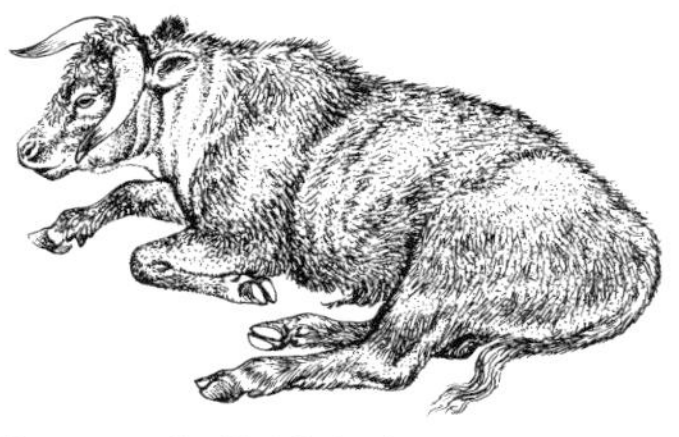

Devon cattle; Red Ruby is the name of the smaller north county breed.

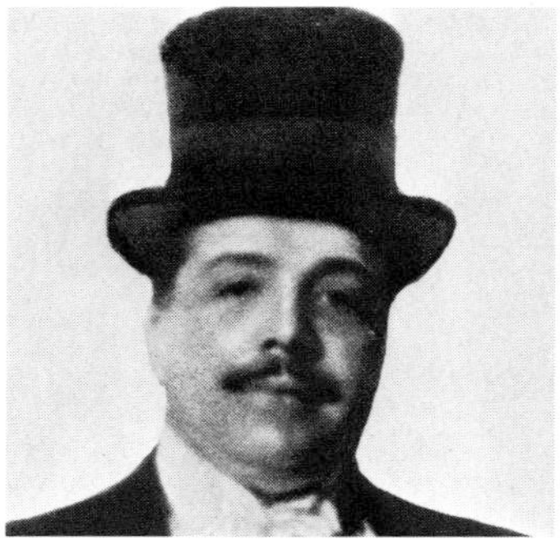

Diaghilev; his production of *The Rite of Spring* caused a riot when it opened in 1913.

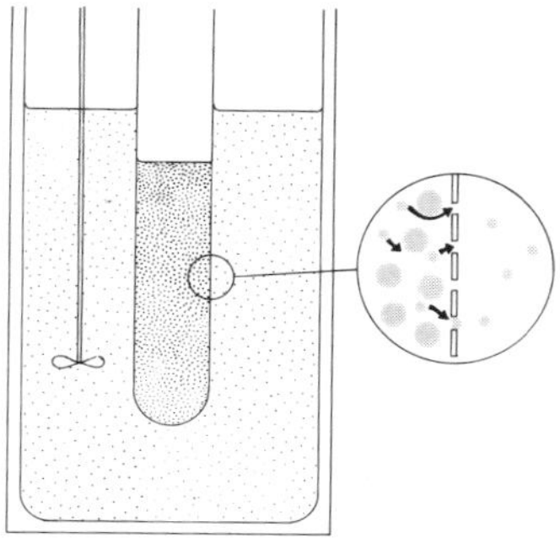

Dialysis; a kidney machine removes waste artificially from the patient's blood.

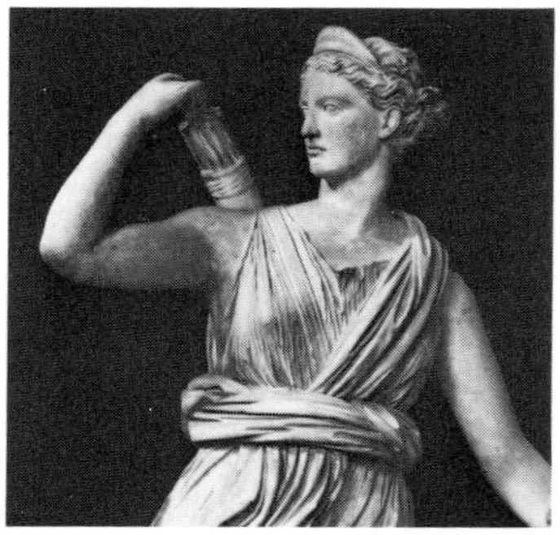

Diana is usually portrayed as a huntress with bow and arrow and hunting dogs.

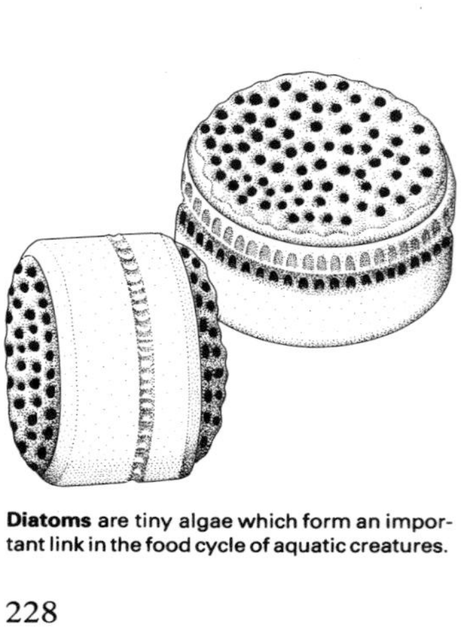

Diatoms are tiny algae which form an important link in the food cycle of aquatic creatures.

and functions. Susceptibility to diabetes mellitus is inherited, although the disease usually develops with obesity or infection, and is slightly more common in males. A non-hereditary form is produced by cancer of the PANCREAS.

Insulin is normally secreted by the islets of Langerhans in the pancreas. In diabetes caused by a diseased pancreas, too little insulin is produced and severe symptoms result. In diabetes mellitus that begins in adult life (generally after age 40), the effectiveness and speed of release of insulin from the pancreas is often disturbed, producing minor (in some cases, almost no) symptoms. In diabetes mellitus, the body cannot handle the sugar end-products of CARBOHYDRATE and convert them to energy compounds. The excess sugar is excreted in the urine and signs such as frequent urination, a dry mouth, extreme thirst, weakness, loss in weight and blurred vision can result. Diagnosis depends on urine and blood tests as well as special glucose-tolerance tests. The disease cannot be cured but it can be treated with carbohydrate-limited diet, exercise and the administration of drugs – either insulin injection or synthetic oral drugs – to lower blood-sugar levels. *See also* MS pp.65, 100, *101*.

Diaghilev, Sergei Pavlovich (1872–1929), Russian ballet impressario. He was active in the Russian artistic avant-garde after 1898 and moved to Paris, where he formed the revolutionary BALLETS RUSSES company in 1909. He attempted to unite music and scenery with the movement of the dance. His company assembled many talented artists, dancers and musicians, including NIJINSKY, STRAVINSKY and FOKINE. *See also* HC2 pp.274–275.

Dialectical logic, philosophical concept of G.W.F. HEGEL (1770–1831). Hegel argued that ordinary logic, governed by the law of contradiction, is static and lifeless. In the *Science of Logic* (1812–16) he claimed to satisfy the need for a dynamic method, whose two moments of thesis and antithesis are cancelled and reconciled in a higher synthesis. Logic was to be dialectical, or a process (movement) of resolution by means of conflict of opposing categories. In short, thought was as "living" as organic nature itself. *See also* DIALECTICAL MATERIALISM.

Dialectical materialism, the philosophical basis of Marxism. Karl MARX (1818–83) agreed with G.W.F. HEGEL that the course of history was logically dialectical – ie change occurred in terms of the opposition of thesis and antithesis, leading to synthesis. Marx believed that Hegel was wrong, however, to define the basis of dialectics as spirit or reason. For Marx, the proper dialectical subject was material experience. According to his theory of historical materialism, mind (soul, reason) was derived from material, economic or social realities. *See also* DIALECTICAL LOGIC.

Dialecticians, Chinese school of Forms and Names (400–220 BC), of which *Hui Shih* and *Kung-Sun Lung* are typical representatives. They analysed the relations of things to their names. The longest and most authentic text known is the *Kung-Sun Lung Tzu*. The sophisticated work of this group was largely disregarded by later Chinese schools.

Dialysis, process for separating a COLLOID from a dissolved substance by virtue of their different rates of diffusion through a semi-permeable membrane. In the ARTIFICIAL KIDNEY the unwanted (smaller) molecules are separated out. Electrodialysis employs a direct electric current to accelerate the process, especially useful for isolating proteins. *See also* MS p.102.

Diamond, native element, crystalline form of carbon (C). It is found in volcanic pipes and in alluvial deposits as cubic system octahedral (diamond-shaped) crystals. It is brilliant, transparent to translucent, colourless or of many hues including yellow, green, blue and brown, depending on the impurities contained. This form of carbon is the hardest natural substance known; its hardness and brilliance make it unsurpassed as a gem. Bort, a variety of diamond inferior in crystal and colour, and carborondo, an opaque grey to black variety called black diamond, as well as all other non-gem varities, have applications in industry. Industrial diamonds are used as abrasives, bearings in precision instruments such as watches, and in the cutting heads of drills for mining. Other uses for them are as cutting heads of diffraction grating-ruling engines and as the styli of high-fidelity sound record-players. Synthetic diamonds, made by subjecting graphite with a catalyst to about 7×10^5 N/sq m (1 million lb/sq in) pressure and temperatures of about 3,000°C (5,400°F), have been made since 1955, but are fit only for industrial applications. Diamonds are weighed in carats (0.2gm) and in points (1/100 carat). The largest diamond mines are in South Africa. Hardness 10; s.g.3.5. *See also* PE p.98; SU p.*139*.

Diamond Challenge Sculls, the blue riband of singles sculling. It has been held annually at the Henley Royal Regatta since 1844, at which time it was of domestic interest only. Since the 1890s it has been dominated by non-British oarsmen. From 1957, the Australian Stuart MACKENZIE won the event six consecutive times.

Diamond Lil (1928), theatrical comedy written by and starring Mae WEST, set in the Californian Gold Rush.

Diana, in Roman mythology, the virgin huntress and patroness of domestic animals. Initially a woodland goddess, she was rapidly identified with the Greek ARTEMIS, the moon goddess and sister of APOLLO. With strong associations as a fertility deity she was invoked by women to aid conception and childbirth. The lower classes and slaves regarded her as their protector.

Diana of the Ephesians, goddess worshipped at Ephesus, Asia Minor. She was originally derived from a Greek earth goddess but later became merged with the Roman goddess Diana. Her temple was one of the wonders of the ancient World. *See also* MS p.*210*.

Diane de Poitiers, Duchesse de Valentinois (1499–1566), mistress of HENRY II of France. Although she was much older than the king, his love for her served to overshadow the queen, CATHERINE DE' MEDICI.

Dianthus. *See* CARNATION.

Diapason, in Greek and medieval musical theory meaning "through all the notes", ie the octave. The diapason stop on an ORGAN is the main foundation stop which produces the most characteristic tone of the instrument.

Diaphragm, sheet of muscle that separates the abdominal cavity from the cavity of the chest. During breathing out it relaxes and allows the chest to subside; when breathing in it contracts and bears down, causing the chest cavity to enlarge. *See also* MS pp.66–67.

Diaphragm. *See* BIRTH CONTROL.

Diarbekir. *See* DIYARBAKIR.

Diarrhoea, the frequent elimination of loose, watery stools, often accompanied by cramps and stomach pains. Diarrhoea is a symptom, caused by a functional disorder, fatigue, food allergy or lack of vitamins; by a generalized bodily disorder such as kidney disturbance or overactivity of the thyroid gland, or inflammation or infection of the lower bowel caused by bacteria, viruses or other agents. A mild short attack of diarrhoea, serious in children but not in adults, can be treated by a bland diet; more severe and longer-lasting attacks and those accompanied by fever or other signs should be treated by a doctor. *See also* MS pp.105, 107.

Diary, literary record of events and observations kept by an individual at the time of their occurrence, either for his private satisfaction or self-consciously for later publication. The earliest known diary of real worth is CAESAR's account of the Gallic wars. Diaries are of interest either for the information which they contain for historians or for the beauty of their prose. Of the former C.C.Greville's diaries of the reign of Queen VICTORIA are unsurpassed. Of the latter there is none more popular than Francis KILVERT's diary of a country parson. When the two qualities are combined, as in the diaries of Samuel PEPYS and those of Jules and Edmund GONCOURT, the result is a literary masterpiece. *See also* LETTERS; MEMOIRS.

Diary of Anne Frank, record of the two years (1942–44) spent by Anne Frank (1929–45) and her family in a sealed-off room in Amsterdam to escape Nazi persecution. It was published in 1947. It is a poignant account of Jewish suffering.

Diary of a Nobody, book by George and Weedon GROSSMITH, originally serialized in *Punch*. The diary is Mr Pooter's, a lower-middle-class clerk, and its laconic comic style pokes fun at his pathetic attempts to remain dignified through the ups and downs of suburban life.

Diaspora, Jewish communities outside PALESTINE. The dispersion of the Jews began when large numbers of them were sent into exile as a result of the Assyrian and Babylonian conquests (722 and 597 BC). Although CYRUS THE GREAT allowed Jews to return from Babylonia in 538 BC, some of the exiles remained behind. In the 3rd century BC significant Jewish communities existed in Alexandria and Antioch. The destruction of Jersualem in AD 70 by the Romans accelerated the process, and Diaspora Jews spread to all parts of the world, far outnumbering those within Palestine. Their religious and cultural centre, however, remained Palestine, where they finally succeeded in establishing the state of ISRAEL as a Jewish national home in 1948.

Diastole, the part of the cardiac cycle during which the HEART muscle is relaxed and the heart is filling with blood. *See also* MS pp.62–63.

Diastrophism, large-scale changes in the earth's crust. It includes INTRUSION and METAMORPHISM and the large movements that produce mountain ranges, ocean basins and continents. In the past diastrophism was sometimes used to describe a localized event, but the term now refers to large-scale phenomena only.

Diathermy, medical treatment which uses heat generated by high-frequency (short wave) alternating electric current. The heat stimulates local blood circulation and tissue repair. It is used to treat back pain, to aid muscle and tendon repair, and is often used in eye and neurosurgery.

Diatom, any of a group of tiny microscopic single-celled algae (class Bacillariophyceae) characterized by a shell-like cell wall made of silica. The shell (frustule) consists of two halves that fit together. Diatom shells occur in a wide variety of highly symmetrical shapes. They live in nearly every environment that has water and is exposed to sunlight, including virtually all bodies of salt and fresh water and even soil, damp rocks and tree bark. The microscopic shells of long-dead diatoms accumulate in, for example, diatomite (kieselguhr), a mineral with abrasive, absorbent and refractory uses.

Diatomaceous earth, sediment formed from the skeletons of diatoms, microscopic marine plants. The deposits are almost pure silica and often form large, thick beds on the ocean floor.

Diatonic, musical scale which uses seven of the 12 notes of the OCTAVE, the notes moving in the TONIC SOL-FA progression. It has been the basic scale of Western POLYPHONIC music since the 16th century. *See also* CHROMATIC; MUSICAL NOTATION.

Diaz, Bartholomew (*c.*1450–1500), also known as Bartolomeu Dias, Portuguese navigator, the first European to round the CAPE OF GOOD HOPE. In 1487, under the commission of John II of Portugal, Diaz sailed three ships around the African continent, thereby opening the route to India. He was part of the expedition of 1500 of Pedro Álvares CABRAL that discovered Brazil, but he was drowned on the voyage. *See also* HC1 pp.234–235.

Diaz de la Peña, Narcisse-Virgile (1808–76), French landscape painter, a member of the BARBIZON SCHOOL. He also painted mythological scenes, a favourite subject being a nude Venus, with Cupid and nymphs.

Díaz del Castillo, Bernal (*c.*1492–*c.*1581), solder who served with CORTÉS, known for his *The True History of the Conquest of New Spain,* written 40 years after the event but not published until 1632. Díaz put less emphasis on the role of Cortés in the conquest of Mexico than had earlier writers.

Diazepan, tranquillizer in widespread use as Valium. It is a benzodiazepine, as is Librium. It acts as a skeletal muscle relaxant and has the side-effects of drowsiness and fatigue, and possibly ataxia (inability to co-ordinate movements).

Dibdin, Charles (1745–1814), British composer and singer. He wrote many sea-songs (eg *Tom Bowling*) that gained wide popularity. He also composed stage entertainments containing songs that had considerable public appeal.

Dibdin, Thomas Frognall (1776–1847), British bibliographer, whose books included *Bibliomania* (1809),*Library Companion* (1824) and *Bibliographical, Antiquarian and Picturesque Tour in the Northern Counties of England and Scotland* (1838). He catalogued what became the John Rylands Library, Manchester.

Dibiasi, Klaus (1947–), Austrian-born Italian diver who, after winning a silver medal in 1964, dominated the highboard at the next three Olympic Games (1968, 1972, 1976), the first such gold medal hat-trick in diving history. Also a silver medallist at springboard (1968), he won the world and European titles.

Dice, small cubes of wood, ivory, bone or stone used in board games or in gambling. A cube has its six faces numbered by dots, from 1 to 6, so placed that the numbers on opposite faces add to 7. The British learned to gamble with dice from their Roman conquerors. Such games continued to be popular in the Middle Ages, although frowned upon by the Church.

Dichloromethane, colourless liquid which is used as a solvent for cellulose acetate, as a cleaning fluid and as an inhalation anaesthetic. Its formula is CH_2Cl_2, with a molecular weight of 84.94. It is prepared by chlorinating methane. Properties: b.p. 39.75°C (103.5°F); m.p. −95°C (−139°F): and s.g. 1.34 at 15°C. *See also* SU p.41.

Dichromatic vision. *See* COLOUR BLINDNESS.

Dickens, Charles (1812–70), British novelist. He began his writing career as a parliamentary reporter for the *Morning Chronicle.* His first great success was the series of satirical pieces which appeared in the press after 1833, collected in 1836 as *Sketches by Boz.* They were followed by the sporting sketches collected as *The Posthumous Papers of the Pickwick Club* (1836–37). His first novel was *Oliver Twist* (1838); his other novels include *Dombey and Son* (1848), *David Copperfield* (1850), *Bleak House* (1853) and *Great Expectations* (1861). *See also* individual titles; HC2 pp.98–99.

Dickens, Monica (1915–), British writer, resident in the USA, the great granddaughter of Charles DICKENS. She wrote amusing autobiographies based on her life as a cook, ie *One Pair of Hands* (1939) and as a nurse, ie *One Pair of Feet* (1942) and *Time to Make the Tea* (1951). Her novels include *Mariana* (1940) and *The Heart of London* (1961).

Dickinson, Emily Elizabeth (1830–86), US poet. Although she lived an active social life to the age of 23, she then became a total recluse, writing more than 1000 short, mystical poems in secrecy. Considered among the finest written in the USA, these exploited rich imagery to explore a world of emotion and beauty in simple things. *See also* HC2 p.288.

Dickinson, Goldsworthy Lowes (1862–1932), British writer and political theorist. He wrote *The Greek Way of Life* (1896) and was involved in the creation of the League of Nations. His *The International Anarchy 1904–14* was published in 1926.

Dick-Read, Grantly (1890–1959), British obstetrician whose theories revolutionized obstetrics. In his book *Natural Childbirth* (1933) he suggested that anaesthetics should not be relied upon in childbirth, which need not be unduly painful if the mother follows a course of prenatal relaxation exercises. The book caused much controversy. Between 1949 and 1953 he practised in South Africa.

Dicotyledons, larger of the two subclasses of flowering plants (ANGIOSPERMS) characterized by two seed leaves (cotyledons) in the seed embryo. The leaves of dicotyledons are usually net-veined and their flower parts are in fours or fives. Most common garden plants are dicotyledons. The smaller subclass contains MONOCOTYLEDONS. *See also* NW pp.58–65.

Dicoumarin, or dicoumarol, anticoagulant drug used to reduce or retard blood clots. *See also* MS p.91.

Dictator, ruler of a state whose power is not limited by law or constitution. The word is Roman in origin, when it meant an extraordinary magistrate in the empire. He was appointed to quell civil disturbances or to meet a military crisis before which the normal civil authorities felt themselves incompetent. His term of appointment was limitedh originally, to only six months. The modern dictator shares with his Roman ancestor the ability to control the nation's armed forces, but also extends his authority over every aspect of the national life in order to exercise a TOTALITARIAN control.

Dictatorship, absolute rule by an individual or group without the consent of the governed. In many modern dictatorships, all power resides in the dictator, with representative assemblies either abolished or existing as mere formalities. Personal freedom is severely limited; censorship is generally enforced; education is tightly controlled; and legal restraints on governmental authority are abolished. *See also* MS pp.276, *277.*

Dictatorship of the proletariat, stage that Karl MARX felt must precede the introduction of pure Communism, during which all remaining capitalistic thoughts and attitudes would be weeded out. In this stage the state owns the means of production and directs the production of goods and services. The few capitalistic procedures, eg wage payment based on productivity, that survive to this stage are limited.

Dictionary, book that lists, generally in alphabetical order, the meanings of words. Some enable words in one language to be translated into words of equivalent meaning in another language. A dictionary may be general – including all the commonly used words in a language – or specialized – containing words used in a particular discipline such as science or music. *See also* MM pp.214–215.

Dictionary of National Biography, biographical encylopaedia of important British historical figures. Work on it was started in 1882, and its editor until 1891 was Sir Leslie STEPHEN, who contributed many articles to the first 26 volumes. It was completed in 1901 and reissued in 22 volumes in 1908–09; supplements have been published every ten years.

Dictum, in law, both the judgment in a case settled by arbitration and the saying or opinion of a magistrate uttered during the hearing of a case. A dictum not immediately relevant to the case before the magistrate is called an *obiter dictum.*

Dictyoptera, insect order including MANTIDS and COCKROACHES. It is comprised of two sub-orders, Blattaria (cockroaches) with front legs adapted for running, and Mantodea (mantids) with front legs adapted for seizing prey. Some species may attain a length of 10cm (4in). *See also* NW pp.106–107, *110, 213.*

Diderot, Denis (1713–84), French philosopher and man of letters. He was imprisoned in 1749 for irreligious writings, and later assumed direction of the French *Encyclopédia* (1751–72). *On the Interpretation of Nature* (1754) and *D'Alembert's Dream (1760)* reveal his scientific materialism, and *Jacques the Fatalist* (1796) and *Rameau's Nephew* illustrate his determinism. He also made noteworthy contributions to art and literary criticism. *See also* HC2 pp.22–23.

Didjeridu, musical instrument of Australian ABORIGINES. It is a hollow piece of wood of about 1.5m (5ft), which is blown.

Dido, in Greek and Roman legend the founder of Carthage. Carthage prospered and Dido's hand was sought by the King of Libya. To escape him she stabbed herself and died on a funeral pyre. VIRGIL made Dido a contemporary of AENEAS, and attributes her suicide to Aeneas's decision to abandon her at Jupiter's command.

Dido and Aeneas (1869), only opera by Henry PURCELL, with libretto by Nahum Tate, based on the story in VIRGIL's *Aeneid.* It is considered an early masterpiece of English opera, notable for its dramatic characterization and beautiful melodies. *See also* HC1 pp.318, *319.*

Didot, Firmin (1764–1836), most eminent member of a distinguished French family firm of printers, founded in 1713. He developed the first successful STEREOTYPE process (*c.* 1795); his father, François-Ambroise Didot (1730–1804) invented a system, which is still in use, for establishing type sizes.

Didrikson, Mildred ("Babe") (1914–56), US athlete. She won two gold medals in track and field events in the 1932 Olympic Games, and after 1934 turned to golf. She won the British amateur title in 1947 and the US Women's Open three times.

Diederichs, Nicolaas (1903–), South African economist and politician. He represented the Losberg constituency in 1958–74, and has been Minister of Economic Affairs, Mines and Finance.

Diefenbaker, John George (1895–), Canadian politician. A homesteader and lawyer in Saskatchewan, he was elected to the House of Commons in 1940. He served as the Progressive-Conservative Prime Minister (1957–63) and had a reputation for his oratory and skill in foreign affairs. He was opposition leader in the Commons (1963–67).

Diégo-Suarez (Antsirane), town in N Malagasy on Diégo-Suarez Bay; location of a French naval base. It was discovered in 1543 by Diégo Soares. Exports: coffee, maize and cattle. Pop. (1975 est.) 41,200.

Dieldrin, brown, solid, chlorinated NAPHTHALENE derivative ($C_{12}H_8OCl_6$) widely used as a contact insecticide and prepared by the oxidation of ALDRIN with peracids. It is insoluble in water and is prepared as an emulsion or powder.

Dielectric, electrical insulator, especially one that separates two conductors, as in a CAPACITOR. The PERMITTIVITY of a dielectric is a measure of the extent to which it can resist the flow of charge. The dielectric strength (usually measured in V/mm) is the maximum field that the dielectric can withstand without breaking down, ie becoming ionized. For many low-power applications, such as tuning capacitors in radios, air is used as the dielectric. *See also* SU p.*126.*

Diels, Otto Paul Hermann (1876–1954), German chemist. He discovered (1906) the sub-oxide of carbon (C_3O_2), studied the structure and synthesis of cantharidine (a poison contained in the body fluid of blister beetles), and did research on sterols (solid, higher alcohols such as cholesterol). He was professor of chemistry (1916–48) at Kiel University, and was jointly awarded the Nobel Prize for chemistry (1950) with Kurt ALDER with whom he discovered (1928) the synthesis of dienes (organic compounds containing two double bonds), known as the Diels-Alder reaction.

Diem, Ngo Dinh (1901–63), Prime Minister of South Vietnam (1954–63). A nationalist opposed to both the Communists and the French, he was appointed premier of South Vietnam in 1954. At first he received strong US support, but corruption and setbacks in the war against the Communists led to growing discontent with his government. With covert US support, army generals staged a coup in 1963, in which Diem was murdered.

Diemen, Anthony (Anton) van (1593–1645), Dutch colonial administrator, governor-general in the East Indies (1636–45). He sponsored TASMAN's voyages of exploration. Tasman named after him the island (now Tasmania) that he discovered in 1642. *See also* HC2 p.124.

Dien-Bien-Phu, site of a decisive battle, fought in 1954, in which the Viet Minh defeated French forces and secured the independence of South-East Asia from

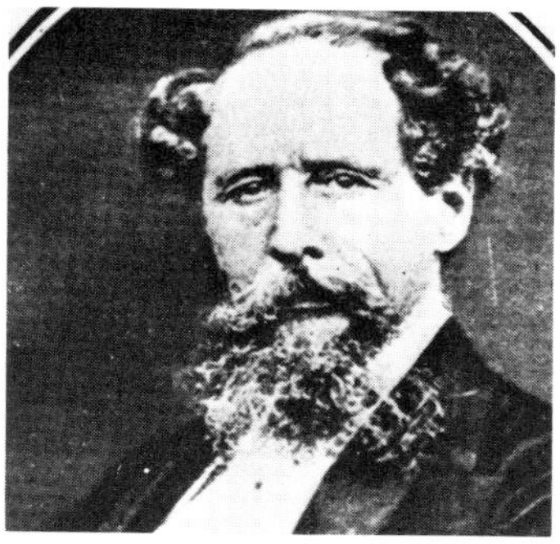

Charles Dickens is honoured as a supreme novelist and biting critic of Victorian society.

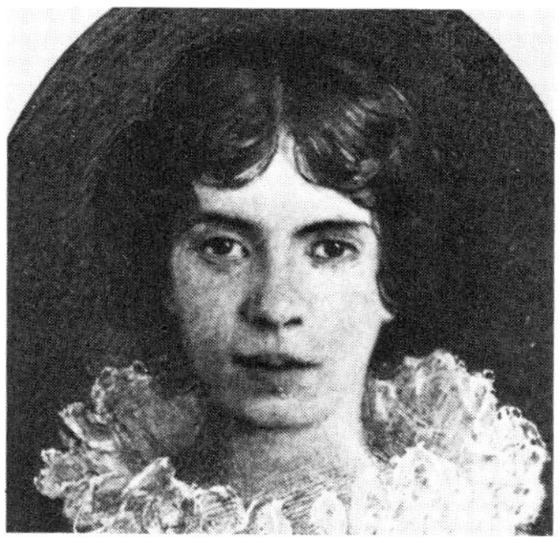

Emily Dickinson received her inspiration from the Bible and the natural world.

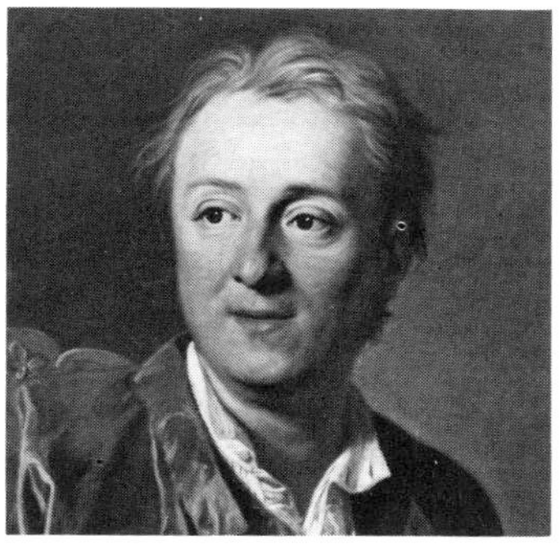

Denis Diderot devoted much of his life's work to compiling the French encyclopaedia.

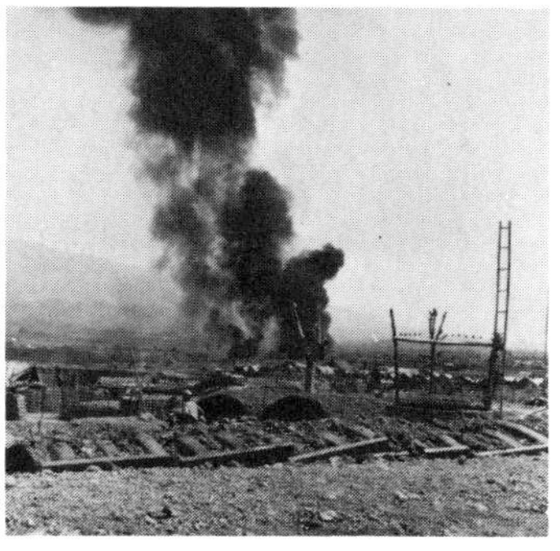

Dien-Bien-Phu; the bitter struggle that ended French presence in Indochina.

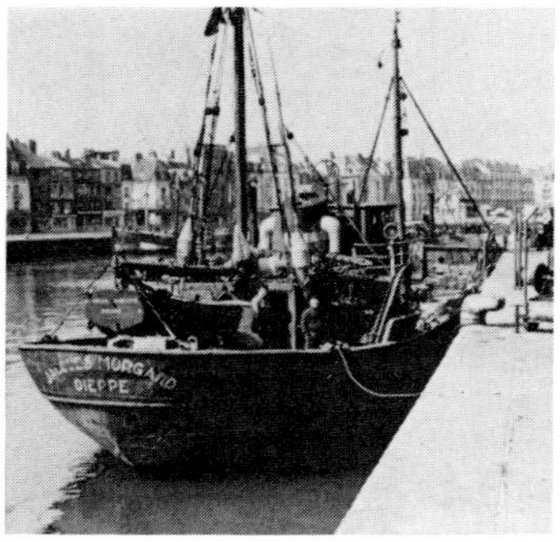

Dieppe, the French Channel port, was the scene of a dramatic raid during World War II.

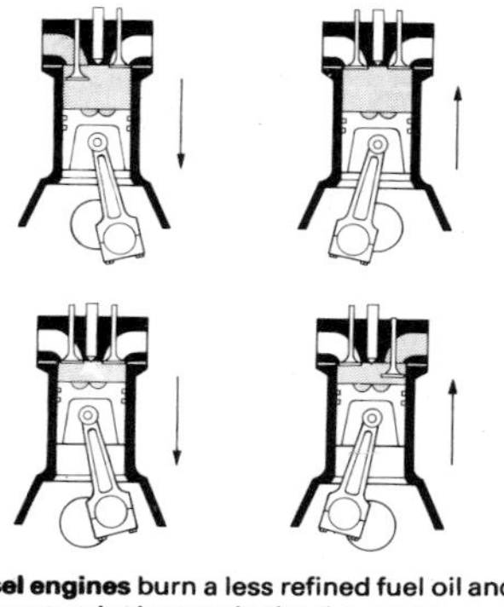

Diesel engines burn a less refined fuel oil and use no spark plugs to ignite the gases.

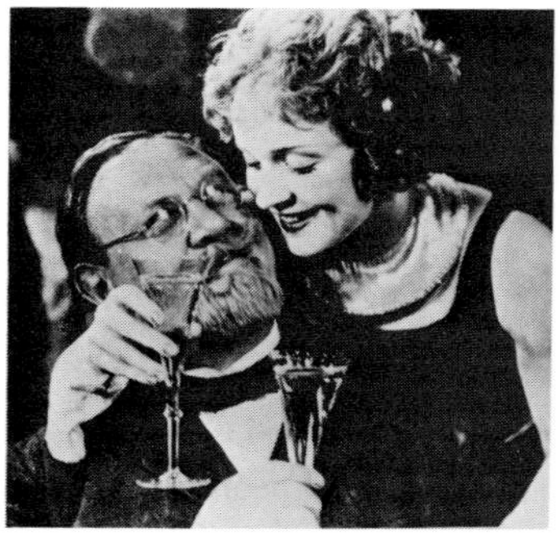

Marlene Dietrich in a scene from her famous German film *The Blue Angel*, made in 1930.

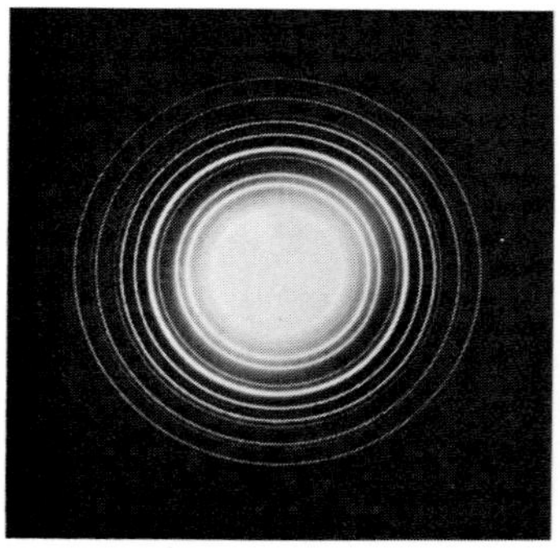

Diffraction rings, a pattern caused by interference as light travels through a tiny hole.

French rule. The French established a military stronghold at Dien-Bien-Phu in 1953, hoping to lure the Viet Minh into battle. In a masterpiece of logistics, the Vietnamese (under General GIAP) surrounded the French forces and used heavy artillery to batter them into submission in a siege lasting 55 days.

Dieppe, town in Normandy, N France, at the mouth of the River Arques on the English Channel. Of strategic importance in the wars between England and France, it was raided by Allied troops, mainly Canadians, in 1942. It has a 13th-century church and a 15th-century chateau. A commercial centre, it has fishing and tourist industries. Pop. 30,000.

Diesel, Rudolf (1858–1913), German inventor who developed, patented and built the diesel internal combustion engine (named after him). He established a factory, in Augsburg, which made DIESEL ENGINES. *See also* ENGINE; RAILWAYS; DIESEL FUEL; MM pp.62–63, 69, 141.

Diesel-electric railway. *See* RAILWAYS.

Diesel engine, internal combustion engine in which air for combustion is first compressed so that its temperature increases sufficiently to ignite fuel injected directly into the cylinders. For this reason it is also called a compression-ignition engine. The fuel and air mixture burns rapidly and expands to drive the pistons. Diesel engines usually have an electrical circuit for heating the cylinders during starting; once the engine has fired this circuit may be switched off. The engine is stopped by cutting off the fuel supply. *See also* MM pp.62, 68–69, *69*.

Diesel fuel, or diesel oil, petroleum product heavier than paraffin but lighter than heating oil, used to power diesel engines in industrial and agricultural vehicles such as lorries, buses, tractors, locomotives and ships. There are many grades of diesel fuels which, unlike petrol, burn unevenly. They are graded against standardized mixtures of hexadecane and alpha methylnaphthalene to establish a cetane number. A cetane number of 30 to 45 is desirable. *See also* MM p.78.

Diet, food and drink consumed by a person or animal. The human diet falls into main groups of nutrients necessary for the maintenance of health: PROTEINS, CARBOHYDRATES, FATS, VITAMINS and MINERALS. An adult requires daily about one gramme of protein for each kilogramme of body weight. Beans, peas, fish, eggs, milk and meat are important protein sources. The body breaks these down into AMINO ACIDS from which it synthesizes its own protein. Carbohydrates (starches and sugars), stored in the body as GLYCOGEN and fat, are the chief sources of energy and are found in cereals, root vegetables and sugars. Carbohydrates make up the bulk of most diets. Fats in the diet, such as butter and vegetable oils, are a concentrated source of energy and aid in the absorption of the fat-soluble vitamins (vitamins A, D, E and K). Vitamins function as COENZYMES in important body processes. Minerals such as iron, calcium, potassium sodium are also essential.

Diet, legislative assembly or administrative council, principally important in German history. CHARLES IV established the diet of the Holy Roman Empire by his Golden Bull of 1356. The diet comprised three estates – the seven electors (of the Holy Roman Emperor), other lay and church nobility, and representatives of the imperial cities – each of which met separately. Approval by each estate and the consent of the emperor were required on all matters. The most important of the diet's infrequent assemblies were at Nuremburg (1467), WORMS (1521) and AUGSBURG (1530). After the Treaty of Westphalia (1648), the diet lost much of its legislative power and importance. *See also* HC1 p.268.

Dietary laws, instructions, either secular or religious, which stipulate what foods may or may not be consumed under certain conditions. Such laws are one of the many ways in which a social group maintains its identity. Many Hindus, for example, practise vegetarianism, and Muslims undertake ritual fasting. In Judaism, such laws are called *Kashrut*. They prohibit certain foods entirely and indicate that others must be prepared in a certain way. The term kosher signifies acceptable foods.

Dietetics, specialized study of the human DIET and nutrition. A dietician plans what people should eat when they are ill, making sure they get what they need to make them well.

Diethylstilbestrol (DES), non-steroid, synthetic oestrogen (female sex hormone). It is used as a drug in cattle feeds as a growth stimulant, and has been tried experimentally on women in a "morning after" contraceptive pill and (in the 1950s) as an agent to prevent miscarriage. The drug was, however, found to have cancer-causing potential and its use is now strictly limited. Some girls born to women who took DES during pregnancy developed a rare and often fatal form of vaginal cancer.

Dietrich, Marlene (1904–), film-star and cabaret singer, *b.* Maria Magdalena von Losch, in Germany. Her glamorous image evolved in films directed by Josef von STERNBERG, eg *The Blue Angel* (1930) and *Blonde Venus* (1932). Other notable films included *Destry Rides Again* (1939) and *Rancho Notorious* (1956). *See also* HC2 pp.268–269, *269*.

Dietz, Robert Sinclair (1914–), US geophysicist. He proposed a theory of sea-floor spreading in 1961, which has since been confirmed. He is also known for his studies of the Moon's physical features and of meteorite impact on rocks.

Differential, small change occurring in the value of a mathematical expression due to a small change in a variable. If $f(x)$ is a function of x, the differential of the function, written df, is given by $f^1(x)dx$, where $f^1(x)$ is the DERIVATIVE of $f(x)$. *See also* SU p.42.

Differential, in a motor-car, a set of circular gears that connect the half-shafts and the propeller shaft. It allows for the difference in the speeds of rotation of the drive-wheels while cornering, and also transmits power from the engine to the wheels. *See also* MM pp.*89*, *131*.

Differential association, social theory of Edwin H. Sutherland (1883–1950) which states that criminal behaviour is learned in much the same way as other kinds of behaviour: exposed to criminal attitudes individuals learn to break the law. *See also* MS pp.288–289.

Differential calculus. *See* CALCULUS

Differential equation, equation containing derivatives, eg $dN/dt = AN$, where N is the number of people in a population, t the time, A a constant and dN/dt the DERIVATIVE of population with respect to time; this differential is a simplified equation for population growth. Differential equations are sometimes solved by INTEGRATION. *See also* CALCULUS; PARTIAL DIFFERENTIAL EQUATION.

Differential geometry, type of GEOMETRY which uses CALCULUS notation to analyse geometric concepts such as curves and surfaces. For example, a curve, such as the path of a projectile, or the orbit of a spaceship, can be described mathematically in terms of three mutually perpendicular VECTORS which vary independently along the length of the curve.

Diffraction, spreading of a wave such as a light beam or water on passing through a narrow opening or by the edge of an obstacle. It is evidence for the wave nature of light and is explained by INTERFERENCE. Diffraction is the reason that the shadow of an object merges from dark through grey to light. The interference pattern produced by Fresnel diffraction can be viewed on a screen placed before the light source and the diffracting object. Fraunhofer diffraction uses a parallel beam of light which, after diffraction, is focused by a lens onto a screen. Diffraction is used to provide information on the wavelength of light and the structure of crystals. All waves, including sound and radio waves and X-rays are diffracted at obstacles. Diffraction accounts, for example, for the audibility of sound around corners. *See also* SU pp.80, 102, 108.

Diffraction grating, substrate consisting of parallel equidistant lines (as many as 1,500 per mm) for producing spectra by diffraction of light. Transmission gratings are ruled on glass and are transparent; reflection gratings are opaque – they are ruled on metal films. Such gratings are much used in SPECTROSCOPY. *See also* DIFFRACTION; SU p.*102*.

Diffusion, spontaneous flow of a substance in a mixture from regions of high concentration to regions of low concentration, due to the random motion of the individual atoms or molecules. Diffusion apparently ceases when there is no longer a concentration gradient; there is no net migration between regions. Its rate increases with temperature, since average molecular speed also increases with temperature. The process occurs quickly in gases, more slowly in solids. *See also* SU p.84.

Diffusionism, in anthropology, theory of the spread of a culture or its artefacts from one culture to another. This spread may be achieved by migration, political control, trade or religious contact. The elements of a culture that are diffused will vary according to the manner in which contact between the cultures is achieved. The diffusion of techniques or ideas is often taken as evidence for contact between cultures where other evidence is lacking.

Digby, Sir Kenelm (1603–65), English diplomat, scientist and writer. He is said to have realized in 1661 that oxygen is necessary for plant life, but many of his other "discoveries" are no longer highly regarded. He was one of the first members of the ROYAL SOCIETY and a friend of DESCARTES and Sir Thomas BROWNE.

Digenis Akrites, 10th-century epic poem, perhaps the most well-known literary production of the Byzantine Empire. It concerns the exploits of the hero Basil Digenis Akrites, who defended the empire's eastern frontiers.

Digestion, natural process of breaking-down food into simpler chemical substances that can be absorbed by an organism. It provides nutrients and energy to keep an organism alive. Digestion occurs mainly by means of chemical agents called ENZYMES. *See also* MS pp.68–69.

Digestive system, group of organs of the body concerned with the DIGESTION of foodstuffs; also known as the alimentary system. It begins with the mouth cavity, which includes the teeth, tongue and salivary glands and continues into the pharynx, which connects with the oesophagus (gullet) that carries food into the stomach. The stomach leads to the small intestine, which then opens into the large intestine, or colon. After food is swallowed it is pushed through about 9m (30ft) of digestive tract by rhythmic muscle contractions and relaxations known as peristalsis. On its journey the food is transformed into a liquid that can be absorbed into the bloodstream and carried to the tissues of the body; carbohydrates are changed to sugars (glucose), proteins to amino acids, and fats to fatty acids and glycerol. The indigestible parts are eventually eliminated from the body (as faeces) through the rectum, at the end of the colon. *See also* MS pp.68–69.

Diggers, millenarian social and religious sect in England in 1649–50, an extreme group of the LEVELLERS, who emerged in the NEW MODEL ARMY. They formed an egalitarian agrarian community at St George's Hill, Surrey, in 1649; it was destroyed the following year by local farmers. The main Digger theorist was Gerrard Winstanley, who proposed an immediate communalization of property to establish social equality in his book *Law of Freedom* (1652).

Diggers, name given to the gold prospectors from Europe and North America who went to Australia after the discovery of gold there in 1852. It was also a name given to New Zealand and Australian troops in WWI.

Digit. *See* NUMBERS.

Digit, significant. *See* SIGNIFICANT DIGIT.

Digital clock. *See* CLOCK.

Digital computer. *See* COMPUTER.

Digitalis, drug obtained from the leaves of the FOXGLOVE (*Digitalis purpureal*), used

to treat heart disease. It increases contractions of the heart muscle and slows the cardiac rate. *See also* MS p.*86*, 90.
Digital signals, signals representing zeros and ones of the BINARY SYSTEM, transmitted by radio and translated by computer into dots of varying shades to produce pictures similar to half-tone newspaper photographs. *See also* MM p.226.
Dik-dik, tiny African antelope with a soft grey to red coat and a tuft of hair on its forehead; its name is derived from its call. It may live singly or as part of a family or large group. The males have horns. Height: 41cm (16in) at the shoulder. Family Bovidae; genus *Madoqua. See also* NW pp.*201.*
Dike. *See* DYKE.
Dill, aromatic annual herb native to Europe and cultivated widely. Its small oval seeds and feathery leaves are used in cooking to impart a flavour similar to aniseed or caraway. Family Umbelliferae; species *Anethum graveolens. See also* PE pp.*210, 212.*
Dillard, Harrison (1923–), American high hurdler who, as world record-holder, failed to qualify for his event in the 1948 US Olympic team, entered the 100m instead, and won two gold medals (100m; 4 by 100m). In 1952 he won his own event, 110m hurdles, and another gold medal in the relay.
Dillon, John (1851–1927), Irish politician. He was a supporter of PARNELL and MP in 1880–83 and 1885–1918. He was chairman of the Irish Nationalist Federation (1896) and became leader of the Irish Nationalist Party in 1918, just before it was eclipsed by SINN FEIN.
Dilthey, Wilhelm, (1833–1911), German philosopher and one of the first to postulate a separation of the natural sciences and the structures of experience. As a result, he formulated a distinct methodology for the social sciences which emphasized the individual in the context of his past and present environment. Dilthey also developed the treatment of history from a cultural viewpoint which has been influential in the study of literature.
DiMaggio, Joseph Paul ("Joe"), (1914–), US baseball player. A hitter and centre-fielder for the New York Yankees (1936–42; 1946–51), DiMaggio scored a hit in a record 56 consecutive games in 1941 and had a lifetime batting average of 0.325. He was elected to the Baseball Hall of Fame in 1955.
Dimbleby, Richard (1913–65), British broadcaster. He was the BBC's first war correspondent and later presented current affairs TV programmes. He possessed great dignity and authority and was the BBC's radio and TV commentator on important state occasions.
Dimensions, in mathematics, properties called length, area and volume. A figure having length only is said to be one-dimensional; a figure having area but not volume, two-dimensional; and a figure having volume, three-dimensional. The number of dimensions of a figure is the same as the number of co-ordinates that are needed to determine the points of the figure. For example, in a plane which is two-dimensional, two co-ordinates are required (x,y). In physics, the fundamental dimensions are mass, length and time. *See also* SU pp.32–33.
Dimetrodon, extinct predatory reptile once found in N USA during the early and middle Permian period (225–280 million years ago). Its large dorsal "sail", formed by elongated vertebrae, may have served as a device for regulating the animal's body temperature. Length: 3.5m (11ft). *See also* NW pp.184–185, 186–187.
Diminishing returns, law of (law of increasing costs), in economics, states that as more and more of a variable input, eg labour, is added to the production process, while all other factors are held constant, the addition to total output per unit begins to decline after some point. While the first unit of labour, for example, might produce ten units of output, the second unit of labour may produce only eight units of output; the third, only six units, etc. While the total output tends to increase, the marginal output (addition to total output) declines after some point. *See also* MS p.310, *310.*
Dimitrov. *See* PERNIK.
Dinaric Alps (Dinara Planina), SE extension of the Eastern Alps in Yugoslavia, along the E coast of the Adriatic Sea. They extend from Istria to Albania, and include peaks over 2,400m (7,900ft). Length: 640km (400 miles).
Dinaric subrace, hypothetical subdivision of the CAUCASIAN race, characterized by medium to tall stature, swarthy skin, usually black hair and eyes, a large convex nose, and flattened occipital regions of the skull. While not regarded as a distinct racial entity by most anthropologists, this type is seen as a variant of the Alpine race.
Dine, Jim (1935–), US painter, known for attaching objects, such as tools or shoes, to a painted canvas. His works include *Name Painting (1935–63)[1]*, painted 1968–69, which has the names of the people he knew during those years charcoaled across it.
Dinesen, Isak (1885–1962), pseudonym of Karen, Baroness Blixen-Finecke, Danish writer. Fascinated by Africa, she described her life on a coffee plantation in Kenya in *Out of Africa* (1937). Her collections of short stories include *Seven Gothic Tales* (1934), *Winter's Tales* (1942) and *Shadows on the Grass* (1960).
Dinghy, general term for any of a variety of small rowboats or sailboats originally used along the coasts of India. It is now also used for an auxiliary boat on yachts.
Dingle, the northernmost peninsula in County Kerry, sw Ireland. Slieve Mish is the chief mountain range. The town of Dingle, once a walled stronghold, is now a fishing centre. Pop. 1,683.
Dingo, yellowish-brown wild DOG found in Australia; it is thought to be a descendant of early domestic dogs that were introduced by Aborigines. It feeds mainly on rabbits and other small mammals, but may also attack sheep. Family Canidae; species *Canis dingo. See also* NW pp.204–205.
Dinosaur, any of the large number of REPTILES that lived during the Mesozoic era, between 225 and 65 million years ago. They first appeared during the Triassic period, survived the Jurassic and disappeared inexplicably at the end of the Cretaceous. There were two orders. The Saurischia ("lizard hips") included the bipedal carnivores and the giant herbivores; the Ornithiscia ("bird hips") were smaller herbivores. Many theories have been advanced to account for the disappearance of the dinosaurs, the "terrible lizards". It is possible that, as the climate changed, swamps drained and vegetation altered, they were incapable of the sophisticated and swift adaptation required by their environments. Diplodocus, at 25m (82ft) long, was the longest land animal that has ever lived. *See also* NW pp.24–25, 184–187.
d'Inzeo, name of two Italian brothers, Piero (1923–) and Raimondo (1925–), who between them won most major honours in the sport of showjumping. Piero, European champion in 1959, followed an Olympic bronze medal in 1956 with a silver in 1960; Raimondo, world champion in 1956 and 1960, won the 1956 silver and the 1960 gold. With the Italian team, they won a silver (1956) and three bronzes (1960, 1964, 1972). Piero won the coveted King George V Gold Cup in 1957, 1961 and 1962.
Diocese, administrative area over which a BISHOP is responsible. Larger dioceses may have two or more deans to help in administration, each responsible for several parishes.
Diocletian, Caius Aurelius Valerius (245–313), Roman emperor (*r.* 284–305). He was of humble birth and was proclaimed emperor by the army. He reorganized the structure of the empire to resist the barbarian threat, and ruled jointly with Maximian, Constantius I and Galerius. In 303 he ordered the last great persecution of the Christians. He retired in 305.
Diode, electronic component with two electrodes, used mainly as a rectifier. The semiconductor diode, which has largely replaced the electron-tube type, usually has a single p-n junction. It allows current to flow freely in only one direction (positive or negative), but only a small current flows in the reverse voltage direction. A zener diode blocks current flow until a critical voltage is reached, when it breaks down and conducts. *See also* SU pp.128–130.
Dioecious plant, plant bearing either female, pistillate flowers (with carpels only) or male, staminate flowers (with stamens only); but not both.
Diogenes (*fl.* 4th century BC), Greek CYNIC philospher. As a youth he went to Athens and studied under Antisthenes. Diogenes' teachings founded the Cynic school of philosophy. He believed that the virtuous and happy life could be achieved only by rejecting all possible restrictions on personal freedom – material possession, emotions and conventional values – and attaining self-sufficiency. By reducing personal needs to the minimum one can have mastery over the one real thing – one's soul.
Diogenes of Apollonia (5th century BC), Greek natural philosopher. He studied and taught in Athens during a transitional period of Greek thought, and tried to combine ancient ideas with the new biological observations. Like ANAXAGORAS, he believed that all things in the world are modifications of air, and further that this common harmony of air was due to an all-encompassing intelligence.
Diomede Islands, two islands in the Bering Strait. Big Diomede Island (Ratmanova) is a possession of the USSR and Little Diomede Island belongs to the USA. Between the two islands lies the USSR-US boundary and the INTERNATIONAL DATE LINE. The islands were discovered on 16 Aug. 1728 (St Diomede's Day) by Vitus Bering.
Diomedes, the name of two figures in Greek mythology. Diomedes, son of Tydeus and hero of ARGOS, was famous for his deeds at Troy where he wounded Aphrodite and Ares and captured the city's sacred image, the PALLADIUM. Diomedes, King of the Bistones, was thrown by HERCULES to his own man-eating mares.
Dione, one of the ten known satellites of Saturn, the fifth of the ten, between Tethys and Rhea. Dione's period is 2 days, 17 hours and 41 minutes and its mean distance from Saturn is 377,000km (234,000 miles). It was discovered by Giovanni CASSINI in 1684. *See also* SU p.213.
Dionne, Narcisse Eutrope (1848–1917), Canadian historian and bibliographer who wrote a history of early Canada and compiled a definitive bibliography of Quebec, *Inventaire chronologique* (1905–09). He also published historical studies of Jacques CARTIER and Samuel de CHAMPLAIN.
Dionysia, Greek religious festivals of Dionysus, the god of wine, corresponding but not equivalent to the Roman Bacchanalia. The great, or city, Dionysia were the most abandoned. Lesser festivals were the Lenaea, the Anthesteria and the little, or rustic, Dionysia.
Dionysius, the Areopagite (*fl.* 1st century AD), first bishop of Athens, converted by St Paul. His name was used by a Palestinian writer of *c.*500 now known as Pseudo-Dionysius, whose NEO-PLANTONIC mystical works had a great influence on the thinking of various scholars in medieval times.
Dionysius Exiguus (*c.* 500–*c.* 550), Roman monk and theologian, who worked out the method of calculating the date of Easter that was adopted by the Roman Church and is still in use. He compiled a collection of canon law that was widely used in the early Middle Ages.
Dionysus. *See* BACCHUS.
Diophantus (AD 250), Greek mathematician who pioneered the solution of a type of indeterminate algebraic equation. The work in this area is known as Diophantine analysis. Of the 13 books with which Diophantus is credited, only six have survived. The standard edition in Greek was edited by Paul Tannery (2 vols., 1893–95).
Dioptre, optical unit of magnifying power of a lens system. The power of a lens is equal to one metre divided by the focal length in metres. An algebraic sign (+

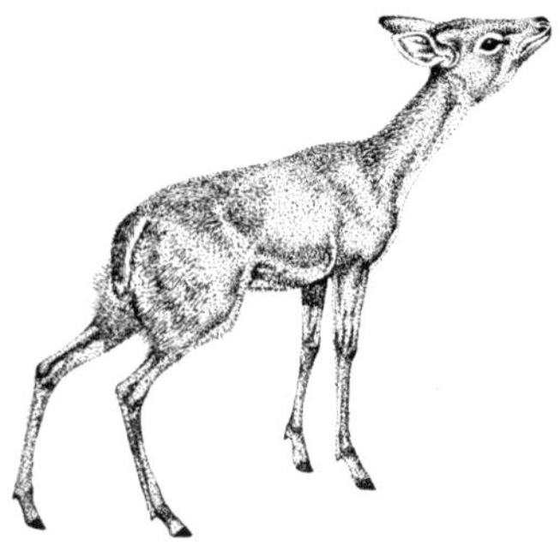

Dik-Dik, the miniature African antelope which gets its name from its curious call.

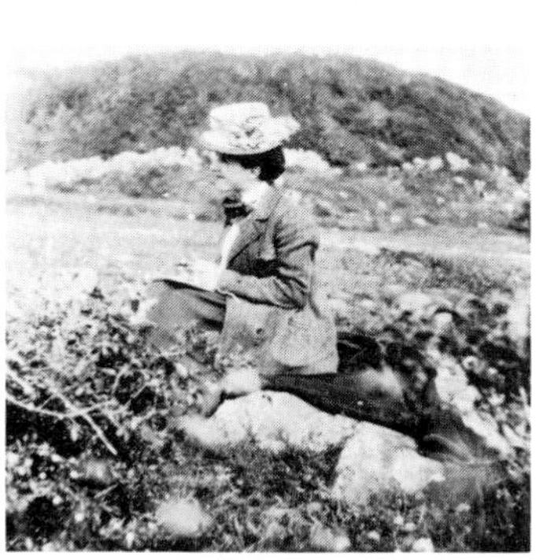

Isak Dinesen was the pseudonym of the Danish authoress Baroness Blixen-Finecke.

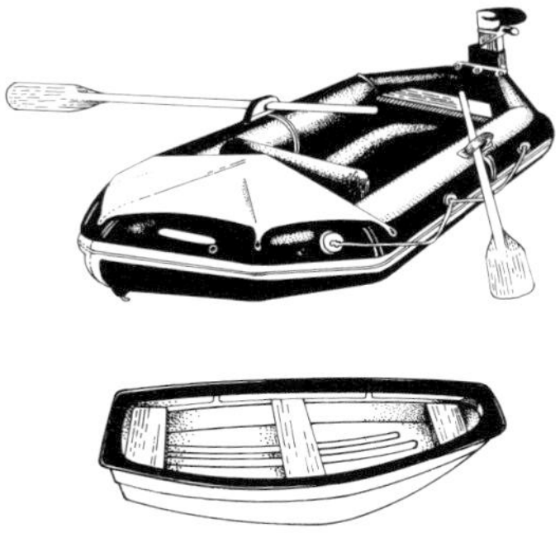

Dinghy comes from the Hindi word *dingi*, the small boat used along the Indian coast.

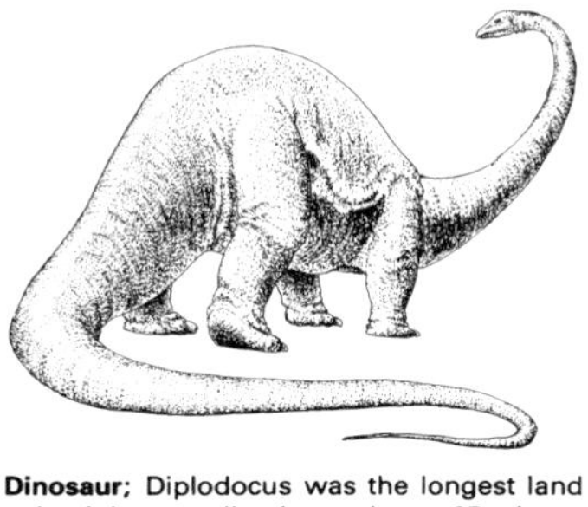

Dinosaur; Diplodocus was the longest land animal that ever lived, growing to 25m long.

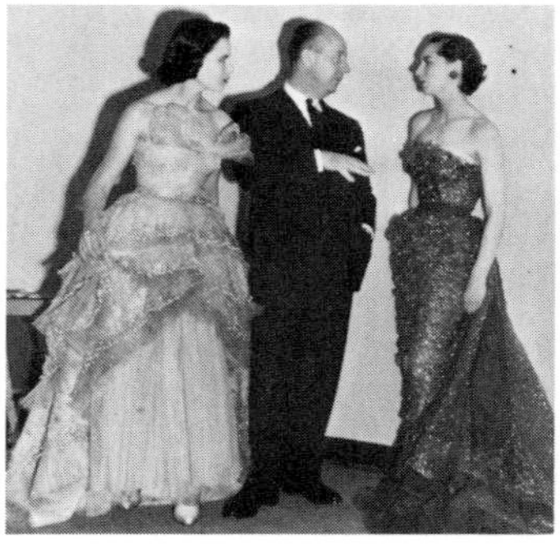

Christian Dior with two of his models at a fashion show in London (1950).

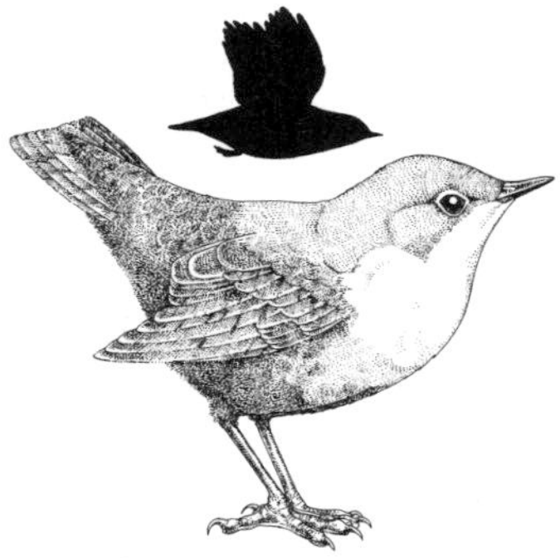

Dipper dive for small fish in the waters of fast-flowing mountain streams.

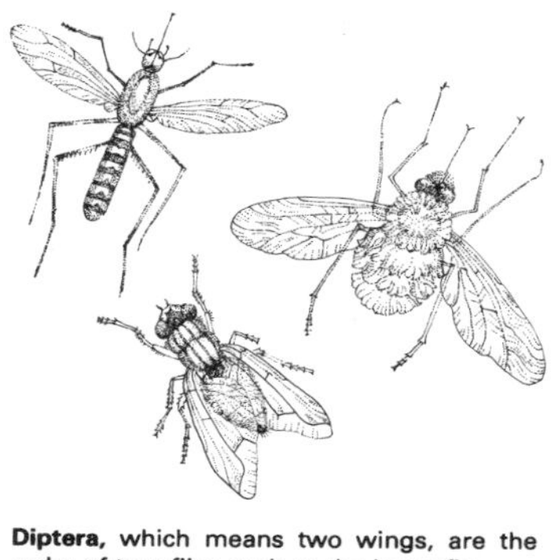

Diptera, which means two wings, are the order of true flies such as the housefly.

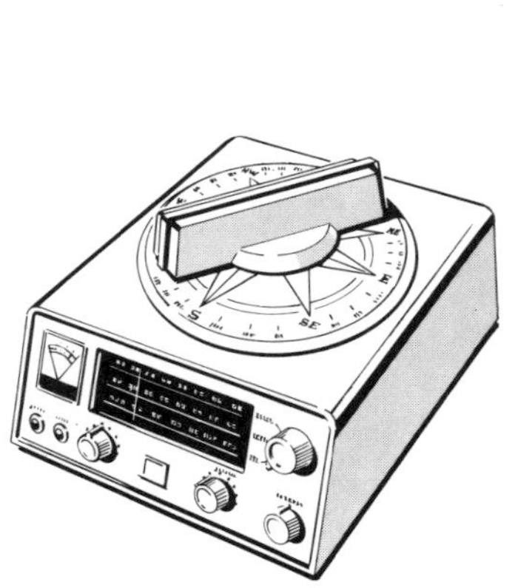

Directional aerials receive maximum signal when they are set at 90° to the transmitter.

or −) indicates whether the system is convergent or divergent – for example, a diverging lens of focal length 1/3 metre has a power of −3 dioptres. The power of a combination of lenses is the sum of their individual powers.

Dior, Christian (1905–57), French fashion designer. In the spring of 1947 he launched the NEW LOOK which swept the fashion world. His was considered the leading fashion design house between 1945 and the mid-1960s.

Diorite, deep-seated IGNEOUS rock similar to GRANITE in its texture but made-up mainly of plagioclase feldspar and hornblende, BIOTITE or augite. It is usually dark grey. *See also* PE pp.100–101, *101*.

Dioscorides Pedanius (*c*. AD 40–*c*. 90), Greek botanist, physician and pharmacologist. He wrote *De materia medica*, the leading classical text on drugs and their use. It included detailed descriptions of plants and information on the specific use, dosage and method administration of drugs made from them.

Diouf, Abdou (1935–), Prime Minister of Senegal since 1970. He was educated at St Louis, Dakar and Paris, and became a member of the Senegal Progressive Union in 1961. He was Minister of Planning and Industry (1968–70), and became a member of the National Assembly in 1973.

Dip, in geology, acute angle between the bedding plane of a rock strata and the horizontal surface of the earth. It is measured in degrees with a CLINOMETER. *See also* PE pp.129.

Dip, (or inclination) magnetic, angle between the direction of the earth's magnetic field and the horizontal. A freely suspended magnetic needle dips, with its north pole pointing down, at an angle of 71.5° to the horizontal in London. *See also* PE p.*22*.

Dip poles, imaginary points on the earth's surface where the direction of the earth's magnetic field is vertical – downwards at the north pole and upwards at the south pole – and are themselves offset in respect to the geomagnetic poles, each by a different amount so that the S dip pole is not exactly opposite the N dip pole. *See also* PE pp.*22*–23.

Diphda or Beta Ceti, brightest star in the constellation of Cetus. An orange giant, it is believed to be variable in nature. Characteristics: apparent mag. 2.04; absolute mag. 0.7; spectral type K1; distance 59 light-years. *See also* SU pp.226–227, 262–263.

Diphilus (*fl. c*. 360 BC), Greek playwright. He wrote 100 comedies, of which 60 survive. He was imitated by PLAUTUS and TERENCE, and many of his plays were later reworked by the Romans.

Diphtheria, acute, contagious infection, chiefly affecting children, and once common throughout temperate regions. The disease is caused by a bacterium, *Corynebacterium diphtheriae,* which often enters through the upper respiratory tract. There it releases an exotoxin that produces symptoms of fever, chills, malaise, mild sore throat, brassy cough and a thick coating of the upper respiratory tract by dead cells and bacteria. The body responds by producing antitoxin and recovery usually follows. Complications, including impaired function of the heart and peripheral nerves, may occur temporarily. Vaccination of children with diphtheria toxoid confers immunity. *See also* MS pp.96, 112.

Diplococcus, genus of BACTERIA characterized by gram-positive, spherical cells that grow in pairs. Some species are parthenogenic, eg *Diplococcus pneumoniae* which causes pneumonia.

Diplodocus, extinct reptile that lived in N USA during the Jurassic period (135–195 million years ago); the longest land animal that has ever lived. It has a long slender neck and tail, and was a swamp-dwelling herbivore. Length: 25m (82ft). *See also* NW pp.24–25, 184–185.

Diploid, term to describe a nucleus which has its CHROMOSOMES in pairs, as in almost all animal cells except GAMETES.

Diplomatic service, corps of agents who are the official, accredited representatives of a government in a foreign, host state. Diplomats are appointed by the sovereign or chief executive and enjoy special protection and privileges. They are prohibited from activities such as espionage and are subject to expulsion for violating the laws of the country in which they are stationed. In cases where countries have no diplomatic relations, their interests may be represented by diplomats of other powers. *See also* AMBASSADOR; CHARGÉ D'AFFAIRES.

Diplopia, double vision, a disorder that can result from various diseases or from the action of certain drugs (including alcohol) on the central nervous system.

Diplopoda, class of arthropods found throughout the world; its members are called MILLIPEDES. Some attack plants, others are predatory. They may have as many as 200 pairs of legs.

Diplura, insect order including japygids and CAMPODEIDS, the two-pronged bristle-tails. They are pale, blind insects that live in soil and feed on dying and living plant matter, often damaging growing plants. Length: 5cm (2in). *See also* NW pp.106–107.

Dipnoi, order of CROSSOPTERYGIAN fish found in tropical waters of Australia, Africa and South America; it includes the COELACANTH, with its lobed limb-like fins, and the LUNGFISH, with its primitive lungs. *See also* NW p.124.

Dipole, molecular, separation of electric charge in a molecule. In a COVALENT BOND between two atoms the electron pair is not equally shared between them. In hydrogen chloride, HCl, the electrons are attracted towards the more electronegative chlorine atom, giving it a partial negative charge and leaving an equal positive charge on the hydrogen atom. Such dipoles contribute to the chemical properties of molecules. Magnetic substances have dipoles consisting of north and south poles; they may be ordered or disordered to give strong or weak magnetic properties. *See also* SU pp.140–141.

Dipper, bird associated with fast-flowing mountain streams, where it swims and dives for small fish and aquatic invertebrates. It has a thin straight bill, short wings and greyish-brown plumage. Length: to 19cm (7.5in). Family Cinclidae; genus *Cinclus.*

Dipsomania. *See* ALCOHOLISM.

Diptera, order of true FLIES. They have soft bodies and one pair of wings, the other being reduced to knob-like halteres. They have a complete life cycle: the adult lays eggs that hatch into LARVAE (maggots); these pupate and become adults. Within this order are many important pests, such as MOSQUITOES, HOUSE FLIES and others that attack human beings, animals or crops or carry diseases. *See also* NW pp.106–107, 112–113.

Dirac, Paul Adrien Maurice (1902–), British physicist who devised a new version of QUANTUM MECHANICS. His equation (the Dirac equation) combines relativity and quantum-mechanical descriptions of electron properties. This results in accurate values and relates them to fundamental principles. He shared the Nobel Prize in Physics in 1933. *See also* SU p.66 –*66*.

Direct evidence, in law a statement by a witness that an event or action did or did not occur. It is distinguished from indirect or CIRCUMSTANTIAL EVIDENCE, in which the witness infers from one set of facts that another must or must not be true.

Directional aerial, radar or radio aerial for receiving or transmitting signals in one prime direction. A radio direction-finder for example, has a rectangular loop antenna which receives maximum signal when it is broadside to the station, and minimum signal when it faces the station end-on. The orientation of the antenna is indicated on a direction scale.

Direction finding (DF), in navigation, a method that determines position by the intersection of two projected bearing lines obtained from known landmarks. Radio DF instruments tune-in using a directional antenna to two radio signals from transmitters at known points.

Direct motion, orbital motion of a planet, comet or other heavenly body around the Sun or of a satellite around its primary in a west-to-east direction. Also the apparent west-to-east movement of a planet against a stellar background, as seen from the N Pole.

Directoire style, art style named after the DIRECTORY which ruled France from 1795 to 1799. It marked a transition between the rococco style of Louis XVI and the more decorative style of the Empire. Neo-classical elements, derived partly from the recent excavations at POMPEII, were combined with contemporary ideas, especially in dress and fashion. In all its aspects, particularly furniture, the style is exemplified by simple shapes which possess an economy of line.

Directory, Government of France according to the constitution of the year III (1795). It was headed by five directors who in general lacked the great political skill necessary to balance the conflicts of the age. They came to rely increasingly on the army, lost popularity and achieved little. After an army coup in Nov. 1799 the Directory was replaced by a CONSULATE led by NAPOLEON. *See also* HC2 p.75.

Dire Dawa, city in E Ethiopia on the Addis-Ababa-Djibouti railway. The city was founded in 1902 when the railway reached that point and its growth has resulted from trade brought by the railway. Industries: food processing, textiles, cement. Pop. (1970 est.) 60,900.

Dirigible, steerable airship. Circular balloons can be made to rise by throwing off ballast, or descend by venting gas from the envelope, but they are not steerable. The first dirigible, powered by steam, was invented in 1852 by Henri GIFFARD. *See also* MM pp.146–147.

Disaccharide, class of sugars (including common sugar) formed by the condensation of two monosaccharides with the removal of water. Cane-sugar, sucrose, $C_{12}H_{22}O_6$, is a disaccharide which, on hydrolysis with dilute acid, yields both glucose and fructose, monosaccharides each having the formula $C_6H_{12}O_6$. Lactose and maltose are other important disaccharides. *See also* SU p.152.

Disarmament, the reduction of armaments by nation states. The term refers principally to events since 1918 and especially to attempts since 1945 to reach international agreements to control arms production. The United Nations established the Atomic Energy Commission in 1946 and the Commission for Conventional Armaments in 1947. In 1952 the two were joined in the Disarmament Commission. It produced no results and the USSR withdrew in 1957. In Aug. 1963 a Test Ban Treaty, banning the testing of nuclear weapons above the ground, in outer space and underwater, was signed by the USSR and the USA. They also signed a Non-Proliferation Treaty in 1968, which provided for an international inspectorate. The SALT talks between the USSR and the USA, which began in 1969, have produced the 1972 treaty on the limitation of anti-ballistic missile systems. *See also* HC2 pp.306–307.

Disasters of War, series of 65 powerful etchings by GOYA made during the Napoleonic invasion of Spain (1810–13). Breaking new ground technically, their brutal realism expresses impassioned outrage at the violence and suffering of war.

Disc, in astronomy, circular appearance of the Sun, Moon or a planet, especially when viewed through a telescope. It contrasts markedly with the sharp point-source image of a star. *See also* SU p.224.

Disc, gramophone, grooved vinyl pressing containing recorded sound. The lateral disc was invented in 1887 by Emile BERLINER and 78rpm shellac records were marketed by 1900. The long-playing 33⅓ rpm vinyl disc (1948) revolutionized the industry. Stereophonic sound came in 1956 and quadrophony some 15 years later. *See also* GRAMOPHONE.

Disc cam, mechanical component that converts rotating motion into reciprocating (back-and-forth) motion. Most internal combustion engines use oval-shaped disc cams mounted on a rotating cam shaft to open and close the valves by displacing

HC1 = History and Culture Vol. 1 HC2 = History and Culture Vol. 2 MS = Man and Society MM = Man and Machines

push-rods (cam followers). *See also* MM pp.*68–69*; *86*.

Discharge, in law, freeing of an offender at the discretion of a judge or magistrate. An offender may be discharged absolutely and treated as if he had not been convicted. Or he may be discharged conditionally without penalty, but told that if he is convicted within a given time (in Britain one to three years), he will be sentenced both for the original offence and the new one. When the sentence is only suspended, the original penalty is added automatically to a subsequent conviction.

Discharge, in medicine, any normal or abnormal loss of fluid from a part of the body. Normal discharges include the slight loss of fluid from the vagina or the expected discharge of mucus from the nose which accompanies a common cold or an allergy such as hay fever. An unexpected discharge, eg from the ear, vagina or penis, can be an early symptom of a serious disorder and should immediately be referred to a doctor.

Discharge tube, glass envelope containing gas at low pressure, which gives light due to the collesion of electrons with gas molecules. Discharge lamps, filled with one or more of various gases, are used to give coloured light: mercury vapour gives purple, sodium vapour gives yellow and neon gives red. Early discharge tubes (called Geissler tubes) were used as toys. A FLUORESCENT LAMP is a discharge tube coated with a fluorescent substance. *See also* SU pp.*63*, *109*, *137*.

Disciple, one of 12 close friends and associates of Jesus Christ during his lifetime, most of whom later became APOSTLES. They were: Peter, Andrew, James the Greater, John, Thomas, James the Lesser, Jude (or Thaddaeus), Philip, Bartholomew, Matthew, Simon and Judas Iscariot. *See also* HC1 pp.110–111.

Disconformity, in geology, the hiatus or eroded surface between two layers of rock. The time interval represented by the hiatus is more difficult to estimate than the rate of deposition of a layer. Nevertheless the hiatus must be considered when calculating the age of a rock formation. *See also* UNCONFORMITY; PE p.124.

Discovery, HMS, ship used by R.F. SCOTT for a voyage of exploration to the Antarctic (1901–04). The journey explored the ROSS SEA and reached farther S than ever before. The *Discovery* was later moored permanently in the River Thames, London, and opened to the public.

Discovery Bay, bay on the S coast at Australia, on the boundary between Victoria and South Australia, on the Indian Ocean. Port MacDonnell is located on the W shore. Length: 72km (45 miles); width: 13km (8 miles).

Discrimination, prejudicial treatment of an individual or group on the basis of race, religion, ethnic background, sex or age. In the broader, public sense, discrimination may take the form of housing restrictions, segregated community facilities and limited employment and educational opportunities. *See also* MS 268–271.

Discus, in athletics field events, wooden or metallic disc weighing 2kg (4lb 6.4oz) with a diameter of 22cm (8.75in), thrown by the competitor. Originally an ancient Greek athletic event, it was revived in 1896 for the first modern Olympic Games held at Athens.

Disease, impairment of health or abnormal functioning of an organism, affecting the entire organism or one organ or system of the body. A disease may be acute, producing severe symptoms for a short time; chronic, lasting a long time; or recurrent, with symptoms returning periodically. There are many types and causes of disease: infectious diseases, caused by harmful bacteria, viruses, or other agents; hereditary and metabolic diseases; diseases of growth and development; diseases of the immunological system; neoplastic (tumour-producing) diseases; nutritional diseases; DEFICIENCY DISEASES; endocrine (hormonal) diseases; diseases due to particular physical agents, eg lead poisoning; circulatory diseases; and mental illness.

Treatment depends on the cause and course of the disease but, in general, may be symptomatic (relieving symptoms but not necessarily combating the cause of the disease) or specific (attempting to cure the underlying cause of the disease using drug therapy). Surgery is also sometimes a method of treatment, as are radiation therapy, physiotherapy and psychotherapy. Prevention of disease involves eradication of disease-producing organisms, vaccines to confer immunity against disease, public health measures, careful medical attention and routine medical examinations. *See also* MS pp.82–148.

Disestablishment, the severing of the legal connection between the Church of England and the state. The movement in favour of it, led by Radicals and Dissenters, was powerful in the 19th century. The Irish Church was disestablished in 1869, the Welsh in 1914, although the latter act did not take effect until after WWI.

Disinfectant, usually liquid or solid substance used to kill micro-organisms that cause disease. The term is most often applied to fairly strong reagents that are used on inanimate objects, as distinguished from ANTISEPTICS, which are used on living tissues.

Disjunction, logical proposition produced by joining two simple propositions by the word "or". An example is the proposition "John is intelligent or John is modest"; it is false if both parts are separately false, otherwise it is true. The disjunction is used in mathematics – in which the proposition is true if *both* components are true. In ordinary speech a second type, the exclusive disjunction, is also used expressing an alternative between the two components. The disjunction of two simple propositions, *P* and *Q*, is written *PvQ*, and read "*P* or *Q*". *See also* SU pp.40–41.

Dislocation, in medicine, complete displacement of bones forming a joint, accompanied by damage to supporting ligaments and the enclosing capsule. In physics a dislocation is a fault in the structure (lattice) of a CRYSTAL. *See* also MS p.95; SU pp.88–89.

Dislocation of crystals, lattice flaw in a crystal structure which is classified according to type. The flaw is one dimensional and forms a line in the crystal. The two basic types of dislocation are the edge and the screw. The screw dislocation plays an important part in crystal growth, forming them into spiral ramps.

Disney, Walter Elias ("Walt") (1901–66), US film animator and studio executive. His cartoon features, animal, fantasy and adventure films are internationally renowned. His first success, *Steamboat Willie* (1928), was the first cartoon to use sound. It featured Mickey Mouse, who became the world's most famous cartoon character, rivalled only by another Disney character, Donald Duck. Among his notable films are *Snow White and the Seven Dwarfs* (1937), *Fantasia* (1940), *Dumbo* (1941), *Treasure Island* (1950), *The Living Desert* (1953) and *Mary Poppins* (1964).

Disneyland, US amusement park located in Anaheim, California. Created by film producer Walt DISNEY and opened in 1955, it features four main amusement areas: Adventureland, Frontierland, Fantasyland and Tomorrowland. It is visited by several million people each year.

Dispersion, colloidal. *See* COLLOIDAL DISPERSION.

Dispersion, wave. *See* WAVE DISPERSION.

Displaced persons, Europeans left homeless after WWII. Most displaced persons emigrated to the USA, and others returned to their homeland, or moved to Britain or Israel. Between 1948 and 1951, almost half a million refugees were allowed to enter the USA.

Displacement, in chemistry, replacement of one atom in a compound by an atom of a different element. *See* SUBSTITUTION.

Displacement, in psychoanalysis, the mechanism in which there is a mental shift of meaning, fantasy or emotion away from one person or object (towards which it was originally directed) to another, usually neutral or less dangerous. A common instance is the displacement of anger, eg when a mother, angry at her husband, begins to shout at her child. In BEHAVIORISM, displacement is the substitution of one response for another when the former behaviour is prevented in some way.

Displacement, in geology, the relative movements of two adjacent types of rock. It incorporates the direction of change and the specific amount of the movement. Lateral displacement is described as strike slip and strike separation, whereas vertical displacement is known as dip slip and dip separation. *See also* FAULT.

Displacement, in nautical engineering, a measure of the size (TONNAGE) of a ship. *See also* MM p.114.

Disposable personal income, in economics, portion of a person's earnings that remains after all taxes and financial commitments have been deducted.

Disproportionation, simultaneous oxidation and reduction of the same chemical substance. An example is the disproportionation of copper I chloride, involving oxidation to copper II chloride and reduction to metallic copper: $2CuCl \rightarrow CuCl_2 + Cu$. *See also* OXIDATION-REDUCTION.

Disraeli, Benjamin, 1st Earl of Beaconsfield (1804–81), British Conservative politician and novelist. He helped to overthrow Robert PEEL when the CORN LAWS were repealed in 1846. As Conservative leader in the House of Commons (1849–68), Disraeli was several times Chancellor of the Exchequer and guided the 1867 REFORM ACT through Parliament. He was Prime Minister in 1868 and again in 1874–80. He secured Britain's half-share in the Suez Canal in 1875 and at the Congress of BERLIN (1878) forced Russia to surrender Turkish lands and gained Cyprus for Britain. His most famous novels are *Coningsby*, *Sybil* and *Tancred*. *See also* HC2 pp.112–113.

Dissection, systematic cutting into plant or animal tissue, usually after death, to explore its anatomy or to discover abnormalities which may help in the understanding of the cause and effect of disease. It is the foundation of a proper understanding of how the healthy body works. *See also* POST MORTEM; MS pp.*85*, 126–127.

Dissenters. *See* NONCONFORMITY.

Dissociation, mental process in which some thoughts, attitudes experiences or parts of the personality lose their normal relationship to the rest of the mind and split off to function independently and separately. This occurs in reaction to some intolerable stress, anxiety or insurmountable difficulty. It enables the mind to cope, as the dissociated incompatible areas of experience do not then come into conflict. Externally, however, signs of psychological disorder will be apparent in such behaviour as HYSTERIA, sleep-walking, FUGUE states, automatic writing and delusions. It may also lead on to the "split" or multiple personality. Whole areas of experience may also be repressed, leading to AMNESIA. *See also* MS pp.140–141.

Dissolution of the Monasteries (1536–40), abolition of English monasticism in the reign of HENRY VIII, devised and carried out by Thomas CROMWELL. The dissolution completed the break with the Church of Rome, but the main motive was financial, the confiscated property reverting to the king's possession. By an Act of Parliament of 1536, Cromwell sent commissioners to close the smaller monasteries and the larger ones were closed piecemeal, 1538–40. The dissolution caused some social disruption, since the monasteries were the greatest landowners in the country, but it is probable that the contemporary stories of ex-monks starving were exaggerated. New secular schools were set up to replace the education formerly provided by the monks and much of the land was sold by the king to the newly wealthy rural middle class. *See also* HC1 pp.*241*, 270–271.

di Stefano, Alfredo (1926–), Argentine-born footballer rated by many as the most "complete" player ever. From River Plate he went to the Millonarios club in Bogotá and then Spain, where he dictated the play and fortunes of Real Madrid from 1953–64. He played seven times for

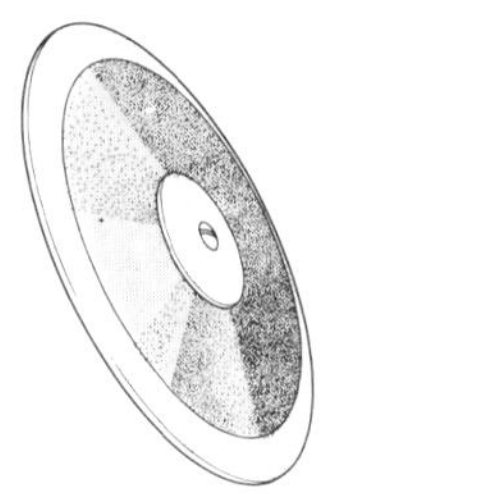

Discus; the first throw of over 61m (200ft) was by the US athlete Alfred Oerter in 1962.

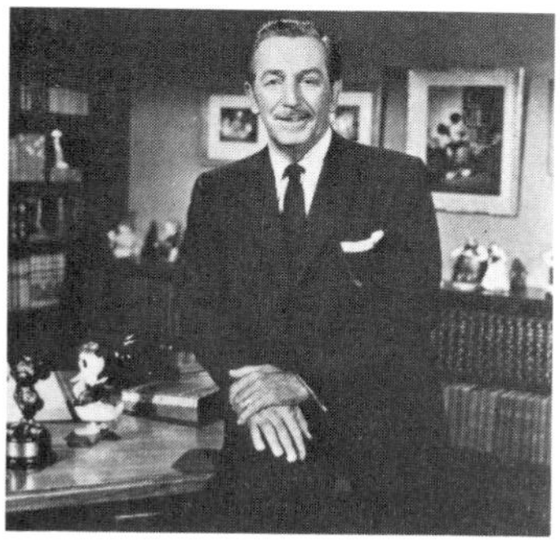

Walt Disney originally visualised Disneyland as a prototype for an urban community.

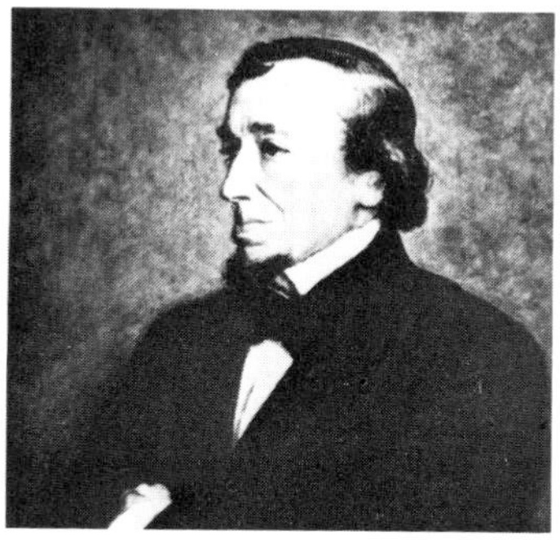

Benjamin Disraeli, the brilliant, flamboyant politician who remains an enigma to this day.

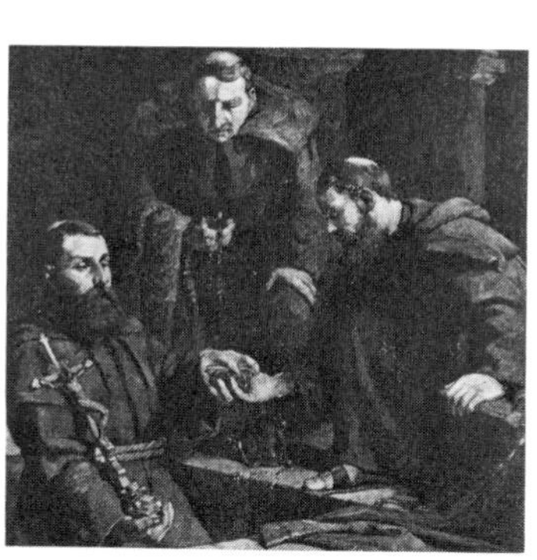

Dissolution of the Monasteries; monks hiding treasure from Cromwell's agents.

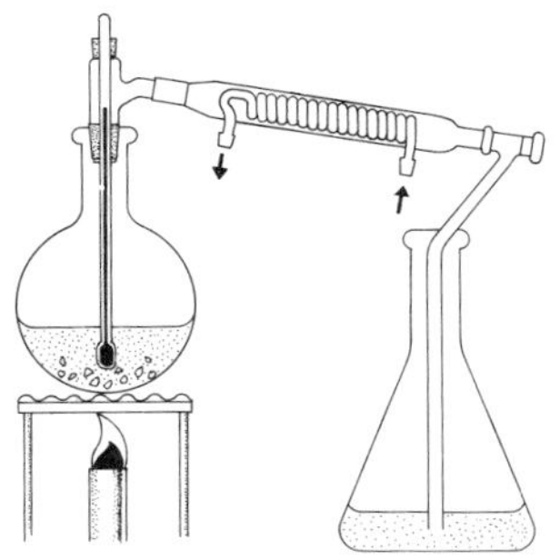

Distillation; the liquid into which the vapour condenses is free from dissolved impurities.

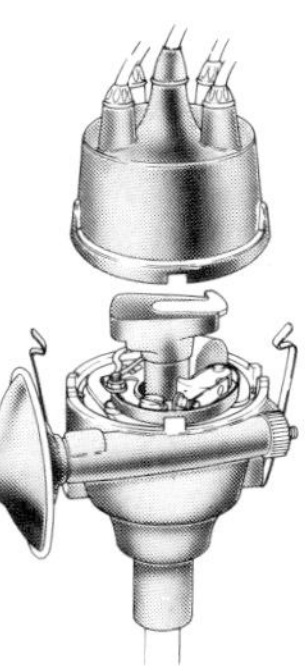

Distributor, the device that ensures the cylinders in an engine fire in the correct order.

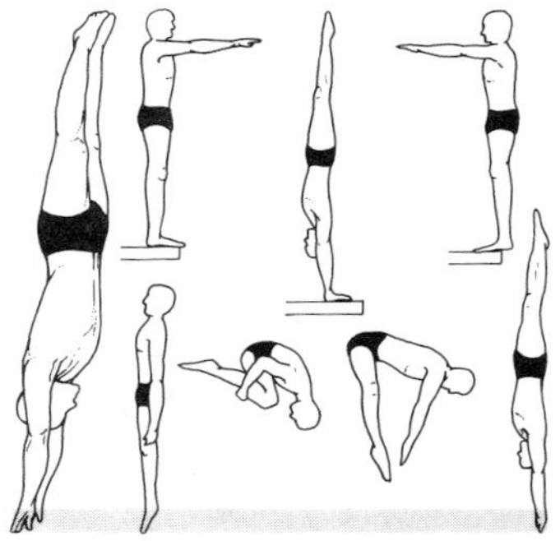

Diving; a good high diver tucks himself into a tight knot if he loses control of a dive.

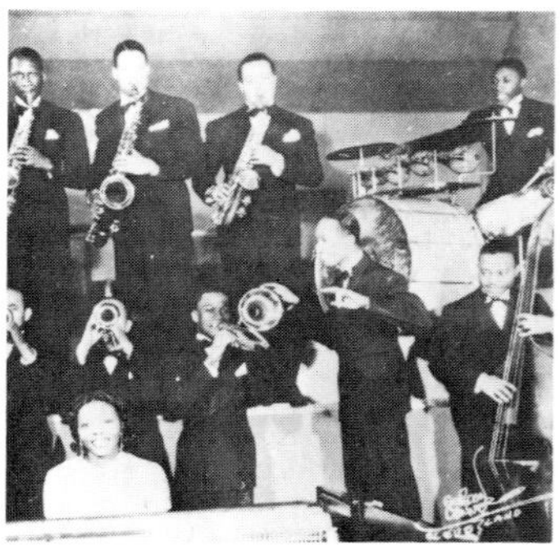

Dixieland is the traditional jazz music of New Orleans; The Original Jazz Band, 1922.

Argentina, 31 for Spain, and was European Footballer of the Year in 1957 and 1959.

Distemper, contagious, often fatal, disease of young dogs, wild canines and members of the weasel family. Symptoms: fever, shivering, muscular spasms and loss of appetite. Death is commonly caused by inflammation of the brain. Puppies can be immunized against distemper.

Distillation, extraction of a liquid by boiling a solution in which it is contained, and cooling the vapour so that it condenses and can be collected. The method is used to separate liquids that are in solution, or liquid solvents from dissolved solids. Fractional distillation is the method used in oil refineries to separate the various fractions of crude oil. *See also* SU pp.144–*145*; MM pp.80–81; PE pp.206–207.

Distilled water, pure water prepared by boiling tap water and condensing the steam. It is essential for some chemical reactions, in which even the small traces of dissolved salts (such as the carbonates of calcium and magnesium) and other impurities present in tap water are intolerable. For many applications it is being replaced by de-ionized water. *See also* WATER SOFTENER.

Distilling, production of spiritous liquors by DISTILLATION, especially of alcohol (ETHYL ALCOHOL). This concentrates the alcohol in the distilled spirit, as yeast fermentation gives an alcoholic content of only about 15% in such drinks as wine. In distilling the alcohol is boiled off and may be later added as needed for the spirit's desired proof. *See also* PE pp.206–207.

Distortion, sound. *See* SOUND DISTORTION.

Distribution, in economics, portion of the total amount of the goods and services a society produces that each individual or group receives. Sometimes called personal distribution or income distribution in order to distinguish it from the marketing of commodities (physical distribution), it has been an important aspect of economic analysis since Adam SMITH focused on the issue in the 18th century.

Distributive law, rule of combination in mathematics in which an operation applied to a combination of terms is equal to the combination of the operation applied to each individual term. Thus, in algebra and arithmetic, $3 \times (2 + 1) = (3 \times 2) + (3 \times 1)$; the multiplication is distributed over the addition. *See also* SU p.28.

Distributor, in a motor vehicle, an electrical device for distributing synchronized pulses of high-voltage secondary current from the induction coil, via a rotating contact (rotor arm), to the various sparking plugs of an engine in their proper firing order. *See also* MM pp.68, *130*.

District Council, local governing body in England and Wales of a county district which is not a borough. There are both urban and rural districts. Councillors are elected for a four-year term; metropolitan district elections are held for one-third of the seats for each year when there are no county council elections. Non-metropolitan districts can adopt the same system or choose to have elections for all the seats at once. The councils deal with matters such as public health, council-house building and the maintenance of minor roads.

District of Columbia, the state of the city of Washington, capital of the USA. It was created from the states of Maryland and Virginia and was originally 260sq km (100sq miles) in area. The part in Virginia was given back in 1846 and it is now 179sq km (69sq miles). The capital covers the entire area.

Ditching, aircraft, emergency method of landing a land-plane on water. If the wind is heavy and seas are light, the ditching is made into the wind. If the seas are heavy, the aircraft is ditched parallel to the swell regardless of the wind. In either case the undercarriage is left in the retracted position.

Dithyramb, irregular poem or chant of a wild or inspired nature. Dithyrambs originated in ancient Greece as improvised choral lyrics sung at banquets in honour of Dionysus, the god of wine, and flourished between about 600 BC and the 2nd century AD. Later other gods were honoured and dithyrambs became important parts of theatrical presentations and festivals.

Dittersdorf, Carl Ditters von (1739–99), Austrian composer. His musical output was huge – 34 operas, more than 100 symphonies, and many concertos, sonatas and choral works. He was ennobled in 1773.

Diuretic, drug used to increase the flow of urine and, usually, its salt content. Diuretics are used to treat OEDEMA, an over-accumulation of fluid caused by heart disease or other diseases, and abnormal kidney function.

Diurnal rhythm. *See* CIRCADIAN RHYTHM.

Dive, in aeronautics, steep descent of an aircraft with or without power at a greater airspeed than that normal for level flight. Dive bombing during WWII was accomplished by pointing the nose of the aircraft at a ground target, releasing the bomb, and executing a steep ascent. Steep dives or ascents produce stresses which can damage the airframe, unless it is specially designed to resist them. *See also* MM pp.*152*–153.

Diver (bird). *See* LOON.

Divergence, mathematical property of an infinite series (or sequence) of not having a finite limiting value. Such a series is said to diverge. The harmonic series, $1 + 1/2 + 1/3 + 1/4 + \ldots$, is an example of a divergent series. *See also* CONVERGENCE.

Diverging lens. *See* LENS.

Divers. *See* DIVING BIRDS.

Diverticulitis, illness caused by inflammation of diverticula, (small "pouches" on the wall of the intestine), often caused by faecal matter obstructing the neck of the pouch. Symptoms include pain in the lower left side, cramp, nausea, vomiting, sometimes fever, malaise and alternating constipation and diarrhoea. If untreated (with antibiotics and a bland diet), abcess, haemorrhage and perforation of the intestinal wall can occur, and surgery becomes urgently necessary. *See also* MS p.*93*.

Diverticulosis, common, often symptomless condition whose incidence increases with age, in which small spherical pouches protrude from the lower intestinal wall, most often from the sigmoid colon (just above the rectum). Inflammation of these pouches produces DIVERTICULITIS. It is thought to be caused by the low "bulk" content of diet. *See also* MS p.*92*.

Divertimento, name for a collection of musical pieces for chamber orchestra, used especially by HAYDN and MOZART to indicate that the collection did not meet the formal criteria of a SUITE.

Dividend, that part of the net earnings of a public company that is paid to its stockholders. Usually paid regularly, the dividend is a percentage of the par value of the stock and is paid in cash in Britain, whereas in the USA a dividend may be paid in other forms, such as bonds or stock.

Divination, foretelling the future or discovering what is unknown by interpreting various signs. Divination is a form of magic with worldwide distribution. Signs of the future are often thought to be found in the entrails of animals that are specially sacrificed. Other techniques include casting lots and palmistry. *See also* AUGURY; HARUSPICATION; OMEN; RHABDOMANCY; SCAPULISMANCY; MS p.196.

Divine Comedy (*c*. 1307–21), allegorical, narrative poem by DANTE ALIGHIERI. Through this work Dante established Tuscan as the literary language of Italy. It is divided into three parts, *Inferno, Purgatorio* and *Paradiso*, and consists of the author's imaginary tour of Hell, Purgatory and Heaven. He meets his contemporaries, historical figures and characters from mythology, the Bible and classical literature. It is written in *terza rima*, a complex verse form. *See also* HC1 p.*207*.

Divine right of kings, political theory, popular in 16th and 17th centuries in various European countries, that anointed kings derive absolute and irresistible authority directly from God. Law is an instrument of grace, not a contrivance of human wisdom, so that the king is answerable only to God and is above all promulgated laws, including his own.

Diving, water sport in which acrobatic manoeuvres are performed off a springboard or highboard. The several types of competition include the 1- and 3-m springboards and the 5-, 7.5- and 10-m firm highboards. The judging, based on points, is complicated and depends not only on the difficulty of the dive but also on the diver's movement at the start, the technique and grace of the flight and the entry into the water. *See also* SKIN DIVING; SWIMMING.

Diving, deep-sea, commercial or leisure activity dating from antiquity but popularized with the use of the diving-bell, diving-suit and SCUBA (self-contained underwater breathing apparatus). Scuba-diving's growth dates from WWII with the use of the aqualung, patented by Jacques COUSTEAU and Emil Gagnan in 1942. Divers receive air via a demand regulator from cylinders of compressed air worn on the back, and using masks, flippers and heat-retaining foam-rubber wet suits can reach depths of 50–60m (165–195ft). Underwater sports include spear-fishing and photography.

Diving beetle, predaceous aquatic beetle found throughout most of the world. It has thread-like antennae and long hind legs adapted for swimming. One of the most ferocious fresh-water carnivores, the adult and larva feed on insects, tadpoles and small fish. Family Dytiscidae; genus *Dytiscus*. *See also* NW p.*230*.

Diving-bell, hollow structure providing a dry environment for underwater workers. Early diving-bells were bell-shaped, filled with compressed air, and open at the bottom to give access to the sea-bed. The BATHYSPHERE, which made its first dive in 1930, was spherical, made of steel, and could withstand considerable pressures, but it was restricted to depths within reach of supply and winch cables. It has been replaced by the bathyscaphe. *See also* PE pp.92–93.

Diving birds, any of various species of water birds that dive for their food. Loons are adept divers – they can dive to depths of 61m (200ft). Grebes, albatrosses, cormorants, kingfishers, pelicans and dippers are also typical divers. Others include diving petrels, boobies and some ducks and geese.

Divisionism. *See* NEO-IMPRESSIONISM.

Division of labour, in economics, plan of production in which each individual or group of workers specializes in a single phase of the production process. The performance of one, or a limited number of operations, is characteristic of today's mass production in both capitalistic and socialistic economies. *See also* MS p.262.

Divorce, legal dissolution of a marriage. In Britain divorce was obtained by private Act of Parliament until 1857, when the Divorce Court was established. Adultery was the only ground for the action until 1937, when desertion, insanity and mental cruelty were added. Since 1971 the only ground has been the irretrievable breakdown of the marriage.

Diwali, Hindu festival during which homes are lit with numerous tiny clay lamps in commemoration of RAMA's defeat of RAVANA, a demon who sought to destroy the world. The story is symbolic of the return of light after the rainy season and the festival marks the resumption of pilgrimages, marriages and other social activities.

Dix, Otto (1891–1969), German painter and engraver but known for his series of etchings, *War* (1923) based on his experiences in WWI. He later developed into an ardent EXPRESSIONIST and satirist and, like George GROSZ, attacked the corruption of post-WWI Germany. Dix suffered persecution during the Hitler regime. After WWII he painted numerous religious subjects. *See also* HC2 p.175.

Dixieland, style of jazz music originating in New Orleans in the 1900s. It usually consisted of a steady beat with interweaving melodic lines and was played by a small group, typically clarinet, trumpet, trombone and rhythm section. King OLIVER and Louis ARMSTRONG were two of its most famous exponents. *See also* HC2 p.*272*.

Diyarbakir, city in SE Turkey, on the River Tigris; capital of Diyarkakir province. The city was made a colony in AD 230 by the Romans, who named it Amida. It is an agricultural trade centre for a region producing fruit, cereal crops and cotton. Industries: textiles, gold- and silverwork, copper products. Pop. (1973) 180,237.

Dizziness. *See* VERTIGO.

Djakarta, capital of Indonesia, on the NW coast of Java. It was founded (as Batavia) by the Dutch *c.*1619 as a fort and trading post, and it became the headquarters of the Dutch EAST INDIA COMPANY. It became the capital after Indonesia gained its independence in 1949. An administrative, cultural, and educational centre, the University of Indonesia (1950) is in the city. Industries: ironworking, printing, timber. Exports: rubber, tea, quinine. Pop. (1977 est.) 6,178,500.

Djerba, Île de, island off the SE coast of Tunisia, in the central Mediterranean Sea. An administrative district of Tunisia, it has Roman ruins and is believed to be the island of the lotus-eaters described in the ODYSSEY. Exports: olive oil, dates. The main industry is fishing. Area: 510sq km (197sq miles). Pop. (1966) 62,445.

Djerid, Chott, salt-water lake in SW central Tunisia. It was known in Greek mythology as the birthplace of Athena. Area: approx. 4,920sq km (1,900sq miles).

Djibouti, independent nation in E Africa on the Red Sea, formerly the French territory of the Afars and Issas. A small country that gained independence in 1977, it consists mainly of stony desert. More than half of the population is nomadic, herding cattle, sheep and goats. There is some industry in the capital, Djibouti, which has developed as a trade centre at the terminus of a railway from Ethiopia. Area: 22,000sq km (8,494sq miles). Pop. (country) 226,000; (city) 70,000 *See also* MW p.65.

Djilas, Milovan (1911–), Yugoslav political writer and political leader. One of Tito's leading ministers, he supported his country's break with Moscow in 1948, but his criticisms of Tito's regime ended his political career (1954). He was jailed and on the publication of his book *The New Class: An Analysis of the Communist System* (1957) his prison term was extended; he was released in 1961. In the following year he was again imprisoned for his book *Conversations with Stalin.* He was finally released in 1966.

D-Lysergic acid. *See* LSD.

Dmitri (*d.* 1606), pretender to the throne of Russia, *b.* Yury Otrepyev. After Tsar Fyodor I died in 1598 and was succeeded by Boris GODUNOV, Otrepyev (then a monk) claimed to be Dmitri, Fyodor's son and heir. The real Dmitri had died in 1591. Boris Godunov died in 1605 and Dmitri was proclaimed tsar after bringing about the death of Fyodor II, son of Boris. In 1606 Dmitri Vasily Shuysky led a revolt in which Dmitri was murdered.

DNA (deoxyribonucleic acid), molecule found in chromosomes and viruses that is responsible for storing the genetic code. It consists of two long-chain polynucleotides shaped like a twisted rope ladder, the sides of which consist of sugar-phosphate chains and the rungs of linked nitrogenous bases. The sugar is 2-deoxy-D-ribose and the four bases are adenine, cytosine, guanine and thymine. The genetic code is stored in terms of the sequence of the bases, three bases coding for one amino acid. *See also* NW pp.28–29; SU pp.153, *157.*

Dnepr. *See* DNIEPER.

Dnepropetrovsk, city in the Ukraine (Ukrainskaja SSR), USSR, on the DNIEPER (Dnepr) river; capital of Dnepropetrovsk Øblast. It was founded in 1787 by Grigori Potemkin for Catherine II and named after the Ukrainian Bolshevik, Petrovski. It has a university and several colleges. Industries: iron and steel, mechanical engineering, chemicals, cement. Pop. (1975) 958,000.

Dnestr. *See* DNIESTER.

Dnieper (Dnepr), river in Ukrainian Republic (Ukrainskaja SSR), USSR. Rising in the Valdai Hills, W of Moscow, it flows S through Belorussia and the Ukraine to the Black Sea; it is the third-longest river in Europe. The Dneproges dam, completed in 1932, made the river navigable for its entire course. The Dnieper is linked by canal to the Bug River, and has several hydroelectric power stations. Length: 2,286km (1,420 miles).

Dniester (Dnestr), river in the Ukraine (Ukrainskaja SSR), USSR. It rises on the slopes of the Carpathian Mts and flows SE to the Black Sea SW of Odessa; part of its course forms the border between Ukrainskaja and Moldavskaja. Navigation is hampered by irregular water levels. The Dniester formed the border between the USSR and Romania from 1918 until 1940. Length: 1,412km (877 miles).

Dobell, Sir William (1899–1970), Australian painter, sometimes regarded as the nominal leader of modern art in Australia. Dobell, who studied in London and Holland from 1929 to 1939, excelled in cruelly realistic portraits, influenced by HOGARTH. He was knighted in 1966.

Doberman pinscher, strong guard and police dog bred in Germany in the late 19th century. It has a long, wedge-shaped head and short erect ears. Its deep-chested body is set on straight legs. The smooth coat may be black, red or fawn. Height: to 71cm (28in) at the shoulder.

Döblin, Alfred (1878–1957), German novelist. He was an EXPRESOIONIST writer and a socialist. In 1933 he left Germany to live in Palestine and the USA, although he returned after WWII. His work includes *Wadzek's Battle with the Steam Turbine* (1918) and *Mountains, Oceans and Giants* (1931) which deal with man's struggle with machines. His style of talking to himself was developed in the novel *Berlin Alexanderplatz* (1929).

Docetism, ancient Christian heresy; the doctrine that Christ did not have a material human body but that his birth, death and other earthly manifestations were merely illusions. This belief, regarded as the first Christian heresy, reached its height in GNOSTICISM.

Dock, any of more than 200 species of flowering plants native to N USA and Europe, especially curled dock (*Rumex crispus*). It has scaly brown flowers and oblong leaves with curly margins, from which its name is derived. Dock leaves are a country remedy for nettle stings. Family Polygonaceae.

Dock, in marine engineering, artificial basin, floating or fixed, where ships are tended; also a wharf, or pier, or the waterway between two wharves, or piers. In a dry dock, water must be excluded by lock-gates, or ships must be hauled out of the water on to slipways for repairs; floating docks can tend ships at sea although it is more common that they are used in sheltered waters. *See also* MM pp.194–195.

Dr Jekyll and Mr Hyde, The Strange Case of (1886), Victorian thriller by Robert Louis STEVENSON. The good Dr Jekyll changes himself at intervals by means of a potion into the loathsome Mr Hyde, and recovers with an antidote. The story turns on the discovery that the two characters are, in fact, two aspects of the same man.

Doctor Zhivago (1957) novel by Boris PASTERNAK. It records the life of Yuri Zhivago, a Russian physician, from 1903 through the revolution and civil war until his death in 1929. The Soviet authorities made strenuous efforts to suppress the work and it was first published in Italy. In 1965 it was filmed by David Lean.

Doctrine of Four Causes, propounded by Aristotle in the *Physica.* Four causes concern the physicist; the material, the formal, the efficient and the final, although the last three often coincide and a physical explanation usually states the final cause or end of a process or its antecedent necessity. *See also* MS p.*229.*

Doctrine of signatures, principle of early medicine or magic whereby parts of the body are cured by means of natural objects with which they seem to have some physical characteristics in common. The theory is also called the principle of correspondences. *See also* MS p.116.

Documentary film, unscripted or "non-fiction" film. The term was first used in 1929 by John Grierson of Robert Flaherty's *Nanook of the North* (1921), which portrayed at first hand Flaherty's experience of living among the Alaskan Eskimos. *Nanook* received world-wide acclaim and the documentary form was born. The documentary in the form of newsreels rivalled popular newspapers and now, in the days of television, has become the major means of news presentation. Donn Alan Pennebaker's *Don't Look Back* (1967) is another well-known documentary film, as is Marcel Ophul's *A Sense of Loss* (1972).

Dod, Charlotte ("Lottie") (1871–1960), British all-round sportswoman who won five Wimbledon singles titles (1887, 1888, 1891, 1892, 1893), retired from competitive tennis at the age of 22, and went on to become All-England All-comers' golf champion. She represented England at golf and hockey and also excelled at archery and skating.

Dodd, Charles Harold (1884–1973), British theologian. He was professor of theology at Cambridge University (1935–49) and wrote *History of the Gospel* (1938). He helped to organize the New Translation of the Bible in the 1950s and 1960s.

Dodd, Sir Charles (1884–), British theologian. His view that the coming of God's kingdom was fulfilled in the Incarnation was given in his book *The Apostolic Preaching and its Developments* (1936).

Dodder, leafless, parasitic, twining plant with a thread-like stem and clusters of small yellow flowers. It feeds using haustoria, modified roots that enter the host plant. The dodder then releases its contact with the ground. Family Convolvulaceae; species *Cuscuta europaea.*

Dodecanese (Dhodhekánisos), group of about 20 islands in Greece, in the SE Aegean Sea, between W Turkey and E Crete. The capital and largest island is Rhodes (Ródos). The islands have been conquered and ruled since 1600 BC by many peoples including Greeks, Romans, the Crusaders, and the Knights of St John. Under Turkish control from 1500 until 1912, they were seized by Italy in 1912 and passed to Greece in 1947. The main occupation is agriculture, including fruit growing, livestock raising, and diving for sponges. Pop. (1971) 121,017.

Dodge City, city in SW Kansas, USA, on the Arkansas River. It was founded in 1872 near Fort Dodge on the Santa Fe Trail, and it became a cowboy town, with Wyatt EARP and Bat Masterson among its marshalls. The distribution centre for a livestock rearing and wheat-producing region, its industries include farm tools and tourism. Pop. (1970) 14,127.

Dodgson, Charles Lutwidge (1832–98), British mathematics lecturer and author, better known by his pen-name Lewis CARROLL.

Dodgson, Stephen (1924–), British composer. His largest orchestral work is the *Sinfonietta* (1964). He has written many CONCERTOS, including one for guitar (1956) and a *Serenade* for viola and orchestra (1956).

Dodo, extinct, flightless bird that lived on the Mascarene Islands in the Indian Ocean. The last dodo died in about 1790. The true dodo (*Raphus cucullatus*) of Mauritius and the similar Réunion solitaire (*Raphus solitarius*) were heavy-bodied birds with large heads and large hooked bills. Weight: to 23kg (50lb).

Doenitz, Karl. *See* DÖNITZ, KARL.

Doesburg, Theo van (1883–1931), Dutch painter, writer, and critic, leader of the De STIJL movement and founder of its journal. He collaborated with architects such as J.J. OUD to extend De Stijl principles to architecture and interior design. Doesburg taught at the BAUHAUS (1921–23) and publicized DADAISM in The Netherlands.

Dog, domesticated carnivorous mammal closely related to the jackal, wolf and fox. Typically it has a slender, muscular body; long head with slender snout and triangular ears; small paws with five toes on the forefeet and four on the hind; non-retractile claws; and well-developed teeth. The dog walks on its toes with the heel, or hock, raised off the ground. Smell is the dog's most important

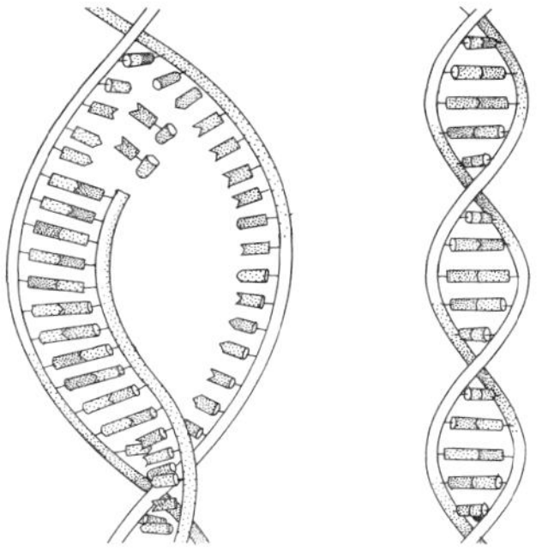

DNA, the master molecule of life; its structure contains the genetic code.

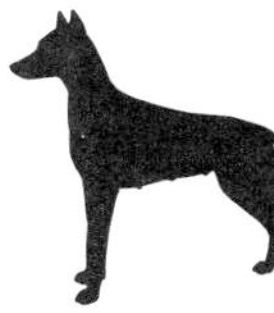

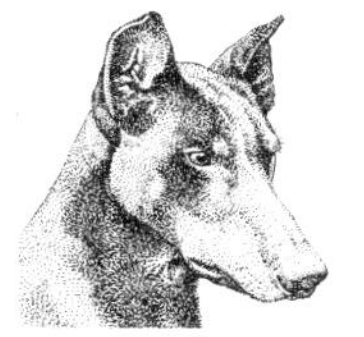

Doberman pinscher are named after Louis Doberman, who developed the breed.

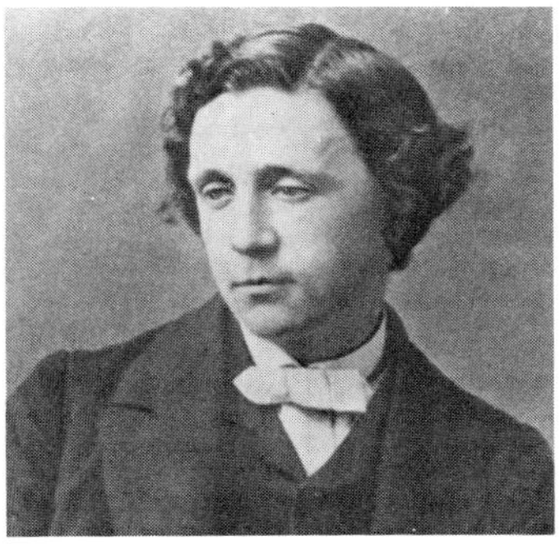

Charles Lutwidge Dodgson, better known as Lewis Carroll, creator of *Alice in Wonderland.*

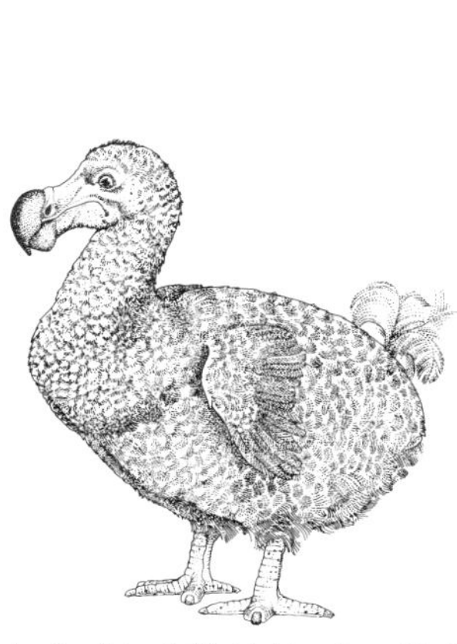

Dodo; the fate of this bird is relevant to the aims and principles of modern conservation.

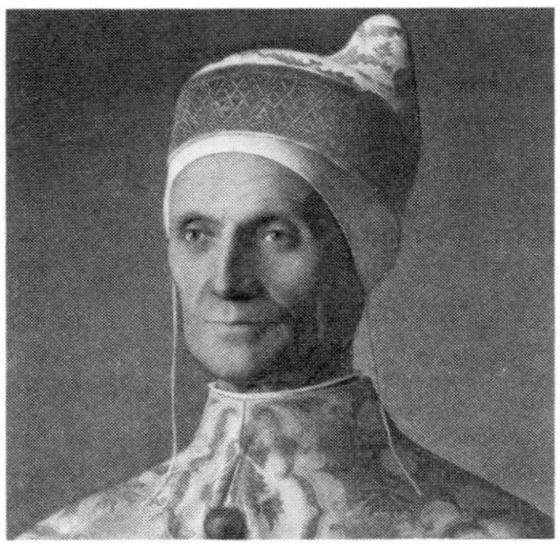

Doge; Giovanni Bellini's portrait of Doge Leonardo Loredan in the National Gallery.

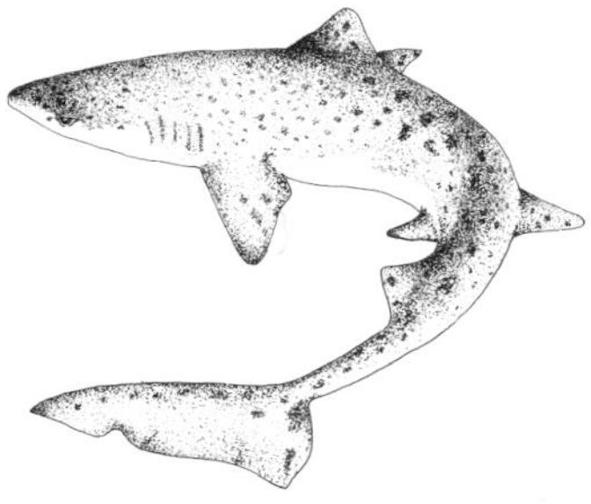

Dogfish are probably so-called from the way they hunt voraciously in large packs.

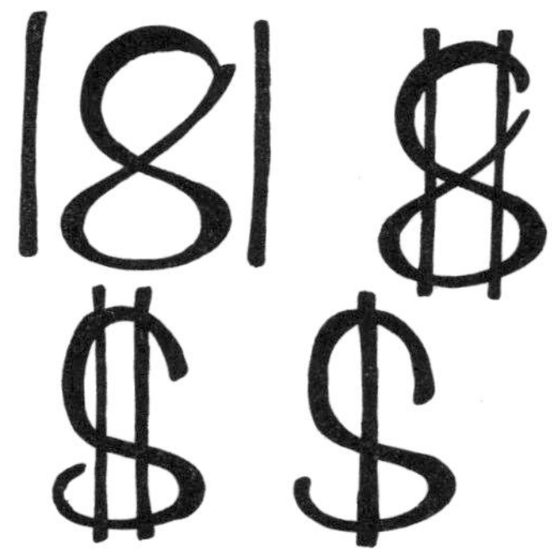

Dollar; the sign is thought to have originated from "pieces-of-eight", written /8/.

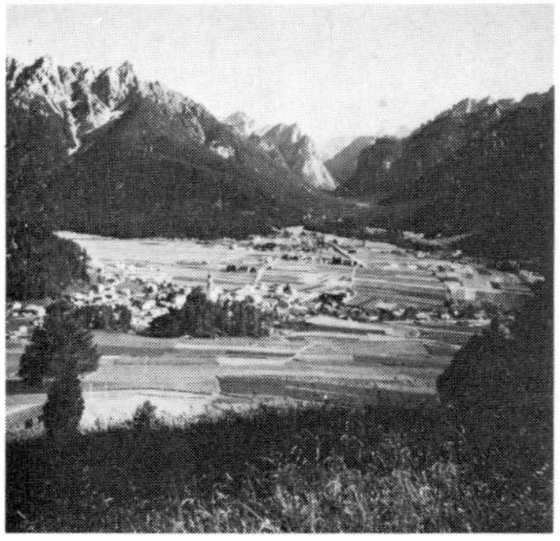

Dolomites, the region of the Alps composed of the magnesium-calcium rock dolomite.

sense; its hearing is also acute. The gestation period is 49–70 days and one or more young are born. Dogs developed from the tree-dwelling *miacis*, which lived about 40 million years ago, through intermediate forms to *tomarctus*, which lived 15 million years ago. The dog was domesticated about 10–14 thousand years ago. There are approx. 400 breeds; one of the oldest is the Saluki, in existence for 5,000 years. Dog breeds are classified into sporting, hound, terrier, working, toy and non-sporting groups. Length: body 34–135cm (13.4–53.2in); tail 11–54cm (4.3–21.3in); weight: 0.9kg–68kg (2–150lb). Family Canidae; species *Canis familiaris*. *See also* individual breeds.

Dog-cart, light two-wheeled horse-drawn vehicle, with two transverse seats back to back. It was originally designed to carry sportsmen and their dogs. It is also the name of a cart drawn by a dog or dogs. These were sometimes used as small delivery carts or for children to play with. *See also* MM p.*121*.

Doge, title of the chief magistrate of Venice from 697 to 1797, and of Genoa 1339–1805. Despite an attempt in Venice in the 12th century to make the office hereditary, it remained elective; after the 14th century it carried an increasingly limited power.

Dogfish, SHARK found worldwide in marine waters. Generally greyish with white spots, it lacks a lower tail lobe. Dogfish are usually divided into two groups: spiny dogs, with a stout, sharp spine in front of each dorsal fin, and spineless dogs which lack a spine in front of the second dorsal fin. Length: spiny, 0.6–1.2m (2–4ft); spineless, 7.3m (24ft). Suborder Squalidae. *See also* Chondrichthyes; NW pp.126–127; PE pp.246–247, *247*.

Dogger Bank, extensive sandbank in the central North Sea between Great Britain and Denmark. It is an important breeding ground for a variety of fish, especially cod and herring. The water is shallow, 17m–36m (55–120ft) deep. Area: 17,610sq km (6,800sq miles).

Doggerel, trivial verse written for comic or burlesque effect, generally loosely styled, irregular in metre and often badly written. The word can be applied to serious writing as a term of abuse.

Doggett, Thomas, Irish comedian who in 1715 originated DOGGETT'S COAT AND BADGE RACE on the River Thames for professional watermen.

Doggett's Coat and Badge Race, traditional sculling race on London's River Thames for watermen who have just finished their apprenticeship. Originated by Thomas DOGGETT and first rowed on 1 Aug. 1715 from London Bridge to Chelsea, it is the oldest sculling race in the world and carries as its prize a scarlet (formerly orange) livery with a silver arm badge.

Dogon, Negroid people whose traditional ancestral dwellings are in remote cave-villages in the Bandiagara district of the Mali Republic. Their patrilineal village society is based on subsistence agriculture, principal foods being millet and sorghum. Their religion is notable for its abstract concepts and a powerful creation myth.

Dog rose, wild ROSE that occurs in many varieties inwoods and hedges; it is one of the commonest species in Britain. It has serrated leaflets, strongly curved thorns and white or pink flowers. Family Rosaceae.

Dog sled racing, sport popular in Alaska, Labrador and other Arctic regions of North America. Teams vary, as do the length and rules of the events, but five-dog teams predominate. These comprise a lead dog (point) who sets the pace for the two swing and two wheel (rear) dogs. The Alaskan Malamute, Husky, Samoyed and Eskimo are the most used breeds. An annual event is the World Championship Sled Dog Race in Anchorage, Alaska.

Dogwood, any of several small trees and shrubs in the genus *Cornus* of the dogwood family (Cornaceae). In the wild, flowering dogwoods are graceful, sparsely-leaved inhabitants of the dimly lit undergrowth of deciduous forests. Their small flowers, enclosed by four large, petal-like, white bracts, bloom before the leaves open.

Doha (Ad-Dawhah), capital of Qatar, an independent Arab state on the Persian Gulf. It was a small fishing village until oil production began in 1949, since when it has developed into a modern city and trade centre. It has a Turkish fort dating from 1850. Pop. 95,000.

Doherty, Charles Joseph (1855–1931), Canadian jurist and political leader. He was Canadian minister of justice (1911–21). In WWI he worked to organize Canada's army; he was a signatory of the Treaty of Versailles (1919) and a delegate to the League of Nations (1920–21).

Doherty, name of two British brothers, champion tennis players, Reginald Frank ("Big Do") (1876–1919) and Hugh Lawrence ("Little Do") (1874–1910). Between them they won ten major singles titles, Reggie winning four consecutive Wimbledon championships (1897–1900) and Laurie five (1902–06); together they won eight Wimbledon doubles. In 1900 Laurie won the Olympic singles, Reggie the mixed doubles, and their superiority was such that Britain won the Davis Cup 1903–06.

Doherty, Peter (1914–), Irish footballer who played 16 times for Northern Ireland and was manager of the side that reached the 1958 World Cup quarter-finals. A gifted inside-forward, he helped Manchester City win the Football League (1937) and Derby County the FA Cup (1946).

Dohnányi, Ernö (1877–1960), Hungarian composer, conductor and pianist. His works sometimes display elements of Hungarian folk music, as in the piano suite *Ruralia Hungarica* (1926). He also composed operas, concertos and orchestral pieces.

Doisy, Edward Adelbert (1893–), US biochemist. He did research which helped in the understanding of blood buffers, vitamins and metabolism; he isolated the female sex hormones estrone (1929), and estradiol (1935); was professor of biochemistry (1923–65) at St Louis University; and was awarded, with Henrik DAM, the 1943 Nobel Prize in physiology and medicine for his chemical analysis of vitamin K.

Dokuchaev, Vasily Vasilyevich (1846–1903), Russian geologist who, at the close of the 19th century, identified the basic determining factors in the morphology – structure or form – of soils, and thereby furthered the science of pedology (the study of soil and its unique biological, chemical and physical properties).

Dolce Vita, La (1959), Italian film directed by Federico FELLINI. It starred Marcello MASTROIANNI, Anouk Aimée, Anita Ekberg and Yvonne Furneaux, and was a frank view of the empty pleasures of members of Roman society; it caused much controversy.

Dolci, Danilo, (1924–), Italian social reformer who was trained as an architect but in 1950 committed his life to working for the poor. After witnessing the death from starvation of a girl in Sicily, he fasted for a week to force the government to take action. He raised money for schools and community centres in Sicily, and campaigned for reform in the face of opposition from the government, the Church and the MAFIA. In 1958 he received the Lenin Peace Prize.

Doldrums, region of the ocean near the Equator, characterized by calms, light and variable winds, and squalls. It corresponds approximately to the equatorial trough, a belt of low pressure around the Equator.

Dole, distribution as a charity of food, money or clothing to the poor, a practice which dates from the Middle Ages. In Britain since WWI the term has been applied to the weekly payments from the state to the unemployed.

Dolerites, medium-grained INTRUSIVE ROCKS found in thin extensive sheet-like masses that are injected in or between the sedimentary rock layers; they lie vertically and horizontally and are called dikes and sills respectively. *See also* PE p.*101*.

Dolichocephalic. *See* CEPHALIC INDEX.

Dolin, Anton (1904–), British ballet dancer, real name Patrick Healy-Kay. He joined Diaghilev's BALLETS RUSSES in 1921, becoming a principal dancer in 1924. He also danced with the Vic-Wells Ballet in London and the Ballet Theatre in New York. He was director and principal male dancer in companies he formed with Alicia MARKOVA (1935–38, 1945–48) and in 1950 they formed London's Festival Ballet.

Dollar, standard monetary unit of the USA since 1792. It was derived from the decimal system of Spanish coinage based on the "dolar", which was the most widely used coin in the American colonies. Divided into a hundred cents, the value of the US dollar was based on the price of gold until 1934. Many other countries have adopted the dollar as their unit, including Canada, Hong Kong, New Zealand, Singapore, Australia and Liberia.

Dollfus, Audouin-Charles (1924–), French astronomer, a pioneer of high-altitude observation from balloons. An expert in planetary studies, he discovered Janus, the tenth satellite of SATURN, in 1966. *See also* SU pp.*191*, *212–213*, 213.

Dollfuss, Englebert (1892–1934), Austrian chancellor (1932–34) who took office at a time when his country was close to economic collapse. In 1933 he dissolved the National Socialist Party, which had been calling for union with Nazi Germany. In 1934 he crushed the Social Democratic Party and assumed dictatorial powers. He was assassinated by Austrian Nazis.

Döllinger, Johann Joseph Ignaz von (1799–1890), distinguished German Roman Catholic church historian who held the chair of church history at the University of Munich from 1826 to 1873. He opposed the dogma of papal infallibility defined at the first VATICAN COUNCIL in 1870 and was excommunicated for it in 1871. He subsequently became identified with the independent German OLD CATHOLIC CHURCH, although he did not formally join it.

Dolland, John (1707–61), English optician and inventor. Self-taught in science, mathematics and languages, he devoted himself to the invention of an achromatic telescope, his efforts being rewarded with the Copley Medal of the Royal Society in 1758.

Doll's House, A (1879), four-act drama by Henrik IBSEN. Its story of a woman breaking away from her husband and family shows Ibsen's concern for the position of women in society and condemns of the 19th-century bourgeois family.

Dolmen, megalithic monument comprising a large stone lintel supported by three or more upright stones. Dolmens were originally used as burial chambers and covered by mounds. They are most common in Cornwall and Brittany.

Dolmetsch, name of a family of British musicians. Arnold (1858–1940) began restoring old instruments and making copies in the 19th century. He gave authentic performances of little-known early music, mainly Renaissance and Baroque. Carl (1911–), a virtuoso recorder player, became director of the annual music festival at Haslemere, Surrey, in 1940, where the family make copies of old instruments, notably recorders and early flutes.

Dolomite, pearly-white or pink sedimentary rock, probably formed by the alteration of limestone by seawater. Also a carbonate mineral, calcium-magnesium carbonate, $CaMg(CO_3)_2$, found in dolomite rocks and metamorphosed rocks. Calcite-like rhombohedral system prismatic crystals, often intergrown, are found in hydrothermal veins. Hardness 3.5–4; s.g. 2.8. *See also* PE pp.110–111.

Dolomites (Dolomiti or Dolomiten), part of the Italian Alps, in NE Italy. They are composed of dolomitic limestone which has eroded to form a striking landscape. First climbed by the English in the 19th century, they are very popular with mountain climbers and tourists. There are several hydroelectric power stations in the region. The highest peak is the Marmolada which rises to 3,342m (10,964ft).

Dolphin, small, toothed WHALE with a distinct beak and slender body. Larger than the PORPOISE, it is the fastest and most agile and playful of the whales. In captivity, the highly intelligent, bottle-nosed dolphin readily learns complicated tricks. Length: to 4m (13ft). Family Delphinidae; species *Tursiops truncatus*. *See also* NW pp.*157*, 166–167.

Dolphin fish. *See* DORADO.

Domagk, Gerhardt (1895–1964), German chemist. In 1927 he was made director of the research institute of the I. G. Farben industrial works. He is known for his discovery of the drug Prontosil, the forerunner of sulphanilamide, the first of the "wonder drugs" used to combat infectious diseases. He was awarded the Nobel Prize in physiology and medicine in 1939 for his discovery. *See also* MS pp.120, *120*.

Domain, in mathematics, a set of values that can be assigned to the independent variable in a function or relation; the values of the dependent variable are called the range. For example, the function can be $y = x^2$. If x is 0, 1, 2, 3, −3, etc. then y is 0, 1, 4, 9, 9, etc. The domain is {0,1,2,3,−3,...}, and the range is {0,1,4,9,9,...}.

Dombey and Son, (1847–48), novel by Charles DICKENS. Written at a time of extensive industrial growth, it is set in the world of trade and commerce, and the effects of the development of railways are important to the plot.

Dome, in architecture, hemispherical roof. A development of the arch, it is most commonly used in cathedral architecture, and was an important element in Byzantine styles. One of the earliest monumental domes belongs to the Pantheon, Rome. Eclipsed in importance in Gothic architecture, it was a significant element in Renaissance and Baroque styles and has survived the modern reinforced concrete slab used in vaulting.

Dome, lunar, any of several broad-based low mountains on the surface of the Moon, with gentle slopes and often a summit craterlet.

Domenichino (Zampieri) (1581–1641), leading Italian Baroque painter and architect. In 1602 he worked with Annibale CARRACCI on the Farnese Palace. Between 1621–23 he was chief architect of the Vatican. His landscape paintings, including *The Hunt of Diana* and *Landscape with St John Baptizing*, influenced Nicolas POUSSIN and CLAUDE LORRAIN.

Domenico Veneziano (*c*.1410–61), Florentine painter noted for his strong sense of colour. His work has been reassessed in recent times and his influence on the pictures of PIERO DELLA FRANCESCA is now generally recognized.

Dome of the Rock, also known as Kubbet es-Sakhra, mosque and shrine built (685–705) by Abd al-Malik on the Jewish temple site in Jerusalem. The dome covers the summit of Mt Moriah, from which the prophet is believed to have ascended to Heaven. The rock is also that on which Abraham was to have sacrificed Isaac. It is octagonal in plan; the large magnificent dome is made entirely of wood. *See also* HC1 p.*148*.

Domesday Book, two-volume village-by-village account of the population and wealth of England ordered by WILLIAM THE CONQUEROR in 1085 and completed the following year. The book is a unique record of medieval economic conditions and survives almost intact in the Public Record Office, London. The survey was intended to provide an accurate record of land ownership and of the value of each village and manor for the purposes of taxation, although some counties escaped it. The values of estates are compared with their values in the reign of Edward the Confessor; the social status of their inhabitants and number of plough-teams or value of the crops are also included. The survey was carried out by royal agents, each covering a hundred (division of the shire). *See also* HC1 pp.167–168, *168*.

Domestication of animals, breeding, training, taming and use of animals by man as pets, draught animals or for hides, wool, meat, milk and by-products such as manure. Animals that fit into one or more of these categories include CATTLE, SHEEP, DEER, CAMELS, PIGS, HORSES, BUFFALOES, OXEN, POULTRY, FISH, MINK and other fur animals, BEES and SILKWORMS, and household pets such as CATS and DOGS. As early as 9000 BC man began to organize settlements and kept a limited range of animals that suited his needs. Today SELECTIVE BREEDING is practised to improve the quality of farm stock. In the light of current predictions of human population growth, selective breeding is essential if demands are to be met. Totally new breeds may have to be developed, or man may have to look farther afield towards the domestication of alternative meat-producing animals. *See also* PE pp.224–253.

Domett, Alfred (1811–87), British writer and New Zealand Prime Minister (1862–63). His period of residence in New Zealand (1842–71) inspired his epic poem *Ranolf and Amohia* (1872).

Dominance, in genetics, the tendency of one trait to be reproduced in preference to another. Brown eyes represent a dominant trait while blue eye colouring is a RECESSIVE trait. A child inheriting each of these traits from its parents will have brown eyes although retain the ability to pass on recessive genes to its children. *See also* NW p.*30*.

Dominance relationship, or pecking order, system by which different individuals within a social group are ranked or ordered in terms of status or "dominance". Most such systems in animal societies are based on strength or aggressiveness. In human societies, status commonly depends more on the acquisition of possessions or prestige.

Domingo, Placido (1941–), Spanish TENOR. He made his operatic debut at Monterrey, in Mexico, in 1961. He made his Metropolitan debut in 1968 and his Covent Garden debut in 1971, in TOSCA.

Dominic, Saint (*c*.1170–1221), real name Domingo de Guzmán Spanish priest, founder of the DOMINICAN Order. In 1203 Pope Innocent III sent him to S France to preach to the Albigensians, who had fallen into heresy. He led a life renouned for sanctity, austerity and humility, and based his order on scholastic and democratic principles.

Dominica, largest island of the Windward group in the West Indies, in the Caribbean Sea, between Guadeloupe and Martinique islands; the capital and chief port is Roseau. It was named after "dies dominica" (Sunday), on which day it was discovered by Christopher Columbus in 1493. Products: copra, bananas, fruit and tobacco. Area: 290sq km (750sq miles). Pop. 75,000. *See also* MW p.65.

Dominican Republic, independent nation occupying the E two-thirds of the mountainous island of Hispaniola in the West Indies. Mineral deposits are becoming an increasingly important export, although agriculture is still the mainstay of the economy. The main crops are sugar cane, coffee, fruit, cocoa and tobacco. The capital is Santa Domingo. Area: 48,442sq km (18,703sq miles). Pop. (1975 est.) 4,697,000. *See* MW p.65.

Dominican friars. *See* DOMINICANS.

Dominicans, members of a Roman Catholic religious order, officially known as *Ordo Praedicatorum* (O.P.), founded by St DOMINIC, who gave definite shape to it at two general chapters at Bologna in 1220–1221. They are also known as Friars Preachers or, in England, Black Friars (from the black mantle worn by them over a white habit) or, in France, Jacobins (from their first house in Paris which was under the patronage of St James – Jacobus in Latin). They are specially devoted to preaching and study.

Dominion, until 1947, title of some of the self-governing nations within the British COMMONWEALTH OF NATIONS after the Statute of Westminster of 1931. *See* WESTMINSTER, STATUTES OF.

Dominion Day (1 July), national holiday in Canada. It commemorates the establishment of the DOMINION OF CANADA on 1 July 1867.

Dominion of Canada, official name of CANADA since the BRITISH NORTH AMERICAN ACT of 1867. Under confederation, the central government assumed powers of tariff, taxation, defence and criminal law. Confederation paved the way for the inclusion in Canada of British Columbia (1871), Prince Edward Island (1873) and Newfoundland (1949). *See also* HC2 pp.136–137; MW pp.45–50.

Dominoes, game played with rectangular pieces. The standard game, played by 2 to 6 players, uses 28 pieces. Each piece is divided in half, each containing from 0 to 6 dots in every combination – 0–0, 1–1, 1–0, etc. The dominoes are played one at a time and must be placed next to a domino which has a corresponding number. There are various methods of play from winning simply by laying all one's pieces to a complicated scoring based on the number of factors of 3 or 5 that divide into the number formed by the sum of the dots of the end dominoes.

Domino, Fats (1928–), US pianist and singer, real name Antoine Domino. A New Orleans-born rhythm-and-blues performer, he sold 23 million records between 1949 and 1960, most of which he also wrote. The most popular included *Ain't that a Shame* (1955) and *Blueberry Hill* (1956). Only Elvis PRESLEY and the BEATLES have sold more records.

Domino theory, tenet of US foreign policy formulated after WWII; often applied to South-East Asia. It is based on the assumption that if one country falls to Communist rule, its neighbours will inevitably succumb as well. The domino theory was one reason for US involvement in Vietnam and was subscribed to by the successive administrations of presidents Eisenhower, Kennedy, Johnson and Nixon.

Domitian (51–96), Roman emperor (81–96), second son of VESPASIAN, successor to TITUS. His rule was at first orderly but became cruel and tyrannical. He recalled AGRICOLA from Britain, overpowered the senate and ruled as an absolute monarch. His repressive politics led to plots against him and a reign of terror. His wife, Domitia, arranged his assassination.

Domrémy-la-Pucelle, village in E France, on the Meuse River. Joan of Arc was born there in *c*.1412, and her home is now preserved as a museum.

Don, Celtic mother goddess, the Welsh equivalent of Anu or Danu in Irish tradition. Her children included gods of the sky, the sea, and poetry and were locked in battle with the powers of darkness known as the Children as Llyr.

Don, river in Ukrainian Republic (Ukrainskaja SSR) USSR; rising SE of Tula, it flows S then SW to the Sea of Azov. Rostov-na-Donu is the major port, near the mouth of the river. Annual floods are controlled by the Ciml'anskoje Reservoir. The river is navigable for 1,370km (850 miles) and is an important shipping route for grain, timber and coal. Length: 1,930km (1,200 miles).

Donald, William Henry (1875–1946), Australian journalist (editor of the *Far Eastern Review*) and adviser to Chinese national leaders including SUN YAT-SEN and CHIANG KAI-SHEK. After Chiang was kidnapped in 1936 Donald helped to negotiate his release.

Donald Bane, King of Scotland (*r*.1093–97). The first of a succession of weak kings to rule after the death of MALCOLM III in 1093. As Malcolm's brother he was supported in his claims to the throne, and he successfully seized Edinburgh castle. He was deposed by DUNCAN II, but returned after Duncan's murder, only to be dethroned by Edgar in 1097. *See also* HC1 p.182.

Donat, Robert (1905–58), British actor whose career was cut short through asthma. His sensitive performances were typified by *Goodbye Mr Chips* (1939), for which he won an Oscar. He also acted in *The Thirty-Nine Steps* (1935), *Lease of Life* (1954), which he also directed, and *The Inn of the Sixth Happiness* (1958).

Donatello (*c*.1386–1466), Italian sculptor, who worked in Florence and Padua and exercised a profound influence on Renaissance art. His wooden statue *Mary Magdalen* (1455), in the Baptistery, Florence, reflects the expressive and emotional qualities of his style. His *Zuccone*

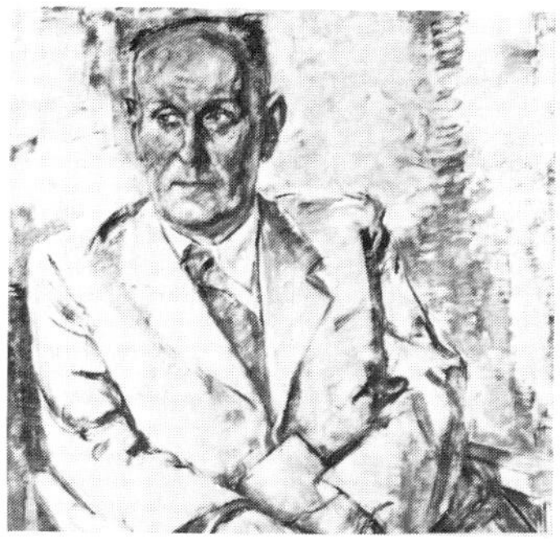

Gerhardt Domagk won the 1939 Nobel Prize for discovering the so-called "wonder" drug.

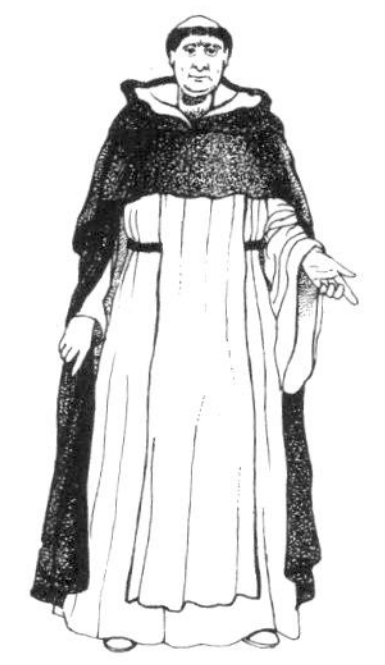

Dominicans; their emphasis on study produced such scholars as Thomas Aquinas.

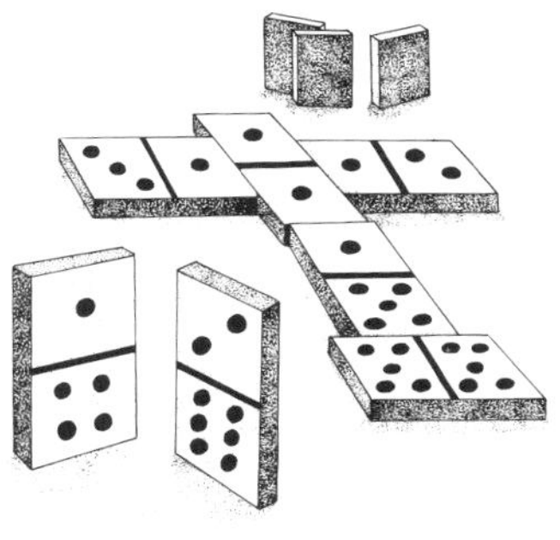

Dominoes, although fairly new to Europe, were known to the ancient Chinese.

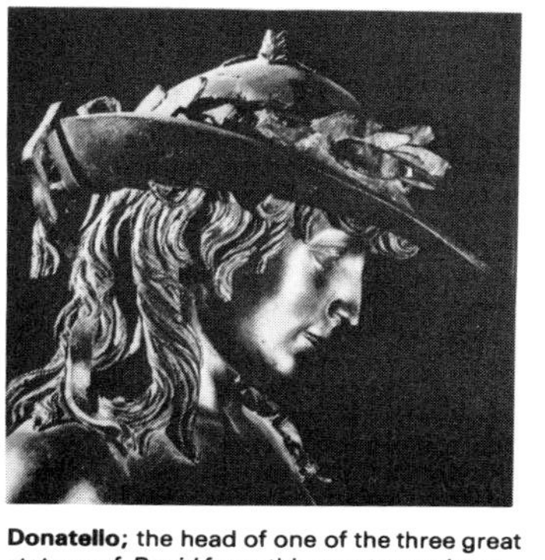

Donatello; the head of one of the three great statues of *David* from this master sculptor.

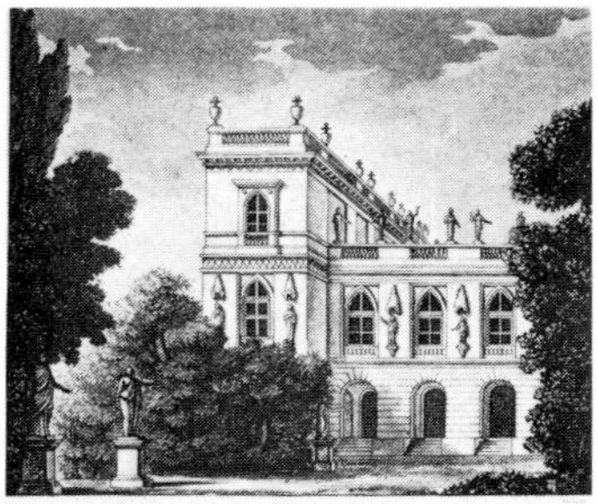

Don Giovanni; sketch design for the garden scene of Mozart's two-act opera.

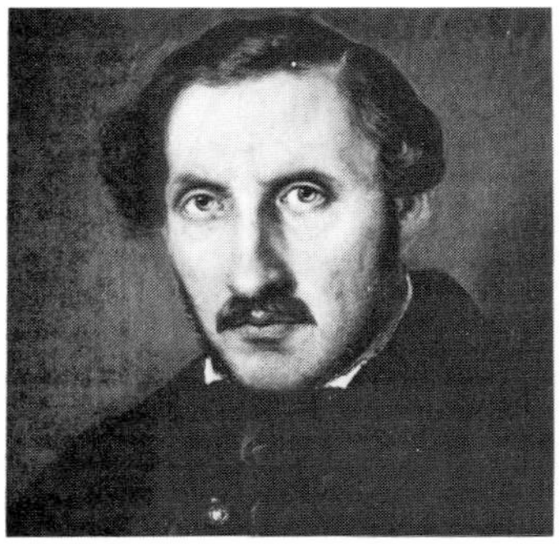

Gaetano Donizetti is renowned for the quantity of operas he composed.

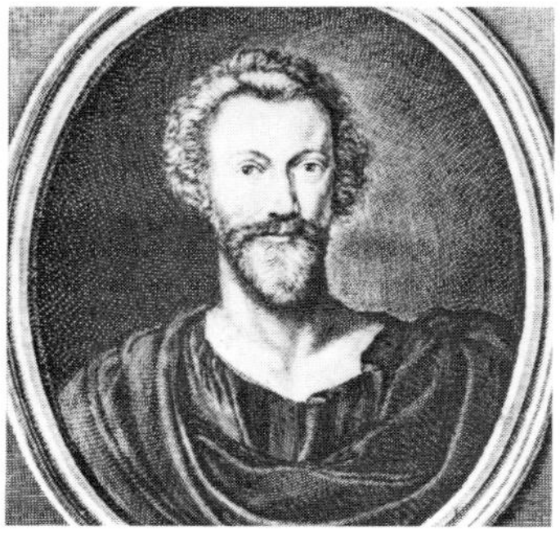

John Donne was a preacher and one of the greatest of the metaphysical poets.

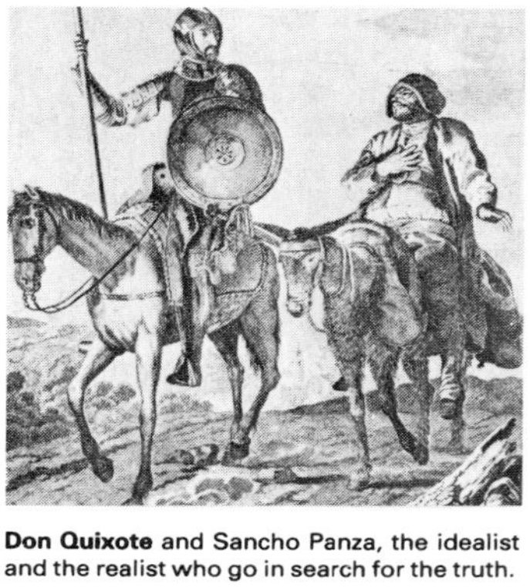

Don Quixote and Sancho Panza, the idealist and the realist who go in search for the truth.

(bald-pate) *prophet* (*c.* 1436) exemplifies his use of realism in its portrayal of an ugly subject, while the bronze *David* (1435) shows his knowledge of Classical sculpture. Almost every major Florentine Renaissance artist has been influenced by Donatello, notably MASACCIO, CASTAGNO, BOTTICELLI and, above all, MICHELANGELO. Paduan artists such as MANTEGNA, learned from the technical skill of Donatello's work. Almost all subsequent schools have used some aspect of his work.

Donati, Giovanni Battista, (1826–73), Italian astronomer who pioneered the spectroscopic study of the Sun and the stars. One of the first to analyze the spectrum of a comet, Donati concluded that comets are partly gaseous in their composition. He discovered six comets, including Donati's comet (1858).

Donatism, doctrine held by a schismatic body in the 4th century Christian Church in Africa that sacraments conferred by unworthy bishops or priests were invalid. The schism arose because of the refusal of the Donatists to accept Caecilian as Bishop of Carthage on his appointment in 311 on the grounds that he had been consecrated by bishops who had compromised the faith during the persecutions of the Emperor DIOCLETIAN. Donatism was condemned by the Synod of Arles (314), which asserted that the validity of the sacraments did not depend on the merits of the clergy administering them, Christ himself being the true minister of the sacraments.

Donatus, Aelius (mid-4th century AD), Roman grammarian and literary critic. He taught St JEROME, and in the Middle Ages his grammatical works *Ars Minor* and *Ars Secunda* were widely used, becoming the foundation of Latin grammar.

Donau glaciation, stage in the last ice age, the Pleistocene, which lasted from 250,000 years ago until 10,000 years ago. This age was characterized by several stages of glaciation separated by periods of milder climate. The Donau glaciation stage or Donau Glacial may be related to the Eburon glacial stage of N Europe and Thurnian sequence of marine strata in Britain. *See also* PE p. *118.*

Donbas. *See* DONETS.

Doncaster, city in South Yorkshire, NE England, on the River Don, 27km (17 miles) NE of Sheffield. It has a famous racecourse with an 18th-century grandstand. The Mansion House in the city centre is a fine example of Georgian architecture. Industries: coal-mining, railway engineering, mechanical engineering. Pop. (1971) 82,500.

Donec. *See* DONETS.

Doneck. *See* DONETSK.

Donegal, county in NW Republic of Ireland, bounded by Northern Ireland (E) and the Atlantic Ocean (N and W). There is a rocky indented coastline and much of the county is hilly, with the Derryveagh Mts in the NW and the Blue Stack Mts in the W. The chief rivers are the Finn, Foyle and Erne. Agriculture is the main occupation but only one-third of the land is fit for cultivation, mainly in the river valleys where oats and potatoes are grown. Tourism and fishing are also important. Area: 4,830sq km (1,865sq miles). Pop. (1971) 108,000.

Donets Basin, also called Donbas or Donec, major industrial region in the Ukraine (Ukrainskaja SSR), USSR, N of the Sea of Azov (Azovskoje More) and SW of the River Donets. It lies mainly in Doneck (Donetsk) and Vorosilovgrad oblasts, and extends E into Rostov oblast. The region produces 35% of the USSR's coal and is a major steel producer, being close to deposits of ferrous metals in the E Ukraine. Development of the region began *c.* 1870 and it is now one of the most concentrated industrial areas in the world. Area 25,900sq km (10,000sq miles).

Donets (Donec)), river in the Ukraine (Ukrainskaja SSR), USSR. It rises NE of Belgorod and flows SE to join the River Don; its lower course is navigable. Length: 1,015km (631 miles).

Donetsk (Doneck), city in the Ukraine (Ukrainskaja SSR), USSR, on the River Kal'mius; capital of Doneck oblast. It is the largest city in the Donets Basin, a highly industrialized region. Formerly known as Yuzovka, it was developed after 1870 when British entrepreneur John Hughes founded an ironworks. Industries: iron and steel, engineering, chemicals. Pop. (1975) 950,000.

Dong, Pham Van (1902–), Prime Minister of North Vietnam (1954–). Active in Communist and nationalist organizations from the 1920s, he was imprisoned by the French (1929–36). He was a founder of the VIET MINH (1941), and fought against the Japanese and French. In 1954 he led the Viet Minh delegation at the Geneva Peace Conference and was appointed premier of North Vietnam. After Ho Chi-minh's death (1969), Dong's influence increased. *See also* HC2 p.*293.*

Dongen, Kees van (1877–1968), Dutch painter who settled in Paris and became a French citizen in 1929. His sensual use of colour showed the influence of FAUVISM. He became a fashionable portrait painter and created a feminine type who was thin and pale with vivid lipstick and an aura of wit and sophistication.

Don Giovanni (1787), two-act opera by Wolfgang Amadeus MOZART, commissioned by the city of Prague; Italian libretto by Lorenzo da PONTE, after Giovanni Bertati's opera and a medieval Spanish legend. Don Giovanni (baritone) tries to seduce Donna Anna (soprano). He kills her father, who is avenged by her fiancé Don Ottavio (tenor). A statue of the victim comes to life, and finally drags the villain to hell. *See also* HC1 p.319.

Dongola (Dunqulah), region in Northern province, Sudan, N 120km (75 miles) of Old Dongola (Dunqalah al-Qadimah), which was of historic importance because of its strategic position on a hill overlooking the River Nile. The first settlement there was established by the Egyptians during the New Kingdom (1570–1075 BC). It became the capital of the Nubian kingdoms in the 4th century AD. It was attacked by Muslims from Egypt in 641, and captured by the MAMELUKES in 1275. The capital was abandoned in 1366 when the Muslims recaptured it. Area of region: 44,308sq km (27,520sq miles).

Dönitz, Karl (1891–), German naval officer. In WWII he was commander of the submarine fleet until 1943. He then became grand admiral and commander-in-chief of the German navy until 1945, when Hitler named him as his successor to the Reich. He was sentenced to 10 years in prison by the Nuremberg tribunal in 1945.

Donizetti, Gaetano (1797–1848), Italian operatic composer. He wrote 75 operas, both comic and serious. These include *L'Elisir d'Amore* (1832), *Lucia di Lammermoor* (1835), *Roberto Devereux* (1837), *La Fille du Régiment* (1840) and *Don Pasquale* (1843). *See also* HC2 pp.*106*, 120.

Don Juan, legendary Spanish philanderer. There are similar libertine figures in the legends and literature of many peoples. The story originated in the Middle Ages, but the earliest printed version is *The Rake of Seville* (1630) by Tirso de Molina. The story tells how Don Juan caps his amorous adventures by seducing the daughter of the commander of Seville whom he kills in a duel. Later, his victim's statue comes to life and drags him off to hell. Don Juan has been the hero of many different versions of his legend, eg MOLIÈRE's play *The Stone Feast*; MOZART's opera *Don Giovanni*; and BYRON's satirical poem *Don Juan.*

Donkey, domesticated ASS, used by man since well before 3000 BC. Crossed with a horse it produces a MULE or a HINNY.

Donleavy, James Patrick (1926–), US-born Irish author. His first novel *The Ginger Man* was published in Paris in 1955 but did not reach Britain and the USA in unexpurgated form until 1963. It was produced in London as a play in 1959. His other works include *A Singular Man* (1963) and *The Onion Eaters* (1971).

Donne, John (*c.* 1572–1631), English poet and cleric. He was originally a Roman Catholic but was converted to Anglicanism and ordained in 1615. In 1621 he became dean of St Paul's Cathedral, London. His poems include love poems, satires and religious sonnets and are noted for their wit, extravagant imagery and passion. Although his work was well-known in his lifetime, the poems for which he is now famous were not published until 1633. *See also* HC1 p.283.

Donnelly, Martin (1917–), New Zealand cricketer whose left-handed stroke-play won post-war acclaim in England, where he played for Oxford University and Warwickshire as well as representing England once at rugby union. In seven Test Matches he scored 582 runs, at an average of 52.90.

Donoghue, Steve (1884–1945), British jockey. Champion jockey ten times (1914–23) and a great favourite with race goers, he rode six Derby winners (1915, 1917, 1921, 1922, 1923, 1925) and twice won the Oaks (1918, 1937) and St Leger (1915, 1917). His most famous mount was *Brown Jack.*

Don Quixote de la Mancha (1605, 1615), novel by Miguel de CERVANTES, published in two parts. Cervantes combined tragedy and comedy in his portrayal of the adventures of an elderly country gentleman, Don Quixote, and his simple squire Sancho Panza. Don Quixote is an avid reader of chivalric romances and, like a knight of old, sets out to redress the wrongs of the world. Together they pass through a series of adventures which combine pathos with humour. The novel had a profound influence on later writers.

Doolittle, Dr. *See* LOFTING, HUGH.

Doolittle, Hilda (1886–1961), US poet. Her work appeared under the initials H.D. Her collections of verse include *Sea Garden* (1916), and *The Flowering of the Rod* (1946).

Doolittle, James Harold (1896–), US aircraft pilot who served in both world wars. Between the wars he became famous for his speed records. He commanded the first bombers that attacked Japan in 1942 and later, the 8th Air Force against Germany.

Doomsday Book. *See* DOMESDAY BOOK.

Doone, legendary family which lived on Exmoor, SW England, where its members roamed at will plundering local farmers. Described in R. D. Blackmore's novel *Lorna Doone* (1869), they had disappeared by the 17th century.

Doornkop, village of Transvaäl, South Africa, 24km (15 miles) W of Johannesburg, famous because the forces of Dr Starr Jameson surrendered there on 2 Jan. 1896. The JAMESON RAID was launched on 29 Dec. 1895 from Bechuanaland to help the Uitlanders (foreigners) unrepresented in the Transvaal Parliament.

Doppelgänger, ghostly counterpart of a person. An encounter with one's double, who is invisible to others, signifies imminent death.

Doppler, Christian Johann (1803–53), Austrian physicist and mathematician, famous for his discovery of the DOPPLER EFFECT, which he first described in a paper on double stars published in 1842. He was educated in Vienna and he became professor of physics there in 1850.

Doppler effect, change in frequency of a wave, usually sound, light or radar, when there is relative motion between the wave source and the observer or detector. The amount of change depends on the velocities of the wave, source and observer. With a sound wave the effect is demonstrated by the drop in pitch of a vehicle's siren as it passes the observer. With light the velocity of the source or observer must be large for an appreciable effect to occur, as when light is received from a rapidly receding galaxy, which has its spectral lines shifted toward the red end of the spectrum. *See also* RED SHIFT; DOPPLER RADAR; NAVIGATION.

Doppler radar navigational system, essentially a range-finding radar navigational aid which relies on the DOPPLER EFFECT, ie a change in frequency (or wavelength) due to motion of an object relative to an observer. Electronic accessories are used to measure differences in frequencies, or the time taken by the echo of a signal to return (both are effectively the same), and interpret them in terms of distances. Bats and dolphins locate prey and navigate by unconsciously making similar measurements from the echoes of the high-pitched sounds they emit.

DORA, full name Defence of the Realm Act (1914). Act conferring special, arbitrary powers upon the British Government for prosecuting the war against Germany. It gave the government extraordinary control over such matters as the press, employment in munitions factories and prices.

Dorado, tropical offshore marine fish. A favourite game fish, it has a squarish head and a forked tail; it eats FLYING FISH and its silvery, blue and yellow colours change when it is taken from the water. Length: to 182cm (72in); weight: 30kg (60lb). Family Coryphaenidae.

Dorado, or the Swordfish, southern circumpolar constellation. It has no stars brighter than the third magnitude but it contains most of the Large MAGELLANIC CLOUD (Nubecula Major). *See also* SU p.263, *263*.

Dorat, Jean (1508–88), French teacher and poet. His humanist ideas and knowledge of Classical literature greatly influenced the doctrines of the group known as the PLÉIADE. He wrote Latin poems, some in imitation of PINDAR.

Dorati, Antal (1906–), Hungarian conductor and composer. He was principal conductor of the BBC Symphony Orchestra (1963–66) and the Stockholm Philharmonic Orchestra (1966–74). In 1975 he was appointed principal conductor of the Royal Philharmonic Orchestra. His compositions include the ballet *Magdalena*, and the cantata *The Way of the Cross*.

Dordrecht, city in SW Netherlands, on the River Mass (Meuse), 19km (12 miles) ESE of Rotterdam. Founded in 1008, it was the scene of the first congress of the Protestant provinces of The Netherlands in 1572, and of the Synod of Dort (1618–19). An important rail junction and river port, it has shipbuilding, machinery, clothing and chemical industries. Pop. 101,000.

Doré, Gustave (1832–83), French illustrator, painter and sculptor. Known best for his engraved book illustrations, many of them grotesque fantasies, he illustrated editions of Dante's *Inferno* (1861), *Don Quixote* (1862), and the Bible (1866).

Dorians, people who settled N Greece and conquered MYCENAE *c.* 1200 BC. This began a 300-year "dark age" in Greek history, of which little record remains. The Dorians added significantly to the development of Greek culture, especially its architecture. *See also* HC1 p.*68*.

Doric, earliest and simplest of the three Classical ORDERS of architecture invented by the Greeks and imitated by the Romans. A typical Doric column had no base, a relatively short shaft with surface fluting meeting in a sharp arris (or edge) and a simple, unornamented capital. *See also* HC1 pp.76, *76*, *78*, 79.

d'Oriola, Christian (1928–), French fencer. A left-hander, he won two Olympic gold medals (1952, 1956), four world championships (1947, 1949, 1953, 1954) and shared in four world and two Olympic team titles.

d'Oriola, Pierre (1920–), French showjumper who was the first civilian to ride in the national team and went on to become the first showjumper to win two Olympic individual gold medals: 1952 on *Ali Baba*, and 1964 on *Lutteur*. In 1966 he won the world championship on *Pomone*.

Dorman, Sir Arthur (1848–1931), British engineer, co-founder of the steel manufacturing company of Dorman and Long. The company has built many major steel structures, particularly bridges (such as Sydney Harbour Bridge).

Dormancy, temporary state of inaction or reduced metabolism. Animals may become dormant by hibernating; dormant plant seeds for a time cease to grow or develop. An organism can return to a fully active state when conditions, such as temperature, moisture or day length, change. *See also* NW p.206.

Dormouse, mouse-sized squirrel-like RODENT of Eurasia and Africa that hibernates. Most dormice are active at night and sleep by day. They eat nuts, fruit, seeds, eggs, insects and other tiny animals. Length: 10–20cm (4–8in) excluding tail. Family Gliridae. *See also* NW p.*209*.

Dornier, Claude, or Claudius (1884–1969), German aircraft manufacturer who designed and manufactured the first all-metal aeroplane. While working with Ferdinand von Zeppelin, the airship manufacturer, Dornier founded an aeroplane company and built wooden and metal planes which served in WWI. In 1929 he designed the DO-X, a 12-engined passenger aeroplane. After WWII, his company built US-designed aircraft.

Dorset, county in SW England, on the English Channel. It is traversed W to E by the North Dorset Downs and the South Dorset Downs (nearer the coast) and drained by the rivers Frome and Stour. The chief towns are Dorchester, the county town, Poole, Bournemouth and Weymouth. Agriculture is important and includes the cultivation of cereal crops and vegetables, and the raising of sheep, cattle, pigs and poultry. Industries: tourism, marble quarrying. Area: 2,520sq km (973sq miles). Pop. (1971) 361,919.

Dorsey, name of two brothers, both popular US bandleaders. Jimmy (1904–57) was a clarinettist and saxophonist, and Tommy (1905–56) a trombone player. In 1953 they joined to form The Fabulous Dorseys.

Dort. *See* DORDRECHT.

Dortmund, city in W West Germany; a port on the Dortmund-Ems Canal. In the 13th century Dortmund flourished as a member of the HANSEATIC LEAGUE. It declined in the late 17th century but grew as an industrial centre from the mid-19th century. Coal is mined nearby and the city is an important iron and steel centre in the Ruhr industrial district. It was badly damaged in WWII. Pop. (1970) 632,317.

Dory, also called John Dory, marine fish found throughout the world. It is deep-bodied and has a large mouth. The species *Zeus faber* of the Mediterranean Sea and Atlantic Ocean is a valuable food fish. Length: to 1m (3.3ft). Family Zeidae. *See also* PE p.247, *247*.

Dory, small narrow fishing-boat, about 6m (20ft) long. It has pointed ends, high flaring sides and a flat bottom. Engines, sails or oars are used for power, but dories are usually auxiliaries of larger craft.

Dosimeter, instrument used for measuring radiation dose, usually a pocket electroscope. A quartz fibre, after being charged, is viewed against a scale; its deflection across the scale on discharge gives a measure of the dosage of radiation to which it was exposed.

Dos Passos, John (1896–1970), US novelist. His first novel *Three Soldiers* appeared in 1921. In his later work – the trilogy *USA* (1937) – he developed various innovatory techniques, including stream-of-consciousness writing and the use of contemporary headlines and biographies of prominent Americans. *See also* HC2 p.288.

Dostoevsky, Fyodor Mikhailovich (1821–81), Russian novelist. After writing *Poor Folk* (1846) and *The Double* (1846) he joined a revolutionary group, was arrested, and sentenced to death in 1849. He was reprieved just before the time set for his execution and sentenced to four years' hard labour. He returned to St Petersburg in 1859 where he wrote *Notes from the Underground* (1864). After *Crime and Punishment* (1866) appeared, he left Russia and travelled in Europe, partly to escape his creditors. While abroad, he wrote *The Idiot* (1868) and *The Possessed* (1871–72). His last major work was *The Brothers Karamazov* (1879–80).

Dotrice, Roy (1925–), British actor. He was with the Royal Shakespeare Company (1957–65). His one-man show, *Brief Lives*, ran for 200 performances in London in 1969, establishing a world record.

Dotterel, wading bird of the plover family. The Eurasian dotterel (*Eudromias morinellus*) has a stocky body, short tail and mottled-brown plumage with a rust-coloured breast. Length: 22cm (8.5.in). Family Charadriidae.

Douai, town in N France, on the River Scarpe 30km (19 miles) S of Lille. The town passed to France in 1668, having been a possession of the dukes of Burgundy and the Spanish Hapsburgs. At its Roman Catholic college the Old Testament of the Douai Bible was prepared in 1609. Industries: coal-mining, chemicals, iron products. Pop. (1968) 49,187.

Douai Bible, English translation (from the Latin Vulgate) of the Bible, authorized by the Roman Catholic Church for use after the REFORMATION. Gregory Martin, an Oxford scholar living in exile at the English college at Douai, France, was the main translator. The New Testament was published at Reims in 1582, the Old Testament at Douai in 1609–10. It was revised in 1749–50 by Richard Challoner.

Douala, chief port of Cameroon, W Africa, on the Bight of Biafra. It was the capital of the German Kamerun Protectorate from 1901 until 1916. Exports include coffee, cocoa and bauxite. Pop. (1970) 250,000.

Double bass, largest stringed instrument, usually with four strings tuned in fourths (E-A-D-G) and played one octave below the musical notation. It resembles a large violin but has sloping shoulders (it was originally a member of the VIOL family). The double bass is held vertically, with the player standing or sitting behind. A bow is generally used for classical music, but the strings are usually plucked in jazz. *See also* HC2 p.104, *104*.

Double bassoon, lowest-pitched woodwind instrument, sounding an octave below the BASSOON; also called contrabassoon. It consists of a tube 5m (16ft) long doubled back on itself four times. The modern form of the instrument dates from the late 19th century.

Double galaxy, two adjacent galaxies orbiting around a common centre of gravity, rather like a BINARY STAR. The components are often linked by tenuous bridges of intergalactic matter.

Double helix, structure of DNA (deoxyribonucleic acid), the basic store of genetic information in the cells of each living organism. First demonstrated in 1953 by Francis CRICK and James WATSON, the knowledge of the structure of the DNA molecule has since revolutionized biological science. *See also* SU pp.*153*, 157, *157*.

Double star, star that appears single when viewed with the naked eye but is really two stars close together. Double stars are either gravitationally associated BINARY STARS or simply the results of optical effects – two completely separate objects that happen to lie in or near the same line of sight when viewed from Earth. *See also* SU pp.236–237.

Doublet, or gipon, close-fitting upper garment laced or buttoned down the front. It was worn by men over a linen shirt in the period 1400–1600. At times slits were cut to allow the blouse to puff through, and fur or other trim was added.

Double Vision. *See* DIPLOPIA.

Doughty, Charles (1843–1926), British explorer, pravel writer and poet. He travelled from Damascus to Mecca (1876–78), an account of which appears in *Travels in Arabia Deserta* (2 vols, 1888). His poetry includes *The Dawn in Britain* (6 vols, 1906) and *The Clouds* (1912).

Douglas, Lord Alfred Bruce (1870–1945), British poet, whose work includes the volume of verse *In Excelsis* (1924), and his *Autobiography*, (1929). He was an intimate friend of Oscar WILDE.

Douglas, Archibald, 6th Earl of Angus (*c.* 1489–1557), Scottish noble. In 1514 he married Margaret Tudor, sister of Henry VIII of England and mother by a previous marriage of James V, boy-King of Scotland. With Henry's aid Angus ruled Scotland from 1526–28, but he was exiled in 1529 when James asserted his own authority. On James' death in 1542, Angus returned and helped to repel the English invasions of 1547–48.

Douglas, Gavin (*c.* 1474–1522), Scottish poet, important in the emergence of Scots as a language distinct from English or Gaelic. One of the most proficient medieval poets, Douglas completed a rhymed-couplet version of Virgil's *Aeneid* in Scots in 1513, the first translation of a classical

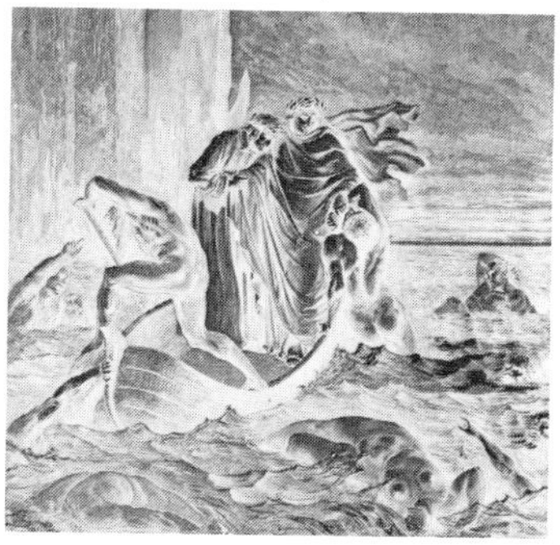

Gustave Doré; one of his fantastic engravings illustrating *Dante's Inferno*.

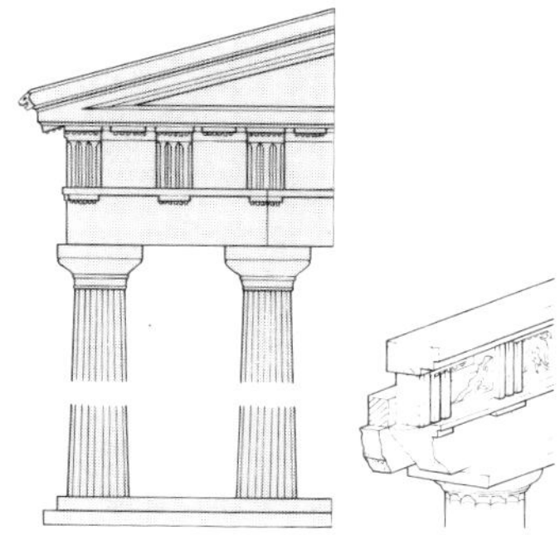

Doric; is the earliest and the simplest of the three orders of Greek architecture.

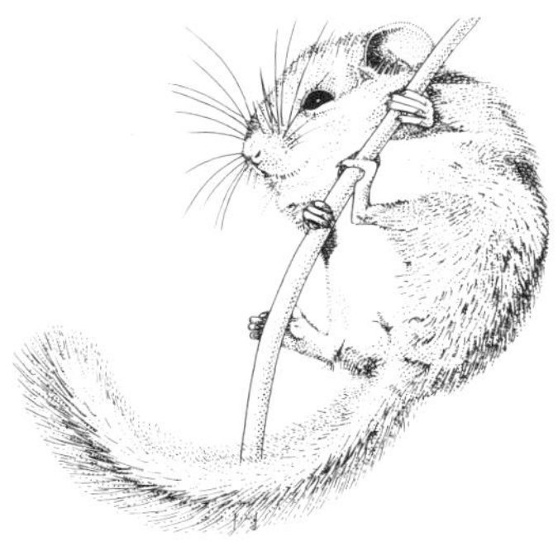

Dormouse spends most of the day sleeping and is active only at night.

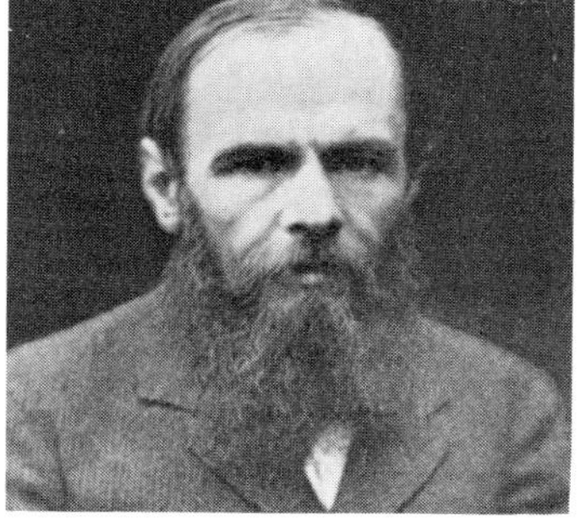

Dostoevsky believed that evil was in man and could not be cured by any political system.

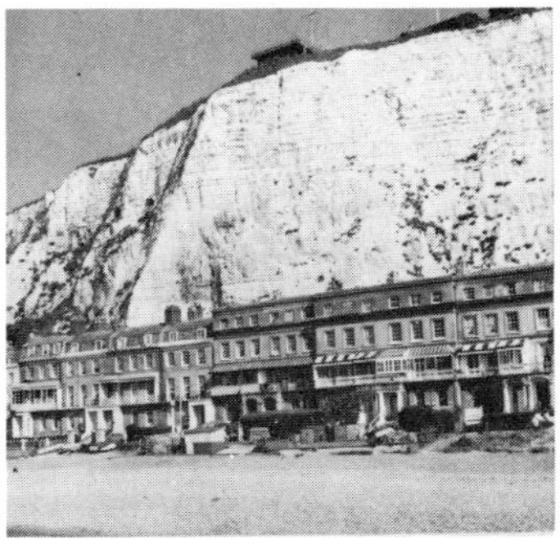

Dover's white cliffs, the first sight of "home" for Britons returning from the continent.

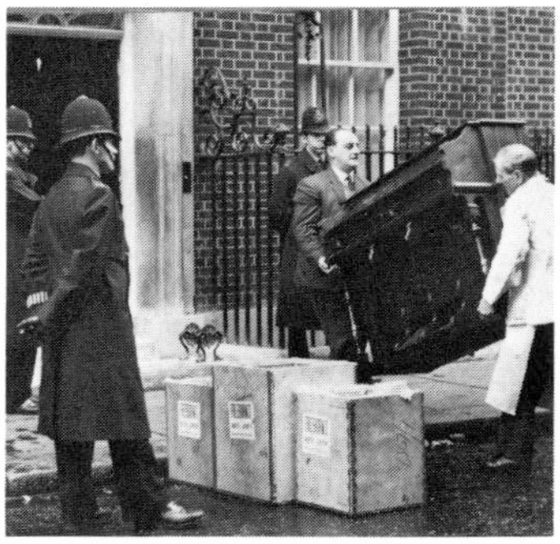

Downing Street; a harmonium arrives at number ten for a new prime minister.

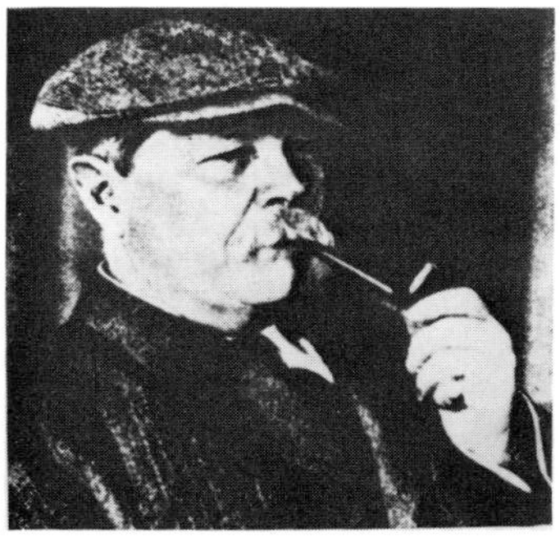

Sir Arthur Conan Doyle smoking a more prosaic pipe than his famous detective character.

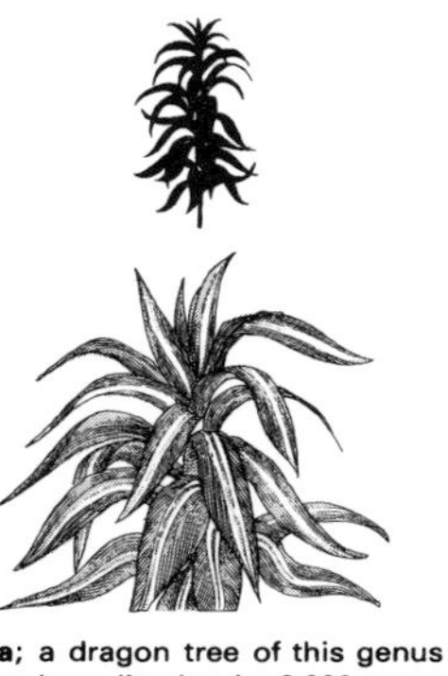

Dracaena; a dragon tree of this genus was reputed to have lived to be 6,000 years old.

poem into an English-based language. *See also* HC2 p.30.

Douglas, James, 4th Earl of Morton. *See* MORTON, JAMES DOUGLAS, 4TH EARL OF.

Douglas, Sir James (1803–77), Canadian fur trader and political leader. He worked for the Hudson's Bay Company (1821–58) and established Fort Connolly in 1827 and Fort Victoria in 1842. He served as governor of Vancouver Island (1852–64) and of British Columbia (1858–64).

Douglas, Sir James de, Lord of Douglas (1286–*c.*1330), Scottish noble. He was Robert BRUCE's greatest captain in his struggles against England. After Bruce died, Douglas took Bruce's heart on a pilgrimage to Jerusalem, and died crusading in Spain. *See also* HC1 p.244.

Douglas, John Sholto (1844–1900), 9th Marquess of Queensberry who *c.*1867 gave his name and patronage to the rules of boxing drafted by John Graham Chambers. In 1895 he was acquitted of libelling the poet and dramatist Oscar WILDE, whose downfall followed.

Douglas, Kirk (1916–), US actor and producer, real name Issur Danielovitch Demsky. Throughout his career he has specialized in tough or dramatic parts, as in *Detective Story* (1951), *The Bad and the Beautiful* (1952), *Gunfight at the OK Corral* (1957), *Paths of Glory* (1957) *Spartacus* (1960), *The Arrangement* (1969) and *A Gunfight* (1971).

Douglas, Lloyd Cassel (1887–1951), US author. He was a Lutheran clergyman and wrote a number of novels, including *Magnificent Obsession* (1929). Several of his novels were based on the New Testament, such as *The Robe* (1942) and *The Big Fisherman* (1948).

Douglas, Norman (1868–1952), British author, best known for his first novel *South Wind* (1917), a satire on modern morality. He also wrote two non-fictional works, *Siren Land* (1911) and *Old Calabria* (1915).

Douglas, Thomas, 5th Earl of Selkirk. *See* SELKIRK, THOMAS DOUGLAS 5TH EARL OF.

Douglas, noble Scottish family of obscure origins. It first rose to prominence in about 1200 with Sir William de Douglas, a powerful landowner in Douglasdale, Lanarkshire. The title Earl of Douglas was first given in 1358 and another branch of the family were earls of Angus (1389) and Morton (1458). The family was prominent in Scottish politics until the Act of Union (1707).

Douglas, main town on the Isle of Man. A popular resort on the Irish Sea, it has the Tower of Refuge (1832) built by William Hilary, the founder of the Royal National Lifeboat Institution, and the Manx Museum. Industries include light engineering and fishing. Pop. (1970 prelim.) 20,400.

Douglas DC-3, early airliner. It first flew in 1935 and over the next ten years became the world standard airliner, and the standard Allied transport in WWII. *See also* MM p.149, *149.*

Douglas fir, evergreen tree native to NW USA and Canada. An important timber pine, it is also grown in the E USA as an ornamental. Its bark is thick and corky and deeply grooved. Height: to more than 76m (250ft). Family Pinaceae; species *Pseudotsuga taxifolia. See also* NW p.55, *55*; PE p.*219.*

Douglas-Home, Sir Alec (1903–), British Conservative politician. Entering Parliament in 1931, he became Neville Chamberlain's parliamentary private secretary (1937–39) and subsequently held ministerial posts. He became 14th Earl of Home in 1951. He was appointed Foreign Secretary (1960–63), but had to renounce his peerage to become Prime Minister (1963–64). *See also* HC2 p.237.

Douglas of Kirtleside, William Sholto Douglas, Lord (1893–1969), RAF commander. He was assistant chief of air staff in 1938 and became an air marshal in 1946. He served as chairman of British European Airways (BEA) from 1949 to 1964. He was raised to the peerage in 1948.

Douglas scales, two scales of numbers indicating surface conditions of the sea. One scale indicates the amount of swell, the other the conditions on the surface of the sea. In both scales numbers range from 0 (calm) to 9 (confused).

Doukhobors, Russian-Canadian religious sect. The name means literally "spirit-wrestlers". The Doukhobors seem to have originated in 18th-century Russia, preaching the inherent goodness of man without the intercession of organized religion. Persecution of them in Russia encouraged Leo TOLSTOY to petition the Tsar to allow them to emigrate. With further help from the QUAKERS, 7,500 settled in Saskatchewan, Canada in 1899. They lived communally, following pacifist and vegetarian precepts. Now known as the Union of Spiritual Communities of Christ, their anarchistic nonconformity has tended to prevent their full assimilation into Canadian society.

Doulton, Sir Henry, (1820–97), British pottery manufacturer who introduced in 1846 stoneware drain-pipes instead of flat-bottomed brick drains. He later founded, near Dudley, Staffordshire, what were to become the largest pottery works in the world.

Douro (Duero), river in Spain and Portugal. It rises in N central Spain, flows W across Spain to form part of the border with Portugal, then through Portugal to the Atlantic Ocean near Porto. There are hydroelectric power plants along its lower course. Length: 895km (556 miles).

Dove, cooing, plump-bodied bird found throughout the world except in polar and subpolar areas and on some remote islands. Doves are related to PIGEONS and have small heads, short legs and dense, varied plumage. They feed mostly on vegetable matter. Length: 15–83cm (6–33in). Family Columbidae.

Dover, town in Kent, SE England, on the Strait of Dover. One of the CINQUE PORTS, Dover is a resort and an important cross-Channel ferry port. During WWI it was the centre of the British defence of the English Channel and an important naval base. Pop. (1971) 34,322.

Dover, Strait of, sea passage between Dover and Calais, at its narrowest 32km (20 miles) across. Many invasions of both Britain and Europe have been centred on the Strait, which now forms one of the busiest shipping lanes in the world.

Dowding, Hugh Caswell Tremenheere (1882–1970), RAF commander. He served in the Royal Flying Corps in WWI, commanded Fighter Command (1936–40), a period including the Battle of Britain. He retired in 1942.

Dowiyogo, Bernard (1947–), President of Nauru since 1976. He is a member of the Nauru Party, set up in 1968 when Nauru became independent.

Dowland, John (1563–1626), English composer of songs and lute music. The most famous of his songs are the *Lachrymae.* He was also the most celebrated lutenist of his age. *See also* HC1 p.*248.*

Down, county in SE Northern Ireland, on the Irish Sea coast. A hilly region, it rises to the Mountains of Mourne in the SE, and is drained by the Upper Bann and Lagan rivers. The chief towns are Downpatrick, the county town, Bangor, Newry and Newtownards. Agriculture is important and includes the cultivation of cereal crops, potatoes and flax, and the rearing of sheep, cattle, pigs and poultry. Industries: textiles, food processing. Area: 2,466sq km (952sq miles). Pop. (1971) 311,266.

Down and Out in Paris and London (1933), first book by George ORWELL. In it he describes his experiences when he lived with some of the poorest members of society, first as a dishwasher in Paris and later as a tramp in London.

Downhill racing. *See* SKIING.

Downing, Sir George (1623–84), British diplomat. He was an MP (1654–59) and was appointed British minister at The Hague in 1657. DOWNING STREET is named after him. His grandson, also Sir George, endowed the Cambridge college which bears their name.

Downing Street, street in London, off Whitehall, containing the official residence of the British Prime Minister at No. 10, the Chancellor of the Exchequer at No. 11 and chief whip at No. 12. It was named after Sir George DOWNING.

Downpatrick, market town in E Northern Ireland, approx. 34km (21 miles) SE of Belfast. It is a pilgrimage centre and St PATRICK is thought to have founded a church there *c.*440; St Patrick, St COLUMBA and St BRIDGET were long thought to be buried there. Industry: textiles. Pop. 8,400.

Downs, North and South, two chalk hill ranges in SE England, running parallel and separated by The Weald, an area approx. 48km (30 miles) wide. The North Downs extend SE approx. 161km (100 miles) from the S outskirts of London, through Surrey and Kent; the South Downs extend approx. 100km (65 miles), from E Hampshire through W Sussex to E Sussex. The hills provide some excellent pasture for sheep. The highest point is Leith Hill, rising to 294m (965ft).

Downs, The, anchorage off Deal, Kent, SE England, between North Foreland and South Foreland in the English Channel. The area is sheltered by the Goodwin Sands. It was the scene of a naval battle between the Dutch and the Spanish in 1639 and between the English and the Dutch in 1666. Length: approx. 13km (8 miles); width 9.5m (6 miles).

Down's syndrome, commonly called mongolism, disorder which may include some of the following symptoms: thickened hands and feet, enlarged tongue, mental retardation, slanted eyes, small nose and heart or kidney malformations. Usually occuring in the first children of older women it is an autosomal abnormality, in which most cells have 47 rather than 46 chromosomes. *See also* MS pp.84, 143.

Dowry, economic transaction in which money or goods are given to the bridegroom on marriage by his father-in-law. This usually occurs in societies where women are considered economic burdens. The dowry system is not recognized in law in England and the US (except in Louisiana). *See also* MARRIAGE.

Dowsing, searching for underground water or minerals by using a divining-rod, usually a forked willow twig. Still widely used in many parts of the world, its actual basis is still disputed. The method is to hold the forks of the stick close to the body, and the horizontal stem is pulled down when the dowser walks over the water or mineral.

Dowson, Ernest Christopher (1867–1900), British poet. He was a member of the Decadent group, and a friend of W. B. YEATS. His works were published in 1896 and 1899. He died of consumption.

Doyle, Sir Arthur Conan (1859–1930), British novelist and physician. His novel *A Study in Scarlet* (1887) featured the first appearance of his famous character SHERLOCK HOLMES. Other Sherlock Holmes stories appeared in *The Adventures of Sherlock Holmes* (1892), *Memoirs of Sherlock Holmes* (1894) and *The Return of Sherlock Holmes* (1905). Among his other works were *The Lost World* (1912) and *The White Company* (1891).

D'Oyly Carte, Richard. *See* CARTE, RICHARD D'OYLY.

Drabble, Margaret (1939–), British novelist. Her first book was *The Summer Birdcage* (1963). *The Millstone* (1965) was filmed as *A Touch of Love* (1969) and in 1974 she wrote a biography of Arnold BENNETT.

Dracaena, genus of ornamental plants. Most species have short stalks and long, pointed, oval leaves. The leaves are often striped with pink or purple along their length and the flowers, when present, are red, green or yellow. Family Agavaceae.

Drachenfels, peak in the Siebengebirge range, W West Germany, on the E bank of the River Rhine. According to legend it is the site where SIEGFRIED slew the dragon. The Drachenburg, a fortress now in ruins, was built there in 1117. Height: 321m (1,053ft).

Drachenlock, Switzerland, site of a cave in which remains of Neanderthal man have been discovered. *See also* MS p.27.

Draco, or the Dragon, northern circumpolar constellation between the Great Bear and the Little Bear (Ursa Major and Minor). The brightest star is Gamma

Draconis, or Etamin, of about the second magnitude. *See also* SU p.256.
Dracon, Athenian lawgiver. In 621 BC he drew up laws famous for their severity, in which death was the punishment even for minor crimes. Most of his laws were repealed by SOLON.
Dracula, Count, central character and archfiend of the Gothic horror novel *Dracula* (1897) by Bram Stoker. He is depicted as a vampire who rests as a corpse by day, but emerges at night to feed on the blood of human beings. Dracula has more recently been identified with Prince Vlad "the Impaler", who ruled Romania in the 15th century.
Draft. *See* CONSCRIPTION.
Drag, aerodynamic, force opposing the motion of an aircraft through the air either as the rearward component of the lifting force or as the friction of air over external surfaces and other parts of the aircraft (such as a fixed undercarriage) not associated with the development of lift. *See also* MM pp.*152*.
Dragon, mythical scaly lizard, snake or worm-like fire-breathing monster. It is often depicted with bat-like wings, talons and a lashing tail, although in some traditions it has many heads or may change shape at will. It is often shown ravaging the countryside and slaying the inhabitants. Sometimes, as in the tale of St GEORGE and the dragon, it is used symbolically as the personification of Evil that Good must fight and conquer. In China and Japan the dragon is identified with a beneficent force of nature. Today the name can refer to certain species of lizards such as the KOMODO DRAGON, a monitor lizard. *See also* MS p.*206*.
Dragonet, bottom-dwelling fish related to the GOBY. It has a flattened body, a short snout and spines on its gill-covers. It burrows into sand and propels itself with strong fins. Order Perciformes; genus *Callionymus*.
Dragonetti, Domenico (1763–1846), Italian double-bass player and minor composer. He was one of the great virtuoso performers of the 19th century. He wrote several SONATAS, CONCERTOS and capriccios for the double-bass.
Dragonfly, swift-flying insect of the order Odonata. It has a long slender abdomen that may be brightly coloured and two pairs of large membranous wings. Like the DAMSELFLY, it mates while flying in tandem. The nymphs, which emerge from eggs laid on water plants, are aquatic. Wingspan: to 17cm (7in). *See also* NW pp.*106, 111, 230*.
Dragoon, mounted infantryman originating in the late 16th century. The name derived from the short musket that they carried. Dragoons, who originally rode into battle but fought on foot, came to use tactics inseparable from those of the cavalry in the 18th century.
Drag Racing, American derivative of motor racing in which two matched machines accelerate over a straight quarter-mile strip from a standing start, reaching speeds of 320km/h (230mph) or more. It also has adherents in Europe, Australasia and Japan. Categories established by the American National Hot-Rod Association include Top Fuel and Top Gas (petrol) Eliminators, Funny Cars and Stock. The drag begins with orange flame and smoke enveloping the dragster as squealing tyres grab for traction; it ends seconds later with the billowing of a parachute.
Dragún, Osvaldo (1929–), Argentine playwright. His dramas criticize what he believes to be the problems of Latin American society – corruption, the generation gap and purposeless violence. His work includes *Historias para ser contadas* (1957), a series of one-act plays.
Drainage basin, also called a catchment area, region from which all precipitation such as rain and melted snow flows to a single stream or system of streams. By identifying such a basin, scientists can calculate DENUDATION rates and moisture balances from various hydrological measurements such as evaporation rates.
Drainage system, in geology, the system by which surface water is collected and removed by streams, rivers and lakes. The pattern of drainage is determined by the type of rock and the slope of the land over which the water flows. *See also* PE pp. 114–115.
Drais, Karl von, (1785–1851), German engineer who developed the hobby-horse or *draisienne*. His invention was exhibited for the first time in 1818 in Paris and it enjoyed great popularity until about 1830. The draisienne was the first practical form of the bicycle. *See also* MM p.122.
Drake, Edwin Laurentine (1819–80), US oil well drilling expert whose well, started in 1858 near Titusville, Pennsylvania, USA was first ever to produce oil. *See also* MM p.78.
Drake, Sir Francis (*c.* 1540–96), English admiral and navigator, the first Englishman to sail round the world. He achieved fame raiding Spanish shipping and colonies in the Caribbean (1570–72). In 1577–80 he sailed west around the world in his ship the *Golden Hind*. He was knighted by Elizabeth I and made mayor of Plymouth in 1581. He made further raids against Spain (1585–87) and his seamanship and daring contributed greatly to the defeat of the Spanish Armada. *See also* HC1 pp.276–277, 279, *279*.
Drakensberg Range, mountains in South Africa, extending through Natal, Lesotho, Orange Free State and Transvaal. The highest peak is Thabana Ntlenyana in Lesotho, rising to 3,485m (11,425ft). Length: approx. 1,130km (700 miles).
Drama, art form which probably derived from primitive religious rituals in which early man sought increased control over his environment. In the West, Classical Greek drama reached its peak in Athenian festivals held each spring and winter in honour of Dionysus (BACCHUS). Of these plays, which reached their peak in the 5th century BC, some 35 tragedies survive, representing the works of AESCHYLUS, SOPHOCLES and EURIPIDES, and the 11 comedies of ARISTOPHANES. Greek tragedy maintained the unity of action, defined by ARISTOTLE in his *Poetics*, in the production of such works as *Agamemnon, Oedipus Rex* and *Medea*. Classical Roman drama, such as SENECA's stoical tragedies and PLAUTUS' comedies, relied heavily on Greek models and these, in turn, strongly influenced Renaissance drama; this saw its greatest flowering in Elizabethan and Jacobean England, but was also significant in Spain. Drama of this period also had religious origins in the medieval MYSTERY PLAYS, which were based on Christian themes.

In the late 16th and early 17th centuries London saw the greatest and most varied works of drama since those of the Greeks, with the plays of KYD, BEAUMONT and FLETCHER, MARLOWE's *Doctor Faustus* and *Tamburlaine the Great*, and above all the tragedies of SHAKESPEARE, who also wrote lasting comedies and a series of history plays. His contemporary, Ben JONSON, wrote in the genre of the Comedy of Humours, examples of which are *Volpone* and *The Alchemist*, plays in which the protagonists personify physiological humours determining their personalities and behaviour. The *Revenger's Tragedy,* by Cyril TOURNEUR, was a common type of Jacobean drama known as the REVENGE PLAY of which *Hamlet* is also an example. In Spain at this time LOPE DE VEGA wrote hundreds of plays on a variety of themes.

Drama also flourished in the France of Louis XIV with the neo-classical poetic tragedies of CORNEILLE and RACINE, examples of which are *Le Cid* and *Phèdre,* plays which adhered to the three unities of time, place and action, the 16th-century development of the Aristotelian unities. The comedies of MOLIÈRE reflected the influence of the COMMEDIA DELL'ARTE.

The twentieth century has seen another revival of drama, receiving its impetus from the Naturalistic plays of CHEKHOV, IBSEN and STRINDBERG, which deal with themes of alienation, and status of women, and other modern preoccupations. Modern drama is characterized by experiments in forms and styles, ranging through ARTAUD's THEATRE OF CRUELTY, T. S. ELIOT's verse dramas and PIRANDELLO's surrealism to the brevity of Samuel BECKETT's *Breath*, which lasts for only 30 seconds.
Drammen town in SE Norway at the head of Drammens Fjord, the western branch of the Oslo Fjord, 32km (20 miles) SW of Oslo. It is an important timber exporting port. Pop. (1970 est.) 49,300.
Draper, John William (1811–82), US chemist, pioneer in spectral analysis and in photography. He took the first photographs of the Moon, in 1839, and was one of the first people to use DAGUERRE's photographic process, taking the first successful photographic portrait in sunlight.
Draper, Ruth (1884–1956), US actress, noted for her gifted mimicry and dramatic monologues that she wrote herself. She used only a bare stage with very few props. She made her professional stage debut in New York in 1915.
Draughts, board game, called checkers in the USA, played between two people on a chess board (an eight by eight array of alternate light and dark squares). Each player starts with a set of 12 discs, called men, arranged on dark squares of the first three rows of his side of the board. The players take it in turn to move men one square diagonally forwards. A player may not move a man to a square already occupied by one of his own pieces; if that square is occupied by an opponent's piece, it may be "jumped" (providing the next square on that diagonal is empty) and the opponent's piece removed from the board. A man reaching the opponent's back line can be "crowned" as a king (generally denoted by stacking one disc on top of another), which is able to move diagonally backwards as well as forwards. The object of the game is to capture all the opponent's men or to block them in such a way that none can move.
Dravidian, family of languages spoken in S India by nearly ten million people. The four major Dravidian languages are Telugu, Tamil, Kannada (Kanarese) and Malayalam. Tamil is also spoken in Sri Lanka; another Dravidian language, Brahui, is spoken in Pakistan.
Drawbridge, or bascule, bridge with one or more spans that are hinged and counter-weighted, allowing the raising of the span, so that vessels may pass. Bascules have their origin in castle moat drawbridges. This type of bridge is common on canals in Britain and The Netherlands; the most famous example is probably Tower Bridge, London.
Drawing, the art of representation in chalk, crayon, charcoal, pen or pencil. The Egyptians made brush-drawn sketches on potsherds. During much of the Middle Ages drawing as an autonomous technique was mainly restricted to the pattern book used in workshops.

Drawing achieved independence as a means of artistic expression with LEONARDO DA VINCI. He considered his sketches like the rough drafts of poems; his unfinished drawings were used to suggest fresh ideas for major works. RAPHAEL was influenced by him and was considered a great natural draughtsman. MICHELANGELO's drawing technique of close-hatching resembled the marks made by the chisel. At this time Giorgio VASARI collected drawings to keep a record of the various styles of the artists. In the academy of the CARRACCI drawing was systematically cultivated. Among north Italians, Tintoretto produced some of the greatest drawings. In N Europe, Albrecht DÜRER was famed for his superb and varied drawings and Pieter BRUEGHEL for his studies of genre figures and landscapes. REMBRANDT, the Pre-Raphaelites, Edgar DEGAS, Vincent Van GOGH, Henri MATISSE, Paul KLEE and Pablo PICASSO were all particularly interested in the art of drawing, as were the sculptors Auguste RODIN and Aristide MAILLOL. Among more recent artists who have shown interest is Jim DINE.
Drayton, Michael (1563–1631), English poet. He was the author of a great number of historical, religious, pastoral and other verse which included the fine lyric *Since*

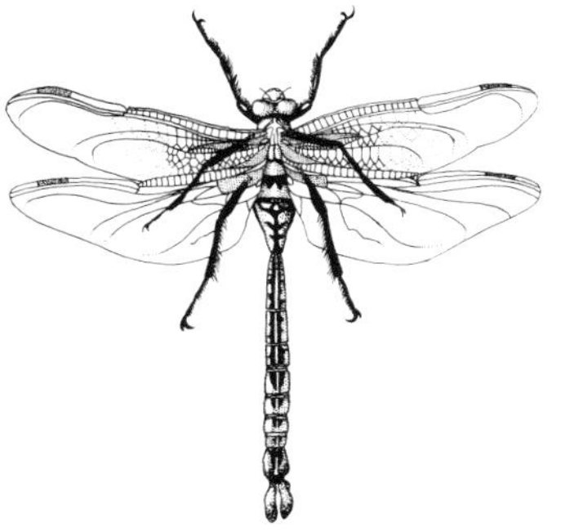

Dragonfly; huge compound eyes give the insect extremely sensitive "mosaic" vision.

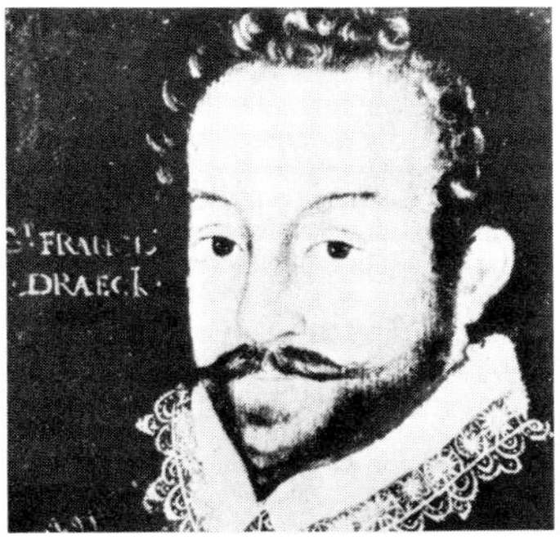

Sir Francis Drake; his total tactical genius and leadership won many naval battles.

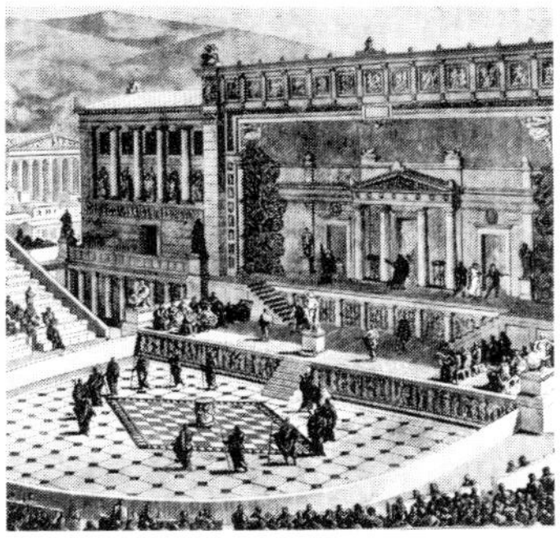

Drama; the theatre of Dionysius as it probably was in Athens in the 5th century BC.

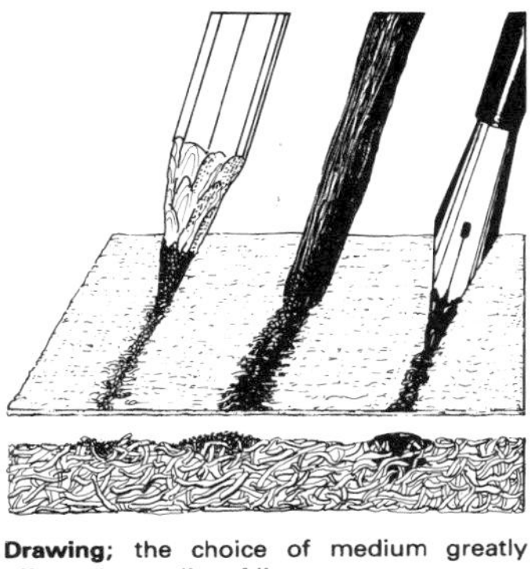

Drawing; the choice of medium greatly affects the quality of line.

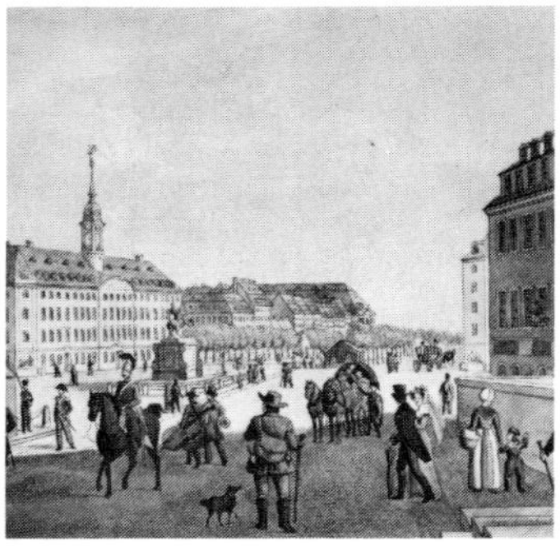

Dresden; an 18th-century print of the beautiful city devastated by Allied bombs in WWII.

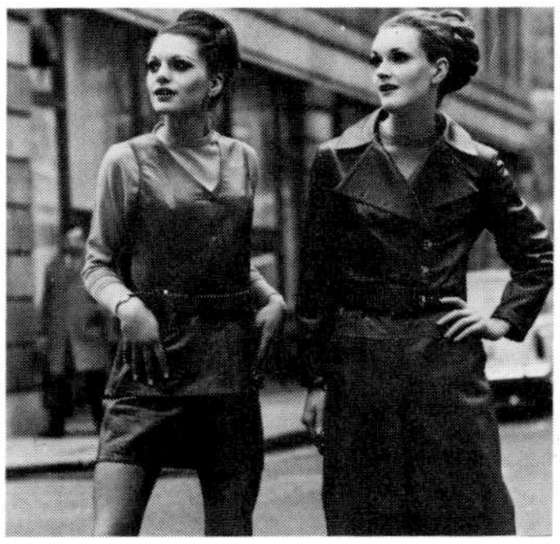

Dress; leather was probably one of the first materials people wore next to their skins.

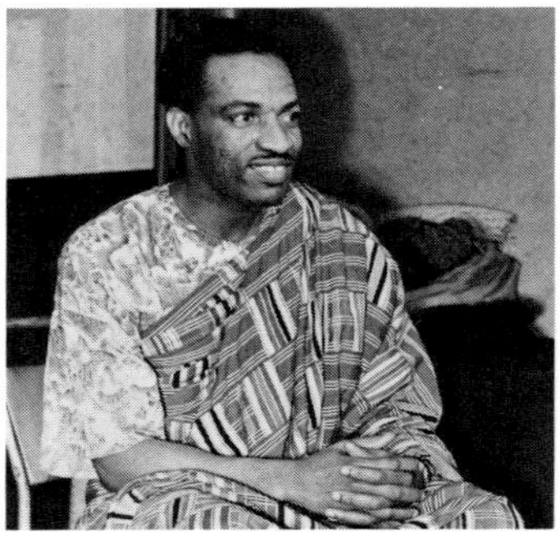

Dress instantly marks national differences as well as indicating status within a group.

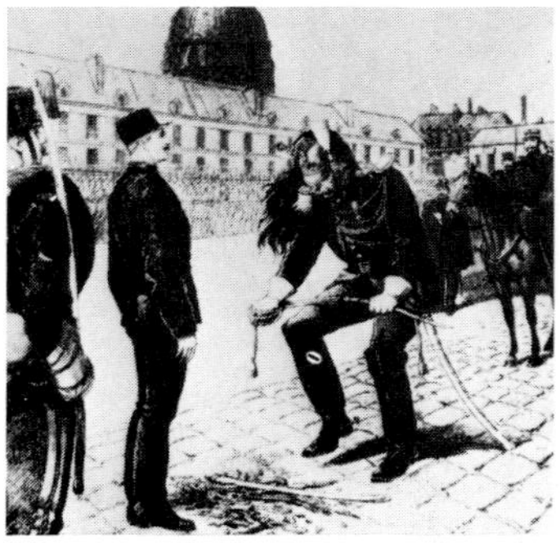

Dreyfus Affair, a crisis which ultimately led to the separation of church and state in France.

There's No Help (1594) and *Polyolbion* (1612–22).

Dreadnought, HMS, one of the first of a class of British battleships launched in 1906. It was faster (maximum speed 21 knots), more heavily armoured and larger than its predecessors (displacement 21,407 tonnes), with steam turbine engines and a main armament of ten 12in calibre guns. These changes enabled the battleships to direct fire over long ranges and reduce the danger of torpedo attack. The *Dreadnought* class was followed by a class known as *Superdreadnoughts*, with even larger guns and displacements of about 27,000 tonnes. *See also* MM pp.174–175.

Dream, mental activity associated with the rapid-eye-movement (REM) period of sleep. It is usually a train of thoughts, scenes and fancies expressed in visual images and symbols rather than sound or language. On average, a person dreams for one-and-a-half to two hours during eight hours of sleep. The dream content is thought to be connected with body changes, eg eye movements become "watching" in the dream. Dreaming is a necessary restorative and assimilative process. People deprived of dream-sleep become irritable and disturbed. Since ancient times, dreams have been a source of prophecy and visionary insight, or seen as soul-wandering or visitation by the gods. Although dreams are sometimes regarded as sinister and amoral, and are thus repressed, modern psychology (especially PSYCHOANALYSIS) aims at bringing people to terms with their dreams, seeing them as creative, educative, the playground of the mind, and an essential part of the whole personality. *See also* MS pp.42–44, *148*, *198*.

Dream of Gerontius, The, oratorio by Edward ELGAR. A setting of the poem by Cardinal Henry NEWMAN, it is scored for three solo voices, mixed chorus and orchestra. It was first performed at the Birmingham Festival in 1900.

Dream of the Rood (*c.* 8th century), Old English poem about the Crucifixion. In it the Cross itself speaks, telling of Christ's agonies in harrowing detail. It occurs as fragmentary runic inscriptions on the 8th century Ruthwell Cross in Dumfriesshire, but the complete version is in the later Vercelli Book.

Drebbel, Cornelius Jacobszoon (1572–1633), Dutch inventor who built the first submarine in 1620. It travelled along the River Thames, London, at a depth of 4–5m (12–15ft). James I is reputed to have ridden in it. Covered with greased leather, the craft was propelled by oars through watertight flaps.

Dredger, ship or floating platform equipped for dredging, either to keep docks, harbours and river channels free from silt or for mining underwater. Dredgers are also used to rake up minerals or molluscs, crustaceans and other edible sea creatures from the sea-bed. *See also* MM pp.98–99.

Dredging, excavation of material from the bed of a river, harbour or other area of water to deepen it or remove a blockage. Dredging is also used in some surface-mining, eg gold and tin, and it is sometimes profitable to flood an area in order to let DREDGERS operate. Huge dredgers are used in lakes for tin-mining in Malaysia. *See also* MM pp.98–99.

Dreikanter, or ventifact, desert pebble with several flattened surfaces giving it a pyramidal shape, due to erosion by wind-blown particles. *See also* PE p.121.

Dreiser, Theodore Herman Albert (1871–1945), US writer, one of the foremost exponents of American naturalism. Many of his works describe man as a victim of biological and social forces. His greatest work is considered to be *An American Tragedy* (1925), about a poor man driven to murder by his dreams of success. *See also* HC2 p.288.

Dresden, city in SE East Germany, on the River Elbe, 161km (100 miles) S of Berlin; capital of Dresden province. Settled by the Germans in the 9th century, it was occupied by Prussia during the Second Silesian War and the SEVEN YEARS WAR. It suffered severe damage from Allied bombing during WWII. Dresden china has been famous since the 18th century, although it is in fact manufactured in Meissen. Industries: optical and precision instruments, food processing, glass, chemicals and clothing. Pop. 506,100.

Dresden, common English misnomer, since the 18th century, for the porcelain ware MEISSEN, named after its place of manufacture, near Dresden in Germany.

Dress, clothing and decorating of the human body, practised since earliest times in most civilizations. The first use of dress is not known, but tools have been found on Neanderthal sites that were probably used for softening leather for use as clothing. The ability to weave was generally one of the earliest skills developed by agricultural, rather than pastoral, societies.

The social and psychological purposes of dress have been much debated. The evidence of cave paintings and that derived from anthropological studies of primitive societies suggest that little distinction can be drawn between dress and other forms of body ornamentation such as painting and jewellery. The commonness of clothes in regions where they are not dictated by the climate suggests that warmth was not their primary purpose, although protection from thorns and from the sun may have been important. The convenience of having pockets and pouches may have been of equai practical importance to that of body-covering. It seems unlikely that dress is connected with any innate sense of modesty, since the parts of the body covered or exposed by dress vary greatly between cultures.

It is hard to study in detail the total history of dress within a culture, since records of clothing styles are rarely complete, but it is an apparently universal phenomenon that dress is a fundamental means of indicating status within a group and of preserving its identity in relation to outsiders. Thus the dress of the leading members of a society has habitually been heavily ornamented. In many cases, such as noble Chinese women whose feet were bound, or 18th-century European women who wore model ships in their hair or huge hooped skirts, dress has been a means of conspicuously indicating that the wearer was a member of the leisured classes. By contrast, the clothes of the less prominent have been practical and often dull in colour (since bright dyes were usually expensive and rare until modern times). Nevertheless, the existence of many peasant traditions of decorated clothes shows that probably the most basic psychological role of dress is to make the wearer attractive in the eyes of his or her peers. The history of Western dress is usually told in terms of the changing fashions of the upper classes, whose clothes have sometimes been preserved or well documented in sculpture and painting. Despite the often extravagant vagaries of fashion, the dress of most of the population did not dramatically change until the Industrial Revolution introduced the first cheap mass-produced cotton clothes.

In ancient times, from the rise of Meospotamia to the fall of Rome, the upper classes wore variations on two basic styles: a square of cloth wrapped around the body, either as a KILT as in Egypt or as a TOGA in Rome, and a tunic, worn either thigh-length or to the ground. Trousers were known in early times in India, Persia and Japan, and among the Scythians, but they were not adopted in the West until the Roman Empire extended to the colder climates of Britain and Germany. Nakedness was not unusual in ancient societies, particularly at sporting and religious festivals.

Trousers, worn under an abbreviated Roman tunic, were adopted in most of the barbarian kingdoms. The noble and warrior class tended to indicate their social superiority in their military dress, such as armour, until the 14th century. Then clothes began to be shaped to the body and the idea of fashion emerged, dominated until the 19th century by the styles adopted in the European courts. In the royal courts there arose a tradition of fantastic and fast-changing fashions that often had no connection with utility or convenience and were generally dominated by topical concepts of masculinity and femininity or current tastes in art or aesthetics. Laws delineating the type of dress that could be worn, and prohibiting extravagance, usually for moral or religious reasons (the sumptuary laws), had been common in medieval times, perhaps indicating that they were hard to enforce. In 17th-century England the Puritans, denouncing worldliness in dress, attempted to revive them.

In the 19th century the typical dress of the middle classes, with grey or black trousers, frockcoat and top hat for men, gradually became accepted by the nobility, and courtly styles were worn only on the most formal, usually evening, occasions. Working-class clothes, which had not substantially changed since the Middle Ages, also came to be based on middle class models. The technological achievements of the 19th and 20th centuries, such as the development of synthetic materials, have made possible the availability of "fashion" to the population as a whole. But much fashion is still dictated by designers catering for the most wealthy, and there is little indication that they are any less powerful than before. *See also* MS pp.192–193.

Dressage, complex manoeuvres executed by a horse in response to the subtle movements of the rider's hands, legs and weight. It has been adopted by the equestrian world generally as a test of horsemanship and of a horse's development and state of training. Dressage was first included in the Olympic Games in 1912.

Drew, Charles Richard (1904–50), US physician. His research at the Columbia Medical Center in 1940 led to the discovery that blood plasma could replace whole blood transfusions. During WWII he supervised the American Red Cross blood-donor project but was not allowed to donate blood himself because he was black; his continuing protest led to a change in policy.

Drew, George Alexander (1894–1973), Canadian politician. He was a lawyer, field-commander in WWI and a jurist. He served as prime minister of Ontario (1943–48) and later led the Progressive Conservative Party in the Canadian House of Commons (1949–56). He was Canadian High Commissioner in Britain (1957–64).

Dreyfus Affair (1894), French scandal in which Alfred Dreyfus, an army officer and a Jew, was charged with treason. Convicted under forged evidence of sending military information to the Germans, Dreyfus was deported for life. Evidence incriminating a Major Esterhazy was suppressed, but under pressure from Dreyfus' supporters, Major Hubert Henri, an accomplice, confessed to the forgeries and committed suicide. After a second trial Dreyfus was pardoned in 1899, but it was not until 1906 that he was fully cleared. *See also* HC2 p.181, *181*.

Dreyse, Johann Nikolaus von (1787–1867), German gunsmith. He invented a breech-loading needlegun in 1836, which was used in the Prussian army after 1848. *See also* MM p.163.

Drier, or drying machine, in industrial processes, device to remove liquids, usually water, from wet solids, using direct, indirect or radiant heat. Direct driers use hot gases flowing over the solid. Indirect drying is done by passage of heat to the wet solid through a wall, as in passing material through internally heated rollers. In radiant-heat driers the liquid evaporates upon absorption of infra-red rays.

Driers, substances added to DRYING OILS to accelerate the rate at which they harden. They are used in paints, varnishes, etc. Commonly used compounds include the naphthenate or oleate salts of lead, cobalt or manganese.

Drift, in aeronautics, change in an aircraft's flight path over the ground caused by a crosswind. To correct for this drift, the pilot "crabs" or takes a heading some-

what upwind of his required course to offset the movement due to the wind.
Drift, in geology, gradual change in the land mass, related to soil CREEP. In oceanography it indicates slow oceanic circulation. Sedimentary drift is a general description of surface debris, which is carried by either a river or glacier. It may also indicate an accumulation such as a snowdrift or sand drift. CONTINENTAL DRIFT is the movement of continents.
Drill, large, gregarious, ground-foraging MONKEY found in the rain forests of Central w Africa. It has a black face, dog-like muzzle and large teeth. Smaller and less brightly coloured than the MANDRILL, it is nevertheless powerful and aggressive. Length: 82cm (32in). Family Cercopithecidae. *See also* BABOON.
Drilling fluid, in drilling oil wells, mud pumped down to cool the drill and which carries the loose debris to the surface. Drilling mud is pre-mixed to ensure the correct viscosity. *See also* MM p.78.
Drilling rig, platform carrying a derrick and all the associated equipment used for drilling for oil or natural gas below the sea floor. Most rigs have long legs (usually three or four) located on the sea-bed, with a working platform up to 30m (98ft) above the water. They are sited up to 200km (125 miles) offshore, often connected to the mainland by underwater pipelines. *See also* MM pp.78–79, *78–79*; PE pp.138–139.
Drilling ship, vessel equipped with modified oil-drilling rigs, designed to take core samples of ocean-bed sediments, and used for both scientific research and commercial exploration. *See also* PE pp.*25, 91.*
Drinkwater, John (1882–1937), British poet and dramatist. He wrote several successful historical dramas such as *Mary Stuart* (1921), and was a founder of the Birmingham Repertory Company.
Drip-feeding, introduction of liquid nourishment directly into the veins of a patient who is unable to eat or drink due to unconsciousness, weakness or illness. Glucose sugar solution is commonly drip-fed; it is contained in an inverted bottle, and passes under gravity through a tube which terminates in a vein – usually in the forearm.
Driscoll, Jim (1880–1925), Welsh featherweight boxer. An exponent of the classic British style based on an upright stance and a straight left, he won British and European titles but a "no decision" verdict prevented him from winning the world championship from Abe Attell in 1909.
Driver ant. *See* ARMY ANT.
Droeshout, Martin (1601–1650), English portrait engraver of Dutch parentage. His engraving of William Shakespeare, which appeared in the first folio of his plays (1623), is one of two authenticated portraits of the poet.
Drogheda (Droichead Atha), town in NE Republic of Ireland, in s County Louth. It was a Danish town in the 10th century. In 1395 the Irish princes of Leinster and Ulster surrendered there to RICHARD II. Oliver CROMWELL stormed Drogheda in 1649 and most of the inhabitants were killed. The Battle of the BOYNE was fought there in 1690 and the town surrendered to William III. Industries: textiles, brewing, engineering, chemicals, fertilizers. Pop. (1971) 19,744.
Dromedary, large domesticated CAMEL, a pack and riding animal valued also for its hide, wool, milk and meat. It has a long neck and legs, wide feet suited to walking on sand and snow, and a single fatty hump on its back. Height: to 2m (7ft) at the shoulder. *See also* NW pp.220, *221.*
Drone, male BEE or ANT, a member of a social order of insects. Its function is to mate with the queen and it plays no part in the everyday activities of the hive or nest. For this reason, anyone who lives by the work of others can also be referred to as a drone. *See also* NW p.*113.*
Drone aircraft, pilotless aircraft, remotely controlled by radio signals from the ground or from another aircraft. Drones may be used to tow targets for gunnery practice or in aerodynamic research. They can also carry explosives and be used, for example, in anti-submarine warfare.
Dronefly, two-winged fly of the HOVERFLY family Syrphidae. It is black and yellow, resembling a stinging BEE, and this mimicry provides effective protection from predators. Species *Eristalis tenax.*
Drongo, noisy, pugnacious, insect-eating bird of South Africa, SE Asia and Australia. It has a thick, hooked bill, bristled nostrils, a long forked tail, iridescent blackish plumage and, in some species, ornamental feathers and crests. Length: 18–38cm (7–15in). Family Dicruridae.
Drop hammer, tool employed in drop forging. The falling weight (often powered with steam or air pressure) of the hammer and the upper die forces heated, soft metal into a lower die, forging it to the desired shape.
Dropsy, old name for OEDEMA.
Drosophila, genus of about 1,000 species of small flies, commonly known as fruit-flies. They are short-lived and their cells contain only four pairs of chromosomes. They are much used in breeding experiments by geneticists because they reproduce rapidly and their lines of heredity can easily be traced after chromosome damage or mutation. Order Diptera. *See also* NW p.*31.*
Drought, condition that occurs when EVAPORATION and TRANSPIRATION exceed PRECIPITATION for long periods. Four kinds are recognized: permanent, typical of arid and semi-arid regions; seasonal, in climates with well-defined dry and rainy seasons; unpredictable, an abnormal failure of expected rainfall; and invisible, when even frequent showers do not restore sufficient moisture.
Drowned coast, or submerged shoreline, once a term indicating a complicated landform that had been above sea-level and therefore exposed to wind and water erosion but was subsequently submerged. More recent theory suggests that all continental shorelines are submerged or drowned coasts or estuaries.
Drowning, death caused by suffocation in water or other liquid. It can occur in only a few inches of water, and most drownings among non-swimmers happen in shallow water, often quite close to shore and safety. The suffocation is caused both by water preventing air from being taken in and by water being drawn into the lungs. After loss of consciousness, a drowning person's heart may continue to beat for several minutes. For this reason, artificial respiration should be attempted immediately after rescue. For first aid treatment, *see* MS p.*132.*
Drug, in medicine, a chemical substance used to cure, prevent or alleviate a disease or deficiency (or their symptoms), either physical or mental. Drugs can be taken orally, injected, inhaled or applied to the skin. Today most drugs are synthesized in the pharmaceutical industry, although some are still obtained from plants, animals or minerals. There are now an enormous number that act in many different ways. Almost all (except eye drops and local anaesthetics applied to the skin) enter the blood stream and circulate to the site of drug action. As a result various reactions may accompany the main action. These side-effects vary in severity but can be serious, eg the pain-killer MORPHINE causes vomiting, constipation and other undesired results. Dosages must be carefully controlled since some drugs are toxic, and all are poisonous if administered in large quantities. Also some people have an ALLERGY to particular drugs. Drugs are now given extensive clinical trials and are tested on animals before passing into use.
Essentially, drugs act by altering the speed of cell activities. CHEMOTHERAPEUTIC drugs kill or inhibit the growth of pathogenic organisms such as bacteria, viruses and fungi. They include ANTIBIOTICS, and Quinacrine and various synthetics which act against malaria and other parasitic infections. Other drugs affect various systems in the body. For example, stimulants such as AMPHETAMINES and depressants such as ANALGESICS, NARCOTICS, BARBITURATES and ANAESTHETICS act on various parts of the nervous system; DIURETICS increase the flow of urine; anticoagulants inhibit blood clotting, probably by preventing the formation of FIBRIN or PROTHROMBIN or by decreasing the availability of THROMBIN; muscle relaxants and stimulants; hormones such as INSULIN and THYROXINE; CORTISONE; immunological agents used in disease prevention such as vaccines. Sedatives, HYPNOTIC DRUGS, anti-depressants and HALLUCINOGENS are used for treating emotional and mental disorders. These control the symptoms rather than cure the illness but can be effective when combined with other forms of treatment.
Drugs are also used to alter states of the healthy body and mind. Many natural drugs have been used like this for centuries, eg MARIJUANA, OPIUM, morphine, CAFFEINE and COCA. But whether they are condoned and what constitutes abuse varies from culture to culture. Continued taking of some of them, and also of some synthetic drugs, can lead to physical and psychological dependence and hence DRUG ADDICTION. *See also* MS pp.88, *91,* 104–105, 112–121, 138, 144–145, 194.
Drug addiction, the chronic (continual) use of and physical dependence on a drug that is initially taken for its pleasurable effect on mind and body. If the drug dose is decreased or stopped the addict experiences withdrawal symptoms, vomiting, muscle cramps, convulsions and delirium. Addicts also develop a TOLERANCE to the drug so that increasing doses are required to achieve the same effect. Physically addictive drugs include narcotics, eg HEROIN and MORPHINE, and depressants, eg alcohol and BARBITURATES. Other drugs can induce psychological dependence. *See also* MS pp.104–105.
Druids, pre-Christian Celtic priests in ancient Britain, Ireland and Gaul, who also served as judges, magicians, diviners, healers and teachers. Their religion, which was strongly ritualistic, was polytheistic and included belief in the immortality of the soul. The earliest Druistic records date from the 3rd century BC, but the Druids probably existed far earlier. They enjoyed a high social position and held considerable political power, but were suppressed in Roman territories. *See also* HC1 p.140.
Drum, percussion instrument, generally a hollow cylinder or vessel with a skin stretched across the openings and struck with hands or beaters. They were among the earliest musical instruments; examples have been found dating from 6,000 BC. Drums have a crucial role in African music, in which large groups of drummers achieve complex rhythmic effects. Drums often also have an important social role, as in the "talking drums" used to send messages. In India a pair of tunable drums is one of the basic instruments of the classical tradition of music. Drums first appeared in European Classical music as Turkish band instruments around 1750. During the 19th century by far the most important drums were TIMPANI (kettle-drums), although military drums such as the snare drum and bass drum were sometimes used for effects. In the 20th century the role of drums in Western music has greatly expanded.
Drumfish, or croaker, bottom-dwelling tropical and temperate marine fish. It uses its air bladder and attached muscles to make drumming sounds. The marine black drum (*Pogonias cromis*) generally grows to 1.2m (4ft) and weighs up to 65.7kg (29lb). Family Sciaenidae.
Drumlin, hill created by a GLACIER out of either debris or bedrock. Drumlins usually occur in groups. The head end points towards the retreating glacier and is steeper and higher than the tapering tail. They are ellipsoidal in shape and the long axis is parallel to the movement of the parent glacier. *See also* DEPOSITION; PE p.*116.*
Drummond, William of Hawthornden (1585–1649), Scottish writer, chiefly remembered for his verbatim notes of Ben Jonson's visit to Scotland in 1618 and for his personal tragedy – his fiancée died on the eve of their wedding.
Drummond, William Henry (1854–1907), Irish-Canadian poet. He began his career as a physician practising in the Canadian backwoods, and his poems

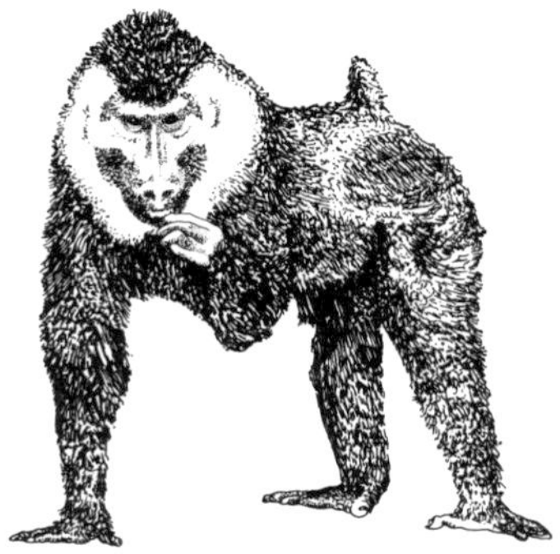

Drills are powerful aggressive monkeys living in the rain forests of central west Africa.

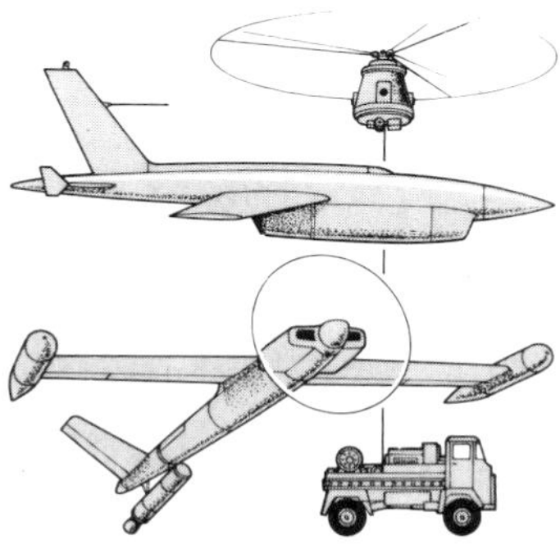

Drone aircraft are remotely controlled and so are useful for towing gunnery targets.

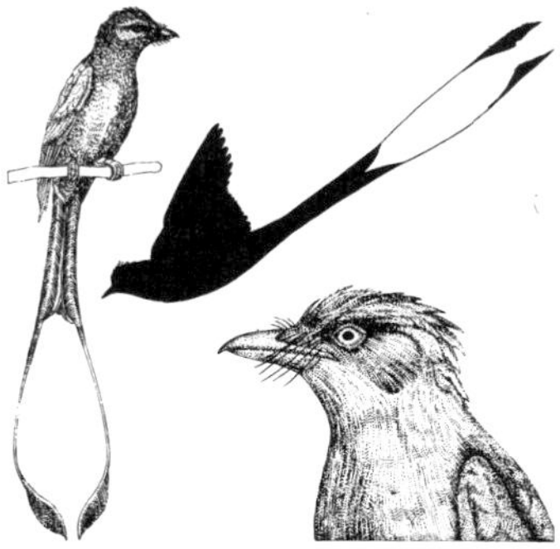

Drongo; these glossy fork-tailed birds are sometimes known as king crows or shrikes.

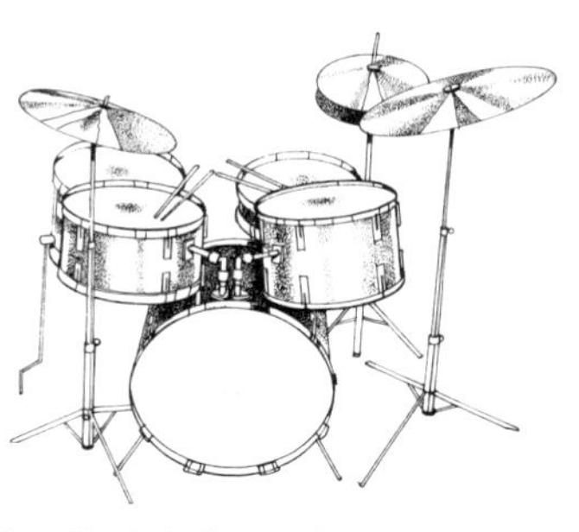

Drum kits, including the skins or "heads", are now often made out of transparent plastics.

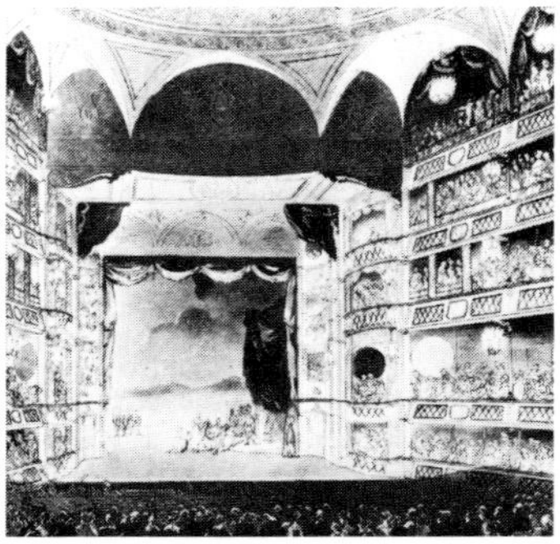

Drury Lane Theatre, London's oldest existing theatre, was built originally in 1663.

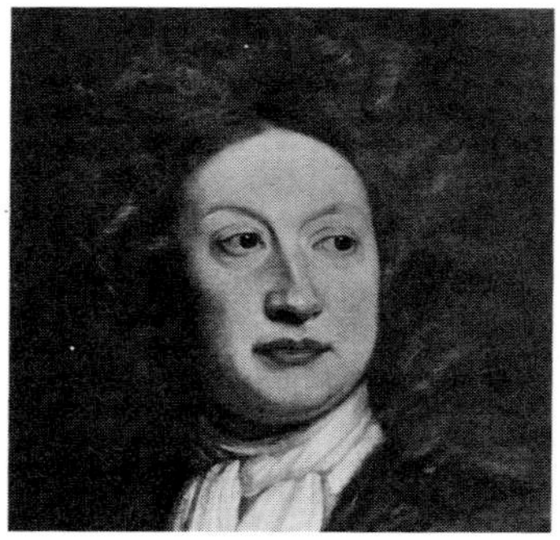

John Dryden wrote biting satires in support of the newly restored King Charles II.

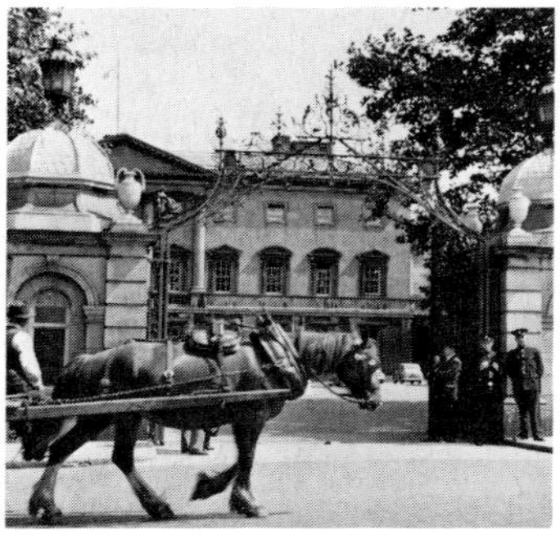

Dublin; the Dáil buildings, the lower house of parliament of the Irish Republic.

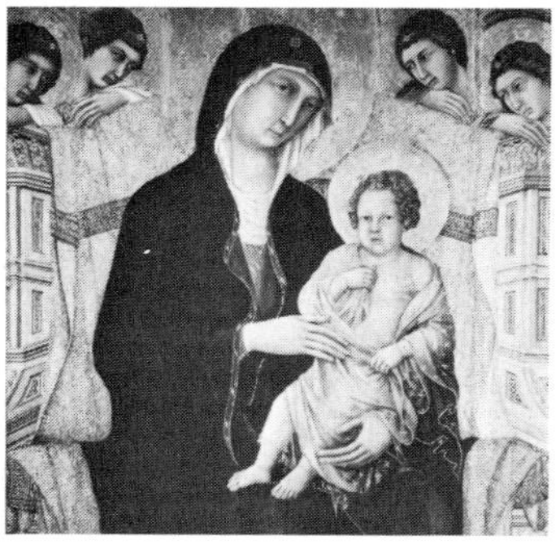

Duccio; his religious works show a loosening and softening of the rigid Byzantine style.

mirror the outlook of rural French Canadians. His works include *The Habitant* (1897), *Johnny Courteau* (1901) and *The Voyageur* (1905).

Drupe, or stone fruit, any fruit with a thin skin, fleshy pulp and hard stone or pip enclosing a single seed. Examples are plums, cherries, peaches, olives, almonds and coconuts. *See also* PE p.*192*.

Drury Lane Theatre, London's oldest existing theatre. It was built in 1663 as the Theatre Royal and rebuilt in 1674 by Christopher Wren after being burnt down in 1672. The present theatre, re-styled in 1812 to the design of Benjamin Wyatt, has housed most forms of entertainment from opera to the circus.

Druses, or Druzes, Middle Eastern religious sect. An offspring of the ISMA'ILI Muslims, it includes elements of belief from other religions. The Druses originated in the reign of al-Hakim (996–1021), the sixth Fatimid CALIPH of Egypt. Al-Hakim claimed to be divine, and a cult grew up about him of which the Druses are a continuation. They are named after al-Darazi, the first to proclaim the cult publicly. Stressing pure monotheism, they maintained that al-Hakim would live in hiding until his re-appearance for the Last Judgment. They also emphasized, however, the possibilities of direct communication with divinity as a living presence. They were persecuted in Egypt and fought many wars against both Turks and local Christians, and revolted against French rule in Syria in the 1920s. Their number in the mid-1970s was estimated at about 320,000.

Dryads, in Greek mythology, nymphs of the woodlands and guardian spirits of trees. Depicted crowned with leaves and sometimes carrying axes; they are particularly protective of oaks.

Dry cell, electric battery, a type of small LECLANCHÉ CELL containing no free fluid. In the commonest type the electrolyte is ammonium chloride paste, the positive electrode a central carbon rod and the negative electrode the zinc casing. Dry cells are widely used in torches and portable radios. *See also* SU pp.*115, 148*.

Dry cleaning, method of cleaning fabrics using special solvent fluids and soaps without water. It was discovered by accident in 1849 by a French tailor, Jolly-Belin, when he noticed the cleaning effect of some spilt turpentine. Introduced into Britain in 1866, it now uses non-inflammable solvents in special machines (washing by hand was originally used). Clothes are washed with solvent and dried in a warm-air tumbler. Special solvents are used for some stains. *See also* SU p.*144*.

Dryden, John (1631–1700), English poet and playwright. He became known with his *Heroic Stanzas* on Oliver Cromwell's death in 1658; this was followed in 1660 by *Astraea Redux*, praising Charles II. He was poet laureate (1668–88) and wrote numerous fine plays, poems and essays. His poems include *Annus Mirabilis* (1667), *Absalom and Achitophel* (1681), *Mac Flecknoe* (1682), *The Hind and the Panther* (1687), and *Alexander's Feast* (1697). His best-known plays include *All for Love* (1677) and *Marriage à la mode* (1673).

Dry-dock. *See* DOCK.

Dry farming, growing crops without irrigation where the rainfall is below 50cm (20in) a year. Water loss and soil erosion are minimized, eg every other year the land is not used for crops, in order to conserve moisture. Crop density is adjusted to suit the amount of water available and drought-resistant varieties of plants are used. *See also* PE p.*168*.

Drygalski, Erich Dagobert von (1865–1949), German geophysicist. In 1892 he led a voyage to Greenland and headed the German Antarctic expedition (1901–03), reaching the area that he named Kaiser Wilhelm II Land.

Drygalski Island, small island off the Queen Mary Coast of Antarctica. It was named after the German explorer Erich von DRYGALSKI who first observed the island from a balloon in 1902.

Drying oil, natural oil, such as linseed oil or cottonseed oil, that slowly hardens in air to form a tough film. Drying oils are extensively used in paints, varnies, lacquers, printing inks and putty. They are unsaturated compounds that harden by oxidation or polymerization, a process accelerated by adding DRIERS.

Dryopithecus, extinct group of apelike animals, the ancestor of modern APES and of man. The Dryopithecines lived about 30 million years ago, mostly in tree-houses, and remains have been found in Europe, Africa and Asia. *See also* MS pp.20–21, *21*.

Drypoint, engraving technique characterized by a furry line produced by the burr or ridge thrown up along the edge of the incision made on the copper plate. REMBRANDT was the greatest master of this medium. *See also* ENGRAVING; PRINTMAKING.

Dry rot, FUNGUS "disease" that attacks timber, reducing it to a dry, crumbly mass. Despite its name it thrives in damp, unventilated places. It spreads rapidly, carrying its own supply of moisture, and can be prevented by treating timber with fungicides.

Drysdale, George Russell (1912–), English-born painter who emigrated in childhood to Australia. He was among the first painters to depict the Australian landscape and its inhabitants in new, semi-abstract terms.

DSDP (Deep-sea drilling project), US scientific programme sponsored by the National Science Foundation to obtain a core from the mantle of the Earth by drilling through the crust. (The moho, or base of the crust, is thinnest under deep oceans.) The core was expected to carry a continuous fossil and sediment record of the Earth's history. The project was suspended in 1966 but drilling was resumed in 1968. *See also* PE pp.*25*, 91.

DSL. *See* DEEP SCATTERING LAYER.

DSRT, abbreviation of "deep-sea reversing thermometer", used for determining the temperature at depth. See also PE p.*91*.

DTs (delirium tremens), serious condition occurring most often when alcohol is abruptly withdrawn from an alcoholic, occasionally as a reaction to barbiturates or other drugs. It produces tremor, loss of appetite, terrifying dreams, various mental and nervous-system disturbances and, if severe, delirium. It is thought up to 20% of sufferers die. *See also* MS p.104.

Dualism, doctrine in philosophy and metaphysics that recognizes two basic and mutually independent principles – such as mind and matter, body and soul, or good and evil. Characterized by precise definition of concepts, dualism contrasts with MONISM, in which reality has a single ultimate nature. Both PLATO and DESCARTES were dualists, but more modern philosophers, influenced by the discoveries of science, have tended towards monism.

Dual Monarchy. *See* AUSTRO-HUNGARIAN EMPIRE.

Duan, Le. *See* LE DUAN.

Dubai (Dubayy), one of seven states forming the federation of United Arab Emirates, in E Arabia, on the Persian Gulf. A dependency of Abu Dhabi until 1833, it became a British protectorate in the 19th century. Oil was discovered in the early 1960s and its production is now the chief economic activity. The capital is Dubai. Area: approx. 3,885sq km (1,500sq miles). Pop. (1968) 59,092.

Du Barry, Marie Jeanne Bécu, Comtesse (1743–93), French adventuress. She was mistress of, among others, Jean du Barry, who facilitated her rise under the false title of Comtesse du Barry, eventually engineering, through a marriage to his brother, her acceptance as last mistress of Louis XV of France. A great patron of the arts and normally politically inactive, she was executed by the Revolutionary tribunal for associations with the British and her aid to the émigrés.

Dubawnt Lake, lake in North-West Territories, N central Canada. Located N of the tree line, it is icebound for most of the summer. One of Canada's largest lakes, it covers 2,576sq km (1,600sq miles). The Dubawnt River flows through the lake, then E to Baker Lake at the head of Chesterfield Inlet on Hudson Bay. Length: 934km (580 miles).

Dubček, Alexander (1921–), Czechoslovak Communist Party secretary, leader of liberal reform movement during the late 1960s. He earned enthusiastic national support with his commitment to "the widest possible democratization". The USSR, however, viewed the reform programme as a threat to their economic domination of the country, and on 20–21 Aug. 1968 Warsaw Pact forces occupied Czechoslovakia. A purge of party leaders followed and Dubček was removed from office. *See also* HC2 p.242.

Dublin, county in E Republic of Ireland, in Leinster province, on the Irish Sea. Low-lying in the N, the land gradually rises to the Wicklow Mts in the S and is drained chiefly by the River Liffey. Beef and dairy cattle are raised and wheat, barley and potatoes are grown. The county town is Dublin, the capital of the Republic. Area: 922sq km (356sq miles). Pop. (1971 prelim.) 849,500.

Dublin (Baile Átha Cliath), capital of the Republic of Ireland, at the mouth of the River Liffey on Dublin Bay. It was a Danish town until 1014 when Brian BORU defeated the Danes. They regained control, however, until 1170 when Richard Strongbow took Dublin for the English, and the city became the seat of English government in Ireland. In the 19th century Dublin suffered much bloodshed in nationalist attempts to free Ireland from English rule. Strikes beginning in 1913 finally resulted in the EASTER RISING of 1916. The city has the Christ Church Cathedral (1053), St Patrick's Cathedral (1190), Trinity College (1591), University College (1908) and the ABBEY THEATRE (1904), and was the birthplace of George Bernard SHAW, James JOYCE and Oscar WILDE. Industries: brewing, textiles, clothing, footwear, fertilizers. Pop. (1971) 567,900. *See also* HC1 p.180; HC2 pp.25–27, 283; MW p.102.

Dublin Bay prawn, also called Norway LOBSTER, commercially valuable lobster. It is often sold as "scampi". Order: Decapoda; species *Nephrops norvegicus*. *See also* NW p.*101*; PE p.*248*.

Dubliners (1914), volume of short stories by James JOYCE set in Dublin and presenting a "moral history" of Ireland. With precision and irony, the author evokes what he saw as the spiritual paralysis afflicting Dublin society. *See also* HC2 pp.282, 290.

Dubois, Marie Eugène François Thomas (1858–1940), Dutch anatomist and geneticist. He discovered the remains of JAVA MAN in 1890 while excavating caves on the islands of Sumatra and Java. He published his findings and returned to Europe, where he became professor of geology at the University of Amsterdam in 1895. *See also* MS p.*24*.

Dubuffet, Jean (1901–), French painter and sculptor. Among his best-known works are assemblages of glass, sand, rope and other junk arranged into crude shapes, which he called *pâtes*. He also collected the work of psychotics and others who were untrained (*art brut*, or raw art).

Duccio di Buoninsegna (*c.*1265–1315), Italian painter, the first great painter of the SIENESE SCHOOL. He infused the rigid Byzantine style of figure painting with a new humanity and lyricism seen in that era only in GIOTTO's work, and with a superlative colour sense, feeling for composition and dramatic rendering of religious subjects. His major surviving works are the *Rucellai Madonna* (1285; Uffizi, Florence) and the Maestà altarpiece (1308–11; cathedral museum, Siena).

Duce, name taken by MUSSOLINI as leader (in Latin *dux*) of the Italian nation. Its Latin origin was intended to make the title evocative of the past glories of Imperial Rome.

Duchamp, Marcel (1887–1968), French painter who caused a sensation in New York at the ARMORY SHOW (1913) with his *Nude Descending a Staircase*. He later helped found the DADA movement in New York; invented "ready-made" art, which treats commonplace objects as works of art; and he constructed many non-functional machines. Most of his works are in Philadelphia, including his celebrated *The Bride stripped bare by her bachelors, even* (1915–23). *See also* HC2 pp.202–203, *202*.

Ducharme, Réjean (1942–), Canadian novelist. His novels, which combine reality and fantasy, include *The Swallower Swallowed* (1966), *L'océantume* (1968) and *La fille de Christophe Colombe* (1969).

Duchess of Malfi, The, revenge tragedy by JOHN WEBSTER, first performed in 1613. Its powerful poetry evokes a uniquely macabre view of Renaissance corruption and violence. It has been performed often since its revival in the Romantic era.

Duck, worldwide waterfowl valued as game and domesticated for its eggs and meat, which is high in nutritional value. Most ducks nest in cool areas and migrate to warm areas in winter. All have large bills, short legs, and webbed feet. Their colour is varied, and their dense plumage is underlaid by down and waterproof feathers. Dabbling ducks feed from the water surface; others dive for food. All strain seeds, aquatic insects, crustaceans and molluscs from the water with their flat bills. Most engage in complex courtship, lay a large clutch of eggs and are flightless during a post-breeding moult. There are seven tribes: eiders, shelducks, dabbling ducks, perching ducks, pochards, sea ducks and stiff-tailed ducks. Length: 30–60cm (1–2ft); weight: to 7.2kg (16lb). Family Anatidae. *See also* NW p.*148*, 227.

Duckbill. *See* PLATYPUS.

Duckweed, family (Lemnaceae) of four genera including 25 species of tiny, aquatic, monocotyledonous flowering plants. The flowers are almost invisible; small flat discs replace the leaves. The watermeal (*Wolffia arrhiza*) is the smallest of all flowering plants.

Ducommun, Élie (1833–1906), Swiss journalist who advocated PACIFISM. In 1891 he founded the International Peace Bureau at Berne, and with his fellow countryman Charles GOBAT shared the 1902 Nobel Peace Prize.

Ductless glands. *See* ENDOCRINE SYSTEM.

Dudek, Louis (1918–), Canadian poet and publisher. In addition to writing his own poetry he founded the Contact Press (1952–67) and Delta Canada (1964–72), both of which published the work of young Canadian poets.

Dudintsev, Vladimir Dmitriyevich (1918–), Soviet novelist. His works include the collected stories *With Seven Brothers* (1952) and the novels *Not by Bread Alone* (1956) and *Poplar on the Other Bank* (1967).

Dudley, Sir Edmund (*c.*1462–1510), English lawyer. Speaker of the House of Commons in 1504, he was a ruthless collector of taxes for HENRY VII. He was executed for treason by HENRY VIII.

Dudley, John, Duke of Northumberland. *See* NORTHUMBERLAND, JOHN DUDLEY, DUKE OF.

Dudley, Robert, Earl of Leicester. *See* LEICESTER, ROBERT DUDLEY, EARL OF.

Dudley, town and metropolitan district of the W central Midlands, England, 16km (10 miles) W of Birmingham on a ridge overlooking the Black Country. It is dominated by a castle. Today Dudley is a major coal-mining centre. Pop. (1971) 185,535.

Duesenberg, US car. In 1930 when it was introduced, it was one of America's most expensive cars. It had a "straight-eight" 6.9 litre engine which gave it a top speed of more than 175km/h (110mph). *See also* MM p.*128*.

Dufay, Guillaume (*c.*1400–74), Burgundian composer, the leading member of the Netherlands school which then dominated Church music. The bulk of his compositions are MOTETS and settings of the liturgy.

Duff, Alexander (1806–78), Scottish missionary to India who wanted to end Hinduism and persuade the people to accept the traditions and philosophy of the West. *See also* HC2 p.*139*.

Duff, Roger Shepherd (1912–), New Zealand antropologist. His excavations led him to believe that the "moa hunter period" was an early phase of MAORI (ie Polynesian) culture, rather than representing a pre-Polynesian one, as had previously been thought.

Duffy, Sir Charles Gavan (1816–1903), Irish-Australian statesman and writer. He helped found and edit the *Nation* (1842) and was tried for his political activities. He was acquited and emigrated to Australia, where he entered politics, becoming Prime Minister of Victoria (1871–72). He wrote *Ballad Poetry of Ireland* (1845), *Young Ireland – 1840–50* (1880–83) and *Conversations with Thomas Carlyle* (1892).

Duffy blood groups, method of "typing" blood based on three genes, Fy^a, Fy^b and Fy. Fy^a and Fy^b are non-dominant alleles and Fy is recessive. Gene Fy is most frequent in Negroes (about 85%); only 3% of Europeans have it.

Dufour, Guillaume-Henri (1787–1875), Swiss general and cartographer. As commander of the Swiss army he suppressed the 1847 SONDERBUND insurrection. He was one of the founders of the RED CROSS.

Dufy, Raoul (1877–1953), French painter. An IMPRESSIONIST, Dufy converted to the style of FAUVISM early in his career (*c.*1905), under the influence of Henri MATISSE. His style changed again (*c.*1909) while he was with Georges BRAQUE at L'Estaque. He developed a bright, decorative, calligraphic style well suited to his subjects, such as racing and boating scenes.

Duggan, Maurice (1922–), New Zealand writer. His short stories, noted for their experimental style, appeared in a collection, *Immanuel's Land* (1956).

Dugong, or sea cow, large plant-eating aquatic mammal found in shallow coastal waters of Africa, Asia and Australia. Grey and hairless, the dugong has no hind legs, and its forelegs have been modified into weak flippers. Length: 2.5–4m (8–13ft); weight: 270kg (600lb). Family Dugongidae. *See also* NW p.*155*.

Dugout canoe, type of boat formed from hollowed-out trees, found all over the world in primitive maritime and riverine communities. The hull is hollowed by burning, chiselling or scraping and is streamlined on the exterior. An OUTRIGGER is sometimes added for stability.

Duhamel, Georges (1884–1966), French playwright and novelist. He was a member of the Abbaye group, and his works reflect a deep humanism. *Civilisation: 1914–17* (1918) won the Prix Goncourt in 1918.

Duiker, or duikerbok, small sub-Saharan African ANTELOPE usually found in scrubland. The female is larger than the male and occasionally carries stunted horns; the horns of the male are short and spiky. Duikers are grey to reddish yellow. Height: up to 66cm (26in) at the shoulder; weight: up to 17kg (37lb). Family Bovidae; species *Sylvicapra grimmia. See also* NW p.*212*.

Duikerbok. *See* DUIKER.

Duisburg, city in W West Germany, at the confluence of the Rhine (Rhein) and Ruhr rivers. During WWII it was the centre of the German armaments industry, and suffered extensive damage. Today it is Europe's largest inland port and one of Germany's leading iron and steel producers. Other industries: textiles, chemicals, metal products. Pop. (1969 est.) 460,517.

Dukas, Paul (1865–1935), French composer of orchestral music and the opera *Ariane et Barbe-Bleue* (1907). His best-known work is the orchestral piece *The Sorcerer's Apprentice* (1897).

Duke, European aristocratic title, ranking just below a prince. In the Middle Ages he was a leader in battle and the ruler of a county or small estate. The first English duke was Edward, the Black Prince, made Duke of Cornwall in 1337.

Duke, Geoff (1923–), British motor-cyclist who dominated grand prix circuits in the 1950s, first with Norton and later Gilera. Four times 500cc world champion (1951, 1953, 1954, 1955) and twice 350cc (1951, 1952) he brought a new approach to riding with his crouching style and one-piece leather clothing.

Duke, Benjamin Newton and James Buchanan (1855–1929, 1856–1925), US industrialists, founders of the American Tobacco Company (1890). They contributed heavily to Trinity College, Durham, in North Carolina, renamed Duke University after them.

Duke of Edinburgh. *See* PHILIP, PRINCE.

Dulac, Edmund (1882–1953), French-born English illustrator, designer and painter. He is famous for his rich, fantasy-ridden watercolour illustrations for *The Arabian Nights* (1907), *Omar Khayyam* (1909), *Treasure Island* (1927) and many books of fairy tales.

Dulbecco Renato (1914–), US virologist. He shared the 1975 Nobel Prize in physiology and medicine with David BALTIMORE and Howard TEMIN for his contributions to an understanding of the interaction between tumour viruses and the genetic material of the cell.

Dulcimer, medieval stringed instrument originally Persian, with a flat, triangular sounding board and ten or more strings struck with hand-held hammers. It was the prototype of the pantaleon and cimbalon.

Dulles, John Foster (1888–1959), US Republican political leader. Before WWII he held various diplomatic posts. He helped to form the UN at the San Francisco Conference in 1945 and was US delegate there (1946, 1947, 1950). He was Secretary of State (1953–59) and a major influence on US policy during the COLD WAR. *See also* HC2 p.*255*.

Dulong, Pierre Louis (1785–1838), French chemist and physicist. He discovered the explosive nitrogen trichloride, and in 1819 he helped formulate DULONG AND PETIT'S LAW of specific heats which aided in the determination of atomic weights.

Dulong and Petit's law, physical rule stating that the product of SPECIFIC HEAT and ATOMIC WEIGHT is constant (about 6.2) for the heavier solid elements. The specific heat of an element was one of the easier values to measure during the early days of chemistry, and an approximation of the atomic weight could be made by dividing the specific heat by 6.2.

Dulse, any of a group of large red seaweeds (genus *Rhodymenia*), especially *R. palmata*, that are used as food condiments. Dulses grow chiefly in cold northern seas. *See also* RED ALGAE.

Duluth, Daniel Greysolon, Sieur (1636–1710), French-born Canadian explorer. He explored Lake Superior in 1678, founded Fort St Joseph in 1686, and was commandant of Fort Frontenac (1695–96). The city of Duluth, founded as a fort in 1679, is named after him.

Duma, Russian representative council or parliament, established in 1906 in response to the political agitation of the previous year. The Duma met four times, in 1906, 1907, 1907–12, 1912–17, but the tsar refused it any real power. It was abolished after the revolution of Oct. 1917. *See also* HC2 p.169.

Dumas, Alexandre (père) (1802–70), French novelist and dramatist. Largely self-educated, his success began with his numerous romantic historical plays, such as *La Tour de Nesle* (1832). He won a large following with swashbuckling historical novels such as *The Three Musketeers* (1844), *The Count of Monte Cristo* (1844) and *The Black Tulip* (1850). *See also* HC2 pp.98, 101.

Dumas, Alexandre (fils) (1824–95), French dramatist and novelist. The illegitimate son of Alexandre DUMAS (père), his first great success was *La Dame aux Camélias* (1852), a realistic view of the *demi-monde* milieu of Paris. His didactic later plays, such as *Les idées de Madame Aubray* (1867), helped to provoke changes in French social laws. *See also* HC2 pp.98, 101.

Du Maurier, Dame Daphne (1907–), British novelist, granddaughter of George DU MAURIER. She also wrote plays, short stories, and a biography of Branwell Brontë. Her popular novels include *The Loving Spirit* (1931), *Jamaica Inn* (1936), *The Glass Blowers* (1936), *Rebecca* (1938) and *Frenchman's Creek* (1941).

Du Maurier, George Louis Palmella Busson (1834–96), British novelist, poet and artist. His major novels, based on his childhood in France, are *Peter Ibbetson* (1891) and *Trilby* (1894). His illustra-

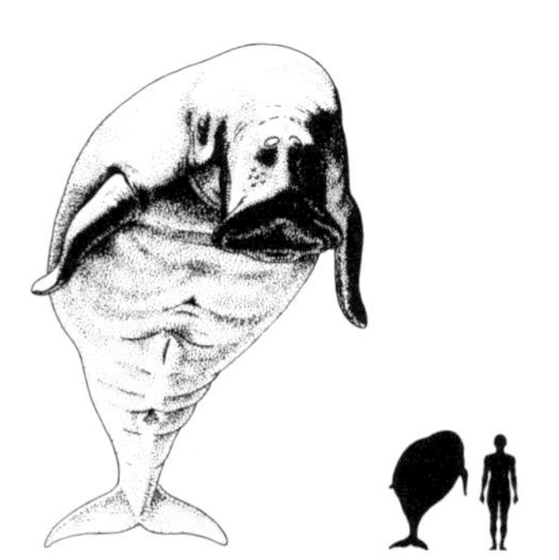

Dugongs "breast-feed" their calves and may have inspired the mermaid myth.

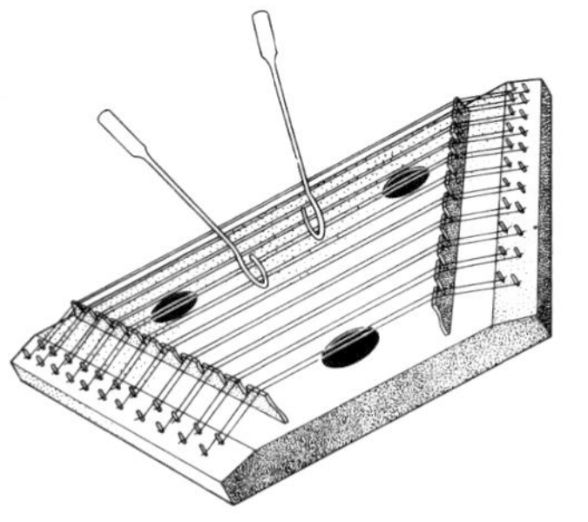

Dulcimer, an instrument which developed, via the clavichord, ultimately into the piano.

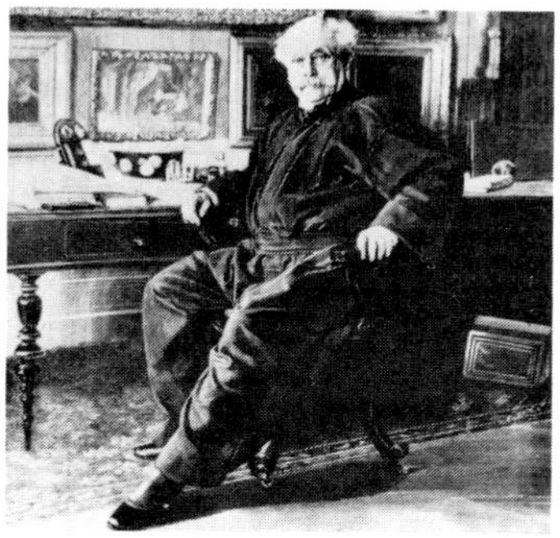

Alexandre Dumas (fils); his illegitimacy explains the didactic tone in his work.

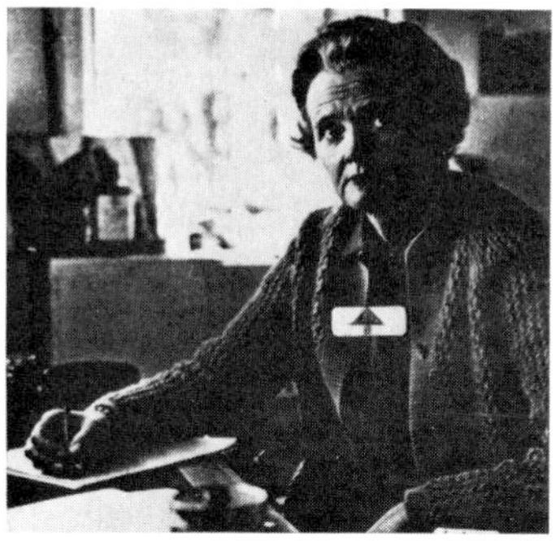

Daphne du Maurier is one of a family of highly creative English writers, actors and artists.

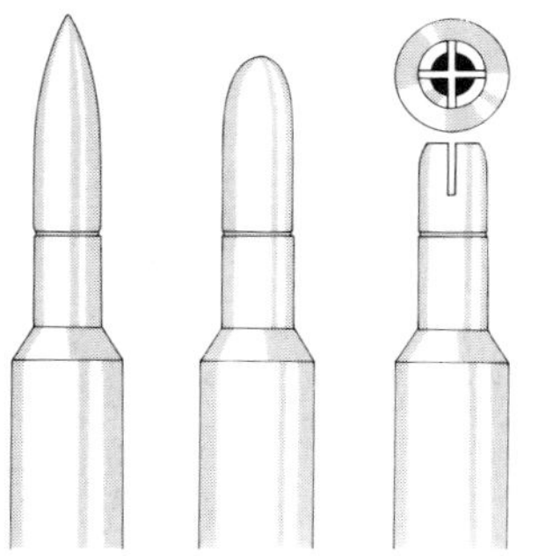

Dumdum; this type of bullet which fragments on impact is now banned.

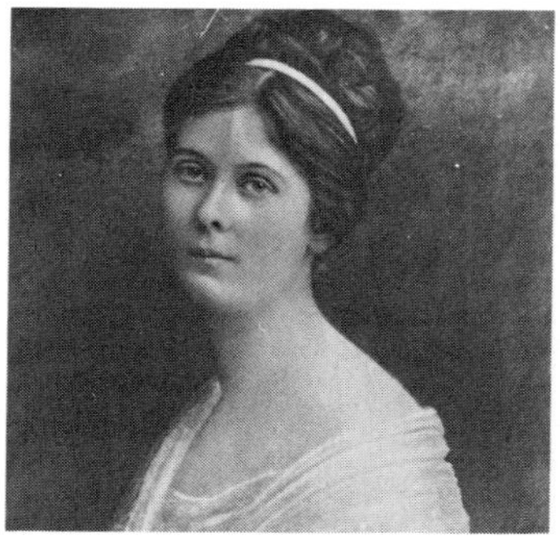

Isadora Duncan abandoned the restrictions of formal dance for self-expression.

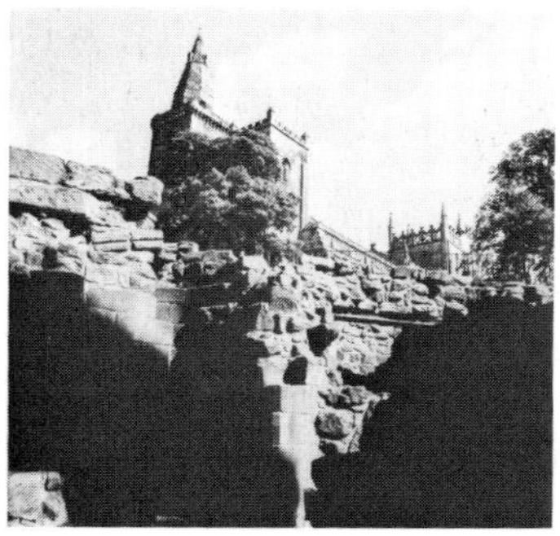

Dunfermline is the last resting place of many of the great kings and queens of Scotland.

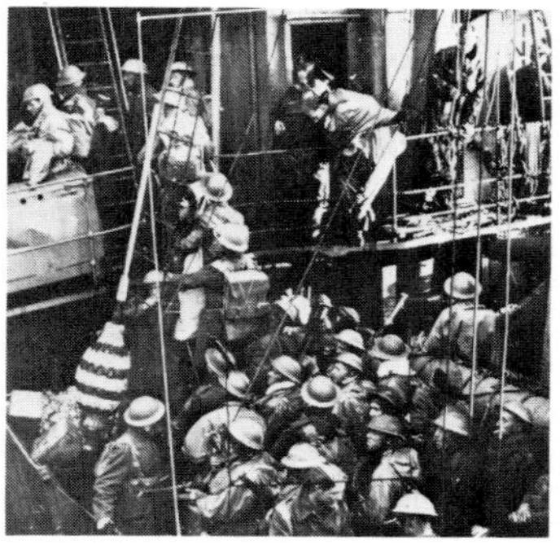

Dunkirk; a flotilla of craft rescued the British Expeditionary Force from its beaches in 1940.

tions, which appeared in *Punch* and *Cornhill Magazine*, re-create the mild social satire of the novels.

Du Maurier, Sir Gerald (1873–1934), English actor-manager, the son of George DU MAURIER and father of Daphne DU MAURIER. He specialized in light comedy roles, and he managed Wyndham's Theatre (1910–25). He was knighted in 1922.

Dumbarton Oaks Conference (1944), meeting held near Washington, DC, by representatives of the USA, Britain, the USSR and China. The six-week meeting resulted in a plan for an international organization to preserve world peace after WWII. The structural proposals made at that meeting, especially on the composition and powers of the Security Council, became the basis for the UN charter of 1945. *See also* HC2 p.298.

Dumbbell Nebula (M27, NGC 6853), planetary nebula in the constellation of Vulpecula. Irregular in shape, it is of about the 8th magnitude. It was discovered in 1764 by Charles Messier. *See also* SU p.233.

Dum-Dum, town in West Bengal state, E India, a suburb of Calcutta. In the 19th century its arsenal was the first to produce a type of lead-nosed bullet (dumdums) shaped so that they inflict tearing wounds. Pop. (1970) 31,363.

Dumfries and Galloway, the southernmost Scottish region, formed in 1975 from the former countries of Dumfrieshire, Kircudbrightshire and Wigtownshire. It stretches from the S and SW coasts of Scotland to the Southern Uplands. The chief towns are Dumfries, Lockerbie, Kirkudbright and Stranraer. Pop. (1974) 143,711.

Dumfries, county town of Dumfries and Galloway Region, S Scotland, on the River Nith. During the wars of Scottish Independence it was raided many times by the English because of its position close to the border. Robert BURNS lived there and was buried in St Michael's Church in 1796; his house is now a museum. Industries: knitwear, hosiery, chemicals Pop. 29,400.

Dumfriesshire, former county in S Scotland, N of the Solway Firth on the border with England; now part of Dumfries and Galloway Region. Sheep are raised on the uplands, and barlry, oats and potatoes are grown in the valleys. Dumfries is the county town. Industries include coal-mining, limestone and sandstone quarrying, and salmon fishing. Area: 2,784sq km (1,075sq miles).

Dumortierite, silicate mineral, hydrous aluminum borosilicate, $Al_8BSi_3O_{19}(OH)$. It is found scattered in metamorphic rocks, and occurs usually in fibrous masses, rarely as orthorhombic crystals. It is glassy to pearly violet or blue. Properties: hardness 7; s.g. 3.3.

Dumping, in economics, practice of selling goods abroad at prices below those in exporter's home market (after allowance for transport and other costs). Dumping is a competitive measure employed to shore up production levels during a business depression. It is also the method used to eliminate competing domestic producers in the export markets.

Dunant, Jean Henri (1828–1910), Swiss philanthropist. His account of the sufferings of the wounded at the Battle of SOLFERINO appeared in 1862 with a plea for relief for wartime wounded. His campaign, to which he devoted all his fortune, succeeded in bringing about the GENEVA CONVENTION in 1864 which set down humane rules of conduct in war and established the international RED CROSS. He received the first Nobel Peace Prize in 1901 with Frédéric PASSY. *See also* HC2 p.171.

Dunaway, Faye, (1941–), US actress whose rise to stardom was ensured by the success of Arthur Penn's film *Bonnie and Clyde* (1967). Her roles have revealed a flair for comic irony and for her part as a fanatical television producer in *Network* (1976) she received an Academy Award.

Dunbar, Paul Laurence (1872–1906), US author. His poems written in the dialect of Black people earned him the title "poet of his race". He demonstrated a facility for a mixture of sadness and humour in *Lyrics of Lowly Life* (1896), about Southern Black life before the Civil War.

Dunbar, William (*c.* 1460–*c.* 1520), Scottish poet. He was a Franciscan, possibly a friar, who later became a diplomat in the court of JAMES IV. Dunbar was a poet of great versatility. His works include coarse satire – *The Twa Maryit Women* – polished allegory – *The Goldyn Targe* – and moving elegy – *Lament for the Makaris. See also* HC2 p.31.

Dunbar, Battle of (1650), victory of the English army under Cromwell over the Scots, after the Scottish estates had proclaimed Charles II king; 3,000 Scots were killed.

Dunbartonshire, former county in W central Scotland, E of Loch Long, now part of Strathclyde Region. It has a mountainous terrain and Loch Lomond in the N is a great tourist attraction. The River Clyde flows through the S; the county town is Dumbarton. Industries: shipbuilding, textiles, light engineering. Area: 627sq km (242sq miles).

Duncan, name of two kings of Scotland. Duncan I was the grandson of MALCOLM II and was killed in a feud with MACBETH in 1040. Duncan II (*d.* 1094), his grandson, was given as a hostage by his father MALCOLM III to William I of England. With the help of the English and Normans he recaptured the Scottish throne briefly in 1093 from Donald Bane, but was killed the following year after his followers had been driven out. *See also* HC1 p.182.

Duncan, Adam, 1st Viscount Duncan of Camperdown (1731–1804), British naval commander. He commanded HMS *Valiant* at the capture of Havana (1762) and was made an admiral in 1795. He was commander-in-chief of the North Sea fleet from 1795 to 1801.

Duncan, Isadora (1878–1927), US dancer, one of the greatest pioneers of, and influences on, modern dance. She lived in Europe for most of her life and achieved fame for her style of dancing, which was based on Greek Classical art. She died tragically when a scarf she was wearing caught in the wheel of a car and strangled her. She wrote an autobiography, *My Life* (1926–27). *See also* HC2 p.275.

Dunciad, The (1728 and 1743), satirical poem by Alexander POPE ridiculing dullness in general, those authors he considers to be dull and other literary vices. In four books, Bayes (the contemporary poet laureate, Colley CIBBER) is enthroned as king and succeeds in spreading soporific dullness over every aspect of contemporary life. *See also* HC2 p.313.

Dundalk, port in NE Republic of Ireland, in County Louth, near the mouth of Castletown River. Throughout its history Dundalk has been of strategic importance as a result of its location in a natural pass into Northern Ireland. Industries: brewing, engineering, textiles; exports: cattle and grain. Pop. (1971) 21,672.

Dundas, Henry, 1st Viscount Melville (1742–1811), British politician. He was a member of Parliament from 1774 to 1802 and the chief electoral manager for PITT's government in Scotland. In 1806 he was the last British official to be impeached. He was acquitted.

Dundee, city in Tayside Region, E Scotland, on the N shore of the Firth of Tay. It is an important port and a university town. It was a centre of the Reformation in Scotland in the 16th century. Industries: textiles, food processing, shipbuilding, engineering. Pop. (1974) 181,243.

Dundee, John Graham of Claverhouse 1st Viscount. *See* CLAVERHOUSE, JOHN GRAHAM OF.

Dune, hill or ridge of wind-blown particles, most often sand. Dunes are found wherever sandy particles carried by the wind are deposited. They occur in a variety of shapes depending on the direction of the wind, whether or not it is constant, and the surrounding landforms. *See also* PE p.121, *121.*

Dunedin, city in Otago, a province in South Island, New Zealand. When Dunedin was founded in 1848 by Scottish Free Church settlers, the Gaelic name for Edinburgh was preferred in place of the planned "New Edinburgh". It is a hilly town on Otago harbour, enriched by gold-mining, and with modern industries such as chemical production, food processing and brewing. It is the site of the University of Otago (1871). Pop. (1971) 82,216.

Dunes, Battle of the (June 1658), engagement near the beach at Dunkirk in which the French, aided by English Commonwealth troops and led by the Vicomte de Turenne, defeated the Spaniards, assisted by English royalists under the Duke of York.

Dunfermline, town in Fife Region, E central Scotland, 21km (13 miles) NW of Edinburgh across the Firth of Forth. It has an 11th-century abbey and was the birthplace of Andrew CARNEGIE: Dunfermline has the headquarters of Carnegie Trusts. The Rosyth Royal Naval dockyards are nearby. Industries include textiles, coal-mining and engineering. Pop. 49,900.

Dung beetle, small to medium-sized SCARAB BEETLE that feeds on dung. Some species form balls of dung as food for their larvae. The beetles may roll the balls some distance before burying them in the ground. Family Scarabaeidae; typical genus *Onthophagus. See also* NW pp. *107,* 113.

Dungeness, promontory in the most southerly part of Kent. It is a bank of shingle 24sq km (9.5sq miles) in area which extends 46cm (18in) each year. There is a lighthouse, signalling station, bird sanctuary and a narrow-gauge railway.

Dunham, Katherine (1914–), US dancer and choreographer. In 1945 she founded the Katherine Dunham Dance Company and the Katherine Dunham School of Cultural Arts in New York City. Her choreography is based on ethnic ritual, folk-stories and the everyday lives of Blacks in Africa, the Caribbean and the USA.

Dunite, ultrabasic igneous rock of colour ranging from light yellowish green to an emerald green, composed almost entirely of OLIVINE. It occurs in South Africa, Sweden and the Dun Mountain in New Zealand, from which it takes its name. *See also* PE p. 101, *101.*

Dunkirk (Dunkerque), city in Nord département, N France, on the Strait of Dover, 71km (44 miles) NW of Lille. Founded before the 7th century it came under French rule in 1662. During WWII more than 300,000 Allied troops were evacuated from its beaches between 29 May and 3 June 1940, when the Germans broke through to the English Channel. Today it is a leading French port and a major iron- and steel-producing centre of Western Europe. Pop. (1968) 27,504. *See also* HC2 pp.228, 230.

Dun Laoghaire, port in E Republic of Ireland on the Irish Sea. It is a yachting centre and the main passenger port for Dublin. Formerly known as Kingstown, it prospered after the completion of a railway to Dublin in 1834. Fishing is the chief industry. Pop. (1971) 53,000.

Dunlin, small wading bird, the most common in Britain. It has a long downward-curved bill and plumage that varies seasonally from mottled brown in summer to grey in winter. Length: to 20cm (8in). Species *Calidris alpina. See also* NW p.*227.*

Dunlop, John Boyd, (1840–1921), Scottish inventor and pioneer of the pneumatic tyre. He was a veterinary surgeon in Belfast until, in 1888 he re-invented the pneumatic tyre (previously patented in 1846 by Robert Thompson but undeveloped). His invention replaced solid tyres.

Dunmow flitch award, ceremony still held at Dunmow in Essex. It originated in the early Middle Ages when Fitzwalter, a local squire, offered a flitch (side) of bacon to any man who, a year and a day after his marriage, would swear before local worthies that he did not repent of it.

Dunsany, Edward John Moreton Drax Plunkett, Lord (1878–1957), Irish playwright and novelist. He was active in the Abbey Theatre, and his plays include *The Golden Doom* (1912) and *A Night at the Inn* (1916). Dunsany's mysterious characters move through worlds of fantasy.

Dunsinane, the most westerly hill of the Sidlaw Hills, in central Scotland. It was the scene of the defeat of MACBETH by Siward in 1054 and it has the ruins of a fort called Macbeth's Castle. Height: 308m (1,012ft).

Duns Scotus, John (*c.* 1265–1308), Scottish theologian and scholastic philosopher. A member of the Franciscan order, he was ordained in 1291 and subsequently lectured at Cambridge, Oxford and Paris. His principal works were commentaries on the writings of Peter LOMBARD. He founded a school of SCHOLASTICISM called Scotism. *See also* HC1 pp.*194*, 346; HC2 p.30.

Dunstable, John (*d.* 1453), English composer of whom little is known. He gained European recognition in his time for his early experiments in COUNTERPOINT. Manuscripts of his works have been found in Italy.

Dunstan, Saint (*c.* 925–88), English monk and Archbishop of Canterbury (959–88). He was the first of a line of clerical advisers to royalty and held great power under King EDRED. He spent time in exile under King EDWY and on his recall by King EDGAR brought Cluniac reforms to England and rose in his career to Bishop of London (957), then Archbishop of Canterbury. *See also* HC1 pp.154, 155.

Dunster, Henry (*c.* 1612–59), English-born educationalist, first president of Harvard University, USA. He emigrated to New England in 1640 and was appointed president of the newly-founded Harvard University. He patterned the university on English secondary education but when he became a Baptist in 1654 was forced to resign.

Duodecimal system, number system with twelve as its base. It has advantages over the decimal system (base 10) inasmuch as one-third is recurring (0.3333...), as is two-thirds (0.6666...), but in duodecimal they would be 0.4 and 0.8 respectively.

Duodenum, first section of the small intestine following the stomach, shaped like a horseshoe. The pyloric sphincter separates it from the stomach. Alkaline BILE and pancreatic juices enter the duodenum and mix with intestinal secretions to aid the DIGESTION of food. *See also* MS pp.*68*, 69.

Duparc, Henri (1848–1933), French composer. He was a pupil of César FRANCK and, although not a prolific composer, he is remembered for the songs he composed of poems by Charles BAUDELAIRE, LECONTE DE LISLE and others.

Dupleix, Joseph François (1697–1763), French colonial administrator in India. He enlisted the Indians to aid the French in driving out the British in 1746. He was governor of Chandernagor (1731–42) and of all French possessions in India (1742–54). *See also* HC2 p.49.

Duplessis, Maurice Le Noblet (1890–1959), Prime Minister of Quebec (1936–39; 1944–59). He was elected to the Quebec parliament in 1927 and became leader of the Conservative Party (1933–35). He founded the Union Nationale Party which was nationalist, anti-labour and pro-farmer.

Duplicators, or copiers, machines that reproduce images such as the written word, drawings and photographs. They vary in size, operating process and quality of reproduction, but all are intended for quick, small-quantity copying where the high quality of large, cumbersome printing presses are not essential. However some duplicators, such as the offset-litho press, are capable of high-quality duplicating; some modern photostatic copiers give good-quality copies; others are capable of making coloured copies. *See also* MM pp.208–209.

Du Pont, major US industrial company. E. I. Du Pont built a gun-powder mill near Wilmington, Delaware (1802). When the family business became a corporation in 1899, it was one of the world's largest manufacturers of explosives. After WWI, the company diversified and began to make chemicals and other industrial materials.

du Pré, Jacqueline (1945–), British cellist, wife of Daniel BARENBOIM. Soon after her London debut (1961) she was acknowledged throughout the world as a remarkable talent with a vigorous technique. Her interpretation of Elgar, Beethoven and Brahms drew special acclaim before illness cut short her career.

Dupré, Jules (1811–89), French painter, a member of the BARBIZON SCHOOL of painting. His work often showed a sombre or tragic interpretation of nature.

Dupré, Marcel (1886–1971), French organist and composer. He was a pupil of Charles WIDOR and won first prize in both piano and organ at the Paris Conservatory. He also composed many organ works.

du Preez, Frik (1935–), South African rugby union lock forward who made a record 38 appearances for his country (1960–71). A superb lineout exponent, he also used his strength and size to formidable effect in loose play for both the Springboks and his province, Northern Transvaal.

Duque de Caxias, city in Rio de Janeiro state, SE Brazil, on Guanabara Bay. It is an industrial suburb of Rio de Janeiro. Pop. (1970) 256, 582.

Durable goods, consumer goods with a useful economic life of more than one year, eg houses, motor vehicles, refrigerators and other household appliances. During recessions purchases of durable goods are postponed (existing ones can be repaired), which prolongs the reduction in demand.

Duralumin, alloy of aluminium with copper magnesium and manganese composed within the following limits: aluminium – over 90%; copper – about 4%; magnesium – 0.5% to 1.5%; manganese – less than 1%.

Durand, Asher B. (1796–1886), US landscape painter, with Thomas COLE and others, a leading member of the HUDSON RIVER SCHOOL. He was a successful landscape engraver before becoming a painter, first of portraits and religious themes and later of Romantic landscapes influenced by 17th-century Dutch painters, eg HOBBEMA.

Durango, state in NW Mexico. In the W, the Sierra Madre Occidentale contains rich mineral deposits including silver, gold and lead. The plains of the E provide excellent pastures and in the fertile valley of the Nazas River cereal crops, cotton, sugar cane, tobacco and vines are cultivated. The capital is the city of Durango, which has timber, food processing, tanning and textile industries and is the leading commercial centre of the state. Area: (state) 119,648sq km (46,196sq miles). Pop. (state 1970) 919,381; (city 1975) 191,034.

Durante, Jimmy ("Schnozzle"), (1893–), US commedian, full name James Francis Durante. He worked in music hall, theatre, films and television. As a member of the nightclub team Clayton, Jackson and Durante (1923–30), he appeared in the plays *Get-Rich-Quick Wallingford* (1932) and *Jumbo* (1935) and in the film version of *Jumbo* (1962).

Duras, Marguérite (1914–), French novelist and screenwriter. Her novels include *The Sea Wall* (1950), *The Sailor from Gibraltar* (1952), *Vice-Consul* (1966) and *Destroy, She Said* (1969); her screenplays, *Hiroshima Mon Amour* (1959).

Durazzo. *See* DURRËS.

Durban, chief port of South Africa, on the N shore of Durban Bay, 483km (300 miles) SE of Johannesburg. The national convention initiating the 1910 Union of South Africa was held there in 1908–09. It has the University of Natal (1949) and the Natal University College (1960). Exports: sugar, oranges, pineapples, wool, coal, maize. Industries: petroleum, textiles, motor vehicles, paint, sugar-refining. Pop.721,265.

Durban July Handicap, South African weight-for-age horse race run over 10½ furlongs at Greyville. First run in 1894, it is the richest event on the South African turf calendar, attracting millions of rands in betting.

Durbar, word used in India for court occasions or assemblies of notables. In the British era it was used for the festival which marked Queen VICTORIA's becoming Empress (1876) and for the state visit of GEORGE V and Queen Mary (1911).

Dürer, Albrecht (1471–1528), German painter, engraver and designer of woodcuts who worked in Nuremburg. Two visits to Italy at the time when it was being changed by the ideas of Leonardo and other Renaissance revolutionaries profoundly affected the work of Dürer, who made a personal synthesis of the N and S European traditions, one that deeply affected European art. His greatest single achievement was his book of woodcuts *The Apocalypse*, which established him as the supreme graphic artist. His masterpieces of painting include *The Feast of the Rose Garlands, Adoration of the Trinity* and *Four Apostles. See also* HC1 pp.*239*, 260, *260*, *261*.

Durey, Louis (1888–), French composer. He was, for a time, a member of LES SIX and composed predominantly small-scale chamber works and songs.

Durga, in the Hindu pantheon, one of the names of the wife of SHIVA. Depicted as a 10-armed goddess, she is both destructive and beneficent but is worshipped today as a warrior against evil. Her festival, the Durga-puja, which occurs in September or October, is an occasion for family reunions. *See also* DEVI; HC1 p.*121*.

Durham, John George Lambton, 1st Earl of (1792–1840), British Whig statesman. A radical, he promoted reform in Britain, and served briefly as governor-general of Canada (1838). He produced a report in 1839 recommending internal self-government for Canada, which also became the basis of the British policy in other colonies. *See also* HC2 p.220.

Durham, town in Durham county, NE England, on the River Wear, 24km (15 miles) S of Newcastle-upon-Tyne. An episcopal seat, it is noted for its cathedral (1093), which contains the tomb of the Venerable Bede, a Norman castle (1072) and university (1832). The chief industry is carpet weaving. Pop. (1971 prelim.) 24,700.

Durham Report (1839), report on the government of Canada, written after the 1837 rebellion by Lord DURHAM. He was sent to Canada as governor-general in 1838. The report advocated the union of Lower and Upper Canada, internal self-government and the extension of the British system of responsible government (in which the cabinet is responsible to the legislature) to Canada. *See also* HC2 pp.132, *132*, 136, 220, *220*.

Durian, tree and its fruit native to South-East Asia. The tree has oblong leaves and yellowish-green flowers. The oval fruit contains a delicate, creamy-white pulp which has a sweet taste, although it has a pungent, repellent odour. Family Bombacaceae; species *Durio zibethinus. See also* PE p.*195*.

Durkheim, Emile (1858–1917), French sociologist. With COMTE he believed that the methods of physical science could be used for the study of human society and is therefore considered to be one of the fathers of modern SOCIOLOGY. One of his most important theoretical works was *The Rules of the Sociological Method* (1895). *See also* MS pp.262–263.

Durrell, Gerald Malcolm (1925–), British naturalist and author, born in India. He has written many books about his collecting expeditions including *My Family and Other Animals* (1956), which also tells of his boyhood in Corfu, and *A Zoo in My Luggage* (1960).

Durrell, Lawrence George (1912–), British novelist and poet. He has lived most of his life in Greece, Egypt and other Mediterranean countries and they have provided the inspiration for most of his writing. His major work is *The Alexandria Quartet*, a novel published in four parts: *Justine* (1957), *Balthazar* (1958), *Mountolive* (1958) and *Clea* (1960); other novels include *Tunc* (1968) and *Numquam* (1970).

Dürrenmatt, Friedrich (1921–), Swiss dramatist. His works are characteristically ironic and display a nihilist, black humour. They include *The Visit* (1956), and *The Physicists* (1962). He has also written novels such as *The Pledge* (1958).

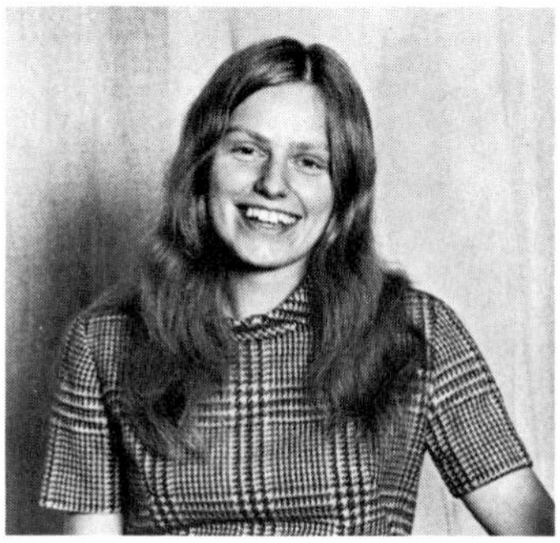

Jacqueline du Pré, whose brilliant musical career was cut short by multiple sclerosis.

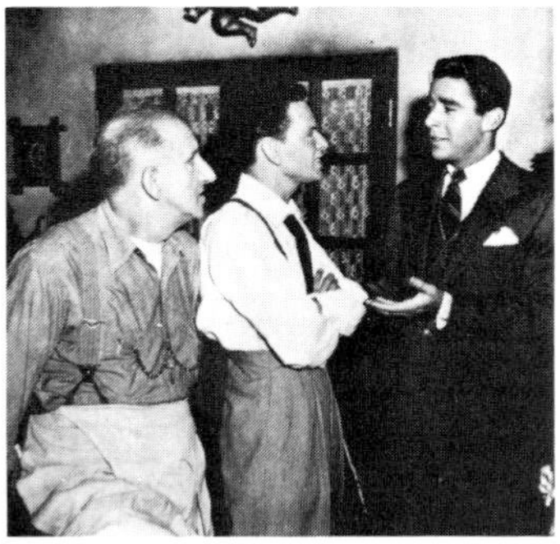

Jimmy Durante, the American musician and comedian in *It Happened in Brooklyn.*

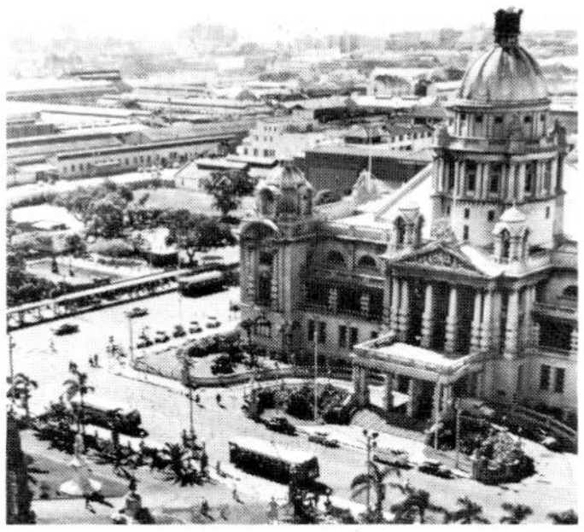

Durban; this busy commercial port is also a popular holiday resort in South Africa.

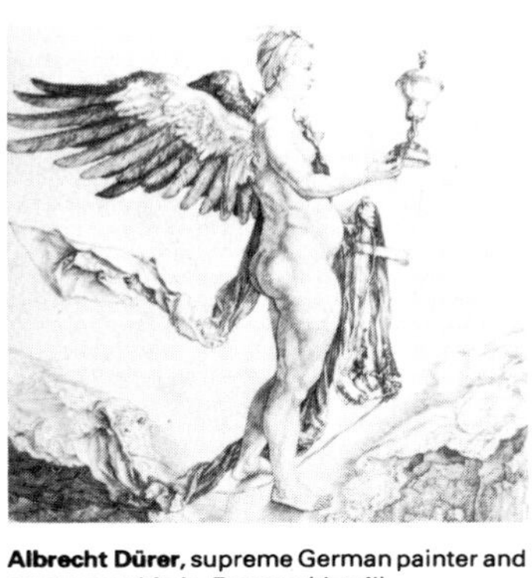

Albrecht Dürer, supreme German painter and engraver; this is *Fortune* (detail).

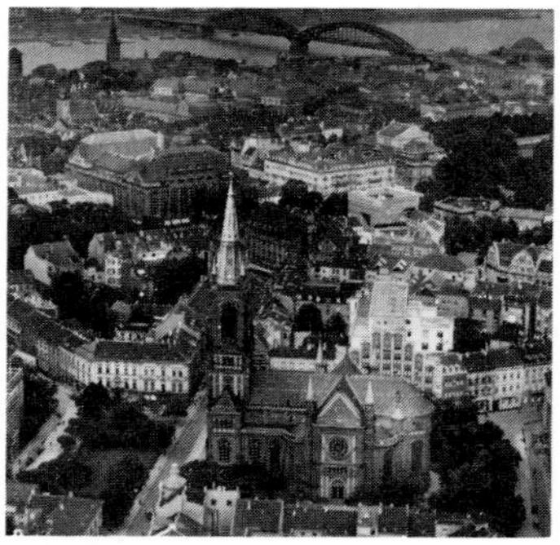

Düsseldorf; an aerial view of this graceful industrial city showing the Rhine Bridge.

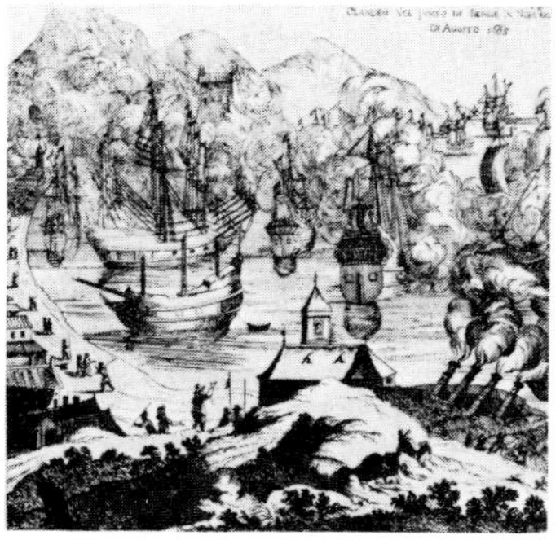

Dutch Wars, conflicts which resulted in the emergence of English naval power.

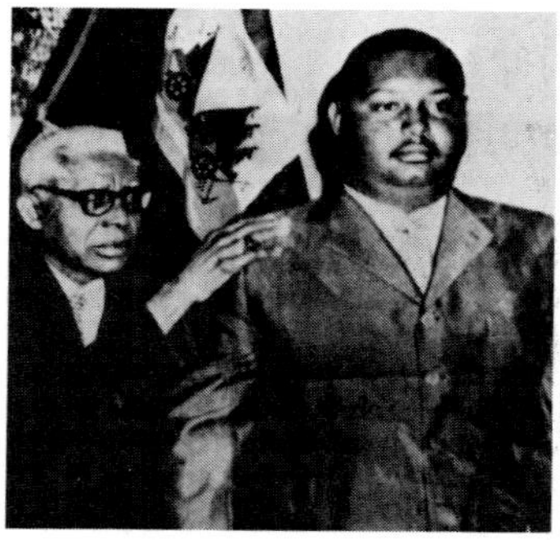

"Papa Doc" Duvalier with his son "Baby Doc", who relaxed his father's regime.

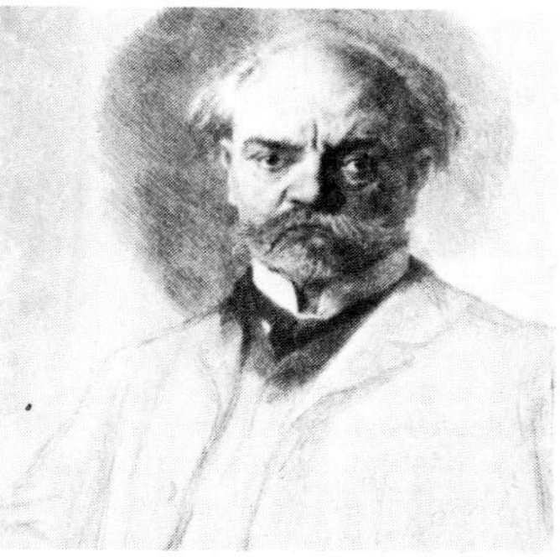

Antonín Dvořák, the Czech composer best known for his *New World Symphony*.

Durrës, city in W Albania on the Adriatic coast; capital of Durrës province. Founded in 625 BC as a joint colony of Corcyra and Corinth, it became an important trade centre. It is Albania's chief port and exports include grain, olive oil and tobacco. Industries: food processing, textiles and leather. Pop. 57,000.

Duse, Eleanora (1858–1924), Italian actress, She made her debut at the age of four in *Les Misérables*; at 14 she played Juliet. She acted in many countries in such plays as *Thérèse Raquin* and *La Dame aux Camélias*. She introduced several plays written by D'Annunzio and also gave notable performances in many of the works of IBSEN.

Düsseldorf, city in W West Germany at the confluence of the rivers Rhine (Rhein) and Düssel; capital of North Rhine-Westphalia state. From the 14th to the 16th century it was the capital and residence of the dukes of Berg. It became part of Prussia in 1815 and was occupied by France from 1921 until 1925. Industries: chemicals, textiles, iron, steel. Pop. (1970) 663,586.

Dust Bowl, area of approximately 40.4 million ha (100 million acres) of the GREAT PLAINS in the USA that have suffered extensively from wind erosion. Due to drought, overplanting and mismanagement, much of the topsoil was blown away in the 1930s. Subsequent government soil conservation programmes, such as crop rotation, and strip planting have helped to restore productivity.

Dust devil, or dust whirl, brief, small-scale whirlwind containing sand or dust. Only a few yards in diameter, the funnel may extend upward as far as 914m (3,000ft). It is caused by local atmospheric instability, eg by intense heating of the earth on a hot day.

Dust, galactic, dust found in the outer arms of spiral GALAXIES. It appears to be made up of minute particles, perhaps of graphite and ice.

Dust, interplanetary, material made up of minute meteoric particles orbiting the Sun. It is believed that sunlight reflected by such dust is the cause of ZODIACAL LIGHT.

Dust, interstellar. *See* INTERSTELLAR MATTER.

Dust, zodiacal. *See* DUST, INTERPLANETARY.

Dust collector, device used in industrial plants to collect dusts, such as silica, coal dust and asbestos, which can cause or aggravate respiratory diseases. Usually the exhaust ventilation of machinery is filtered and the harmful dust collected in bags. *See also* MS p.*89*.

Dust extraction, removal of particles that are suspended in an atmosphere. It is essential in planetariums where the presence of dust would render the projected light beams visible, and in some industrial premises, eg some electronic assembly factories where satisfactory results depend on dust-free assembly. One method of extraction employs filters through which air in the atmosphere being controlled is continuously circulated. A second method is to scrub, or wash, the dust-laden air with water sprays. In electrostatic extractors, dust is attracted to charged plates arranged in a grid. *See also* AIR CONDITIONING.

Dust storm, violent storm laden with fine dust picked up by high winds sweeping an arid region, where the soil is loose. Duststorms can smother crops and destroy pasturage. *See also* PE p.100.

Dutch barn, large oblong farm building, often open-sided, of simple modern frame and cladding construction and usually with a semicircular roof. Such barns have largely replaced haystacks for storing hay. *See also* PE p.165.

Dutch cap. *See* BIRTH CONTROL.

Dutch elm disease, highly infective fungus infection that attacks the bark of elm trees and spreads inwards until it kills the tree. It has been rampant since WWII.

Dutch East India Company. *See* EAST INDIA COMPANY.

Dutch East Indiaman, sailing ship which was introduced in the early 18th century; it developed from the GALLEON. These broad, heavily armed and extremely robust merchant ships could be used as men-of-war, which suited their use by the Dutch EAST INDIA COMPANY. *See also* MM p.*113*.

Dutch East Indies, until 1949 the part of South-East Asia that is now Indonesia. This overseas territory of The Netherlands comprised the whole archipelago except Borneo and E Timor. Lying between the Pacific and Indian oceans, the islands were colonized by the Dutch from 1602.

Dutch Guiana. *See* SURINAM.

Dutch Wars, three 17th-century Anglo-Dutch naval conflicts arising from commercial rivalry. The first war (1652–54) stemmed from efforts to exclude the Dutch from England's trade. England was more successful in the fighting, but the peace treaty was inconclusive. The second war (1665–67) followed England's seizure of New Amsterdam (New York). The Dutch inflicted heavy losses and England had to modify her trade laws, but by the Treaty of BREDA (1667) both sides kept their colonial conquests. The third war (1672–74) arose from French ambitions in the Low Countries. France invaded The Netherlands with English support but the Dutch were victorious at sea and stemmed the French advance on land. England made peace (1674) and the war ended with French territorial gains in the Spanish Netherlands and with Dutch trade gains. *See also* HC1 p.290.

Dutch West India Company. *See* WEST INDIA COMPANY.

Dutton, Clarence Edward, (1841–1912), US geologist who developed the principle of isostasy, according to which the level of the Earth's crust is determined by its density. The rise of light materials forms continents and mountains, and sinking heavy materials form oceans and basins.

Duun, Olav (1876–1939), Norwegian novelist. He wrote in Nynorsk (New Norwegian) and used peasant dialects. His work dealt with the difficulties experienced by primitive people in adapting to modern conditions. *The People of Juvik* (1918–23), a series of novels, is his best-known work.

Duval, Claude (1643–70), French highwayman who went to England in 1660 in the service of the Duke of Richmond. He was famous for his daring and his gallantry to the women he robbed. He was hanged at Tyburn and buried in Covent Garden Church, after lying in state in a tavern.

Duvalier, François ("Papa Doc") (1907–71), President of Haiti (1957–71), whose prominence as a public health specialist was a springboard to politics. Once elected, Papa Doc declared himself president-for-life and used voodoo worship and the feared TONTONS MACOUTES (an extra-legal vigilante group) to consolidate his dictatorship. Under his ruthless regime, the longest in Haiti's history, the country's economy severely declined.

Duvalier, Jean-Claude (1951–), President of Haiti (1971–). He succeeded his father and, like him, was declared president-for-life. He introduced several important reforms and disbanded the feared TONTONS MACOUTES.

Duve, Christian René de (1917–), Belgian cell biologist who shared with Albert CLAUDE and George PALADE the 1974 Nobel Prize in medicine for a detailed description of the structure and function of the cell and its parts. Analysis of biochemical activity in a cell led him to discover the lysosome, an organelle that acts as the "stomach of the cell".

Duveen, Joseph, Baron Duveen of Millbank (1869–1939), British art dealer, influential in determining art tastes during his lifetime, especially in the USA. He financed extensive additions to the TATE GALLERY, London, and subscribed to a new wing at the NATIONAL GALLERY and a wing for the Elgin Marbles at the BRITISH MUSEUM.

Du Vigneaud, Vincent. *See* VIGNEAUD, VINCENT DU.

Dvina, or Northern Dvina (Severnaya Dvina), river in N European USSR, formed at the confluence of the Suchona and Jug rivers. It flows NW into Dvina Bay in the White Sea not far from Archangel (Archangel'sk). Length: 750km (465 miles).

Dvina, or Western Dvina (Zapadnaya Dvina) river in NW European USSR; rises in the Valdai Hills, flows S and then W through Belorussia and Latvia into the Gulf of Riga (Rižskij Zaliv), an arm of the Baltic Sea. It is connected by canal to the Dnepr (Dnieper) River. Length: 1,020km (635 miles).

Dvořák, Antonín (1841–1904), Czech composer of the Romantic period. He adapted the spirit of Czech nationalism and folk music to a classical style. He composed in every form, but is especially known for his orchestral works, which include nine symphonies, two sets of *Slavonic Dances* and a number of suites and symphonic poems. His *Cello Concerto* (1895) is regarded as one of the supreme achievements in that form. He lived in the USA from 1892 to 1895, a stay which inspired his most popular work, the *Symphony in E minor* (*From the New World*). *See also* HC2 p.*106*, 107.

Dwarf, in European mythology, a short, ugly evil but clever creature who hid from the light of day in rocks and caves. Dwarfs were skilled craftsmen and armourers, guardians of mines and minerals. The seven dwarfs in the stories of Snow White are probably the best-known in literature.

Dwarfism, condition in which a person is much below normal size and lacks the capacity for normal growth. Dwarfism is associated with several inherited disorders including CRETINISM, TURNER'S SYNDROME and ACHONDROPLASIA, a condition in which there is normal mentality and normal trunk but short arms and legs. It is also caused by chronic kidney disease and potentially treatable pituitary gland malfunctions in which too little growth hormone is secreted. Pituitary dwarfs generally have normal body proportions. *See also* MS p.100.

Dwarf pea. *See* CHICKPEA.

Dwarf star, low-magnitude star in the main sequence of the HERTZSPRUNG-RUSSELL diagram. Dwarfs belong to the spectral classes G, K, and M, and are characterized by a small diameter and extremely high density compared with giant stars of the same spectral types. *See also* SU pp.226–229.

Dwarf star, carbon. *See* CARBON DWARF STAR.

Dwarf water buffalo. *See* ANOA.

Dyak. *See* DAYAK.

Dyce, William (1806–64), British landscape painter. He was influenced early in his career by the NAZERENES and introduced their ideas to the PRE-RAPHAELITE BROTHERHOOD, founded in 1848. His best-known work is *Pegwell Bay* (1860), a painting of extreme realism.

Dye, substance, natural or synthetic, used to impart colour to textiles, hair, wood, etc. Their use dates back to the earliest times. Dyes are classified according to the way they are applied, which depends on the fibre dyed, or by their chemical composition. Direct dyes can be applied directly to the fabric; they are acidic or basic compounds that bind to fibres such as wool and silk. Indirect dyes require a secondary process to fix the dye in the fabric. Substantive dyes, sulphur dyes and vat dyes act directly, ingrain dyes and mordant dyes act indirectly. *See also* MM pp.56–57, 244–245, *247*.

Dyeing, colouring of various materials especially textiles, leather and food. The natural dyes have been largely replaced by synthetic dyes, most of which are derived from coal tar. Alizarin comes from anthracene and indigo from aniline. Some materials such as silk and wool may be dyed by merely dipping them in the dye, but cotton, for instance, requires the use of a mordant, as do some dyes, such as alizarin. The mordant fixes the dye and may be common salt. Dyeing is an ancient industry, and the Phoenicians traded extensively in cloth dyed with Tyrian purple. The secret of the dye, which came from a species of mollusc, was known only to them. *See also* MM p.244.

Dyer, Jack (1913–), Australian Rules

footballer whose aggressive spirit and iron-hard physique earned him the name "Captain Blood". During 19 years with the Melbourne club Richmond he played 310 games, as a ruckman or in attack, and was a noted tactician and innovator.

Dyfed, county in sw Wales, formed in 1974 from the counties of Cardigan, Carmarthen and Pembroke, and occupying a peninsula bounded by St George's Channel, Cardigan Bay and the Bristol Channel. It has a rocky, indented coastline where the Cambrian Mts reach the coast in the Mynydd Prescelly range. Agriculture is based on sheep and cattle rearing, and the cultivation of oats, wheat and potatoes. Industries include fishing, timber, woollen textiles, tourism and oil refining. Area: 5,765sq km (2,226sq miles). Pop. (1975 est.) 321,700.

Dyke, in engineering, barrier or embankment, usually constructed of earth, designed to confine or regulate the flow of water. Dykes are used in reclaiming land from the sea by sedimentation, as practised in The Netherlands, and are also of value as controls against river flooding (when they are called artificial levees). In early English usage, the term dyke also refers to a drainage ditch or a raised earthwork defence, as in OFFA'S DYKE. In geology, a dyke (or dike) is an intrusion of igneous rock whose surface is different from that of the adjoining material. Dykes are usually vertical, and the patterns they exhibit are indicative of the stress fractures of the bed rock that they intruded. *See also* PE pp.*30*, *100*.

Dyke, Sir Anthony van. *See* VAN DYKE, SIR ANTHONY.

Dylan, Bob (1941–), US popular singer and composer. He taught himself to play the guitar, piano, autoharp and harmonica and became popular on concert tours and in recordings in the 1960s. One of the originators of the folk-rock style of popular music, he has composed many songs, including *Blowin' in the Wind* and *The Times They Are A-Changin'*. *See also* HC2 p.273, *273*.

Dynamics, in economics, change or changes occurring in economic conditions over a period of time. Dynamics is often used in equilibrium analysis in order to reveal the movement of the economic situation over time, such as the different rates of growth of population and food supplies. Dynamics is also important in simulation models, where changes affect the relationship through the movement over time. *See also* MS p.310.

Dynamic testing, measurement of the forces exerted by moving bodies on resisting members. Such examples as the effects of cars moving over a bridge, landing shock on an aircraft's undercarriage and moving machine parts are all examples which require dynamic testing.

Dynamite, solid, blasting explosive that contains NITROGLYCERIN incorporated in an absorbent base such as charcoal or wood-pulp. Shock-resistant but easily detonated by heat or percussion, it is used in mining, quarrying and engineering. Its properties can be varied by adding ammonium nitrate or sodium nitrate. It was invented by Alfred NOBEL in 1866. *See also* MM p.243.

Dynamo, or generator, device that converts mechanical energy into electricity by the principle of ELECTROMAGNETIC INDUCTION. It consists of a number of copper coils each terminating on diagonally opposite sides of a COMMUTATOR, formed on a cylindrical spindle; the whole is called an armature. The armature is rotated within a magnetic field produced by a permanent magnet or, more usually, a pair of copper coils through which current, from the dynamo, is passed. Rotation of the armature causes a current to be induced in its coils. *See also* SU pp.*115*, *118*–119, 122–123, *124*.

Dynamometer, electrical measuring instrument in which a pointer is deflected as a result of the force exerted between fixed and moving coils, the pointer being attached to the latter. It has applications in ammeters, wattmeters and voltmeters. The term is also used for a torque meter, measuring the power of rotating engines, eg the brake HORSEPOWER of a car engine.

Dyne, unit of force in the cgs (metric centimetre gramme-second) system of units. One dyne is the force that gives a mass of one gramme an acceleration of one centimetre per second per second. One NEWTON equals 100,000 dynes.

Dysentery, infectious disease characterized by DIARRHOEA, intestinal bleeding, fever and, in severe cases, intestinal perforation, cramp and nausea. It is spread in contaminated food and water and can occur in epidemic form in crowded areas with poor sanitation, especially in the tropics. Bacillary dysentery, caused by BACTERIA, is usually treated with antibiotics. Amoebic dysentery, caused by a type of AMOEBA, is treated with the drug emetine.

Dysfunction, distinction in the highly refined sociological theory of STRUCTURAL FUNCTIONALISM that means any function, or consequence of a social system, that lessens the system's adaptation to its setting, thereby reducing its ability to survive.

Dyslexia, inability to read properly. Its specific causes are disputed, but it is probably due to some defect in the speech centres of the brain. Symptoms may include difficulty in writing, especially in spelling correctly. It is not a sign of low intelligence and some cases may benefit from special teaching. *See also* MS p.*143*.

Dysmenorrhea, painful menstruation, as distinct from normal menstrual discomfort or premenstrual tension. It can occur shortly after the first menstruation or later in life, and is characterized by cramp-like pain in the lower abdomen, and sometimes nausea.

Dyspepsia, indigestion or upset stomach occurring during or after a meal. The symptoms include wind, heartburn, excess acidity and, in severe cases, vomiting. It can be caused by eating too much too quickly, or by various disorders, such as peptic ulcers.

Dyspnoea, difficulty in breathing. It is normal after strenuous exertion, but can be a sign of various disorders.

Dysprosium, metallic element (symbol Dy) of the LANTHANIDE group, first identified in 1886 by Lecoq de Boisbaudran. Its chief ores are monazite and bastnasite. It has few commercial uses. Properties: at. no. 66; at. wt. 162.5; s.g. 8.54 (25°C); m.p. 1,409°C; (2,568°F); b.p. 2,335°C (4,235°F); most common isotope Dy^{164} (28.18%).

Dystrophy, muscular, progressive degenerative disorder associated with the breakdown of muscle cells and of unknown cause. It is an hereditary complaint which begins in early childhood and affects boys more than girls. In most cases death occurs before adulthood, but there is a form whose onset is in adolescence and which may persist until middle age.

Dzerzhinksky, Ivan (1909–), Russian composer, an occasional pupil of SHOSTAKOVICH. His operas, especially those based on SHOLOKHOV's *Don* trilogy, have been extremely successful in the USSR.

Dzungarian Basin. *See* ZHUANGAERPENDI.

Dzungarian Gates, pass in the Dzungarian Ala-Tau mountain range in NW China that served as an important invasion route from Russia to China. The narrow and inhospitable pass was used by GENGHIS KHAN, among others.

E

E, the fifth letter of the alphabet, derived from the Semitic *he*, which the Greeks adopted as the letter epsilon. E is a vowel and the most frequently used letter in written English. It has various pronunciations, depending on its position in a word. It may be long as in *me* (although this sound is much more frequently denoted by a double *e*, as in *feed*) or short, as in *fed*. At the end of a word it often modifies the sound of a preceding vowel, eg the short *a* in *fat* becomes a long *a* in *fate*. In a few English words *e* is pronounced like an *a*, as in *clerk* and *sergeant*.

Ea, or Enki, in Mesopotamian mythology, the god of freshwater (Apsu), which together with saltwater (Tiamat) was the source of all life. He became the lord of knowledge, magic art and science. He gave kings their wisdom and artisans their skill. According to one account, at the creation Ea was responsible for forming man out of clay. His earthly residence was the holy city of ERIDU. *See also* MS p.213.

Eadfrith (*d.* 721), bishop of Lindisfarne in Northumbria from 698. A disciple of St CUTHBERT, he encouraged the writing of a biography of the saint by the Venerable BEDE. The LINDISFARNE GOSPELS are thought to be the work of Eadfrith. *See also* HC1 p.164.

Eadmer, or Edmer, of Canterbury (*c.* 1060–*c.* 1128), English monk, theologian and historian. An Anglo-Saxon by birth, Eadmer was a friend and confidant of St ANSELM of Canterbury. His most important writings were a history of England for the previous 50 years (*Historiae novorum in Anglia*), biographies of Anselm and other English saints, and a tract on the IMMACULATE CONCEPTION.

Eads, James Buchanan (1820–87), US engineer and inventor. He invented and used the diving bell to salvage sunken steamboats and their cargoes, and in 1842 formed the first ship salvaging business on the Mississippi River. Early in the US Civil War he built a fleet of armour-clad gunboats to patrol the Mississippi.

Eagle, strong, carnivorous diurnal BIRD OF PREY. Sea and fishing eagles, including the bald and stellar eagles, are large birds, frequenting American sea-coasts where they dive for fish and feed on small animals and carrion. Serpent eagles are stocky reptile-eating birds; the large HARPY EAGLES inhabit tropical forests; some eagles indigenous to Asia and Africa are open-country predators. True eagles (*Aquila*) have long, hooked bills, broad wings, and powerful toes with long curved claws. They are usually brownish, black or grey with light or white markings. They nest high on sea-coasts or island mountains, building massive stick nests lined with grass and leaves, called eyries. One or two light-brown or spotted eggs are laid. Length: 40–100cm (16–40in.) Family Falconidae. *See also* FALCON; NW pp.*142*, *200*, *217*, *222*, 234, *244–245*.

Eakins, Thomas (1844–1916), US painter and photographer. Unrecognized for most of his lifetime, he is now regarded as one of the finest US portrait painters of the 19th century. Among his most famous paintings are *The Gross Clinic* (1875), *The Chess Players* (1876) and *The Swimming Hole* (1883). *See also* HC2 pp.*117*.

Ealdorman, Anglo-Saxon official appointed by the king to organize the defence of the shire. The office was not hereditary and carried no automatic grant of land. The ealdorman usually also presided over the shire courts. In the 11th century, the office was overtaken by that of the EARL, with which often came the authority over several counties. The word is now *Alderman*. *See also* HC1 p.165.

Ealing Studios, British film studios founded in 1929, especially remembered for its production (chiefly supervised by Michael BALCON) in the decade after WWII. The highly popular "Ealing comedies" such as *Passport to Pimlico* (1949), *The Lavender Hill Mob* (1951) and *The Ladykillers* (1955) with original screenplays, realistic backgrounds, location exteriors and consistently fine performances from a nucleus of actors led by Alec GUINNESS, typified the company's output. The studios themselves were sold in 1952.

Eames, Charles (1907–), US architect and designer. Eames is best known for his chairs of moulded plywood and reinforced plastic. He has also designed film-sets. He collaborates with his wife, and together they won the Kauffmann International Design Award in 1960.

Eanes, General Antonio dos Santos Ramalho (1935–), President of Portugal since 1976. He had a military career overseas and became close friend of Gen. Antonio Spinola, who was then president. He became Chief-of-Staff in Nov. 1975 and president on Spinola's resignation.

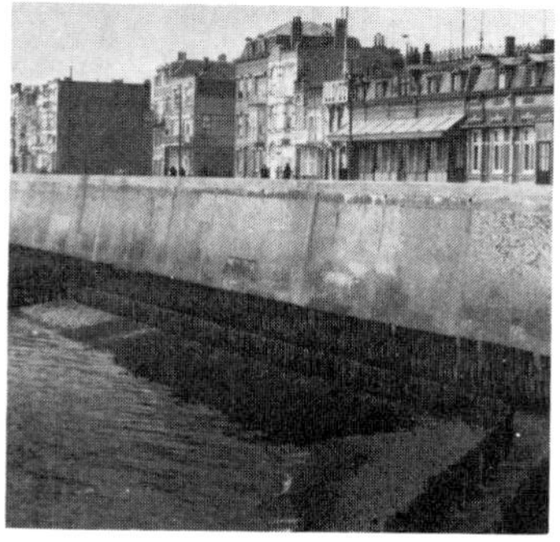

Dyke: the Great Dyke at Flushing, The Netherlands, has rows of protective wooden piles.

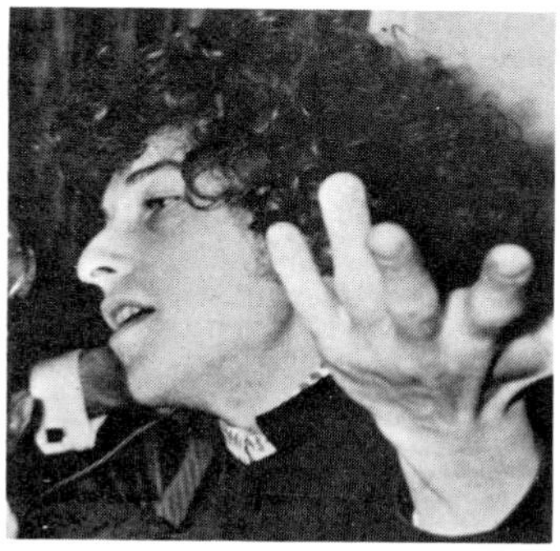

Bob Dylan, seen here talking to journalists at a press conference in Paris.

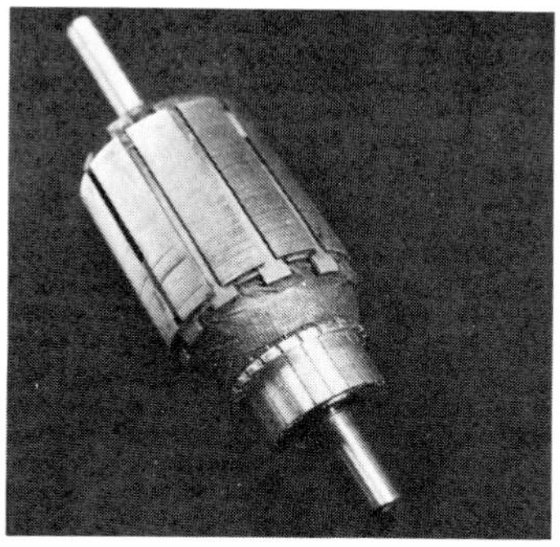

Dynamos convert the mechanical energy of a rotating armature into electric energy.

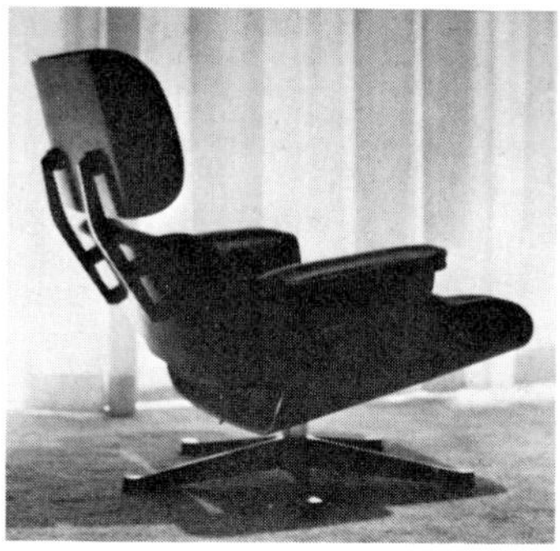

Charles Eames is an original and versatile designer, best known for his moulded chairs.

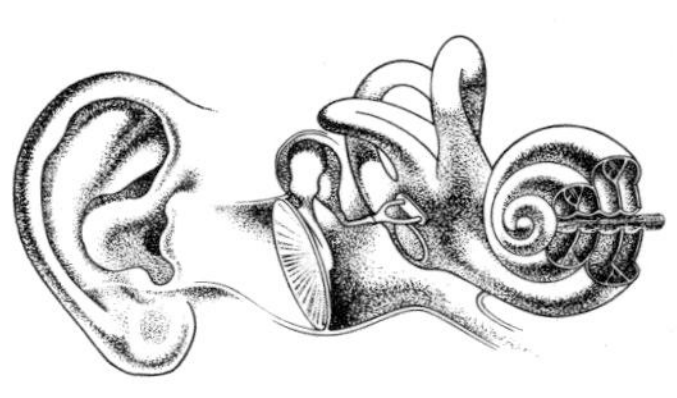

Ear, man's second most important sense organ, only the eyes being of greater service.

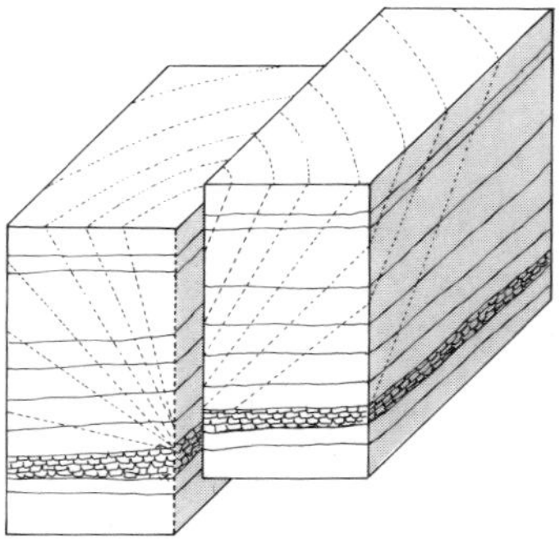

Earthquake, sudden shock felt at the Earth's surface; there may be a million in a year.

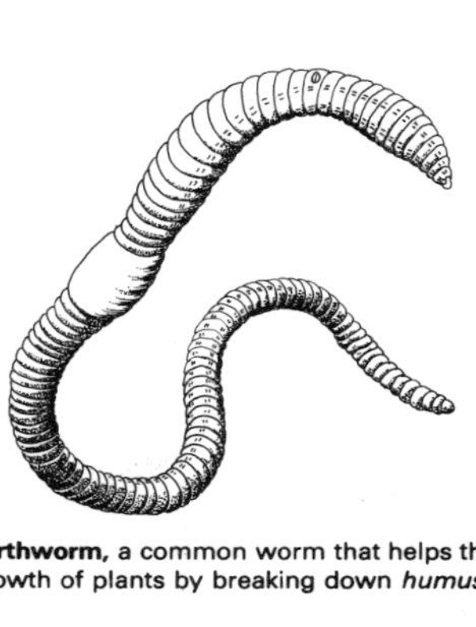

Earthworm, a common worm that helps the growth of plants by breaking down *humus.*

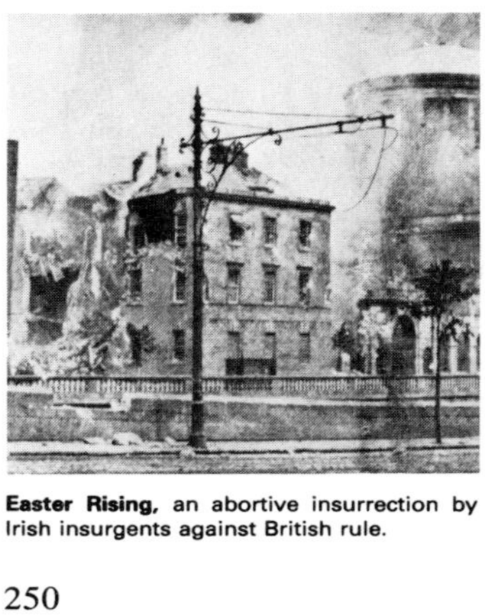

Easter Rising, an abortive insurrection by Irish insurgents against British rule.

Ear, organ of hearing and balance. It converts sound waves to nerve impulses that are carried to the brain, and maintains a sense of orientation and balance. In most mammals it consists of the outer, middle and inner ear. The outer ear carries sound to the eardrum, which separates the outer and middle ears. The middle ear has three tiny bones that pass on the sound vibrations to the inner ear, which contains the cochlea and organ of Corti, the essential hearing organ. Vibrations set up here stimulate the auditory nerve that transmits impulses to the brain. The inner ear also has organs that maintain orientation and balance. *See also* MS pp.50–51.

Earhart, Amelia (1898–1937), US aviator. The first woman to cross the Atlantic as a passenger in 1928, she became the first woman pilot to make solo flights across the Atlantic in 1932 and from Honolulu to Oakland, California in 1935. In an attempt to fly around the world, she disappeared between New Guinea and Howland Island in the Pacific in 1937.

Earl, British or Irish peer, next in rank above a VISCOUNT and below a MARQUIS; the title dates back to the early 10th century, but it no longer confers any official power. The territory under the jurisdiction of an earl is called an earldom.

Earl Marshal, in heraldry, the head of the English COLLEGE OF HERALDS; the office is held in heredity by the Dukes of Norfolk. The modern functions of heralds are to trace pedigrees, grant coats of arms and armorial insignia and to take part in official functions. The Duke of Norfolk is in charge of coronations and issues regulations on ceremonial costume.

Earlom, Richard (1743–1822), British engraver who united the techniques of mezzotint with engraving. His engravings reproduced contemporary paintings.

Early Bird, first commercial communications satellite, launched on 6 April 1965. It was a stationary satellite, ie, in a synchronous orbit so that it remained always over the same place about 35,400km (22,000 miles) above the mid-Atlantic. It could relay 240 telephone conversations simultaneously between North America and Europe.

Early English, term for the first phase of English GOTHIC architecture. It followed the NORMAN style and preceded the DECORATED phase of English Gothic. Introduced in England through the spread of the French monastic orders, Early English began with Wells Cathedral (*c.* 1180) and Lincoln (1192) and lasted until the late 13th century. The purest expression of Early English is Salisbury Cathedral (begun in 1220), the richest is Lincoln. It is characterized by longer, lower lines and less compact plans than are found in French Gothic; by the pointed arch, lancet windows without mullions, grouped in threes, fives and sevens; and piers made up of groups of clustered columns.

Earp, Wyatt Berry Stapp (1848–1929), US law officer. In 1879 he went to the silver mining camp at Tombstone, Arizona, as the deputy sheriff. In 1881 he and his two brothers took part in the famous gunfight at the O.K. Corral. He also served as US marshal in Dodge City and in Wichita.

Earth, third planet from the Sun, with one natural satellite, the Moon. The earth has outer radiation belts (VAN ALLEN RADIATION BELTS), an oxygen-rich atmosphere, and a lithosphere, or solid crust, beneath which is the mantle and the outer and inner core. Mean distance from the Sun, 149,600,000km (92,950,000 miles); mass, 5.976×10^{27}g; volume, 1.083×10^{27}cu cm; equatorial diameter, 12,756km (7,926 miles); polar diameter, 12,714km (7,896 miles); rotation period, 23hr 56min; period of sidereal revolution, 1.00004 years; the composition of the Earth's crust in order of abundance is: oxygen, silicon, aluminium, iron, calcium, sodium, potassium, magnesium and titanium. *See also* SOLAR SYSTEM; PE pp.20–25, 36–37, 66–67; SU pp.192–193.

Earthenware, vessels and other utensils or ornaments made of clay, fired at relatively low temperatures, resulting in porous, opaque pieces. Such items can be made waterproof by glazing the surface. *See also* MM p.44, 45.

"Earth grazers", asteroids whose orbits cause them to pass close to the earth. The asteroids Eros and Hermes have come close to the earth. In 1937 Hermes brushed past the earth only 780,000km (485,000 miles) away.

Earthlight. *See* EARTHSHINE.

Earth pillars, structures developed on valley slopes by rain denudation. They are columns of earth or clay often 6 to 10m (20–33ft) high capped by boulders which protect the material below from further erosion. Of frequent occurrence in mountain valleys, earth pillars are best exemplified in the Tyrol Mountains of Austria.

Earthquake, number of rapid, consecutive, elastic waves in the earth. A major quake is usually preceded by a few foreshocks (small quakes) and followed by many minor aftershocks. The source of a quake may be shallow or up to 690km (430 miles) deep. The shallow quakes are thought to be the rapid release of slowly accumulated strain along fault lines extending over a wide region. The rupture of a fault and the friction between faulting rock surfaces produce the elastic waves. The origin of the accumulated strain is the subject of some debate. *See also* PE pp.28–29.

Earthquake engineering, term used to describe the designing of structures such as buildings, dams and roads to minimize damage to them during quakes. Constructions over fault lines are avoided and cushions of concrete or polymeric materials are used as foundations to help buildings float or slide during a quake without breaking in areas where strain build-up is evident.

Earthquake prediction, branch of SEISMOLOGY dealing with the projection of possible quakes and their magnitude and location using past history of a region and measurement of the build-up of the strains in it and the time of the build-up. *See also* FAULT; SEISMOGRAPH; PE p.28.

Earthshine, or earthlight, phenomenon most easily observed during the crescent phase of the Moon, when the darkened portion of the lunar disc is illuminated by an ashen light reflected onto it by the Earth. *See also* SU p.*178.*

Earthworm, terrestrial and semi-terrestrial ANNELID having a cylindrical, segmented body with tiny bristles underneath. Most worms are a uniform red, pink or brown, and are mainly subterranean in moist soil. Their burrowing loosens and aerates the soil, helping to make it fertile. Length: 5cm–33m (2in–11ft). There are several hundred species. Class Oligochaeta; genus *Lumbricuus. See also* NW p.*75.* 88–89.

Earwig, slender, flattened, brownish-black insect found in dark, dry crevices and under the bark of trees. There are some 900 species worldwide, winged and wingless; all have a pair of forceps at the hind end of the abdomen. Order Dermaptera; genus *Forficula. See also* NW pp.*106, 110.*

Easement, legal right to use land belonging to another for a particular purpose. Common examples are access to land and the right to run a ditch for draining through it. It is also a right that can be invoked to prevent the owner of land from using his property in a particular way.

East, Edward Murray (1879–1938), US plant geneticist, botanist and chemist whose work influenced in the development of hybrid maize. He worked to determine and control the fat and protein in maize.

East, cardinal point on the horizon where the sun rises and therefore a term for the lands in that direction, especially east of Europe. The near east includes Turkey, Syria and Israel; the middle east Iraq, Iran and Arabia; the far east China, Japan and the East Indies.

East Africa, part of Africa that includes Kenya, Uganda, Tanzania and Mozambique. Kenya and Uganda were British colonies, Tanganyika (now Tanzania) was German, and Mozambique Portuguese. In WWI the Allies took Tanganyika after Germany invaded Kenya.

East African Community, association of E African nations, comprising Tanzania, Kenya and Uganda. The association was formed in 1967 to develop common economic goals and trade as well as social policies and services, such as transport and agricultural research. By 1974, it had virtually disintegrated.

East Anglia, flat region of E England, made up of the counties of Norfolk and Suffolk. An Anglo-Saxon kingdom, its large area and the protection afforded by the fenlands made it one of the most powerful English kingdoms in the late 6th century. After the Vikings were defeated in 917, East Anglia became an earldom. The fertile agricultural land produces cereals, sugar-beet and vegetables, and cattle, poultry and horses are reared. Industries include market-gardening, tourism and fishing.

East Bengal, region of the NE Indian subcontinent, on the Bay of Bengal. It was made part of East Pakistan in 1947, which became Bangladesh in 1971. The population is mainly Muslim. Area: 141,191sq km (54,514sq miles).

East Berlin. *See* BERLIN.

Eastbourne, town in East Sussex, SE England, on the English Channel at the foot of the South Downs, 5km (3 miles) NE of Beachy Head. A popular resort, its industries include printing, light engineering and plastics. Pop. (1971) 70,500.

East Coast, statistical area in the North Island of New Zealand. It has a jagged coastline and a broad inland valley; the chief city is Gisborne. It has a large Maori population, whose farming is concentrated in the Ruatoria district.

East China Sea, northern branch of the China Sea, bordered by Korea and Japan (N), China (W), Taiwan (S) and the Ryukyu Islands (E). Area: approx. 1,249,160sq km (482,300sq miles) Depth (max.): approx. 2,780m (9,120ft).

East Devon, county district in SE DEVON, SW England; created in 1974 under the Local Government Act (1972). Area: 817sq km (315sq miles). Pop. (1974 est.) 100,300.

Easter, in the Christian liturgical calendar, feast of the resurrection of Christ from the dead on the third day after His crucifixion. It is the oldest and greatest Christian feast and is celebrated on the Sunday following the first full moon between 21 March and 25 April. It is generally believed to have superseded an old pagan festival for renewed life. The name "Easter" is of uncertain origin but has been connected with the Anglo-Saxon spring goddess Eostre. The popular custom of exchanging Easter eggs dates back to pre-Christian times.

Easter Island (Isla de Pascua), island in the SE Pacific Ocean, approx. 3,200km (2,000 miles) off the W coast of Chile, to which it belongs. Inhabited mostly by Polynesian farmers, the island is famous for its curious hieroglyphs and formidable statues carved in stone standing up to 12m (40ft) tall. Area: 119sq km (46sq miles). Pop. 1,100.

Easterlies, broad currents or persistent patterns of winds from the east, such as the tropical easterlies or trade winds and the equatorial and polar easterlies. The trade winds occur in the N and S margins of the tropics during the summer and cover most of the tropics during the winter. *See also* WESTERLIES.

Easter Rising, rebellion by Irish nationalists against British rule, launched on 24 April 1916 (Easter Monday). Led by Patrick PEARSE, Joseph PLUNKETT and James CONNOLLY, about 1,200 men from para-military groups, chiefly the Irish Citizen Army, seized the General Post Office and other buildings in Dublin and proclaimed Ireland a republic. The British crushed the rising within a week and executed 15 of the ringleaders. Nationalist sentiment upsurged; renewed guerrilla fighting led to the establishment of the Irish Free State in 1921. *See also* HC2 p.163.

Easter Rite, ceremony performed in the Latin Church on EASTER eve at which a new fire and a paschal candle, representing the new light of Christ, are lit. It may derive from the annual renewal of the sacred fire in the Temple of VESTA which took place at the beginning of the year in Rome.

Easter tables, means of determining the date of Easter, first established by the Council of Nicaea (325) as the Sunday immediately following the 14th day of the paschal moon (the moon whose 14th day followed the vernal equinox). Since the Gregorian calendar (1582) Easter has fallen on the first Sunday after the full moon following the vernal equinox, hence not earlier than 22 March, nor later than 25 April.

East Germany. *See* GERMANY, EAST.

East Hertfordshire, county district in E HERTFORDSHIRE, England; created in 1974 under the Local Government Act (1972). Area: 477sq km (184sq miles). Pop. (1974 est.) 104,400.

East India Company, name of several organizations set up by various W European countries in the 17th century to trade east of Africa. The British company was set up in 1600 to compete for the East Indian spice trade, but competition with the Dutch led it to concentrate on India, where it gradually won a monopoly. Its supremacy over the French was assured by 1763. Although the British government assumed responsibility for its political direction in 1773, the company continued to administer the British colony in India until the mutiny (1857); after 1873 its functions were entirely taken over by the government. The Dutch company was founded in 1602, and set up its headquarters in Batavia (Djakarta) in 1619, exploiting the spice trade. It established a colony at the Cape of Good Hope in 1652. The company was dissolved in 1799, by which time its possessions had been incorporated into the Dutch empire and the company was almost bankrupt. The French company was founded by Louis XIV in 1664 and set up colonies on several islands of the Indian Ocean. It was established as a trading company in India in the early 18th century but, defeated by the English company for control of that region, it was abolished in 1789. *See also* HC1 pp.*279*, 301.

East Indies, archipelago of islands of various sizes, occupying a triangular area between the Malay peninsula, China, New Guinea and Australia. They range in size from the large islands of Borneo, Sumatra, Java, Celebes and Luzon to tiny islets. The main chain runs from Sumatra and Java to Timor; Borneo and Celebes are to the N across the Java and Banda seas; and the Philippines (Luzon, Samar, Mindanao, etc.) lie even farther N across the Celebes and Sulu seas. Most once belonged to The Netherlands; the Philippines to first Spain and then to the USA; Sarawak and Brunei (in NW Borneo) to Britain; and half of Timor was Portuguese. All are now part of independent nations, most of them in INDONESIA.

East Kilbride, town in the Strathclyde Region, S central Scotland. Established by the New Towns Act of 1946, its industries now include motor vehicle and aircraft engines and electronic equipment. Pop.63,500.

East Lindsey, county district in E LINCOLNSHIRE, England; created in 1974 under the Local Government Act (1972). Area: 1,746sq km (674sq miles). Pop. (1974 est.) 99,800.

East London, (Oos-Londen), port of Cape province, South Africa, on the Indian Ocean. Founded in 1847 as a British military base during the KAFFIR WAR, its harbour was developed after 1886. The main exports are wool and fruit and the port's industries include fishing, textiles and food processing. Pop. 36,800.

East Lothian, former county in SE Scotland, E of Edinburgh between the Firth of Forth and the Lammermuir Hills; now part of Lothian Region. The major river is the Tyne. Sheep are grazed on the highlands and wheat, barley and potatoes are grown on the coastal lowlands. The main industries are fishing, distilling and coal-mining. The administrative centre is Haddington. Area: 692sq km (267sq miles). Pop. 55,900.

Eastman, George (1854–1932), US photographic inventor and manufacturer, who created the basic materials for still and motion picture photography. He introduced machine-coated dry plates in 1880, paper roll film in 1884, celluloid roll film and the Kodak camera in 1888, and the Brownie, for children, in 1900. In 1892 he founded the Eastman Kodak Company. *See also* MM p.218.

East Pacific Rise, part of the mid-oceanic ridge and a region of seismic activity in the E Pacific Ocean. It is also known as the Albatross Cordillera. Shallow-focus earthquakes occur along the crest of the rise which is an area of SEA-FLOOR SPREADING. *See also* PE p.24.

East Riding, administrative area in the former county of YORKSHIRE, England; since 1974 most of the area has been part of HUMBERSIDE.

East Staffordshire, county district in E STAFFORDSHIRE England; created in 1974 under the Local Government Act (1972). Area: 388sq km (150sq miles). Pop. (1974 est.) 96,500.

Eastwood, Clint (1930–), US film actor and director. He made his name in Westerns with the television series *Rawhide* and later a series of Italian films including *The Good, the Bad and the Ugly* (1967). He then turned successfully to directing, with such films as *Play Misty for Me* (1971), *The Outlaw Josey Wales* (1976) and *The Gauntlet* (1977).

Easy Rider (1969), low-budget film produced by and starring Peter Fonda, directed by Dennis Hopper. Its story of two young drug pedlars on expensive motorbikes crossing the southern US mirrored the contradictions in the rebellious mood of American youth at the time.

Eau de Cologne, also called toilet water, scented solution consisting of alcohol and a perfume concentrate. Toilet waters were originally weak solutions of perfumes.

Ebbinghaus, Hermann (1850–1909), German psychologist whose work *On Memory* (1885) founded the scientific study of memory. Using himself as a research subject, he succeeded in describing the processes of learning, remembering and forgetting.

Ebbw Vale, urban district in Gwent, SE Wales, on the River Ebbw, 32km (20 miles) N of Cardiff. It is the centre of a region with industries which include coal-mining and steel. Pop. 26,000.

Ebionites, ascetic Judaeo-Christians who lived in communal poverty (the name means "the poor") E of the River Jordan, from the 2nd to the 4th century. Converted from Judaism originally by Jewish Christians rather than by Hellenistic Christians (such as St Paul), they used only St MATTHEW'S GOSPEL, emphasized Mosaic Law and stressed Christ's humanity and fulfilment of Old Testament prophecies. Two distinct groups developed: Pharisaic Ebionites and the Essenes, who tended more towards GNOSTICISM.

Ebonite, black vulcanized rubber, a hard material produced by combining rubber and sulphur; the sulphur forms numerous cross-links between the long polymer molecules, resulting in a rigid structure. It is commonly used in the manufacture of musical instruments. *See also* MM p.54.

Ebony, hard, fine-grained dark heartwood of various Asian and African trees of the genus *Diospyros* in the ebony family (Ebenaceae). The major commercial source of ebony is the macassar ebony (*D. ebenum*) of S India and Malaysia. Ebony is valued for woodcarving, cabinetwork, and parts of musical instruments.

Ebro, river in Spain which rises at Fontibre in the Catabrian Mts and flows ESE. At Reinosa it receives the Hijar in a reservoir, and flows through Miranda de Ebro, Tudela, Mora and Tortosa. Formerly it was called the Iberus or Hiberus. Length: 910km (565 miles).

Eccles, Sir John Carew (1903–), Australian physiologist. He made fundamental discoveries concerning the interaction of neurons, or nerve cells in the transmission of a nerve impulse. He shared the 1963 Nobel prize in physiology and medicine with Alan L. HODGKIN and Andrew F. HUXLEY.

Ecclesiastes, Old Testament book of aphorisms, probably by several authors, compiled under the literary pseudonym "the Preacher, the son of David". This appellation implies SOLOMON, but internal evidence makes quite clear that the book dates from after the BABYLONIAN CAPTIVITY. The single theme of the work is the vanity and emptiness of human life and aspirations; only faith in God relieves the cheerless and illusory conditions of the present life.

Ecclesiastical Commissioners. *See* CHURCH COMMISSIONERS.

Ecclesiastical Courts, system of courts set up after the Norman Conquest to deal with matters involving the Church, the clergy or religious offences, and some secular matters (until 1857). The highest penalty available to the courts was excommunication. In the 16th century appeals to Rome were forbidden, and the PRIVY COUNCIL became the highest ecclesiastical court. High Commission was also used as a means to ensure religious conformity.

Ecclesiastical History of the English People (*Historia Ecclesiastica Gentis Anglorum*) *See* HISTORY OF THE ENGLISH CHURCH AND PEOPLE.

Ecclesiasticus, book of the APOCRYPHA. The work of Jesus ben Sirach (or ben Sira, or Siracides) in about 190 BC, and edited by his grandson in about 132, it was originally in Hebrew but found its way into the Greek bible and not the Jewish canon. Its theme is zeal for the Law, the liturgy of the Temple and the traditions of the Jewish wisdom literature.

Eccrine sweat gland, one of two types of sweat gland in mammals. In man and some apes, eccrine glands are the more numerous and are distributed generally over the body, not associated only with hair, as are APOCRINE GLANDS. *See also* MS p.61.

Echegaray y Eizaguirre, José (1832–1916), Spanish dramatist. A versatile and important figure, he contributed to the scientific, political and literary life of Spain. It was as a playwright that Echegaray was most influential; he won the Nobel prize in 1904. His plays dealt with issues of morality and social concern; among them were *O locura o santidad* (1877) and *El gran Galeoto* (1881).

Echidna, or spiny anteater, MONOTREME related to the PLATYPUS, found in Australia, Tasmania and New Guinea. The upper part of the body is spiny, and its snout forms an elongated beak. Length: 30–77cm (12–30in). *See also* NW pp.*156*, 204–205.

Echinoderm, phylum of spiny-skinned marine invertebrate animals thought to be related to the evolutionary stock that produces chordates. It is the only major phylum made up entirely of animals. They are radially symmetrical with five axes, and have calcareous skeletal plates in their skin. Their hollow body cavity (COELOM) includes a water vascular system and tube feet. They reproduce sexually, and produce a bilaterally symmetrical larva resembling that of chordates; regeneration also occurs. The more than 5,500 species include SEA URCHINS, SEA-CUCUMBERS, and STARFISH. *See also* NW pp.72, 118–119, 179.

Echo, in Greek mythology, an oread or mountain nymph condemned to speak only in echoes because her chattering had distracted the goddess HERA from the infidelity of her husband ZEUS. Unable to declare her love for the young NARCISSUS, Echo pined away in solitude until her bones turned to stone and only her voice remained.

Echo, reflected portion of a wave such as SOUND or radar from a surface so that it returns to the source and is heard or observed after a short interval. Sound echoes are usually heard as the distorted repetition of a voice in a large empty room or over a valley. High notes provide a better echo than low notes. Echoes are useful in echo-sounding (used by bats and whales and by navigational equipment) but are objectionable in auditoriums, where they are eliminated by using absorbent material on the walls and avoiding curved surfaces that can focus echoes like a mirror. *See also* SU p.80; MM p.236.

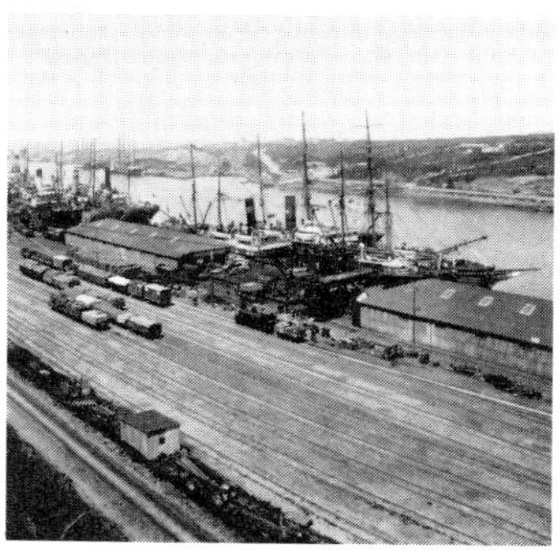

East London, an early view of the fourth-largest port of the Republic of South Africa.

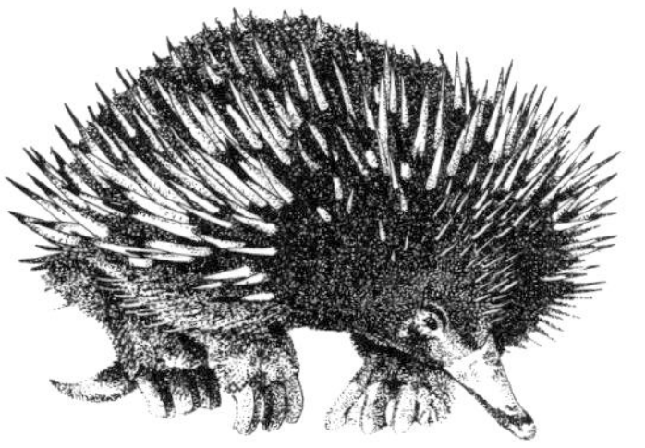

Echidna, a mammal that uses its strong claws to dig rapidly and bury itself for protection.

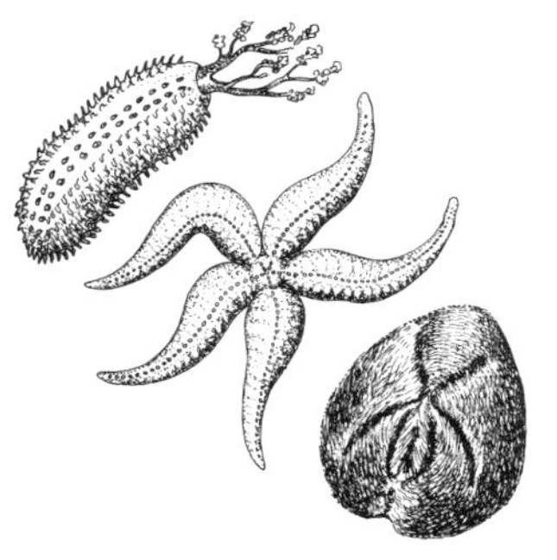

Echinoderm, marine invertebrates, common on temperate and tropical seashores.

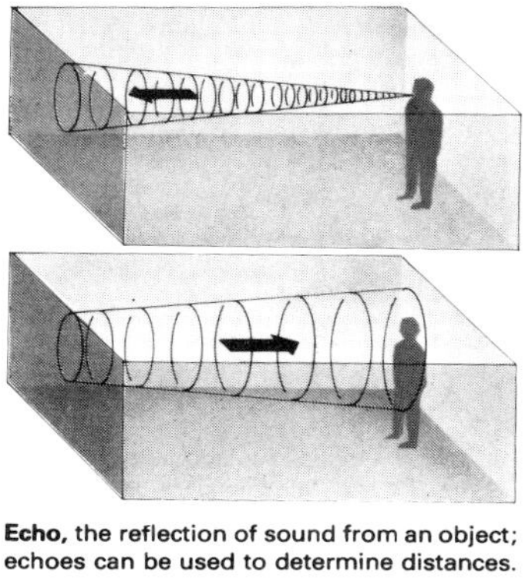

Echo, the reflection of sound from an object; echoes can be used to determine distances.

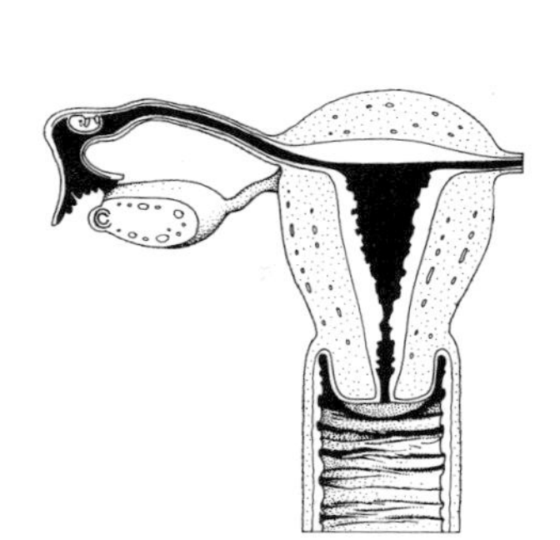

Ectopic pregnancy, a misplacement of a fertilized ovum necessitating early termination.

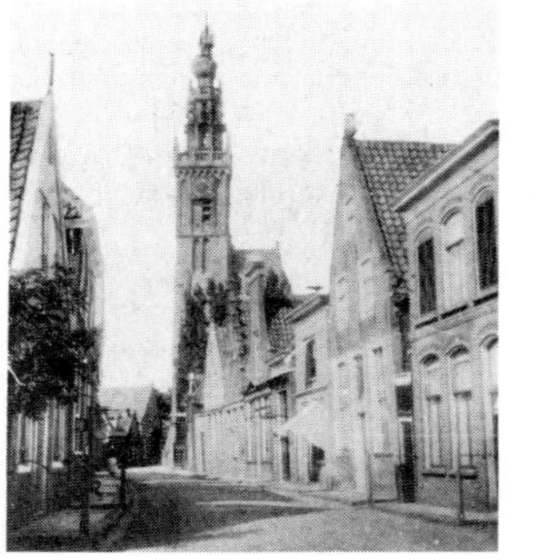

Edam; a view of the town showing the church of St Nicholas, rebuilt in 1602 after a fire.

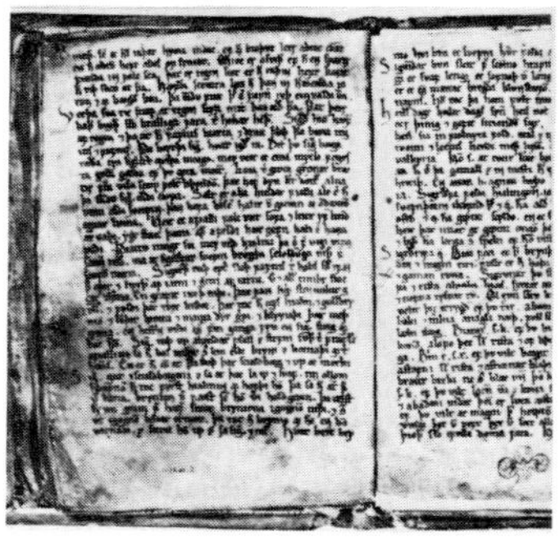

Edda; a page of manuscript from this work, probably written during 1222–23.

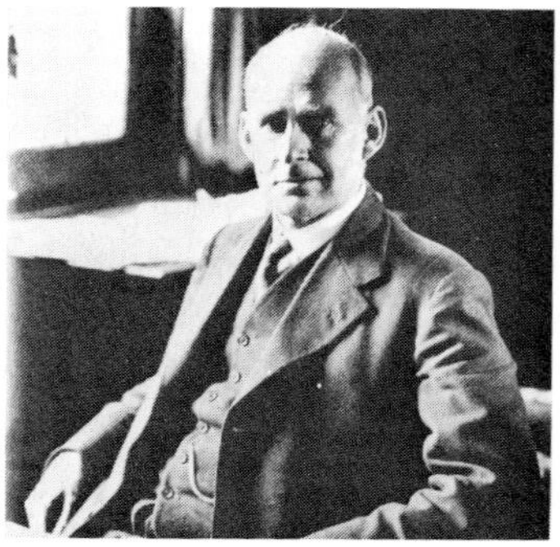

Sir Arthur Eddington, a British astronomer renowned for his studies of stellar motion.

Echolocation, in animals, system of orientation used principally by whales and bats. Such animals emit a series of short, high-frequency sounds, most of which are beyond the range of human hearing. From the returning echoes that result from these sounds, the animals can accurately gauge the range and direction of nearby obstacles, enemies or prey. *See also* NW pp.126, 161.

Echo sounder, device that sends ultrasonic sound pulses through water and detects their reflection – from the sea bottom, schools of fish or any submerged object. Continuous chart recordings can provide a profile of the sea bottom. *See also* SONAR; PE p.*91*; MM p.236.

ECHO viruses, group of viruses found in the faeces of apparently healthy individuals, having the name Enteric Cytopathogenic Human Orphan. There are at least 28 types of these RNA-containing viruses. They are known to cause diseases such as aseptic meningitis and various respiratory tract diseases.

Eck, Johann (1486–1543), German theologian and defender of the papacy against German Protestant reformers. He publicly debated with Martin LUTHER in 1519 and was largely instrumental in securing the papal bull which condemned Luther in 1520. In 1530 he drafted the refutation of Lutheranism according to the AUGSBURG CONFESSION.

Eckermann, Johann Peter (1792–1854), German writer. Although himself an author and poet, he is best known for his relationship with Johann Wolfgang von GOETHE. His *Gespräche mit Goethe*, a biographical study of Goethe, has been compared to BOSWELL's *Life of Johnson.*

Eckhart, Johannes (*c.* 1260–1327), German Dominican theologian and mystic, also known as Meister Eckhart (or Eckehart), whose speculations on the union of the soul with God led to his being tried and condemned for heresy by the Papacy. His ideas influenced later Protestant thinkers.

Eclampsia, rare disorder occurring in the last weeks of pregnancy, characterized by high blood pressure, swelling, excessive weight gain, convulsions, and albumin in urine. The cause is unknown. Treatment includes various drugs to control the symptoms. Delivery may be hastened or caesarean section performed.

Eclecticism, in philosophy, the combination of elements from different systems of thought without resolving conflicts among the systems. The method was favoured by Roman philosophers, including CICERO, some Renaissance thinkers and 19th-century philosophers led by Victor Cousin, who coined the term. Similar principles have applied to painting and sculpture since the 16th century.

Eclipse, in astronomy, occurs when a celestial body temporarily obscures another, as seen from the Earth. The most familiar kinds are solar and lunar eclipses. A solar eclipse happens when the Moon passes between the Earth and the Sun so that the Sun's light is blocked from the part of the Earth on which the Moon's shadow, or umbra, falls. A lunar eclipse is caused by the Earth when it moves between Sun and Moon so that the Moon passes into the Earth's umbra, and cannot shine by reflected sunlight. Both kinds of eclipses can be total, when Earth or Moon pass completely into the other's umbra; or partial, when Earth or Moon remain partly in the other's partial shadow, or penumbra. If a solar eclipse happens when the Moon is at apogee (furthest point from Earth), its apparent size is less than the Sun's, and an annular or ring eclipse results, with the Sun appearing as a bright ring around the dark Moon. If Earth and Moon's orbits were in the same plane, solar and lunar eclipses would be monthly, occurring at new and full moons. But because the Moon's orbit is at an angle to Earth's, eclipses are possible only when the Moon crosses Earth's orbital plane and is in line with Earth and Sun. These conditions happen seven times a year at the most. To early peoples eclipses, especially of the Sun, were awe-inspiring events. It is not surprising that the knowledge that eclipses can be predicted added greatly to the authority of its discoverers, the astronomer-priests of Chaldea (Mesopotamia). Today solar eclipses enable astronomers to make studies which are not normally possible, such as checking Einstein's theory of RELATIVITY. *See also* SU pp.*178*, 224–225.

Eclipsing variable or binary, regular variable star in which the light variations are the result of the star being a BINARY STAR, ie, consisting of a bright component with a darker companion. The two stars regularly pass in front of each other and are at maximum brightness when one is not eclipsing the other. The prototype of the best-known class of eclipsing variables is Beta Persei, or Algol. *See also* SU p.237.

Ecliptic, great circle on the CELESTIAL SPHERE, inclined at 23.5° to the CELESTIAL EQUATOR, ie, the yearly path of the Sun as seen from Earth or the Earth's orbit as seen from the Sun. The plane of the ecliptic thus passes through the centre of both the Earth and the Sun. The planets (except PLUTO) are always located near the ecliptic. *See also* SU p.*254*.

Ecliptic co-ordinate system, astronomical co-ordinate system that refers to the plane of the ECLIPTIC. The co-ordinates used are celestial latitude and longitude. Celestial latitude is the angular distance of a celestial body above (positive value) or below (negative value) the ecliptic, from 0° to 90°. Celestial longitude is the angular distance eastward along the ecliptic from the First Point of Aries or vernal EQUINOX to the vertical plane through the celestial body, from 0° to 360°.

Ecology, or environmental biology, bionomics, biological study of relationships between living things and their environment. It is also the interactions of groups of organisms with each other and with their surroundings. *See also* NW pp.192–194.

Econometrics, quantitative branch of economics, involving the application of statistics to economic problems, usually with the aid of computers.

Economics, study of how individuals in a particular society choose to allocate resources in order to produce the right proportion of goods demanded by that society. It involves studying methods of production to obtain maximum efficiency in the use of resources and deciding how material wealth is to be distributed. Ideally, economics also helps societies plan in such a way that future needs will be met. *See also* MS pp.308–11.

Economy, financial organization of the production and distribution of goods and services within a society or economic unit such as a household. Economic systems have varied greatly depending on the nature of available resources, labour and demand, the lines of communication, the forms of exchange and the level and type of technology. The two dominant and competing economic systems today are private-enterprise economy, or capitalism, and the centrally-planned economy.

Ecosphere, similar to BIOSPHERE, the total of all the ECOSYSTEMS of the Earth. The term BIOSPHERE is used solely to indicate the zone of life, but the term ecosphere includes the interaction of living organisms with their environment. *See also* NW pp.194–195.

Ecosystem, or ecological system, functioning community of living things and their environment. It is a complete ecosystem only if it recycles elements, has a constant energy source, and can incorporate energy into organic compounds and pass it from organism to organism. *See also* NW p.194.

ECT (electroconvulsive therapy), electrical stimulation of the brain leading to convulsions; used primarily in the treatment of emotional disturbances. When current is applied the patient immediately loses consciousness; his body becomes rigid, and his breathing stops for a few seconds. Then a brief period of muscular convulsions occurs. After treatment, the patient has a temporary memory loss and may be confused. Six to eight treatments are often sufficient to affect a severe depression. *See also* MS p.145.

Ectoderm, one of three so-called germ layers of tissue formed in the early development of a fertilized egg. It is the outer layer of the BLASTULA and later develops, in most animals, into a skin or shell, a nervous system, lining tissue, parts of some sense organs, and various miscellaneous tissues. Other germ layers are the ENDODERM and MESODERM.

Ectomorph, type of human being of slight or delicate build, usually with a thin face, high forehead and receding chin. Most people are a combination of ectomorph, ENDOMORPH and MESOMORPH. *See also* MS p.*189*.

Ectopic pregnancy, occurrence of a fertilized ovum outside the uterus – in the FALLOPIAN TUBE or elsewhere. The embryo cannot develop normally, and spontaneous termination of the pregnancy usually occurs. If it does not, serious injury for the mother may result if the condition goes unrecognized.

Ectoplasm, in biology, outer layer of the CYTOPLASM of a cell; it is usually semi-solid and transparent. The term is also used to refer to the apparently solid emanation that is believed to be produced by a spiritual medium in a trance.

Ecuador, republic in NW South America, which includes the GALAPAGOS ISLANDS. Until recently the country's economy depended largely on the export of bananas, but the discovery of oil in the late 1960s should strengthen it. The capital is Quito. Area: 270,670sq km (104,506sq miles). Pop. (1976 est.) 7,305,000. *See also* MW p.66.

Ecumenical Council, ecclesiastical convention of worldwide Roman Catholic Church representatives, restricted to members of that Church since the REFORMATION. The pronouncements of such a council are considered infallible by Catholics. Twenty-one ecumenical councils have been called by various popes, the last being VATICAN II (1962–65). All Christians recognize the first seven councils, the last of which was held in NICAEA in 787. *See also* HC2 p.304.

Ecumenical movement, movement aiming at the restoration of the lost unity of Christendom. In its modern sense the movement began with the Edinburgh Missionary Conference of 1910 and has continued to grow in strength, leading to the foundation of the WORLD COUNCIL OF CHURCHES in 1948. For a long time the Roman Catholic Church stood apart, but its attitude changed after the Second VATICAN COUNCIL (1962–65) and now it is as committed to the movement as are the other branches of Christendom.

Eczema, form of chronic DERMATITIS characterized by redness, oozing, blisters and itching. It can be caused by contact with a substance, such as poison ivy or detergent, to which the skin has been sensitized. More general eczema may occur with no identifiable cause, often in persons with histories of allergies. The treatment is local medication. *See also* ALLERGY; MS p.98.

Edam, town in North Holland, Netherlands, 19km (12 miles) NE of Amsterdam, near the Zuider Zee. Once a great port, it has many fine old buildings. The local cheese is also called Edam. Pop. (1970 est.) 18,200.

Edda, term applied to two manuscripts, one a collection of Old Norse poems – *Older Edda* or *Poetic Edda* – and the other a work by Snorri Sturluson – *Younger Edda* or *Prose Edda*. The *Older Edda* is dated *c.* 1270, but includes poems as old as of the 8th century. It contains epic poetic narrative featuring the traditional Germanic heroes and mythological subjects. The *Younger Edda* (early 13th century) was written as a manual of instruction for professional poets. It includes a section of myth and a section called the *Skalda*, which explains the use of diction, metre, alliteration, etc.

Eddery, Pat (1952–), Irish-born jockey who was Britain's champion jockey for four successive seasons (1974–77). In 1975, riding *Grundy*, he won the Derby, Irish 2,000 Guineas, Irish Derby and the King George VI and Queen Elizabeth Diamond Stakes.

Eddington, Sir Arthur Stanley (1882–

1944), British scientist who contributed to mathematics, relativity, cosmology and astronomy. He was professor of astronomy at Cambridge University and researched into the structure of stars. He also made significant contributions to the general theory of relativity, and was an eloquent popularizer of science.

Eddy, Mary Baker (1821–1910), American founder of CHRISTIAN SCIENCE (1879). She claimed to have rediscovered the secret of primitive Christian healing after an instantaneous recovery from serious injury in 1866. She expounded her system in the CS textbook, *Science and Health with Key to the Scriptures* (1875).

Eddy, Nelson (1901–67), US film star and singer. The highest paid singer in the US in the early 1940s, Eddy starred, often with Jeanette Macdonald, in many musical films including *Naughty Marietta* (1935), and *Bitter Sweet* (1940).

Eddy current, circulatory electric current induced in a conductor when subjected to a varying magnetic field. Eddy currents cause a loss of energy in AC generators and motors; the reaction between the eddy currents in a moving conductor and the field in which it moves retards the motion of the conductor. *See also* SU p.120–121.

Eddystone Lighthouse, stands on isolated rocks in the English Channel, S of Plymouth, SW England. The first Eddystone lighthouse was built in 1696. The present one is the fourth and was completed in 1882.

Ede, town in Gelderland, Netherlands, centre of the Dutch rayon industry and on the railway from Amsterdam and Utrecht to Arnhem. The nearby St Hubertus castle has an art collection. Pop. (1970 est.). 72,000.

Edelman, Gerald Maurice (1929–), US molecular biologist. He shared with R.R. PORTER in 1972 Nobel prize in physiology and medicine for his work on unravelling the chemical structure of the antibody gamma globulin. The determination of the structure of gamma globulin was essential to research on how antibodies function in the immunization system which recognizes and destroys invaders in the body.

Edelweiss, small perennial plant native to the Alps and other high Eurasian mountains. It has white, downy leaves and its small yellow flower heads are enclosed in whitish-yellow bracts. Family Compositae; species *Leontopodium alpinum. See also* NW pp.222, *223*.

Edema. *See* DROPSY.

Eden, Sir Anthony. *See* AVON, LORD.

Eden, in the Bible, garden created by God as the home of Adam and Eve, until they were banished for eating the forbidden fruit from the tree of knowledge. It is often equated with Paradise. *See also* MS p.184.

Edentate, any of a small order of North and South American mammals found from Kansas to Patagonia. The approximately 30 species include ARMADILLOS, SLOTHS and ANT-EATERS. *Edentate* means "with all the teeth removed", but only the ant-eaters are truly toothless. *See also* AARDVARK; NW pp.*154*, 155.

Edgar (*d.*1107), King of Scotland, crowned in 1097 after an English expedition led by his uncle, EDGAR (THE) AETHELING, deposed Donald Bane, King of Scotland. This victory established the dominance of the English language in Scotland. Edgar developed Edinburgh as his capital.

Edgar the Aetheling (*c.*1050–*c.*1130) Anglo-Saxon prince, grandson of EDMUND IRONSIDE. Heir-elect to the English throne after HAROLD's death at Hastings in 1066, he submitted to the Normans, but was later involved in several unsuccessful raids on England from Scotland and Flanders. *See also* HC1 p.166.

Edgar the Peaceable (943/4–75), King of the English from 959 when he succeeded his brother as King of Wessex. A promoter of ecclesiastical reform, he was also the first English king to be crowned at what is still the coronation service. *See also* HC1 p.*155*.

Edgehill, Battle of, first encounter of Parliamentarians and Royalists in the ENGLISH CIVIL WAR. It took place on 23 October 1642. Although the Royalists were outnumbered (11,000 men to the Parliamentarians' 13,000), the result was inconclusive. *See also* HC1 p.*289*.

Edgeworth, Maria (1767–1849), British novelist. She wrote *Practical Education* (1798) jointly with her father, Richard Lovell Edgeworth. Her novels, largely depicting Irish life, include *Castle Rackrent* (1800), *Belinda* (1801), *The Absentee* (1812) and *Ormond* (1817).

Edinburgh, capital city of Scotland, in Lothian Region, on the S shore of the Firth of Forth; Leith serves ts its port. The town grew steadily from the 11th century when Malcolm III made the castle his residence, despite being attacked by the English during the border wars. It became capital in 1437. JAMES IV was the first monarch to make Edinburgh his regular seat. After the Act of Union with England in 1707, Edinburgh retained the supreme courts of law. It flourished as a cultural centre in the 18th and 19th centuries around such figures as David HUME, Adam SMITH, Robert BURNS, and Sir Walter SCOTT. Places of interest include Holyrood palace, home of MARY QUEEN OF SCOTS, the Chapel of St Margaret, the city's oldest building, the home of Protestant reformer John KNOX, Princes Street and the castle. The University of Edinburgh was founded 1583. Industries: brewing, tourism, shipbuilding, chemicals, printing and publishing, and electrical engineering. Pop. 475,042. *See also* UNION, ACT OF (1707); HC2 pp.28–29, 284–285.

Edinburgh, Duke of. *See* PHILIP, PRINCE.

Edinburgh International Festival of Music and Drama (founded 1947), annual festival held in August-September in Edinburgh, Scotland. Rudolf BING was its first artistic director. It quickly became one of Europe's most highly regarded festivals. A variety of "fringe" activities (drama, art and film exhibitions) has added to its appeal. *See also* HC2 pp.284, *285*.

Edirne (Adrianople), fortified city in NW European Turkey, 209km (130 miles) WNW of Istanbul, at the confluence of the Meric and Tundzha rivers. Founded by Hadrian in *c.* AD 125, the city passed to the Ottoman Turks in 1361 and was their capital until 1453. Captured by the Russians in 1829 and again in 1879, the Bulgarians in 1913 and ceded to Greece in 1920, the city was returned to Turkey in 1923. It is an agricultural trading centre, and its industries include textiles and tanning. Pop. (1965) 46,091.

Edison, Thomas Alva (1847–1931), US inventor. Although he received little formal education, he made many important inventions, including the telegraph, the phonograph (1877), the first commercial electric light (1879), and many improvements to the electricity distribution system. He worked for the US government during WWI on anti-submarine weapons. He lost control of most of his companies which were merged into the General Electric Company in 1892. *See also* HC2 p.*153*; MM pp.226, *232*.

Edmonton, capital of Alberta, Canada, on the N Saskatchewan river. It is an industrial and commercial centre, with coalmining, natural gas and agriculture. Named after the original settlement Fort Edmonton, the town is also a railway centre. Pop. (1971) 434,116.

Edmund Ironside (*c.*993–1016), English king. After the death of his father, ETHELRED II the Unready, the rather unpopular Edmund was proclaimed king in 1016. Edmund won several victories over his former barons and the rival claimant, the Dane CANUTE, before Canute defeated him. The two divided England, but Edmund, then ruler only of Wessex, died a month later.

Edmund, St (*d.*869), King of East Anglia, canonized having allegedly been put to death by the Danes for refusing to give up his Christian faith.

Edmund of Abingdon, Saint (*c.*1175–1240), English churchman and scholar, also known as Edmund Rich. Renowned as a teacher at Oxford, he preached in favour of the Sixth Crusade (1227) and subsequently became Archbishop of Canterbury (1234–40). He opposed King Henry III's favouritism towards foreign counsellors and died on his way to Rome to state his case. He was canonized in 1247.

Edom, ancient kingdom of Palestine (12th century to 6th century BC) which was located astride the modern Jordan-Israel border, between the Dead Sea and the Gulf of Aqaba; it is sometimes called Idumea. Known for its iron and copper mines (Edom means "red earth"), it was supposed to have been originally settled by the descendants of ESAU.

Edred, or Eadred (*d.*955) English king. He was crowned in 946 and strove successfully against the Norsemen to take back Northumbria as part of England.

Education Acts, legislation on which the British education system is based. The most important Acts are those of 1870, 1902, 1918, 1944 and 1976. The 1870 Act established a system of compulsory and free elementary education. In 1902 education became the responsibility of local education authorities. The 1918 Act set the school-leaving age at 14. The Act of 1944 established free secondary education within a system of grammar and secondary modern schools. And finally the 1976 Act required local education authorities to provide secondary education in comprehensive schools, raising the school-leaving age to 16. *See also* HC2 pp.97, 225.

Educational psychology, branch of psychology that deals with the process of learning and the whole context in which this takes place – social, institutional and personal (including both teachers and pupils). It is generally taken to include attempts to measure intelligence and ability. *See also* MS pp.152–153.

Education and Science, Department of (DES), British government department responsible for the promotion of education and the fostering of civil science in England. It is headed by the Secretary of State for Education and Science and its specific functions are the broad allocation of capital resources for education, the provision and training of teachers and the setting of basic standards in education. The Department works in co-operation with local education authorities which administer the day-to-day running of schools, and with the University Grants Committee which administers the universities. The Department derives from the Board of Education and was set up as the Ministry of Education by the EDUCATION ACT of 1944.

Education sentimentale, L', novel (1869) by Gustave FLAUBERT. Dealing with the passion of a young man for an older woman, the work is largely autobiographical.

Edward I (1239–1307), King of England (*r.*1272–1307). He won influence and fame suppressing the baronial revolt of 1263–65 against his father, HENRY III, and on a crusade (1270–72). He carried out important administrative, judicial and financial reforms, and contributed greatly to the development of Parliament by summoning frequent sittings and including commoners in them. Edward conquered Wales and incorporated it into England (1275–84). Although he conquered Scotland in 1296, the remainder of his reign was occupied with further Scottish revolts. *See also* HC1 pp.179, 182–185, 210.

Edward II (1284–1327), King of England, (*r.*1307–27). Edward's weak rule and reliance on favourites alienated his barons, who increasingly took control of the government, especially after the Scots decisively defeated Edward at BANNOCKBURN in 1314. He regained control in 1322 only to rely on new favourites. He alienated his queen, ISABELLA, who became the mistress of the exiled baron Roger Mortimer. These two invaded England in 1326, deposed and murdered Edward, and crowned his son Edward III. *See also* HC1 p.179, *183*.

Edward III (1312–77), King of England (*r.*1327–77). He became involved in unsuccessful wars with Scotland at the start of his reign, and his claim to the French throne after 1328 led to the outbreak of the HUNDRED YEARS WAR in 1337. Edward led several campaigns to France during which he took part in the battle of CRÉCY and the siege of Calais in 1346–47.

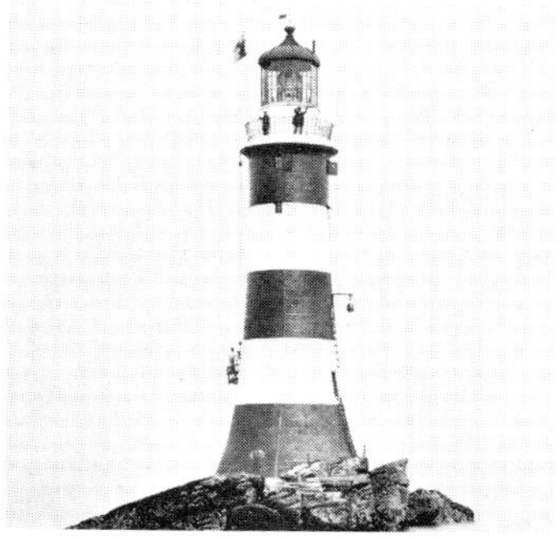

Eddystone Lighthouse: the fourth structure at its completion in 1882.

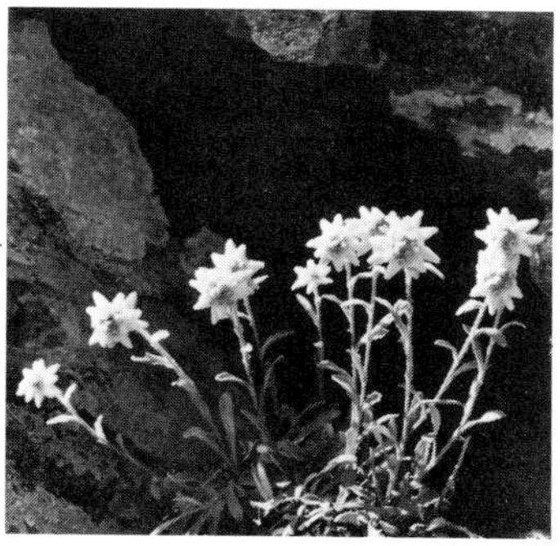

Edelweiss is an alpine plant that grows well in gardens under lowland conditions.

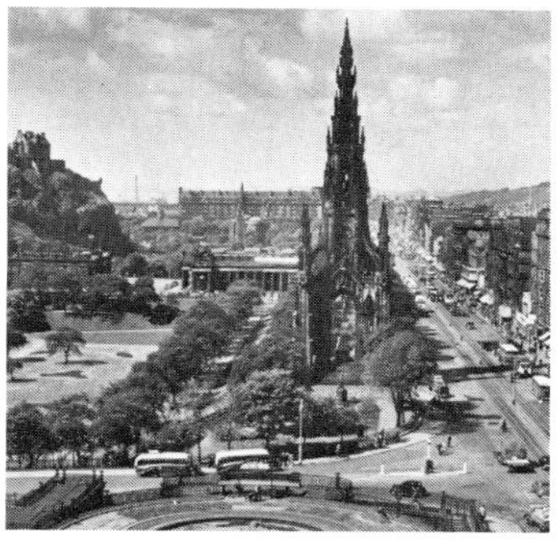

Edinburgh; a view of the city showing Princes Street and the Scott Memorial.

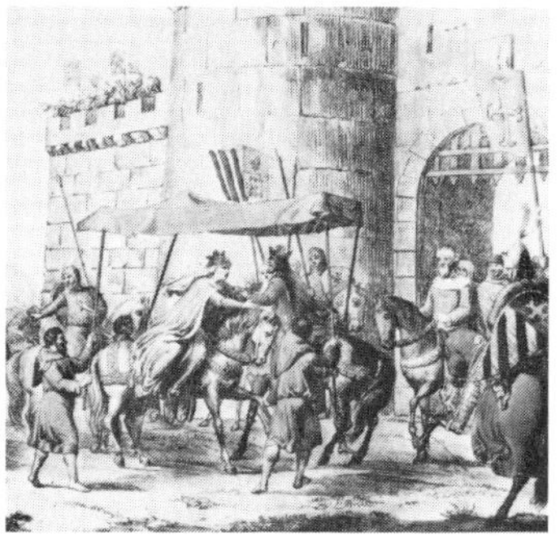

Edward I; a 19th-century lithograph of his first meeting his bride, Eleanor of Castile.

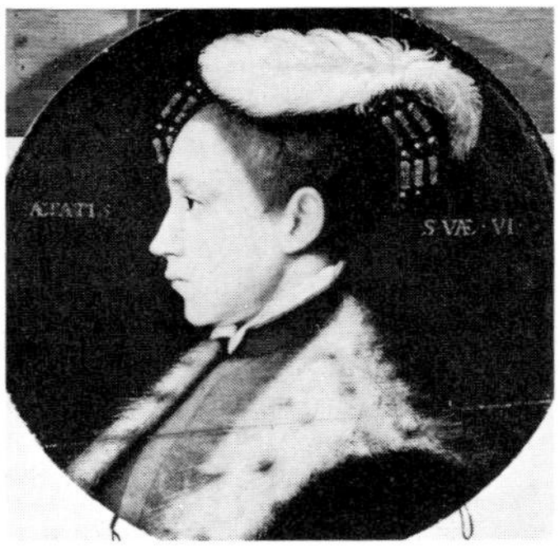
Edward VI, a Protestant, tried to exclude his Catholic sister, Mary, from the succession.

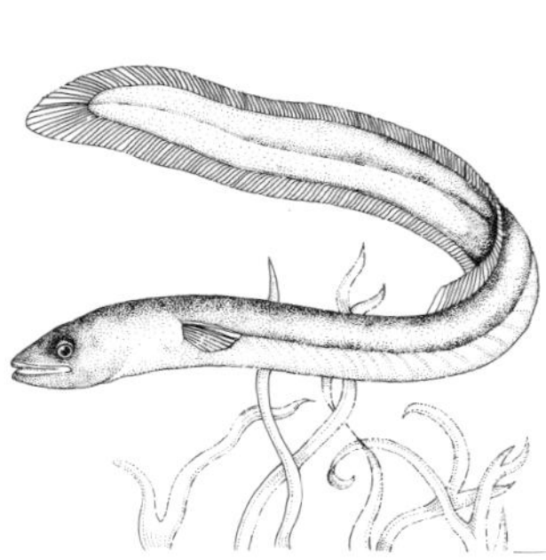
Eels are slippery and difficult to hold because of their copious covering of mucus.

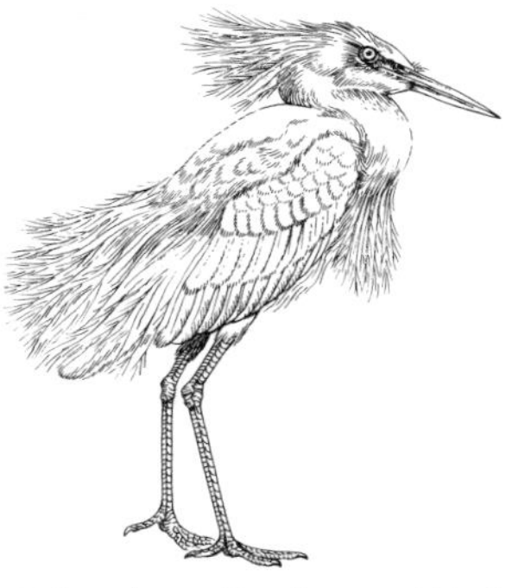
Egrets have long, silky plumes, which they employ in elaborate courtship rituals.

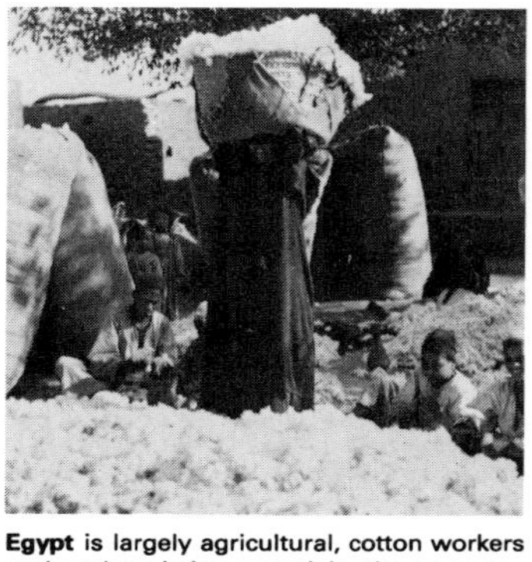
Egypt is largely agricultural, cotton workers such as these being essential to the economy.

At home, he rallied the nobility behind his wars; he increased the scope of Parliament to improve its administration; and he enacted legislation limiting the powers of the papacy in 1351–53. Towards the end of his reign he fell under the influence of his mistress Alice Perrers; government was increasingly in the hands of Edward's sons JOHN OF GAUNT and EDWARD THE BLACK PRINCE. *See also* HC1 pp.210–215.

Edward IV (1442–83), King of England (*r.* 1461–70; 1471–83), He became leader of the Yorkist faction in the WARS OF THE ROSES in 1460 and became king the following year after defeating the Lancastrians at the battle of Mortimer's Cross. He relied on the support of Warwick, who allied with the exiled Henry VI in 1470 and forced Edward himself into exile. Edward returned to defeat Warwick and Henry at Barnet in 1471, and kept his throne thereafter in relative peace. He was responsible for the reorganization of the Crown lands and attempted to build up the power of the Crown independently of the nobility. *See also* HC1 pp.242–243.

Edward V (1470–83), King of England. He succeeded his father, EDWARD IV, in April 1483. His uncle Richard, Duke of Gloucester, the regent, housed Edward and his younger brother in the Tower; the Lords and Commons proclaimed them illegitimate and crowned the duke RICHARD III. The two boys were probably murdered in August 1483 and have become known as "the Princes in the Tower". *See also* HC1 p.242.

Edward VI (1537–53), King of England, only legitimate son of HENRY VIII, who came to the throne aged only nine. His uncle the Duke of Somerset was his regent (1547–49), but after the display of popular dissatisfaction with his rule and religious policy shown in KET's rebellion of 1549, he was overthrown by the duke of Northumberland, who introduced a more fully Protestant policy. Edward died of tuberculosis at the age of 15. *See also* HC1 pp.270–271.

Edward VII, (1841–1910), King of Britain and Ireland (*r.* 1901–10). The eldest son of Queen VICTORIA, he was generally excluded from government affairs by his mother. He turned his energies to social life, travel and sport, and was involved in several scandals. As king he restored court pageantry and became popular. He attempted to maintain European peace through personal contacts between rulers and contributed particularly to the growth of the Anglo-French alliance. *See also* HC2 p.183.

Edward VIII (1894–1972), King of Britain and Ireland, subsequently Duke of Windsor. In WWI he served in the army. Soon after becoming king in 1936 he abdicated in order to marry an American divorcee. During WWII he was governor of the Bahamas. *See also* ABDICATION; HC2 p.225.

Edward of Woodstock. *See* BLACK PRINCE.

Edward, Prince Antony Richard Louis (1964–), third son and fourth child of Queen ELIZABETH II of Britain. He is third in line of succession to the British throne.

Edward the Black Prince (1330–76), outstanding English military commander, eldest son of EDWARD III. He distinguished himself in France at CRÉCY (1346) and led the English to victory at Poitiers (1356). He led several other expeditions in France, but as viceroy in Aquitaine (1362–71), he proved an unsuccessful ruler. In the 1370s he built up a faction against his brother JOHN OF GAUNT, but he died before he could ascend the throne.

Edward the Confessor (*c.* 1002–66), King of England (*r.* 1042–66). Edward was the half-Norman son of Ethelred II, and spent much of his life in Normandy before succeeding to the throne. He suffered a serious revolt from earl GODWIN in 1051–52. He also introduced many Normans to the English court and may have offered the throne to William of Normandy who later certainly claimed the offer had been made. He supervised the rebuilding of WESTMINSTER ABBEY. *See also* HC1 pp.166–167.

Edward the Elder (*d.* 925), King of Wessex (*r.* 899–925). He was son and successor to ALFRED THE GREAT and after his father's death was responsible for the reconquest of the DANELAW, in 920. He was considered overlord by the rulers of Northumbria and Wales. *See also* HC1 p.154.

Edward the Martyr (*d.* 978), King of England (*r.* 975–78). He was murdered, perhaps by his stepmother, after failing to establish control of his kingdom. After his death he was popularly regarded as a saint.

Edward (Idi Amin Dada), lake in central Africa, on the Zaire-Uganda border, connected to Lake Albert (Mobutusese Seko) by the River Semliki. It was discovered in 1889 by Henry STANLEY. Area: 2,150sq km (830sq miles).

Edwards, Duncan (1936–58), British footballer. A strongly built wing-half of prodigious talent, he played 18 times for England (1955–57) and twice won League honours (1956, 1957) with Manchester United. He and seven of the famous "Busby Babes" from the same team died in a plane crash at Munich airport in 1958.

Edwards, Gareth (1947–), Welsh rugby union scrum-half, at 20 the youngest captain of Wales. He later lost the captaincy but became Wales's most capped player, with 49 appearances (1967–77). A member of the Cardiff club, he toured South Africa (1968, 1974) and New Zealand (1971) with the British Lions.

Edwin, King of Northumbria (*r.* 616–33). Overlord of all the English kings of 626, he was converted to Christianity in 627, bringing Roman Christianity to Northumbria. He was killed in battle by Penda of Mercia.

Edwy (*d.* 959), King of Wessex (*r.* 955–59). He quarrelled with St DUNSTAN, who was subsequently exiled. He was succeeded by his younger brother Edgar.

EEC (European Economic Community), multinational economic and political organization dedicated to European development. Also known as the Common Market, its founder members were France, West Germany, Italy, Belgium, The Netherlands and Luxembourg; the UK, Irish Republic and Denmark joined in 1973. Established by the Treaty of Rome (1957), its general purpose is to create an economic union of common policies in areas such as agriculture, trade and employment and give Western Europe greater influence in world affairs through close political co-operation. *See also* HC2 p.259.

Eeckhout, Gerbrand van den (1621–74), Dutch painter, a close friend, pupil and imitator of REMBRANDT. At first he mostly painted portraits based closely on the style of Rembrandt, but later he broadened his repertoire to include genre subjects in the manner of G. TER BORCH.

Eel, marine and freshwater fish found worldwide in shallow temperate and tropical waters. Eels have snake-like bodies, dorsal and anal fins continuous with the tail, and an air bladder connected to the throat. Length: up to 3m (10ft). The various types include freshwater, moray, conger and snake eels. Order Anguilliformes. *See also* NW pp. *125–126*, 129, *130–131*, *233*, *240–241*.

Eel grass, or grass wrack, flowering plant that grows in shallow water and on mud flats. It has long, grass-like leaves and spikes of inconspicuous flowers. Family Potamogetonaceae; species *Zostera marina*. *See also* NW p.*234*.

Eelworm, tiny, thread-like NEMATODE found throughout the world in soil and fresh and salt water. Unlike the earthworm, it is not segmented. Most species are parasitic on plants or other animals.

EFL (English as a Foreign Language), teaching methods through which foreigners are taught English – different from teaching English to English people. In Britain English is taught widely in private schools for adults; methods vary between direct audiovisual; and conventional traditional grammar and translation.

EFTA (European Free Trade Association), multinational customs union established in 1959 in Stockholm. Comprised of Austria, Iceland, Norway, Portugal, Sweden and Switzerland, it seeks to promote free trade among its members. Competition has existed between the group and the EEC (European Economic Community) since both have essentially the same objectives, although the latter is more politically oriented. *See also* HC2 p.259/

Egan, Patrick (1841–1919), Irish nationalist and US politician. He was an active member of the Irish Land League, but emigrated to the USA in 1883 to avoid arrest. There he gained political prominence, first as a Republican and after 1896 as a Democrat.

Egbert (*d.* 839), King of Wessex, (*r.* 802–39), sometimes considered to be the first king of all England, after 828, when he defeated Beornwulf of Mercia. After 836 he had to defend his lands against the first Danish invasions.

Egg, Augustus (1816–63), British painter of social history subjects, whose popularity revived in the 20th-century fashion for Victoriana. Typical of his style is the series of three paintings *Present and Past* (1858).

Egg, or ovum, reproductive cell of female animals surrounded by protective jelly, ALBUMIN, shell, CHORION, egg case or MEMBRANE, depending upon the species. It supplies a reserve of food in the form of a yolk for the EMBRYO; its nucleus supplies half the chromosome complement of a future embryo; and supplies almost all the CYTOPLASM upon union with the SPERM. The amount of yolk in an egg depends on when the embryo actively begins to feed. Bird and insect eggs each have a large yolk, mammalian eggs a much smaller one. The life-span of a mature human egg is 12–24 hours; sea urchin eggs 40 hours; and those of most invertebrates, amphibians and fish, a few minutes. *See also* MS pp.*74–75*; NW p.*145*.

Eggplant. *See* AUBERGINE.

Eglantine, or sweetbrier, wild rose native to Europe. It has soft pink flowers, and its leaves and flowers have a spicy odour. Height: to 1.8m (6ft). Family Rosaceae; species *Rosa eglanteria*.

Egmond, Lamoraal, 4th Count of (1522–68), Flemish general and statesman. In the service of PHILIP II OF SPAIN he defeated the French at Saint-Quentin (1557) and Gravelines (1558). Although himself a Roman Catholic, he protested against the Spanish persecution of Protestants in the Low Countries. In 1565 he took his protest to the king of Spain, to no avail. The new Spanish governor of the Low Countries, the Duke of Alba, had Count Egmond and Count Hoorn arrested on false charges of treason in 1567 and publicly beheaded in 1568. This led to open revolt in the Low Countries.

Egmont, Mt, dormant volcano near New Plymouth, North Island, New Zealand. Height: 2,518m (8,260ft).

Ego, the self or the "I" which the individual consciously experiences. In psychoanalysis, according to Sigmund FREUD, it is that conscious level of the personality that deals with all the demands and difficulties of the external world, and also mediates the internal demands made by the impulses of the ID and by the SUPEREGO. There are many differing interpretations of the role, structure, development and disorders of the ego in the various schools of psychoanalysis. *See also* MS pp.161, 187.

Egret, white HERON of temperate and tropical marshy regions. It is known for its plumes, once popular for decorating hats. Egrets are long-legged, long-necked, slender-bodied wading birds with dagger-like bills. They feed on small animals and nest in colonies. Height: 50–100cm (20–40in). Family Ardeidae; genus *Egretta*.

Egypt, independent nation in NE Africa which also claims the Sinai Peninsula in SW Asia. Most of the working population is engaged in agriculture, cotton being the most valuable crop. Toll charges for the Suez Canal are still an important source of revenue, and tourism also provides a high income. Recently industrialization has increased and most industries are now nationalized. The capital is Cairo. Area: 1,001, 449sq km (386,659sq miles). Pop. (1976 est). 38,067,000. *See* MW pp. 66.

Egypt, ancient, civilization that emerged in the region of the Nile valley in the 4th millenium BC and continued until 30 BC, when the region was annexed to the Roman empire. The region comprised two separate kingdoms: Lower Egypt, in the Nile delta, with its capital at Heliopolis, and Upper Egypt, on the Nile N of the 2nd Cataract, with its capital at Thebes. The two kingdoms were united by Menes in *c.* 3100 BC. *See also* HC1 pp. 34–35, 48–49, 50–51.

Egyptian plover. *See* CROCODILE BIRD.

Egyptology, study of ancient Egypt, its people and, primarily, its antiquities. Mystery still surrounds the famous pyramids, tombs, temples, art and religion of the ancient Egyptians. Important landmarks in the exploration and understanding of Egypt include the discovery of the ROSETTA STONE and the tomb of TUTANKHAMEN; and the moving of the temple at ABU-SIMBEL.

Ehrenburg, Christian Gottfried (1795–1876), German biologist and founder of the science of micro-palaeontology. Ehrenburg studied at Berlin University and travelled widely as a naturalist, identifying and classifying many terrestrial and marine plants and micro-organisms. He advanced the theory of "complete organisms", stating that all animals – even microscopic infusoria – have complete organ systems; it was later refuted.

Ehrenburg, Ilya (Grigoryevich) (1891–1967), Soviet novelist and journalist. He lived in Western Europe (1908–17, 1921–40) working as a journalist for several Russian newspapers. His novels, introducing Western European trends into Soviet literature, include the satiric *Julio Jurenito* (1919), *The Storm* (1948), and *The Thaw* (1954). *See also* THAW, THE.

Ehrenstahl, David Kloker (1629–98), German born Swedish painter. His work, which includes allegorical portraits, still-lifes and landscapes won him the title "father of Swedish painting".

Ehrlich, Paul (1854–1915), German bacteriologist. He shared with E. METCHNIKOFF the 1908 Nobel prize in physiology and medicine for his work on immunization, which included the development of basic standards and methods for studying toxins and antitoxins, with special reference to diphtheria antitoxins. His subsequent search for a "magic bullet" against disease and his discovery of SALVARSAN, a chemical effective against syphilis micro-organisms, introduced the modern era of chemotherapy (a term he coined). *See also* MS p.120.

Eichendorff, Joseph Freiherr von (1788–1857), German novelist and lyric poet. Among the greatest of German Romantic poets, his works inspired many composers. His main prose work is *Memoirs of a Good-for-Nothing* (1826).

Eichler, August Wilhelm (1839–87), German botanist who developed a system of plant classification eventually accepted worldwide. It included division of plants into four major classes. He helped to edit some 15 volumes on the flora of Brazil and published a 2-volume study of the comparative structure of flowers.

Eichmann, Adolf (1906–62), Austrian Nazi, head of subsection IV-B-4 of the Reich Central Security Office in WWII. He supervised fulfilment of the Nazi policies of deportation, slave labour, and mass murder in the concentration camps, which led to the death of some 6,000,000 Jews during the war. He escaped to Argentina in 1945, but was abducted by Israelis in 1960, tried and executed in Israel.

Eider, large sea DUCK found in northern regions of Europe and North America. Its down is used as a filling for pillows and quilts. In the breeding season the male grows striking black and white plumage. Family Anatidae; genus *Somateria.*

Eidetic imagery. *See* PHOTOGRAPHIC MEMORY.

Eiffel, Alexandre-Gustave (1832–1923), French engineer who established metal as an architectural material. His EIFFEL TOWER was the world's tallest structure until 1930.

Eiffel Tower, landmark built for the Paris *exposition* of 1889. Designed by Alexandre-Gustave EIFFEL, the tower rises 300m (984ft) and has an iron frame. Lifts and stairs lead to observation platforms, and at the top is a TV transmitter. *See also* HC2 p.178.

Eigen, Manfred (1927–), German chemist who shared the 1967 Nobel Prize in chemistry with R. G. W. NORRISH and G. PORTER. The techniques devised by Eigen is to disturb the balance by a chemical reaction near equilibrium and make measurements of colours emitted as the system relaxes into a new equilibrium state. These techniques have been used in the study of RADIATION chemistry, and in reactions that use ENZYMES as CATALYSTS.

Eiger, mountain peak in W central Switzerland, in the Bernese Alps, approx. 16km (10 miles) SE of Interlaken. Height 3,975m (13,040ft).

Eigg, island of NW Scotland, one of the Inner Hebrides, S of Skye, W of Morar; Mallaig is the largest mainland port nearby. Area: 20sq km (12sq miles). Pop. (1974 est.) 70.

Eight, The, group of US painters formed in 1907 to protest against the policies of the National Academy of Design. The group had little coherence but several members later established the ASHCAN SCHOOL who, in 1913, organized the ARMORY SHOW in New York. This introduced modern European art to America, shocking audiences and critics.

Eight Masters of T'ang and Sung, The, term traditionally used in Chinese schools for eight outstanding prose writers during the T'ANG (618–907) and SUNG (960–1279) dynasties. During the T'ang, Han Yü (768–824) and Liu Tsung-yüan (773–819) instituted a return to the simpler style of several centuries earlier. The six other masters furthered this reform during the Sung. They were: Ou-yang Hsiu, Wang An-shih, Su Shih, Su Hsün, Su Chê and Tsêng Kung.

Eijkman, Christian (1858–1930), Dutch medical researcher and physician. In 1929 he shared with F.G. HOPKINS the Nobel Prize in physiology and medicine for his discovery of the antineuritic vitamin. Eijkman was the first to recognize a dietary deficiency disease, demonstrating that BERIBERI was produced by a lack of a certain dietary substance, later identified as vitamin B_1. *See also* MS pp.84–85.

Eindhoven, city in S Netherlands, on the Dommel River, approx. 88km (55 miles) SE of Rotterdam. The city developed into an industrial centre after 1891 when the Philips Electrical Company was founded there. Industries: radio, electrical equipment, textiles. Pop. (1974) 191, 942.

Einhard (770–840), historian of the medieval Frankish empire. Born in Germany, Einhard was educated in Fulda, and later became an important scholar and diplomat at the court of CHARLEMAGNE. He is best known as author of the *Life of Charlemagne* (*Vita Caroli Magni*)

Einstein, Albert (1879–1955), German-American physicist, *b.* Germany. He published three important theoretical papers; the first contained a mathematical analysis of BROWNIAN MOVEMENT: the second concerned the application of QUANTUM THEORY to photoelectricity, for which he was awarded the Nobel Prize for physics in 1921; and the third contained the first publication of the Special Theory of RELATIVITY – a paper that completely revolutionized physics and led, through its equation of mass and energy, to the discovery of the atomic bomb. In 1916 Einstein produced his General Theory of Relativity, but died before completing his work on a unified field theory. Being a Jew, he left Germany when Hitler came to power, spending the rest of his life in the USA, becoming a US citizen in 1940. *See also* SU p.106, *106.*

Einsteinium, radioactive metallic element (symbol Es) of the ACTINIDES, first identified in 1952 as a decay product of U^{238} produced in the first large hydrogen-bomb explosion. Properties: at.no. 99; most stable isotope Es^{254} (half-life 276 days). *See also* TRANSURANIC ELEMENTS.

Einthoven, Willem (1860–1927), Dutch physiologist. He became professor at Leiden University in 1886 and was awarded the 1924 Nobel prize in physiology and medicine for his work on the string galvanometer, the mechanism for the ELECTROCARDIOGRAM.

Eire. *See* IRELAND.

Eisenhower, Dwight David (1890–1969), 34th US president (1953–61). A professional soldier, he commanded the invasion of N Africa (1942) and the victorious Allied offensive in Europe (1944) to become a national hero. He was later appointed US army chief of staff, then NATO commander. As president he shared Harry S. Truman's global view of US responsibilities, often clashed with Russian leaders and presided over rising affluence at home. He used troops to force school integration in Arkansas and although he was humiliated by the U-2 INCIDENT (1960) and bequeathed the abortive BAY OF PIGS invasion of Cuba (1961) to his successor, he left office one of the most popular of all presidents. *See also* HC2 pp.229–264, 306.

Eisenstein, Sergei (1898–1948), Soviet film director, technical innovator and theorist. Although he completed just six films in 25 years (he frequently clashed with disapproving authorities), he remains one of the most influential artists in the history of film-making. He developed a strong intellectual and aesthetic style, enhanced by the incisive use of creative editing for narrative and expressive effect. His films are *Strike* (1924), *The* BATTLESHIP POTEMKIN (1925), *October* (or *Ten Days That Shook the World,* 1928), *The General Line* (or *Old and New,* 1929), *Que Viva Mexico* (unfinished, 1932), *Alexander Nevsky* (1938) and *Ivan the Terrible* (two of three parts completed, 1944–46). His translated writings include *The Film Sense* (1942) and *Film Form* (1949). *See also* MONTAGE; HC2 p.201.

Eisteddfod, Welsh music and poetry competition held annually. Dating from the 7th century, eisteddfodau were revived in the 19th and have become important in preserving the Welsh language and cultural traditions. International eisteddfodau are popular tourist attractions and are not restricted to Welsh participants.

Eitoku, Kano (1543–90), Japanese painter. Probably trained by his grandfather Motonobu, he is best known for his decorative works of gigantic forms painted on gold-leaf backgrounds. The rulers Nobunaga and Hideyoshi were among his patrons.

Ejaculation, in biology, the sudden emission or spouting of fluid or seed from either the animal or vegetable system.

Ejector seat, device for escaping from an aircraft in an emergency. In order to PARACHUTE successfully from high-speed aircraft it is necessary to blow the seat and the pilot clear of the fuselage and tail section with an explosive charge. In hypersonic craft the pilot can be protected by separating the entire cockpit from the fuselage and parachuting the capsule and occupant together to the ground.

Ekaterinburg, city in the Russian Republic (Rossijskaja SFSR) in the E foothills of the Urals. In 1918 the Russian royal family was imprisoned and executed there. Renamed Sverdlovsk in 1924, it is now a leading producer of machinery. Other industries include gem cutting and metallurgy. Pop. (1970) 1,026,000.

El, supreme god of the western Semites in ancient times, depicted by the Phoenicians as an elderly figure with a long beard. An all-encompassing nature deity with patriarchal authority over all the gods, he was the husband of Asherah and father of MARDUK; the Romans identified him with Chronos. By the time of the RAS SHAMRA texts, El had become the all-wise, all-just Creator.

Elahi, Chaudhri Fazal (1904–), President of Pakistan from 1973. He became a lawyer in 1929 and joined the Punjab government (1947–56). He was a member of the National Assembly from 1962, becoming Deputy Speaker (1965) and Speaker (1971). He succeeded President Bhutto.

El Alamein (Al-'Alamayn), village in N Egypt, 104km (65 miles) W of Alexandria.

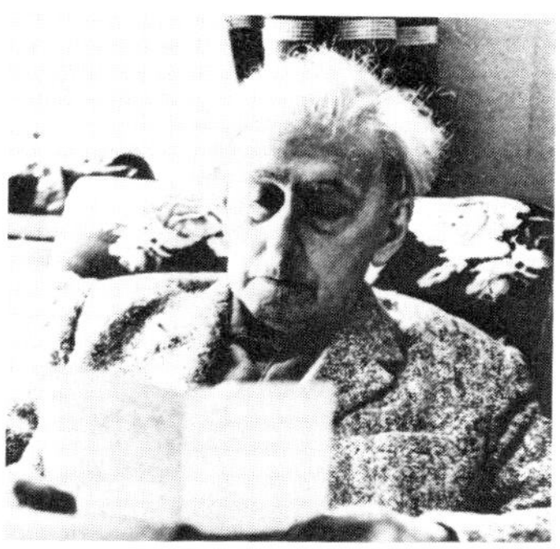

Ilya Ehrenburg, a Soviet writer who was among the first to criticize Stalin's regime.

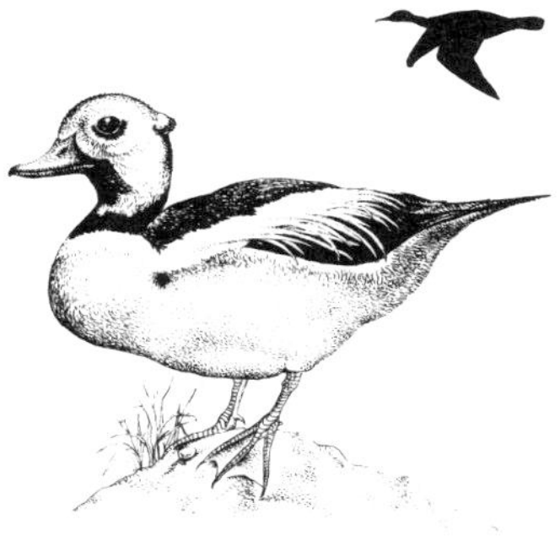

Eider; the female lays four to six eggs and covers them with down during incubation.

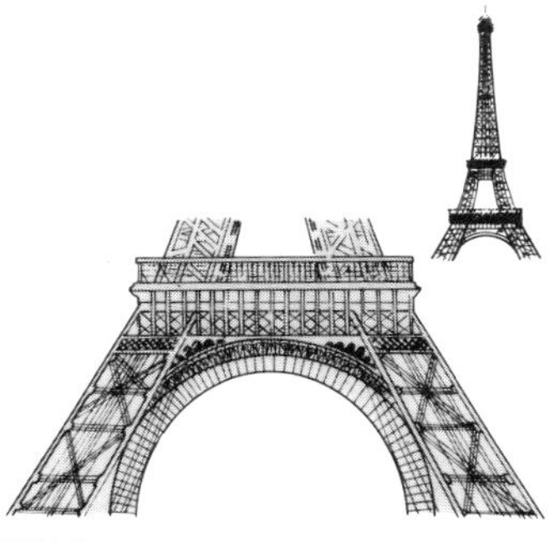

Eiffel Tower, once the world's highest structure, was an observation post during WWI.

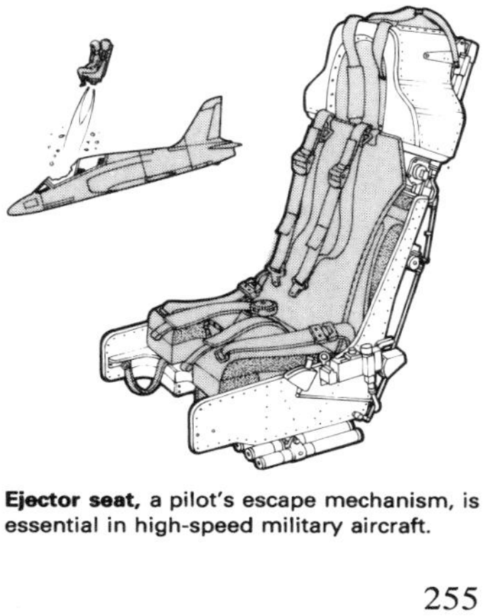

Ejector seat, a pilot's escape mechanism, is essential in high-speed military aircraft.

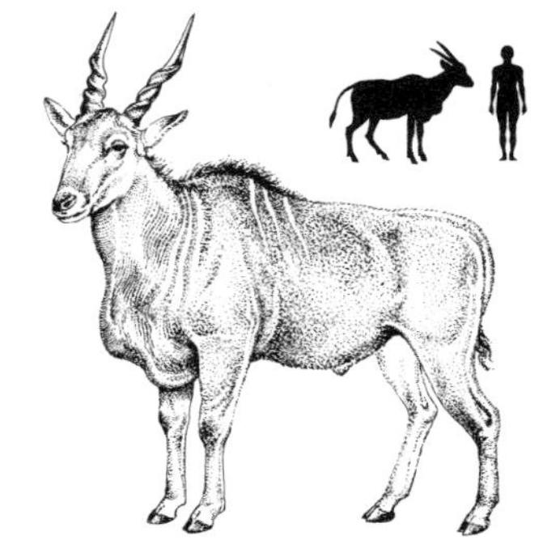

Elands browse in herds of up to 200 and can live for weeks without water during droughts.

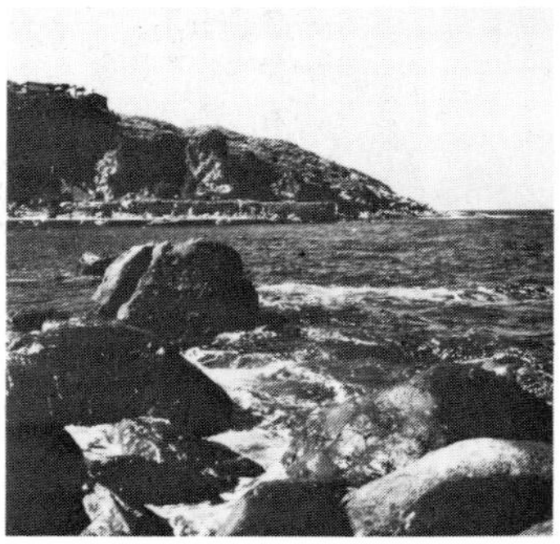

Elba, an Italian island of mild climate, supports rich olive groves and vineyards.

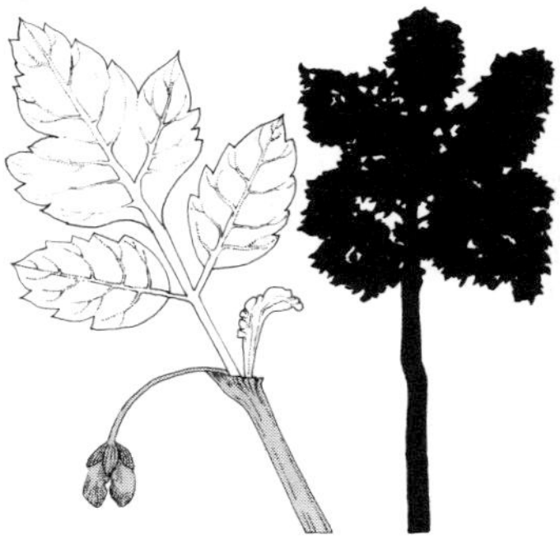

Eder; from the stem of which the Greeks made a musical instrument called a *sambuke.*

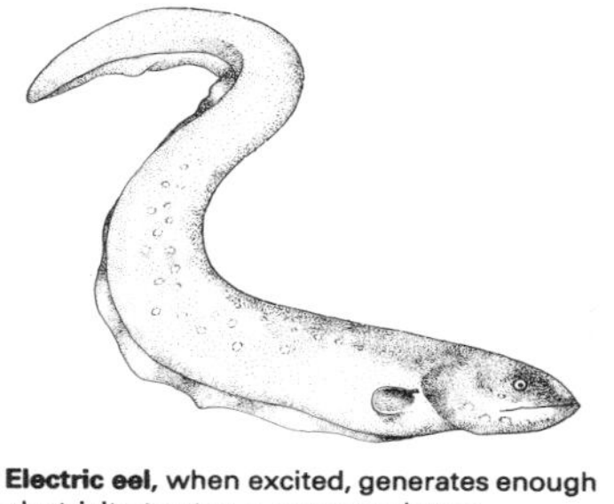

Electric eel, when excited, generates enough electricity to stun a man or a horse.

Gen. Bernard MONTGOMERY successfully attacked AXIS forces there and eventually drove them back to Tunisia, frustrating Axis efforts to take Egypt. *See also* HC2 pp.*228*, 229, 231, *231.*

Elam, ancient country of Mesopotamia, with its capital at SUSA. The Elamite civilization emerged around the 4th millennium BC, but did not attain prominence until *c.* 2000 BC when the Elamites took BABYLON. Their civilisation flourished until the 7th century BC, when it succumbed to ASHURBANIPAL the Assyrain king. The Elamites were racially and culturally independent from most of the other peoples of Mesopotamia, but they adopted cuneiform characters. *See also* HC1 pp.32–33.

Eland, largest living ANTELOPE, native to central and southern Africa. Gregarious and slow-moving, elands are nevertheless good jumpers. Both sexes carry heavy, spiralled horns. Height: up to 1.8m (5.8ft) at the shoulder; weight: up to 900kg (1,984lb). Family Bovidae.

Elasmobranch. *See* CHONDRICHTHYES.

Elastic materials. *See* ELASTOMERS.

Elasticity, capability of a strained material to recover its size and shape after deformation. STRAIN is determined by molecular structure. When external force (STRESS) is applied, molecular spacing changes. Stress is proportional to strain within the elastic limit, which depends on the material's composition. The ratio of stress to strain is a material's YOUNG'S MODULUS. *See also* HOOKE'S LAW.

Elastomer, substance that regains its original size and shape after being deformed. Elastomers include natural RUBBER and various synthetic materials with similar properties. All are polymers in which the molecular chains are folded; stretching the elastomer straightens the chains. *See also* MM p.23, 54.

Elat, seaport town in S Israel, on the Gulf of AQABA. It is the site of a pipeline terminal sending oil to the Haifa refinery. Industries: fishing, tourism. Pop. 14,600.

Elâziğ (Kharput), town in E Turkey, capital of Elâziğ province. It is bounded by the Murat, Peri and Euphrates rivers. Industries include copper mining and hydroelectric power. Pop. (1973) 127,003.

Elba (Isola d'Elba), Italian island in the Tyrrhenian Sea; largest of the Tuscan Archipelago. The chief port and town is Portoferraio, on the N coast. The island is mountainous, and is a major supplier of Italy's iron ore, which has been mined since Etruscan and Roman times. NAPOLEON I was exiled there (1814–15). Industries: fisheries, wine, tourism, Area: 223sq km (86sq miles). Pop. 27,500.

Elbe, river in central Europe. It rises as the Labe on the slopes of the Riesengebirge, NW Czechoslovakia, flows through Czechoslovakia, East and West Germany, entering the North Sea at Cuxhaven. In 1945 the river was made part of the demarcation line between East and West Germany. Length: 1,167km (725 miles).

Elberfeld. *See* WUPPERTAL.

Elbrus, Mt (Gora El'Brus), two peaks in the Caucasus Mts, SW USSR, formed by two extinct volcanoes. The W peak is the highest in Europe, 5,633m (18,481ft). The E peak is 5,595m (18,356ft) high.

Elburz Mts (Alborz or Reshteh-ye Kūhhā-ye Aeborz), narrow mountain range in N Iran, along the S coast of the Caspian Sea, separating the dry inland plateau from the agriculturally rich coastal lowlands. The range includes Mt Damāvand, the highest peak in Iran, rising to 5,771m (8,934ft). Length: 900km (560 miles).

El Cid. *See* CID, RODRIGO DIAZ DE BIVAR.

Elder, in the Bible, man of authority among any of the twelve tribes of Israel, not specifically of religious importance, but with a voice in the tribal council. The New Testament "elders" of the early Christian Church were later known as PRESBYTERS or priests.

Elder, shrub and small tree found worldwide in temperate and subtropical areas. They have divided leaves and clusters of tiny white flowers. Their small berries are eaten by wildlife; they are also used in making wine, jellies and medicine. The common European elderberry shrub (*Sambucus nigra*) has coarse-toothed leaflets, white flower clusters and purple berries; height: 4m (13ft). There are 40 species. Family Caprifoliaceae. *See also* NW p.*64.*

Eldjárn, Kristján (1916–), Icelandic statesman and archaeologist. He was curator of the National Museum of Iceland (1947–68) and was elected president of Iceland (1968–).

Eldon, John Scott, 1st Earl of (1751–1838) British jurist. He was solicitor-general (1788–93), attorney-general (1793–99), chief justice of Court of Common Pleas (1799–1801) and chancellor (1801–27). He encouraged action to crush radical movements.

El Dorado, mythical city of fabulous wealth, supposedly located in the interior of South America, the focus of many Spanish expeditions in the 16th century. The name (meaning "The Gilded" or "The Golden One") also refers to a legendary South American king who daily powdered himself all over with gold dust.

Eleanor crosses. *See* ELEANOR OF CASTILE.

Eleanor of Aquitaine (*c.*1122–1204), Queen consort of France, and later of England. She married LOUIS VII of France, and accompanied him on the Second Crusade (1147–49). She was divorced in 1152 and married Henry, Duke of Normandy (later Henry II of England), and was the mother of Richard I and John.

Eleanor of Castile (*c.*1246–90), Queen consort of England. She married EDWARD I in 1254 and gave him her half-brother's claim to Gascony. Edward made crosses to mark her funeral progress from Nottingham to London, and gave her a fine tomb in WESTMINSTER ABBEY.

Eleanor of Provence (*c.*1223–91), Queen consort of England who married Henry III in 1236, and was a great influence on him. Her French relatives and courtiers were unpopular at the English court. She returned to a convent in 1286.

Eleaticism, teachings of the Eleatic school of Greek philosophy. Founded in the 5th century BC by PARMENIDES and including ZENO OF ELEA, the school taught that absolute reality is immobile, immutable and indivisible. Change in the world, which is perceived by the senses, is only apparent; reason alone knows the real essence.

Elecampane, stout, hardy perennial of the Compositae family, native to Eurasia and now common in many other parts of the world. It has a few large, yellow, daisy-like flowers, hairy stems and aromatic leaves and root. Height: up to 1.2m (4ft). Species *Inula helenium.*

Election, a process of choosing candidates for political office. There are usually two stages: a party's candidate is chosen by local constituency party members; registered electors in the constituency then choose between the various party candidates by secret ballot. Depending on the system, voters may make only one choice (as in Britain) or rank the candidates in order of preference (as in Australia). Age, race and residency qualifications, set by law, govern a person's eligibility to vote; candidates must also meet certain requirements. The maximum period between elections is determined by law or the constitution. In the USA important judicial officers in some states are elected to office. In Totalitarian countries, elections are simply between candidates of the only permitted party. *See also* MS p.276.

Electoral College, the body of US electors who, chosen by the electorates of the states, cast the votes which actually elect the president and vice-president of the USA. The system was devised in 1787 because the size of the country made it difficult for voters to know the candidates for national office. They therefore elected local men to choose them for them. Despite modern communications the college has survived.

Electors, in the Holy Roman Empire, German princes (usually seven) who chose the king of Germany and the emperor. The practice arose in the 13th century as the succession was often disputed. *See also* HC1 pp.160–161.

Electra (*c.*418–414 BC), tragedy by SOPHOCLES. The heroine, Electra, helps her brother Orestes avenge their father Agamemnon's death by plotting to kill their mother Clytemnestra and stepfather Aegisthus. There is controversy about the historical and literary origins of this play. EURIPIDES wrote a similar play with the same title in 413 BC.

Electrical branch circuit, any electrical circuit that is an interconnected branch of the main circuit where Kirchhoff's network laws apply. These state that at any branch junction the sum of the currents flowing to that point is equal to the sum of the currents flowing away.

Electrical capacity. *See* CAPACITANCE, ELECTRICAL.

Electrical circuit, path provided for an electric current, composed of conducting devices and including a source of ELECTROMOTIVE FORCE that drives the current. Current flows according to several definite laws, the most important is OHM'S LAW. *See also* SU pp.54, 59.

Electrical engineering, branch of ENGINEERING that deals with the practical application of ELECTRICITY, especially as related to illumination, communication, COMPUTERS and automatic control of machinery. Electrical engineers are fully trained in the mathematics of electrical circuits and are involved in research, development, design, production, supervision and improvement of production methods. *See also* MM pp.70–71, 109.

Electrical panel box, wall-mounted junction for all the main and branch CIRCUITS of a house. Within it are usually terminals from the main power source and switches to all the outlets, along with the corresponding fuses or CIRCUIT BREAKERS.

Electrical switch, any device used to stop and restart the flow of CURRENT within an electrical CIRCUIT. The basic principle always involves an interruption and restarting of the conducting medium, usually the wiring. *See also* MM p.32; SU p.54.

Electric arc furnace. *See* ELECTRIC FURNACE.

Electric cars, vehicles powered by electricity supplied by storage batteries. Displaced by cars with petrol engines after the 1920s, they caused interest again during the fuel shortage of the 1970s. They are still considered impractical, however, because of their relatively short travelling distances between recharges and their low speeds. *See also* MM pp.132–133.

Electric chair, device used in CAPITAL PUNISHMENT. The prisoner is strapped into the chair and electrodes are fastened to the crown of his head, and one leg; through these is transmitted a high voltage shock. The electric chair was first used in New York in 1890.

Electric current, flow of ELECTRONS in a material, most familiarly in a metal wire. The current in a circuit was thought to flow from positive to negative, or from live to neutral; this convention is still used, but because electrons are negatively charged, the flow is really in the opposite direction. Electric current is measured in AMPERES, one ampere being the passage through the medium of 6.25×10^{18} electrons per second.

Electric eel, fresh-water tropical fish found in South America. It is not a true eel. Its ribbon-like body is dark-brown to black and is bordered by an anal fin extending along its underside. Air is breathed at the waters surface. Electric organs make up 80 per cent of its body and produce charges of up to 600 volts. Length: 2.9m (9.5ft). Family Electrophoridae (also called Gymnotidae); species *Electrophorus electricus. See also* NW pp.129, *233.*

Electric, or electrostatic, field, region surrounding an electric charge in which a force would be experienced by another charged particle. The force is attractive if the charges differ in polarity and repulsive if they are the same. The strength of the field due to charge Q at a distance r is equal to $Q/4\pi\varepsilon_0 r^2$ where ε_0 is the permittivity of free space. The force that a charge q experiences in an electric field of strength E is equal to qE. *See also* SU pp.112–113.

Electric fish, several unrelated species of cartilaginous and bony fish that possess electric organs capable of producing abnormally high voltages. These can be used for attack, defence or navigation by ECHO-LOCATION. The ELECTRIC EEL (*Electrophorus electricus*) can deliver one or two amperes at about 600 volts, which could be enough to disable or even kill, a man. *See also* PE pp.129, *129, 133.*

Electric flux, quantity of electricity displaced across an area in a DIELECTRIC medium, expressed as the product of the area and the component of the electric vector at right-angles to the area. *See also* GAUSS' LAW.

Electric furnace, enclosure heated by ELECTRIC CURRENT. Electric furnaces are used for melting and producing metals such as alloy steels and refractory materials. Three main methods of heating are used: striking an arc between electrodes in the furnace; inducing EDDY CURRENTS in the material to be melted using an alternating magnetic field; and by passing a high current through the material, heat being produced by its resistance. An electric arc furnace is used for very high temperatures. *See also* MM p.31.

Electric guitar, six or twelve-stringed instrument whose sounds are produced electronically. Electric guitars differ from acoustic guitars in having one or more electromagnetic devices (pickups) which generate a signal when the strings above them are plucked. The signal is then amplified and played through a loudspeaker. Electric guitars are widely used by pop groups.

Electricity, form of energy associated with static or moving CHARGES. Charge has two forms; positive and negative. Like charges repel each other and unlike attract; these forces are described by COULOMB'S LAW. Electric charges are acted upon by forces when they move in a MAGNETIC FIELD and this movement in turn generates an opposing magnetic field (Faraday's laws). Electricity and MAGNETISM are different aspects of the same phenomenon, ELECTROMAGNETISM. The flow of charges constitutes a CURRENT, which consists of negatively charged ELECTRONS travelling through a CONDUCTOR. For a current to exist in a conductor there must be an ELECTROMOTIVE FORCE (EMF) or POTENTIAL DIFFERENCE between the ends of the conductor. If the source of potential difference is a battery the current flows in one direction only (direct current, DC), whereas if the source is the mains the current changes direction twice every cycle (alternating current, AC). The AMPERE is the unit of current, the COULOMB is the unit of charge, the OHM the unit of RESISTANCE and the VOLT is the unit of electromotive force. OHM'S LAW and KIRCHHOFF'S LAWS (the summing of voltages and currents in a circuit) are the basic means of calculating circuit values. *See also* SU 112–115, 124–127.

Electricity sources, supplies of energy that are converted into electricity. Most of our electricity comes from the chemical energy of fossil fuels – coal, oil and natural gas. A small proportion is converted from the nuclear energy of atoms. Chemical batteries and FUEL CELLS convert chemical energy into electricity directly. SOLAR CELLS convert the heat and light of the Sun's rays into electricity. *See also* ENERGY SOURCES; MM pp.66–67, 70–75.

Electricity supply. *See* NATIONAL GRID.

Electric light, artificial light produced by the flow of ELECTRONS in a wire or gas. Incandescent light, produced when a filament, such as tungsten-alloy wire, is heated, is richer in red light than is light from the Sun. In a fluorescent tube or vapour lamp, the electric current is carried by ions, electrically charged atoms, which also emit light.

Electric motor, electric rotating machine that converts electrical energy into mechanical energy by the interaction of a MAGNETIC FIELD with an ELECTRIC FIELD. Electric motors are convenient and comparatively quiet, and have replaced many other forms of motive power. They may use alternating current (AC) or direct current (DC). The stationary part of the motor is called the stator, and the moving assembly of wire loops is known as the rotor or armature. *See* SU p.122.

Electric ray, or torpedo, flatfish related to the SKATE, found in all tropical and temperate seas. Electric rays stun their prey with electrical charges of up to 200 volts produced by two large electric organs located on either side of the head. Family Torpedinidae; there are about 30 species. *See also* ELECTRIC EEL; ELECTRIC FISH; NW p.129.

Electric shock, passage of high voltage electricity through the body, resulting in muscular spasms which can cause injuries such as broken bones and which may prevent an electrocuted person from letting go of a live wire accidentally grasped. Other injuries to the body can include severe burns at the points of contact, brain concussion and stoppage of the heart and breathing. Electric shock may be fatal unless treated immediately. For first aid treatment, *see* MS p.132.

Electric storm. *See also* LIGHTNING, THUNDERSTORM; PE p.69; SU p.112.

Electric unit, standard quantity in which electricity is measured. The domestic unit of electricity is the kilowatt hour. A fire rated at 1 kilowatt (1,000 watts) consumes 1 unit of electricity when it is switched on for 1 hour. A WATT is the power developed in a circuit when one AMPERE of electricity flows across a POTENTIAL DIFFERENCE of one VOLT.

Electrocardiogram, or ECG, amplified recording of small voltage changes occurring in the heart made with an instrument called an electrocardiograph. It is used for measuring stress to the heart, and monitoring cardiovascular diseases. *See also* SU p.*113.*

Electrochemical analysis, analytical techniques used by chemists in which ELECTROLYSIS of a solution is used to precipitate solids or release gases, the quantities of which correspond exactly to the amounts of electricity passed through the solutions. *See also* ELECTROCHEMICAL EQUIVALENT.

Electrochemical equivalent, amount of any substance that is precipitated or consumed when 96,500 coulombs of electricity is passed during ELECTROLYSIS of a solution of the substance. This amount of electricity equals one FARADAY, named after its discoverer.

Electrochemical series, list of the metallic elements in order of their reactivity. The more reactive, such as sodium, occur near the top of the table, and the less reactive, such as gold, occur lower down. The gas hydrogen frequently behaves chemically as a metal and is placed in the table as a reference: metals that are more electropositive than hydrogen will displace it from its solutions; less electropositive metals will not.

Electrochemistry, branch of physical chemistry concerned with ELECTROLYTES. It includes such topics as certain properties and reactions of IONS in solution, the CONDUCTIVITY of electrolytes and the study of the processes occurring in electrochemical cells and in ELECTROLYSIS. *See also* SU p.148.

Electroconvulsive therapy. *See* ECT.

Electrocution, in CAPITAL PUNISHMENT, the infliction of the death penalty by passing high voltage electricity under controlled conditions through the body. Accidental electrocution can be fatal, depending on the voltage. An ELECTRIC SHOCK tends to be more severe if the victim is in contact with water. For first aid treatment, *See* MS p.132. *See also* ELECTRIC CHAIR.

Electrode, conductor through which an electric current flows into or leaves a medium. In ELECTROLYSIS, two electrodes – a positive (ANODE) and a negative (CATHODE) – are immersed in a liquid (ELECTROLYTE). In an electric arc furnace, arcing between two electrodes heats up the surrounding gas space. *See also* SU p.149.

Electrodeposition, deposition of an adhering metallic coating onto an ELECTRODE by passing a direct-current (DC) low-voltage electric current through an ELECTROLYTE. Its most common application is ELECTROPLATING. Zinc, nickel and chromium plate prevent corrosion on cars and household appliances; silver protects tableware; copper prevents case-hardening in steel. In this case the object to be coated is the electrode. *See also* ANODIZING.

Electrode potential, measure of the tendency of a reaction at an ELECTRODE. An electrode of an element (M) placed in a solution of its ions (M^+) constitutes a half-cell. In general a POTENTIAL DIFFERENCE exists between the electrode and the solution, caused by reactions of the type $M \rightleftharpoons M^+ + e$. In practice it cannot be measured absolutely and standard electrode potentials are defined with reference to a hydrogen electrode under specified conditions of concentration, temperature and pressure. Such reactions are oxidations, and so the term OXIDATION POTENTIAL is often also used. *See also* ELECTROCHEMICAL SERIES.

Electrodialysis. *See* DIALYSIS.

Electrodynamics, in physics, study of moving electric currents and the relations between electric and magnetic fields. It began in the 19th century with the theoretical work of James Clerk MAXWELL, and later became part of QUANTUM MECHANICS.

Electroencephalogram. *See* ELECTROENCEPHALOGRAPHY.

Electroencephalography, study of the electrical activity of the brain. Electrodes are attached to the scalp to pick up the tiny oscillating currents produced by brain activity. The brainwaves are recorded as a continuous trace on a paper strip called an electroencephalogram (EEG). The instrument is used in brain research and in the diagnosis of EPILEPSY and other brain disorders. *See also* ELECTROCARDIOGRAM; MS pp. 194–195.

Electroforming, making of metal articles by deposition of the metal in a mould by ELECTROLYSIS. A notable application is the manufacture of metal negative replica moulds for gramophone records, where the accuracy of the deposition process provides faithful sound reproduction. *See also* ELECTRODEPOSITION.

Electroluminescence, production of light by certain substances, particularly phosphors, when they are placed in an alternating electric field. Part of the light from a fluorescent lamp is due to electroluminescence; the rest is due to PHOTOLUMINESCENCE.

Electrolysis, chemical reaction caused by passing a direct electric current (DC) through an ELECTROLYTE. The reaction is the result of transfer of electrons at the electrode surfaces. The type of electron-transfer reaction occurring depends on the ELECTRODE POTENTIALS of ions present, and the electrode material may play a part in the reaction. For example, in electrolysis of copper salts with a copper anode, atoms of the electrode ionize and enter into solution $Cu \rightarrow Cu^{2+} + 2e$. Electrolysis is an important method of obtaining chemicals, particularly extracting reactive elements such as sodium, magnesium, aluminium and chlorine. *See also* MM p.34; SU pp.136, 148.

Electrolyte, liquid that can conduct electricity. In electrolytes the current is carried by positive and negative IONS rather than by electrons. These are present in fused ionic compounds, eg magnesium is extracted from molten magnesium chloride, in solutions of ionic compounds and in solutions of acids and bases, which dissociate into ions. *See also* ELECTROLYSIS; SU p.148.

Electrolytic solution, solution that is an ELECTROLYTE, ie a conductor of electricity. For example, a solution of sodium chloride contains sodium ions (Na^+) and chloride ions (Cl^-), which transport the current.

Electromagnet, magnet constructed from a soft iron core around which is wound a coil of metal wire. A magnetic field is set up when an electric current is passed through the wire, and disappears when the current is switched off. *See also* SU pp.118, *119.*

Electromagnetic field, region in which the

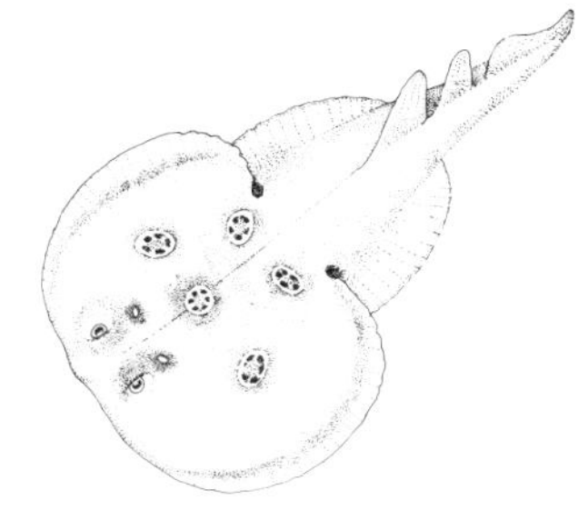

Electric fish generate sizeable voltages, which some use for navigation.

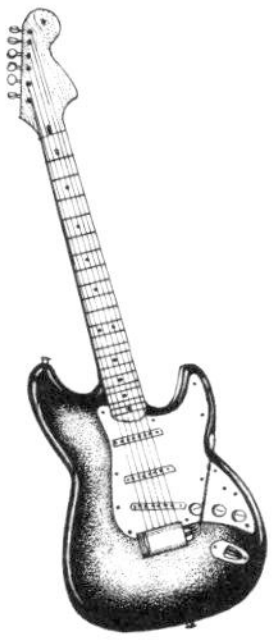

Electric guitars are cut from a solid piece of timber to avoid acoustic feedback.

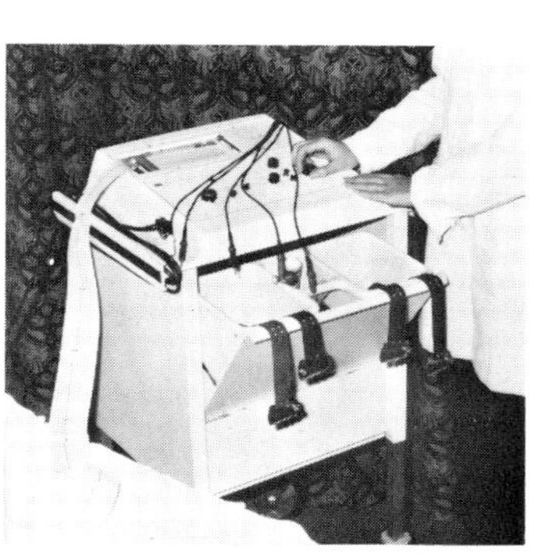

Electrocardiogram is a record of a patient's heartbeat as a continuous trace on paper.

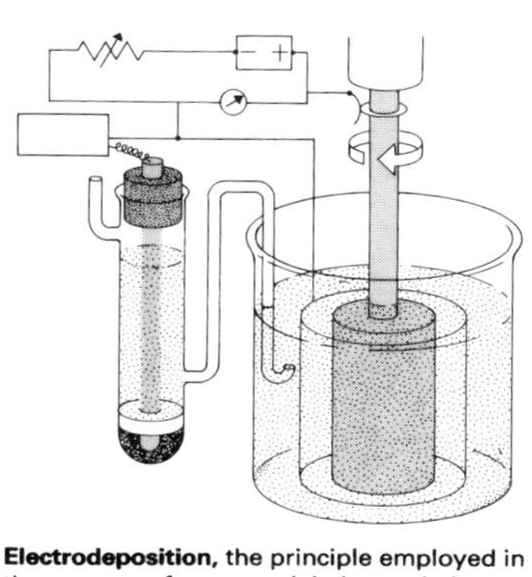

Electrodeposition, the principle employed in the process of commercial electroplating.

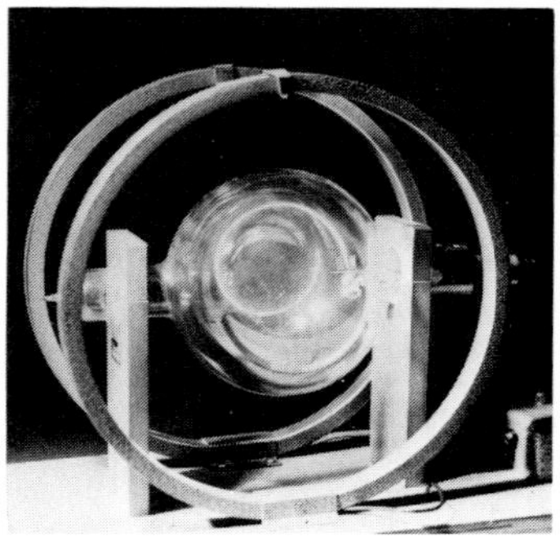

Electron: demonstration apparatus used to measure the ratio of charge to mass.

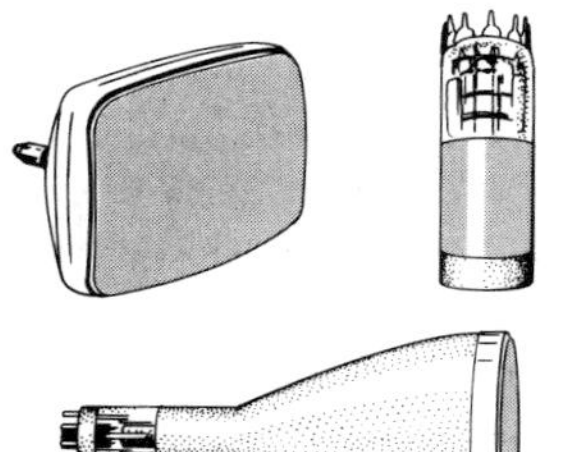

Electron tube: the most familiar form of this device is the television cathode-ray tube.

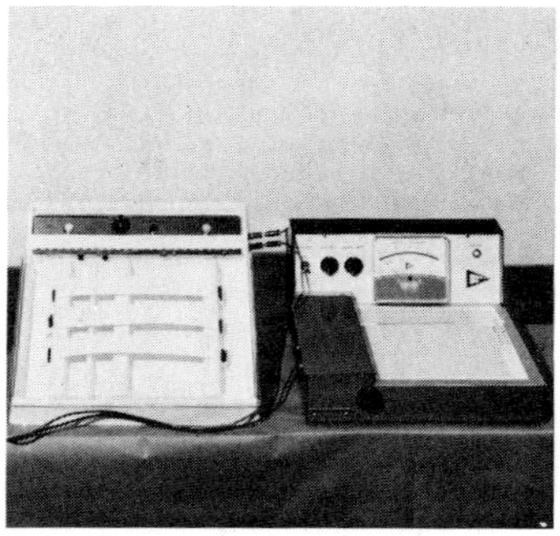

Electrophoresis is a way of electrically separating particles suspended in a liquid.

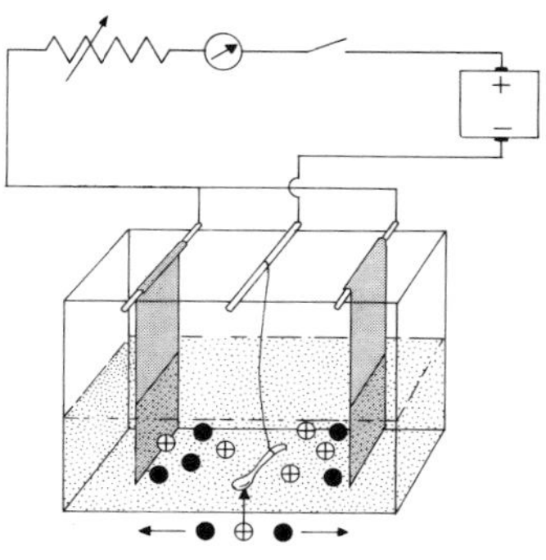

Electroplating: the rate of metal deposition depends on the current density.

effect of an electromagnetic system can be detected. When a magnetic field of force varies or changes, an electric field can always be detected. Conversely, when an electric field varies, a magnetic field can always be detected. Either type of energy field can, therefore, be regarded as an example of an electromagnetic field.

Electromagnetic induction, use of MAGNETISM to produce electricity. If a bar magnet is pushed through a wire coil, an electric current is set up, or induced, in the coil, as long as the magnet is moving. This is the basic working principle of electricity GENERATORS, electric MOTORS and TRANSFORMERS. *See also* SU pp.118–123.

Electromagnetic radiation, energy in the form of waves of a wide range of frequencies that travels through empty space at the speed of light, 299,792.58km/s (186,201 miles per second), and through material media at different speeds. Light, radio waves, infra-red (heat), ultra-violet and X-rays are all examples of electromagnetic radiation. In general, electromagnetic waves are set up by electrical and magnetic vibrations, which occur universally in the atoms of matter. *See also* ELECTROMAGNETIC SPECTRUM.

Electromagnetic spectrum, distribution of different types of ELECTROMAGNETIC RADIATION with regard to either frequency or wavelength. It ranges from low-frequency (high-wavelength) radio waves, through infra-red (heat) waves, light (the visible spectrum), ultra-violet waves, X-rays, to very high frequency gamma rays. *See also* ELECTROMAGNETIC WAVES; SU pp.98–105.

Electromagnetic system of units. *See* ELECTROSTATIC AND ELECTROMAGNETIC SYSTEMS OF UNITS.

Electromagnetic waves, waves of energy composed of electric and magnetic fields vibrating sinusoidally at right-angles to each other and to the direction of motion; they are thus transverse waves. They travel in free space at a constant speed of 299,792.58km/s (the speed of light), which is reduced when travelling through a denser medium, such as air or glass. These waves, which make up the ELECTROMAGNETIC SPECTRUM, are produced by the accelerations of charged particles. Electromagnetic waves can undergo REFLECTION, REFRACTION, INTERFERENCE, DIFFRACTION and polarization. Other phenomena, such as the absorption or emission of light, can be explained only by assuming the radiation to be composed of QUANTUM of energy rather than waves. *See also* SU pp.98–105.

Electromagnetism, branch of physics dealing with the laws and phenomena that involve the interaction or interdependence of electricity and magnetism, such as the magnetic field produced by a moving charge. *See also* SU pp.112–123.

Electrometallurgy, applications of ELECTROCHEMISTRY to METALLURGY. It includes the production and refining of metals by ELECTROLYSIS and such techniques as ELECTROPLATING, electrolytic machining and polishing, and ELECTROFORMING. In a wider sense, electrometallurgy includes other uses of electric current, as in alloy-steel production using an electric furnace. *See also* MM pp.34–35; SU pp.148–149.

Electrometer, instrument having an electrical circuit for measuring differences of electric potential (voltages) without drawing appreciable current. Modern electrometers are essentially voltage AMPLIFIERS. *See also* VOLTMETER.

Electromotive force (EMF), sum of the potential differences in a circuit, measured in volts. It is equal to the energy liberated when unit charge passes completely round the circuit in the direction of the resultant EMF. *See also* SU pp.114–115, 118–119, 124–127, 130–131.

Electromotive series, table of chemical elements arranged vertically in decreasing order of their ELECTRODE POTENTIALS. The series illustrates the relative tendencies of metals to form positive ions in solution, the more electropositive metals being higher up the series. For example, metals higher than hydrogen displace hydrogen from acids by reactions of the type $Ca + 2H^{+} \rightarrow Ca^{2+} + H_2$. The series is also called the ELECTROCHEMICAL SERIES, especially in the context of relative abilities of elements to form ions in chemical reactions. *See also* SU p.148.

Electromyogram, record of the electrical activity of muscles by means of electromyography (EMG). Muscles produce no currents when at rest, but during activity the currents generated enable a continuous trace of action potentials to be recorded. These traces are valuable for research and in diagnosis of muscle dysfunction.

Electron, lightest stable elementary particle (symbol e) with a negative charge, a rest mass of 9×10^{-31} kg (1/1836 that of the PROTON), and SPIN ½. Discovered by J.J. Thomson in 1897, electrons are constituents of matter, moving around the NUCLEUS of an atom in complex orbits. In a neutral atom, their total charge balances that of the protons in the nucleus. Removal or addition of an atomic electron produces a charged ion. Chemical bonds are formed by the transfer or sharing of electrons between atoms. When not bound to an atom electrons are responsible for electrical conduction. Beams of electrons are used in several electronic devices, such as television tubes, oscilloscopes and electron microscopes. High-energy electron beams, from particle accelerators, are used in nuclear research. *See also* SU pp.62–67, 112–115.

Electron configuration. *See* CONFIGURATION, ELECTRON.

Electron emission, liberation of electrons from the surface of a substance. It can occur as a result of heat (THERMIONIC EMISSION), light (PHOTOELECTRIC EMISSION), high electric field (field emission), bombardment by ions or other electrons (SECONDARY EMISSION), or it may result from RADIOACTIVE DECAY. In all cases, the electrons must acquire energy from the outside source in excess of the WORK FUNCTION of the substance. Most valves and cathode-ray tubes depend on thermionic emission, whereas photoelectric cells rely on photoelectric emission. Field emission is important in the field-emission microscope and secondary emission is the principle used by electron multipliers and storage tubes. *See also* SU pp.128–131.

Electron gun, in a CATHODE RAY TUBE such as that in a television receiver or an oscilloscope, device that emits electrons. The arrangement also focuses the electrons in a scanning beam on a fluorescent screen. A similar device in a television camera produces the video signal required to transmit the picture. *See also* MM p.*230*.

Electronic brain, early name for the COMPUTER. The first completely electronic brain was ENIAC, developed at the University of Pennsylvania in 1945. ENIAC had some 18,000 vacuum tubes which made it unreliable and cumbersome. It was not until the invention of the TRANSISTOR in 1948 that computers of a significant capacity and reliability were built. With the growth of silicon-chip technology computers have become smaller, cheaper and more widely used. *See also* INTEGRATED CIRCUITS; MM pp.106, 109; SU pp.*97*, 128–129.

Electronic circuits, electronic components wired together to form a unit capable of performing a particular function, such as detection or amplification of a signal or as a GATE in a logic circuit. The components commonly used in electronic circuits are resistors, capacitors, inductors and transformers in conjunction with thermionic valves or semiconductor devices (which have largely replaced valves). Wiring between components is largely by printed circuits, in which components are soldered to a board on which connections are made by narrow "tracks" of copper. *See also* SU pp.126–131.

Electronic control system, control system based on ELECTRONIC CIRCUITS. Complex control systems rely upon computers, the control functions being carried out by logic circuits. These consist of GATES, which give a high output current when the input currents conform to a predetermined pattern. *See also* MM p.104.

Electronic music, 20th-century genre of music employing electronic methods to generate or modulate sounds. Although the first pieces produced on tape recorders were composed in the 1920s, the development of tapes after WWII stimulated much more complex electronic music. The invention of the music synthesizer, capable of generating required sounds and filtering or modulating other sounds, was greatly explored, particularly by Karlheinz STOCKHAUSEN, and in the 1960s it also became possible to use computers in the manipulation of complex electronic sounds. As well as pure electronic music, many composers such as Luciano BERIO have added electronic taped music to the conventional orchestra.

Electronic musical instruments, 20th-century inventions producing sounds by means of electronic oscillators, photocells, electromagnetics, tape systems, etc. They include the Hammond, Novachord and Solovox organs, with variations such as the Theramin, Ondes Martenot, Moog synthesizer, and amplified ELECTRIC GUITAR popular in rock music.

Electronics, study and use of circuits based on the conduction of electricity through valves and semiconducting devices. John Fleming (1849–1945) invented the DIODE valve which was modified into the TRIODE by Lee de Forest (1873–1961) in 1907. These devices, with further modifications and improvements, provided the basic components for all the electronics of radio, television, and radar until the end of WWII. A major revolution occurred in 1948 when a team at Bell Telephone Laboratories, led by William SHOCKLEY, produced the first semiconducting TRANSISTOR. Semiconductor devices are much lighter, smaller and more reliable than vacuum tubes. They do not require the high operating voltages of valves and they lend themselves to miniaturization in the form of integrated circuits. These characteristics have enabled electronic computers and automatic control devices to change the face of both industry and scientific research. *See also* MM pp.102, 106, 108, 228, 230; SU pp.128–131.

Electron microscope. *See* MICROSCOPE.

Electron tube, electronic device consisting of electrodes arranged within an evacuated glass tube; for special purposes a gas at low pressure may be introduced into the tube. The DIODE, used for rectification, consists of a negative CATHODE, which emits electrons when heated, and a positive ANODE or plate. The TRIODE, used for amplification, has a perforated control grid between the cathode and the anode; a signal fed to the grid provides an amplified signal at the anode. Electron tubes have been largely replaced by TRANSISTORS and other semiconductor devices. *See also* SU pp.128–129.

Electron volt, unit of energy (symbol eV) equal to the energy acquired by an ELECTRON in falling freely through a POTENTIAL DIFFERENCE of one volt. It is equal to 1.601×10^{-19} joules.

Electro-osmosis, flow of water caused when an electric current is passed through a porous clay or other porous material, in a watery suspension. This phenomenon is caused by the formation of positive and negative IONS, one type of which is bound to the clay while the other (in the water) moves towards the opposite electric pole. *See also* OSMOSIS; SU p.145.

Electrophoresis, migration of electrically charged colloidal particles through a fluid from one ELECTRODE to another when an electromotive force is applied across the electrodes. It is used in the analysis and separation of colloidal suspensions, especially of colloidal proteins. It is also used as a means of depositing coatings of one material on another. *See also* COLLOID.

Electrophysiology, cardiac, study of the electrical activity of the heart muscle. When muscles contract and relax they produce electric currents. The heart produces the principal muscular currents and these are measured for diagnostic purposes by attaching electrodes to the outside of the body and connecting them to an ELECTROCARDIOGRAPH (ECG). *See also* ELECTROMYOGRAM.

Electroplating, deposition of a coating of

one metal on another by making the object to be coated the CATHODE in an electrolytic cell. Positive ions in the ELECTROLYTE are discharged at the cathode and deposited as metal ($M^+ + e \rightarrow M$). Electroplating is used to produce a decorative or corrosion-resistant layer, as in silver-plated tableware and chromium-plated motor-car parts. *See also* MM pp.32–33; SU pp.148–149.

Electropolishing, electrolytic treatment of metals and alloys, usually in strong acid solutions, to produce a smooth, bright surface. It is the final surface treatment for some stainless steels and for polishing inaccessible surfaces of metal parts, eg inside gun barrels. Some alloys are electropolished before ELECTROPLATING. See also SU pp.124–5, 149.

Electrorefining, purification of a metal by ELECTROLYSIS. Electrorefining is used to obtain 99.9 per cent pure copper. The cell has a copper sulphate ELECTROLYTE with a thin pure copper cathode; the impure copper is used as the anode. At the anode copper enters solution ($Cu - 2e \rightarrow Cu^{2+}$) and the reverse reaction occurs at the cathode. Thus the net result is a transfer of pure copper from anode to cathode.

Electroscope, instrument for detecting the presence of an electric charge. The commonest device is the gold-leaf electroscope, in which two gold leaves hang from a conducting support insulated from the case. A charge applied to the support causes the leaves to separate. *See also* MM p.224.

Electrostatic field. *See* ELECTRIC, OR ELECTROSTATIC, FIELD.

Electrostatic induction. *See* INDUCTION.

Electrostatic and electromagnetic system of units, in electricity and magnetism, any of four systems of UNITS, based on different definitions of fundamental quantities, still in use. These include the centimetre-gram-second (cgs) electrostatic system, applied particularly to electrostatic problems, and the cgs electromagnetic system, for problems involving magnetic fields. These systems are combined in the Gaussian system of units and the international or SI SYSTEM. *See also* CGS SYSTEM; MKS SYSTEM.

Electrostatics, branch of physics which studies electrical charges, usually electrons, at rest, as on a charged metal sphere insulated from its surroundings, or on the insulated plates of a condenser or CAPACITOR. *See also* SU pp.73, 112–113.

Electrotype, name of a PRINTING process and also of a print made using it. In the process, a negative mould of the typeface or other surface to be printed is dipped in a bath of acid solutions where copper is electrodeposited onto it. The copper typeface is backed with TYPEMETAL to make the printing plate used on a press. *See also* ELECTRODEPOSITION; MM pp.204–209.

Elegiac tradition, a literary form that originated in Greece in the 7th century BC. In classical literature, the term referred to poetry written in elegiac couplets concerning grand themes such as war, friendship and death. In modern usage, poems written in elegiac tradition need not follow a prescribed metrical pattern, but generally deal with the subject of death.

Elegy Written in a Country Churchyard (1750), contemplative poem by Thomas GRAY in quatrains of iambic pentameters. The poet, alone one evening in a country churchyard, reflects on the melancholy tombs around him, the ultimate futility of human endeavour and his own ultimate destiny.

Element, substance that cannot be split into simpler substances by chemical means. All atoms of a given element have the same ATOMIC NUMBER, and thus the same number of electrons – the factor which will determine chemical behaviour. The atoms can have different MASS NUMBERS and a natural sample of an element is generally a mixture of ISOTOPES. The known elements range from hydrogen (at. no. 1) to Lawrencium (at. no. 103). Other highly unstable elements have been prepared, but in insufficient quantity to study their chemistry. *See also* SU pp.134–137.

Element 104, element with ATOMIC NUMBER 104, first claimed in 1964 by a Soviet team at the Joint Institute for Nuclear Research am Dubna. They obtained the ISOTOPE of mass number 260 (half-life 0.3 seconds) by bombarding plutonium with neon ions. The element was named Kurchatovium after Igor Vasilevich Kurchatov, the former head of Soviet nuclear research. In 1969 an American team at Berkeley, California, obtained the isotope with mass number 257 (half-life 4–5 seconds) by bombarding californium with carbon nuclei. They proposed the name Rutherfordium after the New Zealand physicist, Ernest RUTHERFORD.

Element 105, element with ATOMIC NUMBER 105, first reported by a Soviet team at the Joint Institute for Nuclear Research at Dubna. They claimed the ISOTOPES of mass numbers 260 and 261, as a result of bombarding americium with neon ions. In 1970 a team at Berkeley, California claimed the isotope 260 (half-life 1.6 seconds) obtained by bombarding californium with nitrogen nuclei. The Americans have suggested the name Hahnium after Otto HARN.

Elementary particles, "pieces" of matter that have not been subdivided. They are the basic constituents of matter and are distinguished from each other by their mass (usually expressed in equivalent energy units) and a set of QUANTUM NUMBERS, including charge and spin. They may be classified by their interactions into either HADRONS (mesons and baryons), which are subject to the strong interaction, or LEPTONS (electrons and neutrinos), which are subject to the weak interaction. Charged particles also undergo electromagnetic interactions. Many elementary particles have an associated antiparticle, which has the same mass, and a charge, BARYON number, and STRANGENESS equal in magnitude but opposite in sign. Of the large number of particles known, only the proton, electron, neutrino, neutron (when in a nucleus), their antiparticles and the photon are stable. The others decay after a characteristic lifetime to form stabler particles. When an elementary particle collides with its own antiparticle, mutual annihilation occurs, with the production of radiant energy. At high energies, particle-antiparticle pairs are produced. *See also* SU pp.62–67.

Elementary subparticles. *See* SUBPARTICLES, ELEMENTARY.

Elephant, largest land animal and the only living member of the mammal family Proboscidea. It is native to Africa and India, the African bush elephant (*Loxodonta africana*) being larger than the Indian or Asian (*Elephas maximus* or *E. indicus*). A bull elephant may weigh as much as 7,000kg (15,400lb). They are herbivores, and browse widely in herds of up to 100, each elephant eating about 225kg (102lb) of forage daily. The tusks, the source of ivory, are elongated upper incisors with a length of about 3.3m (11ft) and a weight of up to 107kg (236lb). The trunk is an elongated nose and upper lip; at its tip are nostrils and finger-like projections. An elephant has acute senses of hearing, smell and touch. As an ENDANGERED SPECIES, it is now protected by law. In the wild it may live to the age of 80 but in captivity the life span is reduced to 60 years. Its only enemy is man. *See also* NW pp.155, 162.

Elephant bird, one of a group of huge, extinct, flightless birds that lived in Madagascar up to about the mid-17th century. Height: to about 3m (10ft); weight: about 453kg (1,000lb). Genera *Aepyornis* and *Mullerornis*. *See also* NW p.145.

Elephantiasis, tropical disease caused by parasitic invasion of lymph vessels, resulting in the swelling of legs and external genitals, and the thickening and fissuring of skin. The most common cause is a disease called FILARIASIS which results from infestation with small roundworms (*Filaria*) carried by mosquitoes. The adult worms inhabit the lymphatic system. *See also* MS p.106.

Elephantine, island in s Egypt, in the River Nile below the Aswan Dam. It is the site of many ancient ruins and important archaeological finds have included the Elephantine papyri, describing a Jewish colony (*c.*5th century BC), and the Nilometer, dating from the time of the Ptolemies, used to measure the depth of the Nile.

Elephant seal, largest type of SEAL, which breeds on the s California coast and in sub-Antarctic regions; it is so-called because of its large trunk-like proboscis. Elephant seals grow up to 5.5m (18ft) long and males weigh as much as 2.3 tonnes. The northern species is *Mirounga angustirostris*; the more numerous southern species is *M. leonina.*

Elephant's foot, tropical climbing vine native to South Africa. It belongs to the YAM family and has edible tuberous roots. Length: 3m (10ft). Family Dioscoreaceae; species *Dioscorea elephantipes.*

Elephant shrew, any of approx. 20 species of small insect-eating African mammals. They have long, pointed snouts, long tails and powerful hind legs. Length 9–32cm (3.5–12.6in). Family Macroscelididae. *See also* INSECTIVORE.

Elevator. *See* LIFT.

Elevator stage, theatre system of two stages vertically aligned inside a lift shaft that facilitates the speedy change of sets. While the set at stage level is being used, the other stage, either above in the attic or below in the basement, is prepared for the following scene. Devised in 1819 by Steele MacKaye for the Madison Square Theater, New York, it marked the beginning of modern mechanical stage-shifting devices.

Elf, in Germanic mythology small, mischievous fairy possessing great magic. Evil elves are grotesque creatures of the darkness. They milk farmers' cows and ride their horses all night, snuff out candles and prevent bread from rising. Superstition attributes to elves the practice of stealing human children and leaving instead a deformed or unpleasant changeling. Good elves love the woods and fields, where they dance and sing to the music of magic harps. They help a farmer's butter to form and his beer to brew.

Elgar, Sir Edward (1857–1934), British composer. His compositions cover a wide range: two symphonies, a violin concerto, a cello concerto and several orchestral and choral works, the grandest of the last being THE DREAM OF GERONTIUS. Of the five *Pomp and Circumstance* marches (1901–30), the middle section of the first is famous as the song *Land of Hope and Glory.* The *"Enigma" Variations* is his most often played work. *See also* HC2 p.107, 270, *270.*

Elgin, James Bruce, 8th Earl of (1811–63), Governor-General of Canada (1847–54). As MP he advocated responsible government for Canada. He encouraged trade with the USA and introduced liberal reforms.

Elgin, Thomas Bruce, 7th Earl of (1766–1841), British diplomat. He took the ELGIN MARBLES from Athens while he was on a mission in Constantinople. *See also* HC2 p.42.

Elgin, former county town of Morayshire, NE Scotland, on the Lossie River; since 1974 it has been part of Grampian Region. There is a 13th-century Gothic cathedral and Gordonstoun School is nearby. A market town, it has whisky distilling and woollen textile industries. Pop. 16,400.

Elgin Marbles, group of sculptures from the Acropolis of Athens including many of the friezes and the pediments of the PARTHENON and one of the caryatids of the Erechtheum, collected by the 7th Earl of ELGIN and sold to the British Government in 1816. They are now on display in the British Museum, London. They form the largest surviving group of Classical Greek sculpture.

Elginshire. *See* MORAYSHIRE.

El Greco. *See* GRECO, EL.

Elhuyar, Juan José d', (1754–96) and **Fausto d',** (1755–1833), Spanish scientists whose studies in mineralogy and metallurgy led to their discovery of TUNGSTEN in 1783. Subsequently Juan José perfected a method for amalgamating silver and mercury.

Eli, biblical high priest at Shiloh who

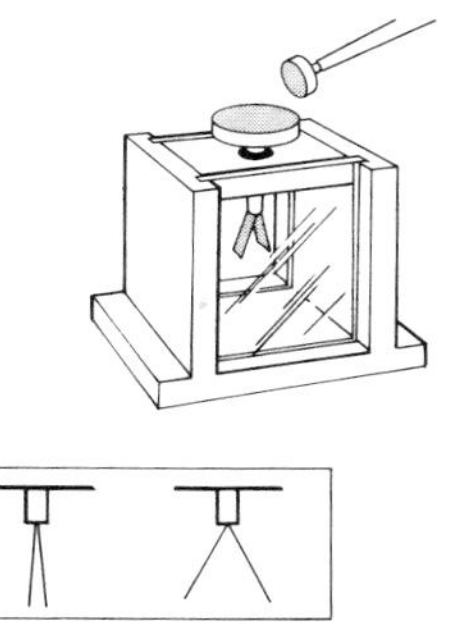

Electroscope's two gold leaves receive the same charge and mutually repel one another.

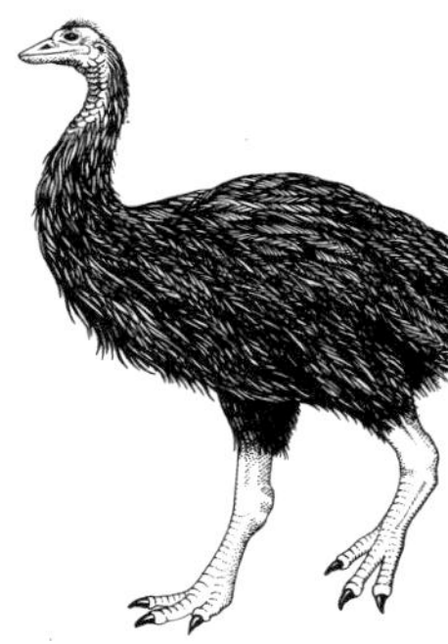

Elephant bird, an extinct creature whose huge eggs held 450kg (2 gallons) of liquid.

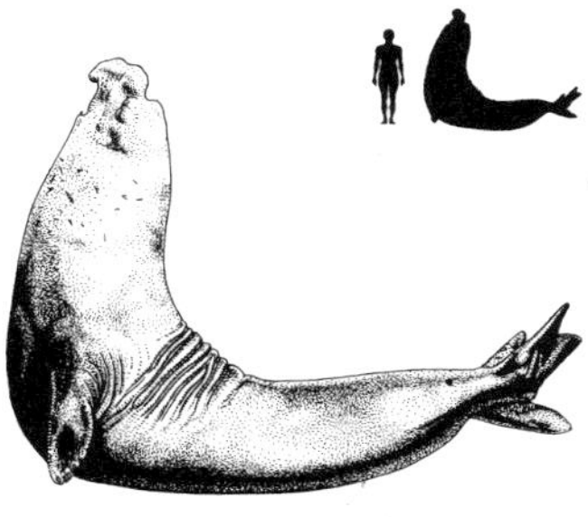

Elephant seal, almost exterminated through over-hunting, is now back in numbers.

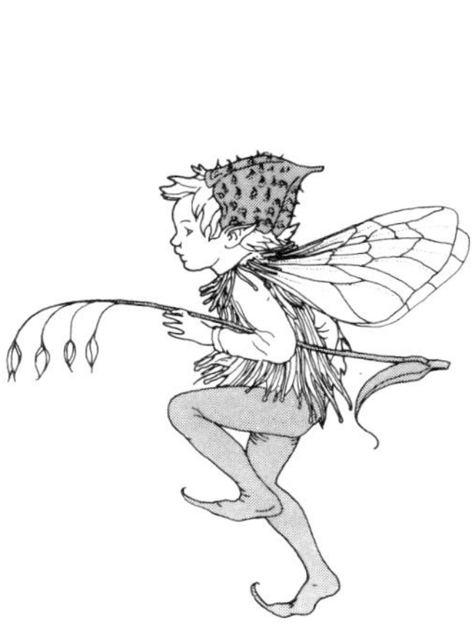

Elf, a small being of mythology, thought to be responsible for many misfortunes.

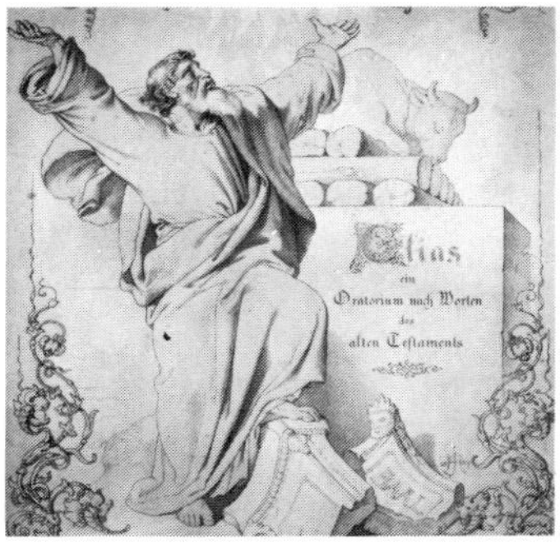
Elijah, according to the Old Testament, ended a drought inflicted on the Jews by God.

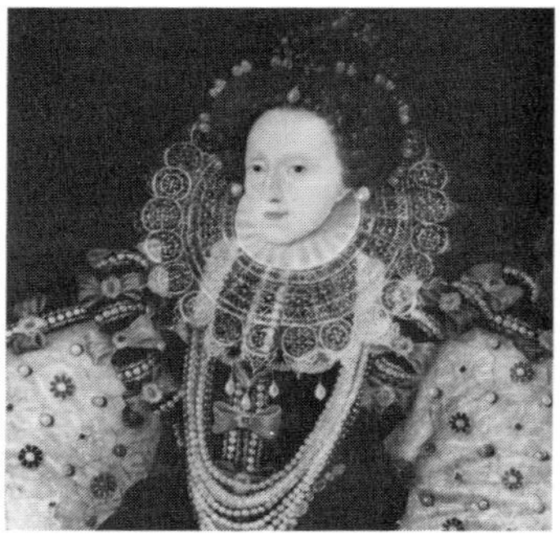
Elizabeth I was 70 when she died, older than any English sovereign before her.

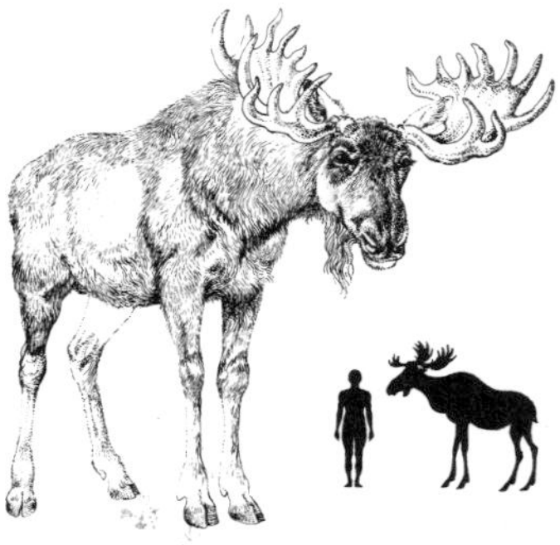
Elk; the American species winter in valleys, returning to the higher mountains in spring.

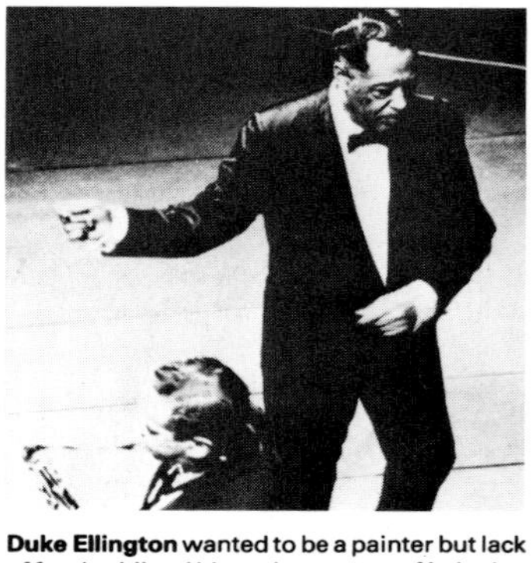
Duke Ellington wanted to be a painter but lack of funds obliged him to become a café pianist.

tutored the young Samuel in the service to God. The news of his sons' deaths and the capture of the Ark of the Covenant by the Philistines caused his death.

Elijah, biblical Tishbite prophet and teacher of ELISHA. He was bent on destroying idolatry and lived in poverty, performing miracles. He was fed by ravens in the wilderness and departed from the earth in a whirlwind. *See also* HC1 p.59.

Elim Foursquare Gospel Alliance, one of the PENTECOSTAL sects, founded in 1915 by George Jeffreys in Monaghan, Ireland. Whereas most Pentecostal groups maintain a congregational form of government, Elim differs from them by being more centralized.

Eliot, George (1819–80), British novelist, whose real name was Mary Ann Evans. Her romantic union with G.H. Lewes had a decisive influence on her work. Her novels, all realistic works about the problems of the provincial middle class, include *Adam Bede* (1859), *The Mill on the Floss* (1860) and *Silas Marner* (1861). *Middlemarch* (1871–72) is often considered her best work. *See also* HC1 p.98.

Eliot, Thomas Stearns (1888–1965), British poet, *b.* USA. He moved to England in 1914 and became a British citizen in 1927, the same year he converted to Anglo-Catholicism. *The Waste Land* (1922) created a literary sensation with its unique, complex language utilizing literary allusions and mythical and religious symbolism to descry the emptiness of contemporary life. Later poems, notably *Ash Wednesday* (1930) and the *Four Quartets* (1936–43), held out hope through religious faith. *See also* HC2 p.289.

Elisabethville. *See* LUBUMBASHI.

Elisha, biblical prophet of Israel, a disciple of ELIJAH. He anointed Jehu king over Israel, thus fulfilling the curse on AHAB.

Elite, people at the top of any hierarchy, eg intellectual, social or political. Elites may contain the best in a particular human group – eg the strongest, the most highly trained, the most intelligent – or they may be made up of those who exercise a major share of authority or influence. *See also* MS p.*275*.

Elizabeth I (1533–1603), Queen of England (*r.* 1558–1603). She was the daughter of HENRY VIII and Anne BOLEYN. During the reigns of EDWARD VI and MARY she was careful to avoid implication in political disputes and ascended the throne peacefully on Mary's death. She reintroduced Protestantism in 1559, broadly interpreted to ensure wide support. Throughout her reign she adhered to a small group of advisers, such as BURGHLEY and WALSINGHAM; and despite constant demands on all sides that she should marry, she remained single. She led the country in its opposition to the threat of Spanish invasion in 1588. By a close identification between herself and the people, nurtured by regular journeys throughout the country, she won enormous prestige and loyalty that enabled her to withstand growing opposition in Parliament. *See also* HC1 pp.271, 274–285.

Elizabeth II (1926–), Queen of the United Kingdom and head of the COMMONWEALTH OF NATIONS (*r.* 1952–). She is the daughter of GEORGE VI, and married Philip Mountbatten, Duke of Edinburgh, in 1947. She served as a mechanic and lorry driver during WWII. She was crowned in 1953. Throughout her reign she has travelled extensively, especially around the Commonwealth, and she has encouraged closer contact than previously between the monarch and the people. She has four children, CHARLES, ANNE, ANDREW and EDWARD.

Elizabeth (1900–), Queen consort of GEORGE VI of Britain. She was Lady Elizabeth Bowes-Lyon until her marriage in 1923. She is the mother of Queen Elizabeth II of England and Princess Margaret.

Elizabeth of Valois (1545–68), Spanish queen, married in 1560 to PHILIP II, although originally considered for Philip's mentally unstable son, Carlos. She later became a figure of legend, in which she and Carlos were involved in an improbable, ill-fated love affair.

Elizabeth of York (1465–1503), Queen of England, wife of HENRY VII after 1486. By marrying her Henry aimed to reconcile the Yorkist and Lancastrian factions in the WARS OF THE ROSES. She had four children. *See also* HC1 p.*266*.

Elizabeth, in the New Testament, wife of Zacharias and mother of JOHN THE BAPTIST. She was related to Mary, mother of Jesus.

Elizabeth, city in NE New Jersey USA on Newark Bay, 8km (5 miles) S of Newark. Settled in 1664 on land purchased from the Delaware Indians and a provincial centre in the 17th century, it was later the scene of important manoeuvres in the AMERICAN WAR OF INDEPENDENCE. Today it is a transport centre whose industries include chemicals and sewing machines. Pop. (1970) 112,654.

Elizabethan drama, drama staged in England during the reign of Elizabeth I (1558–1603). Elizabethan drama combines two movements in Western art and thought: classical and medieval. Also drawing from native forms of folk drama, Elizabethan drama is characterized by a spiritual vitality and the beginnings of doubt that the universe is harmonious and hierarchically ordered. Masters of the period include William SHAKESPEARE (1564–1616), Christopher MARLOWE (1564–93) and Ben JONSON (1572–1637). *See also* HC1 p.282–285, *282–285*.

El-Jadida, seaport town in W Morocco, SW of Casablanca, on the Atlantic Ocean. Formerly called Mazagan, it was taken in 1502 by the Portuguese and reconquered by the Moroccans in 1769. Pop. 40,300.

Elk, name of two different species of DEER: the European elk (*Alces alces*), known in North America as the MOOSE; and the American elk, or WAPITI. The elk, found in northern Eurasia, is the largest of all deer. Height at the shoulder: to 1.9m (6ft); weight: 816kg (1,800lb). Family Cervidae. *See also* NW pp.*193*, 206–207.

Elkington, George Richards, (1801–65), British chemist and industrialist who, with his cousin Henry Elkington, introduced the ELECTROPLATING and electrogilding industries to Britain in 1840. He also established a copper-smelting works at Pembrey, S Wales.

Ellesmere Island, ice-capped island of North-west Territories, Canada, in the Arctic Ocean, NW of Greenland; second largest and northernmost island of the Arctic Archipelago. It has been the site of many geological, glaciological and geographical expeditions. Area: 212,688sq km (82,119sq miles).

Ellice Islands. *See* GILBERT AND ELLICE ISLANDS.

Ellington, Edward Kennedy ("Duke") (1899–1974), US jazz pianist and composer. One of the great figures of jazz history, he organized his first band in 1918 and continued at the forefront of the jazz world until the 1970s. His many compositions include piano suites, classic jazz band arrangements and many songs such as "Mood Indigo" (1930), "Caravan" (1937) and "I Got It Bad" (1941). *See also* HC2 pp.272, *272*.

Elliott, Herb (1938–), Australian athlete. He lowered the world record in the mile to 3min 54.5sec and also established a world record at the 1,500-metre distance in 1958. At the 1960 Olympics he won a gold medal by improving his world record for 1,500 metres to 3min 35.6sec.

Ellipse, conic section formed by cutting a right circular cone with a plane inclined at such an angle that the plane does not intersect the base of the cone. When the intersecting plane is parallel to the base, the conic section is a circle. In rectangular Cartesian co-ordinates its standard equation is $x^2/a^2 + y^2/b^2 = 1$. Most planetary orbits are ellipses. *See also* SU p.36.

Ellipsoidal reflector, floodlight reflector that has two focal points, used in theatrical lighting.

Elliptical galaxy, type of regular GALAXY having either a globular or lenticular structure and characterized by the absence of spiral arms. Graded E0 to E7 according to increasing ellipticity, elliptical galaxies consist of old stars free of gas and dust. *See also* SU p.248.

Ellis, Henry Havelock (1859–1939), British psychologist and author. His seven-volume *Studies in the Psychology of Sex* (1897–1928) promoted the scientific study of sex and was important in changing public attitudes. He was also a pioneer in the study of dreams.

Ellis, Jan (1943–), South African rugby union loose-forward whose fast, tigerish displays and constructive forward play won him 38 international caps (1965–76), thus equalling du Preez's South African record. He played for South West Africa.

Ellis, Ruth (1926–55), last women to be hanged in Britain before the suspension of capital punishment as the penalty for murder in 1965. A model, she was convicted of the murder of 25-year-old racing-driver David Blakely.

Ellis Park, rugby union ground in Johannesburg, South Africa, named after a local councillor. First used for rugby in 1928, it is Transvaal's home ground and the venue of South Africa's international matches. In 1955 a crowd of 95,000 people (a world record for a rugby match) watched the British Lions beat South Africa there.

Ellison, Ralph Waldo (1914–), US author. A short-story writer and essayist, he won a National Book Award in 1953 for his first novel, *Invisible Man* (1952). The book deals with the prejudice and hostility faced by a young black man in the USA.

Ellora, Shrines of, series of rock temples cut from a hill (6th–8th century). They serve the Buddhist, Hindu and Jain religions. The Hindu Kailasa temple, dedicated to the god Shiva, is the most magnificent. *See also* HC1 p.*121*.

Ellsworth, Lincoln (1880–1951), US polar explorer. He financed the Norwegian explorer Roald AMUNDSEN, in 1911 the first person to reach the South Pole, and made a successful airship flight with Amundsen from Spitzbergen over the North Pole to Alaska in 1926. In 1931 he explored vast regions of the Arctic Ocean and in 1935 made the first flight over Antarctica.

Ellsworth Land, region of W Antarctica extending E from Byrd Land to the W coast of the Weddell Sea.

Elm, hardy, deciduous tree of north-temperate zones, often planted as a shade tree. Varieties include the American (*Ulmus americana*), English (*U. procera* and Scotch elm (*U. glabra*). All are susceptible to the deadly DUTCH ELM DISEASE. Height: over 30m (100ft). The smaller Chinese elm (*U. parvifolia*) and Siberian elm (*U. pumila*) are resistant to the disease. Family Ulmaceae. *See also* NW p.*209*.

Elmbridge, county district in N central SURREY, England, bordering on Greater London; created in 1974 under the Local Government Act (1972). Area: 96sq km (37sq miles). Pop. (1974 est.) 112,800.

Elmer Gantry (1927), novel by Sinclair LEWIS that exposes hypocrisy in the ministry through the career of a man who uses religion to gain himself fame and fortune.

Elongation, in astronomy, difference measured in degrees between the celestial longitude of the Sun and that of a planet or the Moon. In the case of inferior or superior conjunction, the elongation is almost zero; for quadrature, it equals 90°; for opposition it equals 180°.

El Paso, city and port of entry in W Texas, USA, across the Rio Grande from Ciudad Juárez, Mexico. Although there was a settlement nearby in 1598 (El Paso de Río) there was no permanent settlement until 1827. Now a commercial centre, the city's industries include oil and copper refining and food processing. Pop. (1970) 322,261.

Elphinstone, William (1431–1514), Scottish prelate and Bishop of Aberdeen (1488) who was responsible for introducing the first printing press (Chapman and Millar's) into Scotland. In 1488 JAMES III made him Lord High Chancellor. Elphinstone was ambassador to France in 1491, and keeper of the privy seal from 1492. He founded King's College in 1494 which later became the University of Aberdeen.

El Salvador, republic in Central America bordered by Guatemala to the W and

260 HC1 = History and Culture Vol. 1 HC2 = History and Culture Vol. 2 MS = Man and Society MM = Man and Machines

Honduras to the N and E. The fertility of the upland plains allows the cultivation of coffee and sugar cane and agriculture is the chief occupation, although industrialization is progressing. The capital is San Salvador. Area: 21,393sq km (8,260sq miles). Pop. (1976 est.) 4,240,000. *See* MW p.68.

Elsasser, Walter Maurice (1904–), US theoretical physicist and geophysicist. He is noted for his investigation of the upper mantle of the earth. In 1925 he predicted electron diffraction and, in 1936, neutron DIFFRACTION.

Elsene. *See* IXELLES.

Elsheimer, Adam (1578–1610), German painter. His most characteristic works are small-scale landscapes painted on copper, with biblical or mythological themes.

Elsinore (Helsingør), city in E Denmark. Its castle, redesigned in the 17th century, was the setting for Shakespeare's HAMLET. Pop. 7,560.

Éluard, Paul (1895–1952), French poet, real name Eugène Grindel. When a SURREALIST (1919–38) he wrote *Capital of Grief* (1926) and *The Public Rose* (1934). He joined the Communist Party (1942) and fought in the Resistance. Later poems include *Poetry and Truth* (1942).

Elvström, Paul (1928–), Danish yachtsman whose dedicated approach to his sport brought him four Olympic gold medals (in the *Firefly* class 1948, and *Finn* 1952, 1956, 1960) and 11 world championships: *505* (1957, 1958), *Finn* (1958, 1959), *Snipe* (1959), *Flying Dutchman* (1962), *Star* (1966, 1967, 1974), *5.5m* (1966) and *Soling* (1969).

Ely, Isle of. *See* ISLE OF ELY.

Elyot, Sir Thomas (*c.*1499–1546), diplomat and author, who served as ambassador to the court of the Holy Roman Emperor CHARLES V. On the first occasion (1531) his primary brief was to obtain Charles' consent to HENRY VIII's divorce. He wrote the *Boke called the Governour* (1531), a discussion of the education of a statesman, dedicated to Henry VIII. *See also* HC1 p.282.

Elysium, in Greek mythology, the Elysian fields; the abode of blessed mortals after their removal from the Earth. It was not the place of the dead, but a realm to which heroes departed to live a life of happiness. HOMER located Elysium at the farthest ends of the earth on the banks of the river OCEANUS.

Elysium Planitia, volcanic plane of intermediate geological age on the planet MARS. It contains two large volcanic craters (calderas), Hecate tholus and Albor tholus, as well as a clearly marked dome, Elysium Mons. *See also* SU pp.*195,* 199, *199.*

Emancipation, freeing from restriction, especially the granting of freedom to slaves, but also the improvement of the legal status of women and the increase in religious tolerance for Roman Catholics in Britain, during the last 150 years. In Russia the Edict of Emancipation (1861) was ALEXANDER II's proclamation of freedom to the serfs; under the edict the serfs were also granted land in return for redemption payments made by them to the state over the next 49 years. The scheme was not a success (*see* HC2 p.168, *168*). In the USA, a proclamation of Emancipation was made by Lincoln on 1 January 1863, technically freeing only those slaves in the rebel CONFEDERATE STATES; but emancipation was made general by the 13th amendment to the constitution passed in 1865 (*see also* HC2 pp.151–152). In Britain the emancipation of slaves is usually referred to as the abolition of slavery.

Embargo, obstruction of the movement of cargo to prevent its delivery. In modern terms, it refers to complete suspension of trade with a country or withholding crucial goods, such as oil.

Embolism, blocking of a blood vessel usually by a blood clot, but also by a foreign body, air bubble or fat globule. Symptoms vary according to the organs affected and may be severe, eg a heart attack. ANTICOAGULANTS and surgery are treatments. *See also* ARTERIOSCLEROSIS; MS p.90.

Embroidery, art of ornamenting textiles with NEEDLEWORK, although many other decorative materials can also be added. Embroidery is not woven into a fabric but is sewn on an already finished cloth. About 300 different embroidery stitches exist, of four main types: flat, looped, chained and knotted. Decorative embroidery is an ancient art that has been used throughout the world to convey magnificence; sometimes, as in the BAYEUX TAPESTRY, it has also served as a means to record real or imaginary events. In medieval times England was renowned for its embroidery, which was mainly ecclesiastical in inspiration; and during the Renaissance embroidery was an important art of many royal or ducal courts. There was also a tradition of less sumptuous peasant and folk embroidery, particularly in E Europe. A fine example of this is the quilting of the early English settlers in America.

Embryo, multicellular organism, the developing stage of an animal or plant from its fertilization until the moment (in animals, hatching or birth; in plants, germination) when it is structurally able to live as an independent organism. In man, the term applies only during the first seven weeks of pregnancy; thereafter the term FOETUS is applicable. An embryo may also be formed in the cleavage of an unfertilized egg by natural PARTHENOGENESIS. In animals which reproduce sexually the embryo is formed when the nuclei of an egg (produced by the female) and a spermatozoon (produced by the male) fuse to form a single cell, called a ZYGOTE (the fertilized egg). The zygote then begins to divide into an embryo. The embryo undergoes rapid changes in which the cells differentiate themselves to form limbs and organs, according to both their genetic predisposition and the place in the developing structure in which they find themselves. In plants the embryo is found in the seed, the young bud or at the end of the root. In some plants it may be found in the seed leaves. *See also* MS pp.74–76; NW pp.70–71, 76–77.

Embryology, biological study of the origin, development and activities of an EMBRYO. This science, in tracing the sequence of events from ovum (egg) to birth, follows the ZYGOTE through CLEAVAGE, MORULA stage, BLASTULA stage, and GASTRULA stage when two and then three layers, precursors of body organs, appear. *See also* MS p.75.

Emerald, variety of BERYL, varying in colour from light to deep green and highly valued as a gemstone. The colour is due to the presence of small amounts of chromium but the stone may lose its colour if heated. Emeralds were mined in Upper Egypt in 1650 BC; now they are found mainly in Colombia. *See also* PE p.99.

Emerson, Ralph Waldo (1803–82), US essayist and poet. In 1832 he resigned his pastorate and travelled to Europe where he met CARLYLE, COLERIDGE and WORDSWORTH and came into contact with German Romanticism. Emerson's book *Nature* (1836) expressed the principles of TRANSCENDENTAL thought. His belief in the soul, the unity of God with man and nature, self-reliance and hope appear in his *Essays* (1841, 1844), *Poems* (1847), *Society and Solitude* (1870) and many other works. *See also* HC2 p.288.

Emery, impure form of the mineral CORUNDUM, (aluminium oxide, Al_2O_3), that occurs as dark granules with MAGNETITE and HAEMATITE in them. An unusually hard mineral, it is used as an abrasive.

Emetine, ALKALOID ($C_{29}H_{40}N_2O_4$) used to induce vomiting. It is extracted from IPECAC root and is used in the treatment of some human parasitic diseases.

Emil and the Detectives, children's story by Erich KÄSTNER, which has proved lastingly popular with boys and girls in many countries. Published in Germany in 1929 it tells of the efforts of Emil and a group of friends to regain stolen money.

Eminence Grise, name given to Père JOSEPH, French diplomat, in reference to his pervasive influence over Cardinal RICHELIEU, principal minister of LOUIS XIII.

Eminent Victorians (1918), biographical work by the British writer Lytton STRACHEY. It debunks the myths surrounding four great Victorians: Cardinal MANNING, Dr Thomas ARNOLD, Florence NIGHTINGALE and General GORDON.

Emma (1816), novel by Jane AUSTEN concerned with the smug, but lively and entertainingly interfering Emma Woodhouse, her misguided schemes for arranging the lives of her acquaintances, and her gradual realization of the consequences of her behaviour. *See also* HC2 p.*98*.

Emmanuel, or Immanuel, name meaning "God (is) with us" given by the biblical prophet ISAIAH to the child who would be a sign from God of deliverance. In the New Testament, the Apostle Matthew refers to Jesus as Emmanuel. Devotional literature and hymns occasionally use Emmanuel synonymously with Jesus.

Emmen, city in Drenthe province, NE Netherlands. It is a market centre and textiles and electronic equipment are manufactured. Pop. (1970 est.) 79,700.

Emmental, fine Swiss cheese that takes its name from the valley of the River Emme in central Switzerland, a dairy-farming region where the cheese is produced.

Emmet, Robert (1778–1803), Irish nationalist leader, who hoped to destroy the 1801 Act of Union which placed Ireland under the British Parliament. In July 1803 he led an attack upon Dublin Castle, which was intended as a prelude to a French invasion to help the nationalist movement. His plot failed and he was arrested, tried and executed.

Emotion, human feelings involving complex mental and physical reactions. Primary emotions are anger, fear, grief, joy and pain. The subtlety and complexity of emotions mean that intuitive understanding (EMPATHY) or the systematic study of subjective experience is often the best way of comprehending their nature. However, emotions are associated with predictable physiological changes such as increased heart and breathing rates, sweating, dryness of the mouth and trembling. Physiological studies have indicated that the reticular formation in the brain is important for emotional changes: greater emotional intensity involves greater nervous activity there. Some expressions of emotions, such as crying and smiling, appear to be unlearned. Other expressions are acquired from environmental culture, eg some people when angry react with violence, others may show anger only in their facial expression. *See also* MS pp.40, 135, 158–159, 236, 237.

Empathy, ability to know and experience what someone else feels by mentally putting oneself in that person's place. This feeling is part of a person's responses to works of art, especially novels and poetry, and also contributes to an actor's interpretation of a character.

Empedocles (*c.*490–430 BC), Greek philosopher. He attempted to harmonize ELEATICISM, the concept of permanent being, with HERACLEITUS' teaching of constant flux. Teaching the doctrine of the four elements – earth, water, air and fire – and anticipating modern physics, he explained change as being alterations in the proportions of the four elements in the object. *See also* HC1 p.82.

Emperor, title of the supreme head of an empire, deriving from the Roman *imperator*. The title was first given to Julius CAESAR, and was adopted again by CHARLEMAGNE when the HOLY ROMAN EMPIRE was set up; it was adopted by several European monarchs in the 18th century.

Emphysema, accumulation of air in tissues, most often occurring in the lungs (pulmonary emphysema). Causes are unknown but air pollution and heavy smoking exacerbate the symptoms, which include wheezing, coughing and shortness of breath. Treatment can include ANTIBIOTICS and inhalants to relieve spasms and secretions, and breathing exercises. *See also* MS p.88.

Empire State Building, skyscraper in New York. From its completion in 1931 to 1972, it was the highest building in the world, at 381m (1,250ft), or 449m (1,472ft) to the top of its television mast. It was designed by Shreve, Lamb and Harmon and is used for offices. Its name derives from the nickname of New York State. *See also* MM p.*49*.

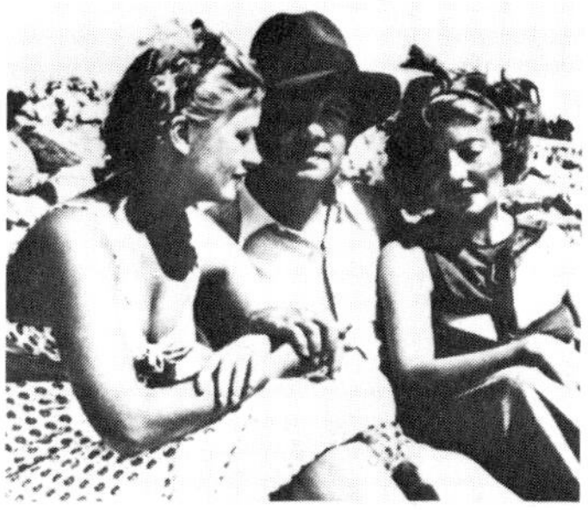

Paul Éluard; his experiences in WWI gave his work a heightened sympathy with suffering.

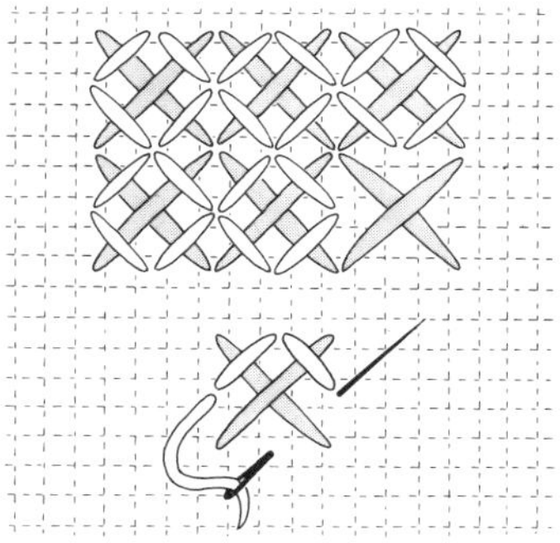

Embroidery is thought to have its origins in the human need to join fabrics for clothing.

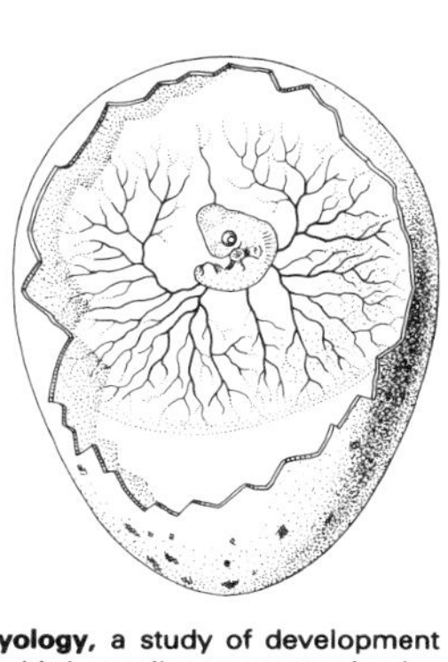

Embryology, a study of development from egg to birth, applies to most animals.

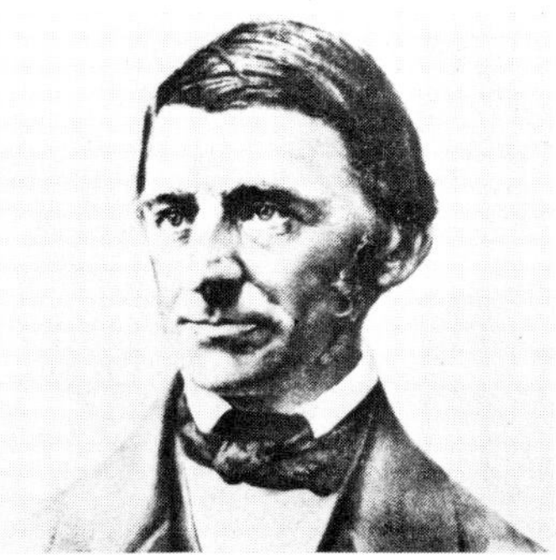

Ralph Waldo Emerson, despite ill-health, developed a philosophy of self-reliance.

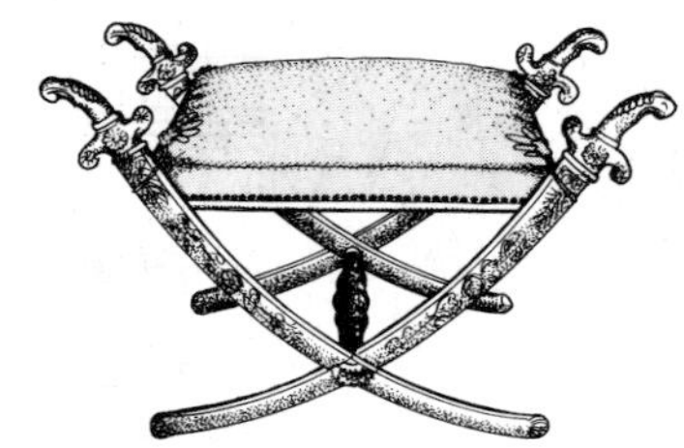

Empire style, a phase of neo-classical art encouraged by Napoleon.

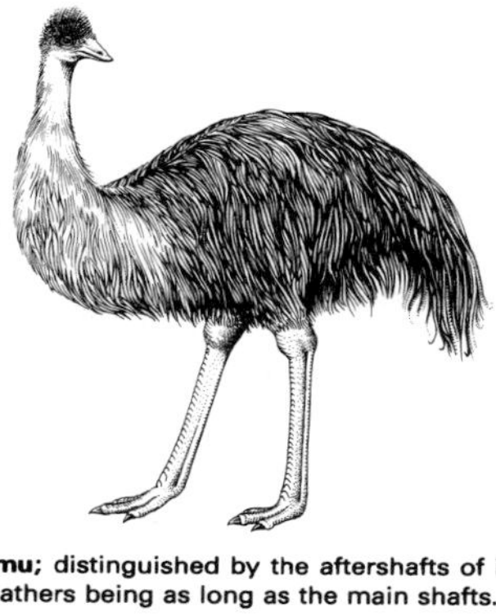

Emu; distinguished by the aftershafts of its feathers being as long as the main shafts.

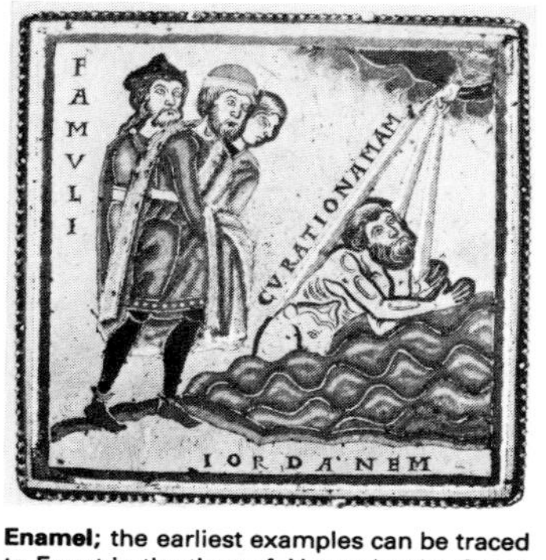

Enamel; the earliest examples can be traced to Egypt in the time of Alexander the Great.

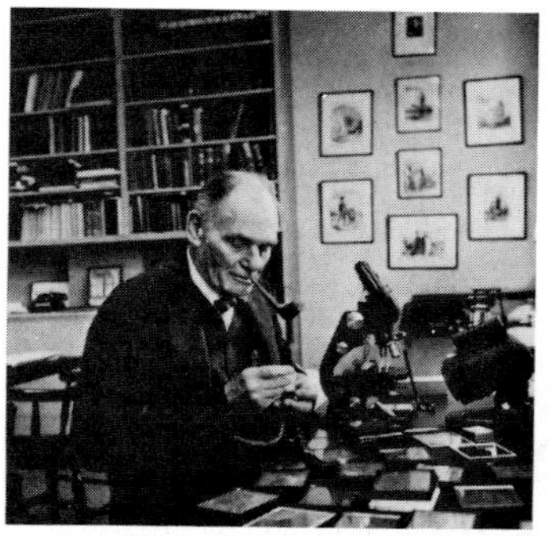

John Franklin Enders, his early researches were in ailments such as measles.

Empire style, neo-classical style in interior decoration which started in Paris in about 1800 and spread throughout Europe by 1820. It made affected use of Egyptian and other ancient decorative motifs. In England it corresponded to the REGENCY STYLE. In women's fashion it was exemplified by high-waisted dresses embellished with embroidery.

Empiricism, philosophical doctrine that all knowledge is derived from experience. It has been mainly developed by a school of British philosophers, LOCKE, BERKELEY and HUME, in reaction to the RATIONALISM of DESCARTES, SPINOZA and LEIBNIZ, who claimed that there is such a thing as *a priori* knowledge (or "innate ideas"). Thoroughgoing empiricists, such as the LOGICAL POSITIVISTS in this century, would argue that all ideas are reducible to sense impressions, with the exception of mathematics and logic which are simply the elaboration of certain rules, otherwise they are meaningless. *See also* MS pp.231, 233.

Empson, William (1906–), British poet and critic. Empson expanded the ideas of I. A. RICHARDS in the critical work *Seven Types of Ambiguity* (1930). He wrote extremely detailed analyses of specific texts and poems, a technique that became known as the New Criticism. Empson's other critical works include *Some Versions of Pastoral* (1935), *The Structure of Complex Words* (1951) and *Milton's God* (1961).

Empyema, infection of the pleural cavity of the lungs which yields large amounts of pus. It is usually secondary to a lung infection and its treatment includes ANTIBIOTICS and drainage of the cavity. *See also* MS p.88.

Ems Dispatch (1870), final cause of the FRANCO-PRUSSIAN War. The French were alarmed at the candidacy for the Spanish throne of Prince Leopold, a relative of WILHELM I of Prussia, and their ambassador requested assurance of the permanence of Leopold's refusal. Wilhelm declined and informed his prime minister, BISMARCK, of the conversation, who in turn published an insulting version of the conversation in a telegram, thus inflaming the French to war. *See also* HC2 p.180.

Emu, large, dark-plumed, flightless Australian bird. A strong runner with powerful legs, it lives in groups and feeds mostly on plants. Large greenish eggs (8–10) are hatched by the male in a ground nest of grass and leaves. Height: 1.5m (5ft); weight: to 54kg (120lb). Species *Dromiceius novaehollandiae. See also* NW p.*205*.

Emulsion, dispersion of fine droplets of one liquid in a larger volume of another liquid. Two types are generally distinguished: oil-in-water emulsions and water-in-oil emulsions. To stop the liquids separating out again it is necessary to add an emulsifying agent, such as soap. In milk, a natural oil-in-water emulsion, proteins are the emulsifying agents. In photography, a suspension of silver oxide or salts in a liquid is called, erroneously, an emulsion.

Enamel, decorative or protective glazed coating produced on metal surfaces, or a type of paint. CERAMIC enamels are made from powdered glass with the addition of various metal oxides to give colour and calx, a mixture of tin and lead, for opacity. The mixture is first melted, quenched and finely ground, and applied to the surface. Then it is fired to give a fused vitreous coating. Enamel paints consist of zinc oxide and lithopone, brown linseed oil, and high-grade varnish. The finish is hard, glossy and highly durable. The term "enamel paint" is derived from its resemblance when dry to the finish found on ceramic-enamel products. *See also* MM pp.44, 245.

Enamel, in mammals, hard covering of the crown of the tooth; it is the hardest body tissue, but is not living and contains no nerves. Strongest at the biting edges, enamel varies in thickness and density over the tooth. *See also* MS pp.130–131.

Encaustic painting, method of painting in the ancient world and early Christian era, using pigments mixed with hot wax. The technique, which has proved particularly durable, was used especially in Roman Egypt.

Encephalitis, viral disease of the brain and spinal cord which is usually EPIDEMIC. It is transmitted from animal to man by insects. Similar to the bacterial infection MENINGITIS, its symptoms include fever, headache, vomiting and a stiff neck and back, increasing to convulsions and possible paralysis. Accurate diagnosis by analysis of the spinal fluid is necessary to differentiate encephalitis from forms of meningitis which can be treated by ANTIBIOTICS. Complete and spontaneous recovery is frequent.

Encina, Juan del (*c.* 1468–*c.* 1529), generally held to be the earliest important Spanish dramatic writer. His works include adaptations of VIRGIL's *Eclogues* in Spanish dialect (1498–1507 and 1513–14) and much music and lyrics, with which he closed his plays.

Encke, Johann Franz (1791–1865), German astronomer noted for his study of comets, one of which bears his name. Encke's comet has the smallest known orbit, passing close to the Sun every 3.30 years. Encke was director of the Berlin Observatory (1825–63). *See also* SU pp.216, *216*.

Enclosure, in English history, the fencing-in and appropriation by an individual of open fields previously subject to common rights, or of common grazing land. Enclosure began in the mid-12th century, reached its medieval peak in the 15th and early 16th centuries to create fenced pastureland, and recurred in the late 17th century and in 1750–1870, when it was endorsed by Parliament as a necessary prerequisite of introducing improved crop rotation. Enclosure was usually carried out by the local landowner or large farmers, and the loss of rights on the common land sometimes caused severe hardship to the peasantry. *See also* HC1 pp.196–197, 274–275; HC2 pp.20–21.

Encomienda, right granted to the early Spaniards in Latin America to demand tribute, and initially also labour, from local Indians of a specified area in return for "civilizing" them. It did not imply a grant of land. Attempts to abolish the system failed, although it became less profitable in the 1600s. *See also* HC1 pp.236–237.

Encounter therapy, in psychotherapy, relatively informal and unstructured kind of group THERAPY that replaces analysis with action, eg games, PSYCHODRAMA, confession, body touching and discussion. It is mainly beneficial to those who do not suffer from severe psychological disorders and aims at developing spontaneity and deeper inter-personal relationships. *See also* MS pp.148–149.

Encyclical, letter sent to all churches of a particular area either, in the Anglican Church, by the bishops at the conclusion of LAMBETH CONFERENCES, or, in the Roman Catholic Church, by the POPE. A papal encyclical, although dealing with doctrinal matters, is not held to be infallible. Well-known modern encyclicals include Pope Leo XIII's *Rerum Novarum* (1891) on social justice, Pius X's *Pascendi* (1907) against MODERNISM, Pius XI's *Mit brennender Sorge* (1937) against German Nazis, and Paul VI's *Humanae Vitae* condemning artificial means of contraception.

Encyclopaedia, compendium of knowledge, containing information in all fields (general) or in a particular field (specialist). Some of the first encyclopaedic works were by ARISTOTLE and PLINY, but the first modern work was probably John Harris's *Lexicon Technicum* (1704), which contained excellent bibliographies and cross-referencing. *See also* MM pp.214–215.

Encyclopaedia Britannica, major reference book first published in three volumes (1768–71), edited by William Smellie. It has grown in size and reputation since then, and has been published in the USA since 1929. It was revised in 1974 into a 30-volume three-part structure: *Propaedia*, short-entry *Micropaedia* and long-entry *Macropaedia*..

Encyclopédie; ou, Dictionnaire raisonné des sciences, des arts, et des métiers (1751–72), literary work of the 18th century, an embodiment of the spirit of ENLIGHTENMENT. The French *Encyclopédie* was intended to be a complete guide to useful knowledge. Its principal director, Denis DIDEROT, and eminent contributors hoped that the work would combat superstition and systematize knowledge. *See also* MM p.*214*; HC2 pp.22–23.

Encyclopedists, French philosophers who presented their rationalist, humanitarian and deist views that epitomize ENLIGHTENMENT thought through the ENCYCLOPÉDIE in the latter half of the 18th century. Encountering severe opposition from the religious and political establishment, the main editor, Denis DIDEROT, and such prominent thinkers as VOLTAIRE, ROUSSEAU and D'ALEMBERT helped to prepare the philosophical basis of the French Revolution. *See also* MM p.214; HC2 pp.22–30.

Endangered species, animals or plants threatened with extinction in the foreseeable future as a result of man's activities: nearly 1,000 different species of animals throughout the world, and 20,000 plants. Notable examples of animals at risk are porpoises, elephants and whales. *See also* NW p.251.

Endeavour, ship in which Capt. James COOK made his first voyage of Pacific exploration (1768–71). He circumnavigated the two main islands of New Zealand, charted the E coast of Australia and returned through the Torres Strait. The ship was not used for his later voyages. *See also* HC2 pp.124–125.

Endell, August (1871–1925), German architect. He was one of the pioneers of JUGENDSTIL architecture, and his best-known work was the Elvira Studio at Munich (1897–98), the exterior of which relied heavily on oriental styles of decoration.

Endemic, presence of a disease within a closed population, peculiar to that population. There may or may not be any clinical symptoms. For instance, cholera and plague are endemic in some parts of Asia.

Ender, Kornelia (1958–), East German swimmer. She set 23 individual world records at freestyle, backstroke, butterfly and medley and won four Olympic (1976), eight world (1973, 1975) and four European (1974) gold medals.

Enders, John Franklin (1897–), US microbiologist. He shared the 1954 Nobel Prize in physiology and medicine with Frederick C. ROBBINS and Thomas H. WELLER for their discovery of the ability of poliomyelitis viruses to grow in cultures of various types of tissues. This work was fundamental to the later development of the polio vaccine.

Endgame (1957, Fr. *Fin de Partie*), play By Samuel Beckett, translated by him into English in 1958. Three of its four characters are immobilized – two are in dustbins and one chair-ridden. Its bleak symbolism, stark setting and grotesque comedy powerfully evoke Beckett's nihilistic vision.

Endive, leafy annual or biennial plant widely cultivated for its sharp-flavoured leaves that are cooked or used raw in salads. It resembles LETTUCE, but its leaves are more substantial. There are two main types: curly endive, or escarole, with slender, wavy-edged leaves and a variety with broad, flat leaves. Family Asteraceae; species *Cichorium endivia. See also* PE p.190.

Endocarditis, inflammation of the lining of the heart. It is often caused by bacteria and is also associated with rheumatic fever. *See also* MS pp.90–*91*.

Endocrine system, body system made up of all the endocrine (ductless) glands that secrete hormones directly into the bloodstream to control body functions. The endocrine system (together with the nervous system) controls and regulates all body functions. It differs from other body systems in that its ductless glands are not structurally connected to one another. The chief endocrine glands are: the PITUITARY GLAND, located at the base of the brain; the THYROID GLAND, located in the throat; the PARATHYROID GLAND, also

located in the throat; the ADRENAL GLANDS, situated on top of the kidneys; the ISLET OF LANGERHANS in the pancreas; the sex glands (GONADS) in males and OVARIES in females. *See also* MS pp.64–65.
Endoderm, or entoderm, innermost cell layer of embryos of higher animals. It forms the epithelial lining of the liver, pancreas, digestive tract and respiratory system. It is also the inner cell layer of a simple animal body.
Endogamy, in anthropology, marriage within a specific tribe or other social unit such as class or caste. It is basically an obligation, and may be strictly defined and enforced or merely be a social tendency. *See also* EXOGAMY; MS pp.250–251.
Endometriosis, condition in which tissue resembling the uterine mucous membrane appears in other areas of the pelvic cavity, sometimes in the form of cysts or nodules.
Endometrium, highly vascularized tissue that lines the uterus (womb), shed each month during MENSTRUATION. Upon conception it forms part of the placenta to maintain the developing foetus during pregnancy. *See also* MS p.*75*.
Endomorph, type of human being of round or stout build, usually with a round face and short arms and legs. Most people are a combination of endomorph, ECTOMORPH and MESOMORPH. *See also* MS p.189.
Endoscope, instrument used to examine the interior of the body through a natural opening. Generally a light source and lenses are included in a flexible tube. Examples include a gastroscope (for examining the stomach) and a cystoscope (for examining the urinary bladder).
Endosperm, tissue that surrounds the developing embryo of a seed and provides food for growth.
Endothermic reaction, chemical reaction in which heat is absorbed from the surroundings, causing a fall in temperature – eg in the manufacture of WATER-GAS from coal and steam. *See also* SU p.154.
Energy, one of the great unifying concepts of physics. Energy is defined as the capacity for doing work and has many forms: mechanical, atomic, heat, chemical and others. It undergoes transformations: thermonuclear reactions in the Sun release solar energy; photosynthesis in plants stores this energy in chemical form; ingestion of the plant by animals allows muscles to transform this energy yet again into physical action. The concept of energy came into being with Galileo and Newton. Its conservation through all its transformations was established almost simultaneously by Joule, Rumford and Kelvin in the mid-19th century. The relationship between energy and mass of a particle was established in 1905 by EINSTEIN, who recognized that energy (E) and mass (m) could be transformed into each other according to the relation $E = mc^2$, where c is the velocity of light. *See also* SU p.68.
Energy, conservation. *See* CONSERVATION OF ENERGY.
Energy sources, supply of energy for heat, light and power which we derive, ultimately, from the Sun. They include the fossil fuels such as coal, oil and natural gas, which are the remains of life that was dependent for growth in its day on solar energy, just as all forms of life are today. HYDROELECTRICITY also derives from solar energy, which maintains the circulation of water vapour in the atmosphere; wind power has the same source. The movements of tides and waves depend both upon solar thermal energy and also on the gravitational pulls of the Sun and Moon. We use solar energy directly for heating domestic water supplies, and for providing electricity from PHOTOCELLS. Other major sources are radioactive metals such as uranium and thorium, which provide NUCLEAR ENERGY. Future possibilities include the extraction of energy from water by thermonuclear processes, and tapping the heat of the oceans and the Earth's interior crust on a much larger scale than the geothermal exploitation of today. *See also* MM pp.62–84.
Enesco, Georges (1881–1955), Romanian virtuoso violinist and composer. He studied in Paris with MASSENET and FAURÉ. His compositions include three symphonies and an opera, *Oedipe*. One of his pupils was Yehudi MENUHIN.
Enfants Terribles, Les (1929), novel by Jean COCTEAU. Brother and sister, Paul and Elisabeth, create their own, unbalanced world, where they must follow the rules of the "game" that eventually leads them to destruction.
Engadine, mountainous region in E Switzerland in the valley of the River Inn, in the Rhaetian Alps. It consists of Lower Engadine (NE) and Upper Engadine (SW) and extends NE approx. 100km (60 miles) from the Maloja Pass to the Austrian border. A region of spectacular scenery, it has several health and mountain resorts, including St Moritz.
Engelbrektsson, Engelbrekt (1390–1436), Swedish national hero. He led a revolt against Eric of Pomerania, King of Denmark, Sweden and Norway. Engelbrektsson was a mine owner, but in 1434 he became leader of a peasants' and miners' uprising against the king. Engelbrektsson seized castles throughout eastern and southern Sweden until the diet of 1435 accepted his demands and made him regent.
Engels, Friedrich (1820–95), German political writer. He was a disciple of Karl MARX, with whom he formulated the theory of DIALECTICAL MATERIALISM. As agent in England of his father's textile business (1842–44) he wrote *The Condition of the Working Classes in England* (1845). He had met Marx in Europe during the early 1840s, and together they wrote the *Communist Manifesto* (1848). From 1870 to Marx's death in 1883, Engels supported Marx's research financially and continued to help him with his writings. Engel's materialist reorientation of HEGEL's dialectics is most evident in his *Socialism, Utopian and Scientific* (1882) and *Anti-Dühring* (1878). *See also* HC2 pp.109, 172.
Engine, any device or machine that converts one form of energy into another to provide useful mechanical motion. The term is, however, usually restricted to machines that burn fuels to provide power. Such machines include steam, petrol, jet and rocket engines, all of which convert the chemical energy of fossil or other fuels, and nuclear engines, which convert the nuclear energy of the atoms of their radioactive fuels. These engines are distinguished from electric motors and generators, energy converters which, in providing their power, do not alter the chemical or physical composition of matter. However, some engines of the near future such as ION ENGINES and SOLAR ENGINES, will not fit into this restrictive definition. Combustion engines of the present day are of two main kinds, external combustion engines and INTERNAL COMBUSTION ENGINES. External combustion engines burn their fuels externally to the chamber in which power is developed: in the steam locomotive, this chamber is the boiler. Steam raising with a boiler is the method also employed in marine nuclear engines such as those fitted in Soviet icebreakers and Polaris submarines. Most conventional ships are at present fitted with oil-fired steam TURBINES. In both types, steam at high pressure, raised in boilers, is fed to a turbine housing where it expands to turn the turbine wheels. In gas turbines employed widely in industry, gases from fuels burned in a combustor, or other source, are fed to a compressor before being admitted to the turbine. In contrast to these external combustion turbine engines, the turbojet engines of aircraft are really internal combustion engines. In the standard turbojet, air enters at the front and is compressed by a rotary compressor before passing to a combustion chamber where it causes the fierce combustion of injected KEROSENE fuel. The exhaust blast not only provides thrust for the aircraft but also turns a turbine, which is coupled to and drives the AIR COMPRESSOR. The turbofan engine differs in that air is also drawn into the engine by a fan, driven by the turbine, so that it passes along an annular space surrounding the combustion chamber, expanding by heat and so providing extra thrust at the exhaust outlet. Ramjet engines have no moving parts, the air being compressed only by the fast forward movement of the aircraft; these are used only experimentally and can operate only at high speeds. Combustion reactions in a large rocket engine take place between liquid oxygen (oxidant) and a liquid fuel such as kerosene; smaller rockets usually employ solid chemical fuels. Because rockets carry their own oxidant, they, unlike jetplanes, can travel in space, by the principle of REACTIVE THRUST. Most familiar of internal combustion engines are those of road vehicles. Most car engines are driven by petrol, the vapour of which, together with air, is ignited in the engine cylinders by a timed electrical spark. The expanding gases thrust a piston along the length of each cylinder, in a reciprocating movement, which, by the movement of various linked shafts and gears, is transformed into the rotary movement of the car wheels. In DIESEL ENGINES the explosion in the cylinder is achieved by compression only; diesels are generally rather heavier engines. The Wankel engine is a later development of the petrol engine and has, not many reciprocating pistons, but a single, rotary one. This is triangular in shape and rotates under the thrust of the combustion gases so that, at one point in its cycle, the petrol mixture is admitted, at another the gases are combusted, and at a third point they are exhausted from the cylinder. *See alsot* MM pp.62–75, *130–131*, 132–133, *141, 153*, 156.
Engineering, application of scientific principles for many practical purposes such as the design and building of structures and the design and operation of machines and processes. For example, mechanical engineers design and test industrial machinery and vehicle engines; civil engineers prepare sites, design and construct bridges, tunnels and harbours; electrical engineers design and install mains electrical systems; electronic engineers design and build scientific instruments and design and install control systems; nuclear engineers have special knowledge of the installation and operation of nuclear reactors; and chemical engineers of the equipment and methods needed to contain large-scale chemical reactions. Between these many fields of engineering there is some overlap of interest and expertise. For this reason the academic training of all engineers starts with a thorough grounding in the fundamentals of science and continues with an education in general engineering subjects which overlaps to varying degrees the specialized training in the student's chosen field.
Engineering, chemical. *See* CHEMICAL ENGINEERING.
Engineering, genetic, deliberate alteration in the characteristics of an organism by controlled manipulation of its genetic make-up. From the 1940s onwards, knowledge of the hereditary or genetic make-up of simple organisms such as bacteria and viruses accelerated considerably. It was revolutionized in 1953 by the explanation of the structure of DNA – the "molecule of life" – by WATSON, CRICK and WILKINS. Not long after this genetic experiments with certain viruses and bacteria enabled microbiologists to characterize their genetic make-up more or less completely – that is, to state the structure of every one of their GENES, their positions in the DNA OR RNA, and their certain or probable function in the life and reproduction of the microbe. With such exact knowlege of the genetic machinery of these simple forms of life, microbiologists could now hope to alter them in controlled and specific ways. To date, many completely novel viruses and radically altered strains of bacteria and fungi have been made in this way by artificial means. They have been manufactured either for purposes of pure research, or for practical reasons, including the increased production of antibiotic drugs, the investigation of drug resistance passed on between bacteria, and for microbiological warfare. *See also* HEREDITY; PE pp.176–177.

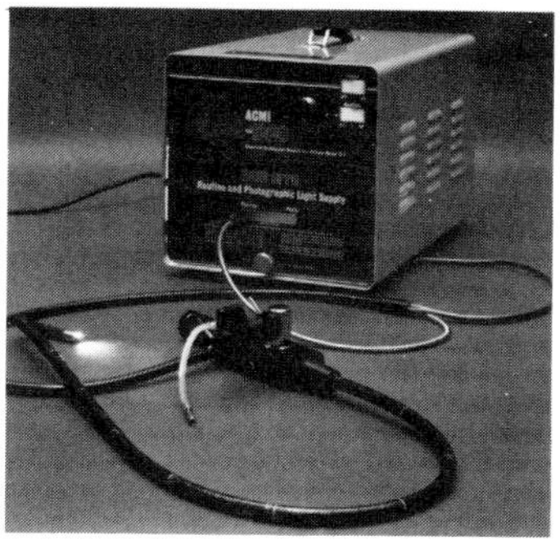

Endoscopes are used without anaesthetics, unless an incision into the body is made.

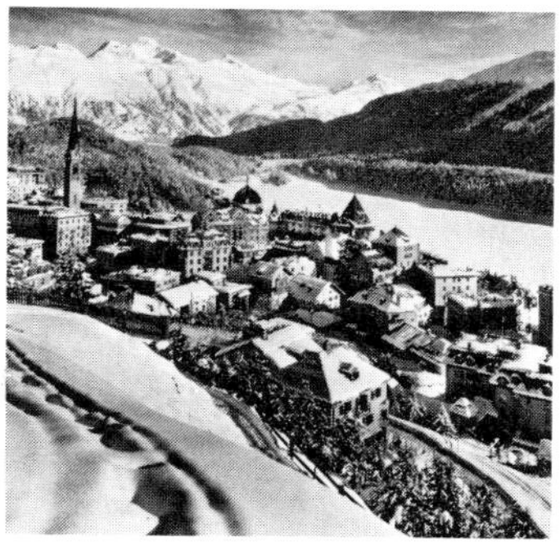

Engadine; a winter view of St Moritz, a resort in this spectacular region of Switzerland.

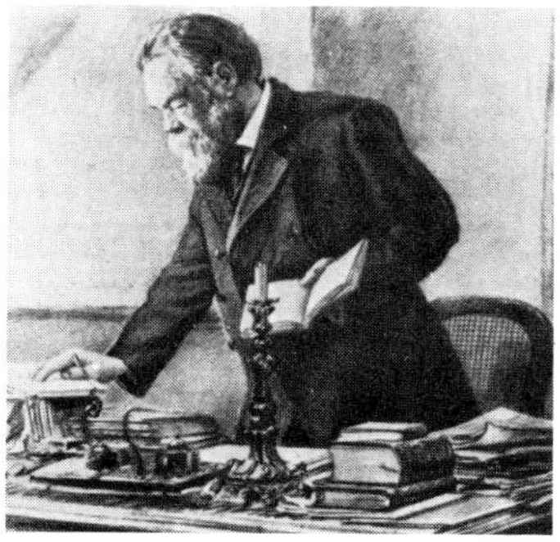

Friedrich Engels predicted that war would become obsolete in an industrialized world.

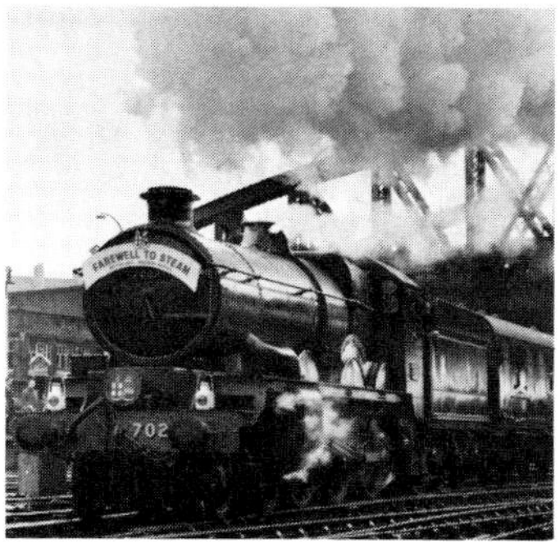

Engine; the last steam train in main-line service in Britain leaves Paddington, 1965.

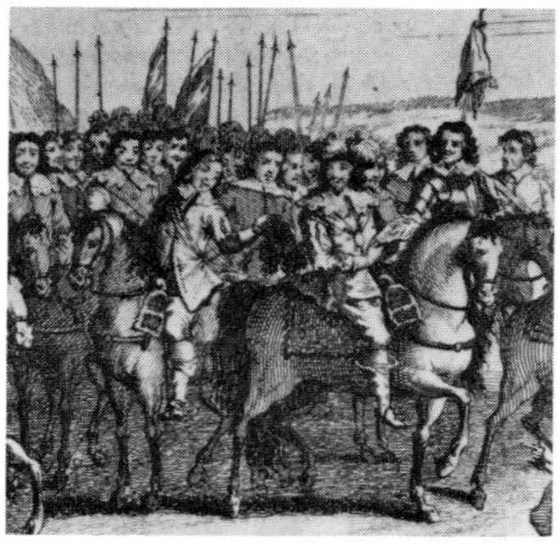

English Civil Wars; an engraving of the King's Declaration to his gentry and army in 1642.

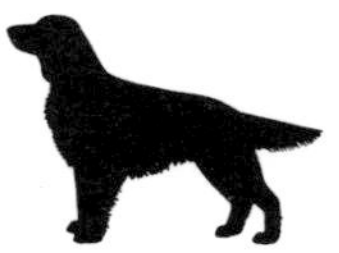

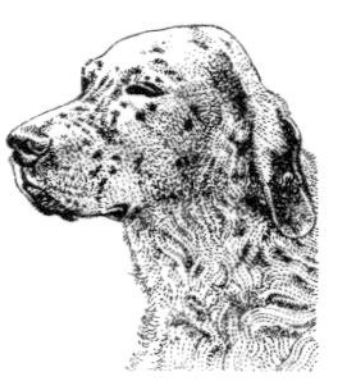

English setter is a retrieving dog trained to locate shot game on the ground.

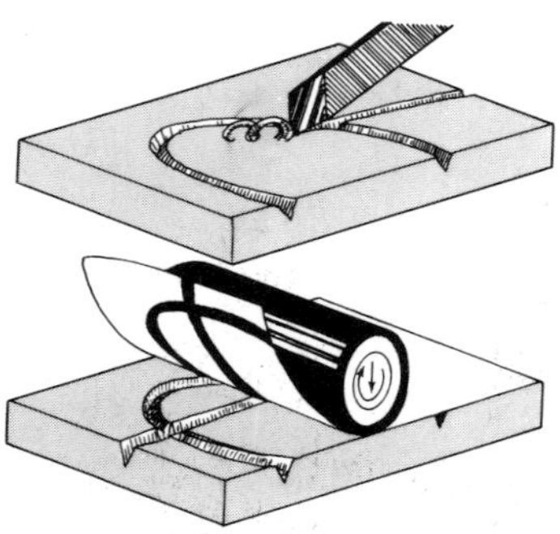

Engraving, a process by which designs can be reproduced accurately and in any quantity.

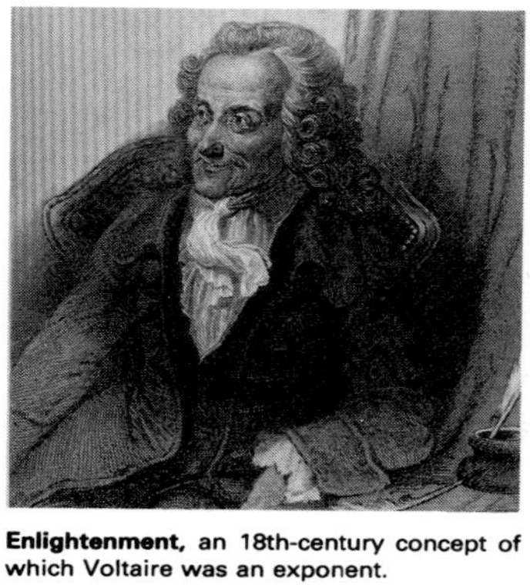

Enlightenment, an 18th-century concept of which Voltaire was an exponent.

England, largest nation within the United Kingdom bounded by the North Sea (E), the English channel (S), Wales and the Irish Sea (W) and Scotland (N). The landscape is complex although in general the N and W is higher and geologically older than the S and E. Dairying is the most important agricultural activity. Industries are varied, but engineering and coal-mining are of great importance. The country trades mostly within the EEC which it joined as part of Britain in 1973. The capital is London. Area: 130,362sq km (50,333sq miles). Pop. (1976) 44,600,000. *See also* MW pp.68–74.

England, Church of. *See* CHURCH OF ENGLAND.

English Channel, arm of the Atlantic Ocean between France and Britain; it joins the North Sea at the Strait of Dover. A cross-channel train-ferry service between Dover and Dunkirk was started in 1936. Width: 30–160km (20–100 miles); length: 564km (350 miles).

English Civil Wars (1642–46; 1648), conflicts between CHARLES I and his opposition in Parliament. The wars were originally fought between companies organized by individual commanders on each side, until Jan. 1645 when the Parliamentarian army was reorganized into the centralized NEW MODEL ARMY. The first war comprised a number of separate campaigns marked by many battles and skirmishes. The king was based in Oxford, and drew his main support from the north and west, and the Parliamentarians had their centre in London, and much of their support came from the home counties. The first main battle, at EDGEHILL in Oct. 1642, was indecisive, and little was achieved in the following year. In 1644 a Scottish army entered England on the Parliamentarian side, and Charles's army, led by his nephew Prince RUPERT, was beaten at MARSTON MOOR near York in July. The SELF-DENYING ORDINANCE of 1645 made Sir Thomas FAIRFAX head of the Parliamentarian army in the place of the Earl of ESSEX; its demand that all the Parliamentarian officers should give up their commands was necessary for the reorganization of the army. Charles met a serious defeat at the hands of Oliver CROMWELL at NASEBY (June 1645), and eventually surrendered to the Scots in May 1646. The second civil war broke out in Feb. 1648 after Charles escaped from custody and concluded an alliance with the Scots to support PRESBYTERIANISM. The uprising was crushed by Cromwell at PRESTON in Aug. 1648. *See also* HC1 pp.288–289.

"England expects that every man will do his duty", message given by Nelson before the Battle of Trafalgar (Oct. 1805). *See also* HC2 pp.78, *79*; MS p.*242*.

English setter, retrieving DOG (sporting group), first bred 400 years ago in England. An outdoor dog, it has a long, lean head with a square muzzle, hanging lips and rounded ears that hang close to the head. The medium-length body and legs are graceful, and the straight, feathered tail tapers to a point. Average height: 63.5cm (25in) at the shoulder; weight: 27kg (60lb).

English Speaking Union, society founded in 1918 by Sir Evelyn Wrench to further the fellowship of the English-speaking peoples of the world.

English Stage Company, company formed in 1956 to produce plays by new playwrights. Its first director was George DEVINE, its first success OSBORNE's *Look Back in Anger*, produced at the company's home, the Royal Court Theatre, London, in May 1956.

Engraver beetle. *See* BARK BEETLE.

Engraving, intaglio (incised) printing process. Prints are made from metal plates into which linear designs have been made by a cutting tool. Ink is rubbed into the lines, and the remaining surface is cleaned. A sheet of damp paper is placed on the plate, backed by several layers of felt. The plate is then passed through an etching press which applies pressure enough to force the paper into the lines and receive the ink. The various intaglio processes such as ETCHING, AQUATINT, LINE ENGRAVING differ only in the way of incising the copper plate. In modern engraving, different processes are frequently combined in a single plate. *See also* PRINTMAKING.

Enigma cipher machine, electrical machine with a typewriter keyboard which transposed the typed characters according to a prearranged random setting. Enigma was invented by Arthur SCHERBIUS in the 1920s and was the means by which the Germans transmitted their most secret information during WWII. The British could decipher Enigma messages early in the war but had to be careful not to make obvious use of the information received this way, so that the Germans would not stop using the system and thereby deprive the Allies of further information. *See also* MS p.*243*.

Enki. *See* EA.

Enkidu, in the EPIC OF GILGAMESH, a wild man created by the god Anu who at first lived among animals. Having attained some education he travelled to Uruk (the biblical Erech) to meet Gilgamesh. The two later killed a divine bull sent by Ishtar, after which Anu ended Enkidu's life. At the end of the epic, Enkidu's spirit returns to regale Gilgamesh with grim tales of the underworld. *See also* MS pp.*209*, 211.

Enlightened Despotism, term for the monarchical rule in 18th-century European states whose absolute rulers took pride in following the rational precepts of the ENLIGHTENMENT and thereby reforming the antiquated structure of feudal society. The two most famous examples are FREDERICK THE GREAT of Prussia and MARIA THERESA of Austria. *See also* HC2 pp.22–23.

Enlightenment, The, word used to describe the intellectual temper of Western Europe in the 18th century. It developed from the spirit of rational enquiry of the SCIENTIFIC REVOLUTION and from political theorists of the late 17th century AGE OF REASON such as LOCKE. Its centre was France, intellectually dominated by DIDEROT, VOLTAIRE and ROUSSEAU; but it had its representatives in Britain (HUME, ADAM SMITH), Germany (KANT) and America (FRANKLIN, JEFFERSON). Enlightenment thought supposed the susceptibility of nature to rational human investigation, opposed obscurantism and superstition, and therefore tended to DEISM in religion. Its belief in the perfectibility of man gave it its note of optimism. It found some political expression in ENLIGHTENED DESPOTISM but it also had a profound influence on the attitudes which produced the French and American revolutions. *See also* HC2 pp.22–23.

Enlil, chief god of the Sumerian pantheon and later of Babylon and Assyria. He was guardian of the city of Nippur, the political and religious centre of southern Mesopotamia. As the god of mountains, air, storm and winds Enlil shared his dominion with first two then three great deities, but he alone was responsible for bringing the Me, or laws governing all existence. He was eventually displaced by MARDUK

Ennius, Quintus (239–169 BC), early Latin poet, sometimes known as father of Roman poetry. He spoke Oscan, Greek and Latin, and taught as well as producing adaptations of Greek plays. The *Annales* was his principal work. *See also* HC1 p.112.

Enoch, name of several Old Testament figures. One was the father of METHUSELAH, to whom the pseudepigraphical Books of Enoch are ascribed (*see also* PSEUDEPIGRAPHA). Another was CAIN's eldest son, whose name was given to the city built by Cain.

Enosis, Greek Cypriot demand, originating in 1878, for political union with Greece, which after WWII included a campaign of violence. In the late 1950s the Turks, alarmed at the prospect of enosis, put forward a counter demand for partition of the island, which they achieved by invasion in 1974. The movement found its greatest leader in Archbishop MAKARIOS III; it remains a vital political issue.

Enright, Dennis Joseph (1920–), British author. Collections of his poetry include *The Laughing Hyena* (1953), *Some Men are Brothers* (1960) and *The Terrible Shears* (1973). His novels include *Academic Year* (1955) and *Insufficient Poppy* (1960).

Enriquez Gomes, Antonio (1602–63), Spanish poet, dramatist and satirist. While living in France he attacked the INQUISITION in *Politica angelica* (1647). On his return to Spain he worked chiefly as a playwright, but in 1660 his effigy was burnt at an AUTO DA FÉ, and in the following year he was arrested by the Inquisition. He died in prison.

ENSA (Entertainments National Service Association), British WWII organization established in 1938 to provide morale-boosting diversion for troops and civilians, and directed by Basil DEAN.

Enschede, city in E Netherlands near the border with West Germany, on the Twente Canal. Founded in 1118, it was devastated by fire in 1862. It has a university (1961) and a natural history museum. Industries: pharmaceuticals, textiles, paper, dairy products, brewing. Pop. (1974) 141,575.

Enstatite ($MgSiO_3$), orthorhombic mineral of the pyroxene group, commonly found in ultrabasic igneous rocks such as norites, pyroxenites, gabbros and peridotites. It varies from colourless to yellowish grey, shading to green if iron is present. Hardness, 5.5; s.g. 3.2–3.5.

Entail, in law, restriction of inheritance to a limited class of descendants (eg eldest sons) for at least several generations, its object being to preserve large estates which would disintegrate if inherited in equal parts by all the descendants. In the absence of descendants the entail terminates. The creation of entail estates was abolished in 1925.

Entebbe, town in S central Uganda, E Africa, on NW shore of Lake Victoria; scene of Israeli commando raid in 1976 to rescue a hijacked jet liner. Founded in 1893 it was the capital of the British Protectorate of Uganda 1894–1962. The surrounding area produces coffee and cotton. Pop. (1969) 10,900.

Entente, diplomatic term first used in 1844 in the phrase *Entente Cordiale*, or cordial understanding (rather than a formal alliance), between France and England. It is more usually related to the TRIPLE ENTENTE brought about by agreements between France and Britain (1904) (which also became known as the ENTENTE CORDIALE) and Britain and Russia (1907). *See also* HC2 pp.180, 183, *183*.

Entente Cordiale, name given to a series of agreements signed by France and Britain in April 1904. Quarrels about fishing rights off Newfoundland and about various spheres of colonial interest were settled. British paramountcy in Egypt and French in Morocco were recognized. The *entente* was the first step leading to the TRIPLE ENTENTE. *See also* HC2 pp.180, 183.

Enteritis, chronic or acute inflammation of the lining of the intestine. Its causes include the ingestion of irritant poisons, or infectious disease; mild to extreme diarrhoea and abdominal pain are symptoms. Treatment usually includes a bland diet. *See also* GASTROENTERITIS; MS p.92.

Enterokinase, enzyme released by the small intestine during digestion. It activates the digestive enzyme TRYPSIN.

Entoderm. *See* ENDODERM.

Entomology, scientific study of INSECTS, including their relation to man. The ancient Greeks of the 4th century BC were the first serious entomologists, and ARISTOTLE coined the term *entoma* after which the science is named.

Entropy, quantity specifying the disorder or randomness of a system containing either energy or information. In THERMODYNAMICS it expresses the degree to which thermal energy is available for work – the less available it is, the greater the entropy. Energy can be extracted from a system only as it changes from a more ordered to a less ordered state. According to the second law of thermodynamics, in any process a system's change in entropy is either zero or positive. Thus the entropy of the universe is increasing. In INFORMATION THEORY, the entropy of a system is proportional to the lack of information about that system. *See also* SU p.93.

Enugu, city in SE Nigeria; capital of East-Central state. It developed as a coal-mining town in the early 20th century. It is linked by rail to Port Harcourt, and its industries include textiles, steel, furniture and cement. Pop. 182,000.

Enuma Elish, Old-Babylonian poem written in the 11th century BC. This epic on the creation of the world is sometimes known as the Babylonian Genesis. It describes the battle of the Babylonian god MARDUK against Tiamat (the force of chaos), Marduk's victory and his elevation to the status of ruling deity.

Enumerated goods, products of the English colonies listed under the NAVIGATION ACT to be exported only through the mother country. Products affected included many raw materials such as tobacco, sugar and furs, as well as naval stores.

Enver Pasha (1881–1922), Turkish military and political leader. Involved in the Young Turk revolution (1908), he became virtual dictator through a coup in 1913. He was instrumental in bringing Turkey into WWI as an ally of Germany. When Turkey signed an armistice (1918), Enver fled to Berlin. He was killed leading an anti-Soviet expedition in Bukhara.

Environment, forces and conditions that surround and influence living and non-living things (biotic and abiotic environments). Factors such as temperature, soil, atmosphere and radiation compose the abiotic environment, while food, plants, organisms and animals compose the biotic environment. *See also* NW p.194.

Environment, Department of the (DOE), British government department responsible for a wide range of functions relating to the physical environment. Headed by a secretary of state, it is responsible for statutory and regional planning, inner city renewal, land policy, new towns, local government structure and finance, water and minerals, conservation of historic monuments, control of pollution and future planning. The secretary is assisted by the minister for housing as well as by the Property Services Agency, which provides government services relating to land, property and building.

Enzymes, group of proteins that function as catalysts in biochemical reactions. Since they are not used up in these reactions they are effective in tiny quantities and, because they are highly specific, enormous numbers of them occur in nature. Many enzymes require the presence of accessory substances (COENZYMES) in order to function effectively. Enzymes are important in heredity; many genes function by producing specific enzymes. The names of most enzymes end in the letters "-ase" except for a few, such as pepsin, that retain older names. *See also* SU pp.154, 156; MS pp.65, 68, 69, 92.

Eocene Period, the second of the five epochs of the TERTIARY PERIOD from about 60–30 million years ago. The name implies the "dawn" of life in which the modern families appeared. The fossil record shows members of modern plant genera, including beeches, walnuts and elms, and indicates the apparent dominance of mammals, including the ancestors of camels, horses (notably Eohippus), rodents, bats and monkeys. The world climate was warmer than at the present time. *See also* PE pp.130–131; NW p.190.

EOKA (Ethniki Organosis Kipriakou Agonos, National Organization of Cypriot Fighters), organization formed in Cyprus by Gen. GRIVAS, with the secret assistance of Archbishop MAKARIOS, in 1955. Its aim was to drive out the British rulers by guerrilla war and then to achieve union with Greece (ENOSIS). After heavy fighting the British left in 1959 and Cyprus became an independent nation.

Eolian (or aeolian) formation, in geology, structure created by wind-transported material. It may be a dune on a riverbank or ripple marks in sand on a beach or DESERT, or the growth phase of DUNE building. It also can be used to describe shapes carved in rock by the wearing away of softer materials. *See also* BUTTE.

Eolithic Age, or "Dawn Stone" Age, name usually given to the earliest period of human history, in which man, or near-man, used fractured stone tools. These tools were so primitive that they are often hard to distinguish from naturally broken stones.

Eoliths, crudely chipped stone flakes from very early or pre-PLEISTOCENE deposits. Once thought to be the oldest man-made tools, it is now generally accepted that they were chipped by natural agencies.

Eos, in Greek mythology, the dawn-goddess, daughter of HYPERION and THEA. She drove through the sky in a horse-drawn chariot preceding Helios, the sun, her brother. Homer and other poets describe her as "rosy-fingered" and "saffron-robed". Cursed by APHRODITE because she dallied with Ares, Eos was involved in a constant stream of hopeless love affairs.

Eosinophil, white BLOOD CELL with an affinity for eosin, the red dye. In certain diseases, such cells increase in number.

Eothen (1844), travelogue by A. W. KINGLAKE. The name means "towards the dawn", and the piece is a sympathetic and imaginative account of the author's travels in the Middle East.

Eotvös, József, Baron Von Vásárosnemény (1813–71), Hungarian statesman and author. He devoted his life to the democratization of Hungarian society and as education minister (1848; 1867–71) achieved useful reforms. His writings include the novels *A karthausi* (1839) and *A növérek* (1857).

Epée, sharp-pointed narrow sword, without a cutting edge, developed in the 19th century for duelling and fencing practice. The modern epée is triangular in section; the handguard is bowl-shaped.

Epeirogeny, in geology, form of DIASTROPHISM that results in the formation of large features of the Earth's crust such as continents and oceans, and the creation of large areas such as plateaus and basins within them. The movements that constitute epeirogeny are primarily vertical ones. In some processes that result in the formation (or deformation) of mountain topography, epeirogeny and OROGENY (main process by which mountains are formed) interact and overlap, making distinctions difficult. *See also* TECTONICS; PE p.106.

Ephemeroptera, mayflies, which live for a long time as nymphs, but only a few hours as adults. The adult cannot eat or drink.

Ephedrine, widely used drug, chemically similar to EPINEPHRINE (adrenaline). It stimulates the autonomic nervous system and is used to treat some allergies, to treat bronchial asthma by dilating bronchioles, to dilate pupils of the eyes, as a nasal decongestant and to treat low blood pressure.

Ephesians, New Testament epistle dictated by St PAUL during his captivity in Rome. Addressed to the Christian Church at Ephesus, it outlines the profound doctrine of the mystical body of Christ and stresses unity in love and faith.

Ephesus, ancient Ionian city of W Asia Minor. It was a prosperous port under the Greeks and Romans. Croesus, king of Lydia, captured it (*c.* 550 BC), and Cyrus the Great (*c.* 546 BC), Alexander the Great (334 BC), and the Romans (133 BC) later took the city. It was sacked by the Goths in AD 262. The COUNCIL OF EPHESUS was held there in 431. It has a noted temple of Artemis (Diana).

Ephesus, Councils of, two assemblies of the early Christian Church. The first council (431) was called by THEODOSIUS II and condemned NESTORIANISM. The second council of 449, the Robber Council, was also called by Theodosius and acquitted EUTYCHES, an early MONOPHYSITE, of heresy, deposing instead his opponent Flavian, patriarch of Constantinople.

Ephod, linen garment used in religious services in ancient Israel. A tunic worn by the high priest, it was sometimes also used for divination or for obtaining oracles showing God's will.

Ephraem Syrus (*c.* 308–373), Syrian churchman, a saint in the Roman Catholic and Eastern Orthodox churches. He wrote biblical commentaries and sacred verses, which he used in converting the Syrians to Christianity and in combating heresies. Feast: 18 June.

Ephraim, Old Testament figure, younger son of Joseph, grandson of Jacob. The eponymous founder of one of the 12 tribes of Israel, Ephraim seized a large, fruitful tract of land for his people.

Epic, long narrative poem in grandiose style in which heroes perform superhuman tasks of strength. The earliest known form of Greek literature, epics were originally used to transmit history orally. Using highly formalized language, they often involved gods, men and legendary battles. HOMER is the author of the two most famous epics, the *Iliad* and the *Odyssey*. Later examples include BEOWULF, VIRGIL's *Aeneid*, John MILTON's *Paradise Lost* and Edmund SPENSER's *Faerie Queene*.

Epicanthic fold, or Mongolian eyefold, downward and inward fold of the upper eyelid over the inner corner of the eye, producing the so-called "slant" eye characteristic of numerous peoples of Asiatic origin, some American Indians and the Khoisan groups of southern Africa. *See also* MS p.32.

Epicentre, spot on the Earth's surface directly above the focus of an earthquake. Depending on the character of the focus, the epicentre may be a small circle or a line. *See also* PE pp.28, *29*.

Epic of Gilgamesh, incomplete Mesopotamian epic poem of the third millennium BC, in which the tragic hero GILGAMESH searches for the means to restore his friend Enkidu to life; but having found the flower of immortality with the help of his ancestor Utnapishtim (the Babylonian Noah), he loses it, and his misery is compounded by Enkidu's grim descriptions of the place of the dead. *See also* HC1 p.30.

Epictetus (*fl.* *c.* 520–500 BC), ancient Greek painter. A cup painter, he was one of the first to use the red-figure style. His work shows great draughtsmanship, perfectly fitting figures to the insides of cups.

Epictetus, (AD *c.* 55–*c.* 135), Greek STOIC philosopher. His teachings were recorded in *Discourses* and *Enchiridion* by his disciple, Arrian. An admirer of SOCRATES and DIOGENES, he stressed the brotherhood of man, so influencing Christian thought.

Epic theatre, theory of dramatic presentation formulated in the late 1920s by Bertolt BRECHT and Edwin PISCATOR. It tries to undermine the theatrical illusion through "distancing" effects in the use of costume, sets, songs, argument, "montage narrative" and explicative soliloquies. The audience is meant to view the events on stage objectively and critically. Epic theatre often carried a socialist message.

Epicureanism, school of Greek philosophy founded by EPICURUS in the 4th century BC. Opposing the idealistic and sceptical mood of the times, Epicurus wanted to provide security in an unsure world. He grounded his system on the uncontestability of sense experience, postulating pleasure and pain as the ultimate measures of good and evil. Intelligent choice from experience is necessary for the good life. The last known member of the school was Diogenes of Oenoanda (*fl.* AD 200).

Epicurus (342–270 BC), Greek philosopher, founder of EPICUREANISM. Although only fragments of his works remain, his loyal disciples passed on his belief in man's freedom of action and his doctrines of friendship, peace of mind and spiritual enjoyment as goals of the good life.

Epidaurus, ancient city of Greece, in the NE Peloponnese. It has a 4th century BC theatre built on a hillside near the town, which is famous for its exceptional acoustics. Performances of Greek plays are still held regularly in the theatre. Epidaurus was also the site of a temple of Asclepius, the god of healing. *See also* HC1 p.*74*.

Epidemic, uncontained rapid spread of a disease through a population. The study of epidemics includes the causes, patterns of contagion and methods of containing disease. Bubonic plague, smallpox and typhoid have been causes of epidemics; hepatitis, influenza and venereal disease are now concerns of epidemiologists.

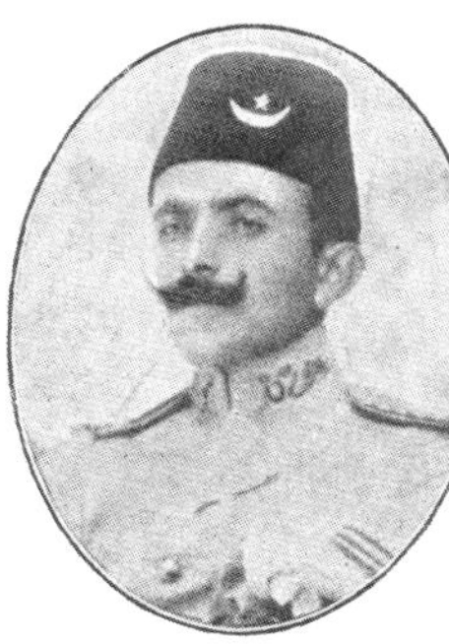

Enver Pasha sought to unite the Turkic people of Central Asia with the metropolitan Turks.

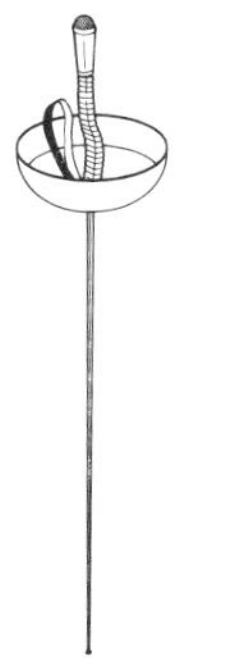

Epée, a sword weighing up to 765 grammes (27oz) and 109cm (43in) long.

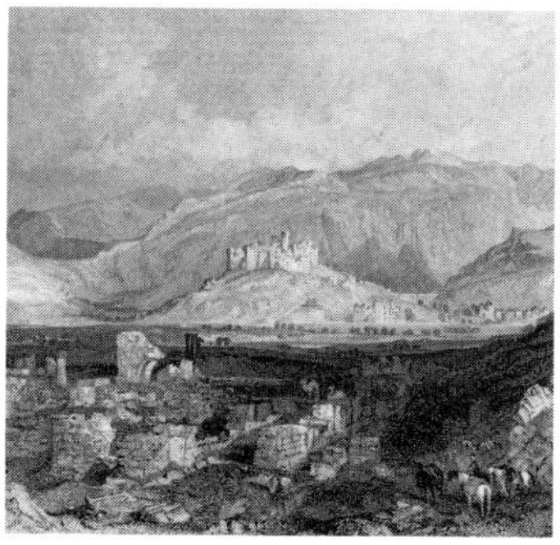

Ephesus, a 19th-century lithograph of the ruined city with the castle of Aiasaluk.

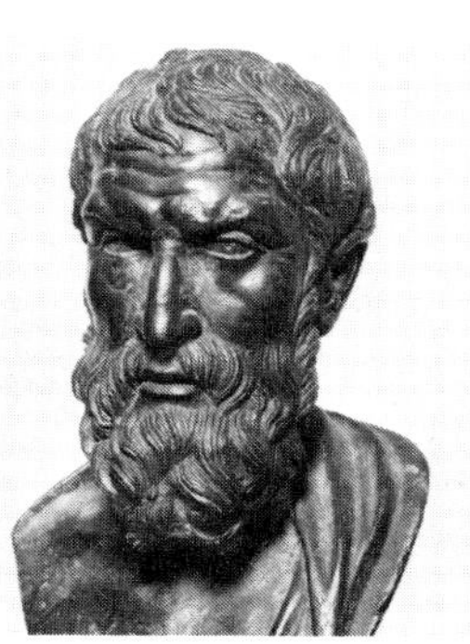

Epicurus; a bust of the celebrated Greek philosopher in the Museo Nazionale in Naples.

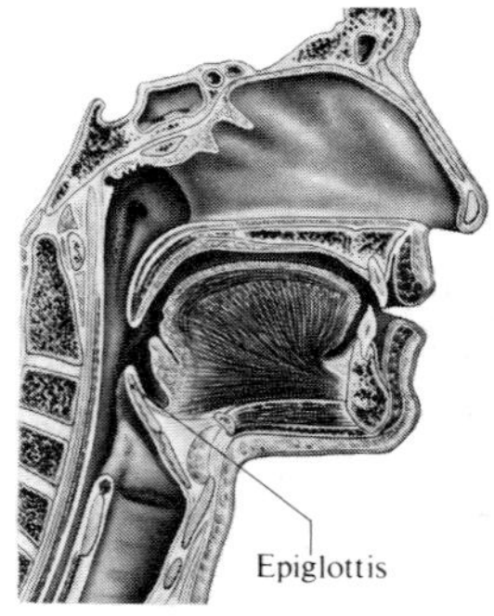

Epiglottis: diagram showing the location of this flap of cartilage in the back of the throat.

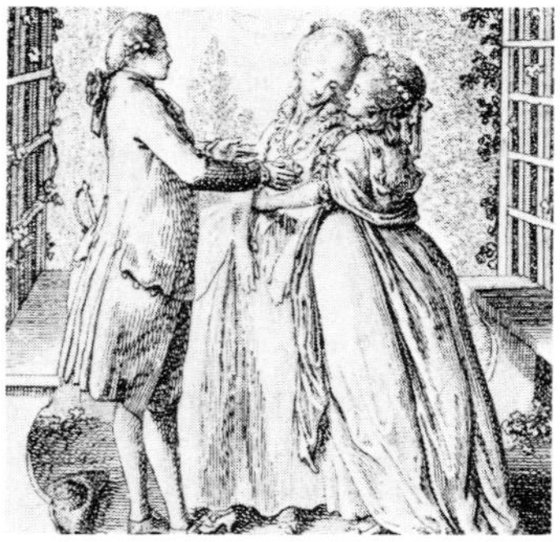

Epistolary novel; engraving by D. Chodowieck for Rousseau's *La Nouvelle Héloïse*.

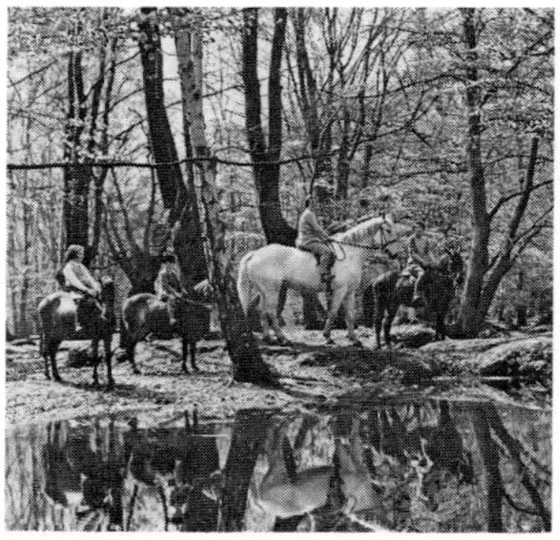

Epping Forest attracts early morning riders, seen here in a typical springtime setting.

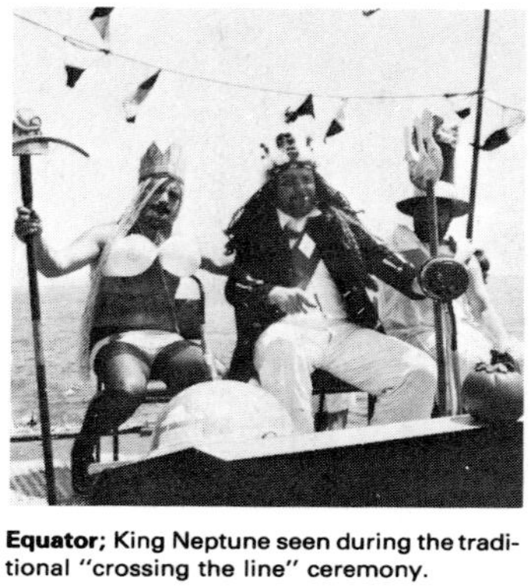

Equator; King Neptune seen during the traditional "crossing the line" ceremony.

Epidermis, outer layer of skin that contains no blood vessels. It is made up of four cell layers, including the outer horny stratum corneum, which protects the delicate underlayers from injury and infection, and the inner Malpighian layer, containing cells to replace spent outer cells and the pigments responsible for skin colour. *See also* MS pp.60, *60–61*

Epidiascope, optical instrument that projects an enlarged image of an object onto a screen. It is used to project transparent images such as slides and also opaque images such as the pages of a book.

Epididymis, network of ducts in the TESTES, where sperm cells mature and are stored. See also VAS DEFERENS; MS p.74, *74*.

Epidote, orthosilicate mineral, hydrated calcium iron-aluminium silicate $[Ca_2Fe_3(Al_2O)(OH)(Si_2O_7)(Si_2O_4)]$. It is found in metamorphic and igneous rocks as monoclinic system prismatic crystals and fibrous or granular masses; typically pistachio green, glassy and brittle. Certain large crystals, 7.5–25cm (3–10in), are collector's items. Hardness 6–7; s.g. 3.4.

Epidural anaesthesia, regional anaesthesia resulting from the disposition of a local anaesthetic such as procaine into the epidural space of the spinal cord. This space is between the fibrous membranes which surround and protect the spinal cord, and the vertebral canal. Epidural anaesthesia is increasingly being used to lessen or prevent pain during childbirth. *See also* MS p.*79*.

Epiglottis, thin ridge of CARTILAGE projecting upwards behind the root of the tongue. It blocks off the LARYNX during swallowing to avoid choking, ensuring that food passes into the OESOPHAGUS. *See also* MS pp.*67–68*.

Epigram, Greek word meaning "inscription". In classical literature, the term refers to a brief Greek or Latin poem expressing, in a pointed, witty manner, a single thought.

Epigraphy, study of epigraphs (inscriptions on durable material such as stone and metal or citations in books). The science of epigraphy is particularly important to classical archaeologists who learn much about life in Greece and Rome through inscriptions on statues, monuments and buildings.

Epilepsy, brain disorder characterized by disturbances in CONSCIOUSNESS, motor and sensory functions, often accompanied by CONVULSIONS (once commonly called fits). Epileptic seizures usually first manifest themselves in children between 3 and 15 years old, slightly more often in boys than in girls. The most familiar categories are *grand mal, petit mal* and pyschomotor. *Grand mal* seizures, up to five minutes long, may be preceded by so-called auras, and may involve calling out, loss of consciousness and loss of muscular control. *Petit mal* attacks last up to 15 seconds and are milder, although there may be an almost unnoticeable loss of consciousness. Pyschomotor attacks last up to three minutes, with confusion of motor and sensory abilities. Treatment may be with anti-convulsant drugs or education of the patient. *See also* MS pp.*97*, 139, *145*.

Epinephrine, or adrenalin, hormone produced by the medulla of the adrenal glands. It is chemically a catecholamine, $C_6H_3(OH)_2CHOHCH_2NHCH_3$ and is secreted under conditions of stress to prepare the body for "flight or fight" by dilating the blood vessels, increasing the heart beat rate and blood-sugar level. Synthetic epinephine, made from catechol, and the extract obtained from the adrenal glands of sheep and cattle are used in medicine. *See also* MS p.64.

Epiphany, Christian feast, celebrated on 6 Jan. It originated in the East as an observance of the baptism of Jesus, sometimes also of his birth. In the West it became associated with the manifestation of Christ to the Gentiles.

Epiphyte, or air plant, plant that grows on another plant but is not a parasite. Epiphytes usually have aerial roots and produce their own food by PHOTOSYNTHESIS. They are common in tropical forests. Examples are some ferns, orchids and Spanish moss.

Epirus (Ipeiros) province on the mainland of NW Greece, bounded by the Pindus Mts, (E) Albania (N and W) and the Ionian Sea (W). Arta is the administrative centre. This province occupies the southern portion of a region known in ancient times as the home of the oracle of Dodona. United under Pyrrhus in the 3rd century BC it was made a republic *c.*200 BC and fought with Macedonia against Rome. Plundered by Aemilius Paulus in AD 167 and subsequently occupied by the Serbs, the Albanians and the Turks in 1430, it became a semi-independent state controlled by Ali Pasha of Ioannina in the late 18th century; E Epirus passed to Greece in 1881; N Epirus remains part of Albania. Products include dairy produce, olives, citrus fruit and rice. Pop. (1971) 11,000.

Episcopacy, system of church government in which bishops (Greek *episkopoi*), regarded as the successors of the original twelve apostles, are responsible for pastoral care in their own DIOCESES. The Anglican, Roman Catholic and Eastern Orthodox Churches maintain an episcopal structure. *See also* APOSTOLIC SUCCESSION.

Epistemology, branch of philosophy that critically examines the nature, limits and validity of knowledge and the difference between knowledge and belief. Although it dates from the early Greek philosophers, in the 17th century DESCARTES showed that many previously "philosophical" questions would be better studied scientifically, and that what remained of metaphysics should be absorbed into epistemology. *See also* MS pp.226, 232–233.

Epistles, 20 letters forming most of the middle section of the New Testament. More than half of them are attributed to the apostle PAUL. (The Epistle to the Romans contains the single most complete formulation of Paul's teachings). Written in response to problems facing the first Hellenistic Christian congregations, some epistles contain instructions to specific communities, others were addressed to all Christians.

Epistolary novel, novel in the form of a letter or series of letters, popular in the 18th century. Samuel RICHARDSON established the English vogue for it with *Pamela* (1740) and ROUSSEAU used the form in *La Nouvelle Héloïse* (1761).

Epithalamium, nuptial poem derived from Fescennine verses, written to honour a bride and bridegroom and pray for their prosperity. The form was perfected by the classical poets Sappho, Anacreon, Pindar, Theocritus and Catullus. The most famous examples in English literature are Edmund SPENSER's *Epithalamion* and *Prothalamion*.

Epithelium, layer of cells, closely connected to form a membrane that covers every surface of the body to give protection from contact with foreign matter. Epithelium covers not only the skin, but also various internal organs and surfaces such as the intestines, nasal passages and mouth. There are various types of epithelial cells, including ciliated, columnar and squamous or flattened. Membranes may be one cell layer thick or many layers such as on the skin. Epithelial cells may also produce protective modifications such as hair and nails, or secrete substances such as enzymes and mucus. *See also* MS p.60.

Epode, form of lyric poetry in which a long line of poetry is followed by a shorter one. It is often preceded by stasima, a pair of elaborate stanzas. Its invention is attributed to ARCHILOCHUS in 7th-century BC Greece.

Epoxy resin, any of a group of thermosetting polymers with outstandingly good mechanical and electrical properties; stability, heat and chemical resistance, and adhesion. Epoxy resins are used in casting and protective coatings. Popular epoxy resins are sold in two separate components, a viscous resin and an amine or anhydride hardener, which are mixed just before use. *See also* MM p.55.

Epping Forest, county district in SW Essex, England, created in 1974 under the Local Government Act (1972). Area: 345sq km (133sq miles). Pop. (1974 est.) 114,800.

Epping Forest, originally part of the great forest of ESSEX, England, famous for its hunting. The forest was almost entirely destroyed by ENCLOSURES, but a small part of it, now in NE London, was saved by the Epping Forest Act of 1871.

Epsom and Ewell, municipal borough in Surrey, SE England bordering on Greater London. In the 17th and 18th centuries Epsom's mineral springs made it a popular spa town, and EPSOM SALTS (magnesium sulphate) was prepared there in about 1618. The town is also noted for its racecourse on Epsom Downs and its public school, Epsom College, founded in 1855. Pop. 72,000.

Epsom salts, hydrated form of magnesium sulphate ($MgSO_4.7H_2O$) found in nature in the mineral epsomite and in mineral waters; used in medicine as a cathartic. It was first prepared from mineral springs at Epsom, England.

Epstein, Sir Jacob (1880–1959), US sculptor who settled in Britain in 1905. His first major works were the 18 symbolical figures which decorated the BMA building in London. Other works are the bronze *Visitation* (1926), the marble *Genesis* (1930), the stone *Ecce Homo* (1934–35) and the alabaster *Adam* (1939).

Equator, imaginary circle on the Earth's surface that lies midway between the N and S poles and is the zero line from which latitude is measured. It divides the Earth into the Northern and Southern hemispheres.

Equator, celestial, great circle on the CELESTIAL SPHERE that lies directly above the Earth's equator. It is used as a reference to determine the position of a star using the astronomical co-ordinate system of right ascension and declination.

Equatorial bulge, enlargement in the equatorial region of a planet or the Sun as a result of distortion of the body caused by rotation. The equatorial diameter is thus greater than the polar diameter and the object is an oblate spheroid rather than a sphere. The bulge is most noticeable in rapidly rotating non-solid objects such as Jupiter. *See also* PE p.32.

Equatorial co-ordinate system, astronomical co-ordinate system that refers to the plane of the CELESTIAL EQUATOR. Two sets of co-ordinates are used: right ascension and declination, and hour angle and declination.

Equatorial currents, currents of the Atlantic and Pacific oceans that flow near the Equator. As they move W, their waters deflect either N or S in a clockwise or anti-clockwise direction. Nearer the Equator is the equatorial countercurrent which flows E between the North and South Equatorial currents. *See also* PE p.79.

Equatorial Guinea, Republic of, independent nation in W Africa. It consists of mainland Rio Muni, which supports 75 per cent of the population although it is largely underdeveloped, and the island of Macias Niguema Biyoga, where cocoa and coffee are grown on fertile volcanic soil. The capital is Malabo. Area: 28,051sq km (10,830sq miles). Pop. (1976 est.) 316,000. *See also* MW p.74.

Equatorial mounting, common telescope mounting in which the telescope rotates about two perpendicular axes, one of which the polar axis, is parallel to the Earth's axis, and so points towards the CELESTIAL POLE. The steady movement of celestial bodies, due to the Earth's rotation, can be followed by a daily rotation of the telescope about this axis, usually by means of a clock drive.

Equatorial orbit, orbit in the plane of the equator of a rotating celestial body. Equatorial orbits for artificial Earth satellites are the most economical to achieve, since the spacecraft already has a velocity of about 1,600km/h (1,000mph) caused by the Earth's rotation. Only restricted portions of the Earth's surface may be visible in such an orbit. *See also* SU p.268.

Equestrian sports, term used to describe horse sports. Although it applies to flat racing and National Hunt racing, and embraces hunting, point-to-point and polo, it is commonly used with reference to the three Olympic equestrian disciplines: dressage, show-jumping and trials (or eventing). Dressage tests a horse's training, development and ability to execute defined movements; show-jumping tests its speed and jumping ability over obstacles set in a confined area; trials, held over 1–3 days, tests its all-round ability at dressage, over obstacles across country and in show-jumping.

Equidae, HORSE family including one genus, *Equus*, with five subgenera – true zebra, Grevy's zebra, Asiatic wild ass, African wild (and domestic) ass, and wild (and domestic) horse. Class Mammalia; order Perrissodactyla.

Equigravitational point, location between two celestial bodies, such as the Earth and Moon, at which the sum of the two gravitational forces is zero. A space vehicle reaching this point will begin to accelerate towards the body it is approaching.

Equilibrium, in economics, position at which the total demand for goods and services equals the total supply of those goods and services. In such a situation there tends to be neither inflation nor recession. The market price is set at such a level that the quantity of goods producers are willing to produce equals the quantity that consumers are willing to buy.

Equilibrium, chemical. *See* CHEMICAL EQUILIBRIUM.

Equilibrium constant, ratio of concentrations of products to those of reactants, characterizing the CHEMICAL EQUILIBRIUM of a particular reversible reaction at a specified temperature.

Equinox, either of the two days of the year when, everywhere on Earth, day and night are of equal duration. They occur on the two occasions when the Sun crosses the CELESTIAL EQUATOR, moving in either a northerly or southerly direction.

Equisetales. *See* HORSETAIL.

Equity, in economics, value of an item or business less any amount owed on it. Equity normally refers to the difference between a firm's assets and its liabilities. As the asset value increases relative to liabilities, the equity is greater. The ordinary shares of limited companies are known as equity shares.

Equivalence principle, concept that ENERGY and mass are equivalent and interconvertible according to the equation $E=mc^2$ (c is the velocity of light). *See also* RELATIVITY; SU p.106.

Equivalent, electrochemical. *See* ELECTROCHEMICAL EQUIVALENT.

Equivalent weight, weight of an element, in grammes, that combines with 8gm of oxygen or its equivalent, eg the equivalent weight of hydrogen is 1 in forming water (H_2O). The equivalent weight of an acid is the weight that contains one gramme of acidic hydrogen. A similar definition is used for bases.

Érard, Sébastien (1752–1831), member of a French family of musical instrument makers. The son of a cabinet-maker, in 1777 he constructed the first piano to be built in France and nine years later set up a branch workshop in London. Today, the firm's name of Érard is highly regarded among HARP and PIANO makers.

Erasistratus (*fl.c.*250 BC), Greek physician. He made important discoveries concerning the heart and brain, among which were his description of the heart valves and his idea of the heart as a pump. He described the motor and sensory nerves and the function of the epiglottis. *See also* HC1 p.83.

Erastianism, complete control of church affairs by the state. It is named after Thomas Erastus (1524–85), a Swiss physician and theologian, who denied that the Church alone had disciplinary powers, especially of excommunication. Hence "erastianism" is a distortion of his position, which assumed co-operation between Church and state.

Erasmus, Desiderius (*c.*1466–1536), Dutch scholar, considered the greatest of the RENAISSANCE humanists. He was ordained as a Catholic priest in 1492. His *Enchiridion militis* (*Manual of the Christian Knight*) (1503) emphasized simple piety as an ideal of CHRISTIANITY and called for reform of the Church. *Praise of Folly* (1509) is a satire of late medieval society. His works had an early influence on LUTHER and other Protestant reformers, but he himself sought change from within the Catholic Church and found the course of the REFORMATION at least as upsetting as the faults of the Catholic Church that he had criticized. In *On Free Will* (1524) he openly clashed with Luther. *See also* HC1 pp.247, *268*.

Eratosthenes (*c.*276–*c.*194 BC), Greek scholar who first measured the earth's circumference by geometry. Eratosthenes administered the LIBRARY OF ALEXANDRIA and was renowned for his work in mathematics, geography, philosophy and literature. *See also* SU pp.*44*, *166*; HC1 pp.83, 336S.

Erbium, metallic element (symbol Er) of the LANTHANIDE SERIES, first isolated in 1843 by C. G. Mosander. Its chief ores are monazite (a phosphate) and bastnasite (fluorocarbonates). The element is used in some specialized alloys and erbium salts are used as pink colourants for glass. Properties: at. no. 68; at. wt. 167.26; m.p. 1,522°C (2,772°F); s.g. 9.045 (25°C); b.p. 2,510°C (4,550°F); most common isotope Er^{166} (33.41%).

Ercilla y Zuniga, Alonso de (1533–94), Spanish writer remembered for his epic poem *La Araucana* (1569–89). The poem concerns the uprising of the Araucanian Indians of Chile against their Spanish conquerors.

Erech (Uruk), ancient Sumerian city of S Mesopotamia, on the River Euphrates. It is the site of modern Warka, Iraq. It prospered *c.*5000 BC, and became the capital of Lower Babylonia. *See also* HC1 p.*31*.

Erechtheum, temple in the ACROPOLIS, built between 420 BC and 405 BC. It is made of Pentelic marble, and may have been designed by MNESICLES. It is perhaps the best example extant of the Greek IONIC order.

Erection, stiffening of the PENIS caused by a rush of blood into its spongy tissue.

Erewash, county district in SE DERBYSHIRE, England; created in 1974 under the Local Government Act (1972). Area: 109sq km (42sq miles). Pop. (1974 est.) 100,600.

Erewhon (1872), satirical novel by Samuel BUTLER. Higgs, the narrator, discovers the utopian country of Erewhon (an anagram of "nowhere"); Butler exposes the hypocrisy of Victorian society by means of an ingenious paradox.

Erfurt, city in SW East Germany, 102km (64 miles) WSW of Leipzig, on the River Gera; capital of Erfurt province. One of Germany's oldest cities, first mentioned by St. Boniface in the 8th century, it has the site of the Kränerbrücke (Merchants' Bridge) dating from 1325. Martin LUTHER lived there as an Augustinian monk (1505–08) and there is a 12th-century cathedral. Industries: optical instruments, precision tools. Pop. (1975) 203,190.

Erg, unit of energy in the metric cgs (centimetre-gramme-second) system of units. One erg is the work done by a force of one DYNE acting through a distance of one centimetre. One JOULE equals 10 million ergs.

Ergonomics, application of physiological and psychological principles to man-machine systems. It is used to design machines, tools, and work areas that take into account the physical and psychological limitations of human beings.

Ergosterol, organic chemical compound, a STEROID, found particularly in yeast and other fungi. When irradiated with ultraviolet light, it reacts to form many compounds.

Ergot, fungus (*Claviceps*) disease of rye plants and other small grasses. Part of the fungal body contains alkaloids that are generally poisonous to man but when purified and in appropriate doses can be used medicinally: ergotamine is used to treat migraine headaches, and ergonovine to induce uterine contractions to eject the afterbirth.

Erhard, Ludwig (1897–1977), German politician and economist, largely responsible for West German economic recovery after WWII. He was chancellor of West Germany from 1963 to 1966 and after his resignation was made honorary chairman of the CHRISTIAN DEMOCRATS.

Erica, genus of more than 500 species of mostly low, evergreen shrubs comprising true heaths and heathers. Most of the species are native to Africa, but many grow on moors in Britain and other parts of Europe. Blossoms are colourful and tube-shaped or bell-shaped. Family Ericaceae.

Ericsson, John (1803–89), US inventor. He went to the USA from Sweden in 1839 to build ships for the navy. During the AMERICAN CIVIL WAR, he constructed a new type of ironclad ship, the *Monitor*. The battle between the *Monitor* and the Confederate ironclad ship *Virginia* (formerly *Merrimac*) made him a Union hero.

Ericsson, Leif (*fl.* 1000), Norse explorer, son of ERIC THE RED. He is said to have discovered and wintered in Vinland on the North American continent (*c.*1000) when, on a voyage from Norway to bring Christianity to Greenland, he was blown off course. The probable site of his landing is in Nova Scotia. *See also* HC1 p.156.

Eric the Red (*fl.* 10th century), Norse explorer and discoverer of Greenland. He was exiled from Norway and Iceland for manslaughter, and went on a voyage of discovery during which he found Greenland in 982. He took colonists from Iceland to establish permanent settlements in 986. *See also* HC1 p.156.

Eridu, ancient Sumerian city and the modern site of Abu Sharein, S Iraq. Iraqi excavations (1946–49) indicate that Eridu dates from 5000 BC, making it the oldest known settlement in S Mesopotamia. Ruined temples decorated with silver, lapis lazuli and painted pottery dating from 3500 BC have been found. *See also* HC1 pp.*26*, 30.

Erie, city in NW Pennsylvania, USA, on Lake Erie. It was first settled by the French in 1753 and then occupied by the British in 1760. Pennsylvania's only port on the Great Lakes, it exports timber, coal, iron ore, petroleum, grain and fish. Industries: machinery, plastics, paper. Pop. (1970) 129,321.

Erie, Lake, one of the Great Lakes in North America, bordered by Ontario (W), New York (E), Ohio and Pennsylvania (S) and Michigan (SW); part of the Great Lakes-St Lawrence waterway. Discovered in 1669 by the French explorer Louis Jolliet, it is the shallowest and second smallest of the Lakes. Industrial cities on its shores have polluted it, but government regulations are now aiding its recovery. Area: 25,667sq km (9,910sq miles); max. depth: 64m (210ft).

Erie Indians, also known as the Cat Nation, sedentary tribe of Iroquoian-speaking North American indians who once occupied N Ohio, W New York and NW Pennsylvania. Formerly numbering 15,000, they were almost wiped out in a war with the IROQUOIS (1653–56). The few hundred survivors joined the Seneca tribe.

Erigena, Johannes Scotus (*c.*810–77), Irish philosopher and theologian. Little is known of his life. His major work, *De Divisione Naturae* (*c.*862–66), discusses the doctrine of creation.

Erik II Magnusson (1268–99), King of Norway (1280–99), also called "Priest-Hater". He continued the war against Denmark (1280–95) begun by his father MAGNUS VI. In 1282 he married Margaret of Scotland; in 1293 he married Isabella Bruce, sister of Robert BRUCE of Scotland.

Erik Bloodaxe (*d.*954), King of Denmark, Norway and Sweden (*r.*930–34). In 934 he was driven from Norway for his cruelty and injustice. He was given charge of Northumbria by ATHELSTAN, and ruled at York until slain in battle.

Erikson, Erik Homburger (1902–), US psychoanalyst and historian, *b.* Germany. He pioneered the use of Freudian psychoanalysis in treating children. He is a leading exponent of the psycho-historical school of history, having written the psychoanalytical studies *Young Man Luther* (1958) and *Gandhi's Truth* (1970).

Erin, ancient Gaelic name of Ireland, still often used poetically. According to legend, Erin was a mythical Irish queen.

Erinyes. *See* FURIES, THE.

Eris, in Greek mythology, the spirit of discord. She appeared as the only uninvited goddess at the wedding of Thetis and Peleus and threw among the guests an

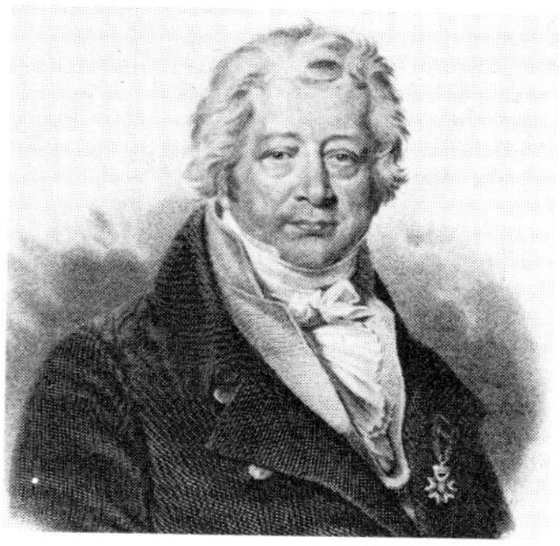

Erard, an instrument maker, fled to England during the French Revolution.

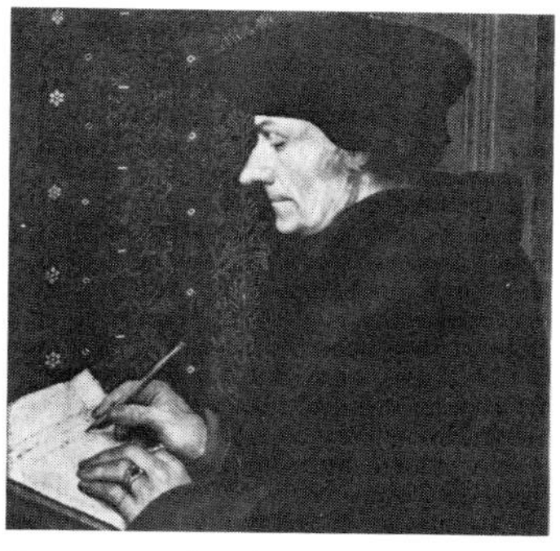

Erasmus; seen here in a portrait by Hans Holbein the Younger in the Louvre, Paris.

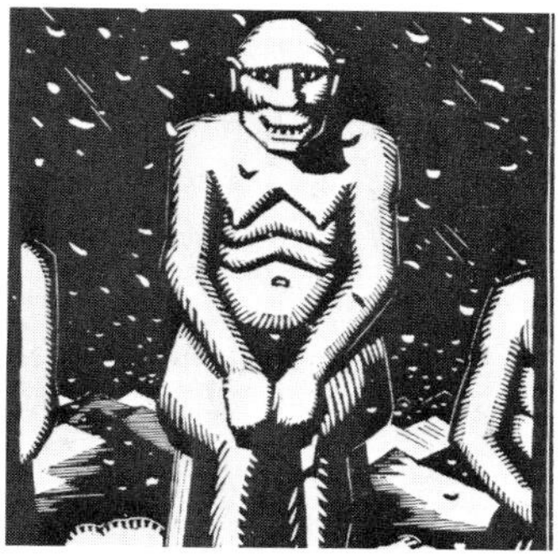

Erewhon; an illustration to an 1872 edition of Samuel Butler's famous work.

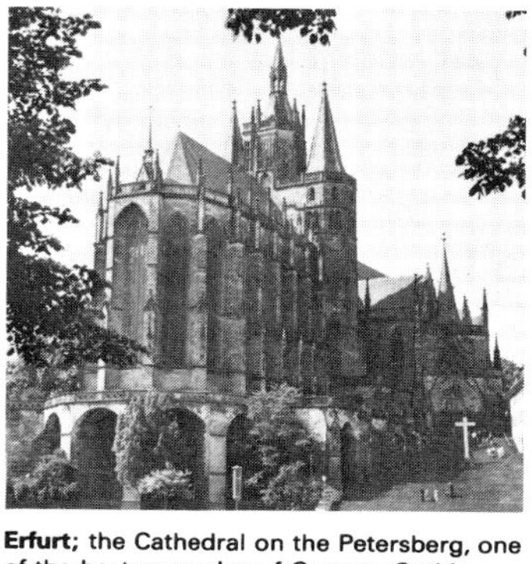

Erfurt; the Cathedral on the Petersberg, one of the best examples of German Gothic.

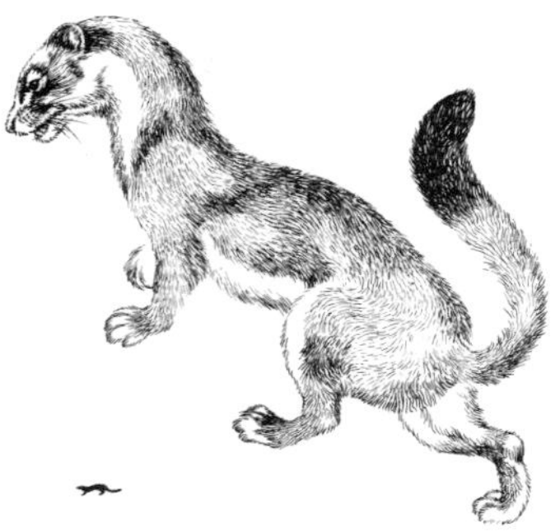

Ermine once provided the fur for trimming the robes of the European nobility.

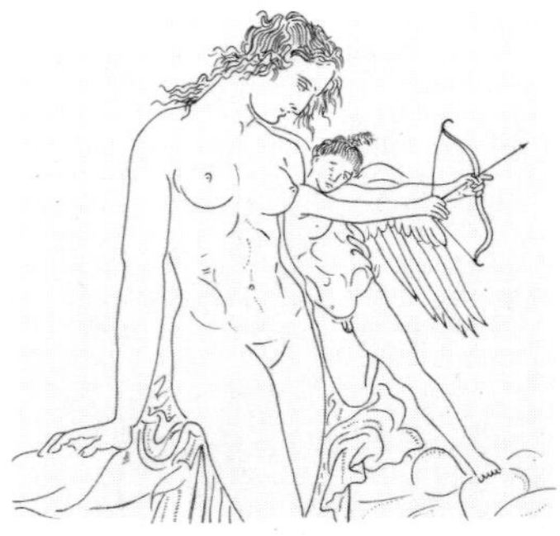

Eros, in the art of antiquity, was depicted first as a youth but later as an infant.

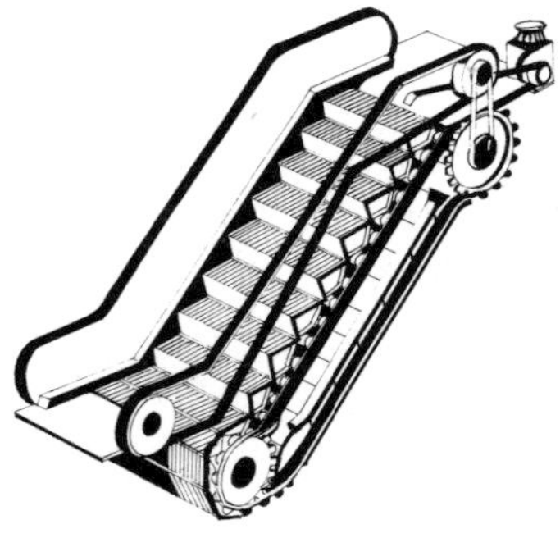

Escalator; the first inclined elevator was patented by Jesse W. Reno in 1891.

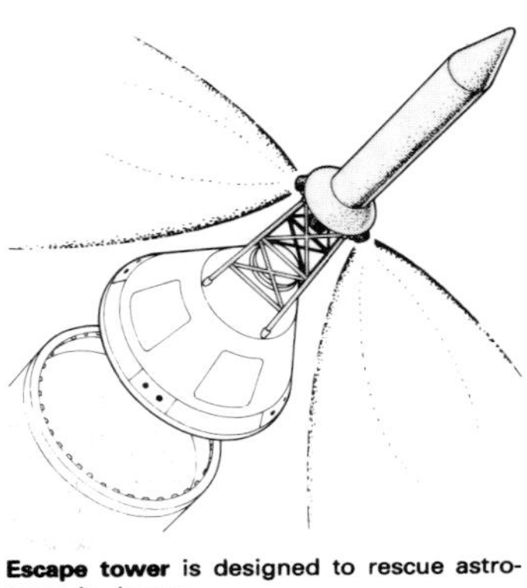

Escape tower is designed to rescue astronauts in danger.

apple addressed "To the fairest". When Hera, Athena and Aphrodite each claimed it, Zeus ordered the Trojan prince Paris to decide. His choice of Aphrodite led to the Trojan War.

Eritrea, province in N Ethiopia, on the Red Sea. The capital is Asmara and the chief ports are Aseb and Mesewa. It was under the control of Ethiopia until the Ottoman Empire took it in the 16th century. During the 19th century Ethiopia fought Egypt and Italy for control of the region, but Italy claimed it after 1890, and used it as a base from which to attack Ethiopia in 1935. Since 1962 Eritrea has been part of Ethiopia, but Eritrean separatists do not accept the union, and fighting between Eritrean nationalists and Ethiopian troops was particularly savage in the mid-1970s. Area: 117,599sq km (45,405sq miles). Pop. 1,836,800.

Erlach, J.B. Fischer von. *See* FISCHER VON ERLACH, J.B.

Erlanger, Joseph (1874–1965), US physiologist. In 1964 he shared the Nobel prize in physiology and medicine with H. S. GASSER for discoveries regarding the highly differentiated functions of single ner e fibres.

Erlkönig, in German legend a goblin king who haunted the Black Forest and exercised a malignant and fatal influence upon people, and expecially children, by offering alluring promises that led to their destruction.

Ermine, small, slender mammal called a stoat in Eurasia and short-tailed WEASEL in North America. Ermines have short black-tipped tails and a brown coat that turns white in winter. Length: 23cm (9in); weight: to 280gm (10oz). Family Mustelidae; species *Mustela erminea.*

Ermine Street, Roman road that ran from London through Ware, Royston, Huntingdon, Ancaster and Lincoln to York. It was one of the four roads given special protection by William I, and the name was applied indiscriminately to other Roman roads. Ermine was probably a Saxon personal name, given centuries after the road was built.

Ernest Augustus I of Hanover (1629–98), the first elector of HANOVER (1692–98). He created the ninth imperial electorate by uniting Hanover and Brunswick-Lüneberg. His son became King GEORGE I, first king of both Hanover and Great Britain.

"Ernie", acronym of *Electric Random Number Indicator Equipment,* the device housed at Lytham St Annes in Lancashire, England, which selects the numbers of winning PREMIUM SAVINGS BONDS. Numbers are selected every week and the holders of the numbered bonds win cash prizes. In addition, specially large prizes are distributed once each month.

Ernst, Max (1891–1976), German painter and sculptor, Founder of a DADA group in Cologne (1919), he later became prominent in the SURREALIST movement. He developed the form known as frottage, in which rubbings are made on paper held over various textured surfaces, to express his often fantastic and disturbing visions. His most important works include *L'Eléphant Célèbes* (1921) and *Two Children Threatened by a Nightingale* (1924). *See also* HC2 pp.202, 203.

Eros, in Greek mythology, god of love, identical with the Roman Cupid. Initially a personification of cosmic harmony being the son of Chaos, he was later depicted as a beautiful and playful youth with a bow and arrows, servant of his mother Aphrodite and inspirer of passion. He married Psyche, a mortal.

Eros, elongated asteroid with irregular-shaped orbit, discovered in 1898 by Carl Witt. In 1931 and 1975 it approached to within 24 million km (15 million miles) of the Earth. Longer diameter 27km (17 miles); mean distance from the Sun 232 million km (144 million miles); mean sidereal period 1.76 yr. *See also* SU p.204.

Eros, popular name for the Shaftesbury Memorial Fountain at Piccadilly Circus, London. Built in honour of the philanthropist Lord Shaftesbury and executed by the sculptor Sir Albert Gilbert, it was unveiled in 1893.

Erosion, in geology, alteration of landforms by gradually wearing them away and transport of the debris via wind, water, glacial movement, gravity and living organisms. Erosion can have disastrous economic results, eg the blowing away of topsoil, the weathering of man-made structures and the alteration of water systems. *See also* DENUDATION; GEOMORPHOLOGY; PE pp.112–114, 120.

Erosion channel, trench cut in the landscape due to rapid runoff of surface water, generally in areas unprotected by vegetation. In arid zones this form of erosion produces flat-floored channels called *arroyos*; in humid areas V-shaped gullies are the usual shape.

Erosion control, protection against loss of surface soil for agriculture, forestry, landscaping and recreation. Agricultural mismanagement, overgrazing and deforestation have destroyed major portions of the Earth's surface by exposing them to erosion by water and wind. Methods to prevent erosion include: zoning of land to limit grazing, TERRACING, contour cultivation, strip-cropping, litter-covering of cultivated soil, and the planting of trees as wind-breaks. *See also* SOIL CONSERVATION.

Erratic, or erratics, in geology, unstratified and frequently loose rocks, eg a rocking boulder, of all sizes. They are too large to have been stream-carried and are assumed to have been carried to their present locations by glacial action.

Erse, name given by Lowland Scots to the CELTIC LANGUAGE of the people of the W Highlands which is Irish in origin (the Middle English word *erisch* means "Irish").

Erucic acid, fatty acid ($C_{22}H_{42}O_2$) occurring in many vegetable oils such as rapeseed and mustard. When pure it is a colourless, crystalline solid, insoluble in water. Properties: s.g. 0.86; m.p. 33.4°C (92.1°F); b.p. 381.5°C (718.7°F).

Eruption, emission of volcanic materials either on land or under the sea. Any volcanic material constitutes an eruption, whether it is violent or calm, eg leaking of laval material from volcanic fissures. Constructive processes (such as FOLD and FAULT formation) resulting in the appearance of new material is also eruptive. *See also* PE pp.30–31, 104.

Ervine, St John Greer (1883–1971), Irish playwright, novelist and critic. He was manager of the ABBEY THEATRE, Dublin (1915–16). His plays, often set in Ulster, included *Mixed Marriage,* first produced in 1911, *The First Mrs Fraser* (1928) and *Boyd's Shop* (1936). He worked as a drama critic on both the *Observer* and the *Morning Post.*

Erysipelas, contagious skin infection caused by a STREPTOCOCCUS bacterium. Symptoms include pain and heat in the affected part, and coarse skin rashes which become red and shiny and appear swollen. *See also* MS pp. 98–99.

Erythema, redness of the skin caused by congestion of the capillaries, sometimes due to infection. Symptoms include tingling and pain. *See also* MS pp.98–99.

Erythrocyte, non-nucleated (usually disc-shaped) red blood cell, containing the pigment haemoglobin, that carries oxygen to the tissues and gives the blood its red colour. Normal human blood contains an average of five million such cells per cubic millimetre of blood, but the number is generally slightly higher in men and lower in women. *See also* MS pp.*62*–63.

Erythromycin, generic name of an antibiotic used to treat infections caused by streptococci, staphylococci, pneumococci and other gram-positive bacteria.

Erzgebirge (Krušnéhory, or Ore Mts), range extending along the border of Czechoslovakia and East Germany. Uranium, lead, zinc, tungsten, tin, copper, bismuth, antimony and arsenic are the chief metals whose ores are now mined there. The highest peak is Klínovec, 1,244m (4,080ft). Length: 161km (100 miles).

Erzurum, city in NE Asian Turkey; capital of Erzurum province. It was known as Theodosiopolis in the 5th century AD and was an important Byzantine frontier fortress. It was captured by the Ottoman Turks in the early 16th century. The first Turkish Nationalist congress was held there in 1919. Industries: agriculture, metal goods. Pop. (1973) 151,590.

Esaki, Leo (1925–), Japanese physicist who developed the tunnel diode, a semiconductor which allows electrons to cross normally impassable electronic barriers. Ivar GIAEVER extended Esako's research to the field of superconductivity, which led to the Josephson effect. For this work they shared the 1973 Nobel Prize in physics with Brian JOSEPHSON. The tunnel diode, also called Esaki diode, has found extensive applications which include its use in computer information storage.

Esarhaddon, King of Assyria (*r.* 681–669 BC), son of SENNACHERIB. He crushed revolts and defeated the Chaldaeans, who ruled BABYLON. He conquered Egypt (675–669 BC) and dominated ELAM. His son ASHURBANIPAL succeeded him. *See also* HC1 p.57, *57.*

Esau, Old Testament figure who, after a hard day's work, sold his birthright (his future inheritance as elder son) for refreshment to his scheming brother Jacob, later called Israel. The story probably derives from an attempt to give an ancient background to the enmity between the Israelites and the EDOMITES.

Esbjerg, port in SW Denmark, on the North Sea, on the Jutland peninsula. The city grew in the 19th century when its port was constructed. Industries: shipbuilding, fishing, cement. Pop. 76,000.

Escalator, electrically powered moving stairs, driven by chain and sprocket and held in the correct plane by two tracks. It is usually inclined at 30° and limited to a total rise of up to 18m (60ft). As the steps approach the landing, they pass through a protective comb-like device. Escalators are used to carry pedestrians between floors in busy areas such as large stores, office buildings and underground railway stations. The Otis Elevator Company exhibited the first escalator in 1900 at the Paris Exposition. *See also* MM pp.97, *97.*

Escalator clause, stipulation in a union-management work agreement that provides for an automatic upward adjustment in wages when the retail price index (or similar cost-of-living gauge) rises by a predetermined amount. It is designed to protect workers from the effects of inflation.

Escape energy, rocket, energy required by a rocket to reach ESCAPE VELOCITY and become free from the gravitational field of a star, planet, satellite or stellar system. Disregarding atmospheric friction, the escape energy at any distance R from a mass M for a rocket of mass m is mMG/R, where G is the gravitational constant. *See also* MM p.157.

Escapement, mechanical device for the interaction of oscillating and circular motion, in which a toothed wheel alternately engages and escapes the oscillating member. The mechanism is used in clocks and watches in which the escapement intervenes between the drive (spring or weight) and the regulating device (balance wheel or pendulum).

Escape tower, spacecraft, launching-pad structure attached to the top of a manned space vehicle. It contains an escape rocket used to pull the CAPSULE containing the astronauts away from the launch vehicle in an emergency. The blast from the escape rocket is vented to the side to protect the astronauts. The tower is jettisoned after normal ascent.

Escape velocity, rocket, minimum velocity required to free a rocket of the gravitational field of a celestial body or stellar system. Escape velocities are, for the Earth 11.2km/sec (7mps) and Moon 2.4km/sec (1.5mps). They can be calculated from the formula: $v=(2GM/R)^{\frac{1}{2}}$, where G is the gravitational constant, M the mass of the planet or system and R the distance of the rocket from the centre of mass of the system. *See also* MM p.157.

Escarpment, or scarp, steep slope of a continuous cliff face or a plateau, produced by faulting and differential erosion. Loosening of rock by wind or water produces spectacular cliff faces such as the Grand Canyon. *See also* PE p.114, 115.

Eschatology, in systematic theology, the

formalized doctrine concerning the end of time. It comprises the study of teaching and theory on the coming of the kingdom of God and the consequent final destiny of each individual soul. The term was first used in the 19th century.

Escheat, in feudal English law, the legal right of the lord of the land to claim property where there is no apparent heir. The law of escheat was abolished in England in 1925.

Esch-sur-Alzette, town in Luxembourg, 16km (10 miles) SW of the city of Luxembourg, close to the French border, on the River Alzette. It is an industrial centre with iron and steel works and railway communications with France, Belgium, Germany. Pop. (1970 est.) 27,600.

Escorial, Spanish monastery and palace near Madrid. Built 1563–84 for PHILIP II by the architects Juan de Toledo and Juan de Herrera, it comprises a massive and austere group of buildings arranged in a square plan and dominated by church towers and a dome. The palace has a notable art collection of Spanish and Netherlandish work.

Esdras, two books of the Bible, at the beginning of the Apocrypha. Esdras I includes parts of Chronicles II, Ezra, and Nehemiah. Esdras II, also known as the Ezra Apocalypse, is the product of Jewish Christian apocalyptic thought and employs the typical imagery of apocalyptic literature.

Esenin, Sergey. *See* YESENIN.

Esfahān. *See* ISFAHAN.

Esk, river in SW Scotland formed at the confluence of the Black Esk and White Esk rivers in Dumfries. It flows roughly S and enters the Solway Firth in Cumbria. Length: 45km (28 miles).

Esker, sand and gravel ridge of gentle slope. It is formed from debris carried by streams that ran under or through an old, almost stationary glacier or a retreating one. *See also* PE pp.116, 117.

Eskilstuna, city in SE Sweden, 72km (45 miles) W of Stockholm. A commercial centre in the 12th century, it prospered in the 17th and 18th centuries when an iron and steel industry was developed. There is a 12th-century church and a technical college in the city. Industries: steel, machine tools, engineering. Pop. 67,500.

Eskimo, Algonquian Indian for "eaters of raw flesh", referring to the aboriginal inhabitants of Arctic and sub-Arctic regions. They have developed cultural and linguistic characteristics distinct from North American Indians. Their language, for example, is related only to that of the Aleut. Eskimoes have Mongoloid features and originally migrated from Asia. They have adapted themselves extremely well to harsh climates and are some of the most proficient hunters in the world. They rely on sea mammals, particularly seals, for food, tools, clothes and oil, and they also catch reindeer and fish. They have considerable artistic skill and fashion objects from stone, ivory and bone. Today approx. 25,000 live in Alaska, 15,000 in Canada and 40,000 in Greenland. *See also* MS pp.33, *35, 252, 254.*

Eskişehir, city in NW central Turkey, capital of Eskişehir province. It is the site of the ancient Phrygian city of Dorylaeum. Industries: farm and railway equipment, sugar-refining, cement. Pop. 173,900.

Esmeraldas, river, town and most northerly province of Ecuador. The river is 242km (150 miles) long and its chief tributary is the Guallabamba. The town, pop. (1972 est.) 67,022, is on the coast; it is a trading centre. The province, area 14,711sq km (5,680sq miles), consists of a coastal plain and foothills; pop. (1971) 184,800.

ESP, extra-sensory perception, a parapsychological phenomenon. The term covers alleged psychical cognitive such as clairvoyance, telepathy and precognition. The events that believers in the existence of ESP posit, such as the perception of one person of the thoughts of another, or the ability to predict what will happen in the future, are not explainable by the traditional methods of physical science. They have, even so, been the subject of serious investigation, beginning with the establishment in 1882 in London of the Society for Psychical Research. *See also* SPIRITUALISM; MS pp.198–199.

Esparto, or needlegrass, coarse grass, native to Spain and N Africa, used for making ropes, cord and paper. There are about 150 species. Heights: to 0.9m (3ft). Family Gramineae; genera *Stipa* and *Lygeum.*

Esperanto, artificial language devized in 1887 by a Polish doctor, Ludwik Zamenhof, in the hope that it would become the language of international communication. Its spelling and grammar are consistent, and its vocabulary is based mainly on that of W European languages. There are 22 international professional organizations that use Esperanto. *See also* MS pp.*240,* 241.

Espinel, Vicente (1550–1624 much-travelled Spanish novelist and poet who is said to have invented the *decima.* This stanza form consists of 10 lines of eight syllables each. Espinel's best known work is a picaresque novel *Vida de Marcos de Obregón.*

Espinosa, Pedro (1578–1650), Spanish poet who took holy orders and lived for a time as a hermit. He is best known for *Fábula del Genil* and for his translation of the psalms. He also wrote prose satires and published an important anthology of contemporary poetry (1605).

Espionage, the act of obtaining secret information, especially for one nation about the political, military and industrial matters of a rival. It was engaged in by both the Egyptians and the Greeks. Although regarded nowadays as accepted practice, the risks are great and penalties for those agents who are detected are severe. It is an activity in which, in peacetime and war, a single individual can prove highly effective, aided as he is today by all manner of sophisticated technical devices. *See also* COUNTER-ESPIONAGE.

Espoo (Esbo), town of Uusimaa province, Finland, 18km (11 miles) WNW of Helsinki. It is in an area of flat valleys and clay hills. By 1968 it was connected to Helsinki by a motorway. The town is growing rapidly. Pop. (1973) 110,107.

Espronceda, José de (1808–1842), Spanish Romantic poet. Active in the liberal revolutions of the 1830s, he fought in France (1830) and Spain (1835, 1836) and wrote many poems on the themes of patriotism and freedom. The autobiographical *Canto a Teresa* (1841) is a fine example of Spanish ROMANTICISM.

Esquire, or squire, in FEUDALISM, term for a knight's assistant or for an apprentice knight. The word orginally meant "one who bears arms". In the 17th century it came to mean a country gentleman, below the nobility.

Esquirol, Jean Etienne Dominique (1772–1840), French pioneer in the humane treatment of the mentally disturbed. He was appointed inspector-general for the University of Paris medical faculty (1823) after founding the first instructional clinic in psychiatry (1871). He wrote the first modern work on clinical psychology, *Des Maladies Mentales* (1938).

Essad Pasha (*c.*1863–1920), Albanian political leader who aided the YOUNG TURKS in their agitation of 1908 for reform of the OTTOMAN EMPIRE. He represented Albania in the new legislature but later turned against the Turks in search of Albanian independence. When this was achieved in 1913, he had a chequered career in the new state, finally being exiled when the Austrians invaded in 1916. He was assassinated in France.

Essay, short, non-fictional composition, written expressing a personal point of view. The essay form originated with the French writer Montaigne in the 16th century. Famous British essayists include Abraham Cowley and Francis Bacon in the 17th century; Joseph Addison and Henry Steele, Henry Fielding, Dr. Samuel Johnson and Oliver Goldsmith in the 18th century; Matthew Arnold, Charles Lamb and William Morris in the 19th century. Noted US essayists include in the 19th century Ralph Waldo Emerson, Henry David Thoreau and Oliver Wendell Holmes; and in the 20th century Clarence Day, James Thurber, George Santayana, Dorothy Parker, Christopher Morley and E. B. White.

Essay Concerning Human Understanding, An (1690), philosophical treatise by John LOCKE. Locke argued that all human knowledge is derived from experience; without the senses, nothing can be known. The senses supply the data that the mind extends into ideas by reflection. By restricting knowledge to possible experience, Locke suggested the path of modern EPISTEMOLOGY. *See also* MS pp.232–233.

Essay on Man (1734), long poem in four parts, written in rhyming couplets of IAMBIC pentameter by Alexander POPE. It attempts to give a poetic summation of the prevailing philosophical "optimism" of the AGE OF REASON.

Essen, city in W West Germany on the River Ruhr, 30km (18 miles) NNE of Düsseldorf. The city grew up around a 9th-century Benedictine convent. From the 13th to the 18th century it was a small imperial state ruled by the abbess of the convent, before being annexed to Prussia in 1803. The city has an 11th-century cathedral. Industries: iron and steel, glass, textiles, chemicals. Pop. 674,000.

Essenes, Jewish religious sect which existed in Palestine from the 2nd century BC to the end of the 1st century AD. The members of the sect, usually composed entirely of men, lived in communal groups isolated from the rest of society. Sharing all their possessions, they stressed ritual purity and were stricter than the Pharisees in their observance. A secrecy developed about the sect, and they shunned public life as well as temple worship. The Dead Sea Scrolls are considered to have been their work.

Essex, Robert Devereux, 2nd Earl of (1566–1601), English courtier and soldier. He won great favour with ELIZABETH I by a successful attack on Cadiz in 1596. He was made earl marshal in 1597 and lord-lieutenant of Ireland in 1599. He led a unsuccessful rebellion against Elizabeth in 1601 and was executed for treason. *See also* HC1 p.*275.*

Essex, Robert Devereux, 3rd Earl of (1591–1646), British soldier. He took command of the Parliamentary armies at the onset of the English Civil War in 1642. He resigned in 1645 when the Parliamentary forces were reorganized into the NEW MODEL ARMY.

Essex, county in SE England. Low lying on the E coast, the land rises to the NW providing pasture for dairy- and sheep-farming. Wheat, barley and sugar-beet are all important crops and there is some market gardening supplying the London area. Industries include machinery and electrical goods. The main towns are Chelmsford, the county town, Colchester and resorts such as Southend-on-Sea and Clacton. Area: 3,674sq km (1,419sq miles). Pop. (1976) 1,426,200.

Estaing, Valéry Giscard d' (1926–), French politician. He was born into a patrician, landowning family and in 1956 was first elected as a *deputé.* He was minister of finance in 1962–66 and 1969–74. In May 1974, as the candidate of the Right – his party, the Independent Republicans, are the allies of the Gaullists – he defeated François MITTERAND to become the third president of the Fifth Republic.

Estate, property or interest held by a person in a property, usually land. The term applies especially to the property, possessions and effects bequeathed in a will, but applies also to modes of tenure such as FREEHOLD and LEASEHOLD – the principle in that case being that no one except the Crown can own land absolutely in England.

Estate, social, in feudal societies, a rigidly defined social stratum. The population is divided into a hierarchy of ruler, nobles, clergy, vassals and serfs. In France the Third Estate comprised all those who were neither nobility nor clergy.

Estates-General, national assembly composed of separate divisions, or "estates", each historically representing a different social class. In France the Assembly was

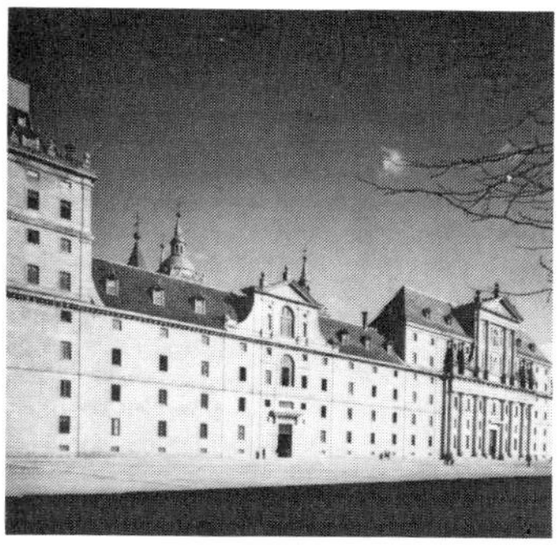

Escorial has an art collection that includes works by El Greco, Titian and Velazquez.

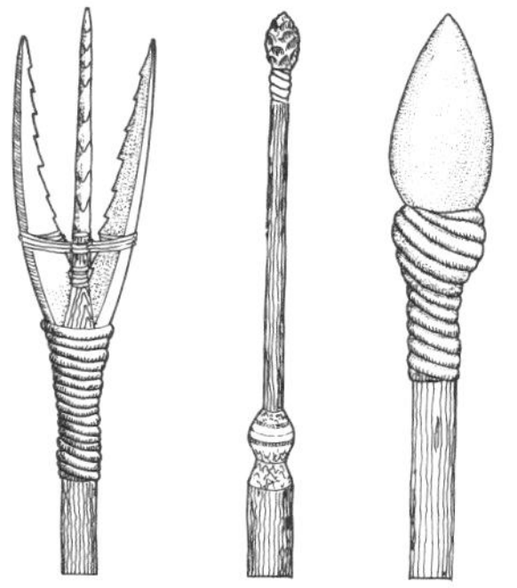

Eskimo; spear tips fashioned for hunting marine mammals, their principal diet.

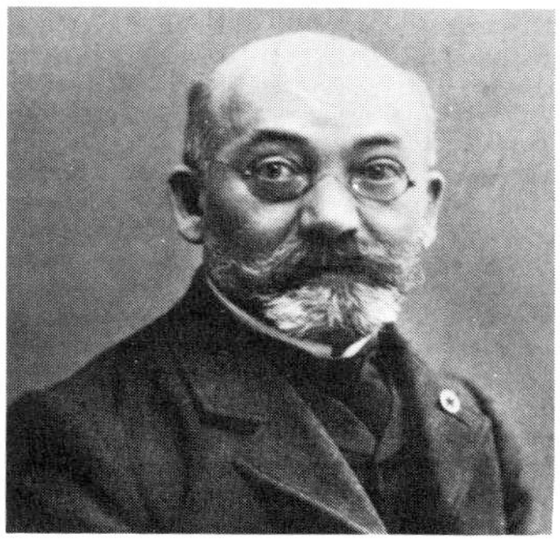

Esperanto, devised by Ludwik Zamenhof, means in that language "one who hopes".

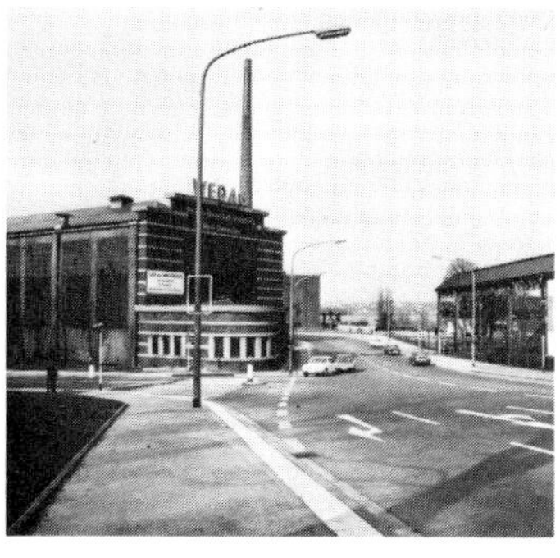

Essen, badly damaged by Allied bombing during WWII, has been largely rebuilt.

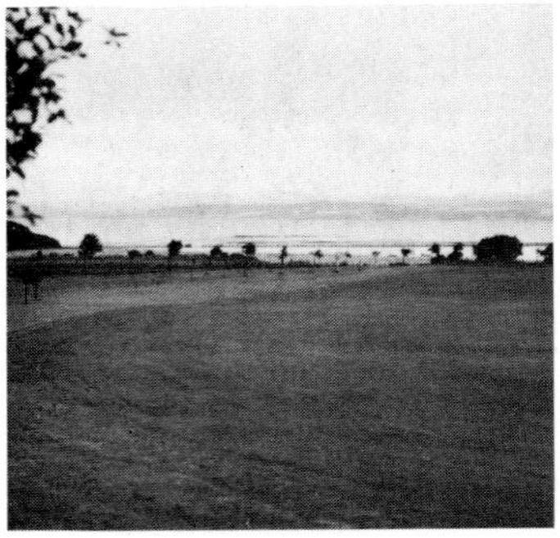

Estuary of the River Forth, one of the most famous in the world, is at Edinburgh.

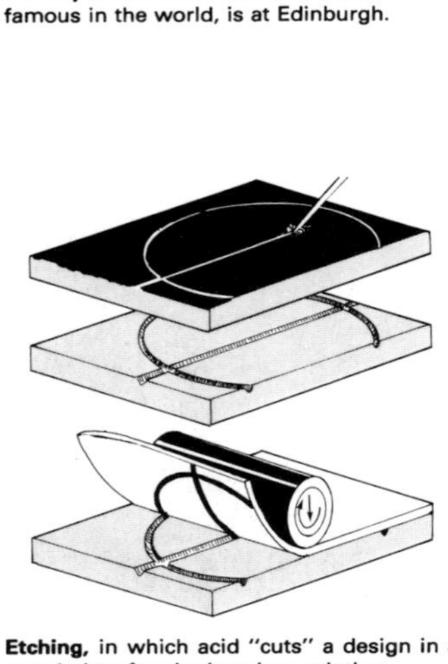

Etching, in which acid "cuts" a design in a metal plate for single-colour printing.

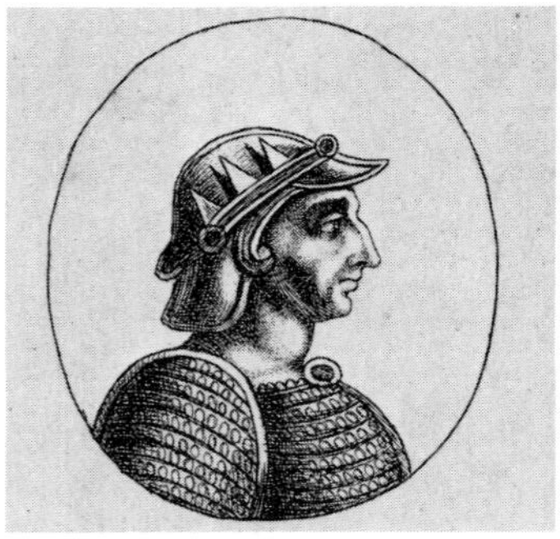

Ethelred II; a portrait of this early English king taken from a rare coin of the time.

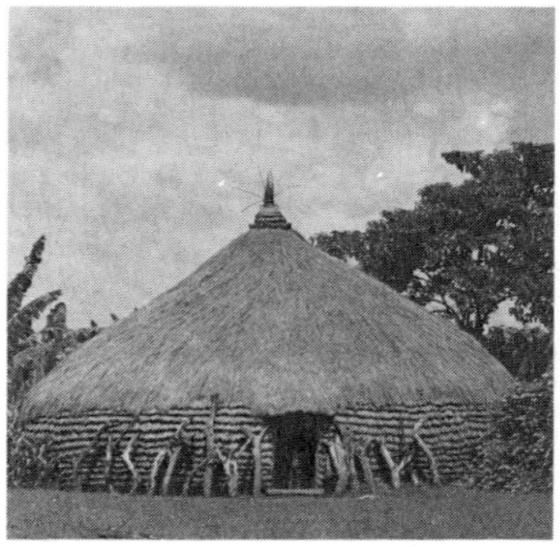

Ethiopia; a dwelling typical of those found in the Rift Valley at Sidamo, southern Ethiopia.

divided into three estates – clergy, nobility and commoners – representing the three major divisions of European society before the FRENCH REVOLUTION (1789). The upper classes traditionally allied against the Third Estate but in 1789 all three united in their refusal to dissolve the assembly at the command of Louis XVI, thus precipitating the revolution. The Dutch parliament still retains the name Estates-General. *See also* HC2 p.74.

Estavenico (*c.* 1500–39), Moroccan guide for explorers Panfilo de NARVAEZ and Cabeza de VACA. He was one of four survivors of the party that explored the Florida coast in 1528. In 1539 he guided Fray MARCOS into New Mexico, but was killed by Indians.

Este, Italian aristocratic family that ruled in Ferrara (13th–16th centuries) and in Modena and Reggio (15th–18th centuries). An important GUELF family, with the rule of Niccolo III (1393–1441) the Este were established as one of the foremost families in Europe. Ercole I (*r.* 1471–1505) and his son, Cardinal Ippolito I (*d.* 1520), were both patrons of the poet Ludovico ARIOSTO, who dedicated his *Orlando Furioso* to the cardinal. Alfonso II (*r.* 1559–97) was connected with the patronage of the poet Torquato TASSO.

Ester, any of a class of organic compounds formed by reaction between an alcohol and an acid. The commonest type, those formed from carboxylic acids, have the general formula RCO.OR′. Simple esters are fragrant and volatile compounds, and are used as flavourings. FATS are esters of glycerol and long-chain carboxylic acids. *See also* SAPONIFICATION.

Esterházy family, Magyar clan whose many prominent members since the 16th century contributed greatly to the histories of Austria and Hungary. Paul (1635–1713), elected palatine of Hungary in 1681, was prominent in the defence of Vienna and the reconquest of Hungary from the Turks. His grandsons, Paul Anton (*d.* 1762) and Nicholas Joseph (*d.* 1790) were great art patrons, notably of Joseph HAYDN.

Estes, Sleepy John (1904–77), US blues singer and guitarist. With Robert JOHNSON and Blind Willie MCTELL, Estes established a tradition of unsentimental but highly personal and moving lyrical blues writing.

Esther, Old Testament book narrating how the legendary heroine queen Esther averted the mass killing of her people, the Jews, by the Persians in Babylon. The Persian king had been advised by his grand vizier Haman (Aman) that the Jews were a pernicious race and should be exterminated. Haman's overthrow is celebrated at the Jewish feast of Purim, though the feast is older than the book. Nothing is known of the author.

Estivation, ability of certain organisms, including snails and some rodents, to spend the summer in a DORMANT state. In desert areas it serves as a survival mechanism during water and food shortages.

Estournelles de Constant, Paul Henri Benjamin Balluat (1852–1924), French diplomat and politician. He worked for international conciliation and disarmament first as a diplomat and then as a politician, becoming a *deputé* in 1895 and being elected to the French senate in 1904. He was a delegate at the HAGUE PEACE CONFERENCES of 1907, and in 1909 with Auguste BEERNAERT he was awarded the Nobel Peace Prize.

Estremadura (Extremadura), region of W central Spain, on the Portuguese border; crossed by the Tagus and the Guadiana rivers. It was the birthplace of the CONQUISTADORS Francisco PIZARRO and Hernán CORTÉS. Today sheep and pigs are reared in the area and its industries include timber and coal-mining. Pop. (1970 est.) 2,656,200.

Estuary, coastal region where a river mouth opens into the ocean and fresh water from the land is mixed with salt water from the sea. Many estuaries are drowned river valleys, perhaps formed after a rise in sea-level at the end of an ice age. They usually provide good harbours and are often breeding grounds for many kinds of marine life.

Eta, Japanese minority group, generally regarded as the lowest caste in traditional Japanese society. Thought to be descendants of groups such as butchers and tanners, associated with the taking of life, they are still shunned by many Japanese.

Eta Carinae, irregular variable star in the constellation of Carina. Surrounded by nebulosity, it reached magnitude −0.8 in 1843 and was the second brightest star in the sky, but it is now invisible to the naked eye. It is an extremely remote object of an unusual spectral class not yet fully analysed. Apparent mag. 7.7. *See also* SU pp.226, 240–*241*, 260–261, 266.

Eta meson, uncharged ELEMENTARY PARTICLE (η) with zero spin. It is grouped under the HADRONS (one of the three main groups).

Etching, method of INTAGLIO (incised) printing used especially for reproducing black-and-white designs. The etching process allows a more freely drawn figure than does an ENGRAVING process. First the artist covers the metal plate, usually copper, with an acid-proof ground made of a mixture containing bitumen, beeswax and resin. Next, the design is drawn on to the grounded plate with an etching needle so that the lines penetrate the ground. The plate is then placed in an acid that eats away the exposed line. To create shading, the etcher places an acid-resisting varnish over the desired areas and once again immerses the plate to allow the acid to incise more deeply the still exposed lines. When the plate is finished, it is rolled with ink and placed in an etching press to be printed. Corrections and changes can be made by covering the plate with a new ground and reworking it. *See also* PRINTMAKING.

Ethane, gas with the chemical formula CH_3CH_3 and which is therefore a member of the alkane group of HYDROCARBONS. With no taste or odour, it is a minor constitutent of natural gas. *See also* SATURATED COMPOUND.

Ethanol. *See* ETHYL ALCOHOL.

Ethelbald (*d.* 757), King of Mercia (716–57). By 731 he controlled all of England S of the Humber River. He also encouraged the development of the church by making large grants of land and freeing ecclesiastical lands from most obligations to the king.

Ethelbert (*d.* 616), King of Kent who came to power in 560. His attempt to extend his kingdom westwards was thwarted in 568 by the West Saxons, but by the late 6th century he was the strongest ruler in England S of the Humber River. He was the first Christian king in Anglo-Saxon England and allowed AUGUSTINE and his monks to settle and preach in Canterbury. He also founded the see of Rochester.

Ethelbert (*d.* 866), King of Kent and Wessex, an elder brother of ALFRED THE GREAT. He succeeded to the throne of Kent in 858 and to that of Wessex in 860, thus uniting the two kingdoms. During his reign the Danes sacked Winchester.

Ethelfleda (*d.* 918), daughter of ALFRED THE GREAT, known as "Lady of the Mercians". She married Ethelred, Ealdorman of the Mercians, whom she succeeded in 911. She joined her brother, EDWARD THE ELDER, to recover English territory from the Danes and captured Derby in 917 and Leicester in 918.

Ethelfrith (*d.* 616), King of Northumbria. He united the kingdoms of Bernicia and Deira, inflicted defeats on the Britons near the Forth in 603 and again near Chester (613–16) and laid the foundations of Northumbrian political dominance in England. He was killed by supporters of his successor, EDWIN of Deira.

Ethelred (*d.* 871), King of Wessex and Kent (865–71). With his younger brother ALFRED, he assisted the Mercians in resisting a Danish invasion in 868. When the Danes attacked Wessex, he defeated them at Ashdown in 871. He was succeeded by Alfred.

Ethelred II (968–1016), King of England (978–1013; 1014–16), called the Unready (from the Old English "evil *rede* or counsel"). He suffered continually from Danish attacks, and in 994 he began to pay off the raiders with money raised by the DANEGELD. The Danes returned nevertheless in 997 and a massacre of Danes in 1002 brought retaliation from the Danish King Sweyn who conquered England in 1013. Ethelred was made king again on Sweyn's death, but was succeeded by Sweyn's son Canute. *See also* HC1 p.155.

Ethelwold, Saint (*c.* 908–84), Bishop of Winchester after 963, and leader of the Benedictine monastic reform. He was a friend of St Dunstan and of Oswald, and earned the name "The Father of Monks" by founding many abbeys, among them Chertsey and Ely. *See also* HC1 p.54.

Ethelwulf (*d.* 858), King of Wessex (*r.* 839–55). He successfully defended his realm against Danish attack, and in 852 he subdued N Wales. In 855 he travelled to Rome with his fifth son ALFRED. As he returned from that pilgrimage he married Judith, daughter of Charles II of France. Thereafter he allowed his son Ethelbald to rule Wessex, while he ruled in Kent where a third son, ETHELBERT, succeeded him.

Ether (diethyl ether), colourless volatile inflammable liquid ($C_2H_5OC_2H_5$) prepared by the action of sulphuric acid on ethanol followed by distillation. It is used as an ANAESTHETIC (although less than previously), industrial solvent and fuel additive. Diethyl ether is a typical member of the ethers with the general formula ROR′, where R,R′ are hydrocarbon radicals. Properties: m.p. −116.2°C (−117.2°F); b.p. 34.5°C (94.1°F).

Ether, in physics, hypothetical medium that was supposed to fill all space, even inside matter, and to offer no resistance to motion. It was postulated as a medium to support the propagation of electromagnetic radiations, but its existence was disproved by the MICHELSON-MORLEY EXPERIMENT. *See also* SU pp.104–105, *105*.

Etherege (Etheredge), Sir George (*c.* 1635–91), English dramatist. He borrowed from Molière the mixed verse and prose form of his *The Comical Revenge; or Love in a Tub* (1664). His most famous play, *The Man of Mode* (1676), satirized the new dandyism.

Ethical Movement, international movement founded in 1876 in New York by Felix Adler, emphasizing the supreme importance of moral values independent of religious belief. The membership is small but intellectually influential and encourages community service. It enforces no definite ethical system, and other religious affiliations may be held. The first English branch, the South Place Ethical Society, was founded in 1888.

Ethics, study of human conduct in the light of moral principles, also called moral philosophy. Because moral statements, such as "Abortions are wrong", differ fundamentally from factual statements, such as "It is not raining today", they are a source of philosophical debate, and moral philosophers have sought to establish basic principles for making moral judgements. These may be metaphysical, such as KANT's system; religious; social, such as the UTILITARIAN's "the greatest good for the greatest number"; or individual, such as the intuitionists who claim that everyone has an innate moral sense. *See also* MS pp.182–183, 234–235.

Ethiopia, independent nation in NE Africa, on the Red Sea, formerly an ancient empire. Its ruler HAILE SELASSIE was deposed in 1974 and replaced by a left-wing military junta. Coffee is the most valuable export although barley and maize are also grown and cattle are raised. Industries include brewing and cement, and some gold is mined. The capital is Addis Ababa. Area: 1,221,900sq km (471,776sq miles). Pop. (1975 est.) 27,946,000. *See also* MW p.75.

Ethnic group, in sociology, any social group that shares a complex of characteristics distinguishing it from the larger society of which it is a part. Such groups are usually based on national origins, religion, language, culture or race. In many instances people of one ethnic group prefer to live in the same neighbourhood.

Ethnocentrism, preference for one's own

culture. All human groups have an unconscious and sometimes a conscious tendency to assume that their own culture is superior to others. Ethnocentrism is an automatic, emotional response, not a rational one. *See also* DISCRIMINATION; PREJUDICE; MS p.268.

Ethnography, study of the culture of a race of human beings, generally a single ethnic group or society. Ethnographers gather anthropological data by direct observation during a period of residential fieldwork. They participate in the group's economic and social life and interview its members. *See also* ANTHROPOLOGY; ETHNOLOGY; MS p.249.

Ethnolinguistics, study of the interrelationship of language and culture in the present as well as the ancient past. Social organization and lifestyles of ancient peoples are deduced from studying their vocabularies. Edward Sapir, the US anthropologist, suggested that people see the world as their language presents it to them.

Ethnology, comparative study of cultures. Using material from two or more societies, ethnology can attempt to cover the entire cultural range or concentrate on a single trait. Historical ethnology was developed in the late 19th century in an attempt to trace cultural diffusion. Ethnologists now concentrate on cross-cultural studies. *See also* MS pp.34–35; 248–249.

Ethology, study of animal behaviour, first outlined in the 1920s by Konrad LORENZ of Austria and Nikolaas TINBERGEN of The Netherlands. Ethologists study natural processes that range across all animal groups, such as courtship, mating and self-defence. Field observations and laboratory experiments are both used. *See also* NW pp.78–79.

Ethyl alcohol, or ethanol, colourless volatile liquid (C_2H_5OH) produced by the fermentation of various items including molasses, grains, fruits and vegetables or by the catalytic hydrogenation of ethylene. Its many uses include beverages, cleaning solutions, rocket fuels, cosmetics and pharmaceuticals. Properties: s.g. 0.789; m.p. −117.3°C (−179.1°F); b.p. 78.5°C (173.3°F).

Ethyl chloride, anaesthetic agent (C_2H_5Cl), less irritating than ETHER, but explosive and used only in limited ways; eg to produce sleep before ether is administered.

Ethylene (ethene), colourless gas (CH_2CH_2) derived from the cracking of propane and other compounds. Vast quantities of the gas are used annually for the manufacture of polyethylene, or POLYTHENE. Ethylene is also used widely for many other chemical syntheses.

Ethyl ether. *See* ETHER.

Etna, Mount, active volcano on the E coast of Sicily, Italy. It is the highest active volcano in Europe and the highest mountain in Italy, S of the Alps; its height fluctuates because of volcanic activity. Pindar and Aeschylus described the first known eruption in 475 BC and other major eruptions occurred in 1169, 1669 and 1971. The fertile lower slopes are used for agriculture. Height: approx. 3,340m (10,958ft).

Eton College, English public school founded in 1440 by Henry VI, and situated in Eton, near Windsor, Berkshire. Eton has educated a high proportion of Britain's statesmen, writers and nobility.

Eton fives. *See* FIVES.

Eton Wall Game, form of football unique to the famous British Public School. For two teams of ten players (originally 11), it is fought on a narrow strip 3.6–4.5m (12–15ft) wide and 108m (354ft) long alongside a brick wall, the object being to reach the opponents' end and touch the ball against the wall (a *shy*). This achievement merits a throw or kick at goal, but with goals a rarity, shies invariably determine the result.

Etruria, ancient region in Italy, bounded by the River Tiber, the Apennines, and the Tyrrhenian Sea. The ETRUSCANS migrated probably from Asia Minor *c.* 900 BC and formed several city-states. Their civilization reached a peak *c.* 500 BC but was gradually taken over by Rome. *See also* HC1 pp.88–89.

Etruscans, ancient inhabitants of ETRURIA, who developed a sophisticated society and empire by 500 BC. Their racial origins are obscure. They first developed a religious confederation of independent city-states based on Volsinii, and attained cultural unity by the 7th century BC. Much of their naturalistic art and skilled metalwork, like their language, derives from traditions quite unlike those of the rest of the Mediterranean world. By 500 BC their influence was spread throughout the major islands of the W Mediterranean and coastal Spain, and they controlled Umbria and central Italy. They came into conflict with the Greeks, and despite early successes, their authority began to wane in the late 5th century. At the same time Celtic invasions halted their northward expansion and the Samnites forced them from Campagna. The Romans adopted many features of Etruscan civilization before they overtook the Etruscan strongholds, such as VEII in 396 BC. Etruscan independence ended entirely in 88 BC during the struggle between SULLA and MARIUS. *See also* HC1 pp.88–90.

Etty, William (1787–1849), British painter. Known primarily for his studies of nudes, he was greatly influenced by the work of RUBENS and TITIAN.

Etymologiae, or *Twenty Books on Origins,* 6th-century encyclopaedia by St ISIDORE of Seville (570–636). It collated much of the work of previous encyclopaedias, and for its time is noteworthy for its emphasis on the liberal arts and medicine rather than on the Bible.

Etymology, branch of PHILOLOGY dealing with the history and derivation of words. The word *telephone*, for example, is a combination of the Greek derivatives *tele* (distant) and *phone* (sound). The word *coach*, by contrast, is derived from the city of Kocs, in Hungary, where coaches were first used.

Euboea (Évvoia), mountainous island of SE central Greece, in the Aegean Sea, separated from the mainland by the Gulf of Euboea. It is the second-largest island in Greece, and Khalkís is the administrative centre. It was under Athenian domination 506–411 BC and taken by Philip II of Macedon 338–191 BC. After the fall of Rome, it was held successively by the Byzantines, the Venetians and the Turks (1470–1830), and it was incorporated into Greece after independence was declared (1830). Today its industries include livestock, grapes, timber, grain, marble-quarrying, lignite and magnesite-mining. Area 3,654sq km (1,411sq miles). Pop. (1971) 163,017.

Eucalyptus, group of trees commonly known as gum trees, native to Australia and cultivated in warm and temperate regions. They are valuable sources of hardwood and oils. Generally they have tall, slender trunks, sometimes covered with exuded gum, bluish or whitish leaves, flowers without petals and woody fruits. Height: to 122m (400ft). Included in some 600 species are the Australian mountain ash (*Eucalyptus regnans*), Tasmanian blue gum (*E. globulus*), ghost gum (*E. papuana*) and the ironbark (*E. leucoxylon*). Family Myrtaceae. *See also* NW p.*210*.

Eucharist, from the Greek for "thanksgiving", central act of Christian worship and thanksgiving at which the priest and congregation partake in Holy Communion – one of the principal SACRAMENTS. The Eucharist is a commemorative re-enactment of the Last Supper at which Christ blessed bread and wine and gave them to his disciples saying, "Take and eat: this is my body ... Drink this, all of you, for this is my blood ... Do this as a memorial of me". Among Roman Catholics the rite is also called Mass; among Protestants, the Lord's Supper. Since the REFORMATION, the mode of Christ's presence in the eucharistic elements has been one of the chief points of controversy among the Churches, but recent years have seen an increasing doctrinal widening of horizons. *See also* CONSUBSTANTIATION; TRANSUBSTANTIATION.

Eucken, Rudolf Christoph (1846–1926), German philosopher who was awarded the 1908 Nobel Prize for literature. He believed that a transcendental spirit and nature unite in man. His works include *The Meaning and Value of Life* (1909), *Individual and Society* (1923) and *Socialism: An Analysis* (1921).

Euclid (*fl. c.* 300 BC), ancient Greek mathematician about whom little is known except that he taught at Alexandria during the reign of Ptolemy. He is remembered for his text books on geometry, especially *The Elements*, which was first printed in 1482 in a Latin translation from the Arabic. His other works include *Data* (on geometry) and *Phaenomena* (on astronomy). Several books have been lost. *See also* HC1 p. 83; SU p. 21, 26.

Euclidean geometry. *See* GEOMETRY.

Euclid of Megara, (*c.* 450–374 BC), founder of the Megarian school of philosophy, the main influence on which was SOCRATES. The influence of ELEATICISM is also evident in Euclid's emphasis on the unity of goodness.

Eugène of Savoy (1663–1736), French prince and general in the service of the HOLY ROMAN EMPIRE. He entered Austrian service in 1683 and fought the Turks at Vienna (1683) and Zenta (1697). In the War of the SPANISH SUCCESSION (1702–13), his victories over the French included BLENHEIM (1704), Oudenarde (1708) and Malplaquet (1709), all won with the Duke of MARLBOROUGH. His greatest victory was over the Turks at Belgrade in 1718.

Eugene Onegin (1823–33), romantic novel in verse by Alexander PUSHKIN. It develops the character of Onegin as a prime example of the "superfluous man" – detached, arrogant and cynical. It inspired the three-act opera (1879) of the same name by Peter Ilyich TCHAIKOVSKY.

Eugenics, study of human improvement by genetic means, founded in the 19th century by Francis GALTON. Its main proposed means of improving the inherited characteristics of the human species is through the careful selection of parents. Positive eugenics encourages parents who are above average mentally and physically to have more children. Negative eugenics proposes that those with less desirable or below average qualities should have fewer. What should be considered "desirable" traits remains a problematical and difficult ethical judgement. As a social movement eugenics was discredited in the early 20th century due to its association with racist views. Advances in genetics, psychology, medicine and demography have meant that eugenics has become more specific in its proposals and more aware of its limits. People known to have defective genes that could cause physical or mental disorders in offspring can be warned of the facts in terms of social responsibility and may even be encouraged to avoid having children. However, the genetic inheritance of personality traits cannot yet be accurately predicted. *See also* MS p.183; NW pp.30–31.

Eugénie (1826–1920), consort of Napoleon III, and French empress. Born of a Spanish father and American mother, she became the wife of Louis Napoleon shortly after he declared the second empire in 1852. Regent in her husband's absences at war (1859, 1865, 1870), her influence as a Catholic and conservative was often felt in French affairs. After being deposed in 1870 she fled to England, with the Prince Imperial (her only son). After his death (1879), she retired from public life and, apart from frequent travels abroad, remained in England.

Eugenius, name of four POPES. Of the two most notable, Eugenius III (*r.*1145–53), born as Bernardo Paganelli, was a Cistercian who tried to reform the clergy but was driven out of Rome (1146–49, 1150–52) by Arnold of Brescia. He promoted the disastrous Second CRUSADE. Eugenius IV (*r.*1431–47), born as Gabriele Condulmer in *c.*1383, disputed the authority of the Church hierarchy meeting at the Council of Basle (1431–37) and tried to uphold the supremacy of the papacy, despite

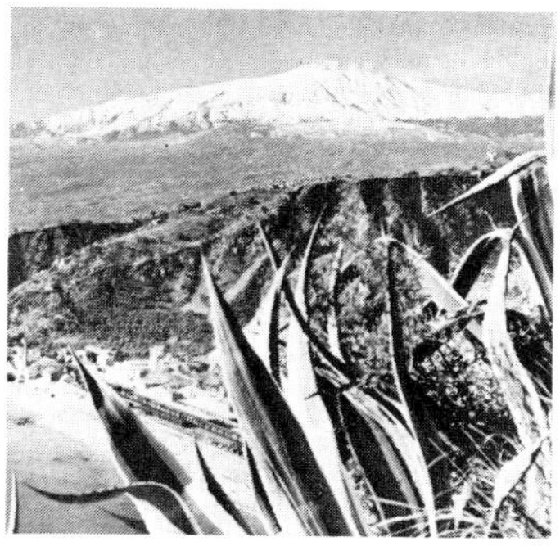

Etna, on which trees and hardy shrubs grow to within 1,000m (3,000ft) of the top.

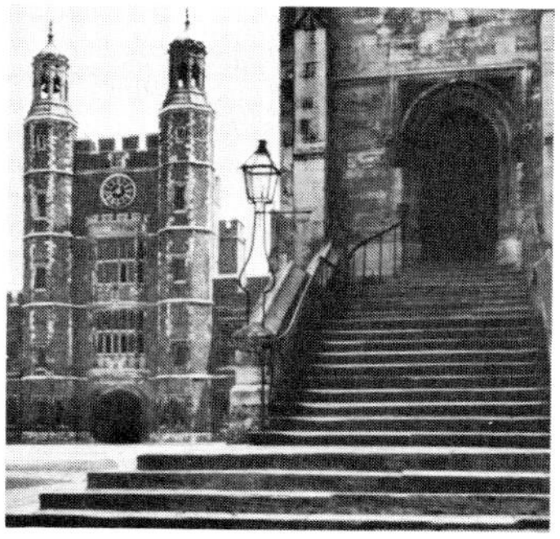

Eton Colleges chapel steps have been worn down by generations of schoolboys.

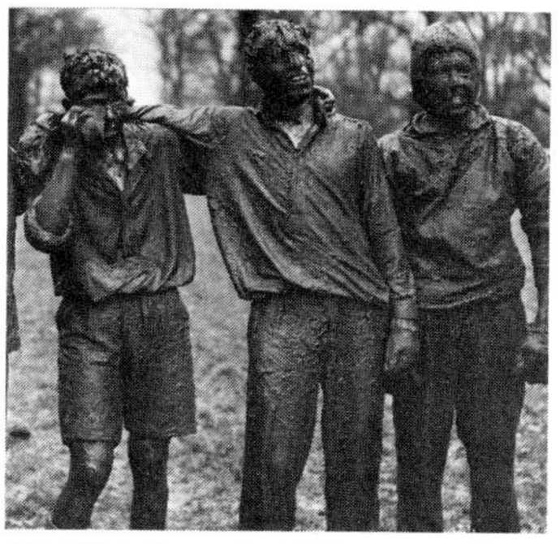

Eton Wall Game; the 1954 team testifies to the hazards of the game on a wet day.

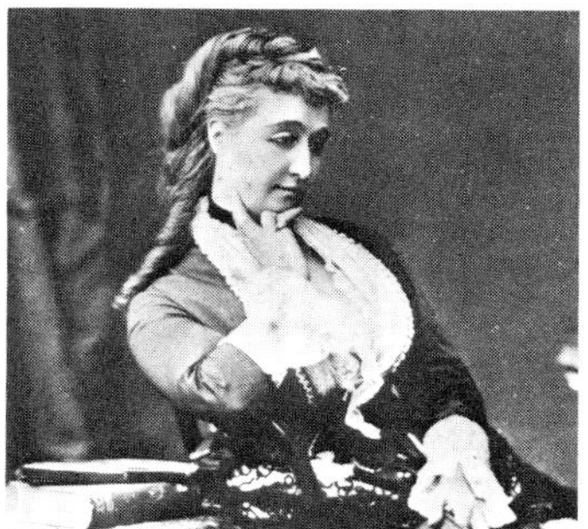

Eugénie, French empress of great beauty whose political influence was calamitous.

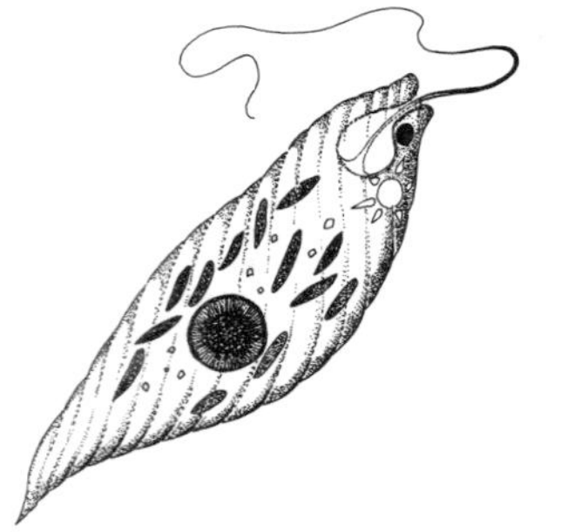

Euglena can develop in such numbers that it forms green or red patches on water.

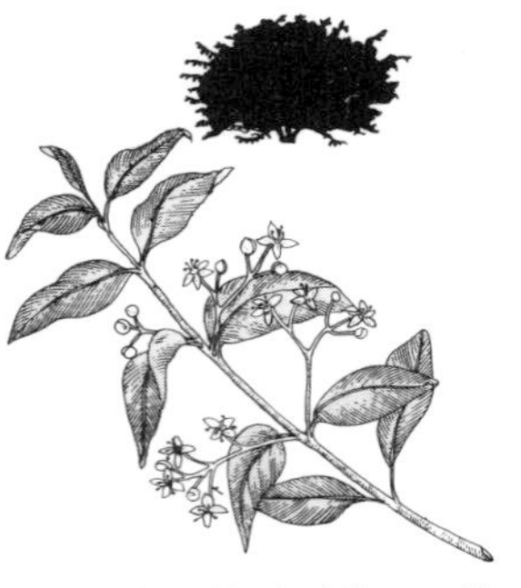

Euonymus; when this shrub flowered it was said in the Middle Ages to fortell plague.

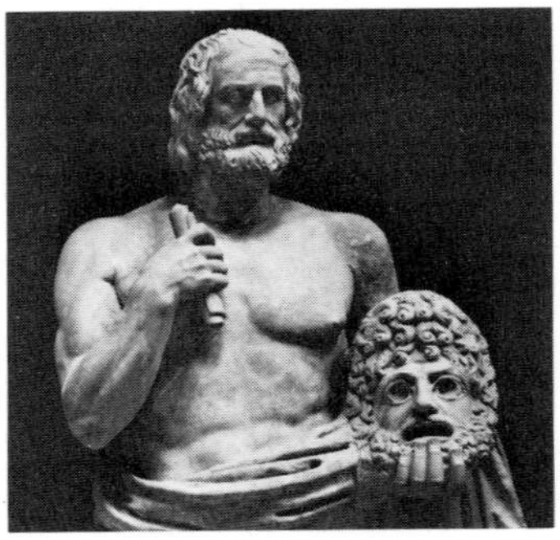

Euripides holds the mask of tragedy in this statue in the Museo Vaticano, Rome.

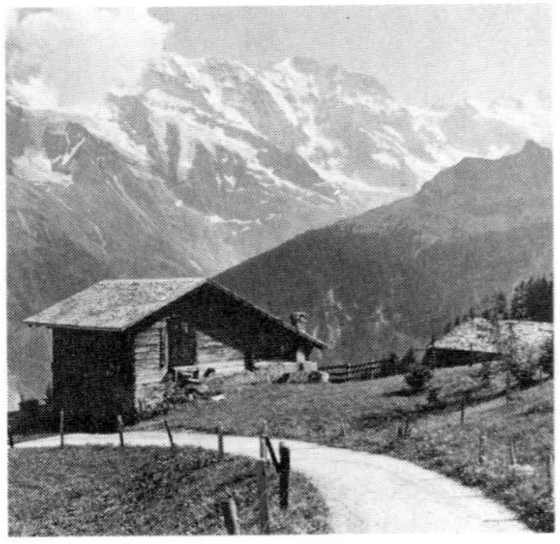

Europe is a continent of varied terrain, the Bernese Alps being typical of Switzerland.

being driven from Rome in 1434–43.

Euglena, flagellate protozoan found in fresh water. It has an elongated body that appears green because of its approx. 15 chloroplasts. There is a characteristic "eyespot" and a single flagellum. It moves by beating the flagellum and by alternately elongating and contracting its body to produce a squirming motion. It has both plant and animal features. Most common is *Euglena gracilis.* Class Mastigophora. *See also* NW pp.*21, 38.*

Eulachon, or candlefish, marine SMELT of inshore temperate waters or cold seas of the Northern Hemisphere. It has oily flesh and was used by American Indians to make torches. Length: 30cm (12in). Family Osmeridae; species *Thaleichthys pacificus.*

Eulalia, tall perennial grass native to SE Asia and widely cultivated for lawn or border ornamentals. It has white, plume-like flower clusters and striped leaves. Species *Miscanthus sinensis.* Also, perennial grass of Australia and SE Asia, important as fodder, Genus *Eulalia.* Family Gramineae.

Eulalius (*d.*423), antipope from 418–419. He and BONIFACE I (418–422) were chosen by different factions of the clergy to succeed ZOSIMUS as pope. Although his claim was initially supported by the Emperor HONORIUS, he disobeyed the latter by entering Rome before a council had settled the dispute. He was banished to Campania, and Boniface was elected.

Euler, Leonard (1707–83), Swiss mathematician. After studying under BERNOULLI in Basle he was appointed professor in St Petersburg and later in Berlin. His mathematical expertise was wide-ranging and he published more than 800 papers on subjects such as mechanics, algebra, optics and astronomy. *See also* EULER DIAGRAM; EULER'S THEOREM; SU p.52.

Euler, Ulf Svante von (1905–), Swedish physiologist. He shared the 1970 Nobel Prize in physiology and medicine with Julius AXELROD and Bernard KATZ for work on the chemistry of nerve transmission. Euler demonstrated that the nerve endings of sympathetic nerves release the chemical noradrenaline, which transmits the nerve impulse.

Euler-Chelpin, Hans Karl August von (1873–1964), Swedish bio-chemist who researched into the effects of ENZYMES in the fermentation of sugars. For this work he shared the 1929 Nobel Prize in chemistry with Sir Arthur HARDEN. Euler-Chelpin also investigated the chemical structure of several VITAMINS. In 1906 he became professor of chemistry at Stockholm University.

Euler diagram, simple diagram used in logic to illustrate SYLLOGISMS. Classes of objects are represented by circles so that, for example, a premise of the type "some *a* is *b* can be represented by overlap of these circles. *See also* VENN DIAGRAM; SU p.*52.*

Euler's theorem, in solid geometry, states that for any polyhedron (many-sided solid figure) $V-E+F=2$, where V is the number of vertices, E the number of edges and F the number of faces of the polyhedron. The theorem is named after the Swiss mathematician Leonard EULER (1707–83). *See also* SU pp.48, 52.

Eunuch, castrated man, once frequently used as the keeper of a harem in the Orient. Employed since ancient times as servants in royal and wealthy households, especially in the Byzantine and Ottoman empires, eunuchs were often obtained through the African slave trade. A eunuch who sang in a choir or an opera was called a CASTRATO.

Eunuchoidism, deficiency of testicular function which, before puberty, retards development of genitals, and of secondary sex characteristics (facial hair, deepening voice). It can also occur after puberty with milder effect. *See also* MS p.164.

Euonymus, genus of deciduous or evergreen shrubs and woody vines found in Europe, E Asia and North and Central America. Most have green branches, opposite (and sometimes variegated) leaves and inconspicuous flowers. The fruits are orange-red. There are about 176 species. Height: to 6m (20ft). Family Celastraceae.

Euphonium, brass musical instrument with valves. Invented in 1843, it was derived from the cornet and the valved bugle. It is pitched in C or B♭ in England, and orchestral parts for tenor tuba are often played on it. It is related to the TUBA, which it resembles in shape, and is the highest in pitch of that group of instruments.

Euphorbia, genus of widespread, varied plants of the SPURGE family. Most grow as herbs or shrubs and often have an acrid, milky juice in the stems. Flowers are usually small and inconspicuous with colourful bracts. Family Euphorbiaceae.

Euphotic zone, uppermost layer of oceans. Much light penetrates this comparatively shallow zone, and many green plants and herbivores are found there, and often sea-dwelling mammals. *See also* NW pp.240, 241.

Euphranor (*fl. c.*360 BC), Greek painter and sculptor. He painted great canvases for the Stoa of ZEUS at Athens. He sculpted in both bronze and marble.

Euphuism, highly mannered style of English prose, heavy in SIMILES, METAPHORS, ALLITERATION and other literary devices. The word derives from the *Euphues* of John LYLY, published in 1580.

Euphrates (Firat, or Al-Furāt), river formed by the confluence of the rivers Murat and Karasu. It flows from E Turkey across Syria into central Iraq, where it joins the River Tigris. The ancient civilizations of Babylonia and Assyria developed along the lower Euphrates, and it was the site of the cities of BABYLON and UR. Length: 3,598km (2,235 miles). *See also* HC1 pp.*26,* 27, 29.

Eupolis (*c.*455–*c.*410 BC), Greek playwright. Considered a major writer of comedy, he earned praise for his inventiveness, patriotism, and satirical humour. Titles of 17 plays and fragments survive.

Eureka Stockade, name given to the armed rebellion of Australian gold-diggers at Ballarat, Victoria, on 3 Dec. 1854. Miners' grievances about exploitative administration of the goldfields culminated in some 150 diggers forming a stockade to resist government authority. The diggers opened fire on a contingent of 280 police and troops but were quickly overcome with about 30 men killed. None of the rebels was subsequently convicted.

Eurhythmics, system of musical and dance training which has influenced ballet and acting. Developed by the Swiss Emile JAQUES-DALCROZE in the early 20th century, it is developed from a set of gymnastic exercises in response to music.

Euripides (*c.*480–450 BC), Greek playwright. With AESCHYLUS and SOPHOCLES, he is considered to be one of the three great writers of Greek tragic poetry. He was married and lived in Athens, but otherwise little is known of his personal life. The plots of his plays are complicated and his ideas were sometimes controversial and held to be offensive. His language is simple. His heroes, whether gsds or mortals, are portrayed with sceptical candour. Only 18 (or perhaps 19) of his 92 plays have survived. His first play was produced in 455. He won the competition for tragedy at the annual festival of Dionysus only four times, but his reputation grew after his death. Among the extant plays are *Alcestis* (438), *Iphigenia in Tauris* (*c.*411) and *Phoenician Women* (*c.*408).

Eurobond, bearer security to underwrite a loan in the EUROCURRENCY market, made for a greater amount and longer period than can be accommodated in a normal Eurocurrency operation. A Eurobond is usually underwritten by an international syndicate.

Eurocurrency, currency redeposited or lent, usually for not more than six months, in a country in which it is not the domestic currency. The Eurocurrency market is centred in Europe, chiefly London. *See also* HC2 p.*301.*

Eurodollar, dollar redeposited in a bank outside the USA, usually in Europe. Because of the relative stability of the dollar, it is the currency most prevalent in the EUROCURRENCY market, which is often also called the Eurodollar market. *See also* HC2 p.301.

Europa, beautiful Phoenician princess of Greek legend. She was abducted and ravished by ZEUS who appeared to her as a white bull and carried her across the sea to Crete after she playfully climbed upon his back. She bore three sons, including MINOS, King of Crete, where she was worshipped as Hellotis.

Europa, satellite of Jupiter, one of the GALILEAN SATELLITES. Diameter: 3,600km (2,200 miles); mean distance from Jupiter 671,000km (417,000 miles); mean sidereal period 3.55 days. *See also* SU p.212.

Europa Nostra ("Our Europe"), organization formed in 1963 to foster the preservation of national monuments and historic sites. It was formed as a federation of many organizations with similar aims in 17 European countries. Its principal function is to rally public opinion in support of its objectives.

Europe, second smallest continent, comprising the western fifth of the Eurasian land mass. It is separated from Asia by the Urals (E), the Caspian Sea and the Caucasus (SE), the Black Sea and the Dardanelles (S), and from Africa by the Mediterranean Sea.

Land. Europe is dominated by the great alpine mountain chain, the principal links of which are the Pyrenees, Alps, Carpathians, Balkans and the Caucasus, traversing the continent from W to E. Mt. Elbrus, 5,633m (18,481ft), in the Caucasus and Mont Blanc 4,807m (15,771ft), in the Alps are the two highest peaks. Between the Scandinavian peninsula and the Alpine chain is the great European plain, which extends from the Atlantic coast in France to the Urals. Much of the plain is fertile farm land, but it also includes areas of forest, steppe, lakes and tundra. To the S of the Alpine chain are the Iberian, Italian and Balkan peninsulas. Major European islands include the British Isles, Sicily, Sardinia, Corsica and Iceland.

Structure and geology. Much of N Europe is made up of large sedimentary plains overlying an ancient pre-Cambrian shield area, outcrops of which remain in N Scandinavia, Scotland and the Urals. There are worn down Palaezoic highlands in places. Many upland areas of N Europe, N of the Alps, were formed during the Carboniferous period, including Ireland, the moorlands of Devon and Cornwall, and the Pennine chain in England. S Europe is more youthful, geologically speaking. Alpine folding began in the Oligocene period and Europe's major mountain systems were formed at this time.

Lakes and rivers. The major rivers of Europe are, from W to E, the Tagus, Garonne, Loire, Rhône, Rhine (Rhein), Elbe (Labe), Oder (Odra), Danube (Donau) and the Volga (3,750km; 2,330 miles long), Europe's longest river. The Caspian is the world's largest lake with an area of 393,896sq km (152,083sq miles).

Climate and Vegetation. Europe's climate varies from sub-tropical to polar. The Mediterranean climate of the S is dry and warm. Much of the land is scrub, especially maquis, and there are some hardwood forests. Further N the climate is mild and quite humid, being moderated by prevailing westerly winds and the Gulf Stream of the N Atlantic. The natural vegetation is mixed forest but this has been extensively changed by man. In central Europe the climate is continental and there is a much greater range of temperature. Mixed forest merges into boreal, or northern, forest with large stands of conifers. In SE European USSR there is wooded steppe and grass steppe merging into semidesert to the N of the Caspian Sea. In the far N lies the tundra, an almost permanently snow-covered area.

Animal life. Domestic animals are of native origin, although the wild ancestors of the dog, horse and cow are now extinct. Carnivorous mammals include the wolf, fox, brown bear, lynx, stoat, wildcat, otter, shrew and several species of bat. Rodents include squirrels, rats, lemmings and voles. There are several species of deer, and wild sheep and goats in the Mediterranean areas. The tortoise is found in the SE and Gibraltar has the only European monkey (BARBARY APE). There are great numbers of birds and insects, and all the common species of amphibians. Reptiles include various species of snakes and lizards. There are many freshwater fish, including salmon, eel, pike, sturgeon, trout and perch.

People. The racial origin of European peoples is not clear-cut. They are usually characterized according to what is called "ethnic type" but this is based on physical traits of the present population. The majority of European languages fall into three groups, Germanic, Latin (Romance) and Slavic, all of which are Indo-European in origin. Other languages include Finno-Ugric, spoken in Finland, Hungary and parts of European USSR, Maltese (Semitic) and Basque. Christianity is dominant among religious faiths. In general, S and central Europe is Roman Catholic, N Europe is for the most part Protestant and the SE, Greece, Romania and Bulgaria, is Orthodox. The most important non-Christian religion is Islam, practised in Yugoslavia, Albania, Bulgaria and Turkey.

Economy. Approx. half the land of Europe is agriculturally unproductive because of climate, relief, soil, or urbanization. A quarter is forested, and timber and its associated industries are particularly important in Scandinavia and the mountainous areas of E Europe. Fishing is of moderate importance in the Mediterranean, but a major industry of countries bordering the Atlantic Ocean and the North Sea. Of cultivated land, two-thirds is arable and cereals are the principal crop. Wheat is the most important, replaced by oats in the N and sometimes maize in the S. Rice is grown with the aid of irrigation. Sheep are grazed on many upland areas but dairy farming is by far the most important form of animal husbandry. In Mediterranean areas many fruits, early vegetables and vines (mainly for wine) are cultivated.

Europe produces over a third of the world's coal and three-quarters of that is mined in Britain, West Germany and Poland. Iron ore is mined in many parts of Europe, in particular in France and N Sweden. Other mineral deposits include bauxite, mercury, lead, zinc and potash. Romania was the largest producer of oil in Europe, until the countries bordering the North Sea, especially Britain, began to exploit their resources. Several countries in central Europe also have oil fields. Europe is highly industrialized and manufacturing employs a high proportion of the work force. There are many industrial areas, but the largest are to be found in W central Europe, in particular N and NE France, the Ruhr district of West Germany and around the North Sea ports of Antwerp, Amsterdam, Rotterdam and Hamburg. There are other major industrial regions in Britain, N Italy and central European USSR.

Recent history. After WWII the countries of Europe became divided into two ideological blocs: Eastern Europe, dominated by the USSR, and Western Europe, closely aligned with the USA. The resulting rivalry was known as the COLD WAR. NATO was established to act as a deterrent to the spread of COMMUNISM; the WARSAW PACT was formed in reaction to this by the eastern nations. Several economic organizations, in particular the EEC (Common Market), have worked towards economic unity. Eastern European countries have an equivalent organization called COMECON. At the end of the 1960s and during the 1970s, however, tension between East and West eased and relations greatly improved.

Area approx. 10,360,000sq km (4,000,000sq miles)
Highest mountain Mt Elbrus (USSR) 5,633m (18,481ft)
Longest river Volga 3,750km (2,330 miles)
Population (1973 est.) 640,000,000
Largest cities Moscow (7,734,000); London (7,028,000); Paris (2,289,000)
See also NW pp.198–199, 206–209, 222-223, 226–227; PE pp.40–41; articles on individual countries in *The Modern World.*

Europe, Statute of the Council of (1949), agreement which established the COUNCIL OF EUROPE. During WWII, calls for a European council came from several nations and in 1947 various bodies joined to form the International Committee of the Movements for European Unity. Its work led to the first Congress of Europe which met at The Hague in May 1948. The 16 nations which sent delegates to the Congress agreed in principle to an economic and political union. The Council of Europe formally came into existence in May 1949, constituted, by the statute, on the British plan of government-appointed ministers, rather than the Franco-Belgian plan of a supra-nationally elected assembly. The statute omitted defence from the Council's competence, which covered economic, social, cultural, scientific, legal and administrative matters.

European Athletics Championships, tournament in which athletes from European countries compete in the recognized track and field events, plus the marathon. Gold, silver and bronze medals are awarded for 1st, 2nd and 3rd places. The championships were first held in 1934 in Turin – for men only; in 1938, men went to Paris, women to Vienna; they held the first combined meeting at Oslo in 1946. The championships were held every four years until 1966, when a three-year cycle was adopted, only for the four-year cycle to be resumed after the 1971 championships in Helsinki.

European Atomic Energy Community (Euratom), economic organization founded in 1958. The community was formed in order to co-ordinate nuclear research and production among West European nations. The member states are pledged to provide for the free movement of nuclear raw materials, capital for investment, specialists and equipment. The community has wide executive powers to act on behalf of its members. It is administered by the Commission of European Communities and operates nuclear reactors in Belguim, West Germany, Italy and The Netherlands. *See also* HC2 pp.258–259.

European Coal and Steel Community (ECSC) (1951), body formed according to the Schuman Plan, so named after the French foreign minister who proposed the idea in 1950. The member states were originally the same six who formed the EUROPEAN ECONOMIC COMMUNITY. They pledged themselves to co-operate in the production of steel and coal by providing a unified market for coal and steel products and a unified labour force. Restrictions on imports and exports were removed. Between 1953 and 1961 steel production by the ECSC increased by over 80 per cent while its price rose by only 4 per cent compared with 40 per cent in the USA. The executive machinery which the Council established paved the way for the formation of the EEC, into which it was incorporated in 1967. *See also* HC2 pp.258–259.

European Convention on Human Rights, agreement to protect the rights of the individual, signed by the COUNCIL OF EUROPE in 1950. It arose from the postwar desire to mitigate the action of national dictatorial regimes. In 1948 the Congress meeting at The Hague proposed the convention. It came into force in 1953 and has been ratified by 15 states. The convention listed 12 basic rights, including the right to life, to a fair trial, to peaceful assembly and association, and to freedom from slavery and torture. There have been five additional protocols adding seven further rights, the fourth (in force from 1968) including the guarantee of the right to freedom of movement within a country and freedom of residence. *See also* HUMAN RIGHTS.

European Cup (football), familiar name of the European Champion Clubs' Cup, a knockout soccer competition for clubs who have won their national League the preceding season, plus the holder. On each leg of the competition teams drawn together play each other twice (at home and away) until the final, which is held at a neutral venue. Real Madrid of Spain won the first five finals (1956–60).

European Cup (athletics), official name the Bruno Zauli European Cup, an international team championship in which six countries qualify for separate men's and women's finals. Each team has one representative per track and field event, the result being determined by awarding from 6 to 1 points for finishing 1st to 6th. Designed to assess a country's all-round strength, it began in 1965 as the Europa Cup and was held three-yearly from 1967–73, when a four-year cycle was adopted.

European Cup-Winners' Cup, knockout soccer competition for clubs who have won their national cup the preceding season, plus the current holder. Like the EUROPEAN CUP it is played on a home-and-away basis until the final, which is held at a neutral venue. It began in season 1960–61.

European Defence Community, attempt in the early 1950s to form an integrated, supranational army in Western Europe. The idea arose from the French desire to control German rearmament and the concern of the USA to combat the USSR. Belguim, France, West Germany, Italy, Luxembourg and The Netherlands signed a treaty in May 1952 providing that each country should contribute troops to a unified army. But in France a two-year struggle with the conservative opposition, led by Charles DE GAULLE, ended in the failure of the French assembly to ratify the treaty. Combined with Britain's refusal to join, the French decision killed the plan.

European Economic Community. *See* EEC.

European Free Trade Association. *See* EFTA.

European Football Championships, soccer competition for national teams of UEFA countries, contested every four years over a two-year period. It began in 1958–60 as the European Nations Cup. The first two championships used a knockout system, but with its increased popularity a league system was introduced from 1966–68, the winner of each group qualifying for the quarter-finals. In these and the group matches teams meet each other twice, at home and away; the semi-finals and final are staged in one country.

European Nuclear Energy Agency, body to promote international co-operation in the use of nuclear energy for peaceful purposes. It was formed by the Organization for European Economic Co-operation in December 1957, the same year as the European Atomic Energy Community, on the advice of the report written by Louis Armand, chairman of the French State Railways. That report drew attention to Europe's dwindling energy resources and advised that nuclear energy could be properly developed only by co-operation in technical matters and research. In 1969 the agency began an ambitious programme to develop fuels for high-temperature power reactors. In 1972 it became the OECD (Organization for Economic Co-operation and Development) Nuclear Energy Agency.

European Postal Union, body to co-ordinate postal services, established in 1959. It issued the first European stamp at a preliminary meeting in 1956. It was joined by the "Six", the member nations of the COUNCIL OF EUROPE, and by eight other nations.

European Southern Observatory, astronomical observatory at Cerro la Silla, a mountain peak in Chile. It is run by a group of European nations. It has a 3.6m (11.9ft) reflecting telescope, one of the largest in the world.

European Space Research Organization (ESRO), organization founded by several European nations in 1962 to promote international co-operation in space research. Australia was admitted in 1965.

Europium, metallic element (Eu) of the lanthanide group, first isolated as the oxide in 1896 by Eugène Demarçay. Its chief ores are monazite (a phosphate) and bastnäsite (a fluorocarbonate). The metal is used in the manufacture of television screens and as a neutron absorber in

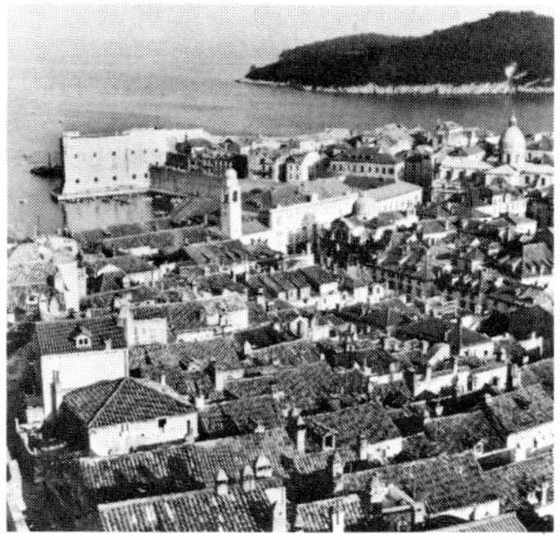

Europe; a view of the old city of Dubrovnik on the Dalmatian Coast in Yugoslavia.

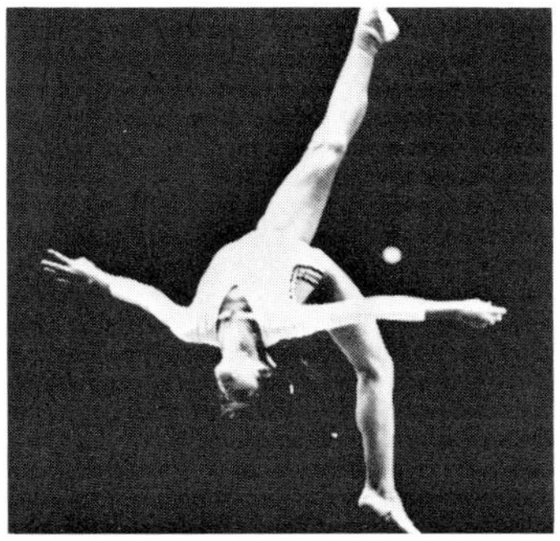

European Athletics Championships, 1977; Romania's Nadia Comaneci in the finals.

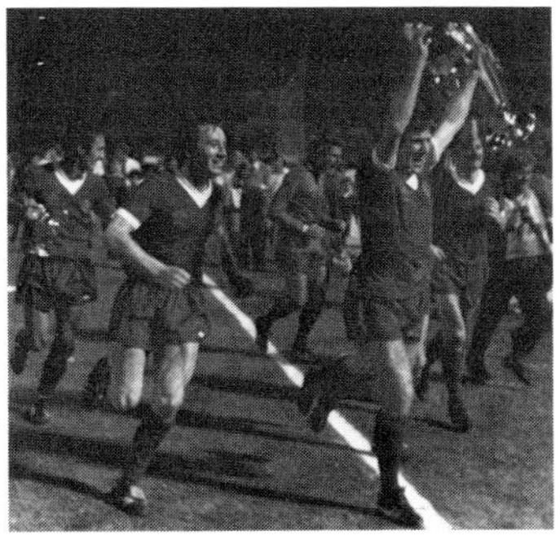

European Cup; Emlyn Hughes raises the cup after Liverpool defeated Borussia in 1977.

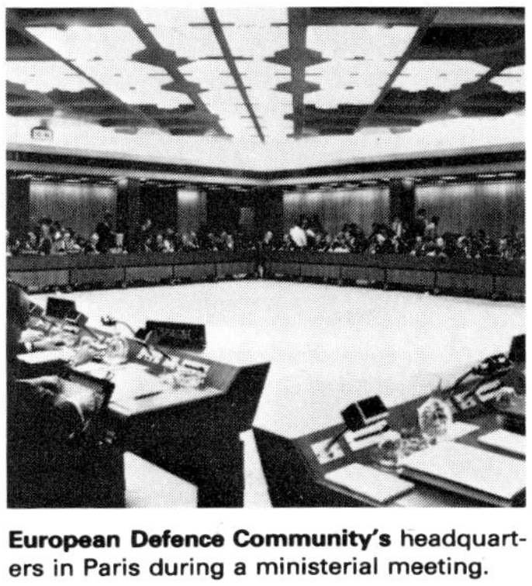

European Defence Community's headquarters in Paris during a ministerial meeting.

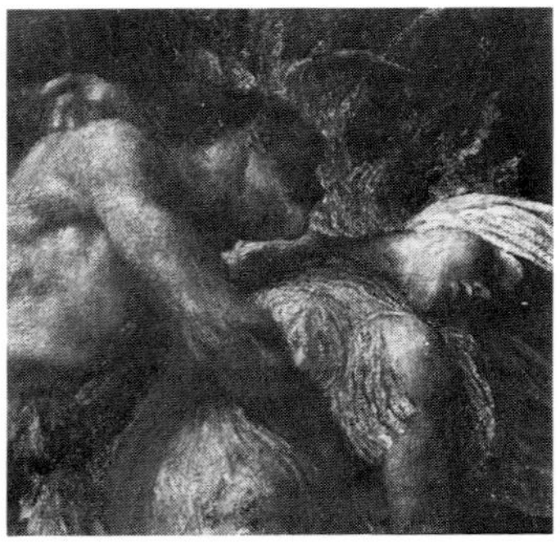

Eurydice; a painting by G. F. Watts of one of the greatest love stories in Greek mythology.

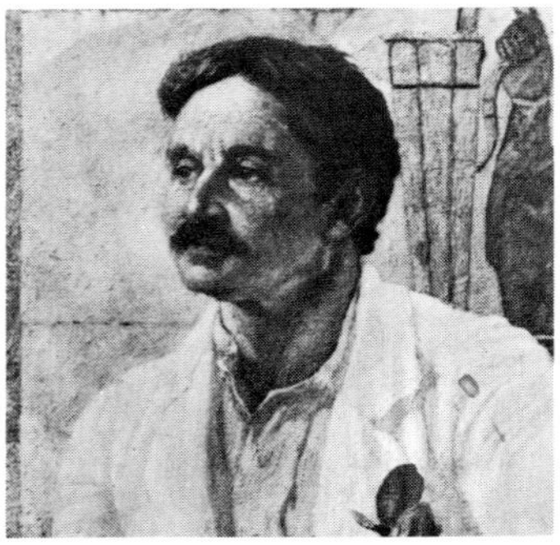

Sir Arthur Evans by W. Richmond; Evans was president of the Society of Antiquaries.

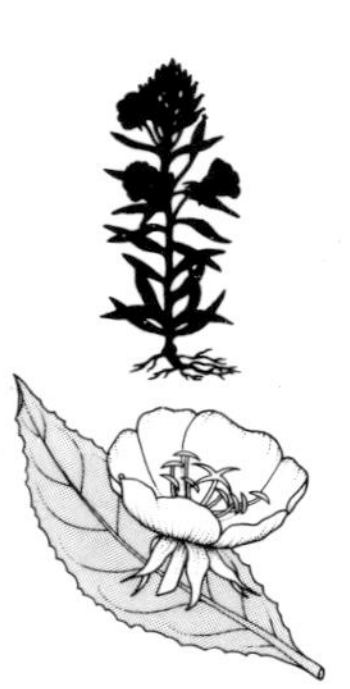

Evening primrose has stalks of scented yellow flowers 3 to 10cm (1–4in) across.

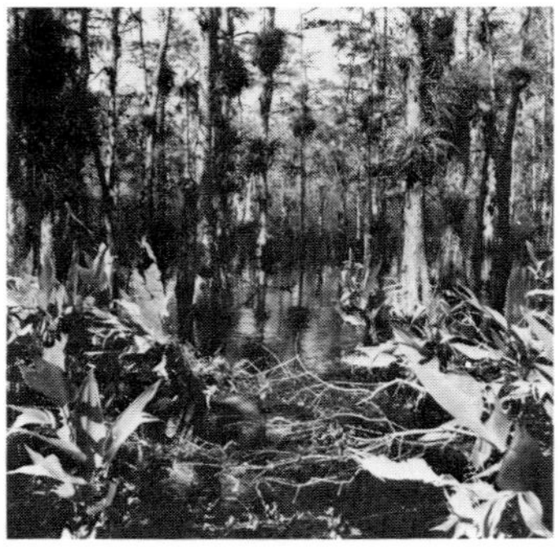

Everglades; water-diversion and building in this area has endangered many animals.

reactors. Properties: at. no. 63; at. wt. 151.96; s.g. 5.25 (25°C); m.p. 822°C (1,512°F); b.p. 1,597°C (2,907°F); most common isotope Eu^{153} (52.18 per cent).

Eurydice, in Greek mythology, a nymph married to the semi-divine singer and lyre-player ORPHEUS. When she died from a snake-bite, the inconsolable Orpheus braved the journey to the Underworld and charmed HADES into agreeing to release Eurydice. But Orpheus lost her for ever when in impatient excitement he broke his promise not to look at her before they emerged from Hades. *See also* MS pp.214–215.

Eusebio, Ferreira da Silva (1942–), Portuguese footballer. Known as the "Black Panther", he was the top scorer in the 1966 World Cup (9 goals) and his precise shooting made his club Benfica a European force in the 1960s. He was named European Footballer of the Year in 1965.

Eustachian tube, mucus-lined tube that connects the middle ear and the pharynx, equalizing internal and external pressures. It may also carry infection from the throat to the middle ear. *See also* MS p.50.

Eustachio, Bartolommeo (1520–74), Italian anatomist. A professor of medicine in Rome and the pope's physician, he introduced the study of anatomical variations. The EUSTACHIAN TUBE which leads from the middle ear to the throat is named after him. *See also* HC1 p.303; MS p.50.

Euston Road School, school of painting and drawing founded in London in 1937 by William COLDSTREAM, Victor PASMORE and Lawrence GOWING. They stressed the value of an objective approach to nature, influenced by SICKERT and CÉZANNE, rather than the prevalent abstract or surrealist styles. The school was closed in 1939.

Euthanasia, inducing the painless death of a person, often through the administration of a drug. Commonly known as mercy killing, it is illegal in most countries. An associated practice is the withholding of treatment which would uselessly prolong life.

Eutrophication, in geology, process by which a stream or lake becomes rich in inorganic nutrients by run-off from the land and by artificial means. Compounds of nitrogen, phosphorus, iron, sulphur and potassium are vital for plant growth in water; in excess, however, they overstimulate the growth of surface ALGAE and micro-organisms. Light penetration and oxygen absorption are also necessary for eutrophication. *See also* PE pp.150–151.

Eutyches (*c.*378–*c.*454), early church leader and heretic. In 448 he was accused of the heresy of denying the human nature of Christ and recognizing only his divine nature. As the first real MONOPHYSITE, he was deposed by St Flavian, Patriarch of Constantinople; he was acquitted by the Robber Synod at Ephesus (449), but was deposed and exiled at the Council of Chalcedon (451).

Eutychianus, Saint, POPE (*r.*275–83) of whom almost nothing is known.

Evacuation, withdrawal of troops or inhabitants from an area in an emergency where injury or loss of life is threatening. Evacuation procedures are planned by civil defence specialists where there is danger of such calamities as earthquakes, volcanic eruptions, flooding, the escape of noxious materials or enemy attack.

Evangelicalism, in Christian usage, a term with several connotations: (a) in a broad sense it has been applied to PROTESTANTISM as a whole because of its claim to base its doctrines strictly on the Gospel (Greek *euangelos*, "good news" or "gospel"); (b) in Germany and Switzerland the term "Evangelical Church" is sometimes used to denote the Lutheran denomination as distinct from Calvinist bodies, which are termed "Reformed"; (c) in the Church of England, evangelicalism denotes the school – often called low church – which stresses personal conversion and witness of salvation by faith in the atoning death of Jesus Christ.

Evangeline (1849), narrative poem by Henry Wadsworth LONGFELLOW. Based on the expulsion of Acadian settlers from Canada during the French and Indian Wars, it is a story of two lovers, Evangeline and Gebriel, who are separated.

Evangelist, from the Greek for "bringer of good news", one who preaches the Gospel, announcing the good news of redemption through Jesus Christ, and the hope of everlasting life. The word also applies by extension to the authors of the four gospels: MATTHEW, MARK, LUKE and JOHN.

Evans, Sir Arthur John (1851–1941), English archaeologist. He excavated the ruins of the city of KNOSSOS in Crete and found evidence of a Bronze Age civilization, which he named the MINOAN AGE. He also made several discoveries of pre-PHOENICIAN script. He wrote *The Palace of Minos* (4 vols, 1921–36).

Evans, Bill (1929–), US jazz pianist. He played with Tony Scott, George Russell, Charlie MINGUS and Miles DAVIS before forming his own successful trio in 1959.

Evans, Caradoc (1878–1945), Welsh novelist (real name David Evans) whose bitterly satirical attacks on the bigotry and parsimony of his compatriots appeared in *My People: Stories of the Peasantry of West Wales* (1915) and his novels *Nothing to Pay* (1930) and *Wasps* (1934). They were deeply resented by the Welsh. After 1940, however, he wrote short stories generally praising his countrymen.

Evans, Dame Edith (1888–1976), British stage and screen actress. While with the Old Vic (1925–26; 1936) she played a variety of roles, including Katharina in *The Taming of the Shrew* and the Nurse in *Romeo and Juliet.* Some of her best remembered roles were Mrs Millamant in Congreve's *Way of the World* (1924, 27) and Lady Bracknell in Wilde's *The Importance of Being Ernest* (1939; filmed in 1952). She received great acclaim for her West End role in Enid Bagnole's *The Chalk Garden*, and was awarded the New York Film Critic's Award for her performance in *The Whisperers* in 1967. Her last stage appearance was a lively one-woman show in 1974.

Evans, Sir Geraint (1922–), Welsh baritone. After studying at the Guildhall School of Music, London, he made his debut at Covent Garden in 1948. He has sung with all the famous leading European and US opera companies and has developed a large repertoire of modern and traditional roles. *See also* HC2 p.*287*.

Evans, Gil (1912–), US jazz pianist, composer and arranger, *b.* Ian Ernest Gilmore Green. He arranged music for Claude Thornhill and others in the 1940s and for Miles DAVIS in the 1950s.

Evans, Godfrey (1920–), Kent and England cricketer who in 91 Test Matches (1946–59) made 219 wicket-keeping dismissals (173 caught, 46 stumped), a Test record that stood until Alan KNOTT beat it in 1976. During his first-class career he dismissed 1,060 batsmen (811 caught, 249 stumped).

Evans, Mary Ann. *See* ELIOT, GEORGE.

Evans, William John (Bill) (1928–), US jazz pianist. He played with Tony Scott and Miles DAVIS in the 1950s, then led his own trio and is regarded as one of the most original and significant jazz piano stylists of the 1960s.

Evaporated milk, tinned milk product being between 25 and 33% solids and having 8% fat, more than twice as concentrated as fresh milk. It is made by sterilizing milk concentrate in the tin at 116°C (240°F). This process gives it the off-white colour and particular taste. It is used in cooking and has the advantage of keeping well after the tin has been opened.

Evaporation, or vaporization, process by which a liquid or solid becomes a vapour. The reverse process is CONDENSATION. Solids and liquids cool when they evaporate because they give up energy (LATENT HEAT) to the escaping molecules. In chemistry, evaporation is the concentration of a liquid by boiling off vapour, usually prior to the formation of crystals. The rate of evaporation is speeded up by increased heat, stirring and by prompt vapour removal. *See also* SU p.86.

Evaporator, area to be cooled – such as the freezing compartment and the interior of refrigerators. The refrigerant (eg FREON or ammonia) evaporates, absorbing heat from the surroundings. Evaporators are built with large surface areas to allow maximum heat absorption. *See also* MM p.*253*.

Evaporite, mineral deposit of precipitated salts, formed by the evaporation of saline lakes or confined volumes of salt water usually in previous geological eras. They are important sources of GYPSUM, anhydrite, rock-salt, sylvite and small amounts of nitrates and borates.

Evapotranspiration, combined processes of EVAPORATION and TRANSPIRATION in which water is transferred from the Earth's surface to the atmosphere. It is a key factor in the water balance. Water or ice is evaporated by the Sun's rays and by the wind, and plants are cooled by transpiration. *See also* SU p.86.

Evaristus, St, POPE (*r.*99–107) who appointed clergy to the 25 parishes in Rome. He is said to have been martyred.

Evatt, Herbert Vere (1894–1965), Australian politician. He was attorney-general and minister for external affairs (1941–1949) and later a delegate to the United Nations General Assembly (1946–48), where he was president. Between 1951 and 1960 he was leader of the Australian Labor Party.

Eve, in GENESIS, first woman, created by God from Adam's rib to be his companion and wife. Her name probably means "life". *See also* ADAM AND EVE; MS pp. *184, 219*.

Evelina, or *The History of a Young Lady's Entrance into the World,* EPISTOLARY NOVEL published anonymously by Fanny BURNEY in 1778. It completely abandoned the contemporary picaresque style and in its spontaneity, acute social observation and detailed descriptions of domestic life anticipated the work of Jane AUSTEN.

Evelyn, John (1620–1706), English diarist. His writings include *Sculptura* (1662) on engraving, *Sylva* (1664) on tree-growing, *Navigation and Commerce* (1674) and his *Diary* (first published 1818), which is a vivid account of life in 17th-century England. *See also* HC1 p.*294*.

Evening primrose, any of various annual, biennial or perennial plants of the genus *Oenothera*, many of which are native to w North America. They have yellow, pink or white flowers that open in the evening. Height: 1.8m (5.3ft). Family Onagraceae.

Evening star, planet, not star, visible near the horizon in the early evening. It appears as a brightly shining object that does not twinkle. Although Mars, Jupiter and Saturn occasionally appear as evening stars, the term most often refers to Venus, which shines so brightly as to be sometimes visible during daylight.

Everest, Sir George (1790–1866), British surveyor-geographer after whom Mt EVEREST is named. He went to India when he was only 16 and began his career of exploration and surveying in that country. Many of the boundaries of modern India are based on his work.

Everest, Mount, highest mountain in the world, in the central Himalayas on the borders of Tibet and Nepal. The first successful attempt to reach the top was accomplished on 29 May 1953 by a British expedition led by Sir Edmund HILLARY and Tenzing Norgay of Nepal. There had been eight previous attempts. Named after George Everest, the first surveyor-general of India, its Tibetan name is Chomo-Langma, or Mother Goddess of the World. Height: 8,848m (29,029ft).

Everglades, large tract of marshland in s Florida, USA, extending from Lake Okeechobee to Florida Bay, it includes the Everglades National Park. The region is made up of mangrove forests, saw grass, hummocks (island masses of vegetation) and water, and supports tropical animal life including crocodiles, alligators, egrets and bald eagles. Area: approx. 10,000sq km (4,000sq miles).

Evergreen, plant that retain its green foliage for a year or more (deciduous plants lose their leaves every autumn). Evergreens are divided into two groups: narrow-leaved, or CONIFERS, and broad-leaved. Conifers include fir, spruce, pine, hemlock and juniper. Among the broad-leaved evergreens are holly, magnolia, box, cherry laurel and rhododendron. But not all conifers are evergreens; an exception is the decidous larch.

Everlasting flowers, types of flowers that retain their colour and shape when dried. Best known are those of the everlasting flower or immortelle (*Helichrysum bracteatum*), with daisy-like yellow, brown, purple or white blooms. Other popular plants include globe amaranth, *Statice, Lunaria* and *Xeranthemum*.

Evershed, John (1864–1956), British astronomer who, in 1919, discovered the horizontal flow of gases from the centre of sunspots, called the Evershed effect. He studied in various Indian observatories, later building his own at Ewhurst (1925).

Evert, Christine Marie (1954–), US tennis player. One of the world's top women players in the mid-1970s, she has won numerous titles, among them the US (1975), French (1974–75) and Wimbledon women's singles in 1974 and 1976.

Everyman's Library, successful series of universal classics founded by J.M. DENT and named after the morality play line, "Everyman, I will go with thee, and be thy guide". The first fifty books were published in 1906 at one shilling each; the thousandth volume appeared fifty years later. By 1977 total sales exceeded 55 million copies.

Evesham, Battle of (1265), final battle of the BARONS' WARS, in which Simon de MONTFORT, the rebel leader, was defeated and killed by Edward, son of Henry III. *See also* HC1 p.*178*.

Evidence, testimony by witnesses, items from the scene of a crime, or forensic or scientific information given by experts in a court of law, to establish the facts of a case. Evidence is chiefly of two kinds: DIRECT EVIDENCE and CIRCUMSTANTIAL EVIDENCE.

Evil, man's concept of wickedness, wrong-doing and sin; it is a relative term, the meaning of which depends on the nature of the good it opposes. This good, in turn, is the perfection or integrity of being; moral, material and spiritual. Evil therefore functions on three levels. Moral evil is regarded as a sin; an action committed with the conscious intention of doing wrong; physical evil affects a nature; and metaphysical evil results from absence of perfection; the mere finitude of created beings. A theological dilemma arises from the contradictory nature of good and evil, ie God is almighty and good, yet evil exists. The Devil is commonly used to personify the source of all evil, which was once also associated with dragons and other monsters, insanity and physical deformity. Over the ages the conflict between good and evil – light against the darkness – has dominated man's beliefs and imagination.

Evil Eye, belief in the power of a human glance to inflict harm. This belief is widespread in Christian, Jewish and Muslim traditions and in primitive societies. *See also* MS pp.196–197.

Evolution, theory that organisms originate from simpler forms of another organism and that a new species is the end of gradual development and change from the simpler forms. Early work on evolutionary theory was initiated by Jean LAMARCK during the early 1800s, but it was not until Charles DARWIN wrote *The Origin of Species* during the mid-1800s that the theory was considered worthy of argument. Present-day evolutionary theory is derived from the work of Darwin and MENDEL and maintains that in any population or a gene pool, there are random MUTATIONS in genetic forms and characteristics. Most species reproduce in greater quantities than their environment can support, so only those members best adapted to the environment survive. When mutated characteristics provide survival advantages, mutants survive to pass on these new characteristics. In this way a species effects gradual changes to adapt and survive in a competitive, and often changing, environment. *See also* NATURAL SELECTION; NW pp.22–25, 32–35, 188–191.

Evolutionary socialism, the belief that SOCIALISM can be introduced through the ballot box, ie that government can be an instrument of reform. This gradual approach contrasts with the traditional Marxist view that socialism can be brought about only by the violent overthrow of capitalism.

Evora, market town in SE central Portugal; capital of Evora district. It has a ruined Temple of Diana, a Romanesque 13th-century cathedral and a Roman aqueduct. Pop. (1970) 47,806.

Ewald, Johannes (1743–81), Danish lyric poet. His dramatic poem *Adam and Eve* (1769) was followed by *Rolf Krage* (1770), a drama based on legend. The song "King Christian stood by the Lofty Mast", from Ewald's opera *The Fishermen* (1779), is Denmark's national anthem.

Ewbank, Thomas (1792–1870), inventor of the household carpet sweeper, *b.* Durham, England. Emigrating to New York in 1819, he made his money manufacturing metal tubing and retired in 1836 to concentrate on writing books on mechanics and science. After travelling in South America (1845–48) he helped to found the American Ethnological Society. *See also* MM p.252.

Ewing, James Alfred (1855–1935), Scottish physicist and engineer. He observed and identified hysteresis, the lag in effect when forces acting on an object are changed, and invented a number of instruments to test magnetic properties.

Ewing, William Maurice (1906–74), US geophysicist. First to take seismic measurements in open seas (1935), he aided understanding of marine sediments and ocean basins. He proposed that earthquakes are associated with central oceanic rifts and took the first deep-sea photographs (1939).

Ewins, Arthur James (1882–1957), British chemist; he was one of the discoverers of sulphapyridine, a SULPHONAMIDE derivative used to treat pneumonia. He also discovered other medicinal compounds including pentamide which was one of the first drugs to combat sleeping sickness.

Eworth, Hans (*c.* 1520–after 1573), Flemish painter. Known primarily for his precise portraits of English nobility, he was greatly influenced by Hans HOLBEIN who preceded him as Henry VIII's court painter.

Ewry, Ray (1873–1937), US athlete who overcame paralysis to win eight Olympic gold medals in the now defunct standing jump events: high, long and triple jumps in 1900 and 1904; high and long jumps in 1908. He also won the high and long jumps at the 1906 Interim Olympic Games.

Exchange, Bill of. *See* BILL OF EXCHANGE.

Exchange rate, in finance, the rate at which one nation's currency can be converted to that of another. It varies according to the fluctuations registered on the world's foreign exchange markets. Changes in the exchange rate can be influenced by such factors as a nation's BALANCE OF PAYMENTS, political developments and speculation in money markets. *See also* MS pp.314–315.

Exchange theory, theory of social behaviour, associated with Georg SIMNEL, stating that people enter into and maintain relationships because doing so brings them a reward. The reward may be intrinsic to the relationship, eg love or friendship, or extrinsic to it, eg advice, help or economic advancement. *See also* MS pp.262–263.

Exchequer, branch of the medieval CURIA REGIS, which kept the royal accounts in England. In the mid-13th century the increase in its business required it to stay in one place, not move about with the king's HOUSEHOLD. It "moved out of court" to become its own separate department of finance. Its chief officer is called "chancellor" because it was originally a court; but its legal function was abolished in 1873. It gets its name from the chequered cloth on which its accounts were done. *See also* HC1 p.178.

Exchequer, Chancellor of the. *See* CHANCELLOR OF THE EXCHEQUER.

Exchequer Court of Canada, one of two Canadian federal courts. It has jurisdiction over revenue, property and other affairs of the crown. In certain cases an appeal can be made from the Exchequer Court to the Supreme Court, its companion federal court.

Excise. *See* CUSTOMS AND EXCISE.

Excited state, condition of an atom, ion or molecule, when its energy level is higher than that of the ground (lowest) state. For example, an atom can be in an excited state having absorbed a photon. The increased energy causes one of the electrons to occupy an orbital of higher energy; the atom may restore its former state by various emissions. *See also* SU pp.62–63.

Exclusion principle, Pauli, basic law of quantum mechanics, proposed by Wolfgang PAULI in 1925, stating that no two electrons in an atom can possess the same energy and spin. More precisely, the set of four quantum numbers characterizing certain elementary particles called fermions must be unique. In atoms, these numbers specify an electron's spin direction, orbital shape and the energy level at which it resides, or would reside, in a magnetic field. *See also* SU p.133.

Exclusive Brethren, religious sect formed when the PLYMOUTH BRETHREN split into the Exclusive and Open Brethren in 1849, over a controversy on the human nature of Christ and on church government. Their teaching is the same as that of the Plymouth Brethren, and they have a conservative outlook on the Bible, and puritanical moral views.

Excommunication, formal expulsion from the community, sacraments and rites of a religious body, largely abandoned by Protestants but retained by Jewish congregations and the Roman Catholic Church. In the days when the Church held great temporal (as well as spiritual) authority, excommunication was a severe punishment for heresy or blasphemy.

Excretion, elimination of waste materials from the body, particularly nitrogeneous wastes which would be toxic if allowed to accumulate. In mammals these wastes are excreted mainly as urine, and to some extent also by sweating. Carbon dioxide, a waste product of metabolism, is excreted mainly through the lungs during breathing. Defaecation, strictly speaking, is not excretion; faeces are mostly material that has never been part of the body.

Executor, person on whom responsibility for execution (or carrying out of the provisions) of a will rests. Normally the executor is named in the will by the TESTATOR. The executor's duties are to arrange the funeral of the deceased, to pay outstanding debts and to distribute the property among the beneficiaries according to the deceased's wishes, in addition to settling any disputes about the will.

Executive privilege, right invoked by the US president to justify withholding information from Congress or the courts, often on the grounds of confidentiality, national security or the public interest. The precedent was set by George Washington in 1794 when he refused to give Congress certain documents. During the WATERGATE scandal (1973–74) Richard Nixon claimed executive privilege initially in refusing to surrender tapes of White House conversations.

Exekias (*fl.* 6th century BC), Athenian vase painter, the most famous and probably the best of the black-figure painters. His known works include such scenes as Ajax and Achilles playing dice and Dionysus sitting in his boat.

Exeter, county town of Devonshire, England, a city on the River Exe 60km (37 miles) NE of Plymouth. Despite bombing during WWII, many ancient buildings remain, including the twin-towered cathedral and a guildhall. Pop. (1971) 95,598.

Exeter Book, manuscript, copied *c.* 975, containing the largest extant collection of Old English poetry. The manuscript was probably copied from an earlier book, and was given to Exeter Cathedral by Bishop Leofric. It contains both religious and secular verse, as well as 95 riddles.

Exhibition, The Great (1851), display of British and foreign manufactured goods held in Hyde Park, London, and

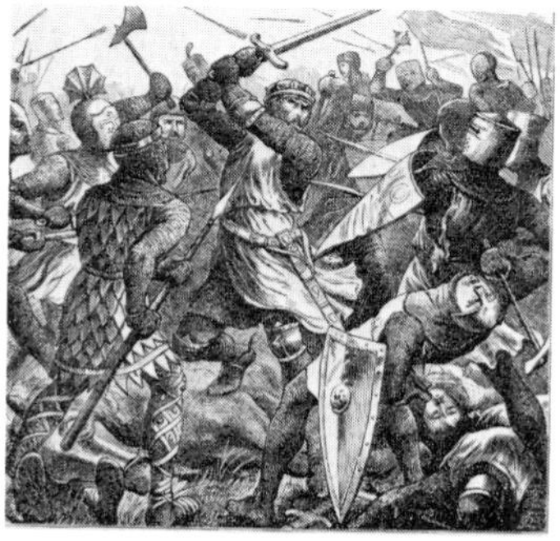

Evesham, Battle of, where the body of de Montfort was grossly mutilated.

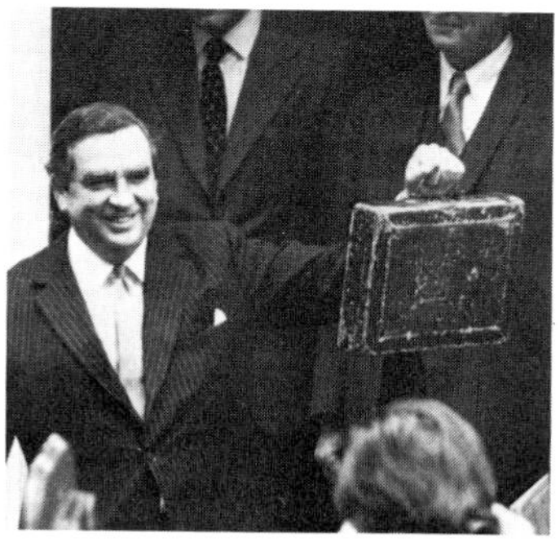

Exchequer; the British Chancellor, Denis Healey, leaving to present his budget.

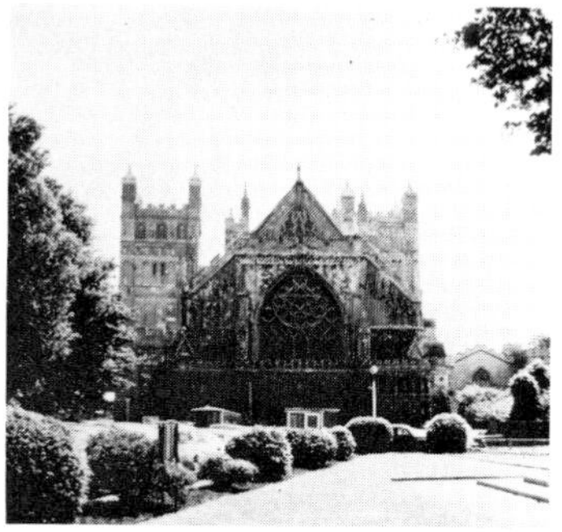

Exeter Cathedral is the most westerly Gothic cathedral in England.

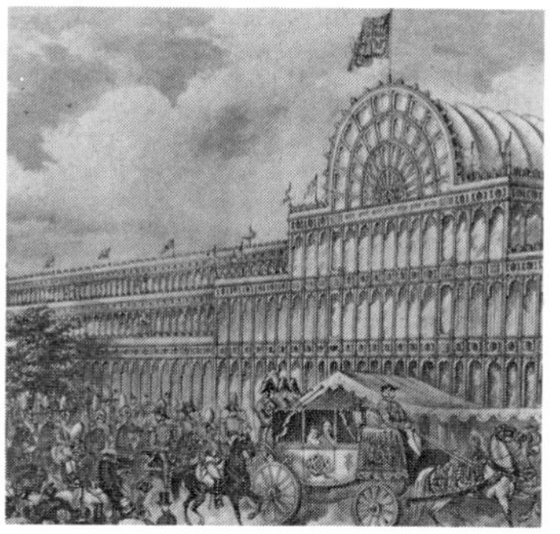

Exhibition, The Great; Queen Victoria and Prince Albert arriving at the Crystal Palace.

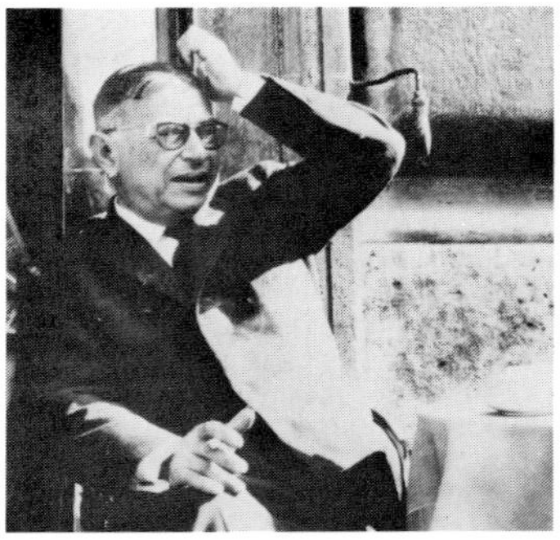

Existentialism; Jean-Paul Sartre, one of the principal exponents of this philosophy.

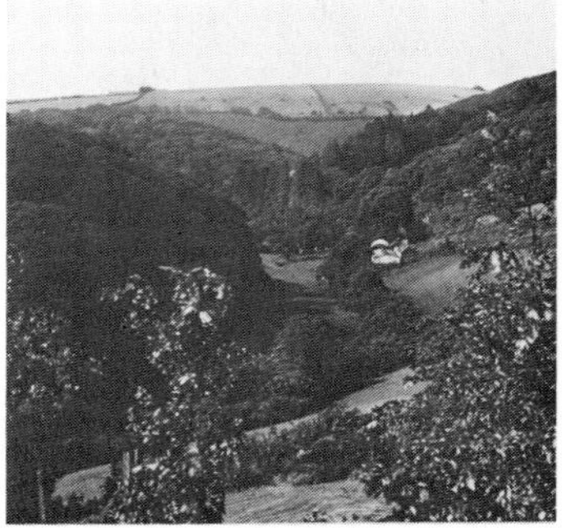

Exmoor National Park; much of it lies more than 300m (1,000ft) above sea-level.

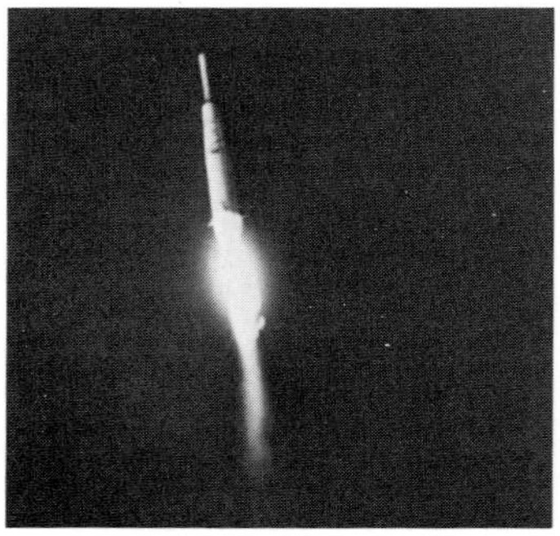

Explorer I exploded at an altitude of 15,000m (50,000ft) after 75 minutes of flight.

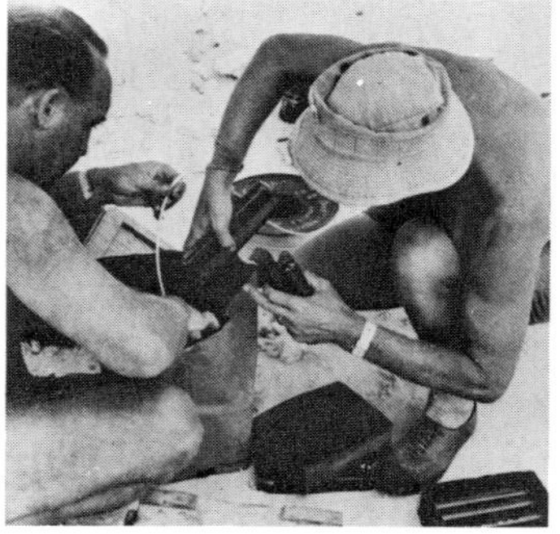

Explosives; preparations for a hydrogen bomb test on Christmas Island in 1957.

organized by Prince ALBERT. The exhibition was housed in the CRYSTAL PALACE, and was intended to demonstrate the benefits of industry and international peace and trade; it had more than 6 million visitors. *See also* HC2 p.*112*.

Existentialism, term associated with various philosophers and writers, all of whom are concerned with the individual and his relationship with the universe or with God. Most of its adherents hold the belief that "existence precedes essence" – ie, that man is completely free to create his own destiny and is in no way determined by forces outside his control. The beginnings of the modern movement can be seen in the theological writings of Søren KIERKEGAARD, later developed by Karl JASPERS. Martin HEIDEGGER's and Jean-Paul SARTRE's writings show the influence of PHENOMENOLOGY. The novelist Albert CAMUS and the Christian thinker Gabriel MARCEL are also linked with existentialism. *See also* MS p.231.

Exit the King (Le Roi se meurt) (1962), long one-act play by IONESCO in which he explores the nightmare of ultimate death as an imminent necessity. In a relatively straightforward style departing somewhat from his totally absurdist manner, he gives a controlled allegorical account of the progressive demise of the supposedly ageless King Bérenger and his court. In the London production of 1963, Alec GUINNESS gave a powerful performance as the king.

Exmoor, moorland plateau in NW Somerset and N Devon, SW England. It is mainly rough open pasture supporting sheep and wild ponies. It lies within Exmoor National Park and its highest point is Dunkery Beacon, 520m (1,705ft).

Exobiology, study of environmental conditions and possible biochemical and evolutionary pathways to life beyond Earth. It is concerned with such experiments as creation of amino acids from electrical discharges in methane-ammonia atmosphere, eg primeval Earth or present Jupiter, or survival of bacteria or mosses under Martian conditions. The *Viking* lander (1976) was designed to test Martian soil for gaseous byproducts of metabolic activity. *See also* VIKING MISSION.

Exodus, biblical book, second book of the PENTATEUCH, named by Greek translators after its account of the flight of the Israelites from slavery in Egypt after the plagues had forced the pharaoh to release them. The book is divided into two sections, the first historical narrative and the second legislative directions. *See also* HC1 pp.58–59.

Exogamy, in anthropology, the practice of marrying outside a particular social group. This restriction always applies to close relatives and in some cultures is extended to wider kinship groups. Some have explicit rules about who cannot marry whom, including INCEST TABOOS, whereas in others it is a vaguer obligation. *See also* ENDOGAMY; MS pp.250–251.

Exophthalmos, abnormal protrusion of the eyeball caused by oedema (DROPSY), ANEURYSM, or disorder in the ENDOCRINE SYSTEM. Onset may be sudden or gradual depending on the cause.

Exopterygota, sub-class of insects which develop into adults by a gradual series of moultings, such as EPHEMEROPTERA.

Exorcism, ritual expulsion of evil spirits from a person, place or thing, usually performed by a priest, witch doctor or sorcerer. Exorcism is a practice common to many religions. In the Christian church it is performed by means of the LAYING-ON OF HANDS and incantation; in other religions whippings or sacrifices may be necessary in addition.

Exoskeleton, protective and supporting outer covering of an animal's body. It may be made of CHITIN, as in the case of crustaceans, or of horny plates, as in the carapace of the tortoise.

Exosphere, outer shell in the atmosphere from which light gases can escape. *See* ATMOSPHERE.

Exothermic reaction, CHEMICAL REACTION in which heat is evolved, causing a rise in temperature. A common example is COMBUSTION. *See also* ENDOTHERMIC REACTION; SU pp.154–155.

Expanding universe, theory of the origin and direction in time of the Universe. Physicists have attempted to explain the red-shift phenomena of some stars as resulting from a single, huge explosion which causes these stars to be moving away from our section of the Universe. The red-shift occurs when, due to the DOPPLER EFFECT, the perceived wave lengths of light from some stars are lengthened because of their outwards movement. There is also the opposite effect, a blue-shift, but this does not occur as often. Today the balance of opinion is in favour of the theory of the expanding universe. *See also* "BIG BANG," THE; SU pp.*105*, 164–165, *249*.

Expansion, mathematical process of replacing an expression by a sum of a finite number of terms, or by an infinite series. For example, the expression $(x + 1)(x + 3)$ can be expanded to $x^2 + 4x + 3$; the function $\sin x$ can be expanded into the converging series $x - x^3/3! + x^5/5! - \ldots$. *See also* BINOMIAL THEOREM.

Expansion, coefficient of, ratio of the rates of change of volume to temperature (at constant pressure), or of volume to pressure (at constant temperature). For a gas, the coefficient of expansion is usually large; for a solid, it is much smaller.

Expansion chamber. *See* CLOUD CHAMBER.

Ex parte, application in a judicial proceeding made by someone who is not a party to the proceeding but who has an interest in the matter. It can also apply to an application made by someone in the absence of the person against whom the application is made, as in an ex parte INJUNCTION.

Experimental psychology, use of experimental methods in psychological investigations. Close observation, careful recording and other scientific techniques are easiest to carry out in a laboratory, but psychologists also use them in clinics, schools or the community at large.

Explorer I, first of a series of US scientific satellites. It was launched in 1958, and the programme continued into the 1970s. The early Explorers provided information about the radiation zones surrounding the Earth that are now known as the VAN ALLEN BELTS. *See also* SU pp.268–269.

Explosive decompression, sudden drop in pressure of an aircraft or spacecraft cabin due to meteorite puncture or system failure. A pressure drop to below 47mm Hg (pressure of water vapour at 38°C) results in the boiling of body liquids. Lungs collapse completely within a few seconds, blood pressure drops and the large bowel relaxes. Anoxemia (lack of oxygen in blood) and embolisms (blood-clots blocking blood vessels) result.

Explosives, substances that react rapidly and violently releasing heat, light, sound and shock waves. Chemical explosives are mostly highly nitrated compounds or mixtures that are unstable and decompose violently with the evolution of much gas. Nuclear explosives are radioactive metals, the atoms of which can undergo fission or fusion to release vast amounts of radiant energy and shock waves. *See also* MM pp.242–243.

Exponent, superscript number placed to the right of a symbol indicating its POWER; eg in $a^4 (= a \times a \times a \times a)$, 4 is the exponent. Certain laws of exponents apply in mathematical operations. For example, $3^2 \times 3^3 = x^{(3+2)} = 3^5$; $3^4 \div 3^3 = 3^{(4-3)} = 3^1$; $(3^2)^3 = 3^{(2\times3)} = 3^6$; $3^{-5} = 1/3$

Ex post facto law, law of retrospective effect that punishes a person on conviction for an offence that was not punishable at the time it occurred.

Expressionism, movement in the arts in the early 20th century, mainly in Germany. It was characterized by its stress on heightened and violent emotions and an emphasis on inner vision; balance of design was replaced by distortion for this purpose. It represented a reaction to naturalism and realism, opposed any form of idealism and was influenced by psychoanalysis. Many expressionists were violently anti-bourgeois. The movement in painting used dramatic colours and agonized scenes; it was developed by the BLAUE REITER and die BRÜCKE groups before WWI; after 1945 in the USA it lost its illustrative content and developed into ABSTRACT EXPRESSIONISM. Expressionist film laid stress on heavily contrasted light and shade; it was best achieved in the CABINET OF DR. CALIGARI, and in the works of Fritz LANG. STRINDBERG and KAFKA are often considered expressionist writers, and SCHOENBERG and WEBERN are typical expressionist musicians. *See also* HC2 pp.174–175.

Expressionist theatre, theatrical style originating in Germany and popular in Europe and America throughout the 1920s. A reaction against theatrical realism, its beginnings are in August STRINDBERG's later works, especially *The Ghost Sonata* (1916). It attempted to present emotional rather than apparent reality and used symbols and bold psychological interpretations of people and events. Two important expressionist playwrights are Ernst TOLLER (1893–1939) and Elmer RICE (1892–1967).

Expresso Bongo (1958), British musical play by Wolf Mankowitz and Julian More which satirized the personalities and manipulations of the popular music industry. The stage production starred Paul SCOFIELD; a film with Cliff RICHARD and Lawrence HARVEY appeared in 1959.

External combustion engine. *See* ENGINE.

Extinction, in behaviouristic psychology, the gradual diminution of the conditioned response resulting from the withholding of the unconditioned stimulus or the reinforcing reward.

Extinction, part of the evolutionary process of natural selection in which certain species of plants and animals die out to be replaced by others. All organic life is enriched by this process, as opposed to wanton destruction by man, which depletes irreplaceable species.

Extraction, in chemistry, physical separation of a liquid or solid mixture by selectively dissolving some components with a solvent. Specific ingredients for perfumes and flavourings may be extracted from plant oils. Proteins are separated from carbohydrates in soya beans by controlled solvent extraction to produce soya protein isolates. *See also* SU pp.144, *144*, 148.

Extrapolation, in mathematics, method of finding values beyond those that are measured. Most of economics is extrapolation, in that statistics are compiled up to the present year, and using them as a guide, decisions are made concerning future years. A simple graph such as a straight line can be extrapolated because it is assumed to be continuous. *See also* INTERPOLATION; SU p.*35*.

Extrasensory perception. *See* ESP.

Extrinsic factor, or Vitamin B_{12}, provides cobalt, a trace element needed in ERYTHROCYTE formation; deficiency results in PERNICIOUS ANAEMIA. *See also* INTRINSIC FACTOR; MS p.*91*.

Extrovert, personality type characterized by "out-going" behaviour; the opposite of INTROVERT. According to Hans EYSENCK, extroversion-introversion is one of the basic dimensions of PERSONALITY. This theory was based on statistical analyses. The term was popularized by Carl JUNG. *See also* MS p.188–189.

Extrusion, in geology, the breaking-out of igneous material from below the Earth's surface. Any volcanic product reaching the surface becomes extrusive material whether it is ejected through a volcano's cone or through pipe-like channels or fissures in its crust. In industry, extrusion is the forcing of metals (eg magnesium, copper, aluminium, their alloys or plastics) at optimum temperature through a die to make rods, tubes and various hollow or solid sections. *See also* IGNEOUS ROCK; VOLCANO; MM pp.55, *55*.

Eyadema, Gnassingbe (1935–), President of Togo since 1969. He was in the French Army (1953–61), mostly in Indo-China and Algeria; he was commissioned in 1963.

Eyck, van, two brothers, Flemish painters. Jan (*d.* 1441), acclaimed founder of Flemish painting, worked mainly at the courts of John of Bavaria and Philip the Good until 1430, when he settled in Bruges. His best-known works are the altarpiece of the Church of St Bavon, Ghent, which includes the *Adoration of the Lamb* (completed in 1432), and the *Arnolfini Wedding* (1434), both of which display intricate detail and clear realism. He is said to have perfected the manufacture and technique of oil paint. His elder brother Hubert (*d.*1426) worked in Ghent and assisted his brother on the St Bavon alterpiece. No other works are known definitely to have been painted by him. *See also* HC1 p.252, *252*.

Eye, sense organ of vision. It converts light energy to nerve impulses that are transmitted to the visual centre of the brain. Most of the mass of each eye lies in a bony protective socket, called the orbital cavity, which also includes muscles and other tissues to hold and move the eye and associated structures, such as the lachrymal apparatus which produces TEARS. The eyeball is spherical and composed of three layers; the sclera (white of the eye), which contains the transparent cornea; the choroid, which connects with the iris, pupil lens and contains blood vessels to provide food and oxygen; and the retina, which contains RODS AND CONES for converting the image into nerve impulses. The aqueous humour (a watery liquid between the cornea and iris) and the vitreous humour (a jelly-like substance behind the lens) both help to maintain the shape of the eye. *See also* SIGHT; MS pp.48–49.

Eyebright, any of several small annual and perennial plants widely distributed in N and S temperate and subarctic regions. They have terminal spikes of white, yellow or purple flowers. European eyebright (*Euphrasia officinalis*) got its name because it was formerly used to treat eye diseases. Family Scrophulariaceae.

Eyre, Edward John (1815–1901), British explorer and colonial administrator. He began explorations in Australia in 1833, gaining an intimate knowledge of the Aborigines. Later, positions in the governments of New Zealand and some lesser islands led to the governorship of Jamaica in 1864. His allegedly brutal suppression of a black uprising in 1865 caused his controversial dismissal.

Eyre, Lake, salt lake in NE South Australia. It is the lowest point on the continent, 12m (39ft) below sea-level, and the largest salt lake in Australia. Area: 9,324sq km (3,600sq miles); max. depth: 1.2m (4ft).

Eyre Peninsula, long peninsula in S South Australia, on the Great Australian Bight W of Spencer Gulf. Sheep are reared and there are large deposits of iron ore. Length: approx. 320km (198 miles).

Eysenck, Hans Jurgen (1916–), English psychologist. He devised the Eysenck Personality Inventory, to isolate the components of personality. He is also widely known as an advocate of BEHAVIOUR THERAPY. *See also* MS pp.187–189.

Ezekiel, Old Testament prophet to whom the Book of Ezekiel is ascribed. Before he went into exile he was violently opposed to apostasy. During the exile he received God's message and became the third and last of the "greater" Old Testament prophets, the successor of ISAIAH and JEREMIAH.

Ezra, in the Old Testament, a continuation of Chronicles I and II. It records the priest Ezra's journey from Babylon to Jerusalem to spread the law of Moses. It also includes an account of the rebuilding of the Temple, part of the city's restoration after it was destroyed by Nebuchadrezzar, and a census of Ezra's companions on his trip to the Holy City.

F

F, sixth letter of the alphabet, derived from the hook-shaped Semitic letter *vaw*. It is said to have had the sound of a *w* in pre-classical Greek (the letter *digamma*) and it was the Romans who first gave it an *f* sound. It almost always has the same sound in English (and is sometimes doubled), although it is pronounced like a *v* in *of*. In some English words ending in *f* (such as *hoof*) the *f* changes to a *v* in the plural (*hooves*).

Fabbri, Diego (1911–), Italian religious dramatist, strongly influenced by PIRANDELLO, who expressed his devout beliefs and concept of "tragic Christianity" in plays such as *Inquisition* (1950), *Family Trial* (1954) and *Between Two Thieves* (1955). Although these have been widely performed in Europe and South America, they have seldom been presented to English-speaking audiences.

Fabergé, Peter Carl (1846–1920), Russian jeweller. Following training as a goldsmith and jeweller he was apprenticed in Frankfurt-on-Main. In 1870, he took over his father's business, making decorative objects in gold and precious stones, and winning international repute for his designs of flowers and animals. He made many jewelled Easter eggs for European royalty, designing the first for Tsar ALEXANDER III in 1884. Fabergé worked until he left Russia after the revolution of 1917. *See also* SU p.*137*.

Fabian, Saint, Roman pope (236–50). He reorganized the Church in Rome and provided for ecclesiastical government by presbyters and deacons. He was martyred during the persecution of Christians by the Emperor DECIUS.

Fabian Society, British socialist society of non-Marxists founded in 1883, who believed that SOCIALISM should be attained through gradual political change. With George Bernard SHAW and Sidney and Beatrice WEBB as members, the society gained widespread recognition and helped found the LABOUR PARTY (1906). *See also* HC2 p.*212*.

Fabius Maximus Verrucosus, Quintus, called *Cunctator* ("delayer") (*d.*203 BC), Roman consul and dictator. He is famed for his strategy of avoiding pitched battle while conducting harrassing raids during the Second PUNIC WAR, a tactic that wore HANNIBAL's forces to exhaustion. *See also* HC1 p.91.

Fable, literary genre in the form of a short allegorical tale which is intended to convey a moral. The characters are often animals, whose words and deeds are used to satirize those of human beings. The oldest extant fables are the Greek tales of AESOP and the Indian stories of the *Panchatantra*. Other collections of fables were made by Jean de LA FONTAINE, John GAY and Ivan KRYLOV.

Fabre, Jean Henri (1823–1915), French entomologist. He made accurate and important studies of the anatomy and behaviour of insects and arachnids, especially bees, ants, beetles, grasshoppers and spiders. He emphasized the importance of the theory of inherited instincts in insects. His most important work was embodied in the ten volumes of his *Souvenirs Entomologiques* (1879–1907).

Fabriano. *See* GENTILE DA FABRIANO.

Fabricius, Hieronymus (1537–1619), Italian anatomist, also called Girolamo Fabrici. He was a pupil of Gabriello FALLOPIUS, whom he succeeded as professor of anatomy at Padua in 1562. His book, *On the Formed Foetus* (1600), describes his pioneering research in embryology. Fabricius also gave the first complete description of the valves in veins, although he misunderstood their function.

Fabritius, Carel (1622–54), Dutch painter. An outstanding pupil of REMBRANDT, his works include portraits, still lifes and animals. He died in the disastrous explosion of the Delft powder magazine, which also destroyed most of his paintings.

Facial expressions, form of non-verbal communication which can give information to an individual concerning the emotions and feelings of another person. Facial expressions are similar across a wide range of cultures; each of the primary emotions, such as fear, happiness and anger, has a unique expression that can be recognized world-wide. Nonverbal communication preceded speech in the evolution of man; Charles DARWIN suggested that emotions and their expression played a central role in the development of man and the primates, enabling them to build complex social structures. *See also* MS pp.236–237.

Facies, in geology, all the features of a rock or stratum of rock that show the history of the rock's formation. The concern is often to distinguish the age by the facies. The term is also applied to gradations of igneous rock. *See also* PE p.126.

Facsimile transmission, system by which graphic material such as printed matter, photographs or drawings can be transmitted by telephone or radio. The graphic matter is scanned and translated into electrical impulses that are transmitted and retranslated on a synchronized receiver, which prints a facsimile copy. *See also* MM p.*225*.

Factor analysis, in statistics and PSYCHOMETRICS, mathematical method for reducing a large number of measurements or tests to a smaller number of "factors" that can completely account for the results obtained on all the tests, as well as for the CORRELATIONS between them. *See also* INTELLIGENCE TEST.

Factories, buildings erected for the efficient manufacture of large quantities of goods by a group of workers. The name derives from "factor", meaning an agent who buys and sells for an employer. Although existing before the Industrial Revolution, factories became common at the end of the 18th century with the development of the textile industry in N England. They quickly replaced cottage industry, hitherto the production system, and workers thereafter used the tools and worked the hours of their employers, rather than their own. Factory manufacturing was revolutionized in the 1790s by the American Eli WHITNEY who introduced interchangeable parts, a development that led to the moving assembly line of Frederick W. Taylor and Henry FORD's notion of mass production. These steps to improve the efficiency of factories were based upon the need for scientific management, and the integration in one building of all aspects of the production of goods. In recent times, the task of an individual worker in a factory has become increasingly that of a controller of mechanical effort. *See also* MM pp.22–23, 94–95.

Factory Acts, series of laws in Britain regulating hours and conditions in factories. The first acts concerned only the textile trades. The Act of 1802, the work of the elder Peel, limited the hours of work for children and the Act of 1819 forbade the employment of children under the age of nine. They were ineffective, because enforcement was left to local magistrates. The 1833 Act, applying to all textile works except those weaving silk, set up a central body of inspection and was therefore more effective. In 1847 the hours for women and children were restricted to ten per day. In 1850 and 1853 a limit was also placed on working hours for male labour. Since then there have been many Factory Acts for all industries. *See also* HC2 pp.96–97.

Factory farming, rearing of livestock such as calves for veal, poultry and pigs in large, densely populated factory-type enclosures. Feeding is usually regulated and automatically dispensed, and the emphasis is on "mass-production". *See* PE pp.162–163.

Factory ship, ship equipped to process whales or fish at sea. Fishing and whaling vessels bring their catch to the factory ship instead of having to return to port with it.

Faculae. *See* SUNSPOT.

FA Cup, annual knockout football competition for member clubs of England's Football Association. It was inaugurated in 1872. Qualifying rounds begin early in the season but 1st and 2nd Division clubs do not enter until the 3rd round in January. The final at Wembley in May is seen by millions in many countries on television.

Fadden, Sir Arthur William (1895–1973), Australian politician. He became leader of the Country Party early in 1941, and served as prime minister, August–October 1941. He retired from the leadership of the party in 1958.

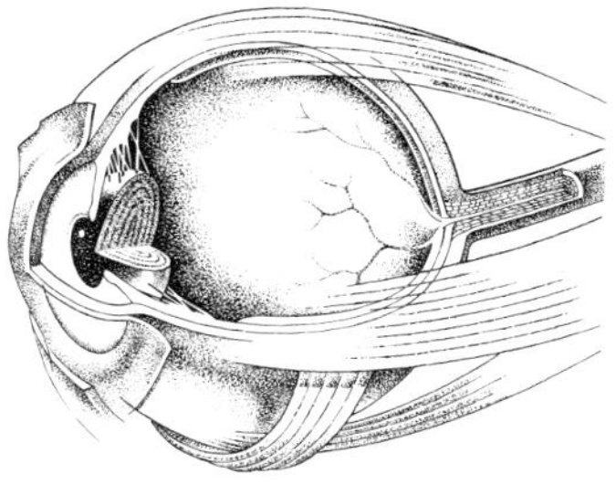

Eyes consist, in essence, of an iris, a lens, and a light-sensitive retina.

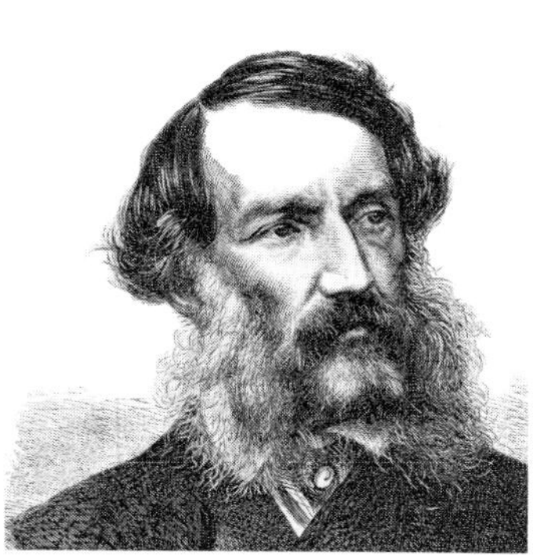

Edward Eyre, after whom a lake and a major highway in Australia are named.

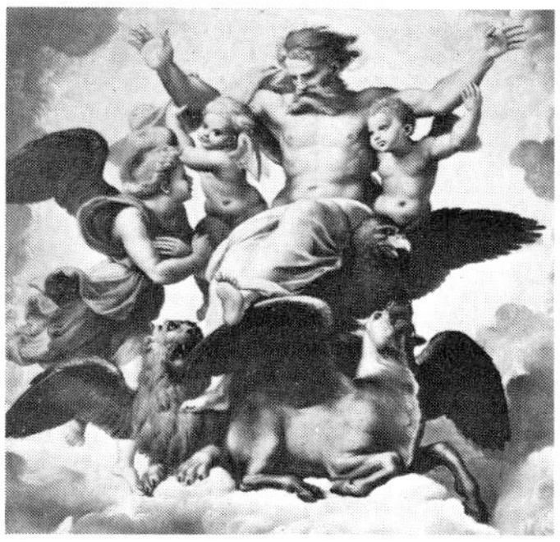

Ezekiel, a jewish prophet who lived at the time of Nebuchadrezzar.

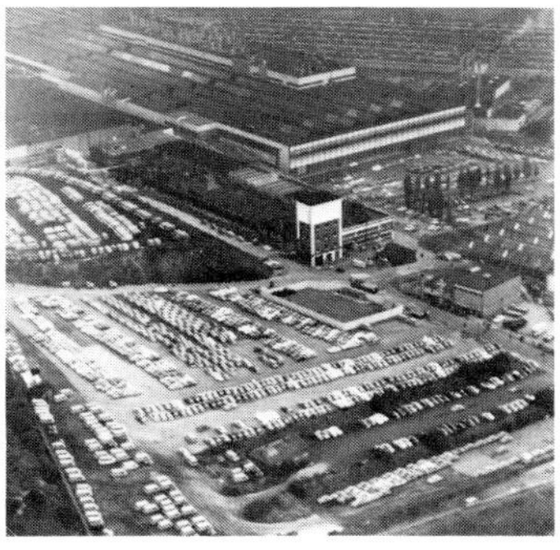

Factories; an aerial view taken in 1960 of the extensive Vauxhall Motor Works at Luton.

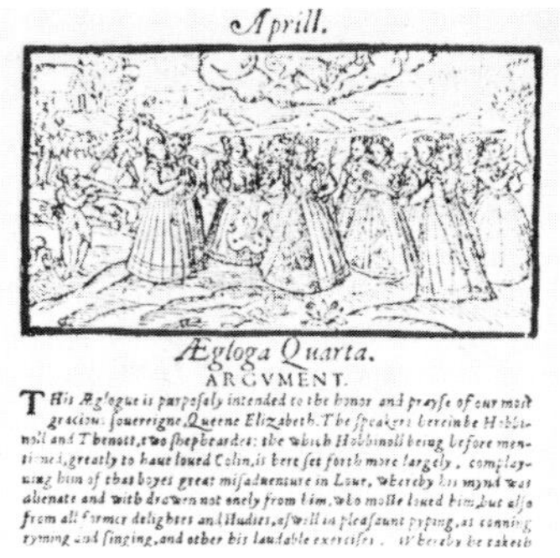

The Faerie Queene; an early woodcut to "Aprill", a section of this Elizabethan poem.

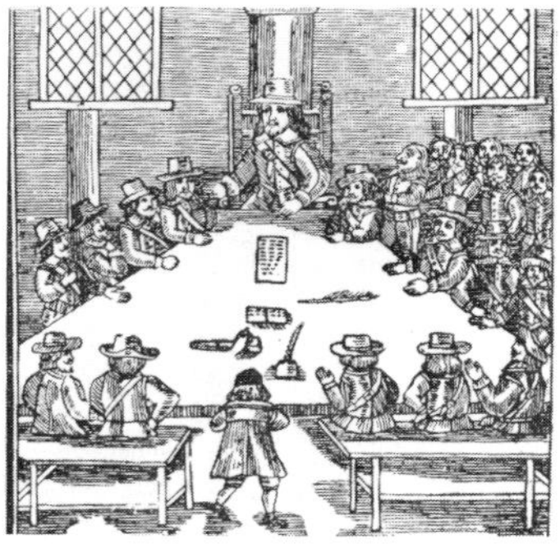

Fairfax, a parliamentarian who, disillusioned by the Protectorate, assisted the Restoration.

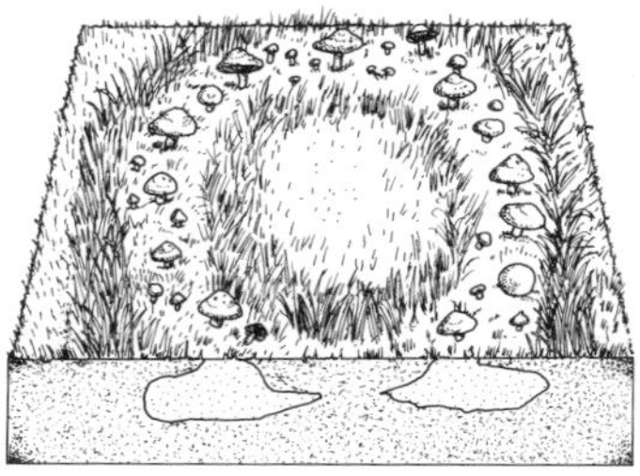

Fairy rings gradually grow larger, rings up to 65m (213ft) wide having been found.

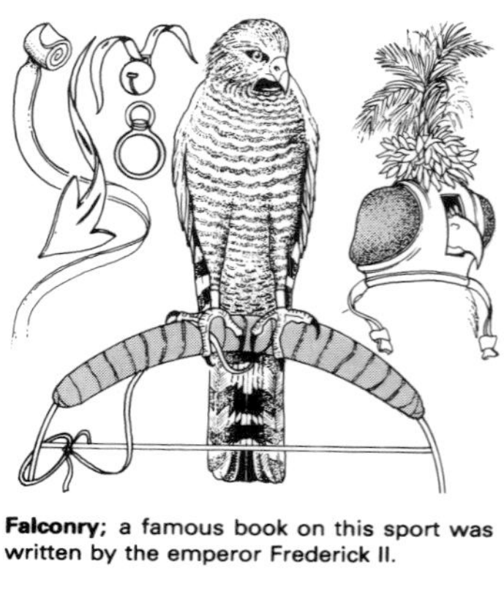

Falconry; a famous book on this sport was written by the emperor Frederick II.

Fadeyev, Alexander Alexandrovich (1901–56), Russian novelist. His military experiences in the civil war are reflected in *The Nineteen* (1927). *The Young Guard* (1945), although revised several times, was criticized by the Communist Party and Fadeyev lost his status in the Party. In 1956 he committed suicide.

Faeces. *See* EXCRETION.

Faenza, city in N central Italy on the River Lamone. FAÏENCE or MAJOLICA, a type of ceramic, has been made there since the 15th century. Pop. (1971) 54,733.

Faerie Queene, The (1589–96), unfinished allegorical poem by Edmund SPENSER. The six published books of the planned 12 relate the allegorical story of Prince Arthur's quest to Fairyland, and his encounters. The form of the poem is Spenser's invention – known as the Spenserian stanza – and *The Faerie Queene* is the most successful example of this verse form. *See also* HC1 pp.282–283.

Faeroe Islands, group of 22 volcanic islands in the N Atlantic Ocean between Iceland and the Shetland Islands. They have belonged to Denmark since 1380 and were granted home rule in 1948. Fishing, whaling and sheep-rearing are the most important activities. Area: 1,339sq km (540sq miles). Pop. (1975 est.) 41,000. *See* MW pp.75–76.

Fafnir, in Scandinavian mythology, a giant who turned himself into a dragon to guard a pile of gold he had obtained by murdering his father, Hreidmar. Siegfried slew him and by tasting his blood understood the speech of birds.

Fahrenheit, Gabriel Daniel (1686–1736), German physicist and instrument-maker. He invented the alcohol THERMOMETER (1709), the first mercury thermometer (1714) and devised the FAHRENHEIT TEMPERATURE SCALE, for which he is chiefly remembered. He also showed that the boiling points of liquids vary with changes in atmospheric pressure and that water can remain liquid below its freezing point.

Fahrenheit temperature scale, system for measuring temperature based on the freezing point of water (32°F) and the boiling point of water (212°F). The interval between them is divided into 180 equal parts. To convert °C to °F: °C = (°F–32) × 5/9.

Faïence, EARTHENWARE covered with a decorative opaque white GLAZE made with tin oxide. The technique and designs of 15th-century Italian MAJOLICA influenced the development and refinement of French faïence in subsequent centuries. Fine baroque figuring, elaborate scroll-work and floral designs were characteristic of 18th-century work, and the Rouen factories produced distinctive stiff lace-work patterns. Until that century, colours were restricted to the few that could withstand high kiln temperatures. Because of the greater durability of creamware and PORCELAIN, little faïence was manufactured after the early 19th century.

Fainting, or syncope, temporary impairment of consciousness accompanied by general weakness of the muscles. An attack may be preceded by giddiness, sensory distortions, nausea, pallor and a profuse cold sweat. Its causes may include an insufficient flow of blood to the brain, change in the blood's composition, emotional disturbances, and injury to the heart or other organs. *See also* MS p.*132*.

Fairbairn, Steve (1862–1938), Australian oarsman whose controversial coaching methods revolutionized rowing in the early 20th century. In 1926 he founded London's Head of the River race on the Thames.

Fairbanks, Douglas, two US film stars. Douglas Sr (1883–1939) founded UNITED ARTISTS films (1919) with Charlie CHAPLIN, D.W. GRIFFITH and Mary Pickford, whom he married. His swashbuckling acrobatics and breezy charm made him an idol for millions and enhanced such adventures as *The Mark of Zorro* (1920), *The Three Musketeers* (1921), *Robin Hood* (1922) and *The Thief of Baghdad* (1924). Douglas Jr (1909–) had a very successful career through films such as *The Dawn Patrol* (1930), *Catherine the Great* (1934), *The Prisoner of Zenda* (1937), *Gunga Din* (1939) and *That Lady in Ermine* (1948).

Fairbanks, city in central Alaska, on the Tanana and Chena rivers, 403km (250 miles) N of Anchorage. It was founded in 1902 after the discovery of gold. The oil pipeline laid in the 1970s has accelerated the city's growth. Industries include gold, timber and coal-mining. Pop. (1970) 22,640.

Fairbridge, Kingsley (1885–1924), South African explorer. His family moved to Rhodesia in 1896 and much of his life was spent in journeys around that country. His autobiography was published in 1927.

Fairburn, Arthur Rex Dugard (A. R. D. Fairburn) (1904–57), one of the first distinguished New Zealand poets. His satirical and lyric verse collections include *Dominion, The Voyager, Strange Rendezvous* and *Three Poems*.

Fairey, Sir Charles Richard (1887–1956), British aircraft manufacturer, who founded the Fairey Aviation Co. in 1915. This company produced such famous aircraft as the Firefly, Albacore and Swordfish. Fairey also invented the wing flap.

Fairfax of Cameron, Thomas, 3rd Baron (1612–71), English soldier. He was commander-in-chief of the Parliamentary Army (1645–50) at the end of the Civil War. A popular commander, he won the decisive victory at Naseby (1645). *See also* HC1 p.288.

Fairs Cup, European association football competition. It began in 1955 as an inter-cities competition and in 1971 was renamed the UEFA Cup.

Fairy, in mythology, magical, often mischievous being, usually depicted as a tiny person with wings. In recent time fairies have been shown as pretty and gentle creatures, but their past is far more sinister. Once they were genuinely feared and were believed capable of frightening revenge on anyone who offended them. *See also* ELF.

Fairy ring, circle or ring of fungi commonly *Marasmius oreades*, that appears seasonally in lawns or meadows. In folklore the area enclosed was said to be the dancing ground of fairies. *See also* NW p.*42*.

Fairy tale, fantastic story involving wonderous, often magical elements, characters and occurrences. Many such tales have descended from a worldwide oral tradition, from literary origins or have interchanged between the two, undergoing numerous adaptations in the process. The term includes such popular folktales as *Little Red Ridinghood* and *Cinderella,* both of which were collected by Charles PERRAULT in his *Stories or Tales of Olden Times: Tales of Mother Goose* (1697), and the stories recorded by the Brothers GRIMM, in their *Fairy Tales* (1812–22). The form was popular with 19th-century writers such as Oscar WILDE, Charles KINGSLEY, John RUSKIN and Hans ANDERSON, whose work derives from folk legends.

Faisal, name of two kings of Iraq. Faisal I (1885–1933) fought against the Turks with T.E. LAWRENCE in WWI. In 1920 he was proclaimed King of Syria, but in the same year was ousted by the French. He was made King of Iraq by the British in 1921. On his death Faisal I was succeeded by his son Ghazi, who died in 1939 and was followed by his young son, Faisal II (1935–58). He was killed in the revolution which overthrew the Iraqi monarchy.

Faith healing, use of some inner or spiritual force to effect a cure. In Christianity present-day healing can be traced back to the miracles of the Holy Spirit performed through Christ and his apostles, as recorded in the New Testament. Prayers and rituals for the purpose are found throughout the history of man. *See also* MS pp.122–123.

Fakir, Muslim or Hindu monk or wandering mendicant. Fakirs are commonly thought to possess special powers, and to be able to perform magic and incredible feats of endurance, such as walking on fire. *See also* MS p.*195*.

Falange, Spanish political party founded in 1933 by José Antonio Primo de Rivera (son of the Spanish dictator). Modelled on other European FASCIST parties, it became the sole legal political party after the forces of Francisco FRANCO won the SPANISH CIVIL WAR. Its power declined in later years and during free elections in 1977 it suffered a major defeat. *See also* HC2 p.223.

Falashas, ethnic group in Ethiopia, probably descendants of early converts to JUDAISM. Their form of religion relies solely on observance of the OLD TESTAMENT works with no later traditions or interpretations. They speak local dialects and form a sort of inferior caste; some Falashas have emigrated to Israel.

Falcon, widely-distributed bold, hawk-like bird of prey, sometimes trained by man to hunt game. Falcons have keen eyesight, short hooked bills, long pointed wings, streamlined bodies, strong legs with hooked claws, longish tails and grey or brownish plumage with lighter markings. The females are much larger than the males. Falcons hunt by day, feeding on insects, smaller birds, rodents and other small animals on the ground. They can kill on the wing, with their feet. They lay two to five brown-spotted white eggs, often in abandoned nests. Length: 15–64cm (6–25in). Family Falconidae. *See also* NW pp.*140*, *146*, 199, *221*, *225*.

Falconiformes, order of birds of prey, including VULTURES, HAWKS, EAGLES and FALCONS. *See also* NW pp. 140–141.

Falconry, sport in which FALCONS are used to hunt birds and small animals. The falcon is taken when young to be trained. The falconer wears a glove upon which the hooded falcon sits. When the hood is taken off, the falcon makes straight for the quarry, but leaves the prey untouched after the kill, returning to the falconer's wrist. Falconry attained its greatest popularity in late medieval and early modern Europe, and was one of the chief pastimes of royalty.

Falkirk, largest town of Central Region, Scotland, lying on a ridge S of the Firth of Forth 18km (11 miles) SE of Stirling. Its chief industry is coal mining. Edward I defeated Wallace (1298) and Bonnie Prince Charlie defeated General Hawley (1746) there. Pop. (1974 est.) 36,589.

Falkland Islands (Islas Malvinas), group of islands E of Argentina in the S Atlantic Ocean. It includes two large islands, East and West Falkland, and 200 smaller islands, administered as a British Crown colony. The main activity is sheep-farming and wool and hides are exported. The capital is Stanley. Area: 11,961sq km (4,618sq miles). Pop. (1975 est.) 2,000. *See* MW p.76.

Falkner, John Meade (1858–1932), British poet and novelist. He is best known for his adventure story, *Moonfleet* (1898), but he also wrote the historical works *A History of Oxfordshire* (1899) and *Durham Cathedral* (1929).

Falla, Manuel de (1876–1946), Spanish composer who developed the Spanish nationalistic style by using Spanish folk songs as the basis for many of his compositions. Among his popular works are the opera *La Vida Breve* (1905), *Nights in the Gardens of Spain* (1916) for piano and orchestra, and the music for the ballets *El Amor Brujo* (1915) and *The Three-Cornered Hat* (1919).

Fall of the House of Usher, The (1839), tale of terror by Edgar Allen POE. It is about the last descendant of the House of Usher, Roderick, who is driven mad by the sense of impending doom that pervades his ancestral home.

Fallopian tube, or oviduct, either of two narrow ducts leading from the upper part of the uterus into the pelvic cavity and ending near each ovary. After ovulation, the ovum enters and travels through the fallopian tube where fertilization can occur. The fertilized ovum, or embryo, continues into the uterus where it becomes implanted. If the fertilized ovum remains in the tube, an ECTOPIC (or tubal) PREGNANCY occurs. If fertilization does not occur, the ovum is shed along with uterine lining at menstruation. Conception can be prevented by removing or somehow closing the fallopian tubes. *See also* BIRTH CONTROL MS pp.74–75.

Fallopius, Gabriello (1523–62), Italian anatomist who became professor of anat-

omy and botany at Padua in 1551. His book *Anatomical Observations* (1561) contains the first descriptions of the FALLOPIAN TUBES (from the ovaries to the womb) and the SEMI-CIRCULAR CANALS.
Fallout, atomic, radioactive contamination in the atmosphere following a leakage or accident at a nuclear reactor, or explosion of a nuclear weapon. Large windborne particles fall to earth after a few hours, sometimes up to several hundred km from the source; lighter particles entering the troposphere are detected after a longer period at about the same latitude as the source. Any particles entering the stratosphere eventually fall over the earth's surface, often many years later. *See also* MM pp.*180–181*.
Fallow deer, medium-sized DEER native to Asia Minor and parts of Europe. The coat is usually spotted white in symmetrical rows, with white patches on the underparts and rump; the spots tend to disappear in winter. The males have broad antlers. Height: 91cm (3ft) at the shoulder. Species *Dama dama.*
Falmininus, Titus Quinctius (*c.*238–179 BC), Roman statesman and military leader who helped to establish the Roman protectorate over Greece. His victory at Cynoscephalae in Macedonia (197) against Philip V proved the superior tactics of the Roman legions over the Macedonian phalanxes.
False pregnancy, also called pseudocyesis, a rare phenomenon that occurs in women who greatly desire a baby. Menstruation ceases and there may be an enlargement of the breasts and abdomen, "morning sickness" and, later, labour pains. The affected woman believes she is pregnant. It is an example of the mind influencing hormone secretion; treatment is by psychotherapy.
False teeth. *See* DENTURES.
Falsetto, register of the voice specially produced at the LARYNX to enable a male adult to sing in the ALTO range, or to yodel. All males are capable of producing this high voice, but the technique must be practised. *See also* COUNTER TENOR.
Falstaff, (1893), opera in three acts by Giuseppe VERDI, libretto by Arrigo Boito. It is based on the Shakespearean plays, *The Merry Wives of Windsor* and *Henry IV* in which Falstaff was a protagonist. It was first produced at La Scala, Milan.
Famagusta (Ammokhostos), town on the E coast of Cyprus; it has a natural harbour and is connected to Nicosia by rail. Various fortifications, a castle, a cathedral (now a mosque) and other buildings remain of its medieval greatness. Pop. (1971 est.) 43,600.
Fame, Georgie (1943–), British singer and jazz organist, real name Clive Powell. During the 1960s he played popular versions of American urban BLUES and now works mainly in cabaret.
Familiar spirit, small demon said to attend a witch. It is commonly shown as a cat, toad or an imaginary being that lives on the witch's blood drawn through a special teat. In witch trials these teats, which in reality were probably warts or moles, were expected to be insensitive to pain, although their very presence was enough to convince authorities of the witch's guilt.
Family, in biology, the systematic classification of living organisms, a taxonomic category ranking above a genus and below an order. The earliest use of this form of classification appears in the work of Carl Linnaeus (*Systema Naturae*, 1758). In 1901 the International Rules of Zoological Nomenclature were established; the Commission for which now acts as a court to determine new or altered classifications. Family names are printed in Roman (ordinary) letters with an initial capital (eg, Felidae, the cat family), whereas genus names are usually printed in italic letters, also with a capital (eg, *Felis*, the genus to which the domestic cat belongs).
Family, unit of social organization comprising in its simplest form parents and their children. This form of the family, known as the nuclear family, has been regarded as the basis of all societies. In many parts of the world, close ties, often deriving from the cohabitation of several related nuclear families, have created the extended family. The role of the family is both reproductive and economic – in Europe until the 19th century the family was often dominated by a head of the family who assumed responsibility for all its other members. Changing economic relationships introduced by the Industrial Revolution, the emancipation of women and the growth of state education have tended to alter this traditional family structure. *See also* MS pp.250–251, 254.
Family planning. *See* BIRTH CONTROL.
Family therapy, in psychotherapy, treatment of emotional disturbance or mental illness in the context of the family, not as a disorder of an individual member. It involves direct involvement between the family and the therapist, often for a considerable time. *See also* MS p.*149*.
Fan, light, flat manual costume accessory, especially used by women for cooling the face. Rigid fans, usually made from feathers, were used by the Assyrians, Egyptians, Romans and the medieval church. More elaborate folding fans probably originated in Japan, reached Europe by the 9th century and arrived in England from Italy during the reign of Henry VIII. By the 17th and 18th centuries, fans had become ornate and expensively fashionable accessories with ivory, gold and silver sticks and mounts of paper, parchment or lace. France was always the chief centre of production.
Fan. *See* ALLUVIUM.
Fangio, Juan Manuel (1911–), Argentine racing driver. One of the best drivers in the sport's history, he was five-times winner of the world championship (1951, 1954–57) and on his retirement in 1958 had won a total of 24 grand prix.
Fanny by Gaslight (1940), romantic historical novel by Michael Sadleir describing the career of a British cabinet minister's illegitimate daughter.
Fanny Hill (1748–49), novel by John CLELAND, first issued in two volumes. It is an account, told in her own letters, of the seduction and subsequent career of a London courtesan. Suppressed on publication, it was seized as pornography as recently as 1963 in England.
Fanon, Frantz Omar (1925–61), French West Indian psychiatrist and theorist of Third World revolution. He left Martinique in 1956 to work for the Algerian nationalists, and wrote *Black Skin, White Masks* (1952) and *The Wretched of the Earth* (1961), in which he outlined his hopes for a peasant revolution against Western colonialism.
Fanshawe, Sir Richard (1608–66), English politician and writer. He assisted the Royalists during the ENGLISH CIVIL WARS and made a verse translation of *The Luciads* from the Portuguese in 1655.
Fantail. *See* PIGEON.
Fantasia (1940), US animated film, directed by Walt DISNEY, that visually interpreted themes from classical music (conducted by Leopold Stokowski) in eight cartoon sequences. It was one of the first films with stereophonic sound.
Fantasy, in psychology, spontaneous activity of the imagination, including daydreaming and hallucination. It may involve several of the senses. Controlled or directed activity of the imagination is generally regarded as creativity. Fantasy is not directed towards a definite goal, but is part of ordinary thinking. It is commonly associated with AUTISM and is an integral part of play in children and in adults. *See also* MS p.304.
Fanti, black African people of Ghana. Numbering approx. 250,000, they follow a matrilineal system of political succession and material inheritance, and a patrilineal system of military and spiritual succession. They were middlemen in trade between the African interior and Europeans on the coast and they became embroiled in conflicts with the Ashanti. They were first aided and later dominated by British colonists.
Fantin-Latour, Ignace Henri Jean Théodore (1836–1904), French painter. Noted for his realistic group portraits, including *Hommage à Eugène Delacroix* (1864); he also did still lifes and lithographs illustrating the music of Wagner and others.
Fanzogo, Cosimo (1591–1678), Italian architect and sculptor. A master of the Baroque style, among his fine work is the church of S. Giuseppe degli Scalzi, Naples (*c.*1660).
FAO. *See* FOOD AND AGRICULTURAL ORGANIZATION.
Faraday, Michael (1791–1867), British physicist and chemist. He acquired his scientific education through reading and from lectures given by Sir Humphrey DAVY at the Royal Institution in London, where in 1825 he became director of the laboratories. He liquefied chlorine, discovered benzene and two "chlorides" of carbon and enunciated the laws of electrolysis (FARADAY'S LAWS). Moving from chemistry to electricity, he discovered electromagnetic induction, made the first dynamo, built a primitive electric motor, and studied non-conducting materials (dielectrics). The unit of capacitance (the farad) is named after him. *See also* SU pp.*149*; HC2 pp.*156*–157.
Faraday's laws, two fundamental principles in science. Faraday's laws of electrolysis state that (1) the mass of a substance liberated (or the extent of chemical change) at an electrode in an ELECTROLYTE is proportional to the current passing and the time for which it passes; and (2) the masses of different substances liberated or deposited are in proportion to their chemical equivalent weights. Faraday's law of induction states that, when the magnetic flux through a circuit changes, an electromotive force (emf) is induced in the circuit proportional to the rate of decrease of magnetic flux. *See also* SU pp.148–149.
Farce, light comic drama typified by its unrealistic and exaggerated characterizations, its improbable plot lines and an emphasis on simple humour. Modern farce is a 19th-century invention and was developed by Arthur PINERO and Ben TRAVERS in England and Eugène LABICHE and Georges FEYDEAU in France.
Fard, Wallace D. (*c.*1877–1934), US politician. He moved to the USA from Arabia before 1930 and founded the BLACK MUSLIM movement before his disappearance in 1934.
Far East, countries of E and SE Asia. They include China and Japan, Korea, Manchuria, Mongolia, eastern Siberia, Vietnam, Laos, Cambodia, Thailand, Malaysia, Burma, the East Indies (including the Philippines) and various other former European dependencies.
Farewell to Arms, A (1929), novel by Ernest HEMINGWAY. Frederic Henry, an American ambulance driver in Italy during WWI, falls in love with Catherine Barkley, an English nurse. Eventually he and Catherine desert and escape to Switzerland, where she dies giving birth to their child.
Far From the Madding Crowd (1874), romantic novel by Thomas HARDY. Bathsheba Everdene marries the dashing Sgt Troy, who is murdered by a jealous farmer, Boldwood. The tale ends happily, with Bathsheba's marriage to the shepherd Gabriel Oak, who loves her selflessly throughout.
Fargo, William George (1818–81), US businessman. Having been a messenger and post rider, he organized with Henry WELLS a carrier service with routes between Buffalo and the West in 1844. Wells, Fargo & Company then set up an express service between New York and San Francisco to cater especially for the gold rush. Fargo was the secretary of the company, which merged with two others to form the American Express Company in 1850. Wells Fargo still operates as a San Francisco bank.
Farinelli, Carlo Broschi (1705–82), Italian male soprano, one of the most notable of the 18th-century "castrati" – Italian male singers who were sopranos as the result of childhood castration. His debut in 1722 was a sensation and from 1737 to 1759 he was the official singer to the Spanish royal court.
Farman, Henri (1874–1958), French aviation pioneer and manufacturer. In

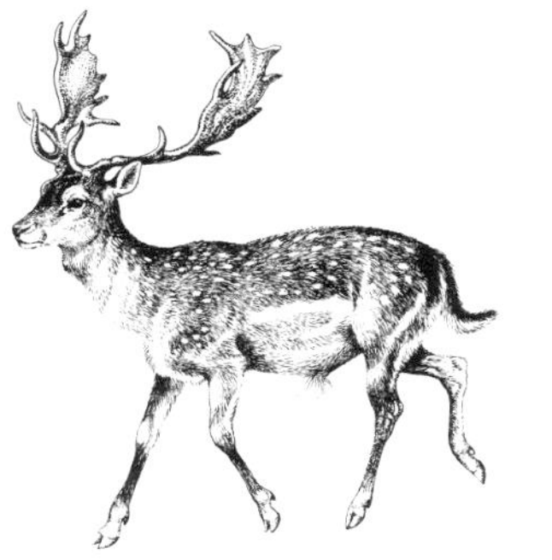

Fallow deer, a species now semi-domesticated in British parks and reserves.

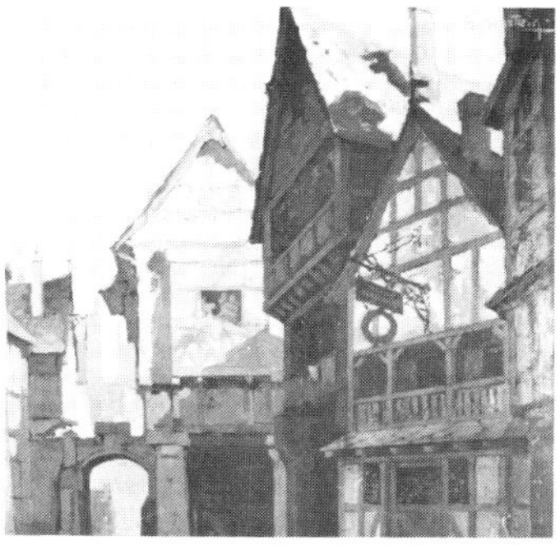

Falstaff; an 1893 design for Act III, Scene I of Giuseppe Verdi's opera.

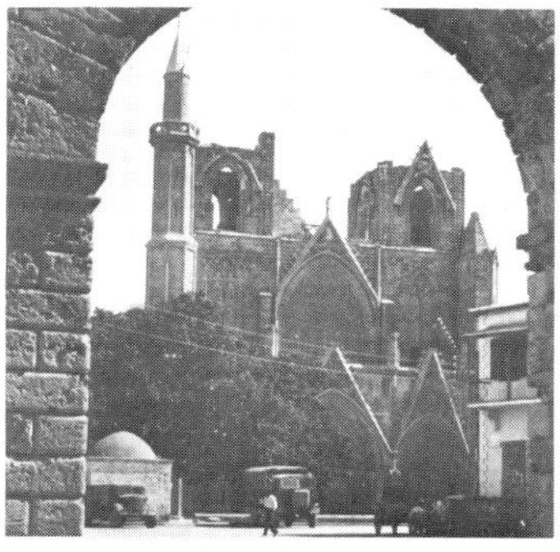

Famagusta; a view of the Church of St Nicholas, now the mosque of St Sophia.

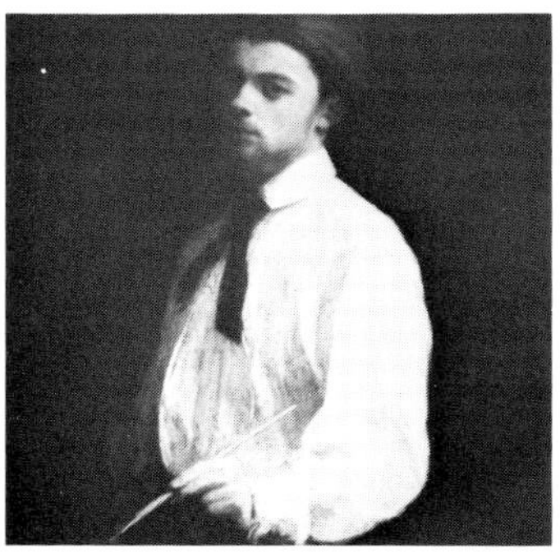

Fantin-Latour, a self-portrait by this painter friend of Corot, Delacroix, Ingres and others.

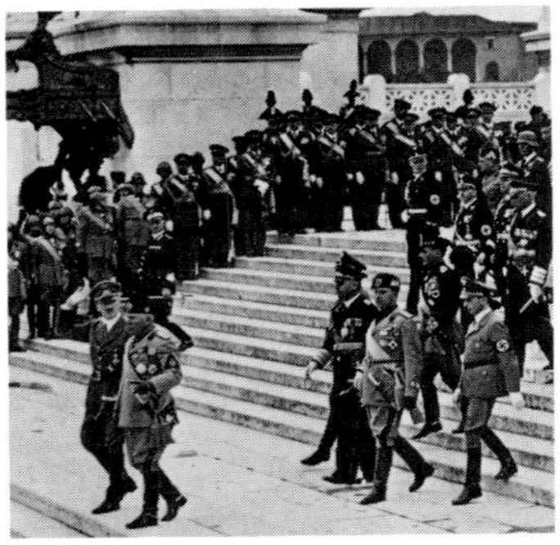

Fascism; Mussolini and Adolf Hitler in Rome during the Führer's state visit in 1938.

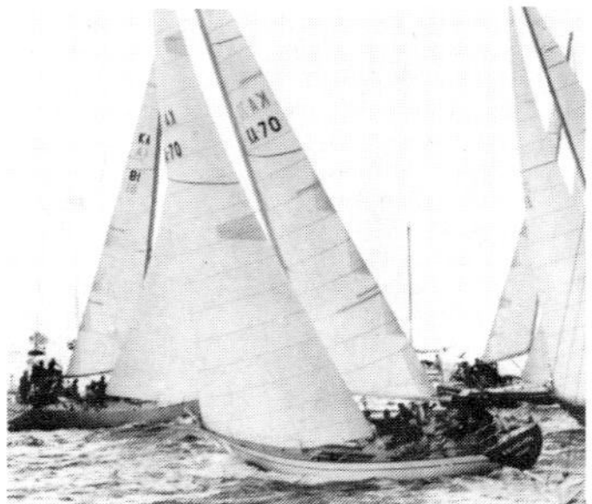

Fastnet race in 1977; a view of yachts jockeying for position on the starting line.

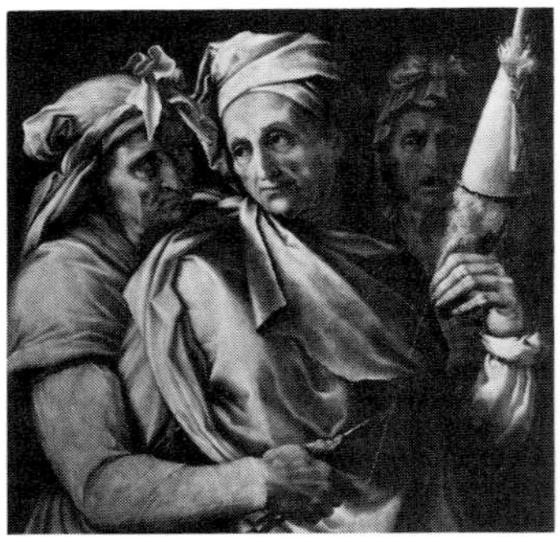

Fates; a painting of the three goddesses by Michelangelo in the Pitti Gallery, Florence.

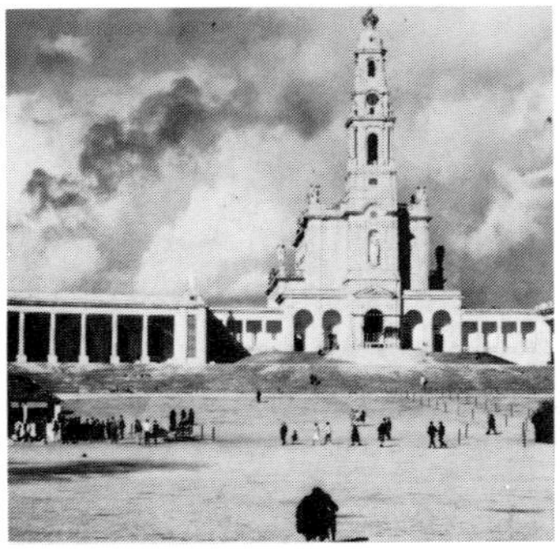

Fatima; the first pilgrimage took place in 1927 and the basilica was begun in 1928.

1908 he won a prize for the first circular flight of 1km (0.6 miles) and in 1909 he established a flight record of 179km (112 miles). In 1912 he founded an aircraft factory which later became one of the largest in Europe and with his brother Maurice established the first air passenger service between London and Paris.

Farmer, Ken (1910–), Australian rules footballer of great goal-kicking prowess. He kicked 100 goals a season 11 times, was South Australia's top goalscorer 1930–40, and in a 224-games league career kicked 1,419 goals.

Farmer's Wife, The (1916), play by Eden PHILLPOTTS. A rural comedy first produced in Birmingham, it later ran at the Royal Court Theatre, London, for more than 1,300 performances.

Farming. *See* AGRICULTURE.

Farming, collective, socialized farming in which a number of smallholdings are worked co-operatively as a single unit and ownership vested either in the community or the state. Collectivization of farms was introduced in the USSR in the 1930s and in the People's Republic of China in the 1950s. A similar system – the KIBBUTZIM – prevails in Israel.

Farnborough, town in N Hampshire, England, famous for the Farnborough Air Show. About 51km (32 miles) SW of London, it is the site of the Royal Aircraft Establishment, where experimental work in aeronautics is carried out. Pop. (1971 est.) 41,233.

Farne Islands, group of islands in NE England, off the coast of Northumberland. The National Trust maintains a bird sanctuary on them.

Farnese, celebrated Italian family which established itself among the Roman aristocracy. Through the military skill of Ranuccio Farnese (*d.c.* 1460), who defended the PAPAL STATES and won the gratitude of EUGENIUS IV, his son Alessandro became Pope PAUL III in 1534 and his illegitimate son Pier Luigi (1503–47) was created first duke of Parma and of Piacenza after 1545. Pier Luigi's grandson Alessandro (1545–92), also duke of Parma and Piacenza, served PHILIP II of Spain as governor-general of The Netherlands from 1578. The line ended with the death of Antonio in 1731.

Faro, the most southerly town of Portugal, situated on the Atlantic coast; capital of Faro province. It has a large shallow harbour, from which agricultural products are exported. Pop. (1970) 30,269.

Faroe Islands, Faroes. *See* FAEROE ISLANDS.

Farouk (1920–65), King of Egypt (*r.* 1936–52), son and successor of King FUAD I. He opposed the Wafd party and failed to expel the British; defeat in the Arab-Israeli conflict (1948) lead to his abdication after a coup by dissident military officers in 1952. Egypt became a republic less than a year later.

Farquhar, George (1678–1707), Irish dramatist. His comedies were distinguished by humour combined with depth of character. *The Beaux Stratagem* (1707), still frequently revived, opened at the Haymarket Theatre, London, shortly before he died. *See also* HC2 p.27.

Farrar, Frederic William (1831–1903), British clergyman. He was headmaster of Marlborough College (1871–76), archdeacon of Westminster (1883–95) and then dean of Canterbury until his death. He wrote a *Life of Christ* (1874) and *Life of St Paul* (1879).

Farrell, James Gordon (1935–), British novelist. He won the Faber prize for *Troubles* (1970), set in Ireland in the 1920s. He won the Booker prize for *Siege of Krishnapur* (1973).

Farrell, James Thomas (1904–), US novelist. His trilogy about Studs Lonigan (1932–35), set in a poor Irish community in Chicago, is typical of his harshly realistic treatment of modern city life. Much of his work is in a subjective, stream-of-consciousness style.

Farrelly, Bernard ("Midget") (1944–), Australian surfer who won the world championships in 1964 (Sydney) and was runner-up in 1968 (Puerto Rico) and 1970 (Sydney).

Farrer, William James (1845–1906), Australian agriculturalist, *b.* England. He emigrated in 1870 and developed several new varieties of wheat in New South Wales after 1886.

Fārs (Farsistan), mountainous province of SW Iran. The ruins of Persepolis, an early Persian capital, are in this region. The present capital of the area is Shirāz. Area: 133,385sq km (51,500sq miles). Pop. (1966) 1,439,804.

Farthing, British coin worth a quarter of a penny or 1/960 of a pound sterling. It was introduced in 1279 and was a silver coin until 1613. After 1856 farthings were the coins of smallest value; they were withdrawn from circulation in 1960.

Farthingale, padded roll or a heavy metal frame worn around the hips by women from the 16th century to make their wide skirts stand out. A form of farthingale known as a pannier or hoop skirt, made of osier reeds or whalebone, reappeared in the early 18th century. Farthingales were were revived again in the 1830s, when they became round and even bigger.

Fasces, symbol of state power in ancient Rome, depicted as a bundle of rods into which an axe is set. The emblem was adopted by the Italian FASCIST Party in 1919. *See also* HC1 p.92.

Fascism, nationalistic, totalitarian and anti-communist movement founded in Italy by Benito MUSSOLINI in 1919. The term was also used of later regimes established by Adolf HITLER in Germany (1933) and Francisco FRANCO in Spain (1936). A reaction to the Russian Revolution (1917) and the subsequent spread of communist influence, the movement based its appeal on the fear of instability among the middle-class financial and property-owning interests and on a wider social discontent. Basic to fascist ideas were glorification of the state and total subordination to its authority; suppression of all political opposition; preservation of a rigid class structure; stern enforcement of law and order through a powerful police system; and the supremacy of the leader as the embodiment of high ideals. An aggressive militarism aimed at achieving national greatness was also generally stressed. Unlike communism, it lacked a consistent, rational philosophy and the character of fascist regimes varied accordingly. In Italy the Fascist Party, which governed 1922–43, was organized in a military manner, its black-shirted members using the ancient Roman salute. The name was derived from FASCES, symbol of authority in the Roman Empire. Discredited by defeat in WWII, fascism has been relegated to a minor role in the politics of western Europe. *See also* NATIONAL SOCIALISM; HC2 pp.222–223.

Fashoda Incident (1898), diplomatic struggle between France and Britain for control of Egypt's Upper Nile. Britain sought control of continuous territory from Egypt to South Africa, and France wanted a route from the Atlantic Ocean to the Red Sea. Their respective expeditions, led by Britain's KITCHENER and Major MARCHAND, met at Fashoda, Sudan. Wishing to maintain equable relations with Britain because of growing German power, the French withdrew.

Fassbinder, Rainer Werner (1946–), German film director. He began to make films in 1969, and his many productions are made in Munich on a small budget with a regular group of actors. He became known internationally for *The Bitter Tears of Petra von Kant* (1972), and *Fear Eats the Soul* (1974).

Fast, Howard (1914–), US author. A prolific writer, many of his novels are about the American Revolution, including *Conceived in Liberty* (1939) and *April Morning* (1961).

Fast Breeder Reactor. *See* REACTOR, FAST BREEDER.

Fastnet Race, classic off-shore race for ocean yachts. It was first held in 1925. Sailed every two years during Cowes Week, it covers a distance of 968km (605 miles) from the Isle of Wight to the Fastnet Rock off the SW coast of Ireland and back to Plymouth. Since 1957 it has been part of the Admiral's Cup series.

Fastolf, Sir John (*c.* 1378–1459), English soldier and administrator. He fought at AGINCOURT (1415) and elsewhere in France (1417–40). He featured in the Paston letters, which detail his investment of large war profits in English estates. Shakespeare borrowed his name, and no doubt some of his attributes, for Falstaff.

Fat, semi-solid organic substance made and used by animals to store energy and shield them from the cold. Fats are soluble in organic solvents such as ether, carbon tetrachloride, chloroform and benzene. They are esters of glycerin with a carboxylic (fatty) acid such as palmitic, lauric and stearic acid, which have 12 to 18 carbon atoms. Vegetable oils are similar to fats, but are viscous liquids rather than semi-solids, and have a higher proportion of molecules with double chemical bonds in the carbon chain – ie, they are unsaturated. *See also* LIPID; SOAP; MS pp.68–69, 70, 85; SU pp.152–155.

Fates, in Greek mythology, the three goddesses of human destiny. Called the *Moirae* by the Greeks, they correspond to the Roman *Parcae* and the Germanic *Norns.* Clotho spun the thread of life; Lachesis, the element of chance, measured it; and Atropos, the inevitable, cut it.

Father Brown, The Innocence of (1911), collection of short stories by G.K. CHESTERTON, in which a mild middle-aged priest, Father Brown, solves a series of crimes and mysteries through his quick observation and understanding of human nature.

Father lasher, short-spined, marine species of bullhead, common in the E Arctic and Atlantic Oceans. It has a large head and lacks a swimbladder. It is a voracious predatory fish that feeds on crustaceans and the eggs and larvae of commercial fish. Species *Myoxephalus scorpius.*

Fathers and Sons (1862), novel by Ivan TURGENEV which analyses the social changes that were taking place in Russia in the mid-19th century.

Fathers of the Church, ecclesiastical writers of exceptional orthodoxy and holiness from *c.* 90 to *c.* 750. The term derives from the Greek notion of the teacher as father and the early church's view of the bishop as the spiritual father of his flock. The term was first used in the 4th century in reference to the bishops of the Council of Nicaea (325), and in the 5th century the Fathers were cited in the Christological controversies. Augustine was the first so to refer to a layman, Jerome. Other great Fathers include Ambrose and Gregory the Great in the west and Basil the Great in the east.

Fathom, unit used in measuring depth, especially of water. One fathom equals 1.83m (6ft). It is also a quantity of material which has a cross-section six feet square but varies in length. Originally it was the distance spanned by a man's arms.

Fatigue, in physiology, inability to function at normal levels of physical and mental activity. Muscle fatigue results from the accumulation of LACTIC ACID in the muscle tissue and the depletion of GLYCOGEN (stored carbohydrates). It is often associated with depression or with illnesses such as HEPATITIS and ANAEMIA.

Fatigue, metal, weakening of the crystalline structure of a metal due to repeated rhythmic straining, bending or vibration. It can cause superficial cracks which may spread inwards, causing the metal to crumble. Components have to be designed to reduce and delay fracture due to metal fatigue. *See also* SU pp.88, *89.*

Fatima (606–632), daughter of the prophet MOHAMMED, wife of ALI. Fatima and Ali felt deprived of their rightful inheritance by ABU-BAKR, first Muslim Caliph after Mohammed's death. Their disappointed followers, the SHI'A sect of ISLAM, honour Ali as the rightful successor to Mohammed and offer devotion to Fatima similar to that offered the Virgin Mary in Roman Catholicism.

Fatima, village of W central Portugal where three children had a vision of the Blessed Virgin Mary in 1917. It is now the site of the shrine of Our Lady of the Rosary of Fatima. It was visited in 1967 by Pope Paul VI.

Fatty acids, organic chemical compounds, so called because they are present widely in nature as constituents of fats. They are monobasic acids (ie, they contain a single carboxyl acid group (−COOH). The term fatty acids is sometimes restricted to the series of saturated acids having the general formula $C_nH_{2n+1}COOH$, eg, acetic acid, CH_3COOH, and palmitic acid, $CH_3(CH_2)_{14}COOH$, the latter being a common fat constituent. Also present in fats, and also often called fatty acids, are unsaturated acids having one or more double bonds. These include oleic acid, $CH_3(CH_2)_7CH{=}CH(CH_2)_7COOH$; both types have molecules shaped like a long, straight chain. *See also* FATS; LIPIDS; SATURATED COMPOUNDS; SU p.*152*.

Faulkner, Brian (1921–77), Northern Ireland politician. A member of the Unionist Party (Protestant), he was Minister of Home Affairs (1959–63), Commerce (1963–69), and Development (1969–71). He was Prime Minister of Northern Ireland (1971–72) and helped establish a new coalition administration of Catholics and Protestants, which he headed in 1974. This was brought down by a general strike later that year. *See also* HC2 *p.295*.

Faulkner, William (1897–1962), US author. With *Sartoris* (1929), his third novel, he created Yoknapatawpha County, the setting of most of his future works. The primary themes of the so-called Yoknapatawpha Saga include the relationship of the past to the present and the effects of the disintegration of traditional Southern US society. He was awarded the 1949 Nobel Prize in literature. His other works include *The Sound and the Fury* (1929), *Sanctuary* (1931), *Absalom, Absalom!* (1936), and *The Reivers* (1962). *See also* HC2 pp.288, *289*.

Fault, in geology, a fracture in the Earth's crust along which movement has occurred. Many EARTHQUAKES are caused by the rapid slipping of TECTONIC plates along faults, eg the San Francisco earthquake of 1906. *See also* PE pp.24, *24–25*, 104–106, *128*.

Fauna Preservation Society, organization formed to help to conserve wildlife throughout the world. In the British Isles it is particularly concerned with reptiles, mammals and amphibians. It was founded in 1903 as the Society for the Preservation of the Wild Fauna of the Empire.

Fauré, Gabriel Urbain (1845–1924), French Romantic composer whose works are characterized by their intimate and restrained quality. They include many songs, such as *Clair de lune* (1889); chamber music, such as his *Elégie* (1883) for cello and piano; and the *Requiem Mass* (1887), in memory of his father. His pupils included Maurice RAVEL and Nadia BOULANGER. *See also* HC2 p.*106*.

Faust (1808; 1831), drama by Johann Wolfgang von GOETHE based on the legend of Dr Johann Faustus (1488–1541). There is also a play by Christopher MARLOWE (*c.* 1588) and an opera by GOUNOD (1859) on this theme. The Goethe play is in two parts with a prologue. Faust promises to forfeit his soul to Mephistopheles in exchange for one moment of perfect contentment. Only finally does Faust realize that contentment lies in helping others; he pronounces himself perfectly contented and dies. Although he should really forfeit it, however, his soul is taken into heaven. *See also* HC2 pp.*72*, 101.

Fauves, term coined in 1905 by the art critic Louis Vauxcelles to describe the group of artists led by MATISSE. *See also* FAUVISM.

Fauvism, art movement of Paris in the early 1900s. It had little artistic vogue and lasted only a few years. Fauvist paintings are characterized by their rapid brushwork and brilliant flat colours, based on the work of GAUGUIN and van GOGH but conveying a higher degree of violence. The movement originated when a group of painters around MATISSE, most of whom were pupils of MOREAU, exhibited in 1905 and were dubbed *fauves* (wild beasts) by the critics. The artists involved included ROUAULT, MARQUET, VLAMINCK, DERAIN, BRAQUE, DUFY and van DONGEN. Their paintings were mostly land- or townscapes, still lifes and figure compositions. The group exhibited together again in 1906 but subsequently lost its coherence. Some of the group turned to CUBISM and others to EXPRESSIONISM. *See also* HC2 pp.174–175, *174–175*.

Favart, Charles-Simon (1710–92), French playwright. He was the author of several short farces and one of the originators of a new form of light musical comedy, the OPÉRA-COMIQUE. His works include *La Chercheuse d'Esprit* (1741), and *La Belle Arsène* (1773).

Fawcett, Dame Millicent Garrett (1847–1929), British suffragette leader, from 1897 to 1919 the president of the National Union of Women's Suffrage Societies. She was also one of the founders of Newnham College, Cambridge, one of the first women's colleges in Britain.

Fawcett, Percy Harrison (1867–*c.* 1925), British explorer. He surveyed the frontier between Brazil and Bolivia in 1906–08, and returned to South America after WWI. He disappeared with his son on an expedition to the interior of Brazil.

Fawkes, Guy (1570–1606), English conspirator in the GUNPOWDER PLOT, who was discovered with barrels of gunpowder in the Houses of Parliament on the night of 4–5 Nov. 1605 for which he was tried and executed in 1606. He was a Roman Catholic who fought in the Spanish Netherlands from 1593 to 1604. *See also* HC1 p.*286*.

Fayum, region of N Egypt, W of the River Nile. Archaeological remains date back to the Neolithic period. Canals for irrigation were dug in the early 2nd millennium BC. *See also* HC1 *p.26*.

Fazzān, region in Libya, in the Sahara, bordering Algeria. It is mostly desert with some oasis settlement. Exports include palms and dates. Area: approx. 551,171sq km (212,807sq miles).

FBI (Federal Bureau of Investigation), US organization for investigating violations of federal law, especially those concerning internal security. Its findings are reported to the attorney-general and various attorneys throughout the USA for decisions on prosecution. It was established in 1908, when it was called the Bureau of Investigation. Under the directorship of J. Edgar HOOVER (1924–72) it was reorganized and renamed the Federal Bureau of Investigation in 1933.

"FE". *See* BIRKENHEAD, F. E. SMITH.

Fealty, in the FEUDAL SYSTEM, the loyalty and obligations due to a king or lord by his VASSAL, or the specific oath of loyalty and consent taken by the vassal. In the 9th century fealty meant refraining from participation in any action that endangered the lord's life or property. By the 11th century the positive duties of a vassal to his lord were established, including personal military service, financial obligations and other forms of personal service. The oath of fealty was followed by an act of HOMAGE and, if the granting of a FIEF was involved, by the rite of investiture. *See also* HC1 p.204.

Fear, intense emotional state aroused by anticipation of pain or injury from some event. Some capacity for fear is desirable and adaptive because it can lead to the avoidance of or escape from harmful events. Abnormally strong or inappropriate fears, however, can become PHOBIAS. *See also* MS pp.*65*, *159*.

Feather, one of the skin appendages that makes up the plumage of birds. Feathers are composed of the fibrous protein KERATIN. Body contour feathers grow in demarcated skin tracts separated by bare areas. Short, fluffy down feathers insulate the body and long contour feathers make up the wing and tail surfaces. Contour feathers have a central shaft with paired, interlocking branches. These are moulted (shed and replaced) at least once a year. *See also* NW pp.142–143.

Feathering, in aviation, adjusting the propeller of an aircraft in flight so that the blades are aligned most nearly to the direction of flight. Feathering is usually done to reduce drag in the event of engine failure so that the propeller does not continue to "wind-mill".

February, the second month in the Gregorian calendar, consisting of 28 days except in leap years, when it has 29. FEBRUUS was the Roman God of purification and February, as the last month in the reformed Roman calendar (*c.* 790 BC), thus represented purification before the new year. The 29th day was added to every fourth year in the Julian calendar to make it agree better with the solar year. In the French revolutionary calendar February corresponded to parts of the months of "rain" (Pluviôse) and of "wind" (Ventôse).

February Revolution (1848), French insurrection that overthrew the government of LOUIS-PHILIPPE and set up the SECOND REPUBLIC. The Revolution was the result of a rising in Paris following the economic crisis of 1847–48 and agitation for parliamentary reform; the leadership comprised bourgeois radicals and working-class revolutionaries. The revolution inspired similar uprisings throughout Europe in the same year; but the republic failed by 1851. *See also* HC2 p.108.

Februus, in Roman mythology, a god of purification, probably adopted from an Etruscan god of the dead. February was the month of the dead in Rome.

Fechner, Gustav Theodor (1801–87), German physician and psychologist who helped found experimental psychology by using objective, precise methods to study psychophysics – the relationships of physical stimuli to sensation and perception. Fechner's law states that the relationship between the strength of a stimulus and the perceived intensity of a sensation is logarithmic.

Federal Bureau of Investigation. *See* FBI.

Federalism, political system that allows states united under a central government to maintain a measure of independence. The USA is the best-known example of a federal state, although Australia, Canada and India also have federal systems. A federal government has supreme authority, but the component states have a considerable amount of autonomy in such matters as education and health.

Federal Republic of Germany. *See* GERMANY, WEST.

Federation Cup, women's international team tennis championship contested annually on a knockout basis. Teams are limited to three players; contests are decided by two singles and a doubles. First held in London in 1963, it has been dominated by the USA and Australia.

Federation of British Industries. *See* CBI.

Federmann, Nikolaus (*c.* 1501–42), German explorer who trekked through the Andes in the 1530s.

Fee, in the FEUDAL SYSTEM, a FIEF or grant of land to a knight in exchange for specific military services to his lord. A fee varied in size according to the quality of the land, but in Norman England it often corresponded to five hides (an Anglo-Saxon unit of land theoretically equalling the amount of land needed to provide for a single peasant family).

Feedback, in technology, the process of returning a part of the output energy of a device to the input. In negative feedback the output energy is arranged to cause a decrease in the input energy. A governor is a negative feedback device, the output being coupled to the input so that constant speed is obtained, irrespective of load. In positive feedback, the output energy reinforces the input energy. This occurs when a loudspeaker feeds into a microphone coupled to the same amplifier as the loud speaker. The amplifier oscillates producing a high-pitched "scream" in the loudspeaker. *See also* MM pp. 104–105; SU p. *131*.

Feed line, theatrical technique often used in comedy, whereby a character speaks a line of which the sole purpose is to permit a humorous reply.

Feijoa, small genus of South American shrubs or trees closely related to the GUAVA. It has opposite leaves and whitish blossoms that develop into edible fruits about 5cm (2in) long, oblong, and green marked with red. Family Myrtaceae; species *Feijoa sellowiana*.

Feininger, Lyonel (1871–1956), US

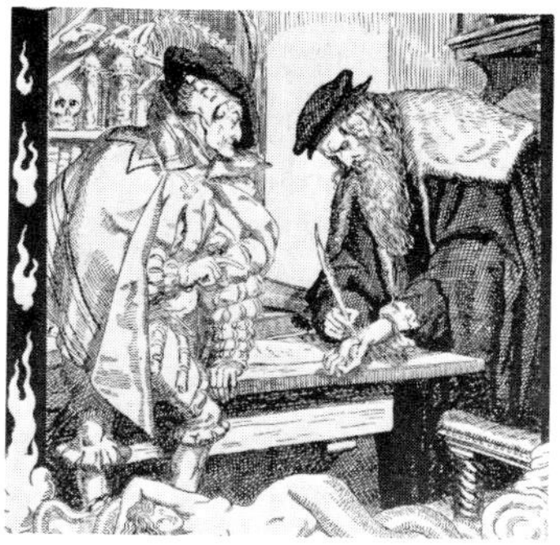

Faust, in a drawing by Franz Stássen, entering into his covenant with Mephistopheles.

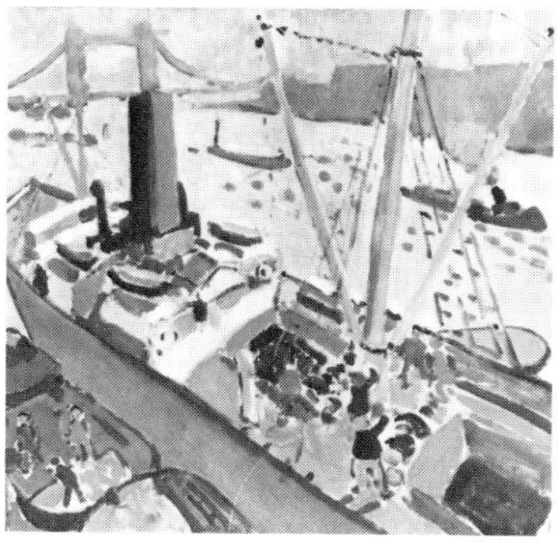

Fauvism, a typical example of this movement is a landscape by the French artist Derain.

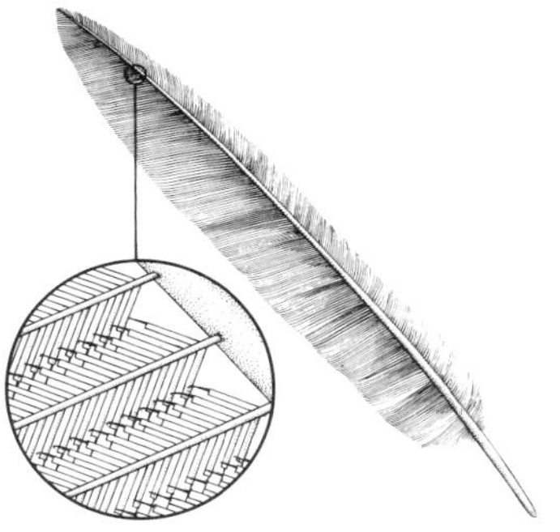

Feather; the barbs branch out from the shaft like the branches of a tree.

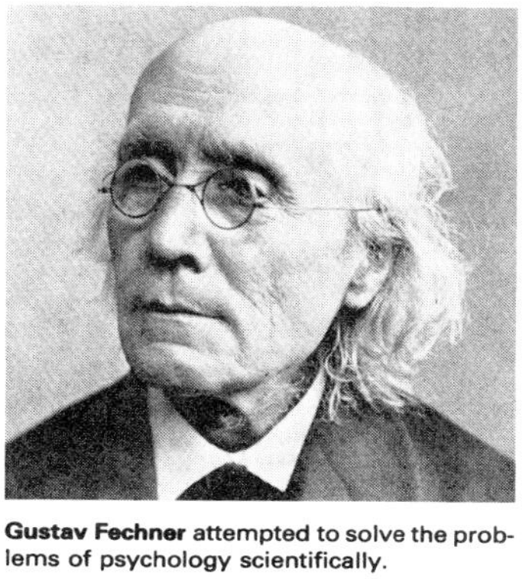

Gustav Fechner attempted to solve the problems of psychology scientifically.

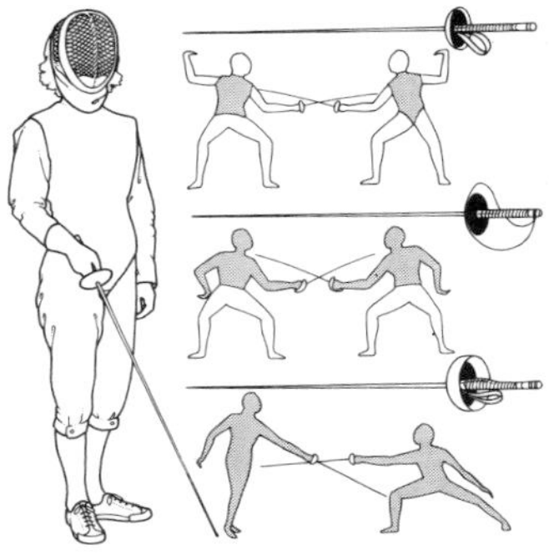

Fencing; shaded areas indicate targets for (top to bottom) foil, sabre and épée.

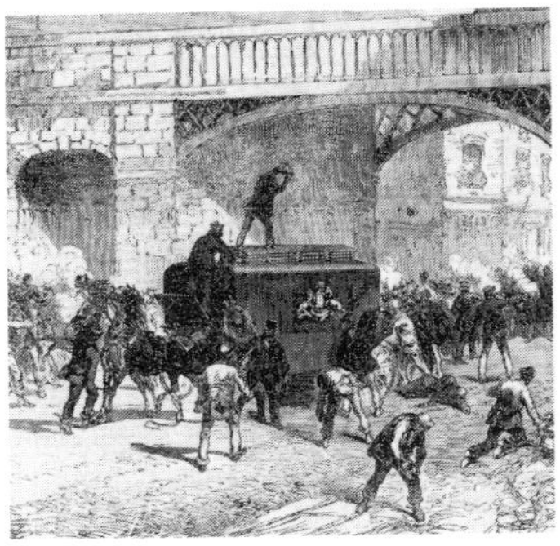

Fenian movement; leaders being rescued from a police van in Manchester in 1867.

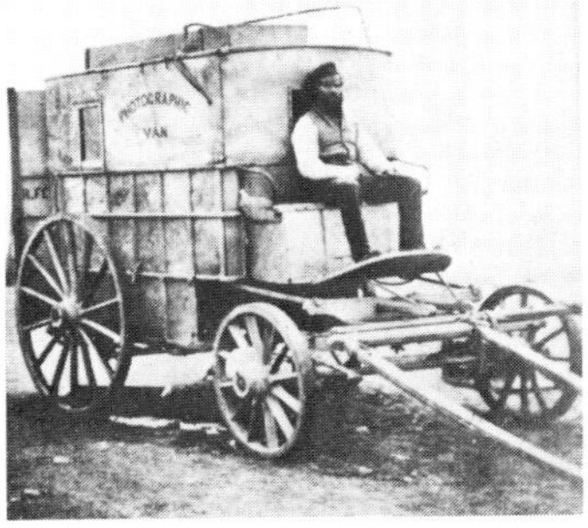

Roger Fenton; an early photograph of the pioneer photographer and his darkroom.

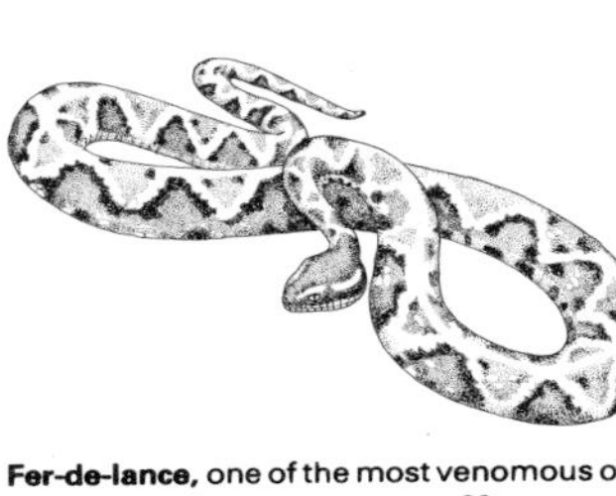

Fer-de-lance, one of the most venomous of all snakes, produces as many as 60 young.

painter who taught at the BAUHAUS (1919–33). His work shows a strong CUBIST influence. In 1937 he returned to the USA, where his style reached its richest form in such watercolours as *Dawn* (1938).

Feisal I. *See* FAISAL.

Felidae, cat family usually taken to consist of six genera (there is disagreement on the exact classifications) and 36 species of carnivores, ranging from the domestic cat to the tiger. The so-called big cats include the lion, tiger, leopard, jaguar, puma and cheetah, the last-named being the only member of the family with non-retractable claws. *See also* NW pp.217, 220.

Felipe, León, pen name of the Spanish poet León Felipe Camino Galicia (1884–1968). He wrote simple, direct verse on moral and religious themes. His works include *Versos y oraciones de caminante* (1917) and *Antología rota* (1920–47).

Felix, the name of five popes and antipopes. Little is known about Felix I, Saint (*r.*269–74). Felix II (*d.*365; antipope 355–58) was elected after the enforced exile of Pope Liberius and forced to retire on his return. Felix III, Saint (*d.*492; *r.*483–92) instigated the Acacian Schism (484–519) by excommunicating Acacius, the Patriarch of Constantinople (for supporting the Monophysite Peter Mongus). Felix IV (*d.*530; *r.*526–30) is remembered for the church of Saints Cosmas and Damian in Rome, formed from two pagan shrines. Felix V (1383–1451; antipope (1440–49) formed the order of St Maurice and was elected by the Council of Basel in 1439. On his abdication he was made a cardinal.

Fellini, Federico (1920–), Italian film director, famous for the macabre satire of his films which were often autobiographical. His major films include *La Strada* (1954), *La Dolce Vita* (1960), *8½* (1963), *Satyricon* (1969), *Roma* (1972), *Amarcord* (1974) and *Casanova* (1977). *See also* HC2 p.277.

Fell running, demanding form of cross-country running practised mostly in the highland regions of N England and Scotland. Races over "out and home" and circuit courses vary in distance from 2.4–64km (1½–40 miles), but as not all routes are defined, map- and compass-reading are further attributes of the experienced fell runner.

Felony, in British law, indictable criminal offence. Originally punishable by death, felonies were for long distinguished from misdemeanours, ie crimes of a less serious nature. The distinction was abolished by the Criminal Law Act (1967).

Felspars, or feldspars, group of common aluminium silicate minerals; principal constituents of igneous rocks. Orthoclase and microcline are potassium felspars of monoclinic and triclinic system crystals, respectively. Members of the plagioclase series (sodium and calcium felspars) have physical properties similar to microcline, but with crystals frequently twinned. Several are cut as gems: amazonite, a green form of microcline; moonstone, white with a bluish stain, is an alkali felspar; labradorite, an iridescent red, blue or green is a plagioclase variety; and sunstone is a spangled variety, frequently reddish. Hardness 6–6.5; s.g. 2.5–2.8. *See also* PE pp.96–*97*, 98, *101*; SU p.140.

Felucca, lateen-rigged narrow sailing boat used in the Mediterranean and on the Nile. A felucca may have two or three masts, a rudder at either end and can be propelled by oars. Shallow-draft vessels, they are light and fast and have been used since ancient times.

Feminism, movement which aims at political, social and economic equality of women with men. Feminism is rooted in the ideas of the Enlightenment of the late 18th century; it gathered momentum in the 19th century with the rapid economic and social changes arising from the INDUSTRIAL REVOLUTION. In 19th-century Britain, women were legally forbidden to hold public office, to vote or to own property if married until the MARRIED WOMEN'S PROPERTY ACT. Women were regarded as physically, socially and intellectually inferior to men. The SUFFRAGETTES aimed at universal suffrage, or a vote for each man and each woman, and they were linked with early socalism. The PANKHURSTS, Emmeline and her daughter Christabel, Millicent FAWCETT, and her sister Elizabeth Garratt ANDERSON were leading members of the feminist movement. In 1928 universal suffrage was finally granted. In the 1960s came the next resurgence in feminism, known at first as WOMEN'S LIBERATION. This movement sought deeper changes in economic, social and political structures, and a need was seen to eliminate sexual preconceptions of female dependence. In the 1970s, various equal pay acts were passed in many countries, and legislation was enacted to end discrimination against women in respect of goods, services and employment.

Feminists, women who actively advocate equality with men in all respects. The first important feminist document in the English language was *The Vindication of the Rights of Women* (1792) by Mary Wollstonecraft. The early feminists believed that equality would follow if they obtained the vote for women, an aim which was fulfilled in 1928 in the UK. This failed to achieve true equality, and the 1960s wave of feminists aimed for the total psychological, social, economic and political emancipation of women and their acceptance on equal terms with men. Leading feminists and their written works include Simone de BEAUVOIR (*The Second Sex*, 1949), Betty Friedan (*The Feminine Mystique* 1963), Kate Millet (*Sexual Politics*, 1970) and Germaine Greer (*The Female Eunuch*, 1970).

Femur, upper-leg bone, extending from the pelvis to the knee. It is the longest and strongest bone of the human skeleton. Its rounded smooth head articulates with the pelvis at the acetabulum, or hip socket; its large flattened lower end – which can be felt on both sides of the knee – articulates with the tibia, the larger of the lower leg bones. *See also* MS pp.56–*57*.

Fen, tract of low-lying marshy land where peat is formed below the surface. The soil is only slightly acid and much drainage is needed before a fen can become arable. The term is usually applied to the swampy Wash area (The FENS) in E England where most of the land is at or below sea-level.

Fenby, Eric William (1906–), British composer and arranger who for six years acted as musical amanuensis to Fredrick DELIUS and assisted in the completion of his last works such as *A Song of Summer* and the third violin sonata (both 1930). Fenby's own studies of Delius appeared in 1936 and 1971.

Fencing, sport of attack and defence with FOIL, ÉPÉE OR SABRE. It is conducted on a strip or mat (*piste*) 14m (46ft) long and 2m (6ft 7in) wide; in 1973 a *piste* of 24m (78ft 9in) was allowed for the sabre. Fencers wear wire-mesh masks, and jackets, gloves and breeches generally made of canvas. The tip of the weapon is blunted and points are scored by touching the opponent.

Fénélon, François de Salignac de la Mothe (1651–1715), French churchman and philosopher. He was tutor to the Duke of Burgundy in 1689 but lost favour owing to his espousal of QUIETISM – a variety of Roman Catholic mysticism – and his *Télémaque* (1699), a satirical work critical of the government of Louis XIV.

Fenian movement (Irish Republican Brotherhood), Irish nationalist organization set up in 1858 by James STEPHENS. It sought independence from Britain by revolution, and most of its support came from the urban lower classes. After several abortive plots the leaders were arrested in 1867, and the focus of Fenian activity moved to the USA, where there were many Irish who had left Ireland during the famine of the 1840s. Under the leadership of John Devoy and John O'Neill, the Irish Fenians invaded Canada in 1866. The movement continued underground until WWI, when it was superseded by SINN FEIN. *See also* HC2 p.162.

Fenian Uprising, attempts to invade Canada in June 1866 and May 1870 by the FENIAN MOVEMENT. The US Government arrested the Fenian leaders and sent a military force to halt the raids in order to appease British interests.

Fennel, tall, pereniial herb of the parsley family, native to S Europe. All parts are aromatic, and the seeds and extracted oil are used to add a liquorice flavour to medicines, liqueurs and foods. The height of the cultivated plant about 1m (3.2ft). Family Umbelliferae; species *Foeniculum vulgare*. *See also* PE pp.*210*, *212*, 213.

Fens, lowland region of E England 117km (73 miles) long and 56km (35 miles) wide lying W and S of the Wash. This marshy area was first drained in the 17th century and is now under intensive cultivation, producing fruit and vegetables.

Fenshan. *See* KAOHSIUNG.

Fenton, Roger (1819–69), British pioneer photographer whose carefully composed portraits and landscape studies earned him enduring acclaim. In 1855 he became one of the first war photographers with a series of more than 350 plate photographs of the CRIMEAN WAR, many of them taken under very dangerous conditions, including *The Valley of the Shadow of Death*.

Feodor, name of three tsars of Russia. Feodor I (1557–98) became tsar in 1584; he was the last of the Rurik dynasty. He took little part in government affairs, which were controlled by Boris GODUNOV. Feodor II (1589–1605) was the son of Boris and ruled only briefly, on his father's death, from April to June 1605. He was murdered by supporters of the "false Dmitry", who took the imperial throne. Feodor III (1661–82) became tsar in 1676. In his reign the Westernization of Russia was begun, especially the introduction of Roman Catholic religious doctrines and Latin literature.

Ferber, Edna (1887–1968), US author. Her novels include *So Big* (1924), *Show Boat* (1926), which was made into a musical, and *Giant* (1952). She also wrote several successful plays with George S. KAUFMAN, including *Dinner at Eight* (1932) and *Stage Door* (1936).

Fer-de-lance, widely distributed Central and South American lance-headed PIT-VIPER. It has black-edged, light diamond markings on a brown ground colour. Its fast-acting venom is usually fatal to humans. Length: to 2.1m (6.9ft). Family Viperidae; species *Bothrops atrix*. *See also* SNAKE.

Ferdinand, name of three Holy Roman Emperors. Ferdinand I (1503–64) was emperor (1556–64) and King of Bohemia and Hungary (1526–64). He never really controlled Hungary, where he had to pay tribute to Sultan SULEIMAN I to retain his title. He had a strong hold on Bohemia and began the process of re-conversion to Catholicism, while in Germany he warred against the Protestants with varying success, finally ending in the religious truce of the Peace of AUGSBURG (1555). In 1556 his elder brother, CHARLES V, abdicated and Ferdinand became emperor. Ferdinand II (1578–1637) was Holy Roman Emperor (1619–37) and King of Bohemia (1617–37) and Hungary (1618–37). The THIRTY YEARS WAR, precipated in 1618 by a revolt against his rule in Bohemia, dominated his reign. Ferdinand III (1608–57) was Holy Roman Emperor (1637–57), King of Hungary (1626–57) and Bohemia (1627–57). In 1648 he accepted the Peace of WESTPHALIA, ending the Thirty Years War. *See also* HC1 p.273.

Ferdinand I (1793–1875), Emperor of Austria (1835–48), King of Hungary (1830–48). This weak sovereign let Prince METTERNICH govern for him. Faced with revolutions in Hungary, Italy and Vienna, he was forced to abdicate and flee in 1848.

Ferdinand, name of two kings of Aragon and Sicily. Ferdinand I (*c.*1379–1416) was King of Aragon and Sicily (1412–16). In 1410 his uncle, Martin, died leaving vacant the thrones of Aragon and Sicily which Ferdinand eventually took in 1412. ALFONSO V, his son, succeeded him. Ferdinand II (Ferdinand the Catholic) (1452–1516) was King of Aragon (1479–1516), of Castile and Leon (as Ferdinand V) (1474–1504), of Sicily (1468–1516) and of Naples (1504–16). In

1469 he married ISABELLA I and in 1474 he became joint ruler of Castile and Leon; in 1479 he inherited Aragon from his father JOHN II. Ferdinand and Isabella became rulers of a united Spain after they had expelled the Moors from Granada in 1492. In the same year they also expelled the Jews and sponsored the voyage of Christopher COLUMBUS to the New World. In 1478 they had established the Spanish INQUISITION. Ferdinand gained much territory in Italy during his struggle there for supremacy over France in the Italian Wars (1511–13); in 1512, he occupied the kingdom of Navarre and absorbed it into that of Castile. *See also* HC1 pp.148–149.

Ferdinand I (1861–1948), Prince (1887–1908) and Tsar of Bulgaria (1908–18). In 1908 he declared Bulgaria independent of the Ottoman Empire and himself the tsar. With Russian backing he allied Bulgaria with Serbia, Greece and Montenegro in the first BALKAN WAR (1912–13), which ended Turkish dominance in the Balkans. But in the second Balkan War (1913), Greece and Serbia joined with Romania and Turkey in defeating Bulgaria. Most of Macedonia was lost to Greece and Serbia. In 1915 Bulgaria joined the CENTRAL POWERS in WWI. After defeat in the war, Ferdinand abdicated in favour of his son BORIS III. *See also* HC2 pp. 184–185.

Ferdinand, name of five kings of Castile and Leon. Ferdinand I, or Ferdinand the Great, (*d.* 1065) was King of Castile (1035–65) and Leon (1037–65). He successfully fought the Moors, making vassals of the rulers of Seville, Toledo and Saragossa. Ferdinand II (*d.* 1188) was King of Leon (1157–88) and successor of ALFONSO VII. Ferdinand III (1199–1252) was King of Castile (1217–52) and Leon (1230–52). His mother renounced her rights to Castile in his favour in 1217 and when his father, ALFONSO IX, died in 1230 Ferdinand united the two kingdoms. He had a marked success against the Moors; at his death all of Spain except Granada had been Christianized. He was canonized in 1671. Ferdinand IV (1289–1312) was King of Castile and Leon (1295–1312). He took Gibraltar from the Moors in 1309. For Ferdinand V, *see* FERDINAND II of Aragon. *See also* HC1 pp.148–49.

Ferdinand V. *See* FERDINAND II of Aragon.

Ferdinand, name of four kings of Naples. Ferdinand I (1423–94) was King of Naples from 1458 to 1494. His succession was not recognized at first, but after war with the pretender John of Anjou, Pope PIUS II recognized him. A rebellion by nobles in 1485, backed by Pope INNOCENT VIII, was suppressed. Ferdinand II (1467–96) was King of Naples from 1495 to 1496. With Spanish aid he expelled French occupation forces in the Italian Wars. His sudden death the same year allowed the Spanish to usurp the throne. For Ferdinand III, *see* FERDINAND II of Aragon, and for Ferdinand IV, *see* FERDINAND I, King of the Two Sicilies.

Ferdinand, name of two kings of Portugal. Ferdinand I (1345–83) reigned from 1367 to 1383. His overwhelming ambition for the throne of Castile kept Portugal in almost continuous warfare with that country. A series of crushing settlements were ended when his daughter and heir married JOHN I of Castile. Ferdinand II (1816–85), king consort of Portugal (1836–53), was regent to his son, PETER V, until he came of age. In later years he was offered the Greek (1862) and then the Spanish (1869) crowns.

Ferdinand I (1865–1927), King of Romania (1914–27). He became king when his uncle, CAROL I, died in 1914. Although the Romanians were crushed by the armies of the CENTRAL POWERS in WWI, Ferdinand had won the loyalty of his people and he returned from exile in 1918. He was crowned in 1922. By the terms of the peace treaties, Romania more than doubled its territory, although many of the settlements were disputed.

Ferdinand, name of two kings of Spain. Ferdinand VI (1713–59; *r.* 1746–59) succeeded Philip V and forced his stepmother Elizabeth FARNESE into retirement. He kept Spain out of the SEVEN YEARS WAR until he died. Ferdinand VII (1784–1833) became king in 1808, was deposed in the same year and was restored in 1814. His rule grew more reactionary and he set off the CARLIST wars by abolishing the law of succession to allow his daughter Isabella to succeed him. *See also* HC2 pp.77, *86.*

Ferdinand, name of two kings of the Two Sicilies. Ferdinand I (1751–1825; *r.* 1815–25) was king of Naples as Ferdinand IV (1759–1806) and of Sicily as Ferdinand III (1806–1815). His reign in Naples was interrupted in 1799 and 1806–15 by a French republican occupation. A repressive reactionary ruler, he combined his kingdoms in 1816 to form the Two Sicilies. Ferdinand II (1810–59; *r.* 1830–59), initially considered a liberal, relapsed into repressive despotism. The popular revolution of 1848 led to a constitution that he soon revoked. His isolationist rule weakened his kingdom, which joined a united Italy in 1860.

Ferdinand, name of three grand dukes of Tuscany. Ferdinand I de Medici (*c.* 1549–1609, *r.* 1587–1609) resigned his cardinalship to succeed his brother Francesco. His marriage to Christine of Lorraine in 1589 provided a counterbalance to Spanish influence in Italy. Ferdinand II de Medici (1610–70, *r.* 1627–70) was a weak ruler, and Medici extravagance was allowed to drain the family fortune. In 1657 he set up the Academia del Cimento, the first academic institution for the sciences. Ferdinand III (also Archduke of Austria) (1769–1824, *r.* 1790–1824) had his reign interrupted by French occupation (1799–1814); he was noted for his enlightened and liberal rule.

Ferenczi, Sandor (1873–1933), Hungarian psychoanalyst. Influenced by FREUD, Ferenczi extended psychoanalysis to include permissive therapy, in which neurotics were encouraged to release their pent-up emotions.

Ferguson, Adam (1723–1816), Scottish philosopher and historian. Professor of philosophy at Edinburgh University from 1759 to 1785, he was associated with the "common-sense" school of philosophy. His major work was *The Principles of Moral and Political Science* (1792).

Ferguson, Harry (1884–1960), British engineer who designed and pioneered the development of agricultural machinery, especially the Ferguson tractor. In the late 1930s he joined Henry FORD in the manufacture of tractors in the USA.

Ferguson, Howard (1908–), British composer. His first published works were performed at the Gloucester Festival in 1934. He is best known for his violin and piano sonatas and the *Partita for orchestra* (1935–36).

Ferguson, Sir Samuel (1810–86), Irish poet and antiquary. His poetry, including *Lays of the Western Gael* (1865), *Conary* (1880) and *Deirdre* (1880), was based on Irish legends.

Ferguson, William Gow (*c.* 1632–*c.* 95), Scottish painter of still lifes; he spent most of his career in The Netherlands.

Fergusson, Sir Bernard Edward (1911–), British soldier. A brigade commander in Burma in WWII, he was director of combined operations of the British army in 1945–46. He served as Governor-General of New Zealand from 1962 to 1967.

Ferlinghetti, Lawrence (1919–), US author. A BEAT GENERATION poet, in 1953 he opened the City Lights bookstore in San Francisco and began publishing the works of Beat authors such as Allen GINSBERG. His own works include *A Coney Island of the Mind* (1958) and *Starting from San Francisco* (1961).

Fermanagh, county in SW Northern Ireland. It is hilly in the NE and SW and these areas are devoted largely to grazing. It is an agricultural region and the county town is Enniskillen. Area: 1,852sq km (715sq miles). Pop. 50,000.

Fermat, Pierre de (1601–65), French mathematician. With Blaise PASCAL he helped to formulate the theory of probability and, by showing that light travels along the shortest optical path (Fermat's principle), he laid the foundation for geometric optics.

Fermentation, energy-yielding process by which sugar and starch molecules, catalyzed by enzymes or micro-organisms such as yeast, are broken down anaerobically. Old-established uses, where the major products are carbon dioxide and ethanol, include bread-making, wine- and beer-brewing, cheese maturation and drug manufacture. Fermentation is a major metabolic degrading process where the products may differ due to different enzymes directing the last stages. The intoxicating effect of crushed fruits stored in a warm place may have been known as early as 4000 BC. *See also* PE pp.*183,* 202–207, 250.

Fermi, Enrico (1901–54), Italian physicist who worked mainly in the fields of atomic behaviour and structure, and QUANTUM THEORY. He showed that transmutations may be caused by neutron bombardment of elements and constructed the first atomic pile. He was awarded the 1938 Nobel Prize in physics; the element FERMIUM was named after him.

Fermium, radioactive metallic element (symbol Fm) of the ACTINIDE group, first identified in 1952 as a decay product of U^{255} after it was produced in the first large hydrogen bomb explosion (1952). Properties: at. no. 100; most stable isotope Fm^{257} (half-life 80 days). *See also* TRANSURANIC ELEMENTS.

Fern, TRACHEOPHYTE or non-flowering plant that produces spores instead of seeds. They take many forms. Most ferns grow in warm, moist areas; there are about 10,000 species. The best-known genus *Pteridium* (BRACKEN) grows on moorland and in open woodland. Ferns are characterized by two perennial generations: the conspicuous sporophyte that possesses leafy fronds, stems, rhizomes and roots and reproduces by minute spores usually clustered on the leaves, and the inconspicuous gametophyte that resembles tiny moss and produces sperm and ova. Fronds unroll from curled "fiddle-heads" and may be divided into leaflets. Ferns were growing during the Devonian period, some 400 million years ago. Class Filicinae. *See also* NW pp.38–39, 52–53.

Fernandel (1903–71), French film comedian, real name Fernand-Joseph Desiré Constantin. He came to prominence in 1932 in *Le Rosier de Madame Husson,* and won renown with his portrayals of Don Camillo during the 1950s.

Fernández de Córdoba, Gonzalo (1453–1515), Spanish general, known as the Great Captain, who negotiated the surrender of the Moors in Granada in 1492. During the Italian wars he was a commander of the troops of FERDINAND and ISABELLA. He became the first viceroy of Naples after 1502.

Fernandez, Juan (*c.* 1536–*c.* 1604), Spanish navigator and explorer. He discovered and tried to colonize the Juan Fernandez Islands W of Chile; descendants of the goats left by colonists were found by Alexander SELKIRK 150 years later.

Fernando Póo (Macías Nguema Biyogo), island in the Bight of Biafra, off the coast of W Africa. Discovered in 1472 by Fernão do Po, the island was ceded to Spain from Portugal in 1778 and is now a province of EQUATORIAL GUINEA. It exports cocoa, coffee and copra. The capital is Malabo formerly Santa Isabel. Area: 2,018sq km (779sq miles). Pop. 61,200. *See* MW p.74.

Ferrar, Nicholas (1592–1637), English divine. After working for the Virginia Company (1618–25), he founded a religious community at Little Gidding, Huntingdonshire, where he studied the scriptures. The community was closed in 1647 for its HIGH CHURCH tendencies.

Ferrarese School, artistic school of the northern Italian Renaissance, originating in the late 15th century. Its leading artists included Cosimo TURA and Ercole de' ROBERTI, and in the early 16th century the Dosso brothers. Its style was austere, influenced by the work of MANTEGNA.

Ferreira, António (*c.* 1528–69), Portuguese playwright and poet. He was greatly influenced by the Italian Renaissance and his studies of the classics, and

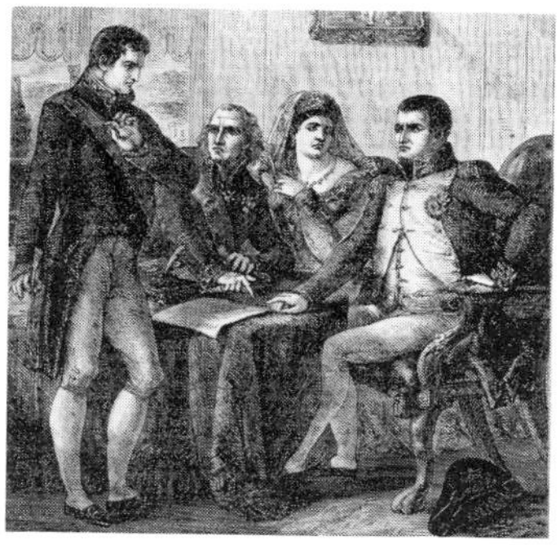

Ferdinand VII of Spain abdicating his throne in 1808 at the order of the Emperor Napoleon.

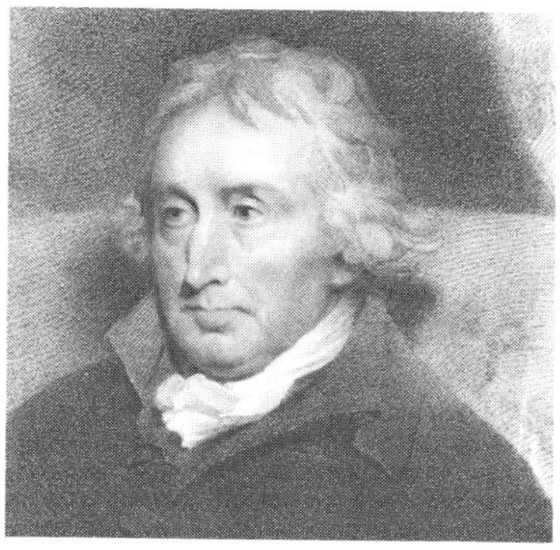

Adam Ferguson served on a commission sent to reconcile the American colonists.

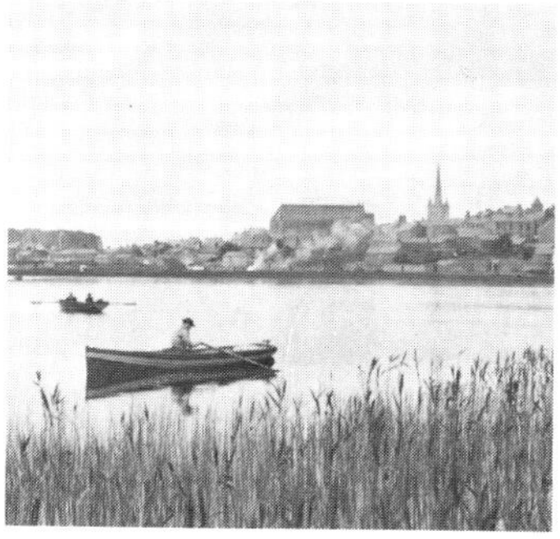

Fermanagh; a view of Enniskillen, the county town, where clothing is manufactured.

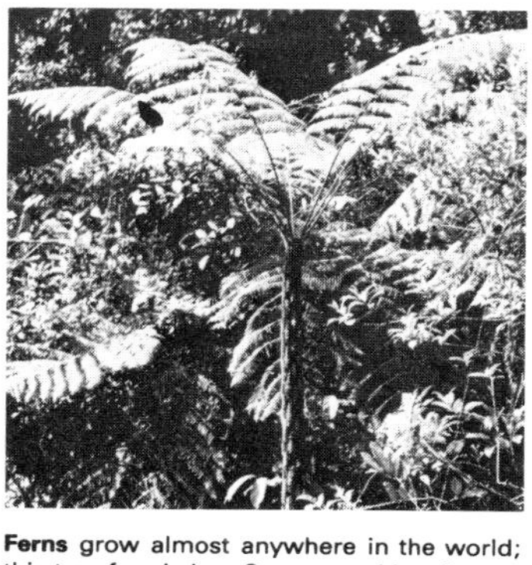

Ferns grow almost anywhere in the world; this tree fern is in a Cameroons' jungle.

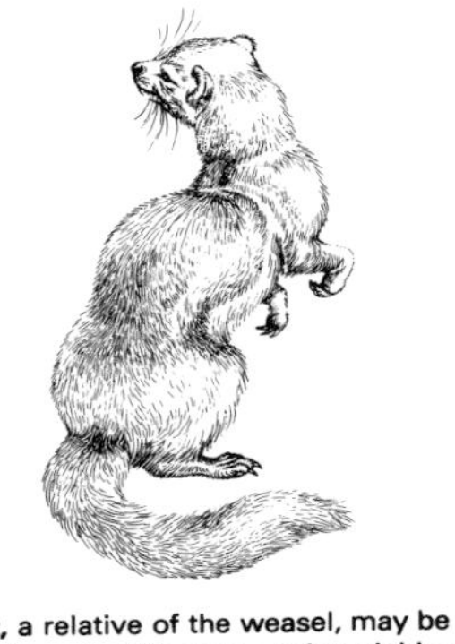

Ferret, a relative of the weasel, may be various colours but its eyes are invariably pink.

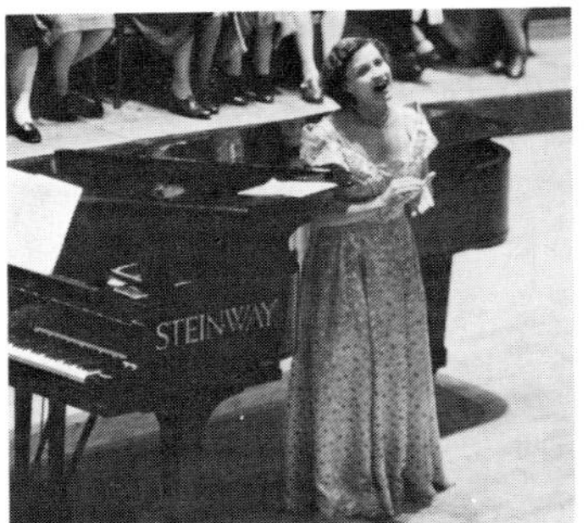

Kathleen Ferrier performing at the Usher Hall during the Edinburgh Festival of 1949.

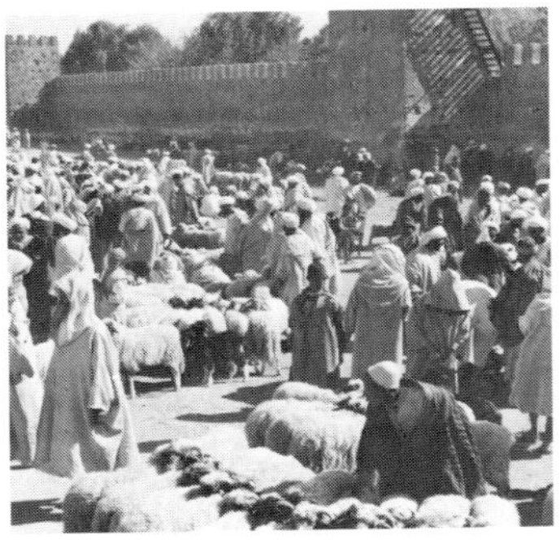

Fès, showing the sheep market beside the ramparts in this ancient Moroccan capital.

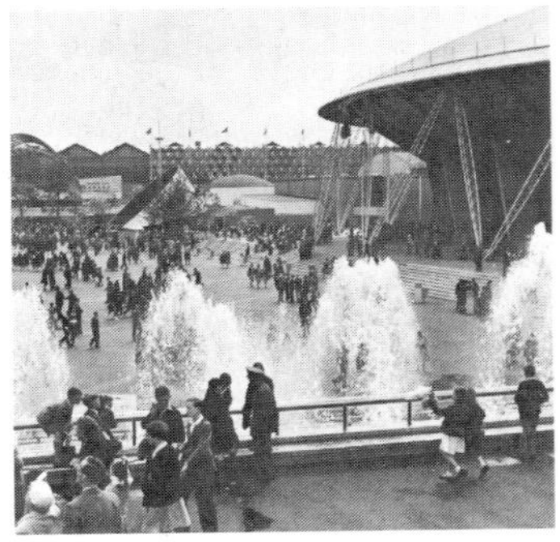

Festival of Britain; a view of the Fairway, with the Dome of Discovery on the right.

produced the earliest Portuguese tragedy, *Ignez de Castro* (1558). He wrote several comedies and a volume of poetry, *Poemas Lusitanos* containing over 100 sonnets.

Ferrer, José (1909–), US producer, director and actor. On stage he acted in *Phello* (1943), *Cyrano de Bergerac* (1946) and *The Shrike* (1952) and played in many films, notably *Cyrano de Bergerac* (1950), for which he received an ACADEMY AWARD, *The Caine Mutiny* (1954) and *Enter Laughing* (1967).

Ferrera, Andrea (or Andrew Ferrera), colloquialism for a high quality Scottish broad-sword, greatly prized by Highlanders in the 17th and 18th centuries. There is much controversy about its origins: Sir Walter Scott conjectured that such swords were named after a specific Anrea dei Ferrera; others hold the name derived simply from the Latin for "smith".

Ferret, semi-domesticated albino form of the POLECAT. Ferrets are small, carnivorous weasel-like animals. They have a long necks, slender bodies, long tails, short legs, pink eyes and all white fur. They are agile killers, used by hunters to kill rats and flush rabbits from their burrows. Body length: 36cm (14in); weight: 700g (1.5lb). Family Mustelidae; species *Mustela putorius*. *See also* WEASEL.

Ferri, Ciro (1634–89), Italian Baroque painter from Rome. He completed unfinished frescoes of his master Pietro da CORTONA in the Pitti Palace, Florence, and produced religious frescoes of his own in Bergamo and the altarpiece of St Ambrose, Rome.

Ferrier, Johan Henri Eliza (1910–), Surinam politician. He was prime minister of Surinam (1955–58), and became president in 1975.

Ferrier, Kathleen (1912–53), British contralto. The beauty of her voice brought her international fame as a concert and opera singer before her early death from cancer. Benjamin BRITTEN, in particular, wrote for her and she sang the title rôle in the first performance of *The Rape of Lucretia* (1946) by him at Glyndebourne, where she also received acclaim as Orpheus in GLUCK'S ORFEO.

Ferrite, one of the crystalline forms (ALLOTROPES) of the metal iron (Fe), present together with other forms in steel, wrought iron and cast iron. It is also called α-iron, and has highly magnetic properties. The name ferrite is also given to chemical compounds such as nickel ferrite ($NiFe_2O_4$), and zinc ferrite ($ZnFe_2O_4$), found naturally in rocks and also synthesized as magnetic materials. *See also* FERROMAGNETISM.

Ferro-alloys, combinations of silicon, manganese, chromium, molybdenum, vanadium, titanium and several other elements, added to molten steel to confer such properties as greater strength and corrosion resistance. Individually they are named after their major constituents; eg ferrochromium contains about 70% chromium, about 6% carbon and about 2% silicon as well as iron. *See also* ALLOY.

Ferroelectrics, crystalline materials which are naturally electrically polarized. Within the crystal of such a material lie regions or domains which are spontaneously polarized in specific directions, although these directions can often be changed by the application of an electric field. All ferroelectrics are also PIEZOELECTRICS; this leads to many applications of the materials in research and industry, eg as special ceramics. *See also* SU p.114.

Ferromagnetism, form of MAGNETISM exhibited by substances (such as iron, cobalt and nickel), with high MAGNETIC PERMEABILITIES. *See* SU pp.116–119.

Ferron, Jacques (1926–), Canadian author. A doctor, he wrote many plays, as well as novels and stories. His works include the short-story collection *Tales from the Uncertain Country*, which won the Prix du Gouverneur Général in 1964.

Fertile Crescent, historic region in the Middle East. It extends across the N part of the Syrian desert, and is watered by the rivers Tigris and Euphrates. The first great civilizations developed there.

Fertility, in mythology and religion, the sacred power of procreation in nature; it is associated with fruitfulness and abundance. Fertility rites are common in agricultural societies where rituals may be performed to ensure a plentiful harvest. The rituals and associated images make great symbolic use of human sexuality. *See also* MS pp.*207*, 212.

Fertility drugs, substances administered to increase the likelihood of conception and pregnancy. One of the many causes of female sterility results from insufficient secretion of pituitary hormones, and this malfunction is often treated with either human chorionic gonadotropin or clomiphene citrate, although use of the latter has resulted in multiple births. In males, sterility may be due to sperm deficiency, although there are many causes; treatment depends on the cause of sterility but in some cases involves the administration of ANDROGENS. In cases where fertilization of the ovum does occur, but where the uterine lining is unable to support the developing foetus, the hormone progesterone may be used. But there are many cases of infertility which drugs cannot correct. Examples are those arising from anatomical disorders such as blocked FALLOPIAN TUBES in females or obstructed sperm ducts in males.

Fertilization, process in the REPRODUCTION of plants and animals, in which impregnation of an egg nucleus by a sperm nucleus forms a ZYGOTE. Stages of fertilization are: penetration – sperm enters the egg – and fusion of egg and sperm nuclei. After fertilization, the zygote begins to divide. Fertilization can be external (as in fish and amphibians) or internal (reptiles, birds and mammals). *See also* EMBRYO; MS pp.74–75; NW pp.70–71, 76–*77*.

Fertilizer, natural or artificial substance added to soil, containing chemicals to improve plant growth. Manure and compost were the first fertilizers. Other natural substances, such as bonemeal, ashes, guano and fish, have been used for centuries. Modern chemical fertilizers, containing principally compounds of nitrogen, phosphorus and potassium in powder or liquid form are now widely used. Specialized fertilizers also contain other, including trace, elements. *See also* PE pp.156, 166–167, 170–171, 174–175.

Fès (Fez), city in N central Morocco, approx. 242km (150 miles) ENE of Casablanca. Founded in 790, it is a sacred city of Islam containing many mosques. Industries: leather goods, metal-working. Pop. 290,000.

Fescue, GRASS native to the Northern Hemisphere and widely cultivated for pasture and fodder. Some species, such as red fescue (*Festuca rubra*), are also used in lawns. The short, five-leafed sheep fescue (*F. ovina*) grows in dense tufts on mountains and forms turf in sandy soil. Family Gramineae. There are about 100 species.

Fessenden, Reginald Aubrey (1866–1932), US engineer and physicist who was a pioneer in depth-finding and radio. Fessenden developed a new type of wireless system using continuous waves. He invented the high frequency alternator, the electrolytic detector, a system of radio telephony, the heterodyne system of radio reception and the fathometer.

Festival of Britain (1951), exhibition of British trades and arts, held to celebrate the centenary of the Great Exhibition. It was held on the South Bank of the River Thames. Built for the occasion, the Royal Festival Hall remains the centre of London's musical life. *See also* HC2 p.*237*.

Fête galante, French 18th-century genre of painting in which courtiers are depicted amusing themselves in dancing and general dalliance in parks and other sylvan settings. WATTEAU, of whose work the term was first used (1717), was the outstanding painter in this genre; LANCRET and J. B. F. PATER were his principal imitators.

Feti, Domenico (1589–1624), Italian painter. His painting, mainly in the Venetian style, displayed the CHIAROSCURO technique and much of his work comprised small genre paintings of contemporary life taken from biblical themes.

Fetish, object possessing supernatural powers. Its power derives either from a deity or consecration or from a spirit lodged within it. Claws or amulets may be fetishes. They are often carried around, especially by witch doctors, as sources of magical power.

Fetishism, in psychiatry, sexual perversion in which a particular object, eg a shoe, or a part of the body, eg the foot, becomes an essential aspect of sexual arousal and gratification. The fetish may replace a man or a woman as a sexual object. *See also* MS p.141.

Feudal system, social system that prevailed in most of Europe from the 9th century to the late Middle Ages, based on the tenure of land according to the mutual personal obligation between a VASSAL and his lord. The system varied widely in practice from country to country and in England was most uniformly practised after 1066. The feudal system originated in the necessity to provide for a permanent group of knights to assist the king in his wars. All land was theoretically owned by the monarch and leased out to his tenants-in-chief in return for their loyalty, attendance at the king's court and military assistance; and they in turn let out FIEFS to knights in return for military service and other obligations. The Church too was sometimes required to render military service for the land it held. Many men owed FEALTY to more than one lord, and as the estates that carried specific obligations changed hands, men sometimes became tenants-in-chief for one estate while still vassals for another. In the later Middle Ages military service was often commuted to money payments; as war became more highly organized during the HUNDRED YEARS WAR, a new system ("bastard feudalism") of temporary obligations based on indentures replaced the more permanent land-based system. *See also* HC1 pp.*158*, 204–205.

Feuerbach, Ludwig Andreas (1804–72), German philosopher. He developed G.W.F. HEGEL'S "idealism" in a materialistic direction, and applied Hegelian canons to a critique of religion in *The Essence of Christianity* (1840). God, he argued, was the alienated essence of man. Karl MARX extended Feuerbach's thesis from religion to society as a whole.

Fever, elevation of the body temperature above normal – 37°C (98.6°F) for adults – caused by infection and numerous other disorders. Fever can be reduced medically (with drugs) or mechanically (by sweating or cooling), but the cause should be determined first.

Feverfew, bushy Eurasian perennial plant now widely naturalized. It has fine-lobed aromatic leaves and small white flower heads borne in open clusters. It was formerly used as a remedy for fever, hence the name. Height: to 60cm (23in). Family Compositae; species *Chrysanthemum parthenium.*

Feydeau, Georges (1862–1921), French playwright. He wrote many tightly-constructed and extremely popular FARCES, with absurd plots and sparkling dialogue. Amongst these plays were *La Dame de chez Maxim* (1899) and *L'Hotel du Libre Échange* (1894).

Feynman, Richard Phillip (1918–) US physicist. He worked on the atomic bomb during WWII, then on quantum electrodynamics, where his invention of Feynman diagrams greatly facilitated the solution of electromagnetic interactions between elementary particles. For this work he shared the 1965 Nobel Prize in physics with Julian SCHWINGER and Shin'ichirō TOMONAGA.

Fez. *See* FÈS.

Fianna Fáil (Warriors of Eyre), Irish political party formed by Eamon DE VALERA in 1926 to oppose the treaty of 1921 that created the Irish Free State. The party controlled Irish politics almost continuously from the 1930s to 1973, and has sought complete independence of all of Ireland, revitalization of the Gaelic language, and economic improvement in the Republic of IRELAND. *See also* HC2 pp.294–295.

Fiat, international conglomerate, based in Italy. In terms of sales in the early 1970s, it is one of the top three motor vehicle manufacturers in Europe, also producing iron and steel. It employs about 330,000 people. *See also* MM p.*127*.

Fibiger, Johannes (Andreas Grib) (1867–1928), Danish pathologist. He was awarded the 1926 Nobel Prize in physiology and medicine for his discovery of a type of rat CANCER that he produced experimentally by constant irritation of a nematode worm. The work suggested that further research would be worthwhile.

Fibonacci, Leonardo (*c.*1170–1240), Italian mathematician. He wrote *Liber abaci* *c.*1200, the first Western work to propose the adoption of the Arabic numerical system. He produced the mathematical series known as the FIBONACCI SERIES.

Fibonacci series, sequence of numbers each term of which is formed by the addition of the two terms preceding it: thus 0, 1, 1, 2, 3, 5, 8, 13, 21 ... the next number being 34, the sum of 13 and 21 and so on. The sequence is named after Leonardo FIBONACCI, the Italian mathematician who devised it. The sum of the ratios of each Fibonacci number to the preceding one converges to the GOLDEN MEAN which is $\frac{1}{2}(\sqrt{5} + 1)$. Many natural forms – spiral shells and leaf systems – are delimited by the Fibonacci series. *See also* SU p.*27*.

Fibre, man-made, fibre made from a synthetic resin (plastic) by forcing it through a fine nozzle (spinneret). The resin is melted and extruded through the spinneret or first dissolved in a solvent which is removed, either by hot air or by a liquid coagulating bath. The result is a monofilament which can be woven into textiles, made into rope, etc. Many textiles, particularly for clothing, use both man-made and natural polymer fibres woven together. Synthetic fibres are polymeric materials having long-chain molecules. Many types, with various properties, exist, including nylon and other polyamides, polyesters and acrylics. Nylon, the first synthetic fibre, was introduced in 1938. *See also* MM pp.56–58; SU p.142.

Fibre, natural, naturally occurring fibrous material that can be made into yarn, textiles, carpets, rope, felt, etc. Natural fibres are made-up of long narrow cells. Animal products are based on protein molecules; they include wool, silk, mohair, angora and horsehair. Vegetable fibres are based mainly on cellulose; they include cotton, linen, flax, jute, sisal and kapok. Asbestos is a natural inorganic fibre. Another class of fibres, including rayon and acetate, is obtained from natural products (usually cellulose) modified chemically. *See also* MM pp.56–58.

Fibreglass, spun glass used as a continuous filament in textiles and electrical insulation, and in a fibrous form to reinforce plastics or for sound or heat insulation. Molten glass is drawn through spinnerets or spun through holes in a revolving dish. Combined with layers of resin, fibreglass is a popular medium for car bodies, boats, aircraft parts and containers. It resists heat, corrosion, rot and most chemicals and can be, weight for weight, stronger than steel. *See also* MM pp.37, *57*.

Fibrillation, small involuntary contraction of muscle, most often associated with heart disorders. Symptoms of the more common atrial fibrillation include irregular heart rate and pulse. Ventricular fibrillation can be fatal.

Fibrin, insoluble fibrous protein that polymerizes during the BLOOD CLOTTING process to form the basic meshwork of the blood clot. *See also* FIBRINOGEN; MS pp.114–115.

Fibrinogen, soluble protein synthesized by the liver and released into the bloodstream. It is converted to FIBRIN (an insoluble protein) by THROMBIN (an enzyme) during the BLOOD CLOTTING process. *See also* MS pp.114–115.

Fibroblast, type of living cell found in the connective tissues of the body. Fibroblasts are mobilized to restore tissue damaged as a result of injuries. The elongated or irregularly shaped cells lay down the fibrous protein COLLAGEN and other structural materials of the CONNECTIVE TISSUES. *See also* MS p.115.

Fibro-cartilage, form of CARTILAGE found mainly in parts of the skeleton that are subject to extreme physical tension or compression. These include intervertebral discs and the parts of TENDONS that are attached to the ends of the long bones. Fibro-cartilage consists largely of the fibrous protein COLLAGEN.

Fibroid, synonymous with fibromyoma but referring usually to benign uterine tumours. The tumours are mixtures of fibre and muscle.

Fibrositis, term describing a type of muscular rheumatism resulting from inflammation of fibrous tissue or a strained muscle going into spasm, and characterized by general or localized pain and muscle stiffness. The term is rarely used by doctors.

Fibula, smaller of the two lower leg bones. It extends from the knee region to the ankle, ending in the projection that may be felt on the outer side of the ankle. *See also* TIBIA; MS p.*57*.

Fichte, Johann Gottlieb (1762–1814), German philosopher. He explored transcendental idealism in his *Critique of Practical Reason* (1788) and embraced romantic nationalism in his *Addresses to the German Nation* (1807–08). He stressed the role of the "ego", which becomes aware of its own freedom and its unity with the absolute.

Ficino, Marsilio (1433–99), Italian philosopher. He was a Greek scholar and founder of the Florentine Academy and promoted the study of Plato. Although he was a humanist, he had leanings toward mysticism. His *Theologica Platonica*, a synthesis of Greek mysticism and Christianity, was influential in the 16th century. *See also* HC1 p.246.

Fiddler crab, crustacean found throughout the world that burrows in sandy beaches and drier parts of salt marshes. It is named after the male's huge claw used for signalling during courtship and mating season battles. The other claw (the "bow") is small. Width: to 25mm (1in). Family Ocypodidae; genus *Uca*. *See also* NW p.*237*.

Fidei Defensor. *See* DEFENDER OF THE FAITH.

Fidelio, full name *Fidelio oder die eheliche Liebe* ("Fidelio, or Wedded Love"), opera by BEETHOVEN, first performed at Vienna in 1805 with the Leonore overture No.2. The final version, with the Fidelio overture, was not produced until 1814.

Fiduciary, relationship in which a person holds something in trust for another and has rights and powers which he is obliged to exercise for that other person. He may not derive any benefit or profit from the relationship except with the other's knowledge. The relationship of a solicitor and client is fiduciary.

Fiduciary issue, issue of banknotes without the bullion reserve to back them. The Currency and Banknotes Act 1954 authorizes the Bank of England to issue notes up to a limit set by the Treasury. The issue of notes without adequate reserves can lead to chronic inflation, as occurred in Germany in the 1920s.

Fief, in the FEUDAL SYSTEM, an area of land granted by a lord to his VASSAL as a reward for past services or in exchange for future military and other services and loyalty. The lord kept the ultimate rights to the land, while the vassal had its use and most of the profits from it. *See also* HC1 p.204.

Field, Cyrus W. (1819–92), US financier and promoter of the first trans-Atlantic telegraph cable. After two unsuccessful attempts the cable was laid by the steamship, *The Great Eastern*, in July 1866. Field also developed the Wabash railway with Jay GOULD. *See also* MM p.*225*.

Field, John (1782–1837), Irish composer and pianist who settled in Russia. He wrote mostly piano music, including seven concertos and 18 nocturnes that influenced Frederic CHOPIN. *See also* HC2 pp.27, *106*.

Field artillery, light- and medium-sized ARTILLERY pieces, such as guns, mortars and HOWITZERS, used in close support of troops engaged in battle. *See also* MM pp.166–169.

Field emission. *See* ELECTRON EMISSION.

Fieldfare, large European THRUSH that frequents wooded regions but feeds in open country in winter. It has a blue-grey head and rump, chestnut back and white under-wing flashes. Length: 25.5cm (10in). Species *Turdus pilaris*.

Fielding, Henry (1707–54), British novelist. He wrote comedies such as *Historical Register for the Year 1736* and later took up political journalism. His novels include *Joseph Andrews* (1742) and *Tom Jones* (1749). *See also* HC2 pp.34, *35*.

Fielding, William Stevens (1848–1929), Prime Minister of Nova Scotia (1884–96), and Canadian Minister of Finance (1896–1911; 1921–25). Fielding was a Liberal and supported trade with the USA in the Knox-Fielding Pact (1911).

Field Marshal, senior rank in most European armies, symbolized by the award of a decorated baton. The modern rank dates from the early 19th century, when NAPOLEON I named some of his generals *maréchal de l'Empire*.

Field mouse. *See* MOUSE.

Field of the Cloth of Gold (1520), conference between HENRY VIII of England and FRANCIS I of France held near Calais. Despite the great ostentation that won the occasion its name, the two kings failed to make the hoped-for alliance against the Holy Roman Emperor CHARLES V. *See also* HC1 p.*240*.

Fields, Gracie (1898–), British comedienne best known for her performances of comedy songs and sentimental ballads. She began her career in music hall as a child and became popular during WWII. She retired to the Isle of Capri with her third husband, Boris Alperovici.

Fields, W. C. (1880–1946), US music hall and film comedian, real name William Claude Dukenfield. He was famous for his portrayal of hard-drinking, misanthropic braggarts in such films as *Tillie's Punctured Romance* (1928), *My Little Chickadee* (1940) and *Never Give a Sucker an Even Break* (1941).

Field spaniel, breed of sporting dog developed in Britain by crossing the cocker and Sussex spaniels. Its silky coat may be flat or wavy, always a solid colour, usually black, but also red-brown. Height: 46cm (18in); weight: 18kg (40lb).

Field sports, term embracing those activities involving the pursuit of game. Fox, hare, otter, and stag hunting, beagling, hare coursing and deer stalking, each with its own unique traditions and rituals, are all field sports. They are also called blood sports and come under heavy criticism from humanitarian opponents to the killing of animals. Those practising field sports claim they are performing an essential task by reducing numbers. Field sports also include equestrian events, angling, and shooting.

Field trials, competition for hunting dogs. They are divided into five categories: beagle, hound, pointing dog, retriever and spaniel trials. In each of these the animal, on land and/or in water, must perform one or more manoeuvres in the sighting, retrieving and returning of game. Field trials originated in the 17th century in England, where events are now governed by the Kennel Club.

Fiennes, Celia (1662–1741), English diarist. Her diaries, published in 1888, give a vivid description of England. Between 1685 and 1703 she travelled extensively in England and enthusiastically detailed the places she visited. She also described the coronations of JAMES II, WILLIAM AND MARY and Queen ANNE.

Fieschi, noble medieval family of Genoa. In the mid-13th century they developed GUELPH inclinations and alliances with Angevin kings of Sicily, when Sinibaldo Fieschi became Pope INNOCENT IV. These factors shaped the family destiny until the great statesman Andrea Doria put Genoa into the control of the Emperor in 1528 and the line ended. Ottobono Fieschi became pope as ADRIAN V in 1276, and Caterina Fieschi (1447–1510) was later canonized as St Catherine of Genoa.

FIFA, Fédération Internationale de Football Association), the governing body of soccer. It was formed in 1904 by representatives from seven European nations; today it is world-wide with six confederations: Africa, Asia, Europe (UEFA), North and Central America and the Caribbean

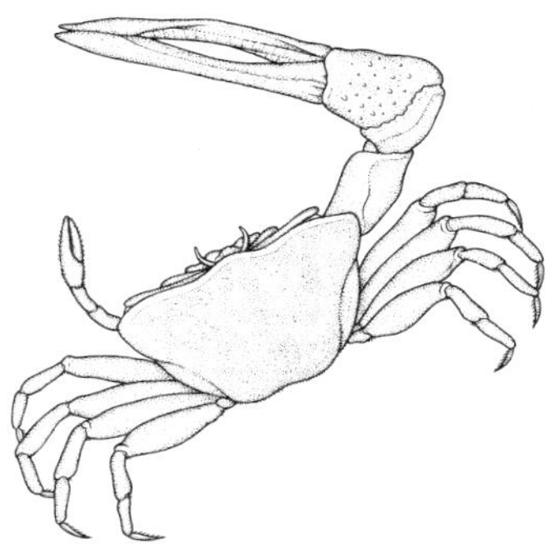

Fiddler crab's large claw, if caught during fighting, can be broken off to allow escape.

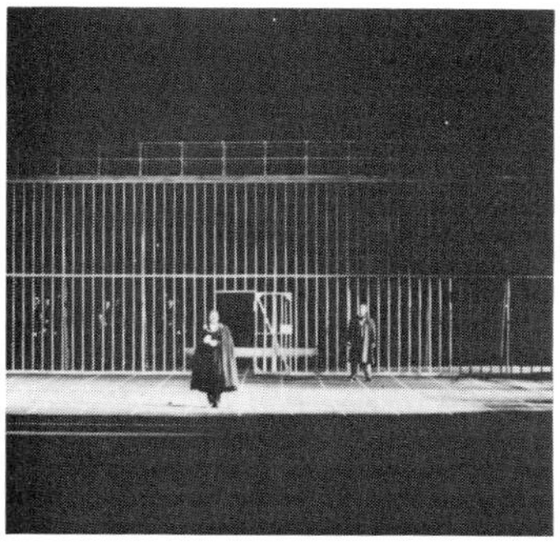

Fidelio; a scene from the production of the opera at La Scala, Milan, in 1960–61.

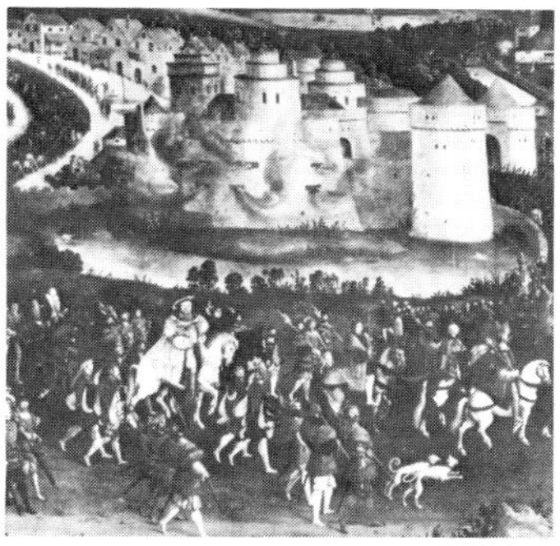

Field of the Cloth of Gold in a painting by Hans Holbein at Hampton Court.

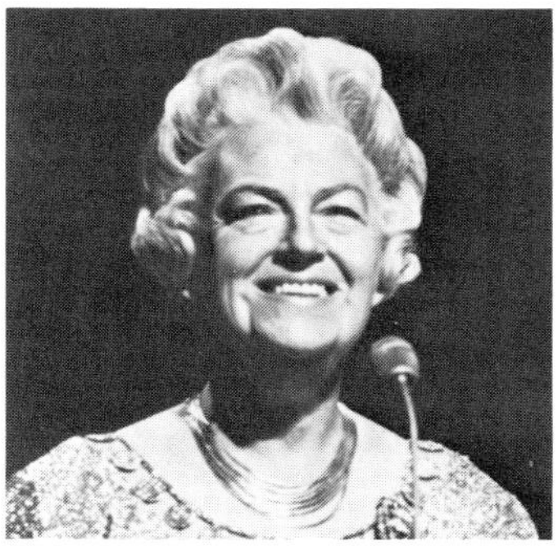

Gracie Fields, when aged 66, rehearsing for the Royal Command Performance of 1964.

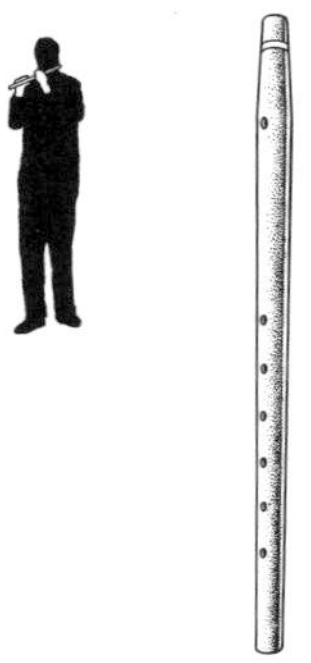

Fife, an instrument thought to have been taken to Britain from Switzerland in the 1500s.

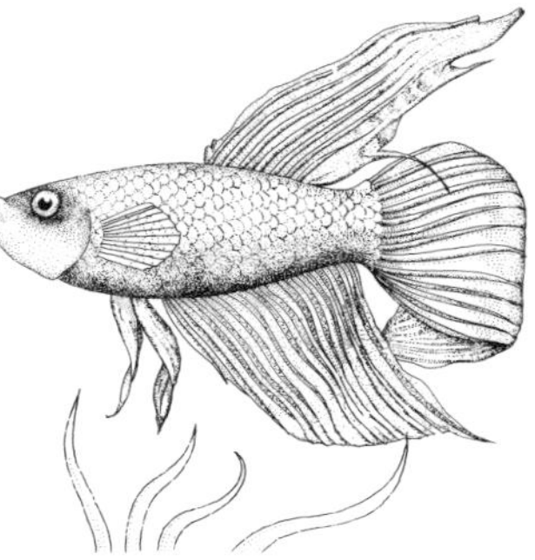

Fighting fish are so belligerent that one will even attack its own reflection in a mirror.

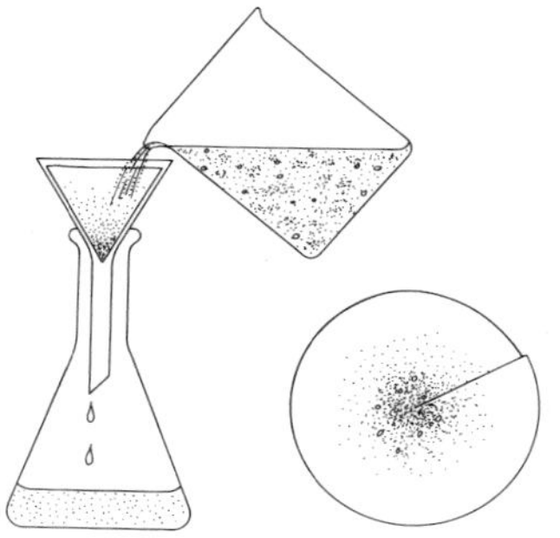

Filtration using paper and a funnel, still commonly used in chemistry laboratories.

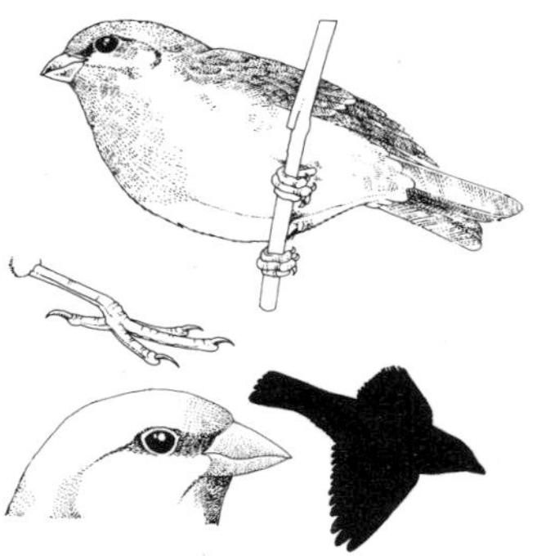

Finch, some of whose species are brilliantly coloured although most are dull; all sing well.

(CONCACAF), Oceania and South America (CONMEBOL). It organizes the four-yearly FIFA World Cup.

Fife, former county and, since 1975, region in E central Scotland between the firths of Tay and Forth. The land is mostly low-lying and the principal crops are cereals, sugar-beet and potatoes; cattle and sheep are also reared. Industries include coal mining and shipbuilding. The main towns are Kirkcaldy and Dunfermline. Area: 1,305sq km (504sq km). Pop. (1975 est.) 336,300.

Fife, shrill-toned musical instrument related to the FLUTE, but with a smaller barrel and usually six fingerholes, sometimes with keys like the PICCOLO. It has been used with drums in military music since the Crusades.

Fifteen, The. *See* JACOBITE REBELLIONS.

Fifth Column, saboteurs, spies and other non-uniformed para-military elements active behind the battle area, working to undermine the enemy's cause. The term dates from the SPANISH CIVIL WAR (1936–39) and described Republican sympathizers in Madrid at the time when four Republican columns were advancing on the city.

Fifth Monarchy Men, religious sect which flourished in England during the COMMONWEALTH and PROTECTORATE. The members' belief, derived from the fifth kingdom prophesied in Daniel 2: 36–45, was in the imminent reappearance of Christ and the establishment of his new monarchy on earth. After two attempted uprisings, in 1657 and 1661, the sect's leaders were executed.

Fig, tree or shrub of the mulberry family, growing in warm regions, especially from the eastern Mediterranean to India and Malaysia. The common fig (*Ficus carica*) has tiny flowers without petals that grow inside fleshy receptacles; these become the thick outer covering holding the seeds, the true fruit of the fig tree. Height: to 11.8m (39ft). Family Moraceae. *See also* NW p.64.

Fighters. *See* AEROPLANE.

Fighting fish, also called betta, or Siamese fighting fish, fresh-water tropical fish of Indo-China and the Malay Peninsula. It is popular in home aquariums because selective breeding has produced brilliantly coloured specimens with long, flowing fins. Males will fight each other until exhausted or injured. Length: 5–7.5cm (2–3in). Family Anabantidae; species *Betta splendens.*

Figurative art, term used to apply to paintings and sculptures that represent recognizable objects or human beings. The term non-figurative art is often used instead of the term "abstract art". Semi-abstract paintings such as those of the Cubists are figurative paintings, insofar as they were loosely based on an objective image.

Figure skating. *See* ICE SKATING.

Figwort, common name for any of 3,000 or more plant species of the genus *Scrophularia.* They are perennial herbacious plants distributed throughout the world. Most species have a strong smell and bear small, greenish-yellow or purple flowers. Family Scrophulariaceae.

Fiji, republic made up of more than 800 islands and islets in the S Pacific Ocean. Discovered by TASMAN in 1643, the islands were annexed by Britain in 1874. It became independent in 1970 and now has dominion status within the Commonwealth. The main products are copra, sugar and rice. The capital is Suva. Area: 18,272sq km (7,055sq miles). Pop. (1975 est.) 573,000. *See also* HC2 pp.*124*, 125, *220*; MW p.76.

Filament lamp, incandescent electric light first developed by Thomas Alva EDISON. Edison's lamp used a carbon filament and was made in 1879. The bulb was partially evacuated. Modern filament lamps comprise tungsten coiled filaments inside an evacuated glass envelope or bulb.

Filariasis, group of tropical disorders caused by infection with a nematode worm, *Filaria,* carried by mosquitoes. The lymph glands are often involved, with swelling and impaired circulation in the infected region preceding lymphatic inflammation. Drug treatment reduces the symptoms. *See also* ELEPHANTIASIS.

Filibuster, method of frustrating the action of a legislative assembly by making long speeches. It has particular reference to debates in the US senate, where the device of reading long passages from the Bible has been used by conservative senators from the south to prevent the passing of liberal legislation.

Filippo, Eduardo de (1900–), Italian playwright and actor. His dialectical comedies, most of which deal with his life in his birthplace, Naples, include *Questi fantasmi* (1946) and *Napoli milionaria* (1945). He also wrote *Saturday Sunday, Monday* and *Filumena,* produced in London in 1973 and 1977 respectively. *Il paese di Pulcinella,* a volume of verse, was published in 1951.

Film festivals, gatherings at which new films are shown to critics and members of the industry; prizes are usually awarded. These important gatherings provide a showcase for new productions and a spur to foreign sales. The Venice Film Festival was first held in 1932, Cannes following in 1947. The other top festivals include West Berlin (from 1951) and Moscow (1935; revived 1957), which alternates with Karlovy Vary, Czechoslovakia (1954). New York, Cork and Edinburgh also hold highly regarded festivals. There are also specialist festivals, such as those held at Trieste (for science fiction) and Oberhausen, West Germany (short films).

Film, photographic, sensitized strips of cellulose acetate or other plastic, coated on one side with a light-sensitive emulsion, used to record photographic images. The emulsion of a black-and-white film consists of a suspension of finely divided grains of silver bromide in gelatin. After exposure the film is kept in darkness until the latent image is made visible by developing and fixing. Film is rated according to its "speed" or sensitivity to light. This is a measure of the size of the silver bromide grains contained in the emulsion. A "fast" black-and-white film (high ASA or DIN numbers) gives rise to a grainy, high-contrast image, whereas "slower" film captures a greater range of tones. Within the two rating systems an ASA number of 50 is equivalent to a DIN number of 18. *See also* MM pp.218–223.

Filter, device for separating solid particles from a liquid or gas. The process is known as filtration. Many complex forms of filter have been devised for various uses. Most cars have a number of filters, for air, petrol and oil. These operate either by trapping solid particles in porous materials such as paper or meshes, or by circulating the material to be filtered through a maze, the pockets of which trap particles, as in the air filter.

Filtration, process of removing solids from liquids by passage through a suitable medium such as filter paper, glass wool or sand. *See also* SU pp.144–*145*.

Final Solution, policy adopted by HITLER by 1942 to exterminate the Jewish race systematically. Before this time he planned other means of dealing with the Jews, such as transporting them to Madagascar. The adoption of the final solution led to the full utilization of extermination camps such as AUSCHWITZ.

Finance, in ECONOMICS, loaning and borrowing of capital to facilitate the purchase, manufacture, development or distribution of goods and services. Finance takes many forms, ranging from the supply of capital necessary to build a power station to that needed to buy furniture. Loans of money are paid back with interest by the borrower.

Finbackwhale. *See* RORQUAL.

Finch, Peter (1916–77), British actor. He played in many stage productions after 1949, but he was most famous for his strong film performances, including roles in *The Trials of Oscar Wilde* (1960) and *Far From the Madding Crowd* (1967). He died shortly after completing *Network,* for which he was awarded a posthumous Oscar.

Finch, any of a family (Fringillidae) of small or medium-sized birds, including SPARROWS, CARDINALS, CANARIES, BUNTINGS and GROSBEAKS. They are found in most parts of the world, except for Australia, New Zealand and the Pacific islands. Most have a cone-shaped bill and feed on seeds, although some eat fruit or insects. Some British "finches", such as the bullfinch and goldfinch, belong to another family, Ploceidae.

Fine Gael, Irish political party. It was founded in 1933 as a successor to the party under William COSGRAVE which had held power since the inception of the IRISH FREE STATE. The party has three times held office in coalition with the Labour Party, in 1948–51, 1954–57 and 1973–77. In the last government its leader, Liam COSGRAVE, was prime minister. *See also* HC2 pp.294–295.

Fingerprint, pattern of ridges in the dermis or deeper skin on the end of the fingers and thumbs. Fingerprints are specific to an individual and remain unchanged in pattern throughout life; for this reason they are useful as a means of identification. Criminological use was first made in Argentina in 1888. The Gatton-Henry system was adopted by Britain's Scotland Yard in 1901, and is the most widely-employed system in the world. Dactyloscopy, the technique of fingerprinting, involves the cleaning of the fingertips in a solvent such as ether, drying them and then rolling each on a glass surface coated with black printer's ink. Each may then be "printed" on to a prepared index card. They may be categorized by the loops, arches and whorls made by the ridges in the deimis. Methods of classifying and filing fingerprints using a computer are being introduced. *See also* MM p.*217*; MS pp. *61*, 190–191, 294–295.

Finland (Suomi), republic in N Europe. Most of the country is low-lying, characterized by many lakes and rivers. There are also thousands of offshore islands. Only a small percentage of land is cultivated, as the economy has always depended on timber and forest-based industries. Area: 337,009sq km (130,092sq miles). Pop. (1976 est.) 4,734,000. *See* MW p.76.

Finland, Gulf of, E part of the Baltic Sea, between Finland and the USSR. The chief ports are Leningrad and Tallinn in the USSR, and Helsinki in Finland. Width: 72–137km (45–85 miles); length: 419km (260 miles).

Finlay, Carlos Juan (1833–1915), Cuban physician who suggested in 1881 that yellow fever was spread by the mosquito. In 1900 a US medical delegation headed by Walter Reed went to Cuba to help confirm the hypothesis.

Finnegans Wake (1939), novel by James JOYCE. A Dublin pub-keeper's dreams portray the cyclical history of civilization, in which Joyce employs the stream-of-consciousness technique. Its linguistic complexity makes it demanding for the reader. *See also* HC2 p.290.

Finney, Albert (1936–), British stage and film actor. He became known for his performances in modern plays such as *Billy Liar* (1960), and John OSBORNE's *Luther* (1961), and has made a number of films including *Tom Jones* (1963) and *Gumshoe* (1971). He has also acted in many classical productions, such as *Hamlet* and *Tamburlaine* with the National Theatre of Great Britain as well as directing the film *Charlie Bubbles.*

Finney, Tom (1922–), British footballer who won 76 national caps (1946–58) in four different positions, scoring 30 goals. He played for Preston North End from 1946–60 and is best remembered as a skilful winger.

Finn Mac Cumhail, or Finn MacCool (*fl.* 2nd or 3rd century AD), semi-mythical Irish leader of a group of soldiers known as the Fenians. Their exploits were recorded in many ballads and poems, including those said to have been by OSSIAN.

Finnmark, most northerly county in Norway, bounded by Finland (S), the Arctic Ocean (N), the Barents Sea (E) and the USSR (SE). The chief occupations are fishing, farming and mining. The capital is Vadsø. Area: 48,648sq km (18,783sq miles). Pop. (1972 est.) 77,100.

Finno-Ugric languages, group of AGGLUTINATIVE LANGUAGES spoken by more than 22 million people in Finland and N Norway, in Estonia and Karelia (in the USSR), in various areas at the N end of the Volga river and each side of the Ural Mts (also USSR) and in Hungary. The Finnic branch includes Finnish, Estonian, Lappish, Mordvinian, Mari, Komi, Votyak, Cheremiss and Zyrian; the Ugric branch comprises Hungarian, Ostyak and Mansi (Vogul). Although together with the SAMOYED languages, Finno-Ugric is said to make up the URALIC sub-family, efforts have been made to relate the group to several ancient tongues, notably Sumerian.

Finsen, Niels Ryberg (1860–1904), Danish physician. He studied the physiological effects of light, particularly the blue end of the spectrum. He set up a clinic in Copenhagen to study light therapy for skin diseases, and was awarded the 1903 Nobel Prize in physiology and medicine.

Finzi, Gerald (1901–56), British composer. He wrote chiefly vocal works, including *Dies Natalis* (1939), a setting of passages from Thomas Traherne, and *Intimations of Immortality* (1950), a setting for tenor, chorus and orchestra of the WORDSWORTH ode.

Fiord, or fjord, narrow, steep-walled inlet on a sea coast. Fiords are found in glacial regions, and so it is assumed that these deeply-cut valleys were formed by GLACIERS as they moved towards the sea. *See also* PE pp.116–117, *116–117.*

Fir, any of a number of evergreen trees of the PINE family, native to cooler, temperate regions of the world. They are pyramid-shaped and have flat needles and erect cones. Species include the silver and balsam firs. Height: 15–91m (50–300ft). Family Pinaceae; genus *Abies.*

Firbank, Ronald (1886–1926), English novelist. His novels, predominantly in dialogue, have little plot or characterization and are marked by an absurdist wit. They include *Vainglory* (1915), *Caprice* (1917), *The Flower Beneath the Foot* (1923) and *Sorrow in Sunlight* (1925).

Firdausi (935–1020), Persian poet, real name Abul Kasim Mansur. Little is known about his life, but he wrote the *Shah Nama* (Book of Kings), an epic poem of more than 50,000 couplets about the history of Persia. The work, which created the traditions of Persian poetry, was presented to Mahmud of Ghazni in 1010.

Fire, combustion of inflammable materials, usually accompanied by flames or smoke. Chemically it is an example of rapid oxidation, and an abundant supply of air or oxygen is generally necessary for a fire to continue to burn. Primitive man learned to control fire for warmth, cooking, making pottery and metal-working. Although fundamental to much technology, uncontrolled it can cause great devastation. The power of fire has always fascinated man and influenced his beliefs and imagination. *See also* MM pp.*21,* 26–27, *53.*

Firearm, weapon from which a projectile is fired, generally by the expansion of gases after the rapid combustion of gunpowder or other explosive. Although occasionally used to describe an ARTILLERY piece, the term generally means a small arm – a weapon carried and fired by one man or a small group of men.

Firearms were used in Europe in the 14th century. They were, however, ineffective in close combat until *c.*1425, when a primitive trigger to bring a lighted match into contact with the gunpowder charge was invented. Such firearms, called MATCHLOCKS, were heavy and cumbersome, and needed a constantly lit match. The lighter FLINTLOCK (which used the spark produced by flint striking steel to ignite the powder) superseded the matchlock in the mid-17th century and became the main infantry weapon for more than 100 years. Cavalry of this period often used the efficient, but more expensive, WHEEL-LOCK.

At the end of the 18th century most firearms were still single-shot, muzzle-loading and smoothbore, working on much the same principle as 14th-century guns. During the 19th century there were great changes. In 1805 the Rev Alexander FORSYTH discovered the explosive properties of mercury fulminate, and together with the percussion cap invented in 1815 it provided a surer, more efficient means of detonation, permitting the development by 1865 of both the centre-fire cartridge (which has basically been the type of ammunition used in firearms ever since) and breech loading, not previously practicable.

Another major 19th-century advance was rifling, the cutting of spiral grooves along the inside of a barrel to make the bullet spin in flight, thus vastly increasing accuracy. The technique had been tried centuries before, but it was not until 1849 and the invention of the MINIÉ rifle that rifling became practical for a mass-produced weapon.

During the 1830s Samuel COLT perfected the REVOLVER, a PISTOL which could fire several shots without the need to reload. By the 1880s magazine RIFLES were also in use, and were made more effective when a bolt action was incorporated after 1889.

The next step was towards a weapon that could fire a continuous stream of bullets. Manually operated systems had been tried (eg the GATLING GUN), but the first modern MACHINE GUN was the MAXIM GUN, invented in the 1880s, which used the recoil energy of the fired bullet to push the next round into the breech and recock the weapon. Guns of this type dominated the trench warfare of WWI, and by WWII more portable automatic weapons, light machine guns such as the BREN GUN and SUB-MACHINE GUNS, were in use.

Most 20th-century firearms operate on principles established in the 19th century. Newer developments, under the stimulus of the emergence of aerial warfare and the TANK, include gas-operated rifles, recoilless rifles, firearms with several rotating barrels and extremely high rates of fire and small firearms that use explosive bullets. *See also* MM pp.162–165, *162–165;* HC2 pp.*188, 322.*

Firebird (1910), ballet in three scenes by Michel FOKINE with music by Igor STRAVINSKY, first produced in Paris by the BALLETS RUSSES. The story is taken from a Russian fairy-tale about Ivan, a prince who captures the Firebird. In return for her freedom she gives him a magical feather with which he may summon her in time of danger.

Fireblight, highly infectious and destructive disease that attacks apples, pears and related fruit trees, causing a blackened, scorched appearance of leaves and twigs. Other symptoms of the disease, caused by the bacterium *Erwinia amylovora,* include cankers on the stems and discoloured flowers and fruit. Control of the disease is difficult and involves spraying the affected plants with antibiotics. Some tree varieties are resistant to the disease.

Firebrick, brick formed in a variety of shapes for use in structures, such as furnace linings, which are exposed to high temperatures. Firebrick is composed of FIRECLAY and other non-metallic, high-melting-point minerals, particularly those rich in silica, aluminium oxide, magnesium and carbon.

Fire brigade, body of professional FIREFIGHTING personnel. Although references to such bodies date possibly back to 4000 BC in China and to the 1st century BC in Rome and while English legislation paid special attention to the use of fire-resistant building materials in 1189 and 1212, it was not until after the Great Fire of London (1666) that regular bodies of firefighters drawn from the ranks of Thames watermen were established. Even these, such as the Phenix (1680) and the Hand-in-Hand (1698) were not officially appointed bodies but affiliated to the fire assurance companies who retained them, and strictly forbidden to assist householders whose property was not insured with their respective employers. In 1709 and 1774, Parliament insisted that London parishes should provide engines and "proper ladders of one, two and three storeys high", but no real provision was made for operating such equipment until in 1832 the brigades of more than 30 rival insurance companies were merged into the London Fire-Engines Establishment.

In 1904, the London Fire Brigade came under the aegis of the LCC and further legislation in 1938 anticipated the severe demands of WWII and insisted on keener co-operation between local brigades supported by well-trained part-time volunteers. In most countries this formula has been adopted and endorsed by the OECD and the International Technical Committee for the Prevention and Extinction of Fire (CTIF).

In Britain the 63 fire authorities employ about 34,000 professional firemen assisted by 17,500 (1977) part-timers; West Germany has 59 such brigades; in addition to the Brigade des Sapeurs-Pompiers in Paris, which was founded by Napoleon in 1811, France maintains forces whose maximum operational radius is no more than 11km (6.8 miles). Australian protection is in the hands of local boards comprising state government, local authority and insurance interests.

Fireclay, clay that can withstand high temperatures without becoming deformed. It is used for making FIREBRICK, crucibles and many refractory shapes. Fireclay approaches KAOLIN in composition; better grades contain at least 35% alumina (Al_2O_3) when fired.

Firedamp, in coal mining, inflammable and explosive gas emitted by coal seams. It is composed mostly of methane (CH_4) but also contains some hydrogen, oxygen and carbon dioxide, and occasionally a little ethane (CH_3CH_3). Firedamp has caused many disastrous pit explosions; it is detectable with a Davy lamp (after Sir Humphry DAVY), the flame of which elongates when the gas is present.

Fire extinguisher, any device used to put out a fire – including a blanket or a bucket of water or sand – but especially a canister filled with chemicals, usually including liquid carbon dioxide, under high pressure, and halogenated hydrocarbons such as carbon tetrachloride, the vapours of which are heavy and so effective in smothering flames. A different kind of chemical extinguisher sprays powdered sodium bicarbonate which, when heated by the flames, releases carbon dioxide and water. Others spray a mixture of water and a foaming agent. *See also* MM p.*249.*

Firefighting, broad term that includes the prevention, detection and extinguishing of fire, especially when lives, property or ecosystems are threatened. Fire prevention involves the control of fire hazards in industry and the home; it includes regulations to produce fireproof materials for the manufacture of goods. Fire protection involves the detection and extinguishing of fires and includes measures aimed at the reduction of losses of life and property. It therefore involves the compulsory provision of fire escapes, fire extinguishers, organized fire drills, firefighting personnel, and overhead heat-sensitive equipment in large buildings, designed to sound an alarm or turn on sprinklers if a fire starts. Public firefighting vehicles carry water, flame-retarding foam, ladders and heavy equipment to deal with most problems that could arise at the scene of a fire. At large airports these appliances or tenders may be specialized to carry enormous quantities of foam-producing chemicals to smother fires that result from the spillage of fuel. *See also* MM p.249.

Firefly, light-emitting beetle found in moist places of temperate and tropical regions. Organs underneath the abdomen usually give off rhythmic flashes of light that are typical of the species. The luminous larvae and wingless females of some species are called GLOW-WORMS. Length: to 25mm (0.9in). There are 1,000 species. Family Lampyridae.

Firenze. *See* FLORENCE.

Fire of London (2–6 Sept. 1666), fire that destroyed most of the City of London. It started in a baker's shop in Pudding Lane, on a site now marked by The Monument, and a strong east wind spread it quickly through the closely-packed wooden

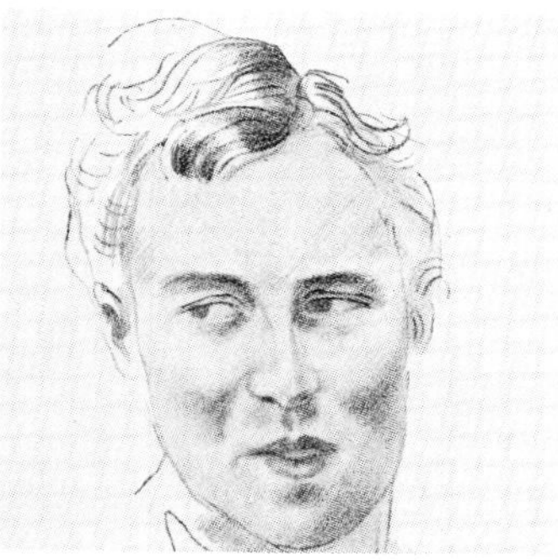

Ronald Firbank was little regarded in his lifetime, but his work is now more popular.

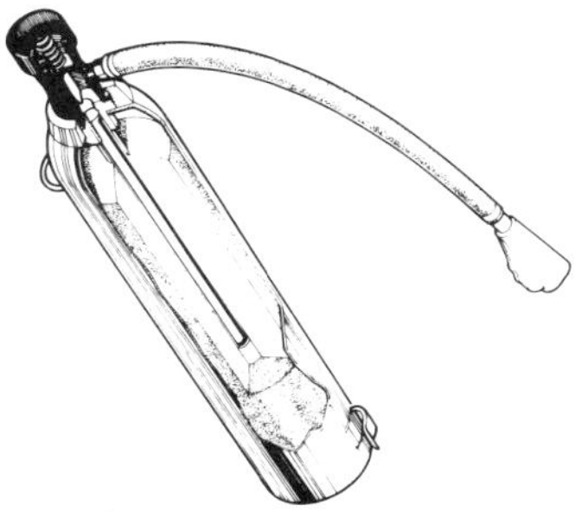

Fire extinguisher; different types are required, depending on the material burning.

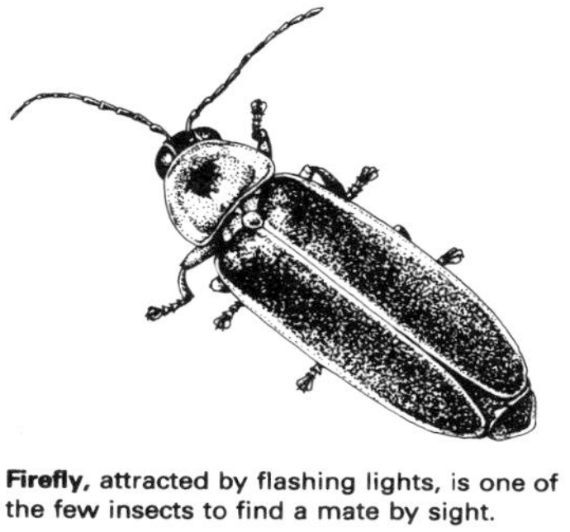

Firefly, attracted by flashing lights, is one of the few insects to find a mate by sight.

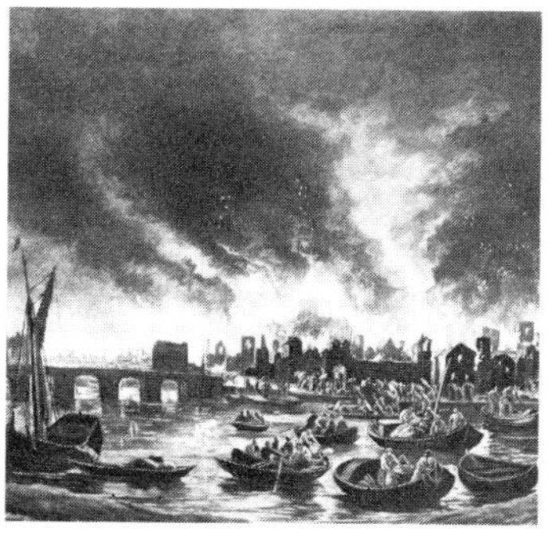

Fire of London in an engraving after a painting of the great disaster by Lieven Verschour.

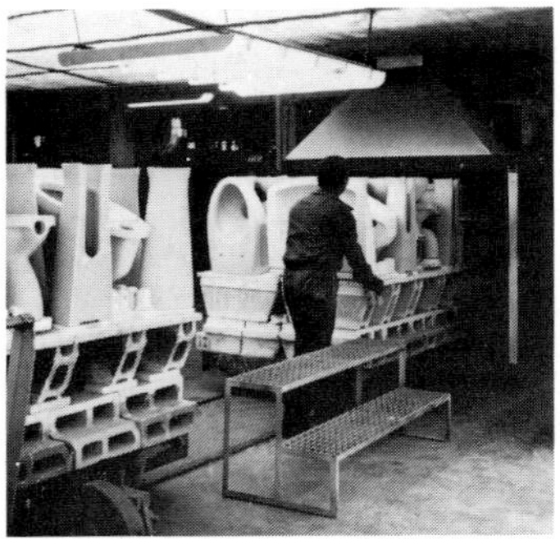

Firing of china and ceramics is today carried out under highly mechanized conditions.

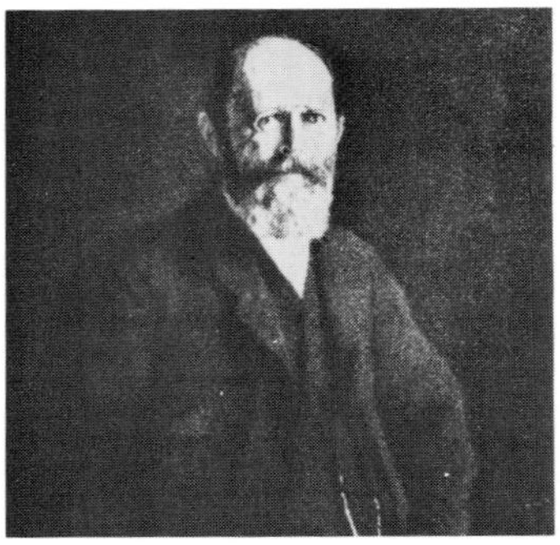

Emil Fischer was a chemist who taught at the university of Berlin from 1892 until his death.

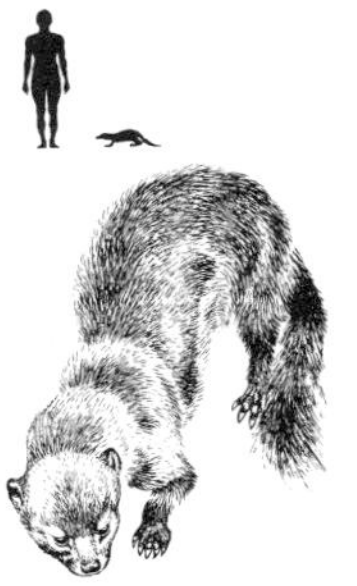

Fisher, a member of the weasel family, also known as Pennant's marten and black cat.

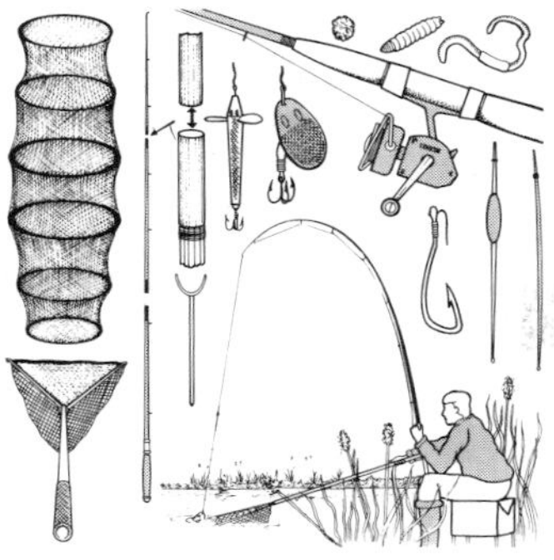

Fishing; some bait, hooks, floats, nets, rods and other tackle used in this popular sport.

houses. The fire provided an opportunity (which was never completely realized) for rebuilding London on a more spacious plan. *See also* HC1 p.295.

Fire-proofing, impregnation of inflammable materials such as household carpets, curtains and theatre hangings and scenery with fire-retarding chemical solutions containing such salts as ammonium sulphate and ammonium phosphate. Lightweight textiles can be fire-proofed with similar solutions. *See also* ASBESTOS.

Firestone, Harvey Samuel (1868–1938), US industrialist. He founded the Firestone Co. in Akron in 1900, and was the first to manufacture the pneumatic tyres used on the Ford Model T car. In 1926 he founded rubber plantations in Liberia.

Fireworks, or pyrotechnics, controlled EXPLOSIVES (and their spectacular display) that are intended for visual rather than destructive effects. They range from light- and sparkle-emitting capsules and coils, to rockets that burst into miniature "galaxies of stars" after a short near-vertical flight. Fireworks began with the ancient Chinese, who first used them in the 8th or 9th centuries. They spread to Europe in the 12th and 13th centuries, along with the military uses of GUNPOWDER. Besides gunpowder, potassium chlorate mixtures came to be used as explosives and propellants; iron filings and magnesium and aluminium powders were incorporated to provide sparkle and brilliance; and fireworks were coloured brightly by the inclusion of salts of the metals sodium (yellow), barium (green), strontium (red) and copper (blue). Fireworks find serious applications in Very lights and distress rockets and flares. *See also* MM pp.242–*243*.

Firing, heating of ceramics until they are chemically changed; the process prevents a return to the plastic state. Many ceramic clays contain matter that must vitrify (fuse) to render the ware non-porous. This may require temperatures of up to 1,450°C (2,650°F). Firing is done in KILNS, or ovens. *See also* MM pp.44–45, *52*.

Firn, hard-packed mountain snow that has been converted into granular ice in a mountain glacier and, with an accumulation of broken rock materials at its base, digs out round basins called CIRQUES. *See also* PE p.116, *116*.

First aid, emergency attention administered by a person without sophisticated medical training. Some form of training is, however, advisable in order to learn the few basic techniques that may help to save life. *See* MS.p.132–133.

First of June, Battle of the (1794), naval engagement between British and French fleets off the coast of Brittany. The French under Louis Villaret de Joyeuse, protecting a convoy of US ships carrying grain to Brest, were attacked by Admiral Richard Howe. The convoy escaped but the French lost six ships.

First World War. *See* WORLD WAR I.

Firth, Raymond William (1901–). British anthropologist. Born in New Zealand, he carried out much of his work in the Pacific region. He was professor of anthropology at London 1944–68, and wrote *Human Types* (1938) and *Social Change in Tikopia* (1959).

Firth of Clyde. *See* CLYDE, FIRTH OF.

Firth of Forth. *See* FORTH, FIRTH OF.

Fischer, Emil Hermann (1852–1919), German chemist who was awarded the 1902 Nobel Prize in chemistry for his work on the synthesis of sugars and PURINE substances. His important organic chemistry research contributed substantially to the knowledge of purines. He was the first to recognize the importance of STEREOCHEMISTRY, and he was fundamental in establishing ENZYME chemistry. He synthesized glucose and fructose in addition to several other sugars.

Fischer, Ernst Otto (1918–), German chemist. He became professor of chemistry in Munich in 1957 and was awarded the Nobel Prize in chemistry in 1973 jointly with Geoffrey WILKINSON for their work on organometallic chemistry.

Fischer, Hans (1881–1945), German biochemist who received the 1930 Nobel Prize in chemistry for his structural studies of CHLOROPHYLL and of the red blood pigment haemin. His research indicated the close relationship between these two substances, and he was able to synthesize haemin and almost completely to synthesize one of the chlorophylls. He also studied CAROTENE.

Fischer, Johann Michael (1692–1766), German architect. His best-known work is the BENEDICTINE abbey church at Ottobeuren (1748–67) which has an exuberantly designed interior. His ROCOCO style is also seen in the church at Rott-am-Inn (1760) and the Church of St Anna in Munich (1727–36).

Fischer, Robert James ("Bobby") (1943–), US chess player, world champion (1972–75) and US champion (1958–60, 1962–63). A temperamental and controversial competitor, in 1975 he refused to defend his world title.

Fischer von Erlach, Johann Bernhard (1656–1723), Austrian architect who combined PALLADIAN and other styles to create a new style, Austrian BAROQUE. His many notable palaces and churches include the Schönbrunn Palace (1696–1711), and the Karlskirche (1716), both in Vienna.

Fischer-Dieskau, Dietrich (1925–), German baritone. One of the foremost operatic singers of the 20th century, he was an extremely versatile singer, appearing in recitals, as soloist with orchestras, in operatic roles and in recordings. He is also an outstanding interpreter of LIEDER.

Fish, cold-blooded, aquatic vertebrate animal characterized by fins, gills for breathing, a streamlined body almost always covered by scales or bony plates on to which a layer of mucus is secreted, and a four-chambered heart. Fish are the most ancient form of vertebrate life, with a history of about 450 million years. They reproduce bisexually and fertilization may be external or internal. The eggs develop in water or inside the female, according to species. Fish have lateral line organs, which are fluid-filled pits and channels that run under the skin of the body. Sensitive fibres link these channels to the central nervous system and detect changes of pressure in the water and changes of strength and direction in currents.

About three-quarters of all fish live in the sea; the remainder are freshwater species that live in lakes, rivers and streams. A few fish, such as SALMON and EELS migrate freely between salt and fresh-water habitats. There are more than 22,000 species of bony fish and they represent about 40% of all living vertebrates. They are divided into 34 orders and 48 families. The classification of fish varies. They are usually divided into two superclasses: Agnatha, which are jawless fish, including the HAGFISH and LAMPREY; and Pisces. Pisces are divided into two main classes: Chondrichthyes (cartilaginous fish), including the subclasses Elasmobranchii (SHARKS, SKATES and RAYS) and Holocephali (CHIMERAS); Osteichthyes (bony fish), including subclasses of soft-rayed fish (LUNGFISH and lobefin), and the higher bony fish. *See also* NW pp.*24*, *75*, 123–129, *131*, *180*, 241; PE pp.150, *156*, 240–47.

Fishbourne, Roman palace in Sussex, England, dating from the 1st century AD. It is one of the largest Roman palaces outside Italy, and was probably built for a British chieftain, Cogidubnus, who supported the Romans. It has several fine mosaic floors and a formal garden. The palace was destroyed by fire in the 3rd century and not rediscovered until 1960.

Fisher, Saint John (*c.* 1469–1535), English Roman Catholic prelate. Fisher opposed HENRY VIII's proposed divorce from CATHERINE OF ARAGON in 1529. He was tried and executed for denying that Henry was supreme head of the church under the Act of Supremacy. He was canonized in 1935.

Fisher, Andrew (1862–1928), Australian politician, *b.* Scotland. He entered the first federal parliament in 1901 as a Labor member and was Prime Minister in 1908–09 and 1910–13. He was Australian high commissioner in London 1916–21.

Fisher, Herbert Albert Laurens (1865–1940), British statesman and historian. As President of the Board of Education (1916–22) his education bill of 1918 established compulsory education in England to the age of 14.

Fisher, John Arbuthnot ("Jackie"), 1st Baron Fisher of Kilverstone (1841–1920), British naval officer. He achieved prominence in the Crimean and China wars (1859–60). As First Sea Lord (1904–15), he reorganized and re-equipped the Royal Navy. He resigned in opposition to the Gallipoli campaign.

Fisher, large, long-tailed MARTEN of North America that has commercially valuable fur, which is brown to black with white-tipped outer hairs. Good climbers and carnivorous, fishers are among the few known predators of porcupines. Length: 1m (3.5ft); weight: to 6.8kg (15lb). Family Mustelidae; species *Martes pennanti. See also* SABLE.

Fishing, popular fresh-water or marine sport. The two basic types of fresh-water fishing are fly-casting and bait-casting. The object is to "play" the fish rather than reel it in forcibly, so the equipment used for rods and reels is light. Bait is either live (worms, insects or minnows) or artificial (flies or lures), and bait-casting requires a sturdy rod and reel. Salt-water fishing generally requires heavier rods and reels, and includes trolling and casting from the beach, or trolling and sea-bed fishing. Fishing is also a major industry and provides food and employment for many maritime nations. *See also* PE pp.*46*, 240–1, 246–7.

Fishing cat, small wild cat of forests and grasslands of South-East Asia. It lives on the banks of streams from which it catches fish; rodents and birds are also taken as prey. Length: 1.6m (3.4ft) overall. Family Felidae; species *Felis viverrina.*

Fishing eagle. *See* EAGLE; OSPREY.

Fish louse, common parasitic CRUSTACEAN found on the skin or in the gill cavities of fresh-water fish. It has a flattened body, one pair of compound eyes and a shield-like carapace. It uses a poisonous spine and two suckers on its jaws to attach itself to the host. Order Branchiura.

Fiske, Bradley Allen (1854–1942), US naval officer and inventor. He invented an electrically powered turret, turbine-driven torpedo, telescopic sight and electric rangefinder, the latter used successfully in the battle of Manila Bay in 1898.

Fission, form of asexual reproduction in which the parent cell divides into two or more daughter cells. Binary fission produces two equal daughter cells (as in bacteria and blue-green algae). Multiple fission produces 4, 8 or 16 daughter cells, each developing into a new organism. *See also* NW pp.80–81.

Fission, nuclear. *See* NUCLEAR ENERGY.

Fistoulari, Anatol Grigorevich (1907–), Russian conductor. At the age of seven, he conducted Tchaikovsky's sixth symphony in Kiev. In 1937 he made his first tour of the USA; after WWII he was associated with the London Philharmonic Orchestra.

Fitch, John (1743–98), US inventor. In 1787 he built what is believed to be the first US steamboat. He constructed and operated another steamboat on the Delaware River (1787–90), having secured exclusive rights to operate in New Jersey, Pennsylvania, New York, Delaware and Virginia.

Fitch, Ralph (*fl.* 1583–1611), English explorer. He travelled overland to India in 1583, and traded with Mogul emperor AKBAR. Three years later he became the first European to visit Burma and Siam.

Fitness, physical, capacity of the body to withstand stress, to perform work and to resist disease. The type of fitness required by an individual depends on the types of stress he must overcome. Short spells of maximum effort lasting less than 10 seconds require anaerobic fitness, which is the state in which the body can function without oxygen in the blood. Aerobic fitness is required for efforts of longer duration. Orthostatic fitness gives the body the ability to adjust to a sudden change in posture.

Fitt, Gerard (1926–), Northern Irish politician. He has represented Belfast West at Westminster as a Social and

Democratic Labour Party member since 1966. He has been leader of the party since 1970 and was the only SDLP candidate to be returned at the two elections of 1974. He was also a member of the Northern Irish Constitutional Convention of 1975–76.

Fitzgerald, Edward (1809–83), British author and translator. His most noted achievement was his free translation from the Persian of the *Rubáiyat of Omar Khayyám* (1859). He also translated *Calderon* (1853) and *Aeschylus* (1865).

Fitzgerald, Ella (1918–), US jazz singer who won world acclaim for her smooth, effortless style in jazz, blues and popular "standards" by George GERSHWIN and Cole PORTER. Her first hit song was *A Tisket a Tasket* (1938). A cabaret and concert-hall artist, she has toured many countries and made numerous recordings.

Fitzgerald, Francis Scott Key (1896–1940), US author. He began his first novel, *This Side of Paradise* (1920), while in the army, which he entered in 1917. This book, with *The Beautiful and the Damned* (1922), established him as a chronicler of the "Jazz Age". During most of the 1920s he lived in Europe mingling with wealthy and sophisticated expatriates. His masterpiece, *The Great Gatsby*, was published in 1925. His last novels were *Tender is the Night* (1934) and the unfinished *The Last Tycoon* (1941). *See also* HC2 p.*289*.

Fitzgerald, George Francis (1851–1901), Irish physicist who researched into ELECTROLYSIS and electric waves and who is noted for his electromagnetic theory of radiation. As an explanation of the MICHELSON-MORLEY EXPERIMENT, he suggested the theory that objects change length (the Lorentz-Fitzgerald contraction) due to their movement through the ETHER.

Fitzgerald, James Edward (1818–1896), New Zealand politician and journalist, *b.* Britain. He was leader of the House of Representatives in New Zealand's first parliament. He founded the Christchurch newspaper *The Press* in 1857.

Fitzgerald, Robert David (1902–), Australian poet. His work, such as *Between Two Tides* (1952) and *This Night's Orbit* (1953), explores the problems of action and responsibility.

Fitzherbert, Maria Anna (1756–1837), wife of GEORGE IV of England when he was Prince of Wales. They were wed secretly in 1785, but the marriage was illegal by the Royal Marriages Act (he being under age). She lived with him until 1803 and remained close to him after his official marriage to CAROLINE OF BRUNSWICK.

Fitzroy, Robert (1805–65), British naval commander, explorer and meteorologist. He was captain of the *Beagle* (1828–36), on which Charles DARWIN served as naturalist, and assisted Darwin in writing an account of the voyages. He later served as governor-general of New Zealand. (1843–45).

Fitzroy, two rivers in Australia. One, in E central Queensland, is formed by the confluence of the Dawson and Mackenzie rivers. It flows E to the Pacific Ocean at Rockhampton. Length: 290km (180 miles). The second, in N Western Australia, rises in the King Leopold Mts and flows W and NW to King Sound in the Indian Ocean. Length: 564km (350 miles).

Fitzsimmons, Robert ("Bob") (1862–1917), British-born boxer who began his career in New Zealand and earned world fame in the USA. He was world middleweight champion (1891–97), and took the world heavyweight title from James J. CORBETT (1897) but lost it to James J. JEFFRIES (1899). He later became world light-heavyweight champion (1903–05).

Fitzwilliam, William (1526–99), English political figure. Lord deputy of Ireland (1572–75, 1588–94), he suppressed rebellions caused by the "plantation" scheme of settling Scots and English in Ireland.

Fiume. *See* RIJEKA.

Five, The, or "The Russian Five", group of prominent Russian composers who consciously promoted nationalism in Russian music in the late 19th century. Its members were Mili BALAKIREV, Alexander BORODIN, Cesar CUI, Modest MUSSORGSKY and Nikolai RIMSKY-KORSAKOV. *See also* HC2 p.107.

Five-leaved sheep fescue. *See* FESCUE.

Five Nations Indians. *See* SIX NATIONS INDIANS.

Fives, game in which players alternately hit a small cork-and-rubber ball against a wall with a gloved hand. There are three major kinds: Eton, Rugby and Winchester, named after the British schools where they were devised. Eton fives is played to eccentric rules by two pairs in a three-walled court incorporating a buttress and step. This resembles the playing conditions of the early 19th century, when boys hit a ball against the chapel wall. Only the serving side can score; first to score 12 wins, usually in five games. Rugby and Winchester fives are played as singles or doubles in a four-walled court, the Winchester variation having a small buttress on the left-hand wall. Usually the first to score 15 (or sometimes 11) wins in Rugby fives and only the receiver can score; in Winchester fives it is the server.

Five-year Plan, series of economic goals, especially those set by the USSR. Introduced by Joseph STALIN in 1928 to develop the country as quickly as possible, the ultimate aim was an agriculturally and industrially self-sufficient nation. The idea was to increase production by setting targets for manufactured goods and agricultural products; bonuses were given when quotas were reached ahead of time. Other Communist countries as well as some developing nations have adopted the practice as a spur to economic growth. *See also* HC2 p.*198*.

Fixation of nitrogen, chemical or biological process that converts atmospheric nitrogen into useful or life-supporting chemical compounds. In industry, nitrogen is fixed using the HABER PROCESS to make ammonia. In biology, certain bacteria and blue-green algae fix nitrogen, either freely in the soil or as symbionts in the roots and other parts of higher plants. *See also* NITROGEN CYCLE.

Fixer, photographic, solution in which photographic film or paper is immersed after development to remove unexposed and unreduced silver halide and render the image stable. Sodium thiosulphate (hypo) is usually used, often acidified to avoid staining. *See also* MM p.219, *219*.

Fizeau, Armand Hippolyte Louis (1819–96), French physicist, the first to accurately determine the speed of light in both air and water. Fizeau also took (with Léon Foucault) the first clear photograph of the sun. He researched the polarization of light, the expansion of crystals and the DOPPLER EFFECT, and looked for methods of increasing the life of Daguerrotypes.

Flag. *See* IRIS.

Flag, symbol of national identity deriving from earlier standards of personal or local significance. The modern national flag has its origin in the standards of the rulers and armies of ancient Middle Eastern civilizations, the oldest flag in existence being a metal one from Iran, about 5,000 years old. *See also* MW pp.17–23.

Flagellants, sinners who regard flagellation, or being flogged, as a means of doing penance. The now almost obsolete practice has at various times been part of many religions. The earliest Christian flagellants were active in the 4th century; in the mid-13th century they became widespread in Germany and Italy. Fear of the BLACK DEATH in the 1340s caused itinerant flagellant groups to become common throughout Europe; but as they went from town to town imploring the populace in general to repent, mortify themselves and be saved, usually under the direction of a priest, they may have been disease-carriers themselves. They were condemned by the pope in 1349. Flagellation reappeared for a time under the auspices of the JESUITS in the 16th century.

Flagellate, any of numerous single-celled organisms that possess, at some stage of their development, one or several whip-like structures (flagella) for locomotion and sensation. Most have a single nucleus and many have a thin firm covering (pellicle) or a jelly-like coating composed of CELLULOSE or CHITIN. They are divided into two major groups; the phytoflagellates resemble plants, the zooflagellates resemble animals. Reproduction is by FISSION (asexual) or sexual, involving the production of GAMETES. Flagellates may be solitary or colonial. *See also* NW pp.26–27.

Flageolet, originally a French 17th century instrument, although English flageolets were produced in the 19th century. Similar to the recorder and penny whistle, it is now largely obsolete.

Flagstad, Kirsten (1895–1962), Norwegian soprano. She first performed in 1913, but was little known outside Scandinavia until her debut at the METROPOLITAN OPERA in 1935. She was famous for her performances of WAGNER and was the first director of the Royal Norwegian Opera (1958–60).

Flaherty, Robert Joseph (1884–1951), pioneer US director of documentary films. In Canada he made *Nanook of the North* (1922) about Eskimo life, followed by *Moana* (1926), an idyllic treatment of Samoa. Other major films include *Industrial Britain* (1932) and *Louisiana Story* (1948). *See also* HC2 pp.276, *276*.

Flambard, Ranulf (*d.* 1128), English state official and ecclesiastic. He was the keeper of the seal under WILLIAM I and the chief minister of WILLIAM II. In 1099 he was made Bishop of Durham, but fled to France to escape the persecution of HENRY I. In 1101 he was restored to his bishopric.

Flamboyant style, final phase of French GOTHIC architecture (14–16th century). The name comes from the flame-like forms of the elaborate tracery used in cathedrals, as on the west façade of Rouen cathedral (1370). *See also* HC1 p.218.

Flamen, priest dedicated to a single god in the polytheistic religion of ancient Rome. A patrician, he would offer sacrifices under the supervision of a chief priest, wearing a conical cap called an apex.

Flamenco, traditional song, dance and instrumental music of Andalusia, s Spain. Flamenco consists of improvisation within strict rules. There are three types of song, of which the most demanding is the *cante hondo*. The dances epitomize pride, poise and sensuality. Songs and dances are accompanied by handclaps, finger-snapping and a series of complicated and rhythmic rolls on the guitar.

Flame test, in chemistry, test for the presence of metallic elements whose main spectral emission lines give characteristic colours in a Bunsen flame. A salt of the metal is introduced into the flame by means of platinum wire first dipped in hydrochloric acid. Some metals and their colours are: lithium, red; sodium, yellow; potassium, lilac; strontium, crimson; barium, apple-green; copper, blue-green; lead and arsenic, blue. *See also* SU p.150.

Flamingo, long-necked, long-legged wading bird of tropical and subtropical lagoons and lakes. The birds have webbed feet and a plumage that varies in colour from pale to deep pink; their wings have black feathers at the edges. Their bills have fine hair-like filters which strain muddy water from the aquatic plants and small marine animals on which the birds feed. Flamingos nest and wade in groups. Height: to 1.5m (5ft). Family Phoenicopteridae.

Flammarion, Nicolas Camille (1842–1925), French astronomer and popularizer of his subject. He studied the Moon's craters and the canals of Mars. In later life he turned to psychical research.

Flamsteed, John (1646–1719), British astronomer, the first Astronomer Royal (1675). His book *British Catalogue of Stars* contained a record of his observations and listed nearly 3,000 stars; it was the most accurate of the time and became the standard work for many years.

Flanagan, Bud (1896–1968), British comedian, real name Robert Winthrop, famous for his partnership with Chesney Allen from 1920 and their later association with the Crazy Gang. With his old fur coat and battered straw boater, Flanagan popularized many songs, including *Run Rabbit Run* and *Underneath the Arches*.

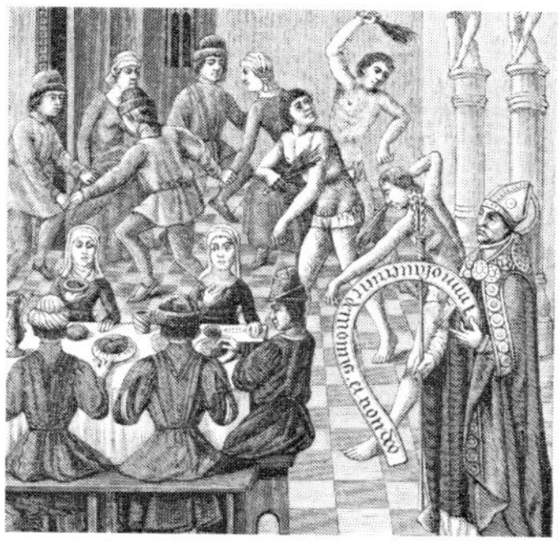

Flagellants; the bishop's streamer reads: "They sacrifice to Satan, and not to God."

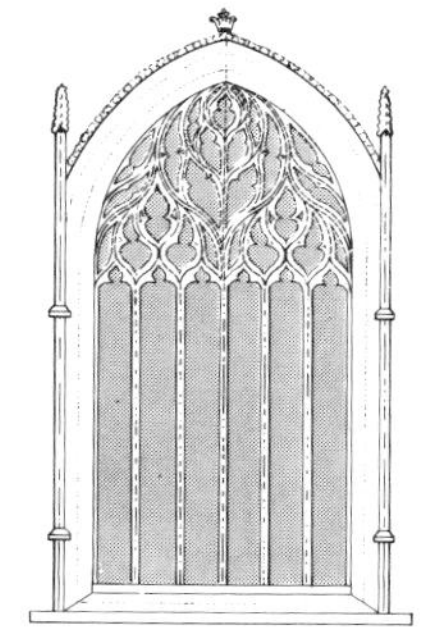

Flamboyant style, by the middle of the 15th century, dominated French architecture.

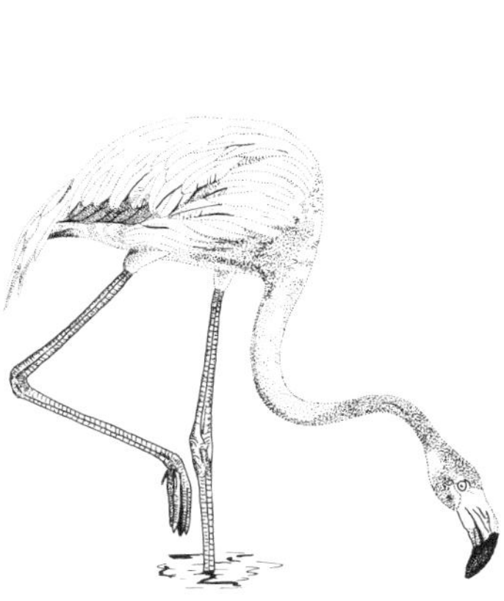

Flamingo mates once a year, its single egg taking about 30 days to hatch.

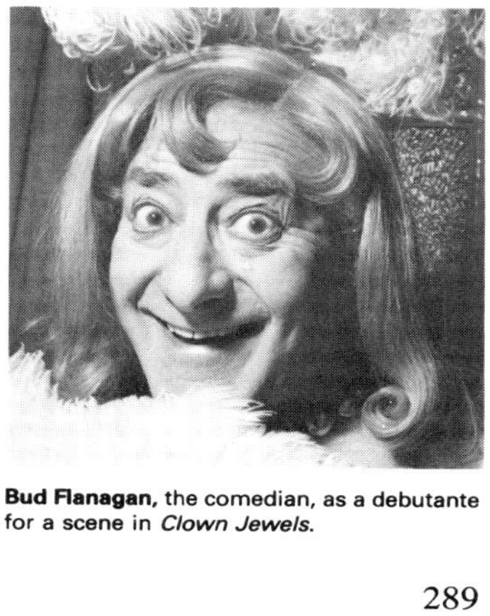

Bud Flanagan, the comedian, as a debutante for a scene in *Clown Jewels*.

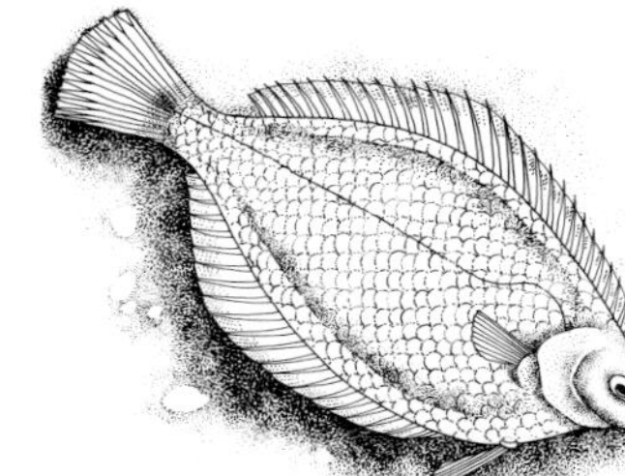

Flatfish lie on one side, both eyes being located on the "upper" side of the head.

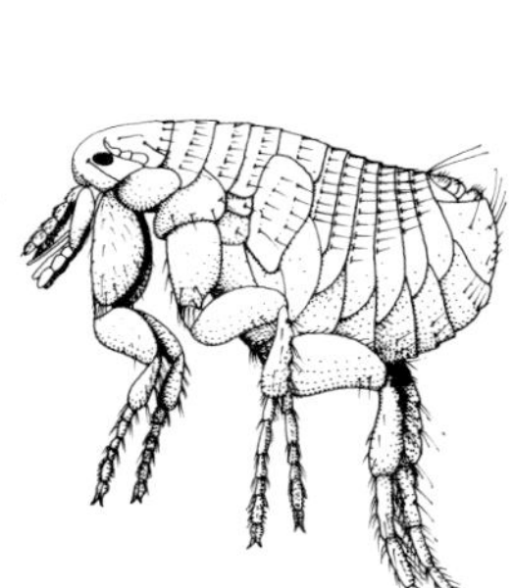

Flea; the species that lives on human beings can jump as far as 33cm (13in).

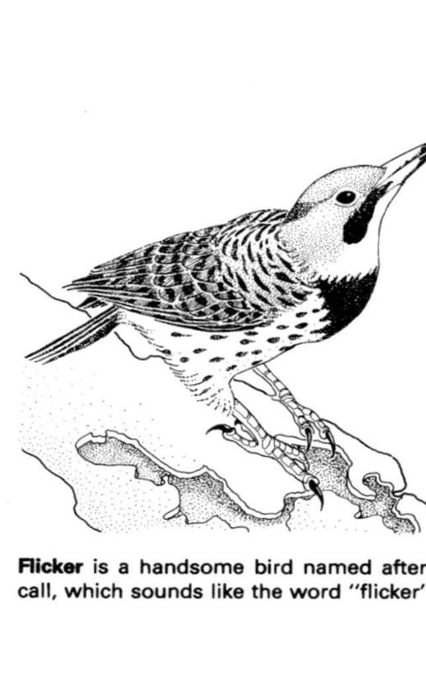

Flicker is a handsome bird named after its call, which sounds like the word "flicker".

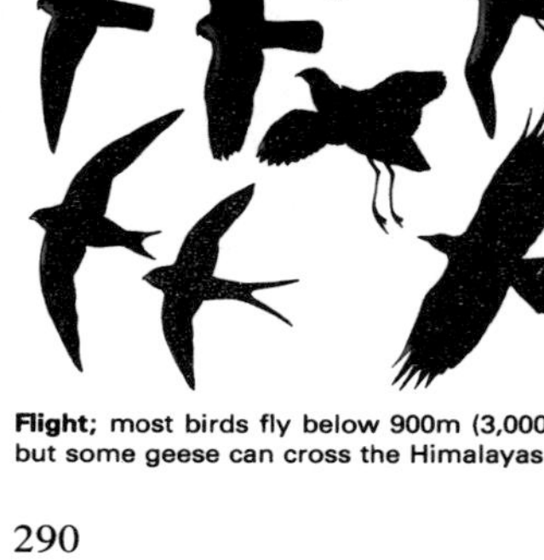

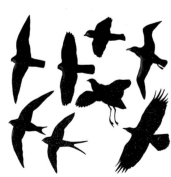

Flight; most birds fly below 900m (3,000ft), but some geese can cross the Himalayas.

Flanders (Vlaanderen, or Flandre), former county in W Belgium and France, encompassing the modern boundaries of E and W Flanders provinces, Belgium, and a portion of France's Nord département. By the 13th century the Flemish cloth industry was the most important in Europe, and the area prospered. The industry declined in the late 15th century and the area was incorporated into the Spanish Netherlands in 1584. Louis XIV annexed portions in 1668 and part of the region was ceded to France (1797), but was later awarded to The Netherlands. Its strategic position has made it a battleground since the Middle Ages. *See also* HC1 pp.252–253, *252–253*.

Flannan Islands (Seven Hunters), group of seven uninhabited islands off NW Scotland, 32km (20 miles) NW of the Isle of Lewis.

Flare, solar. *See* SUN.

Flashback, film technique in which chronological continuity is broken to shown relevant action from the past. Visual signs such as momentary fades are often used to indicate a flashback. The technique has been used in many films since the 1930s, notably in CITIZEN KANE (1941).

Flash bulb, in photography, small glass bulb filled with finely shredded aluminium and a small amount of magnesium; it is ignited by electricity to produce a high-intensity flash of light of short duration as a photograph is taken. It is used either as a substitute for or supplement to available light. *See also* MM p.*221*.

Flashlight. *See* FLASH BULB; TORCH.

Flashpoint, lowest temperature at which an inflammable liquid heated under test conditions gives off sufficient vapour to be ignited (as a flash) when a flame is applied.

Flat, in musical notation, an accidental or sign placed before a note or immediately after the clef to indicate that the note it refers to should be sounded a semitone lower. It is designated by the sign♭.

Flat feet, condition in which the arches of the feet are lowered, often accompanied by other distortions in foot structure. It frequently causes pain in the instep, and arch supports may be prescribed to alleviate the condition.

Flatfish, any of more than 500 species of bottom-dwelling, mainly marine fish found throughout the world. Most flatfish have oval flattened bodies. Both eyes are on the upper side; the "blind" lower side is generally white. Examples include the halibut, flounder, plaice, dab, turbot and sole. Order Pleuronectiformes. *See also* NW p.*130*.

Flatford Mill on the River Stour, oil on canvas painting by John CONSTABLE, dated 1817. *Flatford Mill* is a development of the traditional realistic qualities of the earlier *Boat Building* (1815) and is infused with an exhilarating, original and truthful treatment of light peculiar to the English countryside. It is now in the Tate Gallery, London.

Flathead Indians, term applied to many North American Indian tribes, from their custom of deforming the heads of infants to develop an elongated skull to a socially desirable shape. The term is used most commonly to refer to the CHINOOK. Inhabitants of the Flathead Reservation in Montana, also called Salish Indians, never followed this practice; although they were referred to as "flatheads" by neighbouring tribes that shaped their heads in a pointed style.

Flats, in the theatre, units of scenery made of stretched canvas or hardboard mounted on wooden batten frames and usually erected in various combinations to provide a three-dimensional stage set.

Flatworm, simple, carnivorous, ribbon-like creature which, having no circulatory system and sometimes no mouth or gut, feeds by absorption through its body wall. Most are aquatic. The FLUKE and TAPEWORM are both parasites of man and animals. Order Platyhelminthes. *See also* NW pp.86–87; MS pp.*85*, 93, 106–107.

Flaubert, Gustave (1821–80), French novelist. He spent most of his life in Rouen among the provincial bourgeoisie who inhabit most of his novels. He wrote *The Temptation of St Anthony* (1847), *Madame Bovary* (1857), *Salammbô* (1862) and *Sentimental Education* (1869).

Flax, slender, erect, flowering plant cultivated for its fibres and seeds. After harvesting the stems are retted (soaked in water) to soften the fibres, which are spun into yarn to make linen. The seeds yield linseed oil. Family Linaceae. *See also* PE pp.216–217.

Flaxman, John (1755–1826), British artist and sculptor. He is best known for his memorial sculptures, including those of Sir Joshua Reynolds and Lord Nelson (in St Paul's Cathedral, London); he also illustrated the works of Homer, Dante and others.

Flea, any of 1,000 species of wingless, leaping insects found throughout the world. All fleas are external parasites on warm-blooded animals. In moving from one host to another they can be important carriers of disease. Length: to 1cm (0.4in). Order Siphonaptera. *See also* NW pp.106–107.

Fleabane, any of about 250 species of plants of the genus *Erigeron* that grow in temperature climates. Most have lance-shaped leaves and daisy-like flowers with yellow central discs and white, yellow, pink or purple ray florets. Some species are cultivated in gardens. Height: to 1m (3.3ft). Family Compositae.

Flea-beetle, any of several small beetles, found throughout the world, whose enlarged hindlegs make them excellent jumpers. They feed on leaves and some are regarded as serious pests of crops. Family Chrysomelidae.

Flecker, Herman James Elroy (1884–1915), British poet and playwright. His Foreign Office service in the Middle East influenced the character of his poetry, already evident in *Bridge of Fire* (1907). His verse play *Hassan* was extremely successful when it was produced in 1922 with music by DELIUS. He died of tuberculosis.

Fledermaus, Die (1874), three-act opera by Johann Strauss junior, German libretto by C. Haffner and Richard Genée. Baron von Eisenstein (tenor) is wanted by the police, who go to his house and mistakenly arrest Alfred (tenor), lover of his wife Rosalinde (soprano). Eisenstein and his friend Falke (baritone) then attend a ball given by Prince Orlofsky (mezzo-soprano). Rosalinde and her maid Adèle (soprano) are also there, and much champagne and revelry lead to complications for all.

Fleet prison, historic prison set up in London in the 12th century. It was a frequent object of attack during London rebellions, and later became notorious as a debtors' prison. Fleet prison was closed in 1842 and demolished in 1844.

Fleet Street, London street which, since the late 17th century, has been the centre of British newspaper journalism. In the early 18th century it was the home of the coffee-house literary circles associated with such men as Jonathan SWIFT, Alexander POPE and Dr Samuel JOHNSON.

Fleming, Sir Alexander (1881–1955), British bacteriologist. He shared with Howard FLOREY and Ernst CHAIN the 1945 Nobel Prize in physiology and medicine for his part in the discovery of penicillin and its therapeutic effect. In 1928 Fleming noticed that a mould, identified as *Penicillium notatum*, liberated a substance that inhibited the growth of some bacteria. He named it penicillin. However, the importance of this discovery was not recognized until Florey and Chain had done further research. *See also* MS p.120.

Fleming, Ian Lancaster (1908–64), British novelist. After a career as a journalist and banker, he wrote 13 escapist spy thrillers about James Bond, secret agent "007", which won great popularity for their realistic detail, and sexual and violent fantasy. They include *From Russia with Love* (1957), and *Goldfinger* (1959). Many were later filmed.

Fleming, Sir John Ambrose (1849–1945), British electrical engineer. He invented the thermionic valve which was the basis of almost all early radio receivers and transmitters, television receivers and computers. The first valves were rectifiers, or diodes (two electrodes in an evacuated glass envelope, which permitted current to flow in one direction only). *See also* SU p.130.

Fleming's rules, in physics, ways of remembering the relationships between the directions of the current, field and mechanical rotation in electric motors and generators. In the left-hand rule (for motors) the forefinger represents field, the second finger the current, and the thumb, motion; when extended at right-angles to each other the appropriate directions are indicated. The right-hand rule applies the same principles to generators. *See also* SU pp.122–123.

Flemington, famous racecourse in Melbourne, Australia, where on the first Tuesday of November the world-renowned Melbourne Cup is run. In winter it is the venue of Australia's Grand National Steeplechase. The course dates from 1840 and was named after a local butcher whose shop was opposite.

Flemish, one of the two official languages of Belgium (the other being French). It is spoken mainly in the northern half of the country, by about half the population. Flemish is virtually the same language as Dutch, but for historical and cultural reasons is called Flemish in Belgium and Dutch in The Netherlands. *See also* MS p.240, *240*.

Flemming, Walther (1843–1905), German pioneer in the study of CYTOLOGY and expert in anatomy. He researched and published material on the fatty tissues of the body and, in 1880, was first to describe the longitudinal splitting of chromosomes.

Fletcher, Andrew (1655–1716), Scottish politician. He was adviser to the Duke of Monmouth on his invasion of England (1685). He opposed union of Scotland and England under English rule and worked for a federal union. After the Act of Union (1707) he retired from politics.

Fletcher, Sir Banister Flight (1866–1953), British art historian. He published his best-known work, *History of Architecture on the Comparative Method*, in 1896. It is still a standard work.

Fletcher, John (1579–1625), English dramatist and poet. With Francis BEAUMONT from about 1607 to 1616 he wrote romantic tragicomedies, including *The Knight of the Burning Pestle, Philaster, The Maid's Tragedy, A King and No King* and *The Scornful Lady.* He may have collaborated with Shakespeare on *Henry VIII* and *The Two Noble Kinsmen. See also* HC1 p.285.

Fleur-de-lis, in heraldry, symbol used in ancient India, Egypt and many other countries, but most often associated with the French royal family. It is said to represent three lily petals tied together.

Fleurs du Mal, collection of poems by Charles BAUDELAIRE, published in 1857 (revised 1861 and 1868). In style the poems herald the SYMBOLIST age; in content they celebrate the symbiosis of beauty and evil. *See also* HC2 p.*101*.

Flicker, type of WOODPECKER found in the USA. It cuts nest-holes in trees but does not drill into wood for food. Its slender, curved bill is used to find insects on the ground. Family Picidae.

Flight, travel through the air. The two main requirements for flight are THRUST – to give forward motion and overcome air resistance (DRAG), and LIFT – to overcome the earthward pull of gravity. A bird's wing, powered by muscles anchored to the breastbone, provides both thrust and lift, mostly on the downstroke. A bird's flight is controlled by manipulation of its flight feathers; balance and steering are provided by the tail feathers. In an aeroplane, thrust is provided by an engine-driven propeller or by the rapid emission of hot expanding gases from jet engines. Lift is provided by specially shaped wings (AEROFOILS) which pierce the air so that it passes the aerofoils faster on the top surfaces (where it exerts reduced pressure), and slower on the under surfaces (where it exerts increased pressure). *See also* HELICOPTER; MM pp.146–147, 152–155; NW pp.142–143.

Flightless birds, large, non-flying birds; often they have only weak or poorly-developed wings. Most have strong legs, and have evolved some way for efficient movement by walking, running or swimming. The ostrich, rhea, cassowary, emu, kiwi and penguin are all flightless birds. Others, such as the New Zealand wrens and some rails, fly only with difficulty. The MOA of New Zealand and the DODO of Mauritius were both flightless birds, but were hunted to extinction by man. *See also* NW pp.140–141, 229, 244; PE p.144.

Flight simulator, device that duplicates the instrument behaviour and physical attitude of an aircraft in flight, used for training pilots and aircrew. A more sophisticated simulator, in addition to having an exact replica of the controls of a particular aircraft, may also have a visual display of the terrain being "flown over" to contribute to realism.

Flight testing, method of determining capabilities and limitations of an aircraft or component part under actual conditions of flight. Although most research and experiment is done in the laboratory or by computations of a machine (computer), eventually all equipment must be tested in its true environment. For example, although the LUNAR MODULE flew satisfactorily in earth orbit, a test mission was flown in lunar orbit before the actual moon landing.

Flinders, Matthew (1774–1814), British navigator. He explored and charted the Australian coast (1795–1803) and sailed round Tasmania (1798).

Flinders Island, island off the NE coast of Tasmania and Australia in the Bass Strait, the largest of the Furneaux group. Its industries include tin-mining. Area: 1,992sq km (769sq miles). Pop. 1,000.

Flinders Ranges, mountain system in S Australia; extending NNE from Gladstone to the area between the Torrens and Frome lakes. It is a rich mining area. The highest point is St Mary's peak, 1,189m (3,900ft). Length: 419km (260 miles).

Flinders reefs, coral group outside the Great Barrier Reef, off NE Australia. It lies between the coastal cities of Cairns and Townsville.

Flinders, river in N Australia that rises in the Great Dividing Range. It flows NW and N to the Gulf of Carpentaria and its main tributaries are the Saxby and Cloncurry rivers. Length: 837km (520 miles).

Flint, Sir William Russell (1880–1969), British painter. His best-known works are watercolours of semi-uudes in Spanish or French settings.

Flint, city in S Michigan, USA. Founded in 1819 as a fur-trading post, it is now one of the world's major car manufacturing centres. GENERAL MOTORS CORP. was founded there in 1908; the city now ranks second to Detroit in motor car production. Pop. (1973) 181,684.

Flint, SILICA rock, a granular variety of QUARTZ of a fine crystalline structure. It is usually smokey brown or dark grey, although the variety known as chert is a paler grey. It commonly occurs in rounded modules and is found in chalk or other sedimentary rocks containing calcium carbonate. Flint was used by Stone Age peoples to make weapons and tools.

Flint, mineral of great importance to man during the STONE AGE. When struck a glancing blow, flint can be flaked, leaving sharp edges appropriate for tools and weapons; two flints struck together produce a spark which can be used to make fire. During the PALAEOLITHIC AGE man learnt how to use the flakes, as well as the central core. So great was the need for flint that flint mines were sometimes dug, eg Grimes Graves in Norfolk. *See also* HC1 pp*23, 42*; MM p.*25*; SU pp.*20–21*.

Flint clay, hard, flinty fireclay. It is a KAOLINITE, usually found at greater depths than most clays. It is used almost exclusively in the production of firebrick and crucibles.

Flintlock, muzzle-loading firearm, invented *c.*1550. The firing mechanism consisted of a flint held in a vice (called the cock) which struck a piece of steel (the frizzen or battery) when the trigger was pulled; the resulting spark ignited gunpowder in a priming pan which then set off the charge in the breech of the barrel. Cheaper and lighter than its predecessor, the MATCHLOCK, the flintlock was the main weapon of European armies from 1700–1830. *See also* MM pp.162, *162*.

Flintshire (y Fflint), former county of NE Wales, since 1974 part of Clwyd. It had two separate parts, and ran from the Clwydian Hills to the Dee estuary. The capital was Mold. Pop. (1971) 175,396.

Float glass process. *See* GLASS.

Floating currency, in economics, modern trend whereby a currency, such as the dollar or the pound, is neither devalued nor revalued (upwards), but is left to increase, or decrease, in relation to other currencies according to its worth on the foreign exchange market. Sterling is a floating currency, unlike some other European currencies which are fixed until forced to devalue, or revalue.

Flocculi, or plages, cloudy markings on the Sun's disc which are visible on spectroheliograms. They appear to be chromospheric phenomena, clouds of calcium or hydrogen associated with SUNSPOT. *See also* SU p.222.

Flodden, field in N Northumberland, NE England, scene of the Battle of Flodden (1513), in which an English force led by the Earl of Surrey defeated JAMES IV of Scotland. *See also* HC1 p.245.

Flood, The, primeval deluge, according to the Bible sent by God as a punishment on all the inhabitants of the Earth. Only NOAH, his family and a pair of every living creature, contained in the floating Ark, were spared to start Creation anew. Similar myths occur in many cultures, from the American Indians to the Australian aborigines; another version is the Mesopotamian EPIC OF GILGAMESH. Together with this anthropological evidence, some archaeological and geological indications would seem to suggest that a catastrophe of this nature and magnitude may actually have taken place.

Flood, Henry (1732–91), Irish politician. He entered the Irish Parliament in 1759 and took leadership of the nationalist movement. His influence was weakened by his accepting office in the British government in 1775 and by his opposition to CATHOLIC EMANCIPATION.

Floodlight, light beams of high intensity, produced by electric lamps with reflectors. Most often used to illuminate the stage in theatres and concert halls, floodlights are used to illuminate buildings, monuments and outdoor night-time games.

Floodplain, level land alongside a river consisting of alluvium deposited by the river when in flood. Such plains usually have extremely fertile soil and are often used, as near the River Nile, for intensive cultivation. *See also* PE pp.112–113.

Flora, in Roman mythology, personification and goddess of springtime and of budding fruits, flowers and crops. Depicted garlanded with flowers, she was honoured as a fertility goddess in the Floralia at the end of May, a bawdy festival.

Florence (Firenze), city in central Italy, on the Arno River; capital of Firenze province and Tuscany Region. It was the site of a Roman military colony and by the 12th century had become a trading and industrial centre. Although in following years the GUELPHS and GHIBELLINES fought for control of the city, under MEDICI rule in the 13th and 14th centuries it became the cultural and artistic centre of western Europe. Notable buildings include the Church of Santa Croce and the Uffizi gallery. Industries: ornamental glass and pottery, tourism. Pop. 457,000. *See also* HC1 pp.208, *208, 246–247,* 250–251, *250–251,* 256, *257.*

Florence, school of, artistic movement of the Renaissance which began with GIOTTO in the 14th century and included Fra ANGELICO, LEONARDO, MICHELANGELO, BOTTICELLI and RAPHAEL. It reached its finest achievements in the early 15th century and again in the decades around 1500. Not all the artists of the school were born in Florence but all found patronage there and worked in a recognizably Florentine style, which laid stress on the purity of line and composition rather than on colour. *See also* HC1 pp.250–251; *250–251,* 256–257.

Florey, Baron Howard Walter (1898–1968), British pathologist, *b.* Australia. He shared, with A. FLEMING and E. B. CHAIN, the 1945 Nobel Prize in physiology and medicine for his part in the development of PENICILLIN. Florey isolated the antibacterial agent from the mould discovered by Alexander Fleming. This made possible the large-scale preparation of penicillin. *See also* MS p.120.

Florida, state in the extreme SE USA, occupying a peninsula between the Atlantic Ocean and the Gulf of Mexico. At the S tip there is a chain of small islands, the FLORIDA KEYS, stretching W. The subtropical climate has encouraged both tourism and agriculture, the chief products being citrus fruits, sugar cane and maize. Industries have developed since WWII and focus on the John F. Kennedy Space Center at CAPE CANAVERAL. The state capital is Tallahassee. Discovered in 1513, the first permanent settlement in Florida was at St Augustine. Originally Spanish, the land passed to the English in 1763 and was returned to the Spanish in 1783. The Americans purchased Florida in 1819 and although the state seceded from the Union in 1861 it was little affected by the AMERICAN CIVIL WAR. It developed rapidly after 1880 when forest clearing and drainage schemes were begun. Area: 151,670sq km (58,560sq miles). Pop. (1975 est.) 8,357,000. *See also* MW p.175.

Florida Keys, chain of small coral and limestone islands extending off the S tip of Florida in a curve to the SW. The more significant islands are Key West, Key Largo, Long Key, Vaca Key and Big Pine Key. It is a resort area, with some commercial fishing. Length: approx. 242km (150 miles).

Florin, coin, originally gold, first used in Florence in the 13th century. Florins have been used in several European countries, including The Netherlands and Britain. The florin was introduced into England by EDWARD III with a value of six shillings; between 1848 and 1971 it was worth two shillings (10 new pence).

Florio, John (*c.*1553–1625), English writer, of Italian parents. He compiled an Italian-English dictionary, *A Worlde of Wordes* (1598), published a translation of MONTAIGNE's essays in 1603, and taught Italian at the court of James I.

Flory, Paul John (1910–), US chemist whose discovery of a method of analysing POLYMERS accelerated the development of plastics and earned him the 1974 Nobel Prize in chemistry. With Wallace H. CAROTHERS he developed the first nylon and a synthetic rubber, neoprene. Flory also discovered similarities between the elastic properties of organic tissues and plastics.

Flotation, process used to separate minerals in which the ore is treated so that it floats and can be skimmed off. Crushed rock and powdered ore is dosed with chemicals which cause the ore particles to become water-repellent. The aqueous suspension is then aerated. The ore particles cling to the air bubbles and rise to the surface, forming a foam which is skimmed off, the waste sinking to the bottom. It is used to concentrate sulphide and oxide ores.

Flotilla, fleet of small ships, or a small fleet. The word is Spanish in origin, a diminutive of *flota*, a fleet. In a navy, a flotilla is two or more squadrons of small warships.

Flotsam and jetsam, items of property found abandoned at sea. They, and the finder's legal rights to them are defined in Britain by the Merchant Shipping Act (1894). This defines flotsam as goods found floating on the sea's surface, jetsam as goods specifically jettisoned in order to lighten a vessel in danger of sinking. The phrase "flotsam and jetsam" is also used frequently in a figurative sense for unwanted articles.

Flounder, marine flatfish found in the Arctic, Atlantic and Pacific oceans. It is grey, brown or green on the upper, sighted, side; the blind underside is nearly white. It is an important food fish. Length: to 90cm (35in). Order Pleuronectiformes; species *Platichthys flesus. See also* NW p.*130*; PE p.*152*.

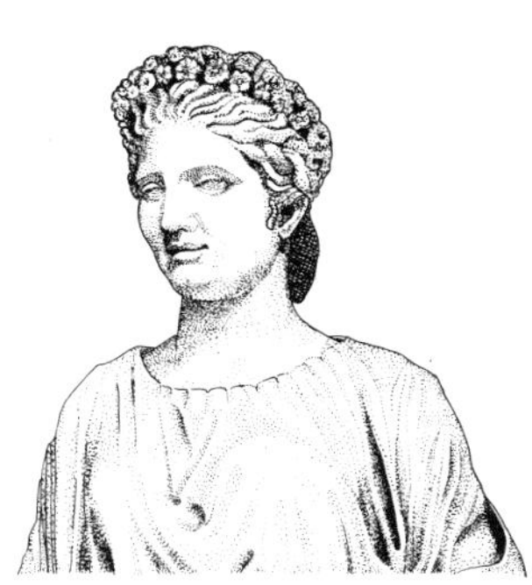

Flora, her head distinguished by a floral crown, adorned many Roman coins.

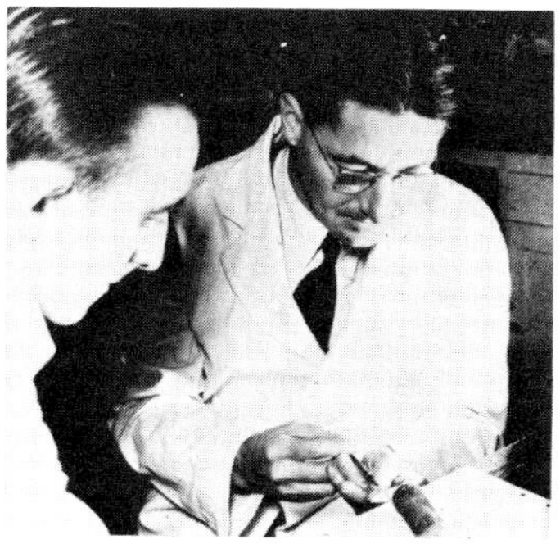

Howard Florey travelled widely during WWII, studying possible uses of penicillin.

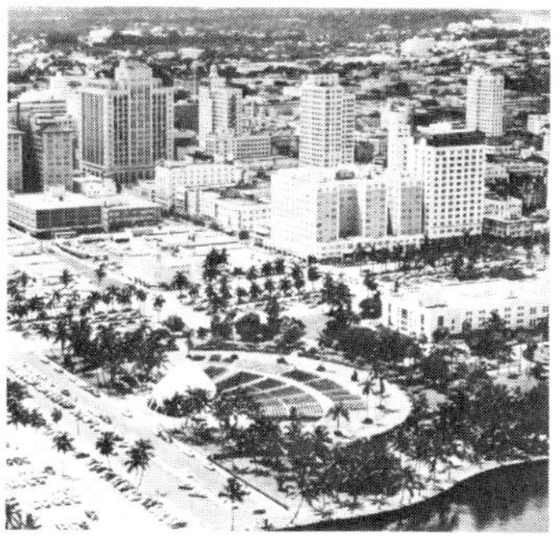

Florida; an aerial view of the Miami resort area, including part of Miami beach.

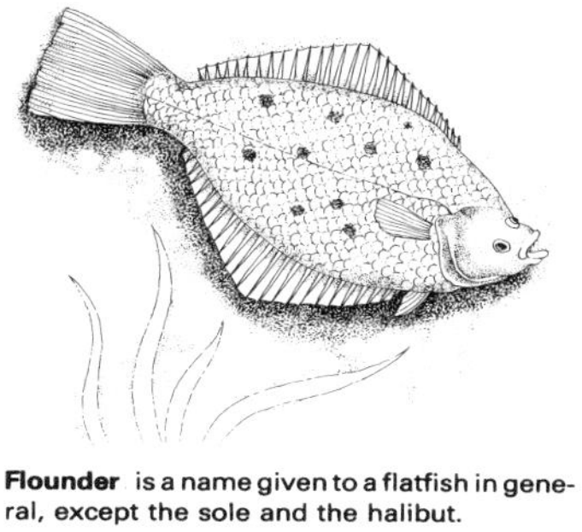

Flounder is a name given to a flatfish in general, except the sole and the halibut.

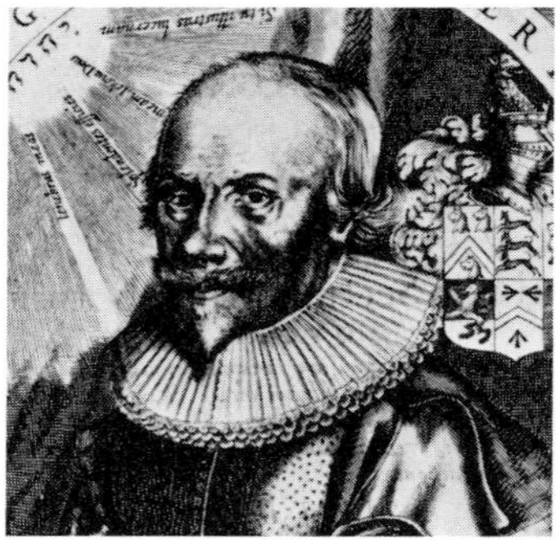

Robert Fludd used faith-healing as well as orthodox medical treatment.

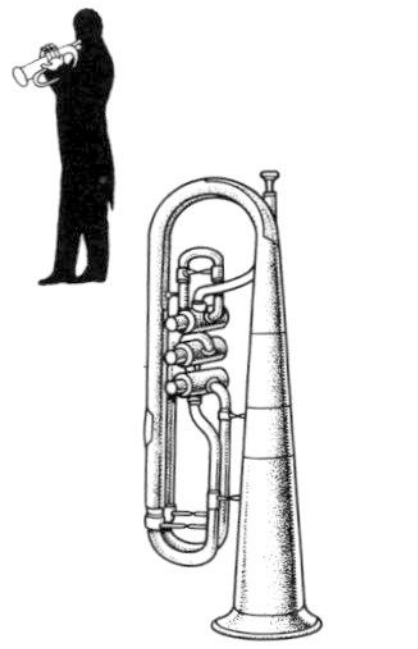

Flugelhorn is a brass instrument in b-flat with a range of some 2½ octaves.

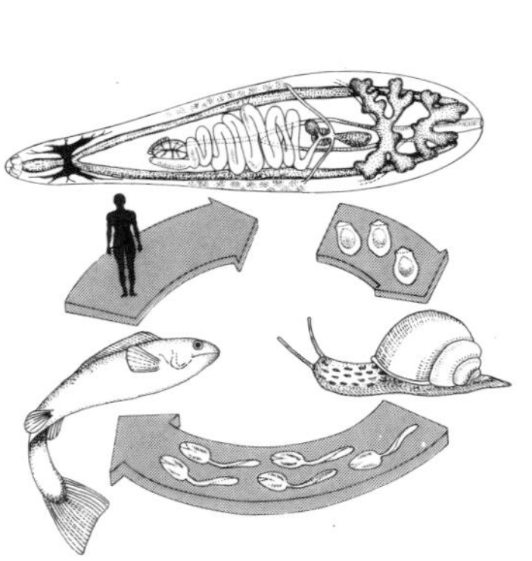

Fluke; the diagram shows the progress of a fluke from snail, through fish to man.

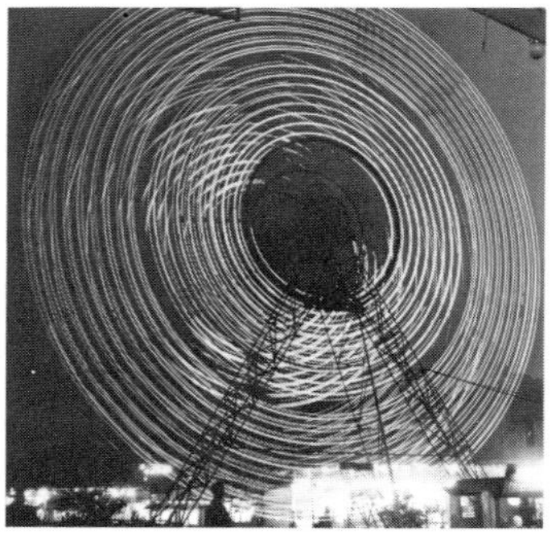

Fluorescent lighting is often used for decorative illumination, as in Luna Park, Rome.

Flour, finely ground meal made from cereal grains, seeds of leguminous plants or various nuts. Flour used for baking bread, cakes and biscuits comes from cereals. The degree of whiteness varies according to the bran content and some commercial flours are "bleached" to make them whiter. Self-raising flour contains added BAKING POWDER. Flour-milling has been practised for at least 8,000 years. *See also* PE p.182.

Flow, solid, in geology, the slide, flow or creep of solid, unsuspended material downwards on a slope. The movement within the solid is achieved by rearrangement between or within its particles.

Flow chart, graphical method used in scheduling computer programs and other complex tasks involving several interdependent stages. Various tasks or activities are listed within circles interconnected by directional time-sequence (flow) lines. Critical path analysis determines the minimum program time. Flow charts must be updated as variations in predictions occur. *See also* MM p.108.

Flower, Robin Ernest William (1881–1946), writer and translator, *b.* England of Irish parents. He worked at the British Museum (1906–44) and wrote a fragment of a history of Irish literature, *The Irish Tradition* (1947). Among his other works are *Poems and Translations* (1931) and *The Western Island* (1944).

Flower, reproductive structure of a flowering plant. It has four sets of organs set in whorls on a short apex (receptacle). Typically the sepals are leaf-like structures that protect the bud; they form the calyx. The petals, often brightly coloured, form the corolla; the stamens are stalks tipped by anthers (pollen sacs); the carpels form the pistil with an ovary, style and stigma. Flowers are bisexual if they contain stamens and carpels, and unisexual if only one of these is present. Reproduction occurs when pollen is transferred from the anthers to the stigma. A pollen tube grows down into the ovary where fertilization occurs and a seed is produced. The ovary bearing the seed ripens into a fruit and the other parts of the flower wilt and fall. *See also* NW pp.70–71.

Flower animal. *See* ANTHOZOA.

Flowering plant, any of about 250,000 species of plants that produce FLOWERS, FRUITS and SEEDS. Such plants include most herbs, shrubs, trees, fruits, vegetables and cereals. Their seeds are protected by an outer covering and as a result botanists classify them as ANGIOSPERMS, meaning "plants with enclosed seeds". Angiosperms are further subdivided into two main groups; MONOCOTYLEDONS, plants that grow from seeds with only one seed leaf; and DICOTYLEDONS, plants with two leaves for each seed. Many flowering plants are valuable for food, timber and their medicinal properties. *See* NW pp.58–59.

Flu. *See* INFLUENZA.

Fludd, Robert (1574–1637), English mystic philosopher who was strongly influenced by Paracelsus. Fludd became a ROSICRUCIAN and helped to spread Rosicrucian doctrines in England at the same time attempting to reconcile them with 17th century science. He believed that an all-pervading substance called ether was also present in human blood. Some of his ideas were given in his *Anatomiae Amphitheatrum* (1623).

Flugelhorn, brass musical instrument similar to the CORNET, but with a wider bore, larger bell and a mellower tone. It is most often used in military bands and jazz ensembles.

Fluid flow, behaviour of a moving fluid, determined by its velocity, pressure and density. These three quantities are related by three basic equations: the equation of continuity, which relates the amount of fluid flowing into a given space with the amount flowing out of that space; EULER's equation of motion, which shows how the velocity of the fluid changes with time at a given point in space; and the ADIABATIC equation, which describes the exchange of heat between different parts of the fluid. In incompressible fluid flow, which applies to most liquids, these equations take on a particularly simple form. Compressible flow equations are necessary for high-speed aerodynamic calculations. Often a fluid is treated as "ideal", meaning that no internal friction or viscosity is supposed. The equations for realistic fluids are so complicated that complete solutions to most problems do not exist; numerical solutions must be attempted by computer techniques. *See also* SU p.78.

Fluidics, use of fluids – gases or liquids – in controlling and actuating devices, to carry out switching and amplifying operations more familiarly associated with electronic circuits. Fluidic circuits were developed in the USA in the 1960s for use in rocket and aircraft guidance. *See also* SU p.*79*; MM p.*45*.

Fluidization, powdering of a solid so that it can be processed as if it were a fluid. The technique not only allows solids to be conveniently transported, but also hastens gas-solid reactions – the gas is injected from below and the powder is suspended to form a fluidized bed, an ideal condition for industrial drying or roasting.

Fluid mechanics, study of the behaviour of liquids and gases. Fluid statics includes the study of pressure, density and the principles of PASCAL and ARCHIMEDES. Fluid dynamics includes the study of streamlines, BERNOULLI's equation, and the propagation of waves. Engineers use fluid mechanics in the design of bridges, dams and ships. Physicists use fluid mechanics in studying the structure of the atomic nucleus and it has been used by astronomers to explain the spiral structure of the galaxies.

Fluid mining, method of obtaining minerals which involves dredging or HYDRAULIC MINING. Gravel (placer) deposits containing ore can be broken down with high-pressure streams of water or flooded so that dredgers with digging and processing equipment can operate. Many off-shore deposits, including gold, tin, iron-bearing sands, shell and gravel, are mined by dredging. *See also* MM p.99.

Fluke, FLATWORM and an external or internal parasite of man and other animals of the phylum Platyhelminthes, class Trematoda. Adult flukes have suckers for attachment to the host, and a complicated reproductive system. Human infection can result from eating uncooked food containing encysted larvae, or penetration of the skin by larvae in infected waters. The worms may enter various body organs such as the liver, lungs and intestines, causing oedema (swelling) and decreased function; or the flukes may remain in the bloodstream. Treatment is difficult. *See also* NW pp.86–87.

Fluorescence, emission of radiation, usually light, from a substance, the atoms of which have acquired energy from a bombarding source of radiation, usually ultra-violet light or electrons. When the source of energy is removed the fluorescence ceases. With phosphorescence, which is produced by a similar process, the emission persists for a short time. Mercury vapour is a fluorescent substance used in motorway lights; television tubes use fluorescent screens. *See also* SU pp.109, 137.

Fluorescent lamp, glass tube coated on the inside with a chemical phosphor and containing, at low pressure, small quantities of mercury. When an electric current is passed through the tube, the atoms of mercury emit ultra-violet radiation, which impinges on the phosphor coating, causing it to glow brightly. *See also* DISCHARGE TUBE; FLUORESCENCE; SU p.*109*.

Fluoridation, addition of inorganic fluorides, usually sodium fluoride, to the water supply to about one part per million, with the intention of strengthening teeth and reducing their decay. Since its inception in the 1930s fluoridation has been adopted in many countries, including Britain, the USA, Canada, Australia and New Zealand. *See also* MS pp.71, 111, 130.

Fluoride, any salt of hydrofluoric acid (HF); more particularly, fluoride compounds added to drinking water or toothpaste in order to build up resistance to tooth decay. This protection appears to result from the formation of a fluorophosphate complex in the outer tooth layers, which become resistant to penetration by acids made by mouth bacteria. *See also* MS p.130.

Fluorine, gaseous element (symbol F) of the halogen group, isolated in 1886 by Henri Moissan. Chief sources are FLUORSPAR and CRYOLITE. The element, obtained by ELECTROLYSIS, is the most electronegative of all elements and attacks many compounds. It is used in making FLUOROCARBONS and in extracting URANIUM. Properties: at.no. 9; at.wt. 18.9984; density 1.696g dm^{-3}; m.p. −219.6°C (−363°F); b.p. −188.14°C (−306.65°F); most common isotope F^{19} (100%). *See also* HALOGEN; SU p.137; MS pp.71, 130.

Fluorite, halide mineral, calcium fluoride (CaF_2) found in sedimentary rocks and pegmatites. It has cubic system crystals with granular and fibrous masses and is brittle, glassy, and colourless when pure. Hardness 4; s.g. 3.1. It is used as a flux in steel production where it is called fluorspar or fluor.

Fluorocarbon plastics, plastics made from a class of chemically inert compounds composed entirely of carbon and fluorine. The best-known is the resin polytetrafluoroethylene, or PFTE. They are valued for their non-flammability, low chemical activity, low resistance to friction and low toxicity. *See also* MM p.55.

Fluorocarbons, technically chlorofluoromethanes, used as propellants in some AEROSOL spray cans and as refrigerants (freons). They are highly volatile and inert gases, yet in the STRATOSPHERE they are broken down by sunlight to release chlorine atoms. These can react with ozone, so reducing the OZONE LAYER that protects organisms from dangerous quantities of solar ultra-violet rays. Due to this effect, new propellants have been developed for aerosols. *See also* PE p.147.

Fluorspar. *See* FLUORITE.

Flute, woodwind musical instrument. Air is blown across a mouth-hole near one end of a straight tube held horizontally across the mouth; holes covered by keys arranged in the BOEHM system provide a range of three octaves, permitting rapid scales and trills. The tone is mellow in the lower register and brighter in the higher. *See also* HC2 p.104.

Flux, in ceramics, any substance that promotes VITRIFICATION when mixed with clay. When the ware is fired, the flux melts, filling the porous clay form. As the piece cools, it hardens, becoming glossy and non-porous. Fluxes include felsphathic rock, silica, and borax. In METALLURGY, a flux is added to the charge of a smelting furnace to purge impurities from the ore and to lower the melting point of the slag. *See also* MM p.44.

Flux, magnetic, lines of force or of magnetic induction in a magnetic field. These lines can be seen as the closed curves followed by iron filings placed near a magnet. The direction of the flux at any point is the magnetic field, and the closeness of the flux (number of flux lines in a given area) is a measure of the magnetic field strength. *See also* MAGNETISM; SU pp.*73*, 116–*117*.

Fly, any of a large order (Diptera) of two-winged insects that range from midges 1.6mm (0.06in) long to robber flies more than 76mm (3in) in length; the order includes mosquitoes, horseflies, fruitflies, gnats and tsetseflies. There are between 60,000 and 100,000 species and they are found in every part of the world. Adult flies have compound eyes and sucking mouthparts. Many are pests and spreaders of disease, especially horseflies, mosquitoes and tsetseflies. The common HOUSEFLY is species *Musca domestica. See also* NW pp.*31, 107, 112, 113*.

Fly, river in Papua New Guinea, in the SE of New Guinea island. It rises in the Victor Emmanuel Range, flows S and SE into the Gulf of Papua and forms part of the boundary with West Irian, Indonesia. Length: 1,046km (650 miles).

Fly agaric, also called fly amanita, poisonous (but rarely fatal) toadstool, common in open woods and pastures. It has a broad orange or scarlet cap with prominent white "warts". The stem is white with rings at the base. Species *Amanita muscaria. See also* NW pp.*38, 43, 209*.

Fly-ball governor, mechanism which controls the rate at which an engine operates first invented by James WATT in 1788. Two weights suspended on rods from a vertical shaft – which is connected to the part of the engine whose rotational speed is to be governed, eg road speed engine speed, – will move outwards under centrifugal force, causing the rods to activate a control valve which will reduce the required rotational speed. *See also* MM p.*105*.
Flycatcher, any of several small birds of the order Passeriformes, found throughout the world, that catch insects in midflight. The most common species in Britain is the spotted flycatcher (*Muscicapa striata*). It is greyish-brown and inhabits gardens and woodlands. It feeds from more exposed branches than other flycatchers, flying erratically with frequent changes of direction when catching insects. It rarely alights on the ground, preferring to perch on fences and low branches. Length: 14cm (5.5in).
Flying. *See* FLIGHT.
Flying boat, aeroplane designed to take-off from and land on water. It has a boat-shaped fuselage strong enough to withstand the impact of the water and of sufficient buoyancy to remain afloat. Usually each wing has a stabilizing pontoon float, which is retractable in the latest flying-boats. *See also* MM p.148.
Flying bomb, also known as buzz-bomb, or doodlebug, popular names for the German V-1 missile, launched against England in 1944. The V-1 was a pilotless aircraft, powered by a pulse-jet engine with a guidance system composed of a distance-measuring device, a gyro-compass and an altimeter. In 1944 Germany also developed the V-2, a long-range ballistic missile carrying a 1-tonne warhead to a range of 320km (200 miles) on a ballistic arc trajectory with an altitude of 95–110km (60–70 miles). It was powered by a mixture of liquid oxygen and ethyl alcohol, and it was the precursor of postwar missiles. *See also* MM p.169.
Flying dragon, gliding lizard native to South-East Asia and the East Indies. It has elongated ribs that support extensible skin folds; these are spread for gliding from tree to tree. Length: approx. 20cm (8in). Family Agamidae; species *Draco melanopogon*. *See also* NW p.*139*.
Flying Dutchman (1843), three-act opera by Richard WAGNER, with the composer's German libretto after Heinrich HEINE. A Dutch ship's captain, Vanderdecken (baritone), is under a curse to sail until he finds a maiden faithful unto death. He sails to the home of Norwegian Captain Daland (bass) and is betrothed to his daughter Senta (soprano). Believing her to be unfaithful, he sails away. Senta affirms her faithfulness by drowning herself; the cursed ship disappears and the ghosts of the lovers are united forever.
Flying fish, tropical marine fish found worldwide. It is dark blue and silver and uses its enlarged spineless pectoral and pelvic fins to glide above the water surface for several metres. Length: to 45.7cm (18in). Family Exocoetidae; species *Cypselurus opisthopus*. *See also* NW p.128, *128*.
Flying fox, fruit-eating bat with a fox-like head that lives in South-East Asia. The largest of all bats, it does substantial damage to fruit crops. Length: to 40cm (16in); wingspan: to 1.5m (5ft). Genus *Pteropus*. *See also* NW p.214.
Flying lemur, or colugo, nocturnal gliding mammal of SE Asia. It climbs trees and can glide from branch to branch on "wings" formed from the membraneous skin between its outstretched limbs. Its common name comes from its resemblance to the LEMUR. Order Dermoptera; genus *Cynocephalus*. *See also* NW p.214.
Flying saucers, also called unidentified flying objects (UFOS), unusual phenomena in the sky, commonly believed to be of extra-terrestrial origin. The term is not restricted to saucer-shaped objects, nor does it encompass only aerial phenomena. Reports have been documented, often pictorially, since ancient times. With the development of aeronautics and astronautics the number of sightings has increased enormously. There have been various rational explanations, including optical floaters (in the observer's eye), weather balloons, aircraft, fire balls, clouds and artificial satellites. Some of these are unsatisfactory.
Flying shuttle, re-usable space-craft system developed in the late 1970s. The first test flight occurred in 1977 when the shuttle rocket (unpowered) was released from on top of a modified Boeing 747. The shuttle is designed to separate from the 747 and fly into orbit, and then have the capacity to land. It is expected to inaugurate commercial space flights.
Flying snake, small arboreal snake of South-East Asia, India and Sri Lanka whose spectacular leaps from tree to tree have inspired its inaccurate name. It glides rather than flies, launching itself almost horizontally, flattening its body against wind resistance to land gently in the branches. Species *Chrysopelea ornata*.
Flying squirrel, small gliding rodent that lives in forests of Eurasia and the USA. It glides by means of furry flaps of skin that stretch out flat and taut on both sides of the body when the limbs are extended. Genus *Pteromys*. The African flying squirrel is of a separate genus (*Anomalurus*). *See also* NW pp.160, *206*, 213.
Flynn, Errol (1909–59), US film actor, *b.*Tasmania. He made his name with *Captain Blood* (1935), and won worldwide fame for his romantic, swashbuckling heroes, as in *The Adventures of Robin Hood* (1938). His autobiography, *My Wicked, Wicked Ways* was published in 1959.
Flywheel, massive solid or heavy-rimmed wheel attached to a machine's drive shaft to minimize fluctuations in rotational velocity and to store energy. The inertia of the large wheel tends to absorb energy in the effective portion of an engine's cycle and to release energy in the least effective portion of the cycle. The flywheel was initially developed by James WATT.
Foam, suspension of gas bubbles separated from each other by thin films (0.1–1mm thick) of liquid or solid. Foaming is not possible in a pure liquid and a promoter must be added – such as soap or proteins, which are used in such edible foams as marshmallow.
FOB, or free on board, in business, stipulation that the buyer of a product assumes responsibility for paying the product's transport charges. The buyer also chooses the method of transport.
Focal length, distance from the midpoint of a curved mirror on the centre of a thin lens to the FOCAL POINT of the system. For converging systems it is given a positive value, for diverging systems, a negative value. *See also* SU pp.100–101.
Focal point, point on the axis of a lens or curved mirror to which incident light rays, parallel and close to the axis, are converged (real focus) or from which they appear to be diverged (virtual focus) after reflection or refraction. *See also* SU pp.100–101.
Foch, Ferdinand (1851–1929), French marshal. In WWI he was a commander in the battles of the Marne (1914), Ypres (1914, 1915) and the Somme (1916). In 1918 he became commander-in-chief of the allied armies, shaping their victory over the Germans. *See also* HC2 p.*193*.
Focus, either of two points on the major axis of an ELLIPSE such that the distance from one focus to any point on the ellipse and back to the other focus is constant. *See also* SU pp.164–165.
Foetus, or fetus, EMBRYO in a mammal after the main adult features are recognizable. In human beings it dates from about 8 weeks after conception. *See also* MS pp.76–77.
Fog, or mist, water vapour in the atmosphere condensed at or near the ground, as opposed to water vapour condensed as clouds. Fog forms when moist air is cooled below its DEW POINT. *See also* PE p.71.
Föhn, warm, dry wind on the lee or down-wind side of mountains tending to produce aridity. Mistral, sirocco and chinook are names for Föhn winds.
Foil, light weapon with a tapering quadrangular blade and small bell-shaped guard used in FENCING. The target area in foil is the trunk of the body. Women are restricted to fencing with the foil only.
Fokine, Michel (1880–1942), Russian-born choreographer. His concern in ballet for unity of music, drama, dancing and décor was revolutionary in the early 1900s. He became chief choreographer for DIAGHILEV'S BALLETS RUSSES in Paris (1909). Leaving Russia in 1918 he lived in New York from 1923, becoming naturalized in 1932. His best-known works include *Les Sylphides, Firebird, Petrushka* and *Don Juan*. *See also* HC2 pp.274–275.
Fokker, Anton Herman Gerard (1890–1939), pioneer Dutch aircraft designer and industrialist. He founded his own aircraft works in Germany in 1912, which made fighter planes used by Germany in WWI, and designed an interrupter gear system that enabled a machine gun to be fired through the propeller arc. In 1922 he emigrated to the USA where he concentrated on making commercial aircraft.
Fold, in geology, pronounced bending in a layer of rock. Folds are defined according to their axes. Thus an upfold, which is an arch, is an ANTICLINE; a downfold, a SYNCLINE. The fold system may be symmetrical (in neat waves), asymmetrical, overturned or recumbent (with the axis of the fold parallel to the horizon). A single folding is a MONOCLINE. *See also* PE p.104.
Foley, John Henry (1818–74) Irish sculptor. He executed the statue of Prince Albert in the Albert Memorial, London.
Foliation, crude layering of rocks produced under compression. The layering is approximately parallel to the bisecting planes of folds, and often results in the rock splitting because of the parallel orientation of the mineral layers. Mica and slate are good examples of foliation.
Folic acid, yellow crystalline derivative of GLUTAMIC ACID (formula $C_{19}H_{19}N_7O_6$) forming part of the VITAMIN B complex and used in the treatment of ANAEMIA. The COENZYME tetrahydrofolic acid is derived from folic acid.
Folie à deux, literally "double madness", name in psychology for a delusion shared by two people, usually a husband and wife or two sisters.
Folies-Bergère, Parisian music hall famous for its extravagant revues. Built in 1869, it has provided the setting for many great French entertainers, including Maurice CHEVALIER and FERNANDEL.
Folio, largest sheet of paper used in publishing. A book made of folio sheets folded once is a folio edition. In English law a folio is a document of 72 words or, for parliamentary and chancery documents, 90 words. In US it is one of 100 words.
Folk-dance, local traditional dance form, sometimes with roots in an ancient ritual or festival. The term applies to the traditional dances of the peoples of any area, large or small, from a town to a nation. Examples are the Helston Furry (Floral) Dance and the Irish jig.
Folklore, the lore of the common people, or the traditions, customs and beliefs of the people as expressed through non-literary tales, songs and sayings. In contrast to "literature", which is transmitted through the printed page, "folk literature" has an oral source and is transmitted primarily through memory and tradition. The best-known study of folklore is Sir James Frazer's anthropological study *The Golden Bough* (1890).
Folk-music, music deriving from, and expressive of, a particular national, ethnic or regional culture, nearly always originally vocal and usually (some would say always) unable to be attributed to a composer or even a definite period. Its main theme is usually the history of a people, or dramatic or everyday events in that history, so that folk-songs are usually narrative in content. Their origin is almost always peasant (as distinct from the urban provenance of "art songs"). The musical structure is the simple repetition of a tune (with or without chorus), sometimes with a freedom of rhythm which adheres more to the natural metre of the word than to the more formal requirements of composition. Nearly always the main musical

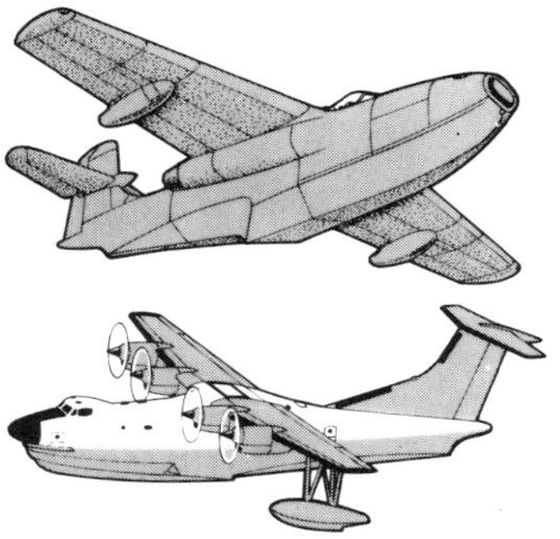

Flying boats, now little used, were highly influential on aircraft design before WWII.

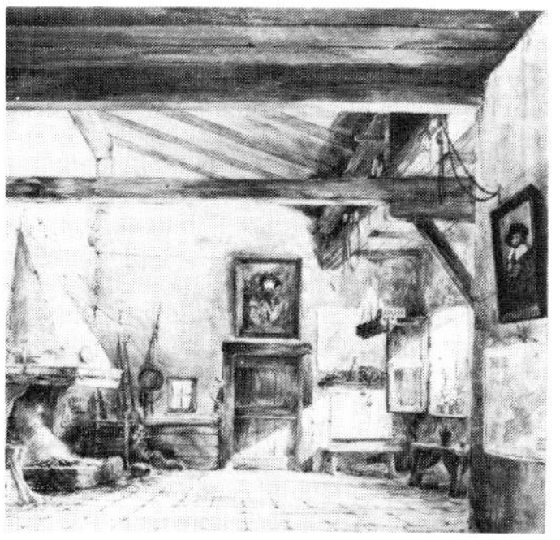

Flying Dutchman; a sketch by Johann Kantsky for a production of Wagner's opera.

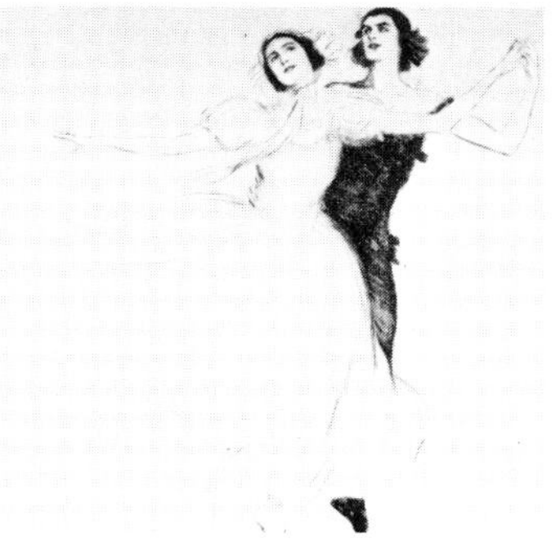

Michel Fokine; a drawing of Tamara Karsavina, one of the great interpreters of his work.

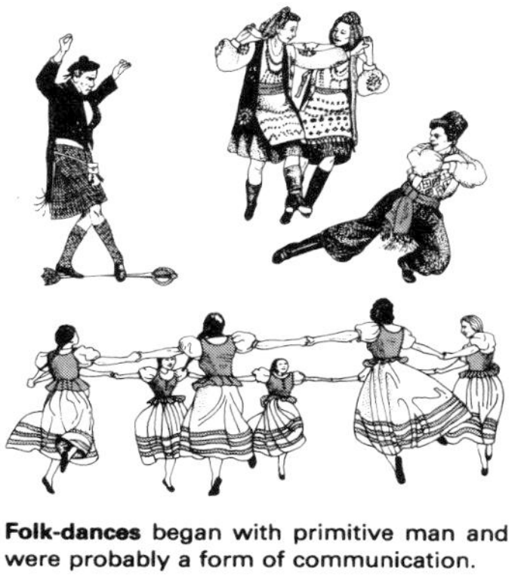

Folk-dances began with primitive man and were probably a form of communication.

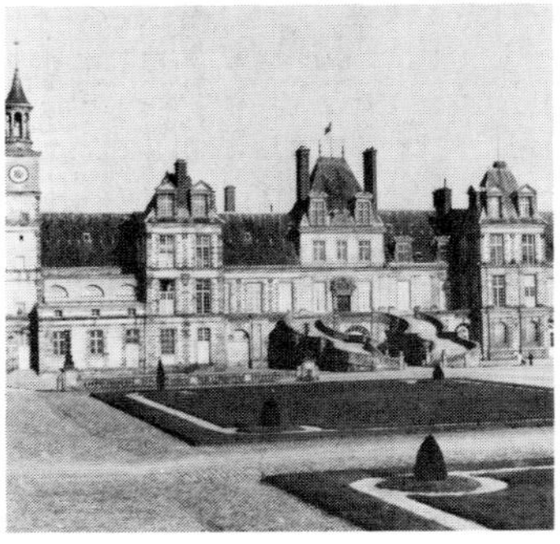

Fontainebleau; a view of the palace and its historic front court and stairway.

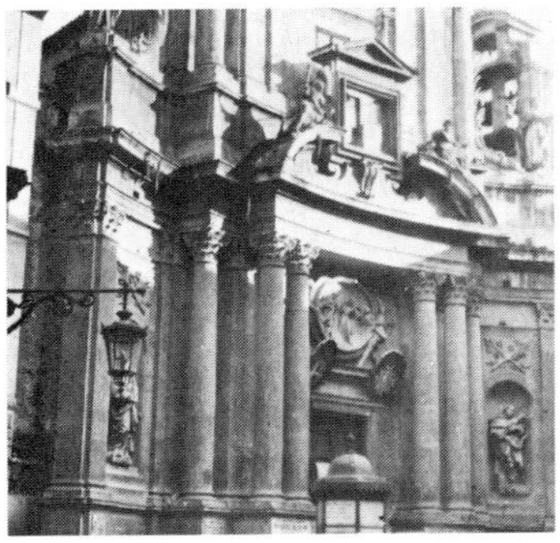

Carlo Fontana; a detail of the façade of the Church of S. Marcello in Rome.

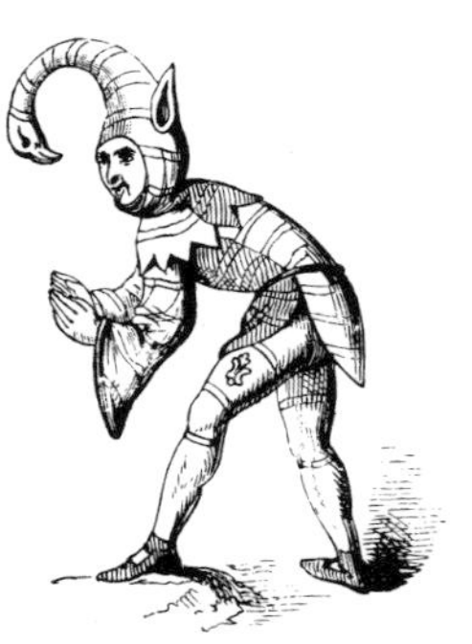

Fool; the origin of this character in drama can be found in Muslim and early Irish times.

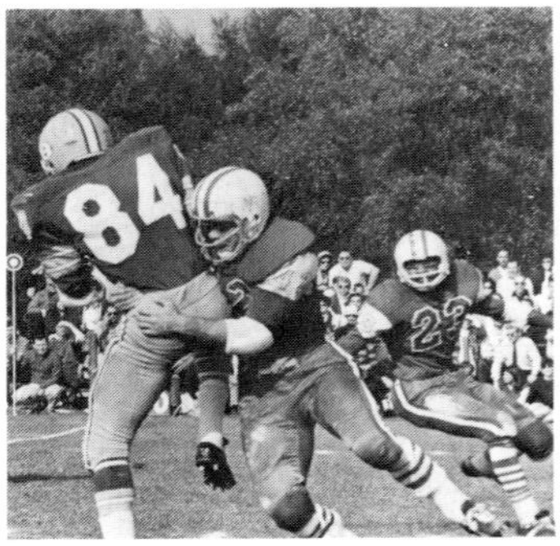

Football, American style, being played with customary vigour in a London park in 1969.

interest in folk-song is in the melodic line, although POLYPHONIC vocal folk-music occurs more often in Eastern European countries. The words and music of the same folk-song may show extreme variation from region to region. As unselfconcious expression of common experience, folk-tunes are often incorporated into the art of formal composition by composers: BARTÓK and KODÁLY in Hungary, BRITTEN and VAUGHAN WILLIAMS in England, GRIEG in Norway, DVOŘÁK in Bohemia and ALBÉNIZ and FALLA in Spain. Some modern writers of popular music, such as Bob DYLAN, have applied the folk idiom to their compositions.

Folk-tale, the most prevalent type of FOLKLORE literature. Tolk-tales are stories that have developed independently of the written word, and which deal with a wide variety of subjects – myths, fables, fairy tales and, more rarely, stories loosely based on historical characters and events.

Folk theatre, drama or entertainment that uses folklore, traditional and regional material and non-professional actors. It is generally performed by natives of rural areas and may be impromptu. Elements of folk drama – music, dance or social themes – are often incorporated in more professional dramatic works.

Folkways, traditional patterns of behaviour including habits and customs, which characterize a particular culture or social group. They exercise a strong though unconscious influence on the behaviour of each member. The term was first used by W.G. SUMNER in 1906.

Folsom Man, prehistoric inhabitants of North America who fashioned a characteristic fluted stone spear-point. The first such "Folsom point" was found near Folsom, New Mexico, in 1926 along with the bones of extinct mammals such as the mastodon. The Folsom finds were of great importance, raising anew the question of how long man has lived in North America. Some authorities believe Folsom Man lived approx. 10,000 years ago.

Fon, Kwa-speaking people of S Benin (Dahomey) and Nigeria. Their polygamous, patrilineal society is based on subsistence farming with a market system using cowrie shells as money. Hunters form a class with special social and religious status, while ancestor-worship is an important element in their religion.

Fonda, Henry (1905–), US actor. His first film was made in 1935; he has received acclaim for his roles in many films including *Young Mr Lincoln* (1939), *The Grapes of Wrath* (1940), *Twelve Angry Men* (1957) and *Firecreek* (1967). His stage successes include *The Caine Muting Court Martial* (1953) and *Two for the Seesaw* (1958).

Fonda, Jane (1937–), US film actress. The daughter of Henry FONDA, she has starred in such films as *Period of Adjustment* (1962), *Joy House* (1965), *Barefoot in the Park* (1967), *They Shoot Horses, Don't They?* (1969) and *Klute* (1971).

Fontaine, Jean de la. *See* LA FONTAINE, JEAN DE.

Fontainebleau, resort town in N France, in the Forest of Fontainebleau, 56km (35 miles) SE of Paris. Its palace, long a royal residence, was begun by FRANCIS I and became one of the flories of French Renaissance architecture; it is now the presidential summer residence. The town was headquarters of the military branch of NATO from 1945 to 1965. Pop. 18,100.

Fontana, Carlo (1634–1714), Italian architect. An apprentice of BERNINI, he designed many chapels, tombs and altars. Typical of his work is the façade for S. Marcello al Corso (1683) in Rome.

Fontana, Domenico (1543–1607), Italian architect and engineer who undertook much replanning of Rome. He designed the Lateran Palace and parts of the VATICAN and helped finish the dome of St Peter's Cathedral. With his brother he designed the great aqueduct of Acqua Felice (1587).

Fontane, Theodor (1819–98), German novelist. He wrote journalism, poetry, theatre criticism and travel books before his first novel, which was written at the age of 56. His masterpiece is *Effi Briest* (1895), about the decay of Berlin society.

Fontanelle, membranous space between the edges of the cranial bones in the SKULL of an infant. The fontanelle closes as the cranial bones grow towards each other. By the age of two years they are joined but the seams between the bones do not completely fuse until old age.

Fontanne, Lynn. *See* LUNTS, THE.

Fonteyn, Dame Margot (1919–), British ballerina. Trained at the Sadler's Wells Ballet School, she became a member of the ROYAL BALLET (1934–59). She has been a guest artist with every major US and European ballet company. Late in her career she continued to dazzle audiences, especially in her appearances with Rudolf NUREYEV. She has been acclaimed as one of the most exquisite classical dancers of this century. *See also* HC2 pp.274–275.

Foochow (Fuzhou or Fu-chou), port in SE China on the Min Chiang river; capital of Fukien province. The city received its name during the T'ang dynasty (618–907). It was one of the first treaty ports to be opened to foreign trade (1842) and thereafter it flourished as a major port and China's largest tea-exporting centre. It declined, however, in the early 20th century because of silting of the river and a lessening demand for tea. In 1949, after the Communist takeover, the port was blockaded by the USA and Chinese Nationalists. Industries: chemicals, textiles, food processing, paper, tea. Pop. 900,000.

Food, material containing essential nutrients taken into an organism to maintain life and growth; these include PROTEINS, FATS, VITAMINS, MINERALS and CARBOHYDRATES. Foods from animals include meat, eggs, fish, shellfish, milk and fat; plant foods include cereals, tubers, legumes, nuts, vegetables, fruits, oils and sugars. Plants themselves produce carbohydrates through the process of PHOTOSYNTHESIS. *See also* PE pp.156–157, 252–253.

Food additive, substance introduced into food for a variety of purposes. Additives fall into four categories: some enhance the flavour; some, such as sodium benzoate, are preservatives; some, such as colourings, enhance the appearance; and some restore or increase the nutritional value.

Food and Agriculture Organization (FAO), oldest of the UN specialized agencies, established at the end of WWII to try to improve world nutrition and eliminate hunger; technical aid is given on coordinated projects. There is a biennial FAO conference.

Food chain, transfer of food energy through a series of organisms, each organism eating the member below it. Its main sequence is from green plants (producers) to herbivores (primary consumers) and then to carnivores (secondary consumers). Decomposers such as acids, bacteria and enzymes act at each stage and at the end of the chain, breaking down waste and dead matter into forms that can be absorbed by plants, so perpetuating the chain. *See also* PE pp.*147*, *151*, *153*.

Food poisoning, disorder that can be caused by a number of organisms, the most common being SALMONELLA. Such organisms are most frequently ingested from animal products such as meat, seafood and eggs. Symptoms include abdominal pain, DIARRHOEA, nausea and fever; vomiting may also occur. The symptoms usually appear within 8 to 48 hours after eating the infected food and usually subside within two to five days, although diarrhoea may persist for longer. Treatment includes rest, fluids to prevent dehydration and no food until cramps and vomiting subside. *See also* BOTULISM; GASTROENTERITIS; MS p.110.

Food preservation, treatment of foodstuffs to prolong the time for which they can be kept before spoiling. The oldest methods are those of smoke-curing and heat-drying – both of which preserve meat by removing water and adding protective outer layers – and salting, pickling and fermentation, which preserve food chemically. Chemical preservatives, such as sodium benzoate, can also be added to foods. In CANNING, meats and vegetables are sterilized by heat after being sealed into airtight tins. Storage at 5°C (41°F) prolongs the life of foods temporarily, and DEEP-FREEZING at −5°C (23°F) or below for much longer periods. In the modern technique of freeze drying, water is removed from foods without raising their temperature, so that they can be fully reconstituted when required. The packing of foods in sealed plastic containers is a method of temporary preservation. *See also* PE pp.234, 250–251.

Fool, character in Elizabethan drama based on the traditional court jester or fool. He was usually dressed in "motley", or parti-coloured costume with close-fitting cap and bells, and was expected to comment satirically on the actions and concerns of his principals. Typical fools are found in Shakespeare's *King Lear* and *Twelfth Night*. *See also* HC1 p.285.

Foolscap, sheet size of writing or printing paper, 13½ by 17in (34.2 × 41.2cm), or 13½ by 8½in when folded. It originally bore a watermark that depicted a jester's or fool's cap. This sheet size is gradually losing favour as the international paper sizes are brought into use; the accepted equivalent is A4, 29.7 by 21cm (11¾ × 8¼in).

Foot, family name of five people who have made distinguished contributions to British public life. Isaac (1880–1960) was a Liberal politician who resigned from government office in 1932 in protest against protectionist policies. His sons include Sir Dingle (1905–), a Liberal MP (1931–45) who joined the Labour Party in 1956 and was solicitor-general (1964–67); Hugh, Lord Caradon (1907–), who after a distinguished career in the colonial service became Minister of State for Foreign and Commonwealth Affairs and UK representative at the United Nations (1964–70); John, Baron Foot (1909–), solicitor who was created a life peer in 1967; and Michael (1913–), Labour MP and journalist who was acting editor of the London *Evening Standard* (1942) and twice editor of the *Tribune* (1948–52; 1955–60). He was secretary of state for employment (1974–76) and then became leader of the House of Commons.

Foot, in poetry, unit of verse metre. Each foot is composed of a group of two or more syllables, some of which are stressed. Most commonly used feet are anapest, DACTYL, IAMB and TROCHEE.

Foot-and-mouth disease, also known as aphthous fever, contagious viral disease of cattle, pigs, sheep and other cloven-hooved animals. Its symptoms include fever, blisters on the mucous membranes (especially the mouth and hooves), loss of weight and appetite and drooling. A vaccine is available, but it does not guarantee prevention. Foot-and-mouth disease rarely occurs in man, although he can be a carrier, as can rats, dogs, birds and frozen meats. Epidemics cause losses of livestock but effective inspections, quarantines, the slaughter of diseased animals and sanitation help control the disease.

Football, American, game unique to the USA. It is played over four 15-minute quarters between two teams of 11 heavily padded players using an oval, rugby-type ball. Free substitution is allowed; from up to 40 in professional football. The field of play is rectangular, 100.5 × 48.8m (330 × 160ft), including the end zone behind the goal-lines. The area between the goal-lines 91.4m (300ft) is divided at 4.57m (15ft) intervals by lines marked across the pitch so that it resembles a gridiron. In college football, the H-shaped goal-posts stand on the end line; in the professional game they overhang the goal-line. Points are scored by touchdown (6), field goal (3), or conversion (1 or 2). A safety, when a defender is caught in possession in his end zone, is worth two points. Play moves in a series of downs, which begin with a scrimmage line. The team in possession has four downs in which to gain 9.1m (30ft) by running or passing, or the team loses possession. Players protect the ball-carrier by blocking with their forearms or bodies, but he is the only one who may be tackled. The touchdown is scored by running with the ball over the goal-line or catching a forward pass in the end zone.

Football, association, also called soccer, ball game played in most parts of the world in which two teams of 11 players attempt to force a round ball into their opponents' goal. It is played on a rectangular pitch of maximum size 120 by 90m (390 × 300ft), minimum 90 by 45m (300 × 150ft). The goals, two uprights surmounted by a crossbar, are 7.32m (24ft) wide by 2.44m (8ft). Only the goalkeeper may handle the ball, and then only in the penalty area of the goal he is defending; the other players may play the ball in any direction with any other part of the body, although essentially it is kicked or headed. Infringements of the laws, such as foul play, handling, offside and obstruction, are penalized by a direct or indirect free kick. A direct free kick to the attacking side in the defending penalty area is a penalty – a direct kick at goal from 11m (36ft) with only the goalkeeper defending. The game is played over two 45-minute periods and is controlled by a referee, who may caution or even send off players guilty of serious offences or persistent infringements. Football as known today developed in 19th-century England, where the first rules were formulated and in 1863 the Football Association was founded. In 1872 England played Scotland in the first-ever international match; the Scots were to have an important influence on the game, introducing the passing game and professionalism. The legalization of professionalism in 1885 led to the inauguration of the FOOTBALL LEAGUE Championship in 1888. The game was soon to spread beyond Britain, and in 1904 FIFA was formed to control the sport at world level. Football has been played at the Olympic Games since 1908, and in 1930 the four-yearly World Cup was first held. Football tactics have changed greatly since the early days with the old player-formation of goalkeeper, two full-backs, three half-backs, and five forwards giving way to a more fluid manner of positioning in which players found themselves labelled defenders, midfield men and strikers. Substitution of players for tactical reasons or in event of injury is permitted, the number varying with competition rules.

Football, Australian. *See* AUSTRALIAN RULES FOOTBALL.

Football, Canadian, game similar to American football but with variations to the rules. The Grey Cup is the highlight of the professional season. The principal differences are that teams have 12 players, are allowed only three downs and play on a larger field – 100 by 59.4m (330 × 195 ft). *See* FOOTBALL, AMERICAN.

Football, Gaelic. *See* GAELIC FOOTBALL.

Football, rugby, ball game for two teams in which the oval ball may be handled as well as kicked. There are two codes, union and league, but the purpose in each is the same; to touch the ball down in the opposition in-goal area for a try, which allows a kick at the H-shaped goal (a conversion). Kicks must pass over the crossbar between the line of the posts. Players may not pass the ball forward or knock it on to the ground when attempting to catch it. The field of play is rectangular, 100m (330ft) long and 55–68m (180–225ft) wide, and play consists of two 40-minute halves.

Rugby union, which developed as part of football until the 1860s, is a 15-a-side game restricted to amateurs. A team comprises eight forwards and seven backs: replacements (two) are allowed in the event of injury. Breakdowns in play are restarted with a scrum or a lineout, both contested by the forwards, and infringements are penalized by a scrum or an indirect or direct penalty kick. Points are awarded for a try (4), conversion (2), penalty and dropped goals (3 each). Rugby union is most popular in Britain, France, South Africa, New Zealand and Australia, but its following is increasing in other countries.

Rugby league, which began as a breakaway movement from rugby union in northern England in 1895, is a 13-a-side game for professionals and amateurs. There are six forwards and seven backs: tactical substitutions (two) are allowed. Played mostly in England, Australia, New Zealand and France, it differs from union in permitting tackled players to retain possession and play the ball back to a team-mate for a number of tackles limited by the "play-the-ball" rule. Breakdowns in play are restarted by a scrum; there are no lineouts. Points are awarded for a try (3), goal (2) and dropped goal (1).

Football League, annual championship administered by the body of the same name for 92 English and Welsh member clubs divided into four divisions: 22 each in I and II, 24 each in III and IV. Teams within a division play all the others twice, at home and away, getting two points for a win and one for a draw. A system of relegation and promotion operates between the divisions. The League was first contested in the 1888–89 season.

Foot binding, the practice of compressing girls' feet with tight bandages to restrict foot growth. This custom made the feet deformed and almost totally useless, forcing women to remain in the home. Common in all classes of Chinese society, the practice was abolished by the Communists when they came to power. *See also* MS p.*192*.

Foote, Robert Bruce, (1834–1912), British geologist and archaeologist who spent 33 years in India on its geological survey. He founded the study of the subcontinent's prehistory and discovered many historic sites. Many of his postulates were confirmed by later excavations.

Footlights Club, theatrical company at Cambridge University founded in 1883, which presents its own revue annually. It has been a vehicle for many talented British writers and actors, including Alan Bennett, Eleanor Bron, Peter Cook and John Cleese.

Foppa, Vincenzo (*c.*1427–1515), Italian painter. The dominant painter of Lombardy prior to Leonardo da Vinci, he painted religious subjects. In his treatment of colour and light, he was influenced by Jacopo BELLINI.

Forain, Jean Louis (1852–1931), French illustrator and painter. He is best known for his cartoons and caricatures attacking social injustices and for his etchings, largely on religious subjects. In style, he is highly reminiscent of DAUMIER.

Foramen magnum, cavity at the base of the skull through which the spine passes. In the gorilla it is positioned towards the back, whereas in man it is set well forward. *See also* MS p.*56*.

Foraminifera, amoeboid protozoan animals that live among plankton in the sea. They usually have multi-chambered chalky shells called tests which may be spiral, straight or clustered and vary in size from microscopic to 5cm (2in) across, according to species. Many survive as fossils and are useful in geological dating. When they die their shells sink to the ocean-floor to form large deposits, which are the source of chalk and limestone. Order Foraminiferida. *See also* NW p.*121*; PE pp.*83, 90, 119, 129*.

Forbes, Bryan (1926–), British film director, real name John Clarke. Starting as an actor, he became a script-writer, notably for *The League of Gentlemen* (1959) and *The Angry Silence* (1959). As director his films included *Whistle Down The Wind* (1961), *The L-Shaped Room* (1962) and *The Whisperers* (1966). His authorized biography of Edith EVANS, *Ned's Girl*, appeared in 1977.

Forbes, George William (1869–1947), New Zealand politician. He became leader of the United Party and Prime Minister in 1930, and led a coalition government (1931–35). He set up work camps for the unemployed during the Depression.

Forbes-Robertson, Sir Johnston (1853–1937), British actor-manager. He made his first stage appearance in 1874, and later toured England and America. In 1895 he became manager of the Lyceum Theatre in London, where he played *Hamlet* in 1898 and many other roles until his retirement in 1913.

Forbes, Stanhope Alexander (1857–1947), Irish painter of rustic genre scenes, landscapes and historical subjects. After studying in France, he founded a school of art in Newlyn, Cornwall, in 1899. Typical of his work is *The Fish Sale on a Cornish Beach*.

Forbidden City, walled area of Peking, China. It contains the former imperial palaces of the Ming and Manchu dynasties dating from the 15th century, and was so named because the public used not to be able to enter. It is now a large museum, containing many art treasures.

Force, loosely speaking, a push or a pull. A force acting on a body may (1) balance an equal but opposite force or combination of forces to maintain the body in equilibrium; (2) change the state of motion of the body (in magnitude or direction); or (3) change the shape or state of the body. There are four basic forces in nature. The most familiar, and the weakest, is the gravitational force, a force that attracts inversely as the square of the distance between any two masses. The gravitational force between the Earth and an object accounts for the objects weight. Much stronger is the electromagnetic force, which also follows the inverse-square law and may attract or repulse. Two other forces are recognized, both operating only on the sub-atomic level. The weak nuclear force associated with the decay of particles is intermediate in strength between the gravitational and electromagnetic force, whereas the strong nuclear force associated with the "glue" that holds nuclei together is the strongest force known in nature. *See also* SU pp.70–74.

Forcing, in horticulture, speeding up the development of a plant or a part of a plant, usually by providing heat and moisture. Forcing, using a greenhouse, is a method by which vegetable growers can get produce to market before those who raise plants in the open. It is still often used to accelerate the blooming of plants (eg daffodils and tulips) raised from bulbs.

Ford, Ford Madox (1873–1939), British novelist, poet and critic, real name Ford Madox Hueffer. He influenced such writers as Ezra POUND, Joseph CONRAD and D.H. LAWRENCE through his editorship of *English Review*. His chief work is the tetralogy *Parade's End* (1924–28).

Ford, Gerald Rudolph (1913–), 38th President of the USA (1974–77). He trained as a lawyer, and after naval service in WWII he was elected (1948) as a Republican to the US House of Representatives. He became Vice-President in Dec. 1973, and replaced Richard NIXON as President in Aug. 1974. He was defeated by Jimmy CARTER in 1977. *See also* HC2 pp.264–265.

Ford, Henry (1863–1947), car manufacturer and industrialist. He developed a petrol-engined car in 1892 and founded FORD MOTORS in 1903. He brought out the economical Model T in 1908. He initiated the conveyor-belt assembly line in 1913 and introduced the eight-hour day with a $5 minimum wage. In 1936 he established the FORD FOUNDATION, now worth more than $3,000 million. *See also* MM p.*126*.

Ford, John (*c.*1586–1640), English playwright who, with Cyril TOURNEUR, pioneered post-Jacobean drama. His major plays included *The Broken Heart* (1630), *'Tis Pity She's a Whore* (1633), *Love's Sacrifice* (1633) and *Perkin Warbeck* (1634). Common themes are incest and thwarted passion, and the plays emphasize differences between public and private morality.

Ford, John (1895–1973), US film director. He won Academy Awards for best director for *The Informer* (1935), *The Grapes of Wrath* (1940), *How Green Was My Valley* (1941) and *The Quiet Man* (1952). His other films include *Stagecoach* (1939), *The Horse Soldiers* (1959) and *Cheyenne Autumn* (1964). *See also* HC2 p.*269*..

Forde, Daryll (1902–73), British anthropologist. His work on North American Indians and on various ethnic groups in Nigeria, described in his book *Habitat, Economy and Society* (1934), was extremely influential.

Ford Foundation, philanthropic body that makes grants to individuals and institutions, mainly in the USA with the aim of

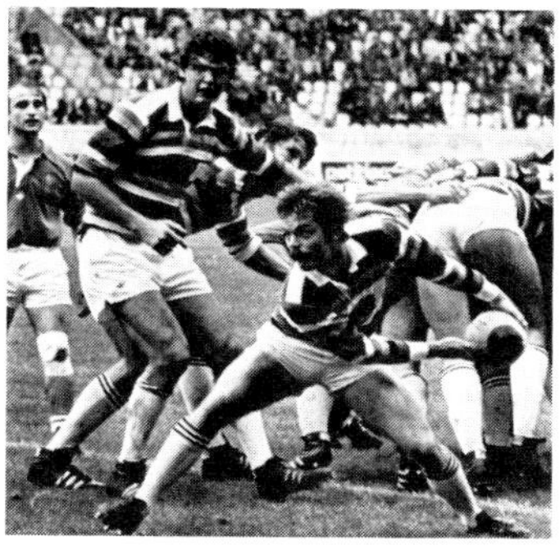

Football, rugby; a moment during the game France won against a world all-star team.

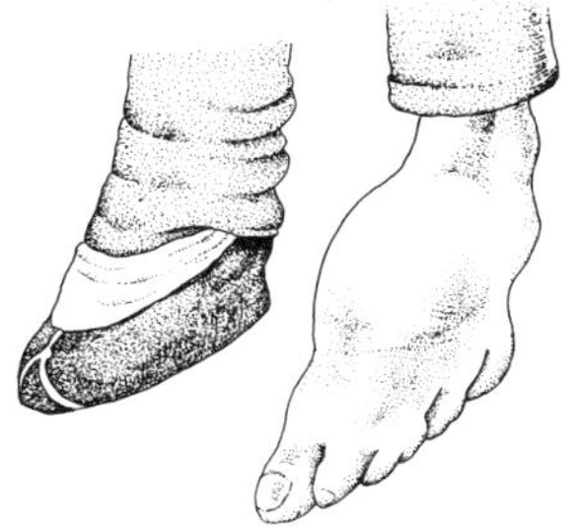

Foot binding; illustration of the method of binding and the resulting deformity.

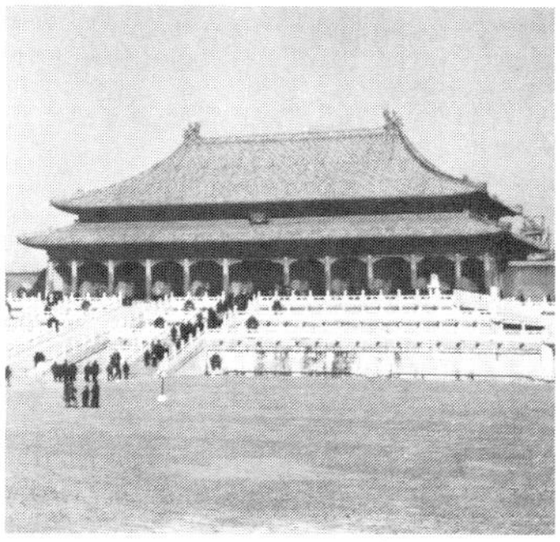

Forbidden City; a winter view of the former home of the emperors.

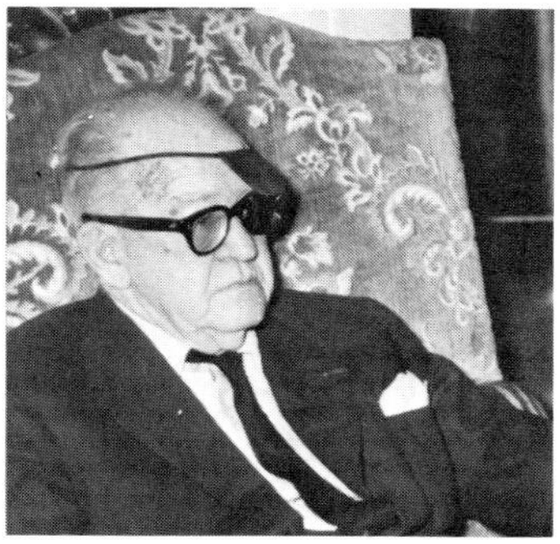

John Ford was awarded the Presidential Medal of Freedom in 1973.

Ford Motor Company

Foreign Legion soldiers, mostly Europeans and Americans, in Paris in 1939.

Forget-me-not is a favourite flower of poets and is a symbol of constancy between lovers.

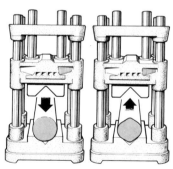

Forging is the hammering process by which metal, hot or cold, can be shaped.

George Formby with his dog, Punch, rehearsing for a number in *Zip Goes a Million* in 1951.

advancing human welfare. Its main areas of involvement are education, social matters and the arts. Henry and Edsel FORD set up the foundation in 1936.

Ford Motor Company, major US-based manufacturer of motor cars, trucks, industrial machinery and sophisticated products for use in electronics and space exploration. Founded by Henry FORD in 1903, it is now a public company with numerous plants in the USA and abroad.

Forebrain, one of the three primary parts of the developing brain, clearly distinguishable, together with the MIDBRAIN and HINDBRAIN, in the early embryo, but which became overlaid in the adult human by the cerebral hemispheres, which are massive developments from the forebrain. *See also* MS p.40.

Forecasting, weather, technique of anticipating and describing future weather for a given time and place. There is a three-fold classification depending on the length of the period covered. Short-term forecasts cover the next 24 hours and include wind velocity, cloud cover and temperature. Medium-range forecasts look two to five days ahead and contain information on the dominant circulatory conditions – the paths of cyclones and anticyclones. Long-range forecasts cover periods of five days and more ahead and are really more extensive medium-range forecasts. Pressures and circulatory patterns are usually given as averages. Artificial satellites have increased the accuracy of weather forecasting, especially when dealing with severe turbulences such as hurricanes.

Foreclosure, deprivation of the right to redeem or continue to hold a MORTGAGE. When a person has failed to pay a mortgage on time, the mortgagee (the one who has lent the money) is legally entitled to foreclose, ie to take possession of the mortgaged property and sell it to recover the amount lent.

Foreign and Commonwealth Office, British government department. In 1964 the Plowden Report recommended that the overseas services of the FOREIGN OFFICE and the COMMONWEALTH (RELATIONS) OFFICE be joined. In 1965 the two offices were combined in a single diplomatic service, managed by the Diplomatic Service Administration Office. In 1968 that office and the Foreign and Commonwealth offices were merged in a single Foreign and Commonwealth Office under one secretary of state, the first of whom was the Labour minister Michael Stewart.

Foreign Legion, French, skilled professional military group of mixed national origin, created in 1831 to serve in French colonies. After fighting in the two world wars and later French colonial struggles, the Legion moved its headquarters from Algeria to s France in 1962.

Foreign Office, British Government department which ceased to exist in 1968 when it was joined with the COMMONWEALTH (RELATIONS) OFFICE. It began as an independent department in 1782, when the Secretary of State for the Northern Department became the Secretary of State for Foreign Affairs, and after that date was one of the three chief departments of state, along with the Treasury and the Home Office. *See also* HC2 p.*122.*

Foreland, North and South, two chalk headlands in E Kent. North Foreland is the NE corner of Thanet; South Foreland, 5km (3 miles) NE of Dover, is the E extremity of the North Downs.

Foreman, George (1949–), US boxer. He won the Olympic gold medal (heavyweight) in 1968. He defeated Joe Frazier for the world heavyweight championship in 1973 and lost it to Muhammed ALI in 1974.

Forensic medicine, branch of science that deals with the relations and applications of medical facts to legal matters. It mainly concerns itself with cases of insanity, injury, paternity or violent death. *See also* MS p.294.

Forensic science, also called medical jurisprudence, the application of medical, scientific or technological knowledge to the investigation of crimes. It permits minute examination of available evidence on the basis that every criminal leaves

clues of some kind, however microscopic. Forensic medicine involves examination of living victims and suspects, as well as the pathology of the dead. The cause of death, if there is doubt, is established at an autopsy. Forensic science developed in the early 1900s in England as a product of police work and medicine. Most branches of the sciences may be involved in some way. *See also* MS pp.294–295.

Foreshortening, in painting, the illusion of depth achieved by recording the distortion seen by the eye when an object or figure is seen in the distance or at an unusual angle. The closest object or part of it may be unusually large and the more distant object or part unusually small. This skill was mastered by Renaissance painters, beginning with MASACCIO's application of scientific perspective in 1425.

Forest, extensive wooded area preserving some primitive wildness. Tropical rain forests lie in the equatorial rain belt and are made up mainly of closely packed, broad-leaved EVERGREEN trees and vines. Hardwood forests comprise mainly DECIDUOUS trees with a long growing period in warm, moist regions. Softwood forests are found in colder and temperate areas and are mainly of CONIFERS. *See* NW pp.*194, 206.*

Forest Hills, tennis stadium on Long Island, New York, that staged the US lawn tennis championships 1915–20 and 1924–77. The grass courts were replaced by clay in 1975. A feature of Forest Hills is its horseshoe-shaped stand.

Forest, Lee de. *See* DE FOREST, LEE.

Forester, Cecil Scott (1899–1966), British author best known for his sea stories. He gave up a career in medicine and turned to writing fiction. His popular naval saga about Horatio Hornblower, a naval officer during the Napoleonic Wars, began with *The Happy Return* (1937). His other works include *The African Queen* (1935) and *The Gun* (1933).

Forest of Dean. *See* DEAN, FOREST OF.

Forestry, science of managing areas of woodland with their associated waters and wastelands. The main aim of forestry is to raise timber, but conservation of soil, water and wildlife is also a consideration. Systematic management probably began in Germany in the 16th century, where forests were divided into sections for timber-felling and regeneration, to sustain annual yields. Education in technical forestry began in western Europe in the 19th century. Natural forests once covered nearly two-thirds of the world's land surface, but clearances for farming have reduced this figure to barely a third today. *See also* PE pp.218–219.

Forestry Commission, UK national forestry authority charged with promoting the interests of forestry, the development of afforestation and the production and supply of timber in the UK. The primary afforestation programme is being developed in the Highlands of Scotland.

Forests, lands in Britain which, from the time of WILLIAM I, were set aside for hunting and shooting and were subject to the forest laws. Forest laws and the special privileges granted to landowners by them fell into disuse in the late 17th century. New Forest, Hampshire, is an ancient royal forest. *See also* HC1 p.196.

Forever Amber (1944), best-selling English novel by Kathleen Winsor. Set in Restoration England, it is the epic story of Amber St Clare, a fictional mistress of Charles II. It was made into a film in 1947.

Forfar, market and county town in E Scotland. In 1975 it became part of the Tayside region. Its industries include jute, linen and rayon. Pop. (1971) 10,500.

Forfarshire (Angus), former Scottish county N of the River Tay, incorporated in Tayside in 1975. It comprised part of the Grampians in the NW, with Sidlaws to the s. Dundee, Forfar, Arbroath and Montrose are the chief towns.

Forgery, making of a fraudulent immitation of a document or artefact. In the UK forgery is a serious crime punishable by imprisonment, and the forgery of a deed, will or banknote may be punishable with imprisonment for life.

Forget-me-not, any of about 50 species of

hardy perennial and annual herbs of the BORAGE family, found in temperate parts of Europe, Asia, Australasia and North America. The typical five-petalled flowers are sky blue but may change colour with age. Genus *Myosotis*.

Forging, shaping of metal articles by hammering or pressing metal blanks between pairs of forging dies. The upper die is attached to the ram of a forging hammer or press so that it can be raised and dropped (with or without additional pressure) against the rigidly supported lower die. Most metals are forged hot, but cold forging is also practised. *See also* MM pp.40, 42.

Form, in philosophy, can refer to various concepts. According to PLATO's theory of Forms or Ideas, forms are eternal, immutable objects of the intellect, not part of the world as perceived by the senses. ARISTOTLE believed that every object consisted of matter which was shaped into a form. This form could change, but the basic matter from which it is composed could not. In LOGIC, the form of a proposition is the type to which it belongs, such as the negative or the universal. It is contrasted with the content, the subject matter of a proposition. *See also* MS pp.226–227.

Formaldehyde, colourless suffocating and poisonous gas (HCHO) prepared commercially by the catalytic oxidation of METHANE or METHANOL. It was discovered by August von HOFMANN in 1867. It is used in the manufacture of plastics, and as a germicide, preservative, reducing agent and corrosion inhibiter. Most formaldehyde is in the form of formalin, an aqueous solution containing 35-40% of formaldehyde. Chief properties: m.p. $-92°C$ ($-133.6°F$), b.p. $-21°C$ ($-6°F$).

Formalhaut, or Alpha Piscis Austrini, giant star in the constellation Piscis Austrinus. Characteristics: apparent magnitude: 1.16; absolute magnitude: 1.9; spectral class: A3; distance: 23 light years. *See also* SU pp.226, 262.

Formby, George Jr (1904–61), British music-hall comedian noted for his direct Lancashire humour and saucy songs such as *When I'm Cleaning Windows,* which he performed to his own high-speed ukelele accompaniments. Primarily a performer in variety, he also made 22 films between 1936 and 1948.

Forman, Milos (1932–), Czech film director whose films present a humorous view of fundamentally serious problems. He made several films in Czechoslovakia, including *Fireman's Ball* (1967), before moving to the USA in 1968. Since then he has made *Taking Off* (1971), about the generation gap between a young girl and her parents, and the award-winning *One Flew Over the Cuckoo's Nest* (1976), based on a novel by Ken Kesey.

Formica, trademark for a plastic material that forms a hard, smooth, heat- and stain-resistant surface for furniture and wallboards. Layers of resin-impregnated paper are bonded together under heat and pressure. The top sheet is patterned and coloured, frequently with a wood grain. *See also* MM p.54.

Formic acid (methanoic acid), colourless fuming liquid (HCOOH) prepared by treating sodium formate with sulphuric acid and distilling it. It occurs in the stings of ants. It is used in the making of paper, textiles and leather. Properties: s.g. 1.22; m.p. 8.3°C (46.9°F); b.p. 100.8°C (213.5°F).

Formosa. *See* TAÏWAN.

Fornix, in anatomy, arch or fold of tissue, many of which occur in the body, eg in the brain and the innermost region of the vagina. *See also* MS p.41.

Forrest, Sir John, 1st Baron Forrest of Bunbury (1847–1918), Australian politician and explorer. He explored much of Australia's interior (1869–70, 1874), becoming surveyor general of Western Australia in 1883; he was also Western Australia's first premier (1890–1901). He held several posts in the Australian Commonwealth government.

Forssmann, Werner (1904–), German physician and physiologist. He shared the 1956 Nobel Prize in physiology and medicine with A. F. COURNAND and D. W.

RICHARDS. This was belated recognition for his development of the cardiac catheter, a tube which is inserted into a vein in the arm and pushed through it until it reaches the heart. It is used in the diagnosis of heart and lung diseases.

Forster, Edward Morgan (1879–1970), British novelist. He wrote six novels: *Where Angels Fear to Tread* (1905), *The Longest Journey* (1907), *A Room with a View* (1908), *Howards End* (1910), *A Passage to India* (1924) and the posthumously published *Maurice* (1971). *Aspects of the Novel* (1927) is a collection of lectures in literary criticism. *Abinger Harvest* (1936) and *Two Cheers for Democracy* (1951) are collections of essays on literature, society and politics.

Forster, John (1812–76), British journalist and biographer. He wrote an extensive survey of contemporary politicians and was appointed editor of the *Daily News* in 1846. He is best known for his memoir of Charles DICKENS (1872–74).

Forster, William Edward (1818–86), British Liberal politican who entered Parliament in 1861. He was the minister responsible for the 1870 Education Act, which established compulsory state elementary education.

Forsyth, Rev. Alexander John (1769–1843), Scottish inventor of the first operable PERCUSSION CAP for the ignition of gunpowder. He developed his first percussion cap, which used mercury FULMINATE, in 1805 and by 1807 he had improved the system to work in existing weapons. The cap greatly increased the efficacy of firearms, and Forsyth received a pension from the British government. *See also* MM p.162.

Forsyth, James (1913–), British poet and dramatist. His plays, many with religious themes, include *Heloise* (1951), *The Pier* (1958) and a nativity play, *Emmanuel* (1960). He also dramatized C. S. LEWIS's *The Screwtape Letters* (1942) as *Dear Wormwood* (1961).

Forsythia, genus of hardy deciduous shrubs of the OLIVE family Oleaceae, named after the British botanist William Forsyth. They are commonly cultivated in temperate regions. The masses of small yellow flowers look like golden bells and appear in early spring before the leaves. Height: to 3m (9.8ft).

Fort Albany, fur-trading post of the HUDSON'S BAY COMPANY in Ontario. The fort was established in 1679 by Charles Bayly who had started trading there in 1675. It was held by the French (1686–93), and was a key trading centre dominating the fur trade on the Albany River.

Fortaleza (Ceará), port city in NE Brazil, 435km (270 miles) NW of Natal. Founded in 1609 it is the capital of Ceavá Industries: sugar-refining, textiles, soap, shipping. Pop. 842,200.

Fort-de-France, port city and capital of Martinique, French West Indies, on Fort-de-France Bay. It was settled in 1762 by the French although it remained undeveloped until the beginning of the twentieth century. It is now a popular tourist resort. Pop. 99,000.

Fort Garry. *See* WINNIPEG.

Forth, river in Scotland, formed by the junction of Duchray Water and the Avondhu, 1.5km (1 mile) W of Aberfoyle. It meanders down the Carse of Forth W of Stirling to the Firth at Kincardine.

Forth, Firth of, estuary of the Forth, beginning at Kincardine and extending 77km (48 miles) to the Isle of May. It widens to 30.5km (19 miles) N of Musselburgh, but is only 13.5km (8.5 miles) wide N of North Berwick.

Forth Bridge, railway bridge over the Forth estuary, Scotland, opened in 1890. It is a cantilever structure with towers reaching to 110m (361ft) above the water. Length: 2,498m (8,196ft). The adjacent road bridge, opened in 1964, is a suspension span 1,006m (3,300ft) long.

For the Fallen (1914), poem by Laurence BINYON dealing with the unfading glory of those who died in WWI. A patriotic poem, it can be contrasted with the later, disillusioned war poetry of Wilfred OWEN.

Fort Knox, US Army post and depository of most of the nation's gold bullion. The fort, in Kentucky, was set up as a military establishment in 1917, and its vaults for the department of the treasury were built in 1937.

Fort Sumter, fort in South Carolina, USA, the scene of the first hostilities of the AMERICAN CIVIL WAR. In 1861 it was the only post in South Carolina still controlled by the federal government. LINCOLN sent reinforcements but the Confederates attacked and took it in two days. *See also* HC2 pp.150–151.

wFortuna, originally Roman fertility goddess. Later, after being identified with the Greek Tyche, she became goddess of chance or luck and was worshipped as Jupiter's first-born daughter, bearer of prosperity and increase.

Fortune Theatre, London playhouse opened in 1600, managed by Edward ALLEYN and Philip HENSLOWE. Thomas DEKKER, George CHAPMAN, and Thomas HEYWOOD all wrote plays for the Fortune in competition with SHAKESPEARE, who was at the Globe Theatre. It was demolished in 1649. *See also* HC1 p.284.

Fort Worth, city in N central Texas, USA, 53km (33 miles) W of Dallas. It was settled in 1843 and the US army established a post there in 1847. The area is famous for its oil and cattle, and since WWII an aircraft industry has also developed. Other products include processed food. Pop. (1973) 359,542.

Forty-ninth parallel, boundary line between the USA and Canada from Lake Superior to the Pacific coast. It was agreed in 1818, but only as far as the Rocky Mts, the Oregon Territory being left to the joint administration of Britain and the USA. In 1846 it was extended to the coast by the Treaty of Oregon.

Forum, in Roman towns, chief market and public gathering place. In Rome it originated in the 6th century BC and was set in a valley from the Capitoline hill along the Quirinal, Oppian and Palatine hills. It held many civic buildings including basilicas and temples, the *curia* (senate-house), treasury and triumphal arches. *See also* HC1 pp.90, 93, *98*.

For Whom the Bell Tolls (1940), novel by Ernest HEMINGWAY. Taking its title from a poem by John DONNE, it presents an optimistic vision of men's inevitable involvement with each other. It takes place during the SPANISH CIVIL WAR and concerns an American hiding in the mountains with a band of guerilla fighters.

Foss, Lukas (1922–), US composer and conductor, *b.* Germany. He is known for his AVANT-GARDE compositions, particularly those, such as *Elytres* (1964), that experiment with ALEATORIC music.

Fosse Way, British Roman road, running between Lincoln and the S Devon coast. The line of the road in AD 47 marked the boundary of the original Roman province of Britain which was guarded by a line of forts. Its name derived from the *fosse*, or ditch, that formed the frontier. *See also* HC1 pp.*100*, 101, *104*.

Fossil, any direct evidence of the existence of an organism more than 10,000 years old. Fossils mostly consist of original structures, such as bones or shells, or wood, often altered through mineralization or preserved as moulds and casts. Imprints such as tracks and footprints are also fossils. Leaves are often preserved as a carbonized film outlining their form. Occasionally organisms are totally preserved in frozen soil (mammoths), peat bogs and asphalt lakes (woolly rhinoceroses), or trapped in hardened resin (insects in amber). Fossil excrement, called coprolites, frequently contains undigested and recognizable hard parts. Very few animals and plants that die become fossilized. Since fossils reveal evolutionary changes through time, they are essential clues for geologic dating. *See also* NW 174–191, *174–191*; PE pp.124–127.

Foster, Brendan (1948–), British long- and middle-distance runner. A strong-running strategist, he won the 5,000m in the 1974 European Championships and was third in the 1976 Olympic Games 10,000m. He held world records at 2 miles and 3,000m.

Foster, Myles Birket (1825–99), British painter and engraver. In the 1850s he illustrated many books, including Longfellow's *Hyperion* (1853), but in about 1860 turned to landscape watercolours.

Foster, Stephen Collins (1826–64), US songwriter. Influenced by the Negro spiritual, his songs were extremely popular but he had little business sense and died in poverty. They include *Camptown Races* (1850), *Old Folks at Home* (1851), *My Old Kentucky Home* (1853) and *Jeanie with the Light Brown Hair* (1854).

Fotheringhay, village in Northamptonshire, central England, on the River Nene. It has the ruins of a 12th-century castle which was the birthplace of RICHARD III and the scene of the execution in 1586 of MARY, QUEEN OF SCOTS. Pop. 172.

Foucault, Jean Bernard Léon (1819–68), French physician and physicist. He proved that the Earth spins on its axis, worked on a method to measure the absolute velocity of light and in 1850 showed that it is slower in water than in air. He also noted the occurrence of eddy currents ("Foucault currents"). *See also* SU pp.104–105.

Foucault pendulum, heavy metal bob hung from a long, fine wire, first used by Jean Foucault to demonstrate the Earth's rotation. As the Earth turns on its axis, the plane of swing of the pendulum, as observed from the Earth's surface, rotates because of the heavy bob's inertial resistance to change of absolute direction, until it has returned to its original orientation. Its period of rotation depends on its latitude; in London it rotates in 30 hours. *See also* INERTIA; MM p.91.

Fougasse, (1887–1965), British cartoonist, real name Kenneth Bird. He is remembered chiefly for the small comic stick figures in his cartoons for *Punch*, of which he was editor (1949–53). During WWII his posters promoting various national causes gained him widespread fame.

Foundry, workshop in which metals are processed by melting and casting in moulds. Up to the 18th century, foundries were usually small, mainly casting gun barrels and bells. From 1760, however, they grew in size as the use of coke provided an efficient fuel to heat large furnaces. Foundaries became increasingly sophisticated, especially where iron and steel were concerned, after the innovations of men such as CORT and BESSEMER. *See also* MM pp.30–31, 42–43.

Fountains Abbey, Cistercian abbey, now in ruins, 5km (8 miles) N of Harrogate in the West Riding of Yorkshire, England. Founded *c.* 1132, it was suppressed in 1539 during the Reformation, at which time it housed 30 members in addition to an abbot and prior.

Fouquet (Foucquet), Jean (*c.* 1420–*c.* 80), French court painter. His work is monumental and sculptural in character, with figurings modelled in broad planes. Notable works include his portrait of CHARLES VII (*c.* 1447), BOOKS OF HOURS (1450–60) and the *Pietà* at Nouans. *See also* HC1 pp.*153*, *203*, *206*, 262.

Four Freedoms, expression of post-WWII goals made by Franklin D. ROOSEVELT in his State of the Union Address of Jan. 1941. They were: freedom of speech and expression; freedom of worship; freedom from want; and freedom from fear. Some of these were echoed in the ATLANTIC CHARTER of 1941. *See also* MS p.*191*.

Four Horsemen of the Apocalypse, allegorical figures described in the biblical Book of REVELATION (6: 1-8). The first horseman rides on a white horse; he carries a bow and is given a crown of conquest. The second is on a red horse; he has the power to take peace from the earth, and is given a sword. The third is on a black horse and carries a pair of balances; and the fourth is on a pale horse and is Death, who has unlimited power to destroy.

Fourier, Jean (1763–1830), French mathematician and physicist, scientific adviser to Napoleon in Egypt from 1798 to 1801. His later work on the mathematical analysis of heat flow led to his devising what is known as the FOURIER SERIES. *See also* HC2 p.316.

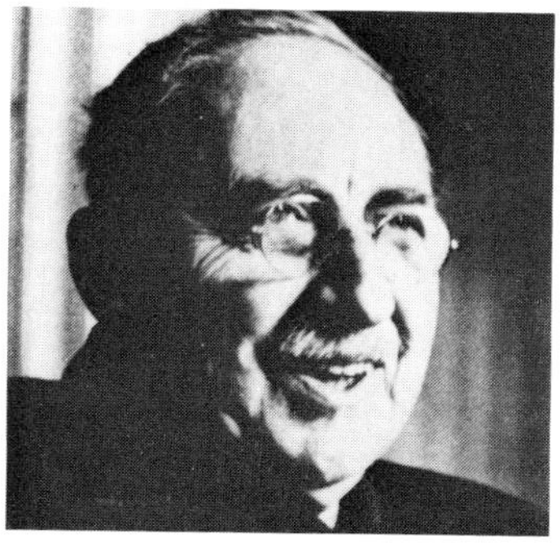

E. M. Forster's works contrast those who live by convention with those who live by instinct.

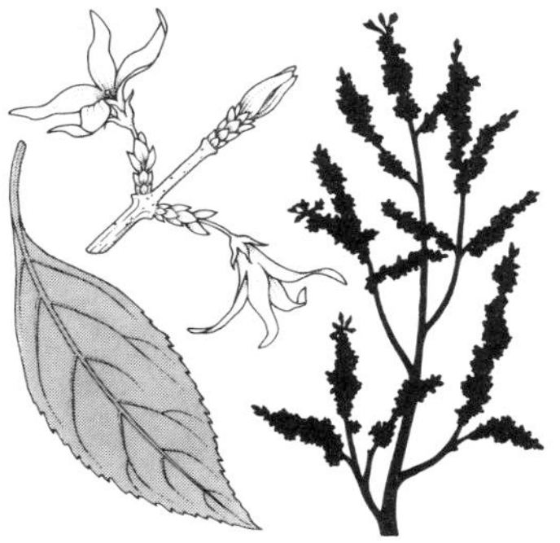

Forsythia is a popular shrub with gardeners because it grows well in almost any soil.

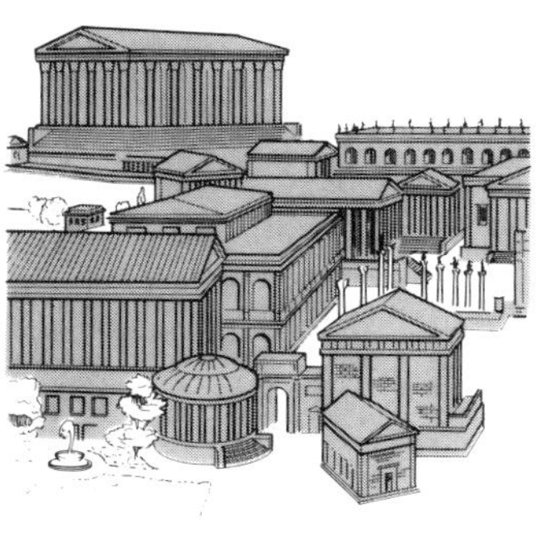

Forum, in Rome, was used for meetings and athletics and had galleries for spectators.

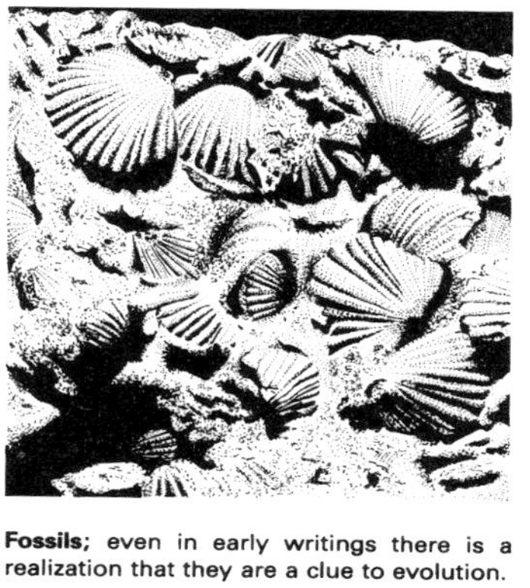

Fossils; even in early writings there is a realization that they are a clue to evolution.

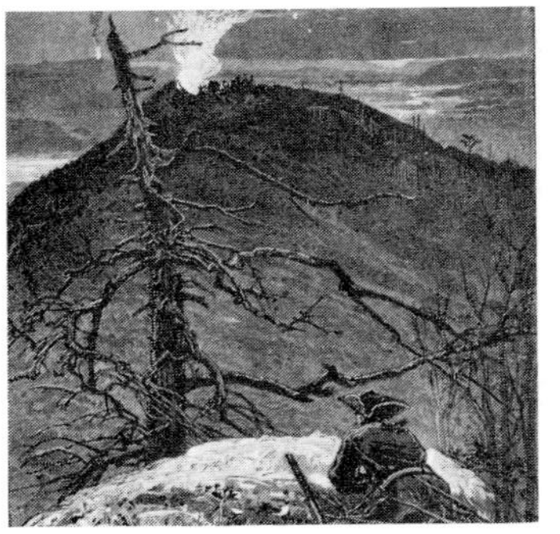

Fourth of July; an American soldier watches beacon fires lit in celebration of peace.

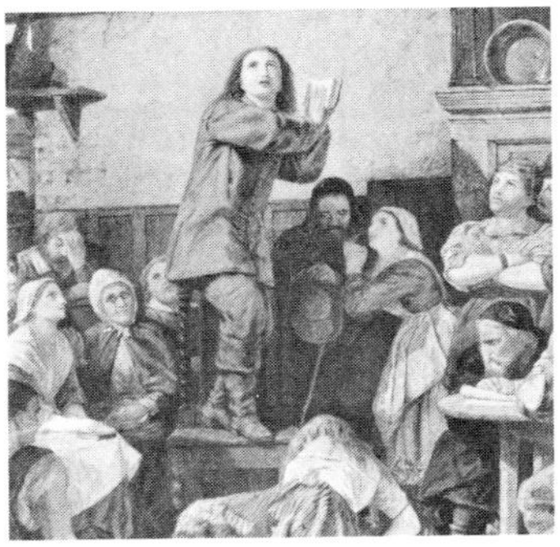

George Fox; Quakers were named from his advice to "tremble at the word of the Lord".

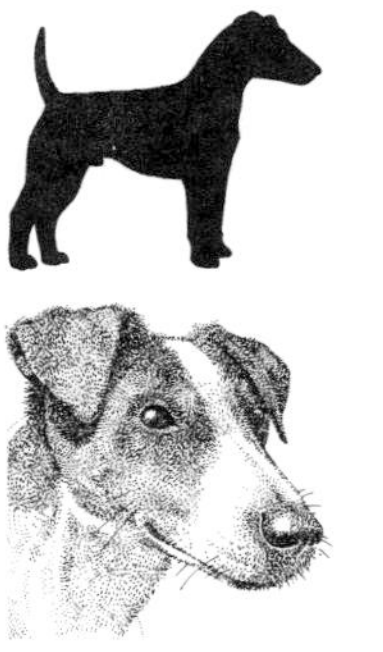

Fox terrier was originally bred to follow a fox into its burrow and then drive it out.

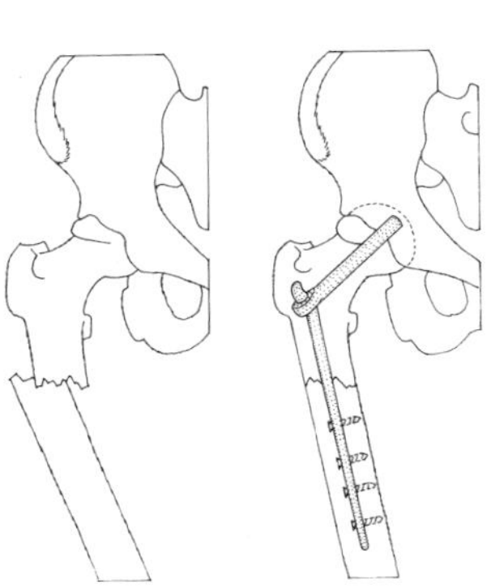

Fractures are generally located by X-ray and may sometimes need fixing with pins.

Fournier, Pierre Simon (1712–68), French typefounder and typographer who was the first to modernize traditional typefaces. He contributed to DIDEROT's *Encyclopédie.*
Fournier, Pierre (1906–), French cellist. He studied at the Paris Conservatory and became a teacher there (1941–49). He made his debut as a soloist in 1928 and was acclaimed for his performances of works by ELGAR, BACH, BRAHMS and DEBUSSY.
Four Quartets (1943), poem by T. S. ELIOT. Its four sections, originally published individually, are *Burnt Norton* (1936), *East Coker* (1940), *The Dry Salvages* (1941), and *Little Gidding* (1942). They reflect the poet's conversion to Anglo-Catholicism.
Foursquare Gospel Alliance. *See* MCPHERSON, AIMÉE SEMPLE.
Four-stroke cycle, power cycle that is completed after four journeys by a reciprocating piston, used in most motor car and lorry engines. First, the piston descends to admit the fuel-air mixture (intake stroke). Second, the piston rises, compressing the mixture (compression stroke). Third, the mixture is ignited by spark or compression, and expanding gases from the explosion force the piston downwards (ignition or power stroke). Fourth, the piston again rises to expel the spent gases from the cylinder (exhaust stroke). *See also* TWO-STROKE CYCLE; MM pp.62–63.
Four-stroke engine. *See* ENGINE.
Fourteen Points (1918), Woodrow WILSON's unsuccessful plan for peace after WWI. Several points were included in the Versailles treaty, and Wilson's dream of a LEAGUE OF NATIONS was realized. *See also* HC2 p.192.
Fourth dimension, time considered as an additional dimension, together with the three dimensions of space, in a full description of the motion of a particle. In RELATIVITY theory this four-dimensional framework is called SPACE-TIME. *See also* SU p.106.
Fourth estate, name often given to the press – people who gather, write and edit news. The phrase was first used by Thomas Babington MACAULAY when he wrote (1828) of the House of Commons that "The gallery in which the reporters sit has become a fourth estate of the realm", thus making an addition to the term THREE ESTATES – the lords spiritual, lords temporal and commons.
Fourth of July, US Independence Day and national holiday in celebration cf the adoption of the American Declaration of Independence of 4 July 1776. The day has been a holiday since that time.
Fowl, generally any gallinaceous or similar bird such as the pheasant or turkey; or more commonly the domestic chicken. *See* POULTRY.
Fowler, Henry Watson (1858–1933), British lexicographer and grammarian. He is known for *A Dictionary of Modern English Usage* (1926), and other writings such as *The King's English* (1906).
Fowles, John (1926–), British writer whose novels make strong comments on English ethical and social mores. *The Collector* (1963) and *The Magus* (1966) have both been made into films; *The French Lieutenant's Woman* (1969) and *Daniel Martin* (1977) have also been bestsellers.
Fox, Charles James (1749–1806), British WHIG politician who entered Parliament in 1768. In 1770–72 he was a lord of the Admiralty and in 1773–74 a lord of the Treasury. In 1782 he became foreign secretary in ROCKINGHAM's government and in 1783 formed a coalition government with Lord NORTH. Thereafter he led the small Whig opposition to the long government of PITT, returning to office as foreign secretary briefly in 1806. *See also* HC2 pp.68–69.
Fox, George (1624–91), English religious leader, founder of the Society of Friends (QUAKERS). He embarked upon his evangelical calling in 1646 in response to an "inner light". He was imprisoned eight times between 1649 and 1673. In 1671–72 he travelled to America to visit Quaker colonists there.
Fox, Neil (1939–), British rugby league player who, as a powerful centre, won 29 caps for Britain (1959–69). He began his career in 1956 with Wakefield Trinity and by the mid-1970s had amassed more than 5,000 points.
Fox, Sir William (1812–93), New Zealand politician. As Prime Minister he opposed moves to abolish New Zealand's provincial government and staunchly supported prohibition.
Fox, any of several carnivores of the DOG family. The red fox (*Vulpes vulpes*) is typical. Distinguished by its sharp features, rather large ears and long bushy tail, it feeds on insects, fruit, carrion and any small animal it can overpower. Height: 38cm (15in) at the shoulder; weight: about 9kg (19.8lb). Family Canidae. *See also* NW pp.*157*, *206*, *209*, *220*, 224.
Foxe, John (1516–87), English Anglican clergyman and historian. He was exiled during Mary I's persecutions, returning in Elizabeth I's reign to write his monumental *Actes and Monuments of these latter and perillous Dayes,* known as *Foxe's Book of Martyrs* (1563), a graphic description of religious persecutions from John WYCLIFFE to Thomas CRANMER. *See also* HC1 p.*271.*
Foxglove, any of a genus (*Digitalis*) of hardy Eurasian biennial and perennial plants with long, spiky clusters of two-lipped, tubular flowers. The common biennial foxglove (*D. purpurea*), source of the heart stimulant DIGITALIS is widely grown for its showy white, rose, purple or blue flowers. Family Scrophulariaceae.
Foxhound, medium-sized dog (sporting group) used in foxhunting. The coat is short and smooth, the ears droop and the tail is carried erect. The colour is black, tan and white. Foxhounds are noted for their speed and stamina. The American foxhound, recognized as a separate breed, is slighter than the English variety. Height: 53.3–63.5cm (21–25in) at the shoulder.
Fox hunting, field sport in which a fox is pursued across country by hounds, horsemen and horsewomen. A hunt is controlled by the master of hounds; the hounds by the huntsman, helped by whippers-in. Traditionally, if a fox is killed, its head, feet and tail (mask, pads and brush) are cut off and presented to members of the hunt, and its body given to the hounds.
Fox terrier, popular hunting dog (TERRIER group) recognized in two varieties – the smooth and the wire-haired. It has a narrow, tapered head, V-shaped, drooping ears, a short, straight-backed body, straight legs and a high-set tail carried erect. The coat is predominantly white in both varieties. Standard height: 39.5cm (15.5in) at the shoulder; weight: 7–8kg (15—18lb).
Fox-trot, ballroom dance popularized by the husband-and-wife dancing team of Vernon and Irene Castle in the early 20th century. Performed to a 4/4 beat, it is based on the two-step, but has a syncopated, rather than even, rhythm.
Foyle, river and lough of N Ireland. The River Foyle is formed from the rivers Finn and Mourne, which come together at Lifford. It flows past Londonderry and enters the tidal Lough Foyle.
Fraction, quotient written in the form of one number divided by another, eg $\frac{3}{4}$. In general, a fraction is $\frac{a}{b}$ where a is the numerator and b the denominator. If a and b are whole numbers the quotient is a simple fraction. If a is smaller than b, it is a proper fraction; if b is smaller than a, it is an improper fraction. In an algebraic fraction the denominator, or the numerator and denominator, are algebraic expressions, eg $\frac{x}{y+2}$. In a complex fraction both the numerator and denominator are themselves fractions. *See also* SU pp.28–29.
Fracture, break in a BONE. A compound fracture is one in which the bone has broken through the skin. During healing the break must be immobilized for a period of time that depends on the age and size of the bone, and the complexity of the fracture. *See also* MS pp.*115*, *133.*
Fragonard, Jean-Honoré (1732–1806), French painter. He was a student of Jean CHARDIN and François BOUCHER. He used many different styles, but is best known for the lighthearted spontaneity of his amorous scenes, rustic landscapes and decorative panels.
Frame, Janet (1924–), New Zealand short-story writer and novelist. Her works, set in New Zealand, explore the situation of contemporary women. They include *The Lagoon* (1951), *A State of Siege* (1966) and *The Rainbirds* (1968).
Frame of Reference, mathematical coordinate system for describing events in space and time with respect to a given observer. In the theory of RELATIVITY, this frame of reference is four-dimensional, and the description of events in other frames of reference depends on the relative velocities and accelerations of those frames with respect to the frame of reference of the observer. *See also* SU p.106.
Frampton, Sir George James (1860–1928), British sculptor. His work includes the statue of *Peter Pan* (1912) in Kensington Gardens, London.
Franc, monetary unit of France, Belgium, Switzerland and Luxembourg as well as of the African Financial Community (CFA) and the French Pacific Community. It is divided into 100 centimes.
France, Anatole (1844–1924), real name Anatole François Thibault, French author. He achieved recognition with the novels *The Crime of Sylvester Bonnard* (1881) and *Thaïs* (1890). He supported Emile ZOLA in the DREYFUS AFFAIR, and his writing grew more political, eg in the novels *Contemporary History* (1896–1901) and *Penguin Island* (1908). He was awarded the 1921 Nobel Prize in literature.
France, republic in W Europe; S of Britain, N of Spain, and W of Germany, Italy, Switzerland and the Low Countries. It is lowlying in the N and W with highlands to the S and E. The country's richest resource is its soil, and important products include wheat, grapes, soft fruits and butter and cheese from dairy herds. Although the industrial areas were devastated during WWII, post-war reconstruction turned France into a leading industrial nation, productng steel, pig iron and chemicals. The capital is Paris. Area; 547,026sq km (211,207sq miles). Pop. (1976 est.) 52,904,000 *See* MW p.77.
Francesca, Piero della. *See* PIERO DELLA FRANCESCA.
Franche-Comté, historic region of E France; its capital was Dôle until 1674 and Besançon thereafter. It was founded in the 12th century as the "free county" of the Burgundians, and throughout the Middle Ages was disputed between the Holy Roman Empire, France, Burgundy, Spain and Switzerland. After LOUIS XIV's conquest of 1674, it was finally recognized as part of France in 1678.
Franchise, business activity based upon an agreement between two parties that one will market the product of the other under specific conditions. It is common in the marketing of convenience foods (such as ice cream) where the supplying company may furnish almost everything except labour and some of the capital.
Franchise, right or privilege conferred on an individual or body by government, principally, in politics, the right to vote. In Britain the modern basis of the franchise dates from the 1832 REFORM ACT, which replaced the hotch-potch of medieval qualifications by a uniform set of qualifications. Broadly, the 1832 Act enfranchised the urban middle class, the 1867 Act the urban working class, and the 1884 Act agricultural labourers. All adult males (age 21) and women of age 30 were enfranchised in 1918, women of age 21 in 1928. (The first country to give women the vote was New Zealand, in 1893.) The voting age in Britain was lowered to 18 in 1969. *See also* HC2 pp.68–69, *95*, 160–161.
Francis, name of two Holy Roman emperors. Francis I (1708–65) was also Duke of Lorraine (1729–35) and of Tuscany (1737–65). In 1736 he married the Hapsburg heiress MARIA THERESA. Her accession in 1740 precipitated the War of the AUSTRIAN SUCCESSION. In 1745 Francis suc-

ceeded Charles VII as emperor, but was ineffectual; the real ruler was his wife. Francis II (1768–1835) was the last Holy Roman emperor (1792–1806) and Emperor of Austria (1804–35). Repeatedly defeated by France, in 1806 NAPOLEON forced him to dissolve the empire, but he had already proclaimed himself Austrian emperor. In 1810 his daughter Marie-Louise married Napoleon, but in 1813 Austria rejoined the anti-French coalition. Although Francis presided over the Congress of Vienna, since 1809 Austrian affairs had been run by Prince METTERNICH. *See also* HC2 p.*84*.

Francis, name of two kings of France. Francis I (1494–1547; *r.*1515–47) was a candidate for Holy Roman Emperor in 1519 but was defeated by CHARLES V of Spain. He then fought four wars against Charles – 1521–25, 1527–29, 1536–38 and 1542–44 – mainly in Italy, allying himself at different times with England, the papacy, Venice, Florence and the Turkish Sultan Suleiman I. He lost all the wars and much territory, including Burgundy. His absolutist rule saw the flourishing of the French Renaissance and the persecution of the WALDENSES. Francis II (1544–60; *r.*1559–60) reigned for only 17 months. He married Mary Stuart whose uncles Francis, Duc de Guise, and Charles, Cardinal of Lorraine, ruled the kingdom. *See also* HC1 pp.240, *240*, 263, *263*, 298, *298*.

Francis, name of two kings of the Two Sicilies. Francis I (1777–1830) became king in 1825. He showed liberal sympathies towards the CARBONARI rising of 1820 and opposed Austrian intervention in Naples, but on his accession he became an extreme reactionary and asked for greater Austrian presence. Francis II (1836–94) acceded to the throne in 1859 and was the last Bourbon King of Naples. He fled before GARIBALDI's army in 1860, was deposed by the plebiscite of 1861 and went into exile in Rome, France and Austria.

Franciscans, orders of friars following the rule of St FRANCIS OF ASSISI, which was approved by Pope Innocent III in 1209. They comprise the Observants, now known as the Friars Minor; the Friars Minor Capuchin, who were allowed to return to the strict observance of the primitive rule early in the 16th century; the Conventuals, and the Poor Clares, an order of nuns founded by St Francis and St Clare. Originally called Greyfriars, Franciscans now wear brown robes. *See also* HC1 p.187, *187*.

Francis, Dick (1920–), British writer of crime fiction. He was once a steeple-chase jockey and his novels, such as *Dead Cert* (1962) and *Bonecrack* (1971), are often about people and situations connected with horse racing.

Francis Joseph I, (1830–1916), Emperor of Austria (1848–1916), King of Hungary (1867–1916). He succeeded his uncle Ferdinand, who abdicated during the REVOLUTIONS OF 1848 and quickly brought the revolutions under control, defeating the Hungarians under KOSSUTH and the Italians under VICTOR EMMANUEL II of Savoy (both in 1849). But he lost Lombardy to Savoy in 1859 and in the AUSTRO-PRUSSIAN WAR (1866) lost Venetia to Italy, and Austria's prestige among the German states declined. In 1867 he was forced to grant Hungary co-equal status with Austria in the Dual Monarchy. He died in the midst of WWI two years before the complete collapse of his empire. *See also* HC2 p.*85*.

Francis of Assisi (*c.*1182–1226) founder of the itinerant order of the FRANCISCAN Friars, Roman Catholic saint (1228). Born Giovanni de Bernardone, the son of a wealthy merchant, in 1205 he renounced his worldly life for one of poverty and prayer. In 1209 he received permission from Pope Innocent III to begin a monastic order. The Franciscans were vowed to humility, poverty and devotion to aiding mankind. In 1212 he established an order for women, the Poor Clares, and in 1221 a lay fraternity. Like his brother friars he travelled widely, going to Egypt, Spain and to the Holy Land in 1219–20. In 1221 he gave up leadership of his order and later retired to his birthplace, Assisi in Italy. In 1224 he received the STIGMATA. He became revered for his love of man and nature, and is often depicted preaching to the birds. *See also* HC1 pp.187.

Francis of Paola, Saint (1416–1507), founder of the Order of Minim Friars, formed in 1435. Charles VIII of France built a friary for the Order at Plessis-les-Tours, where his dying father, Louis XI, had been assisted by Francis in 1482. The friars were vowed to perpetual fasting. Francis was canonized in 1519.

Francis of Sales, Saint, (1567–1622), Roman Catholic divine. A renowned preacher, he was a leader of the COUNTER-REFORMATION in Savoy. His first mission was to Chablais where he converted many from CALVINISM. In 1602 he was appointed Bishop (in exile) of Geneva. With Jeanne de Chantal he founded the Visitation Nuns. *Introduction to the Devout Life* (1609) is his best-known work.

Francistown, city in NE Botswana, on the railway from Cape Town (South Africa) to Bulawayo and Salisbury in Zimbabwe (Rhodesia). It is situated 161km (100 miles) SW of Bulawayo. Pop. (1971) 19,000.

Francis Xavier, Saint (1506–52), JESUIT missionary, often called the Apostle to the Indies. He was an associate of St IGNATIUS OF LOYOLA, with whom he took the vow founding the Society of Jesus. From 1541 he travelled through India, Japan and the East Indies, making many converts. He died while on a journey to China.

Francium, radioactive metallic element (symbol Fr), discovered in 1939 by Marguerite Perey. It occurs naturally in uranium ores and is a decay product of actinium. It is quite rare and its chemical properties are unknown, but it is thought to resemble CAESIUM. Properties: at.no. 87; most stable isotope Fr^{223} (half-life 22 min). *See also* ALKALI ELEMENTS.

Franck, César Auguste (1822–90), French Romantic composer, *b.* Belgium. He wrote major works for the organ and is best remembered for the *Symphonic Variations* for piano and orchestra (1885), and the popular *Symphony in D Minor* (1888). *See also* HC2 pp.106–107.

Franck, James (1882–1964), US physicist, *b.* Germany. Franck studied and taught at German universities. With Gustav HERTZ he experimented with electron bombardment of gases, providing support for Niels BOHR's theory of atomic structure and information for Max PLANCK's quantum theory. He and Hertz shared the 1925 Nobel Prize in physics. In 1935 he went to the USA, became a US citizen and ultimately worked on the development of the atomic bomb.

Franco, Francisco (1892–1975), Spanish general and dictator of Spain (1939–75). He joined the 1936 military uprising that led to the SPANISH CIVIL WAR and assumed leadership of the FALANGE party. By 1939, with the aid of Nazi Germany and Fascist Italy, he had won the war and became Spain's dictator. He kept Spain neutral in WWII, after which he presided over Spain's accelerating economic development and kept rigid control over its politics. He declared Spain a monarchy in 1947 with himself as regent. In 1969 he designated JUAN CARLOS as heir to the throne, and he became king upon Franco's death. *See also* HC2 p.223.

Franconia, historic region of Germany around the River Main. It was a duchy of the East Frankish kingdom after 843 and was later divided among several ecclesiastical princes, of whom the bishop of Würzburg was one of the most powerful. Much of Franconia became part of Bavaria in the 19th century.

Franco-Prussian War (1870–71), conflict in which BISMARCK, Chancellor of Prussia, engineered a dispute with France on the Spanish succession as a pretext for invading France, in alliance with the other German states, in Aug. 1870. The French were disastrously defeated at SEDAN in Sept. and NAPOLEON III abdicated. According to the terms of the peace of March 1871 Alsace and Lorraine were ceded to the new German Empire. *See also* HC2 pp.110, 180.

Frangipani, group of shrubs and small trees native to Central America and the West Indies and now grown in other warm regions. They have fragrant white, yellow, pink or red flowers and a poisonous milky sap. A perfume of the same name is prepared from one species. Family Apocynaceae; genus *Plumeria*.

Frank, Anne. *See* DIARY OF ANNE FRANK.

Frankau, Gilbert (1884–1952), British poet and novelist. After experimenting with novels in verse and poems in *Poetical Works* (1923), he wrote various prose novels, including *Peter Jackson, Cigar Merchant* (1919) and *The Love Story of Aliette Brunton* (1922).

Frankel, Benjamin (1906–), British composer. An accomplished composer of film scores, he wrote music for *The Importance of Being Earnest* (1952) and *London Belongs to Me* (1948). His other compositions include orchestral and chamber works that display technical versatility and marked emotional introspection.

Frankenstein (1818), novel by Mary Wollstonecraft SHELLEY. Its "gothick" horror story centres around a monster which Frankenstein created from corpses. Unloved because of his revolting appearance, the monster takes revenge on Frankenstein. The monster has been the inspiration for several films and has been most notably played by Boris KARLOFF, who starred in the definitive 1931 film version.

Frankfurt-on-Main (Frankfurt-am-Main), city and port in central West Germany, on the River Main 27km (17 miles) N of Darmstadt. Founded as a Roman town in the 1st century, it later became one of the royal residences of CHARLEMAGNE. It was annexed by Prussia after 1866. Industries: chemicals, electrical equipment. Pop. (1974) 663,422.

Frankincense, also called olibanum, gum resin extracted from the bark of trees of the genus *Boswellia*, found in Africa and Arabia. It is burned as incense, and the fine spicy oil extracted from the resin is used as a fixative in perfumes.

Frankland, Sir Edward (1825–99), British chemist who formulated the theory of valence which states that each element may be assigned a whole number (eg 1,2 or 3) or valency which represents the number of hydrogen atoms with which an atom of the element will combine. He also discovered, with Sir Joseph N. LOCKYER, the gas helium.

Franklin, Aretha (1942–), US singer. She rose to stardom in 1966 with *I never loved a man (the way I love you)*, a million-selling record. She is known as "The Queen of Soul".

Franklin, Benjamin (1706–90), US inventor. He published *Poor Richard's Almanac* (1732–57). He invented the Franklin stove and experimented with electricity. He spent a total of 16 years in England before the American War of Independence, attempting to reconcile Britain and the colonies. He was a delegate to the Second Continental Congress and helped to draft the Declaration of Independence. He was postmaster general in 1775–76. Sent to France (1776–85), he helped to bring that country into the war on the American colonists' side. *See also* HC2 p.22.

Franklin, Sir John (1786–1847), British rear admiral and arctic explorer. He fought at the Battle of Copenhagen (1801) and the Battle of Trafalgar (1805). He later commanded two explorations of the North American coast (1819–22 and 1825–27), for which he was knighted. In 1845 he led an arctic exploration in search of a northwest passage in which he and all his crew died.

Franklin, Stella Maria Miles (1879–1954), Australian novelist. *My Brilliant Career* (1901), is a fictionalized account of her early life. She travelled widely, returning home to write *All That Swagger* (1936), probably her best work.

Franklin, district and northernmost region in Canada. Founded in 1895, it is part of Canada's North-West Territories. It encompasses all the numerous islands N of

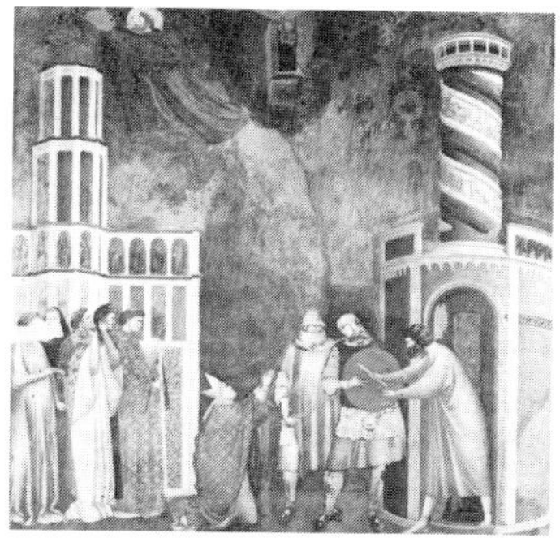

Francis of Assisi was portrayed by a friar in *The Little Flowers of St Francis.*

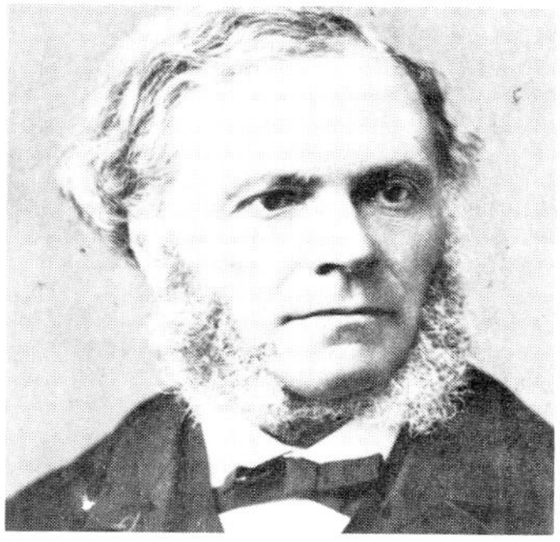

César Franck received recognition in his later years only but his admirers include Debussy.

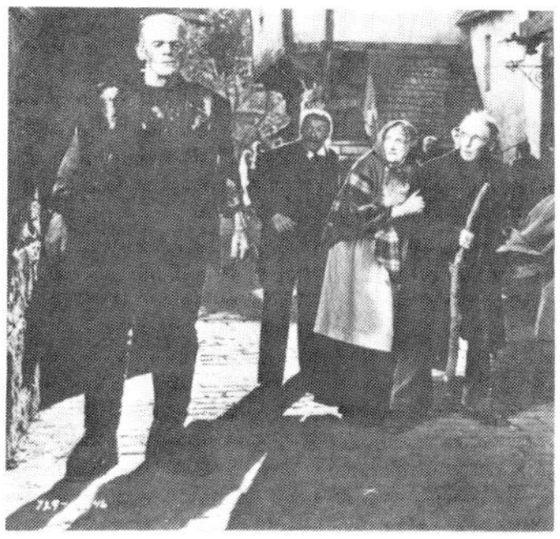

Frankenstein; a still from the film of 1931, with Boris Karloff as the monster.

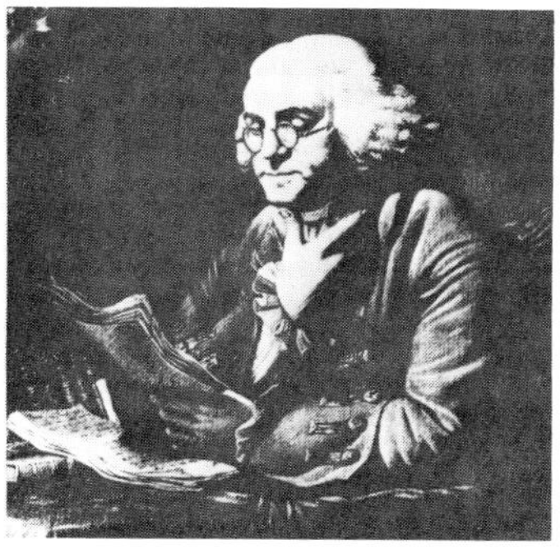

Benjamin Franklin never sought public office but was one of the USA's best diplomats.

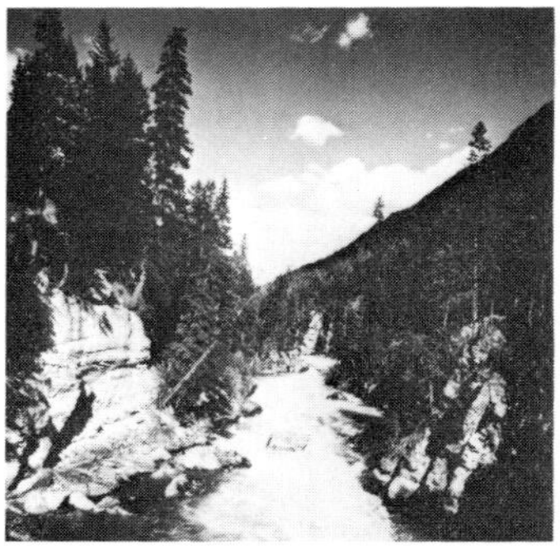

Fraser river, famous for its salmon, drains almost all of southern British Columbia.

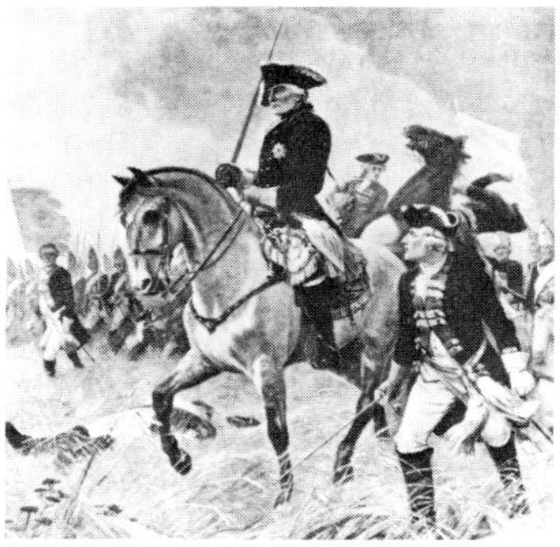

Frederick the Great at the Battle of Hohenfriedberg where he defeated the Austrians.

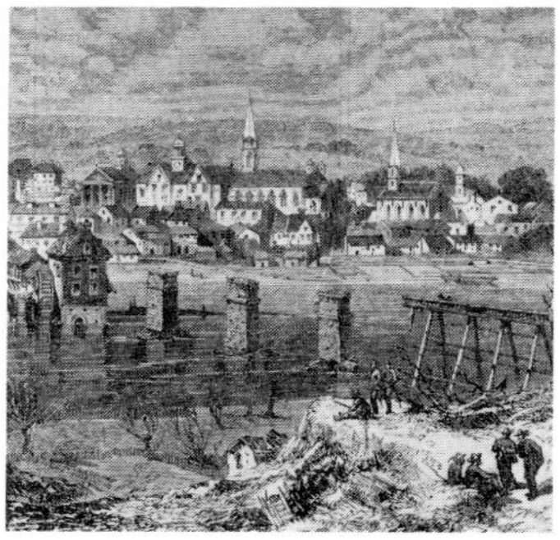

Fredericksburg; a view of the town, with demolished bridge, after the Civil War battle.

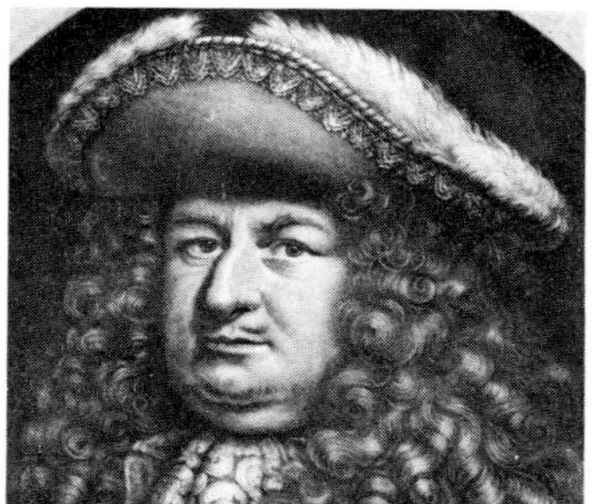

Frederick William's policies laid the foundations of Prussian dominance.

the Canadian mainland, the Boothia and Melville peninsulas and the districts of Mackenzie and Keewatin. Area: 1,422,644sq km (549,253sq miles). *See* MW p.50.

Franks, Germanic people who settled in the region of the River Rhine in the 3rd century. Under CLOVIS they overthrew the remnants of Roman rule in Gaul in the late 5th century and established the MEROVINGIAN empire. The empire was later divided into the kingdoms of Austrasia, Neustria and Burgundy, but was reunited by the CAROLINGIANS, notably by CHARLEMAGNE. The partition of his empire into the East and West Frankish kingdoms is the origin of Germany and France. *See also* HC1 pp.134–135, 152–153.

Franzén, Frans Mikael (1772–1847), Swedish poet and scholar, *b.* Finland. He is best known for the poems such as *Det nya Eden* (The New Eden, 1794).

Franz Josef Land (Zemlya Franca-iosifa), archipelago in the Arctic Ocean; part of Archangel'sk oblast, USSR. A group of approx. 187 islands, it includes Alexandra Land, George Land and Graham Bell Island. Area: 20,720sq km (8,000sq miles).

Frasch process, named after the German-born chemist Herman Frasch, a method of mining sulphur by pumping superheated water and air into the sulphur deposits, melting the mineral, and forcing it to the surface. The process was first put to practical use in Louisiana and made the USA independent of imported sulphur.

Fraser, Dawn (1937–), Australian swimmer who won the 100m freestyle event at three successive Olympic Games (1956, 1960, 1964), plus a 4 × 100m relay gold medal in 1956. The first woman to swim 100m in less than 1 minute, she set 27 individual world records.

Fraser, John Malcolm (1930–), Australian politician. He entered Parliament in 1955 and after a series of cabinet appointments from 1966 to 1971, he became both leader of the Liberal Party and Prime Minister.

Fraser, Peter (1884–1950), New Zealand politician, *b.* Scotland. He emigrated to New Zealand in 1910. He helped to organize the SOCIAL DEMOCRATIC Party and its successor, the LABOUR Party. He was elected to Parliament in 1918 and became minister of education, health, marine and police in the Labour government in 1935. He was prime minister from 1940 to 1949.

Fraser, Simon (1776–1862), Canadian explorer and fur trader. He moved to Canada from the USA in 1784 and joined the Northwest Company in 1792. He extended their trade routes west to British Columbia (1805–08) and founded a string of trading posts. He also explored the Fraser River and the Red River.

Fraser, river in S British Columbia, Canada. It rises in the Rocky Mts and flows NW then S around the Cariboo Mts and into the Strait of Georgia. It was discovered in 1793 by Alexander Mackenzie and explored in 1808 by Simon Fraser. Length: 1,368km (850 miles).

Fraud, in law, deception or misrepresentation of facts in order to obtain an advantage by unfair means. It is commonly an element of specific crimes such as impersonation, misrepresentation or obtaining money by false pretences. Withholding or concealing facts injurious to another person may also constitute criminal fraud.

Fraunhofer, Joseph von (1787–1826), German physicist and optical instrument maker. His studies of the dark lines (Fraunhofer lines) in the solar spectrum helped to establish the science of spectroscopy. Although he mapped the positions of these lines, he was unable to explain them. He also invented a DIFFRACTION grating device. *See also* SU pp.63, 226.

Frayn, Michael (1933–), British writer. His first novel was *The Tin Men* (1965). He also wrote *Towards the End of the Morning* (1967) and the plays *The Two of Us* (1970) and *Alphabetical Order* (1975).

Frazer, Sir James George (1854–1941), Scottish anthropologist, folklorist and classical scholar. His major work is *The Golden Bough: a Study in Magic and Religion* (1890) which held that the history of thought is a logical progression from the magical through the religious to the scientific.

Frechette, Louis-Honoré (1839–1908), Canadian poet and politician. He served in the Canadian Parliament (1874–78). His poetry includes *La voix d'un exilé* (1866–68), *Les fleures boréales* (1879) and *La Légende d'un peuple* (1887).

Frederick, name of three Holy Roman emperors. Frederick I (*c.* 1123–90) was a HOHENSTAUFEN, Holy Roman Emperor (1155–90), King of Germany (1152–90) and King of Italy, called "Barbarossa" (Red Beard). He restored order in Germany by appeasing the feuding nobles. He spent 30 years trying to restore imperial power in N Italy and was in conflict with successive popes before the Lombard League defeated him in 1176 and he was reconciled with pope Alexander III. Frederick II (1194–1250), also a Hohenstaufen, Holy Roman Emperor (1220–50), King of Germany (1211–20), King of Sicily (1198–1250) and King of Jerusalem (1229–50), continued the power struggle with the popes and maintained his control of Germany. His rule in Sicily showed him to be a brilliant lawmaker, administrator, warrior, multilingual diplomat and patron of the arts and sciences. Frederick III (1415–93), Holy Roman Emperor (1452–93) and German king (1440–93), lost several territories early in his reign which were later regained. He reconciled his power with that of the papacy, and by marrying his son Maximilian to Mary, heiress of BURGUNDY, gained an enormous inheritance for the HAPSBURGS. *See* HC1 pp.160–161, 176, 177.

Frederick V (1596–1632), elector palatine (1610–23) and King of Bohemia (1619–20), called the Winter King. In 1619 the Bohemian nobles deposed Emperor Ferdinand II and replaced him with Frederick. He lost both titles at The Battle of the White Mountain (1620).

Frederick, name of nine kings of Denmark and Norway. Frederick I (1471–1533; *r.* Denmark 1523–33, Norway 1524–33) discouraged war with Sweden and tolerated the spread of Lutheranism in Denmark. In the reign of Frederick II (1534–88; *r.* 1559–88) Denmark prospered peacefully. Frederick III (1609–70; *r.* 1648–70) fought unsuccessful wars with Sweden and established absolute monarchy. Frederick IV (1671–1730; *r.* 1699–1730) failed to recover Sweden, but gained Schleswig and, at home, instituted reforms. Frederick V (1723–66, *r.* 1746–66) was ineffective but his ministers introduced successful economic policies. Frederick VI (1768–1839; *r.* Denmark 1808–39, Norway 1808–14) became regent in 1784 and introduced land reforms. In the Napoleonic Wars he was at first neutral, then supported France. He had to cede Norway to Sweden in 1814, and in 1834 set up elected provincial assemblies. Frederick VII (1808–63; *r.* Denmark 1848–63) introduced a constitution and was involved in the SCHLESWIG-HOLSTEIN question. Frederick VIII (1843–1912, *r.* 1906–12); Frederick IX (1899–1972), who ruled 1947–72, altered the succession law so that his daughter, Margaret, could succeed him.

Frederick, name of two kings of Prussia. Frederick I (1657–1713), was elector of Brandenburg as Frederick III (1688–1713) and the first King of Prussia (1701–13). He assumed the title of king with the approval of his ally the Holy Roman Emperor Leopold I. Frederick II (1712–86; *r.* 1740–86), called Frederick the Great, adopted an aggressive policy towards Austria. He made Prussia a major European power through his involvement in the War of the AUSTRIAN SUCCESSION (1740–48), the SEVEN YEARS WAR (1756–63) and the War of the Bavarian Succession (1777–79). He acquired Polish Prussia in the first partition of Poland (1772). Frederick carried out many internal reforms but his government was autocratic and over-centralized. A great patron of the arts, he wrote extensively in French and was a good musician.

Frederick Augustus, name of two kings of Saxony. Frederick Augustus I (1750–1827) was first elector (1768–1806) and then king (1806–27). He entered the war against France, but after the Prussian defeat at Jena in 1806 he made a separate peace with Napoleon, who approved the title King of Saxony and made him Grand Duke of Warsaw. He lost much of his kingdom to Prussia at the Congress of VIENNA (1815). Frederick Augustus II (1797–1854; *r.* 1836–54) was co-regent with his uncle Anton from 1830 and instituted the 1831 constitution, but as king resisted further change. He repressed a revolt in 1849 with the aid of Prussia.

Frederick Henry (1584–1647), Prince of Orange-Nassau. Son of WILLIAM THE SILENT, in 1625 he became stadtholder of the United Provinces. Under his rule the stadtholdership was accepted as hereditary for the House of ORANGE. In 1635 he allied with France and Sweden against the Hapsburgs during the THIRTY YEARS WAR and campaigned against Spanish strongholds in The Netherlands.

Fredericksburg, Battle of (1862), victory for Confederate Gen. Robert E. LEE's Army over Maj. Gen. Ambrose Burnside's Union Army. Lee's men stopped 14 attacks, killing or wounding nearly 13,000 of the 114,000 Union men. Lee lost about 5,300 of his 72,500 troops.

Frederick William, name of four kings of Prussia. Frederick William I (1688–1740; *r.* 1713–40) founded its rigidly organized military and administrative systems. He doubled his standing army to 80,000 men, further centralized the government and seized part of Swedish Pomerania. Frederick William II (1744–97; *r.* 1786–97) joined the alliance against France in 1792 but made peace in 1795 to consolidate his acquisitions in the east as a result of the partitions of Poland (1793 and 1795). He kept an extravagant court and left the country virtually bankrupt. His son, Frederick William III (1770–1840; *r.* 1797–1840), was forced to declare war on France in 1806, but suffered a crushing defeat at Jena. After the Peace of Tilsit in 1807, major reforms were carried out by his ministers, Barons Stein and Hardenburg. Later, allied with Russia, Prussia took part in the final defeat of Napoleon. After 1815 he joined the HOLY ALLIANCE and, growing more reactionary, refused to grant a constitution. His son Frederick William IV (1795–1861; *r.* 1840–61) gave way at first to the 1848 revolution, calling a constituent assembly, but he later dissolved this and issued a conservative constitution. His schemes for German unity foundered and because of mental problems, following a stroke, his brother William became regent in 1858.

Frederick William (1620–88), elector of Brandenburg (1640–88), called the Great Elector. At the Peace of Westphalia (1648), which ended the THIRTY YEARS WAR, he acquired Eastern Pomerania and, by intervention in the war (1655–60) between Poland and Sweden, won recognition of his sovereignty over Prussia, formerly a Polish fief. He also built up the Prussian army, curtailed the privileges of the nobility and fostered trade.

Fredro, Alexander (1793–1876), Polish dramatist who wrote witty ironic comedies such as *Sluby Panienski* (*Maiden's Vows* 1832). He was successful until silenced in 1835 by a patriotic attack on his cynicism.

Free Churches, Protestant Churches which are independent of the established Church of a country. In 1896 in England, where the established Church is ANGLICAN, the BAPTISTS, CONGREGATIONALISTS, METHODISTS and PRESBYTERIANS formed a National Council of the Evangelical Free Churches. Such Churches generally have a minimum of hierarchy, are largely organized by their congregation, and emphasize the importance of preaching and witness.

Free Church of Scotland, Church formed as a result of the secession of nearly a third of the Established Church of Scotland at the Disruption of 1843. After joining with the United Presbyterian Church in 1900 and becoming the United Free Church of Scotland, in 1929 a minority of this group, opposed reunion with the Established Church, retained their independence and kept the name United Free Church.

Free city, description used since the Middle Ages of European cities recognized as autonomous states, exempt from duties and taxes and under imperial or international protection. Hamburg, Bremen and Lübeck held this status in Germany until the 1930s. Danzig (Poland) and Fiume (Yugoslavia) were, for a time, free cities under the LEAGUE OF NATIONS.

Freedman, Barnett (1901–58), British painter and lithographer. He designed many posters and book illustrations and the postage stamps for the Jubilee of George V in 1935. He was a war artist during WWII.

Freedom of a city, honour inherited or bestowed by a town or city corporation on distinguished individuals. It dates from the Middle Ages when it was acquired by birth, marriage, apprenticeship to a freeman, gift or purchase, and this is still so in the acquisition of the freedom of the city of London. In the modern ceremony a person is granted the freedom of a city by being presented with a key symbolizing his right to come and go at will.

Freedom of the seas, fundamental principle of international law affirming that no state has sovereignty over the seas beyond its territorial waters. It guarantees the right to fish and sail on the high seas, to fly over them and to lay cables and pipelines.

Freedom of Worship. *See* RELIGIOUS TOLERATION.

Free enterprise, in economics, system in which market forces alone decide what goods are produced and the prices at which they are sold and who consumes them. Individual firms may combine resources for production, and individual consumers may buy what they wish. Significant government control of the economy is absent.

Free-fall parachuting, or skydiving, sporting activity in which parachutists delay opening their parachutes until a series of acrobatic manoeuvres have been performed. Competitions are for solo, pairs and team jumps.

Free French, group formed by Charles DE GAULLE on the creation of the VICHY GOVERNMENT in 1940. Its purpose was to continue French opposition to Germany. Operating outside France, the group was soon aligned with internal resistance groups. The Free French aided the Allies throughout the war, forming a provisional government after the D-DAY invasion.

Freehold, legal term describing an estate held for an indefinite period, hence in practice implying absolute ownership. The idea of freehold dates back to feudal times, when only the monarch could own land. An unlimited, inheritable, tenancy of this land was known as an *estate in fee simple*, or freehold. *See also* LEASEHOLD.

Freeling, Nicolas (1927–), British writer of DETECTIVE FICTION. His first novel was *Love in Amsterdam* (1962), in which he introduced the hero of his stories, the Dutch detective, van der Valk.

Freemasonry, secret fraternal order, most popular in Britain and countries once within the British Empire. It evolved from the medieval guilds of stonemasons and cathedral builders. When cathedral building declined, honorary members were admitted to increase the numbers. In 1717 the first Grand Lodge (meeting place) was founded in England. Historically associated with liberalism and although not a formally Christian institution, freemasonry teaches morality, charity and law-abiding behaviour. Freemasons, all adult males, believe in God and the immortality of the soul. A member enters the order as an apprentice, becomes a fellow of the craft and finally a master mason. It is estimated that there are one million masons in Britain.

Free radicals, highly reactive molecules containing an unpaired electron, formed by the splitting of a chemical bond (usually by short-wave radiation). Such radicals are indicated by a dot, eg methyl $CH_3\cdot$. They are usually short-lived (less than 1ms) and are important intermediates in such reactions as combustion.

Freesia, genus of perennial herbs of the IRIS family, native to South Africa. Species of freesia are widely cultivated for their fragrant yellow, white or pink tubular flowers. They are grown in cool greenhouses for winter blooming.

Free speech, in Elizabethan England, the right of members of Parliament to initiate discussion on any issue. During the 17th century the term came to mean the right of anyone to discuss any question without hindrance. John MILTON was an early proponent of this concept of free speech in AREOPAGITICA (1644).

Freetown, seaport and capital city of Sierra Leone, W Africa. It was founded in 1787 by freed slaves from England, Nova Scotia and Jamaica and was the capital of British West Africa 1808–74. It exports diamonds and its industries include cigarettes and oil-refining. Pop. 178,600.

Free Trade, term usually used to describe commerce conducted between nations without restrictions on imports and exports. In modern history its origins lie in the 19th-century attack, especially in Britain, on the traditional MERCANTILIST control of trade. The repeal of the CORN LAWS (1846) and the Anglo-French free-trade treaty (1860) were the chief marks of the mid-Victorian faith in free trade. After WWI Britain again became a protectionist nation. Free-trade agreements in the 20th-century have been made within limited areas – EFTA and the EEC – or have been limited in scope – GATT.

Free verse, verse with no regular metre and no apparent form, relying primarily on cadence. The unsystematized rhythm is close to that of prose. WHITMAN and RIMBAUD were early users of free verse, which has become common in the 20th century.

Freeway. *See* ROADS.

Free will, capacity to choose a course of action, where such choice exists. It has been asserted as the basis of man's superiority among living creatures, and its long tradition in Western law and moral thought has Greek origins in the work of SOCRATES. It is frequently contrasted with DETERMINISM.

Freeze-drying, technique used to preserve foods. Water is removed from the frozen substance at a low temperature under high vacuum, avoiding the concentration effect that occurs when a solution is evaporated slowly in normal freezing. Freeze-drying is better at retaining the flavour and nutritional value of foods and is used commercially for meat, fish and instant coffee. *See also* FROZEN FOODS; PE p.251.

Freezing, solid phase in the reduction of temperature of a liquid. The steady removal of heat from a liquid is accompanied by a steady drop in temperature until the liquid's FREEZING POINT is reached. Freezing points of liquids are always given at standard or atmospheric pressure, and the Celsius temperature scale gives the freezing point of water as 0°C. In the Fahrenheit scale (F) it is 32° and in the Kelvin scale (K) it is 273°. The quantity of heat extracted from one kilogramme of water as it freezes is known as the latent heat of water. Absolute zero (0°K; −273.16°C) is the point at which all things freeze and all motion stops.

Freezing point, temperature at which a substance changes phase from liquid to solid. The freezing point for most substances increases somewhat as pressure increases. The reverse process, from solid to liquid, is melting; melting point is the same as freezing point. *See also* SU p.86.

Frege, Gottlob (1848–1945), German philosopher. He was a professor of mathematics at Jena from 1879 until he retired during WWI, and with George BOOLE was one of the founders of modern symbolic LOGIC. Frege attempted to derive all mathematics from logical axioms in his *Foundations of Arithmetic* (1884).

Freighter, ship designed to carry dry cargo or freight. The most modern cargo freighters are CONTAINER SHIPS, which carry pre-packed steel containers delivered to the quayside by trains or lorries, and the BACAT (barge aboard catamaran) vessels, which carry steel lighters or barges. *See also* MM p.*114*.

Fremantle, seaport in SW Australia, at the mouth of the Swan River. Its exports are wool and wheat. Pop. 25,300.

Fremont, John Charles (1813–90), US explorer and general, best known for his exploration and mapping of the OREGON TRAIL in 1842. He served as senator from California (1850–51) and was the first Republican presidential candidate.

French and Indian War (1754–63), name given to the SEVEN YEARS WAR by the American colonists, referring particularly to the part of the war fought in America, in which the French and the Indians were allies against Britain. It began two years before the general European conflict.

French Antarctica, small enclave in Australian territory known as Adélie Land, between 136°E and 142°E. In Jan. 1840 J. S. C. Dumont d'Urville discovered the coast when attempting to reach the S magnetic pole.

French bulldog, good-tempered dog bred from toy English bulldogs in France in the 1860s. It has a large, square bulldog face with a short nose, prominent lower jaw and thick, hanging lips. Its broad-based, erect ears distinguish it from the larger BULLDOG. The body is short, the legs are stout and muscular and the short tail is straight. Average height: 30.5cm (12in) at the shoulder; weight: 8.5–12.7kg (19–28lb).

French Canadians, Canadians whose first language is French. The French founded the first settlement in Canada in 1605. Immigration declined after 1675, yet today they comprise 31% of the population. After 1763 French Canadians defended their language and culture with success. But the RIEL rebellions, opposition to WWI and urban industrialization after WWII weakened their influence. Only in Quebec have they succeeded in preserving their social autonomy.

French Guiana, French overseas département on the NE coast of South America. Most of the population lives along the coastal region as tropical forest renders much of the inland area uninhabitable. Economically the country is dependent on France although the exploitation of bauxite deposits could alter this. The capital is Cayenne. Area: 91,000sq km (35,135sq miles). Pop. (1975 est.) 60,000. *See* MW p.81.

French Guinea. *See* GUINEA.

French horn, brass musical instrument. It has a flared bell, long coiled conical tube, three or four valves and a funnel-shaped mouthpiece. Its romantic, mellow tones were favoured by Richard WAGNER, Johann BRAHMS and Richard STRAUSS. *See also* HC2 p.105, *105*.

French India, French colonies in India. The French East Indian Company (1664–1769) acquired Pondicherry on the coast below Madras. Pondicherry remained a French post until 1954.

French marigold. *See* MARIGOLD.

French Polynesia, group of more than 100 islands in the S Pacific Ocean, including the Society Islands and the Marquesas. *See* MW p.81.

French Revolution, set of events which took place in France between 1789 and 1799. It began in June 1789 when an ESTATES GENERAL met at Versailles during a political crisis caused by attempts to tax the nobility. Representatives of the Bourgeoisie demanded reform and proclaimed themselves a NATIONAL ASSEMBLY; the government could not resist because the people of town and country rose in revolt. In October 1791 the LEGISLATIVE ASSEMBLY was installed. Faced with growing internal and external pressure, it declared war on Austria in April 1792, and was soon in conflict with most other European states. The war hastened political change: in August 1792 LOUIS XVI was deposed, and the National CONVENTION met in September to proclaim a republic. After a period of rivalry between JACOBINS and GIRONDINS (Nov. 1792–June 1793) strong central government was imposed during the REIGN OF TERROR and Louis was executed. This was followed by the confused THERMIDOREAN REACTION (July 1794–Oct. 1795). In 1795 rule by the DIRECTORY began, and continued until 1799 when the CONSULATE brought the

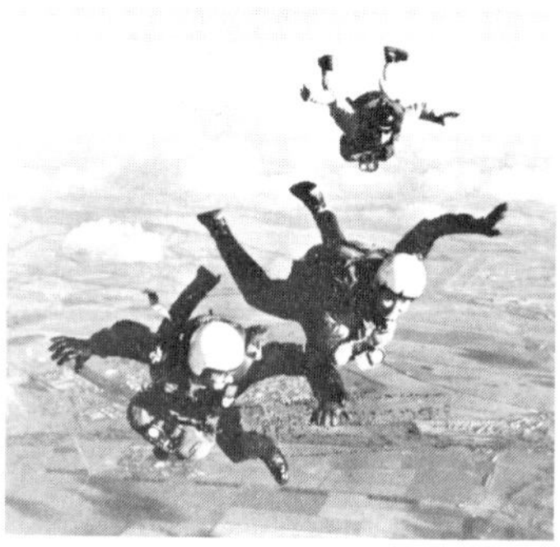

Free-fall parachuting; low temperatures and heavy equipment make this a hardy sport.

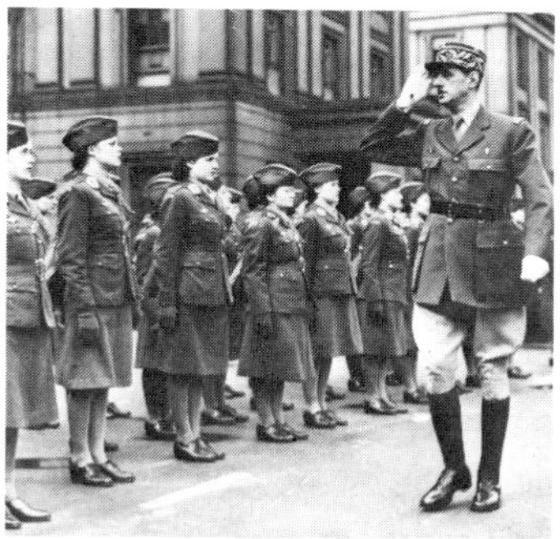

Free French; members of the Women's Army being saluted by General de Gaulle.

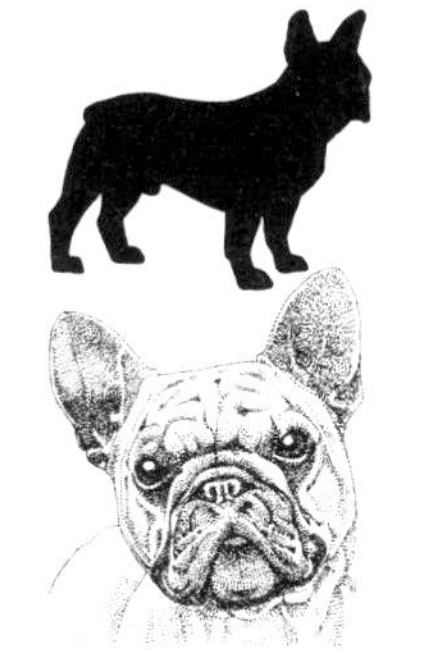

French bulldog, whose coat is usually brindle with white patches but may be mainly white.

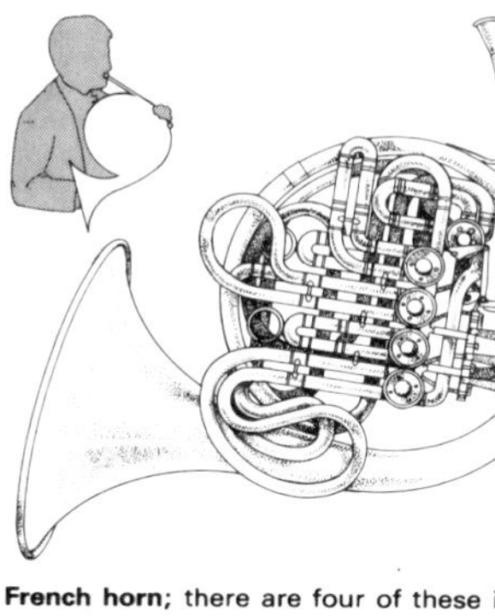

French horn; there are four of these instruments in most modern symphony orchestras.

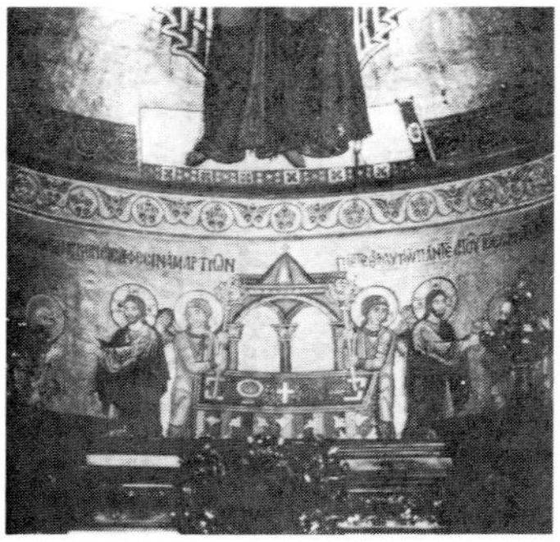

Fresco painting; this example of the art form is a detail in the Cathedral of St Sophia, Kiev.

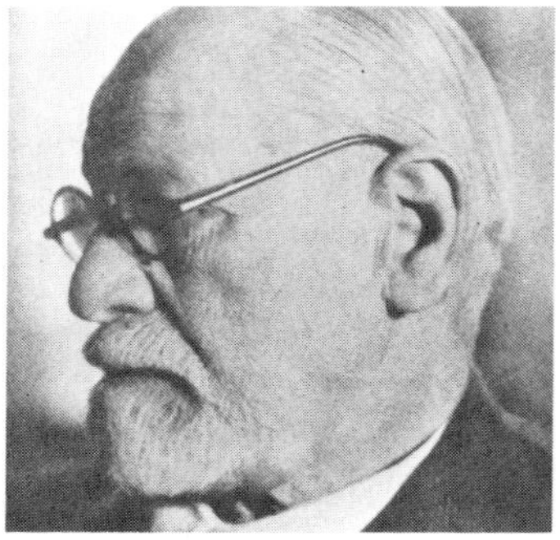

Sigmund Freud's *The Interpretation of Dreams* caused a storm in medical circles.

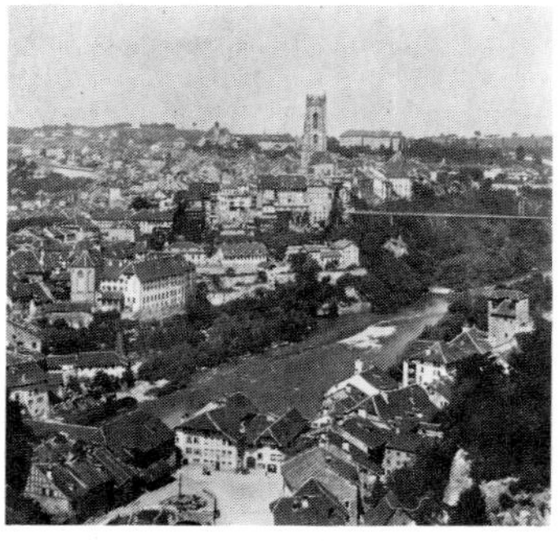

Fribourg; a general view of the Swiss city showing the River Saane.

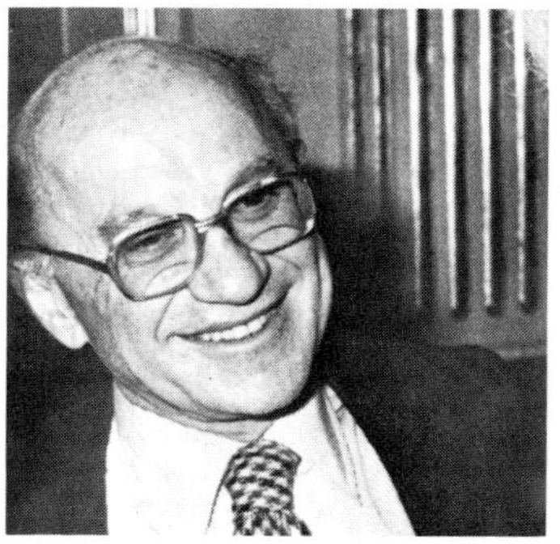

Milton Friedman has been sharply critical of Britain's economic policies.

decade of revolution to an end. *See also* HC2 pp.74–75, *74–75.*

French Revolutionary Wars (1792–1802), series of wars between France and other European states. France declared war on Austria in April 1792, and defeated an invading army at VALMY in September. In 1793 more states, including Britain, entered the war, forming the First Coalition. Although in desperate straits during 1793, the French government managed to keep its forces intact and gradually moved over to the offensive, winning the battle of Fleurus in June 1794, after which the First Coalition broke up. Austria was forced to make peace at Campo Formio (1797), leaving only Britain in the war against France. In 1798, a second Coalition was formed, including Russia, Austria and Britain. Russia withdrew in 1799, however; the Austrians, defeated at MARENGO and Hohenlinden, concluded the Treaty of LUNÉVILLE in 1801, and the British signed the Treaty of AMIENS in 1802. *See also* HC2 pp.74–75, *75*, 76.

French Shore Question, Anglo-French dispute over fishermen's rights off Newfoundland. The Treaty of UTRECHT (1713) ended French territorial claims to Newfoundland, but allowed French fishermen to use parts of the coast for drying and processing. The ENTENTE CORDIALE (1904) eliminated shore rights, but permitted some French fishing in Newfoundland waters.

French Somaliland. *See* DJIBOUTI.

French West Africa, former federation of eight French overseas territories. It includes the modern republics of Dahomey, Guinea, Ivory Coast, Mauritania, Niger, Mali, Upper Volta and Senegal. The federation was dissolved in 1959.

Freneau, Philip (1752–1832), US poet and newspaper editor. He became known for his satirical anti-British verse, such as *The British Prison Ship* (1781), during the AMERICAN WAR OF INDEPENDENCE.

Freons, trade name for certain compounds of carbon, fluorine and sometimes other elements used as refrigerants AEROSOL propellants, cleaning fluids and solvents. They are all clear, stable and inert liquids. Examples are Freon-11 (CCl_3F), Freon-12 (CCl_2F_2) and Freon-14 (CF_4). Freons have been implicated in the destruction of the ozone in the ionosphere. *See also* PE p. 147; MM p. *253.*

Frequency, rate of occurrence. In statistics, the number of times a numerical value, event, or special property occurs in a population in a given time. In physics, the number of oscillations occuring in a given time, including those of sound and light waves, swinging PENDULUMS and vibrating springs. Frequency is the reciprocal of PERIOD. *See also* HERTZ; SU pp.*47, 76–77, 80, 110;* MM p.*228.*

Frequency modulation (FM), variation of the frequency of a transmitted radio CARRIER WAVE by the signal being broadcast. The technique gives radio reception fairly free from static interference. *See also* MM pp.228–229, *228.*

Frere, John (1740–1807), British antiquarian who discovered Stone Age implements at Hoxne, Suffolk, in 1790 and discerningly attributed them to "a very remote period indeed, even beyond that of the present world".

Frères du Pont, religious order formed in France by a group of priests to design and build lasting bridges. The Pont d'Avignon, built in 1177 over the River Rhône with 21 arches, was the most famous of this order's work. *See also* MM pp.190–191.

Frescobaldi, Girolamo (1583–1643), Italian composer and organist, reputedly the greatest organist of his age. He was organist at St Peter's Rome, 1608–28. Most of his compositions were for the organ.

Fresco painting, method of painting on freshly spread plaster while it is still damp. In true fresco, or *buon fresco,* the paint combines chemically with the moist plaster so that, when dry, the painted surface does not peel. Dry fresco, or *fresco secco,* involves the application of paint in a water and glue medium to a dry plaster wall. It does not last as well as true fresco.

Fresnay, Pierre (1897–1975), French actor and producer, real name Pierre-Jules-Louis Laudenbach. He established himself as a leading actor at the Comédie-Française in 1915 and thenceforth pursued a long and varied career both on the stage and in films, most notably in Jean RENOIR's *La Grande Illusion* (1937).

Fresnel, Augustin Jean (1788–1827), French physicist and engineer. His pioneer work in optics helped to establish the wave theory of light. He researched into the conditions governing interference fringes in POLARIZED LIGHT, studied double refraction and devised a way of producing circularly polarized light.

Frets, in music, the raised lines across the finger-boards of stringed instruments (such as the guitar), signifying the position of notes on the scale. They are not simply guides to intonation; they also give to the strings, when "stopped", the resonance of "open" strings by counteracting the softening effect of the finger tips.

Freud, Anna (1895–   ), psychoanalyst, youngest of Sigmund FREUD's six children, *b.*Austria. She has spent most of her adult life in Britain. She applied PSYCHOANALYSIS to the development of children, was an early user of play THERAPY and wrote a number of books, including *Normality and Pathology in Childhood* (1968).

Freud, Lucian (1922–   ), British painter. He had his first one-man exhibition in 1944. He paints with a meticulous realism, chiefly portraits, but also surrealist-like canvases of plants and animals.

Freud, Sigmund (1856–1939), Austrian physician and founder of PSYCHOANALYSIS. With Josef BREUER he developed new methods of treating mental disorders – free association and the interpretation of dreams. These methods derived from his positing the existence of the ID, EGO and SUPER-EGO and therefore emphasizing the unconscious and subconscious as agents of human behaviour. He developed theories of the NEUROSES involving childhood relationships to one's parents and stressed the importance of sexuality in both normal and abnormal behaviour. He thus established PSYCHOLOGY and PSYCHIATRY on a pseudo-scientific basis. His works include *The Psychopathology of Everyday Life* (1904), *The Ego and the Id* (1923) and *Civilization and its Discontents* (1930). *See also* MS pp.134–148.

Freudian psychology, theoretical framework developed by Sigmund FREUD in this practice of the therapeutic method of psychoanalysis. Freud believed that each personality had a tripartite structure: the ID, the unconscious emotions, desires and fears which may surface in dreams or madness; the EGO, the conscious rationalizing section of the mind; and the SUPER-EGO, which may be compared to the conscience. As he saw it, a very young baby is largely id, full of unchecked desires; the ego develops from the id, enabling the child to negotiate realistically with the exterior world. The super-ego evolves as the child adopts (internalizes) the moral values of society. The ego comes to mediate the selfish needs of the id and the idealistic demands of the super-ego. The adoption of a satisfactory super-ego is dependent on the resolution of the OEDIPUS COMPLEX. *See also* MS pp.186, *187.*

Freya, in Nordic mythology a fertility and mother goddess, one of the most ancient of Scandinavian deities; her name means "Lady". Perhaps originally even a moon goddess, drawn across the sky by two cats or two boars, she eventually became goddess of love and was often confused with the Teutonic equivalent goddess FRIGGA.

Freyberg, Bernard Cyril, 1st Baron Freyberg, (1889–1963), military figure of the Commonwealth. Born in Britain and educated in New Zealand, he won a VICTORIA CROSS in WWI and commanded New Zealand troops during WWII. He was governor-general of New Zealand from 1946 to 1952.

Freycinet, Louis-Claude de Saulces de (1779–1842), French explorer. He explored the S Australian coast (1800–1805), made maps and wrote a report of this expedition. In 1817 he commanded another expedition on the *Uranie,* and gained valuable additions to natural history, published in *Voyage Around the World* (13 vols, beginning 1824).

Freyja. *See* FREYA.

Friar, member of certain religious orders. The four main orders, the DOMINICANS, FRANCISCANS, CARMELITES and AUGUSTINIANS, were founded in the 13th century. Friars differ from cloistered monks in their widespread outside activity and greater centralization. *See also* HC1 p.187, *187.*

Friar's balsam, compound tincture of benzoin. It is used: as an inhalant in boiling water; internally, a few drops are swallowed with sugar against colds; and externally, it is used to cover abrasions.

Fribourg, town in W Switzerland, 27km (17 miles) SW of Berne on the River Saane. It is the capital of the Fribourg canton. Founded in 1157, the town passed to the houses of Kyburg (1218), Hapsburg (1277) and Savoy (1452), finally becoming a member of the Swiss Confederation in 1481. Today its products include cheese and chocolate. Industries: metal-working, chemicals. Pop. (1970) 39,659.

Frick, Wilhelm (1877–1946), German politician. He was the Nazi parliamentary leader and minister of the interior (1933–43). The chief drafter of the 1935 NUREMBERG LAW, he was convicted of war crimes and hanged.

Fricker, Peter Racine (1920–   ), British composer living in the USA. His works include concertos for the violin and the viola, four symphonies and an oratorio, *The Vision of Judgement.*

Friction, resistance encountered when surfaces in contact slide or roll against each other, or when a fluid flows along a surface. Friction is directly proportional to the force pressing the surfaces together and the surface roughness. The friction opposing motion equals the moving force up to a certain point, called the limiting friction, after which slipping occurs. Static friction is the value of the limiting friction just before slipping; kinetic friction is the value just after slipping and is slightly less than static friction. Fluid-viscous friction is velocity-dependent as well as affected by the materials. *See also* FRICTION, COEFFICIENT OF; SU pp.70, 93.

Friction, coefficient of, number associated with any two materials characterizing the force necessary to slide or roll one along the surface of the other. If an object has a weight N and the coefficient of FRICTION is μ, then the force f necessary to move it without acceleration along a level surface is $f = \mu N$. The coefficient of static friction determines the force necessary to initiate movement; the coefficient of kinetic friction determines the (lesser) force necessary to maintain movement.

Friday, sixth day of the week. The English name is derived from that of the Norse and Teutonic goddess Frigg or FRIGGA. The crucifixion of Jesus Christ on the sixth day has given Friday its penitential nature in the Christian Church, and until 1966 Roman Catholics were not supposed to eat meat on that day.

Fried, Alfred Hermann (1864–1921), Austrian pacifist. He founded the German Peace Society in 1892 and tried to introduce a legislative means of maintaining peace in the world. He won the Nobel Peace Prize with Tobias ASSER in 1911.

Friedman, Milton (1912–   ), US economist. An important and influential member of the Chicago school of economics, he supported monetary policy as the best means of controlling the economy. His works include *A Monetary History of the United States 1867–1960* (1963), written with Anna Schwartz and a key book in monetary economics; *A Theory of the Consumption Function* (1957); *Essays in Positive Economics* (1953) and *Capitalism and Freedom* (1962). He was awarded the 1976 Nobel Prize in economics. *See also* MONETARISM.

Friedrich, Caspar David (1774–1840), German painter. One of the greatest German Romantic painters, he created eerie, symbolic landscapes, such as *Shipwreck on the Ice* (1822) and *Man and Woman Gazing at the Moon* (1824). *See also* HC2 p.102.

Friendly societies, associations established in Britain to provide insurance against sickness, old age and funeral expenses. They were started in the 17th century and in the 18th century became a conventional alternative to parish relief and charitable assistance. Thereafter they spread quickly and were, in the Victorian age, the most important form of working-class insurance.
Friends, Society of. *See* QUAKERS.
Fries, Elias Magnus (1794–1878), Swedish botanist who developed one of the first systems for the classification of fungi. His system is still a basis for classification. *See also* NW pp.40–41.
Friese-Greene, William (1855–1921), English inventor. In 1890 he patented a combination camera-projector that used sensitized material on rolls – the first practicable motion picture camera.
Friesz, Achille Émile Othon (1879–1949), French painter. His most successful paintings were FAUVIST in style, most notable among these being the *Portrait of Fernand Fleuret* (1907).
Frigate, small WARSHIP used to protect fleet and merchant ships from submarine attack. Most frigates are less costly than DESTROYERS, and they are usually less well-armed, although some modern vessels carry guided missiles. In the 18th century a frigate was a three-masted sailing vessel with up to 50 guns, the forerunner of the modern CRUISER. In WWII the term applied to versatile swift escort ships. *See also* MM pp.*172, 175.*
Frigatebird, powerful sea bird that soars over tropical and subtropical oceans and steals food from other birds. It has a small, dark body; the male has a scarlet throat sac that inflates in display. It lays one chalky white egg in a nest on a bush or rock on an oceanic island. Length: 101cm (40in). Family Fregatidae. *See also* NW p.*144.*
Frigga, in Norse mythology, the wife of the great god ODIN and the supreme goddess. She was depicted as the loving mother of BALDER but also as an argumentative and deceitful wife.
Frigidity, lack of sexual desire in women, or the inability to enjoy sexual intercourse. Failure to achieve ORGASM is a narrow definition of the term. Occasional frigidity is a normal reaction to various temporary stresses. Habitual frigidity almost invariably stems from deep-seated psychological causes. Treatment usually takes the form of counselling or psychoanalysis. *See also* IMPOTENCE.
Frilled lizard, pale brown Australian lizard with a fold of skin that spreads into a ruff when the mouth is opened in aggressive display. The cartilaginous frill has serrated edges with red, black and brown spots. It can be raised to 20cm (10in). Length: to 90cm (35in). Family Agamidae; species *Chlamydosaurus kingi.*
Friml, Charles Rudolf (1879–1972), US composer, *b.*Prague. He moved to the USA in 1906. He was chiefly a writer of musical comedies and operettas, such as *The Firefly, You're in Love* and *Rose Marie.*
Fringe benefits, compensation to employees in addition to wages, involving non-cash payments. They may be granted as part of a COLLECTIVE BARGAINING contract or freely provided by the employer. They include such things as insurance policies paid for by the employer, a company car, time off with pay, special buying privileges, etc. Their value may equal as much as 25% of annual salary.
Fringe medicine, non-orthodox medical treatments which may or may not be accepted by the current medical establishment. Acceptability depends on the authority of the diagnosis. Examples include OSTEOPATHY, CHIROPRACTIC, HOMEOPATHY and ACUPUNCTURE, practitioners of which may also have conventional medical training. *See also* MS p.123.
Fringillidae, bird family of about 125 species comprising finches, crossbills, seed eaters and bramblings. They occur in Europe, Asia, Africa and the Americas, and have sturdy, seed-eating bills, cup-shaped nests and pale blue eggs spotted with brown. *See also* NW pp.*206, 223, 229.*
Frisch, Karl von (1886–), Austrian zoologist. He shared with K. LORENZ and N. TINBERGEN the 1973 Nobel Prize in physiology and medicine for his pioneering work in ETHOLOGY. He deciphered the "language of bees" by studying their dance patterns in which one bee tells others of the hive the direction and distance of a food source. In his earlier work he showed that fish and bees see colours, fish can hear and that bees can distinguish various flower scents. *See also* NW p.78.
Frisch, Max (1911–), Swiss novelist and dramatist. His plays are experimental in form and often satirical. For example, he attacked dictators in *The Chinese Wall* (1946); the average man's unquestioning acceptance of things in *The Fire Raisers* (1953); and anti-semitism in *Andorra* (1961). The novels *Stiller* (1954) and *A Wilderness of Mirrors* (1964) are concerned with man's quest for identity.
Frisch, Ragner (1895–1973), Norwegian economist who aided the development of ECONOMETRICS by his application of statistics to economic theory. Innovation in this field earned Frisch and Jan TINBERGEN the first Nobel Memorial Prize in economics in 1969. Frisch founded the Econometric Society in 1931 and was professor of economics at Oslo from 1927 to 1965.
Frisian Islands, chain of islands in the North Sea, off the coast of Western Europe, owned by The Netherlands, West Germany and Denmark. Stock-raising and fishing are important to most of the islands, which are also popular as tourist resorts. *See* MW p.81; PE p.*44.*
Frith, William Powell (1819–1909), British painter. His best-known works are minutely detailed crowd scenes from contemporary life, such as *Derby Day* (1858). *See also* HC2 p.*117.*
Fritillary, common name for several genera of butterflies including large fritillaries, or silverspots, of the genus *Speyeria,* which have silver markings on the underside of their wings, and small fritillaries of the genus *Boloria.* The larvae (caterpillars) are largely nocturnal. Family Nymphalidae.
Fritillary, common name for numerous species of hardy, perennial plants of the genus *Fritillaria* of north temperate regions. In many species the large, drooping, often solitary flowers have a strikingly chequered appearance. Family Liliaceae.
Friuli, historic region of NE Italy, bordering Austria and Yugoslavia (N and E), the Adriatic Sea (S) and the Veneto region (W). It was under Roman rule from the 2nd to the 6th century AD, when it became a Lombard duchy. It later belonged in turn to the Hapsburgs, Venetians and Austrians. In 1866 and 1918 Italy received those portions of the territory it now holds.
Friuli-Venezia Giulia, region in NE Italy. Formed after WWII, it encompasses the provinces of Udine, Pardenone, Gorizia and Trieste. It was granted limited autonomy in 1963. The capital is Trieste. Agriculture is most important, although there are some industries including oil refining and textiles. Area: 7,846sq km (3,029sq miles). Pop. 1,225,900.
Frobenius, Leo Viktor (1873–1938), German ethnologist and authority on prehistoric art. He developed a three-stage theory of cultural evolution, and made many research trips to Africa. He wrote more than 60 important works, eg *The Voice of Africa* (1912–13).
Frobisher, Sir Martin (*c.*1535–94), English navigator and mariner. He attempted to discover the NORTH-WEST PASSAGE and on an expedition in 1576 discovered Frobisher Bay, Canada. He returned twice (1577–78), primarily in search of gold. He served with DRAKE and HAWKINS in the defeat of the Spanish ARMADA.
Fröding, Gustaf (1860–1911), Swedish poet, noted as an innovator, as in his use of colloquial vocabulary in lyric poetry. His works include two volumes of poems, *Guitar and Concertina* (1891) and *New Poems* (1894).
Froebel, Friedrich Wilhelm August (1782–1852), German educator and influential educational theorist. His main interest was in pre-school age children, and in 1841 he opened the first KINDERGARTEN. He stressed the importance of pleasant surroundings, self-directed activity, physical training and play in the development of the child.
Frog, tailless AMPHIBIAN, found throughout the world. Frogs have long hind limbs, webbed feet and external eardrums behind the eyes. Most begin life as fish-like larvae (TADPOLES) after hatching from gelatinous eggs usually laid in water. Some frogs remain aquatic, some are terrestrial, some live in trees and some burrow underground. Most have teeth in the upper jaw and all have long sticky tongues attached at the front of the mouth to capture live food, usually insects. Length: 2.5–30cm (1–12in). Subclass Salientia (or Anura), divided into 17 families; the most typical genus is *Rana. See also* TOAD; NW pp.73, *75,* 78, *79,* 132–133, 138, 205, 210, *210, 215, 230, 246.*
Frog-bit, floating aquatic plant of ponds and ditches in Europe and Asia. The smooth, rounded leaves and small, white flowers are borne on long stalks. Species *Hydrocharis morsus-ranae.*
Frog hopper, any of various small, hopping insects whose eggs and young are covered with a protective frothy mass called cuckoo spit. Adults are triangular and grey, greenish or brown. They feed on plants. Length: to 1.5cm (0.6in). Order Homoptera; family Cercopidae.
Frogmouth, bird related to the NIGHTJAR and named after the gape of its mouth. It is a native of bush and forested regions of South-East Asia and Australia. Family Podargidae. *See also* NW pp.*205, 211.*
Froissart, Jean (1337–*c.*1404), French poet and chronicler. He travelled widely in Europe, visiting several famous courts in Scotland, England, Italy and France. He is perhaps best known for his *Chronicle,* a lively though inaccurate account of Europe between 1325 and 1400.
Fromm, Erich (1900–), psychoanalyst and writer. Born in Germany, he moved to the USA in 1934. Fromm applied PSYCHOANALYSIS to the study of peoples and cultures, stressing the importance of interpersonal relationships in an impersonal, industrialized society. His books include *Escape from Freedom* (1941) and *The Art of Loving* (1956).
Fronde (1648–53), series of civil reactions against the growing power of the French monarchy. The Fronde of the PARLEMENT (1648–49) started when ANNE OF AUSTRIA, acting as regent for Louis XIV, proposed to reduce the salaries of high court officials. The Fronde of the Princes (1650–53) was a rebellion of the nobility. The Great CONDÉ inspired riots and war against the king but was defeated. The crown's victory established absolute monarchy in France. *See also* HC1 pp.314, 353.
Front, in meteorology, the interface between two air masses of different temperatures or of different densities. A polar front separates cold and warm air masses that have originated in polar and tropical regions; it often creates cyclonic disturbances that dominate the weather. Cold fronts occur as a relatively cold and dense air mass moves under warmer air. With a warm front, warmer air is pushing over colder air and replacing it. An occluded front is composed of two fronts: a cold front overtakes a warm or stationary front, occlusion occurs and a wave cyclone often develops, with cyclonic weather changes. With a stationary front, air masses remain in the same areas and the weather is mostly unchanged. Fronts of various kinds are often depicted on weather maps. *See also* PE pp.68–73.
Front de Libération de Québec, neo-Marxist separatist movement in the Canadian province of Quebec. The Front was started by students who were dissatisfied with the *Parti Québecois.* In 1963 its members set bombs in urban areas and in 1970 they kidnapped James Cross, the British trade commissioner, and murdered Pierre Laporte. The movement was then driven underground by the War Measures Act of the federal government.
Frontenac (et Palluau), **Louis de Baude, comte de** (1620–98), Governor-General

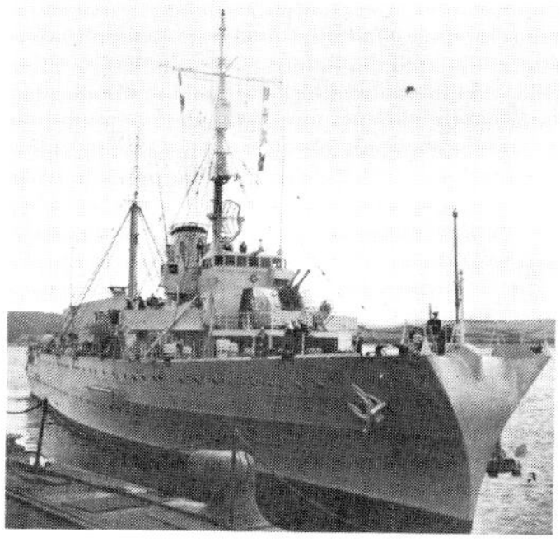

Frigates were first built in England in 1652; this is HMS *Protector* ready for Arctic duty.

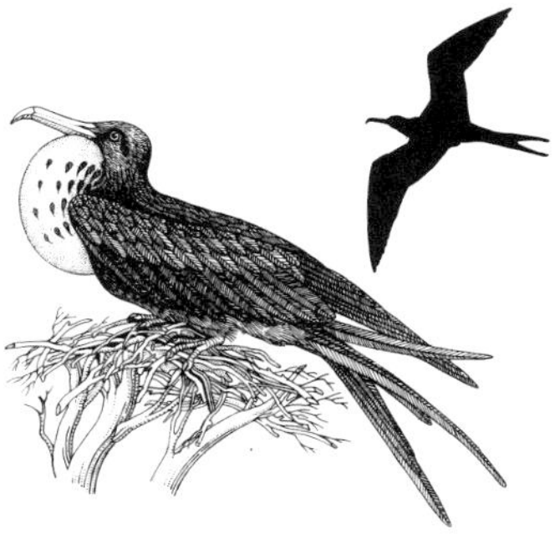

Frigatebird, a sea bird that can blow up the scarlet pouch under its bill like a balloon.

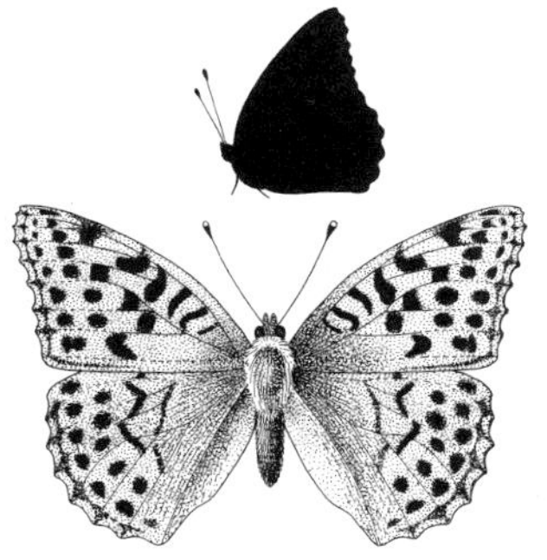

Fritillary, most species of which fly from June to August and are found in light woods.

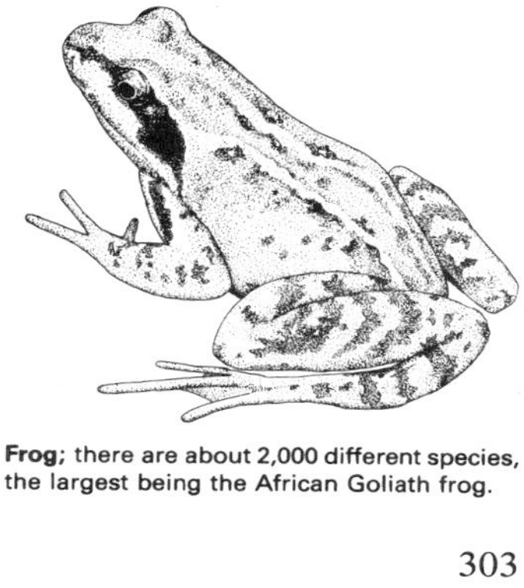

Frog; there are about 2,000 different species, the largest being the African Goliath frog.

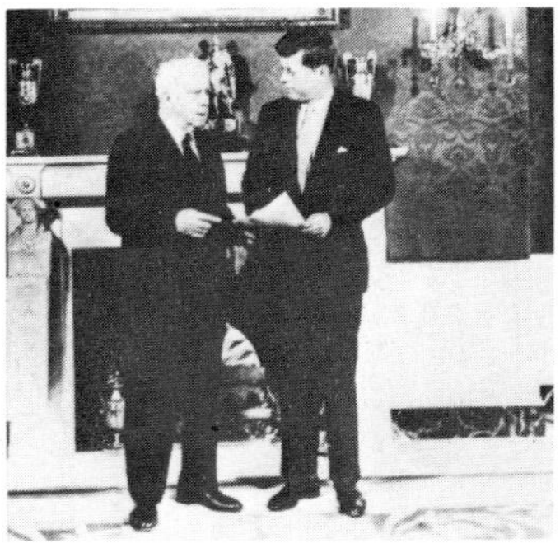

Robert Frost (left), possibly America's most popular poet, with President Kennedy.

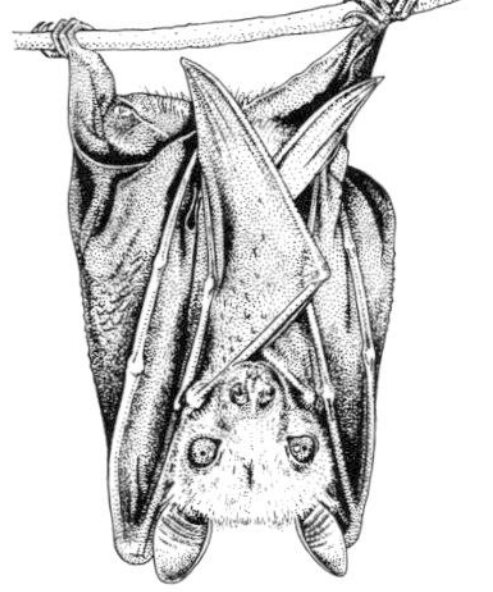

Fruit bat, large groups of which hanging in a tree make it look laden with fruit.

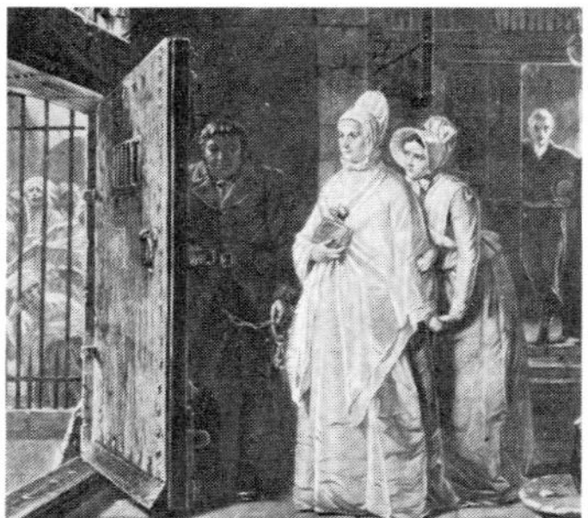

Elizabeth Fry visiting prisoners in Newgate Prison (from a painting by Mrs E. M. Ward).

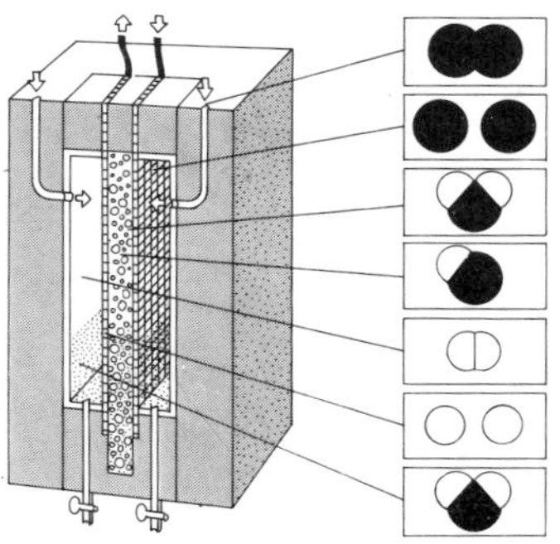

Fuel cell; scientists are now working to produce cells that run on cheap fuels.

of New France (1672–82, 1689–98). His rule was autocratic and he was recalled in 1682. In his second term, Frontenac repulsed an English attack in 1690 and briefly attempted an attack on New York. He encouraged LA SALLE's explorations and extended French rule to Lake Winnipeg and the Gulf of Mexico.

Frontennis. *See* PELOTA.

Frost, in meteorology, atmospheric temperatures below 0°C. The visible result of a frost is usually a deposit of minute ice crystals formed on exposed surfaces from DEW and water vapour. In freezing weather the "degree of frost" indicates the number of degrees below freezing point. When white hoar-frost is formed, water vapour changes from its gaseous state to a solid, without becoming a liquid. A frost is referred to as white or black, depending on whether or not white hoar-frost is present.

Frost, Robert Lee (1874–1963), US poet. His volume of lyric poems *A Boy's Will* (1913) and that of narrative poems *North of Boston* (1914) were enthusiastically received in Britain; establishing his reputation. He received the Pulitzer Prize for poetry in 1924, 1931, 1937 and 1943.

Frost, Terry (1915–), British painter. He worked in the abstract style, in a group that was centred in St Ives, Cornwall, in the 1950s, simplifying natural images to flat shapes and colours.

Frostbite, freezing of living body-tissue, either superficially or penetrating beneath surface cells. It causes defective circulation and the breakdown of the tissue. In severe cases the tissue dies and GANGRENE may set in. First-aid treatment involves rapid rewarming of the affected area.

Froude, James Anthony (1818–94), British historian. His 12-volume *History of England from 1529 to 1588* was the first scholarly treatment of the Tudors. He was regius professor of history at Oxford University (1892–94).

Frozen foods, foodstuffs preserved by freezing. Food kept at 5°C (41°F) deteriorates only slowly because bacterial growth is greatly retarded. Deep-frozen at −5°C (23°F) or below, many foods will keep indefinitely. Delicate foodstuffs such as soft fruits can be preserved by rapid DEEP-FREEZING methods which prevent the growth of large ice crystals in the fruits that would otherwise destroy their texture. In FREEZE-DRYING, water is evaporated from foodstuffs at low temperatures, to preserve them indefinitely. *See also* FOOD PRESERVATION.

Fructose, white crystalline sugar ($C_6H_{12}O_6$) that occurs in fruit and honey. It is made commercially by the HYDROLYSIS of beet or cane sugar and is used in foods and medicine. *See also* SU p.152.

Fruit, seed-containing mature OVARY of a flowering plant. Fruits serve to reproduce and spread plants and are important to human beings and animals as food. They can be classified as simple, aggregate or multiple. Simple fruits, dry or fleshy, are produced by one ripened ovary of one pistil and include legumes (peas and beans), nuts, apples, pears and citrus fruits. Aggregate fruits develop from several simple pistils; examples are raspberry and blackberry. Multiple fruits develop from a flower cluster; each flower produces a fruit which merges into a single mass at maturity; examples are pineapples and figs. Fruits provide vitamins, acids and salts, and as such form an important part of the human diet. Vitamin C, found especially in citrus fruits, helps to develop sound bones and teeth. Calcium, iron and phosphorus are also provided by fruits for a healthy, well-balanced diet. *See also* PE pp.192–195, 214.

Fruit bat, any of about 160 species of nocturnal, fruit- or nectar-eating, tropical BATS. Species have an independent, clawed second digit. They rely on sight, rather than echo location for orientation, and are capable of powerful, sustained flight. Wingspan: to 1.5m (5ft). Family Pteropodidae. *See also* FLYING FOX.

Fruit fly. *See* DROSOPHILA.

Frustration, prevention of the satisfaction of an aroused physiological, psychological or social need. It may be imposed from the outside or may originate from within a person, as in setting goals beyond one's ability. Frustration may lead to increased effort, to anger or to aggressive behaviour. According to some psychoanalytic theories AGGRESSION is always a sign of some sort of frustration.

Fry, Christopher (1907–), British dramatist, real name Christopher Harris. His blank-verse plays are often set in ancient or medieval times. They include *A Phoenix Too Frequent* (1946), *The Lady's Not for Burning* (1948) and *Venus Observed* (1950).

Fry, Elizabeth (1780–1845), British social worker and prison reformer. The daughter of John Gurney, a rich Quaker banker, she married Joseph Fry (a London merchant) in 1800. She agitated for more humane treatment of women prisoners and of convicts sentenced to transportation to Australia. She later became active in other fields of reform, notably improving standards for nurses and facilities for women's education.

Fry, Maxwell (1899–), British architect. He introduced the modern style of the BAUHAUS to Britain, designing several domestic homes in London in the 1930s. *See also* HC2 p.281.

Fry, Roger Eliot (1866–1934), British art critic and painter. He painted mostly landscapes, many of which were exhibited in London in 1920. He helped to introduce to England the works of CÉZANNE and the POST-IMPRESSIONISTS. He wrote many books, including studies of *Bellini* (1899) and *Cézanne* (1927) and *Vision and Design* (1920).

Frye, Northrop (1912–), Canadian literary critic. His first book, *Fearful Symmetry* (1947), is a masterly study of William BLAKE's poetry. Frye set forth his principles of criticism in *Anatomy of Criticism* (1957). He has taught at the University of Toronto since 1939.

Fuad, name of two kings of Egypt. Fuad I (1868–1936), was sultan (*r.* 1917–22) and first king of modern Egypt (*r.* 1922–36). He founded the University of Cairo in 1906. He suspended the constitution in 1930 and restored it in 1935. Fuad II (1952–), his grandson, was king (1952–53) until the republic was set up.

Fuchs, Klaus (1911–), German physicist. Interned in Britain at the start of WWII, he carried out nuclear research there and in 1944 was sent to the USA to work on the atom bomb. He was imprisoned for passing secrets to the USSR. Released in 1959, he went to East Germany.

Fuchs, Sir Vivian Ernest (1908–), British geologist and explorer who made the first land crossing of the Antarctic. He led the Falkland Island Dependencies Survey in the Antarctic (1947–50). In 1957 he headed the British section of the Commonwealth Transarctic expedition and made the hazardous 3,473km (2,158 miles) journey across the Antartic, which earned him a knighthood.

Fuchsia, shrubby plant found wild mainly in tropical and subtropical America, parts of New Zealand and, as a variant form, in Ireland. It is also widely cultivated. It has crisp, oval leaves, trailing stems and trumpet-shaped, waxy flowers. The 100 or so species include the crimson-purple *Fuchsia procumbens* and cultivated *F. speciosa.* Family Onagraceae.

Fuel cell, electrochemical cell for direct conversion of the energy of oxidation of a fuel to electrical energy. Suitably designed electrodes are immersed in an ELECTROLYTE, and the fuel, eg hydrogen, is supplied to one and the oxidizer, eg oxygen, to the other. Electrode reactions occur leading to oxidation of the fuel, with production of electric current. Fuel cells are used in space vehicles. *See also* SU p.149.

Fuentes, Carlos (1928–), Mexican novelist and short-story writer. His novels include *Where the Air is Clean* (1958) and *The Death of Artemio Cruz* (1962), which share a critical view of Mexican society. He also wrote in a style of mixed realism and fantasy, eg *Change of Skin* (1967).

Fugard, Athol (1932–), South African dramatist whose plays sympathize strongly with the position of non-whites and include *Boesman and Lena* (1970), *Sizwe Banzi is Dead* (1973) and *Statements after an Arrest under the Immorality Act* (1974). Fugard's passport was withdrawn by his government in 1967.

Fugger, German merchant and banking family, the origin of whose wealth was laid by Hans of Augsburg in the 14th century. In the late 15th and 16th centuries it was the richest family in Europe and played a major role in arranging credit for the Hapsburg emperors, notably Charles V. *See also* HC1 p.239.

Fugue, in psychology, pathological loss of memory associated with dissociative HYSTERIA. The patient is apparently conscious of his actions, however uncharacteristic these may be, but when the fugue ends has no recollection of them. *See also* MS p.140.

Fugue, in music, a composition of several simultaneous parts or voices where the same melodic line or theme is stated and developed in each voice so that interest in its overall development becomes cumulative. Generally the theme begins in one part and others are added in sequence. Fugue writing, popular in the BAROQUE period, reached its peak in the music of Johann Sebastian BACH. There has been a revival of interest in fugal writing by composers of the 20th century.

Führer, Der, name used by HITLER as leader (its meaning in German) of the German people. It was more evocative of racial nationalism and one-man rule than the official title of chancellor.

Fujiwara, strong, rich and cultured Japanese family since the 7th century, which between 857 and 1160 dominated the Heian period and had a sculptural style named after it. By marrying Fujiwara women into the royal family they gained great influence as "advisers" to the emperor. The family reached its peak of power under Michinaga Fujiwara (966–1027). *See also* HC1 pp.130–131.

Fujiyama, (Fuji-san), highest mountain in Japan, 113km (70 miles) WSW of Tokyo, in the Fuji-Hakone National Park. An extinct volcano, it is regarded as the most sacred mountain in Japan. It is also a summer and winter sports area. Height: 3,776m (12,389ft).

Fukien (Fu-chien or Fujian), province in SE China, on the Formosa Strait opposite the island of Taiwan; the capital is Foochow (Fuzhou). It has a warm, moist climate and a mountainous terrain which has hampered communications. Its people are predominantly Chinese and four main dialects are spoken. Rice, sweet potatoes, tea and wheat are grown in upland areas, and fruit, silk, sugar and jute are produced in the lowlands. Industries include food processing, timber, textiles, cement and ceramics. As a result of its strategic location near Taiwan, a number of military posts have been maintained there since 1950. Area: approx. 123,000sq km (47,500sq miles). Pop. 18,000,000.

Fukuda, Takeo (1905–), Japanese politician. He became a member of the House of Representatives for the Liberal-Democratic Party in 1952, and following several ministerial posts from 1965 became Prime Minister in Dec. 1976.

Fukuoka, city in N Kyūshū, Japan, on the SE shore of Hakata Bay. In medieval times the area of Hakata was one of the chief ports of Japan. There is a rich agricultural region to the N; industries include textiles and chemicals. Pop. (1970) 853,270.

Fulani (Fulah or Fulbe), African people of mixed Negro and Berber origins, scattered through W Africa and numbering approx. six million. Their language belongs to the W Atlantic group of the Niger-Congo family. Originally a pastoral people, they helped to spread Islam throughout W Africa from the 16th century and established areas of empire until defeated by the British in the 19th century.

Fulbright, James William (1905–), US DEMOCRATIC politician. He was a representative from Arkansas (1943–45) and senator (1945–74). He was chairman of the senate committee on Foreign Relations from 1959 to 1974, on which he was a frank and persistent critic of US military involvement overseas. In 1977 he was awarded the Benjamin Franklin medal. He has published *Old Myths and New Realities* (1964), *The Arrogance of Power* (1967) and *The Crippled Giant* (1972).

Fulcrum, point about which a lever pivots. Its use in the PRINCIPLE OF MOMENTS was recognized by ARCHIMEDES, who is reputed to have said: "Give me a firm place on which to stand and I will move the earth". *See also* MM pp.86, *86*, 100; SU p.*70*.

Fuller, Isaac (*c.* 1606–72), English portraitist and decorative painter. Few of his works survive, but five *Self Portraits* display a certain boldness of form.

Fuller, Richard Buckminster (1895–), US architect and engineer. Believing that only technology can solve modern world problems, he invented several revolutionary designs. The best known, and widely used, is the GEODESIC DOME, a spherical structure composed of light, strong, triangular parts. His books include *Operating Manual for Spaceship Earth* (1969) and *Earth Inc.* (1973). *See also* SU p.*45*.

Fuller, Roy (1912–), British poet and novelist, who for many years wrote in his spare time from being a solicitor. His verse includes the war poetry of *The Middle of a War* (1942) and *A Lost Season* (1944). *Epitaphs and Occasions* (1949) and *Counterparts* (1954) are later collections of poetry. Among his novels are *Image of a Society* (1956) and *My Child, My Sister* (1965).

Fuller's earth, clay-like substance that contains more than half SILICA. Originally used to remove oil and grease from wool, (the process of fullering), it is now used to bleach petroleum and in refining vegetable oils.

Fulmar, scavenging oceanic bird of the Arctic, Antarctic and N Atlantic, related to the SHEARWATER. Heavily built and with grey feathers, it has a large head, hooked bill, short neck, a throat pouch, long narrow wings and a short tail. It spits foul-smelling oil when threatened. Length: 30–45cm (12–18in). Family Procellariidae. Genus *Fulmarus.*

Fulminate, explosive, a salt of fulminic acid (HONC), especially fulminate of mercury, $Hg(ONC)_2$, which is formed by the action of nitric acid on mercury metal in the presence of alcohol. It is a highly unstable compound used in DETONATORS and blasting caps. *See also* MM p.162.

Fulton, Robert (1765–1815), US inventor and engineer. He patented designs for torpedoes and other naval weapons. His main interest was in navigation and, as early as 1796, he was urging the USA to build canals. His great triumph was the steamboat *Clermont*, whose 1807 voyage between New York City and Albany pioneered the use of the steamboat for carrying passengers and freight.

Fumarole, vent in the ground that emits gases and vapours, usually found in volcanic areas. The term also refers to a hot spring or geyser that emits steam. A fumarole is sometimes defined in terms of the composition of its gases, such as a chlorine fumarole. *See also* PE pp.30–31.

Fumigation, use of toxic gases to kill insects and other pests in houses, industrial and agricultural storage buildings, burrows and soil. The fumigants *o*- and *p*-dichlorobenzene are often used to kill such household pests as clothes moths, termites and carpet beetles. Grain fumigation may be carried out using a mixture of carbon disulphide and tetrachloromethane (carbon tetrachloride). Hydrogen cyanide gas is often used as a fumigant, although its intense toxicity necessitates extreme caution.

Fumitory, common name for a family of herbaceous plants (Fumaricaceae) that includes more than 400 species native to northern temperate regions. The common fumitory (*Fumaria officinalis*) is a small, tufted bush with weak, slender stems, feathery leaves and white flowers tipped with purple.

Funchal, port in Portugal, on the SE coast of the island of Madeira. Founded in 1421, it is now a trade and resort centre for all the islands in the Madeira archipelago. Pop. (1970) 33,750.

Functional disorders, mental disorders that cannot be accounted for by an organic disturbance. They include SCHIZOPHRENIA, MANIC-DEPRESSIVE psychosis and PARANOIA. Although their precise nature is unknown, functional disorders are thought to be caused by psychological factors. *See also* MS pp.138–139.

Functionalism, in art and architecture, an early 20th-century style based on utilitarianism that emphasized the purpose of the building or piece of equipment. Functionalism rejected ornamentation and stressed instead the basic structure of the work and of the materials used. Major proponents of functionalism included GROPIUS, members of the BAUHAUS school and LE CORBUSIER. *See also* HC2 p.281.

Functionalism, sociological and anthropological theory. Its fundamentals were outlined by Emile DURKHEIM. It is a theory of the relationships of the parts of a society – eg customs, institutions, objects, roles, religion – to the whole and of one part to another. The contribution that each part makes to the total cultural system is its function. The theory also tries to understand the "needs" of the social organism to which the cultural phenomena correspond. *See also* A. R. RADCLIFFE-BROWN; HC2 pp.266–267, 281.

Functional psychology, late 19th century movement, founded by William JAMES and John DEWEY, that emphasized the adjustment of the organism to the environment and the operations of conscious activity, eg thinking. It was a forerunner of BEHAVIOURISM.

Fundamentalism, movement within some Protestant denominations, particularly in the USA, which originated at the turn of this century as a reaction against biblical criticism and contemporary theories of evolution. The name is derived from *The Fundamentals,* a series of 12 tracts published between 1909 and 1915 by eminent evangelical leaders. The doctrines most emphasized by fundamentalists are: the inspiration and infallible truth of the Bible; the divinity of Christ; the VIRGIN BIRTH; ATONEMENT by Christ bringing expiation and salvation for all; and the physical RESURRECTION and SECOND COMING. *See also* MS p.225.

Fundamental particles. *See* ELEMENTARY PARTICLES.

Fundin, Ove (1933–), Swedish speedway rider. He won five world titles (1956, 1960, 1961, 1963, 1967) and helped Sweden to win six world team titles (1960, 1962–64, 1967, 1970).

Fundy, Bay of, inlet of N Atlantic Ocean which divides Nova Scotia from New Brunswick, Canada. Passamaquoddy Bay to the NW divides Canada from the USA. Tides there reach 19m (70ft). Length: 151km (94 miles); width: 51km (32 miles).

Funen. *See* FYN.

Funfkirchen. *See* PÉCS.

Fungicides, in agriculture and gardening, chemicals that kill fungi, used to prevent or reduce losses from FUNGUS diseases of plants. The most important group of fungicides – including a majority of copper, sulphur and organic compounds – are used to protect healthy but susceptible plants from fungus infections. The other main group – including dinitro compounds and organic sulphur or mercury compounds – are used to eradicate fungus infections already established in plants. Fungicides used on wood, such as creosote, prevent DRY ROT

Fungus, any of a wide variety of plants that cannot make their own food by photosynthesis, including mushrooms, truffles, moulds, smuts and yeasts. Fungi have relatively simple structures, with no roots, stems or leaves. The main body, or thallus, of a typical multicellular fungus consists of a usually inconspicuous network of fine filaments called a mycelium. The mycelia occasionally develop spore-producing, often conspicuous, fruiting bodies, as in mushrooms and toadstools. Fungal PARASITES depend on living animals or plants; SAPROPHYTES utilize the materials of dead plants and animals; and symbionts obtain food in the mutually beneficial relationship with other plants. All three groups are of great importance to man. *See also* NW pp.40–43; PE pp.*173, 200,* 201, *223*.

Funk, Casimir (1884–1967), US biochemist who discovered VITAMINS. In 1912 he found vitamins B_1, B_2, C and D, coined the term "vitamine" (the AMINES of life) and presented a paper formulating the idea of vitamin deficiency disorders. Funk also contributed to the knowledge of cancer and of the hormones of the sex glands.

Fur, soft, dense hair covering the skin or pelt, of certain animals. Such animals include mink, fox, ermine, musquash, wolf, bear, squirrel and rabbit. Most of these animals are hunted and killed for their pelts which, when manufactured into coats and other garments, may command high prices. But some fur-bearing animals are now protected by law because over-hunting has threatened them with extinction. Some, such as mink, are also reared on farms.

Furie, Sidney, (1933–), Canadian film director trained in television whose films were especially noted for their spirited camerawork and accomplished editing. Best-known examples include *The Ipcress File* (1965) and *Lady Sings the Blues* (1972), a successful cinematic biography of Billie HOLIDAY.

Furies, The, in Greek mythology, three hideous and terrible goddesses of vengeance whose main task was to visit torment upon those who had committed social crimes.

Furlong, imperial unit of measurement, equal to 220yds (201m). There are eight furlongs to a mile. The word derives from a "furrowlong"; it represented the standard length of a furrow on a square field of 10 acres in medieval times.

Furnace, enclosed space which is raised to high temperatures by the combustion of fuels or by electric heating. Most furnaces are used in the extraction of metals or the making of alloys, although their heat may be used to fire kilns (for "baking" ceramics), ovens and boilers. Even a domestic boiler – especially if it burns solid fuel – is sometimes loosely described as a furnace.

There are three main types of electric furnaces. An arc furnace, eg as used in the extraction of phosphorus, relies on the heat generated by an electric arc (spark), often between two large carbon electrodes, which are slowly consumed. A resistance furnace is heated by radiation from coils or windings carrying an electric current, as in a domestic oven. An induction furnace melts a metallic charge by inducing a heating current in it. *See also* ELECTROMAGNETIC INDUCTION; MM pp. 30–31, 40, *72*.

Furneaux Islands, group of islands off the NE coast of Tasmania at the end of Bass Strait, separated from Tasmania by the Banks Strait. The group includes Flinders Island (the largest), Cape Barren Island and many smaller islands. Industries: diary products, tin-mining. Area: approx. 2,330sq km (900sq miles. Pop. (1969 est.) 1,240.

Furniture, movable items of domestic equipment, especially chairs, tables, beds and other such large pieces. Furniture has been used since earliest times, and until the 20th century wood has been the most common material used, both for the construction and decoration of furniture. The use of metals has increased since the Industrial Revolution and of plastics since WWII. As well as its simple function of supporting the body at rest or at work, furniture, particularly the chair, has played an important role in reinforcing social relationships – in medieval times, for instance, it was rare for even the most wealthy to own more than a few chairs, and highly decorated ones such as thrones denoted particular social importance. The advent of the generally available comfortably upholstered chair perhaps coincided with the achievement of the conveniences of middle-class life in Georgian England (a period often considered a golden age of domestic furniture). Furniture has been decorated since Classical times either to conceal the structure of the piece or with ornamentation designed to refer to its symbolic functions; since Renaissance

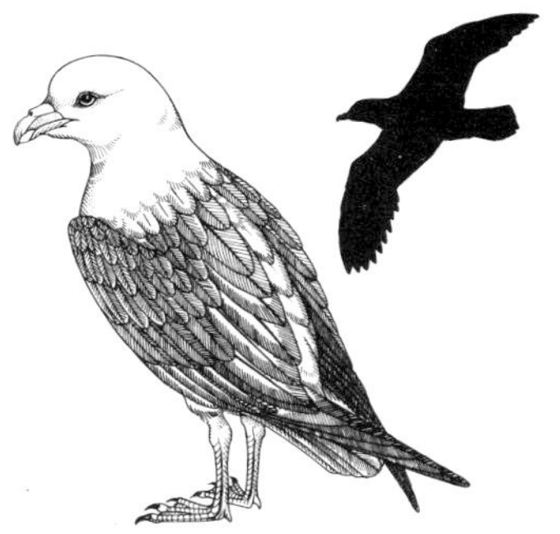

Fulmar builds its nest in high, rocky crevices, where it lays only one egg.

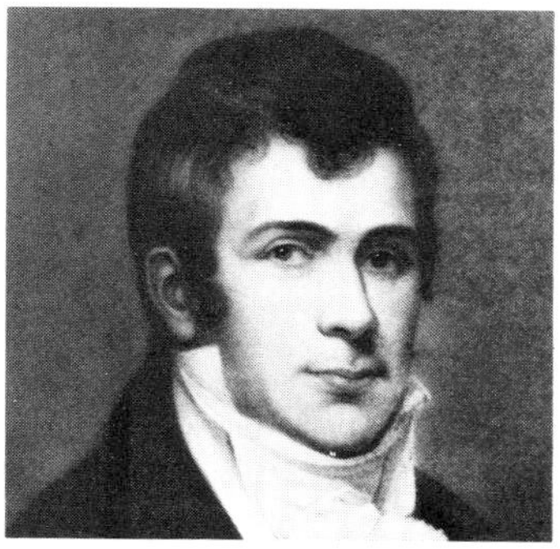

Robert Fulton designed a warship to defend New York Harbour in the War of 1812.

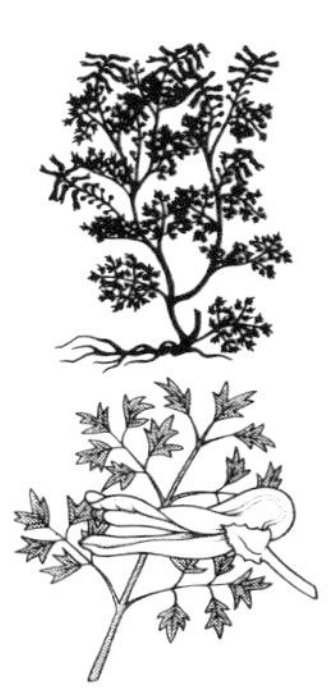

Fumitory was esteemed in earlier times for its supposed medicinal and cosmetic qualities.

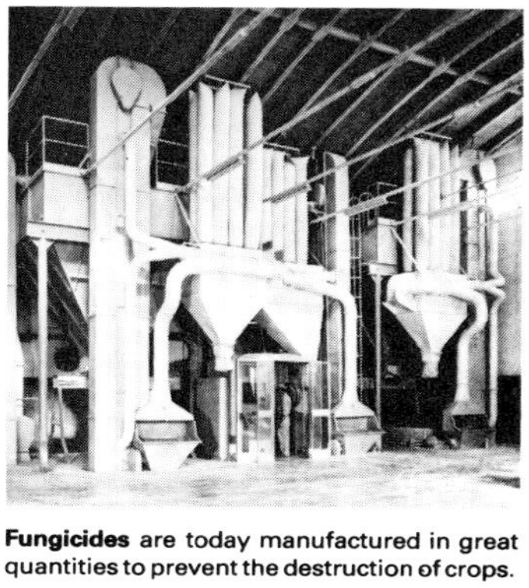

Fungicides are today manufactured in great quantities to prevent the destruction of crops.

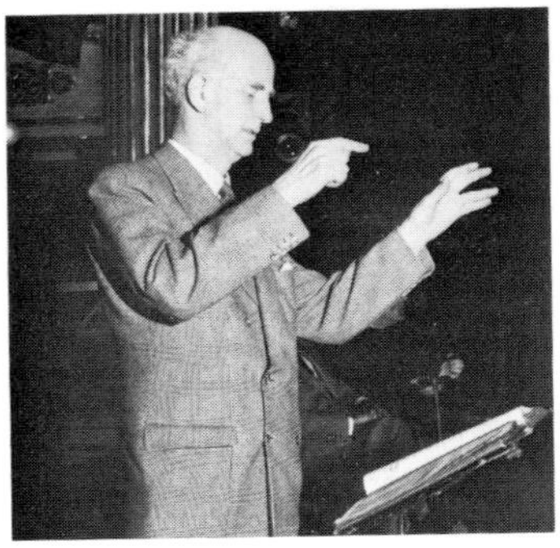

Wilhelm Furtwängler succeeded Richard Strauss at the Berlin State Opera in 1920.

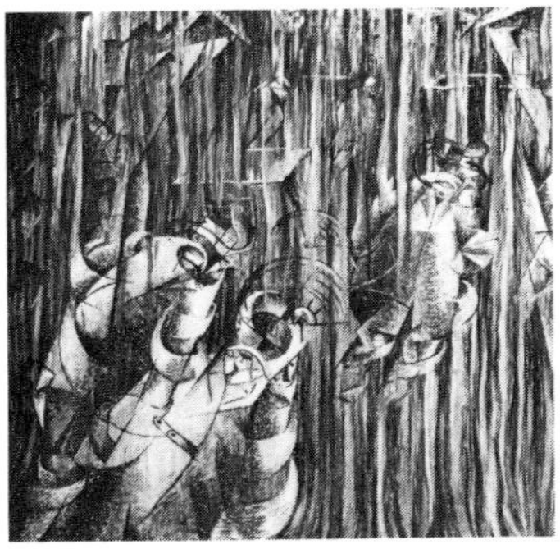

Futurism; a painting by Boccioni, one of the signatories of the Futurist Manifesto.

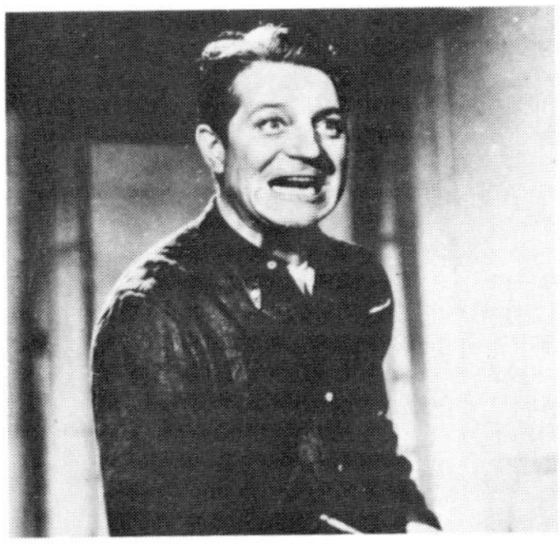

Jean Gabin, the popular French film actor, as he appeared in *Le Jour se Lève.*

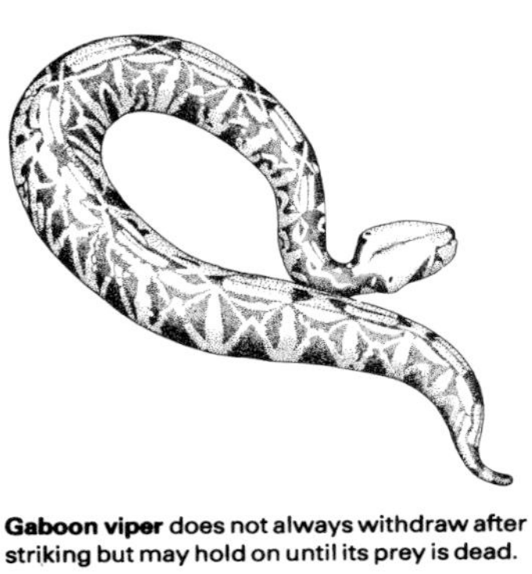

Gaboon viper does not always withdraw after striking but may hold on until its prey is dead.

times this decoration has generally echoed current architectural designs. This tendency has continued in the 20th century: Gerrit RIETVELD designed a de STIJL chair, and the use of steel in furniture construction was pioneered at the BAUHAUS.

Furniture beetle. *See* WOODWORM.

Furphy, Joseph (1843–1912), Australian novelist, pen-name Tom Collins. His unconventional but subtle work underwent a revival in the 1940s, and his major novel *Such is Life* (1903) describing episodes in the life of a solitary wayfarer, rece: ed much critical acclaim.

Furtseva, Ekaterina Alekseyevna (1910–74), USSR politician. From 1952 to 1956 she was a member of the Central Committee and from 1957 to 1960 of the Praesidium. In 1955 she became a member of the USSR Supreme Soviet. From 1960 she was the minister of culture.

Furtwängler, Wilhelm (1886–1954), German conductor. He became conductor of the Berlin Philharmonic Orchestra in 1922 (conductor for life in 1952), and of the Vienna Philharmonic Orchestra in 1930. He appeared frequently at the Bayreuth and Salzburg festivals and was a specialist in the works of Beethoven and Wagner.

Furze. *See* GORSE.

Fusan. *See* PUSAN.

Fuse, in electrical engineering, a safety device to protect against overloading. Fuses are commonly strips of easily melting metal placed in series in an electrical circuit such that when overloaded, the fuse melts, breaking the circuit and preventing damage to the rest of the system. *See also* SU p.*115.*

Fused-salt electrolysis, ELECTROLYSIS of molten ionic salts as a method of extracting elements. The technique is used for producing electropositive metals, such as aluminium and magnesium, which are higher than hydrogen in the ELECTROMOTIVE SERIES. (Electrolysis of aqueous solutions of their salts cannot be used because hydrogen ions would be discharged at the cathode in preference to metal ions.) *See also* MM p.34; SU p.149.

Fuselage, body of an aircraft, to which the wings, tail assembly and landing gear are attached; it houses the crew, cargo, passengers and controls. Its structural strength lies in a stress-bearing skin, internal bulkheads, lengthwise stringers and formers. *See also* MM pp.148–153.

Fuseli, Henry (1741–1825), British painter *b.* Switzerland. An admirer of the work of MICHELANGELO and a friend of William BLAKE, he painted visionary and grotesque illustrations of SHAKESPEARE's plays and *The Nightmare* (1782). *See also* HC2 pp.*72, 80.*

Fusel oil, poisonous, clear, colourless liquid with a disagreeable smell; a mixture of amyl alcohols obtained as a by-product of the fermentation of plant materials containing sugar and starch. It occurs as a dangerous impurity in badly made spirit drinks. It is used as a solvent for waxes, resins, fats and oils and in the manufacture of explosives and pure amyl alcohols.

Fushun, city in Liaoning province, NE China, on the Hun Ho river, 40km (30 miles) NE of Shenyang (Mukden). The city was developed as a mining centre by the Russians from 1902 to 1908, when it came under Japanese control until after WWII. It has one of the largest open-cast mines in the world. Industries: oil-refining, aluminium, chemicals, machinery. Pop. 1,700,000.

Fusion, nuclear. *See* NUCLEAR ENERGY.

Fust, Johann (*c.*1400–66), German printer. When Johann GUTENBERG was unable to repay a loan made by Fust, he took over Gutenberg's machinery and with a partner, Peter Schoeffer, established a commercial printing press. Among the works published were the *Psalter* (1457), a Benedictine psalter (1459) and Cicero's *De officiis* (1465).

Futabatei, Shimei (1864–1909), Japanese author and translator. His novel *The Drifting Cloud* (1887–89) was never completed, but is generally accepted as the first modern Japanese novel in both style and content. Its description of Japan in the 1880s borders on caricature.

Future shock, term coined by Alvin Toffler, who used it as the title of his 1970 bestseller, to describe the impact of rapid change on people and societies. Characterized by disorientation and anxiety, and generated by urbanization and rootlessness, future shock results from the sudden breakdown of old social systems and values.

Futurism, art movement that originated in Italy in 1909 with the publication of the first FUTURIST MANIFESTO. It aimed to glorify machines and to depict speed and motion in painting and sculpture by means of an adapted version of CUBISM. It was violently opposed to the study of the art of the past, and proclaimed the values of modernity. The leading futurists included the poet MARINETTI, SEVERINI and BOCCIONI in Italy, and Marcel DUCHAMP in France. After WWI the movement became linked with FASCISM through its advocacy of an artistic elite and its wholesale rejection of the past, and artistically its ideas were absorbed by DADAISM and SURREALISM. *See also* HC2 pp.176–177.

Futurist Manifestos (1909–14), series of articles (1909–12) that announced the objectives of FUTURISM. The first, written by F. T. MARINETTI, for the French paper *Le Figaro*, appeared in Feb. 1909 and proclaimed the new beauty of mechanical speed; two following manifestos, published in 1910, discussed the implications of this aesthetic for painting.

Fuzhon. *See* FOOCHOW.

Fyfe, David Patrick Maxwell, 1st Earl of Kilmuir (1900–67), British lawyer and politician. He became a Conservative MP in 1935 and was attorney-general in 1945. He served as deputy chief prosecutor at the NUREMBERG TRIALS, was home secretary (1951–54) and lord high chancellor (1954–62). He was made an earl in 1962.

Fyffe, Will (1885–1947), Scots comedian. He began his acting career with his father's stock company but by 1921 had achieved great personal success in music-halls with his character sketches. Among his most popular songs was *I Belong to Glasgow.*

Fyn, island of Denmark, between the Jutland peninsula (W) and Sjaelland Island (E). It is the second-largest of the Danish islands and is connected to the mainland by a bridge. It produces dairy goods and wheat. Area: 3,486sq km (1,346sq miles). Pop. 389,400.

G

G, seventh letter of the alphabet, derived from the Greek *gamma,* which entered the early Roman alphabet as a letter that stood for both *g* and *k.* This Roman letter resembled a *c* and later had a vertical line added to form the modern hand-written form of the letter *g.* In English a *g* may be hard, as in *game,* or soft (pronounced like a *j*), as in *page.* A following *h* gives it a variety of sounds (like a *w* in *bough,* like an *f* in *rough* or silent, as in *high*); *g* is also silent in some other words, eg *sign.*

g, unit of acceleration based on the acceleration of falling bodies near the Earth's surface: 1g = 9.807m/sec^2 (32ft/sec^2). Great forces are experienced by bodies travelling at accelerations greater than g. *See also* GRAVITY.

G, universal constant of gravitation, equal to 6.67×10^{-11} newton-m^2/kg^2. It is the constant of proportionality in Sir Isaac Newton's law on GRAVITATION.

Ga, black African people on Ghana's SE coast. They number approx. 625,000 and follow a system of patrilineal political and material inheritance for men and matrilineal inheritance for women.

Gabbro, coarse-grained basic igneous rock. It can be regarded as the plutonic equivalent of BASALT, being much coarser because of its slow crystallization. The constituents are sodium and calcium FELSPARS and the dark minerals OLIVINE and PYROXENE, which impart a green hue to the rock. *See also* PE p.*101.*

Gabelentz, Hans Conon von der (1807–74), German linguist, ethnologist, and government official. Best known for his linguistic scholarship, he published research on the Malayo-Polynesian, Mongolian, Gothic, Dakota and many other languages.

Gabin, Jean (1904–76), French film actor, real name Alexis Moncourgé. He is famous for his roles as a disillusioned but heroic survivor. His major films include *La Grand Illusion* (1937), *Quai des Brumes* (1938), *Le Jour se Lève* (1939), *Maigret Tend un Piège* (1958), and *Fin de Journée* (1969).

Gable, Clark (1901–60), US film actor. His impudent, virile magnetism made him a screen idol for 30 years. His films included *Red Dust* (1932), *It Happened One Night* (1934), *Gone With the Wind* (1939), *The Tall Men* (1955) and *The Misfits* (1961), his last film.

Gabo, Naum (1890–1977), US sculptor and architect, *b.* Russia, real name Naum Pevsner. A founder of CONSTRUCTIVISM, he published the *Realist Manifesto* (1920) with his brother Antoine Pevsner, a work explaining the principles of that style, works of which were often transparent, geometrical abstractions composed in plastic. His works include a huge public sculpture in Rotterdam (1957).

Gabon, nation in western central Africa. The tropical climate creates rain forest throughout the country and although coffee and cocoa are grown, the economy is based on timber and mineral deposits. Exports include ebony, crude oil, manganese and uranium. The capital is Libreville. Area: 267,677sq km (103,346sq miles). Pop. (1975 est.) 1,155,800. *See* MW p.81.

Gaboon viper, highly venomous but docile VIPER native to central Africa and closely related to the PUFF ADDER. The snake has a stocky body and its head is twice as wide as its neck. A brilliant geometric pattern of yellow, blue, pale purple and brown over its body provides a highly effective camouflage. The Gaboon viper has enlarged, horn-like scales between its nostrils. Length: up to 2m (7ft). Family Viperidae; species *Bitis gabonica.*

Gabor, Dennis (1900–), British physicist *b.* Hungary, who was awarded the 1971 Nobel Prize in physics for his invention of HOLOGRAPHY. He developed the basic technique in 1947 but it was not until the invention of the laser, by Charles H. TOWNES in 1960, that holography (a process of three-dimensional photography) became commercially feasible. Gabor has also researched into optics and communication theory.

Gaboriau, Émile (1832–73), French novelist. He wrote a number of early popular detective stories, including *L'Affaire Lerouge* (1866), *Monsieur Lecoq* (1869) and *La Corde au Cou* (1873).

Gaborone, capital city of Botswana, 240km (150 miles) NW of Pretoria, South Africa. The city served as the administrative headquarters of former Bechuanaland Protectorate and became the capital when the Protectorate gained its independence in 1966. Pop. (1971) 17,718.

Gabriel, one of the four major archangels, mentioned in both the Old and New Testaments. In the Old Testament account he helps DANIEL to interpret his visions. In the New Testament he foretells the birth of St JOHN THE BAPTIST to his father, ZACHARIAS, and that of Jesus to his mother, the Blessed Virgin Mary.

Gabriel, Jacques Ange (1698–1782), French architect. He perfected the French Classical style. Gabriel became first architect to Louis XV in 1742 and built or enlarged many chateaux and palaces under royal commission. His work includes the Petit Trianon at Versailles, the École Militaire in Paris, and the Place de la Concorde.

Gabrieli, family name of two Italian composers, uncle and nephew. Andrea Gabrieli (*c.*1510–86), a pupil of WILLAERT, was organist at St Mark's, Venice. He wrote vocal music (sacred and secular) and organ music, developing the antiphonal use of several choirs. His nephew and student Giovanni Gabrieli (*c.* 1555–1612) succeeded him as organist at St Mark's. Giovanni's varied output included large works for voices and orchestra, from which the orchestral sections emerged as independent pieces in the new CONCERTO style. He was a major influence on the early BAROQUE period, particularly (as teacher of Heinrich SCHÜTZ) in Germany. *See also* HC2 p.104.

Gad, two biblical figures, one the seventh son of JACOB, whose tribe settled in Gilead. The other was a prophet and historian during DAVID's reign.

Gaddi family, Florentine artists of the early Renaissance. Gaddo Gaddi (Gaddo di Zanobi) (*c.*1259–*c.*1330) made mosaics in many Florentine churches, some of which show the influence of CIMABUE. His son, Taddeo (*c.*1300–*c*1366), was trained by and worked with GIOTTO. His best-known work is the fresco series *Life of the Virgin* (completed in 1338) in the Baroncelli Chapel, Santa Croce, Florence. Other works include the Ponte Vecchio bridge, altarpieces and panel paintings. Taddeo's son, Agnolo (*d.*1396), also painted frescoes; the most famous is the *Legend of the True Cross* (*c.*1380) in Santa Croce, Florence. Agnolo has also had many panel paintings attributed to him. *See also* MM p.191.

Gadidae, family of fish containing about 70 species, some of which – including cod, haddock and hake – are caught for food. *See also* PE pp.246–247.

Gadolinium, metallic element (Gd) of the LANTHANIDE SERIES, first isolated as the oxide in 1880. Chief ores are monazite (a phosphate) and bastnäsite (a fluorocarbonate). The element has some specialized uses including neutron absorption and the manufacture of certain alloys. Properties: a.n. 64; a.w. 157.25; s.g. 7.898 (25°C); m.p. 1,311°C (2,392°F); b.p. 3,233°C (5,851°F); most common isotope Gd^{158} (24.87%).

Gaea, in Greek mythology, mother goddess of the earth who was less actively worshipped than goddesses of later origin. Wife (and in some legends, mother) of URANUS, she bore the Titans, the Cyclopes and the Hecatoncheires ("those of a hundred hands"). When Uranus hid all her children from her, she persuaded the Titan Cronus to castrate his father.

Gaelic, language spoken in scattered parts of Ireland and Scotland. The two branches diverged in the 15th century and are mutually unintelligible. The Irish variety is one of the official languages of the Irish Republic and is taught in schools but the number of speakers is diminishing. In Scotland Gaelic has no official status and is gradually dying out. Gaelic is a CELTIC LANGUAGE.

Gaelic football, sport popular in Ireland. Each side has 15 men who may kick, punch or pass the ball, but not throw it. Players may not pick the ball up directly from the ground with the hands; it may be carried for four paces but then has to be bounced, or kicked or punched away. The pitch is between 128m (420ft) and 146m (480ft) long and between 77m (252ft) and 91m (300ft) wide. There are goalposts at each end. One point is scored for putting the ball over the bar and three for driving it under the bar. The game lasts 60 minutes, except in the All-Ireland semi-finals and final when it lasts 80 minutes, with two halves, and is controlled by a referee and four goal umpires. The sport was established in Ireland in the 16th century and the ruling body, the Gaelic Athletic Association, was formed in 1884.

Gagarin, Yuri Alekseyevich (1934–68), Russian cosmonaut and national hero, the first man to orbit the earth. His historic flight took place on 12 April 1961, in the five-ton spacecraft *Vostok* ("East"). He attained a height of 300km (188 miles), and made his single orbit in 1 hr. 29 min.; he landed safely in the Soviet Union. Gagarin died seven years later in a plane crash. *See also* SU p.268.

Gage, Thomas (1721–87), British general, and administrator in North America. He became governor of Montreal in 1760, and was made head of the British forces in North America in 1763 and governor of Massachusetts in 1774. His soldiers fought the patriots at Lexington (April 1775), the battle that began the AMERICAN WAR OF INDEPENDENCE. He resigned in October of the same year.

Gagging Acts, popular name for a series of acts passed by the British parliament in 1817 to restrict the radical agitation which was the product of postwar unemployment and high food prices. After Orator Hunt's mass meeting at Spa Fields, London, in November 1816 and an attack on the Prince Regent in December, the Tory government suspended the right of HABEAS CORPUS and outlawed the holding of "seditious" meetings.

Gag rules, series of rules adopted by the US Congress in the late 1830s to prevent the discussion of slavery. The first, and most important, was the resolution of 1836, which declared that all petitions relating to slavery should be "laid on the table of the House" without debate. For eight years John Quincy ADAMS led the fight against the rules and in 1844, with the support of the northern abolitionist states, he succeeded in getting them repealed.

Gaia. *See* GAEA.

Gaillardia, also called blanketflower, a genus of annual and perennial flowering plants of the composite family. They are native to North America and are popular garden flowers. They have floral heads of a yellow, red or purple colour.

Gainsborough, Thomas (1727–88), British portrait and landscape painter. He made skilful use of various influences, including VAN DYCK, RUBENS and the Dutch landscape painters, to develop a personal style that is remarkable for its characterization and use of colour. His portraits, such as *Viscount Kilmorey* (1768) rivalled those of Sir Joshua REYNOLDS. Among his best landscapes is *The Watering Place* (1777). He also painted pastoral genre scenes or "fancy pictures", eg *The Harvest Waggon* (*c.*1770).

Gainsford, John (1938–), South African rugby union player. A tall, strongly-built centre-threequarter, he played in 33 internationals (1960–67) – then a Springbok record – scoring 8 tries. He represented Western Province and South-West Districts.

Gairdner, dry salt lake N of Eyre Peninsula, in South Australia. Area: 4,766sq km (1,840sq miles).

Gairy, Eric Matthew (1922–), Grenada politician who became a member of the legislative council in 1951, and Prime Minister in 1967. He was Prime Minister at and after Grenada's independence in 1974.

Gaitskell, Hugh Todd Naylor (1906–63), British politician. He entered Parliament as a Labour MP in 1945, was minister of fuel and power (1947–50), minister of state for economic affairs in 1950, and in the same year, at the age of 44, became the youngest chancellor of the exchequer since Austen CHAMBERLAIN (in 1903). His 1950 budget, by imposing some charges on National Health treatment, brought him the leadership of the right wing of the Labour Party against the Bevanites. He became treasurer of the party in 1953 and 1954, defeating Aneurin BEVAN, and in 1955 was elected leader of the party. At the 1960 party conference he distinguished himself by his resolute defiance of the conference's vote in favour of unilateral nuclear disarmament.

Gaius. *See* CAIUS.

Gajdusek, Daniel Carleton (1923–), US physiologist who shared the 1976 Nobel Prize in physiology and medicine with Baruch S. BLUMBERG for work on the neurological disease kuru. Working among tribes in New Guinea, which were being decimated by this disease, he postulated its transmission by the ritual eating of human brains. Further study implanting kuru in animals led him to conclude that it was caused by a slowly acting virus which could remain dormant for years. This finding implicated viruses in other diseases such as multiple sclerosis and Parkinson's disease.

Gal, little-used unit, abbreviated from Galileo, measure of acceleration equal to 1 centimetre per second per second.

Galactic co-ordinate system, astronomical co-ordinate system that refers to the plane of the galaxy. The co-ordinates are galactic latitude and longitude. Galactic latitude is the angular distance of a celestial object above or below the galactic plane. Galactic longitude is the angular distance around the galactic equator from a defined zero point. This point is at right ascension 17hr 42.4min, declination −28°55′, and is the direction of the presumed galactic centre. The galactic north pole is at RA 12hr 49min, dec +27°24′.

Galactosemia, genetic inability to convert galactose (in milk) to usable glucose because a particular enzyme is missing. Symptoms, appearing in infants within a few days of birth, include vomiting, possible oedema and feeding difficulty. It is controlled by eliminating milk and milk products from the diet.

Galago, also called bush baby, any of several African species of small, nocturnal and tree-living PRIMATES of the subfamily Galaginae of the LORIS family (Lorisidae). At night galagos leap between branches like squirrels, searching for fruit and insects. They have large, light-gathering eyes and long fingers, toes and bushy tails. *See also* NW pp.*168, 212.*

Galah, bright pink and grey COCKATOO that lives in large numbers in Australia and is often kept there as a cage bird. Species *Kakatoe roseicapilla. See also* NW p.205.

Galahad, in Arthurian legend, son of LANCELOT and Elaine. He qualified as the best knight by passing the test of the Perilous Seat and drawing a sword from a marble and iron stone. He was a late addition to the legends, replacing Percival as the major seeker of the Holy GRAIL. Galahad was successful in the quest because he was a pure knight.

Galápagos Islands, volcanic archipelago in the Pacific Ocean astride the Equator near Ecuador, to which country they belong. They are famous for the visit in 1835 of the naturalist Charles DARWIN in HMS *Beagle.* Darwin noted that the dominant animals were not mammals but reptiles and birds. These include species found nowhere else, such as the GALAPAGOS TORTOISE and the marine IGUANA. SEABIRDS include FRIGATEBIRDS, GANNETS and a flightless CORMORANT. The GALÁPAGOS FINCHES, a group of birds that show radiative adaptation to various ways of feeding, gave Darwin strong evidence for his theory of evolution by natural selection. *See also* MW p.81; NW pp.32–33.

Galapagos tortoise, any of several tortoises, all subspecies of *Testudo elephantopus*; they are found solely on the GALÁPAGOS ISLANDS. Animals introduced to the islands are robbing the tortoises of their staple food, but a conservation programme is in progress. Length: to 1.1m (3.7ft); weight: to 180kg (397lb).

Galatea, in Greek mythology, a sea nymph. She was in love with Acis, the son of a river nymph, but was loved by the Cyclops, POLYPHEMUS, who, when he found her with Acis, crushed Acis under a huge stone. To release Acis, Galatea turned him into a river. By some legends, Galatea is also the name of the woman brought to life from a statue.

Galati, port in E Romania, on the Danube (Donau) River; capital of Galati county. It was the seat of the European Danube Commission from 1856 until 1945. Its major exports are grain and timber, and industries include iron and steel, shipbuilding, chemicals and textiles. Pop. (1974) 197,853.

Galatia, ancient region of Asia Minor near modern ANKARA in Turkey. It was named after the Celts who invaded the area in the 3rd century BC. Galatia became subject to the Romans in 189 BC and in 25 BC its name was given to a Roman province larger than the original region.

Galatians, Epistle to the, letter in the New Testament written by the apostle Paul in indignation at the increase in false teachings among his Galatian converts. Paul stressed his apostolic authority and the commission which he had received directly from God, and argued against teachers who exhorted the Galatians to adhere strictly to Jewish Law.

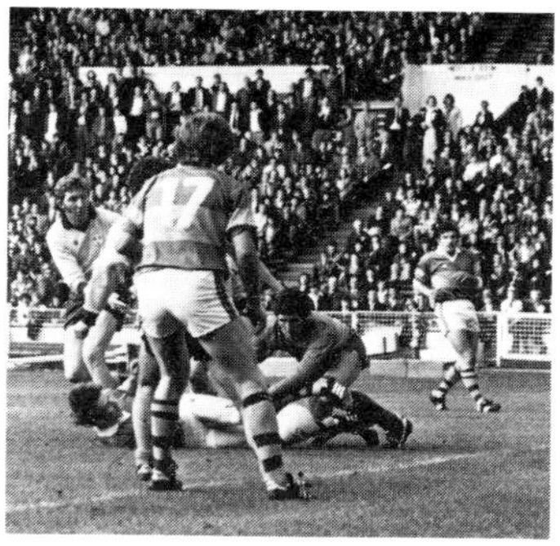

Gaelic football; the All Ireland Senior final between Kerry and Dublin, 1976.

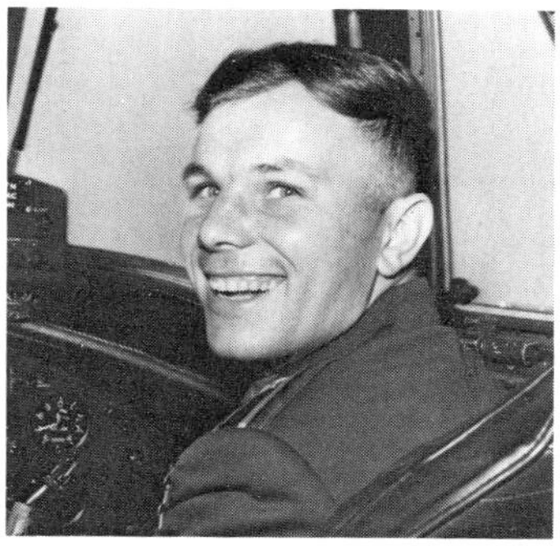

Yuri Gagarin, photographed in Britain in 1961 while visiting the Soviet Exhibition.

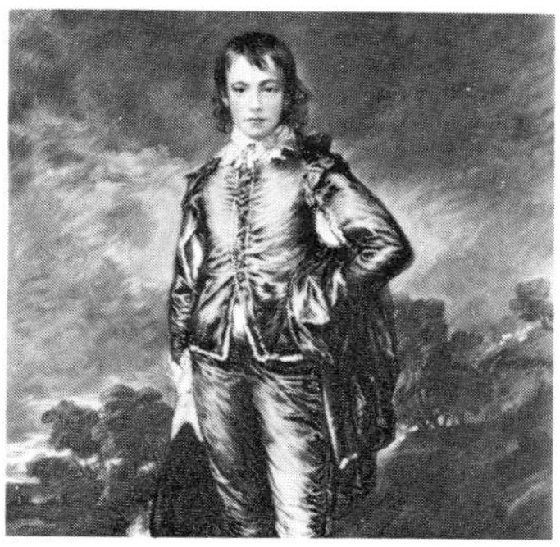

Gainsborough's *Blue Boy* rebuffed Reynolds' dogma against areas of blue.

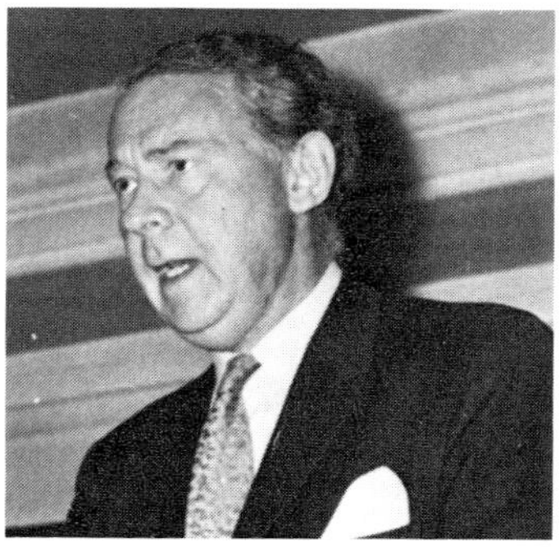

Hugh Gaitskell explaining the Labour Party manifesto at a press conference in 1961.

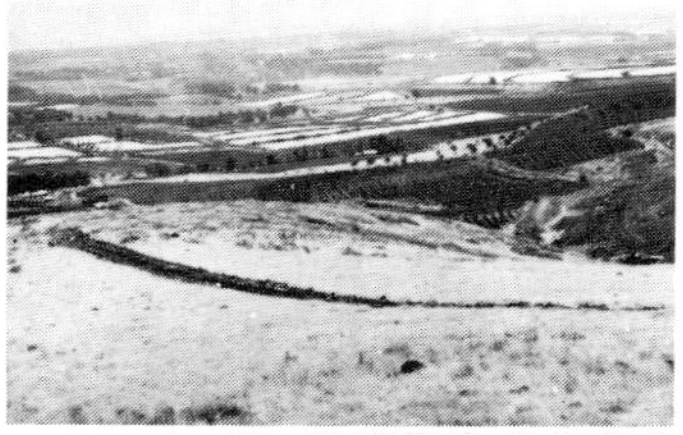

Galilee; many Kibbutzim in this fertile area have built artificial ponds for fish farming.

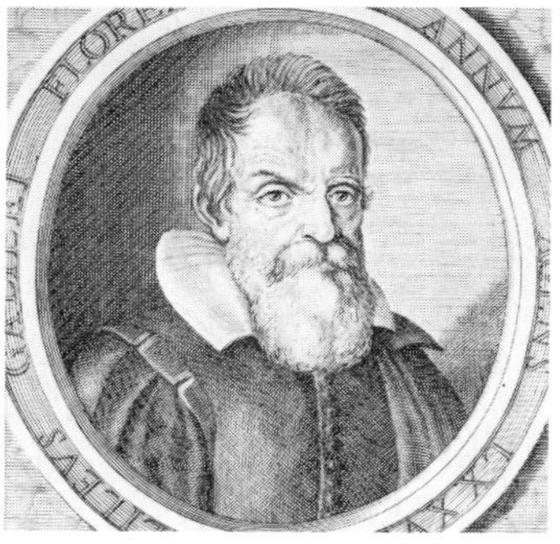

Galileo used actual experiments to prove his theories concerning the rate of falling bodies.

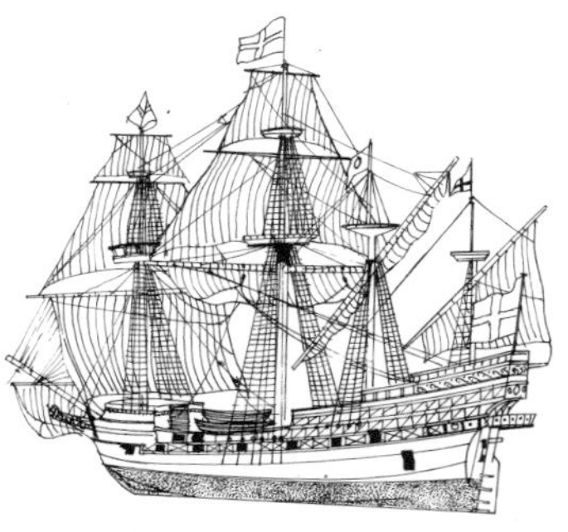

Galleons were the large fully rigged warships developed in the 15th and 16th centuries.

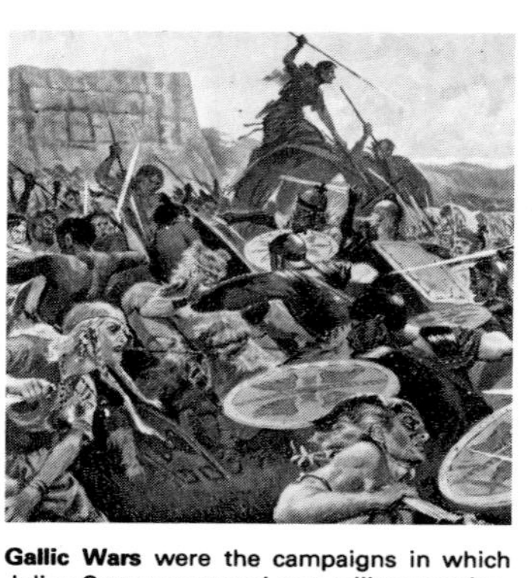

Gallic Wars were the campaigns in which Julius Caesar emerged as a military genius.

Galaxy, large collection of stars, gas and dust, held together by gravitational attraction of the component parts, and prevented from collapsing in on itself by its rotational movement. Galaxies usually contain millions of stars and are classified according to their shape, a system originated by E. P. HUBBLE. The majority of galaxies are spiral or elliptical. A spiral galaxy is shaped like a flat disc with a central bulge, or nucleus, made up of old stars, with spiral arms consisting of gas, dust and young stars. This type is further classified into normal and barred spirals, the latter having a central bar of stars from which the arms project. Our Galaxy, the MILKY WAY, is a typical spiral galaxy. Elliptical galaxies have no spiral arms and resemble the nuclei of spiral galaxies. They contain no gas or dust and vary greatly in size and mass. Some galaxies, composed wholly of young stars, and with no shape or nucleus, are known as irregular galaxies, an example being the MAGELLANIC CLOUDS. Galaxies often occur in clusters, although they are apparently retreating from each other at great speed, demonstrated by red shifts in their spectra. The more distant galaxies seem to be retreating at greater velocities, evidence in support of the BIG BANG theory of cosmology. Some galaxies emit energy in forms other than visible light, and many radio galaxies have now been detected. *See also* SU pp.244–251.

Galaxy cluster, group of associated galaxies, consisting of several separate systems moving together through space. Our own Galaxy (the Milky Way) belongs to the LOCAL GROUP OF GALAXIES which includes the ANDROMEDA spiral and the MAGELLANIC CLOUDS. A concentration of galaxy clusters is termed a galaxy supercluster. *See also* SU pp.246–247, *249*.

Galbraith, John Kenneth (1908–), US economist, *b.* Canada. His works have made him well known to the general public. Three of his most famous books are *American Capitalism: The Concept of Countervailing Power* (1952); *The Affluent Society* (1958); and *The New Industrial State* (1967). In general, Galbraith takes the position that many accepted theories about consumption are outmoded. An early supporter of and adviser to John F. Kennedy, he was ambassador to India from 1961 to 1963.

Galen (*c.* AD129–*c.* 199), Greek physician. His work and writings provided much of the foundation for the development of medicine. He tried to synthesize all that was known of medical practice and to develop a theoretical framework for an explanation of the body and its disorders. He made numerous anatomical and physiological discoveries, including ones concerning heart valves, secretions of the kidney, respiration and nervous-system function. He was among the first to study physiology by means of detailed and ingenious animal experimentation. Galen's theories influenced medical practice for centuries. *See also* MS pp.*82, 85,* 188; HC1 p.116.

Galena, lead-grey, brittle metallic mineral, lead sulphide (PbS); a major ore of lead in igneous and sedimentary rocks. It occurs as granular masses, and commonly as cubic system octahedral crystals; sometimes fibrous. Hardness 2.5–2.7; s.g. 7.5.

Galicia, historic region in SE Poland (Western Galicia) and W Ukraine (Eastern Galicia), on the slopes of the Carpathian Mts N of Czechoslovakia. It is mainly an agricultural region, producing grain, flax, hops, potatoes and tobacco, but there are some oilfields. It was part of Poland from the 14th century until the partitions of Poland in 1772, 1795 and 1815 when Austria took possession. In 1919 Poland took W Galicia and gained E Galicia in 1923. The 1939 partition of Poland gave E Galicia to the Ukraine. Area: 78,500sq km (30,309sq miles).

Galicia, region in NW Spain, comprising the provinces of La Coruña, Lugo, Orense and Pontevedra. Galicia has an indented coastline and a mountainous interior. The economy is based on the raising of livestock. The region has always been known for its spirit of independence; there were frequent rebellions against the crown in the Middle Ages and an important cultural revival in the 19th century. Pop. (1970) 2,584,000.

Galilean satellites. *See* CALLISTO; EUROPA; GANYMEDE; IO.

Galilee, region in N Israel, bounded by the River Jordan and the Sea of Galilee (E) and the Plain of Esdraelon (S). Irrigation has made this a fertile agricultural area, and olives and grain are the chief crops. Fishing is the most important industry. Nazareth is the major town of the region. The home of JESUS CHRIST, it was the scene of His ministry and His disciples were local fishermen.

Galilee, Sea of (Lake Tiberius or Yam Kinneret), freshwater lake in N Israel, near the border of Syria and Israel. It receives most of its water from and is drained by the River Jordan. Israel's major reservoir, it is an important fishing ground and the source of water for irrigation of the Negev Desert via the "National Water Carrier". It has been the site of several archaeological excavations. Area: 166sq km (64sq miles).

Galileo Galilei (1564–1642), Italian scientist, lecturer at Pisa, later moving to Florence and then to Padua. He deduced the formula for the period of a pendulum from the oscillation of a hanging lamp in Pisa Cathedral. He later studied falling bodies and disproved Aristotle's view that the rate of fall is proportional to the weight. He also discovered the parabolic flight path of projectiles. He developed the telescope, which enabled him to discover sunspots, lunar craters, Jupiter's satellites and the phases of Venus. In *Sidereus Muncius* (1610) he announced his support for the Copernican view of the universe, with the earth moving around the sun. This was declared a heresy by Cardinal BELLARMINE. In *Dialogo Sopra i Due Massimi Sistemi del Mondo* (1632) he defied the pope by making his views even more explicit; as a result he was brought before the INQUISITION at the age of 69 and forced to recant. *See also* MM p.90; SU pp.24, 212.

Gall, Franz Joseph (1758–1828), German anatomist and physiologist, who correctly identified the function of several areas of the brain and suggested that these areas controlled or were related to certain parts of the body. He extrapolated from this and founded PHRENOLOGY, the study of the external structure of the skull to determine the character of an individual.

Gall, abnormal swelling or protuberance of plant tissue stimulated by an invasion of any of a wide variety of parasitic or symbiotic organisms, including bacteria, fungi, insects and nematodes. Most gall organisms stunt but do not kill the affected plants. The gall wasp larva makes a spongy "apple" gall on oak trees, which contains tannin. These galls are used in leather tanning and made into inks and dyes.

Gallacher, Hughie (1903–57), Scottish footballer. A small, quick-witted centre-forward, he played 19 times for Scotland (1924–35), scoring 22 goals. During a tempestuous career he scored 387 league goals for Airdrieonians, Newcastle United, Chelsea, Derby County, Notts County, Grimsby Town and Gateshead.

Gall bladder, muscular sac found in most vertebrates. It stores and concentrates BILE which it receives from the LIVER. It is well supplied with blood vessels, nerves and lymphatic tissue. When stimulated by the vagus nerve, the gall bladder discharges bile into the duodenum via the bile duct. *See also* MS p.69, *69*.

Gallé, Émile (1846–1904), French designer and technical innovator in art glass, a leading force in the ART NOUVEAU movement. His glassware, in which the influence of Japanese art is evident, made a vital contribution to the evolution of asymmetrical forms and symbolic overtones associated with ART NOUVEAU. It was rich in special textures obtained with air bubbles and metallic foil, and with special effects produced by mixing varying thicknesses of layered glass which was carved or etched to create plant forms.

Galle, Johann Gottfried (1812–1910), German astronomer, the first to observe and identify Neptune as a planet (1846), although its presence had been postulated by other scientists. Galle also suggested a system for determining the scale of the solar system based on the observation of asteroids.

Galleon, general-purpose wooden sailing ship dating from the 16th century and larger than the earlier CARRACK and CARAVEL. It featured a larger forecastle and quarterdeck, and was rigged with a bowsprit sail, two main masts with several square sails and one or two lateen masts at the rear. *See also* MM pp.112–113.

Gallery, topmost seats in a theatre or cinema, most usually the upper balcony or balconies and known colloquially as "the gods". Usually the cheapest part of a theatre, its occupants were once noted for their unreservedly critical reactions to the performance on stage. A gallery can also be any raised platform at the rear or side of the stage.

Galley, oared Mediterranean warship of ancient origin used by the Greeks and Romans, as well as by the Italian, French and Turkish navies up to the 17th century. They usually had from one to three rows of oars on each side. Later galleys carried guns and had a crew of several hundred. *See also* TRIREME; MM pp.172–173, *172*.

Galliard or Gaillard, court dance in moderate triple time, full of quick turns and intricate steps. It was popular in 16th-century Europe and in Italy replaced the earlier Saltarello.

Gallicanism, nationalist movement within the French Roman Catholic Church, opposed to ULTRAMONTANISM. It affirmed the supreme authority of the French bishops and Crown at the expense of the papacy. The movement began in the 13th century, and was enshrined in the Pragmatic Sanction of Bourges (1438) and the Concordat of Bologna (1516). The controversy continued in several forms, such as JANSENISM, until modern times.

Gallico, Paul (1897–1976), US writer of Italo-Austrian parentage. He was a prominent US sports journalist before turning to fiction writing in 1936. His books, many of them enchanting stories about animals and children, include *The Snow Goose* (1941), *The Small Miracle* (1952) and *Thomasina* (1958).

Galli-Curci, Amelita (1882–1963), US SOPRANO, *b.* Italy. She studied in Milan and made her debut in 1909 as Gilda in Verdi's *Rigoletto*. She became a famous soprano in the Italian repertoire and spent much of her career with the Metropolitan Opera Company, New York (1921–30).

Gallic Wars (58–51 BC), campaigns in which the Romans, led by Julius Caesar, conquered the Gauls. By 57 he had subdued SW and N Gaul and extended Roman influence to the River Rhine and N France. In 56 he conquered the Veneti, leaders of an anti-Roman confederation, and in 55–54 invaded Germany and Britain. He defeated a united Gallic force under Vercingetorix in 52 BC. Caesar's *The Gallic Wars* is a classic account of the campaigns. *See also* HC1 p.*97*.

Galliformes, order of six families of GAME BIRDS, including TURKEYS, GUINEA FOWL, PHEASANTS and PARTRIDGES.

Gallipoli (Gelibolu), city in SW European Turkey, on the Gallipoli Peninsula; port at the E end of the Dardanelles. First colonized by the ancient Greeks, it has been of strategic importance throughout history in the defence of Istanbul (Constantinople). It was the first European city to be conquered by the Ottoman Turks, in 1354. Pop. (1970) 14,600.

Gallipoli Campaign (1915), Allied attempt during WWI to defeat Turkey and establish a Black Sea supply route to Russia by capturing the DARDANELLES. Some 45,000 British and French and 30,000 Anzac troops were involved. In April British and ANZAC forces established a beach-head along the E coast of the Gallipoli Peninsula; French troops landed on the Asiatic side of the BOSPORUS Strait. After eight months of fighting and more than 144,800 casualties, the Allies were ordered to withdraw. *See also* HC2 pp.*127*, 190.

Gallium, metallic element (symbol Ga) of

group IIIA of the periodic table, predicted by MENDELEYEV (as ekaaluminium) and discovered spectroscopically in 1875 by Lecoq de Boisbaudran. Chief sources are as a by-product from bauxite and some zinc ores. The metal is used in high-temperature thermometers and in semiconductors. Properties: at.no. 31; at.wt. 69.72; s.g. 5.9 (29.6°C); m.p. 29.78°C (85.6°F); b.p. 2,403°C (4,357°F); most common isotope Ga^{69} (60.4%).

Galloway, region of SW Scotland, made up of the former counties of Wigtownshire and Kirkudbrightshire, and now part of Dumfries and Galloway Region. The area includes the Mull of Galloway, the most southerly part in Scotland. Galloway is famous for its black, hornless cattle. Dairy farming and tourism are the principal economic activities.

Gallstone, or cholelithiasis, stonelike formation, usually containing cholesterol, found in the gall bladder. It is more common in women than men. Gallstone formation is thought to be related to liver malfunction, and may be due to fatty foods, but its cause is not positively known. Symptoms range from none to excruciating pain (biliary colic). *See also* MS pp.*92*, 93.

Gallup, George Horace (1901–), US statistician and public opinion pollster. He taught journalism and then, in the 1930s, embarked on a career sampling public opinion on social, political and business matters. He correctly forecast the outcome of the 1936 presidential election and since then, with the notable exception of 1948, when he predicted a win for Thomas Dewey over President Truman, the Gallup Poll has acquired a reputation for accuracy. His methods are used extensively in advertising and market research.

Gall-wasp, small brown wasp found worldwide. The female lays eggs in plant tissues and a GALL develops as the larvae hatch and mature. The abnormal plant tissues provide the larvae with food and shelter. The galls are usually found on oak trees ("oak apples") and roses ("robin's pincushions"). Length 6–8mm (0.25–0.32in). Family Cynipidae. *See also* NW pp.*116*, *208*.

Galois, Évariste (1811–1832), French mathematician who laid the foundation of the algebraic GROUP THEORY. His work was dismissed by the mathematical establishment as incomprehensible and he turned to political activism, being arrested twice. He died after a duel.

Galsworthy, John (1867–1933), British novelist and playwright. His novels deal with the contemporary English upper middle class. The most noted of his novels are those about the Forsyte family, grouped in three trilogies: *The Forsyte Saga* (1906–21), *A Modern Comedy* (1924–28) and *End of the Chapter* (1931–33).

Galt, Sir Alexander Tilloch (1817–93), Canadian politician. He sat in the Legislative Assembly (1849–50, 1853–67) and promoted the Grand Trunk Railway. As minister of finance in 1858, he urged confederation on the British and was influential at the Quebec Conference as chief spokesman for the English of Lower Canada.

Galt, John (1779–1839), Scottish writer. Galt produced poems, dramas and historical novels, but particularly remembered are his studies of life in Scotland: *The Ayrshire Legatees* (1821), *Annals of the Parish* (1821) and *The Entail* (1823).

Galton, Sir Francis (1822–1911), British scientist and scholar. He pioneered the study of human differences, mental tests and statistical analysis of data. In *Hereditary Genius* (1869) he described his theories of HEREDITY and advocated a science of EUGENICS – selective breeding of persons with desirable traits.

Galty Mountains, range of mountains in S central Republic of Ireland, extending W to E through S Limerick and S Tipperary counties. The highest peak is Galtymore, rising to 920m (3,018ft) in Tipperary. Length: 24km (15 miles).

Galvani, Luigi (1737–98), Italian physician and physicist who became lecturer of anatomy at Bologna and did pioneer studies in electrophysiology. His experiments with frogs' legs indicated a connection between muscular contraction and electricity, although the correct explanation was given by VOLTA.

Galvanism, early name for an electric current that results from chemical action, so called after Luigi GALVANI.

Galvanizing, the coating of iron or steel articles with zinc, either applied directly in a bath of molten zinc, electrodeposited from cold zinc sulphate solutions, or dusted on and baked. Corrugated sheets, dustbins, nails, pails and wire netting may be protected from the corrosive effects of atmospheric carbonic acid. The metal to be protected is first derusted but if, after galvanizing, the zinc coating is pierced protection is still provided because of the preferential attack by corrosion on zinc rather than on iron.

Galvanometer, instrument for detecting, comparing, or measuring electric currents. It is based on the principle that a current through a conductor (usually a coil) creates a magnetic field which reacts with a magnet giving a deflection. The main types are the moving-coil galvanometer (modern and most commonly used) and the moving-magnet instrument. *See also* SU pp.118–119.

Galway, county in the W Republic of Ireland. Bounded by the Atlantic (W) it has an indented coastline with many islands. It is a farming region, mountainous in the W, lowlying in the E and drained by the River Shannon. The chief towns are Galway, Tuam and Ballinasloe. Area: 5,939sq km (2,293sq miles). Pop. (1971) 148,220.

Gama, Vasco da (*c.*1469–1524), Portuguese navigator and discoverer of the sea route to India. In 1497 he led the historic expedition to establish a maritime route to the Indies. He reached South Africa, sailed around the Cape and across the Indian Ocean to Calicut, India. The route is still used by ships today, and opened up the resources of Asia to the Western European powers. In 1524, he went to India as viceroy, becoming head of the first European enclave in Asia. He died there only months later. *See also* HC1 p.234.

Gambetta, Léon Michel (1838–82), French politician. He was a parliamentary opponent of Napoleon III, organized French resistance in the Franco-Prussian War (1870–71) and helped form the Third Republic. He was Prime Minister from 1881 to 1882.

Gambia, republic in W Africa. It is Africa's smallest nation, lying on either side of the Gambia River for about 464km (290 miles) and varying in width from 24–48km (15–30 miles). The economy is dependent on groundnuts and associated products, and these together account for 95% of the country's exports. The capital is Banjul. Area: 11,295sq km (4,361sq miles). Pop. (1975 est.) 524,000. *See* MW p.81.

Gambia, river and major trade route in W Africa. It rises in the Fonta Djalon Mountains, Guinea, and flows NW through Senegal and W into the Atlantic Ocean at Banjul. It is navigable by ocean-going ships for 300km (185 miles) of its 1,120km (700 miles).

Gambier Islands, island group of FRENCH POLYNESIA, S Pacific Ocean. It consists of four inhabited islands, known as the Mangareva group, and numerous uninhabited atolls used for nuclear testing. Industries: copra, coffee and pearls. Area: 31sq km (12sq miles). *See also* MW p.81.

Gambling, pursuit in which people bet money on a contest with the aim of winning back more than their initial outlay. It takes a large number of forms: a "flutter" on the football pools or Derby sweepstake; a bet against defined odds put up by a bookmaker on sports events or, say, a general election; a stake on personal success, as at cards, roulette, or the humble but avaricious "fruit machine". Chance is the main ingredient of all gambling; luck more often than skill the ingredient of success. With more fortunes lost than won through gambling, and with crime and poverty sometimes closely associated with it, it is not surprising that some countries view it as a social evil and declare it illegal. In others the state derives considerable income from taxes on gambling or from the profits on state-run lotteries, such as the British Premium Savings Bonds. Gambling has been described as "a way of buying hope on credit". *See also* SU pp.58–59.

Game bird, bird hunted by humans for food, especially birds of the two major orders Galliformes and Anseriformes. Galliformes include the chicken, turkey, quail, pheasant, partridge, guan and curassow. Typically, they are ground birds with strong legs adapted for walking and running, and strong toes to scratch the ground for fruits and seeds. They often have abundant plumage and elevated tails and make simple ground-depression nests. Anseriformes include the duck, goose and swan. They are waterfowl and have rounded, open nostrils, dense undercoats of down, and special glands to waterproof their plumage. *See also* individual species; PE pp.238–239.

Gamelan, traditional village percussion orchestra of Indonesia, consisting of tuned and untuned percussion instruments (mainly xylophones, marimbas, gongs and drums), played by up to 30 musicians. The music is based on various PENTATONIC scales, and is rhythmically complex.

Game Laws, series of laws in Britain from the 14th to the 20th centuries controlling the possession, shooting and sale of animals classified as game. The first act (1389) forbade persons below a certain rank and fortune (a landed income of 40 shillings a year) from shooting hares, deer or conies. From then until the comprehensive Game Acts of 1816 and 1831 there were 50 acts of parliament on the subject. By then game included hares, pheasants, partridges, grouse, blackgame and bustards. These acts, the basis of the present law, prescribed severe penalties for poaching and restricted the shooting and sale of each animal to a few weeks of the year (called the open season). *See also* PE pp.238–239.

Gamete, sexual reproductive cell that joins with another cell to form a new organism. Female gametes (ova) are motionless; male gametes (sperm) have a tail enabling them to swim. *See also* MS pp.74–75; NW p.*30*.

Game theory, in mathematics, the analysis of problems involving conflict. Its application includes problems in business management, sociology, economics and military strategy (they involve situations in which there is a conflict of interest, incomplete information and an element of chance) as well as "true" games such as poker and chess. The theory was first introduced by Émile Borel and developed by John von Neumann in 1928. *See also* SU pp.58–59.

Gametophyte, generation of plants that bears the female and male gametes (sexual reproductive cells). In flowering plants these are the germinated pollen grains (male) and ovules containing the embryo sac (female). *See also* ALTERNATION OF GENERATIONS; FERN; MOSS; NW pp.38–39, 52–53.

Gamma globulin, one of the protein components of the serum of mammalian blood. It contains approximately 85% of the circulating ANTIBODIES of the blood. It gives temporary immunity in patients who have been exposed to certain diseases such as measles. *See also* MS p.62.

Gamma radiation, or γ rays, form of ELECTROMAGNETIC RADIATION emitted from the nuclei of radioactive atoms, or extremely short wavelength, ie high FREQUENCY. High energy gamma rays have even greater powers of penetration than hard X-RAYS, so that sources of this radiation must be stored inside thick lead containers. Gamma rays can be detected with a GEIGER COUNTER. *See also* RADIOACTIVITY; SU pp.*99*, 173, 222.

Gammer Gurton's Needle (*c.*1557), play believed to be by William Stevenson. An early and somewhat coarse comedy, it realistically portrays hearty, rustic English contemporary life, employing racy, idiomatic dialogue.

Gamow, George (1904–68), US nuclear physicist, cosmologist and author,

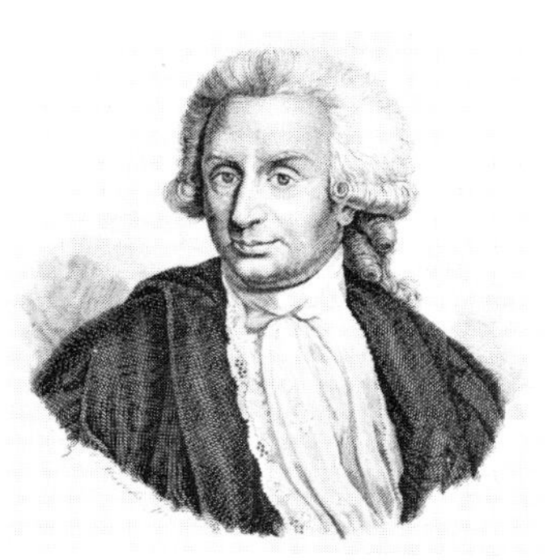

Galvani believed that nerve juices caused the electricity residing in an animal.

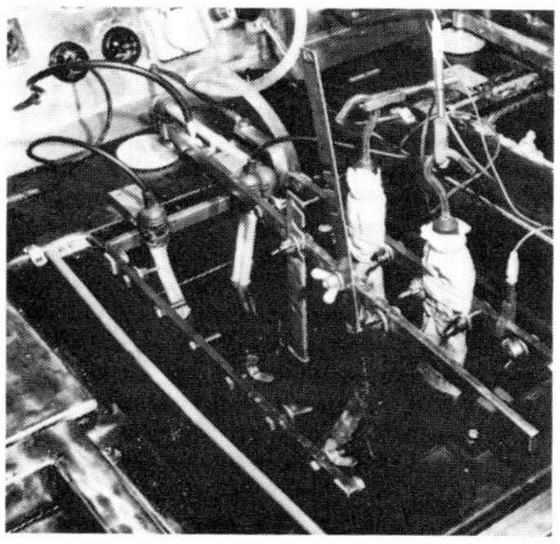

Galvanizing is a method of protecting iron or steel from the corrosive effects of weather.

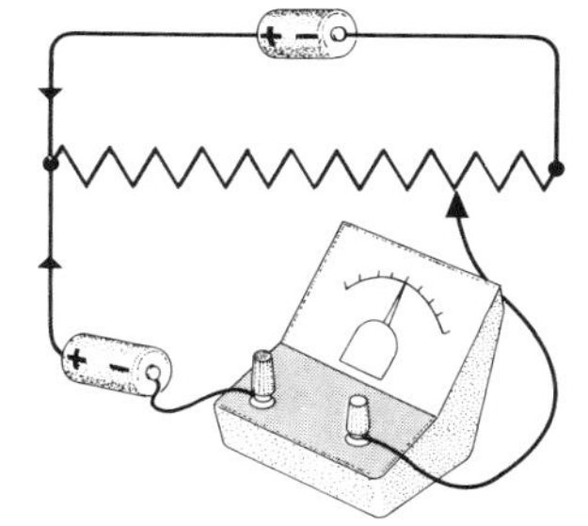

Galvanometers may be used to find the balance point in bridge circuits.

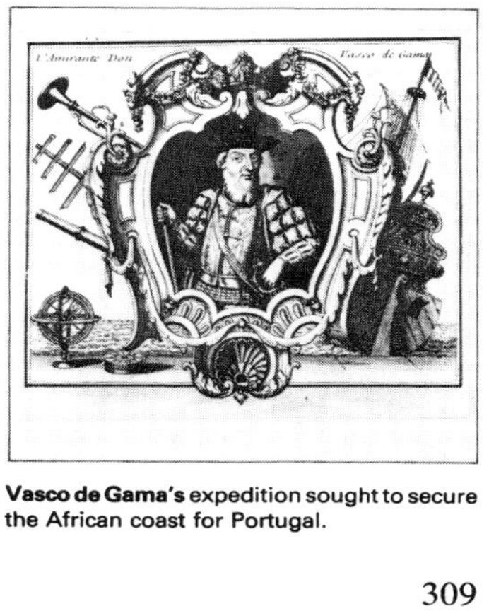

Vasco de Gama's expedition sought to secure the African coast for Portugal.

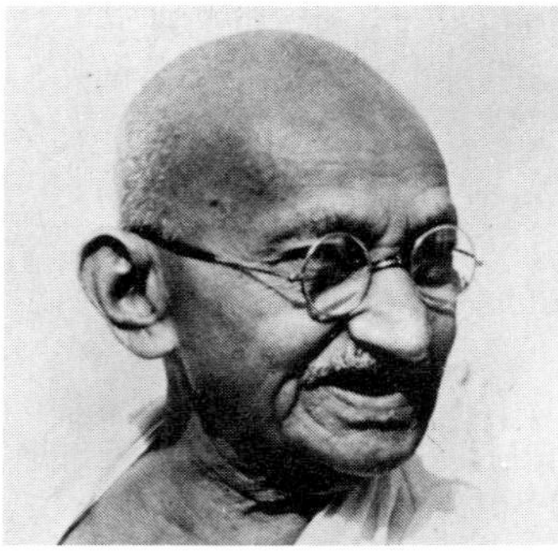

Gandhi led the people of India in a non-violent struggle for independence.

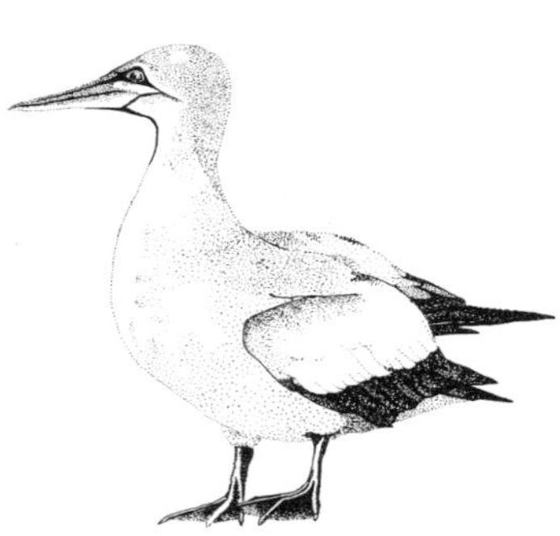

Gannets have air sacs under their skin which cushions their impact when landing on water.

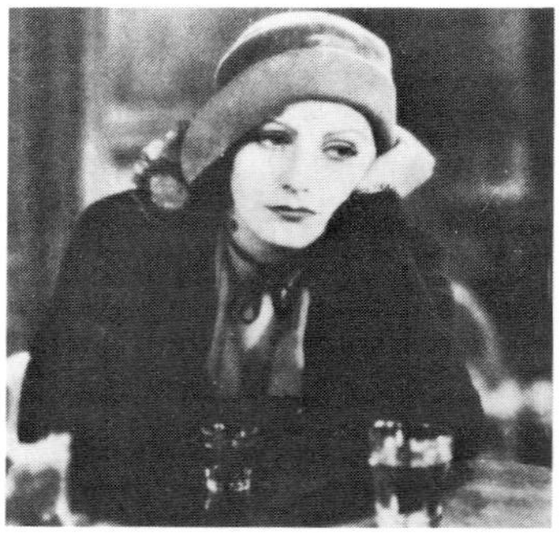

Greta Garbo's withdrawal from the limelight was described as "conspicuous isolation".

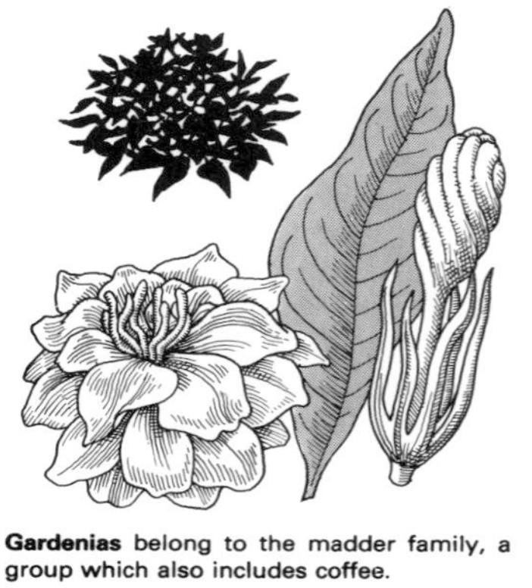

Gardenias belong to the madder family, a group which also includes coffee.

b. Russia. He was a proponent of the "BIG-BANG" theory of the creation of the universe and he contributed to the deciphering of the genetic code. He also developed the quantum theory of radioactivity and proposed the liquid-drop model of atomic nuclei. With Edward TELLER, he established the Gamow-Teller theory of beta decay and the internal structure of red giant stars.

Gandhara, historic area in modern NW Pakistan, on the Indus river. A Persian colony (6th century BC), it passed to the MAURYA EMPIRE of India (*c.* 303 BC); under ASHOKA (*c.* 265–238 BC) Gandhara flourished as a cultural and Buddhist centre. Its greatest prosperity came during the rule of the KUSHANS (1st–3rd centuries AD), who developed the Gandhara School of art, noted for Buddhist sculptures and reliefs. In the 6th century, the area was raided by the HUNS.

Gandhi, Indira (1917–), Indian political figure, the first woman elected (1966) Prime Minister of India. The daughter of Jawaharlal NEHRU, she served as president of the Indian National Congress Party in 1959–60. In 1975 she was found guilty of breaking electoral rules in the 1971 elections. She refused to resign, invoked emergency powers and imprisoned many of her opponents. In the 1977 elections her party was defeated.

Gandhi, Mohandas Karamchand "Mahatma" (1869–1948), Indian leader. Known as the Mahatma ("Great soul"), he was regarded as the father of India because of his leadership of the country's nationalist movement from 1919 to 1947, when independence was granted. His method, called *Satyagraha* ("truth-keeping") included all forms of non-violent resistance to British rule, such as strikes, refusal to pay taxes, and refusal to respect courts. His experiences in South Africa, where he spent 21 years trying to end oppression of the Indians, and the massacre of a mob in Amritsar by the British in 1919, led him to believe that freedom could not be gained by force. In 1930 he made a dramatic (388km, 241-mile) protest march to the sea inspiring widespread demonstrations. His methods succeeded, and he came to be considered a moral as well as actual leader. He was assassinated by a Hindu Brahmin who objected to his religious tolerance. *See also* HC2 pp.216, 220.

Ganeśa, elephant-headed Hindu god, son of SHIVA and PARVATI; he is considered to be able to remove obstacles, relieve difficulties and is the patron of learning said to have written down the MĀHABHĀRATA. He is the leader of Shiva's attendants and is depicted with a pot-belly and a broken tusk. His birth festival is in the lunar month Bhadrapada.

Ganges (Ganga), sacred river in India. It rises in the Himalayas, formed by the confluence of two headstreams: the Bhāgirathi and Alaknanda. It then flows SE and empties into the Bay of Bengal through the combined Brahmaputra – Ganges delta. The plains of the Ganges are extremely fertile and support one of the world's most densely populated areas. In Hindu religion and legend, the Ganges is the earthly form of the Goddess Ganga, and pilgrims purify themselves in its waters. Length: 2,512km (1,560 miles).

Ganglion, small mass of nervous tissue preponderant in the nervous system of invertebrates, peripheral in vertebrates.

Gangrene, death of body tissues associated with loss of blood supply and bacterial infection. It can occur as a result of injury, freezing or in people with diabetes. In dry gangrene, found most often in old people with diseased arteries, the affected part gradually turns black, with inflammation and skin ulcers. Moist gangrene is characterized by fever, inflammation and effusion of fluid from the diseased limb; it can be fatal. Gas gangrene occurs when open wounds become infected with gas-producing bacteria (*Clostridium welchii*). Treatment consists of antibiotics and, in severe cases, amputation.

Gangster film, melodramatic film, many made in the USA, depicting the exploits of a gangster or a gang who carries out robberies with murder, or indulges in warfare with a rival gang. Such bloodthirsty films began with Sternberg's *Underworld* (1927), followed by the classic *Quick Millions* (1931), *The Roaring Twenties* (1939) and *White Heat* (1949). The style was revived with *Bonnie and Clyde* (1967) and continued into the 1970s with *The Godfather* (1971) and *Lucky Luciano* (1973).

Gangtok, capital of Sikkim, S central Asia, situated in the Himalayas, 28km (17 miles) NE of Darjeeling, India, one of the world's wettest regions. Gangtok has a Buddhist monastery. There is a little light industry. Pop. (1968 est.) 9,000.

Gangue, waste material in an ore of deposit, as opposed to metal-containing or other useful minerals.

Ganivet, Angel (1865–98), Spanish novelist. He analysed the problems of Spanish culture and empire in *Spain: An Interpretation* (1897), and introduced Scandinavian writers including STRINDBERG and IBSEN to the Spanish public.

Gannet, fast-diving marine bird of cooler offshore waters, related to tropical boobies. Gannets are heavy-bodied with tapering bills, long pointed wings, short legs and webbed feet. Their plumage is white with a yellowish head and black wing tips. They feed on fish and nest in huge colonies on rocky islands. Length: 63–101cm (25–40in). Family Sulidae. *See also* NW pp.*144, 149.*

Ganymede, in Greek legend, the son of Tros, King of Troy. Because of his adolescent beauty, he was carried off by ZEUS to serve as cupbearer to the gods.

Ganymede, largest of Jupiter's satellites, one of the Galilean satellites; it is larger than Mercury. Diameter: approx. 5,000km (3,100 miles); mean distance from Jupiter: 1,000,000km (621,000 miles); mean sidereal period: 7.15 days. *See also* SU pp.212, 278.

Garamond, Claude (*c.* 1480–1561), French type-cutter. With Robert Estienne (1503–1559) he designed the famous Greek typeface *Grecs du Roi* (in recognition of the patronage of King Francis I). Garamond based his own typeface on designs of the Italian printer Aldus Manutius (1449–1515) and the earliest examples are found in books printed in Paris in about 1532. Many of the modern versions of this typeface such as those by GOUDY are based on the *Typi Academiae* of Jean Jannon, cut in Sedan in about 1615.

Garbanzo. *See* CHICKPEA.

Garbo, Greta (1905–), Swedish film actress, real name Greta Gustafsson. She became famous for her aura of mystery and legendary romantic beauty. Her silent films included *Torrent* (1926) and *Flesh and the Devil* (1927), but her greatest successes were the sound films *Anna Christie* (1930), *Grand Hotel* (1932), *Queen Christina* (1933), *Anna Karenina* (1935), *Camille* (1936) and the comedy *Ninotchka* (1939). She retired in 1941 and since then has eschewed all publicity.

Garborg, Arne Evenson (1851–1924), Norwegian novelist, poet, playwright and essayist. His works were inspired by the peasant society in which he grew up. His book *Bondestudentar* (1883) describes the life of a peasant-student in the city. His most popular work is the poetic cycle *Haugtussa* (1895).

García Calderón, Ventura (1886–1959), Peruvian author and one of the leading Latin American writers of the early 20th century. His best-known collection of stories, *The Vengeance of Condor* (1924), deals with rural Peru and the plight of the South American Indian.

García de la Huerta, Vincente Antonio (1734–87), Spanish playwright, poet and critic whose most celebrated work is the neo-classical tragedy *Raquel* (1778). He translated Greek and French drama and also published an anthology of plays from the 16th and 17th centuries, *Spanish Theatre* (1785–86).

García Gutiérrez, Antonio (1819–84), Spanish playwright and poet. His play *El Trovador* (1836) inspired an opera by VERDI. His other plays included *Venganza Catalana* (1864) and *Juan Lorenzo* (1865). He also wrote much lyrical poetry.

García Lorca, Federico (1898–1936), Spanish poet and dramatist. His poetry, from *Gypsy Ballads* (1928) to *The Poet in New York* (1940), was internationally acclaimed. His early balletic farces gave way to tragedies of frustrated womanhood, such as *Blood Wedding* (1933) and *The House of Bemoela Alba* (1936). He was killed by Nationalist soldiers at the outbreak of the Spanish Civil War.

García Márquez, Gabriel (1928–), Colombian novelist. His popular novel *One Hundred Years of Solitude* (1967), set in the mythical town of Macondo (as are his previous novels), achieves a unique combination of earthy realism, lyricism, wild comedy and mythical fantasy. *The Autumn of the Patriarch* (1977) marks a new departure in style and content.

Garcilaso de la Vega (1503–36), Spanish poet, courtier and soldier. He helped to introduce Italian metrical forms into Spain. His poems, principally concerning love and nature, include sonnets, *canciones* and elegies and were published with those of Juan BOSCÁN in 1543.

Garcilaso de la Vega (1539–1616), Peruvian historian. Calling himself "El Inca", he was one of the first accomplished writers of the New World. His best-known work is *The Royal Commentaries of Peru* (1609–17), a history of the Inca Empire.

Garda, Lake (Lago di Garda), lake in N Italy fed by the River Sarca and drained by the River Mincio. It is the largest in Italy. Area: 370sq km (143sq miles).

Garden city, planned urban residential and industrial area, with a fixed population size and mix, and with as much open space as possible. The British concept of garden cities as a cure for the social ills of industrialization arose early in the 19th century, but the first such community was not built until Letchworth was founded in 1903. A second, Welwyn Garden City, was founded in 1919. The idea of a fully integrated and almost self-sufficient garden city lost popularity after the 1950s. *See also* HC2 p.*97.*

Gardenia, genus of more than 60 species of evergreen shrubs and small trees of the MADDER family, native to tropical and sub-tropical Asia and Africa. They have white or yellow fragrant, waxy flowers and are widely cultivated. Height: to 5.5m (18ft). Family Rubiaceae.

Gardening, cultivation of flowers, shrubs, trees and vegetables for pleasure or practical benefit. The development of the garden as an extension of the dwelling place, a design feature and a place of relaxation prompted the growth of a scientific approach to gardening both domestic and commercial. The Egyptians, Persians, Romans, and the Chinese all made notable contributions to the art. In the Middle Ages the enclosed gardens of monasteries gave impetus to the private garden. In England gardening flourished under the Tudors, and Renaissance Italian and French design emphasized symmetry and incorporated waterfalls and fountains. A reaction against this formalism led, in England, to the creation of parkland settings accompanied by the Victorian liking for "Gothic" ruins, grottoes and other devices, all intended to surprise. Chinese and Japanese elements were also introduced. With the decline of the great houses in Europe, gardening has become a small-scale domestic pastime of great popularity. The type of plants grown is determined by climate, site and soil.

Garden of Eden. *See* EDEN.

Garden Party, The (1922), collection of short stories by Katherine MANSFIELD, in which she captures with quiet clarity of detail and subtlety of characterization the atmosphere of her childhood in New Zealand.

Gardiner, Stephen (*c.* 1483–1555), English prelate and statesman. He became secretary to HENRY VIII (1534) and was appointed Lord CHANCELLOR by MARY (1553), supporting her persecution of Protestants.

Gardner, Earl Stanley (1889–1970), US writer who invented the detective lawyer, Perry Mason. Beginning in 1933 with *The Case of the Velvet Claws*, Gardner wrote 80 Perry Mason novels, some of which were made into a popular television series. He also wrote under two pseudonyms of A. A. Fair and Charles J. Kenny.

Garfish, marine NEEDLEFISH found in all tropical and temperate waters, also in bays and coastal rivers. Its long silvery body has a dark green or blue-black stripe; the jaws are elongated and pointed, with sharp teeth. The flesh is edible. Length: to 1.2m (4ft). Family Belonidae.

Gargantua and Pantagruel, two comic and satirical works by the French writer, humanist and physician François RABELAIS. *Pantagruel* (1532) and *Gargantua* (1534), which are now generally combined in one volume, depict the foolhardiness and superstition of the Middle Ages with much ribaldry. These themes were extended into three more volumes, culminating in *Le Cinquiesme Livre* (1564).

Gargoyle, stone waterspout, often carved in the shape of a grotesque human and animal figure, used on medieval church and cathedral roofs.

Garibaldi, Giuseppe (1807–82), Italian patriot and guerrilla general who helped to bring about Italian unification. He was influenced by MAZZINI. After participating in a naval mutiny in 1834 Garibaldi fled to South America, where he fought in the war between Uruguay and Argentina. Returning in 1848, his defence of the Roman Republic against the French (1849) made him a national hero. In 1860 he successfully led his 1,000 strong guerrilla army against Sicily and Naples, uniting Italy under King Victor Emmanuel II of Sardinia-Piedmont. He failed to capture Rome in 1862 and 1867, and was involved in the Franco-Prussian War (1870–71). *See also* HC2 pp.110–*111*.

Garland, Judy (1922–69), US singer and film actress. She began her film career at 13, gaining popularity in the Andy Hardy films and *The Wizard of Oz* (1939). Her other films included *Meet Me in St Louis* (1944), *Easter Parade* (1948) and *A Star is Born* (1954). *See also* HC2 p.*268*.

Garlic, bulbous herb native to s Europe and central Asia. It has onion-like foliage and a bulb made up of sections called CLOVES that are used for flavouring. It is also claimed to have medicinal properties. Family Liliaceae; species *Allium sativum*. *See also* PE pp.189, 212, 213.

Garneau, François Xavier (1809–66), Canadian historian. He worked as the town clerk of Quebec while writing his major work, *Histoire du Canada depuis sa Découverte jusq'à Jours* (4 vols. 1845–48, 1852), a history of Canada to 1840. It has provided source material and inspiration for generations of Canadian writers.

Garneau, St Denys (1912–43), Canadian poet. He wrote art criticism for several years but gradually withdrew to the isolation of his childhood home. His poems are about death and suicide, such as *Regards et Jeux dans l'Espace* (1937).

Garner, Alan (1935–), British writer. His books, some of them for children, weave together folklore and the supernatural. They include *Weirdstone of Brisingamen* (1965) and *Red Shift* (1973).

Garner, Erroll Louis (1921–77), US jazz pianist and composer. Self-taught, he developed a unique "stride" piano style featuring full chords in the left hand. He was one of the most popular jazz pianists of the postwar era. His most famous composition was *Misty* (1959).

Garnet, two series of common orthosilicate minerals: the pyralspite series (pyrope, almandite and spessartite); and the ugradite series (uvarovite, grossularite and andralite). Garnet is found in metamorphic rocks and pegmatites as cubic system crystals, rounded grains and granual masses. It is brittle, glassy and occurs in many hues; some varieties (particularly the red form) are important as gemstones. Hardness 6.5–7.5; s.g. 4.

Garnier, Francis (1839–73), French naval officer and explorer. He served (1859–62) in French campaigns against China and became governor of French-ruled Saigon in 1862. He went on a hazardous expedition (1866–68) through Vietnam, Cambodia, Laos and southern China which showed that the Mekong River was not a trading route into China. He was killed in 1873 during the first French attempt to conquer northern Vietnam.

Garnier, Jean Louis Charles (1825–98), French architect. The designer of the famous Opéra in Paris, he combined the neo-Baroque style with Classical elements to create elaborate decorative effects. *See also* HC2 p.*123*.

Garnier, Tony (1867–1948), French architect. Along with Auguste PERRET, he explored the architectural possibilities of the then new material, reinforced concrete. Most of his work is in Lyon, including the stockyards, cattle market and abattoirs (1913) and a stadium (1913–18). *See also* HC2 p.178.

Garnierite, ore of nickel. It is a serpentine, of a more or less lustrous green colour, also containing magnesium and silicon. It occurs in ultrabasic rocks as a decomposition product of OLIVINE. Externally it resembles chrysoprase and this is its main difference from CHRYSOTILE.

Garrick, David (1717–79), English actor. He is credited with replacing the formal declamatory style of acting with easy, natural speech. After making his reputation in the title role of Shakespeare's *Richard III* in 1741 he was hired by the Drury Lane Theatre in 1742, where he remained until his retirement in 1776. He became its manager in 1747, and pioneered the use of concealed lighting and banished spectators from the stage. His final performance was in *The Wonder: A Woman Keeps a Secret* (1776).

Garrotte, method of CAPITAL PUNISHMENT still used in Spain. Originally a string around the throat, tightened by twisting a stick, it now consists of an iron collar, attached to an iron post, which is placed round the condemned person's neck. A screw is then tightened until the victim dies of strangulation.

Garson, Greer (1908–), Anglo-Irish actress who, after appearing on the London stage, starred in her first film *Goodbye Mr Chips* (1939). Thereafter she became established in roles of intelligent, high-principled women in such Hollywood films as *Mrs Miniver* (1942) and *Madame Curie* (1943), a pattern culminating in her portrayal of Eleanor Roosevelt in *Sunrise at Campobello* (1960).

Garter, Order of the, most ancient of chivalric orders in Britain. It was the creation of EDWARD III and held its first meeting in 1348, on St George's day, at Windsor Castle (which remains its home). The monarch is the Grand Master. Originally there were 25 other members, among whom were some of the great feudal barons of the land, but in 1831 the order was enlarged to include sons of the monarch and some foreign rulers. The emblem, a dark blue garter edged in gold, and the motto *Honi soit qui mal y pense* ("The shame be his who thinks badly of it") are traced to the story that at a ball at Calais, Edward III spoke the words when returning, to Joan, Fair Maid of Kent, a garter which she had dropped. The garter, the personal gift of the monarch, is worn on ceremonial occasions, below the knee on the left leg.

Garter snake, non-venomous SNAKE, usually striped, ranging from s Canada through Central America. The ground colour is usually olive-brown with yellow, orange, red or blue stripes often spotted with black. It feeds on frogs, insects and earthworms. Length: to 60cm (24in). Family Colubridae; genus *Thamnophis*.

Garvin, James Louis (1868–1947), British journalist and historian. He was editor of *Outlook* (1905–06), *The Observer* (1908–42) and the *Pall Mall Gazette* (1912–15). When he died he had completed the first three volumes of a biography of Joseph CHAMBERLAIN.

Gas, state of matter in which molecules are free to move in any direction, so that a gas always expands to fill a container of any size. Eleven of the chemical elements are gases at room temperature. Some, such as hydrogen and chlorine, have molecules containing two atoms (diatomic), and others, such as neon, are monatomic (composed of single atoms). Many simple chemical compounds are gases at room temperature, including ammonia, methane and carbon dioxide. When cooled, gases become liquids. Pressure assists in liquefaction and some gases, such as carbon dioxide, can be liquefied at room temperature by pressure alone. Most gases, however, require cooling before they can be liquefied, and the temperature above which a gas cannot be liquefied by pressure alone is called the critical temperature of that gas. All gases follow certain laws which have long been established in physical science; Boyle's law states that a volume of gas varies inversely with the pressure upon it, if the temperature remains constant; Charles's law states that the volume of a gas varies directly with the absolute temperature, if the pressure remains constant; Avogadro's law states that equal volumes of gases at equal temperatures and pressures contain equal numbers of molecules; Graham's law states that the rate of diffusion, or spreading through an orifice, of a gas is inversely proportional to the square root of its density – a gas of density "1" will diffuse twice as quickly as a gas of density "4". Because of their low densities, most gases are poor conductors of heat and electricity. *See also* SOLID; LIQUID; PLASMA; SU pp.84–90.

Gas analysis, determination of the nature and quantity of constituents of gas mixtures. It is carried out widely in National Coal Board laboratories to analyse mine gases and by the Gas Boards. Three methods of analysis are available; the gases can be selectively absorbed in chemical solutions and the decrease in volume is measured; in gas chromatography the rates of diffusion of gases through such media as charcoal is utilized; and there is the instrumental method where such physical properties of the gases as density are used as the basis of analysis. *See also* SU pp.150–151.

Gas chamber, airtight compartment into which lethal gas is pumped to execute the occupant. It was used until recently in ten states of the USA as a means of capital punishment, and as a method of mass-killing used by Adolf HITLER against JEWS and others during WWII. *See also* CAPITAL PUNISHMENT; MS p.*297*.

Gascoigne, George (*c*.1525–77), English poet, essayist and playwright. His *Spoyle of Antwerpe* (1576) anticipated modern war-correspondence, but he is chiefly remembered for his poetry, which includes *A Hundred Sundrie Flowers* (1573) and *The Poesies of George Gascoigne* (1575). He also wrote a dramatic tragi-comedy, *The Glasse of Government* (1575). He was an MP from 1557–59 and fought with English troops in The Netherlands (1572–74).

Gascony, province of sw France. The region was part of Roman AQUITAINE, and was conquered by the Visigoths in the 5th century and the FRANKS in the 6th century. In about 700 the region was settled by the Basque-speaking Vascones tribe, who gave their name to the region. Most of the region was reunited with Aquitaine in 1058, became an English possession in 1154 disputed in the HUNDRED YEARS WAR. It became part of France in 1451.

Gas engines. *See* ENGINE.

Gaskell, Elizabeth Cleghorn (1810–65), British writer. She spent her adult life in Manchester and became familiar with the problems of the industrial poor, which she explored in her novels *Mary Barton* (1848) and *North and South* (1855). Other works include *Cranford* (1835), *Wives and Daughters* (unfinished, 1866) and *The Life of Charlotte Brontë* (1857).

Gaskill, William (1930–), British stage director. He established his reputation in the 1950s at the ROYAL COURT THEATRE, London, and consolidated it with both the ROYAL SHAKESPEARE COMPANY and the NATIONAL THEATRE, where his many successful classical and modern productions included Farquhar's *The Recruiting Officer* (1963). He returned to the Royal Court as director of the English Stage Company (1965–72) and subsequently worked widely as a freelance.

Gas mask, protective device worn over the nose and mouth to prevent inhalation of poisonous or irritating gases, germs, or

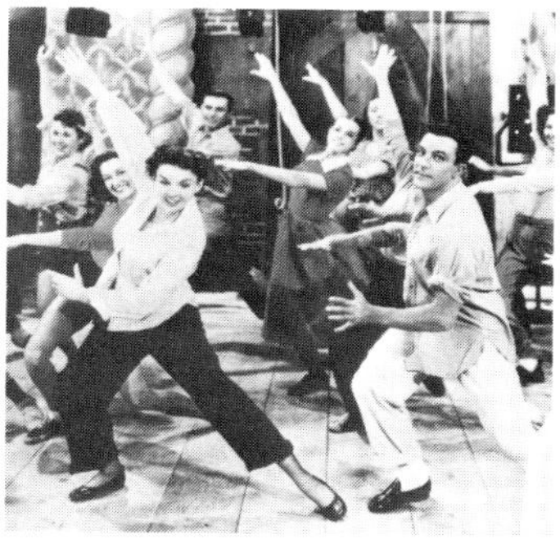

Judy Garland's personal life reflected the emotional stresses of the Hollywood star.

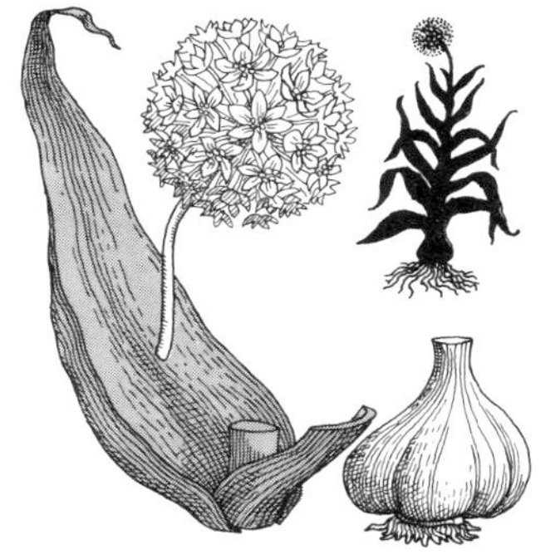

Garlic oil was used medicinally by the Romans as a stimulant for their soldiers.

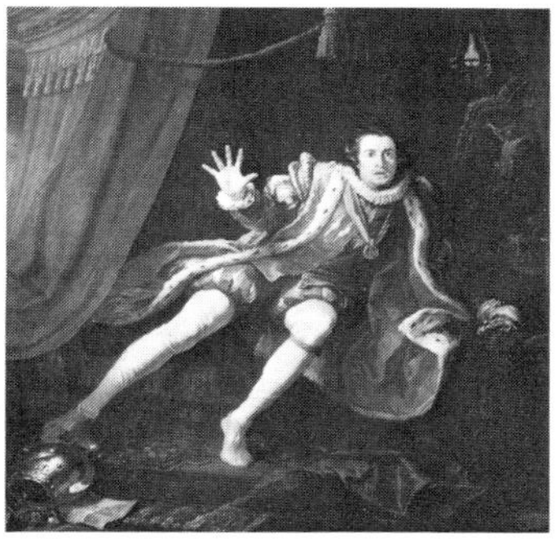

David Garrick, portrayed here by Hogarth, revolutionized 18th-century English theatre.

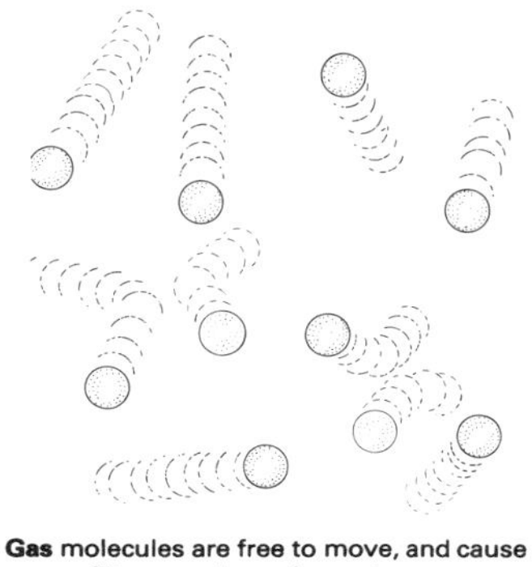

Gas molecules are free to move, and cause a gas to fill a container of any size.

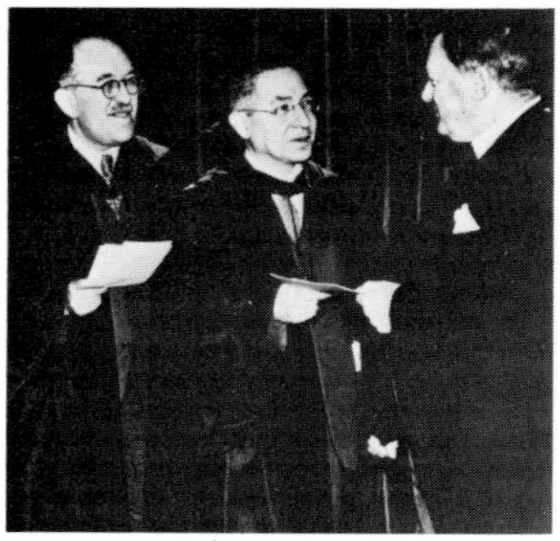

Gasser demonstrated that different nerves carried different sensations to the brain.

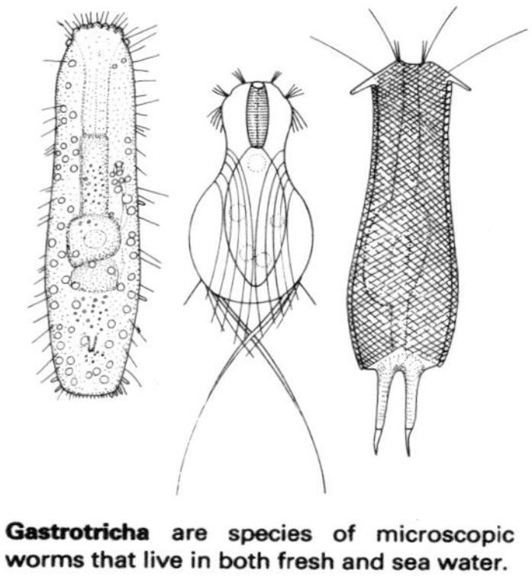

Gastrotricha are species of microscopic worms that live in both fresh and sea water.

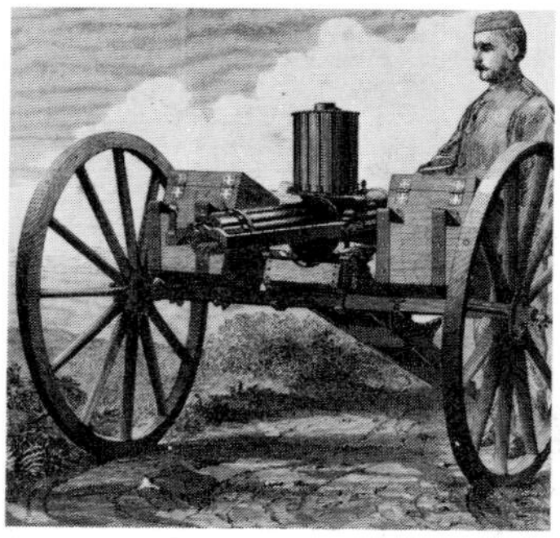

Gatling gun; multi-barrelled machine gun immediately adopted by the US army.

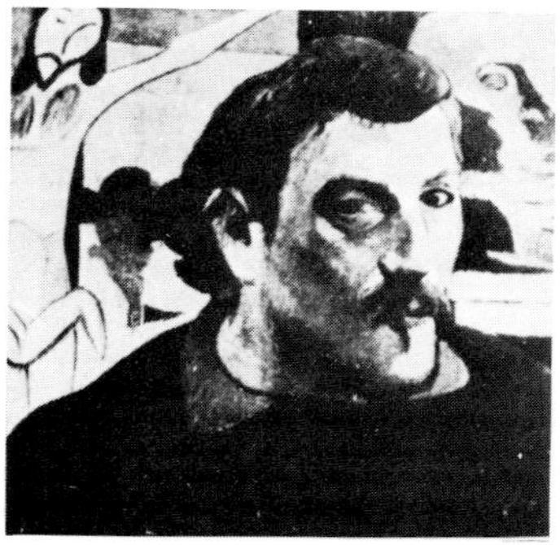

Paul Gaugin, the French post-impressionist painter, in his self portrait of 1890.

dust. It consists of a valve which ensures that air is inhaled through purifying filters only, and is exhaled through a separate duct. It is used by many armies, civil police (during tear gas raids) and in industry.

Gasnier, Reg (1939–), Australian rugby league player. A member of Sydney's St George club, he played 39 times for his country, scoring 28 tries and winning fame as a centre of outstanding physique, speed and courage. In 1962, aged 23, he became Australia's youngest captain.

Gasolene. *See* PETROLEUM.

Gasometer, or gas-holder, large container for storing fuel gases for domestic and industrial consumption. Most familiar are the telescopic gas-holders in which gas is stored in a cylindrical vessel that moves up and down on guides, ascending from and descending into a cylindrical steel or brick tank, the gas being contained by a water seal between these two vessels.

Gasparini, Francesco (1668–1727), Italian composer. He was a pupil of CORELLI and one of the most popular opera composers of his day. His first opera, *Il Roderico*, was performed at Rome in 1694. The most famous (he wrote about 65) was *Ambleto* (1705), the first opera about HAMLET.

Gas poisoning, illness resulting from the effects of toxic gases of many kinds. Most widespread until recent times was coal gas poisoning, caused by the carbon monoxide part of that gas. Carbon monoxide was also responsible for many deaths in coalmines. In WWI poison gases were used to cause illness and death; they included the gases chlorine and phosgene, and the volatile liquids MUSTARD GAS and lewisite. Tear gases cause lachrymation and temporary incapacitation. *See also* GAS WARFARE.

Gasser, Herber Spencer (1888–1963), US physiologist and medical researcher. He was director of the Rockefeller Institute (1935–55). He shared the 1944 Nobel Prize in physiology and medicine with Joseph ERLANGER for their discoveries regarding the highly differentiated functions of single nerve fibres.

Gastric juice, mixture of substances secreted into the stomach; they break down complex proteins and carbohydrates into simpler units during digestion. They include hydrochloric acid, the enzyme PEPSIN and mucus. *See also* MS p.68.

Gastritis, inflammation of the lining of the stomach, chronic or acute. It may be caused by chemicals, irritant foods or disease.

Gastroenteritis, inflammation of the lining of the stomach and intestine. It may be caused by viruses, bacteria, chemicals or an allergy. Treatment is aimed at alleviating symptoms, which include vomiting and DIARRHOEA.

Gastroenterology, branch of medicine that deals with the diagnosis and treatment of diseases and disorders of the gastrointestinal tract. *See also* MS p.92.

Gastrolith, stone swallowed by birds and reptiles to help grind up their food in a crop or gizzard. Such stones have been found with the fossils of dinosaurs.

Gastropods, any of a class of MOLLUSCS including SNAILS, SLUGS, WINKLES, WHELKS, LIMPETS, CONE SHELLS, ABALONES and SEA SLUGS. Many possess a single shell which is coiled into a flat or conical spiral and has been secreted by the mantle, or skin covering the body. In gastropods with larger shells the internal organs follow the spiral twist of the shell. The foot and head can be extended from and withdrawn into the shell. Many types of gastropods live either totally or periodically immersed in sea-water, breathing through gills. Some freshwater snails, paradoxically, breathe through lungs and need to surface periodically for air. Sea butterflies (pteropods) have delicate, glassy shells and swim using fins developed from the foot. Sea slugs are entirely without shells and are often brilliantly coloured. *See also* NW pp.72, 90, *90*, 92, 96.

Gastrotricha, phylum of microscopic, multi-cellular animals similar to ROTIFERS. Structurally similar to simple worms, they have bristles covering the entire body. Reproduction is HERMAPHRODITIC and PARTHENOGENETIC.

Gastrula, an early stage in the embryonic development of many animals. It is a hollow sac of two layers of cells, the inner endoderm and the outer ectoderm. The sac cavity is called the archenteron and its mouth the blastopore. *See* EMBRYO.

Gas warfare, offensive use of noxious gases as tactical weapons. First used in WWI the major gases used by both sides were MUSTARD GAS – a vesicant and lung irritant which causes severe blistering on all body surfaces, blindness and death (which may be delayed some days) and chlorine – a lachrymator (like tear gas) and lung irritant which brings pulmonary oedema and death. In trench warfare the most efficient means of delivery was the gas shell, developed by the French. There was widespread revulsion to the use of gas and, although much research has gone into the development of more refined and deadly gases, such as NERVE GAS (which attacks the nervous system causing paralysis and death), gas was not used as a weapon in WWII. *See also* GAS POISONING; MM pp.180–181.

Gate, in electronics and FLUIDICS, circuit having two or more inputs but a single output energized only under specific input conditions. Gates are used extensively in LOGIC CIRCUITS in which the sequence of operations, or their combinations, are determined by the rules of SYMBOLIC LOGIC.

Gates, Horatio (*c*1727–1806), US general. Born in England, he served in the British army until he emigrated to Virginia in 1772 and joined the patriots' cause in the American War of Independence. In 1776 he became commander of the army in the north, and with Benedict ARNOLD and Daniel MORGAN decisively defeated the British at Saratoga, NY in 1777. He was relieved of his command after his defeat at Cowden, South Carolina (1780).

Gates, Sir Thomas (died *c.* 1621), member of the London Company, which organized the first settlement of Virginia. En route from England in 1609 he got lost and was shipwrecked, rejoining the other colonists in 1610. He was Governor of Virginia (1611–14).

Gateshead, county district in W TYNE AND WEAR, England, created in 1974 under the Local Government Act (1972). Area: 143sq km (55sq miles). Pop. (1974 est.) 222,300.

Gathas, collection of hymns, believed to be the work of Zoroaster, that are the basis of the AVESTA or sacred book of ZOROASTRIANISM. They contain the fundamental teachings of the prophet and are concerned with man's duty in the conquest of evil.

Gatling, Richard Jordan (1818–1903), US inventor. He invented and manufactured machines for sowing cottonseed, rice and wheat, later perfecting a revolving machine gun (1862). The GATLING gun, at first rejected by the Union army, was improved (1865) and adopted by the US government in 1866. He devised a gun metal of steel and aluminium in 1886.

Gatling gun, early MACHINE GUN invented by Richard GATLING, the US inventor. It consisted of several barrels mounted in a cylindrical chamber that was rotated manually by a crank so that each barrel, in turn, was positioned to fire a cartridge. The gun was mounted on a carriage; one model had ten barrels and was capable of firing 1,000 rounds per minute. *See also* MM p.164.

GATT (General Agreement on Tariffs and Trade), UN agency of international trade. Founded in 1948, it is designed to prevent "tariff wars" and to work towards the gradual and orderly reduction of TARIFF levels. It is based on the most-favoured nation principles: any reduction granted by one nation to another must be extended to all members of the group. Most non-communist nations are party to GATT. *See also* MS p.316.

Gaucho, colourful COWBOY of Argentine and Uruguayan history and legend, and an important political force in the 18th and 19th centuries. At first proud nomads of the PAMPAS, the mixed-blood gauchos became farmhands and superb horse soldiers as civilization advanced and fenced their lands. They later became the subject of a distinctive South American literature.

Gaudi, Antoni (1852–1926), Spanish architect. He built the Casa Vicens in Barcelona (1878) in a startlingly individual style. His work employs bizarre sculptural and sinuous forms, and in its plasticity is often associated with ART NOUVEAU. His works include the Palau Guell (1885–89), the Caso Battlo (1905–07) and the Church of the Sagrada Familia (unfinished), all in Barcelona. *See also* HC2 p.178.

Gaudier-Brzeska, Henri (1891–1915), French sculptor, who lived in England from 1911. His work was highly experimental; he was a friend of Roger FRY and Ezra POUND, and he was part of the pre-war VORTICIST avant-garde movement. His works include abstracts such as *The Dancer* and many sensitive animal sculptures. He was killed in WWI. *See also* HC2 p.280.

Gauge, term for many kinds of measuring device. For example, calipers are width gauges, dipsticks are depth gauges and thermometers are temperature gauges, although here the term is restricted usually to mechanical thermometers. Pressure gauges are of various kinds, the Bourdon gauge being the type used to measure fluctuations of air pressure in aneroid barometers and variations in gas and liquid pressure in industry. The term is also used of the perpendicular distance between railway lines, from the largest actual gauge (the "5-foot gauge") to miniature and model.

Gauguin, Eugène Henri Paul (1848–1903), French painter. Early in his career as a painter, he exhibited in four IMPRESSIONIST exhibitions from 1880. However he reacted against the realism of the Impressionists, and the use of colour solely for its representational function. For him, form and pattern should represent mental images and these ideas influenced the SYMBOLIST movement, though after 1889 Gauguin himself repudiated Symbolism. In 1891 he left France for Tahiti and there he executed his most famous paintings – primitive and exotic, using strong outlines and flat, gold colours depicting native figures and landscapes. *See also* HC2 p.174.

Gaul, old name for the land of what is now France, Belgium, northern Italy and part of W Germany. It was conquered (58–51 BC) by Julius CAESAR. By the 5th century AD German tribes had wrested control from the Romans. *See also* HC1 pp.*97*, 136–137.

Gaulle, Charles André Joseph Marie de. *See* DE GAULLE.

Gauls, Celtic tribes who moved W across the River Rhine in *c.* 1500 BC and had occupied the whole of modern France by 400 BC. They invaded Italy, and sacked Rome in 390 but were confined N of the Alps by 250. Gaul was conquered by the Romans in the 50s BC, and during the next century it was fully Romanized. There was a revival of Gallic civilization during the 3rd century AD, until the Frankish invasions of Gaul in the 5th century.

Gaumont, British, film production and distributing company formed in 1927 from the Gaumont Film Company, which was established in 1898. It was not until new studios were opened at Shepherd's Bush in 1932 and Gaumont became linked with the Gainsborough company and Michael BALCON that it enjoyed major successes. These included Alfred HITCHCOCK's *The Thirty-Nine Steps* (1935) and *Sabotage* (1936). Although Gaumont has survived as a name for cinemas, the company ceased production and distribution after 1936.

Gaunt, John of. *See* JOHN OF GAUNT.

Gaur, species of wild cattle found in forested hilly country in India and Malaysia. Gaurs, also called seladangs, are dark brown in colour with a white "sock" on each leg. An adult bull may grow up to 3.8m (12.4ft) long and weigh more than a tonne. Gaurs range in small herds, feeding

HC1 = History and Culture Vol. 1 HC2 = History and Culture Vol. 2 MS = Man and Society MM = Man and Machines

in the morning and evening. Family Bovidae; species *Bos gaurus. See also* NW p.*196.*
Gauss, Karl Friedrich (1777–1855), German mathematician. As a child prodigy from a poor family his education was sponsored by the Duke of Brunswick. He made studies of electricity and magnetism and advanced mathematics in areas such as number theory and the theory of series. The unit of magnetic induction is named after him. *See also* HC2 p.156.
Gauss's law, the total electric flux, φ, of a closed surface in an electric field equals the electric charge, q, within that surface divided by the permittivity of the medium, ε:φ=q/ε. The law also applies to surfaces in a magnetic field and similar statements can be made for a gravitation field.
Gautama Buddha. *See* BUDDHA.
Gautier, Théophile (1811–72), French poet, novelist and critic. He turned from painting to write Romantic poems, such as *Albertus* (1833), macabre stories, *La Morte Amoureuse* (1836) and the novel *Mademoiselle de Maupin* (1835). He was an early exponent of the formalist "aesthetic" theory of art that influenced the PARNASSIANS and SYMBOLISTS. *See also* HC2 p.100.
Gavelkind, system of inheritance common in England before the NORMAN CONQUEST and abolished in 1926. As opposed to primogeniture, by which the eldest son inherited his father's estate, the custom of gavelkind entitled all sons to share equally in the estate.
Gaveston, Piers (*d.*1312), English favourite of Edward II. His arrogance, relatively lowly birth and the fact that he was a foreigner (his father was a Gascon knight) brought baronial opposition while he was keeper of the realm (1308), and Edward was forced to agree to his banishment. He returned to England the next year, but further opposition led again to a brief exile in 1311. He was executed by the barons in 1312. *See also* HC1 p.179.
Gavial, crocodilian native to N India. It has a long, narrow, rod-like snout, an olive or brownish back and a lighter belly. It is harmless to man, feeding almost exclusively on fish. Length: to 5m (15.4ft). Family Gavialidae; species *Gavialis gangeticus. See also* CROCODILE.
Gaviiformes. *See* LOON.
Gävle, city on the Gulf of Bothnia, 161km (100 miles) NNW of Stockholm. Founded in 1446, the city was rebuilt several times after fires swept the area. Although icebound for part of the year, Gävle has an important timber and iron ore export trade. Pop. (1970) 2,987.
Gavotte, originally a peasant folk dance of the 15th century. It was popularized and became fashionable in French court society in the 18th century. Graceful and stately, it is similar to the minuet, but more lively and in 4/4 rhythm.
Gawain and the Green Knight, Sir. *See* SIR GAWAIN AND THE GREEN KNIGHT.
Gay, *See* HOMOSEXUAL.
Gay, John (1685–1732), English poet and dramatist. His best-known work is the ballad-opera *The Beggar's Opera* (1728), a political satire burlesquing Italian opera style, and mirroring the moral degradation of society in its characters of highwaymen and thieves. His other works include the poem *Trivia* (1716), a delightful description of London life at the time.
Gay, Noel (1898–1954), English musical comedy composer. He is best remembered for the Cockney musical *Me and My Girl* (1937), which introduced "The Lambeth Walk".
Gay-Lussac, Joseph Louis (1778–1850), French chemist and physicist who did pioneer research on the behaviour of gases. He discovered the law of combining gas volumes (Gay-Lussac's Law) and the law of gas expansion, often also attributed to J. A. C. CHARLES (who discovered it earlier but did not publish his results). In chemistry he prepared (with Louis-Jacques Thenard) the elements potassium and boron, investigated fermentation and hydrocyanic (prussic) acid, and invented a hydrometer.
Gay-Lussac laws. *See* CHARLES'S LAW.
Gaza Strip, small region in NE Egypt, bordering on the SE Mediterranean Sea. It was part of Britain's Palestine Mandate after WWI although by 1947 Britain intended to give up the area, and the settlement after the ARAB-ISRAELI WAR (1948–49) made it an Egyptian possession. It has served as a Palestinian Arab refugee centre since WWII and it has been occupied by Israel since 1967. Area: 36sq km (130sq miles). Pop. (1971) 365,000. *See also* HC2 pp.296–297; MW p.82.
Gazelle, any of a dozen species of fast, graceful, small-to-medium antelopes native to Africa and Asia, frequently inhabiting plains and treeless areas. The lyre-shaped horns, common to both sexes in most species, are generally lacking in females of the species *Gazelle subgutturosa.* Most animals are light brown with a white rump. Bedouins hunt them with falcons and dogs – some gazelles can run at 80km/h (50mph) for more than 15 minutes. Family Bovidae; genus *Gazella. See also* NW pp.*201,* 220, *222.*
Gaziantep, city in S Asian Turkey, located between the Taurus Mountains and the River Euphrates; capital of Gaziantep province. It is an agricultural trade centre, and was formerly known as Aintab. An ancient Hittite city, it was conquered by the Ottomans in the early 16th century. It resisted French occupation from 1920 until 1921, when it was returned to Turkey. Products: pistachio nuts, grapes, textiles. Pop. 275,000.
Gdańsk (Danzig), port in N Poland, on a branch of the River Vistula and the Gulf of Danzig; capital of Gdańsk province. Settled by Slavs in the 10th century, it was a member of the HANSEATIC LEAGUE and became an important Baltic port. It was taken by Poland in the 15th century but passed to Prussia in 1793. The Treaty of VERSAILLES (1919) established Gdańsk as a free city serving as Poland's port. HITLER's demand for the return of the city to Germany was a major cause of the German invasion of Poland and thus of WWII. Its shipyards are among the largest in the world and other industries include metallurgy, chemicals, food processing, machinery and timber. Pop. (1974) 402,000.
Gear, toothed wheel, usually attached to a rotating shaft. Operating in pairs, the teeth of one gear engage those of the other to transmit and modify rotary motion and torque. The smaller member of a pair of gears is called a pinion. If the pinion is on the driving shaft, speed is reduced and torque amplified; if the gear is on the shaft, speed is increased and torque reduced. A screw-type gear, called a worm, may have only one tooth; a pinion must have at least five. *See also* MM pp.88–89.
Geb, in Egyptian mythology, the earth god, son of Shu and Tefnut, husband and brother of NUT and father of OSIRIS, ISIS, SETH and NEPHTHYS. He is sometimes depicted as a goose, or as a man with a goose on his head. In the Egyptian myth of creation, the air separates Geb, the earth, from Nut, the sky.
GEC (General Electric Company), Britain's largest electrical engineering company. It was founded in 1889, is a public company and has offices and factories in some 40 countries with a total staff of almost 200,000. It manufactures a wide range of products, from computers, radar equipment and telephone exchange systems to domestic appliances, cables, wire and electric lamps.
Gecko, any of about 650 species of small to medium LIZARDS that are common in most warm regions of the world and live in a variety of habitats, even in houses. They owe their remarkable climbing ability to minute hooks on their feet. They make chirping or barking calls. Length: 3–15cm (1–6in). Family Gekkonidae. *See also* NW pp.*137, 219.*
Gedda, Nicolai (1925–), Swedish operatic tenor. He made his début at Stockholm in 1952, his Covent Garden début in RIGOLETTO in 1954 and his Metropolitan Opera debut in FAUST in 1957. He has remained a leading tenor with the Metropolitan Opera Company, New York.
Gedling, county district in S central NOTTINGHAMSHIRE, England, created in 1974 under the Local Government Act (1972). Area: 112sq km (43sq miles). Pop. (1974 est.) 100,200.
Geelong, city in Victoria, SE Australia, on an inlet of Port Philip Bay. A major port, it exports wool, wheat, meat and hides, and imports oil. Industries: safety glass, fertilizers, motor vehicles. Pop. 17,775.
Gefle. *See* GÄVLE.
Geiger, Hans Wilhelm (1882–1945), German physicist who, with Ernest Rutherford in 1908, devised a method of detecting and counting alpha particles. This device, with modifications, became the GEIGER COUNTER. Geiger and E. Marsden noticed the deflection of alpha particles by thin metal foil in 1909, and this phenomenon was the basis of Rutherford's planetary theory of the atom.
Geiger counter, also called Geiger-Müller counter, instrument used to detect and measure the strength of radiation, or the numbers of particles. It is a type of IONIZATION CHAMBER in which a high voltage is applied across a pair of electrodes. Radiation or particles entering the chamber ionize gas atoms and the resulting ions, gaining energy from the electric field between the electrodes, magnify the effect by producing many more ions. These constitute a current which quickly subsides so that a pulse of current is produced for each particle. Each pulse activates a counting circuit enabling several thousand particles per second to be counted.
Geijer, Erik Gustaf (1783–1847), Swedish historian and poet; professor of history at Uppsala from 1817. Originally a conservative, he adopted reformist liberal ideas in 1838. He also wrote lyrics and hymns set to his own music. His best known work is *History of the Swedes* (trans. 1845).
Geisel, Ernesto (1908–), President of Brazil (1974–). Originally an army officer, Geisel inaugurated a policy that slightly relaxed parts of the authoritarian political and social system that had been in effect since the military took power in 1964.
Geisha, in Japan, a woman who is a member of a professional class employed to entertain and attend men at restaurants and parties. Traditionally she may sing, dance, play a musical instrument or simply converse. After training for a period of years, she must display delicate manners and be exquisitely dressed.
Geissler tube, old name for a discharge tube, a glass electronic tube used in the study of the light emitted by various substances in a gaseous form. The tube has an electrode at each end. The tube is filled with a gas at low pressure, and the current which flows through the tube when a high voltage is applied between the electrodes causes the gas to glow with a distinctive colour. *See also* SU p.*63.*
Gel, homogeneous mass consisting of minute particles dispersed or arranged in a liquid to form a fine network throughout the mass. Their appearance may be notably elastic or jellylike (as in GELATIN or fruit jelly) or quite rigid and solid (as in silica gel, a material resembling coarse white sand used as a dehumidifier in the manufacture of silicone and rubber).
Gelasius, name of two Popes. Gelasius I, saint and Pope (*r.*492–96), upheld papal supremacy in a dispute with the Byzantine emperor Anastasius. He produced more than 100 treatises, including attacks on PELAGIANISM, and introduced the feast of the Purification. Gelasius II was Pope from 1118 to 1119. He was twice driven out of Rome by Emperor Henry V, who appointed an antipope, known as GREGORY VIII, in opposition to him.
Gelatin, colourless or yellowish protein obtained from collagen in animal cartilages and bones by boiling in water. It is used in photographic film, size, capsules for medical drugs as a culture medium for bacteria and in foodstuffs such as jellies.
Geld, land tax in England, first systematically assessed in the 10th century. ETHELRED II used it from 991 to 1012 to buy peace from the Danes. For the next 50 years it was used to maintain an army and navy and was called the *heregeld.* It later

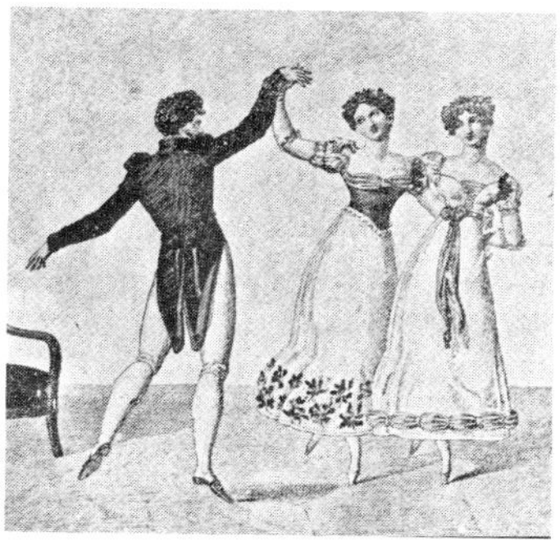

Gavotte; a restoration print showing this fashionable court dance of the 18th century.

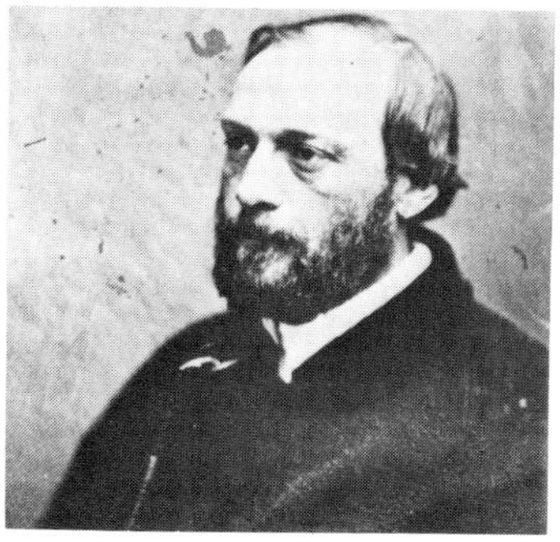

Gay-Lussac, the French chemist and physicist who made important studies of gases.

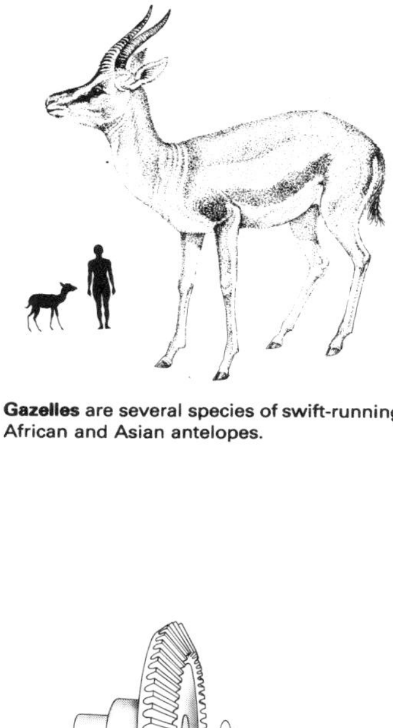

Gazelles are several species of swift-running African and Asian antelopes.

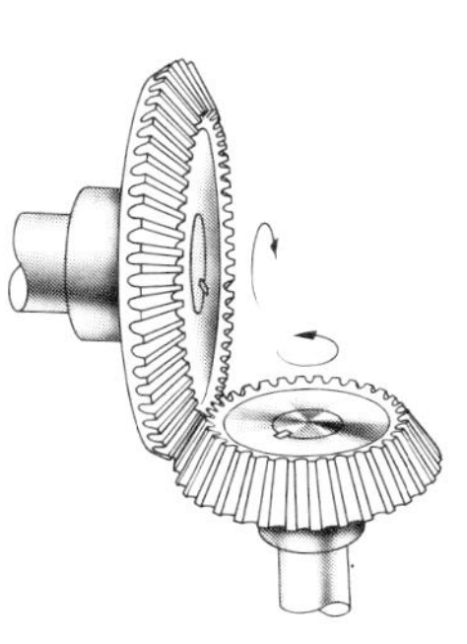

Gears are used to modify either the turning force or speed of rotary mechanical motion.

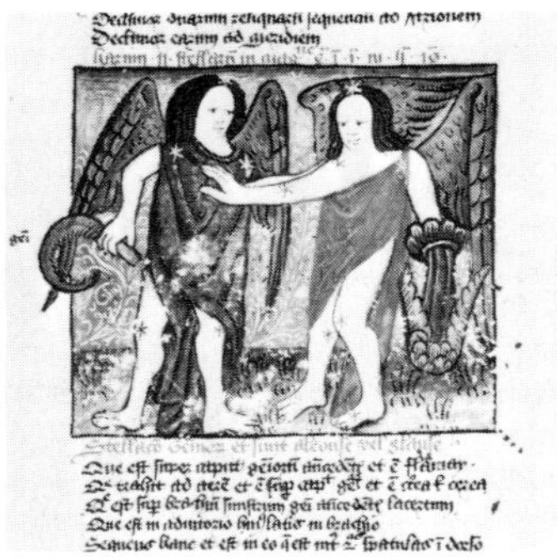

Gemini – the twins, who in Arabian astrology were represented by a pair of peacocks.

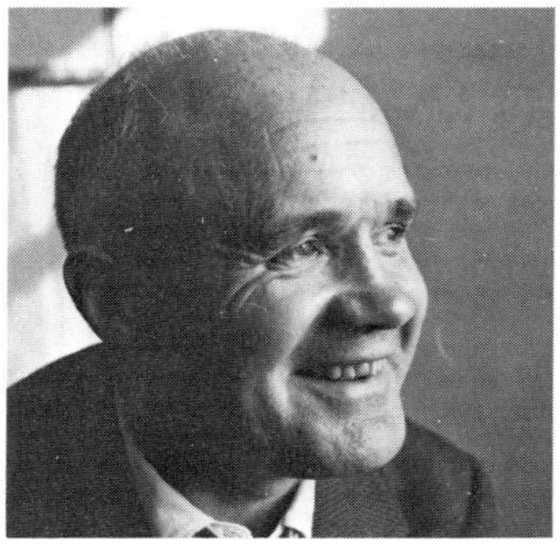

Jean Genet draws freely on the degrading and criminal experiences of his own life.

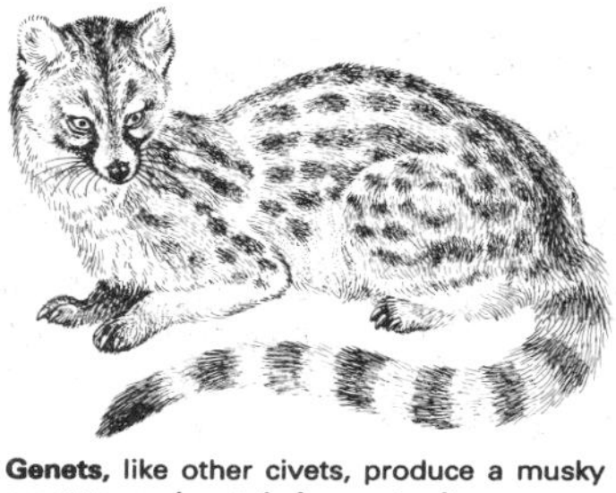

Genets, like other civets, produce a musky scent to mark out their own territory.

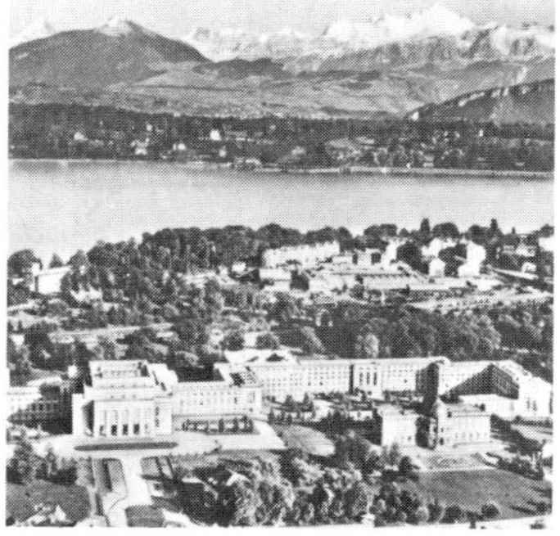

Geneva; a view of the city with the UN buildings and the Jura mountains beyond.

became generally described as the DANEGOLD.

Gelderland, province of The Netherlands, stretching from the German frontier to the IJSSELMEER; the capital is Arnhem. Fertile in the SW, the region is known for its agricultural produce. The Veluwe, heathland to the N and W, is popular as a resort area. Area: 5,130sq km (1,981sq miles). Pop. (1971 est.) 1,533,700.

Gelibolu. *See* GALLIPOLI.

Gellert, Christian Fürchtegott (1715–69), German poet and moralist, prolific writer of fables, stories and hymns. His best-known works are the collection *Fables and Tales* (1746–48) and the hymn *The Heavens Praise the Creator's Glory*, which was set to music by Beethoven.

Gell-Mann, Murray (1929–), US physicist who was awarded the 1969 Nobel Prize in physics for his application of group theory to elementary particles, which led to the prediction of QUARKS as the basic constituents of baryons and mesons. His theory also predicted the existence of an unknown particle called the omega minus (Ω^-), subsequently discovered in 1964. He also introduced, in 1953, the concept of strangeness to explain the longevity of certain particles.

Gelsenkirchen, city of W West Germany on the River Emscher 24km (15 miles) W of Dortmund. After the development of the RUHR district in the 1860s, the city grew rapidly and became an industrial and coal-mining centre. Its manufactures include chemicals, iron, steel and glass. Pop. (1974) 333,202.

Gem, any of about 100 minerals, either opaque, transparent or translucent, valued for their beauty, rarity and durability. Transparent stones, such as diamond, ruby, emerald and sapphire, are the most highly valued. Pearl, amber and coral are gems of organic origin. During the Middle Ages, many gems were thought to have magical powers. The art of cutting and polishing gemstones to bring out their colour and brilliance was developed in the 15th century, particularly in Italy. Stones with a design cut into them are intaglios; with a design in relief, cameos. *See also* LAPIDARY; PE pp.98–99.

Gem, artificial, man-made imitation of natural gemstone composed of any of various substances. Glass is frequently used; the best quality contains high lead content. Pearls are simulated by coating glass beads with pearl essence, a derivative of fish scales. Imitation diamonds are made of strontium titanate, rutile or yttrium GARNET. Ruby, sapphire, emerald and spinel are also made synthetically.

Gemini, or the Twins, northern constellation, situated on the ecliptic between Taurus and Cancer; the third sign of the zodiac. It contains the star cluster M 35 (NGC 2168) and the planetary nebula NGC 2392. The brightest star is Beta Geminorum (Pollux). *See also* MS pp.200–201; SU pp.*254*, 257, *257*.

Gemini Programme, series of US manned experimental space flights that followed the Mercury and preceded the Apollo programmes. Gemini 3 was a two-person craft first manned by Maj. Virgil Grissom and Lt. Cmdr. John Young on 23 March 1965; they made three earth orbits. Subsequent flights and experiments ending with Gemini 12 (11–15 Nov. 1966) demonstrated space walks, space docking manoeuvres and tests of longevity including a 14-day flight by Lt. Col. Frank Borman and Cmdr. James Lovell, Jr, in Dec. 1965. *See also* MM p.*158;* SU pp.268–269.

Gemmology, study of gems. A gem is regarded as any precious or semi-precious stone, and is usually of mineral origin although it may be organic (eg, pearl, coral and amber). The appearance of a gem is greatly improved by polishing, and this may be done in either of two ways. The cabochon cut, in which the surface of the gem is rounded, is used mainly for opaque materials; whereas the faceted cut, in which reflective faces are cut into the surface, is used for transparent stones. *See also* PE pp.98–99.

Gemsbok. *See* ORYX.

Gene, unit by which hereditary characteristics are passed on from one generation to another in plants and animals. Genes are found in a line in CHROMOSOMES. The universal chemical constituent of a gene is DNA. Genes control both the morphology and the metabolism of a cell and hence the organism. *See also* MW pp.28–31.

Genealogy, study of family origins and history. A genealogist compiles lists of ancestors and arranges them in pedigree charts. In Europe, the study began to develop in its present form in the early 16th century.

Genée, Dame Adeline (1878–1970), British dancer, *b.* Denmark, real name Anita Jensen. She made her debut in Oslo in 1888 and later toured Australia and the USA. She is especially remembered for her portrayal of Swanilda in *Coppélia*. A vivacious charming dancer, she retired in 1917 and was first president of The Association of Operatic Dancing of Great Britain (1920–35) and its successor, the Royal Academy (1935–54).

General, commander or divisional commander of an army, usually of rank immediately below a FIELD MARSHALL and above lieutenant-general.

General Agreement of Tariffs and Trade. *See* GATT.

General Assembly. *See* CHURCH OF SCOTLAND.

General Council. *See* ECUMENICAL COUNCIL.

General Electric Co. *See* GEC.

General Motors Corporation, massive US-based international industrial concern. It is the world's largest manufacturer of motor vehicles and has overseas branches or subsidiaries in West Germany, Canada, Britain and Australia. Apart from cars, buses and trucks, General Motors also produces refrigerators, diesel locomotives and a wide range of engines. In 1976 it employed an average of 748,000 people throughout the world.

General Strike, nationwide strike in Britain in May 1926, resulting from the failure of miners and mine owners to reach agreement on terms of employment. Economic difficulties led the mine owners to propose reduced wages and longer hours. The Miners' Federation refused to accept them and the owners ordered a lockout for 1 May, which was answered by the TUC's call for a national strike. It lasted from 3–12 May but was a failure. The miners, who remained on strike thoughout the summer, returned to work on the employers' terms.

General Synod, formerly the Church Assembly, which in 1969 became the governing body of the CHURCH OF ENGLAND. It consists of three houses: bishops, clergy and laity. The body meets at least twice a year, and its members (except bishops) are elected on a diocesan basis.

General Theory of Relativity. *See* RELATIVITY.

Generation of '98, group of Spanish writers of the early 20th century, so called because they aimed to face up to the implications of Spain's defeat in the Spanish-American War. The leading writers associated with the movement were José MARTÍNEZ RUIZ and Pio Baroja. They sought the essence of Spanish culture within Spanish history.

Generator, electric, device for producing electrical energy. The most common is a machine that converts the mechanical energy of a turbine or internal combustion engine into electricity by employing ELECTROMAGNETIC INDUCTION. There are two types: alternating current (AC) and direct current (DC) generators, often called an alternator and a dynamo. Each has an armature (or ring) which rotates within a magnetic field creating an induced current. The direct current generator has a commutator on the armature which divides the induced current as it changes direction, giving rise to a pulsating direct current. *See also* MM p.84; SU p.122.

Genesis, first book of the Old Testament and of the PENTATEUCH, written following three separate strains of tradition which occasionally contradict each other: the Priestly, the Yahwist and the Elohist. There are three sections: the creation of the universe (two stories), from ADAM and EVE to ABRAHAM, and from Abraham to JOSEPH and the descent into Egypt.

Genet, Jean (1910–), French dramatist and novelist. The hardships of his childhood led him into delinquency and crime. In books such as *Our Lady of the Flowers* (1944) and *Thief's Journal* (1948) he records his experiences as a homosexual in brothels and prisons. His plays, which include *The Maids* (1947) and *The Balcony* (1956), are concerned with a world of illusions, masks and mirrors.

Genet, cat-like carnivore of the CIVET family native to W Europe and S and E Africa. Solitary and nocturnal, genets have long, slender bodies, short legs, grey to brown fur with black or brown spots and banded tails. Length: body – to 58cm (22in); tail – to 53cm (20.8in); weight: to 2kg (4.4lb). Family Viverridae; genus *Genetta*. *See also* NW pp.*165, 212.*

Genetic code, the arrangement of information in GENES that specifies exactly the way in which all the complex substances in living cells are made. It also specifies the manner of cell reproduction and is, therefore, the ultimate basis of heredity. In molecular biology the genetic code is the arrangement of NUCLEOTIDES – complex chemical groups – in the long molecules of nucleic acids in the cell CHROMOSOMES. These nucleotides, in groups of three, constitute the code words, each of which specifies an amino acid or an action such as "start" or "stop". Together, the code words constitute the genetic code.

Genetics, biological science and study of HEREDITY, mutation and development in plants and animals. Geneticists study molecular structures involved in heredity and evolution and the genes involved in the structure or alteration of an individual or a population. They also examine the effects of heredity or environment on personality and how these two factors interact. Heredity is also examined relative to behaviour, learning ability and physiology. The application of genetics has provided improved plant and animal stocks. *See also* NW pp.28–30.

Geneva (Genève), city in SW Switzerland, on the River Rhône, at the S end of Lake Geneva; capital of Genève canton. A former seat of the Burgundian kingdom, it was taken by the Franks in the 6th century, and passed to the HOLY ROMAN EMPIRE in the 12th century. The city accepted the REFORMATION in 1536 and became the centre of PROTESTANTISM under John CALVIN in 1541. It became part of the Swiss Confederation in 1815 and was the scene of the GENEVA CONVENTION in 1864. The city was the headquarters of the LEAGUE OF NATIONS from 1920 until 1946, and is the European centre of the UNITED NATIONS. It has a university, founded in 1559 by Calvin, and a Gothic cathedral. Industries: banking, jewellery, iron goods, tourism, enamelware. Pop. 173,618. *See also* HC1 p.*269*; HC2 pp.*171, 218.*

Geneva, Lake (Lac de Genève, Lac Léman), crescent-shaped lake in SW Switzerland. Lying between the ALPS and the JURA mountains, the S section is part of E France and it is drained to the W by the River Rhône. Length: 72km (45 miles); width: up to 14km (9 miles). Area: 580sq km (224sq miles).

Geneva Conventions, series of agreements on the treatment of wounded soldiers and prisoners during war, and on the neutrality of the medical services. The first convention was held in 1864. Later conventions have changed and updated its rules. *See also* HC2 p.*171.*

Genghis Khan (1167–1227), conqueror and Emperor of the MONGOL Empire stretching across central Asia from the Caspian Sea to the Sea of Japan. Mongol Emperor from 1206, he united the Mongol tribes and demonstrated his military genius and ruthlessness by capturing Peking (1215), annexing Iran and invading Russia as far as Moscow. He established law codes, tolerated ethnic and religious minorities and fostered contact between the East and West. His empire was divided and expanded by his sons and grandsons. *See also* HC1 pp.222, 224.

Genizah, room in a synagogue designated for the storage of holy books and utensils that are no longer in use. Jewish law forbids the destruction of such objects.
Gennesaret, Lake of. *See* GALILEE, SEA OF.
Genoa (Genova), port in NW Italy, on the Gulf of Genoa; capital of Genoa province and Liguria region. An important commercial centre in the Middle Ages, its fortunes declined in the 15th century and it came under foreign control. Occupied by Napoleon in 1796, it passed to France in 1805 and Sardinia in 1815. It was the birthplace of Christopher COLUMBUS *c.* 1451. It has a university (1471) and an Academy of Fine Arts (1751). Exports: rice, wine, olive oil, silk, coral, marble, macaroni. Industries: iron and steel, textiles, shipbuilding, chemicals. Pop. (1975) 805,855.
Genocide, deliberate governmental policy aimed at destroying a racial, religious or ethnic group. The word has become synonymous with the Nazi extermination of Jews during WWII, although the practice has existed for centuries. The UN General Assembly has defined genocide as an international crime, but no court with international criminal jurisdiction exists. *See also* ANTI-SEMITISM.
Genotype, genetic or hereditary makeup of an individual (the particular set of genes present in each cell of an organism). This is contrasted with PHENOTYPE, the observable characteristics of the organism.
Genoux, Claude (*d.* 1835), French printer who made important improvements to the STEREOTYPE process. In 1829 he patented a papier mâché sheet (a flong) which could be beaten or rolled into shape to form the stereotype. It was a great improvement on the late 18th century methods of using clay, stucco or molten metal.
Genova. *See* GENOA.
Genre painting, art term used to define realistic painting of scenes of everyday life. It was popularized in 16th-century Flanders by Pieter BRUEGEL THE ELDER and flourished in 17th-century Holland in the works of DE HOOCH, TER BORCH, METSU, VERMEER and many others, extending in the 18th and 19th centuries to France and England, where its major exponents included CHARDIN, WATTEAU, MORLAND and WILKIE. In Italy CARAVAGGIO and the CARRACCI were prominent among genre painters. More recently, the IMPRESSIONISTS frequently painted genre subjects, as did artists of the ASHCAN SCHOOL in the USA.
Gent. *See* GHENT.
Gentian, perennial herb native to temperate regions, although many species are alpines. It has heart-shaped leaves and usually blue, tubular flowers. Among 500 species are the dark blue *Gentiana clusii*, fringed *G. crinita* and yellow *G. lutea*, whose bitter root is used as a gastro-intestinal tonic. Family Gentianaceae. *See also* NW p.*223*.
Gentian violet, purple dye used in biology as a bacterial stain and in medicine as an antiseptic applied to the skin.
Gentile, Giovanni (1875–1944), Italian philosopher and educator. He founded an important journal of philosophy and literary criticism in 1920. His philosophy, "actual idealism", was an extreme version of HEGEL's idealism. He supported the Fascists in Italy and was minister for education (1922–24) under them, and editor of the *Enciclopedia italiana* (1925–43). He was killed by anti-Fascist partisans.
Gentile da Fabriano (*c.* 1370–*c.* 1427), Italian painter. A leader of the INTERNATIONAL GOTHIC revival, he greatly influenced Florentine art with his elegant frescoes and decorative altarpiece for the Church of Sta Trinita, Florence, depicting the *Adoration of the Magi* (1423).
Gentileschi, name of two Italian painters. Orazio Gentileschi (1563–*c.* 1647) was a follower of CARAVAGGIO, and is best known for his portraits and historical paintings. In 1626 he went t. England as the court painter to Charles I, and he spread the style of Caravaggio in northern Europe. He was accompanied by his daughter, Artemisia (*c.* 1597–*c.* 1652). who also became noted for her portraits and depictions of violent scenes.
Gentili, Alberico (1552–1608), Italian jurist. He is regarded as the first to expound the principles of international law, which he said should rest on the actions of civilized states and moral considerations. He divorced secular law from that of the Roman Catholic Church. Exiled from Italy because of his Protestantism, he taught at Oxford University from 1581.
Gento, Francisco (1933–), Spanish footballer. A stocky left winger of remarkable speed and ball control, he played in all Real Madrid's European finals from 1956 to 1971, captaining them in 1966 when they won the European Cup.
Gentofte, one of the largest suburbs of Copenhagen, Denmark, to which it is connected by an underground railway. It includes the lake Gentofte Sö. Chiefly a residential area, Gentofte is the site of Bernstorff Castle and a sports stadium. Pop. (1971 est.) 71,683.
Genus, group of closely related biological species with common characteristics. The genus name is usually a Latin or Greek noun, normally printed in italic letters. Example: genus *Quercus* denotes oak trees and *Felis* denotes all cats. A genus contains from one to several species. It is the sixth major category in taxonomy, the biological system of classification. The seven main categories are: Kingdom, Phylum, Class, Order, Family, Genus and Species. *See also* NW p.22.
Geochemistry, study of the chemical composition of the Earth and the changes that have resulted in it from chemical and physical processes.
Geochronology, the dating of rocks or of Earth processes. Various techniques are used, such as the measurement of radioactive decay, the search for fossils of a known age and the study of the sequence of deformation of a system. *See also* PE p.130.
Geode, small hollow rock nodule with inner walls lined with crystals, generally quartz or calcite. It is formed by gelatinous silica and mineral-bearing water within a cavity.
Geodesic dome, architectural structure of plastic, metal or even of cardboard, based in shape upon triangular or polygonal facets which evenly distribute the tension. Originated (1947) and perfected by R. Buckminster FULLER, geodesic domes in their use of prefabricated standardized parts are a recent descendant of the assembly methods first used by Sir Joseph PAXTON in the CRYSTAL PALACE. They may be used for housing. The best-known example is the US Pavilion at Montreal's Expo 67. *See also* SU p.*45*.
Geodesic surveying, method of surveying that covers areas large enough to involve consideration of the Earth's curvature. It is carried out in order to establish such geographical features as national boundaries, and as a basis for the mapping of whole states or countries. The maps are made using various projections, such as Mercator's or polar azimuthal, which transfer the Earth's curved surface to a plane surface.
Geodesy, in geophysics, the determination of the size and shape of the Earth, its gravitational field and the location of fixed points. Unlike surveying in civil engineering, ie plane surveying, geodesic surveying takes into account the curvature of the Earth. *See also* PE pp.34–35.
Geoffrey of Anjou (1113–51), ancestor of the PLANTAGENET kings of England. He married Henry I's daughter Matilda in 1128, and in 1129 became Count of Anjou, Maine and Touraine. He became Duke of Normandy in 1144. He had three sons, the eldest of whom became Henry II of England.
Geoffrey of Monmouth (*c.* 1100–54), English chronicler best known for his *Historia Regum Britanniae* (History of the Kings of Britain). Based on Latin manuscripts, Welsh genealogies and oral tradition, it is primarily a fictional account but was accepted as a historical document until the 17th century. It directly inspired Shakespeare's *King Lear* and *Cymbeline*, and was translated into many languages.
Geography, science that studies the relationship between the surface of the Earth and mankind. It includes the size and distribution of land masses, seas and resources, climatic zones and plant and animal life. Because it seeks to relate all the Earth's features to man's existence, geography differs from other earth sciences such as geology, meteorology and oceanography, which study this planet's features as specific phenomena. *See also The Modern World* and *The Physical Earth*.
Geological survey, the study of the geology of an area, usually with some other end in view, such as the evaluation of the area's agricultural potential, its mineral resources or its suitability as building land. *See also* PE p.128.
Geology, study of the materials of the Earth, their origin, arrangement, classification, change and history. Geology is divided into several categories, the major ones being mineralogy (arrangement of minerals), petrology (rocks and their combination of minerals), stratigraphy (arrangement and succession of rocks in layers), palaeontology (study of fossilized plant and animal remains), geomorphology (study of landforms), structural geology (classification of rocks and the forces that produced them), hydrology (study of surface and sub-surface waters), environmental geology (geological study applied to the best use of the environment by man) and oceanography (combination of several fields as they relate to the total study of oceans). *See also* PE pp.124–125.
Geomagnetism, the physical properties of the Earth's magnetic field. A compass needle points to magnetic north, which differs from geographical north by an amount that varies over geological periods of time as the Earth's magnetic field shifts in direction. Geomagnetism is attributed to the metallic composition of the Earth's core, and the movements of magnetic north is a result of the Earth's rotation and currents within the mantle.
Geometric mean, square root of the product of two numbers. For example, the geometric mean of 8 and 2 is $\sqrt{8 \times 2} = 4$. The geometric mean of n numbers is the nth root of their product $\sqrt[n]{a.b.c.\ ...}$.
Geometric progression, sequence of numbers in which the ratio of each term to the preceding one is a constant (called the common ratio). It has the form a, ar, ar^2, ar^3, ... where r is the common ratio. The sum of these terms, $a + ar + ar^2$ ..., is a geometric series. If there are n terms the sum equals $a\ (1-r^n)/(1-r)$. Infinite geometric series converge to $a/(1-r)$ if r lies between -1 and $+1$. *See also* SU p.38.
Geometry, branch of mathematics concerned broadly with studies of shape and size. To most people geometry is the Euclidean geometry of simple plane and solid figures. It is, however, a much wider and more abstract field with many subdivisions. Analytic geometry (also called co-ordinate geometry), introduced in 1637 by René DESCARTES, applies algebra to geometry and allows the study of more complex curves than those of Euclidean geometry. Projective geometry is, in its simplest form, concerned with projection of shapes – operations of the type involved in drawing maps and in perspective painting – and with properties that are independent of such changes. It was introduced by Jean-Victor Poncelet in 1822. Even more abstraction occurred in the early 19th century with formulations of non-Euclidean geometry by Janos Bolyai and N.I. Lobachevsky. Differential geometry – based on the application of calculus and ideas such as the curvature and lengths of curves in space – was also developed during this period. Geometric reasoning was also applied to spaces with more than three dimensions. TOPOLOGY is a general form of geometry, concerned with properties that are independent of any continuous deformation of shape. *See also* SU pp.44, 48–52.
Geomorphology, the study of features of the Earth's surface that have been formed as the result of wind and water erosion. It includes the formation of river valleys and estuaries, the formation of sand dunes and glacial moraines, and the creation of other

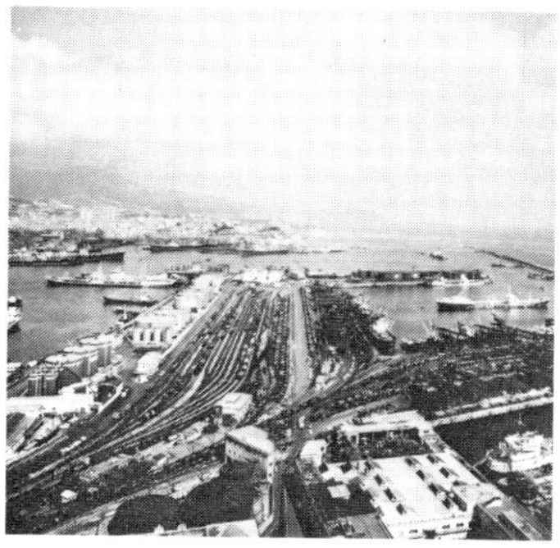

Genoa, birthplace of Christopher Columbus, was a vital medieval commercial port.

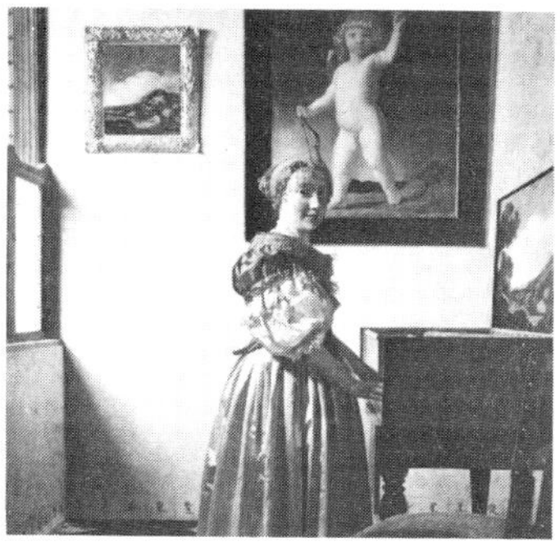

Genre painting; Vermeer's works are superb examples of the Dutch genre.

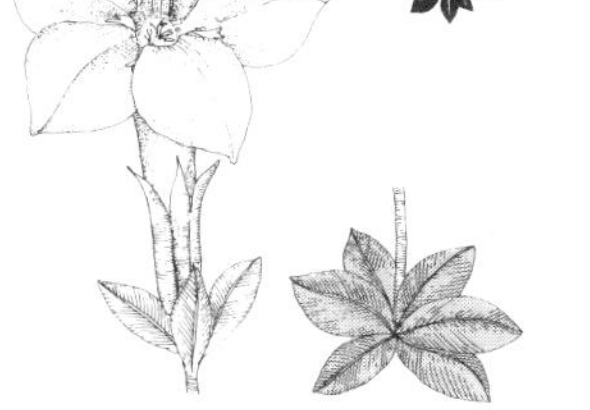

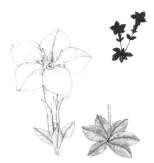

Gentian, a perennial flower whose roots are used to produce medicinal compounds.

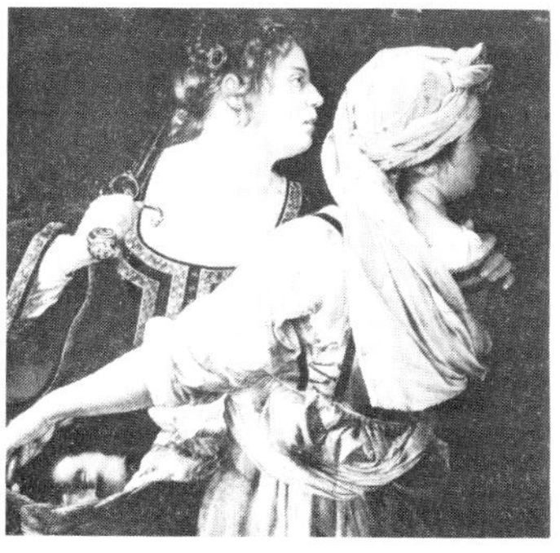

Artemisia Gentileschi; detail from her painting of Judith, the biblical Jewish Heroine.

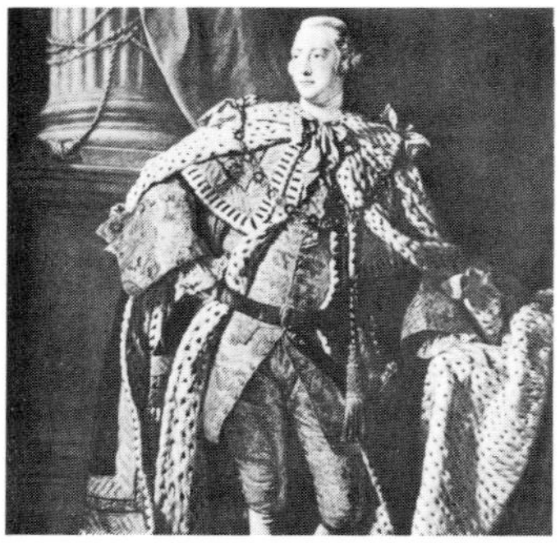

George III's unfortunate political meddlings led to the loss of the American colonies.

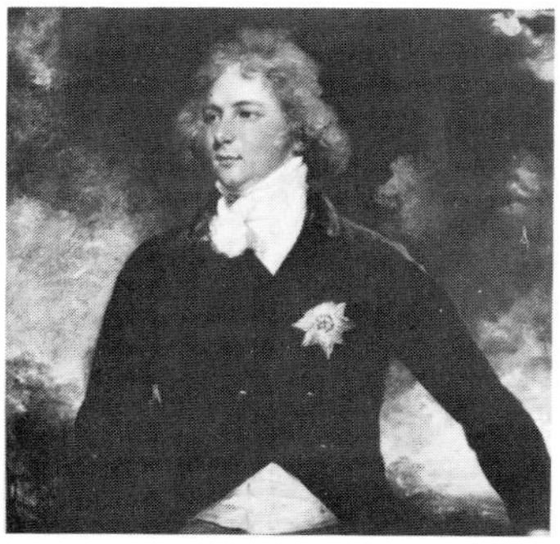

George IV, the dissolute British monarch who was, however, patron of the arts.

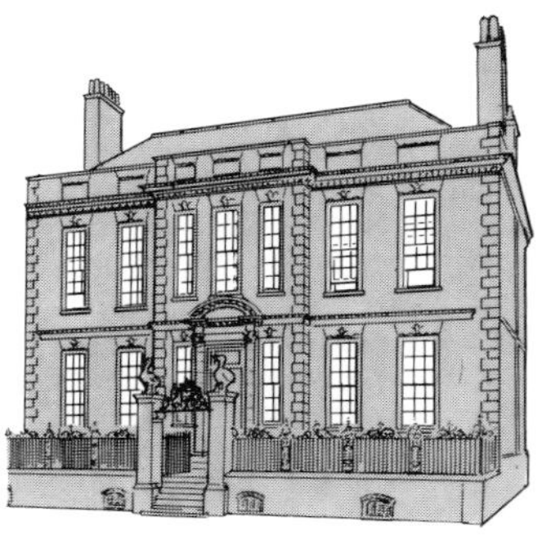

Georgian architecture was inspired initially by the principles of Andrea Palladio.

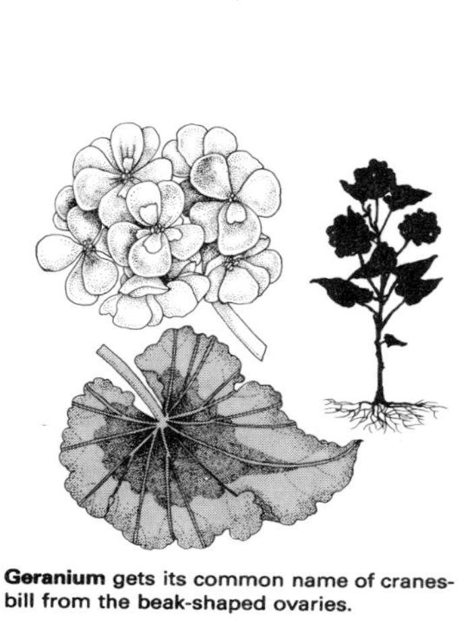

Geranium gets its common name of cranesbill from the beak-shaped ovaries.

topographical features by the accretion of eroded materials.

Geophone, seismic detection device placed on or in the ground to measure the echoes produced by volcanic or seismic (earthquake) activity.

Geophysics, study of the characteristic physical properties of the Earth as a whole system. It uses parts of chemistry, geology, astronomy, SEISMOLOGY, METEOROLOGY and many other disciplines. From the study of seismic waves geophysicists have deduced the structure of the Earth's interior.

George, Saint, early Christian martyr who became patron Saint of England in the late Middle Ages. According to tradition he was born in Palestine and martyred at Lydda some time before 323. Many stories grew up about him including the 12th-century tale of his killing a dragon to save a maiden. He is one of the great saints in the Eastern Church and is the ancient patron of soldiers. His feast day is April 23, and he remains a revered martyr.

George I (1660–1727), King of Great Britain and Ireland (1714–27) and Elector of Hanover (1698–1727). Great-grandson of James I and a Protestant, he succeeded Queen Anne and was the first Hanoverian monarch. He favoured the Whigs over the Tories, suspecting the latter of Jacobite sympathies. In 1715 and 1719 he put down Jacobite uprisings. In 1717–18 he formed alliances with Holland, France and Austria that guaranteed Hanoverian succession. He was disliked in England because he did not speak English and spent much of his time in Hanover. *See also* HC1 p.313; HC2 p.18.

George II (1683–1760), King of Great Britain and Ireland (1727–1760) and Elector of Hanover (1727–1760). Robert WALPOLE (in office 1727–42) dominated the early part of the reign. George brought Britain into the War of the AUSTRIAN SUCCESSION (1740–48) to protect Hanover, personally commanding victorious forces at Dettingen (1743). He suppressed the last Jacobite rebellion (1745–46). In the last years of his reign, during the SEVEN YEARS WAR (1756–63), William PITT the Elder was largely responsible for imperial acquisitions in Canada and India. *See also* HC1 p.*324*; HC2 pp.18, *22*, 68.

George III (1738–1820), King of Great Britain and Ireland (1760–1820); Elector and then King of Hanover (1760–1820); grandson of George II. He initially sought an active role in government during the ministries of BUTE, GRENVILLE, PITT the Elder, GRAFTON and Lord NORTH (1760–82), influencing the disastrous colonial policy that led to American independence (1776) but effectively suppressing the anti-Catholic GORDON RIOTS (1780). He consolidated Tory power by calling William PITT the Younger to office (1783–1801, 1804–06), yet defeating Pitt's plans for Catholic emancipation (1801). Suffering increasingly from bouts of insanity after 1765 (probably caused by the disease porphyria) he became nearly blind in 1805 and completely insane in 1811. Under the Regency Act (1811) his son (later GEORGE IV) acted as regent (1811–20). *See also* HC2 pp.18, *19–20*, *47*, 63, *68–69*, 162.

George IV (1762–1830), King of Great Britain and Ireland (1820–30). He served as regent during the periods of George III's madness (1788–89; 1811–20). In 1785 he secretly married Maria FITZHERBERT, but because he was under 25 and the king had not consented, the marriage was invalid. In 1795 he married CAROLINE OF BRUNSWICK in order to obtain parliamentary settlement of his debts; they separated within a year. When limitations on his powers as regent were removed in 1812 George decided to retain his father's Tory advisers instead of replacing them with the Whigs, whom he had supported earlier. A patron of the arts, he was, however, disliked for his extravagances and dissolute habits. He was succeeded by his brother WILLIAM IV.

George V (1865–1936), King of Great Britain and Northern Ireland and Emperor of India (1910–36). He had taken up a naval career but became heir apparent after his elder brother, Albert, Duke of Clarence, died in 1892. He married Princess Mary of Teck in 1893. In 1917 he changed the name of the royal house from the German SAXE-COBURG-GOTHA to Windsor. He maintained a strong personal interest in the British Empire throughout his reign and was occasionally active in domestic politics.

George VI (1895–1952), King of Great Britain and Northern Ireland (1936–52) and Emperor of India (1936–47). He was proclaimed king when his brother, EDWARD VIII, abdicated. In 1923 he married Lady Elizabeth Bowes-Lyon. To boost the morale of his people during WWII he and his family toured bombed areas and inspected mines and munitions factories, and he visited several battle fronts. In 1949 he was recognized as the head of the Commonwealth of Nations.

George I and II, kings of Greece. George I (1845–1913), King of the Hellenes (1863–1913), was appointed by Great Britain, France and Russia. He gained territory for Greece in the Balkan Wars but was assassinated in 1913 and succeeded by his son Constantine I. George II (1890–1947), king (1922–23 and 1935–47), was deposed in 1923 and Greece was declared a republic (1924). He was reinstated in 1935 whereupon he dissolved parliament and suspended constitutional rights. He fled the Germans in 1941, but ruled again from 1946 until his death.

George, Stefan (1868–1933), German poet. Influenced by the French SYMBOLISTS, he strove to achieve perfection of form, eg in *The Year of the Soul* (1897) and *The Carpet of Life* (1899). The Nazis misinterpreted his visions of noble youth and a new Reich in *The Seventh Ring* (1907) and *The New Reich* (1928), so he went voluntarily into exile.

George Cross, decoration first awarded in 1941 by King George VI for "the greatest heroism or the most conspicuous courage in circumstances of extreme danger". It ranks next to the Victoria Cross and was intended primarily for civilians, replacing the Empire Gallantry medal.

George Medal, decoration first awarded in 1940 by King George VI. It is presented for bravery in similar, but less outstanding, circumstances to the George Cross. Its insignia is a red ribbon with five narrow blue stripes. In 1942 King George VI awarded it to the entire population of Malta for bravery.

Georgetown, largest city and capital of Guyana, at the mouth of the Demerara River. Founded in 1781 by the British, it was the capital of the united colonies of Essequibo and Demerara, and known as Stabroek during Dutch occupation. Renamed Georgetown in 1812, it is the country's major port, exporting sugar, rice, timber, bauxite, gold and diamonds. Industries include shipbuilding, food processing, brewing and rum distilling. Pop. 63,200.

George Town. *See* PENANG.

Georgia, state in SE USA, on the Atlantic Ocean, N of Florida. In the S and E of the state is a broad coastal plain. The central area consists of the Piedmont plateau beyond which, in the N, are the Blue Ridge Mts and the Appalachian plateau. The area is drained by the Savannah, Ogeechee and Altamaha rivers. Cotton, once the chief crop, has declined in favour of tobacco, grown in the SE, and peanuts, grown in the SW. Livestock and poultry are now important. Textile manufacture has long been a major industry, but others include transport equipment, chemicals, paper and timber. Atlanta is the capital and the largest city. The first settlement of Georgia was on the Savannah River by James Oglethorpe in 1732. In the AMERICAN CIVIL WAR, it was one of the original six states of the Confederacy. The state was ravaged by the armies of General Sherman in 1864. Re-admitted to the Union in 1870, the recovery of the state economy was very slow. Area: 152,488sq km (58,876sq miles). Pop. (1975 est.) 4,926,000. *See also* MW p.175.

Georgia (Gruzinya SSR), one of the 15 union republics of the USSR, bounded by Turkey (S), the Black Sea (W) and the Armenian, Azerbaijan and Russian republics. It is a mountainous region on the slopes of the Caucasus, and the climate varies from the lowlands near the Black Sea, where it is subtropical, to the dry steppes of the E. Most of the people are farmers. The warmer parts of the region produce tea, citrus fruits, tobacco and grapes. Sheep, pig and poultry raising are important throughout the area. There are rich mineral deposits, including manganese, coal, lignite, iron and oil; there are also large areas of peat. The chief industries are iron and steel, railway and mining equipment, chemicals, machinery and building materials. The region has abundant hydroelectric power. The capital is Tbilisi. Area: 69,000sq km (26,910sq miles). Pop. (1976) 4,965,000. *See also* HC1 p.224; MW p.169.

Georgian architecture, building style in Britain and its colonies in the 18th and early 19th centuries. The name derives from the Hanoverian kings who reigned during this period. Based on classical forms, Georgian architecture stresses symmetry and makes use of brick and stone. A typical small Georgian building is rectangular in shape, built around a central stair-hall, and often with an imposing main door which employs a projecting hood or porch supported with columns. Many churches, particularly in London, were built in the Georgian style.

Georgian language, language spoken principally in Georgia, USSR. It is the most important member of the South Caucasian (Kartvelian) language family which is used by about 3 million people south of the Caucasus. The Georgian alphabet dates from the 5th century AD.

Georgian Poetry, series of anthologies in the conservative tradition, begun in 1912 and edited by Sir Edward Marsh; five volumes were published in London between 1912 and 1922. Noted contributors included Rupert BROOKE, W.H. DAVIES, Lascelles Abercrombie, James Elroy FLECKER, and Edmund BLUNDEN, Walter DE LA MARE and Robert GRAVES.

Georgics, instructive work in four books (29 BC) by VIRGIL. It vividly depicts the hard struggles and great rewards of all the activities of a farmer's life, as part of its purpose in persuading freemen to return to Italy's depopulated farms.

Geostrophic current, general term for an ocean or wind current whose direction is affected by the meeting of its pressure gradient with the CORIOLIS FORCE. *See also* PE pp.68, *68*, 78, *79*.

Geosyncline, great basin or trough in which deposits of sediments and volcanic rock, thousands of metres thick, have accumulated during slow subsidence over long geologic periods. It is an older and more extensive form of a SYNCLINE. *See also* PE pp.106–107.

Geothermal energy, heat contained in the Earth's crust. It is naturally released by GEYSERS and VOLCANOES, and is used as a power source for generating electricity in Lardorello in Italy, Wairakei in New Zealand and in N California, USA.

Geotropism, in plant growth, the response to the stimulus of gravity. Plant stems are generally negatively geotropic and grow upwards; roots are positively geotropic and grow downwards. For example, growth curvature is caused by the accumulation of the plant hormone AUXIN in the tissue on the lower side of the stem; growth increases on that side and the stem bends upwards. *See* NW p.45.

Gera, city in S East Germany, 56km (35 miles) SSW of Leipzig. One of the country's oldest cities, it was the capital of the principality of Reuss, 1564–1918. Today it is a communications and industrial centre, whose manufactures include textiles and metal products. Pop. (1975) 114,117.

Gerald of Wales. *See* GIRALDUS CAMBRENSIS.

Geranium, shrubby or trailing house and garden plant native to S Africa. It is densely branched with hairy, fan-shaped leaves that in some varieties emit a spicy aroma. Red, pink or white flower clusters are borne on stalks above the leaves. Its structure favours cross-pollination.

Height: 10–80cm (4–33in). Family Geraniaceae; genera *Pelargonium* and *Geranium*.

Gerard, John (1545–1612), English herbalist and author of *The Herball, or generall historie of plantes* (1597), in which he listed thousands of plants and their healing properties. It was a popular work, divided into 800 chapters. He also recorded much of the folklore associated with the plants. *See also* PE p.212.

Gerbil, small, mainly nocturnal rodent native to arid areas of Asia and Africa, and a popular pet. It has large eyes and ears, long hind legs and long tail. Its fur may be fawn, grey, brown or red. In its natural habitat it is a subterranean herbivore and often hoards food; it requires little water. Length: to 12cm (5in). Family Cricetidae. *See also* NW p.*220*.

Gerhard, Roberto (1896–1970), Spanish composer, *b.* Switzerland. After studying with GRANADOS and SCHOENBERG he later moved to Cambridge, England, in 1939. His works, which include five ballets, symphonies and chamber music, mingle Spanish idioms with the 12-tone technique and, later, serialism.

Gerhardt, Charles-Frédéric (1816–1856), French chemist best known for his attempt to systematize organic chemistry under the Theory of Types. This based all compounds on four main types and was influential in the development of structural chemistry. He published this and other ideas in *Traité de Chimie Organique* (4 vols, 1853–1856).

Geriatrics, branch of medicine that deals with the disorders and other medical problems of the elderly, who are subject to degeneration and ageing of certain tissues and other disorders not common in younger people. Arteriosclerosis and arthritis occur more frequently in old age, as does SENILITY. *See also* MS pp.176–180.

Géricault, Jean Louis André Théodore (1791–1824), French painter. A forerunner of the Romantic movement, he began as a painter of battle scenes. His most famous work was *Raft of the Medusa* (1817), depicting the survivors of a shipwreck who, after 12 days on a raft, had thrown the others overboard or eaten them. Out of 147, only 15 remained.

Gerkhin. *See* CUCUMBER.

Germ, word popularly denoting any infectious agent of microscopic or ultramicroscopic size. Germs can be pathogenic bacteria, fungi or viruses. The word germ is used in biology to denote a rudimentary stage in plant growth, such as an embryo in a seed, or a bud.

Germain, Saint (*c.*496–576), Bishop of Paris. According to legend, he both cured and saved King Childebert I from licentiousness, in compensation for which the king built the monastery of St Vincent in 558, later renamed Saint-Germain-des-Prés. Feast: 28 May.

German, Sir Edward (1862–1936), British composer, real name Edward German Jones. He wrote *Merrie England* (1902), *Tom Jones* (1907) and other light operas. He also composed two symphonies and a *Welsh Rhapsody*. He completed SULLIVAN's *The Emerald Isle*.

German Confederation (1815–66), federation of 39 German principalities set up by the Congress of Vienna to replace the HOLY ROMAN EMPIRE. It had few formal powers, beyond a mutual defence pact, and was dominated by Austria. It collapsed in 1848 but was restored two years later; after the Prussians defeated Austria in 1866 it was dissolved and replaced with the North German Confederation. *See also* HC2 pp.82, *110*.

German Democratic Republic. *See* GERMANY, EAST.

German Federal Republic. *See* GERMANY, WEST.

Germanic language, group of languages forming a sub-division of the Indo-European family. One branch includes English, German, Yiddish, Dutch, Flemish, Frisian and Afrikaans; another includes Swedish, Danish, Norwegian, Icelandic and Faroese. Gothic, the language of the ancient Goths, but long extinct, was a third branch.

Germanium, metalloid element (symbol Ge) of group IVA of the periodic table, predicted (as ekasilicon) by Mendeleyev and discovered in 1886. Germanium is a by-product of smelting zinc ores or may be obtained from the combustion of certain coals. It is important in transistors, rectifiers and similar semiconductor devices. Properties: at.no. 32; at.wt. 72.59; s.g. 5.32 (25°C); m.p. 937.4°C; (1,719°F); b.p. 2,830°C (5,126°F); most common isotope Ge^{74} (36.54%).

German measles, or rubella, virus-caused contagious disease characterized by a light pink rash beginning on the face and spreading down. The disease is mild, requiring only symptomatic relief, usually of itching. Young girls who have not had the disease are frequently immunized against rubella to prevent contagion to women in childbearing years, because rubella during pregnancy can damage a foetus. *See also* MS p.99.

German shepherd, breed of working dog developed in Germany by about 1900. It has wooly underhair and a slightly wavy or straight outer coat. Its commonest colours are black, grey or black and tan. Height: approx. 64cm (25in) at the shoulder; weight: 27–38kg (60–85lb).

Germanus, Saint (*c.*378–448), Gallic churchman. He became Bishop of Auxerre in 418, and visited Britain on papal instructions twice, in 429 and 447. In 447 he probably helped the British defeat an invasion by the Picts and Saxons. He may also have sent bishops to Ireland to assist St PATRICK. *See also* HC1 p.138.

Germany, former nation in central Europe, divided since 1945 into two independent countries, East GERMANY and West GERMANY. Some territory also became part of Poland and the USSR. A unified German nation existed from the end of the Franco-Prussian War in 1871 until 1945. On two occasions in the 20th century Germany initiated and was defeated in world wars. *See* MW pp.82–87.

Germany, East, Communist country in N Europe, official name the German Democratic Republic, formed after WWII from the NE part of Germany. Devastated during the war, it is now one of the richest Communist countries. The principal crops, produced on collective farms, are rye, sugar beet, potatoes, wheat barley and oats. Most raw materials have to be imported although East Germany produces approx. one-third of the world's brown coal (lignite). Industries include steel, chemicals, heavy machinery, motor vehicles and textiles. The capital is East Berlin. Area: 108,178sq km (41,610sq miles). Pop. (1976 est.) 16,850,000. *See* MW p.83.

Germany, West, nation in W Europe, official name the Federal Republic of Germany. It has made an astonishingly rapid recovery since WWII and now has one of the highest standards of living in the world. Many foodstuffs have to be imported, but wheat, barley, oats, sugar beet and rye are grown. West Germany is also noted for its hops and vines. The country is, however, overwhelmingly industrial. Iron and steel, motor vehicles, chemicals, electrical goods, oil refining and food processing are of great importance. The capital is Bonn. Area: 248,577 sq km (95,976sq miles). Pop. (1976 est.) 61,000,000. *See also* MW p.85.

Germicide, any substance for destroying disease-causing micro-organisms. Germicides include antiseptics, disinfectants and antibiotics.

Germinal (1885), naturalistic novel by Émile ZOLA which graphically describes the struggle of Lantier, a socialist miner, against an indifferent and oppressive social system. The result is not only a well-balanced and complex study of labour problems, but also a psychological drama of considerable power. *See also* HC2 pp.98, *99*.

Germination, growth of the embryo of a plant after the seed ripens and is detached from the parent plant. It may occur immediately or after a period of DORMANCY. In order to germinate, a seed or spore needs favourable conditions of temperature, light, moisture and oxygen. The process begins with the rehydration of the protoplasm of the embryo and the production of the amino acids and energy that stimulate growth. Germination is complete when a root appears outside the seed coat. *See also* DICOTYLEDON; MONOCOTYLEDON; PE pp.178–179.

Germiston, city in Transvaal province, NE South Africa, 13km (8 miles) E of Johannesburg in the Witwatersrand. It has the world's largest gold refinery. Industries: chemicals, textiles, engineering. Pop. (1970) 210,298.

Germ theory of disease, the attribution of the causes of infectious disease to micro-organisms, such as bacteria, viruses and microscopic fungi. In the 1850s Louis PASTEUR demonstrated that bacteria could infect a nutrient solution only if it was exposed to air or any other infecting medium. This destroyed the old but widely held idea of spontaneous generation of bacteria. In 1876 Robert KOCH carried out experiments that demonstrated conclusively the bacterial aetiology of the disease anthrax and, by inference, that of many other diseases. *See also* MS p.85.

Germ warfare, or biological warfare, the deliberate use of pathogenic micro-organisms, such as bacteria, viruses and microscopic fungi, and their toxins, to produce disease in an enemies' population, domestic animals or food crops. Microbiologists are now able to grow such organisms on a large scale and, by genetic manipulation, even to increase their virulence. Guided missiles are capable of firing a "package" of disease across the world; large-scale germ warfare is now a possibility. The widespread use of DEFOLIANTS by the US armed forces in Vietnam, in an attempt to undermine that country's economy and deprive enemy troops of cover, is a modern application of biological warfare. *See also* MM pp.180–181.

Geronimo (1829–1908), chief of the Chiricahua Apaches. He led his tribe against white settlers in Arizona for more than 10 years. In 1886 he surrendered his tribe to General Miles and they were taken to Fort Sill, Oklahoma. Geronimo became a prosperous farmer and national celebrity.

Gerontology, the study of ageing. The capacity of an organism to repair tissues effectively, by the replacement of worn out cells, diminishes with age, so that "growing old" is inevitable (even when, as in many large trees, it is delayed for some thousands of years). The effect of GERIATRIC medicine has been to relieve and treat the disease burdens of age. It has not noticeably increased life expectancy. *See also* MS p.176.

Gerrymander, practice of rearranging electoral districts in such a way as to favour a particular party. It was a common means by which parties sought to retain power. The manoeuvre is named after Elbridge Gerry, governor of Massachusetts (1810–12), whose party employed the practice. One of his redefined districts was said to resemble a salamander, hence by combination the verb gerrymander.

Gershwin, George (1898–1937), US composer who wrote many popular songs, for which his brother Ira Gershwin (1896–) mostly wrote the lyrics. The scores for several musicals, eg *Lady Be Good* (1924) and a Negro opera *Porgy and Bess* (1935) were by him, as were also some serious orchestral works that contain elements of jazz and popular music: *Rhapsody in Blue* (1923), originally for piano and jazz band (later reorchestrated), and the tone poem *An American in Paris* (1928). *See also* HC2 p.271.

Gesner, Abraham (1797–1864), Canadian geologist and inventor. He is noted for his exploration and geological mapping of Nova Scotia, and his invention of a process for the distillation of kerosene from petroleum.

Gesner, Konrad von (1516–65), Swiss scientist who is best remembered for his diverse scientific knowledge. He taught physics and practised medicine. He compiled a dictionary of animals called *Historiae animalium* (1551–58).

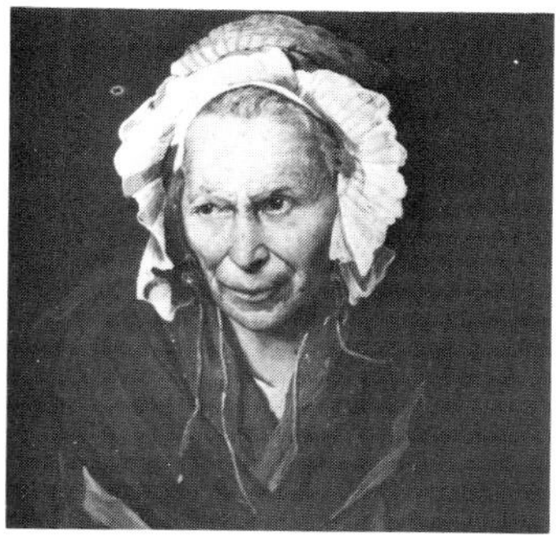

Géricault; *A Mad Woman with the Mania of Envy* from his paintings of the insane.

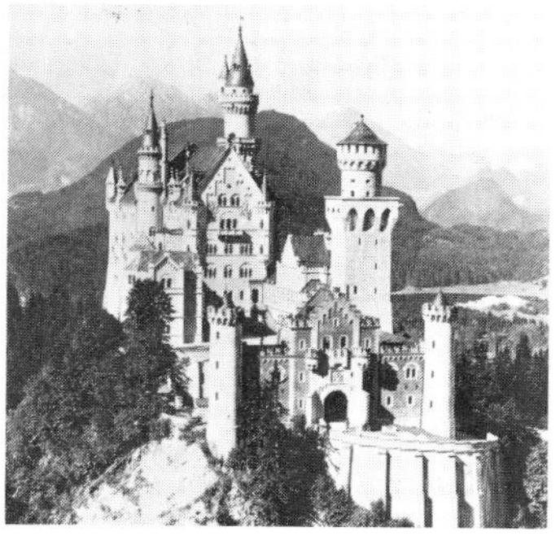

Germany; the Bavarian royal castle at Neuschwanstein built in the 19th century.

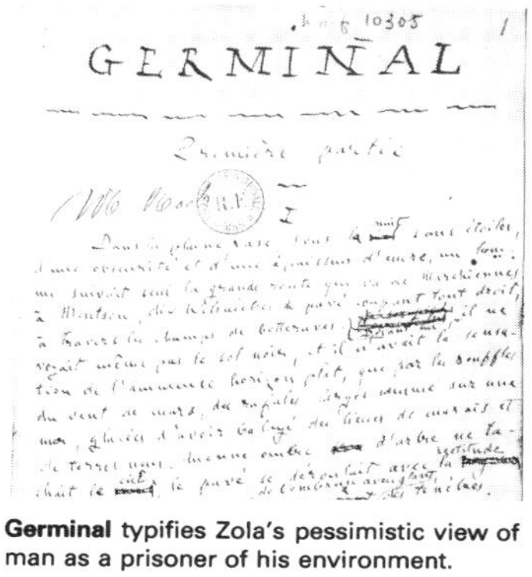

Germinal typifies Zola's pessimistic view of man as a prisoner of his environment.

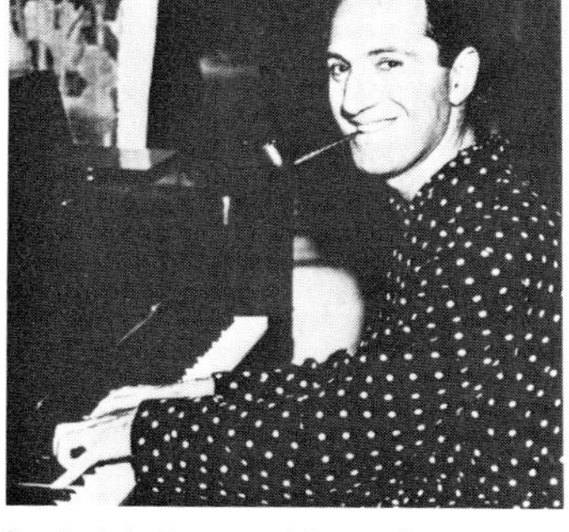

Gershwin's *Porgy and Bess* reflects a deep study of black customs and music.

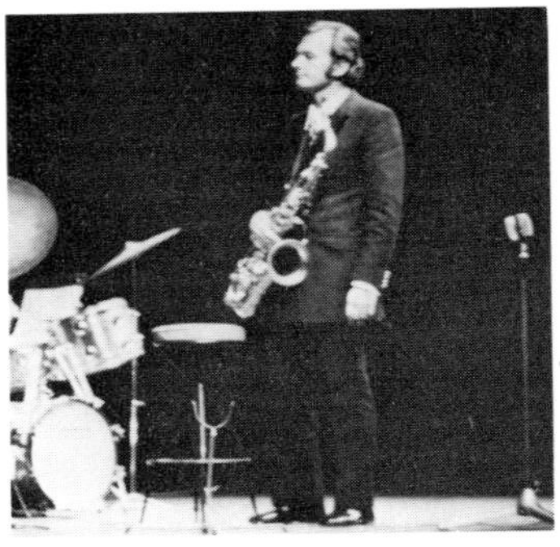

Stan Getz has recently fused the new latin rhythms with his own jazz style.

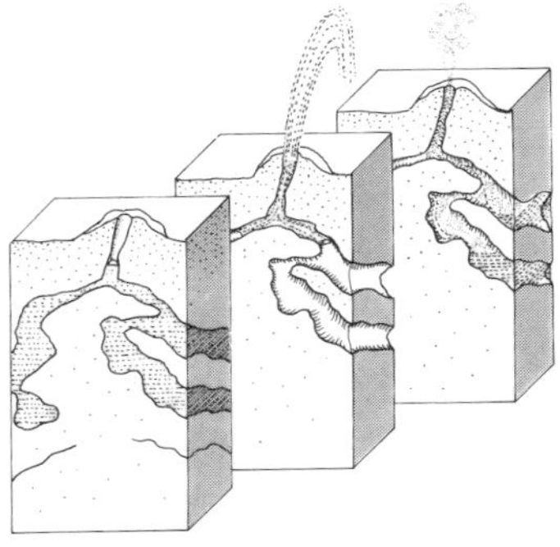

Geysers operate like giant safety valves for powerful underground volcanic activity

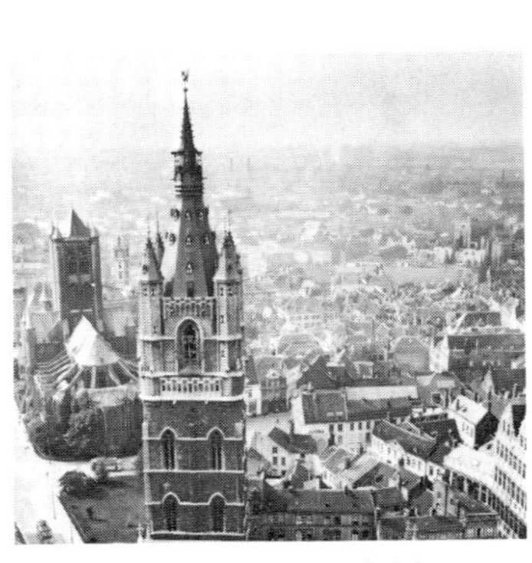

Ghent, more than any other Belgian town, has retained a feudal atmosphere.

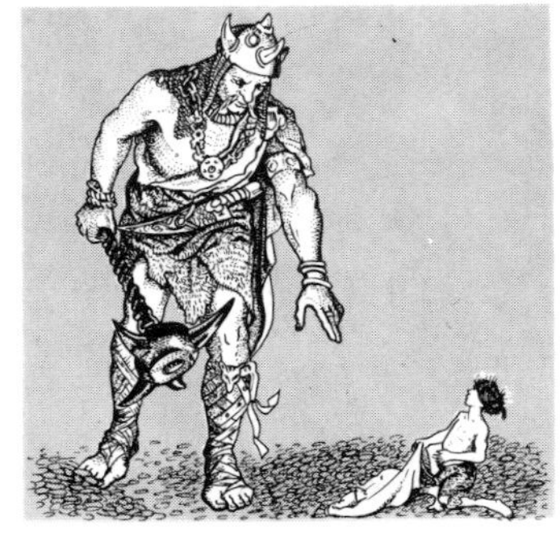

Giants are common mythological figures, one of the most famous being Goliath.

Gesso, in art, a ground applied TEMPERA, Oil Paint or GILDING; it is a mixture of gypsum or chalk, and size. The first layer, *gesso grosso*, is coarse, heavy and absorbent; second, *gesso sottile*, is a mixture of size and slaked plaster of paris and is applied in several fine coats to provide a brilliant-white, smooth surface. *Gesso grosso* may be reapplied to strengthen the surface. Furniture manufacturers indent the gesso, or mould it (*gesso rilievo*), after which painting or gilding is done.
Gestalt psychology, school of psychology based on the theory that man perceives phenomena as relating to a configuration, a whole or Gestalt. Thus the whole is more than the sum of its parts. From the end of the 19th century, in Germany Gestalt psychology was developed by Max WERTHEIMER, Wilhelm WUNDT, Wolfgang KÖHLER and Kurt KOFFKA. Using mainly introspective methods, they formulated several principles which were essentially refinements of the original concept. According to Gestalt psychologists, these principles govern man's perception of the world. They also did important research into the neurological basis of perception. *See also* MS pp.46–47.
Gestapo (Geheime Staatspolizei), state secret police of NAZI Germany. Originally founded in 1933 by GOERING in Prussia, it soon became a national organization. It was taken over by HIMMLER in 1934 and became in effect a unit of the SS (Schutzstaffel). It had virtually unlimited powers and, together with SS, ran the Nazi concentration and extermination camps.
Gestation, period of carrying a developing EMBRYO in a uterus between conception and birth. Gestation periods are specific to each mammalian species and range from 12 days (Virginia opossum) to 22 months (Indian elephant). In man and many apes the period is approximately 38 weeks.
Gestring, Marjorie (1923–), US diver who became the youngest individual champion of the modern Olympic Games when, aged 13, she won the springboard gold medal at Berlin in 1936.
Gethsemane, in the New Testament, olive grove at the foot of the Mount of Olives, E of Jerusalem; the name means "oil-press". A favourite place for Jesus to pray, it was there that the three disciples could not remain awake during the night of Jesus's agony (or Passion). The next morning Jesus was confronted there by Judas Iscariot and "a number of men carrying sticks and clubs", the chief priests and the Temple guard, the preliminary to his being led off to crucifixion.
Getty, Jean Paul (1892–1976), US businessman and art collector. He inherited his father's oil business, George F. Getty, Inc., becoming its president in 1930. After 1959 he lived in England. He was one of the world's richest men, with a fortune estimated at more than £1,000 million.
Gettysburg, town in S Pennsylvania, USA. It was the scene of the historic battle in 1863 during the AMERICAN CIVIL WAR in which Robert E. LEE and his Confederate troops were defeated by the Union army led by George Meade. The battle proved a turning point in the war, stopping Lee's invasion of the North. It was also the scene of Lincoln's GETTYSBURG ADDRESS in Nov. 1863. There are several monuments commemorating the battle. Tourism is a major industry. Pop. (1970) 7,275.
Gettysburg Address (19 Nov. 1863), speech by Abraham LINCOLN at the dedication of the national cemetery on the site of the battle of GETTYSBURG. It has become famous for its eloquence and brevity. The final sentence contains a phrase that has become a definition of democracy: "government of the people, by the people and for the people".
Getz, Stan (1927–), US jazz saxophonist. He came to fame with Woody Herman in the 1940s and since then has led his own groups. Although popular, he has usually managed to avoid vulgarization. A creative stylist strongly influenced by Lester YOUNG, his sensitive tone control has made him influential..
Geum, or avens, perennial herb of the rose family. Most species have orange, red, yellow or white flowers and deeply indented basal leaves. Height: to 60cm (24in). Family Rosaceae; genus *Geum.*
Geyser, hot spring that erupts intermittently, throwing up jets of superheated water and steam. Before eruption, the water occupies a natural crooked tube reaching deep into the earth. Pressure, at eruption, forces columns of water into the air to a height commonly of 60 metres (197ft) which are followed by a shaft of steam emitted with a thunderous roar. Most geysers occur in Iceland, New Zealand and the USA. *See also* MM p.73; PE p.30.
Gezelle, Guido (1830–99), Flemish lyric poet and priest-journalist. He was disapproved of by the state and the Church for his Flemish nationalism, which is revealed in poetry such as *Kleengedichtjes* (1860) and *Laatste verzen* (1901).
Ghaghra (Gogra), river in Asia which rises in the Himalayan Mts in Tibet, China, and flows SE through Nepal to join the River Ganges in Bihar state, E India. Length: approx. 920km (570 miles).
Ghana, nation in W Africa, known as the Gold Coast before independence in 1957. Most of the inhabitants depend on agriculture, producing cassava, groundnuts and guinea corn. Ghana is also the world's leading cocoa producer. It has little industry although gold and diamonds are mined. The capital is Accra. Area: 238,537sq km (92,099sq miles). Pop. (1975 est.) 9,866,000. *See* MW p.87.
Ghats, two mountain systems in peninsular India. The Western Ghats extend from the Tapti River to Cape Comorin and form the W edge of the Deccan Plateau; the Eastern Ghats extend from the Mahānadi River to the Nilgiri Hills and form the E edge of the Deccan Plateau. Height: (Western) 900–1,500m (2,950–4,920ft); (Eastern) 600m (1,970ft). Length: (Western) 1,600km (1,000 miles); (Eastern) 1,400km (875 miles).
Ghent (Gent), city in NW central Belgium, 50km (31 miles) NW of Brussels. It was a major cloth centre in the 13th century and the power of the guilds made the city virtually independent. The Pacification of Ghent was signed there in 1576. The city's development was disrupted by war in the following century as it was captured by France in 1698, 1708 and 1745. Its prosperity revived after the FRENCH REVOLUTIONARY WARS when textile factories were established. The city was occupied in WWI and WWII. Industries: plastics, chemicals. Pop. 224,728.
Ghent, Treaty of (1814), treaty which ended the WAR OF 1812 between the British and the USA. It made no mention of the maritime issues which were the ostensible cause of the war – notably the US ships' ignoring of the blockade set up by the British against the French during the NAPOLEONIC WARS. Instead it appointed a commission to settle the dispute over the boundary dividing the USA and British North America.
Ghetto, section of a city inhabited almost exclusively by one ethnic group. The term originated in Europe, designating a separate area of a city for Jews. Characterized by homogeneity, cultural cohesion and shared economic conditions, ghettos are founded on the basis of religion, race or culture. Ghettos may generate alternative life-styles that differ from those of the larger society. The term has come to have a pejorative connotation, indicating a poor, dilapidated area.
Ghibellines, political faction in 13th century Italy that supported the HOHENSTAUFEN dynasty of the HOLY ROMAN EMPIRE, opposed to the pro-papal GUELPHS. The name derived from Waiblingen castle which belonged to the Hohenstaufens. During the struggles that occurred in north and central Italy between Emperor Frederick II and the popes of the mid-13th century, the term came to designate those on the imperial side.
Ghiberti, Lorenzo (1378–1455), Italian sculptor, goldsmith, architect, painter and writer; a major transitional figure between the late Gothic and Renaissance worlds. He made two pairs of richly gilded bronze doors for the Baptistery in Florence. The first (1403–24) depicts 28 New Testament scenes; the second (1425–47) is his own choice of 10 scenes from the Old Testament. The latter, known as the "Doors of Paradise", are considered his masterpiece. *See also* HC1 p.250, *251.*
Ghirlandaio, Domenico (*c.* 1449–94), Italian Florentine painter. A prolific fresco artist, he typified the trend towards detailed realism in figures, settings and landscapes. He worked on the Sistine Chapel with BOTTICELLI and others, his major contribution being *Christ Calling the First Apostles* (1482).
Ghost, phantom or spectre of a dead person, animal, or possibly both simultaneously (as with ghosts of highwaymen on horseback). Occasionally only heard, not seen, ghosts may appear as likenesses of people who died in any former time, in full or in part, and with reasonable definition or faint and shadowy. Much belief in ghosts stems from the idea that violent death may cause the deceased to haunt the living; this fear has given rise to many folktales and has influenced the religious beliefs of societies since primitive times. A popular modern theory is that ghosts may be some kind of "image-memory" in the fabric of particular places, imprinted during the deceased's lifetime by his repeating an action time after time – which would account for the number of ghost priests in churches and prisoners in castles. A noisy but unseen ghost that moves objects and furniture is called a POLTERGEIST.
Ghosts (1881), three-act play by Henrik IBSEN, showing how moral diseases from the past – symbolized by hereditary venereal disease – can haunt the present. The author's uncompromising presentation of this subject led to riots at its first performance in Chicago. Critical and popular reactions to its first public performances in Oslo (1883) and London (1914) were equally vitriolic. *See also* HC2 p.10.
Giacometti, Alberto (1901–66), Swiss sculptor and painter. In the 1930s he worked on SURREALIST sculpture. During the 1940s and 1950s he produced his greatest works – emaciated, dreamlike figures built of plaster of paris on a wire base. His paintings and drawings have the same agitated, visionary quality.
Giaever, Ivar (1929–), US physicist, *b.* Norway, who shared the 1973 Nobel prize in physics with Brian JOSEPHSON and Leo ESAKI for their research into tunnelling in semiconductors and superconductors. Esaki developed the tunnel diode, which enables electrons to cross normally impassable electronic barriers, and Giaever applied this to superconductors, demonstrating new effects which led to a better understanding of SUPERCONDUCTIVITY. *See also* SEMICONDUCTIVITY.
Giambologna, or Giovanni Bologna (1529–1608), Flemish sculptor, active in Florence. A master of MANNERISM, he executed his *Rape of the Sabine* in 1582 and *Astronomy* in *c.* 1573. *See also* HC1 p.*265.*
Giant, in mythology, huge being of enormous strength and human form. In Norse mythology giants existed before the gods who overcame them; in Greek mythology the TITANS were giants who repeatedly attacked Olympus. Most medieval European giants were portrayed as clumsy, greedy cannibals, dominating whole districts. Traditionally, a giant could not be overcome by might, but could be defeated by cunning and trickery.
Giant's Causeway, promontory on the N coast of Northern Ireland in County Antrim. It extends 5km (3 miles) along the coast and consists of thousands of basalt columns of varying height.
Giant star, star belonging to a luminosity class midway between main-sequence stars and supergiants. Giant stars lie directly above the main sequence on the HERTZSPRUNG-RUSSELL DIAGRAM and are characterized by large dimensions, high luminosity, and low density. They are found throughout the entire surface-temperature range. Those of spectral type G-M (the red giants) contrast with corresponding DWARF STARS of the main sequence. *See also* SU pp.226–229.

Giap, Vo Nguyen (1912–), Vietnamese general and politician. A brilliant guerrilla commander, he led the VIETMINH forces that entered Hanoi in 1945 and that later defeated the French at Dien Bien Phu (1954). He commanded North Vietnamese forces in the VIETNAM WAR (1961–75), and organized the 1968 Tet offensive. He is now deputy premier of a united Vietnam.

Giauque, William Francis (1895–), US chemist. Giauque is noted for discovering the isotopes of oxygen and for his studies of phenomena at extremely low temperatures. In 1926 he suggested a method for producing temperatures approaching absolute zero, until then believed impossible in practice. He received the 1949 Nobel Prize for chemistry.

Gibberd, Sir Frederick (1908–), British architect and town planner, one of the first in Britain to accept the INTERNATIONAL STYLE. His best-known works include the plan and some major buildings for Harlow New Town, Essex (1947), London Airport (1955) and the prize-winning design for the Roman Catholic Cathedral, Liverpool (1960), influenced by Oscar NIEMEYER's Brasilia Cathedral.

Gibberellins, group of organic compounds that stimulate stem elongation, dormancy and plant response to light and temperature. Originally isolated from the fungus *Gibberella fujikuroi*, they interact with some AUXINS to promote cell enlargement and have been used to increase crop yields substantially. *See also* NW p.45.

Gibbon, Edward (1737–94), British historian. A man of independent means, he travelled widely, and it was during a visit to the Forum in Rome in 1764 that he decided to write his great work *The History of the Decline and Fall of the Roman Empire* (6 vols., 1776–88). Its magisterial sweep and cynical vision of history render it one of the most widely known historical works of modern times.

Gibbon, Lewis Grassic (1901–35), Scottish writer; the pen-name of James Leslie Mitchell. He wrote with feeling about Scottish rural life, especially in his trilogy *Sunset Song* (1932), *Cloud Howe* (1933) and *Grey Granite* (1934).

Gibbon, small, slender, long-limbed ape that lives in forests in SE Asia. It has a shaggy brown, black or silvery coat and is the most agile of the mammals that live in trees. It travels from branch to branch by swinging with its long, powerful arms. Height: 41–66cm (16–26in). Family Pongidae, genus *Hyloblates.* See also NW pp.*169, 214.*

Gibbons, Grinling (1648–1721), English wood carver of fruit, flower and lacy decorations. There are fine examples of his work at St Paul's Cathedral, London, Windsor Castle and many country houses, especially Petworth House, Sussex, which has a magnificent room decorated by him. Gibbons, whose patrons included Charles II and George I, also worked in conjunction with Christopher WREN.

Gibbons, Orlando (1583–1625), English composer. He was organist of the CHAPEL ROYAL (1605–25) and of Westminster Abbey (1623–25). Although he composed viol fantasies and madrigals, he was, above all, a composer of church music and a master of POLYPHONY (as in *Hosanna to the Son of David* and *O Clap Your Hands*).

Gibbons, Stella Dorothea. *See* COLD COMFORT FARM.

Gibbs, Cecil Armstrong (1889–1960), British composer. He is best known for his songs, in particular his setting of poems by Walter DE LA MARE. He also composed large choral works, such as *Deborah and Barak* (1937) and the choral symphony *Odysseus* (1938).

Gibbs, James (1682–1754), Scottish architect whose best-known work is the church of St Martin in the Fields, London (1722–26). He was influenced by Italian architecture and the work of Sir Christopher WREN. He also designed the Radcliffe Camera at Oxford (1737–1749).

Gibbs, Josiah Willard (1839–1903), US theoretical physicist and chemist. While a professor at Yale, he devoted himself to establishing the basics of physical chemistry. His application of thermodynamics to physical processes led to statistical mechanics. He evolved the concepts of free energy and chemical equilibrium, devised the phase rule and developed vector analysis.

Gibbs, Lance (1934–), West Indian cricketer. He is a tall off-spin bowler whose immaculate control and deceptive flight brought him a world record 309 wickets in 79 Test matches for the West Indies (1957–76). He played for Guyana, Warwickshire, and South Australia.

Gibraltar, British Crown colony on the S coast of Spain. Its name comes from the Moorish *Djebel Tariq* ("mountain of Tariq"). It was from Gibraltar that the MUSLIM conquest of Spain by TARIQ was begun in 711, and it remained under Moorish control until it fell to the Castilians in 1462. In 1704 it was captured by an Anglo-Dutch fleet and was formally ceded to Britain by the Treaty of UTRECHT (1713); it has remained a crown colony ever since. In 1964 it was granted extensive self-government, and in 1967 a referendum revealed the almost unanimous wish of Gibraltarians to remain British. *See also* MW p.88, HC2 p.*47.*

Gibraltar, Strait of, channel connecting the Mediterranean Sea with the Atlantic Ocean between Gibraltar (N) and Ceuta (S) at the E end and capes Trafalgar (N) and Spartel (S) at the W end. Width: 13–37km (8–23 miles); length: 58km (36 miles).

Gibson, Sir Alexander (1926–), British conductor. He was assistant conductor of the BBC Scottish Orchestra 1952–54 and has been the principal conductor of the Scottish National Orchestra since 1959 and of the Scottish Opera, which he founded, since 1962.

Gibson, Althea (1927–), US tennis player. The first black player to win a major championship (the French in 1956), she went on to win the Wimbledon and US singles in 1957 and 1958, the years she was ranked No. 1 in the world. She turned professional in 1959.

Gibson, Charles Dana (1867–1944), US illustrator and artist. He worked for, among others, the magazines *Life* and *Collier's Weekly* and his depiction of the American feminine ideal became known as the Gibson Girl. He illustrated Anthony HOPE's *Prisoner of Zenda* and other novels and also published books of drawings, eg *The Social Ladder* (1902) and *Our Neighbours* (1905).

Gibson, Mike (1942–), Irish rugby union player, an equally gifted fly-half or centre, who between 1964 and 1977 won 62 caps (only one less than the Irish record). A Cambridge blue and a British Lions tourist to New Zealand (1966, 1971, 1977) and South Africa (1968, 1974), he played for North of Ireland FC in Belfast.

Gibson desert, arid region in E and central Western Australia state, Australia. It is noted for its salt lakes. Length: 402km (250 miles), width: 837km (520 miles).

Gide, André (1869–1951), French novelist, playwright and critic. His novels and his *Journals* (1885–1949) show him to be constantly divided by the puritan and pagan elements within himself. Works such as *The Immoralist* (1902) and the experimental *The Counterfeiters* (1926) dramatize a parallel search for spiritual truth and individual freedom. He was awarded the Nobel Prize in literature in 1947. *See also* HC2 p.291.

Gideon, biblical Judge, Israelite hero and father of Abimelech. Called by an angel of God (Yahweh), he destroyed the Canaanite altar of BAAL. After a victorious attack on the Midianite camp with only 300 soldiers (chosen by God) he refused to be made titular king, although as a Judge he was already not far removed, and his son's name means "son of the king".

Gideons, The, interdenominational religious body of laymen founded in the USA in 1899. It is best known for donating Bibles to places such as hospitals, hotels and prisons. It has about 23,500 members throughout the world.

Giedion, Sigfried (1893–1968), Swiss historian who specialized in architecture. He was closely associated with the International Congress of Modern Architecture, which first met in 1928. In lectures which he gave at HARVARD UNIVERSITY he presented history in terms of constancy and change.

Gielgud, Sir Arthur John (1904–), British stage actor whose consistently excellent performances in both modern and classical roles after 1921 established him as one of the century's finest actors. He played almost every major Shakespearian role and his outstanding Hamlet, first performed in 1929, delighted audiences on more than 500 occasions. Other major appearances were made in *The Importance of Being Earnest* (1939), *The Lady's Not For Burning* (1948) and *The Cherry Orchard* (1954). For the NATIONAL THEATRE he won wide acclaim for the rôles he created in *No man's Land* (1975) and *Half-Life* (1977).

Gierek, Edward (1913–), Polish Communist political leader. After periods in France and Belgium before and during WWII, he returned to Poland in 1948 and rose through the party hierarchy. When riots over increased food prices and shortages broke out in Gdánsk and other port cities in 1970, Gierek succeeded Wladyslaw Gomulka as party chief. He attempted to satisfy the demands of workers, and to improve relations with the Roman Catholic Church. *See also* HC2 p.243.

Gieseking, Walter (1895–1956), German pianist, born in France. He made his debut in 1915 and his first European tour in 1920; he made his London début in 1923. He was later accused of collaboration with the Nazi government in the 1930s. He was highly regarded as a player of the music of DEBUSSY and SCHUBERT..

Giffard, Henri (1823–1882), French engineer who in 1852 constructed a steam-driven dirigible (steerable airship). His steam engine was the first power source light and powerful enough to have application in lighter-than-air ships. It drove a 3.5m (11ft) long propeller at the rate of 110rpm to power a 44m (143ft) airship at about 9km/h (5.5mph). *See also* MM p.146.

Gigantism, generalized over-growth of an individual, believed to be caused by PITUITARY GLAND disturbance resulting in pre-pubescent overproduction of the GROWTH HORMONE. The body may remain in proportion or have distorted extremities and head. *See also* MM pp.*100–101.*

Gigli, Beniamino (1890–1957), Italian tenor. After his début in 1914, he became a favourite in Italian opera houses until 1920, when he succeeded CARUSO at the Metropolitan Opera, New York. He made his début at Covent Garden in 1930, and after 1946 often appeared in opera with his daughter, the soprano Rina Gigli.

Gila monster, poisonous nocturnal LIZARD that lives near water in deserts of SW USA and N Mexico. It has a stout body, massive head, flat tail and bead-like scales of orange, yellow and black. It eats small mammals and eggs. Length: 50cm (20in). Family Helodermatidae; species *Heloderma suspectum. See also* NW p.*137.*

Gilbert, Cass (1859–1934), US architect. He designed New York's 52-storey Woolworth Building (1913), which influenced the development of the skyscraper. He also designed the US Supreme Court Building in Washington DC. His styles were not highly original but exemplified the Neoclassical derivative style which then predominated.

Gilbert, Sir Humphrey (*c.*1539–83), English soldier and explorer. A brilliant navigator, Gilbert wrote his *Discourse* on the Northwest Passage (1576) and made expeditions to Canada in 1578 and 1583. He established the first British colony in North America at St John's, Newfoundland in 1583. Gilbert used his private means in searching for a passage to the Pacific Ocean. *See also* HC1 pp.278–279.

Gilbert, William (1544–1603), English physicist and physician to Queen Elizabeth I. His *De magnete, magneticisque corporibus* (1600) laid the foundation for the scientific study of magnetism. He was the first to recognize terrestrial magnetism and concluded that a type of magnetism keeps the planets in their orbits. He

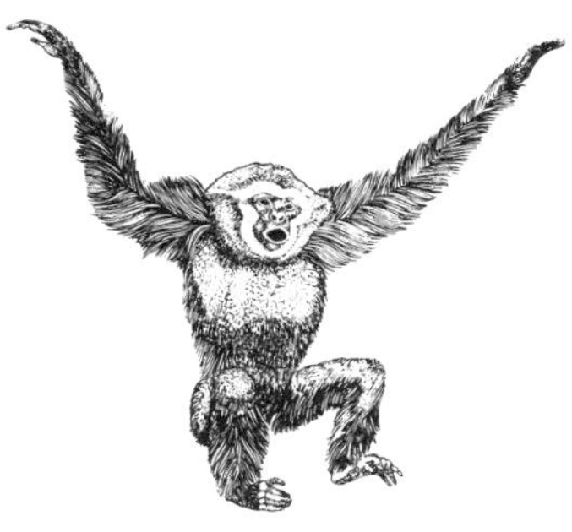

Gibbons swing through the trees but walk erect with arms held aloft or behind.

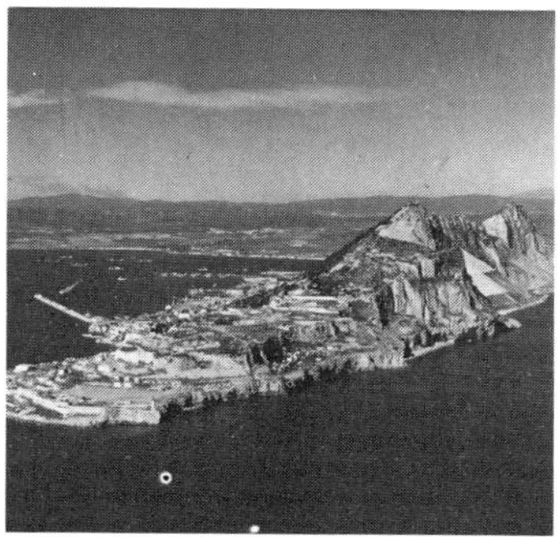

Gibraltar voted almost unanimously to remain a British colony in 1967.

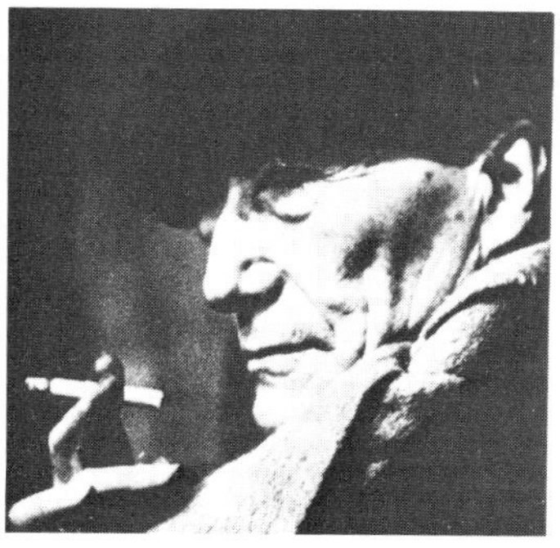

Gide's affection for Soviet socialism declined after his journey to the USSR in 1936.

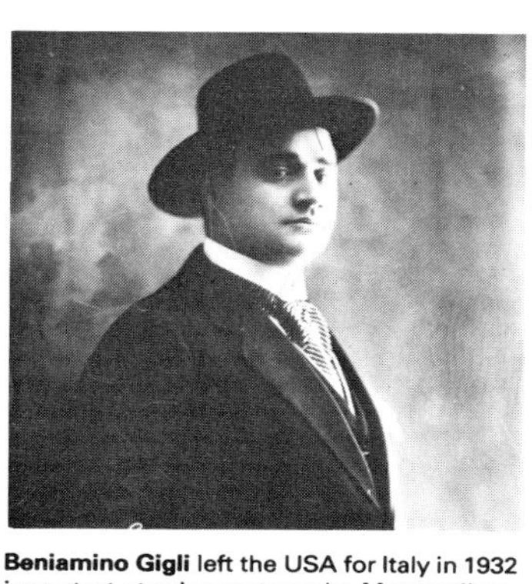

Beniamino Gigli left the USA for Italy in 1932 in protest at salary cuts at the Metropolitan.

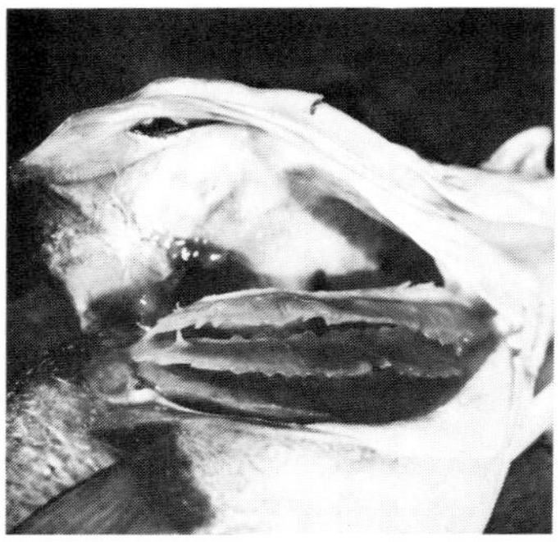

Gills are sometimes used to generate currents which draw food towards the fish.

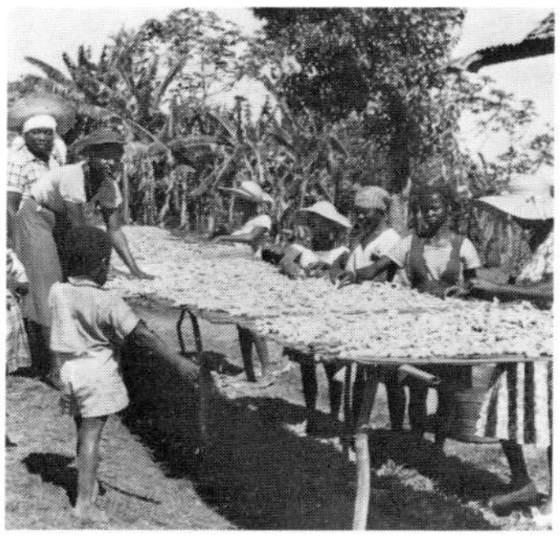

Ginger being laid out to dry in Jamaica, where it is a major commercial crop.

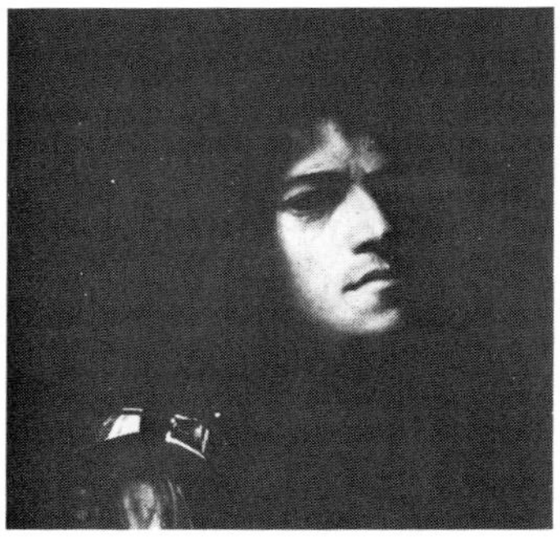

Giorgione shows in this self-portrait the emotional moodiness typical of his paintings.

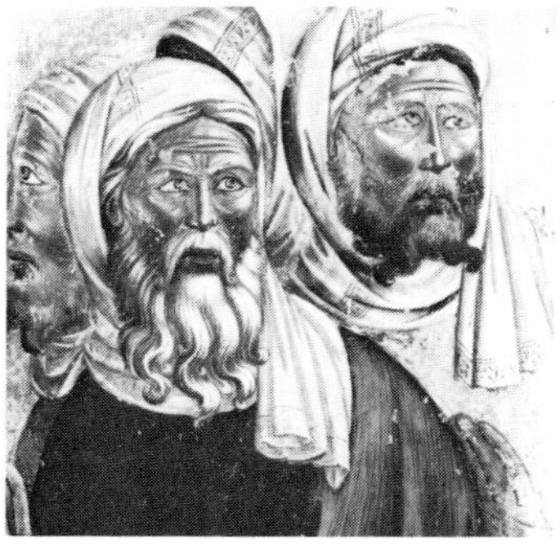

Giotto; detail from the *Story of St Francis*, whose authenticity has caused controversy.

coined the terms magnetic pole, electric attraction and electric force. *See also* SU p.*116*.

Gilbert, Sir William Schwenck (1836–1911), English librettist and playwright. He collaborated with Sir Arthur SULLIVAN on an immensely successful series of 14 comic light operas frequently performed by the D'Oyly CARTE company. Their works include *HMS Pinafore* (1878), *The Pirates of Penzance* (1879) and *The Mikado* (1855). Gilbert's lyrics reveal an exuberant wit and an often macabre humour.

Gilbert and Ellice Islands, British coral island group in the W Pacific Ocean, 4,000km (2,484 miles) NE of Australia. Most are low-lying atolls producing copra and mother-of-pearl for export. The capital is Tarawa. Area: 733sq km (283sq miles). Pop. (1975 est.) 66,000. *See* MW p.88.

Gilbert of Sempringham, Saint (*c.* 1083–1189), English priest who founded the Gilbertines, the only Roman Catholic monastic order of exclusively English origin. He was born in Lincolnshire, the son of a Norman knight. He started the order as a convent for girls, but it grew to have double monasteries, with houses for monks and nuns. Feast: 4 February.

Gilchrist, Percy Carlyle (1852–1935), British chemist who developed, with his cousin Sidney Gilchrist THOMAS, a process for smelting iron ore rich in phosphorous in a BESSEMER converter. The process was patented and extended to the open-hearth furnace.

Gildas (fl. 6th century), British monk and chronicler. In the 540s he wrote *De excidio et conquestu Britanniae* (*The Overthrow and Conquest of Britain*), an account of the Anglo-Saxon invasions, bemoaning the state of the country until the British victory at Mount Badon. It is the earliest surviving record of the invasions, and of the ruler who can be identified as King Arthur. *See also* HC1 pp.20, 138.

Gilding, process by which a thin layer of gold is used to cover another surface. Silver is the metal most commonly gilded, but base metals are also used extensively. The original method of gilding was by a chemical process, but in the 19th century ELECTROPLATING, a cheaper if less effective method, was introduced.

Gilds. *See* GUILDS.

Gilead, mountainous region in Jordan, E of the River Jordan, between the Dead Sea and the Sea of Galilee. Traditionally the place of reconciliation between JACOB and LABAN, it was also the birthplace of the prophet ELIJAH and the spot where jephthah was made Judge over Israel.

Gilgamesh, hero of the great Assyro-Babylonian myth, the EPIC OF GILGAMESH, a story similar in theme and construction to the Greek story of Orpheus. Gilgamesh, king of the city of Uruk (biblical Erech), was a hero of divine birth who went, sorrowing for his dead friend ENKIDU, in search of the secret of immortality. After overcoming monsters and gods and difficult journeys he accomplished his goal and found the flower of life, only to have immortality denied him by a serpent that snatched the magic plant from him.

Gill, (Arthur) Eric (Rowton) (1882–1940), British engraver and sculptor. He designed many typefaces, including Gill sans serif (1927). He is best known for his carved sculptures, including the *Stations of the Cross* (1914–18), in Westminster Cathedral, and *Prospero and Ariel* (Broadcasting House, London, 1931).

Gillen, Francis James (1856–1912), Australian anthropologist. He did pioneering research on Australian Aborigines and worked for many years with the Aranda people. With Sir Walter Baldwin SPENCER he wrote *The Native Tribes of Central Australia* (1899) and *The Northern Tribes of Central Australia* (1904).

Gillespie, John Birks "Dizzy" (1917–), US jazz trumpeter and bandleader. With Charlie (Bird) PARKER he founded the BEBOP style in the 1940s. After 1950 he led his own groups and made many recordings with other jazz performers. Arrangements he made for his big bands of the 1940s greatly influenced other jazz musicians. *See also* HC2 p.272.

Gillette Cup, annual knockout cricket competition for the 17 first-class English counties and the top five Minor Counties. A team has one innings limited to 60 overs, bowlers being restricted to 12 overs each. The final is held in September at Lord's. It began in 1963; since then Gillette Cup competitions have also been instituted in the West Indies, South Africa, Australia and New Zealand.

Gillette, King Camp (1885–1932), US inventor and manufacturer of the first safety razor. Patented in Dec. 1901, his concept of a thin, double-edged blade was not an instant success, but by the end of 1904 he had produced 90,000 razors and almost 12.5 million steel blades.

Gillingham, county district in N central KENT, England; created in 1974 under the Local Government Act (1972). Area: 34sq km (13sq miles). Pop. (1974 est.) 93,000.

Gillray, James (1757–1815), English caricaturist. His work was wider in scope in its political and social satire than that of HOGARTH; the vital, witty and vitriolic cartoons were famous throughout Europe at a time when England's prestige was pre-eminent. He displayed a certain artistic naïveté and rivalled Fuseli in his rich and fanciful imagination. Among his caricatures are those of "Farmer George" (George III) and *Temperance Enjoying a Frugal Meal*.

Gills, breathing organs through which most fish and some larval amphibians obtain oxygen from water. When a fish breathes it opens its mouth, draws in water and shuts its mouth again. Water is forced through the gill slits, over the gills and out into the surrounding water. Oxygen is absorbed into small capillary blood vessels, and carried to larger blood vessels. At the same time, waste products carried by the blood are released and diffused through the gills. *See also* NW p.*126*.

Gilman, Harold (1876–1919), British painter. He was a leading British post-Impressionist, and was a member of the CAMDEN TOWN GROUP and first president of the LONDON GROUP (1913). His best works are his vividly coloured landscapes, interiors with figures and portraits.

Gilmore, Dame Mary (1865–1962), Australian poet. Her best poetry, such as *The Myall in Prison* and *Old Botany Bay*, gives humanist expression to her sympathy with the Aborigines and Australia's convict pioneers.

Gilpin, Sawrey (1733–1807), British painter and draughtsman. He specialized in sporting scenes and horses, sometimes assisting other artists, such as TURNER, by painting animals in their pictures. He was the younger brother of Rev. William Gilpin (1724–1804), writer on the PICTURESQUE.

Gilroy, Cardinal Sir Norman Thomas (1896–1977), first Australian-born Cardinal of the Roman Catholic church. Ordained in 1923, he became a Bishop in 1934, Archbishop of Sydney in 1940, and Cardinal in 1946.

Gin, distilled alcohol containing flavouring substances from the berry of the JUNIPER tree, *Juniperus communis*. English and American gins are alcohol distilled from fermented grain, diluted to the required strength – between 80° and 94° proof spirit – and flavoured with juniper and small amounts of orris, cassia, lemon and other aromatic substances. Dutch gin is distilled from barley malt and has a lower alcoholic content. *See also* PE p.207.

Ginger, herbaceous, perennial plant native to tropical E Asia and Indonesia and grown commercially in Jamaica and elsewhere. It has fat; tuberous roots and yellow-green flowers with purple edges spotted with yellow. The kitchen spice is made from the tubers of *Zingiber officinale*. Family Zingiberaceae. *See also* NW p.*67*; PE p.211, *211*.

Ginger ale and beer, beverages having little or no alcoholic content, flavoured principally with the rhizome (underground stem) of the ginger plant, *Zingiber officinale*; they are saturated with carbon dioxide gas, which makes them effervescent. Pale, dry ginger ales contain more added acid and capsicum than the darker, more golden brands. Both types are clear liquids, whereas ginger beer is cloudier because of its higher solids content; it is also a sweeter drink. Its effervescence is due to the incomplete fermentation of yeast which generates carbonic acid.

Gingivitis, inflammatory disease of the gums that makes them tender and swollen and causes them to bleed easily. In severe cases ulceration and even anaemia may develop. General infections, bad tooth alignment and faulty dentures may all cause gingivitis; it may also be a symptom of vitamin C deficiency or an allergy.

Gingold, Hermione Ferdinanda (1897–), British actress who made her name as a comedienne in revues of the 1930s and 1940s and made frequent appearances in the theatre, cinema and on television, especially in the USA. In 1973 she created the role of Madame Armfeldt in the New York production of *A Little Night Music* and repeated it in London.

Ginkgo, also called maidenhair tree, oldest living species of tree, native to temperate regions of China, but occurring only rarely in the wild. It dates from the late Permian period. It has delicate fan shaped leaves, small, foul-smelling fruits and edible, nut-like seeds. Each tree bears either male or female flowers. Height: to 30m (100ft). Family Ginkgoceae; species *Ginkoo biloba*. *See also* NW pp.*55*, *187*, 208.

Ginkel, Godard van Reede-Ginkel (1644–1703), distinguished Dutch soldier who went to England with William of Orange in 1688. As commander-in-chief of Ireland in 1691 he subdued Athlone and Galway, and decisively beat the Irish army at Aughrim. For his services he was created 1st Earl of Athlone in 1692.

Gin rummy, card game for two players, who are dealt ten cards from a 52-card pack, the top card of the deck remaining being turned face up. The object is to form matched sets (melds) of three or more cards either of the same number or of consecutive cards of the same suit, so that the value of the upturned card, or to play until one player lays down all ten cards in matched sets (a gin). Either merits the player the value of his opponent's unmatched cards (ace 1, court cards 10). The first to score 150 or more wins.

Ginsberg, Allen (1926–), US poet, major writer of the BEAT GENERATION. His work is influenced by his interest in ZEN BUDDHISM, meditation and the use of drugs. His most famous poems are *Howl* (1956), a condemnation of American society, and *Kaddish for Naomi Ginsberg (1894–1956)* (1961), a lament for his mother, who became insane.

Ginseng, either of two perennial plants found in the USA (*Panax quinquefolius*) and E Asia (*P. schinseng*). It has yellow-green flowers and compound leaves. The dried tuberous roots are used in Chinese traditional medicine. Height: to 51cm (20in). Family Araliaceae.

Gioconda, La. *See* MONA LISA.

Gioconda, La (1876), opera in four acts by Amilcare PONCHIELLI, with libretto by Arrigo Boïto, based on a play by Victor HUGO. It was first performed at La Scala, Milan.

Giorgione, Il (*c.* 1475–1510), Italian painter. He was a pupil of BELLINI, and became one of the major painters of the Venetian High Renaissance. He evolved his own mysterious romantic style, creating a unity of figures and landscape. His *Tempest* (*c.* 1505) is the first painting of the Renaissance in which atmosphere is important. Only a few of the works attributed to him are really his, and many paintings that undoubtedly he began were finished by others, eg TITIAN. *See also* HC1 p.*258*.

Giotto di Bordonne (*c.* 1266–1337), Italian painter and architect. He had profound influence on the development of Western art, and created visually and psychologically convincing human forms and arranged his realistic figures in dramatic relation to each other and to their setting. Probably his best work is the fresco cycle

Lives of the Virgin and Christ (1305–08) in the Arena Chapel at Padua. In these scenes, Giotto broke away from medieval formulas of figure painting: the concern is more for portraying moral fibre than divine splendour. The NATURALISM of the Italian Renaissance owes much to his work. *See also* HC1 pp.*217, 247.*

Giovanni di Paolo (1403–83), Italian painter; one of the most influential and prolific Siennese painters of the 15th century. His ecstatic, often wistful figures have a languid grace which can be seen in the monumental altarpiece *Presentation of Christ in the Temple* (1447–49). In his later work the forms are heavier and distorted and the colours darker.

Giraffe, even-toed, hoofed, ruminant mammal that lives in the savannas of Africa; it is the tallest living mammal. It has a long neck that contains only seven vertebrae (as do the necks of most other mammals) and bears a short tufted mane. On the heads of both sexes are two to four skin-covered horns and sometimes a fifth protuberance between the eyes. The legs are long, slender and bony; in order to drink, the animal must bend or splay its forelegs. Its coat is pale brown and almost covered by characteristic red-brown blotches. Height: to 5.5m (18ft). Family Giraffidae; species *Giraffa camelopardalis. See also* NW pp. 162–163, *200–201.*

Giraldus Cambrensis (*c.*1146–1223), Welsh ecclesiastic and historian, also known as Gerald de Barri. From 1184 to 1195 he was in the service of HENRY II, despite his opposition to the Anglo-Norman control of the Welsh Church. In 1176 and again in 1199 he was nominated for, but never elected to, the bishopric of St David's, which he wished to make independent of Canterbury. His writings include *Expugnatio Hibernica* (*Conquest of Ireland, c.*1189) and *Cambriae descriptio* (*Description of Wales,* 1194).

Girard, Philippe Henri de (1775–1845), French inventor and industrialist. In 1832 he invented a machine for spinning linen thread from flax which was capable of separating long and short fibres. The machine was subsequently improved in England.

Girardon, François (1628–1715), French sculptor in a severely Classical style who worked at Versailles Palace for Louis XIV. His most celebrated works there are *Apollo tended by the Nymphs* (1666) and *Rape of Persephone* (1694–99).

Giraudoux, Jean (1882–1944), French novelist and dramatist who wrote a series of slight novels about adolescence. Louis Jouvet, the French director and actor, recognized the dramatic possibilities of the works. The first international successes were *Amphitryon '38* (1929; trans. and adapted by S. N. Behrman, (1938) and *La Guerra de Troie n'aura pas lieu* (1935, trans. as *Tiger at the Gates* by Christopher FRY, 1955).

Girder, in engineering, a main load-supporting beam. Steel or iron girders may be made of a single piece or of laminated strips built up of plates, latticework or bars. When the cross-section is formed in the shape of an I by riveting and welding plates or by rolling the girder, greater stiffness is achieved and larger spans are possible. Girders may also be made of reinforced or pre-stressed concrete.

Girl Guides, organization for girls founded in England in 1910 by Agnes Baden-Powell, sister of Lord BADEN-POWELL, founder of the BOY SCOUTS. There are about 871,000 guides in Britain, divided into three groups, according to age. Girls between 7 and 11 are eligible to become Brownie Guides; those between 10 and 16 are known as Guides; and girls between 14 and 20 are called Ranger Guides. Girl Guides subscribe to a three-fold promise of loyalty and service to God, their monarch and the Guide Law. They share their motto with the scouts: "Be Prepared". Work and play is organized under a system of patrols of some 6 to 8 girls, each under a leader.

Giro, system of receiving and paying accounts through an account with the Post Office. The practice began in 1883 in Austria, spread throughout W Europe, and to Japan, and reached Britain in 1968. The name derives from the Greek *gyros* meaning ring, since the money recycles.

Girondins, political group of the French Revolution named after legislators from Gironde. Although never an organized party, the name is associated with attempts to prevent the execution of Louis XVI, to reduce the power of Paris over the provinces and an inability to accept the consequences of a revolutionary war. After bitter personal disputes with the JACOBINS they were arrested and their leaders executed in June 1793.

Girtin, Thomas Joseph (1775–1802), British watercolour artist. His evocative use of broad washes of strong colour, offset by darker areas, ushered in the ROMANTIC revolution in watercolour landscape art developed by TURNER and CONSTABLE. *See also* HC2 p.*102.*

Gisborne, town in the North Island of New Zealand, the chief town of East Coast. It is a port for the export of dairy products and wool. Population: (1975) 32,400.

Giscard d'Estaing, Valéry. *See* ESTAING, VALÉRY GISCARD D'.

Giselle, Romantic ballet by Vernoy de Saint Georges, Théo GAUTIER and Jean Coralli with music by Adolphe ADAM. The first production was in Paris in 1841 with Carlotta GRISI in the title role. Famous interpreters of the main role include Alicia MARKOVA, Nora Kaye and Margot FONTEYN. *See also* HC2 p.274.

Gish, Dorothy (1898–1968), US stage and screen star who began as a child actress and reached the height of her popularity in silent films. She appeared with her sister, Lillian, in many films, including *Hearts of the World* (1918), *Orphans of the Storm* (1921) and *Romola* (1925).

Gish, Lillian (1896–), US stage and film actress. She portrayed delicate heroines in such silent films of D. W. GRIFFITH as *The Birth of a Nation* (1915). With MGM in the 1920s, she made films such as *The Scarlet Letter* (1926). Her sound films include *The Night of the Hunter* (1955). She has often appeared on the stage.

Giulini, Carlo Maria (1914–), Italian conductor. He was music director of Radio Italiana from 1946 to 1951. His first major appointment was principal conductor of La Scala, Milan (1951–56). From 1956 he conducted the New Philharmonia Orchestra regularly and also officiated at many operas at COVENT GARDEN.

Giulio Romano (1492–1546), Italian painter and architect. One of the founders of MANNERISM, he was Raphael's chief assistant in his youth. His later work, influenced by Michelangelo, has an exaggerated dramatic quality. He designed pornography and had to flee from Rome for Mantua, where in 1526 he began his famous *Pallazo del Te.*

Giza (Al-Jīzah), city in N Egypt; capital of Al-Jīzah governorate. The Great SPHINX and the pyramid of Khufu (Cheops) are near the city. The University of Cairo (1924) and Egypt's film industry are to be found in Giza. A suburb of Cairo, it is a resort and agricultural centre with cotton textiles, footwear and cigarette manufacturing industries. Pop. (1974) 853,700. *See also* HC1 p.*328,* 329A.

Gjellerup, K. A. (1857–1919), Danish poet and novelist. His first novel, *An Idealist* (1878), was written when he turned to atheism. *Minna* (1889) and *The Pilgrim Kamanita* (1906) represent his interest in Buddhism. Other works include *The Mill* (1896) and a collection of poetry, *Rødtjørn* (1881). He shared with Henrik PONTOPPIDAN the Nobel Prize for literature in 1917.

Glacial groove, deep, wide, usually straight furrow cut in the bedrock. It is caused by the abrasive action of large rock fragments dragged along the base of a moving glacier. The grooves are larger and deeper than glacial striations, ranging in size from a deep scratch to a glacial valley. *See also* PE pp.116–117.

Glacial polish, polish on bedrock resulting from abrasion by rock flour held in the bottom of the overriding ice. *See also* PE pp.116–117.

Glaciation, climatological and geological process in which ice sheets and glaciers advance and retreat with fluctuations in atmospheric temperature, causing topographical changes and great alterations in animal and plant populations. Glacial features of landscape include scooped-out valleys, re-directed rivers, the formation of lakes and the alteration of shorelines. *See also* PE pp.116–119.

Glacier, large mass of ice, consisting mainly of recrystallized snow, which moves slowly by CREEP downslope or outward in all directions due to the stress of its own weight. At its source there is a constant supply of snow and the glacier is broad and deep, although the flow is greatest in the centre as it is retarded by friction at the base and sides. The flow terminates where the rate of loss of ice by ABLATION is equal to the forward advance of the glacier. There are three main types: mountain or valley glaciers, piedmont glaciers and ice sheets and ice caps. *See also* PE pp.116–117, 118–119.

Glaciology, study of ice. No longer restricted to the study of glaciers, this science deals with ice and the action of ice in all its natural forms. Glaciology, therefore, draws upon the knowledge of many other related subjects, notably physics, chemistry, geology and meteorology. *See also* PE pp.116–117, 118–119.

Gladesville Bridge, bridge over the Parramatta River in Sydney, Australia. When completed in 1964 it was the world's longest reinforced concrete arch. It carries an eight-lane roadway and spans 305m (1,000ft). *See also* MM p.*192.*

Gladiators, armed men who fought, usually to the death, for public entertainment. Perhaps originally an Etruscan custom, gladiatorial combats were first recorded in Rome in 264 BC, although they may have begun as an extension of the displays of swordsmanship that were part of the funeral rites given as military honours to heroes killed on the battlefield. Later gladiators were commonly prisoners of war, slaves or condemned convicts, trained to fight one another or wild beasts in the public arenas. The gladiator who lost a battle, unless already dead, could have his life spared by a show of popular approval. Although abolished by Constantine I in AD 325, gladiatorial combats persisted into the 5th century. *See also* HC1 p.95.

Gladiolus, genus of 250 species of flowering plants native to Europe and Africa but cultivated widely. A CORM is planted in early spring to produce a flowering spike of funnel-shaped flowers and tall, lance-shaped leaves. Cultivated hybrid species may be almost any colour. Height: to 0.91m (3ft). Family Iridaceae.

Gladstone, William Ewart (1809–98), British politician. He entered Parliament as a Tory in 1832 and served as president of the Board of Trade in Sir Robert Peel's cabinet (1843–45). He then held several cabinet posts including chancellor of the Exchequer. He joined the Liberal Party in 1859, became its leader in 1867, and was prime minister four times (1868–74, 1880–85, 1886, 1892–94). A social reformer and Christian moralist, his achievements included DISESTABLISHMENT of the Church of Ireland (1869), the Irish Land Act (1870), the Elementary Education Act (1870), introduction of the secret ballot, the reorganization of the judiciary and a third REFORM ACT (1884). His attempts to establish IRISH HOME RULE led to his government's defeat in 1886 and 1894 and shattered the Liberal Party. *See also* HC2 pp.113, *163,* 182–183.

Glâma, river in SE Norway; rises in the highlands of Sør-Trøndelag county and flows S into the Skagerrak at Fredrikstad; its chief tributary is the River Vorma. The longest river in Norway, it has several hydroelectric stations and a timber-floating industry along its course. Length: 612km (380 miles).

Glamorganshire (Morganwg), former county in S Wales and site of the ancient Roman city of Caerlon-upon-Usk. Since 1974 Glamorganshire been divided into West, Mid and South Glamorgan and Gwent. The mountains in the

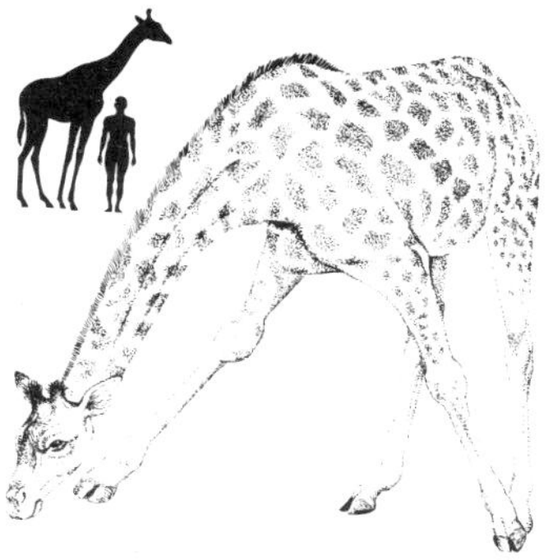

Giraffe, the gentle, almost totally silent animal, produces one fawn at a birth.

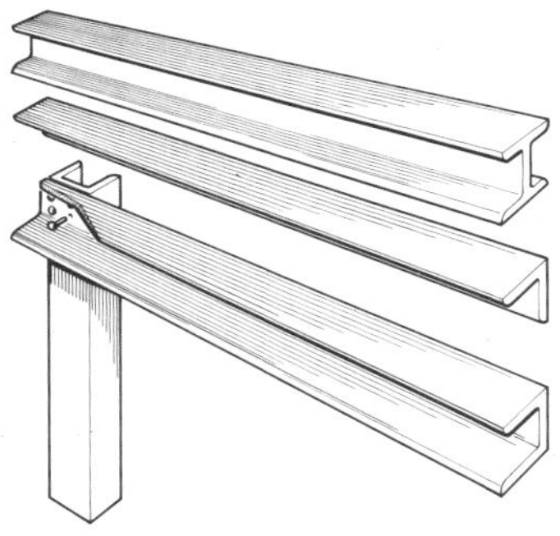

Girders are the main load-bearing beams designed to sustain great lateral stress.

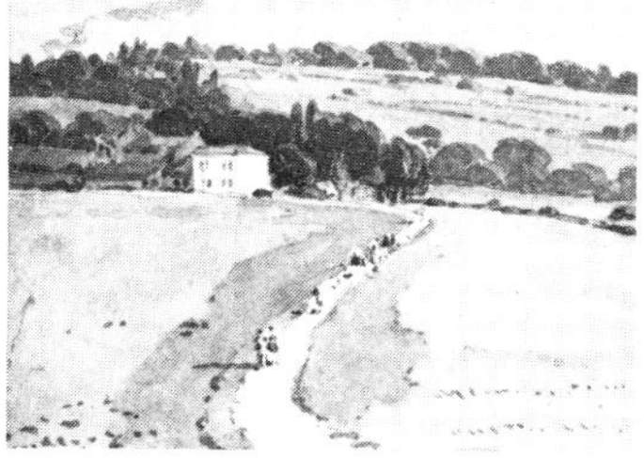

Thomas Girtin; detail from his watercolour of *Copenhagen House,* Islington, London.

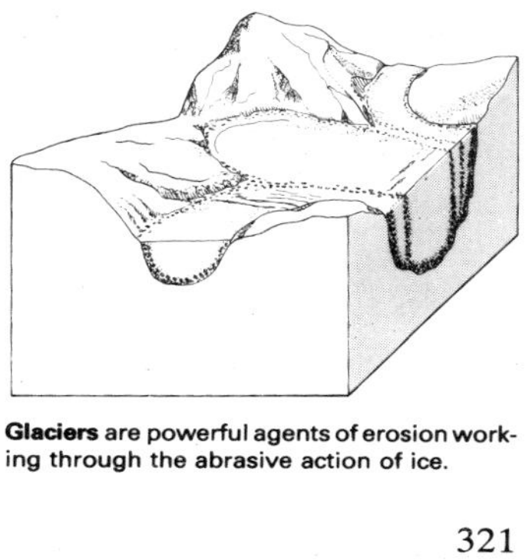

Glaciers are powerful agents of erosion working through the abrasive action of ice.

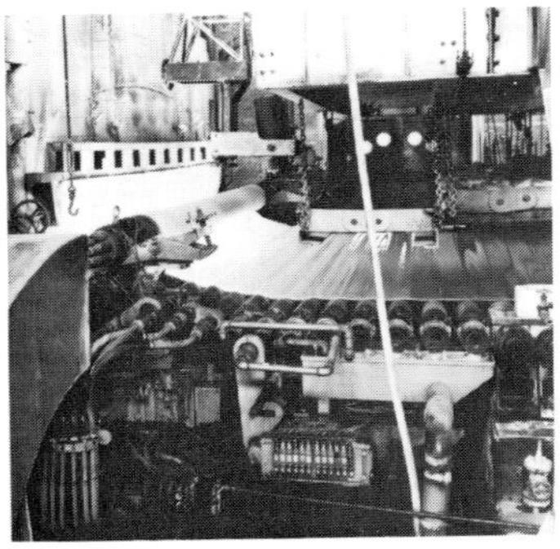

Glass is rolled out in a continuous process from the molten state to polished plate.

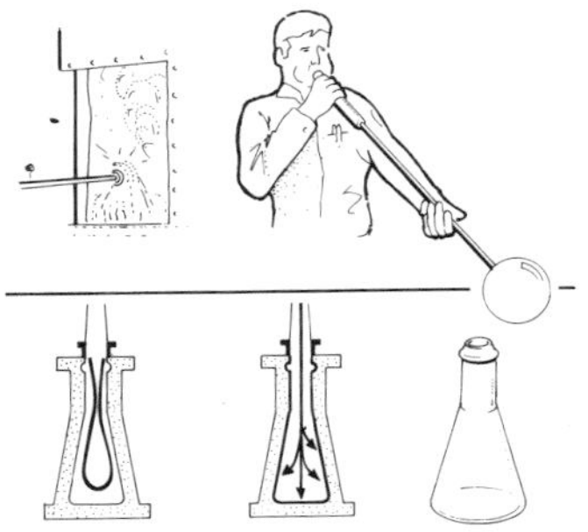

Glass blowing techniques have changed little from those of the early Syrian craftsmen.

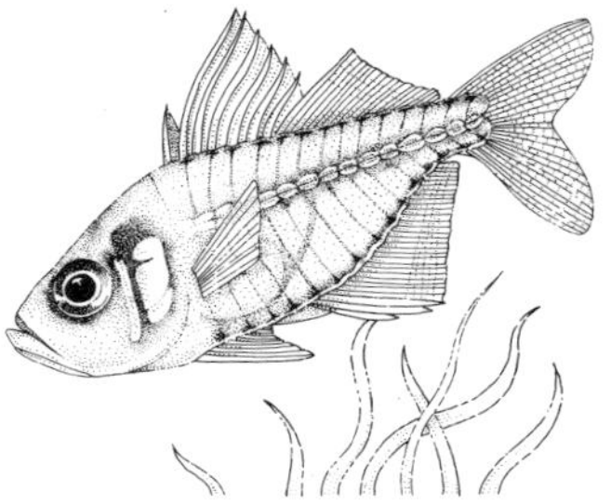

Glass fish, the transparent-bodied aquarium fish known sometimes as glass perch.

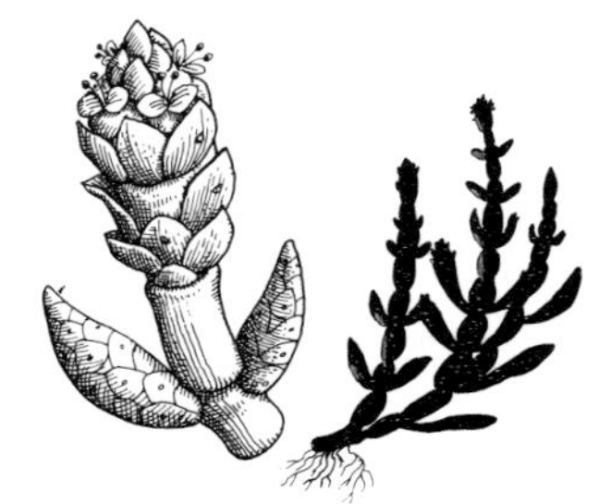

Glasswort is a plant whose ashes contain a chemical that was once used in glass making.

N have rich coal deposits. The fertile coastal plain has wheat and dairy farming, and on the Gower Peninsula in the SW, fruit and vegetables are grown. The region is drained by the Taff, Neath and Tawe rivers. A major industrial region of the British Isles, its chief industries are coal mining, iron and steel and tinplate. The main urban areas are Cardiff, the administrative centre, Swansea, Merthyr Tydfil and Rhondda. Area: 2,119sq km (818sq miles). Pop. (1971) 1,202,591.

Gland, in anatomy, organ or tissue whose cells manufacture and secrete special substances. Many plants bear glands on their leaves, which secrete excess sugars, ENZYMES or sticky liquids for trapping insects. The glands of animals are of two basic types. EXOCRINE GLANDS make such substances as hydrochloric acid, mucus, sweat, sebaceous oil and enzymes, and secrete these usually through ducts to the sites of metabolic function. ENDOCRINE GLANDS contain cells that secrete HORMONES directly into the bloodstream. *See also* MS pp.64, 100.

Glanders, or farcy, contagious disease of horses, donkeys and mules. The organism *Malleomyces mallei* enters the digestive tract, permeates the blood and the lungs and skin, resulting in nasal emissions, hardening of certain lymph glands and ulcers. Diseased animals are usually slaughtered. Infection in man can occur from exposure to the broken skin of infected animals.

Glandular fever, acute ailment usually of young people, the symptoms of which are fever, enlargement of the glands of the neck, and occasionally a rash. It is caused by a virus and is also known as infectious mononucleosis from the increase in numbers of white blood cells, particularly LYMPHOCYTES. *See also* MS p.100.

Glanvill, Ranulf de (*d.*1190), English lawyer. He was chief justiciar of England 1180–89, and wrote a *Treatise on the laws and customs of the kingdom of England*, an early compilation of COMMON LAW. He died on the Third CRUSADE.

Glanville-Hicks, Peggy (1912–), Australian composer who studied under VAUGHAN WILLIAMS, Nadia BOULANGER and Egon WELLESZ. She has written principally orchestral music, including stage works, film scores and a flute concerto. She has lived in the USA and Greece for many years.

Glaser, Donald Arthur (1926–), US physicist who in 1953 invented the BUBBLE CHAMBER and, with it, devised a new method for studying ELEMENTARY PARTICLES; for this work he was awarded the 1960 Nobel Prize in physics. The idea of the bubble chamber is reputed to have occurred to him while he contemplated a glass of beer. In 1964 Glaser became professor of physics at the university of California. *See also* SU p.*87*.

Glasgow, Ellen (1874–1945), US novelist. Her writing dwells on regional values, giving the South what she termed "blood and irony" in such novels as *The Descendant* (1897), *Barren Ground* (1925), *The Romantic Comedians* (1926) and *In This Our Life* (1941, Pulitzer prize winner).

Glasgow, city in Strathclyde Region, SW central Scotland; largest city in Scotland. Located on both banks of the River Clyde 68km (42 miles) W of Edinburgh, it is a major port and industrial region. Founded in the 6th century, its commercial development came with the American tobacco trade in the 18th century and the cotton trade in the 19th century. Nearby coal fields and the Clyde estuary promoted the growth of heavy industry. It has a university (1451) and the Hunterian, a museum (1807). Industries: shipbuilding, heavy engineering, flour milling, brewing, textiles, tobacco, chemicals, printing. Pop (1974) 816,265. *See also* HC2 pp.28–29, 164, 284–285.

Glasgow Citizens' Theatre, theatre in Glasgow. Opened in 1943 with a performance of *The Holy Isle* by James BRIDIE, who helped to found the theatre, it was so successful that it moved in 1945 to larger premises in the Royal Princess Theatre, in the Gorbals, a working-class district of Glasgow. One of the leading Scottish repertory companies, it pursues a policy of making theatre available to everybody with excellent productions and cheap seats.

Glasgow Orpheus Choir, Scottish choral society. It was formed in 1901 by its conductor, Sir Hugh Roberton, and was disbanded on his retirement in 1951. The choir made a speciality of singing folk songs arranged in Victorian harmonies, many of the arrangements by the conductor.

Glass, brittle and usually transparent material made by melting together silica and smaller proportions of an alkali with a base, such as lime or lead oxide. Glass melts slowly, can be worked only while hot and pliable, and must be cooled gradually to prevent strains or breakage. Fused silica is the simplest glass and is preferable when stability against changing temperatures is needed. Soda-lime glass is used in the manufacture of bottles and drinking vessels. Flint glass, which is heavy and refracts light well, is used in lenses and prisms. Glass appears to have been invented in the Eastern Mediterranean, probably Egypt, where glass objects, especially jewellery and small containers, were made *c.*2500 BC. Glass figurines and vessels were common in the Middle East and in Greece during the 8th and 7th centuries BC. The discovery of the process of glass-blowing probably in the 1st century BC in Syria revolutionized the glass-making industry by allowing glassware to be mass-produced in a variety of thicknesses and sizes. From the 12th to the 14th centuries Syria and Egypt had a highly developed industry producing enamel Islamic mosque lamps. During the 13th century Murano, in Venice, rose to prominence as a major centre in the making of thin, coloured glass. It was the Venetians who discovered the art of making clear crystal glass in the 16th century and immediately raised the status of glass vessels. In the late 17th century heavy, lead glass was developed in England. The process of making pressed (or moulded) glass – the greatest technical development in glass since the invention of blowing – was introduced (1826) in the USA and soon adopted elsewhere. During the 19th century E. Gallé in France and L.C. Tiffany in the USA developed cased glass and other techniques for the production of electric-light fittings and attachments in the ART NOUVEAU style. In the 20th century Scandinavia has been a leader in industrial and decorative glass design. *See also* MM pp.44–45.

Glass blowing, art of shaping molten glass by inflating it through a hollow tube or blowpipe. Glass blowing was invented by Syrian craftsmen probably in the 1st century BC. Molten glass is picked up on the end of the blowpipe, inflated to a bubble and then formed by blowing, swinging and rolling on a smooth stone or iron surface. Additions are attached by welding. The glass is reheated to maintain optimum viscosity. Intricate shapes such as glassware for chemistry laboratories, illuminated signs and works of art are blown by skilled glassblowers. Manufacture of large numbers of like pieces such as milk bottles is achieved by blowing glass into rotating moulds. *See also* MM pp.44–45.

Glass fibre, glass in the form of filaments, used widely for heat insulation (as glass wool) and with a plastic resin to make a composite material (fibreglass) for materials and repair kits. Glass fibre for these applications has short filaments made by blasting air or steam into molten glass. Continuous glass fibre of closely controlled quality, for such applications as FIBRE OPTICS, is made by spinning molten glass through fine metal nozzles or spinnerets. *See also* MM p.*57*.

Glass fish, any of several species of deep-bodied freshwater fish of the family Ambassidae, found in shallow waters of N India. A favourite aquarium fish, it has an almost transparent body. Length: to 5cm (2in). Genera, *Centropomus, Chanda.*

Glass Menagerie, The (1945), "memory" play in 7 scenes by Tennessee WILLIAMS. Chiefly concerned with failure and loneliness, and the most lyrical of all the author's works, the play dramatizes the hopes and illusions of Amanda Wingfield and her lame daughter Laura. Many devices, including music and pantomime, heighten the emotion of the play, which is narrated by Tom Wingfield, a figure many identify with Williams himself.

Glass snake, or glass lizard, legless LIZARD found in North America, Eurasia and Africa. The cylindrical body has a groove along each side and is mostly brown or green, although some species are striped. Length: 60–120cm (24–48in). Family Anguidae; genus *Ophisaurus.*

Glasswort, fleshy plant found in salt marshes throughout temperate regions of the Northern Hemisphere. It has succulent stems and inconspicuous leaves and flowers. Family Chenopodiaceae; genera *Salicornia* and *Salsola.*

Glastonbury, ancient and historic market town in Somerset, SW England, 35km (22 miles) SW of Bath. According to legend, it was the site of the first Christian church in England founded by Joseph of Arimathea. Industries: tanning, dairying. Pop. 6,600.

Glastonbury legends, many legends surrounding the ancient town of Glastonbury, England, its ruined abbey and tor. According to tradition the abbey church was built by missionaries from Rome in AD 166. In 1191 the supposed grave of KING ARTHUR and GUINEVERE was found and their remains reinterred at the abbey. It is also believed that St JOSEPH OF ARIMATHEA visited Glastonbury bearing the Holy GRAIL, which was the object of quests by the knights of King Arthur.

Glauber, Johann Rudolf (1604–68), German chemist and physician. He made valuable contributions to chemistry, mainly concerning the preparation of salts. He prepared hydrochloric acid, sodium sulphate (known as Glauber's salt) and tartar emetic.

Glauber's salt, sodium sulphate decahydrate, $Na_2SO_4.10\ H_2O$, once prescribed by doctors as a purgative and diuretic. It has few uses today.

Glaucoma, eye disease characterized by increasing pressure of aqueous humour (the fluid within the eye) leading to progressive loss of vision. Its causes are unknown although heredity seems to be a factor. It occurs most frequently in persons over 40 and is accompanied by the need for frequent changes in corrective lenses, mild headache and occasionally nausea. Chronic glaucoma sets in gradually and can be arrested with drugs that permit greater outflow of aqueous humour. Acute glaucoma sets in suddenly and can lead to total permanent blindness if left untreated.

Glaze, in painting, a transparent coat of oil paint applied over other colours, thus modifying them and giving added richness to the painting. In CERAMICS, a glaze is a glass-like coating fired on to porcelain or earthenware to make it waterproof.

Glazunov, Alexander Constantinovich (1865–1936), Russian composer, in the romantic tradition of TCHAIKOVSKY. His works include eight symphonies, chamber music, two violin concertos and the ballets *Raymonda* (1897) and *The Seasons* (1898). *See also* HC2 p.106.

Glebe, land attached to a parish church for the maintenance of the incumbent. It is part of the endowment of the church and the freehold is in the parson. But under common law the parson may not alienate the land without the consent of the bishop and the patron of the living. By acts of 1842 and 1858 glebe land in Britain may be let on building leases for up to 99 years and on mining leases for up to 60 years.

Gleiwitz. *See* GLIWICE.

Gleizes, Albert (Léon) (1881–1953), French painter and writer. Through his writings, he was the chief disseminator of CUBIST ideas. In 1911 he exhibited with the first Cubist group. In 1912 he and Jean Metzinger published the influential *On Cubism.* By 1919 his paintings had become religious in tone, combining Roman Catholic themes with Cubist ideas. *See also* HC2 p.176.

Glencoe, massacre of (13 Feb. 1692), slaughter of 38 members of the MacDonald clan, including women and children, for the technical failure of their chief to declare allegiance to William III. The massacre was carried out by the Campbells at the instigation of the secretary of state for Scotland, John Dalrymple. Glencoe is situated in N Argyll, S Highland region, Scotland. *See also* HC1 p.*299*.

Glendower, Owen. *See* GLYN DŴR, OWAIN.

Glider, aircraft with no power source of its own, which sustains flight through the controlled loss of altitude. Gliders usually have long narrow wings to provide maximum lift with minimum drag from even weak air currents. They may be launched in a variety of ways: towed by a plane, car or winch; pulled by an elastic shock cord; or pulled by a ground crew, with a rope or cable attached to the front of the glider. GLIDING is a keenly competitive sport requiring skills that are additional to those needed by powered aircraft pilots.

Gliding, unpowered flying in which a GLIDER is launched by a sling or towed into flight by an aeroplane. Gliding depends on the same aerodynamic principles as does the flight of other fixed-wing aircraft, but it is closest to that of the soaring birds. The main difficulty in gliding is the gaining and maintenance of height. This is done in two ways: with thermals and with lift patterns. Thermals are regions of hot air that are rising in relation to the colder surrounding air. Once a glider enters a thermal the pilot may ascend in tight turning circles and heights of more than 10,000m (30,000ft) have been achieved. A lift pattern is formed when the wind blows at close to right-angles to a line of hills or a ridge, along which the glider may fly.

Glinka, Mikhail (1804–57), Russian composer, important as the first of the nationalist school in Russian opera and the first Russian composer to receive acclaim outside his own country. His two operas *A Life for the Tsar* (1836) and *Russlan and Ludmilla* (1841) inspired the composers who were called the "MIGHTY FIVE". *See also* HC2 p.107.

Glissando, rapid playing of a scale (or a slur from one note to another with no definite intervals) on a musical instrument to give a sliding effect (from the French *glisser* – to slide). It is used principally for the trombone, piano, harp and xylophone. On the piano it is played by turning the finger over and running the finger-nail over the keys.

Gliwice, city in SW Poland on the River Klodnitz 75km (47 miles) SW of Opole. The city is the centre of the Katowice region, which produces coal and iron, and its industries include the production of chemicals and machinery. Pop. (1974) 179,900.

Globe artichoke. *See* ARTICHOKE.

Globeflower, perennial flowering plant native to temperate parts of the Northern Hemisphere. The yellow sepals form large blossoms and buttercup-like leaves surround the stem. The European Globeflower (*Trollius europaeus*) has yellow or orange globular blooms. There are about 15 species. Family Ranunculaceae.

Globigerina, genus of one-celled marine PROTOZOA whose empty shells are an important component of ocean floor ooze. The shell is spiralled into a lumpy sphere with needle-like extensions. *See also* FORAMINIFERA.

Globular cluster, stellar CLUSTER that is symmetrical in shape and believed to contain hundreds of thousands of stars. Globular clusters are located near the galactic nucleus and composed largely of POPULATION II stars. *See also* SU pp.242–243.

Globulins, family of globular proteins that are soluble in dilute salt solutions, found in the blood serum. Some globulins serve as carriers of lipids, hormones and inorganic ions. The immunoglobulins are included in this general category. Globulins differ from ALBUMINS in that albumins are more soluble in ammonium sulphate solution. *See also* MS p.62.

Glockenspiel, percussion instrument with a bell-like sound. Its name comes from the German (*Glocken* = bells; *spielen* = to play). Its tuned metal bars are struck with a hammer, either freehand or from a miniature keyboard. The word is occasionally used for a chime of real bells or carillon.

Glorious First of June (1794), British naval victory over the French. The Channel Fleet under Admiral HOWE met the French fleet under Admiral Villaret de Joyeuse 690km (430 miles) W of Ushant on 28 May. After four days six French ships had been taken and one sunk. The rest of the fleet was allowed to retreat to Brest harbour.

Glorious Revolution (1688–89), the abdication of JAMES II of England, and his replacement with WILLIAM III and MARY II. After James had aroused the hostility of much of the political nation with his pro-Catholic policies, the birth of a male heir to the throne prompted seven leading statesmen to inite the Dutch William, Prince of Orange, to take the throne. He invaded England with an army in Nov. 1688, and James's army, led by John Churchill, later Duke of MARLBOROUGH, defected to William's side. James fled to France in Dec. 1688, and William and Mary were made joint rulers the following year. The principles of the revolution, which won its name from the fact that no blood had been shed in achieving it, were enshrined in the BILL OF RIGHTS and the DECLARATION OF RIGHTS (1689). These upheld the rule of law and the principle of toleration. The revolution was the central point of the movement towards the establishment of a constitutional monarchy. *See also* HC1 pp.293, 312.

Glossitis, inflammation of the tongue. There are various causes, including infection and anaemia.

Glossolalia, speaking in tongues, or making sounds, which are usually unintelligible, made by people in a state of religious ecstacy. Pentecostal sects cite the Bible (Acts 2) for authority and there are other references in the New Testament. *See also* PENTECOSTAL CHURCH.

Glottis, aperture less than 25mm (1in) long between the vocal cords at the lower end of the pharynx. It opens into the trachea, and its dimensions are changed by the vibration of the VOCAL CORDS.

Gloucester, county town of Gloucestershire, W England, on the River Severn, 151km (94 miles) WNW of London. Gloucester was the Roman city of Glevum and capital of Mercia in Saxon times. There is an 11th-century cathedral where Edward II is buried. Gloucester is a market town, and has agricultural machinery, aircraft components, railway equipment and fishing industries. Pop. (1971) 90,134.

Gloucestershire, county in SW England. To the E are the Cotswold Hills where dairy and arable farming is important. The fertile valley of the Severn River is also devoted to dairying. To the W is the Forest of Dean and the Wye valley where sheep are raised. Industries include aircraft, engineering and paper. The main towns are Gloucester, the county town, and Cheltenham. Area: 2,642sq km (1,020sq miles). Pop. 491,500.

Glove-box, chamber with a viewing window into which are let, and firmly sealed, rubber gloves. It is used in laboratories for handling toxic and other harmful materials, including radioactive chemicals and metals, and cultures and toxins of pathogenic microbes.

Glover, Denis (1912–), New Zealand poet. He founded the Caxton Press at Christchurch, and began publishing poetry in the 1930s. His volumes include *Cold Tongue, Arawata Bill, Sings Harry* and *Myself When Young.*

Glow-worm, small European BEETLE closely related to the FIREFLY. The male is winged and has tiny light-producing organs. The wingless female flashes her brightly luminous hindquarters to attract a mate. Adults do not eat, but die shortly after mating. Larvae feed on snails. Family Lampyridae, genus Lampynis.

Gloxinia, herbaceous plant with short stems, native to South America. The common gloxinia (*Sinningia speciosa*) has elongated, bell-shaped flowers ranging in colour from purple to violet, sometimes with red or white variations. Family Gesneriaceae.

Glubb, Sir John Bagot (1897–), British commander of Jordan's Arab Legion, known as Glubb Pasha. After WWI he helped the British to oversee Palestine and Trans-Jordan but from 1948 he led a Palestinian force against ISRAELI border raids. HUSSEIN I of Jordan dismissed him in 1956 because of anti-British feeling in the Middle East.

Glucagon, protein hormone secreted by cells in the ISLETS OF LANGERHANS. It helps regulate blood sugar blood glucose levels. *See also* INSULIN.

Glucinum. *See* BERYLLIUM.

Gluck, Christoph Willibald von (1714–87), German operatic composer who studied in Prague and Vienna. After composing his early operas in the Italian tradition, Gluck became dissatisfied with this mannered style and in his opera *Orfeo ed Euridice* (1762) unified musical, emotional and dramatic components into a more coherent whole. This change in operatic tradition influenced, amongst others, MOZART. Gluck's finest work is thought to be *Iphigénie en Tauride* (1779). *See also* HC1 pp.318–19.

Glucose, colourless crystalline sugar ($C_6H_{12}O_6$) that occurs in fruit and honey. It requires no digestion before being absorbed since it is a normal component of blood. Other carbohydrates in the bodies of animals are converted to glucose before being utilized as an energy source. It is prepared commercially by the hydrolysis of starch using hydrochloric acid and is used in confectionery, tanning and pharmaceuticals. *See also* SU pp.152, *152*, 154–155.

Glucoside, a carbohydrate-containing compound that yields a glucose and a non-sugar component (either an alcohol or phenol) when decomposed by the process of hydrolysis. The natural glucosides are important in plant metabolism, and many polysaccharides, such as cellulose, starch and glycogen, are regarded chemically as glucosides. They may be used as drugs, colouring agents and aromatics.

Glue, traditionally a cement made by boiling down animal skin, bones, horns and hooves. It consists of a jelly of hydrolysed collagen protein mixed with many other animal substances. It dries to form a hard, tough skin or film. There are many other types of glue, which range from simple mixtures of flour and water, through rubber adhesives to EPOXY RESINS.

Glutamic acid, colourless AMINO ACID, $COOH(CH_2)_2CH.NH_2.COOH$), commonly found in proteins. One of its functions is to increase the solubility of its associated proteins by providing them with one negative charge. It also helps in the removal of poisonous ammonia from the body. Its sodium salt (sodium glutamate) is used as a food flavouring. *See also* GLUTAMINE; SU p.*153*.

Glutamine, colourless soluble AMINO ACID, $(COOH)CH(NH_2)(CH_2)_2CONH_2$. It is formed when one of the acidic carboxyl groups of GLUTAMIC ACID couples with ammonia, a poison to the body, which is carried safely to the liver where it is converted to urea.

Gluten, protein substance present in wheat flour, grey in colour and elastic in texture. Gluten contributes the elasticity to dough. Being insoluble in water, it can be washed out of flour. It is then used to make gluten bread for diabetics, and as an additive to chocolate and coffee.

Glycerin, glycerine or glycerol (1, 2, 3 propanetriol), thick syrupy sweet liquid ($CH_2OH.CHOH.CH_2OH$) obtained by the saponification of fats and oils in the manufacture of soap or from propylene or acrolein. It is used in the manufacture of various products including plastics, explosives, cosmetics, foods, antifreeze and paper coating. Properties: s.g. 1.26; m.p. 18°C (64.4°F); b.p. 290°C (554°F). *See also* SU pp.152, *152*.

Glycine, colourless soluble crystalline AMINO ACID (NH_2CH_2COOH); the principal amino acid in sugarcane and the simplest, structurally, of the alpha-amino acids.

Glycogen, also known as animal starch, the carbohydrate stored in the body, principally by the liver and the muscles.

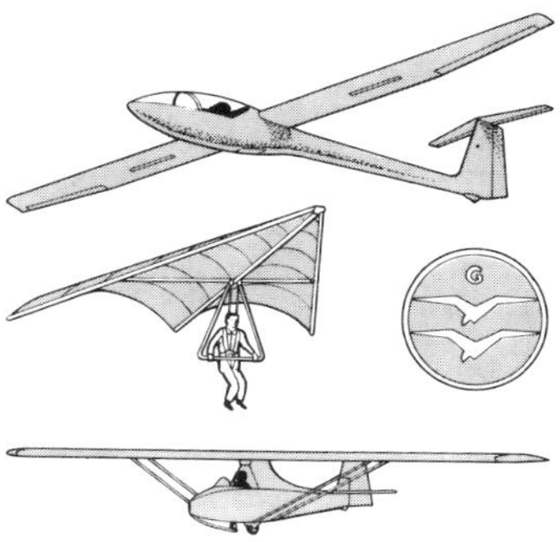

Gliders remain aloft by seeking out the rising currents of warm air known as thermals.

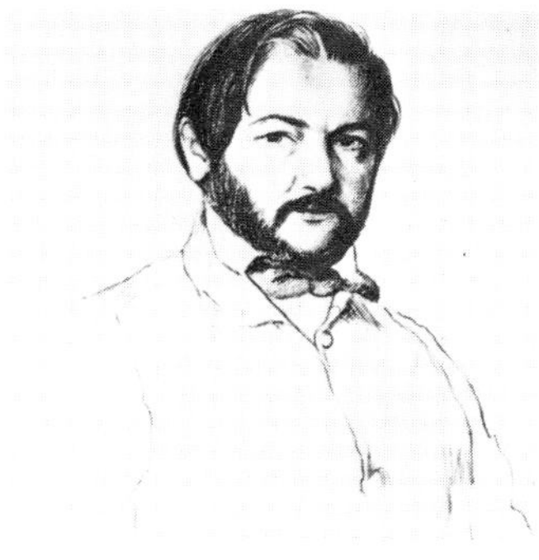

Glinka's great inspiration was the folk music he heard as a child in his native province.

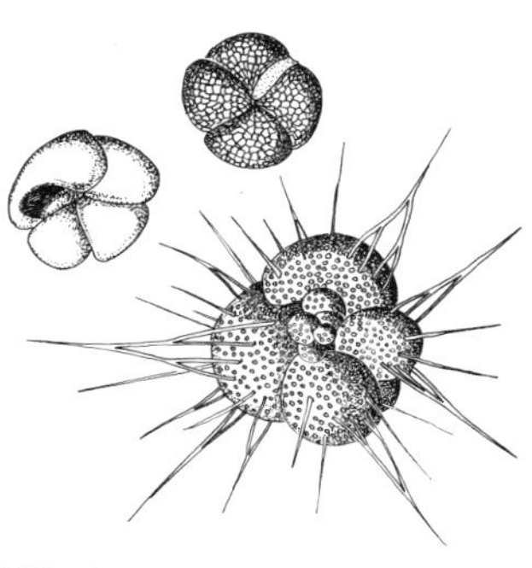

Globigerina are protozoa whose empty shells form part of the deep sea sediment.

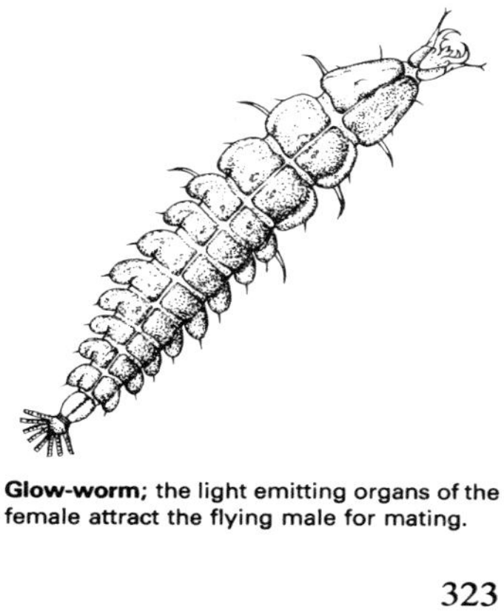

Glow-worm; the light emitting organs of the female attract the flying male for mating.

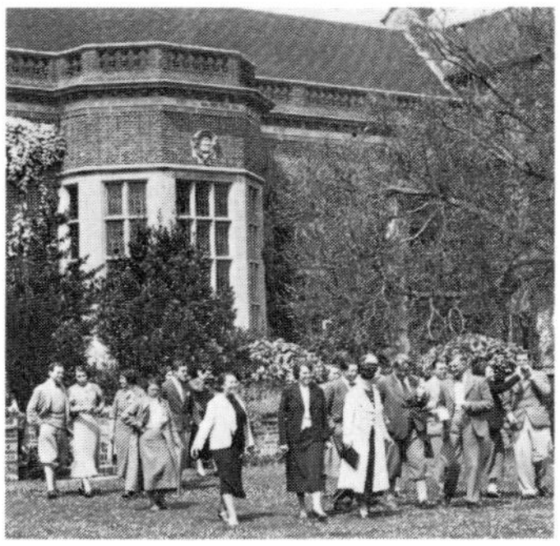

Glyndebourne opera-goers stroll out onto the lawns of the estate to relax between acts.

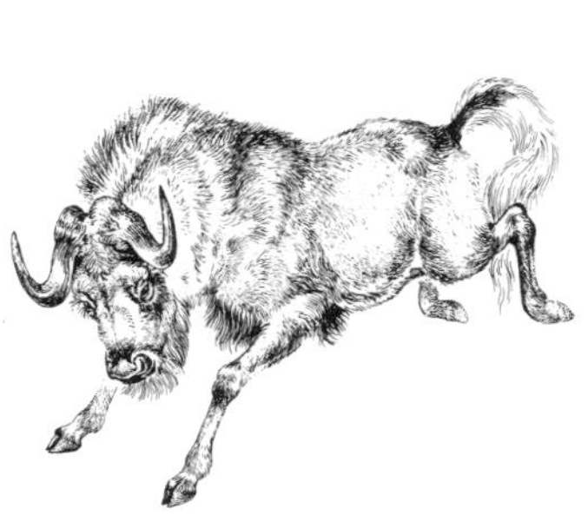

Gnus gallop in a wild extravagant manner, tossing their heads and kicking back

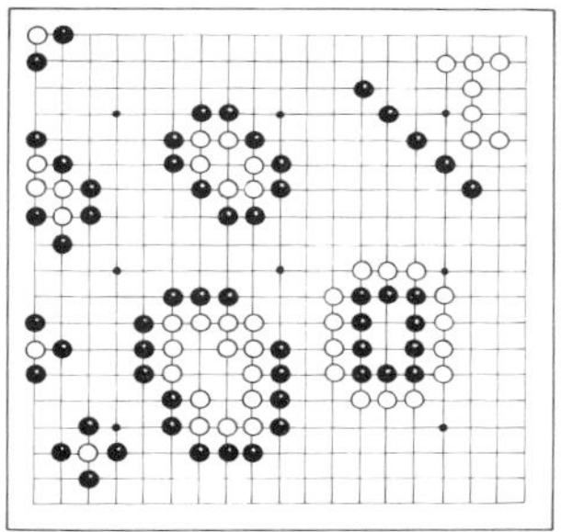

Go is an ancient oriental board game which is currently enjoying renewed popularity.

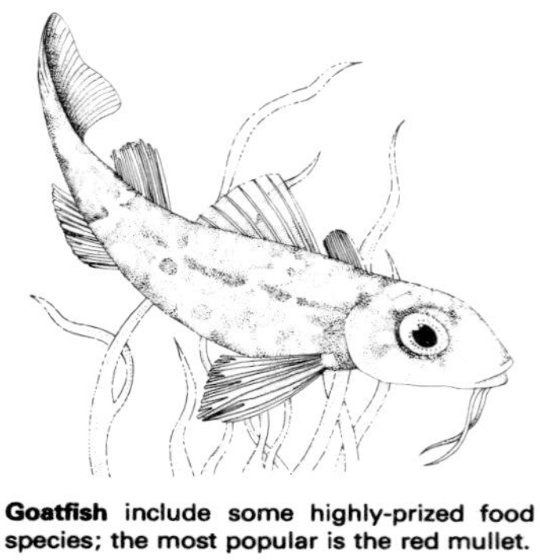

Goatfish include some highly-prized food species; the most popular is the red mullet.

Like starch and cellulose it is a polymer of GLUCOSE. When the body needs energy, glycogen is broken down to glucose, which is further metabolised to carbon dioxide, water and ADENOSINE TRIPHOSPHATE (ATP) (a source of chemical energy). *See also* MS p.70; SU p.157.

Glycol, or diol alcohol containing two hydroxyl groups. The simplest is ethylene glycol, or ethane diol, $C_2H_4(OH)_2$, a viscous liquid used in plastics, antifreeze and artificial fibres.

Glycosuria, excretion of an abnormally large amount of sugar in urine. It is found in disorders such as diabetes.

Glyn, Elinor (1865–1943), British writer, *b.* Jersey, Channel Islands. She shocked contemporary society with the publication, in 1907, of *Three Weeks*, a novel of a torrid love affair. The resulting notoriety prevented critics giving her later works serious consideration. These included *The Career of Catherine Bush* (1917) and *Man and Maid* (1927).

Glyndebourne, estate in East Sussex, England, and the home of the famous annual festival of opera. John CHRISTIE, who once owned the estate and its Elizabethan house, built a theatre for opera there after marrying Audrey Mildmay in 1931. The first performance of Glyndebourne Opera took place in 1934; the festivals are of international standard.

Glyn Dŵr Owain (Glendower, Owen) (*c.* 1359–*c.* 1416), Welsh leader. He was a member of the house of Powys, and led a revolt against English rule in 1400. He was proclaimed Prince of Wales, won temporary alliances with the Mortimer and Percy families in England, and captured Harlech and Aberystwyth castles. He lost both castles by 1409, and retreated to the hills where he carried on a guerrilla war against the English until 1412. *See also* HC1 p.*185*.

Glyn Dŵr Rebellion, Welsh revolt against English rule led by Owain GLYN DŴR (Owen Glendower). It began in N wales in 1400 and by 1403 had spread across the principality. In 1404 Owain declared himself Prince of Wales and summoned a parliament. But by 1409 he had lost control and the revolt withered. *See also* HC1 pp.184–185.

Glyptodont, extinct edentate South American mammal, and the Pleistocene representative of the ARMADILLO family. Its bones have occasionally been found associated with those of human beings. It was up to 3m (10ft) long, with a broad body armoured with tough plates and a stout, clubbed tail. *See also* NW p.*189*.

GMT (Greenwich Mean Time), the local time at Greenwich, London, situated on the PRIME MERIDIAN. It has been used as the basis for calculating standard time in various parts of the world since 1884. GMT corresponds with local time in England during the winter months; British Summer Time (BST) is one hour ahead of GMT. *See also* MW p.188.

Gnägi, Rudolf, (1917–), Swiss lawyer and politician. A member of the Farmers' Tradesmen's and Burgers' Party of Berne, he became a member of the National Council in 1953, a member of the Federal Council in 1966 and in both 1971 and 1976 he was President of the Swiss Confederation.

Gnat, common name for several small flies, mainly of the family Culicidae, the female of which bites human beings. The term is also used to refer to MOSQUITOES, MIDGES and biting midges.

Gneisenau, August Wilhelm Anton Graf Neithardt von (1760–1831), Prussian Field-marshal. After the Prussian defeat by NAPOLEON at Jena (1806), he played a major role in the reorganization of the army with Gerhard von Scharnhorst and Hermann von Boyen. Chief of staff to Marshal BLÜCHER, he devised the strategy that defeated Napoleon in the Wars of Liberation.

Gneiss, general term that describes a coarse-grained rock, laminated with minerals and largely recrystallized, but which lacks the breaking pattern of SCHIST. It is formed by metamorphic processes from IGNEOUS OR SEDIMENTARY ROCKS. *See also* PE pp.102–103.

Gnetales, primitive seed plants of the GYMNOSPERM order, having some feeding and reproductive qualities of ANGIOSPERMS.

Gnome, in western folklore, a subterranean DWARF or GOBLIN who guards mines or hidden treasure, commonly depicted as a small, deformed (often hunch-backed) creature resembling a wizened old man. Gob, traditionally the king of gnomes, ruled with a magic sword.

Gnosticism, religious movement including numerous sects, widespread by the 2nd century AD. Its creed of occult philosophy promised salvation in the form of escape from the powers of evil for its followers alone. The sects incorporated many tenets of Christianity, to which at one time Gnosticism represented a serious competitor.

GNP. *See* GROSS NATIONAL PRODUCT.

Gnu, or wildebeest, large, ox-like African ANTELOPE. The white-tailed gnu (*Connochaetes gnou*) is almost extinct, except for a few protected herds in S Africa. The brindled gnu (*Connochaetes taurinus*) lives in E and S Africa. It has a massive, buffalo-like head and horns, and a slender body. Both sexes are horned. The brindled gnu is silver with brownish bands and black neck, face and shoulder mane. Length: up to 2.4m (7.8ft); height: 1.3m (4ft); weight: up to 275kg (606lb). Family Bovidae.

Go, board game of oriental origin for two players. On a board consisting of 361 intersections, 181 black and 180 white stones are alternately placed one at a time with the object of encircling the opponent's pieces and territory.

Goa, former Portuguese colony in SW India on the Arabian Sea. It was seized by India in 1962 and is now part of a self-governing union territory with Daman and Diu. Its products include rice, cashews and spices. Pop. (1971) 857,180.

Goajiro, tribe of Arawak-speaking South American Indians that live on the Goajira Peninsula in W Colombia. A nomadic, cattle-raising people, they are one of the most numerous tribes of N South America with a population of between 30,000 and 50,000, according to recent estimates.

Goat, horned RUMINANT raised mainly for milk, meat, leather, and hairs. They are closely related to sheep and are brown or grey in colour. The male is a ram or billy, the female a doe or nanny and the young a kid. Wild species are generally nomadic in rugged mountains. The gestation period is five months and usually two young are born. The five species include the ibex (*Capra ibex*), markhor (*Capra falconeri*) and the pasang (*Capra aegagrus*), which is thought to be a forerunner of many domestic breeds. Length: to 1.4m (4.5ft); height: to 0.85m (2.8ft). Family Bovidae; genus *Capra*. *See also* PE p.*233*; NW pp.*222*, 223.

Goatfish, or red mullet, or surmullet, any of 55 species of marine fish found in tropical and temperate inshore, shallow waters. Goatfish are elongated, brilliantly coloured fish, with forked tails and long, fleshy whiskers. Length: up to 60cm (24in). Family Mullidae; species include one British, *Mullus surmuletus*.

Goatsucker, common name for various large-mouthed, nocturnal birds of the order Caprimulgiformes. They are widely distributed in warm areas and include the FROGMOUTH, nighthawk, nightjar, potoo and whippoorwill. They fly with their bristly mouths agape, to catch insects. They lay one to four whitish eggs, on bare ground or a heap of leaves. Length: 15–30cm (6–12in). Family Caprimulgidae. *See also* NW p.141.

Gobat, Charles Albert (1843–1914), Swiss lawyer and philanthropist who played an active role in Swiss politics. He was director of the Bureau International Permanent de la Paix and was awarded the Nobel Peace Prize with Élie DUCOMMUN in 1902.

Gobbi, Tito (1915–), Italian baritone. Since his debut in Rome in 1938 in *La Traviata*, he has sung in all the famous opera houses. Particularly admired as an interpreter of VERDI and PUCCINI, his powerful acting ability has also been highly acclaimed. He has also produced operas, his first being *Simon Boccanegra* at Covent Garden (1965).

Gobelins, Manufacture nationale des, state-controlled TAPESTRY factory in Paris, founded *c.* 1440 by Jean Gobelin as a dye-works and converted in 1601 to a tapestry works. In 1662 Louis XIV bought the premises to create a royal tapestry and furniture works. From 1697 the Gobelins specialized in tapestry, producing in the late 17th and the 18th century panels of unrivalled perfection. Famous examples include a set of tapestries based on RAPHAEL's frescoes in the Vatican and 14 great panels commemorating Louis XIV.

Gobi (Sha-moh), large desert area in central Asia, extending over much of Mongolia and the N part of China; one of the world's largest deserts. It is a plateau region, 910 to 1,520m (3,000–5,000ft) high, and most of the topsoil has been removed by the prevailing north-westerly winds. The desert fringes are grassy and these areas are inhabited by nomadic Mongolian tribes who rear sheep and goats. The desert has cold winters and hot summers, and fierce winds and sand storms are common. Rainfall is intermittent and often in the form of cloudbursts. The desert is crossed by a highway and the Trans-Mongolian railway. Area: approx. 1,295,000sq km (500,000sq miles).

Goblin, in western folklore, a SPRITE who lives in a grotto, but aims its mischief and malice at human beings and their households. Traditionally it creates noise and disturbance and moves objects and furniture at night, only to run away unseen. It is generally depicted as a small figure with pointed ears and a mischievous smile.

Goby, marine and occasionally freshwater fish found in tropical and temperate inshore waters or around coral reefs. Gobies are brightly coloured and have a suction area, formed from fused pelvic fins, on the front of the body which is used to hang on to underwater surfaces. Length: 1–10cm (0.5–4in). Family Gobioidae; species 700, including the neon goby, *Elactinus oceanops*. *See also* NW p.*131*.

God, name given in many religions to the creator and mover of the universe, in others to a variety of supernatural beings. JUDAISM, CHRISTIANITY and ISLAM are monotheistic religions, holding that there is one God. In HINDUISM, BRAHMA is considered the soul of the world, but there are lesser gods. In polytheistic religions, such as those of ancient Greece and Rome, there are many gods and goddesses. Sceptics doubt the existence of any god. *See also* AGNOSTICISM; ALLAH; ATHEISM; BUDDHISM; DEISM; YAHWEH; ZEUS.

Godard, Jean-Luc, (1930–), French film director whose innovative flair revolutionized film-making. He has produced one of the most creditable science-fiction films to date – *Alphaville* (1965). His political sketches have transformed film as propaganda as in *Weekend* (1968) and *Tout va bien* (1972). Godard also made fine thrillers, such as *Breathless* (1959), with Jean-Paul Belmondo, and *Made in USA* (1966). Sophisticated and erudite, his films do not have widespread appeal.

Godavari, river in central India which rises in the Western Ghats and flows SE across the Deccan to the Bay of Bengal, SE of Rajahmundry. Its waters supply hydroelectric power and irrigation schemes. Sacred to the Hindus, there are many pilgrimage centres along its banks. Length: 1,450km (900 miles).

Goddard, Paulette (1911–) US film actress, real name Marian Levee. She worked on the New York stage before rising to stardom in Charlie CHAPLIN's film *Modern Times* (1936). Between 1933 and 1942 she was married to Chaplin. She was at the height of her fame in the 1940s, appearing in 20 films between 1940 and 1950. These included *The Great Dictator* (1940), *Diary of a Chambermaid* (1946) and *An Ideal Husband* (1947).

Goddard, Robert Hutchings (1882–1945), US physicist and pioneer in rocket development. He developed and launched (1926) the first liquid-fuelled rocket, developed the first smokeless powder rocket, and the first automatic steering for rockets. *See also* SU p.268; MM p.156.

Godden, Rumer (1907–), British novelist. She spent much of her childhood and later life in India, as reflected in her novels *Black Narcissus* (1939), *The River* (1946; filmed 1951 by Jean RENOIR) and *Kingfishers Catch Fire* (1953).

Gödel, Kurt (1906–78), US logician, *b.* Czechoslovakia. In 1931 he published the theorem named after him. By uniquely numbering each statement in his Consistency Theorem he proved that in any formal system that can be dealt with using NUMBER THEORY there exist true propositions that cannot be proved within the system. The implication is that the whole of human knowledge can never be systematized within one axiomatic system. Gödel emigrated to the USA in 1940.

Goderich, Frederick John Robinson, Viscount, later 1st Earl of Ripon (1782–1859), British politician. He entered the House of Commons in 1806 and was President of the Board of Trade (1818–23) and Chancellor of the Exchequer (1823–27). He was Prime Minister for five months in 1827–28. He was later a minister in Lord GREY's Whig government (1830–34), becoming Earl of Ripon in 1833, and in Robert PEEL's Conservative government (1841–46).

Godfather, The, (1969), bestselling novel by Mario PUZO, which was later made into two successful films (1971 and 1974) directed by Francis Ford Coppola. It is the story of a young Italian migrant's rise in the competitive world of US crime. Don Corleone's son, Michael (played in the films by Al PACINO), establishes their Family as supreme among the US Mafia, and then channels their ill-gotten gains into other, legitimate, enterprises. *See also* MM p.*212*.

Godfrey of Bouillon (*c.* 1060–1100), French leader in the First CRUSADE (1096). Having sold his possessions to raise an army, Godfrey led about 3,000–4,000 Germans to Palestine. His troops were the first to enter Jerusalem in 1099. He was offered the throne of the city, but out of piety took instead the title Defender of the Holy Sepulchre. Later, in legend, Godfrey was portrayed as the ideal Christian knight.

Godiva, Lady (*d. c.* 1080), English benefactress, wife of Leofric, Earl of Mercia. According to tradition she rode naked through the streets of Coventry in 1040 to obtain the people's relief from taxation by her husband. She founded endowed monasteries at Coventry and Stow.

Godley, John Robert (1814–61), Irish colonizer. He went to New Zealand as a director of the New Zealand Company in the 1850s and stayed there until the granting of self-government in 1852.

Godolphin, Sidney Godolphin, 1st Earl of (1645–1712), English politician. Secretary of State (1684) under James II, he regained office under William III (1688–96) but maintained secret contact with James. As Lord Treasurer (1702–10), he helped finance the military campaigns of the Duke of MARLBOROUGH. A public servant rather than a party politician he was ousted from power in 1710 as party strife became more extreme.

God Save the King/Queen. *See* NATIONAL ANTHEMS.

Godthåb, capital city of Greenland, at the mouth of a group of fjords on the SW coast. Founded in 1721, it is the oldest Danish settlement in Greenland. Industries: fishing and fish processing, scientific research. Pop. 7,000.

Godunov, Boris. *See* BORIS GODUNOV.

Godwin, Earl of Wessex (*d.* 1053), English noble. He aided the accession of Edward the Confessor in 1042. Edward later married Godwin's daughter, Edith. He was outlawed in 1051, but landed in England in 1052 and forced the king to restore him to power. He was the father of King HAROLD. *See also* HC1 p.166, *166*.

Godwin, William (1756–1836), British political philosopher, husband of Mary WOLLSTONECRAFT and father of Mary SHELLEY. A dissenting minister for five years, he subsequently became an atheist and anarchist. His belief in the power of man's reason is expressed in *Enquiry concerning Political Justice* (1793) and in the novels *Caleb Williams* (1794) and *St Leon* (1799).

Godwin-Austen. *See* K2.

Godwit, large wading bird with long, slender bill, related to the SANDPIPER and SNIPE. Nesting on grassland or tundra, it breeds noisily and usually lays four greenish eggs. Godwits feed on insects and their larvae, worms, fish, tadpoles and water snails. Length: 43cm (17in). Family Scolopacidae, genus *Limosa*.

Goebbels, Joseph (1897–1945), German Nazi leader. He joined the Nazi party in 1924 and worked with Gregor Strasser, leader of the left wing of the party. Changing loyalty to HITLER in 1926, Goebbels founded the newspaper *Der Angriff* and became the leading Nazi propagandist. He was elected to the Reichstag in 1928, and when the Nazis came to power in 1933 became Minister of Propaganda. As such he ruled much of Germany's cultural life. He was a brilliant orator and a masterful propagandist. He committed suicide with his entire family in April 1945. *See also* MS p.*279*.

Goehr, Alexander (1932–), British composer who studied under MESSIAEN in Paris. He has written an opera, *Arden Must Die* (1967), a piece of "music theatre", *Naboth's Vineyard* (1968), a symphony, a violin concerto and several cantatas. He was appointed Professor of Music and Fellow of Trinity College, Cambridge, in 1976.

Goerdeler, Karl Friedrich (1884–1945), German rightist politician, who served as mayor of Leipzig until 1937. He opposed HITLER and planned a takeover with other German leaders which led to an attempt to assassinate Hitler in 1944, for which Goerdeler was hanged.

Goering, Hermann Wilhelm (1893–1946), German Nazi leader. A flying ace in WWI, he then joined the Nazi party. Elected to the Reichstag in 1928, he became its President in 1932. Under the Nazis he became Minister for Aviation and Minister of the Interior in Prussia, where he founded the GESTAPO. As virtual creator of the German air force, he enjoyed great prestige at the start of WWII; but its defeat discredited him. Sentenced to death at the NUREMBERG TRIALS, he committed suicide. *See also* HC2 p.228.

Goes, Hugo van der (*fl. c.* 1440–82), Flemish painter. His *Portinari Altarpiece* in Florence, combining realism and monumentality, influenced many Italian painters. He created a popular art in which he introduced lower-class types and greater individuality in figures. His later religious paintings, executed after he had gone mad, are dramatic, powerful and disturbing. *See also* HC1 p.*209*.

Goethe, Johann Wolfgang von (1749–1832), German poet. One of the greatest German writers and thinkers, his range was vast: from simple love poems to profound philosophical poems or scientific theories. In his long life he was lawyer, botanist, politician and civil servant, physicist, zoologist, painter and theatre manager. Johann Gottfried von HERDER taught him to appreciate SHAKESPEARE, and this influenced his *Götz von Berlichingen* (1771–73). His major works include *The Sorrows of Young Werther* (1774), a novel *Italian Journey* (1816–29), the classical drama *Iphigenie auf Tauris* (1787), *Torquato Tasso* (1789), *Egmont* (1787), *Wilhelm Meisters Lehrjahre* (1795–96), *Elective Affinities* (1808) and his most famous work, *Faust* (1808, 1832). *See also* HC2 pp.22, 73, 99–101.

Goethite, hydroxide mineral, iron oxyhydroxide, FeO(OH). It is found in secondary oxidized deposits with orthorhombic system slender plates and velvety needles. It also occurs in a massive fibrous form with uniform surfaces. It is black, brilliant and earthy. Hardness 5–5.5; s.g. 3.3 to 4.3.

Gog and Magog, in REVELATION, two powers that make war on Christ's Kingdom. In Ezekiel Gog, a prince of the land of Magog, leads an assault on Israel. In British legend they were giants chained to a palace on the site of London's Guildhall.

Gogarty, Oliver St John (1878–1957), Irish poet, man of letters and physician. His friend James JOYCE depicted him as Buck Mulligan in *Ulysses*. He was also a friend of W. B. YEATS, A. E. (pseudonym of George RUSSELL), Lady GREGORY and other figures in the Irish literary renaissance, and served in the parliament of the Irish Free State (1922–36). *As I was going down Sackville Street* (1936), an autobiographical volume, exhibits his racy wit.

Gogh, Vincent van (1853–90), Dutch painter, a leading POST-IMPRESSIONIST and a formative influence on modern art, especially on MUNCH and the EXPRESSIONISTS. During his brief and turbulent life he sold only one painting. He began to paint in 1880 and was virtually self-taught, with only occasional tuition. His early works were often sombre pictures of peasants, eg *The Potato Eaters*. In 1886 he left Holland for Paris, where he met GAUGUIN, SEURAT and other leading painters. His work underwent a transformation: he adopted the light, colourful IMPRESSIONIST palette and painted flowers, portraits and Parisian views. Two years later he went to Arles, in Provence, where most of the paintings for which he is remembered were painted, in a frenzy of prolific activity interspersed with bouts of mental illness and depression which ended in suicide. The paintings of these final two years were his most ecstatic – executed with heavy brushwork in heightened, flamelike colour, with passionate expression of light and emotion, and with evident influence of Japanese colour prints. To this period belong his sunflower paintings, *Cypresses by Moonlight*, *The Bridge at Arles*, *The Night Café*, and the swirling *Starry Night*. *See also* HC2 p.174; SU p.*136*.

Gogol, Nikolai (1809–52), Russian novelist and dramatist whose work marks the transition from Romanticism to early Realism. He made his reputation with folktales, such as *Taras Bulba* (1835), the stories *Diary of a Madman* (1835) and *The Nose* (1835), and the drama *The Inspector General* (1836), which already show his grotesque satirical style. Dismayed by reactionary criticism, he turned to religion for spiritual support and lived mostly in Rome from 1836 to 1848. Here he wrote the first part of his major work *Dead Souls* (1842) and the story *The Overcoat* (1842). The second part of *Dead Souls* was destroyed before publication. *See also* HC2 p.99.

Goiânia, city in SE central Brazil, capital of Goiás state. A modern planned city, it is a distribution and processing centre for a cattle-rearing region. It has a federal university (1964). Pop. (1970) 362,152.

Goiás, state in central Brazil; the capital is Goiânia. A plateau region of scrubland and semi-desert, it is largely undeveloped. Settled by emigrants from São Paulo in the 17th century, its mineral deposits, mainly industrial diamonds, are now somewhat depleted and cattle grazing is the chief occupation. There is some grain cultivation in the S. The new national capital of Brasília is located in the centre and has improved the state's economy. Area: 642,092sq km (247,912sq miles). Pop. (1970) 2,989,414.

Going, Sid (1943–), New Zealand rugby union player from North Auckland. A strongly-built scrum-half of Maori birth, he played 29 times for the All Blacks (1967–77). His aggressive bursts around the scrum produced many tries.

Goitre, enlargement of the THYROID GLAND accompanied by swelling at the front of the neck. Caused most frequently by iodine deficiency, it is occasionally accompanied by hypothyroidism or, in areas where goitre is endemic, by CRETINISM in children. The usual treatment is to increase intake of iodides; hormone therapy or surgery is rare. *See also* MS pp.*71*, 100.

Go-karting, also called karting, the cheapest and simplest form of motor sport, which accounts for its almost universal appeal. It began in 1956 when a Los Angeles mechanic, Art Ingels, put a motor-mower engine on a small tubular-frame construction with 13 cm (5in) wheels. By 1958 competition rules had

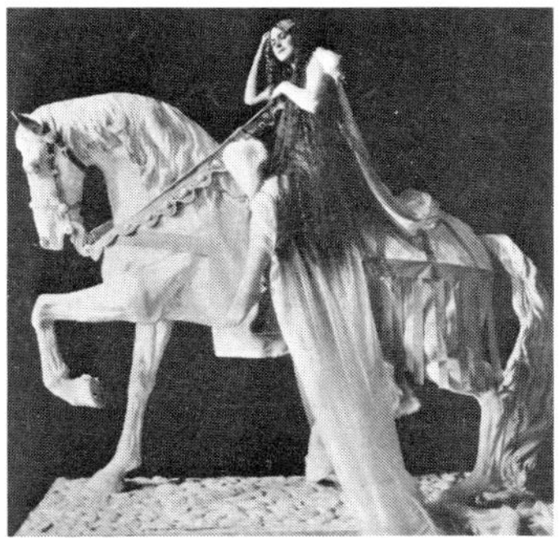

Lady Godiva's ride was commemorated in an annual fair in Coventry until 1826.

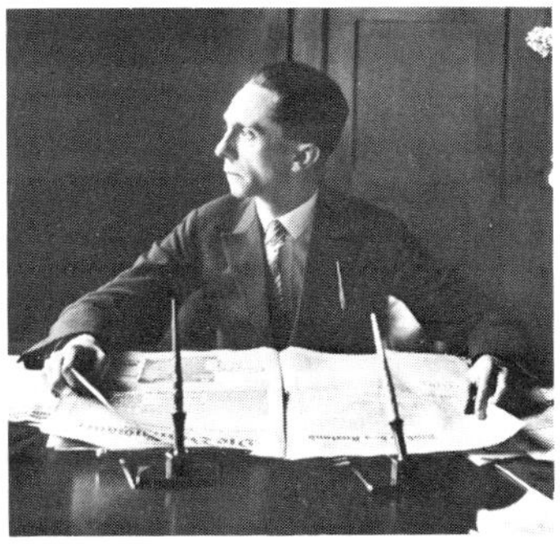

Goebbels used his intellectual powers to dignify the philosophy of National Socialism.

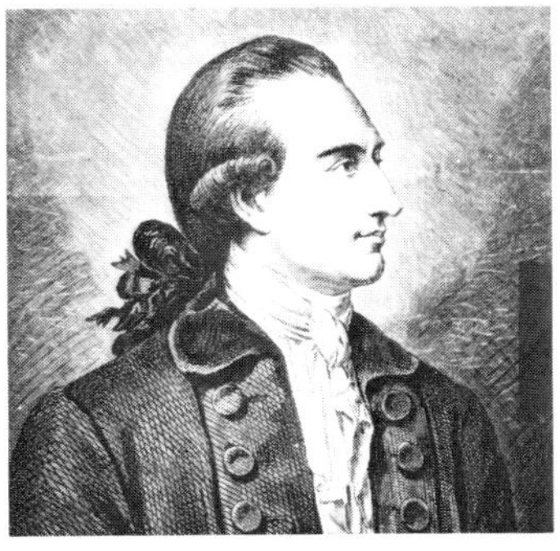

Goethe; universal genius whose greatness lay in interpreting the human character.

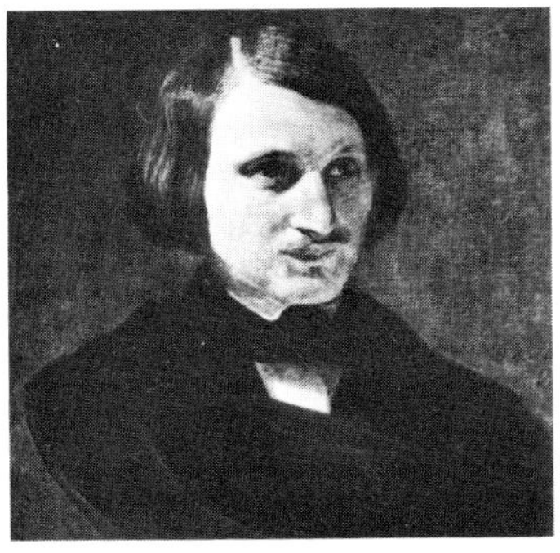

Gogol has been likened to Dickens in the way he presents characters of force and truth.

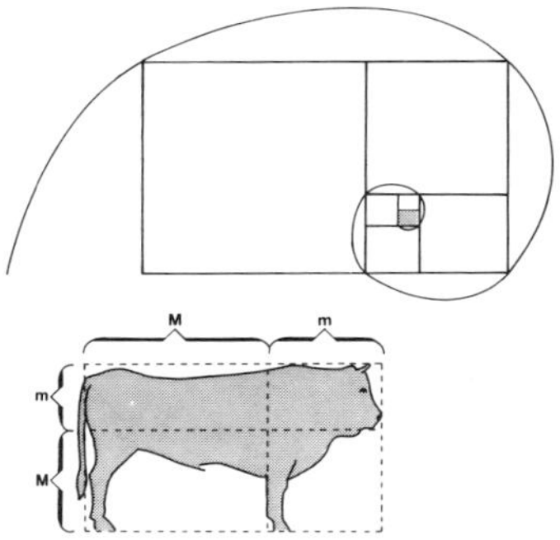

Golden mean; this irrational proportion was once thought to hold some mystic power.

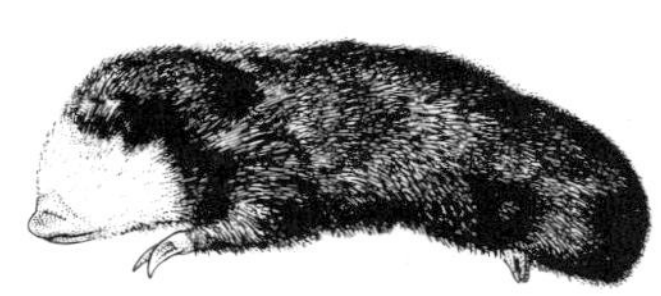

Golden mole; its two pick-like claws are well adapted to digging in the hard local soil.

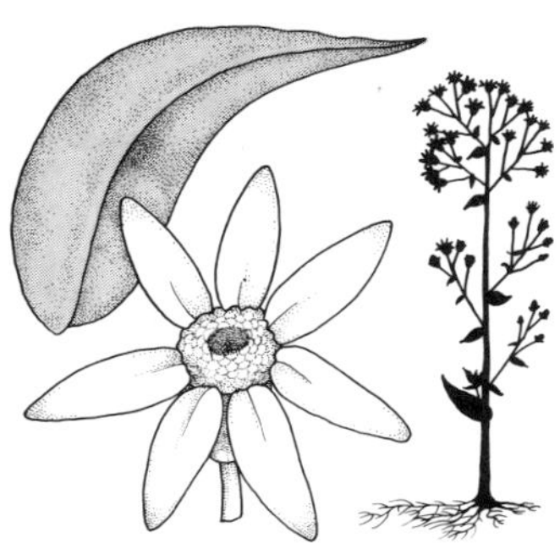

Goldenrods grow up to nearly 3m tall, with clusters of numerous bright yellow flowers.

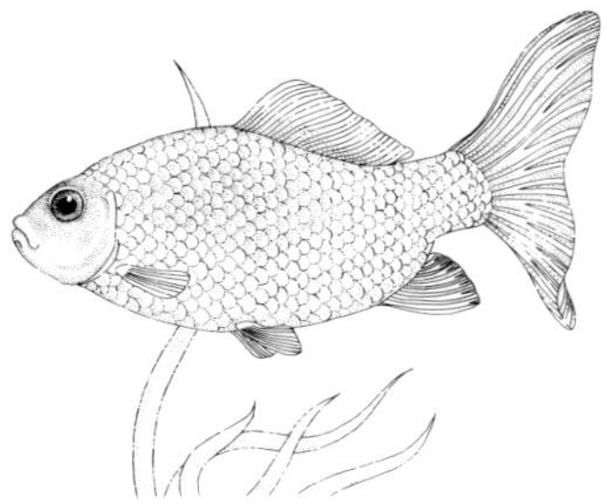

Goldfish which escape back to the wild tend to revert to their original brownish colour.

been formulated. Chassis dimensions are standardized, but constructions vary from simple ladder-shaped frames to complicated multi-tubular affairs. Bodywork is forbidden. Karts are usually powered by single-cylinder two-stroke engines with capacities of 100, 200 or 270cc, yet they can attain speeds in excess of 160km/h (100mph). Large-capacity karts require a gearbox. Races vary in length, with 8km (5 miles) the maximum for shorter races, and there are also 6-, 9- and even 24-hour events.

Golan Heights (Ramat Ha-Golan), disputed region in SW Syria. During the six-day ARAB-ISRAELI WAR (1967), Israel occupied the area and later colonized it. Syria subsequently rejected the United Nations' peace plan (Nov. 1967) and broke off diplomatic ties with Britain and the USA. Sporadic fighting between Syria and Israel has continued, although a cease-fire agreement was signed in 1975. *See also* HC2 pp.296–297.

Golconda, ruined town and fortress in SE India. It was part of the Bahmani kingdom *c.* 1424–1512, and capital of the Muslim sultanate of Golconda, 1512–1687. It was conquered by AURUNGZEBE in 1687. The city was famous for its diamond mines.

Gold, metallic element (symbol Au) of the third transition series, known from earliest times. The metal occurs naturally; some gold is also obtained as a by-product in the electrolytic refining of copper. It is used in jewellery and as a monetary standard. Gold leaf can be made as thin as 0.00001mm. Colloidal gold is sometimes used in colouring glass. The isotope Au^{198} (half-life 2.7 days) is used in radiotherapy. The metal is unreactive, being unaffected by oxygen and common acids. It dissolves in aqua regia. Properties: at. no. 97; at. wt. 196.9665; s.g. 19.30; m.p. 1,063°C (1,945°F); b.p. 2,800°C (5,072°F); most common isotope Au^{197} (100%). *See also* PE pp. 76, *76*, 96, *97*, *132*, 133.

Goldberger, Joseph, (1874–1929), US doctor who proved that PELLAGRA was due to a lack of meat and milk in the diet. These two foods are the main sources of vitamin B. His proof involved denying them to prison inmates who subsequently fell ill with pellagra. He also studied yellow fever and TYPHUS.

Gold Coast, former British colony on the W coast of Africa, now GHANA. The Portuguese began trading there in the 1470s. Britain organized control of the coastal region in 1874, and, after defeating the ASHANTI in 1901, annexed their inland kingdom. It became independent Ghana in 1957. *See also* HC2 pp.130, 220–1, *220–1*.

Goldcrest, smallest British bird. Its head is capped with bright yellow and orange and a black stripe. Its body is olive green and its wings are black with a white stripe. It is related to the Old World warblers. Length: about 8.4cm (3.3in). Family Muscicapidae; species *Regulus regulus*.

Golden Age, The, mythical period believed in classical times to have been the original state of the world. It was a time of innocence when men lived in peace and harmony with each other and with nature. The term has since been used to describe the flourishing years of any group or civilization.

Golden Ass, The, or Metamorphoses (*c.* 2nd century AD), prose work by Lucius APULEIUS. In 11 books it recounts the adventures of Lucius of Patras, who is transformed into an ass and undergoes initiation into the mysteries of Isis and Osiris before he regains his human form. It is the only novel in Latin to survive intact.

Golden Bough, The, (1890–1915), pioneering study of cultural anthropology by Sir James FRAZER. He took as the starting point for this mammoth 12-volume investigation of "primitive" practices and superstitions the mythical Golden Bough in the grove of Diana Nemorensis in Italy – which could be obtained only by killing its guardian priest and assuming that sacred post – and showed how it exemplified the development of an incarnate deity. He then exhibited his phenomenally comprehensive knowledge by comparing and contrasting it with similar customs and concepts from all parts of the world and all periods of history. An abridged one-volume edition of his life's work was published in 1922.

Golden Bowl, The, last long novel of Henry JAMES, published in 1904. It is a treatment of his favourite theme of American innocence exposed to the corruption of the Old World society.

Golden-brown algae, group of mostly microscopic, primarily freshwater plants (division Chrysophyta). The best known members of the group are the tiny single-celled DIATOMS, common among both salt- and freshwater plankton. All members contain characteristic yellow-brown pigments and lack chlorophyll B.

Golden Calf, according to the Old Testament, an idol fashioned by Aaron while MOSES was on Mt Sinai. The Israelites were punished with a plague for worshipping the idol.

Golden eagle. *See* EAGLE.

Golden fleece, in Greek myth, fleece of the winged ram who saved Helle and Phrixus from their step-mother Ino. While the ram flew to Colchis, Helle fell into the sea (henceforth called the HELLESPONT). After arriving, Phrixus killed the ram (which became the constellation ARIES) and hung the fleece in a wood guarded by a dragon. *See also* JASON.

Golden Gate, strait linking the Pacific Ocean and San Francisco Bay on the coast of California, USA. It is believed to have been sighted in 1579 by Sir Francis DRAKE, but the first landing was made in 1769 by Francisco de Ortega. It is spanned by the Golden Gate Bridge, completed in 1937. Length: 8km (5 miles); width: 1.5 to 3km (1 to 2 miles).

Golden Hind, flagship of Sir Francis DRAKE on his circumnavigation of the globe (1577–80). It was renamed (from *The Pelican*) after the promoter of the voyage, Sir Christopher HATTON, whose crest showed a hind standing on gold.

Golden Horde, W MONGOL empire that included most of Russia, also known as the Kipchak Khanate. The lands were given by GENGHIS KHAN to his eldest son, Juchi, but were not actually conquered and ruled until the invasion of Russia by Juchi's son, Batu Khan, in the mid-13th century. The empire was conquered by TAMERLANE and after his death (1405) split into several khanates.

Golden mean, or golden section, Classical ratio created when a line is divided into two parts in such a way that the ratio of the shorter to the longer is as the longer to the whole; ie $a/b = b/(a + b)$ where $a + b$ is the line's length. The FIBONACCI SERIES relates to the golden mean, and it was cited by the Roman historian Vitruvius as the basis of proportion in Classical Greek architecture. The modern architect LE CORBUSIER based his "modulor" on the golden mean. *See also* SU p.*27*.

Golden mole, blind burrowing mammal found in Africa S of the Sahara Desert. It has two pick-like claws on each front paw and a leathery padded snout for pushing through soil. It feeds on worms and other small invertebrates. Length: 8–23cm (3–9in). Family Chrysochloridae.

Golden retriever, hunting dog (sporting group) bred in Scotland in the 19th century for water and land bird retrieving. Ruggedly built, it has a broad head and rectangular muzzle, short, rounded ears hanging flat, a shortish body, medium-length legs, and a straight tail. The flat coat may be straight or wavy with a ruff at the neck and feathering on the legs and tail; its colour is golden. Average height: 58–61cm (23–24in) at the shoulder; weight: 25–32kg (55–70lb). *See also* SPORTING DOG.

Goldenrod, any of numerous species of mainly North American perennial herbs that grow almost everywhere. They have small yellow (sometimes white) flowers in one-sided clusters and they bloom in late summer. Height: 0.3–2.7m (1–9ft). Family Compositae; genus *Solidago*.

Golden Rose, rose-shaped ornament of gold inlaid with gemstones. It is blessed by the pope each fourth Sunday in Lent and later presented to a notable individual or group of people.

Golden wattle, shrub or small tree native to Australia. Its yellow flowers grow in clusters. The wattle is one of the unofficial national symbols of Australia. Height: up to 9m (29ft). Family Leguminosae; species *Acacia longifolia*.

Goldfaden, Abraham (1840–1908), Ukrainian playwright, regarded as one of the founders of the Yiddish theatre. He toured Europe and the USA and settled in New York City in 1903. He wrote such dramas as *Shulamit*, *Bar Kokhba* and *Die Kishufmacherin*, which are classics of the Yiddish stage.

Goldfinch, small, seed-eating, sparrow-like bird that frequents woods and cultivated areas in Bermuda and Europe. It usually lives in flocks, and lays bluish-white eggs (3–6) in a cup-shaped nest. The red-faced European goldfinch (*Carduelis carduelis*) has a brownish body with yellow and black wings. Family FRINGILLIDAE.

Goldfish, freshwater CARP originally found in China. Probably the most popular of all aquarium fish, it was domesticated by the Chinese about 1,000 years ago. The wild form of this hardy, adaptable fish is plain and brownish, but selective breeding has produced a bewildering variety of colours – gold and variegated red, yellow, blue, white and black forms with flowing fins, including the pearlfish, blackmoor, lionhead, comet, eggfish and harlequin. Family Cyprinidae; species *Carassius auratus*.

Goldie, Charles Frederick (1870–1947), New Zealand painter, well-known for his MAORI portraits and scenes of Maori stories, such as *The Arrival of the Maori*.

Golding, William (1911–), British novelist. His books are complex parables of the human condition, with symbolic overtones; they include *Lord of the Flies*.

Goldmark, Peter Carl (1906–), US scientist, *b.* Hungary. He demonstrated (1940) a colour TV system he had devised, and developed the first system to find commercial acceptance. In the late 1940s he invented the 33 1/3 LP record, and later developed an electronic video recorder used as an educational aid, and a system that enabled photographs to be transmitted from space to Earth.

Goldmark, Rubin (1872–1936), US pianist and teacher of composition. A pupil of DVOŘÁK, he taught George GERSHWIN and Aaron COPLAND.

Goldini, Carlo (1707–93), prolific Italian dramatist. He substituted written comedy for the traditional COMMEDIA DELL'ARTE improvisations. Called the MOLIÈRE of Italy, Goldoni ridiculed the aristocracy and endowed women characters with spirited independence. His most famous play is *La Locandiera* (1753).

Gold rush, series of dramatic influxes of population following the reports of the discovery of gold. The largest such rush was in 1848–49, when more than 40,000 prospectors went to California, few of whom found gold. The rush was important in that it influenced the entry of California into the USA in 1850. Many prospectors went from there to Australia in 1851–53. There were also gold rushes to the WITWATERSRAND, South Africa in 1886, and to the KLONDIKE, Canada, in 1897–98. *See also* HC2 p.149.

Goldsmith, Oliver (1730–74), Irish poet, novelist, essayist and dramatist. His works include the essay *The Citizen of the World* (1762), the poems *The Traveller* (1764) and *The Deserted Village* (1770), a novel *The Vicar of Wakefield* (1766), and the play *She Stoops to Conquer* (1773). Goldsmith hated the literary pendantry of his day and sought to achieve a naturalness in his own work. *See also* HC1 p.34.

Goldsmith, Oliver (1794–1861), Canadian poet. A grandnephew of the Irish poet of the same name, he wrote *The Rising Village* (1825), a poem inspired by his great-uncle's *The Deserted Village* (1770).

Gold standard, monetary system in which the gold value of currency is set at a fixed rate and currency is convertible into its gold equivalent on demand. It was adopted by Britain in 1821, by France, Germany and most countries in W Europe in the 1870s and by most of the rest of the world before the 1890s. Internationally it produced nearly fixed exchange rates. It was intended to work so that a large flow of gold out of a country would automatically set in motion a series of correctives. An outflow of gold, by reducing the money supply, would force up interest rates, thus attracting back to the country capital investment in search of high returns, and correcting the original imbalance that had produced the outflow. The intended effects were never satisfactorily realized. When the DEPRESSION produced falling demand without a proportionate fall in wages and prices, countries were forced to depreciate their exchange rate in an attempt to foster trade. By the mid-1930s all countries had followed Britain's lead (1931) and abandoned the gold standard.

Goldwyn, Samuel (1882–1974), US film producer, real name Samuel Goldfish *b.* Poland. He was noted for his commercially successful films, including one of the first feature films, *The Squaw Man* (1913); *Wuthering Heights* (1939); *The Little Foxes* (1941); *The Best Years of Our Lives* (1946); *Guys and Dolls* (1955); and *Porgy and Bess* (1959). He formed Goldwyn Pictures in 1917 and later merged with Louis B. Mayer to form Metro-Goldwyn-Mayer (1924).

Golf, sport played with a ball and clubs with the object of hitting the small, hard ball from the starting point (the tee) into a distant hole in the fewest number of strokes. The course is usually more than 5,450m (17,880ft) long and divided into 18 holes that may vary from 90–595m (295–1,952ft) from tee to putting green – the short, smooth grass in which the holes are sited. Competition may be over 18, 36, 54 or 72 holes and the winner decided by the lowest total of strokes (stroke play) or the most holes won (match play). The area between the tee and green, the mown fairway, can contain such hazards as ponds or streams and be bordered by trees and long grass. Greens are usually set about with sand traps (bunkers). A player may use a maximum of 14 clubs. Those made of wood are used for long drives. The irons, numbered one to nine, are used for accurate shots of shorter range: the higher the number, the greater the angle of the club-face and the higher the flight of the ball. Once the green is reached, the putter is used. Specialized clubs may be substituted for the standard range. A system of handicapping operates in amateur play at club level, allowing golfers of widely varying skill to compete on roughly equal terms. The growth of professionalism and the televising of major tournaments has transformed the game into one of the most popular throughout the world. Professional golfers are among the highest earners of all professional sportsmen. Golf had its origins in 15th-century Scotland. In 1754 the Royal and Ancient Golf Club, St Andrews, Scotland, was formed and the basic rules of the game were drawn up. The Club is the highest authority on matters relating to the sport.

Golgi, Camillo (*c.*1843–1926), Italian histologist. He shared the 1906 Nobel Prize in physiology and medicine with Santiago RAMÓN Y CAJAL for his work on the structure of the NERVOUS SYSTEM. In 1873 Golgi developed a method of staining tissue with silver nitrate for microscopic study. With this he discovered the GOLGI BODY within the cell.

Golgi body, collection of microscopic vesicles or packets observed near the nucleus of many living cells. It is a part of a cell's inner membrane structure, or endoplasmic reticulum, specialized for the purpose of packaging and dispatching proteins made by the cell. *See also* NW pp.26–27, *27*.

Golgotha, a burial-ground, particularly the site outside Jerusalem where Jesus and two others were crucified. It is also called CALVARY.

Goliath, biblical PHILISTINE giant slain by DAVID, the shepherd boy and the only Israelite to accept Goliath's challenge to single combat in front of their respective armies. Goliath was felled by a stone between the eyes from David's sling. The Israelite army thus encouraged routed the Philistines.

Gollancz, Sir Victor. *See* LEFT BOOK CLUB.

Goltzius, Hendrik (1558–1617), Dutch painter and line engraver. He is famed for his exquisite miniature portrait drawings. His portraits, both engraved and painted, show fine character portrayal and sober realism; his superb technique compares favourably with that of DÜRER.

Goma, Maj. Louis Sylvain, (1941–), Congolese army officer and politician who was educated in France. A member of the Parti Congolais du Travail (PCT), he became Chief of General Staff of the Armed Forces in 1974 and a member of the Council of State in 1975. In 1975 he also became Premier under President Marien Ngouabi.

Gombrich, Ernst Hans (1909–), British art historian and theoretician, *b.* Vienna. He was professor of history of the classical tradition at London University (1959–76), and has written *The Story of Art* (1950), *Art and Illusion* (1960), *Meditations on a Hobby Horse* (1963) and *Norm and Form* (1966).

Gombrowicz, Witold (1904–70), Polish novelist and playwright. He emigrated to Argentina in 1939 and moved to Paris in 1963. His two best novels are *Ferdydurke* (1937) and *Trans-Atlantyk* (1953). His plays include *Yvonne, Princess of Burgundy* (1938), *The Wedding* (1946) and *Operetta* (1967).

Gomułka, Władysław (1905–), Polish Communist political leader. He became Poland's deputy Premier after WWII, but was dismissed in 1948 and imprisoned (1951–54) for ideological deviation. Reinstated on the central committee of the Communist Party in 1956, he became first secretary and denounced Russian domination. He also revoked some of the more oppressive Stalinist measures. He supported the USSR in its 1968 invasion of Czechoslovakia. He was forced to resign during the food riots of 1970. *See also* HC2 p.242.

Gonad, the primary reproductive organ of male and female animals, in which develop the GAMETES or sex cells. Thus, the gonad in the male is a testis and in the female an ovary. Hermaphrodite animals possess both types.

Gonçalves, Nuno (*c.*1438–71), the most important Portuguese painter of the 15th century, court painter to Alfonso V. His only known surviving work is a series of six panels (*c.*1465–67) depicting Alfonso, Henry the Navigator and Portuguese citizens praying to St Vincent. A master of colour and composition, Gonçalves shows the influence of wood carving in his modelling of heads, which are painted with sharp psychological insight.

Gonçalves, Vasco dos Santos (1921–), Portuguese army officer and politician. He was a leading member of the armed forces movement that overthrew the government of Marcello Caetano in April 1974. Gonçalves, a leftist, became Premier in July 1974; he continued as Premier after Francisco da Costa Gomez became President in September 1974.

Gonçalves Dias, Antônio (1823–64), Brazilian poet. Considered the best of Brazil's early Romantic poets, he wrote lovingly about his country, especially its Indians and tropical beauty. His patriotic *Song of Exile* from the collection *First Songs* (1847), is one of Brazil's most famous poems. He had an intensely emotional style that has been compared to that of WHITMAN.

Goncharov, Ivan Alexandrovich (1812–91), Russian novelist. A civil servant from 1834–67, he spent many years in the ministry of censorship. His novels include *A Common Story* (1847), *Oblomov* (1859) and *The Precipice* (1869). *The Frigate Pallas* (1858) is based on his voyage to Japan.

Goncourt, de, family name of brothers Edmond (1822–96) and Jules (1830–70), French novelists and social historians. They wrote in collaboration until Jules died of syphilis. Self-absorbed and wealthy, they saw themselves as having a literary and artistic mission. Their joint works include *Art of the Eighteenth Century* (1859–75) and the naturalistic novels *Soeur Philomne* (1861) and *Germinie Lacerteux* (1864), but they are famous for the often malicious *The Journal of the Goncourts* (1836–40). Edmond (1822–96) wrote the novels *La Fille Elisa* (1877) and *Les Frères Zemganno* (1879). The PRIX GONCOURT, France's top literary award, was provided for in his will.

Gondoliers, The, or the King of Barataria, (1889), comic operetta in two acts by Arthur SULLIVAN with libretto by William GILBERT. It was first performed at the Savoy Theatre, London. A satire on the class system and developing democracy, it was the last great success of the Gilbert and Sullivan partnership.

Gondwana, historical region in India, now divided into the states of Andhra Pradesh, Madya Pradesh and Mahārāshtra. The main inhabitants are a Dravidian-speaking people, the Gonds.

Gondwanaland, name given to the southern supercontinent which began to break away from the single land mass Pangaea about 200 million years ago. The name comes from GONDWANA, a historical region in central India. The northern supercontinent, which eventually became North America and Eurasia without India, was Laurasia. The occurrence of tillites (glacial deposits) in separate parts of India, South America and Africa is fair evidence that these were once a single continent. *See also* PE pp.26–27.

Gone to Earth (1917), novel set in Shropshire by Mary WEBB describing "the continuity of country life" with an unusual and sympathetic intensity.

Gone With the Wind (1936), novel by Margaret MITCHELL. It was made into a successful colour film in 1939. Set in Georgia during the Civil War and Reconstruction, it deals with Scarlett O'Hara and her efforts to maintain and restore her plantation home, Tara. The film starred Vivien Leigh as Scarlett, Clark Gable as Rhett Butler and Leslie Howard as the ineffectual Ashley Wilkes. It was mainly directed by Victor Fleming, and won nine Academy Awards. *See also* HC2 pp.268, *269*.

Gong, PERCUSSION instrument sometimes known as a tamtam, a bronze dish-shaped disc, struck with a soft-headed beater. Its origin is oriental. At least 1m (3.3ft) in diameter, it is normally of indefinite pitch, but 20th-century composers have scored parts for sets of tuned gongs which are much smaller.

Góngora y Argote, Luis de (1561–1627), Spanish poet and chaplain to the king (1616–26). His poetry includes *Galatea* (1585), *Panegyrico al duque de Lerma* (1609) and *Las Soledades* (1612–17). His works became increasingly complex, allusive and BAROQUE, giving rise to the term GONGORISM.

Gongorism, literary term originally referring to 17th-century baroque poetry of Luis de GÓNGORA Y ARGOTE. It is deliberately complex and is characterized by Latinized vocabulary, neologism, obscure allusions and unconventional syntax. As a literary phase it reflects the decadence of the late Golden Age in Spain.

Goniatite, type of AMMONITE cephalopod mollusc, with a coiled shell divided into chambers by zigzag partitions. It first appeared in the upper Devonian period, about 350 million years ago. *See also* PE p.*127*.

Goniometer, instrument used mainly by mineral collectors to help in the identification of crystal forms by measuring the critical angles of related sets of crystal faces. These angles are characteristic for certain minerals.

Gonorrhoea, most common venereal disease, caused by a gonococcus and transmitted usually through sexual intercourse. Sometimes carriers of the disease, particularly females, show no symptoms. In males, symptoms usually occur between two and ten days after exposure and include a profuse, purulent discharge from the urethra; homosexual men may also have anal or pharyngeal infections. Females may show increased or painful urination, vaginal discharge or signs of uterine infection. Complications include

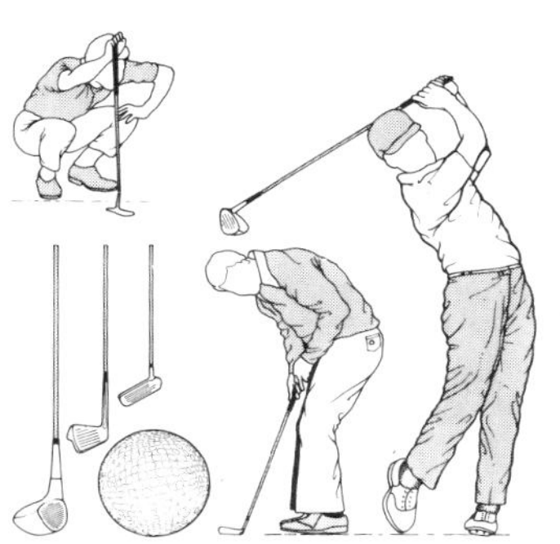

Golf balls were originally made of leather and stuffed with boiled goose feathers.

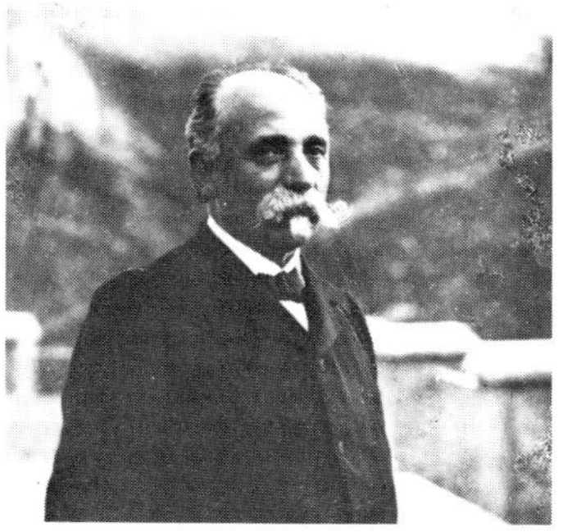

Camillo Golgi made important discoveries in malaria and the causes of mental disease.

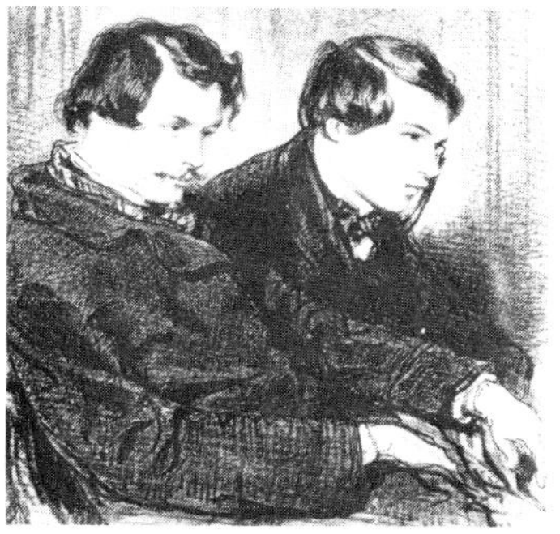

Goncourt brothers; many of their novels have a fragmentary quality.

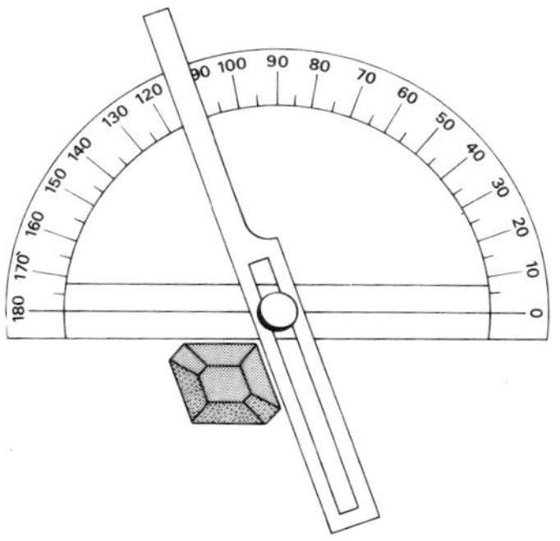

Goniometers are of three kinds; the contact (illustrated), the reflecting and the X-ray.

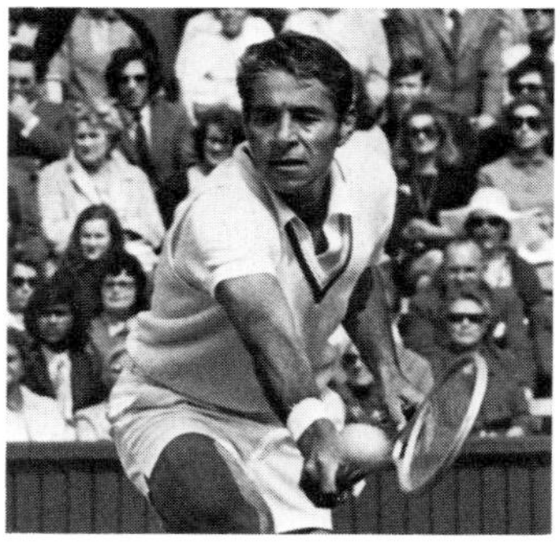

Pancho Gonzales, pictured in action aged 43 on the centre court at Wimbledon (1971).

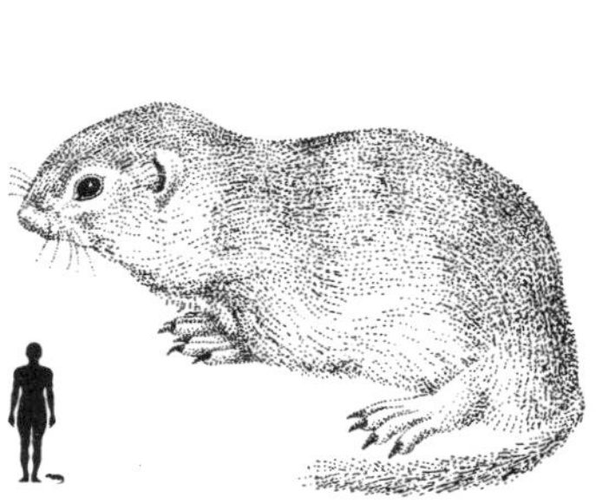

Gopher holes were a hazard to the cowboy, whose horse could accidentally step into one.

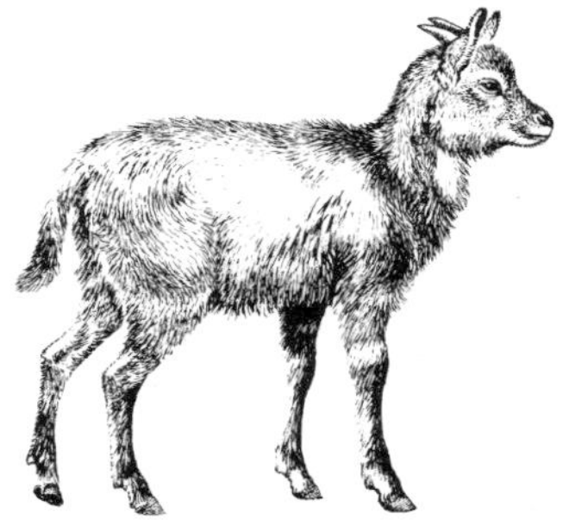

Gorals are goat-like animals which live in the area from the Himalayas to eastern Siberia.

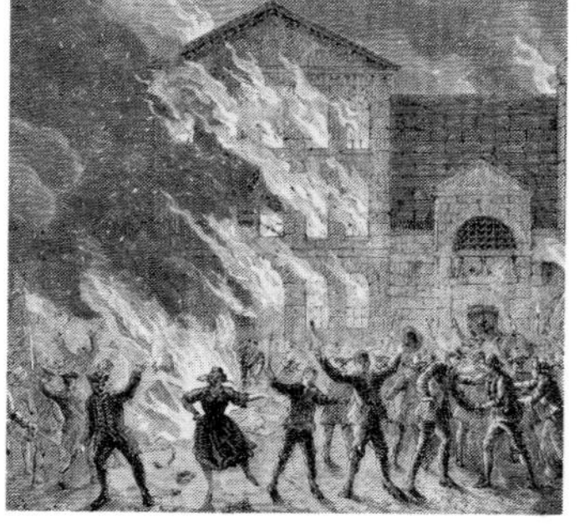

Gordon rioters burning the prison at Newgate during anti-Catholic protests.

infection of other organs in the body, endocarditis and meningitis. Infants of infected parents may be infected at birth. It may be treated with a course of antibiotics. *See also* MS p.*103*.

Gonzaga family, Italian dynasty that ruled Mantua (1328–1707) and Montferrat (1536–1707). The family's power in Mantua was established by Luigi Gonzaga (*c.* 1267–1360), a supporter of the Holy Roman Emperor. Giovanni Francesco in imperial service, was a patron of the humanist Vittorino da Feltre. Giovanni Francesco II (1466–1519) was a leader of Italian defence against Charles VIII's invasion in 1494 and wed Isabella d'Este, a great Renaissance art patron. *See also* HC1 p.258.

Gonzales, Richard ("Pancho") (1928–), US tennis player who, having won the US singles in 1948 and 1949, turned professional. He dominated professional tennis in the 1950s with an aggressive all-round game built on a booming service, powerful volleys and a delicacy of stroke-play remarkable for such a big man. At Wimbledon in 1969, aged 41, he won a 112-game marathon that lasted 5 hours 12 minutes.

Goodbye To All That (1929), autobiographical book by Robert GRAVES in which he recalls his childhood, his schooling and his experiences during WWI and its aftermath. It is a frank, realistic, yet restrained account of the horrors of war.

Goodbye to Berlin (1939), novel by Christopher ISHERWOOD that describes life in Berlin during the early 1930s, based on the author's own experiences. It became the basis of a successful play, *I Am a Camera* (adapted by John van Druten), and a musical play (and later film), *Cabaret*.

Good Companions, The (1929), novel by J. B. PRIESTLEY, awarded the James Tait Black Memorial Prize. In his story, Priestley assembles a small company of people, turns them into a concert party, and lets them loose on England. He turned it into a play (1931) and it was later made into a musical and a film.

Good Friday, the Friday before EASTER Sunday. The most solemn day in the Church calendar, it is observed by all Christians as a time for the remembrance of the death of Jesus Christ on the cross. For many Christians it is a day of fasting and abstinence. A popular devotion on this day is a service of meditational vigil which starts at noon and continues for three hours.

Goodman, Benny (1909–), US clarinettist and bandleader. After a period (1926–30) with Ben Pollack, he formed a big band in 1934 and was immediately successful. He also formed small groups which were the first permanent jazz units to have both white and black musicians. Goodman's own playing, which was marked by an excellent Classical technique, was at its best in these small groups.

Good Parliament (1376), English Parliament noteworthy for its constitutional innovations. The Commons' choice of Peter de la Mare as its spokesman is the origin of the office of SPEAKER. By trying Latimer and other royal servants for misconduct, Parliament took a large step towards the procedure of IMPEACHMENT. It then nominated new royal councillors itself. The Acts of the Parliament were annulled by EDWARD III in 1377. *See also* HC1 p.*210*.

Goods, in economics, the physical products of an economic system that are able to satisfy human desires and needs. Economists usually classify them as durable or non-durable goods and consumer or producer goods.

Goodwill, in business, an intangible asset. For example, a person who pays a premium for the assets of a going concern is in fact purchasing an intangible value, the value attached to the name and reputation of that company.

Goodwin Sands, sandbanks, approx. 16km (10 miles) long, about 9km (6 miles) off the S coast of Kent, SE England. The area is marked by lightships because no lighthouses can be built on the sands.

Goodwood, magnificently-situated racecourse, generally acknowledged to be the most beautiful in Britain, on the Sussex Downs. Horse racing began there in 1801. The Goodwood Cup, first run in 1812, is the feature race of Goodwood's July meeting, known as "Glorious Goodwood". Some miles away is the Goodwood motor racing circuit, which opened in 1948 but closed in 1966 for safety reasons.

Goodyear, Charles (1800–60), US industrial inventor. Despite early business failures, he developed an acid and metal coating process for rubber in 1837 and succeeded in vulcanizing rubber, which process he patented in 1844. Infringements upon his rights allowed others to reap profits from his work, and financial difficulties in France put him in prison.

Goolagong, Evonne. *See* CAWLEY, EVONNE.

Goonhilly Downs, site of Post Office satellite tracking station on the Lizard peninsula, in Cornwall, SW England. It is equipped with a transmitter and receiver for communications satellites and is in permanent contact with most parts of the world. The station is capable of handling 500 transatlantic telephone calls and a television channel simultaneously.

Goosander, also called common merganser, duck of the family Anatidae. It is distinguished from the red-breasted merganser (*Mergus serrator*) mainly by the markings on its head and neck. Found throughout Britain and continental Europe, it flies low and favours lakes, rivers and wooded areas. Length: 67cm (26in). Species *Mergus merganser*.

Goose, widely distributed waterfowl, related to DUCKS and SWANS, valued as game and raised commercially for its dark, protein-rich meat, its feathers, which are used in pillows and quilts, and the delicacy *paté de foie gras* (a paste made from its liver). Heavier than ducks, geese have blunt bills, long thick necks, shortish legs, webbed feet and, in the wild, a combination of grey, brown, black and white dense plumage underlaid by down. They live near fresh or brackish water but spend time on land, grazing on meadow grasses. They fly in flocks with rather laboured wingbeats, in V-shaped formations, making long, noisy migrations. Wild geese breed in colonies, mate for life, and build grass-and-twig down-lined nests for 3–12 eggs. The sexes look alike. Weight 1.4–5.9kg (3–13lb). Family Anatidae. *See also* NW pp.*227*, 235; PE pp.*237–239*, 238.

Gooseberry, hardy, deciduous, spiny shrub and its edible fruit, which is generally green and hairy and fairly acid. Family Grossulariaceae; species *Ribes grossalaria*. *See also* PE p.214.

Goosefish. *See* ANGLER FISH.

Goose flesh (goose pimples), temporary pattern of small bumps on the skin caused by contraction of underlying tissue in response to cold, fear and other emotions. The effect causes hairs to stand erect and trap more air for insulation against cold; long-haired animals become apparently enlarged – a form of deterrent against enemies.

Goosefoot, or pigweed, any of about 120 species of herbs and sub-shrubs, with mealy, often lobed, leaves that look like goose feet, and minute green flowers. The widely distributed species, mostly weeds, also include SPINACH and BEETS. Family Chenopodiaceae.

Goossens family, Belgian and British musicians. Eugène (1845–1906), *b.* Bruges, was appointed conductor of the British touring company, the Carl Rosa Opera, in 1882. His son Eugène (1867–1958) was a violinist and conductor. He succeeded his father at the Carl Rosa in 1899. He became conductor of the British National Opera in 1926. His son Sir Eugene (1893–1962) was a conductor and composer, born in London. He was conductor of the Rochester Philharmonic (1923–31), director of the Cincinnati Orchestra (1931–46) and conductor of the Sydney Symphony (1948–56). He wrote much chamber music and two operas. His brother Leon (1897–) has made a reputation as Britain's foremost oboist.

Gopallawa, William (1897–), Sri Lankan lawyer and politician. Gopallawa served as ambassador to the People's Republic of China from 1958 to 1961, to the USA, Cuba and Mexico between 1961 and 1962 and he was governor-general of Ceylon from 1962 to 1972 when he was appointed president of the Republic of Sri Lanka by Prime Minister Mrs Bandaranaike.

Gopher, small, stout burrowing rodent of North and Central America that has furlined external cheek pouches and long incisor teeth outside the lips. It lives mostly underground, digging shallow tunnels to find roots and tubers, and deeper ones for shelter and food storage. Length: 13–46cm (5–18in). Family Geomyidae.

Goral, shaggy, mountain-dwelling goatlike ruminant found in central Asia, China, Korea and Burma. It has brownish fur, short conical horns and lives in small family groups. Length: to 1.3m (51in). Family Bovidae; genus *Naemorhedus goral*.

Gordian Knot, complicated binding, tying the yolk to the pole of a wagon of Gordius, legendary King of Phrygia. An oracle foretold that whoever could untie the knot would conquer all Asia. In 333 BC ALEXANDER THE GREAT was said to have slashed through the binding with his sword, before going on to fulfill the prophecy.

Gordimer, Nadine (1923–), South African writer of novels and short stories, most of them critical examinations of life in South Africa. Her works are also concerned with the problems of contemporary politics and social morality. Her novels include *The Lying Days* (1953) and *The Conversationalist* (1974), for which she won the Booker Prize for fiction.

Gordon, Adam Lindsay (1833–70), Australian poet. His simple, melancholic verse, often celebrating heroic virtues, is included in the collections *Sea Spray and Smoke Drift* (1867), *Ashtaroth* (1867) and *Bush Ballads and Galloping Rhymes* (1870). There is a memorial to him in Westminster Abbey.

Gordon, Charles George "Chinese" (1833–85), English soldier and administrator. In 1860 he took part in the expedition that captured Peking and was personally responsible for the burning of the Summer Palace. From 1877–80 he was governor of the Sudan, where he attempted to suppress the slave trade. In 1884 he returned to the Sudan and attempted to put down the Mahdi Rebellion. He was killed at Khartoum in 1885 after he and his troops had been besieged for 10 months by insurgents. *See also* HC2 p.131.

Gordon, Lord George. *See* GORDON RIOTS.

Gordon, George Hamilton, 4th Earl of Aberdeen. *See* ABERDEEN, GEORGE HAMILTON GORDON 4TH EARL OF.

Gordon, Richard (1921–), British writer. After leaving medical practice in 1952, he took up writing and produced a series of humorous novels about the medical world, including *Doctor in the House* (1952), *Doctor on the Boil* (1970) and *Doctor in the Nude* (1973). Many of his books have been made into films.

Gordon Riots (1780), reply of Protestant zealots in London to the Roman Catholic Relief Act of 1778. Lord George Gordon formed a Protestant Association to agitate for the repeal of the Act and on 2 June 1780 led a deputation to Parliament. That night rioting began: houses, churches and breweries were sacked and prisons opened. Order was restored by martial law. About 450 persons were killed or injured. Gordon was acquitted, but 21 rioters were executed.

Gordon setter, bird and gun dog that originated in Scotland. It has a heavy head with a long muzzle, broad nose and set ears folded close to the head. The strong body is deep-chested and set on bigboned, feathered legs. The tail is carried horizontally. The flat, straight or slightly waved coat is black with tan markings. Height: to 68.5cm (27in) at the shoulder; weight: 20–32kg (44–70lb).

Gordonstoun, boys' public school near Elgin, Scotland, which lays particular stress on spartan outdoor activities. It was

founded in 1934 by Kurt HAHN and several members of the British royal family were educated there.
Gore, Charles (1853–1932), British theologian, bishop and a dominant figure in the Church of England for nearly 50 years. Principal of Pusey House, Oxford, from 1884–93, and founder of the Community of Resurrection, he combined traditional high churchmanship with liberal social and theological ideas.
Gore, Spencer Frederick (1878–1914), British painter of landscapes, interiors and music-hall scenes, who assimilated the influence of IMPRESSIONISM and POST-IMPRESSIONISM but retained a fresh and original style. With GILMAN, SICKERT and others he was a founder member of the CAMDEN TOWN GROUP, of which he was first president (1911).
Gorgas, William Crawford (1854–1920), US surgeon whose successful mosquito-control programme in Panama eradicated malaria and yellow fever there and made possible the building of the Panama Canal.
Gorges, Sir Ferdinando (*c.*1566–1647), English colonizer. He was a founder of the Plymouth Company (1606), which acquired charter rights to New England. Gorges transferred the charter to the Council for New England in 1620, which granted patents to the Plymouth and Massachusetts Bay colonies.
Gorgons, in Greek mythology, three monsters named Stheno, Euryale and MEDUSA, who had gold wings and snakes for hair, and who turned to stone anyone who looked directly at them. With the help of a reflective surface PERSEUS killed Medusa, the only mortal one. *See also* MS pp.*206, 210.*
Gorgonzola, pungent, pale-yellow cheese with pronounced blue veins. It was originally made in the Italian town of the same name. *See also* PE pp.228–229, *229.*
Gorilla, diurnal, gregarious, powerfully-built great ape that lives in the forests of equatorial Africa. It is the largest primate and is mostly brown or black, with long arms and short legs. It walks on all fours and spends most of its time on the ground, searching for fruits and other vegetarian foods. Generally shy and peaceful, the gorilla builds a nest in a tree each night. Height: to 175cm (70in); weight: 140–180kg (308–396lb). Family Pongidae; species *Gorilla gorilla. See also* MS p.*21;* NW pp.*168,* 213.
Gorki (Gor'kij or Gorky), city in W central USSR, 400km (250 miles) NE of Moscow, at the confluence of the Volga and Oka rivers; capital of Gorki oblast. Formerly known as Nizhny Novgorod, the city was united with Moscow state in 1417. It became a trade and cultural centre in the 18th–19th centuries. It was renamed in 1932 after the Russian writer Maxim GORKY. It has a state university (1918) and a medieval kremlin. Industries: motor vehicles, aircraft, plastics, textiles, shipbuilding, food processing, oil refining. Pop. (1975) 1,283,000.
Gorky, Arshile (1905–48), US painter, *b.* Turkey. His early work was influenced first by CÉZANNE and then by CUBIST primitivism. His mature paintings were brightly coloured washes and tints overlaid with calligraphic black lines, creating a hybrid effect, as in *The Betrothal II* (1947). *See also* HC2 p.203.
Gorky, Maxim (1868–1936), Russian dramatist and writer, *b.* Aleksei Madsimovich Peshkov. Gorky championed the worker and peasant in *Sketches and Stories* (1898), in the play *The Lower Depths* (1902), produced by the Moscow Art Theatre with Anton CHEKHOV's support, and in the novel *Mother* (1907). He also wrote autobiographical volumes (1913–23) and other plays, including *Yegor Bulychov* (1931). He has been called the father of Social REALISM.
Gorky. *See* GORKI.
Gorogstiza, José (1901–), Mexican poet. His wide-ranging verse extends from simple folklore to complex and obscure subject matter. His overriding concerns are with God and death. The collection *Poesía* (1964) contains his best poems.
Gorse, also called furze, any of several dense thorny shrubs found mainly in Europe; all are of the genus *Ulex*; family Leguminosae. The common European species, *U. Europaea,* bears yellow flowers and thrives in open hilly regions. *See also* NW p.*70.*
Gorst, Sir John Eldon (1835–1916), British politician. He was a Conservative MP (1866–68 and 1875–1906) and chief organizer of the Party (1868–80). He was a member of Randolph CHURCHILL's "Fourth Party" (1880–85) and solicitor-general (1885–86). He spent five years in New Zealand (1860–65) and wrote *The Maori King* (1864).
Gort, John Standish Surtees Prendergast Vereker, Viscount (1886–1946), British soldier. He was given command of the British Expeditionary Force sent to France in 1939, and led it in its retreat to Dunkirk in 1940. He was governor of Malta from 1942 to 1944, when it was beseiged by the AXIS powers.
Gorton, John Grey (1911–), Australian politician who was elected to the Senate in 1949. In Jan. 1967 he became leader of the Liberal Party and prime minister, but having lost the support of his party he resigned in 1971. He was Liberal Party spokesman on the environment 1973–75.
Gosford, Sir Archibald Acheson (1776–1849), governor-in-chief of British North America (1835–37). A Whig from Ireland in the British Parliament, he attempted to conciliate French Canadians while delaying confederation. His reports anticipated the Rebellion of 1837.
Goshawk, large hawk with greyish plumage and a long, rounded tail. It feeds on small mammals, including rabbits and squirrels, and on birds. Length: to 61cm (24in); wingspan: to 1m (39in). Family Accipitridae; species *Accipiter gentilis. See also* NW pp.*146, 152,* 207.
Gospel, in Christian theology, term used to denote the central content of the Christian faith, the good news of redemption. Meaning precisely "good news", the term is also used as a title for the first four books of the New Testament, ascribed to Matthew, Mark, Luke and John. The first three gospels are called the "Synoptic Gospels", because they contain approximately the same account in roughly the same order, whereas the Gospel according to St John, which is more in the nature of a theological treatise, is arranged carefully for profound philosophical effect.
Gospel music, term applied to US Negro-style vocal church music, which arose from the fusion of Protestant hymn harmony with originally African rhythmic and melodic features, such as blue notes (*See* BLUES). A powerfully expressive idiom, gospel music is often in call-and-response form (choir answering soloist/preacher). The secular equivalent is known as SOUL MUSIC or RHYTHM-AND-BLUES. "Negro spirituals" are gospel music arranged for concert presentation.
Gosplan, state planning committee of the USSR. It is an important unit in the economic decision-making process. Responsible directly to the Council of Ministers, Gosplan creates and administers plans in all sectors of the economy.
Gossaert, Jan. *See* MABUSE.
Gosse, Sir Edmund William (1849–1928), British man of letters. He was lecturer in English at Cambridge University (1884–90) and librarian of the House of Lords (1904–14). He wrote many biographies and one classic fragment of autobiography, *Father and Son* (1907).
Götaland, traditional name for the S part of Sweden. It was derived from the early settlers of the region, thought to be ancestors of the GOTHS. The area comprises the counties S of Lakes Vänern and Vättern. Area: 92,624sq km (35,762sq miles). Pop. 3,819,800.
Göteborg. *See* GOTHENBURG.
Gothenburg (Göteborg), city in SW Sweden, at the confluence of the Göta and Kattegat rivers. It is the chief seaport and second largest city in Sweden. The present city was founded by Gustavus Adolphus in 1619, and it quickly flourished as a commercial centre with colonies of Dutch and English merchants. Today its industries include shipbuilding, motor cars and lorries, food processing and textiles. Pop. 444,650.
Gothic, term applied to the style in European arts that developed in the 12th century and lasted throughout the remainder of the Middle Ages, following ROMANESQUE and preceding RENAISSANCE. In architecture it began *c.*1140 with the east end of the abbey church of St Denis, Paris, from whence it spread through western Europe. Notre Dame de Paris and Laon are the two great cathedrals in the earliest Gothic style, while Chartres, Bourges, Amiens and Beauvais are among famous examples in the mature style. Gothic architecture is characterized by the pointed arch, soaring spires, elaborate vaults, extensive use of stained glass and sculpture and increasingly intricate stone TRACERY. In contrast to Romanesque, the emphasis in Gothic is on dynamic line (rather than weight and mass) and increased height, in keeping with the new spirit of mysticism of the age. The style spread from France to England (where it developed in the three phases of EARLY ENGLISH, DECORATED STYLE and PERPENDICULAR) and slightly later to Germany. Spanish Gothic, though at first deeply influenced by French, developed a splendidly exuberant national style in the 15th century. Italy remained outside the mainstream, abandoning the Romanesque style for the Gothic reluctantly, and turning to the Renaissance soon after 1400. INTERNATIONAL GOTHIC is a term used in painting. *See also* GOTHIC REVIVAL ARCHITECTURE; HC1 pp.198–201, 216–219.
Gothic novel, genre of English fiction widely popular in the late 18th and early 19th centuries. Although not necessarily historical, Gothic novels often rely on eerie medieval (ie "Gothic") externals, such as old castles, monasteries, hidden trapdoors etc, as symbols of their characters' psychological states. Horace WALPOLE's *The Castle of Otranto* (1765) was an important prototype. Later examples include Mary Wollstonecraft SHELLEY's *Frankenstein* (1818) and Charles Robert Maturin's *Melmoth the Wanderer* (1820). The genre was an important strand of the ROMANTIC movement.
Gothic revival, or neo-Gothic, terms applied to architecture based on the GOTHIC style of the Middle Ages. Beginning in the late 18th century with fanciful remodellings, the revival reached a peak in 19th-century Britain and the USA, and appeared in many European countries. Its two leaders in Britain, the critic John RUSKIN and the writer and architect A. W. N. PUGIN, insisted on the need for authentic, structural recreation of medieval styles. Notable examples of neo-Gothic buildings are Pugin and Sir Charles BARRY's Houses of Parliament in London, and Richard UPJOHN's Trinity Church in New York City.
Gothic script, or black-letter script, style of calligraphy, and later of printing, that emerged in Switzerland in the late 9th century and prevailed until the RENAISSANCE. It was characterized by dense, thick black strokes, and by a rejection of curves in favour of sharp angles.
Goths, Germanic people who settled on the lower Vistula in the 1st century AD. They began to make inroads on the Roman Empire after 238, but were halted by Gallienus and CLAUDIUS. The Visigoths (West Goths) occupied Dacia until resettled by the Emperor Theodosius (382). Under ALARIC they ravaged Greece and sacked Rome (410). The Ostrogoths (East Goths) ruled in the Ukraine until conquered by the Huns (*c.*370). They entered Italy under THEODORIC THE GREAT (489). The Franks forced them into Spain where they survived until defeated by the Moors in 711. *See also* HC1 pp.136–137.
Gotland, island 97km (60 miles) off Oskabharm on the E coast of Sweden in the Baltic Sea. The island belonged to Sweden in the 13th century, became part of Denmark in 1570 and was returned to Sweden in 1645 by the Treaty of Brömsebro. The capital is Visby. Products include sugar-beet processing, barley and rye. Area: 3,172sq km (1,225sq miles). Pop. 54,100.

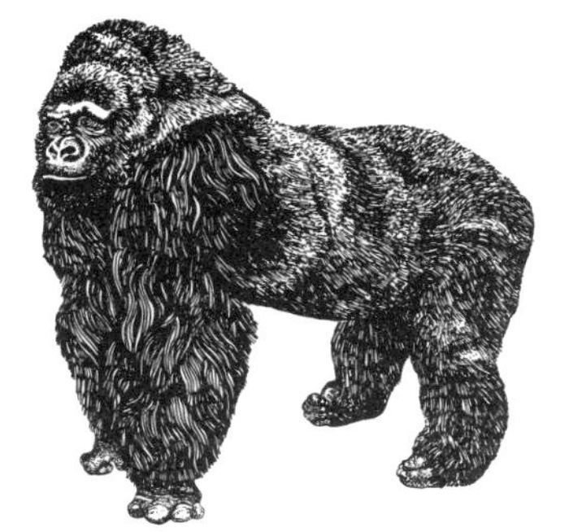

Gorillas, unlike their close relatives the chimpanzees, do not fare well in captivity.

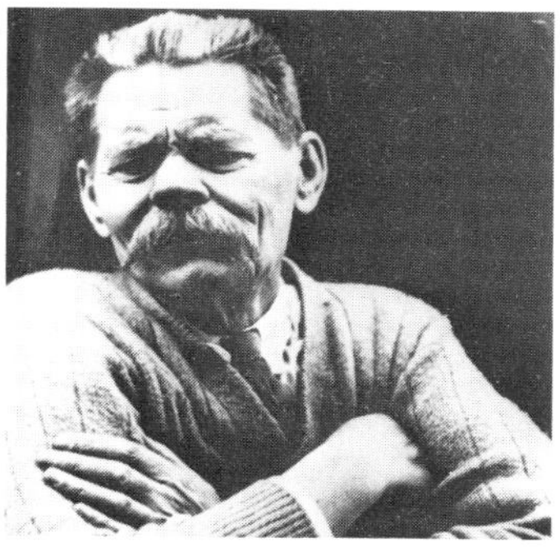

Maxim Gorky championed the workers and subsequently the Bolshevik cause.

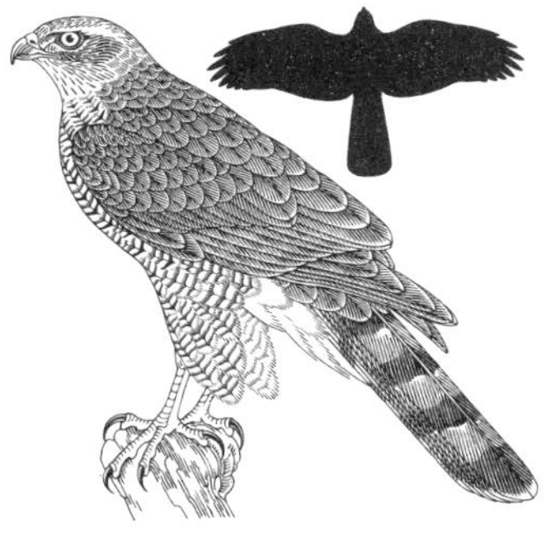

Goshawk (goose hawk) is a large, long-legged hawk which is used in falconry.

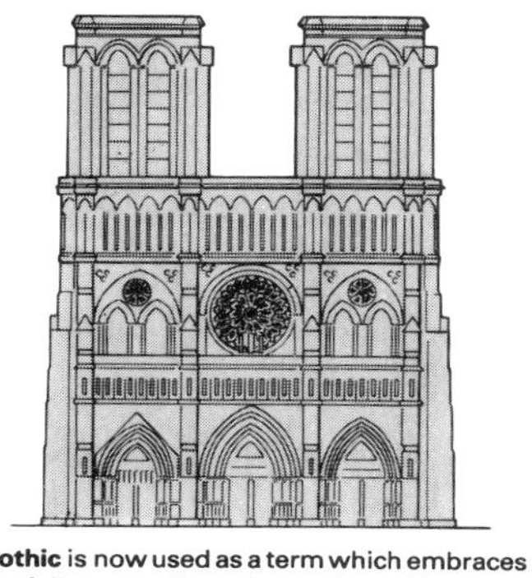

Gothic is now used as a term which embraces the full range of man's creative spirit.

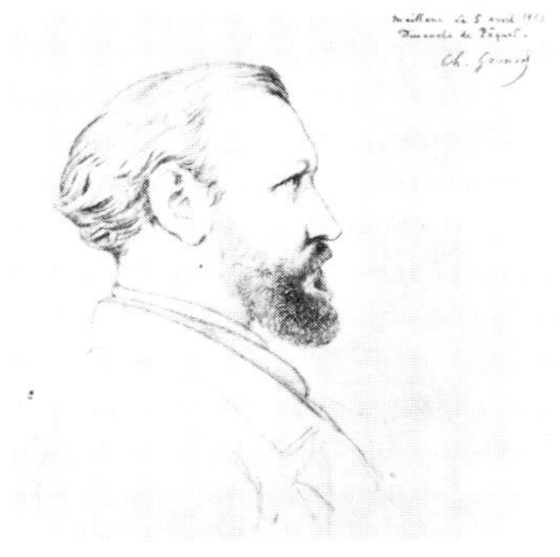

Gounod's lasting fascination for Goethe's *Faust* inspired his most successful opera.

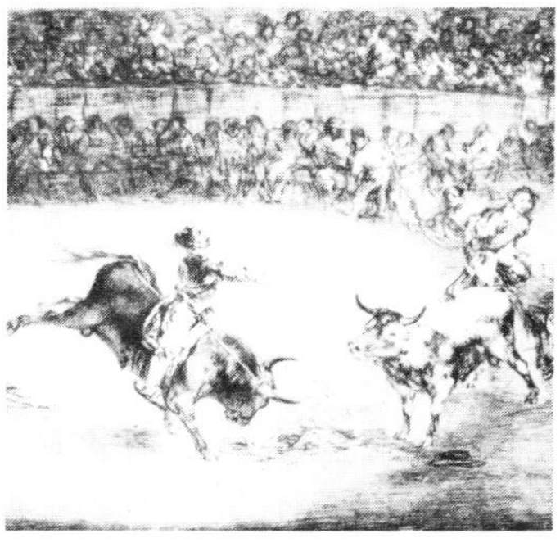

Goya's lithograph of the famous American bullfighter Mariano Ceballos.

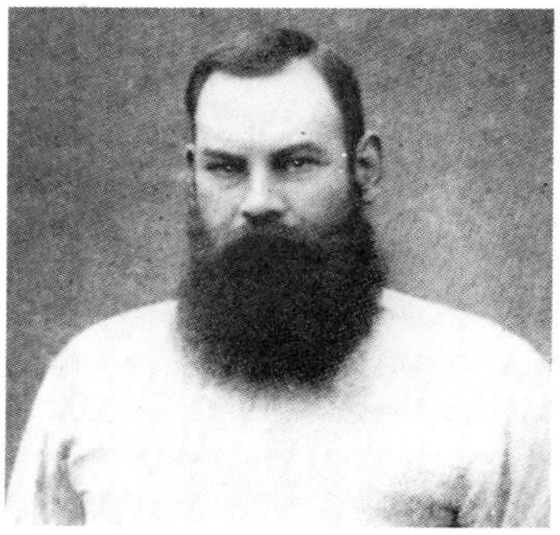

W. G. Grace, the legendary English batsman, played first-class cricket for 36 years.

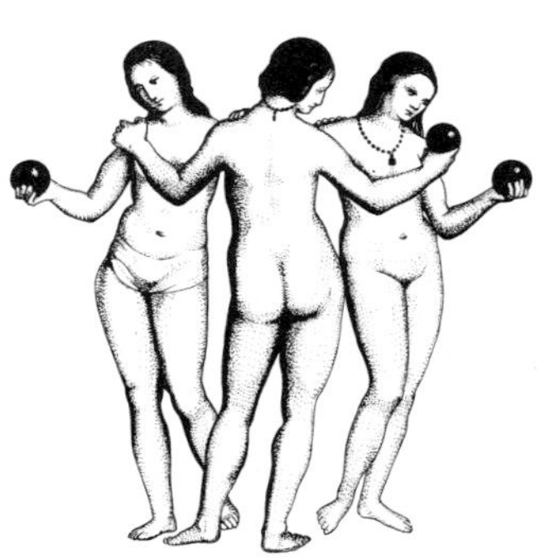

Graces; the three Greek goddesses of fertility thought to be the daughters of Zeus and Hera.

Götterdämmerung ("The Twilight of the Gods"), opera in three acts by Richard WAGNER, the last of the tetralogy, *Der Ring des Nibelungen.* The libretto is by the composer. It was first produced at BAYREUTH in 1876, when it was conducted by Hans RICHTER.

Gottfried von Strassburg (*fl.* 1210), medieval German poet. Little is known of his life, but he was apparently well educated in literature and theology. His Arthurian stories, such as *Tristan und Isolt,* are largely borrowed from French and British sources, but his treatment of characters is often more profound and perceptive than the originals.

Gottlieb, Adolph (1903–74), US ABSTRACT EXPRESSIONIST painter. His works, influenced by primitive art, use Freudian themes and allusions translated into abstract symbols. He was a founder, with ROTHKO and others, of the Ten Group in New York in 1935.

Gouache, type of watercolour paint made opaque by the addition of white. Although somewhat resembling oil paint in effect, gouache tends to lighten in colour when dry and often cracks if used thickly. Poster colour is an inferior variety of gouache. Especially popular among manuscript illuminators in the Middle Ages, gouache has been widely used by 20th-century painters and commercial artists.

Gouda, round, pale-coloured mild cheese that is made from whole or partly skimmed milk; it is usually covered with a protective coating of yellow wax. It was originally made in the town of Gouda, Holland. *See also* PE pp.228–229.

Goudy, Frederic William (1865–1947), US printer and typographer. He established his first press in 1905 and designed more than 100 typefaces, the most popular and influential of which were inspired by Roman and Renaissance letter forms and include Kennerley (1911), Goudy Old Style (1915–16) and Monotype Garamond (1921).

Goujon, Jean (*c.* 1510–68), French Renaissance sculptor and architect known for his decorations in low relief for buildings. He was influenced by Italian MANNERISM and associated with Pierre LESCOT, the architect of the Louvre, where a number of Goujon's works are found today. *See also* HC1 p.263.

Gould, Glenn (1932–), Canadian pianist and composer. A child prodigy, he was a soloist with the Toronto Symphony Orchestra at age 14. He is famous for his interpretations of the Romantic composers, and also of J. S. Bach. His first string quartet was premiered in 1956. In recent years he has concentrated on recording.

Gould, Jay (1836–92), US speculator and financier. In 1869, his attempt to corner the gold market resulted in financial panic. Avoiding prosecution, he later bought control of Union Pacific and other railways, and eventually controlled much of the railroad mileage in SW USA.

Gould, Morton (1913–), US composer and conductor. He is known for his compositions containing elements of jazz, popular and folk music, and has written stage works, film music, orchestral and piano compositions.

Gould, Shane (1956–), Australian swimmer who, in a 2½-year career, won five Olympic medals at Munich in 1972 (including golds for the 200m medley, 200m and 400m freestyle) and broke every freestyle record from 100m to 1,500m plus the 200m medley. In 1973, aged 16, she turned professional.

Gounod, Charles François (1818–93), French composer and organist. He composed church and choral music but is chiefly known for his operas, the most successful of which have been *Faust* (1859), *Mireille* (1863) and *Roméo et Juliette* (1864). *See also* HC2 p.121.

Gour, ridge formed in the bed of a calcite-rich underground stream by the deposition of CALCITE by turbulence. The ridges can grow to the water surface and dam the stream, and a series of them may form a terraced structure resembling paddy fields on a slope. *See also* PE p.*110–111.*

Gourami, also called kissing gourami, white deep-bodied tropical freshwater fish of the Malay Peninsula, Thailand and the Sunda Islands. It has a sucker-like mouth, and two fishes may often join mouths, for unknown reasons. It is a popular aquarium fish. Length: to 30cm (12in). Family Helostomatidae; species *Helestoma temmincki.*

Gourd, annual vine and its ornamental, hard-shelled fruit. These range from almost spherical, as in *Cucurbita pepo,* to irregular or bottle-shaped, as in the bottle gourd, *Lagenaria siceraria.* The rind may be smooth or warty. When hollowed and dried, the fruits of some species make useful containers. Family Cucurbitaceae. *See also* NW p.*61*; PE p.158.

Gournia, ancient Cretan industrial town (1600–1400 BC), the only well-preserved late MINOAN settlement on Crete. It was destroyed by fire in about 1400 BC.

Gout, form of arthritis, possibly hereditary associated with an excess of uric acid. Adult men are primary victims. Its symptoms usually affect one joint, often the big toe, with intense pain that may last for a week. It was once thought to be caused by excessive eating and alcoholic drink. It is partially treated with high liquid intake to increase the urine output.

Goutweed. *See* GROUND ELDER.

Govind Rai, or Govind Singh (1666–1708), tenth and last guru of the SIKHS. He created the military fraternity the Khalsa (the chief Sikh brotherhood, and instituted their strict practices, such as the wearing of a turban and long hair.

Gow, Neil (1727–1807), Scottish violinist and composer. He was famous for his renditions of Scottish melodies, especially strathspeys and reels. He published dance music in six *Collections* (1784–1822).

Gower, John (*c.* 1330–1408), English poet, all of whose works are of didactic or moral intention. *Vox Clamantis* (*c.* 1382) on social injustice and violent rebellion. His most famous work is *Confessio Amantis* (1390), an allegorical collection of tales on the subject of Christian and courtly love.

Goya y Lucientes, Francisco José de (1746–1828), Spanish painter and engraver. Goya sympathized with the French Revolution but was still esteemed at the Spanish court, where he painted a portrait, *The Family of Charles IV* (1800), shocking in its revelation of the corrupt inner life of its subjects. Among Goya's most vivid and expressive works are his portraits and nude studies of his mistress. When Napoleon's occupation of Spain was accompanied by brutal atrocities, Goya's bitter disillusionment was reflected in such brilliantly coloured, dramatic works as *The 3rd of May, 1808,* commemorating the execution of a group of Madrid citizens, and a series of etchings *The Disasters of War* (1810–14). *See also* HC2 pp.*80,* 316.

Goyen, Jan Josephszoon van (1596–1656), Dutch painter. A pioneer of Dutch realistic painting, he attempted to capture natural light and space, and to depict calm atmospheric effects in nearly monochromatic form. Many of more than 1,000 paintings are town views and river scenes. *See also* HC1 p.311.

Gozzi, Carlo (1720–1806), Italian writer. He was an opponent of the theatrical reforms of Carlo GOLDONI, who wished to substitute prepared dialogue for the improvisation of the COMMEDIA DELL'ARTE.

Gozzoli, Benozzo (*c.* 1421–97), Italian painter. His numerous frescoes, such as that of the Medici family as the Magi in the Chapel of the Medici Palace, Florence, faithfully depict 15th century Italian life. He began as an assistant to Fra ANGELICO, but his work is secular in mood and outlook.

GPO. *See* POST OFFICE.

GPU. *See* KGB.

Graaf, Regnier de (1641–73), Dutch anatomist and doctor after whom the Graafian follicles – thin-walled cavities in mammalian ovaries in which eggs develop – were named. De Graaf investigated the functions of the pancreas and the nature of the sexual organs. He was the first user of the term "ovary".

Grace, Christian concept of a frame of mind in which God's power is felt, accepted or even used, and which itself is a free gift from God. Faith, regular worship and the sacraments are all means of receiving grace.

Grace, W. G. (William Gilbert) (1848–1915), British cricketer. A formidable bearded figure with a deserved reputation for psychological tactics, Grace had a prolific career for England, Gloucestershire and London County. He scored a total of 54,904 runs (including 126 centuries), took 2,876 wickets and held 877 catches in first-class matches. He led England in 13 of his 22 Test matches (1880–99). He was also a doctor.

Graces, in Greek mythology, three goddesses who represented intellectual pleasures: beauty, grace and charm. Associated especially with poetry, Aglaia, Euphrosyne and Thalia were often linked with the MUSES. Perhaps originally fertility deities, they were also described as daughters or granddaughters of ZEUS.

Grackle, any of several species of stout-billed, New World blackbirds within the genera *Quiscalus* or *Cassidix* of the family Icteridae. Sometimes called crow-blackbirds, they have blackish, iridescent plumage. The common grackle, *Q. quiscula,* of the USA, may reach 30cm (12in) in length. Species of Asian MYNAH birds of the genus *Gracula* are also called grackles.

Graebner, Fritz (1877–1934), German ethnologist who postulated the theory of the *Kulterkreise* (culture complex), which held that all primitive cultures derived from a single type. His theory founded the culture-historical school of ETHNOLOGY in Europe.

Graf Spee, German POCKET BATTLESHIP launched in 1936. Its main armament was six 11in guns and it displaced 12,500 tonnes. Having sunk many British merchant ships early in WWII, the *Graf Spee* was finely cornered in Montevideo harbour, Uruguay, in Dec. 1939 by three British cruisers – Ajax, Exeter and Achilles – and scuttled by her captain.

Graft, tissue, portion of skin, bone or other tissue removed from its original site and transferred elsewhere in the body to repair a defect. The tissue may be taken from the individual requiring the repair (autograft), from another individual of the same species (homograft or allograft) or from an individual of another species (heterograft). The chief difficulty in grafting is that the recipient's tissues may reject the grafted tissue. Autograft and grafting from an identical twin are less likely to be rejected than heterograft or even homograft.

Grafting, in horticulture, method of plant propagation. A twig of one variety, called the scion, is established on the roots of a related variety, called the stock. Most fruit trees are propagated by a similar process called budding, in which the scion is a single bud. Grafting is a way of producing new plants that are genetically identical to the parent from which the scions are cut, and is carried out when the plant is infertile or will not grow from seed. Dwarf or special varieties may also be produced if desired. *See also* PE pp.178–179, 220.

Grafton, Augustus Henry, 3rd Duke of (1735–1811), British statesman. In 1765 he was Secretary of State under Rockingham and became First Lord of the Treasury under Pitt (Lord Chatham). Having deputized for Pitt during his illness in 1766, he became Prime Minister in 1768. He was forced to resign in 1770, following the crisis in the American colonies and the Wilkes affair, but he later served as Lord Privy Seal under North (1771–75), and under Rockingham and Shelburne (1782–83).

Graf Zeppelin, German airship built in 1928, which provided a passenger and freight service between Germany and South America until 1937. Capable of 124km/h (77mph) it was 236m (776ft) long and had room for 63 passengers. In 1929 it flew around the world in 21 days.

Graham, George (1673–1751), British inventor who in about 1715 invented the first of many pendulums that were compensated for temperature changes. He also invented astronomical instruments. *See also* MM p.92.

Graham, Martha (1893–), US choreographer and dancer, a leading figure in the modern dance movement. In the early 1920s she began to break with traditional ballet forms, employing instead highly individual forms based on natural movement. Her ballets, often based on psychological situations rather than the more narrative form of conventional dance, include *Primitive Mysteries* (1931), *Appalachian Spring* (1944), scored by Aaron COPLAND, and *Archaic Hours* (1969).

Graham, Thomas (1805–69), British physicist who is best remembered for the rule he formulated (GRAHAM'S LAW) which relates the density and rate of diffusion of gases. He also discovered DIALYSIS, a process used in kidney machines.

Graham, William Franklin ("Billy") (1918–), US evangelist. His evangelism is estimated to have reached more than 60 million people. He was the confidant of several presidents including Truman, Eisenhower, Kennedy, Johnson and Nixon. *See also* HC2 p.305; MS p.*225*.

Grahame, Kenneth (1859–1932), British author of children's books. He created Mole, Rat, Badger and Mr Toad in the classic *Wind in the Willows* (1908). Earlier books included *The Golden Age* (1895) and its sequel *Dream Days* (1898). A. A. MILNE based the play *Toad of Toad Hall* (1930) on Grahame's book.

Grahame-White, Claude (1879–1959), British pioneer airman who was the first Briton to receive a certificate of proficiency (1910) in flying. He founded (1909) the first British school of aviation.

Graham Land, or Antarctic Peninsula, northward extension of Antarctica that reaches 1,290km (800 miles) towards South America. It was claimed for Britain in 1831, but Argentina also claimed it (as San Martin Land), as did Chile (as O'Higgins Land). In 1964 the region was called the Antarctic Peninsula by international agreement.

Graham of Claverhouse, John. *See* CLAVERHOUSE, JOHN GRAHAM OF.

Graham's Law, in physics, states that the velocity of the molecules of a gas is inversely proportional to the square root of its density. It has important industrial applications, and can be expressed as follows: rate of diffusion = k/ square root of density, where k is a constant.

Grail, Holy, object of quest of the knights of Arthurian romance. The grail (cup) was supposedly the one used by Jesus at the LAST SUPPER, and possibly by JOSEPH OF ARIMATHEA to catch the blood from Jesus's wounds. The quest for the grail became a search for mystical union with God.

Grainger, Percy Aldridge (1882–1961), Australian composer and pianist. He was a pupil of BUSONI and a protegé of GRIEG, who encouraged him to collect, edit and arrange English and Irish folk- songs. His arrangements of *Country Gardens* and *Shepherd's Hey* were both published in 1908, and he continued to produce other songs and orchestral pieces in the same folk tradition.

Gram. *See* CHICKPEA.

Gramme-atom, quantity of an element whose weight, in grammes, is equal to its atomic weight. It has been replaced by the SI unit, the mole. For example, one gramme-atom of hydrogen (H, atomic weight = 1) is 1g.

Grammar, the branch of linguistics that deals with a language's inflections, its phonetic system and syntax. Rules for the English language were developed on the basis of Latin grammar, which is inflectional (based on variations in the form of words), even though English is more of a syntactical language (based on word order). Grammar is continually evolving in response to popular usage.

Gramme molecular volume, volume occupied by a weight of gas equal to its molecular weight in grammes (eg 2 grammes of hydrogen or 32 grammes of oxygen). At a given temperature and pressure it has approximately the same value for all gases. It is 22.415 litres for an ideal gas at 760mm of mercury pressure and 0°C (STP).

Gramme, Zénobe Théophile (1826–1901), Belgian engineer who developed the first practical industrial dynamo in 1869. His knowledge of electrical theory was limited, but even so he developed an electric motor from his dynamo, and was one of a group of scientists who, in 1872, succeeded in transmitting direct current electricity over long distances.

Gramophone, name of the instrument for reproducing sound, invented by Emile BERLINER in 1887. It was an early form of record player: a stylus traced the spiral indentations of the recording on a horizontal disc. This was a significant advancement on the original phonograph invented by Thomas A. EDISON in 1877, in which a stylus traced vertical indentations upon a rotating cylinder wrapped in tin foil, the weak sound output being amplified by a horn. *See also* MM pp.232–233.

Grampian, region in NE Scotland, formed in 1975 from the former counties of ABERDEEN, KINCARDINE, BANFFSHIRE and most of MORAY. The administrative centre is ABERDEEN. Area: approx. 8,550sq km (3,300sq miles). Pop. (1974 est.) 447,935.

Grampians, mountain range in N central Scotland. It is the highest mountain system in Britain, running SW-NE between Glen More and the Scottish Lowlands. Rivers rising in the Grampians include the Spey, Findhorn (flowing N), Don, Dee (flowing E), Tay and Forth (flowing S). Highest peak: Ben Nevis, 1,343m (4,406ft).

Grampus, also called Risso's dolphin, species of DOLPHIN found in temperate and tropical seas throughout the world. It is dark grey with a lighter belly, has no "beak" and feeds primarily on cuttlefish. Length: 4m (13ft). Family Delphinidae; species *Grampus griseus*.

Gramsci, Antonio (1891–1937), Italian political thinker, a founder of the Italian Communist Party (PCI) and one of its leading theorists. From a poor Sardinian background, he entered Turin University in 1911, but abandoned his studies to become an active socialist and then Marxist. He founded the newspaper *L'Ordine Nuovo* (*The New Order*) in 1919 and was a leader of the 1920 Turin general strike. In 1921 he and his followers left the Socialist Congress at Livorno to form the PCI. In 1924 he became party leader and was elected to the Chamber of Deputies. Arrested in 1926, Gramsci was imprisoned for 11 years, and died soon after his release. His posthumously published *Lettere dal carcere* (*Prison Letters*, 1947) have greatly influenced modern Italian Communism.

Gram stain, in microbiology, a differential staining method named after the Danish physician H.C.J. Gram. It aids in the categorizing and identification of bacteria, which are said to be gram-positive or gram-negative, depending on whether or not they retain the original violet stain at the end of the process. If gram-negative, the stain washes out to a red counterstain.

Granada, province in Andalusia, S Spain in the Andalusia region, bounded in the S by the Mediterranean Sea. It is a fertile area drained by the Genil River, and sugar-beet is the chief crop. There are a few mineral resources. Conquered in the 8th century by the Moors, Granada became an independent kingdom in 1238 and a centre of Moslem learning and civilization. The capital is the city of Granada. Area: 12,530sq km (4,838sq miles). Pop. 733,375.

Granados, Enrique (1867–1916), Spanish composer who, like ALBÉNIZ and FALLA, worked to develop a national style, drawing inspiration from the rhythms and melodies of Spanish folk-music. His most famous work, *Goyescas* (1911), was written for piano, and later arranged as an opera (1916). He wrote six other operas, piano and orchestral music and songs.

Granby, John Manners, Marquis of (1721–70), British soldier. He was commander of the Leicester "blues" (1745–59) and led the British forces in Germany during the SEVEN YEARS WAR. In 1766 he was made commander-in-chief of the British army.

Gran Chaco. *See* CHACO.

Grand Alliance, War of the (1689–97), war between France and the Grand Alliance. In 1688 LOUIS XIV invaded the PALATINATE, and the Holy Roman Emperor LEOPOLD I formed the Alliance primarily with The Netherlands, Spain and England. There were French victories at Namur (1692, 1695) and an English naval victory at La Hogue (1692). Peace was concluded by the Treaty of Rijswijk (1697).

Grand Bank, underwater plateau 564km (350 miles) long and 320km (200 miles) wide in the Atlantic Ocean off the coast of Newfoundland. The flow of the GULF STREAM along its E edge encourages marine life and makes this area one of the world's most productive fishing grounds.

Grandbois, Alain (1900–), Canadian poet. He travelled abroad extensively between the world wars. His innovative poetry includes *Les Îles de la Nuit* (1944) and *Poèmes* (1963). He also wrote *A Life of Jolliet* (1933).

Grand Canal, main waterway in Venice, Italy. It is crossed by three bridges, the most famous of which is the Rialto. It forms, with smaller canals, the major Venetian transport system. Length: 3km (2 miles); width: 30–60m (100–200ft).

Grand Canyon, immense gorge in NW Arizona, USA, carved by the Colorado River. With its multicoloured rocks and magnificent rock formations, the Grand Canyon is considered to be one of the great natural wonders of the world. It is 450km (280 miles) long and varies from 6km (4 miles) to 18km (11 miles) in width. *See also* PE pp.*124*, *127*.

Grande Chartreuse, La. *See* CHARTREUSE, LA GRANDE.

Grand Design, plan attributed by SULLY to HENRY IV of France for setting up a Christian Republic of Europe devoted to ensuring perpetual peace. The Holy Roman Emperor would act as magistrate, with a general council to discuss matters of general interest and tackle any problems that might occur.

Grande, Rio. *See* RIO GRANDE.

Grande Illusion, La (1937), French film directed by Jean RENOIR and written by him with Charles Spaak. Set in a German prison camp, it is a subtle, sympathetic portrait of the dying aristocracy and its outmoded rules of conduct. The actors include Erich von Stroheim, Pierre Fresnay and Jean Gabin.

Grand Guignol, theatrical genre of short melodramatic plays featuring passion, rape, murder and suicide and named after the Parisian Théâtre du Grand Guignol, in which such horrific pieces were strongly exploited in the 1890s and 1900s.

Grandma Moses. *See* MOSES, GRANDMA.

Grand jury, in US law, a group appointed by the law that investigates in secret a crime within its jurisdiction. It hears evidence, then decides whether a person should stand trial. It is so-called because it is usually larger than the trial jury.

Grand mal, type of epileptic attack characterized by loss of consciousness and muscular contractions, lasting up to five minutes. *See also* EPILEPSY; MS p.96.

Grand National, premier steeplechase of the English National Hunt horse-racing season. First run in 1839 over fields at Aintree, near Liverpool, this handicap for six-year-olds and upwards became world famous for the severity of such jumps as Becher's Brook, Valentine's Brook and the Chair. It is raced over 4 miles 856yards (7.2km), with 14 of the 16 obstacles jumped twice.

Grand Piano. *See* PIANO.

Grand Prix de Paris, French classic horse race for three-year-olds. Inaugurated in 1863, it is run over 3.1km (1 mile 7½ furlongs) at Longchamp on the last Sunday in June – traditionally a day at the races for Parisians.

Grand Tour, part of the education of young people of aristocratic or wealthy English families between the 16th and 19th centuries. It lasted from two to three years and went from France to Italy (especially Rome), returning through the German states and the Low Countries.

Grand Remonstrance (22 Nov.1641), statement drawn up by the opposition to

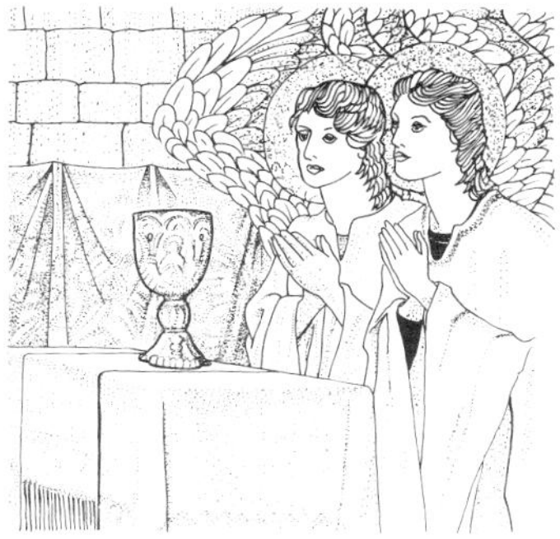

The Holy Grail is thought to carry overtones from the mythological Celtic horns of plenty.

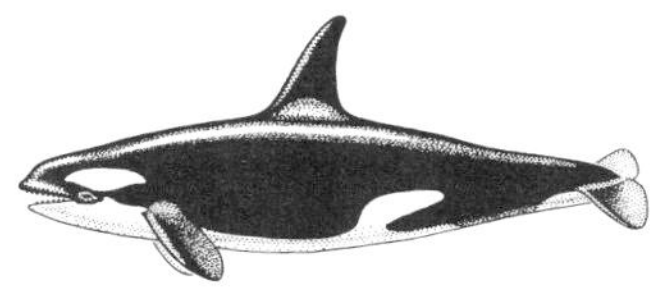

Grampus is the common name sometimes used for the killer whale.

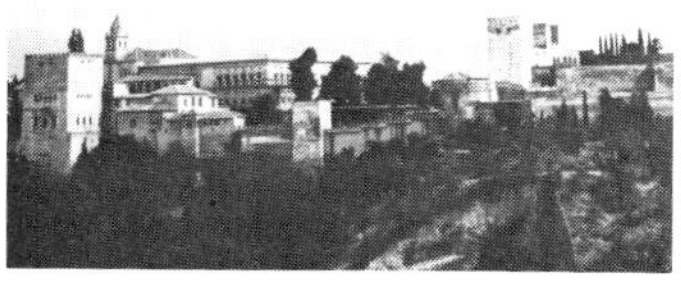

Granada may be so-called from the Spanish word for pomegranate.

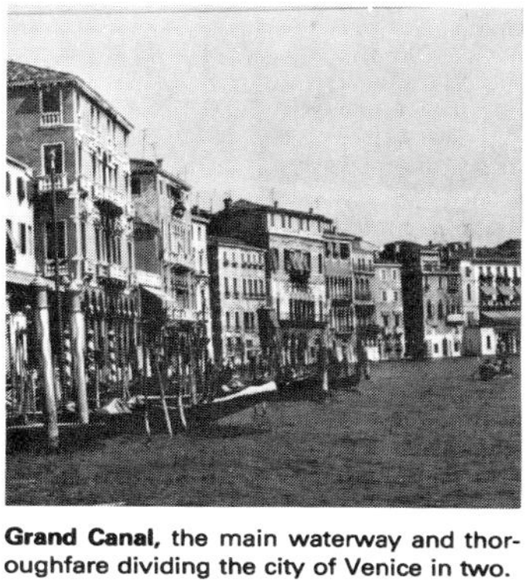

Grand Canal, the main waterway and thoroughfare dividing the city of Venice in two.

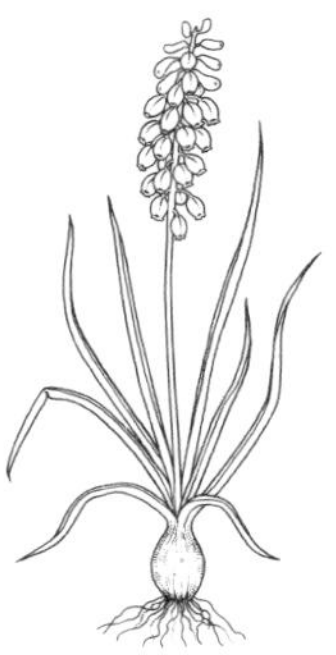

Grape hyacinth; most of the 50 species have clusters of blue, pink or white flowers.

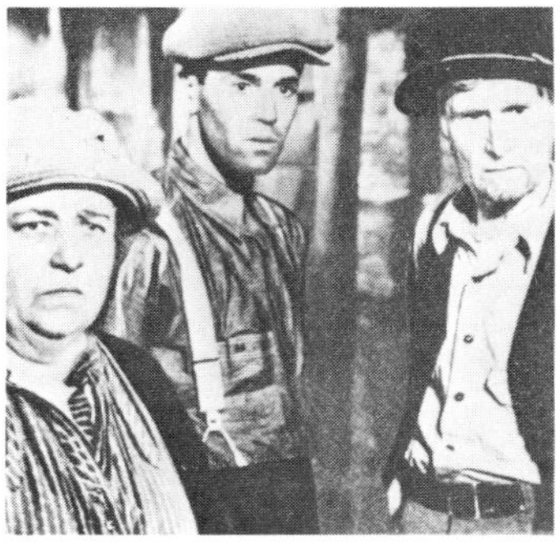

Grapes of Wrath; Henry Fonda (centre) in a scene from the film of Steinbeck's novel.

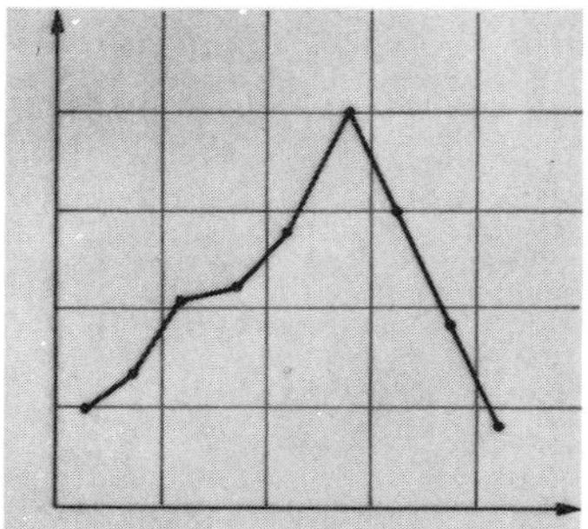

Graphs show an immediate graphic relationship between varying quantities or numbers.

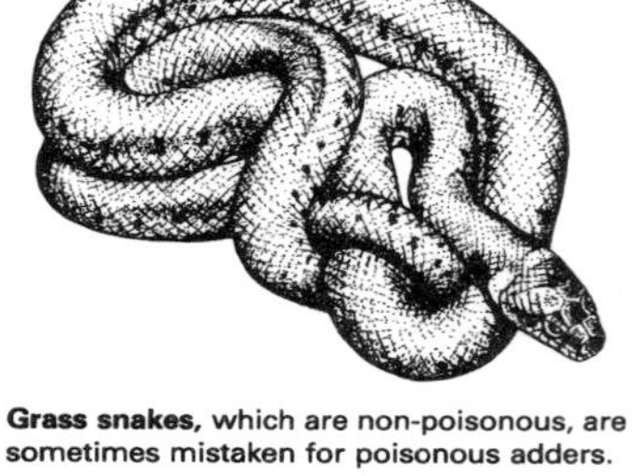

Grass snakes, which are non-poisonous, are sometimes mistaken for poisonous adders.

Charles I in England, declaring Parliament's right to approve ministers employed by the king and laying forth radical proposals for the reform of the Church. It proved to be a test of whether a man were a royalist or a parliamentarian, and it was passed in the House of Commons by only 11 votes.

Grand Trunk Pacific Railway, western part of a Canadian transcontinental railway. It ran from Winnipeg (Saskatchewan) to Prince Rupert (British Columbia) and was completed in 1914. The following year the eastern line, Moncton (New Brunswick) to Winnipeg, was finished. The company that built the line went bankrupt, was taken over by the government in the 1920s and its lines integrated with the Canadian National Railways system.

Grand Union Canal, artificial inland waterway in England which runs from London through Leicester, Birmingham and Loughborough in the Midlands. It is the longest canal in England, with a navigable length of over 422km (262 miles).

Granit, Ragnar (1900–), Swedish neurophysiologist who contributed greatly to an understanding of vision. He shared the 1967 Nobel Prize in physiology and medicine.

Granite, IGNEOUS ROCK from deep within the earth, composed chiefly of felspar and quartz, with some mica or hornblende. Its colour is usually light grey, although felspar may redden it. Its durability makes it a valuable construction material. Granite is thought to have solidified from magma (molten rock), but the occurrence of some granite with features normally associated with rocks of metamorphic origin suggests that not all granites are igneous. It crystallizes at great depths where the pressure is high; it becomes exposed at the earth's surface only by erosion of surface rocks or by movements in the earth's crust. *See also* PE pp.100–103.

Grant, Cary (1904–), US film-star, *b.* Britain, real name Alexander Archibald Leach. His many films include sophisticated comedies such as *Topper* (1937) and *Bringing Up Baby* (1938) and stylish thrillers such as *North by Northwest* (1959) and *Charade* (1963).

Grant, Duncan (1885–), British landscape painter, portraitist and designer, one of the first British artists to be influenced by the POST-IMPRESSIONISTS. He was a member of the BLOOMSBURY GROUP and as a designer was closely associated with Roger FRY and the OMEGA WORKSHOPS.

Grant, George Munro (1835–1902), Canadian educator and writer. Educated in Scotland at Glasgow University, he later joined the Canadian Pacific Railway's expedition to the W of Canada. He recounted his experiences in *Ocean to Ocean* (1873), his most famous book. The interest it aroused helped to encourage the settlement of W Canada. From 1877 to 1902 he was principal of Queen's University, Ontario. Under Grant the university gained in size and importance.

Grant, Ulysses Simpson (1822–85), US soldier and politician. He served in the Mexican War (1846–48) and at the start of the Civil War was colonel of the 21st Illinois Volunteers. After capturing Fort Henry and Fort Donelson in 1862, he was made a major-general. In 1864, as a lieutenant-general, he was given command of the Union forces. In 1866 he was made a general. Chosen as the Republican candidate for president in 1868, he was elected and served two terms in the White House (1869–77).

Grantham, market town and railway junction on the River Witham in Lincolnshire. The Battle of Grantham (1643) was the first Roundhead victory against the Royalists in the ENGLISH CIVIL WAR. Pop. 27,913.

Grant's gazelle, large pale-brown GAZELLE of E African plains. It is noted for its long, ringed horns. Height: to 89cm (35in). Family Bovidae; species *Gazella grantii.*

Granule, in astronomy, any of millions of irregular, frequently polygonal, markings on the Sun's photosphere, imparting to it a bubbly mottled appearance. Granules are transient phenomena – the tops of hot gas clouds set up by subsurface convection currents.

Granulite, granular METAMORPHIC ROCK that derives largely from quartz and felspar. Also called leptites, granulites often have a banded appearance. *See also* PE pp.102–103.

Granville-Barker, Harley (1877–1946), British dramatist-producer and critic who co-managed the Court Theatre in London (1904–07) and was one of the theatrical forces of his day. He produced the works of young playwrights and, as a critic, is known for his *Prefaces to Shakespeare* (1927–45).

Grape, any of numerous species of vines that grow in temperate and subtropical climates, and its important fruit which is eaten raw, dried or used for making WINE. The classical European vine (*Vitis vinifera*) had its origins in Asia. The climate, soil, topography and the methods of cultivation all determine the quality of the crop. Family Vitaceae. *See also* PE pp.192–193, 200–201, 202–203.

Grapefruit, evergreen citrus fruit tree of the family Rutaceae and its popular edible fruit, which is a valuable source of vitamin C. The tree, which may reach 6m (20ft), is grown mainly in subtropical climates in the USA, Israel, South Africa and Argentina. The large, spherical fruit has a thick yellow rind and a juicy, acid pulp.

Grape hyacinth, any of more than 50 Old World, perennial, bulbous plants native to the Mediterranean region. They have long, narrow leaves and deep blue, sometimes white or pink bell-shaped flower clusters. Family Liliaceae; genus *Muscari.*

Grapes of Wrath, The (1939), realistic novel by John STEINBECK about US farmers during the Depression. It deals with the Joad family who leave their drought-ridden Oklahoma farm for California. The novel received a Pulitzer Prize in 1939 and the following year was made into a film directed by John FORD and starring Henry FONDA. *See also* HC2 pp.288–289.

Graph, diagram representing a functional relationship between numbers or quantities, generally using CARTESIAN CO-ORDINATES. Two scales (axes) are drawn at right-angles. The point of intersection (origin) has the value zero and the scales have positive values to the right and above the origin and negative values to the left and below it. Distances along the horizontal axis (abscissa) represent values of the independent variable (x); those along the vertical axis (ordinate) give values of the dependent variable (y). Thus a point on the graph can be represented by a pair of numbers, and a curve is a "plot" of all possible pairs of numbers belonging to the function. *See also* SU pp.34–37, 54, 55.

Graphic art, form of art that depends for its effect mainly on drawing and not on colour. It includes the art of engraving and all forms of drawing, sometimes within the context of painting or PRINTMAKING. In current usage the term is sometimes extended to include the processes of graphic design, TYPOGRAPHY, photography and illustration, which are commonly integrated to meet the needs of industry and commerce. Traditionally, however, graphic art refers to the aesthetic process of drawing, exployed by an artist to create a "work of art".

The first professional engraver, Marcantonio RAIMONDI, interpreted the works of other artists. But as early as the 16th century others, such as Albrecht DÜRER and Lucas van LEYDEN, were creating their own subjects. In the 19th century technical engravers were almost in opposition to the artist-engravers. Some of this feeling has filtered through to today, but this distinction is by no means absolute.

Graphite (plumbago), dark grey, soft crystalline allotrope of CARBON that occurs naturally in deposits of varying purity and is made synthetically by heating petroleum coke. It is used in pencils (a mixture of graphite and clay is the "lead"), lubricants, electrodes, brushes of electrical machines, rocket nozzles and as a moderator in nuclear reactors. It owes its lubricating properties to the overlapping scale-like crystals that tend to slide, giving it a smooth slippery feel. Properties: s.g. 2–2.25.

Graptolite, any of an extinct group of colonial aquatic drifting organisms; sometimes considered a separate phylum but also thought to be related to the CHORDATES. They are found most frequently as flattened fibres of carbon, resembling pencil marks, in black shales of the ORDOVICIAN and SILURIAN ages. Their uncompressed skeletons etched out of limestone show that graptolites were composed of many small tubes regularly arranged along branches, which are presumed to have been attached to a common bladder-like float. *See also* NW pp.*22*, 179, *179*.

Grasmere, village in Cumbria, NW England. It is famous for its literary associations. The Romantic poets William WORDSWORTH and Samuel Taylor COLERIDGE lived there, as did the essayist Thomas DE QUINCEY. Wordsworth's house, Dove Cottage, is now a museum.

Grass, Günter (1927–), German novelist, poet and playwright. His prose narrative combines evocative description with historical documentation in the Mannerist style. He used powerful techniques to effect grotesque comedy in *Tin Drum* (1959) and *Cat and Mouse* (1961) and to satirize the Nazi era, the war and its aftermath, as in *Dog Years* (1963). Other works include *From the Diary of a Snail* (1972) and *Inmary praise* (trans. 1974).

Grass, any of many non-woody plants with fibrous roots that have long, narrow leaves enclosing hollow, jointed stems. The stems may be upright or bent, and may lie on the ground or grow underground. The small flowers, lacking petals and sepals, are arranged in spikelets and in the axils of bracts. Grass grows from the base, and so removal of the tips does not inhibit growth, making it suitable for lawns and pastures. The seed-like fruits store oil and protein, and are called grains. Economically the grasses are the most important plant family. CEREAL grasses such as rice, millet, maize and wheat are cultivated for their seeds. Others are grown as forage for domestic grazing animals, and for erosion control and ornament. Furniture is made from some grasses, such as bamboo. Height: 2.5cm–30m (1in–100ft). Family Gramineae; there are approx 8,000 species. *See also* MONOCOTYLEDON; NW pp.66–68.

Grasshopper, plant-eating insect found throughout the world. Its enlarged hind legs make it a powerful jumper. The forewings are leather-like and the hind wings are membranous and fan-shaped; when the insect is at rest, the wings are folded over its back. Length: 8–11cm (0.3–4.3in). Order Orthoptera; families Acrididae and Tettingoniidae. *See also* CRICKET, LOCUST, ORTHOPTERA; NW pp.*109*, *199*.

Grass of Parnassus, any of about 50 species of the perennial herb *Parnassia* of the SAXIFRAGE family, native to damp, cold to temperate, or mountainous regions of the Northern Hemisphere. The graceful plants bear solitary, showy flowers.

Grass snake, also called European water snake, a non-poisonous snake found in Europe, N Africa and central Asia. It swims readily, but is generally found in long grass and undergrowth. It is greenish-brown with a yellow collar. In Britain it is sometimes mistaken for the ADDER. Length: to 1m (3.3ft). Family Colubridae; species *Natrix natrix. See also* NW pp.*137*, *139*.

Grass track racing. *See* MOTOR-CYCLE SPORT; MOTOR SPORTS.

Grass tree, tree-like perennial plant native to regions of Australia. The long, grass-like leaves grow in tufts on thick stems. Family Xanthorrhoeaceae; genus *Xanthorrhoea.*

Grass wrack. *See* EEL GRASS.

Grateful Dead, US rock group. Formed in 1965 as the Warlocks, they typified the acid-rock movement of the late 1960s. Records from this period include *Aoxomoxoa* (1969) and *Live Dead* (1970). Later recordings in a country-rock vein such as *Workingman's Dead* and *American Beauty* 1970 show an increasing realization of the potential of studio recordings.

Gratianus, Flavius (359–83), Western Roman emperor (367–383). Co-emperor first with his father, Valentinian I (until 375), he later ruled with his brother Valentinian II. Advised by St Ambrose, he tried to stamp out paganism in the empire.

Grattan, Henry (1746–1820), Irish statesman. Trained as a lawyer, he entered the Irish Parliament in 1775 and through his oratory quickly became a leader of the party supporting Ireland's independence from the British Parliament, a goal achieved in 1782.

Grattan's Parliament, popular name given to the Irish parliament of 1782 to 1800, when it was ended by the Act of UNION between Britain and Ireland. It got its name from Henry GRATTAN, leader of the Irish Volunteer Movement, which succeeded in forcing the British Parliament to restore the independence of the Irish legislature and also the appellate jurisdiction of the Irish House of Lords.

Graunt, John (1620–1674), English statistician who prepared the first mortality table. This was published in 1662 under the title *Natural and Political Observations ... Made upon the Bills of Mortality.* Graunt was a founder member of the ROYAL SOCIETY.

Gravel, mixed pebbles and rock fragments, 2mm or more in diameter. Gravel beds are the remains of ancient seashores or river beds. Some are mined for their metal content, such as the California gold-bearing gravels. Usually gravel is used as an aggregate in concrete.

Graveney, Thomas William (1927–), British cricketer who played for Gloucestershire, Worcestershire and England. Noted for the elegance and grace of his batting, Graveney played in 79 Test matches from 1951–69, scoring 4,882 runs (including 11 centuries) at an average of 44.38.

Graves, Robert Ranke (1895–), British poet, novelist and critic. After publishing his WWI autobiography, GOODBYE TO ALL THAT (1929), he emigrated to Majorca. Other works include *I, Claudius* (1934), *Claudius the God* (1934) and *The Crowning Privilege* (1955). In *The White Goddess* (1948), he discusses the importance of religion and myth in the creative process.

Gravesham, county district in W KENT, England, on the Thames estuary, created in 1974 under the Local Government Act (1972). Area: 100sq km (39sq miles). Pop. (1974 est.) 97,300.

Gravettian culture, PALAEOLITHIC culture of *c.*22,000–18,000 BC. It is named after the site of La Gravette, in the Dordogne, France, but is found also in Italy. A related culture, the Eastern Gravettian, flourished in E Europe and Russia at about the same time. *See also* MS pp.*22–28.*

Gravimeter, or gravity meter, instrument used in geophysical surveys. Essentially, it is a heavy mass suspended from a spring. In the vicinity of a dense underground feature such as a metal deposit, the weight of the gravimeter mass increases slightly by gravitational attraction, so causing the spring to extend slightly, a movement recorded by its analogue meter. *See also* PE p.*32.*

Gravimetric analysis, in geology, the study of the magnitude of the earth's gravitational field in a particular area. Small variations in this field can be caused by the density of the rocks beneath the surface and can provide information about structures that are otherwise inaccessible. The instrument used for such a survey is known as a GRAVITY METER. *See also* PE p.*32.* In chemistry, gravimetric analysis is a method of determining the composition of a substance by making weighings. *See also* SU p.150.

Gravireceptors, sensory organs in the utricle and saccule located in the inner EAR (labryinth). They are sensitive to bodily equilibrium and gravity and have been found to be temporarily affected by prolonged weightlessness.

Gravitation, one of the four kinds of known forces (the others being electromagnetism and the weak and strong nuclear forces). Gravitation is extremely weak compared to the others, but it is nonetheless obvious to man because of the great mass of the earth. The gravitational force F between two masses M_1 and M_2 a distance d apart was found by Isaac NEWTON to be $F = DMm/d^2$, where D is a constant of proportionality called the universal constant of gravitation. A more powerful treatment of gravitation was developed by Albert EINSTEIN, who showed in his general theory of RELATIVITY how to understand gravitation as a manifestation of the underlying structure of space time. *See also* SU pp.72–73.

Gravitational red shift, slight shift in the red spectral lines of radiation emanating from a source within a gravitational field. It is predicted by EINSTEIN's general theory of RELATIVITY and has been experimentally observed in the spectra of celestial bodies, most noticeably in massive stars such as white dwarfs.

Gravitational waves, similar to electromagnetic waves, postulated by Einstein's general theory of RELATIVITY as being emitted from a massive accelerating body, such as an exploding or collapsing star, and to travel at the speed of light. Experimental results put forward as evidence for such waves have not yet been generally accepted. *See also* SU pp.106–107.

Graviton, hypothetical elementary particle of zero mass thought to be continuously exchanged between bodies of mass and thus to be the carrier of the gravitational force. The graviton is analogous to the photon – the quantum of electromagnetic waves. Its existence was suggested for the same reason that early physicists postulated an ETHER: to satisfy a theory.

Gravity, gravitational force of attraction at the surface of a planet or other celestial body. The Earth's gravity produces an acceleration of 9.8 m/sec^2 (32ft/sec^2) for any unsupported body. If the mass M and radius R of a planet are known, the acceleration due to its gravity (g) at its surface can be determined from $g = 6M/R^2$, where D is the universal constant of gravitation. The WEIGHT of a body is a measure of the force with which the Earth's gravity attracts it. Unlike MASS, which remains constant at normal speeds, weight (or the force of gravity) varies from place to place. *See also* SU pp.72–73.

Gravity anomaly, deviation in gravity from the expected value. Gravity measurements over deep ocean trenches are lower than average, those in mountainous regions are higher than average. There are two theories to explain this: according to J.H. Pratt mountains are composed of blocks of material of various densities floating at the same level, whereas G.B. AIRY assumes that there are blocks of the same density at various levels. *See also* PE p.32.

Gravity-assisted flight, use of a close approach to a planet to obtain extra velocity from its gravitational pull. A rocket "grazing" a planet is accelerated and whipped off in a new direction with greatly increased velocity, perhaps unattainable by conventional means. This technique will help the two Voyager probes, launched in 1977, on their way to the outer planets.

Gravity corer, device for collecting samples of the sea-bed. A weighted tube is dropped into the sediments and pulled to the ocean surface containing whatever sediment is trapped in the tube. A triggering device is usually incorporated so that the corer can be lowered slowly until it is just above the sea-bed and then dropped the last few metres. *See also* PE p.*91.*

Gravity meter. *See* GRAVIMETER.

Gravity survey, large-scale survey of rock formations that lie close to the surface, using sensitive instruments to measure increases in gravity to indicate possible petroleum reservoirs. Observable formations may be anticlinal folds, fault blocks and salt domes. Gravity surveys are made from the air and are generally used to discover areas for further exploration. *See also* SEISMIC SURVEY.

Gray, Elisha (1835–1901), US inventor. He received his first patent for a self-adjusting telegraph relay in 1867. He also invented and patented the telegraphic switch, telegraphic repeater, type-printing telegraph and telautograph. He claimed priority in inventing the speaking telephone, but Alexander Graham BELL's patent rights were upheld by the US Supreme Court.

Gray, John (1907–), Canadian biographer. His work, typified by *Lord Selkirk of Red River* (1963), combines painstaking research with balanced judgement. His other works include *The One-Eyed Trapper* (1942).

Gray's Elegy. *See* ELEGY WRITTEN IN A COUNTRY CHURCHYARD.

Gray, Sir James (1891–), British zoologist, noted for his research on the movement of cells and animals. He wrote many books, including *How Animals Move* (1953) and *Animal Locomotion* (1968).

Gray, Thomas (1716–71), English poet. His *Elegy Written in a Country Churchyard* (1751) brought him fame. Other poems include *Ode on the Death of a Favourite Cat* (1748), and *The Descent of Odin* (1768). His letters are valued for their witty observations of contemporary life.

Grayling, freshwater food and sporting fish of the salmon group found in N North America and Eurasia. It is characterized by an unusually long, tall dorsal fin and a small mouth. Length: to 60cm (24in). Family Salmonidae; species include *Thymallus thymallus. See also* NW p.*125*; PE p.*245.*

Graz, city in SE Austria, on the River Mur, 140km (87 miles) SSW of Vienna, in the Styrian Alps; second largest city in Austria. It has a 16th-century university where astronomer Johannes KEPLER taught. Industries: iron and steel, machinery, paper, leather, glass, textiles. Pop. 248,500.

Grease, semi-solid lubricant which consists of a mixture of a liquid lubricant with either a saponified fat or a dispersion of metallic soaps. There are five types: water soluble; water resistant; synthetic; special purpose; and multi-purpose. Although liquid lubricants are usually preferred, greases are used where a piece of machinery cannot be relubricated or where there is a need to avoid leakage, which may occur if oil were used.

Great Australian Bight, wide inlet on the S coast of Australia, part of the Indian Ocean. The coast is backed by a continuous line of the 80m (262ft) high cliffs of the arid Nullarbor Plain. During winter months the sea in the area is very stormy. Width: 966km (600 miles).

Great Barrier Reef, largest coral reef in the world, off the NE coast of Queensland, Australia. Made up of several individual reefs, it forms a natural breakwater and is, in places, up to 800m (2,625ft) wide. It is separated from the mainland by a shallow lagoon 11–24km (7–150 miles) wide. Length: 2,000km (1,242 miles).

Great Bear, or Ursa Major, northern circumpolar constellation, nicknamed the Plough, made up of seven stars, six of which are of the 2nd magnitude. It includes Mizar or Zeta Ursae Majoris, in the Bear's tail, which has a faint companion, Alcor. The two stars at the other end of the constellation are "pointers" to the Pole Star (Polaris). *See also* SU pp.*165–166, 237,* 256–257, 264–267.

Great Bear Lake, lake in Northwest Territories, Canada; largest lake in Canada and fourth largest in North America. It is drained in the W by the Great Bear River which flows into the Mackenzie River, but the lake is icebound for eight months of the year. It was first explored in 1825 by John FRANKLIN. Area: approx. 31,800sq km (12,278sq miles).

Great Bible, Thomas Cromwell's edition of English BIBLE which was ordered to be placed in every parish church. Published in 1539, it was an amalgamation of existing vernacular bibles. The second edition of 1540 contains an influential preface by Thomas CRANMER, and is known as "Cranmer's Bible".

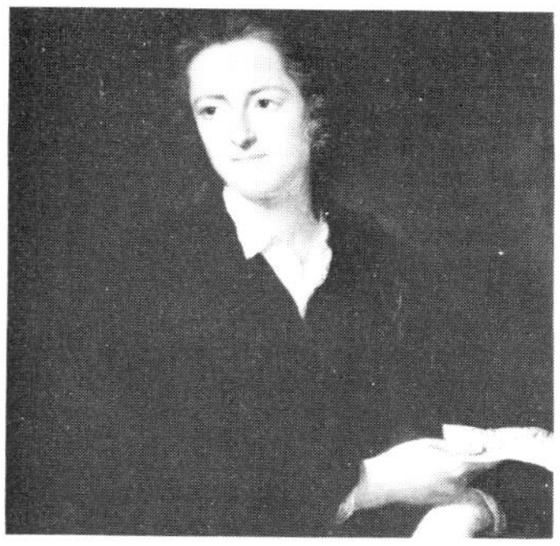

Thomas Gray, who wrote the poem *Elergy Written in a Country Churchyard.*

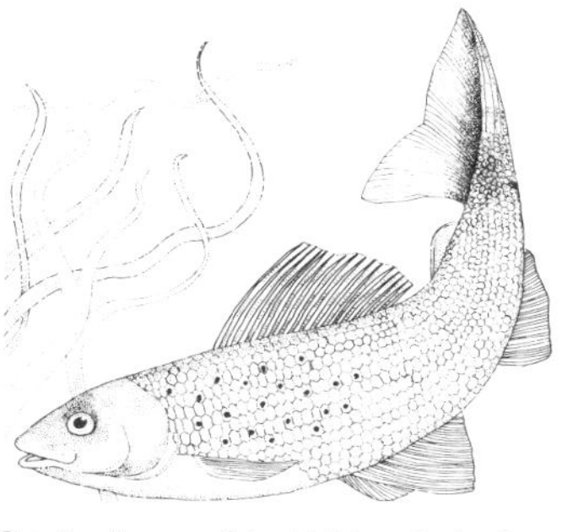

Grayling is game fish which is suffering from the pollution of N American streams.

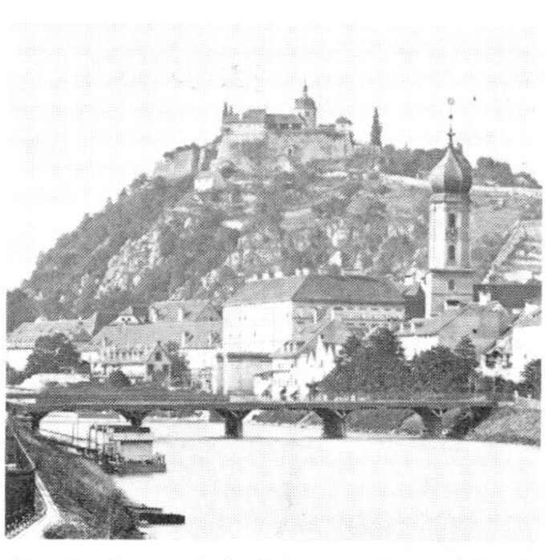

Graz is the capital of the province of Styria and the second largest city in Austria.

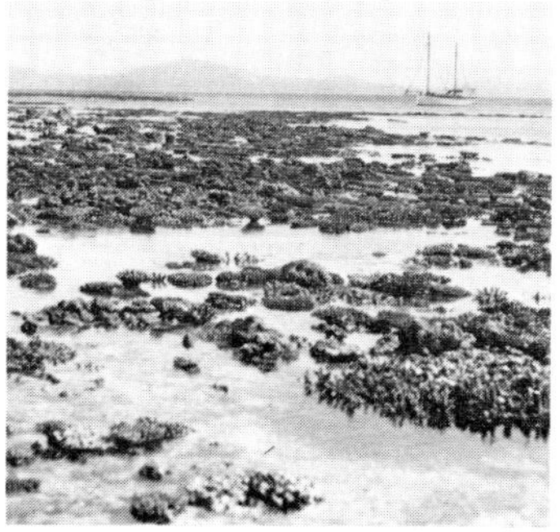

Great Barrier Reef, which faces destruction from the crown-of-thorns starfish.

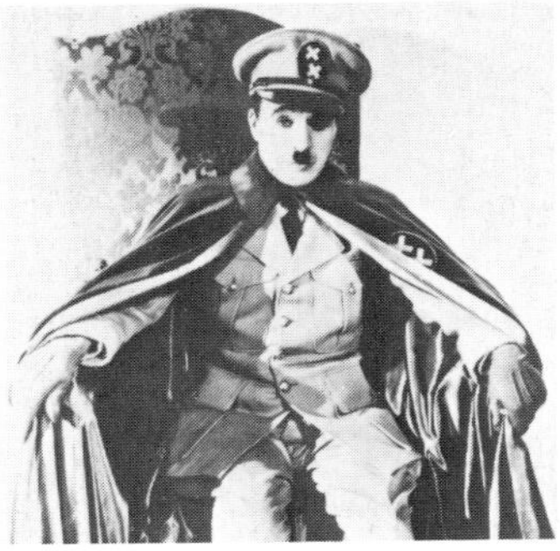

The Great Dictator was the first film in which Chaplin made full use of a soundtrack.

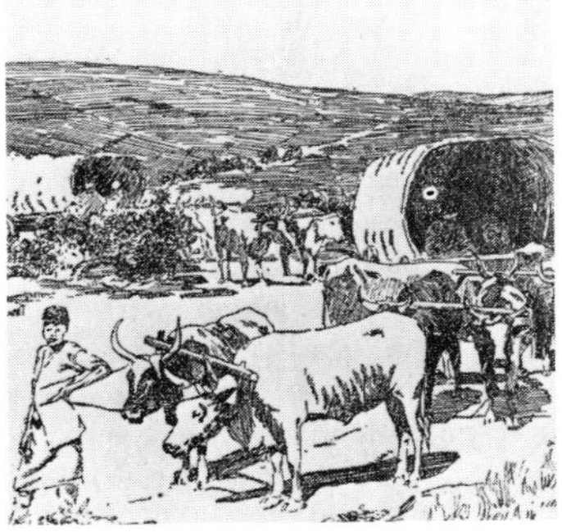

The Great Trek was the migration of the Boer farmers from Cape Colony into the interior.

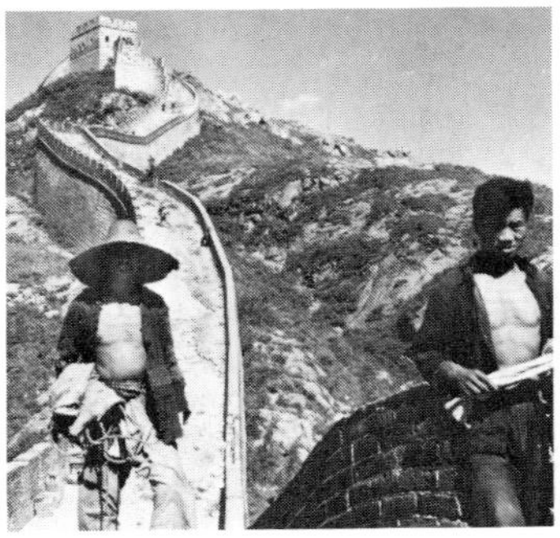

The Great Wall of China, which took centuries to finish, was built to keep out invaders.

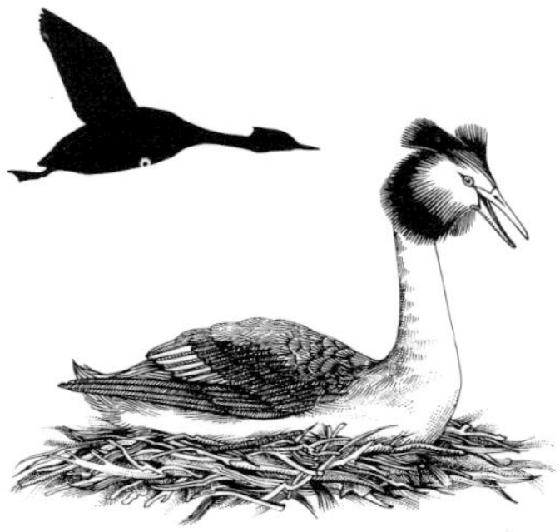

Grebes build nests which sometimes float like rafts in the shallows of lakes or ponds.

Great Bitter Lake, marshy lake of salt water N of Suez, Egypt. Once part of the Red Sea, it was deepened when the Suez Canal opened in 1869.

Great Britain, kingdom in NW Europe, officially named the United Kingdom of Great Britain and Northern Ireland, made up of England, Scotland, Wales and Northern Ireland, the Channel Islands and the Isle of Man. It is commonly known as Britain. *See* MW p.174.

Great circle, circle on a spherical surface whose centre is coincident with the centre of the sphere. Thus lines of longitude lie on great circles; a route above the great circle is the shortest distance between two points on a sphere.

Great Dane, also called German mastiff, a large hunting and fighting dog originally bred in Germany more than 400 years ago for boar hunting. It has a long narrow head with a large blunt muzzle. Its long, broad, deep-chested body is set on long strong legs. The short, smooth coat may be brindle, fawn, blue, black or a mixture called harlequin. Height: at least 76cm (30in) at the shoulder.

Great Dictator, The, US film, released in 1940. Written and directed by Charles CHAPLIN the film starred Chaplin himself, Paulette GODDARD and Jack Oakie. Its plot, the story of how a Jewish barber is mistaken for the dictator Adenoid Hynkel, gave Chaplin the chance to satirize Adolf HITLER and FASCISM.

Great Dividing Range (Eastern Highlands), series of mountain ranges and plateaus along the E coast of Australia, extending from the Atherton Tableland (N) to Victoria (S). The highest peak is Mt Kosciusko, 2,230m (7,316ft). Length: 3,703km (2,300 miles).

Great Eastern, British-built steamship, completed in 1858, for many years the largest ship in existence. Conceived by Isambard BRUNEL, she had a displacement of 27,400 tonnes when fully laden, and a length of 211m (692ft). Built for the England-India trade, she ended up in the North Atlantic, laying the Atlantic cable from Ireland to Newfnundland in 1866. *See also* MM p.*225*.

Greater Antilles, largest of the three major island groups in the West Indies between the Atlantic Ocean and the Caribbean Sea. The group includes Cuba, Hispaniola, Jamaica, Puerto Rico and the Cayman Islands. Puerto Rico is self-governing in association with the USA, the Cayman Islands are a British colony and the other islands are independent, Hispaniola being divided into Haiti and the Dominican Republic. *See* articles on individual islands in *The Modern World*.

Greater London, administrative area in SE England, formed in 1974 from the former county borough of London and the City of London, most of the former county of MIDDLESEX, and parts of the former counties of SURREY, KENT, ESSEX and HERTFORDSHIRE. Greater London includes the Corporation of the City of London plus 32 boroughs. Area: 1,580km (610sq miles). Pop. (1976 est.) 7,028,200.

Greater London Council (GLC), governing body for the metropolitan area of greater London. It replaced the London County Council in 1964, when 87 separate local authorities were abolished and London divided into 12 inner and 20 outer boroughs, each with its own council. The City of London, a corporation, retained its independence. Elections to the GLC are held every four years in May. The GLC has no authority to levy rates or administer education in the outer boroughs, although it does administer education in the inner boroughs through the Inner London Education Authority (ILEA). The chief duties of the GLC are overall planning, the maintenance of main roads, traffic control and public transport, and fire brigade services. The metropolitan police are under the direct control of the HOME OFFICE.

Greater Manchester, metropolitan county in NW England, formed in 1974 from parts of the former counties of CHESHIRE, LANCASHIRE and including the former county borough of Manchester. Area: 1,284sq km (496sq miles). Pop. (1976) 2,684,100.

Great Exhibition (1851). *See* CRYSTAL PALACE.

Great Expectations (1861), novel by Charles DICKENS. Tragi-comic in tone and sporadically autobiographical, the novel differs from Dickens' earlier work in that it concerns itself closely with individuals rather than with society as a whole, examining with profound psychological insight the themes of gratitude, revenge, and the illusions accompanying wealth.

Great Gatsby, The (1925), novel by F. Scott FITZGERALD. Specifically dealing with the gloomy spiritual isolation of Jay Gatsby, the possessor of great wealth dubiously obtained, the novel more generally highlights both the illusory nature of social glamour and, in common with many novels of the period, the failure of the "American Dream".

Greathead, James Henry (1844–96), British engineer, *b.* South Africa. He developed a method of shield tunnelling that is named after him. The shield was designed to complete the building of a subway in 1869, under the River Thames, London, and other projects included the City and South London railway tunnels.

Great Lakes, chain of five freshwater lakes in central North America, between Canada and the USA; they are, from W to E lakes SUPERIOR, MICHIGAN, HURON, ERIE and ONTARIO, and are connected by straits, rivers and canals, providing a continuous waterway. Formed at the end of the ICE AGE, they are drained by the St Lawrence River. The opening of the Erie Canal in 1825 connected Lake Erie with the Hudson River, New York and the Atlantic Ocean. The deepening of the St Lawrence River opened up the lakes to world shipping. The Illinois Waterway connects the lakes with the Mississippi River. Heavy industrialization along their shores has greatly increased pollution, particularly lakes Erie, Ontario and Michigan. Major cities on the lakes' shores include Chicago, Detroit, Buffalo, Cleveland and Milwaukee. The combined surface area of the lakes is 245,300sq km (94,710sq miles). *See also* PE pp.*60*, 151.

Great Leap Forward, name given to a five-year economic plan begun by MAO TSE-TUNG in China in 1958. It aimed to double industrial production and boost agricultural output in record time. Tens of millions of workers were mobilized to smelt iron in primitive handmade furnaces, but much of the iron produced proved useless. Collective farms were merged into communes but initial progress was dashed by a succession of poor harvests. After four years the government was forced to admit that the scheme had failed. *See also* HC2 p.244, *244*.

Great Mammoth Cave, large underground cavity in the Mammoth Caves, Kentucky, USA. Part of the world's largest underground cave network, the cavity was formed in a limestone plateau by surface water seeping through and dissolving the rock. *See also* PE pp.110–111.

Great Ouse, river in S central England; rises in the Northampton Highlands and flows E and NE through Bedfordshire and Cambridgeshire to the Wash near King's Lynn. Its drainage basin extends over the E Midlands and the W Fens. Length: 251km (156 miles).

Great Plains, high, extensive region of grassland in central North America; extends from the central Canadian states of Alberta, Saskatchewan and Manitoba S through W central USA, including North and South Dakota, Nebraska, Kansas, Oklahoma, Montana, Wyoming and New Mexico to Texas. It is a sparsely populated region with a semi-arid climate, and cattle ranching and sheep-rearing are the main economic activities in the W. Farther E, wheat is the principal crop, but sorghum and flax are also grown.

Great Rift Valley, steep-sided, flat-floored valley in SW Asia and E Africa, extending from N Syria, through the Jordan Valley, Dead Sea and the Gulf of Aqaba. It continues as the trough of the Red Sea, through Eritrea, Ethiopia and S across Kenya, Tanzania and Malawi to the lower valley of the Zambezi River in Mozambique. One of the finest examples of a RIFT VALLEY, the Great Rift Valley was formed in the Pleistocene period. Length: approx. 6,400km (4,000 miles).

Great Salt Lake, large, shallow salt-water lake in NW Utah USA. Fed by the Bear, Weber and Jordan rivers, its depth and area vary from year to year with climatic changes. It is believed to be the remnant of the prehistoric Lake Bonneville, which covered much of the Great Basin of North America. Area: approx. 5,180sq km (2,000sq miles).

Great Sandy Desert, large arid region of sand dunes, scrubland and salt marshes in N Western Australia state, Australia. Area: 518,000sq km (200,000sq miles).

Great Schism, division within the Catholic Church (1378–1417). The split reflected political ambition and controversy about the power of the cardinals over the pope. The unpopular URBAN VI was elected pope in 1378 by half the college of cardinals, which later tried to depose him and elect another pope, CLEMENT VII, who was installed in Avignon. Thereafter successive popes held sway in Avignon and Rome. The schism was ended by the Council of CONSTANCE (called in 1414), which established MARTIN V as the only pope. *See also* HC1 p.*187*.

Great Seal, chief seal of the British monarch, used on all important documents. It is normally in the possession of the Lord CHANCELLOR. The seal is circular and double-sided. The earliest impression extant is from EDWARD THE CONFESSOR. A new seal is produced for a monarch on accession.

Great Slave Lake, lake in Northwest Territories, Canada: the fifth largest lake in North America. The British fur trader Samuel Hearne discovered it in 1771, and it was named after the Slave Indians. Gold is mined on its N shore. Area: approx. 28,400sq km (10,980sq miles).

Great Train Robbery, The (1903), US film. This western was the longest narrative film of its time, 92m (302ft), which ran for 11 minutes. In a series of short, interdependent scenes, the director, Edwin S. Porter, made a number of editing innovations, including parallel and overlapping action sequences. *See also* HC2 p.200.

Great Trek (1835–40), migration of Boer farmers from the CAPE COLONY in South Africa northwards into the interior. They were called *voortrekkers*, men of Dutch origin who wished to escape from the British government's attempt to preserve native lands for the Bantu people and to protect the rights of non-European people on the eastern frontier. About 12,000–14,000 farmers and about the same number of slaves and servants made the journey. They founded NATAL, the TRANSVAAL and the ORANGE FREE STATE. *See also* HC2 pp.128–129.

Great Wall of China, defensive wall 2,400km (1,500 miles) long, marking a clear boundary between the settled areas of China and the lands inhabited by nomads. The wall was first unified in 214 BC by the first CH'IN emperor, but many shorter lengths of wall already existed. The present wall was mostly built by the MING DYNASTY. The wall is about 7.6m (25ft) high and up to 9.1m (30ft) thick. *See also* HC1 p.*122*.

Great Western, transatlantic steamship. Designed by Isambard Kingdom BRUNEL, it made its maiden crossing of the Atlantic in 1838 in 15 days, about half the normal time. The vessel displaced 1,340 tonnes, was 65m (213ft) long and could accommodate 148 passengers.

Great Whale, river in Quebec province, Canada which rises E of Lac Bienville, and flows W into Hudson Bay. At its mouth is the Hudson Bay trading post of Great Whale River. Length: 370km (230 miles).

Greaves, Jimmy (1940–), British footballer. A supreme forward with a strong left-foot shot, he scored 491 goals in a 16-season career (1957–71), playing for Chelsea, AC Milan, Tottenham Hotspur and West Ham United.

Grebe, brown, grey and black freshwater diving bird found throughout the world. It flies laboriously and has legs set so far back that it cannot walk on land. There are five common species of glebes in Britain and w Europe. They are either resident or regular visitors. Length: to 48cm (19in). Family Podicepididae; genus *Podiceps*. *See also* NW p.*140*.

Grechko, Andrei Antonovich (1903–76), Soviet military commander. In WWII he was an army commander in the Caucasus and Ukraine. From 1957 to 1960 he was commander-in-chief of the Soviet land forces. In 1967 he became both commander-in-chief of the armed forces of the Warsaw Treaty Powers and Soviet minister of defence.

Greco, El (1541–1614), Spanish painter, real name Domenikos Theotokopoulos, *b.* Crete. His early style was influenced by TITIAN and other Italian MANNERISTS. By 1577 he had settled in Toledo and his earliest work there, *The Assumption of the Virgin*, combines new Spanish influences with the Italian. His intensely personal vision is ecstatically mystical, with elongated, distorted figures, disturbing colour schemes and a disregard for normal rules of perspective. His later paintings, such as *Burial of Count Orgasz* (1586), *Agony in the Garden* (1610) and *Assumption* (1613) express his profound and emotional religious conviction.

Greco, Emilio (1913–), Italian sculptor, *b.* Sicily. His sculptures of female figures and portraits border on the avant garde, with angular mannered rhythms and simplified forms. His works also include the bronze doors of Orvieto Cathedral (1964) and the Pinocchio monument at Collodi.

Greco, José (1918–), US dancer and choreographer, *b.* Italy. He is famed for his flamenco dances. He began his dance career in the New York production of *Carmen* in 1937 and was a partner of the dancer La Argentinita in 1943. In 1948 he organized his own company, the Ballets y Bailes de España.

Greece, nation in the S of the Balkan Peninsula in the E Mediterranean. A magnificent civilization flourished there in the first millennium BC, but later Greece came under foreign domination for centuries, and today it is a largely underdeveloped country that has suffered political unrest in the 20th century. Agriculture is based on grain, tobacco, fruits, cotton and sugar-beet. The chief industries are food processing, chemicals and textiles. It is, however, a leading maritime nation with a large commercial fleet. The capital is Athens. Area: 131,944sq km (50,944sq miles). Pop. (1975 est.) 9,046,000. *See* MW p.88.

Greece, ancient, civilization of the NE Mediterranean that arose in the 3rd millennium BC in Crete, and reached its greatest achievements on the Greek mainland 500–300 BC. Although politically divided into diverse city-states, Greece and its colonies maintained a universal culture that formed the basis of Roman and European art, philosophy and science until modern times. *See also* HC1 pp.38–41, 68–79.

Greek architecture and art evolved after the decline of the MYCENAEANS and the migrations to the Aegean (*c.*1100 BC) of the Dorians.

The architecture of ancient Greece achieved its unique character and its place as a principal influence on European styles until the present century not through great structural innovations (the Greeks used simple TRABEATE construction) but through its unparalleled perfection in form and proportion and refinement of detail. The Greeks regarded beauty as a god-like attribute and the pursuit of beauty as a religious exercise. They evolved many types of building, including the AGORA, or civic centre, around which were grouped buildings such as council chambers, schools, libraries, theatres, gymnasia, public baths and lavatories. From earliest times, however, the Greek architect's chief concern was with temple building, first in wood and later in stone (6th century BC), when the transformation was monumental in every sense and Greek architecture really came into being. Gradually distinct styles or ORDERS of column, each with its own form of entablature, began to emerge – DORIC, IONIC and, lastly, CORINTHIAN. The earliest Doric temple of which there are appreciable remains is the Temple of Hera at Olympia (late 7th century BC). The Temple of Aphaia at Aegina (*c.*490 BC) is perhaps the earliest example of mature Doric, while the PARTHENON, on the ACROPOLIS, Athens, enjoys the reputation of being the most perfect Doric temple ever built. Among Ionic temples, that of Athena Nike (*c.*427 BC), at the gateway of the Acropolis, is an early surviving example and the Erectheion, near the Parthenon, is considered the most perfect. The Temple of Olympian Zeus at Athens (2nd century BC) is among the most important Corinthian buildings; the Corinthian Mausoleum at Helicarnassus (350 BC) was one of the Seven Wonders of the World.

Greek art may for convenience be divided into four chronological periods: Geometric, Archaic, Classical and Hellenistic.

The Geometric period (late 11th to late 8th century BC). There is no extant painting or major sculpture from this period. Numerous terracotta vases, decorated with geometric motifs, survive, also a large number of naively executed figurines and, from the end of the period, a few miniature bronze horses, sculpted in a simple, abstract style in keeping with their size.

The Archaic period (late 8th century to 480 BC). A new feeling, reflecting the growth in civic life and trade, began to enter Greek art. Fresh ideas and motifs were introduced, some of them from the E Mediterranean, particularly Syria, and there was a general spirit of experimentation. Stone sculpture appeared for the first time and painting probably began; vase painting proliferated. The anatomy of the human figure, the main interest of representational artists, was a common subject by the end of the period.

The Classical period (480–323 BC). Civic wealth and pride increased throughout the period. Sculpture, which aimed at ideal beauty of form, proportion and expression, reached its peak of serene perfection; painting experimented with the third dimension, although vase-painting declined; metalwork and engraving of gemstones was excellent.

The Hellenistic period (327–23 BC). Technical skill and variety in the arts still developed, although the art of the Classical period continued without interruption throughout the Hellenistic period. *See also* HC1 pp.68–83.

Greek drama, first form of DRAMA in western civilization, among which are found plays of unparalleled poetry and power. Greek drama took two forms, TRAGEDY and COMEDY. Tragedy developed from religious festivals at which a chorus sang responses to a leader. AESCHYLUS introduced a second actor, allowing for genuine dramatic interaction, and SOPHOCLES added a third. The other main surviving tragedian was EURIPEDES. Greek tragedy usually dealt with mythical subjects, but sometimes, as in Aeschylus' *The Persians*, used recent history for its setting. The subjects are based on the inexorability of fate, the failure of man's attempts to transcend his limitations, and human dilemmas of love and duty. A tradition of Greek comedy arose in the 5th century BC, which was often highly topical and lampooned the conventions of tragedy as well as the actions of politicians. The best-known comedy-writer was ARISTOPHANES. Drama competitions, for both comedy and tragedy, were run by many of the cities at religious festivals. *See also* HC1 pp.74–75.

Greek fire, compound that ignited and burned strongly when brought into contact with water. It was first used by the Byzantine Greeks in sea battles in the 7th century AD. Its constituents probably included sulphur, tar, quicklime and naphtha, but its exact composition remains unknown.

Greek language, Indo-European language spoken in Greece since *c.*2000 BC. In ancient Greece there were several dialects, of which Attic, spoken in Athens, is the most common in literary records. Greek was widely spoken in the Middle East in HELLENISTIC times in a simplified form known as *koine*, and was known throughout the Roman Empire. It was the official language of the Byzantine Empire, and began to evolve into its modern form in *c.*1000 AD. After the fall of Byzantium in the 15th century it was confined to Greece, where it developed two forms: "demotiki", the spoken language and that used in most literary forms, and "katharevousa", used for 18th-century literature in official documents. Ancient Greek is still spoken by Greek Orthodox priests. *See also* MS pp.*240–241*.

Greek literature, one of the longest surviving traditions of literature in the world. Earliest Greek literature was in the form of epic songs, collected by HOMER in the *Iliad* and the *Odyssey*. Throughout classical Greece there was a tradition of fine literature in poetry, both lyric and dramatic, and prose writing, encompassing history, philosophy and oratory. Greek literature continued to flourish until the fall of the Roman Empire, and most of the scientific works of the period were written in Greek. Imaginative literature was less popular than scholarship in the Byzantine Empire, and writing in Greek died out after the Turkish invasions of the 15th century. With the overthrow of the Turks in 1828, Greek literature was revived, and several writers of international significance such as Nikos KAZANTZAKIS and George SEFERIS have written in Greek. *See also* HC1 pp.74–75.

Greek Orthodox Church. *See* ORTHODOX CHURCH.

Green, Julian (1900–), French novelist of American parentage and brother of novelist Anne Green. He expresses deep spiritual anxiety in the face of a violent and sinful society. Among his best-known works are *The Closed Garden* (1927), *Moira* (1950) and *Ce qui reste de jour* (1972).

Green, Thomas Hill (1836–82), British philosopher. A representative of English idealism, he reacted against the English empiricists and stressed self-determination based on free ethical choice. His most important work is *Prolegomena to Ethics* (1883).

Green algae, large group of marine and freshwater algae (division Chlorophyta). Green algae range in size from microscopic single-cell types to large, complex seaweeds. Some of the single-cell types form colonies. Others live in a symbiotic relationship with fungi, forming the plant known as a LICHEN; and yet others live in symbiotic association with certain marine invertebrates. *See also* NW p.46.

Greenaway, Kate (1846–1901), British author and illustrator of books for children. Her illustrations of a joyous world of children are executed with charm and delicacy, but without sentimentality. Her first major success was *Under the Window* (1879). Other titles include *Mother Goose* (1881) and *Language of Flowers* (1884).

Green belt, area of open land as a barrier between adjoining built-up areas. The concept of green belts was first put forward by Ebenezer HOWARD in his plans for Garden Cities. Howard used them to distinguish residential from industrial sections. The green belts provide insulation from ugly factories and intensive commercial areas, they may provide recreational space and they aid in the replenishment of atmospheric oxygen.

Greene, Henry Graham (1904–), British novelist and dramatist. His novels, usually written from the evident viewpoint of a Roman Catholic convert, include *Brighton Rock* (1938), *The Power and the Glory* (1940), *The Quiet American* (1955), *Our Man in Havana* (1958), *Travels with My Aunt* (1969) and *The Honorary Consul* (1973). His plays include *The Living Room* (1953) and *The Potting Shed* (1957).

Greene, Nathanael (1743–86), American Revolutionary general. From 1775–77 he served as an able subordinate to WASHINGTON in Massachussetts, New York and New Jersey. He was appointed commander of the army of the South in 1780.

Greene, Robert (1558–92), English dramatist and pamphleteer. His works include the play *The Honourable History*

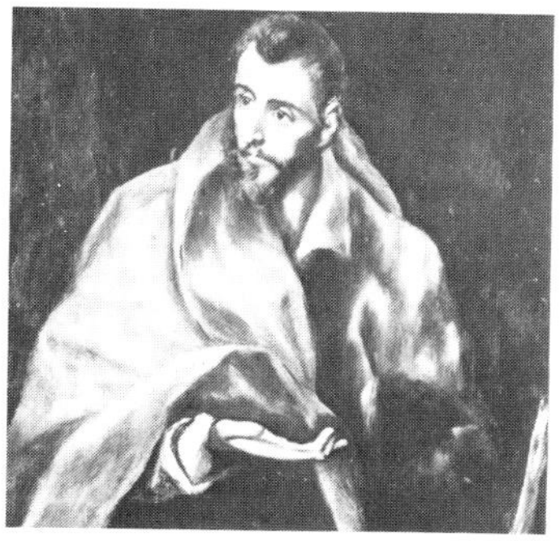

El Greco was born in Crete, studied in Italy, but is regarded as a Spanish painter.

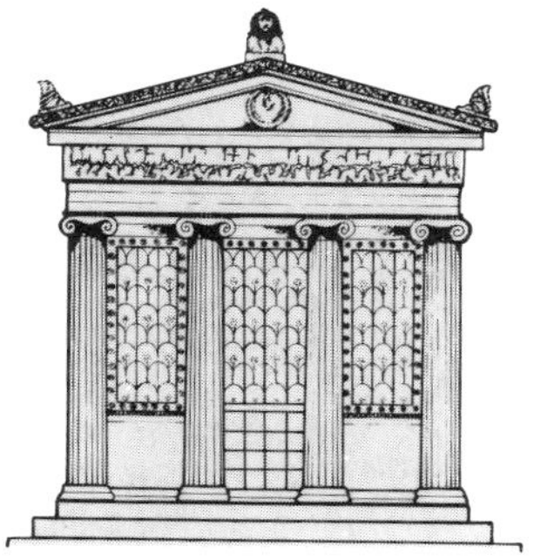

Greek architecture's perfection of form influenced all subsequent European styles.

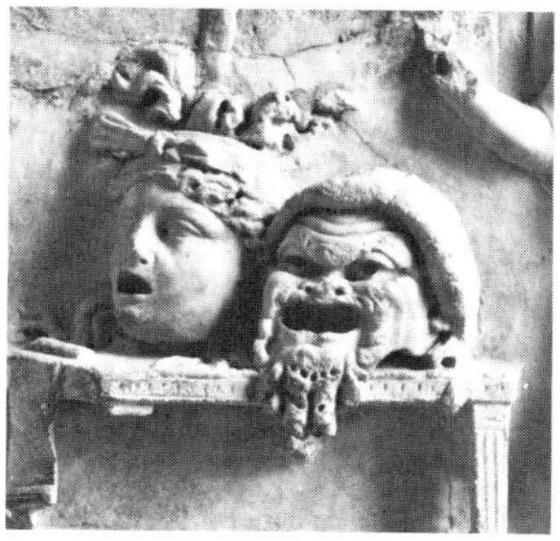

Greek drama marks the introduction of the distinction between tragedy and comedy.

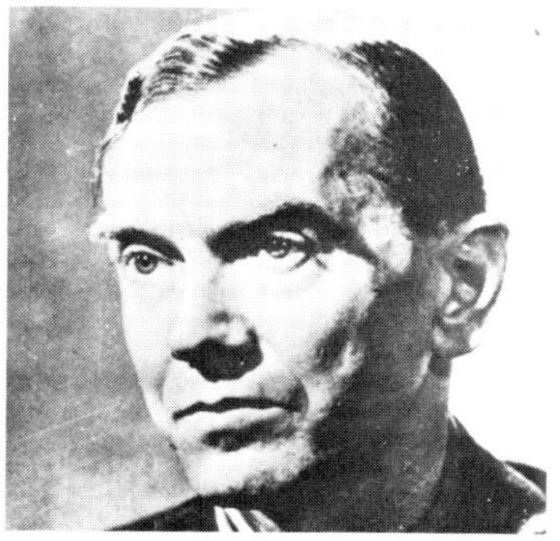

Graham Greene's novels present a recurring theme of the conflict between good and evil.

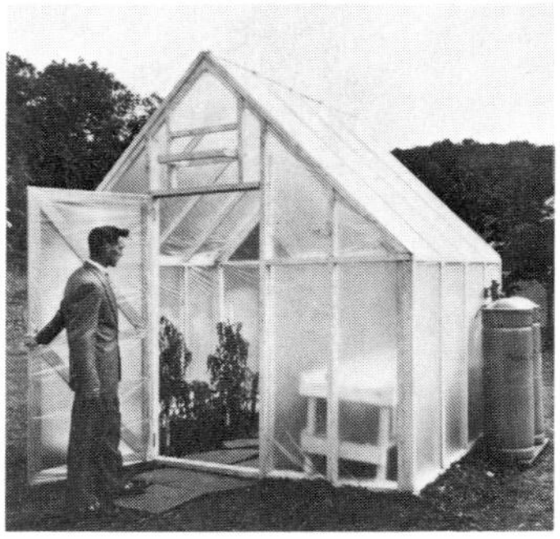

Greenhouses using clear plastic film can be erected quickly by most amateurs.

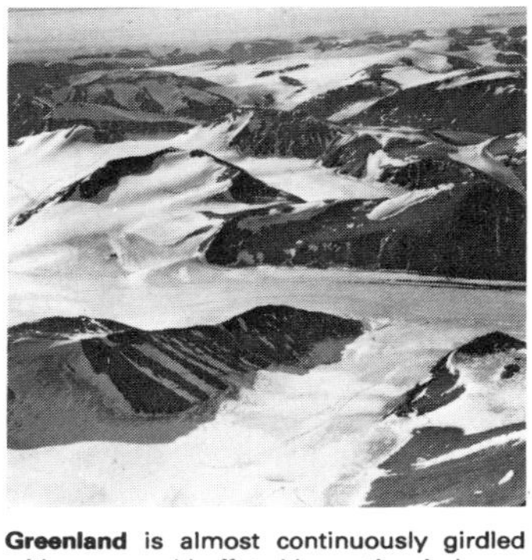

Greenland is almost continuously girdled with snow and buffeted by arctic winds.

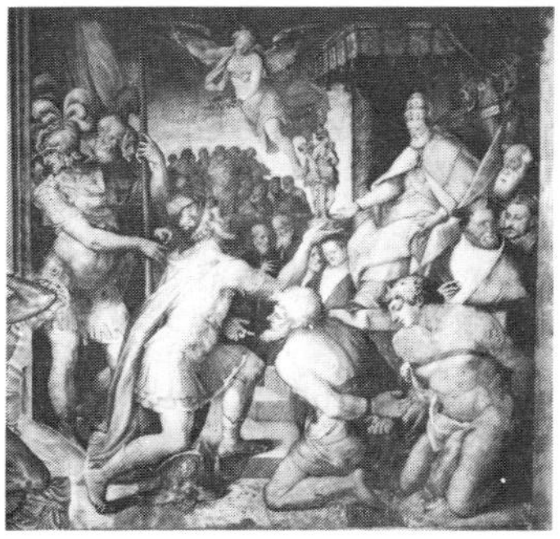

Gregory I delivered a panic stricken Rome from threats of invasion by the Lombard king.

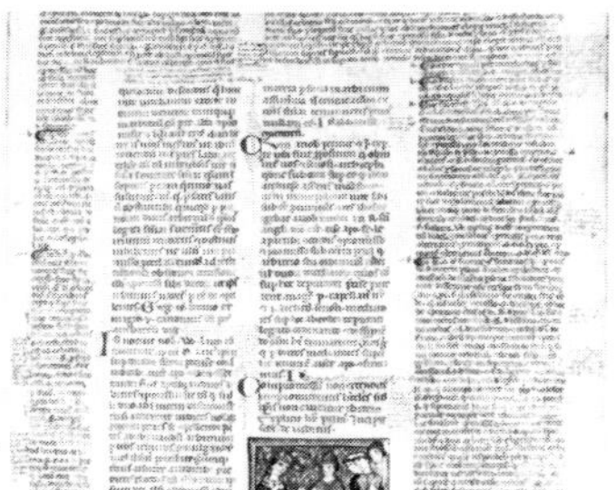

Gregory IX twice excommunicated Frederick II, the emperor of the Holy Roman Empire.

of Friar Bacon and Friar Bungay (acted *c.*1592), the prose romance *Pandosto* (1588) and accounts of London's criminal underworld. His romantic comedies influenced those of SHAKESPEARE, and he was possibly co-author of the *Henry VI* plays on which Shakespeare based his own.

Greenfinch, greenish bird with yellow wing markings; it is resident in Britain, but found also in other parts of Europe and in N Asia. Length: 14.7cm (5.8in). Family Fringillidae; species *Carduelis chloris.*

Green flash, the greenish or bluish hue of the upper rim of the sun seen just as it is about to disappear at setting, or appear at rising, due to refraction, scattering and absorption of light in the atmosphere.

Greenfly, small insect of the order Hemiptera which is, with the blackfly, the most common APHID. These plant lice pierce the leaves and stems of plants with their mouthparts and suck out the juices, thereby helping to spread plant diseases and seriously to deform seedlings. They are preyed upon by LADYBIRDS, but are nurtured by ants for their sticky, sugary excretion called honeydew. Length: about 3mm (0.25in). *See also* NW p.*110.*

Greengage. *See* PLUM.

Greenheart, tropical American tree which yields a heavy dense greenish wood that resists attack by insect and marine borers. It has accordingly been used to build piers and the keels of boats. Family Lauraceae; species *Ocotea rodiaei.*

Greenhouse, also called hothouse, building designed to protect vulnerable plants against extremes of temperature. Most greenhouses have a wooden or metal framework with glass or clear plastic. They may also be used to house germinating seeds and seedlings. Temperature and humidity can be controlled so that out-of-season or exotic plants can be grown.

Greenhouse effect, selective trapping of heat radiation from the sun by the atmosphere causing the earth to be heated. It is so named because the effect is readily demonstrable in a greenhouse in which the glass is analogous to the atmosphere. Of the radiation reaching the earth, or the inside of a greenhouse, only the shorter (ultra-violet) rays can pass back through the atmosphere, or the glass; the longer (infra-red) heat rays are re-reflected within, due to the optical properties of the atmosphere, or glass.

Greenland, in the NW Atlantic Ocean, largest island in the world. Most of the land is ice-covered and the vegetation is limited to mosses and lichens. The majority of the population is Eskimo, who hunt seals and live on the SW coast. Fish and fish products are the basis of the economy although there is some mining for coal, mica, quartz and cryolite. The capital is Godthåb. Area: 2,175,000sq km (840,000sq miles). Pop. (1975 est.) 49,500. *See* MW p.90.

Green Revolution, intensive plan of the 1960s to increase crop yields in THIRD WORLD agriculture by introducing higher-yielding strains of plant and new fertilizers. The scheme began in Mexico in the 1940s and was successfully introduced in parts of India, SE Asia, the Middle East and Latin America. Particularly notable for his work in this sphere is N. E. BORLAUG. *See also* HC2 p.*303.*

Green room, traditional actors' backstage common-room, probably named after the colour of its walls and furnishings or perhaps derived from a corruption of "scene room".

Greenshank, shy wading bird with a long, slightly up-turned bill; it breeds in Scotland and Scandinavia and is a common winter visitor to Britain. It has characteristic olive green legs. Height: 30cm (12in). Family Charadriidae; species *Tringa nebularia. See also* NW p.*206.*

Greenwich, borough in Greater London and site of the Royal Observatory from its foundation in 1675 until the 1950s, when it moved to Herstmonceux, Sussex. It is still used to define the PRIME MERIDIAN. Pop. (1971) 59,755.

Greenwich Mean Time. *See* GMT.

Greenwood, Walter (1903–), British novelist and playwright whose works describing social conditions in pre-war Lancashire, most notably *Love on the Dole* (1933) and *Only Mugs Work* (1938), won him considerable contemporary acclaim.

Gregg, Sir Norman McAlister (1892–1966), Australian ophthalmic surgeon. In 1941 he discovered that rubella – GERMAN MEASLES – in a pregnant woman could cause physical defects in her child. Gregg was knighted in 1953.

Gregorian calendar. *See* CALENDAR.

Gregorian chant, religious PLAINSONG music of the early and medieval Christian Church still, however, sung in some high Anglican and Roman Catholic churches today. Named after Pope GREGORY I (*r.*590–604), it is nevertheless believed to have originated shortly after Gregory's time. Before the REFORMATION, Gregorian chant was sung to the liturgy, psalms and canticles in Latin.

Gregory, name of 16 popes, of which those listed below were the most prominent. Gregory I (*r.*590–604) reformed the administration of the papal patrimony, insisted that the Apostolic see was the head of all churches, codified church music and initiated the conversion of Anglo-Saxons. He was canonized and became known as Gregory the Great. Gregory II (*r.*715–31) travelled with Pope CONSTANTINE I to Constantinople in 710, alienated the Byzantine government by his opposition to iconoclasm and developed new Masses for Lent. Like Gregory I, he was canonized. Gregory VII (family name Hildebrand; *r.*1073–85) twice excommunicated the Roman Emperor Henry IV over a conflict on lay investiture. He considered a crusade against the Seljuk Turks, increased the papacy's temporal power and thought constantly of the rights and duties of rulers. Gregory IX (Ugolino di Anagni *b.c.*1143; *r.*1227–41) was made a cardinal deacon in 1198 by his uncle Pope INNOCENT III and as pope, clashed continuously with Emperor FREDERICK II. He ordered the 1233 INQUISITION, placed the Dominicans in charge of it and published the Decretals in 1234, a code of common law used until 1917. Gregory XI (Pierre Roger de Beaufort, *b.*1329; *r.*1370–78) was the last Avignon pope and his concern to recover the papal lands led to war with Florence. He issued the first condemnation of John WYCLIFFE's teachings. Gregory XII (Angelo Correr, *b.c.*1325; *r.*1406–15) was appointed Latin patriarch of Constantinople in 1390 and later served as secretary to Pope Innocent VII. When he failed to end the schism between Rome and Avignon, he was deposed and died a cardinal bishop in 1417. Gregory XIII (Ugo Boncompagni, *b.*1502; *r.*1572–85) served as papal legate to France and Belgium (1556–57). He supported the training of the clergy, giving special support to the Jesuits, and restored the Roman Catholic Church in Poland. Gregory XVI (Bartolomeo Alberto Cappellari, *b.*1765; *r.*1831–46) lived monastically and revived missionary activity to combat secularization.

Gregory, (Isabella Augusta Lady) (1852–1932), Irish playwright. She recorded the folklore, humour and dialect of the peasants of western Ireland in such one-act plays as *Spreading of the News* (1909) and *The Rising of the Moon* (1909). With W. B. YEATS she organized the ABBEY THEATRE of Dublin and toured the USA with it in 1911.

Gregory of Nazianzus, Saint (*c.*330–*c.*390), bishop, theologian and father of the early Church. For a time Gregory was Patriarch of Constantinople, upholding the NICENE CREED against the ARIAN heresy, but retired to lead a monastic life and write. His most important contribution was his exposition on the Trinity.

Gregory of Nyssa, Saint (*c.*331–*c.*396), bishop, theologian and father of the Eastern Church. At the Council of Constantinople (381) Gregory supported the orthodox stand of GREGORY OF NAZIANZUS against ARIANISM. Gregory of Nyssa's many writings include tracts on asceticism and mysticism. His systematic works on Christian doctrine make him one of the greatest theologians of his period.

Gregory of Tours, Saint (*c.*538–594), bishop and historian of Gaul. After he became bishop of Tours in 573 he used his influence to end various political feuds. He is best known, however, for his writings. His *History of the Franks* consists of three separate sections on current affairs, which are primary sources for a study of his times. He also wrote on miracles, martyrs and church fathers.

Greig, Tony (1946–), England and Sussex cricketer, *b.* South Africa. A tall (2.0m; 6ft 7in), fiercely competitive all-rounder, he first played for England against the Rest of the World in 1970 and won 58 caps (1972–77), 14 as captain. In 1977 he joined the "outlawed" Kerry Packer cricket circus.

Grenada, independent republic of the Commonwealth in the SE Caribbean Sea, 137km (81 miles) N of Trinidad. It consists of Grenada and the smaller islands of the South Grenadines. The economy is largely based on cocoa, bananas and sugar. The capital is Saint George's. Area: 344sq km (133sq miles). Pop. (1975 est.) 105,000. *See* MW p.90.

Grenadier Guards, First Regiment of Foot Guards in the British army. Grenadiers were originally grenade-throwers, chosen for their height. Its troops are today still the tallest in the British army.

Grenade, small hand-thrown or rifle-launched bomb carried by individual soldiers. Grenades may be filled with an explosive charge or substances used in chemical warfare. They are usually fused and are set off by a detonator which is included within the metal case. The early grenadiers were troops trained to use grenades. *See also* MM p.*242.*

Grenfell, Joyce Irene (1910–), British writer and popular film, television and theatre entertainer. She started her career as radio critic for The *Observer* newspaper and made her first stage appearance in London in 1939. Her autobiography was published in 1976.

Grenfell, Sir Wilfred Thomason (1865–1940), Canadian doctor and philanthropist. Grenfell devoted his life to the welfare of residents of Labrador and Newfoundland, using a hospital ship and establishing orphanages, hospitals and small businesses. He wrote about his experiences in *Forty Years for Labrador* (1932) and *The Romance of Labrador* (1934).

Grenville, George (1712–70), British statesman; member of Parliament from 1741; navy treasurer (1756–62), first lord of the Admiralty (1762–63) and prime minister (1763–65). He was responsible for the STAMP ACT, which provoked violent reactions in the colonies, especially the Americas, and eventually caused the downfall of his ministry.

Grenville, Sir Richard (*c.*1541–91), English naval commander and hero. He was fatally wounded and his ship, the *Revenge,* was captured in a sea battle off the Azores in 1591 against a vastly superior Spanish force.

Grenville, William Wyndham, Baron, (1759–1834), British prime minister. A longtime friend of William PITT the younger and a supporter of Roman Catholic emancipation, he formed the "ministry of all the talents" (1806–07) after Pitt's death, which abolished the slave trade in 1807.

Gresham, Sir Thomas (1519–79), English merchant and financier, often sent on diplomatic and financial missions by ELIZABETH I. He was the founder of the ROYAL EXCHANGE and the endower of GRESHAM'S COLLEGE, London. He gave his name to GRESHAM'S LAW, although he did not formulate it.

Gresham's College, English educational establishment in the City of London. Founded in 1597 with money bequeathed for the purpose by Sir Thomas GRESHAM, the college offered open lectures on science in English rather than Latin. It made a notable contribution to the development of scientific thought and was the first home of the ROYAL SOCIETY.

Gresham's law, in economics, is stated as "bad money drives out good money". Specifically, the law means that if two kinds of money, eg, gold and silver coins, are in circulation, and if gold is overvalued while silver is simultaneously undervalued, then people will spend gold coins and hoard silver ones.

Gretna Green, village in Dumfries and Galloway, s Scotland, close to the border with England. It became famous as the destination of eloping English couples after 1754, when English marriage laws were tightened, until 1856 when a law was passed making it necessary that one of the prospective marriage partners reside in Scotland for 21 days prior to issue of the licence.

Greuze, Jean-Baptiste (1725–1805), French painter. He is known for his narrative GENRE PAINTINGS depicting strong passions in his subjects. His later works, mostly mood studies and paintings of nudes, were mawkishly sentimental.

Greville, Charles Cavendish Fulke (1794–1865), British diarist. Clerk to the Privy council, and an intimate of politicians of both parties, his *Memoirs* were published in eight volumes (1875–87). They contain details about public figures and events spanning a 40-year period.

Grew, Nehemiah (1641–1712), English physician, botanist and microscopist whose best-known work, *The Anatomy of Plants* (1682), included a description of the anatomy of flowers and many fine wood engravings of the structures of plant tissues. It also contained ideas on the sexuality of different parts of a flower.

Grey, Albert Henry George, 4th Earl (1851–1917), governor-general of Canada (1904–11). A Liberal from England, Grey devoted himself to Commonwealth unity, the Quebec centenary in 1908, and the establishment of the Grey Cup for rugby.

Grey, Beryl (1927–), British dancer. She studied with Sergeyev and DE VALOIS and was a soloist with Sadlers Wells Ballet (1942–57). She created many roles including ASHTON's *Les Sirènes* (1946) and MASSINE's *Donald of the Burthens* (1951). Her international appearances have included Russia and China, and in 1968 she became artistic director of the London Festival Ballet.

Grey, Charles, 2nd Earl (1764–1845), British prime minister. During his administration (1830–34), the First Reform Bill was passed (1832). Grey supported limited parliamentary reform, though as a WHIG aristocrat he was no radical.

Grey, Sir George (1812–98), British colonial administrator. He explored Western Australia (1837–39) and served as lieutenant governor for South Australia (1841–45). He governed New Zealand (1845–53, 1861–68) and Cape Colony in South Africa (1854–61). He was premier of New Zealand (1877–79).

Grey, Lady Jane (1537–54), Queen of England. A great-granddaughter of Henry VII, she was married to Guildford Dudley, son of the Duke of Northumberland, as part of the duke's scheme to oust the Tudor dynasty. On Edward VI's death in 1553 she was proclaimed queen, but Princess Mary's claim was established quickly and Lady Jane was executed in February 1554.

Grey, Zane (1875–1939), US novelist. One of the best-known writers in the western genre, his most popular novel was *Riders of the Purple Sage* (1912). His cowboy stories present brawny heroes, loyal to the ethics of the frontier, who overcome callous villians.

Grey, river in NW South Island, New Zealand; rises in the Spenser Mountains and flows SW into the Tasman Sea at Greymouth. Length: 121km (75 miles).

Greyhound, coursing dog traditionally used to hunt hares and also used for racing. It has a long tapered head and muzzle with small ears set at the back and dark bright eyes. Its broad muscular back and well-arched loins are set on long lean legs. The tail is long and tapered and the smooth coat may be almost any colour. Height: 66cm (26in) at the shoulder; weight 29kg (65lb).

Greyhound racing, sport in which GREYHOUND dogs race each other around an oval track in pursuit of an electrically operated dummy hare. Races are "graded" or "open" and begin with the traps being opened automatically to release all the dogs at once. Distances vary between 210 and 1,100m (230–1,200 yards), with a maximum of eight dogs, more usually five or six. The greyhound's origins are ancient, but the sport did not begin until 1876 in London, and it was another 43 years before the oval track and mechanical hare were introduced. Popular as a betting sport, it attracts a large following in Britain, the USA, Australia and W Europe.

Grey matter, term used to distinguish brain cells that are not coated with a whitish substance, called MYELIN, from those that are – which are called white matter.

Greymouth, town and port on the W coast of New Zealand's South Island, at the mouth of the Grey River. Exports include coal, gold and timber.

Grey of Fallodon, Viscount (1862–1933), English statesman. As foreign secretary (1905–16) he was a major influence in British policy-making up to and during WWI, supporting France against Germany's expansionism and fostering links between Britain and the USA.

Gribble, isopod crustacean related to WOODLICE. It is a marine animal that bores into the wood of piers and jetties, causing considerable damage. Family Limnoriidae; genus Limnoria. *See also* NW p.100.

Grid, or control grid, perforated electrode placed between the cathode and the anode of a thermionic valve for controlling the flow of electrons in the valve. This effect is the basis of electronic amplification. Grid also refers to the reticulation systems of energy sources such as electricity or gas, as in the NATIONAL GRID.

Grieg, Edvard Hagerup (1843–1907), Norwegian composer. Called the "Chopin of the North", he used Norwegian folk themes in his music, much of which is for the piano or voice. His music manifests some of the most undiluted romantic nationalism, and among his best-known works are the song *I Love Thee* (1864), the two *Peer Gynt* suites for orchestra (1876), and the immensely popular *Piano Concerto in A minor* (1868). *See also* HC2 p.107.

Grierson, John (1898–1972), British critic and film-maker. He coined the "documentary" as a cinematic concept in 1926 and thereafter pioneered its aesthetic development in both Britain and abroad – especially before WWII, when he worked closely with Robert FLAHERTY and administered the output of various official DOCUMENTARY FILM units.

Griess, Johann Peter (1829–88), German chemist who discovered the diazo reaction which enabled azo dies to be prepared from a wide range of intermediate chemical compounds. *See also* AZO AND DIAZO COMPOUNDS; MM pp.245–246.

Griffith, Arthur (1872–1922), Irish politician and a founder of the Irish Free State. He edited "The United Irishman" (1899–1906), which proclaimed the SINN FEIN policy of national self reliance. He was president of the SINN FEIN party (1910) and of DÁIL EIREANN (1922).

Griffith, David Wark (1875–1948), US film maker. His feeling for realistic narrative and characterization and his sense of varied composition, lighting and dramatic editing (montage) established the art of film in the US. His principal feature films include *Enoch Arden* (1911); *The Birth of a Nation* (1915); *Intolerance* (1916); *Broken Blossoms* (1919); *Orphans of the Storm* (1922); and *Isn't Life Wonderful* (1925). *See also* HC2 p.200.

Griffon, also called griffon vulture, carrion-eating bird of prey of Eurasia and N Africa; it has gold or sandy-brown plumage. It is gregarious and nests in large flocks in caves or on cliffs. Length: 1m (3.3ft). Family Accipitridae; species *Gyps fulvus.*

Grignard, Francois Auguste Victor (1871–1935), French chemist who shared the 1912 Nobel Prize in chemistry with Paul SABATIER for his discovery and investigation of GRIGNARD REAGENTS. He also synthesized organic compounds of aluminium and mercury.

Grignard reagents, organic chemical compounds containing the metal magnesium, having the general formula R.Mg.X, where R is an alkyl or aryl group and X is chlorine, bromine or iodine. Examples are methylmagnesium iodide, CH_3MgI, and phenylmagnesium bromide C_6H_5MgBr. Grignard reagents undergo many reactions to form carbon-carbon bonds and for this reason they are invaluable in organic synthesis. They are named after the French chemist and Nobel Prize winner (1912) Victor GRIGNARD.

Grigson, Geoffrey (1905–), British poet and critic. His first publication was *Several Observations* (1939). He won the Duff Cooper Memorial Prize in 1971 for *Discoveries of Bones and Stones and Other Poems.*

Grike, feature of limestone exposed by erosion. Rainwater containing dissolved carbon dioxide is a weak acid that dissolves limestone along its planes of weakness. A blocky surface results, the blocks being called CLINTS and the separating cracks called grikes. *See also* PE pp.100,*110.*

Grillparzer, Franz (1791–1872), Austrian Romantic poet and playwright whose works combined elements of popular STURM UND DRANG historical drama with an expression of the innate conflicts between spiritual serenity and worldly realities. His best-known plays, in a variety of classical metres, include *The Golden Fleece* trilogy (1821), *The Waves of the Sea and of Love* (1831) and *The Jewess of Toledo* (1837).

Grimaldi, Joseph (1779–1837), British clown, singer, dancer and actor. His white-face character, "Joey the Clown", influenced the development of the circus clown. He rose to fame at Covent Garden in 1806 in the pantomime *Harlequin and Mother Goose.* Often regarded as the greatest of clowns, he was also a popular comic singer.

Grimaldi, Genoese GUELPH (pro-papal) family who were lords of Monaco from the 15th century. With the Fieschi, the Grimaldi were leaders in Genoa's 13th-century pro-Angevin struggle against Frederick II, which began a long period of association with the house of Anjou. In 1419, after several earlier seizures of power, a branch of the family took final possession of Monaco and in 1659 assumed the title of prince, now held by Prince Rainier III (*r.* 1949–).

Grime's Graves, NEOLITHIC flint mines, named after the Anglo-Saxon god Grim (or Woden), near Brandon on the Norfolk-Suffolk border, SE England. Remains have been excavated of some 340 shafts, from which flint, mainly for axe blades, was extracted. These were roughly chipped on site and then sold in half-finished condition.

Grimm, the Brothers, two German brothers, Jacob Ludwig Carl Grimm (1785–1863) and Wilhelm Carl Grimm (1786–1859), famous for their collection of folksongs and folktales, in particular *Grimm's Fairy Tales* (1812–22). This was the first systematic compilation of traditional, mostly oral, stories. The brothers' interest in Germanic history and philology led to the publication of Jacob's *Deutsche Grammatik* (1819–37) and the *Deutsches Wörterbuch,* a study of the historical development of the Germanic languages, for which he also formulated GRIMM'S LAW.

Grimmelshausen, Hans Jakob Christoffel von (*c.* 1625–76), German novelist. He wrote *Simplicissimus* (1669), a satirical novel on social conditions during the THIRTY YEARS WAR. He had served in the Holy Roman and Swedish armies and became a Roman Catholic convert.

Grimmett, Clarrie (1891–), Australian cricketer, *b.* New Zealand. An accurate leg-break bowler with a low arm action, he came late to Test cricket yet in 37 Test matches (1925–36) became Australia's leading wicket-taker with 216 dismissals. He played for Wellington (NZ), Victoria and South Australia.

Grimm's law, in philology, series of rules that describes sequences in the development and divergence of related languages. The law of consonantal mutations was first suggested by Jacob GRIMM in his *Deutsche Grammatik* (1819–37); he discovered significant correlations between German and

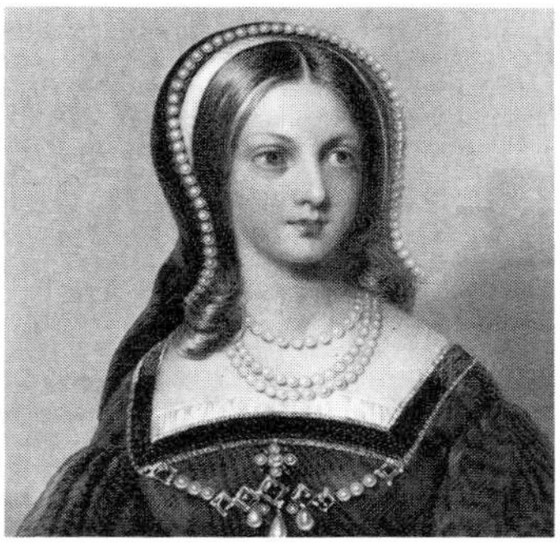

Lady Jane Grey, who was beheaded in the Tower, was Queen for only nine days.

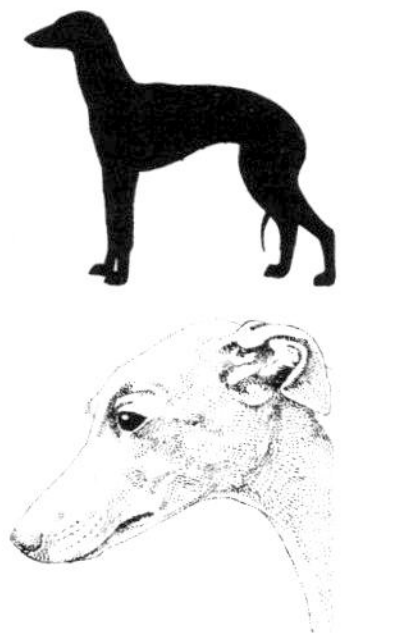

Greyhounds were originally hunting dogs, relying on their speed and keen eyesight.

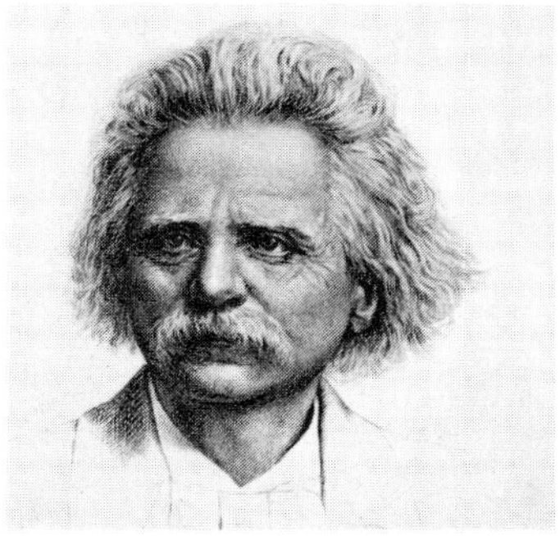

Grieg received an income from the government for the fame he brought to Norway.

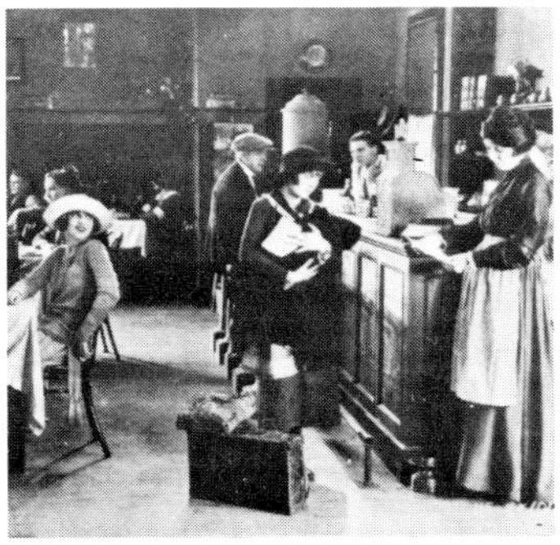

D. W. Griffith; a scene from his film *The White Rose,* a domestic drama made in 1923.

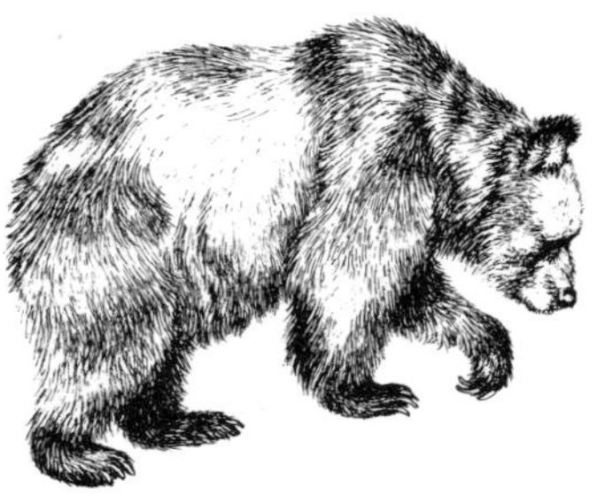

Grizzly bears are so called from the "grizzled" (grey) tips to their otherwise dark fur.

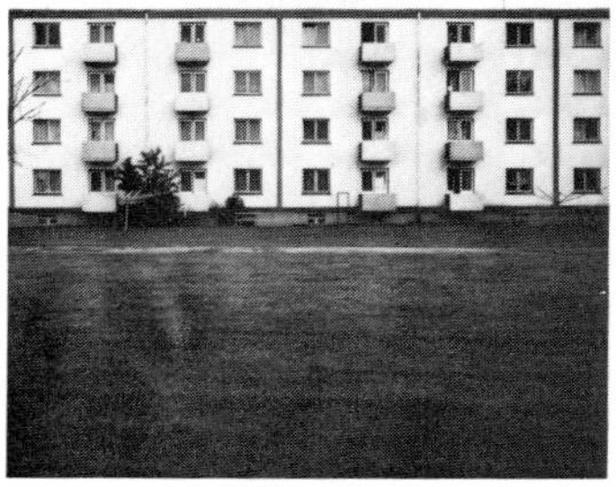

Walter Gropius designed these Proletariat Houses in Karlsruhe, Germany.

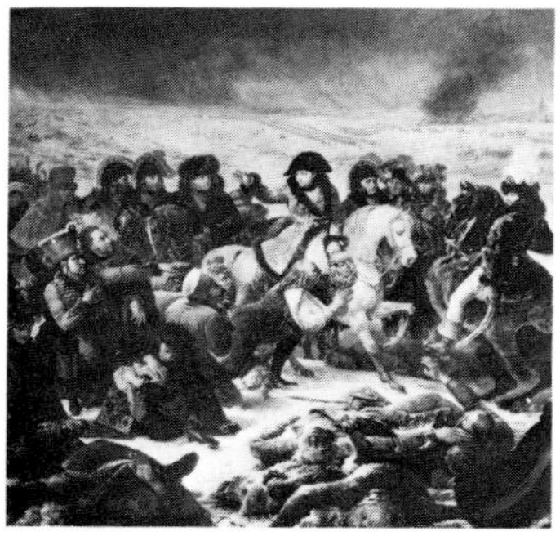

Antoine-Jean Gros' sweeping canvas of *Napoleon on the Battlefield of Eylau* (detail).

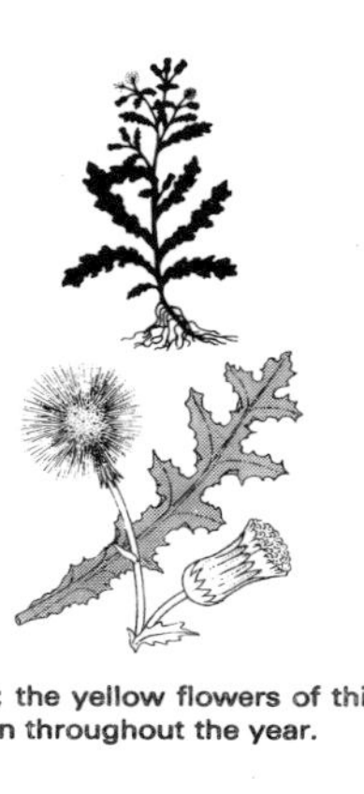

Groundsel; the yellow flowers of this weed can be seen throughout the year.

other INDO-EUROPEAN LANGUAGES, especially Latin, and demonstrated that sound changes are not random but a regular process. The law runs: Hard consonant becomes Aspirate, Aspirate becomes Soft, Soft becomes Hard – mnemonically abbreviated to HAS over ASH.

Grimsby, county district in SE Humberside, England, on the Humber estuary; until 1974 it was in the county of Lincolnshire. The town of Grimsby is one of the world's largest fishing ports. Pop. (1971) 95,685. *See also* HUMBERSIDE.

Grinham, Judy (1939–), English 100m backstroke swimmer who retired when aged 20, having become the first swimmer to hold Olympic (1956), European (1958) and Commonwealth (1958) titles concurrently.

Gris, Juan (1887–1927), Spanish painter, sculptor and writer. He settled in Paris in 1906 and, with PICASSO and BRAQUE, became a leading CUBIST artist. His later works included collages, architectonic paintings, still lifes and stage sets and costumes for DIAGHILEV. A representative work is the oil paint collage *Breakfast* (1914).

Grisaille, monochromatic painting in greys. It may be used in the first stage of an oil painting, or to imitate sculptural features, as in works by such early Netherlandish painters as Jan van EYCK. It is also a type of stained-glass painting, a famous example of which is the *Five Sisters* window in York Minster, England.

Grisi, Carlotta (1819–99), Italian ballerina. Infatuation by her led Théophile GAUTIER to adapt for ballet the legend *Giselle* (music by ADAM). She created the title roles in *La Esmeralda* (1844) and *Paguita* (1846). In 1845 she starred with Marie TAGLIONI in *Pas de Quatre.*

Grisons, or Graubünden, largest and most easterly canton in Switzerland; the capital is Chur. A region of glaciated peaks, forests and fertile valleys, it is a popular tourist area. There is little industry. The majority of the population speak Romansch, the rest either Italian or German. Area: 7,112sq km (2,745sq miles). Pop. (1970) 162,086.

Grist, in the brewing of beer, crushed malt in which the barley husks are retained whole. The next stage in the brewing process is to feed the grist into a mash tun, where hot water is added and the goodness extracted. The spent grain may later be used as an ingredient of cattle cake.

Grit, in geology, a coarse sandstone. It is usually formed in a river delta where material eroded from a landmass has been deposited rapidly before the fragments have been rounded or sorted. The Upper Carboniferous deltas left thick beds of grit in many areas of the British Isles.

Grivas, George (1898–1974), Greek Cypriot general who led the Greeks in Cyprus in rebellion against Britain from 1955 until 1959. He formed the guerrilla force EOKA (National Organization for the Cyprus Struggle) to fight for ENOSIS (union with Greece) but clashed with Archbishop MAKARIOS and retired. He returned in 1964 to head Greek forces in Cyprus, was forced to leave again in 1967, but re-entered the country secretly in 1971.

Grizzly bear, large omnivorous BEAR, generally considered to be a variety of brown bear (*Ursus arctos*) although sometimes classified as a separate species (*Ursus horribilis*). Once widespread in W North America, the grizzly is now rare except in W Canada, Alaska and the Yellowstone and Glacier parks. Length: to 2.5m (7ft); weight: 410kg (900lb).

Groat, medieval English silver coin worth four contemporary pence. First minted in 1351, it lasted for 300 years until the introduction of milled coins. The name is borrowed from an earlier Dutch and Flemish coin and means "large".

Grock (1880–1959), stage name of Charles Adrian Wettach, Swiss clown who during his career built up an international reputation second only to that of GRIMALDI. Especially popular in Paris and London, he exhibited an inimitable and infectious appreciation of his own jokes and pathetic sympathy with himself when in distress.

Groenendael. *See* BELGIAN SHEEPDOG.

Gromyko, Andrei (1909–), Soviet diplomat. In 1943 he was appointed ambassador to the USA and took part in the YALTA and POTSDAM conferences. In 1946 he became Soviet representative to the UN and in 1952 ambassador to Britain. After being appointed to the Communist Party Central Committee in 1956, he was made foreign minister in 1957.

Groningen, NE province of The Netherlands, bordered by West Germany (E) and the North Sea (N); the capital Groningen. The economy is based on algriculture. There is much reclaimed land. Area: 2,419sq km (934sq miles). Pop. (1971 est.) 522,400.

Groombridge 34, binary star in the constellation of Andromeda. Both components are faint red stars. Characteristics: apparent mag. 8.1 (A), 11.0 (B); absolute mag. 10.3 (A), 13.1 (B); spectral type M1 (A), M6 (B); distance 11.7 light-years. *See also* SU p.226.

Groote Eylandt, island off the NE coast of the Northern Territory, Australia, in the Gulf of Carpentaria. It has a rocky, barren terrain and manganese ore is mined. It is part of the Arnhem Land Aboriginal Reserve. Area: 2,460sq km (950sq miles).

Gropius, Walter (1883–1969), German-born architect and founder of the BAUHAUS (1919–28). He pioneered the functional design that became known as the INTERNATIONAL STYLE and his belief in group-work led him to associate with other architects on almost all his buildings. Representative of his work is the Fagus Factory at Alfeld-an-der-Leine (1911) and Impington Village College (1939) near Cambridge, England, which Gropius designed in partnership with Maxwell FRY. *See also* HC2 pp.178–179, *179*,.

Gros, Antoine-Jean (1771–1835), French painter. He was a forerunner of the ROMANTIC MOVEMENT and strongly influenced by the NEO-CLASSICISM of DAVID. His large, dramatic pictures illustrating the NAPOLEONIC WARS influenced GÉRICAULT and DELACROIX, who admired his rich colours and the sweeping movement of his compositions.

Grosbeak, name given to several birds of the FINCH family (FRINGILLIDAE) which have short, thick, seed-cracking beaks. Found in wooded areas of the Americas, Europe and Asia, grosbeaks feed on seeds, fruits and buds. They include the rose-breasted grosbeak (*Pheucticus ludovicianus*) of North and South America; the pine grosbeak (*Pinicolor enucleator*) of Canada and N Europe; and the scarlet grosbeak (*Carpodacus erythrinus*) of Europe. Length: 18–25cm (7–10in).

Grosseteste, Robert (*c.*1175–1253), statesman, scholar and Bishop of Lincoln. He influenced English FRANCISCANS toward biblical study and other academic pursuits. His belief that the Church is superior to the state brought him into conflict with the crown.

Grossmith, name of two brothers, entertainers on the British stage. George (1847–1912) was a singer of light opera who created many of the roles in works by Gilbert and Sullivan, including *The Mikado, Iolanthe* and *Patience.* With his brother Weedon (1854–1919) he wrote *The Diary of a Nobody* (1892), the imaginary diary of an extremely respectable city clerk of the 1890s. Weedon Grossmith was initially a painter and in 1885 went on the stage as an actor and comedian. *The Night of the Party* (1901) was his most successful play.

Gross National Product (GNP), total market value of all goods and services produced by a nation in a specific period, usually one year. GNP is a universal indicator of economic performance and can tell a government how different areas of the economy are faring. GNP is the sum of four types of spending: private consumption (goods and services bought by the community); government expenditure; exports, less the value of imports; and business investment. GNP can be adjusted for changes in prices to produce a "real" figure in terms of the prices of a given base year.

Gross profit, or gross margin, in accounting, the difference between the money received for goods sold and the costs that were incurred in producing them. The gross profit figure is used as a measure of the profitability of a company. A downward trend in the gross profit figure over a period may indicate an inadequate pricing policy.

Grosz, George (1893–1959), German illustrator and painter. A founder of the DADA movement in Berlin, he savagely satirized capitalist and military corruption in books of pen drawings and caricatures, such as *Ecce Homo* (1923). After settling in the USA in 1932, his later works combined satirical with idyllic and then nightmarish qualities which showed some affinity with SURREALISM. *See also* HC2 p.175.

Grotefend, Georg Friedrich (1775–1853), German classical scholar. Although he specialized in Latin and Italian, his greatest achievement was the deciphering (1802) of ancient Persian cuneiform (wedge-shaped) script, first copied at Persepolis in Iran in 1765. He deduced correctly that the inscriptions were in three languages.

Grotius, or De Groot, Hugo (1583–1645), Dutch jurist and statesman. He held the office of chief magistrate of Rotterdam from 1613 until 1618 when he was ousted by his political opponents. He was sentenced to life imprisonment but escaped in 1621 and lived in Paris. His most famous work was *De Jure Belli ac Pacis* (On the Law of War and Peace, 1625), and he is considered the founder of international law.

Grotowski, Jerzy (1933–), Polish theatre director, an influential avant-gardist who advocates a style of "poor theatre" stripped of superfluous effects. He founded the Polish Laboratory Theatre in 1959, and wrote *Towards a Poor Theatre* (translated 1968).

Ground effect, aircraft, reaction of the wing to reduced DRAG when operating close to the ground. When close to touchdown, drag may drop by as much as 40%, allowing an aircraft to fly at a speed lower than its normal STALL speed.

Ground elder, perennial herb whose long RHIZOMES make it a troublesome weed in many temperate regions. It is also called goutweed and is sometimes eaten as a vegetable. Family Umbelliferne; species *Aegopodium podagraria.*

Ground ivy, trailing, perennial herb native to Europe and often considered a weed. It has round leaves and small, violet, clustered flowers, and spreads rapidly in cool, damp places. Family Labiatae; species *Glechoma hederacea.*

Groundling, member of an Elizabethan audience who occupied the promenade pit of a theatre and constituted its most rowdy and vociferous element. *See also* GALLERY.

Ground loop, in aviation, a violent, uncontrollable turn by an aircraft on the ground. If, on taking off or landing, an aircraft is not correctly aligned, a ground loop may be caused if a wing-tip touches the ground.

Groundnut, or peanut, fruit of the plant *Arachis hypogaea* of the pea family (LEGUMINOSAE). It is grown as a valuable food crop in many warmer parts of the world. Groundnuts are not "nuts" at all, but pea-like fruits which ripen in underground pods. The name groundnut is also sometimes given to the edible tubers of other plants, such as the European *Cyperus esculentus* (family Cyperaceae). *See also* PE pp.215, *217.*

Ground pine. *See* CLUB MOSS.

Groundsel, also called ragwort, any of numerous species of plants in the genus *Senecio*; many can be cultivated. More than a dozen wild species are common in Britain, in woods, sandy soils, cultivated land or waste ground. Most of these, including common groundsel (*S. vulgaris*), produce yellow flowerheads. Family Compositae.

Groundspeed, aircraft's actual rate of progress with respect to the ground, rather than the air. It may be calculated from the airspeed by correcting for variations in temperature and pressure and by allowing for the speed of the wind.

Ground squirrel, small terrestrial SQUIRREL native to Eurasia and North America. Ground squirrels, active by day, find shelter in burrows or crevices and eat plants, seeds, insects and other small animals and sometimes eggs. Most have greyish-red to brown fur and some are striped or spotted. Length, excluding tail: to 40.5cm (16in); weight: 85–1,000g (0.1–2.2lb). Family Sciuridae; genus Cittellus (and others). *See also* NW p.*206*.
Ground state, most stable energy state of an atom, ion or molecule. It is the state of an atom when the orbiting electrons move in such orbits that the atom's energy is at a minimum.
Ground water, water that lies in the zone beneath the surface of the earth. The water comes chiefly from the atmosphere, although some is of volcanic or sedimentary origin. Ground water moves through porous rocks and soil and can be trapped by wells. It can dissolve minerals which are in the rocks, precipitating others, creating such geological structures as caves, stalagmites, stalactites and SINKHOLES.
Grouper, tropical marine fish found from the coast of Florida to South America and in the Indian and Pacific oceans. It has a large mouth, sharp teeth, a mottled body and the ability to change colour. Length: to 3.7m (12ft); weight: to 450kg (1,000lb). Family Serranidae; species: giant, *Epinephelus itajara* and the Australian, *Epinephelus lanceolatus. See also* NW p.*129*.
Group theory, branch of abstract algebra applicable to symmetry properties. A group is a collection of entities with associated operations, obeying a specific set of rules (associative law, existence of an inverse, etc). The theory was developed mainly by the French mathematician Évariste GALOIS. The symmetry elements of an object, for example – operations, such as rotations, that bring an object back to its original position – form a group. Group theory is particularly useful in QUANTUM MECHANICS, SPECTROSCOPY and theories of elementary particles. *See also* SU pp.40–41, 50–51.
Group therapy, psychotherapy in which two or more patients and a trained therapist participate to resolve difficulties and effect therapeutic changes. There are several different types often based on different theories, but they all rely on the group generating an atmosphere of mutual trust and support. With discussion, confession and constructive criticism the patients are able to conquer their problems and disorders, develop their interpersonal skills and gain personal understanding. The role of the therapist varies: he can be detached and analytic, limited to interpreting the dynamics of the group, or he can be more involved personally, offering advice, direction and reassurance. *See also* ENCOUNTER GROUP THERAPY; PRIMAL THERAPY; MS pp.148–149.
Grouse, plump game bird of N areas of the Northern Hemisphere. About the size of a small turkey, grouse are fowl-like but have feathered tarsi and toes for walking on snow, feathered nostrils and often distensible, brightly-coloured air sacs on the neck. Some species, such as the PTARMIGAN, are seasonally monogamous. Family Tetraonidae. *See also* CAPERCAILLIE; PRAIRIE CHICKEN; SAGE GROUSE; NW pp.*144, 206*.
Grove, Frederick Philip (1871–1948), Canadian writer, *b.* Sweden. His works, mainly concerned with prairie life, include *Settlers of the Marsh* (1925), *The Yoke of Life* (1930) and *Fruits of the Earth* (1933).
Groves, Sir Charles Barnard (1915–), British conductor. His first appointment was as assistant conductor of the BBC Theatre Orchestra (1942). He was conductor of the Bournemouth Symphony (1954–61), and between 1963 and 1977 was musical director and conductor of the Royal Liverpool Philharmonic. In 1977 he became principal conductor of the English National Opera.
Grove, Sir George (1820–1900), British musical scholar. He discovered parts of SCHUBERT's *Rosamunde* music and edited the authoritative *Dictionary of Music and Musicians* (1879–89).
Growing Up in New Guinea, study of sex and adolescence in a primitive society by the US anthropologist Margaret MEAD, published in 1930.
Growth, progress or development; in biology, the process by which an organism increases in size and weight. It involves cell division or enlargement, or both. It can result from the inclusion of external matter, and is usually dependent on the environment of the organism.
Growth hormone, or somatotropin, protein hormone produced by the anterior PITUITARY; it effects general growth of the body. Over-secretion results in ACROMEGALY in the adult, and GIGANTISM in the young; under-secretion results in "pituitary dwarfism". *See also* MS p.64.
Grub, common term for the LARVA (often legless) of an insect, although fly larvae that infest decaying food are more usually called maggots.
Grub Street, street in London which, in the 18th century, was largely taken over by minor writers and pamphleteers. The term is used to describe literary hackwork.
Gruffydd ap Llywelyn (*d.* 1063), Welsh king. He fought both the Danes and English successfully and became King of all Wales in 1055. After his defeat by Earl HAROLD (future king of England) Wales reverted to a group of princedoms. *See also* HC1 pp.184, *184*.
Gruiformes, order of birds, many of which are aquatic, eg rails, fiafoots or sunbitterns, COOTS and CRANES. Terrestrial species, including BUSTARDS, rarely fly. *See also* NW p.141.
Grundy, Mrs, symbol of conventional British propriety, named after a character in Thomas Morton's *Speed the Plough* (1798). She is continually referred to in this play – "What will Mrs Grundy say?" "What will Mrs Grundy think?" – but never actually appears.
Grünewald, Mathias (*c.* 1480–1528), German painter. Although a contemporary of DÜRER, he applied few Renaissance techniques except in perspective, light and colour. His greatest work was the folding altarpiece for the Antonite monastery in Isenheim (1512–16). It consists of a majestic sequence of religious scenes with mystical overtones in late Gothic linear style. *See also* HC1 pp.260, *260*.
Grunion, marine silverfish found in shallow tropical and temperate waters, particularly along the Baja and S California coast. Shoals of grunion spawn high on the beach at the highest tide, and the eggs hatch at the next high tide. Family Atherinidae; species *Leuresthes tenuis.*
Grunt, marine fish found in shallow tropical waters of the W Atlantic and Pacific. A deep-bodied fish with a large mouth, it makes sounds by grinding its pharyngeal teeth, an air bladder acting as a resonator. Family Pomadasyidae; species includes Bluestripe *Haemulon sciurus.*
Gruyère, popular cheese produced in the Fribourg canton of W Switzerland. It is high in butterfat and has a light yellow colour. *See also* PE pp.228–229, *229*.
Gryphius, Andreas (1616–64), German author. He wrote lyrics, tragedies and comedies in High German and dialect, and is best known for his satirical comedies. These include *Horribilicribrifax* (1663) and *The Beloved Rose Among Thorns* (1660).
Guadalajara, city in SW Mexico; capital of Jalisco state and second largest city in Mexico. Noted for its mountain scenery and mild climate, it is a popular health resort and communications centre, having a direct rail link to the USA. Industries: engineering, food processing, pottery. Pop. (1975) 1,560,805.
Guadalcanal, tropical island in the W central Pacific Ocean, approx. 970km (600 miles) E of New Guinea; largest island of the British Solomon Island Protectorate. The port of Honiara is the centre of government. The island was the scene of heavy fighting between Japanese and US troops in WWII. The chief products are coconuts and timber. Area: 6,475sq km (2,500sq miles). Pop. 24,000.
Guadeloupe, overseas French département in the Leeward Islands, E West Indies; made up of the islands of Basse-Terre (W), and Grande-Terre (E). Basse-Terre is the capital and Pointe-à-Pitre is the chief port. Discovered in 1493 by Columbus, the islands were settled by the French in 1635. The chief crops are sugars and bananas. Industries: distilling, tourism. Area: 1,780sq km (687sq miles). Pop. (1975 est.) 354,000.
Guahibo, tribe of nomadic South American Indians that live in the savannah W of the Orinoco River in E Colombia. They speak their own language and are related to the Chiricoa. Today there are approx. 20,000 people in the tribe.
Guam, unincorporated US territory in the W Pacific Ocean; largest of the Mariana Islands. Discovered by Ferdinand MAGELLAN in 1521, it was ceded to the US by the Treaty of Paris in 1848. Guam was the first US territory to be occupied by the Japanese during WWII. It has a large US military base. Area: 541sq km (209sq miles). Pop (1975 est.) 104,000. *See also* MW p.90.
Guanaco, one of four gregarious South American relatives of the camel; the other three are the LLAMA, alpaca and vicuña. It is a slender-bodied animal with a long neck and long legs. It is prized for its hide, meat, droppings (for fuel) and wool, which is used for high quality textiles. Height: to 110cm (43in) at shoulder. Family Camelidae; species *Lama guanacoe.*
Guangzhou. *See* CANTON.
Guano, dried excrement, mainly of seabirds and bats, that accumulates along coastlines and in caves. A valuable natural fertilizer, containing phosphorus, nitrogen and potassium, it is found mainly on islands off South America and Africa where there is a large population of pelicans, gannets and cormorants. Seal guano is also used.
Guantánamo, city in E Cuba, served by the port of Caimanera on Guantanamo Bay. It is the processing centre for a prosperous coffee and sugar producing region. The USA maintains a naval base on Guantánamo Bay under the terms of a treaty first signed in 1903. Pop.130,100.
Guaraní, tribe of South American Indians speaking the Guaraní tongue. Once numerous, they have declined greatly, although most Paraguayans have some Guaraní blood. Their language has survived, and is the second national tongue of Paraguay. Some 200,000 people are counted as essentially Guaraní.
Guardi, Francesco (1712–93), Italian painter. Like CANALETTO, he specialized in views, but his style is freer and more imaginative. His views of Venice were not highly regarded in his day but his work has since been re-evaluated, first by the IMPRESSIONISTS who praised his treatment of atmosphere and light.
Guards, Brigade of. *See* individual regiments.
Guareschi, Giovanni (1908–68), Italian author whose humorous stories about a village priest, Don Camillo, sympathetically satirized the especially Italian problem of simultaneously acknowledging Roman Catholicism and Communism. *The Little World of Don Camillo* (1950) and its many sequels were widely translated, and adapted into films.
Guarneri, a family of violin makers who worked in Cremona, Italy. The first of these was Andrea (*c.* 1626–1698) who designed and built his instruments in the AMATI style. The greatest craftsman of the family was his grandnephew (or possibly grandson) Giuseppi Antonio (1698–1744). He is known for the original designs of his violins which can be compared to the instruments made by STRADIVARI.
Guatemala, nation in Central America between the Caribbean Sea and Pacific Ocean. The country has a tropical climate which is moderated by several mountain ranges. Although the economy is based on agriculture (coffee and bananas are among the chief crops), mining is becoming increasingly important. The capital is Guatemala City. Area: 108,889sq km (42,042sq miles). Pop. (1973) 5,540,000. *See* MW p.90.
Guatemala City (Ciudad Guatemala),

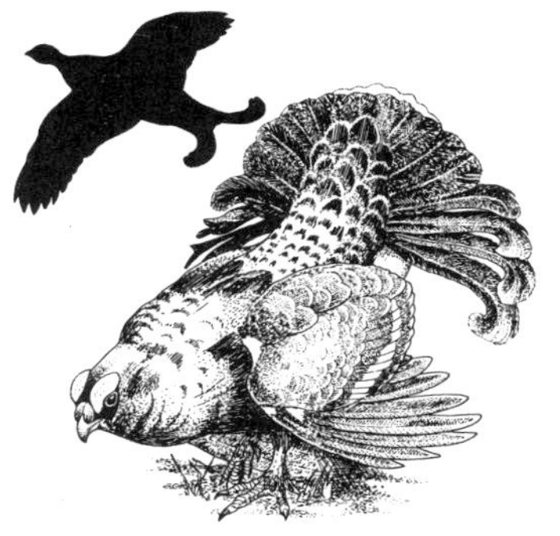

Grouse; the black grouse is a European member of this large family of game birds.

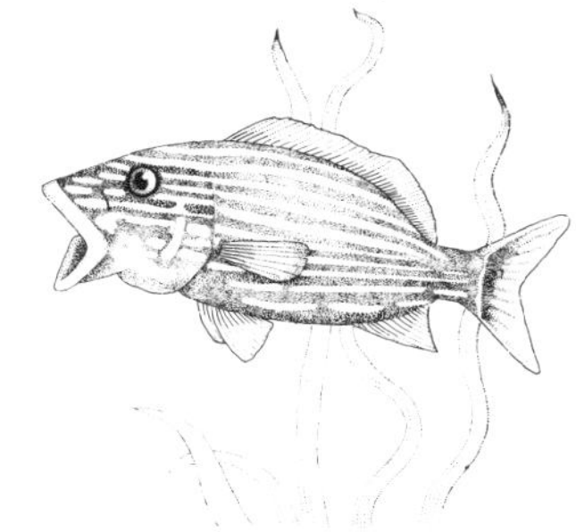

Grunts are so called from the sound which they make when fished out of the water.

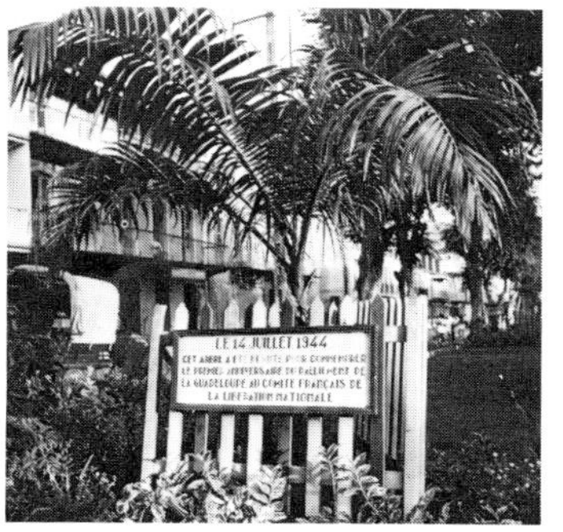

Guadeloupe; a palm tree commemorating Basse-Terre's liberation in 1944.

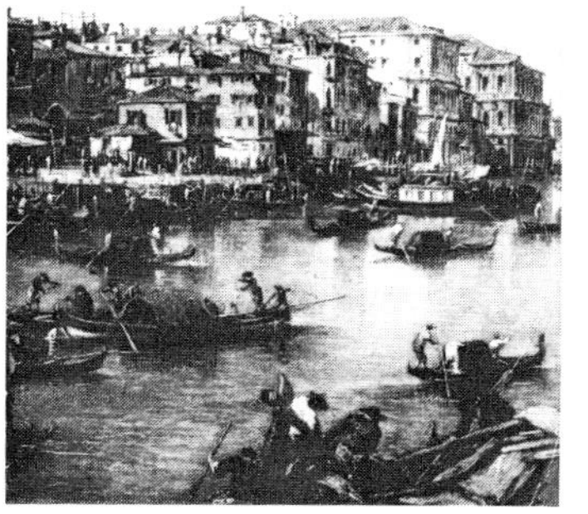

Guardi's treatment of this canal scene is less mechanical than, say, a Canaletto.

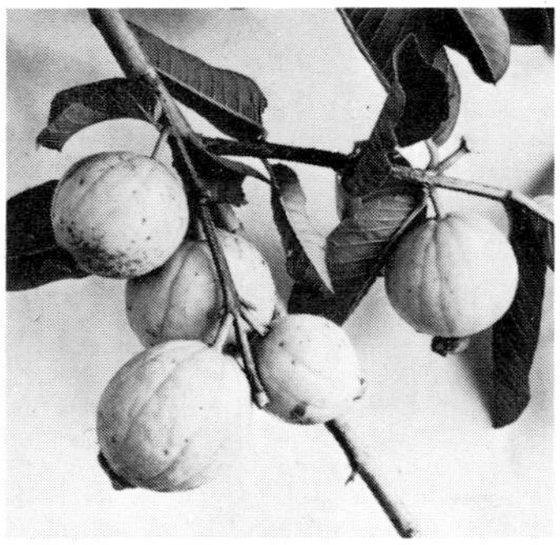

Guavas have a sharp flavour and are used in a variety of ways, including cheese-making.

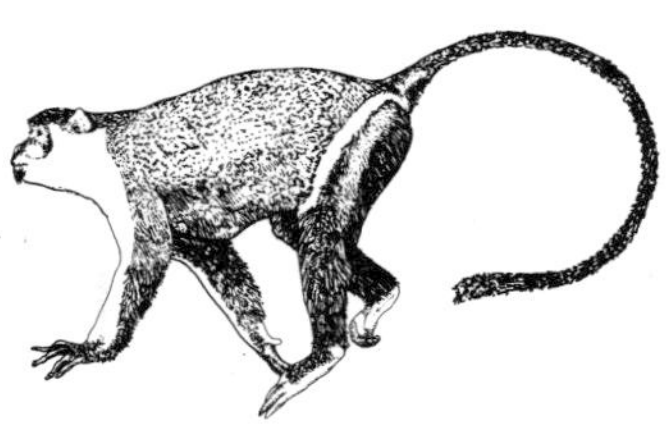

Guenons are like the macaques in that they have cheek pouches.

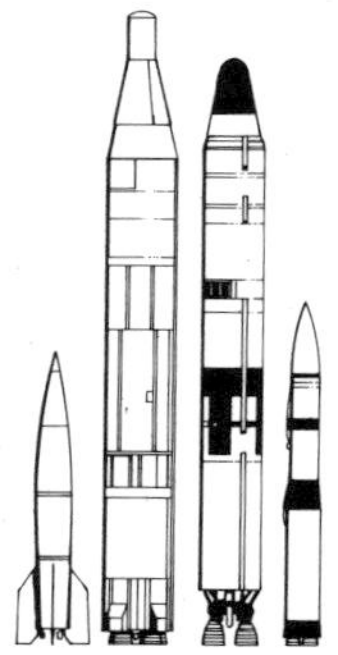

Guided missiles employ a variety of computer systems to take them to their target.

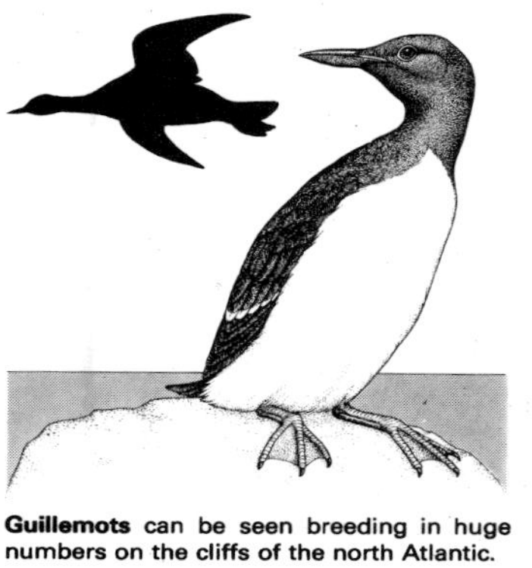

Guillemots can be seen breeding in huge numbers on the cliffs of the north Atlantic.

capital city of Guatemala, on a plateau in the Sierra Madre; largest city in Central America. Founded in 1776 to replace Antigua as the colonial capital of Spanish Central America, the city became the capital of the Central American Federation from 1823 until 1833. It was badly damaged by earthquakes in 1917–18 and 1976. It is the seat of San Carlos University (1676). Exports: coffee, gold, copper, silver, lead. Industries: mining, furniture, textiles, clothing, food processing, handicrafts. Pop. 717,300.

Guava, any of various trees or shrubs native to tropical America and the West Indies, and bearing fruit of the same name. The large white flowers produce a 7.6cm (3in) berry-like fruit, usually yellow with white, pink or yellow flesh. The 100 species include the common guava, *Psidium guajava*, and the strawberry guava (*P. cattleyanum*), with purplish-red fruit. Family Myrtaceae.

Guayaquil, city in W Ecuador, on the River Guayas near its mouth in the Gulf of Guayaquil; capital of Guayas province, chief port and largest city of Ecuador. Founded in 1535 by the Spanish, Guayaquil was frequently attacked by buccaneers in the 17th century. The city used to be plagued by tropical disease as a result of its hot, humid climate and inadequate sanitation. Industries: textiles, leather goods, cement, iron products. Pop. 814,000.

Guaymí, tribe of Indians inhabiting Panama; their language is of the Chibchan group. They are the most numerous Indians in Panama, and may be divided into the Northern Guaymí, who inhabit tropical forests, and the Southern Guaymí. Dependent on agriculture, they are also hunters with the bow and arrow.

Guayule, shrub native to desert regions of N Mexico and Texas. Latex extracted from it is a commercial source of rubber. Height: 0.9m (3ft). Family Asteraceae; species *Parthenium argentatum.*

Gudgeon, freshwater CARP found in rivers from Britain to central China. It has a small mouth with barbels (fleshy whiskers) at each corner, elongated body and variable colour. Length: rarely exceeding 20cm (8in).

Guelder rose, plant of the honeysuckle family grown as a garden ornamental. It has globular clusters of white or pink sterile flowers. Species *Viburnum opulus.*

Guelphs, medieval Italian pro-papal political faction, opposed to the pro-imperial GHIBELLINES. "Guelph" derives from "Welf", the name of the German family contending with the HOHENSTAUFENS for control of the Holy Roman Empire in the 12th and 13th centuries, but the term later applied to the Italian opponents of the Hohenstaufen emperor Frederick II, and, more generally, the supporters of his enemies, the pope and the Angevins.

Guenon, any of 10–20 species of long-tailed, slender, medium-sized African MONKEYS found S of the Sahara Desert. Guenons are day-active tree-dwellers, living in small troops dominated by an old male. Their omnivorous diet consists mainly of fruit, leaves and roots. They make good pets while young but often turn savage as they grow older. Genus Cercopithecus. *See also* MS p.*20.*

Guercino, Francesco Barbieri (1591–1666), Italian painter. Influenced early in his career by Caracci, he worked mainly in Bologna. For Pope Gregory XV in Rome he painted the ceiling fresco *Aurora* in the Villa Ludovisi – a Baroque masterpiece.

Guernica, town in N Spain. It is a centre of Basque nationalism; the oak of Guernica under which the diet of Vizcaya used to meet is a symbol of lost BASQUE liberties. Its bombing in the SPANISH CIVIL WAR aroused international protest and inspired one of Picasso's best known paintings.

Guernsey, second-largest island in the CHANNEL ISLANDS of the United Kingdom, 40km (25 miles) NW of Jersey. It constitutes a bailiwick with several smaller islands, including ALDERNEY and SARK. The mild and sunny climate makes farming and horticulture the most important activities. Tourism is another valuable source of income. Area: 78sq km (30sq miles). Pop. 51,500.

Guernsey, common breed of DAIRY CATTLE originally in the English Channel Island of Guernsey. The cows give rich, yellow milk, second only to the JERSEY breed in butterfat content, but greater in overall volume. Larger than Jerseys, Guernseys are brown and white. Weight: about 770kg (1,700lb).

Guerrilla warfare, small-scale ground combat operations frequently designed to harass rather than destroy the enemy. Such tactics are often employed by insurgents or irregular soldiers, and the term is closely associated with rebellion against an unpopular government or a foreign rule. By conducting limited forays against supply lin1s and small installations, guerrilla forces are able to avoid open engagements with conventional military units, enabling them to tie down a disproportionate quantity of enemy military strength. Guerrilla tactics are especially suited to difficult terrain (although they have been adapted to urban use) and rely on lightning attacks and aid from civilian sympathizers. By itself guerrilla warfare may not be decisive; it often needs to be complemented and consolidated by conventional strategy. In the 20th century guerrilla tactics have been used by many nationalist and/or Communist movements, eg in China, by TITO's Yugoslavian partisans in WWII, in Africa (Algeria, Angola, Mozambique, Zimbabwe) and Indochina (notably Vietnam).

Guevara, Ernesto "Che" (1928–67), revolutionary leader and political theorist; a key figure in CASTRO's Cuba. A physician born in Argentina, Guevara became associated with Castro in Mexico, and returned with him to Cuba in 1956 to conduct guerrilla activities against the regime of Fulgenico BATISTA. When Castro came to power, Guevara was placed in charge of economic planning. He disappeared from public view in 1965. Two years later he was captured and killed while trying to establish a Communist guerrilla base in Bolivia.

Guiana. *See* FRENCH GUIANA; GUYANA; SURINAM.

Guided missile, missile controlled throughout its flight to target either by exterior or interior control systems. There are four types: (1) surface-to-surface, (2) surface-to-air, (3) air-to-air, (4) air-to-surface. The first guided missiles were built in Germany during WWII. The first of these was the V1, which was powered by a pulse-jet engine and flew at quite low speeds which made it easy to destroy in the air. The V2 was a far more sophisticated weapon – rocket-powered, with an automatic pilot and electronic guidance, it could reach a height of 100km (60 miles) and speeds of over 5,800km/h (3,600mph) and deliver a tonne of high explosive. Postwar development improved upon the V2 with missiles ranging from the huge intercontinental ballistic missiles (ICBMS) with ranges of 10,000km (6,000 miles) and nuclear warheads, to small hand-launched anti-tank missiles. The main strategic capability of nuclear missiles resides in the submarine systems developed by the superpowers, the first of which was Polaris. The multiple independently targeted re-entry vehicles (MIRVS) – ICBMS with many independently targetable sub-missiles – were developed in the late 1960s. The USA has built the cruise missile which, like the MIRV, threatens the balance of power. This missile can evade radar by flying at low heights and its computer guidance compares satellite photographs with the terrain over which it flies, bringing the missile to within ten metres of its target. *See also* MM pp.169, 175, 178–179.

Guido d'Arezzo (*died c.*1050), musical theorist and Benedictine monk, *b.* France. While head of the choir school at Arezzo, Italy, he gave the names *ut, re, mi, fa, sol, la* to the notes of the 6-note or hexachord scale then used. This was the basis of SOLMIZATION, used in Italy and France, and its British variant, TONIC SOL-FA. Guido also furthered the use of the STAFF to indicate the pitch of notes.

Guido da Siena (*fl.* mid-13th century), Italian painter. Although little is known of him, he is believed to be one of the first Italian painters to move away from the Byzantine style, and was a forerunner of DUCCIO and the Sienese painters.

Guild, organization formed by special interest or skilled group during the Middle Ages. Guilds, being urban organizations in the age of the FEUDAL SYSTEM, were formed for self-protection, social life and profit by those outside the rural manorial system. In 10th-century England, the London peace-guild was formed to protect urban landowners. In the 12th and 13th centuries, craftsmen in towns throughout Europe organized guilds to maintain the price and quality of goods, to protect their interests and to supervise the training of apprentices. By exercising a monopoly of a craft, they were able to control the amount of labour employed by the craft. By the 14th and 15th centuries, there were also religious guilds, burial guilds, merchant and money-lending guilds. At first self-governing and politically influential, guilds in the later Middle Ages were subject to municipalities. The longest-lasting guilds, those of teachers and students, were responsible for the development of medieval universities.

Guildford, county district in W SURREY, England, bordering Greater London. It was created in 1974 under the Local Government Act (1972). Area: 271sq km (104sq miles). Pop. (1974 est.) 121,600.

Guild socialism, type of socialism in Britain that advocated government control of the means of production and contracting of workers through national GUILDS. The initial theorist, Arthur J. Penty, urged a restoration in the power of guilds. The movement stressed worker-control of industry rather than general political reform. It lasted from 1906 to 1925.

Guillaume, Charles Édouard (1861–1938), Swiss physicist who was awarded the 1920 Nobel Prize in physics for his discovery of invar, an alloy of iron and nickel with an extremely small coefficient of expansion. He also developed another alloy, platinite, which expands at about the same rate as glass.

Guillemot, small, usually black and white seabird of the AUK family (Alcidae). It lives on cold Northern Hemisphere coastlines and dives for food on the sea bed. Nesting in colonies, it lays two oval eggs on rocky coasts. Length: about 43cm (17in). Genera *Cepphus* and *Uria. See also* NW p.*149.*

Guillen, Jorge (1893–   ), Spanish poet. After the civil war he left Spain for the USA. His main work, *Cántico*, appeared in several augmented editions from 1928 to 1950. *Language and Poetry*, a critical work, appeared in 1961.

Guillotine, mechanized beheading device adopted during the FRENCH REVOLUTION after its invention by Dr Guillotin. Following experiments on corpses, it was first used to execute a highwayman on 25 April 1792. Its first political victim was Collenot d'Angremont, who was convicted of being a royalist agent. The term also describes a British parliamentary procedure (first used 1887) by which a set time is allotted to various stages of a bill.

Guimard, Hector (1867–1942), French ART NOUVEAU architect. He designed several of the entrances to the Paris Métro (1899–1901), employing plant-like forms in cast iron, and taught at the École des BEAUX-ARTS. His Castel Béranger, a residential building in Paris (1898), was one of the first examples of Art Nouveau in France. *See also* HC2 p.178.

Guinea, gold coin introduced by Charles II of England in 1663 and then worth 20 shillings. The gold used in its minting came from the Guinea coast of Africa, hence its name. From 1717 the guinea was 21 shillings and in 1817 it was replaced by the gold sovereign (worth 20 shillings). It survives, even after the introduction of "metric" currency in Britain, as a pricing unit in the sale of horses, works of art and various professional fees, its value being taken as 21 shillings (£1.05).

Guinea, nation in W Africa, on the Atlantic coast. The agricultural economy relies heavily on the banana and coffee crops, and a large majority of the population is involved in farming. There is, however, considerable mineral wealth, and bauxite (aluminium ore) accounts for 65% of all exports. The capital is Conakry. Area: 245,857sq km (94,925sq miles). Pop. (1975 est.) 4,416,000. *See* MW p.91.

Guinea, Equatorial. *See* EQUATORIAL GUINEA.

Guinea-Bissau, nation in W Africa. It was formerly known as Portuguese Guinea until independence in 1974. The economy is based on agriculture and more than 80 per cent of the country's exports come from groundnuts and associated products. The capital is Bissau. Area: 36,125sq km (13,948sq miles). Pop. (1976 est.) 534,000. *See* MW p.91.

Guinea Coast, stretch of the W coast of Africa, from Cape Verde in Senegal to Moçâmedes in Angola. It includes the regions formerly known as the Ivory Coast, Gold Coast and Slave Coast, names which originated in early colonial trade.

Guinea fowl, pheasant-like GAME BIRD of Africa and Madagascar typified by the common domestic guinea hen (*Numida meleagris*). It is bluish, greyish or blackish with white spots and an ornamental crest. Other species have spurs, some have feather tufts on the head and one has a long, ornamental tail. Length: to 50cm (20in). Family Phasianidae. *See also* NW pp.*140, 200.*

Guinea pig, type of CAVY found in South America and a popular pet; including the wild guinea pig (*Cavia aperea*) and the domestic strain (*Cavia porcellus*). It has a large head, short legs and no tail. Its fur may be short or long and of any colour. It eats grass and other green plants. Family Caviidae. *See also* NW p.*203.*

Guinevere, in Arthurian legend, King Arthur's queen and the object of LANCELOT's love. In Thomas MALORY's *Morte d'Arthur* she betrayed the king and was sentenced to die, was rescued by Lancelot and later restored to Arthur. Towards the end of her life she became a nun; she was buried with her husband.

Guinness, Sir Alec (1914–), British actor. His first major role was in *Twelfth Night* at London's Old Vic (1936–37). He became world-famous after WWII playing the English eccentric in such EALING Studio films as *Kind Hearts and Coronets, The Lavender Hill Mob* and *The Ladykillers.* He has appeared in *Vicious Circle* (1946); *The Cocktail Party* (1950, 1968); *Exit the King* (1963); *Wise Child* (1967); *Time Out of Mind* (1970). He also played in such films as *Bridge on the River Kwai,* for which he won an Academy Award (1957); *Doctor Zhivago* (1966) and *The Comedians* (1970). More recently he has appeared on the London stage in *The Old Country* (1977) and in the film *Star Wars* (1977).

Guinness, brewery established by the Irish family of the same name. Arthur Guinness founded the firm which brewed porter in Dublin. Its control passed in turn to Benjamin Lee (1798–1868), Arthur Edward (1840–1915) and Edward Cecil Guinness (1847–1927) who, in 1919, became Lord Iveagh.

Guise, Sir John (1914–), politician from Papua New Guinea who was a member of the Legislative Council from 1961 to 1963, its speaker from 1968 until 1971, and deputy chief minister from 1972–75. In 1975 he became governor-general.

Guise, House of, ducal house of Lorraine, the most influential family in 16th-century France. Claude, Duke of Lorraine (1496–1550), founded the house in 1528. His son François (1519–63) supervised the massacre of HUGUENOTS at Vassy in 1562, thus precipitating the French Wars of Religion. His brother Charles (1524–74), Cardinal of Guise, played an important role at the Council of Trent. François' son Henri helped to organize the MASSACRE OF ST BARTHOLOMEW'S DAY in 1572, and led the HOLY LEAGUE, which opposed any toleration of Protestantism. The power of the family declined when HENRY IV became a Catholic in 1593. The male line ended in 1675.

Guitar, plucked stringed musical instrument of great antiquity. It was introduced into Spain by the Moors perhaps as early as the 12th century. Like the lute, the early guitar had four double strings. The popularity of the lute in the 17th century extended also to the guitar of which the famous exponent at that time was Robert de Visée (*c.*1650–*c.*1725). The national instrument of Spain, the modern guitar has six strings and the virtuoso playing of Andrés SEGOVIA has inspired compositions for the instrument by FALLA, VILLA LOBOS and CASTELNUOVO-TEDESCO. As a popular instrument today, it is also used for simple chordal accompaniment to folk song and dance and, as an electric instrument, in jazz and rock groups. *See* ELECTRIC GUITAR.

Guitar fish, cartilaginous RAY found worldwide in tropical and subtropical waters. It travels in schools, feeding off the sea bed. It is usually brown with spots, and its young are born alive. There are 9 genera and 45 species including *Rhinobatos cemiculus.* Family Rhinobatoidae. Length: 1.5–2m (5–6.6ft).

Guitry, Sacha (1885–1957), French actor, director and prolific author of immensely successful, mainly lightweight plays. Their plots often involved famous people such as Pasteur, Napoleon or Mozart, and inevitably starred Guitry himself with one or other of his five wives.

Guizot, François (1787–1874), French leader of the conservative constitutional monarchists and historian. He held several posts during the July Monarchy (1830–48). The Guizot law (1833) promised all citizens secular, primary education. Despite a pacific foreign policy, an economic crisis and his stubborn refusal to extend the limited franchise brought about his fall in the FEBRUARY REVOLUTION of 1848. *See also* HC2 p.170.

Gujarat, state in W India, on the Arabian Sea; the capital is Gandhinagar. It was established in 1960 when the former state of Bombay was separated into Marathiand and Gujarati-speaking areas. Archaeological finds have linked this region to the Indus valley civilization (3000–1500 BC). It was a centre of JAINISM under the Maitraka Dynasty from the 5th to the 8th centuries. The home of Mahatma GANDHI, it was the site of his religious retreats, the first of which was in 1915. Industries: cotton textiles, saltmining, oilseed. Area: 195,984sq km (75,669sq miles). Pop. (1971) 26,697,475.

Gujrānwāla, city in the Punjab, NE Pakistan, 67km (42 miles) N of Lahore. It is a market centre for a district producing wheat, rice, sugar, oilseed and oranges. It was an important centre of SIKH power in the 18th and 19th centuries, particularly under Ranjit Singh. Industries: ironware, textiles, pottery. Pop. 366,000.

Gulag Archipelago, The (1973–74), prose work in two volumes, written between 1958 and 1968 by the Soviet author Alexander SOLZHENITSYN. It is a detailed documentary account of life in Soviet prison camps between 1918 and 1956, derived from the author's own experience and correspondence with more than 200 other survivors of the camps.

Gulbenkian, Turkish-Persian family of financiers. Calouste Sarkis (1869–1955) organized important oil concessions for Britain, France, Holland and the USA in Turkey and the Middle East (1888–1954). He became a nationalized Briton in 1902, but assumed Persian citizenship in 1940 after his oil company was nationalized. On his death an international Gulbenkian Foundation was set up, to which he left a fine art collection. His son Nubar Sarkis (1896–1972) worked in his father's company, and as an Iranian diplomat (1926–51).

Gulf of Mexico. *See* MEXICO, GULF OF.

Gulf Oil Corporation, US company internationally involved in the exploration for and the processing of crude oil and natural-gas liquids. It produces petrochemical products and mines uranium. It is one of the giants of US industry.

Gulf States, name given to countries around the Persian Gulf, namely Iran to the N, Iraq to the NW, Kuwait, Saudi Arabia and Qatar to the W, Trucial Oman to the S and E and the Bahrain Islands between Saudi Arabia and Qatar. These states have gained international importance in recent years because of the discovery of extensive oil reserves within their borders.

Gulf Stream, relatively fast-moving current of the N Atlantic Ocean flowing from the straits of Florida along the E coast of North America, then E across the Atlantic to the NW European coast. Long considered to be one wide mass of water, research now indicates that it is made up of many thin streams which cause local variations in the water temperature. The current has a warming effect on the coastal climates along its course. *See also* PE pp.78–79.

Gull, also called seagull, any of various ground-nesting birds found soaring and gliding along most coastlines. Gregarious, particularly when feeding, gulls eat carrion, refuse, fish, shellfish, eggs and young birds. The herring gull is grey and white with black markings (although the young are mottled brown) and has a hooked bill, pointed wings, a rounded tail and webbed feet. It grows to 56–66cm (22–26in). The black-headed gull is smaller, and has black feathers on the top of the head in summer. Family Laridae; species: herring gull *Larus argentatus,* black-headed gull *Larus ridibundus.*

Gulliver's Travels (1726), prose satire by Jonathan SWIFT. Although the descriptions of the four cultures visited by Gulliver can be enjoyed by both children and adults as pure exercises of imagination, they clearly satirize contemporary political, scientific and moral institutions. The last section in particular, dealing with the Houyhnhnms, has often been seen as a vicious and misanthropic attack on the mental and physical attributes of humanity itself. *See also* HC2 p.27.

Gullstrand, Allvar (1862–1930), Swedish ophthalmologist. He received the Nobel Prize in physiology and medicine in 1911 for his contributions to dioptrics, the study of refraction of light by the eye. He invented many important ophthalmological tools, including the slit lamp, which aided the study of the structure and function of the CORNEA, and improved corrective lenses for use after surgery.

Gum arabic, or acacia gum, soluble yellowish gum obtained from certain species of acacia trees and consisting of a complex carbohydrate POLYMER. It is used in foods, cosmetics and adhesives.

Gums, secretions of plants. Some gums are soluble in water; others absorb water and swell. Gums are chemically complex, consisting mainly of various saccharides bound to organic acids by glycoside linkages. Common examples are GUM ARABIC, agar and tragacanth. Many substances of similar appearance, such as some RESINS, are classed as gums.

Gums, two areas of tissue covering the alveolar arch of the upper and lower jaws. The gums surround the teeth and are quite resistant to damage – their submucosa is well supplied with nerves and blood vessels. Inflammation of the gums is called GINGIVITIS, and is caused by poor mouth hygiene, THRUSH or VITAMIN DEFICIENCY.

Gun, general term for any tubular weapon firing a projectile, usually by force of explosion. The phrase "The guns" was sometimes used in the 19th century to refer to artillery, but the word gun is now used for artillery pieces with a relatively high muzzle velocity and a flat trajectory: thus a MORTAR or HOWITZER is not often described as a gun, but PISTOLS, RIFLES and MACHINE GUNS can all be so described. The word has also been applied to weapons that use compressed air to propel projectiles, ie airguns. *See also* MM pp.162–171, 173–174, 176–179, *176–179.*

Guncotton, nitrocellulose, highly nitrated form of CELLULOSE which is highly explosive. It is made by soaking cotton cellulose in mixed nitric and sulphuric acids. When dry, guncotton is dangerously unstable. It is used mainly as an ingredient of explosive propellants such as CORDITE.

Gunmetal, types of wear-resistant BRONZE once used to make heavy field and naval guns, but now used in gears, bearings and

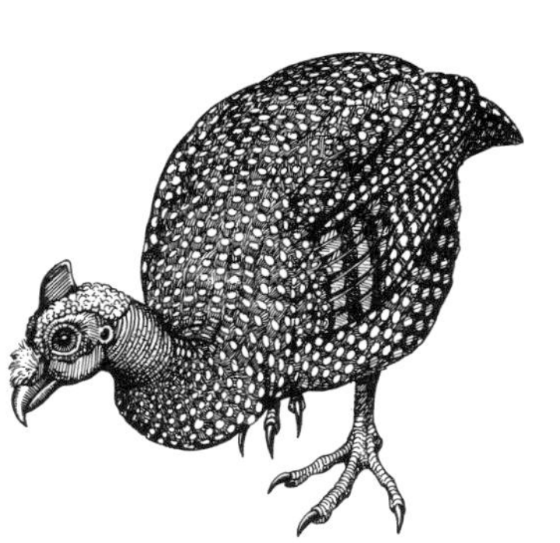

Guinea fowl are pheasant-like birds which can be bred like domestic poultry.

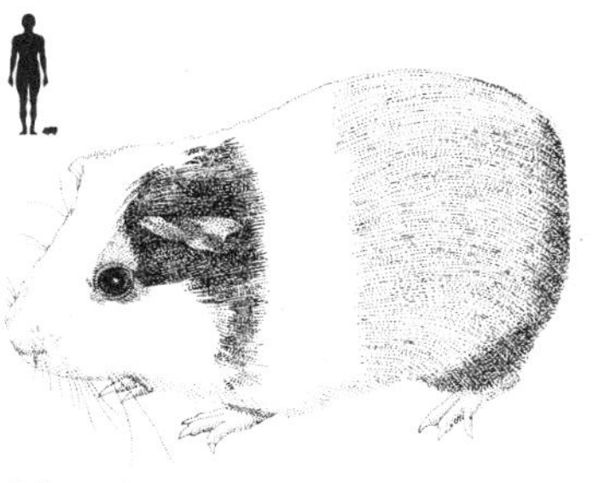

Guinea pigs have lent their name to a person or group who assumes an experimental role.

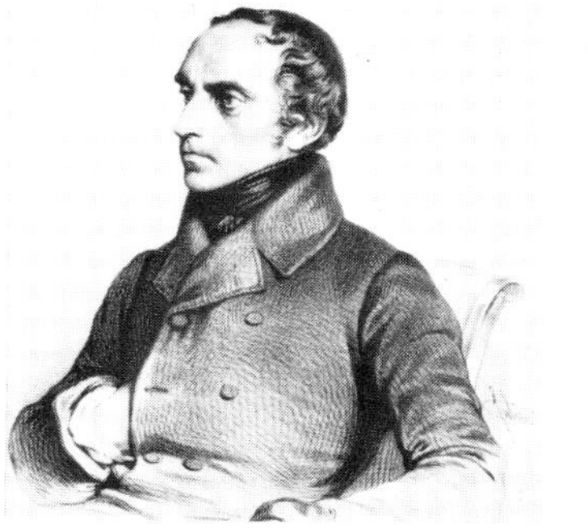

Guizot survived violent changes of regime in a turbulent period of France's history.

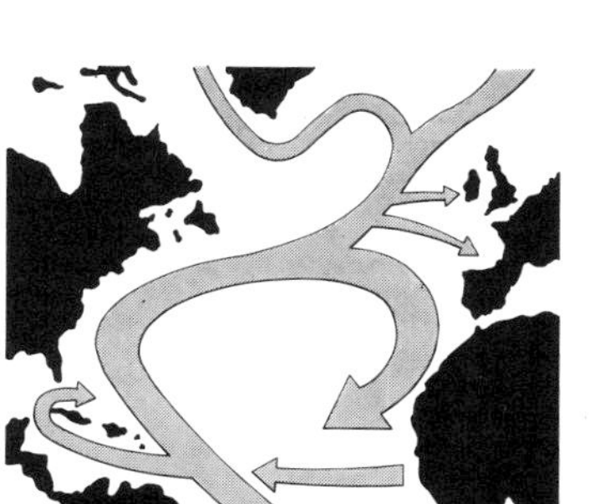

Gulf Stream; a blueness distinguishes it from the colder inshore counter-currents.

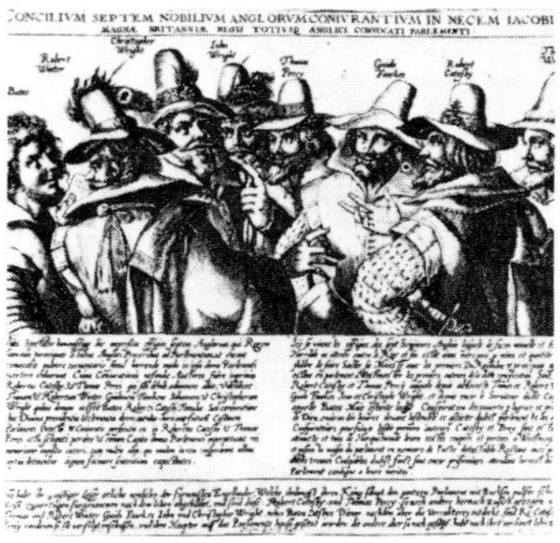

The Gunpowder Plot has became, without its religious aspects, an English festival.

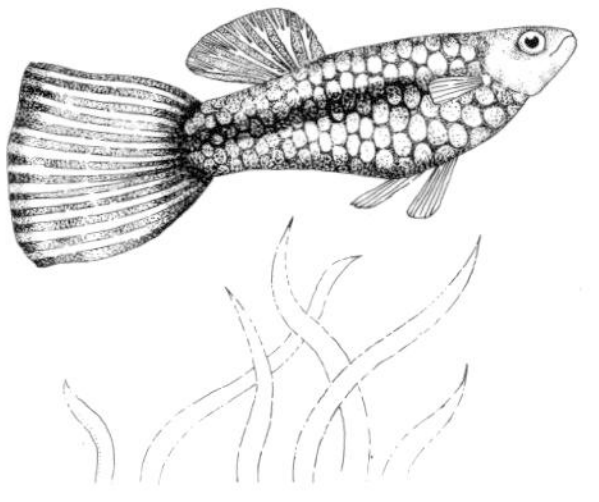

Guppies are a common sight, seen darting excitedly around the waters of home aquaria.

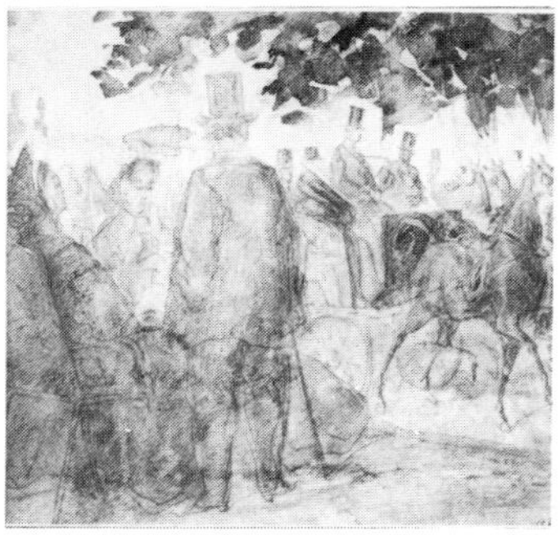

Constantin Guys portrayed fashionable society, as in *The Elysian Fields* (detail).

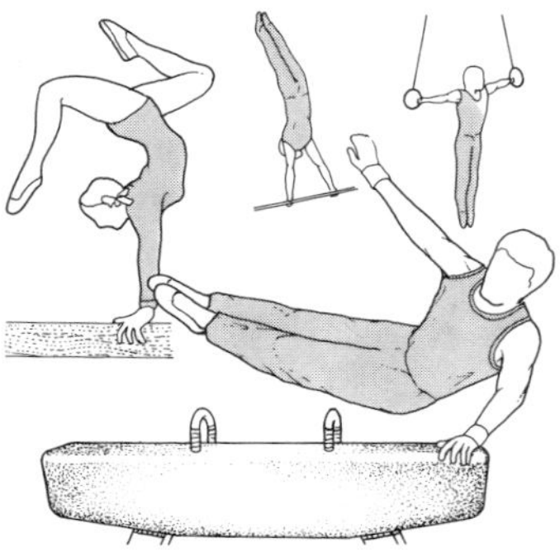

Gymnastics has received a new impetus from the appeal of televised Olympic excellence.

pump spindles. A typical gunmetal alloy contains about 88% copper, 10% zinc and 2% tin.

Gunn, Thom (1929–), British poet. His first poems appeared in *Fighting Terms* (1954) and *The Sense of Movement* (1957). Other collections are *My Sad Captains* (1961), *Positives* (1966) and *Moly* (1971). He now lives in the USA.

Gunpowder, mixture of saltpetre (potassium nitrate), charcoal and sulphur. When ignited, it expands violently due to the almost instantaneous conversion of the solid ingredients into gases such as carbon dioxide, carbon monoxide, nitrogen, oxides of nitrogen, oxides of sulphur and steam. The sudden release of enormous volumes of these gases gives the reaction its explosive force. It was used extensively in firearms until about 1900, after which it was replaced by smokeless powders such as CORDITE. *See also* MM pp.242–243.

Gunpowder Plot (1605), Roman Catholic conspiracy to blow up JAMES I of England and the Houses of Parliament, and to establish Catholicism in England. The plotters, led by Robert CATESBY, took gunpowder into the cellars beneath Parliament, where Guy FAWKES was to ignite it when James opened Parliament on 5 Nov. The authorities, however, were alerted and Fawkes was arrested, tried and executed along with his fellow conspirators. The plot led to increased penalties against Catholics. *See also* HC1 p.*286*.

Gunther, Franz Ignaz (1725–75), Bavarian sculptor in wood. His painted sculptures of religious themes are among the finest and most moving examples of the ROCOCO style. Especially notable are *The Annunciation* (1764) and the *Pietà* (1774), his last work.

Guppy, or millions fish, minnow found in fresh waters of the West Indies, Venezuela, the Guianas and N Brazil, and named after R. J. L. Guppy, a 19th-century clergyman and naturalist. The wild guppy is grey with bright spots but selective breeding has produced many different coloured varieties. The smaller male is brighter than the female, which bears live young. It is a popular aquarium fish. Length: to 3–6cm (1.2–2.5in). Family Poeciliidae; species *Lebistes reticulatis*.

Gupta dynasty (*c*.AD 320–550), ruling dynasty of a kingdom covering most of northern India. The state was the prototype of Indian empires to follow. The Guptas conquered territory and collected tribute from defeated rulers but allowed them to remain on their thrones. The Guptas were considered benevolent, and art and literature flourished under their rule. *See also* HC1 pp.118–119.

Gurkha, HINDU ruling caste of Nepal since 1768. They speak a SANSKRIT language and their racial characteristics are a mixture of Mongoloid and Caucasoid. The name often denotes a Nepalese soldier in the British or Indian army. Gurkha soldiers have a high reputation for combat skills and physical endurance.

Gurnard, tropical marine bottom-dwelling fish. It has a large spiny head and enlarged pectoral fins. It uses its fins to "walk" on the sea-bed. Length: to 50cm (20in). Family Triglidae.

Guru, Sanskrit term for a teacher and spiritual master. In traditional Hindu education, boys lived in the home of a guru, who was their guide in their studies of the sacred books (VEDAS) and saw to their physical health and ethical training. In many Hindu sects the guru is responsible for initiating novices. In SIKHISM the title Guru was assumed by the leaders of the community until the guruship was terminated in 1708.

Gustavus, name of six Swedish kings. Gustavus I (Gustavus Vasa) (*r*.1523–60) founded the VASA dynasty. He promoted a national Protestant church (1527), organized a national army and navy, suppressed clerical and peasant revolts and limited the power of the nobles, thus strengthening the monarchy and founding the modern Swedish state. Gustavus II (Gustavus Adolphus) (*r*.1611–32), the "Lion of the North", spearheaded the Protestant cause in the THIRTY YEARS WAR. Invading Germany in 1630, he won a series of battles against the imperial commanders TILLY and WALLENSTEIN but was killed at Lutzen. His reign saw economic and administrative reform within Sweden, largely due to his chancellor, OXENTIERNA. Gustavus III (*r*.1771–92) ended civil strife, restored royal power, reformed Sweden's finances and built up the navy. He defeated the Danes and Russians but was assassinated by an aristocratic conspiracy. He founded the Swedish Academy (1786). Gustavus IV (*r*.1792–1809) followed a reactionary policy at home. His anti-French foreign policy led to the loss of Swedish Pomerania and Finland to France and Russia, and to his forced abdication. The reign (1907–50) of Gustavus V saw the development of Sweden's advanced welfare state and a policy of international neutrality. Gustavus VI (*r*.1950–73) was a noted botanist and archaeologist. He founded the Swedish Academy in Rome and was a member of the British Royal Society.

Guston, Philip (1912–), US painter. Largely self-taught, he executed many murals for the Federal Art Project (1935–40). He was a prominent ABSTRACT EXPRESSIONIST, and his style is reminiscent of MONET, with colourful subdued tints in patches on a light background.

Gutenberg, Beno (1889–1960), US seismologist, noted for his analyses of earthquake waves. He showed that three-quarters of earthquakes occur in the Circum-Pacific belt. He worked with Charles RICHTER to develop the RICHTER SCALE.

Gutenberg, Johann (*c*.1400–*c*.68), German goldsmith and printer credited with the invention of printing from movable type. He experimented with printing in the 1430s, and his innovations included a new type of press and a type-metal alloy, neither of which were used in the older woodblock printing process. He made the first printed Bible, known as the Gutenberg Bible (*c*.1455).

Guthrie, Sir William Tyrone (1900–71), British director and playwright. He directed the Scottish National Theatre (1926–27), the Festival Theatre, Cambridge (1929–30) and the Old Vic and Sadler's Wells Theatres. He also worked in other countries and directed the theatre named after him (1963) in Minneapolis. He was particularly known for his productions of Shakespeare.

Guthrum (*d*.890), Danish leader. He fought against the English in E Anglia in the 870s, and is said to have lead the first Danish expedition to have wintered in England, in 877. In 878 he was granted a kingdom in East Anglia and agreed to be converted to Christianity. After his baptism he was known as Aethelstan. *See also* HC1 pp.154, *155*.

Gutta-percha, evergreen tree found in Malaya, Sumatra and Borneo. It is the source of a rubber-like gum used in belting, golf-balls and in chewing gum. The tree is flat-topped and has long oval leaves that are green above and coppery with silky hairs below. Height: to 30.5m (100ft). Family Sapotaceae; species *Palaquium gutta*.

Guttuso, Renato (1912–), Italian painter. A SOCIAL REALIST, after WWII he became an influential figure in the left-wing New Art Front. Influenced by Pablo PICASSO, his art became less representational but remained committed to protesting against social injustice.

Gutzkow, Karl Ferdinand (1811–78), German dramatist, journalist and novelist. His works include the comedies *Zopf und Schwert* (1844) and *Der Königsleutnant* (1849); the tragedies *Richard Savage* (1839) and *Uriel Acosta* (1846) and a novel, *Maha Guru* (1833).

Guyana, nation in NE South America, between Venezuela and Surinam. It was formerly British Guiana. The land is covered by tropical forest and savanna, and most of the population inhabits the coastal region. The terrain prevents full exploitation of the country's bauxite deposits, and agriculture remains the basis of the economy with sugar cane and rice as the chief crops. Capital: Georgetown. Area: 214,970sq km (83,000sq miles). Pop. (1975 est.) 794,000. *See* MW p.91.

Guyenne. *See* GUIENNE.

Guy of Lusignan (1140–94), Latin King of Jerusalem (1186–92) and of Cyprus (1192–94). He succeeded BALDWIN V of Jerusalem, but was defeated and captured by SALADIN at Hattin (1187). He later fought in the Third CRUSADE (1189–91), resigned the throne to Conrad of Montferrat (1192) and was granted Cyprus by RICHARD I of England. *See also* HC1 pp.176–177.

Guyot, or tablemount, names given to flat-topped submarine mountains. They rise about 1,000m (3,300ft), with tops about 2.5km (1.5 miles) below sea-level. Before becoming submerged, they may have been volcanic islands with peaks flattened by wave erosion. If so, this is evidence for the subsiding of the ocean floor. *See also* PE p.*83*.

Guys, Constantin (1805–92), French painter and illustrator. Much of his work was published in the *Illustrated London News*. He is best known for his witty drawings of contemporary society.

Guys and Dolls (1950), popular Broadway musical by Frank Loesser based on a Damon RUNYON short story. A similarly successful screen version appeared in 1955.

Gwent, county in SE Wales, formed in 1974 from most of the former county of MONMOUTHSHIRE and a small part of BRECKNOCKSHIRE, bounded by the English border and the Severn estuary. The administrative centre is Cwmbran. Area: 1,376sq km (531sq miles). Pop. (1975 est.) 440,100.

Gwyn, or Gwynne, Nell (1650–87), English actress. She made her first stage appearance at 15 in *The Indian Emperor*. Much in demand as a speaker of prologues and epilogues, she attracted the attention of King CHARLES II while reciting the epilogue to Dryden's *Tyrannic Love* (1669). She later became his mistress and bore him two sons.

Gwynedd, county in NW Wales, on the Irish Sea coast, formed in 1974 from the former counties of ANGLESEY, CAERNARVON, part of DENBIGHSHIRE and most of MERIONETH. The administrative centre is Caernarvon. Area: 3,866sq km (1,493sq miles). Pop. (1975 est.) 224,200.

Gymnastics, sport requiring suppleness, strength and poise in the performance of a variety of athletic exercises. Men and women compete separately in individual and team events. At national and international level, men perform in six events: on the vault, parallel bars, horizontal bars, pommelled-horse, suspended alloy rings and floor exercises. Women take part in four events: the vault, balance beam, floor exercises and asymmetrical bars. Contestants perform twice in each event; they complete a compulsory set of exercises, then a set of their own choosing. Exercises are rated in terms of difficulty, and points for technical skills and visual appeal are awarded by a panel of judges. The combined scores of these individual events give the final result of an all-round event.

Dating back to the ancient Chinese and Greeks, gymnastics became truly international only after WWII, when world championships were begun (1950) and women's events gained Olympic acceptance (1952). The father of the modern sport, Friedrich Ludwig Jan, devised the apparatus and exercises requiring muscular power, while Pehr Henrik Ling, a Swede, stressed rhythmic movement. The exercises performed today are of both these types. The sport has become increasingly popular, and the televised Olympic successes of Olga KORBUT and Nadia COMANECI, transmitted throughout the world, brought thousands of youngsters into sport in the 1970s.

Gymnosperm, seed plant with naked seeds borne on scales, usually in cones. Most trees commonly referred to as EVERGREENS are gymnosperms. All living seed-bearing plants are divided into two main groups: gymnosperms and ANGIOSPERMS (with seeds enclosed in an ovary). Gymnosperms include CYCADS, GINKGO, PINES, SPRUCES, CEDARS and ephedras. *See also* CONIFER; NW pp.*38*, 54–55, 177.

Gynecomastia, inappropriate enlargement of the male breasts, usually at puberty, caused by hormone imbalance – ie, an excess of the female hormone oestrogen. The enlargement often subsides spontaneously.

Györ, city port in NW Hungary, at the confluence of the Rába and Répce rivers. Its location makes the city an important communications centre. Local industries include steel, textiles and distilling. Pop (1974) 114,709.

György, Paul (1893–), US doctor, *b.* Hungary, who was involved in the discovery of riboflavin, vitamin B6 and biotin (vitamin H). He was the chairman of advisory groups to the UN and WHO from 1958 until 1961.

Gypsies, nomadic people, now believed to have originated in N India, now inhabiting Europe, Asia, Siberia, America, Africa and Australia. They were once thought to have come from Egypt, hence their name. They speak the distinctive ROMANY language, from which they are also known as Romanies, and traditionally live in decorated, horse-drawn carriages. Gypsies first appeared in Europe in the 15th century. Since then their reluctance to lead a settled life has caused prejudice, often resulting in persecution. On the other hand, their colourful folklore is part of popular tradition. Other wandering groups who are not true Romanies are also sometimes called gypsies, although strictly speaking, this is incorrect.

Gypsophila, genus of the PINK family containing annual or perennial plants, native to Europe, Asia and North Africa. Growing to 0.9m (3ft), they have narrow leaves and pink or white flowers in single or double blossoms. They are widely cultivated in gardens and for cut flowers. Family Caryophyllaceae.

Gypsum, commonest sulphate mineral, calcium sulphate ($CaSO_4.2H_2O$), and a source of PLASTER OF PARIS. Huge beds of gypsum occur in sedimentary rocks. It crystallizes in the monoclinic system as prismatic or bladed crystals. Varieties are alabaster (massive); selenite (transparent and foliated); and satinspar (silky and fibrous). It can be clear, white or tinted. Hardness 2; s.g. 2.3.

Gypsum processing, production of PLASTER OF PARIS from hydrated calcium sulphate ($CaSO_4.2H_2O$). Partial calcination is accomplished by heating GYPSUM to 120°–180°C (248°–356°F) to produce the hemihydrate, a fine, quick-setting white powder. Hard wall plaster contains an additive to retard the set.

Gypsy moth, small TUSSOCK MOTH with black zigzag markings; the female is larger and lighter in colour. The caterpillar of this species feeds on forest and fruit trees, and can be a serious pest; it is pale brown and covered with tufts of stiff hairs. Length: 5cm (2in). Family Lepidoptera; species *Lymantria dispar.*

Gyre, large circular flow of ocean water with a calm centre region called an eddy. There are three gyres in both the Atlantic and Pacific oceans and one in the Indian Ocean. They are narrowest and swiftest on their western sides and are generally centred on the Horse latitudes (about 30° latitude in both hemispheres). *See also* PE p.79.

Gyrfalcon, bird of prey living mainly in Scandinavia and arctic regions; it is the largest European FALCON. It commonly flies low, catching prey on the ground or small birds in flight; it rarely soars. Plumage is a mottled grey-brown. Length: to 61cm (24in). Family Falconidae; species *Falco rusticolus. See also* NW p.*225*.

Gyrocompass, navigational aid consisting of a continuously driven GYROSCOPE, used where a magnetic compass would be unreliable because of large masses of iron or steel nearby. The spinning axis of the gyroscope is horizontal and its direction indicates true north, irrespective of the course or attitude of the craft to which it is attached. Similar devices are used to "hold" the aim of guns carried by warships and tanks.

Gyropilot, mechanism consisting of devices for detecting and automatically correcting changes in the attitude of an aircraft or the course of a ship in which it is mounted. In an aircraft the gyropilot makes the correction by moving the appropriate control (rudder for azimuth and change in heading, aileron for roll and elevator for pitch). The essential component is the spinning wheel, or GYROSCOPE, which is suspended in gimbals so that it maintains its direction of spin irrespective of the orientation of the craft to which it is secured; the gyroscope constitutes a reference platform. The gyropilot detects changes in orientation and signals affiliated components, such as slave motors, to make corrections. *See also* MM pp.*104*, 105.

Gyroscope, symmetrical spinning body, usually a wheel, mounted in gimbals so that it can spin in any direction. When the gyroscope is spinning, a change in the orientation of the outer gimbals does not change the orientation of the spinning wheel; thus changes in direction aboard, say, a ship can be determined without external references. A torque (twisting force) applied to a fast-spinning gyroscope, eg by leaning it out of the vertical, results in a phenomenon known as PRECESSION: the gyroscope does not fall but rotates about a fixed point with the axis of spin describing a cone around the vertical. This tendency to resist changes in the spin axis accounts partly for the stability of bicycles, and the orbits of heavenly bodies. *See also* MM p.*90*.

H

H, eighth letter of the alphabet, derived from the Semitic letter *heth*, which was used like an English *h* (aspirate) or like the *ch* sound in *loch*. In Greek it became *eta* (pronounced like a short *e*) or an aspirate, in which form it passed into the Roman alphabet. In English an initial *h* may be silent (as in *hour* and *heir*). It modifies the sounds of certain preceding consonants, as in *ch*, *gh*, *ph*, *sh* and *th*, but is virtually silent after *w* (as in *what* and *which*). It is generally silent after a vowel, but lengthens its sound (compare the *a* sounds in *eta* and *bah*).

Haakon I (*c.* 914–961), "the Good", King of Norway, son of Harald I. Brought up a Christian in King Athelstan's court in England, he returned to Norway to take control from his brother, the tyrannical ERIK BLOODAXE.

Haakon IV (1204–63), "the Old", King of Norway, elected 1217, crowned 1247: son of Haakon III. He made legal reforms and acquired Iceland and Greenland. He was patron of the arts and his reign began medieval Norway's "golden age" (1217–1319).

Haakon V Magnusson (1270–1319), King of Norway, son of Magnus VI, succeeded his brother Erik II in 1299. He limited the power of the nobles, and alienated the English by trading with the HANSEATIC LEAGUE.

Haakon VI Magnusson (1339–80), King of Norway. Son of Magnus VII, he ruled from 1355, and was the last king of independent Norway. His reign was weakened by war and the BLACK DEATH.

Haakon VII (1872–1957), King of Norway. Formerly Prince Charles, son of Denmark's King FREDERICK VIII, he was offered the crown in 1905 when Norway separated from Sweden. During WWII he held government while in exile.

Haarlem, city in W Netherlands, on the River Spaarne; capital of North Holland province. Haarlem was a centre of Dutch painting in the 16th and 17th centuries. The city has many old buildings, including the 13th-century Groote Kerk (or St Bavo's Cathedral), which houses a fine organ and where many recitals are held. Haarlem is a centre for the export of tulips and has industries which include electronic equipment and machinery. Pop. (1974) 167,052.

Habakkuk, Book of, Old Testament book by the eighth of the 12 minor prophets. It bemoans the condition of JUDAH and the apparent success of God's enemies.

Habeas Corpus, the most important WRIT in English law for the protection of the liberty of the individual. There are several kinds of writs of *habeas corpus*, but the most important is the *habeas corpus ad subjiciendum*, which commands a person who holds another in custody to bring his captive before the court and to state the cause of his detention.

Haber, Fritz (1868–1934), German physical chemist whose early work involved ELECTROCHEMISTRY and THERMODYNAMIC gas reactions. With Carl BOSCH he invented (1908–09) the HABER PROCESS for converting atmospheric nitrogen into ammonia. He was awarded the 1918 Nobel Prize in chemistry.

Haber process, industrial process in which nitrogen from the atmosphere is "fixed" by synthesizing ammonia. A mixture of nitrogen and hydrogen is passed over a heated catalyst at a pressure of about 1,000 atmospheres. The chemical reaction, $N_2 + 3H_2 \rightarrow 2NH_3$, is exothermic, which in turn speeds up the reaction.

Habsburg. *See* HAPSBURG.

Habyalimana, Maj.-Gen. Juvenal (1937–), Rwandan politician. He became President of Rwanda in 1973, an office he combined with those of Prime Minister and Minister of National Defence.

Hackman, Gene (1931–), US film and television actor. He appeared in various television productions and gained an international reputation with small character parts in such films as *Bonnie and Clyde* (1967) and *Downhill Racer* (1969). In 1972 he won an Academy Award for his performance in *The French Connection* (1971).

Hackney, light HORSE bred for heavy harness and carriage use. An English breed developed during the early 18th century from the Norfolk trotter and the thoroughbred, it has short legs and robust build. Colours are chestnut, bay or brown, with white markings. Its tail is docked and its mane pulled for show. The Hackney pony is a cross between the horse and a Welsh pony. Height: 147–157cm (58–62in); weight: 360–540kg (800–1,200lb).

Hadad. *See* ADAD.

Hadal zone, deepest oceanic environment, particularly that of the deep ocean trenches from 6.5km (4 miles) below sea-level down to the ocean floor.

Haddock, marine food and commercial fish found in cold and temperate waters, primarily in the Northern Hemisphere. Dark grey and silver, it has a large, dark blotch near the pectoral fins. Length: to about 90cm (36in); weight: to 11kg (24.5lb). Family Gadidae; species *melanogrammus aeglefinus. See also* NW p.*131*; PE pp.*241*, 246, *247*.

Hades, in Greek mythology, both another name for PLUTO, god of the underworld, and the world of the dead, ruled by Pluto and PERSEPHONE. The dead were ferried to Hades by CHARON across the river STYX. The entrance was guarded by the dog CERBERUS.

Hadley, John (1682–1744), British inventor who in 1721 constructed the first reflecting telescope sufficiently accurate for astronomical observations. In 1730, independently of Thomas Godfrey, he designed a reflecting quadrant, the forerunner of the sextant, which enabled navigators to make accurate determinations of latitude.

Hadramawt, region in E Yemen, along the coast of Arabian Peninsula. For more than 100 years it was under the British protected Quaiti and Kathiri sultanates. In 1967 these were overthrown and Southern Yemen (the People's Democratic Republic of Yemen) formed. Area: approx. 153,220sq km (58,000sq miles). Pop. 240,000.

Hadrian, Publius Aelius (AD 76–138), Roman emperor (117–138). He crushed a Jewish revolt and destroyed the Temple of Jerusalem in 135 but promoted major building programmes, including the Pantheon in Rome, his villa at Tivoli and HADRIAN'S WALL in Britain. He enlarged and reformed the civil service and

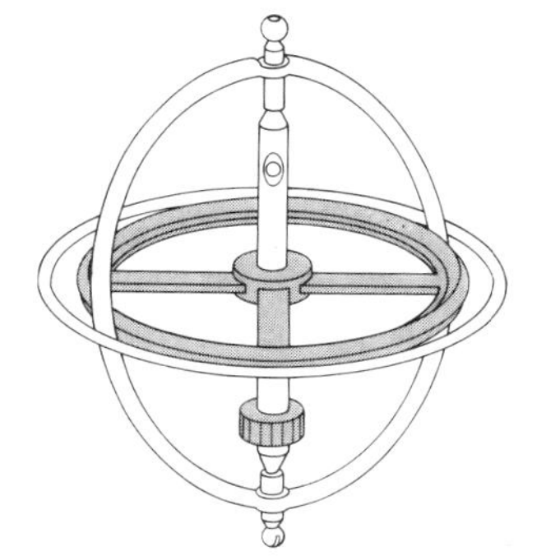

Gyroscopes are one of the scientific toys which have enthralled many children.

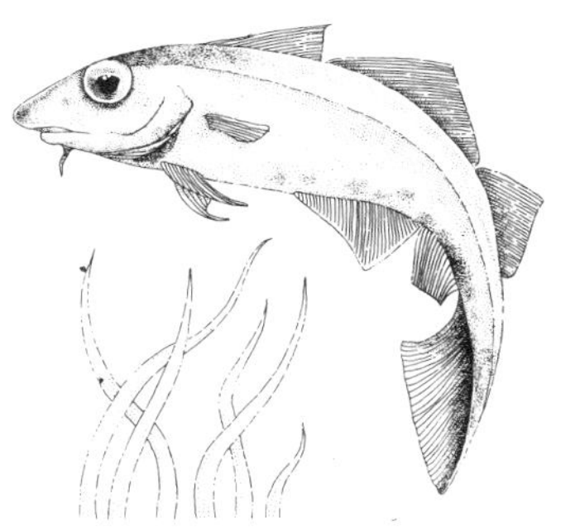

Haddock, one of our most valuable food fish, is trawled extensively in the northern seas.

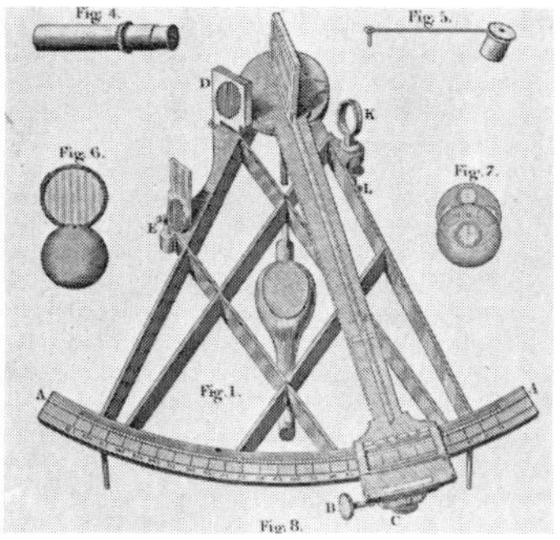

John Hadley; a detail from the illustration of the principal parts of his original quadrant.

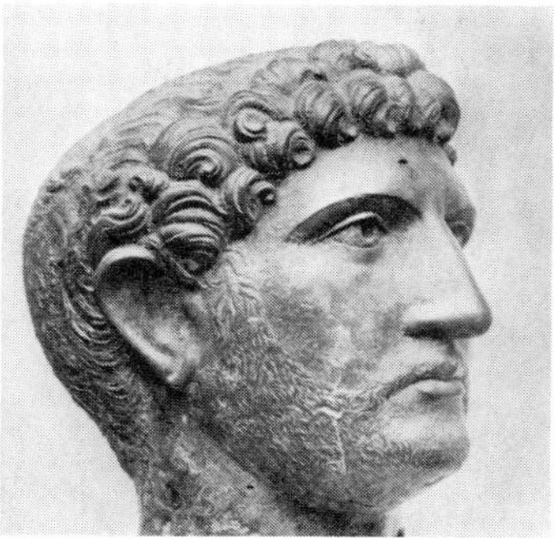

Hadrian; this bronze head was found in the Thames near to London Bridge.

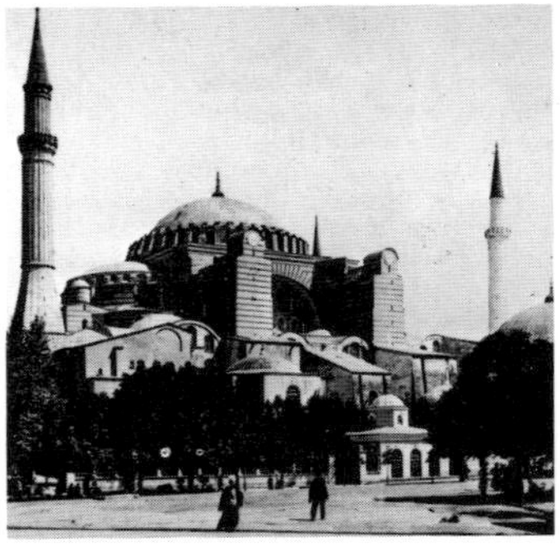
Hagia Sophia, rivalled in splendour only by St Peter's in Rome, took only five years to build.

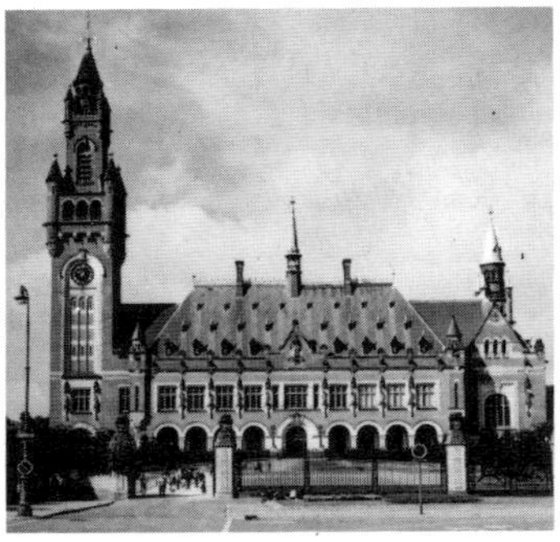
The Hague; the Peace Palace was financed by the US industrialist Andrew Carnegie.

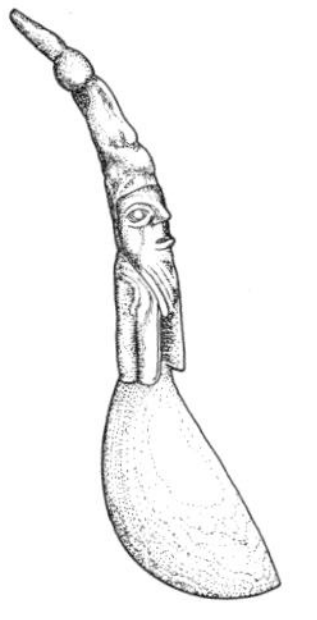
Haida; a carved ladle from the small tribe whose carving and sculpture are renowned.

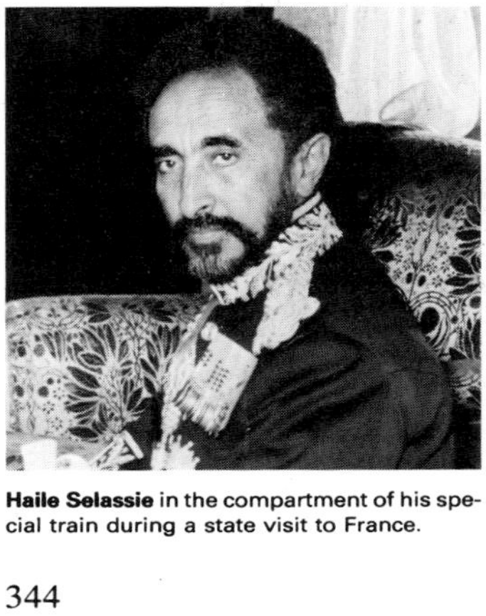
Haile Selassie in the compartment of his special train during a state visit to France.

provided alms and circuses for the poor of Rome. *See also* HC1 pp.99, 108.

Hadrian's Wall, northern boundary wall of Roman Britain erected on the orders of the Emperor Hadrian between AD 122–136. It extended 118.3km (73.5 miles) from Wallsend-on-Tyne to Bowness-on-Solway. About 2.3m (7.5ft) thick and 1.8–4.6m (6–15ft) high, it supported many stone forts along its length. The Romans held it until 383. An extensive ruin survives.

Hadron, class of elementary particle with strong interaction. The group can be divided into BARYONS, such as the neutron and proton, and MESONS, such as the pion and kaon. Over 150 hadrons have been discovered, mostly since about 1950, and with the exception of the proton and antiproton they are all unstable. Unlike LEPTONS, they have a measurable size; experiment indicates a substructure postulated to consist of QUARKS. *See also* STRANGENESS; SU pp.66–67.

Haeckel, Ernst Heinrich (1834–1919), German zoologist. His popular books defended and extended the theories of Charles DARWIN and helped to promote interest in the study of biology.

Haematite, one of the most important iron ores, ferric oxide, Fe_2O_3. It contains 70% of iron by weight. It is blood red in colour and occurs in several forms. Kidney ore is so called because it occurs as red, rounded masses that resemble kidneys. Specular haematite is more obviously crystalline and takes a high polish. Haematite deposits are found in all continents.

Haematoma, localized mass of blood, often clotted, that collects in an organ or tissue when an associated blood vessel breaks. Its treatment depends on location and its size.

Haematuria, blood in the urine. It may have various causes, such as an injury or obstruction in the urinary tract, and should be reported to a doctor immediately.

Haemoglobin, protein present in the red blood cells or ERYTHROCYTES of vertebrates that carries oxygen to all cells in the body. It is scarlet when combined with oxygen to form OXYHAEMOGLOBIN and bluish-red when deoxygenated. Oxygen attaches to the haem part of the protein which contains iron; the globin part is a globular protein. Worn out red blood cells are destroyed by the liver which salvages the iron for making more haemoglobin.

Haemophilia, hereditary defect which can cause severe external or internal bleeding because the blood clots only with difficulty due to the absence of clotting factor VIII, a globulin. The gene for the disease is passed on almost exclusively by the mother; male haemophiliacs, even when they survive long enough, rarely have children. About one in 10,000 boys are born haemophiliac but haemophiliac girls are extremely rare. If a haemophiliac male and a carrier female produce children, half of the girls will be haemophiliac, the other half being carriers. *See also* MS pp.84, 91, 115.

Haemorrhage, bleeding. That from an artery is most serious because blood is forced out by the heartbeat. Internal bleeding can also be dangerous whether from an artery or a vein. Haemoptysis is the spitting of blood from a lung haemorrhage. Haematuria is blood in the urine. Haematemesis is vomiting blood, often caused by a stomach haemorrhage.

Haemorrhoids, piles, varicose veins of the lower rectum. External haemorrhoids are purplish in colour. Internal haemorrhoids, under their coverings of mucous membrane, are bright red in colour and extend farther up the rectum. Both types can protrude from the anus and both can be very painful. The causes of haemorrhoids are many and ill-defined.

Haffkine, Waldemar Mordecai Wolff, (1860–1930), Russian bacteriologist who from 1889 to 1893 was an assistant to Louis PASTEUR in Paris. After founding a research laboratory in Bombay, India, he discovered and used a method of inoculation against cholera by which some 42,000 people were treated.

Hafiz (died *c.* 1388), Persian poet, born as Shams ed-Din Muhammed. He was associated with the DERVISHES and was a SUFI. His verse, in rhyming couplets, was powerful and dealt with sensual pleasures.

Hafnium, metallic element (Hf) of the third transition series, first discovered in 1923. Its chief source is as a by-product in obtaining the element ZIRCONIUM. It is used as a neutron absorber in reactor control rods. Properties: a.n. 72; a.w. 178.49; s.g. 13.31; m.p. 2,220°C (4,031°F); b.p. 4,602°C (8,316°F); most common isotope Hf^{180} (35.24%). *See also* SU pp.134–136.

Haganah, semi-underground ZIONIST army which was formed in the 1920s to protect Jewish interests in Palestine. It allied with the extreme Irgun group in 1945 in an attempt to change British policy on Jewish immigration, and received financial and military aid from American Zionists after that time. *See also* HC2 pp.296–297.

Hagar, in the Old Testament, handmaid given by SARAH to ABRAHAM as a concubine. She bore his first son, Ishmael. Hagar and Ishmael were banished because Sarah feared Ishmael would share in ISAAC's inheritance.

Hagen, Friedrich Heinrich von der (1780–1856), German philologist. His edition of the Norse song cycle *Nibelungenlied* was published in 1810.

Hagen, Walter Charles (1892–1969), US golfer. One of the most colourful personalities in golf history, he helped improve the standing of professional players and their prize money. He won five Professional Golfers' Association titles (1921, 1924–27), four British Open championships (1922, 1924, 1928–29) and two US Opens (1914, 1919).

Hagfish, or slime eel, eel-like, jawless fish found in temperate-to-cold marine waters. It has underdeveloped eyes and four to six fleshy whiskers around its sucking mouth. It is a scavenger and feeds on dead or dying fish. It also secretes a slimy mucus from pores along its sides. Length: to 80cm (32in). Family Myxinidae. *See also* CYCLOSTOMATA; NW p.123.

Hägg, Gunder (1918–), Swedish middle-distance runner who, from 1941 to 1945, ran a series of races in which he set 15 world records for the mile/1,500m, 2,000m, 3,000m, 2 miles and 3 miles/5,000m. In 1945 he lost his amateur status for infringements of the amateur code.

Haggai, biblical author and tenth of the 12 Minor Prophets. After the BABYLONIAN CAPTIVITY, he encouraged the people in rebuilding the TEMPLE in Jerusalem (516 BC).

Haggard, Sir Henry Rider (1856–1925), British novelist. His experiences in the colonial service in the Transvaal (1875–79) and Africa provide the background for his romantic adventure novels, including *King Solomon's Mines* (1885), *She* (1887) and *Allan Quatermain* (1887).

Haggis, traditional Scottish dish, dating at least from the early Middle Ages. It is made of the liver, heart, lungs and other offal of a sheep or a calf. These are mixed with suet, oatmeal, onions and spices, wrapped in the lining of the animal's stomach, and boiled.

Hagia Sophia (532–537), Byzantine church at Constantinople (Istanbul). Built for the Emperor Justinian by Anthemius of Tralles and Isidorus of Miletus, it is the supreme masterpiece of Byzantine architecture. The church was converted into a mosque in 1453 but is now a museum of Byzantine art. *See also* HC1 pp.*143*, 146–147.

Hagiographa, historical and sacred writings in the Old Testament. They comprise the Psalms, Proverbs, Job, Song of Songs, Ruth, Lamentations, Ecclesiastes, Esther, Daniel, Ezra, Nehemiah and Chronicles I and II. In the Jewish scriptures, they form the third and final part.

Hague, The ('s-Gravenhage, or Den Haag), capital of the Netherlands, on the North Sea. Founded in the 15th century, the city had become an important European intellectual and political centre by the 17th century. The country's administrative capital, it has the Dutch supreme court and the headquarters of the Dutch legislature. The Hague, since 1945, has been the seat of the International Court of Justice. Although there is some industry, the the city's economy depends on its diplomatic and administrative activities. Pop. (1976 est.) 550,600.

Hague Peace Conferences (1899, 1907), international meetings that drew up laws on the conduct of warfare and the rights of neutral nations, but failed to reach agreement on arms reduction. The first conference set up the Permanent Court of Arbitration, a forerunner of the International Court of Justice.

Hahn, Kurt (1886–1968), educationist who was influential in emphasizing physical rather than intellectual activities in education. He was born in Germany, went to England in 1933 and in the following year founded a public school at Gordonstoun in Morayshire. Hahn's ideas influenced such establishments as the Outward Bound Schools and Atlantic College.

Hahn, Otto (1879–1968), German chemist who became director of the Kaiser-Wilhelm Institute in 1928. With Lise MEITNER he discovered protoactinium and several isomers. He was later the co-discoverer of nuclear fission (1939) for which he won the 1944 Nobel Prize in chemistry. During WWII he remained in Germany; after the war he was appointed president of the Max PLANCK Institute in Berlin.

Hahnemann, Christian Friedrich Samuel (1755–1843), German physician. He popularized HOMEOPATHY, a method of medical treatment based on the idea that "like cures like", or that a disease should be treated with minute doses of agents that produce the symptoms of the disease.

Hahnium. *See* ELEMENT 105.

Haida, tribe of North American Indians. They are closely related to the Tlingit and the Tsimshian and inhabit the Queen Charlotte Islands, Canada. A small group that moved to Alaska in the 18th century are known as the Kaigani. The Haida are skilled wood-carvers, and are famous for their totem poles and other highly decorative sculptures. Pop. (1970) 1,367.

Haifa, city in NE Israel on Mt Carmel. It is one of the largest Israeli ports, handling ocean-going vessels and local trade. It is also a focus of the Israeli railway system and has an international airport. Pop. (1974) 225,000.

Haig, Douglas, First Earl (1861–1928), British WWI commander. After service in Sudan, South Africa and India, he was sent to France in 1914 and became commander-in-chief of the British Expeditionary Force in Dec. 1915 and field-marshal in 1916. Despite enormous losses, Haig and Marshal FOCH, the French commander, finally broke the German lines in 1918. *See also* HC2 p.188.

Haiku, Japanese poetry form consisting of 17 syllables in five-seven-five pattern, originally evoking a moment in nature. It came into prominence through its mastery by MATSUO Bashō (1644–94), still regarded as the finest practitioner. The form remains popular in Japan.

Hail, precipitation from clouds in the form of balls of ice. Hailstorms are associated with atmospheric turbulence extending to great heights together with warm, moist air nearer the ground. Hailstones are usually less than 1cm across but some have exceeded 13cm. *See also* PE pp.69, *71*.

Haile Selassie (1892–1975), Emperor of Ethiopia (1930–74), original name Lij Tafari Makonnen. When Italy invaded Ethiopia in 1935, he was forced into exile (1936), despite his appeal to the League of Nations for help. He drove out the Italians with British aid in 1941. Subsequently he became a leader among independent African nations, helping to found the Organisation of African Unity (OAU) in 1963. Unrest at lack of reforms led to his being deposed by a military coup in 1974.

Hailey, Arthur (1920–), English-born writer who went to Canada in 1947 and was naturalized in 1952. His best-selling novels have exciting plots and much detailed information about their subject matter. His novels include *Flight into Danger* (1958), *Hotel* (1965), *Airport*

(1968), *Wheels* (1971) and *The Moneychangers* (1975).

Hail Mary, prayer to the Blessed Virgin MARY, the mother of Jesus, widely used in the Roman Catholic Church. The Latin version (beginning *Ave* Maria) has been set to music by GOUNOD and others.

Hailwood, Mike (1940–), British motorcyclist who dominated the first half of the 1960s, winning nine world titles (250cc 1961, 1966, 1967; 350cc 1966, 1967; 500cc 1962–65). His record of 12 wins in the Isle of Man Tourist Trophy remains unbeaten. He retired in 1967 to race cars, but without the same success.

Hainan, island off SE China, in the South China Sea, separated from the mainland by the Hainan Strait; second-largest Chinese island. Under Chinese control since the 2nd century BC, it has long been a place for those seeking political exile. It was taken in 1950 by the Chinese Communists. Products: rubber, coffee, rice, sugar cane, fruit, timber, tin, copper, iron, steel and bauxite. Area: 33,991sq km (13,124sq miles). Pop. 2,900,000.

Hainaut, historic county in the Low Countries, now divided between Belgium (Hainaut province) and France (Nord département). Hainaut and the county of Flanders were united in 1051. They later separated, but reunited in 1191. Later, as part of The Netherlands, it belonged to the Burgundians and then the Hapsburgs. The modern Belgian province has productive farmland and coalfields; its industries include the manufacture of glass and electrical equipment. The capital is Mons. Area: 3,789sq km (1,463sq miles). Pop. (1971) 1,330,789.

Haiphong (Hai-phong), port in N Vietnam, 32km (20 miles) from the Gulf of Tonkin on a branch of the Red River Delta. Founded in 1874, it was developed by the French, and became the chief naval base of French Indochina. It was occupied during WWII by the Japanese, and bombed by the French in 1946 during the French-Indochina war. The city was included in the new state of North Vietnam in 1954. It was heavily bombed by the USA during the Vietnam War. Industries: cement, glass, chemicals, cotton. Pop. 812,000.

Hair, outgrowth of mammalian skin; it has protective and sensory functions. Hair is made up of three layers: an outer flat scale-like cuticle, a middle keratinized cortex that contains the pigment, and an inner medulla layer. Hair grows in a follicle, a tubular structure extending down through the epidermis to the upper dermis. The hair follicle ends in a papilla, a highly vascularized point that supplies nourishment for hair growth. *See also* CILIA; MS pp.34, 60–61.

Hair (1967), rock musical in two acts with book and lyrics by Gerome Ragni and James Rado, and music by Galt McDermot. It was first produced on Broadway, where it ran for more than 1,700 performances, and productions followed throughout the world.

Haire, Norman, (1892–1952), Australian obstetrician, gynaecologist and sexologist. He settled in England in 1919 and helped to found the Walworth Welfare Centre, one of the first establishments in Britain to give advice on contraception.

Hairstreak, any of a group of butterflies of the family Lycaenidae. They are grey and brown and commonly found in open areas on every continent, especially in the tropics. Hairstreaks have a quick erratic flight. Larvae of some species bore into fruit and seeds, often causing damage to growing crops. Genus *Strymon.*

Haiti, independent nation occupying the W third of the Caribbean island of Hispaniola, and including the off-shore islands of Tortuga and Gonâve. Although much of the land is uncultivable, it is one of the most densely populated countries in the world. There is subsistence farming and some mining of bauxite. Area: 27,750sq km (10,714sq miles). Pop. (1975 est.) 4,584,000. *See also* MW p.92.

Haitink, Sir Bernard (1929–), Dutch conductor who was appointed musical director of the Amsterdam Concertgebouw Orchestra in 1964 and principal conductor of the London Philharmonic in 1967. He won a reputation for his fine interpretations of the work of Anton BRUCKNER and Gustav MAHLER. He also worked in many opera houses, notably Covent Garden and Glyndebourne.

Hajj, meaning "setting out", the pilgrimage to Mecca in the 12th month of the Muslim year. The fifth of the Five Pillars of ISLAM, it is the duty of each Muslim to make this pilgrimage at least once. This duty is based on instructions in the KORAN.

Hake, commercial marine fish found in cold and temperate waters. Its elongated, streamlined body is silver and brown. Length: to 1m (40in); weight: to 14kg (30lb). Family Gadidae or Merluccidae; species include Atlantic silver *Merluccius bilinearis* and Pacific *M. productus. See also* NW p.*131.*

Hakluyt, Richard (*c.*1552–1616), British geographer. He was a member of the VIRGINIA COMPANY and a compiler of travel accounts. His most important work was *The Principal Navigations, Voyages, Traffics, and Discoveries of the English Nation* (1589–1600). *See also* HC1 p.*279.*

Halberg, Murray (1933–), New Zealand middle-distance runner who overcame the handicap of a paralysed arm to win the 1960 Olympic Games 5,000m, the Commonwealth Games 3 miles in 1958 and 1962 and set world records for 2 and 3 miles.

Haldane, John Burdon Sanderson (1892–1964), British scientist whose work formed the basis of the mathematical study of population genetics. His book, *The Causes of Evolution* (1933), examined the theory of natural selection in the light of modern genetical research. In 1932 he was the first to estimate the mutation rate of a human gene. His book *Daedalus, or Science and the Future* (1924) was an attempt to popularize science.

Hale, George Ellery (1868–1938), US astronomer who organized a number of observatories. He initiated work on the Mt Palomar observatory, whose 200-inch telescope bears his name. Hale invented the spectroheliograph, an instrument for photographing the Sun, and discovered the Sun's magnetic field.

Hale Observatories. *See* MOUNT WILSON and PALOMAR.

Halévy, Ludovic (1834–1908), French librettist who, in collaboration with Henri Meilhac, wrote for such composers as Offenbach, Delibes and Bizet. Operas for which he was librettist include *Carmen,* (BIZET), *La Belle Hélène* and *La Vie Parisienne* (OFFENBACH) and *Le Petit Duc* (1878) by LECOCQ.

Haley, Bill (1925–), US singer. White idol of the rock'n'roll era in the 1950s, Haley made his first solo recording in 1945, but had to wait until 1953 for his first real success with *Crazy Man Crazy.* In 1954 he achieved world-wide fame with the re-release of *Rock around the Clock,* and between 1955 and 1956 he had a series of successes, including *See you Later, Alligator* and *R-O-C-K.*

Haley, Sir William John (1901–), British journalist. He began his career at the Manchester Evening News in 1922, and was Director-General of the BBC (1944–52) and editor of *The Times* (1952–66).

Half-cell, electrode immersed in an ionic solution. A full electrolytic cell is formed of two connected half-cells – different solutions being separated by a membrane or conducting bridge that allows electricity to flow but prevents mixing. *See also* ELECTRODE POTENTIAL.

Half-life, time taken for one-half of the atoms present in a given amount of radioactive isotope to undergo one disintegration – ie, to change into another element or isotope. Half-lives range from fractions of a second to millions of years. *See also* RADIOACTIVITY.

Half-tone process, the production of zinc or copper plates for printing illustrations. By breaking down the continuous image of the original into separate dots of varying size (which therefore control the amount of ink printed within a specific area), it is possible to reproduce the full tone values of a photograph or original artwork. The image required is photographed through a glass screen bearing ruled lines crossing each other at right-angles, and the resultant image is exposed on a sensitized printing plate.

Fox Talbot and other Victorians experimented with photographic half-tone processes and the first such printed image probably appeared in the *Canadian Illustrated News* in 1869. But Georg Meisenbach of Munich is usually credited as the inventor of the half-tone – which he patented in 1882 – although many authorities credit the Levy brothers of Philadelphia with the first wholesale commercial usage of the half-tone processes. *See also* MM p.207, *207.*

Haliburton, Thomas Chandler (1796–1865), Canadian judge and humorist who wrote several books on law and history. He used the adventures of Sam Slick, a fictional Yankee pedlar, to chide his fellow Nova Scotians for their laziness.

Halibut, flatfish found worldwide in deep cold to temperate seas. An important commercial food fish, it is brownish on the eye side and white below. Family Pleuronectidae; species, Atlantic *Hippoglossus hippoglossus,* giant Pacific *H. stenolepis. See also* NW p.130; PE pp.246, *247.*

Halicarnassus, Ionic Greek city in the extreme SW of Asia Minor (modern Bodrum, Turkey). With an advantageous trading position, the city was a rich port, and the Mausoleum was the site of one of the SEVEN WONDERS OF THE WORLD.

Halide, salt of a HALOGEN, or an organic compound containing a halogen. The halide salts, fluorides, chlorides, bromides and iodides, contain negative ions. The alkyl halides are organic compounds such as methyl chloride (chloromethane, CH_3Cl), containing an alkane radical bound to a halogen atom.

Halifax, Charles Montague, Earl of (1661–1715), English statesman whose political success stemmed from his great financial skills. As a lord of the treasury in 1692 he initiated the national debt and was instrumental in founding the Bank of England. He was twice impeached (1701, 1703) for breach of trust as auditor of the exchequer, but was acquitted.

Halifax, George Savile, First Marquess of (1633–95), English statesman. As a privy councillor (1672–85), he led the opposition to a Bill to prevent Charles II's Roman Catholic brother James from becoming king. He was Lord Privy Seal (1682–85) but was dismissed by James II on his accession.

Halifax, city port and capital of Nova Scotia, Canada, on the Atlantic Ocean. It is the terminus of the country's transcontinental highway and of the two railway networks. Industries include commercial fishing, shipbuilding and oil refining. Pop. (1974) 122,035.

Halite, common salt, most abundant HALIDE mineral, sodium chloride (NaCl). It is found in sedimentary rocks, salt domes and dried lakes, as cubic system interlocking cubic crystals, granules and masses. It is colourless, white or grey with a glassy lustre. Hardness 2.5; s.g. 2.2. It is important as table salt and as a source of CHLORINE.

Halitosis, or bad breath, may have a number of causes including respiratory infections, mouth disorders, dental decay and excessive smoking. Occasionally, odour occurs with no apparent cause.

Hall, Asaph (1829–1907), US astronomer. He was professor of mathematics at the US Naval Observatory, Washington DC (1863–91) and professor of astronomy at Harvard (1896–1901). In 1877 he discovered PHOBOS and DEIMOS, the two moons of Mars. *See also* SU pp.*171,* 202.

Hall, Charles Martin (1863–1914), US chemist who in 1886 discovered (independently of Paul L. T. HÉROULT) the first economical method for extracting aluminium electrolytically from bauxite. *See also* MM pp.34–35.

Hall (Halle), Edward (1498–1547), English chronicler. *The Union of the noble and illustre Famelies of Lancastre and York* is his only famous work. It deals with the court of HENRY VIII and describes the FIELD OF THE CLOTH OF GOLD. *See also* HC1 p.240, *240.*

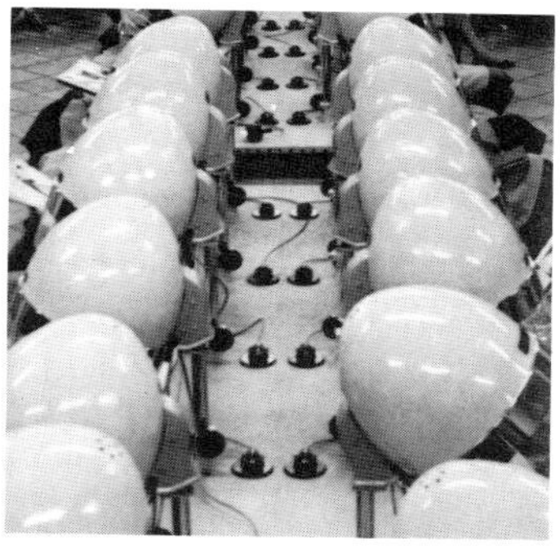

Hair, the styling of which creates its own curious technological landscape.

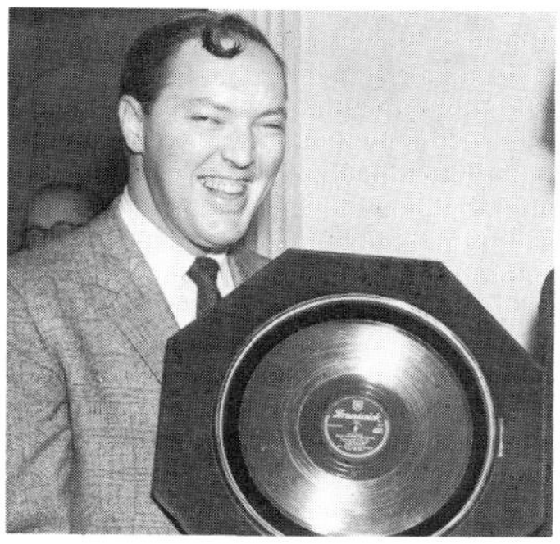

Bill Haley with his golden disc of *Rock Around the Clock,* the first million seller in Britain.

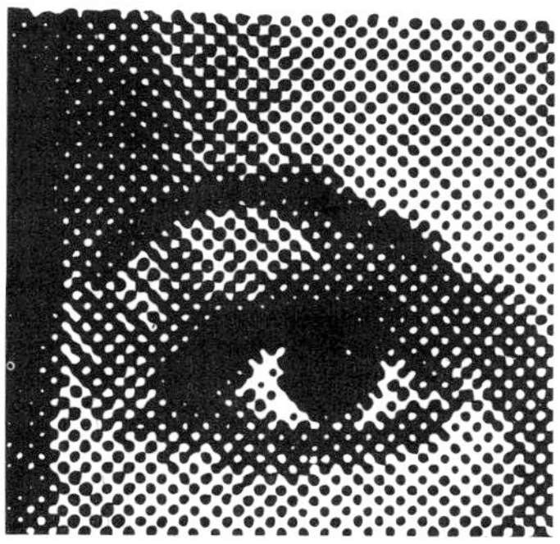

Half-tone process; the mixing of black dots and white paper produces greys.

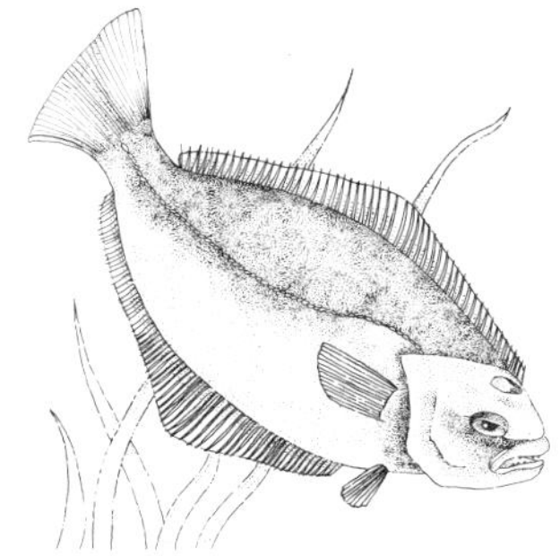

Halibut; the name comes from the word "holy" as the fish was eaten on holy days.

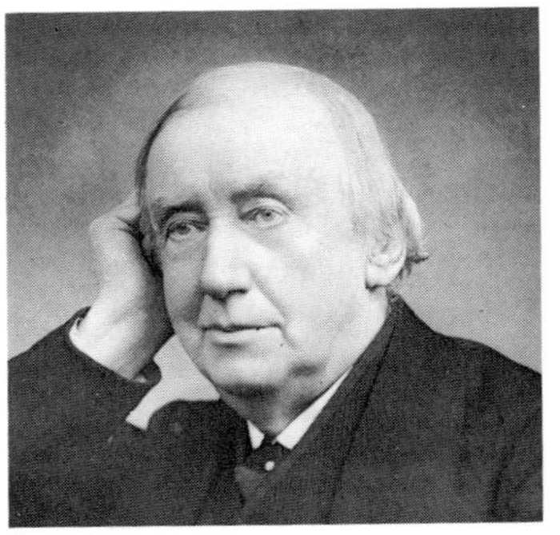

Sir Charles Hallé mixed with many celebrities of his time, including Chopin and Liszt.

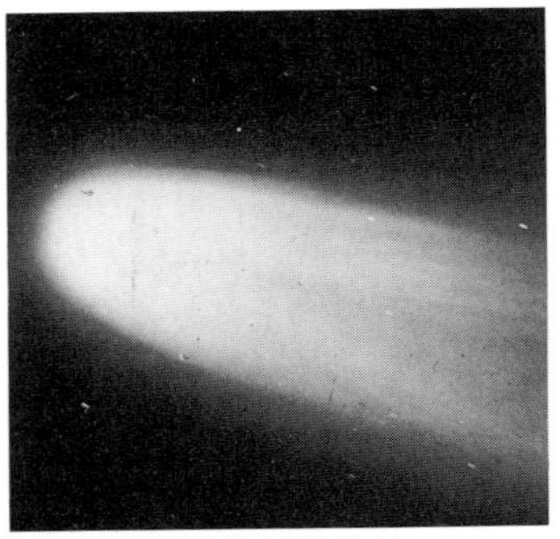

Halley's Comet photographed in 1910 during its last appearance; it returns every 76 years.

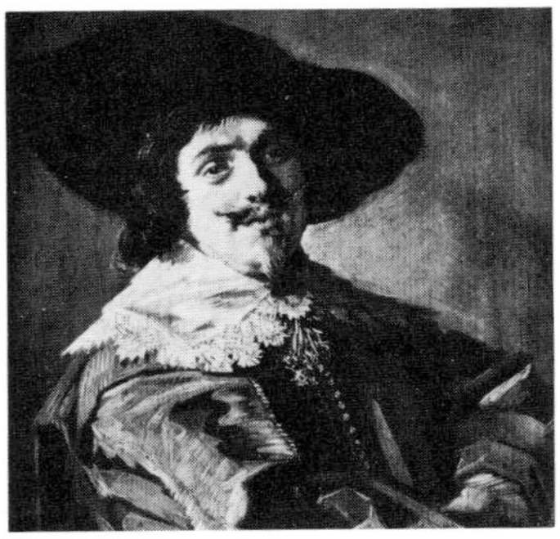

Frans Hals; his *Young Man in Yellow-Grey* is typical of his renderings of robust figures.

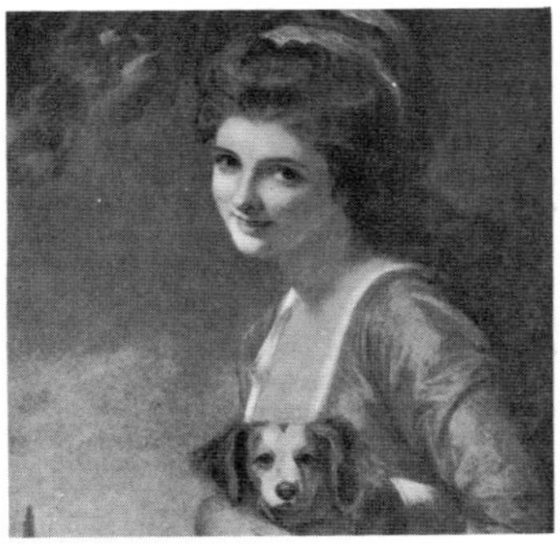

Lady Emma Hamilton as "nature" in one of her *poses plastiques*, by George Romney.

Hall, Marguerite Radclyffe (*c.* 1886–1943), British novelist best known for the *The Well of Loneliness* (1928), a sincere study of lesbianism, originally banned as obscene in Britain. Other novels include *The Unlit Lamp* (1924), *Adam's Breed* (1926) (which was awarded the James Tait Black prize) and *The Sixth Beatitude* (1936).

Hall, Marshall (1790–1857), British physician and physiologist who showed that reflex actions occur even when the nerve cord to the brain is cut. Hall was able to conclude that the nerve cord has a dual function, as producing co-ordinated movements and as an autonomous system. His name is given to a form of artificial respiration.

Hall, Sir Peter Reginald Frederick (1930–), British theatrical director. He was well known for his many Shakespearean productions at the Shakespeare Memorial Theatre at Stratford-upon-Avon. He was director of the ROYAL SHAKESPEARE COMPANY (1960–73) and was responsible for the formation of the permanent company in 1960. He has directed opera at GLYNDEBOURNE and COVENT GARDEN and made several films, including *Akenfield* (1974). In 1973 he became director of the NATIONAL THEATRE of Great Britain.

Hall, Willis (1929–), British dramatist whose reputation was established with the success of his first play, *The Long and the Short and the Tall* (1959). He subsequently worked closely with Keith WATERHOUSE, notably on the stage, screen, musical and television versions of the latter's *Billy Liar.*

Hallam, Henry (1777–1859), British historian. The death of his son, Arthur, was the occasion of TENNYSON's *In Memoriam.* His enduring reputation rests on his studies of early modern European society and letters and his *Constitutional History of England* (1827).

Hallé, Sir Charles (1819–95), British conductor. He began as a concert pianist and in 1857 formed a symphony orchestra in Manchester, England, which subsequently became known as the Hallé Orchestra. He was a founder of the Royal Manchester College of Music, which was established in 1893.

Halle, city in s central East Germany, on the River Saale, capital of the Halle district. It is a transport centre and part of an important industrial region. Manufactures include chemicals, food products and machinery. There is some salt and potash mining in the area. Pop. (1975) 239,181.

Haller, Albrecht von (1708–77), Swiss biologist, physician and poet. As a botanist he was celebrated for his descriptions of alpine flora and as a poet for his glorification of the mountains in his *Die Alpen* (1729). While professor of anatomy, medicine and botany at the University of Göttingen in 1736, he researched the contractile properties of muscle tissue, and his resulting treatise (1757–66) laid the foundations of modern neurology.

Halley, Edmond (1656–1742), British astronomer and mathematician. He accurately predicted the return in 1758 of the comet which has since borne his name. He published a map of the winds in 1686.

Halley's comet, noted periodic comet, observed in 1682 by Edmond HALLEY who identified it as the comet seen in 1531 and 1607. He predicted its return in 1758. It last returned to perihelion in 1910 and is due back in 1986. A bright naked-eye object, it was known before the time of Christ. *See also* SU pp.216, *217.*

Hallgrimsson, Geir (1925–), Icelandic politician, chairman of the Independence Party. He started his career as a lawyer in his father's firm, and entered politics in 1959. He became Prime Minister in 1974.

Hallmark, official stamp used by British government ASSAY offices to mark the standard of gold and silver articles. The mark has four elements: the standard mark, showing the purity of the metal; the office mark, bearing the assay office's cipher; the date mark; and the maker's mark.

Hallowe'en, hallowed or holy evening, in medieval times a holy festival observed on 31 Oct., the eve of All Saints' Day. It was merged with the ancient Celtic festival of Samhain, which was also observed at the end of summer and marked the beginning of the Celtic year. This was the occasion when fires were lit to frighten away evil spirits and to guide the souls of the dead who were supposed to revisit their homes on this day. Hallowe'en is observed today as a social festival.

Hallstatt, town in s Austria, on Lake Hallstätter. Archaeological excavations (1846–99) unearthed cultural relics dating from *c.* 800 BC, now known as the Hallstatt era of the IRON AGE. Today the village is a thriving tourist centre.

Hallucination, apparent perception of something that is not, in fact, present. Although they may occur in any of the five senses, auditory hallucinations (hearing voices or noises) and visual hallucinations (seeing things or people) are the commonest. While they are usually symptomatic of pyschotic disorders, hallucinations may result from fatigue or emotional upsets and can also be a side-effect of certain drugs. *See also* MS pp.47, 105, 134, 138–139.

Hallucinogen, drug that causes HALLUCINATIONS, ie, unusual perceptions without external cause. Hallucinogenic drugs, such as CANNABIS, MESCALINE and lysergic acid diethylamide (LSD), have been used in primitive religious ceremonies and are extensively but illicitly taken today. Some are employed in experimental investigation and treatment of mental illness. *See also* MS pp.104–105, 144.

Halogens, elements (fluorine, chlorine, bromine, iodine and astatine) belonging to group VII of the periodic table. They react with most other elements and with organic compounds; reactivity decreases down the group. The halogens are highly electronegative and react strongly because they require only one electron to achieve the "stable 8" inert gas configuration; they produce crystalline salts containing negative ions of the type F^- and Cl^-. The name halogen means "salt-producer". *See also* SU pp.134–137.

Halogenation, introduction of one of the HALOGEN elements – fluorine, chlorine, bromine, iodine or astatine – into an organic compound either by addition or by substitution of an atom or group of atoms. This reaction is widely used in making pharmaceuticals and dyes.

Halophyte, any plant, usually a seed plant, which is able to live in salty soil and absorb water which is rich in salts.

Hals, Frans (*c.* 1581–1666), Dutch painter. He was unique in his ability to capture fleeting expressions in his paintings of robust, vital figures, such as the *Laughing Cavalier,* and his group portraits. His later works, more subdued in colour and mood, have a dignity and strength approaching those of his contemporary, REMBRANDT. *See also* HC1 p.310.

Halsbury, Hardinge Stanley Giffard, 1st Earl of (1823–1921), British politician and judge. He was appointed Solicitor-General in 1875. From 1877 to 1885 he was a Conservative MP. In 1885 he was raised to the peerage and made lord chancellor. *Halsbury's Laws of England* was published under his direction from 1905 to 1916.

Halsey, William Frederick, Jr. (1882–1959), US admiral. He was a destroyer commander in WWI and led carrier raids against the Japanese-held Marshall and Gilbert Islands early in WWII. The terms of Japanese surrender in 1945 were signed aboard his ship.

Hälsingborg, city port in sw Sweden, on the Øresund opposite Helsingør, Denmark. It is a commercial and industrial centre whose industries include copper, sugar refining and rubber processing. Pop. (1974) 102,137.

Halstead, William Stewart (1852–1922), US physician. He pioneered the use of cocaine as a "block" anaesthetic and expanded on the techniques of antisepsis in surgery by introducing rubber gloves. Halstead experimented on animals to improve surgical procedures, including operations for breast cancer.

Halton, district in N Cheshire, England, on the Mersey estuary; created in 1974 under the Local Government Act (1972). Area: 74sq km (29sq miles). Pop. (1974 est.) 106,200.

Ham, in Genesis, second of NOAH's three sons. After the Flood, his irreverence resulted in a curse by Noah, who predicted that Ham's descendants, called CANAAN, would be subservient to those of his brothers, SHEM and JAPHETH.

Hamadan, city in w Iran, at the foot of Mt Alvand. It was the ancient city of Agbatana. Taken by the Arabs in AD 645, it later passed to the Seljuk Turks and to the Mongols. The modern city is the market centre for a farming region and is known for its rugs and leatherwork. Pop. (1973 est.) 144,000.

Hamadryas, or sacred baboon, small BABOON living in the plains and rocky hills of NE Africa and Arabia. Adults and males have a mane round the neck. The animal was sacred to the ancient Egyptians. Weight: to 18kg (40lb). Family Cercopithecidae; species *Papio hamadryas.*

Hamah (Hama), city in w Central Syria, on the River Orontes. Settled since the Bronze Age, it serves today as a market centre for the nearby irrigated farming region, and produces textiles and silks. Pop. (1970) 137,421.

Hambledon, Hampshire village whose cricket team was one of England's first, and its finest from 1753–87.

Hamburg, city that is also a constituent state of West Germany, on the River Elbe. Founded in AD 808 by CHARLEMAGNE, it became a successful medieval trading port and by 1510 was an imperial free city. Severely damaged during WWII, the city was rebuilt in 1945. It is now the country's largest city and cultural centre. It has shipyards and diverse manufacturing industries including electronic equipment and chemicals. Pop. 1,738,800.

Hamelin, (Hamelyn) town and port in Lower Saxony, N West Germany. Situated at the confluence of the rivers Wesel and Hamel, its industries include the manufacture of carpets, electrical motors, baking powder and pottery. With a history dating back to the 8th century and its famous association with the legend of the PIED PIPER, the town also attracts a valuable tourist trade. Pop. (1970 est.) 47,000.

Hamhŭng, city in E North Korea; capital of South Hamgyŏng province. The city was the scene of heavy fighting during the KOREAN WAR. Today it is a commercial centre; its industries produce sake, fertilizer and cotton textiles. Pop. 420,000.

Hamilcar Barca (*d.* 228 BC), military commander of CARTHAGE, father of HANNIBAL and HASDRUBAL. After quelling a revolt of mercenaries led by Spendius and Mathos (241–38 BC, he conquered S and E Spain.

Hamilton, Alexander (1775–1804), US statesman. During the American War of Independence he became an assistant of George WASHINGTON and served as secretary of the Treasury during Washington's first administration, setting up the Bank of the United States.

Hamilton, Lady Emma (*c.* 1765–1815), wife of the ambassador and archaeologist Sir William Hamilton and, from 1798, mistress to Lord Horatio NELSON, by whom she had two daughters, one of whom, Horatia (1801–1881), survived.

Hamilton, Gavin (1723–98), Scottish neo-classical painter. He spent much of his life in Rome but also lived in London (1753–54). He was an associate of WINCKELMANN. *See also* HC2 p.*42.*

Hamilton, Iain Ellis (1922–), British composer. Influenced early by such contemporaries as Hindemith, Bartók and Stravinsky, his compositions had become serialist in style in 1960 and include the operas *The Royal Hunt of the Sun* (1966–67) and *Tamburlaine* (1977).

Hamilton, Sir Ian Standish Monteith (1853–1947), British general. He led the Mediterranean Expeditionary Force at the GALLIPOLI campaign of WWI. He later became a leading pacifist.

Hamilton, James Hamilton, 1st Duke of (1606–49), Scottish politician. As CHARLES I's commissioner in Scotland (1638–39) he tried to conciliate the COVENANTERS and led Charles's army against them in 1639. He fought for Charles in the Civil War but was imprisoned by him (1644–46); he was executed after leading a Royalist army against CROMWELL at the Battle of Preston (1648). *See also* HC1 pp.298–299.

Hamilton, Richard (1922–), British artist who was a leader of the POP ART movement in the 1950s and 1960s, mainly producing collages of images taken from commercial art. These include *Just what is it that makes today's homes so different, so appealing?* (1956). *See also* HC2 pp.*278*, 279.

Hamilton, Sir William (1788–1856), Scottish philosopher. He became professor of logic at Edinburgh in 1836, and expounded the views of the school of common sense realism in his *Discussions in Philosophy and Literature* (1852).

Hamilton, Sir William Rowan (1805–65), Irish mathematician. He was appointed professor of astronomy at Trinity College, Dublin, and Irish astronomer royal in 1827. His greatest achievement was in the creation of a three-dimensional mathematics (quaternions).

Hamilton, capital and chief seaport of Bermuda Island, at the head of Great Sound. Founded in 1790 and settled by the English, it was incorporated in 1793. It became the capital in 1815 and was made a free port in 1956. Tourism is the major industry. Pop. (1970) 2,127.

Hamilton, city in SE Ontario, Canada, 64km (40 miles) SW of Toronto on Lake Ontario. It is an important centre of communications and is also a large manufacturing city, producing iron, steel and textiles. Pop. (1974) 309,175.

Hamilton, city in North Island, New Zealand, on the Waikato River. It is the commercial centre of the surrounding dairy farming and sheep rearing region. Pop. (1972 est.) 77,600.

Hamito-Semitic languages, family of languages spoken in N Africa, the Sahara, parts of E Africa, central Africa, W Africa and W Asia. About 130 million people speak them. With a few exceptions, notably the Tamechek dialect which uses a Berber alphabet, the family uses the Arabic alphabet. It is the only family of languages common to Asia and Africa.

Hamlet (*c.*1601), five-act tragedy by SHAKESPEARE based on a historical account which had already been dramatized, probably by Thomas KYD. Subject to persistent critical and psychological appraisal, the complicated role of Hamlet is one of the most demanding but rewarding parts an actor can play.

Hamlyn. *See* HAMELIN.

Hammada, rocky desert surface. It is often found on desert plateaus where the surface has been swept clear of sand or rocky debris by the wind. Local patches of sand or rubble are found in sheltered spots, but the distinctive landscape features are yardangs, wind-eroded rocky outcrops. *See also* PE p.121.

Hammarskjöld, Dag (1905–61), Swedish diplomat who succeeded Trygve LIE as Secretary General of the United Nations in 1953. In 1956 he played a leading part in the SUEZ CRISIS by sending a UN emergency force to Egypt. He sent another UN force to the Congo to keep peace in 1960. En route to Katanga for peace talks, he was killed in a plane crash. He was posthumously awarded the 1961 Nobel Peace Prize.

Hammer, in athletics, field event for men in which a ball attached to a spring-steel wire is thrown by a gloved thrower who builds up momentum with a series of 3 rotations within a 2.13m (7ft) circle. The "hammer" weighs 7.26kg (16lb) and is 1.213m (almost 4ft) long. The best athletes make throws around or in excess of 77m (252ft). The hammer has been an Olympic event since 1900.

Hammerbeam roof, late GOTHIC form of roof in which massive beams project from the supporting side walls without meeting their corresponding opposite members. The roof of WESTMINSTER HALL, London (1397–99), is the earliest dated example of the type; that of the 15th-century church of St Margaret, Ipswich, a double hammerbeam, is another example.

Hammer Film Productions, British film company, formed 1948, which enjoyed much success in the 1950s and 1960s, mostly with numerous reworkings of gothic horror themes. Its films include *Dracula* (1958), *The Mummy* (1959), *The Gorgon* (1964) and *Plague of the Zombies* (1965).

Hammerhead shark, aggressive, dangerous fish found in all tropical marine waters and warmer temperate zones. It can be recognized by its unusual head, which is extended laterally in two hammerlike lobes, with one eye and one nostril located at the tip of each lobe. The shark is greyish above and whitish below. Length: to 6.1m (20ft); weight: to 906kg (2,000lb). Family Sphyrnidae; *See also* SHARK.

Hammerstein, Oscar (1846–1919), US opera impresario, *b.* Germany. After emigrating to the USA in the 1860s he amassed a large fortune by means of more than 100 inventions. He built the Manhattan Opera House in 1906, and staged there the first US performances of operas by various composers, including MASSENET, CHARPENTIER and DEBUSSY.

Hammerstein, Oscar II (1895–1960), US lyricist and librettist. He collaborated with Jerome KERN (*Show Boat*, 1927) and Richard RODGERS (*Oklahoma!*, 1943; *Carousel*, 1945; *South Pacific*, 1949 and *The King and I*, 1951). Rodgers and Hammerstein gave the US musical a new direction and substance.

Hammer toe, or claw toe, toe deformed by the flexion of one or more joints. Treatment is sometimes by surgery, although special shoes or pads may help relieve pressure.

Hammett, Dashiell (1894–1961), US author, the originator of hard-boiled, realistic, seamy detective novels. He created Sam Spade, a tough but honest private detective, and Nick Charles, a sophisticated one. His books include *The Maltese Falcon* (1930), *The Glass Key* (1931) and *The Thin Man* (1932).

Hammond, Dame Joan (1912–), Australian lyric soprano *b.* New Zealand. Also a talented violinist, she left Sydney in 1936 to study singing in Vienna and later London, and made her operatic debut in 1938 (London). Thereafter she sang in all the principal opera houses, including those in the USSR, and made numerous recital tours.

Hammond, Walter (1903–65), England and Gloucestershire cricketer who, in 85 Test matches (1927–47), scored 7,249 runs (average 58.45), including a record 336 not out, and took 83 wickets. But it is more for the attractive way in which he scored his 50,551 career runs that Wally Hammond will be remembered.

Hammond organ, electric keyboard instrument producing amplified music with discs rotating in an electromagnetic field. Invented by Laurens Hammond in 1934 to replace pipe organs in small churches, it was later used in jazz and popular music. The size of a small upright piano, it can produce a wide variety of tones.

Hammurabi (18th century BC), King of Babylonia in the first dynasty. He extended his rule in Mesopotamia, organized the empire, built canals and wheat granaries and classified the law (the CODE OF HAMMURABI). *See also* HC1 p.32.

Hammurabi, Code of, ancient code of law compiled under Hammurabi, King of Babylonia (*r.*18th century BC). Found carved on a diorite column in 1901, it is now in the Louvre. It is composed of 282 case laws in CUNEIFORM script dealing with Babylonian social structure, economic conditions, industries, law and family life. *See also* MS p.282.

Hampden, John (1594–1643), English statesman who was influential in Parliament's struggle against CHARLES I. Hampden's refusal to pay SHIP MONEY, and his opposition to royal policies, led the king to make an unsuccessful attempt to arrest him and four other critics (1642), which in turn helped to precipitate the ENGLISH CIVIL WAR.

Hampden Park, football stadium in Glasgow, Scotland, home of the Queen's Park club and venue for Scotland's international matches and Cup finals. With capacity for 134,000 spectators, it is Britain's largest ground and holds attendance records for European matches.

Hampshire, county in S England, bordering the English Channel. Most of the terrain is undulating chalk downland; the Test and Itchen rivers drain into the SOLENT. Predominantly agricultural, Hampshire contains the major port of Southampton and the naval centre at Portsmouth. Its coastal resorts and the New Forest woodlands are tourist attractions. The county town is Winchester. Area: 3,782sq km (1,460sq miles). Pop. (1976) 1,456,100.

Hampstead, former N London village, now part of the borough of Camden. Its fine air and rural milieu have endeared it to literary and artistic residents such as John KEATS, John CONSTABLE and D. H. LAWRENCE.

Hampstead Heath, partly wooded open area of N London that was formerly common land. Attempts to build on it resulted in its gradual acquisition, beginning in 1871, for public use. It now includes adjoining areas such as the grounds of Kenwood and Parliament Hill, covering about 324 hectares (806 acres).

Hampton, Lionel (1913–), US jazz vibraphonist and bandleader. He played with the Benny GOODMAN Orchestra (1936–40), then led his own big bands and small groups which were among the best known of jazz ensembles for almost three decades.

Hampton Court, royal palace begun in 1515 by Cardinal WOLSEY beside the Thames, 23km (14 miles) from Westminster. The Splendour of its architecture and fittings was apparently so envied by HENRY VIII that Wolsey made it over to him in 1526. Henry made considerable extensions and improvements between 1531 and 1536. WREN rebuilt and extended parts between 1696 and 1704. *See also* HC2 pp.*219, 297.*

Hamster, small, mainly nocturnal, burrowing RODENT native to Eurasia and Africa. It has internal cheek pouches for carrying food. Golden hamsters, popular as pets and also used in laboratory experiments, are descendants of a single family discovered in Syria in 1930. Disease-resistant and almost odourless, golden hamsters are easy to handle. They eat fruit, green vegetables, seeds, nuts and meat. Length: up to 18cm (7in). Family Cricetidae; species *Cricetus mesocricetus. See also* NW p.*198.*

Hamstring. *See* ACHILLES TENDON.

Hamsun, Knut (1859–1952), Norwegian naturalist novelist and playwright; *b.* Knut Pedersen. He was awarded the 1920 Nobel Prize for literature for *The Growth of the Soil* (1917). Other important novels include *Hunger* (1890), *Victoria* (1898) and *Vagabonds* (1927). His six plays were influenced by those of IBSEN and STRINDBERG. His pro-German sympathies aroused considerable controversy in both WWI and WWII.

Han, name of two rivers in China. The River Han in E central China rises in SW Shensi (Shanxi) and flows SE to join the River Yangtze (Changjiang) at Hankow. Length: 1,200km (750 miles). The River Han in SE China rises on the border of Fukien (Fujian) and Kaingsi (Jiangxi) provinces, and flows S to the South China Sea at Swatow (Shanton). Length: 160km (100 miles).

Han Chinese, or Han-Jen, Mongoloid people that make up about 94% of the population of China; they inhabit the densely populated eastern half of the country. They consist of various groups sharing the same culture, traditions and written language, although within the Han Chinese language are several dialects. Their ancient hierarchical society, based on Taoist, Confucian and Buddhist tenets, has been reorganized under Communism and their agriculture modernized.

Hancock, Sir Keith (1898–), Australian academic who became professor of history at the University of Birmingham, in 1933. From 1957 to 1965 he was professor of history at the Australian National University at Canberra, and was the civil editor of the official war histories.

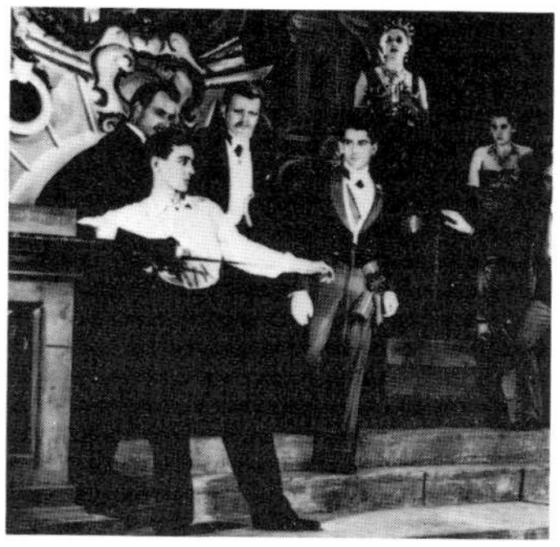

Hamlet, played by Alec Guiness, in the Tyrone Guthrie modern version (1938).

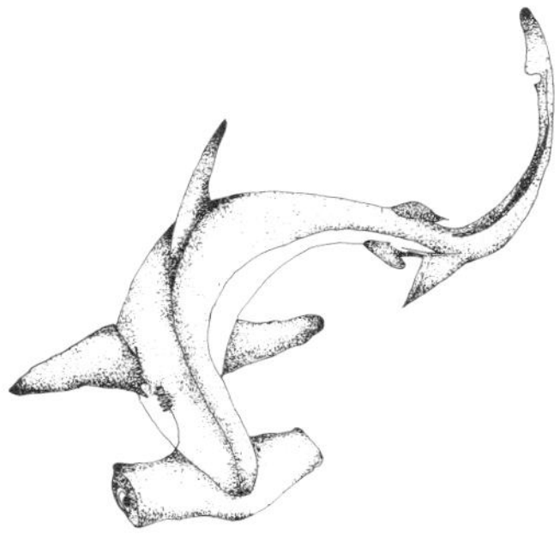

Hammerhead shark: its streamlined body enables it to swim effortlessly at speed.

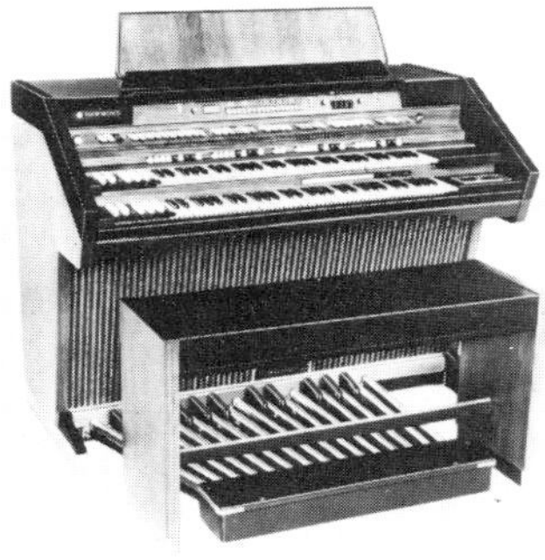

Hammond organs feature built-in rhythm machines and string and brass effects.

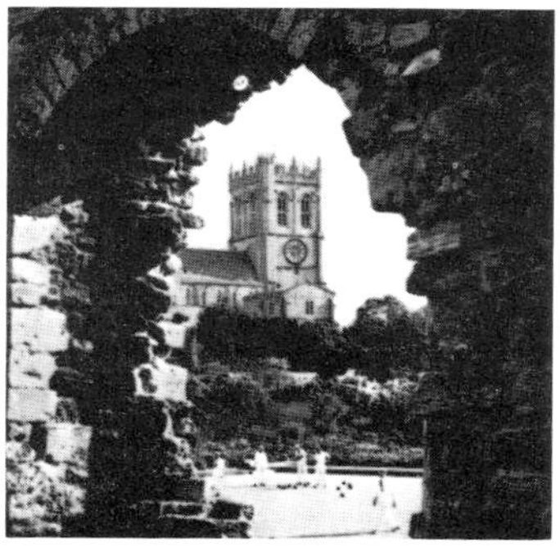

Hampshire; the bowling green, framed in the ruins of the priory at Christchurch.

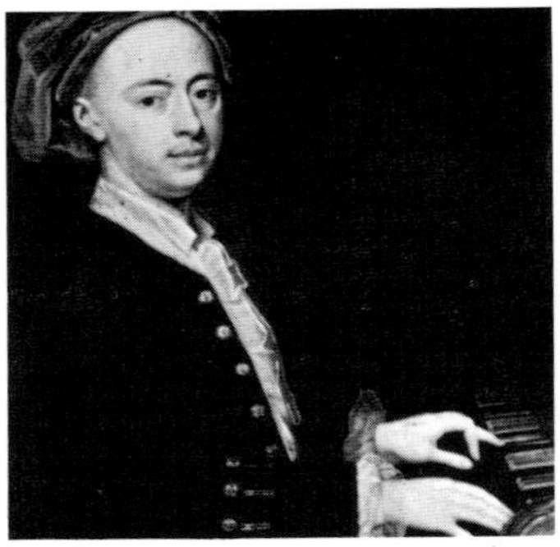

Handel's operas, regained recognition at the beginning of this century.

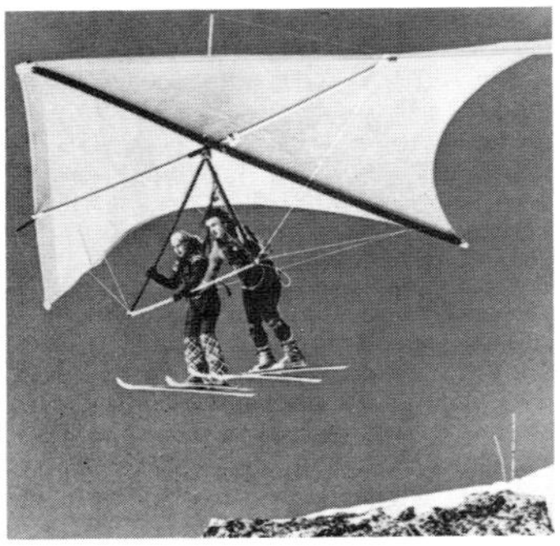

Hang gliding; two skiiers launch themselves from the top of the Weisshorn in Switzerland

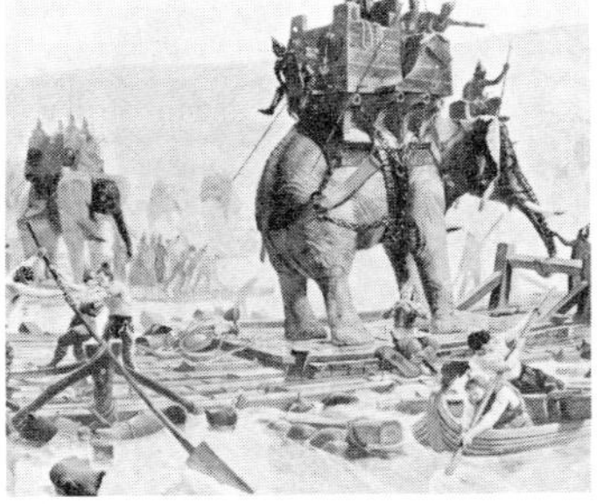

Hannibal: (detail) a painting by Henri Motte of the Carthaginian army crossing the Rhône.

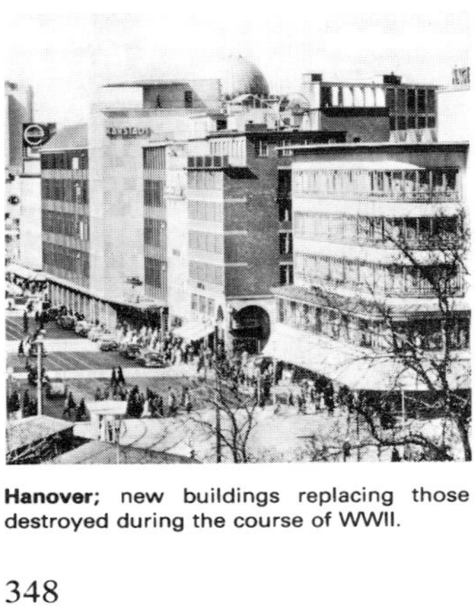

Hanover; new buildings replacing those destroyed during the course of WWII.

Hancock, Tony (1924–68), British comedian. His truculent and self-centred performances in *Hancock's Half Hour* gained a unique and original comic reputation, and he explored new areas of radio and television social comedy. His films included *The Rebel* (1961) and *The Punch and Judy Man* (1963).

Handball, name given to two sports played mostly in Ireland and the USA. One version is a game similar to FIVES and played indoors or outdoors with a hard, small ball by two or four players on courts of one, three or four walls. The other game, sometimes called field handball, is quite different. On a court between two goals and two goalkeepers, players catch, pass and throw a ball like a small football with the object of hurling the ball past the opposing goalkeeper. They may not run more than three steps with the ball or hold it for more than three seconds or approach closer than the semicircular goal area. Outdoors the game is played by teams of eleven; indoors by teams of seven. Dimensions of pitches vary greatly.

Handel, George Frederick (1685–1759), German-born composer who became a naturalized Englishman in 1726. With J. S. BACH, he is regarded as the greatest composer of the BAROQUE period. Among his many works are operas (eg, *Atlanta, Berenice, Serse*), oratorios (eg. *Samson, Esther, Judas Maccabaeus*), organ music, chamber concertos, sonatas and songs. His most popular works include the *Water Music* (*c.* 1717) and the *Fireworks Music* (1749), both composed for outings and holidays promoted by the English royal court. Handel's best-known work is perhaps the oratorio, the *Messiah* (1742), famous for its Hallelujah Chorus. Handel was greatly honoured in his own day, especially in England; HAYDN, MOZART and BEETHOVEN all professed great admiration for his music. He is buried in Westminster Abbey. *See also* HC1 p.318.

Hand grenade. *See* GRENADE.

Handicapped, people with physical or mental disabilities. Depending on the degree of severity of the handicap these people may need special help. Such aid is available in the form of prosthetic limbs, special training and equipment and the persistance and care of others.

Handicapping, system used in some sports to give all competitors an equal chance by placing the better contestants at some disadvantage. It is primarily associated with horse racing, in which entrants carry excess weight (usually up to 19kg; 42lb) related to the previous performances. The first handicap was run at Newmarket, England, in 1785, and the system is today used throughout the world.

Handley, Tommy (1892–1949), British radio comedian who appeared in a succession of programmes from 1926. He became well known in ITMA (It's that man again; 1942), a morale-building series of WWII that established the comedy show formula of stock characters and catchphrases. He also made several films, including *Elstree Calling* (1930) and *It's That Man Again* (1942).

Handley Page, British manufacturer of military aircraft. Its first large bomber, powered by two Rolls-Royce 12-cylinder engines, was introduced in 1918, in time to serve in the latter part of WWI. It was made of wood and fabric, could carry sixteen 50kg (110lb) bombs or one 750kg (1,650lb) bomb, and had a crew of two to five. The most famous Handley Page bomber of WWII was the *Halifax*. *See also* MM p.176–177.

Hands, Terry (1941–), British stage director who worked with the ROYAL SHAKESPEARE COMPANY after 1966. His direct, textual approach to plays was the keynote of many award-winning productions.

Handy, William Christopher (1873–1958), US composer and musician known as the father of the BLUES. He led his own band in 1903 and later composed several hits including *Memphis Blues* (1911) and *St Louis Blues* (1914). After 1923 he devoted his time exclusively to composing and publishing many other classic blues songs.

Han dynasty (206 BC – AD 220), Chinese dynasty. It was founded by Liu Pang and was ruled by his family for more than four centuries. It is considered by the Chinese to be one of their greatest periods of rule. Han rulers laid the administrative and ideological basis for the subsequent greatness of the Chinese Empire. Under the Han the Confucian state cult was formalized through the examination system; art and literary traditions were established and imperial expansion began to spread Chinese influence throughout E Asia. *See also* HC1 pp.122–123.

Hangchow (Hangzhou), capital city of Chekiang (Zhejiang) province, E China, on Hangchow Bay. Founded in 606, the city became an important cultural centre and capital of theuSouthern Sung dynasty (1126–1279). It developed as a major silk-producing centre at the same time. The city's modern prosperity dates from the opening of the Shanghai-Hangchow-Ningbo railway. Industries include iron and steel, fertilizers, motor vehicles, machine tools, electronic equipment and chemicals. Pop. (1970 est.) 1,100,000.

Hang gliding, sport that enables a person to "fly", supported only by a large, generally triangular, kite-like wing, which is stabilized by the weight of his own body. The gliders fall into two categories – the sail wing and the rigid wing – and may weigh as much as 45kg (100lb). Take-off is made from the top of almost any steepish incline, but requires a steady updraught. The pilot sits on, and is harnessed to, a suspended bar. He steers by means of a fixed, triangular, trapeze-like frame, which he uses to help shift his weight from side to side (thereby varying the glider's centre of gravity). For landing, the pilot needs to use his legs. This sport can be dangerous and a number of participants have been killed.

Hanging, method of capital punishment, especially in the Western world. It derives from ancient Teutonic practice and was introduced into England by the Anglo-Saxons.

Hangnest, or Baltimore oriole, North American orange and black bird well known for its clear, musical whistle. It gets its first name from its firmly woven nest built suspended from the tip of a branch, and its second from the orange and black colours of the Calverts, the founding family of Maryland where the bird was first found. Species *Icterus galbula.*

Hangover, results of acute alcoholic intoxication. Symptoms may include headache, nausea, general discomfort and agitation. The precise cause is unknown and no medical cure has been confirmed, although popular remedies abound. *See also* ALCOHOLISM.

Hanif Mohammed (1934–), Pakistani cricketer who dourly amassed a world-record 499 runs for Karachi and played the longest innings ever: 16 hours 13 minutes for 337 runs for Pakistan against the West Indies in 1957–8. He played in 55 Test matches between 1952 and 1969 (3,915 runs, average 43.98), 11 times as captain.

Haniwa, Japanese terracotta sculpture of the YAMATO period. Originally they were cylindrical grave-markers. Later they were modelled to represent retainers and property of the deceased. *See also* HC1 p.*131.*

Han Kan (*c.* 720–80), Chinese painter of the T'ANG DYNASTY, court painter to the emperor. In both his religious art and in secular paintings, eg, of horses, he had a remarkable gift for suggesting mass and perspective.

Hankow. *See* WUHAN.

Hann, Julius (1839–1921), Austrian meteorologist whose data, collected from balloon ascents and from climbing in the Alps and Himalayas, showed that about 90% of the atmosphere's water vapour is found below 6,010m (20,000ft). From this it followed that high mountains were effective barriers against the transport of water vapour.

Hannah, in the Bible, mother of the prophet Samuel. Barren for many years, she kept the promise to dedicate her first son to God by taking Samuel, at the age of three, to the high priest Eli.

Hannay, James Owen. *See* BIRMINGHAM, GEORGE A.

Hannibal (247–183 BC), Carthaginian general, one of the foremost military commanders in history. Commander of the Carthaginian forces in Spain (221 BC), he conquered much of the country. With about 40,000 select troops and elephants he crossed the Alps into Italy in 218 and won brilliant victories at Ticino and Trebia. At Cannae in 216 he wiped out at least 48,000 Romans in his greatest victory but, deprived of support from Carthage, was gradually forced south. In 203 he was ordered to return to Carthage; after 16 years of battle in Roman territory he was finally defeated at Zama in N Africa by SCIPIO Africanus. Political enemies forced him to flee to Syria, then probably to Bithynia where he poisoned himself rather than fall into Roman hands. *See also* HC1 p.91.

Hanoi (Ha-noi), city in Vietnam, on the Red River; former capital of North Vietnam and now capital of the Socialist Republic of Vietnam. The Chinese ruled Vietnam from Hanoi in the 7th century. Taken by the French in 1883, the city became the capital of Indochina from 1887 to 1945. It was liberated by the VIET MINH in 1945. From 1946 to 1954 it was the scene of heavy fighting between the French and the Viet Minh. It was heavily bombed by the USA during the VIETNAM WAR. There is a university (1956). Industries: textiles, rice milling. Pop. (1976 est.) 1,443,500. *See also* HC2 pp.292–293.

Hanover, House of, British royal family from 1714 to 1901. The Electors of Hanover succeeded to the English throne in 1714 under the terms of the Act of Settlement (1701) and the Act of Union (1707). GEORGE I, the first Elector also to be King of England, was succeeded in both England and Hanover by GEORGE II, GEORGE III, GEORGE IV and WILLIAM IV. SALIC LAW forbade Queen Victoria's accession in Hanover, so that the Hanoverian title was inherited by her uncle, the Duke of Cumberland. In 1901 Victoria was succeeded by her son who, as EDWARD VII, took his father's family name, Saxe-Coburg-Gotha.

Hanover (Hannover), city in N West Germany on the River Leine, 56km (35 miles) WNW of Brunswick (Braunschweig). Founded in 1241, the city became the residence in 1636 of the dukes of Brunswick-Lüneberg (predecessors of the House of Hanover, the British royal house 1714–1901). Although badly damaged during WWII, many old buildings were reconstructed in the post-war years. The city is now a centre of industry and communications, holding an annual trade fair. Manufactures include machinery, steel, textiles and chemicals. Pop. (1974) 505,106.

Hanoverian Succession, settlement of the House of Hanover on the British throne by act of parliament (1701), to take effect on the death of Queen ANNE. It was accepted by Scotland in the Act of Union (1707). The claims of the Stuart house were set aside in order to ensure a Protestant monarch. George I became the first Hanoverian king in 1714. *See also* HC2 pp.18–19.

Hansard, colloquial name for the daily record of the proceedings of the British Houses of Parliament. Named after Luke Hansard (1752–1828), printer to the Commons, who compiled unofficial reports, and his son Thomas Curson Hansard (1776–1833) who took over official publication of the reports from William Cobbett in 1812. These verbatim records have continued to be referred to as "Hansard" even though the family sold their publishing interest in 1889 and the responsibility now rests with Her Majesty's Stationery Office.

Hanseatic League, commercial union of German, Dutch and Flemish towns established in the 13th century, which grew from smaller local unions, or Hanse. The League functioned as protector of the merchants of its member towns by controlling the trade routes from the Baltic region to the Atlantic seaboard. The League began to decline in the late 15th century with the opening up of the New World and aggressive trading by the British and Dutch. The League's diet met for the last time in 1669. *See also* HC1 pp.163, 208.

Hansel and Gretel (1893), three-act opera by Engelbert HUMPERDINCK, German libretto by Adelheid Wette, based on the GRIMM brothers' tale. The roles of Hansel and Gretel are always sung by women (mezzo-soprano and soprano respectively).

Hansom cab, horse-drawn cab which was open at the front and had the driver placed at the back and above the passenger. The Hansom safety cab was patented in 1834 by Joseph Aloysius Hansom, (1803–1882), an English architect who also designed Birmingham Town Hall in 1833.

Hanukkah, or Chanukah, meaning consecration or dedication, an eight-day festival celebrated in JUDAISM. It is also known as the Feast of Lights. It is a major ceremony, involving services at home and in synagogues, which commemorates the re-dedication of the TEMPLE in 165 BC and the miracle of a one-day supply of oil lasting for eight days. Gifts are given, and games played.

Hanuman, in Hindu mythology, the monkey general who helped RAMA to find and rescue SITA. His attributes include great strength, agility and wisdom. He remains a favourite deity in many villages.

Hanuman, or entellus LANGUR, leaf-eating MONKEY of S Asia with bristly hairs on its head. It is believed to migrate from higher to lower levels in cold weather. Family Cercopithecidae; species *Presbytis entellus.*

Hanway, Jonas (1712–1786), British traveller and philanthropist. He travelled to Russia and Persia, retiring in 1750 and becoming an advocate of prison reform, and working for other philanthropic causes. He is said to have been the first Englishman regularly to carry an umbrella, which had been considered an unmanly appendage.

Han Yü (768–824), Chinese writer. He was a leader of the reform movement during the T'ANG DYNASTY (618–906) which opposed the inhibiting effect of certain established prose rules and returned to the simpler prose style of the CHOU and HAN dynasties several centuries earlier. He was also a popular poet, much of his verse being macabre.

Haploid cell. *See* MEIOSIS.

Happening, spontaneous or improvised multi-media event emphasizing audience participation and an element of surprise. Most popular in the 1960s, happenings draw on elements of DADA, SURREALIST and POP ART and the THEATRE OF CRUELTY.

Hapsburg (Habsburg), name of a royal Austrian family, one of the principal houses of Europe from the 15th century onwards. From Werner, the first count of Hapsburg in the 11th century, there was a direct male line until 1740, when the PRAGMATIC SANCTION allowed a daughter, MARIA THERESA, to succeed.

FREDERICK III, the Hapsburg King of Germany, was crowned Holy Roman Emperor in 1452, and the title remained in the family until the empire was dissolved in 1806. His descendants gained, by marriage and war, vast territories, including the Netherlands, Spain, Naples, Sicily and Sardinia. But the empire's size proved too unwieldy and the family split into two branches in 1558: the Spanish and the Austrian Hapsburgs. The Spanish line died out in 1700; the last ruling Austrian Hapsburg, Charles I, abdicated in 1918. *See also* HC1 p.273; HC2 pp.83–85, 108–9.

Hapsburg Empire, lands ruled by the Austrian HAPSBURG family from the 13th century to 1918. The heart of the empire was Austria, which the founder of the dynasty, Rudolf I of Germany, gave to his son, Rudolph II of Austria, in 1282. From 1452, when Frederick V was elected emperor, until 1806, the HOLY ROMAN EMPIRE was identical with the Hapsburg. From the 16th to 18th centuries the empire was at its peak, extending over most of Germany, Spain and Italy and including also the Spanish colonies in America. Hapsburg power ended with the disintegration of Austria-Hungary in WWI. *See also* HC1 pp.*268, 312*; HC2 pp.16–17, 83–85, 108–109.

Hara-kiri, Japanese form of ritualized suicide by disembowelment; it is also known as seppuku. It originated with the samurai in the 12th century and was considered an honourable alternative to execution. Later, it was often ordered for acts of insubordination, although it was usually performed voluntarily to avoid becoming prisoner, to prove loyalty or as an expression of protest. Japanese servicemen in WWII often performed hara-kiri.

Harald Hardrada (Harold III) (1015–66), King of Norway (1045–66). After spending his youth in Russia, he served as a mercenary for the Byzantine Empire, returning to Norway in 1045. He made vain attempts to conquer Denmark and was finally killed at Stamford Bridge in 1066 during his invasion of England.

Harappa, ancient city of the INDUS VALLEY CIVILIZATION, now in Pakistan, in the central Punjab. The site was a flourishing town from *c.* 2300 BC to some time after 2000 BC, when it was abandoned. Excavations there began in 1920. *See also* HC1 pp.36–37.

Harari, people of the city and province of Harer (Harar), E Ethiopia. They differ from other Ethiopians in that their language is Semitic and their literature is written in Arabic. The region produces cereals and coffee.

Harbour seal, also called common SEAL or spotted seal (*Phoca vitulina*), North American earless seal usually found in coastal waters of Canada and Alaska. Adults have a spotted grey or black coat, pups are born white or grey. Harbour seals come ashore frequently and congregate in herds when they are on land. Length: about 1.5m (5ft); weight: 116kg (255lb). Family Phocidae.

Hardecanute (*c.* 1019–42), King of Denmark (1028–42), King of England (1040–42), son of King CANUTE. His claim to the English throne was opposed by his half-brother Harold the Harefoot, who, elected king in 1037, died in 1040. Hardecanute was succeeded by his half-brother, EDWARD THE CONFESSOR.

Hard-edge painting, style of abstract art in which geometric forms are executed in a sharp, "hard-edged" manner. It developed in New York City in the late 1960s in reaction to ABSTRACT EXPRESSIONISM. Leading hard-edge painters include Al Held, Ellsworth KELLY, Frank STELLA and Barnett NEWMAN.

Harden, Sir Arthur (1865–1940), British biochemist who showed that each stage in the fermentation of sugar is catalyzed by a specific ENZYME and that the essential first step is the attachment of a phosphorus-containing group to the sugar. For this research he shared the 1929 Nobel Prize in chemistry with Hans von EULER-CHELPIN. He also studied bacterial enzymes and the conversion of glycogen to lactic acid during muscle activity. His work laid the foundation for the elucidation of the KREBS (citric acid) cycle, which describes the process of sugar metabolism.

Hardie, James Keir (1856–1915), British socialist and a founder of the Labour Party. He organized the Ayrshire miners' union, founded the newspaper *Labour Leader* and was chairman of the INDEPENDENT LABOUR PARTY (1893–1900; 1913–14). He was the first Labour Member of Parliament and for three years ((1892–95) was the sole representative of that party in parliament.

Harding, St Stephen. *See* STEPHEN HARDING, SAINT.

Hardness of water, reluctance of water to produce a lather on the addition of soap, due to various kinds of dissolved salts (mainly carbonates and sulphates) such as those of calcium and magnesium. These prevent the soap from lathering by giving rise to an insoluble precipitate and also cause incrustations in boilers and pipes. Lather is inhibited until all the dissolved salts are precipitated as scum, which floats on the surface.

Hardness scales, graduated indications of a material's hardness. The several ways of determining such scales are known as the BRINELL, MOHS and ROCKWELL tests, after the metallurgists who developed them.

Hardouin-Mansart, Jules (1646–1708), chief architect to Louis XIV of France from 1674. His major works include the Hall of Mirrors (1678–84), the Orangerie (1681–86) and the Grand Trianon (1687–88), all at Versailles, and the dome of the Hôtel des Invalides, Paris, (1680–91).

Hard Times (1854), novel by Charles DICKENS describing the de-personalizing effect of the Industrial Revolution. Its memorable characters include the fact-loving Mr Gradgrind and the self-made Mr Bounderby.

Hardwār, city in N India, on the River Ganges. Considered one of the seven most sacred pilgrimage centres in the country, it is the scene of the Kumbh-Mela, a large bathing festival held every twelfth year. Pop. (1971) 77,940.

Hardwick, Elizabeth ("Bess of") (1518–1608), English gentlewoman who married four times, lastly to George Talbot, Earl of Shrewsbury. She inherited all four of her husbands' estates and is remembered for the many fine buildings she commissioned; Chatsworth House and Hardwick Hall were built on her lands. She was also entrusted with the care of Mary, Queen of Scots.

Hardwick, Philip (1792–1870), British architect of a variety of public and private buildings. His most famous works were Euston Station, with its majestic Greek DORIC entrance (Entrance Screen, 1835–37; demolished 1962), and Goldsmiths' Hall (1835), both in London.

Hardy, Thomas (1840–1928), British novelist and poet. His novels are set in a fictitious region of Wessex, and include *Far From the Madding Crowd* (1874), *Tess of the d'Urbervilles* (1891) and *Jude the Obscure* (1896). Hardy later concentrated on poetry, in volumes such as *Wessex Poems* (1898). Much of his earlier writing is emotional and tragic and has strong moral undertones.

Hardy, Sir Thomas Masterman (1769–1839), British naval officer. He twice commanded the flagship of NELSON's fleet and was at Nelson's side when he died at Trafalgar. Hardy became First Sea Lord in 1830.

Hare, large member of the herbivorous RABBIT family (Leporidae), widely distributed around the world. Like the rabbit, it has long ears and large hind feet, but in contrast true hares (genus *Lepus*) have ears that are longer than their heads, and their young are born with open eyes and a full coat of fur. Length: to 76cm (30in); weight: to 4.5kg (10lb). Hares include JACK RABBITS and SNOWSHOE RABBITS. *See also* NW p.160.

Harebell, flowering plant of the BELLFLOWER family (Campanulaceae) widespread as a wild flower of pastures and also cultivated in gardens. It has drooping, bell-shaped, mid-blue flowers. Species *Campanula rotundifolia.*

Hare-lip, congenital cleft in the upper lip caused by the failure of the two parts of the palate to unite. Heredity may be a cause, as may metabolic disorders of the mother. Corrective surgery is usually undertaken successfully when a child is two months old. *See also* CLEFT PALATE; MS p.131.

Harem, women's quarters in a MUSLIM household. It contained a man's wives, concubines and female servants. The most famous harems were those of the Turkish sultans, which often had several hundred women and were guarded by eunuchs. The harem originated with Semitic cultures, and was adopted by Islam, which required women to be segregated.

Harer (Harar), city in E central Ethiopia. In the 16th century a centre for Islamic studies, it was incorporated into Ethiopia in 1857. It is now an important commercial centre and the market for a region which produces coffee and cereals. Fierce fighting between Ethiopians and Somalis occurred there in 1977. Pop. (1970 est.) 45,000. (1970 est.) 45,000.

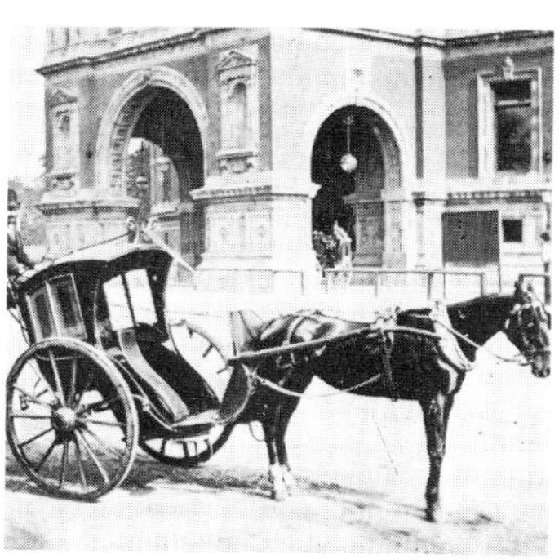

Hansom cab; model of the 1880s, photographed outside the Albert Hall in London.

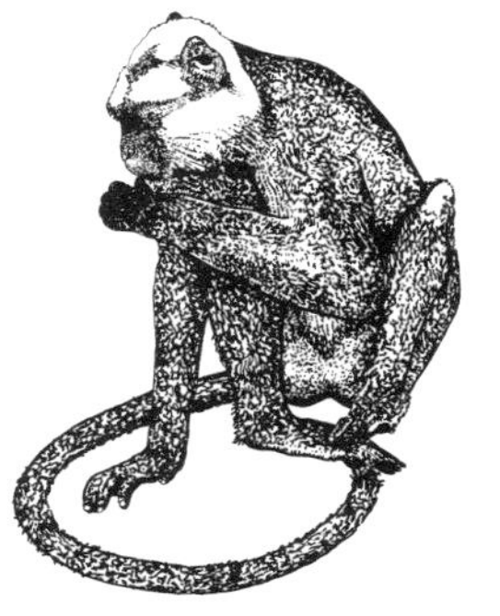

Hanuman is one of the commest Indian monkeys, protected as a protege of the god.

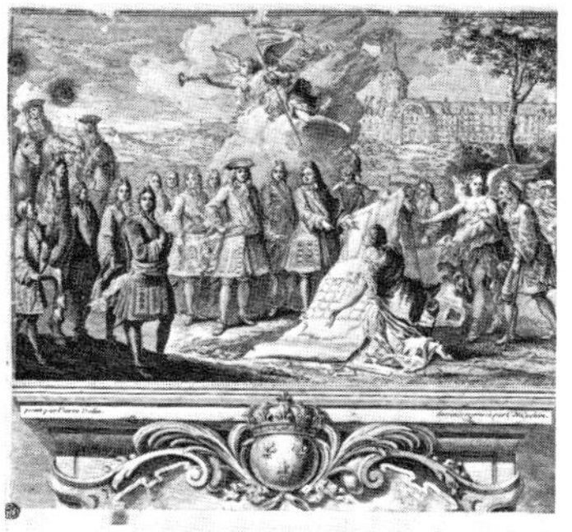

Hardouin-Mansart; an engraving of the architect with his patron, King Louis XIV.

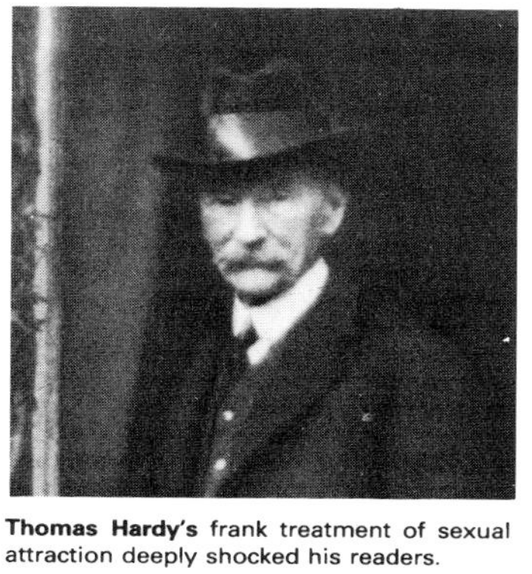

Thomas Hardy's frank treatment of sexual attraction deeply shocked his readers.

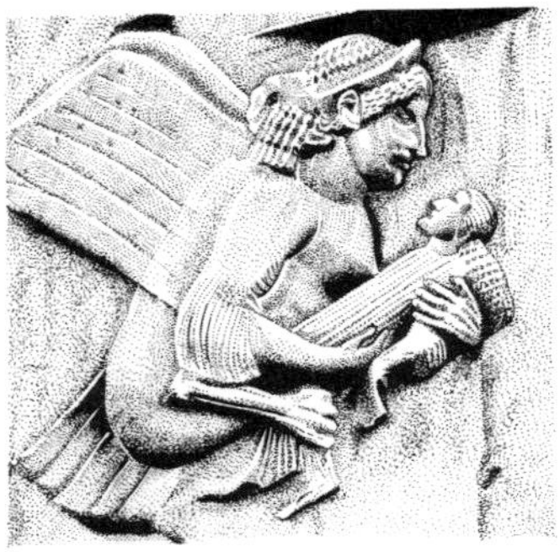

Harpies, regarded as two or three in number, administered the vengeance of the gods.

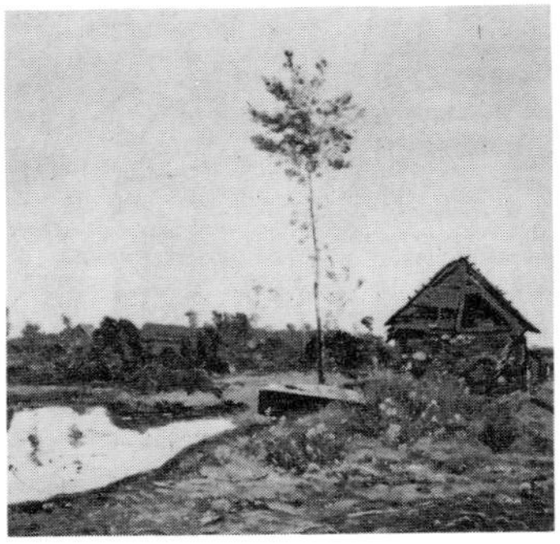

Henri Joseph Harpignies; a detail from one of his pastoral scenes, painted in 1883.

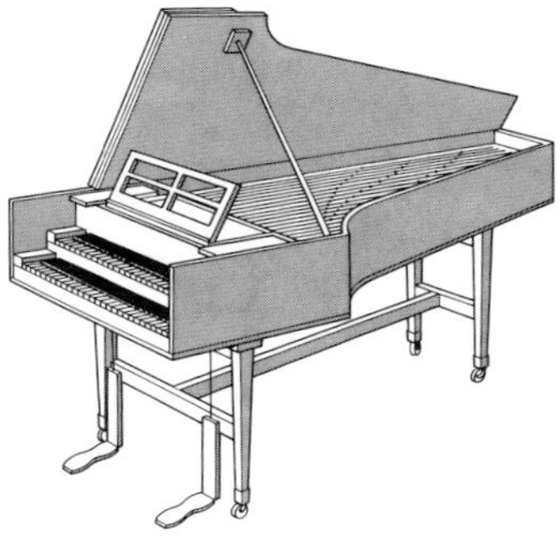

Harpsichord, developed in the late 1300s, was most popular between 1500 and 1700.

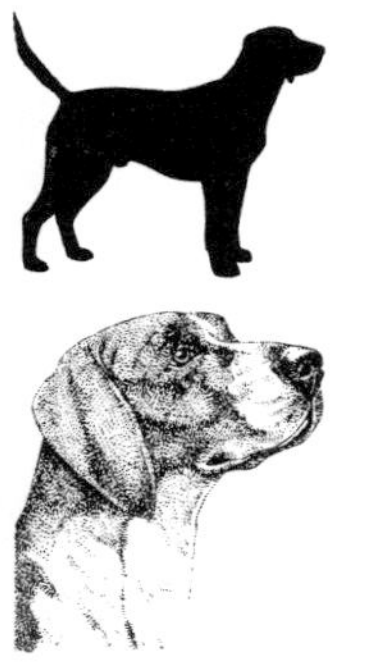

Harrier, dog thought to have developed from a cross between a hound and a greyhound.

Hargeysa, town in N Somalia, E Africa. It was the capital of British Somaliland from 1884 to 1960. It is now the market centre for the surrounding area. Pop. (1963 est.) 40,000.

Hargraves, Edward Hammond (1816–91), Australian gold-digger. One of the first to discover gold in Australia, his success was in the Bathurst district in New South Wales in 1851. He had been involved in the California gold rush in 1849 and was able to find gold in Australia because of the similarity of landforms.

Hargreaves, James (*d.* 1778), British inventor. He was working as a weaver at Stanhill, Blackburn when, in 1764, he invented the spinning jenny, which was able to spin eight threads of cotton at the same time. When in 1768 Blackburn weavers destroyed his machinery and house, he moved to Nottingham and, with Thomas James, built a mill and became one of the first great factory owners. *See also* MM p.58.

Hariana. *See* HARYANA.

Harington, Sir John (1561–1612), English courtier. He wrote many epigrams and poems, translated Ariosto's *Orlando Furioso* in 1591 and wrote *A Short View of the State of Ireland* (1605). He also designed the earliest water closet.

Harkness, Edward. *See* PILGRIM TRUST.

Harlem, residential area of Manhattan, New York City, USA. It was a fashionable 19th-century community, and an influx of blacks *c.* 1905–20 made it one of the largest black settlements in the USA and a political and cultural focus. The Center for Research in Black Culture is located there, next to the Countee Cullen branch Library, which has been a meeting place for black writers since the 1920s.

Harlequin, name derived from the character Arlecchino of the COMMEDIA DELL'ARTE who was a quick-witted, unscrupulous serving man. A harlequin nowadays appears in pantomine and comedy as a mute jester dressed in multi-coloured tights.

Harlequinade, essential 18th-century element in the development of PANTOMIME. A mixture of dance, music and mime, it featured characters from the COMMEDIA DELL'ARTE. But Pantaloon's comic involvement, as developed by clowns such as GRIMALDI, overwhelmed the strictly romantic elements, and the harlequinade slowly declined as the 19th century progressed.

Harley, Robert, 1st Earl of Oxford (1661–1724), British politician. He was a TORY MP (1688–1711) and Speaker of the House of Commons (1701–05). In 1710 he became the leading minister of Queen ANNE, but was unable to form a lasting government. He was appointed Lord High Treasurer in 1711, but dismissed from office in 1714.

Harley Davidson, US motor cycle manufacturer; one of the pioneers in the development of the motor cycle. The characteristic V-twin cylinder engine was first produced in 1909. The Harley Davidson WLA and WLC motor cycles, produced in 1945 for the Canadian Government, have a fine reputation for reliability. *See also* MM p.*124*.

Harlow, Jean (1911–37), US film actress who became known as the "blonde bombshell". An almost legendary figure of Hollywood in the 1930s, she is now considered one of its most tragic victims. Her first major role was in *Hell's Angels* (1930), after which she made more than 20 films in six years until her untimely death from kidney failure in 1937, during the filming of *Saratoga*.

Harmonica, or mouth organ, musical instrument consisting of a metal cassette containing free metal reeds tuned to diatonic or chromatic scale. The reeds are vibrated as the player blows or inhales through slots along one edge of the cassette; on blowing, notes of the home key chord are produced; on inhaling, other notes. It was invented *c.* 1820 and is regarded as a novelty instrument despite being difficult to play expertly.

Harmonic motion, periodic motion, such as that of a pendulum, atomic vibrations or an oscillating electrical circuit. SIMPLE HARMONIC MOTION is governed by a restoring force (F) proportional to the displacement (X) of the vibrating particle from its equilibrium point: $F = -kx$, where k, called the spring constant, determines the strength of the restoring force. The above equation pervades all branches of physics. *See also* SU pp.76–77.

Harmonic progression, sequence of the form $\frac{1}{a}, \frac{1}{b}, \frac{1}{c}, \ldots$, where *a, b, c,* etc, form an ARITHMETICAL PROGRESSION. The simplest is formed by the reciprocals of the positive integers: $\frac{1}{1}, \frac{1}{2}, \frac{1}{3}, \frac{1}{4}, \ldots$ Strings with lengths proportional to these terms (and with identical diameter and tension) vibrate with harmonic musical tones.

Harmonics, in acoustics, additional notes whose frequencies are multiples of a basic (fundamental) note. When a violin string is plucked or a drumskin tapped, the sounds emitted correspond to vibrations of the string or skin. The loudest sound (note) corresponds to the fundamental mode of vibration. But other, weaker notes, corresponding to subsidiary vibrations, also sound at the same time. Together these notes make up a harmonic series. *See also* SU pp.82–83, *82–83*.

Harmonium, keyboard instrument that produces notes when air propelled by a pedal-operated bellows vibrates metal reeds. It is equipped with stops to vary the tone and sometimes levers to control volume. The harmonium was developed in France about 1840, by Alexander Debain.

Harmony, in music, structure of chords and the relationships existing between them. The DIATONIC scale (from one C to the next on a piano, for example) is the basis of chord construction, and a harmonic progression from one chord to the next is defined by the KEY. The tonic, dominant and subdominant chords are the primary chords of a key (eg, C, G and F chords in the key of C) and composers, especially of the 18th and 19th centuries, followed specific rules of harmony. In some 20th-century work, harmony is more a matter of musical suitability than of following accepted formulas. *See also* HC2 p.270.

Harness racing, sport popular in the USA, Australia and New Zealand and increasingly so in Britain. Horses race around an oval circuit and draw a two-wheeled sulky that holds the driver. The horses are classified according to gait: trotters are diagonally gaited and pacers laterally gaited. The distance raced is 1.6km (1 mile) or more, and the horses begin from either a standing or moving start. There are various classes of race, usually dependent on speed. A TOTE betting system pays on first, second and third place, and sometimes on combinations. Harness racing, also known as trotting, began in the USA in the 1830s and was popular in New Zealand and Australia a century later. Famous US races include the Hambletonian and the Roosevelt International Trot. The Inter-Dominion Championship is a highlight of the trotting calendar in New Zealand and Australia.

Harney, Bill (1895–1962), Australian author and amateur anthropologist. He was adviser to many anthropological expeditions and during WWII was Government Protector of Aborigines. His books include *Taboo* (1943), *North of the Twenty-third* (1946) and *Life Among the Aborigines* (1957).

Harold I, or Harold the Harefoot (*d.* 1040), Danish king of the English from 1035 to 1040. He was the illegitimate son of CANUTE. He failed to establish his authority over the Anglo-Saxons, and his reign was one of continual civil strife.

Harold II (*c.* 1022–66), last king of Anglo-Saxon England. He was the son of Godwin, Earl of Wessex and, after King EDWARD THE CONFESSOR, the most powerful man in the kingdom. When Edward died in 1066 he became king, but he was slain in the same year at the Battle of HASTINGS.

Harold, sometimes spelled Harald, the name of four Norwegian Kings. Harold I consolidated his rule by deposing rival chiefs, a process probably completed in the 880s. His harsh taxes led many to emigrate to the British Isles and perhaps Iceland. He abdicated in favour of his son Eric Bloodaxe, who was succeeded by his brother HAAKON I. Harold II (*c.* 930–970), with the aid of his uncle the Danish King Harold Bluetooth, overthrew and killed Haakon I, *c.* 961. A harsh ruler, he forbade pagan worship. Harold III (1015–66), HARALD HARDRADA, served the Byzantines. From 1047 to 1064 he tried to conquer Denmark; he died while aiding Earl TOSTIG in his effort to conquer England in 1066. Harold IV (1103–36) reigned for six years until his death. He feuded with fellow King MAGNUS IV. After capturing and blinding Magnus, he became sole ruler in 1135 but was killed by Sigurd Slembi, a pretender to the throne.

Harp, ancient musical instrument consisting of a frame over which strings are stretched and plucked by hand. Variations have been found in civilizations as diverse as Egyptian, Greek and Celtic. A modern orchestral harp has a large triangular frame that carries 46 strings tuned diatonically, with certain strings coloured for quick identification. Seven pedals alter the home key by half a tone each (thus covering the diatonic range) by means of a double-action mechanism perfected by Sébastien ÉRARD in 1810.

Harpies, in Greek mythology, storm goddesses generally depicted by later writers as loathsome creatures with hag faces and the bodies, wings and talons of birds. Their ravages spread disease and famine and they were foul-smelling. The ARGONAUTS escaped their clutches, and several other heroes battled against them.

Harpignies, Henri Joseph (1819–1916), French painter and graphic artist. Greatly influenced by COROT, he is best known for his poetic watercolour paintings of various regions of France and Italy.

Harpoon, weapon, usually a barbed spear attached to a strong line, used for hunting fish and whales. It has a flat, triangular, sharpened head, sometimes detachable from the shaft. The harpoon may be hurled by hand or fired from a gun; the head of a modern whaling harpoon carries an explosive charge.

Harp seal, North American SEAL that ranges widely over the Arctic seas, with the largest herds found off the W coast of Greenland and the E Arctic Ocean. To whelp, they migrate to Labrador and the Gulf of St Lawrence. Adults are silver with black harp-shaped marks on their backs; pups are pure white. Species *Pagophilus groenlandicus.* Length: to 1m (3.3ft).

Harpsichord, keyboard musical instrument, often ornately decorated, resembling a small grand piano. Its metal strings are mechanically plucked by quill plectrums (not struck by hammers). Unlike the piano, its volume can barely be regulated, although stops may be used to bring extra strings into use. Historic instruments may have had two or, rarely, three keyboards. The harpsichord was the principal keyboard instrument 1500–1750 but was later replaced by the piano. Harpsichord playing has been revived in this century, especially through the masterly playing of Wanda LANDOWSKA, George MALCOLM and Rosalyn Tureck.

Harpur, Charles (1813–68), Australian poet. He used a variety of poetic forms and was the first to versify truly Australian topics. A collection of his work, *Poems of Charles Harpur* (1883), was published by his widow.

Harpy eagle, any of four species of EAGLES of tropical rain forests in New Guinea, the Philippines and South America. Included are the monkey-eating eagle (*Pithecophaga (Pithecophaga jefferyi)* of the Philippines and the harpy (*Harpia harpyja*) of South America that feeds on capuchin monkeys. Family Accipitridae.

Harrier, diurnal bird of prey with an owl-like face. It frequents pastures and grasslands where it swoops on small animals. It has a small bill, long wings, legs and tail, and may be grey, black or brown with a white rump. Length: 38–50cm (15–20in). Family Accipitridae; genus *Circus.*

Harrier, pack hunting dog of the HOUND group. Used for hare hunting, it can be followed on foot. A smaller version of the FOXHOUND, it has a medium-sized head with a pronounced forehead; flat, thin, ears; a muscular body; and straight, well-boned legs. Standard height: 46–48cm (18–19in) at the shoulder; weight: approx. 18kg (40lb).

Harriman, William Averell (1891–). US political leader and diplomat. After a financial career, he went into public life and served under various presidents from Franklin D. ROOSEVELT to Lyndon JOHNSON. His most distinguished work was as ambassador to the USSR during WWII (1943–46) and to Britain (1946). In 1956 he was an unsuccessful candidate for the Democratic presidential nomination.

Harris, Sir Arthur Travers (1892–), British air marshal. He flew with the Royal Flying Corps during WWI; from 1939–41 he was an air vice-marshal, and from 1942 Commander-in-Chief of Bomber Command. He instigated a policy of mass bombing raids.

Harris, Frank (1856–1931), British-American writer, *b.* Ireland. At 15 he emigrated to the USA where he attended the University of Kansas. He is best remembered for his scandalously frank but unreliable autobiography *My Life and Loves*, which appeared in five volumes (1923–27) and was for many years banned in England and the USA.

Harris, Howell (1714–63), Welsh revivalist preacher who, with Daniel Rowlands, founded Welsh Calvinistic Methodism. After a disagreement with Rowlands (1751) he organized his congregation into a communal settlement at Trevecka.

Harris, Joel Chandler (1848–1908), American author known for his retellings of folk-tales of the American Negroes, known as the *Uncle Remus* stories. The character of Brer Rabbit is perhaps the most memorable. Harris's first collection was *Uncle Remus: His Songs and His Sayings* (1880), followed by *Nights with Uncle Remus* (1883) and *Uncle Remus and His Friends* (1892).

Harris, Reg (1920–), British track cyclist who set long-standing world records and won five world sprint titles: as an amateur in 1947, and as a professional in 1949, 1950, 1951, 1954. In 1948, despite a broken arm, he won two Olympic silver medals (1,000m sprint, 2,000m tandem).

Harris, Richard (1932–), leading Irish actor whose stage debut was in Brendan BEHAN's *The Quare Fellow* (1957). He gave a notable performance in J.P. Donleavy's *The Ginger Man* (1959) and then virtually abandoned the theatre for the cinema, appearing in *Mutiny on The Bounty* (1962), *This Sporting Life* (1963). *Camelot* (1967), *Cromwell* (1970), *A Man Called Horse* (1970) and many others.

Harris, Roy Ellsworth (1898–), US composer. He was a pupil of Nadia BOULANGER. His works include seven symphonies, among them *Symphony for Voices* (1936) and the *Folksong Symphony* (1940), a piano quintet (1936) and the *Cumberland Concerto* (1951).

Harris, S part of LEWIS and Harris in the Western Isles, NW Scotland. The main occupations are crofting, fishing and stock raising, although the main shopping and residential area is Stornoway (Lewis), which is also the centre of the Harris tweed industry. Gaelic is the predominant language. Area: 505sq km (195sq miles). Pop. (1971) 2,963.

Harrison, James (1816–93), Australian journalist and inventor in 1851 of the first large practical refrigerator. He recognized the potential of meat exporting for the economy of Australia, which greatly benefited from the introduction of refrigerated ships. *See also* MM p.252.

Harrison, John (1693-1776), British horologist (watch or clock maker) who, in 1753, made a marine chronometer for which he was awarded a Government-sponsored prize of £20,000. The timepiece was tested for accuracy on two sea voyages to Jamaica. *See also* MM p.93.

Harrison, Rex Carey (1908–), British actor who appeared on the stage from 1924 and in films from 1929, both in London and the USA. Probably his best known role was as Prof. Higgins in *My Fair Lady* on Broadway (1956), in London (1958) and in the film (1964), for which he received an Academy Award.

Harrison, Richard Berry (1864–1935), US actor. The grandson of escaped slaves, he made his professional debut in Canada and from 1930 played "De Lawd" in *Green Pastures* for 1,659 consecutive performances.

Harrogate, county district in S North Yorkshire, England, created in 1974 under the Local Government Act (1972). Pop. (1974 est). 134,300.

Harrow School, public school that originated in the 14th century, in Middlesex, England. Its charter was granted in 1571, and after a bequest from John Lyon, a local landowner, the present school buildings were begun in the early 17th century.

Hart, Basil Henry Liddell. *See* LIDDELL HART, BASIL HENRY.

Hart, Doris (1925–), American tennis player who overcame a crippling illness to win six singles (Australian 1949; French 1950, 1952; Wimbledon 1951; USA 1954, 1955) and 29 doubles titles in the four major world championships. Although physically frail, she was a perfect stylist. She became a professional in 1955.

Harte, Francis Bret (1836–1902), US author. In 1868 he became editor of *Overland Monthly* and in 1870 published his most famous work, *The Luck of Roaring Camp and Other Sketches.*

Hartebeest, large ANTELOPE native to African grasslands S of the Sahara Desert. Both sexes are light to dark brown and have lyre-shaped horns united at the base and rising sharply from the forehead. Length: up to 200cm (79in); height: to 150cm (59in); weight: up to 180kg (397lb). Family Bovidae.

Hartford, capital city and port of entry in central Connecticut, USA, on the Connecticut River. Known as the insurance capital of the world, more than 25 companies have their headquarters there. Manufactures include precision instruments and electrical equipment. Pop. (1970) 158,017.

Hartford Wits, The. *See* CONNECTICUT WITS.

Harthacnut. *See* CANUTE.

Hartlepool, county borough in NE England. In 1974 it became part of the new county of Cleveland. A seaport, it exports coal and imports timber. Other industries include shipbuilding and marine engineering. Pop. (1971) 96,898.

Hartley, Lesley Poles "LP" (1895–1972), British novelist. His works include the trilogy *The Shrimp and the Anemone* (1944) *The Sixth Heaven* (1946) and *Eustace and Hilda* (1947), an account of a sibling relationship from childhood to adulthood. He also wrote *The Go-Between* (1953).

Hartline, Haldan Keffer (1903–), US neurophysiologist who shared the 1967 Nobel Prize in physiology and medicine with George WALD and Ragnar GRANIT for their contributions to an understanding of vision. Hartline studied the compound eye of the horseshoe crab and determined the effects of brightness on the eye.

Hartmann, Karl Robert Edward von (1842–1906), German philosopher. His *The Philosophy of the Unconscious* appeared in 1870 and postulates a system by which the human unconscious evolves through two stages before reaching the highest stage, where reason prevails. He was much influenced by HEGEL and SCHOPENHAUER.

Hartmann, Nicolai (1882–1950), German IDEALIST philosopher whose theories were influential in early 20th-century philosophy. Influenced by PLATO and Immanuel KANT, he finally rejected Kantian ideas in his book *New Ways of Ontology* (1942), which proposed that existence is an essential prerequisite for knowledge, a reversal of Kant's idea. He also considered reality to be meaningless, forcing people to live in a world irrelevant to human desires.

Hartono, Rudi (1949–), Indonesian badminton player who won the All-England singles title for an unprecedented seven successive years 1968–74, lost the 1975 final, and in 1976 took the title for a record eighth time.

Hartung, Hans (1904–), French painter of German origin. He developed a truly abstract style using ink-blots and calligraphic pen strokes, often with strong colour to unite the effect.

Harty, Sir Hamilton (1879–1941), Irish conductor, arranger and composer. He was conductor of the Hallé Orchestra in Manchester, England, from 1920 to 1933 and was well known for his performances of works of the Romantic composers.

Harun ar-Rashid (*c.* 764–809), the most famous of all the ABBASID caliphs. His brilliant reign has been given added lustre by the role given him in the stories of the *Thousand and One Nights.* He is known to have had diplomatic relations with CHARLEMAGNE and to have waged successful wars against the BYZANTINE empire. *See also* HC1 p.*149.*

Harunobo, Suzuki (1725–70), Japanese printmaker. He was the first artist to print in a wide range of colours, beginning with the multi-colour calendar prints made from woodcuts in 1765.

Harvard University, oldest US college, founded in 1636 by John Harvard at Cambridge, Massachusetts. Originally intended for the instruction of Puritan ministers, this religious restriction declined in the 18th century as more liberal subjects were introduced.

Harvestman, ARACHNID found worldwide with legs that may be several times its body length. There is little narrowing between head and abdomen. It feeds on dead or living insects and plant juices. Body length: 2.5–13mm (0.1–0.5in). Family Phalangidae. *See also* NW pp.103, *104.*

Harvest mite, any of several species of ARACHNIDS whose larvae are ectoparasites on human beings and animals. Infestation usually results in local dermatitis and severe itching. The animal's mouth parts are borne on a "false head". Length: 1mm (0.04in). *See also* NW p.*104.*

Harvey, Robert Neil (1928–), Australian cricketer. A stylish left-hand batsman and a superb fielder, he played in 79 Test matches between 1946 and 1963 (6,149 runs, average 48.41), the most by an Australian. He represented Victoria and New South Wales and in the 1970s became an Australian selector.

Harvey, William (1578–1657), English physician and anatomist who discovered the circulation of the blood. This landmark in medical history marked the beginning of modern physiology. His findings, published (1628) in ***De Motu Cordis et Sanguinis*** (***On the Motions of the Heart and Blood***), were ridiculed at first and only later generally accepted. Harvey also made important studies in EMBRYOLOGY. *See also* HC1 p.303.

Harwell, research and development centre of the United Kingdom Atomic Energy Authority, situated close to the village of Harwell in Berkshire.

Haryana, state in N central India. Chandīgarh, the capital, is a Union territory and shares its facilities between Haryana and the Punjab. Although there is some agriculture, the land is generally dry and barren. Wheat production is most important. Area: 44,222sq km (17,074sq miles) Pop. (1971) 10,036,808.

Hary Janos (1926), ballad opera by Zoltán KODÁLY, based on Hungarian legend and first performed in Budapest. An orchestral suite drawn from the opera has become well known.

Harz Mountains, mountain range on the border of East and West Germany, extending about 96km (60 miles) between the Elbe and Leine rivers. It is a resort and mining area. The highest peak is Brocken, 1,142m (3,747ft).

Hasdrubal, name of two Carthaginian generals. The elder (*d.* 221 BC) expanded Carthaginian power and founded Cartagena. The younger (*d.* 207 BC) was the son of HAMILCAR BARCA and the brother of HANNIBAL. He took command in Spain when Hannibal marched into Italy. Defeated by Publius Cornelius SCIPIO in 208, he crossed the Alps to join Hannibal but was forced to withdraw to the Metaurus valley in 207, where he was defeated and killed. *See also* HC1 p.91.

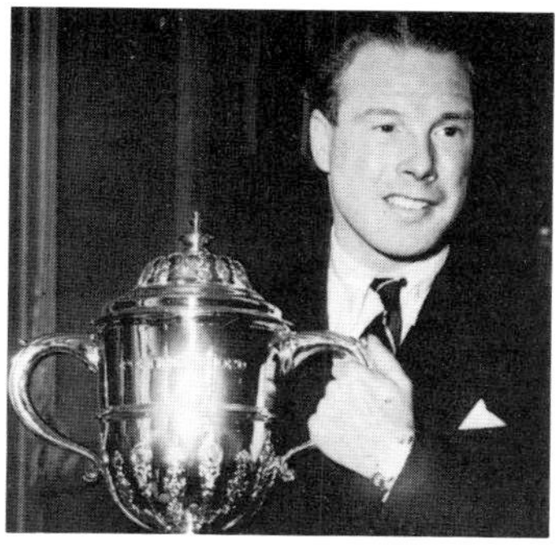

Reg Harris, sprint cyclist of the 1950s, with his Sportsman of the Year trophy in 1951.

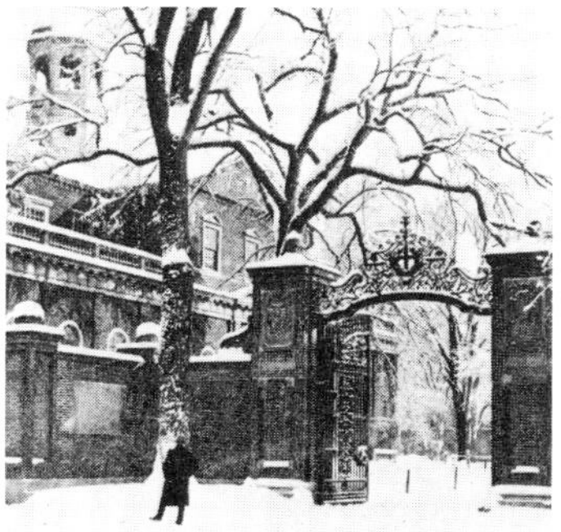

Harvard: the main gateway of the USA's oldest institution of higher education.

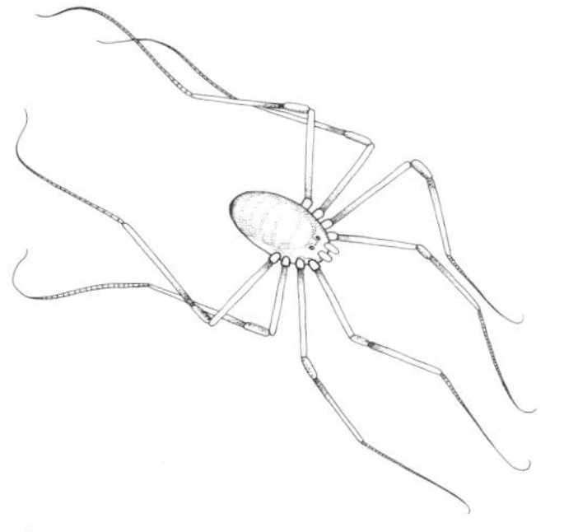

Harvestman, insect popularly known in the UK and USA as a "daddy longlegs".

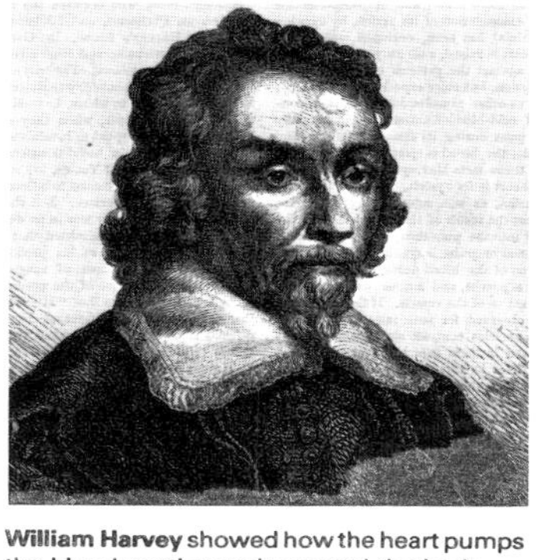

William Harvey showed how the heart pumps the blood continuously around the body.

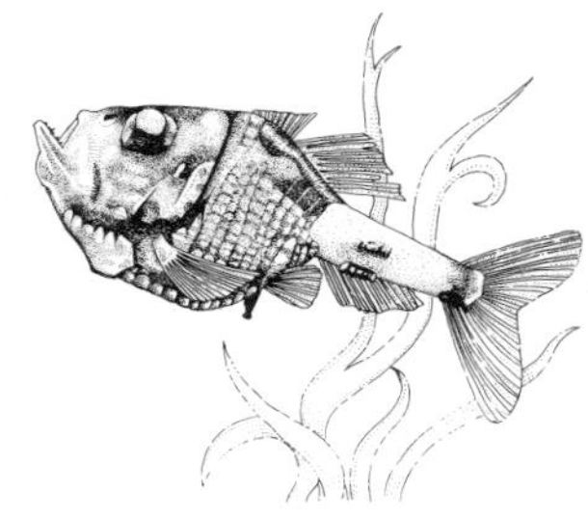

Hatchet fish possess luminous organs that supply light in their dark habitat.

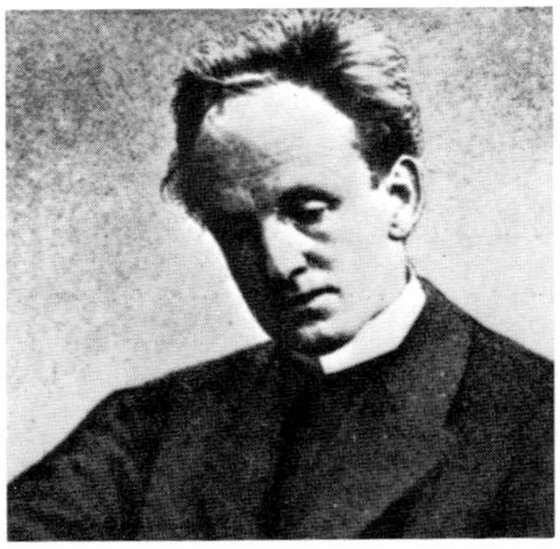

Gerhart Hauptmann: his plays portray man as obliged to act according to his basic drives.

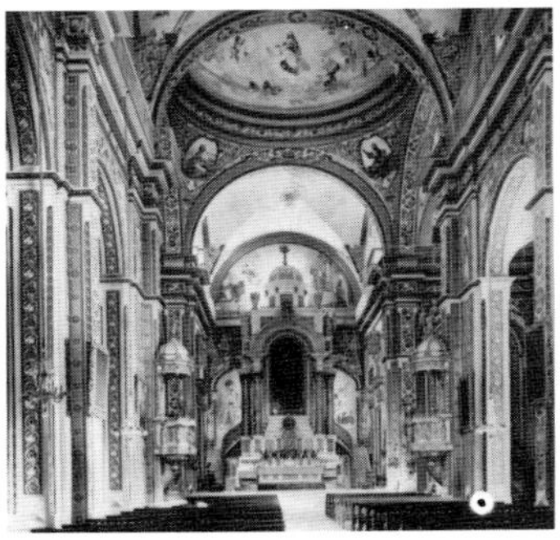

Havana: the lavish interior of the Mercedes Church, built in 1746, and rebuilt in 1792.

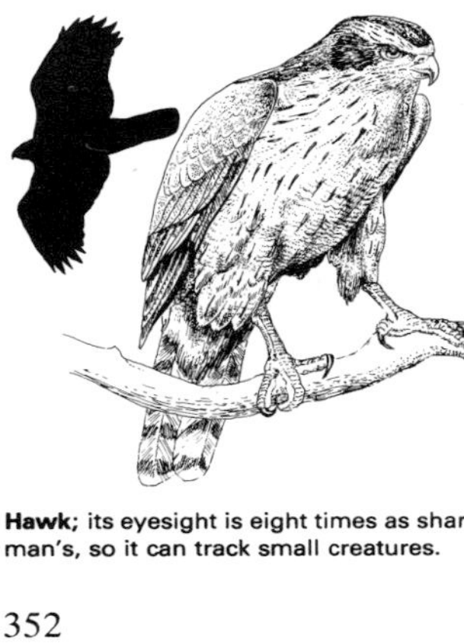

Hawk; its eyesight is eight times as sharp as man's, so it can track small creatures.

Hašek, Jaroslav (1883–1923), Czech satirical novelist and short-story writer, author of the best-selling novel *The Good Soldier Schweik* (four volumes of which were completed by his death). Schweik is an ambivalent character, variously interpreted as a Czech patriot making fun of his Austrian rulers and as the "little man" struggling against bureaucracy.

Hashish, resin obtained from the flowering tops of the hemp plant, *Cannabis sativa*, and used as a psychotropic drug. Its effects vary from user to user, but usually when smoked or eaten it induces heady sensations and often a feeling of carefree detachment. It is not markedly hallucinogenic, nor has it ever proved to be addictive. The legal penalties following discovery of its use are connected with drug smuggling and with the supposition that its use can lead to addiction to HEROIN and other "hard" drugs. *See also* MARIHUANA; MS p.105.

Hashman, Judy, née **Devlin** (1935–), American badminton player. Without equal in the women's game, she won ten All-England singles (1954, 1957, 1958, 1960–64, 1966, 1967) and 7 doubles; 12 USA singles (1954, 1956–63, 1965–67), 10 doubles, and 6 mixed doubles. She was in the winning US Uber Cup team in 1957.

Hasidism, popular pietist movement within JUDAISM founded by Israel Baal-Shem-Tov (*c.* 1699–*c.* 1761). It taught the ability of all men to reach God, and its followers became known for tolerance and glorification of the founder. The movement, centred in E Europe until WWII, strongly supports Orthodox Judaism. Its main centres are now in Israel and the USA.

Haskell, Arnold Lionel (1903–) British writer on ballet. In 1935 he was a ballet critic with the *Daily Telegraph* newspaper and subsequently editor of *The Ballet Annual* (1947–63). His writings, which include *Balletomania* (1934) and *Dancing Round the World* (1937), have done much to popularize the art of dance.

Hassan II (1929–), King of Morocco (1961–), son and successor of MOHAMMED V. He dissolved the National Assembly in 1965, assuming all executive and legislative powers, but in 1970 provided a new constitution by referendum. He eliminated foreign ownership of business in 1973, and in 1975 made claims to much of the Spanish Sahara after organizing a march of hundreds of thousands of his subjects across its border.

Hassan al-Bakr, General Ahmad (1914–), Iraqi military and political figure. After serving as a colonel in WWII he played a key part in the overthrow and execution in 1963 of Gen. Abdul Karim KASSEM, president since 1958. He became Prime Minister under Col. Abdul Salem Arif but was dismissed in 1964 because of Baathist sympathies. The coup of 1968 gave Hassan al-Bakr the presidency and put the Baathists back in office.

Hassel, Odd (1897–), Norwegian chemist who shared the 1969 Nobel prize in chemistry with Derek BARTON for his work on conformational analysis, the study of the three-dimensional structures of molecules. In 1930 he began research on aromatic organic compounds and discovered the two stereo isomers of cyclohexane.

Hassett, Lindsay (1913–), Australian cricketer. A compact, balanced batsman from Victoria, he played in 43 Test matches between 1938 and 1953 (3,073 runs, average 46.56), 24 times as captain. He scored 59 first-class centuries, second only to Don BRADMAN among Australians.

Hastings, Francis Rawdon-Hastings, 1st Marquess of (1754–1826), British soldier, politician and colonial administrator. He fought in the American Revolution, worked actively for the House of Lords and later (1813–23), when governor of Bengal, greatly expanded British control of India. In 1819 he gained Singapore by purchase for Britain.

Hastings, Warren (1732–1818), British colonial administrator, first governor-general (1772–85) of Bengal (British India). He fought at the battle of Plassey with CLIVE (1757), was governor of Fort William and reorganized the revenue collection system. Pitt's India Act of 1784 caused Hastings to resign and return home. In 1786 impeachment proceedings began for corruption in his Indian administration. But, after a seven-year trial, he was acquitted. *See also* HC2 p.47.

Hastings, city in Hawkes Bay province, New Zealand, on Heretaunga Plains on the North Island's E coast. It is a sheep farming and manufacturing centre. Pop. (1972 est.) 30,600.

Hastings, Battle of (1066), battle fought near Hastings, Sussex, between King HAROLD of England and a claimant to his throne, WILLIAM, Duke of Normandy (WILLIAM I "THE CONQUEROR"). Harold's defeat and death in battle led to the establishment of the Norman dynasty by William. *See also* HC1 pp.167–168.

Hatchet fish, marine fish found in deep temperate and tropical seas. Its body is silvery and there are light-emitting organs along the underside of its deep, muscular abdomen. Length: to 10cm (4in). Family Sternoptychidae (or Characidae). *See also* NW pp.*240–241*.

Hathaway, Anne (1555–1623), wife of William SHAKESPEARE. She was born in Shottery near Stratford ("Anne Hathaway's Cottage"), was married in 1582 and had three children. *See also* HC1 pp.284–285.

Hathor, ancient Egyptian goddess of love and happiness, music and dance, depicted as a cow or with the horns of a cow. A personification of the sky, she was thought to appear at the bedside of a newborn child to determine his fate.

Hatshepsut, powerful and well-travelled Queen of Egypt (*c.* 1494–1482 BC). Daughter of THUTMOSE I, she married her half-brother THUTMOSE II, ruled through him, and when he died, ruled as regent for his son THUTMOSE III. She may have been the biblical Queen of Sheba.

Hattin, Battle of (1187), engagement in which the Christian troops of Guy de Lusignan, King of Jerusalem, were defeated by a Muslim army under SALADIN. This defeat, which led to the Muslim reconquest of Jerusalem, Antioch and Tripoli, forced Europe to consider mounting a third crusade.

Hatton, Sir Christopher (1540–91), Lord CHANCELLOR of England. A favourite of ELIZABETH I, he was a leading royal spokesman in the Commons after his election in 1571. He was Chancellor from 1587 to 1591, and prominent in the trials of Catholic plotters against the Queen.

Hauhauism, Christian sect set up by Te Ua Haumene in New Zealand in 1862. He claimed the Maoris to be a lost tribe of Israel. The sect expressed anti-European feeling.

Hauptmann, Gerhart (1862–1946), German dramatist, poet and novelist. His play *Vor Sonnenaufgang* (1889; *Before Dawn*, 1909) was received with great excitement, and marked the birth of German naturalist drama. *Die Weber* (1892; *The Weavers*, 1961) portrayed the human misery of the industrial age. He was awarded the 1912 Nobel prize for literature. He is chiefly remembered for his earthy realistic scenes, rather than for the grim fantasy which pervaded several of his works.

Hausa, Negroid people of Islamic culture, inhabiting NW Nigeria and S Niger. Hausa society is basically feudal and is traditionally based on patrilineal descent. Its language is a member of the Chad group of Afro-Asiatic languages; it is the official language of N Nigeria and a major trading language of W Africa. Hausa crafts, especially weaving, leatherwork and silversmithing, are important aspects of an extensive trade network.

Haussmann, Georges-Eugène, Baron (1809–91), French town planner. He was responsible for the rebuilding of Paris (1851–68) under NAPOLEON III. He planned the broad straight boulevards visible today, said to have been built to enable troops more easily to quell any civil disturbances. *See also* HC2 p.*109*.

Haüy, René Just (1743–1822), French geologist and mineralogist, regarded as the father of CRYSTALLOGRAPHY. He defined the five mineral classes, and formulated the laws governing the structure of crystals. *See also* PE pp.94–95.

Havana (La Habana), capital city on the NW coast of Cuba, 145km (90 miles) SSW of Key West, Florida. The settlement was moved to its present site in 1519 and Havana has remained a strategically and commercially important centre in the Caribbean. Its present industries include oil refining and steel. Pop. (1974 est.) 1,838,000.

Havana brown cat, domestic short-haired cat breed with distinctive pink pads on the feet. It has a long head, large ears, oval chartreuse eyes and a medium-sized body. The tobacco-brown coat is smooth and glossy.

Havilland, Sir Geoffrey de. *See* DE HAVILLAND, SIR GEOFFREY.

Havířov, city in N Czechoslovakia, SE of Ostrava, near the Polish border. Founded in the 1950s, it is now part of the Ostrava-Karvinå industrial complex and an important mining centre. Pop. (1970 est.) 82,200.

Hawaii, state of the USA, in the Pacific Ocean, 3,363km (2,090 miles) WSW of San Francisco, California. Hawaii consists of eight large and 124 small volcanic islands, many of which are uninhabited. The economy is based on valley agriculture and there is an extensive tourist trade. There is an important US naval base at PEARL HARBOR. The islands were annexed by the USA in 1898, became a territory in 1900 and were admitted to the Union in 1959. The capital is Honolulu. Area: 16,705sq km (6,450sq miles). Pop. (1975 est.) 865,000. *See also* MW p.175.

Hawfinch, largest European FINCH, nesting in mixed and deciduous woods in temperate regions. Distinguished by its large bill with which it cracks nuts and fruit stones, it has mostly chestnut plumage, with black and white patches. Length: 18cm (7in). Species *Coccothraustes coccothraustes. See also* NW p.*144*.

Haw-Haw, Lord. *See* JOYCE, WILLIAM.

Hawk, any of several species of diurnal BIRDS OF PREY found in temperate and tropical climates. They have short, hooked bills for tearing meat and strong claws for killing and carrying their prey. The females are larger than the males. Hawks have red, brown, grey or white plumage with streaks and bars on the wings. They lay three to five eggs in a sturdy twig-and-stick nest high in a tree. The downy young, or hawklets, are blind and helpless, and are fed by the parents for six weeks. Length: 28–66 cm (11–26in). Order Falconiformes; genera *Accipiter* and *Buteo. See also* NW p.*217*.

Hawke Bay, inlet of the South Pacific Ocean on the E central coast of North Island, New Zealand. The coastal provincial district of Hawke's Bay is a fertile region producing fruit and vegetables. Its chief city is Napier, on thh SW coast of the inlet.

Hawke of Towton, Edward Hawke, 1st Baron (1705–81), British admiral. Distinguished service off Toulon in 1744 and in the English Channel in 1747 earned Hawke rapid promotion. His greatest victory, at QUIBERON BAY in 1759, saved Britain from the threat of a French invasion.

Hawkins, Coleman (1904–69), US jazz saxophonist. He made his recording debut in 1923 with Fletcher HENDERSON and greatly extended the scope of the improviser by basing his solos on the arpeggios of the chords of a melody rather than on the notes of the melody itself. From 1934–39 he lived in Europe where he recorded with Django REINHARDT.

Hawkins, Jack (1910–73) British actor. He made many stage appearances after his debut in 1924 in SHAW's *St Joan.* After 1932 he appeared in films such as *The Good Companions* (1935), *The Cruel Sea* (1952), *The Bridge on the River Kwai* (1957) and *Lawrence of Arabia* (1962). After recovering from an operation for cancer of the larynx in 1966, he learnt to speak again, but his subsequent minor film appearances were dubbed.

Hawkins, or Hawkyns, Sir John (1532–95), English naval commander. With the support of Queen Elizabeth I, he led two lucrative expeditions to Africa and the West Indies (1562–63, 1564–65), but on his third expedition (1567–69) the Spaniards destroyed most of his ships. He was prominent in plans to improve the navy, both in administration and in the design of its ships, and played an important role in the defeat of the Spanish ARMADA (1588). *See also* HC2 p.134.

Hawkins, Sir Richard (*c.*1560–1622), English seaman, son of Sir John Hawkins. In 1593 he attempted to circumnavigate the globe, but off the coast of Peru he was captured by Spanish warships and was sent to Spain, where he remained prisoner until 1602.

Hawkmoth, or sphinx moth, or humming-bird moth, medium-to-large MOTH characterized by narrow wings, a spindle-shaped body and a long sucking-tube coiled beneath its head. Strong flyers, hawk moths usually feed at dusk, hovering over flowers and sucking nectar through the extended tube. Their larvae – large, smooth-skinned caterpillars – are called hornworms because of a hornlike protrusion on the posterior segment. Family Sphingidae. *See also* NW p.117.

Hawks, Howard (1896–1977), US film director. Famous chiefly for his action dramas and deft comedies, he made more than 40 films in a career spanning the whole history of film-making and employing almost all the stars of Hollywood's heyday. These films include *Bringing Up Baby* (1938), *Sergeant York* (1941), *The Big Sleep* (1946) and *Rio Lobo* (1970).

Hawksbill, or tortoise-shell, turtle, carnivorous marine TURTLE found in tropical seas. It has overlapping plates on its carapace, and is prized for its brown-and-yellow horny plates. Length: to 55cm (22in). Family Cheloniidae; species *Eretmochelys imbricata. See also* NW p.*138.*

Hawksee, Francis, (died *c.*1713), English experimental physicist and student of Robert Boyle. Hawksee was responsible for the double-cylindered air-pump with which he showed that air glows at low pressure when excited by an electric discharge. Hawksee also demonstrated that the transmission of sound through air was dependent on pressure.

Hawksmoor, Nicholas (*c.*1661–1736), English BAROQUE architect who started as an assistant to WREN. He also assisted VANBRUGH at Castle Howard and Blenheim Palace. His own buildings – all extremely innovative in his use of towers, steeples, niches and porticoes for the most exciting effects – are close to Italian Baroque, which he never saw. Among them are the Clarendon Building and Queen's College at Oxford and six outstanding London churches, including St Mary Woolnoth, St Anne, Limehouse, and St George-in-the-East. He also built, in Gothic style, the two W towers of Westminster Abbey.

Hawkweed, creeping perennial plant with a rosette of hairy leaves at ground level. In late summer a leafless stem grows out of the rosette and bears yellow to red flower heads that resemble dandelions. Height: up to 30.5cm (12in). Family Compositae.

Haworth, Sir Walter Norman (1883–1950), British organic chemist and Fellow of the Royal Society. Educated at Manchester and Göttingen, he held academic posts in London, St Andrews and Newcastle and was Director of chemistry at Birmingham from 1925–48. He determined the constitution of vitamin C and various carbohydrates, sharing the 1937 Nobel Prize for chemistry with O. Paul KARRER for this work.

Hawthorn, any of more than 1,000 species of shrubs and trees of the ROSE family, growing in N temperate parts of the world. Their flowers are white or pink, and their berries, shaped like tiny red, black or blue apples, are borne in clusters. Genus *Crataegus. See also* NW p.*61.*

Hawthorne, Mike (1929–59), British motor racing driver. He won the world drivers' championship in a Ferrari in 1958, having finished third in 1954. In 1955, driving a Jaguar, he won the Le Mans 24-hour race.

Hawthorne, Nathaniel (1804–64), US novelist and short story writer. Like Edgar Allan POE, he was a leader in the development of the American short story. His early work received little acclaim but his reputation was made with the publication of *The Scarlet Letter* (1850), a tale of sin and redemption through suffering. Among his other popular works are *The House of Seven Gables* (1851), a novel, and *The Snow Image and Other Thrice-Told Tales* (1851). *See also* HC2 p.288.

Hay, Will (1888–1949), British character comedian who after many years in music hall became a film actor. On screen he portrayed a cheerful incompetent. His films included *Those Were The Days* (1934), *Oh Mr Porter* (1937), *Ask A Policeman* (1938), *The Ghost Of St Michael's* (1941) and *My Learned Friend* (1943).

Haydn, Franz Joseph (1732–1809). Austrian composer. One of the greatest composers of the Classical period, he served from 1761 to 1790 as musical director for the wealthy Esterházy family and composed many of his best works during these years. Later he twice visited England, composing the last 12 of his 104 symphonies for concerts there. Haydn brought the sonata form to masterful fruition in these symphonies, which included the *Military*, the *Clock* and the *London.* One of the most prolific of all composers, he also wrote many songs, string quartets, masses, chamber works, concertos and choral works, the most famous of the latter being the oratorios *The Creation* (1798) and *The Seasons* (1801). He influenced and was in turn influenced by his friend MOZART. *See also* HC2 p.41.

Haydon, Benjamin Robert (1786–1846), English historical painter and writer. His most valuable writing, *Autobiography and Memoirs* (1853), provides important information about notable artists and politicians of the period. His paintings were greatly influenced by the Italian masters, and were executed on a grand scale.

Hayek, Friedrich August von (1899–), British economist, *b.* Vienna. He was professor of economic science, London (1931–50), of social and moral science, Chicago (1950–62) and of economics, Freiburg (1962–69). He has written many books on law, economics and philosophy. In 1974 he won the Nobel Prize in economics.

Hayes, Evelyn. *See* BETHELL, MARY URSULA.

Hayes, Helen (1900–), US actress. She made her stage debut in New York in 1908, but is more famous for her film roles. In 1932 she won an Academy Award for her part in *The Sin of Madelon Claudet.*

Hay fever, seasonal ALLERGY induced by grass pollens (fertilizing dust-like particles in flowers). Its symptoms include asthma, itching of the nose, pharynx and eyes which can develop abruptly, followed by sneezing and watery discharge from the nose and eyes. Headache and coughing may also accompany attacks. The symptoms can often be controlled with ANTIHISTAMINES. *See also* MS pp.87, 89.

Haynes, Johnny (1934–), British footballer who became England's first £100-a-week player. An inside-forward of immaculate passing skills, he spent his entire career (1952–70) with Fulham, winning 56 England caps (1954–62), 22 as captain.

Hazel, any of about 15 bushes or small trees of the BIRCH family, native to temperate regions of Europe, Asia and America. The leaves are large, oval and serrated. There are separate male and female flowers. The fruit is a hazelnut, also called cobnut or filbert. Family Betulaceae. *See also* NW p.*70.*

Hazlitt, William (1778–1930), British writer and critic. He wrote for several periodicals, including the *Edinburgh Review*, and was a political reporter for *The Morning Chronicle*, but he is best known for his essays, particularly those in literary criticism as in *A View of the English Stage* (1818). His most famous collections of essays are *Table Talk, or Original Essays on Men and Manners* (1821–22) and *The Plain Speaker* (1826).

Head, in anatomy, that part of the animal body that contains the brain together with sense organs such as eyes and ears. In all vertebrates and in many invertebrates, the organs of smell and taste, and the mouth, are also located in the head. Positionally the head is anterior, or at the leading end of the body.

Headache, one of the most frequent discomforts suffered by human beings. It may be caused by disease, emotional disorder or distress, pressure on cranial nerves, or by the dilation or contraction of certain blood vessels. The most frequent causes of minor short-duration headaches are daily tensions and fatigue. MIGRAINE is an intense form of headache, usually lasting several hours and often accompanied by vomiting.

Headhunting, taking and sometimes preserving the heads of enemies. Once a widespread custom, it is still sometimes practised in New Guinea and lingered in Europe after 1900. Captured heads were believed to give victors their victims' powers, to prove courage or to be necessary for fertility.

Headingley, cricket ground in Leeds, home of Yorkshire County Cricket Club, and since 1899 a Test match venue. Sir Don Bradman played six innings there, making 963 runs at an average of 192.6. In 1975, vandals dug up the pitch during the England-Australia Test.

Healey, Denis (1917–), British Labour politician. He became a Labour MP in 1952 and was Secretary of State for Defence between 1964 and 1970. He was a member of the Labour Party National Executive Committee from 1970 to 1975, and in 1974 became Chancellor of the Exchequer.

Health and Social Security, Department of, British government department responsible for the administration of the NATIONAL HEALTH SERVICE and the social services provided by local bodies. It also has various related functions, eg the payment of benefits, the assessment of the means of LEGAL AID applicants and the determination of non-contributory benefits. It is headed by the Secretary of State for Social Services, who is assisted by a Minister for Social Security and two Ministers of State for Health.

Health Service. *See* NATIONAL HEALTH SERVICE.

Healy, Timothy Michael (1855–1931), Irish political leader and first governor-general of the Irish Free State (1922–28). He worked closely with PARNELL and showed a remarkable spirit of conciliation in his political duties.

Heany, Seamus (1939–), Irish poet who has written several volumes of poetry, including *Eleven Poems* (1965), *Death of a Naturalist* (1966), *Door to the Dark* (1969) and *North* (1975), for which he won the W. H. Smith Prize.

Heard and McDonald Islands, island group forming an external territory of Australia, situated in the S Indian Ocean 4,000km (2,500 miles) SW of Perth. Heard Island is partly glaciated and inhabited only periodically by research groups. The McDonald islands are situated to the W of Heard Island and are uninhabited.

Hearing, process by which sound waves are experienced. Sound waves are systematic compressions and decompressions of the air. The physical mechanism of hearing begins when sound waves enter the EAR canal and vibrate the eardrum. The vibrations are transmitted by the three small bones of the ossicles to the cochlea, the organ of hearing. Within the cochlea are receptors called hair cells, which generate nerve impulses that pass via the auditory nerve, to the brain, to be interpreted as sounds. Many of the distinctions human beings make among sounds are psychological, eg the difference between noise and music is learned in part, although physical factors do play a role. *See also* MS pp.50–51; SU pp.80–83.

Hearing aid, electronic sound-reproducing device to increase the sound intensity at the ear. Modern aids use a small crystal microphone, a microminiaturized battery-powered amplifier and an earpiece (often shaped to fit into the auditory canal). The device consists of either two parts connected by a thin wire (the battery and amplifier being hidden in the

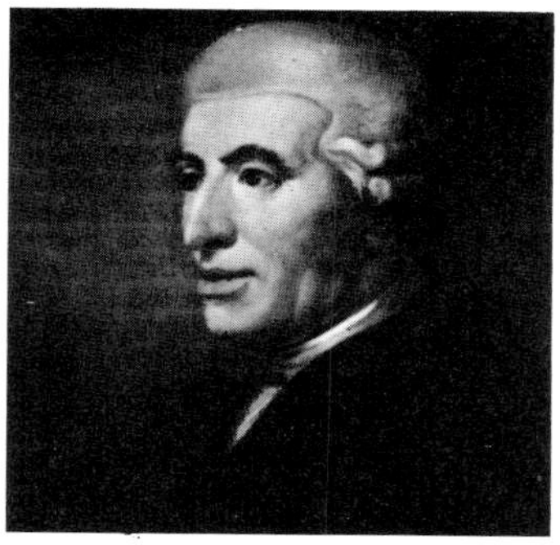

Joseph Haydn's combination of instruments became the basis of the modern orchestra.

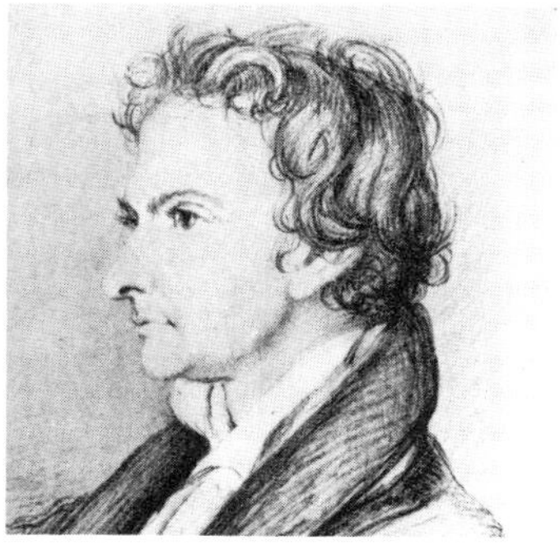

William Hazlitt's "personal" essays, *Table Talk*, were published in two volumes.

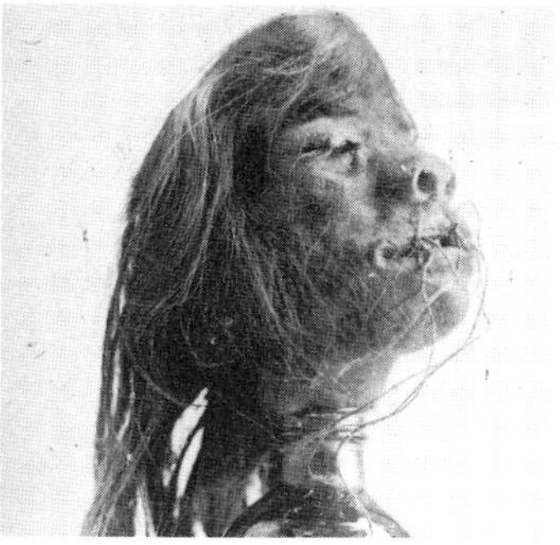

Headhunting; the lips are sewn together to prevent evil spirits escaping.

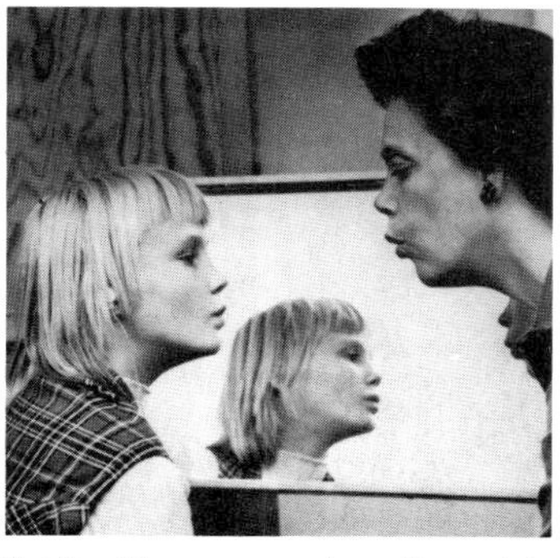

Hearing aids, are now made small enough to be completely hidden from sight.

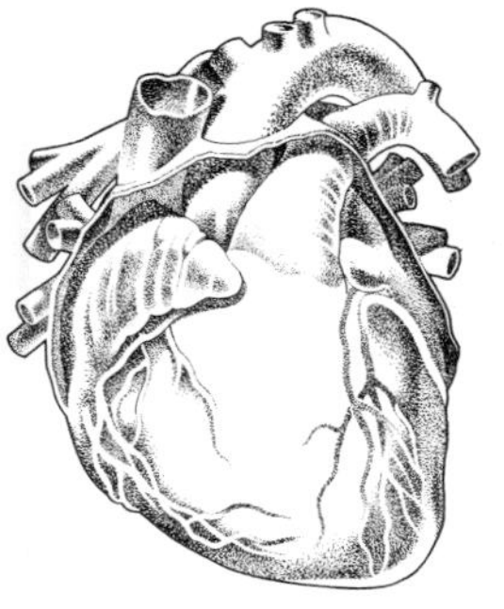

Heart: William Harvey first deduced that blood circulates "constantly in a circle".

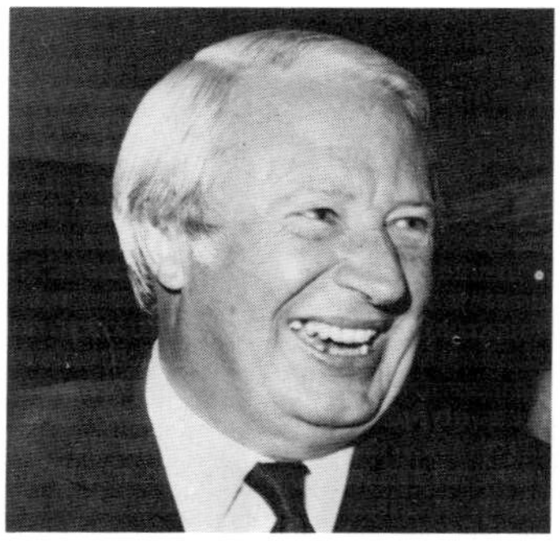

Edward Heath's confrontation with the miners led to a government defeat in 1974.

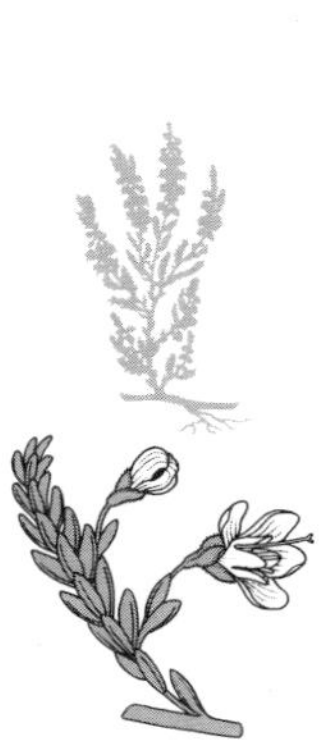

Heather is a common shrub in the Scottish Highlands, thought by some to be lucky.

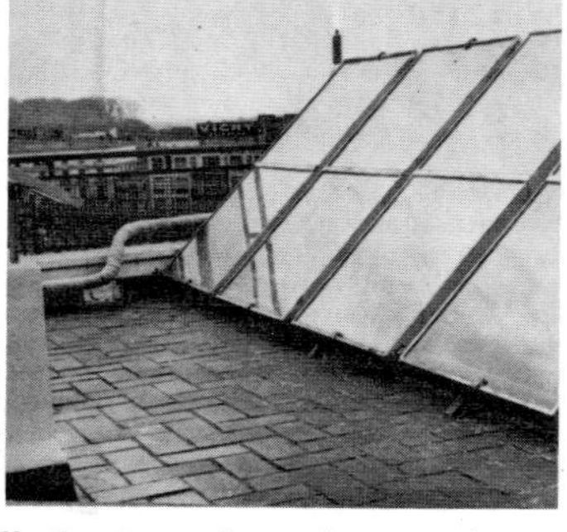

Heating; these solar panels are part of a central heating system in a French hotel.

clothing) or one tiny unit placed in or behind the ear or housed in spectacle frames. *See also* MS pp.50–51.

Hearne, Samuel (1745–92), Canadian fur trader and explorer, *b.* England. Hearne navigated for the HUDSON'S BAY COMPANY (1768–70), in 1770 making the first overland trek to the Arctic Ocean. In 1774 he founded Cumberland House, the first inland trading post of the Hudson's Bay Company.

Hearst, William Randolph (1863–1951), US publisher. He built a countrywide publishing empire that included newspapers, magazines, a syndicated weekly supplement, news services, radio stations and film studios. As with his rival, Joseph PULITZER, he practised sensational journalism and promoted American imperialism.

Heart, muscular organ that pumps blood throughout the body by rhythmic contractions of its unique muscle tissue. In man, the heart is located behind the sternum (breastbone) between the lower parts of the lungs. It lies in a double-walled sac, the pericardium; the walls are separated by pericardial fluid that cushions the heart from shock. The heart is divided longitudinally by a muscular wall, the septum. The right side contains only deoxygenated blood; the left side only oxygenated blood. Each side is divided into two chambers: an atrium and a ventricle, both separated by valves. The rhythmic contractions are maintained by electrical impulses that originate in the sinuatrial node, a bundle of muscle cells, blood vessels and nerves; the average heart rate for an adult is 70–80 beats per minute. *See also* MS pp.62–63.

Heart attack, or myocardial infarction, diminishing or failure of blood supply to the heart, generally although not always the result of CORONARY OCCLUSION or thrombosis. It is accompanied by pain which is typically persistent, described as constricting or oppressive, and commonly by shortness of breath. Vomiting, nausea and pale, cold, moist skin may occur. If the victim survives, immediate hospital treatment is necessary. *See also* ANGINA PECTORIS; MS pp.90–91.

Heartburn, burning sensationg along the oesophagus occurring soon after eating, especially overeating. It is caused by gastric contents spreading back to the oesophagus and throat. Heartburn pain may resemble that of a heart attack. It may be relieved by drinking fluids, or by acid neutralizers.

Heart failure, disorder in which the heart is unable to pump blood at the rate necessary to supply body tissues. Symptoms include respiratory distress, oedema and fatigue. Treatment is with bed rest and avoidance of stress; drugs are sometimes prescribed. *See also* HEART ATTACK; MS pp.90–91.

Heart-lung machine, device that supplies and distributes oxygen to the body when the natural circulation is interrupted during open heart surgery. It consists of an oxygenator, which substitutes for the lungs, and a pump, which performs the circulatory functions of the heart. *See also* MS p.*127*.

Heart murmur, abnormal sounds in the chest heard (using a stethoscope) because of vibrations and turbulence in the heart and blood vessels around it. The intensity, pattern and location of murmurs are used in diagnosis. Murmers are most frequently associated with rheumatic fever and congenital disorders, but they do not always indicate the presence of disease or disorder.

Heat, form of energy associated with the constant vibration of atoms and molecules. It was once thought to be a material substance called caloric, that was contained in all bodies and could flow from one to another. The KINETIC THEORY is the present accepted theory of heat. It holds that the degree of hotness of a body depends on the extent of vibration of its atoms. Heat is distributed in three forms: CONVECTION, through gases and liquids; CONDUCTION, through solids; and RADIATION, mainly through space. Heat and temperature are sometimes confused; temperature is an indication of how much heat a body possesses. Heat and mechanical energy are interchangeable, eg the hands can be warmed by rubbing them, causing friction which produces heat. *See also* SU pp.90–91.

Heat cycle. *See* HEAT PUMP; CARNOT CYCLE.

Heat engine, any engine that converts heat energy into useful mechanical energy. Thus, all engines that burn fuels are heat engines, including steam, petrol, diesel and jet engines.

Heat exchange, or heat transfer, flow of heat energy from one object to another. This flow of energy occurs at all times when two or more bodies at different temperatures are in thermal contact. Three methods of heat transfer may be distinguished: CONDUCTION, CONVECTION and RADIATION. In conduction, heat is transferred from molecule to molecule within a body, as in an iron rod stuck in a fire; in convection, heat is transferred by circulation of fluid, as in boiling; in radiation, heat is transferred in the form of electromagnetic waves, as in sunlight. Heat exchange is essential in many industrial processes where heat may be extracted from one source for use elsewhere. *See also* SU pp.90–91.

Heath, Edward Richard George (1916–), British politician. He entered parliament as a Conservative in 1950 and subsequently held several offices, including government chief whip (1955–59), minister of labour in 1965 and prime minister on winning the general election of 1970. Heath successfully concluded negotiations for Britain's entry into the EEC in 1973 but was defeated by Labour under Harold WILSON in 1974. Margaret THATCHER succeeded him as party leader in 1975. *See also* HC2 p.238.

Heath, family (Ericaceae) of about 2,000 species of evergreen herbs, shrubs and small trees native to temperate zones of Africa, North America, Europe, tropical mountains and the Arctic. The plants have small, thick or needle-like leaves and bell-shaped flowers. The fruit is usually a small berry. The best-known example is HEATHER. *See also* ERICA.

Heather, or ling, small, evergreen shrub native to North America, Europe and Asia Minor. It has scale-like leaves and small bell-shaped flowers of pink, lavender or white. It is common on British moors. Family Ericaceae; species *Calluna vulgaris*. *See also* ERICA.

Heathrow, major international airport to the W of London, one of the busiest in the world. It is situated 24km (14 miles) from the West London Air Terminal, and in 1977 was connected with London Underground railway system. *See also* MM p.186.

Heating, of industrial and domestic buildings and installations, is accomplished either by burning fuels or by tapping heat from available nearby sources. Older types of heating systems for buildings include stoves and open fireplaces burning the solid fuels wood, coal and coke. These often pass part of their heat to a water boiler which supplies hot water for washing and cooking purposes, and in larger installations, also feeds steam to heavy radiators for central heating. More sophisticated fuelled central heating systems burn oil, natural gas or solid fuels more efficiently in a specially-designed burner which transfers the heat to a boiler, which then supplies hot water to efficient, lightweight radiators, usually via pumps. In hot air systems a fan blows air across elements heated either by combusted fuels or by electricity; the heated air passes on through ducting to outlet grills situated in the areas to be heated. Underfloor central heating systems include ducts and electric coils. Electricity can also be supplied at a cheaper, off-peak cost to storage heaters, which release the heat slowly during daylight hours. All these arrangements are combined usually with effective heat insulation such as glass-wool insulation of lofts and double glazing. Near factories, dwellings may be centrally heated by the excess heat generated by an industrial process. In countries situated in regions of geothermal activity, such as Iceland, New Zealand and Italy, hot water and steam can be tapped from springs and geysers and piped to buildings, or a geothermal power station built to supply electricity for this and other purposes. Solar heaters for houses are now effective even where sunshine is, at best, intermittent for most of the year. Solar cookers for heating food are used in many hot countries, particularly where fuel is expensive. These comprise a polished reflector that focuses heat on to a metal food heater. *See also* MM p.53, *53*.

Heat pump, employed mainly in refrigerators and central cooling systems. In a refrigeration cycle, a liquid boiling at about −30°C, called a FREON, is evaporated at low pressure in metal coils. This absorbs heat from the surrounding space, so producing the cooling effect. The freon vapour then passes to a pump driven by an electric motor, which delivers it at raised temperature and pressure to a condenser outside the refrigerated area. As the vapour condenses to a liquid it gives up heat to the surrounding space. The liquid, still under pressure, passes to a receiver, from which the suction intake of the pump withdraws it at lowered pressure back to the evaporator in the refrigerated area, so completing the cycle.

Heat shield, in aerospace technology, plate or apron attached to the leading edge of a spacecraft to absorb or dissipate heat upon re-entry into the Earth's atmosphere. It is constructed of ablative materials, which chip off or vaporize to dissipate heat and provide an insulating layer of gases to protect the spacecraft. Materials used include quartz and various plastics. *See also* ABLATION; NOSE CONE.

Heatstroke, exhaustion or illness brought on by exposure to extreme heat. This can include exposure to intense sunlight and heat, and to the heat of such working-places as boiler rooms and steel foundries. In all cases, damp heat is more injurious than dry heat because it prevents sweat evaporating from the skin. In the end stages of severe heatstroke the body's temperature regulation system fails and collapse, coma and death ensue.

Heat transfer. *See* HEAT EXCHANGE.

Heat treatment, cycle of heating and cooling of a metal or other material to alter its physical properties. In annealing the material is heated to a predetermined temperature, held for a time, then cooled to room temperature. This improves ductility and reduces brittleness in a metal and reduces strains in glass. Annealing is intermittently carried out during the working of a piece of metal, when ductility is lost through hammering.

Heat unit, in physics, quantity of heat energy chosen to be convenient for calculations. The kilocalorie, or calorie, is usually employed, defined as the amount of heat needed to raise the temperature of one kilogram of water one degree Celsius (from 14.5°C to 15.5°C).

Heaven, in most religions, the dwelling-place of God and the angels and of those human beings who have entered into a state of bliss after physical death as a reward for leading a virtuous life on earth. In Christian theology heaven is essentially the fulfilment of the chief end of man, ie to glorify God and to enjoy His presence for ever.

Heaviside layer, obsolete name for the IONOSPHERE. The term Kennelly-Heaviside layer was also used, after the two scientists who first proposed the existence of this atmospheric layer.

Heavy water, deuterium oxide, water in which the hydrogen atoms are replaced by DEUTERIUM, the isotope of HYDROGEN of atomic mass 2 (normal hydrogen has mass 1). It occurs in small proportions in ordinary water, from which it is obtained by electrolysis. It is used as a moderator in some nuclear reactors. Molecular weight: 20.

Hebb, Donald Olding (1904–), Canadian psychologist who wrote *Organization of Behaviour* (1949) in an attempt to relate physiological brain processes to intelligence. It greatly influenced subsequent research and theory of brain processes, learning and memory.

Hebbel, Christian Friedrich (1813–63), German playwright and novelist. Naturally inclined towards tragedy, he nevertheless wrote several comedies, including *The Diamond* (1841). His tragedies, in both verse and prose, include *Maria Magdelene* (1844) and *Julia* (1848). He also write an epic poem *Mother and Child* (1859).

Hebe, in Greek mythology, the goddess of youth, dutiful daughter of ZEUS and HERA, a maiden who attended to the domestic needs of the gods. She married HERCULES.

Hebrew, language in the SEMITIC group of the Hamito-Semitic family. Use of it as a spoken tongue decreased as a result of the BABYLONIAN CAPTIVITY (586 BC), when it was overtaken by the cognate Aramaic; the Aramaic alphabet became Square Hebrew, which is the basis for the modern Hebrew writing. Hebrew continued, however, as the language used by the Jews for religious purposes, especially in exegesis, for over 2,000 years. It was revived as an ordinary, secular spoken language in the 19th century, and in 1948 was declared the official language of the newly-founded state of Israel.

Hebrides (Western Isles), islands in the Atlantic Ocean off the W coast of Scotland. They are divided into the Inner Hebrides (principal islands: Skye, Rhum, Eigg, Islay, Mull), which are part of the Strathclyde and Highland regions, and Outer Hebrides (principal islands: Lewis with Harris, North and South Uist), part of the Western Isles island region. The main occupations are fishing and farming. Pop. 60,000.

Hebron (al-Khalil), town in W Jordan, 32km (20 miles) SSW of Jerusalem. Traditionally one of the oldest cities in the world, it is considered the burial place of ABRAHAM and SARAH. The modern city is surrounded by a grape and vegetable growing area. Its industries include tanning and food processing. Pop. (1968 est.) 38,000.

Hecate, powerful Greek mythological goddess thought to be the daughter of Perses and Asteria. She ruled over heaven as SEMELE, on earth as ARTEMIS, and in the underworld as an attendant of PERSEPHONE. She bestowed the wealth and blessings of daily life and presided over witchcraft, graveyards and cross-roads.

Heckelphone, woodwind instrument developed in 1904 in response to a suggestion from WAGNER for an extended low-register instrument. It has a double reed and a wooden bell, and in tonal quality it is a combination of the oboe and alphorn. It was first used by Richard STRAUSS in the opera *Salome* (1905)

Hector, in Greek mythology, the greatest of the Trojan heroes, eldest son of PRIAM and HECUBA (king and queen of the besieged city) and husband of ANDROMACHE. ACHILLES slew him and dishonoured his body, but Priam persuaded Achilles to return the body for an honourable burial.

Hecuba, in Greek mythology, the consort of PRIAM (King of Troy) and mother of HECTOR. After the fall of Troy, Hecuba was imprisoned by the conquering Greeks, and because of her revenge on King Polymnestor of Thrace (who had killed her youngest son) became the personification of motherly courage.

Hedda Gabler (1890), four-act drama by Henrik IBSEN which emphasizes the danger of adhering to the conventions of society at the expense of individuality. The work revolves round it strong-willed heroine, Hedda, who refuses to come to terms with her own spiritual nature and in so doing brings tragedy upon herself, a former admirer and her husband (whom she has ceased to love).

Hedgehog, small, nocturnal Eurasian mammal of the family Erinaceidae. The common European hedgehog, has short sharp spines above and lighter-coloured, thick fur below, and has a pointed snout. It feeds on insects and other small animals and defends itself by rolling into a ball with the spines outermost. Species *Erinaceus europaeus.*

Hedge-sparrow, or dunnock, small European accentor, with a grey and brown body and grey-tipped wings. The somewhat similar house-sparrow is no relation. Length: to 14.5cm (5.7in). Species *Prunella modularis.*

Hedin, Sven Anders (1865–1952), Swedish geographer and traveller who explored and mapped much of central Asia. In several expeditions between 1891 and 1908 and in 1927–33 he found ruined cities in Turkistan, and explored central Asia's high plateau complex.

Hedonism, from the Greek *hedonē,* "pleasure", may be of three types: that of the moment, as taught by Aristippus; careful discrimination of pleasure sought, as found in EPICUREANISM; or emphasis on complete and lasting happiness. Basically, hedonism springs from the premise that man seeks pleasure in all he does.

Heem, Jan Davidszoon de (1606–84), Dutch still life and portrait painter, who specialized in sumptuous flower paintings. His many pupils and imitators included his son Cornelis (1631–95).

Hegel, Georg Wilhelm Friedrich (1770–1831), German philosopher. He was professor of philosophy at Heidelberg, and subsequently at Berlin, where he became famous for a romantic, metaphysical system that traced the self-realization of spirit by so-called dialectical "movements" towards perfection. First in the *Phenomenology of Mind* (1807) and then in *Science of Logic* (1812–16) Hegel claimed to express the course of universal reason with his METAPHYSICAL DYNAMISM. *See also* HC2 pp.170, 173.

Hegemony, term used to describe the leadership or dominance of one state over others. It originated with the Greek city-states and derives from a Greek word meaning leader.

Hegira, flight of MOHAMMED from the wrath of the merchants of polytheistic Mecca to Medina (then called Yathrib) in AD 622. The Islamic calendar dates from 1 July of this year, as indicated by the letters AH (*Anno Hegirae*). Thus AD 622 is AH 1.

Heian, period of rule in Japanese history from *c.* 794 to 1185, centred on the city of Heian, now Kyoto. Under the FUJIWARA dynasty the period was marked by great advances in Japanese civilization, above all in poetry and prose, which flourished with the development of a phonetic-based script, encouraging writing in Japanese in addition to the traditionally Chinese-based literature. Some of the most important developments of Japanese BUDDHISM also occurred at this time. *See also* HC1 pp.130–131.

Heidegger, Martin (1889–1976), German philosopher who had a major influence on 20th century EXISTENTIALISM. Publishing his principal work, *Being and Time,* in 1927, he sought the "meaning of being" in terms of individual human thought.

Heidelberg Man, species of man (*Homo erectus*) of the type formerly classified as PITHECANTHROPUS, known from a 300,000 to 400,000-year-old jawbone discovered near Heidelberg, Germany, in 1907. The teeth are human in development, but are set in a massive ape-like, chinless jaw. *See also* MS p.25.

Heidenstam, Verner von (1859–1940), Swedish poet, essayist and novelist. In his essay *Renaissance* (1889) he called for a rebirth of literary fantasy and beauty. His verse, published in three volumes, displayed original imagination. He also wrote several historical novels and was awarded the 1916 Nobel Prize in literature.

Heidi (1880–81), classic children's novel by Johanna Spyri. A story containing much autobiographical material of the author's early life in the Swiss Alps, it champions simple virtues and country life. In its first ten years it ran through 13 editions, and it has remained a favourite with children ever since.

Heifetz, Jascha (1901–), US violinist, *b.* Russia. He made his debut at the age of six and first performed in London in 1920, rapidly establishing a reputation for technical virtuosity. He commissioned a number of new violin works, including William WALTON's *Violin Concerto* (1939).

Heilungkiang (Heilongjiang), province in NE China, making up the N part of the region known as Manchuria, bordered by the USSR; the capital is Harbin (Haerbin). Products: wheat, timber, flax, soya beans, coal, oil, gold. Industries: heavy machinery, electrical equipment. Area: 463,790sq km (179,069sq miles). Pop. (1977 est.) 21,000,000.

Heine, Heinrich (1797–1856), German poet and prose writer. In 1826 he published his satirical *Pictures of Travel* and in 1831 he settled in Paris, writing on German life and letters. The pain and fear he suffered in the last eight years of his life from a paralytic illness are recorded in *Poems 1853 & 1854* and *Romanzero* (1851). *See also* HC2 p.100.

Heinkel, Ernst Heinrich (1888–1958). German aircraft designer who founded the Heinkel works in 1922. Initially he specialized in developing sea-planes, and later light passenger aircraft. He designed the HE-178, the first jet aircraft flown in 1939. Also in that year the HE-176 flew, powered by a liquid-fuel rocket motor. During WWII his aircraft were used extensively by the German Luftwaffe, particularly the versatile twin-engined HE-111 bomber.

Heinz, Henry John, (1844–1919), US food packer and founder of the famous firm that still bears his name. With his brother and cousin he founded the firm of F. & J. Heinz to make and sell pickles and other prepared foods in 1876. The firm became famous for its pre-cooked baked beans, which required only light cooking before eating. Heinz was president of the company from 1905 until 1919.

Heisenberg, Werner Karl (1901–76), German physicist and philosopher, professor at Leipzig and later in Berlin. He is best known for his discovery of the uncertainty, or indeterminacy, principle (1927). He was awarded the 1932 Nobel Prize in physics for his work on QUANTUM MECHANICS.

Heisenberg uncertainty principle, in physics, law th at states that it is impossible to measure exactly the position and momentum of a body at the same time; the product of these two uncertainties is always greater than PLANCK'S CONSTANT. This principle was first stated by Werner HEISENBERG in 1927.

Hejaz (Al-Hijáz), region in NW Saudi Arabia, on the Red Sea coast. The centre of ISLAM, it contains the Muslim holy cities of MECCA (birthplace of MOHAMMED) and MEDINA (the first Islamic capital). Proclaimed an independent kingdom under HUSSEIN IBN ALI (1916), it was taken by IBN SAUD in 1924 and has been part of Saudi Arabia since 1932. Area: 388,500sq km (150,000sq miles). Pop. (1963 est.) 2,000,000.

Hejira. *See* HEGIRA.

Heldenlieder, group of short poems performed in song that celebrated dramatic tales of Germanic heroes. Beginning *c.* AD 375 they were transmitted orally, originally by court poets. *Hildebrandlied* (*c.* 800) is one of only few to survive, and such hero songs provided the subject outline for the 13th century epic *Nibelungenlied.*

Helen, in Greek mythology, the daughter of either LÉDA OR NEMESIS and ZEUS, sister of Pollux and half-sister of CASTOR. She was exceptionally beautiful, and her many suitors pledged themselves to aid whoever she should choose to wed. She married Menelaus, King of Sparta, but was carried off three years later by Paris, Prince of TROY. Her former suitors rallied to the King and the TROJAN WAR began.

Helena, Saint (*c.* 250–330), mother of the Roman Emperor CONSTANTINE I and wife of Constantius Chlorus (Constantine's father), who married another woman when he became emperor as Constantius I. Helena's son was named emperor in 306, and she became an ardent patron of Christianity. Early church historians relate that Helena inspired the building of the Church of the Nativity in Bethlehem. Later tradition claims that she found the Cross on which Christ died.

Helicopter, aircraft that derives support from lift provided by power-driven rotor(s) revolving around a vertical axis or axes. It is capable of vertical take-off and

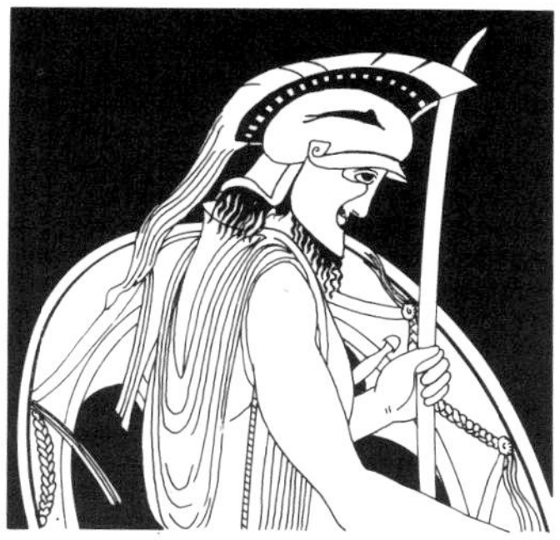

Hector; in his heroic deeds in the Trojan War form a part of Homer's epic, the *Iliad.*

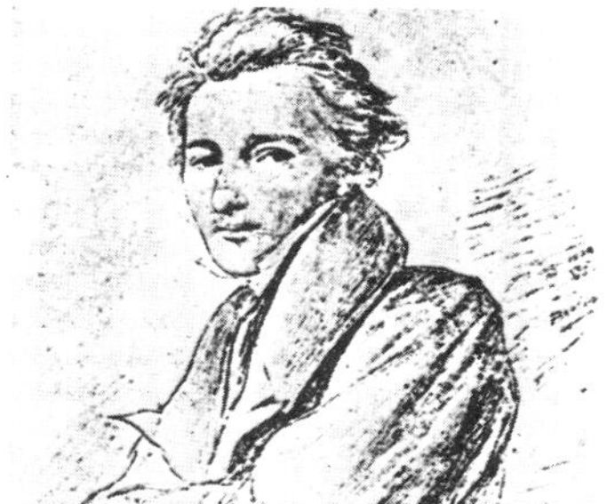

Heinrich Heine; a pastel drawing of the great German poet by Wilhelm Hensel, 1829.

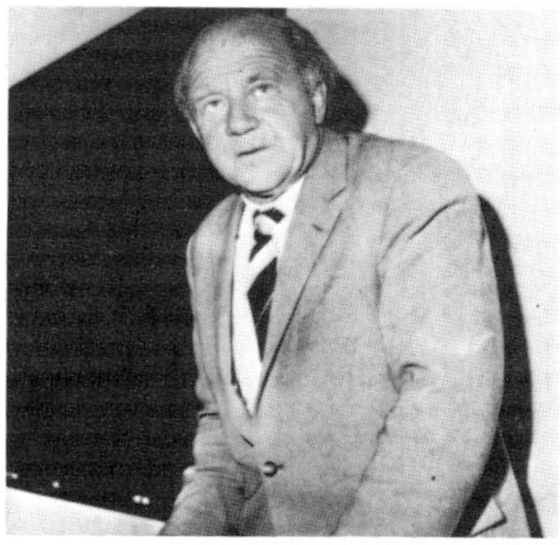

Heisenberg's most influential work is *The Physical Principles of the Quantum Theory.*

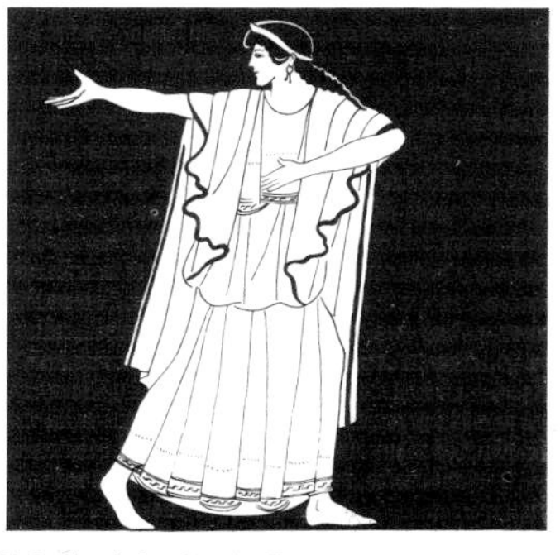

Helen's abduction by Paris caused the Trojan War in which Troy was besieged for ten years.

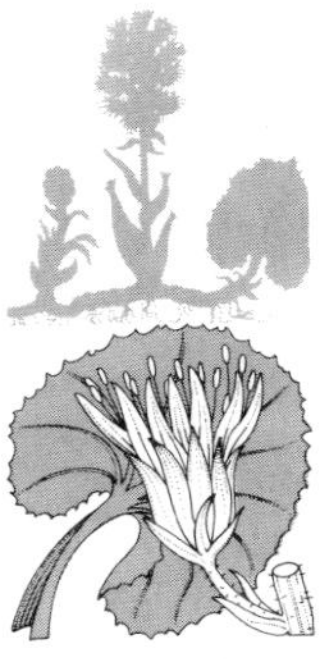

Heliotrope; the name means "turning towards the sun", which these flowers do.

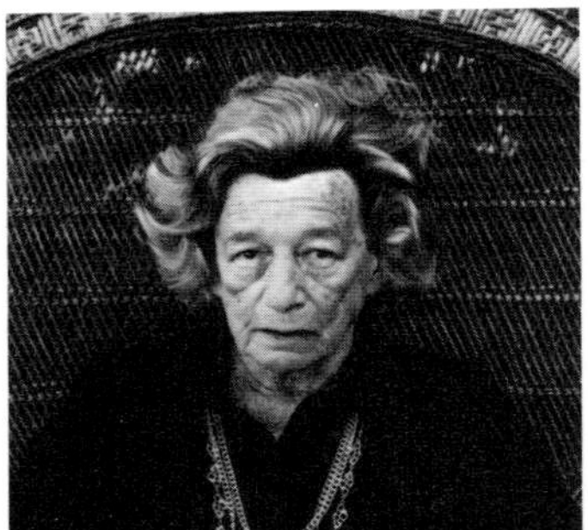

Lillian Hellman is a distinguished screenwriter, adapting many of her own plays.

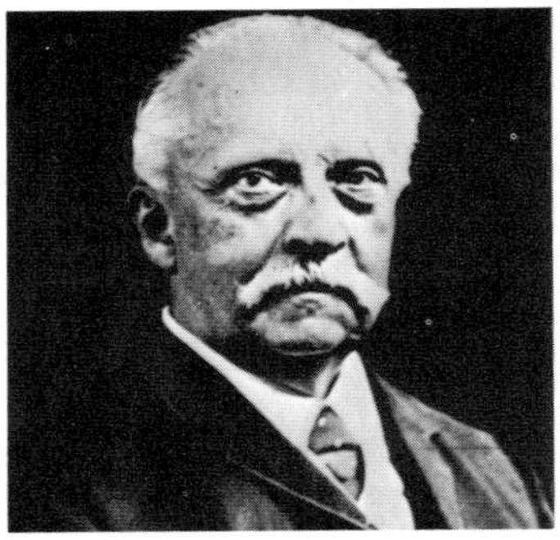

Helmholtz argued that knowledge is derived from experience and not from innate ideas.

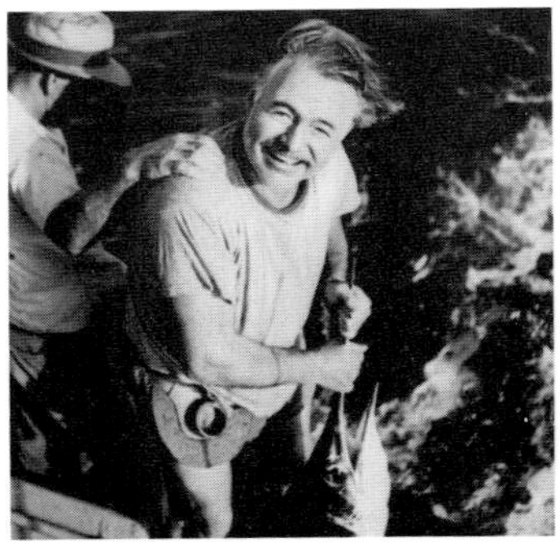

Ernest Hemingway's writings reflect the action and commitment of his own lifestyle.

landing, hovering, and forward, backward and lateral flight. Military applications include rescue, reconnaissance and combat. In civil aviation, it is commonly used for short-haul transport, crop-dusting and pipeline patrolling. *See also* MM p.*111*, 154–155.

Heligoland (Helgoland), island of West Germany in the North Sea, 64km (40 miles) NW of Cuxhaven. It has been under German control since 1890, when Britain exchanged it for Zanzibar. It played a strategic role in WWI and WWII with the installation of German fortifications. It is now a resort and fishing area. Area: 61 hectares (150 acres). Pop. (1971 est.) 2,300.

Heligoland Bight, Battle of (28 August 1914), first naval battle of WWI, off the German island-base of HELIGOLAND, at the mouth of the River Elbe in the North Sea. The British fleet, under Admiral BEATTY, sank three German cruisers and one destroyer.

Heliopolis, ancient city in N lower Egypt, in the Nile delta, 10km (6 miles) NE of Cairo. It was noted as a centre of sun worship for the god RA, from *c.* 1580–1090 BC, and was the site of the obelisks called CLEOPATRA'S NEEDLES. The founding of Alexandria in 332 BC affected the prosperity of the city, although it remained important until the Christian era.

Helios, ancient Greek god who represented the physical presence of the sun in its daily and yearly course, later confused with the Olympian deity APOLLO, whose attributes are spiritual. The offspring of the Titan HYPERION, the god of light, and father of PHAËTON, Helios appears in mythology as the charioteer of the sun driving a four-horse chariot through the sky.

Heliotrope, properly, the name of flowering plants of the BORAGE family, genus *Heliotropium,* which bear clusters of small, white or purple, scented flowers. The name has also been given to plants of the VALERIAN family which bear similar flowers.

Heliozoa, or sun animal, order of fresh water, amoeboid PROTOZOA characterized by a spherical body surrounded by needle-like extensions of protoplasm. Many are encased in a gelatinous capsule or a perforated silica skeleton. Common examples are *Actinophrys sol* and *Actinosphaerium eichhornia.* Length: 0.04–1mm (0.002–0.04in).

Heliport, airport reserved particularly for the use of HELICOPTERS. Because these aircraft are able to land and take-off vertically, a heliport can be quite small, often requiring only the roof of a building or one apron in an airport.

Helium, gaseous non-metallic element (symbol He) of the noble-gas group, discovered in 1868 by Pierre JANSSEN, who noticed its lines in the sun's spectrum. It is the second most common element in the universe. The element was first obtained in 1895 from the mineral clevite; the chief source is from natural gas. Helium is also found in some radioactive minerals and in the Earth's atmosphere (0.0005% by volume). It is a light, colourless noninflammable gas used in balloons, mixed with oxygen to make artificial "air" for divers, in welding, semiconductor preparation, metallurgy and other applications requiring an inert atmosphere. It has the lowest melting point of any element and is extensively used in low-temperature research. The element forms no chemical compounds. Properties: at.no. 2; at.wt. 4.0026; s.g. 0.178 g dm^{-3}; m.p. -272.2°C (-457.96°F) (26 atm.); b.p. -268.9°C (-451.48°F; most common isotope He^4 (100%). *See also* NOBLE GASES.

Helix, curve generated when a point moves over the surface of a cylinder in such a way that the curve it traces is inclined at a constant angle to the axis of the cylinder; as in a coil spring or the thread of a bolt.

Helix, double. *See* DOUBLE HELIX.

Hell, in many religions, place or state of eternal torture and punishment after death for those who have led wicked lives. In modern Christian theology Hell is conceived as the state of eternal separation from God – and consequently from all possibility of happiness – for the unrepentant sinner in consequence of his deliberate rejection of the will of God. Such an exclusion from Heaven is not held to be inconsistent with the idea that God is love, since God does not force response from anyone against his will. See also HADES, HEAVEN, LIMBO, PURGATORY.

Hellbender, large aquatic SALAMANDER of E and central United States. Because it does not completely metamorphose the adults lose their gills, but lack eyelids and retain their larval teeth. The hellbender has a grey or brown, loose, wrinkled skin. Length: up to 76cm (30in). Family Cryptobranchidae; species *Cryptobranchus alleganiensis.*

Hellebore, any of about 20 species of poisonous herbaceous plants that grow in Eurasia. The most familiar is the Christmas rose, *Helleborus niger,* garden hybrids that bear red flowers in mid-winter to early spring. Others have green or white flowers. Family Ranunculaceae.

Hellenes, name by which the ancient Greeks called themselves (after Hellen, grandson of Prometheus). More especially, it means the people who came under the sway of Greek civilization, especially after the conquests of Alexander the Great, and adopted the Greek language and way of life.

Hellenism, culture and ideals of Classical Greece. The term is used especially of the culture of Athens and related cities during the golden age of PERICLES (5th century BC). Hellenism came to symbolize pagan pleasure, freedom, love of life and the pursuit of beauty in the arts. The Hellenic period ended in the 4th century BC, with the conquest of ALEXANDER THE GREAT; it was succeeded by the HELLENISTIC civilization. *See also* HC1 pp.72–73, 78–79.

Hellenistic Age (323–30 BC), E Mediterranean and Near Eastern history between the death of ALEXANDER THE GREAT and the accession of AUGUSTUS. Greek dynasties (the PTOLEMIES and SELEUCIDS) were established in Egypt, Syria and Persia. Alexandria and Pergamum became major cultural and trading centres, adding unique elements to, while preserving much of, Greek culture. Major literary figures were the poets Callimachus and Theocritus and the philosopher Theophrastus. Numerous STOIC and EPICUREAN philosophers flourished. Important works of art included the sculptures the *Venus de Milo* and *The Dying Gaul.* Hellenistic city planning influenced the Romans, who eventually dominated and overshadowed Hellenistic culture. *See also* HC1 pp.78–79.

Heller, Joseph (1923–), US author. His first novel, *Catch-22,* appeared in 1961. Subsequent works include the play *We Bombed in New Haven* (1968) and the novel *Something Happened* (1974).

Hellespont. *See* DARDANELLES.

Hellman, Lillian (1905–), US playwright and author. Her plays, which include *The Children's Hour* (1934) and *The Little Foxes* (1939), deal with psychological and social issues. She has also published three autobiographical volumes: *An Unfinished Woman* (1969), *Pentimento* (1973) and *Scoundrel Time* (1976).

Hello Dolly! (1964), musical play, later a film, with songs by Jerry Harman and book and lyrics by Michael Stewart. Based on a Thornton Wilder play, it tells the story of a matchmaker who seeks a prime catch for herself.

Helmholtz, Hermann Ludwig Ferdinand von (1821–94), German anatomist, physicist and physiologist. He made contributions in ACOUSTICS and OPTICS, expanding Thomas YOUNG's three-colour theory of vision and inventing an OPHTHALMOSCOPE and an ophthalmometer. His experiments on the speed of nerve impulses led to a study of animal heat, which in turn led to work on the principle of conservation of energy.

Helmont, Jan Baptista van (1580–1644), Flemish chemist, physician and physiologist. Although he believed in TRANSMUTATION and that water was the basic substance of the earth, he carried out quantitative experiments and coined the word gas (Greek *chaos*). He also discovered CARBON DIOXIDE, expressed his (mistaken) belief that fermentation caused digestion and nutrition, and proposed the use of alkalis to compensate for excess acidity in the digestive juices.

Héloise. *See* ABÉLARD, PIERRE.

Helots, class of Greeks between free men and slaves, probably indigenous. In SPARTA they outnumbered full Spartan citizens. Often employed as agricultural labourers and as domestic servants, they were owned by the state, which used them as soldiers after the PERSIAN WARS (500–449 BC). They were freed in 369 BC. *See also* HC1 p.79.

Helpmann, Sir Robert (1909–), Australian ballet dancer and actor. He was a principal with the Vic-Wells and Sadler's Wells Ballets (1933–50) and later (1956) co-artistic director and chief choreographer of the Australian Ballet. From 1935 he regularly partnered Margot FONTEYN and appeared in films, including *Henry V* (1944), *The Red Shoes* (1948) and *Tales of Hoffmann* (1950). *See also* HC2 p.*274*.

Helsinki (Helsingfors), seaport and capital of Finland, in the S of the country on the Gulf of Finland. Founded in 1550 by GUSTAVUS I of Sweden, it was rebuilt after a fire in 1808 and became the capital in 1812. It is the commercial and administrative centre of the country. Industries include food processing and textiles. Pop. (1975) 495,287.

Helvellyn, mountain in Cumbria, NW England, between Thirlmere and Ullswater. It has a sharp ridge (Striding Edge) running E. Height: 950m (3,118ft).

Helvetia, old name for the plateau region between the Alps and the Jura Mts, roughly the western part of present-day Switzerland. Its CELTIC inhabitants were called HELVETII by the Romans, who defeated them at Bibracte in 58BC. The name is still used poetically and appears on Swiss postage stamps.

Helvetii, CELTIC people that inhabited S Germany and migrated in the 2nd century BC to the N part of modern Switzerland. In 58BC they invaded SW Gaul but were defeated by CAESAR. They lived thereafter in Belgian Gaul and upper Germany under Roman control until AD 260, when they were subjected by the ALEMANNI.

Helvétius, Claude-Adrien (1715–71), French philosopher whose best-known work, *On the Mind* (1758), attacked the religious basis of morality. The book aroused great opposition, causing him to leave France temporarily. He also claimed that everybody is intellectually equal but some have less desire to learn than others. This belief led him to claim, in *De l'homme* (1772), that all human problems could be solved with education.

Hematite. *See* HAEMATITE.

Hemery, David (1944–), British hurdler who, at the 1968 Olympic Games, won the 400m hurdles and beat the world record of 48.8 seconds by 0.7 seconds. In 1972 he was third in this event and won a silver medal in the 4×400m. He won Commonwealth golds in 1966 (120 yards hurdles) and 1970 (110m hurdles).

Hemichordata, subphylum of the phylum CHORDATA that includes two groups of primitive marine animals, the Enteropneusta or Balanoglossida and the Pterobranchia. Most of the animals do not have common names. Characteristics include a short NOTOCHORD, or primitive backbone; partially or completely solid dorsal nerve chord; and may have gill slits. *See also* NW pp.73, 122.

Hemingway, Ernest Miller (1899–1961), US author. After WWI he became a correspondent in Paris for the Toronto *Star* and was strongly influenced by the work of Gertrude STEIN. With the novel *The Sun Also Rises* (1926) he established his reputation as a writer. This book also established him as the spokesman for the Lost Generation. Later works by Hemingway include *A Farewell to Arms* (1929), *To Have and Have Not* (1937) and *For Whom the Bell Tolls* (1940).

Hemiplegia, paralysis of one side of the body. It can be caused by brain injury, and may be accompanied by spasticity.

Hemiptera, or Heteroptera, order of

INSECTS, made up of true BUGS, found worldwide. They may be winged or wingless and all have three life stages – egg, nymph and adult. The piercing and sucking mouthparts are used to suck liquids from either plants or animals. Length: 1.7–100mm (0.04–4in). *See also* NW pp.106, 114, *115*.

Hemlock, poisonous plant found throughout the world. It has a long taproot, lacy foliage and flat clusters of white flowers. The leaf stalks have conspicuous purple spots. Family Umbelliferae; species *Conium maculatum*.

Hemlock, evergreen tree native to the USA and Asia. Its leaves are long flat blunt-ended needles; the tree bears small pendulous cones and drooping branches. Its bark is used to make tannin and the soft, light timber is used in construction work. Height: to 60m (196ft). Family Pinaceae.

Hémon, Louis (1880–1913), Canadian novelist. He worked as a farm labourer in N Quebec and that area provides the setting for his famous novel, published posthumously, *Maria Chapdelaine* (1915).

Hemp. *See* HASHISH.

Hempel, Carl Gustav (1905–), US philosopher. Trained in physics and mathematics, his LOGICAL POSITIVISM was influenced by Moritz SCHLICK and Rudolph CARNAP. His works include *Fundamentals of Concept Formation in Empirical Science* (1952) and *Philosophy of Natural Science* (1966).

Hen. *See* POULTRY.

Henbane, deadly poisonous plant that grows in the Mediterranean region and W Africa. It contains a powerful ALKALOID that affects the nervous system. The leaves are coarsely toothed and the stems are hairy. The bell-shaped yellow flowers have purple veins and produce black seeds. Height: to 74cm (29in). Family Solanaceae; species *Hyoscyamus niger*. *See also* MS p.*117*.

Hench, Philip Showalter (1896–1965), US physician. He shared the 1950 Nobel Prize in physiology and medicine with Edward KENDALL and Tadeus REICHSTEIN for their pioneering work on hormones of the adrenal cortex, which led to discovery of the treatment of rheumatoid arthritis with CORTISONE.

Hencke, Karl Ludwig (1793–1866), German astronomer who found the fifth and sixth minor planets to be discovered, Astraea in 1830 and Hebe in 1847. Before this, professional astronomers had given up the search for further asteroids.

Henderson, Arthur (1863–1935), British labour leader, one of the chief organizers of the British Labour Party. He was the first Labour politician to hold office in the WWI cabinets (1915–17). He became Home Secretary in the first Labour government in 1924, but grew more and more internationalist in outlook. He served as Foreign Secretary (1929–31) and was awarded the Nobel Peace Prize in 1934. *See also* HC2 p.211.

Henderson, Fletcher (1898–1952), US jazz composer and arranger. Henderson was the first man to write jazz arrangements for more than a small group, and as such had great influence during the 1920s and 1930s.

Henie, Sonja (1913–69), Norwegian figure skater. Olympic chnmpion (1928, 1932, 1936) and world amateur champion (1927–36), she popularized figure skating in the USA through her Hollywood Ice Revues and her starring roles in several films.

Henley Royal Regatta, oldest rowing regatta in the world, begun in 1839 at the prompting of merchants in Henley-on-Thames. The course measures 2.1km (1.3 miles). It is equally famous as a social event and for the quality of rowing for such trophies as the Grand Challenge Cup, Diamond Challenge Sculls, Silver Goblets and Stewards' Challenge Cup.

Henna, also called Egyptian privet, a small shrub native to the Middle East and N Africa and cultivated in Egypt. Since ancient times people have extracted a red-brown dye from the leaves and used it to colour hair and to make patterns on the skin. Family Lythraceae; species *Lawsonia inermis*. *See also* MM p.*247*.

Hennepin, Louis (1640–*c*.1701), Belgian explorer and Franciscan missionary. He sailed to Canada in 1675 with Cavelier de LA SALLE. After doing missionary work among the Indians Hennepin was directed to explore the upper Mississippi. In an account of his trips, he claimed to have explored the river to its mouth, but this false claim discredited him.

Henri, Robert (1865–1929), US painter, a member of the ASHCAN SCHOOL, best known for his realistic urban street scenes.

Henrietta Maria (1609–69), Queen consort of CHARLES I of England, daughter of HENRY IV of France. She married Charles in 1625. Her Catholicism and negotiations with the Pope and the French government increased Parliament's hostility to Charles. After 1644 she lived in France, except for a brief return to England after the Restoration. *See also* HC1 p.*287*.

Henry, the name of seven German kings, all of whom except Henry I were elected emperors of the HOLY ROMAN EMPIRE. Henry II (*r*.1002–24), who was canonized in the mid-12th century, maintained order in Germany, subdued the LOMBARDS and fought constantly against the Poles. Henry III (*r*.1039–56) succeeded his father, Conrad II. Imperial power reached its zenith during his reign. He made the Duke of Bohemia and, for a time, the King of Hungary, vassals of the empire, contained revolts in Germany and effected the election of four popes. He supported reforms in the Roman Catholic Church by denouncing the marriages of priests and the buying of church offices. Henry IV (*r*.1056–1106) became embroiled in controversy with the popes over the lay investiture of clerics. He opposed Pope GREGORY VII but rebellion in the German church made him seek papal absolution at Canossa in 1077. Thereafter, however, he resumed the struggle, setting up the antipope CLEMENT III. In 1104 his son Henry joined a rebellion against him and deposed him. *See also* HC1 pp.160, 186. Henry V (*r*.1099–25), who succeeded him, inherited the quarrel with the papacy over investiture. After a prolonged and violent struggle, he reached a compromise with Pope CALIXTUS II in the Concordat of Worms in 1122. *See also* HC1 p.*161*. Henry VI (*r*.1169–97) married Constance I of Sicily in 1186 and much of his reign was devoted to securing that inheritance. He was finally crowned King of Sicily in 1194. A rebellion in Germany was quelled when the rebels' ally, RICHARD I of England, became his prisoner. *See also* HC1 p.161. Henry VII (*r*.1308–13) acquired Bohemia for his family by marrying his son John to Elizabeth of Bohemia in 1310. Henry revived imperial ambitions in Italy but, although crowned King of the Lombards (1311), failed to keep authority there.

Henry I (1068–1135), King of England, younger son of William I. On William II's death, he was crowned king in 1100. His elder brother Robert, Duke of Normandy, claimed his throne, but Henry defeated him and captured all his lands at Tinchebrai in 1106. Henry, who married an Anglo-Saxon princess reformed the judicial and fiscal administration, but his reign was troubled by unruly barons, wars with the French and Welsh, and the death in 1120 of his heir, William. *See also* HC1 pp.168, *168*, 178, *179*.

Henry II (1133–89), King of England, son of Geoffrey Plantagenet and Matilda, daughter of Henry I. He inherited the Angevin lands, obtained Aquitaine by marrying Eleanor in 1152, and succeeded to the throne in 1154. He reformed the judicial, monetary and military systems, and set up a system of peripatetic royal justices. His attempt in 1164 to bring church courts under secular control through the Constitutions of Clarendon failed. By the Treaty of Montmirail (1169) Henry secured France's sanction for his sons' succession to his territories and Prince Henry was crowned heir in 1170. After the murder of Thomas à BECKET in 1170, Henry's life was beset by trouble with the Church, revolts in Ireland and Normandy, and a continual struggle with his own sons. *See also* HC1 pp.168–169, 178, 186, 194.

Henry III (1207–72), King of England, son of JOHN, whom he succeeded when a minor in 1216. He married Eleanor of Provence in 1236. His favouritism of foreigners led to resentment among his barons, who revolted against him and refused to finance his overseas campaigns. Forced to make substantial constitutional concessions, the PROVISIONS OF OXFORD, by the so-called "MAD PARLIAMENT" in 1258, he enlisted French and papal aid but the barons under Simon de MONTFORT defeated him at Lewes in 1264. His son Edward's victory at Evesham (1265), however, enabled him to retain executive power and grant reforms. *See also* HC1 pp.*168*, 179, 210.

Henry IV (*c*.1367–1413), King of England, son of John of Gaunt and cousin of RICHARD II. He was banished by Richard in 1398, but returned to claim his father's estates in 1399 and, finding Richard campaigning in Ireland and deserted by many of his former supporters in England, claimed the throne for himself. Henry's reign was disturbed by Welsh and Scottish wars, attempts on his life and rebellions (chiefly fomented by the PERCY family). *See also* HC1 pp.179, 242.

Henry V (1387–1422), King of England, eldest son of Henry IV. After fighting on his father's behalf at Shrewsbury in 1403, in Wales and in Scotland, he succeeded him in 1413 and immediately demanded the restoration of territories formerly ceded to France. Invading France, he captured Harfleur and won the decisive victory at Agincourt in 1415. Further military and diplomatic success led to his adoption as the French king's heir by the Treaty of TROYES in 1420. *See also* HC1 pp.*212*, 213, 242.

Henry VI (1421–71), King of England who succeeded his father, Henry V, in 1422 at the age of 8 months. He came of age in 1437, after a sheltered youth spent in study. He had no capacity for government and his reign was characterized not only by military and diplomatic disasters in France (by 1453 nothing remained of the Crown's former French possession except Calais) but also by civil war in England, where his feebleness permitted the Yorkist and Lancastrian factions to instigate the Wars of the ROSES. Deposed by the Yorkists (1461), he was restored in 1470 but was again deposed almost immediately and then murdered. *See also* HC1 pp.242–*243*.

Henry VII (1457–1509), King of England, founder of the TUDOR dynasty. Having come to the throne by killing RICHARD III at Bosworth in 1485, Henry united the warring factions by marrying the Yorkist heiress, Elizabeth. His financial acumen restored England's fortunes after the devastation of civil war and gave the monarchy considerable independence of action. He concluded various advantageous foreign treaties, such as the Treaty of Etaples in 1492, and took effective action against pretenders to his throne, thereby securing the future of his dynasty. *See also* HC1 pp.*185*, *211*, 240, 242, 266.

Henry VIII (1491–1547), King of England who succeeded his father, Henry VII, in 1509. In 1513 victories over the French (at Tomnai) and the Scots (at Flodden) re-established England as a European power, a position maintained by the diplomacy of Cardinal WOLSEY. He, however, was dismissed in 1529 after Henry's decision to divorce Catherine of Aragon (who had not borne a male heir) in favour of Anne Boleyn led to conflict and his eventual excommunication. With the help of Thomas CRANMER, Archbishop of Canterbury from 1533, Henry compelled the clergy to acknowledge him as supreme head of the Church, and executed those, such as Sir Thomas MORE, who protested. Under Thomas CROMWELL's direction he initiated other anti-ecclesiastical legislation in the 1530s, including transferring church revenues to the Crown, and appropriating monastic property. From his six marriages (Catherine of Aragon, Anne Boleyn, Jane

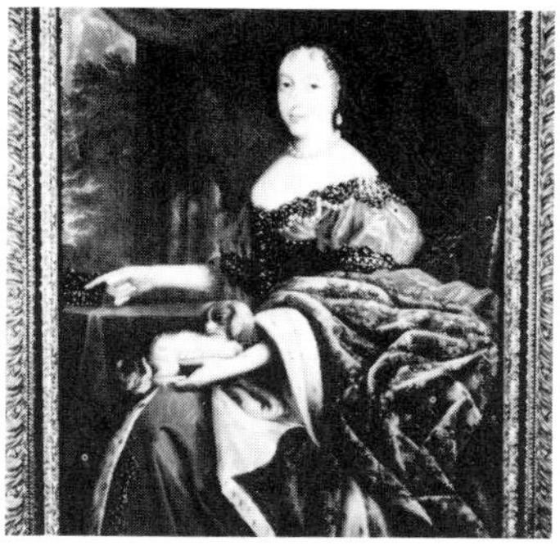

Henrietta Maria was indefatigable in raising money for Charles I during the Civil War.

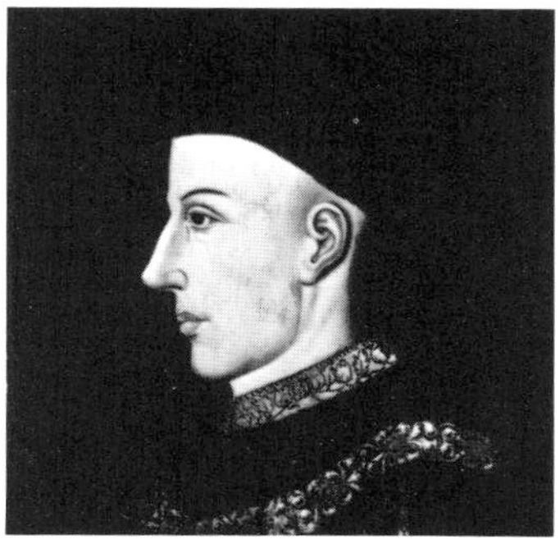

Henry V, had he lived a few months longer, would have succeeded to the French throne.

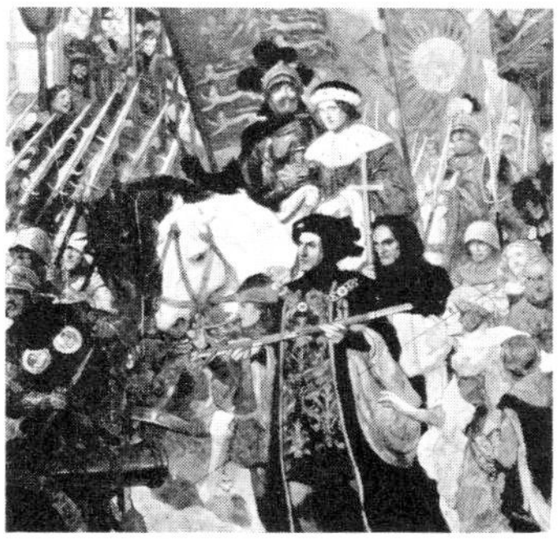

Henry VI, the last Lancastrian king, being taken a virtual prisoner at the Battle of Barnet.

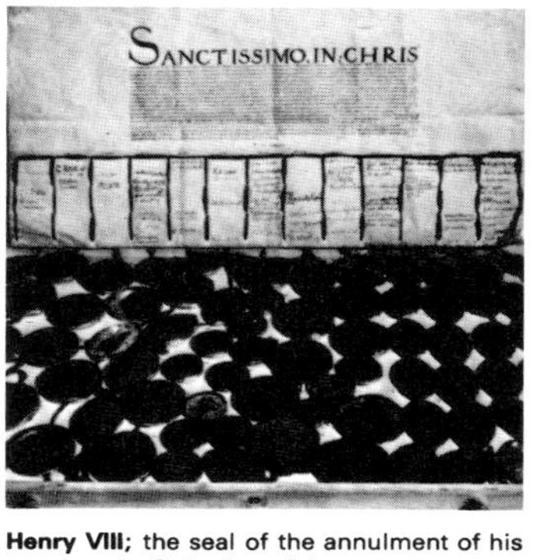

Henry VIII; the seal of the annulment of his marriage to Catherine of Aragon.

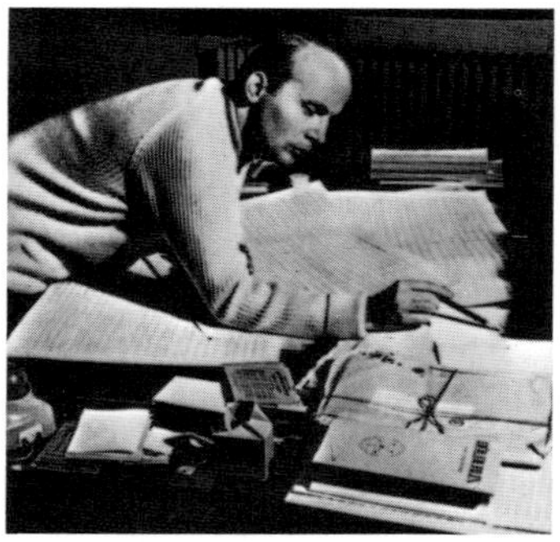

Hans Werner Henze's work has had a great influence on the ballet in post-war Germany.

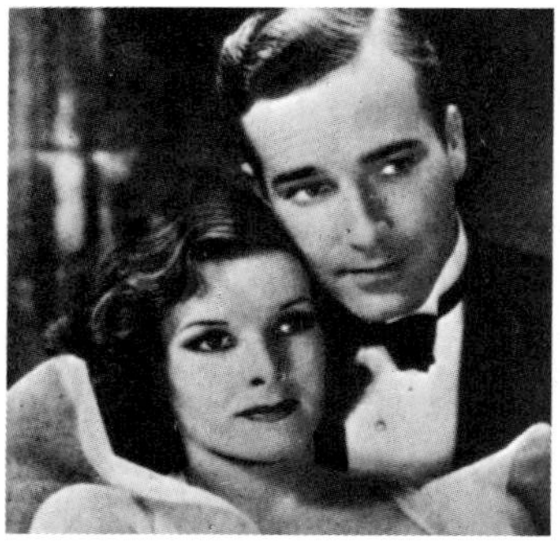

Katherine Hepburn; a scene from one of her great successes, *A Bill of Divorcement* (1932).

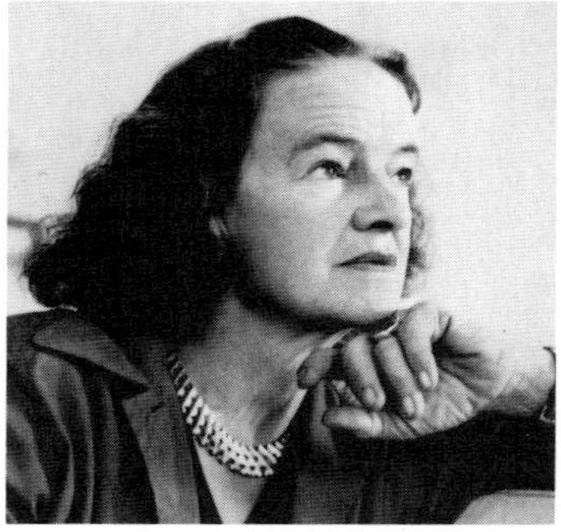

Barbara Hepworth's work is represented in major galleries in Europe and the USA.

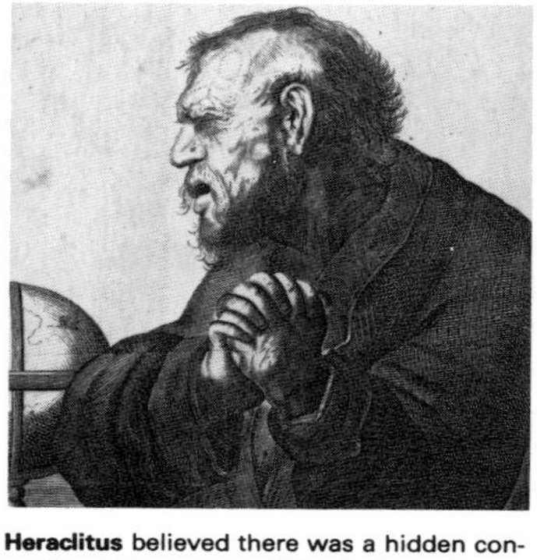

Heraclitus believed there was a hidden connection between everything in the universe.

Seymour, Anne of Cleves, Catherine Howard and Catherine Parr), he had one son and two daughters. *See also* HC1 pp.*240–241*, 266–267, 269–271.

Henry, French *Henri*, the name of four kings of France. The reign of Henry I (1008–60), who ruled from 1031 to 1060, was characterized by the king's struggle to maintain central authority. Henry's younger brother, Robert, claimed the throne and was supported by their mother, Constance of Provence. In the ensuing civil war, Henry was forced to cede Burgundy to Robert. Henry II (1519–59), reigned 1547–59, was the second son of Francis I; he became heir to the throne upon his brother's death. He married Catherine de Medici. As king, Henry continued his father's policies of strengthening the monarchy and effecting administrative reform. A militant Catholic, he initiated harsh, systematic repression of Protestants. Henry III (1551–89), reigned 1574–89, was the last of the Valois dynasty. As Duke of Anjou he defeated the HUGUENOTS in 1569 in the Wars of Religion. With his mother, Catherine de Medici, he instigated the Massacre of Saint BARTHOLOMEWS DAY (1572). Elected King of Poland in 1573, he returned to France to assume the throne on the death of his brother, Charles IX, in 1574. He made peace with the Huguenots in 1576, but when his younger brother Francis died in 1584 and the Protestant Henry of Navarre became heir to the throne, he renewed the wars. Henry IV, or Henry of Navarre (1553–1610), King of Navarre (as Henry III, 1572–1610) was the first Bourbon King of France (1589–1610). Raised as a Huguenot, he nevertheless married Margaret of Valois, the Roman Catholic sister of the French king Charles IX in 1572. He escaped the Massacre of Saint Bartholomew's Day (1572) by agreeing to renounce his Protestantism, and was kept as a virtual prisoner at the French court until he escaped in 1576, to join the Huguenot forces. He became heir to the French throne in 1584 on the death of the younger brother of Henry III. Henry III was persuaded by Henry de Guise, leader of the Catholic League, to deny Henry of Navarre the succession. The War of the Three Henrys resulted. Henry of Navarre defeated the king's forces in 1587 and was reconciled with him after the Catholic League expelled the king from Paris (1588). Henry III was assassinated in 1589, but Henry of Navarre did not gain Paris until after he renounced his Protestantism in 1594. During his reign he reconciled the Huguenots by the Edict of NANTES and laid the foundations of French ABSOLUTISM, before his assassination by a religious fanatic. *See also* HC1 p.*273*.

Henry IV, play in two five-act parts by William SHAKESPEARE. Both parts were first performed in *c.* 1597. *See also* HC1 p.*285*.

Henry V, historical play in five acts by William SHAKESPEARE. Like his other historical plays, the major source was Holinshed's *Chronicles*. *See also* HC1 pp.*284–285*.

Henry VI, historical play in three parts by William SHAKESPEARE. Probably his first play, all the parts were performed *c.* 1590. *See also* HC1 pp.284, *285*.

Henry VIII, five-act play by William SHAKESPEARE, probably written in collaboration with John FLETCHER. Its first performance was in *c.* 1613. *See also* HC1 p.*285*.

Henry, Joseph (1797–1878), US physicist whose contribution to ELECTROMAGNETISM was essential for the development of the commercial telegraph. His work on INDUCTION led to the development of the TRANSFORMER. In 1850 he introduced a system of using the telegraph for sending weather reports, making possible the establishment of the US Weather Bureau. The unit of inductance is named after him.

Henry, O. (1862–1910), a pen-name of William Sydney Porter, a popular US short story writer. His typical surprise ending gave rise to the term the "O. Henry ending". In 1901 he moved to New York City, the scene of much of his fiction.

Henry, Patrick (1736–99), US patriot, orator and lawyer. Elected to the Virginia House of Burgesses (1765–75), he denounced the Stamp Act. He was a member of the Continental Congress (1774–76) and became convinced that war with Britain was inevitable. It was then he delivered his "Give me liberty or give me death" speech that established his reputation as a gifted orator.

Henry of Navarre. *See* HENRY IV (of France).

Henry, William (1774–1836), British chemist and physician whose most important work was his study of the solubility of gases in water under varying temperatures and pressures. This led to his formulation in 1803 of HENRY'S LAW.

Henry's law, principle in physical chemistry which states that the weight of a gas dissolved in a fixed quantity of a liquid is directly proportional to the pressure of the gas on the liquid, at constant temperature. Thus the more a gas is compressed, the more it is absorbed in a liquid.

Henry the Lion (1129–95), Duke of Saxony (1142–80) and of Bavaria (1156–80). He married MATILDA, daughter of HENRY II of England, in 1168. He failed to extend his power beyond the River Elbe.

Henry the Navigator (1394–1460), Portuguese prince and patron of explorers. He was the third son of JOHN I and the uncle of ALFONSO V. In 1419 he established an observatory at Sagres and a school for the study of geography and navigation. He made no exploratory journeys himself, but sponsored numerous Portuguese navigators who made many important discoveries in West Africa that formed the basis for the later Portuguese empire.

Henze, Hans Werner (1926–), German composer. Influenced by TWELVE-TONE MUSIC, he has composed in almost every medium and is known especially for his operas, which include *Boulevard Solitude* (1952), *Elegy for Young Lovers* (1961) and *The Bassarids* (1965). He also composed six symphonies. *See also* HC2 p.*271*.

Hepatitis, inflammation of the liver. It is caused by one of two viruses and takes the form of infectious hepatitis, which is usually spread through faecal contamination, or serum hepatitis, which is spread by blood transfusion or poorly sterilized hypodermic needles. Symptons include lethargy, nausea, fever and perhaps jaundice. Recovery is usually spontaneous although observation in hospital is usual to guard against complications and to provide relief of symptoms.

Hepburn, Audrey (1929–), actress born in Belgium who achieved success in the US. Real name Edda Hepburn van Heemstra. Trained as a dancer, her initial popular success was achieved in ingénue, gamine roles such as *Roman Holiday* (1953), *Sabrina* (1954) and *Funny Face* (1957). After these, her performances matured with starring roles in *My Fair Lady* (1964), *Two for the Road* (1967) and, after a prolonged absence from the screen, that of the ageing romantic heroine in *Robin and Marian* (1976).

Hepburn, Katharine (1909–), US stage and film actress who is famed for her intelligence, wit and noble bearing. She made nine films with Spencer TRACY, including *Adam's Rib* (1949), *Pat and Mike* (1952) and *Guess Who's Coming to Dinner* (1967). Her dramatic films include *The African Queen* (1951), with Humphrey BOGART, *Long Day's Journey into Night* (1962) and *The Lion in Winter* (1968).

Hephaestus, ancient Greek god of fire and crafts. Son of ZEUS and HERA, he is equivalent to the Roman VULCAN. Blacksmith and armourer to the Olympian gods, with a forge under Etna (or Stromboli), he is depicted as crippled and uncouth but clever and able enough to create PANDORA, the first woman, and to wed APHRODITE.

Hepplewhite, George (*d.* 1786), British furniture designer and cabinetmaker. His furniture, light in scale and usually with tapered legs, combined pale woods with mahogany, often in the form of inlay. Hepplewhite was best known for his shield-back chairs.

Heptane, any chemical compound having the formula C_7H_{16}. Such compounds are saturated, or paraffin, hydrocarbons. Normal heptane or *n*-heptane is used in car fuels to determine OCTANE ratings.

Heptarchy, generally recognized term for the seven Anglo-Saxon kingdoms from the 5th century to the Danish invasions of the 9th, including Mercia, Northumbria, Sussex, Kent, East Anglia, Essex and Wessex. *See also* HC1 pp.154–155, 166–167.

Hepworth, Dame Barbara (1903–76), English sculptor. Her carvings, in wood or stone, have a poetic quality in the open and closed form of the abstract works. Much of her later work is in bronze. *See also* HC2 pp.280–281.

Hera, in Greek mythology, the daughter of Cronus and Rhea, queen of the Olympian gods, sister and wife of ZEUS. Depicted with crown and sceptre, she was worshipped as patron of ARGOS and SAMOS. In myths she appears as a jealous scold who persecuted her rivals but helped heroes such as JASON and ACHILLES.

Heraclitus (536–470 BC), pre-Socratic philosopher. He maintained that all things are constantly changing, even the universe as a whole: since only change is real, the orderliness of successive changes, or the world's destiny, is all that remains the same.

Heraclius (*c.* 575–641), Byzantine emperor (*r.* 610–41). One of Byzantium's greatest rulers, he came to power at a time of economic, political and military crisis. Byzantium's enemies had overrun vast territories, but, under Heraclius, far-reaching reforms in the army and administration led to an improvement in the internal situation and to Byzantium's defeat of the Persians (622–628).

Herakles. *See* HERCULES.

Heraklion. *See* IRÁKLION.

Heralds' College. *See* COLLEGE OF HERALDS.

Herāt, city and provincial capital in w Afghanistan, on the Hari Rud. Originally the ancient city of Aria, Herāt served as TAMERLANE's capital in the fifteenth century. Its present industries include textile weaving. Pop. 62,000.

Herb, seed-bearing plant, usually with a soft stem that withers away after one growing season. Most herbs are flowering plants, or ANGIOSPERMS. The term is also applied to any plant used as a flavouring, seasoning or medicine, such as THYME, SAGE and MINT. *See also* PE pp.212–213.

Herbart, Johann Friedrich (1776–1841), German philosopher who maintained a doctrine of "reals" in permanent and objective entities in nature. In his view METAPHYSICS and psychology are unified, and ideas act in much the same way as do forces in physics. His educational doctrine, Herbartianism, became influential in the USA until superseded by the ideas of John DEWEY.

Herbert, Sir Alan (Patrick) (1890–1971), British humorist, novelist and librettist. He was a barrister and was member of parliament for Oxford University from 1935 until university seats were abolished in 1950. His novel *Holy Deadlock* (1934) led to a reform of the British marriage laws. He also campaigned for an improvement in the legal rights of authors.

Herbert, George (1593–1633), English poet. Educated at Cambridge University, he was disappointed in his hopes of a court appointment. After four years in quiet retirement he took full orders in 1630 and became vicar of Bemerton in Wiltshire until his death. His verse, remarkable for its gentle tone, was collected and published after his death as *The Temple*.

Herbert, George Edward Stanhope Molyneux, 5th Earl of Carnarvon (1866–1923), British archaeologist. He joined Howard CARTER in excavating in Egypt in 1907, and together they discovered the tomb of TUTANKHAMEN in 1922.

Herb Gerard. *See* GROUND ELDER.

Herbicide, chemical substance used to kill weeds and other unwanted plants. There are two kinds: selective herbicides, such as 2,4-D, 2,4,5-T and MCPA, which kill the weeds growing with crops, leaving the crops unharmed; and non-selective herbicides, such as sodium arsenite, which kill all the vegetation with which they come into contact.

Herbivore, animal that feeds solely on plants. The term is most often applied to mammals and especially to the ungulates or hoofed mammals. The herbivores are characterized by broad molars and blunt-edged teeth, which they employ in pulling, cutting and grinding their food. Their digestive systems are adapted to the assimilation of cellulose. Cows, for instance, regurgitate their food and have some seven stomachs for this purpose. Cattle, sheep, deer, horses and goats are known as grazers inasmuch as they feed from the ground, cutting the grass, whereas giraffes and elephants tear leaves from bushes and trees.

Herb robert, common weed of the geranium family that grows in temperate regions. It has a strong unpleasant smell, pink flowers and deeply-lobed leaves. Family Geraniaceae; species *Geranium robertianum.*

Hercegovina, Herzegovina. *See* BOSNIA-HERCEGOVINA.

Herculaneum, ancient city in Italy, on the site of modern Resina. Devastated in AD 62 by an earthquake, it was buried in AD 79 with POMPEII by the eruption of Mt VESUVIUS. Archaeological excavations begun in 1709 have unearthed a Villa of the Papyri, which contained a library.

Hercules, Greek hero, renowned for his valour and strength. He spent 12 years at the court of King Eurystheus, where he performed his 12 famous labours: he killed the Nemean lion and the HYDRA; caught the Erymanthian boar and the Cerynean hind; drove away the Stymphalian birds; cleaned the Augean stables; caught the Cretan bull and Diomed's horses; stole the girdle of HIPPOLYTE; killed Geryon; captured CEREBUS; stole the golden apples of Hesperides. *See also* MS p.209.

Herder, Johann Gottfried von (1744–1803), Prussian philosopher and cultural historian. He believed that human society is an organic and secular totality that develops as the result of an historical process. His claim that a nation and its language define an essential cultural unity anticipated "nationalist" sentiment. Herder was also a founder of German Romanticism and an opponent of Immanuel KANT. He wrote *Ideas on the Philosophy of History of Humanity* (1784–91), which applies the concept of history to all areas of human culture. *See also* HC2 pp.72, *72*, 171, *172*, 173.

Heredia, town in central Costa Rica. Founded in 1571, it is noted for its colonial architecture. It is situated on the country's central plateau and is a centre of the coffee and livestock industries. Pop. (1970) 24,021.

Hereditary disorders, abnormal conditions of the body or mind transmitted genetically. They are clearly distinguished from CONGENITAL DISORDERS, which are acquired in the womb or at birth. Their effects are various, depending on which parts of the body they affect. Their frequency of occurrence, however, depends mainly on whether they are handed down as recessive genes or as dominant genes. An example of the first is the disease SICKLE-CELL ANAEMIA, which is much more severe if inherited from both parents. An example of the second is ACHONDROPLASIA, or abnormal shortness of the arms and legs; the gene from only one parent is needed to cause this condition.

Heredity, transmission of physical and other characteristics from one generation of plants or animals to another. These characteristics make up an organism and make it different from others. The combination of characteristics may be specific to the individual, such as blue eyes and blond hair, or it may be typical of the type of organism, such as simply having external ears. These features are passed on by genetic codes from parent to offspring. The first reliable studies of heredity were done during the 19th century by Gregor MENDEL. *See also* NW pp.30–31.

Hereford, widespread breed of BEEF CATTLE. Originally from Herefordshire, there are now numerous herds in various parts of the world, particularly in the USA and Argentina. Herefords gain weight quickly on comparatively little food and adapt well to semi-arid conditions. The animals are red-brown with white faces, and are usually horned. The polled Hereford is a separate breed, without horns. *See also* PE pp.226, *226*, 232.

Hereford and Worcester, county in W central England formed in 1974 from the former counties of Herefordshire and Worcestershire. Area 3,926sq km (1,516sq miles).

Herero, Negroid people of Namibia (South West Africa). By tradition, the Herero are nomadic pastoralists who practise ancestor worship, although European influence and Christianity are now widespread. Both matrilineal and patrilineal descent exist in a society governed by localized autonomous units. Many of the Herero died during a revolt against German rule (1903–07).

Heresy, denial of or deviation from orthodox religious dogma. The concept is found in most organized religions with a rigid dogmatic system. The early Christian Church fought against heresies such as ARIANISM and NESTORIANISM. In the Middle Ages the INQUISITION was established to fight heresy. After the REFORMATION the Roman Catholic Church described Protestants as heretics because of their denial of many papally defined dogmas, while Protestants applied the same term to those who denied their interpretation of the major scriptural doctrines. Persecutions for heresy were common in most parts of Christendom until relatively recent times. In modern usage the term heresy is also applied to deviation from the "orthodox dogmas" of a secular ideology such as Marxism.

Hereward the Wake (*fl.* 11th century), leader of Anglo-Saxon resistance to the NORMAN CONQUEST of WILLIAM I. With the aid of a Danish fleet he sacked Peterborough in 1070 and consolidated his forces on the Isle of Ely. William captured Ely in 1071. *See also* HC1 p.*167.*

Heriot, Anglo-Saxon and FEUDAL death duty. Originally the return of horses and armour (the word "heriot" derived from the Anglo-Saxon for military clothing) lent by a lord to his arms-bearing tenants, it more commonly became a payment in the form of livestock by 1066. In the 12th century heriots became part of the more general concept of feudal reliefs.

Heriot, George, (1563–1624), Scottish goldsmith and philanthropist who was goldsmith to James I in London, where he amassed a fortune and lent the Queen as much as £18,000 at a time. He was the original of "Geordie" in Walter Scott's *Fortunes of Nigel* and left a bequest for founding Heriot's Hospital in Edinburgh.

Herland, Hugh (*fl.* 1350–1405), English master carpenter whose masterpiece was the wooden roof of WESTMINSTER HALL, London (1397–99), the earliest dated example of a HAMMERBEAM ROOF.

Hermaphrodite, organism that has both male and female sexual characteristics. Hermaphroditic plants are called monoecious. Most normally hermaphrodite animals are invertebrates, such as the PLANARIAN, EARTHWORM and SNAIL, and are sessile or slow-moving. They reproduce by the mating of two individuals which exchange sperm, or when one individual's ovum (egg) and sperm unite. Hermaphroditism also occurs as a rare abnormality in higher animals, including humans.

Hermes, in Greek mythology, god identified with the Roman MERCURY, represented with winged hat and sandals and carrying a golden wand. Hermes was the messenger of the gods and patron of travellers and commerce. He conducted the souls of the dead to HADES.

Hermit crab, small, common crab-like CRUSTACEAN found in tidal pools and shallow water worldwide. It uses sea-snail shells to protect its soft abdomen, using larger shells as it grows. Some forms are terrestrial and do not use shells as adults. Family Paguridae. *See also* NW p.*105.*

Hernández, José (1834–86), Argentine poet. His narrative poem *Martín Fierro* is Argentina's national epic and the oustanding poem of the gaucho genre. It was published in two parts: *Departure* (1872) and *Return* (1879).

Hernia, protrusion of an organ, or part of an organ, through its enclosing wall or through connective tissue. Common types of hernias are protrusion of an intestinal loop through the umbilicus (umbilical hernia) or inguinal canal of the groin (inguinal hernia), or protrusion of part of the stomach or oesophagus into the chest cavity through the opening (hiatus) of the oesophagus into the diaphragm (hiatus hernia). *See also* MS p.*95.*

Herod Antipas (21 BC–AD 39), tetrach of Galilee and Petraea (4 BC–AD 39), son of HEROD THE GREAT. He had John the Baptist beheaded at the instigation of his wife Herodias and his step-daughter Salome. He refused to intervene in the trial of Christ, leaving His fate to the Roman procurator Pontius PILATE. The Emperor Caligula banished him to Gaul in AD 39.

Herod Agrippa I (*c.* 10 BC–AD 44), grandson of HEROD THE GREAT and King of Judaea (AD 41–44). He became king as a reward for helping to gain the Roman emperorship for CLAUDIUS. He was a zealous opponent of Christianity.

Herod Agrippa II (AD27–*c.* 93), son of HEROD AGRIPPA I and last of the rulers of the Herodian dynasty. He was King of Chalcis from AD 50 and tetrarch of NE Judaea from AD 53. He tried, in vain, to prevent a rupture between Rome and the Jews.

Herodotus (*c.* 485–425 BC), Greek historian and geographer. He made lengthy journeys through the ancient world and helped to colonize Thurii in S Italy. He is best known for his vivid history of the Persian Wars. Considered the beginning of Western history writing, his work contains much and varied information and is rich in anecdotes. *See also* THUCYDIDES; HC1 pp.55, *56*, 88, *247.*

Herod the Great (73–4 BC), King of Judaea from 40 BC to his death, appointed by MARK ANTONY. His principal achievement was to gain favour for the Jews with the Roman state. Five days before his death, he had his son, Antipater, killed for plotting against him.

Heroic couplet, in English poetry, two consecutive lines of iambic pentameter rhyming verse, used in epic or "heroic" poetry. It was mastered by John DRYDEN and perfected by Alexander POPE. In French poetry it consists of two lines of twelve syllables, the ALEXANDRINE.

Heroin, drug synthetized from MORPHINE. Compared to morphine, heroin requires a smaller dose to produce similar effects more quickly, including reduction of pain, euphoria and depressed respiration; nausea and vomiting are side effects. Heroin produces dependence, ie it is addictive. Its unprescribed use is illegal in many countries, and its abuse has been widely publicized in the richer democracies, such as the United Kingdom and the USA. *See also* MS pp.104–105.

Heron, any of several species of wading birds that live near rivers and estuaries. Herons have white, grey or brown plumage, a long thin neck and legs, broad wings and a sharp, dagger-like bill. They feed mainly on fish, and nest early in large groups, called heronries. Height: to 1.8m (6ft). Family Ardeidae.

Hero of Alexandria (*fl. c.* 1st–2nd century AD), Greek engineer who built an early steam engine, called an aeolipile. He used it to control doors automatically and to power moving statues.

Herophilus (*c.* 335–*c.* 280 BC), Greek anatomist who practised at Alexandria and was one of the first to experiment with post-mortem examinations.

Héroult, Paul-Louis-Toussaint (1863–1914), French chemist who developed the method of extracting aluminium from the electrolysis of cryolite. Héroult also invented an electric-arc furnace for refining steel. *See also* MM p.34.

Herpes, infectious virus. *Herpes simplex* infects the skin and is characterized by blisters. These are called cold sores when they appear on the lips. *Herpes zoster* attacks nerve ganglia, causing SHINGLES.

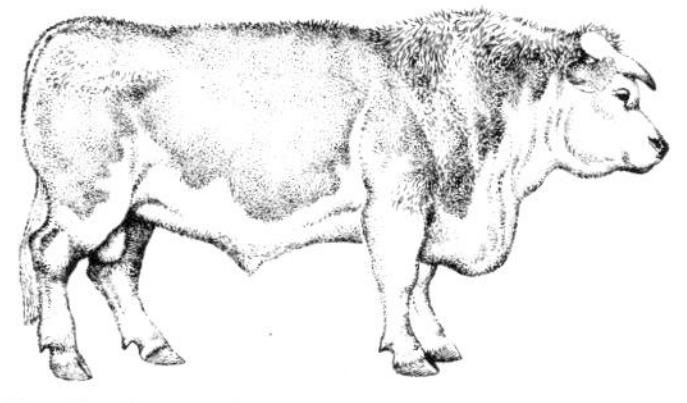

Herefords, native to England, were first exported to the USA in 1817.

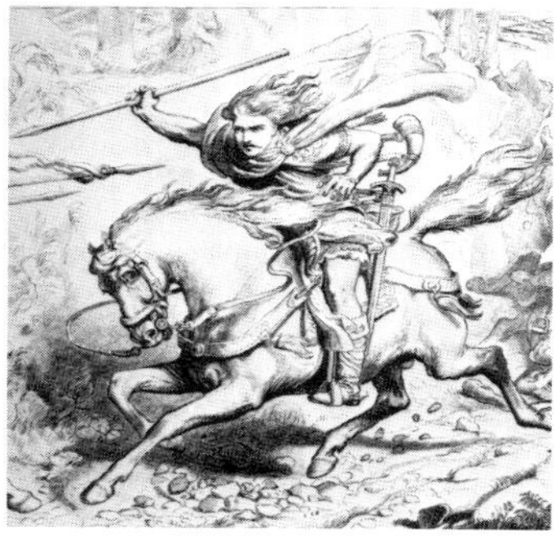

Hereward the Wake's fate is unknown, although he became a legendary hero.

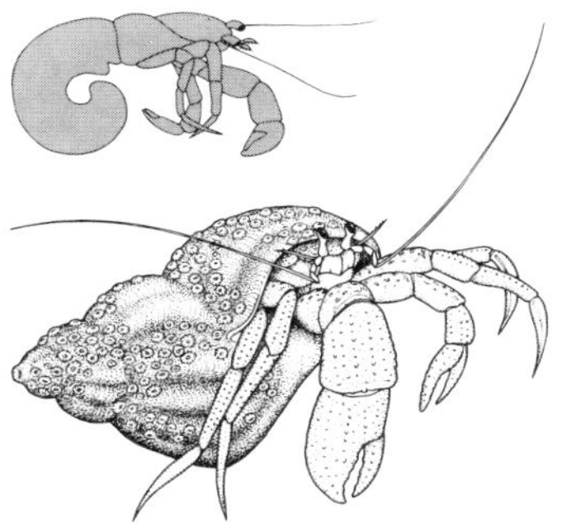

Hermit crab; one kind, the "robber" crab, grows to a size of 15cm (6in) across.

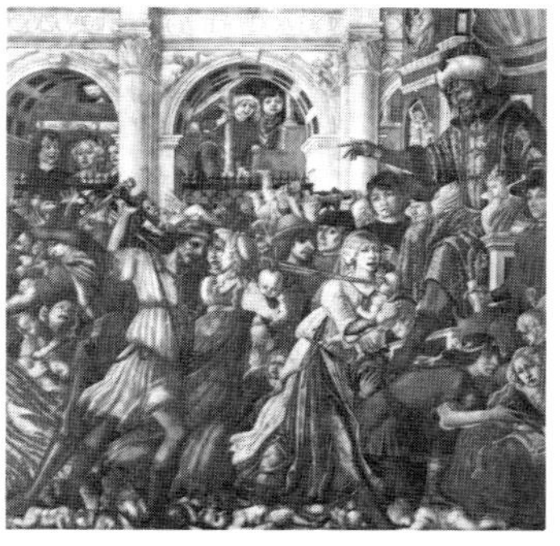

Herod the Great, according to legend, sought to destroy the new-born Messiah.

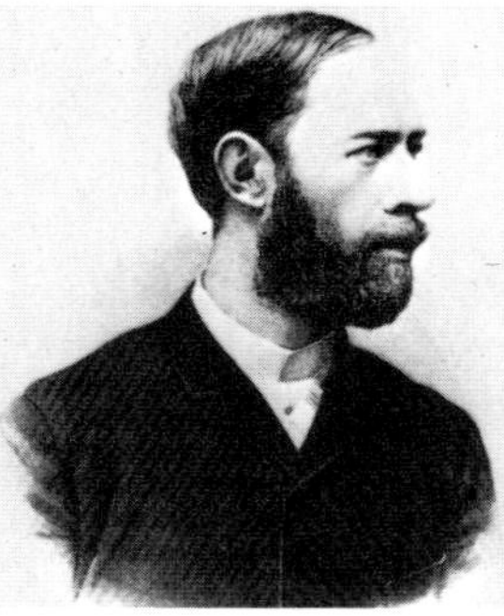

Heinrich Rudolf Hertz, whose researches made radio, television and radar possible.

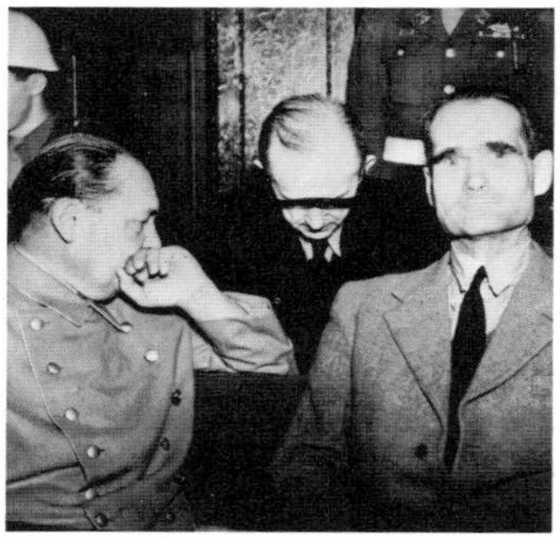

Rudolf Hess, seen with Herman Goering at the Nuremburg Trials in December 1945.

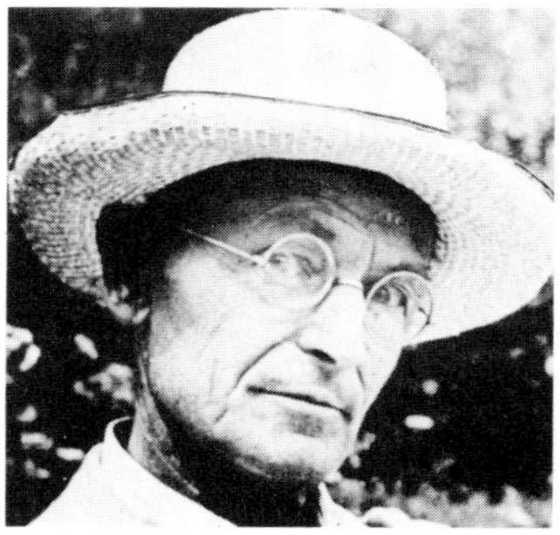

Hermann Hesse left Germany for Switzerland, becoming a Swiss citizen in 1927.

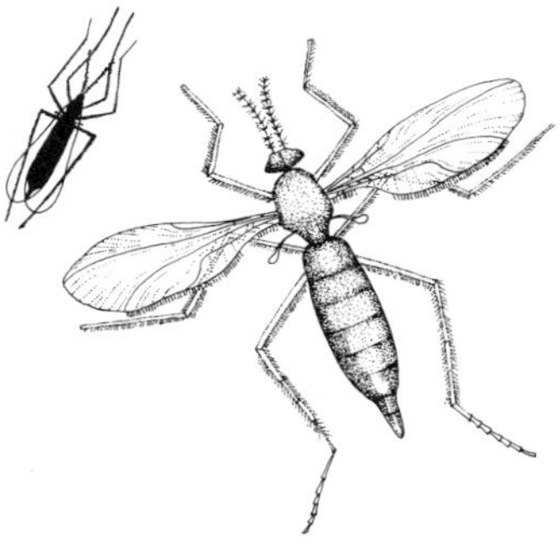

Hessian fly females lay up to 300 eggs, which hatch in five days and devour wheat leaf.

Herpetology, branch of zoology that deals with AMPHIBIANS and REPTILES. Areas of study include taxonomy (classification), life history and geographical distribution. *See also* ZOOLOGY; NW pp.132–139.

Herrera, Juan de (*c.*1530–97), Spanish architect. He succeeded Juan de Toledo in designing the ESCORIAL near Madrid. His partly executed plans for Valladolid cathedral were influential in cathedral architecture in Spain and the New World.

Herrick, Robert (1591–1674), English cavalier poet, disciple of Ben JONSON. Educated at Cambridge University and ordained in 1623, he was ejected from his living (1647–62) for royalist sympathies, but regained his post after the Restoration. His best poems, notably the collection *Hesperides* (1648), have great lyric freshness and simplicity.

Herring, marine schooling fish found worldwide. One of the most important food fish, various species are canned as PILCHARD or SARDINE and sold fresh, pickled or smoked (kippers and bloaters). Herrings have a laterally compressed body, a deeply forked tail fin and a large mouth. Length: 8–46cm (3–18in). Family Clupeidae; the 190 species include *Clupea harengus. See also* NW pp.126, *126*, 130, 240; PE pp.*241*, 246, *246–247*.

Herrings, Battle of the (1429), inconclusive battle in the HUNDRED YEARS WAR at Rouvay between French and English forces. The English, under Sir John FASTOLF, were bringing provisions, mainly herrings, to the besiegers of Orleans.

Herrmann, Bernard (1911–), US composer and conductor of the CBS Symphony Orchestra (1940–55). He made his name as a composer of radio and film music. His many film scores include *Citizen Kane* (1941) and *Psycho* (1960). He also wrote an opera, *Wuthering Heights* (1965).

Herschel, Sir John Frederick William (1792–1871), British mathematician and astronomer. He continued his father's observations of double stars, and discovered many previously unobserved nebulae and stellar clusters in the S sky. His books included *A General Catalogue of Nebulae* (1864), which later was revised as the NEW GENERAL CATALOGUE (NGC). He also contributed to the study of stellar parallax. *See also* SU p.230.

Herschel, Sir William (1738–1822), British astronomer, *b.* Germany. He moved to Britain during the Seven Years War. A renowned maker of telescopes, he made many discoveries (including in 1781 the planet Uranus) and mapped numerous galactic nebulae. *See also* SU pp.*99*, 186, 230, 236, 244, *255*.

Hershey, Alfred Day (1908–), US biologist who shared with M. DELBRÜCK and S.E. LURIA the 1969 Nobel Prize in physiology and medicine for his part in discoveries concerning the way viruses reproduce. He also found evidence that nucleic acid contains the genetic material of the CELL.

Herstmonceux, village in East Sussex, S England. It is the site of a 15th-century castle, a notable example of early brick buildings, and the ROYAL GREENWICH OBSERVATORY, which was moved to the village from Greenwich, London, in 1958. *See also* SU p.171.

Hertford, county town of Hertford(shire), S central England, on the River Lea. Records of the settlement date from AD 672 when it was the site of a general synod. A market town, Hertford's industries include brewing and light engineering. Pop. (1971) 20,370.

Hertsmere, county district in S Hertfordshire, England; created in 1974 under the Local Government Act (1972). Area: 98sq km (38sq miles). Pop. (1974 est.) 90,000.

Hertz, Gustav (1887–1975), German physicist, who shared the 1925 Nobel Prize in physics with James FRANCK for his work on the laws of impact between electrons and atoms. He was Professor of Physics at Berlin and Director of the Siemens Research Laboratory until 1945. He worked as head of a research laboratory in the USSR from 1945–54, returning then to East Germany to become Director of the Physics Institute at Leipzig.

Hertz, Heinrich Rudolf (1857–94), German physicist who discovered radio waves. He was assistant to Hermann HELMHOLTZ and held professorships at Karlsruhe and later at Bonn. He discovered, broadcasted and received the radio waves predicted by James CLERK MAXWELL. He also demonstrated the phenomenon of electromagnetic or electric waves and showed that their velocity and length could be measured and that heat and light are also kinds of electromagnetic waves. The unit of frequency, HERTZ (Hz), is named after him.

Hertz, unit of FREQUENCY named after Heinrich HERTZ. A periodic phenomena that has a PERIOD of one second is equivalent to 1Hz. This unit replaces the cycle per second. Commonly used multiples are the kilohertz (kHz; 1,000Hz) and megahertz (MHz; 1,000,000Hz).

Hertzsprung, Ejnar (1873–1967), Danish astronomer who in 1908 devised a diagram illustrating the relationship between the luminosities, surface temperatures and spectral types of stars. He anticipated the work of Henry RUSSELL in the USA a few years later. The diagram is now known as the HERTZSPRUNG-RUSSELL, or H-R, diagram. *See also* SU pp.226–229, *238*.

Hertzsprung, Ejnar (1873–1967), Danish astronomer who in 1908 devised a diagram illustrating the relationship between the luminosities, surface temperatures and spectral types of stars. He anticipated the work of Henry RUSSELL in the USA a few years later. The diagram is now known as the HERTZSPRUNG-RUSSELL, or H-R, diagram. *See also SU pp.226–229, 238.*

Hertzog, James Barry Munnik (1886–1942), Boer military commander and political figure. He served as a judge in the Orange Free State, a guerrilla leader in the SOUTH AFRICAN WAR (1899–1902) and later became minister of justice for the new Union of South Africa. He was temporarily excluded from the government for his anti-British sentiments but became prime minister in 1924. He resigned in 1939 after Parliament voted to support Britain in WWII.

Herzberg, Gerhard (1904–), scientist and Nobel Prize winner. Born in Hamburg and educated at Darmstadt, Gottingen and Bristol, he settled in Canada in 1935. He joined the National Research Council in Ottawa in 1949, and became their first Distinguished Research Scientist in 1969. He was awarded the 1971 Nobel Prize in chemistry for his work on the electronic structure and geometry of molecules, particularly radicals.

Herzegovina. *See* BOSNIA-HERCEGOVINA.

Herzl, Theodor (1860–1904), Jewish leader and the founder of political ZIONISM, *b.* Austria-Hungary. A lawyer and a journalist, in 1897 he became president of the World Zionist Organization, which worked throughout Europe to establish a Jewish national home in Palestine. Herzl wrote of himself as the founder of the Jewish state, and in 1949 his body was reburied in Israel.

Hesdin, Jacquemart de (*fl.*1384–1411), Flemish manuscript illustrator. His four illuminated manuscripts for Jean, duc de Berry, show both a French and Italian influence.

Heseltine, Philip. *See* WARLOCK, PETER.

Hesiod (8th century BC), classical Greek poet. The first major poet after HOMER and the first to reveal his personality through his poetry, he is best-known for his *Works and Days.* In *Theogony* he traced the mythological history of the gods. *See also* HC1 p.74.

Hesperides, in Greek mythology, daughters of ATLAS and Hesperis who were charged by JUNO with guarding her precious golden apples. As the last and most difficult of his 12 labours, HERCULES was required to obtain the golden apples. He tricked Atlas into helping him, and successfully retrieved the apples.

Hesperidin, vitamin-like substance found in citrus fruits, particularly unripe fruits. It has the chemical formula $C_{28}H_{34}O_{15}$ and is a GLUCOSIDE.

Hesperus (Hesperos), in Greek mythology, the evening star, King of the Western Land and grandfather of the HESPERIDES. Called Vesper by the Romans, Hesperus later became identified with PHOSPHORUS, the bringer of light (Latin Lucifer), the morning star.

Hess, Dame Myra (1890–1965), British pianist. She made her debut in London in 1907 and first performed in the USA in 1922. She was best-known as an interpreter of the Baroque composers Scarlatti and J. S. Bach and of the concertos of Mozart.

Hess, Rudolf (1894–), German Nazi leader. He joined the Nazis in 1921 and took part in the abortive Munich putsch in 1923. He was Adolf HITLER's deputy from 1933, but lacked influence; he flew alone to Scotland in 1941 in an attempt to make peace with the British. Imprisoned for the rest of the war, he was afterwards sentenced to imprisonment for life.

Hess, Victor Francis (1883–1964), US physicist, *b.* Austria. As a result of his investigations into the ionization of air, he suggested that radiation similar to X-rays comes from space, later named COSMIC RAYS. He shared the 1936 Nobel Prize in physics with Carl ANDERSON. Soon after receiving the prize, Hess emigrated to the USA.

Hess, Walter Rudolf (1881–1973), Swiss physiologist. He shared with A. de Egas MONIZ the 1949 Nobel Prize in physiology and medicine for his work on how specific, highly circumscribed areas of the BRAIN control body functions, such as blood circulation, muscle relaxation and breathing rate.

Hesse, Hermann (1877–1962), German novelist and poet. He spent much of his life studying Indian mysticism and Jungian psychology, as expressed in the novels *Demian* (1919), *Siddhartha* (1922), *Steppenwolf* (1927), *Narziss und Goldmund* (1930) and *The Glass Bead Game* (1943). He was awarded the 1946 Nobel Prize in literature.

Hessian fly, brown to black FLY found N of the Tropic of Cancer and in New Zealand. It is a serious pest of wheat and other grains. Length: 4–6mm (0.16–0.24in). Family Cecidomyidae, species *Mayetiola destructor.*

Hess's law, in physical chemistry, law referring to the heat produced or absorbed during chemical reactions leading to the preparation of any chemical compound. It states that the net value of this heat is the same by any chemical route.

Hestia, in Greek mythology goddess of the burning hearth. In the myths, she is the unmarried daughter of Cronus and Rhea who scorned the attentions of Apollo and Poseidon and was installed in Olympus by ZEUS. She was revered as the oldest of the Olympian goddesses. In all Greek towns a flame burned continuously at the Public Hearth. In Rome, virgins (originally two in number) tended the fire at her temple, where she was worshipped as Vesta. *See also* VESTAL VIRGINS.

Heston, Charlton (1924–), US actor noted for his distinctively virile screen performances, originally associated with herioc epics such as *The Ten Commandments* (1956), *Ben Hur* (1959) and *El Cid* (1961). He gave more exacting performances in *The War Lord* (1965), *Will Penny* (1967) and *Khartoum* (1966).

Heterocyclic compounds, in organic chemistry, compounds having a ring structure consisting of atoms of carbon and an atom or atoms of any other element. Pyridine, C_5H_5N, containing a nitrogen atom, is an example.

Heterodyne, in radio, the production of one frequency as the difference of two others. It is used in radiofrequency oscillators and in receivers. The heterodyne system was invented by Reginald A. FESSENDEN in 1905.

Heterosexuality, attraction of a male or female to members of the opposite sex. The word is used to distinguish such attraction from homosexuality.

Heterotroph, organism classified according to its method of obtaining nutrition. Autotrophs can synthesize their own food from inorganic materials, as do most green plants; heterotrophs require organic compounds to sustain life. All animals, includ-

ing man, are heterotrophic.
Heterozygote, organism possessing two different hereditary units in a CHROMOSOME pair. In human beings, for example, one chromosome contains the GENE for dark hair and the other the gene for fair hair. *See also* HOMOZYGOTE.
Hevelius, Johannes (1611–87), Polish astronomer *b.* Danzig, where he used his home observatory to chart the Moon's surface, catalogue more than 1,500 stars and discover four comets. His Moon atlas *Selenographia* charted many lunar features.
Hevesy, George Charles de (1855–1966), Hungarian-Swedish chemist, who was awarded the 1943 Nobel Prize in chemistry. Co-discoverer of the element hafnium (Hf) in 1923, he was also an early researcher into the uses of radioactive ISOTOPES, including their use as "tracers" in living tissue. In the early 1940s he fled from Germany, where he had been teaching, to live in Sweden. He worked with Ernest RUTHERFORD in England and later with Niels BOHR in Copenhagen.
Hewish, Antony (1924–), British radio astronomer who shared with Sir Martin RYLE the 1974 Nobel Prize in physics. After WWII Hewish returned to Cambridge University, where he had been educated, to do research and with S. J. Bell in 1967, while surveying the sky with a radio telescope, he discovered the first PULSAR. Hewish became Professor of Radioastronomy at Cambridge in 1971.
Hexachlorophene, germicide used as a local antiseptic on the skin, usually in combination with soap. It is used in preparations to combat acne and, very rarely, sensitivity reactions may occur to it.
Hexameter, verse line of six metrical feet. DACTYLIC hexameter, the oldest form of Greek verse, characterizes the epic poetry of Homer. An example of the use of the hexameter in English poetry is *Evangeline* (by LONGFELLOW).
Hey, Donald Holroyde, (1904–), Welsh chemist who was professor of chemistry at King's College, University of London from 1945 to 1950. He held many other academic posts and was awarded honorary degrees all over the world.
Heyer, Georgette (1904–74), British popular novelist. Her prodigious output of historical romantic fiction includes *Devil's Cub* (1934), *The Corinthian* (1940) and *The Black Sheep* (1966).
Heyerdahl, Thor (1914–), Norwegian ethnologist who, with five companions, drifted on the balsa raft *Kon Tiki* approximately 8,000km (5,000 miles) across the Pacific Ocean from Peru to Polynesia (1947) in an attempt to prove that the Polynesians came from South America and not from South-East Asia. Pursuing his theory, Heyerdahl led archaeological expeditions to the GALAPAGOS ISLANDS (1953) and to Bolivia, Peru and Colombia (1954). In 1970 he sailed from Africa to the West Indies in the papyrus boat *Ra II.*
Heymans, Corneille (1892–1968), Belgian medical researcher. He was awarded the 1938 Nobel Prize in physiology and medicine for his contributions to an understanding of how breathing and blood pressure are regulated in the body.
Heyrowský, Jaroslav (1890–1967), Czechoslovakian chemist. He was awarded the 1959 Nobel Prize in chemistry for the discovery of polarography, an electrochemical method of analysis that can be used with substances which undergo electrolytic OXIDATION or reduction in solution.
Heyse, Paul Johann Ludwig (1830–1914), German writer. His work is often artificial in style and includes the short story *L'Arrabbiata* (1855), the verse tragedy *Meleager* (1854) and the novel *Children of the World* (1872). He was awarded the Nobel Prize in literature in 1910.
Heywood, John (*c.* 1497–*c.* 1580) English dramatist. His work was popular at the courts of Henry VIII and Mary I but, being an ardent Roman Catholic, he left England on the Accession of Elizabeth I. He wrote dramatic interludes of a comic nature, which mark the beginning of the 16th-century drama of types and HUMOURS. Among the plays attributed to him are *The Pardoner and the Friar* (*c.* 1519) and *The Play of the Weather* (1533).
Heywood, Thomas (*c.* 1574–1641), English dramatist. Despite a busy career as a professional actor, he wrote numerous plays, non-dramatic works in verse and prose, and translations. Much of his writing was hasty and superficial, but some work, eg *A Woman Killed with Kindness* (1603), shows dramatic merit.
Hezekiah, (*r. c.* 720–690 BC), King of Judah who led an unsuccessful revolt against the Assyrians in 701. He built an important watercourse to Jerusalem. The prophets ISAIAH and MICAH preached during his reign. *See also* HC1 p.*56*.
H I and H II regions, interstellar regions made up of neutral (H I) or ionized (H II) hydrogen. H I regions produce characteristic emissions of radio waves at a wavelength of 21cm (8.5in). H II regions, having been excited by nearby hot stars, shine optically as emission NEBULAE. *See also* SU pp.230–231.
Hiatus hernia. *See* HERNIA.
Hiawatha, The Song of (1855) narrative poem by Henry Wadsworth LONGFELLOW based on American Indian folklore. It recounts the adventures of Hiawatha, a leader of the Onondaga tribe.
Hibernation, dormant condition adopted by certain animals to survive the harsh conditions of winter. Adaptive mechanisms to avoid starvation, drying out and extreme temperatures include a reduction in blood pressure, a slower heartbeat and respiration rate and decreased endocrine gland activity. *See also* NW p.206.
Hibiscus, genus of plants, shrubs and small trees native to tropical and temperate regions and cultivated throughout the world. Most species have large white, pink, yellow or red bell-shaped flowers with darker or variegated centres. Family Malvaceae. *See also* NW p.*70*.
Hiccup (hiccough), spasmodic contraction of the DIAPHRAGM followed by a short inhalation that is stopped by closure of the GLOTTIS, producing a typical sound. It is caused by irritation of the nerves leading to the diaphragm and is a symptom of several diseases, such as TYPHOID FEVER and BRIGHT'S DISEASE.
Hickey, William, name given to the gossip columnist of the London newspaper the *Daily Express.* The name was first affixed to the column in the issue of 29 April 1933. Since then the column has been published without a break.
Hickok, James Butler ("Wild Bill") (1837–76), US law enforcement officer. He was a stagecoach driver and marksman. He served in the Union Army during the AMERICAN CIVIL WAR as a guerrilla fighter and was a scout for Gen. George CUSTER in his wars against the American Indians. He served as US Marshal in Kansas (1869–71). In 1872–73 he toured the country with BUFFALO BILL as a sharpshooter and trick rider. He was shot dead in a saloon in Deadwood, South Dakota, while playing poker.
Hickory, deciduous tree of the WALNUT family native to E North America. Hickories are grown for ornament, timber and for their nuts. Height: 25m (80ft). Family Juglandaceae; genus *Carya. See also* PECAN.
Hicks, Sir John Richard (1904–), British economist. He became a fellow of All Souls', Oxford, in 1952, and was professor of political economy, Oxford (1952–65). He has written many books and in 1972 he won the Nobel Prize in economics.
Hidalgo, minor planet discovered by Walter BAADE in 1920. It has an eccentric path that takes it out almost as far as the orbit of Saturn over a period of approx. 14 years. With a diameter of approx. 24–48km (15–30 miles), Hidalgo has the greatest orbital inclination (42.5°) of any known planet. *See also* SU p.205, *205*.
Hide, unit of land area in Britain from Anglo-Saxon times. It was the amount of land considered necessary to support a peasant family and varied from 120 to 140 acres. It was the central unit of the Old English agrarian economy and the basis of taxation until the 14th century.
Hierarchy, in social groups and organizations, ranked system in which the position of members is determined by their relative importance to the group and their proximity to power. In hierarchical societies ranking may be based on such criteria as sex, age and tasks performed. In business it is determined by such factors as position held, personal influence and work effectiveness. *See also* CLASS; MS pp.253, 256–257, 272–273.
Hieratic script, cursive form of Egyptian HIEROGLYPHICS. Hieratic script was developed early for convenient and quick writing, especially on papyrus documents. *See also* MS p.*244*.
Hieroglyphics, type of writing in which meanings are represented by pictures, used in ancient Egypt and also in Crete, Asia Minor, Central America and Mexico. Only the Egyptian system has been fully deciphered. *See also* MS pp.244–245, *244,* 246–247.
Higashiōsaka, city on the SW coast of Honshū island, Japan. It was formed by the union of Kasaka and Kusume in 1967. Industries include engineering and chemicals. Pop. (1970) 500,173.
Higgins, Frederick Robert (1896–1941), Irish poet. Much of his poetry, lyrical in tone, was published by the CUALA PRESS and includes *Island Blood* (1925), *The Dark Breed* (1927) and *Arable Holdings* (1933).
High, area of high pressure, often shown on weather maps, associated in the Northern Hemisphere with anticyclones (clockwise, outward, atmospheric circulation). *See also* LOW, PE pp.68–69.
High blood pressure, elevation of arterial BLOOD PRESSURE above normal levels. In a normal healthy person, systolic blood pressure (maximum pressure reached when the heart contracts) is generally considered to be 120mm of mercury (mm Hg), and diastolic pressure (minimum reached when the heart is relaxed) 80mm Hg. Persistence of high blood pressure, called hypertension, may be of unknown cause (essential, or primary, hypertension) or may be secondary to a variety of conditions, including kidney, cardiovascular or central nervous system diseases, adrenal gland tumours, and toxaemia of pregnancy. Treatment of high blood pressure is by weight reduction, salt restriction and anti-hypertensive drugs. Hypertension shortens life and, if untreated, leads ultimately to damage of vital organs. *See also* MS pp.90–91, *142*.
High Church, term describing the part of the Anglican Church which, by stressing its historical continuity with the pre-Reformation Church, still employs some ceremonial rites and vestments that were allowed to lapse by Protestant Churches. "High" in this sense means "grand" or "main" (as in High priest or High mass). The more Protestant side of the Anglican Church is sometimes called LOW CHURCH. *See also* OXFORD MOVEMENT.
High Commissioner, the appointed representative of a Commonwealth country in the capital of another Commonwealth country.
High Court, in English law the supreme court of judicature, reorganized by the Administration of Justice Act of 1970. It consists of three divisions: the QUEEN'S BENCH, the CHANCERY, and the Family division. As it was originally first formed under the terms of the Judicature Act of 1873, it had ten divisions.
High diving. *See* DIVING.
High explosive (HE), substance which, when detonated, burns rapidly to produce hot gases that expand and exert a violent force on the surrounding space. An example is TNT. *See also* BOMB; GUNPOWDER; MM pp.242–243.
High-fidelity, sound recording and reproduction with the minimum of distortion, usually involving the use of high quality components and circuits. The original sound source may be a gramophone record, magnetic tape, a radio signal or a live performance. An audio amplifier is required to "magnify" the signals, and one or more loudspeakers are needed to make the source audible. Domestic high-fidelity sound systems have been made since the

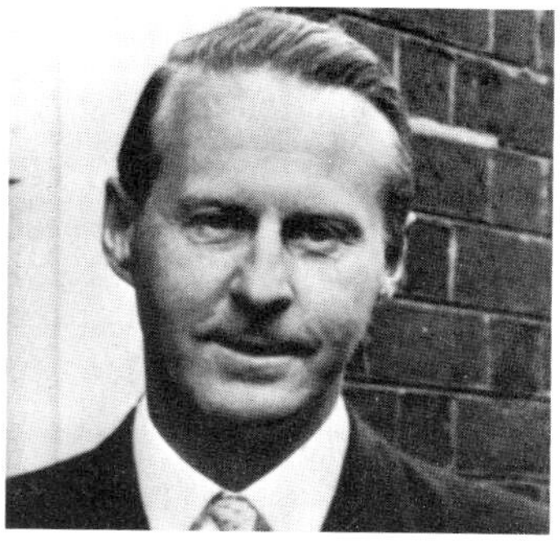

Thor Heyerdahl's *Ra* journey linked Egyptian and Pre-Columbian cultures.

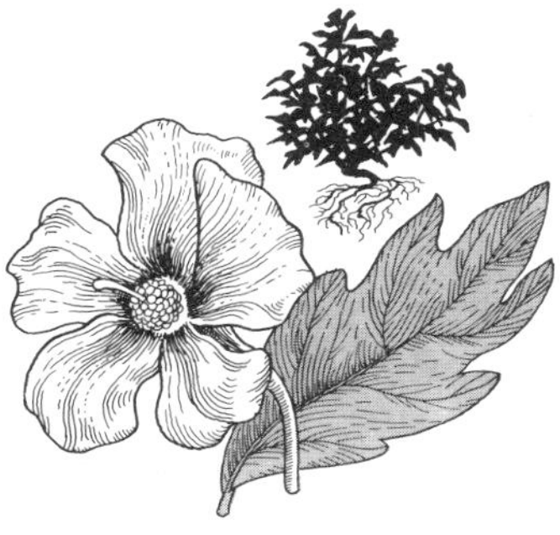

Hibiscus; the Chinese often used the tropical variety to stain their teeth and eyebrows.

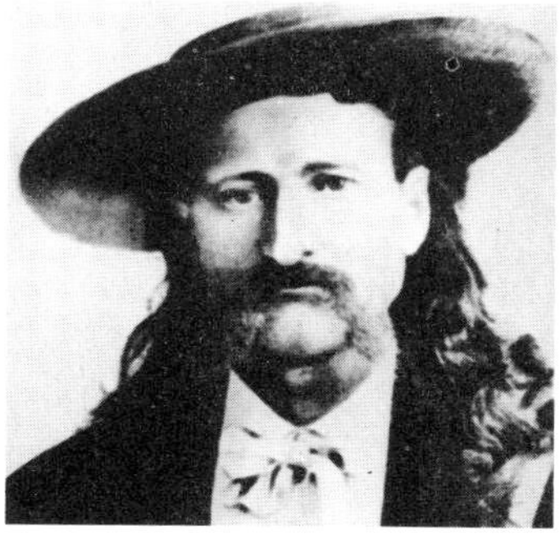

"Wild Bill" Hickok never killed a man except in self-defence or while on official duty.

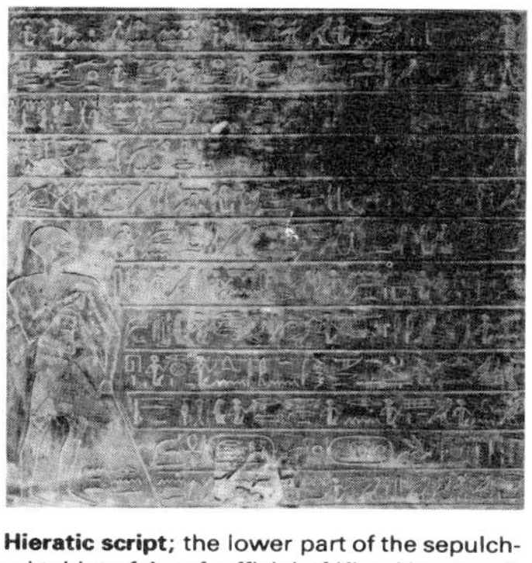

Hieratic script; the lower part of the sepulchral tablet of Antef, official of King Usertsen I.

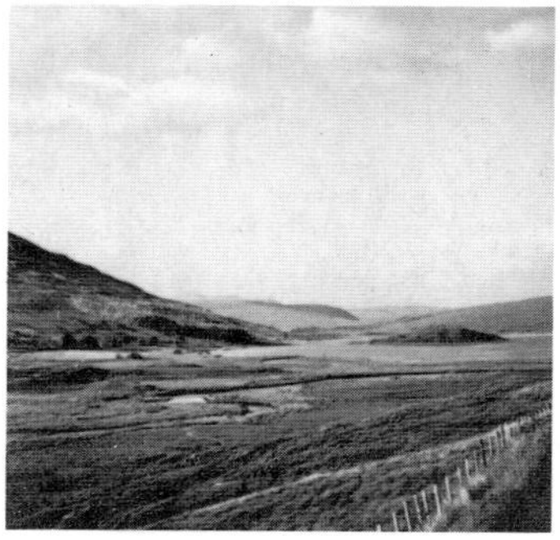

Highlands; a glaciated valley, a view typical of many parts of northern Scotland.

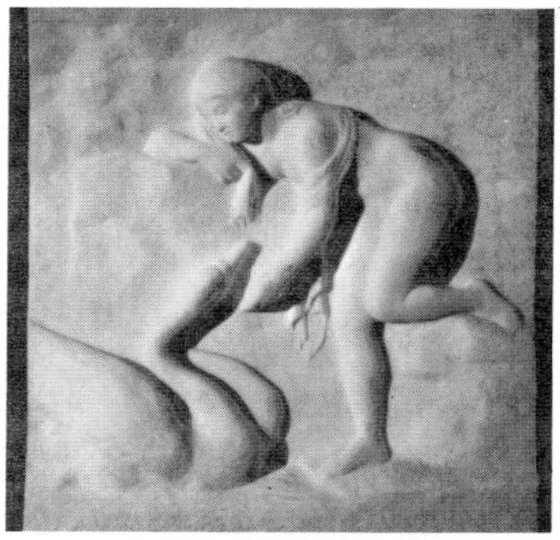

Adolf von Hildebrand; an example of his work, based on classical Greek principles.

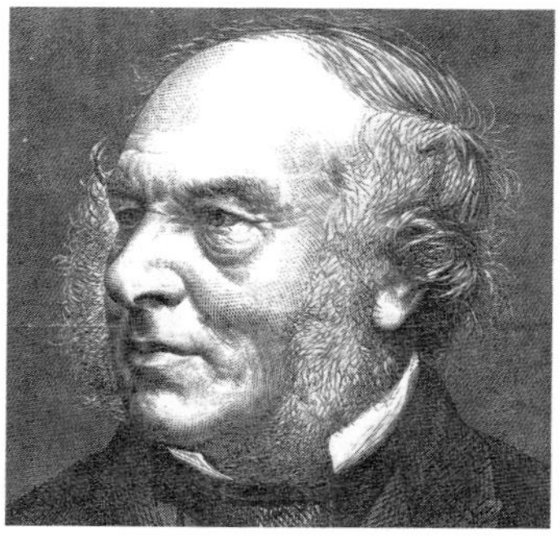

Rowland Hill's postal reforms were the result of his comprehensive analysis of taxation.

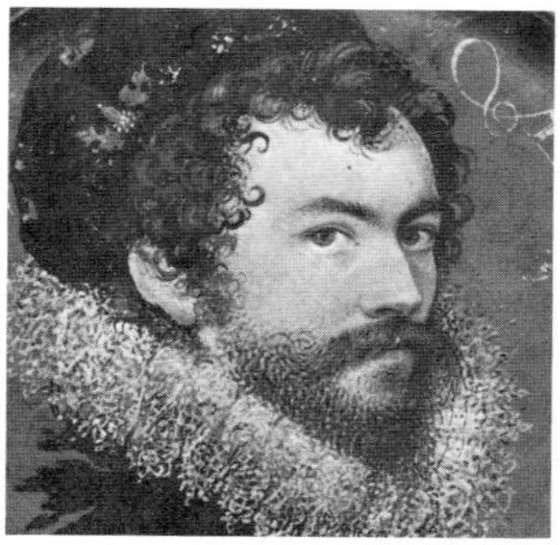

Nicholas Hilliard in a miniature self-portrait made by the artist in 1577 when he was 30.

1920s, but did not become common until the advent of long-playing gramophone records in the 1950s and 1960s. Recent developments have included stereophonic sound, recorded on two channels, and quadraphonic sound, recorded on four. *See also* MM pp.232–233.

Highgate, residential suburb in N London, its name deriving from a toll gate that stood there. Francis BACON and Samuel Taylor COLERIDGE lived there; buried in Highgate Cemetery are Karl MARX, George ELIOT, Michael FARADAY and Herbert SPENCER.

High jump, field athletics event for men and women in which a competitor, taking off from one foot, attempts to jump over a bar suspended between two uprights. If successful, he or she may attempt to clear a new height; if the bar is dislodged, the jump counts as a failure. Under IAAF rules, a competitor has up to three attempts to clear each height. There are three main styles of high jumping: the outmoded Western roll, the straddle and the recently introduced Fosbury flop, in which the jumper clears the bar backwards. With the leading men jumping *c.* 2.30m (7ft 6½in) and the women *c.* 1.96m (6ft 5in), the "air bed" landing mats are essential. The high jump has been an Olympic event since 1896.

Highland, region in N Scotland, formed in 1975 from the former counties of CAITHNESS, ROSS AND CROMARTY, SUTHERLAND, INVERNESS (excluding the Western Isles) and NAIRN and parts of MORAY and ARGYLL. Area: 25,130sq km (9,735sq miles). Pop. (1975 est.) 182,000.

Highland Games, series of athletics meetings, often professional, held during the autumn in the Scottish highlands. Dancing, bagpipe playing, running and field events make up the programme, with pride of place going to tossing the caber, for which entrants wear a kilt. The modern games, principally the Royal Braemar Games, date from the early 19th century.

Highlands, Scottish mountain and moorland region lying N of a line running SW to NE approx. from Dumbarton to Stonehaven. The area is divided geologically into the Northwest Highlands and the Grampian Highlands, separated by Glen More. In an effort to halt the decline in population through emigration caused by poverty, hydroelectric power and forestry schemes have been introduced. Tourism is also an increasing source of income.

High-temperature physics, production and analysis of the effects of temperatures above 50,000°C (90,000°F). At such temperatures atoms begin to be ionized (stripped of their electrons) and a fourth state of matter, called a PLASMA, is achieved. Normal stars are plasmas; so is the region around an exploding hydrogen bomb. To make controlled thermonuclear fusion (joining of light nuclei and release of energy) a reality, physicists must find a way to confine a plasma at temperatures of over a million degrees. *See also* MAGNETIC BOTTLE; SU pp.64–65.

Highway Code, British government publication outlining rules of good conduct on the roads, issued by the Secretary of State for the Environment.

Highwaymen, bandits who specialized in robbing coaches on the highways of 17th- and 18th-century England. Many highwaymen became local heroes, such as John Nevison (1639–84) and Dick TURPIN (1706–39), who operated in the forests around London.

Hijacking, illegal capture usually of an airliner, by one or more of its passengers. The commonest motives are political, and the other passengers are held hostage towards some goal. The first hijacking, in 1968, involved a US airliner which was forced to land in Cuba. The crime reached a peak in the early 1970s, but stricter security measures and some dramatic rescues have decreased its incidence.

Hiking, leisure activity in which people travel about by walking. It grew in popularity between the World Wars as a cheap way of enjoying the countryside and was boosted by the growth of the Youth Hostel and Ramblers' associations. Using detailed maps to avoid main roads, hikers can easily walk 32 to 48km (20–30 miles) a day. Sturdy walking shoes, or boots, and thick socks are recommended, and a rucksack is standard equipment for carrying food, clothes and a first-aid kit.

Hilary of Arles, Saint (403–449), Archbishop of Arles and leader of the theological school of SEMI-PELAGIANISM. Feast: 5 May.

Hilary of Poitiers, Saint (*c.* 315–367), the "ATHANASIUS of the West", known for his defence of Christian orthodoxy against ARIANISM. Feast: 13 January.

Hilda, Saint (614–80), Anglo-Saxon abbess, the great-niece of EDWIN of Northumbria. She founded the monastery of Streaneshalch (now Whitby) in 657. *See also* HC1 p.*165*.

Hildebrand, Adolf von (1847–1921), German sculptor. The Italian classical influence on his style is evident in his many statues, including his equestrian statue of BISMARCK in Bremen, and portrait busts. He designed numerous private and public fountains, the most famous of which is the Wittelsbach Fountain in Munich.

Hildebrandt, Lukas von (1668–1745), Austrian BAROQUE architect. He studied in Italy where he was influenced by Italian Baroque architecture. In 1723 he became First Court Architect in Vienna. Of the many palaces he designed, the Belvedere in Vienna is considered his masterpiece. He also designed the Peterskirche and the Piaristenkirche, Vienna.

Hilgard, Eugene Woldemar (1833–1916), US geologist and agricultural chemist, *b.* Germany. He was the first to recognize the close relationship between climatic conditions and soil type. His geological studies laid the foundation for subsequent studies of the Gulf Coast Plain. He was also influential in developing scientific methods for cultivating cotton.

Hill, Alfred (1870–1960), Australian conductor, composer and violinist. He was a violinist with the Gewendhaus Orchestra and professor at the Sydney Conservatorium (1915–35). His interest in the MAORI music of New Zealand is displayed in such compositions as the opera *The Weird Flute* and the *Maori Symphony*.

Hill, Archibald Vivian (1886–1977), British biophysicist. He shared with O. F. MEYERHOF the 1922 Nobel Prize in physiology and medicine for discoveries relating to the generation of heat in muscles.

Hill, David Octavius. *See* ADAMSON, ROBERT.

Hill, Geoffrey (1932–), British poet. He writes in a markedly dense style on themes of English history. His volumes include *For the Unfallen* (1959), *King Log* (1968) and *Mercian Hymns* (1971).

Hill, Graham (1929–75), British motor racing driver who achieved a unique treble, winning the world drivers' championship in 1962 (BRM) and 1968 (Lotus), the Indianapolis 500 in 1966 (Lola), and the Le Mans 24-hour race in 1972 (Matra). Five times winner of the Monaco Grand Prix, he was killed in an air crash shortly after retiring.

Hill, John, (*c.* 1716–75), English botanist and writer whose book on British flora was the first to be based on the Linnaean system of nomenclature. His *Vegetable System*, in 26 folio volumes, was published from 1759 to 1775.

Hill, John Edward Christopher (1912–), British historian. He was elected master of Balliol College, Oxford, in 1965. His prodigious work on 17th-century Britain has established his pre-eminence in that field.

Hill, Sir Rowland (1795–1879), founder of the penny post in Britain. His invention of the adhesive postage stamp, for which he had some years campaigned, was adopted in the budget of 1839 and introduced in 1840. He was Secretary to the Postmaster General in 1846 and Secretary to the Post Office (1854–1864).

Hill, Susan Elizabeth (1942–), British novelist and playwright. Her first novel was *The Enclosure* (1961) and she established her reputation with her third, *Gentlemen and Ladies* (1969).

Hillary, Sir Edmund Percival (1919–), New Zealand explorer and mountaineer. He participated in the New Zealand and British expeditions to the Himalayas (1951 and 1953). In 1953 he and his Sherpa guide, Tenzing Norkey, were the first to reach the summit of Mt EVEREST, the world's highest mountain. In 1955–58 he led the New Zealand section of the British Commonwealth Trans-Antarctic Expedition. He now spends much time in Nepal where he built a hospital for Sherpa tribesmen in 1966.

Hill climbing. *See* MOTOR SPORTS.

Hiller, Dame Wendy (1912–), British actress (DBE, 1975). In 1936 she played St Joan at the Malvern Festival and made her Broadway début in *Love on the Dole*. Other appearances include roles in *The Aspern Papers* (1962) and *Waters of the Moon* (1951–53). Her film appearances include *Pygmalion* (1938), *Major Barbara* (1941), *Separate Tables*, for which she won an Academy Award (1958), *A Man for All Seasons* (1966) and *Murder on the Orient Express* (1974).

Hillery, Patrick John (1923–), Irish politician and member of the Dáil from 1951 until 1973. He has served as minister of Education, Industry and Commerce, of Labour, and of Foreign Affairs. From 1973 until 1976 he was vice president of the commission of the EEC with special responsibility for social affairs. In December 1976 he was appointed President of the Republic of Ireland.

Hill figures, monuments, some of which date from the pre-Roman period, depicting men or animals cut into the side of chalk hills. Perhaps the oldest hill figure in Britain is the White Horse of Uffington, which is probably of the Iron Age and has given its name to the Vale of the White Horse. The Cerne Abbas giant, in Dorset, was cut about 1,500 years ago. The significance of these figures is not clear. *See also* HC1 p.*103*.

Hill-forts, late Bronze Age and Iron Age defensive sites in Europe, characterized by a ring of earthworks protecting the top of a hill. The earliest hill-forts were introduced by the URNFIELD people, and in Britain they became common after 500 BC, when intertribal warfare become more prevalent. Some of the hill-forts, such as MAIDEN CASTLE or Badbury Rings, had permanent buildings and are considered the first true towns. *See also* HC1 pp.84–87; MM pp.*28–29*.

Hilliard, Nicholas (*c.* 1547–1619), English miniaturist and goldsmith, court painter to ELIZABETH I and JAMES I. A self-taught painter and the first native-born English artist whose life and work is documented, he painted elegant linear miniature portraits of the highest quality on vellum and on the backs of playing cards. His best known works include *Alice Hilliard, Man leaning against a tree with rose bushes* and *Queen Elizabeth. See also* HC1 pp.280–281.

Hilton, Conrad Nicholson (1887–), US businessman who built hotels throughout the USA, Latin America, Europe and the Middle East. He worked in his father's hotel as a child and bought his own first hotel in 1919.

Hilton, James (1900–1954), British novelist and journalist. His works include *Lost Horizon* (1933), a novel set in a Tibetan monastery called Shangri-La, and *Goodbye Mr Chips* (1934), an account of an eccentric schoolmaster at a British public school. Both books were filmed.

Hilversum, municipality in central Netherlands, 27km (17 miles) SE of Amsterdam, of which it is a suburb. It is the centre of Dutch broadcasting and is a summer resort noted for its impressive modern architecture. Its industries include electrical machinery and chemicals. Pop. (1971) 98,948.

Himachal Pradesh, state in NW India in the W Himalayas; the capital is Simla. Although the state is heavily forested, intensive cultivation is practised in the valleys; potatoes and fruit are grown. Timber provides the main source of income. Area: 55,673sq km (21,495sq miles). Pop. (1971) 4,615,176.

Himalayan cat, long-haired domestic CAT developed from Persian and Siamese breeds. Its body resembles that of a Persian, with a round head, small ears, short tail and a long thick coat. The eyes are Siamese blue and the coat is cream or white with seal, lilac, blue or chocolate points.

Himalayas, system of mountains in S Asia, extending approx. 2,400km (1,500 miles) N–S in a long arc between Tibet and India-Pakistan and between the Indus River (W) and the Brahmaputra River (E). The mountains are divided into three ranges: the Greater Himalayas (N), which include Mt EVEREST, the Lesser Himalayas, running parallel to the Greater and the Outer Himalayas (S). The range marks the beginning of the high Tibetan plateau and is difficult to cross, even by air travel. *See also* PE pp.106–107.

Himmler, Heinrich (1900–45), German NAZI leader. He took part in the abortive MUNICH PUTSCH (1923) and in 1929 became head of the SS. After the Nazis came to power in 1933 he assumed control of the entire German police system. A fanatical racist, he controlled the Jewish extermination programme. He became minister of the interior in 1943 and head of the army's home organization in 1944. In April 1945 he tried secretly to negotiate peace with the Allies and was expelled from the party. He was captured by the British, but killed himself. *See also* HC2 pp.222–223.

Hims. *See* HOMS.

Hīnayāna Buddhism, the older of the two major schools of BUDDHISM. The term *Hīnayāna*, meaning "Lesser Vehicle", is a commonly used but derogatory name for *Thervada* ("Doctrine of the Elders") and originated at an early stage in the history of Buddhism as a contrast to *Mahayana* ("Greater Vehicle"), those Buddhists who were dissatisfied with conservative teachings. Hīnayāna Buddhism stresses that sorrow and suffering can be conquered only by the suppression of desire. Desire can be suppressed only if the individual realizes that nothing is permanent, everything is always in a state of flux, and the only stable condition is NIRVANA, an undefinable state of rest. Hīnayāna Buddhism is widespread in Sri Lanka and SE Asia. *See also* MAHAYANA BUDDHISM.

Hindbrain, one of the three primary parts of the BRAIN. In the embryo, the hindbrain develops into the CEREBELLUM, the part of the brain concerned with unconscious muscle co-ordination, and also into the PONS and the MEDULLA oblongata. *See also* FOREBRAIN; MIDBRAIN.

Hindemith, Paul (1895–1963), German composer who emigrated to the USA in 1939, then from 1953 lived in semi-retirement in Switzerland. Hindemith experimented with dissonance and atonality early in his career, but eventually his works became more melodic and tonal in character. He was a master of counterpoint in music, and many of his compositions are Neo-classical in style. Among his works are the song cycle *Das Marienleben* (1924), symphonies, and concertos such as the viola concerto *Der Schwanendreher* (1935), ballets, chamber music, operas and sonatas. In the 1930s, he developed, with Kurt WEILL, *Gebrauchs musik*, or music written for amateur performance. His best-known work is the symphony he derived from his opera *Mathis der Maler* (1934).

Hindenburg, Paul Ludwig Hans von Beneckendorf und von (1847–1934), German general and president (1925–34). Commanding the army on the eastern front in WWI, he defeated the Russians in the Battle of Tannenberg (Aug. 1914). In 1916 he became supreme commander and, with his chief-of-staff, Erich Ludendorff, directed the entire war effort (civilian as well as military) until the end of the war. Elected president in 1925, he held office during the collapse of the WEIMAR REPUBLIC. *See also* HC2 pp.188, 196.

Hindenburg, German airship built in 1936. Like its sister ship, *Graf Zepplin* built in 1938, it had 200,000m^3 (7 million cu ft) of hydrogen giving a lift of about 232 tonnes; they were the largest airships ever built. In 1937, the *Hinddnburg* exploded in flames in the USA with 36 deaths. *See also* MM pp.*146*–147.

Hindi, most widespread language in India, spoken principally in the north-central part of the country by about 154 million people. With English it is an official language. Like the other languages of N India, Hindi derives from SANSKRIT and thus belongs to the Indo-European family.

Hindle Wakes. *See* HOUGHTON, WILLIAM STANLEY.

Hinduism, traditional religion of India, characterized principally by a philosophy and way of life rather than a dogmatic structure. Unlike other religions, it was not founded by any individual. Its birth is almost synonymous with the beginnings of Indian history about 3000 BC and it has been developing gradually ever since, showing a remarkable ability to absorb external influences and arriving at a synthesis with them. There are several divergent schools within Hinduism, but all Hindus recognize the VEDAS as sacred, believe that all living creatures, not merely human beings, have souls, follow the doctrine of TRANSMIGRATION OF SOULS and look upon *moksha*, ie liberation from suffering and rebirth, as the chief end of life. One of the features of Hindu society is the age-old CASTE system, but modern Hindu scholars maintain that it is not part of the Hindu religion. In the mid-1970s Hindus numbered about 500 million.

Hindu Kush, principal Asian mountain range, which extends WSW for 805–965km (500–600 miles) from NE Afghanistan. The mountain system is glaciated and receives heavy snow falls, making the area almost uninhabited. The highest peak is Tirich Mir, 7,700m (25,260ft).

Hindustani. *See* URDU.

Hinemoa, in Maori legend, noblewoman who defied her parents to marry Tutanekai, who lived on an island in Lake Rotorua. She swam the lake to reach him.

Hines, Earl Kenneth (1905–), US jazz pianist and bandleader. He played in Louis ARMSTRONG's band and led his own groups from the 1920s. His "trumpet" style of piano playing – use of the single-note lines in the right hand – was modelled on Armstrong's style and influenced other jazz musicians. He also composed songs and made many recordings.

Hinny, hybrid offspring of a male horse and a female donkey. It is bred less commonly than the MULE to which it is considered inferior as a working animal, but which it resembles in appearance. Like the mule, it is infertile. *See also* NW p.35.

Hinshelwood, Sir Cyril Norman (1897–1967), British chemist, President of the Royal Society from 1955–60. From 1937–64 he was Dr Lee's Professor of Chemistry at Oxford, and Research Fellow at Imperial College, London, from 1964. He shared the 1956 Nobel Prize in chemistry with Nikolai N. SEMENOV for their simultaneous work on chemical reaction kinetics.

Hinton, Christopher, Baron Hinton of Bankside, (1901–), British nuclear engineer. From 1946, as deputy controller of atomic energy production, he created a new industry in Britain with the world's first full-scale atomic power station at Calder Hall, which was opened in 1956.

Hip, joint on each side of the lower trunk, formed at the fusion of three bones, the ilium, ischium, and pubis, that together with the sacrum form the PELVIS. *See also* MS pp.57, 95.

Hipparchus (*fl.* 146–127 BC), Greek astronomer who worked on the island of Rhodes. He estimated the distance of the Moon from the Earth, drew the first accurate star map with more than 800 stars and divided stars into orders of magnitude based on their brightness (a system fundamentally in use today). He also developed an organization of the universe which, although it still had the Earth at the centre, provided for accurate prediction of the positions of the planets. *See also* SU p.254, *254*.

Hippias of Elis (5th century BC), Greek SOPHIST. Only fragments of his writings survive, and he is known mainly through the writings of PLATO. Because of Hippias' claim to have mastered all the fields of learning, Plato regarded him, and all Sophists, as superficial.

Hippies, term used, especially in the 1960s to refer to people who rejected conventional middle-class values. Most were young people who renounced materialism, the work ethic and war, emphasizing brotherhood and love. They had irregular life-styles, often living in communal groups. *See also* BEATNIKS; YIPPIES.

Hippocrates (*c.* 460–377 BC), Greek physician, often called "the father of medicine". Although little is known about him, and the writings known as the *Hippocratic Collection* probably represent the works of several people, he exerted a tremendous influence. He freed medicine from superstition, emphasizing clinical observation and providing guidelines for surgery and for the treatment of fevers. Most important, he is credited with providing the Hippocratic Oath, a code of professional conduct still followed by doctors today. *See also* MS pp.36, 136.

Hippolytus of Rome, Saint (*c.* 170–*c.* 235), author and antipope. When he opposed the policies of Pope CALIXTUS I his followers elected him antipope. He was banished (235) to Sardinia, where he finally resigned his claim to the papacy and died a martyr. Many of his works survive only in fragments, among them his *Apostolic Tradition* and *Refutation of All Heresies*.

Hippolytus, son of the mythical Greek hero Theseus and the Amazon queen Hippolyta. The dramatist EURIPIDES, in his tragedy *Hippolytus*, tells of Hippolytus' refusal to shun other women in order to honour APHRODITE and how this led to divine retribution.

Hipponax (6th century BC), Greek lyric poet, believed to be the inventor of the scazon, or "limping" IAMBIC verse. His poems were bitter, satirical and concerned with love and quarrels between his friends.

Hippopotamus, bulky, herbivorous, even-toed mammal that lives in Africa. *Hippopotamus amphibius* has a massive grey or brown body with a large head, short legs and short tail. Males weigh up to 4.5 tonnes. Hippopotamuses generally live in groups, spending much of their time in water. They can close their nostrils under water but have to rise to the surface to breathe. Pygmy hippopotamuses, *Choeropsis liberiensis*, are much smaller, generally solitary, and spend more time on land. The hippopotamus is valued for its hide and flesh, but the pygmy is protected. Family Hippopotamidae. *See also* NW pp.*155*, *163*, *232*; PE p.*253*.

Hire-purchase, method of acquiring goods by making a down-payment (a deposit), and paying the rest, with interest, in instalments at regular intervals. The vendor usually has an agreement with a bank or financier who pays the full selling price of the goods, at the request of the buyer (usually any credit-worthy member of the public). The financer then hires the goods to the buyer who becomes full owner of the goods only after repaying the financer.

Hirohito (1901–), emperor of Japan (1926–). His visit to Europe in 1921 made him the first Japanese crowned prince to travel abroad. Although he exercised little political power, he persuaded the Japanese government to surrender to the Allies in 1945, announcing that surrender himself on the radio. Under the constitution drawn-up by the occupation forces he lost almost all his remaining power. *See also* HC2 pp.214, *215*.

Hiroshige, Ando (1797–1858), Japanese master of the UKIYO-E (coloured WOODCUT). He is known for his landscapes, the most famous of which are his 53 woodblock prints depicting his trip from Edo (Tokyo) district to Kyoto. His work influenced IMPRESSIONIST and other 19th-century European artists.

Hiroshima, city in the SW of Honshu, Japan, at the W end of the Inland Sea. The River Ota divides the city into six islands connected by 81 bridges. Founded in 1594, it was a military headquarters in several wars and the target, in 1945, of the first atomic bomb dropped on a populated area. Sixty per cent of the city was destroyed, of which a small part was later designated a "Peace City" by the govern-

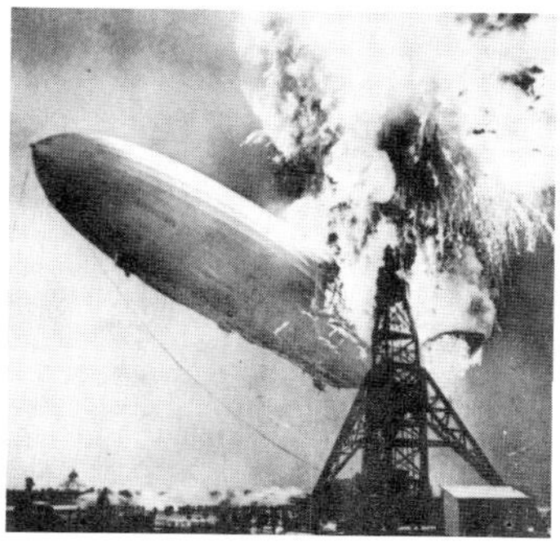

Hindenburg; the German airship bursting into flames at its moorings in the USA in 1937.

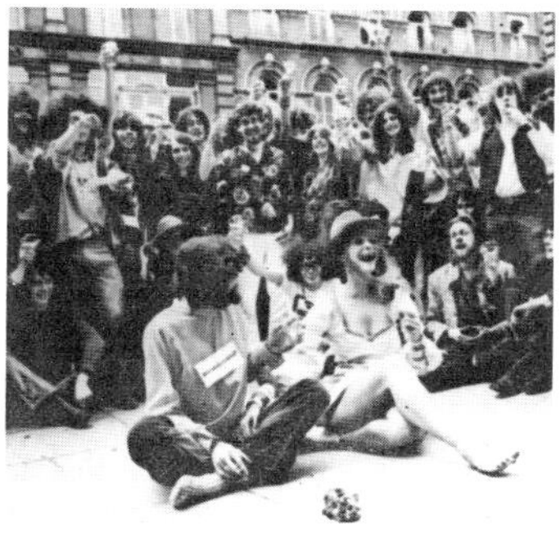

Hippies at a 1968 wedding reception – held, in hippy style, before the wedding itself.

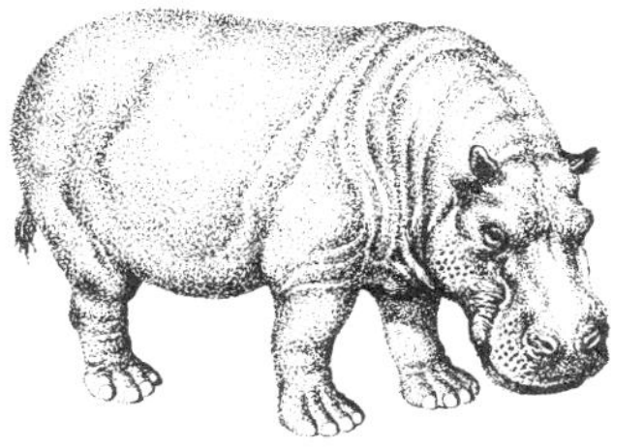

Hippopotamus is the third largest land animal; the elephant and rhinoceros are larger.

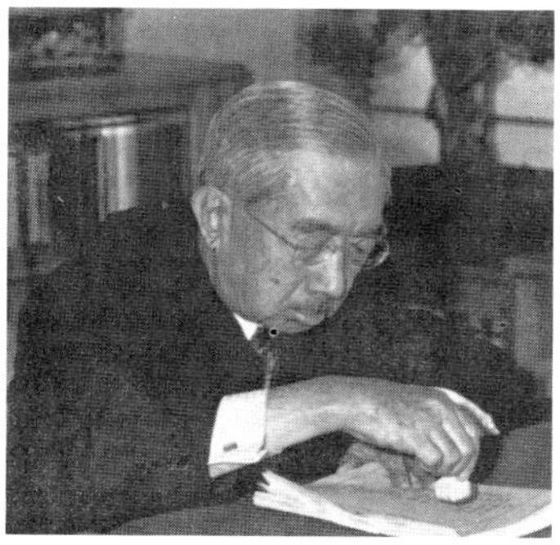

Hirohito, seen here sealing government papers. He has reigned for over 50 years.

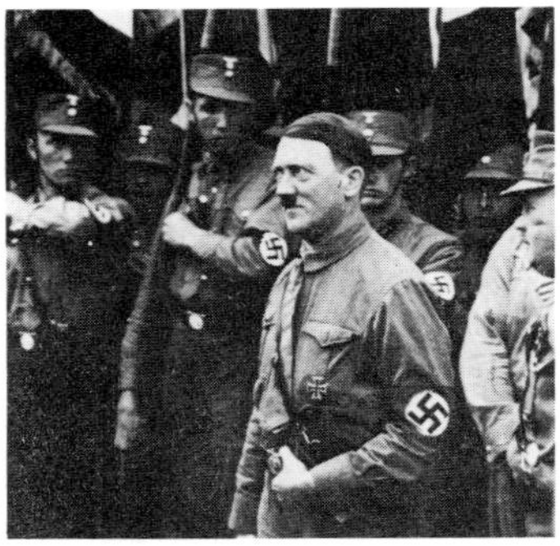

Adolf Hitler at a 1931 rally after the Nazis had won power in the Thuringia government.

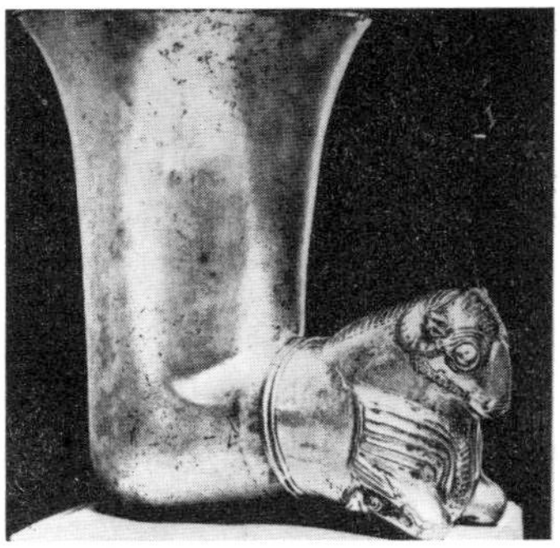

Hittite drinking horn of *c.* 7th century BC, made of silver with a handle of gold.

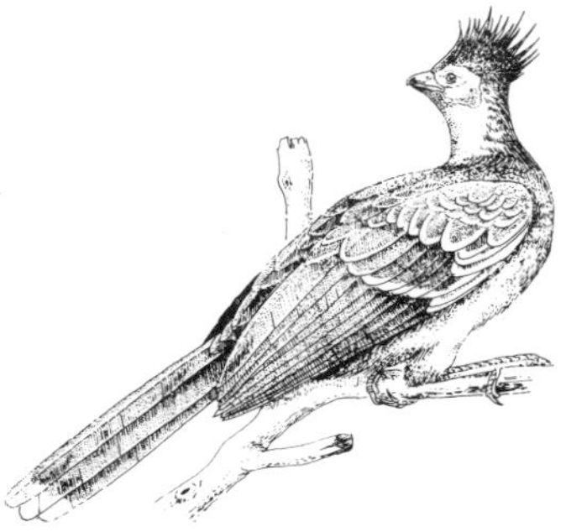

Hoatzin has attractive feathers but its musky odour has earned it the name "stinkbird".

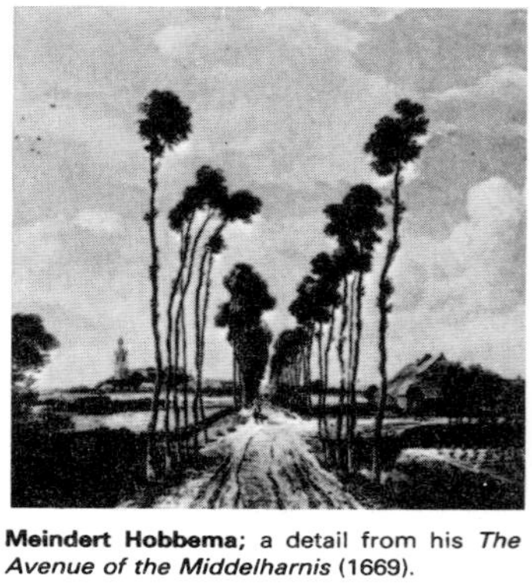

Meindert Hobbema; a detail from his *The Avenue of the Middelharnis* (1669).

ment. An annual conference against nuclear weapons is held in the city. Its industries include brewing, shipbuilding and engineering. Pop. (1974) 761,240.

Hirschvogel, Augustin (1503–53), German etcher, glass painter, enamelist and cartographer. He is best known for his mountain landscapes.

Hirsutism, excessive or abnormally located hair growth, especially in women. It may be caused by ovarian or adrenal tumours and sometimes by drugs.

Hispaniola, second-largest island in the West Indies, between Cuba (W) and Puerto Rico (E), in the N central Caribbean Sea. HAITI occupies the W third of the island and the DOMINICAN REPUBLIC, the remaining eastern portion. It is a mountainous, agricultural region with a subtropical climate. It was discovered in 1492 by Christopher COLUMBUS, who called it Española, the first Spanish colony in the New World. Industries: coffee, cacao, and some mining, particularly bauxite. Area: 76,480sq km (9,559sq miles). Pop. (1975 est.) 9,281,000.

Hispano-Moresque style, type of 14th-century Moorish pottery and tiles made in Spain, especially in Malaga and Granada. These ceramics were usually decorated with gold lustre pigments, often combined with blue.

Histidine, colourless soluble crystalline AMINO ACID, $C_3H_3N_2CH_2CHNH_2COOH$, which is the precursor of histamine.

Histochemistry, study of the distribution of biocmical substances and reactions in living tissue. *See also* BIOCHEMISTRY.

Histoire naturelle (1749–1804), momentous 44-volume work by the French naturalist George-Louis Leclerc, comte de Bufton. Published as *Histoire naturelle, générale et particulière*, it deals with the history of natural science.

Histology, biological, especially microscopic, study of organic tissues and structures in living organisms.

Historical geology, study of sedimentary rocks in which a record of events in the history of the Earth is trapped. The composition of the different layers, and the plant and animal remains they contain, give clues to the stages of evolution and to water, land and temperature conditions that prevailed when a particular stratum was deposited. *See also* PE pp.128–131.

Historicism, view that an adequate account of any subject capable of description in time must be historical. All things must be explained in terms of their origins and comprehended in their development from inception to maturity. The term has been associated with the philosophy of Friedrich HEGEL and Karl MARX. *See also* DETERMINISM.

History, written reconstruction of man's past. The Western historical tradition dates back to the Greek historians HERODOTUS and THUCYDIDES. Most medieval historical research was the work of ecclesiastics such as BEDE, who is often considered the first English historian. Renaissance historians uncritically followed precedents of earlier ones, but rationalism was the chief influence on the historiography of the 18th century. Modern history writing, however, is concerned with objectivity and critical examination of primary sources. It dates from the early 19th-century German school led by Leopold von Ranke and Berthold Niebuhr. It was only after this time that history became a topic in schools and universities, and specialist journals were devoted to it.

History of the English Church and People, (AD 731), account by BEDE of the Anglo-Saxons and the Church. Although mainly an ecclesiastical history, it is an important primary source for the early history of the Britons, and was therefore used for the earlier entries of the *Anglo-Saxon Chronicle*.

History of the English-Speaking Peoples, (1956–58), four-volume work by Winston CHURCHILL dealing with the period from 55 BC to death of Queen VICTORIA. Churchill's theme was his hope that the "contemplation" of past "trials and tribulations" would bring about peace and alliance in the world.

History of the Kings of England (*Historia de Gestis Regum Britanniae*), written account that contains a genealogy of the legendary kings of England from the time of Brutus the Trojan. Produced by Geoffrey of Monmouth, who claimed it was a translation of a Breton manuscript, it is one of the sources for the legends of Arthur and his knights.

Hitachi, Japanese business conglomerate, a major producer of electrical equipment, appliances and machinery. In 1976 it employed about 144,000 persons.

Hitchcock, Alfred (1899–), British film director who has lived in Hollywood since 1940. A master of the droll, sophisticated suspense thriller, he believed strongly in the creation of emotion by purely cinematic means. His films include *Blackmail* (1929), *The Thirty-nine Steps* (1935), *Suspicion* (1941), *Notorious* (1946), *Strangers on a Train* (1951), *Dial M for Murder* (1954), *Rear Window* (1954), *Vertigo* (1958), *North by Northwest* (1959), *Psycho* (1960), *Frenzy* (1972) and *Family Plot* (1976).

Hitler, Adolf (1889–1945), German dictator, *b.* Austria. He served in the ranks of the German army during WWI and was decorated for bravery. After the war he returned to Munich and in 1921 became the leader of the small National Socialist Workers' (or NAZI) Party. In 1923 a Nazi Putsch failed to overthrow the Bavarian government and Hitler was imprisoned. While serving his sentence he set out his extreme racist and nationalist views in MEIN KAMPF. After his release, Hitler worked to revive the Nazi Party and finally, partly in consequence of economic depression and ineffectual democratic government, became Chancellor in a coalition on 30 Jan. 1933. Within a month the REICHSTAG FIRE gave him the excuse to establish a one-party state, and the following year he launched a purge in which all possible rivals were liquidated. In the following years Hitler rearmed Germany and occupied large areas of central Europe. Germany's attack on Poland (Sept. 1939) precipitated WWII, a conflict of global proportions, during which the Jewish people were systematically exterminated by the Germans in all parts of occupied Europe. Hostilities ceased in 1945 with Germany's total defeat and Hilter's suicide (30 April). *See also* HC2 pp.223, 226–227.

Hittites, ancient people who built a powerful empire in Asia Minor and N Syria (*c.* 2000–*c.* 1200 BC). Primarily of Indo-European stock, they invaded BABYLONIA (*c.* 1590 BC), seized Cappadocia and conquered Syria and Palestine. Rameses II of Egypt checked them near Kadesh on the River Orontes (*c.* 1284), which led to a treaty. Boğazköy and Carchemish were their great cities. After 1260 BC the Thracians, Phrygians and Assyrians invaded the Hittite lands, and their loose empire broke up. The Hittites moved southwards, but their culture survived in city states established by refugees in N Syria. By the 8th century BC these last remnants of the Hittites had been entirely absorbed into the Assyrian empire. *See also* HC1 pp.52–53.

Hives, popular term for the transient, itchy reddish or pale raised skin patches of urticaria (nettle-rash). Hives may be caused by ALLERGY to certain foods or drugs, by irritants such as sunlight or animal dander (a form of dandruff), or by emotional stress. *See also* MS pp.*98*, 99.

HMS Pinafore, comic opera in two acts by Arthur SULLIVAN, libretto by William GILBERT. It was first produced at the Opera Comique, London, in 1878. It ran for 700 consecutive performances and became widely popular in Europe and the USA.

Hoad, Lewis Alan ("Lew") (1934–), Australian tennis player. He won the Wimbledon mens singles championship in 1956 and 1957; in 1956 he also took the Australian and French singles titles.

Hoare-Laval plan (1935), plan devised by the British foreign secretary, Sir Samuel Hoare, and the French prime minister, Pierre LAVAL, to avoid war with Italy over MUSSOLINI's invasion of Abyssinia. It ceded two-thirds of the country to Italy. Public outcry led to both Hoare's and Laval's resignation.

Hoatzin, shaggy-crested bird of N South American river valleys. It has a large crop for storing vegetable matter. The hatchlings have claws on their wings and are able to climb trees. The hoatzin is a member of the CUCKOO family but resembles a long slender crow, the brownish adult having rounded wings and a long tail. The female lays two to three oval, spotted, white eggs. Species *Opisthocomus hoazin.*

Hoban, James (*c.* 1762–1831), US architect, *b.* Ireland. He designed the State Capitol, Columbia, and the original White House, Washington, DC (1792).

Hobart, capital and port of the island state of Tasmania, SE Australia. It has one of the best natural harbours in the world, and most of the state's exports leave by sea routes from Hobart. The city's industries include fruit processing, textiles and zinc. Pop. (1970) 52,900.

Hobbema, Meindert (1638–1709), Dutch painter of serene landscapes, a favourite of 18th and early 19th-century English landscape artists. His *The Avenue of Middelharnis* (1669) is among the most popular of all Dutch landscape paintings.

Hobbes, Thomas (1588–1679), English philosopher. In *De Corpore* (Concerning the Body), *De Homine* (Concerning Man) and *De Cive* (Concerning the Citizen) he presented his view that matter and its motion comprise the only valid subject matter of philosophy. His greatest work, *Leviathan* (1651), argued that man is not naturally a social being but most obey moral rules in order to maintain civilized society.

Hobbs, Sir John Berry ("Jack") (1882–1963), England and Surrey cricketer whose records of runs scored (61,237) and centuries (197) remain unbeaten. The most accomplished of opening batsmen, he played in 61 Test matches between 1907 and 1930 (5,410 runs, average 56.94).

Hobby, typical FALCON, a diurnal bird of prey found in temperate regions, especially in Europe. A brown-and-white streaked bird, it lives in or near open woodland country and east small birds and insects. Length: 33cm (13in). Species *Falco subbuteo*. *See also* NW p.*140*.

Hobson, Harold (1904–), British drama critic. He was drama critic of *The Sunday Times* (1947–76) and television critic of *The Listener* (1947–51). He has also written several book on the theatre.

Hobson, Captain William, (1793–1842), British colonist and first governor of New Zealand. A humane and just administrator, he regularized land sales in the colony and helped to draft the Treaty of Waitangi, by which the Maoris accepted British sovereignty. Hobson entered the navy in 1803 and became governor in 1841.

Hochelaga, IROQUOIS name for Montreal, Canada. The village was discovered by Jacques CARTIER in 1535. The name is translated as "at the place of the beaver dam", and it was a centre of Indian trade and government.

Hochhuth, Rolf (1931–), German dramatist whose reputation rests on two controversial documentary plays based on incidents of WWII. *The Representative* (1963) attacked the noncommittal attitude of Pope Pius XII towards Nazi concentration camps. *Soldiers* (1967) implied that Winston Churchill was responsible for the death of the Polish premier-in-exile, Gen. Sikorski. *Guerillas* (1970), *The Midwife* (1972) and *Lysistrata and NATO* (1973) proved somewhat less controversial.

Ho Chi Minh (1890–1969), Vietnamese political figure, *b.* Nguyen That Thanh. In 1911 he left Vietnam and lived successively in the USA, Britain and France. In 1920 he joined the French Communist Party. He returned to Vietnam and presided over the founding of the Vietnamese Communist party in 1930 but, threatened with arrest, fled to Moscow and later China. In 1941 he returned to Vietnam and founded the VIET MINH to fight the Japanese. With the Japanese driven out, he declared Vietnam an independent nation (1945) and was himself appointed president. The French returned and contested Ho's authority until their defeat in 1954. The 1954 Geneva Conference recognized Ho as president of the Democratic Republic of Vietnam (North Vietnam). When the government of the South, backed by the USA, refused to hold reunification elections, Ho helped the NATIONAL LIBERATION FRONT (Viet Cong) in its attempt to gain control of the South. He did not live to see the unification of an independent Vietnam. *See also* HC2 pp.292–293.

Hockey, 11-a-side game, for both sexes, played with curved sticks and a 7–7.3cm (2.8–3in) diameter white ball. The aim is to hit the ball into one of the 3.66 by 2.13m (12 × 7ft) goals centred at each end of the rectangular 92 by 50–55m (100 × 55–60 yards) pitch. To score, a player must be within the striking semicircle in front of the goal. Formations vary with tactics, but basically a team consists of a goalkeeper, two backs, three halves and five forwards. Play commences with a "bully" between two opposing players, who touch sticks twice then go for the ball. After this the ball is dribbled or passed using only the flat side of the stick, which may not be raised above shoulder height. Only the goalkeeper, protected by gloves and pads, may kick or use his body to stop the ball; others may use a flat hand to stop it dead in flight. Infringements are penalized by free hits, penalty corners or penalty strokes. A game comprises two 35-minute halves and is controlled by two umpires. Although hockey's origins are lost in antiquity, the modern game dates from the mid-19th century. A purely amateur sport, it is played throughout the world and has been an Olympic sport, with breaks, since 1908.

Hockey, ice. *See* ICE HOCKEY.

Hockey, roller. *See* ROLLER HOCKEY.

Hockney, David (1937–), British painter, who made his name during the POP ART movement with witty, often deliberately naïve, paintings, such as *Flight into Italy–Swiss Landscape* (1962). In the late 1960 and the 1970s he developed a more realistic, classical style. Typical of this style are his portrait of Celia Birtwell and Ossie Clark (1970) and *A Bigger Splash* (1967). His graphic work, executed with an economical but powerful sense of line, includes many fine portraits and his series of etchings, *A Rake's Progress* (1961–63). *See also* HC2 p.*281*.

Hoddinott, Alun (1929–), Welsh composer. He studied with Arthur Benjamin and was appointed professor at the University College of South Wales in 1967. His compositions include symphonies, concertos for piano, clarinet and viola, an oratorio and chamber music.

Hodgkin, Sir Alan Lloyd (1914–), British physiologist. He shared the 1963 Nobel Prize in physiology and medicine with John ECCLES and Andrew HUXLEY for his part in discoveries concerning the ionic mechanisms involved in the excitation and inhibition of the membranes of nerve cells. This work is fundamental to an understanding of the function of NERVES.

Hodgkin, Dorothy Mary Crowfoot (1910–), British chemist. After teaching at Oxford and Cambridge Universities she spent some time at the University of Ghana before returning to Oxford in 1960. In 1964 she was awarded the Nobel Prize in chemistry for her determination of the structure of VITAMIN B_{12} by X-RAY CRYSTALLOGRAPY. She also determined the structure of PENICILLIN and several other large molecules by the same process.

Hodgkins, Frances (1869–1947), New Zealand-born painter. Arriving in Europe in 1901, she lived in France, especially Paris, and Britain, settling first in St Ives, Cornwall (1914) and later in Dorset. In her most mature work, painted in her later years, she developed a style of still-life and landscape painting that grew increasingly nearer abstraction.

Hodgkin's disease, named after the pathologist Thomas Hodgkin (1798–1866) who first described it, a condition characterized by painless enlargement of the LYMPH GLANDS, lymphatic tissue, and spleen, with subsequent spread to other areas. Fever is a common symptom, and weight loss, anaemia, loss of appetite, and night sweats may occur. The condition is twice as common in males as in females. Treatment varies with the stage reached by the disease but in general consists of RADIOTHERAPY, combinations of drugs, or both. Likelihood of cure or long-term survival is about 50%.

Hodler, Ferdinand (1853–1918), Swiss painter. His early work included naturalistic landscapes; later, he used colour and line in an EXPRESSIONISTIC manner, as in his symbolist painting *Night* (1890).

Hoe, Richard March (1812–86), US inventor of the rotary printing press (1847), which worked at far higher speeds than the traditional "flat-bed" press. Later developments further increased the pace by printing on a roll or "web" of paper, rather than on single sheets. The rotary press and the web feed became the foundations of the newspaper industry. *See also* MM p.*64*.

Hoff, Jacobus Hendricus van't (1852–1911), Dutch physical chemist, professor at Amsterdam, Leipzig and then Berlin. His research involved advanced investigations of the carbon atom, the theory that gas laws are also applicable to dissolved substances, and the chemical application of THERMODYNAMICS. In 1901 he was awarded the first Nobel Prize in chemistry for his studies on the mechanism of chemical equilibrium, reaction rates and osmotic pressure.

Hoffman, Dustin (1937–), US film actor who became a star following his appearance in *The Graduate* (1967). In John Schlesinger's *Midnight Cowboy* (1969) he played Ratso, a derelict; in Sam Peckinpah's *Straw Dogs* (1971) he was an academic who goes berserk; and he portrayed the Jewish comedian Lenny Bruce in *Lenny* (1974). He also starred in *Marathon Man* (1976) and *All the Presidents Men* (1976).

Hoffmann, Ernst Theodor Wilhelm (1776–1822), German Romantic author. He wrote many fantastic stories, several of which were later the basis of the opera *The Tales of Hoffmann* (1881) by OFFENBACH, and was a noted music critic. *The Devil's Elixir* (1813–15) was his only novel.

Hoffmann, Josef (1870–1956), Austrian architect, a pioneer of modern architecture in Vienna. A student of Otto WAGNER, he was a founder of the VIENNA SEZESSION (1897) and the Wiener Werkstätte (1903). His buildings were courageously early examples of the white cube buildings of the INTERNATIONAL STYLE; with his Stoclet House, Brussels (1905–11), he showed that this new, anti-traditional style could be made to look lavish and monumental by means of the materials used.

Hofmann, August Wilhelm von (1818–1892), German chemist and teacher. After serving as an assistant to Justus von LIEBIG he was appointed director of the new Royal College of Chemistry in London. Most of his work was based on the compounds of coal tar and their derivatives. Hofmann discovered a method for converting an amide into an amine – the Hofmann reaction – and classed all amines as formal derivatives of ammonia. One of his pupils was William PERKIN, who made the first aniline dye, the colour mauve.

Hofmann, Melchior (*c.* 1495–*c.* 1543), German ANABAPTIST leader. A mystic, he believed that Christ would soon return to earth for the judgment day and urged his followers to be prepared. He spread Anabaptist beliefs in Holland, where his followers were called Melchiorites.

Hofmannsthal, Hugo von (1874–1929), Austrian dramatist, poet and essayist whose *Jedermann* (*Everyman*; 1911) is a verse drama that is regularly staged at the Salzburg Festival, of which he was a founder. One of Richard STRAUSS's librettists, he collaborated with him on *Der Rosenkavalier* (1911) and several other operas.

Hofstadter, Robert (1915–), US physicist who shared the 1961 Nobel Prize in physics with Rudolf MÖSSBAUER for their investigations of nuclear structure. Hofstandter discovered that both PROTONS and NEUTRONS (which make up the NUCLEUS) have a central positively charged core surrounded by a cloud of PIONS.

Hog. *See* PIG.

Hogan, William Benjamin ("Ben") (1912–), US golfer who overcame a near fatal car accident to become one of the best players in the world. He won four US Open championships (1948, 1950–51, 1953), two Professional Golfers' Association titles (1946, 1948), two Masters' tournaments (1951, 1953) and the British Open (1953).

Hogarth, William (1697–1764), English painter, engraver and caricaturist, most famous for his genius in portraying the English national character in such brilliant story-series of paintings as *The Harlot's Progress* (also made into engravings). Similarly, in the *The Rake's Progress* and *Marriage à la Mode*, he satirized English society. In his treatise *The Analysis of Beauty* (1753) he expounded his theories of art. He also painted fine portraits, such as a self-portrait *The Painter and his Pug* (1745). *See also* HC2 pp.*19*, 70.

Hogben, Lancelot (1895–1975), British scientist and popularizer of mathematics. Hogben was professor of social biology at London from 1930 to 1937, of zoology at Birmingham from 1941 until 1947 and of medical statistics at Birmingham from 1947 to 1961.

Hogg, James (1770–1835), Scottish poet and sheep farmer, known as "The Ettrick Shepherd". Encouraged by Sir Walter SCOTT, he published several poetic works which display an interest in the supernatural. His most enduring prose work is *Private Memoirs and Confusions of a Justified Sinner* (1824).

Hogg, Quintin McGarel (1907–), British lawyer and Conservative politician. After a successful legal career, Hogg succeeded to the title of Viscount Hailsham in 1950, which he resigned in 1963 to pursue his political career in the House of Commons. In 1970, however, he re-entered the Lords as Baron Hailsham. He was Lord Chancellor from 1970–74.

Hogmanay, in Scotland, the eve of New Year's Day. Traditionally more festive than Christmas in Scotland, the Hogmanay celebrations are marked by customs and superstitions dating back to Celtic times. The term is sometimes also applied to presents given at New Year, and possibly derives from the word for such gifts in the French Norman dialect.

Hohenstaufen, German dynasty (also called GHIBELLINE) which exercised great power in Germany and the HOLY ROMAN EMPIRE from 1138 to 1254. Its name comes from the castle of Staufen, built in 1075 by Frederick, Count of Swabia, whose son became King CONRAD III of Germany and Holy Roman Emperor in 1138. From Conrad III to CONRAD IV, who died in 1254, the family occupied the Imperial throne, except for the years 1209–15 (when Otto IV, the representative of their great rivals the GUELPHS, was emperor). The greatest of the Hohenstaufens was FREDERICK II, who firmly shifted the family's interests to Italy. On his death in 1250 the family went into decline. It died out with the death of Conradin in 1268.

Hokkaidō, formerly Yezo, the second largest of the four main islands of Japan, and the country's chief farming region. Forests cover a large part of the land area and are a source of timber and wood pulp. It is also the major coal-mining region of Japan. The capital is Sapporo. Area: 78,511sq km (30,313sq miles). Pop. (1970) 5,184,287.

Hokusai, Katsushika (1760–1849), Japanese master of UKIYO-E (colour WOODCUT), especially famous for his landscapes. Like his contemporary HIROSHIGE, he had enormous influence on late-19th-century European painters. His most famous print is *The Wave*. *See also* HC1 p.*133*..

Holbach, Paul Henri Dietrich, Baron d' (1723–89), French radical materialist philosopher and virulent anti-Christian, who believed that if man would abandon superstition he could achieve universal happiness. In his *System of Nature* (1770) he expounded his materialist philosophy, which reduced everything to the operation

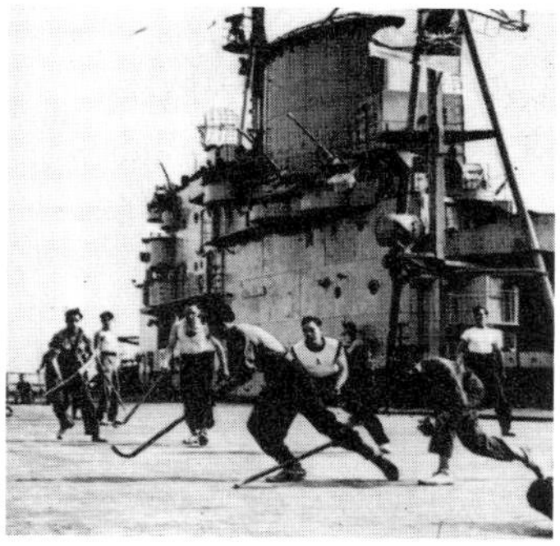

Hockey can be played on many surfaces, as on the deck of the carrier HMS *Illustratious*.

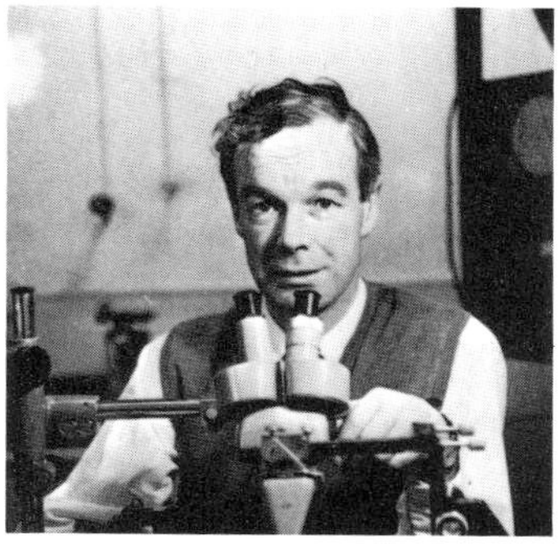

Alan Hodgkin was a government research scientist during WWII, working on radar.

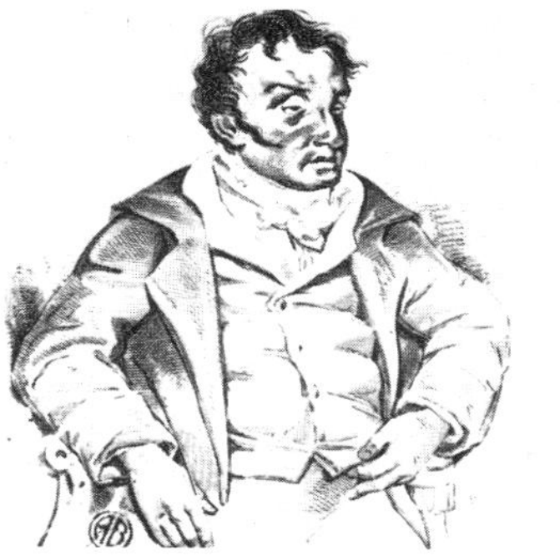

Ernst Hoffmann's *Mademoiselle de Scudéry* (1818) was an early detective story.

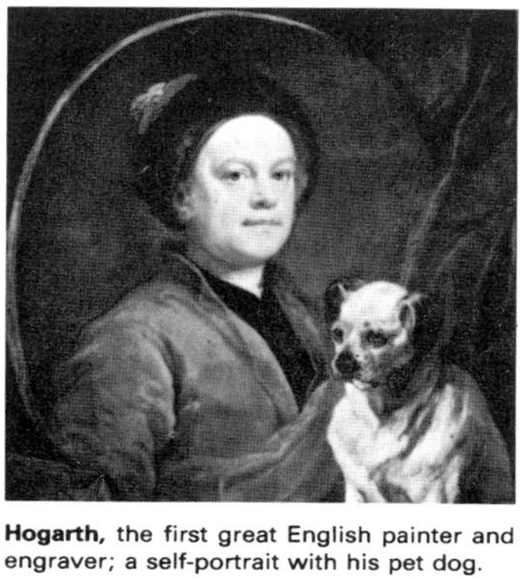

Hogarth, the first great English painter and engraver; a self-portrait with his pet dog.

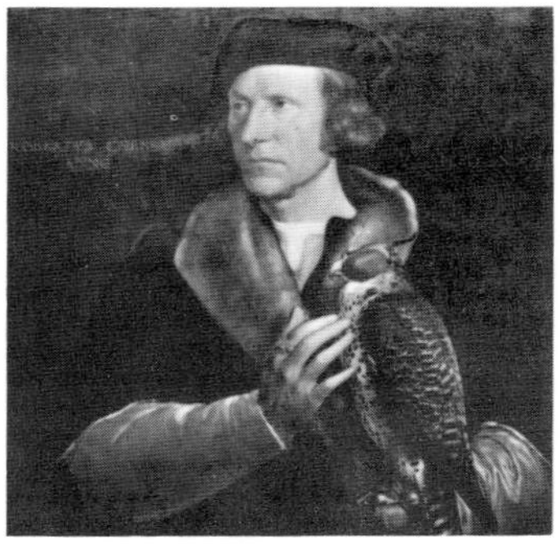

Hans Holbein the Younger; a portrait by him of Robert Cheseman, falconer to Henry VIII.

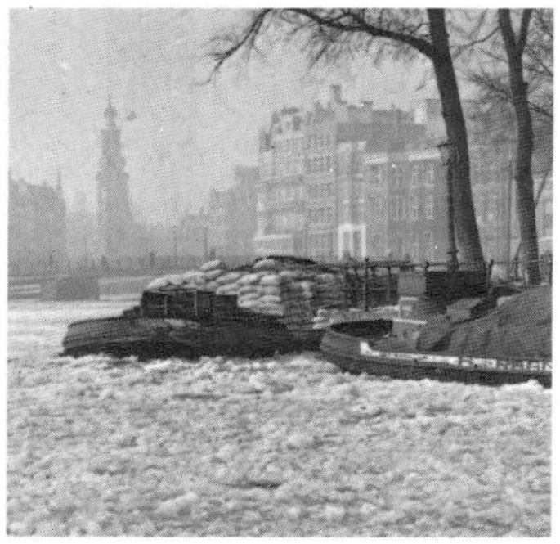

Holland; a winter view of the Amstel, the river by which Amsterdam is built.

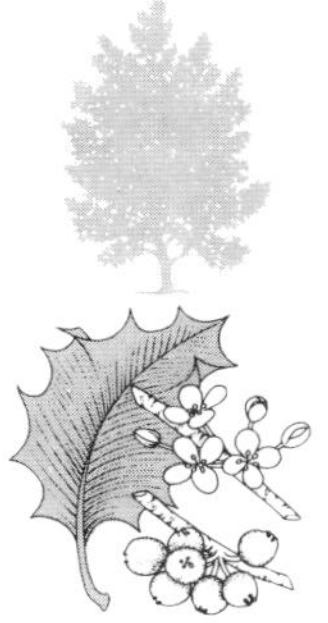

Holly, used in churches at Christmas, was originally called the Holy tree.

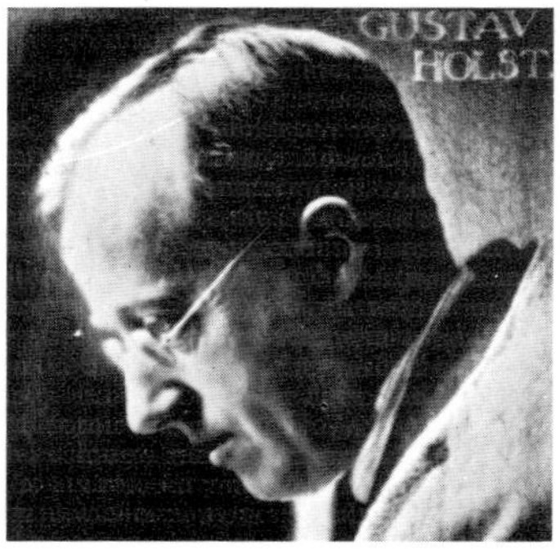

Holst, although influenced by Grieg, Strauss and others, wrote highly original music.

of physical forces as matter; anything else must be illusion.

Holbein, Hans, the Younger (1497–1543), German painter, one of the most penetratingly realist of all European portraitists. He began in the workshop of his father, Holbein the Elder, but about 1514 went to Basel, where he soon won a reputation with his illustrations for the Luther Bible and his wood engravings of the *Dance of Death* (1523–26); his international fame as a portraitist was established with three portraits of his friend Erasmus (1523). During a visit to London in 1526 he painted Sir Thomas MORE and his family. He settled in London in 1532 and from 1536 until his death from the plague he was court painter to Henry VIII. Holbein's masterpieces include his showpiece *The Ambassadors* (1533), and superb easel paintings of *Christina of Denmark, Duchess of Milan* (1538), *Anne of Cleves* (1540), and *Catherine Howard* (1541), all royal sitters. *See also* HC1 pp.260, *260*, 280–281, *280*.

Holberg, Ludwig, Baron von (1684–1754), Danish poet and dramatist, *b.* Norway. His verse includes the mock-heroic poem *Peder Paars* (1719–20), but he is chiefly remembered for his plays, which include *The Political Tinker* (1722), *Jeppe of the Hill* (1722) and *The Fussy Man* (1726).

Holden, Charles, (1875–1960), British architect who is noted for his designs of London Underground stations, especially the facade of Bond Street station. Holden collaborated with sculptors, including EPSTEIN, GILL and MOORE, in urban architecture. He also designed some of the buildings at London University.

Holding company, one which controls the activities of other companies by the acquisition of a majority of their shares. Large public companies are frequently holding companies with many subsidiaries, which individually deal with one section of the trade or industry in which the group deals.

Holford, William Graham (1907–1975), British architect and Lever Professor of Civic Design at Liverpool from 1936, when he worked on the design of nuclear laboratories. From 1948 to 1970 Holford was professor of town planning at London University.

Holiday, Billie (1915–59), US blues and popular jazz singer who sang in nightclubs in the 1930s and later with the bands of Count BASIE and Artie Shaw. Her memorable renditions of *My Man*, *Mean to Me* (1937) and *God Bless the Child* (1941) have a legendary status in the history of American popular and jazz music.

Holiday camp, enclosed area at a seaside resort where holidaymakers pay an overall charge for accommodation, food, recreation facilities and entertainments for one or two weeks. Most activities are organized by the camp staff. The first British holiday camp was opened by Billy BUTLIN at Skegness in 1937. Butlin's camps accommodate between 5,000 and 11,500 people each.

Holidays, Bank. *See* BANK HOLIDAYS.

Holinshed, Raphael (died *c.* 1580), English historian. His historical work, *The Chronicles of England, Scotlande, and Irelande* (2 vols, 1578), provided an invaluable source of information for many early dramatists, notably SHAKESPEARE.

Holland, Henry (1745–1806), British architect; the son-in-law of Capability BROWN, with whom he worked from 1771. His independent works include Carlton House, London (1783–85), and the Marine Pavilion, Brighton (1786–87; later altered to the Royal Pavilion by NASH), both for the Prince Regent. He also built country houses and laid out part of Chelsea, including Sloane Street, but little of this work survives. He worked in a style close to that of the ADAM brothers.

Holland, John Philip, (1840–1914), US inventor of the first modern petrol-drivens submarine. He offered a design to the US Navy Department in 1875 but it was rejected as impracticable. With further work the successful *Fenian Ram* was launched in 1881. This was not practical for extended operations, but further development produced the *Holland* which had an internal combustion engine for surface cruising and an electric motor for submerged cruising. The US government bought the *Holland* in 1900. *See also* MM p.118.

Holland, Sir Sidney George (1893–1961), New Zealand politician and prime minister (1949–57). As head of a National Party administration, he relaxed economic controls, abolished the upper house and settled a five-month-long dockers' strike. *See also* HC2 p.250.

Holland, name popularly given to the entire NETHERLANDS, but properly referring to only one of the country's provinces. A fief of the Holy Roman Empire in the twelfth century, it was seized by the county of Hainaut in 1299 and passed to Burgundy in 1433 and to Austria in 1482. In the next 200 years Holland became a sea power and led the United Provinces of the Netherlands in their long battle for independence from Spain.

Hollar, Wenceslaus (1607–77), Bohemian printmaker. He made numerous topographical and historically important engravings of London before the Great Fire of 1666. His etchings and watercolour drawings of 17th-century English life include a portrait of *Charles I and his Queen* (1691) after VAN DYCK.

Holley, Robert William (1922–), US biochemist. He shared with H.G. KHORANA and M.W. NIRENBERG the 1968 Nobel Prize in physiology and medicine for his work on the way genes determine the function of CELLS. Holley described the first full sequence of sub-units in nucleic acid, the genetic material of a cell. This was an important step towards the understanding of gene action.

Holly, Buddy (1936–59). US singer and songwriter. After an unsuccessful recording session in Nashville in 1956, Holly and his group the Crickets released *That'll be the Day* (1957). The immediate success of this record was emulated in the same year by the hits *Oh Boy* and *Peggy Sue*. He was a pioneer of double-tracking and the standard rock-group four-man line-up. He was killed in an air crash.

Holly, any of 300 species of shrubs and trees that grow in most parts of the world. They have alternate, simple leaves and small flowers; male and female flowers are usually on separate plants. The one-seeded fruit is usually red. The English holly tree (*Ilex aquifolium*) has spiny evergreen leaves. Height: to 15m (50ft). Family Aquifoliaceae.

Hollyhock, biennial plant native to China and cultivated widely throughout the world. It has leafy stems and showy, often double, flowers of red, pink, white, yellow or orange. Height: to 2.7m (9ft). Family Malvaceae; species *Althea rosea*. *See also* PE p.*179*.

Hollywood, suburb of Los Angeles, USA, which was developed after 1910 by the new US film industry because of its fine weather and clear air. With most films now made in studios or on location, Hollywood is no longer the centre it once was, although many film stars still inhabit its most glamorous suburb, Beverly Hills.

Holman Hunt, William. *See* HUNT, WILLIAM HOLMAN.

Holmes, Arthur (1890–1965), British geologist and geophysicist who studied the age of rocks by measuring their radioactivity. He devised the first quantitative geological time scale in 1913 and estimated the Earth's age by means of temperature measurement.

Holmes, Oliver Wendell (1809–94), US author and physician, who studied medicine at Harvard and Paris. He was a gifted conversationalist and much of his best literary work was cast in the form of table-talk, as in *The Autocrat of the Breakfast Table* (1858), *The Professor at the Breakfast Table* (1860) and *The Poet at the Breakfast Table* (1872).

Holmium, metallic element (symbol Ho) of the lanthanide group, first identified spectroscopically in 1878. Its chief ore is monazite (a phosphate). The element has few commercial uses. Properties: at.no. 67 at.wt. 164.930: s.g. 8.803(25°C); m.p. 1,470°C; (2,680°F); b.p. 2,720°C (4,930°F); most common isotope Ho^{165}(100%). *See also* LANTHANIDE SERIES.

Holocene epoch, also called the Recent epoch, division of geological time extending from roughly 10,000 years ago to the present. It therefore includes the emergence of man as a settled member of communities, the first known villages dating from about 8,000 years ago. *See also* NW p.191; PE p.118.

Holocephali, one of three groups of cartilaginous fish. *See* NW p.124.

Holofernes, biblical Assyrian general enlisted by King NEBUCHADNEZZAR to subdue Judaea. He was slain by JUDITH, an attractive and pious Jewish widow, as he slept in his camp during the siege of Bethulia.

Holograph, three-dimensional image formed from information stored as light shifts on a photographic plate called a hologram. Although the concept of holography has been appreciated since about 1940, experiments could not proceed until the development of a sufficiently coherent light source – the LASER. *See also* SU pp.110–111.

Holon, city in W central Israel, in the Tel Aviv-Yafo metropolitan area. Its industries include textiles, metal products and food processing. Pop. (1974) 110,300.

Holothuroidea. *See* SEA CUCUMBER.

Holst, Gustav (1874–1934), British post-Romantic composer. His early works often betray his interest in Hinduism (the opera *Sita*, 1906); other influences were his love of folksong (*Somerset Rhapsody*, 1907) and the music of his friend Ralph VAUGHAN WILLIAMS Among his works are several operas, including *The Perfect Fool* (1922), songs, chamber music and popular orchestral suite, *The Planets* (1914–16).

Holst, Imogen (1907–), British composer, conductor and music educationalist. She has published short choral arrangements of folksongs, an overture and piano pieces, as well as a biography of her father, *Gustav Holst* (1938).

Holstein, Duchy of, former duchy in the S part of the West German state of SCHLESWIG-HOLSTEIN. From the 9th century it was part of the duchy of Saxony until it became a county, and in 1474 a dukedom of the Holy Roman Empire. It became part of Schleswig-Holstein in 1773, and passed from Denmark to Prussia in 1886.

Holt, Harold (1908–67), Australian politician. He became deputy leader of the Liberal Party in 1956 and prime minister on the retirement of Sir Robert MENZIES in 1966. Holt was drowned while swimming.

Holtby, Winifred (1898–1935), British novelist and journalist. Her posthumously published novel *South Riding* (1936) became a best-seller, a Yorkshire novel based in part on her own mother's experiences as a County Councillor. Other novels include *Anderby Wold* (1932) and *Mandoa! Mandoa!* (1933).

Holy Alliance, agreement signed by the crowned heads of Russia, Prussia and Austria in 1815. They pledged themselves to conduct policy on Christian principles and to uphold the existing social and territorial order in Europe, in particular the legitimacy of the BOURBONS in France and Spain. Ultimately it was signed by every European prince except the prince regent, later GEORGE IV, of England, the Pope and the Turkish sultan. *See also* HC2 pp.82–83.

Holy Communion. *See* EUCHARIST.

Holy Ghost, or Holy Spirit, in Christian theology, the third Person of the TRINITY that is God. Consubstantial, co-equal and co-eternal with the Creator and omnipresent Omniscience (the Father) and with the saviour and champion of sinful mankind (Christ), the Holy Ghost represents the spiritual force through which God's free gift of GRACE is given.

Holy Grail. *See* GRAIL, HOLY.

Holyhead, seaport on N coast of Holyhead island off NW Wales. It is a seaside resort and site of a nuclear power station. Pop. (1971) 10,608.

Holy Innocents, children of the age of two and under killed in Bethlehem by order of

HEROD THE GREAT who hoped by so doing to eliminate the infant Jesus, rumoured to be a future "king of the Jews". Only St MATTHEW'S GOSPEL contains this story. Their feast, formerly called Childermas, is observed on 28 December.

Holy Island. *See* LINDISFARNE.

Holy Land. *See* PALESTINE.

Holy League, name for a number of European alliances from the 15th to the 17th century. The purposes of these leagues included papal checks on French power, Spanish checks on the power of the Holy Roman Empire, French Catholic assertions against French Protestants and European defences against invasions by the Muslim Turks.

Holy Loch, small inlet on the W shore of the Firth of Clyde in W Scotland, opposite the mouth of the River Clyde. It is the site of a US Polaris submarine base.

Holyoake, George Jacob (1817–1906), British social reformer and founder of Secularism. He was the last person in England to be jailed for blasphemy (1842). He taught at the Mechanics Institute in Birmingham, lectured on Robert OWEN'S socialism, and promoted a parliamentary bill to legalize secular affirmations.

Holyoake, Sir Keith Jacka (1904–), New Zealand politician and Prime Minister (1957; 1960–72). A skilful leader of the National Party, he provided sound economic management and retained public support by unambitious but beneficent policies. In 1977 it was announced that he would succeed Sir Denis BLUNDELL as governor-general. *See also* HC2 p.250.

Holy Office, in the Roman Catholic Church, the tribunal that sat in Rome originally established in connection with the INQUISITION as the final court of appeal in trials of heresy. In 1965 its name was changed to Congregation for the Doctrine of the Faith and it was entrusted with the more positive role of safeguarding and promoting sound doctrine.

Holy Orders, in the Anglican, Roman Catholic and Orthodox Churches, the duties of the clergy and their hierarchical rank as outlined in the office of ORDINATON. A person is ordained and becomes a deacon, priest or bishop, becoming also a successor of the original apostles through the laying-on of hands by the presiding superior. In Protestant Churches, ordination of ministers is not a SACRAMENT. nor is the maintenance of apostolic succession considered relevant.

Holy Roman Empire, European empire founded in 962, when the German king, OTTO I, was crowned in Rome, and surviving until 1806. Some historians date it from CHARLEMAGNE'S coronation in 800. The emperor claimed to be the temporal sovereign of Christendom, ruling in cooperation with the spiritual sovereign, the POPE. However, the empire never encompassed all of western Christendom and its relations with the papacy were stormy. The imperial authority was based on the German monarchy. Once elected by the German princes, the German king sought papal election as emperor. He did not always receive it; and from MAXIMILIAN I (*r.* 1493–1519) the title Emperor was assumed without papal coronation. By that time, although the office remained elective in theory, the empire had become hereditary in the house of HAPSBURG, which held the office from 1438. Earlier dynasties included the SALIANS and HOHENSTAUFENS, under whom (11th-13th century) the empire was at the height of its power. Under the Hapsburgs it became an increasingly nominal entity, its rulers concentrating on their dynastic interests in Austria while the other German princes pursued their own ends. Pressure from NAPOLEON caused Francis II to resign the imperial title in 1806. *See also* HC1 pp.52–53.

Holyrood House, chief residence of the rulers of Scotland, in Edinburgh. It was begun in 1501 on the site of a 12th-century abbey, was partially destroyed in 1544, rebuilt and then burnt down in 1650. The house was rebuilt in French Renaissance style in the 1670s.

Holy See, one of the names by which the pope's see of Rome, or sometimes just the state of the VATICAN, is known. The term is usually used to denote the PAPACY itself in reference to its authority over the worldwide Roman Catholic Church.

Holy Sepulchre, traditional site of the burial and resurrection of Christ in Jerusalem. It is believed to have been "discovered" by St HELENA, mother of the Emperor CONSTANTINE I who built the first "Church of the Holy Sepulchre" there *c.* 335. Several churches have been built, destroyed and rebuilt on the site over the course of the centuries. Most of the present church dates from 1810.

Holy Shroud, The, sheet of very old linen in Turin Cathedral, by tradition the cloth in which the body of Christ was wrapped after the Crucifixion. It was photographed in 1898 when negatives were seen to show the shape of a human figure. In 1977 a Roman Catholic conference suggested the linen be tested scientifically.

Holy Spirit. *See* HOLY GHOST.

Holy water, water blessed by a priest for use in religious ritual as a symbol of cleansing. Water has been used in ancient Egyptian, Hindu, Greek, Roman, and Jewish rites and in Christian churches for blessing, purification and baptism.

Holy week, in the Christian calendar, the week preceding EASTER. Palm Sunday commemorates Christ's entry into Jerusalem, Maundy Thursday His institution of the Eucharist, and Good Friday His crucifixion.

Homage, feudal ceremony by which a person became a vassal of a lord and which preceded the granting of a FIEF (holding of land) by the lord to his vassal. The vassal knelt before the lord, put his hands in his lord's and declared himself to be his lord's man (Latin *homo,* "man"). The lord then signified his own responsibility to the vassal by kissing him and raising him to his feet. The vassal finally swore an oath of FEALTY to the lord. A similar ceremony takes place during the coronation service. *See also* HC1 p.*204*.

Home Counties, term given to those counties adjacent to London: Hertfordshire, Essex, Kent, Surrey and formerly Middlesex.

Home Guard, British volunteer force of men over military age trained for local defence. It began in 1940 and was first called the Local Defence Volunteers. Winston CHURCHILL called it the Home Guard and the name stuck. At first the men wore civilian clothes and trained with broomsticks, but by the end of 1942, when the threat of a German invasion had passed, the Home Guard had become a well-equipped, well-drilled force.

Home Office, British department of state, which dates from 1782. Before then there were two secretaries of state, for the northern and southern departments. The secretary for the southern department became the secretary of state for the Home Office. His principal duties were to advise the monarch on domestic affairs and the use of the royal prerogative. His responsibilities now cover all matters of national administration that have not been entrusted to another Minister. Relations with the Channel Islands and the Isle of Man are conducted through the Home Office. Until the creation of the Department for Northern Ireland in 1972, the office was also responsible for the affairs of Ulster.

Home of the Hirsel, Baron Alexander (Alec) Frederick Douglas-Home (1903–), British politician. *See* DOUGLAS-HOME, SIR ALEC.

Homeopathy, non-orthodox medical treatment that involves administering minute doses of a drug or remedy which causes effects or symptoms similar to those that are being treated. It is the opposite of ALLOPATHY, in which curatives are administered to create the opposite effect. Homeopathy was popularized in the 18th century by the German physician Christian HAHNEMANN. Although it later fell into disrepute, it is now enjoying a revival in some countries.

Homeostasis, in biology, maintenance of constant conditions within a cell or organism in response to either internal or external changes.

Homer (*c.* 8th century BC), Greek epic poet. He is traditionally considered to be the author of the great epics of the TROJAN WARS, the *Iliad* and the *Odyssey*. Traditionally, too, he is represented as blind, but this may have been because of the false attribution to him of the *Hymn to Apollo,* in which he portrays himself as blind. No definite facts are known about Homer and even his very existence has been the cause of controversy among scholars. However, the works attributed to him are the beginning of Greek, and therefore European, literature. *See also* HC1 pp.74–75.

Homer, Winslow (1836–1910), US painter and illustrator. He won international acclaim for his coverage of the American Civil War for *Harper's Weekly* and particular recognition as a painter with *Prisoners from the Front* (1866). In 1876 he abandoned illustration for painting. He found inspiration in the American landscape, eg *The Country School* (1871), and later in the Maine Coast.

Home Rule (Ireland). *See* IRISH, HOME RULE.

Home Rule Party, Irish political party formed with the aim of winning Ireland's autonomy within the British Empire. It was started by Isaac Butt in the 1870s. In the 1880s, under PARNELL, it controlled Irish politics and converted Gladstone and most of the Liberals to home rule. *See also* IRISH HOME RULE; HC2 pp.162–163.

Homo erectus, species of early man dating from about 1.1 million to 0.6 million years ago. The "Ape Man of Java" was the first early human fossil to be found, late in the 19th century. He was later placed in the genus *Homo.* PEKING MAN, also an early discovery, is a more advanced variety of *Homo erectus. See also* AUSTRALOPITHECUS; MS pp. *21–23*, 24–26, 28, 30, *31*.

Homogenization, process that reduces a substance contained in a fluid (liquid or gas) to small particles and redistributes them evenly through it. For example, the fat in milk can be broken down so thoroughly by homogenization that particles do not recombine and cream will not rise.

Homo habilis, problematic species of early man, discovered by Louis LEAKEY in 1964 in the Olduvai Gorge, East Africa. Its fossil remains have been estimated to be between 1.8 and 1.2 million years old, being contemporary with those of the Australopithecines. But the development of hand and skull is much more like that of modern man. *See also* AUSTRALOPITHECUS; MS pp.*22–23*, 24.

Homology, in biology, similarity in form, function or evolution of living things based on a common genetic heritage. For example a man's arm and a seal's flipper are homologues, having developed from a common origin. The wing of a bird and the wing of a bat are not homologous because they evolved independently. *See also* EVOLUTION.

Homophony, in music originally the sounding in unison of voices or instruments, but in modern terminology meaning HARMONY as opposed to monophony (music in a single part) and POLYPHONY (music with several voices moving independently). Homophonic style is familiar to modern listeners and is generally characteristic of most music since the 18th century.

Homo sapiens, modern man, who first appeared about a quarter of a million years ago. Scattered fossil remains of that age, or somewhat younger, include those of STEINHEIM MAN and SWANSCOMBE MAN, both of whom had skull capacities within the modern range. Also, they both predated NEANDERTHAL MAN, who appears to have arisen contemporaneously with later, indisputably *Homo sapiens* types. For this reason Neanderthal Man is now often regarded as a variety of *Homo sapiens.* In Europe, Neanderthal Man was abruptly replaced by CRO-MAGNON Man about 30,000 years ago. *See* MS pp. *21–23*, 25–26, *27*, 28, 30–32.

Homosexuality, sexual attraction, often leading to sexual activity, between members of the same sex. In women it is known

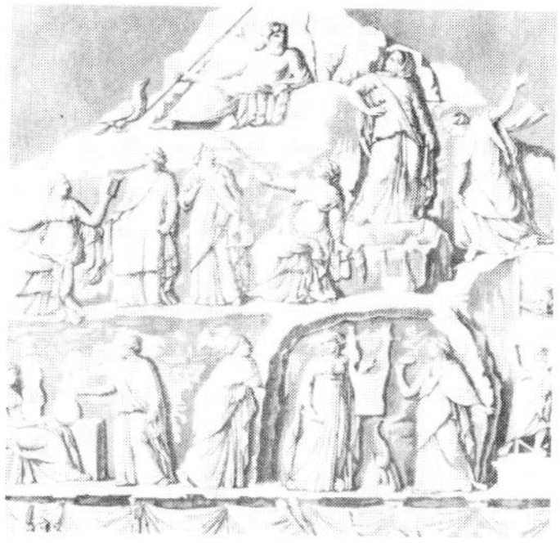

Homer's apotheosis, a 19th-century view of the deification of the great Greek poet.

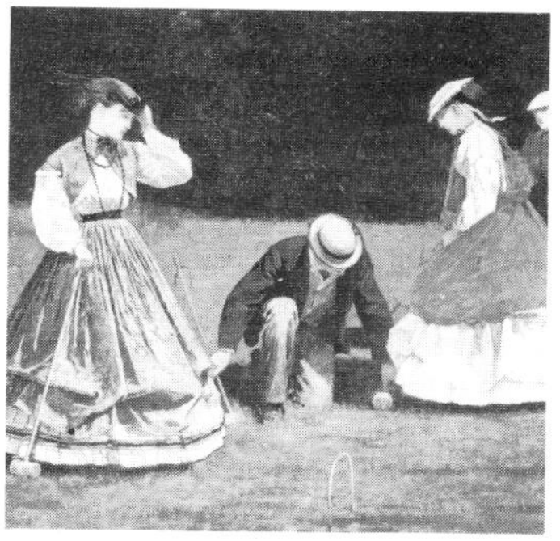

Winslow Homer; a detail from his 1866 painting of people playing a game of croquet.

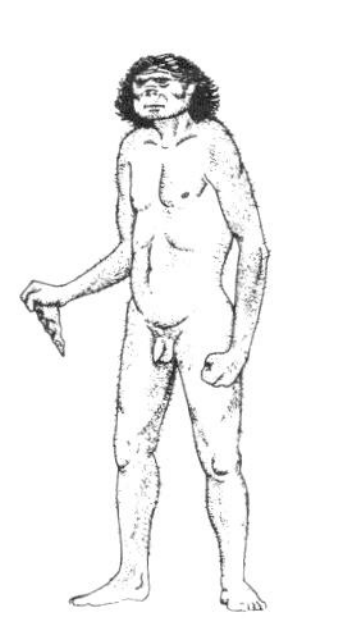

Homo erectus lived in Africa, Asia and Europe and used chopping tools and hand axes.

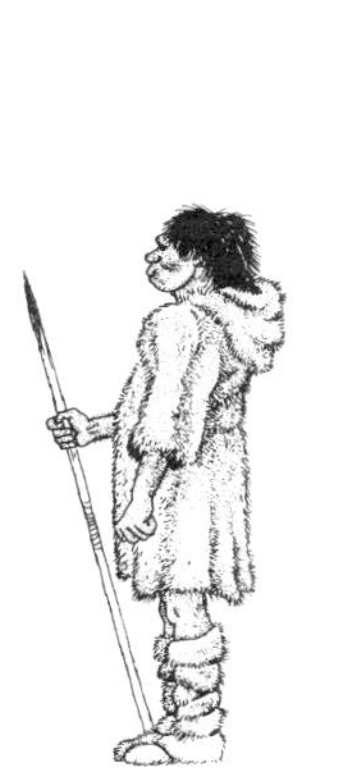

Homo sapiens, followed *Homo erectus,* but little is known about how or when.

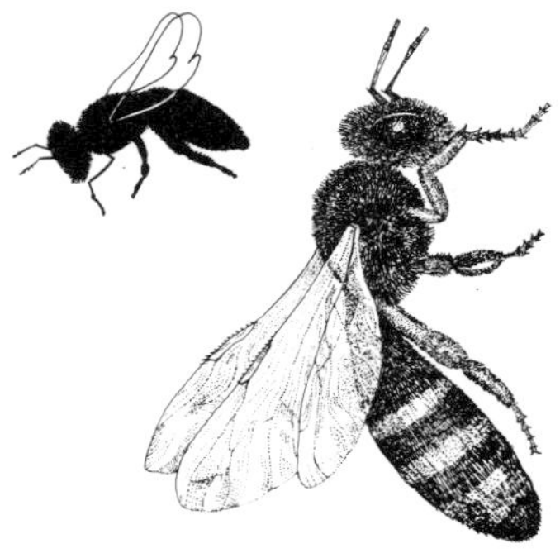

Honeybee; each collects enough nectar in its lifetime to make 45 gramme (1.5oz) of honey.

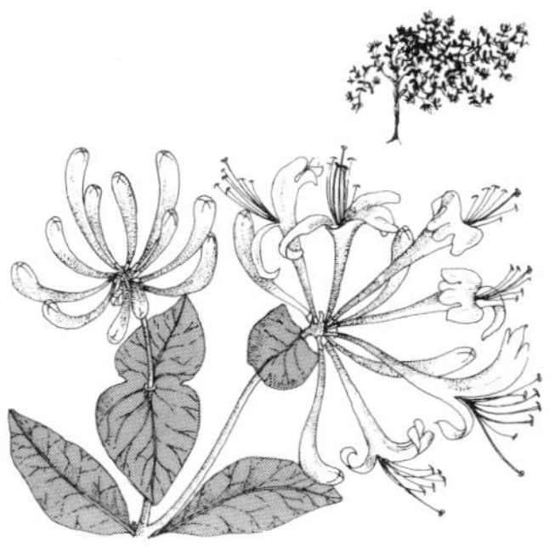

Honeysuckle; some varieties are feeding places for hummingbirds who eat the nectar.

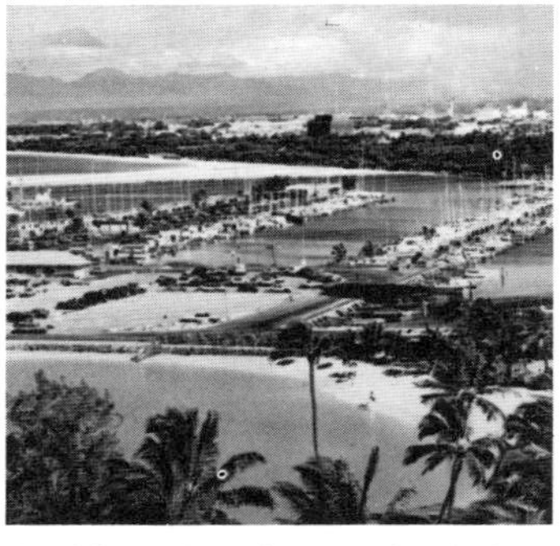

Honolulu; a view of the spacious harbour near the centre of the capital.

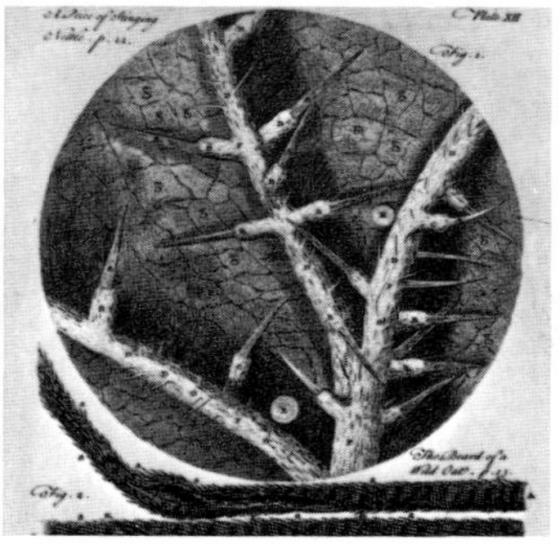

Robert Hooke; a plate from *Micrographia*, in which he described his study of plants.

as lesbianism. Throughout history lesbianism has hardly ever been illegal and recently private homosexual acts between consenting males have been legalized in most Western countries. Homosexual groups have recently publicly campaigned for an end to society's continuing hostility and discrimination. Doctors now agree that homosexuality is not a psychological disorder, but a normal aspect of sexuality. *See also* MS pp.166, *169*.

Homozygote, organism possessing identical alleles (hereditary units) on a CHROMOSOME pair. It is a purebred organism and always produces the same kind of GAMETE. *See also* HETEROZYGOTE.

Homs (Hims), city in W Syria, on the River Orontes. A settlement site since ancient times, the city is now a road and railway junction, serving a fertile farming area. Industries include sugar refining and textiles. Pop. (1970) 215,423.

Honan (Henan), province in E China; the capital is Chengchow (Zhergzhou). It is a mountainous but fertile area, and wheat and cotton are the major crops; rice and tobacco are also grown. Coal and iron ore are mined and abundant hydroelectric power is produced to supply local industries. Drainage and irrigation schemes have further improved the province's economy. Area: 167,090sq km (64,513sq miles). Pop. 50,000,000.

Honduras, independent nation in Central America, between Guatemala (W) and Nicaragua (SE). The damp climate encourages the growth of tropical rain forests in the E. The economy is based on agriculture, with bananas and coffee among the most important crops. Mineral resources have yet to be fully exploited. The capital is Tegucigalpa. Area: 112,088sq km (43,277sq miles) Pop. (1975 est.) 3,037,000. *See also* MW p.92.

Honduras, British. *See* BELIZE.

Honecker, Erich (1912–), East German politician. He was imprisoned by the NAZIS as a Communist but after WWII he was promoted in the East German Communist hierarchy. He succeeded Walter ULBRICHT as party leader in 1971.

Honegger, Arthur (1892–1955), French composer. His works were often religious and mystical in spirit and feeling, but in 1923 he caused a sensation with his *Pacific 231*, an orchestral description of a steam engine, named after a common type of railway locomotive (and its wheel arrangement). His other compositions include five symphonies, a dramatic psalm, *Le Roi David* (1921) and the operas *Judith* (1926) and *Antigone* (1927).

Hone Heke (*d.* 1850), New Zealand Maori chief, the nephew of HONGI HIKA. He opposed British rule and cut down the Union Jack flagstaff at Kororareka (RUSSELL) four times before capturing it in 1845, thus starting the Northern War.

Honesty, widely cultivated, hardy, ornamental biennial plant of the mustard family. It has attractive flat, purple flowers and oval pods. Height: 61–122cm (2–4ft). Family Cruciferae, genus *Lunaria*.

Honey, sweet, viscous liquid, made up mainly of the sugars levulose and dextrose, traces of minerals, and about 17% water. It is manufactured by HONEYBEES, which collect nectar (sweet juices in flowers), partially digest it, and deposit it in the hive cells, where the water is evaporated. *See also* PE pp.196–197.

Honey ant, any of several species of ANTS, found throughout the world, that live on sweet juices or from plant-sucking insects. A number of young ants serve as storage vessels for plant nectar and honeydew, which they feed back to the workers in times of shortage. *See also* NW p.*219*.

Honeybee, insect of the order Hymenoptera. The most common species is *Apis mellifera*, which has long been domesticated for the production of HONEY. It is found throughout the world, and is yellow and black and about 12.5mm (0.5in) long. It constructs its brood cells and honey storage cells from wax and lives in colonies with a social structure. Family Apidae. *See also* NW pp.78–79, 106, *108*, 109, 113.

Honey-creeper, any of a number of small birds of tropical America with thin bills, that feed on nectar and fruit. The name is also given to insect-eating birds, also called liwis, of the family Drepanididae, from Hawaii. *See also* NW p.*229*.

Honydew melon. *See* MELON.

Honey eater, or honey sucker, any of a diverse group of Australian songbirds of the family Meliphagidae. They have long tongues with brush-like tips for feeding on nectar and fruit, and are important pollinators of the flowers they feed on. Australian bellbirds and wattle birds are two of the more familiar types. *See also* NW pp.*71*, *149*, 211, *235*.

Honey-guide, small bird found in Africa and S Asia that leads people and animals to the nests of bees and shares in eating the honey (which it would not otherwise be able to obtain because of its small beak). Adult plumage is typically grey to green to yellowish-green, with brown and white on the tail. Length: to 20.3cm (8in). Family Indicatoridae.

Honey locust, North American tree of the pea family. It has thorny branches, feathery foliage and brown twisted pods about 40cm long. Height: to 40m (131ft). Species *Gleditsia triacanthos*.

Honeysuckle, woody twining plant that grows in temperate regions throughout the world. It has oval leaves and bell-shaped, fragrant flowers with male and female parts. A common species in Eurasia, *Lonicera periclymenum*, climbs to 6m (20ft) and may damage the host tree around which it climbs. Family Caprifoliaceae. *See also* NW pp. *63*, *209*.

Hongi Hika (1777–1828), New Zealand Maori chief. He visited Britain and helped to compile a Maori dictionary. After arming his Ngapuhi tribe with Australian guns he fought rival New Zealand tribes, and took 2,000 prisoners in 1818.

Hong Kong, British Crown colony in S China, 145km (90 miles) SE of Canton. The colony comprises Hong Kong Island, the Kowloon Peninsula, the New Territories on the mainland and some 230 islets in the South China Sea. It is the commercial centre of the Far East and its industries include textiles, plastics and printing. The capital is Victoria. Area: 1,036sq km (400sq miles). Pop. (1975 est.) 4,367,000. *See* MW p.92.

Honnecourt, Villard d' (*c.* 1225–*c.* 1250), French architect. He travelled widely and drew architectural details of Gothic cathedrals. His sketchbook is the only surviving one of its kind made before the 15th century.

Honolulu, capital city of Hawaii, on the SE of Oahu Island. It became the permanent capital of the kingdom of Hawaii in 1850 and remained the capital after the annexation of the islands by the USA in 1898 and the declaration in 1959 of Hawaii as the 50th state. The bombing of Pearl Harbor by the Japanese in 1941 precipitated the USA's entry into WWII. Since then, peacetime defence activity has aided the city's growth. Other industries include sugar refining and pineapple canning. Pop. (1970) 324,871.

Honorius, the name of four popes. Honorius I (*r.* 625–38), an Italian, showed great interest in the church in Spain's Visigothic kingdom and the British Isles and did much to improve church buildings in Rome. He attempted to settle the schism between Rome and the Eastern Church over the MONOPHYSITE and MONOTHELITE controversies, but in a letter to the patriarch of Constantinople he credited Christ with one nature and "one will", thereby appearing to confirm the heresy. At the Third Council of Constantinople he was posthumously declared heretical. Honorius II (*r.* 1124–1130), real name Lamberto Scannabecchi, was instrumental in ending the controversy between the papacy and the Holy Roman Empire over investiture. Honorius III (*r.* 1216–27), real name Cencio Savelli, confirmed the mendicant orders of FRANCISCANS, DOMINICANS and CARMELITES that were to revive Christian spiritual life. Honorius IV (1285–87), real name Giacomo Savelli, encouraged oriental studies at the University of Paris in the cause of re-uniting the Western and Eastern Churches.

Honours list, twice-yearly granting of civil and military honours by the British monarch. Honours lists are published on 1 Jan., on the monarch's official birthday and on other significant occasions such as the changing of the prime minister.

Honshū, largest of Japan's four main islands, between the Sea of Japan and the Pacific Ocean. It produces most of Japan's industrial output and has six of the country's largest cities, including Tōkyō. Industries: shipbuilding, chemicals and textiles. Area: 230,782sq km (89,105sq miles). Pop. (1970) 82,569,581.

Honthorst, Gerard or Gerrit van (1590–1656), Dutch painter. He was influenced by CARAVAGGIO, whose style he introduced into Holland. He achieved international fame as a portrait painter, and went to the English court (1628).

Hooch, or Hoogh, Pieter de (1629–*c.* 1683), Dutch painter, usually of gardens, courtyards and peaceful domestic scenes. His paintings are noted for their deft use of space and light.

Hood, Alexander, 1st Viscount Bridport (1727–1814), British admiral and brother of Viscount Hood. He recaptured the battleship *Warwick* from the French in 1761, and as second-in-command to Howe in the French Revolutionary Wars he served in the Channel and Gibraltar Straits. He was created a Baron in 1796, and Viscount in 1801.

Hood, Robin, *See* ROBIN HOOD.

Hood, Samuel, 1st Viscount (1724–1816), British admiral who served in the SEVEN YEAR WAR and in the American and French revolutionary wars, distinguishing himself especially in the West Indies in 1782. A member of Parliament for Westminster, he became an Admiral in 1794 and was created Viscount Hood in 1796.

Hood, Thomas (1799–1845), British editor and poet. He was editor of various prominent periodicals, much of his work being humorous. But it is his two serious poems, *The Song of the Shirt* and *The Bridge of Sighs*, that reveal his true creative ability.

Hooghly, tributary of the River Ganges, in NE India, formed at the confluence of the Bhagirathi and Jalangi rivers. It is a commercially important trade route and is navigable for almost its entire length of 200km (124 miles).

Hogstraten, Samuel Dircksz van (1627–78), Dutch historical and portrait painter. He studied in Amsterdam with REMBRANDT and his early works were influenced by Rembrandt's style. He was also interested in *trompe l'oeil* painting.

Hooke, Robert (1635–1703), English philosopher and experimental physicist. Active in astronomy, he claimed to have stated the laws of planetary motion before NEWTON, deduced that JUPITER rotated and located the 5th star in ORION. He made many improvements in astronomical instruments and in watches and clocks. He also studied the elastic properties of solids, and formulated HOOKE'S LAW. *See also* HC1 p.303; SU p.88.

Hooker, Sir Joseph Dalton (1817–1911), British surgeon and botanist who went on many expeditions, noting his observations. In 1855 he became assistant director of KEW GARDENS and succeeded his father, Sir William, as director from 1865 to 1885.

Hooker, Richard (*c.* 1554–1600), English theologian, educated at Oxford. His most famous work, *Of the Laws of Ecclesiastical Polity* (1594, 1597), was a learned and powerful defence of the Church of England against PURITAN attacks.

Hooker, Thomas (1586–1647), English colonist in N America and a Puritan clergyman. He fled to Holland in 1630 and then New England in 1633, seeking religious freedom. Pastor of the first church of CAMBRIDGE, Massachusetts, he led colonists in the first western migration to found and settle HARTFORD, Connecticut in 1636. Hooker helped to draft the "Fundamental Orders" in 1639, under which Connecticut was long governed.

Hooker, Sir William Jackson (1785–1865), British botanist and authority on ferns, mosses and fungi. From 1841 he was the first director of KEW GARDENS, where he also founded a museum of economical botany. His son Joseph (1817–1911) succeeded him as director.

Hooke's law, relationship between stress and strain in an elastic material when it is stretched. It states that the stress is proportional to the strain producing it. In mathematical terms, $F = -kx$, where F is the applied force, x is the distance through which the material stretches and k is a constant that describes the strength of the material. *See also* ELASTICITY; SU p.88.
Hookworm, two species of intestinal parasites in man. Larvae usually enter the host by penetrating the skin of the feet and legs, following a circuitous route through the body and finally attaching themselves to the wall of the small intestine. Symptoms can include anaemia, constipation and weakness. It is treated successfully with tetrachloroethylene. Phylum Nematoda; species *Necator americanus* and *Ancyclostoma duodenale.*
Hooper, John (*d.* 1555), English bishop. He became a Protestant follower of ZWINGLI in the 1530s and lived in Zürich (1539–49). He was appointed Bishop of Gloucester in 1550 and of Worcester in 1552. Queen MARY I imprisoned him in 1554 and had him burned for heresy in 1555.
Hoopoe, zebra-striped, fawn-coloured bird that lives in open areas, parks and gardens throughout warmer areas of the Old World. It has a fan-like crest and a long, curved bill. It utters a "hoo-hoo-hoo" call and feeds on small invertebrates. Length: 30cm (12in). Family Upupidae; species *Upupa epops.*
Hoorn, Philip de Montmorency, Count of (1518–68), Flemish stadholder and soldier. With WILLIAM THE SILENT and Count EGMONT, he opposed the policies of the occupying Spanish, especially their cruel treatment of Dutch Protestants. Arrested in 1567, he was condemned as a traitor to Spain and a heretic; both he and Egmont were beheaded the following year. As a result the Dutch rose and eventually gained their independence.
Hoover, John Edgar (1895–1972), US director of the FBI (Federal Bureau of Investigation) (1924–72). He reorganized the bureau, compiling a vast file of fingerprints and building a crime laboratory and training academy. During the 1930s he fought organized crime; after WWII he concentrated on what he saw as the threat of Communist subversion in the USA.
Hoover Dam, one of the world's largest dams, in the USA on the Colorado River between Arizona and Nevada. Opened in 1935, it irrigates land in S California, Arizona and Mexico. Height: 221m (726ft). Length: 379m (1244ft). *See also* PE p.*168.*
Hop, twining vine native to Eurasia and the Americas. It has rough stems, heart-shaped leaves and small male and female flowers borne on separate plants. The female catkins are covered with *lupulin,* a yellow powder used as a sedative. The dried female flowers of *Humulus lupulus* are used for flavouring BEER. Family Cannabiaceae. *See also* NW p.*64*; PE pp.204, *205.*
Hope, Alec Derwent (1907–), Australian poet. He was a scholar of early 18th-century English literature and its rational formality is echoed in his poems, first collected in the volume *The Wandering Islands* in 1955.
Hope, Anthony (1863–1933), real name Sir Anthony Hope Hawkins, British author of the adventure novel *The Prisoner of Zenda* (1894) and of its sequel *Rupert of Hentzau* (1898). Both novels are set in the mythical country of Ruritania, a name invented by Hope.
Hope, Bob (1903–), US comedian, *b.* Leslie Townes Hope in England. He started his career in music hall and in 1938 his *Bob Hope Show* began on radio. From 1950 he has frequently appeared on television. He made more than 50 films, including the *Road* series with Bing CROSBY (1940–52); among his better known are *The Paleface* (1947) and *The Seven Little Foys* (1955). He has entertained US troops all over the world.
Hopei (Hebei), province in NE China, on the Gulf of Chihli; the capital is Shihkiachwang (Shijiashvang). The remains of Peking man found there indicate that Hopei has been inhabited for at least 500,000 years. After the 14th century, agriculture in the region was greatly developed with the introduction of cotton cultivation and extended irrigation schemes. Industries developed after WWI. Communist control was completed in 1949. Products: cotton, wheat, soya beans, corn, millet, sweet potatoes, fruits, nuts, rice, oilseeds. Industries include the manufacture of chemicals, steel, machines, textiles. Area: 202,510km. (78,189sq miles). Pop. 47,000,000.
Hopkins, Frederick Gowland (1861–1947), English biochemist. He shared with Christiaan Eijkman the 1929 Nobel Prize in physiology and medicine for his work on VITAMINS. Hopkins pointed out that some diseases, such as SCURVY and RICKETS, might be caused by the deficiency in the diet of some substance necessary for proper health – the so-called VITAMIN concept. He also investigated the function of LACTIC ACID in muscular activity.
Hopkins, Gerard Manley (1844–89) British poet. He became a Roman Catholic in 1866 and was later ordained a Jesuit priest (1877). The sinking in 1875 of a German ship carrying five nuns inspired his most notable poem, *The Wreck of the Deutschland.* He contributed the principle of SPRUNG RHYTHM to English poetry but his small body of verse (he destroyed much of his work on entering the Jesuit novitiate) was not published until after his death. *See also* HC2 p.100.
Hopkins, Lightnin' (1912–), US BLUES singer. Endlessly inventive, he retained his stylistic integrity through 30 years of performing and recording, perhaps because he refused to leave his home in Houston. His style balanced vivid boogies with slow blues, accompanied by a piano-like guitar-sound.
Hopper, Edward (1882–1967), US painter. A pupil of Robert HENRI and greatly influenced by the ASHCAN SCHOOL, he was a realistic painter of the North American scene.
Hoppner, John (*c.* 1758–1810), British society portraitist, a follower of Joshua REYNOLDS and a rival to Sir Thomas LAWRENCE. He was appointed portrait painter to the Prince of Wales in 1789 and elected to the Royal Academy in 1795.
Hopscotch, children's game with several variants. A set of numbered squares, usually 10, is marked on the ground or pavement. In one variant a stone is thrown into the first square, the player then hops into the second and succeeding squares and back again, picking up the stone on the return to the base line. The process is repeated for each square in numerical sequence. If the player hops on the square with the stone, loses his balance, steps on a line or throws the stone on a line or wrong square, he must try again next time round.
Horace (65–8 BC), Roman poet, full name Quintus Horatius Flaccus. He fought at PHILIPPI (42 BC) with BRUTUS, and later won favour in Augustan Rome. His friend VIRGIL introduced him to Maecenas, who as his patron provided him with an income and a farm. Horace's first *Satires* appeared in *c.* 35 BC, followed by *Epodes* (*c.* 30 BC), *Odes* (*c.* 23 BC), *Epistles* (*c.* 20 BC) and *Ars Poetica* (*c.* 19 BC). His simple, direct Latin lyrics provided a vivid picture of the Augustan age. *See also* HC1 p.112.
Hore-Belisha, Leslie, (1893–1957), British politician and inventor, who, as Minister of Transport from 1934 to 1937 originated the Belisha beacon, a yellow globe atop a pole at pedestrian crossings which flashes regularly. He was Secretary for War from 1937 until 1940.
Horehound, aromatic herb of the mint family which grows in Eurasia and is found as a roadside weed in North America. Its woolly white leaves are used for flavouring cough lozenges and confectionery. Species *Marubium vulgare.*
Horemheb, pharaoh of ancient Egypt (*r.* 1340–*c.* 1320 BC), the last ruler of Dynasty XVIII and successor to TUTANKHAMEN. He served as a notable military commander after *c.* 1365 BC and during his reign restored the old religion after AKHENATON had introduced the worship of the sun god. *See also* HC1 p.48.
Horizon, celestial, GREAT CIRCLE on the CELESTIAL SPHERE, the plane of which contains the line through an observer's position at right angles to the vertical. It lies midway between the observer's ZENITH and NADIR and cuts the observer's meridian at the north and south points. *See also* SU p.264.
Horizon, soil. *See* SOIL PROFILE.
Horizon co-ordinate system, astronomical co-ordinate system referred to the plane of the observer's horizon. The co-ordinates are AZIMUTH and ALTITUDE. *See also* CO-ORDINATE SYSTEMS, ASTRONOMICAL.
Hormisdas, Saint, pope from 514 to 523. After the Acacian schism (484–519) he reunited the Eastern and Western Churches. Feast day 6 August.
Hormones, chemical substances secreted by the ENDOCRINE SYSTEM of the body directly into the bloodstream. They exercise chemical control of body functions, regulating virtually all of them, such as growth, development, sexual maturity and functioning, metabolism and emotional balance (in part). Hormones circulate in the body in minute quantities and often exert their effects at great distances from their point of secretion. Most are slow to take effect, exert widespread action, and are also slow to disappear from the system. The secretion and activity of the various hormones are closely interdependent; one can stimulate or inhibit the secretion of another or two or more can act together to produce a certain effect. In general they maintain a delicate equilibrium which is important to health. Some of the best-known hormones are THYROXINE, ADRENALINE, INSULIN, OESTROGEN, PROGESTERONE and TESTOSTERONE. *See also* MS pp.64–65.
Hormuz. *See* ORMUZ.
Horn, Philip de Montmorency. *See* HOORN, PHILIP DE MONTMORENCY, COUNT OF.
Horn, musical instrument first used for signalling, in hunting and ceremonies. Once made from animal horns and later from metals, different types of horn have normally been made of brass since the Renaissance. They appeared in the opera orchestras of 17th-century Europe and found particular favour in the 19th century with Richard STRAUSS and Richard WAGNER. Also known as the French horn, the modern instrument consists of a coiled tube of conical bore that widens to a flared bell; most have three valves. It has a mellow tone that is controlled by the lips and hand-stopping. *See also* HC2 p.105.
Horn, defensive or offensive structure that grows from the head of some mammals. A typical horn is made up of a central bony core covered by a layer of the skin protein KERATIN; in the rhinoceros, the entire horn is made of keratin. Horns are generally retained for life, although deer shed their ANTLERS annually.
Horn, Cape, most southerly point of South America, situated in the archipelago of Tierra del Fuego. First discovered in 1616, the Horn route is renowned for its rough seas.
Hornbeam, any of a number of small, hardy trees of the genus *Carpinus,* found throughout the N Hemisphere. They have smooth bark, a short trunk, spreading branches and clusters of green nuts. Family Betulaceae.
Hornbill, tropical African and SE Asian brownish and black-and-white bird, so named because of its large brightly-coloured bill. The female lays one to six eggs in a hole high up in a tree trunk and then sometimes erects a barricade, imprisoning herself and her eggs there for 4 to 11 weeks. The male feeds her through a tiny slit in the barricade wall. There are several species. Length: 38–152cm (15–60in). Family Bucerotidae. *See also* NW pp.145, *149, 152, 212,* 214, *214.*
Hornblende, black mineral found widely dispersed in granite and other IGNEOUS ROCKS. It is the commonest form of AMPHIBOLE, and contains iron and silicates of calcium, aluminium and magnesium.
Horned owl, common name for any of 11 species of OWLS with feathery tufts resembling horns on their heads. Fierce and strong, they feed on rodents and other

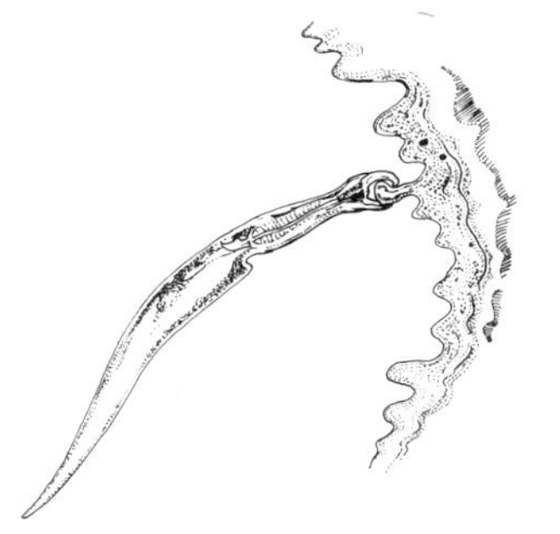

Hookworm larvae can live outside a host but only in warm regions such as the tropics.

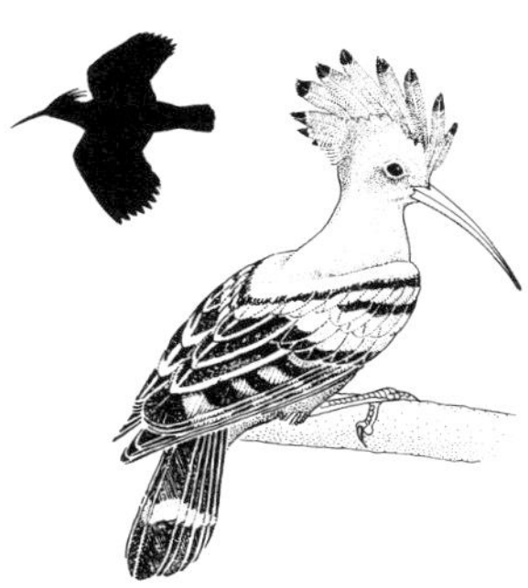

Hoopoes build their nests in trees and walls, the females laying from five to seven eggs.

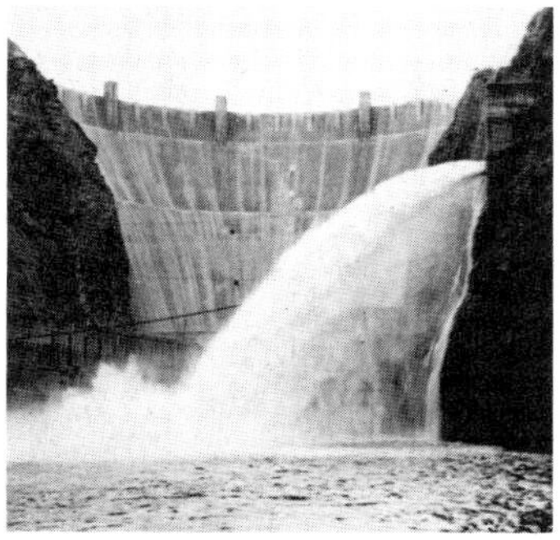

Hoover Dam; it contains enough concrete to pave a two-lane highway across the USA.

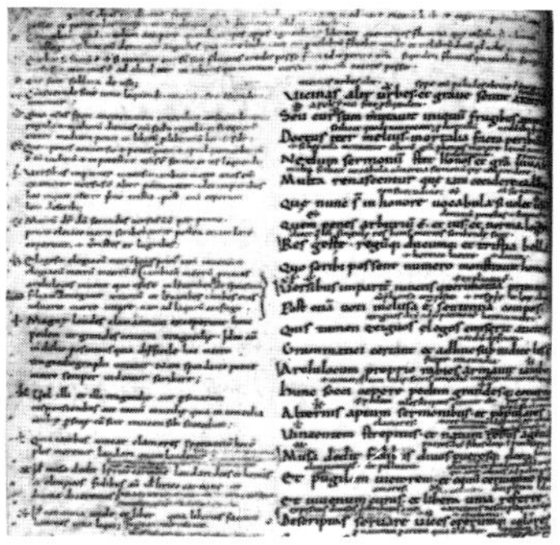

Horace's subjects included friendship and heroism; this is a 12th-century manuscript.

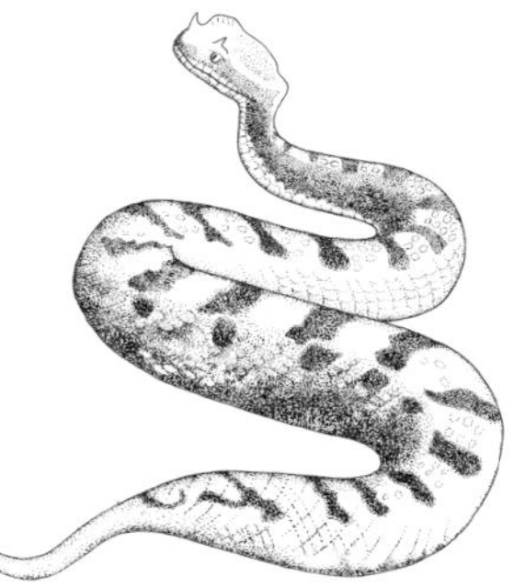

Horned viper's eyes are directed upwards, so that it can see when almost buried in sand.

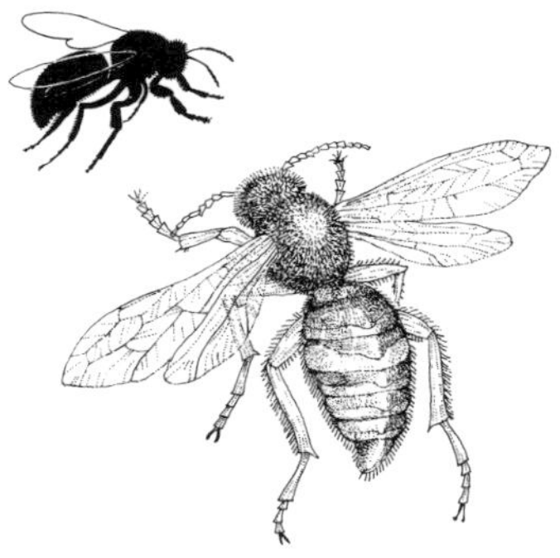

Hornets are useful to man, despite their sting, since the young eat flies and other insects.

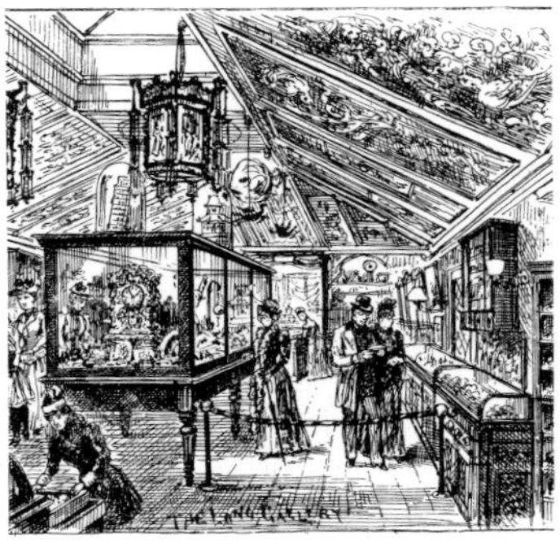

F. J. Horniman; drawing from *The Illustrated London News* of part of his museum.

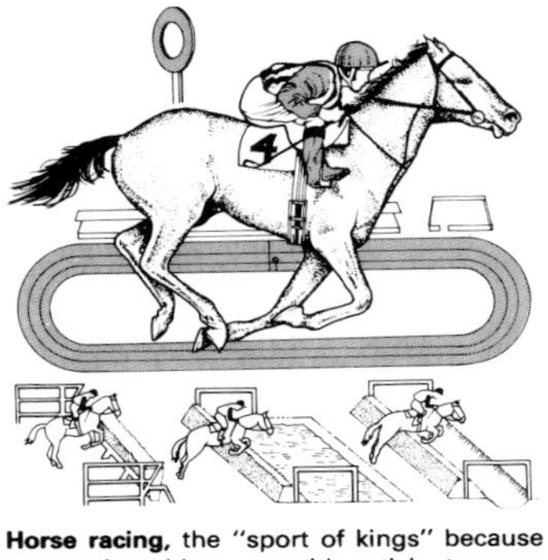

Horse racing, the "sport of kings" because once only noblemen could participate.

small mammals. The eagle owl, *Bubo bubo*, is the largest European species, but the most common is the long-eared owl, *Asio otus.* Family Strigidae.

Horned viper, or horned asp, poisonous SNAKE native to the deserts of N Africa and Arabia. It is brown and black, with a sharp, pointed scale over each eye. Length: to 60cm (2ft). Family Viperidae; species *Cerastes cornutus. See also* VIPER.

Hornet, large dull orange and brown wasp native to Europe. Hornets are social insects. They build egg-shaped paper nests containing one queen and numerous nectar-gathering workers. They have a fearsome reputation and can inflict a powerful sting, but are actually less aggressive than the common wasp and react only when strongly provoked. Family Vespidae. *See also* NW p.*209.*

Horniman, Annie Elizabeth Fredericka (1860–1937), British theatrical benefactress. She founded both the Manchester Repertory Theatre (1908) and Miss Horniman's Company of Actors. She also helped to provide a permanent home in the ABBEY THEATRE, Dublin, for the Irish Literary Theatre Society.

Horniman, Frederick John (1835–1906), British tea importer. In 1897 he founded the Horniman Museum, Forest Hill, London, in which he housed his outstanding collection of curios.

Hornpipe, solo step dance popular in 16th-century England, Ireland and Wales. Probably Celtic in origin, it has more recently been associated with the navy.

Horology, science of measuring time or the art of constructing clocks or dials for measuring time. *See also* MM pp.92–93.

Horoscope, map of the heavens at the time of a person's birth. It shows the position of the celestial bodies in the 12 "houses" through which they pass and their position in relation to the 12 signs of the ZODIAC. It is the basis of ASTROLOGY. *See also* MS pp.200–201.

Horowitz, Vladimir (1904–), US concert pianist, *b.* Russia. He first performed in public in 1921 and was world famous by the age of 20 as a virtuoso of great sensitivity and technique. Since 1950 he has appeared only rarely on the concert platform but continues to make recordings.

Horrocks, General Sir Brian Gwynne (1895–), British soldier. He served in France during WWI and in Russia during 1919. A vigorous corps commander in the western desert and Europe during WWII, he later commanded the British Army of the Rhine (1948–49). Horrocks subsequently followed a successful career as a military journalist and writer.

Horrocks, Jeremiah (1619–41), English astronomer who in 1639 made the first observation of the transit of Venus. He also applied KEPLER'S LAWS of motion to the Moon, and calculated a more accurate value for the solar PARALLAX and the Earth's distance from the Sun.

Horse, hoofed mammal that evolved in North America but became extinct there during late Pleistocene Epoch. Early horse forms crossed the land bridge across the Bering Strait, dispersed throughout Asia, Europe and Africa and produced the modern horse family. The only surviving true wild horse is Przewalski's horse. Hunted by Palaeolithic man for food, the horse was first domesticated about 5,000 years ago in central Asia. Horses returned to the New World with the Spanish conquistadores in the 1500s.

Horses are characterized by one large functional toe; molars with crowns joined by ridges for grazing; an elongated skull and a simple stomach. Fast runners, they usually live in herds and walk, canter, trot or gallop. Gestation lasts for 11 or 12 months; one colt is born and it can walk at birth. All species in the family can interbreed. The true horse is distinguished from other equines (ZEBRAS and ASSES) by its short ears, small head, chestnuts (horny, wart-like growths on the inside hind legs), large hooves and hair-covered tail. Family Equideae; species *Equus caballus. See also* NW pp.162–163, *190,* 191.

Horse chestnut, any of 25 species of deciduous trees that grow in temperate regions, especially the common horse chestnut, *Aesculus hippocastanum.* It has large palmate leaves, long showy flower spikes and round prickly nuts containing one or two inedible kernels (called conkers in Britain). Family Hippocastanaceae. Height: to 30.5m (100ft).

Horse fly, any of several species of flies in the family Tabanidae, especially *Tabanus lineola.* It is a pest to livestock and human beings. The female has blade-like mouthparts, inflicts a painful bite and sucks blood. Length: to 3cm (1.2in).

Horse Guards, building in Whitehall, London, the headquarters of the Household Cavalry regiment. It was built in the 1750s and is the scene of Mounting the Guard, a popular tourist attraction, each morning at 11 am on weekdays and 10 am on Sundays.

Horse mackerel, commercial marine food fish found in the Atlantic Ocean from the North Sea to Africa. Blue-green and silver with a white belly, it swims in shoals. Family Carangidae, species *Trachurus trachurus.*

Horsepower, unit (hp) indicating the rate at which work is done, adopted by James WATT in the 18th century. He defined it as the weight, 250kg (550lb), a horse could raise 0.3m (1ft) in one second, or 550ft-lb per second. At the output shaft of an engine or motor, it is termed "brake horsepower" or "shaft horsepower". In large reciprocating engines it is termed "indicating horsepower" and is determined from the pressure in the cylinders. The electrical equivalent of one horsepower is 746 watts.

Horse racing, sport that consists of races between two or more horses over a (usually grassed) circuit. Most popular is thoroughbred racing, although HARNESS RACING has a large following in some countries. Types of thoroughbred racing include flat races, and steeplechases over a course with obstacles such as hurdles, fences and water jumps. Distances vary from three furlongs (0.6km) (for two-year-olds) upwards, and include a variety of races, determined by age or sex of the horse, or weight handicap. On the starting line the horses are lined up in enclosed starting gates. Bets are placed on a totalisator (and in Britain also with bookmakers). Payment may be made on the first three horses past the winning post, and sometimes on other combinations. Races are controlled by stewards, and finishes are usually photographed and the result declared by a judge. Horse racing began in Assyria in about 1500 BC and the oldest race in existence is the English DERBY, first held in 1780. One of the most famous is the GRAND NATIONAL Steeplechase, contested annually at AINTREE, Liverpool, England, since 1839. In the USA the most popular is the Triple Crown for three-year-olds, comprising the Kentucky Derby, Preakness and Belmont Stakes. Britain, the USA, Australia, New Zealand and France have all produced outstanding thoroughbred race-horses.

Horseradish, perennial plant native to Eastern Europe and is cultivated for its pungent, fleshy root, which is a useful seasoning. Widespread as a weed, it has lance-shaped, toothed leaves, white flower clusters and egg-shaped seed-pods. Height: 1.25m (4.1ft). Family Cruciferae; species *Armoracia lapathifolia.*

Horse's Head Nebula, dark NEBULA close to Zeta Orionis. It forms part of the ORION nebula and obscures some of its light. The dark matter resembles the head of a horse in profile. *See also* SU p.*231.*

Horseshoe, metal plate, usually of iron or steel, fixed to the bottom of horses' hoofs. There is evidence of their use in the 6th century BC, since when they have been made in many designs. They are needed to protect the hoof from becoming worn down by hard surfaces. *See also* MM p.*20.*

Horseshoe crab. *See* KING CRAB.

Horseshoe pitching, game played by two or four people using horseshoes or, more usually, discs of similar shape. The pitching distance is 12.2m (40ft) for men and 9.1m (30ft) for women, the object being to encircle an iron peg 36cm (14in) high in the ground. A game is of 50 points. Encircling the peg (scoring a "ringer") gains three points. If there is no ringer the nearest shoe to the peg – within 15cm (6in) of it – gains one point. Developed from the game of QUOITS, it was originated by Greek and Roman soldiers, and was introduced to North America, where it is widely played.

Horsetail, any of about 30 species of flowerless, rush-like plants that grow in all continents except Australasia. The hollow, round-jointed stems have a whorl of tiny leaves at each joint. Horsetails have existed for more than 300 million years, and their fossils are found in coal from the Carboniferous period. Genus *Equisetum. See also* NW pp.*38,* 52–53, 186.

Horse trials, also known as eventing, an equestrian competition involving three distinct disciplines: dressage, speed and endurance, and show jumping. Trials can be one, two or three-day events, and in the latter a day is devoted to each discipline. The speed and endurance consists of four phases: 1st and 3rd are roads and tracks, a total distance of 16–20km (10–12.5 miles), over which the horse is walked and trotted; 2nd is the steeplechase, over 3.6–4.2km (2.3–2.5 miles); and 4th is the cross-country, over 7.2–8.1km (4.5–5 miles) including 30 to 35 obstacles. The present formula dates from a French cavalry championship in 1902. The three-day event features in the Olympic Games and has a four-yearly world championship for teams and individuals, the places being decided concurrently.

Horsham, county district in central West Sussex, England; created in 1974 under the Local Government Act (1972). Area: 536sq km (206sq miles). Pop. (1974 est.) 90,500.

Horsley, Colin (1920–), New Zealand pianist. He made his debut at Manchester in 1943, his first New Zealand tour in 1947. He is admired especially for his interpretation of the works of CHOPIN.

Horsley, Sir Victor Alexander Haden (1857–1916), British physiologist and surgeon who introduced refinements in NEUROSURGERY. He performed the first successful removal of a tumour of the spinal cord and carried out research on the functions of the thyroid gland, on rabies vaccine and on functions of various regions of the brain.

Horst, in geology, an elongated upthrust block bounded by parallel normal FAULTS on its long sides. *See also* PE pp.104–105.

Horst Wessel Lied, song written by Horst Wessel (1907–30), who joined the NAZI Party in 1927. After 1933 it became the official Nazi hymn.

Horta, Victor, Baron (1861–1947), Belgian architect, one of the leading influences of ART NOUVEAU. His Hotel Tassel in Brussels (1892–93) was one of the earliest buildings in the style. His work featured bold use of exposed iron supports, and metal and glass ornament. He was also noted for interior design, as in the Hotel van Eetvelde house (1895) and his Maison du Peuple (1896–99) in Brussels.

Horticulture, the growing of vegetables, fruits, seeds, herbs, ornamental shrubs and flowers, on a commercial scale, in nurseries, orchards and gardens. The origins of horticulture lie in the small intensive kitchen gardens of the medieval farming system. The techniques employed include asexual, or vegetative, propagation by leaf, stem and root cuttings, and by stem and bud grafting. Fruit trees, shrubs and vines, including those bearing apples, pears, plums, cherries, citrus fruits and grapes, are usually propagated by grafting the fruiting stock on to a hardier rootstock. In the case of apple trees, the rootstock is usually French crab apple. Plants propagated sexually by SEED include some fruits and vegetables including sweet corn, or maize, and many other types that produce seed abundantly. Often the seed needs to be overwintered, or stored at low temperatures and high humidity, before it will germinate. Seed itself is a major horticultural crop. Close scientific control of POLLINATION is essential for producing crops of specific quality. *See also* NW pp.71, *253;* PE pp.170–173, 178–179, 184–195.

Horus, falcon-headed god of ancient Egypt, son of ISIS and OSIRIS. In the myths, he came to rule earth after avenging the murder of his father. Originally the god of lower Egypt, Horus came to be closely identified with all the pharaohs of Egypt, who used his name as the first of their titles and were thought to rule as him on earth. *See also* HC1 p.34.

Horváth, Ödön von (1901–38), German dramatist, *b.* Hungary, whose works such as *Tales from the Vienna Woods* (1931) and *Kasimir and Karoline* (1932), realistically reflect the economic situations and social aspirations of the German-speaking bourgeoisie before the advent of Hitler who subsequently forced Horváth into exile. Neglected in the years after WWII, his plays received renewed critical attention and frequent performances in Germany and other countries in the late 1960s and 1970s.

Hosea, biblical author and first of the 12 minor prophets of the OLD TESTAMENT. He condemned Israel for worshipping false gods and promised mercy to the faithful.

Hoskyns, Bill (1931–), British fencer. The first Briton to win a world title, at épée in 1958, he won two Olympic silver medals at épée (team 1960, individual 1964) and nine gold and one silver at épée, foil, and sabre in three Commonwealth Games (1958, 1966, 1970).

Hospitalet, city in NE Spain. A suburb of Barcelona, it takes its name from its sanctuary that has sheltered travellers since the 12th century. Its chief industries are steel, textiles and chemicals. Pop. (1971 est.) 242,000.

Hospitals, places for the shelter and treatment of the sick and injured. The earliest hospitals in the West may be attributed to the Greeks, where the ill gathered at the temples of Aesculapius – the god of healing – and waited there to be cured. The Romans also used temples as hospitals and after the advent of Christianity Christian hospitals, the origin of modern hospitals, were established throughout the Empire. The monasteries also took in the poor and sick and became centres of pharmaceutical and medical knowledge. This centralization forms the rationale of today's hospitals, which, in the primary function of healing the sick, began to develop in the early 19th century. The modern era has seen the construction of larger and larger general hospitals, which combine treatment with research, teaching and specialization. These hospitals are technologically intensive and have equipment for radiology, bacteriology, haematology, X-ray diagnosis, pathology and many other sciences. There is now a trend away from such centralization.

Host, from the Latin *hostia,* meaning a sacrificial victim, is the term used in the Anglican and Roman Catholic Churches for the consecrated bread or wafer used in the EUCHARIST, or MASS. Any left unconsumed after a service are set aside for the priest's visits to sick parishioners.

Host, organism infected by a parasite, either *definitive* (in which the parasite reaches sexual maturity) or *intermediate* (in which it does not).

Hosta, also called plantain lily or funkia, perennial plant native to E Asia and Japan. It has veined leaves and lily-like flowers ranging from white to blue to lilac. Family Liliaceae; genus *Hosta.*

"Hot line", direct telephone link between the White House in the USA and the Kremlin in Moscow. The agreement to set up the line was signed in 1963. Its purpose is to speed communication between the two superpowers in an emergency, the underlying object being to prevent the outbreak of nuclear war.

Hotspur, Sir Henry Percy (1364–1403), English nobleman, called Hotspur for his zeal in guarding the Scottish-English border. He helped in the overthrow of RICHARD II but quarrelled with the new king, HENRY IV, in 1402. In 1403 he and his father, the Earl of Northumberland, planned to overthrow the king but were defeated by Henry at Shrewsbury.

Hottentot, or Khoikhoi, KHOISAN-speaking people of southern Africa, now almost extinct. Characteristically of short stature, with a dark yellowish skin, they are probably of mixed Bushman and Negro origin. Traditionally they were nomadic pastoralists. Many of them were displaced or exterminated by the early Dutch settlers. Their surviving descendants have mostly been absorbed into the Cape Coloured population of South Africa.

Hottentot fig, succulent vine found in deserts and on seashores in warm regions, and cultivated as a ground cover. Not a true fig, it has woody stems with succulent leaves; and large, daisy-like, yellow or lilac flowers. The fig-shaped fruits are edible but not tasty. Family Aizoaceae.

Hotter, Hans (1909–), Austrian bass baritone, *b.* Germany. After studying at the Munich Academy and making his debut in 1929, he became renowned for his roles in the operas of Wagner, especially in the title role of *The Flying Dutchman.* He had a close association with Richard STRAUSS and created several roles in his friend's operas before retiring in the late 1960s.

Houdini, Harry (1874–1926), US magician, *b.* Erich Weiss in Budapest, Hungary. No packing case or set of handcuffs could contain this escape artist, who also specialized in exposing fraudulent mediums. Author of *The Unmasking of Robert-Houdin* (1908), he had an extensive library on magic, now in the Library of Congress, Washington DC.

Houdon, Jean-Antoine (1741–1828), French sculptor, best known for his portrait busts, including those of Rousseau, Voltaire and George Washington. Houdon worked in a BAROQUE manner for some time but eventually adopted a colder, CLASSICAL style.

Houghton, William Stanley (1881–1913), British playwright. His plays about Lancashire, strongly influenced by the work of Henrik IBSEN, include *The Dear Departed* (1908), *The Younger Generation* (1910), *Fancy Free* (1911) and *Hindle Wakes* (1912). He emigrated to Paris in 1913, but died soon afterwards.

Hound, DOG that hunts with man, either by sight or by ground scent. The sight hunters, including the SALUKI, AFGHAN HOUND, IRISH WOLFHOUND or GREYHOUND, chase quarry at great speed to overtake and kill or capture it. Most are streamlined and deep-chested, with long legs. A trailing hound, commonly a BLOODHOUND, BEAGLE, BASENJI or FOXHOUND, follows game by its scent and flushes it. Most are stocky with large muzzles, long ears and short legs.

Hounslow Heath, area of barren scrubland W of Hounslow, London. Now small (61 hectares; 150 acres) and enclosed, in 1545 it covered 1,739 hectares (4,293 acres). Formerly notorious for its highwaymen, it was also used by British monarchs to assemble troops.

Houphouët-Boigny, Félix (1905–), President of the Ivory Coast Republic from 1960. He served in the government of French West Africa and led his country to independence in 1958.

Hour angle, angle measured westwards along the CELESTIAL EQUATOR from the observer's meridian to the line passing through a celestial body and the celestial poles (hour circle of the body). It is given in hours, minutes and seconds and ranges from 0 to 24 hours. *See also* RIGHT ASCENSION.

Hourglass, instrument used to measure time. It consists of two glass chambers separated by a narrow passage through which fine granules (usually sand) pass. The time taken for the sand contained in one glass to empty through the passage into the other glass is one hour, or a fraction of an hour. They were widely used before the invention of CLOCKS.

Houri, beautiful maiden awaiting a devout Muslim in PARADISE. Having reached paradise, the Muslim is given a large number of houris, with whom he may copulate once for every good work he has done and once for each day he fasted in RAMADAN.

House-fly, black-and-grey fly found throughout the world that lays its eggs in animal waste and decaying vegetable matter. It commonly feeds on the food of human beings, and can transmit several diseases, including TYPHOID FEVER, YAWS, TUBERCULOSIS and intestinal parasites. Order Diptera; species *Musca domestica.* *See also* NW pp.112–113.

Household, royal, corps of officials who were the chief servants of the medieval monarchy in Britain, the forerunners of the Civil Service. The main offices were originally the CHANCERY, the Chamber (from which developed the EXCHEQUER) and the WARDROBE. The Household looked after not only the sovereign's personal affairs but also the great matters of state. The Wardrobe handled the monarch's clothing and domestic supplies – and financed wars. The Chancery protected the king's PREROGATIVE and developed into a court of Equity. The Exchequer shared with the Wardrobe responsibility for revenues.

Housemaid's knee, swelling of the kneecap caused by pressure from kneeling. Technically it is the result of excess liquid in the bursa, or fluid-filled sac, in front of the kneecap bone. If the swelling does not subside naturally the liquid may have to be withdrawn with a syringe. *See also* TENNIS ELBOW; MS pp.57, *94.*

House of Commons, lower elective house of the British PARLIAMENT but with greater powers (especially control over finances) than the HOUSE OF LORDS. Its 635 members are elected by gaining a majority in a constituency election, most in general elections which must be held at least every five years. The Speaker controls debates and is chosen from the dominant party, which provides the government. The Prime Minister is the leader in the Commons of the majority party and members of his CABINET may come from either House. The Commons dates from the 13th century. It is the forum where the people's representatives voice their opinions and question ministers, and where intended legislation is discussed and voted upon. *See also* HC1 pp.210–211.

House of Lords, upper house of the British PARLIAMENT, having both legislative and judicial functions. In its legislative capacity the Lords have been completely subordinate to the HOUSE OF COMMONS since the Parliament Acts of 1911 and 1949 checked virtually all its power, except the right to delay passage of a bill for a year. It has no absolute veto over Commons legislation. All bills except for appropriation may be initiated by the Lords. Life peers, whose titles may not be inherited, and hereditary peers sit in the house. Hereditary peers may resign their titles to run for election to the Commons. There are special "law lords" who act as judges when the House acts as Britain's highest court.

House of Representatives, lower chamber of the US legislature and the name given to the lower chamber in Commonwealth countries such as New Zealand and Australia. In the USA the 435 members of the House are directly elected, and serve two-year terms. The House considers bills and has exclusive authority to originate revenue bills, initiate impeachment proceedings and elect the president should the electoral college be deadlocked. The House of Representatives in Commonwealth countries is usually closely modelled on the HOUSE OF COMMONS. *See also* CONGRESS, AMERICAN; PARLIAMENT; MS pp.276–277.

Housman, Alfred Edward (1859–1936), British poet and classical scholar, best known as the author of three small volumes of poetry, *A Shropshire Lad* (1896), *Last Poems* (1922) and *More Poems* (1936). He treats such general themes as the brevity of life in short, subtle lyrics.

Houssay, Bernardo Alberto (1887–1971), Argentinian physiologist. He shared with C. F. and G. T. CORI the 1947 Nobel Prize in physiology and medicine for discovering the role played by the hormone of the anterior PITUITARY lobe in regulating the metabolism of sugar. He demonstrated the complex interlocking action of various HORMONES of the body – in this case, a pituitary hormone with the

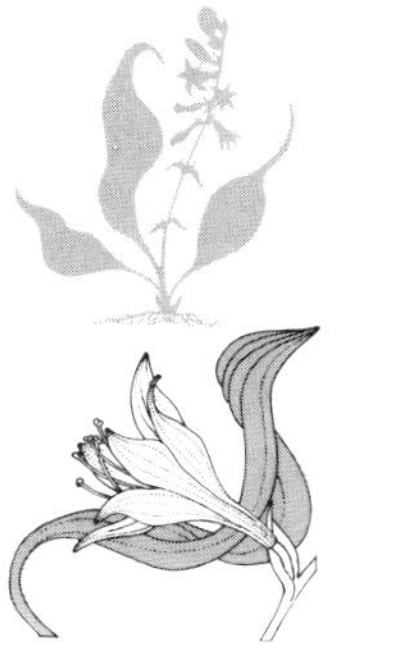

Hosta, a plant much grown in garden borders, flourishes even in partial shade.

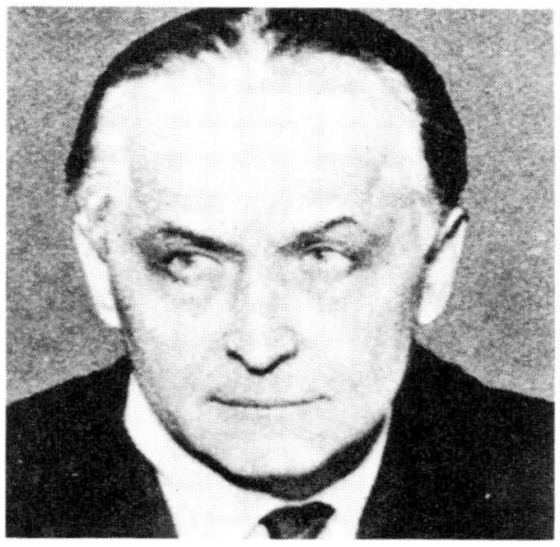

Houdini could escape from all manner of restraints, including even prison cells.

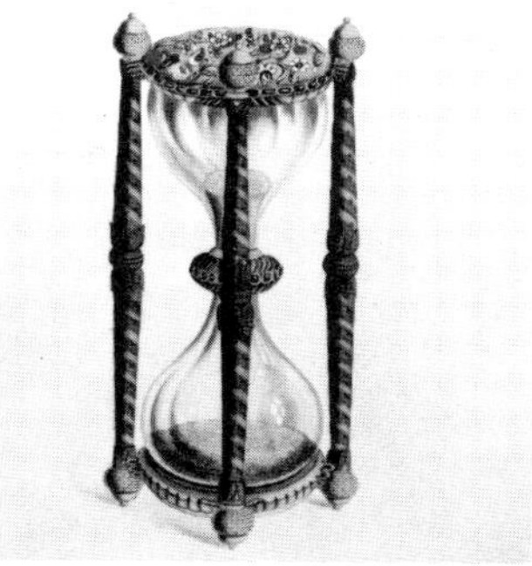

Hourglass; they were used to define the period for which a speaker could talk.

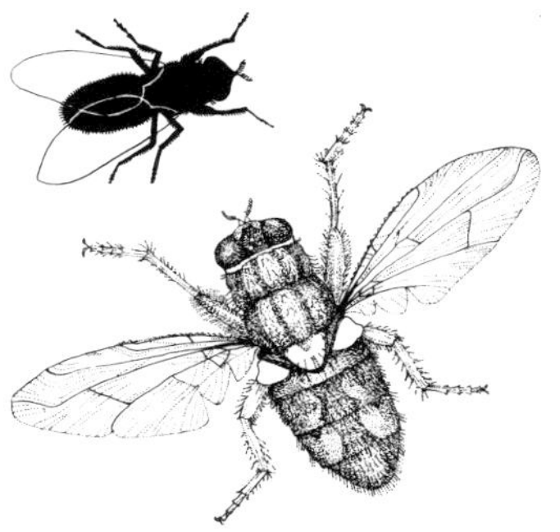

House-fly is one of the fastest of all flying insects; its wings beat 200 times a second.

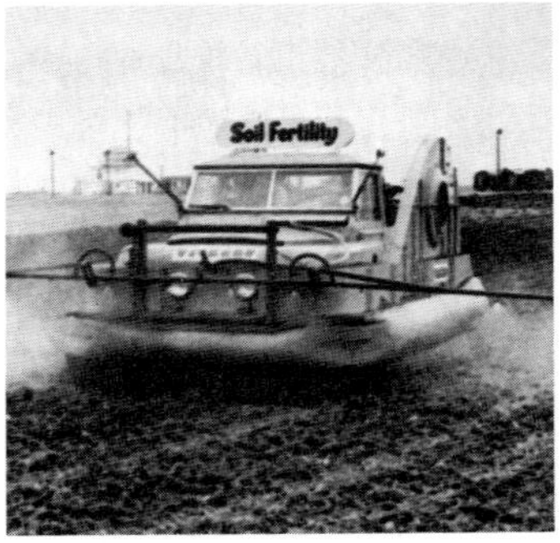

Hovercraft are capable of adaptation; here a farm vehicle is able to cross muddy ground.

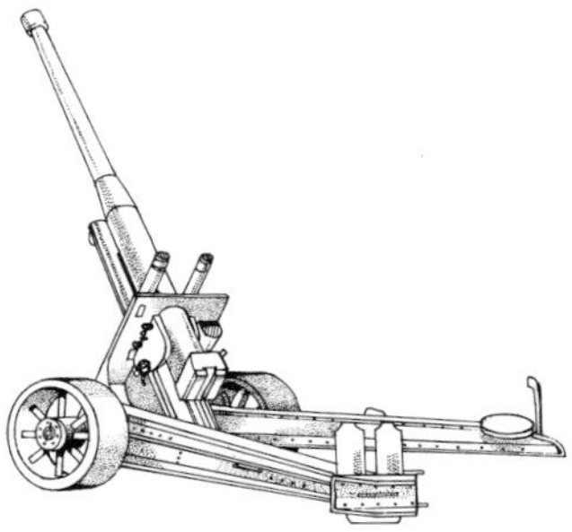

Howitzer; nuclear shells are among the projectiles that this weapon can fire.

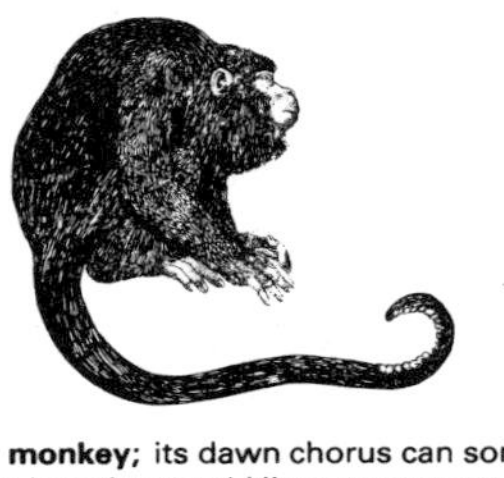

Howler monkey; its dawn chorus can sometimes be heard several kilometres away.

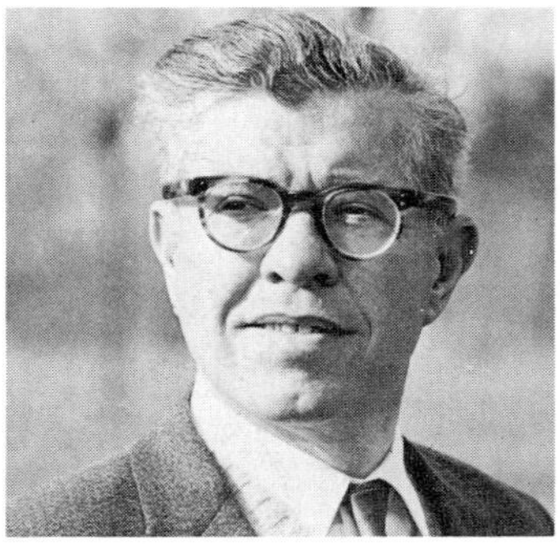

Fred Hoyle; new techniques in radioastronomy disputed his steady-state theory.

sugar-metabolizing hormone INSULIN.

Houston, industrial city and port of entry in SE Texas, 40km (25 miles) NW of Galveston Bay and connected to the Gulf of Mexico by the Houston Ship Canal. Founded in 1836, it served as the capital of the Republic of Texas (1837–39 and 1842–45). Its greatest perio of expansion came after the building of the canal (1912–14), when the exploitation of the coastal oil fields provided a rich source of income. The largest city in the state, its diverse industries include chemicals, rubber and printing. Pop. (1973) 1,320,018.

Hovercraft, or air cushion vehicle (ACV), fast, usually amphibious craft invented by Christopher COCKERELL, a British engineer. Hovercraft are propelled on a cushion of air, usually by turboprop engines similar to those used in aircraft, over land and water at speeds up to 160km/h (100mph). They are invaluable for negotiating swamps, and are used as marine ferries (in Britain) and as military vehicles. Smaller, less speedy craft have been developed as runabouts, and a HOVERTRAIN travelling at more than 480km/h (300mph) has been projected.

Hoverfly, two-winged insect of the large family Syrphidae, easily recognizable from its habit of hovering, then darting forwards. Many hoverflies are banded yellow and black like wasps. Others resemble bees, but none has a sting, their coloration being a form of protective mimicry.

Hovertrain, tracked air-cushion vehicle which is still in the conceptual stage, even though the technology for its operation (it works on the HOVERCRAFT principle) is extensively developed. The advantages that such a train would offer are high speed on elevated, space-saving tracks. *See also* MM pp.144–*145*.

Howard, Catherine (*c.*1520–42), fifth queen of HENRY VIII, granddaughter of Thomas, 2nd Duke of Norfolk. Henry married her in July 1540, but evidence of pre-marital indiscretions was produced against her (Nov. 1541). She was beheaded in February 1542.

Howard, Sir Ebenezer (1850–1928), British town planner. He wrote *Tomorrow: a Peaceful Path to Real Reform* (1898) and founded the Garden City Association in 1899. He was responsible for laying out Letchworth (1903) and Welwyn Garden City (1920), two British GARDEN CITIES.

Howard, Elizabeth Jane (1923–), British novelist, wife of the author, Kingsley AMIS. Among her books are *The Beautiful Visit* (1950), *After Julius* (1965) and *Odd Girl Out* (1971).

Howard, Henry, Earl of Surrey (1517–47), English poet. A cousin of Catherine HOWARD, he too was executed for alleged treason. He wrote some of the earliest English sonnets and translated two books of Virgil's *Aeneid* into blank verse. *See also* HC1 p.282.

Howard, John (1726–90), British philanthropist who devoted much of his efforts to the welfare of prisoners. He was appointed High Sheriff of Bedfordshire in 1773, and instigated two acts of Parliament in 1774 concerning jailers and standards of cleanliness in prisons.

Howard, Leland Ossian (1857–1950), US entomologist. His work helped man to achieve control over parasitic insects, especially the house-fly and the mosquito, and crop destroyers such as the boll weevil (which attacks cotton). His many books include *The Insect Book* (1901) and *The House Fly – Disease Carrier* (1911).

Howard, Luke (1772–1864), English meteorologist who gave names to various types of clouds. He recognized that clouds reflect "the general causes which effect all the variations of the atmosphere, just as the countenance of a person reflects the state of his mind or body". He named cirrus, cumulus, stratus and nimbus and their combinations. *See also* PE p.70.

Howard, Trevor (1916–), British actor. He made his stage début in *Revolt in a Reformatory* (1934), played Shakespearean roles at Stratford-upon-Avon and appeared in US stage productions. He has made numerous films, including *Brief Encounter* (1945), *Ryan's Daughter* (1970) and *Kidnapped* (1971).

Howard, prominent English family, particularly in the Tudor era; Dukes of Norfolk and Earls of Surrey. John Howard was raised to the dukedom of Norfolk by Richard III in 1483 but was killed at BOSWORTH (1485). His son (1443–1524) and grandson (1473–1554), both named Thomas, conquered the Scots at FLODDEN (1513). The younger Thomas's son, Henry, was executed on a spurious charge of treason in 1547, as was the fourth duke in 1572. Catherine Howard, a niece of the 3rd Duke, married HENRY VIII.

Howard of Effingham, Lord Charles (1536–1624), English statesman and admiral. He was ambassador to France (1559) and Lord Chamberlain (1574–85). As Lord High Admiral (1585–1618), he commanded the fleet against the Spanish Armada in 1588 and was the colleague of Essex in the Cadiz expedition of 1596.

Howe, Clarence Decatur (1886–1960), Canadian engineer and politician, who amassed his fortune designing grain elevators. He served as a Liberal member of Parliament (1935–57) and was Minister of Transport (1936). In 1937 he founded Trans-Canada Air Lines.

Howe, Elias (1819–67), US inventor of the sewing machine. In the AMERICAN CIVIL WAR he supported the regiment in which he served with royalties from his patent.

Howe, Edgar Watson (1853–1937), US writer. He edited *Howe's Monthly* (1911–33), but he is most famous for his novel *The Story of a Country Town* (1883). His other works include *Country Town Sayings* (1911) and his autobiography *The Indignations of E.W. Howe* (1933).

Howe, Joseph (1804–73), Canadian journalist and orator, Premier of Nova Scotia (1860–63). A poet and newspaper publisher, he established the freedom of the press in a court suit (1835). He ran Nova Scotia almost single-handedly during his premiership, and was a vigorous opponent of Confederation.

Howe, Julia Ward (1819–1910), US author, lecturer and campaigner for women's rights. She wrote the *Battle Hymn of the Republic* (1862), which first appeared in the *Atlantic Monthly* during the AMERICAN CIVIL WAR.

Howe, Richard Howe, Earl (1726–99), British admiral. After notable service in the Rochefort expedition (1757) and at QUIBERON BAY (1759), he commanded the British navy in North America during the early stages of the American War of Independence. In 1794 he fought and won the action against the French fleet known as the GLORIOUS FIRST OF JUNE.

Howe, Sir William (1729–1814), British general during the American War of Independence. The commander at Bunker Hill, he became supreme commander of British forces in North America in 1775. With his brother Admiral Richard HOWE, he captured New York (1776) and occupied Philadelphia (27 Sept. 1777) but, after defeat at Saratoga (1777), he resigned in May 1778 and returned to England.

Howells, Herbert (1892–), British composer. A pupil of STANFORD, his compositions included several choral works set to religious texts. Prominent among these are the requiem *Hymnus Paradisi* (1938) and *Stabat Mater* (1963). His music, although basically conventional in idiom, was characterized by an individual style of chromaticism.

Howells, William Dean (1837–1920), US novelist and critic, pioneer of American literary realism. As assistant editor (1866–71) and editor (1871–81) of the *Atlantic Monthly*, the leading literary journal of the time, Howells concentrated the magazine's attention more exclusively on literature. His socialist sympathies are reflected in the novels *A Traveler from Altruia* (1894) and *Through the Eye of the Needle* (1907), but his best-known work is *The Rise of Silas Lapham* (1885). *See also* HC2 p.288.

Howitzer, ARTILLERY piece that, because of its low muzzle velocity, is capable of curved fire – hence its projectile may reach targets hidden to high-velocity guns. Howitzers were first used in the late 16th century. *See also* MM pp.166–169.

Howler monkey, mammal that lives in Central and South America; its name is derived from the loud, penetrating call of the male. The largest New World MONKEY, it is a gregarious tree-dweller that feeds chiefly on leaves. Height: to 92cm (36in); weight: 9kg (20lb). Genus *Alouatta. See also* NW p.*216*.

Howlin' Wolf (1910–76), US blues singer. Also known as Chester Burnett, he wrote and performed songs of aggressive intensity right up to his death. He profoundly influenced rock musicians, especially CAPTAIN BEEFHEART and Little Feat. All his major hits were recorded 1954–64.

Howrah, city in E central India, on the River Hooghly opposite Calcutta. It is part of an industrial region and its own products include iron and steel, food processing and textiles. Pop. (1971) 737,877.

Hoxha, Enver (1908–), Albanian Communist leader. He came to prominence in WWII, when he was active in the National Liberation Movement, and in 1941 he established the Albanian Communist Party. In 1944 he became Premier. Following the USSR rift with Communist China in 1960, Hoxha joined Peking in its ideological struggle with Moscow.

Hoy, second largest of the ORKNEY ISLANDS, 23km (14 miles) long and 10km (6 miles) wide, off the NE coast of Scotland. There is some settlement in the NE (pop. 750) but the island is largely barren. The highest point is Ward Hill, 477m (1,564ft).

Hoyle, Sir Fred (1915–), British astronomer and mathematician who worked at Cambridge with Thomas Gold and Hermann Bondi on the development of the STEADY-STATE THEORY, subsequently becoming director of the Institute of Theoretical Astronomy (1966). He held academic posts in the USA and wrote several books, including science fiction novels, sometimes in association with his son Geoffrey. *See also* SU pp.175, 252.

Hoysala (*c.*1006–1346), Indian dynasty that ruled in the southern Deccan and Cauvery valley. Vishnuvardhana won much territory, but his weak son Narasimha I lost it. His grandson Ballala II (*r.*1173–1220) came to his aid. The dynasty's strength or weakness depended upon the merit of the individual on the throne more than its structure of rule.

H-R diagram. *See* HERTZSPRUNG-RUSSELL DIAGRAM.

Hsia dynasty, legendary first dynasty in Chinese history, supposedly prior to the Shang kingdom. Its traditional dates are *c.*2205–*c.*1766 BC, but modern Chinese scholars suggest *c.*1994–1524 BC.

Hsian. *See* XI'AN.

Hsinchu, city in NE Taiwan, 10km (6 miles) inland. Founded *c.*1700 by Chinese settlers from the mainland, it is now a commercial centre with paper, fertilizer and textile industries. Pop. (1970) 208,038.

Hsin-shing, city in China, provincial capital of Kirin province and 282km (175 miles) NNE of Mukden; it is now known as Ch'ang-ch'un. The city was given the name Hsin-ching when it became the capital of the former state of Manchukuo 1932–45. Ch'ang-ch'un is an industrial city producing chemicals, textiles and motor vehicles, and is a large engineering centre. Pop. (1970 est.) 1,500,000.

Hsiung, Shih I (1902–), Chinese playwright. His play *Lady Precious Stream*, based on an ancient Chinese comedy, was produced in London in 1934. Hsiung worked in the theatre in Peking and Shanghai and later taught at Peking University.

Hsüan Tsung (685–762), Chinese emperor (*r.*712–56) of the T'ANG DYNASTY, also known as Ming Huang ("The Enlightened Emperor"). His rule provided the empire with one of its greatest periods of prosperity, grandeur and cultural brilliance, known as the golden age of Chinese poetry. Political dissatisfaction and military revolt followed the development of opposed and powerful factions in his administration, and led to his abdication.

Hsün-tzu (*c.*298–*c.*230 BC), Chinese phi-

losopher. He systematized the work of CONFUCIUS and MENCIUS, thereby securing the continuance of the Confucian philosophical tradition. His importance has been obscured by the stress that later Confucians have placed on the view attributed to him that human nature is basically evil.
Hua Kuo-feng (*c.*1920–), Chinese politician who was appointed Premier of China in April 1976. The previous year he was deputy Premier before being elevated to acting Premier by the death of CHOU EN-LAI. A moderate, he was instrumental in the denunciation of the "gang of four" who made a bid for power following the death of MAO TSE-TUNG in Sept. 1976. He became Chairman of the Chinese Communist Party in Oct. 1976.
Huallaga, river in N and W Peru. It flows from the Andes Mts N to the Marañon River. Length: 1,127km (700 miles).
Huang-ho. *See* HWANG HO.
Huari, (Wari) prehistoric cultural period in Peru, named after a major archaeological site in the Mantaro Basin of the central Highlands. The Huari Empire lasted from about AD 600–1000. Its architecture is characterized chiefly by large stone enclosures. The culture also produced large stone sculptures and naturalistic representations of male and female figures.
Huáscar (*r.*1525–32), Inca King, son of HUAYNA CAPAC, who controlled northern Peru (Cuzco) after his father's death. His younger half-brother, ATAHUALPA, controlled Quito, and the civil war between them (which Huáscar lost) also facilitated their conquest by PIZARRO, who arrived at this time.
Huayna Capac (*d.*1525), last of the great Inca rulers (1493–1525), who extended the Inca Empire to its greatest size. He divided his realm between his two sons, ATAHUALPA and HUÁSCAR; war between the brothers had just ended when the Spanish began their conquest.
Hubble, Edwin Powell (1889–1953), US astronomer. Educated at Chicago and Oxford universities, he thereafter worked at MOUNT WILSON OBSERVATORY. Hubble discovered that galactic NEBULAE were GALAXIES outside the MILKY WAY and also detected and studied their recession. *See also* SU pp.238, 245, 248, 252.
Hubble constant, ratio of the velocity of recession of a GALAXY to its distance. All galaxies beyond the LOCAL GROUP are receding from us and from each other, as indicated by their RED SHIFTS. The limit of the observable universe should thus occur when the recessional velocity equals the velocity of light. Assuming that the Hubble constant holds at large distances this limit is about 10 thousand million (10^{10}) light-years. If the rate of expansion of the universe has always been the same the Hubble constant gives the age of the universe as about 10^{10} years. *See also* SU pp.248–249.
Hubertusburg, Peace of (1763), treaty ending the SEVEN YEARS WAR between Prussia and Austria. Prussia agreed to support the succession of JOSEPH II to the Imperial throne, and in return, Prussia was awarded Silesia.
Huch, Ricarda (1864–1947), German poetess and writer. Her poetry was published in two volumes called *Gedichte* (1891; 1894), but she is remembered chiefly for her historical studies, which include *The Life of Count Federigo Confalieri* (1910), *Wallenstein* (1915) and *Michael Bakunin and Anarchy* (1923).
Huckleberry Finn, The Adventures of, novel by Mark TWAIN, published in 1885. The novel, a sequel to *Tom Sawyer*, is considered to be Twain's most characteristic in characterization, plot and style, and is regarded by some critics as the greatest American novel.
Huddersfield, town in Yorkshire on the River Colne, 24km (15 miles) SW of Leeds. The woollen trade was developed in the 17th century and textiles are now the most important industry. Other products include chemicals and machinery. Pop. (1973) 130,060.
Huddleston, Ernest Urban Trevor (1913–), British churchman. Ordained in 1937, he spent 13 restless years in South Africa, often vociferously opposing the government, before becoming Bishop of Masai (1960–68). Then appointed suffragan Bishop of Stepney, London, in 1969 he became vice-president of the Anti-apartheid Movement. In Oct. 1977 he accepted appointment as Bishop of Mauritius.
Hudibras, verse satire by Samuel BUTLER, published in three parts in 1663, 1664 and 1678. It mocks the 17th-century PRESBYTERIANS and INDEPENDENTS through the adventures of the mutually quarrelsome Hudibras (the presbyterian) and his servant Ralpho (the independent). The work is incomplete. It is written in octosyllabic couplets.
Hudson, Henry (*d.*1611), English navigator and explorer. During his last four years he led several expeditions in search of a passage to China. On his first attempt he reached Newland (Spitsbergen), where he discovered rich fishing grounds. On the third voyage (1609), he reached the American Coast, and, sailing up what was to be called the Hudson River, disproved the possibility of there being a low-latitude sea route across the continent. On his last expedition he passed through the strait which bears his name and entered the inland sea now known as HUDSON BAY. In 1611 he was set adrift by his mutinous crew and never heard of again. *See also* HC2 p.*136*.
Hudson, William Henry (1841–1922), British naturalist writer and novelist who was born in South America and went to England in 1869. His romantic novels include *The Purple Land* (1885) and the popular and haunting *Green Mansions* (1904). He has a talent for observation and description of the English countryside.
Hudson Bay, inland bay in E Northwest Territories, Canada, bounded by Québec (E), Ontario (S) and Manitoba (SW). The bay contains Southampton, Mansel and Coats Islands. The Churchill and Nelson Rivers drain into the bay, which is ice-free from July to October. Area: 1,243,200sq km (480,000sq miles).
Hudson River, river in E New York state which rises near Mount Marcy in the Adirondacks and flows S to New York Bay at New York City. Sighted in 1524 and explored in 1609 by Henry HUDSON, it has become one of the most important waterways of the world. The New York State Barge Canal connects the Hudson with Lake Champlain, the Great Lakes and the St Lawrence River. Length: approx. 493km (306 miles).
Hudson River School, group of US ROMANTIC landscape painters active between 1825 and 1875. They were so named because many painted idealized scenes of the Hudson River Valley. Among the most famous of the group were Thomas COLE, John Kensett, Henry Inman and Asher B. DURAND.
Hudson's Bay Company, corporation chartered in 1670 by CHARLES II of England to promote trade in the HUDSON BAY region of N America and to seek a northwest passage to the Orient. It dealt mainly in furs. In 1821 it absorbed the Montreal-based North West Company. In 1859 it lost its right to govern territories; much of its land was transferred to the new Confederation of Canada in 1870. It then began to expand into diverse business interests. In 1930 it was split up, the fur company remaining in London, the retail shops and diversified businesses in Canada. It remains one of the largest business firms in Canada. *See also* HC2 pp.*46*, *136*.
Hudson Strait, strait in NE Canada, between S Baffin Island and N Québec. It connects Hudson Bay with the Atlantic Ocean and Foxe Channel, and is a passageway to the Arctic Ocean. Length: 725km (450 miles).
Hue, city on the E coast of central Vietnam, on the Hue River. Founded *c.*3rd century AD, the city was occupied by the Chams and the Annamese and it became the capital of Annam. First taken by the French in 1883, Hue witnessed the struggle between the French and the VIET MINH after WWII. Much of the city was destroyed during the Vietnam War. There is a university (1957) in Hue, which is a market centre for rice; it also has cement industries. Pop. (1973) 209,043.
Hueffer, Ford. *See* FORD, FORD MADOX.
Huggins, Charles Brenton (1901–), US physician, *b.* Nova Scotia. He shared the 1966 Nobel Prize in physiology and medicine with F. P. ROUS for his pioneering work in CANCER chemotherapy and his development of ways of investigating and treating cancers through the use of HORMONES.
Huggins, Sir William (1824–1910), British astronomer, the first to use the SPECTROSCOPE to determine the chemical composition of stars, comets and novae. He developed spectroscopic photography and applied the DOPPLER shift of the spectral lines of stars to the measurement of stellar motion. He distinguished between nebulae that are uniformly gaseous and those that contain stellar clusters. *See also* SU p.226.
Hughes, Arthur (1835–1915), British painter. He was a member of the PRE-RAPHAELITE school; his best-known paintings include *April Love* (1856) and *The Eve of St Agnes* (1856).
Hughes, David Edward (1831–1900), Anglo-American inventor and scientist who, in 1879, made the first practical demonstration of what we now call radio waves, but did not publish his findings for 20 years. In 1854 he built the first practical printing telegraph, and is now generally credited as the inventor of the CARBON MICROPHONE. *See also* MM pp.225, 226, 228.
Hughes, Howard (1905–76), US industrialist, aviator and film producer. He inherited an industrial corporation (1923), subsequently becoming one of the wealthiest of US billionaires as head of the Summa Corporation and the Hughes Aircraft Company. In 1935 he set the world speed record of 567km/h (352mph) in an aircraft of his own design. He occasionally produced films, including *Hell's Angels* (1930), in which he made a star of Jean HARLOW, as he did of Jane Russell in *The Outlaw* (1941). He lived the last 20 years of his life in almost total seclusion.
Hughes, Patric ("Spike") (1908–), British jazz composer, arranger and bass player. Hughes was an important force in stimulating jazz interest in Britain during the 1930s. He recorded with well-known US musicians such as Coleman Hawkins during a visit to the USA in 1933.
Hughes, Richard Arthur Warren (1900–76), British novelist. He wrote a number of plays, but is best known for his novels *A High Wind in Jamaica* (1929), a bizarre tale of amiable pirates and malevolent children, *The Fox in the Attic* (1961) and *The Wooden Shepherdess* (1972).
Hughes, Sir Samuel (1853–1921), Canadian soldier and political leader. A member of the Conservative Party, he sat in the House of Commons (1892–1921) and during WWI played an important role in organizing the Canadian expeditionary forces.
Hughes, Ted (1930–), British poet and short story writer whose major works include *Hawk in the Rain* (1957), *Lupercal* (1960), *Wodwo* (1967), the *Crow* poems, beginning in 1970, and *Gaudete* (1977). In these works he explores the theme of man's identity in a hostile universe and uses material from the animal world, mythology and folklore.
Hughes, Thomas (1822–96), British novelist and political writer. An active member of the Christian Socialist Movement, he is chiefly remembered for his popular novel *Tom Brown's Schooldays* (1857) and its sequel *Tom Brown at Oxford* (1861). Among his other works are *The Scouring of The White Horse* (1859) and *The Manliness of Christ* (1879).
Hughes, William Morris (1864–1952), Australian politician, *b.* England. In 1894 he was elected as a Labor member to the New South Wales legislature and he entered the federal parliament in 1901. He was prime minister between 1915 and 1923, and at the Paris Peace Conference

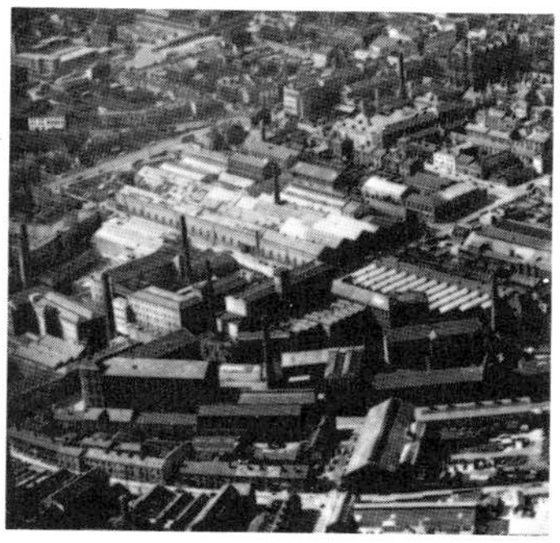

Huddersfield's factories and mills are typical of the landscape of northern industrial towns.

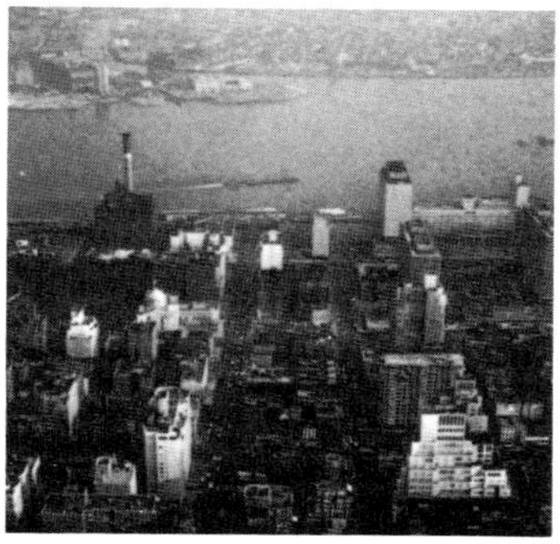

Hudson River; today road tunnels provide links between Manhattan and New Jersey.

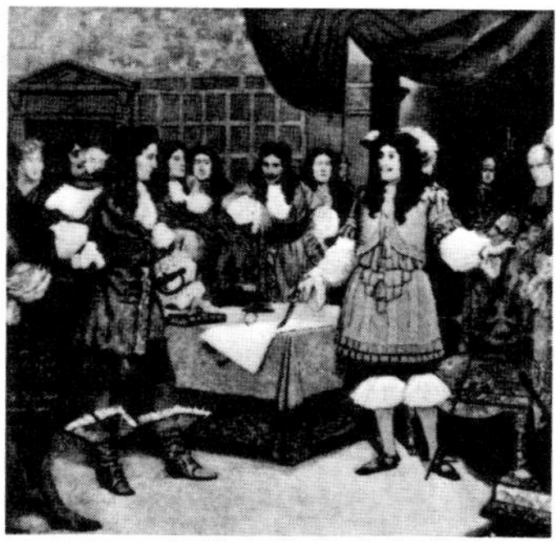

Hudson's Bay Company: Charles II granting a charter for trade to Prince Rupert's syndicate.

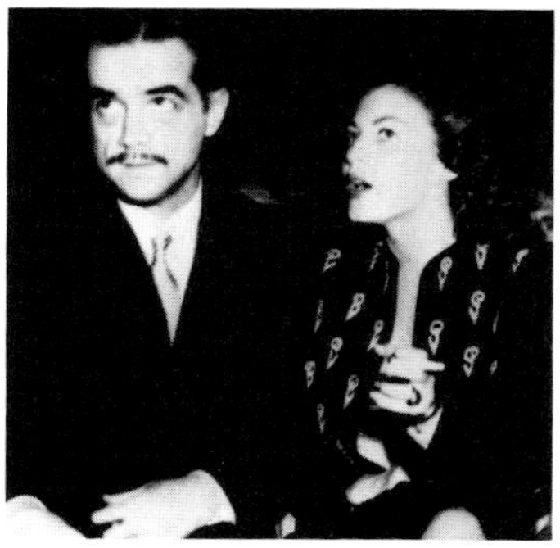

Howard Hughes, the US industrial and film producer who became a recluse.

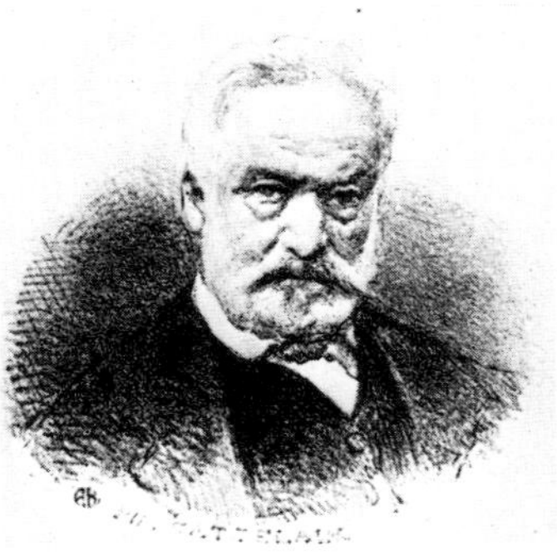

Victor Hugo stood for the French presidency in 1848 but received only derisory support.

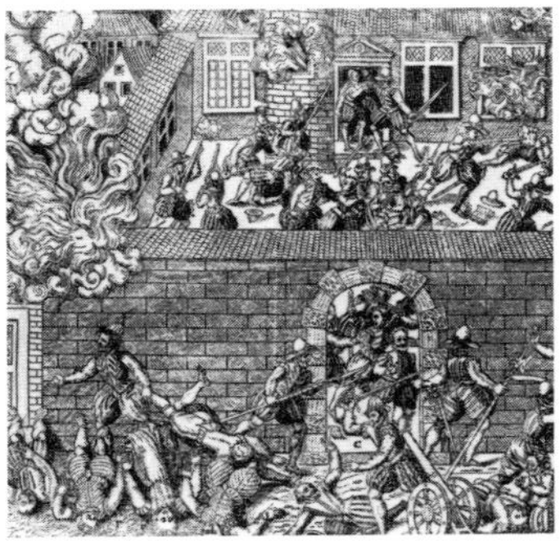

Huguenots; an engraving of a massacre of French protestants at Cahors in 1561.

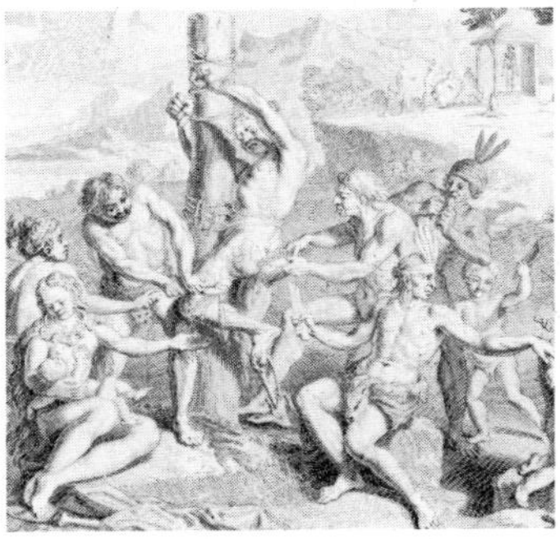

Human sacrifice; an engraving of 1723 of a sacrifice performed by a tribe in the Andes.

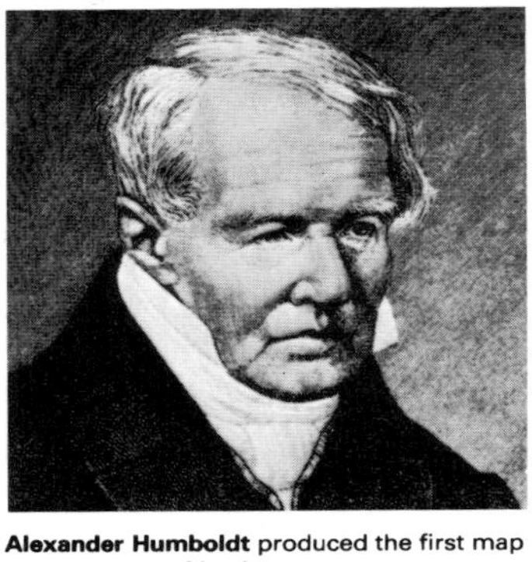

Alexander Humboldt produced the first map showing sets of isotherms.

in 1919 gained German New Guinea for Australia.

Hugh of Avalon, Saint. *See* HUGH OF LINCOLN.

Hugh of Lincoln, Saint (*c.* 1135–1200), English bishop. In 1179 HENRY II appointed him Prior of Witham Friary in Somerset, the first English CARTHUSIAN monastery. He became Bishop of Lincoln in 1186. Courageous and independent, he persistently fought for the interests of ecclesiastical authority in opposition to the Crown.

Hugo, Victor (1802–85), French poet, dramatist and novelist. He received a pension from LOUIS XVIII for his first collection of *Odes* (1822) and presented his manifesto of ROMANTICISM in the preface to his play *Cromwell* (1827). Later works include the plays *Hernani* (1830) and *Ruy Blas* (1838) and the novels *Notre-Dame de Paris* (1831) and *Les Misérables* (1862). Political convictions sent him into exile in the Channel Islands (1851–70) but on the fall of the Second Empire he returned to Paris, where he received a respect bordering on veneration. At his death he was given a state funeral. *See also* HC2 pp.98, 100–101.

Huguenots, French Protestants of the 16th-18th centuries. The name probably comes originally from the German Eidgenossen ("confederates"), but is possibly also influenced by the name of the gate, Roi-Hugen, where the Protestants of Tours assembled at night. In 1559, in the face of persecution, a national Protestant synod adopted a confession of faith and an ecclesiastical structure, influenced by Calvin more than by Luther. During the Wars of Religion the Huguenots continued to be persecuted (*see* BARTHOLEMEW'S DAY MASSACRE). The Protestant HENRY IV came to the throne in 1589, and, despite adopting the Roman faith in 1593, he promulgated the Edict of NANTES (1598). This recognized Catholicism as the official religion, but gave the Huguenots certain rights. It was revoked by LOUIS XIV in 1685 and thousands of Huguenots fled France. In 1789 their civil rights were restored and by the CODE NAPOLÉON (1804) they were guaranteed religious equality.

Huia, extinct New Zealand bird which showed a very unusual form of sexual dimorphism, or specialization of shape between male and female. The male had a short, straight, strong bill for making holes in decaying bark. The female had a long, slender, curved bill for probing crevices and for removing grubs which the male had uncovered but could not reach. Species *Heteralocha acutirostris.*

Huidobro, Vicente (1893–1948), Chilean poet. He founded a literary movement known as *creacionismo,* which attempted to free words from their customary meanings to facilitate original imagery. His most praised poem is *Altazor o el viaje en paracaídas,* an account of what he believed to be modern man's descent from order to chaos.

Hui Tsung (1082–1135), Chinese emperor (*r.* 1101–25). The penultimate emperor of the Northern SUNG DYNASTY, he abdicated under threat from the Jurchen tribes of Manchuria. He founded the first imperial Chinese academy of painting, established imperial porcelain kilns and was an accomplished painter.

Huizinga, Johan (1872–1945), Dutch historian, admired for his social and intellectual history. He was professor of history at the University of Leiden (1915–42). His most famous books are *Erasmus of Rotterdam* (1924), *Homo Ludens* (1938) and *The Waning of the Middle Ages* (1919).

Hulagu Khan (1217–65), Mongol leader, grandson of GENGHIS KHAN. He quelled an uprising in Persia and annihilated the ASSASSIN sect, a Muslim secret society. He sacked Baghdad (1258) and seized Aleppo in Syria (1260). The Mongol advance under his command was checked by the MAMELUKES, an Egyptian military caste.

Hulbert, Jack (1892–1978), British light comedy actor who made his first professional appearance in 1913 and continued to give consistently entertaining performances in plays, musicals and films. He produced and starred – often with his brother Claude – in musicals such as *Lido Lady* (1926) and *Follow a Star* (1930); his films included *The Ghost Train* (1931). He was married to Cicely Courtneidge; his autobiography, *The Little Woman's Always Right,* was published in 1975.

Hull, Cordell (1871–1955), US Secretary of State (1933–44) under Franklin D. ROOSEVELT. He was a member of the House of Representatives (1907–21, 1923–31) and author of the first federal income tax law in 1913. He played a significant part in bringing together the USA and Latin-American states. During WWII he was an important diplomatic figure and was later influential in establishing the preliminary organization of the UNITED NATIONS. In 1945 he was awarded the Nobel Peace Prize.

Hull (Kingston upon Hull), city in Humberside, NE England, on the N shore of the Humber estuary; third largest port and the largest fishing port in Britain. It exports products from the industrial region of NE England. Hull is the only city in Britain to own its own telephone system. Industries: chemicals, iron and steel, food processing, machinery. Pop. (1971) 285,472.

Hulme, Denny (1936–), New Zealand motor racing driver. In 1967 he became the first New Zealander to win the world drivers' championship (in a Brabham), and in 1968 and 1970 won the Can-Am sports car title in a McLaren. In 1967 and 1968 he was fourth in the Indianapolis 500.

Hulme, Thomas Ernest (1883–1917), British philosopher, poet and literary critic. He was a leader of the anti-romantic movement in modern poetry and criticism and a chief figure, with Ezra POUND, of the IMAGIST group of poets, which also included F. S. Flint, H. D. (Hilda Doolittle), Richard Aldington and Amy Lowell. His philosophical writings include *Speculations* (1924) and *Notes on Language and Style* (1929).

Hulst, Hendrik van de (1918–), Dutch astronomer who calculated that the clouds of cold hydrogen gas in space should radiate at a wavelength of 21cm. He also made contributions to the study of light scattering and the solar CORONA. *See also* SU p.245.

Human body, body of HOMO SAPIENS that differs from those of man's close relatives, the great apes, most obviously in the greater cranial development, the S-curved backbones and straight limb bones, a foot development in which the big toe cannot touch more than one other toe, and relative hairlessness. Otherwise the human body, bone for bone, matches those of the chimpanzee, gorilla and orangutan. Genetically, there are more obvious differences as can be seen by examination of the CHROMOSOMES of man and the apes.

Human Comedy. *See* COMÉDIE HUMAINE.

Humanism, philosophical viewpoint based on the belief that "the proper study of mankind is man". Humanist ideas can be found from ancient to modern times, but the flowering of Humanism came during the RENAISSANCE. Medieval scholars had studied the classics to bolster Christian theology; Renaissance men, such as PETRARCH, studied the classics for their own sakes and saw them as a means of educating people. The movement spread northwards from Italy to include such scholars as Sir Thomas MORE, John CALVIN and Desiderius ERASMUS. From the 15th to the 18th centuries Humanism represented the revival of Classical values in philosophy and art. Modern Humanism developed in the 19th and 20th centuries alongside scientific discoveries as an alternative outlook to that of traditional Christian beliefs. This movement, which has been associated with social reform, was championed by Bertrand RUSSELL. *See also* HC1 pp.246–247.

Human rights, freedom which it may be argued that an individual possesses by virtue of being human. The concept of the inalienable rights of the human being has traditionally been linked to the idea of the higher or natural law, on which important commentaries were written by several of the Greek and Roman writers. The concept of human rights was most notably formulated, however, in the American Declaration of Independence (1776), the Constitution (1789) and particularly its first amendments in the Bill Of Rights (1791), and in the French DECLARATION OF THE RIGHTS OF MAN (1789). These documents owed much to the English PETITION OF RIGHT (1628) and BILL OF RIGHTS (1689) which extended the concept of individual freedom proclaimed earlier in the agreement between monarch and barons, MAGNA CARTA (1215). Important also are various international agreements for the protection of rights, most notably the abolition of slavery, including the traffic in women and children during the 19th and 20th centuries. The responsibility of the international community for the protection of human rights is proclaimed in the Charter of the United Nations and the Universal Declaration of Human Rights.

Human Rights, Universal Declaration of, statement drafted by the United Nations Commission on Human Rights and adopted by the general assembly in 1948. It contains 30 articles and sets out basic human rights, including legal, political and economic equality. It declares that all persons should enjoy at least a minimum standard of living, access to health and social services, the right to employment, free education and to pass freely between countries. The declaration does not have the force of international law.

Human sacrifice, sacrifice to a deity usually in an agricultural society to ensure fertility and a good harvest, of at least one human being, usually young. Human life has always been considered more valuable, and so more potent as a sacrifice, than that of an animal. In some societies, such as those of the pre-Roman Celts or ancient Greeks, only pure or noble victims were selected; the rituals of some other societies provided willing volunteers; in yet others mass sacrifices were common, as with the Aztecs. Sometimes the bodies of the victims were eaten to ensure the communality of the rite.

Humberside, county in NE England created in 1974 from parts of Yorkshire, East Riding and North Lincolnshire; HULL is the administrative centre and major port. Area: 3,512sq km (1,356sq miles). Pop. 846,600.

Humble Petition and Advice (1657), second constitution of the English Protectorate, replacing the Instrument of Government. In its original form it made Cromwell king, but he refused the Crown. It restored a second chamber (abolished in 1649) to a Parliament of nominated members and vested executive power in the protector and a privy council. It lasted until the Stuart restoration in 1660.

Humboldt, Baron Alexander von (1769–1859), German scientist and explorer. His special subject was mineralogy but on his scientific trips in Europe and Central and South America he studied volcanoes, the origins of tropical storms and the increase in magnetic intensity from the equator towards the poles. His principal work, *Kosmos* (five vols, pub. 1845–62) is a comprehensive description of the physical universe.

Humboldt (Peru) Current, current in the SE Pacific Ocean. An extension of the West Wind Drift, the Humboldt current flows N along the W coast of South America. A cold current, it lowers temperature along its course until it joins the warm Pacific South Equatorial current. *See also* PE pp.78–79.

Hume, David (1711–76), Scottish philosopher, historian and man of letters. His works include *A Treatise of Human Nature* (1739–40), *History of England* (1754–63) and various essays and philosophical "inquiries". Widely known for his humanitarianism and scepticism, Hume held a form of EMPIRICISM that affirmed the contingency of all phenomenal events. The posthumous *Dialogues Concerning Natural Religion* (1779) indicate the extent of his atheism. *See also* HC2 pp.29, 31; MS pp.226, 229–230, 232–233.

Hume, Joseph (1777–1855), British radical politician. He was an MP in 1812, 1818–41 and 1842–55. He was a forceful advocate of the repeal of the CORN LAWS and of the Combination Laws and a lifelong campaigner for parliamentary reform, including the introduction of universal franchise and the secret ballot.

Humerus, bone in the human upper arm, extending from the scapula (or shoulder blade) to the elbow. A notch, or depression, called the olecranon cavity, on the posterior roughened lower end of the humerus, provides the point of articulation for the ULNA, one of the forearm bones. *See also* MS p.*57*.

Humidity, or relative humidity, measure of the amount of water-vapour in air. It is the ratio of the actual vapour pressure to the saturation vapour pressure, at which water normally condenses, and is usually expressed as a percentage. Humidity is measured by a HYGROMETER. *See also* PE pp.66, 70.

Hummingbird, popular name for small, brilliantly coloured birds of the family *Trochilidae*, found in S and N America. They feed in flight on insects and nectar. Their speed can reach 100km/h (60mph) and their wings, which beat 50–75 times a second, make a humming sound. Length: 6–22cm (2.2–8.6in). *See also* NW pp.149–216.

Humours, the. *See* FOUR HUMOURS, THE.

Humpback whale, finbacked WHALE found in all the world's oceans. It has breast fins that reach a third of its body length, long knobby flippers and a rounded back. Length: to 16.75m (55ft); weight: 32 tonnes. Genus *Megaptera. See also* NW pp.167, *239*.

Humperdinck, Engelbert (1854–1921), German music teacher and composer. His works include incidental music, songs and seven operas, of which HANSEL AND GRETEL (1893), the first, has remained his most popular work. Its simple melodies are used in the heavily orchestrated style of WAGNER, whom Humperdinck helped at Bayreuth in the preparation of *Parsifal* (1880–81), even composing a few bars for the transformation scene.

Humphrey, Hubert Horatio (1911–78), US Vice-President (1965–69). He served as mayor of Minneapolis before entering the Senate as a Democrat. He incurred some hostility for his support of the VIETNAM WAR when Vice-President, but won the Democratic presidential nomination in 1968; he lost the election to Richard NIXON. He was appointed chairman of the Congressional Joint Economic Committee in 1975, and Deputy President *pro tem* of the Senate in 1977.

Humphreys, David. *See* CONNECTICUT WITS.

Humus, dark brown, organic substance resulting from partial decay of plant and animal matter. It improves soil by retaining moisture, releasing protein, aerating and increasing nitrogen content and bacterial activity. Often made in a compost heap or obtained naturally, types include peat moss, leaf mould and soil from woods. *See also* PE pp.166–167.

Hunan, province in SE central China, S of Tung-t'ng Lake. The capital is Changsha. A largely forested region, agriculture is nevertheless important; rice, tea, rape seed and tobacco are produced. The province has valuable mineral resources, including coal, tungsten and antimony. Area: 210,570sq km (81,301sq miles). Pop. 38,000,000.

Hunchback, convex curvature of the upper spine, causing the back to bulge or a person having such curvature. It is generally caused by a disease such as tuberculosis or arthritis, but may be congenital.

Hunchback of Notre-Dame, The, English title of the novel by Victor HUGO, published as *Notre-Dame de Paris* in 1831. It was first published in an English translation in 1833. It was Hugo's first great novel and, with *Les Misérables*, the one that has remained most popular.

Hundred, subdivision of a shire in medieval England, having its origin in the Anglo-Saxon era. Its first official mention occurs in the 10th century. In theory a hundred consisted of 100 HIDES. The hundred court (the hundred's administrative body) met every four weeks under the king's REEVE to deal with small pleas and apportion taxation.

Hundred Days, Napoleon's, interlude between Napoleon's escape from exile on the island of Elba in March 1815 to his defeat at Waterloo in June. The French people received his avowed affection for constitutional rule with scepticism, and the recreated GRAND ALLIANCE defeated him at Waterloo and sent him into permanent exile on St Helena.

Hundred Rolls, records on a variety of matters in 13th-century England, popularly known as Ragman Rolls. Most of them consist of returns from the inquest conducted by EDWARD I in 1274–75 into local administration. The commissioners put their questions to the HUNDRED court, from which the name of the rolls derived.

Hundred Schools, term referring to the classical period of Chinese philosophy (6th–3rd centuries BC). The primary concern of the many philosophical schools of the late CHOU period was ethics. Of the reputed "hundred schools", six were to prove historically significant, and of these CONFUCIANISM was the most important.

Hundred Years War, war between France and England pursued sporadically between the French seizure of English-held Guyenne in 1337 and the English defeat at Castillon in 1453. The refusal of EDWARD III of England to do homage for his French possessions began the war. Early English successes at CRÉCY and Calais and the capture of the French king, JOHN II, in 1356 brought England territorial gains in the Peace of BRÉTIGNY (1360). The French gradually won their lands back and although HENRY V won the Battle of AGINCOURT, subsequent English failures at the siege of Orléans (1428–29) and the Battle of Patay (1429) ensured their ultimate expulsion from most of France. *See also* HC1 pp.212–213.

Hungarian, or Magyar, official language of Hungary, spoken by the country's 10.5 million inhabitants and by 3.5 million more in Romania, Czechoslovakia and elsewhere. It belongs to the Ugric branch of the FINNO-UGRIC LANGUAGES, which are in turn a part of the URALIC family.

Hungary, landlocked nation in central Europe, consisting of two rolling plains divided into three by the rivers Duna and Tisza. It was once a predominantly agricultural country, but the economy is now based on industry. Principal exports include machinery and chemicals. The capital is Budapest. Area: 93,030sq km (35,919sq miles). Pop. (1975 est.) 10,619,000. *See* MW p.93.

Hunger, need or drive for an organism to obtain food. A specific hunger is a need for a particular substance in the DIET, eg vitamin C, to maintain health. In higher animals, eating and cessation of eating are governed by mechanisms in the HYPOTHALAMUS of the brain that respond to blood-sugar levels. In human beings hunger and thirst also reflect complex interactions between physiological clues and past experience with foods and tastes. *See also* MS pp.40–41, 70–71.

Hung Hsiu-Chuan (1814–64), Chinese visionary, leader of the TAIPING REBELLION. He came from KWANGTUNG province and was converted to Christianity in 1843. He believed himself the second son of god and set himself up as head of a new dynasty, centred on Nanking. Captured in 1853, he committed suicide in 1864. *See also* HC2 p.144.

Huns, nomadic Mongol people, probably of Turkish, Tataric or Ugrian stock who spread from the Caspian steppes (present-day USSR) to wage a series of wars on the Roman Empire. Lacking the cultural development attributed to more sedentary peoples, they were very skilled in the arts of war, particularly military horsemanship. By the first half of the 4th century they had conquered the Ostrogoths and the Visigoths, reaching west as far as the River Danube. By about 432 the Huns were collecting an annual tribute from Rome. Their leader ATTILA (*r.* 434–453) invaded the Eastern Empire and then moved still farther westward to Italy and Gaul, but after his death in 453 the power of the Huns was broken. Many took service in the Roman armies; the rest settled on the lower Danube. *See also* HC1 pp.136–137.

Hunt, Geoff (1947–), Australian squash player. The foremost exponent of power squash, he has dominated the game in the 1970s, adding two world professional championships to numerous honours that include the world amateur (1967, 1969, 1971) and the British and Australian Open titles.

Hunt, Henry Cecil John, Baron (1910–) British soldier, mountaineer and explorer who in 1952 led the first successful ascent of Everest, when Sir Edmund HILLARY and Sherpa TENZING NORKEY scaled the peak. His army experience in India and Burma and his organizational skills were largely responsible for the expedition's success. He was made a life peer in 1966.

Hunt, James (1947–), British motor racing driver. After driving for Lord Hesketh's team in 1973–75, he moved to McLaren and won the world drivers' championship in 1976 with six grand prix victories.

Hunt, Leigh (1784–1859), British critic, journalist and poet. A member of literary circles which included SHELLEY and KEATS, he was known in his own time as a literary theorist and political journalist, writing for the contemporary periodicals *The Indicator* and *The Examiner.* He published a memoir of BYRON (2 vols, 1828) and *Poetical Works* (1832). His financial incompetence is satirized in the character of Harold Skimpole in Charles Dickens' *Bleak House.*

Hunt, William Holman (1827–1910), British painter who, with John Everett MILLAIS and Dante Gabriel ROSSETTI, founded the PRE-RAPHAELITE BROTHERHOOD in 1848. From 1854 he journeyed several times to Palestine and Egypt to paint biblical scenes in accurate local settings. His works, which include *The Light of the World* (1854) and *The Scapegoat* (1856) combine meticulous precision with didactic symbolism.

Hunter, John (1728–1793), and his brother William (1718–1783), Scottish anatomists and surgeons. They worked in collaboration for several years during which they studied the lymphatic system, the course of the olfactory nerves and the coagulation of blood. John was the first to ligate an artery in the 1760s.

Hunter, John (1737–1821), British navigator who charted Sydney Harbour. As Governor of New South Wales (1795–1800) his attempts to introduce reforms aroused the enmity of MACARTHUR and Hunter was recalled to London.

Hunting, field sport involving the killing or trapping of small and large game. The three main types of hunting include those with firearms or bows and arrows, trapping and snaring, and coursing and falconry. For small game, hunting dogs (HOUNDS) are sometimes used. Hunting began as a means of survival, but by the Middle Ages in Europe it was considered a sport usually reserved for the privileged class. In Britain it usually refers to the hunting of deer, otters, foxes and hares by a pack of hounds behind huntsmen on horseback. When a deer is cornered it is generally shot; foxes and hares are tracked down by the hounds who then move in for the kill.

Hunting and gathering, practice of small societies in which its members subsist mainly by hunting and by collecting plants rather than by agriculture. There is a low subsistence ratio of people to land, so the groups are always small bands. Although their technology is extremely simple they have sophisticated kinship and ritualistic systems. Today hunting-gathering societies are most numerous in lowland South America and parts of Africa. *See also* MS pp.30, 33, 250–251, 255.

Huntingdon, Selina Hastings, Countess of (1707–91), non-conformist religious leader in Britain and founder of the Calvinist Methodist sect (which broke with WESLEY), called the "Countess of Huntingdon's Connexion". She built 64 chapels as well as a seminary in Wales.

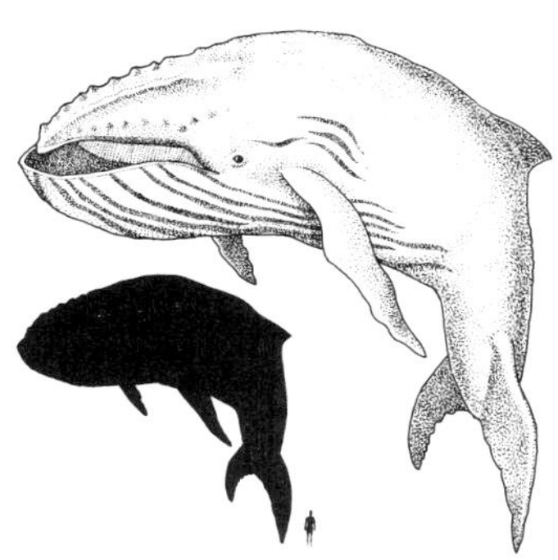

Humpback whale; biologists have made recordings of their "song-like" sounds.

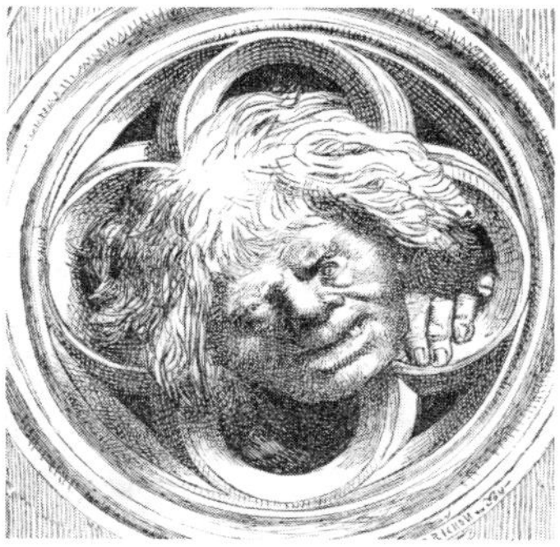

Hunchback of Notre-Dam; Quasimodo taking part in the grinning competition.

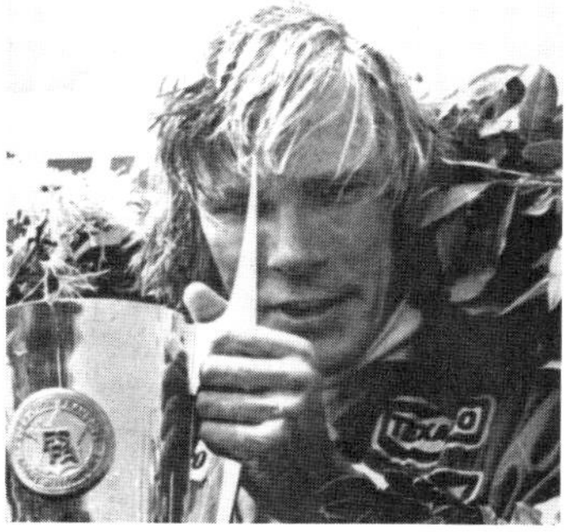

James Hunt with the winner's trophy after his victory in the French Grand Prix in 1976.

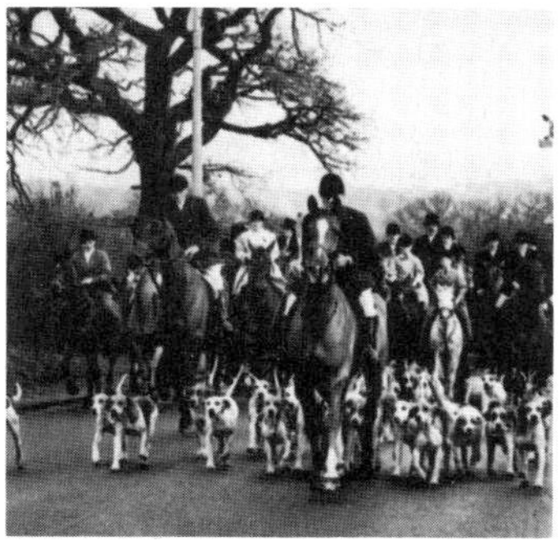

Hunting; the horses and hounds of the Eridge Hunt on Tunbridge Wells common.

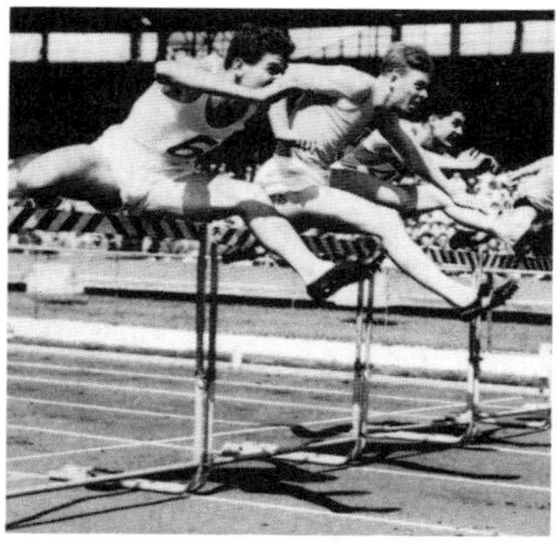

Hurdles; in this event an athlete must make natural strides between each flight of hurdles.

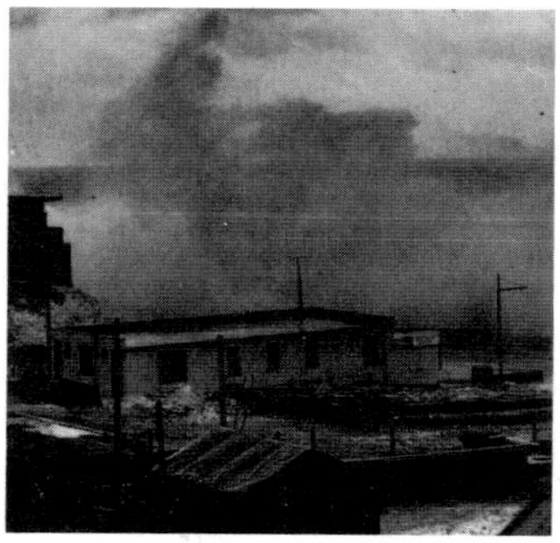

Hurricane force winds battered the south coast of England in 1954.

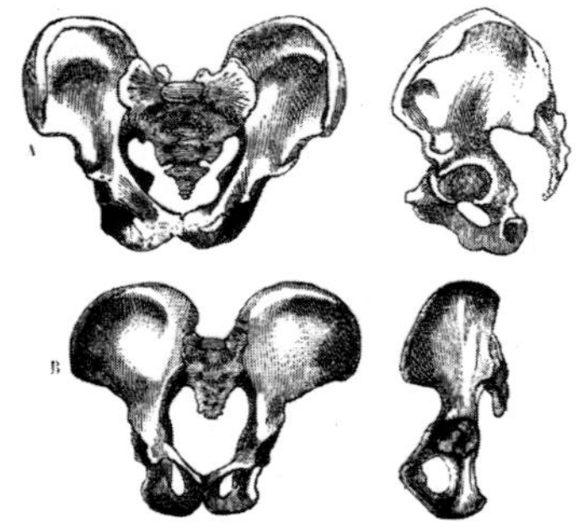

Thomas Huxley; his study of the pelvis was among many used to illustrate his works.

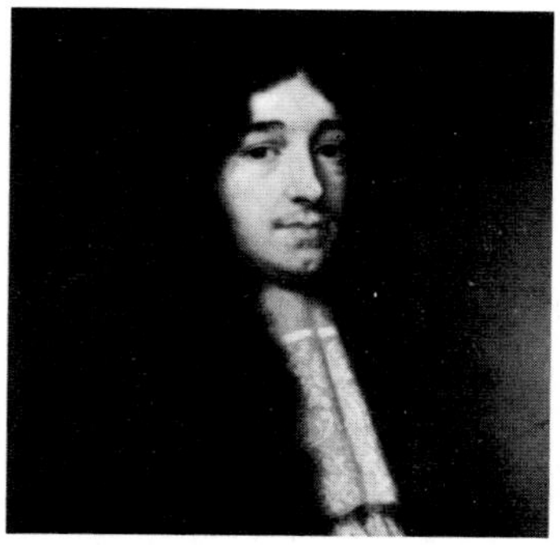

Christiaan Huygens developed an improved method of grinding lenses for his telescopes.

Huntingdon, county district in W CAMBRIDGESHIRE, England; created in 1974 under the Local Government Act (1972). Area: 912sq km (352sq miles). Pop. (1974 est.) 111,300.

Huntingdon and Peterborough, former county in E central England, which became part of Cambridgeshire in 1974.

Hunting leopard. *See* CHEETAH.

Huntington's chorea. *See* CHOREA.

Hunyàdi, János (1387–1456), Hungarian soldier and national hero. He was voivode (governor) of Transylvania (1440) and regent for Ladislas V (1446–52). A brilliant general, he took part in the HUSSITE Wars. In 1456 he defeated the Turkish fleet on the River Danube and broke the siege of Belgrade.

Hunza, people that live in mountainous terrain by the Hunza River, near Gilgit in Jammu, N Pakistan. They are Muslims of the Ismaili sect, followers of the AGA KHAN.

Hupei (Hubei or Hupeh), province in E central China; the capital is Wei-chang. Drained by the Yangtze (Changjiang) and Han rivers, the region is one of the most productive agricultural areas in China. Products: wheat, barley rice, tea, cotton, non-ferrous metals, steel. Area: 187,590sq km (72,430sq miles). Pop. 32,000,000.

Hurdles. *See* HORSE RACING.

Hurdles, track athletic event in which athletes clear ten flights of obstacles while running a prescribed distance. At Olympic and championship level, there are two hurdling events for men (110m, 400m) and one for women (100m, formerly 80m). Imperial distances are sometimes raced, as are events over 200m and 400m (women). The heights of the hurdles depend on the distance: 100m, 84cm (2ft 9in); 110m, 1.07m (3ft 6in); men's 400m, 91.4cm (3ft). Runners may take off from either foot. The event began in the mid-19th century, when sheep hurdles were used – hence the name.

Hurling, game similar to hockey; the national sport of Ireland. It is played by two teams of 15 on a field 137m (450ft) long and 82m (270ft) wide. At each end are goalposts 6.4m (21ft) wide with a crossbar 2.4m (8ft) above the ground. Each player carries a wooden hurley, similar to a hockey stick. The object is to catch the ball on the stick, run with it or hurl it towards a team-mate. Three points are scored for netting the ball under the crossbar, one point for hitting it over the crossbar. The ball may not be picked up or thrown by hand. Hurling, one of the fastest of all team games, is governed by the Gaelic Athletic Association.

Huron, small confederation of Iroquoian-speaking tribes of North American Indians who once occupied the St Lawrence Valley E of Lake Huron from Ontario to Georgian Bay. In wars for control of the fur trade with the IROQUOIS (1648–50) their population was reduced from 15,000 to about 500. They wandered widely, settling finally in Ohio, where they became known as the Wyandot. Others fled to the Great Lakes area and eventually settled in Kansas. Today some 1,250 live on reservations in Ohio, Oklahoma and in Ontario, Canada.

Huron, Lake, second largest of the GREAT LAKES; part of the boundary between the USA and Canada. It drains Lake SUPERIOR and feeds Lake ERIE as part of the Great Lakes–St Lawrence Seaway system and is navigable by ocean-going vessels. Area: 59,596sq km (23,010sq miles); max. depth: 229m (750ft).

Hurrians, ancient people of Mesopotamia. They established a kingdom to the N of the SUMERIANS by 2000 BC. By 1500 BC this had become organized into the kingdom of Mitanni, which established an empire in Syria and warred with Egypt. The power of the Hurrians was eventually destroyed by the ASSYRIANS in *c.* 1200, but they had considerable influence over HITTITE culture. They spoke a language unrelated to any other Mesopotamian language and used a CUNEIFORM script. *See also* HC1 pp.28, 31, *52*.

Hurricane, wind of Force 12 on the BEAUFORT WIND SCALE; intense and devastating tropical cyclone with winds ranging from 120 to 320 km/h (75–200mph), known also as a typhoon in the Pacific. Arising over oceans 10 to 20 degrees from the Equator, hurricanes have a calm central hole, or eye, surrounded by inward spiralling winds and cumulo-nimbus clouds. The winds and waves of hurricanes take many lives and cause extensive damage to shipping and coastal areas, but weather satellites often give adequate warning of their approach. *See also* PE pp.68–69.

Hus, Jan, or Huss, John (*c.* 1369–1415), Bohemian (Czech) religious reformer. A teacher and priest at Prague, he was influenced by the beliefs of the English reformer John WYCLIFFE, became leader of a reform movement, quarreled with the pope and other church authorities and was excommunicated. In 1415 he was burned as a heretic. *See also* HUSSITES.

Husák, Gustáv (1913–), President of Czechoslovakia. He took over as First Secretary of the Communist Party after the fall of DUBČEK in 1969, became its head in 1971, and President in 1975.

Hussein Ibn Ali (1856–1931), Arab religious and political leader. At first an ally of Germany and Turkey in WWI, he later supported the British and led a revolt against the Turks in 1916, proclaiming himself King of the Hejaz. He was defeated by IBN SAUD in 1924 and spent the last years of his life in exile.

Hussein I (1935–), King of Jordan (1953–). He was educated in England and his pro-Western views were attacked by other Arab leaders, especially President NASSER of Egypt. To stress his non-alignment he dismissed (1956) Gen. John Bagot GLUBB (Glubb Pasha), British commander of the Arab Legion (Jordanian Army). In 1967 he led his country into the Arab-Israeli War and lost all of Jordan W of the River Jordan to Israel. At the 1974 Arab summit meeting he was forced to relinquish his country's claim to west-bank Jordan to the Palestinian Liberation Organization (PLO).

Husserl, Edmund (1859–1938), German philosopher, known as the founder of the PHENOMENOLOGICAL MOVEMENT. He studied man's consciousness as it related to objects and the structure of experience. His works include *Ideas: General Introduction to Pure Phenomenology* (1913) and *Cartesian Meditations* (1931).

Hussites, followers of John HUS in Bohemia and Moravia in the 15th century. They worked to reform the Church, demanding freedom of preaching, communion in both wine and bread and a reduction of Church property. The more extreme elements reduced the sacraments to two (BAPTISM and communion) and denied the doctrine of the REAL PRESENCE. Their ideas thus foreshadowed the REFORMATION.

Hustings, platform from which prospective members of parliament spoke in the 18th and 19th centuries. Historically, the court of hustings, officially abolished only in 1977 in London, denoted a medieval open-air tribunal or common gathering.

Huston, John (1906–), US film director, writer and actor, son of the actor Walter Huston. As a scriptwriter he was responsible for several films including *Jezebel* (1938) and *Sergeant York* (1941). His greatest successes as a director were *The Maltese Falcon* (1941), *The African Queen* (1951) and *The Misfits* (1961).

Hutcheson, Francis (1694–1746), Scottish philosopher. In his best-known book, *Inquiry into the Original of Our Ideas of Beauty and Virtue*, Hutcheson referred to an innate "sense" or "feeling", which distinguished the beautiful and the good. His criterion of what is morally right – "the greatest good for the greatest number" – was later utilized by Jeremy BENTHAM.

Hutter, Jakob (*d.* 1536), Austrian ANABAPTIST and founder of the HUTTERITES. When Anabaptists in the Tyrol were persecuted, Hutter led many followers into Moravia. Charged with heresy, he was burned at the stake.

Hutterites, German-speaking Anabaptists practising communal living. The sect originated in Moravia in the 16th century under the leadership of Jakob HUTTER, moved to the Russian Ukraine, and in 1874 to the W USA. Some also live in W Canada. All things are held by them in common ownership and they stress family life, simple ways and pacifism.

Hutton, James (1726–97), Scottish geologist. He sought to formulate theories of the origin of the Earth and of atmospheric changes and concluded that the Earth's history could be explained only by observing current forces at work within it, thereby laying the foundations of modern geological science. *See also* HC2 p.22.

Hutton, Sir Leonard (1916–), England and Yorkshire cricketer who, in 1952, became the first modern professional to captain England. An opening batsman, he played in 79 Test matches between 1937 and 1955 (6,971 runs, average 56.67), 23 as captain. In 1938 he scored a record 364 against Australia in 13 hours 17 minutes, and by his retirement had accumulated 40,140 runs in first-class matches.

Huxley, Aldous Leonard (1894–1963), British novelist. He began his career as a literary journalist and began to satirize the hedonism of the 1920s in novels such as *Crome Yellow* (1921), *Antic Hay* (1923) and *Point Counter Point* (1928). *Brave New World* (1932) presents a nightmarish utopia of the future. His later works include *Eyeless in Gaza* (1936), *The Doors of Perception* (1954) and *Island* (1962).

Huxley, Sir Andrew Fielding (1917–), British physiologist. He analysed the electrical and chemical events in nerve cell discharge and for this work he shared the 1963 Nobel Prize in physiology and medicine with John ECCLES and Alan HODGKIN.

Huxley, Elspeth Josceline (1907–), British writer, *b.* Kenya. She recounted her African childhood in *The Flame Trees of Thika* and *The Mottled Lizard*. Her many novels include *The Merry Hippo* (1963) and *Love Among the Daughters* (1968). *Gallipot Eyes* (1976) recounts a year in her Cotswold village home.

Huxley, Sir Julian Sorell (1887–1975), British biologist, son of Leonard and brother of Aldous Huxley. His researches were chiefly on the behaviour of birds and other animals in relation to evolution; his writings greatly promoted public interest in the subject. He served as secretary of the ZOOLOGICAL SOCIETY of London (1935–48) and as the director general of UNESCO (1946–48). His books include *The Individual in the Animal Kingdom* (1911) and *Evolutionary Ethics* (1943).

Huxley, Thomas Henry (1825–95), British biologist, champion of DARWIN's theory of evolution and the scientific method in research. His works include *Zoological Evidences as to Man's Place in Nature* (1863), *Evolution and Ethics* (1893) and *Manual of the Comparative Anatomy of Vertebrated Animals* (1871).

Huygens, Christiaan (1629–95), Dutch physicist and astronomer. His most notable contributions to science include the wave theory of light, the recognition of Saturn's rings and the use of a pendulum in clocks. *See also* HC1 p.303.

Huysmans, Joris-Karl (1848–1907), French novelist, *b.* Paris of Dutch parentage. He was much admired by Oscar WILDE and other figures of the 1890s for his "decadence", as revealed in his novel *A rebours* (1884; trans. *Against Nature*, 1922), in which the hero pursues perversities to destroy boredom.

Hwang Ho (Huanghe or Yellow), major river in N China, the second longest in China. It rises in Tsinghai (Qinghai) province and flows E and NE through the Ordos desert, before turning due S between Shensi (Shănxi) and Shansi (Shanxi) provinces. The river then flows E through Honan (Heman) and NE through Shantung (Shandong) to enter the Po Hai (Bohai), an arm of the Yellow Sea. The river gets its name from the huge amounts of yellow silt it collects in its middle course. The silting of the river bed makes the river prone to serious flooding, and it is known as "China's Sorrow". Length: approx. 4,830km (3,000 miles). *See also* HC1 p.44, *44*; MW p.53.

Hyacinth, bulbous plant native to the Mediterranean region and Africa. It has long, thin leaves and spikes of flower clusters. The bell-shaped flowers may be white, yellow, red, blue or purple. Family Liliaceae; genus *Hyacinthus*.

Hyades, in Greek mythology, daughters of Atlas, nymphs placed by ZEUS among the stars as reward for the care given the infant Dionysus (BACCHUS), after the death of his mother Semele. Another story has them mourning for their dead brother Hyas until Zeus transformed them into part of the constellation TAURUS.

Hyaena. *See* HYENA.

Hyatt, John Wesley (1837–1920), US inventor who, with his brother Isaac Smith Hyatt, developed CELLULOID patented in 1870. His other inventions include a sewing machine and processes important in sugar refining.

Hybrid, offspring of two true-breeding parents of different gene composition; the cross result of the combination of heterozygous parents. Most inter-species hybrids, plant or animal, are sterile.

Hybridization, cross-breeding of plants or animals between different species, genera or, less commonly, families to produce offspring that differ in genetically determined traits; it is commonly the result of human intervention. Changes in climate or the environment of an organism may give rise to hybridization, but usually man uses specialized techniques to produce hybrids that may be hardier or more resistant to disease than the original forms, or more economical. Most inter-specific hybrids are sterile. *See also* PE pp.176–177, 220, 236, *236*.

Hybrid vigour, the inordinate strength demonstrated in some hybrid offspring, not characteristic of the parents.

Hyde, Anne (1637–71), first wife of James Duke of York (later JAMES II). She was the daughter of Edward Hyde, Earl of CLARENDON, and married James in 1660. She was the mother of Queens MARY II and ANNE.

Hyde, Douglas (1860–1949), Irish nationalist leader, the first President of the Republic of Ireland (1938–45). He was also a major force in reviving Irish literature through the Gaelic League, of which he was first president (1893–1915).

Hyde, Edward. *See* CLARENDON, EDWARD HYDE.

Hyde Park, royal park in the Borough of Westminster, London, between Park Lane and Kensington Gardens. It originally belonged to the manor of Hyde, property of Westminster Abbey until the reign of Henry VIII, who turned it into a deer park. Its most distinctive features are Speaker's Corner (the meeting place of soap-box orators), Marble Arch, Rotten Row (a fashionable bridle path) and the Serpentine (an artificial lake completed 1730). Area: 147 hectares (361 acres).

Hyderābād, city in S India, in the Mūsi River valley, 640km (400 miles) SE of Bombay. It is the capital of Andhra Pradesh state and capital of the former state of Hyderābād (1724–1948). Founded in 1589 as the capital of the GOLCONDA kingdom, it has several notable buildings dating from that time including the Char Minar (1591). It is also the seat of Osniania University (1918). Present day industries include tobacco and textiles. Pop. (1971) 1,607,396.

Hyderābād, city of Sind province, Pakistan, on the River Indus, 144km (90 miles) ENE of Karachi. It is famous for its gold and silver embroidery. Industries include chemicals. Pop. (1972) 628,310.

Hyder Ali (1722–82), Indian ruler. By 1761 he commanded the army of the state of Mysore and had begun to seize land from the Mahratta states and Hyderābād. He defeated the British in 1767 and 1780, although he in turn was defeated near Madras by Sir Eyre COOTE in 1781.

Hydra, popular name for a group of small, cylindrical freshwater organisms including JELLYFISH, CORALS and SEA-ANEMONES.

Hydra (Ídhra or Ydra), Greek island in the Agean Sea, off the E coast of the Peloponnesus. Its chief town, Hydra, on the N coast, became an expatriate artists' colony in the 1950s; it is now a tourist resort. Pop. (1961) (island) 2,766; (town) 2,546.

Hydrangea, any of a number of primarily deciduous woody shrubs and vines of the SAXIFRAGE order, native to the W Hemisphere and Asia. They are grown for their showy clusters of flowers, which may be white, pink or blue. Blue hydrangeas can be obtained by feeding aluminium sulphate to the roots.

Hydration, assimilation of water by an ION or compound. A hydrate is a compound, such as cupric sulphate (blue vitriol) that has a fixed amount of water weakly bonded to each crystal ($CuSO_4.5H_2O$). ETHYLENE can be hydrated to produce ETHYL ALCOHOL (ethanol).

Hydraulic engineering, branch of engineering concerned with the principles of liquid flow and their practical application.

Hydraulic mining, breaking down of earth or rock by high-pressure jets of water delivered through large nozzles (called hydraulic giants). It is mainly used in mining seams that are at or near the surface (surface mining). The large quantities of water transport the loosened materials to sluices, where the minerals are recovered. *See also* COAL MINING; SU p.*78*.

Hydrazine, fuming corrosive liquid ($H_2N.NH_2$) obtained by the reaction of chloramine (NH_2Cl) and ammonia (NH) or by the oxidation of UREA. It is used as a jet and rocket fuel, as a reducing agent and as a corrosion preventer. Properties: s.g. 1.011, m.p. 1.4°C (34.5°F); b.p.113.5°C (236.3°F).

Hydride, chemical compound of HYDROGEN with another ELEMENT, especially a more electropositive element. The hydrides of the electropositive metals, such as lithium hydride (LiH) and sodium hydride (NaH), are salt-like ionic compounds containing the negative ion H^-. They are useful reagents for HYDROGENATION reactions. *See also* ELECTROCHEMICAL SERIES; IONIC BOND.

Hydrocarbon, organic compound containing only CARBON and HYDROGEN. Many thousands of different hydrocarbons exist; they fall into two main classes, aliphatic and aromatic hydrocarbons. The aliphatic hydrocarbons are mainly open-chain compounds, including such groups as the alkanes (paraffins), alkenes (olefins), alkynes (acetylenes) and terpenes. Aromatic hydrocarbons have properties similar to BENZENE; they contain at least one benzene ring, as in NAPHTHALENE and ANTHRACENE. *See also* PE pp.138, 146; MM pp.78, 80–81.

Hydrocele, accumulation of clear liquid in a cavity, most often the scrotum. It builds up in between the tissue covering the testicles and causes a painless swelling.

Hydrocephalus, accumulation of abnormal amounts of liquid in the cranium (skull), usually because of obstruction or excess production, resulting in the increase of head size and mental deterioration.

Hydrochloric acid, solution of the pungent colourless gas hydrogen chloride (HCl) in water. It is obtained by the action of sulphuric acid on common salt, as a byproduct of the chlorination of hydrocarbons, or by combination of hydrogen and chlorine, and is widely used in the chemical, food and metallurgical industries. The concentrated commercial acid contains 38% HCl and has a s.g. of 1.19. *See also* MM p.32, MS p.68.

Hydrocyanic acid, or prussic acid, deadly poisonous weak acid, HCN. It is a liquid with an odour of bitter almonds, sometimes used as a fumigant to destroy rats and other pests of buildings. It also has uses in the chemical industry but is so dangerous to handle that its solid salts potassium and sodium cyanide are preferred, even though these, too, are highly poisonous.

Hydrodynamics, in physics, branch of MECHANICS which deals with the motion of fluids (liquids and gases). It is of great importance in industry, particularly chemical, petroleum and water engineering. The properties of fluids studied include their adhesion, cohesion, viscosity and type of flow (viscous and turbulant). *See also* FLUID MECHANICS.

Hydroelectricity, electricity generated from the motion of water, whether from dams, tides or waves. In all installations this energy of movement, or kinetic energy, is first converted to mechanical energy in the spinning blades of a water turbine, and then to electricity by the spinning rotor of an electric GENERATOR. *See also* MM pp.70, *71*, *85*.

Hydrofluoric acid, colourless corrosive fuming liquid consisting of a solution of the gas hydrogen fluoride (HF) in water, prepared by distilling a mixture of sulphuric acid (H_2SO_4) and fluorspar (FLUORITE). It is used in frosting and etching glass and to make FLUOROCARBONS.

Hydrofoil, speedboat whose hull is lifted out of water by flat or curved plane surfaces that provide lift in water, just as an aeroplane wing generates lift in air. The underwater fin attached to such vessels, seaplanes, or to submarines is also called a hydrofoil. Hydrofoil ships are capable of speeds up to 80 knots. *See also* MM pp.116, *117*.

Hydrogen, gaseous non-metallic element (H), first identified as a separate element by Henry CAVENDISH in 1766. It is usually classified with the ALKALI metals in group IA of the periodic table. Hydrogen is the most abundant element in the universe (70% by weight) and the lightest of all. It is used in the manufacture of AMMONIA and as a rocket fuel. Properties: at.no. 1; at.wt. 1.00797; density 0.0899g cm^{-3} at STP m.p. −259.14°C (−434.45°F); b.p. −252.9°C (−422.5°F); most common isotope H^1 (99.985%). *See also* DEUTERIUM; TRITIUM; SU pp.134–135, *134–135*.

Hydrogenation, chemical reaction between molecular hydrogen (ie atmospheric hydrogen) and an element or compound, sometimes under pressure, usually in the presence of a metal catalyst such as nickel, platinum or palladium. An unsaturated compound, such as benzene, may accommodate the extra hydrogen, but a saturated species will break up (destructive hydrogenation).

Hydrogen bomb, or H-bomb, nuclear weapon developed by the USA in the late 1940s and first exploded by that country in 1952 in the Pacific. Subsequent H-bomb tests by the USA, USSR, Britain, France, China, India and possibly yet other countries have included explosions equivalent in force to that of ten million tons of TNT. These explosions have also greatly added to the poisoning of the atmosphere by radioactive wastes. H-bombs of much greater power, perhaps as much as several hundred million tons of TNT, are now easily within the resources of nuclear technology. Few countries are at present testing H-bombs. These bombs explode by a process of nuclear fusion, in which hydrogen atoms are joined to form atoms of helium, and a huge quantity of left-over energy, which appears as the light, heat, blast and radioactive emission of the bomb. The process is essentially the same as that which takes place in the Sun. *See also* NUCLEAR ENERGY; NUCLEAR WEAPONS; MM pp.180–181.

Hydrogen bond, CHEMICAL BOND formed between certain hydrogen-containing molecules. The hydrogen atom must be bound to an electronegative (electron-withdrawing) atom, the bond being formed between the positive charge on hydrogen and the negative charge on an atom in an adjacent molecule. Hydrogen-bonding occurs in water, and in many biological systems.

Hydrogen peroxide, syrupy liquid (H_2O_2), usually sold in aqueous solution, prepared by electrolytic oxidation of sulphuric acid (H_2SO_4), or from reacting anthraquinone with oxygen. It is used in bleaching, as a disinfectant and as a rocket fuel oxidizer. Properties (anhydrous): s.g. 1.44; m.p. −0.4°C (31.3°F); b.p. 150°C (302°F). *See also* SU p.*140*.

Hydrogen sulphide, colourless poisonous gas (H_2S) with the smell of bad eggs, prepared by the action of sulphuric acid (H_2SO_4) on iron sulphide (FeS). It is used in chemical analysis. Properties: m.p. −85.5°C (−121.9°F), b.p. −60.7°C (−77.3°F). *See also* SU p.*150*.

Hydrograph, graph-like representation of the run-off caused by 25mm (1in) of rainfall falling at a uniform rate and at a specific time over a drainage basin.

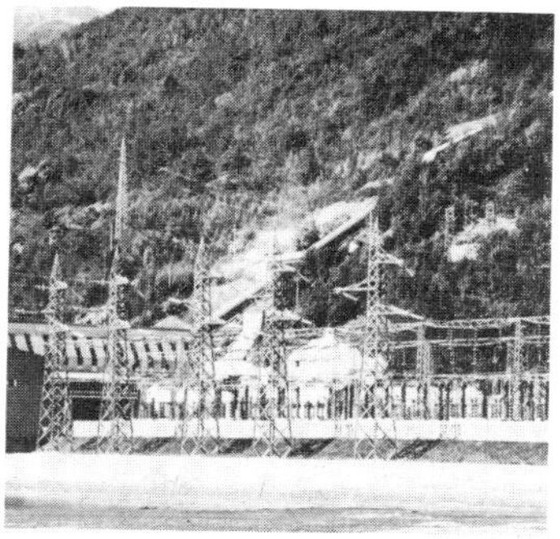

Hydroelectric plants convert the natural energy of falling water into electric power.

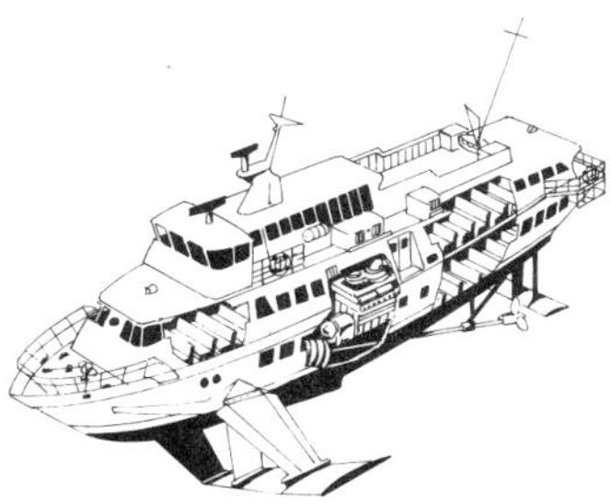

Hydrofoil; the high-speed craft designed originally by the Italian Enrico Felanini in 1906.

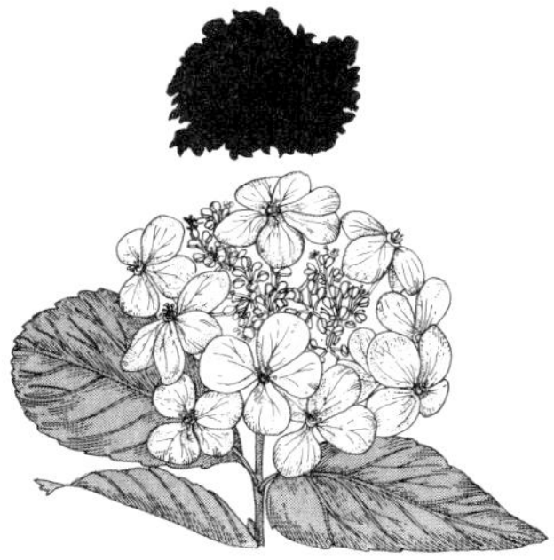

Hydrangeas need a slightly moist, rich soil but grow well even in shaded places.

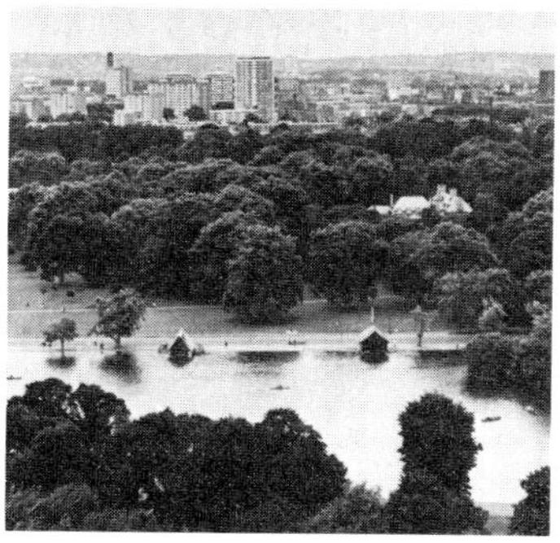

Hyde Park; a view looking north over the Serpentine towards Marble Arch.

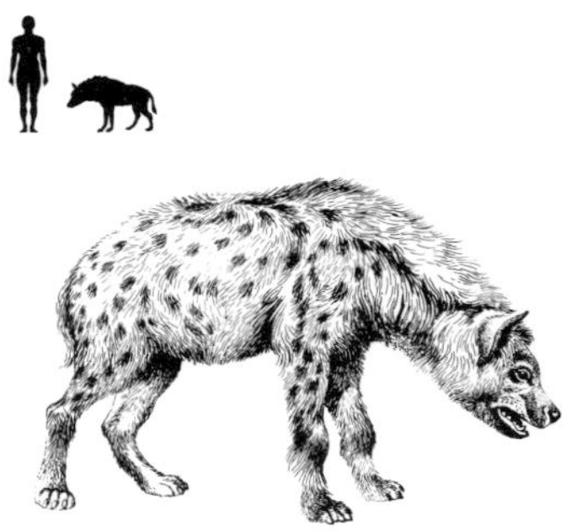

Hyenas have jaws which are as powerful as any in the animal kingdom.

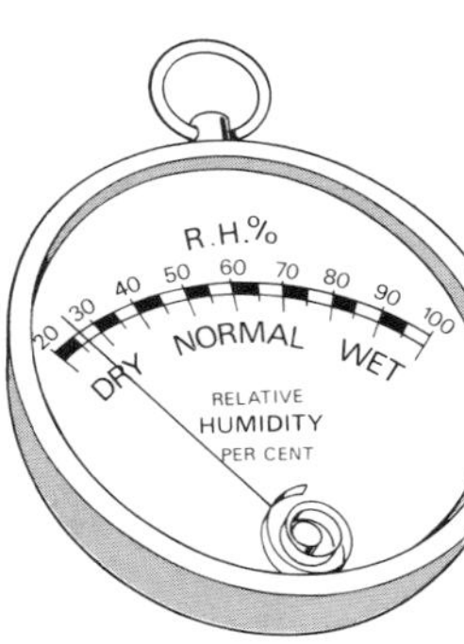

Hygrometers, which work on various principles, all measure the air's moisture content.

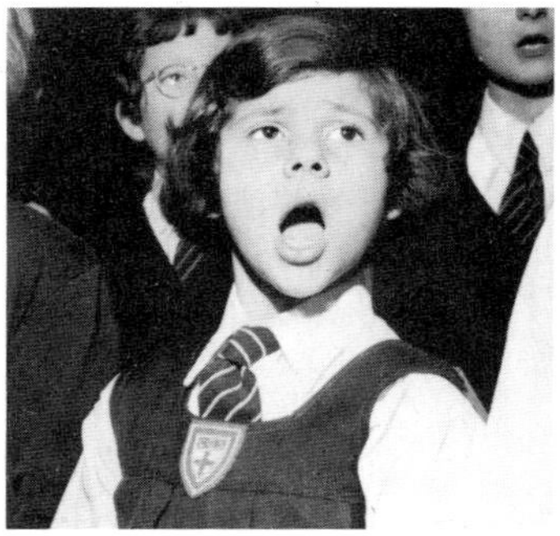

Hymn singing is an activity enjoyed by children more for musical than spiritual reasons.

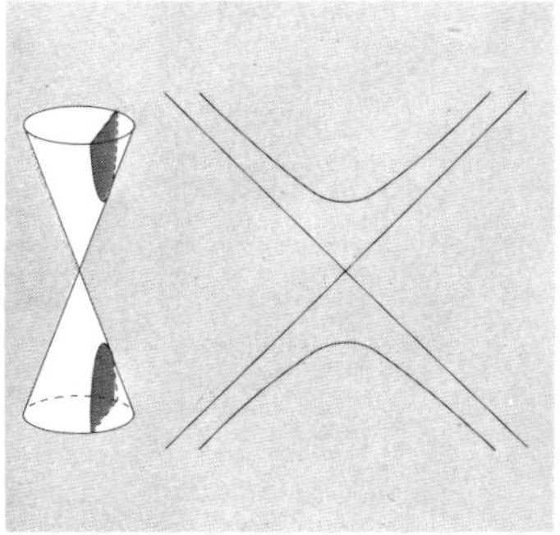

Hyperbola is one of the conic sections obtained when a plane cuts a cone.

Hydrographic chart, or nautical chart, map of the physical features of oceans and adjoining coastal areas. Such charts also contain tide and current information. The most detailed ones exist for coastal areas because more information has been collected there, but new SONAR devices now facilitate the mapping of deep ocean floors.

Hydrography, science of charting the water-covered areas of the earth. Navigational charts have been made since the 13th century, but these were accurate only for sea-coasts. Interest in the charting of oceanic areas away from sea-coasts only developed in the 19th century. Now, detailed bathymetric (deep-sea) surveys are available for geological studies. Hydrographic offices are run by governments of maritime nations to furnish their mariners with nautical charts; the work of these offices is co-ordinated by the International Hydrographic Bureau, founded in 1921. *See also* HYDROGRAPHIC CHART.

Hydrological cycle, also called water cycle, the circulation of water on and near the Earth's surface. Water leaves the oceans by evaporation, passes through the atmosphere as moist air and clouds; precipitates on to the land as rain, snow and hail, and returns to the oceans via lakes, rivers and the water table underground. *See also* PE pp.*108*, 109, 150.

Hydrology, study of the Earth's waters, their sources, circulation, distribution and chemical and physical composition. The hydrological cycle traces the movement of water through various stages of evaporation until it is returned to land, and the continental water systems, both on the surface and underground. *See also* MM pp.200–201; PE pp.108–113.

Hydrolysis, reversible chemical reaction between water and another substance, often assisted by CATALYSTS. It works by a double decomposition reaction, eg $AB + HOH \rightleftarrows AH + BOH$, where A and B are discrete molecules. In digestion, ENZYMES catalyze the hydrolysis of carbohydrates, proteins and fats into forms that the body can assimilate.

Hydrometallurgy, treatment of ores by wet processes to extract their metals. It usually includes LEACHING by water and additives such as sulphuric acid, separation of the waste, purification of leach solution and precipitation of metal from solution by chemicals or electrolytic means. Most metals are extracted by this method.

Hydrometer, instrument for measuring density or SPECIFIC GRAVITY of a liquid. It consists of a long-necked, sealed glass bulb that is weighted. The neck is calibrated to indicate specific gravity which is read off against the surface of the liquid in which it floats. Hydrometers are used to check concentrations of liquids in storage batteries, freezing points of radiator solutions and the "proof" of alcohol.

Hydronephrosis, enlargement of certain kidney structures by distention with urine, resulting from obstruction of the urinary tract. *See also* MS p.102.

Hydrophobia. *See* RABIES.

Hydrophone, microphone used underwater for receiving sound or seismic waves, used extensively in submarine warfare. *See also* SEISMOLOGY; MM p.236.

Hydrophyte, or aquatic plant, plant that grows only in water or damp places. The WATERLILY is considered to be the most important water garden plant. Among the oxygen-producing plants used in home aquariums are anacharis and cabomba. Others that float are azolla, water fern and water hyacinth.

Hydroplane, speedboat able to skim over water by rising out of it at speed until only a small area at the stern remains immersed. This is achieved by means of a flat-bottomed hull, which is powered by a high-performance outboard motor.

Hydroponics, also called soil-less culture or tank farming, growing of plants in a mineral solution or a moist inert medium (such as gravel) containing necessary nutrients, instead of soil. It requires special apparatus including a tank, a solution reservoir, a pump and a timer all installed in a greenhouse. Added nutrients include nitrogen, phosphorus and potassium, with trace elements such as calcium, sulphur and magnesium. Houseplants may be grown hydroponically in ceramic or glass containers filled with water and fed with diluted plant food. *See also* PE p.167.

Hydrostatics, in physics, the branch of mechanics which deals with liquids at rest. Its practical applications are mainly in water engineering and in the design of such equipment as hydraulic presses, rams, lifts and vehicle braking and control systems. *See also* STATICS.

Hydrotherapy, use of water within the body or on its surface to treat disease. It is often used in conjunction with PHYSIOTHERAPY.

Hydrotropism, plant growth in response to water stimulus. It is not a strong tropism and plant responses to higher oxygen and water content, such as the growth of willow roots through river banks, are often confused with it.

Hydroxide, chemical compound containing the group $-OH$, which reacts as a base, ie neutralizes acids. The strong inorganic bases such as potassium hydroxide, KOH, dissociate in water almost completely to provide many hydroxyl ions, OH^-, for chemical reactions. By contrast, such organic hydroxy compounds as phenol, C_6H_5OH, produce no hydroxyl IONS, so are not called hydroxides.

Hydrozoa, class of animals without backbones, all living in water, belonging to the phylum Coelenterata. They vary in shape and size from the large and complex PORTUGUESE MAN-OF-WAR to the small and simple freshwater HYDRA. A few marine hydrozoans are CORAL-like. *See also* NW pp.82–84.

Hyena, predatory and scavenging carnivore native to Africa and s Asia. The spotted or laughing hyena (*Crocuta crocuta*) of the sub-Sahara is the largest, and has sparse grey fur with dark round spots. The brown hyena (*Hyaena brunnea*) of s Africa is smaller, and has dark brown bands round its legs and feet. Weight: 27–80kg (59.5–176.4lb). Family Hyaenidae. *See also* NW p.164.

Hygiene, the means of promoting health in the individual and the community. Private hygiene involves a healthy diet and cleanliness, whereas public hygiene, as it affects public health, is subject to legal regulations. In most Western countries legislation covers health and safety at work, environmental pollution, communicable diseases and the preparation of food for public consumption.

Hygrometer, instrument used to measure the water-vapour content, or HUMIDITY, of the atmosphere. One type, the psychrometer, compares the wet and dry bulb temperatures of the air; other types measure absorption or condensation of moisture from the air, or chemical or electrical changes caused by that moisture.

Hygroscopic, term describing a substance that, on standing, reacts with or absorbs water vapour from the air. Magnesium and calcium chlorides are typical examples. Some hygroscopic solids such as magnesium chloride, said to be deliquescent, absorb sufficient water to dissolve, yielding a concentrated solution.

Hyksos, people who invaded ancient Egypt from Canaan using horse-drawn chariots, an innovation for the time. Probably Semitic, they seized the kingdom from the pharaohs, establishing a new dynasty, ruling from Memphis over the great empire on the lower Nile. They are thought to have been overthrown in about 1570 BC after only one century in occupation. *See also* HC1 p.35.

Hymen, in Greek mythology, god of marriage and personification of the wedding feast or song. Son of APOLLO, he is represented as a brightly-dressed youth in attendance on APHRODITE.

Hymen, in anatomy, thin membrane that partially or completely closes the entrance to the VAGINA of some mammals.

Hymenoptera, insect order containing SAWFLIES, ANTS, WASPS, HORNETS and BEES. All have a complete life cycle – egg, larva, pupa and adult – and two pairs of membranous wings, which move together in flight. They are found worldwide, living solitarily or in social groups. The larvae (grubs or caterpillars) feed on plants or are parasitic or predaceous. *See also* NW pp.*106*, 107, 116.

Hymn, song of praise or gratitude to a god or a hero. The term is normally used for a religious song sung in church, which is not a psalm or a canticle. It was the Reformation that encouraged singing by all worshippers, rather than merely the clergy and choir. Hymns are now regular parts of services; hymnals include songs ranging from translations of Latin poems to modern verses and music.

Hyoscine, or scopolamine, poisonous alkaloid, formula $C_{17}H_{21}O_4N$, obtained in nature from deadly nightshade (belladonna) and other plants of the nightshade family (Solanaceae). It is used in medicine mainly as an hypnotic and to relieve pain caused by muscular spasms.

Hypatia (*c.*370–415), Egyptian NEO-PLATONIST philosopher and mathematician. The daughter of Theon, she became head of the Neo-platonists at Alexandria where she attracted many followers. Although her works are lost, it is thought she wrote critiques on the *Arithmetica* of Diophantus of Alexandria and on Ptolemy's astronomical canon.

Hyperbola, plane curve traced out by a point that moves so that its distance from a fixed point always bears a constant ratio (greater than one) to its distance from a fixed straight line. The fixed point is the focus, the ratio the eccentricity and the fixed line is the directrix. The curve has two branches and is a CONIC SECTION. Its standard equation in CARTESIAN CO-ORDINATES is $x^2/a^2 - y^2/b^2 = 1$. *See also* SU pp.*36–37*.

Hyperbole, rhetorical device in which an obvious exaggeration is used simply to create an effect without being meant literally, such as "The music is loud enough to wake the dead".

Hyperglycaemia, abnormal amount of sugar in the blood, one of the symptoms of DIABETES MELLITUS. *See also* MS pp.100, *101*.

Hypericum, or St John's wort, genus of more than 300 species of shrubby plants and herbs many of which have yellow flowers. Most are native to temperate and warm regions of the Northern Hemisphere, and some are common wild flowers. Well-known garden species include Rose of Sharon (*H. calycinum*) and the Tutsan (*H. androcaemum*). Family Hypericaceae.

Hyperinsulinism, overproduction of insulin, which may result from an INSULINOMA (a tumour in the pancreas), from other organic disturbances such as pituitary dysfunction, or from functional causes such as overexertion or poor nutrition. Hyperinsulinism produces symptoms of HYPOGLYCAEMIA (low blood sugar), such as sweating, dizziness and headaches. *See also* MS pp.65, 100–101.

Hyperion, in Greek mythology, sometimes said to be the original sun god and often confused with his son HELIOS. He was a TITAN, the son of URANUS and GAEA and the father of Helios, the sun, SELENE, the moon, the EOS, the dawn. He drove his chariot across the sky each day and returned each night by the River Oceanus.

Hyperon, class of ELEMENTARY PARTICLES with an anomalously long lifetime. The group includes the lambda particle (Λ), sigma particles (Σ^+, Σ^0, Σ^-), XI particles (Ξ^0, Ξ^-), and omega particle (Ω^-). A lambda can replace a NEUTRON in a nucleus to form a hypernucleus. *See also* BARYON; SU p.67.

Hyperplasia, increase in the normal number of cells in an organ or tissue, as opposed to an increase in the size of the cells (which is called HYPERTROPHY).

Hypersensitivity, condition in which a person reacts excessively or unusually promptly to a stimulus. Most hypersensitive reactions are synonymous with ALLERGIES, the commonest being HAY FEVER, ASTHMA and infantile ECZEMA. Some people become hypersensitive to drugs, such as penicillin, or to chemicals after initial contact.

Hypertension, persistence of HIGH BLOOD PRESSURE.

Hyperthermia, medical treatment, now largely obsolete, in which a patient's temperature was raised to cure him of an infection. It was achieved by injecting the patient with certain vaccines. Less drastic hyperthermic methods involve the use of turkish baths.

Hypertrophy, enlargement of an organ, such as the heart, as a result of an increased amount of work required of it. This refers particularly to muscular tissue. An increase in the number of cells is called HYPERPLASIA.

Hyperventilation, prolonged rapid and shallow breathing, or any condition in which excessive amounts of air enter the ALVEOLI (air cells) of the lungs, reducing carbon dioxide in the blood to undesirably low levels.

Hypnosis, entranced, sleep-like state during which suggestions are readily obeyed. Little has been learned about hypnosis since it was first described two centuries ago. Since the time of F.A. MESMER (1733–1815) it has provoked far more emotional and superstitious concern than serious research. It is, however, fairly well established that hypnosis is physiologically close to a state of relaxed wakefulness; there is increased suggestibility; and hypnosis may be able to affect memory. In deep hypnosis, it is sometimes possible to produce hypnoanaesthetic effects (painlessness); hypnosis can relieve symptoms in hysterical reactions. *See also* MS p.79.

Hypnotic drugs, or soporifics, drugs which induce sleep. The most well known are the BARBITURATES prescribed as sleeping pills. Sodium pentothal, used to induce profound sleep quickly before a surgical operation, is also a barbiturate hypnotic. Other hypnotics include chloral hydrate and paraldehyde

Hypnotism, process of inducing a trance-like state. *See* HYPNOSIS.

Hypo, photographic, popular name for a solution of sodium thiosulphate ($Na_2S_2O_3.5H_2O$) in water (often 200–300g/litre), used as a photographic fixer. It is usually acidified by the addition of sodium metabisulphite (25g/litre of solution). *See also* MM pp.218–219.

Hypoasthesia, inability to feel pain. This rare condition derives from a congenital nervous abnormality. *See also* MS p.53.

Hypochondria (hypochondriasis), exaggerated chronic concern with illness, infection or pain without justification. The illnesses are commonly associated with the internal organs, especially the stomach, liver or heart. Hypochondriacs constantly complain of aches, pains, weakness and fatigue and often consult several doctors in the hope of "cure".

Hypodermic injection, introduction of a liquid under the skin through a hollow needle.

Hypodermic syringe, surgical instrument for the introduction of liquid substances into the body, either under the skin, into muscles or into blood vessels. It comprises a tube containing a piston plunger, connected to a hollow metal needle. The whole is provided sterile – free from micro-organisms – and must be resterilized after use. Many mass-produced hypodermic syringes are used once and then thrown away. *See also* INJECTION.

Hypoglycaemia, abnormally low amount of sugar in the blood, which may result from fasting, excess INSULIN and various metabolic and glandular diseases. Its symptoms are dizziness, headache, cold sweats and, when severe, HALLUCINATIONS, convulsions and coma.

Hypostyle, term for a hall (from Greek *hypo,* meaning under, and *stylos,* meaning pillar), in which the roof – usually flat – is supported by a large number of columns, often arranged to form a wide centre aisle flanked by two or more side aisles. The ruined Egyptian temples of Amon at Luxor (14th century BC) and Khons at Karnak (12th century BC) are celebrated examples.

Hypotension, subnormal blood pressure, not always due to illness or injury. It is a symptom of various diseases, severe haemorrhage, circulatory disturbances or the administration of various drugs. It may also occur on change of position in persons with types of heart or adrenal gland diseases (postural hypotension).

Hypotenuse, side opposite the right angle in a right-angled triangle. It is the longest side of the triangle. *See also* SU p.*44.*

Hypothalamus, principal forebrain structure containing nerve cells controlling the sympathetic and parasympathetic nervous systems. Along with other neural areas, it regulates basic physical and emotional behaviour, including the initiation of HUNGER, thirst and sexual functions. *See also* MS pp.40–41, 52, 100–101.

Hypothermia, lowering of body temperature either deliberately, in surgical operations, or spontaneously as in the HIBERNATION of animals. In harsh conditions with inadequate food or heat, hypothermia is a common cause of death, especially amongst old people.

Hypothyroidism, deficiency of thyroxine, one of the THYROID hormones, most common in women and resulting in slowness, fatigue, menstrual disorders and, if severe, anaemia and mental deterioration. If caused by malfunction of the thyroid gland the condition is called myxoedema in adults and cretinism in children. It can be caused by insufficient iodine in the diet. It is one of the forms of GOITRE. *See also* MS p.100.

Hypsometer, instrument used in forestry to measure heights of tall trees by TRIANGULATION. Hand-held hypsometers contain a bubble spirit level, a sighting device and a vertical scale reading in feet or metres. The name hypsometer is also given to an instrument that measures height above sea-level as a function of the boiling point of water (which drops with increasing height).

Hyracotherium (Eohippus), extinct progenitor of the horse that lived during the Eocene epoch (58 million years ago) in swampy areas of North America. It probably had a small head with large eyes, a short neck and an arched back. Each forefoot had four toes, and each hind foot three. Its teeth were simple and suitable for cropping leaves. Height: up to 50cm (20in) at the shoulder. *See also* NW p.*190.*

Hyrax, small, rodent-like, herbivorous hoofed mammal of Africa and SW Asia, with a squat, furry body and short ears, legs and tail. Rock hyraxes (genus *Procavia*) of deserts and hills live in colonies of about 50 individuals and are larger than the solitary, nocturnal, arboreal hyraxes (genus *Dendrohyrax*), which are the only arboreal hoofed mammals. Length: to 50cm (20in). Family Procaviidae. *See also* NW pp.155, 162–163.

Hyssop, common name for *Hyssopus officinalis,* an aromatic herb of the MINT family. A hardy perennial native to Eurasia, it is used in seasoning food.

Hysterectomy, removal of the WOMB (uterus) and surrounding structures. Hysterectomy may be sub-total, removal of the body of the uterus only; total, removal of the CERVIX; or radical, removal of the entire uterus and its surrounding connective tissues. *See also* MS p.128.

Hysteresis, phenomenon occurring in the magnetic and elastic behaviour of substances in which the STRAIN for a given STRESS is greater when the stress is decreasing than when it is increasing. When the stress is removed a residual strain remains. The phenomenon is particularly important in FERROMAGNETISM; the magnetization of ferromagnetic materials lags behind the magnetizing force. *See also* SU pp.116–117.

Hysteria, in psychology, psychoneurosis characterized by emotional instability, suggestibility, dissociation and psychogenic functional disorders. Conversion has symptoms that resemble organic diseases; DISSOCIATION alters conscious awareness and can manifest itself in such diverse forms as AMNESIA, SLEEPWALKING and withdrawal Leading researchers in this field have included Jean-Martin CHARCOT, Pierre JANET and Sigmund FREUD. *See also* MS pp.*123,* 140, *141,* 148.

Hywel Dda, or Howel the Good (died *c.*950), Welsh king. Notable as an imitator of English ways, he is believed to have drawn up a code of laws, and was the only Welsh ruler to issue his own coins.

I

I, ninth letter of the alphabet, derived from the Semitic letter *yod,* meaning *hand.* It passed through Phoenician unchanged to the Greeks, who called it *iota.* In the Roman alphabet it was pronounced *ee.* In English *i* has two main sounds: short, as in *bit,* and long, as in *wide.* The long *i* has a different sound in some words (eg *police* and *first*) and is pronounced like a *y* in words such as *union* and *onion.* *Seealso* MS pp.244–245.

Iamb, metrical foot consisting of an unstressed followed by a stressed syllable, or a short followed by a long, as in the word *amaze.* The metre is called iambic. Iambic trimeter is characteristic of Greek drama; iambic pentameter is predominant in English-language verse.

Iaşi, city in NE Romania, 16km (10 miles) from the frontier between Romania and the USSR. It was the capital of Romania until 1861 when the capital moved to Bucharest. It remains an important commercial and administrative centre. Industries include textiles, machinery and food products. Pop. (1970 est.) 183,700.

Iatrogenic disease, illness or disorder caused by normal medical treatment. Its most serious aspect today is the mental and physical deterioration which sometimes occurrs among isolated patients in geriatric wards. *See also* MS p.87.

Ibadan, city in SW Nigeria, approx. 145km (90 miles) NNE of Lagos. An industrial and commercial centre, it handles the regional cacao and cotton trades. Its own industries include plastics, cigarettes and food processing. Pop. 847,000.

Ibañez, Vincente Blasco. *See* BLASCO IBÁÑEZ.

Iberia, ancient region S of the Caucasus Mts, USSR, E part of the modern Georgian SSR. Founded as an independent kingdom between the sixth and fourth centuries BC, it became a vassal of the Roman Empire after defeat by the Roman general POMPEY in 65 BC. It became part of Georgia in the 8th century AD.

Iberian Peninsula, the part of SW Europe occupied by Spain and Portugal, separated from Africa by the strait of Gibraltar and from the rest of Europe by the Pyrenees Mountains. It is bordered by the Atlantic Ocean (N and W) and the Mediterranean Sea (E) Area: 596,384sq km (230,264sq miles).

Ibert, Jacques (1890–1962), prolific French composer of songs, chamber music, ballets and operas, perhaps best-known for his orchestral suite *Divertissement* (1928).

Iberville, Pierre le Moyne, Sieur d' (1661–1706), Canadian naval officer and explorer. In 1699, he led an expedition to the Mississippi delta and established Fort Maurepas (now Biloxi), the first permanent French settlement on the coast of the Gulf of Mexico. He was governor of Louisiana from 1703 until his death.

Ibex, any of several species of wild Old World GOATS. The long, backward curving horns grow up to 1.5m (5ft) long on the male, and both sexes have long, yellow-brown hair. Ibexes are renowned for their agility. Height: 85cm (3ft) at shoulder. Family Bovidae. *See also* NW p.*222.*

Ibis, tropical lagoon and marsh wading bird with long down-curved bill, long neck and lanky legs. Closely related to the SPOONBILL, it may be black, whitish or brightly coloured. It feeds on small animals and nests in colonies. The so-called sacred ibis of N Africa was worshipped by the ancient Egyptians. Length: 60–90cm (2–3ft). Subfamily: Threskiornithidae. *See also* NW pp.*140, 216.*

Ibiza, island of Spain, 129km (80 miles) off the E coast, in the W Mediterranean, part of the Balearic group. The mild climate and beautiful scenery have made Ibiza a major tourist resort. Other activities include fishing, salt mining and the cultivation of figs and olives. Area: 572sq

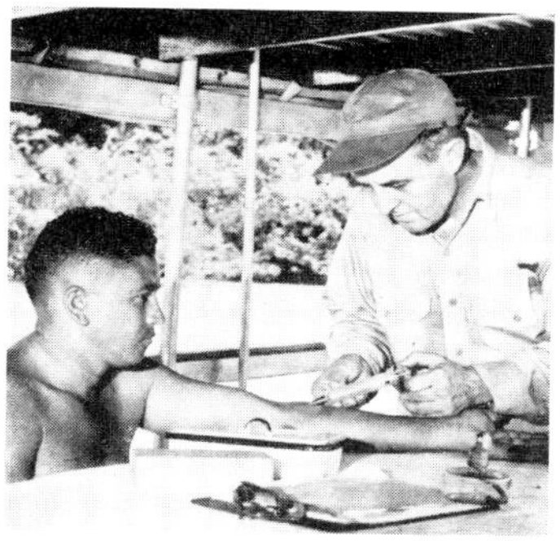

Hypodermic syringe; a doctor on the Amazon taking a blood sample from a fever patient.

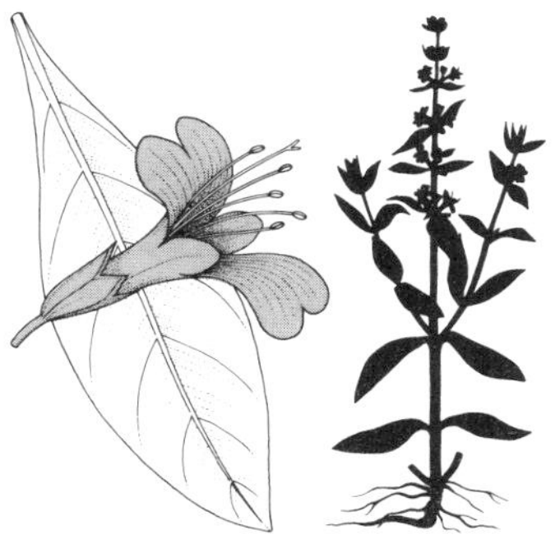

Hyssop has small blue leaves and grows in warmer parts of the USA as well as Europe.

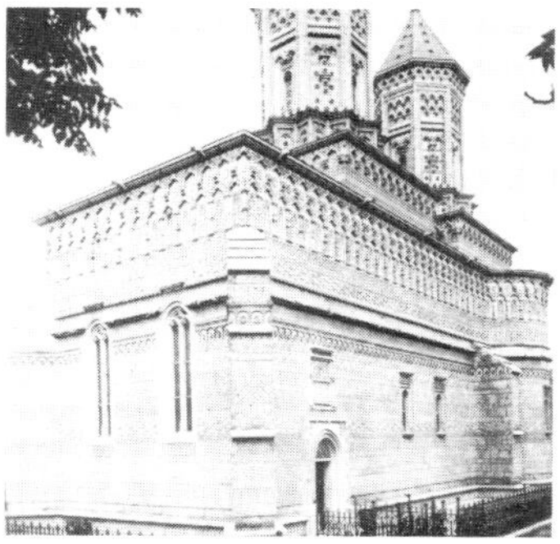

Iaşi; a view of the famous Church of the Three Saints in Romania's old capital city.

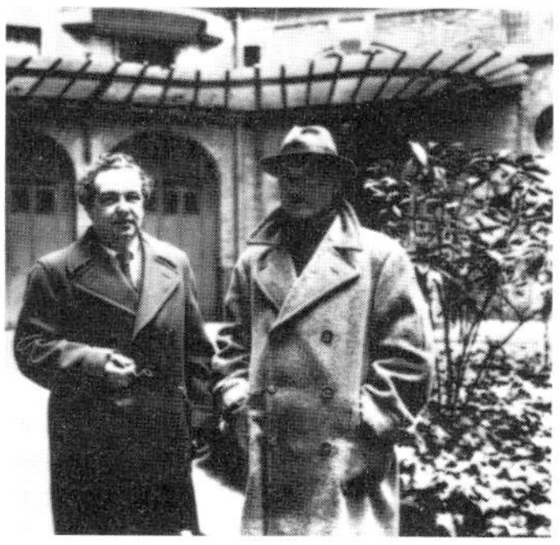

Jacques Ibert (right); his suite, *Ports of Call,* is a representation of Mediterranean seaports.

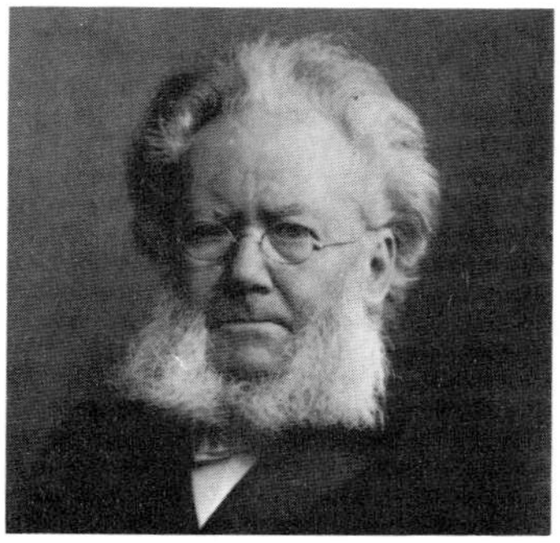

Ibsen believed that man's final sin and ultimate tragedy was simply the denial of love.

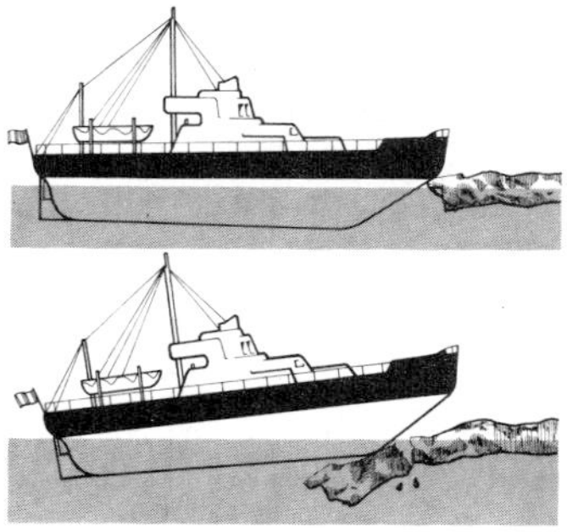

Icebreakers, first used in the 1870s, can break through ice more than 10m (32ft) thick.

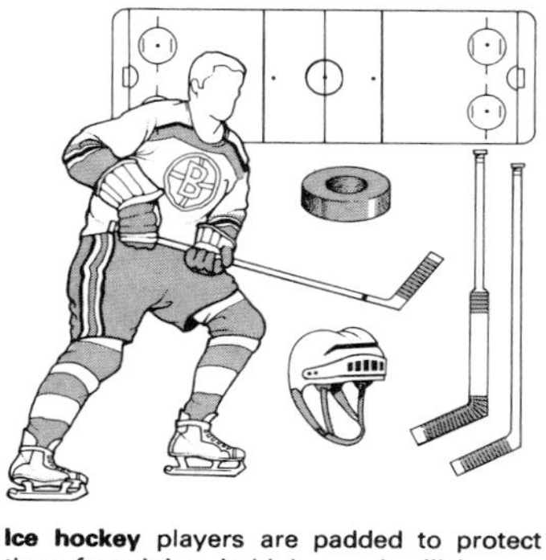

Ice hockey players are padded to protect them from injury in high-speed collisions.

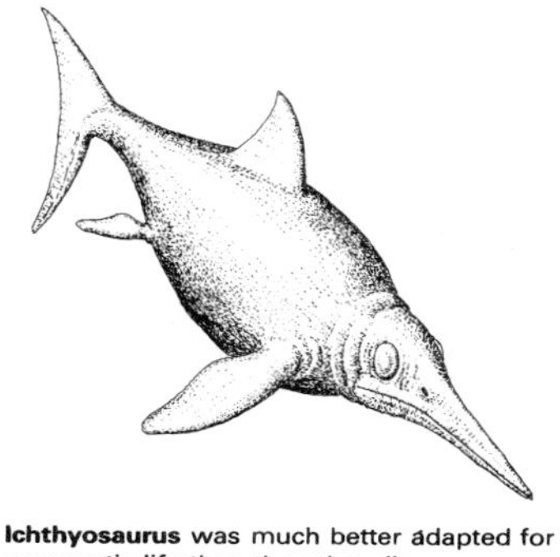

Ichthyosaurus was much better adapted for an aquatic life than the other dinosaurs.

km (221 sq miles). Pop. (1970) 45,075.

Ibn Saud (*c.*1880–1953), founder and first King of Saudi Arabia (*r.*1932–53). Although in exile, his family were considered the leaders of the orthodox WAHHABI movement. . The Wahhabia city, Riyadh was recaptured in 1902 and by 1912 Ibn Saud ruled all of Nejd (central Arabia). He defeated his rival, HUSSEIN IBN ALI, in 1924–25 and constituted his kingdom in 1932.

Ibn Taymiyah. *See* WAHHABISM.

Ibo, or Igbo, Kwa-speaking people of E Nigeria. Originally their patrilineal society consisted of politically and socially autonomous village units, but during the 20th century a political unity developed in reaction to British colonial rule. In 1967 the Ibo attempted to secede from Nigeria as the Republic of BIAFRA.

Ibrahim Pasha (1789–1848), Egyptian general. The son of MOHAMMED ALI, governor of Egypt under the Ottoman Empire, he campaigned against the Wahhabis of Arabia in 1816–18 and later fought the Greek insurgents with great brutality, sending many into slavery in Egypt. When his father defied Ottoman supremacy, Ibrahim conquered Syria (1832–33) and became its governor. In 1841 Turkey, supported by Britain and Austria, forced him to withdraw to Egypt. He was named regent of Egypt in 1848.

Ibsen, Henrik Johan (1828–1906), Norwegian playwright whose works are characterized by a basic questioning of bourgeois morality. *Brand* (1866), *Peer Gynt* (1867), *A Doll's House* (1879), *Ghosts* (1881), *An Enemy of the People* (1882), *The Wild Duck* (1884), *Hedda Gabler* (1890), *The Master Builder* (1892) and *When We Dead Awaken* (1899) are some of his widely translated works. *See also* HC2 p.101, *101.*

Ica, important archaeological period in S Peru centring on the Ica Valley and the surrounding area. It lasted from about AD 1000 to 1475. An unrelated tribe of Chibcha-speaking Indians in Colombia is also known by this name.

Icarus, in Greek mythology, the son of DAEDALUS, architect of the LABYRINTH for MINOS of Crete. Having offended the king, Daedalus made wings of feathers and wax in order to escape to the mainland, and was successful. But Icarus, despite a warning, flew too near the sun, which melted his wings, and he fell into the sea and drowned. He was washed ashore on an island which was named Icaria after him.

Icarus, minor planet, discovered by Walter BAADE in 1949. It has a more eccentric orbit and travels closer to the Sun than any other body in the Solar System with the exception of comets. Icarus approaches to within 6,400,000km (4,000,000 miles) of Earth. *See also* SU pp.204–205.

Icaza, Jorge (1906–), Ecuadorian author. His best-known novel, *Plot of Land* (1934), portrays the exploitation of Indians by a landowner.

ICBM. *See* INTERCONTINENTAL BALLISTIC MISSILE.

Ice, WATER frozen to 0°C (32°F) or below, when it forms complex six-sided crystals. It is less dense than water and floats. When water vapour condenses below freezing point, ice crystals are formed. This occurs mainly in high cirrus clouds, but also in the grey portions of other clouds. Clusters of these ice crystals form snowflakes. *See also* SU p.*89.*

Ice Ages, periods of the Earth's history in which ice sheets and glaciers advance from the polar regions to cover areas previously temperate in climate. The most recent was the Great Ice Age, or Glacial Epoch, which began about 1,000,000 years ago and lasted until the retreat of the ice to about its present polar extent some 10,000 years ago, corresponding roughly to the Pleistocene Epoch of geological time. During this period the ice advanced and retreated not once, but four times. The present time may therefore be an interglacial period. Many of the Earth's features seen today – such as glacial valleys, fiords and moraines – can be attributed to the advance and retreat of the ice. *See also* GLACIER; PE pp.*116–119.*

Iceberg, large drifting piece of ice, broken off from a GLACIER, or polar ice cap. In the Northern Hemisphere the main source of icebergs is the SW coast of Greenland. In the south, the glacial flow from Antarctica releases huge tabular icebergs, some more than 97km (60 miles) long. Icebergs can be dangerous to shipping, since only a small portion is visible above the surface of the water. *See also* PE pp.*56, 119.*

Ice boating. *See* ICE YACHTING.

Icebreaker, ship with a heavy bow and armoured sides, designed with powerful engines which enable it to make a passage through ice. For breaking thick ice, the bow is so designed that the forward motion of the ship drives it up onto the ice, and the weight of the ship breaks it. Propellers fore and aft allow great manoeuvrability. Icebreakers are used regularly to clear channels in the Great Lakes and in the Baltic Sea, and they have also been used in Arctic and Antarctic explorations. The Soviet icebreaker *Lenin,* launched in 1959, was the first nuclear-powered non-naval vessel.

Ice cap, small ICE SHEET, often in the shape of a flattened dome, which spreads over the mountains and valleys of polar islands. The floating ice fields surrounding the North Pole are sometimes incorrectly called an ice cap. *See also* PE pp.*118–119.*

Ice cream, sweet, generally smooth, frozen food made of cream or vegetable and/or animal fats, milk, sugar and an emulsifying agent. The milk is pasteurized, homogenized and blended with fats and other non-milk solids, whipped and then cooled rapidly. At this stage flavourings, fruit or nuts may be added. *See also* PE pp.*228,* 229.

Ice dancing. *See* ICE SKATING.

Ice hockey, fast-action sport, most popular in Canada and the USA. It is played by two teams of six players each on an ice rink usually 61m (200ft) long by 26m (85ft) wide, surrounded by walls about 1.2m (4ft) high. Three to four metres (10–15ft) from each end is a goal net. The rink is evenly divided into three zones – attacking, neutral and defending – each 18.3m (60ft) long. A vulcanized rubber puck is used, the object being to advance it into the opposing goal. Players wear ice skates, carry angled wood sticks similar to hockey sticks, and wear protective equipment. Each goal counts as one point and regulation games consist usually of three 20-minute periods. Substitutions are allowed and the game is controlled by a referee or two linesmen. A penalized player has to leave the ice for two or more minutes. Ice hockey originated in Canada *c.*1860. The amateur sport has been included in the Winter Olympics since 1920 and there are world and European championships as well. The sport is also popular in the USSR, Sweden, Finland and Czechoslovakia.

Iceland, island nation in the N Atlantic Ocean, 290km (180 miles) E of Greenland. Largely composed of lava, the island still shows signs of volcanic activity, such as geysers and mud lakes. The country's economy is based on fishing, with fish products forming 80% of all exports. The capital is Reykjavík. Area: 103,000sq km (39,768sq miles). Pop. (1975 est.) 218,000. *See* MW p.94.

Icelandic, official language of Iceland, spoken by virtually all of the island's 218,000 inhabitants. It is a northern Germanic language, descended from, and still closely resembling, the Old Norse language that was taken to Iceland by the Vikings in the 9th century AD.

Iceland moss, flattened, branched, partly erect LICHEN that grows in arctic and high, cold mountainous regions. In Scandinavia particularly, Iceland moss has been used as a medicine and as food for livestock and human beings. Species *Cetraria islandica.*

Iceland spar, transparent form of CALCITE (calcium carbonate) that has the property of birefringerence, ie it bends light two ways so that an image seen through it appears double. It is used for polarizing prisms and in polarizing microscopes and other optical instruments. *See also* POLARIZED LIGHT.

Iceni, ancient British tribe that occupied the area now known as Norfolk and Suffolk. The territory had been ruled by Prasutagus, a client-king, but on his death (AD 60) the Romans attempted to annex it. This led to a widespread revolt led by Prasutagus's queen, BOUDICCA. The Iceni sacked Colchester, London and St Albans before they were crushed by the Roman governor, Suetonius Paulinus, and their territory reduced to a small area in E Norfolk.

Ice plant, or sea marigold, succulent plant found in warm regions, particularly South Africa. The thick, tongue-shaped leaves are covered with thin, glistening cells that give the plant an icy appearance. The small flowers are yellow or pink. Height: 20cm (8ft). Family Ficoidaceae; species *Cryophytum crystallinum.*

Ice sheet, also described as a continental GLACIER. The term may be used for the vast ICE CAPS covering Greenland and Antarctica. The ICEBERGS formed when ice breaks from the margins of such sheets may themselves be many sq km in area. *See also* PE p.*118.*

Ice skating, winter sport, believed to have originated in Scandinavia *c.*3,000 years ago. The first iron skates were introduced in the 17th century. Previously skates were made of bone and then wood. In the 1850s steel skates, with straps and clamps to fasten them to the shoes, were introduced. This development was soon followed by the permanent skate, in which the skate and the shoe form a single unit. In Britain and North America ice skating became organized in the 17th and 19th centuries respectively. The sport consists of speed skating, figure skating and ice dancing. Speed skating is usually held over distances of 500m, 1500m, 5,000m and 10,000m. In figure skating, compulsory and free-style movements are made.

Ice yachting, winter sport, also known as ice boating. The boats, stiletto-shaped craft with three ski-like runners and a raked mast, are propelled by the wind. The most popular craft is the bow-steered Skeeter class, which is 6.7m (22ft) long, weighs about 135kg (300lb) and is limited to 7sq m (75sq ft) of sail. Competition craft are classified according to sail area and can hold one or two people. The sport was originated in the 18th century by the Dutch and became popular in the USA and Canada in the 1860s. It remains popular in North America, The Netherlands, Germany, Scandinavia and around the Baltic coast.

I Ching. *See* BOOK OF CHANGES.

Ichneumon fly, parasitic insect that attacks other insects and spiders. Found worldwide, they are characterized by an ovipositor that is often longer than its body. They are usually 1cm (0.4in) long, though a North American genus reaches 5cm (2in) in length. Family Ichneumonidae. *See also* HYMENOPTERA.

Ichthyology, zoological study of fish, including their classification, structure, distribution and ecology. The ancient Greeks, particularly Aristotle, are regarded as the pioneers of this science in the West. Although true fish are in the Class Osteichthyes, in some classifications it also includes lampreys, sharks, rays and skates. *See* NW pp.124–131, *124–131.*

Ichthyosaurus, extinct fish-shaped, marine reptile of 65–225 million years ago. These fish-eaters had limbs modified into paddles, a dorsal fin and the start of a fish-like tail. Their fossils suggest that they bore live young. Length: 1–9m (2–30ft). *See also* NW pp.*185–186.*

Ichthyosis, also known as fish-skin disease, a disorder characterized by harshness, dryness and flaking of the skin. Caused by excessive growth of the horny layer, it is often a hereditary condition.

ICI (Imperial Chemical Industries), British industrial company specializing in the manufacture of chemicals. In 1977 it employed about 192,000 people throughout the world.

Icknield Way, prehistoric roadway stretching across England from the Wash, along the Chiltern Hills and Berkshire Downs to Stonehenge on Salisbury Plain. The road divides at Goring to form the Upper and Lower Icknield Way, both of which follow LEY LINES for part of their course.

Icon, type of religious painting or sculpture, often of Christ, the Virgin and Child or individual saints. The term is particularly used of Byzantine pictures and later Russian imitations. They were being produced in the 5th century; from the 6th century they have been used as an aid to prayer. Icons are frequently portable and are usually highly stylized, often with dull gold backgrounds. In later Russian icons the central figure is often framed by a halo of jewels and precious metals.

Iconoclastic Controversy, controversy over the veneration of images or icons in the Byzantine Empire during the 8th and 9th centuries. The controversy began in 726 when the Emperor Leo III issued an edict forbidding the veneration of icons. The edict was opposed by the Church. The Second Council of NICAEA in 787 rejected iconoclasm, but the struggle, which lasted for over a century, ended in 843 with a victory for the proponents of the veneration. Today the Greek Orthodox Church observes the feast of Orthodoxy on the first Sunday of Lent. *See also* HC1 p.142.

Iconography, in art history, the study and interpretation of themes and symbols in the figurative arts. In the 18th century the term referred to the classification of ancient monuments by motifs and subjects, but by the 19th it was more specifically concerned with symbolism in Christian art. Twentieth-century iconographers also study secular art and that of religions other than Christianity. Leading 20th-century iconographers have included Aby Warburg (1866–1929) and Erwin Panofsky (1892–1968). In religion, iconography is the symbolic representation of religious concept and personages central to the worship of Eastern Churches.

Iconoscope, CATHODE-RAY TUBE used in early television cameras, invented by Vladimir ZWORYKIN. Light entering the tube strikes a photoelectric plate, causing it to become positively charged. The other side of the plate is scanned by a beam of electrons from an electron gun. Those electrons not held in the plate bounce back to be collected and transmitted as the television signal. *See also* MM pp.230–231.

Ictinus (5th century BC), Greek architect. After designing the PARTHENON with Callicrates (447–432 BC), he worked on the rebuilding and enlargement of the Temple of Mysteries at Eleusis. He also designed the Temple of Apollo Epicurius at Bassae (*c.* 450–425 BC), most of the columns of which are still in place.

Id, in psychoanalytic theory, the deepest level of the personality that includes primitive drives (eg hunger, anger, sex) demanding instant gratification. Even after the ego and the superego develop and limit these instinctual impulses, the id is a source of motivation and often of unconscious conflicts. The term was coined by Sigmund FREUD. *See also* MS pp.*161*, *187*.

Idaho, state in NW USA on the border with Canada. The terrain is dominated by the Rocky Mts and is drained chiefly by the Snake River, whose waters are used to generate hydro-electricity and for irrigation. The principal crops are potatoes, hay, wheat and sugar-beet, and cattle are reared. Silver, lead and zinc are mined and industries include food processing and timber. The fine scenery attracts many tourists, an important source of income. The state capital and largest city is Boise.

Idaho remained unexplored until 1805 but fur-trading posts had been established within a few years. The discovery of gold in 1860 brought many immigrants although the native Indian population was not subdued until 1877. The state was admitted to the Union in 1890 and by the turn of the century had begun the development of its resources. Area: 216,412sq km (83,557sq miles). Pop. (1975 est.) 820,000. *See also* MW p.175.

Ideal gas law, law relating pressure, temperature and volume of an ideal (perfect) gas: $pV = NkT$, where N is the number of molecules of the gas and k is a constant of proportionality. This law implies that at constant temperature, the product of pressure and volume (pV) is constant (BOYLE's law); and at constant pressure, the volume is proportional to the temperature (CHARLES' LAW). *See also* SU pp.84–85.

Ideal Husband, An (1895), four-act comedy by Oscar WILDE, first performed in London in Jan 1895. It was a merciless satire on Victorian hypocrisy, using brilliant epigrammatic wit and dialogue to drive home its points within a conventional structure. After 100 performances, Wilde's trial forced its closure.

Idealism, doctrine or view that asserts the ideal as fundamental in man's interpretation of experience. It gives preference to mental perceptions (of the soul or spirit) over sensory perceptions and is opposed to materialism and realism. Its history in the west dates from the teachings of Plato and it is found in the teaching of Christianity. Idealism is applied to artistic pursuits to denote a rendering, especially in art, of something "as it ought to be" rather than it actually is (eg the idealization of the human figure in Renaissance painting).

Identical twins. *See* TWINS.

Identity, in psychology, the combination of characteristics that makes each person unique. This concept creates certain anomalies, however, in that to oneself one may be different from the image one projects, and from the image one thinks one projects.

Ideology, strictly the science of ideas. In the 20th century it has been applied to political theories which seek a coherent explanation of all the relationships within a society. It is particularly used to describe theories, such as FASCISM and MARXISM, which are a prescription for political action to change society.

Ides, day in the Roman Republican calendar. They fell on the eighth day after the nones of each month, that is on the 15th of March, May, July and October and on the 13th of the other months. Julius CAESAR was assassinated on the Ides of March.

Idiopathic, in medicine, a term used to describe a disease that arises spontaneously, or a condition whose cause is either unknown or unclear, eg PSORIASIS. *See also* MS p.87.

Idocrase, or vesuvianite, orthosilicate mineral, hydrous calcium, iron, magnesium, aluminium silicate, found in impure limestone. It forms tetragonal system crystals; is glassy green, brown, yellow or blue; hardness 6.5; s.g. 3.4. Its transparent green or brown crystals are cut as gems. *See also* PE pp.98–99.

Idris I (1890–   ), ex-king of Libya, grandson of the leader of the Senussi Muslim sect. He used Italian and British aid to become chief of CYRENAICA, allied his country with the British in WWII and was ruler of Libya when it became independent in 1951. He was deposed in 1969 by a Socialist military junta, and sentenced to death *in absentia* in 1971.

Idrisi, or Edrisi (*c.* 1099–*c.* 1165), Arabian geographer. He worked at the court of Roger of Sicily after 1145 and wrote the *Kitab Rujjar* (Book of Roger, 1154), a geographical study of the world. He also made a map of the world engraved on silver.

Idyll, in Classical Greek literature, a brief poem, generally part of a group of poems describing pastoral scenes or events.

Idylls of the King (1842–85), series of poems by Alfred Lord TENNYSON based on the Arthurian legend. It includes *Morte d'Arthur* (1842), *Guinevere* (1859), *The Holy Grail* (1871), and *Balin and Balan* (1885). The work charts the progress of Arthur's court from nobility to sin and evil, through disillusion.

Ieyasu Tokugawa (1543–1616), Japanese leader who completed the unification of Japan and was made shōgun – military leader – in 1603. By 1615 he had established the Tokugawa shōgunate (1603–1867) as the unchallenged hereditary dynasty which remained in power through tight control of the feudal system and the revival of Confucianism. *See also* HC1 p.133.

If, poem by Rudyard KIPLING, which appeared in *Barrack Room Ballads* (1892). It was popular at the time, but today many people disagree with its imperialist assumptions.

If, French islet 3.2km (2miles) SW of Marseilles. Its fortress, Chateau d'If, has a long history as a prison for political offenders; Honoré MIRABEAU was imprisoned there (1774). Alexandre DUMAS made the castle the scene of the imprisonment of his hero in *The Count of Monte Cristo.*

Ife, historical kingdom in SW Nigeria from the 11th to the 19th centuries when it was conquered by the Oyo tribe. Its capital, Ife, 80km (50 miles) ENE of Ibadan, was the spiritual centre of the YORUBA peoples. It now serves the surrounding farm region as a market centre, exporting mostly cocoa. Pop. (1975) 176,000. *See also* HC2 p.60.

Ife art, art of the Yoruba people of W Nigeria that takes its name from the town of Ife, their spiritual centre, where a number of exquisite sculptured heads in bronze and terracotta have been found during the 20th century. Thought to date from between the 12th and 14th centuries, AD, these Ife heads are of such a high degree of naturalism and technical accomplishment that they have been compared with ancient Greek sculpture. Benin art probably inherited the technique of brass-cutting from Ife sculptors in the late 13th century.

Ifni, region of SW Morocco, on the Atlantic Ocean. Formerly a Spanish overseas territory and controlled by Spain (1860–1969), it was ceded to Morocco in 1969, after border fighting between Spanish and Moroccan forces. Area: 1,502sq km (580sq miles).

Igloo, Eskimo dwelling, especially the snow-house of eastern Eskimos built of blocks of snow stacked into a low dome and welded together by frozen water. Igloos are constructed as temporary dwellings in the winter and provide excellent protection against the cold.

Ignatiev, Count Nikolai Pavlovich (1832–1908), Russian diplomat. The border agreement he negotiated with China in 1859 enabled Russia to become a major Pacific power. Ambassador to Turkey (1864–78), he helped to draw up the Treaty of SAN STEFANO which ended the Russo-Turkish War (1877–78) and gave Russia many advantages in the Balkans.

Ignatius of Antioch, Saint, 1st-century bishop of Antioch. As a condemned prisoner on his way to Rome, where he died for his faith, he wrote his seven *Epistles,* some addressed to St POLYCARP, which are valuable sources for an assessment of the doctrine of the early Church.

Ignatius of Constantinople, Saint (*c.* 799–877), also called Nicetas, a son of Emperor Michael I. He became a monk and was elected Patriarch of Constantinople *c.* 846. He was deposed in 858 and replaced by Photius, but was reinstated in 867.

Ignatius of Loyola, Saint (1491–1556), Spanish soldier, churchman and founder of the JESUITS. Convalescing from a wound received in battle, he read a number of religious works and became inspired to devote his life to the conversion of the heathen. In 1534, with FRANCIS XAVIER and other young men, he made vows of poverty, chastity and obedience. He was ordained to the priesthood in 1537 and moved to Rome where, in 1540, Pope Paul III formally approved his request to found a religious order: the Society of Jesus, or Jesuits. He spent the rest of his life in Rome supervising the rapid growth of the order, which was to become the leading force in the COUNTER-REFORMATION in the second half of the 16th century. His *Spiritual Exercises* was one of the most important books of asceticism and has had a profound influence on religious thought. *See also* HC1 pp.272, *272*, 306, *306–307*.

Igneous rocks, broad class of rocks produced by the cooling and solidifying of the molten magmas deep within the earth. They may take intrusive or extrusive forms. Intrusive rocks, such as GRANITE,

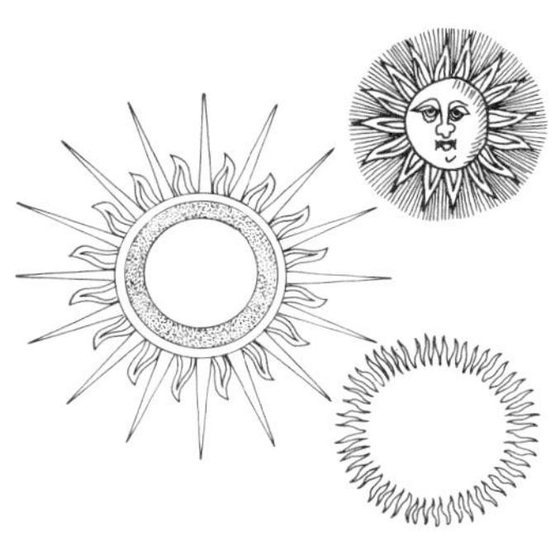

Iconography is the study and classification of symbols (particularly religious) in art history.

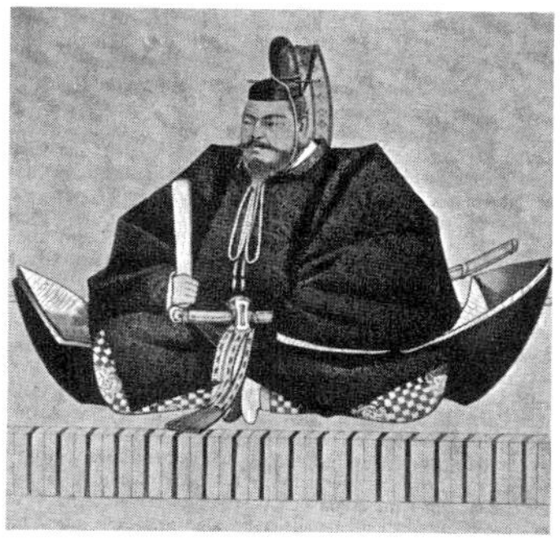

Ieyasu Tokugawa, whose Shogun dynasty ended when the West intruded.

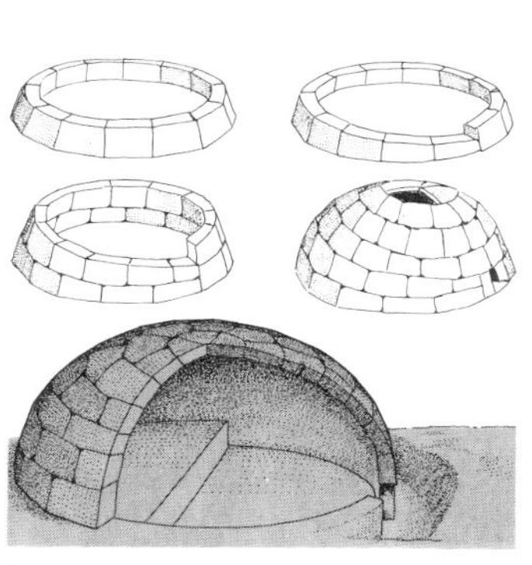

Igloos are constructed in a spiral formation from large blocks of hard packed snow.

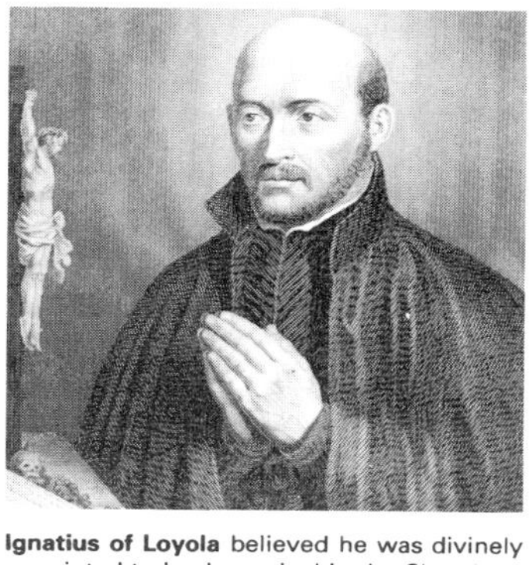

Ignatius of Loyola believed he was divinely appointed to lead a revival in the Church.

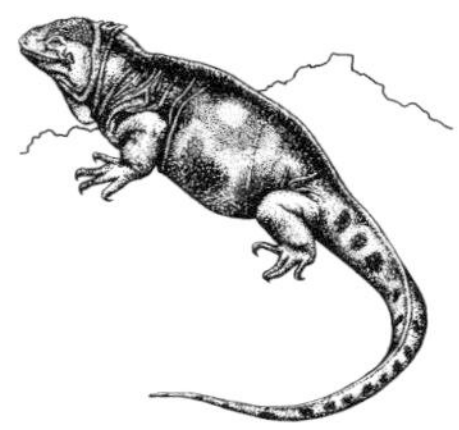

Iguana; members of this group are generally vegetarian despite their large size.

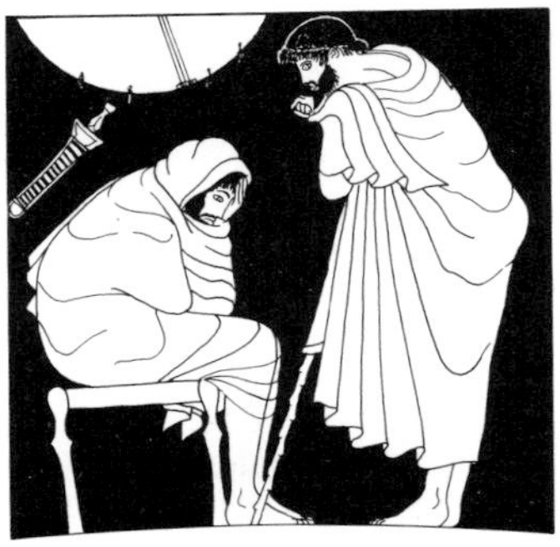

The Iliad describes the final dramatic events in the 10-year war between Greece and Troy.

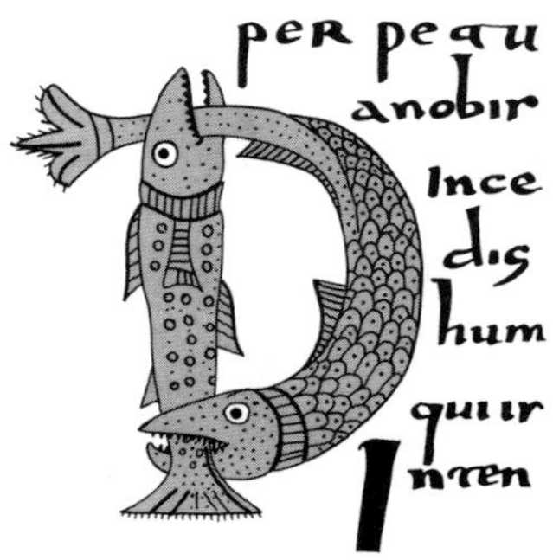

Illuminations allowed medieval artists to make amusing, realistic images.

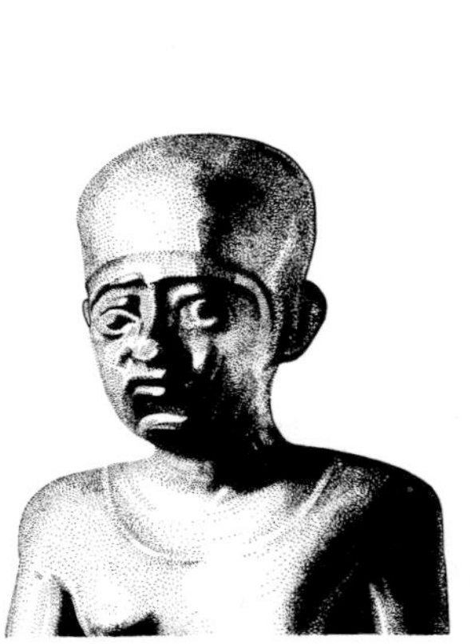

Imhotep, one of few Egyptians to be deified, was merged with the Greek god Asclepius.

are those formed beneath the earth's surface by the gradual cooling of molten material; extrusive rocks, such as BASALT, are formed by the rapid cooling of molten material upon the earth's surface. *See also* PE pp.100–101.

Ignis Fatuus. *See* WILL-O'-THE-WISP.

Ignition, engine, electrical components for igniting fuel in a petrol engine. Air and petrol vapour are mixed in the carburettor and delivered to the cylinder, where the mixture is compressed and ignited by a spark produced by the spark plug. *See also* MM pp.62–63, 68, *69*, *130*.

Iguana, any of numerous species of terrestrial, arboreal, burrowing or aquatic LIZARDS that live in tropical America and the Galapagos Islands. The common iguana (*Iguana iguana*) is greenish-brown, with a serrated dewlap and a crest along its back. Length: to 2m (6.5ft). Family Iguanidae. *See also* NW pp.*33*, *139*.

Iguanodon, primitive bipedal DINOSAUR that lived in Europe during the lower Cretaceous period. It had a spiked thumb, which may have served as a defensive weapon. Its jaws and teeth, like those of later ornithischian dinosaurs, were specialized for grinding plant food. Length: 10m (33ft). *See also* NW p.*185*.

Ihara, Saikaku (1642–93), Japanese poet and novelist. He was renowned for his capacity for rapid verse composition and satires. He wrote many novels, among them *Five Women Who Loved Love* (1686).

IJsselmeer, large freshwater lake in the NW Netherlands, formed in 1932 by the dyke which divided the ZUIDER ZEE into the saline Wadden Zee and the freshwater Ijsselmeer. Large land areas have been reclaimed from the former Zuider Zee since 1932. Length of dyke: 32km (20 miles).

Ikhnaton. *See* AKHENATON.

Ile-de-France, historic region in N central France, bounded by Picardy (N), Champagne (E), Orléanais (S), and Normandy (W). In 987 Hugh CAPET established the first French Crown lands that were to encompass this region, whose capital was Paris. It is regarded as the cradle of the French monarchy. *See also* HC1 p.202.

Ilesha, city of SW Nigeria, 97km (60 miles) NE of Ibadan. It is a commercial centre for the surrounding region. Local crops include nuts, yams and cacao. Pop. (1969 est.) 192,500.

Ileum, part of the small intestine, about 4m (13ft) long, preceding the large intestine. Together with the jejunum (which is nearer the stomach and with which it is continuous), the ileum lies coiled in the front of the abdominal cavity. *See also* DUODENUM; MS pp.*68*, 69.

Ilex. *See* HOLLY.

Iliad, historic Greek epic poem probably written in the 8th century BC, and attributed to HOMER; with the *Odyssey*, it provides a rich source for understanding the religion and people of the period. The *Iliad* describes the activities of the gods and mortals in the last weeks of the ten-year seige of TROY when, after a quarrel with AGAMEMNON, ACHILLES refused to continue the battle. After Achilles' friend PATROCULUS was killed by HECTOR, Achilles led the attack and killed Hector. *See also* HC1 pp.40, 68, 74, *75*, 76.

Ilium, broad flat bone on either side of the PELVIS. Joined by the SACRUM, the fused bones of the base of the spine, it is fused with the ISCHIUM, and PUBIS in a triangular suture at the hip socket. The ilia form the back of the "basin" of the pelvic girdle and anchor the muscles that form the frontal wall of the abdomen. *See also* MS p.*57*.

Illinois, state in N central USA on the E bank of the Mississippi River. The land is virtually level and is drained by many rivers flowing SW to the Mississippi. The state has fertile black loam soil which supports crops such as hay, oats and barley; livestock is also important. Mineral deposits are found in the S. Chicago is a transport centre and its port on Lake Michigan handles domestic commerce through the Great Lakes and ocean-going vessels through the St Lawrence Seaway. The state capital is Springfield.

Illinois was explored first by the French in 1673 and a few settlements were made in the next century. Ceded to the British in 1763, it was occupied by American troops in the American War of Independence. Illinois became a state of the Union in 1818. Area: 146,075sq km (56,400sq miles). Pop. (1975 est.) 11,145,000. *See also* MW p.175.

Illiteracy, inability to read and write. Many people cannot read or write even a simple message; millions more are functionally illiterate – they cannot, for example, read instructions concerning products they buy, or write useful letters. The eradication of illiteracy is one aim of public and compulsory education around the world, and yet the problem remains huge. According to 1973 United Nations statistics, there are about 160 million illiterates in 67 countries.

Illuminations, illustrated manuscripts of the Gospels and other religious books, the earliest dating from about the 5th century. The style ranges from intricate decoration of initial letters and borders to miniatures and full-page illustrations. Glowing colours and the use of gold leaf are common features. Early medieval illuminations were monastic in origin. Gradually, many different schools developed, such as the Hiberno-Saxon, the Carolingian and the WINCHESTER. During the GOTHIC period illumination was used for both religious and secular book illustrations. Illumination was at its height during the 14th and 15th centuries when the INTERNATIONAL GOTHIC style was in use by such Flemish and French artists as the LIMBOURG brothers and Jean FOUQUET. Well-known examples include the BOOK OF KELLS, THE LINDISFARNE GOSPELS and the LUTTRELL PSALTER. *See also* HC1 pp.164–165, *199*.

Illusion, lack of correspondence between the perception of an object and its physical measurement. Illusions include such phenomena as hallucinations and can occur in any of the five senses although optical and visual illusions are the commonest. Optical illusions are caused by physical properties such as refraction, eg a rod lowered into water appears to bend. A visual illusion is the misinterpretation by the brain of something perceived by the eye. Geometric illusions occur when patterns of lines or shapes present conflicts of interpretation, eg the illusion in which two lines of equal length appear unequal because of the diagonal lines that are attached to their ends in different ways. Other visual illusions concern the perception of colour, brightness, motion and depth. *See also* APPARENT MOVEMENT; MIRAGE; PERCEPTION; MS pp.46–47.

Illustrative music, or programme music, type of music that sets out to re-create the emotions aroused by a poem, place or story. It may be contrasted with absolute music, which has no direct references to experiences outside the music itself. An essential concept in the music of the Romantic period, perhaps the earliest example is BEETHOVEN's 6th Symphony (The Pastoral). Symphonic poems by SMETANA and SIBELIUS are more modern instances.

Illyria, ancient region on the N and E shores of the Adriatic Sea that was inhabited by self governing Illyrian tribes of Indo-European origin. They remained free of Greek and Macedonian domination but were defeated by the Romans in 168 BC and their land annexed as Illyricum. In about AD 9 it was divided between the imperial provinces of Dalmatia and Pannonia. Modern Illyria is N of central Albania.

Ilmenite, black oxide mineral, iron titanate ($FeTiO_3$), a major ore of the metal titanium. It is found in basic igneous rocks and beach sands as tabular to fine, scaly crystals in the rhombohedral system, and as compact masses or granules. It has a metallic lustre and is magnetic. Hardness 5-6; s.g.4.7.

ILO (International Labour Organization), specialized agency of the UN to facilitate improved industrial relations and conditions of work. It was formed as an agency of the LEAGUE OF NATIONS in 1919 by the Treaty of Versailles and has a membership comprising government, employer and worker representatives. An annual conference is held, which passes resolutions on such matters as conditions of work, independence of trade unions, migrant workers, equal pay and so on, which member countries agree to abide by. It has a large permanent secretariat in Geneva.

Iloilo, city in the Philippines, in the SE of Panay Island, on Iloilo Strait. Important as a commercial centre since the 17th century, it was declared a foreign trade port in 1855. It now exports sugar, rice and copra and is especially known for its delicate hand-woven fabrics. Pop. (1970 est.) 213,000.

Ilorin, city in W Nigeria, approx. 274km (170 miles) NNE of Lagos. It is a marketing and processing centre for a large agricultural region. Its own industries include cigarettes and palm products. Pop. (1972 est.) 260,474.

Image, optical, points to which light rays from an object converge (real image) or from which they appear to diverge (virtual image) after reflection or refraction. A real image of an object can be projected on to a screen and can be recorded in a photographic emulsion; a virtual image, such as that produced by a plane mirror, cannot. *See also* LENS; MIRROR; SU pp.100–101, *100–101*.

Image intensifier, electronic device in which gamma rays, X-rays, and ultraviolet waves from a source can be converted into a visible image or in which the intensity of a visible image can be increased. The radiation falls on to a special surface and releases electrons that are then accelerated and focused on to a fluorescent screen, producing an enhanced visible image. *See also* PHOTOMULTIPLIER; ELECTROMAGNETIC SPECTRUM; SU p.*109*.

Imaginary numbers, in mathematics, the square roots of negative quantities. The simplest, $\sqrt{-1}$, is usually represented by *i*. The numbers are so called because when first discovered they were widely regarded as meaningless. But they are necessary for the solution of many quadratic equations, the roots of which can be expressed only as complex numbers, which are composed of a real part and an imaginary part. They find applications in AC (alternating current) theory. *See also* NUMBER, COMPLEX.

Imagism, movement in poetry which flourished in the US and England from 1912–17. The Imagists believed that the language of common speech should be used and that new rhythms should be created. They allowed absolute freedom in the choice of subject but demanded that the work should be explicit. Amy LOWELL, the principal exponent of the movement, produced three anthologies called *Some Imagist Poets* (1915–17).

Imago, the adult, reproductive stage of an insect that has undergone full METAMORPHOSIS. Imagos are the winged insects, such as butterflies and dragonflies, that emerge from PUPAS or develop from NYMPHS. *See also* NW p.*109*.

Imam, Arabic word for a leader of the Muslim community, used in several senses. It may describe a man who leads public prayers; he does not usually have the status corresponding to priest in other religions. It is also a title of honour for Islamic theologians and religious leaders, such as the AGA KHAN. Finally, it is the title of a succession of spiritual guides of the SHI'A Muslims.

IMF (International Monetary Fund), guardian body of the international financial situation. It was formed at the BRETTON WOODS CONFERENCE (1944) to secure international monetary co-operation and the stabilization of currency and exchange rates. It is affiliated to the UN and in 1974 had 126 members, who agree to consult the IMF when altering exchange rates (with the exception of one alteration of up to 10%). It also provides a pool of reserves to provide loans to member states.

Imhotep, vizier to Pharaoh Djoser (or Zoser) of Egypt in the Third Dynasty of the Old Kingdom (2680–2258 BC) and architect of the pyramid at Sakkara; also reputed to be a physician and writer. In

525 BC he was deified as the patron of scribes and the son of Ptah, the builder-god of Memphis.
Imipramine, antidepressant drug first synthesized 1951 and introduced into psychiatric use in the 1960s. It was the first of the TRICYCLIC antidepressants and is usually given orally. Its side-effects may include tremors and mental confusion.
Immaculate Conception, the Roman Catholic belief that the Blessed Virgin MARY was free of all ORIGINAL SIN from the moment of her conception. It was defined as a dogma by Pope PIUS IX in 1854.
Immortelle. *See* EVERLASTING FLOWERS.
Immune system, the main method by which the body defends itself against disease. It involves many kinds of cells in the blood, lymph and bone marrow, some of which make ANTIBODIES against invading microbes and other foreign substances, and others (phagocytes) which actively attack and digest such invaders. The total operation of the immune system is exceedingly complex and not fully understood. *See also* MM pp.114–115.
Immunity, in biology, resistance to attack by disease micro-organisms. It can be acquired naturally, as from an infection which stimulates the body to produce protective ANTIBODIES (a newborn baby carries some antibodies from its mother). Alternatively, it can be conferred actively by the injection of an antiserum containing antibodies, or a vaccine containing dead or attenuated disease micro-organisms. *See also* IMMUNIZATION; MS pp.114–115.
Immunity, diplomatic, exemption of diplomats from search, arrest or prosecution in the country in which they serve. It is an essential part of diplomatic practice.
Immunization, practice of conferring immunity against a disease, usually by stimulating the production of ANTIBODIES that combat the disease. In a common type of immunization, weakened forms of infecting organisms are injected into the bloodstream, causing only a mild form of the disease but stimulating antibody production and so providing lasting immunity. *See also* MS pp.87, *89*, 114–115.
Immunoglobulin, protein of a globular shape, found in the bloodstream, that plays a part in the body's immune defence system. ANTIBODIES are immunoglobulins.
Immunological disease, also called an auto-immune disease, a disorder often described as caused by "the body attacking itself". The IMMUNE SYSTEM of the body produces antibodies which are normally defensive but which can, in some circumstances, cause tissue damage. The exact circumstances are often ill-defined. RHEUMATISM and some forms of ARTHRITIS are common examples of such disorders, and there are many others less well known. MULTIPLE SCLEROSIS is possibly at least partly auto-immune. *See also* MS p.87.
Immunology, study of IMMUNITY, auto-immunity and ALLERGY. It is concerned with the provision of active immunity such as vaccination as a means of preventing disease, passive immunity (injections of antitoxins) to treat infection, and diagnosis using various laboratory animals. Auto-immunity is an abnormal injurious reaction which results from overactive immune response to the body's own tissues. Allergic reactions result from an overactive response to harmless foreign substances such as dust, rather than to infective organisms. *See also* MS pp.114–115.
Immunosuppressive drug, any chemical used to prevent or weaken the body's immune response, ie its ability to form ANTIGENS. Such drugs are used so that a beneficial antigen (such as a tissue graft) may be retained or allergic reaction may be prevented.
Impala, or pala, long-legged, medium sized African antelope. Long, lyrate horns are found only on the males, but both sexes have sleek, glossy brown fur with black markings on the rump. Length: to 1.5m (5ft); height: to 1m (3.3ft) at the shoulder. Family Bovidae; species *Aepyceros melampus. See also* NW p.*200*.
Impasto, word of Italian origin used in oil or acrylic painting to describe the thick heavy application of paint to a canvas or panel. When the paint is so heavily applied that it stands out in relief, the term "loaded impasto" is used.
Impatiens, genus of 450 species of succulent annual plants, mostly native to the tropics of Asia and Africa. They have white, red or yellow flowers and seedpods which, when ripe, pop and scatter their seeds, giving the plants their name "impatient". Some species are known as touch-me-not. Family Balsaminaceae.
Impeachment, prosecution of a public official by the legislature of state. In Britain it is conducted by the HOUSE OF COMMONS with the HOUSE OF LORDS as judge and in the USA by the HOUSE OF REPRESENTATIVES with the SENATE as judge. In the USA the last impeachment trial was that of President Andrew JOHNSON; it failed to impeach him. The last person to be impeached in Britain was Lord Melville in 1806.
Imperial Chemical Industries. *See* ICI.
Imperial College of Science and Technology, school of the University of London established in 1907 by royal charter for the study of science, particularly applied to technology and industry. It combined three institutions established in the 19th century: the Royal College of Science, the Royal School of Mines and the City and Guilds College, and became a school of the University of London in 1908.
Imperial Conferences (1887–1937), periodic gatherings of premiers of the countries in the British Empire and representatives of the home government. Early conferences in 1887, 1894 and 1897 emphasized joint political, military and commercial policies, but from 1902 they paid increasing attention to securing preferential trade tariffs. The 1926 Conference defined the British Commonwealth. The 1937 Conference unanimously supported APPEASEMENT of Germany.
Imperialism, domination of one people or country by another. The domination can be economic, cultural, political or religious. Historically, for example, the Roman Empire held sway in Europe to a unique degree. In the wake of the rise of the nation state and the age of exploration came the setting up, from the 16th century, of trading empires by major European powers such as the British, French, Portuguese and Dutch. They penetrated Africa, Asia and North America, their colonies serving as a source of raw materials and providing a market for manufactured goods. With few exceptions imperialism imposed alien cultures on native societies. In the 20th century, although Japan, Germany and Italy exercised imperialist ambitions for a time, and the Communists gained control of E Europe in the 1940s, most former colonies, especially in Africa and Asia, have been granted independence or secured it through wars of liberation. *See also* HC2 pp.130–133; 140–143; 214–215; 246–247.
Imperial War Cabinet (1917–18), special Commonwealth cabinet during WWI. It met in London about 300 times in 1917. It consisted of the inner British war cabinet, the Dominion Prime Ministers and representatives of India. It acted in an advisory capacity, and had no executive power.
Imperial War Museum, London museum founded by the War Cabinet in 1917 to provide a record of the activities of British peoples in WWI. It now illustrates and records all aspects of both world wars, in which the forces of the Commonwealth have been engaged. The museum includes a photographic and film library. It is situated in Lambeth.
Impetigo, contagious bacterial skin infection caused by STREPTOCOCCAL or STAPHYLOCOCCAL infection. It causes multiple, spreading lesions with yellowish-brown crusts and primarily affects the face, hands and feet. *See also* MS p.98.
Importance of Being Earnest, The (1895), three-act play by Oscar WILDE, subtitled "A Trivial Comedy for Serious People". Written in Worthing at considerable speed in late 1894 as a quick way of resolving Wilde's rapidly mounting debts, the work is regarded by many as the greatest English play of the 19th century. It was made into a film in 1952.
Impotence, in men, the inability to perform the act of sexual intercourse. It is the result of organic or psychogenic factors, and is the equivalent of FRIGIDITY in women. It may be a temporary condition brought about emotionally, by anxiety regarding sexual performance, or physiologically, through disease or drugs. The term loosely describes various sorts of sexual dysfunction; the lack or loss of erection, loss of pleasure and the inability to reach orgasm. *See also* MS p.75.
Impressionism, major French anti-academic art movement of the later 19th century. The movement gained its name (originally used as a term of derision) from a painting by MONET entitled *Impression, Sunrise* and exhibited in 1874. Impressionist painters using everyday subjects sought to capture the atmosphere and visual impression of a subject, rather than record it in highly finished, strictly literal style and in the words of Monet, the movement's leading painter, aimed to create "a spontaneous work rather than a calculated one". In the 1860s, Monet, RENOIR and SISLEY formed a close-knit group exploring the possibilities of painting out of doors, with a light, bright palette and closely analysing and interpreting the effects of light on nature. The first Impressionist exhibition took place in 1874 in the studio of the Parisian photographer Nadar. Academics and public alike were unable to accept the shimmering, spontaneous, non-academic paraphrases which these canvasses offered them as being the real effects of light. The movement became widely accepted as an artistic style from the late 1880s and spreading through Europe. Major Impressionists include DEGAS, SEURAT and SIGNAC; PISSARRO organized and exhibited works in all eight Impressionist exhibitions, including the last (1886), and CÉZANNE exhibited with the Impressionists in 1874 and 1887. MANET, never wholly an Impressionist, was influenced by, and in turn influenced, Impressionism. Other Impressionists include Frédéric Bazille, Berthe MORISOT and Mary CASSATT. RODIN has been called Impressionist because of his interest in the effects of light on his sculpture. In music, RAVEL and DEBUSSY are the two composers whose compositions are most often described as Impressionist. *See also* HC2 pp.118–119.
Imprinting, form of learning that occurs within a critical period in very young animals. A complex relationship develops between the newborn infant and the first object it encounters; this is usually, but not always, a parent. The future emotional development of the infant depends upon this relationship. Most animals respond only to their own species; some will respond to inanimate objects. Imprinting in birds has been studied by Konrad LORENZ, who stated that imprinting is an irreversible process. *See also* MS pp.*158*, 159; NW pp.150–151.
Improvisation, in music, performance in which the musician himself invents what he plays, either relating it to a given musical framework or playing totally freely. Classical Indian music and JAZZ have explored many of the formal and aesthetic problems and possibilities involved, and most African music contains some degree of improvisation. Improvisation, especially at the keyboard or in CADENZAS, was an integral part of Western classical music until the 19th century, and was revived in the 20th century in the works of composers such as STOCKHAUSEN. *See also* HC2 p.272, *272*.
Improvisation, in theatre and films, technique in which actors perform with little or no predetermined dialogue or action. It has always played an important role in the theatre, especially in COMMEDIA DELL'ARTE, but its use was not formalized until the work of STANISLAVSKY. He saw it as a way of stimulating a player's observational insights into character, and his followers – especially in theatre workshops such as the New York Actors'

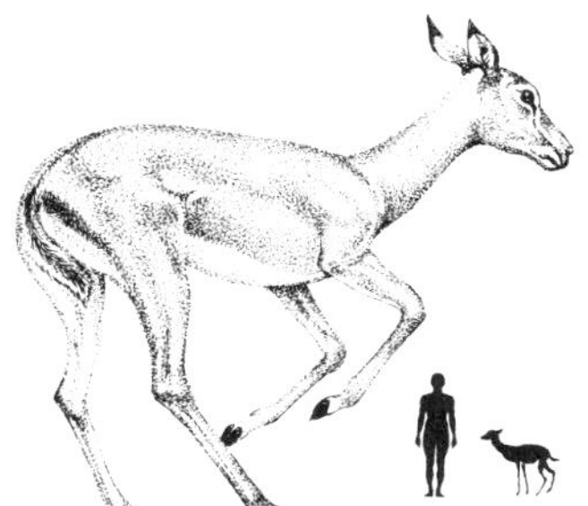

Impalas live in herds in the open country of southern Africa; they can leap 3m (10ft) high.

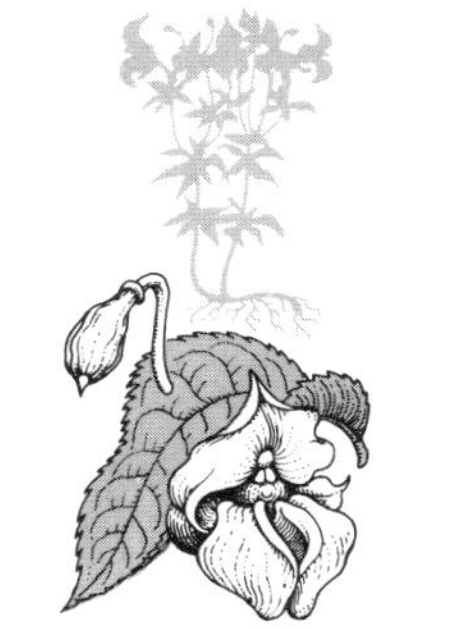

Impatiens; balsam is one of the many species of this plant found widely in N America.

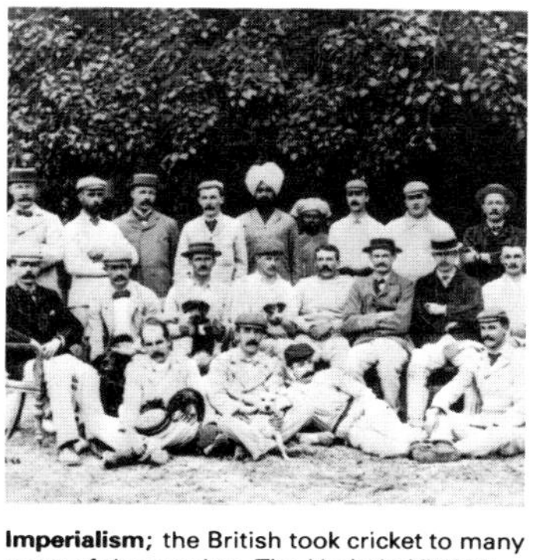

Imperialism; the British took cricket to many parts of the empire: *The Umbala XI* 1903.

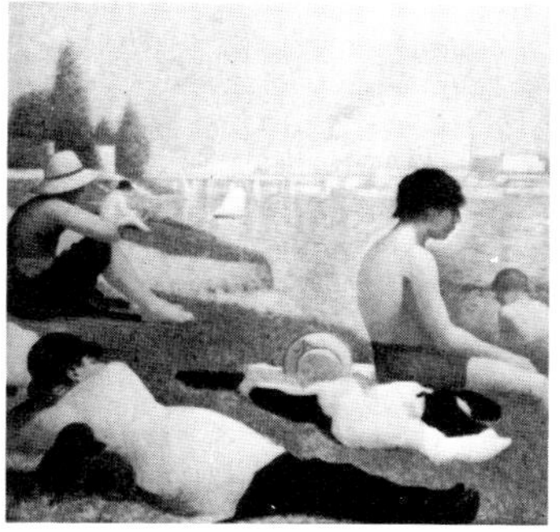

Impressionism: part of Seurat's pointillist painting *The Bathers*, in the National Gallery.

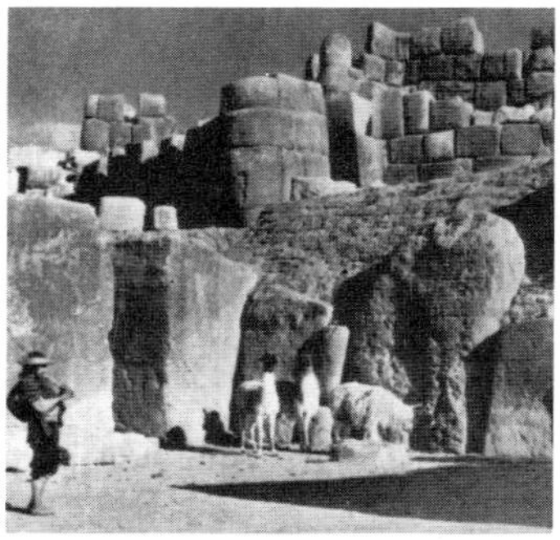

Inca Empire; a shepherd and his llamas at the ruins of Fortaleza de Sacsayhuaman, Peru.

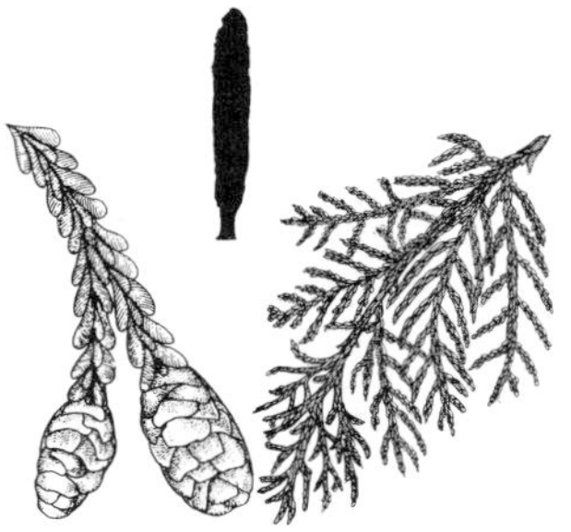

Incense cedar leaves (of the Cypress family) produce a distinctive scent when rubbed.

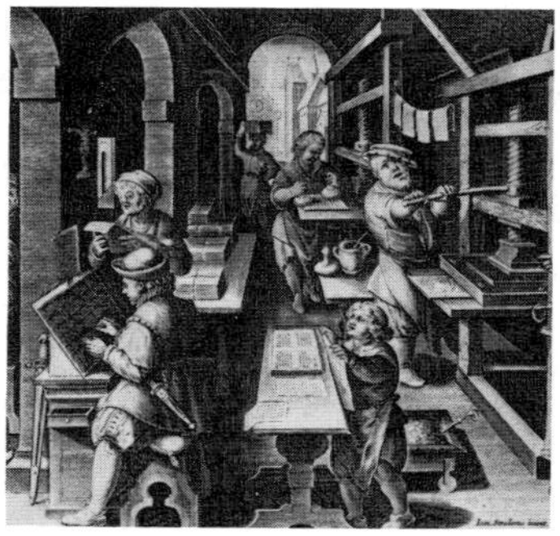

Incunabula, a latin word meaning "birthplace" refers to the earliest printed books.

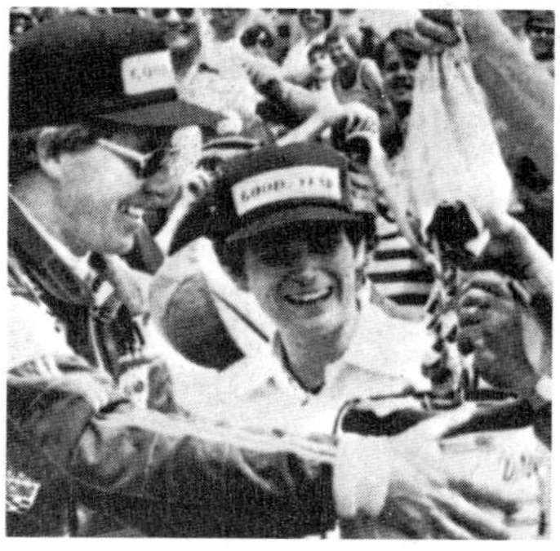

Indianapolis 500; Tom Sneva in 1977 after the first ever lap of 320km/h (200mph).

Studio – called improvisation the METHOD. Today it is not uncommon for whole films or plays to be completely improvised.

Inbreeding, mating of two closely related organisms. It is the opposite of OUTBREEDING and gives a more uniform GENOTYPE and PHENOTYPE. A form of genetic engineering, it can be used to improve breeds in plants and animals. In humans, it can have harmful results, such as the persistance of HAEMOPHILIA in some European royal families. *See also* EUGENICS.

Inca Empire, empire established by a South American Indian group that migrated from the Peruvian highlands into the Cuzco area in about AD 1250. The Incas expanded and consolidated their empire slowly and steadily until the reigns of Pachacuti (*r. c.* 1438–71) and his son Topa (*r. c.* 1471–93), when Inca influence dramatically increased to include the area between Ecuador in the N and Chile, Bolivia and Argentina in the S. The Inca Empire was bureaucratic and militaristic: local leaders were moved to other regions and co-opted into Inca society. Good roads facilitated communication and tax collection. All products were the property of the state. Although the Incas never developed a system of writing, their standards in architecture, pottery, weaving, jewellery-making and other crafts were high. Religious rites included sun worship and the mummification of their dead. When PIZARRO, the Spanish CONQUISTADOR, arrived in 1532, he took advantage of civil war between two Inca claimants to the throne to complete the downfall of an already weakened empire. *See also* HC1 pp.*232,* 233.

Incandescence, emission of light by a substance heated to a high temperature. Whether or not a hot body is seen as incandescent depends to some extent on the dark-adaptation of the human eye, but an incandescent body is never at a temperature below about 400°C (750°F). A body can emit bright light without being incandescent, as in a fluorescent lamp.

Incarnation, in CHRISTIAN doctrine, the tenet that God became man, that the supreme deity became an ordinary mortal human being. The doctrine was confirmed amid controversy by the first general council of the Church at Nicaea in 325. Heresies emphasizing only the god-like or man-like aspects of Christ were condemned by the Council of Chalcedon (451), which expressed the definition that Christ is "truly God and truly man".

Incendiary bomb, bomb designed to burn, rather than destroy by explosion, its target. Incendiary bombs were first used in WWI; in WWII they were used in the Allied bombings of Germany, using phosphorus or thermite as the charge. They were also widely used by the USA in the VIETNAM WAR, in the form of NAPALM.

Incense cedar, widely distributed genus (*Libocedrus*) of evergreen trees native to Chile, North America, New Zealand and China. They may be pyramid-shaped or spreading, and have flat, scale-like leaves. The aromatic wood is used for interior work and furniture. Height: 30–40m (100–150ft). Family Taxodiaceae.

Incest, sexual relations within a family or kinship group, the taboo on which varies between societies. In many countries incest is a crime that carries a prison sentence. It is likely that the rules of many communities of primitive man prohibited marriage between close relatives, long before the genetic effects of such relationships were realized. *See also* ENDOGAMY; EXOGAMY; MS p.250.

Inch. *See* WEIGHTS AND MEASURES.

Inchcape Rock, sandstone reef off the E coast of Scotland. Partly exposed only at low tide, it formerly caused many shipwrecks until a lighthouse, designed by Robert STEVENSON, was erected there (1807–11). Tradition claims that a warning bell was hung there by the Abbot of Aberbrothock (Arbroath); the story is celebrated in Southey's ballad *The Inchcape Rock.*

Inch'on, port city in NW South Korea, on the Yellow Sea. Its economy is largely dependent on the export trade. One of South Korea's major commercial centres, its industries include iron and steel. Pop. (1970 est.) 646,000.

Incisor, any of the chisel-shaped cutting TEETH, in the front of the mouth between the canines in the dentition of mammals. There are eight in humans, two in each half of each jaw.

Inclination, magnetic, or dip, angle made by a free-floating magnet with the Earth's magnetic lines of force. At the north magnetic pole the inclination is zero; at the magnetic equator it is 90°. *See also* DECLINATION, MAGNETIC; PE pp.*22,* 23.

Inclined plane, flat surface that is angled relative to a reference plane. The angle of the plane is the angle between two lines, one in each plane, both at right-angles to their line of intersection. *See also* MM pp. 86–87, *87.*

Income tax, yearly assessment of tax on income, profits and financial gains of any type, administered in Britain by the Board of Inland Revenue. It is a direct tax on money earned or acquired, as distinct from a tax levied on goods or services. In its modern form it was first imposed by William PITT in 1799 as a temporary measure to acquire revenue during the NAPOLEONIC WARS. It took the form of a 10% levy on incomes over £200 per year, with lesser proportions levied on incomes above £60 on a graduated scale. Incomes below £60 were exempt. It was repealed in 1815, but revived in 1842 by Robert PEEL and revised during the late 19th century. Since WWII the taxation rate has varied according to legislation in annual Finance Acts, and until 1972 tax rates were calculated after making an allowance for unearned income. Since then the tax rate has ignored unearned income.

Incubation, process of maintaining stable temperature and humidity conditions to ensure that eggs develop and hatch. Carried out naturally by birds, monotremes and some reptiles, it is accomplished by sitting on the eggs, or using volcanic, solar heat, or that produced by a natural covering such as earth, sand or decaying vegetation.

Incubus, demon lover or nightmare personified as various forms of oppressive night-presence, also known as the Mahr. Said to ride, press on, and even cause death to sleepers, this creature of fantasy can appear as a monstrous being or, more usually, as a desirable sexual partner. The female equivalent is the SUCCUBUS.

Incunabula, books printed from the invention of typography (in the 1450s) to the end of the 15th century. Georg Wolfgang Panzer produced the first catalogue of such books in five volumes (1793–97).

Indemnity, in law, the compensation paid to a person for wrong done to him or for loss or expense suffered by him. It also means the deed in which is contained the undertaking that indemnifies him.

Indépendants, Salon des, society founded in Paris in 1884 by SEURAT, SIGNAC and other artists – many considered avant-garde – who disagreed with academic art and opposed the official annual Salon. The new Salon allowed any artist who so wished to display works in its exhibitions. The artist paid a fee but was not required to have his work judged by a selection committee.

Independence Day. *See* FOURTH OF JULY.

Independent Broadcasting Authority (IBA), British organization responsible for independent television and independent local radio. It appoints programme companies, supervises programmes provided by the contractors and their scheduling, controls advertising and builds, owns and operates transmitting stations. Established as the Independent Television Authority in 1954 to provide an alternative television service to the BBC, the organization appointed companies to provide a programme service. In 1972, it changed its name to the Independent Broadcasting Authority, when its responsibilities were extended to cover the setting up of a network of independent local radio stations. Independent television and radio are financed by the sale of advertising time, but programmes cannot be sponsored and advertisements (commercials) must appear either at the end, the beginning or during a natural break in the programme. National news programmes are provided for Independent Television by a non-profit-making company, Independent Television News (ITN) Independent Radio News, a subsidiary of the London Broadcasting Company (LBC), acts as a news agency for all other independent local radio companies.

Independent Labour Party, British political party, founded at Bradford in 1893. Its first leader was Keir HARDIE. It formed a Labour Representation Committee to return trade union representatives to Parliament. In 1906 that committee became the LABOUR PARTY, which by 1918 completely overshadowed the ILP.

Independents, or Separatists, English Puritan sect which evolved from BROWNISM and sought organizational and intellectual independence as separate congregations from the established Church of England. Separatists established a base in The Netherlands in 1608, and as the PILGRIM FATHERS settled in Plymouth, Massachusetts. The first truly Independent church was founded in Southwark, London, in 1616 by Henry Jacob but the most famous Independent was undoubtedly Oliver CROMWELL. Independents formed the backbone of his army and his support guaranteed their strength during the English Civil War although it was to be eroded after the Restoration by the Act of Uniformity. The name "Independent" was first used during the 1640s and although it continued to be used until the 19th century, the term "Congregationalist" was more common by that time.

Independent Television Authority (ITA). *See* INDEPENDENT BROADCASTING AUTHORITY.

Independent variable. *See* VARIABLE.

Index, in Roman Catholic history, an abbreviation for "Index of Prohibited Books", the official list issued by the Roman Catholic Church of books its members were forbidden to read or possess save in exceptional circumstances and with specific permission. Intended to guard the faithful against moral or spiritual danger, the index was first issued in 1559 and revised at intervals until finally abolished in 1966.

Index of Refraction. *See* REFRACTION.

India, republic in S Asia, occupying the greater part of the Indian subcontinent. One of the most populous countries in the world, its greatest problems are periodic drought and floods producing widespread famine. Agriculture has been improved since independence in 1947, however, and mineral deposits are now being exploited. The capital is New Delhi. Area: 3,275,833sq km (1,266,479sq miles). Pop. (1975 est.) 598,097,000. *See* MW p.95.

Indiana, state in N central USA, S of Lake Michigan. Access to the lake and to the Ohio River in the S ensures efficient distribution of the state's agricultural and manufacturing products. Agriculture remains an important part of the economy and the area is regarded as the country's richest farming region. The development of heavy industry in the NW has made Indiana one of the leading producers of machinery; state capital Indianapolis.

Indiana was explored first by the French who founded several forts there in the early 18th century to protect their fur trade. It was ceded to the British in 1763 and passed to the USA after the American War of Independence. The native Indian population was not subdued until 1811. The state remained a rural area until the late 19th century when industrialization began. Area: 93,993sq km (36,291sq miles). Pop. (1975 est.) 5,311,000. *See also* MW p.175.

Indian antelope. *See* BLACKBUCK.

Indianapolis, capital of Indiana, USA, 282km (175 miles) SE of Chicago on the White River. It is the major cereal and livestock market in a fertile agricultural area. Industries include chemicals, electronic equipment and meat packing. Pop. (1970) 745,739.

Indianapolis 500, most famous motor race in the USA. The distance is 805km (500 miles) and the event has been held annually since 1911. The winner's prize is one of the richest in all motor racing.

Indian art and architecture, can be traced back to the ancient civilization of the Indus Valley which flourished from *c.*2300 to 1750 BC. Excavations at HARAPPA (Punjab) and MOHENJO-DARO (Sind) show fortified cities with a variety of public and domestic buildings and highly sophisticated sanitation. Small sculptures found there in bronze and stone show a considerable understanding of the human form.

MAURYAN art (320–185 BC), intensely Buddhist in motivation, can be seen in *chaitya* (shrines) and *vihara* (monastic halls hollowed out of solid rock) at Ajanta, where there are some rare frescoes. The GUPTA era (AD 320–550) was the golden age of Buddhist art. The Buddhist temple, with a porch and cella (main sanctuary), originated at this time. Religious imagery often combines Buddhist detachment and Hindu passion, in which the portrayal of female figures is often profane.

From the 6th century AD, a typical Hindu temple plan developed: a portico leading through a pillared hall to a cella containing the statue of the deity or the lingam (phallic symbol) of the deity Shiva. In s India (*fl.* 7th and 8th centuries AD) a Dravidian style of Hindu temple emerged: its name came from the language spoken.

Islamic art and architecture were introduced into India after the Muslim conquest (1192). Under MOGUL rule between the 16th and 18th centuries an Indo-Islamic style evolved, influenced by Persian prototypes. The Taj Mahal at Agra, a marvel of symmetry in white marble and precious inlay, stands as the most perfect example of Mogul architecture. Although Persian influence was initially strong in drawing, by the late 16th century Indian taste was emerging in bright colouring and in detailed backgrounds. Under British rule, most Indian art declined to mere craftsmanship until the early 20th century. Major modern painters include Abindranath Tagore, Jamini Roy, Amrita Shir Gil and Francis Souza.

Indian corn. *See* MAIZE.

Indian mutiny (1857–58), also called the Sepoy mutiny, uprising begun by the Indian troops (sepoys) in the Bengal army in India. The revolt occurred when Governor-General Canning continued policies that disregarded the traditions of Hindus and Muslims. The army had cartridges (lubricated with the fat of cows and pigs) which had to be bit open before use, and the outraged sepoys rebelled against their introduction. They gained a stronghold by taking Delhi, and the Mogul Emperor Bahadur Shah II reluctantly took their side. The revolt was eventually suppressed with the aid of Sir Hugh Rose and Sir Colin Campbell.

Indian National Congress, Indian political party, organized in 1885 with British approval; it later became a force for Indian independence. After the Amritsar Massacre in 1919 Mohandas GANDHI became leader of the party and it grew from an elitist group into a mass movement. Non-violent civil disobedience organized by the party brought about the Government of India Act in 1935, which gave India a new constitution. The party agreed to aid the British in WWII, receiving in return the promise of independence for India.

Indian Ocean, world's third largest ocean, bounded by Asia (N), Antarctica (S), Africa (W) and South-East Asia and Australia (E). Branches of the ocean include the Arabian Sea, Bay of Bengal and the Andaman Sea, and its largest islands are Madagascar and Sri Lanka. The average depth is 3,962m (13,000ft) although there is a Mid-Oceanic Ridge or submarine mountain range, extending from Asia to Antarctica; several of its peaks emerge as islands. The ridge encloses a number of deep-sea basins or abyssal plains, the deepest of which is the Java Trench, s of Java, reaching 7,725m (25,344ft). Surface temperatures of the ocean do not reach the extremes experienced in the Atlantic or Pacific oceans, partly because of its landlocked nature. The climate of the nearby land masses is strongly influenced, however, by the ocean's winds and currents. There are three wind belts: the monsoons which pick up moisture from the ocean, bringing heavy rainfall to w India and South-East Asia; the SE trade winds; and the prevailing westerly winds, bringing tropical storms. The currents are governed by these winds, the seasonal shift of the monsoon dictating the flow of water N of the equator. The other circulation system is the regular south equatorial current. The Indian Ocean was the first to be extensively navigated, crossed by Vasco da GAMA on his first voyage from Europe to India in 1479. Area: 73,427,868sq km (28,350,500sq miles). *See also* PE pp.*43, 50–51, 88.*

Indians, American. *See* AMERICAN INDIANS.

India Office, British department of state, responsible for the administration of India until 1947, when India and Pakistan became independent. It came into being in 1858, when it replaced the board of control, which had shared the government of India with the EAST INDIA COMPANY. Its splendid library is now in the keeping of the FOREIGN AND COMMONWEALTH OFFICE.

Indicator, in chemistry, substance applied in minute quantities which, by a change of colour, fluorescence, or by precipitate formation, indicates acidity (usually red) or alkalinity (usually blue). Indicators can detect end-points in reactions involving a change of PH or an OXIDATION-REDUCTION reaction. A universal indicator is a liquid that undergoes a spectral range of colour changes from pH 1 to 13. *See also* SU pp.150–151.

Indictment, written accusation presented to a court in a criminal prosecution, except when the defendant (the accused) is to be tried summarily before a magistrate. The indictment states the offence alleged, the statute (if any) which makes it an offence and other matters to assist the accused in knowing the charge which he has to answer.

Indigestion. *See* DYSPEPSIA.

Indigo (indigotin), violet-blue dye traditionally obtained from plants of the genus *Indigofera*. It has been manufactured synthetically since the late 1890s, and has the chemical formula $C_{16}H_{10}O_2N_2$.

Indigotin. *See* INDIGO.

Indium, metallic element (In) of group IIIA of the periodic table. Its chief source is as a by-product from zinc ores. The element is used in certain low-melting point alloys and in semiconductors. Properties: at.no. 49; at.wt. 114.82; s.g. 7.31; m.p. 156.61°C (313.9°F); b.p. 2,080°C (3,776°F); most common isotope In^{115} (95.72%).

Indo-Aryan languages, sub-group of the INDO-EUROPEAN LANGUAGES comprising the languages of India, Pakistan and some of Nepal. With SANSKRIT as their oldest ancestor, they date from about AD 1100. Geographically, the most important group is the central Indian Hindi group, divided into eastern and western dialects. Western Hindi has the largest number of speakers in the Indian subcontinent and is the source of its two national languages, Hindi and Urdu. Hindi is based on the dialect of the Delhi region and is written in the Sanskrit alphabet. Urdu, which absorbed much more Persian and Arabic during the Mogul period and is written in a form of Perso-Arabic script, became the official language of the Muslims in N India in the 18th century and is now that of Pakistan. The other groups are the eastern group, of which the most important is Bengali; the central group of Rajasthani and Gujarati; the western group, most importantly Punjabi; the southern group, including Sinhalese (of Sri Lanka) and Marathi; and Pahari, the "mountain languages" of the north.

Indo-China, SE peninsula of Asia, including Burma, Thailand, Cambodia, Vietnam, West Malaysia and Laos. The name refers to the former federation of states of Vietnam, Laos and Cambodia, associated with France within the French Union (1945–54). European penetration of the area began in the 16th century. By the 19th century France controlled Cochin China, Cambodia, Annam and Tonkin, which formed the union of Indo-China in 1887; Laos was added in 1893. By the end of WWII France had announced plans for a federation within the French Union, allowing more self-government for the states. Cambodia and Laos accepted the federation, but fighting broke out between French troops and Annamese nationalists, who wanted independence for Annam, Tonkin and Cochin China as Vietnam. The war ended with French defeat at DIEN-BIEN-PHU. French control of Indo-China was officially ended by the Geneva Conference of 1954.

Indoctrination, systematic training intended to implant certain attitudes, beliefs or behaviour in others. It especially applies to political opinion and involves strict control of information given in the media and in education. Although most societies practise subtle forms of conditioning, some such as the USSR and China, use indoctrination for political purposes.

Indo-European languages, world's largest language family, extending over all of Europe, the Western Hemisphere and SW and S Asia. It includes the GERMANIC, Italic, CELTIC, Baltic, Slavonic and Indo-Aryan subgroups, and embraces such disparate languages as English, Spanish, Russian, Greek, Icelandic, Welsh, Albanian, Lithuanian, Armenian, Persian, Sanskrit and Hindi. About half the world's population speaks one or another Indo-European language. *See also* MS pp.240–241.

Indonesia, largest nation in South-East Asia, consisting of more than 3,000 islands and extending 5,150km (3,200 miles) between the Indian and Pacific oceans. Most of the population is engaged in subsistence and cash-crop farming, but other exports now include tin, oil and timber. The capital is Djakarta. Area: 1,919,400sq km (714,080sq miles). Pop. (1977 est.) 138,133,500. *See* MW p.99.

Indore, city in Madhya Pradesh state, W central India, on the Saraswati and Khan rivers, 545km (340 miles) NE of Bombay. It became important in the 18th century as the capital of the Maharajas of Indore. It is now a commercial centre whose industries include iron, steel and chemicals. Pop. (1971) 543,381.

Indra, in Vedic mythology, ruler of heaven, great god of storms, thunder and lightning, worshipped as rain-maker and bringer of fertility to the fields. In the creation myth he slew Vritra, dragon of drought, to produce the sun and water on the earth.

Indri, largest of the LEMURS, an animal that lives in mountain forests of Madagascar but is now extremely rare. It is about 70cm (2.3ft) long and has a blackish-brown body and a rudimentary tail. Family Indriidae; species *Indri indri.* *See also* NW p.*243.*

Inductance, property of an electric circuit which causes a voltage to be induced in it by a change in the current flowing through it (self-inductance) or through a nearby circuit (mutual inductance). *See also* ELECTROMAGNETIC INDUCTION; SU pp.122–123.

Induction, in medicine, the bringing on of LABOUR in childbirth by artificial means. *See also* MS p.79.

Induction, in physics, process by which an ELECTROMOTIVE FORCE (emf) is created in a circuit when the magnetic FLUX through it changes. The direction of the induced current is such that its magnetic field tends to keep constant the number of lines linked with the circuit; and the magnitude of the current is proportional to the rate of change of flux (FARADAY'S LAW of induction). In a transformer the changing magnetic field created by the alternating current in the primary coil induces a current in the secondary coil. A generator consists of a constant magnetic field, created by a permanent magnet or a current-carrying coil (an electromagnet), within which a conducting coil (an armature) is rotated.

Inductive logic, method of reasoning by which a general proposition is supported through consideration of particular cases

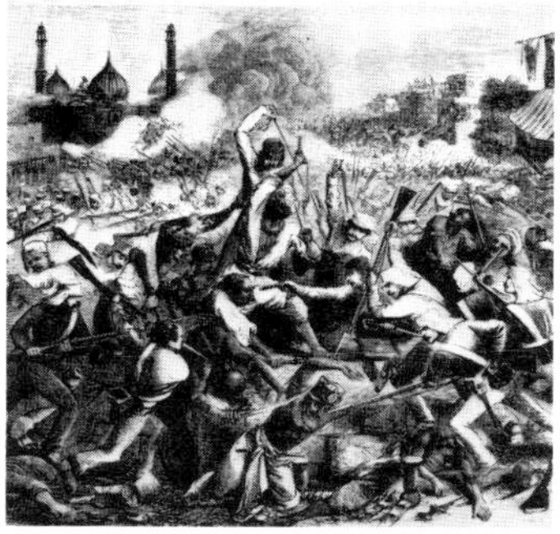

Indian mutiny; this engraving is entitled *Remember the ladies – remember the babies.*

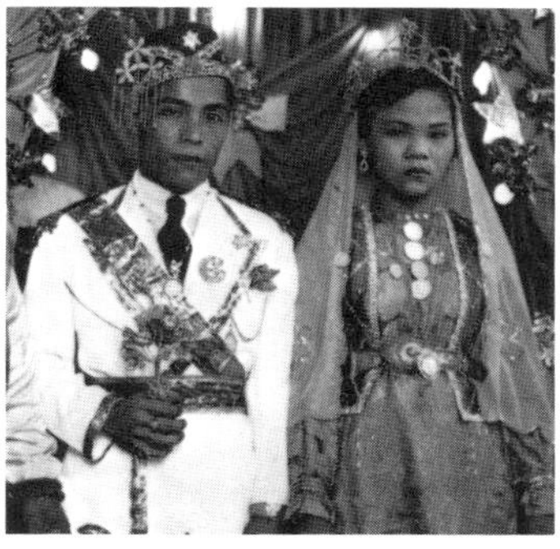

Indonesia; at a Malay-style wedding the couple stand in front of their relatives.

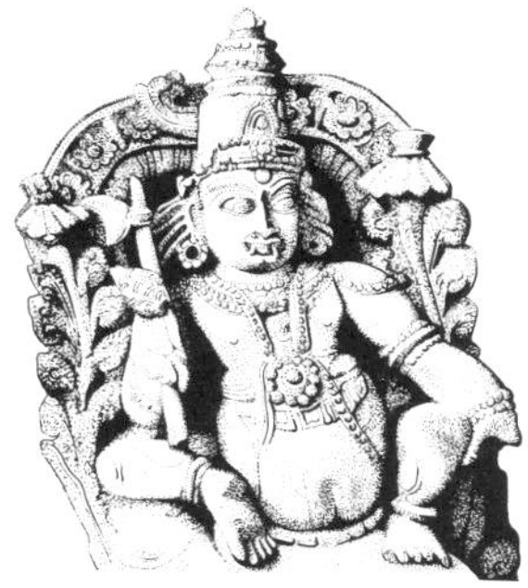

Indra, the chief of the Vedic gods was often depicted riding on a white elephant.

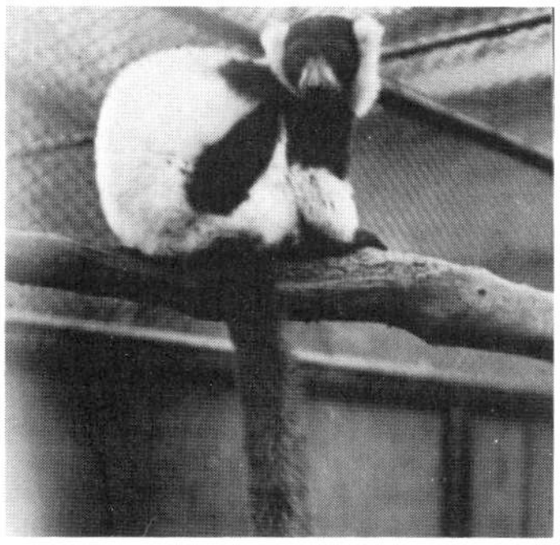

Indri; these tree dwelling lemurs are rare due to the destruction of their forest habitat.

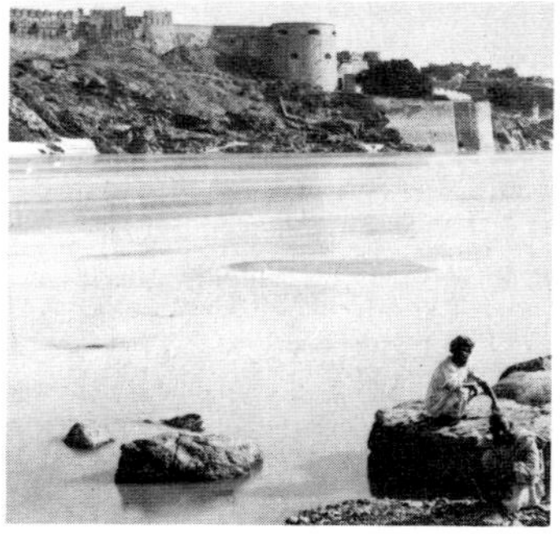

Indus, one of the major rivers of the Indian continent, flows past the fort at Attock.

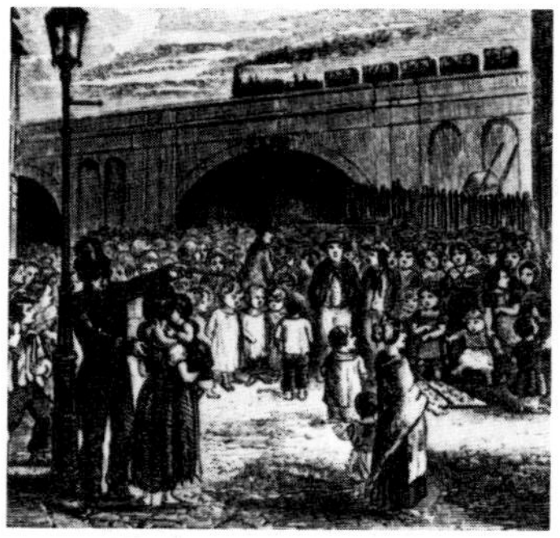

Industrial Revolution produced many tragic scenes such as this market for hiring children.

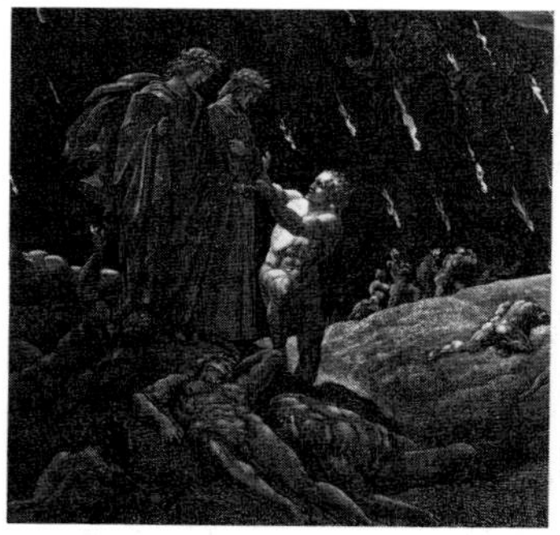

Inferno; Dante meets his former master in the 3rd compartment of the 7th circle of Hell.

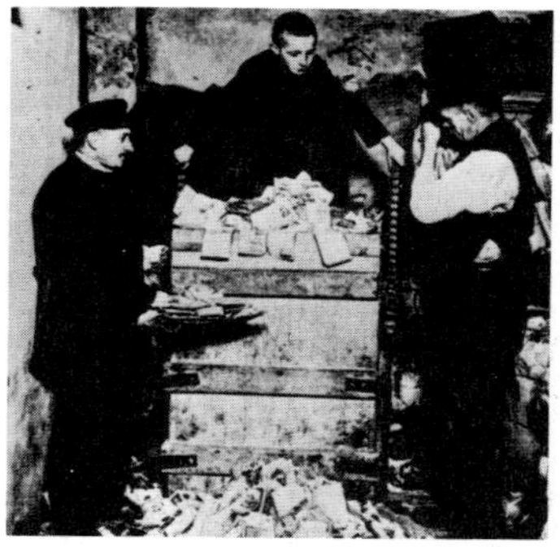

Inflation so devalued currency in Germany that banknotes were sold as waste paper.

that fall under it; often contrasted to DEDUCTIVE LOGIC.

Inductor, device that introduces inductance into an electric circuit. A typical inductor is a torus (doughnut-shaped ring of metallic or ceramic material, around which is wound a coil carrying an electric current). *See also* SU pp.126–127.

Indulgences, in Roman Catholic theology, remission by the Church of temporal punishment for sin. An indulgence, once granted, obviates the need for the sinner to do penance, although it does not necessarily remove guilt, and may itself be only a partial rather than a full (plenary) indulgence. Previously available from bishops, indulgences are today granted only by the pope. Abuses connected with the sale of indulgences in the later Middle Ages were among the principal causes of the REFORMATION. Restrictions were introduced in 1567, and further reforms by Pope PAUL VI in 1967.

Indus, river of India and Pakistan rising in the Kailas mountain range and flowing WNW through the Jammu and Kashmir regions of India, then SW through Pakistan and into the Arabian Sea. Semi-navigable along its shallow lower part, the river is used chiefly for irrigation and hydroelectric power. Length: approx. 3,060km (1,900 miles).

Industrial chemistry, study of the chemical reactions and processes involved in the large-scale manufacture of chemicals in industry. While the engineering aspects of the subject belong to the study of CHEMICAL ENGINEERING, the industrial chemist is concerned with the chemical problems associated with the transfer of small-scale laboratory reactions to industrial plant. *See also* MM pp.238–239.

Industrial psychology, study of the response of industrial workers to the conditions of their environment at work. It examines the effects of factors such as noise and close supervision and seeks to devise strategies to obviate all barriers to increased productivity. An experiment tried in the Volvo car factory in Sweden, in which the assembly line method was disposed of, resulted in reduced absenteeism and improved industrial relations.

Industrial relations, interaction of management and workers within an industrial concern, on questions of wages, conditions of work, and so on. In many firms the workers are represented by trades unions in their dealings with the management. Industrial relations in Britain are only slightly regulated by law; the 1971 Industrial Relations Act, which limited the right to strike, was repealed in 1974. An independent Advisory, Conciliation and Arbitration Service (ACAS) was set up in 1975 to help to settle industrial disputes. *See also* MS pp.300–301.

Industrial Revolution, term applied to the profound economic changes that took place in Britain, Western Europe and the USA from the mid-18th century to WWI. It describes the process by which economies and societies were transformed from being predominantly agricultural to being predominantly industrial. The conditions needed for an industrial revolution include adequate supplies of labour, raw materials and fuel; an efficient transport system; sufficient capital to finance mills and factories; and markets for the sale of goods. All these conditions were met in 18th-century England and were accompanied by several technological innovations. It was the first nation to undergo such a transformation and is generally considered the classic example. Britain's population rose by about one sixth in the first half of the 18th century, there were large deposits of coal and iron ore and an expanding empire provided raw materials (eg cotton from the American colonies) and markets. Textile-making first experienced the impact of change. The flying shuttle was patented in 1733, and the power loom in 1785. Large factories were built to house the machinery and employed hundreds of workers. The use of coal to produce pig iron paved the way for the manufacture of heavy machinery, and the revolution in metallurgy resulted in the development by the 1850s of the BESSEMER PROCESS for making steel. The steam engine provided power for industry and revolutionized transport on land and sea. Along with the great wealth produced, the Industrial Revolution brought social upheaval. The mechanization of agriculture and the enclosure of arable land threw thousands out of work. People flocked to the burgeoning cities, where mills and factories offered work. Living and working conditions were abominable, and wages were so low that children worked to supplement the family income. In the USA the NE became industrialized soon after Britain. But the South remained largely agricultural until after the Civil War, and concerted industrialization did not occur until well into the 20th century. *See also* HC2 pp.66–67; 88–89; MM pp.22–23.

Industrial Workers of the World (IWW) organization founded in Chicago in 1905, which united trade unions and the political left. The organization became unpopular for its disapproval of US policy during WWI; it further alienated itself from the trade unions and political left by developing ideological differences. Eventually in the 1920s it lapsed into insignificance, although at its height it had had branches in Britain, Australia, New Zealand, Canada, South Africa and Norway.

Indus Valley civilization (*c.*2500–1700 BC), ancient civilization of the valley of the River Indus in present-day Pakistan. It was re-discovered by the British archaeologist John MARSHALL in 1921, and is the earliest known urban culture of the Indian subcontinent. Three major cities – Mohenjo-daro, Harappa and Chanhu-daro – have been extensively excavated. It is believed that these cities were overrun by Aryan invaders.

Inert gases. *See* NOBLE GASES.

Inertia, property possessed by all matter, that enables a body to resist changes to its state of motion. NEWTON's first law of motion is sometimes called the law of inertia. The constant of proportionality referred to in Newton's second law is chosen so that the mass of a body equals the numerical value of its inertia. *See also* SU p.74.

Inertial guidance, in aeronautics, system using components that respond to changes in INERTIA to control missiles or spacecraft whose orbits are largely above the Earth's atmosphere. The main components include GYROSCOPES for reference and for detecting changes in orientation, motors or jets for correcting differences between planned and actual flight paths, and ACCELEROMETERS for determining velocity and position. The system can be supplemented by radar observations and control to correct gyro drift. *See also* NAVIGATION.

Infallibility, in Roman Catholic theology, the inability of the POPE to err while officially defining a doctrine regarding faith or morals to be held by the Church. Considered the supreme apostolic authority by Roman Catholics, the pope defines the dogma, previously affirmed by the CURIA, from his throne of state (*ex cathedra*). Papal infallibility itself was defined by the first VATICAN COUNCIL in 1870.

Infanta and infante, titles given to princesses and princes of Spain and Portugal other than the heir apparent to the throne, who throughout the Spanish monarchy was known as the Prince of the Asturias.

Infanticide, killing infants at birth or soon after birth. The custom has been practised by many societies. Reasons vary greatly, and include inadequate food supplies, an abhorrence of weak, deformed or female babies, and CANNIBALISM. Methods used include exposure and suffocation.

Infantile paralysis. *See* POLIO.

Infantry, foot soldiers carrying portable firearms and equipment. Modern infantry forces are organized into platoons, companies and battalions, and are equipped with rifles, machine guns, mortars, grenades, rocket-launchers and other lightweight weapons, as well as supplies for several days of operations. Using voice and hand commands, radios and flares, these units manoeuvre on the battlefield and co-operate with supporting forces. In defence, infantry units rely on earthworks to strengthen their combat power. *See also* MM pp.161–165.

Infarction, death of part of an organ caused by a sudden obstruction in an artery supplying it. This blockage can lead to the formation of a wedge-shaped mass in the organ. The condition can develop from an EMBOLISM and can be serious, as with a myocardial infarction (a HEART ATTACK), in which a section of heart muscle dies.

Infection, invasion of the body by micro-organisms that multiply in the tissues and cause damage to cells or the disease state caused by the invasion. *See also* MS p.126.

Inference, conclusion implicit, but not explicit, from given information. There are two types: conclusions drawn from a single premise and those drawn from two or more independent premises. Logic as a study is concerned with forms of inference.

Inferiority complex, personality pattern marked by feelings of unworthiness and insecurity. The term was coined by Alfred ADLER, who believed that the condition arose from unsuccessful attempts to compensate for childhood feelings of insignificance. A person with an inferiority complex may set extremely high standards for himself, make unrealistic comparisons with others and adopt either sycophantic or aggressive attitudes.

Inferno, first major division, consisting of 34 cantos, of Dante's *The Divine Comedy*. In it Dante relates his journey through hell accompanied by VIRGIL. At the centre is Lucifer, chewing the souls of the Roman traitors Brutus and Cassius, and of Christ's betrayer, Judas.

Infertility, inability to reproduce because FERTILIZATION does not take place, caused in human beings by a variety of medical or psychological factors. Approximately half of the cases of infertility are caused by inadequate sperm production. It can also result from lack of ovulation, an obstruction which prevents sperm reaching the ovum, hormone imbalances or undeveloped sex organs. *See also* MS p.75.

Infinity, without limit or end. Mathematically infinity can be represented in a number of ways. In geometry it is where parallel lines meet. In algebra, where y is any bounded function, then y/x approaches infinity as x approaches zero. In set theory, the set of all integers is only one example of an infinite set. *See also* SU pp.30–31.

Inflammation, reaction of body tissue to infection or injury, with resulting pain, heat, swelling and redness due to the stretching and swelling of small blood vessels and the migration of white blood cells into the affected area.

Inflation, in economics, continual upward movement of prices. Although normally associated with periods of prosperity, inflation may also occur during recessions. It usually occurs when there is relatively full employment. Under cost-push inflation, prices rise because the producers' costs increase. Under demand-pull inflation, prices increase because of excessive consumer demand for goods. Many economists believe that money supply is a major factor in determining the rate of inflation. They contend that the rate of increase of the money supply ultimately controls the consumers' ability to demand goods.

Inflection, in linguistics, a change in word-form which distinguishes tense, person, number, gender, voice or case. In English, this is usually achieved by adding different endings to the word stem ("house, houses"; "jump, jumped"). Another type sees the word stem change ("bring, brought"). Even closely related languages may differ widely in inflection and, depending on the language, some systems are simpler than others.

Inflorescences, FLOWER or flower cluster. Inflorescence are classified according to branching characteristics. A racemose inflorescence has a main axis and lateral flowering branches, with flowers opening from the bottom up or from the outer edge in; types include panicle, raceme, spike

and umbel. A cymose inflorescence has a composite axis with the main stem ending in a flower and lateral branches bearing additional, later-flowering branches.
Influenza, highly infectious virus disease whose symptoms resemble those of the common cold, with fever and general debility. It is treated by bed rest; vaccines are available to confer immunity to some strains.
Information theory, mathematical study of the laws governing communication channels. It is primarily concerned with the measurement of information and the methods of coding, transmitting, storing and processing this information. Some of its concepts have been used in psychology to elucidate the processes involved in sensory perception and memory.
Infra-red astronomy. *See* ASTRONOMY.
Infra-red rays, the part of the electromagnetic spectrum that lies between the red end of the visible spectrum and microwaves. Often called heat radiation, they were first discovered by Sir William Herschel in 1800. Their applications include heat lamps (which radiate infra-red rays), widely used in medicine, and infra-red photography. *See also* PE p.155; SU pp.99, 109.
Infra-red wave, electromagnetic wave that produces a sensation of heat, emitted by hot objects. It is intermediate in energy between light and microwaves. Wavelength range: about 750 nanometers (10^{-9}m) to about 1mm. *See also* ELECTROMAGNETIC SPECTRUM; SU p.*99*.
Infrasound, also called infrasonics, sound waves having a frequency of 15 hertz (cycles per second) or less. This range is also known as the subsonic range, because such low frequency waves are felt as vibrations rather than heard as sounds. *See also* ULTRASONICS.
Ingarden, Roman (1893–), Polish phenomenologist. Studying under Edmund HUSSERL, he came to reject the latter's transcendental idealism, seeing in PHENOMENOLOGY a method leading to realism. His main work is *The Controversy Over the Existence of the World* (2 vols, 1947–48).
Inge, William Ralph (1860–1954), British churchman and writer. He was professor of divinity at Cambridge University (1907–11) and Dean of St Paul's (1911–34). His books include *Christian Mysticism* (1899), *Lay Thoughts of a Dean* (1926) and *Our Present Discontents* (1938).
Inge, William Ralph (1913–73), US playwright, whose first Broadway play, *Come Back, Little Sheba* (1950), examines the relationship between an alcoholic and his wife. *Picnic* (1953) won him a Pulitzer Prize, and he also wrote *Bus Stop* (1955), *The Dark at the Top of the Stairs* (1957), *A Loss of Roses* (1960) and two later plays, *Natural Affection* (1963) and *Where's Daddy?* (1966).
Inge, William Ralph (1860–1954), British churchman and writer. He was professor of divinity at Cambridge (1907–11) and Dean of St Paul's (1911–34). His books include *Christian Mysticism* (1899), *Lay Thoughts of a Dean* (1926) and *Our Present Discontents* (1938).
Ingemann, Bernhard Severin (1789–1862), Danish writer, strongly influenced by Sir Walter SCOTT and the German Romantics. His novels such as *Kong Erik* (1833) and *Prins Otto af Danmark* (1835) glorified Danish medieval greatness. His hymn, *Through the Night of Doubt and Sorrow*, has become popular in English.
Ingénue, in drama, the innocent and naive young heroine of a play. Typical ingénues include Celia in JONSON's *Volpone* and Gwendolen Fairfax in WILDE's *The Importance of Being Earnest.*
Ingersoll, Robert Hawley (1859–1928), US industrialist. He pioneered the application of mass-production techniques to the manufacture of watches and produced a one-dollar watch in 1893.
Ingleborough Hill, one of the major landmarks in the Yorkshire Dales, set in peaty moorland. There are the remains of a hill fort and an Iron Age settlement on this immense natural terrace of water-eroded limestone. Height: 723m (2,373ft).
Ingoldsby, Thomas. *See* BARHAM, RICHARD HARRIS.
Ingres, Jean Auguste Dominique (1780–1867), French painter who painted in the Classical style with emphasis on the careful drawing of figures. He was best known for his portraits, including *Madame d'Haussonville* (1845), and his sensual bathing pictures, such as *Bather of Calpincon* (1808). He also executed large wall paintings. *See also* HC2 p.43, *43*.
Inhibitor, compound that stops or substantially reduces the rate of a chemical reaction. Inhibitors are as specific in their action as CATALYSTS and are widely used to prevent CORROSION, OXIDATION or POLYMERIZATION.
Injection, in medicine, introduction of a fluid (liquid or gas) into body tissues through a needle or CATHETER to treat, diagnose or prevent disease. Injections are either intravenous (into a vein), intramuscular (into a muscle), or intrathecal (into the spinal cord). Injection is an immediate method of introducing medicines into the blood or an organ.
Injunction, in English law, civil WRIT issued by any division of the High Courts enjoining a specified party to refrain from a specified action. Before 1873 the writs were issued only out of CHANCERY. Injunctions are of two kinds, interlocutory (until the hearing of a case) and perpetual (permanent).
Ink, coloured liquid or viscous mixture used for writing, drawing or PRINTING. It may be coloured by a suspended pigment or a soluble dye. Soluble dyes, often based on ANILINE, are used in inks for BALLPOINT PENS. Printing inks usually contain finely divided carbon black suspended in a drying oil, often with added synthetic RESINS. Some inks dry by evaporation of a volatile solvent rather than by hardening of a drying oil. *See also* MS pp.*242*, 246.
Ink cap, any of 100 species of FUNGI found throughout the world, particularly on wood, dung and in grassy areas. After the discharge of the spores, the gills beneath the cap exude a black liquid and the cap deteriorates rapidly. When young, the caps of a few species are edible. Order Agaricales; genus *Coprinus*. *See also* NW p.*43*.
Inkerman, Battle of (5 Nov. 1854), attack in the CRIMEAN WAR by Russian forces against British and French troops who were besieging the naval base at Sevastopol. The Anglo-French troops resisted the attack, forcing the Russians to retreat in disorder. Some 11,000 Russian and 4,000 Allied lives were lost.
Inland Revenue, The Board of, British government department that collects and administers revenue for government expenditure. It was established in 1849. Inland revenue, as defined by legislation, means the revenue of Britain imposed or collected and placed under the management of the Commissioners of Inland Revenue. The specific functions of the board are the collection of all taxes (including income tax, petroleum tax, stamp duty and capital gains tax), advice to the Chancellor of the Exchequer, the collection of rates in Wales, and the valuation in England of land and buildings for compulsory purchase.
Innate ideas, Platonic theory revived by the Rationalists that certain "ideas", such as number and identity, are present in the mind at birth rather than being produced by subsequent experience. *See also* RATIONALISM.
Inner Hebrides. *See* HEBRIDES.
Inner Mongolia. *See* MONGOLIA.
Innes, James Dickson (1887–1914), Welsh landscape painter who worked mainly in Wales and the Pyrenees. He studied in London at the Slade School and became a member of the New English Club. His small landscapes in oil or watercolour were highly regarded and influenced his younger contemporaries.
Innes, Michael (1906–), pseudonym of J. I. M. Stewart, Scottish novelist noted for his detective stories, featuring John Appleby, a gentleman policeman. The novels are erudite and witty, and include *Seven Suspects* (1936), *A Comedy of Terrors* (1940) and *Open House* (1972).
Innocent, the name of 13 popes. Innocent I (*r.*401–17) developed the role of the papacy and excommunicated PELAGIUS in 417. Innocent II, (*r.*1130–43) helped to draft the Concordat of Worms in 1122 and was at the centre of the GREAT SCHISM. Innocent III (*b.c.*1160, *r.*1198–1216) brought the medieval papacy to its height of power. He presided over the Fourth CRUSADE and the ALBIGENSIAN crusade and convoked the fourth LATERAN COUNCIL (1216). Innocent V, (*b.c.*1224, *r.*1276), was the first Dominican pope. Innocent VI (*r.* 1352–62) waged war to regain the papal states. Innocent VIII (*b.*1432, *r.*1484–92) was involved in political disputes and was allegedly elected by bribery. Innocent XI, (*b.*1611, *r.*1676–89) was a pope of high integrity and a sympathizer with JANSENISM. Innocent XII (*b.*1615, *r.*1691–1700) renewed diplomatic relations with France. *See also* HC1 pp.176, 177, 186, 187.
Innocents' Day, also known as Childermas, feast day that commemorates the legendary slaughter, by HEROD THE GREAT, of a large number of baby boys after the visit of the three kings to the infant Jesus Christ. It is celebrated on 28 Dec.
Innsbruck, city in W Austria, on the River Inn 135km (84 miles) SW of Salzburg. Originally a transalpine trading town, it has become a commercial and industrial centre and resort. Its industries include manufacturing, metalworking and food processing. Pop. (1971) 115,200.
Inns of Court, four legal societies in London (Lincoln's Inn, Inner Temple, Middle Temple, Gray's Inn), dating from the 13th century, that have the exclusive right to admit persons to practise as barristers in England. The three grades of membership are benchers (senior members), barristers and students.
Inoculation, introduction of substances, often micro-organisms, into body tissues or laboratory-grown bacteria for therapeutic or experimental purposes. *See also* IMMUNIZATION.
Inönü, Ismet (1884–1973), Turkish military and political leader who became Mustafa Kemal ATATÜRK's Prime Minister (1923–24, 1925–37) and succeeded him as President of Turkey (1938–50). His party lost the first free general election, but after a military coup and a new constitution he became Premier (1961–65).
Inorganic chemistry. *See* CHEMISTRY INORGANIC.
Inquest, inquiry into the manner of death of a person who has been killed, died in prison, died unexpectedly or under suspicious circumstances. In England an inquest is held before a jury of between seven and eleven jurors and is presided over by a coroner, who may in certain cases dispense with the jury.
Inquisition, court set up by the Roman Catholic Church in the Middle Ages to seek out and punish heresy. The inquisitor was authorized by the pope to take testimony, question witnesses and those accused of heresy, and pass judgment. The accused were sometimes questioned under torture. Punishments for the guilty ranged from penances and fines to banishment, imprisonment, and death by fire. Kings and nobles supported what amounted to organized persecution of Jews, Protestants and others considered enemies of Church and state, including those charged with witchcraft. The medieval Inquisition was active in much of Europe from the 12th to the 15th century. A later tribunal, the SPANISH INQUISITION, was instituted in 1483 at the request of the rulers of Spain and was not finally and formally abolished until 1834. *See also* HOLY OFFICE.
Insanity, also called madness or imprecise term for several forms of mental illness. The condition has many manifestations, and is known by various other names which change from culture to culture and from age to age with the fashions in labelling. To psychiatrists there are three types of insanity: psychoses, which include schiziphrenia, manic depression, paronoia and functional psychoses; neuroses, including states of extreme anxiety or phobia, overt obsessional or

THS SNTNC LLSTRTS N NTRSTG ND VTL FTR F NFRMTN T!

Information theory studies choice, and the redundancy of language in printed English.

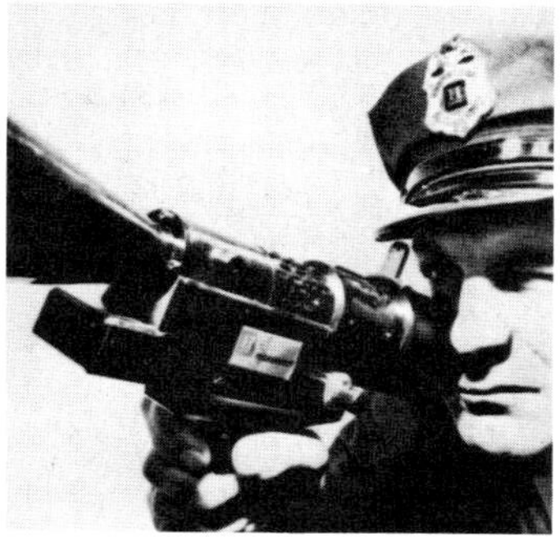

Infra-red rays are used to transmit messages in total security between these devices.

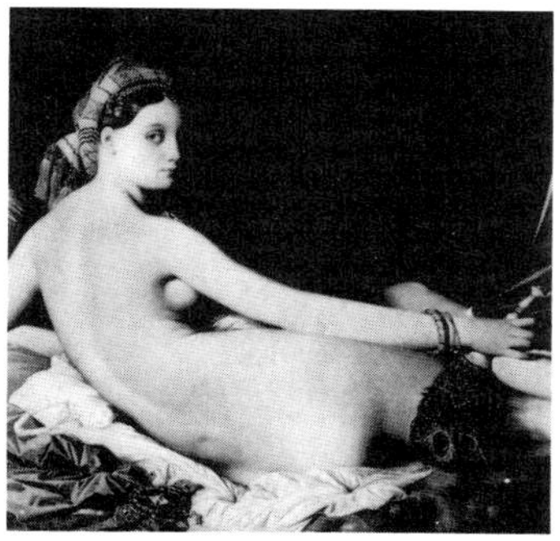

Jean Ingres' nude *Odalisque Couchee*, which hangs in the Louvre Museum, Paris (detail).

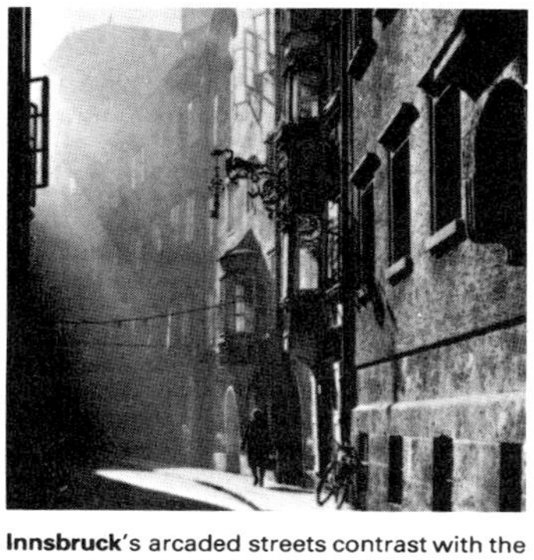

Innsbruck's arcaded streets contrast with the many more modern spacious buildings.

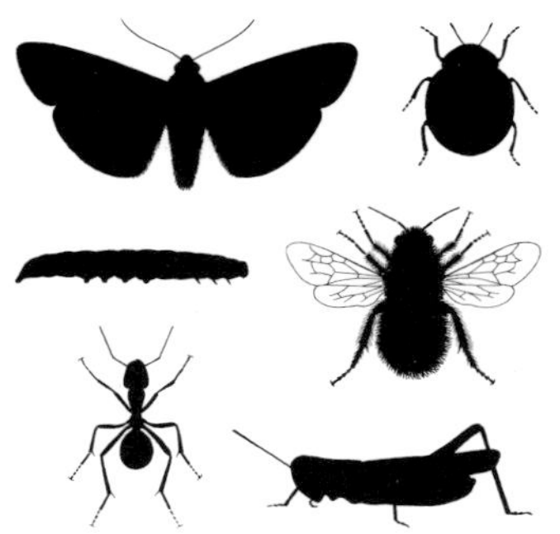

Insects of some species have existed in the same form for over 200,000 million years.

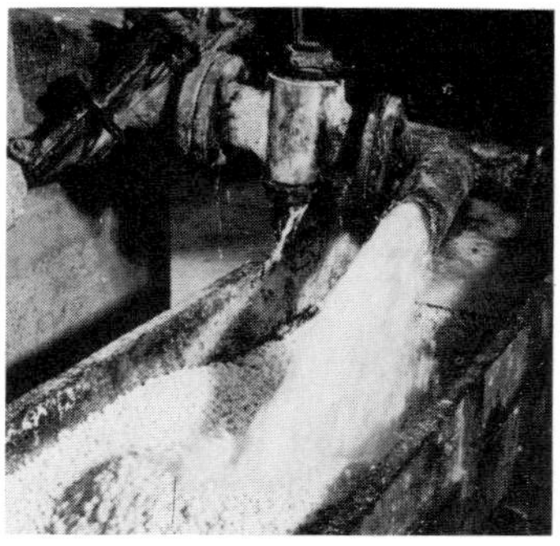

Insecticides can be in liquid or powder form such as DDT, here shown being made.

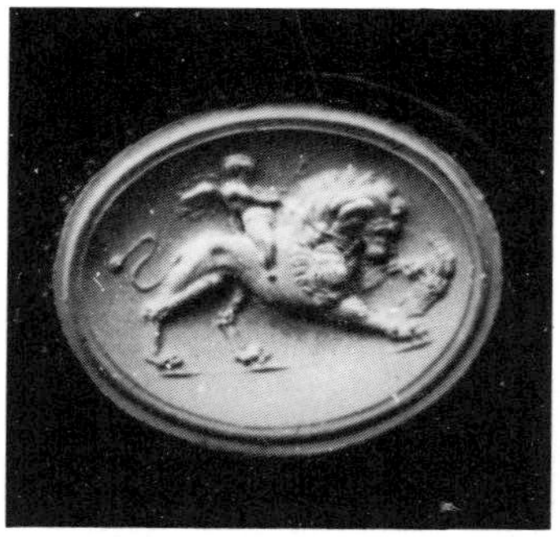

Intaglio carving differs from cameo in that the image is hollowed out below the surface.

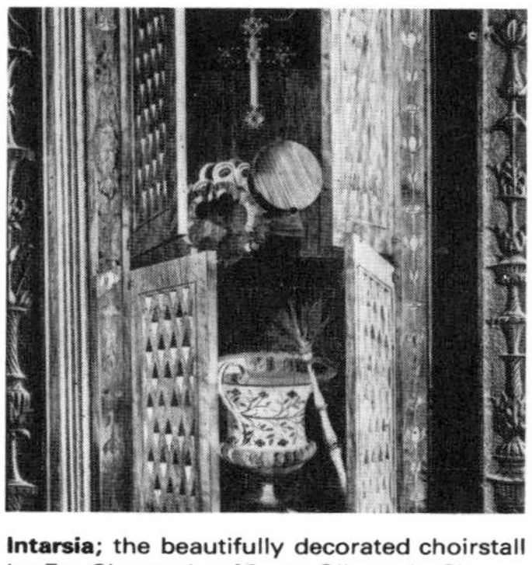

Intarsia; the beautifully decorated choirstall by Fra Giovanni at Monte Oliveto in Siena.

compulsive states and the hysterical or depressive neuroses; and personality disorders, such as the behavioural disorders of childhood, alcoholism and drug addition. *See also* MS p.135.

Insect, any of more than a million known species of small, invertebrate animals, including BEETLES, BUGS, BUTTERFLIES, ANTS and BEES. There are more species of insects than all other animal and plant species combined. They are common in all parts of the world except for the oceans and polar regions. Adult insects have three pairs of jointed legs, usually two pairs of wings, and a segmented body with a horny outer covering or exoskeleton. The head has three pairs of mouthparts, a pair of compound eyes, three pairs of simple eyes and a pair of antennae.

Few insects have true hearing organs or "ears". Most of them can detect a wide range of sounds through ultra-sensitive hairs on various parts of their bodies. Similarly insects do not have voices, but some can "sing" or make sounds by rubbing together parts of their bodies.

Most insects are plant-eaters, many being serious farm and garden pests. Some prey on small animals, especially other insects, and a few are scavengers. There are two main kinds of mouthparts – chewing and sucking. Each order of insects has a variation of one or other of these kinds, or a combination of both. Beetles, for example, chew, butterflies suck, and bugs and bees combine both processes.

Reproduction is usually sexual. Most insects go through four distinct life stages, in which complete METAMORPHOSIS is said to take place. The four stages are egg, larva (caterpillar or grub), pupa and adult (butterflies and beetles). Young grasshoppers and some other insects, called NYMPHS, resemble wingless miniatures of their parents. The nymphs develop during a series of moults (incomplete metamowphosis) and become adults with functional wings at the last moult. SILVERFISH and a few other primitive, wingless insects do not undergo metamorphosis. The newly hatched silverfish is a tiny, sexually immature replica of the adult. Phylum Arthropoda, class Insecta. *See also* ARTHROPOD; NW pp.106–117.

Insecticides, substances used to destroy or control insect pests. They may be stomach poisons, such as lead arsenate and sodium fluoride; contact poisons, such as DDT and ORGANOPHOSPHATES: or systematic poisons, such as octamethylpyrophosphoramide, which are toxic to insects that eat plants into which they have been absorbed. Organophosphates are preferred to chlorinated hydrocarbons (such as DDT) because they eventually break down into non-toxic substances and cause less ecological damage.

Insectivore, small order of carnivorous MAMMALS (Insectivora), many of which eat insects. Almost worldwide in distribution, although none are known in South America, some species live underground, some on the ground and some in streams and ponds. Most insectivores have narrow snouts, long skulls and five-clawed feet. Length: mostly smaller than 45cm (18in); weight: mostly less than 0.5kg (1lb). Three families are always placed in the order: Erinaceidae (moon rats, gymures, HEDGEHOGS); Talpidae (MOLES, shrew moles, DESMANS); and Soricidae (SHREWS). But six other families – including TREE SHREWS, TENRECS and SOLENODONS – are also often included in the order. *See* NW pp.160–161.

Insectivorous plant, also called carnivorous plant, any of several plants that have poorly developed root systems and are often found in nitrogen-deficient sandy or boggy soils. They obtain the missing nutrients by trapping, "digesting" and absorbing insects. Some, such as the Venus's fly-trap (*Dionaea muscipula*), are active insect trappers; when triggered, its hinged leaves close on its prey. The sundews (*Drosera*) snare insects with a sticky substance and then enclose them in their leaves. Bladderworts (*Utricularia*) suck insects into their underwater bladders. Other plants have vase-shaped leaves, such as the pitcher plant (*Sarracenia flava*). *See also* NW pp.*45*, 59.

Inselberg, steep-sided, round-topped hill rising abruptly from a plain, found in semi-arid tropical and subtropical regions. Inselberge are probably formed by exfoliation erosion of old mountains.

Insemination, artificial, placing of SEMEN at the womb's mouth by artificial means, most often a syringe. First developed on animals for livestock breeding purposes, it now has three types of human use. In the first the man may be fertile but unable to complete intercourse. The placing of his semen into the vagina at a suitable time in the menstrual cycle may achieve a successful pregnancy. Secondly, the male's semen may be produced in insufficient quantity, in which case it is collected and frozen over a period of time until enough is obtained. In the third case the male is unable to produce healthy semen and that of another is used. The first two ways are known as AIH (artificial insemination by the husband) and the third as AID (artificial insemination by a donor).

Insomnia, continual difficulty in sleeping. It may be caused by worry, pain or stimulants such as drugs. *See also* MS pp.105, 144.

Instinct, behaviours that are unlearned and innately determined, as opposed to behaviours that are learned from experience. In the 19th century instincts were often cited to explain behaviour, but the term fell into disrepute with the advent of BEHAVIOURISM. The term has recently been revived in the work of such ethologists as Konrad LORENZ. The behaviour of many lower organisms, such as the courting behaviour of birds and aggressive patterns in fish, is instinctive. However, modern research indicates that behaviour previously thought to be instinctive in humans and the higher animals is a result of learning. Consequently it is very difficult to apply the term accurately to these animals. *See also* MS pp.185–187.

Institute of International Law, organization founded to promote progress in international law. It was formed in Belgium in 1873 and in 1904 was awarded the Nobel Peace Prize.

Insulation, material used to reduce heat loss, to confine electric currents within conductors, or to soundproof. Heat insulation may be accomplished by reflective materials (which reduce radiation), such as aluminium foil and coated steel, and bulky materials (which reduce conduction), such as fibre-glass wool, vegetable fibres, paper, foam plastic and firebrick. Some of these bulk materials are also used for sound insulation. Several types of material are used as electrical INSULATORS. Insulation varies according to the intensity of heat or sound, or the voltage to be isolated. *See also* SU pp.113, *113*, 114.

Insulator, in electricity, substance that provides a high resistance to an electric current. Insulators are used to prevent contact between CONDUCTORS in electrical circuits, the thickness of the insulation necessary depending on the voltage. Common insulators are RUBBER, polyvinyl chloride (PVC), MICA, TEFLON, GLASS, ASBESTOS, THERMOPLASTIC and PORCELAIN. *See also* SU pp.113–114.

Insulin, hormone secreted by the ISLETS OF LANGHERHANS in the pancreas and concerned in the maintenance of the blood-glucose level. Insulin has the effect of lowering the blood-glucose level and facilitating the uptake of glucose in the muscles. Sugar (glucose) unmetabolized because of lack of insulin accumulates in excess amounts in the blood and urine, resulting in DIABETES MELLITUS, in which protein and lipid metabolism is also affected. *See also* INSULINOMA; HYPERINSULINISM; MS pp.65, 100–101.

Insulinoma, tumour consisting of tissue from the ISLETS OF LANGERHANS in the pancreas, which can cause a low blood-sugar level. Such tumours may secrete excess insulin and develop into cancers, but are usually removed surgically before this stage.

Insurance, procedure whereby one party (the insured) transfers the financial consequences of risk of loss to another (the insurer) for a consideration (the premium). Insurance is practical because of the loss-sharing principle and the law of averages. Each insured contributes to a common fund, and the losses of the unfortunate few are reimbursed from the fund. Forms of insurance have existed since before Christ; modern practices date back to the 16th and 17th centuries. It covers such things as life, fire, accident and theft. *See also* HC2 p.18.

Insurance, National, system of social security in Britain. It developed from the 1911 National Insurance Act, passed at the instigation of Lloyd George, which provided insurance against sickness. It gradually expanded to include retirement pensions, widows' pensions and insurance against unemployment. It was a self-supporting system with a fund (established by contributions from employers, employees and the government) from which benefits were paid. Employers were responsible for the payment of employees' contributions, which were deducted from wages. In 1937 National Insurance was extended to enable anyone with an annual income of less than £400 to join. The present scheme was established in 1946, when the Ministry of Pensions and National Insurance was set up. In 1966 it became the Ministry of Social Security and is now the Department of Health and Social Security. It offers a comprehensive system of social security for all people over the age of 16 resident in Britain, including unemployment benefits, disablement benefits, maternity grants, sickness benefits, retirement pensions, child allowances and industrial injury grants.

Insurance policy, printed legal document stating the terms of an INSURANCE contract. It is issued to the policy holder by the insurer.

Intaglio, incised carving, the opposite of CAMEO, especially on gemstones, hardstones or glass. In printing, the term is used to describe a process in which ink is applied to incisions and hollows in a printing plate, as in ETCHING.

Intarsia, art of decorating furniture with inlay or MARQUETRY of wood, ivory, mother-of-pearl or tortoiseshell. Developed in Italy during the Renaissance, intarsia reached its peak during the 17th century.

Integer, negative, or positive whole number, eg the numbers ...-3, -2, -1, 0, 1, 2, 3, ..., of which there is a limitless (infinite) number. The positive integers are the natural numbers. The negative integers and zero allow any two numbers to be subtracted. The theory of numbers is concerned with the properties of integers. *See also* SU p.30.

Integral, mathematical function used in CALCULUS. The integral of a curve whose function is $f(x)$, where x is a variable, is the area enclosed between the curve and the x axis. It is written:

$$\int f(x)dx.$$

The symbol for an integral is an elongated "S", standing for "sum". Finding an integral (integration of the function) is equivalent to dividing the area into a number of small rectangles parallel to the y axis, and taking the limit of the sum of their area as the number increases (and each elementary rectangle becomes thinner). A definite integral is the area between given values of x; if these are unspecified the integral is indefinite. The derivative of the indefinite integral of a function gives the original function: thus integration is the inverse of differentiation. *See also* INTEGRAL CALCULUS; SU pp.42–43.

Integral calculus, in mathematics, the branch of calculus that deals with the finding of a function, one or more derivatives of which are given; it is the opposite of differential calculus. To take a simple example, the integral of x is $x^2/2 + c$, the first derivative (dy/dx) of that function being x. The constant c has to be added when integrating to allow for the fact that the derivative of any constant is zero. The applications of integral calculus are many. In mensuration it is used to find complex areas and volumes. In engineering calculations, differential equations are solved by integral calculus. Its principles are incorporated in many measuring and control instruments, eg in flow recorders, in which integrator mechanisms can totalize flows at any moment. *See also* SU p.42.

Integrated circuit (IC), complete electronic circuit incorporating semiconductor devices, such as TRANSISTORS as well as resistors, manufactured in one tiny unit. Hybrid integrated circuits have separate components attached to a ceramic base with interconnections by wire bonds or a conducting film. Monolithic integrated circuits have all the components manufactured into or on top of a single chip of silicon, interconnections between components being by conducting film. *See also* SU pp.128–*129*.

Integration. *See* INTEGRAL CALCULUS.

Intelligence, general ability to learn and to deal with problems, new situations and abstract concepts. It can be manifested in many different ways, eg adaptability, memory, reasoning. Psychologists operationally define intelligence as a score on a test that samples some of the important components of intelligence, especially those related to performance in school. *See also* INTELLIGENCE TEST.

Intelligence, military and political. *See* SECRET SERVICE.

Intelligence Quotient. *See* IQ.

Intelligence test, puzzle or task used to try to categorize degrees of INTELLIGENCE. In 1905 Alfred BINET devised the first successful test, the Binet-Simon scale, to help in identifying mentally deficient pupils in Parisian schools. Subsequent developments included the intelligence quotient (IQ), group tests first used to screen army recruits in WWI, and the Wechsler intelligence scales and Stanford-Binet scales. Modern tests are used for such purposes as predicting success in school, screening job applicants, identifying exceptional children and diagnosing the mentally disturbed. *See also* MS pp.142, *143, 153*.

Intendant, in history, agent of the French king in the provinces. Primarily tax collectors in the 16th century, their power was greatly increased by Louis XIV, who made them his representatives at the local level, dealing with administrative, judicial, financial and police matters. The office was abolished during the FRENCH REVOLUTION.

Intensive care unit, special unit in a hospital for seriously ill patients who require continuous observation and the most up-to-date equipment. Since WWII such units have become a common feature of hospitals in large urban centres.

Intercession, Christian belief that with Christ as the mediator or link between God and man, a congregation or a member of a Church may petition God, especially on behalf of a third party. While Anglicans believe that the Church and its members intercede in this way through Christ, the Roman Catholics hold that the Blessed Virgin Mary and the saints also intercede, and reverence them accordingly.

Intercom, or intercommunication system, system that permits selective loudspeaker voice communication via wires between any pair of several stations, usually in the same building. The stations may be either "master stations", which may initiate calls to any in a group of stations, or "slave stations", which may initiate calls only to a master station.

Intercontinental ballistic missile (ICBM), long-range – more than 8,000km (5,000 miles) – missile for military purposes. Such missiles are installed in scattered, well-protected underground sites (silos), and can deliver thermonuclear warheads across oceans in 30 minutes to a 2km (1 mile) wide error ellipse. Self-contained INERTIAL GUIDANCE systems eliminate JAMMING. ICBMS are also capable of directing multiple warheads to targets hundreds of kilometres apart, and may be equipped with decoys. They are considered to have no effective counterweapon. *See also* MM pp.168–169, 180–181.

Interdict, instrument of punishment in the Roman Catholic Church whereby sacraments and clerical offices are refused. Bishops have this power over individual parishes, but the pope has much wider powers. Medieval popes sometimes placed an interdict on an entire country.

Interest, in economics, price paid to the lender by the borrower for the "use" of money over a specified period of time, usually a percentage of the principal (sum lent). In ancient and medieval Europe the charging of interest was condemned as USURY. With the development of capitalism it became standard practice whenever money was lent in a commercial transaction. There are two types of interest: simple and compound. Simple interest is paid as a percentage of the principal, irrespective of the period of the loan. In compound interest, the interest for one period (eg a year) is added to the principal and the interest for the next period calculated as a percentage of this total.

Interference, in optics, the meeting and mingling of two or more beams of light, or other electromagnetic radiation. The beams totally or partly reinforce or neutralize each other, depending on whether they are more or less in phase or out of phase. This effect can be observed as the appearance of interference patterns or fringes. *See also* SU pp.102–103; 108.

Interferometer, instrument in which a wave, especially a light wave, is split into component waves which are made to travel unequal distances so that on recombination they form INTERFERENCE patterns. The patterns are used for measurement of wavelength, quality control of lenses and prisms, and other purposes. *See also* MICHELSON-MORLEY EXPERIMENT.

Interferon, antiviral protein produced by most cells of the body when infected with certain viruses. It has potential therapeutic value, but work in this field is still in the experimental stage.

Interlude, short theatrical piece prominent in the late 15th and early 16th centuries which provided entertainment during royal and noble banquets. Performed by a travelling company of half-a-dozen players, it combined the didacticism and allegory of morality plays with the clowning of medieval minstrelsy, and as such is sometimes seen as the starting-point for English drama. It was thus the immediate precursor of Elizabethan comedy, and John Heywood (*c.*1497–1580) is usually recognized as the first writer to transform the interlude into a short, specifically secular comedy. The form had completely disappeared by 1580, but its traditions were later incorporated into the 17th-century MASQUE.

Intermezzo, light theatrical entertainment, performed to music between the acts of a drama or opera, which dates from the late 15th century. The 18th-century intermezzi of operas were the basis for the development of OPERA BUFFA. Today the term most commonly refers to an instrumental interlude during the course of an opera.

Internal combustion engine, engine in which fuel is burned within the working cylinder rather than in a separate chamber. Piston and rotary-type petrol and diesel engines are all internal combustion types. The steam-engine is an example of an external combustion engine. *See also* MM pp.62–65.

International, Communist. *See* COMMUNIST INTERNATIONAL.

International Atomic Energy Agency (IAEA), inter-governmental agency founded to promote peaceful uses of atomic energy. It was formed in 1956 to establish international control of nuclear weapons. It attempts to divert atomic energy from military uses and gives advice and assistance for its applications in agriculture, medicine and so on, as well as setting standards of safety. The agency is managed by a 25-member board of governors representing more than 100 members.

International Bank for Reconstruction and Development. *See* WORLD BANK.

International Boundary Commission, for the USA-Canada border, a commission created by a series of treaties between the USA and Britain in 1892, 1908 and 1925. It defines, marks and maintains boundary lines between the USA and Canada.

International Brigades, The, volunteer forces which fought on the Republican side during the SPANISH CIVIL WAR (1936–39). Although the majority of their members were Communists and organized by the COMMUNIST INTERNATIONAL, they were a rallying point for anti-Fascists of all persuasions. They distinguished themselves at the siege of Madrid in 1936, but were too small (never more than 20,000 strong) to influence the result of the war. They were formally withdrawn in 1938.

International Championship (rugby union), annual tournament between England, Ireland, Scotland, Wales (known as the four Home Unions) and France. It is also called the Five Nations' Championship. Each country plays each of the others once, venues alternating yearly, with the placings determined on a league basis: two points for a win, one for a draw. A country which beats all the other four accomplishes the *Grand Slam*; if one of the four Home Unions beats the other three it wins the mythical *Triple Crown*. The championship began in 1884, when all four Home Unions met for the first time. France entered in 1910.

International Civil Aviation Organization (ICAO), specialized agency of the UN that promotes world-wide safety and growth in civil aviation. Its activities include international standards in aircraft design, the development of airport and navigational facilities, and safety in the air. Organized in 1947, its headquarters are in Montreal, Canada.

International Committee of the Red Cross, permanent committee situated in Geneva that negotiates between combatants for the safety and medical treatment of war wounded. It also improves and updates the GENEVA CONVENTIONS. The committee, together with the League of Red Cross Societies, was awarded the Nobel Peace Prize in 1963. *See also* RED CROSS.

International Court of Justice. *See* INTERNATIONAL JUSTICE, PERMANENT COURT OF, THE HAGUE.

International date line, imaginary line extending between the north and south poles (approximately corresponding along most of its length to the 180th MERIDIAN of longitude), that arbitrarily marks off one calendar day from the next. It is a consequence of the various internationally agreed TIME ZONES which are chosen so that noon corresponds approximately to the time at which the Sun crosses the local meridian. *See also* MW p.188.

Internationale, L', socialist and Communist anthem written by Eugène Pottier, a woodworker in Lille, and set to music by P. Degeyter. First sung in France in 1871, it begins *Debout, les damnés de la terre* ("Arise, ye starving from your slumbers"). It was the Soviet national anthem until 1946 and then the official Communist Party song.

International Gothic, style of painting which spread through Europe in the late 14th and 15th centuries. A sophisticated linear style, it originated in French GOTHIC art, particularly illuminated manuscripts, and is characterized by naturalistic detail, elegant elongated figures and jewel-like colour. Examples include the *Très Riches Heures* by the LIMBOURG BROTHERS in Burgundy, and the work of PISANELLO and GENTILE DA FABRIANO in Italy. The style also flourished in Spain, Bohemia and Germany. A variant found in German painting and sculpture is known as the SOFT STYLE.

International Justice, Permanent Court of, The Hague, supreme judicial body of the UN for hearing disputes between countries involving treaties and international law. It developed out of the League of Nations' Permanent Court of Justice, set up in 1921. Its 15 judges are chosen by the UN and each comes from a different country. The UN Security Council may intervene to uphold a judgement of the court, but in fact only a small number of cases have been heard.

International Labour Organization. *See* ILO.

International law, body of rules deemed legally binding that have resulted from

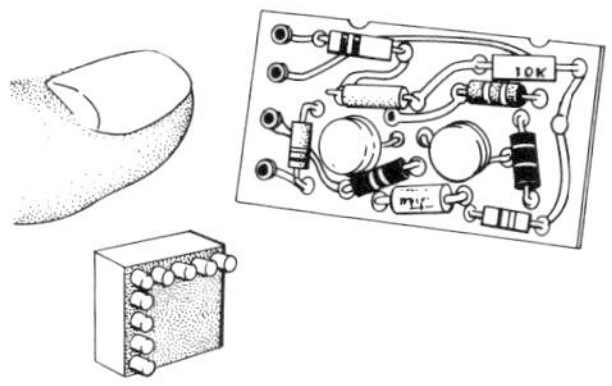

Integrated circuit (left) is much smaller than the printed circuit it replaces.

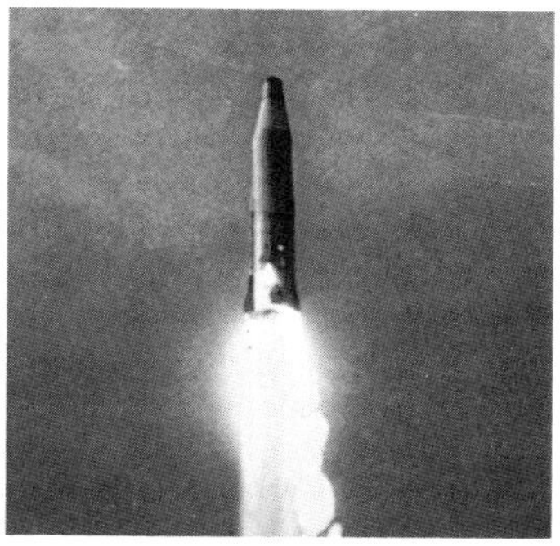

Intercontinental ballistic missiles employ similar technology to space rockets.

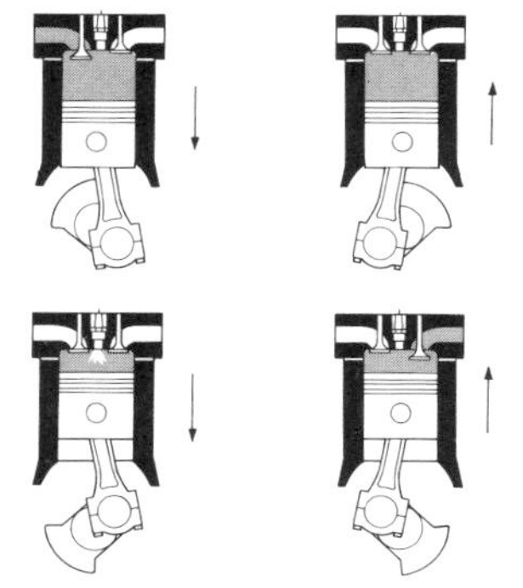

Internal combustion engines derive their power from a mixture of air and fuel.

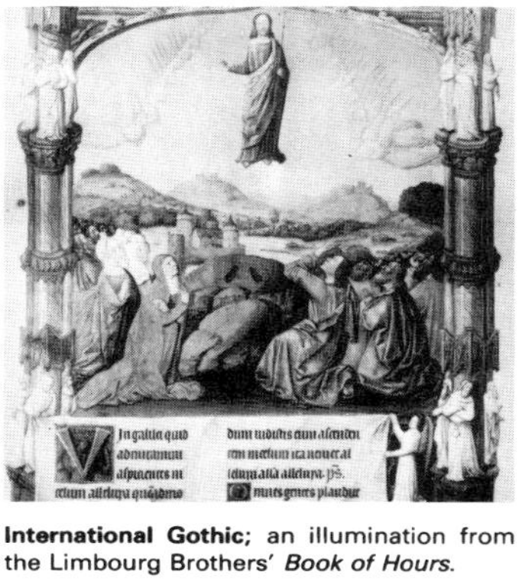

International Gothic; an illumination from the Limbourg Brothers' *Book of Hours*.

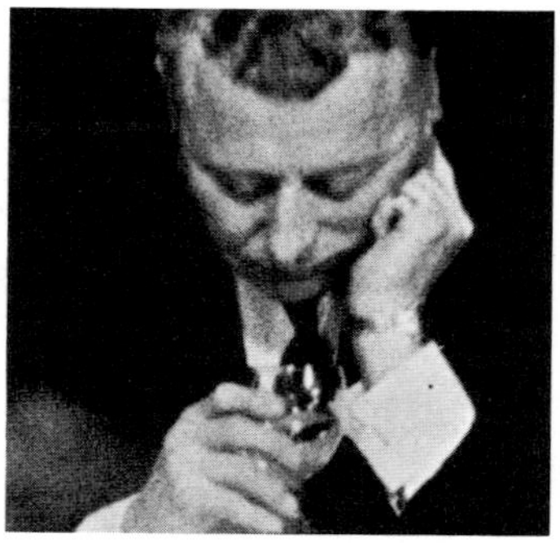

Introversion and introspection are both processes of turning in on oneself.

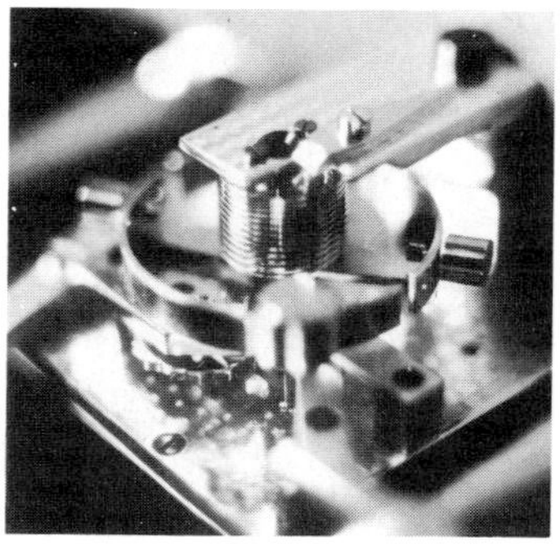

Invar used in watches ensures accurate timekeeping despite temperature changes.

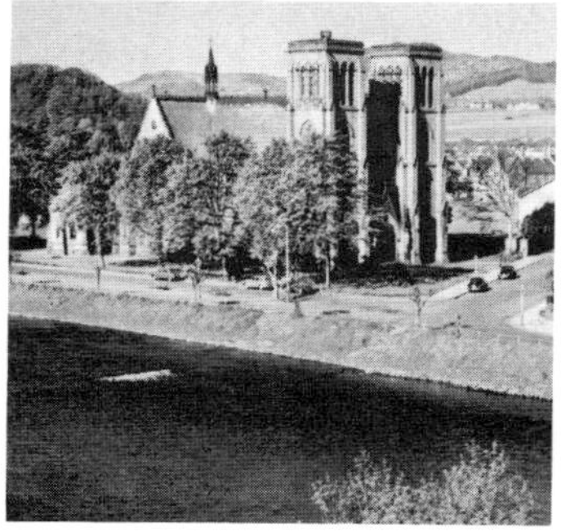

Inverness Cathedral, seen from across the Ness which flows from Loch Ness.

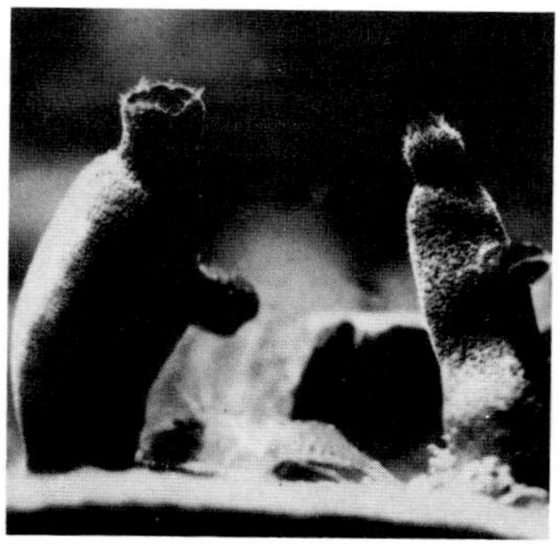

Invertebrate species number more than a million; these are sea squirts.

treaties, agreements and customs between nation states. Its sources are also decisions by agencies, conferences or commissions of international organizations such as the UN, as well as decisions of international tribunals such as those of the International Court of Justice. Instructions and manuals to diplomatic agents and decisions of international law by national courts are further sources. Sanctions for failure to comply with these laws include force of public opinion, intervention by third parties, condemnation by international bodies such as the UN and, in the last resort, armed retaliation. Despite this, it is difficult to enforce international law.

International Monetary Fund. *See* IMF.

International Peace Bureau, body originally formed in 1892 to prepare agenda to be considered by peace conferences. In 1910 it was awarded the Nobel Peace Prize. It was reorganized in 1962 by the International Liaison Committee of Organizations for Peace with the new aim of promoting consultation and co-operation. It has an office in Geneva, Switzerland.

International Style, name for the architectural style developed in Europe in the 1920s and 1930s that stresses function and abhors superfluous decoration in design. It features austere white walls, asymmetrical cubic shapes and large expanses of glass. LE CORBUSIER and Walter GROPIUS were early exponents. The name comes from the book *The International Style* (1932), by Hitchcock and Johnson.

International Whaling Commission, commission organized in 1946 by 16 countries. It promotes conservation of whale stocks, for the common good, encouraging research and updating regulations. It thus encourages the whaling industry to develop in step with availability. Its headquarters are in Cambridge, England.

Interplanetary matter. *See* INTERSTELLAR MATTER.

Interpol (International Criminal Police Organization), organization composed of police forces from more than 100 countries. Established in 1923, it includes most of the countries of the Western world and Yugoslavia (the only Communist member). Its headquarters are in Paris. Interpol's main function is to provide member nations with information about international criminals and to assist in their arrest.

Interpolation, mathematical procedure for finding intermediate unknown values of a function lying between two known values. A common method is to assume that the unknown values lie on the same straight line as do the known values. *See also* EXTRAPOLATION.

Intersection, point, or LOCUS of points, common to two or more geometrical figures. Two non-parallel lines meet in a point; two non-parallel planes meet in a line; the intersection of two curved surfaces is a curve. *See also* SU pp.44–45.

Interstellar cloud, relatively dense concentration of interstellar matter, especially dust, which usually appears in the form of a dark NEBULA. Such clouds are responsible for absorption leading to reddening or dimming of starlight, and they also may be regions in which stars are born.

Interstellar matter, matter within galaxies occupying the space between stars. It includes bright nebulae (clouds of gas excited to luminescence by nearby stars) and dark nebulae (not excited). Farther away from stars, and filling interstellar space, is gas – mostly hydrogen – and particulate matter at exceedingly low densities, about 10–21kg per cu m. The interstellar matter in our galaxy accounts for 5% of its total mass.

Interval, musical term for the space between one note and another, the smallest on keyboard instruments being a semitone.

Intestate, description of a person who dies without leaving a valid will. In such cases, the individual's property is generally divided according to statute, with the next of kin usually the major benefitter.

Intestines, the lower part of the ALIMENTARY CANAL. In the small intestine, food undergoes the final stages of digestion and is absorbed into the bloodstream. In the large intestine, water is absorbed from undigested material. Waste is passed on to the lowest part, the rectum, to be evacuated from the anus. *See also* MS pp.68–69, *68–69*, 85, *85*, 92–93, *92–93*.

Intoxication, condition arising when the body is poisoned by a harmful substance such as drugs (eg alcohol or barbiturates – the common meaning of the term), chemicals (eg lead or mercury accumulations occurring as pollution, or gases) or bacterial toxins. Auto-intoxication can occur in disorders such as hepatitis in which, through prevention of the normal functioning of the liver, body wastes accumulate, leading to skin discoloration.

Intrauterine device. *See* IUD.

Introspection, process in psychology that involves observing one's own mind with the aim of arriving at the principles that govern it. Once regarded as the best means to reach an understanding of the human mind the value of introspection is now realized to be limited by such considerations as maturity and motive. Despite this, it still plays a useful role in scientific psychology.

Introversion, preoccupation with one's own responses and impressions, coupled with a refusal to acknowledge the value of any outside impressions. The term was coined by C. G. JUNG as a polar opposite to EXTROVERSION. In psychiatry, extreme cases of introversion are classified as catatonic, in which the patient has totally withdrawn, neither speaking nor moving. *See also* MS p.188, *188*.

Introvert. *See* INTROVERSION.

Intrusion, in geology, emplacement of rock material which was either forced or flowed into spaces among other rocks. An igneous intrusion, called a pluton, consists of magma which never reached the Earth's surface but filled cracks and faults, then cooled and hardened. *See also* PE pp.101, 103, 106–107, 124.

Intrusive rock, IGNEOUS ROCK that forms by slow cooling under the Earth's surface. In general, they are coarser grained than volcanic rocks which have cooled on the surface. *See also* PE p.101.

Invar, alloy containing about 64% iron, 36% nickel and small quantities of carbon. It has a very low thermal expansion, which leads to its use in instruments for measuring, such as surveying rods.

Invercargill, city in New Zealand, at the extreme S end of South Island. An agricultural trade centre, its industries include timber and food processing. Pop. (1971 est.) 46,700.

Invergordon mutiny, action taken by the British sailors of the Atlantic Fleet based at Invergordon, Scotland, in Sept. 1931 when faced with reductions in pay of more than 10%. The government had passed an economy Bill enacting cuts in all government salaries in an attempt to put national finances in order; the mutiny forced them to suspend the gold standard and introduce a managed currency.

Inverness, town in N Scotland, at the N end of Glen More at the head of the MORAY FIRTH. It is a seaport and centre of a transportation system between the Highlands and the S and E. Its industries include food processing and electrical engineering. Pop. (1974) 36,595.

Inverness-shire, formerly the largest county in Scotland. A mountainous area, the main occupations are forestry, fishing and sheep and cattle rearing. Tourism is also a valuable source of income. Area: 10,906sq km (4,211sq miles). Pop. (1971) 89,545.

Inversion, atmospheric condition in which a property of the air, such as moisture content or temperature, increases with altitude. In a temperature inversion, the air temperature rises with altitude and a cap of hot air encloses the cooler air below. With little wind or turbulence to break up the condition, POLLUTION can build up often to a dangerous extent.

Invertebrate, without a backbone; in zoology, the term for an animal without a backbone. There are more than a million known species of invertebrates, divided into 30 *phyla*, or major groups. One of these is Arthropoda (joint-legged animals), the largest of all animal phyla in numbers of species. Most are INSECTS, but it also includes CRUSTACEANS and ARACHNIDS. MOLLUSCS make up the second largest group of invertebrates. *See also* ARTHROPODS; PHYLUM; NW pp.*23*, 80–121, 178–179.

Investiture, installation in office by a superior authority. In FEUDALISM it was a symbolic act signifying the handing over of a FIEF or office. Following the act of homage and oath of fealty, investiture consisted of the transfer from lord to vassal of a symbolic object, such as a staff or glove. In the late 11th and early 12th centuries the right of lay rulers to invest bishops and abbots became a matter of great dispute between the papacy and European monarchs, particularly the Holy Roman emperors. A compromise to the Investiture Controversy was reached in the Concordat of Worms (1122), providing for secular selection and spiritual investiture.

Investment, employment of money with the object of providing profit or income. An element of risk accompanies investment; generally, the higher the risk the greater the potential profit. Forms of investment include personal savings placed in a bank; factory plant and machinery; insurance; and stocks and shares. The purchase of a house or objet d'art is also an investment, as these can be re-sold, usually at a profit.

Invisible Man, The (1897), science fiction novel by H. G. WELLS. It features the exploits of Griffin, a young scientist who successfully makes himself invisible. His trail of vindictive destruction in the vicinity of London ends with his death.

Involuntary muscle, one of the three types of MUSCLE in the body, so called because, unlike skeletal muscle, it is not under the conscious control of the brain but is stimulated by the autonomic nervous system and by hormones in the bloodstream. It is of two kinds. Smooth muscle is the muscle of the alimentary canal, of blood vessels and of the bladder. Cardiac muscle powers the heart. *See also* MS p.58.

Involuntary nervous system, or autonomic nervous system, complex nerve pathways in the body which are not under the conscious control of the brain. This system is responsible for all the movements of the INVOLUNTARY MUSCLES such as those of the gut, and, together with the HORMONES, it also affects the secretions of glands. The system is in two parts, the sympathetic and parasympathetic autonomic nervous systems, which generally act antagonistically, the one causing a muscle to contract, and the other causing it to relax.

Inwood, name of two British architects. William (*c.* 1771–1843) and his son Henry (1794–1843) co-operated in building many churches in Greek Revival style, including St Pancras Church, London (1819–22). In 1827 Henry published a book on the architecture of the Erechtheum, Athens.

Io, in Greek mythology, a mistress of ZEUS, whom he turned into a heifer in order to prevent her discovery by his wife, HERA. Suspicious Hera had the all-seeing ARGUS guard Io. With the aid of HERMES, who killed Argus, Io escaped, swam the Ionian Sea and the Bosporus, and was finally restored by Zeus.

Io, large innermost satellite of Jupiter. It was discovered by GALILEO in 1609–10 and is larger than the Moon. It has a revolution period of 1.77 days and recent research has confirmed that it has an atmosphere; it is also believed to be coated with ice. It is more than 3,600km (2,200 miles) in diameter and is 421,770km (262,000 miles) above the surface of the planet.

Iodine, non-metallic element (symbol I) of the halogen group, discovered in 1811 by Bernard Courtois. Iodides are found in sea water. The black volatile solid gives a violet vapour. Chemically it resembles CHLORINE, but it is less reactive. It is used as a medical antiseptic and potassium iodide is used in photography. The isotope

I^{131} (half-life eight days) is used in treatment of THYROID GLAND disorders. Properties: at.no. 53; at.wt. 126.9045; s.g. 4.93; m.p. 113.5°C (236°F); b.p. 184.35°C (363.83°F); most stable isotope I^{127} (100%). *See also* SU p.*133*.

Iodoform, yellow, crystalline chemical compound (CHI_3) with a characteristic odour, used as an antiseptic.

Ion, particle of atomic size with a positive or negative charge. Simple ions are formed when atoms gain or lose electrons. More complex ions are charged groups of atoms held together by COVALENT BONDS. Positive ions are called cations (they are drawn to a CATHODE); negative ions are called anions (drawn to an ANODE). Many crystalline solids are composed of arrays of ions of opposite charge. Ions are also responsible for the conduction of electricity by liquids and gases. *See also* SU pp.140, 144–145, 148–149, *148*.

Ion, complex, electrically charged chemical group forming a CO-ORDINATION COMPLEX. It may occur either in solution or in crystal form. The ferrocyanide ion, $Fe(CN)_6^{4-}$, and the cuprommonium ion $Cu(NH_3)_4^{2+}$ are examples.

Iona, island off the coast of W Scotland in the Inner Hebrides. The island has an abbey, founded in AD 563 by St Columba. Tourism is the main source of income. Area: 13sq km (5sq miles). *See also* HC1 pp.*140, 182*.

Ionesco, Eugène (1912–), French dramatist, *b.* Romania. A pioneer of the surrealistic avant-garde, Ionesco had his first success with *The Bald Prima Donna* (1950), a satire on the futility of verbal communication. His other plays include *The Chairs* (1952), *Rhinoceros* (1959) and *Exit the King* (1962).

Ion exchange, method of water-softening employed widely in domestic and industrial units. Water hardness (permanent hardness) is caused mainly by chlorides and sulphates of calcium and magnesium. In ion exchange softeners the calcium and magnesium ions are exchanged by chemical reactions with those of sodium. Since sodium salts are much more soluble, this softens the water.

Ionia, ancient region extending along the W coast of Asia Minor (now Turkey) and including the neighbouring Aegean islands, which are now part of Greece. The area was settled by the Greeks in the 10th and 11th centuries BC. Miletus and Ephesus were the most important cities of the Ionian civilization.

Ionian Islands (Iónioi Nísoi), island group off SW Greece, in the Ionian Sea. It consists of seven main islands, Corfu, Paxos, Leukas, Ithaca, Cephalonia, Zante and Cythera, and several islets. Grouped together as a province under the Byzantine Empire in AD 890 it was captured by the Venetians in 1500, ceded to France under the Treaty of Campo Formio in 1797 and made a British protectorate in 1815. It was ceded to Greece in 1864. Industries include shipping, timber, fruit and wine. Area: 2,248sq km (868sq miles). Pop. (1970 est.) 183,600.

Ionians, in ancient Greece, inhabitants of ATTICA, BOEOTIA and IONIA, who spoke a dialect distinct from that of the DORIANS and AEOLIANS. More narrowly, it also described the inhabitants of Ionia alone, who made great contributions to classical Greek culture, notably in the development of the rational thought that was the basis of Greek philosophy.

Ionian Sea, part of the Mediterranean Sea, between W Greece and the S Italian Peninsula and E Sicily. It is connected to the Adriatic Sea by the Strait of Messina.

Ionic bond, or electrovalent bond, type of chemical bond in which ions of opposite charge are held together by electrostatic attraction. *See also* SU pp.140, *140*, 144, 148, *148*.

Ionic Order, one of the five ORDERS of classical architecture. It developed in the Greek colonies of Asia Minor in the 6th century BC and became known in Greece in the 5th century BC. It is characterized by slender columns with 24 flutes and prominent volutes, or spiral scrolls, on the capitals: the best example is the Erechtheum on the ACROPOLIS.

Ionic radius, effective radius of a particular type of ion. An ionic solid (crystal) is composed of two or more species of ions, which may be regarded as spheres packed together in a regular pattern. By considering the crystal structures and parameters of numbers of compounds, it is possible to obtain a consistent set of ionic radii.

Ionization, process in which neutral atoms or molecules are converted into ions. Positive ions can be formed by supplying energy to detach electrons from the atom, as by the action of X-rays, ultra-violet radiation or high-energy particles. The minimum energy to form an ion is the ionization energy (or potential). The opposite process – electron capture by a neutral species to yield a negative ion – is much less probable. Both types of ions can also be produced by breaking bonds, which can be induced by photons, particles, etc or may occur spontaneously, as in the dissociation of acids and salts when dissolved in water. *See also* SU pp.144, 148, *148*.

Ionization chamber, instrument for measuring the intensity of ionizing particles or radiation, such as X-rays. The gas-filled chamber contains two electrodes across which a voltage is applied. Passage of radiation through the chamber ionizes the gas and the ions formed move towards the charged electrodes. The current thus produced, which is amplified in an associated circuit, is proportional to the radiation intensity. A similar process is used in a GEIGER COUNTER, which detects and measures radioactivity.

Ionizing radiation, electromagnetic radiation having sufficient energy to react with atoms of the atmosphere to produce ions. There are two sources: radioactive elements in the Earth's crust and atmosphere, which emit beta and gamma radiation, and cosmic rays from outer space, which give rise to the IONOSPHERE.

Ion microscope. *See* MICROSCOPE.

Ionosphere, wide region of IONS or charged particles in the ATMOSPHERE. It extends from about 60km (37 miles) above the Earth's surface to the limits of the atmosphere in the VAN ALLEN RADIATION BELTS. Radio waves are deflected from electron layers in the ionosphere, which makes possible long-distance radio communication.

Ion propulsion, method of propelling rockets by heating metals such as CAESIUM to produce IONS and ELECTRONS. The ions are accelerated through a POTENTIAL DIFFERENCE to provide power. In present development, ion propulsion offers advantages of longer acceleration periods, high mass efficiency and increased lifetimes for satellite control systems.

Iowa, state in the N central USA lying between the Missouri and Mississippi rivers. Originally prairie that was ploughed to create farmland, the region is known for its fertile soil. Maize and other cereals are produced and Iowa stands second only to Texas in the raising of prime cattle. Industries include food processing and the production of farm machinery. The state capital is Des Moines.

First discovered by MARQUETTE and Solliet in 1673, the land was claimed for France in 1682. The region was explored by French trappers and hunters until it was sold to the USA in the LOUISIANA PURCHASE of 1803. Iowa was admitted to the Union in 1846. Industrial development was encouraged after WWII. Area: 145,790sq km (56,290sq miles). Pop. (1975 est.) 2,870,000. *See also* MW p.175.

Ipecacuanha, woody tropical plant and the drug obtained from its dried roots, which contain ALKALOIDS. The drug is used in medicine to cause vomiting. Family Rubiaceae.

Iphigenia, in Greek mythology and literature, daughter of AGAMEMNON and CLYTEMNESTRA and sister of Electra, Chrysothemis and ORESTES.

Ipoh, capital city of Perak province, Malaysia, on the Malay Peninsula. It is on the Singapore-Bangkok railway. Ipoh is Malaysia's major tin-mining centre, and dates from the 1890s when immigrant Chinese were brought to work in the tin mines. The city which also has rubber plantations and limestone quarries. Pop. (1970) 247,689.

Ipswich, town and port in Suffolk, E England, on the Orwell estuary. A large wool centre in the 16th century, it now exports barley and malt and imports coal and oil. Other industries include milling and printing. Pop. (1973) 122,670.

IQ, intelligence quotient, classification of the supposed mental power of a person. It is computed by dividing the person's assessed mental age by his real age, then multiplying by 100. The mental age is determined by the average number of questions correctly answered by children of a certain age. If the average number of correct answers for a ten-year-old were 30, and an eight-year-old answered 30 questions correctly, his IQ would be ten divided by eight, multiplied by 100, that is 125.

Iqbal, Sir Muhammad (*c.*1877–1938), Indian MUSLIM political leader, poet and philosopher. He was an advocate of an independent Muslim state and became President of the Muslim League in 1930. His best known poetic work is *The Secrets of the Self* (1915).

Iquitos, inland port city of NE Peru, on the upper River Amazon, approx. 41km (1,268 miles) NE of Lima. It is a commercial shipping centre whose exports include coffee, cotton, timber and rubber. Pop. (1969 est.) 74,500.

IRA (Irish Republican Army), semi-military, primarily Roman Catholic organization dedicated to establishing a united Irish republic. Formed in 1919, the IRA waged guerrilla warfare against British rule. Some members ("Irregulars") rejected the Anglo-Irish settlement of 1921, fighting a civil war until 1923. Periodically active since that time, the "provisional" wing ("Provos"), committed to armed struggle, split in 1969 from the "official" IRA, which emphasized political activities and a Marxist rather than religious approach. Thereafter, the Provos became prominent in the violence among Catholics, Protestants and British troops in Northern Ireland. *See also* HC2 p.295.

Iráklion (Heraklion or Candia), largest city and seaport on the island of Crete, S Greece, in the sea of Crete. Founded in the 9th century by the Saracens, it was conquered by the Byzantines in 961, the Venetians in 1204 and the Turks in 1669. It became part of Greece in 1913. It is near to the ancient ruins of KNOSSOS. Exports include wine, grapes and olives. Pop. (1971) 77,506. *See also* HC1 pp.38–39.

Iran, nation in SW Asia, formerly known as Persia. Although classed as a developing country it draws huge revenues from oil and is the largest oil exporter in the Middle East. The government is sponsoring a programme of modernization and industrial expansion, although village industries are still of major importance. The capital is Teheran. Area: 1,648,000sq km (636,292sq miles). Pop. (1975 est.) 33,957,000. *See* MW p.100.

Iranian languages, subdivision of the Indo-European family. The major Iranian languages are Persian, Pashto, Kurdish, Mazanderani and Gilaki (of Iran), Baluchi (of Iran and Pakistan) and Tadzhik and Ossetic, spoken in the USSR. *See also* MS pp.240–241.

Iraq, nation in SW Asia which includes the ancient region of Mesopotamia. Despite deriving a large income from oil the country is predominantly agricultural, producing cereals, tobacco and fruit. The government has encouraged industrial expansion, but internal politics and inter-Arab disputes have hindered development. The capital is Baghdad. Area: 434,924sq km (167,924sq miles). Pop. (1975 est.) 11,124,000. *See* MW p.101.

Irbil, city in N Iraq, between the Great and Little Zab rivers. It is the site of the ancient city of Urbillum (Arbela). A modern transport and commercial centre, its industries include grain and tobacco. Pop. 90,320.

Ireland, John Nicholson (1879–1962), British composer, influenced by Brahms, Stravinsky, Dvořák and Ravel. His works,

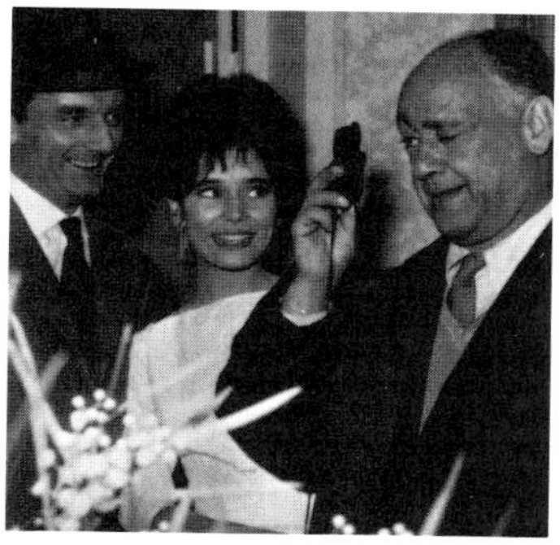

Eugène Ionesco, pretending to squint through a cameraman's "pan" glass filter.

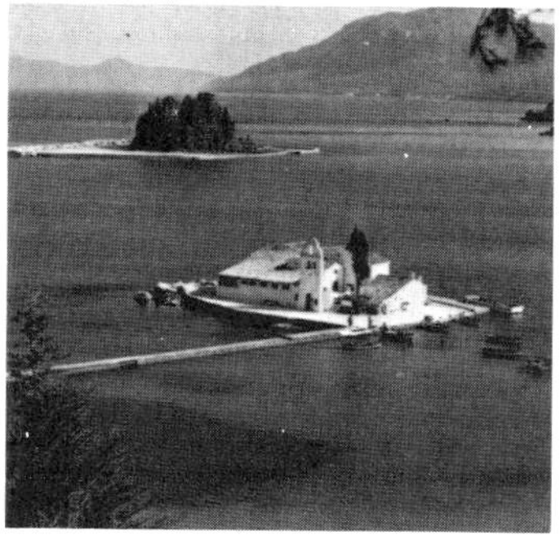

Ionian Islands are noted for beauty spots such as this monastery 8km (5 miles) from Corfu.

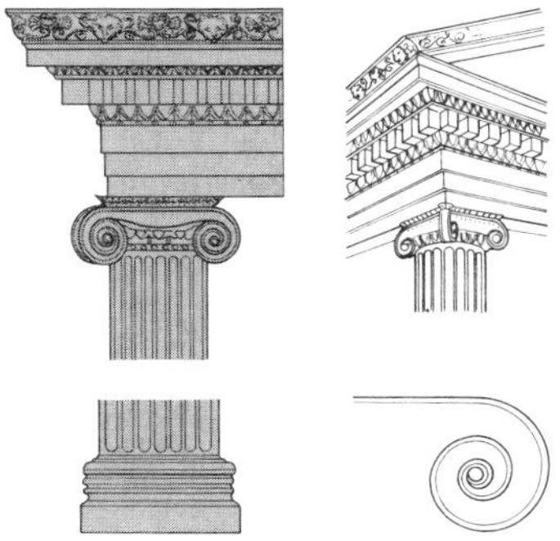

Ionic Order was much used in Baroque buildings as well as in Greek architecture.

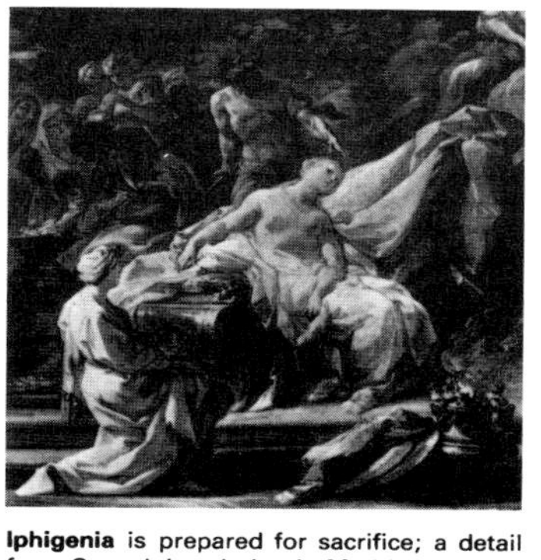

Iphigenia is prepared for sacrifice; a detail from Corrado's painting in Madrid.

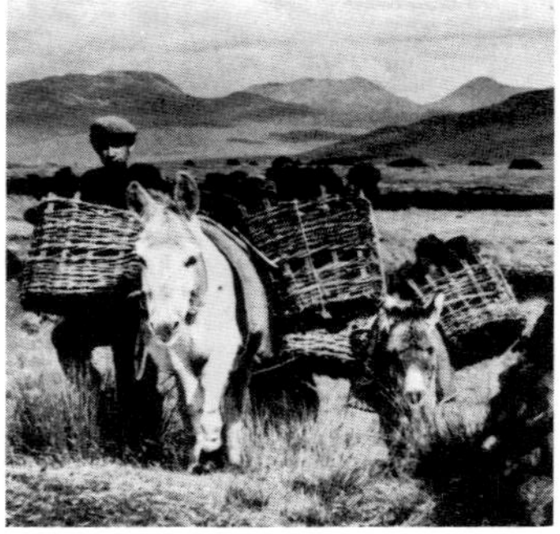

Ireland; donkeys carry peat in County Galway; peat is used as a domestic fuel.

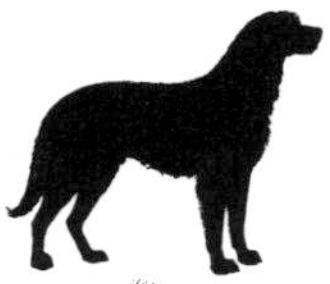

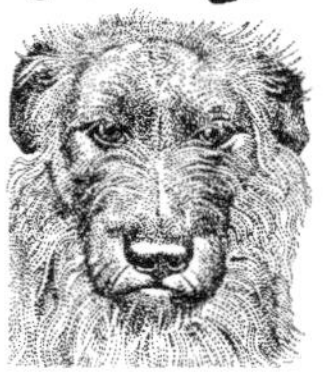

Irish wolfhounds originally hunted elks and wolves; they are the tallest breed of dog.

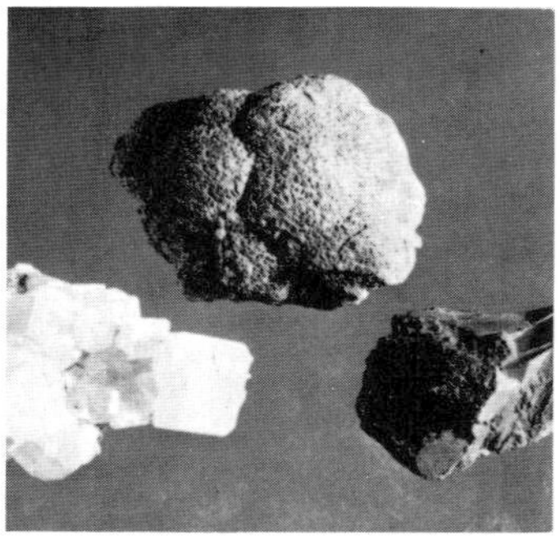

Iron compounds may take various forms, from masses of ores to crystalline salts.

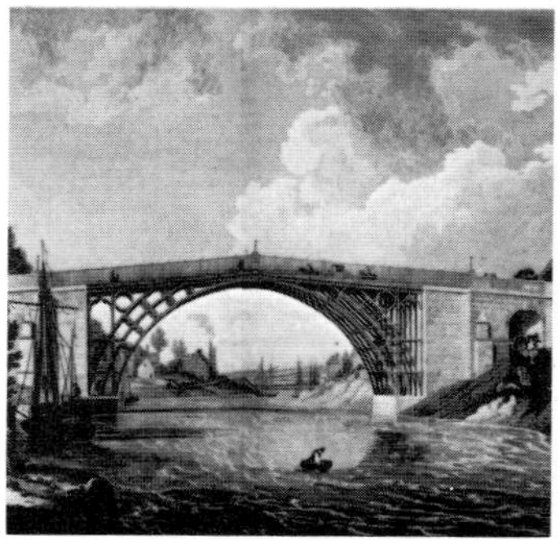

Ironbridge has become a centre for an active growing interest in British industrial history.

firmly grounded in a Romantic tradition and often inspired by places and landscape, include *The Forgotten Rite* (1913), for orchestra; *Mai-Dun* (1921), a symphonic rhapsody; *These Things Shall Be* (1937), for chorus and orchestra; the overture *Satyricon* (1946); and many songs and piano pieces.

Ireland, Home Rule. *See* IRISH HOME RULE.

Ireland, Northern. *See* MW p.136.

Ireland, Partition of, division of Ireland in 1920 into two parts after the breakdown of British government after 1918. By an agreement signed in Dec. 1921 and taking effect in 1922 the six predominantly Protestant counties of Ulster remained part of the UK and the 26 predominantly Catholic southern counties became the Republic of Ireland. *See also* IRISH HOME RULE; HC2 pp.294, *295*.

Ireland, Republic of, country that occupies five-sixths of Ireland, the westernmost island of the British Isles. Since the 1940s it has been changing from an agrarian to an industrial society, although the country's most valuable resource is still its rich farmland and agriculture remains the major factor in the economy. Sea fishing is also important. The capital is Dublin. Area: 70,282sq km (27,136sq miles). Pop. (1976 est.) 3,163,000. *See* MW p.102.

Irenaeus, Saint (*c.* 140–*c.* 200), Church Father and, by tradition, martyr. He probably introduced Christianity to much of Gaul. A tireless opponent of GNOSTICISM, he wrote *Against Heresies* and *Demonstration of the Apostolic Preaching.*

Ireton, Henry (1611–51), English parliamentarian leader, a son-in-law of Oliver CROMWELL. He signed the warrant for the execution of CHARLES I in 1649 and was Cromwell's deputy in Ireland (1649–51).

Irian Barat (West Irian), Indonesian province comprising the W half of New Guinea, formerly Dutch New Guinea. It became independent in 1962 and a part of Indonesia in 1963. Capital: Djajapura. Area: 422,170sq km (163,000sq miles). Pop. 947,000.

Iridium, metallic element (symbol Ir) of the third transition series, discovered in 1803 by Smithson Tennant. It may be used in making pen tips and electrical contacts. Properties: at.no. 77; at.wt. 192.22; s.g. 22.42 (17°C); m.p. 2,410°C (4,370°F); most common isotope Ir^{193} (62.6%).

Iris, in Greek mythology, goddess of the rainbow and messenger of the gods. Depicted as swift-footed, golden-winged and robed in bright colours, she appears in numerous classical writings, including Euripides' *Herakles.* She is also prominent in the myth of Ceyx and HALCYONE.

Iris, the coloured part of the EYE. It controls the amount of light that enters the pupil in the centre of the eye by increasing or decreasing the size of the pupil. The iris is part of the choroid, the middle layer of the wall of the eye. *See also* MS p.48.

Iris, genus of about 200 species of flowering plants widely distributed, mostly in temperate areas. They may be bulbous or rhizomatous. The showy flowers have three erect inner petals, called *standards,* three drooping outer sepals, called *falls,* and flat swordlike leaves. Height: up to 90cm (3ft). *See also* CROCUS; GLADIOLUS.

Irish. *See* GAELIC.

Irish Free State. *See* IRELAND, REPUBLIC OF.

Irish Guards, one of five household regiments in Britain, raised in 1900 to honour the service of Irish regiments in the SOUTH AFRICAN WAR. Their motto is *Quis separabit?* ("Who shall separate us?").

Irish Home Rule, movement to gain Irish legislative independence from the British Parliament in the 19th century, achieved for southern Ireland in 1922. The union of Britain and Ireland (1801) was challenged by O'CONNELL's Repeal Association in the 1830s and 1840s. It failed, but in the 1870s Isaac BUTT began the Home Rule League. His successor, PARNELL, won for the movement the support of Gladstone. His Home Rule Bill of 1886 split the Liberal Party and sent Liberal Unionists into the arms of the Conservatives. That coalition blocked home rule until it was granted by the act of 1914. It was deferred until the end of WWI when, by civil war, Ulster succeeded in retaining the British connection. *See also* HOME RULE PARTY; HC2 pp.162–163.

Irish Literary Renaissance, period of exceptional literary creativity in Ireland in the late 19th and early 20th centuries. An outgrowth of the movement for self-government, it revived Irish literature and fostered Irish drama. Among those involved in the movement were W. B. YEATS, Lady GREGORY, J. M. SYNGE and Seán O'CASEY.

Irish moss, or carrageen, small, dark red seaweed (*Chondrus crispus*) with tufted fronds, common on North Atlantic coasts. Commercial Irish moss, which consists of dried carrageen, is used for thickening or emulsifying foods. *See also* RED ALGAE.

Irish National Land League, organization formed in 1879 by Michael DAVITT and Charles PARNELL to put pressure on Britain to reform the Irish system of land tenure. It arose out of rural depression and a great increase in evictions of Irish tenant farmers for failure to pay rent, mostly to English landlords. It encouraged agrarian outrages for four years, and was a powerful influence on the 1881 Land Act.

Irish Republican Army. *See* IRA.

Irish Sea, part of the Atlantic Ocean, between Ireland and Britain, connected to the Atlantic by the North Channel (N) and by St George's Channel (S). Scotland, Wales and England are on its E shore and Ireland on the W. Area: 103,600sq km (40,000sq miles).

Irish setter, gun dog, originally bred in Ireland as a red-and-white dog from the early 18th century and as the popular solid "red" from the 19th century. It has a long, lean head with a deep muzzle and low-set, pendulous ears. The body and neck are long and the legs straight. Its coat is fine, fringed and coloured chestnut-red or mahogany. Height: to 69cm (27in) at the shoulder; weight: 27–32kg (59–70lb).

Irish Sweeps Derby. *See* DERBY.

Irish terrier, working dog, originally bred in Ireland. It has a long, flat head, squared off by chin whiskers and small, triangular ears that droop forward. The legs and body are moderately long, and the tail is commonly docked. The dense, wiry coat is generally a shade of reddish-brown. Height: to 46cm (18in) at the shoulder; weight: 12kg (27lb).

Irish Volunteers, Protestant force raised by Henry FLOOD in 1779 to defend Ireland against a French invasion during the American revolutionary wars. By 1782 there were 80,000 volunteers. Their presence was used to extract from the British Parliament a free trade agreement in 1779 and legislative independence in 1782. They were disbanded in 1793.

Irish water spaniel, dog commonly used to retrieve ducks. It has a large, domed head with a square muzzle, and long pendulous ears. The medium-length body is slightly raised at the hindquarters and inset on strong legs with large feet. The long tail tapers to a fine point. The coat is usually liver-coloured and in tight ringlets. Height: to 61cm (24in) at the shoulder; weight: 20.5–29kg (45–64lb).

Irish wolfhound, large Celtic hunting dog originally used to hunt Irish wolves and elks. It has a long head with long, pointed muzzle and small ears. The deep and wide-chested body with its long back is set on long, straight legs. It has a long and slightly curved tail; its rough wiry coat may be grey, brindle, reddish-brown, black, white or fawn. Height: at least 79cm (31in) at the shoulder; weight: at least 54.5kg (120lb).

Iron, common metallic element (symbol Fe) of the first transition series, known from the earliest times. Its chief ores are HAEMATITE (Fe_2O_3), magnetite (Fe_3O_4), and IRON PYRITES (FeS_2). It is obtained in a blast furnace by reducing the oxide with carbon monoxide from coke (carbon), using limestone to form a slag. The pure metal – a reactive soft element – is rarely used; most iron is alloyed with carbon and other elements in the various forms of STEEL. The element has four ALLOTROPIC forms, one of which is ferromagnetic. Properties: at. no. 26; at. wt. 55.847; s.g. 7.86; m.p. 1,535°C(2,795°F); b.p. 2,750°C (4,982°F); most common isotope Fe^{56} (91.66%). *See also* MM pp.28–31.

Iron, cast, forms of iron made by remelting steel scrap with pig iron. They contain between 1.5–5% carbon and up to 3% silicon. Although brittle, they are widely used because of their cheapness, notably for the engine blocks of road vehicles.

Iron Age, period succeeding the BRONZE AGE, dating from about 1100 BC, in which man in general learned to smelt iron (although the HITTITES probably developed the first important iron industry in Armenia soon after 2000 BC). Iron's superior strength and cheapness, and the widespread availability of its ore, caused it gradually to supersede bronze. *See also* MM pp.27–29; HC1 pp.66, *67*, 68, 85.

Ironbridge, gorge in Shropshire, central England, where at Coalbrookdale the first iron bridge was built in 1777–79 by Abraham DARBY and John Wilkinson (to the design of Thomas Pritchard). The bridge, which still stands, continued to be used for road traffic until the 1950s. *See also* HC2 p.*314*.

Iron Cross, highest German decoration for military valour. It was the first such award in German history, created by King FREDERICK WILLIAM III in 1813.

Iron Curtain, term coined in 1946 by Winston Churchill in a speech at Fulton, Missouri, USA, to describe the division between Communist eastern Europe and the West. "An iron curtain", he said, "has descended across the Continent." At that time the Communists imposed even more rigid restrictions on communication and the exchange of ideas with the West than they do now.

Iron deficiency. *See* ANAEMIA.

Iron lung, term popularly used for the Drinker respirator, which is a device that provides long-term artificial respiration. It consists of a metal tank in which the patient's body is enclosed (with his head outside). Breathing is sustained by alternating negative and positive air pressure inside the tank.

Iron maiden, medieval torture instrument in the shape of a person. Rather like a sarcophagus, it was hinged in two parts with the interior covered with sharp spikes. The victim was placed inside.

Iron meteorite, type of common meteorite consisting mostly of iron with up to 11% nickel. When they are newly fallen, a thin black crust of IRON OXIDE forms, and quickly rusts. *See also* SU p.*218*.

Iron ore, mineral source of the metal, which is predominantly in the form of IRON OXIDES, particularly HAEMATITE, LIMONITE and MAGNETITE. Other ores include an iron carbonate, SIDERITE, and an iron sulphide, PYRITES. *See also* IRON PYRITES

Iron ore processing, extraction of iron from its ores, mainly by the reduction of iron oxides (principal ores) in blast furnaces. Iron ore, coke and a stony flux are heated in a blast furnace and then subjected to a blast preheated to between 700°–1100°C. This both sustains the temperature, by burning off coke to carbon monoxide (CO), and also reduces the iron ore to the metal (steel), the carbon monoxide reacting with oxygen in the ore to form carbon dioxide (CO_2). *See also* STEEL-MAKING; MM pp.28, 30.

Iron oxides, exist in three forms: iron (II) oxide, or ferrous oxide (FeO); iron (III) oxide, or ferric oxide (Fe_2O_3), and ferrosoferric oxide (Fe_3O_4) which has iron in both forms.

Iron pyrites, mineral composed of iron and sulphur, having the chemical formula FeS_2. It crystallises in large cubes having a yellow lustre that has led to the name "fool's gold". The most widespread of sulphide minerals, it is a valuable source of sulphur for such purposes as making sulphuric acid.

Ironside, William Edmund (1880–1959), British soldier. He served in the SOUTH AFRICAN WAR and commanded the Allied forces at Archangel (1918). He was chief of the imperial general staff (1939–40) and commander of the Home Defence forces (1940).

Ironsides, cavalry regiment led by CROM-

HC1 = History and Culture Vol. 1 HC2 = History and Culture Vol. 2 MS = Man and Society MM = Man and Machines

WELL in the ENGLISH CIVIL WAR, drawn mainly from the yeomen and freeholders of the Eastern Association (formed in the East Anglian counties in 1642 in the parliamentary cause). They were nicknamed "Old Ironsides" by Prince RUPERT, whose royalist army they helped to defeat at MARSTON MOOR.

Ironwood, or hornbeam, two varieties of birch tree in E North America. The *Carpinus carolinia,* or blue beech, has a smooth, silver-grey bark. The *Ostrya virginia* has a ridged, light-brown bark. Various hardwood trees in Australia and the tropics are also called ironwood.

Irony, the use of words to convey, often satirically, the opposite of their literal meaning. It derives from the Socratic method of discussion by feigning ignorance.

Iroquois Confederacy (or League), confederation of tribes of North American Indians occupying the Mohawk valley and Lakes area of New York state. They call themselves Oñgwanósioñi (also spelt Hodinonhsioni) "People of the long house", after the distinctive shape of the bark dwellings they constructed in the 16th century. The original tribes were the Oneida, Mohawk, Seneca, Onondaga and Cayuga; they were later joined by the Tuscarora. The women fulfilled a leading role in society and grew corn, beans and tobacco while the men hunted. The Iroquois had a highly developed political system and were renowned warriors. Their total number has halved since 1600; in the mid-1970s there were 7,500 – 10,000 of them in New York, Wisconsin, Oklahoma and Canada.

Irradiation, exposure to short-wave electromagnetic radiation. Materials are often irradiated with high-energy neutrons in nuclear reactors, to make them temporarily radioactive. More portable sources of such radiation are radioisotopes such as cobalt 60 and caesium 137, whose uses include irradiation treatment for cancer. Treatment also involves the use of particle accelerators, including proton and neutron beam machines. Radioactive sources are used industrially, e.g. in sterilizing food that cannot be heated without deterioration.

Irrational number, in mathematics, any number which cannot be expressed as the ratio of two integers, not including zero. An example is $\sqrt{2}$. Like other irrational numbers, it is infinite and non-repeating when expressed as a decimal. Irrational numbers, together with rational numbers, make up the set of REAL NUMBERS.

Irrawaddy, river in central Burma, formed by the union of the Mali and Nmai rivers. Flowing S through Burma, it serves as a trade and communications route for the cities of Myitkyina, Bhamo and Mandalay. At Henzada a vast delta begins, extending 290km (180 miles) to the Andaman Sea. One of Asia's major rivers, it is also one of the largest rice-producing regions in the world. Length: approx. 2,100km (1,300 miles).

Irredentists, Italian political party formed in 1878, as the *Italia Irredenta* society, whose name, meaning "unredeemed Italy", referred to their intention to gain (or regain) nearby territories such as Trentino and Trieste, which contained large numbers of Italian-speaking people. After Italy's unification (1860–70) they aimed to incorporate similar areas that were controlled by Austria, and worked to keep Italy out of the TRIPLE ALLIANCE. They also influenced Italy's decision to enter WWI on the side of the Allies.

Irregular galaxy, type of GALAXY characterized by an apparent absence of symmetrical or definite structure. Only about 3% of observed galaxies fall into this category, and it is possible that some represent intermediate stages in development, while others may be distorted by internal or external disturbances. *See also* SU p.248.

Irreversible reaction, chemical reaction in which the reactants are completely converted into the products, with no reaction in the opposite direction, from products to reactants. The equation is written using a single arrow, as in $2Na + Cl_2 \rightarrow 2NaCl$.

Irrigation, artificial watering of land to supply the necessary moisture for growing crops. It is used worldwide in regions with inadequate precipitation and dates from 2000 BC in Egypt. Primitive forms, such as buckets and water wheels, are still used in remote areas. Surface water in streams, rivers and lakes or subsurface water from wells are used, depending on the locality. Dykes, sprinklers, surface gravity, canals or underground pipes transport the water to desired locations. Suitable drainage is important when irrigating because concentrations of dissolved salts are harmful to plants and salt-saturated soil is agriculturally worthless. *See also* MM pp.196–197; PE p.168.

Irtysh, river in central USSR rising in the Altay Mts on the Mongolian-Chinese border and flowing across the USSR border into Lake Zaisan. After crossing the Kazakh republic it joins the River Ob near Khanty-Mansiisk in West Siberia. It is the largest tributary of the Ob and is completely navigable. Length: 4,444km (2,760 miles). *See also* MW p.18.

Irving, Sir Henry (1838–1905), British actor-manager, real name John Henry Brodribb. He made his first stage appearance in 1856 and in 1878 engaged Ellen TERRY as his leading lady. He managed the Lyceum Theatre, London (1878–1902), and last appeared on stage in a production of *Becket* in 1905. *See also* HC2 p.101.

Irving, Robert Augustine (1913–), British conductor, especially of ballet music. He was musical director of Sadler's Wells and the Royal Ballet (1949–58), then musical director of the New York City Ballet. He also conducts for the Martha Graham Dance Company.

Irving, Washington (1783–1859), US author, most famous for his stories *Rip Van Winkle* (1819–20) and *The Legend of Sleepy Hollow* (1819–20). He went to Madrid in 1826 and wrote *The Conquest of Granada* (1829) and *The Legends of the Alhambra* (1832). He returned to the USA in 1832 and wrote *Astoria* (1836). *See also* HC2 p.288.

Irvingites. *See* CATHOLIC APOSTOLIC CHURCH.

Isaac, in the Bible, only son of ABRAHAM and SARAH, born when Abraham was 100 and Sarah 90. As a test of faith in God, Abraham was prepared to sacrifice Isaac as commanded, but as the test was successful, the sacrifice was not made. The sons of Isaac and REBECCA were JACOB and ESAU.

Isaacs, Sir Isaac Alfred (1855–1948), Australian political figure. In 1892 he was elected to the legislative assembly of Victoria and helped to draft a Commonwealth Constitution. He became attorney-general in 1905 and the first Australian-born governor-general in 1931.

Isabella (1292–1358), Queen of England (1308–27) and wife of EDWARD II, daughter of Philip IV of France. Neglected by her husband, she formed a liaison with Roger de MORTIMER. They raised armies, deposed Edward II, and in 1327 proclaimed her eldest son, Edward III, king.

Isabella, name of two Spanish queens. Isabella I, Queen of Castile and Aragon (1451–1504, *r.* 1474–1504), was the daughter of John II. She married Ferdinand II of Aragon in 1469 and they ruled their two kingdoms jointly from 1479, forming the basis for a united Spain. Isabella's daughter Joanna ("the Mad") succeeded to the Castilian throne on her death. Isabella II (1830–1904, *r.* 1833–68) was the daughter of Ferdinand VII and Maria Christina. Until she came of age, Isabella's mother and then Baldomero Espartero ruled as regents. Isabella abdicated in 1870, renouncing her claim in favour of her son, Alfonso XII, after a troubled reign.

Isaiah, book of the Old Testament, the first and longest (66 chapters) of the major prophets. Written in both verse and prose, it is generally attributed to at least two authors of different historical background.

Ischaemia, reduction in the blood supply to an area or organ such as the heart. It is caused by constriction or obstruction of blood vessels. *See also* MS pp.*53*, 90–91.

Ischia, volcanic island off S Italy in the Tyrrhenian Sea between the Gulf of Gaeta and the Bay of Naples. Its economy is based on tourism, although fishing and farming are also pursued. Area: 47sq km (18sq miles). Pop. (1971) 14,389.

Ischium, U-shaped bone at the base and on either side of the PELVIS. It is fused with the ILIUM and the PUBIS in the hip socket; its lower edge meets the pubis. In primates the ischium takes most of the body's weight when sitting.

Isfahan (Esfahān), city in central Iran, on the Zaindeh River. The ancient city of Aspadana, it was taken in turn, by the Arabs, Seljuk Turks, Mongols and Safavids. The latter made it their capital, building many mosques and palaces. After capture by the Afghans in 1722, however, the city declined. Today it has steel and textile industries as well as the more traditional crafts of metalwork and silverware. Pop. 605,000.

Isherwood, Christopher William Bradshaw (1904–), British writer. His novels, written in a limpid, economical style, are mainly autobiographical and deal with the sensibility of the homosexual artist in various social contexts. They include *All the Conspirators* (1928) and *Mr. Norris Changes Trains* (1935), set in pre-war Germany, and much praised for its documentary value. The musical *Cabaret* (1966) was based on a short story from *Goodbye to Berlin* (1939). He emigrated to the USA in 1940 and his later works include material on Hinduism and an autobiographical retrospective *Christopher and his Kind* (1977).

Ishihara tests, method of detecting the presence of colour blindness by showing the subject plates that contain dots of various sizes and colours showing gradual tonal changes, forming normally recognizable patterns. An inability to distinguish shapes (usually numerals) on the plates indicates colour blindness.

Ishtar, principal goddess of the Assyro-Babylonian pantheon. In ancient mythology she is both the daughter of ANU, the sky god, and SIN, the moon god. Through the centuries, as she absorbed local deities and her power grew, she came to exhibit diverse attributes, those of a compassionate mother goddess and of a lustful goddess of sex and war. Ishtar is identified with the Sumerian Inanna, Phoenician ASTARTE, and the biblical Ashtoreth.

Isidore of Seville, Saint (*c.* 560–636), archbishop of Seville from *c.* 600 and a distinguished administrator, teacher and author. His works include a history of the world from the Creation to 615 (622–23) and *Origines,* an encyclopaedia.

Isidorus of Miletus. *See* ANTHEMIUS OF TRALLES.

Isinglass, clear, almost pure gelatin that is prepared from the air bladders of sturgeon and other sources. It has a fibrous structure and is used primarily to clarify wines and beers. MUSCOVITE, also called isinglass, is an abundant silicate material; it is used as an electrical and thermal insulator.

Isis, in Egyptian mythology, wife and sister of OSIRIS, and mother of Horus. After the murder of Osiris by his brother SETH (or Set), Isis managed to find and put together the dismembered parts of Osiris's body, and magically revive him. The epitome of fidelity and maternal devotion, veneration of her, particularly as the protectress of children, was spread throughout the ancient world by the Ptolemies and the Romans.

Isis, name applied to the River Thames in its upper course, above and around Oxford.

Iskenderun, Gulf of, formerly the Gulf of Alexandretta, an inlet of the Mediterranean Sea off the coast of S central Turkey. The seaport city of Iskenderun is on the E shore of S Turkey.

Islam, monotheistic religion founded by MOHAMMED in Arabia in the 7th century. There is now a fundamental division of Islam into the SUNNI and Shi'i sects. Members of the faith, called MUSLIMS, date the beginning of the Muslim era from the year in which the HEGIRA took place (AD 622). The KORAN, their sacred book, is believed to be the divine revelation of God to Mohammed, supplemented by the

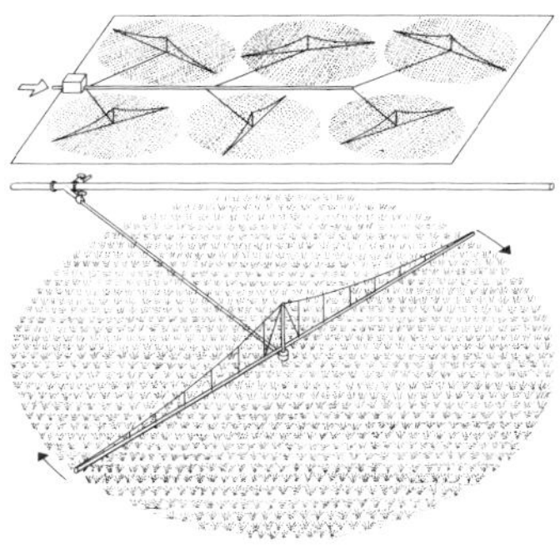

Irrigation techniques include systems of sprinklers which water fields evenly.

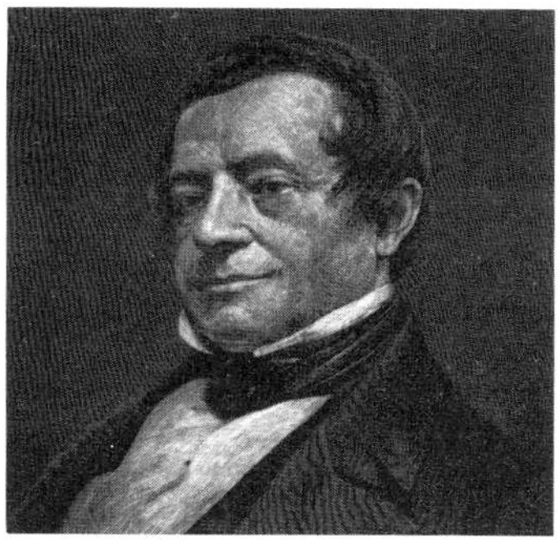

Washington Irving's *Rip Van Winkle* draws from the Dutch character of New York.

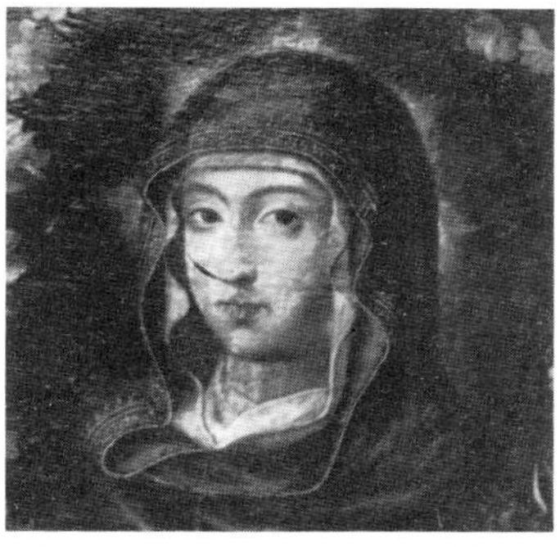

Isabella "The Catholic", Queen of Castile from a painting in the Columbus Museum.

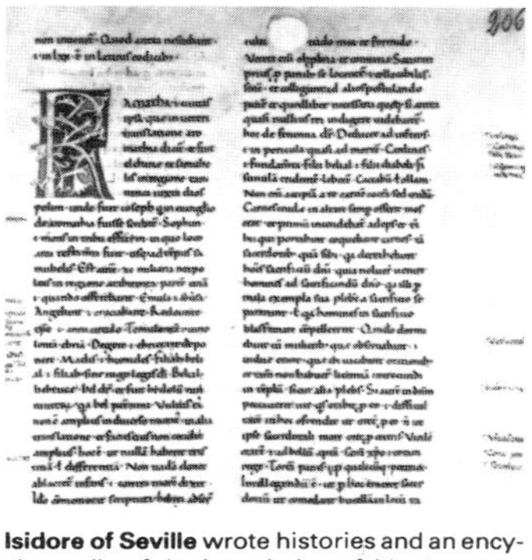

Isidore of Seville wrote histories and an encyclopaedia of the knowledge of his time.

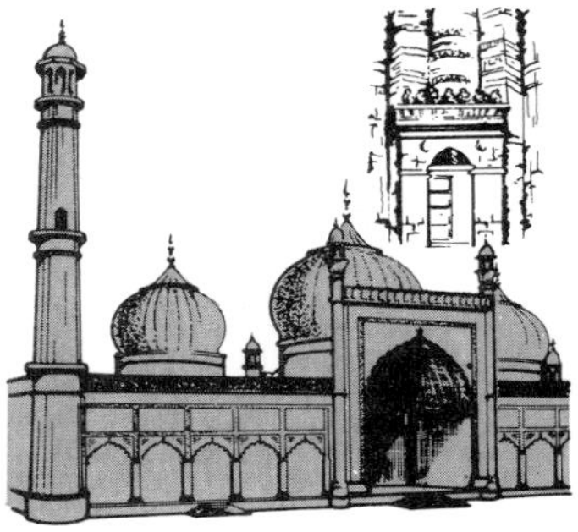

Islamic architecture, centred on forms of the mosque, is usually highly decorated.

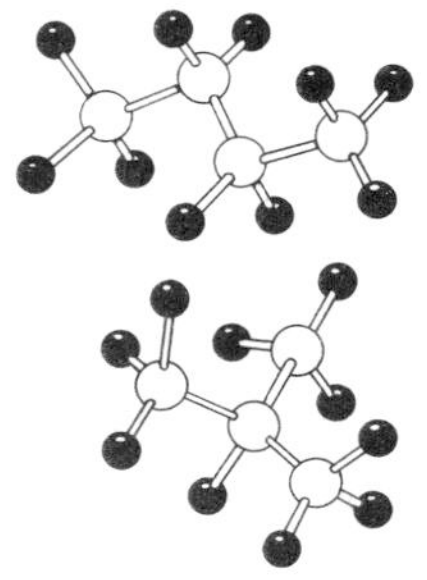

Isomers are chemical compounds with the same formula but different structures.

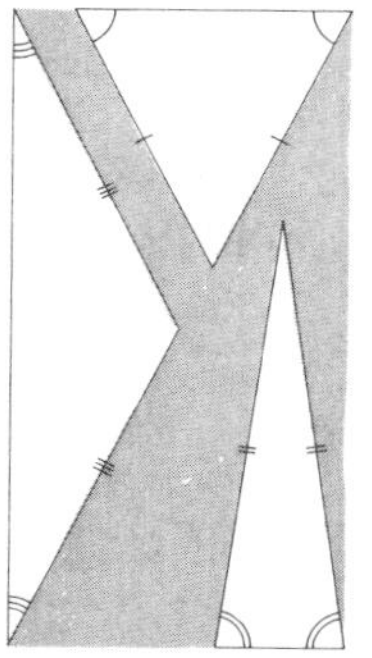

Isosceles triangle has two sides equal; the angles opposite them are also equal.

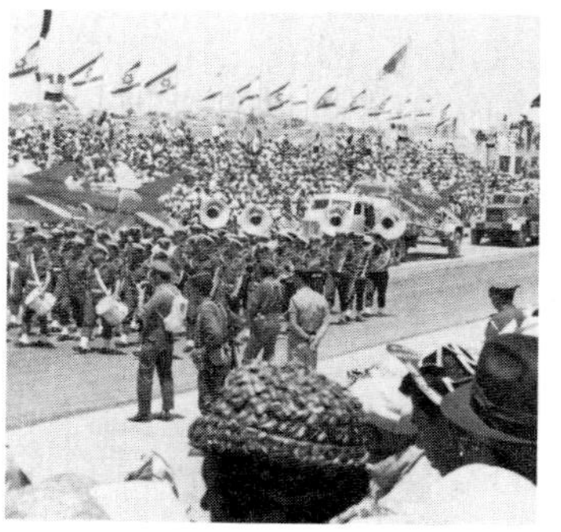

Israel forces parade in celebration of the 20th anniversary of independence in 1968.

Sunni, a collection of Prophet's sayings and deeds. Central themes of Islamic doctrine are belief in the unity of God or ALLAH, in Mohammed's prophetic mission and in the universal Judgement Day to come. The Arabic word "Islam" means "submission" and this should be the believer's attitude in the five duties he must perform. He must also abide by the religious law or Sharia. In theory the Sharia governs the whole life of the individual, but some modern Muslim states have adapted legal codes to replace Muslim law. *See also* HC1 pp.144–145.

Islāmābād, capital of Pakistan 14km (9 miles) NE of Rāwalpindi. Construction of the city to replace Karāchi as the capital began in 1960. Administrative and governmental activities provide most of its income. Pop. (1972) 77,318.

Islamic art and architecture evolved from a fusion of cultures. As the Moors swept through the Middle East and west to Spain in the mid-7th century, they developed a unique style of art based on the influences – Sassanid, Greek, Syrian, Roman, Coptic, Byzantine, Visigoth – of the conquered lands. Islamic art is best illustrated by its architecture. Two surviving examples of the 8th century are the Great Mosque of Damascus and the Dome of the Rock at Jerusalem. The Sassanid tradition of brick and stucco building then characterized Persian Muslim architecture from the Mosque of Tarik Khanah at Damghan (*c.*9th century) to the sumptuous Safavid works of the 17th century. The Seljuk Turks, who defeated the Byzantines in 1071 and overran central Anatolia, left in Asia Minor a bold architectural style derived from Syrian stone carving techniques and the use of Persian decorative brickwork. Moorish architecture in Spain developed somewhat independently, and is characterized by its use of the horseshoe arch, FAIENCE and lacy stone screens. The Suleimanye (1550), Istanbul, is one of the great Ottoman mosques inspired by the Byzantine HAGIA SOPHIA.

Muslim secular art was expressed in pottery, metalwork, textiles and painting. Metalwork flourished from the 12th to the 14th centuries. Many ceremonial silks date from the 9th to 12th centuries, and carpets and rugs had their golden age in 16th and 17th-century Persia. *See also* HC1 pp.144–145, 148–151, 170.

Islamic law, or Sharia, practical ordinances of ISLAM. Defined in the KORAN, it is believed to be the revelations by God to MOHAMMED, the traditional sayings of Mohammed, the consensus of the community in the past, and analogical reasoning. The Sharia is divided into two sections of equal importance: Ibadet, duties owed to God by way of worship; and Muamalet, practical duties towards men and society. Because Islam recognizes no distinction between religious and secular law, the Sharia provides for all aspects of a believer's existence. There are four schools of law: Maliki, Hanifi, Shafi'i and Hanbali, which have come to prominence in different areas of the Islamic world. Muslims were once expected to submit totally to the laws of one of the schools, but modern Muslim states have adopted legal codes limiting the dominance of the Sharia.

Islay, island in W central Scotland, the most southern of the Inner HEBRIDES. The fertile land allows intensive livestock and dairy farming. Fishing, malt whisky production and tourism also provide valuable income. Area: 622sq km (240sq miles). Pop. 5,743.

Isle of Ely, region in N Cambridgeshire, England. Drained chiefly by the Rivers Ouse and Nene, the region rises above low-lying fen country that has been drained to form fertile farmland. Sugar-beet and vegetables are grown, and pigs and poultry are raised. Tourism is important and the main town, Ely, is famous for its 11th-century cathedral.

Isle of Man, island off the NW coast of England, in the Irish Sea. It has been a British Crown possession since 1828 and has its own government, the Tynwald. The basis of the economy is tourism although agriculture is important, the chief products being oats, fruit and vegetables. The capital is Douglas. Area: 572sq km (221sq miles). Pop. (1975 est.) 59,000.

Isle of Wight, island off the S coast of England, separated from the mainland by The Solent. It is an administrative county. The island's mild climate and attractive scenery have made it a popular tourist resort. Other industries: shipbuilding and aircraft construction. Area: 318sq km (147sq miles). Pop. (1976) 112,200.

Islets of Langerhans, clusters of cells in the PANCREAS which produce two hormones: INSULIN, to raise the level of GLUCOSE in the blood and GLUCAGON, to counteract the effect of insulin when necessary. They were discovered by the 19th-century German physician Paul Langerhans.

Ismail, Shah of Persia (*r.*1501–24), founder of the SAFAVID DYNASTY. He re-established Persian independence after centuries of Arab control and established Shi'ite Islam as the state religion of Persia. He warred successfully against the UZBEKS in 1510 but was defeated by the Ottoman sultan SELIM I in 1514.

Ismail Pasha (1830–95), ruler of Egypt (1863–79). In 1867 he received the title khedive. The high price received for Egyptian cotton at the time enabled him to build extensively. Much money was wasted, however, and in 1875 Egypt was forced to sell to Britain its interest in one of the largest constructions, the Suez Canal. Egypt's finances were put in the control of a Franco-British debt commission. The Ottoman sultan replaced Ismail Pasha with his son Tawfiq Pasha in 1879. *See also* HC2 pp.*131, 133.*

Isma'ilis, or Seveners, the smaller of two groups of the SHI'A sect of ISLAM. All Shi'ites believe in the authority of a succession of imams, or spiritual guides, descended from Mohammed's son-in-law, Ali. After the sixth imam had disinherited his eldest son, Isma'il, a dispute arose about the succession. Those who chose Isma'il, and on his death his son Muhammad, are called Isma'ilis or Seveners because they believe that Muhammad was the seventh and last imam.

Isobar, line of constant pressure at the earth's surface or at a constant height above it on a weather map. The patterns of isobars depict the variation in atmospheric pressure, showing areas of high and low pressure on the map. *See also* PE p.72, *72.*

Isocrates (436–338 BC), Athenian rhetorician who wrote speeches and numerous tracts on politics and education, but was himself shy of public speaking. He founded a school in Athens and was an influential teacher and prose stylist.

Isogamy, in biology, reproductive cells that act like sex cells but which are similar in size and structure. It is found in algae, some protozoans, and primitive plants, as distinct from anisogamy, where male and female sex cells differ in appearance.

Isolationism, theme particularly connected with US foreign policy, dating from President George WASHINGTON's farewell address (1796), in which he warned the USA to steer clear of European entanglements. In the 20th century the mood in favour of isolationism has been strong, especially among REPUBLICANS, after WWI, at the start of WWII, during the KOREAN WAR and after the military failure in the VIETNAM WAR.

Isomers, chemical compounds having the same molecular formulas but different properties as a result of having a different arrangement of atoms within the molecules. Structural isomers have different structural formulae. For example, urea, $CO(NH_2)_2$, and ammonium cynate, NH_4CNO, have the same molecular formula (CH_4N_2O) but totally different properties. Geometric isomers differ in their symmetry about a double bond; the cis-form of a compound has certain atoms or groups on the same side of a plane, whereas the trans form has them on the opposite side. For example, maleic acid is the cis-form of fumaric acid. Optical isomers are mirror images of each other. *See also* SU pp.*141,* 147, 152.

Isomorphism, in CRYSTALLOGRAPHY, the resemblance between crystals of chemical compounds having similar crystal structures. In biology, isomorphism refers to the similarity of shape observed in unrelated groups, due to CONVERGENT EVOLUTION.

Isopod, any of about 4,000 species of CRUSTACEANS, including seven aquatic and one terrestrial suborder, characterized by flattened, oval bodies which have several hard-plated segments of similar appearance. The land forms are the familiar WOODLICE. Marine species include wood-borers (gribbles) and specialized fish parasites. *See also* NW p.*105.*

Isoprene, organic chemical compound; formula $CH_2{=}C(CH_3)CH{=}CH_2$. A synthetic product which closely resembles natural rubber can be prepared by the polymerization of isoprene.

Isoptera, TERMITES, an order of insects that lives in large colonies but which are more closely related to COCKROACHES than to the other social INSECTS, ANTS, BEES and WASPS. In tropical countries they damage timber structures because they eat wood, and their bodies harbour microscopic PROTOZOA which can digest CELLULOSE.

Isosceles triangle, triangle having any two of its sides equal in length; the angles opposite these sides are also equal.

Isostasy, theory describing the maintenance of an equilibrium in the total mass of the Earth's crust despite its crustal movement. There exists a balance between the land masses and the mantle of the earth on which the continental plates float so that the plates rise and sink on the semi-molten surface of the mantle in such a fashion that the relative mass weighing upon the Earth's crust is constant. The spread of the continental plates by the upwelling of material from deep within the Earth's crust is balanced by the submergence of the opposite edges of the plates. *See also* CONTINENTAL DRIFT; PLATE TECTONICS; PE pp.26, 32–33.

Isotherm, line of equal temperature on a map (usually a weather map). The patterns of isotherms depict how the temperature changes across the area of the map.

Isotopes, atoms of an element with the same number of electrons or protons (same atomic number) but a different number of neutrons in the nucleus, so that both mass number and mass of the nucleus vary between isotopes. The atomic weight of an element is an average of the isotope masses. The isotopes of an element all have similar chemical properties, but physical properties do vary. Most elements have two or more naturally occurring isotopes, some of which are radioactive (radioisotopes). Many radioisotopes can be produced artificially by bombarding elements with high-energy particles, such as alpha-particles. Radioisotopes are used in medicine, research and industry. Isotopes are also used in the dating of FOSSILS and archaeological remains. *See also* CARBON DATING; SU pp.64, 132–133, *133.*

Isotropic, term meaning the possession of physical properties which are the same regardless of the direction in which they are measured. For example, in water, conductivity and viscosity are isotropic but they may not be so in a very thick oil.

Ispahan. *See* ISFAHAN.

Israel, biblical name: originally that of JACOB after he had wrestled with the mysterious "man" who was either an angel or God himself. Israel was also the name of the territory of the ten northern tribes, as opposed to the two southern tribes of JUDAH, living in Palestine before the BABYLONIAN CAPTIVITY. After the captivity there were no southern tribes left: only Israel returned.

Israel, republic in the E Mediterranean that comprises most of the historic region of Palestine. Most of the agriculture is on a co-operative basis, producing cereal and citrus fruits. Mineral deposits are being exploited and there has been much foreign investment in industry. The economy is heavily depleted by efforts to maintain sovereignty in an area regarded as Arab territory by the surrounding states. The capital is Jerusalem. Area: 20,700sq km (7,992sq miles). Pop. (1976 est.) 3,483,000. *See* ARAB-ISRAELI WARS; MW p.106.

Issachar, in GENESIS, ninth son of Jacob

and Leah. His tribe occupied the fertile land along the River Jordan. Deborah and Barak were members of this tribe.

Issigonis, Sir Alec Arnold Constantine (1906–), British car designer, *b.* Turkey. He began his career in 1933 as a draughtsman. Subsequently a chief engineer and technical director, he became advanced design consultant to British Leyland in 1972. His designs include the Morris Minor (1948), Mini Minor/Austin Seven (1959) and Austin 1100 (1962). *See also* MM p.*127.*

Istanbul, city and seaport in NW Turkey, on both sides of the Bosporus, which links the Black Sea and the Sea of Marmara. It was known as Byzantium until AD 330 when CONSTANTINE chose it as his new capital and renamed it Constantinople. Captured by the OTTOMAN Turks in 1453, the city was largely destroyed by an earthquake in 1509 and rebuilt by Sultan BEYAZID II. Many of the city's mosques date from this period. When the new Turkish Republic was established after WWI, the capital was moved to Ankara and Constantinople renamed Istanbul. Today it is the commercial and financial centre of Turkey, manufacturing glass, textiles and leather goods. It also derives a valuable income from tourism. Pop. (1973) 2,487,100. *See also* HC1 pp.142–143, 176–177, 220–221, 223.

Istria, region of NW Yugoslavia, a peninsula between TRIESTE and FIUME. It became part of the Roman Empire in the 2nd century BC. Incorporated into Austria in 1797, it was ceded to Italy in 1919. In 1947 most of Istria passed to Yugoslavia.

Italian, Romance language of the Indo-European language family and the official language of Italy and of the canton of Ticino, Switzerland. A descendant of Vulgar Latin, its first extant record is in the *Testimonial Formulae of Monte Cassino* (960–63). There are many Italian dialects, and the official language is based on those of central Italy, particularly Tuscan. Tuscany's geographical position between north and south, its commercial importance and cultural dominance – in particular the writing of DANTE, PETRARCH and BOCCACCIO – in the 13th and 14th centuries led to its influence in the development of a single Italian language.

Italian greyhound, miniature breed of GREYHOUND noted for its elegant, prancing gait. It has a long, flat narrow head, a tapering muzzle, folded ears and large eyes. The lean arched body is set on slender, fine-boned legs and the long tail is generally held low. Height: to 25cm (10in) at the shoulder; weight: to 3.6kg (8lb).

Italics, style of handwriting developed by the Florentine humanist Niccolò Niccoli in the 15th century. Known as *antica corsiva* (antique cursive), it was adopted by the papal chancery and by the 16th century had replaced Gothic script in most European countries. It has been revived in the 20th century. In printing it became the model for the Italic type-face which was designed *c.*1501 by Francesco Griffo for Aldus Manutius of Venice. With letters sloping to the right, it is now used for special purposes such as to indicate emphasis or foreign words. *This sentence is printed in italics.*

Italy, country extending from the main continent of Europe SE into the Mediterranean Sea. After devastation during WWII it made the transition from an agrarian to an industrial economy, although industry is concentrated in the N, highlighting the vast regional differences between N and S. Sugar-beet, wheat and rice are produced and exports include machinery and motor vehicles. An adverse balance of trade is reduced by a considerable income from tourism. The capital is Rome. Area: 301,245sq km (116,311sq miles). Pop. (1975 est.) 56,483,000. *See* MW p.107.

Itching, also called pruritus, sensation of irritation on the skin which, if constant, may become unbearable; frequent scratching can result in damage to skin tissue. It may be caused in a variety of ways – materials irritating the skin, the bites of insects or lice, "prickly heat" or allergic reactions. ECZEMA, of which itching is a symptom, is an instance where psychological factors may worsen the condition. Several disorders, including DIABETES MELLITUS and JAUNDICE, can cause various local skin irritations.

Itzá, TOLTEC Indian group that migrated to NE Yucatan (Mexico) between AD 514 and 1200. The ceremonial centre of Chichen was transformed into a city by the Itza, who were subsequently absorbed into MAYA society.

IUD, intrauterine device, plastic or metal loop inserted by a doctor inside a woman's womb as a means of contraception. For those on whom it can be used it is reliable, but it does not suit all women. *See also* MS pp.*80,* 81.

Ivan, name of two grand princes of Moscow and three tsars of Russia. Ivan I (*c.* 1304–41) was Grand Prince of Moscow from 1328 until his death. He enlarged Moscow (Muscovy) and made it the richest province in NE Russia. By allying himself with the Russian Orthodox Church he made Moscow the spiritual centre of Russia. Ivan III (1440–1505) was Grand Prince of Moscow from 1462 until his death. He laid the foundations of a centralized monarchy and began the conquest of the Ukraine from Lithuania and Poland. Ivan IV (1530–84), known as Ivan the Terrible, was the first Tsar of Russia (1547–84). He created a centrally administered Russian state and began the expansion of Russia into non-Slavic lands. He gave Russia its first national assembly (1549). He earned his nickname by the oppression of political opponents in his last years, more than 3,000 of whom died. Ivan V (1666–96) was Tsar of Russia from 1692 to 1696. He was an invalid and mentally retarded and took no part in government affairs. Ivan VI (1740–64) was the infant Tsar in 1740–41. He was deposed by a group led by Elizabeth, daughter of PETER the Great, confined to solitary imprisonment and assassinated during Mirovich's mutiny of 1764.

Ivanhoe, (1819), novel by Sir Walter SCOTT, based on the enmity between Saxon and Norman in England under Richard I. Wilfred of Ivanhoe returns from Richard's crusade, and after various adventures is reunited with Lady Rowena.

Ivanov, Lev (1834–1901), Russian ballet dancer and choreographic assistant to Marius PETIPA, the director of the Imperial Russian Ballet, for which he later staged some 20 works. He based his choreography on the emotional content of the musical score, concentrating on patterns of group movement, as in his snowflake dance in *The Nutcracker* (1892).

Ivanov, Vsevolod Vyacheslavovich (1895–1963), Russian novelist and dramatist whose ability for vivid description and irony was encouraged by Maxim GORKY. The story *Armoured Train 14-69* (1922), which he later dramatized, is regarded as his most important work.

Ivanov, Vyacheslav Ivanovich (1866–1949), Russian poet and philosopher. His poetry displays both symbolism, as in *Pilot Stars* (1901), and mysticism as in *Cor Ardens* (1911). His philosophical works, influenced by Friedrich NIETZSCHE, include *Dionysus and Proto-Dionysianism* (1923).

Ives, Charles (1874–1954), US composer. Although he was a pioneer in experimenting in the use of new harmonic and rhythmic effects he was only gradually acknowledged as the earliest, and one of the most original, of US modern composers. American folk-music is often the thematic basis of his work, as in the *Variations on America* for organ (1891) and the *Symphony No. 2* (1902). His music ranges from symphonies and chamber works to songs and piano music. In 1947 he was awarded the Pulitzer Music Prize. *See also* HC2 p.270.

Ivory, James (1930–), US film director whose work mostly explored the meeting of traditional and modern in Indian life. His early films include *Shakespeare Wallah* (1965) and *Bombay Talkie* (1970). *Savages* (1972), which was set in the USA, marked a departure in content, but Ivory returned to familiar themes in *Autobiography of a Princess* (1975).

Ivory, hard, yellowish-white dentine of an elephant's tusk from which the most highly prized variety is obtained. The term also refers to the teeth of hippopotamuses, walruses, sperm whales and several other mammals.

Ivory Coast, nation in W Africa. The tropical climate produces valuable hardwoods for export although coffee is the country's most important crop. The republic is also a leading producer of cocoa. These exports have produced a high economic growth rate and have encouraged foreign investment in new industries, notably oil and minerals. The capital is Abidjan. Area: 322,463sq km (124,503sq miles). Pop. (1975) 6,673,000. *See* MW p.110.

Ivy, woody, EVERGREEN vine with leathery leaves, native to Europe and Asia. Its long, climbing stems cling to upright surfaces by aerial roots. It may be injurious to trees by becoming virtually parasitic on them. The common English ivy (*Hedera helix*) is propagated by cuttings and grows outdoors in moist shady, or sunny areas. Family Araliaceae.

Iwo Jima, formerly Sulphur Island, the largest of the Japanese Volcano Islands in the W Pacific Ocean. Taken by the USA at great cost in WWII, it was returned to Japan in 1968. Industries include sugar refining and sulphur mining. Area: 21sq km (8sq miles).

Ixelles, city in central Belgium, a SE suburb of Brussels. Its industries include metal-working, chemicals and textiles. Pop. (1971 est.) 87,500.

Izard, Pyrenean IBEX, a surefooted, hardy wild GOAT of the family Bovidae. Also called Spanish ibex, it is regarded as a critically endangered species. Species *Capra pyrenaica.*

Izmir, formerly Smyrna, port city in W Turkey, on the Gulf of Izmir. The city was part of the Ottoman Empire from 1424 until 1919, when it was tentatively assigned to Greece. It passed to Turkey by the terms of the Treaty of Lausanne (1923). It has been the seat of the SE headquarters of NATO since 1952. A commercial centre, it exports fruit, tobacco and silk. Pop. 619,150.

J

J, tenth letter of the alphabet. It evolved from the letter *i* and was the last to be incorporated into the modern alphabet; its early history is therefore the same as that of *i.* The *j* developed from the tailed form of the *i* as often written at the beginnings of words. It is a consonant in English, nearly always pronounced as in *jug*; in some words (such as *hallelujah*) it is pronounced like a *y.* *See also* MS pp.244–245.

Jabberwocky, seven-stanza nonsense poem by Lewis CARROLL, which appeared in *Through The Looking Glass* (1872). The language developed from a mock Anglo-Saxon verse Carroll had first published in 1855, and looked forward to comparable language in *The Hunting of the Snark* (1876). TENNIEL illustrated the jabberwocky itself as a type of dragon – a concept pursued by the film *Jabberwocky* (1977).

Jabiru, the largest stork of the New World, found in tropical swamps from Mexico to Argentina. The head and upper neck are naked. Length: 1.4m (4.6ft). Family Ciconiidae, species *Jabiru mycteria.*

Jaborandi, any of several tropical shrubs (Family Rutaceae) that grow in South America, especially *Pilocarpus pennatifolius* and *P. selloanus.* It is also another name for the ALKALOID pilocarpine, which is derived from the leaves of these plants. This drug stimulates salivation, causes sweating and contracts the iris of the eye.

Jacamar, any of several species of small birds of tropical America with an iridescent black or green back and black or tawny breast, a long sharp bill and a long tapering tail. The common rufous-tailed jacamar (*Galbula ruficauda*)

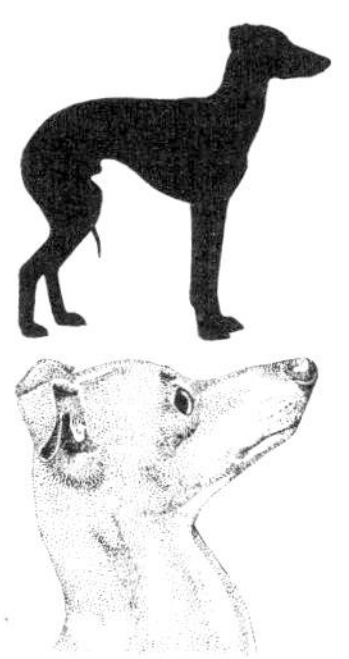

Italian greyhounds have probably been bred in Italy since the days of the Roman Empire.

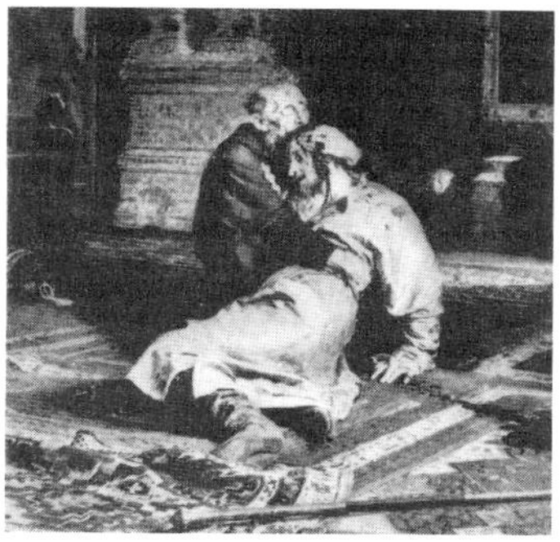

Ivan IV, the "Terrible", portrayed with his dying son who he killed in a fit of rage.

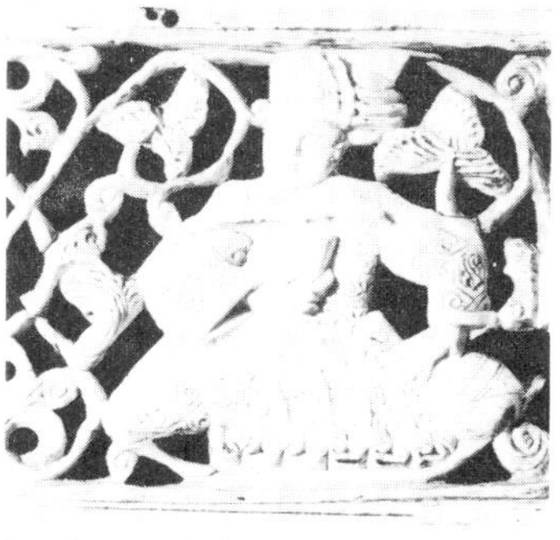

Ivory is often richly carved, as on the side of this 12th-century Mesopotamian jewel box.

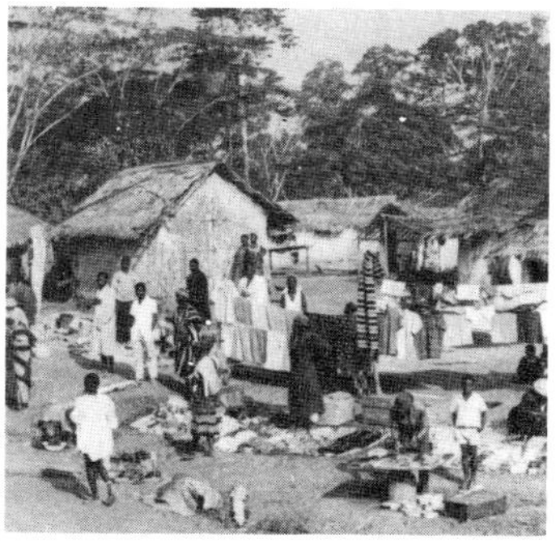

Ivory Coast villagers, at their weekly market, pay serious attention to the photographer.

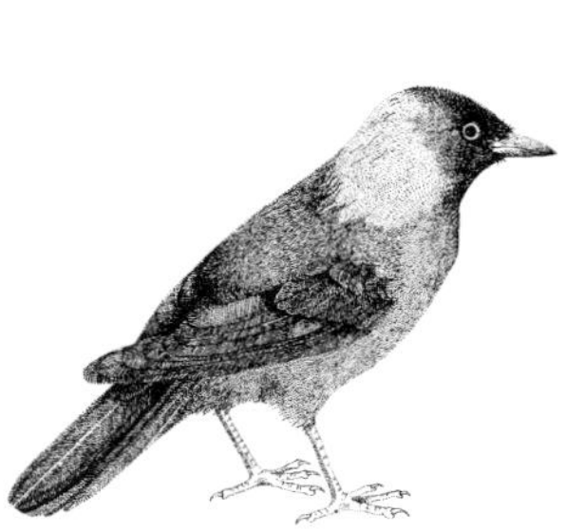

Jackdaws, although inclined to theft, are useful to farmers in destroying insects.

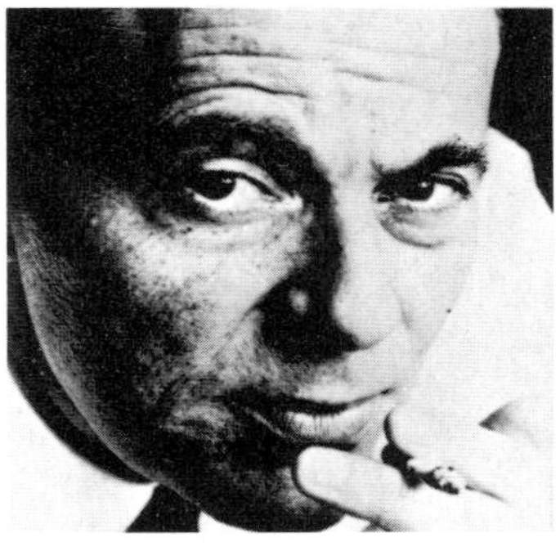

François Jacob became professor of cellular genetics at the Collège de France in 1964.

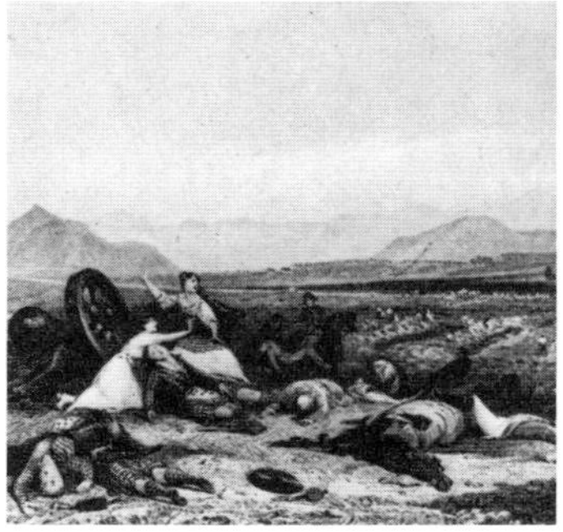

Jacobite rebellions; the Battle of Cullodon Moor, which saw the end of Stewart hopes.

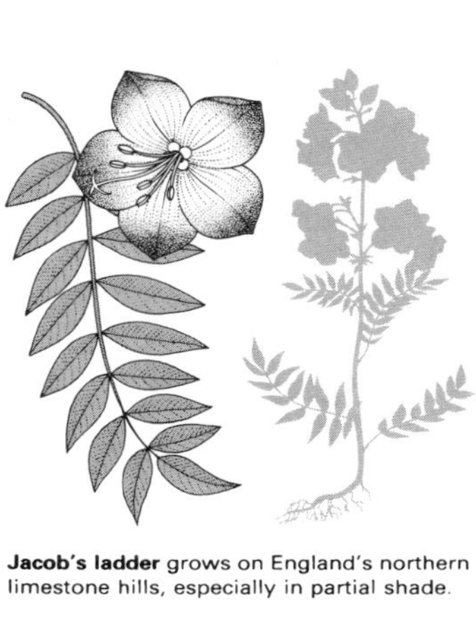

Jacob's ladder grows on England's northern limestone hills, especially in partial shade.

perches in trees along the banks of streams, flying out to catch insects. Length: to 30cm (12in). Family Galbulidae.

Jacana, or lily trotter, long-toed water bird of tropical lakes with a slender body, narrow bill, wrist spurs and tapered claws. It is black or reddish-brown, sometimes with a bright frontal shield. It runs over floating vegetation, feeding on aquatic plants and small animals. Length: to 50.8cm (20in). Family: Jacanidae. *See also* NW p.*233*.

Jacaranda, tree native to tropical America and cultivated in greenhouses throughout the world. The ornamental *Jacaranda mimosifolia* and *J. cuspidifolia* have showy blue flowers. There are 50 species. Family Bignoniaceae.

J'accuse, first two words of an open letter from Émile ZOLA published in the newspaper *L'Aurore* on 13 Jan. 1898. In the letter Zola accused the French government of concealing the true facts of the DREYFUS AFFAIR. The resulting controversy helped re-open the issue.

Jacinth, hyacinth, a rare gemstone, transparent red, orange or yellow in colour, which is a variety of ZIRCON. Deposits are found, notably in Ceylon and New South Wales, where erosion has exposed them.

Jackal, wild dog that resembles a COYOTE in habits, size and general appearance. It preys on small animals and eats carrion, fruit and seeds. The various species, in the genus *Canis*, are distributed throughout Asia and Africa. Length: to 74cm (29.1in). Family Canidae. *See also* NW p.*164*.

Jackdaw, gregarious black-and-grey bird that frequents open country near buildings, ruins or cliffs. Smaller than its relative, the crow, it has a grey head and white-rimmed eyes. It lives in colonies, with both parents constructing the nest and feeding the young. Family Corvidae; species *Corvus monedula*. *See also* NW p.*144*.

Jackeroo, Australian colloquial term for a young man who works as an assistant on large properties and cattle stations. His duties usually include boundary maintenance and supervision. The female counterpart is a jillaroo, a term coined during WWII.

Jack-in-the-box, children's toy consisting of a box, from which a figure on a spring jumps when the box is opened. The name is derived from a phrase used in the 17th century to describe salesmen in market stalls.

Jack-in-the-pulpit. *See* CUCKOO-PINT.

Jacklin, Tony (1944–), British golfer. The highlights of his career came when he won the 1969 British and 1970 US Open Championships. Thereafter his performances became less consistent, although he continued to represent Britain in the Ryder Cup.

Jack rabbit, any of several large, slender, long-eared hares of W North America. Jack rabbits rely on their great speed, powerful leaps and general agility to escape from coyotes and other predators. Most are grey with white underparts, but the common northern white-tailed jack rabbit has a lighter winter coat. Family Leporidae; genus *Lepus*.

Jackson, Andrew (1767–1845), 7th US President (1829–37), general and Indian fighter. At the age of 13 he was captured by the British in the American War of Independence but later as a general in the Battle of New Orleans (1815) he defeated them and became a national hero. A frontiersman, intolerant of formal education, he soon emerged as the symbol of a new egalitarian society. During his presidency the balance of power shifted from the urban East to the farmers and small businessmen of the West.

Jackson, Sir Barry Vincent (1879–1961), British theatre manager and director. He founded the Birmingham Repertory Theatre in 1913 and ran it until his death, and founded the Malvern Festival (1929), notable for productions of plays by George Bernard SHAW. From 1945 to 1948 he was director of the Shakespeare Memorial Theatre, Stratford-on-Avon.

Jackson, Donald (1940–), Canadian figure-skater who, after being a bronze medallist in the 1960 Winter Olympics, won the 1962 world championship with a free-skating routine that included spectacular triple jumps. He turned professional and was world champion in 1970.

Jackson, Glenda (1936–), British actress famed for strong performances in historical and modern dramas. Her films include *Women in Love* (1969), *Sunday, Bloody Sunday* (1971), *Elizabeth R* (for television, 1971), *A Touch of Class* (1972) and *The Romantic Englishwoman* (1974). Her stage roles have included that of the poet Stevie Smith in *Stevie* (1977).

Jackson, John Hughlings (1835–1911), British neurologist. He studied speech defects as a symptom of brain disease; the disease he located in the left cerebral hemisphere. He also traced motor spasms to a brain disorder. Such spasms are now called Jacksonian EPILEPSY.

Jackson, Marjorie (1931–), Australian sprinter. Nicknamed the "Blue Streak", she won the 1952 Olympic 100m and 200m, plus seven British Empire gold medals (1950, 1954). When she retired at age 22, she had established five world records, equalled five and shared in three relay world records.

Jackson, Thomas J. ("Stonewall") (1824–63), US Civil War Confederate general. His stand against overwhelming odds at the first Battle of Bull Run (1861) gained him the nickname "Stonewall". He drove his troops so hard that they were known as "Jackson's Foot Cavalry". He was considered Gen. Robert E. LEE's best general. Jackson was accidentally shot by one of his own men at Chancellorsville, where he had just defeated the Unionists. *See also* HC2 pp.150–151.

Jackson, capital and largest city in SW central Mississippi, on the Pearl River. Originally a trading post established in the 1700s and known as Le Fleur's Bluff, it was chosen as the site of the state capital in 1821. It is the centre for an extensive farm region and has a variety of industries, including food processing, glass and textiles. Pop. (1973) 163,924.

Jacksonville, seaport and largest city in NE Florida, USA, on the St John's River. It served as a CONFEDERATE base during the Civil War, developed as a port in the 19th century and was devastated by fire in 1901. An important centre of commerce and finance in the southern states, it is also a focal point of air, rail and road routes. Industries include cigars, fruit canning and wood products. Pop. (1970) 528,865.

Jack the Ripper (*fl.* 1888), presumed murderer of at least seven prostitutes in the East End of London in late 1888. The name given to the murderer came from his mutilation of his victims. He was never definitely identified.

Jacob, in the Bible, son of ISAAC and REBECCA and younger twin brother of ESAU. While fleeing after tricking Esau out of his birthright, he wrestled with an angel to obtain God's blessing. He married Leah and RACHEL; the descendants of his 12 sons became the 12 tribes of ISRAEL.

Jacob, François (1920–), French biologist. With Jacques MONOD he discovered that a substance that they named messenger RNA carried hereditary information from the cell nucleus to the sites of protein synthesis and that certain genes, called operator genes, control the activity of others. They shared the 1965 Nobel Prize in physiology and medicine with another French biologist, André LWOFF. *See also* SU pp.153, 157.

Jacob, Gordon Percival Septimus (1895–), British composer and conductor. His music has a certain crisp aggressiveness, although much of his vocal music is more lyrical in vein. His compositions include two ballets, *The Jew in the Bush* (1923) and *Uncle Remus* (1930), film music and chamber music.

Jacob, Max (1876–1944), French AVANT-GARDE poet, a close associate of APOLLINAIRE and PICASSO in the early days of CUBISM. Of Jewish descent, he converted to Roman Catholicism in 1915; he lived as a recluse but died in a German concentration camp. Jacob's poetry, a mixture of macabre humour and mysticism, includes *Le Cornet à dés* (1917).

Jacobean, term designating the artistic styles of the reign of JAMES I (1603–25), from whose name in Latin, Jacobus it is derived. The major literary art form was drama, typical examples of which are the works of WEBSTER and TOURNEUR as well as the late plays of SHAKESPEARE. The development of the masque, particularly by JONSON, and the poetry of DONNE and the METAPHYSICALS were further features of the age. In architecture, Italian MANNERISM was a formative influence, but the major achievement of the period lies in the work of Inigo JONES who introduced PALLADIANISM to England. Jacobean painters, such as the miniaturist Isaac OLIVER, did not equal the achievements of other artistic mediums and were to be surpassed by the painters of the following reign. *See also* HC1 p.296.

Jacobin, alternative name in France for a DOMINICAN friar, from the first Dominican house in Paris which was under the patronage of St James – Jacobus in Latin. The JACOBINS of the FRENCH REVOLUTION took their name from this former Dominican convent, in which they used to meet.

Jacobins, French political radicals belonging to a club that played an important role during the FRENCH REVOLUTION. Begun in 1789 by some deputies to protect the revolution against an aristocratic reaction, the club split in 1791 when the moderates left it. Thereafter more popular in orientation, the Jacobin movement developed a network of clubs throughout France. In 1793–94, the club was an instrument of ROBESPIERRE and became part of the government's administration. It was closed soon after Robespierre's downfall in 1794. *See also* HC2 pp.74–75.

Jacobite rebellions, two attempts to overthrow the HANOVERIANS and restore the STUART line to the British throne. The first, led by the Earl of Mar on behalf of the "Old Pretender", James III, began in September 1715. By the time that James arrived in England from Paris in December, Mar had failed to overcome the Duke of Argyle's forces at Sheriffmuir. Sporadic uprisings had occurred throughout the autumn, but by February 1716 the revolt had been put down. James returned to France and Mar also escaped there. Only 26 rebel officers were executed. The second rebellion, led by James' son, the "Young Pretender" Bonnie Prince Charlie began in August 1745. It ended with the overwhelming English victory over the Scots Highlanders at CULLODEN Moor in April 1746, at which the English lost only 310 men and the Scots 1,000. *See also* HC2 p.28.

Jacobites, supporters of JAMES II and his Stuart descendants, who attempted to regain the English throne after the GLORIOUS REVOLUTION of 1688. With unofficial French encouragement, Jacobites were found among Scots (the homeland of the Stuarts), Irish (James II was Catholic) and disgruntled Tories (Whigs dominated the government). *See also* JACOBITE REBELLIONS; HC2 p.28.

Jacobs, Aletta Henriëtte (1854–1929), the first woman doctor in the Netherlands, who ran the medical service set up by the Malthusian League in 1882. Its aim was to provide information on contraception. In 1890 she set up the world's first contraceptive clinic, and the idea spread rapidly to other countries.

Jacobsen, Arne (1902–71), Danish architect and industrial designer in the 1930s, an influential practitioner of the INTERNATIONAL STYLE in Denmark. After WWII he designed brick housing of elegance and originality, and in the 1950s beautifully proportioned CURTAIN WALL office blocks, including the SAS Building, Copenhagen (1959). In England, he was engaged in building the immaculately finished St Catherine's College, Oxford (1964). He designed the "Egg" swivel chair. (1959).

Jacob's ladder, any of 50 species of wild and cultivated plants of temperate areas. It has clusters of delicate blue, violet or white flowers and alternate compound leaves. The European *Polemonium caeruleum* of woodlands and high regions has large blue or white flowers. Height: up to

90cm (3ft). Family Polemoniaceae.

Jacobson, Dan (1929–), British novelist, *b.* South Africa. His first novel was *The Trap* (1955). He has also written *The Rape of Tamar* (1970), *The Wonder-worker* (1973) and *The Confessions of Josef Baisz* (1977).

Jacopo da Lentinio (*fl.* 13th century), Italian poet and notary. His poetry, mostly on the theme of chivalrous love, is technically ingenious. He is credited with inventing the sonnet form and he is mentioned in DANTE's *Divine Comedy*.

Jacopone da Todi (*c.* 1236–1306), Italian poet. After the death of his wife in the 1260s, he became a monk and wrote numerous fervid, intensely personal hymns. His work is notable for the vehemence with which he rejects the temptations of the flesh.

Jacquard, Joseph Marie (1752–1834), French silk weaver, who perfected a loom that could weave patterns automatically (1801–06). It aroused bitter hostility from many silk weavers, who feared for their livelihood. By 1812, there were 11,000 Jacquard looms in use in France. The first automated machine, the loom was controlled by PUNCHED CARDS, the forerunners of those used in modern data storage systems. *See also* MM p.*216*.

Jacquerie, insurrection of peasants against the nobility in NE France in 1358. Enraged by the increased taxes to finance the HUNDRED YEARS WAR and pillaging by English invaders and the French nobility, the peasants and some townsmen revolted. They destroyed several castles. The revolt was defeated by the nobles, who executed the leader Guillaume Carle and massacred thousands of peasants.

Jacques, Reginald (1894–1969), British conductor and organist. In 1926 he was appointed organist at Queens College, Oxford. He was renowned for his choral conducting and in 1947 founded the Jacques String Orchestra.

Jade, a semiprecious silicate mineral of two major types – jadeite, which is often translucent, and nephrite, which has a waxy quality. Both types are extremely hard and durable. Jade is found mainly in Burma and comes in many colours, most commonly green and white.

Jadotville. *See* LIKASI.

Jaffa, port in Israel, 56km (35 miles) NW of Jerusalem. Mentioned in the Bible, it was captured and hellenized by Alexander the Great in 332 BC; taken back by the Jews during the Hasmonean revolt, it was destroyed by Vespasian in AD 68. It changed hands many times in the Middle Ages, and became important in the 20th century as a point of Palestinian resistance to Jewish settlement. In 1948 the Arab inhabitants fled and the town was settled by Israelis.

Jagan, Cheddi (1918–), Prime Minister of British Guiana (1961–64). He founded, with Forbes Burnham, the People's Progressive Party, which came to power in the 1950s. When British Guiana gained independence in 1966 and was renamed Guyana, he and Burnham, had split, the latter becoming the first prime minister and Jagan leading the opposition.

Jagatai (*d. c.* 1242), second son of GENGHIS KHAN, whose kingdom was divided among his three sons and a grandson. Jagatai's area covered modern Turkestan and Afghanistan, and he sternly maintained nomadic traditions. His subjects' language and literature are still known as "Jagatai".

Jagellon, name of a dynasty of Polish kings, beginning with the marriage of Jagello of Lithuania to Queen Jadwiga of Poland (1386) and ending with the death of Sigismund II (1572). Intervening rulers included Władysław III (1434–44), Casimir IV (1444–92), John Albert (1492–1501) and Sigismund I (1506–48).

Jaguar, spotted big CAT found in woody and grassy areas from S USA and New Mexico to Argentina. It has a chunky body, rounded ears and a yellowish coat with black rosettes. This fierce cat eats large mammals, turtles and fish. Length: body to 1.8m (5.9ft); tail to 91cm (35.8in); weight to 136kg (299.8lb). Family Felidae; species *Panthera onca*. *See also* NW pp.*216*, 217.

Jaguarundi, small, ground-dwelling CAT found in Central and South America. Otter-like, it is black, brown, grey, or fox red. Length: to 67cm (26.4in), excluding the tail; weight: to 9kg (19.8lb). Family Felidae; species *Felis yagouaroundi*.

Jahangir (1569–1627), Mogul emperor of India (1605–27). Although he revolted against his father Akbar in 1599, Akbar still named him his successor. He continued the expansion of the empire, conquering Mewar in 1614 and Ahmadnagar in 1616. In 1622, however, the Persians re-took Kandahar. He granted trading privileges to the Portuguese and the British East India Company.

Jahweh. *See* YAHWEH.

Jai alai. *See* PELOTA.

Jainism, an ancient religion of India which originated in the 6th century BC as a reaction against conservative BRAHMANISM. It was founded by Mahavira (599 BC–527 BC). Jains do not accept Hindu scriptures, rituals or priesthood. They believe that salvation can be attained only through rigid self-effort and asceticism, but they do accept, with some modification, the Hindu doctrine of TRANSMIGRATION OF SOULS Jainism lays special stress on *ahimsa*, ie non-injury to all living creatures including animals, birds and insects. The number of Jains in the mid-1970s was estimated at about two million.

Jaipur, city in NW India, 225km (140 miles) W of Agra. Founded in 1727, it was completely enclosed by a wall which still exists, and has a system of wide regular streets which is unusual for a city of its size. A transport and commercial centre, it is famous for its jewellery, enamels and printed cloth. Pop. (1971) 613,144.

Jairzinho, Jair Ventura Filho (1944–), Brazilian footballer, an attacking right winger who, in the 1970 World Cup finals, became the first player to score in every round of the competition. A member of the Botafogo club, he won his first cap in 1964 and also played in the 1966 and 1974 World Cups.

Jakarta. *See* DJAKARTA.

Jamaica, independent island nation in the Caribbean, 145km (90 miles) S of Cuba. It is a largely mountainous country with a tropical maritime climate, and the chief crops are sugar cane, bananas and other fruits. The economy is based on light engineering, construction, and mining (Jamaica is one of the world's producers of the aluminium ore bauxite); tourism is also important. Rural migration to the cities has raised the unemployment rate and there has been much civil unrest. The capital is Kingston. Area: 10,962sq km (4,232sq miles). Pop. (1975 est.) 2,029,000. *See* MW p.110.

James, name of three saints in the New Testament. James the Greater (*d.* 44), one of the Twelve APOSTLES of Jesus, was the brother of the Apostle JOHN. He was beheaded as an exemplary measure by Herod Agrippa I. James the Less, also one of the twelve, was the son of Alphaeus and perhaps of one of the three women named Mary at Christ's cross and later his tomb. James (died *c.* 62) called the "brother of the Lord", a witness to the Resurrection, was a leader of the early Jewish Christian Church in Jerusalem. Allegedly stoned to death or thrown down from a tower, this James is usually identified as the author of the epistle of that name, although there have been suggestions that the author may in fact have been James the son of Alphaeus.

James, the Epistle of, New Testament letter probably written by James called "the brother of the Lord", although it is occasionally attributed to the disciple James the Less. In strictly Jewish Christian terms it exhorts Christians to live righteous lives.

James I (1566–1625), King of England, son of MARY, QUEEN OF SCOTS. Crowned James VI of Scotland on his mother's abdication (1567), James passed his minority mainly under the control of the PRESBYTERIANS, who determined to shield him from Roman Catholic influence. Forced to decide between France and England as an ally for Scotland, James chose Protestant England in 1586. On ELIZABETH I's death in 1603 he became King of England. He supported the ANGLICANS and sponsored a translation of the Bible in 1611 that is known as the King James Version, but his failure to conciliate either the Puritans or the Roman Catholics caused discontent. His reliance upon favourites and his troubled relationship with the House of Commons weakened his effectiveness as a ruler. *See also* HC1 pp.277, *277*, 286–287.

James II (1633–1701), King of England, second son of CHARLES I and younger brother of CHARLES II. After the RESTORATION (1660), James, then Duke of York, played a prominent part in naval affairs and as Lord High Admiral in 1672 defeated the Dutch fleet at Southwold Bay. As a Roman Catholic, however, he was forced to resign all his offices in consequence of the TEST ACT (1673). Despite the rival claim of the Duke of MONMOUTH, an illegitimate but Protestant son of Charles II, James succeeded his brother (1685). His adherence to Roman Catholicism, however, alienated his subjects, and James was forced to abdicate. Whig lords invited WILLIAM III and his wife Mary, James's Protestant daughter, to assume the English throne; he landed at Brixham in 1688. In an unsuccessful campaign (1689–90), James failed to hold Ireland against William. The Stuart cause was carried on hopelessly by his son and grandson, the Old and Young Pretenders. *See also* HC1 pp.293, 299.

James, the name of five kings of the Stuart dynasty of Scotland. James I (1394–1437; *r.* 1406–37) was captured at sea by the English on his way to France and was unable to return to Scotland until 1424. His reign was largely devoted to breaking the power of the nobles, restoring law and order after a long period of disunity and improving commerce and Scotland's military power. Lowland Scotland in particular developed economically during James's reign but his curbing of the nobles had made him many enemies and in 1437 he was murdered. *See also* HC1 p.244. James II (1430–1460; *r.* 1437–60) was only six years old when his father was murdered and for many years of his reign he was under the domination of three vying clans. He was nevertheless able to enhance royal authority and extend the reform of the legal system. A supporter of the cause of the House of LANCASTER in the Wars of the ROSES, he attacked English border outposts and was killed at the siege of Roxburgh. *See also* HC1 pp.244–245. He was succeeded by his son, James III (1452–88; *r.* 1460–88), during whose reign the consolidation of the kingdom was assisted by the acquisition (through his marriage to Margaret of Denmark) of Orkney and Shetland. Opposition to James by a group of Border nobles finally led to an uprising in 1488, during which the king was murdered. *See also* HC1 p.*244*. James IV (1473–1513; *r.* 1488–1513) was the nominal leader of the rebels who killed his father, James III. A strong monarch, he maintained his authority throughout Scotland during his reign and concluded peace with England in 1497, consolidated by his marriage to HENRY VII's daughter, Margaret. In 1513, however, he led an invasion of England and was defeated and killed at FLODDEN. *See also* HC1 p.245. His son James V (1512–42; *r.* 1513–42), like so many of the Stuarts, started his reign as a minor. Efforts to retain control of his nobles and yet remain independent of his uncle, HENRY VIII, occupied much of his reign. His death, it is said from grief, followed the English rout of his forces at SOLWAY MOSS. *See also* HC1 pp.244–245. He was succeeded by his six-day-old daughter MARY, ill-fated Queen of Scots, whose son James VI was in time to become JAMES I of England.

James, the name of two kings of Aragon. James I (1208–76; *r.* 1214–76), called "the Conqueror", became effective ruler in 1227 after a minority disturbed by wars among the nobles. He consolidated royal power and enlarged his realm by seizing the Balearic Islands (1229–35) and Valencia (1233–38). James II (1264–1327; *r.* 1291–1327) became King of

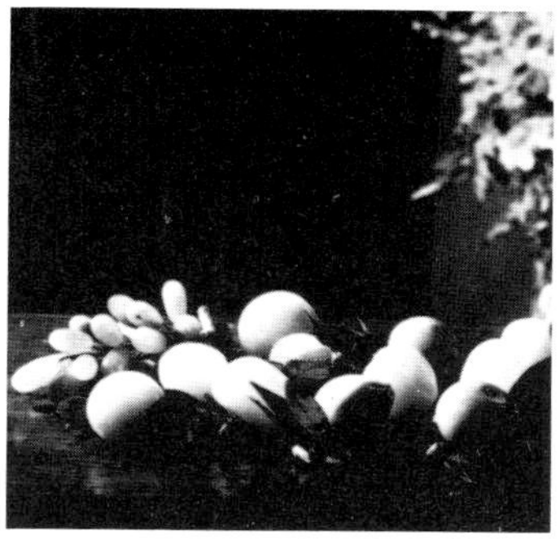

Jade was carved by the Chinese into exquisite jewellery and often buried with the dead.

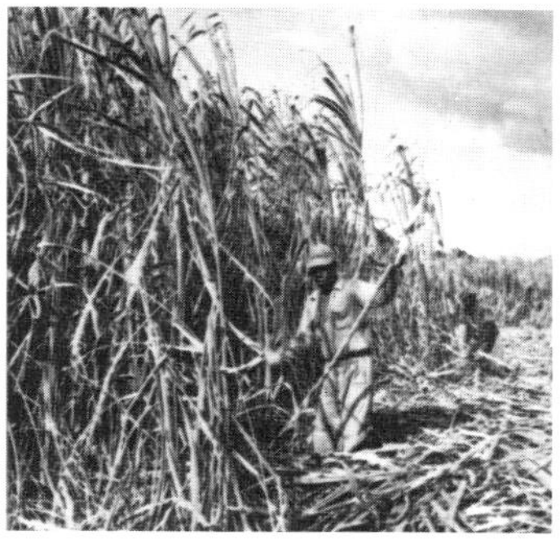

Jamaica; workers on a plantation cutting sugar cane, the main source of income.

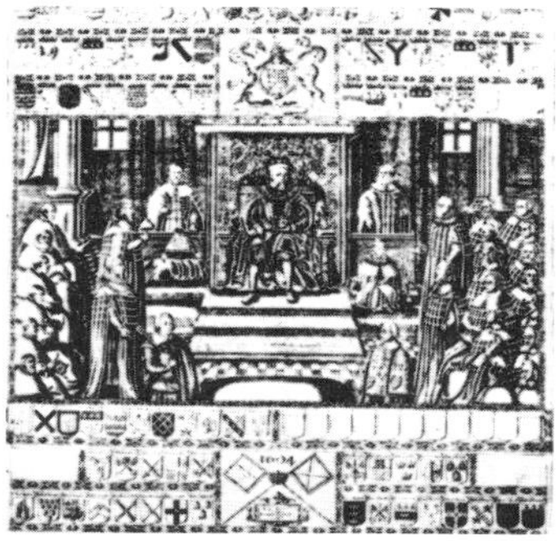

James I persecuted the Puritans and many emigrated to America.

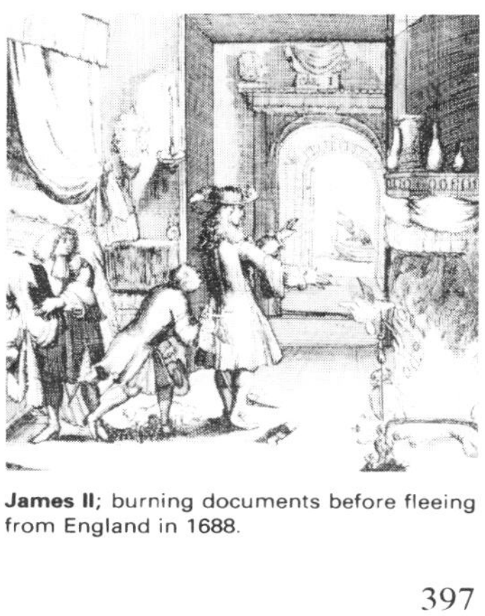

James II; burning documents before fleeing from England in 1688.

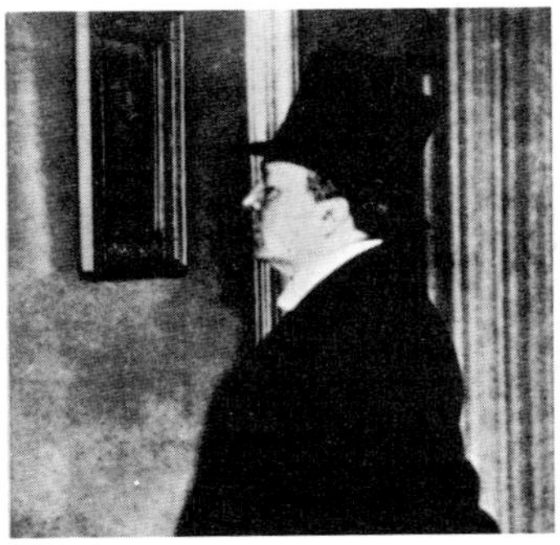

Henry James, one of America's greatest writers, mastered all literary forms except drama.

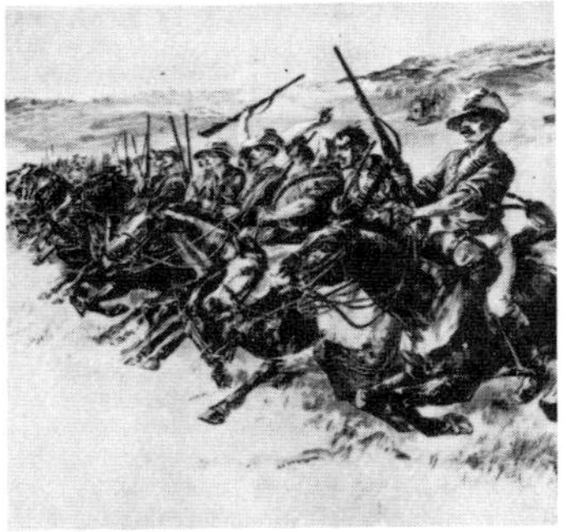

Jameson Raid; a contemporary impression of a cavalry charge during the raid.

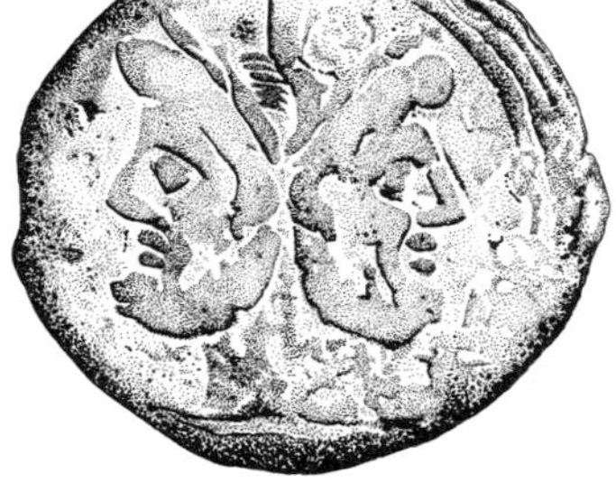

Janus, the Roman god of gates, with one face looking to the past and the other to the future.

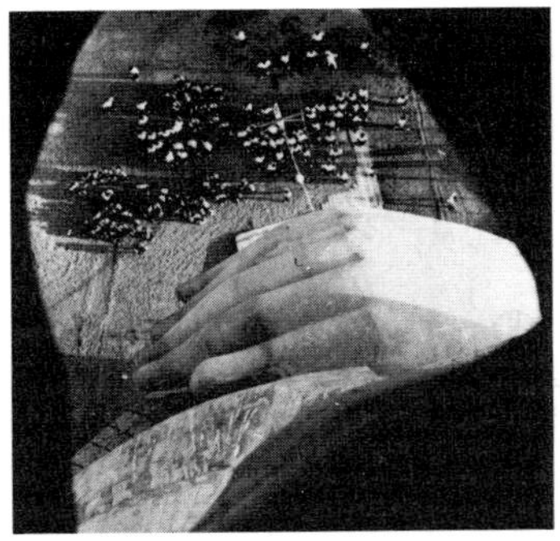

Japan; the view from one of the observation holes in the Goddess of Mercy statue, Tokyo.

Aragon on his brother's death. He gave up his claim to Sicily, which had been conquered by his father, and received Sardinia and Corsica from Naples as compensation. He began the annexation of Sardinia (1323–24) but failed to take Corsica.

James, Frank. *See* JAMES, JESSE WOODSON.

James, Henry (1843–1916), US novelist, short story writer and critic. Brother of William JAMES, he received his early education abroad. In 1915 he became a British subject. James, the master of a complex and convoluted prose style, felt that a writer should "never allow anything to enter a novel which was not represented as a perception or experience of one of the characters". Among his many works are *The Portrait of a Lady* (1881), *The Bostonians* (1886) and *The Ambassadors* (1903). *See also* HC2 pp.99, 288.

James, Jesse Woodson (1847–82), US outlaw. With his brother Frank he fought for the Confederacy during the Civil War. In 1867 they formed an outlaw band and terrorized the frontier, robbing banks and trains in Missouri and nearby states. In 1882 he was shot by Robert Ford, one of the members of his own gang, for a large reward. *See also* HC2 p.*152*.

James, Thomas (*c.* 1593–1635), English navigator. In 1631 he sailed in search of a northwest passage to the Indies and explored James Bay, the southern part of HUDSON BAY. He wrote an account of his exploration, *Strange and Dangerous Voyage* (1633).

James, William (1842–1910), US philosopher and psychologist, the brother of Henry JAMES. Regarded by many as the most distinguished of US psychologists, he pioneered research in many areas, particularly that of the emotions. He held that emotion is the feeling of a state of the body; the bodily state therefore comes first and the emotion follows. His most famous works are *The Principles of Psychology* (1890) and *Varieties of Religious Experience* (1902). *See also* MS pp.*147, 232–233*.

James Bay, extension of Hudson Bay in Canada, between W Quebec and NE Ontario. It receives several rivers including the Nottaway, Albany and La Grande. Length: 450km (280 miles); width: 242km (150 miles).

James Edward Stuart. *See* STUART, JAMES FRANCIS EDWARD.

Jameson, Sir Leander Starr (1853–1917), British political figure in South Africa. He was an associate of Cecil RHODES and led the unsuccessful JAMESON RAID (1895). Later he served as Prime Minister (1904–08) of the CAPE COLONY.

Jameson, Margaret Storm (1897–), British novelist. Her novels, in the family-saga genre, include *The Lovely Ship* (1927), *The Voyage Home* (1930), and *The Early Life of Stephen Hind* (1966).

Jameson Raid, action in South Africa taken by Sir Leander Starr Jameson in 1895. Jameson and Cecil RHODES wished for a federation of South Africa administered by the British, but saw the BOER government of the Transvaal as a threat to this. The raid was a complete failure; Jameson was captured, sent to Britain and imprisoned.

Jamestown settlement, first successful English settlement in America, established in May 1607 under the auspices of the Virginia Company. Despite disease and attacks from the Indians, the leadership of John SMITH and John ROLFE made the colony firm by 1614, when an alliance was made with the local Indians. The town was in decay by 1700. *See also* HC2 p.62.

Jami (1414–92), Persian poet and mystic, the last of Iran's great mystical poets, real name Mowlanā Nùr Od-dīn Abd Orrahamān Ebn Ahmad. He also wrote prose dealing with the Koran, Sufism and music. He is most famous for his seven-part poetic compendium *Haft Owrang* (*The Seven Thrones*; trans. 1856; 1882).

Janáček, Leoš (1854–1928), Czech composer who studied Czech folk music and speech, which greatly influenced his music. His compositions include such orchestral works as *Taras Bulba* (1918) and *Sinfonietta* (1926), two string quartets (1923 and 1928), the cantata *The Eternal Gospel* (1914) and other choral works. He wrote a number of operas, including *Jenufa* (1904), a complex story of tragedy and love, and *Cunning Little Vixen* (1924), a comedy of animals and humans.

Janco, Marcel (1895–), Romanian architect and painter, from 1916 to 1921 at the fore-front of the DADA movement in Zürich, and during the 1920s and 1930s a propagandist of modern art in Romania. In 1940 he emigrated to Israel, where he founded an artists' community.

Jane Eyre (1847), novel by Charlotte BRONTË. It is remarkable as a great romantic novel telling of the relationship between Jane, an orphaned governess of great spirit and wit, and her sardonic but passionate employer, Mr Rochester.

Janet, Pierre Marie Felix (1859–1947), French psychiatrist. He did valuable research in the diagnosis and treatment of HYSTERIA and spent his later years searching for ways of re-educating personalities overwhelmed by seemingly minor anxieties. *See also* MS p.137.

Janissaries, élite corps of soldiers of the Ottoman Empire. The practice of recruiting Christian youths and other war captives who were converted to Islam was begun in the 14th century by the sultan Orkhan. Later membership became hereditary and the corps wielded supreme power within the empire until 1826 when by order of Sultan Mahmud II the corps was massacred. *See also* HC1 p.*221*.

Jan Mayen, Norwegian island in the Greenland Sea of the Arctic Ocean between Greenland and N Norway. First sighted in 1607 by Henry HUDSON, it was annexed by Norway in 1929. The island is barren and uninhabited except for a NATO radio and navigation station. Area: approx. 373sq km (144sq miles).

Jannings, Emil (1884–1950), US film actor, *b.* Germany. He made his stage debut at the age of ten. His films included *Peter the Great* (1923), *The Way of All Flesh* (1928) and *The Blue Angel* (1930).

Janov, Arthur (*c.* 1925–), US psychotherapist who developed primal therapy as a means of treating NEUROSIS. In his book *Primal Scream* (1970) he postulates that neurosis is a defence against pain which may have originated in childhood. It can be treated by reliving "primals" – emotional outbursts in which the patient faces this pain. *See also* MS p.149.

Jansenism, theological school which grew up in the Roman Catholic Church in the 17th and 18th centuries. It is associated with the name of the Dutch theologian Cornelius Jansen (1585–1638), Bishop of Ypres, but the movement grew strongest in France. The main Jansenist tenets may be summed up in the propositions that man is incapable of carrying out the commandments of God without special divine GRACE and that the operation of grace is irresistible. French Jansenists suffered persecution during most of the 18th century. *See also* OLD CATHOLIC CHURCH.

Jansky, Karl (1905–50), US engineer who in 1931, while investigating interference to telephone communications, discovered an unidentifiable radio wave source. He concluded that it was stellar in nature and that the source lay in the direction of SAGITTARIUS, later established as the direction of the centre of our galaxy. *See also* SU pp.172, *173*, 244.

Janssen, Pierre-Jules-Cesar (1824–1907), French astronomer, a pioneer of solar physics and of photography. He made a number of scientific expeditions, including a search for the magnetic equator in Peru (1857–58). In 1893 he established an observatory on Mont Blanc.

Januarius, Saint, or San Gennaro (died *c.* 305), legendary martyr and patron saint of Naples, who suffered under the Emperor Diocletian. A phial said to contain his blood is preserved in Naples Cathedral and 18 times a year the phenomenon of the "liquefaction of the blood" occurs. No natural explanation of this event has ever been put forward. Feast: 1 Jan.

January, first month of the Gregorian calendar, consisting of 31 days. Originally it was the eleventh month of the Roman Republican calendar, but when the Julian version brought calendar date into step with equinoctial time in the first century BC, it became the first month of the year. It was named after JANUS. The birthstone of January is the garnet and its flowers are the snowdrop and the carnation. *See also* NEW YEAR'S DAY.

Janus, in Roman religion, the animistic spirit of doorways and archways. He was regarded as the god of all beginnings. He was normally depicted with two heads facing in opposite directions and was invoked as the first of any gods in regular liturgies.

Japan, independent nation in E Asia, consisting of four large islands and about 3,000 smaller ones. It is a mountainous country with volcanoes and frequent earthquakes. Although there is little arable land, high yields mean that most food is home produced. Japan has few natural resources, having to import many minerals. Despite this it leads the world in shipbuilding. The capital is Tokyo. Area: 377,535sq km (145,766sq miles). Pop. (1976 est.) 112,550,000. *See* MW p.111.

Japan, Sea of, part of the W Pacific Ocean, lying between Japan (E), the Korean peninsula and the coast of the USSR to the W. The shallower areas used to be important fishing grounds but since 1946 the fisheries have become depleted. Area: 1,007sq km (389,100sq miles).

Japanese art, aesthetic tradition which embraces painting, printmaking, sculpture, metalwork, architecture and the decorative arts. The earliest examples are Jomon pottery figurines (*c.* 1000 BC). The Chinese influence was introduced with BUDDHISM in the 6th century. LACQUERWORK, sculpture and ink-painting developed during the NARA period (AD 674–794), at which time T'ANG cultural forms combined with the emergence of characteristically Japanese techniques. The YAMATO-E tradition, which was based on national, rather than Chinese, aesthetic standards, originated in the Kose school of painting in the later HEIAN (FUJIWARA) period and flowered during the KAMAKURA military rule (1185–1333). The profound influence of ZEN Buddhism on Japanese art is particularly apparent in the Muromachi period (1333–1573), when Zen masters used painting as a teaching method. Many of the best-known examples of Japanese art were produced in the Edo (TOKUGAWA) period (*c.* 1600–1868). The UKIYO-E prints of UTAMARO, HOKUSAI, HIROSHIGE and others from this period became known in Europe after the MEIJI Restoration (1868) and influenced Western artists such as Van GOGH, J.M. WHISTLER and some IMPRESSIONISTS. Modern Japanese artists have made important contributions to 20th-century art and design. *See also* HC1 pp.131–132; HC2 pp.56–57.

Japanese spaniel, toy dog, probably bred originally in China, but developed in Japan. Its long, silky coat is usually black and white or red and white. It was brought to the West by Matthew PERRY. Height: 23cm (9in); weight: 3.2kg (7lb).

Japonica, any of several shrubs and their fruit. *Camellia japonica* is also called CAMELLIA; the Japanese quince, *Chaenomeles japonica,* (Family Rosaceae) bears green, aromatic, quince-like fruit. The latter is also cultivated for its orange-red flowers. Height: to 2m (6ft).

Jaques-Dalcroze, Émile (1865–1950), Swiss composer and educator, who from 1892 to 1909 taught at the Geneva Conservatory, where he invented his system of EURYTHMICS. He established a school (1910) devoted to his system which, through his pupils, especially Marie RAMBERT, had great influence on ballet.

Jarmo, archaeological site, now in N Iraq. It contains records of wheat and barley cultivation dating from the 8th millennium BC. Jarmo was excavated in 1948–55, and there is a modern village near by. *See also* HC1 p.*26*.

Jarnach, Philipp (1892–), French-born composer. A student of BUSONI, he arranged piano scores for several of his master's operas.

Jarrah, hardwood timber tree that grows in sandy soils in Australia; it is a type of

EUCALYPTUS. Its leathery leaves are lance-shaped, glossy and dark green above and paler underneath. Height: to 30m (98ft). Family Myrtaceae. Species *Eucalyptus marginata*.

Jarrett, Keith (1945–), US jazz pianist. An introspective and serious musician, he played with Art Blakey and Charles Lloyd before forming a trio with Charlie Haden and Paul Motian in 1966. After a time with Miles DAVIS in 1970–71, he became a solo performer and recording artist.

Jarrow March (1936), progress of unemployed workers from Jarrow, in county Durham, to London. Jarrow, a small shipbuilding town, relied upon one firm, which closed down in 1933. By the end of 1935, nearly three-quarters of the town's insured workers were out of work and 200 of them marched (5–31 October) to draw national attention to their plight. *See also* HC2 p.*209*.

Jarry, Alfred (1873–1907), French playwright and satirist. He is chiefly remembered for his farce *Ubu Roi* (1896), whose principal character, le père Ubu, is the personification of avarice, cowardice and ugliness. Jarry also wrote other works which foreshadowed SURREALISM, including *César-Antéchrist* (1895) and *Supermale* (1902).

Jasmine, climbing shrub known in the Mediterranean region since ancient times. It produces fragrant yellow, pink or white flowers, and an oil that is used in perfumes. Species include *Jasminum sambac* and the white *J. officinale*, which is hardy in temperate regions. Height: to 6.5m (20ft). Family Oleaceae.

Jason, hero in Greek mythology. Sent on a quest for the GOLDEN FLEECE to prevent him from claiming his usurped throne, Jason sailed aboard the Argo with heroes who included HERCULES, THESEUS, ORPHEUS, CASTOR AND POLLUX. After surviving many perils, and despite losing some of his companions, he found the fleece in Colchis, and stole it, with the help of the sourceress MEDES. At the end of a long life he was a wanderer who died under the prow of his old ship, the *Argo*.

Jasper, opaque semiprecious stone, usually red to brown, sometimes yellow or grey to green. Jasper is found in Greece, Siberia, Libya and the River Nile valley. It was once believed that stomach complaints could be cured by wearing these stones. A dark form of jasper was traditionally used as a touchstone to estimate the gold content of precious alloys.

Jaspers, Karl Theodor (1883–1969), German philosopher. His existentialism was influenced by the works of KIERKEGAARD and NIETZSCHE and his own studies in psychopathology. The main themes of his philosophy appear in *Philosophy* (1932); other works include *Philosophical Faith and Revelation* (1962) and *The Future of Germany* (1967).

Jasperware, unglazed stoneware first made in England by Josiah WEDGWOOD *c.* 1775. White in its natural state, it can be stained to various colours with metallic oxides – usually to pale blue, but also to dark blue, lilac, green, black and yellow. White decorations in the neo-Classical style are moulded separately and applied to the jasperware.

Jat, member of an agricultural and pastoral people of the plains of N India, renowned for their fighting prowess. The Jats became a political force in the 17th century. At first Hindu, many later became Muslims or Sikhs.

Jatakas, "birth stories", Buddhist writings which drew moral conclusions from stories of the BUDDHA or some other Buddhist figure in a previous existence. The main character usually appears as an animal whose present circumstances are the result of past acts.

Jaundice, yellowing of the skin and other tissues, especially the whites of the eyes, caused by excess of BILE pigment in the blood. It usually occurs in premature babies; if severe, and if associated with excessive bilirubin in the blood, it may lead to widespread destruction of tissues in the brain. In adults jaundice may occur when the flow of bile from the liver to the intestine is blocked by an obstruction such as a GALLSTONE, or in disease of the liver such as CIRRHOSIS and HEPATITIS. *See also* MS p.93.

Jaurès, Jean Léon (1859–1914), French socialist leader. He helped to form the unified French Socialist Party and founded and edited the socialist journal *L'Humanité*. At the advent of WWI he was assassinated by a fanatical nationalist for advocating arbitration rather than war with Germany.

Java, fourth largest island of Indonesia, lying between the Java Sea and Indian Ocean. It is a mountainous country, having a volcanic belt in the S and an alluvial plain to the N. It has many rivers, and rice, tea and coffee are produced. There is silver, gold and phosphate mining in the N. The largest city is Djakarta. Area: 126,501sq km (48,842sq miles). Pop. 78,201,000.

Java man, extinct race of HOMO ERECTUS, whose skeletal remains were found at Trinil, Java, in 1891. The skull was ape-like but the limb structure was similar to that of modern man. *See also* MS pp.24–25.

Javelin, lightweight spear thrown by hand, used as a weapon since ancient times. The modern javelin used in sport, in athletic field events, may be made of wood or a light alloy. It has a metal tip and weighs a minimum of 800g (28.2oz). Length: to 2.7m (8.9ft). *See also* MM pp.160–161.

Jawara, Sir Dauda Kairaba (1924–), Gambian politician. He served as Minister of Education (1960–61) and Prime Minister (1962–70) of Gambia when it was a British colony, becoming its president when the country became a republic in 1970.

Jawlensky, Alexey von (1864–1941), Russian painter who worked principally in Germany. He was influenced mainly by MATISSE. In Munich he met KANDINSKY; later, with Kandinsky, KLEE and Lyonel FEININGER he formed a group known as the Blue Four, but worked mostly in isolation. Late works, eg *Head* (1935), were deeply expressive, icon-like images.

Jay, any of several species of harsh-voiced birds related to MAGPIES and JACKDAWS, especially the European *Garrulus glandarius*. It is an aggressive bird with characteristic blue wing markings. Length: 34.2cm (13.5in). Family Corvidae. *See also* NW pp.*151, 197*.

Jazz, style of music that evolved in the USA in the late 19th century out of African and European folk music, popular songs and US vaudeville (music hall). It is traditionally characterized by a steady rhythm, usually four beats to the bar; prominence of melody, often with elements derived from the BLUES; and improvisation by the performer. Early jazz was developed in New Orleans in the form of RAGTIME, BLUES and DIXIELAND music. In the 1920s it spread to Chicago and New York City and became known throughout the world as a musical style unique to America. In the 1930s SWING enjoyed great popularity, as did the more sophisticated BEBOP style of the 1940s. The popularity of jazz has decreased as its technical resources and expressive scope have grown. Jazz elements influenced composers such as Maurice RAVEL and Darius MILHAUD and also had an impact on other styles of popular music, such as ROCK-AND-ROLL. *See also* HC2 pp.272–273.

Jazz Singer, The, US film (1927); the first major film to use sound. It was directed by Alan Crosland and starred Al JOLSON. A second version was made in 1953.

Jean, Grand Duke of Luxembourg (1921–). He was a member of the Irish Guards during WWII, and became Grand Duke on the abdication of his mother (1964).

Jeanneret, Charles-Edouard. *See* LE CORBUSIER.

Jeans, Sir James Hopwood (1877–1946), British scientist and author. He investigated STELLAR DYNAMICS and proposed the tidal, or catastrophic, theory of planetary origin, in which he assumed that the matter of the planets was drawn out of the Sun by the attraction of a passing star. His works include *The Universe Around Us* (1929). *See also* SU pp.174–175.

Jedda, port city in Saudi Arabia, on the Red Sea 74km (46 miles) W of Mecca. Under Turkish rule until 1916, when it joined the independent Hejaz, it was taken in 1925 by IBN SAUD. It serves Mecca as a port for pilgrims and as such imports many goods to support this annual influx of people. Since WWII industry has been expanded to include steel rolling, oil refining and pottery manufacture. Pop. (1965 est.) 194,000.

Jedi, Asian tower similar to a STUPA, housing religious relics. Jedis are found throughout SE Asia, dating from any time between pre-Christian and medieval.

Jeep, small, rugged, four-wheel-drive vehicle used by the US Army in WWII as a light general-purpose (GP) form of transport. *See also* MM p.*136*.

Jeeps, Richard Eric Gantrey (Dickie) (1931–), British rugby union player. A solid scrum-half with a quick service and accurate kick to touch, he won 24 caps (1956–62) as a member of the Northampton club and toured South Africa (1955, 1962) and New Zealand (1959) with the British Lions.

Jefferies, Richard (1848–87), British novelist. A naturalist, he wrote several books about the English countryside, including *Wild Life in a Southern County* (1879). Mystical philosophy figures largely in *Wood Magic* (2 vols, 1881), *Bevis* (3 vols, 1882) and *Amaryllis at the Fair* (1887). His autobiography is entitled *Story of My Heart* (1883).

Jefferson, Thomas (1743–1826), third president of the USA (1801–09) and one of the authors of the American Declaration of Independence. A scholar and philosopher, he believed in agrarian democracy. In 1769 he was elected to the Virginia House of Burgesses and, six years later, represented the state at the Second CONTINENTAL CONGRESS. After independence he served as governor of Virginia, represented the USA in Europe, and became the first US secretary of state in 1789. The main achievements of his presidency were the LOUISIANA PURCHASE, the avoidance of US involvement in the NAPOLEONIC WARS, and the abolition of the slave trade. *See also* HC2 pp.22, *64, 71*, 148.

Jeffreys, George, 1st Baron Jeffreys (*c.* 1648–89), English judge. He was made Lord Chief JUSTICE in 1683 and lord CHANCELLOR in 1685. Notorious as a hanging judge, he presided over the assizes which tried participants in MONMOUTH'S REBELLION against JAMES II. For the number of executions he meted out they gained the name BLOODY ASSIZES. After James' overthrow (1688), he was imprisoned in the Tower of London, where he died. *See also* HC1 p.*293*.

Jeffreys, George (*d.* 1685), English composer. A member of the Chapel Royal and organist to Charles I at Oxford (1643) during the Civil war, he wrote anthems, motets and other church music, as well as part-songs and music for masques and plays. The library of the Royal College of Music, London, has a collection of his works.

Jeffreys, Sir Harold (1891–), British astronomer and geophysicist. He ascertained that the four outer planets, JUPITER, SATURN, URANUS and NEPTUNE, are intensely cold and investigated the origin of the solar system. He was the first to suggest that the Earth's core is liquid.

Jeffries, James Jackson (1875–1953), US boxer who reigned unbeaten as world heavyweight champion from 1899 until he retired in 1905.

Jeffries, John (1744–1819), British physicist, *b.* USA. He lived in England after the War of American Independence and conducted experiments on balloons. With the Frenchman Jean-Pierre BLANCHARD, he was the first man to cross the English Channel in a balloon.

Jehovah, misnomer for the name of God. It developed from YHWH (or JHVH or YHVH), the scriptural name of the God of the ancient Israelites as written in Hebrew, whose alphabet at that time contained no vowel symbols. To this framework during the Middle Ages were added the vowels from the Hebrew *adonai*, "my lord", creating the alternative form

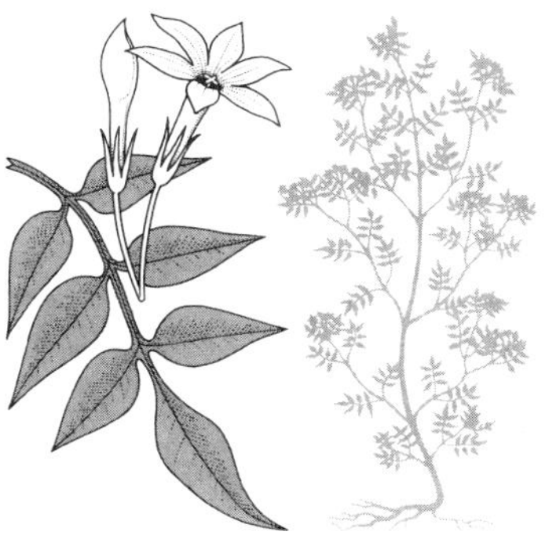

Jasmine; the Spanish variety is larger than common jasmine and is tinged with red.

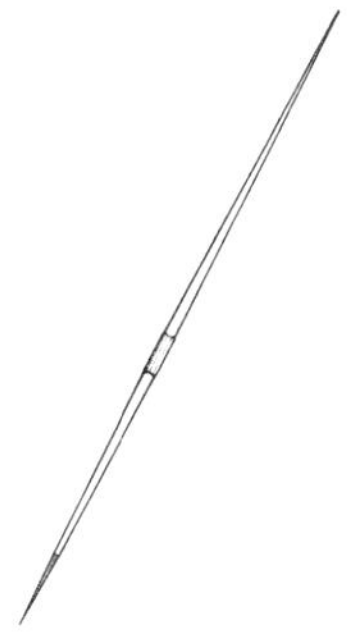

Javelin; apart from modifications to the tip, the weapon altered little over the years.

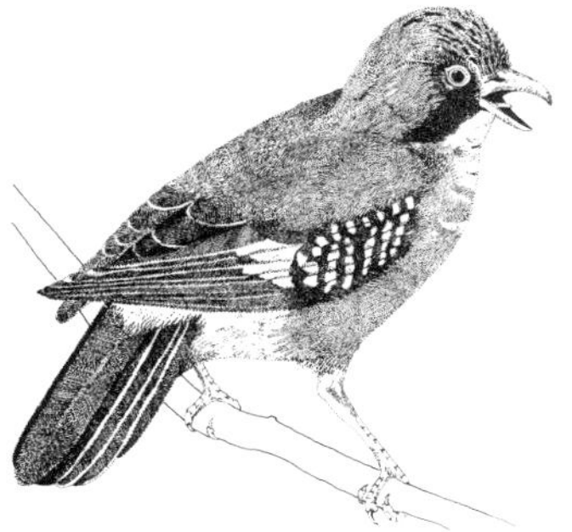

Jay has many nicknames, especially in the USA, because of its mischievous nature.

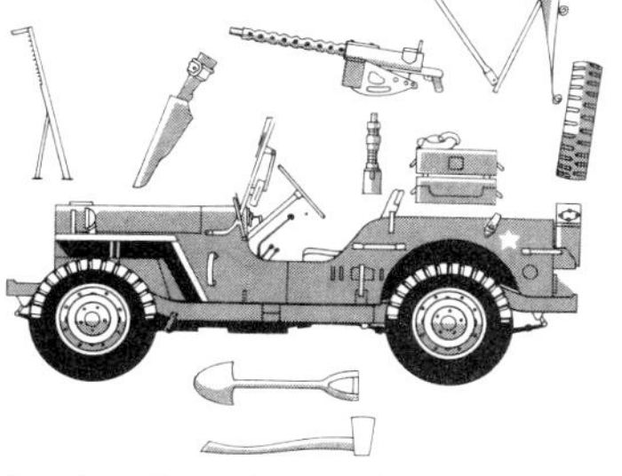

Jeep has a four-cylinder engine, carries up to six people and can travel at 105km/h.

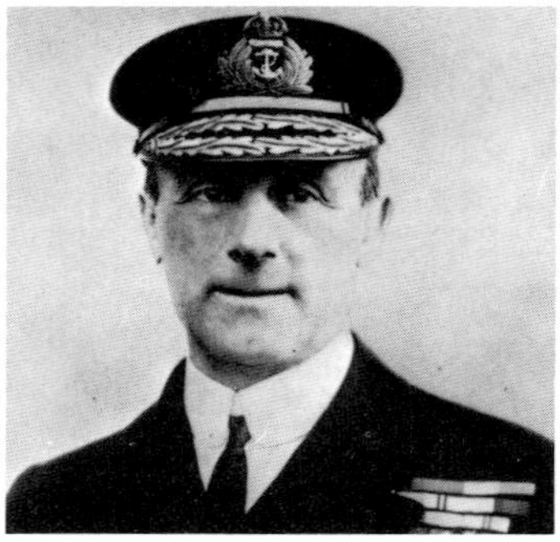

Jellicoe; it was said that he was the only man who could lose WWI in an afternoon.

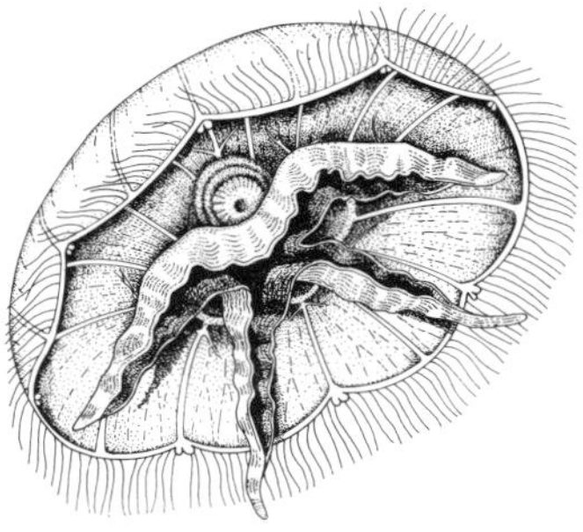

Jellyfish; some small fish are not harmed by their sting and hide among their tentacles.

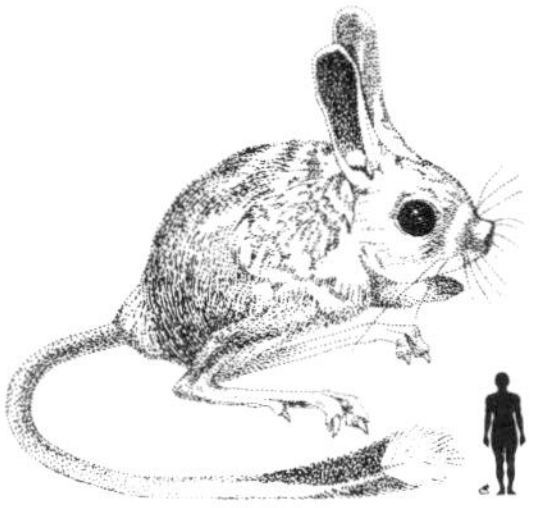

Jerboas, when frightened, escape by jumping, using their tails to balance themselves.

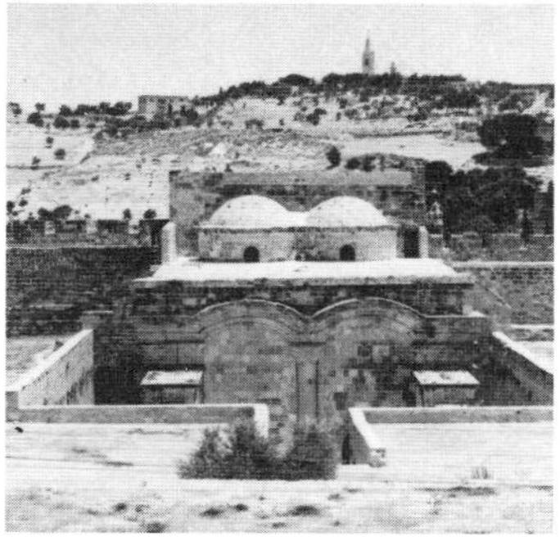

Jerusalem's Golden Gate, rebuilt by Justinian, with the Mount of Olives behind.

Jehovah. From then, both Jehovah and Yahweh came to be used synonymously in the Jewish and the Christian religions. Today, Yahweh is recognized as the basic form.

Jehovah's Witnesses, religious sect founded in the 1870s by Charles Taze Russell (1852–1916) of Pittsburgh, Pennsylvania. The sect believes in the imminent end of the world for all except its own members, who are to be the sole inheritors of the kingdom of God. Their name is derived from a passage in the Old Testament: "Ye are my witnesses, saith Jehovah" (Isaiah 43:10). They hold to the gradually-developed theory of a "theocratic kingdom", membership of which is not to be reconciled with allegiance to any country. In their publication *The Watchtower* they carry out vigorous propaganda against all civil authority and all institutional religion. They deny most of the fundamental Christian doctrines. The sect has now become a worldwide body and is active in preaching and door-to-door missionary work. It is registered in Britain under the name "The Watch Tower Bible and Tract Society".

Jejunum, portion of the small intestine, about 25–30cm (10–12in) long, into which food passes from the DUODENUM. The jejunum precedes the ILEUM, which at the lower end opens into the large intestine. It is generally found empty (jejune) after death. Length: 2.4–2.7m (8–9ft). *See also* MS p.*68*.

Jekyll and Hyde (1866), two main characters from *The Strange Case of Dr Jekyll and Mr Hyde* by Robert Louis STEVENSON. This novel, which greatly widened Stevenson's readership, is both a thriller and a bitter moral allegory. Dr Jekyll, a mild man, seeks an understanding of man's baser instincts and invents a potion to release the "beast within". In a dramatic climax, the doctor's crude alter-ego, Mr Hyde, surfaces unbidden and uncontrollable.

Jellicoe, John Rushworth Jellicoe, 1st Earl (1859–1935), British admiral and gunnery expert. For the first two years of WWI (1914–16), as Commander-in-Chief of the Grand Fleet, he blockaded German naval forces. When the German fleet finally put to sea, Jellicoe skilfully placed his fleet at Jutland between the enemy and its bases. Poor visibility, however, and British mistakes in relaying German signals denied the Grand Fleet an absolute victory. *See also* JUTLAND, BATTLE OF.

Jellyfish, marine COELENTERATE found in coastal waters and characterized by tentacles with stinging cells. The adult form is the MEDUSA. It has a bell-shaped body with a thick layer of jellylike substance between two body cell layers, many tentacles and four mouth lobes surrounding the gut opening. The common *Aurelia* is transparent with four violet circles near its centre. Diameter: 7.5–30.5cm (3in–12in). Class Scyphozoa. *See* NW pp.72, 84–85, *240*.

Jena, Battle of (14 Oct. 1806), victory of NAPOLEON over the Prussian army led by the Prince of Hohenlohe-Ingelfingen. In conjunction with the simultaneous French victory at AUERSTÄDT, it led to the French capture of Berlin and the collapse of Prussia. *See also* HC2 p.*76*.

Jenkins, Roy Harris (1920–), British politician. A member of the Labour Party, he first entered Parliament in 1948. As Home Secretary (1965–67) he sponsored stronger laws against racial discrimination and liberalized laws on ABORTION and HOMOSEXUAL activities. He supported Britain's entry into the Common Market (despite his party's opposition) and in 1976 left Parliament on his appointment for a four-year term as President of the European Commission at the EEC in Brussels.

Jenkins's Ear, War of (1739–41), war between England and Spain arising out of long-term mercantile grievances. War was sparked off by the English outcry at reports of the boarding of Robert Jenkins's ship at Havana in 1731 by a Spanish official, who cut off one of the English captain's ears. *See also* HC2 p.*18*.

Jenner, Edward (1749–1823), British physician who developed VACCINATION. Aware that cowpox, a minor disease, seemed to protect people from smallpox, Jenner in 1796 inoculated a healthy boy with cowpox from the sores of an infected dairymaid. The boy developed the disease but six weeks later, when inoculated with smallpox, was found to be immune to that dreaded infection. This finding established the principle of vaccination as an invaluable technique in medicine. *See also* HC2 p.*33*; MS p.112.

Jenner, Henry (1848–1934), British writer. He initiated the 20th-century revival of the Cornish language and literature, speaking in Cornish in 1903 at a congress in Brittany. He also wrote a *Handbook of the Cornish Language* (1904), a work which rationalizes the language's grammar and spelling.

Jennings, Sarah. *See* MARLBOROUGH, SARAH CHURCHILL, DUCHESS OF.

Jensen, Johannes Vilhelm (1873–1950), Danish novelist, poet and essayist. His works include travel tales, the historical novel *The Fall of the King* (1901), and *Myths* (1906–44). His famous series of six novels, *The Long Journey* (1908–22), follows the development of the Nordic race from before the Ice Age to the time of Columbus. He was awarded the 1944 Nobel Prize in literature.

Jerash, ancient city of the Decapolis, the league of 10 cities E of the River Jordan. It is in present day Jordan. It was rebuilt by the Romans in the 1st century AD and flourished for the next two centuries. It is one of the best-preserved Palestinian cities of Roman times. Many temples and columns still stand.

Jerbil. *See* GERBIL.

Jerboa, nocturnal burrowing RODENT of Eurasian and African deserts, with long hindlegs developed for jumping. It has a satiny, sand-coloured body and a long tail. It is herbivorous and does not usually drink water. Length: to 15cm (5.9in), excluding the tail. Family Dipodidae. *See also* NW pp.*220*, 221.

Jeremiah (*c*.646–*c*.580 BC), Hebrew prophet whose life and teachings are recorded in the Old Testament book of his name. When Babylon invaded Judah (587), Jeremiah saw it as a punishment from God and urged the inhabitants to sue for peace and to trust in God, teaching that they could preserve their worship even in disaster and exile. This attitude was largely construed as treason and ignored. Babylon duly captured Jerusalem and deported most of the Israelites, leaving only a garrison and a skeleton population of trusted individuals, including Jeremiah, who could now see that the only hope for his religion lay with the exiled majority's strength of faith – which he himself had helped to inspire. *See also* HC1 pp.58–59.

Jeremy, the Epistle of, name given to the sixth and last chapter of the Book of BARUCH, placed in the APOCRYPHA in the Authorised Version of the Bible. It is a warning against idolatry.

Jerez de la Frontera, Spanish town in Cadiz province, formerly called Xeres and, even earlier, Ceret. It is best known for sherry wine, to which it has given its name. The numerous wine lodges (bodegas) are a feature of the town.

Jericho, ancient city of Palestine, in the Jordan valley, N of the Dead Sea. Captured by Joshua from the Canaanites in 1550 BC, the city was rebuilt by Herod in the first century BC, S of the old site. In 1950 excavations revealed magnificent Roman remains at the site of Herod's city. Its archaeological importance is further enhanced because it is one of the earliest known continuous settlements, dating from the early NEOLITHIC period.

Jeroboam, name of two kings of Israel, for whose reigns the Bible constitutes the main source. Jeroboam I (10th century BC) led an unsuccessful revolt against SOLOMON, and later established the secessionist kingdom of north Israel, consisting of all Israel except Judah and part of the land of BENJAMIN. Jeroboam II (783–741) succeeded Jehoash and ruled during a period of relative peace.

Jerome, Saint (*c*.347–420), Eusebius Hieronymous, biblical scholar. After a literary education he spent two years of intense study as a hermit in the desert of Chalcis. Later he went to Rome and became secretary to Pope Damasus I. The pope commissioned Jerome to prepare a standard text of the gospels for use by Latin-speaking Christians. Jerome revised the gospels from the Old Latin and later made a new translation of the Psalms and the Old Testament from Greek and Hebrew sources. His work was the basis for what later became known as the Vulgate, which remained the authorized Latin text of the Bible until 1977, when it was superseded by a new version.

Jerome, Jerome Klapka (1859–1927), British humorist whose reputation now rests solely on his best-seller *Three Men in a Boat* (1889) and its successor *Three Men on the Bummel* (1900). His contemporaries knew him as an actor and dramatist whose most successful play, *The Passing of the Third Floor Back* (1908), describes how the inmates of a Bloomsbury boarding house are intimidated by a strange lodger resembling Christ.

Jersey, largest of the Channel Islands of the United Kingdom, lying about 16km (10 miles) off the W coast of France. It is administered as a bailiwick. The official language is French although English is spoken everywhere. The mild, sunny climate makes dairy and fruit farming the basis of the economy. Tourism is also important. The capital is St Helier. Area: 117sq km (45sq miles). Pop. 72,700. *See also* MW p.52.

Jersey, breed of small brown DAIRY CATTLE that originated in France and was developed on the island of Jersey in the Channel Isles. The butterfat content (5.2%) of the milk from Jerseys is the highest of all.

Jerusalem, capital city of Israel, 56km (35 miles) SE of Tel Aviv. It is a sacred city of the Christian, Jewish and Muslim faiths. Originally a Jebusite stronghold (2000–1500 BC), the city was captured by King DAVID after 1000 BC. Destroyed by NEBUCHADNEZZAR *c*.587 BC, it was rebuilt by HEROD *c*.35 BC, but again destroyed by TITUS AD 70. The Roman colony of Aelia Capitolina was established, and Jews were forbidden within the city limits until the fifth century. Christian control was ended by the Persians in AD 614. It was conquered in 1071 by the SELJUK Turks, whose mistreatment of Christians precipitated the CRUSADES, as a result of which the kingdom of Jerusalem 1099–1187 was formed. It was held by the OTTOMAN TURKS 1244–1917, when it became the British mandated territory of Palestine. It was divided in 1948 between Jordan and Israel, the latter taking complete control of the city in 1967. An administrative and cultural centre, the city's industries include tourism and diamond cutting. Pop. (1974) 344,200. *See also* HC1 pp.58–59, 176–177; HC2 pp.296–297.

Jerusalem, Kingdom of, feudal state created in Palestine and Syria by the Crusaders. After Jerusalem fell in the First CRUSADE (1099), GODFREY OF BOUILLON ruled even though the royal title was held by his brother, BALDWIN I. The elected kings also oversaw the Latin counties of Antioch, Edessa and Tripoli, although local lords fought among themselves, as well as for their masters against the MAMELUKES of Egypt, the SELJUK TURKS and the Byzantine emperors. Military orders such as the KNIGHT TEMPLARS gradually undermined royal authority. SALADIN captured Jerusalem in 1187, and the kingdom essentially ended when Jerusalem was sacked by the Turks (1244). *See also* HC1 pp.176–177.

Jerusalem (1804), prophetic poem by William BLAKE in which he explains his theory of the redeeming Imagination: "the world of imagination is the world of eternity" where man goes "after the death of the vegetated body".

Jerusalem artichoke. *See* ARTICHOKE.

Jervis, John, 1st Earl of St Vincent (1735–1823), British naval officer. He held important commands during the French Revolutionary Wars and won a spectacular victory over a larger Spanish fleet off Cape St Vincent in 1797. As first Lord of the Admiralty (1801–04) he initiated many basic and necessary reforms.

Jervis Bay, inlet of the S Pacific Ocean in New South Wales, Australia, approx. 145km (90 miles) SSW of Sydney and the same distance ENE of Canberra. It is the port of the landlocked Australian Capital Territory.

Jessner, Leopold (1878–1945), German theatrical producer and director. His association with the German EXPRESSIONIST THEATRE in the 1920s brought him worldwide fame. His productions included *Hamlet* in modern dress and WEDEKIND's *Der Marquis von Keith*. Nazism forced his emigration to Hollywood in 1933, where he worked anonymously in the film industry.

Jester, professional court fool retained by medieval rulers and nobles. Often deformed and invariably of small stature, jesters were noted for their quick wit and motley costume which included a cap with bells or asses' ears.

Jesuit Martyrs (1648–49), five JESUITS martyred in Canada. The Jesuits began missionary work among the Indians in 1609. Under the leadership of Isaac JOGUES and Jean de Brébeuf, they worked to convert the Hurons and Iroquois to Roman Catholicism. Brébeuf, Antoine Daniel, Gabriel Lalemant, Charles Garnier and Noël Chabanel were killed by the superstitious Iroquois after a series of epidemics in 1648. They were canonized by the Roman Catholic Church in 1930.

Jesuits, officially the Society of Jesus, a Roman Catholic religious order, founded by St IGNATIUS OF LOYOLA in 1540. They played a significant role in the COUNTER-REFORMATION. The Jesuits were often the first Christian missionaries in the New World, and in parts of Asia and Africa. They antagonized many European rulers because they gave allegiance only to their general in Rome and to the pope. In 1773 Pope Clement XIV abolished the order, under pressure from the kings of France, Spain and Portugal, but it continued to exist in Russia. The order was re-established in 1814. Jesuits have distinguished themselves in education, scholarship and missionary work.

Jesus Christ (*c.* 4 BC–*c.* AD 30), the inspiration for Christianity and to Christians the Son of God. "Jesus" is a Greek form of the Hebrew name *Joshua*; "Christ" comes from the Greek translation of the Hebrew *messiah*, the "anointed" whose coming had long been prophesied as the deliverance of the people of Israel. Present knowledge of Jesus's life is based mostly on the biblical gospels of MATTHEW, MARK and LUKE, of which Mark is the earliest and Luke the most detailed. Although BC (before Christ) and AD (*anno domini*, in the year of the Lord) dates are timed from the birth of Christ, Jesus was probably born in 4 BC – the calendar error was made by Christians of the 6th century. It was near the end of the reign of HEROD THE GREAT and was just at the time that the Romans had ordered a census of all their Empire's inhabitants at their places of birth. For the census Jesus's mother MARY had to travel with her husband Joseph from Nazareth in Galilee to his place of birth, Bethlehem in Judaea, where Jesus was also born, in a stable. He probably grew up in Galilee.

In about AD 26 or 27, JOHN THE BAPTIST began preaching his message of repentance and baptism in the area. Jesus was one of many baptized in the River Jordan by John, who may have been a relation. Thereafter Jesus began His own ministry, preaching to large numbers and gathering many followers as He wandered throughout the country. He also taught – through spiritual insights, parables and even miracles – a special group of 12 of His closest disciples who were later to be sent out as the nucleus of the spread of the gospel, and to be called APOSTLES. His teaching was to "love God and love one's neighbour" (comprising all fellow men), and that salvation depended on doing what was patently God's will rather than necessarily adhering to the letter and the contemporary interpretation of the Jewish Law. This tenet did not find approval with the hierarchy of the Jewish religion, particularly those of the TEMPLE in Jerusalem who themselves were the butt of some of Jesus's ridicule.

In about AD 29 or 30 Jesus and His disciples went up to Jerusalem to celebrate the Jewish feast of the PASSOVER. It was a dangerous place for Him, for although the common people loved Him, the chief priests and elders of the Jewish faith were by now trying to devise means of silencing Him in an exemplary manner. A few days later Jesus gathered His disciples for a LAST SUPPER, at which He instituted the EUCHARIST. The next morning, after a night of prayer, He was arrested by agents of the priests and denounced before the Roman governor, Pontius PILATE, on a charge of sedition: that He had claimed to be a king of the Jews. Roman soldiers crucified Jesus on a hill outside the city wall. After His death His body was buried in a sealed rock tomb. Two days later He rose from the dead and appeared several times to His disciples and to other people. Forty days after His resurrection He ascended into heaven, leaving His disciples the promise that His spirit would give them the courage and strength to go on proclaiming His message to all the world.

Christians believe that Christ is at the same time truly man and truly God, and that He came into the world to reconcile sinful man to God by His sacrificial death. *See also* HC1 pp.110–111.

Jésus María, small town in Argentina, site of one of the first JESUIT missions to South America, established in 1618. The town has a fine 18th-century church.

Jet, dense variety of LIGNITE coal formed from wood buried on the sea-floor; it is often polished and used in jewellery. *See also* PE p.98.

JET, Joint European Torus Research Project, nuclear fusion power research centre set up in 1977 at Culham in England. Scientists, sponsored by the EEC, hope to develop a machine which will heat PLASMA to immense temperatures within a MAGNETIC BOTTLE and thereby fuse atoms of hydrogen with the subsequent release of nearly limitless energy. The TOKARNAK fusion machine, developed by the USSR, has shown the small-scale feasibility of this technology.

Jet engine, type of ENGINE that relies for its propulsive power on the thrust provided by the expansion of exhaust gases; also called a gas turbine. Air is taken in at the front, compressed and kerosene vapour added and ignited. The simplest jet engine, the ram jet, uses this principle alone, but can operate only at speeds which force enough air into it. Turbojets and turbofans have a compressor (for the induction of air), driven by a turbine. *See also* MM p.63.

Jet propulsion, movement of a body by way of thrust provided by the backwards discharge of a jet of fluid (gas or liquid), as in JET ENGINES or rockets. In jet engines the ejected gas consists of a mixture of air taken from outside and exhaust gases resulting from internal combustion. *See also* ENGINE; MM pp.63, 69.

Jet streams, narrow, swiftly moving winds between slower currents at altitudes of 10 to 16km (6 to 10 miles) in the upper troposphere or lower stratosphere, principally in the zone of prevailing westerlies. High-flying aircraft may be helped or hindered by the jet stream and the rapid wind variations around it. *See also* ATMOSPHERE.

Jevons, William Stanley (1835–82), British economist. His major contribution to economics was his theory of utility; he held, and demonstrated in mathematical terms, that value was determined by utility. His most important book is *The Theory of Political Economy* (1871).

Jewel, John (1522–71), English religious leader. He spent some time abroad during the reign of Mary I, but returned to England on the accession of Elizabeth I and was made Bishop of Salisbury. His defence of the Church of England against Rome, *Apologia pro Ecclesia Anglicana* (1562), formed the groundwork for all subsequent controversy about the positions of the English and Roman Churches.

Jewison, Norman (1926–), Canadian film maker trained in television whose films include *The Cincinnati Kid* (1965), *The Russians Are Coming* (1966), *The Thomas Crown Affair* (1968) and *Fiddler on the Roof* (1971). His most distinguished film is *In the Heat of the Night* (1967), which won three Oscars.

Jews, people who originated in the ancient Middle East, and lived in kingdoms in Palestine for centuries. After the destruction of Jerusalem by the Romans (AD 70) they were dispersed over the world, sometimes as ghetto minorities, sometimes as citizens (*see* DIASPORA.) In 1948 they established the national state of Israel. Millions more live in other countries. Jews differ among themselves in physical appearance, language and to some extent in customs, so there is no simple definition of Jewishness. Their sense of identity is found in religious beliefs and traditions going back through the Hebrew prophets to the time of MOSES and ABRAHAM. *See also* JUDAISM.

Jew's harp, also called jaw's harp, primitive musical instrument. It is a metal frame which the player holds to his mouth, with a flexible metal strip vibrated by his finger. The player changes tone and pitch by altering the shape of his mouth.

Jex-Blake, Sophia Louisa (1840–1912), British physician who fought vigorously and successfully to get legislation through Parliament enabling women to qualify as doctors and to practise medicine and surgery. She founded a medical school for women in London in 1874 and another in Edinburgh in 1886.

Jezebel (died *c.* 843 BC), in the Bible, Phoenician princess who became wife to AHAB, King of Israel. A haughty foreigner who introduced the worship and priesthood of BAAL, she was disliked intensely by religious Israelites; she clashed most severely with the prophet ELIJAH, who foretold her death at the hand of Jehu, the usurper of her son Jehoram's throne.

Jhabvala, Ruth Prawer (1927–), British writer, *b.* Germany. Her first novel was *To Whom She Will* (1955). In 1973 she published *A New Dominion*. She has also published three sets of short stories.

Jhelum, river in NW India and Pakistan and one of the Five Rivers of the Punjab. It rises in the Himalayas in NW India, flows NW, then SW into Pakistan at the W foot of the Pir Panjāl Range and continues S and W to join the Chenab W of Jhang Maghiāna. Length: approx. 725km (450 miles).

Jidda (Jedda or Juddah), city in Hajaz, W Saudi Arabia, on the Red Sea, 74km (46 miles) W of Mecca; one of the major ports of Saudi Arabia. The port for Mecca, Jidda receives many pilgrims. Pop. (1974 est.) 300,000.

Jig, peasant festival dance in 6/8 time, familiar throughout western Europe. It achieved popularity in the 16th century, especially in Scotland and Ireland, and is still included among the traditional dances of those countries. Usually a dance for couples, it may be accompanied by the bagpipes or fiddle.

Jig-saw, mechanical saw used for cutting shapes in thin materials. It has a short, narrow blade that moves rapidly up and down. The jig-saw puzzle derives its name from the saw used to make it.

Jihād, or Jehād, religious war of Muslims against non-believers. Established in the KORAN as a divine institution, such warfare is a sacred religious duty undertaken especially for the purpose of advancing ISLAM and protecting Muslims from evil. There are four ways in which Muslims may fulfil their Jihād duty: by the heart, by the tongue, by the hand, and by the sword. Jews and Christians, called by Mohammed *ahl al-Kitab*, or people of the book (having a written religious belief), were given special consideration: a choice of conversion or submission to Islamic rule before the declaration of Jihād.

Jiménez, Juan Ramón (1881–1958), Spanish poet. He lived in Spain until 1936, but then went to the USA and later to Puerto Rico. His lyrical work gave way to a simple free verse style. His best known prose work is *Platero and I* (1917). He was awarded to 1956 Nobel Prize in literature.

Jiménez de Quesada, Gonzalo (*c.* 1495–

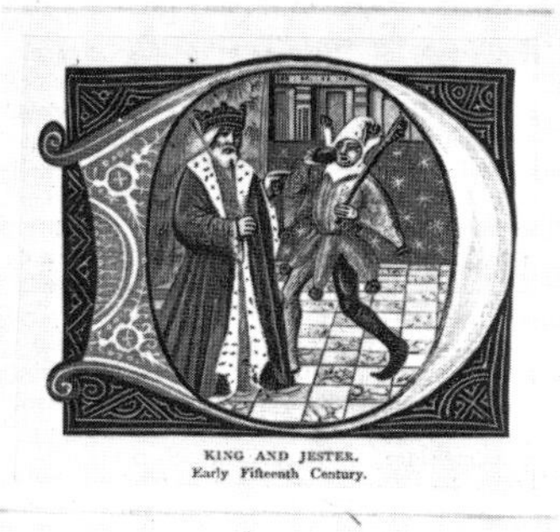

Jester; an early 15th-century impression of a jester entertaining his king.

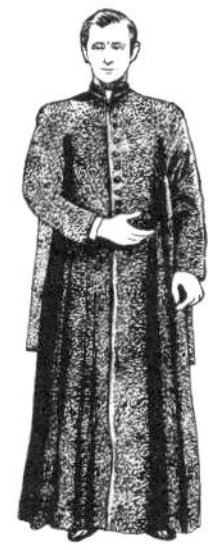

Jesuits have included a great many illustrious explorers, scientists and writers.

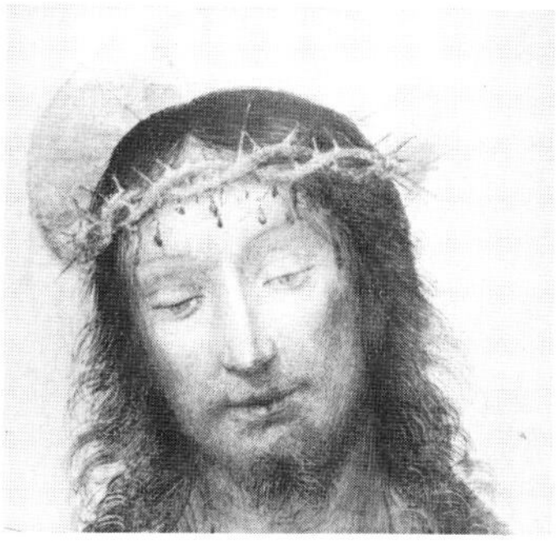

Jesus Christ; Fra Bartolommeo's representation inspired many later portrayals.

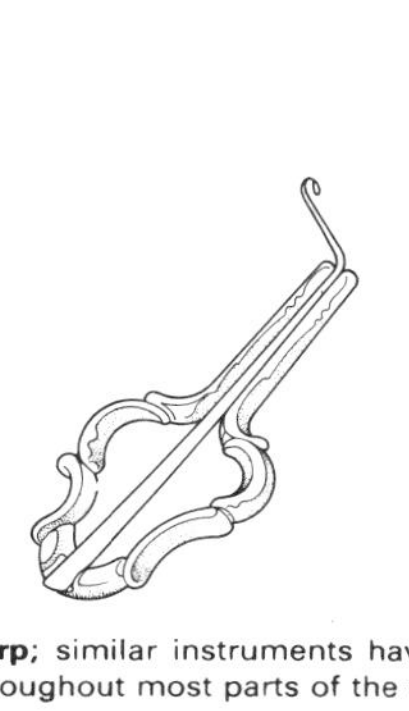

Jew's harp; similar instruments have been found throughout most parts of the world.

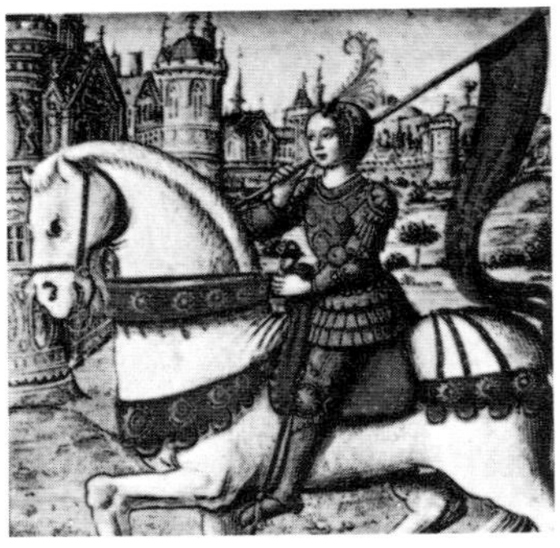

Joan of Arc, like most girls of 15th-century France, never learned to read or write.

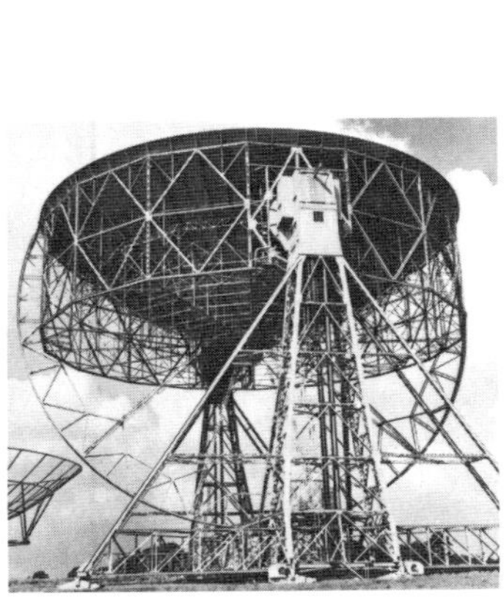

Jodrell Bank's radio telescope began its working life tracking artificial satellites.

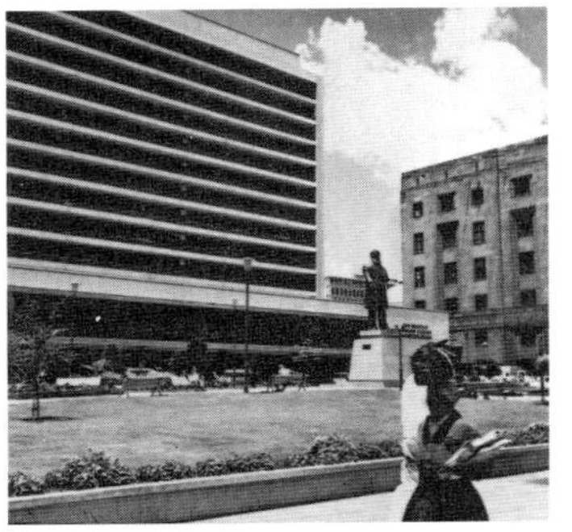

Johannesburg: von Brands Square, named after the first mining commissioner.

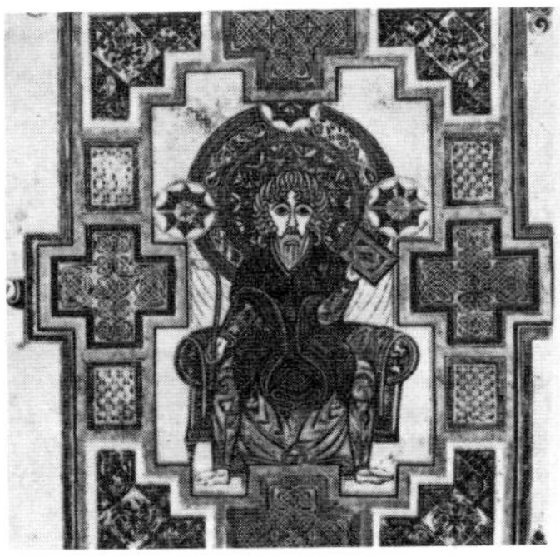

Saint John as depicted in the Book of Kells, an 8th-century illuminated manuscript in Latin.

1579), Spanish soldier and adventurer. When chief magistrate of Santa Marta he was sent to COLOMBIA, where he discovered the source of the Magdalena River, conquered the Chibcha Indians and founded Bogotá (1538).

Jimson weed. *See* THORN APPLE.

Jingoism, chauvinistic and aggressive nationalism. The term originated in the Russo-Turkish War (1877–78) when British supporters of moves to restrain Russia were called jingoists, after a line of a song popular at the time, which ran, "We don't want to fight but, by jingo, if we do/We've got the ships, we've got the men,/We've got the money too!"

Jinja, second largest city in Uganda, on the River Nile, in the SE of the country at an altitude of 1,140m (3,740ft). It was founded by the British in 1901 and its development as an industrial town resulted from the construction of the Owen Falls Dam in 1957. Industries include tobacco, steel, copper, textiles, grain milling and sugar. Pop. 52,000.

Jinn (Djinn), in Arabian mythology, a supernatural spirit composed of air and fire; it may dwell in any inanimate object. Jinns have been variously portrayed as treacherous and vengeful, but it was said that mortals who knew the correct magical procedure could exploit them. The plural form, *jinni,* became Anglicized as *genie.*

Jinnah, Muhammad Ali (1876–1948), founder of PAKISTAN. He obtained a law degree in England and returned to practise in India. In 1906 he joined the Indian National Congress and became a keen advocate of Hindu-Muslim unity, but his views changed over the years and by 1940 he had come to believe that when independence was achieved there must be a separate Muslim state to prevent the Hindu majority from dominating the entire subcontinent.

Jipcho, Ben (1943–), Kenyan middle-distance runner who set a world record in 1973 by running the 3,000m steeplechase in 8min 14.0sec.

Jitterbug, US teenage dance popular in the 1940s and 1950s, usually performed to the syncopated rhythms of JAZZ. A very lively dance, it involved acrobatic twisting and whirling.

Jivaro, warlike South American Indian people of the Montaña region on the E slopes of the Andes. They grow crops for food as a supplement to wild fruits, fishing and game, and live in large community houses. The Jivaro were once noted for their practice of shrinking the heads of their victims. These shrunken heads, called *tsantsas,* were believed to give supernatural power to the taker. *See also* MS p.*252.*

Jive, popular dance which began in the USA in the mid-1950s as the dance of teenagers who followed the new rock and roll beat of William HALEY and Elvis PRESLEY. It soon spread to Europe. The jive does not prescribe a specific footwork.

Joachim, Joseph (1831–1907), Austro-Hungarian violinist. He founded the Joachim Quartet (1869), which presented the conservative quartet repertory of the 19th century in definitive interpretations. He composed CADENZAS for the violin concertos of BEETHOVEN and Brahms.

Joan of Arc (*c.*1412–31), national heroine of France, canonized by the Roman Catholic Church; also known as Joan of Lorraine and the Maid of Orléans. A deeply religious peasant girl, she claimed to hear heavenly voices and see visions of saints urging her to save France, which was then in the midst of the HUNDRED YEARS WAR. In early 1429, wearing men's clothes, Joan and some French troops broke the long English siege of Orléans. She then drove the English from the Loire towns and defeated them at Patay. After this victory she persuaded the indecisive dauphin to proceed to Reims and be crowned. She attempted to liberate Paris but was unsuccessful. In early 1430 she was captured by the Burgundians, handed over to the English and burnt at the stake for witchcraft and heresy (1431). She was declared a saint in 1920. *See also* HC1 p.203, *203,* 204.

Joan of Kent (1328–85), English noblewoman, daughter of Edmund of Woodstock, youngest son of EDWARD I. Early in her life she gained renown for her charm and beauty and in 1361 married Edward the Black Prince, by whom she had two sons, Edward (1365–1370) and Richard, later RICHARD II.

Job, Old Testament wisdom book that describes the crisis in the life of Job. The main theme of the book, which was probably written about 500 BC, is that suffering comes to good and bad people alike. God visits upon the wealthy and happy Job all kinds of deprivations and disease in order to test his faith. Convinced of his own innocence, Job rejects the view that suffering is the result of sin. In the end, his opinion and his faith are justified.

Job's tears, leafy annual grass that grows in Asia and the USA. It is named after the shiny white tear-shaped beads that enclose its edible seeds. Height: to 0.9m (3ft). Family Poaceae; species *Coix lacryma-jobi.*

Jocasta. *See* OEDIPUS.

Jockey Club, the governing body of flat and, since 1969, National Hunt horse racing in Britain. It was formed in 1750 at a Pall Mall inn by influential gentlemen interested in the Turf. Today, through Weatherby's who act as secretary, it attends to the Rules of Racing, discipline, licences, fixtures and publication of the Racing Calendar. There are similar organizations in many other countries.

Jodl, Alfred (*c.*1892–1946), German general and one time chief of the Operations Staff of the German Armed Forces High Command. A brilliant soldier, he was nevertheless utterly subservient to HITLER and did nothing to restrain his military ambitions. In 1945 Jodl signed the unconditional surrender of Germany in Reims and after the Nuremberg trials he was hanged in 1946 for crimes committed during WWII.

Jodrell Bank, experimental station, part of the University of Manchester, England, and the location of one of the world's largest steerable radio telescopes, with a 76m (250ft) parabolic dish. The observatory, built under the supervision (1946–57) of Sir Bernard LOVELL, also contains smaller radio telescopes. It is devoted to astronomy as well as to the observation and tracking of artificial satellites.

Joel, second of the 12 minor prophets of the Old Testament. The book of his name, written about 400 BC, falls into two main sections: part one tells how an invasion of locusts lays JUDAH waste – lamentation and prayer bring the promise of help from YAHWEH; part two describes the Day of Yahweh, and his judgment on the nations.

Joffre, Joseph Jacques Césaire (1852–1931), French general. Joffre was Commander-in-Chief of the French Army at the outbreak of WWI (1914). Determined to advance at all costs and underestimating German strength, he was repulsed, but halted the enemy's counterattack at the battle of the Marne (1914). Joffre was also responsible for the failure of the Anglo-French offensive in the Somme Valley (July-Nov. 1916) and resigned; he was made a Marshal of France.

Joffrey Ballet. *See* ROBERT JOFFREY BALLET

Jogjakarta, city in S Java, Indonesia, 282km (175 miles) WSW of Surabaja, at the foot of Mt Merapi. It served as the capital of a Dutch-controlled sultanate from 1755 and was the scene of a local uprising led by Prince Dipo Negoro, who protested against Dutch forced labour practices and exploitation (1825–30). A Javanese stronghold during the Indonesian Independence Movement of the 1940s, it was the temporary capital of Indonesia (1946–49). Industries include handicrafts, textiles and tanning. Pop. (1971) 342,267.

Jogues, Saint Isaac (1607–46), French Jesuit missionary and martyr. Ordained in 1636, he went to Canada and converted the Huron Indians to Roman Catholicism. The Iroquois captured him but he was rescued by the Dutch. He returned to missionary work in the Great Lakes region and was killed there by the Mohawks. He was canonized in 1930.

Johannesburg, city in NE Republic of South Africa. It was founded in 1886 after the discovery of gold on the Witwatersrand. Today it is the country's largest and leading industrial and commercial city, and the administrative headquarters for the country's gold mining companies. Industries include industrial chemicals, textiles and leather products. Pop. 1,498,700.

John, Saint, one of the 12 APOSTLES of JESUS, the son of Zebedee and brother of the apostle St JAMES the Greater. He is generally believed to be the author of the fourth GOSPEL, and is commonly considered also to have written the three epistles under his name in the New Testament. Together with his brother and St PETER, he belonged to the inner group of disciples who witnessed Jesus's TRANSFIGURATION and His agony in GETHSEMANE. John is also traditionally identified with the anonymous disciple referred to in the fourth gospel as the one "whom Jesus loved", both at the LAST SUPPER and at the crucifixion, where Jesus left the care of His mother to John. Another tradition states that John miraculously escaped martyrdom and died at an old age at Ephesus. Feast day: 27 December.

John, First, Second and Third Epistles of, three New Testament letters often attributed to the Apostle JOHN. They describe the need and benefits of faith, warn against false teachers and call for Church unity.

John, the Gospel According to Saint, fourth and last gospel of the New Testament, believed to have been written by the Apostle JOHN. Although in some ways it supplements the preceding three "synoptic" gospels devoted to JESUS's life and work in Galilee, it differs greatly from them in that it uses no parables, stresses the kingly nature of Jesus, places a unique emphasis on the power of the Holy Spirit, and suggests that Jesus not only fulfilled the Old Jewish liturgy but by doing so brought it to an end. More concerned with the spiritual meaning of events than with historical facts or even historical sequence, it was for centuries identified as the work of the author of the Book of REVELATION (Apocalypse).

John, the name of 21 popes and two ANTIPOPES. John I (*r.*523–526) was sent by the Ostrogothic king, THEODORIC, to Constantinople to gain consent for the toleration of the Arian Christians in northern Italy. John gained imperial recognition of the superiority of the Roman bishop over the patriarch of Constantinople, but failed in his original purpose. On his return, Theodoric threw him into prison, where he died a few days later. John VIII (*r.*872–82) first pope to be assassinated. As pope, he built fortifications to protect Rome, founded the papal navy and fought tirelessly against the SARACENS, although to little purpose since his forces were too weak and help was not forthcoming from Constantinople. He was compelled by the times he lived in to assume an almost entirely political rôle. John XII (*r.*955–64) was only about 18 on his election. He and his court were notorious for depravity and sacrilege and he was deposed in 963. He returned to Rome and regained power but died the following year. John XXI (*r.*1276–77) was a student of medicine and a philosopher of some repute, and the first Portuguese pope. Essentially a man of learning, he nevertheless attempted to organize a crusade against the Saracens in 1276. His *Summulae logicales* became famous as a textbook on logic. John XXII (*r.*1316–34), one of the Avignon popes, condemned (1323) the doctrine of absolute poverty as heretical. His dislike of FRANCISCANS alienated many scholars of the time, but he remained the final arbiter in the affairs of the empire and in 1324 excommunicated LOUIS, KING OF BAVARIA for having himself crowned without papal sanction. During his pontificate, John XXII organized the CURIA in the form which, with minor changes, it is found today. John XXIII (1881–1963) became pope in 1958. Before his election he had served as director of the Society for Propagation of the Faith, had been papal nuncio in France and from 1953 patriarch of Venice. John's place in church history rests on his courage and foresight in calling the Second Vatican Council, which met in 1962 to provide an *aggiornamento* (renewal or updating) of Roman Catholic religious life and doctrine. His reign was also notable for the emphasis he put on questions of peace and justice. *See also* HC2 p.304.

John, the name of eight BYZANTINE emperors. John I Tzimisces (925–76; *r.* 969–76), a former general, defeated both the Bulgarians and the Russians in the Balkans and consolidated Byzantine power in the Near East. John II Comnenus (1088–1143; *r.* 1118–43) gained further military successes in the Balkans and Asia Minor during his rule. John III Dukas Vatatzes (1193–1254; *r.* 1222–54) ruled from Nicaea because Constantinople had been taken by the Crusaders in 1204. He failed to recapture it after a siege in 1235. John IV Lascaris (1250–1300; *r.* 1258–61) was a minor throughout his reign and was deposed by Michael PALAEOLOGUS, the restorer of Byzantine power, who had him blinded and imprisoned. John V Palaeologus (1332–91; *r.* 1341–91), another boy emperor, had a disturbed reign during which he was imprisoned in Venice as a debtor (1369) and he was deposed in 1376, although he regained his throne. From 1347 to 1354, John V was co-emperor with John VI Cantacuzenus (1292–1383) who, in order to resist the Serbs, allied himself with the Turks, with whose help he regained Constantinople in 1347. John VII Palaeologus (1360–*c.* 1410) reigned briefly in 1390 and was regent (1399–1402) for his uncle, MANUEL II, during a time of constant danger from the Turks. John VIII Palaeologus (1390–1448; *r.* 1425–48) made the last desperate attempt to defend the empire against the Turks. In order to get aid from the West, he achieved in 1439 the union of the Greek and Roman churches.

John (*c.* 1167–1216), King of England, youngest son of HENRY II. During RICHARD I's absence on a CRUSADE, John tried to seize control on a crusade, John tried to seize control in 1193 and, on the king's return, had to forfeit all his lands. But Richard soon relented and on his death in 1199 was succeeded by John. His probable murder of his nephew ARTHUR in 1203, the loss of vast territories in France (1204–05) and heavy taxation to finance abortive attempts to regain them made him extremely unpopular. He was forced to submit to the pope after he had been excommunicated. At Runnymede in 1215 he was compelled to accede to the demands of his barons and affix his seal to the draft of MAGNA CARTA. Civil war ensued, during which John died, possibly poisoned. *See also* HC1 pp. *168*, *169*, 169, 178, 186.

John, the name of two kings of France. John I (1316), the posthumous son of LOUIS X, lived only five days. John II, called "the Good" (1319–64), succeeded his father, PHILIP VI, in 1350. At the battle of POITIERS (1356) during the HUNDRED YEARS WAR, he was captured by the English and taken to London. John was later released in exchange for hostages and an enormous ransom. When one of the hostages escaped, John, chivalrous to the last, voluntarily returned to London, where he died. *See also* HC1 pp.203, *209*, 212.

John, the name of two kings of Hungary. John I (1487–1540; *r.* 1526–40), or János Zápolya, was governor of Transylvania (1511–26) and elected king by the diets of Tokaj and Szekespehérvar as a rival to the Hapsburg claimant, Ferdinand I, the Holy Roman emperor. The ensuing civil war ended when John agreed that Ferdinand would determine the succession. Instead, encouraged by the Turks, John I arranged for the succession of his infant son, John II, who was to rule as a vassal of the Sultan.

John, the name of three kings of Poland. John I, or John Albert (1459–1501; *r.* 1492–1501). During his reign, which saw the development of parliamentary government, the nobility and gentry acquired, in return for subsidies, extensive privileges at the expense of the peasants. John I unsuccessfully invaded Moldavia, which incurred a counter-attack by the Turks. John II (1609–72; *r.* 1648–68). He became a JESUIT novice in 1646 but resigned after a year. Upon becoming king, he was almost immediately (1648) faced with rebellion by the Cossacks and their allies, the Tatars. Wars with Russia and Sweden occupied him from 1654–67, during which time the Swedes occupied much of Poland and John was at one time forced to flee to Silesia. Threatened with rebellion by the diet he abdicated (1668) and retired to the abbey of Saint-Germain-des-Prés, France. John III (John Sobieski) (1629–96; *r.* 1674–96), commander of the Polish army. He successfully relieved the Turks' siege of Vienna in 1683. By decisively defeating the Turkish armies, three times the size of his own, he saved Europe from Muslim conquest and was acclaimed the hero of Christendom. He was a notable patron of letters and the arts but the last years of his rule were marred by a decline in his prestige as a result of the country's political stagnation. His death marked the virtual end of Polish independence: foreigners occupied the throne for the next 66 years.

John, the name of six kings of Portugal, the first three of the Aviz family, the others of the BRAGANZA. John I, or John the Great (1357–1433; *r.* 1385–1433), was the illegitimate son of PEDRO I. He forced the King of Castile to raise the siege of Lisbon and leave Portugal; later he defeated the Spaniards several times on their own territory and compelled them to agree to a long-term peace treaty. John II (1455–95; *r.* 1481–95) was a great patron of navigators and explorers and Portugal's great empire had its beginnings during his reign. He was succeeded by a brother-in-law, MANUEL I. John III (1502–57; *r.* 1521–57) was a deeply religious man and during his reign he introduced the INQUISITION into Portugal (1536). Brazil was colonized and the empire reached its greatest extent. He was succeeded by his grandson, SEBASTIAN. John IV (1604–56; *r.* 1640–56) founded the Braganza dynasty and ruled during a period of turmoil. He ascended the throne following a successful revolution against Spanish domination and reconquered Brazil, the coast of which had been seized by the Dutch. John V (1689–1750; *r.* 1706–50) inherited Portuguese involvement in the War of the SPANISH SUCCESSION and suffered military defeats at their hands. He is best remembered for his architectural improvements in Lisbon, made possible by immense riches from Brazil. John VI (1767–1826; *r.* 1816–26) was embroiled during his reign (he was regent from 1799 and effective ruler from 1792) in the upheavals of the NAPOLEONIC WARS and in 1807, when the French occupied Lisbon, was forced to flee to Brazil. He returned in 1821 but was obliged to accept a new, more democratic constitution. In 1825 Brazil became independent.

John III (1537–92), King of Sweden (1568–92), son of Gustavus VASA. A theologian, from 1577 he sought (without success) to establish a synthesis of Catholicism and Lutheranism in Sweden and himself became a Catholic in 1578. He sought to control Russian trade routes by joining Poland in war with Russia (1578–83).

John, Augustus Edwin (1878–1961), British portrait and landscape painter who gained early recognition through his superb draughtsmanship. Always an ardent opponent of academism, he joined the NEW ENGLISH ART CLUB in 1903. Although influenced by the Old Masters and by POST-IMPRESSIONISM, his high-toned colour and solidity of drawing were very much his own. His works include *Galway* (1916) and the brilliant portraits of his wife *Dorelia* and of *Madame Suggia* (*c.* 1923; Tate) and *Bernard Shaw* (*c.* 1914).

John, Barry (1945–), Welsh rugby union player. A fly-half of elusive genius and a skilful goalkicker, he scored a record 90 points for Wales in 25 matches (1966–72) and toured South Africa (1968) and New Zealand (1971) with the British Lions, scoring a record 180 points in New Zealand. He played for the Llanelli and Cardiff clubs.

John, Elton (1947–), British rock singer and pianist, *b.* Reginald Dwight. He began his musical career in 1964 and has since sold millions of records throughout the world. He composes his own music (with lyrics by Bernie Taupin). His records include *Elton John* (1970), *Goodbye Yellow Brick Road* (1973), *Rock of the Westies* (1975) and *Blue Moves* (1976).

John, Gwendolen Mary (1876–1939), British painter. The sister of Augustus JOHN, she is primarily known for her portraits and interiors. Examples of her subtlety in characterization and in tonal relationships include *Self Portrait* (*c.* 1900) and the later *Portrait of a Nun* (*c.* 1920–30).

John Bull, symbolic representation of the typical Englishman and, by extension, of Britain itself. The name became popular after the appearance of the *History of John Bull* (1712) by Dr John Arbuthnot. It advocated a policy of peace with France.

John Chrysostom, Saint (*c.* 350–407), brilliant preacher and greatest of the Greek Church Fathers. In 398 he was made Bishop of Constantinople, where his eloquence, asceticism and charity made him famous. His sermons and writings provide an invaluable record of the 4th century.

John Dory. *See* DORY.

John of Austria, also called Don John (1547–78), Spanish prince and military leader, illegitimate son of Emperor CHARLES V and half-brother of PHILIP II of Spain. In 1571, as head of the naval forces of the Holy League formed by Pope PIUS V, Spain and Venice, he defeated the Turks in the naval Battle of LEPANTO. He took Tunis from the Turks in 1573.

John of Damascus, Saint (*c.* 675–*c.* 749), theologian and doctor of the Church. He was born in Syria and became a Christian priest in the monastery at Mar Saba near Jerusalem. There he wrote hymns and treatises on theology, notably *The Fountain of Wisdom*, which is divided into three parts dealing with philosophy, heresies and the Orthodox faith. Feast day: 4 December.

John of Gaunt (1340–99), fourth son of EDWARD III of England and Duke of Lancaster. His name comes from the Middle English *Gaunt* for Ghent, his birthplace. He led the English army against the French from 1372 to 1374. He was the greatest of medieval "overmighty" subjects and for a brief period in the mid-1370s was the most powerful man in the kingdom. The TUDOR line was descended from him and Catherine Swynford, his third wife. *See also* HC1 pp. *179*, *210*, 214–215.

John of Salisbury (*c.* 1115–80), English churchman and scholar. He was secretary to Theobald, Archbishop of Canterbury, and friend and secretary to St Thomas à BECKET. His most important works were *Policraticus* (1159), a treatise on government, and the *Metalogicon* (1159), in which he presented a picture of the intellectual and scholastic controversies of the time.

John of the Cross, Saint (1542–91), Spanish mystic, poet and doctor of the Roman Catholic Church. He was a monk and then a priest in the Carmelite order, which he tried to reform, becoming co-founder of the Discalced Carmelites. His endeavours aroused opposition and he was deprived of his positions and imprisoned, under torture. He is best known for his spiritual poems, such as *Dark Night of the Soul*, translated with other works in *The Poems of St John of the Cross* (1968). Feast day: 14 December.

John o'Groats, point in Scotland, at the NE tip of the mainland, on the Pentland Firth. It is commonly supposed to be the northernmost point of Scotland, although that is actually Dunnet Head, several miles away. The expression "from Land's End to John o'Groats" is used to denote the longest land distance in Britain, 1,410km (876 miles).

John Player League, sponsored English

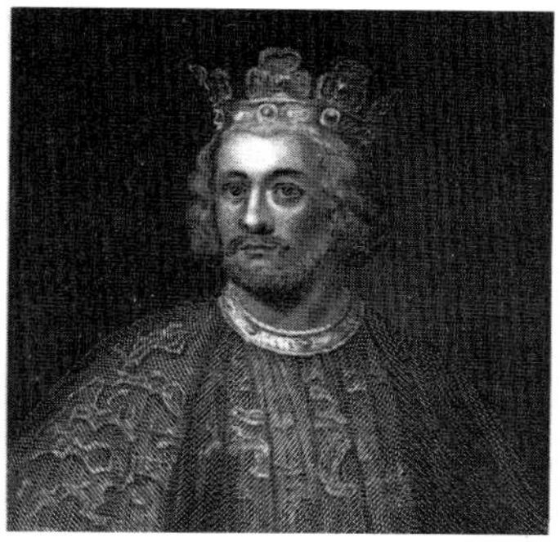

King John, whose death prevented his almost certain victory over the barons.

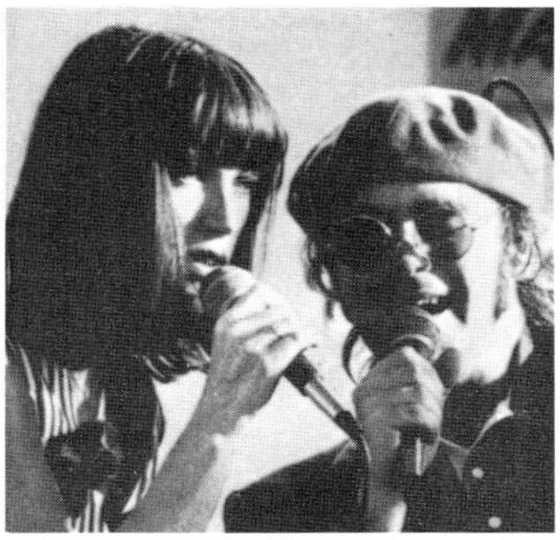

Elton John singing with Kiki Dee at a performance in Central Park, New York, in 1977.

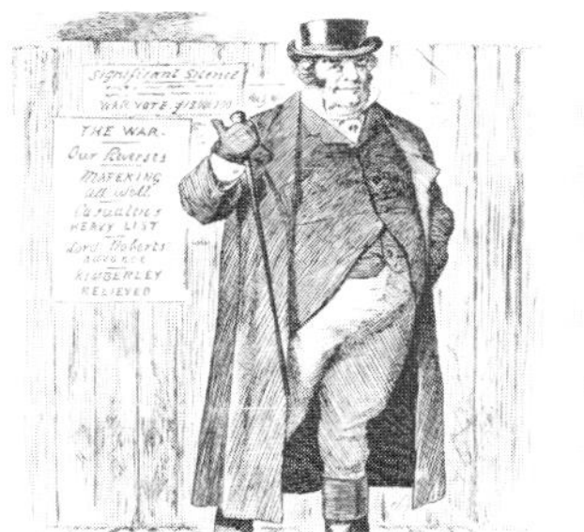

John Bull, a symbol of the English people, was depicted in 19th-century caricatures.

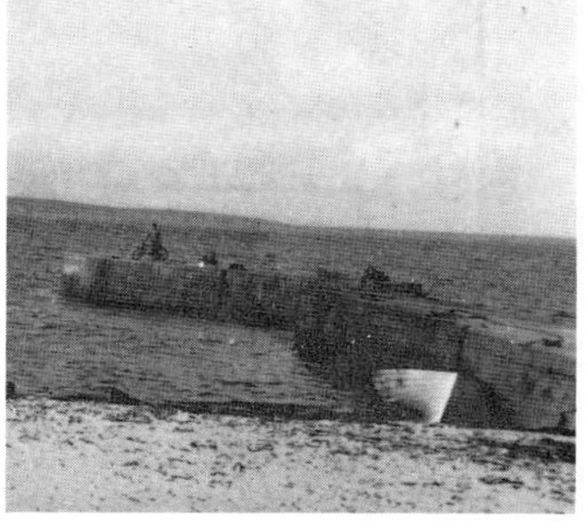

John O'Groats; the pier and northernmost part of the Scottish mainland.

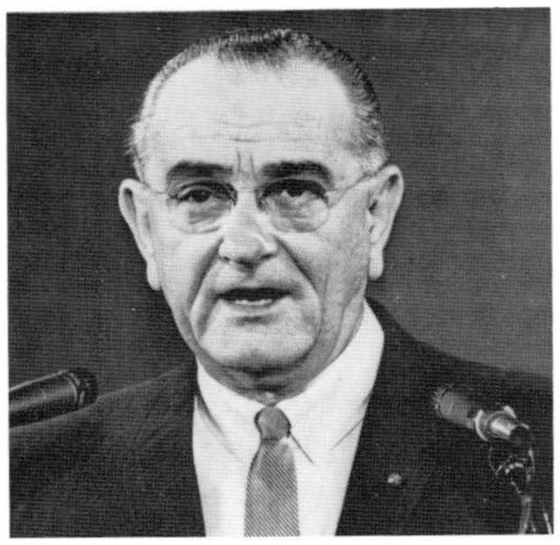

Lyndon B. Johnson's Presidential term was over-shadowed by the Vietnam War.

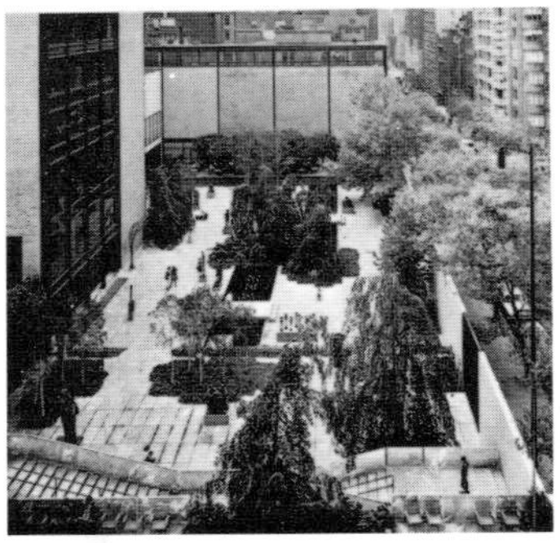

Phil Johnson designed this facade for the Museum of Modern Art in New York City.

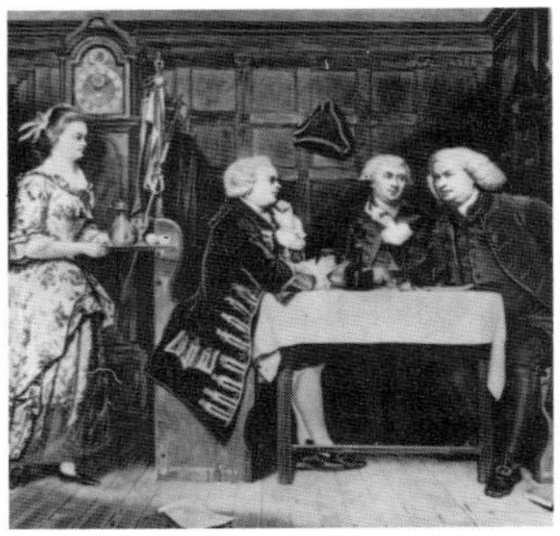

Dr Samuel Johnson with Goldsmith and Boswell at the Mitre Inn, London.

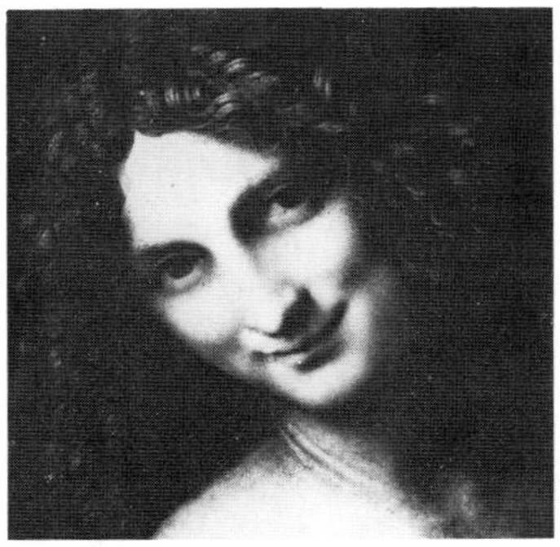

John the Baptist; a detail from Leonardo da Vinci's portrait of him, now in the Louvre.

cricket competition for the 17 first-class counties. Played on Sunday afternoons, matches are of 40-overs innings per side, with bowlers restricted to eight overs each and a run-up of no more than 13.72m (15yd). It commenced in 1969.

John Sobieski. *See* JOHN (KINGS OF POLAND).

Johns, Jasper (1930–), US painter. He abandoned the ABSTRACT EXPRESSIONIST style of his early work to begin painting canvases covered with everyday images (eg flags, targets and numbers) depicted in a highly PAINTERLY style. Examples of his work of this period are *Three Flags* (1958) and *Target With Four Faces* (1955). After 1961 he sometimes attached real objects to the canvas; common street or studio items appeared against painted fields (eg *False Start*, 1959). He also executed many lithographs and drawings that show the influence of COLLAGE and imprint techniques.

Johnson, Amy (1903–41), British pilot who became famous in 1930 for her solo flight from England to Australia. The next year she flew to Tokyo across Siberia and back to Britain, setting another record. In 1932 she broke the record held by her husband (J. A. Mollinson) for a solo flight to the Cape of Good Hope. In 1936 she flew solo to the Cape and back. In WWII she worked as an air ferry pilot and was killed in an air crash near London.

Johnson, Andrew (1808–75), 17th US president (1865–69). Unschooled and a tailor by profession, he entered politics as a supporter of Andrew JACKSON. He was both a pro-slavery southerner and a strong Unionist and as such was nominated running-mate for LINCOLN's re-election in 1864. They won by a large majority, but a month after the inauguration Lincoln was assassinated and Johnson succeeded him as president. Post-Civil War dissension between the president (who favoured a moderate reconstruction policy) and Congress (which advocated a harsh one) culminated in Johnson's impeachment. He was acquitted by one vote. *See also* HC2 p.152.

Johnson, "Bunk" (1879–1949), US jazz trumpeter, real name William Geary Johnson, who helped to create the New Orleans style. He was a member of Buddy Bolden's band, which he led after Bolden's collapse in 1907. None of his early work was recorded.

Johnson, Celia (1908–), British actress best remembered for her WWII film performances in *This Happy Breed* (1944) and *Brief Encounter* (1945). Trained at RADA, she returned to the stage in 1947 as *St Joan* at the Old Vic. Other notable appearances in the theatre were in *The Reluctant Debutante* (1955), *Flowering Cherry* (1957) and *The Dame of Sark* (1974).

Johnson, Cornelius (1593–1661), English painter of Dutch parentage. One of England's foremost portraitists, his popularity waned after the arrival of VAN DYCK (1632), by whom he was increasingly influenced. In 1643 Johnson returned to Holland.

Johnson, Eyvind (1900–76), Swedish novelist. Although his novels contain much political and social comment, he is best known for his autobiographical tetralogy *Romanen om Olof* ("The Novel of Olof", 1934–37), in which he depicts the grim labour conditions of logging in the sub-Arctic. He shared the 1974 Nobel Prize in literature with his fellow countryman Harry MARTINSON.

Johnson, Lyndon Baines (1908–73), 36th President of the USA (1963–69). In the House of Representatives (1937–48) and the Senate (1948–60), he acquired a reputation as a liberal and a skilled representative. As vice-president under John F. KENNEDY he took charge of the space programme, and after Kennedy's assassination embarked on the most ambitious legislative programme since the NEW DEAL. He sought to build a "Great Society" through free medical care for the aged, strong civil rights acts, and anti-poverty and urban renewal projects. His domestic success was over-shadowed by his VIETNAM WAR policy. He increased US commitment to more than 500,000 troops and in 1965 authorized the bombing of North Vietnam. Costs burgeoned and the war became widely unpopular in the USA. In March 1968 Johnson declared that he would not seek re-election and announced a partial halt to the bombing, opening the way to the start of peace talks.

Johnson, Philip Cortelyou (1906–), US architect. He was heavily influenced by MIES VAN DER ROHE, but his style was not as austere. He is noted for his glass-walled New Canaan house (1949) and the New York State Theatre (1962–64).

Johnson, Robert (*c.* 1913–38), US BLUES singer and guitarist. Arguably the greatest bluesman of all time, Johnson combined a highly accomplished but idiosyncratic guitar technique with a passionate improvizational singing style. His death-haunted lyrics in particular can be compared with the best contemporary poetry.

Johnson, Dr Samuel (1709–84), British lexicographer, poet and critic. He settled in London in 1737 and began writing pieces for *Gentleman's Magazine*. He was a prolific writer and witty conversationalist, and his works include the satire *The Vanity of Human Wishes* (1749), *Rasselas* (1759), the 10-volume *Lives of the Poets* (1779–81), the periodical *The Rambler* (1750–52), the *Dictionary of the English Language* (1755) – which established his reputation – and an edition of Shakespeare's plays (1765), and the essays comprising *The Idler* (1758-61). He was a founder (1764) of *The Club*, later known as *The Literary Club* whose members included David GARRICK, James BOSWELL, Edmund BURKE and Oliver GOLDSMITH. Boswell wrote a noted biography of Johnson.

Johnston, Sir Harry Hamilton (1858–1927), British explorer and colonial administrator in Africa. His expedition to Mt Kilimanjaro in 1884 furthered British interests in East Africa, and in 1889 he led an expedition that founded the British Central Africa Protectorate in Nyasaland.

John the Baptist, in the New Testament the herald of Christ's appearance and of the coming of the kingdom of God. The son of ZECHARIAH and ELIZABETH, he was born in Judaea six months before Jesus. At about the age of 30 he went to live in the desert, preaching on the banks of the River Jordan, exhorting his hearers to repent and be baptised for time was short. His baptism of Jesus, although recorded in the New Testament, marks the precise end of the Old, and the beginning of Christ's ministry. John's expressed disapproval of Herod Antipas's marriage (to his brother's ex-wife Herodias) led to his own execution.

Johor Baharu, capital city of Johore state in Malaysia, SE Asia. The city contains the sultan of Johor's residence, the Bukit Serene Palace. It is also a commercial centre for rubber. Pop. (1970) 136,234.

Joint, in anatomy, place where one bone meets another. In moveable joints such as those of the knee, elbow, spine and fingers and toes, the bones are separated and cushioned from one another by pads of CARTILAGE. In fixed joints cartilage may be present in infancy but disappear later as the bones fuse together, as in the FONTANELLES of the skull. *See also* MS pp.56, 57, 94–95.

Joint venture, capital project undertaken by two or more people or companies (usually in the same industry), under the terms of a formal agreement.

Joinville, Jean (1225–1317), French chronicler. A hereditary royal steward, he was a friend of Louis IX, whom he accompanied on his first Crusade (1248–52) and in captivity. He wrote *Histoire de Saint Louis*, a vivid, detailed narrative of the first Crusade and of the pious Louis IX.

Jókai, Mór (Maurus) (1825–1904), Hungarian novelist and journalist. His early radicalism gave way to liberalism, a development reflected in his novels as he moved from the romanticism of *Az Aranyember* (1872) (*Man with the Golden Touch*) to the realism of *Rab Ráby* (1879) (*The Strange Story of Ráby Rab*). His prolific non-journalistic writings occupy 100 volumes.

Jokjakarta. *See* JOGJAKARTA.

Joliot-Curie, name of two French physicists. Irène (1897–1956), daughter of Pierre and Marie CURIE, met Frédéric (1900–1958) when they were both working as assistants to the Curies. She worked on the physical and he on the chemical aspects of RADIOACTIVITY. Their discovery of artificial RADIOISOTOPES was rewarded by the 1935 Nobel Prize in chemistry. They were active in the French resistance during WWII and became Communists. Frédéric was responsible for the construction of France's first nuclear reactor, but he was dismissed for political reasons. *See also* ISOTOPES.

Jolliet, Louis (*c.* 1645–*c.* 1700), French-Canadian explorer who, with Jacques MARQUETTE, was the first white man to travel down the Mississippi River from where it met the Fox River in Wisconsin to the mouth of the Arkansas River. His expedition in 1672 hoped to show that the Mississippi emptied into the Pacific Ocean.

Jolson, Al (1886–1950), US comedian and singer. Sentimentally singing *Swanee* and *Mammy* with his face blacked, this music hall and Broadway stage performer later starred in *The Jazz Singer* (1927), the first talking film.

Jonah, fifth of the 12 minor prophets and subject of the book of his name in the Old Testament. After the fall of Jerusalem (586 BC), he was ordered by God to go and admonish the citizens of Nineveh as a prophet. Reluctant, and foreseeing their hostility, he tried to flee his responsibilities by ship, only to be thrown overboard and swallowed by a fish (usually represented as a whale). Cast ashore, the chastened Jonah went to Nineveh where he was well received and was instrumental in saving the city from the threatened destruction by God.

Jones, Ann, née Haydon (1938–), British table-tennis and tennis player who won the 1969 Wimbledon singles. She was runner-up in the 1957 world table-tennis, 1967 Wimbledon and 1961 and 1967 US finals. A left-hander, she won the French singles (1961, 1966) and shared five major doubles titles.

Jones, Bobby (1902–71), US golfer, full name Robert Tyre Jones jr. Never turning professional, he won the British Open (1926, 1927, 1930), US Open (1923, 1926, 1929, 1930), British Amateur (1930) and US Amateur (1924, 1925, 1927, 1928, 1930) titles. His four 1930 championships constituted an impressive record.

Jones, Daniel Jenkyn (1912–), Welsh composer. He has written nine symphonies, a violin concerto, two operas (*The Knife* and *Orestes*) and an oratorio (*St Peter*).

Jones, David Michael (1895–1974), British artist and writer. During WWI he served in the Royal Welsh Fusiliers. In 1921 he was converted to Roman Catholicism. His paintings were mainly illustrative of Welsh or Christian mythology. With *In Parenthesis* (1937), based on his wartime experience, he became known as a writer. His works include *Anathemata* (1952), *Epoch and Artist* (1959) and *The Tribunes Visitation* (1969).

Jones, Ernest (1897–1958), Welsh psychiatrist. He introduced PSYCHOANALYSIS into Britain and founded the Institute for Psychoanalysis in London in 1924 and the London Clinic for Psychoanalysis in 1926. His best-known book is *The Life and Works of Sigmund Freud* (3 vols, 1953–57).

Jones, Ernest Charles (1819–69), Welsh Chartist, *b.*Germany. He became a Chartist in 1845 and co-edited the *Northern Star* with Feargus O'CONNOR. He was imprisoned for encouraging the use of force (1848–50), and his attempt to revive CHARTISM in the 1850s failed.

Jones, Frederic Wood (1879–1954), British anatomist and physical anthropologist whose career started as anatomy demonstrator at St Thomas's Hospital, London. He became anthropologist to the Egyptian Government, and carried out an archaeological survey of Nubia. Later he was a professor at many universities; Adelaide (1919–26), Hawaii (1927–30), Melbourne (1930–37), Manchester (1938–45) and London at the Royal College of Surgeons (1945–52). His works include: *Mammals of South Australia* and *Trends of Life* (1953).

Jones, Gwyneth (1936–), Welsh dramatic soprano. She has performed at many opera houses in Europe and the USA and is famous as well for her oratorio roles and recitals. She is a principal guest artist at Covent Garden, London and recent roles have included the Marschallin (1975, *Der Rosenkavalier*) and Chrysothemis (1977, *Elektra*).

Jones, Inigo (1573–1652), English architect. He spent his early career painting and designing theatrical sets and costumes for English court masques. During his many journeys to Italy he studied the classical elements of design, which he incorporated into his own architectural work, including the Queen's House, Greenwich (1616–35); the Banqueting House in Whitehall, London (1619–21); and St Paul's, Covent Garden, London (1638). *See also* HC1 pp.*283*, 296.

Jones, James (1921–77), US author. His best-known novels, *From Here to Eternity* (1951) and *The Thin Red Line* (1962), deal with army life. He also wrote *Go to the Widow Maker* (1967).

Jones, John Paul (1747–92), naval officer during the American Revolutionary War. Born in Scotland, he joined the Continental navy in 1775, and proved successful at capturing supplies and enemy vessels. With his flagship *Bonhomme Richard* he engaged the superior British ship *Serapis* in battle off the coast of England in 1779.

Jones, Lewis (1931–), Welsh rugby union and league player. An attacking fullback and goalkicker for Llanelli, he won ten caps for Wales (1950–52) and toured Australia and New Zealand with the 1950 British Lions. In 1952 he joined Leeds Rugby League club for a record fee and set international and domestic scoring records. He played 15 times for Great Britain (1954–57).

Jongkind, Johan Barthold (1819–91), Dutch painter and etcher whose work had close affinities with IMPRESSIONISM. His style was influenced by Louis-Gabriel Isabey and the Dutch masters. Many of his oil paintings were based on landscape watercolours and drawings executed outside his studios. Like VAN GOGH, he was plagued by personal misfortune and, later, madness.

Jongleur, in medieval France, a strolling entertainer. He was a juggler, acrobat and singer of popular songs, unlike a troubadour, whose style was courtly. Much folklore was spread throughout Europe by jongleurs.

Jönköping, city in Sweden, at the S end of Lake Vättern. Since 1844, it has been the centre of Swedish match manufacturing. The safety match was developed there and the city has some of the world's largest match factories. Other industries include textiles and machinery. Pop. (1973 est.) 108,429.

Jonquil. *See* NARCISSUS.

Jonson, Ben (*c.*1572–1637), English dramatist, lyric poet and actor. A friend of Shakespeare, he was popular and influential in Elizabethan and Stuart drama. His comedies of humours include *Everyman in His Humour* (1598), *Everyman Out of His Humour* (1599), *Volpone* (1606), *Epicoene* (1609), *The Alchemist* (1610) and *Bartholomew Fair* (1614). He also wrote the neoclassic tragedies *Sejanus* and *Catiline* and several court masques. His poems include the famous lyric which begins "Drink to me only with thine eyes". *See also* HC1 p.283.

Joplin, Scott (1868–1917), US composer. He wrote RAGTIME piano music such as *Maple Leaf Rag* (1900) and *The Entertainer* (1902), and also the opera *Treemonisha* (1911). His music underwent a revival of popularity in the 1970s. *See also* HC2 p.272.

Joppa. *See* JAFFA.

Jordaens, Jacob (1593–1678), Flemish painter. He is known for his allegorical and mythological works and for his naturalistic depictions of peasant life. He was considered to be Flanders' most eminent painter after the death of Rubens. His works include *The Satyr and the Peasant* and *The King Drinks*.

Jordan, Dorothea (Dorothy) (1761–1816), British actress. She made her debut in Dublin in 1779 and excelled in London in high-spirited roles such as Peggy in *The Country Girl* (1785), and Priscilla Tomboy in *The Romp*, a musical farce. In 1791 she became the mistress of the future William IV by whom she had ten children.

Jordan, Arab monarchy in the Middle East. An arid desert region with a N-S depression forming the River Jordan divides the country into the East and West Banks. The economy has been affected by low agricultural production and a large refugee population after the seizure of the West Bank by Israel in 1967. The capital is Amman. Area: 97,740sq km (37,737sq miles). Pop. (1975 est.) 2,702,000. *See* MW p.114.

Jordan (Al-Urdunn or Hayarden), river in Palestine rising in the Anti-Lebanon Mts at the confluence of the Hasbani, Dan and Baniyas Rivers, flowing S through Israel and the Sea of Galilee and emptying into the Dead Sea. Since 1967 the S part of the river has formed a section of the Israel-Jordan border. Length: 320km (200 miles).

Jorn, Asger (1914–73), Danish painter, a forerunner of ACTION PAINTING in Europe and a founder member of the COBRA group. His painting career reached its peak between 1956 and 1959 with his highly luminous colour compositions, executed with savage brushwork, in which he combined AUTOMATISM with a pictorial vision of immense power. An example from this period is *Letter to my Son* (1957).

Joseph, in Genesis, the youngest son of JACOB and RACHEL. After his father had given him a multicoloured coat, he was sold into slavery by his jealous brothers. In Egypt, by his skill at interpreting dreams, he gained the pharaoh's favour and reached a high position. During the great 7-year famine, the stores laid by from the previous 7 good years by his foresight fed all of Egypt – and his father and brothers in the outlying districts. In the New Testament, Joseph is the name of several men. One was the husband of MARY the mother of Jesus. A descendant of David, he was a carpenter in Nazareth. According to St Matthew (only), he fled with his family to safety in Egypt to escape Herod the Great's massacre of the HOLY INNOCENTS. *See also* JOSEPH OF ARIMATHAEA.

Joseph, name of two Holy Roman Emperors. Joseph I (1678–1711; *r.*1705–11), allied himself with England and Holland in the War of the SPANISH SUCCESSION. Joseph II (1741–90; *r.*1765–90), King of Hungary and Holy Roman Emperor from 1765, was dominated by his mother and co-ruler MARIA THERESA until her death in 1780, but then initiated radical social reforms. His "enlightened despotism", however, was largely reversed by his brother LEOPOLD II. *See also* HC1 pp.324, 325; HC2 p.17.

Joseph Bonaparte (1768–1844), brother of NAPOLEON and King of Naples (1806–08) and Spain (1808–13). He was a member of the French Council of Five Hundred (1798) and a councillor of state (1799). He was placed on the Neapolitan and Spanish thrones by his brother.

Joséphine (1763–1814), consort of NAPOLEON I and empress of the French. Her first marriage, to Vicomte Alexandre de Beauharnais, ended with his death in 1794 in the Reign of Terror. She married Napoleon in 1796 and was crowned with him in 1804. Her inability to bear him a son caused Napoleon to seek and obtain annulment of their marriage in 1810.

Joseph of Arimathea, Saint, in the New Testament, a prosperous Israelite and member of the SANHEDRIN who was converted by Jesus. He begged for and received Jesus's body from Pilate for burial. He is said later to have helped to found the first Christian community at Glastonbury. Feast: 17 March in the West; 31 July in the East.

Josephson, Brian David (1940–), British physicist who shared the 1973 Nobel Prize in physics with Leo ESAKI and Ivar GIAEVER for his discovery of the Josephson effect. In 1962 he predicted that an electric current would flow between two superconductors separated by a thin layer of insulator (the Josephson current), and that none would flow if, instead of insulation, a battery was connected between them. This hypothesis was later verified experimentally, and has helped in the understanding of SUPERCONDUCTIVITY.

Josephus, Flavius (*c.*37–*c.*100), Jewish leader and historian. A Pharisee, he was drawn into the revolt against Rome (66–70) and was appointed military governor of Galilee. The city fell but Josephus won favour with the Roman commander, VESPASIAN, and took Vespasian's family name (Flavius) as his own. In 70 Josephus went to Rome where he remained for the rest of his life and wrote his *History of the Jewish War*. In *The Antiquities of the Jews* he traced their history from the Creation to the outbreak of the revolt; his *Against Apion* defends Judaism.

Joshua, biblical book named after Joshua, the son of Nun, who became leader of the Israelites after the death of MOSES. The book emphasizes that God was responsible for the conquest of CANAAN, the reaching of Israel's Promised Land, and its subsequent apportionment, and ends with Joshua's death.

Josiah, in the Bible, son and successor of AMON as king of JUDAH. He ascended the throne at the age of eight after his father was murdered. During his reign a copy of the Deuteronomic Code was discovered and, guided by its precepts, he vowed to remove all forms of idolatry.

Josquin des Prés (*c.*1445–1521), Flemish composer of masses, motets and chansons. The expressiveness and inventiveness of his music marks him as the most prominent composer of Renaissance Europe. In excellence of composition he was rivalled only by the later 16th century composer, PALESTRINA.

Joubert, Piet (1831–1900), also known as Petrus Jacobus Joubert, Boer political figure. He helped to lead a rebellion to restore Transvaal's independence in 1881, and was defeated four times for the presidency by Paul KRUGER.

Jouhaux, Léon (1879–1954), French labour leader and advocate of international co-operation. He proposed the formation of the International Labour Organization in 1916, and was secretary-general of the French General Confederation of Labour (CGT) (1909–40, 1945–47). In 1949 he helped to found the Confederation of Free Trade Unions, and two years later received the Nobel Peace Prize.

Joule, James Prescott (1818–89), British physicist. Joule's law (1841) related the current flowing through a wire to its heat loss and laid the foundation for the law of conservation of energy. The JOULE is named after him. *See also* SU pp.*75*, 91.

Joule, unit of energy, named after James P. JOULE, in the metre-kilogramme-second (MKS) system of units. One joule is the work done by a force of one newton acting through a distance of one metre. *See also* ERG; SU p.91.

Joust, in the Middle Ages in Western Europe, one of the main attractions at a tournament of knights. Differing from the MÊLÉE, a joust involved single combat on horseback with a lance and a sword, ending in the death or injury of one of the knights. The church condemned jousts, and by the 15th century the winner simply had to unhorse the heavily-armed adversary. *See also* MM p.*161*.

Jowett, Benjamin (1817–93), British classical scholar and liberal thinker. His ideas were in advance of his time; he was in favour of university reform, and in 1860 was tried by the university for heresy after publishing an essay *On the Interpretation of Scripture*. He published authoritative translations of PLATO (1871), THUCYDIDES (1881) and ARISTOTLE (1885).

Joyce, Eileen (1912–), Australian concert pianist, also a harpsichordist. With Percy GRAINGER as her patron, she studied in Germany with Schnabel and later settled in England, where she won great

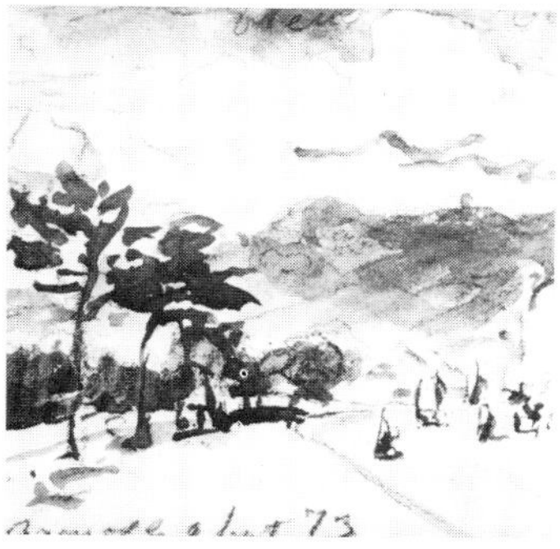

Johan Barthold Jongkind; a detail from a watercolour he painted in 1873.

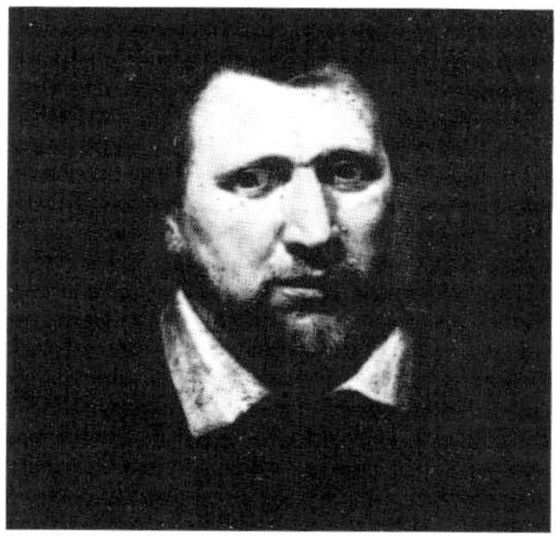

Ben Jonson barely escaped the gallows in 1598, having killed an actor in a duel.

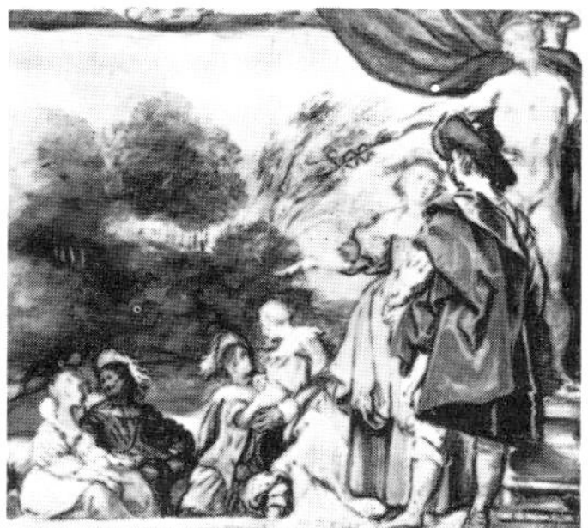

Jacob Jordaens; a detail of his *Boating Party*. His work was influenced by that of Rubens.

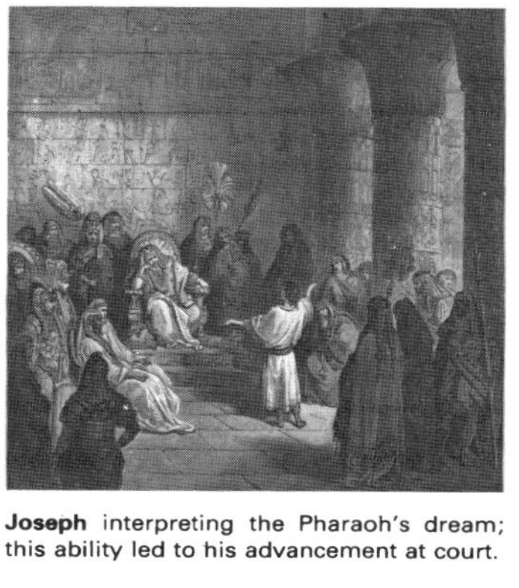

Joseph interpreting the Pharaoh's dream; this ability led to his advancement at court.

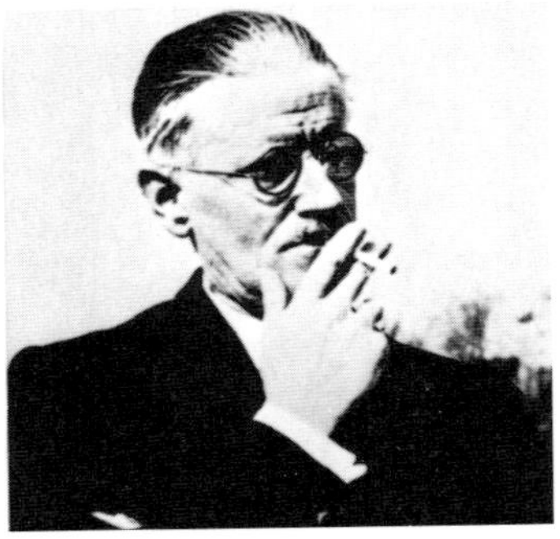

James Joyce, who died almost blind, was one of this century's greatest writers.

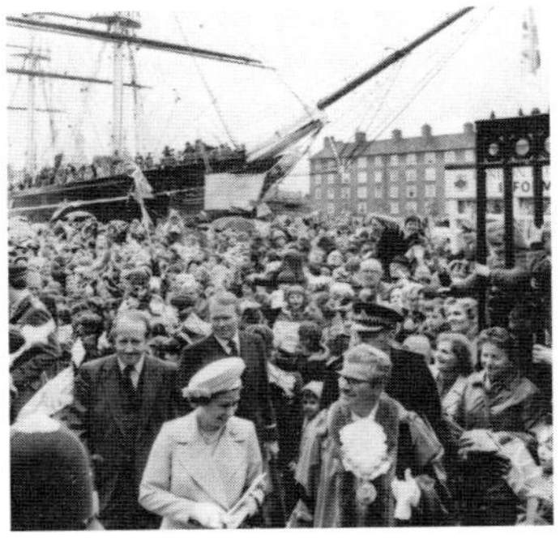

Jubilee; Queen Elizabeth at Greenwich with the Cutty Sark visible in the background.

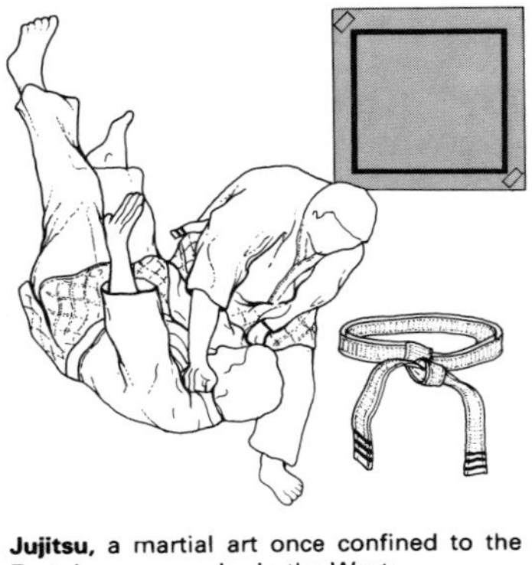

Jujitsu, a martial art once confined to the East, is now popular in the West.

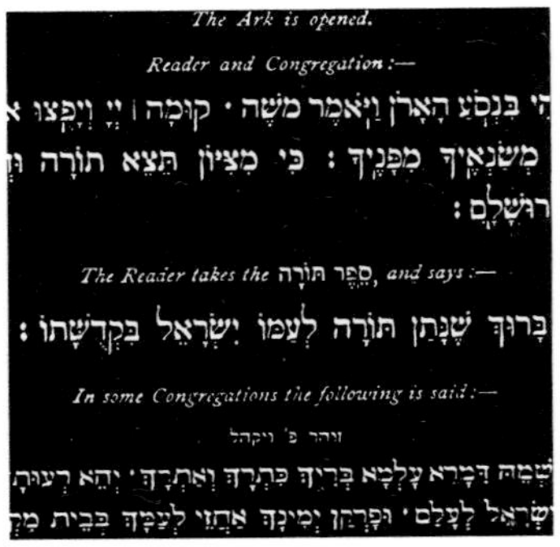

Judaism is a religion of the book in which a "word" acquires significance as an "image".

popularity. Her interpretation of John IRELAND's piano concerto in particular is said to be highly sensitive.

Joyce, James (1882–1941), Irish novelist. He was educated by Jesuits but renounced Roman Catholicism and left Ireland in 1904 to live and work in Europe. Joyce experimented with the form of the novel attempting to convey consciousness itself. The stream-of-consciousness technique became increasingly apparent in Joyce's work, which includes *Dubliners* (1914), *A Portrait of the Artist as a Young Man* (1916), *Ulysses* (1922) and *Finnegan's Wake* (1939), all set in Dublin. *Finnegan's Wake*, perhaps a dream sequence is probably best appreciated read aloud. *See also* HC1 p.290.

Joyce, William (1906–46), anti-British propagandist in WWII. Born in the USA, he grew up in Britain and founded the British National Socialist League (1937). In 1939 he went to Germany and broadcast Nazi propaganda to Britain, and came to be called "Lord Haw-haw". Captured in 1945, he was tried, found guilty of treason and hanged.

Jozsef, Attila (1905–37), Hungarian poet whose work deals with his childhood and working class life, as well as with Marxist and Freudian thought. His first volume of poems, *The Beggar of Beauty*, appeared in 1922, although his work did not gain recognition until after WWII. He committed suicide in 1937.

Juan Carlos I (1938–), King of Spain (1975–). The grandson of Alfonso XIII, the last king, he was named heir to the throne by Francisco FRANCO in 1969. He became king when Franco died in 1975.

Juan de Fuca, Strait of, inlet between S Vancouver Island, SW Canada, and the N shore of W Washington, USA. Length: approx. 160km (100 miles); width: 24–32km (15–20 miles).

Juan Manuel, Infante Don (1282–*c.* 1349), Spanish poet and fabulist. An illustrious nobleman, he is generally accepted as the most artistic prose writer of his time. His work includes *Libro de los Cantaros* (a volume of poetry) and his masterpiece *Libro de Patronio* or *Conde Lucanor*, a collection of 50 moral tales.

Juantorena, Alberto (1951–), Cuban athlete. Tall and powerfully long-striding, he won an unprecedented 400m and 800m double at the 1976 Olympics, setting a world record in the 800m. In 1977 he achieved the same double in the World Cup.

Juárez, Benito Pablo (1806–72), Mexican president. He was elected governor of his native state of Oaxaca in 1847, but was exiled by SANTA ANNA in 1853. He returned in 1855 and joined in Juan Alvarez's rebellion against Santa Anna. He was president of Mexico from 1857 until his death.

Juba, river in E Africa, formed near Dolo, S Ethiopia at the confluence of the Daua and Genale Rivers. It flows S, reaching the Indian Ocean near Kismayu, Somalia. Length: approx. 1,610km (1,000 miles).

Jubilee, celebration of an anniversary, after the Jewish tradition of releasing slaves and cancelling debts every 50th year. In British history it marks a particular number of years a monarch has occupied the throne: silver (25 years), golden (50 years) and diamond (60 years). The first such celebration was for Queen VICTORIA's golden jubilee in 1887. *See also* HC2 p.*113*.

Judaea, Roman province corresponding to S Syria and the old tribal kingdom of JUDAH. The region came under Roman control in 63 BC. The word is also used to apply to the whole region inhabited by the Jews, including the kingdom of ISRAEL. *See also* HC1 pp.58–59, *98*.

Judah, in the Old Testament, fourth son of JACOB and Leah, and forefather of one of the most important tribes of ancient Israel. Of the two kingdoms after the death of SOLOMON, the southern (comprising the tribes of Judah and Benjamin) became known as Judah as opposed to the northern, Israel. It was also prophesied that the MESSIAH would be born of the tribe of Judah.

Judaism, the religion of the Jews. Based entirely on the OLD TESTAMENT, the TALMUD (the body of Jewish Law and legend) and on commentaries on both, it is an ancient monotheistic religion which concentrates on the works of God, past and present, and which stresses man's relationship with God as part of everyday living. Its written authorities cover civil as well as religious regulations; through faith and a correct good life salvation may be attained. Modern Judaism is split into three large groups: Orthodox, Conservative and Reform Judaism. They differ mainly in the practice of rituals and the use of Hebrew. Some elements of belief are formulated differently in each group. Judaism today encompasses an awareness of a long historical development, a rich literature and a strong sense of ethnic identity. *See also* HC1 pp.58–59.

Judas Iscariot, in the New Testament, one of the original 12 apostles of Jesus, always enumerated last. Apparently finding parts of Jesus's teaching incomprehensible he finally betrayed Jesus to the chief priests (and thereby the Romans) for 30 pieces of silver by pointing him out to them with the customary greeting kiss. He subsequently committed suicide in remorse. His name now connotes treachery.

Judas Maccabaeus (*d.* 161 BC), Jewish warrior who led a revolt against Syria. When King Antiochus IV threatened to end Jewish religious practices, Judas used guerrilla tactics to defeat the Syrian armies. The festival of HANUKKAH celebrates his recapture of the Temple of Jerusalem. He was killed in battle, but his brothers continued the fight and made Judaea independent. The story is told in Maccabees I and II, books included in the Old Testament APOCRYPHA in the Greek Bible.

Judas tree, also called redbud, small tree native to S Europe and W Asia. It has round leaves and pink flowers in clusters. Height: to 12m (40ft). Family Leguminosae; species *Cercis siliquastrum.*

Judge, any officer appointed by the state to administer the law, but in England neither a MAGISTRATE nor a JUSTICE OF THE PEACE is properly called a judge. Judges are persons raised from the bar to preside over courts. Their chief duties are to conduct court cases fairly, to arrive at a conclusion (or to direct a jury to a conclusion) and to pass sentence. Judges are removable by the Crown for misconduct. Provided he acts within his judicial authority no action lies against a judge.

Judges, biblical book that originally contained the Book of RUTH. It is an account of events from JOSHUA to SAMSON and is considered a valuable, although highly prejudiced, early history of the Israelites in Palestine.

Judicial separation, separation of man and wife obtained in Britain in a High Court or county court sitting as a divorce court. It differs from separation by a magistrate's court in that a divorce court is competent to apportion property. The grounds are the same as those used to demonstrate irretrievable breakdown of the marriage in a divorce case – adultery, unreasonable conduct, desertion and living apart – but irretrievable breakdown does not have to be shown.

Judith, Old Testament book considered apocryphal by Protestants and Jews. It relates the story of the legendarily beautiful widow Judith, who rescued the city of Bethulia from siege by the Assyrians. Having managed to reach the enemy camp, she advised the Assyrian general Holofernes to expect victory and then murdered him as he slept.

Judo, form of JUJITSU and one of the most popular of the Japanese martial arts; an international competition is held every two years. It is a system of unarmed self-defence that was developed in 1882 by Jigoro Kano, a Japanese jujitsu expert. He modified many of the holds that were considered too dangerous to be used in sport, and developed the system of coloured belts, the method of ranking people who practise judo. A white belt indicates a novice and black an expert. Kano's methods, which place greater emphasis on physical fitness and mental discipline than on self-defence, depend greatly on the skill of using an opponent's weight and strength against him. Judo matches, scored using a points system, begin with a ceremonial bow, after which each contestant grabs the other by the collar and sleeve of his jacket. The techniques used include holds, trips, strangles and falls, with the end of the match signalled by one of the contestants slapping the mat twice to acknowledge defeat.

Judson, Edward Zane Carroll. *See* DIME NOVEL.

Jugendstil, German name for ART NOUVEAU.

Juggernaut, or Jagganath, form of the HINDU god KRISHNA, worshipped in the Indian town of Puri, Orissa. At an annual festival statues of the god are carried around the town on very heavy carts; devotees have been known to throw themselves under the wheels. The word has come to mean any large vehicle.

Jugoslavia. *See* YUGOSLAVIA.

Jugular, in anatomy, term which applies to any structure in the neck and especially to any of several veins. The external jugular veins receive blood from the outside of the cranium, the neck and the deep tissues of the face. Others receive blood from the back of the neck, the larynx, tissues below the lower jaw, the brain and the face.

Jujitsu, system of unarmed self-defence, used in hand-to-hand combat. It involves such techniques as striking, kneeing, holding, throwing, choking and joint locking. There are as many as 50 variations of this system (including JUDO, KARATE and AIKIDO) which have been refined over a period of 2,000 years in Japan, China and Tibet. A fusion of various techniques in 16th-century Japan became what is known in the West as jujitsu. Warriors devised it as a secondary combat system to complement the tactics of their swordsmen. By the early 19th century, when the SAMURAI were forbidden to carry weapons, jujitsu became a highly specialized form of self-defence.

Jujube, either of two species of small thorny trees and their fruit of the genus *Zizyphus*. *Z. jujuba*, native to China, has elliptical leaves and reddish brown, plum-sized fruits, which have a crisp, white, sweet flesh. *Z. mauritiana* of India has smaller fruit. Jujubes may be boiled or baked. Family Rhamnaceae.

Jukebox, coin-operated machine for playing music. The first jukebox, which played cylinder recordings, was installed at the Palais Royal, San Francisco, in 1889. The first pre-selective jukebox was invented by John Dunton, of Michigan, in 1905. The first disc-playing pre-selective jukebox was made in 1906, the first all-electric in 1927. Manufacture of jukeboxes in Britain began in 1947. *See also* MM p.*233*.

Jukskei, team game indigenous to South Africa and Rhodesia in which bottle-shaped pieces of wood (*jukskeis*) are thrown to land as close as possible to a stake in the ground. A team consists of four players. Men throw from 15.8m (52ft), women from 14.0m (46ft). It began as a campsite pastime for Voortrekkers on the great north-bound treks of the 19th century.

Julian (the Apostate) (*c.* 331–366), Roman emperor so named for his attempts to restore paganism without, however, persecuting Christians. Made emperor in 360, he headed successful expeditions against the Persians.

Juliana (1909–), Queen of The Netherlands (1948–). She succeeded to the throne upon the abdication of her mother, Queen Wilhelmina. Married in 1937 to the German prince, Bernhard, she retained the loyalty of the Dutch during WWII. Of her four daughters Beatrix, the eldest, is heiress apparent to the throne.

Julian day, or Julian date (JD), day in the dating system introduced in 1582 by Joseph SCALIGER and named after his father Julius Caesar Scaliger. Julian days, which commence at noon (1200 hrs), are calculated consecutively from 1 Jan. 4713 BC, independently of months and years. Julian dating is used in astronomy, principally in studying long-period phenomena, such as variable stars.

Julian of Norwich (1342–*c.* 1420), English religious writer and mystic, also called Juliana. An anchoress, or hermit, she lived in a cell at St Julian's church, Norwich. Her *Revelations of Divine Love*, completed before 1400, are still regarded as some of the most important expressions of religious mysticism.

Julius, name of several popes. Julius I, Saint (*r.* 337–52), played a major role in increasing Roman and papal authority and condemning Eastern ARIANISM. His attempt to unite the West in opposing Arian heresy failed. Julius II (1443–1513; *r.* 1503–13), a warrior as well as a pope, completed the work begun by Cesare BORGIA of restoring the Papal States to the church and established the Swiss Guard to protect the pope and Rome. A great patron of the arts, he began the building of St Peter's basilica in 1506. *See also* HC1 p.256. Julius III (1487–1555; *r.* 1550–55), was one of three co-presidents of the Council of TRENT and worked with Mary Tudor for the reunion of England with the Church of Rome.

Julius Caesar. *See* CAESAR, GAIUS JULIUS.

Julius Caesar, tragedy in five acts by William SHAKESPEARE, based on PLUTARCH's lives of Caesar, Mark ANTONY and BRUTUS. The play was first performed in *c.* 1599 and has been filmed several times. It deals with the conflicts surrounding the last years of Caesar's life and the events following his assassination. *See also* CAESAR, GAIUS JULIUS.

July, seventh month of the Gregorian calendar, comprising 31 days. It was named after Julius CAESAR, whose birth month was the fifth month of the Roman Republic's Calendar (previously called Quintilis). It is the month when the Sun enters the sign of Leo. Its stone is the ruby.

July Revolution (1830), insurrection in France against the government of the Bourbon King, CHARLES X. The immediate cause was the July Ordinances that dissolved the chamber of deputies, reduced the electorate and imposed rigid press censorship. Street fighting broke out in Paris and Charles was forced to flee. He abdicated and named his grandson Henri his heir, but he was rejected in favour of the Duc D'Orléans who was proclaimed King LOUIS PHILIPPE.

Jumping hare. *See* SPRINGHAAS.

Jumping mouse, any of five species of leaping mice (four from North America, one from China), with long hindlegs and tails. Chiefly nocturnal, they eat insects and seeds and hibernate underground. Length: to 26cm (10in). Family Zapodidae; genera *Zapus, Napaeozapus* and *Eozapus.*

Jumping spider, spider that leaps on its prey trailing a strand of silk by means of which it returns to its place of rest. Most jumping spiders are brightly coloured and active during the day. Length: to 18mm (0.7in). Family Salticidae.

June, sixth month of the Gregorian calendar, comprising 30 days. Its name probably derives from the chief Roman goddess, Juno, who was the patroness of women. In the Northern Hemisphere, June falls in the summer solstice, and in the Southern Hemisphere in the winter solstice. Its flower is the rose and its gemstones are pearl and moonstone.

Jung, Carl Gustav (1875–1961), Swiss psychiatrist. After working with Sigmund FREUD from 1906 to 1914, Jung broke with him to found his school of analytical psychology. His investigations into personality, especially its spiritual and unconscious aspects, led him to his concept of a collective unconscious. He believed introversion and extraversion to be basic personality types, and stressed the importance of personal transformations and self-discovery for the development of a healthy personality. Among his noted works are *Wandlungen und Symbole der Libido* (1912, tr. *Psychology of the Unconscious*; 1952 rev. ed., tr. *Symbols of Transformation*) and *Modern Man in Search of a Soul* (1933). *See also* MS pp.*148–149*, 175, 186, *188*, 189.

Jung, Johann Heinrich (1740–1817), pseudonym of Jung-Stilling, German physician who later became professor of economics at Marburg from 1787 to 1803. As well as a popular autobiography published first in separate parts and later as *Heinrich Stillings Leben* (1806) and *Heinrich Stillings Alter* (1817), he wrote poetry, novels and treatises on medical, veterinary and economic matters.

Jungfrau, mountain peak in S central Switzerland, in the Bernese Alps. It is the site of the Jungfraujoch Pass and an alpine research station. Height: 4,158m (13,642ft).

Jungle Book, The (1894), children's story by Rudyard KIPLING. Like its sequel *The Second Jungle Book* (1895), it relates the adventures of Mowgli, an Indian boy, who gets lost in the jungle and is reared by a family of wolves. Kipling imbued the jungle with its own political and social structure and each animal with a characteristic style of thought and behaviour.

Jungle fowl, ancestor of all domestic poultry, long domesticated by man and bred into many varieties. It resembles a chicken and has a high arched tail. Often known as red jungle fowl (*Gallus gallus*), it is native to South-East Asia, where noisy flocks frequent deep woods and forest edges. *See also* CHICKEN.

Jung-Stilling, Johann Heinrich. *See* JUNG, JOHANN HEINRICH.

Juniper, any of several species of evergreen shrubs and trees native to temperate regions of the Northern Hemisphere. They have needle-like or scale-like leaves and may be tall and upright or low and spreading. These shapes make them popular as ornamentals. The aromatic timber is used for making pencils, and the berry-like cones of common juniper for flavouring gin. Family Cupressaceae. *See also* NW pp.66–67.

Junk, wooden sailing boat, used for thousands of years by the Chinese and Far Eastern peoples. It is a flat-bottomed vessel with a high stern and up to five masts carrying sails made of cloth and bamboo. It can be used as either a transport vessel for cargo or a home. The huge rudder, a feature of the early junks, takes the place of the keel. *See* MM p.112.

Junkers, Hugo (1859–1935), German aircraft designer who founded a factory at Dessau in 1910. He designed the first successful all-metal aeroplane, the J-1 (1915). Later he pioneered the cantilever wing. In 1939 the Junkers factory was the largest in Germany, and in WWII the LUFTWAFFE used many Junkers aircraft, particularly the three-engined JU-52 transport aircraft. *See also* MM p.*149*.

Junkers, the landed aristocracy of Prussia and E Germany which exercised considerable political influence, particularly in the periods 1871–1918 and 1919–33. The Junkers were conservative politically and staffed the Prussian army, which brought about Germany's unification.

Juno, in Roman mythology, the principal female deity and consort of Jupiter, depicted as a statuesque, matronly figure. She was also goddess of light and of childbirth. She became the protective symbol to Imperial Rome after geese sacred to her allegedly warned of an attack on the Capitoline Hill in 390 BC.

Juno, ASTEROID discovered in 1804 by Karl Ludwig Harding. Diameter: 240km (150 miles); mean distance from the Sun: 398,700,000km (247,600,000 miles); mean sidereal period 4.36 yr. *See also* SU pp.204–205.

Junta, ruling administrative council. In contemporary usage, the term generally refers to a ruling faction or clique, often military, which has seized power by force.

Jupiter, king of the Roman gods, protector of Rome, originally god of the sky; identified with the Greek god ZEUS. The Roman games were held in honour of Jupiter, who could take on various forms: the light-bringer (Lucetius), god of lightning and thunderbolts (Fulgur), and god of rain (Jupiter Elicius). Marriages, treaties and oaths were also associated with Jupiter.

Jupiter, largest of the planets and fifth from the Sun; it has 13 known satellites. The temperature under its enveloping cloud of frozen ammonia crystals is estimated to be between −170°C (−274°F) and −110°C (−166°F). Its mass and volume are 318 and 1,300 respectively times that of the Earth; equatorial diameter: 142,800km (188,700 miles); polar diameter: 133,000km (82,800 miles). *See also* SOLAR SYSTEM; SU pp.206–209, 212–213, 278–279.

Jura, island of the Inner Hebrides, Strathclyde, W Scotland. Separated from the mainland (Knapdale and Kintyre) by the Sound of Jura, the island has an airfield and two car ferry ship services. Area: 381sq km (147sq miles). Pop. 230.

Jura mountains, part of the Alpine system in E France and NW Switzerland, extending from the River Rhine at Basel to the River Rhône SW of Geneva. The range has several hydroelectric schemes that supply power to local industries. The highest peak is Crête de la Neige in France, 1,723m (5,652ft).

Jurassic period, in the history of the earth, the central division of the MESOZOIC PERIOD; it lasted from 195–135 million years ago. In this period there were large saurischian DINOSAURS such as *Atlantosaurus* and *Allosaurus*; ornithischian dinosaurs such as *Camptosaurus* and *Stegosaurus.* PLESIOSAURS, PTEROSAURS and ARCHAEOPTERYX (the first known bird) also date from this period. Primitive mammals had begun to evolve; they were the ancestors of later marsupial and placental species. *See also* NW pp.25, 185–187; PE p.*131*.

Jurisdiction, legal power or right of a court to decide a case, limited by the authority that established the court. Some courts have original jurisdiction only, whereas others have the jurisdiction to review decisions of lower courts on appeal.

Jurisprudence, philosophy of the law. It dates at least from the ancient Greeks; both PLATO and ARISTOTLE attempted to answer the question "What is law?". Jurisprudence seeks to discover the source and justification of the law and its scope and function in a particular society. It may be a commentary on a local legal system, such as BLACKSTONE's *Commentaries on the Laws of England* (1765–69), or it may be generally philosophical, as in H.L.A. Hart's *The Concept of Law* (1961). *See also* MS pp.282–286.

Jury, body of laymen summoned to pass judgment under oath. Its origin may be the sworn inquests of CAROLINGIAN kings, at which people answered questions to help to determine royal rights and which were introduced into Britain by the Normans. Or it may come from the Scandinavian "jury of twelve familiars" introduced into Britain by the Danish kings and becoming the Anglo-Saxon trial by compurgation, at which 12 people could acquit the accused by testifying to his honour. The 12-member jury in criminal trials dates from the mid-12th century, but it was only in the 17th century that jurymen ceased to give evidence and simply passed judgment on the basis of evidence heard in court.

Justice, Lord Chief, presiding judge of the QUEEN'S BENCH division in England. He is the second-ranking officer in the hierarchy of English law and presides over the High Court in the absence of the lord CHANCELLOR. He is also an ex-officio judge of the Court of CRIMINAL APPEAL. He has replaced the former Chief Justice, who presided over the former Queen's Bench and the Court of COMMON PLEAS.

Justice of the Peace, subordinate MAGISTRATE in English law, appointed by the Crown on the advice of the lord CHANCELLOR to keep the peace within a local jurisdiction. The office dates from the reign of EDWARD I. It is unpaid and JPS are rarely qualified lawyers. They issue warrants for arrest, commit cases for trial and sit in groups of two or more in the petty sessional courts.

Justiciar, highest royal servant in England in the 12th and 13th centuries. He was not part of the HOUSEHOLD but above it, since he was expected to have competence over all matters, ready to act as regent in the king's absence or incapacity. The most famous, and last of great influence, was Hubert de BURGH, who ruled England during HENRY III's minority.

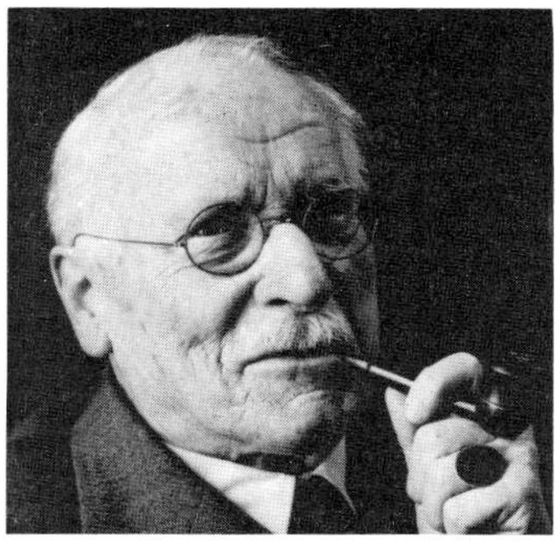

Carl Gustav Jung; the Jung Institute, opened in 1948, trains analytical psychologists.

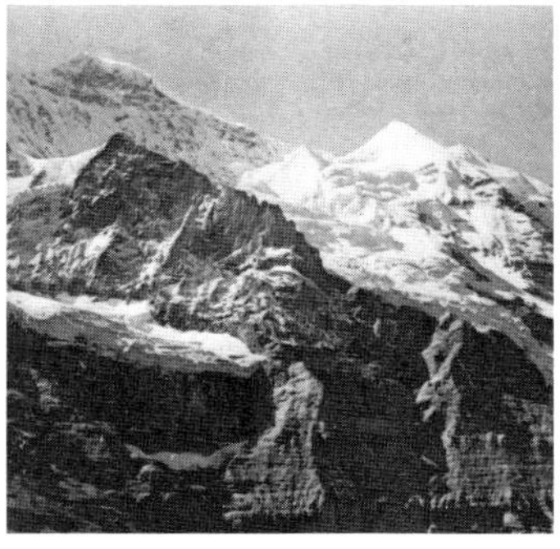

Jungfrau, first climbed in 1811, whose peak can now be reached by a mountain railway.

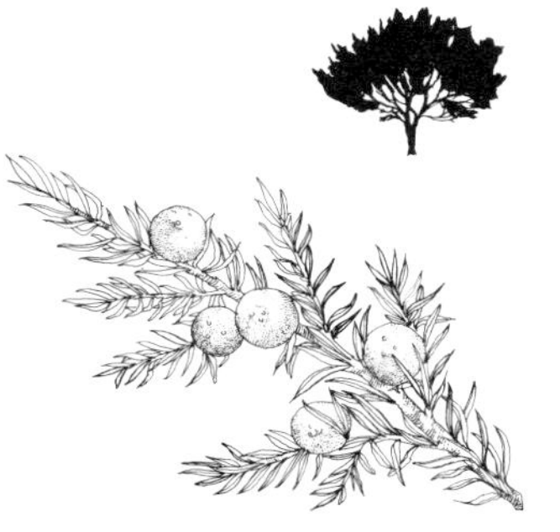

Juniper; of the 60 species growing in many parts of the world, 13 are native to the *USA*.

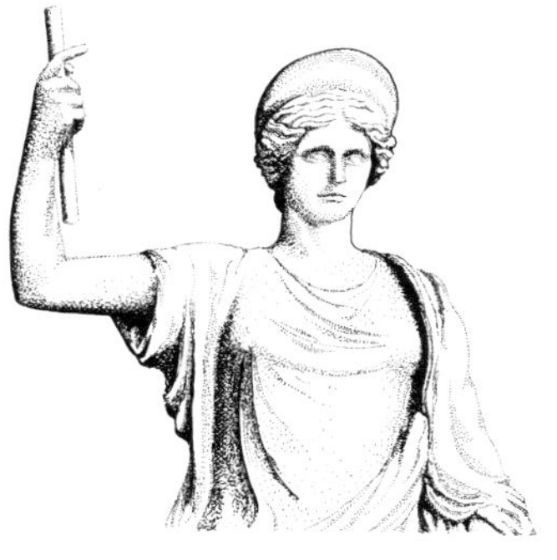

Juno, goddess of marriage and by her Latin name *Juno Lucina,* goddess of childbirth.

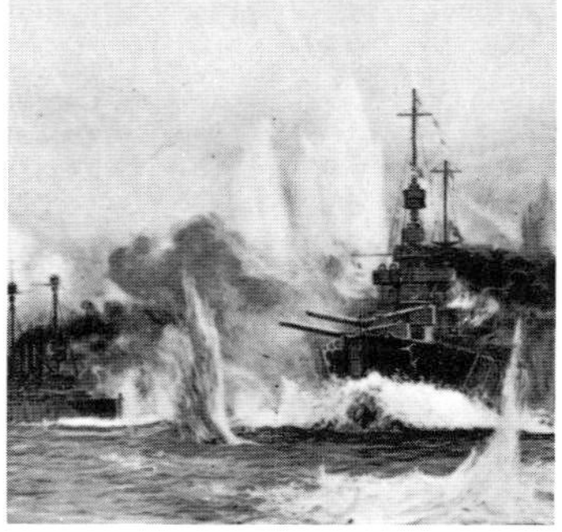

Battle of Jutland; the only naval battle between British and German fleets in WWI.

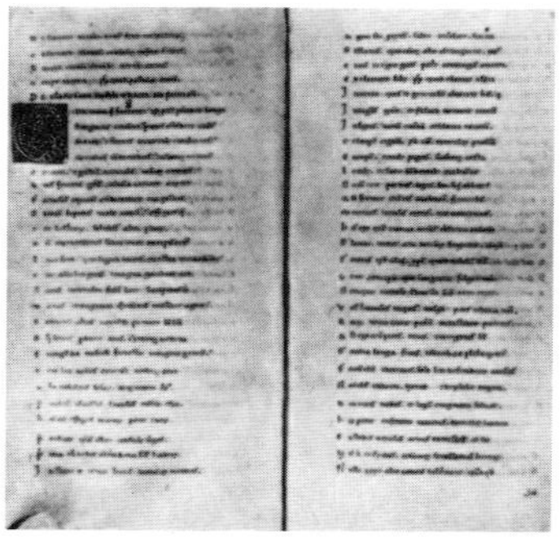

Juvenal's satires against Roman vice influenced many 18th-century English writers.

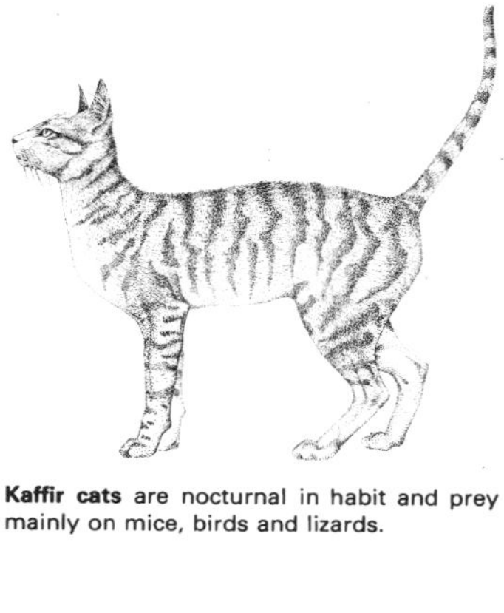

Kaffir cats are nocturnal in habit and prey mainly on mice, birds and lizards.

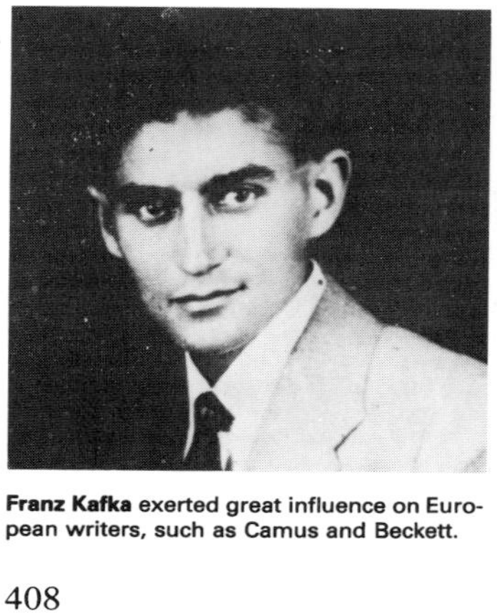

Franz Kafka exerted great influence on European writers, such as Camus and Beckett.

Justinian, name of two Byzantine Emperors. Justinian I, "the Great" (*c.*482–565; *r.*527–565), the son of an Illyrian peasant, became one of the most cultured men of his time and one of the greatest rulers of the Byzantine Empire. During his reign large parts of the old Roman Empire in North Africa, Italy and Spain were reconquered for Byzantium, and his vast building programmes included the erection of the Church of St Sophia in Constantinople. His most lasting legislative achievement was his revision of Roman law. Justinian II (*c.*669–711; *r.*685-95 and 705–11) was surnamed Rhinotmetus ("with a cut-off nose"). A tyrannical ruler, he was deposed in 695, mutilated (hence the surname) and exiled. Ten years later, with the help of the Bulgarians, he regained the throne but was killed in 711. *See also* HC1 pp.137, 142, *142*, *340*, 341; MS p.283.

Justinian Code, monument of Byzantine law and the greatest contribution of the Emperor JUSTINIAN I to posterity. The code was prepared in the 6th century by a commission headed by the legal scholar Tribonian. To the revision of Roman law, Justinian added other legislative works, now known collectively as the *Corpus Juris Civilis* (*Body of Civil Law*). *See also* HC1 p.142; MS p.283, *283*.

Justin Martyr, Saint (*c.*100–*c.*165), Christian scholar. Converted to Christianity, he was also a PLATONIST. A strong defender of Christian doctrine in his *Major Apology* and *Second Apology*, he was put to death in Rome for his faith.

Just So Stories (1902), collection of animal stories for children by Rudyard KIPLING. Included among the stories are *How the Elephant got His Trunk*, *The Camel's Hump* and *The Cat That Walked by Himself*. Kipling first wrote the stories for Mary Mapes Dodge's *St. Nicholas* magazine.

Justus of Ghent (*c.*1435–80), Flemish painter who also worked in Italy. He was influenced by the early Italian Renaissance style, which can be seen in the simplicity of form and idealization of subject in his paintings. His works include the *Adoration of the Magi* (*c.*1466) and a large *Crucifixion* triptych (*c.*1465).

Jute, natural plant fibre obtained from *Corchorus capsularis* and *C. olitorius*, both native to India. Grown as a crop in India and Bangladesh, the plants mature in three months from seed and grow up to 4.6m (15ft) high. The fibre is obtained from the bark by soaking (retting) and beating. Jute is used to make sacking, twine and rope. *See also* PE p.216, *216*.

Jutes, one of the three Germanic-speaking tribes that invaded Britain in the 5th century. They settled around Kent, the Isle of Wight and parts of Hampshire. BEDE called them *Iutae*, and it was believed they came from western Jutland, but the social system of Kent was Frankish in character, differing from that of the other two tribes, the SAXONS and ANGLES. Some modern scholars believe the Jutes may have come from the Rhine delta region rather than Jutland. *See also* HC1 pp.136, 138.

Jutland, Battle of (1916), naval battle between the British Grand Fleet, under Admiral JELLICOE, and the German High Seas Fleet, under Admiral SCHEER. Although inconclusive in itself it was ultimately decisive in that the German surface fleet remained in harbour for the rest of WWI. *See also* HC2 p.189.

Jutland, peninsula in N Europe, comprising Denmark and the N state of Schleswig-Holstein, West Germany. It is bounded by the Skagerrak (N), North Sea (W), Kattegat (E) and the River Eider (S). The land along the E coast is fertile, supporting dairy and livestock farming and the W coast is sand and marshland. There is some mining for iron, marble and limestone. Area: 29,390sq km (11,436sq miles). Pop. (1973 est.) 2,235,848.

Juvarra, Filippo (1678–1736), Italian architect, one of the finest exponents of the BAROQUE style. His highest achievements are the two churches, Superga (1717–31) and the Church of the Carmine (1732), both in Turin, and the four great palaces built at Turin between 1714 and 1726 for King Victor Amadeus II of Savoy.

Juvenal, Decimus Junius (*c.*55–*c.*140), Roman poet. His harsh, bitter and direct satires denounced the affectations and immorality of the Empire. *See also* HC1 pp.95, 113.

Jyväskylä, port city in S central Finland, at the N end of Lake Päijänne. Chartered in 1837, it is the site of the first Finnish-language secondary school. Its industries include paper and wood products. Pop. (1976) 61,596.

K

K, eleventh letter of the alphabet, derived from the Semitic letter *kaph*, possibly from an earlier Egyptian hieroglyph for a hand. In Greek it became *kappa*, and in that form passed to the Romans. In English it generally has the same sound as the hard form of *c*, as in *kitten*, although in front of an *n*, as in *knot* or *knitting*, it is silent. *See also* MS pp.244–245.

K2 (Mount Godwin-Austen), peak in the Karakoram range, N Kashmir: second-highest peak in the world. First scaled in 1954 by the Italian Ardito Desio, it was named after the British surveyor and explorer Henry Godwin-Austen. Height: 8,616m (28,267ft).

Ka, or koi, in Egyptian mythology, a guardian spirit. Born with, and residing in, a person's body, it lives on after the body's death. It is often thought of, and translated, as a double of the person. Food for the Ka was customarily buried with the body. In Indian mythology, Ka is the absolute or BRAHMA.

Kaaba, or Ka'ba, central shrine of ISLAM, in the Great Mosque in MECCA. The object of pilgrimage, it is a cube of stone and marble, in one corner of which rests the Black Stone, which by tradition was given to Adam on his fall. Each pilgrim circles the shrine seven times, touching the Black Stone for forgiveness.

Kabaka, official title of the leader of the Buganda, a tribe in Uganda. The kabakas were among the few African rulers to use European colonization to further their own interests. The last kabaka, Mutesa II (*r.*1939–66), was deposed by Milton Obote, and the office was abolished.

Kabalevsky, Dimitri Borisovich (1904–), Russian post-Romantic composer of songs, piano pieces, concertos and operas including *Colas Breugnon* (1938) and a popular ballet *The Golden Spikes* (1940).

Kabbala, Jewish systematical mysticism, based on an interpretation of the scriptures that perceived mysteries and spiritual revelations in every word, letter or accent, especially in names for God. It achieved some popularity in the 13th century AD as a study of two main sources: the *Sefer Yetzira* (3rd century AD) and the *Sefer ha-Zohar* (allegedly based on a 2nd-century text). By the 15th century the Kabbala had a messianic interpretation, and has since had continuing influence among Hasidic Jews. *See also* MS p.218.

Kabuki Theatre, stylish mixture of dance and music, mime and naturalism; a major form of moralizing entertainment in Japan since the mid-17th century. In contrast to the NŌ theatre, which originated with the nobility, Kabuki was the theatre of the common people. It emphasizes visual appeal and acting skills.

Kābul, city and capital of Afghanistan, on the River Kābul. It was taken by GENGHIS KHAN in the 13th century and became part of the MOGUL EMPIRE 1526–1738. It was occupied by the British in 1842 and 1879 and modernized by the Emir ABD ER-RAHMAN KHAN, in the late 19th century, after the country had become independent. Today its products include textiles, leather goods, furniture and glass. Pop. (1973 est.) 318,094.

Kabyle, Algerian ethnic group of Berber origin living in farming villages in N Algeria. Each village is administered by an assembly of adult males and divided into rival clans. They are MUSLIMS who follow a CASTE system.

Kádár, János (1912–), Hungarian Politician, premier 1956–58 and 1961–65. Active in the Communist Party since his youth, he fought in the resistance movement during WWII. From 1948–50, he served as Minister of the Interior and he was deputy Premier in Imré NAGY's government during the 1956 Hungarian revolution. He replaced Nagy as Premier on 4 Nov 1956, and pursued a policy of accommodation with the Soviets. *See also* HC2 p.243, *243*.

Kaddish, ancient Jewish prayer still in use particularly at services of mourning. It is a formal statement of praise and faith in the coming of God's Kingdom.

Kaden-Bandrowski, Juliusz (1885–1944), Polish short story writer and novelist whose works, including *Black Wings* (1928–29), are realistic portrayals of contemporary Poland.

Kadesh, city in ancient Palestine (W Syria), 24km (15 miles) SW of the modern city of Homs on the River Orontes. It was the scene of the battle between RAMESES II and the HITTITES (*c.*1300 BC), which resulted in a victory for Rameses.

Kaffir, term formerly applied to any member of the Bantu races of South Africa (especially the XHOSA); now considered derogatory. The word derives from the Arabic *kafir* (unbeliever), and was also used to describe a native of Kafiristan (Afghanistan). It may also be spelt Kafir, Kaffer or Caffre. A long series of South African wars (1779–1878) between Bantus and Boers are often called the KAFFIR WARS.

Kaffir cat, also called African wild CAT, small striped cat found in Africa, Asia and S Europe. It is thought to be an ancestor of the domestic cat. Length: to 110cm (43in) overall. Family Felidae; species *Felis ocreata*.

Kaffir Wars, name given by the Cape colonists in southern Africa to the series of wars with the local people, mostly of the Xhosa tribe. African writers now call them the Wars of Dispossession. They began in 1779 and lasted until 1879, and when they ended the Xhosa had lost most of their lands and were confined to the Transkei. In 1853 part of their lands (British Kaffraria) was incorporated into the Cape Colony by the British for white settlement.

Kafirs, or Nuristanis, people of the Hindu Kush mountains in NE Afghanistan, who speak Dardic dialects. The women cultivate cereals; the men are hunters and herdsmen. Islam was introduced in 1895–96 against fierce opposition.

Kafka, Franz (1883–1924), Austrian novelist. The son of a successful Jewish businessman, he suffered under his father's dominance. Little known in his lifetime, he became famous after WWII with the English translation of his novels, such as *Metamorphosis* (1912), *The Trial* (1925), *The Castle* (1926), and *America* (1927). Short stories, with autobiographical undertones, foreshadowed the novels.

Kafre. *See* KHAFRE.

Kagan. *See* BUHARA.

Kagu, extremely rare, almost flightless, heron-sized New Caledonian bird. It has a large head with back-pointing crest, large black-and-white barred wings and orange-red legs. It feeds on insects and worms, and emits harsh calls, chiefly at night. Length: 56cm (22in). Species: *Rhynochetos jubatus*.

Kagu-tsuchi, also called Ho-musubi, the god of fire in Japanese mythology. He was the destructive nature of fire but could be invoked to offer his protection.

Kahn, Gustave (1859–1936), French poet. An inaugurator of VERS LIBRE and a Symbolist, he wrote a preface explaining these terms in *Premiers Poèmes* (1897), a collection comprising his earlier volumes *Palais Nomades* (1887), *Chansons d'amant* (1891) and *Le Livre d'images* (1897).

Kahn, Louis Isadore (1901–74), US architect. His design for the Yale University Art Gallery (1953) included a space-frame ceiling and was considered a depar-

HC1 = History and Culture Vol. 1 HC2 = History and Culture Vol. 2 MS = Man and Society MM = Man and Machines

ture from the International Style. One of his most important works is the Richards Medical Research Centre at the University of Pennsylvania, Philadelphia (1957–61).

Kaieteur Falls, waterfalls on the River Potaro in the Guyana Highlands, central Guyana. They were discovered in 1870 by Barrington Brown of the US Geological Survey. Height: 226m (741ft). The surrounding area became Kaieteur National Park in 1930.

Kaikouras, two parallel mountain ranges in the NE of New Zealand's South Island. The highest peak is Mt Tapuaenuku (2,885m; 9,465ft) in the NW part.

Kaimanawas, mountain range in the centre of New Zealand's North Island, rising to about 1,980m (6,500ft). The mountains are a popular deer-hunting area.

Kaingang. *See* CAINGANG.

Kaiser, German title equal to emperor. It derives from the Roman title Caesar and was first connected with Germany when OTTO I became Emperor of the HOLY ROMAN EMPIRE in 962. The last Kaiser was WILHELM II (*r.* 1888–1918), whose father had adopted the title after the Franco-Prussian war of 1871.

Kaiser, Georg (1878–1945), German Expressionist dramatist. His reputation was achieved with *From Morn to Midnight* (1916). He abandoned realism and attacked the ethical futility of a civilization which he felt was bent on self-destruction. *The Corral* (1917) and *Gas, Parts I & II* (1918, 1920) reiterated this theme. After his work was proscribed by the Nazis in 1933, Kaiser was compelled to emigrate to Switzerland.

Kaiserslautern, city in W West Germany, on the River Lauter. The city was devastated during WWII. It has part of the campus of the University of Trier and Kaiserslautern (1970) and the remains of a 9th-century castle built by CHARLEMAGNE. Industries: ironworks, textiles, furniture, machinery, motor vehicles. Pop. (1974) 102,450.

Kajar dynasty. *See* QAJAR DYNASTY.

Kakapo, largest and most brightly coloured (moss-green and yellow-green with dark barring) of New Zealand parrots. It is now found only in Fiordland and Stewart Is.

Kala-azar, insect-borne disease carrying a high mortality and caused by infection with the parasite *Leishmania donovani*, apparently transmitted by the sandfly. The spleen is particularly affected and becomes enlarged. Additional symptoms include fever, anaemia and wasting. The disease occurs primarily along the Mediterranean coast, in Asia, and in South and Central America and Mexico.

Kalahari, desert region in Namibia, Botswana and South Africa, between the Orange and Zambezi rivers. Thorn scrub and forest grow in some parts of the desert, and it is possible to graze animals during the rainy season. The Kalahari is inhabited by the BUSHMEN, as well as by Africans and Europeans primarily engaged in rearing cattle. Area: 910,000sq km (351,000sq miles).

Kalanchoe, genus of succulent, perennial plants native to Old World tropics. They have oval, waxy leaves and scarlet flower clusters. Often grown as house plants, varieties include *K. pinnata*, with feathery leaves. Height: 17.8cm (7in). Family Crassulaceae.

Kale, hardy crop plant related to the CABBAGE. It is short-stemmed and has large, bluish-green, curly-edged leaves that are eaten as a vegetable. Grown mainly for autumn or winter harvest, it may reach a height of 61cm (24in). Family Brassicaceae; species *Brassica oleracea*. *See also* PE p.188, *188*.

Kalevala, Finnish epic poem, part of Finnish oral tradition. The verses remained in uncollected form until the 19th century, when Elias LÖNNROT edited them and wrote connecting passages. The first collection was published in 1835 and a second in 1849.

Kalgoorlie-Boulder, municipality in S central Western Australia state, Australia, created in 1947 by the merging of two towns. It is the largest settlement of the Western Goldfields which, after a decline in the 1920s, now produces 75 per cent of Australia's gold. The city also serves the nearby Kambalda nickel ore field. Pop. (1971 est.) 20,784.

Kali, supreme mother goddess of India, consort of SHIVA, also known in various aspects as Chandi, DURGA, PARVATI, Sakti, Uma and Mata. As Kali she is her destructive manifestation, depicted as black and many-armed, garlanded with skulls and bearing an iron hook and noose, symbols of death, devouring the life she has produced.

Kalidasa (388–455), Indian poet and dramatist. Considered to be the greatest writer in classical SANSKRIT literature, his work achieved a profoundity and elegance that has never been surpassed. His best-known play is *Sakuntala Recognised*, a drama in verse that tells of romantic love and adversity. *See also* HC1 p.118.

Kalimantan, name of four political divisions of the island of Borneo; the southernmost and largest section of the island, administered by Indonesia. It consists of four provinces: West, South, East and Central Kalimantan. Formerly part of the Netherlands East Indies, it became part of Indonesia in 1950. Economic development is hindered by thick tropical forest. Products: rice, millet, copra, pepper, oil, coal, bauxite, iron, industrial diamonds, timber. Area: 1,100,559sq km (424,926sq miles). Pop. (1970 est.) 5,172,000. *See also* MW p.99.

Kalinin, Mikhail Ivanovich (1875–1946), Soviet political figure, first formal head of state of the Soviet Union (1919–46). He was elected Chairman of the Communist Party Central Committee in 1919 and joined the POLITBURO in 1925.

Kaliningrad (Königsberg), seaport in the Russian Republic (Rossijskaja SFSR), USSR, on the Pregol'a River; capital of Kaliningrad oblast. Founded in 1255 as Königsberg, the city was a member of the HANSEATIC LEAGUE. It became the residence of the dukes of Prussia in 1525 and later the coronation city of the kings of Prussia. The Russians took the city in 1945 after a long siege and its name was changed to Kaliningrad in 1946. Immanuel KANT, who was born in the city, taught in the university, which was founded in 1544. Industries: shipbuilding, food processing, motor vehicle parts. Pop. (1975) 338,000.

Kallio, Kyösti (1873–1940), President of Finland (1937–40). Leader of the Agrarian Party and Member of Parliament (1907–37), he served as Prime Minister four times between 1922 and 1937. He unsuccessfully resisted Russian pressure at the beginning of WWII, despite initial progress.

Kalmar Union (1397–1523), union of Denmark, Norway and Sweden. It began with the crowning of Eric of Pomerania, grand-nephew of Queen Margaret of Norway and Denmark, which was held in Kalmar, Sweden. Queen Margaret had appointed Eric heir after the death of her son Olaf IV. Under the terms of the union, succession was through election from amongst the sons of the late monarch. It established common defences but little else. It lasted until the coronation of Gustavus I as Swedish king in 1523, although Denmark and Norway remained united until 1814.

Kalmuck (Kalmykskaja ASSR), autonomous republic within the Russian Republic (Rossijskaja SFSR) in SE European USSR, on the Caspian Sea. The capital is Elista. The area comprises semi-desert and steppes, and fishing and the rearing of animals are the principal economic activities. During WWII the Kalmucks allegedly collaborated with the Germans in the Battle of Stalingrad. In 1944 the republic was dissolved and the Kalmucks were deported en masse to Soviet Central Asia. They returned in 1957; the republic was re-established in 1958. Area: approx. 75,900sq km (29,300sq miles). Pop. (1970) 268,000.

Kaltenbrunner, Ernst (1901–46), Austrian Nazi leader. He joined HIMMLER's staff after Germany annexed Austria (1938) and was appointed head of the Security Police in 1943. He was convicted at the Nuremberg Trials and hanged for the murder of Allied soldiers and thousands of Jews.

Kalvos, Andreas Ioannides (1792–1869), Greek poet. He benefited from earlier non-Greek Romantic influences, but employed popular Greek metres and forms. His mainly melancholy poetry includes *The Lyre* (1824) and *Odes* (1826).

Kamakura, city on SE Honshū, Japan, on the Sagami Sea at the mouth of Tokyō Bay. An important ancient Japanese city, it was the seat of the Yoritomo shōgunate (1192–1333) and the Ashikaga shōgunate (1333–1573). It has a noted bronze statue of Buddha, a museum of modern art and a museum of national treasures. Today it is mainly a residential and resort area and has a meat processing industry. Pop. 139,249.

Kama Sutra, Hindu text on eroticism, written before AD 500 by Vatsyayana. In it he discusses Kama (sexual pleasure) which, together with its counterparts dharma (religious law) and artha (material prosperity) is considered essential for true fulfilment.

Kamchatka (Kamčatka) Peninsula, peninsula in the far E USSR, separating the Sea of Okhotsk (W) from the Bering Sea and the Pacific Ocean (E). The region has several active volcanoes; mineral resources include oil, coal, gold and peat. Area: 270,034sq km (104,260sq miles).

Kame, conical and low steep-sided knoll or hummock, comprised chiefly of gravel and sand that was deposited by a subglacial stream near the terminal margin of a melting glacier. Long sinuous ridges deposited similarly are called ESKERS.

Kamehameha, name of five kings of Hawaii. Kamehameha I (*c.* 1758–1819) had united all the Hawaiian Islands under the Kamehameha dynasty by 1810. He instituted harsh laws and punishment, but also abolished human sacrifice and offered peasants protection from their landlords. Kamehameha II, or Liholiho (1797–1824) was responsible for admitting the first US missionaries. Kamehameha III, or Kauikeaouli (1813–54), was the brother of Kamehameha II and came to the throne so young that Kaahumanu, Kamehameha I's favourite queen, acted as regent until 1832. Kamehameha III was a liberal ruler who adopted constitutions in 1840 and 1852 and secured foreign recognition of his country's independence. Kamehameha IV, or Alexander Liholiho (1834–63), made social and economic reforms and opposed annexation to the USA. His brother, Kamehameha V (1830–72), the last in the dynasty, was less democratic.

Kamenev, Leo Borisovich (1883–1936). Soviet political figure. Elected to the Communist Party POLITBURO in 1917, he joined the group of his former rival TROTSKY in opposing STALIN in 1926. After 1927 he was thrice expelled from the Party and was eventually tried and executed for treason, a victim of the Stalinist purges. *See also* HC2 pp.*197–198*, 199.

Kamerlingh-Onnes, Heike (1853–1926), Dutch physicist and the first to liquefy HELIUM (He). In the late 1880s he began studying low-temperature gases and in 1908, using a liquid HYDROGEN cooling system, he liquefied helium and found its temperature to be four degrees above absolute zero. He discovered that at this temperature some metals, eg mercury and lead, lose all electrical resistance and become superconductors. He was awarded the Nobel Prize in physics in 1913. *See also* SU p.95.

Kāmet, mountain peak in the Himalayas, in Uttar Pradesh state, N India, on the Indian-Chinese border. When it was first climbed in 1931, by F.S. Smythe and Eric Shipton, it was the highest mountain ever climbed. Height: 7,761m (25,462ft).

Kami, in ancient Japanese religion, the name given to all supernatural beings. Kami were usually beneficent fertility deities. They inhabited SHINTO shrines and sometimes symbolic objects, such as a sword or mirror. When BUDDHISM was introduced to Japan, ancestors and dead heroes were revered as Kami.

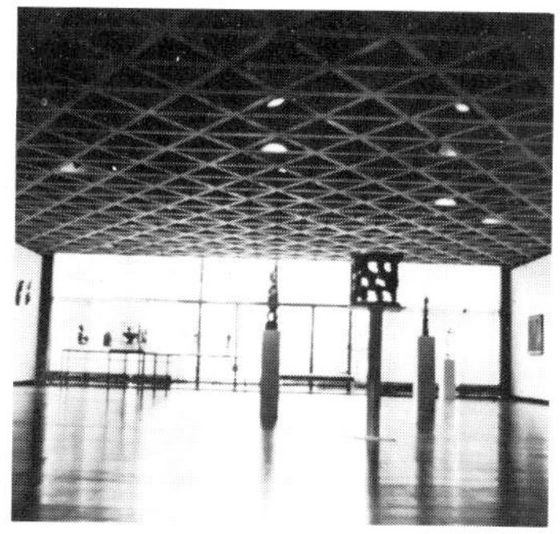

Louis Kahn: interior of the Yale Art Gallery in New Haven Connecticut, built in 1953.

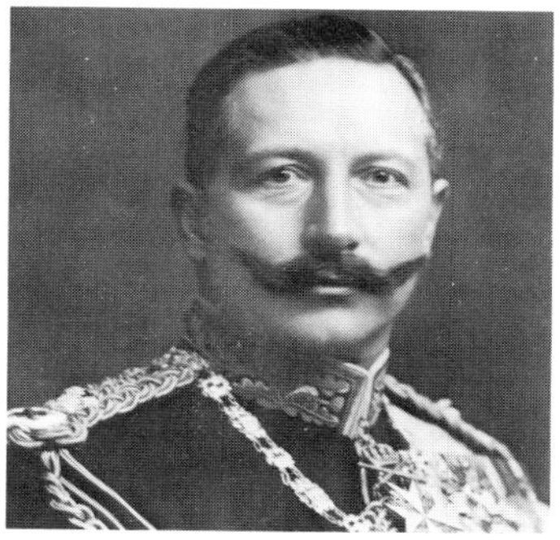

Kaiser William II, the last of the Kaisers who ruled from 1888 to the end of WWI.

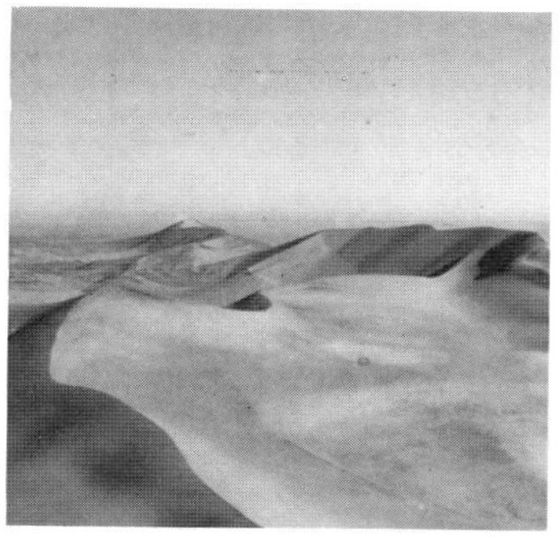

Kalahari; many Boers died in this arid region during the treks of the 19th century.

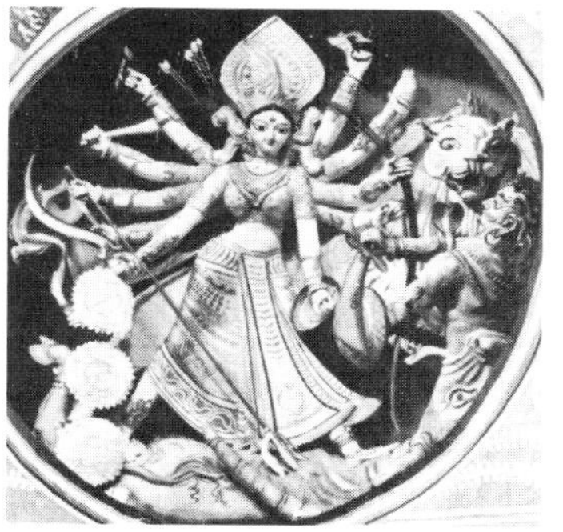

Kali, the sinister goddess in her manifestation as Durga, killing the demon Mahishasura.

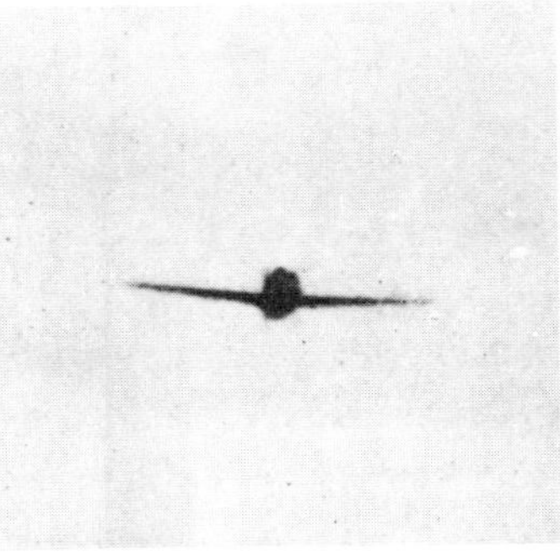

Kamikaze suicide plane as it dived onto the British aircraft carrier *Illustrious* in 1945.

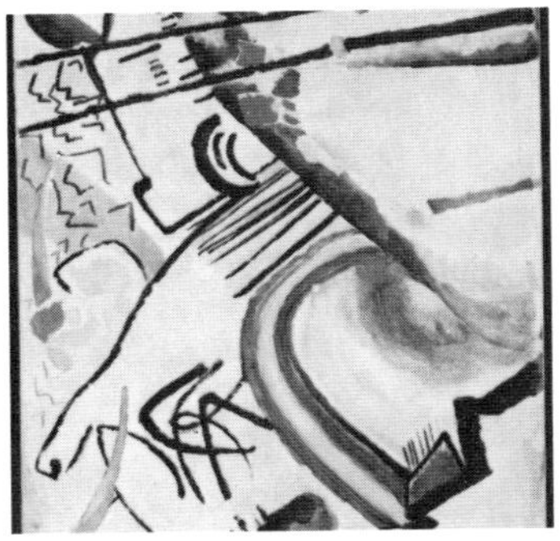

Wassily Kandinsky; a section of his painting *Cossacks* in the Tate Gallery, London.

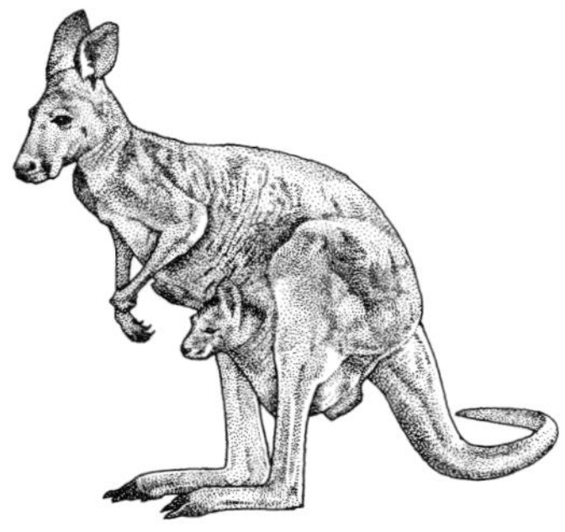

Kangeroos can run, or rather hop, at speeds of up to 64km/h (40mph).

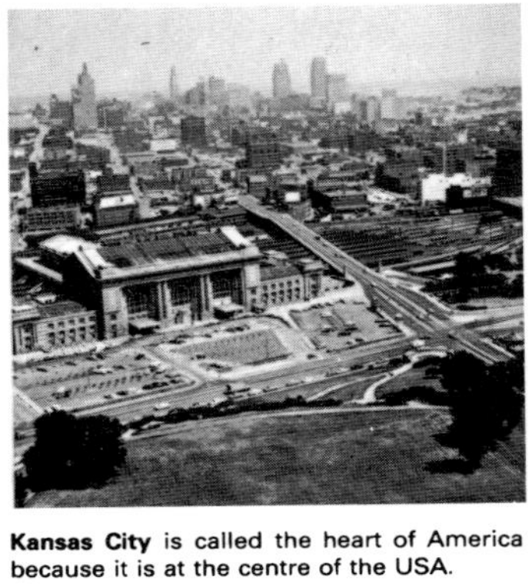

Kansas City is called the heart of America because it is at the centre of the USA.

Kamikaze, name given to flight crews or their explosive-laden aircraft used by the Japanese during WWII. Their method of attack was to dive headlong into ships of the enemy fleet, a tactic first used in late 1944 and in 1945. Serious losses were inflicted on the US Navy at Okinawa. The name means "Divine Wind", and was a reference to the typhoon that destroyed the Mongol invasion fleet in 1281, thus saving Japan from imminent defeat.

Kampala, capital and largest city in Uganda, 34km (21 miles) NNE of Entebbe, the capital of the former British protectorate. Kampala became capital when Uganda attained independence in 1962. A modern city, it is the seat of Makerere University (1963). Linked by rail to Mombasa on the Indian Ocean, it has food processing industries and is the trading centre for the agricultural goods and livestock produced in Uganda. Pop. (1975 est.) 542,000. *See also* MW p.168.

Kamperduin. *See* CAMPERDOWN, BATTLE OF.

Kampf, Mein. *See* MEIN KAMPF.

Kanagawa, Treaty of (1854), treaty of peace, friendship and commerce between the USA and Japan; it was the first treaty between Japan and a Western country. It resulted from an expedition authorized by President Millard Fillmore which sent Commo. Matthew C. PERRY to Japan. Under threat of force, Japan agreed to open two ports for trade and to have a US consul at Shimoda.

Kananga, city in S central Zaire, on the Lulua River; capital of Kasai-Occidental province. Formerly known as Luluabourg (until 1966), the city was founded in 1884 by the German explorer Hermann von WISSMANN. It became a military post and, in 1895, was the scene of a revolt by African troops against the Belgians. The city grew in the early 20th century with the construction of the railways. Kananga is a distribution centre for a region producing cotton, coffee and diamonds. Pop. (1974 est.) 596,954.

Kanarese, or Kannada, language spoken in SW India, principally in the state of Karnataka (formerly Mysore), by about 18 million people. A member of the DRAVIDIAN family, it is one of the constitutional languages of India.

Kanaris, Constantine (1790–1877), Greek naval hero and statesman. His naval exploits against the Turks (1822–25) won him fame in the Greek war of independence. He served as prime minister (1864–65 and 1877), was involved in the overthrow of King Otto in 1862 and served as regent (1862–63).

Kanawa, Kiri Te. *See* TE KANAWA, KIRI.

Kānchenjunga (Kinchinjunga or Kanchanjanga), mountain in the E Himalayas on the border of Nepal and Sikkim. The third-highest mountain in the world, it is the main axis of the Himalayan range. It was climbed in 1955 by a British expedition led by Charles Evans. The highest of its five peaks reaches 8,591m (28,185ft).

Kanchipuram, city in S India, 64km (40 miles) WSW of Madras. One of the seven sacred HINDU cities of India, it has an important BUDDHIST school dating from the 8th century, and numerous temples and shrines built between the 3rd and 16th centuries. It has textile industries and is especially noted for its saris. Pop. (1971) 110,657.

Kandahār, or Qandahār, city and provincial capital in S Afghanistan, approx. 483km (300 miles), SW of Kabul. Situated on important Asian trade routes, it was conquered many times before becoming the capital of the independent Afghani kingdom (1747–73). It is now a commercial centre for the surrounding region, which produces fruit, wool, cotton and tobacco. Pop. 134,000.

Kandinsky, Wassily (1866–1944), Russian painter and theorist whose discoveries and experiments with abstract painting made revolutionary contributions to art. In 1910 he painted his first purely abstract work, generally referred to as *First Abstract Watercolour*. From 1911, he was an active member of the BLAUE REITER, and his writings show the influence of Oriental art philosophy. After WWI his *White Line* (1920) and *In the Black Circle* (1921) demonstrate the beginnings of a refinement of geometrical form which developed during his years at the BAUHAUS (1922–33).

Kandy, city in Sri Lanka, on the Kandy Plateau. The former capital of the ancient kings of Ceylon, it was occupied by the Portuguese in the 16th century and the Dutch in the 18th century before being captured by the British in 1815. It is the site of the Dalada Maligawa, a noted Buddhist temple, which contains what is traditionally believed to be one of Buddha's teeth, brought to Ceylon in the 4th century. The city also has a palace, art museum, oriental library and the University of Sri Lanka (1942): it is a market centre for a region producing tea, rice, rubber and cacao. The chief industry is tourism. Pop. 78,000.

Kane, Elisha Kent (1820–57), US Arctic explorer. He led an unsuccessful expedition to Greenland in 1850 in search of the missing explorer Sir John FRANKLIN, and made a second journey in 1853 in an attempt to discover whether the North Pole was surrounded by sea. He conducted much research while in Greenland but was forced to abandon his ship in 1855. He wrote of his findings in *Arctic Explorations* (1856).

Kane, Paul (1810–71), Canadian painter. He crossed Canada with the HUDSON'S BAY COMPANY (1846–48) and painted many scenes of Indian life.

Kanem, central African empire (9th–19th centuries AD). Formed by the Saharan Sef dynasty in the area of Lake Chad, it became prosperous through trade. Its rulers were Muslim from the 11th century.

Kangaroo, hopping, furry herbivore found only in Australia, New Guinea and adjacent islands. It is the largest living representative of the MARSUPIALS, a group of mammals in which the young feed and develop in a pouch on the female abdomen. The three main types are the grey kangaroo, the red kangaroo and the wallaroo, or euro. The thick, coarse fur is red, brown, grey or black. The front legs are small, the hind legs long and used in leaping. Height: to 1.8m (6ft) at the shoulder; weight: to 70kg (154lb). Family Macropodidae, genus *Macropus*. *See also* NW pp.159, *204–205*, 220.

Kangaroo rat, tiny, desert-dwelling RODENT of W North America that carries seeds in its cheek pouches. It has long hind legs and a long tail, and hops over the ground. It dries and stores seeds and seldom drinks. Length: to 41cm (16in), including the tail. Family Heteromyidae; genus *Dipodomys*.

Kangaroos, the name given to Australia's national rugby league team. They made their first tour in 1908, to Britain, a year after the sport was introduced to New South Wales. Hero of that tour was H.H. "Dally" Messenger, known as "The Master". The Kangaroos tour Britain, France and New Zealand, as well as playing those countries' teams at home and in World Cup Championship series. The greatest interest is generated by matches with Britain for the unofficial title of "world champion". Kangaroos' sides are usually renowned for their tough, hard-running forwards and fast, elusive backs.

K'ang-hsi (1654–1722), Chinese emperor (as Sheng-tsu, 1661–1722). He campaigned deep into Mongolia, conquered three provinces in the north (1662–1705), made a treaty with Russia on the northern border (1689), conquered Yunnan and Formosa (1683) and won control of Tibet (1705–21). While he ruled as a conqueror, keeping the peace with strategically placed garrisons, he adopted Chinese culture, and for a time actively encouraged the Jesuit scholar-missionaries; but in 1717 issued an anti-Christian decree. *See also* HC1 p.354.

Kanhai, Rohan (1935–), West Indian cricketer, *b.* Guyana. An audacious batsman given to improvization, he played in 79 Test matches between 1957 and 1974 (6,227 runs, average 47.53), 13 times as captain. During a long career he played for Guyana, Trinidad, Warwickshire and Western Australia.

Kanin, Garson (1912–), US author, producer and director. He wrote and directed *Born Yesterday* (1946), *The Rat Race* (1949) and the musical *Do Re Mi* (1955). He wrote several books, among them *Tracy and Hepburn* (1971) and *Hollywood* (1974), and directed such plays as *Diary of Anne Frank* (1955), which won a Pulitzer prize, the Antoinette Perry award and the Critics' Circle award; *A Hole in the Head* (1957) and *Idiots' Delight* (1970).

Kanishka (*r. c.* 120–162; died *c.* AD 162), king of what is now the northern part of India and Afghanistan. He convened the fourth BUDDHIST council at which commentaries on Buddhist canon were prepared, yet coins of the period indicate that he honoured Greek and Brahmanic gods. During his reign trade with the Roman empire increased. *See also* HC1 pp.63, *63*.

Kannada. *See* KANARESE.

Kano, city in N central Nigeria; capital of Kano state. The city dates from before the 12th century when it was part of the HAUSA Empire. It became a MUSLIM possession in the 16th century, was conquered by the Fulani in the early 19th century and taken by the British in 1903. Today, Kano is a trading centre for a region producing cotton and nuts, and the city's chief industry is textiles. Pop. 399,000.

Kanō School, school of Japanese painting originating in the 15th century which became the Classical school in Japan. Although showing affinities with Chinese subject matter and ink technique, its style of expression was thoroughly Japanese – usually simple and restrained but occasionally elaborate, as in decorative screen painting. Kanō Masanobu (*c.* 1453–1530), the official painter to the SHŌGUN, was the forerunner of the school. His son Kanō MOTONOBU (*c.* 1476–1539) was the school's founder and one of the foremost Japanese artists. When Motonobu's grandson Kanō EITOKU (154–90) invented the use of gold leaf as a background to screen painting in opaque colour, a new and unparalleled richness was introduced to Japanese art. Eitoku and his followers worked both in Kyoto and in Edo. Artists working in Edo were thenceforth called the Edo Kanō, those in Kyoto being known as the Kyoto Kanō. *See also* HC1 pp.132–133.

Kānpur (Cawnpore), city in Uttar Pradesh state, N India, on the River Ganges, approx. 800km (497 miles) NW of Calcutta; one of the largest cities in India. The city is a major industrial, commercial and transport centre. Kānpur was ceded to the British in 1801, and it became a British frontier post. During the INDIAN MUTINY in 1857, the entire British garrison in Kānpur was massacred by Indian forces. The city has a university, the Indian Institute of Technology and a Hindu temple. Industries: chemicals, leather goods, food processing, textiles. Pop. (1971) 1,154,388.

Kansas, state in central USA. Part of the Great Plains, the land rises from the prairies of the E to the semi-arid high plains of the W, which extend to the Rocky Mts. The area is drained by the Kansas and Arkansas rivers. Kansas is the leading producer of wheat in the USA. Corn, hay and sorghums are also grown and cattle raising is of great importance to the economy. Manufacturing has surpassed agriculture, however, in economic importance, the leading industries being transportation equipment, chemicals, petroleum products and machinery. Other important industries are food processing and aircraft. The major cities are Topeka, the capital, Wichita and Kansas City.

When the area passed from France to the new United States under the LOUISIANA PURCHASE of 1803 it was still Indian country, and not until 1854 was the Territory of Kansas created and the area opened up for settlement. Area: 213,094sq km (82,276sq mi miles). Pop. (1975 est.) 2,267,000. *See also* MW p.175.

Kansas City, name of two adjacent ports in the USA: one in NE Kansas and the other in NW Missouri, both at the confluence of the Missouri and Kansas rivers. Situated on the Oregon and Santa Fe trails in the

19th century, the cities now form a large industrial and commercial centre, and a market for grain and poultry. Industries: food processing, oil refining, farm machinery, motor vehicle assembly, steel. Pop. (Kans.) (1973) 172,944; (Mo.) (1973) 487,799.

Kansas-Nebraska Act (1854), US Congressional measure introduced by Senator Stephen A. Douglas of Illinois which gave states the right to decide for themselves all questions related to slavery. It effectively negated the earlier MISSOURI COMPROMISE of 1820, which declared that all land in the LOUISIANA PURCHASE was to be non-slave, except for the state of Missouri. Written to appease Southern congressmen, the Kansas-Nebraska Act made slavery legally possible in the two vast new territories of Kansas and Nebraska, and revived the bitter slavery controversy. *See also* HC2 pp.150–151.

Kansu (Gansu), province in NW China, on the Chinese-Mongolian border; the capital is Lanchow (Lanzhou). With the aid of irrigation, wheat, cotton, rice, maize and tobacco are grown, particularly in the valley of the Yellow River (Hwang Ho). Livestock are grazed on the mountain slopes. Mineral deposits include iron ore, oil and coal. The province is strategically important, controlling routes to Mongolia and the USSR. Area: 366,625sq km (141,550sq miles). Pop. 13,000,000.

Kant, Immanuel (1724–1804), German philosopher. From 1740–46 he studied at Königsberg University, then worked as a private tutor. In 1755 he returned to the university and was made a professor in 1770. The order, regularity and modesty of his life was undisturbed by the notoriety caused by the publication of his "critical philosophy", particularly *Critique of Pure Reason* (1781), *Critique of Practical Reason* (1788) and *Critique of Judgment* (1790). In addition to his technical treatises, Kant produced several topical essays in support of religious liberalism and ENLIGHTENMENT. *See also* HC2 pp.*172*, 173, 314.

Kantor, MacKinley (1904–1977), US short story writer and novelist. He wrote numerous novels dealing with US history, including *Andersonville* (1955), for which he won the 1956 Pulitzer Prize.

Kantorovich, Leonid Vitalyevich (1912–), Soviet mathematician and economist. In 1939, while working to find ways of making efficient use of the Siberian railway, he devised a method for achieving maximum production despite such difficulties as limited resources. Although ignored at the time because it contradicted the government's economic ideals, it was for this theory of resource allocation that he shared the 1975 Nobel Prize in economics with Tjalling C. KOOPMANS.

Kaohsiung (Kaochiung), city in S Taiwan. Originally a small fishing village, it was developed as a port and manufacturing centre by the Japanese, who occupied Taiwan in 1895. The city has a large naval base, and its industries include shipbuilding, petroleum products, machinery, aluminium, sugar refining. Pop. (1972 est.) 884,200.

Kao K'o-kung (1248–*c.* 1310), Chinese painter. The first notable artist of the YÜAN DYNASTY he is known for his wooded mountain landscapes.

Kaolack, port in W Senegal, on the River Saloum. It is the centre of the SUFI Muslim Tijaniyah brotherhood. An important market for groundnuts, linked by rail to Dakar and the River Niger, Kaolack's industries also include brewing, leather tanning and cotton processing. Pop. (1969 est.) 95,000.

Kaolan. *See* LANCHOW.

Kaoliang, name in China and Manchuria for any of several grain sorghums. They have slender, dry stalks; open, erect panicles; and small white or brown seeds. The grain is used for human food or alcoholic beverages, and the stalks for thatching, fuel or fodder.

Kaolin, or China clay, especially fine and pure clay composed chiefly of the mineral KAOLINITE, a hydrous silicate of aluminium. It is used in the manufacture of ceramics and fine porcelains. *See also* MM p.44.

Kaolinite, sheet silicate mineral of the kaolinite group, hydrous aluminium silicate $[Al_2Si_2O_5(OH)_4]$. It is a product of the weathering of feldspar and has triclinic system tabular crystals, clay-like masses and particles. It is white with a dull lustre and may be tinted by impurities. Hardness 2-2.5; s.g. 2.6. Kaolinite is important in the manufacture of pharmaceuticals, ceramics, and coated paper.

Kao Ming, 14th-century Chinese playwright. He wrote "hsi wên", southern Chinese plays noted for their freedom from foreign influence and featuring folk-songs and numerous scene changes. His most popular play, *Record of the Balloon Guitar*, re-interpreted an old legend.

Kaon, or K meson, ELEMENTARY PARTICLE that is either a charged or neutral meson with zero spin.

Kapilavastu, town in S Nepal just inside the border with India, said to be the birthplace and childhood home of BUDDHA. It is near the modern town of Paderia.

Kapital, Das, (Capital), economic and historical study by Karl MARX, published in three volumes (1867, 1885, 1894), the main exposition of his concept of dialectical materialism. The second and third volumes were edited by ENGELS after Marx's death.

Kapitsa, or Kapitza, Peter Leonidovich (1894–), Russian physicist. He did extensive research in magnetism (in England with Sir Ernest RUTHERFORD) and discovered that helium II (the stable form below -271°C) has almost no resistance to flow – a phenomenon called superfluidity. He subsequently worked on satellite research and thermonuclear FISSION.

Kaplan, Mordecai Menahem (1881–), US rabbi, theologian and religious leader, *b.* Lithuania. He emigrated to the USA and became a teacher at the Jewish Theological Seminary; he settled in Israel in 1972. Kaplan founded the Reconstructionist movement, attempting to change Judaism to meet 20th-century needs. His books include *Judaism as a Civilization* (1934) and *Judaism without Supernaturalism* (1958).

Kapok, tropical tree with palmate leaves and white or pink flowers. Its seed pods burst to release silky fibres which are commonly used for stuffing and insulation. Height: to 50m (165ft). Family Bombacaceae; species *Ceiba pentandra.*

Kapp, Wolfgang (1858–1922), German right-wing politician, *b.* USA. He led a well-supported but ill-fated insurrection against the WEIMAR REPUBLIC in 1920. Kapp fled Germany but returned and died while awaiting trial.

Kapteyn, Jacobus Cornelius (1851–1922), Dutch astronomer noted for his study of stellar motion and the distribution of stars in the MILKY WAY. He discovered that all stars whose PROPER MOTION can be determined, move in one of two streams of stars moving in opposite directions in the plane of the galaxy.

Karāchi, largest city in Pakistan, on the Arabian Sea, NW of the Indus River delta. Ruled for most of its history by Muslim dynasties, it passed in 1843 to the British, who developed it as a major port. It is still an important trading centre for agricultural produce from the surrounding region. Until 1960 it was the capital of Pakistan and it has an international airport. Industries: steel, engineering, textiles, food processing, chemicals, printing and publishing. Pop. 3,442,000.

Karafuto. *See* SAKHALIN.

Karadjordje (*c.* 1768–1817), name, meaning "Black George", assumed by George Petrović, the leader of the Serbs in their fight for independence from Turkey. In 1804 he launched a successful war of independence, with token support from Russia. In 1812, Russia concluded a treaty with Turkey giving Turkey a free hand in Serbia, but the Serbs rose again in 1815. Karadjordje returned from exile in Russia in 1817 but was murdered by Miloš OBRENOVIĆ, the new leader. *See also* HC2 pp.84, *84.*

Karadjordjević dynasty, Serbian dynasty which ruled 1842–58 and 1903–45. It was involved in a long-standing feud with the OBRENOVIĆ dynasty. Whereas the Obrenovićs had kept Serbia within the Austrian sphere of influence since 1881, a coup in 1903 placed PETER I, an avowed Russophile, on the throne and altered the balance of power in the Balkans.

Karadžić, Vuk Stefanović (1787–1864), Serbian scholar and writer. He published his 26,000-word *Serbian Lexicon* in 1818 and spent much time modifying the Cyrillic ALPHABET for Serbian use. He also collected national folk-songs and poems.

Karaism, Karaites, Jewish sect founded in Persia in the 8th century. Rejecting the authority of the TALMUD, the Karaites insisted on interpreting the Bible literally. They accused the talmudists of substituting a man-made law for the TORAH, and developed an oral law of their own which was in many ways more strict. Karaism declined after the 12th century, although some Karaites still exist in Israel and the Crimea.

Karajan, Herbert von (1908–), German conductor. He conducted the Berlin State Opera from 1938–45. In 1954 he became musical director of the Berlin Philharmonic Orchestra and in 1957 became a director of the SALZBURG Festivals. Between 1945–64 he was also director of the Vienna State Opera.

Kara-Kalpak (Karakalpakskaja ASSR), autonomous republic within the Uzbek Republic (Uzbekskaja SSR), in central Asian USSR; Nukus is the capital. The region is one of the USSR's chief producers of lucerne; other crops include rice, cotton, maize and jute. Livestock raising and the breeding of muskrats and silkworms are also important, and there is some light industry. The region came under Russian control at the end of the 19th century. Area: 165,600sq km (63,950sq miles). Pop. (1970) 702,000.

Karakoram, mountain range in India and Pakistan that includes some of the world's highest peaks, among them K2 (Godwin Austen), at 8,616m (28,267ft) the second highest peak in the world. Length: approx. 480km (300 miles).

Karakorum, ancient capital of the Mongol empire, established by Genghis Khan in 1220 in central Mongolia, 322km (200 miles) WSW of modern Ulan Bator. It was abandoned after 1267 when the capital was moved to Khanbaliq. The Russian explorer N. M. Yardrintsev discovered the ruins in 1889 but they were not examined by archaeologists until the late 1940s.

Karakul, breed of SHEEP from Central Asia with coarse fur on the adults and glossy hair on the young. Tightly curled, black or grey pelts taken from lambs are called "Persian lamb". "Broadtail" pelts are obtained from still-born or new-born lambs. *See also* PE p.*231.*

Kara-Kum, desert area in southern USSR, extending from the Caspian Sea (W) to the River Amudarja (E), and including most of the Turkmen Republic (Turkmenskaja SSR). The Kara-Kum Canal carries water approx. 800km (500 miles) from Arnu Darya to Ashkhabad and is used to irrigate a cotton-producing region. Area: 300,000sq km (115,830sq miles).

Karamanlis, Koństantinos (1907–), Greek politician. After practising law in Athens he was elected to Parliament in 1935. He became Prime Minister in 1955 and formed his own party, the National Radical Union, a year later. He reached agreement with Britain and Turkey over Cyprus in 1960 in an attempt to ease strained relations with those countries, but was forced to resign in 1963. During 11 years of self-imposed exile he was an opponent of the Greek military junta, and when it fell in 1974 he returned as Prime Minister.

Karamojong, Nilotic people of NE Uganda. They are semi-nomadic, although living in permanent hut settlements on the arid plains. The women cultivate grain and herd goats. Their economy is based on cattle, with which the men travel in search of water.

Kara Mustafa (1634–83) Turkish grand vizier (1676–83) under Sultan Muhammad IV. Allied with Hungarian rebels under Imré Thokoly against Holy Roman

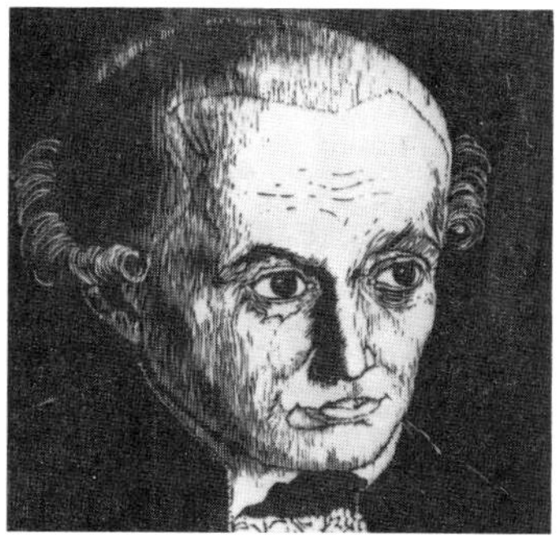

Kant's *Critique of Pure Reason* explores the problems of human knowledge.

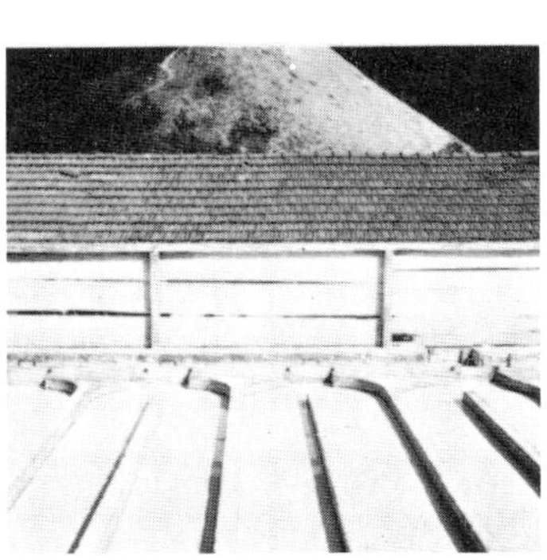

Kaolin, shown here in preparation for purification, is used in ceramics and medicine.

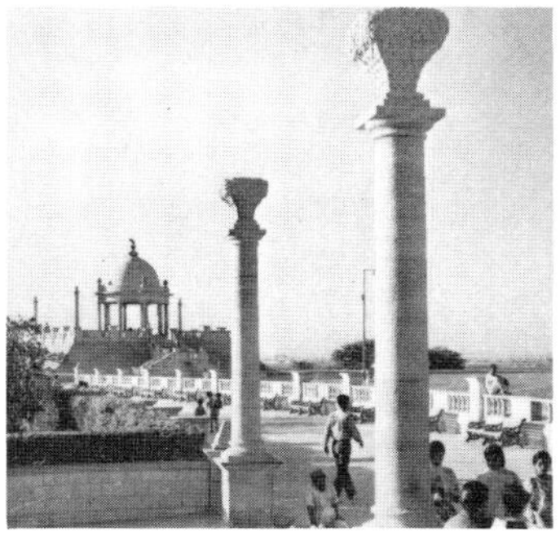

Karachi's Clifton Parade is an example of early 20th-century Mughal architecture.

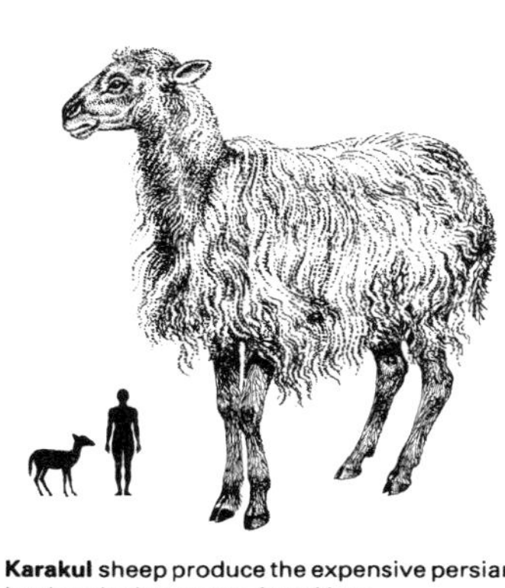

Karakul sheep produce the expensive persian lamb pelts known as Astrakhan.

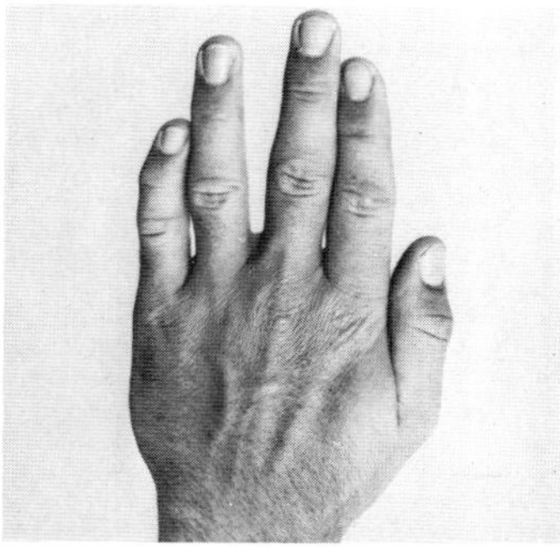

Karate; continuous beating against a wall has distorted the little finger of this hand.

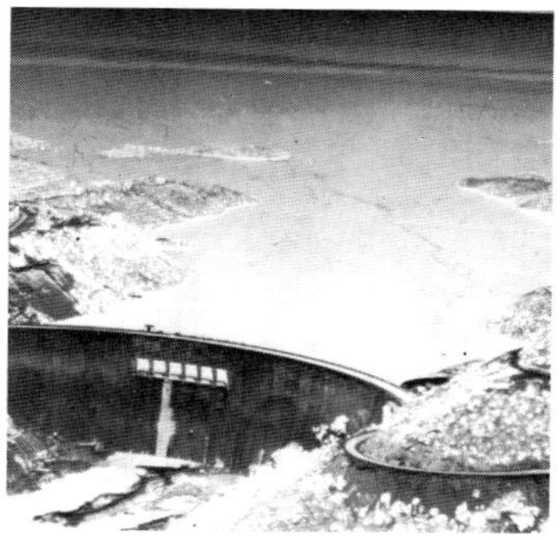

Kariba Dam; animals were saved from the lake behind the dam by Operation Noah.

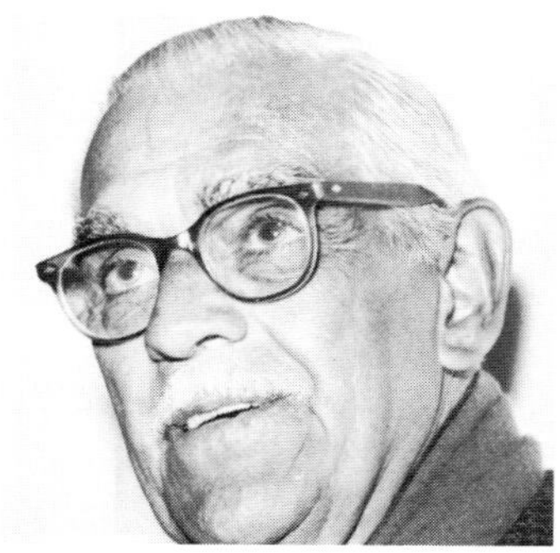

Boris Karloff, whose real name was William Henry Pratt, was born in Dulwich, London.

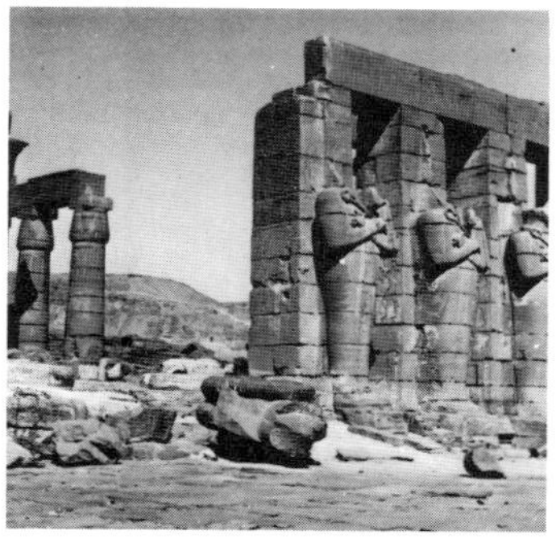

Karnak; Ramesseum Oseiron pillars standing at the site of the ancient city of Thebes.

Emperor Leopold I, he laid siege to Vienna in 1683, but retreated before the relief army of JOHN III SOBIESKI of Poland. When he reached Belgrade the sultan ordered his execution.

Karamzin, Nikolai Mikhailovich (1766–1826), Russian writer, historian and journalist. He was the leader of the Sentimental school of Russian literature, an example of which is his *Poor Lisa* (1792). *Letters of a Russian Traveller* (1789–90) is an account of his European travels. He also wrote the incomplete 12-volume *History of the Russian State* (1816).

Karanga, BANTU-speaking people in Zimbabwe (Rhodesia). Between the 14th and 15th centuries AD they built the city of Zimbabwe (the name commonly given by Africans to Rhodesia). Discovered by European explorers *c.*1870, the ruins of Zimbabwe were believed for a time to be the biblical Ophir where King Solomon had his mines. *See also* HC2 pp.128, *128*.

Kara Sea, part of the Arctic Ocean off the northern USSR between Severnaya Zemlya and Novaya Zemlya. It is an important fishing ground, and main ports are Novyi Port and Dikson. The area is ice-bound except in August and September. Average depth: 127m (417ft).

Karate, martial art popularized in Japan in the 1920s. The technique, which involves a formal method of physical and mental training, includes a variety of blows using the hand, legs, elbows and head. The bony parts of the body in particular are used as weapons. In sport contestants are allowed to use only a few of the techniques so as to avoid serious injuries and all punches, blows or kicks are minimized.

Karavelov, Lyuben (1835–79), Bulgarian writer. He aimed to publicize his country's political difficulties in stories and studies collected in *Pamyatniki narodnago byta bolgar* ("Popular Bulgarian Monuments", 1861) and joined Bulgarian revolutionary émigrés in Bucharest in 1869. He continued his work in the journals *Svoboda* ("Freedom",1869–72) and *Nezavisimost* ("Independence", 1873–74).

Karbalā, city in central Iraq, 89km (55 miles) SSW of Baghdad, on the W edge of the Syrian Desert. A religious centre, it is the point of departure for Iranian pilgrims to Mecca and a holy place for Shi'ite Muslims. Husein, the Shi'ite leader, was murdered in the city in AD 680. Its products include hides, wool, dates and religious objects. Pop. (1970 est.) 107,500.

Karel, Rudolph (1880–1945), Czech composer. Initially Romantic in style, his music later became vigorous, original and richly polyphonic. The symphonic poem *The Demon* (1920) is a masterpiece. Typical of the emotional patriotism of his late works is the *Revolutionary Overture* (1938–41). In 1943 Karel was imprisoned by the Nazis. He died in a concentration camp.

Karelia (Karelskaja SSR), autonomous region in NW European USSR, bounded by the White Sea in the E and Finland in the W. The capital is Petrozavodsk. Established in 1923 as an autonomous republic, it absorbed 36,260sq km (14,000sq miles) of Finnish land after the 1939–40 war between the USSR and Finland, after which its status was raised to a constituent republic, the Karelo-Finnish Republic. It returned to its present status in 1956. Farming is restricted by climate to the S where vegetables and cereal crops are grown and livestock are raised. Fishing and timber are the chief industries. The region has valuable mineral deposits, including lead, zinc, copper and iron. Area: 172,400sq km (66,564sq miles). Pop. (1970) 714,000.

Karens, Thai-Chinese cultural group, mostly farmers, living in Burma. They form about 10% of Burma's population. The hill people practise an animistic religion; the plain-dwellers are Christians and Buddhists. They speak the Karens languages and are deeply opposed to Burmese domination. In 1948–49 a revolt against the Burmese government won for the Karenni state (now Kayah state) a large measure of local autonomy.

Karg-Elert, Siegfried (1877–1933), German composer whose most enduring compositions are those for the harmonium and organ. They combine great harmonic and contrapuntal resourcefulness, despite a tendency to over-chromaticism, and number almost 200 items, most of which place great demands on performer and instrument alike.

Kariba Dam, hydroelectric scheme in S central Africa, in the Kariba Gorge on the River Zambezi, on the border between Zambia and Zimbabwe (Rhodesia). Built between 1955 and 1959, it is one of the world's largest dams. Kariba Lake, the reservoir formed behind the dam, is approx. 280km (175 miles) long and 32km (20 miles) wide. Dam length: 579m (1,900ft); height: 128m (420ft).

Karim Khan (*c.* 1705–79), ruler of Persia (1750–79), founder of the Zand dynasty. He seized control, ruled peacefully as Vakil Al-Roaya, "Regent of the People", and beautified his capital, Shiraz, erecting the Mosque of Vakil and the Bazaar. His dynasty was overthrown in 1794 by the QAJARS, whom he had failed to subdue.

Karitane System, mother- and baby-care system in New Zealand and Australia, founded by Sir Truby KING in New Zealand in 1907. It stresses breast-feeding, or if that is impossible, correct use of cow's milk. There are many Karitane hospitals and clinics in Australia and New Zealand, and some in Britain.

Karlfeldt, Erik Axel (1864–1931), Swedish poet. His verse was an extension of Swedish peasant culture. It appeared in six volumes, including *Songs of Wilderness and Love* (1895), *Fridolin's Songs* (1898) and *The Horn of Autumn* (1927). He was awarded the Nobel Prize in literature in 1931.

Karli caves, Buddhist shrines in Maharashtra, W India. Cut from natural rock as early as the 2nd century BC. The entrance to the caves is famous for the large relief sculptures of amorous couples. The largest cave measures 38m by 14m (124ft by 45ft) and much of its rich decoration survives. *See also* HC1 pp.*63*, 120.

Karl-Marx-Stadt, city in S East Germany, 64km (40 miles) SW of Dresden, on the Chemnitz River; capital of Karl-Marx-Stadt district. Formerly Chemnitz, it was chartered in 1143 and granted a linen-weaving monopoly. Devastated during the THIRTY YEARS WAR, its economy recovered at the end of the 17th century with the introduction of the cotton industry. It has many old buildings including a 12th-century palace and church. Industries: machine tools, carpets, hosiery. Pop. (1974) 302,409.

Karloff, Boris (1887–1969), British character actor noted mainly for his roles in horror films, after his magnificent performance as the monster in *Frankenstein* (1931). He nearly always played evil or sinister characters, representing them as grotesque, but pathetic.

Karlowitz, Treaty of (1699), peace treaty between the Turks on the one side and Venice, Austria and Poland on the other, signed at Karlowitz, N Serbia. Turkey was forced to divide much of its European territory, ceding Transylvania and much of Hungary to Austria, part of the Ukraine and Podolia to Poland and the Peloponnese and most of Dalmatia to Venice. The treaty marked the beginning of the OTTOMAN EMPIRE's fall.

Karlsruhe, city in SW West Germany, on the River Rhine, 56km (35 miles) S of Mannheim. Founded in 1715 by the margrave of Baden-Durlach, it became the capital of the duchy, later the state, of Baden. The city suffered severe damage during WWII. It has a university and several colleges, and has been a centre of atomic research since 1956. Industries: jewellery, chemicals, pharmaceuticals, oil refining. Pop. (1974) 261,250.

Karlstad, city in SW Sweden, on Lake Vänern. Originally called Tingvalla, it was renamed in honour of Charles IX in 1584. After a fire in 1865 it was completely rebuilt and was the scene of negotiations for the treaty in 1905 ending the union of Norway and Sweden. Industries include heavy machinery and wood products. Pop. (1970) 72,290.

Karma, Vedic concept related to belief in reincarnation. According to Karmic law, the acts in past incarnations explain present circumstances, just as acts in this life can affect future lives. Salvation involves cancelling the effects of past evil deeds by virtuous actions in this life. *See also* HINDUISM; REINCARNATION; VEDAS.

Kármán, Jozsef (1769–95), Hungarian writer, author of the sentimental story *Fanny's Testament*, important in the development of the Hungarian novel.

Kármán, Theodore von (1881–1963), US research engineer, *b.* Hungary, best-known for his work in the application of mathematics to aeronautics and space rocketry. He became a US citizen in 1936 and helped found the NASA Jet Propulsion Laboratory, the International Council of the Aeronautical Sciences, and the International Academy of Astronautics.

Karmathians, Muslim sect that ruled by terror and murder. Karmat was an Iraqi peasant and proselytizer who founded a communist-like movement in about AD 890. An independent state on the Persian Gulf was created by his missionary, Jannabi, who proceeded to terrorize Baghdad (899). His successor, Suleiman, seized the sacred Black Stone of Mecca in 930, whose return was demanded by AL-MANSUR and achieved in 951. Some of their traditions passed to the FATIMIDS and ASSASSINS.

Karnak, modern village, 550km (330 miles) SE of Cairo, near the site of Ancient Egyptian THEBES, the chief city of Upper Egypt. Thebes became a political and religious centre during the 11th dynasty, and the base from which the 17th and 18th dynasties drove the HYKSOS from Lower Egypt. Although it declined in importance from the 19th dynasty, many buildings from this period of dominance remain intact. On the east bank of the Nile is a temple to Amon-Re, king of the gods; built over a period of 2,000 years, it is massively imposing. The largest hall has 134 columns, some of which are 24m (78ft) tall. Around this temple was an enclosed area where there were smaller temples and a lake for ritual washing; nearby were temples to Montu (a god of war) and Amon's consort, Mut. An avenue lined with sphinxes led to the temples at LUXOR. On the west bank, the tombs of nobles have been found in cliffs; in valleys farther west, the tombs of kings and queens, including that of Tutankhamen, have been discovered.

Károly, Count Mihály (1875–1955), Hungarian statesman who entered parliament in 1910. He favoured Hungarian autonomy before WWI. He became Prime Minister in Oct. 1918 and then President (Jan. 1919), but resigned in March 1919 after failing to get his reforms adopted. He went into exile until 1946. From 1947 to 1949 he was Hungarian Ambassador to Paris, but resigned in protest against increasingly totalitarian government. Again he went into exile.

Karrer, Paul (1889–1971), Swiss chemist, *b.* Russia, who shared the 1937 Nobel Prize in chemistry with Sir Walter HAWORTH for research on flavins, carotenoids and vitamins. In 1930 he determined the formula of beta CAROTENE, the precursor of vitamin A, and in 1931 elucidated the structure of the vitamin itself. He also studied vitamin E and demonstrated that lactoflavin was part of the vitamin B2 complex.

Karroo, semi-arid region in SW Cape Province, Republic of South Africa. It consists of Little Karroo, which extends east to west approx. 320km (200 miles) and is separated from Great Karroo, which lies by the Swartberg Mts and is approx. 480km (300 miles) long. Parts of the Karoo are well irrigated and fertile, yielding citrus fruits and cereals.

Karsh, Yousuf (1908–), Canadian photographer, *b.* Turkey, who specialized in sensitive portraits of famous people. His outstandingly perceptive photograph of Winston Churchill embodying all the British leader's bulldog determination – and, unusually for Karsh, posed and shot in less than two minutes – made the photographer world famous.

Karst, limestone plateau characterized by

irregular protuberant rocks, sinkholes, caves, disappearing streams and underground drainage. Such topography is named after its most typical site in the Karst region of Yugoslavia; in Britain, the most spectacular example is above Malham, North Yorkshire. *See also* PE p.110.

Karttikeya, also called Skanda, in Hindu mythology, the six-faced god of war, symbolic of the planet Mars. He is the son of SHIVA and PARVATI. He is depicted with a bow and arrow or drum and sword in hand, riding a peacock.

Kasavubu, Joseph (*c.*1915–69), political figure of the Republic of the Congo (now Zaire). A major protagonist in the Congolese quest for independence from Belgium, he became the first President (1960–65) but was obliged to enlist the services of Gen. MOBUTU before emerging successful in a dispute with Premier Patrice LUMUMBA. He was ousted by Mobutu.

Kāshān, city in central Iran. Noted for the production of carpets and ceramic tiles in SAFAVID times, the city was a cultural and artistic centre, and was on an important caravan route. Traditional manufactures include silk textiles, copperware, wool and silk carpets. Pop. (1971 est.) 63,000.

Kashmir, former princely state; now Jammu and Kashmir state in NW India, with its capital in Srīnagar in summer and Jammu in winter, and the Pakistani-controlled Azad Kashmir in NE Pakistan, with its capital in Muzaffarābād. It is a mountainous region and includes parts of the Himalayas and the Karakoram Range. The Vale of Kashmir, in the valley of the River Jhelum, is the most populated area, and wheat and rice are grown. After centuries of Hindu and Buddhist rule, Kashmir was conquered by Muslims in the late 14th century, and most of the population was converted to Islam. Since the partition of India in 1947, Kashmir has been a cause of friction – even war – between India and Pakistan. The situation was further complicated by the intervention of the Chinese in the late 1950s. Area: (India) approx. 139,000sq km (54,000sq miles); (Pakistan) approx. 84,000sq km (32,000sq miles). Pop. (India, 1971) 4,600,000. (Pakistan, 1971) 1,300,000.

Kashmir goat, also called CASHMERE goat, small goat that lives in the Himalayas of India and Tibet. It is domesticated for its silky underwool, which is often used in high-quality textiles.

Kasprowicz, Jan (1860–1926), Polish poet. His first book of poems *Poezje* (1889) contained elements of social reportage using realistic subject-matter and diction. In his later work he used a symbolist technique to explore everyday themes, as in the hymns *To a Dying World* (1901) and *Ballad of the Sunflower* (1908).

Kassalā, city in NE Sudan, NE Africa. It was founded in 1834 as a military camp by MUHAMMED ALI during his conquest of the Sudan, becoming a fort in 1840. The city was taken by the MAHDISTS in 1885 and the Italians in 1894, but was regained by the Egyptians three years later. Industries: cotton, fruit-growing. Pop. (1969) 81,000.

Kassem, Gen. Abdul Karim (1914–63), Iraqi military figure. While pursuing a successful career he assumed the leadership of several disaffected groups within the army. He became the head of the Republic of Iraq after the overthrow of the monarchy in 1958. In an attempt to assert his authority, he purged both right- and left-wing groups, losing the remaining military support when he failed to deal with the Kurdish rebellion of 1961. He was killed in a coup led by Abd as-Salam Arif.

Kasserine Pass, mountain gap 8km (5 miles) NW of the town El Kasserine in W Tunisia. During WWII it was the scene of an AXIS POWERS breakthrough. The pass was retaken by Allied troops in what proved to be a decisive battle of the North Africa campaign. Width: 3.2km (2 miles).

Kassites, or Cassites, ancient people, possibly of Persian origin, who rose to importance in the 3rd millennium BC. By the middle of the 18th century they were impinging on BABYLONIA. Their system of government was policed by a small feudal aristocracy of warriors who used the innovatory horse-drawn chariot. The Elamites eventually forced the Kassites to withdraw to the Zagros Mts in Iran during the 1st millennium. The people disappeared after the beginning of the Christian era. *See also* HC1 p.32.

Kastler, Alfred (1902–), French physicist, *b.* Germany, who was awarded the 1966 Nobel Prize in physics for the discovery and development of optical methods for studying resonance in atoms. He developed the technique of optical pumping, in which gas atoms absorb energy from bombardment with light and radio waves and release it a few milliseconds later, the mode of release varying according to the atomic species. This technique led to a new knowledge of atomic structure and the development of the LASER and MASER.

Kästner, Erich (1899–1974), German satirist, poet and novelist, who was prevented from publishing in Germany by the Nazis in 1933–45. His post-war works lean towards social philosophy but are highly entertaining. He was world famous for the subtlety, charm and humour of his books for children, *Emil and the Detectives* (1929) and *Three Men in the Snow* (1935). His collection of poems, *Lyrical Medicine Chest* (1936), was noted for its satire.

Katanga, southernmost province of Zaire, rich in mineral deposits, notably copper. In 1960, soon after Zaire (formerly the Belgian Congo) became independent, Moise Tshombe led a secessionist movement in Katanga which was finally crushed in 1962, with the help of UN troops and after bitter fighting. In 1972 Katanga was renamed Shaba.

Katayev, Valentin Petrovich (1897–), Soviet author. His lightly satirical novels constitute a chronicle of Soviet society. They include *The Embezzlers* (1926), *Time, Forward!* (1932) *The Son of The Regiment* (1945) and *Winter Wind* (1960). The novel *Lonely White Sail* (1936) depicts the revolution of 1905 as seen by two schoolboys. As a dramatist, he wrote a number of popular plays, including the comedy *Squaring the Circle* (1928) about marriage and housing conditions. *Grass of Oblivion* (1967) is an autobiographical volume.

Katchen, Julius (1926–69), US concert pianist, who made his debut in 1937 with the Philadelphia Orchestra. Having toured Palestine in 1948, he later settled in Paris and gained success in a series of European concert tours.

Katchina, or kachina, divine intermediary between man and god among the Pueblo Indians, or a dancer masked to resemble one. Katchina were believed to be ancestral spirits who brought rain and corn. Elaborate rituals surrounded them.

Kathmandu. *See* KĀTMĀNDU.

Kātmāndu, capital of Nepal, in central Nepal at the N foot of the Mahābhārat mountain range of the E Himalayas. The administrative and commercial centre of the country, it is situated on an ancient pilgrimage route from India to China and Mongolia. Pop. (1971) 150,402.

Kato, Komei Takaaki (1860–1926), Japanese diplomat and political figure. He entered the foreign service in 1887, was ambassador to Britain between 1894–99 and 1908–13, and served briefly as Foreign Minister in 1900, 1906 and 1913. As Foreign Minister in 1914–15 he imposed the "Twenty-one Demands on China", which conferred on Japan economic advantages in China. In 1913 he organized the conservative Kenseikai Party. As Prime Minister from 1924–26 he introduced universal suffrage, reduced government expenditure and the size of the military, and lessened the powers of the House of Peers. He also introduced universal military training and favoured the Peace Preservation Law, which severely penalized political dissent.

Kato, Tomosaburo (1859–1923), Japanese naval and political figure. He was Naval Chief of Staff (1894–95), chief assistant to Admiral Togo during the Russo-Japanese War (1904–05) and navy minister (1915–23)when he directed Japan's navy during WWI and the expansion thereafter. He accepted the principle of naval limitation drawn-up at the Washington Conference in 1921–22. He served as Prime Minister 1922–23.

Katona, József (1791–1830), Hungarian playwright remembered for his five-act tragedy *Bánk Bán* (1815, first performed 1821) which, although set in 13th-century Hungary, reflected contemporary problems.

Katowice, industrial city in S Poland, 72km (45 miles) WNW of Krakow. Founded in the 16th century and chartered in 1865, it passed from Germany to Poland in 1921 but was occupied by the Germans throughout WWII. It is now one of Poland's foremost industrial centres, producing heavy machinery and chemicals. Pop. (1974) 320,400.

Katrine, Loch. *See* LOCH KATRINE.

Katsina, city in N Nigeria, approx. 137km (85 miles) NW of Kano. The former capital of the ancient Katsina kingdom,it was a major city of the Hausa Empire in the 17th and 18th centuries before being taken by the Fulani in the 19th century. The modern city is an agricultural trading centre. It has a Muslim college and many buildings dating from the Hausa period. Products: skins, cotton, peanuts. Pop. (1971) 109,424.

Katsura, Taro (1847–1913), Japanese political figure. He served as Army Minister (1898–1901) and three terms as Prime Minister (1901–06, 1908–11 and 1912–13). During this period as Prime Minister Japan emerged as the major East Asian power by expanding its military forces, defeating Russia in 1904–05, and annexing Korea in 1910.

Kattegat, channel between S Sweden and the Jutland Peninsula of Denmark, in nautical terms between the Skagerrak and the Baltic Sea. Chief ports are Gothenburg (Göteborg) and Arhus.

Katydid, green to brown leaf-like insect found throughout the world, named after its distinctive call. Its wings are arched over its back and it has long antennae. Length: to 3.5.cm (1.4in). Family Tettigoniidae.

Katyn, village in the W Russian Republic (Rossijskaja SFSR). It was occupied by Germany during WWII. In 1943 Germany announced the discovery in a nearby forest of a common grave containing the bodies of 4,250 Polish officers and accused the USSR of their murder during the Soviet infiltration of Poland in 1939. The USSR in turn blamed Germany for the massacre, supporting the charge with the findings of a Soviet investigating committee in 1944. In 1951–52 a special American Congressional committee investigating the allegations found the USSR guilty.

Katz, Sir Bernard (1911–), British bio-physicist, who shared the 1970 Nobel Prize in physiology and medicine with Ulf von EULER and Julius AXELROD for their work on the chemistry of nerve transmission. Katz discovered how the neuro-transmitter, ACETYLCHOLINE, is released by neural impulses, causing muscles to contract.

Katzir, Ephraim (1916–), Israeli head of state and biophysicist. He has been professor of physics at the Weizmann Institute of Science since 1951. In 1966–68 he was the chief scientist at the defence department. He became President of Israel in 1973.

Kauffmann, Angelica (1740–1807), Swiss ROCOCO portrait and decorative painter who worked in England from 1766 to 1782 decorating many interiors in conjunction with Robert ADAM.

Kaufman, George Simon (1889–1961), US playwright. He collaborated on the comedies *Beggar on Horseback* (1924) with Marc CONNELLY; *Dinner at Eight* (1932) and *Stage Door* (1936) with Edna FERBER; *You Can't Take It With You* (1936) and *The Man Who Came To Dinner* (1939) with Moss Hart. He contributed to George GERSHWIN's *Of Thee I Sing* (1932), *Guys and Dolls* (1951) and *Silk Stockings* (1955).

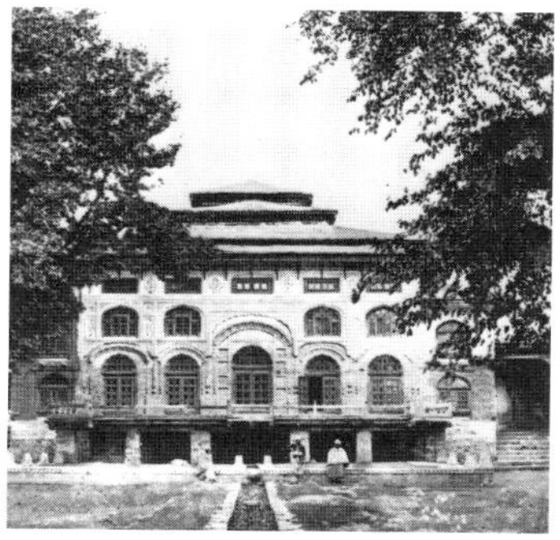

Kashmir: part of the famous Mosque of Hazrat Bal situated on the shores of lake Dal.

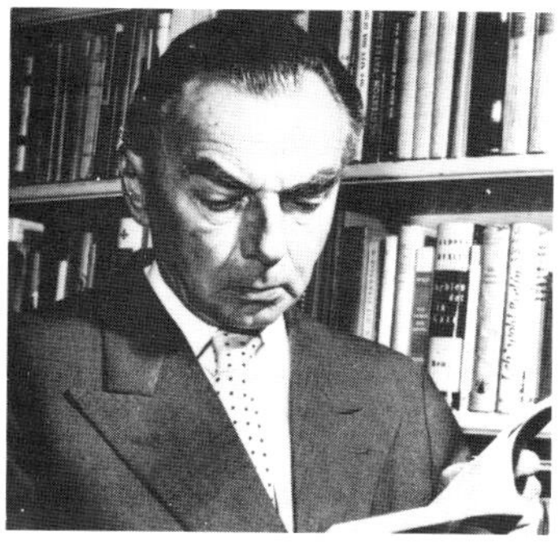

Erich Kästner's satirical books on the early 30s were burned by the Nazis.

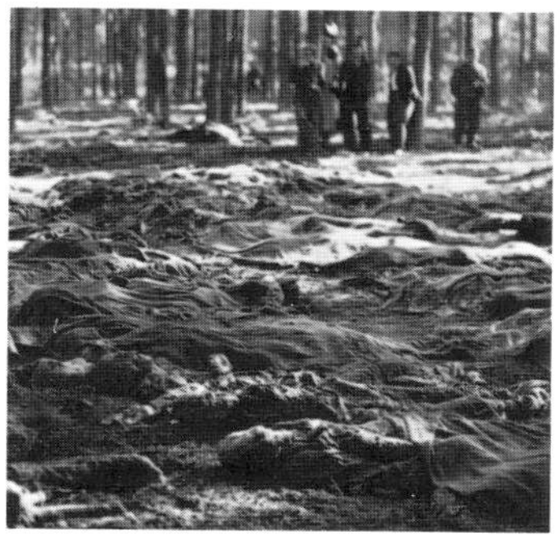

Katyn massacre: the bodies of Polish officers murdered by the Russians prior to WWII.

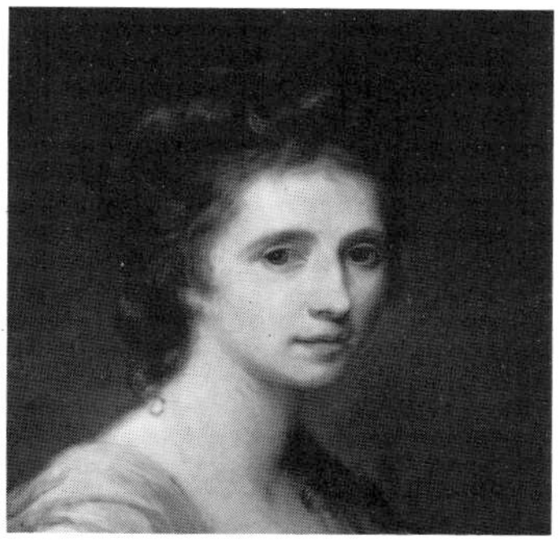

Angelica Kauffman: self portrait by the Swiss artist, now in the National Portrait Galley.

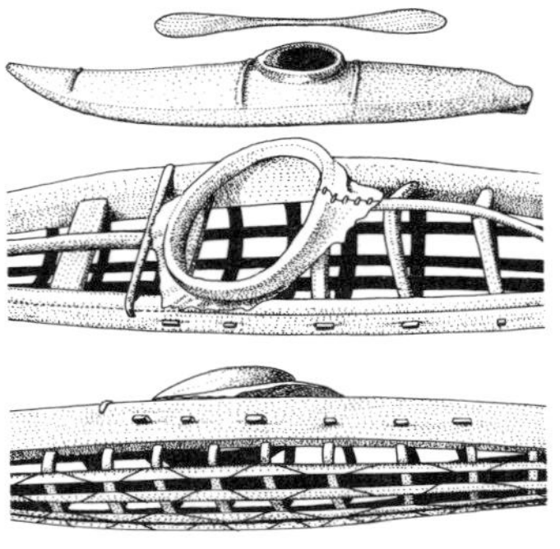

Kayak paddlers, sealed tightly in the canoe, can roll over and then turn upright.

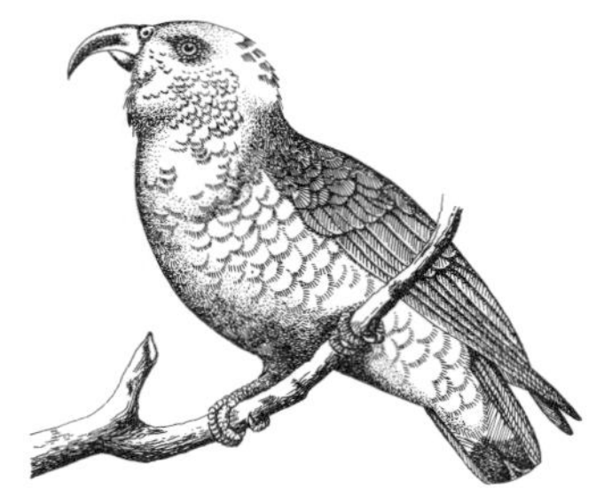

Keas are parrots living in New Zealand; they are also called mountain nestor.

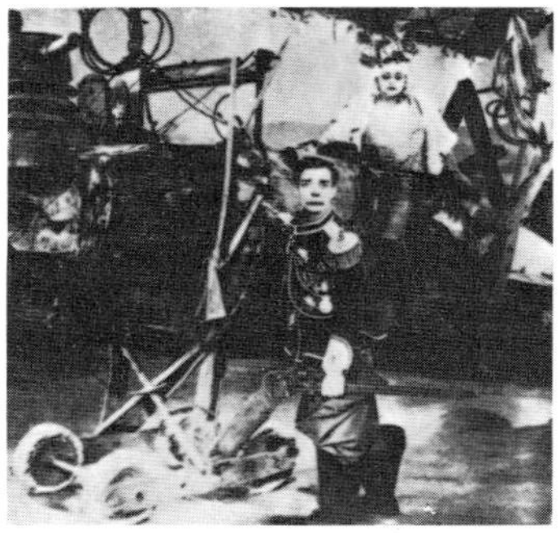

Buster Keaton, shown here in a scene from *Their Honeymoon,* seldom smiled.

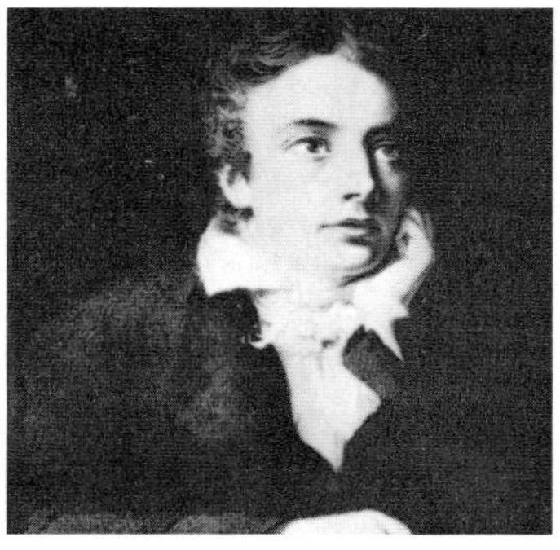

John Keats, the English poet whose odes retain a unique place in English literature.

Kaunas, city and port in Lithuanian Republic (Litovskaja SSR), USSR, on the Neman River. Founded in the 11th century, it became part of Russia in 1795 after the third Partition of Poland. It was captured by the Germans during both World Wars. In between it was the capital of Lithuania. It has a 15th-century church of Vytautas and a university (1922). Industries: iron and steel, chemicals, plastics, textiles. Pop. (1975) 344,000.

Kaunda, Kenneth (1924–), President of Zambia from 1964 when the country gained its independence from Britain. He became leader of the United National Independence Party in 1960, nationalized the copper mines and, in 1973, imposed single party rule. *See also* HC2 *p.253.*

Kaunitz, Wenzel Anton, Count von (1711–94), Austrian statesman. He entered the foreign service in 1740 and in 1748 negotiated the Treaty of AIX-LA-CHAPELLE. He was ambassador to France (1750–53) and as chancellor and foreign minister (1753–92) favoured France over Austria's traditional ally, Prussia. His defensive alliance with France and Russia (1756) precipitated the SEVEN YEARS WAR (1756–63). He secured a share in the partition of Poland in 1772, but the French Revolution destroyed his French alliance.

Kauri pine, evergreen GYMNOSPERM tree native to New Zealand. It has flaky bark, bronze-green leaves and round cones. It was extensively milled by the early settlers of New Zealand. The trees made fine masts and their resin was used in the manufacture of lacquers and varnishes. The Maoris regarded the trees as forest gods and some trees lived for up to 500 years. Height: to 45m (150ft). Family: Araucariaceae. Species *Agathis australis.*

Kava, narcotic drink made from the roots of the kava plant, a variety of pepper (*Piper methysticum*) grown in many South Pacific islands. The roots are chewed or grated to produce a pulp which is placed in a bowl with water or coconut milk and allowed to ferment. Traditionally, ritual surrounded its production and it was consumed in kava ceremonies, but social and medicinal uses are also known.

Kavanagh, Patrick (1905–67), Irish poet. Entirely self-educated, as a young man he worked as a small farmer and a shoemaker. He published *Ploughman and Other Poems* (1936), his first collection of poetry, and *The Green Fool* (1938), an autobiography, before becoming a freelance journalist in Dublin. In 1955 he joined the staff of University College there. A master of rhythm, his later work includes the poem *The Great Hunger* (1942) and the verse collection *Come Dance with Kitty Stobling* (1960).

Kawabata, Yasunari (1899–1972), Japanese novelist. His best-known works, which are influenced by Western literature of the 1920s and Japanese linked verse, are *Snow Country* (1937), *Thousand Cranes* (1947) and *The Sound of the Mountain* (1954). He received the Nobel Prize in literature in 1968.

Kawasaki, city on central Honshū, Japan, on Tokyō Bay. The city suffered extensive damage from Allied bombing during WWII. It has a 12th-century temple. Industries: machinery, motor vehicles, petrochemicals, shipbuilding. Pop. (1970) 973,486.

Kay, John (1704–64), British engineer. In 1733 he patented his famous FLYING SHUTTLE which, by enabling a weaver to throw the shuttle automatically from side to side across the warp of a loom, doubled output. His invention, which was a major step in the development of automatic weaving, was seen as a threat to handloom weavers and he was forced to emigrate to France.

Kay, Ulysses Simpson (1917–), US composer who studied at the Eastman School of Music and at Yale University, under HINDEMITH. He wrote numerous works for chamber ensembles and his later compositions used QUARTAL HARMONY. Included in his works are two one-act operas and *Symphony* (1968).

Kayah State. *See* KARENS.

Kayak, CANOE of Eskimo origin, traditionally built of sealskins stretched over a wooden framework. It is decked over, apart from the cockpit, and propelled by one double-bladed oar. Silent and manoeuvrable, it is still used by Eskimos for fishing and for hunting seals. *See also* CORACLE.

Kaye, Danny (1913–), US comedian and actor, real name David Daniel Kominski. He appeared on Broadway in several plays, including *Lady in the Dark* (1940) and *Let's Face It* (1941). Among his many films are *Up in Arms* (1944), *The Secret Life of Walter Mitty* (1947), *Hans Christian Andersen* (1952) and *The Five Pennies* (1959). Between 1963–67 he appeared regularly on US television in *The Danny Kaye Show.* Since 1953 he has travelled and performed all over the world as a goodwill ambassador for UNICEF.

Kayibanda, Grégoire (1924–), first President of Rwanda (1962–73) after it gained independence from Belgium. As leader of the Hutu tribe, he treated the Tutsi minority with moderation but was deposed by Gen. HABYALIMANA in 1973.

Kayser, Heinrich Gustav Johannes (1853–1940), German physicist known for his work on the properties of sound and his discovery in 1895 of HELIUM gas in the atmosphere. He collaborated with Carl D. T. RUNGE in the development of techniques for determining the characteristic spectra of various elements.

Kayseri, city in central Turkey, at the foot of Mount Erciyas. Originally called Caesarea, it was captured by the Mongols (1243) and the Mamelukes of Egypt (1419); the city became part of the Ottoman Empire in 1515. Its modern industries include textiles, sugar and agriculture. Pop. (1973) 183,128.

Kay-Shuttleworth, Sir James Phillips (1804–77), British educationalist. In 1839 he became secretary of the newly-established Committee of the Privy Council for Education. He increased government grants for education and introduced the system of government school inspection. In 1840 he founded the Battersea Training College for teachers and introduced the pupil-teacher system of training elementary schoolteachers.

Kazakhs, Turkic-speaking Muslim people who inhabit KAZAKHSTAN, USSR, and the adjacent Sinkiang province of China. In 1916 the Kazakhs rebelled against Russia, but the 1917 Bolshevik Revolution prevented the setting up of a Western-style state. Traditionally nomadic, they have become sedentary this century within the Soviet collective farm system.

Kazakhstan (Kazachskaja SSR), constituent republic of southern USSR, bordered by China in the E and the Caspian Sea in the W; the capital is Alma-Ata. The region was gradually taken by Russia between 1730 and 1853. It became an autonomous republic in 1920 and a constituent republic in 1936. The S and E of the region are mountainous, the central area is steppe and there are lowlands in the N and W. The area produces much of the USSR's wheat and wool, and cattle raising is also important. There are large deposits of iron ore and coal, and copper, lead and zinc are also mined. Industries: oil refining, textiles, pharmaceuticals, fertilizers. Area: 2,715,099sq km (1,048,300sq miles). Pop. (1975 est.) 14,200,000.

Kazan, Elia (1909–), US author and director, *b.* Istanbul, Turkey. He was one of the founders of the Actors' Studio and won the New York Drama Critics' Award for his direction of *The Skin of Our Teeth* (1942) and a Tony Award for *JB* in 1958. His work in the cinema includes *A Tree Grows in Brooklyn* (1945), *Gentleman's Agreement* (1947) – for which he received an Academy Award, – and *On the Waterfront* (1954). He wrote two bestsellers, *America, America* (1962) – which he made into a film – (1963), and *The Arrangement* (1967), filmed in 1969.

Kazan', port and state capital of the Tatar Republic (Tatarskaja ASSR), USSR, on the River Volga. Founded in 1437, Kazan' became the capital of the Tatar khanate (1438). Conquered by IVAN IV, it became an 18th-century outpost of Russian colonization in the E. The peasant leader Pugachev burnt the city in 1773, but it was rebuilt by CATHERINE II. Both LENIN and TOLSTOY studied at the university, which was founded in 1804. Industries: electrical equipment, chemicals, footwear. Pop. 946,000.

Kazantzakis, Nikos (1885–1957), Greek politician and writer who studied law at Athens and Paris universities and directed the Greek ministry of public welfare (1919–27). He is best known for his novel *Zorba the Greek* (1946), but he also wrote poetry and analyses of the works of BERGSON and NIETZSCHE.

Kazin, Alfred (1915–), US critic of modern American literature. His first major work was *On Native Grounds* (1942); he has also published studies or edited editions of the works of F. Scott FITZGERALD, Theodore DREISER and Nathaniel HAWTHORNE. His *Bright Book of Life* (1973) is an analysis of US literature up to 1972.

Kazinczy, Ferenc (1759–1831), Hungarian writer and literary innovator who established the radical periodical *Orpheus* (1790). A vigorous champion of the Enlightenment, he was imprisoned for a time for his revolutionary activities and devoted his later life to reforming Hungarian literature. His poetry includes *Poétai epistólák* (1819).

Kea, large parrot with a crossed bill, found in the South Island, New Zealand. Its plumage is olive-green, with green and blue wings. It feeds on buds, fruit, worms and grubs. In winter it frequents sheep-rearing areas, feeding on carcasses. It is sometimes falsely accused of killing sheep. Species *Nestor notabilis.*

Kean, Edmund (1787/90–1833), British actor. His performance as Shylock in *The Merchant of Venice* (1814) launched him on a career of fiery roles, including Macbeth, Iago, Richard III and Barabbas. His last stage appearance (1833) was as Othello to the Iago of his son, Charles.

Kearney, Denis (1847–1907), US labour leader, *b.* Ireland. In 1877 he organized in California the Workingmen's Party in protest against current economic and political evils, including the use of Chinese labour. His followers – the "Sand-Lotters" – packed the state convention and influenced the 1879 Constitution. He later tried to gain support in the eastern states, but was unsuccessful.

Kearton, Cherry (1871–1940), British naturalist, photographer and author. Noted for his films and photographs of wild life, particularly of wild life in Africa and Australia, his books include *Shifting Sands of Algeria* (1924), *The Animals Come to Drink* (1932) and *The Lion's Roar* (1934).

Keaton, Buster (1895–1966), US film comic actor and director, real name Joseph Francis Keaton. His sophisticated, totally visual, slapstick style evolved from a family music-hall background and a series of two-reelers in which he first featured and later directed between 1917 and 1923. *Our Hospitality* (1923), *Seven Chances* (1925) and *The General* (1926), mainly filmed on location with an unusually perfectionist attention to period detail, are pre-eminent among the ten full-length features he released before 1928 and which established Keaton's reputation as a subtle and resourceful originator of silent screen comedy.

Keats, Ezra Jack (1916–), US author and illustrator of children's books. He was one of the first children's authors to create books that focused on children from minority groups. His books include *The Snowy Day* (1962), which was awarded the Caldecott Medal.

Keats, John (1795–1821), British poet whose short life saw the production of verse which has remained popular ever since. Originally intending to be a surgeon, he abandoned this course in his passion for poetry and because of ill-health. Despite the critical disdain with which the long poem *Endymion* (1818) was received, Keats went on to write the restrained *The Eve of St Agnes* and the haunting *La Belle Dame Sans Merci* (both 1819). At this time he also wrote the odes *On a Grecian Urn, To a Nightingale* and *On Melancholy.* He experimented with

verse drama, wrote perceptive letters and completed the long poem *Lamia* (1820) before consumption – of which he knew he was dying – overtook him.
Kebab, preparation of cooked meat, which originated in Arabic countries and is now popular in many parts of the world. Types include shish-kebab (pieces of meat cooked on a skewer) and doner-kebab (slices of mutton in unleavened bread). Both are often served with salad.
Keble, John (1792–1866), British clergyman ordained in 1816 and professor of poetry at Oxford University (1831–41). His sermon entitled *National Apostasy* (1833) is considered to have initiated the OXFORD MOVEMENT, an attempt to revive Catholic ideals within the Anglican Church. *The Christian Year*, published in 1827, and *Lyra Innocentium (Thoughts in Verse on Children)*, published in 1846, are examples of his poetic talent.
Kedah, state of Malaysia, bordered on the N and NE by Thailand. Occupations include fishing and the production of rice and rubber. Area: 9,479sq km (3,660sq miles). Pop. (1970) 955,374.
Keel, central longitudinal part of a boat's bottom; the "backbone" that gives strength to the hull. It extends from stem to stern and the ribs are attached to it. A "fin keel", used on yachts, gives stability by reducing sideways movement.
Keeler, James Edward (1857–1900), US astronomer. As head of the Allegheny Observatory (1891–98) he confirmed that SATURN's rings are not solid units but are composed of meteoric particles. He was director of the Lick Observatory (1898–1900) and using the new Crossley reflecting telescope established that a spiral GALAXY is the most common type of observable galaxy.
Keelhaul, punishment once common in the British and Dutch navies. An offender was dragged by rope underwater, below a ship and across the barnacled keel from side to side. It ceased as a practice during the 18th century and the word became naval slang for any severe reprimand.
Keeling Islands. *See* COCOS ISLANDS.
Keene, Laura (*c.* 1830–73), British actress, who emigrated to the USA in 1855, and became the USA's first woman theatre manager (of Laura Keene's Varieties Theater, New York). In 1856 she opened Laura Keene's Theater and produced and starred in many comedies and melodramas until 1863. Her company was performing Tom Taylor's comedy *Our American Cousin* at Ford's Theatre, Washington, DC, the night Abraham LINCOLN was assassinated there in 1865.
Keeper of the Great Seal, also known as Lord Keeper, originally another name for the Lord Chancellor of England. The two offices were sometimes separated after the reign of Henry II, and in 1562 became the same. The office ceased to exist after 1760, and since then the Great Seal has been kept by the Lord Chancellor.
Keeshond, Dutch dog of Arctic origin; the national dog of Holland during the 18th century. It has a fox-like face with characteristic "spectacles", and small, triangular, erect ears. The compact body is set on straight legs; the tail is curled and high-set. The long, harsh coat is grey, black and cream. Height: to 46cm (18in) at the shoulder.
Kefallinía. *See* CEPHALONIA.
Keflavík, town on the SW coast of Iceland, approx. 35km (22 miles) WSW of Reykjavík, on the SW shore of Faxa Bay. It has an international airport and a NATO base. Fishing is the major industry. Pop. (1970) 5,663.
Keino, Kipchoge ("Kip") (1940–), Kenyan athlete. He set world records in the 3,000m and 5,000m events in 1965. He won the 1,500m at the 1968 Olympics and won the 3,000m steeplechase at the Olympics in 1972.
Keita, Modibo (1915–77), political leader who advocated federation of the French West African states, became President of the federation 1959, and of Mali in 1960. He inaugurated socialist programmes but was overthrown in 1968.
Keitel, Wilhelm (1882–1946), German general. His appointment as Chief-of-Staff of the Supreme Command of the armed forces resulted from Adolf HITLER's assumption of power over the German army. He was Hitler's closest military adviser and ratified the unconditional surrender to the Allies. He was tried and executed as a war criminal.
Keith, Sir Arthur (1866–1955), British anatomist, conservator at the Royal College of Surgeons (1908) and professor of physiology at the Royal Institution, London (1918–23). He carried out work on the anatomy of the heart and applied his knowledge of general anatomy to an important study of human origins, reconstructing prehistoric man from fossil remains. His books include *The Antiquity of Man* (1915) and *A New Theory of Human Evolution* (1948).
Keith, George (*c.* 1639–1716), Scottish Quaker missionary. He was frequently imprisoned for his preaching and emigrated to Philadelphia, USA, in 1689. He was banned from preaching there in 1692, and returned to London and conformed to the Anglican Church in 1700.
Kekkonen, Urho Kaleva (1900–), President of Finland (1956–), and a lawyer, writer and sportsman. He maintained good relations with the USSR and concluded the Finnish-Soviet Treaty in 1948 – extended in 1970 – which guarantees that Finnish territory cannot be used to launch an attack on the USSR.
Kekulé von Stradoniz, Friedrich August (1829–96), German chemist who discovered the ring structure of BENZENE. He became university professor first at Ghent, and later at Bonn. He worked on the structure of organic molecules and on the concept of VALENCY, particularly with respect to benzene and other aromatic compounds.
Kelantan, state in the central Malay Peninsula, Malaysia, on the South China Sea; bounded in the N by Thailand. Ruled by Java in the 14th century, Siam in the 19th and Britain in the 20th, it became part of the Federation of Malaya in 1957, and a state of Malaysia in 1963. Area: 14,970sq km (5,780sq miles). Pop. (1970) 680,626.
Keller, Gottfried (1819–90), Swiss writer. The range of his talent is shown in a collection of ten stories, *Die Leute von Seldwyla* (1856; *The People of Seldwyla*, 1919). Among his subsequent works are *Sieben Legenden* (1872; *Seven Legends*, 1929) and his autobiographical novel *Der grüne Heinrich* (1854; *Green Henry*, 1960).
Keller, Helen Adams (1880–1968), US social worker, writer and lecturer. With the help of her teacher Anne Sullivan, she overcame the loss of sight, hearing and speech, caused by an illness contracted at the age of 19 months. In 1904 she graduated with honours from Radcliffe College. She mastered several languages and lectured throughout the world, raising funds for the training of the handicapped. Her books include *The Story of My Life* (1902), *The World I Live In* (1908), and *The Open Door* (1957).
Kellermann, François Christophe de (1735–1820), French general. Made a *maréchal de camp* in 1788, Kellermann became an army commander in 1792, and it was the union of his troops with those of Dumouriez which led to the victory of Valmy in September of that year. Kellermann became a marshal in 1804. His son was a noted cavalry commander.
Kellogg, Frank Billings (1856–1937), US diplomat. He was the Republican senator for Minnesota (1917–23), an ambassador to Britain (1923–25) and Secretary of State (1925–29). He is best known for his negotiation of the KELLOGG-BRIAND PACT in 1928. He received the Nobel Peace Prize in 1929, later becoming a judge in the Court of International Justice.
Kellogg-Briand Pact (Pact of Paris) (1928), agreement that renounced war as a means of settling international disputes. It was proposed in 1927 by the French Foreign Minister Aristide BRIAND as a treaty between France and the USA and was enlarged in 1928 by the US Secretary of State Frank B. KELLOGG to include all nations. Although 64 countries signed the pact, many qualifications were expressed, in particular about the right to wage war in self-defence. There were no provisions in the pact for enforcing it. After WWII it became part of the legal basis for the Nuremberg trials of war criminals.
Kells, Book of. *See* BOOK OF KELLS.
Kelly, Edward ("Ned") (1855–80), most famous Australian bushranger (outlaw). From 1878 he led a gang which carried out a series of robberies in Victoria and New South Wales. He was captured and hanged after a siege in Glenrowan township, during which the rest of his gang were killed. He was well-known for his use of home-made armour.
Kelly, Ellsworth (1923–), US painter, best known for his HARD-EDGE paintings, such as *Red Blue Green* (1963), and his geometrical sculptures which were manufactured industrially.
Kelly, Emmett (1898–), US circus clown, best known for his role as "Weary Willie", a character which he created as a cartoonist and brought to life in 1923.
Kelly, Gene (1912–), US dancer, choreographer, film star and director. He was a major force in musical films in the 1940s and 1950s, His greatest films, co-directed with Stanley Donen, were *On the Town* (1949), *An American in Paris* (1951) and the popular *Singin' in the Rain* (1951). They featured Kelly's exuberant, athletic dancing and revealed his ambitious directorial style.
Kelly, George (1887–1974), US actor, playwright and director. Many of his plays portray the middle-class American way of life during the 1920s. *The Torchbearers* (1922) was his first Broadway success, followed by the even more successful comedy *The Show-Off* (1924). *Craig's Wife* (1925) won him the Pulitzer Prize and was made into the film *Harriet Craig* (1950).
Kelly, Sir Gerald (1879–1972), British portrait painter, elected to the Royal Academy in 1930. In 1945 he painted official portraits of King George VI and the Queen. He succeeded Sir Alfred MUNNINGS as president of the Royal Academy (1949–54).
Kelly, Grace Patricia (1929–), US film actress until 1956, when she married Prince Rainier of Monaco. She began her film career in 1951 with *Fourteen Hours*. She appeared in *High Noon* (1952) and in 1954 won an Academy Award for her performance in *The Country Girl*. She retired from show business when she got married.
Kelly, Hugh (1739–77), Irish playwright. After moving to London, he edited several magazines. His plays include the comedies *False Delicacy* (1768), *A Word for The Wise* (1770) and *The School for Wives* (1773).
Kelly, John B., Sr (1891–1960), US oarsman who won the Olympic single sculls (1920) and double sculls (1920, 1924). Barred by his own professional status from competing at the amateur Henley Regatta, he had the satisfaction of seeing his son win the Diamond Sculls in 1947 and 1949.
Kelly, William (1811–88), US steelmaker. In *c.* 1850 he invented a method of converting molten iron into steel by oxidization. The process, later known as the BESSEMER PROCESS, was taken up and patented by the British engineer Sir Henry Bessemer in 1856.
Kelmscott Press, founded (1891) by William MORRIS at Hammersmith, London, the first of a number of private presses undertaking experimental work which gradually transformed the standard of commercial typography. Morris based his type on 15th- and 16th-century prototypes, designing three typefaces: the Golden, the Troy and the Chaucer, the last of which was used for the Kelmscott Press edition of *The Works of Geoffrey Chaucer* (1896), its masterpiece.
Kelp, any of several large brown seaweeds commonly found on Atlantic and Pacific coasts, a type of brown ALGA. A typical kelp has a root-like holdfast, stem-like stipes and leaf-like blades. Formerly a principal source of iodine and potassium compounds, it is now used in a number of industrial processes. Giant kelp (*Macro-*

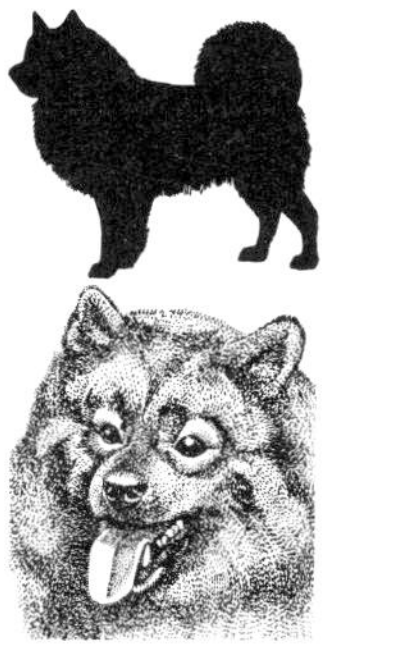

Keeshond; the markings on the eyes of this dog make it look as if it is wearing spectacles.

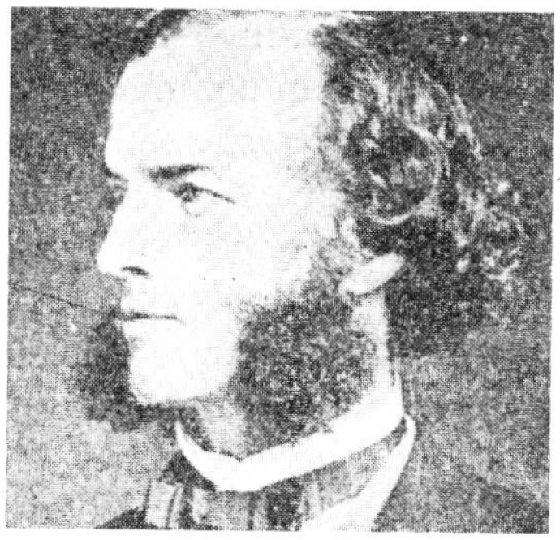

Kekulé von Stradonitz made vital contributions to the theory of chemical structure.

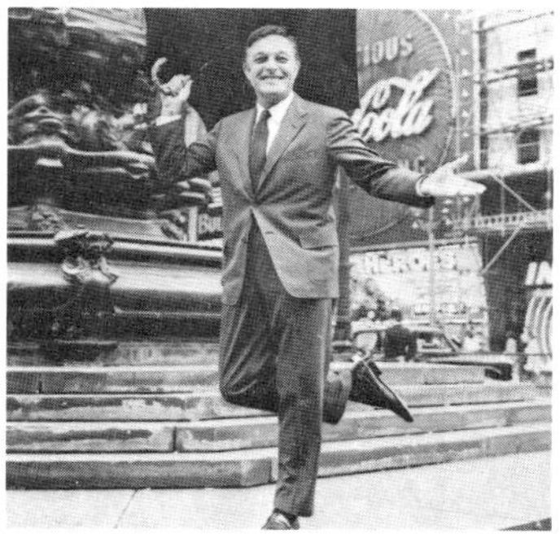

Gene Kelly, no stranger to rain, poses by the statue of Eros in London's Picadilly Circus.

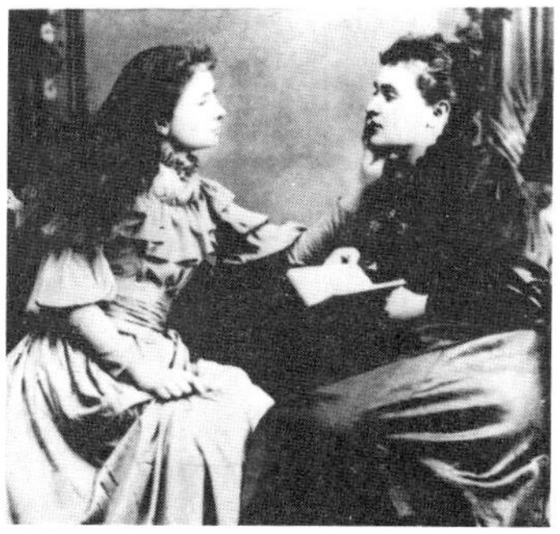

Hellen Keller, with her teacher Anne Sullivan, who communicated via the sense of touch.

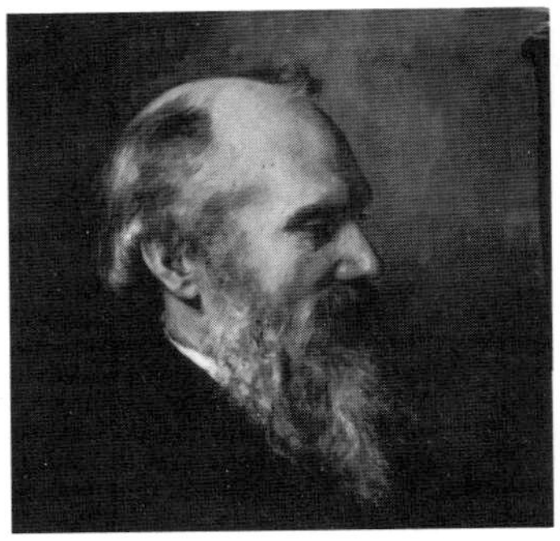

Lord Kelvin's work on the first transatlantic cable earned him a knighthood.

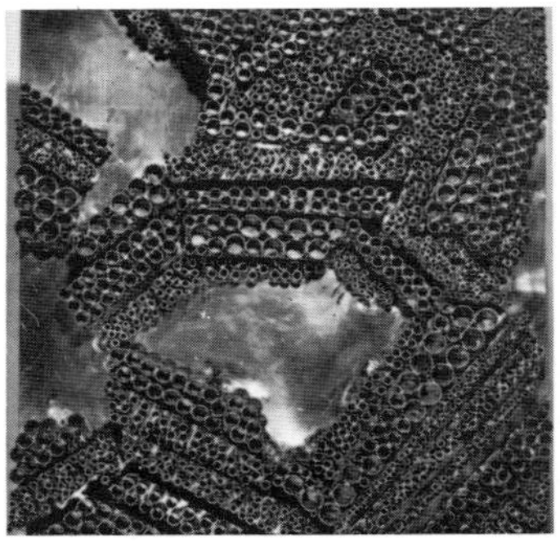

Zoltán Kemény's sculptures produce patterns from the sections of metal tubes.

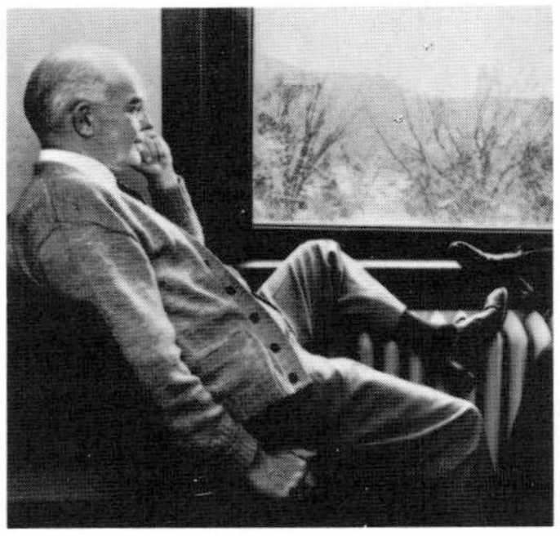

Edward Calvin Kendall won a Nobel Prize in 1950 for his work in isolating cortisone.

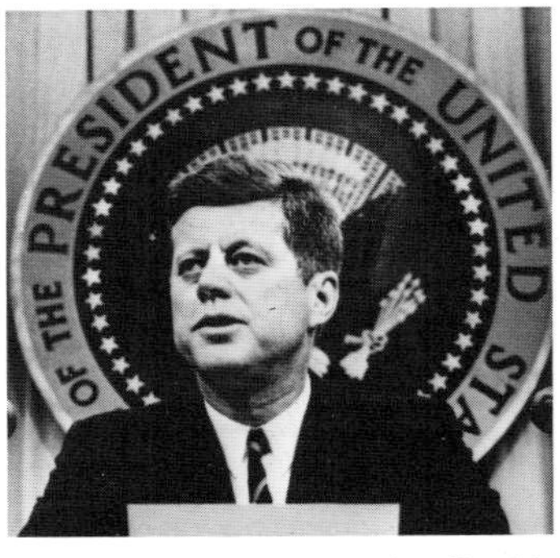

President Kennedy announcing Russia's withdrawal of the Cuban missiles.

cystis) exceeds 46m (150ft) in length. *See also* PE p.*134*; NW p.47.

Kelsen, Hans (1881–1973), US legal philosopher, *b.* Czechoslovakia. He contributed towards the 1920 Austrian constitution and taught at Harvard Law School (1940–42) and the University of California (1942–52). He was noted for his "pure theory of law", which opposes both natural law theory and sociological jurisprudence. His writings include *Legal Technique in International Law* (1939) and *The Law of the United Nations.*

Kelsey, Henry (1670–1729), English explorer and fur trader who began work with the Hudson's Bay Company in 1687 and explored Saskatchewan in 1690. A governor of several important trading posts between 1714–22, he sought a north-west passage, and was captured by the French in 1692. He returned to England in 1722 and died in unknown circumstances.

Kelvin, William Thomson Kelvin, 1st Baron (1824–1907), Scottish physicist and mathematician after whom the absolute scale of temperature is named. The success of the Atlantic submarine telephone cable was due to his researches into the transmission of electric currents for which, in 1866, he was knighted. In THERMODYNAMICS he was able to resolve conflicting interpretations of the first and second laws. He devised a method of measuring the earth's age and published more than 600 scientific papers. The Kelvin temperature scale has absolute zero (−273°C) as its zero point, each degree is the same size as the Celsius degree and the freezing point of water is 273°K. *See also* MM pp.225, 226; SU pp.94, *96*.

Kemal, Yashar (1922–), Turkish novelist. After a number of occupations he worked on the newspaper *Cumhuriyet* (Republic) and published a book of short stories, *Yellow Heat* (1952). His first novel *Mehmed, My Hawk* (1955) won the Varlik Prize. In 1956 Kemal's work explored the experience of the Turkish peasant, using elements of myth and legend and developing themes of such breadth that he was compared with Tolstoy and Hardy. Holding strong political beliefs he was imprisoned for alleged Communist propaganda in the early 1950s and later in 1968, but was released on both occasions.

Kemal, Mustafa. *See* ATATÜRK, KEMAL.

Kemal Atatürk. *See* ATATÜRK, KEMAL.

Kemble, British family of actors of whom the most famous was Sarah SIDDONS, the eldest daughter of Roger (1722–1802), a travelling actor, nine of whose twelve children worked in the theatre. They included John Philip (1757–1823) who, after abandoning ideas of the priesthood, became a tragedian and successfully managed Drury Lane and Covent Garden; Stephen (1758–1822), a large and popular comic actor; and Charles (1775–1854), who was the first to introduce appropriately historical costumes and sets onto the English stage and who successfully played Malcolm to his brother John's Macbeth and excelled in such secondary roles. Frances Ann ("Fanny") (1809–93), the daughter of Charles, made a sensational debut as Juliet at Covent Garden in 1829 and maintained such performances in popular classical parts. She retired from the stage in 1847. Her sister Adelaide (1814–79) sang in opera; her brother John Mitchell (1807–57) was a Cambridge Anglo-Saxon scholar.

Kemény, Baron Zsigmond (1814–75), Hungarian novelist and political journalist. He became editor of the daily newspaper *Pesti Napló* and champion of liberalism and individuality. His novels, such as *Zord Idok (Grim Times)* (1862), are pessimistic in tone.

Kemény, Zoltán (1908–65), Hungarian-Swiss sculptor who also studied painting and architecture. From the 1950s he concentrated on reliefs into which he introduced mass-produced metal articles as well as archaeological and mineralogical materials; in doing so he created what has been regarded as a rhythmic and poetic sculptural style.

Kempe, Margery (*c.* 1373–1440), English writer and mystic. Chiefly famous as the author of probably the first known autobiography in English, *The Book of Margery Kempe*, which was not published in complete form until 1940, she turned to religion after her first pregnancy resulted in an attack of madness, cured by a vision of Christ. She left her husband in 1413 and lived a religious life, travelling to the Holy Land, Italy and Germany before returning to write her autobiography in 1432–36.

Kempe, Rudolph (1910–76), German conductor. Important posts included those with the Bavarian State Opera (1952–61) and the Royal Philharmonic Orchestra, London (1961–75). Renowned for his interpretations of the music of Richard Strauss and Richard Wagner, he was responsible for historic productions of the *Ring* cycle and *Lohengrin* at Bayreuth in the 1960s.

Kempeneer, Pieter (1503–*c.* 1580), Flemish MANNERIST painter and tapestry designer. He studied and painted in Italy for 10 years before settling in Seville, Spain (*c.* 1537), where he became known as Pedro de Campaña. His masterpieces include *Descent from the Cross* (*c.* 1540) and *Presentation in the Temple* (1555), both in Seville Cathedral. In 1563 he returned to Brussels, where he became director of the tapestry factory.

Kempff, Wilhelm (1895–), German pianist and composer. From 1929 he toured throughout the world and received high acclaim for his sensitive interpretations of the music of Beethoven, Schubert and Schumann. His compositions include four operas, two symphonies and various chamber and choral works.

Kempis, Thomas à (*c.* 1379–1471), German spiritual writer. Ordained in 1413, he remained in the same monastery for nearly all the rest of his life. In addition to copying manuscipts, he edited *The Imitation of Christ*, his most famous work, and wrote numerous treatises on the life of the soul. These include *Soliloquium Animae*, concerned with individual spiritual devotion, and *De Tribus Tabernaculis*, which deals with chastity, poverty and humility. He also wrote biographies of many saints.

Kemp-Welch, Lucy Elizabeth (1869–1958), British animal painter who gained popularity both in Britain and abroad with her pictures of horses, such as *Horses Bathing in the Sea*. In 1914 she became the first president of the Society of Animal Painters.

Kemsley, James Gomer Berry, 1st Viscount (1883–1968), British newspaper proprietor. In 1926, with his brother Lord Camrose, he obtained control of Amalgamated Press. He was chairman of Allied Newspapers, later Kemsley Newspapers (1937–59) and editor-in-chief of the *Sunday Times* (1937–59) which he sold to Lord THOMSON in 1959.

Ken, Bishop Thomas (1637–1711), British churchman and religious writer. After ordination, he taught at Winchester College, writing the two famous hymns *Awake my Soul and With the Sun* and *Glory to thee, my God, This Night*. As King's Chaplain, he was made Bishop of Bath and Wells in 1685 and gave absolution to Charles II on his deathbed. In 1691 he was deprived of his see for declining to take the Oath of Allegiance.

Kendal, William Hunter (1843–1917), British actor-manager, real name Grimston, who in 1874 married Margaret ("Madge") Shafto Robertson (1848–1935). By their exemplary acting partnership they helped to raise the status of the Victorian acting profession and while Madge's naturalistic dramatic talents, in such contemporary works as SARDOU's *Dora*, often stole the limelight from William, he acted as an astute manager and nurtured the skills of many young actors in their company. They made regular provincial tours between 1874 and 1908, when both Kendals agreed to retire.

Kendall, Edward Calvin (1886–1972), US chemist who worked on the biological effects of the hormones of the cortex of the ADRENAL GLANDS, in particular the steroid hormone cortisone, which he isolated. He shared the 1950 Nobel Prize in physiology and medicine with Philip Showalter HENCH and Tadeus REICHSTEIN.

Kendall, Henry Clarence (1839–82), Australian poet. His poems have a strong lyrical quality, especially in his descriptions of the forests and plains of New South Wales. *Leaves from Australian Forests* (1869) is generally considered to be his best book of verse.

Kendo, martial art, traditional Japanese form of fencing. The two contestants wear protective armour and fight with swords usually made of bamboo. For formal demonstrations real swords were used. Footwork with short, fast, gliding steps is an important part of the technique.

Kendrew, John Cowdery (1917–), British biochemist who determined the structure of myoglobin, a protein in muscle. Using X-ray DIFFRACTION analysis he was able to elucidate the arrangement of amino acids in the myoglobin helix. For this work he shared the 1962 Nobel Prize in chemistry with Max F. PERUTZ.

Keneally, Thomas Michael (1935–), Australian novelist. His first book was *The Place at Whitton* (1964). *Bring Larks and Heroes* (1967) and *Three Cheers for the Paraclete* (1968) each won the Miles Franklin Award.

Kenilworth castle, near town of the same name in Warwickshire, England. Begun in 1120, the castle passed to the crown in 1359. In 1563, Elizabeth I gave it to Robert Dudley, Earl of Leicester, who turned it into his own private stronghold. Sir Walter SCOTT's novel, *Kenilworth*, deals with this part of the castle's history.

Keniston, Kenneth (1930–), US psychologist. Professor of psychiatry at Yale University School of Medicine since 1962, he has written about US college campuses in the 1960s and 1970s. His books include *The Uncommitted* (1965), *Young Radicals* (1968) and *Youth and Dissent* (1971).

Kennan, George Frost (1904–), US diplomat and author who was largely responsible for the US State Department's policy of containment of the USSR. He was appointed ambassador to the USSR in 1952, and was later ambassador to Yugoslavia (1961–63). He won a Pulitzer Prize for *Memoirs 1925–50* in 1967.

Kennedy, Edward Moore (1932–), US senator, and the youngest of three brothers who were all senators. He was elected to finish his brother John's term as senator from Massachusetts in 1962. Democratic whip from 1969 to 1971, he worked for liberal legislation, particularly in health and welfare. Since his brothers John and Robert were assassinated, he has frequently been mentioned as a presidential candidate.

Kennedy, James (*c.* 1408–65), Bishop of St Andrews and founder of St Salvator's College, Scotland. As adviser to JAMES II, he opposed the growing influence of the DOUGLAS family in Scotland.

Kennedy, John Fitzgerald (1917–63), 35th President of the USA; he held the office from 1961–63. He was the son of Joseph P. Kennedy and the brother of Robert F. Kennedy and Edward M. Kennedy. After distinguished service in the navy in WWII, he was elected to the House of Representatives as a Democrat in 1946. He served there until he entered the Senate in 1953. He made an unsuccessful bid to become vice-presidential candidate in 1956 and immediately began preparations for the presidential nomination of 1960, selecting Lyndon B. JOHNSON as proposed Vice-President. He defeated Richard M. NIXON by a small margin, and at 43 became the second-youngest President. He called for increased federal involvement in civil rights, education and health services. It was foreign affairs, however, that occupied most of his attention. His most spectacular success occurred in Oct. 1962 when, during the CUBAN MISSILE CRISIS, he forced the USSR to remove its missiles from Cuba. In Nov. 1963, Kennedy embarked on a political tour of Texas and was assassinated in Dallas. The WARREN COMMISSION later found that the sniper, Lee Harvey Oswald, had no connection with any conspiracy. *See also* BAY OF PIGS INVASION; VIETNAM WAR.

Kennedy, Margaret (1896–1967), British

writer whose second novel, *The Constant Nymph* (1924), established her reputation and was later dramatized and filmed. Her other light works of fiction included *The Midas Touch* (1938) and *Troy Chimneys* (1953), which was awarded the James Tait Black Memorial Prize. Other works included a biography, *Jane Austen* (1950), and a volume of film criticism, *The Mechanized Muse* (1942).

Kennedy, Robert Francis (1925–68), US lawyer and political leader. In 1960 he managed the successful presidential campaign of his brother John F. Kennedy and became US attorney general from 1961 to 1964, a post in which he vigorously enforced civil rights laws and investigated corruption in organized labour. After his brother's assassination, he left the cabinet and was elected senator for New York in 1964. While a candidate for the Democratic presidential nomination, he was assassinated after a speech in Los Angeles in June 1968.

Kennedy, Cape. *See* CAPE CANAVERAL.

Kennedy Round (1964–67), trade and tariff talks held in Geneva among 54 countries under the General Agreement on Tariffs and Trade (GATT). Named after President John F. Kennedy, who proposed them, the talks were GATT's sixth round of trade negotiations. They resulted in a reduction for the participants of an average 35% in the tariffs on most industrial goods.

Kennelly, Arthur Edwin (1861–1939), US electrical engineer. In 1902, after Guglielmo MARCONI's experiments with radio waves, Kennelly noticed that the waves could reach beyond the Earth's horizon. He proposed that they did this by bouncing off a layer of ions high in the atmosphere. Physicist Oliver Heaviside made a similar proposition, and the layer is called the Kennelly-HEAVISIDE LAYER.

Kennelly-Heaviside layer. *See* HEAVISIDE LAYER.

Kenneth, name of two kings of Scotland. Kenneth I (*d.*858) was the founder of the Scottish dynasty. He defeated the Picts in 846 and moved the seat of government to Scone. Kenneth II (*d.*995), the son of MALCOLM I, took the throne in 971, extended his kingdom N of the River Tay and established his authority over central Scotland.

Kennington, Eric Henri (1888–1960), British painter and sculptor, appointed Official War Artist (1916–19 and 1940–43). He sculpted the British memorial at Soissons, the memorial to Thomas Hardy at Dorchester and bronzes of T.E. Lawrence, including those in St Paul's Cathedral and the Tate Gallery, London.

Kennington Oval. *See* OVAL, THE.

Kenny, Elizabeth (1886–1952), Australian nurse who became famous for her method of stimulating muscles affected by infantile paralysis (POLIOMYELITIS). Initially the method was not received enthusiastically by orthodox physicians, but by the 1940s her procedures had become generally accepted.

Kenny, Seán (1932–73), Irish stage designer who trained as an architect with Frank Lloyd WRIGHT and later designed many notable productions at Stratford-upon-Avon, Chichester and the National Theatre. His revolutionary contribution to theatre design, however, comprised elaborate and adaptable automated sets which moved onstage while performances were in progress and which were used to best effect in the musicals *Oliver!* (1960) and *Blitz* (1962).

Kent, Edward George Alexander Edmund, 2nd duke of. *See* ROYAL FAMILY.

Kent, James (1763–1847), US jurist and legal scholar who was twice elected to the New York legislature. He also served as the first professor of law at Columbia from 1793 to 1798 and as chief justice of the New York Supreme Court from 1804 to 1814. *Commentaries on American Law* (1826–30) was his most important work.

Kent, Rockwell (1882–1971), US painter, author and illustrator whose pictorial works realistically depict vivid dramatic scenes. He lived in Alaska, Newfoundland and Greenland and often painted the inhabitants at work. Three of his best books, known for their harmony of text and illustration, are *Wilderness* (1920), *Voyaging Southward* (1924) and *Greenland Journal* (1962).

Kent, William (1684–1748), English architect, interior designer and painter. He was an exponent of the PALLADIAN style. His best-known works are in London: the Horse Guards Building in Whitehall, the Royal Mews and 44 Berkeley Square.

Kent and Strathearn, Edward Augustus, Duke of (1776–1820), 4th son of GEORGE III. After serving in Gibraltar as Colonel and then Governor, he married Princess Mary Louisa Victoria of Saxe-Coburg-Gotha in 1818 and they produced an heir to the throne; the future Queen VICTORIA was born to them in 1819.

Kent, county in SE England, S of the Thames estuary and NW of the Strait of Dover. Apart from the North Downs, the area is mainly low-lying, with Romney Marsh in the SE. It is drained by the rivers Medway and Stour. Cereals, hops, fruit and vegetables are grown and sheep and cattle are reared. The chief industries are paper making, shipbuilding, chemicals and brewing. The county town is Maidstone. Area: 3,732sq km (1,441sq miles). Pop. (1976) 1,448,100.

Kentigern, Saint (*c.*518–*c.*603), also known as Mungo, which probably means "dear". The first Bishop of Glasgow, he was forced by the pagans to flee to Wales *c.*553, took refuge with St DAVID and founded the monastery of St Asaph. Returning to Scotland in 573, he founded Glasgow Cathedral.

Kentner, Louis (1905–), British pianist and composer who studied at the Royal Academy of Music in Budapest, then embarked on a concert career. His repertoire included works by 20th-century Hungarian composers such as Béla BARTÓK and Zoltán KODÁLY, several of whose pieces he was the first to perform.

Kenton, Simon (1755–1836), US pioneer who was an Indian scout for the governor of Virginia in 1774 and later a scout for Daniel BOONE, helping to fight both the Indians and the British. He was known for his bravery and resourcefulness and once saved Boone's life. He later served as a brigadier general of militia and fought in Kentucky's contingent during the War of 1812.

Kenton, Stanley Newcomb ("Stan") (1912–), US bandleader and composer who led his first band in 1941 and became known nationally with his hit theme *Artistry in Rhythm* in 1945. He continued to lead bands through the 1960s and has promoted the careers of many other jazz musicians and composers.

Kentucky, state in SE central USA. Most of the area consists of rolling plains, including the Bluegrass country for which Kentucky is famous. In the SE the Cumberland Mts dominate a rugged plateau region. The state is drained chiefly by the Ohio and Tennessee rivers. Tobacco is the chief crop, followed by hay, maize and soya beans. Cattle are reared and Kentucky is noted for breeding thoroughbred racehorses. The main industries are electrical equipment, food processing, machinery, chemicals and primary metals. Kentucky is one of the major producers of coal in the country. The main cities are Frankfort, the state capital, Lexington and Louisville.

The region was the first W of the Allegheny Mts to be settled. Daniel BOONE blazed the Wilderness Road from Virginia and North Carolina through the Cumberland Gap in SE Kentucky, and thousands of settlers followed this route. The territory was admitted to the Union in 1792. A border state between the North and the South, its loyalties were divided at the outbreak of the AMERICAN CIVIL WAR. Kentuckians fought in both the Union and Confederate armies and the state was invaded by both. Area: 104,623sq km (40,395sq miles). Pop. (1975 est.) 3,396,000. *See also* MW p.175.

Kentucky Derby. *See* DERBY.

Kenya, independent nation on the E coast of Africa. Most of the population are dependent on agriculture although only a small proportion of the land can be cultivated. The chief cash crops are coffee, tea and sisal. Since independence in 1963, manufacturing has increased with the aid of foreign investment. Tourism is of great importance to the economy. The capital is Nairobi. Area: 582,646sq km (224,960sq miles). Pop. (1975 est.) 13,349,000. *See* MW p.115.

Kenya, Mount, snow-capped, extinct volcanic mountain in central Kenya, second highest mountain in Africa. The fertile slopes are cultivated by the Kikuyu people; at an altitude of between 1,525 and 3,660m (5,000 and 12,000ft) the slopes are forested and inhabited by a variety of big game animals. The highest peak is Batian, rising to 5,200m (17,058ft).

Kenyatta, Jomo (*c.* 1893–), President of Kenya. He entered politics to defend his own tribe, the Kikuyu, and black African rights. He was imprisoned in 1953 for Mau Mau terrorism, exiled and then elected president of the Kenya African National Union (1960). He helped to gain Kenya's independence from Britain in 1963 and became president in 1964, suppressing opposition and outlawing opposing political parties.

Kenyon, Dame Kathleen Mary (1906–), British archaeologist. While Director of the British School of Archaeology in Jerusalem between 1951 and 1966 she showed that the walls of JERICHO, previously associated with JOSHUA, had been built at various periods and that a settlement had existed there in the 7th century BC. Her books include *Digging up Jericho* (1957), *Archaeology in the Holy Land* (1960) and *Digging up Jerusalem* (1974).

Kepler, Johannes (1571–1630), German astronomer who in 1609 put forward the theory that the planets travel round the Sun in elliptical orbits. He was assistant to the Danish astronomer Tycho BRAHE and, on Brahe's death, used his teacher's observations of the positions of the stars and the movements of the planets to formalize three fundamental laws of planetary motion, on which Isaac NEWTON later based his theory of gravitational force, and on which modern astronomy is based. Kepler also revolutionized optics with his ray theory of light to explain vision. *See also* SU pp.*25*, 164–165, *164*, 268.

Kepler's laws, three laws of planetary motion, formulated by Johannes KEPLER and published between 1609 and 1618. The first law states that the orbit of a planet is an ellipse, with the Sun at one of the foci. The second and third laws state that a planet moves fastest when closest to the Sun, and that the SIDEREAL PERIOD of a planet is related to its distance from the Sun. *See also* SU pp.164–165.

Kerala, state of SW India, on the Arabian Sea; Trivandrum is the capital. It is one of India's smallest states and the most densely populated. It was formed in 1956 and a year later elected a Communist government. The central government regained power in 1959, but in the 1967 elections the Communist Party again came into power. Fishing is important, and chief products include rubber, tea, coconuts, cashew nuts, ivory, teak and minerals. Area: 38,864sq km (15,005sq miles). Pop. (1971) 21,347,375.

Keratin, fibrous protein present in large amounts in the superficial cells of the skin, where it serves as a protective layer. Hair and finger nails are made up of modified epidermal cells filled with keratin, which is also the basis of claws, horns and feathers in animals. *See also* MS p.60, *60*.

Keratitis, inflammation of the cornea of the eye. Among its many causes are infection, contact with irritants and physical injury.

Kerekou, Lt.-Col., Mathieu, political and military figure of Benin (formerly Dahomey). He led a military coup in 1972, to become chief of state.

Kerensky, Alexander Feodorovich (1881–1970), Russian political figure and head of the provisional government from July to Nov. 1917. Elected to the DUMA as a moderate socialist in 1912, he became prime minister in July 1917, shortly after

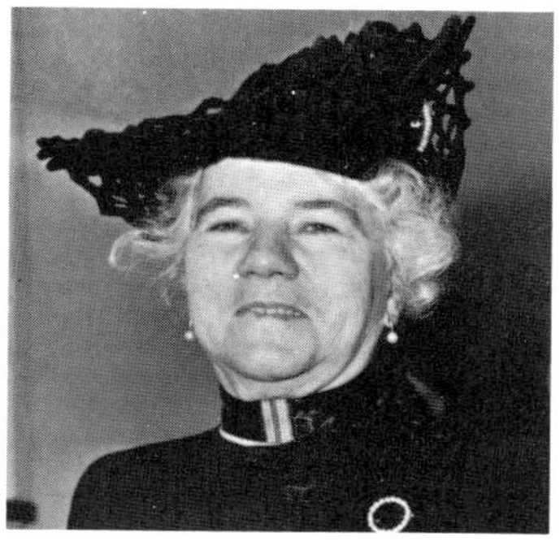

Sister Elizabeth Kenny travelled the world to explain her method of treating polio.

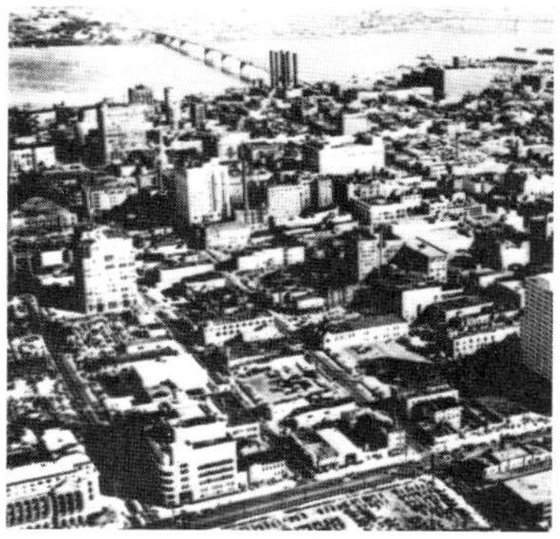

Kentucky; a view of Louisville showing the Ohio River.

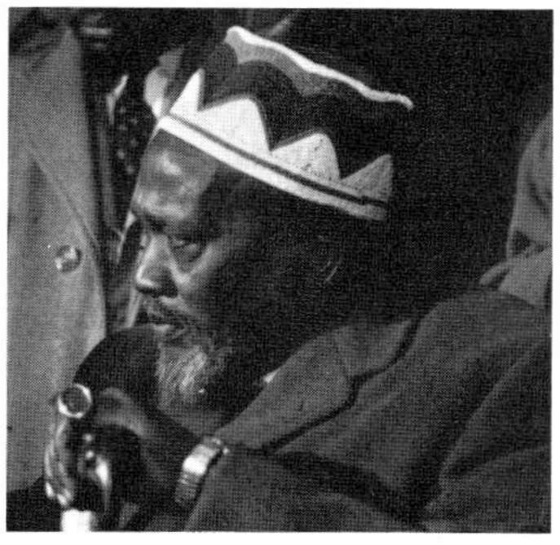

Jomo Kenyatta was Kenya's first president after the country gained independence.

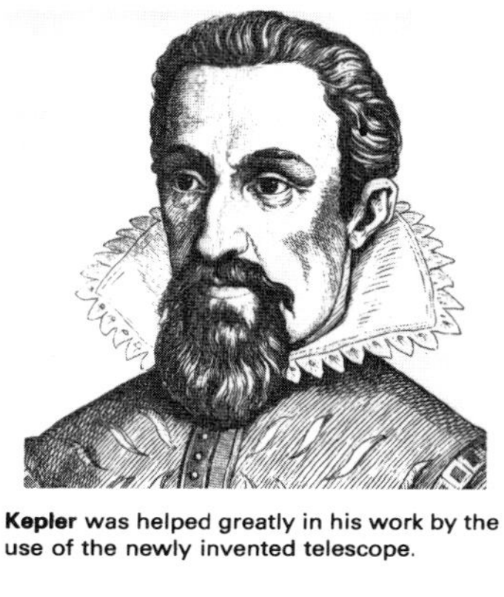

Kepler was helped greatly in his work by the use of the newly invented telescope.

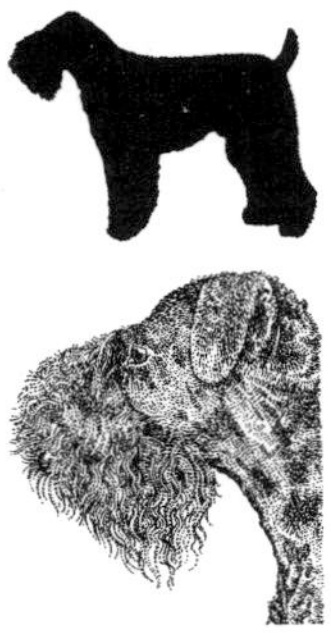

Kerry blue terriers were bred in Ireland as sheepdogs and to destroy small rodents.

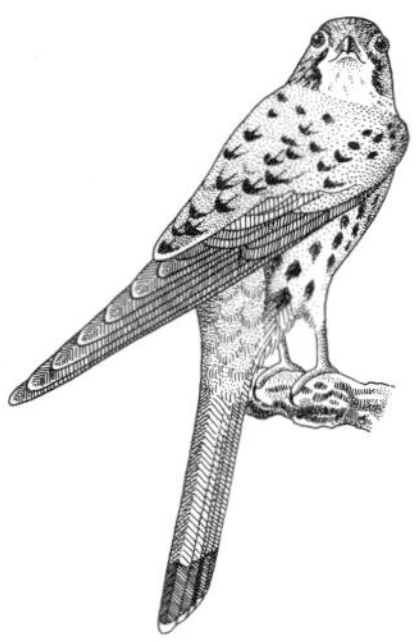

Kestrels are small birds of prey which hover in the wind scanning the ground for food.

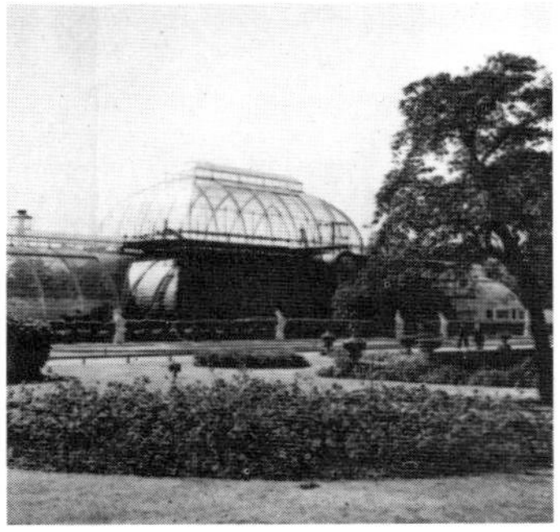

Kew Gardens covers an area of nearly 300 acres on the banks of the River Thames.

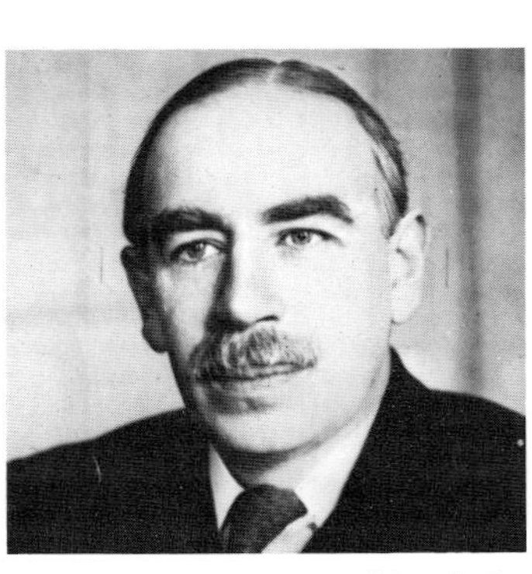

John Maynard Keynes changed his orthodox economic views after the depression.

the overthrow of the tsar. He suppressed KORNILOV's uprising but had to flee after the Bolshevik Revolution of Nov. 1917. *See also* HC2 p.196, *196.*
Kerkira, Kerkyra. *See* CORFU.
Kermadec Islands, group of volcanic islands in the s Pacific Ocean; a dependency of New Zealand since 1887. Sunday Island is the largest and only populated island of the group. Total area: approx. 34sq km (13sq miles). Pop. (1974) 9.
Kermānshāh, city in w Iran situated on the main route from Teheran to Baghdad. It is a trade centre for the surrounding agricultural region which produces cereals and fruits. The city's manufactures include carpets and textiles. Pop. (1971 est.) 190,000.
Kern, Jerome (1885–1945), US songwriter and a leading composer of film and show music, including *Sally* (1920), which launched the song *Look for the Silver Lining*, and *Roberta* (1933), which introduced *Smoke Gets in Your Eyes.* His outstanding musical is *Showboat* (staged 1927; filmed 1936, 1959), which contained the song *Ol' Man River.* His style influenced Richard RODGERS and George GERSHWIN.
Kerosene (paraffin), distilled petroleum product heavier than petrol but lighter than diesel fuel. Kerosene, known historically as an illuminant (paraffin oil), is now used in camping stoves, tractor fuels and turbine fuels for jet and turboprop aircraft. *See also* MM p.81, *81.*
Kerouac, Jack (1922–69), US poet and novelist whose *On the Road* (1957) is considered a pre-eminent work of the BEAT GENERATION. It drew the attention of the public to a subculture of poets, mystics, folksingers and eccentrics. He became a cult figure and a leader in the search for an alternative life-style.
Kerr, Deborah Jane (1921–), British actress who worked mainly in the USA where her refined beauty and formal diction won her roles requiring moral fervour and restrained passion. Her notable film successes, for which she was six times nominated for Oscars, include *Tea and Sympathy* (1956) *The King and I* (1956), *Separate Tables* (1958), *The Innocents* (1961) and *The Arrangement* (1970). Her most powerful performance was perhaps that of the lonely, susceptible army wife in *From Here to Eternity* (1953). Successful London stage performances have included roles in *The Day After the Fair* (1972) and *Candida* (1977).
Kerr, Sir John Robert (1914–), Australian lawyer and public official. He was deputy president of the Trades Practices Tribunal (1966–72), a judge of the Commonwealth Industrial Court and of the Supreme Court of the Australian Central Territories (1966–72), Chief Justice of the Supreme Court of New South Wales (1972–74) and Governor General (1974–77). He created controversy over the role of Governors General in COMMONWEALTH COUNTRIES when, without precedent, he dismissed the Labor government in office (under Gough WHITLAM), in 1975 and precipitated a general election.
Kerr, Walter Francis (1913–), US drama critic for the New York *Herald Tribune* 91951–66 and the New York *Times* from 1966. He wrote the revue *Touch and Go* (1949) and the musical, *Goldilocks* (1958).
Kerry, county in sw Republic of Ireland, in Munster province, on the Atlantic coast. It is a mountainous region with an indented coastline and many lakes, including the Lakes of Killarney. Oats and potatoes are grown and sheep and cattle raised. Industries: tourism, fishing, peat cutting, footwear, woollen goods. The main towns are Tralee, the county town, and Killarney. Area: 4,700sq km (1,815sq miles). Pop. (1971) 112,940.
Kerry blue terrier, working dog bred in Ireland. It has a long head and triangular folded ears. The body, with its short, straight back, is set on powerful legs, and the tail is short. The soft, dense coat is any shade of grey-blue. Height: to 49cm (19.5in) at the shoulder.
Kersh, Gerald (1911–68), US novelist, *b.* Britain. After serving in WWII he wrote *They Die With Their Boots Clean* (1941) and *The Nine Lives of Bill Nelson* (1941) about his experiences. He wrote many other novels, horrific and forceful, and became a US citizen in 1959.
Kesey, Ken (1935–), US novelist who wrote *One Flew Over the Cuckoo's Nest* (1962) about the inmates of a mental hospital. It was made into a highly successful play and film.
Kesselring, Albert (1885–1960), German general. He was air chief of staff from 1936 and commanded air operations in the early years of WWII. He became supreme commander in Italy in 1943 and of the western front in 1945. Convicted as a war criminal, he served five years of a life sentence before he was released.
Kesten, Hermann (1900–), German novelist whose works include *Joseph sucht die Freiheit* (1927; *Joseph Breaks Free,* 1930) and *Der Scharlatan* (1932; "The Charlatan"), a novel attacking Hitler. As a result of the latter book, he was forced to flee from Germany, first going to The Netherlands and then the USA.
Kesteven, The Parts of, region in E England, one of three administrative districts into which Lincolnshire was divided until 1973. It occupied the sw region of the county, with its administrative centre at Sleaford.
Kestrel, also called windhover, small FALCON that lives mainly in Europe, and hovers over its prey before attacking. It feeds mainly on rodents, insects and small birds. Length: 30cm (12in). Species *Falco tinnunculus.*
Keswick Convention, annual summer meeting at Keswick, in England, of evangelical Christians for prayer and Bible study. It was first held in 1875.
Ket, Robert. *See* KETT, ROBERT.
Ketch, John ("Jack") (*d.* 1686), public hangman of England from 1663. He hanged Lord William Russell and the Duke of Monmouth. Such was his fame that the name "Jack Ketch" was used to describe all hangmen for the next two centuries.
Ketch, small two-masted sailing boat used in coastal waters for trade, fishing and pleasure. Rigged fore and aft, it is identifiable from the mizzenmast's position forward of the rudderhead.
Ketchwayo. *See* CETEWAYO.
Ketone bodies, three chemical compounds: acetoacetic acid, β-hydroxybutyric acid and acetone. When present in the blood in high concentrations, they increase the blood's acidity. This occurs in starvation, DIABETES MELLITUS and low-carbohydrate high-fat diet and is known as ketosis. The ketone bodies are products of poor carbohydrate metabolism, and they accumulate in the body tissue and fluids, especially the urine.
Ketones. *See* ALDEHYDES: KETONE BODIES.
Kett, Robert (*d.* 1549), English peasant leader. He was a tanner of an old Norfolk family and led about 12,000 men who gathered at Norwich in 1549 to protest against enclosure. Although their demands were moderate, the rebels were attacked and routed in August by a mercenary army under the Earl of Warwick. Kett was executed as a traitor.
Kettledrum. *See* TIMPANI.
Kettle hole, steep-sided basin formed when a chunk of ice left behind by a receding glacier is covered by rocks and debris previously pushed forward by the glacier. The ice melts and the rocks fall through, creating a kettle-shaped depression. *See also* PE pp.116–117, *116.*
Kew Gardens, official name for Royal Botanic Gardens, collection of plants and trees in sw London. Founded in 1760 by George III's mother, they were given to the nation by Queen Victoria in 1840. Much plant research is carried out there. The gardens include three plant museums, a herbarium and some of the world's largest plant houses, particularly the Palm House (1844–48) and Temperate House (1862, 1899 and 1925). There is also a Chinese pagoda 50m (165ft) high, built in 1761. *See also* NW p.*253.*
Key, Ellen Karoline Sofia (1849–1926), Swedish writer and feminist. Although an advocate of political equality and education for women, she criticized those feminists who insisted that men and women were emotionally and physically equal, emphasizing the importance of motherhood and the home.
Key, Francis Scott (1779–1843), US poet who wrote the US national anthem, *The Star Spangled Banner,* while watching the shelling of Ft McHenry in 1814. The anthem, which was nationally adopted in 1931, first appeared anonymously as a poem, *In Defence of Fort M'Henry.*
Key, in music, term used to indicate tonality in composition, based on one of the major or minor scales. The concept implies relationships between the notes of the scale and the chords built on them. The key of a piece of music is indicated by the key signature at the left hand end of the stave. The key of a passage may, however, change by the addition of accidentals before prescribed notes, which may then define a MODULATION.
Keyboard instruments, large and varied group of musical instruments played by pressing keys on a keyboard. Notes are sounded either by hitting or plucking a string (as in the PIANO or HARPSICHORD), passing air through a pipe or reed (as in the ORGAN or ACCORDION), or electronically (as in the moog synthesizer).
Keyes, Frances Parkinson (1885–1970), US biographer and novelist. She is chiefly famous for her novels, which include *Queen Anne's Lace* (1930), *Dinner at Antoine's* (1948) and *Roses in December* (1960), but she also wrote two biographies: *St Teresa of Lisieux* (1950) and *The Sublime Shepherdess* (1940), a study of Bernadette of Lourdes.
Keyes, Sir Roger John Brownlow, 1st Baron (1872–1945), British admiral who was in charge of submarines at the start of WWI, and subsequently leader of the daring raid on Zeebrugge that crippled the German U-boat campaign in 1918. In 1940 he was given the task of training the first British COMMANDO units.
Keyes, Sidney (1922–43), British poet whose major volumes are *The Iron Laurel* (1942) and *The Cruel Solstice* (1943). His subjects, war, pain, death and guilt, are sensitively conveyed in the poems *The Foreign Gate* and *The Wilderness.*
Keynes, John Maynard (1883–1946), British economist who came to prominence with his book *Economic Consequences of the Peace* (1919), which criticized the economic provisions of the Treaty of VERSAILLES. *The General Theory of Employment, Interest, and Money* (1935) was profoundly influenced by the DEPRESSION. In it Keynes established the foundation of modern MACRO-ECONOMICS. He advocated governmental economic planning and the active intervention of government in the economy to stimulate employment and prosperity. His views had great influence on the BRETTON WOODS CONFERENCE of 1944. *See also* MS p.312.
Keyser, de, name of a family of Dutch artists. Hendrick (1565–1621) was a sculptor and architect to the city of Amsterdam, where he designed the Zuiderkerk and Westerkerk and the Erasmus monument. Three of his sons, Pieter (1595–1676), Willem (1603–*c.* 1674) and Hendrick (1613–65), were sculptors. His son Thomas (*c.* 1596–1667) was a portrait painter and his *Constantin Huygens* (1627, National Gallery, London), anticipates the conversation pieces of the 18th century. His work, always lively and expressive in style also includes the distinguished *Seated Lady* (1676).
Keyserling, Baron Hermann Alexander (1880–1946), German philosopher whose travels throughout the world formed the basis of his best-known work, *The Travel Diary of a Philosopher* (1919). His ideas centred on spiritual themes and the spiritual wisdom of non-European cultures. His works enjoyed considerable popularity after WWI.
Keystone Film Company, US production company established in 1912 which specialized in one-reel comedies, most often directed by Mack SENNETT. The infamous Keystone Kops were developed during the first year of production and typified

the unit's comedy formula: irreverent slapstick, zany situations and strong contributions from ex-music hall stars such as Charlie CHAPLIN, Fatty ARBUCKLE and Buster KEATON, culminating in an inevitable accelerated chase sequence and all consolidated by impeccable pace and timing and the editing skills Sennett had learned from D.W. GRIFFITH. In 1917 Sennett sold his interest in Keystone and took most of his stars with him to PARAMOUNT *See also* HC2 p.201.
KGB, Soviet secret police known as the Committee for State Security (Komitet Gosudarstvennoye Bezhopaznosti). It was first established in 1917 as CHEKA to hunt out political subersives and enemy agents. Later reorganized into the GPU (1923–34) and the NKVD (1934–46), it was instrumental in the purges of the 1930s. From 1946 until 1953 it became the MGB and during WWII began the operation known as SMERSH (death to spies), with the objective of eliminating Soviet enemies. It was also responsible for the political supervision of the army. After STALIN's death in 1953 it was reformed into the KGB. It is supervised by and responsible to the USSR Council of Ministers. Its operations are essentially political in nature, but are less concerned with internal security than were those of its predecessors.
Khachaturian, Aram Ilyich (1903–), Armenian composer whose graduation from Moscow Conservatory in 1934 coincided with the performance of his first symphony which, like much of his music, makes use of folk themes. He wrote a piano concerto in 1936 and a violin concerto in 1940. His best known works are probably the music for the ballets *Gayane* (1942), which includes his famous *Sabre Dance*, and *Spartacus* (1953).
Khadijah (554–619), first wife of MOHAMMED, the founder of Islam, and the first to believe in his mission. A wealthy widow with three children when she married him, she bore him six children and was his confidante and support for 25 years. Only their daughter, FATIMA, survived Mohammed.
Khafre, also known as Khafra, in Greek Chephren or Souphis, pharaoh of Egypt (late 2500s BC). A member of the 4th Dynasty, he was responsible for the building of the second pyramid at GIZA.
Khafre, Great Sphinx of, monumental statue of the SPHINX, situated at GIZA, Egypt. Its name derives from the pharaoh KHAFRE who commissioned the work, and whose portrait is said to be represented by the sphinx's face.
Khaki, normal colour of 20th-century military uniforms, from the Hindu word for dust. Khaki uniforms were first used in battle in the late 19th century by British troops in India, and their camouflage effect became essential because of the increasing accuracy and range of rifles.
Khaled (1913–), Saudi Arabian monarch. While still young he was sent as IBN SAUD's representative to the desert tribes. He also represented Saudi Arabia at various international conferences, and from 1962–75 was vice-president of the Council of Ministers. His interests clearly lay with the BEDOUIN people and their problems. Khaled became crown prince in 1965 and king in 1975 after the assassination of his half-brother King FAISAL.
Khalid (*d.*642), Arab leader. Initially he opposed MOHAMMED and ISLAM. Defeated by Mohammed at Badr in 624 in Islam's first military victory, he won in 625 at Uhud. He was converted to Islam himself in 629 and became, in Mohammed's words, "The Sword of Allah", conquering Syria, Egypt, Iraq and Persia.
Khalifa, The, or Abdullah el Taaisha (1846–99), the ruler of what was Egyptian Sudan from 1885. He was nominated by the MAHDI as his successor in the same year. In 1898 his army was destroyed by Anglo-Egyptian forces at the Battle of Omdurman, although he maintained resistance until the following year.
Khalkhas, ancient nomadic pastoral people who formed the majority of the Mongol nation which invaded Russia and Europe under GENGHIS KHAN. Today they comprise about 75% of the Mongolian People's Republic. They speak the Khalkha language. Their indigenous religion was Shamanism, a spirit-worshipping pantheism, but many of them adopted Tibetan BUDDHISM in the 17th century and after.
Khama, Sir Seretse (1921–), President of Botswana (1966–). After studying in England, he returned to Botswana (then Bechuanaland) but was banished in 1950 after a dispute with the British government over his succession to the chieftaincy of the Bamangwato tribe. He renounced (1956) his claim and became President when Botswana achieved independence in 1966.
Khamsin, hot, dry southerly wind that blows across N Africa from the Sahara during spring and summer. The name means "fifty" in Arabic, the number of days during which the wind is supposed to blow.
Khan, Ayub (1907–74), Pakistani general and politician. In 1951 he became Commander-in-Chief of the army, and proclaimed himself President in 1958. He encouraged agrarian reform and foreign investment and fought a short war against India in 1965. In 1969 he resigned after widespread rioting.
Khaniá (Canea), port on the Gulf of Khaniá, NW Crete, Greece; capital of Khaniá prefecture. One of the oldest Cretan cities, it was held in turn by the Romans, Arabs, Byzantines, Venetians and Ottomans. The Cretan capital since 1841, the port's principal industry is the shipping of olives, citrus fruits and wine. Pop. (1971) 40,452.
Kharkov (Char'kov), city in the Ukraine Republic (Ukrainskaja SSR), USSR, at the confluence of the Kharkov, Lopan and Udy rivers; capital of Kharkov oblast. In the 17th century the city served as the stronghold of the Ukrainian Cossacks in defending Russia's S border, and served as the capital of Ukraine from 1765. It has a university dating from 1805. Industries: food processing, ball-bearings, chemicals, electrical goods. Pop. (1975) 1,357,000.
Khartoum (Al-Khartūm), capital of Sudan, at the junction of the Blue Nile and White Nile rivers; capital of Khartoum province. The city was founded in the 1820s by Mohammed Ali. It was besieged by the Mahdists in 1885, and occupied and rebuilt by Gen. Horatio KITCHENER in 1898. It became the seat of government in 1956 when Sudan gained its independence. The city has the Kitchener School of Medicine (1924) and a university (1956). Industries: cement, gum arabic, chemicals, cotton textiles. Pop. (1972 est.) 300,000.
Khatchaturian, Aram Ilyich. *See* KHACHATURIAN, ARAM ILYICH.
Khayyám, Omar. *See* OMAR KHAYYÁM.
Khazars, Turkic people who first appeared in the lower Volga region *c.*2nd century AD. They allied themselves with the BYZANTINE EMPIRE in fighting the Persians (AD 610–41). Between the 8th and 10th centuries their empire, situated astride important trade routes, was prosperous and extended from N of the Black Sea to the River Volga and from W of the Caspian Sea to the River Dnieper. They conquered the Volga Bulgars, taxed the eastern Slavs and fought the Arabs, Russians and Pechenegs. In the 8th century, their ruling class was converted to JUDAISM, and maintained close relations with Constantinople. Their empire was destroyed in 965 by the army of Sviatoslav, Duke of Kiev. Some scholars believe that they are the ancestors of many Eastern European Jews.
Khedive, unofficial title used by the viceroys of Egypt after the 1820s to stress their autonomy and to indicate superiority over other Ottoman governors. The Ottoman Sultan Abdulaziz conferred the title on Ismail in 1867, having granted the right of hereditary succession in 1866.
Khephren. *See* KHAFRE.
Khepri, or Khepera, in ancient Egyptian mythology, the aspect of RE as the self-created and continuously reborn morning sun, who is also a creator of gods, notably SHU, the air god, and Tefnut, god of rain. Khepri is depicted as a scarab (dung beetle) – a symbol of resurrection – or as a man with a scarab.
Kheraskov, Mikhail Mateyevich (1733–1807), Russian poet. A versatile and prolific writer, he was director of Moscow University from 1763. He is remembered chiefly for the two first Russian epic poems *Rossiada* (1779; "Russian Epic") and *Vladimir Vozrozdionny* (1785; "Vladimir Reborn").
Khirbet Qumrān. *See* QUMRĀN.
Khlebnikov, Viktor (1885–1922), Russian poet and student of mathematics and linguistics who, with the poet Vladimir MAYAKOVSKI, founded the Russian Futurist literary movement. They rejected the art of the past and strongly supported the Bolshevik Revolution of 1917. Khlebnikov, in such poems as *Zaklyatie Smekhom* (1910) and *Poet* (1919), sought to free words of their conventional meanings.
Khmer, language of up to 85% of the inhabitants of Cambodia. It belongs to a group of the Mon-Khmer languages and has given its name to the people who speak it. A Khmer empire was set up between the 9th and 15th centuries AD, and the name was adopted by the Khmer Republic, established in 1970, which fell to the KHMER ROUGE in April 1975. *See also* HC1 pp.226, *227*; HC2 p.293.
Khmer Republic. *See* CAMBODIA.
Khmer Rouge, ruling power in Cambodia, also called the Communist National United Front. After the overthrow of the neutralist Sihanouk government in 1970, the Khmer Rouge turned successfully to armed conflict, taking the capital Phnom Penh in April 1975. Khieu Samphan was named chief of state and Tol Saut premier (April 1976). *See also* HC2 pp.292–293.
Khoisan, group of African languages of South Africa. Hottentots (Khoi, in their tongue) and Bushman (San) are the two largest groups of native speakers. Sandawe and Hadza of Tanzania are also Khoisan. All are characteristically CLICK LANGUAGES.
Khomyakov, Aleksei Stepanovich (1804–60), Russian poet and philosopher. A noble, he retired from the Russian Army in 1829 to devote himself to writing and the management of his estates. His poetry demonstrates his commitment to the Slavophiles and is among the finest Russian political verse. The same commitment is clear in *Neskol'ko slov* (1831; "A few words by an Orthodox Christian about Western Beliefs").
Khorana, Har Gobind (1922–), US biochemist who shared the 1968 Nobel prize in physiology and medicine with Robert W. Holley and Marshall W. Nirenberg for discoveries about the way in which genes determine cell function. They established that most codons, combinations of three of the four different bases found in DNA and RNA, eventually cause the inclusion of a specific AMINO ACID into the cell proteins.
Khorāsān, province in NE Iran; Mashhad is the capital. A mountainous region, its products include farm produce, carpets, turquoise and hides. Area: 313,339sq km (120,980sq miles). Pop. (1971 est.) 2,823,272.
Khorsabad, archaeological site in Iraq, NE of Mosul. Excavations begun in 1843 by the Frenchman Paul-Émile Botta, who unearthed a palace and a temple, have revealed an ancient city thought to be Dur Sharrukin, founded in the 8th century BC by Sargon (Sharrukin) II of ASSYRIA. In 1932, cuneiform tablets in the Elamite language and a list of Assyrian kings from 1700 BC to the mid-11th century were discovered there. *See also* HC1 p.*333*.
Khoshru, name of two kings of Persia. Khoshru I (*d.* AD579) extended his empire, rebuilt cities and expanded commerce. His grandson, Khoshru II (*d.*628), was overthrown by Bahram, the Usurper, but regained the throne. He seized Syria, Palestine and Egypt but lost them to the Emperor HERACLIUS. He was executed after a household revolution and his son, Sheroe, succeeded him to the throne.
Khrushchev, Nikita Sergeyevich (1894–1971), Soviet Policitian who was First Secretary of the Communist Party from 1953 to 1964 and premier of the USSR from

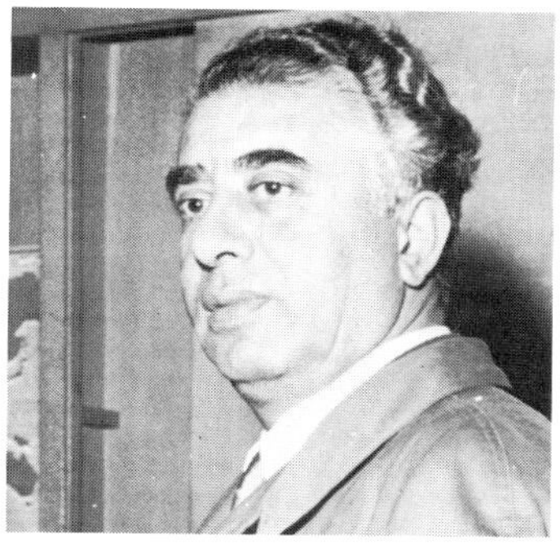
Khachaturian's music entered the British hit parade as theme to the Onedin Line TV series.

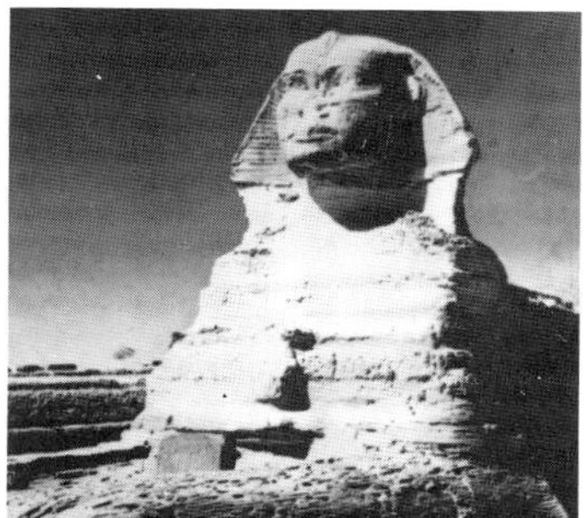
The Great Sphinx of Khafre stands 20m (66ft) high, and is 73m (240ft) long.

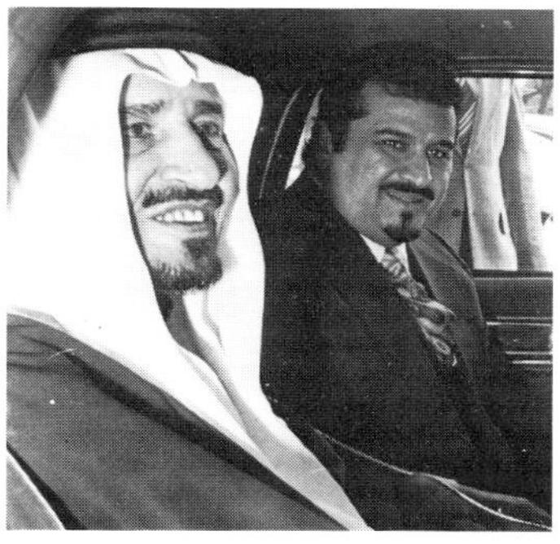
King Khaled with the Saudi Arabian ambassador, while visiting London.

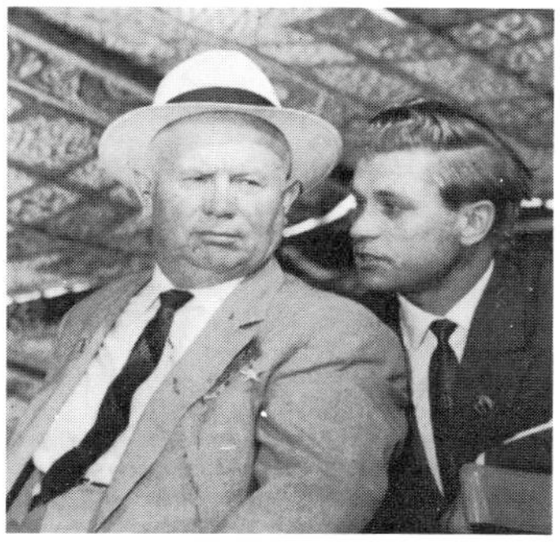
Nikita Khrushchev listens to his interpreter at the opening of the Aswan Dam (1964).

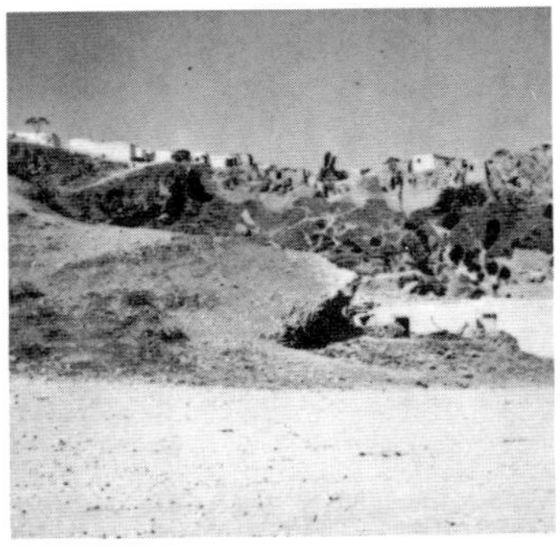

The Khyber Pass has been of vital strategic importance at many different times in history.

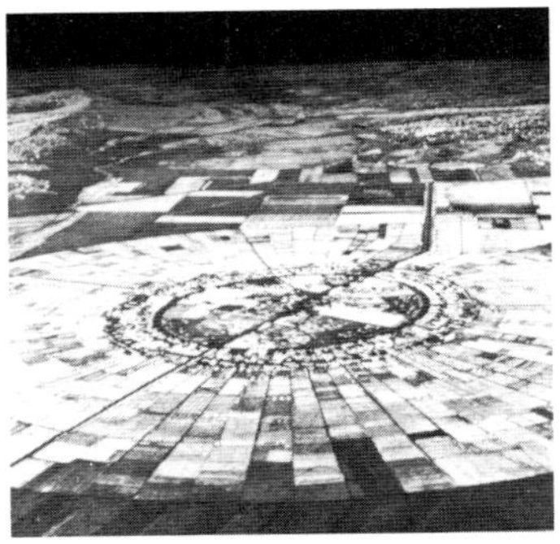

Kibbutz Nahalal, one of the earliest settlements, is the birthplace of Moshe Dayan.

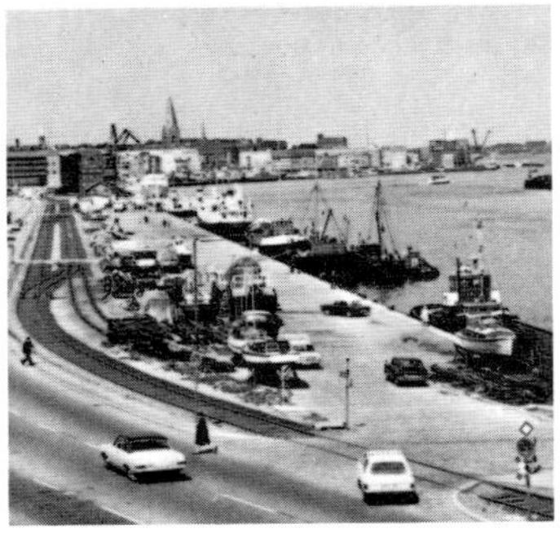

Kiel's harbour lies south of the locks of the famous Kiel Canal, opened in 1895.

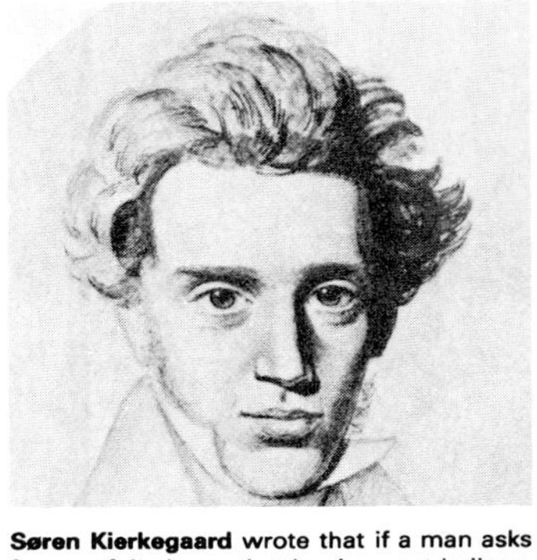

Søren Kierkegaard wrote that if a man asks for proof, it shows that he does not believe.

1958 to 1964. He joined the party in 1918 and was elected to the central committee in 1934. Noted for economic success and ruthless suppression of opposition in the Ukraine, where he was a party secretary, he was elected to the POLITBURO in 1939. After Stalin died he made a speech denouncing him to the Twentieth Party Congress (1956), and expelled his staunchest backers from the central committee. Favouring détente with the West, he yielded to US President John F. KENNEDY in the CUBAN MISSILE CRISIS in 1962. This development, economic setbacks and trouble with China led to his downfall in favour of Leonid BREZHNEV and Alexei KOSYGIN in 1964. *See also* HC2 pp.*240*.

Khufu. *See* CHEOPS.

Khyber Pass, major mountain pass in the Safīd Kūh range, connecting the Kabūl river valley in Afghanistan (W) with Peshāwar in Pakistan (E). A strategic route used for centuries by invaders, merchants and migrating peoples, it was the scene of bitter fighting during the Afghan Wars (1838–42 and 1878–80). Two British outposts, Ali Masjid and Landi Kotal, were situated there. Elevation: 1,073m (3,520ft). Length: 50km (30 miles).

Kiang, also called the Tibetan wild ass, wild Asian ass found in the mountains of Tibet and Sikkim up to 5,486m (18,000ft). The most numerous of all wild asses, it is red and white in summer and dun-coloured in winter. Height: 1.5m (5ft) at the shoulder. Family Equidae; species *Equus hemionus kiang*. *See also* NW p.*222*.

Kiangsi (Jiangxi), province in SE China; the capital is Nanchang. It has a mountainous terrain and fertile areas drained by the Kan River. Originally known as Kan under the Chou dynasty (770–435 BC), the region was ruled by the dynasties of western Ch'in, southern Sung and T'ang, until it came under the Ch'ing dynasty (1644–1911). Products: rice, wheat, beans, sweet potatoes, citrus fruits, tobacco, sugar cane, cotton, peanuts. Industries: timber, fishing, porcelain, mining of tungsten, coal, tin. Area: 164,865sq km (63,654sq miles). Pop. 22,000,000.

Kiangsu (Jiangsu), province in E China, the capital is Nanking (Nanjing). One of China's smallest and most densely populated provinces, it is an extremely fertile region that includes the Yangtze (Changjiang) River delta. It is a highly industrialized region, Shanghai being the chief manufacturing centre of China. Under the rule of the Ming dynasty from 1368 to 1644, it became a separate province in the 18th century. Taken by Japan in 1937, the province was freed by the Chinese Nationalists in 1945 but fell to the Chinese Communists in 1949. Products: rice, cotton, wheat, barley, soya beans, peanuts, tea. Industries: silk, oil refining, textiles, food processing, cement. Area: 102,240sq km (39,474sq miles). Pop. 47,000,000.

Kibbutz, collective settlement in Israel which is owned by its members. The idea developed from the pioneering settlements established by the Jewish settlers in Palestine before it became Israel in 1948. The first kibbutz was set up on the bank of the River Jordan near the Sea of Galilee in 1910. There are now many such settlements, and they have become strategically important in the defence of Israel.

Kibla, or Kiblah, direction of the KAABA in the Great Mosque in Mecca, towards which Muslims face when praying. Inside a mosque this direction is indicated by a niche in the wall called the *mihrab*. *See also* HC1 pp.144–145, *145*.

Kid, Thomas. *See* KYD, THOMAS.

Kidd, Michael (1919–), US dancer and choreographer. After dancing with the Ballet Caravan (1937–40) and the AMERICAN BALLET THEATER (1942–7), he won Tony awards for his choreography of *Finian's Rainbow* (1947), *Guys and Dolls* (1951) and *Can Can* (1953). Later, he choreographed *The Rothschilds* (1972) and the film version of *Hello Dolly* (1969).

Kidd, William (*c.* 1645–1701), sea captain and pirate, commonly known as Captain Kidd. After 1689 he was a privateer for the British against the French and pirates in the West Indies. Later, on commission in Madagascar, he turned pirate himself, prompted in part by the lack of booty. He was denounced and went to New England to seek exoneration, but was sent to England. There he was tried for murder and piracy, and hanged in 1701.

Kiddush, Jewish prayer recited before a meal on the eve of the Sabbath or of a festival. Emphasizing the sanctity of the day that is beginning, the head of the household says the prayer over a cup of wine, which is then passed round to each member to sip.

Kidnapped (1886), novel by Robert Louis STEVENSON. Set in Scotland during the aftermath of the Jacobite Rebellion, which was crushed at Culloden, the novel describes David Balfour's adventures at sea and as a fugitive until he regains his inheritance. He is aided by a volatile Jacobite, Alan Breck.

Kidney, excretory organ that filters water and waste material from the blood, conveying them along the URETER, to the BLADDER as urine. There are two kidneys, one on each side of the body in the small of the back. The human kidneys are made up of about one million highly specialized tubules, each of which contains numerous capillaries that filter the blood entering from tiny branches of the renal artery. *See also* MS pp.68–69, *69*.

Kidney bean. *See* BEAN.

Kidney machine, or artificial kidney, machine for extracting waste matter from blood during kidney failure. Generally it is used once or twice a week for 14-15 hours. The patient is connected to the machine by tubes from his arms or legs through which his blood is pumped. Blood is separated from the waste matter in the machine and returned to the patient.

Kidney stones, small, hard, pebble-like masses formed in the KIDNEY from an accumulation of mineral substances; known medically as calculi. Passage of a stone through the ureter (tube from the kidney to the bladder) causes the excruciating pain of renal colic. They can be removed by surgery or, if the stones are small, they can be passed out in the urine after treatment, which includes drinking large amounts of water.

Kidron, brook or field in biblical times, the present-day Qidron (JORDAN) between Jerusalem and the Mount of Olives. The vale of Kidron has been traditionally identified as the Valley of Jehoshaphat, referred to in JOEL 3 as a place of judgment.

Kiel, seaport city in West Germany, 64km (40 miles) NW of Lübeck, at the head of the Kiel Canal linking the North Sea and the Baltic Sea. The city was ceded to Denmark in 1773, to Prussia in 1866 and was the scene of the mutiny that began the German revolution of 1918. The canal was deepened prior to WWI and given international status in 1919 because of its commercial and military importance. This status was repudiated by HITLER in 1936. Today Kiel is a shipping and industrial city manufacturing textiles, processed food and printed matter. Pop. (1974) 265,587.

Kiel, Treaty of (14 Jan. 1814) dissolved the union of Norway and Denmark that had been established in 1380. After Napoleon's defeat at Leipzig, Swedish Crown Prince Charles (Bernadotte) defeated Denmark (which had sided with France in the Napoleonic Wars). Under the treaty, Frederick VI of Denmark ceded Norway to Sweden but kept Greenland and other Norwegian colonies. Sweden gave up Western Pomerania and Rügen to Denmark.

Kielland, Alexander (1849–1906), Norwegian novelist, dramatist and short story writer. Influenced by Søren KIERKEGAARD, he attacked the church in novels such as *Snow* (1886) and *St John's Festival* (1887). Other works include the novels *Garman and Worse* (1880) and *Jacob* (1891).

Kiely, Benedict (1919–), Irish novelist and historian. His works include *Counties of Contention* (1945), a study of Irish partition, *Modern Irish Fiction: a Critique* (1950) and *Dogs Enjoy the Morning* (1968).

Kierkegaard, Søren Aaby (1813–55), Danish philospher and theologian. Regarded as the forerunner of modern EXISTENTIALISTS, he believed that the individual must make deliberate decisions about the direction of his life. Critical of HEGEL's speculative philosophy, he also opposed organized Christianity. His books include *Either/Or* (1843) and *Philosophical Fragments* (1844).

Kiernan, Tom (1939–), Irish rugby union player. He played 54 times for Ireland (1960–73), the most international appearances by any fullback, and was captain from 1963. He toured South Africa with the British Lions in 1962 and, as captain, again in 1968. An accurate goal-kicker, he scored more than 100 points in internationals.

Kiesinger, Kurt Georg (1904–), West German political leader who was elected to the BUNDESTAG as a Christian Democrat in 1949. In 1958 he became Minister-President of Baden-Württemberg. He was elected federal Chancellor in October 1966 and headed a coalition government with the Social Democrats until 1969, when he resigned, to be replaced by Willy BRANDT.

Kiev, port and capital city of the Ukraine (Ukrainskaja SSR), USSR, on the River Dnieper; capital of Kiev oblast, and third largest city in the USSR. The city belonged to Lithuania in the 14th century, Poland in the 16th century and was taken by Russia in 1686. It served as the capital of the independent Ukrainian Republic from 1917 to 1919. The BOLSHEVIKS took the city in 1920. It is the site of the cathedral of St Sophia, built in 1037 and the oldest church in the USSR, and a university (1834). Industries: shipbuilding, machine tools, food processing, footwear, furniture. Pop. 2,013,000.

Kiffin, William (1616–1701), English merchant and baptist minister who joined a separatist congregation in 1634 and became a baptist in 1638. In 1643 he began a wool business, becoming rich as a result. In 1664 he was arrested and briefly imprisoned on suspicion of plotting against Charles II. He became an alderman of London in 1687.

Kigali, capital of Rwanda, E of Lake Kivu. The chief administrative and commercial centre of the country, its major industries are tin mining, cotton, textiles and coffee. Pop. 60,000.

Kikimora, in Slavic mythology, a female domestic spirit who performed household tasks to assist busy wives. She could be propitiated by washing the kitchen utensils with a brew made from ferns.

Kikuyu, Bantu-speaking people of the fertile highlands of Kenya, E Africa. In pre-colonial times they practised an intensive form of agriculture, in contrast with neighbouring pastoralists such as the Masai. British conquest put severe strains on their political and agricultural system; the result was an outbreak of terrorism during the 1950s known as MAU MAU. After Kenya gained independence they were the country's most important tribe, forming 20% of the population. The first president of the new nation, Jomo Kenyatta, was a Kikuyu.

Kilauea, volcanic crater on central Hawaii Island, Hawaii. It last erupted in 1968 and is the largest active crater in the world. Height: 1,247m (4,090ft), Depth: 152m (500ft).

Kildare, Thomas Fitzgerald, 10th Earl of (1513–37), Deputy-Governor of Ireland in 1534. In that year rumours that his father had been executed in London caused him to renounce his allegiance to King HENRY VIII. He rebelled against the crown, seizing Dublin and murdering Archbishop John Allen. When the rebellion was put down by Sir William Skeffington, he surrendered to Lord Leonard Grey in 1535 and was later executed.

Kildare, county in E central Republic of Ireland. A low-lying region in the central plain of Ireland, it includes the Bog of Allan, and the chief rivers are the Liffey, Boyne and Barrow. Primarily agricultural, Kildare is noted for its breeding of racehorses. Area: 1,694sq km (654sq miles). Pop. (1971) 71,522.

Kiley, Richard Paul (1922–), US stage, film and television actor. After touring with the company of *A Streetcar Named Desire* (1950), he appeared on stage in both dramatic and musical roles. He received Tony awards, in 1959 for *Redhead* and in 1966 for *Man of La Mancha*. His later films include *Blackboard Jungle* (1955) and *Spanish Affair* (1958).
Kilimanjaro, mountain in NE Tanzania, near the border with Kenya. The highest peak in Africa, it is an extinct volcano with twin peaks joined by a broad saddle. Coffee is grown on the intensely cultivated southern slopes. Height: Kibo 5,895m (19,340ft); Mawenzi 5,150m (16,896ft).
Kilkenny, county in SE Republic of Ireland, in Leinster province. Part of the central plain of Ireland, it is drained by the Suir, Barrow and Nore rivers. Farmers grow cereal crops and vegetables, and cattle are reared. The chief industries are food processing, brewing and coal mining. The county town is Kilkenny. Area: 2,062sq km (796sq miles). Pop. (1971) 61,800.
Kilkenny, Statute of (1366), body of laws in Norman French passed in the Irish Parliament called by Lionel, Duke of Clarence, to strengthen English authority in Ireland. It attempted to restrict relations between the Irish and the English – forbidding, for example, intermarriage – and upheld the use of English rather than Brehon law.
Killanin, Baron Michael (1914–), Irish author, film producer and sportsman who in 1972 became president of the International Olympic Committee.
Killdeer, noisy, plover-like shore bird of North American meadows known for its alarm call and distraction displays. Its plumage is white with a double black breast ring and chestnut rump and tail. Family Charadriidac; species *Charadrius vociferus*.
Killer whale, toothed whale that lives in all the world's oceans, especially those in colder regions. A fierce predator of large animals, it is black above and white below, and distinguished by a white patch above each eye and a long, erect, dorsal fin. Length: 9m (30ft). Species: *Orcinus orca*. *See also* NW pp.*167, 224*.
Killiecrankie, Battle of (27 July 1689), JACOBITE victory over the forces of WILLIAM III. On a plain at the top of the pass of Killiecrankie in Perthshire, Scotland, some 3,000 Jacobites under Viscount Dundee fought the troops of Gen. Hugh Mackay, who lost nearly half his force of 4,000 men. Dundee, however, was mortally wounded; near the spot where he died stands Urrard House.
Killigrew, Thomas (1612–83), English playwright who was a page to Charles I and a friend of Charles II, with whom he went into exile in 1647. His plays include *The Prisoners* (1641), *Claracilla* (1641) and *The Parson's Wedding* (1664). In 1663 he built the Theatre Royal in Drury Lane, London. His son, Thomas Killigrew (1657–1719), was also a playwright.
Killy, Jean-Claude (1943–), French skier who won the giant slalom, downhill and slalom races in the 1968 Winter Olympic Games at Grenoble, France. He retired from competitive skiing in 1968.
Kilmer, Alfred Joyce (1886–1918), US poet and critic, who is remembered chiefly for his poem, *Trees* (1913), which is a combination of simple philosophy and sentiment. He was killed in action in WWI, just as his work was beginning to show a greater maturity.
Kilmuir, David Patrick Maxwell Fyfe, 1st Earl. *See* FYFE, DAVID PATRICK MAXWELL.
Kiln, in ceramics, an oven for firing ware. Early kilns were holes in the ground into which the ware was placed and covered by a large fire. Later, special wood- or coal-fired oven-type kilns were built; today most kilns use gas or electricity. *See also* MM pp.44–45, *52*.
Kilpi, Volter (1874–1939), Finnish novelist notable for his use of modern experimental techniques. His works include the long STREAM-OF-CONSCIOUSNESS novel *Alastalon salissa* ("In the Lounge at Alastalo") (1933).
Kilt, knee-length pleated skirt, part of the traditional costume of men from the Highlands of Scotland and also worn in Ireland. Scottish kilts are usually made of fine-spun woollen TARTAN, while the traditional Irish kilt is plain.
Kim (1901), adventure novel by Rudyard KIPLING, regarded by critics as one of his best. It is about Kimball O'Hara, orphaned son of an Irish sergeant in the British army in India. After a vagrant childhood and adoption by his father's old regiment, he joins the secret service.
Kimberley, city in South Africa, 138km (86 miles) WNW of Bloemfontein. It was founded in 1871 after the discovery of diamonds nearby. The diamond fields were taken over by Cecil Rhodes in 1888 for the De Beers company, and it remains one of the world's largest diamond centres. Industries include the mining, cutting and polishing of diamonds, also the processing of gypsum, iron and manganese. Pop. (1970) 103,800.
Kimberlite, ultrabasic rock found in diamond-bearing pipes, mainly in South Africa. It is a mica PERIDOTITE consisting chiefly of olivine and phlogopite, and it weathers to the yellow and blue grounds of diamond mines. *See also* PE p.98.
Kimhi (contraction of Kimchi), family of Jewish grammarians and biblical interpreters whose members were responsible for introducing Hebrew studies to Europe in the Middle Ages. They included Joseph (*c.*1105–*c.*1170) and his sons Moses (*d.c.*1190), author of the important Hebrew grammar *Mahalak Shevile hada'at* (*Way of the Paths of Knowledge*), and David (*c.*1160–*c.*1235), whose greatest work was the *Sefer Mikol* (*Book of Completeness*).
Kim Il-sung, Marshal (1912–), chief of state of the Democratic People's Republic of Korea (North Korea) and chairman of the Korean Workers' Party from 1948; *b.* Kim Sung Chu. He joined the Korean Communist Party in 1931 and led guerilla fighting against the occupying Japanese in the 1930s and a Korean unit in the Soviet army during WWII. In 1950 he led a North Korean invasion of South Korea that precipitated the KOREAN WAR (1950–53).
Kimono, the traditional formal dress of Japanese men and women. It is a single piece of material (usually silk) which is wrapped tightly around the waist, forming loose arms and a flowing skirt. Although still worn it is increasingly being replaced by western styles of dress.
Kinaesthetic sense, also called proprioception, internal sense that conveys information from the muscles and tendons of the body. Specialized receptors connect to a tract of the nervous system which provides information about the contraction and expansion of muscles. It is the position sense, because it allows human beings to know the positions of their limbs without visual confirmation. *See also* CEREBELLUM.
Kincardine(shire), former county in E Scotland; since 1975 it has been part of Grampian Region. The Grampian Mts slope down to a fertile coastal plain in the E. Sheep and dairy and beef cattle are reared, and oats, barley and potatoes are the chief crops. Industries include fishing, woollens, leather goods and whisky distilling. The county town was Stonehaven. Area: 982sq km (379sq miles). Pop. 25,050.
Kinck, Hans Ernst (1865–1926), Norwegian novelist, dramatist and short-story writer. He explored the psychological differences between urban and rural cultures in the short stories collected in *From Sea to Mountain* (1897) and in the trilogy *The Avalanche Broke* (1918–19).
Kindergarten, *See* NURSERY SCHOOL.
Kinetic art, term used to describe art, especially sculpture, in which an element of motion is – or appears to be – present. Examples of kinetic art may be seen in the work of DUCHAMP, CALDER and GABO, and in MOHOLY-NAGY's light modulators. Kinetic art may be mechanical, eg works by Gabo, or non-mechanical, eg *Mobile* (1958) by Calder. Kineticism evolved in response to an increasingly technological modern culture. In painting, OP ART may be regarded as a form of Kineticism. *See also* HC2 p.278.
Kinetic energy, in physics, energy that a body possesses because it is in motion. It is the energy (K) given to a body to set it in motion; it depends on the mass (m) of the body and its velocity (v), according to the equation $K = \frac{1}{2}mv^2$. On impact, it is converted into other forms of energy, such as heat, sound and light. *See also* POTENTIAL ENERGY; SU pp.68–*69, 72, 74*–75.
Kinetics. *See* DYNAMICS.
Kinetic theory, theory in physics dealing with matter in terms of the forces between particles and the energies they possess. There are five principles to the kinetic theory: matter is composed of tiny particles; these are in constant motion; they do not lose energy in collision with each other or the walls of their container; there are no attractive forces between the particles or their container; and at any time the particles in a sample may not all have the same energy. *See also* SU p.84.
Kinetograph and Kinetoscope, camera and peephole viewer invented by Thomas EDISON and William Dickson and patented in 1891. They were early forerunners of the ciné camera and projector. They were superseded by the cinématograph. *See also* CINEMATOGRAPHY; MM p.*222*.
King, Billie Jean, née Moffitt (1943–), US tennis player. She was singles champion of the USA in 1967, 1971–72 and 1974; of Wimbledon in 1966–68, 1972–73 and 1975; of Australia in 1968; and of France in 1972. An outspoken advocate of women's liberation, she heightened interest in women's tennis with her 1973 victory over Bobby Riggs.
King, Carole (1942–), US singer and songwriter, real name Carole Klein. Between 1959 and 1967 she and her husband Gerry Goffin wrote many successful songs, including *Up On the Roof* and *It Might as Well Rain Until September* (1962). Her record *Tapestry* (1971) sold more than 10 million copies.
King, Ernest Joseph (1878–1956), US naval officer. He served as assistant chief of the Bureau of Aeronautics in 1929, was promoted to rear-admiral in 1933 and to vice-admiral in 1938. He was commander-in-chief of the US fleet in 1941 and became chief of US naval operations in 1942. In 1944 he became admiral of the fleet and retired at the end of WWII. He also served as presidential adviser to the ATLANTIC CHARTER Conference in 1941.
King, Francis Henry (1923–), British writer. His first novel was *To the Dark Tower.* His collection of short stories, *The Japanese Umbrella* (1964), won the Katherine Mansfield Prize in 1965.
King, Henry (1592–1669), English poet. Bishop of Chichester (1642–69), he took refuge in Buckinghamshire from CROMWELL's forces (1643–60). His poetry, printed in 1657, includes a magnificent elegy on his wife, *The Exeguy* (*c.*1625).
King, Martin Luther, Jr (1929–68), US clergyman and civil-rights leader. Pastor of a Baptist church in Montgomery, Alabama, he led the Black boycott of Montgomery's segregated transport system in 1956, and subsequently attracted national attention for the passive-resistance protests he advocated. Thereafter he founded and worked through the Southern Christian Leadership Conference to further the cause of national desegregation. He organized the march on Washington in 1963, opposed the VIETNAM WAR and had begun a national compaign against poverty when he was assassinated in Memphis, Tennessee, on 4 April 1968. In 1964 he was awarded the Nobel Peace Prize. *See also* HC2 pp.265, *265*.
King, Sir Truby (1858–1938), doctor who founded the Royal New Zealand Society for the Health of Women and Children in 1907, to combat infant mortality. *See also* KARITANE SYSTEM.
King, William Lyon Mackenzie (1874–1950), Prime Minister of Canada (1921–30 and 1935–48). A lawyer and social worker, he was a successful labour mediator before entering politics. His career was marked by the drive for national unity, concessions to the progressives, and support for the acquisition of French-Canadian rights. Trained by Sir Wilfred Laurier, King led the Liberals

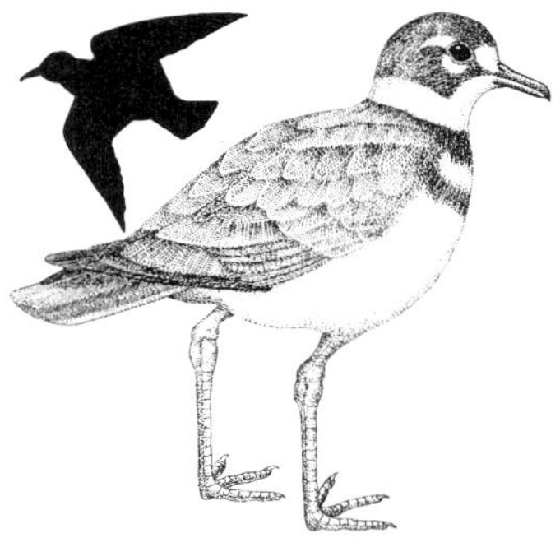

Killdeer, named after its sharp cry, has the scientific name *Charadrius vociferus.*

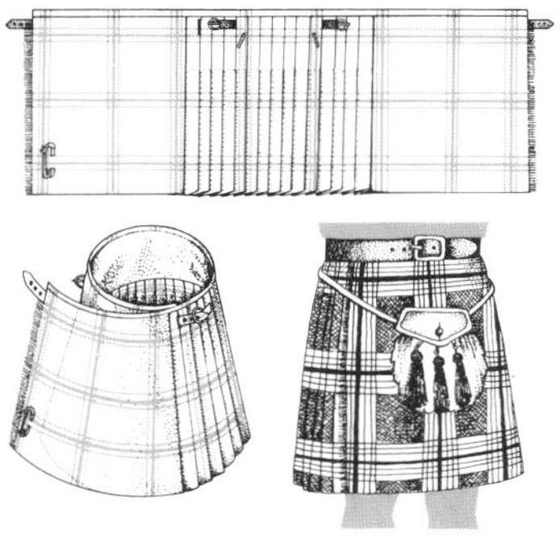

Kilt; the origin of the word is probably the Danish "kilte", which means to tuck up.

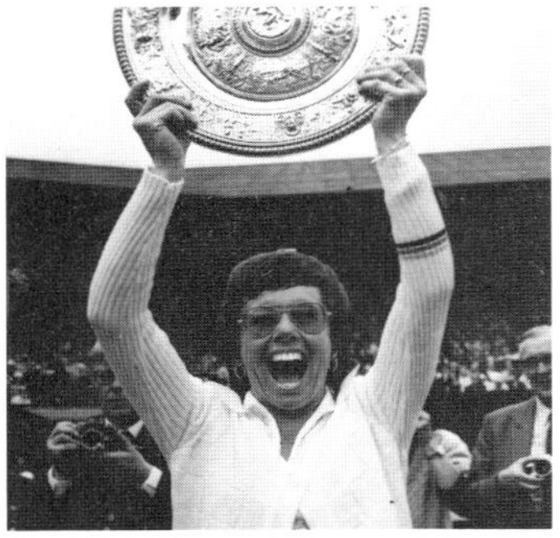

Billie Jean King beat Evonne Goolagong in the 1973 Wimbledon final.

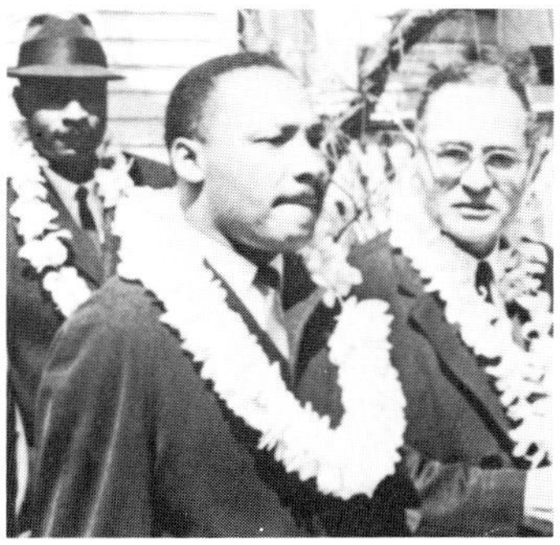

Martin Luther King, with other garlanded leaders in the Selma March, 1965.

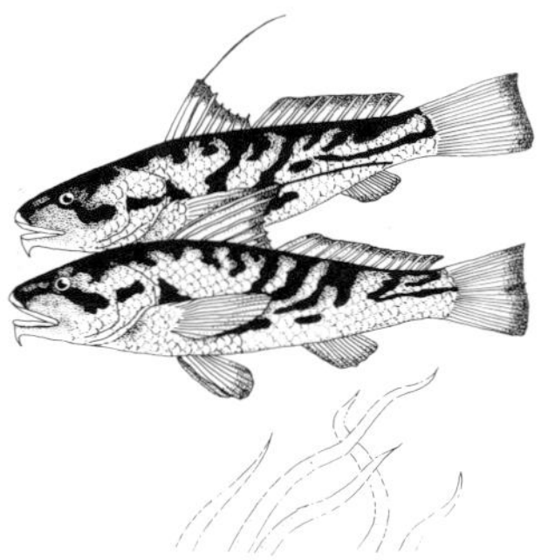

Kingfish, or king whiting, is a green fish with darker green markings, prized by anglers.

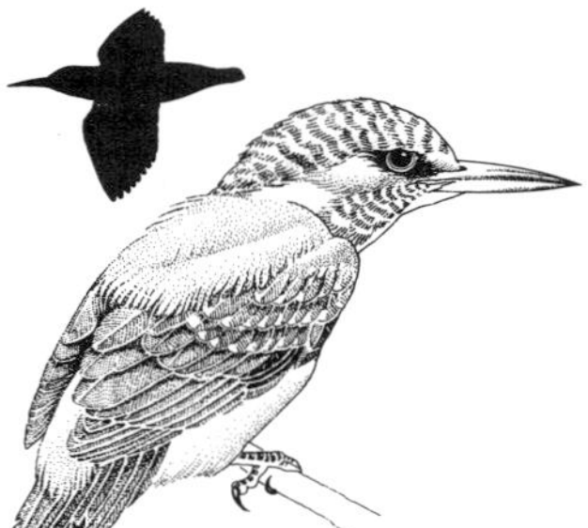

Kingfishers build their nests in river banks from the bones of the fish they eat.

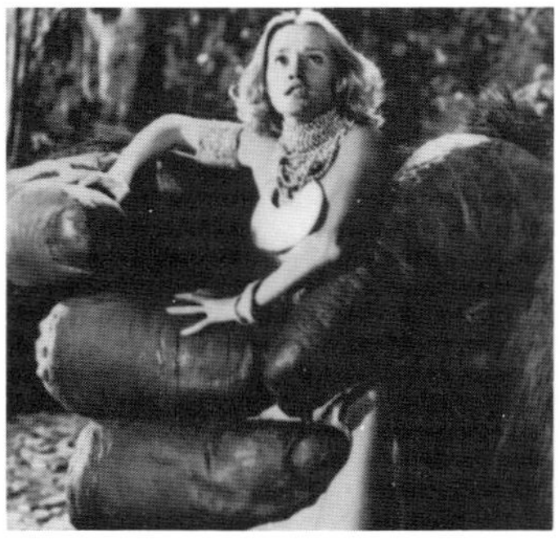

King Kong meets "Dawn", played by Jessica Lange, in the remake of the 1933 film.

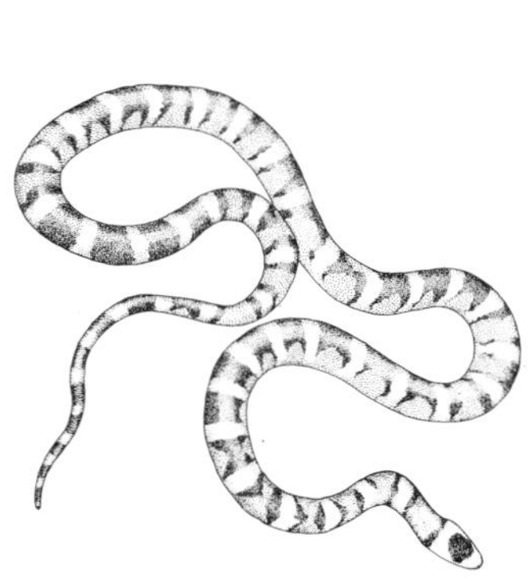

King snakes kill their prey by constriction, and are unharmed by the venom of other snakes.

between 1919 and 1948. He was more interested in foreign policy than social legislation and was a firm supporter of free enterprise.

King and I, The, musical play by Richard RODGERS and Oscar HAMMERSTEIN II, first performed on Broadway in 1951. Based on the story of Margaret Landon, it tells of an English schoolteacher in 19th century Siam who instructs the king's children. Among its songs are *Hello, Young Lovers* and *Getting to Know You.*

King Arthur, legendary British king who was said to rule the Knights of the Round Table. Two medieval chroniclers – Gildas and Nennius – tell of Arthur's fighting against the invading West Saxons and his final defeat of them at Mount Badon (possibly Badbury Hill, Dorset) in the early 6th century. However, these sources are considered by some to be suspect and a modern view is that Arthur was a professional soldier in service to the British kings after the Roman occupation. Geoffrey of Monmouth's *Historia regum Brittaniae,* based on Nennius and Welsh folk-lore and written in the 12th century, gave the Arthurian legend – with the Round Table, Camelot, Lancelot, Guinevere and the Holy Grail – the form in which it was transmitted through the Middle Ages. MALLORY's *Morte D'Arthur* (1470) was based on the version by Geoffrey of Monmouth.

King Cobra. *See* COBRA.

King Country, name given to 10,000 square miles of central North Island, New Zealand in 1857 by adherents of the Maori king who declared the land closed to Europeans.

King crab, or horseshoe crab, marine animal superficially resembling a crab but related to spiders and scorpions. It has a hard, domed shell from which protrudes a sharp tail. *See also* ARACHNIDS; NW p. *104.*

Kingfish, name applied loosely to several varieties of fish valued for food or sport. Species called kingfish include *Seriola grandis*; *Scomberomorus cavalla,* a type of large mackerel; *Menticirrhus saxitalis,* a member of the drum family, also known as a whiting; and *Lampris regius,* also known as the opah or moonfish. *See also* NW p. *130.*

Kingfisher, compact, brightly coloured bird with a straight, sharp bill, which dives for fish along rivers, streams and lakes. It swallows the fish head first when back on its perch. It nests in a deep, horizontal hole in an earth bank, laying white eggs in a nest surrounded by food-scraps. Length: 12.7–43.2cm (5–17in). Family Alcedinidae; there are several species. *See also* NW pp. *144, 214, 230, 232.*

King George's War, hostilities between France and Britain in North America during the War of the AUSTRIAN SUCCESSION (1744–48). Following an attack by the French on Nova Scotia, troops led by William Pepperell laid siege to Louisbourg, which capitulated in June 1745. The fighting elsewhere consisted mainly of skirmishes on the New England–New York border. The Peace of Aix-la-Chapelle (1748) restored Louisbourg to the French in return for Madras in India.

King Horn, hero of a late 13th-century English verse romance, *The Geste of Kyng Horne.* It is the story of the Prince of Suddenne (Isle of Man), who is expelled from his lands by invaders. Eventually he regains them and wins the princess he loves. There is also a French version dating from the 14th century.

King James Bible. *See* AUTHORIZED VERSION.

King John (*c.* 1598), five-act tragedy by William Shakespeare, based on an older drama from Raphael HOLINSHED's *Chronicles.* John, having seized the throne from Prince Arthur is later suspected of murdering him. The lords turn against him and John is poisoned by monks.

King Kong, (1933), US film. This classic thriller about a giant ape who was taken from his natural home to New York was directed by Merian C. Cooper and Ernest Schoedsack with splendid photographic effects and animation by Willis H. O'Brien. It starred Robert Armstrong, with Fay Wray as "beauty" to the "beast". Despite a whole series of imitations, it still remains one of the finest films of its type.

Kinglake, Alexander William (1809–91), British historian. He travelled in the East in 1835 and published *Eöthen, or Traces of Travel Brought Home from the East* in 1844. His most famous work, witten at Lady Raglan's suggestion, was the 8-volume *Invasion of the Crimea* (1863–87).

King Lear (*c.* 1605), five-act tragedy by William SHAKESPEARE, based on an older anonymous play, *King Leir,* and Raphael HOLINSHED's *Chronicles.* Lear, King of Britain, divides his realm between his flattering daughters Goneril and Regan, leaving his youngest and silently sincere daughter, Cordelia, with nothing. The rest of the play describes the consequences of this misguided action through Lear's mental deterioration, belated political success and death in grief and madness.

Kinglet, fearless, active songbird that breeds in cool areas of North America and Eurasia. It has a small crest that reveals a brightly coloured spot when expanded, a short, straight bill and down-like plumage. It feeds on insects. Length: 7.6–10cm (3–4in). Genus *Regulus.*

King Movement, attempted unification by New Zealand Maoris in reaction to European settlement. In 1858 Maori chiefs elected a king, Potatau I. The MAORI WARS followed British refusal to recognize the King Movement.

Kingo, Thomas (1634–1703), Danish poet and cleric. His early poetry, such as *Chrysillis,* depicts rural scenes and village life. He is best remembered for his religious poetry and hymns, which were collected in *Spiritual Chorus* (1674–81).

King Philip's War (1675–76), war between Indians and English settlers in North America. The Wampanoags, under the chief Philip (Metacomet), were originally friendly to the Massachusetts settlers but threatened by increasing colonization feared for their survival. The colonists became suspicious of Philip's intentions, and war was sparked off by the murder of an Indian informer and the execution of three Wamponoags by the English colonists. In the course of the war, the Indians destroyed 12 Massachusetts towns. Philip was killed on Rhode Island (1676) by troops of the New England Confederacy, who had decimated the Narragansett tribe (1675) and defeated the Nipmuck (1676).

Kings I and II, books in the OLD TESTAMENT, called Third and Fourth Kingdoms in the Greek SEPTUAGINT. These books recount the histories of Judah and Israel from the beginning of Solomon's reign (970 BC) to the fall of Judah and destruction of Jerusalem (586 BC). The unknown author interprets events as a revelation of God's presence in the history of Israel.

King's Bench, Court of. *See* QUEEN'S BENCH COURT OF.

King's Counsel. *See* QUEEN'S COUNSEL.

King's Cup (tennis), trophy presented by King Gustav V of Sweden for an annual international indoor championship for men's teams. Inaugurated in 1936, it was contested on a knockout basis until 1976, when a home-and-away league system was introduced with one point awarded for every tie won.

King's Cup Air Race, annual flying event for British-registered aircraft entered and flown by people of British nationality. Raced for on a handicap basis, the Cup was presented by King George V in 1922.

King's Evil, colloquialism for scrofula, ulcerous formations on the skin caused by mineral deficiency. The condition was once thought to be curable at the touch of the sovereign's hand.

Kingsford-Smith, Sir Charles Edward (1897–1935), Australian pilot. In 1928 he made the first flight from the USA to Australia, in a Fokker aircraft. In 1933 he made a record-brecking solo flight from England to Australia of 7 days 4 hours and 43 minutes.

Kingsley, family of British writers. Charles (1819–75) was ordained an Anglican clergyman in 1842 and his Christian Socialist ideas found expression in his influential novels *Alton Locke* (1850) and *Yeast* (1851). He was one of the first clergy openly to support Charles DARWIN, whose ideas he partly incorporated into *The Water Babies* (1863). Other immensely popular novels were *Westward Ho!* (1855) and *Hereward the Wake* (1866), both of which provoked John Henry NEWMAN with their anti-Catholic bias. Both Kingsley's brothers, George Henry (1827–92) and Henry (1830–76), were also writers. The former merely described his extensive travels; the latter wrote powerful fiction about Australian colonial life in novels such as *Geoffry Hamlyn* (1859) and *Ravenshoe* (1861). Kingsley's daughter, Mary St Leger Kingsley (1852–1931), was also a novelist and wrote intense works such as *The Wages of Sin* (1890), using the pseudonym Lucas Malet.

Kingsley, Mary Henrietta (1862–1900). British writer. Widely travelled, she recorded her experiences in *Travels in West Africa* (1897) and *West African Studies* (1899). She died of fever while nursing prisoners in a South African hospital during the SOUTH AFRICAN (BOER) WARS.

Kingsley, Sidney (1906–), US playwright. His *Men in White* (1933) and *Dead End* (1935) are powerful examples of social realism. After *The Patriots* (1942) and *Detective Story* (1949), Kingsley dramatized Arthur Koestler's novel *Darkness at Noon* (1951) and thereby won the New York Drama Critics' Circle award for his characterization of a disillutioned "old Bolshevik".

King's Medal, award first made in 1945 to foreign civilians who assisted Britain during WWII. There are two different citations: for courage or for service in the cause of freedom.

King's Men. *See* CHAMBERLAIN'S MEN.

King snake, non-poisonous shiny SNAKE that lives in the USA. It is generally black with white or yellow markings and feeds on other snakes, including poisonous species. Length: to 1.3m (4.2ft). Family Colubridae, genus *Lampropeltis.*

King Solomon's Mines (1885), popular novel by H. Rider HAGGARD, which brought him immediate fame and enabled him to give up his career as a lawyer for that of authorship. Set in Africa, the book relates the adventures of Allan Quartermain and Sir Henry Curtis during their search for Sir Henry's brother and King Solomon's treasure.

King's Peace (AD 386), treaty ending the Corinthian War, negotiated by Artaxerxes II of Persia with the Spartan Antalcidas and imposed upon the other Greek cities. By the terms of the treaty, Sparta became predominant in Greece, and Persia took possession of the Greek cities in Asia and on the islands, except Lemnos, Imbus and Scyros, which remained Athenian dependencies.

King's Proctor. *See* QUEEN'S PROCTOR.

Kingston, capital and largest city of Jamaica. Founded in 1692, it became the seat of government in 1872. It is one of the finest ports in the West Indies, and its exports include sugar, rum, molasses and bananas. The city is famous for its music, and is the seat of the University College of the West Indies (1946). Industries: tourism, food processing, oil refining. Pop. 550,100.

Kingston-upon-Hull (city). *See* HULL.

Kingston upon Hull, county district in E central Humberside, England; created in 1974 under the Local Government Act (1972). Area: 71sq km (27sq miles). Pop. (1974 est.) 278,800.

Kingston-upon-Thames, borough of SW Greater London, England, S of the River Thames. Several Saxon kings were crowned there, and the coronation stone is preserved in the market place. A residential area, it has light engineering industries. Pop. (1971) 146,615.

Kingstown. *See* DÚN LAOGHAIRE OR ST VINCENT.

Kingu, in Babylonian mythology, god of the powers of darkness, son and consort of the ancient sea goddess Tiamat and leader of her armies of monsters against the forces of EA, led by MARDUK. After the defeat of Kingu – also called Tammuz – Ea used his blood and bone to form man. A lamb, representing Kingu, was sacrificed as

a New Year's ritual by Babylonian kings.
King William's War (1689–97), also known as the first of the FRENCH AND INDIAN WARS, North American part of the war between England and France. In 1690 FRONTENAC, the French Governor of Canada, sent expeditions against the British frontier colonies in New York and what are now New Hampshire and Maine. The English, under Sir William Phips, sailed up the St Lawrence River to take Quebec, but failed. Each side had the support of American Indian allies. Port Royal, Acadia (later Nova Scotia), was captured and restored to the French by the Treaty of Ryswick (1697).
Kinkajou, nocturnal foraging mammal of the RACOON family that lives in forests of Central and South America. Slender-bodied, it has a small round head and a long tongue. Primarily a fruit and insect eater, it lives almost entirely in trees, aided by a long prehensile tail. Length: to 57.5cm (22.7in); weight: to 2.7kg (6lb). Family Procyonidae; species *Potos flavus*. *See also* NW pp.164, *165*.
Kinorhynch, one of a group of microscopic, spiny, worm-like marine animals believed to be closely related to the ROTIFERS. They have tubular bodies of about 13 segments, with a mouth at one end and an anus at the other. They live mainly in the mud of the sea bed. *See also* NW p.*121*.
Kinross(shire), former county in E Scotland; in 1975 it became part of Tayside Region. Hills in the E and the NW border a central plain. Farmers raise beef and dairy cattle and grow oats and barley. Wool and linen weaving are the principal industries. The county town was Kinross. Area: 212sq km (82sq miles). Pop. (1971) 6,422.
Kinsella, Thomas (1928–), Irish poet. Introspective and tightly-controlled, his poetry includes *The Starlit Eye* (1952), *Downstream* (1962), *Nightwalker* (1967) and *One* (1974). He also translated some early Irish poetry.
Kinsey, Alfred Charles (1894–1956), US zoologist, noted for his studies on human sexual behaviour. He was a professor of zoology and later director of the Institute for Sex Research, Indiana University. He is best known for *Sexual Behavior in the Human Male* (1948) and *Sexual Behavior in the Human Female* (1953).
Kinshasa, capital and largest city of Zaire, on the border of Zaire and the Republic of Congo. Formerly known as Leopoldville, it replaced Boma as the capital of the Belgian Congo in 1923, and when Zaire gained independence in 1960 it continued as the capital of the new country. Its name was changed in 1966. A major communications and commercial centre, its industries include food processing, tanning, chemicals and textiles. Pop. 1,633,760.
Kinship, relationship by blood or marriage, sometimes extended to cover relations of affinity. It also refers to a complex of rules in society governing descent, succession, inheritance, residence, marriage and sexual relations. *See also* CLAN; ENDOGAMY; EXOGAMY; FAMILY; INCEST; MS pp.250–251, 254–255.
Kipling, Joseph Rudyard (1865–1936), British author, *b.* India. He achieved recognition with his stories about India, including *Plain Tales from the Hills* (1888), and with his only novel *The Light That Failed* (1891). His *Barrack Room Ballads and Other Verses* (1892), including the poem *If*, underlined his imperialist views. He wrote many children's adventures and animal stories, including *The Jungle Book* (1894), *Captains Courageous* (1897), *Kim* (1901) and *Stalky and Co.* (1899). His post-WWI stories, such as *Debits and Credits* (1926), show a more profound artistry. *See also* HC2 pp.*132*, 133.
Kipnis, Igor (1930–), US harpsichordist, *b.* Germany. He made his debut in 1959, and since 1967 has performed throughout Europe, South America and the Middle East. He has published several editions of harpsichord music and in 1971 became associate professor of music in Connecticut, USA.
Kippenberger, Sir Howard (1897–1957), New Zealand soldier. In WWII he served as an officer in Greece, Crete, North Africa and Italy until seriously wounded in 1944. He later edited New Zealand's official war histories.
Kipps (1905), novel by H. G. WELLS which focuses on the social problems of a young, inarticulate draper's assistant who is suddenly elevated in rank by a legacy. Wells is cynical in his condemnation of the superficiality and opportunism of the society Kipps moves into and the novel argues for friendship and love that is not affected by financial considerations.
Kipp's apparatus, chemical apparatus for generating a stream of any gas that can be made by reacting a liquid with a solid, eg hydrogen sulphide gas from hydrochloric acid and ferrous sulphide or carbon dioxide from hydrochloric acid and calcium carbonate (marble chips). When the outlet tap is turned off, internal gas pressure separates the liquid and solid so that the reaction, and gas generation, cease.
Kirchner, Ernst Ludwig (1880–1938), German painter and printmaker and a leader of the Expressionist artists known as Die BRÜCKE. His most famous works are two versions of *Street, Berlin* (1907, 1913). *See also* HC2 p.174.
Kirchhoff, Gustav Robert (1824–87), German physicist, professor at Heidelberg University and in Berlin. He worked with Robert BUNSEN, and developed the spectroscope, with which he discovered the elements caesium (Cs) and rubidium (Rb) in 1860. He also examined the solar spectrum, worked on BLACK BODY radiation, and enunciated several laws (KIRCHHOFF'S LAWS) relating to electrical circuits. *See also* HC2 p.157; SU pp.221, *221*, *224*, 226, *226*.
Kirchhoff's laws, two rules based on the laws of the conservation of charge and energy, that apply to multiple-loop electric circuits. Essentially they state that (1) charge does not accumulate at one point and thin out at another, and (2) around each loop the sum of the ELECTROMOTIVE FORCES equals the sum of the potential differences (voltages) across each of the resistances.
Kirgiz, Turko-Mongolian people who inhabit Kirgizia (Kirgiz SSR) in central Asian USSR. Of the Muslim faith, they are Turkic-speaking nomadic pastoralists who began to settle in the Tien Shan region of Kirgizia in the 7th century after a long history as one of the chief nomadic groups in Central Asia. They were colonized by the Russians during the 19th century. Having fought against the BOLSHEVIKS in the civil war from 1917 to 1921, many Kirgiz perished from famine that followed.
Kirgizia (Kirgizskaja SSR), constituent republic in central Asian USSR, bordered by China in the SE. The capital is Frunze. Russia annexed this area in 1864. The region resisted BOLSHEVIK control between 1917 and 1921. In 1924 it became an autonomous oblast within the Russian Republic (Rossijskaja SFSR) and a constituent republic in 1936. It is a largely mountainous area, and sugar-beet, cotton, tobacco, fruit cereal crops and poppies are grown by means of irrigation. Sheep, cattle, goats and horses are raised. The chief mineral deposits are coal, lead, uranium, mercury, oil and natural gas. Industries: farm machinery, textiles, sugar refining, agricultural processing. Area: 198,500sq km (76,640sq miles). Pop. (1976) 3,372,000.
Kirin (Jilin), province in NE China, on the Chinese-Soviet border; the capital is Changchun. The region is drained by the Sungari River, which flows across the fertile Manchurian plain. Soya beans, wheat, rice and sweet potatoes are grown. It has some of the best woodland in China, and mineral deposits include iron ore, coal, gold and lead. Area: 187,070sq km (72,228sq miles). Pop. 1,200,000.
Kirk, Scots name for a church building, also often applied to the Presbyterian Church of Scotland, which was recognized as the state Church in 1689.
Kirk, Sir John (1832–1922), British physician and naturalist who is best-known for accompanying David LIVINGSTONE during the latter's second expedition into central Africa (1858–63). He was knighted in 1881.
Kirk, Norman Eric (1923–74), New Zealand politician; Prime Minister (1972–74). With vigour and imagination he led the Labour Party to a landslide victory in 1972. Before the end of his term of office, he laid fresh emphasis on New Zealand's role in the Pacific, recognized Communist China and banned national sports contacts with South Africa. *See also* HC2 p.250.
Kirkaldy of Grange, Sir William (*c.*1520–73), Scottish Protestant leader. Mary, Queen of Scots' marriage to Lord DARNLEY in 1565 provoked him to armed opposition. He received Mary's surrender at Carberry Hill in 1567 and joined her supporters on her promise to divorce her third husband, the Earl of BOTHWELL. James VI's supporters hanged him after the siege of Edinburgh Castle.
Kirkcudbright(shire), former county in S Scotland, now part of the Strathclyde Region. It is a mountainous area, and stock raising and cattle farming are the main occupations. Pop. (1971) 27,450.
Kirke, Sir David (*c.*1597–*c.*1656), English merchant adventurer who, with his brothers, captured a fleet of French ships off Quebec and forced Samuel de CHAMPLAIN to surrender the city in 1629. The territory was later restored to France, but Kirke was knighted nonetheless.
Kirke, Col. Percy (*c.*1646–91), English soldier who was involved in alleged atrocities at the Battle of SEDGEMOOR in 1685. He later fought in Ireland on the side of WILLIAM III, commanding the forces which relieved Londonderry in 1689.
Kirkpatrick, Ian (1946–), New Zealand rugby union player who, as a dynamic, world-class loose-forward, played 39 times for the All Blacks (1967–77), scoring 16 tries. He was New Zealand's captain from 1972 to 1973 and played for Canterbury and Poverty Bay.
Kirkpatrick, Ralph (1911–). US harpsichordist and musicologist. He studied at Harvard University and with Wanda LANDOWSKA and Nadia BOULANGER in Paris.
Kirkūk, city in NE Iraq. It is the centre of the country's oil industry , and has a pipeline connection with ports on the Mediterranean Sea. It is also the market town for the region. Products include cereals, fruit and livestock. Pop. (1970 est.) 207,900.
Kirkwall, administrative, trade and shipping centre for the ORKNEY ISLANDS, on Mainland island. St Magnus' Cathedral was built in 1137, and there are many other ancient ruins. Industries: fishing and tourism. Pop. (1971) 4,618.
Kirov, Sergei Mironovich (1888–1934), Soviet political figure. He was a popular and effective speaker and was elected to the Communist Party POLITBURO in 1930. His murder, probably on STALIN's orders, served as a pretext for the Stalin purges (1934–38). *See also* HC2 p.275.
Kirov Ballet and Opera Company, founded as a dancing company in 1735 in St Petersburg (Leningrad). Under Marius PETIPA the Kirov Ballet was the world's top company, with dancers such as Anna PAVLOVA and Vaslav NIJINSKY. The Opera, too, has made a distinguished contribution to Soviet culture. Among the works it has premiered are Modest Mussorgsky's *Boris Godunov* (1874) and Alexander Borodin's *Prince Igor* (1890). *See also* HC2 p.275.
Kirshon, Vladimir Mihailovich (1902–38), Soviet dramatist. A Bolshevist, he often wrote propagandist plays, including *Rzhavchina* or *Konstantin Terekhin* (1926; tr. *Red Dust*, 1930) and *Khleb* (1930; tr. *Bread*, 1934). He was a leader of the Association of Proletarian Writers in Moscow, was arrested in 1937 during the Stalin purges and was shot in prison.
Kirton. *See* CREDITON.
Kisangani, city and port in N central Zaire, on the River Congo. Formerly known as Stanleyville, it was a stronghold of Patrice LUMUMBA until his assassination in 1961. It has since been the site of several revolts against the central government. Industries include metal goods and textiles. Pop. (1974) 310,705.
Kisfaludy, Károly (1788–1830), Hun-

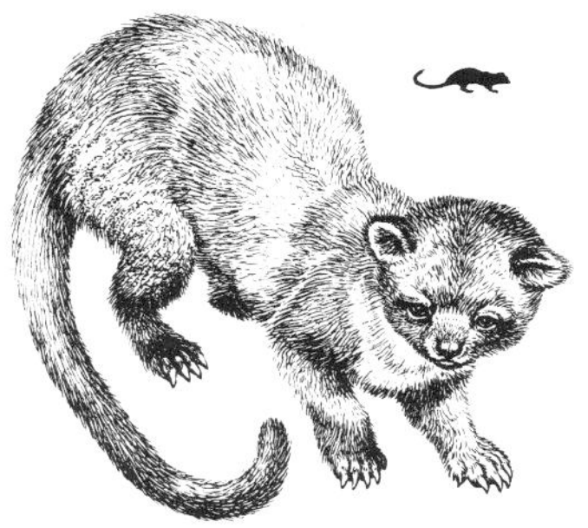

Kinkajous can hang upside down in the trees, holding on tightly with their prehensile tails.

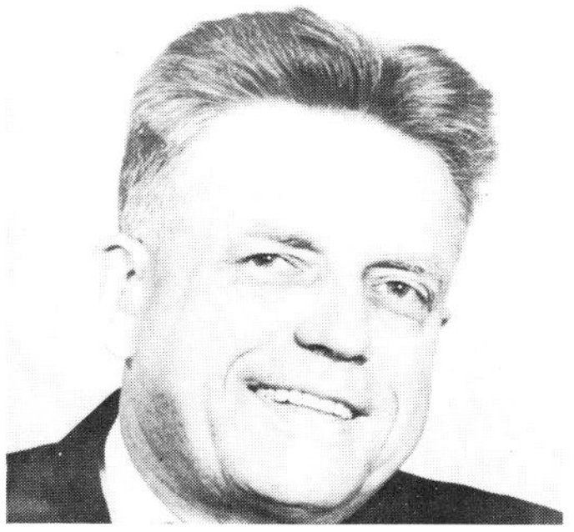

Dr Kinsey's reports produced highly detailed accounts of American sexual behaviour.

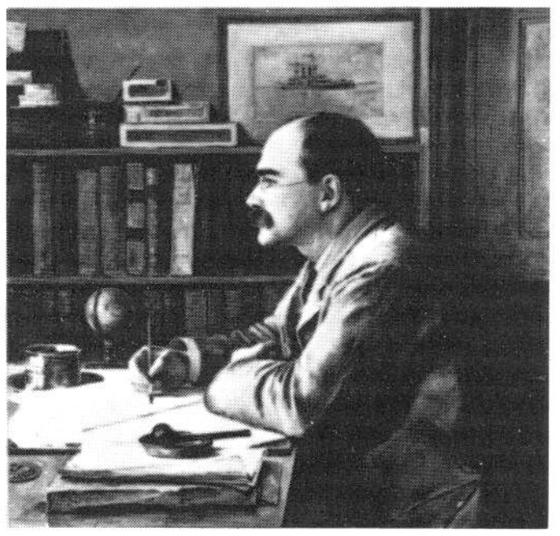

Rudyard Kipling's attitudes to imperialism have often been misinterpreted by his critics.

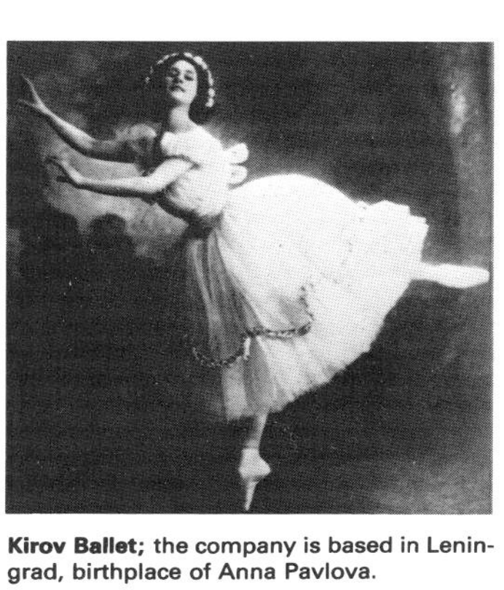

Kirov Ballet; the company is based in Leningrad, birthplace of Anna Pavlova.

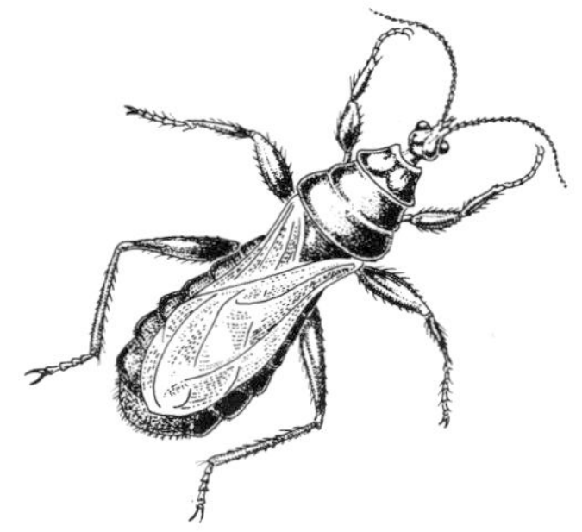

Kissing bugs are the disease-carrying insects that bite animals around the mouth.

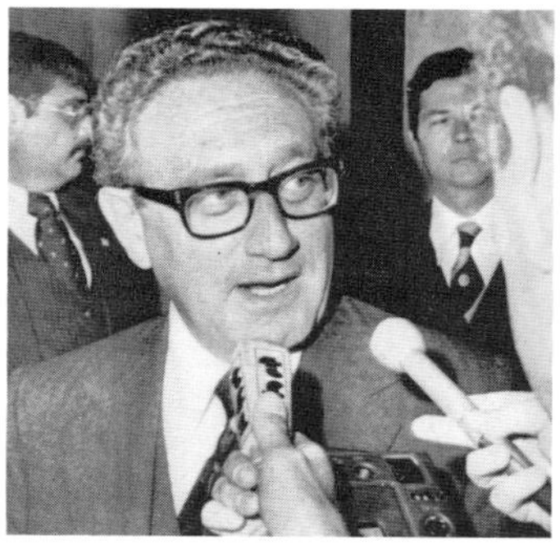

Henry Kissinger, the former American Secretary of State, faces a battery of reporters.

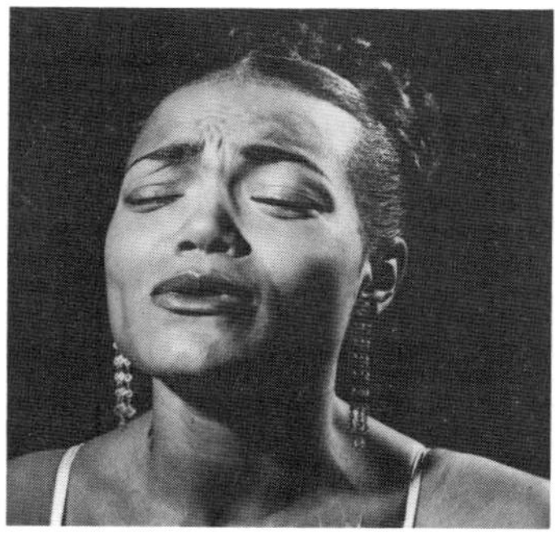

Eartha Kitt, the American singer who perfected her image as a *femme fatale.*

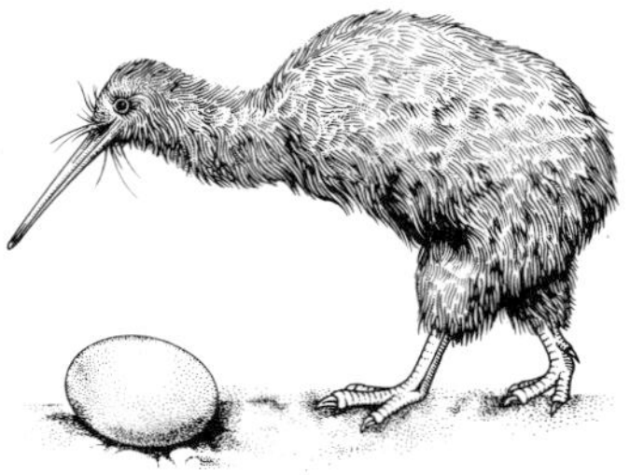

Kiwis are unique birds in that they have nostrils at the tip of their long beaks.

garian playwright, the founder of modern Hungarian drama. A pioneer of Magyar comedy, as well as of national drama, his works include *The Tartars in Hungary* (1819) and *The Suitors* (1819). With his brother, Sándor (1772-1844), a poet, he was a major force in the Hungarian Romantic movement.

Kisfaludy, Sándor (1772–1844), Hungarian poet, dramatist and novelist. His best-known writings, using a highly elaborate verse form, are the cycles *Plaintive Love* (1801) and *Happy Love* (1807).

Kish, ancient city of Mesopotamia. It was located in the Euphrates river valley E of Babylon. In the fourth millennium BC it was a strong Sumerian city. Excavations since 1922 have revealed that SARGON, King of AKKADIA, built a palace *c.*2600 BC and NEBUCHADNEZZAR II and NABONIDUS, kings of BABYLON, erected temples in the 6th century BC.

Kishar, in Sumerian mythology, the personification of the earth at the time of the creation. Anshar the sky and Kishar the earth were born to a pair of serpents who came from the primordial sea. From Anshar and Kishar issued the divinities who filled the sky, the earth and the underworld.

Kismet, Turkish-Arabic word meaning "destiny" or "fate" and the title of an Oriental melodrama by Edward Knoblock (1874–1945), first produced in 1911. In 1953, with additional songs and music arranged from the works of Alexander BORODIN, the work became a Broadway hit whose success was repeated in London in 1955 when *Kismet* was also filmed for the fifth time.

Kissing bug, or conenose, brown to black BUG found in South and Central America, Mexico and Texas. It bites human beings and rodents, usually about the mouth, and is a carrier of CHAGAS' DISEASE. Length: 25–33mm (1–1.3in). Family Reduviidae; genera *Triatoma* and *Rhodinus.*

Kissinger, Henry Alfred (1923–), US political leader, *b.* Germany. While a professor at Harvard University, he wrote several books on political science and served as adviser to various government agencies. He became President Richard NIXON's assistant for National Security in 1969 and became the chief adviser on foreign policy. President Nixon named him Secretary of State in 1973 and he continued in that post under President Gerald Ford. In 1973 he shared the Nobel Peace Prize with Le Duc Tho for his part in negotiating a ceasefire in the Vietnam War, even though fighting continued until 1975. He worked for détente between East and West during the Nixon presidency and acted as mediator in the Middle East crisis of 1973–74. *See also* HC2 pp.254, *255*, 307.

Kissing Gourami. *See* GOURAMI.

Kiss Me Kate (1948), musical by Cole PORTER based on the play by Samuel and Bella Spewack, which in turn was based on Shakespeare's *The Taming of the Shrew.* It was first performed in New York. In 1953 it was made into a 3-D film starring Howard Keele, Kathryn Grayson and Ann Miller.

Kiswah, cloth covering of the KAABA. Renewed each year, the Kiswah is made in Egypt and transported to MECCA by a ceremonial pilgrim caravan. The cloth is black brocade with the Muslim profession of faith woven in gold. The old Kiswah is cut into pieces which are sold to pilgrims. *See also* HC1 pp.144–145, *145.*

Kitaj, Ronald, B. (1932–), US painter who studied and worked in England during the 1950s and 1960s, returning to the USA in 1967. R.B. Kitaj was a leader in Britain of the movement away from the abstraction of the 1950s towards a more figurative kind of painting which attempted to fuse the styles of CUBISM and MATISSE.

Kitakyūshū, industrial city port on N Kyūshū, S Japan. It was formed in 1963 by the union of the cities of Yawata, Tobata, Wakamatsu, Kokura and Moji, and is now one of the country's most important manufacturing regions. Industries: shipping, shipbuilding, iron and steel, and textiles. Pop. (1975) 1,060,000.

Kitasato, Shibasaburo (1852–1931), Japanese bacteriologist who isolated the bacilli that cause the diseases tetanus, anthrax (1889) and dysentery (1898). In 1890 he prepared a diphtheria antitoxin. He also discovered, independently of Alexandre YERSIN, the infectious organism that causes bubonic plague. He trained under Robert KOCH in Germany. *See also* NW pp.36–37.

Kit-cat Club, English literary and political club founded *c.*1700 in London by Whig politicians and leading writers, some of whom were Joseph Addison, William Congreve, Sir Richard Steel and Sir Robert Walpole. The members met in a public house run by Christopher Cat, whose most popular dish was a mutton pie known locally as a kit-cat. The name kit-cat was also applied to portraits – measuring 91×71cm (36×28in) – of the members.

Kitchener, Horatio Herbert, Earl (1850–1916), British soldier involved in the defeat of the MAHDI in the Sudan. As a major in the Egyptian Cavalry, he took part in the relief of Khartoum (1883–85). In 1892 he became a major-general in the Egyptian army and achieved the pacification of the Sudan in 1898 with the victories at Atbara and Omdurman. After service in the South African War, and then in India and Egypt, he was appointed Secretary of State for War in 1914. He was later lost at sea when the cruiser in which he was travelling to Russia sank after hitting a mine.

Kitchener, city in S Ontario, Canada, in the Grand River Valley. Originally known as Berlin, it was renamed in 1916 in honour of Lord Kitchener. It manufactures textiles and rubber products. Pop. (1974) 111,805.

Kitchen midden, also called shell-mound, in archaeology a refuse heap, usually of discarded remains of edible shellfish mixed with human artefacts. It can provide an archaeologist with valuable clues to the nature of a past culture. Most known middens were established in Europe and N Africa after the disappearance of large game animals. *See also* PE p.*149.*

Kitchen sink drama, realistic presentation of true-to-life situations. Beginning in the 1950s, this style of treatment has been applied to plays, films, books and art.

Kite, common name for several diurnal birds of prey, especially the red kite, *Milvus milvus,* which frequents hilly country and wooded slopes in Europe. It has a hooked bill, long wings and a long forked tail. Like the HAWK, it is commonly seen circling, soaring and gliding. Length: 60cm (24in). Family Accipitridae.

Kithara. *See* CITTERN.

Kitimat, district municipality developed around the site of one of the world's largest aluminium smelters completed in 1954. It is at the head of the Douglas Channel to the SE of Prince Rupert, British Columbia, Canada. Bauxite from Jamaica is used to produce aluminium, the process being powered by the Kemano hydroelectric scheme. Pop. (1971) 11,824. *See also* MM p.34.

Kitksan, tribe of North American Indians, occupying an area along the Skeena River in NW British Columbia. Kitksan are closely related to the Niska and Tsimshian peoples and speak the Tsimshian tongue. They are noted for their sculpture.

Kitt, Eartha (1928–), US singer and actress, the seductive singer of many hit songs, including *C'est Si Bon* and *Monotonous* (a showstopper from the New York show *New Faces of 1952,* which brought her fame). She has also starred in films, notably *Accused* (1957), and has appeared internationally on television and in cabaret. She has written an autobiography, *Thursday's Child* (1956).

Kittiwake, Arctic GULL with a greenish-yellow bill, black wing-tips and short dark legs. It flies low over open seas, hunting for fish. The female lays one to three spotted pale eggs in a cup-shaped nest in cliffs. Length: to 41cm (16in); wingspan 91cm (36in). Family Laridae: species *Rissa tridactyla.*

Kittredge, George Lyman (1860–1941), US scholar and critic. He was a professor of English at Harvard University (1894–1936) and a leading writer on the English language. His works include *Chaucer and his Poetry* (1915) and a single-volume edition of *The Complete Works of Shakespeare* (1936).

Kitwe, city in N central Zambia, 290km (180 miles) N of Lusaka. Founded in 1937, it is the main trade and industrial centre of the copperbelt. Pop. (1972) 331,000.

Kiushiu. *See* KYŪSHŪ.

Kiva, underground ceremonial chamber of PUEBLO INDIANS. Each Pueblo Indian religious society has its own kiva, and many of its rites are performed there. Kivas are traditionally circular and are highly decorated.

Kivi, Aleksis (1834–72), pen-name of Aleksis Stenvall, a Finnish writer and dramatist. He wrote *The Seven Brothers* (1870), the first novel to be published in Finnish. His tragedy *Kullervo,* derived from Finland's national epic the *Kalevala,* won a drama competition in 1860. He also wrote a comedy, *The Shoemakers of the Heath* (1864).

Kiwi, any of three species of flightless, mainly nocturnal, fast-running, forest and scrubland bird of New Zealand; especially the common brown kiwi, *Apteryx australis.* It has hair-like feathers and a long, flexible bill with which it probes for food in the ground. The eggs, which are incubated by the male, are laid in a leaf-lined scrape or burrow. Family Apterygidae. *See also* NW pp.*140*, *153*, 211.

Kiwis, the name given to New Zealand's national rugby league team, although the original New Zealand tourists to Britain in 1907 were dubbed the "All Golds" as a comparison with the famous, and amateur, rugby union team, the All Blacks. Although rugby league does not have the same following as rugby union in New Zealand, the Kiwis have enjoyed some international success: they won the Courtney Trophy for the best record in test matches 1960–65.

Kiyonaga, Torii (1752–1815), Japanese ukiyo-e (colour) printmaker. He worked during the great period of Japanese printmaking. He is noted for his woodcuts of beautiful women and warriors, and is ranked as the most brilliant representative of this style.

Kizil. *See* KYZYL-KUM DESERT.

Kjeldahl method, rapid method for measuring the proportion of nitrogen in an organic compound, named after Johan G. C. T. Kjeldahl, the Danish chemist. Nitrogen in the sample is converted into ammonium sulphate by heating it and a catalyst in concentrated sulphuric acid. Sodium hydroxide is added and the whole is boiled, liberating ammonia. This is dissolved in acid and the quantity of ammonia, and therefore the nitrogen, is determined by TITRATION.

Klagenfurt, city in Austria, N of the Karawagen Mts near the Yugoslavian border. It holds an annual wood trade fair and is also a popular sports centre. Industries include woodworking plants, leather and clothing. Pop. (1969 est.) 73,200.

Klaproth, Martin Heinrich (1743–1817), German chemist who began as an apothecary's apprentice. He became the first professor of chemistry at Berlin University. He was a pioneer in analytical techniques, recognizing and naming a number of elements, including uranium (1789). He also recognized and named titanium (1795), tellurium (1798) and cerium (1803), some of which had already been isolated, although left unnamed, by other scientists.

Klaus, Josef (1910–), Austrian lawyer and politician after WWII. He was Governor of Salzburg (1949–61), Minister of Finance (1961–63), and Chancellor of Austria (1964–70).

Klausenburg. *See* CLUJ.

Klavier. *See* CLAVIER.

Kléber, Jean Baptiste (1753–1800), French general. He was an architect, but in 1789, after the outbreak of the Revolution, he joined the National Guard and fought with distinction in the Revolutionary Wars. In 1793 he put down a royalist rebellion in the Vendée. He commanded one of Napoleon's divisions in Egypt (1798–1800); defeated the Turks twice; and recaptured Cairo. He was assassinated by an Egyptian.

Klebs, Edwin (1834–1913), German physician and pathologist known for his work in bacteriology. In 1884 he and Friedrich LÖFFLER discovered the diphtheria bacillus. He held professorships, both in Europe and in the USA. His research included original observations on tuberculosis, syphilis and malaria.

Klee, Paul (1879–1940), Swiss painter who was also a trained musician. He began as a graphic artist and later was influenced in the development of his own pictorial language by CUBISM, hieroglyphs, primitive art and children's drawings. Combining these elements with a sensitive feel for colour, he produced clever, inspirational works of subtle simplicity. He studied in Munich and by the end of WWI was established as a master. He taught at the BAUHAUS (1920–31) and at Düsseldorf Academy (1931–33) but returned to Switzerland in 1933 after the Nazis had condemned his work as degenerate. Characteristic works include *Graduated Shades of Red-Green* (1921) and *A Young Lady's Adventure* (1922), *Around the Fish* (1926) and *Revolutions of the Viaducts* (1937). In his *Pedagogical Sketchbooks* (1925), Klee defined the principles of his art. *See also* HC2 p.175.

Kleiber, Erich (1890–1956), Austrian conductor. He conducted in German opera houses and served as music director of the Berlin Opera (1923–35). During this period he introduced many new works, including Alban BERG's opera *Wozzeck* in 1925. From 1936–49 he conducted German opera in Buenos Aires, and returned (1955) for a brief time as conductor of the Berlin Opera.

Klein, Abraham (1909–72), Canadian poet. His work, full of humour and erudition, often reflects his Jewish heritage. *Hath not a Jew* (1940), draws brilliantly on the richness of Jewish culture; *The Hitleriad* (1944) is a savage attack on anti-Semitism; and his novel *The Second Scroll* vividly recreates the ZIONIST pilgrimage.

Klein, Melanie (1882–1960), British psychoanalyst, *b.* Austria, who developed therapy for young children. In *The Psychoanalysis of Children* (1932) she presented her methods and ideas of child analysis; she believed play was a symbolic way of controlling anxiety and analysed it to gain insight into the psychological processes of early life. Basically Freudian in approach, she emphasized such concepts as the ego, superego and the Oedipus complex in the mental development of children.

Klein, Yves (1928–62), French painter. In his collages of paint and assorted objects he attempted to destroy the concept of paintings as paint on canvas. His work was disliked during his lifetime but his ideas have been much copied since.

Kleist, Bernd Heinrich Wilhelm von (1777–1811), German dramatist. He left the Prussian Army as a young officer to write what are considered to be some of Germany's best dramas: *Amphitryon* (1807) and *Der Zerbrochene Krug* (1808). In *Prinz Friedrich von Homburg* (1810) he praised Prussia. *The Marquise von O. and Other Stories* is a collection of short pieces. He shot himself at the age of 34.

Kleist, Ewald Christian von (1715–59), German poet, chiefly remembered for his long poem *Der Frühling* (1749). He also wrote *Ode an die Preussische Armee* (1757), in praise of Frederick the Great's Prussia. He served as an officer and was fatally wounded at Kunersdorf. Other works include *Seneca* and *Cissides und Paches* (1759).

Kleitman, Nathaniel (1895–), US physiologist, *b.* Russia. His pioneering researches into the study of sleep led him, with his colleague, Eugene Aserinsky, to the discovery in 1952 that rapid eye movements occur in sleep only when a person is dreaming. *See also* MS pp.42, *43*.

Klemperer, Otto (1885–1973), German conductor. He was celebrated for his interpretations of Beethoven, Brahms and Mahler. In 1933, with the rise of Nazism in Germany, he went to the USA and became conductor of the Los Angeles Philharmonic. In 1946 he returned to Europe as director of the Budapest Opera (1947–50). In 1970 in London, aged 85, he conducted the New Philharmonia Orchestra in Mahler's *Das Lied von der Erde*.

Kleptomania, compulsive, pathological desire to steal. Often the stolen objects are of little value to the thief and so seem to have a symbolic value. The causes of kleptomania are unknown; some psychologists believe it is the result of a deprived childhood whereas others see the thefts as aggressive acts. The methods of treatment vary from psychoanalysis to aversion therapy, but most have so far been unsuccessful.

Kleve. *See* CLÈVES.

Klimt, Gustav (1862–1918), Austrian painter and designer, a founder member of the VIENNA SEZESSION group and the foremost ART NOUVEAU painter in Vienna. His style, which owed something to Japanese art, was highly decorative and erotic; it considerably influenced the decorative arts in Austria and the work of the painters Egon SCHIELE and Oskar KOKOSCHKA. Klimt devoted much of his time to architectural decoration, eg *The Kiss* (1908), and murals for Stoclet House, Brussels, designed by Josef HOFFMANN.

Kline, Franz (1910–62), US painter, an important figure in the ABSTRACT EXPRESSIONIST movement. From the 1950s he began to paint large, stark, grid-like compositions, generally in black and white and often reminiscent of Chinese calligraphy. He re-introduced colour in his later works.

Klinger, Friedrich Maximilian von (1752–1831), German playwright. A friend of GOETHE, his drama *Der Wirrwarr; oder Sturm und Drang* (1776) gave its name to the STURM UND DRANG (meaning storm and stress) drama movement. His other works include the play *The Twins* (1776) and the novel *Faust's Life, Deeds, and Journey to Hell* (1791).

Klipspringer, small ANTELOPE, native to rocky areas of Africa S of the Sahara Desert. Usually only the male carries short, spiked horns. The klipspringer has a thick coat of grizzled, bristly hair. Height: to 60cm (23.6in) at the shoulder; weight: to 16kg (35lb). Family Bovidae; species *Oreotragus oreotragus*.

Klondike, region of Yukon Territory in NW Canada, E of the Alaskan border around the Klondike River. It is remembered in connection with the KLONDIKE GOLD RUSH. Some gold is still mined in the region. Area: approx. 2,000sq km (775sq miles).

Klondike Gold Rush (1896–1904), the stampede of prospectors to the Klondike region, following the discovery of gold in the Yukon Territory of NW Canada. George Carmack was the first to find large quantities of gold, in the gravel of Bonanza Creek. Word quickly spread to the USA and by 1898 the mining town of Dawson had grown to 25,000 people. During that year's harsh winter the community was threatened with famine, and all food was commandeered and rationed. About 100 million dollars worth of gold was extracted before the easily accessible lodes were exhausted. Access to the Yukon during this time aggravated a long-standing dispute between Canada and the USA over the Alaska Panhandle boundary.

Kloos, Willem Johan Theodoor (1859–1938), Dutch Romantic poet and critic. In 1885 he founded *The New Guide*, a literary journal, in which he expressed his personal distaste for the effete and excessively rhetorical literature of his day.

Klopstock, Friedrich Gottlieb (1724–1803), German poet. He anticipated the STURM UND DRANG literary movement and influenced other poets such as Goethe, Rilke and Hölderlin. While still a student he began writing *Der Messias* (1748; tr. *The Messiah*, 1826), an epic in 20 cantos. His *Odes* (1747–80) were set to music by GLUCK and SCHUBERT, and others, including MAHLER, set his lyrics to music.

Kloster-Zeven, Convention of (1757), agreement signed by the Duke of Cumberland, commander of the British army early in the SEVEN YEARS WAR, at Zeven, Germany, after his defeat by the French. He agreed to allow the French to occupy Hanover. The British government learned about the document and dismissed Cumberland.

Kluck, Alexander von (1846–1934), German general. In August 1914 he led the German advance in France to within 48km (30 miles) of Paris, but was defeated by British and French forces at the first battle of the MARNE. *See also* HC2 pp.188, 190.

Klystron, ELECTRON TUBE that makes use of a stream of electrons moving at controlled speeds. Klystrons are used in ultra-high-frequency (UHF) circuits, such as radar transmitters, where they operate at frequencies up to 400,000MHz. *See also* RADAR.

Knapweed, flowering plant of the COMPOSITAE family, with deep blue-purple, rayed florets resembling those of THISTLES. Knapweed commonly grows wild in meadows and on path verges, although some species are cultivated. Genus *Centaurea*.

Knave, originally the son of the house (cf the German *Knabe*, "boy") and thus a squire or knight's attendant. In this sense it became the name of the lowest court card of any card suit (also called the Jack). By the 16th century the term described any attendant or servant, and pejoratively, a knowing rogue – which is what it means today.

Kneller, Sir Godfrey (*c.* 1646–1723), German-born painter who settled in London (1674), where he became the foremost portrait painter. His best-known works include 42 portraits known as the *Kit Cat series* (National Portrait Gallery, London). He founded the first English Academy of Painting (1711). Knighted in 1692, he was the first painter to be created an English baronet (1715).

Knickerbocker School, group of writers associated with New York City in the first half of the 19th century (Knickerbocker was an affectionate term given to the elite resident families of New York). Members of the School published individually, and their work also appeared in New York newspapers and in *Knickerbocker* magazine. Among the writers were William Cullen Bryant, Lydia M. Child, James Fenimore Cooper, Joseph R. Drake, Fitz-Greene Halleck, Washington Irving, Clement Moore, James K. Paulding, Nathaniel Willis and Samuel Woodworth. *See also* HC2 p.288.

Knievel, Evel (1949–), US motorcycle stunt rider. His flair for publicity led him to undertake daring stunts, the most famous of which was an (unsuccessful) attempt to leap across Snake River Canyon, Idaho, in 1974.

Knight, Dame Laura (1877–1970), British artist. Remembered for her many studies of ballet, circus and gypsy life painted in a lively style. In 1936 she became the third woman ever to be elected to the Royal Academy.

Knight, Sarah Kemble (1666–1727), colonial American author who became known as an astute businesswoman. In 1704 she travelled by horse from Boston to New York; *The Journal of Mme. Knight*, her humorous diary of the trip and an interesting record of contemporary life, was published in 1825.

Knight, originally a term for a military attendant or close follower of a battle leader. By the 12th century, under the literary ideal of courtly love, the knight had become a romantic figure, the epitome of virtuous manhood. Before the 14th century, however, he was a fully equipped mounted warrior, with a metal helmet and chain mail; and by the 15th century he had a complete suit of steel armour. Under the feudal system, the knight was the retainer of the sovereign, to whom he was bound as a vassal, and whom he was obliged to provide with military service, hospitality or funds. During the 20th century the title has lost much of its glory. Although the dubbing ceremony

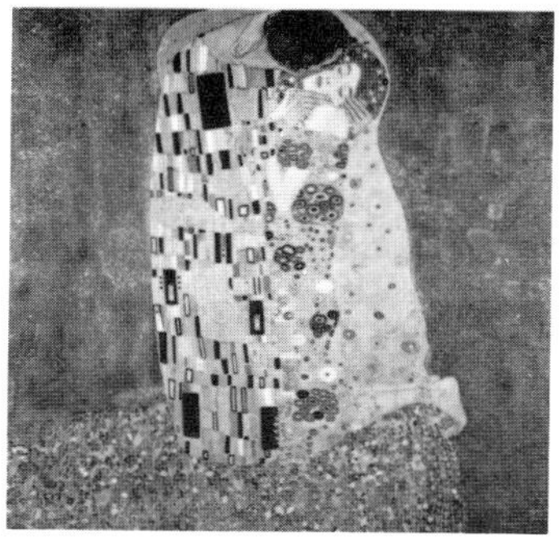

Gustav Klimt produced many decorative mosaics; this is *The Kiss* (1908).

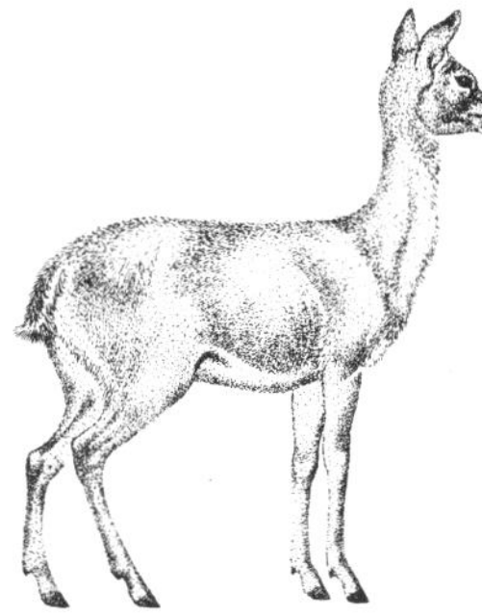

Klipspringers are flecked with gold markings and perform startling antics when alarmed.

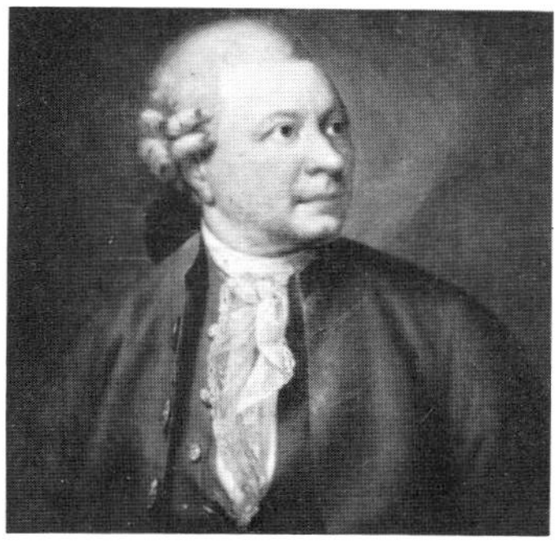

Friedrich Klopstock suffered a tragic loss when his wife died after only four years.

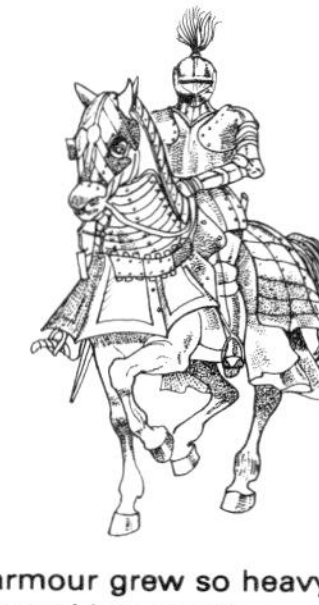

Knights' armour grew so heavy that a crane had to be used in mounting.

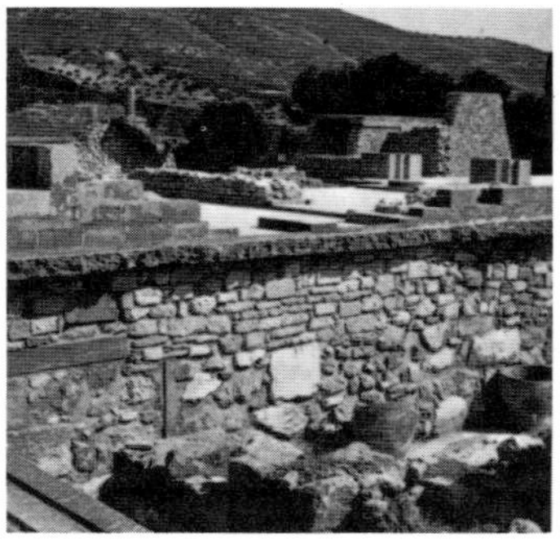

Knossos, whose excavation revealed the splendours of the Minoan civilization.

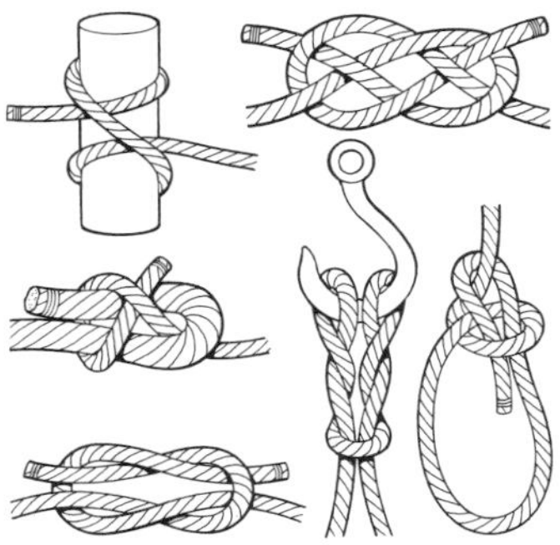

Knots and their applications are still essential knowledge for all sailors on board ship.

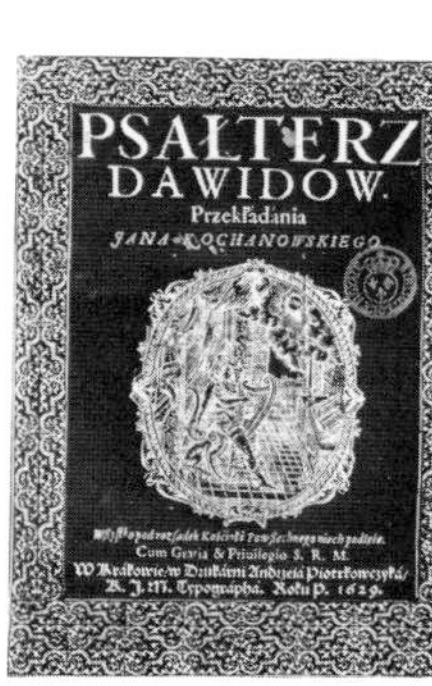

Jan Kochanowski; title page of the *Psalterz Dawidow* (*Psalter of David.*)

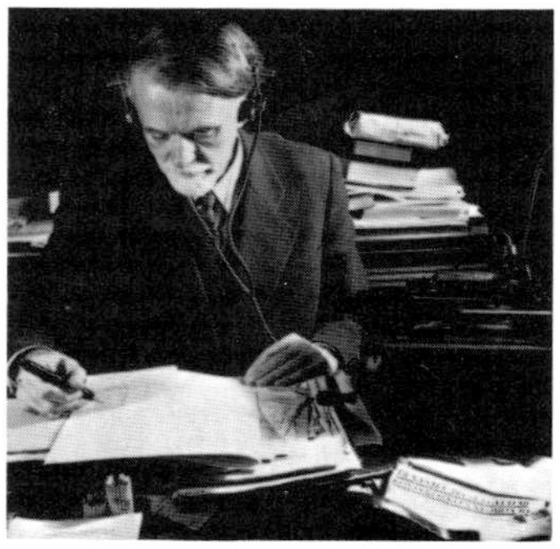

Zoltán Kodaly; his study of Hungarian folk music is evident in many of his works.

has changed little for centuries – the sovereign lightly taps each shoulder of the new knight with the ceremonial sword – military knighthoods are now far less common than those given for political or social services on the various Honours Lists announced during each year. Some of the ancient orders of knighthood still remain, however, including the Order of the Garter (or of St George), the order of the Bath (so called because formerly the knight was ceremonially bathed on the eve of his knighthood), and Knight Bachelor (the most ancient title, and that of lowest rank). *See also* MM p.161, *161.*

Knights Hospitallers, or Knights of St John of Jerusalem, military religious order established early in the 11th century. The knights cared for Christian pilgrims who fell ill in Jerusalem, where they had a hospital and hostel. During the CRUSADES the Hospitallers policed routes to Jerusalem, together with their bitter rivals, the KNIGHTS TEMPLAR. After the end of the crusader states (1291), the Hospitallers fortified Christian strongholds first in Cyprus and then in Rhodes, until 1522. Today there remain two charitable orders in Jerusalem that still maintain a hospital there (one Anglican, the other Roman Catholic). *See also* HC1 pp.176–177.

Knights Templar, military religious order established in 1118, with headquarters in the supposed Temple of SOLOMON in Jerusalem. With the KNIGHTS HOSPITALLERS, the Templars protected routes to Jerusalem for Christians during the CRUSADES and amassed a great fortune for their order; fighting between the two orders contributed to the failure of the Crusades. The possessions of the Templars in France attracted King Philip IV, who urged Pope Clement V to abolish the order in 1312. Their property was confiscated and many members of the order were tortured and executed. *See also* HC1 pp.176–177.

Knipper, Lev Constantinovich (1898–), Russian composer who studied in Berlin under Philipp JARNACH. His early work shows the influence of Igor STRAVINSKY and he has written many symphonies, several operas and chamber music. In 1932 he was appointed music instructor to the Russian army and navy.

Knitting, construction of a fabric by joining loops of yarn with needles. Although it is allied in origin to weaving it was apparently unknown in Europe before the 15th century when it began to be practised in Spain and Italy. It probably came to Europe from the Arab world. Two needles with heads are required for flat work and three or more, pointed at both ends for tubular work. There are two basic stitches, the weft (including the styles known as plain, purl and rib) and warp (which can only be produced on machines). The first knitting machine was invented in England in 1589 by William Lee, but the principle was not applied to a power-driven machine until 1864. *See also* MM pp.58, 59, *59.*

Knockout, blow that renders a person unconscious; in boxing, it is also the stunning of a man so that he is unable to rise from the canvas before the count of ten. A technical knockout also ends a boxing match. It is ruled when an injured boxer cannot properly defend himself or does not come out at the start of a round.

Knossos, ancient city on the NW coast of Crete, 6.4km (4 miles) SE of modern Candia. In 1900 Sir Arthur EVANS began excavations which revealed that Knossos had been inhabited before 3000 BC. His main discovery was of a palace (built *c.*2000 BC and rebuilt *c.*1700), whose existence had hitherto been thought a legend. Planned on a large scale, the palace included a great throne room, a theatre, a central court and many small compartments. Its complexity may well have given rise to the Greek legend of the Labyrinth. Close to the palace were the houses of Cretan nobles. The whole complex also contains many frescoes which are informative about Cretan life. Knossos dominated Crete *c.*1500 BC but the palace was occupied (*c.*1400) by Mycenean invaders from the mainland, who used a form of LINEAR SCRIPT known as Linear B. The city, however, stayed an important centre until the 4th century AD.

Knot, interlacement of ropes used to bind objects together. There are many types. A sheep-shank, for example, shortens a rope, while a splice knot joins two ropes at the ends.

Knot, unit of measurement equal to one nautical mile per hour – 1 knot equals 1.852km/h (1.15mph). The speeds of ships and aircraft are generally expressed in knots, as are those of winds and currents.

Knot, SANDPIPER that nests in the N tundra and winters in temperate coastal areas. It is usually chestnut and brown with black markings. It feeds on small animals. Length: 25.4cm (10in). Species *Calidris canutus. See also* NW p.*227.*

Knott, Alan (1946–), British cricketer who has played for Kent and England. In 1977 he signed for the Kerry Packer cricket circus. Knott became holder of the world record for wicket-keeping dismissals in 1976, when he passed Godfrey Evans' total. In 89 Test matches from 1967–77, Knott claimed 252 victims: 233 caught and 19 stumped.

Knowles, James Sheridan (1784–1862), Irish dramatist. He lived most of his life in London, and became a Baptist in 1844. His plays include *Caius Gracchus* (1815), *William Tell* (1825), *The Hunchback* (1832) and *The Love Chase* (1837).

Knowles, John (1926–), US author. A writer of short stories and travel articles, his first novel, *A Separate Peace,* was published in 1960. Other works include *Indian Summer* (1966) and *Spreading Fires* (1974).

Knox, Henry (1750–1806), US general and America's first secretary of war 1785–94. He took part in every major battle of the American War of Independence and was a close adviser to George WASHINGTON, becoming a brigadier-general in 1776. He founded the Society of the Cincinnati (1783), an organization formed by officers of the Continental Army for patriotic purposes.

Knox, John (*c.*1514–72), leader of the Protestant Reformation in Scotland. Ordained a Catholic priest, he nevertheless took up the cause of the Reformation. Having been imprisoned in France (1547), he lived in exile in England as a Reformed preacher. When the Catholic Mary I came to the throne in 1553 he fled to Switzerland where, in Geneva, he was influenced by CALVIN. In 1559 Knox returned to Scotland, where he continued to promote the Protestant cause through preaching and pamphlets advocating rebellion against tyrannical rulers. In 1560, with military help from England and while the young and Catholic MARY, QUEEN OF SCOTS was away in France, the Scottish Parliament, under Knox's leadership, made Presbyterianism the state religion. *See also* PRESBYTERIANISM; CHURCHES: HC1 p.298, *298.*

Knox, Ronald Arbuthnot Hilary (1888–1957), British priest and writer who translated the Bible from the Vulgate (1939–49). The son of the Bishop of Manchester, he was appointed chaplain of Trinity College, Oxford, in 1912, where he gained a reputation as a religious controversialist. He was received into the Roman Catholic Church in 1917 and ordained two years later.

Knudsen, William Signius (1879–1948), US industrialist and public official, *b.* Denmark. He emigrated to the USA in 1899, joined the Ford Motor Company in 1902 and became its production manager in 1914. He moved to General Motors in 1921, becoming president of the corporation in 1937. From 1940 until the end of WWII he co-ordinated US military supplies for the National Defense Research Committee. Later, he was appointed director of the Office of Production Management.

Knum-Ra, or Khnemu, in Egyptian mythology, the creator of the universe, the gods and man; husband of the sisters Sati and Anuket. The ram-headed Knum-Ra was supposed to have shaped the gods and man on his potter's wheel using the mud of the River Nile as his clay.

Knur and spell, ancient game played in the north of England in which a small ball (knur), weighing 14g (0.5oz), is struck with a bat or stick, the distance hit determining the winner. The ball can be set up for hitting by releasing it from a spring trap (spell), by suspension in a gallows frame, or throwing it up by hand.

Koa, Hawaiian tree valued for its wood, used in cabinet making. It has clustered flowers and 15cm (6in) pods. Height: to 21m (70ft). Family Leguminosae: species *Acacia koa.*

Koala, small MARSUPIAL that lives in eucalyptus trees of Australia, eating their leaves. Regarded as the traditional "teddy bear", it is not actually related to bears. A single young is born at a rudimentary stage of development, is then nurtured in its mother's pouch until fully formed, and is finally carried on her back for a further six months. Length: 85cm (33in). Species *Phascolarctos cinereus. See also* NW pp.*159, 205,* 210.

Koan, in ZEN Buddhism, a question or statement used to train novices through meditation on problems which cannot be resolved analytically. Of perhaps 1,700 examples, one of the best-known is: What is the sound of one hand clapping?

Kobe, city port on SW Honshu, Japan, on the N shore of Osaka Bay. In 1878 Hyogo, an important fishing port for over 1,000 years, became part of Kobe which since then has become a major port of Japan. Largely rebuilt after suffering bomb damage in WWII, the city is now also an industrial centre. Industries include shipbuilding, iron and steel and chemicals. Pop.(1970) 1,288,937.

København. *See* COPENHAGEN.

Koch, Ludwig (1881–1974), German naturalist who was formerly a singer (1905–14). He was the first to record directly the songs and cries of birds and wild animals, and is the originator of "sound books". From 1936 he lived in Britain. His works include *Songs of Wild Birds* (with E.M. Nicholson; 1936–37), *Animal Language* (with J. Huxley; 1938) and *Memoirs of a Birdman* (1955).

Koch, Robert (1843–1910), German bacteriologist. He was awarded the 1905 Nobel Prize in physiology and medicine for his discovery of the bacillus that causes TUBERCULOSIS. This work laid the foundation for methods of determining the causative agent of a disease.

Kochanowski, Jan (1530–84), major poet of the Polish Renaissance. He was mainly a writer of didactic verse and classical drama. Kochanowski's lyrics, his version of the psalms, *Psalterz Dawidów* (1579), and the laments on the death of his daughter in *Treny* (1580) represent his main achievements.

Köchel, Ludwig von (1800–77), Austrian musicographer. He was the first to catalogue the complete works of MOZART in his *Chronological-Thematic Index* (1862). His numbering system, although considerably revised by Alfred Einstein (1937), is the basis of present-day identification of Mozart's works, each number being preceded by the letter K.

Kocher, Emil Theodor (1841–1917), Swiss surgeon who was awarded the 1909 Nobel Prize in physiology and medicine for his work on the physiology, pathology and surgery of the thyroid gland. He was the first to remove the thyroid gland in goitre cases. *See also* MS p.100, *100.*

Kocsis, Sándor (1929–), Hungarian footballer who in 66 matches for his country (1949–56) scored 75 goals from the inside-forward position. Known as the "Golden Head" for his heading ability, he was top scorer in the 1954 World Cup. Having played for Ferencvaros and Honved, he went to Barcelona after the 1956 Hungarian uprising.

Kodak, word invented as a trademark for the cameras manufactured by George EASTMAN and later by Eastman Kodak, the company he founded in 1892. Introduced in 1888, the simplicity of the first Kodak camera did much to promote the growth of amateur photography, and established the name as a household word.

Kodály, Zoltán (1882–1967), Hungarian composer. With BARTÓK he collected and systematized Hungarian folk-music, which was the principal influence in his work. His music uses established forms with great originality and feeling. Among his best-known compositions are the *Psalmus Hungaricus* (1923), the *Concerto for Orchestra* (1939), the comic opera Hary Janos (1927) and the *Missa Brevis* (1945). *See also* HC2 p.270, *270.*

Kodes, Jan (1946–), Czechoslovakian tennis player. He won the French (1970–71) and British (1973) singles championships.

Kodiak bear, Alaskan brown BEAR native to Kodiak Island off the S coast of Alaska. The biggest bear in the world and the largest meat-eating animal that lives on land, it can grow up to 2.8m (9.2ft) in length and weigh more than 780kg (1,720lb). Species: *Ursus arctos middendorffi.*

Kodiak Island, island in the Gulf of Alaska, SE of the Alaska Peninsula. A large area is given over to a national wild life park, the island having two native animals, the KODIAK BEAR and the king crab. The main occupation of the islanders is salmon fishing. Area: 13,890sq km (5,363sq miles). Pop. (1970) 6,357.

Koechlin, Charles (1867–1950), French composer. He entered the Paris Conservatory in 1890 and studied under MASSENET and then FAURÉ. His numerous innovative compositions, in all the standard musical forms, are sensitive and distinguished, and above all individually suited to the idiom and without sensationalism.

Koestler, Arthur (1905–), British novelist and philosopher, *b.* Hungary. After living in many European capitals in the 1920s and 1930s, he went to Spain to report the SPANISH CIVIL WAR. He was a Communist until the mid-1930s, and his novels, such as *Darkness at Noon* (1940), are often concerned with political themes. His works in English include *The Act of Creation* (1964) and two volumes of autobiography, *Scum of the Earth* (1941) and *Arrow in the Blue* (1952).

Koetsu, Honnami (1558–1637), Japanese painter, calligrapher, potter and art patron. He helped further the national style of his time and is noted for the calligraphy he executed on scrolls.

Koffka, Kurt (1886–1941), US psychologist, *b.* Germany. With Wolfgang KÖHLER and Max WERTHEIMER, he was a founder of GESTALT PSYCHOLOGY. He did important work in perception and became spokesman for the Gestalt movement. He wrote *Growth of the Mind* (1921) and *Principles of Gestalt Psychology.* (1935). *See also* MS pp.46–47.

Kogan, Leonid (1924–), Soviet violinist. He studied at the Moscow Conservatory with Abram Yampolsky and won the International Competition in Brussels in 1951. He has been a professor at the Moscow Conservatory since 1952, played many concerts and won the Lenin Prize in 1965.

Koh-i-noor, Indian diamond which has the longest known history; its name is Hindi for Mountain of Light. It is reputed to have been stolen from the Rajah of Malwa in 1304, having been in his family for several generations. After changing hands many times, it was bought by the British Crown in 1849, recut to 109 carats in 1852, and set in the crown of Queen Elizabeth, the consort of George VI, for the coronation of 1937.

Kohlberg, Lawrence (1927–), US psychologist. Studying the moral development of reasoning in children, he has conducted a series of tests among children of different age groups and societies, asking them to respond to a number of moral dilemmas. He has classified three progressive stages in the thinking behind their answers. *See also* MS pp.151, 160, *160.*

Köhler, Wolfgang (1887–1967), US psychologist, *b.* Estonia. He emigrated to the USA in the 1930s. With Kurt KOFFKA and Max WERTHEIMER, he was a key figure in GESTALT PSYCHOLOGY. His work on animal learning and problem solving, is summarized in *The Mentality of Apes* (1917). *See also* MS pp.46–47.

Kohlrabi, edible crop vegetable with lobed leaves and a greenish-white or purple, turnip-like stem. It is unusual in that both the stem and leaves may be eaten. Family Cruciferae; species *Brassica caulorapa. See also* PE p.188.

Kohoutek, long-period comet that last appeared in 1973 but was much less spectacular than expected. It will not return to perihelion for 75,000 years. *See also* SU p.217, *217.*

Koiso, Kuniaki (1880–1950), Japanese Prime Minister (1944–45). After the fall of the TOJO government in July 1944, he attempted to forestall military defeat. Heavy bombings and US landings on Okinawa led to his defeat in April 1945, leaving Admiral Suzuki Kantaro to find honourable grounds for surrender. Koiso was sentenced to life imprisonment as a war criminal in 1948.

Kojiki, with NIHON-SHAKI, chronicles describing the legendary and historical origins of Japan. The texts date from the early 8th century and were mostly written in Chinese ideographs as Japan lacked a literary tradition. Kojiki, the sacred book of SHINTO, deals with traditional mythology; the Nihon-shaki relates historical events.

Kokoschka, Oskar (1886–), Austrian painter. He was influenced by the elegance of KLIMT but later developed his own EXPRESSIONIST style, characterized by forceful, energetic draughtsmanship and restless brushwork. The same tension that permeates his early, portraits is also present in his later, panoramic landscapes. He taught at Dresden Academy (1919–24) and then travelled extensively before moving to London in 1938. He became a British subject in 1947 and a CBE in 1959.

Kolanut, or colanut, fruit of an African tree that bears the same name, from which is extracted the main ingredient of cola soft drinks. The nuts contain CAFFEINE. Species *Cola acuminata. See also* COCA-COLA.

Kolar Gold Fields, area in S India, 233km (145 miles) W of Madras. Founded in the late 19th century and now the centre of India's gold-mining industry, it produces 95% of the country's gold. Pop. (1971) 76,112.

Kolbe, Adolf Wilhelm Hermann (1818–84), German chemist. In *c.* 1843 he converted carbon disulphide to acetic acid, one of the first syntheses of an organic compound from inorganic chemicals. He also developed a theory of radicals and predicted the existence of secondary and tertiary alcohols.

Kolchak, Alexander Vasiliyevich (1874–1920), Russian admiral. He commanded the Baltic and Black Sea fleets during WWI. After the Bolsheviks took power he led White forces in Siberia, and was, at one stage, proclaimed supreme ruler of Russia. He was captured and shot in 1920.

Kölcsey, Ferenc (1790–1838), Hungarian poet, critic and political figure. He used his political position to support the linguistic reforms of Ferenc KAZINCZY and, through his poetry and criticism, helped to develop aesthetics in Hungary. He wrote the Hungarian national anthem, *Himnusz* (1823). His collected works appeared in 1886–87).

Koldewey, Robert (1855–1925), German archaeologist. Excavating at Babylon between 1899 and 1917, he used a technique of stratification, whereby different layers corresponding to different periods of occupation are excavated; this had considerable influence on later archaeological work. Some of the results of his excavations were published in *The Excavations at Babylon* (1914).

Kolehmainen, Hannes (1889–1966), Finnish middle- and long-distance runner who won four Olympic gold medals (1912: 5,000m, 10,000m, cross-country; 1920: marathon), set six world records from 3,000m to 30,000m and began the tradition of Finnish distance running.

Kolkhoz, Russian term for a collective farm. Since 1929 the majority of Soviet farm workers have worked on such collective farms, some of which were converted to *sovkhozy,* or state farms, in the 1950s. A kolkhoz is technically autonomous; its members have a share in its produce in that although since 1961 their produce has been bought by the state at predetermined prices, any surplus is shared between the workers. *See also* HC2 p.*198*; MW p.170.

Kollár, Ján (1793–1852), Slovak poet, an important contributor to Czech cultural revival. He became an evangelical pastor in Pest and in 1849 was appointed professor of Slavonic archaeology in Vienna. His works, written in Czech and often promoting the cause of Slavonic cultural unity, include the sonnet cycle *The Daughter of Slava* (1824).

Kölliker, Rudolph Albert von (1817–1905), Swiss embryologist and histologist. His contributions to medicine include the application of cell theory to tissue structure and embryonic development.

Kollwitz, Käthe (1867–1945), German graphic artist and sculptor. Her best-known works depict suffering, especially of women and children. They include six cycles of etchings, lithographs and woodcuts such as *War* (1922–23) and *Death* (1934–35).

Köln. *See* COLOGNE.

Kolokotrónis, Theódoros (1770–1843), Greek patriot and general in the Greek war for independence from Turkey. His heroism is recorded in a number of Greek folk-songs. In 1825 he invited Sir Richard CHURCH to offer British protection to Greece.

Kolozwvar. *See* CLUJ.

Kölreuter, Josef Gottlieb (1733–1806), German botanist known for his breeding experiments with plants. He was the first to demonstrate the importance of insects and of wind in the cross-fertilization of plants.

Kolyma, river in the far eastern USSR. It rises as several headstreams in the Kolyma and Cherskogo (Čerskogo) ranges, and flows N to the East Siberian Sea. Its lower course is navigable between June and October. Length: approx. 1,780km (1,110 miles).

Komisarjevsky, Theodore (1882–1954), British theatre director, *b.* Russia. His highly stylized productions, especially of Shakespeare's plays such as *Macbeth* (1933) at Stratford-upon-Avon, made him a controversial figure.

Komodo dragon, giant monitor lizard that lives on four islands to the E of Java, Indonesia; it is the largest lizard in the world. Its survival is threatened as the deer and wild pigs on which it feeds are reduced in number by hunting. Of the 2,000–5,000 that exist, only 400 are mature females. Length: 3m (10ft). Family Varanidae; species *Varanus komodoensis. See also* NW pp.*137, 246.*

Komondor, Hungarian guard dog for livestock It has a short, wide head with a straight, broad muzzle, and triangular, pendulous ears. The powerful body is set on muscular legs and the feet are large. The unusual coat is long and white and is comprised of matted, felt-like cords. Height: at least 60cm (24in) at the shoulder; weight: at least 34kg (75lb).

Komorowski, Tadeusz (1895–1966), Polish general. He led the Polish underground forces during the 62-day Warsaw uprising of 1944. The Germans demolished the city in suppressing the revolt. Komorowski had hoped to link up with the advancing Soviet army but it had halted on the outskirts of the city during the uprising.

Komsomol, derived from the Russian for "Communist League of Youth"; organization in Russia for students aged from 14 to 28. Supervised by the Communist Party, the Komsomol helps to spread Communist teachings among young people and to gain members for the Party. It is associated with the organizations known as the Pioneers, and the Little Octobrists, which are for younger children.

Kongo, Negroid people of W Africa, living in the Congo Republic, Zaire and Angola. The Kongo kingdom (14th–17th centuries) had extensive influence. Today the Kongo practise sedentary agriculture raising such staple crops as sweet potatoes and manioc; coffee is a cash crop. Their culture is rich in ORAL LITERATURE, music and sculpture. Ancestor worship and fetish

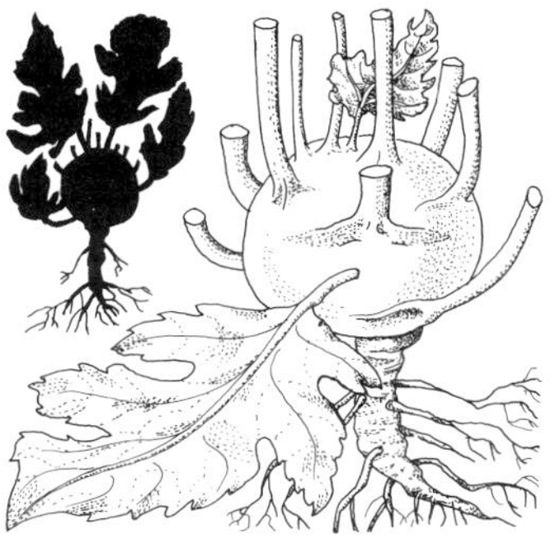

Kohlrabi, *Brassica oleracea,* is a bulbous vegetable closely related to the cabbage.

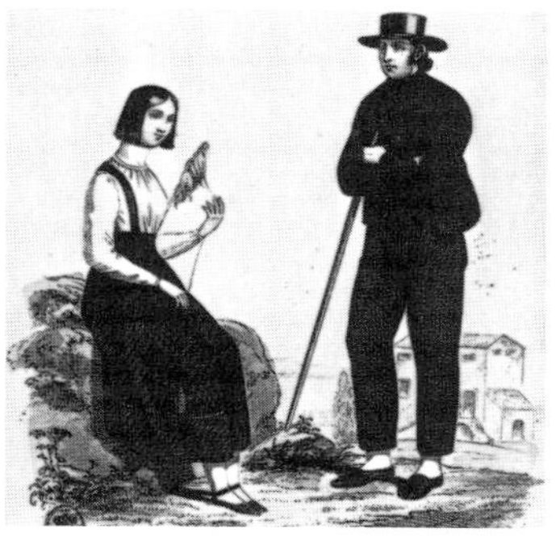

Ján Kollár was a leading Czech poet in the 19th century; an illustration from his diary.

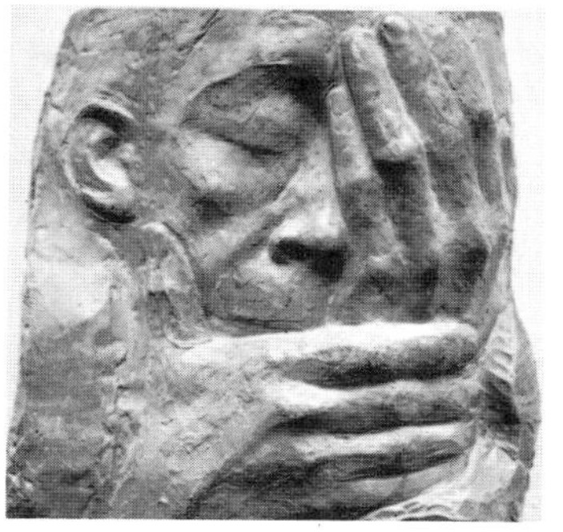

Käthe Kollwitz' carving *Lament for Barbach;* she was noted for her depiction of suffering.

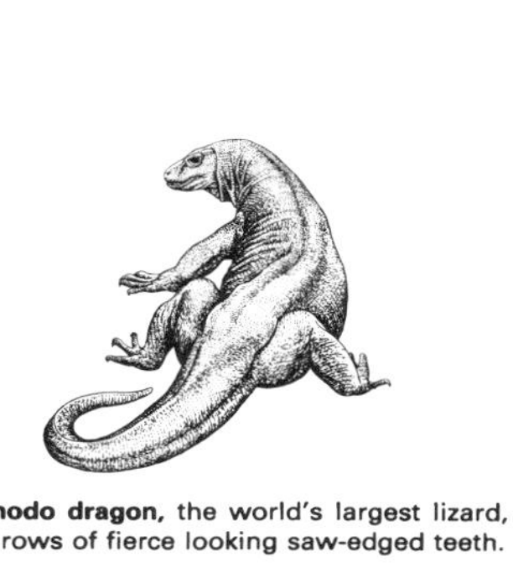

Komodo dragon, the world's largest lizard, has rows of fierce looking saw-edged teeth.

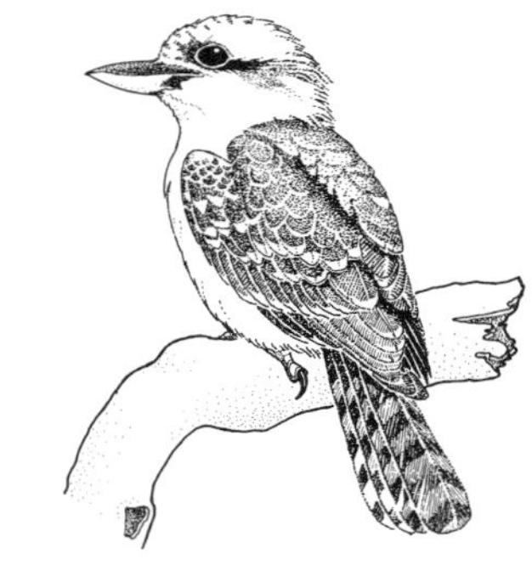

Kookaburras, which eat a variety of small creatures nest in holes in trees.

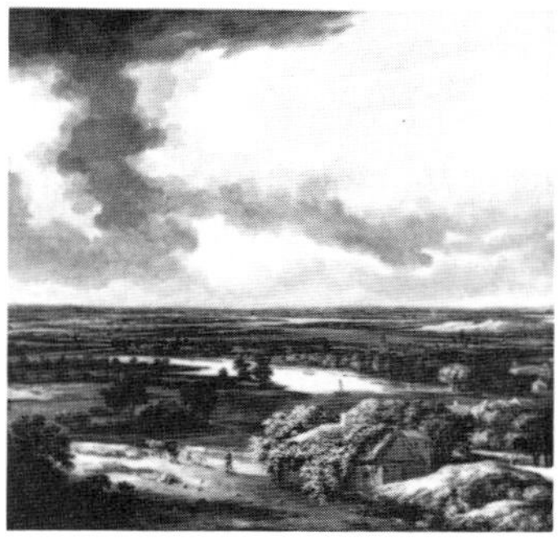

Philips de Koninck; a detail from one of his typical Dutch landscapes.

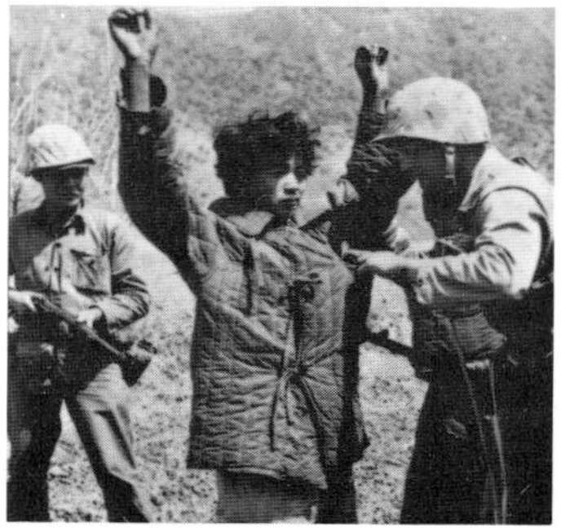

Korean War; a Chinese Communist soldier being searched by US troops.

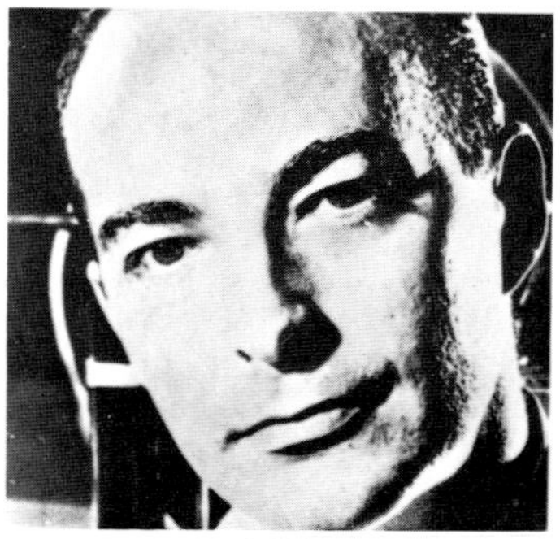

Arthur Kornberg artificially produced a self-reproducing nucleic acid.

cults continue to dominate their religion.

Koniev, Ivan Stepanovich (1897–1973), Soviet general. He was outstanding as a military leader in WWII; his troops recaptured the Ukraine from the Germans in 1944, and were among the first to enter Berlin in 1945. He became a marshal in 1944 and commander-in-chief of the Soviet army in 1946.

König, Friedrich (1774–1833), German printer. He invented the first steam printing press and was co-founder of the König and Bauer Company, manufacturers of steam printing presses, established at Würzburg in 1817.

König Rother, German epic poem, written *c.* 1145. It tells of the adventures of King Anthari in his attempts to marry an Eastern princess.

Königsberg. *See* KALININGRAD.

Koninck, Philips de (1619–88), Dutch painter of genre, historical and landscape themes, especially famous for his panoramic views of low-lying country beneath expansive skies. His drawings have been confused with those of REMBRANDT, whose student he may have been.

Konoye, Fumimaro (1891–1946), Japanese statesman. A member of the ancient FUJIWARA family, he was president of the House of Peers (1933–34). He became Prime Minister in 1937 and served three terms. As Foreign Minister in 1938 he was responsible for much of Japanese policy in the early part of the SINO-JAPANESE WAR (1937–45).

Konrads, John (1942–), and his sister **Ilsa** (1944–), Australian swimmers, *b.* Latvia, who dominated middle-distance freestyle events from 1958 to 1960. John set 26 individual world records and won one Olympic (1960) and three Commonwealth (1958) gold medals. Ilsa set 12 individual world records and won a Commonwealth gold medal in 1958.

Konrad von Soest (*fl.* early 15th century), principal Westphalian painter, active in Dortmund and Soest. A signed polyptych, in Niederwildungen parish church, executed in the SOFT STYLE, is his major work.

Konrad von Würzburg. *See* WÜRZBURG, KONRAD VON.

Konstanz. *See* CONSTANCE, LAKE.

Kon-Tiki Expedition, undertaking by the scientist Thor HEYERDAHL in which he tested his theory that Polynesia could have been colonized by an ancient South American people. With five companions he built a balsa-wood raft and sailed from the W coast of South America in 1947. They reached a group of islands near Tahiti after a voyage of three and a half months during which they travelled about 8,000km (5,000 miles), thus proving that such a migration is possible.

Konya, city in S central Turkey, 233km (145 miles) S of Ankara. The capital of the SELJUK sultanate of RŪM from 1099, it was annexed by the OTTOMAN sultan in 1472. It is a religious centre of the Whirling DERVISHES, an order founded in the 13th century. Manufactures include cotton and leather goods. Pop. (1973) 227,887.

Koo, Vi Kyuin Wellington (1887–), also called Ku Wei-chün, Chinese Nationalist diplomat. He served as China's representative to the Paris Peace Conference in 1919 and then as ambassador to France (1936–41), Britain (1941–46) and the USA (1946–56). He also represented China at the conference that established the UN (1945), and was a justice at the International Court (1957–67).

Kookaburra, also called laughing jackass, large KINGFISHER of Australia known for its call resembling fiendish laughter. Groups often scream in unison at dawn, mid-day and dusk. They feed on rodents, lizards and other land animals. Species *Dacelo gigas. See also* NW pp. *141, 205.*

Kooning, Willem de (1904–), US painter, *b.* Holland. He trained in Europe and was at first influenced by de STIJL, but after moving to the USA in 1926 he turned to abstract painting. After WWII he became a leading action painter. The series *Woman I-IV* (1952–53) and *Woman Acabonic* (1966) are representative of his work.

Koopmans, Tjalling Charles (1910–), US economist *b.* The Netherlands. He was attached to the financial division of the League of Nations (1938–40) and on the staff of the University of Chicago (1945–55). From 1955 he was professor of economics at Yale University. In 1975 he shared the Nobel Prize in economics with the Soviet economist Leonid KANTOROVICH for their contributions towards a theory of optimum allocation of resources.

Kootenay, river in W Canada. It rises in the Rocky Mts of SE British Columbia, flows S into Montana, USA, NW through N Idaho, then N and back into Canada. It flows through Kootenay Lake to join the Columbia River at Castlegar. Length: 655km (407 miles).

Kooyong Stadium, complex of tennis courts in Melbourne, Australia. Built in 1927, it is one of the venues of the Australian tennis championships, and its 12,000-capacity centre court has also been used for Davis Cup challenge rounds and world championship boxing.

Kopernik, Nikolai. *See* COPERNICUS, NICOLAUS.

Köppen, Wladimir Peter (1846–1940), German meteorologist and climatologist, *b.* Russia, who introduced a climate classification still used today. In 1884 he produced a world map of temperature belts. In 1900 he introduced his system of climate classification which divided climate into five major categories according to temperature and rainfall. *See also* PE p. *74.*

Köprülü, Turkish family prominent in the late 17th century. Seven of its members served as Grand Vizier (Chief Minister). Köprülü Pasha (*c.* 1586–1661); *r.* 1656–61), *b.* Albania, consolidated power under the Turkish sultan, Mohammed IV, and expelled the Venetian fleet from the Dardanelles. Later Köprülü viziers were involved in wars with Venice, Austria and Poland which resulted in the extensive loss of territory. *See also* HC1 pp.220–221.

Kops, Bernard (1926–), British dramatist who left school at age 13. Many of his works concern rebellious Jewish youth coming to terms with life, based on his own working-class background in London's East End. His plays include *The Hamlet of Stepney Green* (1958) and *Enter Solly Gold* (1962).

Koran or Qur'ān, sacred scriptures of ISLAM. The canonical text was established AD 651–52 or the year 30 in the Muslim calendar, which dates from the HEGIRA. It was collected under the Caliph OTHMAN who is believed to have destroyed all other existing copies to ensure its uniformity. According to Muslim belief, the Koran contains the actual word of God (Allah) as revealed to the Prophet Mohammed in the 7th century. Its 114 chapters or suras are the source of Islamic belief and a guide for the whole life of the community. *See also* HC1 pp.144–145.

Korbut, Olga (1955–), Soviet gymnast whose charm entranced worldwide audiences as she won three gold medals (beam, floor exercises, team) and a silver medal at the 1972 Olympic Games. In 1976 she won a team gold and a silver.

Korda, Sir Alexander (1893–1956), British film director, *b.* Hungary. He received the first knighthood ever bestowed on a film-maker (1942) for his contributions to the British film industry. He was noted for his lavish productions and somewhat flamboyant business methods. His films of the 1930s and 1940s received international acclaim. Among them were *The Private Life of Henry VIII* (1933), *The Scarlet Pimpernel* (1935), *Lady Hamilton* (1941) and *Anna Karenina* (1948). *See also* HC2 p.269.

Kore, term derived from the Greek word for "maiden" and generally applied to draped, free-standing statues of females in archaic Greek art (*c.* 500 BC). A statue of a male from the same period is called a *kouros.*

Korea, peninsula in Asia now made up of North Korea and South Korea. *See* MW p.115; KOREA, NORTH; KOREA, SOUTH.

Korea, North (Chosŏn Minjujuŭi In'min Konghwaguk), independent nation of NE Asia, occupying the N part of the Korean Peninsula. The country has extreme seasonal temperatures and only a small percentage of the land can be farmed. Its mineral resources, however, are highly developed and tungsten, graphite and magnesite are produced. The capital is P'yŏngyang. Area: 120,538sq km (46,540sq miles). Pop. (1975 est.) 15,852,000. *See* MW p.116.

Korea, South (Taehan-Min'guk), independent nation of NE Asia, occupying the S part of the Korean Peninsula. It is a mountainous country with few natural resources and only 20% of the land area can be cultivated. Economic growth, slow since the Korean War, was adversely affected by the 1974–75 oil price increases. The capital is Seoul. Area: 98,484sq km (38,025sq miles). Pop. (1975 est.) 34,688,000. *See* MW p.116.

Korean, national language of South and North Korea, spoken by a total of 50 million people. It may be related to Japanese but this remains to be proved. The Korean alphabet was developed in the 15th century.

Korean War (1950–53), conflict between Communist (North Korea and People's Republic of China) and non-Communist (South Korea, US and UN) forces. On 25 June 1950, North Korea invaded South Korea. The UN Security Council demanded a halt, in which it called upon the help of member nations. US President Harry TRUMAN, without recourse to Congress, ordered land, sea and air forces to aid South Korea. Token forces from 16 UN countries supported the South Korean and US armies and Gen. Douglas MACARTHUR was appointed commander. British and Commonwealth forces acquitted themselves well; four Victoria Crosses were won, two of them in the heavy fighting on the Imjin River (April 1951), where the 1st Bn The Gloucestershire Regiment were cut off from the brigade. The war tested the air strength of both sides, and marked the appearance of the Soviet MiG-15 fighter. Although the conflict ended inconclusively in a truce (27 July 1953) at the cost of about 4 million casualties, its containment may have prevented worldwide nuclear war. *See also* MW pp.115–116.

Korfball, basketball game of Dutch origin for teams of both sexes, six men and six women per side. It is played over two 45-minute periods on a grass court divided into three zones, goalposts with a cylindrical basket being centred inside the end zones. The aim is to score goals through the basket. Players must pass the ball within a zone or into an adjacent zone. Running with, kicking, punching, or bouncing the ball is illegal, as is bodily contact. After two goals, players move to a different zone.

Korinthos. *See* CORINTH.

Kornberg, Arthur (1918–), US biochemist. He was medical director of the US Public Health Service (1951) and chairman of the department of biochemistry at Stanford University. In 1959 he shared the Nobel Prize in physiology and medicine with Severo OCHOA for their work on the synthesis of RNA and DNA, an important contribution to the study of genetics. *See also* NW pp.28–29.

Kornbluth, Cyril M. (1923–58), US science-fiction writer. His stories, set in the future, often show the effects of domination by big business on social and political life. He wrote his most famous work, *The Space Merchants* (1953), in collaboration with Frederik POHL.

Korneichuk, Alexander Yevdokimovich (1905–72), Ukrainian dramatist. His *Wreck of the Squadron* (1934) was produced by the Red Army Theatre. Other works include *Truth* (1937), *In the Steppes of the Ukraine* (1941), a controversial play *Wings* (1953) and a comedy, *Why do the Stars Smile?* (1956).

Kornilov, Lavr Georgievich (1870–1918), Russian general. Appointed supreme military commander by KERENSKY in Aug. 1917, he rebelled unsuccessfully against the provisional government a month later. After the Bolshevik Revolution in Nov. 1917, he led White Russian forces in the Civil War (1918–20) and was killed while attacking Krasnodar which at

that time was known as Ekaterinodar .
Korolev, Sergei Pavlovich (1906–66), Soviet engineer. He was chief designer at the Scientific Research Institute near Moscow and directed the design and manufacture of the Vostok and SOYUZ manned spacecraft, including VOSTOK I, in which Yuri GAGARIN made the first manned space flight in 1961.
Korutürk, Fahri S. (1903–), Turkish naval officer and politician. Made Commander-in-Chief of the Navy in 1957, he later served as ambassador to the USSR and Spain. He became President of Turkey in 1973.
Koryaks, MONGOLOID people who live on the Kamchatka peninsula of NE Siberia in the USSR. Their way of life is similar to that of the ESKIMOS: subsistence by hunting, fishing and breeding reindeer. They speak a language of the Palaeosiberian family and practise rituals connected with their hunting activities.
Korzeniowski, Josef Konrad. *See* CONRAD, JOSEPH.
Korzybski, Alfred Habdank Skarbek (1879–1950), US scientist, *b.* Poland. He created an influential SEMANTIC system of linguistic philosophy, that distinguishes between a word and the object it describes. He wrote *Science and Sanity: An Introduction to Non-Aristotelian Systems and General Semantics* (1933).
Kós, island in SE Greece, in the Aegean Sea; second-largest of the Dodecanese, near the Turkish coast. Kós is the main town. Fishing, sponge diving and livestock raising are important, and grain, tobacco and grapes are cultivated. In ancient times Kós was ruled by Athenians, Macedonians, Syrians and Egyptians. It was a cultural centre and HIPPOCRATES founded a school of medicine there in the 5th century BC. Area: 287sq km (111sq miles). Pop. (1971) 16,650.
Kosciusko, Thaddeus (1746–1817), Polish patriot and soldier. Championing the ideals of liberal philosophy, he went to America in 1776 to fight with the revolutionary army. He returned to Poland in 1784 and after the second partition of the country in 1793 led a revolutionary movement to regain Polish independence. Initially successful, the invading armies of Russia and Prussia proved too strong and Kosciusko was imprisoned (1794–96) and then exiled.
Kosciusko, Mount, highest peak in Australia and situated in the Australian Alps, SE New South Wales; it is a popular skiing resort. Height: 2,230m (7,316ft).
Kosher, Hebrew word that means ritually correct. It is applied by Orthodox Jews to food that confirms to Jewish dietary laws and customs, many of them based on health considerations. The rituals for the killing and preparation of kosher food are specified in the TALMUD.
Košice, city in E Czechoslovakia on the Hernad River, 217km (135 miles) NE of Budapest. Formerly in Hungary, it was incorporated into Czechoslovakia under the Treaty of Trianon in 1918. Its ancient buildings include a Gothic cathedral and a 14th-century Franciscan monastery. Industries: iron and steel, brewing, textiles. Pop. (1974) 166,240.
Kosinski, Jerzy (1933–), US novelist, *b.* Poland. Two of his works, *The Painted Bird* (1965) and *Steps* (1968; National Book Award 1969), involve a series of incidents of grotesque violence. *Cockpit* was published in 1975. He has also written under the name Joseph Novak.
Kossel, Albrecht (1853–1927), German biochemist who was awarded the 1910 Nobel Prize in physiology and medicine for contributions to the understanding of cell chemistry. He showed that the nucleoprotein of the cell nucleus is made up of a protein and a nitrogen-containing nucleic acid, which in the 1950s was discovered to be the basic hereditary material. *See also* NW pp.28–29.
Kossuth, Louis (Lajos) (1802–94), Hungarian leader. He entered the National Diet in 1830 but was imprisoned (1837–40) for his part in the attempt to achieve a separate constitution for Hungary from that of Austria. He became finance minister and virtual dictator in 1848, and took the title of governor in 1849. Defeated by the Russian and Austrian armies, he fled to Turkey and subsequently travelled to the USA, from whence he went to England and Italy. He refused amnesty in his own country but when he died his body was returned to Budapest where it was buried in state. *See also* HC2 p.109.
Kostelanetz, André (1901–), Russian-born conductor, who emigrated to the USA in 1922 and became a conductor for the Columbia Broadcasting System in 1930. He also conducted his own orchestra and was best known for his arrangements of light music. In 1938 he married the coloratura soprano Lily PONS.
Kostrowitsky, Wilhelm. *See* APOLLINAIRE, GUILLAUME.
Kosygin, Aleksei Nikolayevich (1904–), Soviet politician elected to the Communist Party Central Committee in 1939 and the POLITBURO in 1948. He was removed in 1953 but regained his seat in 1960. After KHRUSHCHEV's fall in 1964, he became Chairman of the Council of Ministers, and was regarded as second to Leonid BREZHNEV. *See also* HC2 p.241.
Köthen, town in central East Germany, 19km (12 miles) SW of Dessau. From 1603 until 1847 Köthen was the residence of the dukes of Anhalt-Köthen, of whose court Johann Sebastian BACH was appointed musical director from 1717 until 1723. Industries: machinery, lignite mining, sugar refining, chemicals, textiles. Pop. (1970 est.) 36,600.
Koto, large 13-stringed ZITHER with moveable bridges used in Japanese music from the earliest times. The thumb and first two fingers of the right hand pluck the strings, while the left hand presses the strings to control pitch.
Kotzebue, August Friedrich Ferdinand von (1761–1819), German diplomat and dramatist, whose murder by a student led to the suppression of German student organizations. A prolific and popular playwright, he wrote over 200 dramatic works, many of them sentimental melodramas. They include *Menschenhass und Reue* (1789; tr. *The Stranger*, 1798) and *Die Indianer in England* (1790; tr. *The Indian Exiles*, 1801).
Koumiss, or kumiss, slightly alcoholic drink made from mares' and camels' milk by central Asian nomads. The milk is fermented by a YEAST and a BACTERIUM. A new batch is started by the addition to a small quantity of milk of a previous batch.
Kountché, Lieutenant-Colonel Seyni (1931–), army officer and head of state, NIGER, W Africa. As Chief of Staff of the armed forces in 1974, he led the *coup* that overthrew the government of Hamani Diori and became President.
Koussevitzky, Sergei Aleksandrovich (1874–1951), Russian musician. A virtuoso double-bass player, he became even more famous as conductor of the Boston Symphony Orchestra (1924–49).
Kowloon, suburb of Hong Kong, on the Kowloon Peninsula of China, connected to Hong Kong Island by a road tunnel and a ferry. It was ceded to Britain by the Chinese in 1860. Shipbuilding is an important industry. Pop. (1971) 715,400.
Kraal, old-fashioned name for the household of the rural Bantu people of South Africa, consisting of a mud thatched hut surrounded by a stockade forming an enclosure for the domestic animals (Dutch *kraal*; cf. English *corral*). Based on a family unit, a kraal was often one of a circle under the authority of a chief, himself under the tribal chief who deferred to the paramount chief.
Kraepelin, Emil (1856–1926), German psychiatrist and pioneer in the classification of mental illness. By studying the symptoms from many case-histories he distinguished two broad classes of psychosis: DEMENTIA PRAECOX (now called SCHIZOPHRENIA) and MANIC-DEPRESSION.
Krafft-Ebing, Richard von, Baron (1840–1902), German psychiatrist. His *Psychopathia Sexualis* (1886) described sexual pathologies and did much to promote open discussion of the sex drive. He also was one of the first to conclude that general PARESIS was caused by syphilis.
Kraft, Adam (*c.*1455–1509), German GOTHIC stone-sculptor. Most of his work is in Nuremberg, including his masterpiece, the great tabernacle in St Lorenz Church (1493–96) and the Schreyer monument in St Sebald's Church.
Krait, highly venomous snake of the *Bungarus* genus. Found in the open country of E Asia, Kraits are usually nocturnal and generally attack only other snakes. Their skins are shiny and distinctively marked.
Krakatoa, volcanic island in W Indonesia 6km (4 miles) in diameter, in the Sunda Strait between Java and Sumatra. In 1883 one of the largest volcanic eruptions of recent times occurred, destroying most of the island. The resulting TSUNAMI caused great destruction on nearby coasts, and volcanic debris was scattered across the Indian Ocean. Height: (of volcano) 813m (2,667ft). *See also* PE p.31.
Kraken, mythical beast thought to appear at times in the sea off Norway. First described in the 1750s by Bishop Pontoppidan, it is said to have a huge back and long arms which drag down ships.
Kraków, city in S Poland, 251km (156 miles) SSW of Warsaw. Taken by BOLESLAV I of Poland in 999, it was made a residence of the Polish kings in the 12th century and ceded to Austria in 1795 in the Third Partition of Poland. It was made part of the grand duchy of Warsaw in 1809, became a republic in 1815 and was restored to Austria in 1946. It became part of Poland after WWI. Today it is a manufacturing centre which produces chemicals, metals and machinery. Pop. 668,300.
Kramer, John Albert ("Jack") (1921–), US tennis player and US singles (1946–47) and British singles (1947) champion. He also won the US doubles (1940–41, 1943 and 1947) and British doubles (1946–47) titles. He turned professional in 1947 and later became a successful promoter.
Kramář, Karel (1860–1937), Czech nationalist and statesman. He was a leader of the liberal Young Czech movement and during WWI was tried for treason by the Austrian authorities. He became the first Prime Minister of Czechoslovakia (1918–19).
Kramer, Stanley (1913–), US independent film producer. He is noted for his excellent low-budget films. His major works include *Champion* (1949), *The Men* (1950), *Death of a Salesman* (1951), *High Noon* (1952), *The Caine Mutiny* (1954) and *Ship of Fools* (1965).
Kraszewski, Jozef I. (1812–87), Polish journalist and novelist. His works mark the transition between the Romantic and Realist periods in Polish literature, and wrote many historical novels. Those translated into English include *Jermola* (1857), *The Countess Cosel* (1901) and *Count Bruehl* (1902).
Kraus, Karl (1874–1936), Austrian satirist and poet. He was founder of *The Torch* and of the Theatre of Poetry, where he gave readings from SHAKESPEARE's works. He produced many essays and dramas, eg *Mankind's Last Day* (1919), which exposed the degeneration of culture, morals and language.
Kraus, Lili (1908–), Hungarian pianist who settled in England. She studied at the Royal Academy in Budapest and also with Béla BARTÓK, Zoltán KODÁLY and Artur SCHNABEL. In 1928 she became a professor at the Vienna Conservatory and toured widely as a concert artist, becoming well known as an interpreter of MOZART.
Krause, Karl Christian Friedrich (1781–1832), German philosopher, whose ideas greatly influenced Spanish education in the late 19th century. He also attempted to reconcile THEISM and PANTHEISM in his notion of "panentheism" in his *System of Morality* (1810), and *Lectures on the System of Philosophy* (1828).
Krebs, Sir Hans Adolf (1900–), British biochemist, *b.* Germany. He shared with F.A. LIPMANN the 1953 Nobel Prize in physiology and medicine for his discovery of the CITRIC ACID CYCLE, the process that results in the production of energy in living organisms.
Krebs' Cycle. *See* CITRIC ACID CYCLE.
Krefeld, city in W West Germany, on the

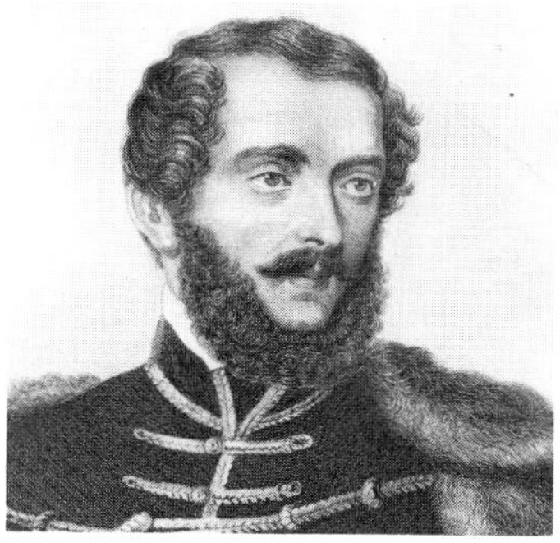

Louis Kossuth, the Hungarian leader and revolutionary who became dictator in 1848.

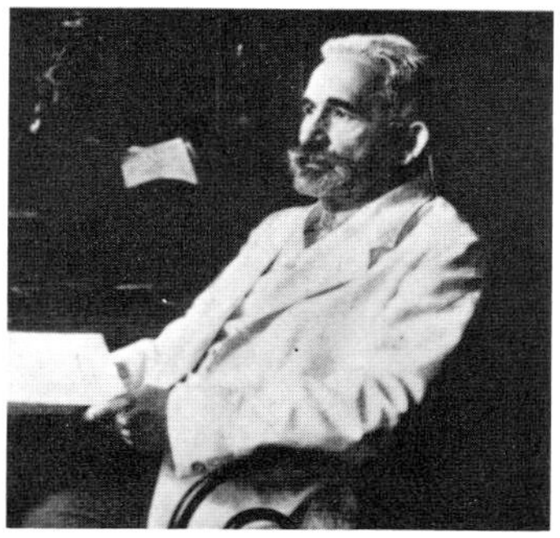

Emil Kraepelin's studies in mental illness are regarded as the foundations of psychiatry.

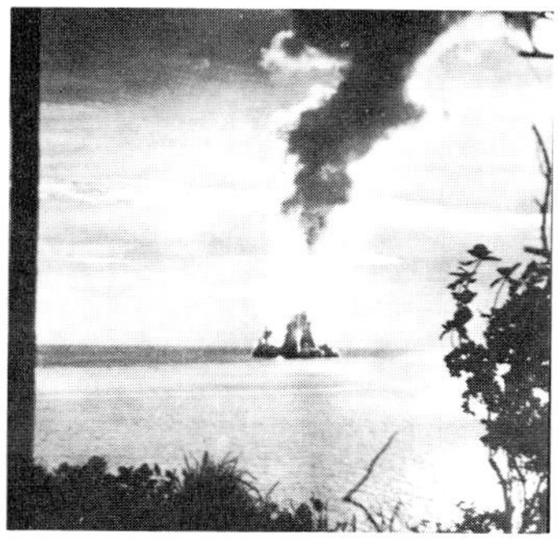

Krakatoa in eruption; when this island exploded in 1883, 36,000 people were killed.

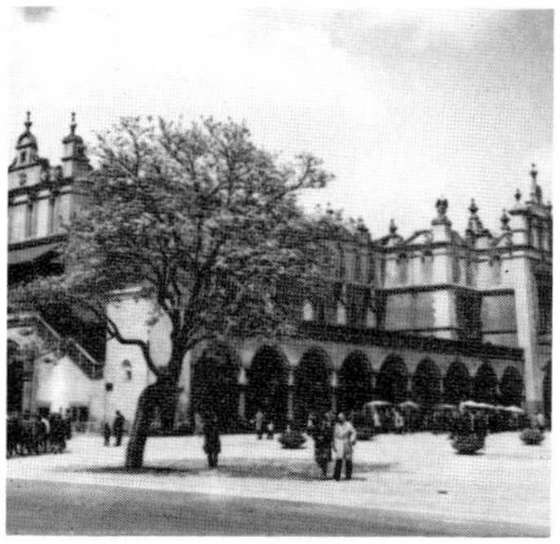

Kraków; a view of the main market square and the 16th century Cloth Hall.

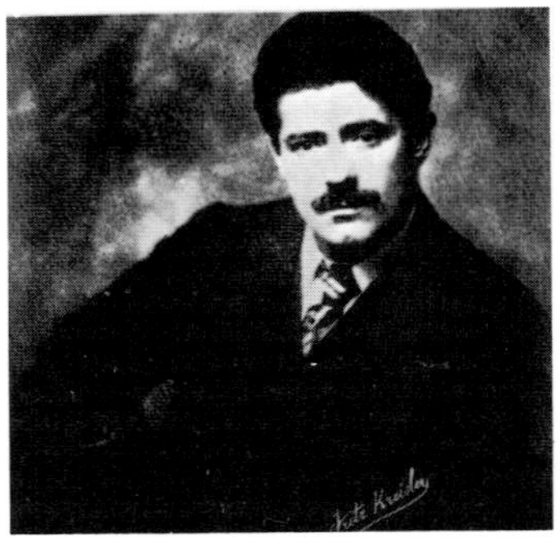

Fritz Kreisler had a prodigous talent as a child and made his New York debut aged 13.

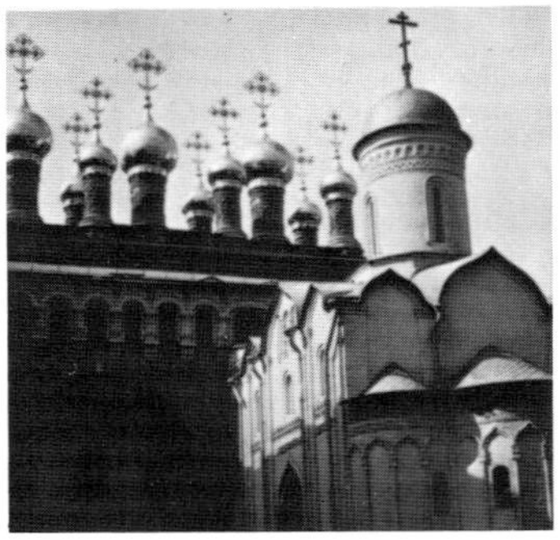

Kremlin, whose golden domes contrast strongly with the walled fortifications.

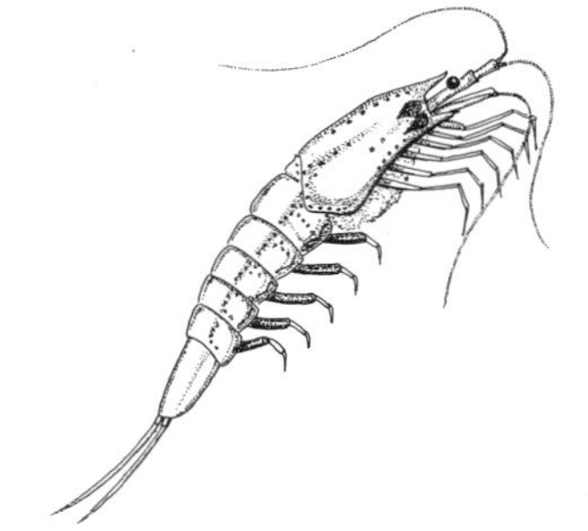

Krill; these shrimp-like creatures may well become a source of food for man.

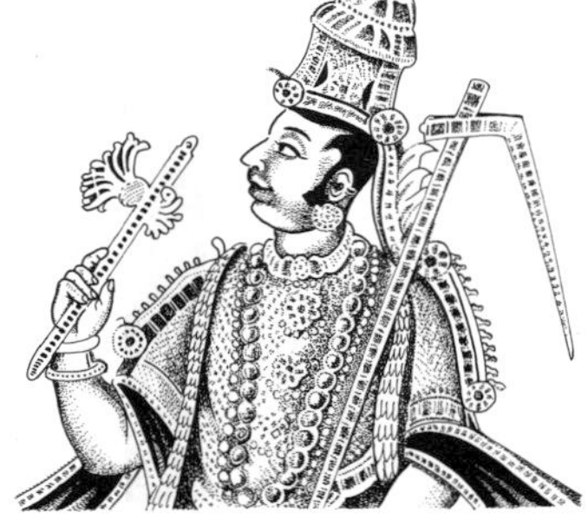

Krishna is one of the physical manifestations of the Hindu god Vishnu, who protects man.

River Rhine, 31km (19 miles) WSW of Essen. An important linen-weaving town centre until it passed to Prussia in 1702, it developed into a centre of the silk industry when given a monopoly by Frederick II. Industries include textiles, steel and dyes. Pop. (1974) 221,240.

Kreisky, Bruno (1911–), Austrian political figure. A social democrat, he lived in Sweden during the Nazi occupation and in 1946 joined the Austrian foreign service. He helped to negotiate the 1955 treaty that guaranteed Austria's independence and neutrality, was elected to Parliament in 1956 and was foreign minister (1959–66). In 1967 he became chairman of the Socialist Party of Austria and was made Chancellor of Austria in 1970.

Kreisler, Fritz (1875–1962), US violinist and composer, *b.* Austria. He studied at the Vienna and Paris conservatories and made his début in the USA in 1889. He was a world-famous violin virtuoso and also composed numerous short violin pieces.

Kremlin, The, historic centre of Moscow. It is a roughly triangular fortress covering approximately 36.5 hectares (90 acres) and is bounded by the River Moscow and Kremlin Quay (S), Red Square and Lenin's tomb (E) and Moscow Historical Museum and St Basil's Cathedral (W). The name "Kremlin" derives from the medieval Russian for "citadel" and was also applied to the central sections of other towns. Moscow's Kremlin walls were first built of timber in the 12th century and its first stone walls were built in 1367. The present stone enclosure has 20 towers and five gates. Within these walls several cathedrals face on to a central square and the largest secular building, the Great Kremlin Palace (1838–49), was the tsar's Moscow residence until the Revolution. In March 1918 the Supreme Soviet established the Kremlin complex as the location of all government offices and its name became synonymous with the government of the USSR. Entry was strictly forbidden to the public, but after Stalin's death (1953) the Kremlin and its buildings were declared a national museum and the Supreme Soviet (parliament) of the USSR and Communist Party conventions continue to be held in the former Great Kremlin Palace.

Křenek, Ernst (1900–), US composer, *b.* Austria, who emigrated to the USA in 1938. From 1920 in Berlin, he experimented with atonal music and after 1930 in Vienna, adopted SCHOENBERG's twelve tone technique. He created a sensation with a jazz opera, *Jonny Spielt Auf* (1925–26), and subsequently wrote for all standard forms of composition.

Kreutzer, Rodolphe (1766–1831), French violinist and composer of studies, sonatas and concertos for the violin, as well as operas. BEETHOVEN dedicated to him his *Sonata in A major* for violin and piano (The "Kreutzer", opus 47).

Krill, collective term for the large variety of marine crustaceans found in all oceans, and in vast quantities in the Antarctic seas, strained and used as a highly nutritious food by the baleen whales. With the extinction of the blue whale threatened, krill trawling has been suggested as a substitute and experiments in krill processing carried out. *See also* NW p.*239*; PE p.241.

Krips, Josef (1902–), Austrian conductor. He made his début with the Vienna Volksoper in 1921 and was conductor of the Vienna State Opera (1933–38). Later he became first conductor of the London Symphony Orchestra (1950–54) and music director of the San Francisco Symphony Orchestra (1963–70). He is a leading interpreter of the operas of Mozart and Wagner.

Krishna, most celebrated hero of Hindu mythology. He was the 8th incarnation of VISHNU and primarily a god of joyfulness and fertility. His amorous adventures with the *gopis,* wives and daughters of cowherds, are well recorded. As a result of a curse uttered by a peevish sage, Krishna was killed by a hunter who mistook him for a deer.

Krishna Menon, Vengali Krishnan (1897–1974), Indian diplomat and political figure. He lived in England between 1924–47 where he joined the Labour Party and served as a secretary of the Indian League (1929–47) which advocated independence. Between 1947–52 he was High Commissioner for India in Britain and served as India's UN delegate (1952–62) when he was sharply critical of US foreign policy. He served in the national legislature (1953–67, 1969–74) and as Minister of Defence (1957–62), but was dismissed after India's poor showing in its border war with China.

Kuan-yin, in Chinese BUDDHISM the goddess of mercy. A Bodhisattva (a person who is potentially a BUDDHA), she intercedes to relieve suffering. She is worshipped in Japan as Kwannon and is called *Bodhisattva Avalokitesvara* in Tibet.

Krishnamurti, Jiddu (1895–), Hindu religious leader. He founded the World Order of Star with Annie BESANT, the theosophist leader, and in 1969 founded and became director of the Krishnamurti Foundation in Ojai, California. His works include *Commentaries on Living* (three volumes, (1956–60) and *The Beginnings of Learning* (1975).

Krivoi Rog, site of rich iron mines worked by the Scythians from *c.*700 BC, now a modern industrial city in the Ukraine. The area had trading links with Greece and the Near East.

Kroeber, Alfred Louis (1876–1960), one of the most important cultural anthropologists of the first half of the 20th century. He helped to advance the study of North American Indian ethnology, linguistics and folklore. His numerous works include the text *Anthropology* (1923).

Krogh, Schack August Steenberg (1874–1949), Danish physiologist. He was professor of animal physiology at Copenhagen University (1916–45) and concentrated on the study of respiration and blood circulation. He was awarded the 1920 Nobel Prize in physiology and medicine for his discovery of the motor-regulating mechanism of capillaries. His writings include *The Anatomy and Physiology of Capillaries* (1922).

Kronstadt, naval base near Leningrad, W USSR. It was the scene of a revolt in Feb. 1921 which was quelled by TROTSKY. In revealing the depths of popular discontent, the rising caused LENIN to introduce new policies, notably the New Economic Policy (1921).

Kroo, or Kru, tribe of W African people who live along the coast of LIBERIA. They work as fishermen and are noted as seamen on cargo ships. There are about 20 subtribes, each traditionally inhabiting an autonomous town with well-developed political and social organizations.

Kropotkin, Peter Alexeievich (1842–1921), Russian anarchist who was jailed for seditious propaganda in 1874; he escaped dramatically into exile in 1876. He was also jailed in France from 1883 to 1886 for anarchist activities, went to London and returned to Russia after the March 1917 revolution. Supporting Alexander KERENSKY and the war against Germany, he denounced Bolshevik centralism and the forcible suppression of opposition.

Krüdener, Barbara Juliane, Baroness von (1764–1824), Russian mystic and novelist who married Baron von Krüdener, a Russian diplomat, in 1782. Her supposedly autobiographical novel *Valérie* (1804) was a literary sensation. She was then converted to the Moravian Church, and preached throughout Europe.

Kruger, Stephanus Johannes Paulus (1825–1904), Boer political figure who helped to settle the Transvaal. After its annexation by the British in 1877 he worked for independence and served as President from 1883 to 1902, organizing continued resistance to British rule. In 1895 he defeated the JAMESON RAID, which was designed to capture the Transvaal. During the Boer War (1899–1902) he represented the Boers in Europe, where he died. *See also* HC2 p.129.

Kruger National Park, large game reserve in Transvaal province, NE South Africa. One of the largest wildlife reserves in the world, it includes most species of animals in southern Africa. Founded in 1898 by S.J.P. KRUGER as the Sabi Game Reserve, it was enlarged and became a national park in 1926. Area: approx. 20,720sq km (8,000sq miles).

Kruger Telegram, on 3 Jan. 1896 message sent to Paul Kruger, President of the Transvaal, by Kaiser WILHELM II of Germany, congratulating the Boers on repelling the JAMESON RAID. The telegram led the Boers to expect direct aid from Germany and stimulated anti-German feeling in Britain.

Krum (*d.* 814), Khan of the Bulgars who successfully engaged Byzantium in warfare (807–13), nearly capturing Constantinople in 813. After killing the Byzantine Emperor NICEPHORUS I in 811, he made his skull into a drinking cup. During his short reign progress was made towards establishing the absolute power of the khan, to the detriment of the Bulgar aristocracy.

Krung Thep. *See* BANGKOK.

Krupa, Gene (1909–73), US jazz drummer and bandleader. He played in the Benny GOODMAN Orchestra until 1938, when he formed his own big band with Roy Eldridge (trumpet) and Anita O'Day (vocalist). In the 1950s he generally led his own jazz combos. He was the first jazz drummer to achieve an international reputation. Krupa appeared in many films and recorded the music for his film biography *The Gene Krupa Story* (1959).

Krupp family, German industrial family who were the world's largest manufacturers of munitions; they had the monopoly for the manufacture of arms in Germany in WWI. Alfred Krupp (1812–87) expanded his father's small iron foundry into a giant industry. He was the first steel-maker to install the BESSEMER process and was one of the leaders in the industrial development of the Ruhr valley. His son Friedrich Alfred Krupp (1854–1902) expanded into shipbuilding and the manufacture of chrome and nickel steel alloys and armour plate. One of their best-known products was Big Bertha, a monstrous but inaccurate gun that shelled the Paris area from a distance of 132km (82 miles). Under Friedrich's son-in-law, Gustav von Bohlen und Halbach, the Krupp works were a mainstay in the NAZI war effort. His son Alfred Krupp (1907–67) was imprisoned for his war activities and was required to sell a portion of his Krupp interests. Alfred's son Arndt decided not to enter the business, and it passed from family control and became a corporation in 1967.

Krylenko, Nikolai Vasilievich (1885–1938), Soviet official who was commander-in-chief of BOLSHEVIK troops in 1917 and became head of the Commissariat of Justice in 1936. He was arrested in 1937 and presumably executed, a victim of STALIN's purges.

Krylov, Ivan Andreyevich (1769–1844), Russian writer who satirized contemporary life by representing social types as various animals. His translations of the fables of LA FONTAINE and AESOP led him to invent his own stories in a similar style. He so captured the Russian character in his own *Fables* (1809; tr. 1869) that his works have become classics.

Kryolite. *See* CRYOLITE.

Krypton, gaseous nonmetallic element (Kr) of the NOBLE GAS group, discovered in 1898. Krypton is present in the Earth's atmosphere (0.000115% by volume) and is obtained by the fractional distillation of liquid air. It is used in FLUORESCENT LAMPS. Chemically it is extremely inert but it does have a well-defined difluoride. The standard linear metre is defined by the wavelength of an emission line in the krypton spectrum. Properties: at.no. 36; at.wt. 83.80; density 3.733gm/litre; m.p. −156.6°C; (−249.88°F; b.p. −152.3°C; (−242.14°F); most common isotope Kr^{84} (56.9%).

Kuala Lumpur, largest city and capital of Malaysia, in Selangor state, 322km (200 miles) NW of Singapore. It was made the capital of the Federated Malay States in 1895, of the Federation of Malaya in 1957 and of Malaysia in 1963. Today it is a commercial centre whose industries include tin and rubber. Pop. (1975 est.) 557,000.

Kuang-hsü (1871–1908), Chinese emperor from 1875 to his death. He was appointed by his aunt, the Empress Dowager Tz'u Hsi. He began his personal rule in 1889, but after the "hundred days of reform" of 1898, his aunt imprisoned him and ruled China herself.

Kubelik, name of two Czech musicians. Jan (1880–1940), was a violinist and composer, and was highly regarded for his technical mastery. He made numerous appearances throughout the world and after the outbreak of WWI he devoted himself to composition. Rafael (1914–), his son, was an eminent conductor as well as a gifted composer. As a conductor he was known especially for his interpretations of Czech composers such as Anton DVOŘÁK and Léos JANÁČEK. From 1973 to 1974 he was musical director of the Metropolitan Opera in New York.

Kubik, Gail Thompson (1914–), US violinist and composer. He studied at the Eastman School of Music, New York. His compositions include orchestral, choral and chamber music as well as *Mirror for the Sky* (1947), a folk opera on the life of John AUDUBON. He has also worked on many film scores, especially in association with the work of William WYLER.

Kubin, Alfred (1877–1959), Austrian draughtsman and illustrator, associated with the BLAUE REITER group. After 1909 he concentrated on book illustration, eg on works by POE and DOSTOEVSKY, and also made thousands of drawings.

Kubitschek, de Oliveira Juscelino (1902–76), President of Brazil from 1956–60. He trained as a doctor; his political career began in the 1930s.

Kublai Khan (1215–94), Mongol emperor (1260–94) who was the grandson of GENGHIS KHAN. In 1279 he completed the conquest of China, deposing the Sung dynasty and founding the Yüan dynasty, which ruled until 1368. Marco POLO visited his court at Peking. *See also* HC1 pp.127, *127, 224,* 225.

Kubla Khan, (1816), incomplete poem by Samuel Taylor COLERIDGE which, according to the author, was inspired by an opium dream.

Kubrick, Stanley (1928–), US film director. His first successful film, *The Killing* (1956), was followed by the astringent *Paths of Glory* (1957), which starred Kirk Douglas. He also directed *Dr Strangelove* (1963), a darkly humorous satire on power politics; *2001: A Space Odyssey* (1968), with a mystical conclusion; *A Clockwork Orange* (1971); and *Barry Lyndon* (1975).

Kuchuk Kainarji, Treaty of (1774), diplomatic agreement ending the Russo-Turkish War of 1768–74. It gave Russia a foothold on the Black Sea. Turkey agreed to Crimean independence, ceded important ports and territories to Russia and guaranteed free passage to Russian ships on the Black Sea.

Kudu, large African ANTELOPE found S of the Sahara. The body is grey-brown with vertical white stripes and the male bears long, spiral horns. There are two species, the greater and the lesser Kudu. Genus *Tragelaphus. See also* NW p.*201.*

Kuhn, Richard (1900–67), German chemist who shared the 1938 Nobel Prize in chemistry with Paul KARRER. They researched CAROTENOIDS and the isolation of vitamin B_2. He was forced by the NAZIS to refuse the award and did not receive it until the end of WWII.

Kuibyshev (Kujbyšev), city and river port in the Russian Republic (Rossijskaja SFSR), USSR, on the River Volga at the mouth of the River Samara; capital of Kuibyshev oblast. It was the scene of Pugachev's rebellion against CATHERINE II (1773–74), a provincial seat and a focus of trade. During WWII, when Moscow was threatened by the German army, Kuibyshev became the temporary capital. It has eight higher education institutions. Industries: motor vehicles, aircraft, ballbearings, flour milling, oil refining. Pop. (1975) 1,164,000.

Kuiper, Gerard Peter (1905–73), US astronomer who emigrated from The Netherlands to the USA in 1933. One of the most influential authorities on the solar system, he made important discoveries about the outer planets and advanced the condensation theory concerning the formation of the planets. *See also* SU pp.*207, 211, 214.*

Kujbyšev. *See* KUIBYSHEV.

Kukai (774–845), real name Kobo Daishi, founder of the SHINGON school of Japanese Buddhism. He renounced CONFUCIANISM, studied in China, and in the *Ten Stages of Consciousness* (830) showed a systematic grasp of major oriental religions. His monastery at Mt Koya is the base for Shingon sects, whose total number of adherents was estimated in the mid-1970s to be approx. 8 million.

Ku Klux Klan, US secret society advocating white supremacy over black people. It was founded (1866) in Pulaski, Tenn., by six confederate veterans after the AMERICAN CIVIL WAR, to prevent newly-enfranchised southern Blacks from voting, and generally to hinder the reconstruction programme. Members dressed up in white sheets and hooded masks, riding at midnight to terrorize and murder their victims. The Klan was formally disbanded in 1869. The Force Acts (1870–71) and the Ku Klux Klan Act (1871) were passed to aid enforcement of the new voting laws. The Klan was revived in 1915, extending its persecutions to immigrants, Catholics and Jews and, this time, was active in the Midwest as well as in the South. By the 1920s membership had reached about five million but it declined to fewer than 9,000 in the 1930s. Membership rose again in the 1960s during the CIVIL RIGHTS activities, but by the mid-1970s the group had little national importance.

Kulak, prosperous Russian peasant. The Kulaks were the dominant force in the countryside and often hired labour. Although they were considered middle-class by the BOLSHEVIKS, their interests were promoted by Lenin's New Economic Policy of 1921. They suffered from the COLLECTIVIZATION of the late 1920s and 1930s, and many were killed or forced into exile. *See also* HC2 pp.168, *198.*

Kulikovo, Battle of (1380), battle between Russians and Mongols. It was fought near the present-day Kurkimo on the upper River Don. Prince Dmitri's victory was the first and only Russian victory over the Golden Horde, but it effectively dispelled the myth of Mongol invincibility.

Kulturkampf, name given to Otto von Bismarck's attempt to subordinate the Roman Catholic Church to the German state (1871–87). The restrictive laws passed were openly resisted, and the Catholic-dominated Zentrumspartei (Centre Party) grew steadily. From 1879 the laws were gradually repealed.

Kumamoto, city in W central Kyūshū, Japan. An important fortified town in the 17th century, it later became an agricultural centre. It also produces ceramics and cotton textiles. Pop. (1970) 440,020.

Kumara, species of SWEET POTATO taken by the Maoris from Polynesia to New Zealand. It became a staple crop and is still widely eaten. Species *Impomoea batheas.*

Kumasi, city in central Ghana, approx. 185km (115 miles) NW of Accra; capital of Ashanti region; second largest city in Ghana. The city flourished as the capital of the Ashanti kingdom after the 18th century. It was occupied by the British in 1874 and 1896, and finally in 1901. Industrial development was spurred by the construction of a railway (*c.* 1903) to major ports on the Gulf of Guinea. Industries: food processing, handicrafts, timber. Pop. (1970) 260,286.

Kumiss. *See* KOUMISS.

Kumquat, hardy evergreen tree or shrub of the RUE family. Growing up to 3.7m (12ft) high, kumquats yield a small citrus fruit, which is orange when ripe. The shrubs are often grown for ornament, and the fruit is used to make jelly or marmalade. Genus *Fortunella.*

Kun, Béla (1886–1937), Hungarian Communist political leader, associate of Lenin, and a Bolshevik. In 1919 he replaced Mihály Károlyi as premier of the newly-formed republic and introduced radical and unpopular changes in the political system of the country, which then became the Hungarian Soviet Republic under his control. Deposed by his countrymen with the aid of the Romanians, he fled to Vienna and finally to the USSR in 1920.

Kung-fu, ancient Chinese martial art that is concerned with the prevention of violence. Literally, it can mean "man who works with art", and its many techniques are based on leg, arm, and trunk exercises derived from the defensive movements of animals. In modern times it has been popularized by the films of Bruce LEE.

K'ung Fu-tzu. *See* CONFUCIUS.

Kung-Sun Lung (*c.* 320–*c.* 250 BC), Chinese DIALECTICIAN and representative of the School of Names. Through such arguments as his famous *Discussion on Two White Horses,* he hoped to align names with their actualities and thereby transform the whole world.

Kuniyoshi, Utagawa (1797–1861) Japanese ukiyo-e (colour) printmaker. He is noted for his prints of historical subjects, warriors, actors of the Kabuki theatre and European-influenced landscapes.

Kuniyoshi, Yasuo (1893–1953), US painter, *b.* Japan. His work, which has been described as Oriental in spirit but Western in technique, includes *Child* (1923), *Landscape* (1924), and *Upside Down Table and Mask* (1940).

Kunming, city in S China, 610km (380 miles) SW of Chungking, on the N shore of Lake Tien, on the Burma road; it is the capital of Yünnan province. A strategic area during WWII, it was used as a US base and Chinese military headquarters. Industries: iron and copper, textiles, chemicals, engineering, food processing. Pop. (1970 est.) 1,700,000.

Kuomintang, or Nationalist Party, the ruling political force in China (1928–49) and subsequently in Taiwan. Initially a foreign-based revolutionary alliance against Manchu rule, it became an open political party (1912) and was reorganized with a Leninist structure and discipline by SUN YAT-SEN with the aid of Soviet advisers. Sun provided it with the programme and doctrine that in large part remain fundamental tenets of the Nationalists in Taiwan. Sun was succeeded by CHIANG KAI-SHEK as head of the organization (1925). *See also* HC2 pp.214–215.

Kupe, legendary Maori discoverer of New Zealand. He is supposed to have arrived by canoe from the Maori homeland in Polynesia (possibly in the Society Islands) *c.* AD 925. On returning to Polynesia he gave his people directions for sailing to New Zealand.

Kupka, František (1871–1957), Czech painter, etcher and illustrator. He inspired the ORPHISM movement, and was among the first painters to develop purely abstract geometric painting. His works include *Fugue in Red and Blue* (1912).

Kuprin, Aleksander Ivanovich (1870–1938), Russian novelist and short story writer. His novel *The Duel* (1905) is about the emptiness of army life; it reflects his service as an officer in the Russian army (1890–94). His best-known work is *The Pit* (1910).

Kurdish language, language of West Iranian origin, spoken by about 7 million inhabitants of Kurdistan. It comprises several dialects. After Persian, it is the second-largest language in the Iranian group. It is written in a modified Cyrillic ALPHABET.

Kurdistan, extensive mountainous region in SW Asia, including parts of E Turkey, NE Iraq, NW Iran and smaller sections of NE Syria and Soviet Armenia. The region lies astride the Zagros Mts and an E extension of the Taurus Mts. It is inhabited by the KURDS. In the 7th century Kurdistan was conquered by the Arabs and converted to Islam. It was ruled by the Mongols from the 13th to the 15th centuries and then by the Ottoman Turks. Since WWI the Kurds have striven for autonomy within Turkey, Iran and Iraq, and this has led to violent clashes on a number of occasions. Area: approx. 191,660sq km (74,000sq miles).

Kurds, semi-nomadic people who live in KURDISTAN, with an estimated total

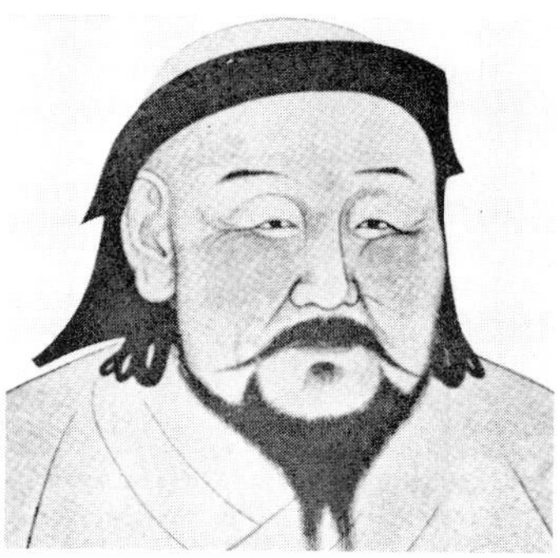

Kublai Khan's empire stretched westwards from the Pacific ocean to the Black Sea.

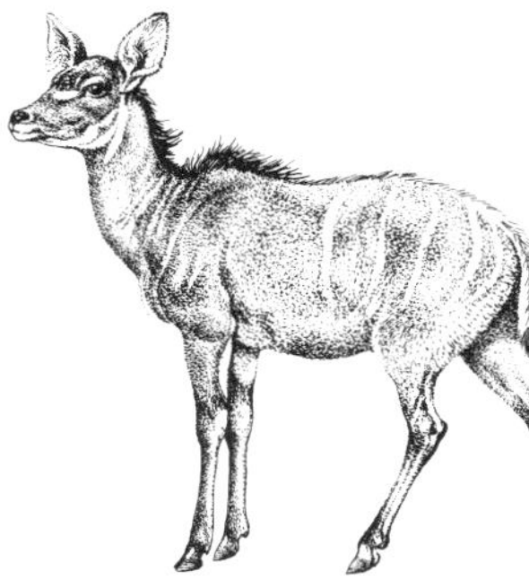

Kudu; the female, shown here, lacks the long spiralling horns of the adult male animal.

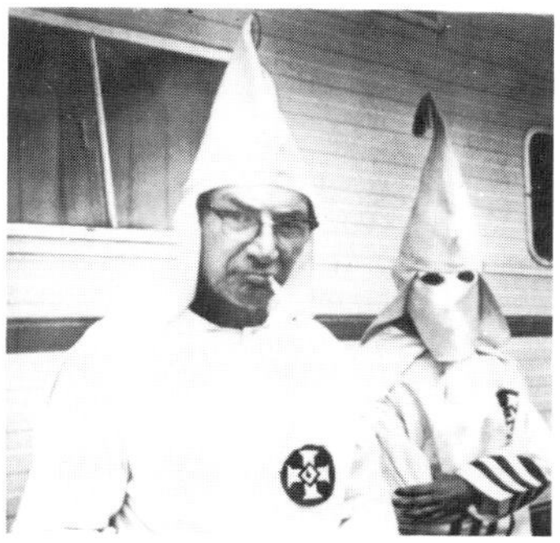

Ku Klux Klan, the sinister face of white racism and bigotry in the southern states of the USA.

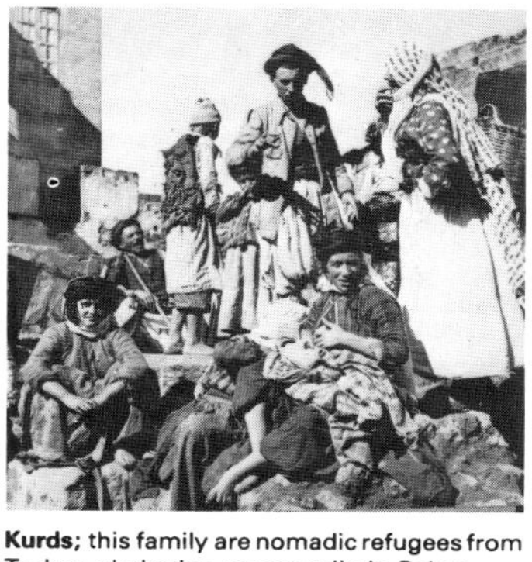

Kurds; this family are nomadic refugees from Turkey, sheltering temporarily in Beirut.

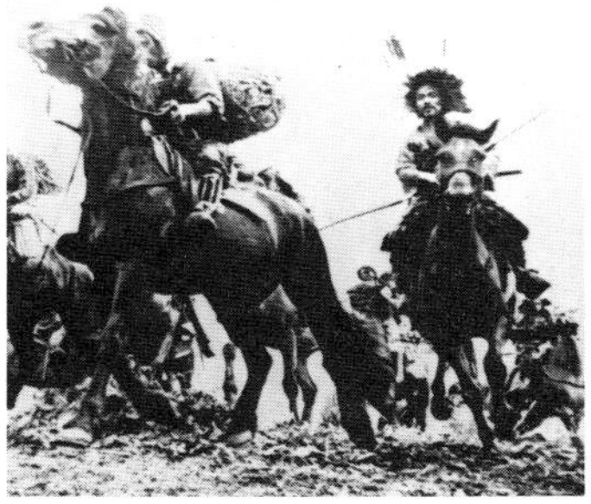

Akira Kurosawa; a scene from his best-known film *The Seven Samurai* (1954).

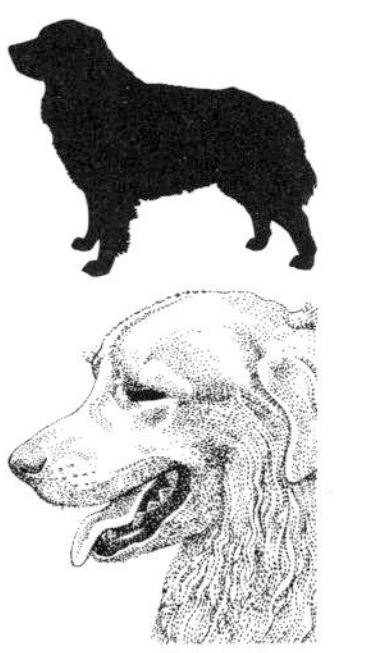

Kuvasz; this working dog was bred mainly in Hungary, but its ancestry is traceable to Tibet.

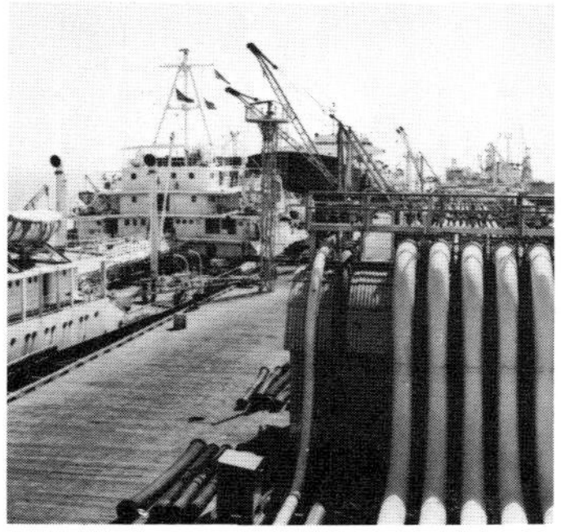

Kuwait; one of the piers, south of Kuwait Town, where oil is piped to tankers.

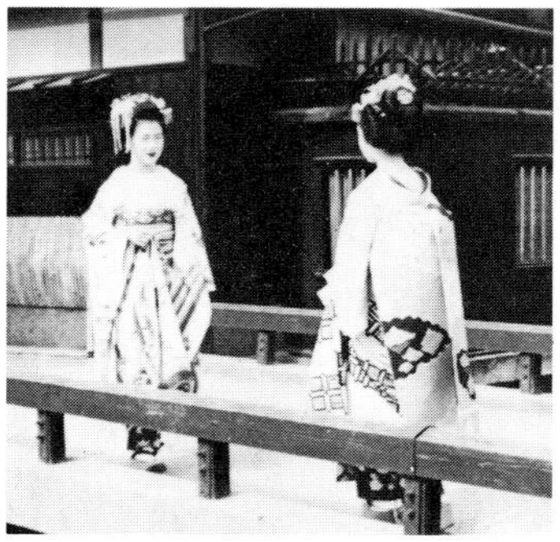

Kyoto: women in traditional dress walking in the Gion district of the city.

population of about 7 million. Traditionally herdsmen, they are Sunnite Muslims and are linguistically close to the Iranians although their ethnic origins are uncertain. Throughout their history the Kurds have resisted domination by other nations. In the 20th century they have striven for autonomy for Kurdistan, and this has led to violence on several occasions.

Kure, city on SW Honshu, Japan 19km (12 miles) SE of Hiroshima, on Hiroshima Bay. It has an excellent natural harbour, being a major Japanese port and an important naval base. During WWII the city was heavily bombed. Industries: shipbuilding, steel, machine tools. Pop. (1974) 241,931.

Kuril (Kuril'skije) Islands, chain of 30 large and many smaller islands, extending 1,200km (750 miles) from S Kamchatka Peninsula, USSR, to NE Hokkaido, Japan, separating the Sea of Okhotsk from the Pacific Ocean. Of volcanic origin, the islands were discovered by the Dutch navigator de Vries in 1634. The N islands were settled by Russians, the S islands by Japanese. After 1945 the islands formerly Japanese were ceded to the USSR, and the population is now entirely Russian. The chief activities are whaling and vegetable growing. Area: 15,600sq km (6,023sq miles). Pop. approx. 15,000.

Kurosawa, Akira (1910–), Japanese film director. In *Rashomon* (1950) he introduced the savage, bloodthirsty world of the SAMURAI warriors to Western audiences. The popularity of this genre was confirmed with *The Seven Samurai* (1954), later remade by John STURGES as *The Magnificent Seven.* He also made films in a modern idiom, notably *Living* (1952). *Dodesukaden* (1970) was his first colour film. *See also* HC2 p.277.

Kurusu, Saburo (1888–1954), Japanese diplomat who was ambassador to Germany from 1939 to 1941. He signed the Berlin Pact (1940), which allied Japan with the AXIS POWERS. He was a special envoy in Washington, USA, when the Japanese attacked PEARL HARBOR. He was interned in the USA until June 1942, when he returned to Japan.

Kusch, Polykarp (1911–), US physicist, *b.*Germany. He shared the 1955 Nobel Prize in physics with Willis LAMB for his precise measurement of the magnetic movement of the ELECTRON, which he discovered had a higher value than was predicted. This led to important developments in nuclear theory.

Kush, kingdom and former state in Nubia. Lasting roughly from 1000 BC to AD 350, it conquered Egypt in the 7th–8th centuries BC. It was thereafter defeated by the Assyrians and moved its capital to Meroë in the Sudan. After Roman and Arab attacks in the north, Meroë was captured by the Axumites around AD 350. The Kushites are thought to have fled west, possibly to the Lake Chad area. *See also* HC1 pp.50–51.

Kushan dynasty, rulers over much of N India, Afghanistan, and parts of Central Asia from *c.*AD 50 to *c.*400. Descended from nomads who ruled over Bactria, they were wealthy and important traders. The decline of their rule followed the rise of the SASSANIDS in Iran.

Kutch, Rann of, area of barren salt and mud flats in N Kutch district, in Gujarat state, W India, on the border with Pakistan. In 1965 it was the scene of fighting between Indian and Pakistani troops during a boundary dispute. Area: 18,000sq km (6,950sq miles)

Kutchuk, Fazil (1906–), Turkish Cypriot doctor and politician. He became involved in politics in the 1940s, leading a party which changed its name to "Cyprus is Turkish" after agitation for ENOSIS grew more violent in the early 1950s. Kutchuk favoured the partition of Cyprus, which became a Republic in 1960 with himself as Vice-President. He was succeeded by Rauf Denktash in 1973.

Kutno, town in central Poland 56km (35 miles) NNW of Łódź. It was the scene of the German defeat of the Polish army on 15 Sept. 1939. Industries: food processing and textiles. Pop. (1970) 30,300.

Kuts, Vladimir (1927–75), Soviet middle-distance runner whose punishing front-running tactics won him the coveted 5,000m and 10,000m double at the 1956 Olympic Games. He won the 1954 European 5,000 and set eight world records at 3 miles, 5,000 and 10,000m.

Kuttner, Henry (1915–58), US science-fiction writer, who used the pseudonym Lewis Padgett. He wrote some stories in collaboration with his wife, Catherine L. Moore. His first short story, *The Graveyard Rats* (1936), became a classic in the horror genre.

Kutusov, Mikhail Illarionovich (1745–1813), Russian general and supreme commander against NAPOLEON. He made the French pay dearly for victory at BORODINO in 1812, then, after abandoning Moscow, he forced the French to retreat in winter through desolate territory, harrying them by guerrilla warfare.

Kuvasz, dog used for guarding and herding livestock. It has an elongated head with a straight muzzle and triangular ears; the broad-backed body is set on medium-length legs and the long tail is carried low. Height: about 66cm (26in) at the shoulder; weight: about 32kg (70lb).

Kuwait, independent Arab nation in the NE Arabian Peninsula, N of the Persian Gulf. Most of Kuwait is desert but huge oil reserves have made it one of the richest countries in the world. Its financial resources have been used to create a comprehensive welfare system and also in loans to other Arab nations. The capital is Kuwait. Area: 17,000sq km (6,560sq miles). Pop. (1975) 994,837. *See* MW p.116.

Kuzbas. *See* KUZNETSK BASIN.

Kuznets, Simon (1901–), US economist, *b.*Russia. He developed the national income accounting system in the 1930s and became known for the study of business cycles. He received the 1971 Nobel Prize in economics for his research into economic growth.

Kuznetsk (Juzneck) Basin, basin in W Siberia, USSR, often called the Kuzbas, between the Kuznetsk Ala-Tau range and the Salair Ridge. Rich coal and iron ore deposits discovered in the 17th and 18th centuries have made it a major industrial region. Area: 25,900sq km (10,000sq miles).

Kuznetsov, Anatoly (1931–), Soviet novelist and short story writer, who changed his name to A. Anatoli after defecting to England in 1969 in protest against Soviet censorship. His works include the novels *Sequel of a Legend* (1957) and *Babiy Yar* (1966), several volumes of short stories and some film scenarios.

Kvass, Russian beer made from a mixture of rye, barley, wheat and other cereals with the addition of sugar or fruit.

Kwajalein, coral atoll, largest island in the Ralik chain, Marshall Islands, in the W Pacific Ocean, formed by 97 islets. Captured by the Americans from the Japanese in WWII, it is now the site of an anti-missile installation. Area: 16sq km (6sq miles).

Kwakiutl, tribe of American Indians on the NW coast speaking the Wakashan tongue, and closely related to the BELLA BELLA. They number approx. 2,000 and occupy northern Vancouver Island in British Columbia, Canada. They are famous for their wooden sculptures, TOTEM POLES and POTLATCH ceremonies.

Kwa languages, branch of the Niger-Kordofan family of African languages. Speakers occupy a large area bordered by the Gulf of Guinea on the south. Most are tonal languages. Important members are Yoruba and Ibo of S Nigeria; Akan of Ivory Coast and Ghana; Ga of Accra city; and Bini of Benin in Nigeria.

Kwangchow. *See* CANTON.

Kwantung (Guang-dong), southernmost province in China, on the South China Sea. Canton is the capital. After 222 BC, Kwangtung came under Chinese suzerainty and was an important centre of China's early foreign trade. The province was the scene of great unrest in the decade before the NATIONALIST Revolution in 1911, staged by the KUOMINTANG (Nationalist People's Party), which Kwangtung supported in the Second Revolution of 1913. CHIANG KAI-SHEK initiated his movement for Chinese unification there during the 1920s. The province fell to the Chinese Communists in 1949. Products: rice, tea, sugar, tobacco, silk, fruit, bamboo. Area: 231,480sq km (89,374sq miles). Pop. 40,000,000.

Kwangsi-Chuang (Guangxi Zhuang Zizhiqu), autonomous region in S China, on the border with North Vietnam; Nanning is the capital. Cultivation is limited by the mountainous terrain, but sugar cane, rice, grain, vegetables, fruits, peanuts and tobacco are grown. Mineral deposits include manganese, zinc, tin, tungsten and antimony. The region was created in 1958 from Kwangsi province, and it has a large non-Chinese minority. Industries: oil refining, fertilizers, dyestuffs, bamboo. Area: 220,495sq km (85,133sq miles). Pop. (1970 est.) 21,000,000.

Kwashiorkor, disease of infants and young children. It occurs primarily in the tropics or subtropics and is caused by a lack of high-quality protein and calories in the diet. The victim's stomach swells and muscles become wasted. There is evidence of retarded growth, mental apathy, anaemia, fatty liver and digestive disorders. Skin pigmentation may change and thick patches form; these may become pinkish and virtually raw. *See also* MS pp.*71*, 107.

Kweichow (Guizhou), province in S China. The capital is Kweiyang. In the rural area the population includes mostly Miao aboriginal tribesmen, who were cast out of other provinces because of their unwillingness to accept Chinese customs. Kweichow came under Chinese suzerainty in the 10th century and became a province under the Ming dynasty. During WWII it served as a military base for the Chinese and Allied forces but was taken by the Chinese Communists in 1950. Crops: rice, corn, wheat, beans, potatoes. Industries: mercury, timber. Area: 174,060sq km (67,204sq miles). Pop. 17,000,000.

Kyd, Thomas (1558–94), English dramatist who achieved popular success with *The Spanish Tragedy* (*c.*1589), a play which has been seen as a forerunner of *Hamlet* because of its theme of revenge and its use of the supernatural. Kyd was a member of the literary circles of the day, which included MARLOWE. In 1593 Kyd was arrested for atheism and blasphemy.

Kyle, Jackie (1926–), Irish rugby union player, *b.* Belfast. A fly-half of instinctive genius, he made a world-record 46 international appearances for Ireland (1947–58) and toured Australia and New Zealand with the 1950 British Lions.

Kyōto, city on W central Honshū, Japan, approx. 42km (26 miles) NE of Ōsaka; capital of Kyōto prefecture. It was the site of the imperial residence for more than 1,000 years and there are many palaces and shrines. Kyōto University dates from 1897. An early centre of the silk industry, its modern industries include porcelain, lacquerware, precision tools and food processing. Pop. 1,461,050.

Kyphosis. *See* HUNCHBACK.

Kyrie eleison, Greek "Lord, have mercy", first words of a three-fold petition for the mercy of God and of Christ, said or sung in Greek or in the vernacular during services in most Christian Churches. The prayer first appeared in the 4th century.

Kyūshū, island in S Japan; third largest and southernmost of the four principal Japanese islands. The terrain is mountainous, and the irregular coastline provides many natural harbours. It is the most densely populated of the Japanese islands, and its main industrial cities include Kitakyūshū, Kumamoto, Kurume and Fukuoka, and the chief port is Nagasaki. Products: rice, tea, tobacco, fruits, soya beans. Industries: mining, textiles, porcelain, metals, machinery. Area: approx. 41,971sq km (16,205sq miles). Pop. (1970) 12,072,179.

Kyzyl-Kum Desert, desert in the UZBEK and KAZAKH republics of the USSR between the Amudarja and Syrdarja rivers. Cotton and rice are grown in the irrigated river valleys and KARAKUL sheep are raised by tribespeople. Area: 230,000sq km (89,000sq miles).